CONTENTS

1995

Japanese army anti-gas chemical warfare unit members decontaminate subway cars that were poisoned by a nerve gas at a Tokyo subway station, March 1995.

	World Affairs	Europe	Africa & the Middle East	The Americas	Asia & the Pacific
Jan.	The World Trade Organization, a global trade-monitoring body, comes into being.	Chechen resistance fighters fight the Russian onslaught as battles that started in December intensify.	A car filled with explosives detonates in Algiers, the capital of Algeria, killing 42 people and wounding 286. The bombing is the single deadliest incident in a three-year struggle between the government and militant fundamentalists.	Peru reportedly mobilizes more than 100,000 soldiers to the disputed frontier with Ecuador.	A powerful earthquake strikes the city of Kobe in Japan, killing more than 5,000 people, collapsing buildings, and sparking fires. It measures 7.2 on the Richter scale and has an epicenter six miles (10 km) beneath Japan's Awaji Island in Osaka Bay.
Feb.	The UN Security Council unanimously authorizes a 7,000-member international peacekeeping contingent for Angola, the largest UN operation in Africa since troops were approved for Somalia in March 1993.	Four Gypsies in Oberwart, a city in eastern Austria, are killed while attempting to remove a booby-trapped anti-Gypsy sign. The incident is one of the country's deadliest terrorist acts since World War II.	Heavy fighting among Somali factions erupts near the airport, halting the retreat of UN troops.	Mexican government forces, backed by air support, occupy 11 formerly EZLN towns.	The Taliban, a faction comprised of religious students who took up arms in 1994, emerges as the most powerful military force in Afghanistan when it routs Premier Gulbuddin Hekmatyar and his Hezb-e-Islami forces from their headquarters in Charasyab, 15 miles (25 km) south of Kabul.
March	The first UN World Summit on Social Development convenes in Copenhagen, Denmark, attracting 118 presidents, vice presidents, and premiers and at least 13,000 other attendees.	In what is described as Turkey's largest military operation ever, a massive Turkish military force crosses into Iraq to eliminate guerrilla strongholds of the PKK.	Burundi is on the verge of a full-scale civil war, prompting the evacuation of foreign nationals.	In an article, a retired naval officer alleges that hundreds of leftist "subversives" were drowned during the later 1970s as part of the military dictatorship's "dirty war" against political opponents in Argentina.	A national public outcry and a diplomatic crisis erupts in the Philippines after the hanging of a Filipina maid in Singapore.
April	As a UN summit on global warming closes, delegates from more than 120 countries approve a compromise plan that establishes a two-year negotiation process regarding the reduction of emissions of carbon dioxide and other greenhouse gases after 2000.	At the third anniversary of the war, Bosnian premier Haris Silajdzic states that the people of Bosnia should be prepared to fight for 10 years to win Bosnia's independence.	Rwandan refugees who fled into Burundi in 1994 fear that ethnic strife in Burundi will send them to neighboring Tanzania as unrest continues.	Cuba and Chile restore full diplomatic relations, which were broken in 1973.	Fighting along Tajikistan's border with Afghanistan spills into Afghanistan when Russian jets bomb the Darwaz district of Afghanistan's Badakhshan region.
May	Representatives from 174 countries at UN headquarters in NYC approve by consensus the indefinite extension of the Treaty on the Nonproliferation of Nuclear Weapons, known as the Nuclear Nonproliferation Treaty.	Croatian forces launch an attack on the Serb-held Krajina region of Croatia, shattering a 14-month-old "permanent cease-fire."	An outbreak of the Ebola virus in Zaire kills more than 150 people.	In Saskatchewan province, Justice James Milliken accepts the recommendation of the Cree community that one of their members, William Bruce Taylor, 28, be banished to a remote area of Canada as punishment for sexual assault. It is only the second time in recent history that a court in North America accepts the recommendation for banishment by a native community.	The legislative assembly of Australia's Northern Territory passes a bill legalizing voluntary euthanasia, or mercy killing, for terminally ill patients. The measure, the Rights of the Terminally Ill bill, is the world's first voluntary euthanasia law.
June	More than 320 UN hostages are being detained in Bosnia-Herzegovina, and UN peacekeepers, unable to protect designated safe areas, abandon many of their posts. The UN Security Council passes a resolution to send as many as 12,500 additional peacekeeping troops to Bosnia.	Fighting for control of Chechnya spills beyond the borders of the republic when 200 rebels attack Budennovsk, a Russian town about 70 miles (110 km) north of the Chechen border.	After two years of feuding, Hamad bin Khalifa al-Thani, Qatar's crown prince and defense minister, wrests the position of emir from his father, Khalifa bin Hamad al-Thani, in a bloodless coup.	Civil strife erupts in the state of Guerrero in southwestern Mexico.	A militant Muslim faction known as the Mohajir Qaumi Movement launches a rampage in Karachi, Pakistan's commercial hub.
July	Thousands of demonstrators in Australia and New Zealand circle French consulates to demand a cancellation of proposed nuclear testing by France in the South Pacific and French Polynesia.	Bosnian Serb forces capture the town of Srebrenica in eastern Bosnia-Herzegovina, one of the UN's safe areas whose civilians the UN vowed to protect. Tens of thousands of Muslim refugees are left to walk across front lines to reach government-held towns.	A suspected Palestinian Islamist detonates a bomb on a public bus in Tel Aviv, Israel's largest city. The deaths raise the tally of Jews killed by Palestinian militants since September 1993 to 130.	Peru and Ecuador agree to demilitarize more than 200 square miles (518 sq km) in the Cordillera del Condor mountains.	As fighting in Sri Lanka continues, military troops kill an estimated 200 Tiger guerrillas on the Jaffna peninsula.
Aug.	The U.S. releases to the UN Security Council spy-satellite photographs allegedly showing mass graves near the Bosnian town of Srebrenica, which Bosnian Serbs captured in July.	The Georgian parliament votes to adopt the country's first constitution since it gained independence from the Soviet Union in 1991. The constitution restores the office of president, which was eliminated after the 1992 coup.	Rebels attempt to launch a bloodless coup against Pres. Miguel Trovoada, Sao Tome and Principe's first freely elected leader. Trovoada is reinstated after signing an amnesty law pardoning the soldiers who took part in the rebellion.	In a crash reported to be the worst in El Salvador's history, all 65 passengers and crew members die when a Guatemalan jetliner hits the side of a volcano in El Salvador. The dead include the Brazilian ambassador to Nicaragua, Gerardo Antonio Muccioli, and the Danish ambassador to Nicaragua, Palle Marker.	Indonesian president Suharto orders the release of three prominent political prisoners who have been held for nearly 30 years because of their alleged roles in an abortive 1965 coup.

A	B	C	D	E
Includes developments that affect more than one world region, international organizations, and important meetings of major world leaders.	Includes all domestic and regional developments in Europe, including the Soviet Union, Turkey, Cyprus, and Malta.	Includes all domestic and regional developments in Africa and the Middle East, including Iraq and Iran and excluding Cyprus, Turkey, and Afghanistan.	Includes all domestic and regional developments in Latin America, the Caribbean, and Canada.	Includes all domestic and regional developments in Asia and Pacific nations, extending from Afghanistan through all the Pacific Islands, except Hawaii.

U.S. Politics & Social Issues	U.S. Foreign Policy & Defense	U.S. Economy & Environment	Science, Technology, & Nature	Culture, Leisure, & Lifestyle	
New York State Supreme Court judge Harold Rothwax sentences a Lebanese immigrant, Rashid Baz, to 141 years and eight months in prison for a 1994 shooting attack on a van carrying 15 Hasidic Jewish students over the Brooklyn Bridge in New York City.	The American Legion veterans group calls for the Smithsonian to cancel or change its planned exhibit featuring the *Enola Gay*, the warplane that dropped an atomic bomb on Hiroshima in 1945.	The Labor Department reports that the nation's seasonally adjusted unemployment rate in December 1994 was 5.4%, the lowest monthly figure since July 1990.	Russian cosmonaut Valery Polyakov completes his 366th day in outer space aboard the *Mir* space station, breaking the record for the longest continuous time spent in outer space.	The WB and UPN become the first national TV networks launched since 1986.	Jan.
The state of Florida files suit against the tobacco industry seeking to recover $1.4 billion in state money spent through Medicaid over a five-year period to care for victims of smoking-related illnesses.	The Clinton administration announces it has declassified as many as 800,000 photographs taken by U.S. spy satellites between 1960 and 1972. It is the first time that the U.S. government makes public any surveillance-satellite photographs.	Officials from the Department of Energy admit that 9,000 people were used as subjects in 154 radiation experiments conducted by the federal government during the cold war.	The U.S. space shuttle *Discovery* blasts off from Kennedy Space Center on a test run for future shuttle dockings aboard the *Mir* space station. The flight includes the first female pilot of a U.S. spacecraft, air force lieutenant colonel Eileen M. Collins.	Sotheby's announces that it will return to the Library of Congress four long-missing notebooks of 19th-century American poet Walt Whitman.	Feb.
New York governor George Pataki (R) signs into law a measure reinstating the death penalty in New York State. By signing the bill, New York becomes the 38th state to currently have capital punishment.	In NYC, federal judge Eugene H. Nickerson strikes down the Defense Department's policy restricting homosexuals' service in the U.S. military, asserting that the "don't ask, don't tell, don't pursue" rule violates free-speech and equal-protection rights provided in the First and Fifth Amendments of the Constitution. Nickerson's decision is the first judicial rejection of the policy.	Pres. Clinton issues an executive order that prohibits the federal government from offering contracts to companies that hire permanent replacements for workers who are legally on strike.	In a historic finding, two competing teams of scientists announce they have found the top quark, the last unknown among the six quark particles thought to be the building blocks of matter.	Popular Mexican-American singer Selena, 23, is fatally shot at a motel in Corpus Christi, Texas, by the founder and former president of Selena's fan club.	March
A massive bomb explodes outside a federal office building in Oklahoma City, Oklahoma, killing more than 100 people. It is the deadliest terrorist attack ever in the U.S.	The Defense Department investigates allegations of U.S. military involvement in Guatemala in the early 1980s. The investigation comes amid accusations that a Guatemalan army officer on the CIA payroll ordered the killing of Efrain Bamaca Velasquez and Michael DeVine. Bamaca's wife, Jennifer Harbury, a U.S. lawyer, conducted a campaign of hunger strikes to press for details on the fate of her husband.	In an unprecedented move, the EEOC affirms that people who have abnormal genes that predispose them to illness but are otherwise healthy cannot be discriminated against by employers concerned about potential medical problems.	U.S. Department of Energy scientists report they have developed a new superconducting tape that carries substantially more current than existing "high-temperature" superconductors.	In Washington, D.C., the Ringling Brothers and Barnum & Bailey Circus stages a one-ring performance in the east parking lot of the Capitol building to mark the circus's 125th anniversary.	April
Alabama revives chain gangs, in which groups of convicts are chained together and made to labor outdoors. The reinstitution of chain gangs is part of an effort by Gov. Forrest (Fob) James Jr. (R) to make prison life tougher.	The Clinton administration ends a 30-year immigration policy when it announces that Cuban boat people seeking asylum in the U.S. will henceforth be summarily repatriated to Cuba.	Some 2,000 members of the United Rubber Workers (URW) union end their 10-month-long strike against Tennessee-based tire manufacturer Bridgestone/Firestone.	Scientists announce that for the first time they have decoded the entire deoxyribonucleic acid (DNA) sequence for the complete gene set, or genome, of a free-living organism.	Christopher Reeve, actor best known as Superman in a series of films, becomes paralyzed from the neck down when he is thrown headlong from his horse during a riding competition in Culpeper, Virginia.	May
In *Miller v. Johnson*, the Supreme Court rules, 5-4, that electoral districts drawn to ensure fair political representation of minorities are unconstitutional if race is used as the "predominant factor" in drawing district boundaries.	Riots erupt at the Esmor Immigration Detention Center in Elizabeth, New Jersey, when 300 detainees awaiting deportation hearings take two guards hostage.	For the first time in his presidential tenure, Pres. Clinton vetoes a bill passed by Congress, which would cut $16.4 billion from spending previously appropriated by Congress for the fiscal year 1995.	The U.S. space shuttle *Atlantis* docks with the Russian space station *Mir*. It is the first of seven dockings scheduled to occur prior to the beginning of construction on the planned international space station.	Members of the Southern Baptist Convention vote overwhelmingly to formally repent for their church's past support of slavery and to ask forgiveness from all blacks.	June
In a case that receives national attention, a circuit court jury in Union, South Carolina, sentences Susan Smith to life in prison for killing her two children.	President Clinton formally reestablishes full diplomatic ties with Vietnam, a move that draws mixed support from veterans groups and U.S. legislators.	The Dow volume of shares traded, 482.9 in millions of shares, is the heaviest since Oct. 20, 1987, and the third highest in the history of the New York Stock Exchange.	More than 800 people nationwide die from a heat wave. It is the highest such toll since 1980.	Pope John Paul II issues a letter addressed to women of all faiths in which he condemns centuries of bias and violence against women and apologizes for the Roman Catholic Church's past discrimination against women.	July
Both *The Washington Post* and *The New York Times* print excerpts from a manuscript by the Unabomber, who has been linked to a series of bombing incidents spanning 17 years.	Officials from the Department of Labor and the INS raid three Los Angeles-area garment factories suspected of employing workers in sweatshop conditions. The agents arrest 55 people, including 39 Thai workers.	Chemical Banking Corp. and Chase Manhattan Corp. announce the largest bank merger in U.S. history, involving a stock swap worth about $10 billion. The deal will create the largest bank in the U.S., which is to be known as Chase Manhattan.	Scientists disclose that fragments of the fossilized remains of humans and stone tools found in Spain are at least 780,000 years old, indicating that humans lived in Europe substantially earlier than previously believed.	Mickey Charles Mantle, 63, New York Yankee who was regarded as one of the greatest baseball players of all time and an American icon, dies in Baylor, Texas, of cancer.	Aug.

F	G	H	I	J
Includes elections, federal-state relations, civil rights and liberties, crime, the judiciary, education, health care, poverty, urban affairs, and population.	*Includes formation and debate of U.S. foreign and defense policies, veterans' affairs, and defense spending. (Relations with specific foreign countries are usually found under the region concerned.)*	*Includes business, labor, agriculture, taxation, transportation, consumer affairs, monetary and fiscal policy, natural resources, and pollution.*	*Includes worldwide scientific, medical, and technological developments; natural phenomena; U.S. weather; natural disasters; and accidents.*	*Includes the arts, religion, scholarship, communications media, sports, entertainments, fashions, fads, and social life.*

	World Affairs	Europe	Africa & the Middle East	The Americas	Asia & the Pacific
Sept.	France detonates a nuclear device at the Mururoa Atoll in the South Pacific. In response, international antinuclear protests are held in several countries, and riots break out during a protest at the main terminal of the international airport in Papeete, the capital of Tahiti.	Some 160,000 Turkish workers strike to protest the government's austerity measures.	A small force led by French mercenary Bob Denard launches a coup in Comoros, an Islamic three-island nation of 4,50,000 people located between Mozambique and Madagascar.	Violence continues to plague the northwestern region of Uraba, Colombia.	The Chinese Communist Party Central Committee removes Chen Xitong, a former Beijing party secretary charged with corruption, from the committee and from the Politburo. Chen is the highest-ranking official to be ousted in the current anticorruption campaign.
Oct.	The largest gathering of world leaders ever assembled convenes at UN headquarters in New York City to commemorate the 50th anniversary of the UN.	Irish prime minister John Bruton meets with David Trimble, leader of Northern Ireland's Ulster Unionist Party, in the first talks between an Irish head of state and a leader of the Ulster Unionists in nearly 30 years.	Zanzibar holds its first-ever multiparty presidential and legislative elections.	An estimated 270 people die due to an outbreak of equine encephalitis in Colombia and Venezuela.	In the first pact brokered between the rebels and the government of Philippine president Fidel Ramos, government negotiators sign a peace accord with representatives from three rebel groups.
Nov.	The presidents of Serbia, Croatia, and Bosnia-Herzegovina agree to a pact to end a nearly four-year-old war among Croats, Muslims, and Serbs in Bosnia that has claimed 250,000 lives. A NATO peacekeeping force of 60,000 troops will be deployed in Bosnia to sustain the accord.	Former Italian premier Giulio Andreotti is charged with murder along with four other people in connection with the 1979 killing of journalist Carmine Pecorelli.	Yitzhak Rabin, 73, Israel's prime minister who shared the 1994 Nobel Peace Prize with Yasser Arafat, is assassinated after delivering a speech at a pro-peace rally in Tel Aviv. The shooting stuns the nation and the world. Foreign Minister Shimon Peres automatically assumes the post of acting prime minister.	In San Salvador, El Salvador's capital, 200 veterans of the country's 12-year civil war occupy a government building to demand land and compensation promised under terms of the 1992 peace accord.	In Afghanistan, Taliban forces, in four separate air strikes, bomb Kabul. Government officials characterize the attack as the heaviest air raid to target the capital in more than a year.
Dec.	Leaders of the Association of Southeast Asian Nations (ASEAN) vote unanimously to extend ASEAN membership to Cambodia, Laos, and Myanmar.	A force of about 800 rebels seizes Gudermes, Chechnya's second-largest city. The clashes are among the worst since July.	For the first time in 29 years, Christmas is celebrated in Bethlehem under Palestinian control.	Police kill three alleged members of the Tupac Amaru Revolutionary Movement when they end a siege in La Molina, a suburb of Lima, Peru's capital. At least one police officer is also killed.	Sri Lankan army troops raise the country's flag in the city of Jaffna, the stronghold of the Liberation Tigers of Tamil Eelam, capping the government's most significant victory in the 12-year-old civil war.

A	B	C	D	E
Includes developments that affect more than one world region, international organizations, and important meetings of major world leaders.	Includes all domestic and regional developments in Europe, including the Soviet Union, Turkey, Cyprus, and Malta.	Includes all domestic and regional developments in Africa and the Middle East, including Iraq and Iran and excluding Cyprus, Turkey, and Afghanistan.	Includes all domestic and regional developments in Latin America, the Caribbean, and Canada.	Includes all domestic and regional developments in Asia and Pacific nations, extending from Afghanistan through all the Pacific Islands, except Hawaii.

U.S. Politics & Social Issues	U.S. Foreign Policy & Defense	U.S. Economy & Environment	Science, Technology, & Nature	Culture, Leisure, & Lifestyle	
The Senate Select Committee on Ethics votes, 6-0, to recommend the expulsion of Sen. Bob Packwood, (R, Oreg.), citing its conclusions that Packwood engaged in sexual misconduct, influence peddling, and obstruction of the committee's investigation of his conduct. In response, Packwood announces his resignation from the Senate.	Defense Secretary William J. Perry orders U.S bases in Okinawa to hold a "day of reflection," in the wake of a rape of a 12-year-old girl by U.S. servicemen in Japan.	Interior Secretary Bruce Babbitt reluctantly signs over the title to 110 acres of federal land in Clark County, Idaho, to a Danish mining company in accordance with the 1872 Mining Act.	Researchers state that fossil remains recently uncovered in Argentina reveal a carnivorous dinosaur that appears to be larger than *Tyrannosaurus rex*.	Philanthropist Paul Mellon donates 85 paintings, sculptures, prints, and drawings to the National Gallery of Art in Washington, D.C. Experts value the works of art at more than $50 million.	Sept.
Hundreds of thousands of black men participate in a rally in Washington, D.C., called the "Million Man March." The demonstration sparks some controversy because it is led by Louis Farrakhan, who has made anti-Semitic remarks, and because it omits women.	A federal jury in New York City convicts 10 militant Muslims on 48 of 50 conspiracy charges stemming from a failed plot to bomb the UN headquarters building and other NYC targets and to assassinate political leaders. The proceedings constitute the biggest terrorism trial in U.S. history.	The Dow closes at a record high of 4802.45, marking the 50th record high registered for the Dow in 1995.	The case of two Ohio girls who underwent an experimental therapy using engineered versions of their own genes to treat a rare, inherited immune-system disease, provides the first evidence of successful gene therapy.	A record 150 million people nationwide watch the acquittal of O. J. Simpson of the June 1994 fatal stabbings of Nicole Brown Simpson and Ronald Goldman.	Oct.
The House votes, 288-139, to approve a bill that will ban a procedure known as intact dilation and evacuation, a rare method used to end pregnancies in their late stages. The bill is the first attempt by Congress to ban an abortion procedure since 1973.	Statistics show that more than 1 million legal immigrants applied for U.S. citizenship in fiscal 1995. That number is nearly double the fiscal 1993 figure and is the highest in the 20th century.	Pres. Clinton vetoes a continuing resolution, or stopgap bill, which forces a temporary, partial shutdown of the federal government.	NASA releases *Hubble Space Telescope* photographs that are said to be the most striking images to date of the birth of stars.	Pope John Paul II and the Vatican Congregation for the Doctrine of Faith reaffirm that the Roman Catholic Church's ban on the ordination of women priests is "infallible" doctrine not open to debate.	Nov.
Pres. Clinton holds the first-ever White House conference on AIDS and HIV, hosting 300 advocates, lobbyists, and doctors.	After heated debate, Congress approves resolutions that give reluctant support to the deployment of American troops in the peace effort in Bosnia-Herzegovina.	Pres. Clinton signs legislation that will abolish the Interstate Commerce Commission.	Astronomers' calculations indicate the presence of a black hole with the mass of 1.2 billion suns, which is located about nine light-years from the center of the galaxy.	NBC agrees to pay $2.3 billion for the rights to broadcast the 2004 Summer Olympic Games, the 2006 Winter Olympic Games, and the 2008 Summer Olympics on TV and cable. The size of the deal is a record in sports TV history.	Dec.

F	G	H	I	J
Includes elections, federal-state relations, civil rights and liberties, crime, the judiciary, education, health care, poverty, urban affairs, and population.	Includes formation and debate of U.S. foreign and defense policies, veterans' affairs, and defense spending. (Relations with specific foreign countries are usually found under the region concerned.)	Includes business, labor, agriculture, taxation, transportation, consumer affairs, monetary and fiscal policy, natural resources, and pollution.	Includes worldwide scientific, medical, and technological developments; natural phenomena; U.S. weather; natural disasters; and accidents.	Includes the arts, religion, scholarship, communications media, sports, entertainments, fashions, fads, and social life.

	World Affairs	Europe	Africa & the Middle East	The Americas	Asia & the Pacific
Jan. 1	The World Trade Organization, a global trade-monitoring body, comes into being. . . . Austria, Finland, and Sweden join the EU. . . . The Southern Common Market (Mercosur) becomes operational. . . . U.S. Trade Representative Mickey Kantor announces that the U.S. and the EU signed a trade agreement with India that will open India's domestic market to exports of textiles.	A cease-fire in Bosnia goes into effect. It is broken sporadically in the region around Bihac, where rebel Muslim forces loyal to renegade Muslim leader Fikret Abdic and Serbs from the Krajina region of Croatia are involved in the fighting. Neither the rebel Muslims nor the Croatian Serbs signed the truce. . . . Frederick West, an alleged killer of 12 women and girls, is found hanged in his jail cell in Birmingham, England, in an apparent suicide.	Militiamen from rival Somali sub-clans battle in Mogadishu, the capital, for control of the Bermuda district, which has access to the seaport currently controlled by the United Nations.	Fernando Henrique Cardoso takes the oath as Brazil's president, succeeding President Itamar Franco.	
Jan. 2		Chechen resistance fighters repel the Russian onslaught that began Dec. 31, 1994, forcing Russian troops back to Grozny's edges and leaving hundreds of Russian soldiers dead, wounded, or captured and Russian tanks incinerated by Chechen grenades. . . . A third party involved in the Bosnian civil war joins the truce when Kresimir Zubak, leader of the Bosnian Croats and president of the Muslim-Croat federation in Bosnia, signs the agreement. . . . A fire damages the west wing of Stormont, Northern Ireland's parliament building, in Belfast.	Three Palestinian policemen are killed near a Gaza-Israel crossing point in an exchange of gunfire with Israeli soldiers who cross into Palestinian territory. In two separate incidents in the West Bank, Israeli troops kill three suspected Islamic militants. . . . Suspected members of the Islamic Group shoot eight policemen to death in four separate attacks in southern Egypt. Three civilians are also killed. . . . Maj. Gen. Mohamed Siad Barre, former Somalian president, 1969–91, whose age was reported as between 75 and 84, dies in Lagos, Nigeria, of a heart attack.		
Jan. 3	WHO reports that the official tally of AIDS cases worldwide for the first time exceeds 1 million.	Russian troops launch an assault on Grozny, bombing and attacking from the ground with army and interior ministry troops. Chechen fighters hit back with rocket fire. . . . Two wings of Everthorpe prison in North Humberside, England, suffers extensive damage in riots. Separately, three dangerous convicts escape from top-security Parkhurst prison on the Isle of Wight, off England's south coast.	Plainclothes Israeli security personnel kill four Palestinians in the Israeli-occupied West Bank town of Beit Liqya, some eight miles (13 km) west of Ramallah, and four other Palestinians are wounded in two clashes near the Erez crossing point in Gaza.		The Sri Lankan government and the Liberation Tigers of Tamil Eelam rebel group reach a cease-fire agreement, which calls for a two-week "cessation of hostilities," to go into effect on Jan. 8. The rebel leader, Velupillai Prabhakaran, agrees to release four policemen held hostage since 1990.
Jan. 4	A panel of scientists claims that it "could find absolutely no reliable intelligence and no medical or biological justification" for allegations that Iraq employed chemical or biological weapons against coalition forces during the Persian Gulf war in 1991. . . . At a meeting of interior ministers from 18 Arab countries, Egypt, Algeria, and Tunisia urge governments from throughout the Arab world to enact practical measures to halt violence by militant Muslim groups.	Statistics show that at least 11 Russian air raids have killed 78 people and wounded 200 others south of Grozny since Jan. 2. Russian president Boris Yeltsin orders the bombing of Grozny to stop, but reports suggest those orders are not obeyed.	Israeli undercover forces kill four members of the PFLP in the West Bank village of Beit Liqya. . . . In Somalia, elders from the Abgal clan, loyal to Ali Mahdi Mohammed, and the Murusade clan, loyal to Gen. Mohammed Farah Aidid, sign a treaty calling for an end to the Bermuda district battles, which has killed 23 people and wounded more than 300. Neither Aidid, who controls much of southern Mogadishu, nor self-styled president Mohammed, who controls much of northern Mogadishu, are present at the signing.	Figures indicate that 650 people died at the hands of leftist guerrillas in Peru in 1994, a 50% decline from similar year-earlier fatalities. . . . The Order of Canada in the 1995 New Year's list names 82 Canadians who achieved outstanding accomplishments or provided special services in various fields.	
Jan. 5		Officials from the United Nations High Commissioner for Refugees (UNHCR) estimate that 100,000 residents of Chechnya have fled the republic.	Reports state that Jordan's King Hussein has appointed Sharif Zeid bin Shaker as the nation's new premier. . . . Hastings Kamuzu Banda, who ruled Malawi, 1964–94, is placed under house arrest in connection with the killing of four political rivals in 1983. . . . The commander of Iran's air force, Brigadier General Mansour Satari, dies in a plane crash near Isfahan, about 200 miles (320 km) south of Teheran, the capital of Iran. Ten other officers, including four generals, also die in the crash.	In Mexico City, Mexico, 30,000 people demonstrate, expressing their concerns over the expected reduction in purchasing power as inflation overtakes wages.	Taiwan's cabinet approves a plan to ease a ban, in effect since 1949, on direct transportation links with China.
Jan. 6	Iraqi deputy premier Tariq Aziz meets in Paris with French foreign minister Alain Juppe in the first formal contacts between France and Iraq since before the 1991 Persian Gulf war. Juppe announces that France will resume limited diplomatic relations with Iraq, sparking criticism that the move violates UN Security Council resolutions.		Joe Slovo, 68, South African Communist Party leader who was instrumental in the fight against the apartheid system of racial segregation and was a longtime ally of current South African president Nelson Mandela, dies in Johannesburg, South Africa, of bone marrow cancer.	Peasants in Colombia end their two-week-long occupation of seven oil wells belonging to the state-owned Empresa Colombiana de Petroleos (Ecopetrol) oil company, which they seized to protest the government's stepped-up campaign to eradicate drug crops.	In the Philippines police arrest two Arab men and seize bomb-making materials from an apartment near the Vatican's papal nunciature in Manila.

A	B	C	D	E
Includes developments that affect more than one world region, international organizations, and important meetings of major world leaders.	*Includes all domestic and regional developments in Europe, including the Soviet Union, Turkey, Cyprus, and Malta.*	*Includes all domestic and regional developments in Africa and the Middle East, including Iraq and Iran and excluding Cyprus, Turkey, and Afghanistan.*	*Includes all domestic and regional developments in Latin America, the Caribbean, and Canada.*	*Includes all domestic and regional developments in Asia and Pacific nations, extending from Afghanistan through all the Pacific Islands, except Hawaii.*

U.S. Politics & Social Issues	U.S. Foreign Policy & Defense	U.S. Economy & Environment	Science, Technology, & Nature	Culture, Leisure, & Lifestyle	
	The U.S. Defense Department reports to Congress that the Clinton administration's Haiti-related expenses totaled about $765 million between Oct. 1, 1993, and Nov. 30, 1994.		Eugene P. Wigner, 92, Hungarian-born physicist who won the 1963 Nobel Prize in physics for his pioneering research in quantum mechanics, dies in Princeton, New Jersey, of pneumonia.	Jess Alexandria Stacy, 90, jazz pianist who played for some of the top "swing era" bands, dies in Los Angeles of congestive heart failure.	Jan. 1
Six convicted murderers escape from the Glades Correctional Institution in Belle Glade, Florida. The six are all Cuban immigrants serving life sentences.					Jan. 2
		Heavy rains begin in California.		Reports state that Don Stine, a rare book dealer from Ocean Township, New Jersey, discovered what may be a previously unknown poem by Edgar Allan Poe.... The U.S. Holocaust Memorial Museum names Steven T. Katz, 50, as its next director.	Jan. 3
The 104th Congress convenes with the Republican Party holding majorities in both the House and the Senate for the first time in 40 years.... Jesse Dewayne Jacobs, 44, convicted of the 1986 abduction and fatal shooting of a paramedic, is executed by lethal injection in Huntsville, Texas. The execution is controversial because prosecutors acknowledge that the crime was committed by his sister. Jacobs is the 86th inmate executed in Texas and the 258th in the U.S. since 1976.		Victor Riesel, 81, syndicated newspaper columnist who crusaded against labor racketeering in the 1950s and was the victim of a notorious acid attack in 1956, which left him blind, dies in New York City of a heart attack.		Brooks Stevens, 83, influential designer who helped launch the industrial design movement in the 1930s, dies in Milwaukee, Wisconsin, of heart failure.... Jim Lee Howell, 80, head coach of the New York Giants professional football team, 1954–60, dies in Lonoke, Arkansas, from an undisclosed illness.	Jan. 4
The House votes on a sweeping package of changes in House rules, which shrink and restructure the chamber's committee system, reduce its work force, and dramatically revise many of its lawmaking procedures.... Pres. Clinton formally names State Department spokesman Michael McCurry as the new White House press secretary.	The Defense Department announces that it will begin shipping 500,000 tons of oil to North Korea.... The U.S. military begins to forcibly repatriate 4,000 Haitian refugees housed at Guantanamo Bay, Cuba.... Ben R. Rich, 69, engineer who helped design some of the U.S.'s most advanced military aircraft, dies in Ventura, California, of cancer.... Pres. Clinton announces that Admiral William O. Studeman will serve as interim director of the CIA when R. James Woolsey Jr. vacates the post Jan. 9.	The House passes a bill, 429-0, that will require Congress to comply with federal civil-rights and occupational-safety laws and other labor statutes.... Crescent Ship Services pleads guilty to criminal charges of polluting the Mississippi River. The company agrees to pay a $250,000 fine, and the executives are the first individuals to face felony charges for violating federal pollution statutes.... Statistics show that the total number of new passenger vehicles sold in the U.S. in 1994 totaled 15.09 million, an 8.6% increase from 1993.	Newt Gingrich (R, Ga.) unveils a computer-data system, accessible through the Internet and other public-access computer networks, through which a wide range of information about congressional activities and legislation will be made available to the public.		Jan. 5
Reports state a 26-year-old Pennsylvania woman who suffers from severe mental retardation was sterilized at her mother's request in December 1994. The mother, Dolores Wasiek, first requested court permission to have her daughter, identified only as Cindy, sterilized in 1987, contending that her daughter, who also suffers from epilepsy, may be harmed or killed by the hormonal changes of pregnancy.		The Labor Department reports that the nation's seasonally adjusted unemployment rate in December 1994 was 5.4%, the lowest monthly figure since July 1990.		In the Boston archdiocese's *Pilot* newspaper, Roman Catholic cardinal Bernard Law reiterates a call for a moratorium on protests outside abortion clinics that he made after the Dec. 30 attacks in Brookline, Massachusetts.	Jan. 6
F	G	H	I	J	
Includes elections, federal-state relations, civil rights and liberties, crime, the judiciary, education, health care, poverty, urban affairs, and population.	*Includes formation and debate of U.S. foreign and defense policies, veterans' affairs, and defense spending. (Relations with specific foreign countries are usually found under the region concerned.)*	*Includes business, labor, agriculture, taxation, transportation, consumer affairs, monetary and fiscal policy, natural resources, and pollution.*	*Includes worldwide scientific, medical, and technological developments; natural phenomena; U.S. weather; natural disasters; and accidents.*	*Includes the arts, religion, scholarship, communications media, sports, entertainments, fashions, fads, and social life.*	

	World Affairs	Europe	Africa & the Middle East	The Americas	Asia & the Pacific
Jan. 7		Maj. Gen. Viktor Vorobyev, commander of Russia's interior ministry troops in Chechnya, is killed by a mortar shell explosion. He is the highest-ranking Russian officer killed in the month-long conflict. . . . Harry Golembek, 83, who represented Britain in several international chess tournaments and who, in 1966, became the first person to receive the title of Officer of the Order of British Empire for contributions to chess, dies. . . . Larry Grayson (born William White), 71, popular British comedian, dies in Nuneaton, England.	In Rwanda, an attack on a refugee camp leaves 12 people dead and 36 wounded. . . . Opposition parties in Niger win a small majority in parliamentary elections.		
Jan. 8		British police capture three convicts who escaped Jan. 3 from the top-security Parkhurst prison on the Isle of Wight, 10 miles (16 km) off the south coast of England.			A cease-fire between Tamil rebels and the Sri Lankan government goes into effect.
Jan. 9	Austria's currency, the schilling, joins the European Union's exchange-rate mechanism (ERM).	Port authorities in the southeastern English city of Shoreham halt livestock shipments to France amid increasing acts of violence by animal-rights activists. . . . Former East German head of state Egon Krenz and six other former Communist Party officials are charged in connection with the deaths of East Germans who attempted to flee to the west when Germany was divided.	The Rwandan army admits its troops were responsible for a Jan. 7 attack on a refugee camp. . . . Israel agrees to recognize passports issued by the PNA.		Data shows the value of foreign investment in South Korea surged 26% in 1994 from 1993, to a total of $1.31 billion. . . . North Korea announces an easing of restrictions on trade ties with the U.S. . . . Prince Souphanouvong, 82, known as the "Red Prince" for leading the Pathet Lao communist guerrilla group for more than two decades in a campaign to overthrow the Laotian rightist government of his half-brother, Prince Souvanna Phouma, dies of heart ailments.
Jan. 10		Bosnian government forces start a blockade of 1,000 UN troops near Tuzla in northern Bosnia. The government forces are protesting the deployment of Colonel Slavko Guzvic, a Serb liaison officer, at the Tuzla airport. . . . The woman with whom Britain's Prince Charles has had a long-standing on-and-off affair, Camilla Parker Bowles, and her husband, Brigadier Andrew Parker Bowles, announce that they are divorcing.	Eleven people are killed when gunmen fire on a bus in Batna, southeast of Algiers. In another incident, four people are killed when gunmen fire on a government-designated mosque in nearby Barika. Militant Muslims are suspected in the attacks. . . . A white doctor from Scotland, Richard McGown, accused of conducting morphine-related medical experiments on black patients in Zimbabwe, is convicted of manslaughter in the deaths of two children. The doctor is acquitted in three other deaths.		Reports confirm that Chinese dissident Wang Dan has returned to his home in Beijing after spending one month in hiding.
Jan. 11	Officials from more than 30 countries agree to form a task force to set guidelines for the creation of a Middle East development bank. . . . U.S. president Clinton and Japanese premier Tomiichi Murayama meet in the first summit between the leaders of the world's two largest economies since February 1994.	The German government announces that Vietnam has agreed to accept the return of up to 40,000 Vietnamese illegal immigrants in exchange for economic aid. . . . Italy's constitutional court announces it has struck down two referendums that could have completely abolished proportional parliamentary representation.	Israeli troops fire stun grenades to disperse Palestinian demonstrators gathered near the West Bank city of Nablus to protest a new building site at the Jewish settlement of Alei Zahav.	Panama's interior minister, Raul Arango, states that 10 members of the national police force were arrested on charges of planning a coup that would have included the assassination of Pres. Ernesto Perez Balladares.	Pope John Paul II begins an extensive Asian tour that includes stops in the Philippines, Papua New Guinea, Australia, and Sri Lanka.
Jan. 12	The UN Security Council votes to retain its oil and general economic embargoes on Iraq during its regular 60-day review of the Iraqi situation. Separately, the Council votes to renew for 100 days the suspension of some sanctions against Yugoslavia. Croatian president Franjo Tudjman informs the UN that Croatia will not renew the UN peacekeeping mandate in Croatia, under which 15,000 UN peacekeeping troops are stationed there as a buffer separating Serb and Croat forces.	Russian forces increase the intensity of their attacks on rebel Chechen forces in Grozny, the capital of the breakaway Russian republic of Chechnya. The Russian assault since the beginning of the year has killed thousands of Chechen rebels and civilians. The Russian army's stepped-up assault comes amidst significant public opposition. . . . Northern Ireland Secretary Patrick Mayhew announces that as of Jan. 16, British troops will no longer carry out daylight street patrols in Belfast, the capital of Northern Ireland, or Ulster.	Nongovernmental relief agencies suspend all nonemergency aid in Mogadishu, Somalia, vowing that they will not resume relief efforts until Rudy Marq, 24, a French aid worker kidnapped in December 1994, is released.	U.S. forces in Haiti suffer their first fatality from hostile fire when a U.S. soldier is killed in a shoot-out at a military checkpoint in Gonaives, a coastal town about 100 miles (160 km) north of Port-au-Prince. A second U.S. soldier is wounded, and one Haitian is killed in the incident.	

A	B	C	D	E
Includes developments that affect more than one world region, international organizations, and important meetings of major world leaders.	*Includes all domestic and regional developments in Europe, including the Soviet Union, Turkey, Cyprus, and Malta.*	*Includes all domestic and regional developments in Africa and the Middle East, including Iraq and Iran and excluding Cyprus, Turkey, and Afghanistan.*	*Includes all domestic and regional developments in Latin America, the Caribbean, and Canada.*	*Includes all domestic and regional developments in Asia and Pacific nations, extending from Afghanistan through all the Pacific Islands, except Hawaii.*

U.S. Politics & Social Issues	U.S. Foreign Policy & Defense	U.S. Economy & Environment	Science, Technology, & Nature	Culture, Leisure, & Lifestyle	
					Jan. 7
				Carlos Monzon, 52, Argentinian boxer who was the world middleweight champion, 1970–77, dies in Santa Fe, Argentina, in an automobile accident while on a furlough from prison.	**Jan. 8**
House Speaker Newt Gingrich (R, Ga.) asks for the resignation of Christina Jeffrey, a political science professor whom he appointed as the House historian. Gingrich dismisses Jeffrey after the public reemergence of comments she made eight years earlier in which she criticized a school history program about the Holocaust for not including "the Nazi point of view."	In Los Angeles, federal judge Mariana Pfaelzer nullifies an August 1993 jury judgment awarding defense contractor Litton Industries Inc. $1.2 billion in damages from rival Honeywell Inc. for violating a Litton patent on an airline-navigation system.	The Arkansas Supreme Court rules, 4–3, that Wal-Mart Stores Inc., the nation's largest retailer, did not violate a state law banning so-called predatory pricing. The decision dismisses an October 1993 lower-court ruling that ordered Wal-Mart to pay a total of $298,407 in damages to three pharmacies in Conway, Arkansas.	Teams of astronomers from the University of Arizona and Los Alamos National Laboratory in New Mexico report they have created for the first time a working computer model for the explosion of a supernova.... Russian cosmonaut Valery Polyakov, 51, completes his 366th day in outer space aboard the *Mir* space station, breaking the record for the longest continuous time spent in outer space. Polyakov is scheduled to remain in orbit until March.	Third baseman Mike Schmidt is elected to the Baseball Hall of Fame in Cooperstown, New York, in his first year of eligibility.... Peter Cook, 57, comedian widely acclaimed as a founder of contemporary British satire, dies in London, England, of a gastrointestinal hemorrhage.	**Jan. 9**
In *Tome v. U.S.*, the Supreme Court rules, 5–4, to limit the use of third-party testimony to rebut a charge that a witness committed perjury during a trial.... Data shows that the death rate from breast cancer in the U.S. declined by 4.7% from 1989 to 1992.		The Senate confirms Robert E. Rubin as secretary of the Treasury.... A group of 26 air traffic controllers, who were among the more than 11,000 fired by then-Pres. Ronald Reagan during a bitter 1981 strike, report for retraining classes in Oklahoma City, Oklahoma. They are the first controllers rehired since Pres. Clinton lifted a ban on their rehiring in August 1993.	Heavy rains that started Jan. 3 cause severe flooding in California. In Sonoma County, the Russian River crests at 15 feet (5 m) above flood level. Pres. Clinton issues a disaster declaration for 24 counties, making them eligible for federal aid.... An Atlas rocket launched from Cape Canaveral, Florida, lifts into orbit a satellite that will relay telephone and television signals worldwide for the International Telecommunications Satellite Organization (Intelsat), a Washington, D.C.-based consortium of 134 countries.		**Jan. 10**
Arlin Adams, the independent prosecutor investigating charges of influence peddling HUD in the 1980s, announces that he will not prosecute Samuel R. Pierce Jr., the former HUD secretary during whose tenure the illegal activity occurred.		The Labor Department reports that the government's index of consumer prices in 1994 rose 2.7% for the second year in a row.... The Senate votes, 98-1, to pass a bill that will end Congress's exemption from 11 federal labor statutes, including occupational-safety and antidiscrimination laws.	A team of U.S. and Japanese astronomers announce that they have gathered the "most direct and definitive evidence to date" of the existence of a supermassive black hole near the center of the NGC 4258 galaxy, about 21 million light years from Earth.... Intel and Advanced Micro Devices announce that they settled a long-running dispute over the interpretation of a 1982 technology-sharing pact.	The WB is the first national TV network launched since 1986.... Josef Gingold, 85, one of the most influential violin teachers in the U.S., dies in Bloomington, Indiana, of a heart attack.... Players and team owners accept a contract in time to avoid cancellation of the 1994–95 National Hockey League season.	**Jan. 11**
Qubilah Bahiyah Shabazz, the daughter of slain black nationalist leader Malcolm X, is arrested in Minneapolis, Minnesota, on federal charges of attempting to hire a hit man to kill Nation of Islam leader Louis Farrakhan, who in the past has been accused of playing a role in Malcolm X's assassination in 1965.		Reports indicate that members of the United Rubber Workers Union of America Local 7 in Akron, Ohio, have agreed to end their strike at a racing-tire production and research facility, and another 800 URW members have crossed picket lines at other plants in the midst of a six-month strike by URW against tire manufacturer Bridgestone/Firestone Inc.	Secretary of Transportation Federico Pena visits Southern California, where he allocates $5 million in emergency funds for initial restoration of storm-damaged roadways and bridges.... Two studies of HIV yield new understanding of the effects of drugs on the virus and of the daily cellular activity that occurs during its progression.	George Price, 93, cartoonist who is credited with helping to establish a new aesthetic in comic illustrations at *The New Yorker* magazine in the 1930s, dies in Englewood, New Jersey, after suffering from a brief, undisclosed illness.	**Jan. 12**

F	G	H	I	J
Includes elections, federal-state relations, civil rights and liberties, crime, the judiciary, education, health care, poverty, urban affairs, and population.	*Includes formation and debate of U.S. foreign and defense policies, veterans' affairs, and defense spending. (Relations with specific foreign countries are usually found under the region concerned.)*	*Includes business, labor, agriculture, taxation, transportation, consumer affairs, monetary and fiscal policy, natural resources, and pollution.*	*Includes worldwide scientific, medical, and technological developments; natural phenomena; U.S. weather; natural disasters; and accidents.*	*Includes the arts, religion, scholarship, communications media, sports, entertainments, fashions, fads, and social life.*

	World Affairs	Europe	Africa & the Middle East	The Americas	Asia & the Pacific
Jan. 13	The UN names Honore Rakotomanana, the former president of Madagascar's supreme court, to serve as chief prosecutor for an international tribunal to try individuals accused of genocide and other war crimes in Rwanda. . . . Representatives of the so-called contact group—the U.S., Russia, Britain, France, and Germany—meet with Bosnian Serb leaders. The meeting is in violation of a UN Security Council resolution since the Bosnian Serb leadership has yet to accept the peace settlement.	Two ETA gunmen in Bilbao, a Basque-region coastal city, allegedly enter a government office and shoot two policemen in the head, killing one. . . . In order to placate protestors, the British Meat and Livestock Commission announces that calves exported from Britain to the Netherlands will not be housed in veal crates. . . . Italian president Oscar Luigi Scalfaro asks a political independent, Lamberto Dini, to be the nation's premier and form a new government.	Algerian opposition groups, including the outlawed Islamic Salvation Front (FIS), jointly issue proposals aimed at ending the civil strife that has plagued Algeria for three years.		China Human Rights states that China's best-known dissident, Wei Jingsheng, was ordered to serve 2½ years of "reeducation through labor." . . . Philippine authorities report they have uncovered an elaborate conspiracy to kill the pope orchestrated by 20 Muslim terrorists.
Jan. 14		A Bosnian government offensive begins, and the Bosnian army seizes the villages of Klokot and Vedro Polje, northwest of Bihac. A Bosnian Serb mortar attack in downtown Bihac kills five people.			Bankrupt Australian businessman Alan Bond, 56, is arrested and charged in an East Perth, Western Australia, court with seven counts of fraud and corporate misconduct.
Jan. 15		Bosnian Serb shelling kills at least two people.	Former South African Communist Party leader Joe Slovo, who died Jan. 6, becomes the first white man to be buried at Avalon cemetery in Soweto, a cradle of the movement against the apartheid system of racial separation. The funeral is marred by a crush of thousands of mourners, most of them black. . . . In Algiers, militant Muslims kill Salah Nour, a member of the National Transitional Council in Ben Omar.	In Mexico, a PRD protest rally in Villahermosa, the Tabasco capital, reportedly attracts 30,000 people.	The Roman Catholic Church's celebration of the 10th World Youth Day draws an enthusiastic crowd of as many as 4 million people in Manila, the Philippines.
Jan. 16		Paul Delouvrier, 80, French civil servant best remembered for leading an extensive urban reconstruction project in Paris during the 1960s, dies of an undisclosed illness in France.			
Jan. 17		Reports reveal that Russia has started to launch daily rocket attacks from the air on Chechen villages south of Grozny. A speaker for the Russian army discloses that nearly 1,200 dead Russian soldiers were counted there. That figure compares with the previous official count of 500 Russian soldiers dead. Some unofficial estimates put the number at 4,000. . . . In Italy, the cabinet of newly appointed premier Lamberto Dini is sworn in.			A powerful earthquake strikes the city of Kobe in Japan, collapsing buildings and sparking fires. It measures 7.2 on the Richter scale and has an epicenter six miles (10 km) beneath Japan's Awaji Island in Osaka Bay. . . . A Singapore high court judge finds a U.S. professor, Christopher Lingle, guilty of contempt of court for an October 1994 article. Lingle is ordered to pay S$10,000 (US$7,000), reportedly the largest fine ever imposed in a Singapore contempt-of-court case.
Jan. 18	In a confidence vote, the EU's parliament votes to approve the new European Commission, led by Jacques Santer. . . . A survey ranks Geneva, Switzerland, as the city that offers the highest quality of life in the world. The survey compares a variety of measures, including political and social stability, security, and health services, in 118 cities worldwide. At the bottom is Algiers, Algeria. . . . A study indicates that Japan was the world's top ship-exporting nation in 1994. South Korea headed the list in 1993.	Russian bombs hit the palace in Chechnya's capital, Grozny, killing dozens of Chechens and wounding Russian soldiers in the hospital in the building's basement. . . . Lamberto Dini officially becomes the head of Italy's 54th post-World War II government.	The South African government declares invalid a secret amnesty granted before elections in April 1994 to 3,500 police officers and former cabinet ministers for crimes committed under the apartheid system of racial separation. . . . An Algerian government spokesman rejects the proposals offered by opposition groups on Jan. 13. . . . Six people are killed, 20 are injured, and four are missing after an explosion on an oil platform in Mobil's offshore Ubit oil field in Nigeria.	The Canadian dollar drops to its lowest point in almost nine years, trading at 70.36 cents to the U.S. dollar.	The Japanese government decides to send 13,000 troops to Kobe and other areas affected by the Jan. 17 earthquake and to build 1,000 temporary homes.

A	B	C	D	E
Includes developments that affect more than one world region, international organizations, and important meetings of major world leaders.	Includes all domestic and regional developments in Europe, including the Soviet Union, Turkey, Cyprus, and Malta.	Includes all domestic and regional developments in Africa and the Middle East, including Iraq and Iran and excluding Cyprus, Turkey, and Afghanistan.	Includes all domestic and regional developments in Latin America, the Caribbean, and Canada.	Includes all domestic and regional developments in Asia and Pacific nations, extending from Afghanistan through all the Pacific Islands, except Hawaii.

U.S. Politics & Social Issues	U.S. Foreign Policy & Defense	U.S. Economy & Environment	Science, Technology, & Nature	Culture, Leisure, & Lifestyle	
In Maryland, Judge Raymond G. Thieme Jr. rejects a lawsuit by former state legislator Ellen Sauerbrey (R) that sought to nullify her narrow loss to Democrat Parris Glendening in the state's 1994 gubernatorial election.		The federal government begins its program to reintroduce the endangered North American gray wolf to Yellowstone National Park in Wyoming and a wilderness area in Idaho.... The Commerce Department reports that the value of retail sales in 1994 totaled about $2.239 trillion, a 7.6% increase from the year-earlier level. The 1994 gain is the largest since 1984.		Reports confirm that a group of investors, including actor Paul Newman and novelist E. L. Doctorow, have purchased *The Nation*, a weekly magazine featuring a progressive political viewpoint. The 130-year-old publication is the oldest continuously published magazine in the U.S.	Jan. 13
			The flooding in California that extends from the Oregon border to deserts located around San Bernardino starts to recede. Statistics reveal that the disaster claimed the lives of 11 people and caused an estimated $735 million in damage. California governor Pete Wilson (R) has declared 37 of the state's 58 counties to be disaster areas, and Pres. Clinton has added 10 federal disaster areas to the ones listed Jan. 10.		Jan. 14
Figures reveal that the rate of deaths resulting from heart disease in the U.S. dropped 24.5% between 1982 and 1992, although the rate of congestive heart failure more than doubled during the same period. Heart disease still causes 42.5% of all deaths in the U.S.			A study finds that electric-utility workers who are exposed to high levels of electromagnetic radiation levels are about twice as likely to die from brain cancer as the average person in the U.S. Researchers argue, however, that the question of whether low-frequency magnetic radiation causes cancer "remains unsolved."	Vera Maxwell, 93, pioneering women's clothes designer, dies in Rincon, Puerto Rico, after a brief illness.... The San Francisco 49ers win the NFC championship over the defending champion Dallas Cowboys. The San Diego Chargers win the AFC championship over the Pittsburgh Steelers.	Jan. 15
			An unmanned Experimental Reentry Space System (Express) capsule is jointly launched by Japanese and German space agencies, but it wobbles out of orbit and splashes down in the Pacific Ocean. The capsule would have tested how reentry into the Earth's atmosphere affects different materials.	A new national television network, United Paramount Network (UPN), is launched.... The St. Louis, Missouri, Symphony orchestra names as its next music director Dutch conductor Hans Vonk.	Jan. 16
		The House clears, 390-0, the Senate's version of the Congressional Accountability Act, a bill that ends Congress's exemption from federal occupational-safety and antidiscrimination laws. It is the first bill passed by the 104th Congress.... The Federal Reserve Board notes that U.S. factories, mines, and utilities operated at 85.4% of capacity in December 1994, the highest level since October 1979.	Pres. Clinton tours flood-stricken Placer County, California, and vows to increase federal flood relief to $65 million, from the $50 million figure established earlier.... DuPont Merck Pharmaceutical reports that the FDA has approved naltrexone, a drug used to treat heroin addiction, for use in treating alcoholism.... The FDA finds that the median time required to approve 62 drugs in 1994 was 19 months, down 21% from 22.9 months in 1993.		Jan. 17
New York State Supreme Court judge Harold Rothwax sentences to 141 years and eight months in prison a Lebanese immigrant, Rashid Baz, who in December 1994 was convicted in a March 1994 shooting attack on a van carrying 15 Hasidic Jewish students over the Brooklyn Bridge in New York City.		In *NationsBank of North Carolina v. Variable Annuity Life Insurance Co.*, the Supreme Court rules unanimously to allow nationally chartered banks to sell annuities.... In *American Airlines v. Wolens*, the Supreme Court rules, 6-2, that travelers may sue airlines for breach of contract over changes made to frequent-flier programs, a decision which allows an Illinois class-action lawsuit to proceed.... At GM's AC Delco East parts-production complex, 6,500 UAW members walk off their jobs.	Researchers suggest that tuberculosis may afflict 90 million people and kill 30 million people in the 1990s if worldwide efforts to stem the spread of the disease are not improved.... Adolf Friedrich Johann Butenandt, 91, German chemist who shared the 1939 Nobel Prize for Chemistry, dies in Munich, Germany, of an undisclosed illness.... Reports confirm that a network of caves containing hundreds of apparently undisturbed paintings thought to date from 17,000 to 20,000 years ago have been discovered in southern France.	Ron Luciano, 57, former MLB umpire known for his flamboyant and combative style, is found dead in the garage of his Endicott, New York, home of carbon monoxide poisoning, an apparent suicide.	Jan. 18

F	G	H	I	J
Includes elections, federal-state relations, civil rights and liberties, crime, the judiciary, education, health care, poverty, urban affairs, and population.	Includes formation and debate of U.S. foreign and defense policies, veterans' affairs, and defense spending. (Relations with specific foreign countries are usually found under the region concerned.)	Includes business, labor, agriculture, taxation, transportation, consumer affairs, monetary and fiscal policy, natural resources, and pollution.	Includes worldwide scientific, medical, and technological developments; natural phenomena; U.S. weather; natural disasters; and accidents.	Includes the arts, religion, scholarship, communications media, sports, entertainments, fashions, fads, and social life.

	World Affairs	Europe	Africa & the Middle East	The Americas	Asia & the Pacific
Jan. 19		The presidential palace in Grozny, the capital of Chechnya, falls to Russian troops, who raise a Russian flag over the palace, one of the most potent symbols of Chechen resistance to the Russian invasion, which began in December 1994. . . . Lord Cowdray (born Weetman John Churchill Pearson), 84, the third Viscount Cowdray and heir to one of Britain's largest family fortunes, dies in Midhurst, England, of bronchial pneumonia.		After news that Mexico may hold new elections, club-wielding PRI supporters in Tabasco stage protests, claiming that the government caved in to leftist demands.	The death toll from the Jan. 17 disaster in Japan is placed at more than 4,100 and is expected to top 5,000 once the bodies of missing people are unearthed. Some 275,000 refugees are living in shelters. The quake was the most deadly to hit Japan since 1923. . . . China's *Daily* newspaper projects that China's population will top 1.2 billion by the middle of February. The population in 1994 grew by 58,000 a day.
Jan. 20		Robert Fryers and Hugh Jack are handed 25- and 40-year prison sentences, respectively, for their roles in a planned London bombing campaign. . . . The Russian ruble falls to its all-time low of 4,004 to the dollar.	South African president Nelson Mandela and deputy president F. W. de Klerk meet to heal a rift that developed between them over a secret immunity deal made in April 1994 that Mandela rejected Jan. 18. . . . Mehdi Bazargan, 87, first premier of Iran after the 1979 Islamic revolution that overthrew the monarchy of Shah Mohammed Reza Pahlevi, dies in Switzerland of heart failure.		
Jan. 21			In separate incidents, three customs employees are shot and killed in Tidjelabine, and the president of the Algerian Soccer Association is shot and killed in Algiers.		Sri Lanka Buddhist leaders boycott a meeting with Pope John Paul II and state they consider his visit an act of aggression They are reportedly angered by comments in the pope's recent book which argue that "Both the Buddhist tradition and the methods deriving from it have an almost exclusively negative soteriology, or doctrine of salvation."
Jan. 22	The interior ministers of Algeria, France, Spain, Italy, Germany, and Tunisia discuss enacting a policy of cooperation between the security forces of their countries to combat and track Islamic fundamentalist militants.	A rally protesting the Chechen invasion is held in Moscow.	Two Palestinian suicide bombers from the Gaza Strip detonate powerful explosions at a military transit point in central Israel, killing at least 18 Israeli soldiers, one Israeli civilian, and themselves. Some 65 others are injured. The terrorist group Islamic Jihad claims that two of its fighters carried out the operation in "general revenge" for Israel's killing of several Palestinians in recent months. . . . Rudy Marq, 24, the French aid worker whose release was demanded by nongovernmental relief agencies in Mogadishu, Somalia, on Jan. 12, is freed unconditionally. . . . Muslim militants shoot and kill a French businessman in Algiers.		A heavy rain falls on Kobe, the site of the Jan. 17 earthquake, prompting the evacuation of some 2,200 families threatened by landslides. Accounts state that Japan has accepted assistance from 11 of 40 countries that offered.
Jan. 23	Cuba and the 13-nation Caribbean Community (Caricom) reach agreement on broad economic and technological cooperation.	Gregorio Ordoñez, a Popular Party spokesman and outspoken critic of ETA, is shot and killed by alleged members of ETA. . . . Russia sends 200 vehicles to Grozny as reinforcements.		Canadian defense minister David Collenette disbands the Canadian Airborne Regiment, a specially trained but scandal-ridden unit of paratroopers, after amateur videotapes of the unit's brutish and racist behavior, widely shown on Canadian television, cause a public outcry.	
Jan. 24		In Chechnya, Russian forces attack Grozny with artillery, tank, and rocket fire. The village of Katiri Yurt is bombed by Russian aircraft. Three people are killed in the raid. . . . Thousands of people demonstrate in the city of San Sebastian in Spain's Basque region to protest the Jan. 23 killing of Gregorio Ordoñez. . . . In an unprecedented admission, Germany's Roman Catholic bishops state that Catholics, the Catholic Church, and other Christians in Germany share responsibility for the Holocaust since they did not act strongly enough.			Two small bombs are thrown at the motorcade of Bangladeshi prime minister Khaleda Zia as she is returning to her office in Dhaka, the capital. In another region of the capital, opposition party leaders hold a 12-hour general strike, marred by violence and bomb throwing. More than 50 people are injured in clashes between police and protesters. . . . Japan reports that its U.S. dollar-denominated trade surplus in 1994 totaled a record $121.2 billion, up 0.8% from the year-earlier figure.

A	B	C	D	E
Includes developments that affect more than one world region, international organizations, and important meetings of major world leaders.	Includes all domestic and regional developments in Europe, including the Soviet Union, Turkey, Cyprus, and Malta.	Includes all domestic and regional developments in Africa and the Middle East, including Iraq and Iran and excluding Cyprus, Turkey, and Afghanistan.	Includes all domestic and regional developments in Latin America, the Caribbean, and Canada.	Includes all domestic and regional developments in Asia and Pacific nations, extending from Afghanistan through all the Pacific Islands, except Hawaii.

U.S. Politics & Social Issues	U.S. Foreign Policy & Defense	U.S. Economy & Environment	Science, Technology, & Nature	Culture, Leisure, & Lifestyle	
	The American Legion veterans group calls for the Smithsonian to cancel its planned exhibit featuring the *Enola Gay*, the warplane that dropped an atomic bomb on Hiroshima in 1945, after learning that Air and Space Museum director Martin Harwit is revising the estimate of U.S. casualties that would have occurred if the U.S. had invaded Japan, to 63,000 from 229,000. Veterans' groups cite figures from 260,000 to 1 million.	Reports indicate that the hiring of permanent replacements has allowed continuous, 24-hour operations at the Bridgestone/Firestone tire manufacturing facilities where URW workers have been striking for six months.		When beatifying a 19th-century nun briefly excommunicated for her feminist views, Pope John Paul II asserts, "The church stands firmly against every form of discrimination which in any way compromises the equal dignity of women and men." However, he also reiterates the church's opposition to the ordination of women priests.	Jan. 19
John Coyle White, 70, chairman of the Democratic National Committee, 1978–81, dies in Washington, D.C. of pneumonia and kidney ailments.	The administration of Pres. Clinton announces that it will ease a 44-year-old trade embargo against North Korea.			The Smithsonian Institution states it has cut off access to nude photographs taken from 1900 to 1960 of college freshmen at prestigious U.S. schools. Initially the photos were taken for posture studies, but they were later used by W. H. Sheldon, who tried to correlate personality types with physical traits, which has been discredited by scientists.	Jan. 20
				Alex Groza, 68, basketball player who helped lead the University of Kentucky team to NCAA championship titles in 1948 and 1949, dies of cancer in San Diego, California.	Jan. 21
Rose Fitzgerald Kennedy, 104, the mother of Pres. John Fitzgerald Kennedy and the matriarch of one of the most prominent families in U.S. politics, dies at the family's home in Hyannisport, Massachusetts, of complications from pneumonia.		Members of the local United Auto Workers union at a GM parts plant in Flint, Michigan, approve a new contract and end their strike, which started Jan. 18.			Jan. 22
In *Schlup v. Delo*, the Supreme Court rules, 5-4, that a death-row inmate may present new evidence to prove that his execution will be "a miscarriage of justice.". . . To mark the 22nd anniversary of the *Roe v. Wade* decision, tens of thousands of abortion foes march in the capital. . . . Albertis Sydney Harrison Jr., 88, former governor of Virginia (D), 1962–66, dies in Lawrenceville, Virginia, of a heart attack.	Pres. Clinton issues an executive order that instructs 500 U.S. banks to search their files for accounts held by groups and individuals with alleged links to terrorist activity in the Middle East and to freeze any accounts found. . . . Lawyers commissioned by Atty. Gen. Janet Reno report they found no evidence to confirm allegations that aides to former president George Bush secretly facilitated arms transfers to Iraq prior to Iraq's invasion of Kuwait in 1990.	Pres. Clinton signs the Congressional Accountability Act. . . . In *McKennon v. Nashville Banner*, the Supreme Court rules unanimously that an employee dismissed due to age discrimination is entitled to back wages, even if the employer later learns that the worker engaged in misconduct on the job that would have led to a legitimate dismissal.	The Computer Emergency Response Team (CERT), a federally funded organization that monitors the global Internet, issues a formal warning to Internet users that public and private computer networks are increasingly vulnerable to illegal entry by outside intruders, known as "hackers." . . . Surgeons in Toronto, Canada, separate Nida and Hira Jamal, two two-year-old Pakistani girls who were born joined at the head.	Edward Shils, 84, internationally acclaimed sociologist who, in 1983, received the Balzan Prize, an award given to scholars in fields not recognized with Nobel Prizes, dies in Chicago, Illinois, of cancer.	Jan. 23
Pres. Clinton gives his State of the Union message, and his centrist speech draws positive responses from members of both major parties, New Jersey governor Christine Todd Whitman delivers the Republican Party's rebuttal. . . . Kermit Smith Jr., 37, convicted of the 1980 kidnapping, rape, and murder of a college cheerleader, is put to death by lethal injection in Raleigh, North Carolina. Smith is only the second white person executed for killing a black person, the seventh person executed in North Carolina, and the 260th in the nation since 1976.		The First U.S. Circuit Court of Appeals in Boston, Massachusetts, rejects a New Hampshire newspaper's claim that many of its staff journalists are not entitled to overtime pay under federal law because they are professionals. The ruling upholds a November 1993 lower court decision that ordered the paper, *The Concord Monitor*, to pay nearly $21,000 in overtime pay to 10 reporters and two photographers.	The director of California's Office of Emergency Services, Richard Andrews, estimates that the storms and flooding that started Jan. 3 caused $735 million in damage, $375 million of which was inflicted on government buildings and roads. He reveals that insured losses to private property totaled $360 million. . . . The FDA urges patients with two heart pacemaker models to undergo special fluoroscopic X-ray examinations to check for possible faulty wires.		Jan. 24

F	G	H	I	J
Includes elections, federal-state relations, civil rights and liberties, crime, the judiciary, education, health care, poverty, urban affairs, and population.	*Includes formation and debate of U.S. foreign and defense policies, veterans' affairs, and defense spending. (Relations with specific foreign countries are usually found under the region concerned.)*	*Includes business, labor, agriculture, taxation, transportation, consumer affairs, monetary and fiscal policy, natural resources, and pollution.*	*Includes worldwide scientific, medical, and technological developments; natural phenomena; U.S. weather; natural disasters; and accidents.*	*Includes the arts, religion, scholarship, communications media, sports, entertainments, fashions, fads, and social life.*

	World Affairs	Europe	Africa & the Middle East	The Americas	Asia & the Pacific
Jan. 25		General Paata Datuashvili, a former Georgian deputy defense minister, is killed, and General Giorgi Karkarashvili, a former Georgian defense minister, is seriously wounded in a shooting attack in Moscow, Russia.	PNA police officers in Gaza disclose that they arrested more than 20 Islamic Jihad militants during the previous two days. Israeli forensic experts confirm Islamic Jihad's assertion that the two Jan. 22 suicide bombers were Salah Shaker, 25, and Anwar Sukkar, 23. . . . Rebel forces attack the town of Kambia in northern Sierra Leone. Separately, the rebels kidnap seven Roman Catholic nuns, six from Italy and one from Brazil.		The death toll from the Jan. 17 earthquake in Japan is 5,063, with 61 people missing and 26,509 injured. . . . China reports that its researchers have discovered three new islets within the Paracel and Spratly island chains in the South China Sea.
Jan. 26	Holocaust survivors and political leaders from around the world gather at the former Nazi concentration camp of Auschwitz-Birkenau near Oswiecim, Poland, to commemorate the 50th anniversary of the liberation of the camp from Nazi Germany. The U.S. delegation is led by Elie Wiesel, a survivor of Auschwitz and Nobel Prize–winning author. German foreign minister Klaus Kinkel calls Auschwitz "the symbol of our deepest shame," and the German parliament remembers the victims of Auschwitz with a moment of silence.	Lt Gen. Rupert Smith of Britain arrives in Sarajevo, capital of Bosnia-Herzegovina, to assume his post as the new commander of UN peacekeeping forces in Bosnia. . . . Reports suggest former Georgian defense minister Tengiz Kitovani tried to invade territory in Abkhazia, but his forces were disarmed by Georgian head of state Eduard Shevardnadze's troops. . . . Officials state that Russian forces control two-thirds of Grozny, which is without water, heat, or electricity. Fighting also reportedly occurs in four other towns in Chechnya.	Jordan's King Hussein and Yasser Arafat, chairman of the Palestine Liberation Organization, sign a wide-ranging accord for mutual cooperation.	Fighting erupts in a mountainous region along the disputed Peruvian-Ecuadorean border. . . . Reports reveal that 6,000 U.S. troops remain in Haiti, down from a force that once totaled about 20,000.	A Chinese-made rocket carrying a U.S. telecommunications satellite explodes above its launch pad in China's Sichuan province. The explosion kills six people and injures 23 others, and it is the fifth mishap in three years to mar China's satellite-launching record. . . . Australia's first pay-television service, Galaxy, is launched.
Jan. 27	To commemorate the 50th anniversary of the liberation of the Nazi concentration camp of Auschwitz-Birkenau, Polish president Lech Walesa presides over a ceremony attended by 5,000 people, and more than 20 countries send delegates, who issue a statement condemning the events of the Holocaust as "the biggest crime in history." Heads of state attending include Czech president Vaclav Havel and German president Roman Herzog.	Sean Kelly, a member of the Provisional IRA, is ordered to serve nine life sentences in prison for his role in a 1993 bombing that killed 10 people. . . . Mediators break off Bosnian peace talks aimed at reaching an agreement between Bosnian Serbs and the Bosnian government to extend the current cease-fire, which began Jan. 1.	Black police officers barricade themselves inside the Orlando police station in Soweto, South Africa, and demand the dismissal of five white officers accused of racism. Jabulani Xaba, a black warrant officer taking part in the protest, is shot and killed by an all-white force of riot police that storm the station.	Clashes between Peruvian and Ecuadorean forces reportedly escalate. Ecuadorean president Sixto Duran Ballen declares a state of national emergency and mobilizes reserve forces.	Reports confirm that Vietnam has reasserted its claim to sovereignty over the Paracel and Spratly island chains in the South China Sea in response to the Jan. 25 statement by Chinese researchers regarding the discovery of three new islets.
Jan. 28	James P. Grant, 72, executive director of the United Nations Children's Fund from 1980 until just before his death, dies in Mount Kisco, New York, of cancer.		Officials in Guinea state that the Jan. 25 attack in Sierra Leone prompted as many as 30,000 people to flee. The refugees' accounts indicate that several people were killed in the attack and that government forces did little to protect them. . . . U.S. soldiers begin arriving in the Kenyan port of Mombasa for a mission to aid the withdrawal of UN troops from Somalia.	George Woodcock, 82, prolific and influential Canadian author who wrote or edited more than 100 books, dies in Vancouver, British Columbia, of heart ailments.	
Jan. 29		Violence breaks out at a soccer match in Italy when Vincenzo Spagnolo, 24, is attacked and killed in Genoa by supporters of rival AC Milan. Following the halftime cancellation of the match, police detain nearly 1,000 Milanese fans at the stadium. At the same time, mobs of Genoese supporters set fires, break windows, and destroy cars with Milan license plates.	South African president Nelson Mandela appoints George Fivaz, a white police general, to take over as national police commissioner. . . . An estimated 10,000 people demonstrate in Algiers in support of Pres. Zeroual and in protest of a peace plan proposed Jan. 13 by opposition groups, which the government rejected on Jan. 18.		
Jan. 30	The UN Security Council authorizes the deployment of a 6,000-member UN peacekeeping contingent to assume security responsibilities in Haiti from U.S. forces by Mar. 31.	Floods force 250,000 Dutch residents to flee their homes in what is the Netherlands' largest peacetime evacuation. . . . Italian sports officials vote to cancel all sporting events on Feb. 5 to protest the Jan. 29 murder of a soccer fan in Genoa. The suspension is reported to be the first of its kind in Italy since the end of World War II. . . . Gerald Malcolm Durrell, 70, British conservationist who was among the first to promote the role of zoos in preserving endangered species, dies in St. Helier, Jersey, of complications from a 1994 liver transplant.	A car filled with explosives detonates in Algiers, the capital of Algeria, killing 42 people and wounding 286. The bombing is the single deadliest incident in a three-year struggle between the government and militant fundamentalists. . . . Israeli forces return three desert enclaves to Jordanian sovereignty in accordance with the peace treaty signed in October 1994. . . . Three people are killed and at least 13 are wounded when militiamen from rival factions battle over a building abandoned by a UN agency in Somalia.	Peru reportedly mobilizes more than 100,000 soldiers to the disputed frontier with Ecuador.	Seven former Allied soldiers who were imprisoned in Japanese labor camps during World War II file suit in Tokyo against the Japanese government, seeking a formal written apology for their treatment. The former soldiers—from Britain, the U.S., Australia, and New Zealand—also seek "token compensation" totaling about $22,000 for each of more than 20,000 surviving former prisoners of war (POWs) in their countries.

A	B	C	D	E
Includes developments that affect more than one world region, international organizations, and important meetings of major world leaders.	Includes all domestic and regional developments in Europe, including the Soviet Union, Turkey, Cyprus, and Malta.	Includes all domestic and regional developments in Africa and the Middle East, including Iraq and Iran and excluding Cyprus, Turkey, and Afghanistan.	Includes all domestic and regional developments in Latin America, the Caribbean, and Canada.	Includes all domestic and regional developments in Asia and Pacific nations, extending from Afghanistan through all the Pacific Islands, except Hawaii.

U.S. Politics & Social Issues	U.S. Foreign Policy & Defense	U.S. Economy & Environment	Science, Technology, & Nature	Culture, Leisure, & Lifestyle	
House Republicans censure Rep. Robert K. Dornan (R, Calif.) for contending that Pres. Clinton "gave aid and comfort to the enemy" during the Vietnam War by protesting the war and making efforts to avoid being drafted. Dornan's remarks are stricken from the *Congressional Record*, and he is barred from taking part in floor debate for 24 hours. The last time the House took the step of barring a member from debate was in 1974.		Data show that sales of existing homes in 1994 totaled 3.97 million units, up 4.3% from the year-earlier level of 3.80 million. The 1994 figure is the second-highest level since 1978.	Albert William Tucker, 89, mathematician credited with establishing the foundations of linear programming, or operations research, whose students include mathematician Jack Milnor and Nobel Prize–winning economist John Forbes Nash Jr., dies in Hightstown, New Jersey, of pneumonia.	Eric Cantona of France, playing for Manchester United, jumps into the stands during a soccer game against Crystal Palace in London and attacks a spectator who reportedly taunted the French star.	Jan. 25
The six winners of the first annual Heinz Awards, established in honor of the late Sen. John Heinz (R, Pa.), are announced. The recipients are Geoffrey Canada, who runs programs for poor children and their families in Harlem; Paul and Anne Ehrlich, both environmentalists; Andrew Grove, the president and CEO of Intel; Henry Hampton, a filmmaker who produced the civil-rights documentary *Eyes on the Prize*; and James Goodby, a former diplomat who had aided in arms-control talks.	In separate cases in Miami, Florida, and Washington, D.C., Teledyne Inc., a California-based military contractor, agrees to pay a total of $13 million to the U.S. government to settle suits related to its export of zirconium to a Chilean arms maker in the 1980s. The material was eventually used in cluster bombs exported to Iraq from Chile.	The House votes, 300-132, in favor of an amendment to the Constitution that will require Congress to balance the annual budgets of the federal government, beginning in the fiscal year 2002.	Studies find that a powerful naturally occurring protein used by the body to spur nerve-cell growth has shown promise in guarding nerve cells from usually lethal damage and in regenerating damaged brain cells.		Jan. 26
Richard A. Moore, 81, TV and attorney who served as special counsel to Pres. Richard Nixon in the early 1970s and who served as ambassador to Ireland, 1989–92, dies in Washington, D.C., of prostate cancer.	Lockheed Corp. pleads guilty in U.S. District Court in Atlanta, Georgia, to charges that it gave an Egyptian legislator a $1 million bribe in 1988 as part of an eventually successful effort to secure a $79 million Egyptian government contract for three cargo jets. Lockheed agrees to pay a $24.8 million fine for violating the 1977 Foreign Corrupt Practices Act, which bars U.S. companies from extending payoffs to foreign officials.	Figures reveal that the U.S. gross domestic product grew at an inflation-adjusted annual rate of 4% in 1994. That is the highest calendar-year growth rate since 1984.		British soccer team Manchester United suspends Eric Cantona of France for the rest of the 1995 season for his Jan. 25 act. . . . At the request of Yale University, the Smithsonian Institution shreds a collection of nude photographs shut off from the public on Jan. 20.	Jan. 27
The National Governors' Association (NGA) holds its annual winter meeting in Washington, D.C., with welfare reform as the gathering's main topic of debate.	The U.S. and Vietnam sign an agreement to exchange diplomats and open liaison offices in each other's capitals. The move is the U.S.'s most significant step toward establishing full diplomatic ties with Vietnam since Pres. Clinton lifted the U.S.'s 19-year-old trade embargo against the country in February 1994.	According to the Congressional Budget Office, about $1.2 trillion in spending cuts and revenue increases will be required to balance the budget by the year 2002.		Mary Pierce of France overcomes Arantxa Sanchez Vicario of Spain to win the women's Australian Open title, her first Grand Slam victory. . . . Steve Largent, Lee Roy Selmon, Kellen Winslow, and the late Henry Jordan are elected to the Pro Football Hall of Fame in Canton, Ohio. Also inducted was the late Jim Finks, former NFL executive.	Jan. 28
		Numbers reveal that the value of orders for U.S.-made machine tools rose 42% in 1994 from 1993, to $4.676 billion. The 1994 total is the highest since 1979. . . . California's insurance commissioner, Charles Quackenbush (R), reaches agreement with Twentieth Century Industries, settling a long-running dispute over refunds mandated by a 1988 insurance-reform law. The amount of the settlement is at least $46 million.		In tennis, Andre Agassi wins the Australian Open men's title over Pete Sampras. . . . The San Francisco 49ers rout the San Diego Chargers, 49-26, in the NFL's Super Bowl XXIX in Miami, Florida. With the victory, the 49ers are the first team in National Football League history to win five Super Bowls.	Jan. 29
The CDC finds that in 1993 AIDS for the first time became the leading cause of death among all people in the U.S. ages 25–44. Unintentional injury was second, followed by cancer, heart disease, and homicides and suicides.	The secretary of the Smithsonian Institution, I. Michael Heyman, announces that the Smithsonian will drastically scale back its planned exhibit featuring the forward fuselage of the *Enola Gay*, the warplane that dropped an atomic bomb on Hiroshima, Japan, in 1945. The Smithsonian decided to change the exhibit because of criticism from veterans groups.		NIH researchers announce that clinical trials have demonstrated the effectiveness of the first preventive treatment for sickle cell anemia. The researchers state that they are issuing a clinical alert to doctors nationwide that the drug hydroxyurea should be considered for treating adult patients who suffer severe sickle cell anemia.	*The Celestine Prophecy* by James Redfield tops the bestseller list.	Jan. 30

F	G	H	I	J
Includes elections, federal-state relations, civil rights and liberties, crime, the judiciary, education, health care, poverty, urban affairs, and population.	Includes formation and debate of U.S. foreign and defense policies, veterans' affairs, and defense spending. (Relations with specific foreign countries are usually found under the region concerned.)	Includes business, labor, agriculture, taxation, transportation, consumer affairs, monetary and fiscal policy, natural resources, and pollution.	Includes worldwide scientific, medical, and technological developments; natural phenomena; U.S. weather; natural disasters; and accidents.	Includes the arts, religion, scholarship, communications media, sports, entertainments, fashions, fads, and social life.

	World Affairs	Europe	Africa & the Middle East	The Americas	Asia & the Pacific
Jan. 31		In Germany, the Rhine reaches near-record levels, flooding such cities as Coblenz, Mainz, and Bonn. In Cologne, the Rhine is 35 feet (11 m) above sea level, and the city's historic downtown area is 6 feet under water. In the French town of Charleville-Mezieres, the River Meuse reaches a record high-water mark. French premier Edouard Balladur visits the besieged town.	A spokesman for the UNHCR states that 24,000 people have fled from Sierra Leone to Guinea since Jan. 25. . . . The official Algerian news agency, APS, reports that security forces claim to have killed 28 armed fundamentalists, 15 of them in Algiers, in the previous 48 hours. Ahmed Kasmi, a member of the opposition National Liberation Front (FLN) central committee, is abducted from his mother's home.		Japan's Emperor Akihito and Empress Michiko visit Kobe, the site of the Jan. 17 earthquake. While touring shelters, the empress clasps hands with and embraces refugees. It is considered rare for a member of the Japanese royal family to have physical contact with ordinary citizens.
Feb. 1	The World Bank discloses that its president, Lewis Preston, has cancer and will retire shortly. Ernest Stern, one of the bank's three managing directors under Preston, is named acting president.	Russian forces pound the western Chechen village of Samashki with rocket, cannon, and helicopter fire. An estimated 20 people are killed and dozens wounded. . . . Rivers begin receding in France, Germany, and Belgium. The European Commission increases its immediate aid to flood victims to 1.5 million European currency units ($1.8 million). . . . Sergei Skorochkin, a member of the Russian Duma, is abducted by four masked gunmen who claim to be police officers.	Somali militiamen loyal to Gen. Mohammed Farah Aidid take over and loot the UN's Mogadishu headquarters after the last remaining peacekeeping contingent withdraws to the nearby airport. . . . TV journalist Ouari Nasser is shot and killed, becoming the 31st journalist killed in Algeria since May 1993.	In Grenada, George Brizan takes the oath as prime minister, succeeding Nicholas Braithwaite.	
Feb. 2		Sergei Skorochkin, 33, a member of the Russian Duma who was abducted Feb. 1, is found dead in a forest near the village of Sarybievo, south of Moscow.			
Feb. 3		The Irish government grants an early release to five incarcerated IRA members in an attempt to bolster the Northern Ireland peace process.	In Algeria, Ahmed Kasmi, a member of the opposition National Liberation Front (FLN) central committee, is found dead at a train station southwest of Algiers.		
Feb. 4	The G-7 finance ministers and central-bank heads meet in Toronto, Canada.	Four Gypsies in Oberwart, a city in eastern Austria, are killed while attempting to remove a booby-trapped anti-Gypsy sign. The incident is one of the country's deadliest terrorist acts since World War II. . . . Chechen forces shoot down a Russian attack jet south of Grozny, killing the pilot.	Reports disclose that between 200 and 300 white officers in Soweto, South Africa, requested transfers out of the black township, saying they were threatened by black officers.		
Feb. 5			Israel eases its restrictions on Palestinian crossings, allowing Palestinian teachers, doctors, nurses, and some merchants to resume work in Israel. . . . Jordan's King Hussein hosts 28 members of the Israeli Knesset at an unprecedented banquet in Amman, the Jordanian capital. . . . The Armed Islamic Group (GIA) claims responsibility for the Jan. 30 car bomb that killed 42 people and wounded nearly 300 in Algiers.	Peruvian president Alberto Fujimori acknowledges that Peru suffered 22 "casualties," but he does not specify the number of dead and wounded in the fighting that erupted Jan. 26 along the disputed Peruvian-Ecuadorian border.	

A	B	C	D	E
Includes developments that affect more than one world region, international organizations, and important meetings of major world leaders.	*Includes all domestic and regional developments in Europe, including the Soviet Union, Turkey, Cyprus, and Malta.*	*Includes all domestic and regional developments in Africa and the Middle East, including Iraq and Iran and excluding Cyprus, Turkey, and Afghanistan.*	*Includes all domestic and regional developments in Latin America, the Caribbean, and Canada.*	*Includes all domestic and regional developments in Asia and Pacific nations, extending from Afghanistan through all the Pacific Islands, except Hawaii.*

U.S. Politics & Social Issues	U.S. Foreign Policy & Defense	U.S. Economy & Environment	Science, Technology, & Nature	Culture, Leisure, & Lifestyle	
For the first time in Texas, two people are executed on the same day when convicted murderers Clifton Russell and Willie Williams become 88th and 89th inmates to be executed in Texas and the 262nd and 263rd in the nation to be put to death since 1976.	The FBI announces it has agreed to pay former agent Suzane J. Doucette nearly $300,000 in an out-of-court settlement of a sexual harassment lawsuit. When Doucette filed the suit in June 1993, it was the first sexual harassment case the FBI faced.... Pres. Clinton invokes presidential emergency authority to provide a $20 billion loan to Mexico to stabilize its falling currency, the peso, and to help Mexico avoid defaulting on its short-term debt.	The Department of Agriculture unveils a proposed new meat-inspection policy that will mandate scientific testing by meat-processing companies. The new policy, described as the most sweeping change in meat-industry monitoring in decades, will replace a 90-year-old method based primarily on visual inspection alone.... Preston Fleet, 60, founder of the Fotomat film-developing company, dies in Santa Barbara, California, of cancer.	Reports confirm that scientists at the Los Alamos National Laboratory have produced preliminary evidence that elusive subatomic particles called neutrinos have a small amount of mass, providing at least a partial explanation for the inability of scientists to locate about 90% of the matter thought to exist in the universe.... George Stibitz, 90, mathematician and inventor of the Model I Complex Calculator, considered the first digital computer, dies in Hanover, N.H., of natural causes.	George Francis Abbott, 107, award-winning playwright, director, and producer whose career in Broadway theater spanned more than 70 years, dies in Miami Beach, Florida, of a stroke.... The publisher Little, Brown reports that a book by O. J. Simpson that was released Jan. 27 has already gone into a second printing.	Jan. 31
The CDC estimates that 9,000 deaths each year can be attributed to food-borne diseases.... A two-year study suggests that 1,800 infants die annually from suffocation as a result of being placed on soft items such as pillows, comforters, and sheepskins.	The State Department releases to Congress its annual human-rights report based on human-rights conditions in more than 160 countries in 1994. China, with whom the U.S. is engaged in a contentious trade dispute, is rebuked in especially harsh terms. Other nations reprimanded include North Korea, Myanmar, Iraq, Iran, and Cuba.	The National Credit Union Administration seizes control of Capital Corporate Federal Credit Union in an attempt to staunch steep losses linked to derivatives contracts. The seizure marks the first time the NCUA has taken over a credit union organization since it was founded in 1970.... The Federal Open Market Committee votes unanimously to increase the federal funds rate to 6% and the discount rate to 5.25%. The Fed has raised rates seven times since February 1994.			Feb. 1
Pres. Clinton nominates Dr. Henry W. Foster Jr., a black physician and former medical school professor and administrator, as the U.S. surgeon general.	Pres. Clinton announces the 17 members of a bipartisan Commission on Roles and Capabilities of the U.S. Intelligence Community, a committee to address agency-wide failures exposed in the Ames espionage case.		Preliminary research shows that an experimental combination of the drug AZT and a new drug called 3TC provide longer suppression of the AIDS virus than other combinations of drugs.	Donald Pleasence, 75, British actor who appeared in more than 100 films, dies in St. Paul de Vence, France, after recently undergoing heart surgery.... Frederick John Perry, 85, the first tennis player to win all four Grand Slam tournaments, dies in Melbourne, Australia, of heart failure.	Feb. 2
A federal jury in Birmingham, Alabama, orders Baxter Healthcare to pay $6 million to Brenda Toole, who claims to have suffered health problems resulting from silicone-filled breast implants that ruptured in 1988.... A male nurse, Bruce Alan Young, 45, pleads guilty to raping seven anesthetized women and girls in an Inverness, Florida, hospital's surgery recovery room. Circuit Judge Hale Stancil sentences Young to 17 years in prison.		The yield on the Treasury Department's benchmark 30-year bond tumbles to 7.62%.... In Arizona, Judge Thomas Dunevan III reduces to $461.8 million, from $1.47 billion, the amount that five current directors and one former director of Amerco Inc. are required to pay to compensate for actions during a 1988 takeover battle for the company.	The U.S. space shuttle Discovery blasts off from Kennedy Space Center on a test run for future shuttle dockings with the Mir space station. The flight includes the first female air force pilot of a U.S. spacecraft, Lt. Col. Eileen M. Collins... German scientists report they have found the physical basis in the brain for perfect pitch, a rare talent that allows musicians to identify any musical note without comparison to a reference note.... Reports confirm that NIH director Dr. Harold E. Varmus has chosen Lt. Col. Wayne Jonas as director of the Office of Alternative Medicine.	Singer and actor Barbra Streisand gives a high-profile speech, entitled "The Artist as Citizen," at Harvard University's John F. Kennedy School of Government.... Baseball owners revoke the salary cap imposed late in 1994 after being informed by the NLRB that they might face a federal unfair-labor-practice charge.	Feb. 3
	U.S. trade representative Mickey Kantor announces the imposition of punitive tariffs of up to 100% on imports of a wide range of Chinese-made goods. China retaliates by slapping 100% tariffs on various U.S.-made goods exported to China.... Reports reveal a former NSC official, Howard Teicher, has charged the CIA "authorized, approved and assisted" the sale of cluster bombs to Iraq by way of a Chilean arms maker in the 1980s.			Patricia Highsmith, 74, crime novelist best known for creating the character of Tom Ripley, a refined murderer who appeared in five of her 20 novels, dies in Locarno, Switzerland, of leukemia.	Feb. 4
Chester (Chet) Holifield, 91, a 16-term Democratic congressman (Calif.), 1942–74, dies in Redlands, California, of pneumonia.				Doug McClure, 59, actor best known for the TV series The Virginian, 1962–70, dies in Sherman Oaks, California, of cancer.	Feb. 5

F	G	H	I	J
Includes elections, federal-state relations, civil rights and liberties, crime, the judiciary, education, health care, poverty, urban affairs, and population.	Includes formation and debate of U.S. foreign and defense policies, veterans' affairs, and defense spending. (Relations with specific foreign countries are usually found under the region concerned.)	Includes business, labor, agriculture, taxation, transportation, consumer affairs, monetary and fiscal policy, natural resources, and pollution.	Includes worldwide scientific, medical, and technological developments; natural phenomena; U.S. weather; natural disasters; and accidents.	Includes the arts, religion, scholarship, communications media, sports, entertainments, fashions, fads, and social life.

	World Affairs	Europe	Africa & the Middle East	The Americas	Asia & the Pacific
Feb. 6		In Great Britain, police announce that they found and dismantled four bombs, which were likely placed by animal-rights activists.	Gunmen kill an Israeli security guard on the outskirts of Gaza City.		
Feb. 7		In Chechnya, Russian forces bomb and shell villages south of Grozny, including the southwestern town of Bamut. . . . Thousands of people gather in Vienna, Austria, to protest the Feb. 4 explosion and other violent acts against Gypsies that are believed to have been committed by members of neo-Nazi "skinhead" groups.	Reports from Algeria reveal that the pesident of the FIS, Abassi Madani, and his deputy, Ali Belhadj, were transferred from house arrest to a military jail. . . . Hamas and the Democratic Front for the Liberation of Palestine claim responsibility for the Feb. 6 murder of an Israeli security guard on the outskirts of Gaza City.	Ecuadorian officials disclose that 11 of their country's soldiers died in the fighting that erupted Jan. 26 along the disputed Peruvian-Ecuadorean border.	Ramzi Ahmed Yousef, 27, who is believed to be the mastermind of the February 1993 bombing of the World Trade Center in New York City, is arrested in Islamabad, Pakistan.
Feb. 8	The UN Security Council unanimously authorizes a 7,000-member international peacekeeping contingent for Angola, the largest UN operation in Africa since troops were approved for Somalia in March 1993.	A Turkish pilot is forced to eject from his crashing F-16 fighter plane after being pursued by two Greek Mirage F1 jets. . . . Spanish premier Felipe Gonzalez rejects calls for his resignation amid charges that his government was involved in an underground antiterrorist war in the mid-1980s. . . . Dzhokhar Dudayev, the separatist president of Chechnya, declares he and his military commanders are leaving Grozny, which effectively gives control of the city to Russian forces.	The head of Nigeria's military government, Gen. Sani Abacha, fires his civilian cabinet, known as the Federal Executive Council. . . . Yasser Arafat, in accordance with his office as PNA president, issues an order establishing a state-security court that will try militants who "threaten the safety and security" of the Palestinian self-rule authority.		The Philippines accuses China of seizing part of the disputed Spratly Islands, a chain of small, uninhabited islands in the South China Sea. . . . . Ramzi Ahmed Yousef, arrested on Feb. 7 in connection with the 1993 bombing of the World Trade Center in New York City, flies from Islamabad, Pakistan, to New York City.
Feb. 9		Belgian defense minister Karel Pinxten announces that mandatory armed service for young people will be discontinued as part of the military's ongoing post–cold war downsizing.		Mexican president Ernesto Zedillo Ponce de León orders the army to launch offensive operations to capture leaders of the rebel Zapatista National Liberation Army (EZLN). Security forces seize one reputed EZLN leader in Mexico City and at least seven people in Veracruz with alleged EZLN links.	
Feb. 10	The leaders of the Commonwealth of Independent States (CIS) gather for a summit meeting in Almaty, capital of Kazakhstan, and sign a nonbinding memorandum to encourage "peace and stability" among member states.		A series of territorial transfers concludes, during which Jordan regained control of a total of more than 130 square miles (340 sq km) of land patches along the Israeli-Jordanian border that were seized by Israel in the 1967 Arab-Israeli war.	Mexican government forces, backed by air support, occupy 11 formerly EZLN towns, including Guadalupe Tepeyac in the Lacandon jungle, which serves as the rebels' headquarters. One army colonel is shot in the head by a sniper. Attorney General Antonio Lozano Gracia states that a man identified as rebel leader Jorge Javier Elorriaga Berdegue was arrested in Chiapas.	The Taliban drives the forces of Afghanistan premier Gulbuddin Hekmatyar from the town of Maidan Shahr, 18 miles (30 km) southwest of Kabul, the capital. . . . A survey finds that Singapore Airlines is the world's best overall airline.
Feb. 11	Foreign Minister Alois Mock announces that Austria has joined NATO's Partnership for Peace program, but it will likely take part in humanitarian and peacekeeping operations only.	Two groups of skinheads destroy candles lit outside a church in Vienna, Austria, in memory of the Feb. 4 bombing victims.	Officials state that the reputed director of assassinations for the Fatah Revolutionary Council, Mahmoud Khaled Eintour, alias Abu Ali Majed, was arrested in Sidon, Lebanon.		The UN's special negotiator in Afghanistan, Mahmoud Mestiri, secures the agreement of nine major mujaheddin factions on an apparent peace arrangement. The mujaheddin, or so-called soldiers of God, are waging armed resistance against the Soviet occupation that began in 1979 when Soviet troops invaded Afghanistan to prop up a communist government.

A	B	C	D	E
Includes developments that affect more than one world region, international organizations, and important meetings of major world leaders.	*Includes all domestic and regional developments in Europe, including the Soviet Union, Turkey, Cyprus, and Malta.*	*Includes all domestic and regional developments in Africa and the Middle East, including Iraq and Iran and excluding Cyprus, Turkey, and Afghanistan.*	*Includes all domestic and regional developments in Latin America, the Caribbean, and Canada.*	*Includes all domestic and regional developments in Asia and Pacific nations, extending from Afghanistan through all the Pacific Islands, except Hawaii.*

U.S. Politics & Social Issues	U.S. Foreign Policy & Defense	U.S. Economy & Environment	Science, Technology, & Nature	Culture, Leisure, & Lifestyle	
A New York City jury evenly splits the blame for the death of Libby Zion, 18, who died eight hours after being admitted to New York Hospital in 1984, between Zion herself and three of her four doctors. The decision culminates a decade-long legal struggle, which led to an overhaul in 1988 of New York State's regulation of the hours of medical residents.	National Australia Bank Ltd., Australia's largest bank, announces that it has agreed to acquire Michigan National Corp. of the U.S. for A$2.07 billion (US$1.56 billion). If approved, the transaction will be one of the largest-ever takeovers of a U.S. bank by a foreign interest.	Pres. Clinton sends to Congress a proposed $1.61 trillion budget for the fiscal year 1996. The budget details plans, first unveiled by Clinton in 1994, for a range of tax cuts designed to benefit middle-class families. . . . The House votes, 294–134, to pass a bill that will give presidents the power to cut spending out of federal budget legislation through the use of a so-called line-item veto.	Statistics reveal that about 31% of all U.S. households owns a personal computer, suggesting that 3.8 million households bought a computer since July 1994, when 27% of all households reportedly owned one.	The 1995 Bollingen Prize in American Poetry is awarded to Kenneth Koch. . . . James Ingram Merrill, 68, Pulitzer Prize–winning poet, dies in Tucson, Arizona, of a heart attack. . . . The American Library Association announces that David Diaz has won the Caldecott Medal and Sharon Creech has won the Newbery Medal.	Feb. 6
Former representative Michael Huffington (R, Calif.) officially concedes his loss to incumbent senator Dianne Feinstein (D) in a November 1994 Senate race. Final, official tallies give the victory to Feinstein by 165,562 votes out of almost 9 million cast, a margin of about 1.8%. . . . TheHouse votes, 430-0, in favor of legislation that will require people convicted of federal crimes to pay restitution to victims harmed physically, emotionally, or financially by those crimes.				Judge Daniel P. Fitzgerald sentences rap performer Tupac Shakur to 1½–4½ years in prison for sexually abusing a woman in November 1993. . . . Pres. Clinton announces that his personal efforts to end the MLB baseball players' strike was unsuccessful and that congressional intervention is likely the only way to settle the dispute.	Feb. 7
More than 500 students hold a protest rally at Rutgers University's main campus in New Brunswick, New Jersey, to call for the resignation of the school's president, Francis L. Lawrence, for remarks that suggest the "genetic, hereditary background" of disadvantaged students is linked to poor performance on college admissions exams. . . . Some Republicans and antiabortion groups continue to harangue Dr. Henry W. Foster Jr., nominated as surgeon general, for his stance on abortion and reproductive rights.	Pres. Clinton nominates Michael P. C. Carns, a retired air force general, as director of central intelligence, to succeed R. James Woolsey, who stepped down in January 1995.		A study suggests that guidelines for desirable body weight issued in 1990 by the federal government classify as acceptable weight gain levels that actually increase a middle-aged woman's chance of suffering a heart attack.	Houston Rockets basketball guard Vernon Maxwell is suspended without pay for at least 10 games and fined $20,000 for running into the stands and punching a heckling fan in Portland, Oregon. The punishment is the most severe imposed by the NBA in nearly 20 years.	Feb. 8
(James) William Fulbright, 89, Democratic senator from Arkansas, 1945–74, who, in 1946, founded the government-sponsored international student exchange program that became known as the Fulbright exchange fellowship and in 1993 was awarded the Presidential Medal of Freedom, dies in Washington, D.C., after suffering a stroke.		A federal grand jury and the federal SEC charges 17 people with violating bans on insider trading in one of the largest cases of its kind. . . . Officials from the Department of Energy admit that 9,000 people were used as subjects in 154 radiation experiments conducted by the federal government during the cold war. . . . Emilio Gabriel (Pete) Collado, 84, who was the U.S.'s first executive director of the World Bank in 1946, dies in Jupiter, Florida, of heart failure.	FBI agents arrest Abraham Jacob Alkhabaz, a University of Michigan student, for posting on the Internet a sexually violent piece of fiction that mentions a female classmate of his by name. . . . Astronauts Bernard Harris Jr. and C. Michael Foale become the first black and first Briton, respectively, to walk in space. . . . Researchers report they have duplicated symptoms of Alzheimer's disease in genetically altered mice. The achievement is hailed as a landmark in Alzheimer's research.		Feb. 9
				At the U.S. Figure Skating Championships in Providence, Rhode Island, Jenni Meno and Todd Sand win the pairs' competition, receiving six perfect scores of six for artistic interpretation, a record for U.S. pairs skaters.	Feb. 10
			The U.S. space shuttle *Discovery* touches down at Kennedy Space Center in Cape Canaveral, Florida. During the mission, the spacecraft flew to within 37 feet (11 m) of the Russian space station *Mir*. The rendezvous is considered a major step in a multibillion-dollar cooperative venture between the U.S. and Russian space agencies.	Nicole Bobek, 17, wins the women's title at the U.S. Figure Skating Championships in Providence, Rhode Island, filling a title vacant since 1994, when the U.S. Figure Skating Association stripped it from then-champion Tonya Harding for her involvement in an assault against rival skater Nancy Kerrigan.	Feb. 11

F	G	H	I	J
Includes elections, federal-state relations, civil rights and liberties, crime, the judiciary, education, health care, poverty, urban affairs, and population.	*Includes formation and debate of U.S. foreign and defense policies, veterans' affairs, and defense spending. (Relations with specific foreign countries are usually found under the region concerned.)*	*Includes business, labor, agriculture, taxation, transportation, consumer affairs, monetary and fiscal policy, natural resources, and pollution.*	*Includes worldwide scientific, medical, and technological developments; natural phenomena; U.S. weather; natural disasters; and accidents.*	*Includes the arts, religion, scholarship, communications media, sports, entertainments, fashions, fads, and social life.*

	World Affairs	Europe	Africa & the Middle East	The Americas	Asia & the Pacific
Feb. 12		Oleg Adolfovich Lyalin, 57, intelligence officer in the KGB whose defection to Great Britain in 1971 was credited with drastically curtailing Soviet spying capacities, dies of an undisclosed illness.	Algerian security forces reveal they have killed 20 militant Muslims, 10 of them in a single operation in Mascara, west of Algiers. . . . In Angola, UNITA agrees to honor the 1994 accord and to welcome the UN peacekeeping force. . . . Human Rights Watch/Middle East accuses the PNA of various human-rights violations, including arbitrary arrests and denial of press freedoms.	Pres. Ernesto Zedillo Ponce de León's Institutional Revolutionary Party (PRI) is dealt its biggest electoral setback in the party's 66 years of uninterrupted rule in Mexico, losing almost all major races in Jalisco state. The results are widely interpreted as a vote of disapproval on Zedillo's handling of the peso crisis.	
Feb. 13	The Yugoslav War Crimes Tribunal indicts Zeljko Meakic, former commander of the Omarska concentration camp run by Serbs in Bosnia, with "genocide and crimes against humanity." The indictment is the first charge of genocide ever made by an international tribunal. . . . In Germany, a ceremony to commemorate the 50th anniversary of Dresden's destruction by a controversial allied bombing raid in World War II is attended by U.S. Joint Chiefs of Staff chairman Gen. John Shalikashvili, German president Roman Herzog, the military chiefs of Britain and Germany, and the Duke of Kent, a cousin of Queen Elizabeth II.	In Sleptsovsk, in the Russian republic of Ingushetia, Col. Gen. Anatoly Kulikov, the commander of Russia's interior ministry troops, and Col. Aslan Maskhadov, the Chechen chief of staff, agree to a limited cease-fire.	Azeddine Medjoubi, the head of Algeria's national theater, is killed in Algiers.		
Feb. 14		Police in Zurich, Switzerland, close down a notorious heroin market in an effort to clamp down on the drug trade that sprung up there due to the city's liberal drug policy. . . . In Grozny, rocket and shell fire breaks out between Russian forces and Chechen rebels. Russian forces shell Chechens near the town of Alkhan Kala. . . . In Britain, the funeral of Jill Phipps, an animal-rights activist who was crushed by a truck while protesting, draws international attention, in part because it is attended by Brigitte Bardot.	About 3,000 black pupils who are bused to an unused school in the Ruyterwacht suburb of Cape Town, South Africa, are met by white protesters, some of them armed. The confrontation is among the most intense to occur since the new academic year began in mid-January. Separately, Pres. Nelson Mandela presides over the inauguration of South Africa's first Constitutional Court.	Mexican president Ernesto Zedillo Ponce de León directs the army to discontinue offensive operations ordered Feb. 9. He calls instead for a resumption of EZLN-government talks to set terms for ending the EZLN's smoldering rebellion.	The Taliban, a faction comprised of religious students who took up arms in 1994, emerges as the most powerful military force in Afghanistan when it routs Premier Gulbuddin Hekmatyar and his Hezb-e-Islami forces from their headquarters in Charasyab, 15 miles (25 km) south of Kabul. . . . U Nu, 87, first prime minister of Burma (now Myanmar), 1948–62, dies in Yangon, Myanmar, of an undisclosed illness.
Feb. 15		Russian and Chechen officials announce a short-term cease-fire agreement. . . . At a soccer match between the English and Irish national teams in Dublin, several English fans riot, reportedly to protest the ongoing Northern Ireland peace process. Nearly 60 people are treated for minor wounds. . . . Lord Taylor (born Francis Taylor), 90, British civil engineer who founded the Taylor Woodrow Group, dies in Sarasota, Florida.	The UN World Food Program estimates that civil strife in Sierra Leone displaced as many as 900,000 people either internally or as refugees in neighboring countries. . . . Nabila Djahnine, president of the feminist group The Cry of Women, is killed in Tizi-Ouzu, capital of the Kabyl region in Algeria.		Gallup Organization Inc. releases results of its first-ever poll conducted in China, and 68% of Chinese surveyed agree that their central philosophy is to "work hard and get rich," while only 4% state they follow the philosophy espoused by former long-time Chinese leader Mao Zedong urging them to "Never think of yourself, give everything in service to society."
Feb. 16		In a speech, Russian president Boris Yeltsin defends Russian military operations against separatists in the breakaway republic of Chechnya, saying that a "dictatorial regime" has taken over there. He admits, however, that human-rights violations have taken place in Chechnya and that both sides have suffered huge losses. . . . An Albanian-run university catering to Macedonia's large ethnic Albanian minority opens in Tetovo.	Burundi premier Anatole Kanyenkiko, a Tutsi, resigns. . . . In response to the busing problems that started Feb. 14 in Cape Town's Ruyterwacht suburb, South Africa education minister Martha Olckers bars the students from attending the school "because it is a health risk." The move sparks protestors to occupy the office of Western Cape premier Hernus Kriel. The sit-in is followed by a rampage of hundreds of black students through Cape Town.		
Feb. 17		In response to the Albanian-run university catering to Macedonia's large ethnic Albanian minority that opened Feb. 16, demonstrations turn violence, and one person is killed and 28 others injured. . . . In Spain, Rafael Vera, a former secretary of security, is remanded in custody for his alleged role in an organization that waged an underground antiterrorist war during the 1980s. Vera is the highest-ranking member of Premier Felipe Gonzalez's government implicated in the widening investigation.	In South Africa, Western Cape premier Hernus Kriel overturns the Feb. 16 ruling made by Education Minister Martha Olckers, saying that he will not allow racial tensions to hamper efforts to educate black students.	Peru and Ecuador sign a pact ending armed clashes that broke out Jan. 26 over a remote stretch of their long-disputed border.	

A	B	C	D	E
Includes developments that affect more than one world region, international organizations, and important meetings of major world leaders.	*Includes all domestic and regional developments in Europe, including the Soviet Union, Turkey, Cyprus, and Malta.*	*Includes all domestic and regional developments in Africa and the Middle East, including Iraq and Iran and excluding Cyprus, Turkey, and Afghanistan.*	*Includes all domestic and regional developments in Latin America, the Caribbean, and Canada.*	*Includes all domestic and regional developments in Asia and Pacific nations, extending from Afghanistan through all the Pacific Islands, except Hawaii.*

U.S. Politics & Social Issues	U.S. Foreign Policy & Defense	U.S. Economy & Environment	Science, Technology, & Nature	Culture, Leisure, & Lifestyle	
				Reports confirm that Jim Mays, a professor in Dublin, Ireland, has discovered 300 poems by 19th-century British poet Samuel Taylor Coleridge.... Todd Eldredge, 23, takes the men's title at the U.S. Figure Skating Championships in Providence, Rhode Island.	Feb. 12
In a 7-2 vote, the Supreme Court refuses to halt an Illinois court order that gives custody of an adopted boy, known as "Baby Richard," to his biological father, Otakar Kirchner.		The Council of Economic Advisers forecasts slowing economic growth in 1995 that will likely lead to lower interest rates, and also notes that surging productivity growth in recent years may herald improvements in Americans' standards of living.			Feb. 13
The House approves, 238-192, anticrime legislation that will authorize more than $10 billion in block grants for local officials. The measure will eliminate federal funding for putting 100,000 new police officers on the streets, which is the centerpiece of a $30.2 billion anticrime law signed in 1994.		Data suggest that the cost of employee health benefits paid by employers in the U.S. in 1994 declined for the first time in a decade.	In Washington, D.C., U.S. District Court judge Stanley Sporkin rejects a proposed consent decree agreed to in July 1994 between the Justice Department and Microsoft Corp. that would have settled government investigations into claims that the company engaged in anticompetitive and monopolistic behavior.	Michael V. Gazzo, 71, playwright best remembered for his groundbreaking drama A Hatful of Rain (1955), dies in Los Angeles, California, of complications from a stroke.	Feb. 14
A jury in Houston, Texas, orders Dow Corning Corp. and Dow Chemical Co. to pay $5.2 million in damages to a couple, Gladys and Robert Laas, who claim that Gladys Laas suffered neurological and other health problems resulting from leaking silicone breast implants made by the two companies. It is the first time that Dow Chemical, a parent company of Dow Corning, is found liable in a breast-implant suit.	Four soldiers in training for the U.S. Army Ranger program, considered the army's most grueling, die from hypothermia during a training exercise. The dead soldiers are Captain Milton Palmer, Second Lieutenant Spencer D. Dodge, Second Lieutenant Curt G. Sansoucie and Sergeant Norman Tillman.		FBI agents arrest Kevin Mitnick, 31, a computer expert accused of stealing thousands of data files and credit card numbers from computer systems, at his apartment in Duraleigh Hills, North Carolina. Mitnick is considered one of the world's most-wanted computer "hackers."		Feb. 15
	The House passes, 241-181, the National Security Revitalization Act, a bill that will reduce U.S. contributions to UN peacekeeping operations around the world.... Figures reveal that the U.S. Coast Guard and Florida law-enforcement officials have intercepted more than 160 Cuban refugees since Feb. 14.	Attorney General Janet Reno announces that the Justice Department has begun a preliminary criminal investigation into the financial affairs of Commerce Secretary Ronald H. Brown.	Researchers from Yale University report they have found evidence that the brains of men and women function differently when processing language.		Feb. 16
A Nassau County, New York, jury convicts Colin Ferguson on 25 counts, including second-degree murder, related to the Dec. 1993 shootings on a Long Island Rail Road train.... In New Orleans, Louisiana, Judge Okla Jones II rules that "all nicotine-dependent persons" in the U.S. may sue the tobacco industry in a class-action lawsuit.... The office of Senate minority leader Thomas Daschle (D, S.Dak.) rebuts allegations that Daschle intervened improperly after a Feb. 1994 plane crash with federal aviation inspectors to benefit a friend who owned B&L Aviation.		In Houston, Texas, Judge Katie Kennedy rejects an August 1994 agreement under which three large chemical companies agreed to reimburse U.S. homeowners who installed defective polybutylene pipes. The agreement was described as the largest property-damage settlement ever reached in the U.S.... The Commerce Department reports the U.S. recorded a $108.1 billion deficit in trade in goods and services in 1994. That is up 42% from the 1993 deficit of $75.7 billion and is the largest calendar-year gap since 1988.		Sotheby's announces that four long-missing notebooks written by 19th-century American poet Walt Whitman have been located. Among the recently found works is an early draft of the poem "Song of Myself." Sotheby's states it will return the notebooks to the Library of Congress.	Feb. 17
F	G	H	I	J	
Includes elections, federal-state relations, civil rights and liberties, crime, the judiciary, education, health care, poverty, urban affairs, and population.	Includes formation and debate of U.S. foreign and defense policies, veterans' affairs, and defense spending. (Relations with specific foreign countries are usually found under the region concerned.)	Includes business, labor, agriculture, taxation, transportation, consumer affairs, monetary and fiscal policy, natural resources, and pollution.	Includes worldwide scientific, medical, and technological developments; natural phenomena; U.S. weather; natural disasters; and accidents.	Includes the arts, religion, scholarship, communications media, sports, entertainments, fashions, fads, and social life.	

	World Affairs	Europe	Africa & the Middle East	The Americas	Asia & the Pacific
Feb. 18			The official Algerian news service reports that security forces have killed five militants suspected in the Feb. 15 slaying of Nabila Djahnine.		
Feb. 19	Serbian president Slobodan Milosevic, effectively the leader of Yugoslavia, rejects a proposal by the contact group—the U.S., Russia, Britain, France, and Germany—trying to negotiate a peace settlement in Bosnia-Herzegovina. The proposal would have lifted all UN-imposed sanctions on what remains of Yugoslavia, the republics of Serbia and Montenegro.	Sir Nicholas Fairbairn, 61, British parliamentarian who has represented the Scottish district of Perth and Kinross since 1974, dies in Dunfermline, Scotland of a liver ailment. . . . Yan Chernyak, 85, Soviet intelligence agent who served in Germany from 1930 until the end of World War II, dies in Moscow of undisclosed causes.	In South Africa, tensions over integration of schools in Cape Town's mostly white, low-income Ruyterwacht suburb continue when the entrance to the school is destroyed by an arson fire, causing about $6,000 worth of damage.		
Feb. 20		Belgian premier Jean-Luc Dehaene announces that general elections will be held seven months sooner than is required by law.			A judge in Perth, Australia, sentences Ray O'Connor, a former premier of Western Australia, to 18 months in jail for stealing a A$25,000 (US$18,500) check from the now-defunct Bond Corp. investment group in 1984. . . . The Australian Stock Exchange introduces 16 indexes designed to improve the means of evaluating the performance of small and medium-sized companies.
Feb. 21		A commission report estimates that 24,400 civilians have died in Chechnya since Russia invaded the republic in December 1994. Sergei Kovalyov, the commission's leader, claims that the figure may be as high as 30,000. . . . Ibrahim Ali, 17, is shot and killed in the southern French city of Marseille, allegedly by campaign workers for France's extremist National Front party.	Zulu chief Mangosuthu Buthelezi leads his Inkatha Freedom Party in a walkout from South Africa's multiparty parliament. He accuses the ANC and the National Party of failing to follow through on an agreement, signed in April 1994, to submit Inkatha political demands to international mediation. . . . Statistics show that, in separate reports of violence, Islamic militants have claimed responsibility for blowing up three bridges in or near Algiers and for killing at least 11 prominent citizens in the arts and civil affairs in a one-week period.	Haitian president Jean-Bertrand Aristide announces that he ordered the forced retirement of 43 senior army officers, including all of the army's generals and lieutenants. The purge effectively removes all remaining officers who held senior positions under the military-led government that ousted Aristide in 1991.	The Australian Bureau of Statistics releases the first detailed, nationwide survey of aboriginal Australians. It finds that the unemployment rate for aborigines is 38%, about four times the national average. The average aboriginal income is below the poverty line, at A$14,406 (US $10,700) annually.
Feb. 22	The UN Security Council selects Arusha, Tanzania, as the site of an international tribunal to try individuals accused of genocide and other war crimes in Rwanda. . . . A U.S.-led seven-nation force of 23 ships, 80 aircraft, and more than 14,000 soldiers assemble off the coast of Mogadishu, Somalia, to aid in the mission to pull out the peacekeepers.	Russian forces renew large-scale attacks in Chechnya, with warplanes bombing Chechen brigades in Gudermes, Argun, and Samashki and on the outskirts of Grozny. . . . The French government announces it has asked the U.S. to recall five Americans, four of them diplomats, for alleged political and economic espionage.	In Burundi, Antoine Nduwayo, a Tutsi and a member of UPRONA, is appointed premier. . . . A UN Development Program convoy is attacked by Somalis in two armed pickup trucks. One Somali is reported killed. . . . Algerian security forces quash a revolt by militant fundamentalist Muslims at the Serkadji prison in Algiers, the capital. Estimates of the number of inmates killed in the revolt vary widely.	A total of 22 observers trek along a 48-mile (80-km) segment of the Cordillera del Condor mountain range, the disputed border between Ecuador and Peru.	
Feb. 23	Russia informs the U.S. that it intends to fulfill a recent nuclear-plant contract with Iran despite U.S. objections that to do so will bolster Iran's weapons capability.	Fighting between Bosnian government forces and Muslim rebels loyal to warlord Fikret Abdic continues in the Bihac region of northwestern Bosnia, despite a Jan. 1 cease-fire.	The Algerian government states that 96 inmates died in the Feb. 22 uprising at the Serkadji prison in Algiers, and that 81 of them were prisoners charged with "terrorist" acts.	U.S. president Clinton makes his first state visit to Canada.	A Pakistani court lifts death sentences that a lower court imposed against two Christians, one a 14-year-old boy, accused of blaspheming Mohammed, the founder of Islam. Citing insufficient evidence, the Lahore High Court dismisses the blasphemy charges and releases the boy, Salamet Masih, and his uncle, Rehmat Masih.

A	B	C	D	E
Includes developments that affect more than one world region, international organizations, and important meetings of major world leaders.	*Includes all domestic and regional developments in Europe, including the Soviet Union, Turkey, Cyprus, and Malta.*	*Includes all domestic and regional developments in Africa and the Middle East, including Iraq and Iran and excluding Cyprus, Turkey, and Afghanistan.*	*Includes all domestic and regional developments in Latin America, the Caribbean, and Canada.*	*Includes all domestic and regional developments in Asia and Pacific nations, extending from Afghanistan through all the Pacific Islands, except Hawaii.*

U.S. Politics & Social Issues	U.S. Foreign Policy & Defense	U.S. Economy & Environment	Science, Technology, & Nature	Culture, Leisure, & Lifestyle	
The NAACP board of directors narrowly elects Myrlie Evers-Williams, the widow of slain civil-rights leader Medgar Evers, as the group's new chair.					Feb. 18
	A U.S. helicopter carrying five marines crashes just after takeoff from the U.S. helicopter carrier *Essex* off the coast of Somalia. Four of the marines are rescued, but Sergeant Justin Harris has yet to be found.			Calder Baynard Willingham Jr., 72, novelist and screenwriter of the film *The Graduate* (1967), dies in Laconia, New Hampshire, of lung cancer.... Sterling Marlin wins his second consecutive Daytona 500 automobile race.	Feb. 19
	U.S. military officials declare U.S. Marine sergeant Justin Harris, whose plane crashed Feb. 19, lost at sea.	The International Ladies' Garment Workers' Union (ILGWU) and the Amalgamated Clothing and Textile Workers Union (ACTWU) announce that they will merge their organizations to form UNITE, an acronym for Union of Needletrades, Industrial and Textile Employees.		Robert Bolt, 70, screenwriter and playwright who won Academy Awards for his screenplays for the films *Dr. Zhivago* (1965) and *A Man for All Seasons* (1966), dies near Petersfield, England, of heart ailments.	Feb. 20
In *O'Neal v. McAninch*, the Supreme Court, 6-3, rules that judges who are unable to determine whether a prisoner's constitutional rights were violated during a state trial should assume that they had been and order a new trial.... The Supreme Court rules, 8-1, that Amtrak, the National Railroad Passenger Corp., is a federal agency and is therefore bound by the Constitution to respect free-speech rights.... The state of Florida files suit against the tobacco industry seeking to recover $1.4 billion in state money spent through Medicaid over a five-year period to care for victims of smoking-related illnesses.	The U.S. and Mexico reach terms on a $20 billion U.S. aid package aimed at stabilizing Mexico's currency, the peso, laying a basis for a gradual recovery of the Mexican economy.	In its quarterly earnings review, *The Wall Street Journal* reports that the net income of 668 major corporations totaled $59.55 billion in the 1994 fourth quarter. That is a 61% gain over those companies' 1993 fourth-quarter profits, which totaled $37.09 billion.... Pres. Clinton promotes Laura D'Andrea Tyson, the CEA chair, to the cabinet-level post of chair of the National Economic Council (NEC). Tyson will succeed Robert E. Rubin.... The House votes, 381-44, to repeal a 1978 FCC program granting tax breaks favoring minority-owned firms that seek to purchase or establish media operations.			Feb. 21
In *Harris v. Alabama*, the Supreme Court rules, 8-1, that an Alabama law that allows judges to overrule juries' sentencing recommendations in death-penalty cases is constitutional.... A grand jury in Washington, D.C., indicts former Rep. Mary Rose Oakar (D, Ohio) on seven felony counts, including conspiracy, filing false financial reports, and lying to the FEC.	The House approves, 262-165, a $3.2 billion defense spending bill.	In *U.S. v. National Treasury Employees Union*, the Supreme Court overturns, 6-3, a federal ethics law that banned federal government employees from accepting honoraria payments for freelance speaking engagements or published articles.... The Supreme Court unanimously dismisses *Anderson v. Green*, a welfare benefits case in which a lower court declared that California's imposition of a one-year residency requirement for eligibility for full welfare benefits violates the constitutional right to travel.	The FDA approves Havrix, the first vaccine for hepatitis A, a liver infection contracted by as many as 150,000 people in the U.S. each year.... A study suggests that optic nerve decompression surgery, which is routinely performed to correct a type of vision loss that affects at least 6,000 people in the U.S. each year, is ineffective and possibly harmful.		Feb. 22
FBI agents in Dallas, Texas, arrest former Rep. Donald E. (Buz) Lukens (R, Ohio) on charges of having taken bribes from two Ohio businessmen in 1990.		Federal prosecutors in New York City announce they have charged three men with arranging a kickback scheme valued at $262,000 with a New Jersey bank seeking to win municipal-bond business from that state in 1990. The case is the most significant to date in the federal government's probe, unveiled in May 1993.... The Dow crosses the psychologically important 4,000-point level for the first time, rising 30.28 points to close at 4003.33.		Melvin Franklin, 52, original member of the music group the Temptations, dies in Los Angeles, California, of heart failure.... James Herriot (born James Alfred Wight), 78, British author of *All Creatures Great and Small* (1974), dies in Yorkshire, England, of cancer.	Feb. 23

F	G	H	I	J
Includes elections, federal-state relations, civil rights and liberties, crime, the judiciary, education, health care, poverty, urban affairs, and population.	Includes formation and debate of U.S. foreign and defense policies, veterans' affairs, and defense spending. (Relations with specific foreign countries are usually found under the region concerned.)	Includes business, labor, agriculture, taxation, transportation, consumer affairs, monetary and fiscal policy, natural resources, and pollution.	Includes worldwide scientific, medical, and technological developments; natural phenomena; U.S. weather; natural disasters; and accidents.	Includes the arts, religion, scholarship, communications media, sports, entertainments, fashions, fads, and social life.

	World Affairs	Europe	Africa & the Middle East	The Americas	Asia & the Pacific
Feb. 24		German interior minister Manfred Kanther bans two neo-Nazi groups after a constitutional court ruled that the organizations are not true political parties. The German government has banned at least four neo-Nazi groups in an effort to cut down on right-wing violence, which, since 1990, has caused the deaths of 30 people, mostly foreigners. Separately, 11,000 members of Germany's largest trade union, IG Metall, go on strike.	UN troops continue boarding planes out of Somalia, and numbers indicate that 4,000 of the 7,900 peacekeepers who were in Somalia in early February remain in the country.	During U.S. president Clinton's visit to Canada, Canada and the U.S. sign a so-called open-skies pact to reduce restrictions on air travel between the countries.	
Feb. 25		In what is called an accidental explosion, 25 Russian soldiers and security service staff are killed in Mozdok, the Russian military headquarters near Grozny, the capital of Chechnya.		Mexican federal agents arrest Othon Cortes Vazquez as an alleged second gunman in the March 1994 slaying of the then-presidential candidate of the ruling PRI party, Luis Donaldo Colosio Murrieta. The arrest signals the apparent determination to reexamine the conclusions made by the previous government that Colosio was murdered by a lone, demented assassin.	In Pakistan, masked gunmen kill 20 Shi'ite Muslims at two mosques in Karachi.... Twelve prominent intellectual dissidents issue a statement urging the parliament to take bold steps to combat corruption in China.... O Jin U, 77, North Korean defense minister who had led the country's army since 1976 and was a leading military figure in the Korean War, dies of cancer.
Feb. 26	Officials from the Group of Seven (G-7) leading industrialized nations pledge to work together closely in developing and building the so-called information superhighway worldwide.	Barings PLC, Britain's oldest merchant bank, declares bankruptcy after discovering that the firm's chief trader in Singapore, Nicholas Leeson, lost approximately £625 million ($1 billion) of the bank's assets on unauthorized futures and options transactions.	Yemen and Saudi Arabia sign an accord that reaffirms the 1934 Taif agreement after month-long talks aimed at settling their 60-year-old border dispute.... The heaviest fighting among Somali factions in recent weeks erupts near the airport, halting the retreat of UN troops. At least one Somali is reported dead.		Pakistani police state they have arrested 36 members of radical Sunni Muslim religious organizations suspected in the Feb. 25 attack.
Feb. 27	In an investigation into the so-called Agusta affair, Willy Claes, the secretary general of NATO, voluntarily submits to questioning to clarify what he knew about alleged bribes paid to the Belgian Socialist Party in 1988 by Italian aircraft manufacturer Agusta S.p.A.... Max van der Stoel, a former Dutch foreign minister monitoring the rights situation in Iraq for the UN Commission on Human Rights, characterizes Iraq as among "the worst offenders of human rights since the Second World War."	Reports state that the predominantly Muslim Bosnian government is restricting the movement of UN troops on government-controlled territory, straining already tense relations between the Bosnian government and the UN mission.... Bernard Cornfeld, 67, international financier noted for his flamboyant and hedonistic lifestyle, dies in London, England, of complications from a 1994 stroke.	Israel deports to Jordan a Palestinian police officer it recently charged with attacks on Israelis and Palestinian collaborators. The deportation is the first of its kind since Palestinian rule was established in Gaza and Jericho in May 1994.... A powerful car bomb rips through the market district of the Kurdish-controlled city of Zakho in northern Iraq, killing more than 50 people and injuring scores of others.		Luis Roldan, former chief of Spain's paramilitary Civil Guard police force, is detained in Laos after a massive 10-month manhunt.... A group of Chinese dissidents issues two statements calling for the establishment of democracy and the guarantee of basic human rights and justice in China.
Feb. 28	A UN force of 1,800 U.S. Marines and 400 Italian soldiers arrive in Mogadishu, Somalia, to aid in the mission to pull out the peacekeepers, and 900 Bangladeshi troops sail from Mogadishu for Tanzania.... Johan Delanghe, top advisor in 1988 to Willy Claes, the NATO secretary general, is arrested in connection with the Agusta scandal.	Luis Roldan, former chief of Spain's paramilitary Civil Guard police force, is returned to Spain by Laos. Roldan fled Spanish charges of economic offenses, and the subsequent investigation uncovered widespread corruption in the interior ministry and sparked a massive scandal.	Reports reveal that the PNA has denounced the Feb. 27 deportation by Israel as a violation of the PLO's accord with Israel.... Amnesty International finds that Kurdish political forces of all ideological persuasions are guilty of widespread human-rights violations in northern Iraq.	Raul Salinas de Gortari, the brother of former Mexican president Carlos Salinas de Gortari, is arrested and charged with planning and arranging the assassination in September 1994 of Jose Francisco Ruiz Massieu, the secretary general of the ruling Institutional Revolutionary Party (PRI). The charges shock most Mexicans.	
March 1		Premier Waldemar Pawlak steps down after losing a vote of confidence in the Polish parliament. ... Pres. Leonid Kuchma announces the resignation of Ukraine's premier, Vitaly Masol. He is replaced by First Deputy Premier Yevhen Marchuk, former head of Ukraine's secret security service.... Vladislav Listyev, 38, general director of Russia's largest state-owned TV channel and one of the country's most famous personalities, is shot to death in Moscow. Police link the murder to organized crime.	About 1,500 Pakistani soldiers pull out of Mogadishu, Somalia, leaving the airport unguarded by international forces for the first time since December 1992. Hundreds of looters move in but are routed by forces loyal to Gen. Mohammed Farah Aidid. His seizure of the airport flouts an accord to hold the airport by a coalition of clan officials.... Police detectives raid the home and offices of Winnie Mandela, the estranged wife of South African president Nelson Mandela, in search of evidence to support allegations of fraud.		

A	B	C	D	E
Includes developments that affect more than one world region, international organizations, and important meetings of major world leaders.	Includes all domestic and regional developments in Europe, including the Soviet Union, Turkey, Cyprus, and Malta.	Includes all domestic and regional developments in Africa and the Middle East, including Iraq and Iran and excluding Cyprus, Turkey, and Afghanistan.	Includes all domestic and regional developments in Latin America, the Caribbean, and Canada.	Includes all domestic and regional developments in Asia and Pacific nations, extending from Afghanistan through all the Pacific Islands, except Hawaii.

U.S. Politics & Social Issues	U.S. Foreign Policy & Defense	U.S. Economy & Environment	Science, Technology, & Nature	Culture, Leisure, & Lifestyle	
	The Clinton administration announces it has declassified as many as 800,000 photographs taken by U.S. spy satellites between 1960 and 1972. The move marks the first time that the U.S. government makes public any surveillance satellite photographs.	The Dow rises 8.41 points to close at 4011.74, its highest closing level ever.	Researchers report that they isolated the first biological clock gene in plants. Experiments in the past have shown that many biological functions in plants and animals are governed by an unexplained internal biological clock.	Greg Louganis, 35, four-time Olympic diving gold medalist and the only male diver ever to win double gold medals at consecutive Olympic Games, acknowledges that he has AIDS.	Feb. 24
				Jack Clayton, 73, British film director best known for *Room at the Top* (1959), dies in Slough, England, of heart and liver ailments. . . . Boxer Gerald McClellan, 27, is hospitalized after being knocked out by Nigel Benn of Great Britain during a bout in London. The brutality of the fight and McClellan's subsequent hospitalization lead to a call for a ban on boxing.	Feb. 25
	Trade negotiators from the U.S. and China sign an accord designed to end a long-running dispute over the Chinese government's inability to halt the widespread production in China of so-called pirated goods—illegal copies of goods protected by international and domestic copyright regulations. The agreement is signed the day that punitive tariffs, announced on Feb. 4, were to go into effect.			The National Book Critics Circle announces its annual awards have gone to Carol Shields for fiction, Lynn H. Nicholas for general nonfiction, Mikal Gilmore for biography, Gerald Early for criticism, and Mark Rudman for poetry.	Feb. 26
		Treasury Secretary Robert E. Rubin unveils a wide-ranging plan to overhaul the nation's complex bank-regulation laws.		*The Celestine Prophecy* by James Redfield tops the bestseller list.	Feb. 27
		The House passes, 286-141, the Risk Assessment and Cost-Benefit Act of 1995, a comprehensive bill that will severely limit the federal government's ability to impose environmental, health and occupational-safety regulations on U.S. industries. . . . In *Gustafson v. Alloyed Co. Inc.*, the Supreme Court rules, 5-4, that a key protection offered to investors under a 1933 statute extends only to those who purchase stock in an initial public offering.	Denver International Airport, the first major commercial airport to be built in the U.S. in 20 years, officially opens. It is the nation's largest airport, covering 53 square miles (137 sq km) of land about 23 miles (40 km) northwest of Denver, Colorado.		Feb. 28
In *Arizona v. Evans*, the Supreme Court, 7-2, rules that evidence obtained by police officers who acted on an invalid arrest warrant can be introduced at trial. . . . Richard Bailey, a former horse trainer accused of soliciting the murder of candy heiress Helen Vorhees Brach, pleads guilty in a federal court in Chicago to a series of charges against him, including racketeering and solicitation of murder, but denies involvement in Brach's murder.	Pres. Clinton's administration downgrades Colombia's rating as an antidrug partner. While the evaluation, issued by the State Department, leaves U.S. aid to Colombia intact, it marks the first time in the report's eight-year history that Colombia has received less than an unqualified certification of its drug-fighting activities. The report draws an angry defense from the Colombian government.	The Commerce Department reports that U.S. gross domestic product grew at a revised annual rate of 4.6% in the 1994 fourth quarter. That compares with an annualized GDP gain of 4% in the third quarter. The U.S. economy in the 1994 calendar year grew at a 4% annual rate, its largest expansion in 10 years.	German entertainment conglomerate Bertelsmann AG announces that it will enter into a joint venture with America Online Inc. of the U.S. to create an on-line computer service in Britain, France, and Germany. . . . Georges J. F. Koehler, 48, German biologist who shared the 1984 Nobel Prize in Medicine and is noted for his techniques in vaccinations, dies in Freiburg, Germany, of heart failure.	At the Grammys, Bruce Springsteen is a big winner, picking up four awards, including best song of the year, best male rock vocal, and best rock song. Singer Tony Bennett wins two Grammys, including the best album of the year, and Sheryl Crow wins three awards, including best record and best new artist.	March 1

F	G	H	I	J
Includes elections, federal-state relations, civil rights and liberties, crime, the judiciary, education, health care, poverty, urban affairs, and population.	*Includes formation and debate of U.S. foreign and defense policies, veterans' affairs, and defense spending. (Relations with specific foreign countries are usually found under the region concerned.)*	*Includes business, labor, agriculture, taxation, transportation, consumer affairs, monetary and fiscal policy, natural resources, and pollution.*	*Includes worldwide scientific, medical, and technological developments; natural phenomena; U.S. weather; natural disasters; and accidents.*	*Includes the arts, religion, scholarship, communications media, sports, entertainments, fashions, fads, and social life.*

	World Affairs	Europe	Africa & the Middle East	The Americas	Asia & the Pacific
March 2		Seven-time Italian premier Giulio Andreotti is indicted for his alleged ties to the Mafia.... Reports confirm that a UN High Commissioner for Refugees (UNHCR) convoy rescued 62 civilians from the isolated Muslim enclave of Gorazde.... Ukrainian authorities disclose they have arrested two doctors accused of stealing newborn babies from Ukrainian parents and selling them to foreigners for adoption abroad.	About 400 Italian soldiers and the remaining Pakistani peacekeepers, along with U.S. military hardware used by the UN, are evacuated from Mogadishu, Somalia.	Jorge Eliecer Rodriguez Orejuela, the brother of Miguel and Gilberto Rodriguez Orejuela, the alleged Cali kingpins, is arrested in Colombia. He reportedly is seized during a wide-ranging sweep carried out by 3,000 police and soldiers that net about 60 other drug-related detentions.... Eric Lamothe, 50, a pro-Aristide member of the Chamber of Deputies, is found dead in his car in Port-au-Prince, Haiti, with two bullet wounds to the head.	
March 3		The House of Commons unanimously passes a bill that largely prohibits game hunting in Britain. ... Tens of thousands of mourners wait outside the Ostankino TV network's Moscow headquarters for hours for a chance to pay their respects to Vladislav Listyev, who was killed Mar. 1. Listyev's execution reportedly causes the greatest display of public mourning in Russia since human-rights activist Andrei D. Sakharov died in 1989.	The last remaining 2,400 UN peacekeeping troops in Somalia depart from a beach in south Mogadishu. Several Somalis are killed by marine gunfire as the last U.S. soldiers depart.	Former Mexican president Carlos Salinas begins a hunger strike, asserting that he will end it only if he is granted meetings with key officials of Pres. Zedillo's government.... In an article, former commander Adolfo Francisco Scilingo, a retired naval officer, alleges that hundreds of leftist "subversives" were drowned during the later 1970s as part of the military dictatorship's "dirty war" against political opponents in Argentina.... In Haiti, a member of a peasant organization that supports Jean-Bertrand Aristide is killed.	
March 4			Pierre-Claver Rwangabo, a moderate Hutu and governor of Rwanda's southern province of Butare, is shot and killed.		
March 5		The AP reports that Russian forces have captured a key road between the Chechen-held villages of Samashki and Achkhoy-Martan, effectively isolating rebels in Samashky.... Voters in Estonia oust the ruling Fatherland Party of reformers and replace it with former communists from the Coalition Party and politicians from the Rural Peoples' Union in general elections.	Inkatha agrees at a party meeting to end its boycott of South Africa's multiparty parliament, which the group started Feb. 21.	Former Mexican president Salinas ends the hunger strike started Mar. 3 after Pres. Zedillo reportedly agrees to publicly absolve him of sole responsibility for having caused Mexico's economic crisis and for having blocked probes into the March 1994 killing of Luis Donaldo Colosio Murrieta.	
March 6	The first UN World Summit on Social Development convenes in Copenhagen, Denmark, attracting 118 presidents, vice presidents, and premiers and at least 13,000 other attendees.... Reports confirm that the G-7 has pledged $4 billion to Ukraine, partly to help dismantle its nuclear weapons.... The EU and Turkey agree to establish a trade alliance.	Reports suggest that Russian forces in Chechnya have driven out the last remaining rebels in Grozny.... Robert Hughes, a junior minister in Britain's Office of Public Service and Science, becomes the 13th member of P.M. Major's Conservative Party government to resign since 1990.... The Dutch financial conglomerate ING announces it will buy most of Barings, a 233-year-old British bank that collapsed.		Reports indicate that violence is escalating in Guatemala and that dead bodies are being discovered each day on the streets of Guatemala City, the capital.	
March 7		Paul-Emile Victor, 87, French polar explorer who first gained fame in 1936 when he crossed Greenland on a dog-drawn sled, dies on Bora-Bora, French Polynesia, of heart ailments.		Longshoremen at ports on both the east and west coasts of Canada begin strikes in disputes with shipping lines over work procedures, job security, and retirement payments. The Montreal labor conflict is the first at that port in 20 years.	Thirteen influential Chinese exiles send an appeal to the congress on behalf of human-rights petitioners, arguing that the parliament should seek to fulfill the dissidents' requests.

A	B	C	D	E
Includes developments that affect more than one world region, international organizations, and important meetings of major world leaders.	Includes all domestic and regional developments in Europe, including the Soviet Union, Turkey, Cyprus, and Malta.	Includes all domestic and regional developments in Africa and the Middle East, including Iraq and Iran and excluding Cyprus, Turkey, and Afghanistan.	Includes all domestic and regional developments in Latin America, the Caribbean, and Canada.	Includes all domestic and regional developments in Asia and Pacific nations, extending from Afghanistan through all the Pacific Islands, except Hawaii.

U.S. Politics & Social Issues	U.S. Foreign Policy & Defense	U.S. Economy & Environment	Science, Technology, & Nature	Culture, Leisure, & Lifestyle	
Under California's "three strikes and you're out" law, Los Angeles Superior Court judge Donald Pitts sentences Jerry Dewayne Williams, 27, to 25 years to life in prison for stealing a slice of pizza from a group of children. The petty theft charge was upgraded to a felony due to Williams's previous convictions. . . . CDC officials report that for the first time they have documented a case of tuberculosis transmitted from one passenger to others aboard a commercial airliner.		A proposed constitutional amendment that would put pressure on Congress to balance the annual federal budget falls just one vote short of the two-thirds majority needed to win passage in the Senate. Sen. Mark Hatfield (R, Oreg.) becomes the only Republican to vote against the measure.	In a historic finding, two competing teams of scientists announce they have found the top quark, the last unknown among the six quark particles thought to be the building blocks of matter. . . . The U.S. space shuttle *Endeavour* blasts off from Kennedy Space Center. . . . Researchers reveal that intermittent infusions of interleukin-2 into the bloodstreams of patients infected with HIV increase the body's production of infection-fighting CD4 lymphocyte cells.	Twenty-seven of 28 MLB clubs begin their circuit of spring-training exhibition games. The Baltimore Orioles does not field a team because its owner, Peter Angelos, refuses to hire replacement players.	March 2
Sen. Ben Nighthorse Campbell, a Colorado Democrat in his first Senate term, announces that he will join the Republican Party, giving the GOP 54 seats in the Senate. . . . Supreme Court justice John Paul Stevens states that officials from Chicago may go ahead with their 1992 plan to ban the sale of spray paint within the city's limits in an effort to curb vandalism. . . . Federal judge Robert Krupansky for the Sixth U.S. Circuit Court of Appeals puts the Cleveland, Ohio, public school system, which is nearly bankrupt, under state control.	U.S. authorities arrest former Mexican deputy attorney general Mario Ruiz Massieu, 44, in Newark, New Jersey, charging him with failing to report that he is carrying $46,000 in cash.	Former representative Mary Rose Oakar (D, Ohio) pleads guilty to seven felony counts, stemming from a federal investigation into the misuse of the now-defunct House Bank. . . . The House passes, 277-141, the Job Creation and Wage Enhancement Act, a package of legislation regarding government regulation practices.	During the *Endeavour* mission, the *Astro-2* observes a stellar explosion, or nova, called Nova Aquilae in the constellation Aquila. . . . R(ussell) E(arl) Marker, 92, chemist who discovered a means of producing a synthetic form of the female hormone progesterone, dies in Wernersville, Pennsylvania, of complications from a broken hip.	Howard William Hunter, 87, who was appointed as leader of the Mormon Church in June 1994, dies in Salt Lake City, Utah, of prostate cancer. . . . The director-designate of the U.S. Holocaust Museum in Washington, D.C., Steven T. Katz, resigns, citing recent news reports of reprimands he received while on the faculty of Cornell University.	March 3
The family of slain civil-rights leader Martin Luther King Jr., in a truce with the U.S. Park Service, reopens King's Atlanta, Georgia, birthplace and tomb to free tours conducted by the service. The family had barred the Park Service in late December 1994. . . . James Bryan McMillan, 78, judge who helped establish a national standard for school desegregation in the U.S. with a 1969 decision that ordered an extensive cross-town busing program in a Charlotte, N.C., school district, dies in Charlotte of cancer.				At an Atlanta, Georgia, indoor track-and-field competition, Michael Johnson of the U.S., runs the 400-meter race in 44.63 seconds, setting a new indoor world record. Also from the U.S., Lance Deal throws the 35-pound (16-kg) weight 84 feet, 10 inches (25.9 m), beating his previous world mark of 81 feet, 8.5 inches (24.9 m).	March 4
Reports indicate that several Supreme Court justices and federal judges accepted gifts from a legal publishing company that has cases pending in lower courts. West Publishing Co. of Eagan, Minnesota, reportedly offered lavish trips to justices and judges who helped the company choose a recipient for its annual Edward J. Devitt Distinguished Service to Justice Award.	Representatives announce a $1 billion deal that Houston, Texas-based Conoco Inc. signed to develop two Iranian oil fields and construct a natural-gas pipeline.		NASA reports that more than 350,000 requests for information have been logged since the *Endeavour* lifted off Mar. 2. During the *Endeavour* mission, NASA for the first time is offering public computer access via the Internet, a global computer network.	The one Australia yacht sinks in the Pacific Ocean during a challengers' semifinal race against Team New Zealand. The yacht's sinking is described as the most dramatic in the 144-year history of America's Cup.	March 5
		In *Curtiss-Wright Corp. v. Schoonejongen*. the Supreme Court rules unanimously that companies have the right to amend employee-benefit plans, even if the change terminates medical benefits for retired workers. . . . In *Mastrobuono v. Shearson Lehman Hutton*, the Supreme Court rules, 8-1, that arbitrators have the authority to award punitive damages to investors.			March 6
New York governor George Pataki (R) signs into law a measure reinstating the death penalty in New York state. By signing the bill, New York becomes the 38th state to currently have capital punishment. . . . The House passes, 232-193, the Attorney Accountability Act, a bill which will apply a "loser pays" principle in some lawsuits to discourage frivolous claims by plaintiffs and to encourage others to settle their cases out of court.		The U.S. dollar plunges to post-World War II lows against the world's two other major currencies, the German mark and the Japanese yen.	During the *Endeavour* mission, telescopes observe the collision of two galaxies about 90 million light years from Earth. Each of the galaxies is about 100 light years in diameter and is thought to have 20 billion times the mass of the sun.	Leon Day, Richie Ashburn, William Hulbert, and Vic Willis are elected to enter the Baseball Hall of Fame, in Cooperstown, New York.	March 7

F	G	H	I	J
Includes elections, federal-state relations, civil rights and liberties, crime, the judiciary, education, health care, poverty, urban affairs, and population.	Includes formation and debate of U.S. foreign and defense policies, veterans' affairs, and defense spending. (Relations with specific foreign countries are usually found under the region concerned.)	Includes business, labor, agriculture, taxation, transportation, consumer affairs, monetary and fiscal policy, natural resources, and pollution.	Includes worldwide scientific, medical, and technological developments; natural phenomena; U.S. weather; natural disasters; and accidents.	Includes the arts, religion, scholarship, communications media, sports, entertainments, fashions, fads, and social life.

	World Affairs	Europe	Africa & the Middle East	The Americas	Asia & the Pacific
March 8	At the first UN World Summit on Social Development, delegates mark International Women's Day. . . . The UN Human Rights Commission rejects an unprecedented measure to censure China for its human-rights record. It votes to condemn several governments, including Sudan and Iran, for their poor human-rights records.	The Greek parliament elects Costis Stefanopoulos to be the country's president, a largely ceremonial position. . . . British home secretary Michael Howard announces that 16 people banned from entering the British mainland from Northern Ireland will also be given the freedom to travel where they wish. All of the people banned from travel are suspected terrorists.			Two Americans, Jackie van Landingham, 33, and Gary C. Durell, 45, are killed and another one, Mark McCloy, is wounded when drive-by gunmen open fire on a van taking the three to the U.S. consulate in Karachi, Pakistan's financial and commercial hub.
March 9	Canadian authorities capture a Spanish trawler off the coast of Newfoundland and arrest the ship's captain. The incident aggravates long-simmering international tensions over fishing rights in the North Atlantic Ocean. . . . Officials from the U.S., South Korea, and Japan announce the establishment of the Korean Peninsula Energy Development Organization, a multinational consortium that will control the raising of funds to complete the nuclear-replacement project.	Queen Elizabeth II makes her first visit to Northern Ireland since the IRA declared a cease-fire in August 1994. . . . Members of Germany's largest trade union, IG Metall, ratify a two-year labor contract, ending a limited strike that started Feb. 24. . . . Reports reveal that war crimes were committed by all sides in the war in Bosnia-Herzegovina, but 90% of the "ethnic cleansing," or the deliberate elimination of an ethnic group through murder, forcible expulsion, and persecution, was carried out by Serbs.			
March 10	Japan holds a memorial service marking the 50th anniversary of the Allied firebombing of Tokyo during World War II. The service is attended by several people, including Walter Mondale, the first U.S. ambassador ever to attend a public ceremony commemorating the firebombing. He apologizes for the attack, which he describes as "that great human tragedy."		A car bomb explodes in Algiers, the capital of Algeria, near a residence for police and their families. At least 63 people are injured. . . . Nigeria's military government confirms for the first time that it had foiled a coup attempt and detained 29 military officers and some civilians in connection with the planned coup. . . . Mattityahu Peled, 71, Israeli army general and member of Israel's Knesset, 1984–88, dies of cancer.	Brazil's central bank devalues the nation's eight-month-old currency, the real, altering the real's trading band for the second time in less than a week.	
March 11		Nursultan Nazarbayev, the president of Kazakhstan, dissolves the country's parliament and states he will rule by decree until new elections can be held. The government resigns. . . . Police in Zurich, Switzerland, report they have arrested about 200 heroin dealers, many of them foreigners who were deported, since the Feb. 14 shutdown of a notorious heroin market. . . . Gunfire and mortar attacks erupt in Sarajevo.	In Burundi, Energy Minister Ernest Kabusheye, a moderate Hutu, is assassinated.		India's ruling Congress (I) Party loses control of parliaments in the country's two most industrialized states in elections.
March 12	U.S. president Clinton nominates James Wolfensohn as the new president of the World Bank. . . . About 6,000 angry Canadians gather in St. John's, Newfoundland, to meet the *Estai*, the Spanish trawler seized Mar. 9. The Canadians shout and throw eggs at the captain, Enrique Davila Gonzalez, and at EU representatives and ambassadors.	As gunfire and shelling continue in Sarajevo, six people are killed and seven wounded in the worst violence since a general cease-fire took effect in Bosnia on Jan 1. . . . Riots erupt when gunmen open fire on several Alawite Muslims in Istanbul, killing two. . . . Croatian president Franjo Tudjman agrees to a new mandate to allow UN peacekeeping forces to remain in Croatia after Mar. 31, the scheduled expiration date.	Data show that several donor nations have failed to honor pledges they made in November 1994 for an emergency fund aimed at meeting the PNA's operating expenses through March 1995. The shortfall, which reportedly leaves the fund depleted, jeopardizes salary payments to the PNA's 24,000 employees.		
March 13	The first UN World Summit on Social Development closes, and delegates from more than 180 countries endorse by consensus a plan aimed at eradicating poverty worldwide and combating social injustice.	In Baku, the capital of Azerbaijan, the forces of Rovshan Javadov take over a police station. Street fighting erupts, killing several people. . . . Cuban president Fidel Castro Ruz makes his first visit to France since the early 1960s. . . . In Bosnia, gunfire breaks out at the Sarajevo airport while a plane tries pick up Indonesian president Suharto. . . . Odette Hallowes (born Odette Marie Celine Brailly), 82, British special operations agent who was tortured by the Gestapo and became the first woman awarded Britain's George Cross medal, dies in Walton-on-Thames, England.	In Burundi, Lucien Sakubu, a Tutsi adviser to the interior ministry and a former mayor of Bujumbura, is kidnapped. . . . Retired general Olusegun Obasanjo is arrested near Lagos in connection with the alleged coup plot the Nigerian government disclosed on Mar. 10.	A UN mission monitoring human rights in Guatemala decries the Guatemalan government for its failure to prosecute security officials who allegedly were involved in widespread rights abuses, including death-squad operations and drug trafficking. . . . About 480 foremen of the International Longshoremen's and Warehousemen's Union go on strike in Vancouver, British Columbia, and other ports on Canada's Pacific coast.	

A	B	C	D	E
Includes developments that affect more than one world region, international organizations, and important meetings of major world leaders.	Includes all domestic and regional developments in Europe, including the Soviet Union, Turkey, Cyprus, and Malta.	Includes all domestic and regional developments in Africa and the Middle East, including Iraq and Iran and excluding Cyprus, Turkey, and Afghanistan.	Includes all domestic and regional developments in Latin America, the Caribbean, and Canada.	Includes all domestic and regional developments in Asia and Pacific nations, extending from Afghanistan through all the Pacific Islands, except Hawaii.

U.S. Politics & Social Issues	U.S. Foreign Policy & Defense	U.S. Economy & Environment	Science, Technology, & Nature	Culture, Leisure, & Lifestyle	
		Pres. Clinton issues an executive order that prohibits the federal government from offering contracts to companies that hire permanent replacements for workers who are legally on strike.... The House clears, 325-99, the Securities Litigation Reform Act, which is designed to discourage shareholders from filing lawsuits that unfairly charge companies with securities fraud when the price of the companies' stock declines.	Heavy rains begin in California.... A study finds that infants who live in homes where people smoke tobacco products are more than twice as likely to die of SIDS as infants in smoke-free homes.... A jury rules in favor of IBM in a lawsuit brought by Nancy Urbanski, who claims that her use of the company's keyboards caused repetitive stress injuries (RSI). The case is the first RSI-liability suit against IBM to go to trial and is watched as a potential benchmark for pending RSI suits.	Paul George Vincent O'Shaughnessy Horgan, 91, Pulitzer Prize-winning author, dies in Middletown, Connecticut, of cardiac arrest.... Reports state the John M. Templeton Prize for Progress in Religion will go to physicist Paul Davies.... At the World Figure Skating Championships, in Birmingham, England, Czechs Radka Kovarikova and Rene Novotny win the gold in pairs.	March 8
		Neal Ainley pleads not guilty on five felony counts stemming from an investigation by prosecutor Kenneth Starr into the Whitewater affair.... Six large securities firms release details of a plan in which they volunteer to submit their currently unregulated derivatives operations to federal scrutiny.... Edward L. Bernays, 103, the "father of public relations" whose clients included Procter & Gamble, GE, GM, and American Tobacco, dies in Cambridge, Massachusetts, of bladder cancer.	During the *Endeavour* mission, the *Astro-2* teams with the *Hubble Space Telescope* to examine the effects on Jupiter's atmosphere of volcanic eruptions on Jupiter's moon Io. The shuttle telescopes are capable of detecting certain frequencies and properties of ultraviolet light that are out of *Hubble's* range.... A study suggests that the bodies of both fat and thin people alter their metabolism in an effort to maintain a set weight.	Ian Ballantine, 79, publishing pioneer who founded three major paperback book houses, dies in Bearsville, New York, of cardiac arrest.... The artistic director of Russia's Bolshoi Ballet, Yuri Grigorovich, submits his resignation.... Elvis Stojko of Canada wins the men's title at the World Figure Skating Championships.	March 9
The House passes, 265-261, the Common Sense Product Liability and Legal Reform Act, a bill designed to prevent courts from assessing disproportionately high damages in personal-injury and malpractice suits.... Former Alabama governor George Wallace (D), a one-time opponent of racial integration, attends a ceremony marking the 30th anniversary of a 50-mile (80-km) civil-rights march from Selma to Montgomery. Wallace has recanted his earlier stance since 1985.	The State Department announces that it is suspending its military-aid program to Guatemala to protest what it calls Guatemala's human-rights abuses.... Retired air force general Michael P. C. Carns, Pres. Clinton's nominee to be director of central intelligence, withdraws from consideration after FBI agents confronted him with allegations that he and his wife violated labor and immigration laws when they brought a Filipino citizen to the U.S.	The Dow closes at a record high of 4035.61, up 52.22 points.	A study finds that people who take calcium channel blockers to lower their blood pressure face up to a 60% higher risk of suffering a heart attack than people taking other types of blood-pressure drugs.... Researchers report they have isolated two genes that, when mutant, cause a relatively rare inherited heart disorder known as long QT syndrome.... A 180-mile (290-km) section of I-5 is closed after a bridge in Coalinga, California, collapses due to floods.	Jonathan Schmitz, 24, who admits to slaying his homosexual admirer, Scott Amedure, 32, out of anger, pleads not guilty to first-degree murder. Amedure revealed his crush on Schmitz during a taping of *The Jenny Jones Show*.... Russians Oksana Gritschuk and Yevgeny Platov win the ice-dancing title at the World Figure Skating Championships.	March 10
				At the World Figure Skating Championships, Chen Lu places first in the women's competition to become the first Chinese skater to win a world title.	March 11
	Judge Philip M. Pro of U.S. District Court in Las Vegas, Nevada, reduces to $5.2 million from $6.7 million the judgment awarded to Paula Coughlin, the whistle-blower in the U.S. Navy's Tailhook convention sexual-assault scandal.		On the *Endeavour* mission, *Astro-2* makes the first-ever ultraviolet observations of Earth's moon.	Gordon B. Hinckley is ordained as the 15th president of the Church of Jesus Christ of Latter-day Saints, commonly known as the Mormon Church. Hinckley, 84, succeeds Howard William Hunter.	March 12
	Attorney General Janet Reno submits a request to a panel of federal judges to appoint an independent counsel to determine whether HUD Secretary Henry Cisneros acted criminally by misleading federal investigators about support payments he made to his former mistress, Linda Medlar.		Pres. Clinton declares federal emergencies due to flooding in 39 of California's 58 counties, making them eligible for federal aid.... The FCC concludes a three-month-long auction for wireless-telephone service licenses. The agency reportedly raised $7 billion, a sum that exceeds most initial estimates.	Leon Day, 78, baseball player who was a star pitcher in the Negro leagues in the 1930s and 1940s, before the major leagues were integrated, and who was selected for induction into the Baseball Hall of Fame on Mar. 7, dies in Baltimore, Maryland, of heart ailments, diabetes, and gout.	March 13

F	G	H	I	J
Includes elections, federal-state relations, civil rights and liberties, crime, the judiciary, education, health care, poverty, urban affairs, and population.	Includes formation and debate of U.S. foreign and defense policies, veterans' affairs, and defense spending. (Relations with specific foreign countries are usually found under the region concerned.)	Includes business, labor, agriculture, taxation, transportation, consumer affairs, monetary and fiscal policy, natural resources, and pollution.	Includes worldwide scientific, medical, and technological developments; natural phenomena; U.S. weather; natural disasters; and accidents.	Includes the arts, religion, scholarship, communications media, sports, entertainments, fashions, fads, and social life.

	World Affairs	Europe	Africa & the Middle East	The Americas	Asia & the Pacific
March 14	U.S. first lady Hillary Rodham Clinton addresses a conference, called "Women and the United Nations," at UN headquarters in New York City.	Ireland's parliament gives final approval to a controversial bill that would liberalize the country's strict antiabortion laws.... France arrests 13 Algerians and one Frenchman of Algerian descent suspected of having ties to militant Muslim groups. ... Nine French UN peacekeeping soldiers are killed and four wounded when their vehicle falls off a slippery road on Mount Igman, south of Sarajevo, the capital of Bosnia-Herzegovina.	In Burundi, the mutilated body of Lucien Sakubu, a Tutsi kidnapped Mar. 13, is found, prompting Tutsi youths to attack Hutus in the capital with hand grenades and knives. A large number of Hutus reportedly are wounded before police intervene.		
March 15	UN figures suggest that total foreign direct investment in 1994 totaled about $204 billion worldwide.	Riots that broke out Mar. 12 in Turkey calm, and data shows that some 30 people were killed. The government states that 1,500 people took part in the demonstrations.... Lord Frederick William Mulley, 76, British Labour Party chairman, 1974–75, and defense secretary, 1976–79, dies of an undisclosed illness.		Carlitos Menem, the only son of Argentine president Carlos Saul Menem, dies in a helicopter crash.... In Bedford, Nova Scotia, former Nova Scotia premier Gerald Regan is charged with 16 counts of sex crimes, including rape, unlawful detention, and indecent assault.	
March 16		Italian premier Lamberto Dini wins a confidence vote when the Chamber of Deputies, in two votes, narrowly approves his proposed "minibudget."... Lord Simon Christopher Joseph Fraser Lovat, 83, British war hero who led a Scottish commando unit onto the Normandy beaches in the Allied forces' 1944 D-Day attack, dies in Beauly, Scotland, of an undisclosed illness.	Canadian Forces captain Michael Sox is convicted by court-martial of negligent performance of duty. Sox is the last remaining defendant in the 1993 torture and beating death of a 16-year-old Somali in the custody of Canadian soldiers on a UN peacekeeping mission in Somalia.		The Australian High Court upholds the federal government's Native Title Act, a controversial 1993 law establishing a system to protect aboriginal land where indigenous people can prove a continuing association with the land in question.
March 17		Azeri government troops storm the headquarters of a rebel police unit about five miles (eight km) north of Baku, the capital of Azerbaijan, crushing the Mar. 13 coup attempt against Azeri president Heydar Aliyev. The leader of the police unit, Deputy Interior Minister Rovshan Javadov, is killed in the attack, along with 80 other people.... Ukraine's parliament passes a resolution that abolishes the constitution of the autonomous republic of Crimea and ousts Crimea's president, Yuri Meshkov. Ukraine deploys 200 riot police to Simferopol, but no unrest is reported.	In Kigali, 24 Rwandan prisoners held on charges of participating in the 1994 massacres are found dead, apparently from suffocation, in a jail cell.... Ahmad Khomeini, 50, son of the late Ayatollah Ruhollah Khomeini, who led Iran's 1979 Islamic revolution and played a key role when Iran held 52 Americans in 1979–81, dies in Teheran, Iran, of a heart attack.		A national public outcry erupts in the Philippines after the hanging of a Filipina maid in Singapore. The maid, Flor Contemplacion, was hanged for the 1991 murders of another Filipina maid and a four-year-old Singaporean boy. Despite international pleas and new testimony suggesting that the woman was innocent, the Singaporean government refused to delay the hanging, and thousands of Filipino citizens take to the streets in what are considered the most emotional public demonstrations since 1986.
March 18		A group of PKK guerrillas cross the border from Iraq to attack a Turkish convoy of 40 vehicles carrying 800 soldiers. An estimated 18 Turkish troops are killed.... Pres. Mary Robinson asks the Irish Supreme Court to review a controversial bill passed Mar. 14 that would liberalize the country's strict antiabortion laws.... Spain's Princess Elena, 31, weds Jaime de Marichalar y Saenz de Tejada, 31, in a Roman Catholic ceremony at the Cathedral of Seville. The ceremony is the first Spanish royal wedding in Spain in 89 years.		Canada's railroad employees begin a nationwide rail strike, bringing to a virtual halt freight and passenger rail service across the country and threatening to damage Canada's economy.	
March 19		The Social Democrat Party defeats the ruling Center Party in general elections, becoming Finland's largest parliamentary party.	Snipers perched on a rooftop in Hebron spray an Israeli bus with automatic-weapons fire, killing two Jewish settlers and wounding several others.... Eight Belgians in a convoy are attacked by suspected Hutu extremists in Burundi. Two soldiers in Burundi's army and three Belgians, including a four-year-old girl, are killed in the attack..... Britain's Queen Elizabeth II visits South Africa for the first time since 1947.		The protests that erupted Mar. 17 escalate when Philippine officials announce the postponement of an April visit by Singaporean prime minister Goh Chok Tong.

A	B	C	D	E
Includes developments that affect more than one world region, international organizations, and important meetings of major world leaders.	*Includes all domestic and regional developments in Europe, including the Soviet Union, Turkey, Cyprus, and Malta.*	*Includes all domestic and regional developments in Africa and the Middle East, including Iraq and Iran and excluding Cyprus, Turkey, and Afghanistan.*	*Includes all domestic and regional developments in Latin America, the Caribbean, and Canada.*	*Includes all domestic and regional developments in Asia and Pacific nations, extending from Afghanistan through all the Pacific Islands, except Hawaii.*

U.S. Politics & Social Issues	U.S. Foreign Policy & Defense	U.S. Economy & Environment	Science, Technology, & Nature	Culture, Leisure, & Lifestyle	
Harvard University discloses that retired investment banker John L. Loeb and his wife, Frances Lehman Loeb, have given $70.5 million to the school in one of the 10 largest private gifts ever made to a U.S. college or university.		The Commerce Department reports that the nation's current-account deficit totaled $155.7 billion in 1994, up 33% from the 1993 calendar-year deficit of $103.9 billion.... Nuclear Regulatory Commission chairman Ivan Selin announces that he will resign from his post on July 1, a year before his term ends.	Researchers report that frogs born in space in September 1992 have borne healthy offspring.... A Russian *Soyuz* rocket, carrying two cosmonauts and Norman E. Thagard, the first U.S. astronaut launched in a Russian spacecraft, lifts off in Kazakhstan.... William Alfred Fowler, 83, astrophysicist who won the 1983 Nobel Prize for developing "a complete theory for the formation of the chemical elements of the universe," dies in Pasadena, California, of kidney failure.	In Alaska, Doug Swingley wins the 1,049-mile (1,689-km) Iditarod Trail Sled Dog Race. Swingley, who is from Simms, Montana, completes the race in nine days, two hours, and 43 minutes. He is the first non-Alaskan to win the race in its 22-year history.	March 14
	U.S. president Clinton signs an executive order barring U.S. companies from engaging in petroleum-production activities in Iran, a country the U.S. has long branded as an instigator of international terrorism. Clinton's moves effectively quash a $1 billion deal, announced Mar. 5, between Conoco and Iran.	The Senate passes, 91-9, a bill designed to deter Congress from passing "unfunded mandates," or laws and regulations that the federal government imposes on states without providing funds for their enforcement.... The Glass Ceiling Commission, a bipartisan federal panel, reveals that women and minorities are extremely underrepresented in senior management posts, despite three decades of affirmative-action efforts.	The heavy rains that started Mar. 8 and spurred severe flooding in much of California begin to end. The disaster has claimed the lives of at least 15 people and caused an estimated $2 billion in damage.	Picabo Street, 23, becomes the first U.S. woman skier awarded the World Cup downhill title.	March 15
The Mississippi House of Representatives approves a resolution ratifying the 130-year-old 13th Amendment to the Constitution, which abolishes slavery. It was discovered earlier in 1995 that Mississippi never ratified the measure.... Atty. Gen. Janet Reno announces the Justice Department has found no improprieties in the awarding of a local-government contract to an investment firm that Transportation Secretary Federico Pena founded.	The Senate passes, 97-3, a $3 billion supplemental defense-appropriations bill that allocates funds to defense accounts drained by peacekeeping operations.... The U.S. lobby group TransAfrica announces it will lead an effort backed by prominent U.S. blacks to pressure Nigeria's military government to restore democracy. It is believed to be the first time a group of African Americans undertakes a large-scale effort against a black-led African government.	The House passes, 227-200, a bill outlining more than $17 billion in spending cuts. The body also approves, 394-28, a bill designed to deter Congress from passing "unfunded mandates," or laws and regulations that the federal government imposes on states without providing funds for their enforcement.	A study suggests that the practice of donating one's own blood for possible transfusion during surgery is more expensive and less efficient than ordinary blood donation because of increased record keeping and waste.... A panel of eight experts report they have found "no evidence of negligence or carelessness" on the part of NIH scientists who ran a 1993 study of a hepatitis B drug called fialuridine. In the testing, five of the 15 people enrolled died, and two needed liver transplants.	Albert Hackett, 95, playwright who collaborated with his wife, Frances Goodrich, on numerous films and plays, dies in New York City of pneumonia.... Rap star Eazy-E, 31, discloses that he has AIDS.	March 16
In Chicago, a panel of judges on the Seventh U.S. Circuit Court of Appeals rules, 2-1, that a group of hemophiliacs who claim to have contracted HIV from blood-clotting treatments cannot proceed as a class with a lawsuit against drug companies because differing laws in the 50 states make the class action unworkable. The decision reverses an August 1994 lower-court ruling.	In Washington, D.C., Pres. Clinton meets with Gerry Adams, leader of Sinn Fein, the political wing of the Provisional IRA, in the second of two controversial meetings.		The FDA approves the first vaccine in the U.S. to prevent chicken pox, which is contracted by 3.7 million people in the U.S. each year.	Reports confirm that the former director of NYC's Museum of Modern Art, Richard Oldenburg, has been named chair of American operations at the U.S.-based Sotheby's Holdings Inc. auction house.	March 17
			The U.S. space shuttle *Endeavour* completes the longest flight in shuttle history when it touches down at Edwards Air Force Base, California, after carrying out a mission to conduct astronomical research.	The director of the Kremlin Ballet, Vladimir Vasilyev, is appointed the artistic director of Russia's Bolshoi Theater.... Former NBA superstar guard Michael Jordan announces that he is returning to professional basketball after a 17-month hiatus.	March 18
					March 19

F	G	H	I	J
Includes elections, federal-state relations, civil rights and liberties, crime, the judiciary, education, health care, poverty, urban affairs, and population.	*Includes formation and debate of U.S. foreign and defense policies, veterans' affairs, and defense spending. (Relations with specific foreign countries are usually found under the region concerned.)*	*Includes business, labor, agriculture, taxation, transportation, consumer affairs, monetary and fiscal policy, natural resources, and pollution.*	*Includes worldwide scientific, medical, and technological developments; natural phenomena; U.S. weather; natural disasters; and accidents.*	*Includes the arts, religion, scholarship, communications media, sports, entertainments, fashions, fads, and social life.*

	World Affairs	Europe	Africa & the Middle East	The Americas	Asia & the Pacific
March 20		The predominantly Muslim Bosnian government launches an offensive against Bosnian Serb positions, shattering a Jan. 1 truce. The government attacks areas near the Muslim enclave of Tuzla in northeastern Bosnia and the city of Travnik in central Bosnia. . . . Danish police arrest Gary Lauck, an American suspected of supplying propaganda to German neo-Nazis. . . . In response to the Mar. 18 attack, a massive Turkish military force crosses into Iraq to eliminate guerrilla strongholds of the PKK. It is described as Turkey's largest military operation ever.	Rachida Hammadi, one of the few female reporters for Algeria's state-run television, is injured by gunmen in Algiers, and her sister, Houria Hammadi, is killed. . . . In Burundi's capital, Bujumbura, clashes erupt as Tutsis apparently seek retribution for the Mar. 19 killings. At least four people are killed. . . . Data reveal that more than 50 opposition lawmakers have been arrested in Kenya since 1993, although most of them were detained for only a short time. . . . Reports find that the Liberian cease-fire signed in December 1994 has been shattered.	Canada's Immigration Ministry begins legal proceedings against Erichs Tobiass, a Canadian citizen born in Latvia who currently lives in Toronto, as part of an effort to deport him and revoke his citizenship. Tobiass, 84, is accused of war crimes, including the execution of civilians, during World War II.	A deadly nerve-gas attack paralyzes Tokyo's subway system, one of the world's busiest. The nation's major mass-transit systems are placed on alert against other possible terrorist incidents. . . . A land-mine blast kills 12 people in Uri, in India's disputed Jammu and Kashmir region near the Pakistani border. Brigadier Venugopal Sridharan, 49, and nine of his troops are among the dead, along with two civilians. . . . Tensions continue to rise when the mayor of the Davao City, the Philippines' fourth-largest city, leads officials in burning a Singaporean flag.
March 21	Belgian police raid the European Commission's headquarters in Brussels to clamp down on alleged EU fraud. At the request of the commission, the police arrest three EU tourism officials accused of taking $492,000 in bribes from private companies seeking EU contracts.		The seven Roman Catholic nuns kidnapped by rebel forces on Jan. 25 in Sierra Leone are released.	Argentine interior minister Carlos Corach states that the government has no list of victims of the navy's "death flights," which were perpetrated in the later 1970s as part of the military regime's "dirty war" of repression against presumed leftist dissidents. Corach's statement comes amid renewed controversy after the remarks made Mar. 3 by a retired naval officer.	
March 22		Peter Holmes Woods, 64, British journalist and news anchor for the BBC, dies in Yeovil, England, of cancer.	In South Africa, Judge Piet Streicher of the Rand Supreme Court declares invalid warrants obtained by police for a Mar. 1 raid of Winnie Mandela's home and offices.		Philippine president Fidel Ramos recalls his ambassador to Singapore, bars women from the Philippines from working as maids in Singapore, and threatens to sever all ties with Singapore if a Philippine inquiry shows that Flor Contemplacion, whose Mar. 17 hanging sparked a diplomatic crisis, was wrongly convicted. Singapore recalls its ambassador to the Philippines. . . . Some 2,500 Japanese police officers raid 25 offices of the Aum Shinrikyo sect.
March 23	The World Trade Organization (WTO) formally names Renato Ruggiero, a former Italian trade minister, as its new director general.	German officials raid the homes of 80 of the followers of Gary Lauck, an American arrested Mar. 20. Police confiscate guns and neo-Nazi racist propaganda. . . . Unidentified Turkish senior officials state that 35,000 soldiers will remain in Iraq until a buffer zone free of Kurds is set up along the Turkish-Iraqi border. . . . Bosnian president Alija Izetbegovic informs the UN that he will extend the UN peacekeeping mandate in Bosnia, set to expire Mar. 31, by only 30 days.	In the Soweto township, Britain's Queen Elizabeth II and South African president Nelson Mandela unveil a monument to 656 black members of the South African Native Labor Contingent who died in World War I. . . . Nigerian information minister Walter Ofonagoro reveals that the government will release Olusegun Obasanjo, who was arrested Mar. 13, in response to pleas made by former U.S. president Jimmy Carter, who is touring Africa.	In the port of Montreal, Quebec, the longshoremen's union and the affected shipping lines both accept a federal mediator's work-resumption proposal, and the longshoremen return to work, ending a job action that started Mar. 7.	The death toll from the Mar. 20 deadly nerve-gas attack in Tokyo is at 10, and more than 5,000 people have been injured.
March 24			In Burundi, at least one man is killed as fighting worsens. Tutsi soldiers and civilians attack suburban areas near Bujumbura, the capital. The office of the United Nations High Commissioner for Refugees discloses that fighting in Bujumbura has prompted 24,000 people to flee to neighboring Tanzania. Up to one-third of the refugees are said to be Rwandans who earlier fled to Burundi.		Onoe Baiko (born Seizo Terashima), 79, prominent Japanese actor in the traditional dramatic art of Kabuki who was designated a Living National Treasure by the Japanese government in 1968, dies in Tokyo of complications from pneumonia.
March 25	Cuba signs the 1967 Treaty of Tlatelolco, a pact among South American, Central American, and Caribbean nations that commits its signatories to refrain from using nuclear weapons. . . . Reports disclose that many developed nations indicated in 1994 that they will not meet the requirement of reducing emissions of carbon dioxide and other so-called greenhouse gases in 2000 to 1990 levels. Among those nations are the U.S., Australia, Austria, Canada, Norway, Spain, and Sweden.		An Iraqi court sentences two U.S. citizens, William Barloon, 39, and David Daliberti, 41, to eight-year prison terms on charges that they illegally entered Iraq. The U.S. administration maintains that they accidentally strayed into the six-mile-wide demilitarized zone on the border with Kuwait. . . . More than 100 people are killed in Karosi, a village near Gasorwe in Burundi. Officials suggest that the death toll in the prior two weeks in the Muyinga region is at 200.	Reports estimate that 20 suspected robbers have been stoned, beaten, or hacked to death in incidents in Port-au-Prince, the capital of Haiti, since the beginning of the month. Data indicate that Haitian courts have convicted only about 100 of some 6,000 crime suspects arrested during the first stage of peacekeeping operations.	

A	B	C	D	E
Includes developments that affect more than one world region, international organizations, and important meetings of major world leaders.	Includes all domestic and regional developments in Europe, including the Soviet Union, Turkey, Cyprus, and Malta.	Includes all domestic and regional developments in Africa and the Middle East, including Iraq and Iran and excluding Cyprus, Turkey, and Afghanistan.	Includes all domestic and regional developments in Latin America, the Caribbean, and Canada.	Includes all domestic and regional developments in Asia and Pacific nations, extending from Afghanistan through all the Pacific Islands, except Hawaii.

U.S. Politics & Social Issues	U.S. Foreign Policy & Defense	U.S. Economy & Environment	Science, Technology, & Nature	Culture, Leisure, & Lifestyle	
		In New Orleans, Louisiana, federal judge Morey Sear throws out a proposed settlement of a class-action lawsuit filed against Ford Motor Co. by owners of the Bronco II, arguing that the settlement is "of little or no value" to Bronco owners.		Sidney Kingsley, 88, playwright whose dramas center on urban social problems, dies in Oakland, New Jersey, of a stroke.	March 20
In *Director v. Newport News Shipbuilding & Dry Dock Co.*, the Supreme Court rules unanimously to limit the authority of federal agencies to file federal-court appeals on behalf of injured individuals.	Loral Corp. agrees to buy the military and aerospace businesses of Unisys Corp. for $800 million in cash. The deal will reportedly boost Loral's operations in military information systems, satellite communications, and radar.	Chris V. Wade, an Arkansas real-estate agent and former manager of Whitewater Development Corp., pleads guilty to two counts of fraud related to his 1990 bankruptcy filing. . . . James L. (Bud) Walton, 73, cofounder of Wal-Mart Stores Inc. whose wealth is estimated at $1 billion, dies in Miami, Florida, of an aneurysm.			March 21
Judge Donald Belfi sentences Colin Ferguson, a Jamaican immigrant convicted of the December 1993 murder of six people aboard a Long Island Rail Road train, to 200 years to life in prison. . . . In *Anderson v. Edwards*, the Supreme Court upholds a California welfare regulation that curbs benefits by classifying as a single family group children living under the care of a single relative in the same household, regardless of whether the children are siblings.	Rep. Robert Torricelli (D, N.J.) alleges that a Guatemalan army officer on the CIA payroll ordered the killing of Efrain Bamaca Velasquez, a rebel commander who was tortured and murdered by the Guatemalan army in 1992, and Michael DeVine, a U.S. citizen who owned an inn in the Guatemalan rain forest and was slain in 1990. Bamaca's wife, Jennifer Harbury, a U.S. lawyer, had conducted a campaign of hunger strikes to press for details as to the fate of her husband.	The Commerce Department reports that the U.S. recorded a $12.23 billion deficit in trade in goods and services in January. That figure—a record high—is 40% larger than the revised December 1994 deficit figure of $7.26 billion. . . . Pres. Clinton signs the final version of a bill designed to deter Congress from passing "unfunded mandates," or laws and regulations that the federal government imposes on states without providing funds for their enforcement.	Russian cosmonaut Valery Polyakov, 52, returns to Earth aboard a *Soyuz* descent module after spending a record 439 days in space while on *Mir*. . . . A study compares the safety effects of pediatric ibuprofen with those of pediatric acetaminophen and finds no significant differences.		March 22
Pres. Clinton outlines plans to review federal affirmative-action programs to confirm that they have not led to "reverse discrimination."	In response to allegations made by Rep. Robert Torricelli (D, N.J.) on Mar. 22, the CIA denies that it had any knowledge of the killings "at the time the deaths occurred."	The Senate passes, 69-29, a bill that will grant the president the power to limit federal spending through the use of the so-called line-item veto.	Researchers report that they treated a brain disease in mice similar to one that occurs in humans by transplanting immature brain cells into the brains of the mice. The researchers suggest that the technique may eventually lead to the development of treatments in humans for Sly disease, which is relatively rare, and for Gaucher's and Tay-Sachs diseases, which are more common.	Irving Shulman, 81, who wrote the original treatment for the screenplay of the movie *Rebel Without a Cause* (1955), dies in Los Angeles of Alzheimer's disease.	March 23
The House votes, 234-199, in favor of a broad overhaul of the current federal welfare system. The bill, the Personal Responsibility Act, will institute the broadest overhaul of the U.S. social welfare system in 60 years and will cut projected welfare spending by some $66 billion over the next five years.		The Senate approves by voice vote a bill that will repeal a 1978 Federal Communications Commission program granting tax breaks to minority-owned firms that seek to purchase or establish media operations, as well as to nonminority firms that do business with them.	Scientists report they have developed a paste made from inorganic calcium and phosphate sources that can be injected into broken bone to form a hard substance similar to natural bone, potentially aiding the rehabilitation of damaged bones. . . . (Noel) Joseph Terence Montgomery Needham, 94, British biochemist who wrote an acclaimed book, dies in Cambridge, England, of an undisclosed illness.		March 24
James Samuel Coleman, 68, sociologist whose findings show that disadvantaged black students perform better in integrated classrooms, which shaped the debate on school desegregation in the 1960s and 1970s, dies in Chicago, Illinois, of prostate cancer.				House Speaker Newt Gingrich (R, Ga.) admits he "totally mishandled" a controversial book contract, a venture that drew accusations of unethical behavior. It is Gingrich's first formal response regarding the contract. . . . Former boxing champion Mike Tyson, 28, is released from the Indiana Youth Center prison after serving three years of a 1992 rape conviction.	March 25
F	G	H	I	J	
Includes elections, federal-state relations, civil rights and liberties, crime, the judiciary, education, health care, poverty, urban affairs, and population.	Includes formation and debate of U.S. foreign and defense policies, veterans' affairs, and defense spending. (Relations with specific foreign countries are usually found under the region concerned.)	Includes business, labor, agriculture, taxation, transportation, consumer affairs, monetary and fiscal policy, natural resources, and pollution.	Includes worldwide scientific, medical, and technological developments; natural phenomena; U.S. weather; natural disasters; and accidents.	Includes the arts, religion, scholarship, communications media, sports, entertainments, fashions, fads, and social life.	

	World Affairs	Europe	Africa & the Middle East	The Americas	Asia & the Pacific
March 26	Seven European Union nations—Belgium, France, Germany, Luxembourg, the Netherlands, Portugal, and Spain—eliminate their internal border controls to adhere to a 1985 open-border pact. As part of that agreement, the seven countries also enact a system of tighter controls on their external borders.	Bosnian Serb leader Radovan Karadzic orders a general mobilization of the entire population of Serb-held Bosnia to counter the government offensives that started Mar. 20. . . . Vladimir Yemelyanovich Maximov (born Leon Samsonov), 64, Russian author who was a leading Soviet dissident in the 1960s and 1970s, dies in Paris, France, of cancer.	Pres. Sylvestre Ntibantunganya admits that fighting between the Hutu and Tutsi ethnic groups in and around Burundi's capital, Bujumbura, has killed at least 150 people and has prompted an exodus of 50,000 others. Other estimates place the number of people killed as high as 500. . . . Algerian papers report that security forces in a five-day offensive killed at least 300 of an estimated 1,000 GIA members.	A series of unexplained explosions at La Aurora military base, located outside Guatemala City, the capital of Guatemala, leaves four people dead. . . . Canada's Parliament passes back-to-work legislation to force striking railroad workers to return to their jobs.	Public protests continue in the Philippines during funeral ceremonies for Flor Contemplacion, who was hanged in Singapore on Mar. 17. In Manila, the Philippines' capital, grenades explode near a Singapore Airlines office and outside the Philippines foreign ministry building. No injuries are reported.
March 27		Hanns Joachim Friedrichs, 68, highly respected German journalist for the country's two national television networks, dies in Hamburg, Germany, of cancer. . . . Maurizio Gucci, former chair of the leather and fashion company that bears his name, is shot and killed in Milan, Italy.	South African president Nelson Mandela dismisses his estranged wife, Winnie Mandela, from her cabinet post. The first cabinet minister ousted from the coalition government, she has been involved in a series of scandals. . . . Unknown armed attackers assault a refugee camp at Magara, Burundi, leaving 12 dead and 22 wounded. The attack prompts 41,000 Rwandans to flee. . . . The Sudanese government announces a two-month cease-fire in response to pleas made by former U.S. president Jimmy Carter, who is touring Africa.	After the labor bill passed on Mar. 26, railroads in Canada resume operations, ending a shutdown caused by a labor strike that started March 18.	
March 28	A UN summit on global warming, the Conference of the Parties to the United Nations Framework Convention on Climate Change, convenes in Berlin, Germany.	In raids in Frankfurt and Aachen, German police arrest two Algerians suspected of smuggling firearms into Algeria. . . . A Dutch UN soldier is killed in northern Bosnia. . . . Italian magistrates file arrest warrants for 35 politicians, businessmen, and reputed mobsters linked to alleged corruption in the healthcare system.		Mireille Durocher Bertin, a prominent critic of Jean-Bertrand Aristide, is shot to death by three unidentified gunmen while in her car in Port-au-Prince, the capital of Haiti.	Mitsubishi Bank Ltd. and Bank of Tokyo Ltd. announce plans to merge, a deal that will create the world's largest bank in terms of assets held.
March 29	Faced with the possibility of a full-scale civil war in Burundi, foreign nationals from the U.S., France, Belgium, Spain, and Italy begin evacuating Bujumbura. . . . The European Commission, the executive branch of the EU, announces that losses due to fraud increased in 1994 to around 1 billion European currency units ($1.3 billion), from about half that in 1993. The rise in detected fraud largely stems from better accounting methods and an increase in organized crime.	Officials in the Netherlands release Jacob Luitjens, 75, the country's last remaining war criminal from World War II. Luitjens was convicted in absentia in 1948, sentenced to life, and starting serving his sentence in November 1992. A Dutch justice minister recommended the early release, citing Luitjen's age and sentence reductions given to similar offenders.		The Canadian government admits that it was wrong to move nine Inuit families, comprising about 100 people, to a remote area north of the Arctic Circle during a relocation project in the 1950s.	
March 30		Reports suggest that the offensive launched Mar. 20 against Bosnian Serb positions has resulted in dozens of civilian casualties. Hundreds of soldiers on both sides have been killed in the battles. . . . About 15,000 more Turkish troops are sent into the Tunceli province of Turkey to root out PKK guerrillas. . . . Russian forces in the breakaway republic of Chechnya in southern Russia capture the town of Gudermes.	Residents of Burao, a town in the breakaway republic of Somaliland in northwest Somalia, estimate that 60 gunmen were killed a few days earlier in battles between rival clans. . . . In response to the government's March 27 announcement, Sudan's largest southern rebel group, the SPLA, declares a two-month "unilateral cease-fire.". . . Reports confirm the Algerian government has launched a major offensive against militant fundamentalists.		The Australian cabinet agrees to protect 264 forest areas from logging and introduces a plan to improve the country's forest reserve system.
March 31	In a ceremony in Port-au-Prince, Boutros Boutros-Ghali, the UN secretary general, and U.S. president Clinton formally transfer peacekeeping responsibilities in Haiti from U.S.-led troops to forces of the UN Mission in Haiti (UNMIH). The UNMIH is composed of 6,000 military personnel and 900 police civilians, drawn from more than 30 countries. . . . The UN Security Council votes to renew until Nov. 30 its peacekeeping mission in the former Yugoslavia, hours before the mandate is to expire.	Russian forces in the breakaway republic of Chechnya in southern Russia capture the town of Shali, considered the last urban stronghold of Chechen resistance. . . . A Romanian airliner crashes shortly after takeoff from Bucharest, the Romanian capital, killing all 60 people on board.	The Tanzanian government closes its border with Burundi, saying it is already overwhelmed with more than 700,000 Rwandan refugees currently living in camps there.	The Guatemalan government and the rebel Guatemalan National Revolutionary Union (URNG) sign an accord to guarantee the rights of Guatemala's Indians. Under terms of the pact, the Guatemalan constitution will be amended to grant recognition to the nation's Maya, Garifuna, and Xinca peoples.	During a tour by U.S. first lady Hillary Rodham Clinton, an estimated 2,000 protesters in Dhaka, the capital of Bangladesh, take to the streets to denounce organizations that espouse women's rights. Protesters in Nepal denounce their government's ties with Western countries, and 23 protesters are arrested for throwing rocks at the first lady's motorcade. . . . In Thailand, thousands of supporters of Yantra Ammarobhikkhu, a Thai monk, protest his expulsion from his religious order over his involvement in a sex scandal.

A	B	C	D	E
Includes developments that affect more than one world region, international organizations, and important meetings of major world leaders.	*Includes all domestic and regional developments in Europe, including the Soviet Union, Turkey, Cyprus, and Malta.*	*Includes all domestic and regional developments in Africa and the Middle East, including Iraq and Iran and excluding Cyprus, Turkey, and Afghanistan.*	*Includes all domestic and regional developments in Latin America, the Caribbean, and Canada.*	*Includes all domestic and regional developments in Asia and Pacific nations, extending from Afghanistan through all the Pacific Islands, except Hawaii.*

U.S. Politics & Social Issues	U.S. Foreign Policy & Defense	U.S. Economy & Environment	Science, Technology, & Nature	Culture, Leisure, & Lifestyle	
				Eric (Eazy-E) Wright, 31, rap singer who led the "gangsta" rap group N.W.A., an acronym for Niggaz Wit Attitude, dies in Los Angeles of complications from AIDS.... The Pan American Games, held in Mar del Plata, Argentina, close, and the U.S. won a record 424 medals. Cuba won 238, and Canada won 117.	March 26
Maryland's legislature enacts a ban on smoking in most workplaces.	Col. Julio Roberto Alpirez, the Guatemalan military officer accused Mar. 22 by Rep. Robert Torricelli (D, N.J.), insists that he is "totally innocent" of involvement in the killings and denies that he ever worked for the CIA.	John P. LaWare, one of the Federal Reserve Board's 12 governors, announces his retirement, effective April 30.		The Celestine Prophecy by James Redfield tops the bestseller list. ... At the Oscars, Forrest Gump wins six awards, including best picture, best director, and best actor. Clint Eastwood receives the Irving G. Thalberg Memorial Award, and musical producer Quincy Jones receives the Jean Hersholt Humanitarian Award.	March 27
Harris County, Texas, district judge Michael Schneider removes Dow Chemical Co. from a Feb. 15 jury verdict that ordered the company and its affiliate, Dow Corning Corp., to pay $5.2 million to a couple, Robert and Gladys Laas.... Statistics show that black women living in poverty and uneducated women of all races are more likely to have mildly retarded children than other mothers.		In Qualitex Co. v. Jacobson Products Co., the Supreme Court rules unanimously that companies can gain trademark protection for colors that they use specifically to distinguish their products or packaging from competitors' goods.			March 28
The House defeats four bills that would have set limits on the number of terms that members of Congress can serve. The votes reportedly are the first ever held in either the House or Senate on seeking a constitutional amendment to restrict legislators' terms.	The U.S. Army discloses that nine instructors will be disciplined in connection with the February deaths of four soldiers in training.... In response to the Mar. 22 allegations regarding deaths in Guatemala, Pres. Clinton orders the Intelligence Oversight Board to conduct an inquiry into the killings.... The CIA reveals that it will pay more than $1 million to settle sexual discrimination charges lodged between 1986 and 1994 by several hundred women in its clandestine operations division.	The Senate unanimously approves a measure to delay for 45 days the implementation of federal agency regulations that will have an economic impact of $100 million or more.... The Commerce Department and HUD report that sales of new homes nationwide plunged 14% in February from January, to a seasonally adjusted annual rate of 551,000 units. The February rate is the lowest since April 1992.			March 29
	In New York City, federal judge Eugene H. Nickerson strikes down the Defense Department's policy restricting homosexuals' service in the U.S. military, asserting that the "don't ask, don't tell, don't pursue" rule, violates free-speech and equal-protection rights provided in the First and Fifth amendments of the Constitution. Nickerson's decision is the first judicial rejection of the policy, which was endorsed by Pres. Clinton in 1993.	The Commerce Department reports after-tax profits of U.S. corporations rose 10.2% in 1994 from 1993, to $322 billion. That compares with 1993 profits of $289.2 billion.... The House passes by voice vote a bill that makes minor adjustments to the federal tax code, including one that reinstates a tax deduction for self-employed people who pay for their own health insurance.	Research shows that a Los Angeles boy tested positive for HIV who shortly after birth apparently shed the virus by age one. The boy, whose mother is HIV-positive, currently is healthy and apparently HIV-negative at age five.... Studies suggest that high doses of the nonprescription painkiller ibuprofen may significantly slow the damage that cystic fibrosis causes to the lungs, especially in children.	Pope John Paul II issues an encyclical in which he stakes out his opposition to abortion, birth control, in vitro fertilization, genetic manipulation, and euthanasia. His statement also includes the church's strongest language to date against capital punishment.	March 30
	Dan Glickman is sworn in as secretary of agriculture, succeeding Mike Espy.... Reports state that an Alaska state judge, Brian Shortell, has ruled that Exxon Corp. does not have to pay $9.7 million in punitive damages to five Alaska native corporations. The ruling has no effect on the $5 billion in punitive damages that Exxon was ordered to pay to 14,000 Alaskan natives, fishermen, and property owners.			Popular Mexican-American singer Selena, 23, is fatally shot at a motel in Corpus Christi, Texas. Police arrest Yolanda Saldivar, the founder and former president of Selena's fan club, and charge her with murder.	March 31

F	G	H	I	J
Includes elections, federal-state relations, civil rights and liberties, crime, the judiciary, education, health care, poverty, urban affairs, and population.	Includes formation and debate of U.S. foreign and defense policies, veterans' affairs, and defense spending. (Relations with specific foreign countries are usually found under the region concerned.)	Includes business, labor, agriculture, taxation, transportation, consumer affairs, monetary and fiscal policy, natural resources, and pollution.	Includes worldwide scientific, medical, and technological developments; natural phenomena; U.S. weather; natural disasters; and accidents.	Includes the arts, religion, scholarship, communications media, sports, entertainments, fashions, fads, and social life.

	World Affairs	Europe	Africa & the Middle East	The Americas	Asia & the Pacific
April 1		Irma Hadzimuratovic, a critically wounded Bosnian girl who attracted international attention when she was rescued from Sarajevo in August 1993 at the age of five, dies in Great Ormond Street Hospital in London, England.		In Peru, Shining Path rebels massacre 11 peasants in the village of Calemar, affixing signs to the dead bodies which read, "We will kill those who vote."	In Tokyo, Japan, the death toll from the Mar. 20 nerve-gas attack increases to 11.
April 2	The Islamic Conference Organization meeting, attended by 300 delegates from more than 80 countries, closes, and delegates urge Islamic nations to continue the armed struggle against Israel.	Data show that Turkey killed 399 of the 2,800 PKK guerrillas hiding out in northern Iraq during the first three weeks of the invasion. Forty Turkish troops were killed in the fighting. . . . Fighting intensifies in the UN-designated safe area of Bihac in northwest Bosnia.	An estimated 50,000 Rwandan refugees, who fled into Burundi in 1994 amid ethnic violence in Rwanda, halt their flight from Burundi into neighboring Tanzania when they are reassured by UN officials that they will be protected by Burundi's army. . . . An explosion in Gaza City destroys the middle floor of a three-story concrete building, killing eight people, including Kamal Kheil, a senior leader of Hamas's military wing, the Izzedine al-Qassam Brigades. More than 30 other people are injured in the blast. . . . Rachida Hammadi, who was injured by gunmen in Algiers Mar. 20, dies, bringing the number of journalists killed by suspected Muslim militants since May 1993 to 31.		
April 3	European Union finance ministers and the governors of many of Europe's central banks hold the first high-level discussions and determine that the EMU is unlikely to be in place until at least five years after the target date of 1997.	In an unprecedented move, a Scottish appeals court upholds a ruling that forces the government-owned BBC to black out a telecast of an interview with P.M. John Major in some parts of the country. The Labour and Liberal Democrat Parties sought an injunction to halt the broadcast in Scotland, arguing that the BBC would violate its impartiality mandate by giving the Conservative Party an unfair campaigning edge.	Western diplomats state that up to 1,500 people in Burundi have been killed in each of the prior three weeks, a marked increase from the usual rate of about 100 civilian deaths a week.		
April 4		Bosnian government forces, aided by Croats, capture most of Mount Vlasic near the town of Travnik. Fighting between Bosnian government and Bosnian Serb forces peaks in the Majevica Mountains near Tuzla. . . . Ukraine's parliament votes to dismiss the country's cabinet in a no-confidence motion. The ministers will remain in their positions until Pres. Leonid Kuchma names a new cabinet. . . . Kenny Everett (born Maurice James Christopher Cole), 50, British disc jockey and TV comedian, dies of an AIDS-related illness.	One man reportedly is killed and dozens of people injured when riot police try to disperse demonstrators protesting the government's economic policies, in Islam-shahr, a working-class suburb located 12 miles (20 km) southwest of Teheran, the capital of Iran. . . . Kenyan police arrest two leading opposition members of Parliament, Paul Muite and Kiraitu Murungi, in Nairobi, the capital.		A band of 200 heavily armed Muslim separatists attack the town of Ipil on the southern Philippine island of Mindanao, killing dozens of citizens, robbing banks, and setting the town's commercial center ablaze. As many as 52 people are killed in the violence. Pres. Fidel Ramos sends troops to the area. . . . China's first nuclear power plant, at Daya Bay in southern Guangdong province, is shut down indefinitely after control rods in one of its two reactors are found in violation of international safety standards.
April 5	Officials from Thailand, Cambodia, Laos, and Vietnam sign a water-use pact that creates the Mekong Commission and replaces the Mekong Secretariat, established in 1958. . . . The U.S. Federal Reserve and the central banks of Japan and Germany attempt to halt the U.S. dollar's sharp decline against the yen and the mark, but the dollar closes at 86.05 yen, down from 86.20 yen, and at 1.3733 marks compared with 1.3780 marks.	Bosnians mark the third anniversary of the war, and Bosnian premier Haris Silajdzic states that the people of Bosnia should be prepared to fight for 10 years to win Bosnia's independence. . . . Christian Paul Francis Pineau, 90, French foreign minister, 1956–58, who signed the 1957 Treaty of Rome to establish the European Economic Community, which evolved into the European Union, dies in Paris.	The UN special representative to Burundi, Ahmedou Ould Abdallah, warns that unsubstantiated death-toll reports made by the international community, including the UN, are helping to push the country toward genocide.		
April 6		Fighting begins in Tajikistan between a Russian-led unit patrolling the border and Tajik rebels opposed to the current Russia-backed Tajikistan government. . . . Great Britain's ruling Conservative Party fails to retain or take control of a single Scottish governing council in local elections.	The Rwandan government in Kigali, the capital, opens the trial of the first six of at least 30,000 people currently detained on charges of participating in massacres during an ethnic civil war in 1994. The trial, however, is delayed indefinitely so that prosecutors and defense lawyers can better prepare their cases.	In Peru, a scheme to mark 3,000 ballots in advance of the election is uncovered in Huanuco, located some 150 miles (240 km) northeast of Lima, leading to the arrest of 15 people.	A Philippine investigative commission submits a report citing evidence that strongly suggests that Flor Contemplacion, a maid whose hanging in March severely strained relations between Singapore and the Philippines, was innocent. The panel asserts that one of the murder victims, Delia Maga, had injuries so severe that Contemplacion would not have been strong enough to have inflicted them.

A	B	C	D	E
Includes developments that affect more than one world region, international organizations, and important meetings of major world leaders.	Includes all domestic and regional developments in Europe, including the Soviet Union, Turkey, Cyprus, and Malta.	Includes all domestic and regional developments in Africa and the Middle East, including Iraq and Iran and excluding Cyprus, Turkey, and Afghanistan.	Includes all domestic and regional developments in Latin America, the Caribbean, and Canada.	Includes all domestic and regional developments in Asia and Pacific nations, extending from Afghanistan through all the Pacific Islands, except Hawaii.

U.S. Politics & Social Issues	U.S. Foreign Policy & Defense	U.S. Economy & Environment	Science, Technology, & Nature	Culture, Leisure, & Lifestyle	
	Deputy Defense Secretary John Deutch announces that the Defense Department has ordered a wide-ranging investigation into U.S. military involvement in Guatemala since the early 1980s, prompted by allegations made Mar. 22 by Rep. Robert Torricelli (D, N.J.).			Francisco Moncion, 76, charter member of the New York City Ballet who danced leading roles for the troupe for nearly 40 years, dies in Woodstock, New York, of cancer.	April 1
			Hannes Olof Gosta Alfven, 86, physicist who won the Nobel Prize in physics in 1970 for establishing the field of magnetohydrodynamics, which focuses on the relationship between electricity-conducting fluids and magnetic fields, dies in Djursholm, Sweden, after suffering from influenza.	The MLB players' strike ends when team owners accept the players' unconditional offer to return to work. . . . Tens of thousands of mourners flock to Corpus Christi, Texas, to view the coffin of singer Selena, 23, who was fatally shot Mar. 31. . . . Harvey Penick, 90, influential golf instructor, dies of unrevealed causes in Austin, Texas. . . . Julius Hemphill, 57, saxophonist who co-founded the World Saxophone Quartet. dies in New York City of complications from diabetes.	April 2
Supreme Court justice Sandra Day O'Connor becomes the first woman in U.S. history to preside over the high court when she takes control for a brief period during the absence of Chief Justice Rehnquist and Justice Stevens, second in seniority. . . . A federal jury in Alexandria, Virginia, finds the former president of the United Way of America, William Aramony, 67, guilty of stealing hundreds of thousands of dollars from the charity.		The Senate passes, by voice vote, a bill that makes adjustments to the federal tax code, including a measure that reinstates a tax deduction for self-employed people who pay for their health insurance. . . . In *Oklahoma Tax Commission v. Jefferson Lines*, the Supreme Court rules, 7-2, that a state can impose a sales tax on the full-fare price of bus tickets sold for interstate travel, as long as the trip begins within that state.		German judge Gertraut Goering upholds a suspended sentence against Guenter Parche, who stabbed tennis star Monica Seles in 1993. . . . Marion Tinsley, 68, considered the best checkers player in the history of the game, dies in Humble, Texas, of cancer.	April 3
A U.S. district court jury in Washington, D.C., convicts Francisco Martin Duran, 26, of attempting to assassinate Pres. Clinton in an Oct. 29, 1994, shooting incident at the White House. The jury also finds Duran guilty on nine other federal criminal counts. . . . Wallace (Gator) Bradley and Hal Baskin, two former members of Chicago's largest black street gang, the Gangster Disciples, are defeated in nonpartisan run-off elections for seats on the Chicago city council.	The Department of Defense announces that it will award the Purple Heart to 14 Americans killed in April 1994 when their U.S. Army helicopters were mistakenly shot down over northern Iraq by two U.S. fighter jets. . . . Reports state that Pakistan has extradited Iqbal Baig and Anwar Khattak, two of its most infamous drug traffickers, to the U.S., where they face 102 counts of heroin and hashish smuggling.	The Dow Jones Industrial Average on the New York Stock Exchange closes at a record high of 4201.61.			April 4
The Justice Department agrees to censure the FBI's acting deputy director, Larry Potts, for his managerial failures during a 1992 siege of the Idaho cabin of white supremacist Randall Weaver. Three people were killed in the raid. . . . In 24 cities, customs officials raid 44 stores that sell electronic surveillance equipment. They charge 15 people with participating in an international conspiracy to smuggle illegal spying devices into the U.S.		The House votes, 246-188, to pass a package of tax breaks for individuals and corporations that is expected to reduce federal tax revenue by $189 billion over five years.		In Washington, D.C., the Ringling Brothers and Barnum & Bailey Circus stage a one-ring performance in the east parking lot of the Capitol building to mark the circus's 125th anniversary.	April 5
The CDC finds that the percentage of babies born with fetal alcohol syndrome rose sixfold between 1979 and 1993. . . . The Senate by voice vote clears the final version of the Paperwork Reduction Bill of 1995, a bill designed to decrease the paperwork requirements placed on small businesses and individuals by the federal government. The House votes, 423-0, to approve the measure.	Both houses of Congress approve a $3 billion supplemental defense appropriations bill that allocates funds to resupply defense accounts drained by peacekeeping and humanitarian operations in Haiti, Bosnia-Herzegovina, Somalia, Kuwait, Cuba, and South Korea.	The Senate, by voice vote, passes legislation that will put the financial affairs of the District of Columbia under the control of a presidentially appointed review board through at least the fiscal year 1999. . . . The Senate votes, 99-0, to pass a bill that will cut about $16 billion in funding that Congress previously approved to pay for a wide range of federal programs in fiscal 1995, which ends Sept. 30.	A prominent transplant surgeon, Dr. John Najarian, and his former colleague, Dr. Richard Condie, are indicted on federal charges of marketing and selling an antirejection drug called antilymphocyte globulin, or ALG, while concealing information on the drug's potentially fatal side effects. . . . Two studies confirm the effectiveness of two types of currently standard breast cancer treatment.		April 6

F	G	H	I	J
Includes elections, federal-state relations, civil rights and liberties, crime, the judiciary, education, health care, poverty, urban affairs, and population.	Includes formation and debate of U.S. foreign and defense policies, veterans' affairs, and defense spending. (Relations with specific foreign countries are usually found under the region concerned.)	Includes business, labor, agriculture, taxation, transportation, consumer affairs, monetary and fiscal policy, natural resources, and pollution.	Includes worldwide scientific, medical, and technological developments; natural phenomena; U.S. weather; natural disasters; and accidents.	Includes the arts, religion, scholarship, communications media, sports, entertainments, fashions, fads, and social life.

	World Affairs	Europe	Africa & the Middle East	The Americas	Asia & the Pacific
April 7	A UN summit on global warming closes, and delegates from more than 120 countries approve a compromise plan that establishes a two-year negotiation process regarding the reduction of emissions of carbon dioxide and other greenhouse gases after 2000. . . . Belgian police raid the home and office of Willy Claes, NATO's secretary general, in connection with an inquiry into the 1988 sale of helicopters by the Italian company Agusta S.p.A. to the Belgian government. Claes maintains his innocence and rejects calls for his resignation.	The Russian military attacks the Chechen village of Samashki, killing scores of civilians.			In the town of Ipil on the southern Philippine island of Mindanao, military officials state that at least 20 people, including five civilian hostages, have been killed in fighting between the rebels and government troops. Hundreds of civilians are reportedly fleeing the area.
April 8		Fighting continues in the Chechen town of Samashki, where hundreds of people are reported killed. . . . Countess Edda Mussolini Ciano, 84, daughter of Benito Mussolini, the fascist dictator of Italy from 1922 to 1943, dies in Rome of cardiac arrest.			
April 9	More than 1,000 Holocaust survivors commemorate the 50th anniversary of the liberation of a Nazi concentration camp in Buchenwald, Germany, by Allied forces. It is one of several anniversary observations in April to mark such anniversaries.	In Sarajevo, the capital of Bosnia-Herzegovina, mortar attacks are launched. . . . Voters in Liechtenstein vote in a referendum to join the European Economic Area (EEA) free-trade union.	At least 62 people are killed when unidentified guerrillas armed with machetes attack the village of Yosi in Liberia. . . . Two Islamic militants carry out separate suicide car-bombing attacks in the Gaza Strip, killing seven Israeli soldiers and a U.S. Jewish student. At least 45 other Jews, mostly soldiers, are injured. Hamas and the Islamic Jihad claim responsibility. Yasser Arafat, head of the PNA, initiates a crackdown on the militant groups.	Peru's Pres. Alberto Fujimori wins reelection to a second five-year term.	
April 10	UN secretary general Boutros Boutros-Ghali announces he has selected U.S. candidate Carol Bellamy to be executive director of UNICEF, despite a challenge for the post from the European Union.	At the UN's request, NATO warplanes begin flying over Sarajevo in response to the mortar attacks that started Apr. 9. . . . Athens, the capital of Greece, begins a temporary trial ban of automobiles in the city's business district. . . . Guenter Guillaume, 68, spy for East Germany whose discovery in 1974 led to the resignation of then-West German chancellor Willy Brandt, dies in Eggersdorf, Germany, of a heart attack. . . . Premier David Oddsson's ruling coalition maintains its majority in Iceland's Althing in general elections.	Statistics show that 125 Jews have died in attacks by Palestinians since May 1994. PNA officials announce that for the first time, the PNA has meted out a prison sentence to an Islamist accused of anti-Israel violence when it sentenced Samir Ali al-Jedi, from the Islamic Jihad, to 15 years in prison for recruiting youths for suicide operations. The trial is the first case ever heard by the PNA's Higher Court for State Security, a military court. Separately, isolated exchanges of gunfire occur in Gaza City and in the southern Gaza town of Rafah.	Reports confirm that Cuba and Chile have restored full diplomatic relations, which were broken in 1973, soon after Chile's military seized power in a coup overthrowing the socialist regime of Salvador Allende Gossens.	Morarji Ranchodji Desai, 99, prime minister of India, 1977–79, dies in Bombay, India, after undergoing surgery on a blood clot in his brain. . . . Chen Yun (born Liao Chengyun), 89, one of China's "eight immortals," a group of elite revolutionaries who led the People's Republic of China after its founding in 1949, dies of an undisclosed illness.
April 11	The UN Security Council unanimously approves a resolution to help nonnuclear countries in the event that they come under nuclear attack. The nuclear states pledge not to use nuclear arms against nonnuclear states that have signed the Nuclear Nonproliferation Treaty unless those countries attack in cooperation with a nuclear state. . . . The World Bank approves a $114 million loan to help support an overhaul of Ukraine's electricity industry.	Russian helicopter gunships attack rebel forces near the town of Khorog along Tajikistan's border with Afghanistan with rocket fire in two separate raids. A CIS spokesperson states that the raids are in retaliation for attacks by rebels on a CIS border post. At least 17 rebels are killed in the first raid and 30 in the second.	Gunmen open fire on a Rwandan refugee camp near Lake Kivu in eastern Zaire, killing 31 refugees and wounding 52. . . . The PNA announces that an Islamic Jihad member, Omar Shallah, 29, has been given a life prison sentence for inciting Palestinians to enlist as suicide bombers. . . . The Zimbabwe government announces that the ruling ZANUPF party of Pres. Robert Mugabe has won an overwhelming victory in parliamentary elections.		Six aborigines mount a High Court lawsuit against the Australian government for forcibly removing them from their families during their childhoods. The six are among thousands of aboriginal people, known as the "stolen generation," who were removed from their homes in the Northern Territory as children under an "assimilation" policy in effect from 1918 to 1953.
April 12		Data from Bosnia show that, in Sarajevo, the mortar attacks that started Apr. 9 have killed three people and wounded 14. . . . Turkish officials announce that 21 Kurds and two Turkish soldiers were killed in the fighting in Tunceli. The joint Iraqi and Tunceli attacks are described as the largest military operation in Turkey's history. The Kurdish parliament in exile, at its opening session, condemns Turkey's invasion into Iraq. . . . The Red Cross estimates that Russian forces have killed at least 250 people in the Chechen Samashki during the assault that started Apr. 7.	Figures indicate that the PNA has arrested 300 members and supporters of Hamas and Islamic Jihad since Apr. 9.		

A	B	C	D	E
Includes developments that affect more than one world region, international organizations, and important meetings of major world leaders.	Includes all domestic and regional developments in Europe, including the Soviet Union, Turkey, Cyprus, and Malta.	Includes all domestic and regional developments in Africa and the Middle East, including Iraq and Iran and excluding Cyprus, Turkey, and Afghanistan.	Includes all domestic and regional developments in Latin America, the Caribbean, and Canada.	Includes all domestic and regional developments in Asia and Pacific nations, extending from Afghanistan through all the Pacific Islands, except Hawaii.

U.S. Politics & Social Issues	U.S. Foreign Policy & Defense	U.S. Economy & Environment	Science, Technology, & Nature	Culture, Leisure, & Lifestyle	
House Republicans rally in Washington, D.C., to mark the fulfillment of their 1994 "Contract with America" campaign manifesto. . . . State regulators from the Florida Agency for Health Care Administration order University Community Hospital in Tampa, Florida, to discontinue elective surgery. The hospital was involved in a series of recent medical errors, including the accidental amputation of the left foot of a diabetic man, Willie King, 51, who was supposed to have surgery to remove his diseased right foot.	Nicholas Lee Ingram, 31, a British American convicted of the 1983 slaying of a man during a robbery in Cobb County, Georgia, is put to death in the electric chair in Jackson, Georgia, despite statements of protest from 53 members of the British Parliament, the archbishop of Canterbury, and the president of the European Parliament, Klaus Haensch. Ingram is the 272nd inmate in the U.S. and the 19th in Georgia to be put to death since 1976.	The House, by voice vote, approves legislation that will put the financial affairs of the District of Columbia under the control of a presidentially appointed review board through at least the fiscal year 1999. . . . Reports confirm that, in an unprecedented move, the EEOC has affirmed that people who have abnormal genes that predispose them to illness but are otherwise healthy cannot be discriminated against by employers concerned about potential medical problems.	Researchers report that a mystery illness that killed 14 horses and a horse trainer in Australia in fall 1994 has been traced to a still-unnamed new virus that belongs to the family that includes the measles and canine distemper viruses.		April 7
			For the first time, the America Online computer network temporarily suspends a forum. The site, dedicated to Hole, a rock band, is spurred by repeated infractions by users, including a death threat. . . . Reports indicate that thousands of kangaroos in the state of South Australia have been infected with an unknown disease that renders them blind.	Royal Athlete wins the Grand National steeplechase at Aintree race course in Liverpool, England.	April 8
	Reports confirm that former secretary of defense Robert McNamara, who was a staunch proponent of U.S. involvement in the Vietnam War in the 1960s, asserts in a new book, *In Retrospect: The Tragedy and Lessons of Vietnam*, that U.S. policy in Vietnam was a mistake.			Ben Crenshaw wins his second Masters tournament at the Augusta, Georgia, National Golf Club.	April 9
Rep. Nathan Deal of Georgia announces that he will leave the Democratic Party to join the GOP. . . . In San Francisco, Superior Court judge James Warren rules that the maker of guns used in a 1993 shooting spree by Gian Luigi Ferri, who killed eight people in a San Francisco law firm, may be sued for the deaths. The decision reportedly is the first to hold that an assault-weapon maker might be liable for the criminal use of its product. . . . A New York City statute that bans smoking in almost all public places takes effect.		Transit workers in Philadelphia, Pennsylvania, return to work, ending a two-week strike that crippled the city's sprawling network of bus, subway, trolley, and train lines.	The world's first national DNA database becomes operational in Britain.		April 10
	Pres. Clinton signs a $3 billion supplemental defense-appropriations bill that allocates funds to resupply defense accounts drained by peacekeeping and humanitarian operations in Haiti, Bosnia-Herzegovina, Somalia, Kuwait, Cuba, and South Korea.	Pres. Clinton signs into law a bill that makes several minor adjustments to the federal tax code. Most prominent among the changes is a popular measure that reinstates a tax deduction for self-employed people who pay for their own health insurance.			April 11
The Massachusetts Supreme Judicial Court unanimously upholds a 1993 jury decision supporting Boston University's ownership claim to about one-third of slain civil-rights leader Rev. Martin Luther King Jr.'s personal papers. . . . A study suggests that smoking by pregnant women results in about 5,600 infant deaths and between 19,000 and 141,000 miscarriages each year in the U.S.	The U.S. expels Edmundo Suarez Hernandez and Saul Hermida Griego, Cuban UN diplomats who refuse to waive their diplomatic immunity and face criminal charges for an alleged assault on a New York City police officer. . . . In Boston, Massachusetts, federal judge Douglas Woodlock orders Gen. Hector Gramajo to pay a total of $47.5 million to Roman Catholic nun Dianna Ortiz and eight Guatemalan Indians terrorized by the Guatemalan military during the late 1980s. Gramajo was Guatemala's defense minister at the time.		Researchers state that middle-aged men who consume large amounts of fruits and vegetables are less likely to suffer strokes later in life than are other men.	Reports state that author David Guterson has been awarded the PEN/Faulkner Award for Fiction for his first novel, *Snow Falling on Cedars*.	April 12
F	G	H	I	J
Includes elections, federal-state relations, civil rights and liberties, crime, the judiciary, education, health care, poverty, urban affairs, and population.	*Includes formation and debate of U.S. foreign and defense policies, veterans' affairs, and defense spending. (Relations with specific foreign countries are usually found under the region concerned.)*	*Includes business, labor, agriculture, taxation, transportation, consumer affairs, monetary and fiscal policy, natural resources, and pollution.*	*Includes worldwide scientific, medical, and technological developments; natural phenomena; U.S. weather; natural disasters; and accidents.*	*Includes the arts, religion, scholarship, communications media, sports, entertainments, fashions, fads, and social life.*

	World Affairs	Europe	Africa & the Middle East	The Americas	Asia & the Pacific
April 13	Reports suggest that a former agent of the Serbian secret police has provided the Yugoslav War Crimes Tribunal with documents implicating Serbian president Slobodan Milosevic in war crimes committed in Bosnia-Herzegovina.	The Royal Ulster Constabulary, Northern Ireland's police force, arrest two men and a woman after raiding an alleged weapons factory of the Ulster Volunteer Force, an outlawed unionist group, near Belfast. Police confiscate about 40 rifles, pistols, and machine-guns, the largest cache found since cease-fires were declared in 1994. . . . Paavo Lipponen is sworn in as Finland's new premier at the head of a five-party governing coalition.			Clashes that started Apr. 6 between Russian-led forces and Islamic Tajik rebels along Tajikistan's border with Afghanistan spill over into the northern town of Taloqan in Afghanistan when Russian jets kill 125 civilians and wound 250. . . . Japanese authorities conduct searches at various sites associated with Aum Shinrikyo, a Japanese religious sect linked to the production of sarin, the nerve gas used in the Mar. 20 attack in Tokyo.
April 14	The UN Security Council passes a resolution to allow Iraq to sell up to $2 billion worth of oil to help alleviate pervasive shortages of food and medicine among its most economically pressed citizens. . . . In a dispute over fishing rights that has raged between Canada and Spain since March, Spain refuses a final settlement that was accepted by other members of the EU.	Sergeant Ralph Gunther, a French peacekeeper, is killed by sniper fire in Sarajevo, the Bosnian capital. . . . Jacques Mellick, a member of France's parliament and mayor of the northern town of Bethune, is barred from office for two years and handed a six-month suspended sentence after admitting that he lied under oath to protect businessman Bernard Tapie, a former Socialist Party minister who is one of several leading public figures brought to trial as a result of a sweeping anticorruption campaign.	Eight residents of the village of Nyabishungu in southwestern Rwanda allegedly attack two government soldiers, prompting the Rwandan army to shoot and kill 16 Hutu villagers.	Haitian police arrest Claudy Lacroix, a suspect in the Mar. 28 slaying of Mireille Durocher Bertin, a prominent rightist opponent of Pres. Jean-Bertrand Aristide.	Shintaro Ishihara, one of Japan's best-known legislators, resigns his seat in the lower house of the country's Diet due to frustration over the state of the Japanese political system.
April 15	In response to Spain's Apr. 14 rejection of a settlement over fishing rights, Canadian prime minister Jean Chretien orders two heavily armed naval gunboats to the disputed waters, where six Canadian fisheries patrol and Coast Guard boats are already stationed.	In Bosnia, a French soldier, Corporal Eric Hardoin, 30, is killed by sniper fire while working on an anti-sniping barrier outside the Sarajevo Holiday Inn, a common site for shootings of civilians.			Members of the militant Muslim group Abu Sayyaf kill 14 people taken hostage in the Apr. 4 raid on the southern Philippine town of Ipil.
April 16	Iraqi president Saddam Hussein's cabinet formally turns down the Apr. 14 UN Security Council offer to allow Iraq to sell up to $2 billion worth of oil to help alleviate pervasive shortages of food and medicine among its most economically pressed citizens. In explaining the rejection, Iraq's state-run radio argues, "The [UN] resolution seriously compromises Iraq's sovereignty and national unity.". . . Canada and the European Union reach a fishing agreement, ending a six-week-long dispute over fishing rights that raged between Canada and Spain.	Stewart Miles MacPherson, 86, British radio commentator known for his coverage of sports events, dies of unreported causes.	Israeli security agents reportedly disguised as Arabs shoot three Hamas members to death in an ambush in Hebron, the West Bank's second-largest city. Separately, the PNA's military court imposes its first sentences against Hamas militants when it orders two-year incarcerations for Mohammed Abu Shamala, 26, and Riad Atar, 24, for illegal weapons training and weapons use.		Iqbal Masih, 12, who gained international attention for his criticism of child-labor practices in Pakistan, is shot dead. Masih, sold into labor as a carpet weaver by his parents at the age of four, spent nearly six years shackled to a carpet loom before escaping at the age of 10 and speaking to an international labor conference in Sweden in 1994. . . . A controversial sculpture that portrays Britain's Queen Elizabeth II and her husband, Prince Philip, sitting naked on a park bench is removed from public view in Canberra, Australia, after vandalism to the sculpture nearly destroyed it.
April 17	Representatives from more than 170 nations meet at UN headquarters in New York City for the beginning of a four-week conference aimed at renewing the Treaty on the Nonproliferation of Nuclear Weapons (commonly known as the Nuclear Nonproliferation Treaty, or NPT).		In Burundi, three people are killed and 32 wounded when attackers throw grenades into a market in Ngozi. . . . Bahrain's government announces it has released 120 political prisoners arrested during prodemocracy disturbances that started in December 1994 after the arrest of a popular Shi'ite Muslim leader, Sheik Ali Salman.		Rustico Secundo, who was taken hostage by a militant Muslim group during the Apr. 4 raid on Philippine town of Ipil, tells reporters that the extremists mutilated and beheaded their captives in a mass execution Apr. 15, and one woman is still being held captive. . . . Philippine foreign minister Roberto Romulo resigns from his post in an attempt to calm the ongoing political furor over the March 17 execution of Flor Contemplacion.
April 18		In Spain Judge Baltasar Garzón indicts 14 people in connection with the government's alleged "dirty war" against Basque separatists in the 1980s. Some of those charged are former government officials and state security personnel.	Two soldiers and five Hutu gunmen are killed when Hutu gunmen attack an army post in Gasorwe, Burundi. . . . At least 10 refugees are killed in a stampede that occurs after soldiers from the Rwandan army surround a refugee camp at Kibeho, Rwanda, and fire shots into the air.	The Bolivian government declares a 90-day state of siege after the collapse of union-government talks aimed at ending several weeks of strikes and civil unrest. . . . Arturo Frondizi, 86, president of Argentina, 1958–62, dies in Buenos Aires, Argentina, of a heart ailment.	

A	B	C	D	E
Includes developments that affect more than one world region, international organizations, and important meetings of major world leaders.	*Includes all domestic and regional developments in Europe, including the Soviet Union, Turkey, Cyprus, and Malta.*	*Includes all domestic and regional developments in Africa and the Middle East, including Iraq and Iran and excluding Cyprus, Turkey, and Afghanistan.*	*Includes all domestic and regional developments in Latin America, the Caribbean, and Canada.*	*Includes all domestic and regional developments in Asia and Pacific nations, extending from Afghanistan through all the Pacific Islands, except Hawaii.*

U.S. Politics & Social Issues	U.S. Foreign Policy & Defense	U.S. Economy & Environment	Science, Technology, & Nature	Culture, Leisure, & Lifestyle	
The Joint Commission on the Accreditation of Healthcare Organizations, a private hospital-certification group, strips University Community Hospital in Tampa, Florida, of its accreditation. The hospital was barred from elective surgery by state regulators from the Florida Agency for Health Care Administration on Apr. 7.	The U.S. Fourth Circuit Court of Appeals in Richmond, Virginia, upholds a lower court's ruling that the Citadel, a currently all-male military academy in Charleston, South Carolina, is required to admit a female student, Shannon Faulkner, to its Corps of Cadets.		A strong earthquake strikes west Texas and New Mexico. The quake measures 5.6 on the Richter scale and is the strongest to hit Texas in 64 years. Its epicenter is located in Marathon, Texas. . . . Researchers conclude that the largest-ever study of the possible heart benefits of consuming large amounts of fish fails to find any link between consumption of fish or fish oil and risk of heart disease.		April 13
				Burl Icle Ivanhoe Ives, 85, folk singer and actor who earned an Academy Award for best supporting actor in 1958, dies in Anacortes, Washington, of cancer.	April 14
		FEC data indicates that Sen. Phil Gramm (R, Tex.) leads all candidates for the 1996 Republican presidential nomination in fund-raising and campaign spending to date. Gramm has raised $8.7 million and spent about $4.7 million on his campaign through the first three months of 1995.			April 15
				Reports confirm that the 17th annual Pritzker Architecture Prize for lifetime achievement has been awarded to Tadeo Ando, a Japanese architect. . . . Cy Endfield, 80, film director whose left-leaning movies brought about his censure in 1951 by the U.S. House Un-American Activities Committee, dies in Shipston-on-Stour, England, of an undisclosed illness.	April 16
		A U.S. District Court jury in Uniondale, New York, awards $19 million to Faith Pescatore, the widow of one of 270 people killed in the 1988 bombing of Pan Am Flight 103. The judgment is the fourth to come in the case and is considered among the largest ever awarded to an individual in a commercial airline disaster. . . . Pres. Clinton signs legislation that will put the financial affairs of the District of Columbia under the control of a review board through at least the fiscal year 1999.		Cosmas N'Deti of Kenya wins his third consecutive Boston Marathon with a time of two hours, nine minutes, and 22 seconds. N'Deti is the third person ever to win three consecutive Boston Marathons.	April 17
In *Plaut v. Spendthrift Farm Inc.*, the Supreme Court rules, 7-2, that Congress does not have the constitutional authority to reopen cases on which federal courts have already passed judgment.	The U.S. State Department announces that Frederick C. Cuny, an American disaster-relief expert, has disappeared in Chechnya, the breakaway southern Russian republic embroiled in a war with Russian forces.	The dollar reaches a postwar low of 80.63 yen in New York trading. . . . In *Freightliner Corp. v. Myrick*, the Supreme Court rules unanimously that lawsuits against two trucking companies can go forward under a Georgia law that requires tractor trailers to have antilock brakes.	U.S. Department of Energy scientists at Los Alamos National Laboratory in New Mexico report that they have developed a new superconducting tape comprising metal and ceramic materials that carries substantially more current than existing "high-temperature" superconductors. The three-layer tape has zero resistance to electricity at -320°F (-196°C), the temperature of liquid nitrogen, and can carry more than 1 million amperes per square centimeter.	Philip M. Foisie, 73, journalist who helped establish the foreign news desk for *The Washington Post* newspaper, dies in Alexandria, Virginia, of a heart attack. . . . Pulitzer Prizes are awarded to Carol Shields, Jonathan Weiner, Horton Foote, Joan D. Hedrick, Philip Levine, and Morton Gould, as well as others.	April 18
F	G	H	I	J	
Includes elections, federal-state relations, civil rights and liberties, crime, the judiciary, education, health care, poverty, urban affairs, and population.	Includes formation and debate of U.S. foreign and defense policies, veterans' affairs, and defense spending. (Relations with specific foreign countries are usually found under the region concerned.)	Includes business, labor, agriculture, taxation, transportation, consumer affairs, monetary and fiscal policy, natural resources, and pollution.	Includes worldwide scientific, medical, and technological developments; natural phenomena; U.S. weather; natural disasters; and accidents.	Includes the arts, religion, scholarship, communications media, sports, entertainments, fashions, fads, and social life.	

	World Affairs	Europe	Africa & the Middle East	The Americas	Asia & the Pacific
April 19	Libya has defied a UN ban by flying 150 Mecca-bound pilgrims to Saudi Arabia aboard an unauthorized Libyan plane. The UN sanctions committee eases its ban on flights to and from Libya to allow Libyans to take part in the hajj, or annual pilgrimage to Mecca, Saudi Arabia, Islam's most holy site, stipulating that Libyan pilgrims may fly between Libya and Saudi Arabia on Egyptian aircraft.	In Madrid, Spain, Jose Maria Aznar, the leader of the opposition Popular Party, is slightly injured in a blast from a car bomb. The explosion also injures 12 others and causes extensive damage to buildings and cars in the area.	Soldiers expel more than 100,000 people from a refugee camp at Kibeho, Rwanda, the country's largest. The refugees, most of them Hutu, are ordered to return to their homes. Several other camps close. . . . Reports reveal that hundreds of civilians were arrested in recurrent rioting and that at least three policemen and 10 civilians died in clashes in Bahrain. The unrest largely occurred in Shi'ite neighborhoods, a number of which were torched by rioters.	The Bolivian government discloses that some 380 union members have been arrested since the onset of the siege in March.	More than 300 people are taken to hospitals in Yokohama, Japan, after a poisonous gas is released in a crowded train that spreads throughout the city's main railroad station. . . . Rebel forces from the Liberation Tigers of Tamil Eelam break a 14-week-long cease-fire agreement by blowing up two Sri Lankan government gunboats at a naval base in the eastern port of Trincomalee. Twelve sailors and four rebels are killed in the attack, and another 21 people are wounded.
April 20		In France, in a highly publicized case, Michel Noir, the mayor of Lyons, and Michel Mouillot, the mayor of Cannes, are handed 15-month suspended sentences and barred from seeking public office for five years. . . . Milovan Djilas, 83, Yugoslav communist revolutionary who became the country's leading political dissident after denouncing his former comrades, dies in Belgrade, Serbia, of heart ailments.	Ten Europeans kidnapped by rebels in Sierra Leone between November 1994 and January 1995 are freed unconditionally at Sierra Leone's border with Guinea. Six of those freed are British, three are Swiss, and one is German. Six Sierra Leone citizens also are freed.	In Canada, a bomb explodes at Province House, the provincial legislature building in Charlottetown, Prince Edward Island, injuring one person.	Fighting along Tajikistan's border with Afghanistan spills into Afghanistan when Russian jets bomb the Darwaz district of Afghanistan's Badakhshan region, killing 12 civilians and wounding 16. Statistics show that at least 200 Tajik rebels and 41 members of the Russian-led border unit have been killed in clashes that started Apr. 6 along border.
April 21		The Slovak Internal Affairs Ministry discloses that Slovak authorities have seized 37.4 pounds (17 kg) of uranium and arrested nine people near Poprad, Slovakia. The seizure is the latest in a series of incidents involving radioactive material, including weapons-grade plutonium and uranium, smuggled from countries of the former Soviet Union to Eastern or Western Europe.	At least 22 refugees are killed and 40 are wounded in the Kibeho camp, which houses as many as 100,000 refugees in Rwanda, when government soldiers open fire after a small group of refugees attempt to take a gun from a soldier.	Several Argentine unions stage a general strike to protest the government's free-market policies.	
April 22		Rauf Denktash is reelected to his third term as president of the breakaway ethnic Turkish section of Cyprus.	An estimated 2,000 refugees are killed in two incidents by gunfire or machetes or subsequent stampedes, when government soldiers attempting to close refugee camps in southwest Rwanda fire on refugees who rushed military lines. The outbreaks of violence are the deadliest since the end of Rwanda's civil war in July 1994.		Four Russian helicopter gunships attack the Afghan village of Maymay as fighting along the border continues.
April 23	The IMF projects that world economic output will rise 3.8% in 1995 and 4.2% in 1996. These figures show a modest increase over 1994, when the world economy grew by 3.7%.	Socialist Party candidate Lionel Jospin is the surprise top finisher in the first round of French presidential elections.			Hideo Murai, 36, a top leader of the Aum Shinrikyo cult, suspected in recent gas attacks in Japan, is stabbed to death in Tokyo.
April 24	The UN-sponsored Yugoslav War Crimes Tribunal names Bosnian Serb leader Radovan Karadzic and General Ratko Mladic, the commander of the Bosnian Serb army, as suspects in war crimes allegedly committed in Bosnia. The tribunal also names Mico Stanisic, a former chief of the Bosnian Serb secret police, as a war-crimes suspect.	Britain's Conservative Party prime minister John Major invites eight suspended Tory members of Parliament back into his parliamentary party. Major also urges one MP who voluntarily gave up his parliamentary privileges to rejoin the Tories.			

A	B	C	D	E
Includes developments that affect more than one world region, international organizations, and important meetings of major world leaders.	Includes all domestic and regional developments in Europe, including the Soviet Union, Turkey, Cyprus, and Malta.	Includes all domestic and regional developments in Africa and the Middle East, including Iraq and Iran and excluding Cyprus, Turkey, and Afghanistan.	Includes all domestic and regional developments in Latin America, the Caribbean, and Canada.	Includes all domestic and regional developments in Asia and Pacific nations, extending from Afghanistan through all the Pacific Islands, except Hawaii.

U.S. Politics & Social Issues	U.S. Foreign Policy & Defense	U.S. Economy & Environment	Science, Technology, & Nature	Culture, Leisure, & Lifestyle	
A massive car bomb explodes outside a federal office building in Oklahoma City, Okla., The blast's death toll is expected to top 200. More than 400 people are injured, and 150 of the building's estimated 550 workers are missing. Several children are thought to be dead since the building houses a day-care facility. It is the deadliest terrorist attack ever in the U.S. . . . In *McIntyre v. Ohio Elections Commission*, the Supreme Court strikes down, 7-2, an Ohio statute that bans the distribution of anonymous political literature.		J(oseph) Peter Grace Jr., 81, chair of W. R. Grace & Co., a specialty chemicals and health-care company founded by his grandfather in 1854, dies in New York City of cancer. . . . Mary Caperton Bingham, 90, matriarch of a Louisville, Kentucky-based media empire, dies in Louisville after suffering a heart attack while attending a banquet in her honor.	A long-term study of 17,300 middle-aged male Harvard graduates indicates that vigorous exercise, but not moderate exercise, increases life expectancy.		April 19
In Oklahoma City, Oklahoma, workers install supports to keep the bombed building from crumbling. The FBI states that authorities have two suspects, described as white males. . . . The CDC finds that the suicide rate among adolescents ages 10–14 increased by 120% between 1980 and 1992, to 1.7 per 100,000 from 0.8 per 100,000.					April 20
Federal authorities take Timothy J. McVeigh, 27, a suspect in the Apr. 19 car-bombing attack in Oklahoma City, into custody. Officials also take into custody two brothers, Terry Lynn Nichols and James Nichols, described as potential witnesses, not suspects. . . . An Oswego, N.Y., jury convicts Waneta Hoyt of fatally smothering her five babies between 1965 and 1971. The deaths of the children initially were attributed to SIDS. . . . A University Community Hospital in Tampa, Fla., spokesman states that the Apr. 7 ban on elective surgery in the hospital was removed.				Tessie O'Shea, 82, British actress and music-hall singer who won a 1965 Tony, dies in Leesburg, Florida, of congestive heart failure.	April 21
Margaret (Maggie) Kuhn, 89, founder of the Gray Panthers, an organization that champions the rights of the elderly and fights age discrimination, dies in Philadelphia, Pennsylvania, of numerous ailments.		Kenneth Starr, the independent counsel investigating the Whitewater affair, interviews Pres. Clinton and First Lady Hillary Rodham Clinton to collect testimony to present to a federal grand jury in Little Rock, Arkansas.		Naomi Nover (born Naomi Goll), 84, news columnist who covered the White House and Congress, dies in Washington, D.C., after undergoing surgery for an aneurysm.	April 22
Pres. Clinton and First Lady Hillary Rodham Clinton attend a memorial service for victims of the Apr.19 bombing at the Oklahoma City State Fair Grounds arena, along with more than 10,000 people. . . . John Cornelius Stennis, 93, conservative Democrat who represented Mississippi in the Senate for more than 40 years and was first elected to the Senate in 1947, dies in Jackson, Mississippi, of complications from pneumonia.				Eight of the 16 living Nobel Prize laureates in literature gather in Atlanta, Georgia, to for a series of discussions. . . . In Britain, the Alexander Korda Award for best British film goes to *Shallow Grave*. . . . Howard Cosell (born Howard William Cohen), 77, one of the best-known personalities in TV sports who gained national attention as the commentator for *Monday Night Football*, dies in New York City of a heart embolism.	April 23
Gilbert B. Murray, the chief lobbyist for the California Forestry Association, is killed when a mail bomb explodes in the group's Sacramento, California, offices. Federal investigators blame the incident on the Unabomber, who has been linked to 15 other bombing incidents since 1978.	The U.S. dispatches two diplomats to Chechnya to look for Frederick C. Cuny, an American disaster-relief expert whose disappearance was confirmed Apr. 18. The decision to send American diplomats to Chechnya is a change of policy for the U.S., which has sharply criticized the Russian military operation in the republic.	*Business Week*'s 45th annual survey of the two highest-paid executives at 371 companies finds that average salary and bonus compensation for the 742 executives is $1,399,698, a 10% increase from 1993. A record 537 of those executives earn more than $1 million. Charles Locke, chair and CEO of Morton International Inc., tops the list with earnings of $25,928,000.		The MLB season opens with several labor issues still unresolved after a 234-day players' strike. . . . *The Rainmaker* by John Grisham tops the bestseller list.	April 24

F	G	H	I	J
Includes elections, federal-state relations, civil rights and liberties, crime, the judiciary, education, health care, poverty, urban affairs, and population.	Includes formation and debate of U.S. foreign and defense policies, veterans' affairs, and defense spending. (Relations with specific foreign countries are usually found under the region concerned.)	Includes business, labor, agriculture, taxation, transportation, consumer affairs, monetary and fiscal policy, natural resources, and pollution.	Includes worldwide scientific, medical, and technological developments; natural phenomena; U.S. weather; natural disasters; and accidents.	Includes the arts, religion, scholarship, communications media, sports, entertainments, fashions, fads, and social life.

	World Affairs	Europe	Africa & the Middle East	The Americas	Asia & the Pacific
April 25	Thousands of people in Australia and Turkey commemorate the 80th anniversary of the Allied invasion of Turkey at Gallipoli during World War I. . . . The finance ministers and central-bank heads of the Group of Seven (G-7) leading industrialized nations meet in Washington, D.C.	A commemoration of the 50th anniversary of Italy's uprising against Nazi German forces is held in Milan. Pres. Oscar Luigi Scalfaro attends mass in honor of the 335 Italians executed by Germans following the uprising. . . . The first shipment of nuclear waste to be stored permanently in Germany arrives in Lower Saxony. . . . Turkey claims success in its military operation against Kurds in northern Iraq and announces that most of force was withdrawn.	Abd al-Samed Harizat, 30, a Palestinian, dies in Israel while in custody of Israeli security agents. He had been detained on suspicion of leading a branch of the Qassem Brigades, the armed wing of Hamas. . . . The Dutch government suspends $30 million in direct aid to the Rwandan government in the wake of recent massacres.		Malaysia's ruling party, the National Front, increases its parliamentary majority in national elections.
April 26		The British government announces that it will pay the family of Winston Churchill, Britain's prime minister during World War II, £13.25 million ($21 million) for Churchill's pre-1945 writings.	Twenty Rwandan refugees are found dead in a crowded jail cell just north of Butare. They were awaiting clearance to return home.		A British tanker carrying 14 tons (12.6 metric tons) of nuclear waste docks in the harbor of Rokkasho, Japan.
April 27		A major gas pipeline explodes in a remote area of north-central Russia near the town of Ukhta. No injuries are reported, but the pipeline explosion is the third disaster in less than a year involving Russia's oil and gas industry. . . . Peter Wright, 78, British intelligence officer whose memoir *Spycatcher* (1987) generated a storm of controversy, dies in Tasmania, Australia, of complications from Alzheimer's disease.	Fourteen Hutu refugees are stoned or beaten to death after returning home to the village of Huye, outside the southwestern city of Butare. . . . The Israeli government discloses a plan to confiscate 135 acres (55 hectares) of mainly Arab-owned land in disputed East Jerusalem as a site for Jewish housing units and an Israeli police station. The self-rule PNA and Arab countries promptly denounce the plan.		
April 28	Austria formally becomes the 10th member of the Schengen group, a border-free region within the European Union.		Amnesty International states that it is "gravely concerned at the sharp increase" in executions in Saudi Arabia in recent months. Some 90 people reportedly were executed in Saudi Arabia between Jan. 20 and Apr. 19, compared with 53 executions during all of 1994. . . . A forensic pathologist from Scotland, Derrick Pounder, reports that that the Palestinian who died Apr. 25, Abd al-Samed Harizat, 30, suffered fatal brain damage while being tortured.		Rebel forces from the Liberation Tigers of Tamil Eelam down two Sri Lankan government air force planes, killing all 97 people aboard. The planes crash near the Palaly Air Base on the rebel-controlled Jaffna peninsula. . . . A leaking gas pipeline at a Taegu, South Korea, subway construction site explodes, killing at least 100 people and injuring about 200. Officials estimate that 60 of the fatalities were teenage students on their way to school.
April 29		In Kazakhstan, voters approve in a referendum a mandate to extend Pres. Nursultan Nazarbayev's term until 2000. . . . Fighting is reported on at least three fronts in Bosnia. . . . Data suggest that in the military operation that Turkey started in March, 505 PKK guerrillas and 58 Turkish soldiers were killed.			In a ceremony in Hanoi, the country's capital, Vietnamese prime minister Vo Van Kiet recalls "genocidal crimes" committed by U.S. troops during the war, including the notorious 1968 My Lai massacre.
April 30		The predominantly Muslim government of Bosnia and leaders of the Bosnian Serbs refuse to extend a four-month cease-fire, set to expire May 1 at noon local time.	The last of the refugee camps in Rwanda close, as thousands of refugees are trucked home from the Ndera camp near Kigali, the capital.		The Vietnamese government celebrates the 20th anniversary of the fall of Saigon—now called Ho Chi Minh City—which ended the Vietnam War. Thousands of Vietnamese military personnel and civilians turn out to view a parade.

A	B	C	D	E
Includes developments that affect more than one world region, international organizations, and important meetings of major world leaders.	Includes all domestic and regional developments in Europe, including the Soviet Union, Turkey, Cyprus, and Malta.	Includes all domestic and regional developments in Africa and the Middle East, including Iraq and Iran and excluding Cyprus, Turkey, and Afghanistan.	Includes all domestic and regional developments in Latin America, the Caribbean, and Canada.	Includes all domestic and regional developments in Asia and Pacific nations, extending from Afghanistan through all the Pacific Islands, except Hawaii.

U.S. Politics & Social Issues	U.S. Foreign Policy & Defense	U.S. Economy & Environment	Science, Technology, & Nature	Culture, Leisure, & Lifestyle	
In *California Department of Corrections v. Morales*, the Supreme Court rules, 7-2, to uphold a change in California parole law that reduces the frequency of parole hearings for some inmates.... In Birmingham, Alabama, U.S. district judge Sam Pointer Jr. rules that Dow Chemical can be held liable in federal court for health problems allegedly resulting from silicone breast implants made by Dow Corning. The ruling reverses an earlier decision.				Art Fazzin Fleming, 70, the original host of the TV game show *Jeopardy!*, dies in Crystal River, Florida, of pancreatic cancer.... Ginger Rogers (born Virginia Katherine McMath), 83, film star and the glamorous dance partner of Fred Astaire, dies in Rancho Mirage, California, of natural causes.	April 25
People across the nation observe a minute of silence at 9:02 A.M., exactly a week after the blast in Oklahoma City. Pres. Clinton declares Oklahoma City a major disaster area, allowing residents to receive longer-term federal aid. ...In *U.S. v. Lopez*, the Supreme Court rules, 5-4, that the Gun-Free School Zones Act of 1990, which makes possession of a firearm within 1,000 feet (300 m) of a school a federal offense, is unconstitutional.... Corliss Lamont, 93, authority on humanist philosophy and director of the ACLU, 1932–54, dies in Ossining, N.Y., of heart failure.			Hira Jamal, a Pakistani conjoined twin who was separated from her sister in January, is released from the hospital. Her twin died in February.... An uncompleted study of heart-attack victims given cardiopulmonary resuscitation (CPR) with a device resembling a toilet plunger shows the device is slightly less effective than standard CPR.	Reports confirm that Poet A. R. Ammons, a professor at Cornell University, has won the Ruth Lilly Poetry Prize.	April 26
The death toll from the Apr. 19 explosion in Oklahoma City, Oklahoma, stands at 110, and 15 of those are children. As many as 94 people are unaccounted for and presumed dead. Local officials state that 200 buildings in the downtown Oklahoma City area incurred structural damage. Ten buildings in the area collapsed.			Researchers report that cells from fetuses implanted into the brain of a 59-year-old man who had Parkinson's disease began to reverse the effects of the disease prior to his death from an unrelated cause. ...A study finds of 134,088 pregnancies suggests that biological factors put teenage mothers at a higher than average risk of having babies who are premature or have other health complications.	In Charlotte, South Carolina, Christophe Auguin of France wins the BOC Challenge solo round-the-world yacht race, finishing with a time of 121 days, 17 hours, 11 minutes, and 46 seconds.	April 27
		The Dow closes at a record high of 4321.27.	Researchers report they have found in Zaire tools made from animal bones, including barbed points and blades, that are 75,000–90,000 years old. The tools are about 60,000 years older than similar artifacts found in Europe, where scientists previously believed humans first developed the ability to use such sophisticated tools. Some scientists, however, challenge the accuracy of the techniques used to date the Zairean tools.	World Wide Christian Radio, a powerful short-wave station in Nashville, Tennessee, removes from the air indefinitely Mark Koernke, the host of the "Intelligence Report" who suggested on the air that the government itself blew up the Oklahoma federal building on Apr. 19.	April 28
	Angier Biddle Duke, 79, diplomat and scion of two wealthy and influential U.S. families who was noted for his work in protecting nonwhite foreign diplomats against racial prejudice in the U.S. during the 1960s, dies in Southampton, New York, after being struck by a car while in-line skating.				April 29
In a case that received national attention, the adoptive parents of a four-year-old boy known as Baby Richard hand over the child to his biological parents, Otakar and Daniela Kirchner. Daniela Kirchner had told Otakar Kirchner that the baby was dead while they were estranged. When they reconciled, he learned the truth and filed for custody of the child, who had never met his biological father. The case sparked debate over the rights of adoptive parents.	Pres. Clinton announces an executive order to suspend all U.S. trade with Iran, citing what he calls Iran's efforts to acquire nuclear weapons, its continued support for terrorism, and concern over a Russian-Iranian agreement that calls for Russia to construct one or more nuclear power reactors in Iran and provide nuclear training to Iranian technicians.... In Washington, D.C., hundreds of U.S. war veterans are joined by Vietnamese refugees and former South Vietnamese soldiers to mark the anniversary of the war's end. About 500 Vietnamese refugees, including a group of 15 Buddhist monks, gather outside the White House to call for political and religious freedom in their homeland.			Eric Berger, 88, editor for Scholastic Magazines Inc., an educational publisher, dies in New York City of lung cancer.	April 30
F	G	H	I	J	
Includes elections, federal-state relations, civil rights and liberties, crime, the judiciary, education, health care, poverty, urban affairs, and population.	*Includes formation and debate of U.S. foreign and defense policies, veterans' affairs, and defense spending. (Relations with specific foreign countries are usually found under the region concerned.)*	*Includes business, labor, agriculture, taxation, transportation, consumer affairs, monetary and fiscal policy, natural resources, and pollution.*	*Includes worldwide scientific, medical, and technological developments; natural phenomena; U.S. weather; natural disasters; and accidents.*	*Includes the arts, religion, scholarship, communications media, sports, entertainments, fashions, fads, and social life.*	

	World Affairs	Europe	Africa & the Middle East	The Americas	Asia & the Pacific
May 1	The UN World Health Organization (WHO) issues its first annual survey of global health. The report cites poverty as the primary underlying cause of disease and death worldwide. According to WHO, 2 billion of the world's 5.6 billion people have been ill at any one time, and many have died from preventable causes.	Croatian forces launch an attack on the Serb-held Krajina region of Croatia, shattering a 14-month-old "permanent cease-fire" and ending more than three years of relative calm in Croatia since January 1992.... Clashes are reported in Grozny, the Chechen capital.... Thousands of communist protesters march in Moscow, St. Petersburg, and as many as 60 other cities across Russia to celebrate May Day. The demonstrators call for the removal of Pres. Boris Yeltsin.	A UN speaker reveals that four murdered Hutus were found dumped into a latrine in Huye, Rwanda.		The Sri Lankan government's air force jets bomb rebel strongholds in the Jaffna region.... The Hindu-dominated government of India's Maharashtra state officially changes the name of Bombay, India's financial hub, to its traditional name, Mumbai. The federal government and some newspapers refuse to recognize the name change.
May 2		Croatian Serbs retaliate for the May 1 offensive by firing rocket-propelled cluster bombs on downtown Zagreb and near the airport south of the city, killing five people and injuring at least 134.... Salvatore Riina, the reputed head of the Sicilian Mafia, and 40 other alleged mob bosses go on trial for the 1992 murder of prosecutor Giovanni Falcone, his wife, and three of his bodyguards. The trial is considered the most damaging blow to the Mafia since 1987, when Falcone won jail sentences for 338 mobsters.	A Rwandan military court opens the trial of 14 soldiers from the Tutsi-led army accused of aggravated murder and other crimes against members of the Hutu majority.		Reports reveal that Yao Daorong, a farmer who trapped and killed a rare giant panda in a nature reserve in China's southwestern province of Sichuan, has been given an 18-year prison sentence.
May 3		Croatian Serbs hit Zagreb with five rockets, killing one policeman and wounding 40 civilians.... In Northern Ireland, Republican protesters, many of whom are reportedly affiliated with Sinn Fein, clash with police, injuring at least 12.... In a tribute attended by 10,000 people, French president Mitterrand throws a bouquet of flowers into the Seine River, where Brahim Bouarrem, a Moroccan immigrant, was drowned, allegedly by a rightist skinheads hours before a rally for the presidential candidate Jean-Marie Le Pen from the National Front.		The British government names John Owen as the next governor general of the Cayman Islands, a British territory.... In Brazil, 48,000 oil workers go on strike to demand higher wages and to protest government proposals to privatize state-owned companies.	
May 4		Croatian forces continue their offensive in western Slavonia, where clashes are reported near the town of Pakrac.	Jordan and the Palestinian National Authority sign a trade pact that sets the stage for an upsurge in trade between Jordan and the Palestinian territories.	Jose Estenssoro, president and CEO of Argentine oil company YPF SA, dies in an aircraft crash in Ecuador.	
May 5		Chechen rebels shoot down a Russian reconnaissance plane in eastern Chechnya, killing the pilot. ... The Turkish army claims it has killed 555 PKK guerrillas in the six-week operation that started in March.... The Italian justice ministry announces that it is investigating Italy's anticorruption prosecutors for allegedly abusing their powers. The decision draws fire.	Iran and Turkey sign a $20 billion, 23-year deal under which Iran will supply natural gas to Turkey. The pact also calls for the two sides to construct a 1,000-mile-long pipeline for transporting gas to Ankara, Turkey, from Tabriz, Iran.		
May 6	In Hyde Park, London, HRM Elizabeth, the Queen Mother, opens three days of celebrations in Britain commemorating the 50th anniversary of Victory in Europe Day. The tributes are attended by leading figures from about 60 nations, including U.S. vice president Al Gore, British prime minister John Major, Canadian prime minister Jean Chretien, German chancellor Helmut Kohl, and Russian premier Viktor Chernomyrdin.	Chechen rebels launch an attack on a column of Russian forces near the village of Novogroznensky in eastern Chechnya, killing three Russian soldiers and wounding 15.			

A	B	C	D	E
Includes developments that affect more than one world region, international organizations, and important meetings of major world leaders.	*Includes all domestic and regional developments in Europe, including the Soviet Union, Turkey, Cyprus, and Malta.*	*Includes all domestic and regional developments in Africa and the Middle East, including Iraq and Iran and excluding Cyprus, Turkey, and Afghanistan.*	*Includes all domestic and regional developments in Latin America, the Caribbean, and Canada.*	*Includes all domestic and regional developments in Asia and Pacific nations, extending from Afghanistan through all the Pacific Islands, except Hawaii.*

U.S. Politics & Social Issues	U.S. Foreign Policy & Defense	U.S. Economy & Environment	Science, Technology, & Nature	Culture, Leisure, & Lifestyle	
In Minneapolis, Minn., Federal District Court judge James Rosenbaum approves an agreement under which Qubilah Bahiyah Shabazz, the daughter of slain black nationalist leader Malcolm X, accepts responsibility and is placed on two years probation for her involvement in a plot to kill Nation of Islam leader Louis Farrakhan..... In NYC, Judge Elliott Wilk sets aside the part of a February jury verdict that found hospital patient Libby Zion partly responsible for her own death.				Officials from the Episcopal Church accuse former church treasurer Ellen F. Cooke of embezzling $2.2 million from the church since 1990.	May 1
Keith Zettlemoyer, 39, convicted of the 1980 murder of a friend who had planned to testify against him in a robbery trial, becomes the first inmate executed in Pennsylvania since 1962 and the 275th in the nation since 1976, when the Supreme Court allowed states to resume capital punishment.... The North Carolina Court of Appeals orders new trials for Robert Kelly Jr. and Kathryn Dawn Wilson, two workers convicted of molesting children at an Edenton, North Carolina, day-care center.	The Clinton administration ends a 30-year immigration policy when it announces that Cuban boat people seeking asylum in the U.S. will henceforth be summarily repatriated to Cuba. The 21,000 Cuban rafters currently detained at the U.S. naval base at Guantanamo Bay, Cuba will be admitted into the U.S.... Hugh E. (Ted) Price announces his retirement from his post as chief of the CIA clandestine operations division, effective May 5. Admiral William Studeman names Price's deputy, John J. Devine, as acting director of clandestine operations.	Neal Ainley pleads guilty in U.S. District Court in Little Rock, Arkansas, to two misdemeanor violations of federal financial disclosure laws. Ainley's plea is related to transactions involving the 1990 reelection campaign of Bill Clinton, who was then Arkansas's governor, from a 16-month-old investigation, currently led by independent prosecutor Kenneth Starr into the Whitewater affair.		The auction houses of Christie's and Sotheby's open their major New York City auctions.... Martin Harwit, the director of the Smithsonian Institution's National Air and Space Museum, resigns due to "continuing controversy and divisiveness" over a planned exhibit of the *Enola Gay*.	May 2
Alabama revives chain gangs, in which groups of convicts are chained together and made to labor outdoors, and more than 300 Alabama inmates are shackled together and made to clear ditches, cut weeds, and pick up litter along a state highway. The reinstitution of chain gangs is part of an effort by Gov. Forrest (Fob) James Jr. (R) to make prison life tougher.		California governor Pete Wilson (R) acknowledges that in the late 1970s he employed an undocumented Mexican immigrant as a maid and failed to pay Social Security taxes on her wages.			May 3
The death toll from the Apr. 19 car-bombing attack in Oklahoma City stands at 164, with two people unaccounted for and presumed dead. Nineteen children died in the blast. One rescue worker, a nurse, also died. The rescue operation concludes.		Lewis Thompson Preston, 68, financier and banker who was president of the World Bank from 1991 until just before his death and who had a 40-year-long career with commercial bank J. P. Morgan & Co., dies in Washington, D.C., of cancer.			May 4
A memorial service for victims of the Apr. 19 attack in Oklahoma City, Oklahoma, is held at the blast site.				Mikhail Moisseyevich Botvinnik, 83, legendary Russian chess grandmaster, dies in Moscow of an undisclosed illness.	May 5
At a benefit attended by 1,400 people at the Apollo Theater in NYC to raise money for the legal defense of Qubilah Shabazz, the daughter of slain civil rights activist Malcolm X, the Nation of Islam leader, Louis Farrakhan acknowledges that "members of the Nation of Islam were involved in the assassination of Malcolm" and calls for forgiveness. ... Ron Kirk (D), an attorney and former Texas secretary of state, is elected mayor of Dallas, Texas. Kirk, 40, will become the city's first black mayor and the first black ever to lead a major Texas city.			A Danish study shows that a group of people who drank wine daily were less likely to die during the study period than a group who drank beer, hard liquor, or no alcohol at all.	Finland defeats Sweden, 4-1, to capture the world hockey championship in Stockholm, Sweden. It is Finland's first-ever world title.... Thunder Gulch wins the 121st running of the Kentucky Derby at Churchill Downs in Louisville, Kentucky.	May 6

F	G	H	I	J
Includes elections, federal-state relations, civil rights and liberties, crime, the judiciary, education, health care, poverty, urban affairs, and population.	*Includes formation and debate of U.S. foreign and defense policies, veterans' affairs, and defense spending. (Relations with specific foreign countries are usually found under the region concerned.)*	*Includes business, labor, agriculture, taxation, transportation, consumer affairs, monetary and fiscal policy, natural resources, and pollution.*	*Includes worldwide scientific, medical, and technological developments; natural phenomena; U.S. weather; natural disasters; and accidents.*	*Includes the arts, religion, scholarship, communications media, sports, entertainments, fashions, fads, and social life.*

	World Affairs	Europe	Africa & the Middle East	The Americas	Asia & the Pacific
May 7		Paris mayor Jacques Chirac, leader of the neo-Gaullist Rally for the Republic (RPR) party, is elected to a seven-year term as president of France in a runoff election.... Bosnian Serbs shell Sarajevo, killing at least 10 people. Franjo Komarica, the Catholic bishop of Banja Luka, reports that a church near Bihac in the northwest was blown up and that Serbs attempted to burn down a church in the town of Vujnovici.	In Kenya, prominent paleontologist and conservationist Richard Leakey announces that he is forming a new political party to challenge longtime Pres. Daniel arap Moi and his ruling Kenya African National Union (KANU). Leakey forms the party, dubbed Safina (or Ark), with Paul Muite and others from the banned group Mwangaza Trust.		
May 8	Thousands of World War II veterans and about 80 international leaders mark the 50th anniversary of Victory in Europe Day. The world figures travel together through London, Paris, Berlin, and Moscow in the largest of dozens of V-E Day celebrations. V-E Day commemorative events are also held in Austria, Belgium, the Netherlands, Poland, and Vatican City.	Reports confirm that Bosnian Serbs blew up a Roman Catholic church and monastery in Banja Luka, northwest Bosnia, killing a nun and a priest.... Reports reveal that international human-rights organizations have determined that the Russian military's attack on the Chechen village of Samashki that started Apr. 7 was a massacre of civilians and that many of the Russian soldiers who participated in it were intoxicated. More than 100 people were killed in Samashki when 3,000 Russian troops fired on civilians at point-blank range, threw grenades and torched houses, according to survivors.			Fires gut the town of Charar-e-Sharief in India's disputed Jammu and Kashmir region as fighting between government troops and Islamic separatists escalate.... Voters in the Philippines cast ballots to fill half of the country's 24-seat Senate, the entire body of the House of Representatives, and thousands of local government posts.... Teresa (Deng Lijun) Teng, 40, Japanese singer known throughout East Asia for her romantic ballads, dies in Ching Mai, Thailand, reportedly of heart failure after suffering an asthmatic attack.
May 9		The UN begins relocating Serb civilians and soldiers from the western Slavonia region of Croatia, which Croatian forces recaptured from Serbs in the May 1 offensive. ... French president François Mitterrand of the Socialist Party, who has held office for an unprecedented 14 years, announces that he will hand over the reins of the presidency to Jacques Chirac prior to the official expiration of his term.	The last of the Hutu refugees who remain ensconced in the Kibeho camp in southwest Rwanda abandon the camp.	Judge David Nevins of Canada's Ontario Court's Provincial Division strikes down an Ontario law that prevents homosexual couples from applying to adopt children.	
May 10	U.S. president Bill Clinton and Russian president Boris Yeltsin state they have reached partial agreements on security in Europe after concluding a much-anticipated and debated summit meeting. The two leaders fail, however, to iron out their differences on more substantive issues.	According to a Reuters report, five Russian helicopters fire rockets at the Chechen village of Serzhen-Yurt. The attack reportedly comes shortly after Yeltsin claims that no Russian military actions are taking place in Chechnya.... Michael Ancram, the British government minister for Northern Ireland, meets with representatives of Sinn Fein. It is the first public encounter between a government minister and Sinn Fein since 1973.... Tajikistan introduces its own currency, making it the last of the ruble, which is pegged at 100 to the Russian ruble.	In South Africa, more than 100 workers die when an underground train falls into a shaft and crashes on top of an elevator in the Vaal Reefs gold mine near Orkney, 112 miles (180 km) southwest of Johannesburg. The train and the elevator plunge more than 1,000 feet (300 m) to the bottom of the 7,500-foot shaft, and the accident is considered one of the worst mine disasters in South Africa's history.	Canadian immigration officials reveal that as many as 75 of 87 members of a delegation of businesspeople from China are missing.	
May 11	Representatives from 174 countries at UN headquarters in New York City by consensus approve the indefinite extension of the Treaty on the Nonproliferation of Nuclear Weapons, known as the Nuclear Nonproliferation Treaty. The NPT, which took effect in 1970 for a 25-year period, is considered to be the key to global nuclear nonproliferation efforts.	The world's tallest concrete structure, a gas-production platform standing 1,549 feet (472 m) high and weighing 1 million tons, is towed 200 miles (320 km) to a North Sea drilling location, setting a terrestrial record.... A French peacekeeper in Sarajevo is shot in the head by a sniper. Heavy fighting is reported near the Posavina corridor, which links Yugoslavia with Serb-held territory in Bosnia and Croatia.	Scientists from the CDC and WHO confirm that a mysterious disease that broke out in the city of Kikwit, 250 miles (400 km) east of Kinshasa, Zaire's capital, is caused by the Ebola virus, one of the world's deadliest virus. WHO states 49 people contracted the virus, and 27 of them died. The news sparks quarantine efforts.		Fires sweep the town of Charar-e-Sharief in India's disputed Jammu and Kashmir region as fighting between government troops and Islamic separatists continues. The Indian government imposes 24-hour curfews in cities throughout the Kashmir region. A 600-year-old mosque dedicated to Sheik Noorudin Noorani, a 14th-century Sufi poet and philosopher considered Kashmir's patron saint, is destroyed in the fire.

A	B	C	D	E
Includes developments that affect more than one world region, international organizations, and important meetings of major world leaders.	*Includes all domestic and regional developments in Europe, including the Soviet Union, Turkey, Cyprus, and Malta.*	*Includes all domestic and regional developments in Africa and the Middle East, including Iraq and Iran and excluding Cyprus, Turkey, and Afghanistan.*	*Includes all domestic and regional developments in Latin America, the Caribbean, and Canada.*	*Includes all domestic and regional developments in Asia and Pacific nations, extending from Afghanistan through all the Pacific Islands, except Hawaii.*

U.S. Politics & Social Issues	U.S. Foreign Policy & Defense	U.S. Economy & Environment	Science, Technology, & Nature	Culture, Leisure, & Lifestyle	
				The librarian of Congress, James H. Billington, announces that Robert Hass has been named poet laureate of the U.S., succeeding Rita Dove.	May 7
	In the first test of the U.S. policy announced May 2, the U.S. Coast Guard returns 13 Cuban boat people to Cuba. . . . Before flying to V-E Day ceremonies in Moscow, Pres. Clinton thanks the "extraordinary generation" that fought in the war. . . . Pres. Clinton signs an executive order announced Apr. 30 that imposes a trade embargo against Iran, effective for U.S. companies in 30 days.	Thomas Donahue announces that he will step down from his post as secretary treasurer of the AFL-CIO labor-union federation at the end of his term in October.		Marshal Walton Royal, 82, lead alto saxophonist for the Count Basie Orchestra, dies in Inglewood, California, of cancer. . . . Bill Spivey, 66, all-American basketball star, is found dead in Quepos, Costa Rica, of reportedly natural causes.	May 8
	The Senate confirms, 98-0, John Deutch as the director of central intelligence. . . . A federal judge in Chicago, Illinois, sentences Claude Marks and Donna Willmott, who surrendered in 1994 after admitting to conspiring to transport explosives for use by the Puerto Rican separatist group Armed Forces of National Liberation. Marks is sentenced to six years' imprisonment, and Willmott is sentenced to three years.	A URW local votes to end its 10-month-long strike at a Decatur, Illinois, Bridgestone/Firestone Inc. tiremaking plant.			May 9
Duncan McKenzie Jr., 43, convicted of murdering a teacher in Montana in the early 1970s, becomes the first person to be executed in Montana since 1943 and the 277th in the nation since 1976. . . . Terry Lynn Nichols, a material witness in the Apr. 19 car-bombing attack on a federal office building in Oklahoma City, is formally charged in the bombing.	U.S. Trade Representative Mickey Kantor announces that the U.S. is filing a grievance with the World Trade Organization (WTO) accusing Japan of unfair trade practices. At the same time, he discloses the U.S. will impose sanctions unilaterally on imports from Japan unless Japan opens its automobile and auto-parts markets.				May 10
Reports indicate that former president George Bush, a lifetime member of the NRA, has quit the gun-rights organization. . . . Evelyn Norton Lincoln, 85, personal secretary to President John F. Kennedy, dies in Washington, D.C., of complications from a recent cancer surgery.		The board of Coors Brewing Co., a company with a reputation for supporting conservative causes, unanimously approves full benefits to employees' unmarried domestic partners, including homosexual companions.	A study finds that women who consume one to three drinks a week of any type of alcohol have greater benefits for longevity than women who drink at any other rate of consumption.	At the end of the NYC fall auctions by Christie's and Sotheby's, art experts note that the total sales tallies are the highest since late 1990. Sotheby's took in $143.7 million during the auctions, while Christie's raised $126.3 million.	May 11

F	G	H	I	J
Includes elections, federal-state relations, civil rights and liberties, crime, the judiciary, education, health care, poverty, urban affairs, and population.	*Includes formation and debate of U.S. foreign and defense policies, veterans' affairs, and defense spending. (Relations with specific foreign countries are usually found under the region concerned.)*	*Includes business, labor, agriculture, taxation, transportation, consumer affairs, monetary and fiscal policy, natural resources, and pollution.*	*Includes worldwide scientific, medical, and technological developments; natural phenomena; U.S. weather; natural disasters; and accidents.*	*Includes the arts, religion, scholarship, communications media, sports, entertainments, fashions, fads, and social life.*

	World Affairs	Europe	Africa & the Middle East	The Americas	Asia & the Pacific
May 12	Belgium's highest court questions Willy Claes, secretary general of NATO, regarding allegations that his Flemish Socialist Party accepted bribes from a defense contractor in the late 1980s.	The UN tells its peacekeeping troops in Bosnia to shoot to kill to protect themselves.... The Irish Supreme Court approves a law that will liberalize strict antiabortion law. Under the new law, doctors may advise women on where to seek abortions outside Ireland.... About 20,000 demonstrators and several government ministers protest a German court ruling that will force an outdoor beer garden to close at 9:30 P.M.... Lord Arnold Abraham Goodman, 81, British newspaper publisher, arts patron, and political adviser, dies in London, England.		Native leaders of the Innu community of Davis Inlet, Newfoundland, and the Newfoundland government agree to settle a dispute over the Davis Inlet court system. The local Innu leaders forcibly evicted court officers from Davis Inlet in December 1993.	
May 13			Said Abu Musameh, a senior official of Hamas and editor of the *Al-Watan* newspaper, is arrested and convicted for publishing "seditious" articles in *Al-Watan*.		
May 14		Croatian troops fail to fulfill a pledge to the UN to withdraw from a UN-protected zone in western Slavonia.	The self-rule Palestinian National Authority's security court in Gaza metes out a two-year prison sentence to Said Abu Musameh, a senior official of Hamas and editor of the *Al-Watan* newspaper, convicted May 13. The court also orders the newspaper closed for three months.	Argentine president Carlos Saul Menem wins reelection outright in balloting, as voters apparently signal a preference for a continuation of free-market policies instituted under his administration.	Muslim gunmen raid the village of Bharat, some 150 miles (240 km) south of Srinigar. The rebels kill a Hindu family of eight in what is seen as retaliation for the May 11 mosque burning. Data suggest that, since May 8, some 30 separatist fighters and two government soldiers have been killed in gun battles in India's disputed Jammu and Kashmir region.
May 15		Bernard Tapie, who was a cabinet member in 1992 under French president François Mitterrand, is sentenced to one year in prison and an additional one-year suspended term for his role in fixing a soccer match in 1993. Tapie has been a subject in an ongoing corruption scandal in France.... Eric Richard Porter, 67, British actor best known for his TV role in *The Forsyte Saga*, which garnered one of the biggest viewing audiences in BBC history, dies in London of colon cancer.			
May 16		The Muslim-led government army in Bosnia-Herzegovina and Bosnian Serb forces battle in Sarajevo, around the northwestern town of Bihac, and in the northeastern town of Brcko, near the strategic Posavina corridor, in what is called the worst fighting in Bosnia in two years.... Figures show Milan prosecutors have requested criminal trials for 160 politicians and businessmen, including former premier Bettino Craxi.... Lola Flores (born Dolores Flores Ruiz), 72, Spanish flamenco singer, dies in Madrid, Spain, of breast cancer.			Japanese authorities arrest Shoko Asahara, the leader of Aum Shinrikyo, a Japanese religious cult linked to a March nerve-gas attack on Tokyo's subway system that killed 12 people and injured 5,000 others. More than 100 other Aum Shinrikyo sites are raided by authorities with arrest warrants. Separately, a bomb explodes in the office of Yukio Aoshima, the new governor of Tokyo, seriously injuring an aide.
May 17		Hundreds of shells are fired into and out of Sarajevo. At least 11 civilians are killed and dozens wounded. Two UN peacekeepers, one Russian and one French, are wounded.... Jacques Chirac is inaugurated as France's new president. Chirac picks Alain Juppe, a former foreign affairs minister, to be the country's premier.	Rioting erupts in Ramadi, the provincial capital, after Iraqi authorities hand over the bruised and decapitated body of Gen. Mohammed Dulaimi to his family. The strife reportedly spreads to other parts of Al Anbar.	Reports confirm that the Jesuit Fathers of Upper Canada have paid more than C$1.5 million in compensation to the victims of Rev. George Epoch, a priest who allegedly sexually abused at least 97 Native American boys at a Nawash Chippewa reserve at Cape Croker, Ontario, between 1972 and 1983.	

A	B	C	D	E
Includes developments that affect more than one world region, international organizations, and important meetings of major world leaders.	Includes all domestic and regional developments in Europe, including the Soviet Union, Turkey, Cyprus, and Malta.	Includes all domestic and regional developments in Africa and the Middle East, including Iraq and Iran and excluding Cyprus, Turkey, and Afghanistan.	Includes all domestic and regional developments in Latin America, the Caribbean, and Canada.	Includes all domestic and regional developments in Asia and Pacific nations, extending from Afghanistan through all the Pacific Islands, except Hawaii.

U.S. Politics & Social Issues	U.S. Foreign Policy & Defense	U.S. Economy & Environment	Science, Technology, & Nature	Culture, Leisure, & Lifestyle	
A three-judge panel on the Michigan Court of Appeals upholds a 1991 injunction barring Dr. Jack Kevorkian from assisting in suicides. . . . Reports confirm that judges in Texas declared mistrials in two separate breast-implant lawsuits after Dow Corning ran a nationwide ad defending implants. The judges decide that finding an unbiased jury will be too difficult. Meanwhile, in Reno, Nev., Judge Connie Steinheimer rules that Dow Corning has a right to publish the ads and that a breast-implant suit will begin as scheduled on May 16.	The INS announces the arrest of Emmanuel Constant, head of the Front for the Advancement and Progress of Haiti (FRAPH), a rightist paramilitary group known for its human-rights violations in Haiti during the former military-led regime. . . . The U.S. Coast Guard returns a group of 11 Cubans picked up in the Straits of Florida to Cabanas.			CBS announces that golf commentator Bon Wright will not be fired for allegedly making statements regarding homosexuality in women's golf. Wright allegedly told a reporter that "lesbians in the sport hurt women's golf." Wright vehemently denies making the statements.	May 12
	An army court-martial convicts Captain Lawrence P. Rockwood, 36, a military intelligence officer who, in 1994, made an unauthorized visit to the National Penitentiary in Port-au-Prince, the Haitian capital, on four charges. He claims he made the visit since prisoners were being mistreated by the Haitian military and his superiors ignored his reports of alleged abuses. Rockwood is acquitted of a fifth charge, dereliction of duty.			Alison Hargreaves of Great Britain becomes the first woman to reach the peak of Mount Everest without the assistance of oxygen tanks. Hargreaves is only the second person to climb Everest's 29,028-foot-high (8,847.7-m) North Ridge alone. . . . Team New Zealand's *Black Magic 1* yacht wins the America's Cup.	May 13
The widow of slain civil-rights leader Medgar Evers, Myrlie Evers-Williams, is sworn in as chairwoman of the NAACP.	An army court-martial sentences Captain Lawrence P. Rockwood, convicted May 13, to discharge from the army and the loss of pay and benefits because of his actions in Haiti during the U.S. intervention there in September 1994.		Christian Boehmer Anfinsen, 79, who shared the 1972 Nobel Prize for his work in the field of protein structure and who was head of the chemical biology laboratory at the NIH, 1963–81, dies in Randallstown, Maryland, after suffering a heart attack.		May 14
In *Hubbard v. U.S.*, the Supreme Court overturns, 6-3, a 40-year-old precedent and asserts a federal criminal law governing false statements does not apply to statements made in court or to Congress. . . . In *City of Edmonds v. Oxford House*, the Supreme Court rules, 6-3, that residential zoning ordinances cannot be used to discriminate against the establishment of group homes for handicapped people. . . . Arizona revives chain gangs in its prison system.		According to *Fortune* magazine, the nation's 500 largest corporations registered aggregate profits of $215 billion in 1994. The figure represents a 54% rise over 1993 profit margins. The rise in profits stems in part from *Fortune*'s decision to allow the inclusion of service businesses on its list. . . . Dow Corning Corp., overwhelmed by lawsuits over silicone breast implants, files for protection from creditors under Chapter 11 of the U.S. Bankruptcy Code.	Archaeologists announce the discovery of a vast underground tomb with at least 67 chambers that they believe is the burial place of 50 of the 52 sons of Ramses II, a powerful Pharoah who ruled Egypt from 1279 B.C. to 1212 B.C. The tomb is the largest yet found in the Egyptian necropolis known as the Valley of the Kings.		May 15
	U.S. officials announce the imposition of punitive tariffs of 100% on 13 Japanese-made luxury-class car models. . . . Harry Earl Bergold Jr., 63, ambassador to Hungary, 1980–83 and to Nicaragua, 1984–87, dies in Paris, France, of cancer.	The Senate passes, 94-6, a measure that will expand states' powers to limit their acceptance of out-of-state municipal waste. . . . The Senate votes, 74-25, to repeal a current ban on exporting oil from the North Slope region of Alaska. . . . The House approves, 240-185, a dramatically scaled-back version of the 1972 Clean Water Act that will ease regulations that prevent industry and municipalities from discharging polluted runoff into lakes and rivers. It includes a controversial amendment that will sharply reduce wetlands protection.			May 16
The Senate Select Committee on Ethics announces it has found "substantial credible evidence" to support allegations of sexual harassment, obstruction of justice and influence peddling against Sen. Bob Packwood (R, Oreg.). . . . Girvies L. Davis, 37, convicted of the 1978 slaying of an elderly, wheelchair-bound man, becomes the fifth inmate executed in Illinois and the 280th person in the U.S. since 1976.	Nora Slatkin is sworn as the director of the CIA. She is the first woman to hold a senior post at the CIA.	The Senate approves, 96-3, a resolution creating a special committee to hold public hearings examining the conduct of Pres. Clinton, First Lady Hillary Rodham Clinton, and key members of the administration in the Whitewater affair. . . . Attorney General Janet Reno asks a panel of federal appeals judges to appoint an independent counsel to investigate the personal finances of Commerce Secretary Ronald Brown.			May 17

F	G	H	I	J
Includes elections, federal-state relations, civil rights and liberties, crime, the judiciary, education, health care, poverty, urban affairs, and population.	Includes formation and debate of U.S. foreign and defense policies, veterans' affairs, and defense spending. (Relations with specific foreign countries are usually found under the region concerned.)	Includes business, labor, agriculture, taxation, transportation, consumer affairs, monetary and fiscal policy, natural resources, and pollution.	Includes worldwide scientific, medical, and technological developments; natural phenomena; U.S. weather; natural disasters; and accidents.	Includes the arts, religion, scholarship, communications media, sports, entertainments, fashions, fads, and social life.

	World Affairs	Europe	Africa & the Middle East	The Americas	Asia & the Pacific
May 18		Russian premier Viktor Chernomyrdin visits Bulgaria, reaching two accords with Premier Zhan Videnov, a former communist elected in December 1994.	At least 3,000 people traveling to Kinshasa, Zaire, are stranded at the roadblocks to quarantine the region after an outbreak of the Ebola virus in the country.		
May 19		Tajikistan president Imamali Rakhmanov and opposition leader Said Abdullo Nuri meet for the first time in Kabul, the capital of Afghanistan. They extended by three months a truce implemented in September 1994.	Reports confirm that the Ebola virus broke out in the Ivory Coast in November 1994. The outbreak killed 20 chimpanzees and infected one laboratory worker. Scientists state the strain of the Ebola virus in the Ivory Coast outbreak differs from the strain in the current outbreak in Zaire.		Thai premier Chuan Leekpai is forced to dissolve Parliament after the Palang Dharma Party withdraws from his ruling coalition.
May 20		Pope John Paul II makes his seventh visit since 1989 to the Czech Republic and Poland.... Italy's anticorruption magistrates in Milan request the indictment of former premier Silvio Berlusconi on bribery charges.		Police in Toronto, Canada, discover a pipe bomb mailed to the home of Ernst Zundel, a denier of the Holocaust and a publisher of anti-Semitic literature.	Nearly 200 people are injured in demonstrations mounted by thousands of refugees housed at the Whitehead Detention Center in Hong Kong. The refugees try to block police from transferring a group of 1,500 detainees to a smaller camp as a prelude to their deportation to Vietnam.
May 21		Belgian premier Jean-Luc Dehaene's center-left ruling coalition retains a majority of seats in the Chamber of Representatives, Belgium's lower parliamentary house, in the first elections held there under a new Belgian constitution, enacted in February 1993.	Lebanese premier Rafik al-Hariri begins a second term in office after emerging triumphant from a showdown with political opponents who stymied his plans for large-scale reconstruction in postwar Lebanon.		
May 22		Pope John Paul II holds a mass in his native Skoczow, Poland. The ceremony is attended by 200,000 enthusiastic supporters.	The Israeli cabinet suspends a government plan to confiscate 135 acres (55 hectares) of mainly Arab-owned land in disputed East Jerusalem in the face of international pressures and imminent no-confidence resolutions.		Thousands of workers at Mount Isa Mines return to work, ending an impasse that followed more than three months of labor unrest at the Australian mining giant.
May 23		Bosnian Serbs defy a UN ultimatum by seizing heavy weaponry from a UN-guarded weapons depot near Sarajevo..... The German federal Constitutional Court rules that spies who worked in the former East Germany during the cold war cannot now be prosecuted in the unified Germany. The ruling affects more than 6,300 alleged East German spies.		Judge Keith Ritter of the Alberta Court of Queen's Bench acquits Marilyn Tan of charges that she had injected her former lover, Conrad Boland, with HIV-infected blood. In the highly publicized case, Tan is convicted on a lesser charge and sentenced to three months in prison for that offense.	

A	B	C	D	E
Includes developments that affect more than one world region, international organizations, and important meetings of major world leaders.	Includes all domestic and regional developments in Europe, including the Soviet Union, Turkey, Cyprus, and Malta.	Includes all domestic and regional developments in Africa and the Middle East, including Iraq and Iran and excluding Cyprus, Turkey, and Afghanistan.	Includes all domestic and regional developments in Latin America, the Caribbean, and Canada.	Includes all domestic and regional developments in Asia and Pacific nations, extending from Afghanistan through all the Pacific Islands, except Hawaii.

U.S. Politics & Social Issues	U.S. Foreign Policy & Defense	U.S. Economy & Environment	Science, Technology, & Nature	Culture, Leisure, & Lifestyle	
The official death toll in the Apr. 19 bombing of a federal office building in Oklahoma City, Oklahoma, stands at 166, including 19 children. In addition, a nurse involved in the rescue operation died of a head injury incurred during the effort.	Juergen Schneider and his wife, Claudia, considered Germany's most wanted white-collar fugitives, are arrested in Miami, Florida, by U.S. and German police. The Schneiders, who have been in hiding for 13 months, are held in the U.S. pending extradition to Germany on charges of fraud and falsification of documents.	The Dow closes at 4340.64, down 81.96 points, or 1.85%. The decline is the index's largest single-day fall since November 22, 1994. . . . The House passes, 235-189, the final version of a bill that will cut $16.4 billion in funding that Congress previously approved to pay for a wide range of federal programs in fiscal 1995, which ends Sept. 30. . . . The House passes, 238-193, its version of the balanced-budget blueprint.	in Baltimore, Maryland, U.S. district judge Edward Northrop orders the University of Alabama and four of its scientists to pay the U.S. government and researcher Pamela Berge a total of $1.6 million for stealing Berge's work and using it to obtain federal funds.	Elisha Cook Jr., 92, character actor, dies in Big Pine, California, of an undisclosed illness. . . . Elizabeth Montgomery, 57 or 62, actress known for the TV show *Bewitched*, dies in Los Angeles of cancer. . . . (Boris) Alexander Godunov, 45, Soviet ballet dancer who defected to the U.S. in 1979, is found dead in Hollywood, California, from effects of alcoholism.	May 18
Edward Rollins Jr., a political consultant working with Senate Majority Leader Robert J. Dole (R, Kans.), apologizes for what he calls a "totally inappropriate remark" made at a dinner in which he referred to Representatives Howard Berman (D, Calif.) and Henry Waxman (D, Calif.) as "Hymie boys." Several Jewish and black House Democrats call on Dole to sever his ties with Rollins immediately.		Kenneth Starr, the independent prosecutor investigating the Whitewater affair, makes clear that he will not indict White House deputy counsel Bruce Lindsey for banking violations related to Pres. Clinton's 1990 gubernatorial reelection campaign in Arkansas.	Researchers report they have restored to life a dormant state bacteria from the stomachs of bees encased in amber believed to be at least 25 million years old. Many other scientists dispute the findings. . . . NASA administrator Daniel Goldin announces a plan to cut thousands of jobs. . . . Robert Sinclair Dietz, 80, geologist known for his pioneering research of the ocean floors, dies in Tempe, Arizona, of a heart attack.	Jimmy Garcia of Colombia dies of brain injuries sustained two weeks earlier during a World Boxing Council championship fight. The boxer's death leads to renewed calls to reform the sport.	May 19
Workers put up barricades to close a two-block stretch of Washington, D.C.'s Pennsylvania Avenue—a six-lane street that passes within 150 feet of the north face of the White House—to all but pedestrian traffic. The closure, the first such measures ever taken to protect the White House, is part of a package of new presidential security provisions.			Levees on the Mississippi and Missouri rivers overflow.	CBS announces that Connie Chung will no longer coanchor the *CBS Evening News*. Chung was named coanchor in May 1993, and she and Barbara Walters are the only women to coanchor an evening news show on a major network. . . . Ulysses Kay, 78, leading black classical composer, dies in Englewood, New Jersey, of Parkinson's disease.	May 20
	Les(lie) Aspin Jr., 56, U.S. secretary of defense from January 1993 to February 1994 who served 22 years as a Democratic representative from Wisconsin, dies in Washington, D.C., after suffering a stroke.				May 21
In *Wilson v. Arkansas*, the Supreme Court rules unanimously that police officers who hold search warrants are required by the Constitution to announce themselves before entering a home to conduct a search. . . . In *U.S. Term Limits Inc. v. Thornton*, the Supreme Court, 5-4, hands down a significant ruling that blocks states and Congress from passing legislation limiting the number of terms that members of Congress can serve. The decision is considered among the court's most important rulings on the balance of state and federal powers. . . . Attorney General Janet Reno appoints Joseph H. Hartzler to head the prosecution team in the Oklahoma bombing case.		Some 2,000 members of the United Rubber Workers (URW) union end their 10-month-long strike against Tennessee-based tire manufacturer Bridgestone/Firestone.		Bartholomew Torpey, a pool mechanic, is indicted on charges of criminally negligent homicide in the 1994 death of tennis star Vitas Gerulaitis.	May 22
In Washington, D.C., a man armed with an unloaded handgun is shot and wounded by a Secret Service agent on the South Lawn of the White House. . . . A Charleston, West Virginia, jury hands down the first conviction for violating the federal Violence Against Women Act when it convicts Christopher Bailey of kidnapping his wife, Sonya Bailey, after beating her into a coma. . . . The federal building bombed Apr. 19 in Oklahoma City, Oklahoma, is razed.		The Transportation Department announces that nine U.S. and Japanese automobile makers have agreed to voluntarily recall more than 8 million cars sold between 1986 and 1991 to repair or replace seat belt buckles found to have design flaws. The action is the second-largest auto recall in 30 years, and some industry analysts expect that the total cost of the recall may reach $1 billion.		The Kennedy family sells its house in Palm Beach, Florida, to New York City banker John K. Castle for an undisclosed sum. The famed seaside estate gained notoriety as the site of an alleged rape by William Kennedy Smith in 1991.	May 23

F	G	H	I	J
Includes elections, federal-state relations, civil rights and liberties, crime, the judiciary, education, health care, poverty, urban affairs, and population.	*Includes formation and debate of U.S. foreign and defense policies, veterans' affairs, and defense spending. (Relations with specific foreign countries are usually found under the region concerned.)*	*Includes business, labor, agriculture, taxation, transportation, consumer affairs, monetary and fiscal policy, natural resources, and pollution.*	*Includes worldwide scientific, medical, and technological developments; natural phenomena; U.S. weather; natural disasters; and accidents.*	*Includes the arts, religion, scholarship, communications media, sports, entertainments, fashions, fads, and social life.*

	World Affairs	Europe	Africa & the Middle East	The Americas	Asia & the Pacific
May 24		At a conference in the U.S., British Northern Ireland Secretary Sir Patrick Mayhew meets with Gerry Adams, leader of Sinn Fein, the political wing of the Provisional IRA. The conference brings together high-ranking republicans, unionists, and British government representatives for the first time since peace negotiations began in 1994. . . . Lord (James) Harold Wilson, 79, British Labour Party leader who served as prime minister, 1964–70, 1974–76, dies in London after suffering from cancer and Alzheimer's disease for several years.		Reports confirm that five Canadian automobile manufacturers have recalled 900,000 vehicles because of faulty seat belts. The automakers agree to repair the seat belts without charge to the owners, at an estimated cost in the tens of millions of dollars. The auto recall is the largest ever in Canada. . . . Five members of a delegation of Chinese business-people who were reported missing in Ontario on May 10 apply for refugee status in Canada. . . . The Brazilian army occupies four strike-torn refineries owned by Petroleo Brasileiro (Petrobras), Brazil's state-run oil monopoly.	
May 25	NATO begins air strikes against Bosnian Serbs in response to the May 23 actions by Bosnian Serbs. Bosnian Serbs begin taking as hostages UN peacekeepers from Britain, France, Canada, Ukraine, and Russia.	NATO bombs the weapons depot near Pale. It is the first time NATO air strikes are launched so close to the Bosnian Serb headquarters. Bosnian Serbs respond by shelling five of the six safe areas in Bosnia, including Tuzla. The death toll of at least 71 is the worst in any single shelling incident since the Bosnian war began in 1992.		The Supreme Court of Canada rules that protection from discrimination under Canada's Charter of Rights and Freedoms extends to homosexuals, even though sexual orientation is not specifically mentioned in the charter. The court, however, also decides that the government can deny benefits to homosexual couples.	Returns from the May 8 election in the Philippines show that the ruling Lakas-Laban coalition of Philippine president Fidel Ramos scored a decisive victory. . . . The legislative assembly of Australia's Northern Territory passes a bill legalizing voluntary euthanasia, or mercy killing, for terminally ill patients. The measure, the Rights of the Terminally Ill bill, is the world's first voluntary euthanasia law.
May 26		In Bosnia, NATO launches air strikes, bombing anew the weapons depot near Pale.	Officials from the World Health Organization state that the number of people who died in a recent outbreak of the Ebola virus in Zaire is 121. WHO reveals that the outbreak of the Ebola virus, one of the deadliest known viruses, occurred in Kikwit, a city of some 600,000 people located about 300 miles (480 km) east of Kinshasa, Zaire's capital.		Rebels from the Liberation Tigers of Tamil Eelam kill at least 42 civilians during an attack on the village of Kallarawa, about 155 miles (250 km) northeast of Colombo, the capital of Sri Lanka. The attack is the most deadly raid by the rebels, who have been fighting for a separate homeland for the country's Tamil minority since 1992.
May 27		In Sarajevo, two French peacekeepers are killed when their unit is drawn into a direct battle with Bosnian Serbs over control of the Vrbanja Bridge in the center of the city. Four rebel Serbs are also killed.			
May 28		A powerful earthquake strikes the large island of Sakhalin, off Russia's east coast that is located in eight time zones and is 4,500 miles (7,200 km) east of Moscow. The earthquake measures 7.5 on the Richter scale, and its epicenter is off the shore of the island's sparsely populated northern tip. . . . Serb forces near the town of Cetingrad in Serb-held territory of Croatia shoot down a helicopter carrying Bosnia's foreign minister, Irfan Ljubijankic, killing him and five others. Separately, Britain announces it is sending 6,000 additional troops to Bosnia.		Mexico's ruling party, the Institutional Revolutionary Party (PRI), suffers its worst defeat in 66 years when it loses by a 2-1 margin to the right-wing National Action Party (PAN) in the state of Guanajuato. The governorship of Guanajuato is won by Vicente Fox Quesada.	

A	B	C	D	E
Includes developments that affect more than one world region, international organizations, and important meetings of major world leaders.	*Includes all domestic and regional developments in Europe, including the Soviet Union, Turkey, Cyprus, and Malta.*	*Includes all domestic and regional developments in Africa and the Middle East, including Iraq and Iran and excluding Cyprus, Turkey, and Afghanistan.*	*Includes all domestic and regional developments in Latin America, the Caribbean, and Canada.*	*Includes all domestic and regional developments in Asia and Pacific nations, extending from Afghanistan through all the Pacific Islands, except Hawaii.*

U.S. Politics & Social Issues	U.S. Foreign Policy & Defense	U.S. Economy & Environment	Science, Technology, & Nature	Culture, Leisure, & Lifestyle	
Leland W. Modjeski, the man who was shot and wounded May 23 on the South Lawn of the White House. is charged with assaulting federal officers and illegally transporting a weapon across state lines. . . . A panel of federal appellate judges appoint David Barrett as the independent counsel to head an inquiry into the conduct of Housing and Urban Development (HUD) secretary Henry Cisneros.		Statistics shows that charitable giving among U.S. individuals, corporations, and foundations totaled $130 billion in 1994. The 1994 sum is an increase of 3.6% over the revised 1993 figure of $125.3 billion.	Scientists announce that for the first time they have decoded the entire deoxyribonucleic acid (DNA) sequence for the complete gene set, or genome, of a free-living organism.	Los Angeles Superior Court judge Judith Champagne sentences Heidi Fleiss, convicted of running an exclusive Hollywood prostitution service, to three years in prison and a $1,500 fine.	May 24
		The Senate passes, 61-38, the final version of a bill that will cut $16.4 billion in funding that Congress previously approved to pay for a wide range of federal programs in fiscal 1995, which ends Sept. 30. . . . The Senate votes, 57-42, to approve a budget resolution that comprises the broad outlines of a plan to balance the federal budget by the year 2002.			May 25
The U.S. Court of Appeals for the District of Columbia partially reverses the 1993 conviction of Deborah Gore Dean, who was found guilty of perjury, defrauding the government, and accepting bribes while at HUD. The appeals court strikes down five of the 12 charges on which Dean was convicted and orders Dean to be resentenced.		Locomotive engineers for the Long Island Rail Road stage a wildcat walkout that leaves more than 100,000 riders stranded and causes a nearly complete shutdown of the commuter line. The railroad obtains a court order to halt the strike, and the strikers return to their jobs that evening. . . . Philip Morris Cos. Inc. announces that it is issuing a voluntary recall of more than 8 billion filter cigarettes because manufacturing defects caused some of the filters to become contaminated with a chemical used in a commercial pesticide.	Scientists who analyzed a segment of the Y chromosome, the male sex chromosome, of 38 men of all major ethnic groups worldwide report that the most likely explanation for a lack of genetic variability found in the men is that they had a relatively small and recent group of common ancestors. The researchers suggest that the current worldwide male population descended from a group of a few thousand men who lived in an undetermined location about 270,000 years ago.	Isadore (Friz) Freleng, 89, cartoon animator who had a 30-year career with Warner Brothers studios, dies in Los Angeles of heart ailments.	May 26
			Flooding in Missouri and Illinois, spurred by record rains, prompts Illinois governor Jim Edgar (R) to dispatch 160 National Guard members to aid in sandbagging efforts in rural Scott and Morgan counties, located on the Illinois River. More than 200 prison inmates also prepare levees in Illinois. The Missouri Emergency Management Agency estimates damage to public facilities at over $10 million.	Christopher Reeve, best known as Superman in a series of films, becomes paralyzed from the neck down when he is thrown headlong from his horse during a riding competition in Culpeper, Virginia.	May 27
A student at Harvard University, Sinedu Tadesse, stabs her roommate, Trang Phuong Ho, to death in their dormitory room and then hangs herself in one of the residence hall's bathrooms. Tadesse and Ho were both 20-year-old juniors.				At the Cannes (France) film festival, the Palme d'Or goes to *Underground*, a film by Bosnian director Emir Kusturica. . . . Jean Elizabeth Muir, 66, British fashion designer, dies in London of breast cancer. . . . Auto racer Michael Schumacher of Germany wins the Monaco Grand Prix in Monte Carlo. . . . Jacques Villeneuve, 24, wins the 79th Indianapolis 500. Villeneuve is the first Canadian to win the auto-racing event.	May 28

F	G	H	I	J
Includes elections, federal-state relations, civil rights and liberties, crime, the judiciary, education, health care, poverty, urban affairs, and population.	*Includes formation and debate of U.S. foreign and defense policies, veterans' affairs, and defense spending. (Relations with specific foreign countries are usually found under the region concerned.)*	*Includes business, labor, agriculture, taxation, transportation, consumer affairs, monetary and fiscal policy, natural resources, and pollution.*	*Includes worldwide scientific, medical, and technological developments; natural phenomena; U.S. weather; natural disasters; and accidents.*	*Includes the arts, religion, scholarship, communications media, sports, entertainments, fashions, fads, and social life.*

	World Affairs	Europe	Africa & the Middle East	The Americas	Asia & the Pacific
May 29		Russia's construction minister, Yefim Basin, states that Neftegorsk, a town almost entirely flattened by the May 28 quake and 40 miles northwest of the epicenter, will not be rebuilt. Many of the town's 3,200 people were crushed as they slept during the disaster.		Justice James Milliken of the Court of Queen's Bench in Canada's Saskatchewan province accepts the recommendation of the Cree community that William Bruce Taylor, 28, a member of the community, be banished to a remote area of Canada as punishment for sexual assault. The case reportedly marks the second time in recent history that a court in North America accepts the recommendation for banishment by a native community.	
May 30		Final results in Spain's regional and municipal elections show that the conservative Popular Party dominated the voting, which marks a radical shift in governing authority away from the Socialist Party, which has won every municipal election since coming to power in 1983.	Fighting erupts in suburban areas around Bujumbura, the Burundi capital, between militiamen from the majority Hutu ethnic group and soldiers from Burundi's army, made up primarily of members of the minority Tutsi ethnic group. . . . Officials from the World Health Organization state the number of people who died in a recent outbreak of the Ebola virus in Zaire is 153, and the number of suspected or confirmed cases of infection, including the 153 deaths, is 205.	Chile's Supreme Court unanimously upholds prison sentences meted out to retired general Manuel Contreras Sepulveda, the former head of the military secret police, and Brigadier Pedro Espinoza Bravo, his deputy, for directing the assassination of Orlando Letelier in Washington, D.C., in 1976. The ruling means that for the first time, high-ranking Chilean military officers will face prison terms for rights abuses perpetrated during the reign of Gen. Augusto Pinochet.	
May 31	The EU issues its first detailed report outlining the gradual implementation of economic and monetary union (EMU).	Britain's Prince Charles becomes the first member of the British royal family to visit Ireland since 1922 and the first to visit Dublin, the capital of Ireland, since 1911. He meets with Irish prime minister John Bruton. . . . NATO warplanes continue to circle Sarajevo in spite of Serb threats to shoot them down. . . . Russia observes an official day of mourning for the May 28 earthquake victims.			
June 1	Russian foreign minister Andrei Kozyrev announces that Russia has agreed to become an active member of NATO's Partnership for Peace, a program to give Eastern European countries associate status in NATO. . . . The Greek parliament ratifies the Law of the Sea, which extends Greece's territorial waters through much of the Aegean Sea.	Heavy fighting between Bosnian Serbs and Bosnian government troops breaks out in Gorazde. Data shows that more than 320 UN hostages are being detained in Bosnia-Herzegovina and that UN peacekeepers, unable to protect designated safe areas, abandoned many of their posts. Lord David Owen, a mediator in the conflict since 1992, announces he is resigning. . . . The Austrian parliament approves a 500 million schilling ($50 million) compensation package for an estimated 30,000 surviving Jewish victims of Nazi persecution between 1938 and 1945.			
June 2		Bosnian Serbs shoot down a U.S. fighter jet near Banja Luka, a Serb stronghold in Bosnia-Herzegovina. The U.S dispatches rescue teams to look for its pilot, air force captain Scott O'Grady. Bosnian Serbs release 121 of the UN hostages but seize 45 Canadians near Ilijas, north of Sarajevo. The number of UN hostages is estimated at 370. . . . Alexandre De Marenches, 73, former top French intelligence official, dies in Monaco of a heart attack.	The Israeli army kills a suspected Hamas militant, Hamed Yaghmour, in the West Bank city of Hebron.	Members of Brazil's Oil Workers Federation vote to end their 31-day strike of Petroleo Brasileiro (Petrobras), Brazil's state-owned oil monopoly. In response, Pres. Fernando Henrique Cardoso orders the withdrawal of troops that have been occupying the refineries since May 24.	
June 3	The defense ministers of 15 Western allied nations agree to form a multinational rapid-deployment force, composed of 10,000 troops and aimed at bolstering the UN mission in Bosnia and protecting it from attack. The force will operate under the UN command now in place, directed by French general Bernard Janvier, the UN commander in the former Yugoslavia, and British lieutenant general Rupert Smith, the UN commander in Bosnia.	The death toll from the May 28 earthquake on the large island of Sakhalin, off Russia's east coast, numbers 866, with more than 1,100 others believed dead and hundreds more injured.			

A	B	C	D	E
Includes developments that affect more than one world region, international organizations, and important meetings of major world leaders.	*Includes all domestic and regional developments in Europe, including the Soviet Union, Turkey, Cyprus, and Malta.*	*Includes all domestic and regional developments in Africa and the Middle East, including Iraq and Iran and excluding Cyprus, Turkey, and Afghanistan.*	*Includes all domestic and regional developments in Latin America, the Caribbean, and Canada.*	*Includes all domestic and regional developments in Asia and Pacific nations, extending from Afghanistan through all the Pacific Islands, except Hawaii.*

U.S. Politics & Social Issues	U.S. Foreign Policy & Defense	U.S. Economy & Environment	Science, Technology, & Nature	Culture, Leisure, & Lifestyle	
Searchers find the last three victims' bodies in the rubble of the federal building bombed Apr. 19 in Oklahoma City. The official death toll is 167, including 19 children.... A spokesman confirms that Edward Rollins Jr. quit his post in the campaign of Sen. Bob Dole (R, Kans.). . . . Margaret Madeline Chase Smith, 97, (R, Maine), the first woman to win election to both houses of Congress, dies in Skowhegan, Maine, of complications from a stroke.	U.S. national security adviser Anthony Lake announces that U.S. forces are being moved to the Balkans as a "precautionary measure."		Flooding in Missouri and Illinois begins to ease. The floods have claimed at least three lives in Missouri.	*The Rainmaker* by John Grisham is at the top of the bestseller list.	May 29
The HUD assumes control of the Chicago Housing Authority (CHA), the largest public-housing agency ever taken over by the federal government. Crime and drug-trafficking are reportedly rampant in CHA's buildings, and seven of the 10 poorest neighborhoods in the U.S. are in Chicago housing projects.... The Health Care Financing Administration cites Boston's Dana-Farber Cancer Institute, in the midst of controversy over patient drug overdoses, for deficiencies in patient care.	The U.S. moves seven ships, a nuclear-powered combat submarine, and some 12,000 marines and sailors to the Adriatic Sea, although there are no immediate plans to deploy U.S. military power in Bosnia.				May 30
		Interior Secretary Bruce Babbitt agrees to transfer 1,000 acres (400 hectare) of federal land to the state of California to use as a burial site for radioactive waste. The tract is about 20 miles (30 km) from the Colorado River, which supplies much of southern California's drinking water.... The Dow closes at a record 4465.14, up 86.46 points, or 1.97% in the largest single-day increase since Dec. 23, 1991,		Stanley Elkin, 65, writer who won a National Book Critics Circle Award, dies in St. Louis, Missouri, of heart failure. . . . Sen. Bob Dole (R, Kans.), attacks the entertainers for producing movies and music that "debase our nation and threaten our children."	May 31
Arlin Adams announces that he is stepping down, effective July 3, as the independent counsel in charge of an inquiry into influence peddling at the HUD during the 1980s, suggesting that the probe is nearing its end.... California governor Pete Wilson (R) issues an executive order curbing the use of affirmative action in some hiring and contracting done by the state.	Secretary of State Warren Christopher renews a 44-year-old U.S. pact with Portugal that allows the U.S. to use the Lajes air base in the Azores Islands for another five years, until the year 2000. Portugal will receive millions of dollars in aid for allowing the U.S. to use the islands, which are 800 miles (1,300 km) west of Lisbon, Portugal's capital.	Two major environmental groups release studies based on 1993–94 EPA statistics and information from local water utilities. Their findings assert that more than one-fifth of the U.S. population drinks tap water contaminated by lead, fecal bacteria, toxic waste, and other pollutants.	The FDA approves the use of Depakote, a popular epileptic seizure medicine, to treat manic episodes caused by bipolar disorder, or manic depression. The drug is the first approved for manic depression, which afflicts more than 2 million people in the U.S., in 25 years.	Justin Carroll, 14, wins the 68th National Spelling Bee by correctly spelling "xanthosis.". . . The U.S. Postal Service issues a stamp featuring the late Marilyn Monroe.... In response to Sen. Bob Dole's May 31 attack, Oliver Stone, film director, claims it is "the height of hypocrisy for Sen. Dole, who wants to repeal the (1994) assault weapons ban, to blame Hollywood for the violence in our society."	June 1
			NASA officials state the planned June 8 liftoff of the U.S. space shuttle *Discovery* has been delayed indefinitely because of repairs required to fix dozens of holes poked in the shuttle's fuel-tank insulation by woodpeckers.	Data show that ticket sales in NYC's Broadway theater district for the 1994–95 season reached a record $406 million. Attendance for the 1994–95 season was 9 million, up 12% from the previous season's 8.1 million figure.	June 2
The University of California at Irvine closes the Center for Reproductive Health, a leading fertility clinic, after filing a lawsuit charging that the clinic's doctors transplanted patients' eggs and embryos into other women without first notifying the patients or receiving their consent.			Colorado scientists, led by Carl E. Weiman and Eric A. Cornell, create BEC, or Bose-Einstein condensate, a new state of matter first postulated 70 years ago by Albert Einstein, whose theory is based on work by Indian physicist Satyendra Nath Bose. They create BEC by cooling rubidium atoms to what is believed to be the coldest temperature ever reached in the universe, billionths of a degree above absolute zero.... J(ohn) Presper Eckert Jr., 76, co-inventor of Eniac, the first electronic digital computer, dies in Bryn Mawr, Pennsylvania, of complications from leukemia.	Dilys Powell, 93, British film and TV critic who is considered to be one of the most influential critics in the history of film, dies in London after suffering several strokes.	June 3

F	G	H	I	J
Includes elections, federal-state relations, civil rights and liberties, crime, the judiciary, education, health care, poverty, urban affairs, and population.	*Includes formation and debate of U.S. foreign and defense policies, veterans' affairs, and defense spending. (Relations with specific foreign countries are usually found under the region concerned.)*	*Includes business, labor, agriculture, taxation, transportation, consumer affairs, monetary and fiscal policy, natural resources, and pollution.*	*Includes worldwide scientific, medical, and technological developments; natural phenomena; U.S. weather; natural disasters; and accidents.*	*Includes the arts, religion, scholarship, communications media, sports, entertainments, fashions, fads, and social life.*

	World Affairs	Europe	Africa & the Middle East	The Americas	Asia & the Pacific
June 4	Johannes Weinrich, an alleged accomplice to the terrorist known as Carlos the Jackal, is extradited to Berlin, Germany, from Yemen. Weinrich is allegedly Carlos's right-hand man and was sought on charges of attempted murder and illegal use of explosives in connection with several terrorist bombings worldwide throughout the 1970s and 1980s.	Antonio Di Pietro, one of Italy's most famous anticorruption magistrates, admits he took loans from a businessman now under criminal investigation. Di Pietro also announces he will resign from several special parliamentary posts in an effort to fight charges of corruption.			
June 5		The BBC discloses extracts of a long-awaited report detailing Britain's role in selling arms to Iraq in the late 1980s that implicates former prime minister Margaret Thatcher in addition to several current members of P.M. John Major's Conservative Party government.	Antoine Nduwayo, the premier in Burundi's coalition government, orders troops to flush out armed militiamen who held off the army in Kamenge, one of the last remaining Hutu areas. Reports indicate 33 people have been killed since fighting broke out May 30.... The Israeli army states that Israeli security forces arrested 45 suspected members of the militant Islamic Resistance Movement, known as Hamas, in the East Jerusalem area.		About 3,000 refugees escape the Sungei Besi detention camp near Kuala Lumpur, the Malaysian capital. Malaysian police armed with tear gas and riot gear force 600 Vietnamese refugees to return to the camp, and 13 people are injured in the clash.
June 6	The European Union and Japan reach agreements on measures designed to increase the EU's access to Japanese auto and auto-parts markets.		Reports suggest at least 20,000 of the estimated 40,000–50,000 Hutu in Kamenge, Burundi, have fled. ... South African judge Braam Lategan sentences Ntombeko Peni, 19, to 18 years in jail for the murder of Amy Elizabeth Biehl, 26, a white Fulbright scholar slain in August 1993. Separately, in its first case, South Africa's highest court abolishes the death penalty, ruling that capital punishment is inconsistent with the human rights guaranteed in the country's interim constitution.	Members of the Upper Nicola Indian tribe agree to end a blockade, started in May, of the Douglas Lake Ranch, Canada's largest ranch and a popular resort, in exchange for promised talks with the British Columbia government over fishing rights. The ranch is located near Kelowna, about 155 miles (250 km) east of Vancouver.	After internal debate, the Japanese governing coalition agrees on a declaration of "deep remorse," but not an apology, for Japan's "acts of aggression" against other Asian nations during World War II.... Sect leader Shoko Asahara is indicted on charges of masterminding a fatal March nerve-gas attack on Tokyo's subway system.
June 7		In Bosnia, 111 UN peacekeepers are released.... The Czech government announces that it is canceling a trade-clearing agreement reached with Slovakia in April 1993.	Burundian army soldiers with tanks and armored vehicles move into Kamenge and the nearby Kinama and Gasenyi districts. Nine people, eight of them Tutsi, are killed by Hutu gunmen in Musaga, a Tutsi area.		P.M. Paul Keating outlines his plan to transform the Australian system of government from a constitutional monarchy to a federal republic.
June 8		Data show that Bosnian Serbs have released 232 UN peacekeepers. At least 53 UN troops remain in Bosnian Serb custody, and 93 are surrounded by Bosnian Serb forces. The UN for the first time begins moving heavy artillery to Mount Igman, a strategic position near Sarajevo. The pilot of the jet shot down June 2, U.S. Air Force Captain Scott O'Grady, is rescued by U.S. Marines backed by NATO air support.	Witnesses state about 40 Hutu civilians, many of them women, children, or elderly persons, were shot or killed with machetes by soldiers in Burundi.	Juan Carlos Ongania, 81, president of Argentina, 1966–70, dies in Buenos Aires, Argentina, of a heart attack.	
June 9		In response to Croatian shelling of Serb villages in Krajina, Serbs respond by bombing Croatian army positions.... Two police officers trying to arrest two Asian youths for obstructing a path while playing soccer spark a mob of 300 Asian youths to riot in Bradford, England. Rioters loot several stores and firebomb several cars. Three police officers are injured, and 21 people are arrested.		Gilberto Rodriguez Orejuela, reputed leader of the Cali cartel, the world's largest drug cartel, is arrested by an elite police force in the southwestern Colombian city of Cali.... Record floods in Canada force about 5,000 people from their homes in Medicine Hat, Alberta.... Reports state that Robert Vesco, an American former financier wanted in the U.S. on fraud and cocaine trafficking charges, is being detained by Cuban authorities.	

A	B	C	D	E
Includes developments that affect more than one world region, international organizations, and important meetings of major world leaders.	Includes all domestic and regional developments in Europe, including the Soviet Union, Turkey, Cyprus, and Malta.	Includes all domestic and regional developments in Africa and the Middle East, including Iraq and Iran and excluding Cyprus, Turkey, and Afghanistan.	Includes all domestic and regional developments in Latin America, the Caribbean, and Canada.	Includes all domestic and regional developments in Asia and Pacific nations, extending from Afghanistan through all the Pacific Islands, except Hawaii.

U.S. Politics & Social Issues	U.S. Foreign Policy & Defense	U.S. Economy & Environment	Science, Technology, & Nature	Culture, Leisure, & Lifestyle	
				At the Tony Awards, *Sunset Boulevard* receives a total of seven awards, including best musical. *Love! Valour! Compassion!* wins for best play. Lifetime achievement awards go to Carol Channing and to Harvey Sabinson.	June 4
In *Reno v. Koray*, the Supreme Court rules, 8-1, that federal inmates cannot count time spent in community centers or halfway houses as a credit to reduce their overall prison sentence.			Beatrix T(ugendhut) Gardner, 61, Austrian-born psychologist who taught sign language to a chimpanzee in a renowned experiment, dies while traveling in Padua, Italy, of a central nervous infection.	Data show that PACs from entertainment groups have given $3 million in donations to the national Democratic Party since Pres. Clinton's nomination in July 1992, while giving only $361,000 to the GOP over the same period.	June 5
Philip Morris Cos. Inc. reaches an agreement with the federal government that requires the company to remove its billboards and other advertisements from the view of TV cameras at baseball, basketball, football, and hockey games in sports arenas and stadiums nationwide. . . . In Rochester, New York, federal judge Michael Telesca sentences Michael Stevens to seven life sentences for the December 1993 package bomb slayings of five people in New York State.			NASA releases images taken in 1994 by the *Hubble Space Telescope* that astronomers call the most detailed observations yet seen of the violent birth of stars.		June 6
The Senate passes, 91-8, a bill that will broaden the government's powers in fighting domestic terrorism. In addition, the measure limits the number of appeals death-row prisoners can make. . . . The Census Bureau reports that the percentage of low-income Americans who voted in the November 1994 congressional elections is significantly lower than the turnout four years earlier. Overall, the proportion of all Americans of voting age who went to the polls in 1994 was 44.6%, down from 45% in 1990 and 46% in 1986.	Taiwan's president, Lee Teng-hui, makes his first private visit as president to the U.S. to attend an alumni reunion at Cornell University. The Chinese government, which regards Taiwan as a renegade province of China, expresses anger over the visit, which the Clinton administration allowed under heavy pressure from the U.S. Congress. Lee's visit is the first by a Taiwanese leader since the U.S. severed relations with Taiwan in 1979, recognizing mainland communist China as the sole Chinese government.	For the first time in his presidential tenure, Pres. Clinton vetoes a bill passed by Congress, a bill that would cut $16.4 billion from spending previously appropriated by Congress for the fiscal year 1995, which ends Sept. 30. . . . A federal grand jury in Little Rock, Arkansas, issues an indictment that accused, the state's governor, Jim Guy Tucker (D), of conspiring to defraud the IRS and the federal Small Business Administration (SBA) in schemes involving cable-television firms.			June 7
Long Island, New York, automobile mechanic Joseph Buttafuoco, who served more than four months in jail for the statutory rape of teenager Amy Fisher, who herself is serving a jail sentence for shooting Buttafuoco's wife, is charged with solicitation of a prostitute.	The FBI arrests Vyacheslav Kirillovich Ivankov, considered to be the most powerful Russian organized-crime leader currently in the U.S. . . . The House passes, 222-192, the American Overseas Interests Act, a foreign-aid bill that will institute broad policy guidelines. . . . A former congressman, William Hendon (R, N.C.), is expelled from Vietnam after alleging that U.S. service members are being held in an underground jail near Hanoi. Vietnamese officials deny the charge.	Thomas D. Cabot, 98, industrialist who built Cabot Corp. into a leading multinational chemical company, contributed to a number of conservationist causes, and purchased 50 small islands off the coast of Maine to ensure their preservation, dies in Weston, Massachusetts, of an undisclosed illness.	A study shows the antidepressant drug Prozac is effective in relieving tension and irritability associated with severe premenstrual syndrome (PMS).	Baseball Hall of Fame outfielder Mickey Mantle, 63, undergoes surgery to replace a liver ravaged by cancer, hepatitis, and years of alcohol abuse.	June 8
	In Alexandria, Virginia, U.S. district judge Albert Bryan Jr. approves a March settlement in which the CIA pays a total of $990,000 to 450 women from clandestine services. . . . In Belgrade, the Serbian and Yugoslav capital, U.S. citizen Shayna Lazarevich is reunited with her two children after trying for six years to retrieve them from her ex-husband, Dragisa Lazarevich, who abducted and hid them in his native Yugoslavia in 1989.				June 9

F	G	H	I	J
Includes elections, federal-state relations, civil rights and liberties, crime, the judiciary, education, health care, poverty, urban affairs, and population.	Includes formation and debate of U.S. foreign and defense policies, veterans' affairs, and defense spending. (Relations with specific foreign countries are usually found under the region concerned.)	Includes business, labor, agriculture, taxation, transportation, consumer affairs, monetary and fiscal policy, natural resources, and pollution.	Includes worldwide scientific, medical, and technological developments; natural phenomena; U.S. weather; natural disasters; and accidents.	Includes the arts, religion, scholarship, communications media, sports, entertainments, fashions, fads, and social life.

	World Affairs	Europe	Africa & the Middle East	The Americas	Asia & the Pacific
June 10		Fighting between Croats and Croatian Serbs breaks out in Croatia. . . . Riots that started June 9 in Bradford, England, begin to calm.		In Medellín, Colombia's second-largest city, 29 people are killed and more than 200 are injured when a bomb explodes at an outdoor music festival.	Masaya Hanai, 82, director of Toyota Motor Co. starting in 1959 and board chairman, 1978–82, dies in Toyoda, Japan, of kidney failure.
June 11		In a series of referendums, Italian citizens vote against curbs on media ownership, thereby allowing former premier Silvio Berlusconi to maintain full control of his media empire, Fininvest S.p.A. . . . Reports state that at least three UN convoys have been turned back or confiscated by Bosnian Serbs.			
June 12	Representatives of Estonia, Lithuania, and Latvia sign so-called association agreements with the European Union (EU). The accords include trade and cooperation arrangements and may eventually lead to full membership in the EU for the three former Soviet republics.	The first humanitarian aid convoy in three weeks reaches Sarajevo. The UN confirms that a peacekeeper from Kenya was killed by Croatian Serb gunmen near Knin while trying to prevent Croatian Serbs from hijacking an earlier UN convoy. . . . Arturo Benedetti Michelangeli, 75, Italian concert pianist, dies in Lugano, Switzerland, of unreported causes.		Parliamentary elections are held in the eastern Caribbean island of Dominica, and the United Workers' Party (UWP) wins a majority in the House of Assembly, taking control of the body from the Dominica Freedom Party (DFP).	
June 13	French president Jacques Chirac announces his country will resume underground testing of nuclear weapons in the South Pacific. . . . The International Confederation of Free Trade Unions reports that 98 countries routinely committed workers' rights violations during 1994. That figure is the highest number ever recorded by the organization.	Bosnian Serbs release most of the 144 remaining UN peacekeepers taken hostage by the Serbs after NATO bombings began May 25. . . . Spain's defense ministry confirms that the military's espionage service eavesdropped on hundreds of mobile-telephone conversations in the 1980s and early 1990s.	Reports reveal that Tutsi students with grenades and automatic weapons attacked Hutu classmates at Bujumbura University in Burundi. School officials state that at least nine people were killed in the attack.	Forest fires rage in several western Canadian provinces. In the Northwest Territories, at least 43 forest fires are reported, forcing the evacuation of 2,000 people.	Data show that 500 lives have been claimed in clashes since the Liberation Tigers of Tamil Eelam broke an internationally monitored cease-fire in April. . . . King Birendra of Nepal dissolves the country's parliament and schedules a general election for Nov. 23.
June 14	In response to France's June 13 announcement, New Zealand prime minister James Bolger breaks defense links with France and denounces the planned nuclear tests as "the arrogant action of a European colonial power." Japanese foreign minister Yohei Kono states that France has "betrayed the trust of nonnuclear nations."	Some 200 rebels, led by Shamil Basayev, attack Budennovsk, a Russian town about 70 miles (110 km) north of the Chechen border. They kill at least 20 police officers. The attack marks the first time that fighting for control of Chechnya spills beyond the borders of the republic, where a war has raged since December 1994. . . . Pilots for Italy's state-owned airline, Alitalia, begin a series of illegal "wildcat" strikes.	Israeli undercover soldiers at the border of the Gaza Strip and Egypt shoot and kill two members of Force 17, the elite Palestinian unit.	Data suggest that 3,628,430 acres of Canadian forest have been destroyed by fire to date in 1995. . . . Steve and Lorelei Turner are convicted of manslaughter in the starvation death of their three-year-old son, John Ryan Turner. It is said to be the first time in Canadian history that parents are convicted of manslaughter for failing to provide the necessities of life for a child.	Reports disclose that officials from India have agreed to provide military support for the Sri Lankan government after recent rebel attacks.
June 15	Leaders of the world's seven wealthiest industrialized nations, the Group of Seven (G-7), meet in Halifax, Canada, for their 21st annual summit.	Chechen fighters, pressing for their demands, reportedly execute at least five hostages in a Budennovsk hospital. . . . UN officials report that Bosnian government troops attacked Serb positions north of Sarajevo with at least 1,600 detonations. The Bosnian Serb assembly votes to unify Serb-held territory in Bosnia with Serb-held territory in Croatia. Data indicates that at least 15 UN peacekeepers are still in Bosnian Serb custody and as many as 10 others are unaccounted for.	Reports disclose that a convoy of diplomats, including Robert Krueger, the U.S. ambassador to Burundi, were ambushed in the Cibitoke province in northwestern Burundi. No diplomats were hurt.		Monsoon storms begin in India, Bangladesh, and Nepal. The storms break a deadly three-week-long heat wave in India and Pakistan that has killed more than 550 people.

A	B	C	D	E
Includes developments that affect more than one world region, international organizations, and important meetings of major world leaders.	Includes all domestic and regional developments in Europe, including the Soviet Union, Turkey, Cyprus, and Malta.	Includes all domestic and regional developments in Africa and the Middle East, including Iraq and Iran and excluding Cyprus, Turkey, and Afghanistan.	Includes all domestic and regional developments in Latin America, the Caribbean, and Canada.	Includes all domestic and regional developments in Asia and Pacific nations, extending from Afghanistan through all the Pacific Islands, except Hawaii.

U.S. Politics & Social Issues	U.S. Foreign Policy & Defense	U.S. Economy & Environment	Science, Technology, & Nature	Culture, Leisure, & Lifestyle	
				Lindsey Nelson, 76, Hall of Fame sportscaster, dies in Atlanta, Georgia, of complications from Parkinson's disease and pneumonia. . . . Thunder Gulch, ridden by Gary Stevens, wins the 127th running of the Belmont Stakes in Elmont, New York. . . . Steffi Graf of Germany defeats Arantxa Sanchez Vicario of Spain to capture the women's tennis title at the French Open.	June 10
Pres. Clinton and House Speaker Newt Gingrich (R, Ga.) hold an hour-long public discussion of policy issues and answer questions from an audience of 300 people at a senior citizens' center in Claremont, New Hampshire.				Thomas Muster of Austria beats Michael Chang to win the French Open men's tennis title.	June 11
In *Missouri v. Jenkins*, the Supreme Court rules, 5-4, that a federal judge exceeded his authority when he ordered the state of Missouri to fund teacher salary raises and magnet schools as part of a program to remedy past segregation. . . . In *Adarand Constructors v. Pena*, the Supreme Court rules, 5-4, that the federal government must adhere to the same strict constitutional standards that states have to obey when implementing affirmative action programs. . . . Arthur J. Kropp, 37, president of the civil-liberties group People for the American Way, dies from AIDS in Washington, D.C.			Astronomers announce they have made the first definitive detection of primordial helium in space, confirming predictions founded on the Big Bang theory of the universe's origin. The findings are based on the observations of a telescope package known as *Astro-2*. . . . The U.S. biotechnology company Cephalon Inc. reports that its genetically engineered drug Myotrophin has helped to ease the symptoms and slow the progression of amyotrophic lateral sclerosis (ALS), known as Lou Gehrig's disease, which affects about 30,000 people in the U.S.	The John D. and Catherine T. MacArthur Foundation of Chicago awards its annual MacArthur Fellowships, or so-called genius grants, to 24 people in various fields. That is four more than what was granted in 1994.	June 12
Mother Teresa of Calcutta, India, the Roman Catholic nun who received a Nobel Peace Prize in 1979, opens a shelter for poor women suffering from AIDS in Atlanta, Georgia.		In a nationally televised address, Pres. Clinton proposes a budget plan that includes $1.1 trillion in spending cuts, spread out over 10 years, designed to bring the federal budget into balance by the fiscal year 2005. Clinton's plan will reduce spending on Medicare, education, and other social services, but will seek to shield those programs from the deeper cuts favored by congressional Republicans.		The African-Americans Against Violence group protests plans to hold a parade and festival in New York City to honor former boxing champion Mike Tyson, who was convicted of rape in 1992.	June 13
Five white seniors at Greenwich High School in the affluent suburban town of Greenwich, Connecticut, are suspended after a coded racial slur is found in messages they included in their yearbook captions. . . . In *Witte v. U.S.*, the Supreme Court rules, 8-1, that evidence that was already considered by a judge to lengthen a defendant's prison sentence can be used as grounds for prosecution of a separate criminal offense.		The UAW union elects Stephen Yokich as its president. . . . In *Oklahoma Tax Commission v. Chickasaw Nation*, the Supreme Court rules unanimously that sales made on Indian tribal territories cannot be subjected to state excise taxes. . . . In *Commissioner of Internal Revenue v. Schleier*, the Supreme Court rules, 6-3, that the federal government can tax awards paid out in age-discrimination suits brought under the federal Age Discrimination in Employment Act.	A team of astronomers announce they have detected, in images taken by the *Hubble Space Telescope*, the first direct evidence of the Kuiper Belt, a ring of objects believed to be located on the edge of the solar system.	Roger Zelazny, 58, science fiction writer, dies in Sante Fe, New Mexico, of kidney failure associated with cancer. . . . The Houston Rockets win their second consecutive NBA title over the Orlando Magic, 113-101.	June 14
A federal judge in Chicago, Illinois, sentences Richard Bailey to 30 years in prison for his alleged involvement in the death of candy heiress Helen Vorhees Brach, who was last seen in 1977 at the age of 65. . . . Five leaders of militia groups testify before the Senate Judiciary Subcommittee on Terrorism, Technology and Government Information. The hearing, led by Sen. Arlen Specter (R, Pa.), marks the first time that militia members have testified before Congress.			Research suggests that women who receive treatments to replace the hormone estrogen after menopause are slightly more likely to develop breast cancer than were other women. . . . John Vincent Atanasoff, 91, coinventor of the first electronic computer in 1939, dies in Monrovia, Maryland, after suffering a stroke.	Charles Bennett, 95, screenwriter and director who collaborated with Alfred Hitchcock, dies in Los Angeles of unreported causes. . . . The Senate approves, 81-18, legislation that will ease restrictions on TV and radio broadcasts and will outlaw the distribution of "indecent" materials over on-line services and the Internet.	June 15

F	G	H	I	J
Includes elections, federal-state relations, civil rights and liberties, crime, the judiciary, education, health care, poverty, urban affairs, and population.	Includes formation and debate of U.S. foreign and defense policies, veterans' affairs, and defense spending. (Relations with specific foreign countries are usually found under the region concerned.)	Includes business, labor, agriculture, taxation, transportation, consumer affairs, monetary and fiscal policy, natural resources, and pollution.	Includes worldwide scientific, medical, and technological developments; natural phenomena; U.S. weather; natural disasters; and accidents.	Includes the arts, religion, scholarship, communications media, sports, entertainments, fashions, fads, and social life.

	World Affairs	Europe	Africa & the Middle East	The Americas	Asia & the Pacific
June 16	The UN Security Council passes a resolution to send as many as 12,500 additional peacekeeping troops to Bosnia. . . . The Nordic Union, comprising Denmark, Finland, and Sweden, agrees to join the Schengen group, the European Union's passport-free zone, at an unspecified future date.	The Bosnian government army launches an attack to break the Serbian siege of Sarajevo. . . . Queen Elizabeth II marks the official celebration of her 69th birthday by granting 1,055 knighthoods, peerages, and other honors.			In response to France's June 13 announcement, a peaceful demonstration of about 80 protesters is held outside the office of Robert Pearce, a Perth plastic surgeon who is also the French honorary consul.
June 17		Heavily armed Russian troops backed by tanks storm the hospital in Budennovsk, Russia. Floor-by-floor fighting between Russian troops and the Chechen rebels continues for hours, and the Russian troops manage to free about 50 hostages. The Chechen fighters release about 150 more hostages but use others, including women and children, as human shields. . . . Lord (David Henley Ennals) Ennals, 72, secretary of state for the British Department of Social Services, 1976–79, dies in London after a long illness.			The office of Robert Pearce, a plastic surgeon in Perth, Australia, who is also the French honorary consul, is burned down, allegedly by antinuclear activists.
June 18		Negotiations between Shamil Basayev, who attacked Budennovsk June 14, and Russian premier Viktor Chernomyrdin are broadcast live on TV throughout Russia. . . . Bosnian Serbs release the 26 remaining UN hostages. . . . Harry Tisch, 68, trade union leader in East Germany, 1975–89, dies in Berlin of cancer.			
June 19	Finance ministers from European Union member states agree to postpone the launch of economic and monetary union (EMU) until 1999, from 1997.	After freeing most of their hostages, the Chechen fighters leave Budennovsk in a convoy of several buses. The rebels take 150 hostages with them to the Chechen border to ensure their own safe arrival in Chechnya. . . . Peter Wooldridge Townsend, 80, British World War II fighter pilot who in 1955 was prevented from marrying Princess Margaret, the sister of Queen Elizabeth II, because he was divorced, dies in Paris, France, of cancer.		Colombian officials launch a crackdown on the Cali drug cartel. Henry Loaiza Ceballos, the alleged "military leader" of the Cali cartel who is notorious for his alleged role in the torture and killing of 107 peasants over several months in 1990, turns himself in at an army base in Bogota.	The International Committee of the Red Cross announces that it will close its office in Yangon, Myanmar—formerly Rangoon, Burma—because the country's military government denied its petition for access to political prisoners.
June 20		The new EU mediator, Carl Bildt, holds his first meeting with officials of the Bosnian government. Separately, Bosnian government troops trap more than 600 Canadian UN peacekeepers in the town of Visoko. . . . Rebels from Chechnya release the last of 2,000 hostages seized in Budennovsk, Russia, on June 14 before crossing the Chechen border. . . . French police arrest 140 people allegedly affiliated with Islamic terrorist groups.	Harry Gwala, 74, militant leader of the African National Congress in South Africa, dies in Pietermaritzburg, South Africa, of heart failure.	The Canadian House of Commons approves a bill to prevent suspects accused of assault or sexual assault from using extreme drunkenness as a defense. . . . The New National Party wins a slim parliamentary majority in Grenada. . . . The bodies of Timothy Van Dyke and Stephen Welch, two Americans kidnapped by FARC in 1994, are found buried near the town of Medina, Colombia.	Data shows that the monsoon storms that started June 15 have caused massive flooding in India, Bangladesh, and Nepal. Nearly 2 million people were stranded by flood waters, and the storms have claimed 50 lives in Bangladesh and 60 people in Nepal. Another 35 people are reportedly missing. . . . The Australian cabinet votes to recognize the aborigine and Torres Strait Islander flags as official flags of the Commonwealth of Australia.
June 21		A multidenominational gathering of religious leaders holds a ceremony to mark the opening of the first Muslim mosque ever built in Rome. . . . The Bosnian army allows UN convoys to deliver 600 tons of food. . . . Chechen leaders agree to help Russian investigators find Shamil Basayev, who attacked Budennovsk on June 14. . . . Tristan Jones, 71, British author and adventurer famous for his sailing expeditions, dies in Phuket, Thailand, after suffering a stroke.			

A	B	C	D	E
Includes developments that affect more than one world region, international organizations, and important meetings of major world leaders.	Includes all domestic and regional developments in Europe, including the Soviet Union, Turkey, Cyprus, and Malta.	Includes all domestic and regional developments in Africa and the Middle East, including Iraq and Iran and excluding Cyprus, Turkey, and Afghanistan.	Includes all domestic and regional developments in Latin America, the Caribbean, and Canada.	Includes all domestic and regional developments in Asia and Pacific nations, extending from Afghanistan through all the Pacific Islands, except Hawaii.

U.S. Politics & Social Issues	U.S. Foreign Policy & Defense	U.S. Economy & Environment	Science, Technology, & Nature	Culture, Leisure, & Lifestyle	
In Tallahassee, Florida, Circuit Court judge F. E. Steinmeyer III upholds a law on which the state of Florida is basing a lawsuit filed against the tobacco industry to recover money spent by the state through Medicaid to care for victims of smoking-related illnesses.			A study of prostitutes in Senegal shows that infection with a milder type of HIV seems to help prevent infection with a more virulent type of HIV.... Research suggests that people who try to quit smoking gradually on a preset schedule are twice as successful as those who quit abruptly.	Charles Elmer Martin, 85, artist best known for his cartoons for the *New Yorker* magazine, dies in Portland, Maine, of unreported causes.... The International Olympic Committee overwhelmingly elects Salt Lake City, Utah, to be the site of the Winter Olympics in the year 2002.	June 16
					June 17
	Riots erupt at the Esmor Immigration Detention Center in Elizabeth, New Jersey, when 300 detainees awaiting deportation hearings take two guards hostage for nearly six hours. Police reportedly use pepper spray on the detainees to end the standoff. Twenty inmates receive minor injuries.			Corey Pavin wins the U.S. Open golf tournament at the Shinnecock Hills Golf Club in Southampton, New York.	June 18
In *Hurley v. Irish-American Gay, Lesbian and Bisexual Group of Boston*, the Supreme Court rules unanimously that constitutional free-speech guarantees give organizers of a St. Patrick's Day parade the right to limit messages conveyed in their event and therefore permit them to exclude a group of homosexual marchers. The court unanimously holds that the central issue in the case is free speech, not gay rights.... In *Sandin v. Connor*, the Supreme Court rules, 5-4, that inmates cannot sue prison officials unless they have subjected the inmates to "atypical and significant hardship."... Mother Teresa dedicates a shelter for women and newborn infants in Washington, D.C.					June 19
	A military tribunal acquits air force captain James Wang on three counts of dereliction of duty in the friendly-fire downing of two U.S. Army helicopters over Iraq in April 1994.... The State Department confirms that Cuba has refused to extradite fugitive U.S. financier Robert Vesco.... Laurence McKinley Gould, 98, who explored Antarctica with Admiral Richard E. Byrd and led the U.S. in an effort to prevent future territorial claims on Antarctica, dies in Tucson, Arizona.	The Senate votes, 65-35, to repeal the 55-mile-per-hour speed limit set for automobiles on federal highways and allow states to set their own speed limits for passenger vehicles.	Pres. Clinton's Advisory Committee on Human Radiation Experiments admits that during the 1950s the federal government secretly collected tissue samples from human cadavers to measure the effects of radioactive fallout from nuclear weapons tests. The tissue was taken without the knowledge of or permission from families or doctors.	Former boxing champion Mike Tyson, convicted of rape in 1992, is welcomed back to his hometown, New York City, by thousands of fans.... Members of the Southern Baptist Convention vote overwhelmingly to formally repent for their church's past support of slavery and to ask forgiveness from all blacks.	June 20
In *U.S. v. Aguilar*, the Supreme Court, 8-1, upholds the government's prosecution of U.S. District Judge Robert Aguilar for illegally disclosing a government wiretap to a former mobster.... In *Florida Bar v. Went For It Inc.*, the Supreme Court rules, 5-4, to uphold a Florida state law that bars lawyers from soliciting business from accident victims and their relatives by direct mail within 30 days of an accident.		The Commerce Department reports that in April the U.S. recorded a seasonally adjusted $11.37 billion deficit in trade in goods and services, the largest deficit since the department began recording a combined sum in January 1992. The April figure marks a sharp jump from a revised gap of $9.79 billion in March.	In Detroit, Michigan, federal judge Avern Cohn dismisses all charges against Abraham Jacob Alkhabaz, a former University of Michigan student who posted a sexually violent story that mentions a female classmate of his by name on the Internet.... Reports confirm that Hoffmann-La Roche Inc. plans to offer its experimental drug Invirase to 2,280 people with AIDS.		June 21

F	G	H	I	J
Includes elections, federal-state relations, civil rights and liberties, crime, the judiciary, education, health care, poverty, urban affairs, and population.	*Includes formation and debate of U.S. foreign and defense policies, veterans' affairs, and defense spending. (Relations with specific foreign countries are usually found under the region concerned.)*	*Includes business, labor, agriculture, taxation, transportation, consumer affairs, monetary and fiscal policy, natural resources, and pollution.*	*Includes worldwide scientific, medical, and technological developments; natural phenomena; U.S. weather; natural disasters; and accidents.*	*Includes the arts, religion, scholarship, communications media, sports, entertainments, fashions, fads, and social life.*

	World Affairs	Europe	Africa & the Middle East	The Americas	Asia & the Pacific
June 22		British prime minister John Major resigns as head of the Conservative Party following months of dissension within the party over his government's policy on the European Union. . . . Numbers indicate that troops of the predominantly Muslim Bosnian government army have surrounded and detained more than 600 UN peacekeepers.	An Israeli bombardment reportedly kills a young girl in the Lebanese village of Shaqra. . . .The government of Iran leaves standing a fatwa, or religious dictum, issued in 1989 by Iran's then-ruler and spiritual authority Ayatollah Khomeini, which calls upon Muslims to kill the Indian-born British novelist Salman Rushdie. The move surprises EU representatives who had expected to receive a written revocation of the dictum.		A militant Muslim faction known as the Mohajir Qaumi Movement launches a rampage in Karachi, Pakistan's commercial hub. Police report that the group has fired grenade launchers, burns several buildings in the city's financial district and tortured several victims. . . . Cambodia's National Assembly expels Sam Rainsy, an outspoken opposition member and former finance minister who accused the government of corruption and human-rights violations.
June 23	The World Bank and international conservation groups announce a plan that will establish or improve the environmental management of 155 marine protection areas, or MPAs, around the world.	Jean-Luc Dehaene is appointed to a second term as Belgium's premier at the head of a center-left ruling coalition. . . . Morris Cohen (alias Peter Kroger), 84, spy who funneled information about the U.S. development of the atomic bomb to Soviet officials during the 1940s, dies in Moscow of heart failure.	In retaliation for the June 22 attack, Hezbollah (Party of God) Shi'ite guerrillas launch a rocket attack against Israel's northwest coast, hitting a facility of the Paris-based Club Med tourist resort and killing a French chef employed there.	Riots erupt in Cordoba, Argentina's second-largest city, prompted by the failure of the government of the province of Cordoba to pay state wages and pensions during the previous two months.	Australian prime minister Paul Keating temporarily recalls his ambassador to France to protest France's expected resumption of nuclear testing in the French Polynesia area of the South Pacific.
June 24		Italian anti-Mafia police in Palermo, Sicily, arrest Leoluca Bagarella, the reputed head of the Cosa Nostra organized-crime group, who is considered Italy's most-wanted fugitive.	Meir Zorea, 72, Israeli general and politician who, after World War II, belonged to the "Avengers," a Jewish group that sought to identify and kill alleged former members of Germany's Nazi party, dies of unreported causes.		
June 25	Seven of the 15 EU nations—Greece, Spain, the Netherlands, Sweden, Finland, Denmark, and Austria—sign a statement that assails France's decision to resume nuclear testing in the South Pacific.	Bulgarian-American artist Christo and his French wife, Jeanne-Claude, officially present Wrapped Reichstag, a work of art in which the Reichstag building in Berlin, Germany is wrapped in a million square feet (93,000 sq m) of silver fabric. The German parliament approved the controversial project, for which the artist has been campaigning for more than 20 years, in February 1994.	Israeli soldiers in the northern West Bank city of Nablus open fire on Arab demonstrators, killing two and wounding 50. Separately, a Hamas suicide bomber on a donkey cart dies in a failed attack against Israeli soldiers near Khan Younis in the south-central Gaza Strip.	Haiti holds its first elections since the October 1994 resignation of Lt. Gen. Raoul Cedras, leader of a military junta, and the return of the democratically elected president he had ousted, Jean-Bertrand Aristide. Election observers describe the voting process as "chaotic" and state that official procedures are not being followed during the counting phase.	The violence that was started June 22 by a militant Muslim faction known as the Mohajir Qaumi Movement in Karachi, Pakistan's commercial hub, has killed nearly 75 people. City officials state that over the past five weeks more than 300 people have been killed in factional fighting between rival Muslim groups and in attacks on police and security forces.
June 26	Representatives from more than 100 nations gather in San Francisco, California, to mark the 50th anniversary of the signing of the United Nations Charter. Events to mark the signing include speeches by U.S president Clinton and UN secretary general Boutros Boutros-Ghali. . . . The leaders of the EU's 15 member states approve granting 6.69 billion European currency units (ECUs) ($8.83 billion) through the year 2000 to aid Eastern European countries seeking EU membership.		Egypt's Pres. Hosni Mubarak escapes an assassination attempt without injury when gunmen open fire on his motorcade in the Ethiopian capital, Addis Ababa. Four people die in the attack. . . . The PNA intensifies its crackdown on Hamas militants in the Gaza Strip with arrests of more than two dozen Hamas leaders, including Mahmoud Zahar and Ahmed Bahar, both senior Hamas officials.		
June 27		Gordon Wilson, 67, Protestant who was injured in an IRA bombing in which 11 Protestants, including his daughter, were killed and who publicly forgave the bombers before he launched a campaign for peace, dies in Enniskillen, Northern Ireland, of a heart attack.	After two years of feuding, Hamad bin Khalifa al-Thani, Qatar's crown prince and defense minister, wrests the position of emir from his father, Khalifa bin Hamad al-Thani, in a bloodless coup.		

A	B	C	D	E
Includes developments that affect more than one world region, international organizations, and important meetings of major world leaders.	Includes all domestic and regional developments in Europe, including the Soviet Union, Turkey, Cyprus, and Malta.	Includes all domestic and regional developments in Africa and the Middle East, including Iraq and Iran and excluding Cyprus, Turkey, and Afghanistan.	Includes all domestic and regional developments in Latin America, the Caribbean, and Canada.	Includes all domestic and regional developments in Asia and Pacific nations, extending from Afghanistan through all the Pacific Islands, except Hawaii.

U.S. Politics & Social Issues	U.S. Foreign Policy & Defense	U.S. Economy & Environment	Science, Technology, & Nature	Culture, Leisure, & Lifestyle	
The Senate effectively rejects Pres. Clinton's choice of Dr. Henry W. Foster Jr. to be surgeon general when Foster's supporters fail to muster the 60 votes needed to end debate over his nomination, which has been embroiled in discussions of abortion rights.... In Alexandria, Virginia, federal judge Claude M. Hilton sentences the former president of the United Way of America, William Aramony, to seven years in prison and three years' probation for stealing hundreds of thousands of dollars from the charity that he spent on himself and his girlfriends.	In Newark, New Jersey, federal district judge Ronald Hedges denies the Mexican government's request to extradite Mario Ruiz Massieu, a former Mexican deputy attorney general who is wanted on charges of covering up information in the assassination of his brother, Jose Francisco Ruiz Massieu.	The Defense Base Closure and Realignment Commission delivers its final recommendations on the closure and realignment of military bases around the country. The commission recommends the closure of nine bases that the Defense Department had not intended to close and votes to keep open 15 bases that the department wanted to close.	Research does not demonstrate a link between silicone breast implants and connective-tissue diseases, according to a medical study.		June 22
A Florida jury convicts Anthony Williams, 21, of murder and strong-arm robbery in the highly publicized 1993 slaying of a German tourist, Barbara Meller Jensen, in Miami, Florida.			Dr. Jonas Edward Salk, 80, virologist who in the 1950s developed a vaccine for poliomyelitis, or polio, which, during the six years following its introduction to the general public, caused the incidence of polio to fall by 95%, dies in La Jolla, California, of heart failure.		June 23
Esther Rome, 49, author and advocate of women's health issues who, in 1969, helped form the Boston Women's Health Collective, dies in Somerville, Massachusetts, of breast cancer.	The U.S. and Japan reach an accord in a two-year trade dispute involving automobiles and auto parts hours before a U.S. deadline for imposing billions of dollars in punitive tariffs on Japan.	The Conference Board business research organization reports that its index of consumer confidence fell to 92.8 in June, down from a revised level of 102 in May. The unexpectedly large fall in the index is the steepest in almost three years and brings it to its lowest level since October 1994.		In hockey, the New Jersey Devils win their first NHL Stanley Cup over the heavily favored Detroit Red Wings. The Devils are the first team since the NHL expanded in 1967 to win the title without enjoying home-ice advantage in any playoff round.	June 24
Warren Earl Burger, 87, former chief justice of the U.S. Supreme Court who had the longest tenure of any chief justice in the 20th century, 1969–86, dies in Washington, D.C., of congestive heart failure.			Ernest T(homas) S(inton) Walton, 91, Irish physicist who shared the 1951 Nobel Prize for his work in splitting atoms, which has had a major influence on nuclear research, dies in Belfast, Northern Ireland, of unreported causes.	The U.S. wins the U.S. Cup soccer title, with a 0-0 tie against Colombia in the final game.	June 25
In *Vernonia School District v. Acton*, the Supreme Court upholds, 6-3, a random drug-testing program for student athletes in an Oregon school district.... Rep. Greg Laughlin (Tex.) announces he will switch to the Republican Party after Republican leaders promised to create a new seat for him on the House Ways and Means Committee. Democrats vociferously object to the creation of a new seat without a corresponding seat for a Democrat.... The Senate, by voice vote, passes a bill that will extend a program intended to encourage senior citizens to use managed-care providers of health insurance to 50 states and the District of Columbia.	The Senate confirms by voice vote George J. Tenet as the new deputy director of the CIA.	A confidential study commissioned by the RTC finds that Pres. Clinton and First Lady Hillary Rodham Clinton were passive investors in the Whitewater Development Corp. real-estate venture. The study states that the couple had "little direct involvement" in legally questionable transactions in the 1980s related to the venture.		*Publishers Weekly* puts *The Rainmaker* by John Grisham at the top of its bestseller list.	June 26
The American Bar Association (ABA), under the threat of a lawsuit from the U.S. Justice Department's antitrust division, agrees to modify the criteria used to accredit law schools.			The U.S. space shuttle *Atlantis* blasts off from Kennedy Space Center in Cape Canaveral, Florida, to carry out a mission to dock with the Russian space station *Mir*.		June 27

F	G	H	I	J
Includes elections, federal-state relations, civil rights and liberties, crime, the judiciary, education, health care, poverty, urban affairs, and population.	*Includes formation and debate of U.S. foreign and defense policies, veterans' affairs, and defense spending. (Relations with specific foreign countries are usually found under the region concerned.)*	*Includes business, labor, agriculture, taxation, transportation, consumer affairs, monetary and fiscal policy, natural resources, and pollution.*	*Includes worldwide scientific, medical, and technological developments; natural phenomena; U.S. weather; natural disasters; and accidents.*	*Includes the arts, religion, scholarship, communications media, sports, entertainments, fashions, fads, and social life.*

	World Affairs	Europe	Africa & the Middle East	The Americas	Asia & the Pacific
June 28	The member nations of the Gulf Cooperation Council, including Saudi Arabia, recognize Hamad bin Khalifa al-Thani as the new emir of Qatar, as does Iran.	Bosnian Serb forces fire rockets into central Sarajevo, killing five civilians and wounding dozens of people, including foreign journalists. . . . Spanish premier Felipe Gonzalez accepts the resignations of two cabinet ministers in connection with a recent electronic wire-tapping scandal.		Civil strife in the state of Guerrero in southwestern Mexico begins when two trucks, each containing between 40 and 60 peasants, are stopped at a police checkpoint near the town of Coyuca de Benitez. Accounts of what provokes the ensuing violence vary widely.	In Sri Lanka, an attack by the Liberation Tigers of Tamil Eelam on Mandaithivu Island, located west of their Jaffna stronghold, claims the lives of an estimated 50 rebels and 75 government troops.
June 29	The U.S. declines to accept an interim global financial-services pact under the auspices of the WTO when it announces that it will not open access to its financial-services markets on a nondiscriminatory (most-favored-nation) basis. The EU steps in to fill the leadership vacuum. . . . Six nations of the Schengen group—Belgium, Germany, Luxembourg, the Netherlands, Portugal, and Spain—agree to eliminate frontier controls permanently, effective June 30. France states it will temporarily maintain border controls despite its participation in the Schengen group.			Retired general Juan Manuel Contreras Sepulveda, former Chilean chief of police who, in November 1993, was sentenced to seven years in prison for directing the 1976 car-bomb assassination of Chilean opposition leader Orlando Letelier and his secretary Ronni Moffitt in Washington, D.C., is put under arrest at a naval hospital after he forestalled his capture for nearly a month.	A five-story wing of a department store complex in Seoul, South Korea, collapses, killing hundreds of workers and shoppers in the worst peacetime disaster in modern Korean history.
June 30	The UN Security Council votes unanimously to extend until Sept. 15 its 70-member observer mission in Liberia. . . . Trade ministers from 34 countries discuss plans for the creation of a free-trade zone, the Free Trade Area of the Americas (FTAA), by the year 2005. . . . The IMF releases to Mexico the remaining $10.7 billion in aid it offered in February, making $2 billion available immediately.	The German parliament ratifies a decision by the cabinet of German chancellor Helmut Kohl to send warplanes and 1,500 troops to Bosnia to support UN peacekeepers there. The decision is controversial because Nazi German forces during World War II committed widespread atrocities in Yugoslavia.		In the state of Guerrero in southwestern Mexico, peasants and members of the Institutional Democratic Revolutionary Party (PRD), angry over the June 28 violence, raid and set fire to the town hall of Coyuca de Benitez.	The Australian Treasury reports a record-high current account deficit of A$2.9 billion (US$2 billion) for the month of May.
July 1		Greece's former crown prince Pavlos, 28, weds American heiress Marie-Chantal Miller, 26, in a ceremony at the Cathedral of Saint Sophia in London, England. . . . Princess Stephanie of Monaco weds Daniel Ducruet, a former bodyguard for the royal family, in a ceremony in Monte Carlo, Monaco. The princess, 30, and Ducruet, 32, have two children together.		Chilean officials announce that the government will buy a tract of forest land in southern Chile in order to prevent a U.S. businessman, Douglas Tompkins, from purchasing it. . . . After the June 30 protests, the attorney general of Guerrero, Antonio Alcocer Salazar, announces that 10 policemen have been charged with homicide, but he does not retract the government's earlier statement that the peasants initiated the June 28 attack.	
July 2		The UN compound in Sarajevo is hit by a mortar shell, apparently fired from Bosnian Serb positions. Shrapnel hits the U.S. embassy. One Canadian and two British peacekeepers are wounded.			Thailand's Chart Thai (Thai Nation) party wins 92 seats in the country's 391-seat House of Representatives, gaining control from incumbent premier Chuan Leekpai and his Democrat Party, which garners 86 seats.
July 3		Private Lee Clegg, a Northern Ireland border guard convicted of killing a Roman Catholic girl, Karen Reilly, in 1990, is released from prison. In response, groups of armed men in Belfast and Londonderry, the largest cities in Ulster, begin rioting.		The opposition Labour Party defeats the ruling People's Action Movement in parliamentary elections in the Caribbean nation of St. Christopher and Nevis.	

A	B	C	D	E
Includes developments that affect more than one world region, international organizations, and important meetings of major world leaders.	*Includes all domestic and regional developments in Europe, including the Soviet Union, Turkey, Cyprus, and Malta.*	*Includes all domestic and regional developments in Africa and the Middle East, including Iraq and Iran and excluding Cyprus, Turkey, and Afghanistan.*	*Includes all domestic and regional developments in Latin America, the Caribbean, and Canada.*	*Includes all domestic and regional developments in Asia and Pacific nations, extending from Afghanistan through all the Pacific Islands, except Hawaii.*

U.S. Politics & Social Issues	U.S. Foreign Policy & Defense	U.S. Economy & Environment	Science, Technology, & Nature	Culture, Leisure, & Lifestyle	
The House votes, 312-120, in favor of a constitutional amendment that will allow federal and state authorities to prosecute people who burn, damage, or otherwise desecrate the U.S. flag.... Pres. Clinton orders federal agencies to institute minimum-security standards recommended by the Justice Department in the wake of the Apr. 19 blast in Oklahoma City.	An exhibit at the Smithsonian Air and Space Museum in Washington, D.C., featuring the forward fuselage of the *Enola Gay*, the warplane that in 1945 dropped an atomic bomb on Hiroshima, Japan, opens to the public. The exhibit had received much attention from veterans groups before its opening.	The Senate votes, 70-29, to pass a bill that will discourage shareholders in companies from filing lawsuits alleging fraud by stockbrokers, corporate officials, or accountants. ... In Little Rock, Arkansas, U.S. district judge George Howard Jr. sentences Webster Hubbell, the most prominent person to be convicted thus far as a result of the federal inquiry into the Whitewater affair, to 21 months in prison for tax evasion and mail fraud.		A white polyester suit worn by actor John Travolta in the 1977 disco film *Saturday Night Fever* is sold for $145,500 to an anonymous telephone bidder at a sale by Christie's auction house in New York City.	June 28
In *Miller v. Johnson*, the Supreme Court rules, 5-4, that electoral districts drawn to ensure fair political representation of minorities are unconstitutional if race is used as the "predominant factor" in drawing district boundaries.... In *Capitol Square v. Pinette*, the Supreme Court rules, 7-2, that an Ohio Ku Klux Klan chapter has a constitutional right to erect a cross in a public park.... In *Rosenberger v. Rector and Visitors of University of Virginia*, the Supreme Court rules, 5-4, that the University of Virginia must provide funds for a student-run Christian journal.		The House, 239-194, and the Senate, 54-46, approve a historic fiscal-policy blueprint that seeks to balance the federal budget by 2002 by implementing $900 billion in cuts in federal spending.... In *Babbitt v. Sweet Home*, the Supreme Court rules, 6-3, that the Clinton administration applied a justifiably broad interpretation of the 1973 Endangered Species Act when it sought to safeguard the habitat of the endangered northern spotted owl.... The House passes, 276-151, a bill that cuts $16.3 billion from spending previously appropriated by Congress for the fiscal 1995.	The U.S. space shuttle *Atlantis* docks with the Russian space station *Mir*. It is the first of seven dockings scheduled to occur prior to the beginning of construction on the planned international space station. ... An international team of oceanographers state that adding large quantities of iron sulfate to the oceans may slow global warming. British and U.S. researchers reportedly have found that the introduction of iron sulfate between Tahiti and the Galapagos Islands stimulates growth of algae which absorb substantial amounts of carbon from the ocean water.	Lana Turner (born Julia Jean Mildred Frances Turner), 75, actress who was one of Hollywood's most glamorous film stars from the 1940s until the 1960s, dies in Century City, California, after suffering from throat cancer.	June 29
Reports disclose that a serial bomber known as the Unabomber sent *The New York Times* and *The Washington Post* a manifesto that he asked be printed in exchange for his ending a series of bombing attacks that span 17 years.... The House passes, 350-68, legislation that extends to all 50 states and the District of Columbia a program intended to encourage senior citizens to use managed-care providers of health insurance.		The U.S. Treasury Department agrees to loan $146.7 million to Washington, D.C., to help carry it through the end of the 1995 fiscal year, which ends Sept. 30.... Statistics show that after-tax profits of U.S. corporations rose 3.8% in the first quarter from the previous quarter, to an annual rate of $350.7 billion. After-tax profits in the 1994 fourth quarter were calculated at a $337.9 billion annual rate.	On *Mir*, the U.S. shuttle astronauts give their Russian colleagues chocolates and flowers and in return receive a traditional Russian greeting of bread and salt. The crew is congratulated by U.S. vice president Al Gore and Russian premier Viktor Chernomyrdin.... Reports state that scientists are suggesting that fossils of a squirrel-sized primate found in the Fayum Desert of Egypt are the earliest known common ancestor of the higher primates.	Gale Gordon (born Charles T. Aldrich Jr.), 89, comic actor best known for his work with Lucille Ball, dies in Escondido, California, of cancer.... NBA Commissioner David Stern imposes a lockout after basketball players fail to ratify a collective-bargaining agreement.	June 30
				The National Basketball Association lockout formally begins, the first work stoppage in NBA history.... Wolfman Jack (born Robert Smith), 57, rock-and-roll disc jockey famous during the late 1960s, dies in Belvidere, North Carolina, of a heart attack.	July 1
				George Seldes, 104, publisher and innovator in the field of journalism criticism, dies in Windsor, Vermont, of heart ailments.... Yugoslavia's basketball team beats the Lithuanian team, 96-90, to win the European championship. Yugoslavia's appearance is its first since the UN eased sanctions imposed in 1992. Players of the Croatian national team, the third-place finishers, walk off the podium while Yugoslavia's national anthem is played.	July 2
Judge Fredricka Smith of Dade County, Florida, Circuit Court sentences Leroy Rogers and Anthony Williams to life in prison for the high-profile 1993 slaying of a German tourist, Barbara Meller Jensen, in Miami. Williams is sentenced to another 30 years and Rogers an additional 15 years on robbery counts.		Data show that the purchasing managers' index decreased to 45.7% in June, down from the revised May rate of 46.1%. Prior to May, the index rose for 20 consecutive months. A measure above 50% indicates an expanding manufacturing sector.	While in orbit aboard *Mir*, Russian and U.S. astronauts take questions from reporters at U.S. and Russian ground stations.	Richard (Pancho) Gonzalez, 67, tennis player famed during the 1940s and 1950s, dies in Las Vegas, Nevada, of stomach cancer.	July 3

F	G	H	I	J
Includes elections, federal-state relations, civil rights and liberties, crime, the judiciary, education, health care, poverty, urban affairs, and population.	*Includes formation and debate of U.S. foreign and defense policies, veterans' affairs, and defense spending. (Relations with specific foreign countries are usually found under the region concerned.)*	*Includes business, labor, agriculture, taxation, transportation, consumer affairs, monetary and fiscal policy, natural resources, and pollution.*	*Includes worldwide scientific, medical, and technological developments; natural phenomena; U.S. weather; natural disasters; and accidents.*	*Includes the arts, religion, scholarship, communications media, sports, entertainments, fashions, fads, and social life.*

	World Affairs	Europe	Africa & the Middle East	The Americas	Asia & the Pacific
July 4		British prime minister John Major emerges as the winner in an unprecedented parliamentary election for leadership of the ruling Conservative Party.... Data suggest that in the first 20 hours of the disturbances that started July 3 in Ulster, 160 vehicles that were destroyed and 32 people were arrested.	Israel and the Palestine Liberation Organization (PLO) outline an accord on the principles of the next phase of their peace agreement, including the redeployment of Israeli soldiers away from Palestinian population centers in the West Bank and a prisoner release.	Labour Party leader Denzil Douglas is sworn in as prime minister of the Caribbean nation of St. Christopher and Nevis.... Colombian officials arrest Jose Santacruz Londoño, reputedly a founder of the Cali drug cartel and its third-highest-ranking leader.	An extremist guerrilla group in India's disputed Jammu and Kashmir state takes Britons Paul Wells and Keith Mangan and Americans John Childs and Donald Hutchings hostage.
July 5	The UN Security Council votes to renew for 75 days the easing of some UN-imposed sanctions against Yugoslavia.	In Armenia's first post-Soviet parliamentary elections, the progovernment Hanrapetutiun (Republic) bloc of parties wins a majority of seats. Voters approve a draft of a constitution.... Turkey sends 3,000 troops backed by warplanes and heavy artillery into northern Iraq to destroy strongholds of Kurdish guerrillas in the region.... Gerry Adams, leader of Sinn Fein, the political wing of the IRA, urges an end to the violence that started July 3. The move causes riots to calm.		Twelve members of a peasant family near the village of Ajuchitlan del Progreso in Guerrero, Mexico, allegedly are forced to lie in a ditch and then are shot to death by unidentified assailants. The sole survivor of the attack, a 14-year-old boy, states that six armed men stopped the truck the family was riding in and that three of the men wore police clothing.	Takeo Fukuda, 90, Japanese premier, 1976–78, who worked to bring Japan into peaceful relations with several Asian countries, dies in Tokyo of chronic emphysema.
July 6		Bosnian Serbs begin to advance on Srebrenica.... In response to the July 5 attack by Turkey, an Iraqi Kurdish group alleges that Turkish troops attacked several villages, wounding three civilians and forcing 3,000 Iraqi Kurds to flee. Turkey maintains that no civilians have been hurt in the operation.		Pres. Rafael Caldera Rodriguez of Venezuela officially restores six constitutional rights suspended in June 1994.... Due to the riots that erupted June 23 in Argentina, the governor of Cordoba, Eduardo Angeloz, resigns after 13 years in office.	
July 7	The member nations of the Caribbean Community and Common Market (Caricom) hold their annual summit meeting in Georgetown, the capital of Guyana, to discuss the creation of a single market in the Caribbean region by 1997.	A popular figure tried in Italy's anticorruption sweep, former foreign minister Gianni De Michelis is convicted of illegal party financing and sentenced to four years in prison.... Government officials in the British colony of Gibraltar seize more than 50 speedboats as part of an antismuggling campaign, spurring riots by hundreds of youths. ...The cabinet of Spanish premier Felipe Gonzalez approves legislation that will liberalize strict abortion laws.... Norway states that the Royal Dutch/Shell Group may temporarily store an idle oil platform in a Norwegian fjord.	The Iraqi government issues a statement demanding that Turkey withdraw its troops immediately, calling the offensive that started July 5 a "flagrant violation of Iraqi sovereignty." Iraq also rejects "the pretexts cited by the Turkish government to justify its military operations inside Iraqi territory."	In civil strife that started June 28 in the state of Guerrero in southwestern Mexico, five officers are killed when a police convoy is ambushed by unidentified gunmen near the town of San Rafael.	
July 8		All of the speedboats seized July 7 in Gibraltar are impounded, prompting rioters to destroy one police car and smash several shop windows. More than 30 people are arrested.... A Dutch UN soldier is killed by the predominantly Muslim Bosnian government army.	Two Lebanese girls, ages 11 and 16, are killed when Israeli forces shell a town in southern Lebanon.	In the Upper Huallaga region in Peru, a guerrilla attack on the town of Nuevo Progreso leaves four policemen and 15 guerrillas dead. ...Argentine president Carlos Saul Menem is sworn in to a second term in office.... Phanor Arizabaleta surrenders to Colombian police in Bogota, becoming the fifth Cali cartel leader taken into custody during the crackdown that began June 19.	Harry Wu, a Chinese-American human-rights activist detained as he tried to enter China from Kazakhstan, is accused by China of being a spy.... American John Childs, captured July 4 by an extremist guerrilla group in India's disputed Jammu and Kashmir state, escapes. However, the militants abduct Hans Christian Ostro, 27, of Norway and Dirk Hasert, 26, of Germany, so they now have five Western hostages.
July 9	French navy commandos in the South Pacific storm the *Rainbow Warrior II*, the flagship vessel of the international environmental group Greenpeace, to avert a protest against France's planned resumption of nuclear testing in region. When the Greenpeace ship passes the 12-mile (20-km) exclusionary zone surrounding the Muroroa Atoll, French commandos fire tear gas and detain many of the ship's 22 crew members.	Turkey reports that its troops have killed 110 members of the separatist Kurdistan Workers' Party (PKK) and has advanced 12 miles (20 km) into Iraq.	Hezbollah guerrillas lob rockets into northern Israel in retaliation for the July 8 deaths of two Lebanese girls. Hezbollah claims both girls died from injuries sustained from Israeli antipersonnel shells, which are prohibited under international warfare conventions. Israeli army officials state they targeted the town by mistake and are examining allegations about antipersonnel weapons.... A PLO spokesman in Jerusalem confirms that 3,500 of the Palestinians detained in Israeli-run prisons have ended a hunger strike after learning the July 4 accord includes a prisoner release.		Rescue workers find a young man alive while searching through the rubble of the department store complex in Seoul, South Korea, that collapsed June 29.

A	B	C	D	E
Includes developments that affect more than one world region, international organizations, and important meetings of major world leaders.	*Includes all domestic and regional developments in Europe, including the Soviet Union, Turkey, Cyprus, and Malta.*	*Includes all domestic and regional developments in Africa and the Middle East, including Iraq and Iran and excluding Cyprus, Turkey, and Afghanistan.*	*Includes all domestic and regional developments in Latin America, the Caribbean, and Canada.*	*Includes all domestic and regional developments in Asia and Pacific nations, extending from Afghanistan through all the Pacific Islands, except Hawaii.*

U.S. Politics & Social Issues	U.S. Foreign Policy & Defense	U.S. Economy & Environment	Science, Technology, & Nature	Culture, Leisure, & Lifestyle	
			In space, a *Soyuz* capsule detaches and backs away by about 200 feet in order to photograph the *Mir-Atlantis* orbital structure. Fifteen minutes later the American shuttle detaches from *Mir*.	Bob Ross, 52, host of the PBS show *Joy of Painting*, dies in Orlando, Florida, of cancer. . . . Eva Gabor, 74, Hungarian-born TV and film actress, dies in Los Angeles of respiratory distress and other infections.	**July 4**
The New Jersey Board of Education rules that the local school board should no longer control the school district of the town of Newark, the state's largest school system. . . . Researchers suggest that many drug-related errors committed at two Boston hospitals during a six-month-long study period may have been avoided with improved communication and information systems, such as a computer bar-code system. . . . Foster Furcolo, 83, governor of Massachusetts, 1957–61, and the first Italian-American to hold that post, dies in Cambridge, Massachusetts, of heart failure.	The U.S. Treasury Department extends a loan of $2.5 billion to Mexico.	The 113-year old typewriter company Smith Corona Corp. files for Chapter 11 bankruptcy.	A study shows that the antianxiety drug alprazolam, known by its brand name Xanax, is "significantly better" at easing the symptoms of premenstrual syndrome (PMS) than is progestin.		**July 5**
The mayor of Washington, D.C., Marion Barry (D), signs into law a curfew designed to fight street crime by and against young people. Nearly 150 cities nationwide currently have youth curfews.		A special panel of federal appeals court judges announce they have selected Daniel Pearson as independent counsel to lead the criminal investigation into the financial dealings of Commerce Secretary Ronald Brown. . . . The Federal Open Market Committee votes to reduce the federal funds rate, the interest rate banks charge on overnight loans made to one another, to 5.75%, from 6%.	A study shows that some people who think they are lactose intolerant actually are not and that those who are intolerant can digest small amounts of milk without suffering digestive problems. . . . The FDA approves the marketing of alprostadil, with a brand name of Caverject, the first prescription drug for diagnosing and treating impotence, a condition that affects between 10 million and 20 million U.S. men.		**July 6**
Pres. Clinton signs into law legislation that will extend Medicare Select, a program intended to encourage senior citizens to use managed-care providers of health insurance in all 50 states and the District of Columbia. . . . The CDC formally recommends that all pregnant women in the U.S. be counseled by doctors about HIV. . . . Joseph Buttafuoco, who served four months in jail for the statutory rape of teenager Amy Fisher, pleads no contest to soliciting sex from an undercover police officer posing as a prostitute and is sentenced to two years' probation.			The U.S. space shuttle *Atlantis* touches down at Kennedy Space Center in Cape Canaveral, Florida, after carrying out a mission during which it docked with the Russian space station *Mir*. Norman E. Thagard, 41, a physician aboard *Mir* since March, returns to Earth after spending 115 days in space, a U.S. record.	Helene Johnson, 89, poet involved in the Harlem Renaissance literary movement in the 1920s and 1930s, dies in New York City after suffering from osteoporosis.	**July 7**
				Steffi Graf of Germany wins the women's tennis title when she takes her sixth singles championship at Wimbledon, England.	**July 8**
Statistics show that the U.S. infant mortality rate in 1994 reached a record low, but the gap between rates for whites and blacks increased.				Pete Sampras wins his third consecutive men's singles tennis title at Wimbledon, England.	**July 9**

F	G	H	I	J
Includes elections, federal-state relations, civil rights and liberties, crime, the judiciary, education, health care, poverty, urban affairs, and population.	Includes formation and debate of U.S. foreign and defense policies, veterans' affairs, and defense spending. (Relations with specific foreign countries are usually found under the region concerned.)	Includes business, labor, agriculture, taxation, transportation, consumer affairs, monetary and fiscal policy, natural resources, and pollution.	Includes worldwide scientific, medical, and technological developments; natural phenomena; U.S. weather; natural disasters; and accidents.	Includes the arts, religion, scholarship, communications media, sports, entertainments, fashions, fads, and social life.

	World Affairs	Europe	Africa & the Middle East	The Americas	Asia & the Pacific
July 10		In Portadown, a town south of Belfast, Northern Ireland, several hundred members of the Orange Order, a group of staunch Protestant loyalists, clash with police during one of the order's yearly parades to celebrate the Battle of the Boyne, fought on July 12, 1690. . . .Turkey announces that it has begun withdrawing its soldiers from northern Iraq.			An Australian ship runs aground on a reef near the Tasmanian shore, spilling over 200,000 gallons (800,000 liters) of heavy fuel oil. It is one of the worst oil spills in Australia's history. . . . Nobel Peace Prize winner and prodemocracy dissident Aung San Suu Kyi is freed by the military leaders of Myanmar, who have kept her under house arrest since 1989.
July 11		Bosnian Serb forces capture the town of Srebrenica in eastern Bosnia-Herzegovina, one of the UN's safe areas whose civilians the UN has vowed to protect. Thousands of refugees from Srebrenica flee to Potocari, surrounding the UN's compound, where they are trapped with 430 Dutch peacekeepers. Bosnian Serbs shell Potocari until NATO and the UN comply with a demand to withdraw NATO planes circling the area. . . . Mihai Botez, 54, Romanian ambassador to the U.S. and former anticommunist dissident, dies in Bucharest of internal hemorrhaging after suffering from cirrhosis of the liver.	Sheik Abdel-Baki Saharaoui, a co-founder of the radical Islamic militant group FIS, is shot to death at a mosque in Paris, France.		Rescue workers find a young woman alive in the rubble of a department store complex in Seoul, South Korea, that collapsed June 29. . . . The 19 crew members aboard the Australian ship that ran aground on July 10 are evacuated.
July 12		Tens of thousands of Muslim refugees from Srebrenica make their way to Tuzla as Bosnian Serbs begin busing refugees toward Bosnian government territory and leave them to walk across front lines to reach government-held towns. Bosnian Serbs detain draft-age men to be investigated for what the Serbs call possible war crimes.	Israeli police arrest 38 ultranationalist Jewish settlers when they block the main Jerusalem-Hebron road in the occupied West Bank. At the same time, hundreds of other settlers reoccupy abandoned houses in the West Bank town of Efrat, which was built a decade earlier for Jewish settlers.	Returns show that the Lavalas Party, endorsed by Pres. Jean-Bertrand Aristide, won the majority in parliamentary elections June 25. Most of Haiti's 28 opposition parties denounce the elections as fraudulent, claiming that the electoral council manipulated the vote count in favor of Lavalas. . . . The Toronto Stock Exchange 300 composite index hits a record high of 4,710.31.	
July 13	The European Union states it will resume its aid to Rwanda as a result of vows by the Rwandan government to promote national unity and the return of refugees.	Szymon Serafinowicz, 84, is charged under the War Crimes Act for killing four Jews in Eastern Europe during World War II. He is the first person in Britain to be accused of Nazi war crimes under the act. . . . U.S. tourist Matthew Peter Tassio, 22 is killed during the running of the bulls at the San Fermin festival in Pamplona, Spain. While every year there are nearly a dozen gorings and trampling injuries, no one had died during the run in the past 15 years. . . . Italian premier Lamberto Dini's government wins a confidence vote in the Chamber of Deputies on a pension-reform package.			In Sri Lanka, reports indicate that hundreds of thousands of Tamils have begun fleeing to the eastern coast of the Jaffna peninsula since the government renewed its military campaign against the Tiger rebels. . . . In Thailand, Chart Thai leader Banharn Silpa-archa is appointed premier by King Bhumibol Adulyadej in a ceremony in Bangkok, the capital.
July 14	Thousands of demonstrators in Australia and New Zealand circle French consulates on France's Bastille Day to demand a cancellation of the proposed nuclear testing in the South Pacific and French Polynesia. Air France is forced to cancel most of its flights between France and Australia because of a 24-hour ban on French flights by transportation workers in Sydney, Australia, and in New Caledonia.	Bosnian Serb forces launch an offensive on the eastern Bosnian town of Zepa, one of the six so-called safe areas of Bosnia-Herzegovina. . . . The German parliament passes a law that illegalizes most abortions but does not provide for punishments for women who seek abortions or doctors who perform them.			
July 15					Rescuers find Park Sung Hyon, 19, alive in rubble after she was trapped without food or drinking water since the June 29 collapse of department store complex in an affluent section of Seoul, South Korea.

A	B	C	D	E
Includes developments that affect more than one world region, international organizations, and important meetings of major world leaders.	Includes all domestic and regional developments in Europe, including the Soviet Union, Turkey, Cyprus, and Malta.	Includes all domestic and regional developments in Africa and the Middle East, including Iraq and Iran and excluding Cyprus, Turkey, and Afghanistan.	Includes all domestic and regional developments in Latin America, the Caribbean, and Canada.	Includes all domestic and regional developments in Asia and Pacific nations, extending from Afghanistan through all the Pacific Islands, except Hawaii.

U.S. Politics & Social Issues	U.S. Foreign Policy & Defense	U.S. Economy & Environment	Science, Technology, & Nature	Culture, Leisure, & Lifestyle	
Alfonso Joseph Zirpoli, 90, federal judge who gained attention when he intervened in the 1974 investigation of the Zebra murders and barred the police from questioning anyone who merely fit the "profile of the Zebra killer," which encompassed most young black men, dies in San Francisco, California, of unreported causes.		The Standard & Poor's Corp. credit rating agency declares Orange County, California, to be in default on municipal bonds worth $600 million. The default is the third-largest in the history of the U.S. municipal bond market.		Pope John Paul II issues a letter addressed to women of all faiths in which he condemns centuries of bias and violence against women and apologizes for the Roman Catholic Church's past discrimination against women.	July 10
	Pres. Clinton formally reestablishes full diplomatic ties with Vietnam, a move that draws mixed support from veterans groups and U.S. legislators. . . . The House votes, 333-89, to approve a foreign-aid appropriations bill of nearly $12 billion for fiscal 1996, which begins Oct. 1. . . . The NSA makes public for the first time 49 coded messages that the former Soviet Union used to communicate with a U.S. spy network of around 200 members, including convicted spies Julius and Ethel Rosenberg, during and after World War II.			In baseball the National League wins its second consecutive All-Star game, 3-2, over the American League.	July 11
	The House Ethics Committee announces that it will not take action against Rep. Robert G. Torricelli (D, N.J.) for revealing to the public in March evidence of CIA involvement in the murders in Guatemala of Michael DeVine and of Guatemalan rebel leader Efrain Bamaca Velasquez.	On the New York Stock Exchange, the Dow Jones industrial average closes at a record high of 4,727.29.	A heat wave strikes the Midwest and Northeast. . . . A study in the *Journal of the American Medical Association* asserts that women who receive treatments to replace the hormone estrogen after menopause are no more likely to develop breast cancer than are other women, a finding which contradicts the findings of a separate Harvard University analysis reported less than one month earlier.		July 12
The Bureau of Alcohol, Tobacco and Firearms (ATF) Director John Magaw announces an ATF probe into allegations that active and retired ATF agents helped organize an annual campout for law-enforcement officers marked by racist incidents. He states that six active and between 10 and 15 retired ATF agents participated in the May event.	Pres. Clinton accepts the recommendations of the Defense Base Closure and Realignment Commission to close 79 military bases across the country and consolidate 26 others. The list is sent to Congress for its approval.		The temperature in Chicago, Illinois, reaches a record 106°F (41°C), and the death toll overwhelms the Chicago morgue. . . . The U.S. space shuttle *Discovery* blasts off from Kennedy Space Center in Cape Canaveral, Florida. . . . Clinical trials in Europe show that a new type of vaccine for pertussis, or whooping cough, is more effective and causes fewer side effects than the version of the vaccine currently in use. . . . The *Galileo* spacecraft launches a probe that is scheduled to enter the planet Jupiter's atmosphere in December.		July 13
Louis Freeh, the director of the FBI, demotes Deputy Director Larry Potts amid growing controversy over Potts's role in a 1992 standoff with Randall Weaver, a white supremacist. During the standoff in Idaho, two people were killed by federal agents.			An international panel of scientists concludes that the presence in the atmosphere of a major ozone-depleting chemical, the man-made chemical methyl chloroform, is beginning to decrease. The substance has declined to 120 parts per trillion molecules of air in 1994, from a high of 150 parts per trillion in 1990. . . . The FDA approves an experimental transplant of baboon bone marrow into a patient with AIDS. Baboons are the only primates that are naturally resistant to HIV-1, the virus strain that causes most AIDS cases worldwide.		July 14
		The NCSL reports that state economies for fiscal 1994–95, which ended July 1 in most states, were "the best they had been since the early 1980s."	Reports confirm that thousands of cattle and tens of thousands of chickens in the Midwest and Plains States have died because of the heat wave that started July 12. Iowa's livestock industry is especially hard-hit, with the deaths of 2,600 cattle and 150,000 chickens.		July 15

F	G	H	I	J
Includes elections, federal-state relations, civil rights and liberties, crime, the judiciary, education, health care, poverty, urban affairs, and population.	*Includes formation and debate of U.S. foreign and defense policies, veterans' affairs, and defense spending. (Relations with specific foreign countries are usually found under the region concerned.)*	*Includes business, labor, agriculture, taxation, transportation, consumer affairs, monetary and fiscal policy, natural resources, and pollution.*	*Includes worldwide scientific, medical, and technological developments; natural phenomena; U.S. weather; natural disasters; and accidents.*	*Includes the arts, religion, scholarship, communications media, sports, entertainments, fashions, fads, and social life.*

	World Affairs	Europe	Africa & the Middle East	The Americas	Asia & the Pacific
July 16		At a ceremony commemorating the 53rd anniversary of the first mass roundup of Jews in Paris, French president Jacques Chirac admits France was responsible for the deportation of thousands of Jews to Nazi concentration camps in Germany and Poland during World War II.... Reports disclose that incarcerated members of the Provisional IRA have begun a series of "dirty protests" in an effort to expedite their transfers to a prison in Northern Ireland, or Ulster.	After meeting with U.S. Rep. Bill Richardson (D, N.Mex.), Iraqi president Saddam Hussein rescinds the eight-year prison sentences that an Iraqi court meted out to William Barloon, 39, and David Daliberti, 41, two Americans arrested in March for illegally crossing into Iraq from Kuwait.... Mordechai (Motta) Gur, 65, who has served in Israel's Knesset since 1978 and was named deputy defense minister in 1992, dies in Tel Aviv, Israel, of a self-inflicted gunshot wound; he was suffering from cancer.		
July 17		More than 4,000 people from Srebrenica, many of them Bosnian government soldiers, arrive in Tuzla after walking 30 miles (50 km) through Serb lines.... The governments of Sweden and Denmark award a 3.8 billion Danish krona ($680 million) contract to a European consortium to build the Oresund Tunnel. The 2.3-mile-long tunnel will connect Malmo, Sweden, and Copenhagen, Denmark.			
July 18		France expels a planeload of 43 illegal African immigrants to Kinshasa, Zaire, drawing fire from human-rights activists.... Russian president Boris Yeltsin appears on Russian television and admits that he suffered a heart attack a week ago.	Two 19-year-old Israeli hikers, one of whom is a soldier, are shot to death in Wadi Kelt, a dry riverbed 10 miles (16 km) east of Jerusalem in the Israeli-occupied West Bank.	Ontario immigration adjudicator Ed MacNamara rules that accused war criminal Joseph Nemsila cannot be deported from Canada, regardless of whether he lied to immigration officers upon entering the country in 1950.	Ryoichi Sasakawa, 96, Japanese right-wing nationalist and entrepreneur who formed the Patriotic Masses Party in 1931, dies in Tokyo of a heart attack.
July 19	Iraq reverses an earlier position when it agrees to a UN demand that it destroy five pieces of equipment used to make engines for ballistic missiles.		South African president Nelson Mandela signs into law legislation creating a Truth and Reconciliation Commission to investigate human-rights abuses committed during the decades when South Africa was ruled under the apartheid system of racial segregation.		An ethnic battle between paramilitary forces and factions of the Mohajir Qaumi Movement claims at least 30 lives in Karachi, Pakistan's violence-torn commercial hub. The incident raises the number of deaths caused by ethnic fighting in Karachi in July to more than 200.... Philippine president Fidel Ramos announces that his administration will restore diplomatic ties with Singapore, ending several months of hostilities between the countries that stemmed from Singapore's hanging of a Filipina maid, Flor Contemplacion, on murder charges.
July 20		As the battle for Zepa continues, Serbs launch a separate military thrust in the Bihac region of northwestern Bosnia near the Croatian border. The Bihac region is controlled by Bosnian government forces but surrounded on all sides by Serb-controlled land in Bosnia and Croatia. Statistics show that, of the 45,000 people who lived in Srebrenica, at least 11,000 are unaccounted for.		In the Upper Huallaga valley in northern Peru, 16 Peruvian soldiers are killed in an ambush by Maoist Sendero Luminoso (Shining Path) guerrillas. Twenty guerrillas are also killed.... The Supreme Court of Canada upholds a C$1.6 million (US$1.2 million) libel award, the largest in Canada's history, against the Church of Scientology and Toronto lawyer Morris Manning.	The death toll from the June 29 collapse of a five-story wing of a department store complex in Seoul, South Korea, stands at 458, with more than 900 injured and 154 still thought to be trapped in the debris.... The Equal Opportunity Tribunal of New South Wales, a state in Australia, orders an insurance company to allow a same-sex couple and their son to receive family coverage.
July 21	The foreign ministers of the Organization of the Islamic Conference (OIC) eight-member contact group on Bosnia meet with Bosnian foreign minister Muhamed Sacirbey and state that the group considers the international arms embargo against the Bosnian government to be "invalid." Members of the OIC contact group are Egypt, Iran, Malaysia, Morocco, Pakistan, Saudi Arabia, Senegal, and Turkey.	Bosnian Serbs release more than 300 Dutch troops held since the Bosnian Serb assault on Srebrenica.... Viktor P. Barannikov, 54, former Russian security minister who in 1993 participated in an armed rebellion against Russian president Boris Yeltsin, dies near Moscow of a heart attack.... Italian anticorruption magistrates formally declare that former premier Bettino Craxi, who is living in self-imposed exile in Tunisia after being sentenced in absentia twice in 1994, is a "fugitive."		Eight officers and two enlisted men are indicted by a Honduran civilian court for a 1982 week-long kidnapping and torture of six student activists in 1982. All 10 of those indicted had been members of an elite army unit called Battalion 316, which was allegedly trained by the U.S. Central Intelligence Agency (CIA). Battalion 316 and other Honduran army units are believed by human-rights observers to have been responsible for the disappearances of at least 184 leftists during the 1980s.	China tests surface-to-surface ballistic missiles, firing them at targets in the sea about 80 miles north of Taiwan.... Sri Lankan police arrest U.S. relief worker Kenneth Mulder for alleged involvement with the Tiger rebels.

A	B	C	D	E
Includes developments that affect more than one world region, international organizations, and important meetings of major world leaders.	Includes all domestic and regional developments in Europe, including the Soviet Union, Turkey, Cyprus, and Malta.	Includes all domestic and regional developments in Africa and the Middle East, including Iraq and Iran and excluding Cyprus, Turkey, and Afghanistan.	Includes all domestic and regional developments in Latin America, the Caribbean, and Canada.	Includes all domestic and regional developments in Asia and Pacific nations, extending from Afghanistan through all the Pacific Islands, except Hawaii.

U.S. Politics & Social Issues	U.S. Foreign Policy & Defense	U.S. Economy & Environment	Science, Technology, & Nature	Culture, Leisure, & Lifestyle	
				Sir Stephen Harold Spender, 86, British writer and poet, dies in London of a heart ailment.... May (Eleanore Marie) Sarton, 83, poet and novelist, dies in York, Maine, of breast cancer.... Auto racer Johnny Herbert of Britain wins the British Grand Prix Formula One race. ... The Times Mirror Co. closes down the 10-year-old tabloid newspaper *New York Newsday*.	July 16
	The U.S. uses a NAFTA provision to challenge heavy tariffs imposed by Canada earlier in 1995 on imports of poultry, eggs, dairy, and other farm products.	The Dow closes at a record high of 4736.29, up 27.47 points, or 0.58%, from the previous trading day's close. This marks the sixth record high for the Dow during a period of nine trading days.... According to *Forbes* magazine, William Gates of Microsoft Corp. is the richest individual in the world with a fortune estimated at $12.9 billion.	Reports confirm that Merck & Co. Inc. has stated it will offer its experimental AIDS drug indinavir sulfate, known by the brand name Crixivan, free to 1,400 people in the late stages of the disease.	Juan Manuel Fangio, 84, Argentine grand prix race-car driver who dominated the circuit during the 1950s, dies in Buenos Aires, Argentina, after suffering from kidney failure and pneumonia.	July 17
		A special Senate committee holds the first of a new round of hearings examining the Whitewater affair, the complex tangle of financial and real-estate dealings involving Pres. Clinton and First Lady Hillary Rodham Clinton.		Seattle Seahawks football receiver Brian Blades, 29, is charged with the manslaughter of his cousin, Charles Blades.... Fabio Casartelli, 24, Italian cyclist who won a gold medal at the 1992 Olympics, dies from head wounds sustained on a crash during the Tour de France.	July 18
After an administration review concluded that most affirmative-action programs are justifiable, Pres. Clinton signs an executive order that directs all federal agencies to ensure that their programs meet stringent judicial standards. The order also opposes programs that create quota systems or reverse discrimination. At the same time, 200 students, led by Rev. Jesse Jackson, protest a meeting of the Board of Regents for the University of California, which is considering an end to affirmative action admissions system.... Congressional hearings into a 1993 siege on a cult compound outside of Waco, Texas, open.		The Dow volume of shares traded, 482.9 in millions of shares, is the heaviest since October 20, 1987, and the third highest in the history of the New York Stock Exchange.	A study finds that women who receive hormone replacement therapy after menopause appear to have a reduced risk of getting colon cancer.		July 19
The Census Bureau reports that black Americans, people under the age of 18, and members of "female-householder families" had a much higher rate of chronic poverty than the American population as a whole between Jan. 1991 and Dec. 1992.... The Board of Regents for the University of California system votes to end by January 1997 the consideration of race, sex, religion, color, ethnicity, or national origin in its admissions.					July 20
The Senate Judiciary Committee holds a hearing on reports that active and retired ATF agents attended or helped organize a May campout marked by racist incidents.... The Common Fund, which manages investments for universities, announces that its recent losses, due to a rogue trader, are at $138 million, larger than originally estimated..... Jon C(lifton) Hinson, 53, former Mississippi congressman who became active in the gay-rights movement during the 1980s, dies in Silver Spring, Maryland, of respiratory failure resulting from AIDS.		The Senate passes, 90-7, a bill that cuts a total of $16.3 billion from spending previously appropriated by Congress for the fiscal year 1995, which ends Sept. 30.	Pres. Clinton announces that $100 million in federal emergency aid will be distributed to 19 states affected by the heat wave that started July 12.	Minnesota Vikings football quarterback Warren Moon is charged with a misdemeanor for assaulting his wife.... NFL team owners approve the Los Angeles Raiders' proposed move to Oakland, California. The relocation will leave the Los Angeles area without a football franchise for the first time in 50 years, as the Rams plan to move to St. Louis, Missouri.	July 21

F	G	H	I	J
Includes elections, federal-state relations, civil rights and liberties, crime, the judiciary, education, health care, poverty, urban affairs, and population.	*Includes formation and debate of U.S. foreign and defense policies, veterans' affairs, and defense spending. (Relations with specific foreign countries are usually found under the region concerned.)*	*Includes business, labor, agriculture, taxation, transportation, consumer affairs, monetary and fiscal policy, natural resources, and pollution.*	*Includes worldwide scientific, medical, and technological developments; natural phenomena; U.S. weather; natural disasters; and accidents.*	*Includes the arts, religion, scholarship, communications media, sports, entertainments, fashions, fads, and social life.*

	World Affairs	Europe	Africa & the Middle East	The Americas	Asia & the Pacific
July 22				Some 1,500 people, most of them army personnel and their families, stage a rally outside a military prison near Santiago, the capital of Chile, in a show of support for former brigadier general Pedro Espinoza Bravo, who was imprisoned for his role in the 1976 assassination in Washington, D.C., of Chilean exile Orlando Letelier.	
July 23		Hundreds of masked youths, mostly of North African origin, riot in the depressed Paris suburb of Montataire, France. One person is killed and several injured in the violence. Some 200 riot police are called in, and five policemen are injured in the ensuing clashes, in which the rioters hurl rocks and gasoline bombs. . . . Turkey's parliament approves a package of constitutional amendments intended to broaden the country's voting and labor laws.			The ruling coalition of Japanese premier Tomiichi Murayama is weakened in general elections for seats in the upper house of the Diet. The New Frontier Party (NFP) is considered the big winner in the contest.
July 24	The Paris Club of donor nations links all further aid to Kenya to progress on political, economic, and human-rights matters.	In France, the riots that started July 23 in the Paris suburb of Montataire begin to calm after one policeman is injured and the rioters burn several cars and loot stores. . . . Tadeusz Mazowiecki, the UN representative for human rights in the former Yugoslavia, states that Bosnian Serb actions in Srebrenica involved "very serious violations of human rights on an enormous scale that can only be described as barbarous."	A suspected Palestinian Islamist detonates a bomb on a public bus in Tel Aviv, Israel's largest city. The blast kills six Jews as well as the bomber and injures more than 30 other people, at least two of them critically. The deaths raise the tally of Jews killed by Palestinian militants since September 1993 to 130.	Justice Thomas Riordan of the New Brunswick Court of Queen's Bench sentences Steven and Lorelei Turner to 16 years in prison for manslaughter in the starvation death of their three-year-old son, John Ryan Turner, who prosecutors said was bound and gagged in his bed during the last six months of his life before dying of starvation. The sentence reportedly is the longest in a child-abuse case in Canadian history.	Taiwan's governor, James Soong, demands an end to the Chinese missile tests that started July 21, comparing them to China's "bloody crackdown on the democratic movement in Tiananmen Square" in 1989. The tests are seen as an attempt to intimidate Taiwan and its leader, Pres. Lee Teng-hui, and discourage the country from trying to seek a more prominent international profile.
July 25	The Yugoslav War Crimes Tribunal in The Hague indicts Bosnian Serb leader Radovan Karadzic and General Ratko Mladic, the Bosnian Serb military commander, on charges of genocide and crimes against humanity. The tribunal states that international warrants for the arrest of Karadzic and Mladic have been issued.	The eastern Bosnian town of Zepa, one of the six safe areas of Bosnia-Herzegovina, is captured by Bosnian Serb forces. The UN evacuates 150 wounded civilians from Zepa to Sarajevo. The Bihac enclave comes under a three-pronged assault from Bosnian Serbs, Croatian Serbs, and rebel Muslims led by Fikret Abdic, whose stronghold is in the Bihac region. . . . A bomb explodes on a crowded commuter train in Paris, France, killing four people and injuring at least 80 people, 14 of whom are listed in critical condition.		Peru and Ecuador agree to demilitarize more than 200 square miles (518 sq km) in the Cordillera del Condor mountains, the site of a border skirmish between the two countries in February.	
July 26		Three people die from severe burns suffered in the July 25 blast in Paris, France, bringing the death toll from the explosion to seven. Mass-transit systems are shut down as a result of several bomb scares, and 8,000 people are evacuated from the Louvre museum when a threat is made.			
July 27	Foreign ministers of the Association of Southeast Asian Nations (ASEAN) hold a summit in Brunei to discuss trade and security issues in the region.	Tadeusz Mazowiecki, the UN's chief human-rights representative in the former Yugoslavia, resigns because of what he calls the international community's "hypocrisy" and inaction after the "horrendous tragedy which has beset the population" of Srebrenica and Zepa.		Pres. Alberto Fujimori of Peru names former education minister Dante Cordova as the new premier. . . . Anselme Remy, the head of Haiti's Provisional Electoral Council, resigns amid harsh criticism of his handling of Haitian elections in June.	The Parliament of the Australian state of South Australia rejects a bill that would have legalized voluntary euthanasia, or mercy killing, for terminally ill patients.

A	B	C	D	E
Includes developments that affect more than one world region, international organizations, and important meetings of major world leaders.	Includes all domestic and regional developments in Europe, including the Soviet Union, Turkey, Cyprus, and Malta.	Includes all domestic and regional developments in Africa and the Middle East, including Iraq and Iran and excluding Cyprus, Turkey, and Afghanistan.	Includes all domestic and regional developments in Latin America, the Caribbean, and Canada.	Includes all domestic and regional developments in Asia and Pacific nations, extending from Afghanistan through all the Pacific Islands, except Hawaii.

U.S. Politics & Social Issues	U.S. Foreign Policy & Defense	U.S. Economy & Environment	Science, Technology, & Nature	Culture, Leisure, & Lifestyle	
A circuit court jury in Union, South Carolina, convicts Susan Smith, 33, a woman who had confessed to drowning her two young sons, on two counts of first-degree murder. Smith gained nationwide attention when she told police that a black carjacker had kidnapped her boys, Michael, 3, and Alexander, 14 months, before confessing to letting her car roll down a boat ramp into John D. Long Lake with her sons locked inside.			After carrying out a mission during which the crew deployed a communications satellite, the U.S. space shuttle *Discovery* touches down at the airstrip at Kennedy Space Center in Cape Canaveral, Florida.		July 22
			Alan Hale and Thomas Bopp, two amateur astronomers working separately, discover a comet thought to be farther from the sun than any yet found by amateurs. The find raises speculation that the comet, called the Hale-Bopp comet C/1995 O1, will be brightly visible from Earth in spring 1997. The last comet visible to the unaided eye was Comet West in 1976.	Uruguay wins the finals of the South American soccer championship, the Copa America, 5-3, over Brazil. . . . Miguel Indurain of Spain wins the Tour de France cycling race in a record fifth consecutive victory. . . . John Daly captures the 124th British Open golf title.	July 23
					July 24
The Senate passes, 98-0, a bill that will require more lobbyists to register with the government and will force registered lobbyists to publicly report whom they represent, whom in the government they contact, and how much they earn. . . . Reports confirm that the Justice Department is investigating Philip Morris Cos. Inc. to determine if the company hid from the public and federal regulators research on the pharmacological effects of nicotine, and it is expanding a preliminary investigation to determine whether tobacco executives committed perjury in testimony before a House subcommittee in April 1994.	A report by Frederick P. Hitz, the inspector general of the CIA, is made public. The report finds that CIA field commanders, or station chiefs, in Guatemala did not violate any U.S. laws in relation to the deaths of Michael DeVine and of Guatemalan rebel leader Efrain Bamaca Velasquez. However, the report criticizes CIA officials for errors in judgment and failure to follow procedure. . . . Mousa Mohammed Abu Marzook, an alleged Palestinian terrorist with ties to Hamas, is arrested in New York City.			Charlie Rich, 62, baritone country singer known as the "Silver Fox," who had several hits in the 1970s, dies in Hammond, Louisiana, of a blood clot in his lung.	July 25
The Fifth Circuit Court of Appeals agrees to consider whether the largest class-action suit in U.S. history can continue against tobacco companies. . . . George W(ilcken) Romney, 88, former chairman of AMC and Republican governor of Michigan, dies in Bloomfield Hills, Mich. of a heart attack. . . . Baruch Korff, 81, rabbi known for his staunch support of Pres. Richard Nixon during the Watergate scandal, dies in Providence, R.I., of pancreatic cancer.	The Senate passes, 69-29, a bill to end U.S. participation in the arms embargo against the Bosnian government.			Data show that a posthumously released album by Selena is the first album by a Latin artist to top the popular music charts. . . . . George Rodger, 87, known for his photographs of the 1944 liberation of Paris and of the Bergen-Belsen concentration camp, dies in England.	July 26
The Senate votes, 97-3, to reauthorize for five years a federal program that funds the care and treatment of people with AIDS.		Leaders of the U.S.'s three largest industrial labor unions—the UAW, the USW and the IAM—announce that they will merge their unions by 2000 and create a labor organization with an estimated 2 million members in North America. . . . Pres. Clinton signs a bill that cuts a total of $16.3 billion from spending previously appropriated by Congress for the fiscal year 1995. In June, Clinton had vetoed an earlier version of the bill; the new version restores some funding for programs favored by his administration.	Two astronomers report they have discovered at least two new moons, and possibly four, orbiting the planet Saturn. . . . Researchers announce that the FDA has approved a series of experimental procedures in which genetically altered pig livers will be attached to the circulatory systems of humans. Genetically altered animal organs have never been used in humans. . . . Data show that more than 800 people nationwide have died from the heat wave that started July 12. It is the highest such toll since a 1980. In Chicago, the death toll is 529.	Miklos Rozsa, 88, composer of film scores who won three Academy Awards, dies in Los Angeles after suffering a stroke. . . . Rick Ferrell, 89, record-setting baseball catcher who was elected to the Hall of Fame in 1984, dies in Bloomfield Hills, Michigan, of arrhythmia.	July 27

F	G	H	I	J
Includes elections, federal-state relations, civil rights and liberties, crime, the judiciary, education, health care, poverty, urban affairs, and population.	*Includes formation and debate of U.S. foreign and defense policies, veterans' affairs, and defense spending. (Relations with specific foreign countries are usually found under the region concerned.)*	*Includes business, labor, agriculture, taxation, transportation, consumer affairs, monetary and fiscal policy, natural resources, and pollution.*	*Includes worldwide scientific, medical, and technological developments; natural phenomena; U.S. weather; natural disasters; and accidents.*	*Includes the arts, religion, scholarship, communications media, sports, entertainments, fashions, fads, and social life.*

	World Affairs	Europe	Africa & the Middle East	The Americas	Asia & the Pacific
July 28	An interim global financial-services pact is concluded under the auspices of the World Trade Organization (WTO). It seeks to widen the access that the more than 90 WTO full-member nations allow foreign companies to have into their securities, banking, and insurance markets. . . . ASEAN ministers admit Vietnam as the group's seventh member. Vietnam is the only communist nation in the trade group.	Some 10,000 Croatian and Bosnian Croat troops capture the Serb-held towns of Bosansko Grahovo and Glamoc, cutting off Serb supply lines to Krajina. . . . Nora Owen, the justice minister for Ireland, announces that 12 people affiliated with the IRA will be released from a prison south of Dublin. . . . German commando police in Cologne kill Leon Bor after he kills the driver of a tourist bus and one woman before taking 19 hostages.		Pres. Alberto Fujimori of Peru is inaugurated for his second five-year term in office.	Military troops kill an estimated 200 Tiger guerrillas on the Jaffna peninsula. The offensive is the deadliest battle since a June 28 raid by Tiger rebels on Mandaithivu Island, located west of their Jaffna stronghold.
July 29		UN spokesman Alexander Ivanko discloses that Bosnian Serbs have torched the town of Zepa and executed the Bosnian government army's regional commander, Avdo Palic, who in 1992 led an assault on Bosnian Serb forces described as one of their most crushing defeats.		A major natural-gas pipeline in the Canadian Prairies ruptures, causing a large explosion and disrupting gas deliveries to central Canada and the midwestern and northeastern U.S. No injuries are reported in the blast.	
July 30		Russian and Chechen negotiators reach an accord they claim will end the war. Estimates suggest that, in the fighting in Chechnya since December 1994, 1,800 Russian soldiers have been killed, 250 are missing, and 6,500 were wounded. About 20,000 civilians, Chechens, and ethnic Russians, have died. . . . Croatian Serb leaders agree to withdraw from the Bihac enclave under a UN-brokered deal aimed at averting a wider war between Serbs and Croats.	Hezbollah fighters ambush an Israeli mechanized convoy in southern Lebanon, killing one Israeli soldier. The attack prompts Israeli troops and the South Lebanon Army to shell and fire on Hezbollah Shi'ite guerrilla positions in southern Lebanon. . . . Eyad Ismoil, who is believed to be the driver of the van containing explosives detonated in the 1993 bombing of the World Trade Center in NYC, is arrested by Jordanian authorities.		
July 31		At least six Russian soldiers are killed after Chechen fighters ignore the July 30 truce. Retaliatory strikes by Russian soldiers leave several Chechens dead. . . . Spain's Supreme Court announces it will assign a special prosecutor to determine whether Premier Felipe Gonzalez will be indicted for his alleged role in forming antiterrorist death squads in the 1980s. . . . A special joint assembly of the French parliament approves constitutional reforms that are considered the most sweeping in France in about 30 years.	Israeli troops and border police dismantle tents and temporary structures erected by settlers on a hilltop encampment at al-Khader on the West Bank, just west of the city of Bethlehem.		New Zealand's most wanted criminal, Joseph Stephenson Thompson, pleads guilty to 129 sex-related crimes committed during an 11-year period. . . . Ferdinand Marcos Jr., son of the late Philippine president Ferdinand Marcos, is convicted of tax evasion and sentenced to nine years in prison.
Aug. 1	NATO threatens Serbs in Bosnia-Herzegovina and Croatia with a broad air campaign if they attack any of the four remaining UN-designated safe areas in Bosnia: Gorazde, Bihac, Tuzla, and Sarajevo. . . . France recalls its ambassador to Australia amid growing international protests against Pres. Jacques Chirac's decision to resume nuclear testing in the South Pacific.				
Aug. 2		Chechen leader Dzhokhar Dudayev approves the July 30 agreement and orders his soldiers to stop fighting. Russia and Chechnya carry out their first exchange of prisoners.		Colombian defense minister Fernando Botero resigns due to a pending investigation into charges that he accepted money from the Cali drug cartel when he was campaign manager for Pres. Ernesto Samper Pizano's election in 1994. . . . Statistics Canada reports that Canada's violent crime rate dropped by 3% in 1994. The decline in violent crime is the first substantial drop in 15 years and the largest since Statistics Canada began tracking the crime rate in 1962.	Reports confirm that China has arrested two U.S. Air Force officers, Colonel Joseph Wei Chan and Captain Dwayne Howard Florenzie, for spying and will expel the pair within 24 hours.

A	B	C	D	E
Includes developments that affect more than one world region, international organizations, and important meetings of major world leaders.	*Includes all domestic and regional developments in Europe, including the Soviet Union, Turkey, Cyprus, and Malta.*	*Includes all domestic and regional developments in Africa and the Middle East, including Iraq and Iran and excluding Cyprus, Turkey, and Afghanistan.*	*Includes all domestic and regional developments in Latin America, the Caribbean, and Canada.*	*Includes all domestic and regional developments in Asia and Pacific nations, extending from Afghanistan through all the Pacific Islands, except Hawaii.*

U.S. Politics & Social Issues	U.S. Foreign Policy & Defense	U.S. Economy & Environment	Science, Technology, & Nature	Culture, Leisure, & Lifestyle	
In a case that received national attention, a circuit court jury in Union, South Carolina, opts to sentence Susan Smith to life in prison rather than sentence her to death. . . . The Senate votes, 98-0, in favor of new rules that will bar senators and their staff from substantial gifts from anyone other than close friends and relatives. The rules apply only to the Senate and do not require approval by the House or the president.			Scientists suggest that fossils of foot bones found in South Africa belong to a human ancestor some 3–3.5 million years old and are adapted to both upright walking and tree climbing. . . . Reports confirm that researchers in three separate laboratories have found daily injections of a natural hormone into obese mice suppresses the animals' appetites and increases their metabolisms, causing them to burn fat.		July 28
				The Pro Football Hall of Fame inducts Steve Largent, Lee Roy Selmon, Kellen Winslow, the late Henry Jordan, and Jim Finks. Following the induction, the Carolina Panthers beat the Jacksonville Jaguars, both expansion teams, 20-14, in their first exhibition game. . . . Monica Seles plays her first public tennis match, an exhibition event, since she left the tour in 1993.	July 29
				The Baseball Hall of Fame inducts Mike Schmidt, Richie Ashburn, the late Leon Day, Vic Willis, and National League founder William Hulbert.	July 30
In Atlanta, Georgia, district judge Frank Mays Hull upholds a state law that requires a minute of silent meditation at the beginning of each school day. . . . The Census Bureau reports that the number of births in the U.S. fell during 1994, and a record number of U.S. residents died that year. There were 3.949 million births in 1994, the first time since 1988 that the number of births fell below 4 million. . . . Dr. Thomas Ellsworth Morgan, 88, (D, Pa.), who served in Congress for 32 years, dies in Waynesburg, Pennsylvania, of congestive heart failure.	Jennifer Harbury, an American lawyer whose husband, Guatemalan rebel leader Efrain Bamaca Velasquez, disappeared in Guatemala in 1992, files a lawsuit against the CIA for failing to provide her with information about her husband.	The House approves a $79.4 billion fiscal 1996 appropriations bill for the VA, HUD, and independent agencies. The bill, known as the VA-HUD appropriations bill, includes severe spending cuts for EPA programs. . . . The White House revises its estimate of growth for the 1995 calendar year downward to 1.9%, from the 2.4% forecast issued in February.		Memnoch the Devil by Anne Rice is at the top of the bestseller list. . . . Reports reveal that the Walt Disney Co. has agreed to purchase Capital Cities/ABC Inc., a takeover that will create the world's largest media and entertainment company. The merger is the second largest ever.	July 31
The U.S. George Washington Elementary School in Sherman, Texas, is the first school to open while participating in the Edison Project, a new program guided by the philosophy that public schools will be more effective if they are privately run. . . . Congressional hearings into the 1993 siege on a cult compound outside of Waco, Texas, close after producing little new information.	U.S. secretary of state Warren Christopher and Chinese foreign minister Qian Qichen agree to continue high-level talks on Sino-U.S. relations, which have been deteriorating since the Clinton administration approved the June visit of Taiwanese president Lee Teng-hui to the U.S. . . . The House approves, 298-128, a bill that will require Pres. Clinton to end U.S. participation in the international arms embargo against Bosnia.	Thomas Donahue is elected interim president of the AFL-CIO labor federation. He will complete the current term of Lane Kirkland. . . . The purchasing managers' index increases to 50.5% in July, up from the revised June rate of 45.7%. Generally, a measure above 50% indicates an expanding manufacturing sector, and a reading of 44.5% or higher indicates overall economic expansion.	A study reveals that people who work in high-stress jobs are not more likely to suffer heart disease than those with low-stress jobs.	Former New York Yankees outfielder Mickey Mantle, 63, discloses that he has terminal lung cancer.	Aug. 1
The Senate votes, 52-48, against a proposal to force public hearings into charges of sexual harassment and official misconduct against Sen. Bob Packwood (R, Oreg.). Since May, the charges against Packwood have been the subject of particularly sharp public debate, during which several Democratic and women senators accused the Senate's Republican majority of exercising a sexist double standard. . . . Both The Washington Post and The New York Times print excerpts from a manuscript by the Unabomber, who has been linked to a series of bombing incidents spanning 17 years.	Officials from the California Department of Industrial Relations raid a garment factory in El Monte, a working-class suburb of Los Angeles, California, and free nearly 70 immigrant workers from Thailand who have been held there against their will. All are in the U.S. illegally and reportedly were forced to work under squalid conditions. . . . Eyad Ismoil, who is believed to be the driver of the van containing explosives detonated in the 1993 bombing of the World Trade Center in New York City, and who was arrested in Jordan July 30, is turned over to the FBI and flown to New York.	The EPA announces that chemical manufacturer E. I. DuPont de Nemours & Co. has agreed to phase out production of cyanazine, a herbicide that the EPA suspects of posing a cancer threat to consumers and to workers who handle the chemical.			Aug. 2

F	G	H	I	J
Includes elections, federal-state relations, civil rights and liberties, crime, the judiciary, education, health care, poverty, urban affairs, and population.	Includes formation and debate of U.S. foreign and defense policies, veterans' affairs, and defense spending. (Relations with specific foreign countries are usually found under the region concerned.)	Includes business, labor, agriculture, taxation, transportation, consumer affairs, monetary and fiscal policy, natural resources, and pollution.	Includes worldwide scientific, medical, and technological developments; natural phenomena; U.S. weather; natural disasters; and accidents.	Includes the arts, religion, scholarship, communications media, sports, entertainments, fashions, fads, and social life.

	World Affairs	Europe	Africa & the Middle East	The Americas	Asia & the Pacific
Aug. 3					India's Maharashtra state government decides to abandon the development of a $2.8 billion electrical power plant already under construction by a U.S. business consortium led by Enron Corp. . . . As expected, China expels Col. Joseph Wei Chan and Capt. Dwayne Howard Florenzie, the two U.S. Air Force officers arrested Aug. 2. The officers are thought to be the first U.S. officials expelled from China since 1979.
Aug. 4	Governments from more than 100 countries approve a UN-sponsored global fishing accord aimed at slowing the depletion of the world's fish stocks and averting international conflicts over fishing rights on the high seas. The agreement is the first international treaty to regulate fishing practices in international waters.	Tens of thousands of Croatian troops, backed by tanks, artillery, and jet aircraft, enter the self-declared Serbian Republic of Krajina in Croatia, a region held by rebel Serbs since 1992, from at least five major fronts in an offensive that spans more than 700 miles (1,100 km). Bosnian Serb leader Karadzic dismisses Gen. Ratko Mladic as commander of Bosnian Serb forces. . . . Hundreds of punk youths in Hanover, Germany, stage their annual "Chaos Days."		On the first day of a general strike called by 49 union organizations in Panama City, a demonstration turns violent when riot police attempt to break down barricades set up by protesters that block off the city's major streets. At least four people are reported killed, dozens injured, and 500 arrested. . . . Retired general Efrain Rios Montt, who led a coup in Guatemala in 1982 and installed himself as president for 18 months, is ruled by Guatemala's Supreme Electoral Tribunal to be ineligible to run in the next presidential election.	
Aug. 5		Croatian troops capture the capital of Krajina, Knin, reportedly without much resistance from Croatian Serb forces. General Ratko Mladic, who was dismissed Aug. 4 by Bosnian Serb leader Karadzic, refuses to step down.			Warren Christopher becomes the first U.S. secretary of state ever to visit Hanoi and the first secretary to visit Vietnam since 1975 when he arrives to formally restore diplomatic relations. . . . Agha Hasan Abedi, 73, Pakistani businessman who in 1972 founded the Bank of Commerce and Credit International (BCCI), which collapsed in 1991, dies in Karachi, Pakistan, of renal failure with blood clotting.
Aug. 6	The World Bank reports that a "worldwide water crisis" is imminent, due to rapid population growth and increasing water pollution from industry, household waste, and agricultural chemicals. The organization estimates that $600 billion will be needed for water projects over the next decade.	The Bosnian government army joins with Croatian government troops to attack Serb forces in the republic of Krajina. Eighteen Bosnian Serb generals announce their support for Gen. Ratko Mladic, who refused to step down Aug. 5. . . . In Hanover, Germany, the "Chaos Days," which began Aug. 4, attracting hundreds of punk youths, end. During that period, riots led to more than 600 arrests, and 94 police officers were injured. . . . Lord Harold Lever, 81, former cabinet minister and economic adviser to two British prime ministers, dies in London of unreported causes.	A bomb on a truck explodes at a power plant outside the town of Boufarik in Algeria, killing 11 people and wounding 25.	Miguel Rodriguez Orejuela, the alleged coleader of the Cali drug cartel, is captured by police in the city of Cali, southwestern Colombia. In a separate incident, the southeastern Colombian town of Miraflores is besieged by rebel leftist FARC guerrillas.	Some 100,000 people gather in Peace Memorial Park in Hiroshima, Japan, to mark the 50th anniversary of the U.S. atomic bombing of the city during World War II. A flock of 1,500 doves is released in Hiroshima to mark the 1945 explosion.
Aug. 7		Croatian defense minister Gojko Susak acknowledges that Croatian soldiers have killed at least three UN peacekeepers in the offensive that started Aug. 4. Separately, the Bosnian government army regains the last remnants of Serb-held territory in the region of Bihac. . . . Brigid Brophy, 66, British writer famous for her experimental and controversial fiction, dies in Lincolnshire, England, after suffering from multiple sclerosis.			A bomb blast near Sri Lanka's landmark Independence Memorial Hall in Colombo, the capital, kills at least 22 people and wounds more than 50 others. Police state that the bomber, who died in the blast, was a member of the Liberation Tigers of Tamil Eelam.
Aug. 8	The UN High Commissioner for Refugees (UNHCR) estimates that the Croatian takeover of Krajina, combined with the Bosnian Serb capture of Srebrenica and Zepa in previous weeks, has forced 185,000 civilians from their homes. That figure is in addition to some 735,000 refugees who have already fled Croatia and Bosnia since 1991.		Two of Iraqi president Saddam Hussein's top military aides who are also his sons-in-law, Lt. Col. Saddam Kamel Hassan al-Majid and Lt. Gen. Hussein Kamel Hassan al-Majid, defect from Iraq with their wives. They are joined by more than a score of senior army officers. . . . A bomb attack on a train south of Algiers kills seven people and wounds 11. . . . Orthodox Jews opposed to expanding Palestinian autonomy stage demonstrations on major motor-vehicle arteries in Israel, snarling traffic in Jerusalem, Tel Aviv, and 18 other locations.		

A	B	C	D	E
Includes developments that affect more than one world region, international organizations, and important meetings of major world leaders.	Includes all domestic and regional developments in Europe, including the Soviet Union, Turkey, Cyprus, and Malta.	Includes all domestic and regional developments in Africa and the Middle East, including Iraq and Iran and excluding Cyprus, Turkey, and Afghanistan.	Includes all domestic and regional developments in Latin America, the Caribbean, and Canada.	Includes all domestic and regional developments in Asia and Pacific nations, extending from Afghanistan through all the Pacific Islands, except Hawaii.

U.S. Politics & Social Issues	U.S. Foreign Policy & Defense	U.S. Economy & Environment	Science, Technology, & Nature	Culture, Leisure, & Lifestyle	
In Portland, Oregon, U.S. district judge Michael Hogan rules unconstitutional an Oregon law that would have allowed doctors to prescribe lethal overdoses of medication to dying patients. The law was approved by Oregon voters in November 1994, but implementation was delayed pending court review.		Pres. Clinton announces his approval of a $53 million disaster-relief package for the U.S. fishing industry, which is suffering due to severe declines in fish stocks or seabed obstructions caused by flooding.	The journal *Nature* reports that Antarctic ozone depletion has increased steadily over the past decade.... Researchers announce that an analysis of 38 prior studies found that consumption of soy protein lowers cholesterol levels in people who have moderately high to high cholesterol.	Ida Lupino, 77, English-born movie actress and director who garnered broad critical acclaim throughout her career, dies in Burbank, California, after suffering a stroke.	Aug. 3
	Matarawy Mohammed Said Saleh, an immigrant from Egypt, pleads guilty to a minor conspiracy charge related to the February bombing of the World Trade Center in New York City. Saleh, 39, admits that he agreed to find stolen cars for the other alleged plotters to use to move various explosives, and in return, prosecutors agree to drop charges of attempted bombing against him.	The House passes, 219-208, a $256 billion fiscal 1996 appropriations bill to fund the Departments of Labor, Health and Human Services, and Education.... The California Labor Department reveals that a 1994 survey of 69 garment manufacturers and contractors found that 50% pay their workers below the minimum wage, 68% violate overtime requirements, and almost 93% violate child labor and workplace safety regulations.		The House approves, 305-117, a major overhaul of telecommunications laws. The House bill will relax regulations governing the ownership and operation of TV and radio stations, cable TV networks, and telephone services. The bill also addresses the issue of violent and pornographic materials on TV and on the Internet.	Aug. 4
					Aug. 5
Democratic representative W. J. (Billy) Tauzin (La.) announces in Thibodaux, Louisiana, that he is switching to the Republican Party. The move means that there are 233 Republicans, 201 Democrats, and one independent in the House. Tauzin is the fifth congressional Democrat to switch to the GOP since the Republicans won a congressional majority in the 1994 elections. The others are Sen. Ben Nighthorse Campbell (Colo.), Sen. Richard Shelby (Ala.), Rep. Nathan Deal (Ga.) and Rep. Greg Laughlin (Tex.).				The World Track & Field Championships open in Goteborg, Sweden. They are the last major outdoor track and field events to be held prior to the 1996 Summer Olympic Games.	Aug. 6
	The U.S. Congressional Research Service discloses that in 1994 France surpassed the U.S. in arms sales to developing nations. The study reports that sales from France grew to $11.4 billion in 1994, from $3.8 billion in 1993. U.S. sales decreased to $6.1 billion in 1994, from $15.4 billion in 1993.	Webster L. Hubbell, who served briefly as associate attorney general in the Clinton administration, begins a 21-month prison term at a minimum-security federal prison in Cumberland, Maryland. In June, Hubbell was sentenced for embezzling from clients at the Rose firm, which is related to the Whitewater scandal.		The Library of Congress states it has acquired the archives of Gordon Parks, a black writer, photographer, filmmaker, and composer. ...NBC states it has secured the rights to air the upcoming summer and winter Olympic Games for a record $1.27 billion.	Aug. 7
Louis J. Freeh, the director of the FBI, names Weldon Kennedy, 56, to replace Larry Potts as deputy FBI director.... Philip Morris Cos. Inc. announces that its U.S. unit will begin to voluntarily label all cigarette packs and cartons with the warning "Underage Sale Prohibited."		Pres. Clinton issues an executive order that requires federal contractors to continue to disclose their toxic emissions to the government.		The NBA and the basketball players' union agree to a six-year labor contract that will end a management lockout. The deal is reached minutes before the union would have been eliminated, or decertified itself, as the players' collective-bargaining representative.	Aug. 8

F	G	H	I	J
Includes elections, federal-state relations, civil rights and liberties, crime, the judiciary, education, health care, poverty, urban affairs, and population.	Includes formation and debate of U.S. foreign and defense policies, veterans' affairs, and defense spending. (Relations with specific foreign countries are usually found under the region concerned.)	Includes business, labor, agriculture, taxation, transportation, consumer affairs, monetary and fiscal policy, natural resources, and pollution.	Includes worldwide scientific, medical, and technological developments; natural phenomena; U.S. weather; natural disasters; and accidents.	Includes the arts, religion, scholarship, communications media, sports, entertainments, fashions, fads, and social life.

	World Affairs	Europe	Africa & the Middle East	The Americas	Asia & the Pacific
Aug. 9		A peace pact is signed by the Croatian army and a local Serb commander. . . . Spanish police arrest three alleged Basque guerrillas planning to assassinate a member of the Spanish royal family, possibly King Juan Carlos. . . . German prosecutors announce two business executives have been charged with three counts of murder and 5,837 counts of attempted murder for their roles in distributing blood contaminated with HIV in the late 1980s.		At least 10 people are killed and 350 arrested in a clash between farmers and 200 police officers in Brazil. . . . In a crash reported to be the worst in El Salvador's history, all 65 passengers and crew members die when a Guatemalan jetliner hits the side of a volcano in El Salvador. The dead include the Brazilian ambassador to Nicaragua, Gerardo Antonio Muccioli, and the Danish ambassador to Nicaragua, Palle Marker.	
Aug. 10	The U.S. releases to the UN Security Council spy-satellite photographs allegedly showing mass graves near the Bosnian town of Srebrenica, which Bosnian Serbs captured in July. The U.S. claims the Bosnian Serbs committed massive atrocities in the capture of Srebrenica, including the mass execution of draft-age Muslim men. As many as 4,000 Muslim men and boys are thought to be still missing.	The French defense ministry announces that France would back a ban on all further nuclear testing after a planned series of tests are completed in 1996. France's move is widely viewed as an attempt to derail growing protests against the country's decision to resume nuclear testing in French Polynesia. . . . Germany's federal constitutional court rules that the crucifix, a symbol of Christianity, must be removed from all public classrooms.	Reports confirm that Jordan has given asylum to the military aides and senior army officers who defected from Iraq on Aug. 8. . . . Richard Leakey and others, including Paul Muite, who formed the party Safina in May in Kenya, are attacked and beaten by a group of youths who Leakey alleges has ties to the ruling KANU, which denies any role in the attack.	FARC rebels pull out of the southeastern Colombian town of Miraflores, which was attacked Aug. 6. The rebels are pursued in the jungle by Colombian authorities. A total of 26 people—13 rebels, seven police officers, and six civilians—died in the rebel assault. The Red Cross airlifts aid to the town.	The Philippines and China agree to a bilateral pact to resolve without force their territorial disputes over the Spratly Islands chain in the South China Sea.
Aug. 11	In response to the Aug. 10 spy-satellite photographs, the U.N. announces an investigation into accusations that 2,700 men and boys were shot and buried in mass graves near the Bosnian town of Srebrenica, which Bosnian Serbs captured in July.	Thousands of Serb refugees who fled Krajina make their way to Serb-held territory in Bosnia and to Serbia, including Belgrade.	Rival Kurdish factions operating in the Western-protected zone of Iraq north of the 36th parallel reach terms on a draft peace agreement to end 15 months of hostilities that reportedly has taken the lives of at least 4,500 people. . . . Saudi Arabia executes two Turkish nationals for allegedly smuggling Captagon, a stimulant containing an amphetamine used as an aphrodisiac, into Saudi territory.	Two subway trains in Toronto, Canada, collide during rush hour, killing three passengers and injuring 36. Toronto Transit Commission officials call it the worst crash in the subway system's 42-year history.	
Aug. 12		Croatian forces attack Bosnian Serb forces around the city of Dubrovnik, Croatia. Bosnian Serbs in nearby Trebinje, Bosnia, shell the area. On another front, the mainly Muslim Bosnian government army, aided by Bosnian Croats, launches an offensive around the Serb-held town of Donji Vakuf, in central Bosnia. . . . In Londonderry and Belfast, Northern Ireland, a total of 30 people are injured in clashes over a Protestant unionist group's march to celebrate the 310-year anniversary of the defeat of King James II at the hands of William of Orange.		Eighteen people are killed when 40 gunmen enter a crowded bar in the small town of Chigorodo, Colombia, and open fire. Separately, Trevor Catton, 22, a British student kidnapped by left-wing guerrillas in June, is found shot dead near the town of Caqueza.	
Aug. 13		French drivers of Eurostar trains, which run between London and Paris, end a labor strike that started earlier in the week. . . . The Russian Duma, or lower house of parliament, passes a resolution to lift international trade sanctions imposed by the UN against Yugoslavia in 1992.		At least 20 people are killed during a series of raids by leftist guerrillas and right-wing paramilitary groups in the Uraba region in northwestern Colombia. . . . In Haiti, makeup elections are held for 41 races in which irregularities in the original June balloting caused results to be declared invalid.	The body of Hans Christian Ostro, 27, of Norway is found decapitated on a road in a Himalayan village southeast of Srinagar. Ostro was one of five Western tourists taken hostage by members of an extremist guerrilla group in India's disputed Jammu and Kashmir state in July. The guerrillas threaten to kill their four remaining captives if the Indian government refuses to release 15 jailed Kashmiri separatists.
Aug. 14			Israeli planes carry out a rocket attack against a Lebanese base of the Popular Front for the Liberation of Palestine-General Command, the Ahmed Jabril-led Palestinian guerrilla group that opposes peace negotiations between Israel and Yasser Arafat's PLO. . . . Saudi Arabia executes another two Turkish nationals for allegedly smuggling into Saudi territory Captagon, a stimulant containing an amphetamine used as an aphrodisiac.	Mexico's National Human Rights Commission charges that police in the western state of Guerrero murdered 17 peasants in June. The shootings sparked a wave of violence that has left more than 30 people dead in the state over a two-week period.	The All-Party Hurriyat Conference, a coalition of more than 30 Kashmiri militant separatist factions, calls for a general strike in the region to protest the killing of Hans Christian Ostro, 27, of Norway. His body was found Aug. 13.

A	B	C	D	E
Includes developments that affect more than one world region, international organizations, and important meetings of major world leaders.	Includes all domestic and regional developments in Europe, including the Soviet Union, Turkey, Cyprus, and Malta.	Includes all domestic and regional developments in Africa and the Middle East, including Iraq and Iran and excluding Cyprus, Turkey, and Afghanistan.	Includes all domestic and regional developments in Latin America, the Caribbean, and Canada.	Includes all domestic and regional developments in Asia and Pacific nations, extending from Afghanistan through all the Pacific Islands, except Hawaii.

U.S. Politics & Social Issues	U.S. Foreign Policy & Defense	U.S. Economy & Environment	Science, Technology, & Nature	Culture, Leisure, & Lifestyle	
Entertainment magnate David Geffen states he is donating $4 million to two leading New York City-based groups that provide services to people with AIDS. The donation reportedly is the largest ever to AIDS-services groups.		The EPA authorizes two pesticide developers, Mycogen Corp. and Ciba Seeds, to market a genetically modified corn seed in the U.S. It is the first corn seed ever to be genetically altered for pest resistance. . . Judge Paul Friedman sentences Walter Fauntroy, a former delegate to Congress for the District of Columbia, to two years' probation, a $1,000 fine, and 300 hours of community service for falsifying a financial report.		Jerry (Jerome John) Garcia, 53, singer, guitarist, and songwriter for the San Francisco-based rock band the Grateful Dead, an extremely popular touring band whose fans follow them on tour, dies in Forest Knolls, California, reportedly of a heart attack.	Aug. 9
A federal grand jury in Oklahoma City, Oklahoma, indicts Timothy McVeigh and Terry Nichols on charges stemming from the April 19 car-bombing attack in Oklahoma City that killed at least 167 people. . . . Pres. Clinton states he is authorizing proposed FDA rules on the advertising and sale of tobacco products that are intended to curb tobacco use among teenagers. The five largest U.S. tobacco companies, along with an advertising agency, file suit, claiming that the FDA is exceeding both its legal rights and the intent of Congress.		A special Senate committee and the House Banking and Financial Services Committee conclude their respective rounds of new public hearings into aspects of the Whitewater affair without exposing clear evidence of wrongdoing by the presidential couple or by members of the Clinton administration.	Three studies reveal that for the first time researchers have isolated a human gene linked to adult-onset diabetes, which is closely associated with obesity.		Aug. 10
Robert Brecheen, 40, convicted of a 1983 murder, is the sixth person in Oklahoma and the 291st in the U.S. to be executed since 1976. Brecheen's case receives attention since he is executed after being revived from an earlier suicide attempt. . . . FBI director Louis Freeh suspends four high-ranking bureau officials indefinitely with pay due to a probe of the siege at white supremacist Randy Weaver's cabin in Idaho.	Pres. Clinton vetoes a bill, passed by the House and the Senate, to end U.S. participation in the arms embargo against the Bosnian government. The veto is the second of Clinton's presidency. . . . U.S. officials hold a lottery to determine the order in which 10,000 of the 13,000 Cuban refugees held at the U.S. Naval Base at Guantanamo Bay in Cuba will be admitted into the U.S.		Scientists disclose that fragments of the fossilized remains of humans and stone tools found in Spain are at least 780,000 years old, indicating that humans lived in Europe substantially earlier than previously believed.	Kenneth (Lo Hsiao Chien) Lo, 81, Chinese chef who wrote more than 30 books on cooking, dies in London, England, of cancer. . . . Phil Harris, 91, radio comedian, band leader, and movie actor, dies in Rancho Mirage, California, after suffering a heart attack.	Aug. 11
Ten Republicans who hope to be named the GOP presidential candidate speak at a convention organized by Ross Perot, a Texas billionaire and 1992 independent candidate for U.S. president, and United We Stand America, a grassroots political association founded by Perot.					Aug. 12
	The FAA orders officials at airports in the New York City metropolitan area to raise their security measures to the most stringent level since the 1991 Persian Gulf war after federal officials reportedly uncover two terrorist threats from Islamic militant groups.			Mickey Charles Mantle, 63, New York Yankee who was regarded as one of the greatest baseball players of all time, dies in Baylor, Texas, of cancer. . . . Alison Hargreaves, 33, who was the first woman to climb solo to the top of Mount Everest without carrying oxygen, dies in the Himalayas while climbing K2, the second-tallest mountain in the world.	Aug. 13
	Shannon Faulkner becomes the first female cadet at the Citadel, a state-supported military academy in Charleston, South Carolina, after having spent more than two years in legal battle with the school. Demonstrators both supporting and opposing Faulkner await her at the academy's entrance.			The Grateful Dead rock band announces that it is canceling all of its scheduled fall concerts in the wake of the Aug. 9 death of group cofounder Jerry Garcia.	Aug. 14

F	G	H	I	J
Includes elections, federal-state relations, civil rights and liberties, crime, the judiciary, education, health care, poverty, urban affairs, and population.	Includes formation and debate of U.S. foreign and defense policies, veterans' affairs, and defense spending. (Relations with specific foreign countries are usually found under the region concerned.)	Includes business, labor, agriculture, taxation, transportation, consumer affairs, monetary and fiscal policy, natural resources, and pollution.	Includes worldwide scientific, medical, and technological developments; natural phenomena; U.S. weather; natural disasters; and accidents.	Includes the arts, religion, scholarship, communications media, sports, entertainments, fashions, fads, and social life.

	World Affairs	Europe	Africa & the Middle East	The Americas	Asia & the Pacific
Aug. 15			Rebel soldiers led by a five-man commission of army officers arrest Pres. Miguel Trovoada, Sao Tome and Principe's first freely elected leader. In a bloodless coup, the rebels seize control of the government, disband parliament, and suspend the democratic constitution, which had taken effect four years earlier.		A Vietnamese court sentences Thich Quang Do, the secretary general of the Unified Buddhist Church, to five years in prison. . . . Japanese premier Tomiichi Murayama offers a "heartfelt apology" for his country's acts of "colonial rule and aggression" against other countries during World War II. In doing so, Murayama becomes the first Japanese leader to use the word "apology" in regard to the war.
Aug. 16	The UN Security Council votes to suspend for one year an arms embargo on the Rwandan government.	The Croatian government refuses to allow the UN and other humanitarian aid workers to reach 30,000 Muslim refugees trapped in Croatia.	After the Aug. 11 and Aug. 14 executions of Turkish nationals in Saudi Arabia, Turkey warns Saudi Arabia not to execute any more Turks. Amnesty International charges that defendants facing capital offenses in Saudi courts are being denied judicial due process.	Bermuda, a self-governing British island colony in the mid-Atlantic Ocean, votes in a referendum to reject becoming independent from Great Britain. . . . A strike by 50,000 teachers, begun in July in Costa Rica, ends. . . . Colombian president Ernesto Samper Pizano announces a 90-day state of emergency, amid increasing violence and civil strife and amid accusations that Samper accepted money from the Cali drug cartel for his 1994 presidential election campaign.	Indonesian president Suharto orders the release of three prominent political prisoners, Foreign Minister Subandrio, 81, former air force commander Omar Dhani, 71, and former intelligence official Raden Sugent Sutarto, 77. The prisoners have been held for nearly 30 years because of their alleged roles in an abortive 1965 coup. . . . The All-Party Hurriyat Conference, a coalition of more than 30 Kashmiri militant separatist factions, holds a general strike to protest the killing of Western hostage Hans Christian Ostro by another militant Muslim group.
Aug. 17	The UN's Human Development Report 1995, which this year focuses on women's issues, finds that, while the world's women in recent decades have gained significantly in areas such as education and health care, they still lack political and economic power and equality under the law. . . . The Association of Caribbean States (ACS) holds its first summit. . . . Iraq begins to disclose data on its biological- and nuclear-weapons programs to the UN.	A bomb explodes in a crowded tourist section of Paris, injuring 17 people. . . . Family members of Frederick C. Cuny, a U.S. disaster-relief expert reported missing in the breakaway Russian republic of Chechnya in April, announce that they have called off their search for Cuny, concluding that he was executed April 14 by Chechen rebels whom they believe were set up by the Russians.	The rebel soldiers who seized control of the government in Sao Tome and Principe on Aug. 15 name the parliamentary president, Francisco Fortunato Pires, as interim president. . . . Reports confirm that South African president Nelson Mandela has initiated proceedings to divorce his estranged wife, Winnie Mandela.		China announces that it exploded a nuclear bomb in an underground test. China's announcement does not specify where the test occurred or how powerful it was.
Aug. 18	The UN announces that it is withdrawing its peacekeepers from the UN-declared safe area of Gorazde, in eastern Bosnia. The protection of Gorazde's roughly 60,000 Muslim inhabitants will fall to NATO.	Swedish premier Ingvar Carlsson announces that he will step down from his post in March 1996. . . . Spain's Supreme Court announces that it will take over a probe into Premier Felipe Gonzalez's alleged role in organizing antiterrorist death squads in the 1980s.	Reports indicate that a family of five was killed in a bomb attack at their home near Blida, Algeria. Two car bombs explode outside Algiers, the capital, killing one girl. Hours later, the Algerian government announces that it will conduct a presidential election on Nov. 16. . . . The coup leaders in Sao Tome and Principe, after meeting with Angolan mediators, release Pres. Miguel Trovoada from an army barracks. . . . Hamas supporters in Gaza burn U.S. flags to protest the July arrest of Mousa Mohammed Abu Marzook, in NYC.		
Aug. 19		Three of the key American peace negotiators in Bosnia-Herzegovina—Robert C. Frasure, 53; Joseph J. Kruzel, 50; and Samuel Nelson Drew, 47—are killed when their armored personnel carrier plunges from a road on Mount Igman outside Sarajevo, the Bosnian capital.	The leaders of Liberia's warring factions agree to a peace pact aimed at ending the country's civil war, which began in December 1989, has taken more than 150,000 lives, and has outlasted a dozen cease-fire agreements. . . . Zaire begins to forcibly expel Rwandan and Burundian refugees. . . . In Guyana, the Essequibo River is fouled with cyanide-tainted water and clay when a reservoir holding effluent from a gold mine collapses.	María de los Angeles Moreno, president of the ruling Mexican Institutional Revolutionary Party (PRI), resigns. PRI secretary general Pedro Joaquín Coldwell also resigns, leaving the top two positions in the party open.	
Aug. 20	The government of Iraq closes discussions with Rolf Ekeus, chair of the UN Special Commission on Iraq responsible for overseeing the elimination of Iraq's weapons of mass destruction. In the talks, Iraq disclosed extensive information on its biological- and nuclear-weapons programs. Iraq's sudden decision to release the data follows the Aug. 8 defection of more than 20 officers, including Lt. Gen. Hussein Kamel Hassan al-Majid, director of Iraq's weapons program since 1987.	A British helicopter that is part of a new UN rapid reaction force crashes into the Adriatic Sea off the coast of Croatia, killing four British soldiers. One soldier is rescued from the sea by a Croatian fishing boat. . . . French police confirm that they are investigating a letter from Algeria's Armed Islamic Group (GIA), claiming responsibility for bomb blasts in July and August.	The government of Israeli prime minister Yitzhak Rabin decides that it will not order an investigation into the alleged atrocities in the slayings of Egyptian prisoners in the 1956 and 1967 wars, which were recently disclosed by former Israeli officers.	An overcrowded smuggling boat carrying Haitian migrants lands in the Bahamas after being intercepted by Bahamian authorities and the U.S. Coast Guard. According to witnesses, the boat originally carried 600 people, only 457 of whom arrive in the Bahamas.	Hundreds of people are killed when a passenger train hits another train stopped in Firozabad, India. The accident, blamed on the error of a signalman, is one of the worst rail disasters in India's history.
	A	B	C	D	E
	Includes developments that affect more than one world region, international organizations, and important meetings of major world leaders.	Includes all domestic and regional developments in Europe, including the Soviet Union, Turkey, Cyprus, and Malta.	Includes all domestic and regional developments in Africa and the Middle East, including Iraq and Iran and excluding Cyprus, Turkey, and Afghanistan.	Includes all domestic and regional developments in Latin America, the Caribbean, and Canada.	Includes all domestic and regional developments in Asia and Pacific nations, extending from Afghanistan through all the Pacific Islands, except Hawaii.

U.S. Politics & Social Issues	U.S. Foreign Policy & Defense	U.S. Economy & Environment	Science, Technology, & Nature	Culture, Leisure, & Lifestyle	
The Justice Department agrees to pay $3.1 million to the family of Randall Weaver, a white separatist whose wife and son were killed by federal agents during a 1992 standoff in Idaho.	U.S. Air Force chief of staff General Ronald Fogleman announces he has issued "letters of evaluation" rebuking seven officers involved in the April 1994 accidental downing of two U.S. Army helicopters over Iraq. The action comes amid criticism that the U.S. Air Force was too lenient in its initial assessment of the officers' conduct.			John Cameron Swayze, 89, early television news anchor and spokesman for Timex Corp., dies in Sarasota, Florida, of unreported causes.	Aug. 15
Leon Moser, 52, convicted of killing his ex-wife and two daughters in 1985, is put to death by lethal injection in Bellefonte, Pennsylvannia. Moser is only the second person executed in Pennsylvania and the 293rd in the nation since 1976. . . . Oveta Culp Hobby, 90, who in 1941 created the Women's Auxiliary Army Corps (WAAC), and who was the second female cabinet member in U.S. history, serving as head of the Department of Health, Education and Welfare, 1953–55, dies in Houston, Texas, after suffering a stroke.	Reports confirm that the Labor Department has reached an agreement with Syntel Inc., a Troy, Michigan-based software-consulting firm, in which the company agrees to make reparations for paying its foreign employees in the U.S. below-market wages. The settlement marks the first major agreement in the federal government's effort to prevent U.S.-based companies from exploiting foreigners in professional-level jobs by paying them lower wages than U.S. workers would command.	The Federal Trade Commission (FTC) announces new regulations designed to curb telemarketing fraud.			Aug. 16
	A federal grand jury in Los Angeles indicts nine Thai nationals suspected of running the El Monte sweatshop, which was raided Aug. 2.	A federal grand jury in Little Rock, Arkansas, indicts James B. McDougal and his ex-wife, Susan McDougal, on bank-fraud and conspiracy charges. The McDougals were the main partners of Pres. Clinton and First Lady Hillary Rodham Clinton in the Whitewater Development Corp. real-estate venture.	Scientists report that fossil remains unearthed near Lake Turkana in Kenya represent a new species of human ancestor that walked on two legs about 3.9–4.2 million years ago. . . . The Department of Energy reveals that an estimated 16,000 people were subjects in radiation experiments conducted by the U.S. government from World War II through the mid-1970s. It is nearly double the figure estimated in February.	Howard Koch, 93, screenwriter best known for his collaboration with Julian and Philip Epstein on the screenplay of *Casablanca* (1942), dies in Kingston, New York, after suffering from pneumonia.	Aug. 17
Sylvester Adams, 39, convicted of the 1979 strangulation death of a teenage neighbor, is executed by lethal injection in Columbia, South Carolina. He is the first inmate to take advantage of a recently passed state law allowing condemned prisoners to choose injection over the electric chair and is only the sixth executed in South Carolina since 1976. He is the 294th person executed in the U.S. since 1976.	Shannon Faulkner, the first female cadet at the Citadel in Charleston, South Carolina, withdraws from the military academy she entered just five days earlier, citing the stress of her legal confrontations with the Citadel. Faulkner is one of 35 new cadets to quit the Citadel during the first week of training, out of the 592 who entered.				Aug. 18
		Reports confirm that the Justice Department's antitrust division is preparing to press a major price-fixing case against some large securities dealers in connection with alleged practices that artificially inflated their profits from trades made on the NASDAQ exchange of over-the-counter stocks.	Research shows that smokers in their 30s and 40s suffer five times as many heart attacks as nonsmokers in the same age group.		Aug. 19
Reports reveal that the State Regents for Higher Education has coordinated a collective effort by scholarship funds, local and state officials and universities to raise money for the 174 children who were injured in the April bombing in Oklahoma City, Oklahoma, or whose parents were injured or killed in the blast. The fund of a total of $7.5 million will provided the children with financial assistance for college.					Aug. 20

F	G	H	I	J
Includes elections, federal-state relations, civil rights and liberties, crime, the judiciary, education, health care, poverty, urban affairs, and population.	Includes formation and debate of U.S. foreign and defense policies, veterans' affairs, and defense spending. (Relations with specific foreign countries are usually found under the region concerned.)	Includes business, labor, agriculture, taxation, transportation, consumer affairs, monetary and fiscal policy, natural resources, and pollution.	Includes worldwide scientific, medical, and technological developments; natural phenomena; U.S. weather; natural disasters; and accidents.	Includes the arts, religion, scholarship, communications media, sports, entertainments, fashions, fads, and social life.

	World Affairs	Europe	Africa & the Middle East	The Americas	Asia & the Pacific
Aug. 21		UN and human-rights investigators state that they have obtained evidence of mass graves in Krajina, a formerly Serb-held region of Croatia, and that Serbs were executed in that area. Human-rights officials also reveal that Croatians continue to burn formerly Serb villages to prevent the Serb population from returning.	A Hamas suicide bomber detonates a powerful explosive in Jerusalem, killing at least five Jews as well as the bomber and injuring some 100 other people. Soon after the explosion, several hundred Jewish rightists gather at the bombing site to demonstrate against the Israeli-PLO talks.		The death toll from the Aug. 20 train crash in in Firozabad, India, stands at more than 340, with more than 400 injured.... Australian prime minister Paul Keating announces his decision to name Sir William Deane, 64, a High Court judge, as Australia's new governor general.
Aug. 22	UN officials report that the Iraqis have provided Rolf Ekeus, chairman of the UN Special Commission on Iraq responsible for overseeing the elimination of Iraq's weapons of mass destruction, with detailed information on substantial quantities of stockpiled germ weapons, such as botulin and anthrax.	Six people are killed and 38 wounded in Sarajevo by shells fired from Bosnian Serb positions. ... Christopher Brain, an ordained priest of the Church of England, admits that he had improper sexual contact with about 20 women belonging to his Nine O'Clock Service church, which reportedly has taken on many characteristics of a fringe cult.	Pres. Miguel Trovoada of Sao Tome and Principe resumes his post, bringing to a close the Aug. 15 bloodless coup. Trovoada is reinstated after signing an amnesty law pardoning the soldiers who took part in the rebellion.... A new parliament in Ethiopia is sworn in for a five-year term, replacing the 1991 transitional government. Parliament elects Negasso Ghidada president.... Guyanese president Cheddi Jagan declares the zone around the Aug. 19 effluent spill an "environmental disaster area."	The Guatemalan National Revolutionary Union (URNG), a coalition of four leftist guerrilla groups in Guatemala, announces a two-week cease-fire to coincide with general elections scheduled for Nov. 12. It will be the first cease-fire between the rebels and the government in 30 years.... Thomas Hargrove, a U.S. citizen kidnapped in Colombia by leftist guerrillas 11 months earlier, is released from captivity and returns to his home in a suburb of Cali, Colombia.	
Aug. 23		Lord Vincent Gordon Lindsay White, 72, cofounder of British conglomerate Hanson PLC, dies in Los Angeles, California, of a respiratory ailment.	Iraq's official TV network broadcasts a speech by Jordan's King Hussein which criticizes policies of Saddam Hussein. It is the first time in about 20 years that Iraq allows criticism of Iraqi leaders on its national TV system.... Meles Zenawi, head of Ethiopia's transitional government, is chosen as premier by Parliament.... The Israeli government announces it has seized more than 30 members of the Hamas cell behind the Aug. 21 bombing in Jerusalem and the July 24 attack in Tel Aviv.	An appellate court in Argentina refuses a request by Italy to extradite Erich Priebke, a former Nazi special-forces officer, in connection with crimes committed during World War II.	Troops loyal to Pres. Burhanuddin Rabbani attack the Taliban at Delaram, a town in Afghanistan's southwestern plains.
Aug. 24	WHO declares an end to a recent outbreak of the Ebola virus in Zaire because 42 days, the time equal to two maximum incubation periods for the virus, has passed without any newly reported cases. In the outbreak, 244 of the 315 people known to have contracted the virus died.	British peacekeepers shoot and kill two men in Bosnian army uniforms who are attempting to raid a UN base in Gorazde. ... The Georgian parliament votes to adopt the country's first constitution since it gained independence from the Soviet Union in 1991. The constitution restores the office of president, which was eliminated after the 1992 coup.... Russia's banking system is thrown into a crisis when the country's banks stop lending to one another.	Under international criticism, Zaire agrees to temporarily halt the forced expulsion of Rwandan and Burundian refugees.... Engineers plug a breach in the wall of the reservoir that collapsed Aug. 19 and fouled Guyana's Essequibo River.... Reports suggest that Iraqi president Saddam Hussein has ordered the arrest of hundreds of officials deemed politically unreliable and restructured his personal security contingent in an apparent effort to consolidate power in the wake of the Aug. 8 defections.	In response to the mayor's approval of the construction of a golf course near the village of Tepoztlan, 30 miles (50 km) south of Mexico City, a coalition of peasants, small business owners, and environmentalists in Tepoztlan seize the town hall.... Germany requests the extradition from Argentina of Erich Priebke, a former Nazi special-forces officer, in connection with crimes committed during World War II. The request comes the day after Argentina refused to extradite Priebke to Italy.	A court in Wuhan, China, convicts Harry Wu, a Chinese-American human-rights activist, of spying and sentences him to 15 years in jail and expulsion. However, China expels Wu without making him serve his sentence. The release of Wu, who worked to document abuses in China's prison system, serves to ease tensions in Sino-U.S. relations.
Aug. 25	Rolf Ekeus, chairman of the UN Special Commission on Iraq that is responsible for overseeing the elimination of Iraq's weapons of mass destruction, reveals that newly disclosed Iraqi documents show that Iraq has around 10 times more anthrax available for use than previously acknowledged. Ekeus states Iraq has admitted that it also produced a third deadly chemical, aflatoxin.	The Sejm, the lower house in the Polish parliament, passes an anti-smoking law with a large majority.	Israeli undercover forces kill two presumed Hamas militants during a gunfight in Hebron.	David Saul is named Bermuda's new prime minister after defeating C. V. Woolridge in a secret ballot of Bermuda's legislators.... Reports state that a Colombian military intelligence agency admits that 87 foreign hostages are being held in Colombia. Other reports note a U.S. State Department speaker has claimed that there are currently four U.S. citizens being held hostage in Colombia, all of whom are missionaries.	
Aug. 26				The British Foreign Office confirms that Timothy Cowley, assistant to the defense attaché at the British embassy in Colombia, has been kidnapped by leftist guerrillas.	

A	B	C	D	E
Includes developments that affect more than one world region, international organizations, and important meetings of major world leaders.	Includes all domestic and regional developments in Europe, including the Soviet Union, Turkey, Cyprus, and Malta.	Includes all domestic and regional developments in Africa and the Middle East, including Iraq and Iran and excluding Cyprus, Turkey, and Afghanistan.	Includes all domestic and regional developments in Latin America, the Caribbean, and Canada.	Includes all domestic and regional developments in Asia and Pacific nations, extending from Afghanistan through all the Pacific Islands, except Hawaii.

U.S. Politics & Social Issues	U.S. Foreign Policy & Defense	U.S. Economy & Environment	Science, Technology, & Nature	Culture, Leisure, & Lifestyle	
Spy Factory Inc., the U.S.'s largest chain of "spy shops," or stores that sell electronic surveillance equipment, is indicted in a federal court for bringing illegal eavesdropping devices into the U.S. and selling them to the public. . . . Dr. Jack Kevorkian, who advocates physician-assisted suicide, attends his 25th suicide when Esther Cohan, 46, of Skokie, Illinois, who was suffering from multiple sclerosis and painful ulcers, dies.		Judge J. Robert Elliott of the U.S. District Court in Columbus, Georgia, imposes a $115 million fine on E. I. du Pont de Nemours & Co. for concealing evidence during a 1993 trial about potential crop and plant damage caused by the company's Benlate fungicide.	Judge Thomas Jackson approves a 1994 antitrust settlement between the Justice Department and Microsoft Corp. . . . A commuter plane crash-lands near Carollton, Georgia, killing five people and injuring the other 24 passengers and crew. . . . Subrahmanyan Chandrasekhar, 84, Indian-born astrophysicist who won the 1983 Nobel Prize and is known for his studies on dying stars, dies in Chicago, Illinois, of a heart attack.		Aug. 21
Rep. Mel Reynolds (D, Ill.) is convicted by a Cook County jury in Chicago of sexual assault, criminal sexual abuse, solicitation of child pornography, and obstruction of justice. The charges stem from accusations that he had sex with a teenage campaign worker.		Former Sen. David Durenberger (R, Minn.) pleads guilty to five misdemeanor charges of cheating on his Senate expense account. As a result of a plea arrangement with the Justice Department, the felony charges against Durenberger are dropped and no prison sentence is recommended. . . . A three-judge panel of the U.S. Fourth Circuit Court of Appeals in Richmond, Virginia, agree to let the federal government store 157 spent nuclear-fuel rods at a South Carolina military installation.		Helen Darville, the 1995 winner of Australia's top literary prize, the Miles Franklin Award, reveals that she had assumed a false name, ethnic identity, and cultural background when she wrote the prize-winning book that depicts Ukraine during World War II. Observers claim that her misrepresentations may have deceptively influenced judges.	Aug. 22
The FDA proposes a new program under which pharmacies will voluntarily provide to patients information on the side effects of prescription drugs. . . . Statistics show that scores on the Scholastic Assessment Test (SAT) increased in 1995 after the College Board changed the test's format. The average score on the verbal section went from 423 to 428 while the average math score went from 479 to 482, the highest score since 1973.	Assistant Secretary of State Richard Holbrooke names U.S. Army brigadier general Donald Kerrick, James Pardew, Christopher Hill, and Roberts Owen to replace the diplomats who died Aug. 19 in a car crash near Sarajevo, Bosnia. . . . Officials from the Department of Labor and the INS raid three Los Angeles–area garment factories suspected of employing workers in sweatshop conditions. The agents arrest 55 people, including 39 Thai workers.			Alfred Eisenstaedt, 96, photographer who contributed to *Life* magazine for nearly 60 years and was most famous for a photograph of a sailor kissing a nurse in NYC's Times Square during celebrations at the end of World War II, dies in Martha's Vineyard, Massachusetts, of unreported causes.	Aug. 23
At least nine members of Congress call on Rep. Mel Reynolds (D, Ill.), convicted Aug. 22, to resign from the House. . . . The CDC reports that more toddlers have been vaccinated than previously believed, but that a quarter of toddlers in the U.S. still are not adequately immunized.			Reports show that the ratio of strains of a common disease-causing bacterium that are resistant to antibiotics has risen significantly in recent years. . . . Microsoft launches the retail sale of Windows 95 amid what many experts call the largest product advertising campaign ever.	Vatican officials report that Pope John Paul II has chosen Mary Ann Glendon as the first woman to head the Vatican's delegation to the UN Conference on Women to be held in Beijing. . . Gary Evan Crosby, 62, singer, actor, author, and son of Bing Crosby, dies in Burbank, California, of lung cancer.	Aug. 24
The Wisconsin Supreme Court orders the suspension of a program that gives poor students in the city of Milwaukee public funds to pay for tuition at private religious schools. The program will be suspended until the court makes a ruling on its constitutionality. The Wisconsin voucher program would have been the first in the U.S. to provide vouchers for religious schools.	The Clinton administration announces that First Lady Hillary Rodham Clinton will attend an international conference on women's issues in China.				Aug. 25
The campaign spokesman for Sen. Robert Dole (R, Kans.), Nelson Warfield, announces that the Dole campaign returned a donation from the Log Cabin Republicans, a group of homosexual Republicans. Warfield states that the senator felt obligated to return the $1,000 contribution because he disagrees with some of the group's political positions, particularly the Log Cabin group's support for lifting the ban on homosexuals in the military.		Officials from the Justice Department report that the government has signed an agreement with the Hotel Employees and Restaurant Employees International Union that calls for a monitoring board to scrutinize the union's alleged corruption and purported ties to organized crime.		Evelyn Wood, 86, creator of a world-renowned method for learning speed reading, dies in Tucson, Arizona, of unreported causes. . . . Ronnie White, 57, songwriter and musician, dies in Detroit, Michigan, of leukemia. . . . A team from Taiwan wins baseball's Little League World Series over a team from Spring, Texas.	Aug. 26

F	G	H	I	J
Includes elections, federal-state relations, civil rights and liberties, crime, the judiciary, education, health care, poverty, urban affairs, and population.	Includes formation and debate of U.S. foreign and defense policies, veterans' affairs, and defense spending. (Relations with specific foreign countries are usually found under the region concerned.)	Includes business, labor, agriculture, taxation, transportation, consumer affairs, monetary and fiscal policy, natural resources, and pollution.	Includes worldwide scientific, medical, and technological developments; natural phenomena; U.S. weather; natural disasters; and accidents.	Includes the arts, religion, scholarship, communications media, sports, entertainments, fashions, fads, and social life.

	World Affairs	Europe	Africa & the Middle East	The Americas	Asia & the Pacific
Aug. 27	The Inter-Parliamentary Union, a Geneva-based organization, finds that the percentage of women elected to national legislatures worldwide declined by almost 25% in the previous seven years.	French police find an undetonated bomb containing 55 pounds (25 kg) of explosives on railroad tracks outside Lyons. . . . Carl Ronald Giles, 78, British cartoonist for London's *Daily Express* and *Sunday Express* newspapers, dies in London after suffering a stroke.		Members of a renegade native group, the Shushwap Traditionalists, who are occupying a campsite in British Columbia, exchange gunfire with police officers. The dispute revolves around claims that the area is sacred Indian land. . . . In an unofficial EZLN-sponsored nationwide referendum, Mexicans vote in favor of the EZLN gaining political status. However, only 1.2 million people, or 3% of Mexico's eligible voters, participate in the referendum.	
Aug. 28		Thirty-seven civilians are killed and more than 80 are wounded when two mortar shells, apparently fired by Bosnian Serbs, hit a marketplace in Sarajevo, the besieged capital of Bosnia-Herzegovina. Separately, a detachment of 250 British, Ukrainian, and Norwegian peacekeepers complete their withdrawal from the Gorazde safe area in southeastern Bosnia. . . . Michael Ende, 65, German author of children's books who is best known for his book *The Neverending Story* (1979), dies in Stuttgart, Germany, of stomach cancer.	The Rwandan parliament votes to back a motion, proposed by Pres. Pasteur Bizimungu, for the dismissal of Premier Faustin Twagiramungu. The departure of Twagiramungu, a moderate Hutu, comes amid a growing crisis involving refugees in neighboring Zaire and heightened fears among Hutu refugees who have refused to return to Rwanda.		
Aug. 29		Georgian head of state Eduard Shevardnadze is slightly wounded when a car bomb goes off near his motorcade in the capital city, Tbilisi, in an apparent assassination attempt. . . . A state court in Berlin, Germany, sentences neo-Nazi Bela Ewald Althans to 3½ years in prison for denying that the Holocaust ever took place, a crime under German law.		At least 16 banana plantation workers are killed by gunmen in the region of Uraba in northwestern Colombia. Officials believe that the Revolutionary Armed Forces of Colombia (FARC) is responsible for the massacre and that the guerrillas also kidnapped seven people.	Liberation Tigers of Tamil Eelam guerrillas hijack a ferry near Mullaittivu, a village on the northeast coast of Sri Lanka. The vessel, is carrying approximately 130 passengers. . . . Japan announces that it will suspend direct foreign aid to China as a form of protest against China's testing of nuclear weapons, particularly the Aug. 17 test.
Aug. 30	In retaliation for the Aug. 28 attack in Sarajevo, more than 60 NATO warplanes bomb Bosnian Serb military positions near the city, in the largest action by NATO forces in the alliance's history. Forty-eight of the warplanes are U.S. Air Force or Navy craft, with the rest provided by Britain, France, Spain, and the Netherlands. . . . A UN-sanctioned gathering that parallels the upcoming United Nations Fourth World Conference on Women opens in the Chinese town of Huairou.	NATO forces launch their first air strike in darkness at about 2:00 A.M. local time. That bombing run is the first of six flown by NATO jets before sundown. One NATO plane, a French Mirage 2000 fighter jet, is downed near Pale by a hand-held surface-to-air missile.		In response to the Aug. 29 killings of plantation workers in Uraba, northwestern Colombia, a general strike is held by the 11,000-member Union of Agrarian Workers in an attempt to pressure the government to provide better security in the violent Uraba region.	Rebels from the Liberation Tigers of Tamil Eelam who seized a ferry on Aug. 29 sink two Sri Lankan military vessels investigating why the ferry is anchored offshore. Most of the 28 members of the two gunboats' crew are thought to have been killed in the attack.
Aug. 31		At least two NATO air strikes are flown over Sarajevo in Bosnia-Herzegovina. . . . French police in Lyons and Paris arrest 20 Muslim fundamentalists, reportedly in connection with recent bombings.	Pierre Celestin Rwigema, a moderate Hutu and the former education minister, is sworn in as Rwanda's new premier. . . . Tens of thousands of Liberians gather in the streets of Monrovia, Liberia's capital, to celebrate the peace agreement signed Aug. 19.		Beant Singh, chief minister of India's Punjab state, is killed by a car bomb outside the main government building in Chandigarh, the state capital. The blast kills at least 12 other people and injures 18 others. Leaders of Babbar Khalsa International, a militant Sikh separatist group, claim responsibility for the bombing. H. S. Brar, Punjab's health and family welfare minister, is sworn in as Singh's successor.
Sept. 1	French navy commandos in the South Pacific storm two protest ships belonging to Greenpeace to prevent the vessels from approaching the site of planned nuclear tests.	NATO forces bring the round of bombing that started Aug. 30 to a halt at 5:00 A.M. local time at the request of French lieutenant general Bernard Janvier, the commander of UN forces in the former Yugoslavia. . . . In Paris, 260 protesters attempting to deliver an anti-nuclear testing petition with 3.3 million signatures to Pres. Chirac are detained during a banned rally.	In Liberia, a new six-member interim ruling council is formally sworn in under the terms of the Aug. 19 peace plan. The council members include Liberia's three primary militia leaders—Charles Taylor, George E. Boley, and Alhaji Kromah—as well as three civilians. . . . Libyan head of state Colonel Muammer Gadhafi announces his intention to expel thousands of Palestinians in protest of efforts by the PLO to achieve peace with Israel.	An Ontario Court finds Paul Bernardo, 31, guilty of the kidnapping, rape, torture, and first-degree murder of two teenaged girls in 1991 and 1992. The sensational trial received much attention, partially because of Bernardo's ex-wife, Karla Homolka, 25, who described helping Bernardo kidnap and sexually abuse Leslie Mahaffy, 14, and Kristen French, 15. Homolka, as a result of a 1993 plea bargain, is serving a 12-year sentence, a bargain struck before the discovery of videotapes that show Homolka taking part in the torture of the victims.	In Lhasa, the capital of Tibet, China holds ceremonies marking the 30th anniversary of its formal rule over Tibet, vowing to quash the separatist movement led by the Dalai Lama, the exiled Buddhist spiritual leader. Nine women exiles from Tibet stage a demonstration protesting repressive Chinese rule in Tibet, wearing silk scarves as symbolic gags.

A	B	C	D	E
Includes developments that affect more than one world region, international organizations, and important meetings of major world leaders.	*Includes all domestic and regional developments in Europe, including the Soviet Union, Turkey, Cyprus, and Malta.*	*Includes all domestic and regional developments in Africa and the Middle East, including Iraq and Iran and excluding Cyprus, Turkey, and Afghanistan.*	*Includes all domestic and regional developments in Latin America, the Caribbean, and Canada.*	*Includes all domestic and regional developments in Asia and Pacific nations, extending from Afghanistan through all the Pacific Islands, except Hawaii.*

U.S. Politics & Social Issues	U.S. Foreign Policy & Defense	U.S. Economy & Environment	Science, Technology, & Nature	Culture, Leisure, & Lifestyle	
			The SEC announces that it will continue to offer its database of corporate information free on the Internet global computer network after current funding for project expires Sept. 30.		Aug. 27
		Chemical Banking Corp. and Chase Manhattan Corp. announce the largest bank merger in U.S. history, involving a stock swap worth about $10 billion. The deal will create the largest bank in the U.S., which is to be known as Chase Manhattan.		Fashion designer Calvin Klein withdraws a controversial advertising campaign, which critics argued resembled auditions for pornographic films. . . . At the top of the bestseller list is *From Potter's Field* by Patricia Cornwell.	Aug. 28
The Consortium on Productivity in the Schools states that U.S. public schools do not use effectively the $285 billion received yearly from the federal government. One of its recommendations is to give schools and teachers more autonomy. . . . The Census Bureau finds that the proportion of people in the U.S. who were born in foreign countries increased to 8.7% in 1994, up from 7.9% four years earlier. The 1994 figure is the highest foreign-born percentage since 1940.					Aug. 29
A severed leg and foot are discovered in the rubble of the federal building in Oklahoma City that was bombed in April. Officials determine that the decomposed leg is not that of any of the 167 known blast victims, thus bringing the death toll to 168, not including a nurse who died of a head injury incurred during the rescue effort.				Sterling Morrison, 53, rock guitarist and cofounder of the New York City–based band the Velvet Underground, dies in Poughkeepsie, New York, of non-Hodgkin's lymphoma.	Aug. 30
	In Washington, D.C., federal district judge Royce C. Lamberth rules that a provision of a 1848 law allowing U.S. citizens to be extradited to foreign countries to face prosecution is unconstitutional. . . . Federal prosecutors present a check for more than $500,000 to the Justice Department's Crime Victims Fund. The money comes from assets confiscated from convicted spy Aldrich Hazen Ames after his February 1994 arrest.		Reports indicate that a combination of two widely available prescription drugs can be used to safely and effectively induce abortions in the early stages of pregnancy. Researchers caution doctors not to perform the procedure until further research has been done. . . . A unit of the NIH advises that high doses of the short-acting form of the heart drug nifedipine should be used "with great caution, if at all."		Aug. 31
Rep. Mel Reynolds (D, Ill.) announces his resignation from the House, prompted by his Aug. 22 conviction of charges of sexual assault, soliciting child pornography, and obstructing justice stemming from his sexual relationship with an underage campaign worker.	U.S. immigration judge John Gossart rules in Baltimore, Maryland, that Emmanuel Constant, a former Haitian paramilitary leader, be deported to Haiti to face criminal charges. Constant is wanted in Haiti on charges of rape, torture, and murder. . . . Statistics suggest that the number of applicants for naturalization rose 225% in the previous five years. . . . The Army Criminal Investigation Command reveals that no commanders or instructors involved in the February deaths of four U.S. Army Ranger trainees are guilty of criminal wrongdoing.	SEC rules that make it mandatory for mutual-fund companies to disclose the average commission rate they pay brokerage firms for buying and selling stocks and bonds go into effect. . . . Data shows that the purchasing managers' index dropped to 46.9% in August, a decline from the revised July rate of 50.5%. A measure above 50% indicates an expanding manufacturing sector, and 44.5% or higher indicates overall economic expansion.		The Rock and Roll Hall of Fame and Museum in Cleveland, Ohio, is inaugurated in a ribbon-cutting ceremony attended by 50,000 people.	Sept. 1
F	G	H	I	J	
Includes elections, federal-state relations, civil rights and liberties, crime, the judiciary, education, health care, poverty, urban affairs, and population.	*Includes formation and debate of U.S. foreign and defense policies, veterans' affairs, and defense spending. (Relations with specific foreign countries are usually found under the region concerned.)*	*Includes business, labor, agriculture, taxation, transportation, consumer affairs, monetary and fiscal policy, natural resources, and pollution.*	*Includes worldwide scientific, medical, and technological developments; natural phenomena; U.S. weather; natural disasters; and accidents.*	*Includes the arts, religion, scholarship, communications media, sports, entertainments, fashions, fads, and social life.*	

	World Affairs	Europe	Africa & the Middle East	The Americas	Asia & the Pacific
Sept. 2		Vaclav Neumann, 74, chief conductor of the Czech Philharmonic Orchestra, 1968–90, dies in Vienna, Austria, of unreported causes.		A British Royal Air Force airplane nose-dives into Lake Ontario near Toronto, Canada, crashing within sight of hundreds of spectators at an aircraft exhibition. The crash kills all seven of the plane's British crewmen.... The U.S. officially turns over two bases, Fort Davis and Fort Espinar, to Panama, as provided for in the 1977 Panama Canal Treaties. ... A boat carrying 47 Cuban exiles on their way to a protest at the edge of Cuban territorial waters sinks. One person dies.	The Hezb-e-Islami forces of renegade Gen. Abdul Rashid Doestam reportedly launch air attacks on the Shindand air base in Afghanistan.... Data shows that Sydney, the capital of New South Wales, has set a city record of 48 days without rain.
Sept. 3	Protests against France's plans for nuclear testing in the South Pacific continue as French commandos board a third protest ship, the *Kidu* sailboat. An unidentified 33-year-old Spaniard hijacks a French airplane en route to Paris in an apparent protest against the testing. The hijacker surrenders in Geneva, Switzerland, freeing all 298 people aboard the plane.	UN peacekeeping troops open a road through Sarajevo's airport that links Sarajevo to the Bosnian government-controlled road across nearby Mount Igman. The move is considered significant because UN troops previously have not taken any such action without permission from Bosnian Serbs. A food convoy enters the city.... In France, a detonator on a malfunctioning bomb explodes in a Paris market, causing minor injuries to four people.		In the northwestern region of Uraba, Colombia violence continues, and leftist guerrillas are suspected of the murders of 10 soldiers.... In the village of Tepoztlán, 30 miles (50 km) south of Mexico City, Mexico's capital, provincial authorities send riot police to activists demonstrating against the planned construction of a golf course and computer center. The protesters take six state government officials hostage and barricade the town.	The Hezb-e-Islami forces of renegade general Abdul Rashid Doestam launch air attacks on Herat in Afghanistan.... Reports confirm that the Indian publisher of the Salman Rushdie's latest novel, which presents a highly critical parody of Bal Thackeray, leader of Shiv Sena, an extreme nationalist and anti-Muslim political party, has decided not to release the book in India's Maharashtra state. Rushdie has been living under police protection since his 1989 novel *The Satanic Verses* prompted Islamic fundamentalists to order his execution.
Sept. 4	The UN Fourth World Conference on Women convenes in Beijing, China's capital, and is attended by official delegations from 185 countries.... In the South Pacific, four protestors in two inflatable rafts are detained by French commandos. The four protesters, all members of Greenpeace, carry a protest letter addressed to Vice Admiral Philippe Euverte, the head of French naval forces in the South Pacific.	Bosnian Serbs fail to meet a NATO deadline to remove heavy artillery that surrounded the besieged capital of Sarajevo.... General Edmond Jouhaud, 90, French military leader who was involved in a 1961 attempted coup against Pres. Charles de Gaulle over the issue of Algerian independence, dies in Royan, France, of unreported causes.	The city of Jerusalem, under the leadership of right-wing mayor Ehud Olmert, opens a 15-month-long celebration of the 3,000th anniversary of the conquest of Jerusalem by King David, the second monarch of the ancient kingdom of Israel. Palestinian Arabs and Western European governments boycott the event, maintaining that its symbolism is skewed in favor of Jewish interests.	Members of the 11,000-member Union of Agrarian Workers, striking since Aug. 30 in an attempt to pressure the government to provide better security in the violent Uraba region in Colombia, return to their jobs.... Gunfire is exchanged between Canadian police and the Shushwap Traditionalists, a renegade native group occupying a campsite in British Columbia. Separately, Chippewa protestors occupy Ipperwash Park, contending it is a sacred Indian burial ground.	Separatist fighters in India's disputed Jammu and Kashmir state detonate a car bomb that kills at least 13 people and wounds 25 others in Srinagar, the state capital. Members of the guerrilla group Hizbul Mujaheddin, or Fighters of the Party of God, claim responsibility.... Afghanistan government troops reportedly initiate a counteroffensive in an effort to retake the Shindand base, which was the government's second-largest air base.
Sept. 5	French defense minister Charles Millon announces that France has detonated a nuclear device in the first of a series of planned tests. The underground explosion was conducted at the Mururoa Atoll in the South Pacific, where an international flotilla of ships has gathered to protest France's decision to resume nuclear testing.	NATO warplanes resume their bombing raids against Bosnian Serb military positions near Sarajevo, the capital of Bosnia-Herzegovina.		The Royal Canadian Mounted Police move four armored vehicles to a remote area near Gustafsen Lake, about 280 miles (450 km) northeast of Vancouver, British Columbia, to protect its lines and try to force an end to a confrontation between police and the Shushwap Traditionalists.	The opposition Taliban militia captures Herat, a strategic city in western Afghanistan, as government troops flee the largely student militia without firing a shot. The Taliban militia establishes a new local government in Herat. Pres. Rabbani accuses Pakistan of backing Taliban rebels fighting government forces in the western regions of Afghanistan.
Sept. 6	In response to the Sept. 5 announcement, of France's detonation of a nuclear device, international antinuclear protests are held in several countries, and activists in The Hague, the Netherlands, attempt to block the entrance to the French embassy. Riots break out during a protest at the main terminal of the international airport in Papeete, the capital of Tahiti. Austrian police are forced to use tear gas to prevent demonstrators from scaling the walls of the French embassy in Vienna. New Zealand and Chile recall their ambassadors to France for consultation.	Ten people are arrested in the town of Torquay, in southern England, in connection with an international fraud ring, which allegedly bilked investors of an estimated £100 million ($156 million) largely through the sale of bogus certificates of credit.... The London Stock Exchange announces that it will unilaterally terminate a contract with a stock-brokerage firm and computer company that would have allowed customers to buy and sell shares on the Internet global computer network.	In the Libyan city of Benghazi, violence breaks out between Muslim militants and Libyan security forces. The clashes stem from Libyan security forces' attempts to gather foreign workers for deportation.	Police in Ontario, Canada, shoot and kill Anthony George, a member of the Chippewa Indian nation during a standoff started Sept. 4 at the Ipperwash Provincial Park near the border with the U.S. state of Michigan. The fatal shooting is thought to be the first of an Indian by Canadian authorities in about 100 years. ... Protesters who took hostages Sept. 3 in the village of Tepoztlán, 30 miles (50 km) south of Mexico City, agree to release the hostages in exchange for the resignation of Mayor Morales, who steps down. ... Haitian officials allege that the smugglers who landed in the Bahamas on Aug. 20 threw at least 100 migrants overboard when the vessel began to take on water.... Hurricane Luis, a 700-mile-wide storm, wreaks havoc on eastern Caribbean islands. Hardest hit are Antigua and Barbuda, where some 75% of buildings are damaged and initial damage estimates are placed at $300 million.	In Sri Lanka, Liberation Tigers of Tamil Eelam who hijacked a ferry near Mullaittivu on Aug. 29 release most of the ferry passengers to Red Cross officials.... Although reports confirm that Pakistan has denied any involvement in the fighting in Afghanistan, several thousand Afghan protesters, armed with clubs and steel rods, descend upon Pakistan's embassy in Kabul. The demonstrators break into the embassy and set fire to the building. One embassy worker and one protester are killed, and more than 20 other embassy employees are injured.

A	B	C	D	E
Includes developments that affect more than one world region, international organizations, and important meetings of major world leaders.	*Includes all domestic and regional developments in Europe, including the Soviet Union, Turkey, Cyprus, and Malta.*	*Includes all domestic and regional developments in Africa and the Middle East, including Iraq and Iran and excluding Cyprus, Turkey, and Afghanistan.*	*Includes all domestic and regional developments in Latin America, the Caribbean, and Canada.*	*Includes all domestic and regional developments in Asia and Pacific nations, extending from Afghanistan through all the Pacific Islands, except Hawaii.*

U.S. Politics & Social Issues	U.S. Foreign Policy & Defense	U.S. Economy & Environment	Science, Technology, & Nature	Culture, Leisure, & Lifestyle	
		A strike against the *Detroit Free Press* and the *Detroit News* takes a violent turn as protestors clash with police.		At the Rock and Roll Hall of Fame, 57,000 people attend a seven-hour concert. . . . Infinity Broadcasting Corp., the company that employs Howard Stern, agrees to pay $1.715 million to settle charges brought by the FCC in the largest settlement ever involving allegations of indecent broadcasts.	**Sept. 2**
					Sept. 3
William Moses Kunstler, 76, radical lawyer best known for his defense of political activists and high-profile defendants during the 1960s, such as Rev. Martin Luther King Jr., dies in New York City of cardiac arrest.		In a speech in Pleasanton, California, Pres. Clinton announces that the federal government will award $3.4 million to a consortium to help it convert the defunct Alameda Naval Air Station into an electric car plant. . . . Violence during the strikes against the *Detroit Free Press* and the *Detroit News* reportedly draws police in riot gear to use tear gas to disperse the strikers trying to block trucks from delivering newspapers. Several strikers are injured, and more than 30 are arrested.			**Sept. 4**
Reports confirm that one school each in Wichita, Kansas; Boston, Massachusetts; and Mount Clemens, Michigan, have adopted Whittle Communications L.P.'s Edison Project, a new program guided by the philosophy that public schools will be more effective if they were privately run. The U.S. George Washington Elementary School in Sherman, Texas, is the fourth school in the project and opened Aug. 1.	The Senate passes, 62-35, a $242.7 billion fiscal 1996 appropriations bill for the Defense Department. . . . The Dalai Lama of Tibet begins a tour of several U.S. cities.	A GAO study finds that 80% of the people who live within 1 mile (1.6 km) of an urban waste site in the U.S. are white. This study compares to a widely reported 1987 survey conducted by the United Church of Christ which asserted that minorities are more likely than whites to live near dump sites.	A task force appointed by Pres. Clinton recommends that information transmitted over computer networks be subject to copyright laws.	Reports confirm that Swedish film director Ingmar Bergman has won the second annual Dorothy and Lillian Gish Prize.	**Sept. 5**
The Senate Select Committee on Ethics votes, 6-0, to recommend the expulsion of Sen. Bob Packwood, (R, Oreg.), citing its conclusions that Packwood engaged in sexual misconduct, influence peddling, and obstruction of the committee's investigation of his conduct. Under Senate rules, expulsion is the most severe punishment that the panel can recommend. No senators have been expelled since the Civil War. . . . The Senate Judiciary subcommittee on terrorism, technology, and government information opens hearings into a 1992 standoff between federal agents and white separatist Randall Weaver that took place at Weaver's cabin in Idaho's remote Ruby Ridge area.	The Senate passes, 64-34, a $265.3 billion defense-authorization bill, which sets policy and specifies the programs that the military will develop.	Interior Secretary Bruce Babbitt reluctantly signs over the title to 110 acres of federal land in Clark County, Idaho, to a Danish mining company. In accordance with the 1872 Mining Act, the land, estimated to hold more than $1 billion worth of minerals, was sold to Faxe Kalk Inc. for $275. At a news conference in Washington, D.C., Babbitt calls the failure of the Congress to revise the law a "flagrant abuse of the public trust.". . . The House passes, 305-101, a $2.2 billion fiscal 1996 appropriations bill for the legislative branch.		Buster Mathis, 51, heavyweight boxer who defeated Joe Frazier in the final heavyweight bout of the 1964 U.S. Olympic trials but was prevented from competing in the games due to an injury, dies in Grand Rapids, Michigan, of heart failure. . . . The FCC decides to lift immediately all rules that prevented national TV networks from competing in the syndicated TV market. . . . Shortstop Cal Ripken Jr. plays in his 2,131st consecutive game, breaking one of MLB's most celebrated records. Pres. Clinton, Vice Pres. Al Gore, Joe DiMaggio, and a capacity crowd of 46,272 attend the game in Camden Yards, Maryland.	**Sept. 6**

F	G	H	I	J
Includes elections, federal-state relations, civil rights and liberties, crime, the judiciary, education, health care, poverty, urban affairs, and population.	*Includes formation and debate of U.S. foreign and defense policies, veterans' affairs, and defense spending. (Relations with specific foreign countries are usually found under the region concerned.)*	*Includes business, labor, agriculture, taxation, transportation, consumer affairs, monetary and fiscal policy, natural resources, and pollution.*	*Includes worldwide scientific, medical, and technological developments; natural phenomena; U.S. weather; natural disasters; and accidents.*	*Includes the arts, religion, scholarship, communications media, sports, entertainments, fashions, fads, and social life.*

	World Affairs	Europe	Africa & the Middle East	The Americas	Asia & the Pacific
Sept. 7	French Foreign Legionnaires are sent to Tahiti, from the Mururoa Atoll, to quell riots that started Sept. 6 in apparent protest of France's nuclear tests.	A bomb 20 yards (18 m) from the entrance of the Jewish School of Lyons explodes only minutes before 700 children are scheduled to leave the building. The blast injures 14 people. The French government launches several emergency security measures. . . . The Supreme Court, Spain's highest court, announces that Premier Felipe Gonzalez will not be subpoenaed in connection with antiterrorist death squads that operated in the 1980s. . . . British author Salman Rushdie makes his first preannounced public appearance since 1989 when he attends a literary panel discussion in London. The meeting is marked by high security.	In the northeastern city of Benghazi, at least 30 people reportedly are killed in clashes between Muslim militants and Libyan security forces that started Sept. 6.		A package bomb explodes in the BBC's office in Srinagar, India. Three journalists are wounded in the blast.
Sept. 8	The UN Security Council, in its review of Iraqi compliance with UN resolutions, extends trade sanctions against Iraq for at least 60 days. . . . The riots that started Sept. 6 in Tahiti come to an end when Oscar Temaru, leader of an independence movement in Tahiti, tells protesters to go home. The French government insists the riots were a protest against French rule in Tahiti organized by Temaru's independence group. In the riots, the protesters set fire to cars, stores and the main terminal of the airport. More than 20 people were injured and 50 arrested.	The combatants in the conflicts in the former Yugoslavia agree to a pact aimed at ending the fighting in Bosnia-Herzegovina. The peace plan will divide Bosnia into two parts, one controlled by a Muslim-Croat federation and the other controlled by Serbs. The agreement is endorsed by the Muslim-dominated Bosnian government; Croatia; and Yugoslavia, acting on behalf of the Bosnian Serbs. NATO warplanes continue to bomb Bosnian Serb targets because the Bosnian Serb military has not removed any of the weapons from the zone.	Five masked assailants posing as Israeli army soldiers shoot dead one 25-year-old Palestinian man and terrorize others in the village of Halhoul, located just north of Hebron. The militant anti-Arab group Eyal, an offshoot of the late Meir Kahane's Kach movement, claims responsibility for the attacks. Separately, Israeli and Palestinian negotiators acknowledge that talks for expanding limited Arab self-rule to wide areas of the West Bank have reached an impasse over Jewish settlers in the southern West Bank city of Hebron.	The Mexican federal government orders developers to temporarily suspend the planned construction of a golf course and computer center on the western border of the village of Tepoztlán, 30 miles (50 km) south of Mexico City, Mexico's capital. The government's action follows angry and often violent protests by residents of Tepoztlán that led to the resignation of the town's mayor Sept. 6.	
Sept. 9		French police arrest 31 suspected Muslim militants in the Lyons area.		Some 30 gunmen open fire on a crowd at an Independence Day party in the Turano Hill shantytown in Rio de Janeiro, Brazil, killing at least 10 people.	
Sept. 10		The U.S. warship USS *Normandy*, under NATO command, fires 13 self-propelled Tomahawk cruise missiles at Serb targets near Banja Luka to compel the Bosnian Serb military to remove its weapons from Sarajevo, Bosnia-Herzegovina.	Jewish settlers in Hebron, with the intention of taking down a Palestinian flag displayed at a Palestinian girls school, reportedly beat the school's headmistress and also injure four students during a student demonstration.		The Nepalese parliament ousts the ruling Communist Party of Nepal (UML), in a no-confidence vote.
Sept. 11	UN secretary general Boutros Boutros-Ghali contends that UN finances are diminishing in part because members pay their dues late or not at all, and that the safety of UN peacekeeping personnel worldwide is in jeopardy.	The Bosnian government army, the Croatian army, and Bosnian Croat forces launch a new offensive in western Bosnia. . . . French police in Paris, Lyons, and Grenoble arrest 40 alleged Muslim fundamentalists, reportedly in connection with recent bombings. . . . Repola Oy and Kymmene Corp. announce that they will merge their holdings to create the largest forest pulp and paper company in Europe. The merged group, UPM-Kymmene Corp., based in Helsinki, Finland, will be the third-largest forestry company in the world.	After a Rwandan army lieutenant is killed in an ambush, the Rwandan army sweeps through villages in northwestern Rwanda, near the border with Zaire. More than 100 men, women, and children are killed in the raids, which take place about 20 miles (32 km) east of the village of Gisenyi.		King Birendra appoints Nepal Congress leader Sher Bahadur Deuba, 49, to succeed Man Mohan Adhikary as prime minister.
Sept. 12	The World Meteorological Organization, the UN's weather agency, reports that the hole in the Earth's ozone layer that appears seasonally over Antarctica is expanding at a record rate and is twice as large as it was in September 1994.	The Swiss Bankers' Association, which represents all banks in Switzerland, announces that it has uncovered 40.9 million Swiss francs ($34 million) in 893 dormant accounts that belonged to victims of the Nazi Holocaust. . . . A Belarusian military helicopter shoots down a hydrogen balloon flying over Belarus during an international balloon race, killing the two Americans aboard, Alan Fraenckel, 55, and John Stuart-Jervis, 68. The two other U.S. teams, each of which comprises two crew members, are taken into custody.	Hundreds of Palestinians are stranded at the border with Egypt after being expelled from Libya.	A bomb explodes in a bar in Montreal, Canada, injuring nine people, in an incident allegedly linked to a motorcycle-gang war.	The Philippine Supreme Court votes to uphold former first lady Imelda Marcos's victory in congressional elections held in May.

A	B	C	D	E
Includes developments that affect more than one world region, international organizations, and important meetings of major world leaders.	*Includes all domestic and regional developments in Europe, including the Soviet Union, Turkey, Cyprus, and Malta.*	*Includes all domestic and regional developments in Africa and the Middle East, including Iraq and Iran and excluding Cyprus, Turkey, and Afghanistan.*	*Includes all domestic and regional developments in Latin America, the Caribbean, and Canada.*	*Includes all domestic and regional developments in Asia and Pacific nations, extending from Afghanistan through all the Pacific Islands, except Hawaii.*

U.S. Politics & Social Issues	U.S. Foreign Policy & Defense	U.S. Economy & Environment	Science, Technology, & Nature	Culture, Leisure, & Lifestyle	
Sen. Bob Packwood (R, Oreg.) announces his resignation from the Senate after the Sept. 6 Senate vote to expel him. Packwood has served in the Senate since 1969. The Senate Select Committee on Ethics releases thousands of pages of information it uncovered during the investigation. . . . In New York City the Second Circuit Court of Appeals overturns a 1994 ruling that found that Vassar College in Poughkeepsie, New York, had discriminated against biology professor Cynthia J. Fisher when it denied her tenure in 1985.	The House passes, 294-125, a $244 billion fiscal 1996 appropriations bill for the Defense Department.	Some 5,000 truck drivers affiliated with the International Brotherhood of Teamsters union go on strike against Ryder System Inc., after months of contract negotiations.	Research shows that people who take four to six aspirin weekly for 20 years significantly reduce their risk of developing colon and rectal cancer. . . . Data suggest that wider use of a blood-thinning drug, warfarin, may prevent 40,000 strokes each year in the U.S.	The first issue of *George*, a political magazine founded by John F. Kennedy Jr. and Michael J. Berman, is publicly unveiled in a press conference in New York City.	**Sept. 7**
Sen. Bob Packwood (R, Oreg.) announces that his resignation from the Senate will take effect Oct. 1, and that he will immediately relinquish his position as chair of the Senate Finance Committee. . . . In Portland, Oregon, federal judge James Redden sentences Rachelle (Shelley) Shannon—who pled guilty in June to setting fires at and vandalizing six abortion clinics in California, Nevada, and Oregon in 1992 and 1993—to 20 years in prison. She is currently serving a 10-year state prison term for the 1993 attempted murder of a Wichita, Kansas, abortion doctor.	Officials indict six Thai and Laotian nationals on charges of harboring and employing illegal immigrants at the three California factories that were raided by the Department of Labor and the INS on Aug. 23.		The U.S. space shuttle *Endeavour* blasts off from Kennedy Space Center in Cape Canaveral, Florida, to conduct a mission to deploy and retrieve two satellites.	Candidates for the Republican presidential nomination address members of the Christian Coalition, a group of politically active conservative Christians, during its annual two-day convention.	**Sept. 8**
Jamie Lloyd Whitten, 85, former Democratic congressman from Mississippi who served for 53 years in the House, the longest tenure ever, dies in Oxford, Mississippi, after suffering from heart problems and kidney failure.				Steffi Graf of Germany wins the women's tennis title at the U.S. Open. . . . Figure skater Nancy Kerrigan, 25, weds her agent, Jerry Solomon, 41, in Boston, Massachusetts. . . . Reports state that the Interfaith Alliance has blasted the Christian Coalition for its "extreme agenda and its efforts to gain control of the Republican Party."	**Sept. 9**
				Pete Sampras wins the men's tennis title at the U.S. Open. . . . At the Emmys, *NYPD Blue* wins for Best Drama Series, and *Frasier* for Comedy Series. The show *E.R.* wins a total of eight awards for its first season, tying a record set in 1981 by the drama *Hill Street Blues*.	**Sept. 10**
In Oswego, New York, Judge Vincent Sgueglia sentences Waneta Hoyt, who was convicted in April of fatally smothering five of her infant children between 1965 and 1971, to 75 years to life in prison. . . . Charles J(ohnston) Hitch, 85, former president of the University of California, 1967–75, and official in the administrations of Presidents John Kennedy and Lyndon Johnson, dies in San Leandro, California, after suffering from Alzheimer's disease.		Due to planned cuts in the appropriations bill for the Department of the Interior which will lessen funds for the Bureau of Indian Affairs (BIA), tribal leaders begin lobbying Congress and the White House and hold a protest vigil on the Mall in Washington, D.C.		*The Weekly Standard*, a weekly political magazine whose editor and publisher is Republican strategist William Kristol, premieres. The magazine was founded by Kristol, former *New Republic* editor Fred Barnes, and former White House speech writer John Podhoretz.	**Sept. 11**
The Senate Finance Committee formally asks Sen. William Roth (R, Del.) to take over as chair, succeeding Sen. Bob Packwood (R, Oreg.). Sen. Ted Stevens (R, Ark.) takes over Roth's chairmanship of the Governmental Affairs Committee.		The U.S. Postal Service announces that it will end fiscal 1995 with a budget surplus of $1.8 billion.		Jeremy Brett (born Peter Jeremy Huggins), 59, British actor best known for his portrayal of Sherlock Holmes, dies in London of heart failure. . . . In Denver, Colorado, Judge John Kane in orders the Church of Scientology to return computer disks it seized from Lawrence Wollersheim and Robert Penny, who had criticized the church on an on-line computer bulletin board.	**Sept. 12**

F	G	H	I	J
Includes elections, federal-state relations, civil rights and liberties, crime, the judiciary, education, health care, poverty, urban affairs, and population.	*Includes formation and debate of U.S. foreign and defense policies, veterans' affairs, and defense spending. (Relations with specific foreign countries are usually found under the region concerned.)*	*Includes business, labor, agriculture, taxation, transportation, consumer affairs, monetary and fiscal policy, natural resources, and pollution.*	*Includes worldwide scientific, medical, and technological developments; natural phenomena; U.S. weather; natural disasters; and accidents.*	*Includes the arts, religion, scholarship, communications media, sports, entertainments, fashions, fads, and social life.*

	World Affairs	Europe	Africa & the Middle East	The Americas	Asia & the Pacific
Sept. 13	Greece announces that it will formally recognize the former Yugoslav republic of Macedonia and end a 19-month-long trade embargo against that Slavic country.	The U.S. embassy in central Moscow, Russia, is hit by a rocket-propelled grenade. The embassy is evacuated, but no injuries are reported.... Two of the U.S. balloonists taken into custody by Belarus on Sept. 12 are released.	A powerful blast damages an apartment building in Gaza City, killing Ibrahim Naffar, who is reportedly a member of the military wing of Hamas.	Hurricane Marilyn strikes the Caribbean island of Barbados.	A military transport plane crashes off the western coast of Sri Lanka, killing all 80 military personnel aboard.... The Philippine government signs an agreement under which people who suffered human-rights abuses during the tenure of Pres. Ferdinand Marcos, which ended in 1986, will receive $100 million.
Sept. 14	Ukraine officially joins the Partnership for Peace initiative, a program to involve countries of Eastern Europe and the former Soviet Union in NATO without giving them full membership.	Bosnian Serb general Ratko Mladic agrees to withdraw the Bosnian Serbs' heavy weapons from within a 12.5-mile (20 km) exclusion zone around Sarajevo within six days. In response, NATO suspends its air strikes.... In Britain, Nuclear Electric PLC, a state-owned power company, is given a record fine of £250,000 ($388,750) for a 1993 incident.... Belarus apologizes for the Sept. 12 deaths of two U.S. balloonist, but argues that their balloon flew into close proximity to military bases.	Pope John Paul II begins a tour of Africa.	Hurricane Ismael, a Pacific Ocean storm, strikes the state of Sinaloa in northwestern Mexico, killing more than 100 people.	
Sept. 15	The United Nations Fourth World Conference on Women closes, and after contentious debate, delegates representing more than 180 nations endorse by consensus a nonbinding "Platform for Action" intended to serve as a blueprint for promoting women's rights worldwide into the next century.... The Northwest Atlantic Fisheries Organization ratifies an agreement that settles a six-month dispute between Canada and the EU over fishing in international waters.	Belarus releases the last U.S. balloon team it took into custody Sept. 12.... Sarajevo's airport reopens to humanitarian aid flights.		Hurricane Marilyn hits the U.S. Virgin Islands with sustained winds of 100 miles per hour, destroying about a third of the homes on the island of St. Thomas.	Michio Watanabe, 72, former foreign minister of Japan who was elected to the Japanese Diet in 1963 and remained in office until his death, dies in Tokyo of heart failure.
Sept. 16		Bosnian Serbs begin removing their heavy weapons from around Sarajevo, the capital of Bosnia-Herzegovina, in compliance with a NATO ultimatum.	An Islamic court in the United Arab Emirates sentences a Filipina maid, Sarah Balabagan, 16, to death for the 1994 murder of her employer, Almas Al-Baloushi. Balabagan's death sentence draws strong protests from Filipinos, who, since the March hanging of a Filipina maid in Singapore, have been pressing the Philippine government to take measures to ensure the safety of maids working abroad.	In the wake of Hurricane Marilyn, Pres. Clinton declares the U.S. Virgin Islands a disaster area. In all, the storm killed at least eight people.	
Sept. 17		Parties opposing Sweden's membership in the European Union make significant advances in the country's first national vote for the European Parliament, the legislative branch of the EU.... Hundreds of people gather outside the U.S. embassy in Moscow to protest the NATO air raids against Serbs in Bosnia-Herzegovina.	An independent candidate for upcoming elections, Abdelmajid Benhadid, 50, is shot to death in Boudouaou, east of Algiers, the capital of Algeria.	A tense standoff between armed Native American protesters and the Royal Canadian Mounted Police in the Gustafsen Lake area of British Columbia ends without violence after medicine man John Stevens meets with the rebel group. In a separate instance, native protesters occupying the Ipperwash Provincial Park in southern Ontario reach an agreement with provincial police to allow a civilian special investigation unit to look into the fatal shooting of Anthony George by police on Sept. 6.	In legislative elections, Hong Kong voters deal a blow to China-backed candidates. Shortly after polls open, the New China News Agency reiterates the Chinese government's vow to dissolve the new legislature in 1997 and to replace it with a provisional body with deputies selected by China.
Sept. 18	The Intergovernmental Panel on Climate Change, a United Nations-sponsored organization of 2,500 scientists responsible for advising signatories to a 1992 environmental pact, assert that a current trend in the warming of the Earth's atmosphere is likely to cause significant economic, social, and environmental upheavals by the end of the 21st century, if emissions of greenhouse gases are not reduced.	Georgian head of state Eduard Shevardnadze announces a plan to introduce a new Georgian currency, the lari, which will be pegged to the U.S. dollar, to replace Georgia's provisional currency, the coupon, by Oct. 2.... The German government agrees to pay 11 U.S. survivors of Nazi concentration camps $2.1 million in reparations. The agreement comes after a 41-year legal battle by one of the survivors, Hugo Princz.			Final tallies show that Hong Kong's Democratic Party, led by lawyer Martin Lee, took 19 of the 25 seats its members had contested, making it the largest single party in the legislature.

A	B	C	D	E
Includes developments that affect more than one world region, international organizations, and important meetings of major world leaders.	*Includes all domestic and regional developments in Europe, including the Soviet Union, Turkey, Cyprus, and Malta.*	*Includes all domestic and regional developments in Africa and the Middle East, including Iraq and Iran and excluding Cyprus, Turkey, and Afghanistan.*	*Includes all domestic and regional developments in Latin America, the Caribbean, and Canada.*	*Includes all domestic and regional developments in Asia and Pacific nations, extending from Afghanistan through all the Pacific Islands, except Hawaii.*

U.S. Politics & Social Issues	U.S. Foreign Policy & Defense	U.S. Economy & Environment	Science, Technology, & Nature	Culture, Leisure, & Lifestyle	
Jimmie Wayne Jeffers, 49, convicted of killing his former girlfriend in 1976 in a Tucson, Arizona, motel room, is executed by lethal injection in Florence, Arizona. Jeffers is only the fourth inmate in Arizona and the 296th in the U.S. to be put to death since 1976.		In Eugene, Oregon, U.S. District Court judge Michael Hogan rules that a budget resolution passed by Congress in July mandates the release of forests that the administration has since set aside for the protection of wildlife and water quality.			Sept. 13
House Republican leaders unveil details of their proposed legislation to overhaul Medicare, the federal health-insurance program for the elderly, and it ignites rancorous partisan disagreement.	Government lawyers file a notice in U.S. District Court in Washington, D.C., stating that the government will resume extraditing accused criminals to foreign countries, pending the outcome of an appeal of Judge Royce Lamberth's ruling in August.	The Dow closes at a record high of 4801.80. It is the third consecutive day that the Dow reaches a record high at closing.	Research suggests that the use of the anti-AIDS drug AZT (zidovudine) alone is less effective than another drug, didanosine (ddI), and less effective than AZT used in combination with either ddI or zalcitabine (ddC). . . . A study finds that women who are mildly to moderately overweight, or who experience mild to moderate weight gain in middle age, increase their risk of premature death. A separate study finds that nonsmoking men who are 20–40 pounds over their optimal weight increase their mortality rates.		Sept. 14
In Nassau County, New York, Judge Jack Mackston sentences Joseph Buttafuoco, who is on probation for the statutory rape of teenager Amy Fisher, to a minimum of 67 days in jail for violating his probation when he solicited a Los Angeles police officer posing as a prostitute in May.	U.S. District Court judge Royce C. Lamberth, who in August struck down a law that allowed the U.S. to extradite accused criminals to other countries, widens that ruling to bar the government from sending any suspects to another country. The decision applies to both U.S. citizens wanted in foreign countries and foreign fugitives who have fled to the U.S.		Major electronics companies agree on a standard format for digital disks that will be capable of storing video, sound, and computer data.		Sept. 15
			Astronauts James S. Voss, 46, and Michael L. Gernhardt, 39, leave the space shuttle Endeavour for six hours and 46 minutes while they walk in space.		Sept. 16
					Sept. 17
A Suffolk County, New York, judge, John J. Jones Jr., sentences serial killer Joel Rifkin to 50 years in prison for the fatal strangulations of two women whom he buried in Southampton, New York. The sentence will be served after Rifkin finishes a 27-year term he received in June in a separate murder case.			The U.S. space shuttle Endeavour touches down on the airstrip at Kennedy Space Center in Cape Canaveral, Florida, after carrying out a mission during which the crew deployed and retrieved two satellites and two astronauts walked in space, in preparation for the planned construction of an internationally operated space station.	Donald Alfred Davie, 73, British poet and literary critic, dies in Exeter, England, of cancer. . . . NBA team owners end their 79-day player lockout after both sides approve a six-year, $5 billion labor contract.	Sept. 18

F	G	H	I	J
Includes elections, federal-state relations, civil rights and liberties, crime, the judiciary, education, health care, poverty, urban affairs, and population.	*Includes formation and debate of U.S. foreign and defense policies, veterans' affairs, and defense spending. (Relations with specific foreign countries are usually found under the region concerned.)*	*Includes business, labor, agriculture, taxation, transportation, consumer affairs, monetary and fiscal policy, natural resources, and pollution.*	*Includes worldwide scientific, medical, and technological developments; natural phenomena; U.S. weather; natural disasters; and accidents.*	*Includes the arts, religion, scholarship, communications media, sports, entertainments, fashions, fads, and social life.*

	World Affairs	Europe	Africa & the Middle East	The Americas	Asia & the Pacific
Sept. 19	Delegates from the 185 member nations of the United Nations convene in New York City for the opening of the 50th UN General Assembly. Among the assembly's first actions is the election of Diogo Freitas do Amaral, former deputy premier of Portugal, as president, succeding Amara Essy of the Ivory Coast.	The Bosnian government and the Bosnian Croats, under intense pressure from the Western allies, agree to halt the offensive in western and central Bosnia. . . . Reports confirm that Pres. Nursultan Nazarbayev has issued a decree that will move Kazakhstan's capital from its current location, Almaty, in the south to Akmola, in the country's northern tip. Analysts suggest the planned move is a bid by Nazarbayev to thwart separatist sentiment among Kazakhstan's ethnic Russians, who make up the majority of the population in the region around Akmola.	Jabari Rizah, 29, commandeers an airliner while en route from Teheran, Iran's capital, to the Iranian island resort of Kish in the Persian Gulf. Rizah forces the pilot of the plane to land at Israel's Ovda air force base, located about 18 miles (30 km) north of Eilat, a resort town. Rizah surrenders to Israeli authorities immediately upon landing. . . . An estimated 300,000 people attend an outdoor mass held by Pope John Paul in Nairobi, Kenya's capital.	The death toll from Hurricane Ismael, which struck the state of Sinaloa in northwestern Mexico on Sept. 14 stands at more than 90, many of whom were fishermen on ships off the coast of Sinaloa taken by surprise by the storm that arrived hours earlier than expected.	
Sept. 20		Some 160,000 Turkish workers strike to protest the government's austerity measures. The CHP, part of the ruling coalition, breaks with the government. Tansu Ciller, Turkey's first female premier, resigns. . . . A bomb explodes on a bridge, injuring one official and one guard in the convoy carrying Russian diplomats to the Chechnya talks. . . . In Makhachkala, the capital of the Russian republic of Dagestan, two gunmen take 18 hostages aboard a bus.	The government of Israel allows the Iranian jet that was hijacked Sept. 19 to return to Iran with all of its passengers and crew. Five passengers reportedly had asylum requests turned down by Israeli authorities. . . . The government of Egypt discloses that two mass graves were discovered in the Sinai Desert that contain the remains of as many as 60 Egyptian POWs and unarmed noncombatants shot to death by Israeli troops during the 1967 Arab-Israeli war.	At least 24 banana plantation workers are killed while on their way to work in the northwestern region of Uraba, Colombia, in an apparent attack by leftist guerrillas.	Japan unveils its largest-ever economic-stimulus package, worth 14.2 trillion yen ($137 billion).
Sept. 21	UN and NATO officials confirm that Serb weapons have been removed from around Sarajevo in Bosnia-Herzegovina, and that NATO has no plans to resume its bombing campaign.	In Bosnia-Herzegovina, fighting is reported around the Serb-held stronghold of Banja Luka, which the Serbs have vowed to defend if attacked. Separately, regular ground shipments of relief supplies begin to reach Sarajevo. . . . Russian commandos free the 18 hostages aboard a bus that was hijacked on Sept. 20 in Makhachkala, the capital of the southern Russian republic of Dagestan.		Three members of the Jokers motorcycle gang, affiliated with the Hells Angels, are killed in Montreal, Canada. The incident brings to 25 the number of deaths in the past year, and half are related to Montreal's ongoing motorcycle gang war. . . . The Canadian Supreme Court rules that the Tobacco Products Control Act, a 1988 law that banned tobacco advertising, violates free expression and is unconstitutional.	
Sept. 22	The UN International Court of Justice in The Hague, the Netherlands, decides not to grant New Zealand's request to place an interim ban on France's nuclear tests.		A constituent assembly elected in March 1994 in Uganda enacts a new constitution.	The Alberta government announces that in the future it will pay for abortions only in cases in which the procedure is determined to be "medically necessary." Alberta's decision makes it the first province in Canada to pledge to restrict a woman's access to abortion.	
Sept. 23	Leaders of the European Union's 15 member nations affirm that they will adhere to the current guidelines for attaining economic and monetary union (EMU) by 1999.	The Albanian parliament passes legislation to bar from office members of Albania's former communist government, which was in power until 1991. The new law also bars from public office people who collaborated with the secret police, known as the Sigurimi.		It is the first day free of tropical storms in nearly two months in the Caribbean.	Reports suggest that, earlier in September, anti-Muslim demonstrators burned the Comoro market in Dili, East Timor. Reports also state that rioting occurred in the towns of Viqueque and Maliana, after a Muslim warden at a Maliana jail allegedly insulted the Roman Catholic religion, the predominant faith among East Timorese. . . . The Mount Ruapehu volcano on New Zealand's North Island erupts.
Sept. 24		A French teenager on a rampage kills 11 people and then himself in what are described as the worst multiple murders in France since 1989. The teenager is identified by police as Eric Borel, 16.	Israel and the Palestine Liberation Organization (PLO) reach agreement on the pivotal second stage of interim Palestinian autonomy, setting terms for an Israeli military pullback from Palestinian cities and villages in the West Bank and the transfer of administrative authority to some 1 million Arabs, as a prelude to elections for a Palestinian legislative council.		

A	B	C	D	E
Includes developments that affect more than one world region, international organizations, and important meetings of major world leaders.	Includes all domestic and regional developments in Europe, including the Soviet Union, Turkey, Cyprus, and Malta.	Includes all domestic and regional developments in Africa and the Middle East, including Iraq and Iran and excluding Cyprus, Turkey, and Afghanistan.	Includes all domestic and regional developments in Latin America, the Caribbean, and Canada.	Includes all domestic and regional developments in Asia and Pacific nations, extending from Afghanistan through all the Pacific Islands, except Hawaii.

U.S. Politics & Social Issues	U.S. Foreign Policy & Defense	U.S. Economy & Environment	Science, Technology, & Nature	Culture, Leisure, & Lifestyle	
The Senate approves, 87-12, the broadest overhaul of the social welfare system in 60 years, which will save an estimated $65 billion over seven years... *The Washington Post* publishes a manifesto by the Unabomber, who is linked to bombing incidents spanning 17 years. The bomber sent the manuscript in late June, seeking its publication in return for an end to his fatal bombings.... Data shows that programs that encourage drug addicts to exchange used needles for new ones greatly reduces the spread of HIV, and does not increase drug use.		An independent panel led by former Sen. Warren Rudman (R, N.H.) recommends that the National Association of Securities Dealers (NASD) separate from the NASDAQ stock market, which is overseen by NASD, in order to restore investor confidence in NASDAQ.... Orville Redenbacher, 88, businessman who developed and sold the most popular brand of popcorn in the U.S. and is widely recognized from TV commercials, is found dead in Coronado, California, where he drowned in a bathtub following a heart attack.	Sir Rudolph Ernst Peierls, 88, German-born physicist whose discoveries contributed to the development of the first atomic bomb and who later became a leading advocate of arms control, dies in Oxford, England, after suffering from a kidney ailment.	The Academy of American Poets awards the 1995 Tanning Prize for outstanding and proven mastery in the art of poetry to James Tate. The award, which is worth $100,000, is the largest literary prize given annually in the U.S.	**Sept. 19**
Charles Albanese, 58, convicted of the 1980 fatal poisonings of his father and two other relatives, is executed by lethal injection in Joliet, Illinois. He is only the sixth convict executed in Illinois and is the 298th executed in the U.S. since 1976.	The House passes, 236-98, the final version of an appropriations bill allocating $11.2 billion for spending on military construction in fiscal 1996.	AT&T Corp., the world's largest telecommunications company, announces a plan to divide its operations into three separate companies. It will be the largest breakup of a corporation in U.S. history.... Walter A(braham) Haas Jr., 79, former president, CEO, and chairman of the board at Levi Strauss & Co., dies in San Francisco, California, of prostate cancer.	In a case that prompted worldwide concern about the vulnerability of electronic banking systems to tampering and theft, British authorities agree to extradite to the U.S. a Russian computer hacker, Vladimir Levin, accused of stealing about $400,000 from corporate accounts at New York City branches of the U.S. bank Citicorp. Levin allegedly tapped into the accounts from his office in St. Petersburg using a laptop computer.		**Sept. 20**
The U.S. Second Circuit Court of Appeals rules that the Village of Airmont, New York, violated provisions of the Fair Housing Act and the First Amendment rights of Hasidic Jews by passing zoning rules that ban rabbis from holding prayer services in their homes.... Data shows the total value of federal college loans in 1994 reached $23.1 billion, a significant increase over the 1984 figure of $7.9 billion.... Rudy George Perpich, 67, former governor of Minnesota, (D), 1977–79, 1983–91, dies near St. Paul, Minnesota, of colon cancer.	The House votes, 294-130, to tighten the U.S. economic embargo against Cuba.... The Senate votes, 91-9, to approve a $12.3 billion foreign-aid appropriations bill for fiscal 1996.... Reports confirm that the U.S. State Department has Guillermo Pallomari-Gonzalez, the alleged treasurer for the Cali (Colombia) drug cartel, in U.S. custody.		Researchers state that fossil remains recently discovered reveal a carnivorous dinosaur that appears to be larger than *Tyrannosaurus rex*. The newly discovered dinosaur is dubbed *Giganotosaurus carolinii*, after Ruben D. Carolini, an amateur fossil hunter who found the remains.... The NIH, acting on the results of a federal study, issues a clinical alert to physicians recommending that coronary bypass surgery, rather than angioplasty, be performed on diabetics with coronary artery disease.		**Sept. 21**
Phillip Lee Ingle, 34, convicted of the 1991 slayings of two elderly couples, is executed by lethal injection in Raleigh, North Carolina. Ingle becomes the 299th person put to death in the U.S. and the eighth in North Carolina since 1976.... The University of Maryland convenes a controversial conference on the links between genetics and criminal behavior.... A survey shows that 33% of ob-gyn doctors performed abortions in 1994, compared with a 42% rate in 1983.	A U.S. Air Force AWACS surveillance airplane crashes and explodes shortly after takeoff from Elmendorf Air Force Base in Alaska. The entire crew, which comprises 22 Americans and two Canadians, is killed. ... The Senate votes, 86-14, to clear an appropriations bill allocating $11.2 billion for spending on military construction in fiscal 1996.	Pres. Clinton announces a $364 million package of federal assistance for Los Angeles County, California, aimed at easing the county's fiscal crisis.... The Senate passes, 94-4, a $2.2 billion fiscal 1996 appropriations bill for the legislative branch.	Researchers at the Columbia-Presbyterian Medical Center in NYC report they have located the brain mechanism that is acted upon by nicotine.	Time Warner Inc. and Turner Broadcasting System Inc. announce they have agreed to a merger, creating the world's largest media company. ... *Showgirls*, a film about strippers, is the first big-budget, major studio film to be released with an NC-17 rating.	**Sept. 22**
The University of Maryland's controversial conference on the links between genetics and criminal behavior is interrupted for about two hours by protesters, who accuse the forum of promoting racist "pseudoscience."				Rookie pitcher Carlos Perez, 24, of the Montreal Expos baseball team is arrested on charges of rape and aggravated sodomy of an unidentified 20-year-old woman.	**Sept. 23**
	Reports confirm that the National Reconnaissance Office (NRO), a secret intelligence agency for the government, has hoarded at least $1.5 billion in unspent budget appropriations from Congress. The discovery provokes outrage from many members of Congress at a time when drastic cuts are being made in programs such as welfare, Medicare, and Medicaid, in order to reduce the deficit.			A European team of professional golfers wins the 31st Ryder Cup over the U.S.	**Sept. 24**

F	G	H	I	J
Includes elections, federal-state relations, civil rights and liberties, crime, the judiciary, education, health care, poverty, urban affairs, and population.	Includes formation and debate of U.S. foreign and defense policies, veterans' affairs, and defense spending. (Relations with specific foreign countries are usually found under the region concerned.)	Includes business, labor, agriculture, taxation, transportation, consumer affairs, monetary and fiscal policy, natural resources, and pollution.	Includes worldwide scientific, medical, and technological developments; natural phenomena; U.S. weather; natural disasters; and accidents.	Includes the arts, religion, scholarship, communications media, sports, entertainments, fashions, fads, and social life.

	World Affairs	Europe	Africa & the Middle East	The Americas	Asia & the Pacific
Sept. 25	The United Nations begins its annual period of general debate.		Two Israeli soldiers die when artillery fire hits their fortified military post in southern Lebanon. The incident raises to 14 the number of Israeli troops killed in Lebanon in the year to date.		Five East Timorese men file requests for political asylum at the British embassy in Jakarta, Indonesia's capital, claiming that their lives are threatened by Indonesian military forces occupying the island. . . . Authorities ban flights under 25,000 feet (7,620 m) over Mount Ruapehu, a volcano that started erupting Sept. 23. A military base and ski resorts are evacuated.
Sept. 26		The three rivals for control of Bosnia-Herzegovina—Bosnian Serbs, Croats, and the Muslim-dominated Bosnian government—reach an agreement to establish a collective presidency and parliament in Bosnia. Important differences remain among the belligerents, however. . . . The trial of former Italian premier Giulio Andreotti, accused of trading favors to the Mafia, opens in Palermo.			Volcanologist Colin Wilson states that the eruption of Mount Ruapehu, which began Sept. 23, is New Zealand's largest in 50 years.
Sept. 27	The European Court of Human Rights in Strasbourg, France, rules that British soldiers acted unlawfully when they killed three unarmed Provisional Irish Republican Army (IRA) guerrillas in Gibraltar in 1988. . . . Great Britain and Argentina sign an accord on the controversial issue of oil rights in waters surrounding the Falkland Islands, located 300 miles (480 km) off the southern coast of Argentina and known in Argentina as the Malvinas.	The mainly Muslim Bosnian army reportedly is still advancing in the area around Kljuc in northwestern Bosnia. Separately, France confirms that the two French fighter pilots downed over Bosnia in August, Capt. Frederic Chiffot and Lt. Jose Souvignet, are alive and being detained by the Bosnian Serb military.	The Sierra Leone government reports that Revolutionary United Front (RUF) rebels have seized four villages in the Bo region, after several days of fighting in which more than 100 civilians and seven soldiers died.	Antonio Jose Cancino, an attorney representing Pres. Ernesto Samper in a probe into government corruption, is wounded in an apparent assassination attempt in Bogota, the capital of Colombia. Two of Cancino's bodyguards are killed, and one is seriously wounded. A previously unknown group identifying itself as the Movement for Colombian Dignity claims responsibility for the attack. . . . About 5,000 protesters gather at Queen's Park in Toronto to oppose government cutbacks. Several people are injured when some of the demonstrators clash with police.	The Russian coast guard seizes two Japanese fishing trawlers in disputed waters between the Japanese island of Hokkaido and the Russian island of Sakhalin. The captain of one of the trawlers is reportedly injured when a Russian vessel fires at the fishing boats.
Sept. 28	The Sept. 24 accord reached by Israel and the Palestine Liberation Organization (PLO), which sets up the pivotal second stage of interim Palestinian autonomy, is formally signed in a ceremony at the White House in Washington, D.C. U.S. president Bill Clinton and a host of foreign dignitaries hail the accord as an historic achievement.	Despite the latest cease-fire agreement, fighting in Bosnia continues.	In Sierra Leone, government troops kill 200 RUF soldiers in an ambush. . . . Aboubakr Belkaid, a former interior minister and opponent of Muslim militants, is shot dead in Algiers, Algeria. . . . A small force led by French mercenary Bob Denard launches a coup on Comoros, an Islamic three-island nation of 450,000 people located between Mozambique and Madagascar. Rebels seize Pres. Said Mohamed Djohar in Moroni, the capital, and free Captain Combo Ayouba, who is named to head the junta. Two civilians are killed.	Cumulative results from three rounds of voting for congressional and local positions in Haiti show that the Lavalas movement, a three-party bloc endorsed by Pres. Jean-Bertrand Aristide, garnered an overwhelming majority of the votes and of the contested seats. . . . Romulo Escobar Bethancourt, 68, Panamanian political figure who led Panama's negotiations with the U.S. over the 1977 Panama Canal Treaties, dies in Panama City, Panama, of throat cancer.	The Chinese Communist Party Central Committee removes from the committee and from the Politburo Chen Xitong, a former Beijing party secretary charged with corruption. Chen is the highest-ranking official to be ousted in the current anticorruption campaign, launched by Pres. Jiang Zemin in 1993. . . . In response to the rape of a Japanese girl by U.S. servicemen, the governor of Okinawa, Masahide Ota, states that he will not renew the leases for some land now used by the American bases when they expire in March 1996.
Sept. 29		French police in a town outside Lyons, France, shoot and kill Khaled Kelkal, an Algerian Muslim wanted in connection with a recent spate of bombings throughout France.	Two mercenaries and five government soldiers are killed on Comoros as the coup that started Sept. 28 continues.		Three U.S. servicemen—Marine Pfc. Rodrico Harp, Marine Pfc. Kendrick M. Ledet and Navy Seaman Marcus D. Gill—are charged with the abduction and rape of a 12-year-old girl on Okinawa and taken into custody by Japanese police.

A	B	C	D	E
Includes developments that affect more than one world region, international organizations, and important meetings of major world leaders.	*Includes all domestic and regional developments in Europe, including the Soviet Union, Turkey, Cyprus, and Malta.*	*Includes all domestic and regional developments in Africa and the Middle East, including Iraq and Iran and excluding Cyprus, Turkey, and Afghanistan.*	*Includes all domestic and regional developments in Latin America, the Caribbean, and Canada.*	*Includes all domestic and regional developments in Asia and Pacific nations, extending from Afghanistan through all the Pacific Islands, except Hawaii.*

U.S. Politics & Social Issues	U.S. Foreign Policy & Defense	U.S. Economy & Environment	Science, Technology, & Nature	Culture, Leisure, & Lifestyle	
Texas billionaire Ross Perot announces that he intends to establish a third political party, called the Independence Party.	An administration-ordered review of the nuclear-weapons research laboratories concludes that they provide "essential services to the nation in fundamental science, national security, environmental protection and cleanup, and industrial competitiveness." The report prompts Pres. Clinton to order the Energy Department to keep all three of its nuclear-weapons research laboratories open.	Daiwa Bank in Japan discloses that an executive in its NYC office has conducted more than 30,000 unauthorized trades since 1984 and concealed about $1.1 billion in losses.	The Albert and Mary Lasker Foundation gives its clinical medical research award to Barry Marshall, of the University of Virginia Medical Center. The award for basic medical research goes to five scientists: Jack Strominger of Harvard; Peter Doherty of the St. Jude Children's Hospital in Memphis, Tenn.; Rolf Zinkernagel of the Institute of Experimental Immunology at the University of Zurich; Emil Unanue of the Washington University School of Medicine in St. Louis, Mo.; and Don C. Wiley of the Howard Hughes Medical Institute and Harvard. Sen. Mark Hatfield (R, Oreg.) is named the public service award winner.	*Forbes* magazine lists Steven Spielberg, with earnings for 1994 estimated at $285 million, as the world's highest-paid entertainer.... Dick Steinberg, 60, manager of the New York Jets, dies in Hempstead, New York, of stomach cancer.... Bessie (Annie Elizabeth) Delany, 104, author, dies in Mount Vernon, New York.... *The Horse Whisperer*, by Nicholas Evans, tops the bestseller list.	Sept. 25
		The U.S. Justice Department files a preliminary complaint charging Toshihide Iguchi, the trader whose misdeeds were revealed Sept. 25, with fraudulent trading and forgery.	A clinical trial finds that AIDS patients who take either of two drug combinations, AZT with ddI or AZT with ddC, have a 38% lower rate of death over two years than do patients who take AZT alone.		Sept. 26
Dennis W. Stockton, 54, convicted of the 1978 contract killing of a teenage boy, is executed by lethal injection in Jarratt, Virginia. Stockton becomes the 300th person executed since the Supreme Court reinstated capital punishment in 1976. He is the 27th person executed in Virginia since 1976.... Statistics show that the number of babies born in the U.S. infected with HIV has leveled off for the first time since the start of the AIDS epidemic. The CDC estimates that in 1993, a total of 1,630 HIV-infected babies were born, down from 1,760 in 1991.	Defense Secretary William J. Perry orders U.S bases in Okinawa to hold a "day of reflection," featuring lectures and discussions about cultural and conduct issues raised by the rape of a 12-year-old girl by U.S. servicemen in Japan. The suspects—Marine Pfc. Rodrico Harp, 21, Marine Pfc. Kendrick M. Ledet, 20, and Navy Seaman Marcus D. Gill, 22—are being held in a U.S. military jail in Japan.... U.S. officials estimate that deploying American troops to Bosnia to aid in the implementation of a peace agreement will cost at least $1 billion.	Treasury Secretary Robert Rubin discloses that the Treasury Department will introduce a redesigned $100 bill into circulation in early 1996.		Time Warner states it has agreed to sell back its 50% stake in the Los Angeles-based rap music label Interscope Records Inc. to the label's founders, Ted Field and Jimmy Iovine. Time Warner has come under fire for its part-ownership of the record label's distribution of so-called gangsta rap, in which performers often use misogynistic lyrics and boast of violent crime.	Sept. 27
In Cook County, Illinois, Judge Fred Suria sentences Rep. Mel Reynolds (D, Ill.) to five years in prison on charges of sexual misconduct, solicitation of child pornography, and obstruction of justice.... Statistics show that costs at four-year colleges rose 6% in the 1995–96 school year from the previous year. The 6% rise is more than double the nationwide rate of inflation. The survey finds that students paid an average of $12,432 a year in tuition and fees at private four-year colleges, and an average of $2,860 at public four-year colleges.		The House approves a continuing resolution—or stopgap bill—that will provide funding for federal government programs and agencies for the first 44 days of the 1996 fiscal year, which begins Oct. 1. ... Reports suggest that one in every three Fortune 500 companies has at least two female directors, compared with one in four companies in 1993.... Exxon Corp. and the National Fish and Wildlife Foundation launch a multimillion-dollar campaign to save the world's five remaining tiger species from extinction.		Greg Harris of the Montreal Expos becomes the first pitcher in the modern era to pitch with both hands in the same game.	Sept. 28
Pres. Clinton and First Lady Hillary Rodham Clinton present the Presidential Medal of Freedom, the highest honor that a civilian in the U.S. can receive, to about a dozen people.... The Senate passes by voice vote a bill that maintains stiffer prison penalties for individuals convicted of crack cocaine offenses than for individuals convicted of similar offenses involving powdered cocaine.	The director of Central Intelligence, John Deutch, announces that he has fired two CIA officers and reprimanded eight others over their mishandling of covert operations in Guatemala in the early 1990s.	The Senate approves a continuing resolution—or stopgap bill—that will provide funding for federal government programs and agencies for the first 44 days of the 1996 fiscal year, which begins Oct. 1.	Research suggests that a small percentage of women of Jewish ancestry in the U.S. carry a gene mutation believed to predispose them to breast cancer.	Philanthropist Paul Mellon donates 85 paintings, sculptures, prints, and drawings to the National Gallery of Art in Washington, D.C. Experts value the works of art at more than $50 million.... The NBA enacts a lockout against basketball referees, effective Oct. 1.	Sept. 29

F	G	H	I	J
Includes elections, federal-state relations, civil rights and liberties, crime, the judiciary, education, health care, poverty, urban affairs, and population.	Includes formation and debate of U.S. foreign and defense policies, veterans' affairs, and defense spending. (Relations with specific foreign countries are usually found under the region concerned.)	Includes business, labor, agriculture, taxation, transportation, consumer affairs, monetary and fiscal policy, natural resources, and pollution.	Includes worldwide scientific, medical, and technological developments; natural phenomena; U.S. weather; natural disasters; and accidents.	Includes the arts, religion, scholarship, communications media, sports, entertainments, fashions, fads, and social life.

	World Affairs	Europe	Africa & the Middle East	The Americas	Asia & the Pacific
Sept. 30		Documents prepared by UN and EU monitors reveal that Croatian troops are executing Serb civilians and burning Croatian Serb villages. UN officials suggest the killings and arson are part of a campaign by the Croatian military to drive several thousand Serbs who remain in Krajina from their homes and prevent the 120,000 Serbs who fled from returning.	In response to the coup attempt of Sept. 28, 200 South African tourists who were vacationing on Comoros board a flight home.		
Oct. 1	Finance ministers for European Union member states agree to abide by strict economic criteria to create a single European currency.	Portugal's Socialist Party emerges the winner in general elections, ending the 10-year reign of the Social Democratic Party (PSD)....Voters in Latvia in parliamentary elections divide their support among the left-wing party, the ruling centrist party and a party led by a German expatriate with ties to far-right groups in Germany....Youths in Vaulx-en-Velin, a suburb of Lyons, France, largely populated by immigrants, riot in protest of the Sept. 29 death of Khaled Kelkal. About 60 cars are burned. Police detain 12 of the youths for questioning.	Gunmen kill 18 people in an attack on a bus in Algeria....In Nigeria, Gen. Abacha, bowing to international pressure, details a plan to implement democratic civilian rule by October 1998. He also commutes the sentences of some 40 people convicted in July of plotting a coup in March.		
Oct. 2	France conducts the second in a series of underground nuclear tests in the South Pacific, provoking a renewed wave of international protests. Australia, Japan, and New Zealand summon their French ambassadors to condemn the tests. Most foreign ministers for EU member states criticize the tests, along with the U.S. and Russia.	Irish prime minister John Bruton meets with David Trimble, leader of Northern Ireland's Ulster Unionist Party, in the first talks between an Irish head of state and a leader of the Ulster Unionists in nearly 30 years.	In Kenya, Koigi wa Wamwere is sentenced with two other men to four years in prison and six lashes for trying to steal weapons from police. The trial has been watched closely by human-rights groups, which claim the charges were fabricated.	Statistics reveal that, despite the Venezuelan government's efforts, inflation rose 71% from June 1994 to October 1995....Reports suggest that a delegation of more than 80 Chinese businessmen who disappeared in Canada in May actually entered Canada as part of an elaborate C$5 million (US$3.7 million) scheme by organized-crime members to smuggle illegal aliens into the country.	Police officers in Queensland conduct raids targeting computer child pornography in several cities in the Australian state. The officers seize 15 computers and begin questioning 18 suspects in what is considered the first operation of the investigation of child pornography under the Classification of Computer Games and Images Act, which the Queensland parliament passed in April.
Oct. 3		Macedonian president Kiro Gligorov is seriously injured in a car-bomb attack in Skopje, the Macedonian capital. Gligorov's driver is killed, and five bystanders are injured in the incident, at least two of them seriously....The trial of Rosemary West, charged with 10 counts of murder, begins in the town of Winchester, England. The case received publicity when police uncovered the remains of at least 11 bodies underneath the couple's home in Gloucester. Frederick West hanged himself in prison earlier in 1995.	Soldiers loyal to the military government of Captain Valentine E. M. Strasser quash an attempted coup in Sierra Leone. The government states that six officers and several civilians opposed to a plan to return to civilian rule were arrested in the coup.	Hurricane Opal assails Mexico, and it reportedly kills at least 10 people in the states of Campeche and Tabasco....Former brigadier general Henri Max Mayard, who was the fourth-highest-ranking officer in Haiti's now defunct military, is murdered by unidentified gunmen in a suburb of Port-au-Prince, Haiti's capital. Mayard is one of at least 20 supporters or officials of the former military who have been killed in what international human-rights officials term "commando-style executions" since the military junta was ousted in October 1994.	Hee Lon Tan, 55, is found guilty of charges stemming from a drug bust that netted about A$40 million (US$30 million) worth of heroin, the largest heroin seizure ever in the state of Victoria. Tan is suspected of leading an international drug syndicate.
Oct. 4	The IMF projects that global economic output will expand by 3.7% through 1995, from 3.6% in 1994. That marks a slight downward revision from the previous IMF forecast in April, which estimated 1995 growth to be 3.8%. The IMF also states that it expects the world economy to expand by 4.1% in 1996.	Due to the Oct. 3 injuries of Macedonian president Kiro Gligorov, the government names Stojan Andov, the speaker of parliament, as acting president....Serb surface-to-air missile sites lock their radar onto NATO planes flying a routine patrol over a no-fly zone in Bosnia. In response, NATO warplanes bomb Bosnian Serb targets....Reports state that walkouts protesting the Turkish government have closed many Turkish ports and businesses.	Some 1,000 French soldiers in Comoros, a former French colony, help to put down a coup launched Sept. 28 by Bob Denard. Four or five Comorans are reported killed, and 10 are wounded. Comoran premier Caabi El Yachourtu Mohamed announces the formation of a new coalition government to replace the government of Pres. Djohar, who has grown unpopular since taking power in 1989.	Carlos Alonso Lucio reveals to a televised session of the Colombian Congress transcripts of what he states are wiretapped telephone conversations between a DEA agent from the U.S. in Colombia and his superiors in the U.S. On the tapes, the agents call Colombian officials "idiots." The incident damages the already strained relationship between the two countries.	Angered by the September rape of a 12-year-old girl by U.S. servicemen in Okinawa, 4,000 people, including several Japanese parliament members, march on the streets of Tokyo calling for reform of a bilateral agreement between Japan and the U.S. regarding military bases.

A	B	C	D	E
Includes developments that affect more than one world region, international organizations, and important meetings of major world leaders.	*Includes all domestic and regional developments in Europe, including the Soviet Union, Turkey, Cyprus, and Malta.*	*Includes all domestic and regional developments in Africa and the Middle East, including Iraq and Iran and excluding Cyprus, Turkey, and Afghanistan.*	*Includes all domestic and regional developments in Latin America, the Caribbean, and Canada.*	*Includes all domestic and regional developments in Asia and Pacific nations, extending from Afghanistan through all the Pacific Islands, except Hawaii.*

U.S. Politics & Social Issues	U.S. Foreign Policy & Defense	U.S. Economy & Environment	Science, Technology, & Nature	Culture, Leisure, & Lifestyle	
		Virginia transportation officials open the first privately financed toll road built in the U.S. in a century. The toll road, the Dulles Greenway, is a 14.1-mile-long highway that links Washington Dulles International Airport with the rural suburb of Leesburg, Virginia. . . . Pres. Clinton signs into law a stopgap bill that will provide funding for the federal government for the first 44 days of the 1996 fiscal year, which begins Oct. 1.		A conference of Episcopalian bishops in Portland, Oregon, votes to compel four bishops to allow the ordination of women priests in their dioceses. . . . George Kirby, 71, comedian, singer, and impersonator, dies in Las Vegas, Nevada, after suffering from Parkinson's disease.	Sept. 30
Michael Bloomberg, the founder and owner of the Bloomberg L.P. news and information service, announces that he will donate $55 million to Johns Hopkins University in Baltimore, Maryland. . . . The resignation of Rep. Mel Reynolds (D, Ill.), sentenced Sept. 28 to five years in prison, from his House seat goes into effect.	A federal jury in New York City convicts 10 militant Muslims on 48 of 50 conspiracy charges stemming from a failed plot to bomb the UN headquarters building and other NYC targets and to assassinate political leaders. The militants include Sheik Omar Abdel Rahman, a blind cleric from Egypt, accused of leading his fellow defendants in plotting a "war of urban terrorism" in response to the U.S. government's support of Israel and of Egypt's current secular regime. The proceedings constitute the biggest terrorism trial in U.S. history.	After failing in November 1994 to reach an agreement on a new contract, the U.S. Postal Service and the American Postal Workers Union (APWU) agree to a federal arbitration board's new contract.		Ernie Irvan competes in his first NASCAR race since leaving the circuit after a near-fatal crash in 1994. . . . Margaret Gorman Cahill, 90, winner of the first Miss America contest in 1921, dies in Bowie, Maryland, of cardiac arrest and pneumonia.	Oct. 1
The Supreme Court opens its 1995–96 term with 43 cases on the docket. In *Rural West Tennessee African-American Affairs Council v. Sundquist*, the justices affirm, without comment, a ruling issued by a panel of federal judges in Nashville, Tennessee, that approves a redistricting plan for the Tennessee state senate. In *American Life League v. Reno*, the justices reject without comment a constitutional challenge to the 1994 Freedom of Access to Clinic Entrances Act.		Figures disclose that the purchasing managers' index rose to 48.3% in September, an increase from the August reading of 46.9%. Generally, a measure above 50% indicates an expanding manufacturing sector, and a reading of 44.5% or higher indicates overall economic expansion.	The FDA states it has approved the drug alendronate sodium for treating the bone-thinning disease osteoporosis. The drug is the first of a class of hormone-free drugs to gain FDA approval for treating the disease.	In Major League Baseball, Seattle Mariners win their first-ever division title when they beat the California Angels. . . . The NHL, its players' union, and the International Ice Hockey Federation jointly announce that NHL players will be able to take part in the 1998 Winter Olympics, in Nagano, Japan.	Oct. 2
In a televised trial that captivated the nation, O. J. Simpson is acquitted of the June 1994 fatal stabbings of Nicole Brown Simpson and Ronald Goldman. Dubbed the "Trial of the Century," the verdict sparks debate. . . . Washington State Superior Court judge James Allendoerfer sentences Simon Roberts and Adrian Guthrie to prison rather than banishment. He had allowed the teens, who are members of the Tlingit Indian tribe, to be banished for a 1993 beating and robbing incident, as per a tribal court. He now argues the banishment is flawed.	Pres. Clinton signs an executive order easing restrictions on travel and money transfers between the U.S. and Cuba and on humanitarian aid to Cuba by U.S. organizations. . . . Pres. Clinton signs an appropriations bill allocating $11.2 billion for spending on military construction in fiscal 1996. The bill is the first of the 13 appropriations bills for fiscal 1996, which began October 1, to be signed into law.	In the third veto of his presidency, Pres. Clinton vetoes the $2.2 billion fiscal 1996 appropriations bill for the legislative branch. Clinton states he supports the content of the bill, which will reduce Congress's spending on its own functions, but he rejects the measure as a matter of principle, faulting Congress for passing its own budget before completing work that funds government agencies and services.	Wildfires ignite on the Pacific coastline in northern California. . . . About 100,000 people flee from coastal cities in Florida, Alabama, and Mississippi in anticipation of Hurricane Opal as it moves across the Gulf of Mexico. . . . The FDA approves the prescription sale of a patch, called Androderm, to deliver the male sex hormone testosterone to men whose bodies produce insufficient amounts of the hormone, a condition called hypogonadism.		Oct. 3
Harold Joe Lane, 50, convicted for the slaying of a teenage girl in a 1982 robbery, is executed by lethal injection in Huntsville, Texas. Lane becomes the 100th person put to death in Texas since the state resumed executions in 1982. Lane is the 301st person put to death in the U.S. since 1976.		John Clemens, accused of accepting bribes from a vendor, is ousted as president of a Baltimore, Maryland, local chapter of the International Brotherhood of Teamsters. He is one of several top union officials dismissed from the Teamsters in a government-led campaign to root out corruption in the union.	Hurricane Opal comes ashore east of Pensacola, Florida. The hurricane kills at least 19 people in Florida, North Carolina, Georgia, and Alabama. It causes at least $1.8 billion in damage to insured property in Florida alone, making it the U.S.'s third-costliest storm. . . . Wildfires in Northern California destroy at least 40 homes in the small town of Inverness, located around 35 miles (60 km) north of San Francisco.	Pope John Paul II begins a tour of the U.S., with stops planned in Newark, New Jersey; New York City; and Baltimore, Maryland. . . . Estimates suggest that a record 150 million people nationwide watched the Oct. 3 handing down of the verdict in the O. J. Simpson trial.	Oct. 4

F	G	H	I	J
Includes elections, federal-state relations, civil rights and liberties, crime, the judiciary, education, health care, poverty, urban affairs, and population.	Includes formation and debate of U.S. foreign and defense policies, veterans' affairs, and defense spending. (Relations with specific foreign countries are usually found under the region concerned.)	Includes business, labor, agriculture, taxation, transportation, consumer affairs, monetary and fiscal policy, natural resources, and pollution.	Includes worldwide scientific, medical, and technological developments; natural phenomena; U.S. weather; natural disasters; and accidents.	Includes the arts, religion, scholarship, communications media, sports, entertainments, fashions, fads, and social life.

	World Affairs	Europe	Africa & the Middle East	The Americas	Asia & the Pacific
Oct. 5	Pope John Paul II addresses the United Nations General Assembly as part of the UN's 50th anniversary celebration. It is the pontiff's second address at the UN during his papacy. In his speech, the pontiff denounces countries' mingling of nationalism and religious fundamentalism and urges the UN to rise above its bureaucratic role and act as a moral force to discourage ethnic and religious enmity within and between nations.	A cease-fire agreement is reached in the war pitting the mainly Muslim Bosnian government and its Croat allies against the Bosnian Serbs in Bosnia-Herzegovina. Separately, the UN announces that it will reduce the number of UN peacekeeping troops in Bosnia to approximately 21,000, from the current 30,500.... As per an agreement with Greece to end an embargo, Macedonia's parliament approves a new flag, which replaces the ancient Greek symbol previously chosen.	A car bomb explodes in eastern Algiers, killing nine people and wounding 19.... Thousands of Israeli rightists hold a torch-lit protest march through Jerusalem. The march is organized by the Likud party and six smaller rightist political parties in protest of the second-phase accord with the PLO.... On the island of Comoros, French mercenary Bob Denard, who attempted a coup Sept. 28, and his force surrender.... An officer is arrested in Sierra Leone, bringing the number of people arrested in the Oct. 3 attempted coup to seven.	In the village of Aurora 8 de Octubre in the northern Guatemalan province of Alta Verapaz, an attack by soldiers leaves at least 11 Indian peasants dead and 17 injured.	
Oct. 6	The International Energy Agency estimates that the global demand for petroleum will grow to 71.4 million barrels a day in 1996. That figure is about 500,000 barrels a day above the estimated consumption level for 1995.... Belgium's highest court requests permission from parliament to indict Willy Claes, secretary general of NATO, on corruption charges. The request triggers renewed calls for Claes's resignation.	A bomb explodes near a subway station in Paris, injuring 13 people. The explosion comes hours after the funeral of Khaled Kelkal, an Algerian Muslim suspected in other bombings.... Two remote-controlled bombs explode in Grozny as a convoy carrying Lt. Gen. Anatoly Romanov, a strong advocate of the peace talks in Chechnya, passes. Romanov is severely injured and left in a coma. His driver and an aide are killed, and 15 others are wounded.... Hugh Charles (born Charles Hugh Owen Ferry), 88, British songwriter who composed more than 50 songs associated with World War II, dies of unreported causes.			
Oct. 7		An Algerian terrorist organization, the Armed Islamic Group (GIA), claims responsibility for the recent bombings in France.			A powerful earthquake strikes the Indonesian island of Sumatra. The quake measures 7.0 on the Richter scale and is centered 10 miles (16 km) west of the town of Sungaipenuh, in northwestern Indonesia. The temblor, which kills scores of people and destroys or damages thousands of buildings, is considered to be the area's worst since 1909.
Oct. 8		John Cairncross, 82, the "fifth man" in a group of British spies recruited by the Soviet Union during the 1930s, dies in western England after suffering a stroke.	Yasser Arafat's PNA frees Mahmoud Zahar, a prominent political leader of Hamas in the Gaza Strip, from detention.... Uganda's new constitution takes effect.	Guatemalan defense minister General Mario Enriquez Morales resigns amid controversy over the Oct. 5 massacre in Alta Verapaz.	Estimates put the death toll from the Oct. 7 earthquake on the Indonesian island of Sumatra at about 100. Hundreds more were injured.
Oct. 9	The Yugoslav War Crimes Tribunal in The Hague, the Netherlands, opens the trial of Dragan Nikolic, the Serb commander of the Susica prison camp, which operated in Bosnia from June to September 1992. Nikolic is believed to be in hiding in Serb-held Bosnia.	In response to shelling by Bosnian Serbs in which one Norwegian UN peacekeeper dies, NATO warplanes bomb Bosnian Serb targets.... Lord Alexander Frederick Douglas-Home, 92, former prime minister, 1963–64, and foreign secretary of Great Britain, 1960–63, 1970–74, dies in Berwickshire, Scotland, of unreported causes.	Tunisian authorities arrest Mohammed Moada, the head of the leading opposition group, the Movement of Democratic Socialists (MDS).	An earthquake measuring 7.6 on the Richter scale rocks Jalisco and Colima states in western Mexico. The epicenter of the quake is located 3 miles (5 km) off the Pacific coastline. It is Mexico's worst earthquake since 1985.	Militants launch several rocket attacks on the Sindh Secretariat Office, a government building in Karachi, Pakistan. At least five people are wounded in the blasts.... Kukrit Pramoj, 84, former premier of Thailand, 1975–76, dies in Bangkok, Thailand, after suffering from heart disease and diabetes.... Four members of the militant Mohajir Qaumi Movement are killed in Pakistan.
Oct. 10	The IMF holds a meeting in conjunction with the World Bank, its sister organization. Brunei becomes the 180th member of the IMF.	UN officials report that Serbs have renewed ethnic cleansing, or the forced expulsion of civilians from their homes, in the area of Banja Luka. Some 10,000 Muslims and Croats reportedly have been expelled since Oct. 7 from Bosanski Novi, Sanski Most, and Prijedor.... More than half of France's 5 million public-sector workers stage walkouts, and some hold demonstrations to protest a salary freeze for fiscal 1996.	Israel releases about 900 Palestinians held in Israeli prisons and begins its military pullout from Palestinian towns, taking the first concrete steps toward implementation of the Sept. 24 accord on interim Palestinian autonomy.... Nigeria's Information Minister Walter Ofonagoro discloses that the life sentences given to Olesegun Obasanjo and others who attempted a coup have been reduced to 15 years and that the 14 originally sentenced to death instead will be jailed for life or 25 years.	Mexican government officials state that at least 48 people died in the Oct. 9 quake, and more than 100 were injured.... Tropical storm Roxanne, located in the Caribbean Sea, strengthens into a full hurricane, bringing the number of hurricanes in the Atlantic Ocean region's current storm season to an unusually high 10.	Dissident and Nobel Prize winner Aung San Suu Kyi is appointed as general secretary of the National League for Democracy (NLD), a party that she helped found in 1988.... Reports confirm that Pakistan's government has expelled Masood Khalili, Afghanistan's envoy to Pakistan's capital of Islamabad, indicating increasing tensions between the countries.

A	B	C	D	E
Includes developments that affect more than one world region, international organizations, and important meetings of major world leaders.	Includes all domestic and regional developments in Europe, including the Soviet Union, Turkey, Cyprus, and Malta.	Includes all domestic and regional developments in Africa and the Middle East, including Iraq and Iran and excluding Cyprus, Turkey, and Afghanistan.	Includes all domestic and regional developments in Latin America, the Caribbean, and Canada.	Includes all domestic and regional developments in Asia and Pacific nations, extending from Afghanistan through all the Pacific Islands, except Hawaii.

U.S. Politics & Social Issues	U.S. Foreign Policy & Defense	U.S. Economy & Environment	Science, Technology, & Nature	Culture, Leisure, & Lifestyle	
Data show that 827,440 black men in their 20s, or 32.2% of black males in that age group, are under judicial supervision. That figure compares with 6.7% of white men in their 20s and 12.3% of Hispanic males in the same age group. It also compares with a 1990 figure that estimated nearly one in four black men ages 20–29 were under the supervision of the criminal justice system. . . . Dan Peavy, a school board member in Dallas, Texas, resigns as a result of accusations that he used racial slurs during taped private conversations.	Deputy Secretary of Defense John White orders the army to end production of a rifle-mounted weapon capable of blinding enemy troops. . . . The Mexican government announces that it will repay, a few weeks ahead of its scheduled due date of Oct. 31, $700 million of the money it borrowed from the U.S.	The Census Bureau finds that 38.1 million people live in poverty, a drop of 1.2 million from the number of poor reported in 1993. According to the bureau, that decrease is the first in five years. The poverty rate, which measures the percentage of Americans living in poverty, was 14.5% in 1994, down from 15.1% in 1993. Preliminary estimates put the percentage of Americans without health insurance coverage at 15.2% in 1994, slightly down from 15.3% figure reported in 1993. . . . Congress has yet to pass 11 of 13 appropriations bills.	Pres. Clinton approves emergency federal disaster assistance to 15 Florida counties and parts of southeastern Alabama that were hit by Hurricane Opal. . . . Medical research shows that orthopedic surgeons, family doctors, and chiropractors are almost equally successful at treating lower-back pain.	Pres. Clinton confers National Medals of Arts and the Charles Frankel Prizes for humanities on 17 American cultural figures and one arts organization. . . . The Nobel Prize in Literature is awarded to poet Seamus Heaney, the third Irishman to win the prize. . . . A mass held by Pope John Paul II is attended by 80,000 people at Giants Stadium in New Jersey.	Oct. 5
	Pres. Clinton scales back federal restrictions on the sale of high-performance computers to customers in foreign countries.	Some 32,500 workers from the International Association of Machinists and Aerospace Workers union go on strike against Boeing Co. after rejecting a three-year contract. The striking machinists make up about 31% of Boeing's total workforce. . . . Data suggest that in terms of income, the bottom 80% of the population have earnings well below the 1989 prerecession level.	A study finds that women during the early months of pregnancy who consume more than 10,000 international units (IUs) of vitamin A per day, twice the daily allowance recommended by the U.S. government, increase their risk of having babies with serious birth defects. . . . Swiss astronomers in Italy report finding the first evidence of a planet outside the solar system orbiting a "live" star—51 Pegasi, 40 light-years from Earth.	Pope John Paul holds an outdoor mass at the Aqueduct Race Track in New York City, and some 75,000 people attend.	Oct. 6
The New York City Board of Education votes, 5-2, to select Rudolph Franklin Crew, superintendent of the Tacoma, Washington, school system, to be the new schools chancellor in New York City. The vote ends a long and difficult search hampered by political struggles between the mayor and the school board.			Wildfires in Northern California continue to rage out of control. Since Oct. 3, a total of around 12,000 acres (5,000 hectares) on the Pacific coastline have been burned.	In New York City's Central Park, 125,000 people gather to hear a mass by Pope John Paul II.	Oct. 7
			Reports suggest that fires in California have caused more than $40 million in damage.	Christopher Keene, 48, conductor who served as general director for the New York City Opera, dies in New York of lymphoma arising from AIDS. . . . Pope John Paul II holds a mass for 50,000 in Baltimore, Maryland. An estimated 300,000 people attend a parade afterwards.	Oct. 8
	John Alfred Scali, 77, former television news correspondent and U.S. ambassador to the UN who helped resolve the Cuban missile crisis, dies in Washington, D.C., of heart failure.	California governor Pete Wilson (R) signs into law legislation that will allow officials in Orange County, which declared bankruptcy in December 1994, to divert more than $800 million in funding to the payment of the county's debts. . . . Members of the International Brotherhood of Teamsters union agree to end their month-long strike against Ryder System Inc.	An Amtrak train derails as it passes over a trestle over a remote desert gulch 27 miles (40 km) east of Hyder, Arizona. One person is killed and some 100 others are injured. . . . The Karolinska Institute for Medicine in Stockholm awards the Nobel Prize in Physiology to two Americans, Edward Lewis and Eric Wieschaus, and a German, Christiane Nuesslein-Volhard, for their discoveries regarding genetic control of the body's early development.		Oct. 9
		The Nobel Prize in Economic Science is awarded to Robert E. Lucas Jr., who is the fifth professor from the University of Chicago in six years to win the economics prize and the eighth overall from that institution. . . . Energy Secretary Hazel O'Leary announces that the Department of Energy has abandoned its plans to build a nuclear reactor for making tritium, a radioactive gas needed to produce nuclear weapons, and will instead leasing or purchasing a commercial reactor.		Paolo Gucci, 64, of Gucci leather goods, dies in London, England, after suffering from chronic hepatitis. . . . Reports state that Bill Gates has bought the Bettmann Archive, which contains millions of historical photographs. . . . Garry Kasparov of Russia successfully defends his world chess title over Viswanathan Anand of India.	Oct. 10

F	G	H	I	J
Includes elections, federal-state relations, civil rights and liberties, crime, the judiciary, education, health care, poverty, urban affairs, and population.	Includes formation and debate of U.S. foreign and defense policies, veterans' affairs, and defense spending. (Relations with specific foreign countries are usually found under the region concerned.)	Includes business, labor, agriculture, taxation, transportation, consumer affairs, monetary and fiscal policy, natural resources, and pollution.	Includes worldwide scientific, medical, and technological developments; natural phenomena; U.S. weather; natural disasters; and accidents.	Includes the arts, religion, scholarship, communications media, sports, entertainments, fashions, fads, and social life.

	World Affairs	Europe	Africa & the Middle East	The Americas	Asia & the Pacific
Oct. 11	Rolf Ekeus, head of the UN Commission on Iraq overseeing the dismantlement of Iraqi weapons of mass destruction, discloses in a six-month report to the Security Council that the Iraqi government concealed the extent of advances it made in its nuclear, chemical, and biological weapons programs.	The Bosnian government army, joined by Croat forces, recapture the towns of Sanski Most and Mrkonjic Grad in that region. . . . Lloyds Bank PLC and TSB Group PLC announce that they will merge, creating Britain's largest retail bank, the U.K.'s third-largest bank overall, and one of the 30 largest banks in the world. . . . Estonian premier Tiit Vahi hands in his resignation and that of his cabinet because of a wiretapping scandal involving Estonia's interior minister, Edgar Savisaar.		Tropical storm Roxanne crosses the Mexico's Yucatan Peninsula with winds of 110 miles per hour. At least four people die. . . . Ecuador's vice president, Alberto Dahik Garzoni, resigns and then flees to Costa Rica after Ecuador's Supreme Court orders him arrested on criminal charges of misusing state funds.	Reports reveal that the Australian Stock Exchange and New Zealand's stock market have agreed to create a joint stock index.
Oct. 12		A cease-fire agreed to on Oct. 5 in the war in Bosnia-Herzegovina between the mainly Muslim Bosnian government and its Croat allies against the Bosnian Serbs goes into effect at 12:01 A.M. local time. . . . Austria's governing coalition collapses after failing to agree on a fiscal 1996 budget.		International researchers announce they have documented a dramatic increase in the number of fires in Amazon rain forests in recent months. Weather satellites spotted 39,900 fires in the region in July—four times as many blazes as were detected in July 1994. . . . U.S. first lady Hillary Rodham Clinton launches a tour of Latin America.	Data shows that monsoon floods have claimed 171 lives and caused an estimated 3 billion Thai bahts ($117 million) in damage in Thailand since July. . . . Business activity in Karachi, Pakistan, is disrupted by a strike called by the militant Mohajir Qaumi Movement to protest the Oct. 9 killings. Six people die in violence during the strike. It is the 17th strike called by the group since January.
Oct. 13	The Norwegian Nobel Committee awards the Nobel Peace Prize to Joseph Rotblat, a British physicist who helped develop the atomic bomb but went on to campaign against nuclear weapons; and the antinuclear group he heads, the Pugwash Conferences on Science and World Affairs.	Austria's parliament votes to dissolve itself to make way for general elections in December. . . . A German judge in Dusseldorf sentences four men described as neo-Nazi sympathizers to jail for their roles in setting a 1993 fire that killed five female members of a single Turkish family. Three of the defendants—Felix Koehnen, 18; Christian Reher, 19; and Christian Buchholz, 22—are tried as juveniles and given the maximum sentence of 10 years in prison. Markus Gartmann, 25, is sentenced to 15 years in jail.	Results from a September referendum in Madagascar are announced, and voters decided the president, rather than parliament, should be granted power to appoint or dismiss the premier. In response, Premier Francisque Ravony, whose clashes with Pres. Albert Zafy compelled the referendum, resigns.	On the 25th anniversary of diplomatic relations between China and Canada, Canadian prime minister Jean Chrétien and Chinese premier Li Peng hold a state dinner in Montreal with several of Canada's provincial premiers. The event is protested by several hundred people, who decry Li for his role in the massacre of prodemocracy students in Tiananmen Square in Beijing in 1989.	In the first pact brokered between the rebels and the government of Philippine president Fidel Ramos, government negotiators sign a peace accord with representatives from three rebel groups—the Revolutionary Alliance of the Masses, the Soldiers of the Filipino People and the Young Officers Union. . . . In Weipa, a town in the state of Queensland, Australia, 76 miners go on strike at a CRA bauxite mine.
Oct. 14		An armed gunman seizes a bus carrying 25 South Korean tourists and a Russian driver and tour guide in Moscow's Red Square. The hijacking is reportedly the first hostage-taking incident to occur in Moscow. . . . In Italy, Judge Fabio Paparella rules that former premier Silvio Berlusconi will stand trial on corruption charges. . . . Helen Vlachos, 83, Greek newspaper publisher who opposed Greece's military dictatorship, dies of unreported causes.	The head of the opposition Zimbabwe African National Union-Ndonga, Rev. Ndabaningi Sithole, and others are arrested and charged with plotting to kill Pres. Robert Mugabe and bring down the government.		Six Tibetans protesting the Chinese rule of Tibet, begin a hunger strike. . . . Pakistani prime minister Benazir Bhutto confirms in a meeting with journalists that a group of army officers has secretly been arrested, although she will not discuss with journalists any details of the investigation.
Oct. 15		The armed gunman who seized a bus Oct. 14 releases all but four of the hostages. Russian commandos storm the bus and kill the hijacker, freeing the four captives. . . . A new minority government proposed by caretaker premier Tansu Ciller loses a vote of confidence in Turkey's parliament. . . . Greece lifts a 19-month-long trade embargo on The Former Yugoslav Republic of Macedonia.	Iraqi president Saddam Hussein wins overwhelming backing in a presidential referendum in which he is the sole candidate. . . . Hezbollah (Party of God) guerrillas kill six Israeli soldiers in an ambush in Israel's self-declared security zone in southern Lebanon. The attack is the deadliest suffered by Israel in a single attack in southern Lebanon in two years, and it raises to 22 the number of Israeli troops killed in Lebanon in the year to date.	Tropical storm Roxanne causes the sinking of a barge off Campeche that claims at least five lives. The barge, which services petroleum platforms and pipelines, was carrying about 245 oil workers, the majority of whom are rescued. . . . UN secretary general Boutros Boutros-Ghali and U.S. vice president Al Gore attend a ceremony marking the one-year anniversary of Jean-Bertrand Aristide's return to power in Haiti. Rioters in Cite Soleil, a slum neighborhood in Port-au-Prince, Haiti's capital, throw stones at a car in the motorcade of Mary (Tipper) Gore, wife of Vice Pres. Gore.	
Oct. 16		In Austria, two people are seriously injured in two separate letter-bomb attacks. . . . In light of the Oct. 15 vote, Turkish premier Tansu Ciller states that she will forge an interim government with her old coalition partner until elections take place.	The PNA, in an effort to smooth its relations with Hamas, releases Ahmed Bahar, a prominent Hamas leader in Gaza imprisoned by the PNA in late June. . . . An Algerian journalist and her chauffeur are shot and killed by unidentified gunmen in Algiers, raising the number of journalists killed in Algeria over two years to more than 50.	Haitian premier Smarck Michel submits his resignation to the Haitian cabinet and congress. . . . Three Honduran army officers—Col. Alexander Hernandez, retired major Manuel de Jesus Trejo, and retired Captain Billy Joya Almendola—disappear after a court orders their arrest for the week-long kidnapping and torture of six student activists in 1982. The three officers are among the ten members of Battalion 316, who were indicted on July 21.	

A	B	C	D	E
Includes developments that affect more than one world region, international organizations, and important meetings of major world leaders.	Includes all domestic and regional developments in Europe, including the Soviet Union, Turkey, Cyprus, and Malta.	Includes all domestic and regional developments in Africa and the Middle East, including Iraq and Iran and excluding Cyprus, Turkey, and Afghanistan.	Includes all domestic and regional developments in Latin America, the Caribbean, and Canada.	Includes all domestic and regional developments in Asia and Pacific nations, extending from Afghanistan through all the Pacific Islands, except Hawaii.

U.S. Politics & Social Issues	U.S. Foreign Policy & Defense	U.S. Economy & Environment	Science, Technology, & Nature	Culture, Leisure, & Lifestyle	
Police take into custody 15 senior citizens who were shouting questions during a meeting of the House Commerce Committee planning a Medicare overhaul. . . . Ten Republican presidential candidates participate in a televised forum in Manchester, New Hampshire.			The Royal Swedish Academy of Sciences awards the Nobel Prize in Physics to Americans Martin L. Perl and Frederick Reines for their separate discoveries of subatomic particles. The Nobel Prize in Chemistry is awarded to two Americans, F. Sherwood Rowland and Mario Molina, and a Dutch citizen based in Germany, Paul Crutzen, for their discoveries about depletion of the ozone layer. The three reportedly are the first to receive a Nobel for work related to environmental sciences.		Oct. 11
		The House, 288-132, and the Senate, by voice vote, approve the final version of a $63.2 billion spending bill that funds the Department of Agriculture, rural development programs, the FDA, and other related agencies for fiscal year 1996.			Oct. 12
			Henry Roth, 89, writer best known for his 1934 autobiographical novel *Call It Sleep* who made a literary comeback 60 years later, dies in Albuquerque, New Mexico, of unreported causes.		Oct. 13
President Clinton alludes to the O. J. Simpson case, during which Simpson admitted to beating his ex-wife, and to his own experience growing up with an abusive stepfather when he calls on men in the U.S. to pledge never to strike women. . . . Frank Lilly, 65, geneticist and one of the first openly homosexual presidential appointees when president Ronald Reagan selected him in 1987 to work on a panel to study AIDS, dies in NYC of prostate cancer.				Edith (Ellis Peters) Pargeter, 82, British author of mysteries who, under the pseudonym Ellis Peters, wrote 90 books between 1936 and 1994, dies in Shropshire, England, after suffering a stroke.	Oct. 14
				Father John Calicott returns to the Holy Angels Church in Chicago, Illinois, after having been suspended for molesting two boys in 1976. Calicott is the first priest in Chicago to be reinstated to a parish after such a suspension. . . . John Walker III, 88, former chief curator and director of the National Gallery of Art, dies in Amberley, England, of cardiopulmonary arrest.	Oct. 15
Hundreds of thousands of black men participate in a rally in Washington, D.C., called the "Million Man March." The march sparks some controversy because it is led by Louis Farrakhan who has made anti-Semitic remarks, and because it omits women. . . . The Census Bureau reports that 30.8% of U.S. families were headed by a single parent in 1994, up from 28% in 1990, 22% in 1980, and 13% in 1970.		The FEC makes public campaign-spending reports from the Republican presidential candidates that show that Senate Majority Leader Robert Dole (R, Kans.), the current front-runner, raised $5.6 million in the third quarter, more than twice as much as any other candidate.		Actor Christopher Reeve makes his first public appearance since he was paralyzed from the neck down in a May horseback-riding accident.	Oct. 16

F	G	H	I	J
Includes elections, federal-state relations, civil rights and liberties, crime, the judiciary, education, health care, poverty, urban affairs, and population.	*Includes formation and debate of U.S. foreign and defense policies, veterans' affairs, and defense spending. (Relations with specific foreign countries are usually found under the region concerned.)*	*Includes business, labor, agriculture, taxation, transportation, consumer affairs, monetary and fiscal policy, natural resources, and pollution.*	*Includes worldwide scientific, medical, and technological developments; natural phenomena; U.S. weather; natural disasters; and accidents.*	*Includes the arts, religion, scholarship, communications media, sports, entertainments, fashions, fads, and social life.*

	World Affairs	Europe	Africa & the Middle East	The Americas	Asia & the Pacific
Oct. 17	Nineteen heads of state and 23 foreign ministers from Spain, Portugal, and Latin American countries close the fifth annual Ibero-American Summit. The participants issue a final document condemning the U.S. economic embargo against Cuba.... The European Court of Justice, the judicial arm of the European Union, rules that setting quotas to increase the hiring and promotion of women is discriminatory.	A suspected terrorist bomb explodes on a crowded subway train in Paris, injuring 29 people, five of them seriously.... Striking air-traffic controllers reach a salary agreement with the Italian government, ending several weeks of labor unrest which delayed most flights into and out of Italy and forced the cancellation of domestic flights.	Iraqi president Saddam Hussein takes the oath of office for his new term during a nationally televised ceremony.... Winnie Mandela files papers with the Rand Supreme Court contesting her divorce from South African president Nelson Mandela, a move that raises the possibility of a public divorce trial.		Sri Lankan president Chandrika Bandaranaike Kumaratunga launches a stepped-up military offensive against the Tigers after they reject a government plan.... In Uttar Pradesh, India's most populous state, chief minister Mayawati resigns after the hard-line Hindu Bharatiya Janata Party (BJP) withdraws its support for the ruling coalition and her Bahujan Samaj Party.
Oct. 18		The GIA, an Algerian militant group suspected in the Oct. 17 bombing and others, threatens to increase the bombings unless France cuts many of its ties to Algeria.... Italy's Constitutional Court rules that Italian judges may imprison criminals suffering from AIDS or infected with HIV.... Germany's Federal Court of Justice overturns the conviction of former East German espionage chief Markus Wolf and recommends another trial.	South African police wound and arrest Moses Sithole, 31, a man suspected of killing some 40 women over an 18-month period. ...Reports confirm that former Palestinian guerrilla Mohammed Daoud Odeh—better known as Abu Daoud—has for the first time admitted that he oversaw the Black September commando group's 1972 massacre of 11 Israeli athletes at the Olympic Games.	Congress approves Eduardo Peña Triviño as the new vice president of Ecuador, succeeding Alberto Dahik Garzoni, who fled Oct. 11.... Gen. Luis Alonso Discua, head of the Honduran armed forces, states that the officers who disappeared Oct. 16 and others cannot be prosecuted for their crimes because of two amnesty agreements in 1987 and 1991 that cover human-rights abuses committed during the 1980s.	India's national government imposes direct rule over Uttar Pradesh, the country's most populous state, after its ruling coalition collapsed on Oct. 17.
Oct. 19	The European Court of Justice, the judicial arm of the EU, rules that the British government's policy of setting different ages for men and women to receive free drug prescriptions is discriminatory. The ruling sparks charges that the European court is undermining British sovereignty.... Belgium's parliament approves the recommendation to deny Willy Claes, secretary general of NATO, immunity amid a domestic bribery scandal in his home country of Belgium.	The Senate, Italy's upper house of parliament, passes a vote of no confidence against Finance Minister Filippo Mancuso. But Mancuso refuses to resign, forcing Pres. Oscar Luigi Scalfaro to relieve him of his portfolio. Scalfaro's dismissal of Mancuso is described as unprecedented in modern Italian politics.	The Lebanese parliament passes a constitutional amendment that extends Pres. Elias Hrawi's six-year presidential term for three years without new elections.		
Oct. 20	The Nonaligned Movement closes the 11th summit of nonaligned nations. During the proceedings, a declaration was adopted that calls for developing nations to be given greater representation on the UN Security Council and for the UN to focus more on ending poverty.... Willy Claes resigns as secretary general of NATO amid a domestic bribery scandal in Belgium.			Thousands of people in Guatemala City cheer the return of the remains of the late leftist president Jacobo Arbenz Guzman, which are reburied in Guatemala after being exhumed from a grave in El Salvador.	
Oct. 21				The former leader of Chile's secret police, retired general Juan Manuel Contreras Sepulveda, is imprisoned. Contreras, 66, was sentenced in May to seven years in prison for the 1976 assassination of Chilean exile Orlando Letelier in Washington, D.C.	Spurred by the September abduction and rape of a 12-year-old girl by U.S. servicemen in Japan, tens of thousands of Okinawans gather in Ginowan, Okinawa, as part of the largest-ever protest against the presence of U.S. military bases on their island.
Oct. 22	The largest gathering of world leaders ever assembled convenes at UN headquarters in New York City to commemorate the 50th anniversary of the UN. The anniversary celebration includes speeches from 178 representatives of member nations as well as from 23 observers, such as the PLO and the Vatican. Speakers also include Cuban president Fidel Castro, who has not addressed the UN since 1979. U.S. president Bill Clinton delivers the opening address.	Switzerland's ruling coalition increases its parliamentary strength in general elections.	A car bombing in Relizane, Algeria, kills eight people and wounds 82 others.... In the Ivory Coast's second-ever multiparty presidential elections, Pres. Henri Konan Bedie is reelected in a vote boycotted by the opposition parties. Two protesters are fatally shot by government forces, and reports indicate that at least eight other people were killed in political violence prior to the election.... Zanzibar holds its first ever multiparty presidential and legislative elections.	The Nicaraguan National Assembly elects Julia Mena, a former legislator, as the country's new vice president.	Police in Colombo reimpose a night curfew in the city in Sri Lanka after rebels blow up two of the city's three major oil depots. More than 23 security forces and three rebels are killed in the attack. Officials estimate that more than $30 million in petroleum products are destroyed in the explosions.

A	B	C	D	E
Includes developments that affect more than one world region, international organizations, and important meetings of major world leaders.	Includes all domestic and regional developments in Europe, including the Soviet Union, Turkey, Cyprus, and Malta.	Includes all domestic and regional developments in Africa and the Middle East, including Iraq and Iran and excluding Cyprus, Turkey, and Afghanistan.	Includes all domestic and regional developments in Latin America, the Caribbean, and Canada.	Includes all domestic and regional developments in Asia and Pacific nations, extending from Afghanistan through all the Pacific Islands, except Hawaii.

U.S. Politics & Social Issues	U.S. Foreign Policy & Defense	U.S. Economy & Environment	Science, Technology, & Nature	Culture, Leisure, & Lifestyle	
Demonstrators protesting the elimination of affirmative-action admissions policies within the eight-campus University of California system erect tents in front of an administration building in Irvine, Calif., and they launch a hunger strike. . . . Attorney General Janet Reno signs an order that revises the rules on the use of deadly force by agents in nine federal law-enforcement agencies. The order is prompted by the 1992 standoff between federal agents and white separatist Randall Weaver.		Robert E. Rubin, secretary of the Treasury, announces that he will reduce government borrowing in an effort to prevent a default on government payments. Rubin states that, to avoid surpassing the U.S.'s $4.9 trillion debt limit, the Treasury Department will offer $6 billion in three-month Treasury bills at the next weekly auction. That figure is about half the amount usually offered.	Representatives of CNN disclose that the network has signed an exclusive agreement with AT&T Corp. to make CNN business and financial news available on a new AT&T on-line computer service, which will be called the AT&T Business Network.	Frenchwoman Jeanne Calment becomes recorded history's longest-living person when she reaches the age of 120 years and 238 days. . . . The Cleveland Indians defeat the Seattle Mariners, 4-0, in the sixth and deciding game of MLB's American League Championship Series.	Oct. 17
The House passes, 332-83, its version of a bill that maintains stiffer prison penalties for individuals convicted of crack cocaine offenses rather than powdered cocaine offenses. The body then clears by voice vote an identical Senate bill. . . . In Chicago, Illinois, Judge Carol Kelly finds two unidentified boys, who in 1994 dropped five-year-old Eric Morse to his death because he refused to steal candy for them, guilty of murder.		The Commerce Department reports that in August the U.S. recorded a seasonally adjusted $8.82 billion deficit in trade in goods and services. That is the smallest monthly deficit in 1995, and it represents a sharp decline from a revised gap of $11.19 billion in July.			Oct. 18
The House approves, 231-201, a plan authorizing an overhaul of Medicare. The plan is the largest and most controversial provision in the congressional Republicans' plan to balance the federal budget within seven years. . . . Fights involving 150 prisoners break out at the Talladega Federal Correctional Institution in Alabama. At least eight people are injured. . . . Pres. Clinton endorses pending legislation that will bar employers from discriminating against individuals on the basis of their sexual orientation.	A military court at the Washington Navy Yard in Washington, D.C., acquits navy captain Everett L. Greene, 47, of charges that he sexually harassed a female junior officer, Lt. Mary Felix. Greene's case receives particular attention because he is the head of the equal opportunity office at the Navy and the highest-ranking naval officer in 50 years to undergo court-martial proceedings. . . . The U.S. Senate passes, 74-24, a watered-down version of a House bill that sought to strengthen the U.S.'s 33-year-old economic embargo against Cuba.	The Dow closes at a record high of 4802.45, marking the 50th record high registered for the Dow in 1995.	Paleontologists report that fossil remains uncovered in China in 1994 represent a new species of the earliest known bird with a toothless beak. Scientists dubbed the new species Confuciusornis sanctus, or "holy Confucius bird."	Rev. Thomas Schaefer, a Roman Catholic priest in the Washington, D.C., archdiocese, is sentenced to 16 years in prison for sexually abusing five boys between 1966 and 1982. Schaefer pled guilty to the charges. . . . Don Cherry, 58, jazz trumpeter and pioneer in the "world music" genre, dies in Malaga, Spain, of liver failure.	Oct. 19
In Memphis, Tennessee, several prison buildings are set on fire. In Allenwood, Pennsylvania, a melee involving 150 inmates leads to the minor injury of a staff member. The Justice Department declares a lockdown at most federal prisons nationwide. In Greenville, Illinois, a riot breaks out when inmates refuse to obey that lockdown. Inmates set fires and take over parts of the prison. At least 10 staff members and prisoners are injured.			A study of two Ohio girls who underwent an experimental therapy using engineered versions of their own genes to treat a rare, inherited immune-system disease provides the first evidence of successful gene therapy. . . . The U.S. space shuttle Columbia blasts off from Kennedy Space Center in Cape Canaveral, Florida, to conduct scientific experiments on the effects of near-weightlessness.		Oct. 20
	A presidential order that freezes the U.S. assets of dozens of companies and individuals believed to be linked to the Cali cocaine cartel in Colombia goes into effect at midnight.	Pres. Clinton signs a $63.2 billion bill funding the Department of Agriculture, various rural development programs, the FDA, and other related agencies for the 1996 fiscal year.		(Richard) Shannon Hoon, 28, lead singer of Blind Melon, a popular rock group, is found dead on the band's tour bus in New Orleans, La., apparently of an accidental drug overdose. . . . Maxene Andrews, 79, a member of the Andrews Sisters, a singing trio whose popularity peaked during the 1940s, dies in Hyannis, Mass., after suffering a heart attack.	Oct. 21
	Cuban president Fidel Castro, who was granted a strictly limited visa allowing him to visit the U.S. and address the UN, speaks at the Abyssinian Baptist Church in the predominantly black Harlem area of New York City.			Sir Kingsley Amis, 73, British novelist, poet, and cultural satirist who won Britain's Booker Prize in 1986, dies in a London hospital after breaking two vertebrae in a fall. . . . Michael Schumacher of Germany, 26, clinches his second straight Formula One racing title in the Pacific Gran Prix in Aida, Japan, and is the youngest driver ever to have won two titles.	Oct. 22

F	G	H	I	J
Includes elections, federal-state relations, civil rights and liberties, crime, the judiciary, education, health care, poverty, urban affairs, and population.	Includes formation and debate of U.S. foreign and defense policies, veterans' affairs, and defense spending. (Relations with specific foreign countries are usually found under the region concerned.)	Includes business, labor, agriculture, taxation, transportation, consumer affairs, monetary and fiscal policy, natural resources, and pollution.	Includes worldwide scientific, medical, and technological developments; natural phenomena; U.S. weather; natural disasters; and accidents.	Includes the arts, religion, scholarship, communications media, sports, entertainments, fashions, fads, and social life.

	World Affairs	Europe	Africa & the Middle East	The Americas	Asia & the Pacific
Oct. 23	French president Chirac on a live TV interview broadcast states that France will conduct four more underground tests in the South Pacific, bringing the expected total to six. A protester from the group Greenpeace is arrested after using a jet-powered parachute to sail near the UN building displaying a banner that reads, "Stop Nuclear Testing." The flight, timed to coincide with a speech by Chirac, is aimed at drawing attention to French nuclear testing.			Pres. Jean-Bertrand Aristide names Foreign Minister Claudette Werleigh to be Haiti's new premier. . . . A Salvadoran group called the Democratic Peasant Alliance organizes the takeovers of 59 properties that are among 285 identified by a government registry as being in excess of the legal limit of 621 acres per landholder.	
Oct. 24	Prior to adjourning its anniversary celebration, the 185 UN member nations unanimously reaffirm the principles of the UN Charter and adopt a pledge to reform the often-criticized, financially troubled organization. . . . . The European Commission, the executive arm of the EU, announces that it will not attempt to block nuclear tests in the South Pacific planned by France by suing France in an international court.	Eighteen Russian soldiers are killed in an ambush of their convoy in Chechnya.	Preliminary returns from Zanzibar's first-ever multiparty presidential and legislative elections suggest that Pres. Salmin Amour was reelected by a close margin. Opposition parties, alleging that the elections were rigged by the ruling CCM, demand a recount, and protesters clash with police.	Emile Jonassaint, 82, former Haitian Supreme Court justice who served as Haiti's military-backed president for four months beginning in May 1994, dies in Port-au-Prince, reportedly of natural causes.	Reports disclose that Myanmar's military government has ruled that the Oct. 10 appointment of dissident Aung San Suu Kyi as general secretary of the National League for Democracy (NLD), a party that she helped found in 1988, is illegal. . . . A shoot-out with police in Puyo, 100 miles (160 km) from the North Korean border, leads to the death of one policeman and the beginning of a manhunt for a North Korean spy in South Korea.
Oct. 25		Spain's parliament rejects a proposed budget for fiscal 1996, reportedly to protest the government's alleged involvement in a violent antiterrorist campaign in the 1980s. The vote marks the first serious parliamentary defeat for Premier Felipe Gonzalez's 13-year-old Socialist Party government.	In Sudan, rebel forces launch an offensive. . . . a Libyan head of state Col. Muammar Gadhafi suspends the expulsion of 30,000 Palestinians. Egypt has strongly lobbied Gadhafi to halt the expulsions.		
Oct. 26		International news organizations report new information that supports accusations that Bosnian Serbs in July massacred thousands of Muslim men and boys around the eastern Bosnian town of Srebrenica. . . . Turkish trade union leaders for public-sector workers accept the government's proposed wage increases and promise to end a series of devastating strikes. . . . Russian president Boris Yeltsin, 64, is hospitalized after suffering chest pains.	Two men on a motorcycle fatally shoot Fathi al-Shiqaqi, 44, the leader of the militant Islamic Jihad movement in the Gaza Strip, in the town of Sliema, located 6 miles (10 km) northwest of Valletta, the capital of Malta. He is not immediately identified. . . . Election returns from Zanzibar show that Pres. Salmin Amour of the CCM has won 165,271 votes, topping Seif Sharif Hamad of the CUF, which won 163,706.	Reports state that an estimated 270 people have died due to an outbreak of equine encephalitis in Colombia and Venezuela.	Tamil Tiger rebels raid two Sinhalese villages in the Welioya district in northeastern Sri Lanka. The rebels reportedly shoot or hack to death more than 20 civilians in the raids.
Oct. 27	France explodes a nuclear device in a series of tests being conducted in the South Pacific. . . . Russian defense minister Pavel S. Grachev and U.S. secretary of defense William J. Perry announce that a "special operations unit" made up of Russian and American troops will be established to help implement a peace in Bosnia.	Former Italian premier Bettino Craxi is sentenced in absentia to four years in prison for illegal party financing. . . . Turkey's parliament eases the country's antiterrorism laws, including those regarding free speech.	Six government soldiers are killed in an ambush by the Movement of Democratic Forces of Casamance in Senegal. . . . More than 250 Hutus are slain near Ngozi, Burundi.	Tens of thousands of people from all over Canada demonstrate in Montreal for Canadian unity on the question of whether Quebec should form its own nation.	Former South Korean president Roh Tae Woo confesses that while president from 1988 to 1993, he illegally collected 500 billion won ($654 million) in secret political donations. . . . Imelda Marcos, widow of former Philippine president Fidel Marcos, is sworn in as a member of the Philippines' House of Representatives. . . . South Korean troops fatally shoot an alleged North Korean spy, Park Kwang Nam, who eluded a massive manhunt that began Oct. 24.
Oct. 28		About 300 people are killed and at least 250 are injured when a crowded subway train catches fire in Baku, Azerbaijan's capital city.	In Niger, negotiations between the government and the Organization of Armed Resistance (ORA), which represents Taureg rebels, reconvenes with the goal of implementing a peace accord signed by the two parties, effective Apr. 25. The pact is aimed at ending a four-year conflict that has caused more than 200 deaths.	Enrique Haroldo Gorriaran Merlo, the former leader of the Argentine leftist guerrilla group known as the People's Revolutionary Army (ERP) who has been a fugitive for 25 years, is captured by Mexican authorities in Mexico City.	Vietnam's National Assembly adopts a national civil code, which lays out personal property, inheritance, and intellectual rights for the country's 72 million citizens. The landmark legislation, drafted over a 10-year period, is the first legal-rights code ever adopted by the country's communist government.
	A	**B**	**C**	**D**	**E**
	Includes developments that affect more than one world region, international organizations, and important meetings of major world leaders.	*Includes all domestic and regional developments in Europe, including the Soviet Union, Turkey, Cyprus, and Malta.*	*Includes all domestic and regional developments in Africa and the Middle East, including Iraq and Iran and excluding Cyprus, Turkey, and Afghanistan.*	*Includes all domestic and regional developments in Latin America, the Caribbean, and Canada.*	*Includes all domestic and regional developments in Asia and Pacific nations, extending from Afghanistan through all the Pacific Islands, except Hawaii.*

U.S. Politics & Social Issues	U.S. Foreign Policy & Defense	U.S. Economy & Environment	Science, Technology, & Nature	Culture, Leisure, & Lifestyle	
	The Defense Department announces that it will end a program designed to help minority-owned firms win defense contracts. The decision marks the first significant action taken by the Clinton administration following its review of federal affirmative-action programs.	A federal judge in Boston, Massachusetts, fines Conrail Inc. $2.5 million in criminal charges for spilling oil into the Charles River over a 15-year period.... The AFL-CIO labor federation holds its 21st constitutional convention.	A private, unmanned Conestoga rocket explodes 45 seconds after liftoff in the first launch from a NASA facility on Virginia's coast. The rocket, made for $14 million by Vienna-based EER Systems Corp., carried science experiments.	At the request of NYC mayor Rudolph Giuliani (R), Yasser Arafat is expelled from a concert for world leaders given by the New York Philharmonic at Lincoln Center.... A jury in Houston, Texas, convicts Yolanda Saldivar for the March murder of popular Mexican-American singer Selena in Corpus Christi, Texas.	Oct. 23
	Both houses of Congress pass a Republican-led bill to force the U.S. administration to move its embassy in Israel to Jerusalem from Tel Aviv, its current site. At the urging of Democratic senators, however, the measure allows the president to indefinitely postpone the move beyond its target date of mid-1999.		Scientists reveal that the corpses of three Inca children sacrificed about 500 years ago were found alongside rare Inca artifacts on Mt. Ampato in the Peruvian Andes.... The board of directors of the American College of Rheumatology claims there is no proof that silicone breast implants cause disease.	NYC mayor Rudolph Giuliani (R) is criticized by Pres. Clinton for expelling PNA head Yasser Arafat from a concert Oct. 23 as a breach of international diplomacy. Giuliani defends the expulsion, calling Arafat a murderer due to ties between the PLO and past terrorist actions.	Oct. 24
A federal jury in Dallas, Texas, orders abortion protesters to pay $8.6 million to Dr. Norman Tompkins, who claims that he and his wife were followed and harassed by the protesters. The jury's award is a record amount for a judgment against abortion protesters.... James Lake, a prominent lobbyist and Republican campaign strategist, pleads guilty to one felony fraud charge and two election-law misdemeanor charges. The charges stem from his participation in an illegal scheme to help pay off the campaign debts of Henry Espy.		The House approves, 393-29, a $13.1 billion appropriations bill for the Department of Transportation and other agencies for fiscal 1996. ...John J. Sweeney is elected president of the AFL-CIO federation, defeating incumbent Thomas Donahue in the first openly contested battle for the presidency in the organization's 40-year history. ...A three-judge appellate panel upholds a ruling that a budget resolution passed by Congress in July mandates the release of forests in the Pacific Northwest that the Clinton administration has since set aside for protection.	Seven high-school students, ages 14 to 18, are killed and more than two dozen others are injured when a commuter train crashes into the tail end of a school bus in Fox River Grove, Illinois, located about 40 miles (60 km) northwest of Chicago. The accident is the worst in the 21-year history of Metra, the commuter train line.... Researchers report they have grown a human ear on the back of a hairless mouse, in an experiment they hope will help them to regrow human tissues for people with missing body parts.	Bobby (Robert Lorimer) Riggs, 77, tennis player best known for his 1973 loss to Wimbledon champion Billie Jean King in the so-called battle of the sexes, dies in Leucadia, California, of prostate cancer.	Oct. 25
Dr. Hamilton Earl Holmes, 54, one of two students who integrated the University of Georgia by becoming the school's first black students in 1961, dies in Atlanta after suffering from a heart ailment.		The House passes, 227-203, its versions of the budget reconciliation bill that calls for the elimination of the federal budget deficit by the fiscal year 2002 via nearly $1 trillion dollars in spending cuts.... In light of the Oct. 25 decision, Pres. Clinton lifts a ban on logging in thousands of acres of old-growth forest in the Pacific Northwest.	Lars Ramskold of the University of Uppsala in Sweden reports finding in China fossils of a 525-million-year-old fishlike creature dubbed Yunnanozoon lividum. Researchers assert that the creature appears to be the oldest known to belong to the phylum Chordata, which includes vertebrates.	Reports state that the Vatican Library has approved commercial licensing projects.... Former education secretary William Bennett and Sen. Joseph Lieberman (D, Conn.), launch a campaign against what they call offensive subject matter on daytime TV talk shows.	Oct. 26
State health officials in Florida disclose that Elmer Hutto became infected with HIV at age 91 when he was bitten in August 1994 by a prostitute, Naomi Morrison, trying to rob him. The officials state it is the first confirmed case of transmission through a bite, but that the virus was transmitted through blood, not saliva.... Researchers estimate that 837,000 people attended the Oct. 16 "Million Man March." The recount comes because the Nation of Islam has threatened to sue the National Park Service regarding its estimates.	A sniper opens fire on hundreds of soldiers on a field at an Army base in Fort Bragg, North Carolina, killing Major Stephen Badger. In the attack, 18 others are wounded. The gunman, subdued by unarmed Special Forces soldiers jogging nearby, is identified as Sergeant William Kreutzer, a member of the 82nd Airborne Division, an elite unit.	Figures show that U.S. gross domestic product grew at a seasonally adjusted annual rate of 4.2% in the third quarter. That rate, the fastest since the fourth quarter of 1994, compares with an economic expansion of 1.3% in the April-June quarter.	Chinese scientists report that they found, near Jixian in China, more than 300 fossils of leaflike multicellular plants that lived in the sea more than 1.7 billion years ago, some 700,000 years earlier than the plants previously thought to be the oldest.		Oct. 27
A jury in state court in Reno, Nevada, finds Dow Chemical Co. liable for health problems that a plaintiff, Charlotte Mahlum, 46, claims she suffered because of her breast implants. The jury orders the company to pay Mahlum and her husband, Marvin Mahlum, $4.1 million in compensatory damages. It is the first time that Dow Chemical is found solely liable in a breast-implant case.		The Senate passes, 52-47, its version of the budget reconciliation bill. While the bill passed by the House Oct. 26 is very similar to this measure, observers believe it probably will take several weeks before a compromise version of the bill is complete.		The Atlanta Braves win MLB's 91st World Series with a 1-0 victory over the Cleveland Indians in Atlanta, Georgia.... Cigar wins the 12th running of the Breeders' Cup Classic with a record time of 1 minute and 59.4 seconds.	Oct. 28
F	G	H	I	J	
Includes elections, federal-state relations, civil rights and liberties, crime, the judiciary, education, health care, poverty, urban affairs, and population.	Includes formation and debate of U.S. foreign and defense policies, veterans' affairs, and defense spending. (Relations with specific foreign countries are usually found under the region concerned.)	Includes business, labor, agriculture, taxation, transportation, consumer affairs, monetary and fiscal policy, natural resources, and pollution.	Includes worldwide scientific, medical, and technological developments; natural phenomena; U.S. weather; natural disasters; and accidents.	Includes the arts, religion, scholarship, communications media, sports, entertainments, fashions, fads, and social life.	

	World Affairs	Europe	Africa & the Middle East	The Americas	Asia & the Pacific
Oct. 29		Pres. Tudjman's party, the Croatian Democratic Union (HDZ), wins a majority of seats in parliamentary elections in Croatia.	Red Cross officials state that some 2,330 inmates have died from disease in overcrowded Rwandan jails during a 15-month period. The jails, which hold 57,000 suspects tied to the 1994 massacres, were built to hold about 12,000 people. . . . Six people are killed and 83 others are wounded when a car bomb explodes in front of a police station in Rouiba, Algeria. . . . The militant Islamic Jihad movement in the Gaza Strip confirms that its leader, Fathi al-Shiqaqi, was killed on Oct. 26. Followers of Shiqaqi burn Israeli and U.S. flags in Gaza City and throw stones at Israeli soldiers in the city of Hebron.	Enrique Haroldo Gorriaran Merlo, the former leader of the Argentine leftist guerrilla group known as the People's Revolutionary Army (ERP) who was arrested Oct. 28 in Mexico, is extradited to Argentina. Gorriaran is wanted in Argentina in connection with numerous crimes, including a 1989 guerrilla attack on an Argentine army barracks that left 40 dead and 100 injured.	Reports reveal that the 425-member state assembly in Uttar Pradesh was disbanded by India's central government.
Oct. 30	An international war crimes tribunal indicts Gen. Mile Mrksic, Maj. Veselin Sljivancanin, and Capt. Miroslav Radic for involvement in the mass executions of Croatian men in November 1991. While other indictments have been handed down against Serbs in Bosnia, these are the first indictments for officials in Serbia. . . . After a summit, French president Jacques Chirac and British prime minister John Major announce a decision to coordinate their nuclear-defense policies.	The Socialist Party government of recently elected premier, Antonio Guterres, takes office in Portugal.	Emmanuel Rakotovahiny is named premier of Madagascar. . . . A Nigerian special tribunal in Port Harcourt in the Ogoni region convicts and sentences to death five MOSOP (Movement for the Survival of the Ogoni Peoples) members. . . . Reports suggest that the Gaza-based Islamic Jihad has named Ramadan Abdallah, 42, exiled in Syria, to replace Fathi al-Shiqaqi, killed on Oct. 26, as head of the movement.	Voters in the predominantly French-speaking Canadian province of Quebec, by a margin of a little more than 1%, reject a proposal for sovereignty that would have led to Quebec's separating from Canada to form its own nation.	
Oct. 31	An economic summit conference attended by 1,500 businesspeople and scores of political leaders and diplomats from the Middle East and North Africa concludes after delegates endorse a resolution, spearheaded by the U.S., to establish a Middle East and North Africa Development Bank, based in Cairo, Egypt.		A Nigerian tribunal convicts and sentences Ken Saro-Wiwa, 54, and three other members of the Movement for the Survival of the Ogoni Peoples (MOSOP) to death. MOSOP seeks to protect the Ogoni ethnic group.	In response to the Oct. 30 returns, Quebec premier Jacques Parizeau, the leader of the province's separatist Parti Quebecois, announces that he will resign and leave political life as of Dec. 22, the last day of Quebec's autumn legislative session.	In a pivotal battle with the Liberation Tigers of Tamil Eelam, Sri Lankan government forces take control of Neerveli, a small village 4 miles from Jaffna. . . . Sir Wallace Edward Rowling, 67, former New Zealand diplomat who served briefly as prime minister, 1974–75, dies in Nelson, New Zealand, of a brain tumor.
Nov. 1	The presidents of Serbia, Croatia, and Bosnia—Slobodan Milosevic, Alija Izetbegovic, and Franjo Tudjman, respectively, gather at U.S. Wright-Patterson Air Force Base outside Dayton, Ohio, for the beginning of peace talks aimed to build on principles agreed to by all three warring parties in September to divide Bosnia into two entities, a Muslim-Croat federation and a Serb republic.	French police conduct raids in Paris, Lyons, and Lille and seize grenades, machine-guns, pistols, documents and computers. Police in Paris arrest an Algerian man suspected of overseeing a recent bombing campaign in several metropolitan areas. . . . Brian Lenihan, 64, who served as former foreign minister and deputy prime minister of Ireland, dies in Dublin, Ireland, of a liver ailment.	The African National Congress wins a majority in South Africa's first-ever democratic local government elections.		An estimated 25,000 Sri Lankan government troops are consolidating their position some 3 miles (5 km) outside of Jaffna.
Nov. 2	For the fourth consecutive year, the UN General Assembly condemns the U.S. economic embargo of Cuba.		Two Palestinian suicide bombers launch separate but apparently synchronized attacks against Israeli convoys in the Gaza Strip. Eleven Israelis are slightly wounded, and the two bombers die in the incidents. . . . In South Africa, former defense minister Magnus Malan and 10 other retired senior military officers are arrested and charged in connection with killings that took place in 1987. The 11 officers are the highest-ranking government officials yet charged in investigations of apartheid-era abuses.	Alvaro Gomez Hurtado, a prominent member of the opposition Conservative Party, is gunned down in Bogota, Colombia's capital city. Pres. Ernesto Samper Pizano declares a 90-day state of emergency. A group calling itself National Dignity claims responsibility for the attack. . . . Argentina's Supreme Court overturns a lower court's ruling and approves the extradition of Erich Priebke, a former Nazi special-forces officer, to Italy in connection with crimes committed during World War II.	Typhoon Angela ravages the Philippines. Angela is the 14th such storm to hit the Philippines in 1995.

A	B	C	D	E
Includes developments that affect more than one world region, international organizations, and important meetings of major world leaders.	Includes all domestic and regional developments in Europe, including the Soviet Union, Turkey, Cyprus, and Malta.	Includes all domestic and regional developments in Africa and the Middle East, including Iraq and Iran and excluding Cyprus, Turkey, and Afghanistan.	Includes all domestic and regional developments in Latin America, the Caribbean, and Canada.	Includes all domestic and regional developments in Asia and Pacific nations, extending from Afghanistan through all the Pacific Islands, except Hawaii.

U.S. Politics & Social Issues	U.S. Foreign Policy & Defense	U.S. Economy & Environment	Science, Technology, & Nature	Culture, Leisure, & Lifestyle	
Police in Irvine, California, arrest five protestors who have been on hunger strikes since Oct. 17 for obstructing a police officer when the strikers refuse to leave their makeshift encampment. The strikers are protesting the elimination of affirmative-action admissions policies within the eight-campus University of California system.				Golfer Billy Mayfair wins the PGA's Tour Championship at the Southern Hills Country Club in Tulsa, Oklahoma. . . . Terry Southern, 71, novelist and screenwriter best known as a coauthor of *Dr. Strangelove* (1964) and *Easy Rider* (1969), dies in New York City, reportedly of respiratory failure.	Oct. 29
Pres. Clinton signs into law a bill that maintains stiffer prison penalties for individuals convicted of crack cocaine offenses rather than offenses involving powdered cocaine. . . . A jury in state court in Reno, Nevada, orders Dow Chemical to pay $10 million in punitive damages to Charlotte Mahlum, 46. When combined with the Oct. 28 compensation, the award is among the largest ever in cases involving silicone breast implants.		Standard & Poor's Corp. finds that the U.S. insurance industry faces $40 billion in environmental related claims. . . . A state court jury in Indianapolis, Indiana, awards Vicki Ammerman and Alana Cuskaden a total of $62.4 million in damages against Ford Motor Co. in connection with a 1991 rollover accident involving a 1986 Ford Bronco II. The jury states that the vehicle's design makes Ford liable for the accident.	A survey indicates that approximately 37 million people in the U.S. and Canada, or 17% of the adult population of those countries, have access to the Internet global computer network. The survey also finds that about 11% of adults in the U.S. and Canada, or 24 million people, have used the Internet during the previous three months.	*The Lost World* by Michael Crichton tops the bestseller list.	Oct. 30
In *Citizens Bank of Maryland v. Strumpf*, the Supreme Court rules unanimously that banks may temporarily freeze the assets of depositors who default on loans, even if those customers had previously filed for bankruptcy protection. . . . In *Louisiana v. Mississippi*, the Supreme Court rules unanimously that a stretch of land along the Louisiana bank of the Mississippi River known as Stack Island belongs to Mississippi. . . . Some 35,000 volunteers in Detroit, Mich., help to put out about 60 arson fires set on Oct. 30, or Devil's Night.	CIA director John M. Deutch testifies in closed-door hearings before the House and Senate select committees on intelligence on the results of an 18-month investigation into the damage caused by convicted spy Aldrich Hazen Ames.	The House, 402-24, and the Senate, 89-6, approve a $19.7 billion fiscal 1996 appropriations bill to fund energy, water-development and nuclear-weapons programs. . . . The Senate, 87-10, passes a $13.1 billion fiscal 1996 appropriations bill for the Department of Transportation. . . . The House approves, 315-106, a $2.2 billion for fiscal 1996 to fund for the legislative branch. . . . The Energy Department states it will conduct six underground nuclear explosions at its Nevada Test Site over a two-year period.	A research report finds new evidence that genetic material on one segment of the X chromosome appears to influence the likelihood of homosexuality in males. The finding does not apply to females. . . . Data show that Compaq Computer Corp. continues to lead computer manufacturers in the number of personal computers (PCs) shipped during the third quarter of 1995.	Soul singer James Brown, 62, is arrested at his Aiken, South Carolina, home on charges of criminal domestic violence.	Oct. 31
The House votes, 288-139, to approve a bill that will ban a procedure known as intact dilation and evacuation, a rare method used to end pregnancies in their late stages. The bill is the first attempt by Congress to ban an abortion procedure since 1973. . . . In what is considered the most comprehensive study of students' U.S. history knowledge, the Department of Education finds that about 64% of fourth-graders, 61% of eighth-graders, and only 43% of high-school seniors have attained at least the basic level of historical knowledge.	In Tokyo, Defense Secretary William J. Perry expresses his "deep sorrow and anger" for the rape of a 12-year-old girl by U.S. servicemen in Okinawa. Pres. Clinton and U.S. ambassador to Japan Walter F. Mondale have also apologized for the incident.	Some 1,000 members of the United Automobile Workers (UAW) union walk off their jobs at Chrysler Corp.'s McGraw Glass Division plant in Detroit, Michigan.	Research suggests that people who each week consume the equivalent of 3.5 ounces (109 grams) of fish rich in two types of omega-3 fatty acids are half as likely to suffer cardiac arrest as those who eat no fish.		Nov. 1
The New York State Court of Appeals rules, 4-3, in favor of extending to unwed couples, homosexual or heterosexual, the right to adopt children. The ruling makes New York the third state whose highest court grants unwed couples the right to adopt children. . . . A hostage rescue team in Miami Beach, Florida, fatally shoots Catalino (Nick) Sang, after he hijacks a school bus carrying 13 disabled children and leads authorities on a 25-mile (40-km), low-speed chase. No hostages are seriously hurt.	The U.S. Justice Department indicts Daiwa Bank Ltd., a major Japanese commercial bank, on 24 counts of fraud and conspiracy. In September Daiwa admitted that its chief trader of U.S. Treasury bonds, Toshihide Iguchi, had amassed and concealed huge losses over an 11-year period.	The Senate approves by voice vote a $2.2 billion fiscal 1996 appropriations bill for the legislative branch. . . . Congress clears a $712 million fiscal 1996 appropriations bill for the District of Columbia.	NASA releases *Hubble Space Telescope* photographs that are said to be the most striking images to date of the birth of stars. The images of about 50 stars in the Eagle Nebula, or M16, about 7,000 light-years from Earth, reveal evaporating gaseous globules from which stars will form at the tips of columns of gas 6 trillion miles high. . . . A study finds that a small area in the hypothalamus brain region of transsexual men is significantly smaller than the same brain area in other men.		Nov. 2

F	G	H	I	J
Includes elections, federal-state relations, civil rights and liberties, crime, the judiciary, education, health care, poverty, urban affairs, and population.	*Includes formation and debate of U.S. foreign and defense policies, veterans' affairs, and defense spending. (Relations with specific foreign countries are usually found under the region concerned.)*	*Includes business, labor, agriculture, taxation, transportation, consumer affairs, monetary and fiscal policy, natural resources, and pollution.*	*Includes worldwide scientific, medical, and technological developments; natural phenomena; U.S. weather; natural disasters; and accidents.*	*Includes the arts, religion, scholarship, communications media, sports, entertainments, fashions, fads, and social life.*

	World Affairs	Europe	Africa & the Middle East	The Americas	Asia & the Pacific
Nov. 3				At least 13 people are killed and 330 injured when a fire in a military munitions plant in the town of Rio Tercera in Argentina touches off a series of explosions. Many of the town's 3,000 residents flee. . . . Paul Bernardo, convicted of first-degree murder in a sensational trial in September, admits that he committed 13 brutal rapes in Scarborough, a Toronto, Canada, suburb in the late 1980s.	Typhoon Angela, the most powerful storm to hit the Philippines since 1984, tears through the archipelago, leaving more than 600 people dead. . . . In the longest and most expensive criminal trial in the history of the Australian territory, David Eastman, 50, a former official of the federal treasury, is convicted of the 1989 murder of Colin Winchester of the Australian Federal Police.
Nov. 4		Police in Great Britain arrest Abdelkader Benouif, reportedly a high-ranking member of the GIA and a suspect in recent bombings in France. . . . Former Italian premier Giulio Andreotti is charged with murder along with four other people in connection with the 1979 killing of a journalist, Carmine Pecorelli. . . . Paul Eddington (born Paul Clark-Eddington), 68, British actor known for TV situation comedies, dies in London of a rare skin cancer.	Yitzhak Rabin, 73, Israel's prime minister who shared the 1994 Nobel Peace Prize with Yasser Arafat, is assassinated after delivering a speech at a pro-peace rally in Tel Aviv. The assailant, identified as Yigal Amir, 24, a Jewish right-wing extremist, is immediately seized by security officers and placed in custody. The shooting stuns the nation. Foreign Minister Shimon Peres automatically assumes the post of acting prime minister. . . . Rwandan government soldiers launch a raid against Hutu rebels on the small island of Iwawa in Lake Kivu near Zaire.		More than 10,000 protesters in Seoul demand that former South Korean president Roh Tae Woo, who confessed to amassing a slush fund while president, be arrested and that Pres. Kim's alleged links to the slush fund be investigated.
Nov. 5		Eduard Shevardnadze, 67, currently Georgia's head of state, is elected president to serve a five-year term under the new constitution approved during the summer. Preliminary returns show that Shevardnadze's party, the Citizens' Union, has won a large number of seats in the parliament. . . . An interim government formed by Turkish premier Tansu Ciller easily wins a vote of confidence in Parliament.	In Sudan, rebel forces seize the Pagere village following the capture of eight other villages in an offensive begun Oct. 25.	A man armed with a knife breaks into the official Ottawa, Ontario, residence of Canadian prime minister Jean Chrétien and his wife, Aline Chretien. Aline Chretien barricades the bedroom and calls the police, who apprehend the intruder, Andre Dallaire, 34.	In Sri Lanka, international relief agencies, citing heavy civilian casualties in Jaffna, estimate that between 300,000 and 400,000 people have fled the region to escape the fighting. The plight of many of the refugees, who reportedly have no shelter, is exacerbated by monsoon storms that begin hitting the region.
Nov. 6	The funeral for Israeli prime minister Yitzhak Rabin is attended by 5,000 mourners, including scores of heads of state. Among those assembled are U.S. president Clinton, King Hussein of Jordan, British prime minister Major, French president Chirac, Russian premier Chernomyrdin, German chancellor Kohl, Italian premier Dini, and Canadian prime minister Chrétien. Premier Gonzalez of Spain also represents the EU, and the UN's Boutros Boutros-Ghali attends. Egypt's president Mubarak makes his first visit to Jerusalem to attend. The PNA, Oman, and Qatar send representatives as well.			The Court Martial Appeal Court of the Canadian Armed Forces voids the 1994 acquittal of retired Lt. Col. Carol Mathieu, who commanded the now-disbanded Canadian Airborne Regiment when it took part in a humanitarian relief operation in Somalia in 1992 and 1993. The appellate court orders that Mathieu be tried again on charges of negligence of duty related to the killings of four Somalis by members of his regiment in 1993.	Franklin Castillo, a director at the Philippines' Office of Civil Defense, states that the provinces hardest hit by Typhoon Angela Nov. 2–3 are inaccessible to rescue workers because of flooding and landslides. He estimates that 636,000 people have fled to government shelters. Castillo also estimates that Angela destroyed or damaged more than 96,000 houses and caused at least $77 million in damage to the country's infrastructure.
Nov. 7		Estonian president Lennart Meri approves a new coalition government and cabinet led by Premier Tiit Vahi. . . . In Portugal, the government halts construction of a dam that reportedly may damage carvings dating back to the Stone Age. . . . A British court of appeals overturns the 1992 convictions of four men found guilty of illegally selling arms to Iraq, finding that the government withheld crucial documents during the 1992 trial.	Rwandan government officials disclose that its soldiers, who are predominately of Tutsi extraction, have killed about half of a 600-strong force of Hutu rebels in a raid that started Nov. 4 on the small island of Iwawa in Lake Kivu, near the Zaire border. Other sources state that a rebel force of 300 was routed, 171 of them were killed, and five Rwandan army soldiers were killed. . . . An attack on an Egyptian passenger train wounds 10 Egyptian citizens.	Jean-Hubert Feuille, a member of Haiti's legislature and a cousin of Pres. Jean-Bertrand Aristide, is fatally shot while riding in a car in broad daylight in Port-au-Prince, Haiti's capital. Rep. Gabriel Fortune, a passenger in the car, is wounded. Separately, Claudette Werleigh is sworn in and becomes Haiti's first female premier.	Three U.S. servicemen plead guilty to conspiring to abduct and rape a 12-year-old girl in Okinawa. Seaman Marcus Gill, 22, admits beating and raping the girl. Pfc. Kendrick M. Ledet, 20, denies raping or beating the girl. Pfc. Rodrico Harp, 21, states he did not rape the girl, but admits to hitting her a single time. . . . The Sri Lankan government states that since early October, approximately 100,000 civilians have fled Jaffna.
Nov. 8	The 185-member UN General Assembly holds a secret ballot to fill the five Security Council seats that will be vacated in 1996. The five countries selected are Chile, Egypt, Guinea-Bissau, Poland, and South Korea.	French judge Pierre Renard-Peyen orders that British Airways pay some $4.8 million in cash damages to 61 French passengers who were taken hostage by Iraq just after that country's invasion of Kuwait in August 1990. The plaintiffs are among 360 passengers and crew members aboard a flight that made an unscheduled landing in Kuwait on the day of the invasion.	Israeli police arrest extremist group Eyal's leader, Avishai Raviv, and a Tel Aviv court orders him held on suspicion of conspiracy in the assassination of P.M. Rabin. . . . An attack on an Egyptian passenger train slightly wounds three people. . . . Despite international pleas for clemency in the case, the Nigerian government gives final approval to convictions and death sentences of the nine members of the Movement for the Survival of the Ogoni Peoples (MOSOP).	The Brazilian Senate approves a constitutional amendment ending the 42-year-old monopoly that state-run oil company Petroleo Brasileiro (Petrobras) has held over oil production, refining, and transport. . . . An Argentine air force plane crashes during a rainstorm in a remote mountainous region in central Argentina, killing all 53 people on board.	Robert S. McNamara, the U.S. secretary of defense during the Vietnam War, makes his first visit to Vietnam since the war.

A	B	C	D	E
Includes developments that affect more than one world region, international organizations, and important meetings of major world leaders.	Includes all domestic and regional developments in Europe, including the Soviet Union, Turkey, Cyprus, and Malta.	Includes all domestic and regional developments in Africa and the Middle East, including Iraq and Iran and excluding Cyprus, Turkey, and Afghanistan.	Includes all domestic and regional developments in Latin America, the Caribbean, and Canada.	Includes all domestic and regional developments in Asia and Pacific nations, extending from Afghanistan through all the Pacific Islands, except Hawaii.

U.S. Politics & Social Issues	U.S. Foreign Policy & Defense	U.S. Economy & Environment	Science, Technology, & Nature	Culture, Leisure, & Lifestyle	
	More than 2,000 people attend a memorial ceremony at Arlington National Cemetery in Arlington, Virginia, for the 270 victims of the 1988 terrorist bombing of Pan Am Flight 103 over Lockerbie, Scotland. . . . . In Monticello, Florida, Judge Nikki Clark sentences teenager John (Billy Joe) Crumitie to life in prison for the 1993 slaying of a British tourist, Gary Colley, at a highway rest stop in northern Florida.	Some 120 people are hospitalized when an accident at a Seattle, Washington, manufacturing plant of the Boeing Co. creates a cloud of toxic gas outside the plant. About 2,300 workers at the plant are evacuated because of the accident.	Research suggests that a gene mutation that previously was thought to cause only a portion of familial breast cancer cases also is linked to noninherited cases, which far outnumber familial cases.		Nov. 3
					Nov. 4
		Some 1,000 members of the United Automobile Workers (UAW) union vote to end the strike begun Nov. 1 at Chrysler Corp.'s McGraw Glass Division plant in Detroit, MI.	The U.S. space shuttle *Columbia* touches down at Kennedy Space Center in Cape Canaveral, Florida, with the crew having completed scientific experiments on the effects of near-weightlessness in a microgravity laboratory in the shuttle's cargo bay.		Nov. 5
The American Medical Association (AMA) issues two sets of guidelines regarding sexual assault and family violence. The organization's statistics reveal that more than 700,000 women are sexually assaulted each year, or one every 45 seconds. The AMA finds that 61% of female rape victims are under age 18, that three-quarters of sexual assaults are committed by friends or acquaintances, and that males are victims in 5% of sexual assaults.	The U.S. Air Force at NASA's Kennedy Space Center launches a *Titan 4*, the most powerful U.S. unmanned rocket, carrying the second in a Defense Department series of $1 billion *Milstar* communications satellites.	*The Wall Street Journal* reports in its quarterly earnings review that the net income of 711 major corporations totaled $63.25 billion in the third quarter of 1995. That is a 5% gain over those companies' revised 1994 third-quarter profits, which totaled $60.22 billion. . . . Los Angeles–based First Interstate Bancorp agrees to be acquired by First Bank System of Minneapolis, Minnesota, for an estimated $9.8 billion. The sale will be the second-largest bank purchase to date in the U.S.		Maryland governor Parris N. Glendening (D) announces that the NFL's Cleveland Browns have agreed to move to Baltimore, Maryland, prior to the start of the 1996–97 season. The popularity of the Browns among Cleveland fans sparks unprecedented protests against team owner Art Modell and the National Football League.	Nov. 6
In *Libretti v. U.S.*, the Supreme Court rules, 8-1, that convicted drug traffickers who agree to forfeit property to the government under plea-bargaining pacts with prosecutors are not entitled to have a judge independently determine how much of their property the government may legitimately seize. . . . Maine voters reject a ballot initiative that would have prohibited Maine from enacting laws designed specifically to protect homosexuals as a group.				Slappy White (born Melvin White), 74, black stand-up comedian, dies in Brigantine, New Jersey, after suffering a heart attack. . . . John Patrick, 90, playwright who won the 1954 Pulitzer Prize, is found dead in Delray Beach, Florida, in an apparent suicide. . . . Novelist Pat Barker wins the 1995 Booker Prize for *The Ghost Road*.	Nov. 7
The National Education Goals Panel, a bipartisan committee created to oversee a 10-year plan to improve education nationwide, reports that limited progress toward U.S. education goals has been achieved midway through the program. Members of the panel indicate that few, if any, of the panel's goals will be met by the year 2000 if progress continues at the current rate.	A three-judge panel of the U.S. Ninth Circuit Court of Appeals in San Francisco, California, rules that foreigners in the U.S. share the same free-speech rights as U.S. citizens. The ruling strikes down a provision of the 1952 Immigration and Nationality Act, known as the McCarran-Walter Act. . . . A U.S. federal judge in Miami, Florida, orders the extradition of real-estate magnate Juergen Schneider and his wife, Claudia Schneider, to Germany from the U.S.	The House passes, 289-134, a measure that lifts a 22-year-old ban on exports of crude oil from Alaska's North Slope to foreign countries.		Officials announces that William Franklin Graham III will succeed his father, the evangelist preacher Rev. Billy Graham, as head of the Billy Graham Evangelistic Association.	Nov. 8

F	G	H	I	J
Includes elections, federal-state relations, civil rights and liberties, crime, the judiciary, education, health care, poverty, urban affairs, and population.	*Includes formation and debate of U.S. foreign and defense policies, veterans' affairs, and defense spending. (Relations with specific foreign countries are usually found under the region concerned.)*	*Includes business, labor, agriculture, taxation, transportation, consumer affairs, monetary and fiscal policy, natural resources, and pollution.*	*Includes worldwide scientific, medical, and technological developments; natural phenomena; U.S. weather; natural disasters; and accidents.*	*Includes the arts, religion, scholarship, communications media, sports, entertainments, fashions, fads, and social life.*

	World Affairs	Europe	Africa & the Middle East	The Americas	Asia & the Pacific
Nov. 9		A Turkish court acquits an American journalist working for Britain's Reuters news service who was charged with breaching the country's antiterrorist laws. The reporter, Aliza Marcus, is the first foreign journalist to be prosecuted under Turkey's strict freedom-of-expression statutes.	In Tel Aviv, PLO chairman Yasser Arafat visits the widow of P.M. Yitzhak Rabin, Leah Rabin, to offer condolences over the Nov. 4 assassination. It is the first publicly known visit by Arafat to Israel. Speculation on a right-wing conspiracy to kill Rabin intensifies with the arrests of two more suspects, Dror Adani, 26, and Ohad Skornick, 23. . . . The Islamic Group claims responsibility for the Nov. 8 attack on a train in Egypt.	The U.S. State Department announces that it is holding up a $4.5 million aid package to Haiti because of that country's slowness in privatizing state enterprises and enacting civil-service reform. . . . Basdeo Panday is sworn in as Trinidad and Tobago's new prime minister after his United National Congress (UNC) party agrees to form a coalition government with the smaller National Alliance for Reconstruction (NAR).	
Nov. 10	An international war-crimes tribunal indicts six Bosnian Croats for "the persecution on political, racial and religious grounds" of Muslim civilians in Bosnia during 1992 and 1993. . . . Leaders from most of the British Commonwealth's 52 member nations, the majority of which are former colonies of Britain, attend a summit and release a statement condemning France's recent resumption of nuclear testing in the South Pacific.	Irish police in the border town of Carrickmacross intercept a van bound for Ulster containing 1,300 pounds (585 kg) of explosives.	Nigeria hangs writer Ken Saro-Wiwa and eight other minority-rights and environmental activists convicted of inciting the murder of four leaders of their Ogoni ethnic group in 1994. Saro-Wiwa maintained that he was framed in the killings. The hangings, carried out despite pleas from the international community for leniency, prompt many nations, including Britain, the U.S., South Africa, Germany, and Austria, to recall their ambassadors to Nigeria. . . . Gunmen in Algiers, Algeria, shoot dead a French nun and wound another.	Brazilian president Fernando Henrique Cardoso signs 40 decrees expropriating 250,000 acres (101,000 hectares) of unused land from large private estates, vowing to allocate the land to some 3,600 landless farming families.	Government troops participating in a stepped-up military campaign against the Liberation Tigers of Tamil Eelam rebel group advance into the outskirts of the rebel-held city of Jaffna on the northeastern peninsula of Sri Lanka.
Nov. 11	In the wake of the Nov. 10 hangings in Nigeria, the 52-member British Commonwealth, meeting at its biennial summit, decide to suspend Nigeria from the organization for human-rights abuses.	Corneliu Coposu, 79, Romanian politician who, in 1989, revived the National Peasant Party, dies in Bucharest, Romania, after a heart attack.	McDonald's Corp. opens the first of its planned restaurants in Johannesburg, South Africa.	At funeral ceremonies for Jean-Hubert Feuille, a member of Haiti's legislature assassinated Nov. 7, Pres. Jean-Bertrand Aristide criticizes the UN peacekeeping force in Haiti for not completely disarming supporters of the ousted military regime.	Tamil rebels carry out two terrorist bombings in Colombo, Sri Lanka's capital, killing an estimated 20 people and injuring at least 40 others. Fighting in Jaffna causes 900 casualties. . . . Afghanistan's state-controlled radio reports that Taliban forces have launched an attack against Kabul, killing 35 civilians and wounding 50. The Taliban refuses to claim responsibility for the offensive. . . . At least 56 people die in what is described as one of the worst avalanches in Nepal's history. More than 500 others are stranded and rescued.
Nov. 12	At a summit of the British Commonwealth's 52 member nations, Mozambique is admitted into the Commonwealth and will become the only member not to have former colonial ties to Britain. . . . The 15 member states of the European Union opt to remove their ambassadors to Nigeria in reaction to the Nov. 10 hangings.	In Azerbaijan's first parliamentary elections, the New Azerbaijan Party—aligned with Pres. Heydar Aliyev—wins the majority. . . . Sir Robert Stephens, 64, British actor regarded a master of Shakespearean performance, dies in London after suffering from liver and kidney ailments. . . . Jack Mann, 81, former British hostage held in Beirut, Lebanon, from in May 1989 to September 1991, dies in Nicosia, Cyprus, after suffering from heart and lung ailments.	The Polisario Front, a rebel group that had been backed by Algeria, turns over to the Red Cross 185 long-held Moroccan prisoners of war taken in a dispute over Western Sahara, which is claimed by both Morocco and the front. . . . Israelis end their formal mourning period for P.M. Yitzhak Rabin with a demonstration that draws 300,000 people to the square in Tel Aviv where he was assassinated Nov. 4.	Guatemala holds government-announced presidential elections. . . . Emmett Matthew Hall, 96, Canadian lawyer and judge who, in 1962, was appointed to Canada's Supreme Court, dies in Saskatoon, Saskatchewan, of unreported causes.	Heavy rains in Nepal cause falling earth to crush houses and tourist lodges in the Himalayan region districts of Manang and Panchathar, killing 17 people. . . . China's official New China News Agency reports that the Chinese government has rejected the Dalai Lama's appointee and will select a new Panchen Lama. The dispute over the designate underscores China's continuing determination to assert authority over Tibet.
Nov. 13	In response to the EU's Nov. 12 decision regarding Nigeria, Nigeria recalls its envoys to those countries, defends the hangings of Nov. 10 as justified, and accuses foreign nations of meddling in its internal affairs.	An Egyptian envoy, Ahmed Ala Nazmi, 42, is shot to death in Geneva, Switzerland. An Islamic group takes responsibility the attack.	The Israeli military withdraws from the West Bank Arab city of Jenin, transferring control to the PNA, headed by Yasser Arafat, after 28 years of Israeli military occupation. . . . Two explosions rock a military training and communications center in Riyadh, the Saudi Arabian capital, killing seven people, including five Americans and injuring about 60 others. . . . In Tanzania, a coalition of all 10 opposition parties withdraws from the election process.		A Japanese cabinet minister, Takami Eto, resigns over controversial remarks made a month earlier regarding Japan's brutal occupation of Korea, which lasted from 1910 to 1945. Eto, the head of the Management and Coordination Agency, said that the occupation had done "some good things" for Korea.
Nov. 14	The World Trade Organization projects that trade in 1995 will continue a marked tendency toward globalization, with the volume of international merchandise trade for the year increasing 8% from 1994 levels.	Several workers' unions hold a series of demonstrations to protest a package of spending cuts and tax hikes in France. . . . International observers claim that the Nov. 12 elections in Azerbaijan were seriously flawed.			Kashmiri militants holding four Western tourists hostage since July disclose that two of their captives are ill, one of whom is "struggling for life."

A	B	C	D	E
Includes developments that affect more than one world region, international organizations, and important meetings of major world leaders.	*Includes all domestic and regional developments in Europe, including the Soviet Union, Turkey, Cyprus, and Malta.*	*Includes all domestic and regional developments in Africa and the Middle East, including Iraq and Iran and excluding Cyprus, Turkey, and Afghanistan.*	*Includes all domestic and regional developments in Latin America, the Caribbean, and Canada.*	*Includes all domestic and regional developments in Asia and Pacific nations, extending from Afghanistan through all the Pacific Islands, except Hawaii.*

U.S. Politics & Social Issues	U.S. Foreign Policy & Defense	U.S. Economy & Environment	Science, Technology, & Nature	Culture, Leisure, & Lifestyle	
	Statistics show that more than 1 million legal immigrants applied for U.S. citizenship in fiscal 1995. That number is nearly double the fiscal 1993 figure and is the highest in the 20th century. . . . One of Hong Kong's richest developers, Gordon Y. S. Wu, announces that he will donate $100 million to the School of Engineering and Applied Science at Princeton University. It is the largest cash donation ever by a foreigner to a university in the U.S.	The NRC grants a low-power permit to the TVA to operate its Watts Bar 1 nuclear power plant, ending a 23-year TVA effort to gain a license for the only commercial nuclear power facility still under construction in the U.S. . . . The Senate passes, 49-47, a bill to increase the debt-limit for federal government funding.		Marcia Clark, lead prosecutor in the O. J. Simpson trial, receives a $4.2 million advance offer, which is the third-largest nonfiction book advance in U.S. publishing history. . . . Cartoonist Bill Watterson states he will stop drawing his strip, *Calvin and Hobbes*, in print since 1986, on Dec. 31.	Nov. 9
One of the most conservative Democrats in the House, Rep. Mike Parker (Miss.), announces that he will switch to the Republican Party. Since the Republicans won control of Congress after the 1994 elections, three other House Democrats have joined the GOP. Parker's switch leaves the House with 234 Republicans, 198 Democrats, one independent, and two vacancies.	Citing several cases of sexual misconduct by navy personnel, Chief of Naval Operations Admiral Jeremy Boorda announces that he has called for a one-day "stand down"—or cessation of normal duties—for the navy. Boorda discloses that navy units will spend that day discussing drug and alcohol abuse, sexual harassment, and the responsibilities of leadership. The stand-down will affect the Navy's 430,000 active-duty personnel.	The House passes, 219-185, a measure to increase the debt limit. The body also approves, 224-172, a continuing resolution. Both measures are designed to fund the federal government past deadlines while Congress works on appropriation bills.	Researchers report that a small group of Australians who have been infected with HIV for 11–14 years have remained healthy without developing AIDS because they are infected with a genetically weak strain of the virus.		Nov. 10
			Scientists claim they have found fossils in 45-million-year-old rocks in China of a small mammal called Eosimias, which is the oldest known anthropoid, the higher primates that includes humans, monkeys, and apes.	Charles Scribner Jr., 74, former head of the Charles Scribner's Sons book-publishing company who was the personal editor for Ernest Hemingway, dies in New York City of pneumonia. . . . The NBA suspends a record 16 players for fighting during a Nov. 10 basketball game between the Indiana Pacers and the Sacramento Kings.	Nov. 11
		John J. Sweeney, the recently elected president of the AFL-CIO labor federation, meets with Boeing workers, striking since Oct. 6, in Everett, Washington, and he leads a march of 300–400 Boeing strikers to a rally attended by several thousand people at Everett Memorial Stadium.	The U.S. space shuttle *Atlantis* lifts off from Kennedy Space Center in Cape Canaveral, Florida, to carry out a mission to dock with the Russian space station *Mir*.	Jeff Gordon becomes the second-youngest NASCAR champion when he clinches the Winston Cup. . . . German Silva of Mexico and Tegla Loroupe of Kenya successfully defend their titles at the New York City Marathon. . . . U.S. golfers win a record fourth consecutive World Cup title.	Nov. 12
A suspected serial killer, Glen Rogers, is arrested in Waco, Kentucky, after leading police on a high-speed chase. Rogers, the subject of a nationwide manhunt, is suspected of killing four women—in California, Mississippi, Florida, and Louisiana—since September and of slaying an elderly man in Ohio.	After a year-long review of the cases of 2,202 servicemen still listed as MIA, the Defense Department discloses there is "virtually no possibility" that the bodies of 567 servicemen killed in the Vietnam War will ever be recovered.	The Senate passes a stopgap bill by voice vote. However, Pres. Clinton vetoes it, which forces a partial shutdown of the federal government. Clinton also vetoes a bill to increase the debt limit. Secretary of the Treasury Robert Rubin states he will tap into two federal retirement funds to avoid government default on $102 billion. Clinton signs a $19.7 billion appropriations bill for energy, water development, and nuclear weapons programs.		Russian-born novelist Andrei Makine is awarded the Goncourt Prize for his novel *Le Testament Français* (*The French Will*). Since Makine had already received France's Medicis prize for *Le Testament Français*, he becomes the first writer to be awarded those two prizes for the same book.	Nov. 13
A study focusing on nine school districts from 1967 to 1991 shows that 38% of new school funding assisted the needs of disabled students and 19% went to other types of special education, while 26% was used for regular education costs.	Aundra Akins, 16, is sentenced to 27 years in prison for the 1993 slaying of a British tourist, Gary Colley, at a highway rest stop in northern Florida. The attack received international attention and called attention to problems facing tourism and safety in the U.S.	The Senate passes, 69-29, a measure that lifts a 22-year-old ban on exports of crude oil from Alaska's North Slope to foreign countries. . . . The failure of Pres. Clinton and Republican leaders to reach an agreement on a continuing resolution bill forces a shutdown of federal agencies around the country.			Nov. 14

F	G	H	I	J
Includes elections, federal-state relations, civil rights and liberties, crime, the judiciary, education, health care, poverty, urban affairs, and population.	*Includes formation and debate of U.S. foreign and defense policies, veterans' affairs, and defense spending. (Relations with specific foreign countries are usually found under the region concerned.)*	*Includes business, labor, agriculture, taxation, transportation, consumer affairs, monetary and fiscal policy, natural resources, and pollution.*	*Includes worldwide scientific, medical, and technological developments; natural phenomena; U.S. weather; natural disasters; and accidents.*	*Includes the arts, religion, scholarship, communications media, sports, entertainments, fashions, fads, and social life.*

	World Affairs	Europe	Africa & the Middle East	The Americas	Asia & the Pacific
Nov. 15		Slovakia's parliament passes a law that declares Slovak the only state language and bars the use of other languages in official communications, ceremonies, broadcasting, and advertising . . . French premier Alain Juppe wins parliamentary support for a sweeping package of spending cuts and tax hikes intended to reduce the country's massive social-security deficit.		Coca growers in the Chapare region of Bolivia clash with police who are enforcing the government's plan to eradicate coca crops, the plant used to make cocaine. A 13-year-old girl is killed. . . . Guatemala announces that the two candidates in Nov. 12 presidential elections, Alvaro Arzu Irigoyen and Alfonso Portillo Cabrera, will face a runoff vote. . . . Reports indicate that seven people have died in clashes during demonstrations in Haiti.	The Australian government agrees to provide funding for the first bridge to cross the Mekong River in Vietnam. About 20 million of Vietnam's 72 million people currently rely on ferries across the Mekong for their transportation needs.
Nov. 16	Russia reaches an accord with the so-called London Club of 600 Western creditor banks to reschedule, over the next 25 years, $32.5 billion in debts incurred by the former Soviet Union. . . . The Yugoslav War Crimes Tribunal in The Hague indicts Radovan Karadzic and Gen. Ratko Mladic on new charges of genocide and crimes against humanity in connection with the capture of the Bosnian town of Srebrenica, which some analysts characterize as the worst massacre in Europe since World War II.	In France, Alain Carignon, a former communications minister and mayor of Grenoble, is sentenced to three years in prison on charges of corruption. Carignon is the most senior official jailed during France's recent anticorruption campaign.	Algerian president Lamine Zeroual wins election to a five-year term in Algeria's first contested presidential election since the country gained its independence from France in 1962. According to the government, nearly 75% of the country's 16 million eligible voters turned out to vote, despite Islamic fundamentalist groups' threats to kill voters at the polls. Several opposition parties boycotted the election. . . . Nigeria's Committee for the Defense of Human Rights reveals that Nigeria has seized nine of its members to stifle protests.		Former South Korean president Roh Tae Woo is arrested for accepting hundreds of millions of dollars in bribes during his tenure as president, from 1988 to 1993. . . . Dockworkers embark on a series of national strikes coordinated by the Australian Council of Trade Unions (ACTU). . . . The official New China News Agency issues China's first major policy statement on arms control, which states that China is committed to peace, will not "threaten or invade" another country, and will not substantially raise its defense spending without a serious threat to its security.
Nov. 17				U.S. president Clinton, in a lengthy interview broadcast on Japanese TV, apologizes for the September rape of a Japanese girl by U.S. servicemen. U.S. Navy admiral Richard C. Macke, commander of U.S. forces in the Pacific region, is forced to retire after telling reporters, "I've said several times, for the price they paid to rent the car, they could have had a girl.". . . Reports confirm that Lee Peng Fei, the alleged organizer of a 1993 attempt to smuggle 300 Chinese immigrants into the U.S. on a freighter called the *Golden Venture*, has been arrested in Bangkok, Thailand.	
Nov. 18		Italian president Oscar Luigi Scalfaro signs a decree that attempts to restrict illegal immigration and allow for the expulsion of some immigrants convicted of crimes. The decree is criticized by the Vatican, which claims that elements of the law are racist. . . . Prince Joachim, 26, second in line to the throne of Denmark, marries former Hong Kong businesswoman Alexandra Manley, 31, at Frederiksborg Castle.		Reports disclose that, in the city of Gonaives, Haiti, pro-Aristide demonstrators have clashed with UN peacekeepers from Nepal.	
Nov. 19	Leaders of the 18 member nations of the six-year-old Asia-Pacific Economic Cooperation group sign a framework agreement on principles for achieving free trade among APEC countries by the year 2020.	Aleksander Kwasniewski, 41, the leader of the formerly communist Democratic Left Alliance (SLD), narrowly defeats incumbent president Lech Walesa in Poland's presidential runoff election.	An important minority of Hamas members publicly announce their intention to establish a political party named Hizb al-Khalas al-Watani al-Islami, or National Islamic Salvation Party, which they characterize as standing in opposition to the Israeli-PLO peace accords.	The Cerro Negro volcano in western Nicaragua begins to erupt, spewing lava, rocks, and gases, and covering the area within a 30-mile (48-km) radius with volcanic ash.	A suicide car bomb destroys the Egyptian embassy in Islamabad, the capital of Pakistan, killing 18 people and wounding 75 others. Three Egyptian Islamic groups claim responsibility. . . . U.S. vice president Al Gore meets with Japanese premier Tomiichi Murayama in Osaka, Japan, and states that the U.S. will keep its troop level in Japan at 47,000, but may relocate some troops from Okinawa.

A	B	C	D	E
Includes developments that affect more than one world region, international organizations, and important meetings of major world leaders.	Includes all domestic and regional developments in Europe, including the Soviet Union, Turkey, Cyprus, and Malta.	Includes all domestic and regional developments in Africa and the Middle East, including Iraq and Iran and excluding Cyprus, Turkey, and Afghanistan.	Includes all domestic and regional developments in Latin America, the Caribbean, and Canada.	Includes all domestic and regional developments in Asia and Pacific nations, extending from Afghanistan through all the Pacific Islands, except Hawaii.

U.S. Politics & Social Issues	U.S. Foreign Policy & Defense	U.S. Economy & Environment	Science, Technology, & Nature	Culture, Leisure, & Lifestyle	
The health department of New York State issues a report stating that "systematic deficiencies" at Memorial Sloan-Kettering Cancer Center in New York City, one of the nation's leading cancer-treatment centers, led its chief of neurosurgery, Dr. Ehud Arbit, to operate on the wrong side of a patient's brain.		Pres. Clinton signs a $13.1 billion fiscal 1996 appropriations bill for the Department of Transportation and other transportation-related agencies. . . . The House, 374-52, and the Senate, 63-35, approve a Treasury and U.S. Postal Service appropriations bill for fiscal 1996. The bill provides $23.2 billion to the White House, the Postal Service, the Treasury Department, and Treasury agencies such as the IRS, the Secret Service, and the ATF.	Reports disclose that a study has shown for the first time that a cholesterol-lowering drug can cut rates of heart attacks and coronary deaths in men with high cholesterol levels who otherwise seem healthy. . . . The shuttle *Atlantis* docks with *Mir*.	The National Book Foundation presents awards to novelist Philip Roth and poet Stanley Kunitz. Tina Rosenberg receives the nonfiction award, and the Medal for Distinguished Contribution to American Letters is awarded to David McCullough.	Nov. 15
The House passes, 422-6, a measure prohibiting its members and their staff from accepting gifts, free meals, and expense-paid trips from anyone except close friends and relatives. The new rule, which does not require approval from the Senate or the president, will take effect Jan. 1, 1996. . . . Attorney General Janet Reno discloses that she has Parkinson's disease. . . . Billy R. Dale, the former director of the White House travel office, is acquitted of embezzlement charges by a federal jury in Washington, D.C.	The House, 270-158, and the Senate, 59-39, vote to approve a $243.3 billion fiscal 1996 Defense Department appropriations bill.	The House, 277-151, the Senate, 60-37, approve a new stopgap measure. . . . To date, Congress has sent the president only five of the 13 appropriations bills that provide funding for government offices and programs.	Researchers announce that fossil remains and stone tools found near the Yangtze River in China provide evidence that human ancestors lived in Asia at least 1.9 million years ago, much earlier than migration to Asia from Africa is believed to have occurred. The find may upset the prevailing theory, which holds that *Homo erectus* originated in Africa almost 2 million years ago and gradually migrated outward, reaching Asia about half a million years later.	Sales figures from the New York City fall auctions held by Sotheby's and Christie's reach a combined total of $255.7 million, indicating a continuing recovery from a slump in the art market that started in 1990. The auctions mark the first time since May 1990 that both houses collected more than $100 million in sales of modern and impressionist art.	Nov. 16
The Connecticut State Senate rejects, 24-10, a proposal by Gov. John G. Rowland (R) to allow casino gambling in Bridgeport. The vote effectively halts plans by the Mashantucket Pequot Indian tribe to build an $875 million casino in the economically troubled city.	The U.S. House passes, 243-171, a bill that will prohibit the U.S. Defense Department from spending money on a Bosnian peacekeeping mission without specific permission from Congress.	The Senate passes, 52-47, a massive Republican reconciliation bill designed to eliminate the federal budget deficit by the year 2002. The bill also authorizes funding for government entitlement programs, which collectively account for about two-thirds of all federal outlays. . . . The Senate passes, 80-16, a measure that will repeal the federal 55 mile-per-hour highway speed limit.	The European Space Agency launches an *Ariane 4* rocket carrying the Infrared Space Observatory. . . . Researchers claim that an experimental drug prevented monkeys from becoming infected with simian immunodeficiency virus (SIV), which is usually lethal and resembles HIV. The drug, known as PMPA, is chemically similar to the anti-AIDS drug AZT, or zidovudine.	Charles Gordone, 68, Pulitzer Prize–winning playwright, dies in College Station, Texas, of cancer. . . . (Ernest) Francis Brown, 91, editor of the *New York Times Book Review*, 1949–71, dies in Brunswick, Maine, of unreported causes. . . . Judge Lawrence McKenna declares a mistrial in the federal fraud case against boxing promoter Don King.	Nov. 17
Republican Mike Foster, a Louisiana state senator, defeats Rep. Cleo Fields (D, La.) in the Louisiana governor's election. Foster is only the second Republican since the Reconstruction era to win the gubernatorial race in Louisiana.			The House passes without debate by "unanimous consent" legislation that will repeal the federal 55 mile-per-hour highway speed limit.	The Vatican Congregation for the Doctrine of Faith announces that the Roman Catholic Church's ban on the ordination of women priests is "infallible" doctrine not open to debate.	Nov. 18
Authorities charge Jacqueline Williams, Fedel Caffey, and Levern Ward in a triple slaying in Addison, Illinois, in which Deborah Evans was fatally shot and stabbed and had a live, full-term baby cut from her womb. Evans's daughter, Samantha, 10, and her son, Joshua, eight, were also killed.		The Senate approves a compromise stopgap measure by voice vote.		Germans Steffi Graf and Boris Becker win the season-ending events on the women's and men's tennis tours. . . . The Baltimore Stallions becomes the first U.S. team to win the Canadian Football League's Grey Cup with a win, 37-20, over Calgary.	Nov. 19

F	G	H	I	J
Includes elections, federal-state relations, civil rights and liberties, crime, the judiciary, education, health care, poverty, urban affairs, and population.	*Includes formation and debate of U.S. foreign and defense policies, veterans' affairs, and defense spending. (Relations with specific foreign countries are usually found under the region concerned.)*	*Includes business, labor, agriculture, taxation, transportation, consumer affairs, monetary and fiscal policy, natural resources, and pollution.*	*Includes worldwide scientific, medical, and technological developments; natural phenomena; U.S. weather; natural disasters; and accidents.*	*Includes the arts, religion, scholarship, communications media, sports, entertainments, fashions, fads, and social life.*

	World Affairs	Europe	Africa & the Middle East	The Americas	Asia & the Pacific
Nov. 20	The European Union and Israel finalize a trade and cooperation pact negotiated in July. The agreement supersedes an accord signed in 1975.... The EU votes to back an arms embargo and an aid freeze against Nigeria.	Two remote-controlled roadside bombs explode in Grozny as a motorcade carrying Doku Zavgayev, the Russian-appointed head of Chechnya's government, passes by. In a coordinated action, rooftop snipers open fire as soon as the bombs go off. Six people, including Zavgayev, are injured.... Greek premier Andreas Papandreou, 76, is admitted into intensive care after suffering from breathing problems brought on by pneumonia.		Labor unions and opposition parties hold a rally outside the government center in Buenos Aires, Argentina's capital, to protest proposed economic reforms, drawing a crowd of between 15,000 and 40,000 people.	
Nov. 21	The presidents of Serbia, Croatia, and Bosnia-Herzegovina agree to a pact to end a nearly four-year-old war among Croats, Muslims, and Serbs in Bosnia that has claimed 250,000 lives. A NATO peacekeeping force of 60,000 troops will be deployed in Bosnia to sustain the accord.... France detonates a nuclear weapon beneath the Mururoa Atoll in the South Pacific despite international protests.	In one of the most highly publicized murder trials in modern Britain, Rosemary West is found guilty of 10 counts of murder. The remains of 11 girls and women were discovered at the convicted killer's Gloucester home.... Thousands of French college students begin a series of demonstrations to protest insufficient education funding.		An interview is published in which retired Bolivian general Mario Vargas Salinas discloses that the body of guerrilla leader Ernesto "Che" Guevara was cremated and buried in a mass unmarked grave in the village of Valle Grande, Bolivia, in 1967.	Nineteen people are injured when a bomb explodes in New Delhi, the capital of India. The Jammu-Kashmir Islamic Front claims responsibility.... Prince Norodom Sirivuddh of Cambodia is jailed on charges that he plotted to assassinate Cambodia's second premier, Hun Sen Sirivuddh.... The strike that began Nov. 16 in Australia ends, but the Weipa miners continue to strike. ...China formally arrests Wei Jingsheng and charges him with attempting to overthrow the Chinese government.
Nov. 22	In response to the Nov. 21 accord, the UN Security Council votes to suspend its economic sanctions in effect since May 1992 against Serbia.... Japan, New Zealand, and Australia formally lodge complaints with their French ambassadors regarding the Nov. 21 nuclear test.	Rosemary West, convicted on 10 counts of murder Nov. 21, is sentenced to life in prison. The West case, which involved the remains of 11 girls and women, is one of the most highly publicized murder trials in modern Britain.	Israel, Jordan, Egypt, and Saudi Arabia are rocked by an earthquake with an epicenter in the Gulf of Aqaba some 70 miles (110 km) south of Eilat, Israel, and Aqaba (Jordan). At least 10 deaths are caused by the quake, which measures between 5.7 and 7.2 on the Richter scale. It is reportedly the most powerful tremor to hit the Jordan Rift Valley since 1927.... Shimon Peres takes the oath as prime minister of Israel.	The Canadian Senate passes and enacts into law a bill that will ban some handguns and require all firearms in Canada to be licensed and registered by the year 2003. The bill is Canada's toughest gun-control measure.	Khun Sa, head of an ethnic Shan rebel group known as the Mong Tai Army, formally tenders his resignation. Khun Sa is considered one of the world's largest heroin traffickers, and U.S. officials have been seeking his arrest since March 1990, when they charged him with attempting to import 3,500 pounds (1,600 kg) of heroin into the U.S. between 1986 and 1988.
Nov. 23		Spain's parliament votes to lift the immunity from prosecution enjoyed by former interior minister Jose Barrionuevo, clearing the way for Barrionuevo to be investigated by Spain's Supreme Court for his alleged involvement with antiterrorist death squads in the 1980s.	Benjamin W. Mkapa is sworn in as president of Tanzania.... A government military court metes out jail terms to 54 members of the Muslim Brotherhood Society and shuts down the society's Cairo headquarters. The convicted Muslims, many of whom are doctors, academics, and community leaders, receive sentences of from three to five years for alleged political activities that include holding clandestine meetings and distributing antigovernment pamphlets.	In San Salvador, El Salvador's capital, 200 veterans of the country's 12-year civil war occupy a government building to demand land and compensation promised under terms of the 1992 peace accord. One person is killed and at least 15 people are injured when police open fire on the protestors.... A six-year-old girl is shot and killed when she is caught in the cross fire involving the police in Cite Soleil, a slum area of Port-au-Prince, Haiti. The incident sparks clashes, killing at least three people.	
Nov. 24		Irish citizens vote in a national referendum to eliminate the country's constitutional ban on divorce.... Most of France's trade unions representing public-sector workers hold a series of strikes and demonstrations to protest Premier Alain Juppe's plans to cut welfare spending. Some 300,000 people also take to the streets to protest the proposed cuts.			Four people are shot dead and another 16 are wounded during a Muslim ceremonial parade led by members of the Jammu and Kashmir Liberation Front in Kashmir. ... Nicholas Leeson is charged in a Singapore court with three counts of forgery and eight counts of cheating for his role in bringing down Britain's Barings PLC bank. ... Three people die and one person is injured when their yacht is hit by a large ship 30 miles (50 km) off the coast of New Zealand.

A	B	C	D	E
Includes developments that affect more than one world region, international organizations, and important meetings of major world leaders.	Includes all domestic and regional developments in Europe, including the Soviet Union, Turkey, Cyprus, and Malta.	Includes all domestic and regional developments in Africa and the Middle East, including Iraq and Iran and excluding Cyprus, Turkey, and Afghanistan.	Includes all domestic and regional developments in Latin America, the Caribbean, and Canada.	Includes all domestic and regional developments in Asia and Pacific nations, extending from Afghanistan through all the Pacific Islands, except Hawaii.

U.S. Politics & Social Issues	U.S. Foreign Policy & Defense	U.S. Economy & Environment	Science, Technology, & Nature	Culture, Leisure, & Lifestyle	
U.S. District Court judge Mariana R. Pfaelzer rules that major sections of California's Proposition 187 are unconstitutional because the measures usurp the exclusive authority of federal immigration officials to regulate immigration. Proposition 187, approved in November 1994, sought to deny education, health, and welfare benefits to illegal immigrants. . . . A federal grand jury in Houston, Texas, indicts Dr. Stanislaw Burzynski, 53, on 75 counts stemming from his development and use of a drug he calls antineoplaston, which has not been certified by the FDA.	The GAO finds that blacks in the military are less likely to be promoted than whites. The GAO reaches no conclusion as to whether the disparity is caused by racism, but it recommends that the Defense Department improve its monitoring of minority promotions.	The House approves, 421-4, the compromise continuing resolution passed by the Senate on Nov. 19. Pres. Clinton signs it into law, thereby allowing the federal government to function through Dec. 15. . . . The House passes, 235-192, a massive budget reconciliation bill. The bill authorizes funding for government entitlement programs, which collectively account for about two-thirds of all federal outlays, and seeks to eliminate the federal budget deficit by the year 2002.	The U.S. space shuttle *Atlantis*, after docking with the Russian space station *Mir* earlier, touches down on the airstrip at Kennedy Space Center in Cape Canaveral, Florida. . . . The FDA approves a new anti-AIDS drug, 3TC, for use in combination with the drug AZT, or zidovudine.	Sergei Grinkov, 28, Russian pairs figure skater who won two Olympic gold medals with his wife and skating partner, Ekaterina Gordeeva, dies in Lake Placid, New York, of a heart attack after collapsing on the ice during training.	Nov. 20
A jury in Philadelphia, Pennsylvania, convicts John Stanfa, the purported boss of a Philadelphia organized-crime faction, on 33 counts, including murder. Seven of his associates are also convicted. . . . Statistics show that public school teachers' salaries in the 1994–95 school year increased by an average of 2.7% nationwide from the previous school year. The annual increase is slightly lower than the annual rate of inflation. . . . George Delvecchio, 47, convicted of a 1977 rape and murder, becomes the 305th person executed in the U.S. and the seventh in Illinois since 1976.		The Dow tops the 5000-point level at the close of trading			Nov. 21
Police arrest photographer Charles Rathbun in connection with the disappearance of Linda Sobek, a model and former cheerleader for the Los Angeles Raiders football team. . . . Research indicates that doctors often ignore the wishes of terminally ill patients.		To date, only six of the 13 appropriations bills that fund the federal government for fiscal 1996, which started Oct. 1, have passed.		The FCC approves a plan by Westinghouse Electric Corp. to purchase the CBS Inc. television network for $5.4 billion in cash. The deal will make Westinghouse the leading broadcasting company in the U.S., with 16 TV stations and 39 radio stations.	Nov. 22
A black gunman, Randall Craig Tolbert, bursts into the Rubidoux, California, halfway house where a former Los Angeles police sergeant, Stacey Koon, who was convicted for his part in the 1991 videotaped beating of black motorist Rodney King, is being held and demands to see Koon. Tolbert kills a hostage before he is shot and killed by police.			Bernard M(ore) Oliver, 79, former director of research for the Hewlett-Packard Co. computer and electronics company who designed the first hand-held calculator in the early 1970s, dies in Los Altos Hills, California, of heart failure.	Junior Walker (born Autry DeWalt Jr.), 53, popular saxophonist and vocalist who founded the band Junior Walker and the All Stars, dies in Battle Creek, Michigan, of cancer. . . . Louis Malle, 63, French film director whose style was characterized as both romantic and skeptical, dies in Beverly Hills, California, of lymphoma.	Nov. 23
Data reveal that in 1993, an estimated one in 92 U.S. men between the ages of 27 and 39 were suffering infection with HIV, the virus that caused AIDS.		Pres. Clinton signs into law a measure that lifts a 22-year-old ban on exports of crude oil from Alaska's North Slope to foreign countries.		Pope John Paul II reaffirms his commitment to the Roman Catholic Church's ban on the ordination of women priests. . . . Ohio judge Kenneth Callahan orders an injunction against the move by NFL's Cleveland Browns to Maryland, pending a Cleveland lawsuit against the team.	Nov. 24

F	G	H	I	J
Includes elections, federal-state relations, civil rights and liberties, crime, the judiciary, education, health care, poverty, urban affairs, and population.	*Includes formation and debate of U.S. foreign and defense policies, veterans' affairs, and defense spending. (Relations with specific foreign countries are usually found under the region concerned.)*	*Includes business, labor, agriculture, taxation, transportation, consumer affairs, monetary and fiscal policy, natural resources, and pollution.*	*Includes worldwide scientific, medical, and technological developments; natural phenomena; U.S. weather; natural disasters; and accidents.*	*Includes the arts, religion, scholarship, communications media, sports, entertainments, fashions, fads, and social life.*

	World Affairs	Europe	Africa & the Middle East	The Americas	Asia & the Pacific
Nov. 25		Bosnian Serbs in Serb-held neighborhoods and suburbs of Sarajevo, the Bosnian capital, stage angry demonstrations against the Nov. 21 peace plan, which, in a transfer of some territory, will put an estimated 60,000 Serbs under Muslim-Croat governance. . . . In Ireland, a referendum to eliminate a constitutional ban on divorce passes by a 50.3% to 49.7%. The margin of victory is some 9,100 votes out of 1.6 million ballots cast.	Lebanese president Elias Hrawi begins an additional three years in office.		
Nov. 26		Eduard Shevardnadze is sworn in as Georgia's first president since 1992. . . . Reports confirm that the Armenian government has restarted the nuclear reactor at Metsamor. . . . Sergei Markidonov, 34, an incumbent of the Russian Duma who belongs to the small Stability party, is shot to death by his bodyguard during a campaign visit to Petrovsk-Zabaikalsky in Siberia. Markidonov is the fourth member of the Duma to be killed since 1993 parliamentary elections.	The Ivory Coast's ruling Democratic Party wins a large majority in the country's second multiparty legislative elections. . . . The Egyptian government steps up a clampdown on moderate Islamic activists, launching a nationwide sweep against those with ties to the Muslim Brotherhood Society, a technically outlawed organization that has operated openly in Egyptian society and eschews violence as a political means.	Voters in Ecuador reject a package of 11 constitutional reforms proposed by Pres. Sixto Duran Ballen.	Taliban forces, in four separate airstrikes, bomb Kabul, killing an estimated 37 people and wounding more than 140. Government officials characterize the attack as the heaviest air raid to target the capital in more than a year. . . . The sole survivor from the Nov. 24 yachting crash near New Zealand, Judith Sleavin, 43, is found on the east coast of North Island.
Nov. 27		Reports state that Bosnian Croat soldiers are burning the towns of Mrkonjic Grad and Sipovo, which are slated under the Nov. 21 accord to be returned to the Serbs in a swap for land around Sarajevo. . . . Russian president Boris Yeltsin, who in October suffered his second heart attack of the year, is released from the Moscow Clinic Hospital. . . . Great Britain's Financial Times-Stock Exchange 100 climbs to a record high of 3,649.	In Algeria, Pres. Lamine Zeroual is sworn in. Separately, Gen. Mohammed Boutaghene, the coast guard commander, is shot dead in Algiers. He is the highest-ranking officer yet slain in the Islamic uprising. . . . The Muslim Brotherhood reveals that about 300 of its members who were detained in the Nov. 26 crackdown were slated to serve as poll observers in upcoming elections in Egypt.	Canadian prime minister Jean Chrétien introduces legislation that will give the predominantly French-speaking province of Quebec greater autonomy within the Canadian federation.	The *International Herald Tribune* newspaper agrees to pay S$152,000 (US$214,000) to former Singapore prime minister Lee Kuan Yew to settle a civil libel suit he brought over an October 1994 *Tribune* article that was critical of unidentified Asian governments and their judicial systems.
Nov. 28	The EU reaches an agreement with 12 Middle Eastern and North African nations intended to foster closer economic and political relations. The pact, known as the Barcelona Declaration, will pave the way for a European-Mediterranean free-trade zone by the year 2010. . . . The Czech Republic becomes the first former communist state to sign on as a new member of the Organization for Economic Cooperation and Development.	Despite strong protests from the Slovak's ethnic Hungarian minority and from the Hungarian government, Pres. Michal Kovac signs a law that declares Slovak the only state language and bars the use of other languages in official communications, ceremonies, broadcasting, and advertising. . . . Germany's government agrees to provide about 4,000 troops to the NATO peacekeeping mission in the former Yugoslav republics. The detachment will be the largest German military unit deployed outside the country since World War II.			Myanmar's opposition National League for Democracy (NLD) delivers a letter to leaders of the ruling military regime, the State Law and Order Restoration Council (SLORC), notifying them that the NLD will not participate in talks to draft a new national constitution. The military leaders reopen their constitutional convention in Myanmar's capital, Yangon, and reaffirm their rejection of a dialogue with opposition forces. . . . A group of 15 Chinese dissidents, in a letter to Parliament, calls for the release of Wei Jingsheng, one of China's best-known dissidents, and of other political prisoners.
Nov. 29	Leaders from Rwanda, Burundi, Zaire, Uganda, and Tanzania agree on a plan to return home some 1.8 million Rwandan refugees scattered throughout the region at a conference sponsored by former U.S. president Jimmy Carter. . . . The UN condemns Bosnian Serbs for such atrocities as "executions, rape, mass expulsion, arbitrary detentions, forced labor and large-scale disappearances." The report is a rare UN condemnation of an entire ethnic or national group.	Bosnian Serbs in Serb-held neighborhoods and suburbs of Sarajevo, the Bosnian capital, stage demonstrations against the Nov. 21 peace plan since it will place an estimated 60,000 Serbs under Muslim-Croat governance. . . . Russian defense minister Pavel Grachev agrees to a plan under which up to 1,500 Russian troops will be included in a "consultative committee" of NATO members supervising the Bosnia operation.	South Africa's president Nelson Mandela announces the appointment of 17 people to serve on the Truth and Reconciliation Commission, which will be headed by Anglican archbishop Desmond Tutu. The commission is to continue for at least 18 months in its efforts to investigate abuses by both the government and groups such as Mandela's African National Congress during the apartheid era of racial segregation.	Thousands of residents of the city of Leon and surrounding villages are evacuated from their homes after the Cerro Negro volcano in western Nicaragua rains debris on the area. The volcano has been erupting since Nov. 19.	Cuban president Fidel Castro Ruz visits China for the first time. Separately, China's communist government holds an elaborate ceremony in Lhasa, the capital of Tibet, and names six-year-old Gyaincain Norbu as the 11th Panchen Lama, the second-highest monk in Tibetan Buddhism. By naming the boy to the religious post, China rejects another boy previously chosen for the spot by the Dalai Lama, Tibet's exiled leader.
Nov. 30	The 1995 Atlantic hurricane season closes, ending the third-worst season since record keeping began in 1871. A total of 19 tropical storms caused 137 deaths in the entire Atlantic region. The death toll in the U.S. mainland, Puerto Rico, and the U.S. Virgin Islands was 58, with an estimated $5.2 billion in property damage. . . . The UN Security Council sets a timetable for the withdrawal of most of its peacekeepers from the Balkans, clearing the way for the arrival of the new NATO force.	U.S. president Bill Clinton becomes the first sitting U.S. president to visit Northern Ireland.	King Fahd of Saudi Arabia suffers a stroke. . . . Militants in the village of Qabatiya, south of Jenin, prevent Israeli soldiers from arresting Samir Zakarneh by taking two Israeli border policemen hostage in Jenin. Following negotiations between Israel and PNA officials, the two Israelis are freed, and Zakarneh surrenders to Palestinian police. Separately, 17 Palestinians are wounded in clashes with Israeli troops in Nablus, and gunmen open fire on an Israeli jeep near Jenin.	Alleged members of the Tupac Amaru Revolutionary Movement, a Marxist guerrilla group in Peru, start a standoff at the guerrilla's hideout in La Molina, a suburb of Lima, Peru's capital.	Reports disclose that Chinese officials have detained 32 monks who are unsupportive of their decision to appoint a new Panchen Lama. Gedhun Choekyi Nyima, who was designated by the Dalai Lama as the 11th incarnation of the Panchen Lama, and his family are also reportedly detained by Chinese authorities.

A	B	C	D	E
Includes developments that affect more than one world region, international organizations, and important meetings of major world leaders.	Includes all domestic and regional developments in Europe, including the Soviet Union, Turkey, Cyprus, and Malta.	Includes all domestic and regional developments in Africa and the Middle East, including Iraq and Iran and excluding Cyprus, Turkey, and Afghanistan.	Includes all domestic and regional developments in Latin America, the Caribbean, and Canada.	Includes all domestic and regional developments in Asia and Pacific nations, extending from Afghanistan through all the Pacific Islands, except Hawaii.

U.S. Politics & Social Issues	U.S. Foreign Policy & Defense	U.S. Economy & Environment	Science, Technology, & Nature	Culture, Leisure, & Lifestyle	
					Nov. 25
An arson fire seriously burns a subway token clerk in New York City.				Jockey Jerry Bailey sets the U.S. earnings record in horse racing for a year, with $16,153,065.	Nov. 26
Reports confirm that the California attorney general's office has launched an investigation into whether a prominent prosecution witness in the O. J. Simpson trial, former police detective Mark Fuhrman, committed perjury during the proceedings. . . . The FBI joins the search for a missing Vicksburg, Mississippi, furniture heiress, Jacqueline Levitz, who was last seen on Nov. 18.	In a nationally televised address, President Clinton urges Congress and the American public to support the deployment of 20,000 U.S. troops in Bosnia-Herzegovina as part of a NATO mission to enforce a peace treaty in the former Yugoslav republic.	Figures show that sales of existing homes dropped 1.9% in October from September, to a seasonally adjusted annual rate of 4.07 million units. The decline is the first after five consecutive monthly advances.		The murder trial of rap singer Snoop Doggy Dogg (Calvin Broadus) opens in Los Angeles, California. . . . *The Lost World*, by Michael Crichton, is at the top of the bestseller list.	Nov. 27
In Chicago, Illinois, Juvenile Court judge Carol Kelly sentences two unidentified boys—now 11 and 12—who in 1994 dropped five-year-old Eric Morse to his death to be confined to a youth home for up to 10 years.		In *National Labor Relations Board v. Town & Country Electric Inc.*, the Supreme Court rules unanimously that union organizers who seek or hold jobs in nonunionized companies are entitled to the same protection under federal labor laws as nonunionized employees. . . . Pres. Clinton signs legislation that will repeal the federal 55 mile-per-hour highway speed limit. The measure also designates 160,955 miles (259,040 km) of U.S. highways as the National Highway System and allocates $6.5 billion for the system's maintenance.	Reports confirm that in 1999, NASA plans to launch a relatively small, low-cost craft called *Stardust* to fly within about 60 miles of the comet Wild-2 in the year 2004 to gather dust samples and return to Earth. . . . Robert Dean Cardin, a nine-year old Michigan boy who in June 1986 received the sixth successful infant heart transplant in the U.S., dies after his immune system rejects the transplanted heart. The boy was known only as "Baby Calvin" at the time of the transplant.	Controversial British artist Damien Hirst, whose work displays pickled animals, is awarded Great Britain's Turner Prize for contemporary art.	Nov. 28
In *Thompson v. Keohane*, the Supreme Court rules, 7-2, that federal judges have the authority to make their own determinations as to whether inmates were placed under police custody before being interrogated. . . . Former senator David Durenberger (R, Minn.) is sentenced to one year's probation and fined $1,000 for political corruption charges. . . . The House passes, 421-0, a bill that will mandate broader definitions of lobbying and will force lobbyists to disclose more information about their employment.	Data suggest that the U.S. Coast Guard has intercepted more than 1,100 Haitian refugees to date in November. That number is greater than the total number of Haitian refugees intercepted during the previous 12 months. . . . Pres. Clinton embarks on a tour of Europe. . . . The CIA releases a study that shows the use of psychics by U.S. military and intelligence agencies to gather information was largely unsuccessful, and it recommends funding for the program be discontinued.	The Dow closes at a record high of 5105.56, marking the 65th record high for the Dow in 1995 and the 14th record high set in the current month.	Astronomers report finding a planetlike object orbiting a nearby star, providing what they call the first undeniable evidence of a brown dwarf. The find caps a three-decade-long search for the "failed stars," which lack the mass to sustain a star's nuclear fusion. The object, GL229B, orbits the star Gliese 229 some 19 light-years from Earth.		Nov. 29
Independent counsel Joseph diGenova reveals he has found no evidence of criminal wrongdoing in allegations that aides of former president George Bush improperly searched the passport files of then Arkansas governor Bill Clinton. . . . St. Jude Children's Research Hospital in Memphis, Tennessee, receives an anonymous $1 million donation in the form of a winning ticket from a game sponsored by McDonald's. St. Jude's, which accepts patients regardless of their ability to pay, will receive $50,000 a year for the next 20 years.		The House passes, 406-4, a bill that will reduce federal subsidies to Amtrak, the national passenger railroad, and give the company more authority to seek alternate sources of funding. . . . General Motors Corp. agrees to pay $45 million and recall more than 470,000 Cadillac model automobiles to settle a federal lawsuit charging that it intentionally skirted federal auto-emissions standards in order to correct a design flaw in 1991 through 1995 models of its 4.9-liter-engine Cadillacs.			Nov. 30
F	G	H	I	J	
Includes elections, federal-state relations, civil rights and liberties, crime, the judiciary, education, health care, poverty, urban affairs, and population.	*Includes formation and debate of U.S. foreign and defense policies, veterans' affairs, and defense spending. (Relations with specific foreign countries are usually found under the region concerned.)*	*Includes business, labor, agriculture, taxation, transportation, consumer affairs, monetary and fiscal policy, natural resources, and pollution.*	*Includes worldwide scientific, medical, and technological developments; natural phenomena; U.S. weather; natural disasters; and accidents.*	*Includes the arts, religion, scholarship, communications media, sports, entertainments, fashions, fads, and social life.*	

	World Affairs	Europe	Africa & the Middle East	The Americas	Asia & the Pacific
Dec. 1	Foreign and defense ministers of NATO choose Javier Solana, the foreign minister of Spain, as NATO's new secretary general. . . . Reports confirm that the World Bank and the IMF have halted a $45 million loan package to Haiti, citing the nation's lack of progress on economic reforms.			Peruvian police kill three alleged members of the Tupac Amaru Revolutionary Movement and arrest at least 15 after a siege that began Nov. 30 in La Molina, a suburb of Lima. At least one police officer is also killed. . . . The government of Montserrat begins the evacuation of 4,000 residents of Plymouth, the capital city, because of renewed activity in the Chances Peak volcano. . . . Argentine officials arrest 12 people in connection with the 1994 bombing of a Jewish community center that left 87 people dead.	The Australian Medical Association reveals that its code of ethics no longer implicitly gives physicians the right to refuse to treat patients who were infected with HIV. Before the change, the code suggested that doctors with safety concerns or moral objections could refuse to treat HIV patients. . . . Weipa miners, striking since Nov. 16 in Australia, end the job action.
Dec. 2			Raul Salinas de Gortari, older brother of former Mexican president Carlos Salinas de Gortari, is charged by federal prosecutors in Mexico with falsifying bank documents. Raul Salinas has been jailed in Mexico since February in connection with the 1994 assassination of Jose Francisco Ruiz Massieu, a former top official of Mexico's ruling Institutional Revolutionary Party (PRI).		Taiwan's ruling Nationalist Party maintains a slim majority in Parliament, but it loses ground to opposition parties in parliamentary elections. . . . A criminal court in Singapore sentences Nicholas Leeson, accused of making covert derivatives trades, to 6½ years in prison for his role in bringing down Britain's Barings PLC merchant bank.
Dec. 3	U.S. president Bill Clinton and Spanish premier Felipe Gonzalez, who holds the rotating presidency of the EU, sign a broad agreement that pledge closer economic and political ties between the U.S. and the EU.	Jimmy Jewel (born James Arthur Thomas Jewel Marsh), 82, British actor and comedian, dies of unreported causes.	A Cameroon Airlines Boeing 737 jetliner crashes near the airport in the city of Douala, killing 72 of the 78 people on board.	The Cerro Negro volcano in western Nicaragua, erupting since Nov. 19, ceases activity.	Former South Korean president Chun Doo Hwan, who ruled from 1980 to 1988, is arrested on charges of staging the December 1979 military coup that brought him to power. Upon his arrest, Chun begins a hunger strike.
Dec. 4		A huge car bomb explodes outside the headquarters of the Russian administration headquarters in the center of Grozny, killing at least 11 people and wounding more than 60. . . . The first sizable NATO units begin arriving in Sarajevo.	Reports confirm that a journalist, Hamid Mahiout, has been found stabbed to death in Algeria.		
Dec. 5	NATO ministers formally elect Javier Solana, the foreign minister of Spain, to the leadership post at a meeting at the alliance's headquarters in Brussels, Belgium. France announces that it will rejoin NATO's military planning committee, ending a 29-year-old rift.	In Russia, a bomb explodes at the Moscow parliament building. No one is hurt in the blast. . . . Tens of thousands of protesters hold demonstrations in Paris and other French cities to protest a government plan to trim welfare spending. . . . Sir (Robert) Charles Evans, 77, Welsh mountain climber who was the deputy leader of the first expedition to climb Mt. Everest, in 1953, dies after suffering from multiple sclerosis.	U.S. vice president Al Gore and South African deputy president Thabo Mbeki sign agreements on cooperation and trade in the first-ever meeting of a new binational commission. The pacts allow the U.S. Peace Corps into South Africa for the first time and create cabinet-level binational groups to deal with cooperation on issues such as business, the environment, science, energy, education, and agriculture.		Sri Lankan army troops raise the country's flag in the city of Jaffna, the stronghold of the Liberation Tigers of Tamil Eelam, capping the government's most significant victory in the 12-year-old civil war. . . . Former South Korean president Roh Tae Woo is indicted on charges of accepting at least 282 billion won ($370 million) in bribes during his tenure as president. Seven of South Korea's most prominent business leaders are also indicted.
Dec. 6	Qatar boycotts the final session of the 16th summit of the six-nation Gulf Cooperation Council (GCC) to protest the GCC's rejection of Abdul-Rahman al-Attiyah, its nominee for secretary general of the organization.	Col. Gen. Dmitri Antonovich Volkogonov, 67, Russian historian known for harsh biographies of Soviet communist leaders who was widely considered a heretic and a traitor in the USSR, dies near Moscow of stomach cancer.	Official tallies show that Egypt's ruling National Democratic Party (NDP) has won a commanding majority in parliamentary elections.	The U.S. government agrees to return more than 150,000 pages of documents seized by U.S. soldiers from the headquarters of the Haitian armed forces in September and October 1994.	Sri Lankan government officials estimate that nearly 2,000 rebels were killed and 5,000 were wounded during the offensive. It states that 400 government troops were killed and 1,600 soldiers were wounded. . . . Japanese authorities arrest former labor minister Toshio Yamaguchi on charges of breach of trust. Yamaguchi, now an independent member of the Diet, is accused of using his political clout to obtain 2.7 billion yen (US$26.7 million) in collateral-free loans for family members, knowing that the loans could not be repaid.

A	B	C	D	E
Includes developments that affect more than one world region, international organizations, and important meetings of major world leaders.	Includes all domestic and regional developments in Europe, including the Soviet Union, Turkey, Cyprus, and Malta.	Includes all domestic and regional developments in Africa and the Middle East, including Iraq and Iran and excluding Cyprus, Turkey, and Afghanistan.	Includes all domestic and regional developments in Latin America, the Caribbean, and Canada.	Includes all domestic and regional developments in Asia and Pacific nations, extending from Afghanistan through all the Pacific Islands, except Hawaii.

U.S. Politics & Social Issues	U.S. Foreign Policy & Defense	U.S. Economy & Environment	Science, Technology, & Nature	Culture, Leisure, & Lifestyle	
Rep. James A. Hayes of Louisiana announces his switch to the Republican Party, becoming the fifth House Democrat to do so since the Republicans won a majority in Congress in 1994. . . . Civil-rights leader Jesse Jackson announces he will resume his position as head of Operation PUSH. . . . Oklahoma's regents of higher education approve an endowed professorship at the University of Oklahoma College of Law named for professor Anita F. Hill.	A $243.3 billion 1996 Defense Department appropriations bill becomes law without Pres. Clinton's signature. When Congress is in session, any legislation that it clears becomes law within 10 days—excluding Sundays—if the president does not veto it. Clinton had repeatedly vowed to veto the defense bill, but, fearing that if he rejected the bill Republicans may retaliate by denying him funding to send U.S. troops to enforce a peace agreement for Bosnia-Herzegovina, Clinton agreed to accept the legislation.			A Christie's auction of 250 items owned by singer Frank Sinatra and his wife, Barbara, fetches a total of $2.07 million, far more than the $1.5 million expected.	Dec. 1
Reports confirm that Yeshiva University in New York City has received a bequest of $22 million from Anne Scheiber, a retired stockbroker who had died in January and was never been affiliated with the university. . . . A Florida doctor, Rolando Sanchez, who in February amputated the wrong leg of a patient and in July removed another patient's toe without consent, is fined $10,000 and barred from practicing medicine for six months by the state Board of Medicine.			NASA launches an Atlas-2AS rocket carrying the *Solar and Heliospheric Observatory* (SOHO), a craft designed to spend two years or more at 92 million miles from the sun relaying to Earth observations of that star. The $1 billion mission is a joint NASA-European Space Agency project. . . . A study finds that a group of people who adhered to a traditional Mediterranean diet had half the death rate as those who ate more Westernized diets.	(William) Robertson Davies, 82, Canadian writer, critic and professor, dies in Orangeville, Ontario, after suffering a stroke.	Dec. 2
Statistics indicate that the state and federal prison population has grown since June 30 by a record 89,707 inmates, to reach a record total of more than 1.1 million.				The 18th annual Kennedy Center Honors are awarded to Sidney Poitier, Neil Simon, B. B. King, Marilyn Horne, and Jacques d'Amboise. . . . The U.S. wins tennis's Davis Cup with a victory over the Russian team in Moscow, Russia.	Dec. 3
A group of eight Michigan doctors calling themselves Physicians for Mercy offer assisted suicide advocate Dr. Jack Kevorkian his first-ever organized support. Kevorkian receives $20,000 from the Sovereign Fund, a private Los Angeles foundation, for what the group calls his work to guard individual rights. . . . Abbott Laboratories announce that in January 1996 it will hold a lottery to offer its experimental AIDS drug ritonavir free to 2,000 people in the U.S. and other countries who are in the late stages of the disease.	The Cambodian government returns to U.S military officials what are believed to be the remains of U.S. Marines who died in a failed military mission during the Vietnam War.	Chrysler Corp. sues Lee Iacocca, its former chairman, charging that Iacocca funneled confidential corporate information to Kirk Kerkorian, a dissident Chrysler shareholder who in the spring waged an unsuccessful battle to take over the company. . . . The NASDAQ index reaches a record high, closing at 1069.79. . . . The United Automobile Workers (UAW) union calls off its 17-month-long strike against Peoria, Illinois-based Caterpillar Inc.		A lawyer for actress Kim Basinger announces that Basinger has settled out of court for an undisclosed amount with Main Line Pictures Inc., whose 1993 award of $8.1 million was struck down by the California Court of Appeals in September 1994. . . . NBA referees narrowly approve a new labor contract that ends a two-month-long management-imposed lockout.	Dec. 4
Reports suggest that an Arizona state court judge has ruled that a public-school district has the right to require students to wear school uniforms. Lawyers characterize the ruling as the first to uphold a public-school uniform requirement that cannot be overruled by parents.		The Senate approves, 65-30. a bill to curb the ability of stockholders to file securities-fraud suits.	Astronomers' calculations indicate the presence of a black hole with the mass of 1.2 billion suns which is located about nine light-years from the center of the galaxy. . . . Clair Cameron Patterson, 73, geochemist known for determining the Earth's age at 4.6 billion years from his study of metals in rocks, a figure that is still accepted at the time of his death, dies in Sea Ranch, California, of an asthma attack.	Officials announce that the ABC television network will launch a 24-hour all-news television channel in 1997. ABC is the latest in a series of companies to announce plans for a 24-hour news service to compete with the CNN.	Dec. 5
Pres. Clinton holds the first-ever White House conference on AIDS and HIV, hosting 300 advocates, lobbyists, and doctors. . . . Marion P. Hammer becomes the first female president of the NRA gun lobby. . . . In *Bailey v. U.S.*, the Supreme Court rules unanimously that the government can invoke a 1988 federal law that mandates a minimum of five years extra for prison sentences of drug traffickers who use or carry firearms, only if the government proves that the defendant actively used the firearm in the commission of the crime.		Pres. Clinton vetoes the massive Republican reconciliation bill, designed to eliminate the federal budget deficit by the year 2002. Clinton says the bill mandates unacceptable cuts in social programs. . . . The House passes, 256-166, a $27.3 billion fiscal 1996 appropriations bill for the Departments of Commerce, Justice, and State and the federal judiciary. . . . The House Committee on Ethics votes unanimously to appoint a special counsel to investigate allegations that House Speaker Newt Gingrich (R, Ga.) violated tax laws when he taught a college class.	Researchers report they have discovered several immune-system chemicals that in laboratory experiments stopped growth of HIV, the AIDS-causing virus.	James Barrett Reston Jr., 86, Scottish-born journalist at *The New York Times* for 50 years who earned Pulitzer Prizes for journalism in 1945 and 1957, dies in Washington, D.C., of cancer.	Dec. 6

F	G	H	I	J
Includes elections, federal-state relations, civil rights and liberties, crime, the judiciary, education, health care, poverty, urban affairs, and population.	Includes formation and debate of U.S. foreign and defense policies, veterans' affairs, and defense spending. (Relations with specific foreign countries are usually found under the region concerned.)	Includes business, labor, agriculture, taxation, transportation, consumer affairs, monetary and fiscal policy, natural resources, and pollution.	Includes worldwide scientific, medical, and technological developments; natural phenomena; U.S. weather; natural disasters; and accidents.	Includes the arts, religion, scholarship, communications media, sports, entertainments, fashions, fads, and social life.

	World Affairs	Europe	Africa & the Middle East	The Americas	Asia & the Pacific
Dec. 7	Estonia, Latvia, and Lithuania sign a free-trade accord with the European Free Trade Association (EFTA), which comprises Iceland, Switzerland, Norway, and Liechtenstein.... Reports confirm that the six-nation Gulf Cooperation Council (GCC) has backed Jamil al-Hujilan, a Saudi citizen, for GCC secretary general.	British prime minister John Major, responding to reports of infected beef products, states that widespread fears over the so-called mad cow disease are largely unfounded.... Protests are held in Paris, Grenoble, Marseilles, and Bordeaux, where French premier Alain Juppe was mayor. Figures suggest that 700,000 of France's 2 million public-sector workers are taking part in the strikes that started Nov. 24.	Senior Jordanian sources reveal that Jordanian authorities have intercepted "very sophisticated" missile-guidance components slated for shipment to Iraq in violation of United Nations sanctions.		More than 100 East Timorese protesters stage sit-ins at the Dutch and Russian embassies in Jakarta, Indonesia's capital, to mark the 20th anniversary of Indonesia's invasion of East Timor, a former colony of Portugal.... The Japanese government files a lawsuit to force 35 landowners—who oppose U.S. bases in Okinawa because of the September rape of a 12-year-old girl by three U.S. servicemen—to renew their leases with the U.S. military.
Dec. 8	Representatives of more than 50 countries and international organizations meet in London, England, to discuss nonmilitary issues related to the Bosnian peace plan.	Mikhail Lezhnev, 48, a candidate for Our Home Is Russia party, is found dead of a gunshot wound on the doorstep of his home near Chelyabinsk, in the Ural region.... Philip Lawrence, the principal of a secondary school in London, England, is fatally stabbed during what is believed to be an incident of gang-related violence.... Some 4,000 striking miners in eastern Lorraine, France, set fire to a mine office building. One policeman and 28 miners are injured in the violence.		Colombian police free British diplomat Timothy Cowley, who was kidnapped by the Revolutionary Armed Forces of Colombia (FARC) guerrilla group in August.... Data reveals that in 1995 Central America was struck by at least four major disease epidemics. In the most severe outbreak, more than 100,000 cases of dengue fever, an often-fatal mosquito-borne disease, were reported in 1995 in Latin America and the Caribbean, with the highest concentration in Central America.	A nuclear reactor in Monju, Japan, is shut down indefinitely after a sodium coolant leak occurs.... Chinese government officials hold a ceremony in Shigatse, Tibet, and install six-year-old Gyaincain Norbu as the 11th Panchen Lama, the second-highest figure in Tibetan Buddhism. China chose the boy in late November after rebuffing a boy chosen earlier by the Dalai Lama, Tibet's exiled leader.
Dec. 9		Voters in Kazakhstan cast ballots to elect members of the 67-seat lower house of the country's new parliament. Candidates earn the absolute majority required for victory in races for only 43 of the seats, leaving the chamber short of the two-thirds quorum necessary to begin a session. Another round is scheduled for 1996.	Jordanian officials arrest Laith Shubailat, an Islamist who led the opposition in Jordan against the peace treaty that King Hussein signed with Israel in October 1994.... A drive-by gunman south of Bethlehem wounds a Jewish settler and his 10-year-old daughter.		In Bangladesh, activists demanding the ouster of P.M. Khaleda Zia call for a general strike. It is the 75th work stoppage called for since April 1994.
Dec. 10		Voters in Belarus go to the polls to complete balloting to elect the country's first post-Soviet parliament.	Israel transfers administrative authority to Palestinians in Tulkarm, on the Israeli border to the northwest of Nablus. The move is met with an outpouring of joy in Tulkarm.		
Dec. 11	UNICEF reveals that some 2 million children were killed and 4 million disabled over the previous decade, as young people increasingly became participants, targets, and victims in a growing number of ethnic wars and violent conflicts. UNICEF proposes 10 antiwar measures, including a ban on land mines, a system for reporting war crimes against women and children, barring conscription of children younger than 18, and "carefully monitoring" the effects of UN economic sanctions against countries such as Iraq.	A remote-controlled car bomb is detonated in Madrid, Spain, killing six people.... Peace rallies are staged in both Moscow and Grozny to mark the first anniversary of the Russian invasion of the breakaway Russian republic of Chechnya.... At least one letter bomb explodes in a mail-box in the southern city of Graz, Austria. No one is injured.... Physicians in Athens, Greece, describe the medical condition of ailing Greek premier Andreas Papandreou as "dangerous" and put him back on a respirator. Papandreou has been receiving constant medical treatment since Nov. 20.	Israeli troops pull out of Nablus, the West Bank's largest city, under terms of the Sept. 28 second-phase agreement on interim Palestinian self-rule. The pullback ends Israel's 28-year-old military occupation of Nablus and signals Israeli prime minister Shimon Peres's determination to continue with peace plans negotiated by former prime minister Yitzhak Rabin. Tens of thousands of Palestinians take to the streets to celebrate.	Venezuelan finance minister Luis Matos Azocar announces a devaluation of the bolivar, Venezuela's currency, by 41.4%, to 290 to the U.S. dollar from 170 to the dollar. Matos reveals that the devaluation is part of an attempt to secure a loan of up to $3 billion from the IMF to help fight Venezuela's current recession.	A three-member panel of India's Supreme Court upholds a 1951 law that prohibits politicians from appealing to individuals' religious convictions to gain votes.... Scores of people are injured in Dhaka, Bangladesh, when armed militants from the governing Bangladesh Nationalist Party clash with rival opposition parties and police.

A	B	C	D	E
Includes developments that affect more than one world region, international organizations, and important meetings of major world leaders.	*Includes all domestic and regional developments in Europe, including the Soviet Union, Turkey, Cyprus, and Malta.*	*Includes all domestic and regional developments in Africa and the Middle East, including Iraq and Iran and excluding Cyprus, Turkey, and Afghanistan.*	*Includes all domestic and regional developments in Latin America, the Caribbean, and Canada.*	*Includes all domestic and regional developments in Asia and Pacific nations, extending from Afghanistan through all the Pacific Islands, except Hawaii.*

U.S. Politics & Social Issues	U.S. Foreign Policy & Defense	U.S. Economy & Environment	Science, Technology, & Nature	Culture, Leisure, & Lifestyle	
Bryan Freeman, 17, a neo-Nazi skinhead accused of slaying his parents and younger brother in February, pleads guilty to killing his mother, Brenda Freeman, and is sentenced to life without parole. ...The Senate votes, 54-44, to approve a bill that will ban a rare procedure known as intact dilation and evacuation, to end pregnancies in their late stages. The bill will render performance of the abortion procedure by doctors a felony offense.	Pres. Jose Eduardo dos Santos becomes Angola's first president to visit the U.S.... Michael James and Jackie Burden, a black couple from Fayetteville, North Carolina, are slain, and police arrest Pvts. Malcolm Wright and James Burmeister, two white army soldiers stationed at Fort Bragg, North Carolina, who allegedly harbor white supremacist views.	The Senate approves, 50-48, a $27.3 billion fiscal 1996 appropriations bill for the Departments of Commerce, Justice and State and the federal judiciary.... The House approves, 227-190, a $80.6 billion fiscal 1996 appropriations bill for the VA, HUD, NASA, the EPA, and FEMA.... Pres. Clinton releases the White House's plan for balancing the budget within seven years as an alternative to the Republican-sponsored proposal that he vetoed Dec. 6.	The *Galileo* spacecraft fires its main engine and enters an orbit of Jupiter for a planned two-year study of the planet, the largest in the solar system. *Galileo* has traveled 2.3 billion miles (3.7 billion km) since its launching in 1989.... The FDA approves the use of a new anti-AIDS drug, saquinavir, the first approval worldwide for the class of drugs known as protease inhibitors.		Dec. 7
Roland Smith, 51, storms a Jewish-owned store in Harlem, shoots and wounds four people, sets a blaze that kills seven people, and then fatally shoots himself. Police state that Smith, who is black, allowed blacks to leave the store, which has been protested since its expansion plans led to the closure of a black-owned store next door.... Ernest LeRoy Boyer, 67, former president of the Carnegie Foundation and U.S. commissioner of education, dies in Princeton, New Jersey, after suffering from lymphoma.	The U.S. Navy announces that Rear Admiral Ralph L. Tindal, 55, was found guilty of sexual harassment, adultery, fraternization, and conduct unbecoming an officer. The charges against Tindal stemmed from his involvement with an unidentified enlisted woman who had worked for him.	A U.S. District Court jury in Compton, California, convicts Rep. Walter R. Tucker III (D, Calif.) on seven counts of extortion and two counts of tax evasion.... A Senate panel investigating the Whitewater affair votes, 10-8, along party lines to subpoena documents that concern a 1993 White House meeting.			Dec. 8
The board of the NAACP unanimously elects Rep. Kweisi Mfume (D, Md.) as its top officer.... Walter Gellhorn, 89, law professor and scholar who served as member director of the ACLU and of the NAACP Legal Defense Fund, dies in New York City of unreported causes.	Sergeant Randy Lee Meadows is charged with conspiracy for allegedly driving a car carrying Pvts. Malcolm Wright and James N. Burmeister in what police call the racially motivated slayings of a black couple in Fayetteville, North Carolina, on Dec. 7.			Running back Eddie George of Ohio State wins the Heisman Trophy.... Douglas Corrigan, 88, known as "Wrong Way Corrigan" since he flew his plane from NYC to Dublin, Ireland, instead of Los Angeles, when he made an error later thought intentional, dies in Orange, California, of unreported causes.	Dec. 9
A subway token clerk in New York City, Harry Kaufman, who was burned in an attack in which arsonists poured lighting fluid onto his booth before igniting it, dies from wounds sustained in the Nov. 26 fire.		Reports disclose that many investors who brought fraud suits against Prudential Securities Inc. are claiming that they did not know about a settlement that was finalized Nov. 17. The company states it informed thousands of investors that their cases were settled according to terms of a class action suit, finalized Nov. 17, unless they opted out of the settlement in writing by an Oct. 30 court-imposed deadline. The legal tactic adopted by Prudential, if successful, will enable the company to escape millions of dollars in claims.			Dec. 10
United Cerebral Palsy presents the Humanitarian Award to Diana, the Princess of Wales, and the Award for Outstanding Achievement to retired army general Colin Powell. ...An official states that court-approved administrators have determined that 294,537 individuals nationwide will share a $46 million settlement in two federal class-action lawsuits accusing Denny's restaurant chain of racial discrimination.		Utah representative Enid Greene Waldholtz (R) holds an emotional press conference during which she admits that her 1994 campaign was financed in violation of FEC rules and accuses Joseph Waldholtz, her estranged husband and the campaign's treasurer, of bilking her father of $4 million used to fund her campaign.... Energy Secretary Hazel O'Leary is reprimanded by senior White House officials for making extravagant travel expenditures on trips overseas.... At least 25 people are injured when an explosion causes a fire at the Malden Mills textile factory, the largest employer in Methuen, Massachusetts.... The Commerce Department reports the number of businesses owned by black Americans grew 46% between 1987 and 1992, compared with a 26% rise in the total number of U.S. firms during the same period. However, the average revenue of black-owned businesses stood at only $51,000 at the end of 1992, compared with a $192,000 figure for U.S. businesses overall.		A jury in Waterville, Washington, acquits a Pentecostal lay preacher and his wife, Robert Roberson and Connie Roberson, of 14 counts of child molestation. The Robersons are among 28 adults charged with child molestation in a two-year investigation that led to the arrest of 40 people, at least 20 of whom are in prison.	Dec. 11

F	G	H	I	J
Includes elections, federal-state relations, civil rights and liberties, crime, the judiciary, education, health care, poverty, urban affairs, and population.	*Includes formation and debate of U.S. foreign and defense policies, veterans' affairs, and defense spending. (Relations with specific foreign countries are usually found under the region concerned.)*	*Includes business, labor, agriculture, taxation, transportation, consumer affairs, monetary and fiscal policy, natural resources, and pollution.*	*Includes worldwide scientific, medical, and technological developments; natural phenomena; U.S. weather; natural disasters; and accidents.*	*Includes the arts, religion, scholarship, communications media, sports, entertainments, fashions, fads, and social life.*

	World Affairs	Europe	Africa & the Middle East	The Americas	Asia & the Pacific
Dec. 12	The UN General Assembly passes a resolution condemning all nuclear testing and urging an end to all such programs.... Judge Richard Goldstone of South Africa, who is heading the UN tribunal to investigate and try individuals suspected of taking part in acts of genocide in 1994 in Rwanda, announces that the tribunal has issued its first indictments, charging eight people with planning or participating in four mass killings near Kibuye. Separately, the UN Security Council votes to extend its Rwandan peacekeeping mission for three months but will reduce its force to 1,200 troops and 200 military monitors.	Striking public-sector workers in France hold large demonstrations in major French cities, including Bordeaux, Toulouse, Rouen, and Le Havre. The strikes bring commuter traffic in and around Paris to a near standstill, and 100,000 marchers in Marseilles and 150,000 in Paris call for Premier Alain Juppe's resignation.... About 90% of voters in Serb-dominated suburbs of Sarajevo vote against the November treaty in a nonbinding referendum. The Serbs oppose provisions in the pact that will transfer control of the districts where they live to the Muslim-Croat federation. Separately, Bosnian Serb soldiers release Capt. Frederic Chiffot and Lt. Jose Souvignet, French pilots whose plane was shot down during a NATO bombing raid in August.	A car bomb explodes in Algiers, the capital of Algeria, killing 15 people and wounding 40.	Demonstrators calling for more government funding for universities take over Nicaragua's Sandino Airport for four hours, forcing incoming flights to be diverted.	David Marshall, 87, chief minister in the government of Singapore, 1955–56, and a strong advocate for human rights, dies in Singapore after suffering from lung cancer.
Dec. 13	The legislative branch of the EU, the European Parliament, overwhelmingly approves a customs pact with Turkey under which Turkey will become part of the EU market by adopting many of its trade laws and external tariffs.	Hundreds of youths in the working-class London borough of Brixton riot over the death of Wayne Douglas, a black man who died in police custody on Dec. 5.... Three policemen are injured, 50 stores are damaged, and 22 people are arrested.... Alfons Noviks, the chief of security forces in then-Soviet Latvia in the 1940s and 1950s, is found guilty of genocide and sentenced to life in prison by a Latvian court.		About 200 students demonstrating for more government funding for universities reportedly hold hostages outside the residence of Pres. Violeta de Barrios Chamorro in Managua, Nicaragua's capital. Riot police fire on the crowd, killing a university professor and wounding 19 people. Although it is not reported, a student is also fatally shot during the demonstration.	One of China's best-known dissidents, Wei Jingsheng, is convicted of "conspiring to subvert the government" and sentenced to 14 years in prison. Wei has spent all but six months of the last 16 years in prison for his writings.... A coroner in Australia's Northern Territory announces that the cause of death of Azaria Chamberlain, whose mother Lindy Chamberlain claimed that her daughter was taken and killed by a dingo, cannot be determined.
Dec. 14	Leaders of the Association of Southeast Asian Nations (ASEAN) vote unanimously to extend ASEAN membership to Cambodia, Laos, and Myanmar.... In Paris, France, leaders of the rival factions in the Bosnian civil war sign a pact to end the nearly four-year-old conflict, formally approving the pact initialed in November. In an important diplomatic breakthrough, the Federal Republic of Yugoslavia, which comprises Serbia and Montenegro, and the Bosnian government agree to establish formal relations.	Islamic fundamentalist paramilitary troops engage in a shoot-out with Croat militiamen at Zepce, Bosnia, that leaves five of the Muslims dead.... A force of about 800 rebels seizes Gudermes, Chechnya's second-largest city, as part of campaign to disrupt local elections intended to ratify a Russian-backed government in Chechnya. The clashes are among the worst since Russian government and Chechen rebel officials signed an accord that was supposed to have ended the secessionist war in July.	Leah Rabin, widow of the late Israeli prime minister Yitzhak Rabin, who was assassinated Nov. 4, holds a private meeting with Pope John Paul II in Rome, during which he reportedly backs Israel's claim that Jerusalem was its capital for the first time.... In Nigeria, more than 450 opposition politicians gather to push for a meeting with Gen. Sani Abacha and a restoration of civilian rule.	The Commission of Accusations, a Colombian congressional panel investigating allegations that Pres. Ernesto Samper Pizano accepted nearly $6 million from the Cali drug cartel to finance his 1994 presidential campaign, closes its preliminary investigation, citing a lack of evidence against Samper.	Japanese premier Tomiichi Murayama endorses a justice ministry request to proceed with efforts to disband Aum Shinrikyo, a Japanese religious cult linked to a fatal March nerve-gas attack on Tokyo's subway system, under a 1952 antisubversion law. The law has never before been used against a group.... Amnesty International accuses the Indonesian military of raping and executing women human-rights activists in East Timor.
Dec. 15	North Korea and an international group sign a $4.5 billion agreement for the construction of two light-water nuclear reactors in exchange for North Korea's agreement to halt its suspected nuclear arms program.... An international body studying the possible disarmament of paramilitary groups in Northern Ireland meets for the first time.... EU leaders agree to call the proposed single currency the "euro" and set the launch date for 1999.... ASEAN leaders sign a pact that declares their region a nuclear-free zone.	In Chechnya, rebels attack the town of Urus Martan, claiming the government is allowing open ballot fraud to take place there.... Many public sector employees of France decide to return to work following a 22-day strike.	Eritrean forces launch an attack against Yemeni troops on the disputed Greater Hanish island, located at the mouth of the Red Sea.... In South Africa, 10 people are killed near Port Shepstone, south of Durban.... The International Committee of the Red Cross states it has suspended its activities in Burundi after a series of grenade attacks on its offices there.		

A	B	C	D	E
Includes developments that affect more than one world region, international organizations, and important meetings of major world leaders.	Includes all domestic and regional developments in Europe, including the Soviet Union, Turkey, Cyprus, and Malta.	Includes all domestic and regional developments in Africa and the Middle East, including Iraq and Iran and excluding Cyprus, Turkey, and Afghanistan.	Includes all domestic and regional developments in Latin America, the Caribbean, and Canada.	Includes all domestic and regional developments in Asia and Pacific nations, extending from Afghanistan through all the Pacific Islands, except Hawaii.

U.S. Politics & Social Issues	U.S. Foreign Policy & Defense	U.S. Economy & Environment	Science, Technology, & Nature	Culture, Leisure, & Lifestyle	
The House passes by unanimous consent an amended bill that will increase sentences for child pornography and child prostitution. . . . Rep. Walter R. Tucker III (D, Calif.), convicted Dec. 8 on seven counts of extortion and two counts of tax evasion, announces his resignation from the House. . . . Convicted murderer James Michael Briddle is executed by lethal injection in Huntsville, Texas. He is the 56th and final inmate to be put to death in 1995. The year's 56 executions are the most since the Supreme Court reinstated capital punishment in 1976. . . . (William) Homer Thornberry, 86, who served in Congress (D, Tex.) 1949–63, and was a 1968 Supreme Court justice nominee, dies in Austin, Texas, of cancer. . . . The Senate rejects a proposed amendment to the Constitution that would have barred desecration of the U.S. flag. The final tally is 62 for the amendment and 36 against, three votes short of the two-thirds majority needed. . . . Jesse Jackson Jr., son of civil-rights activist Rev. Jesse Jackson, wins election to the House in a special election called to fill the seat vacated by former Rep. Mel Reynolds (D, Ill.), who resigned in September after being sentenced to five years in prison.		The Senate and the House, both by voice vote, agree to repeal a provision from the Clean Air Act of 1990 that requires businesses located in high-pollution areas to compel their workers to carpool to work. . . . The White House, citing lawyer-client and executive privilege, refuses to hand over documents subpoenaed Dec. 8 by the Senate panel investigating the Whitewater affair.	Researchers using the *Hubble Space Telescope* estimate that the Hale-Bopp comet has a nucleus up to 25 miles across, far larger than Halley's comet. . . . The FDA approves riluzole, sold by Rhone-Poulenc Rhorer Inc. as Rilutek, the first approval worldwide of a drug to treat amyotrophic lateral sclerosis (ALS), known as Lou Gehrig's disease, which at any given time afflicts 30,000 people in the U.S. Separately, the FDA asserts that it is not slower in approving new drugs than agencies in other countries.	Andrew Nelson Lytle, 92, writer involved in the "agrarian" literary movement in the southern U.S., dies in Monteagle, Tennessee, of systemic failure. . . . NBC agrees to pay $2.3 billion for the rights to broadcast the 2004 Summer Olympic Games, the 2006 Winter Olympic Games, and the 2008 Summer Olympics on TV and cable. The size of the deal is a record in sports TV history.	Dec. 12
The U.S. Court of Appeals for the 11th Circuit approves, 2-1, a redistricting plan for the state of Georgia that will eliminate two of Georgia's three majority-black congressional districts. . . . Laurence Powell, who was convicted for his involvement in the 1991 videotaped beating of black motorist Rodney King, is released from prison.	Wali Khan Amin Shah is indicted in the U.S. on charges that he participated in an aborted scheme, uncovered in January, to bomb 11 American airliners over the Far East. . . . The U.S. Congress, after heated debate, approves resolutions that give reluctant support to the deployment of American troops in the peace effort in Bosnia-Herzegovina. The Senate measure passes by a 69-30 vote, the House resolution by a 287-141 vote.	The House passes, 244-181, a $12.2 billion appropriations bill for the Interior Department for fiscal 1996. . . . The Dow closes at 5216.47, the 69th record high registered for the Dow in 1995. . . . Workers end a 69-day strike against Boeing. Co.			Dec. 13
Former Los Angeles police sergeant Stacey Koon, who was convicted for his involvement in the 1991 videotaped beating of black motorist Rodney King, is released from federal custody after serving more than two years of his sentence. . . . Police arrest three teenagers—James Irons, Vincent Ellerbe, and Thomas Malik—suspected in the Nov. 26 arson attack that fatally burned Harry Kaufman, a subway token clerk in New York City.	The Senate approves, 82-16, the appointment of 18 ambassadors whose confirmations have been held up for months by Sen. Jesse Helms (R, N.C.).	The Senate clears, 54-44, an $80.6 billion fiscal 1996 appropriations bill for the VA, HUD, EPA, NASA, and FEMA. . . . The Senate clears, 58-40, a $12.2 billion fiscal 1996 appropriations bill for the Interior Department. . . . The family of the late Senator H. John Heinz III (R, Pa.) announces a $20 million donation from a family philanthropic trust to establish a research center devoted to environmental policy studies.	A California AIDS activist in the late stages of the disease, Jeff Getty, 38, undergoes an experimental procedure in which baboon bone marrow is transferred into his circulatory system. Baboons are immune to HIV-1. . . . Researchers report they have found a new animal in the mouths of Norwegian lobsters that has a life cycle and anatomy so unusual that it belongs to a new phylum. It is the first new phyla reported since 1983 and about the 36th overall. The researchers assign it to the new phylum Cycliophora and dub the new species *Symbion pandora*.	The FBI releases files on the agency's attempts to deport John Lennon in 1972–73. The files are released after a 12-year court fight led by Jonathan Wiener, a history professor at the University of California. . . . NBC and Microsoft announce that they will jointly launch a 24-hour all-news television channel, MSNBC, in 1996.	Dec. 14
David Freeman, 16, a neo-Nazi skinhead accused of slaying his parents and younger brother in February, pleads guilty to murdering his father, Dennis Freeman, and is sentenced to life in prison without parole. Freeman's brother, Bryan Freeman, 17, pled guilty to related charges on Dec. 7. . . . Statistics reveal that illegal drug use among teenagers rose for the fourth consecutive year in 1995.	The House, 267-149, passes a $265.3 billion fiscal 1996 bill for military spending.	The Dow volume of shares traded is 636.8 million, the heaviest in the 203-year history of the New York Stock Exchange.	Researchers report that they have for the first time genetically engineered disease-resistant rice, the leading food source worldwide. . . . NASA transmits signals to *Pioneer 6*, which returns the transmission, confirming that it is still operable. The craft, launched in December 1965, has circled the sun 35 times and covered 18 billion miles.		Dec. 15

F	G	H	I	J
Includes elections, federal-state relations, civil rights and liberties, crime, the judiciary, education, health care, poverty, urban affairs, and population.	*Includes formation and debate of U.S. foreign and defense policies, veterans' affairs, and defense spending. (Relations with specific foreign countries are usually found under the region concerned.)*	*Includes business, labor, agriculture, taxation, transportation, consumer affairs, monetary and fiscal policy, natural resources, and pollution.*	*Includes worldwide scientific, medical, and technological developments; natural phenomena; U.S. weather; natural disasters; and accidents.*	*Includes the arts, religion, scholarship, communications media, sports, entertainments, fashions, fads, and social life.*

	World Affairs	Europe	Africa & the Middle East	The Americas	Asia & the Pacific
Dec. 16	EU leaders reach an agreement over the possible expansion of the EU. The summit is attended by leaders from countries seeking entry into the union, including 10 former members of the eastern bloc of communist countries, Malta, and Cyprus. Of the Eastern European nations, Poland, Hungary, Bulgaria, Romania, Slovakia, Estonia, Lithuania, and Latvia have formally requested entry.	Public-sector trade unions hold demonstrations throughout most of France's largest metropolitan areas.	Cape Verde holds its second-ever multiparty legislative elections, and the ruling Movement for Democracy wins a clear majority. . . . The state-run press reports that Mohammed Saeed and Abdrrezak Redjam, two top Islamic leaders who had distanced themselves from acts of violence, were executed a month earlier by the GIA of Algeria. . . . Reports confirm that Ethiopia has appealed to Western donors to help feed 3.2 million of its citizens expected to face hunger in 1996.	Manoel Ribeiro, a councilman in the town of Corumbiará in Rondonia state, Brazil, is shot dead in front of his home.	
Dec. 17		Russian voters cast ballots to elect the 450 members of the State Duma, the lower house of the Russian parliament. . . . Chancellor Franz Vranitzky's Social Democratic Party maintains its status as Austria's dominant political party in general elections.	Yemen and Eritrea engage warships and aircraft in battle. . . . Three people die from toxic fumes caused by a sulfur fire at a chemical plant near the South African town of Somerset West. Poisonous sulfur dioxide clouds force the evacuation of 2,500 residents of the nearby town of Macassar.	René Preval, candidate for the Lavalas party, wins presidential elections in Haiti.	
Dec. 18	WHO estimates that at the end of 1994 there were 17 million worldwide cases of infection with HIV, the AIDS-causing virus, with some 6 million of those already advanced to AIDS. . . . The UN warns that North Korea is beginning to experience a severe winter famine—a problem exacerbated by devastating summer floods—that will worsen as temperatures fall.	Russian troops begin pounding Gudermes, the second-largest city in Chechnya, which was seized by rebels on Dec. 14, with artillery and missiles. . . . The wreckage of a Khabarovsk Airlines plane carrying 97 people, missing since Dec. 6, is discovered by a pilot over the remote Bo-Jaus mountains in eastern Russia. There are no survivors. . . . Francis Collins, a former IRA terrorist suspected of drug dealing, is fatally shot in Belfast, allegedly by an IRA hitman. . . . Sir Colville Deverell, 88, British governor of Mauritius, 1959–62, dies in Wokingham, England, after suffering from Alzheimer's disease.	At least 136 people die when a Zairian passenger jet crashes in Angola.	The Nova Scotia provincial Supreme Court sentences Mary Jane Fogarty, 39, to three years' probation for aiding and abetting the suicide of her friend Brenda Barnes. Fogarty is the first person in Canadian history convicted of assisting a suicide. . . . Canadian fisheries minister Brian Tobin announces that the government will raise its limits on seal hunting along Canada's Atlantic coast by about 30%, beginning in 1996.	In Australia, Minister for Foreign Affairs Gareth Evans and his Indonesian counterpart, Ali Alatas, sign a security treaty between the two countries.
Dec. 19	The UN Security Council votes to approve holding a referendum to decide the fate of Western Sahara, which is claimed by both Morocco and the Polisario Front, a rebel group backed by Algeria.	Employees of Belgium's state-owned airline and railroad hold massive strikes, bringing public transportation in the country to a near standstill. . . . Great Britain's parliament rejects the government's request for formal approval of British participation in the European Union's Common Fisheries Policy.	Zairian officials report that there are five survivors from the Dec. 18 crash in Angola.	Reports disclose that 11 Peruvian soldiers were killed in a clash with members of the Sendero Luminoso (Shining Path) guerrilla group in the Huallaga Valley coca-growing region in northern Peru. . . . Dame (Ruth) Nita Barrow, 79, governor general of Barbados since 1990 and the only woman ever to hold that post, dies in Bridgetown, Barbados, after suffering a stroke.	
Dec. 20	Ukraine and the Group of Seven leading industrial nations agree to close the Chernobyl nuclear power plant by 2000. . . Gen. Bernard Janvier of France, the commander of UN forces in Yugoslavia, formally relinquishes control over international military operations in the Balkans to U.S. admiral Leighton W. Smith Jr. of NATO.	Fabio Salamone, a public prosecutor in Brescia, Italy, requests the prosecution of Antonio Di Pietro, Italy's former leading anticorruption magistrate, on charges of blackmail. . . . One of Lithuania's largest commercial banks, Innovation Bank, is declared insolvent by the country's central bank. . . . In England, Buckingham Palace discloses that Queen Elizabeth II has urged Prince Charles and Princess Diana to divorce.	In Mauritius, the main opposition group wins a landslide victory in general elections, ending the 13-year rule of Prime Minister Aneerood Jugnauth.	An American Airlines jet crashes into a mountain near Buga, Colombia, killing 159 of the 163 people on board. The crash of Flight 965 is the first American Airlines crash involving fatalities since 1979 and is the first-ever fatal crash of a Boeing 757.	The U.S. agrees to reduce the amount of Okinawan land occupied by U.S. forces by 2% within three years as part of negotiations to remain in Okinawa after the September rape of a 12-year-old girl by U.S. servicemen.
Dec. 21	International donors at a conference in Brussels, Belgium, pledge $500 million in aid to begin reconstruction efforts in Bosnia. The chairman of the conference, European Union external-affairs commissioner Hans van den Broek, warns that Bosnia's Serbs can expect no aid for rebuilding unless they cooperate in handing over indicted war criminals for prosecution by an international tribunal in The Hague, the Netherlands.	The parliament of Latvia votes to approve Andris Skele, an entrepreneur who belongs to no political party, as the country's next premier. . . . Sir (George) Trenchard Cox, 90, director and secretary of London's Victoria and Albert Museum, 1956–66, dies of unreported causes.	Palestinian police assume control of the city of Bethlehem on the West Bank as Israel withdraws its troops under the terms of a second-phase agreement on interim Palestinian self-rule. Separately, Hamas concludes talks with the PNA by reiterating that it will not participate in Palestinian elections nor halt attacks against Israelis. . . . Hutu guerrillas reportedly slay 30 people and kill Bede Nzobonimpa, governor of the northern Ngozi province.		More than 40 people are killed and at least 125 are injured when a car bomb explodes in Peshawar, Pakistan. . . . Prosecutors indict former South Korean presidents Chun Doo Hwan and Roh Tae Woo for their alleged roles in the 1979 coup. . . . Prince Norodom Sirivuddh travels to Singapore on his way to France, where he has agreed to live in exile after being accused of plotting to assassinate Cambodian second premier Hun Sen.

A	B	C	D	E
Includes developments that affect more than one world region, international organizations, and important meetings of major world leaders.	Includes all domestic and regional developments in Europe, including the Soviet Union, Turkey, Cyprus, and Malta.	Includes all domestic and regional developments in Africa and the Middle East, including Iraq and Iran and excluding Cyprus, Turkey, and Afghanistan.	Includes all domestic and regional developments in Latin America, the Caribbean, and Canada.	Includes all domestic and regional developments in Asia and Pacific nations, extending from Afghanistan through all the Pacific Islands, except Hawaii.

U.S. Politics & Social Issues	U.S. Foreign Policy & Defense	U.S. Economy & Environment	Science, Technology, & Nature	Culture, Leisure, & Lifestyle	
		The federal government is partially shut down because a continuing resolution funding parts of the government expired on Dec. 15. . . . Reports confirm that the Labor Department has ordered the VA to pay $21,500 annually to Philip Wiley, ruling that the death of his wife, Mildred Wiley, was at least partly caused by inhalation of secondhand smoke while working for that department.			Dec. 16
The FBI reveals that murders reported to police dropped 12% during the first six months of 1995, compared with the same period in 1994. . . . Senate majority leader Robert Dole (R, Kans.), the front-runner in the Republican presidential nomination race, reverses an earlier stance when he vows he will not back a constitutional amendment prohibiting all abortions.					Dec. 17
Pres. Clinton signs an executive order that requires all people arrested on federal criminal charges to face drug testing.	Transportation Secretary Federico Pena announces that the U.S. and Mexico will delay implementation of a provision of NAFTA to grant trucks from Mexico unlimited access to U.S. highways in California, Texas, New Mexico, and Arizona.	Pres. Clinton vetoes a $12.2 billion fiscal 1996 appropriations bill for the Interior Department, arguing that it offers inadequate funding. . . . Pres. Clinton vetoes an $80.6 billion fiscal 1996 appropriations bill for the VA, EPA, HJUD, NASA, and FEMA, objecting to the bill's reductions in environmental spending and its elimination of his national service program for college students. . . . The Dow closes at 5075.21, down 101.52 points, or 1.96%. The decline is the index's largest single-day fall since Nov. 22, 1994.	IBM scientists report that they have shown the existence of "glueballs," hypothetical subnuclear particles, after solving a million trillion arithmetic problems using 448 computers for two years. . . . Konrad Zuse, 85, German scientist credited with developing the first working computer, the Z3 program-controlled calculator, in 1941, dies in Hunfeld, Germany, of unreported causes.	*The Christmas Box* by Richard Paul Evans is at the top of the best-seller list.	Dec. 18
Massachusetts becomes the fifth state to sue tobacco companies to recover state money spent through Medicaid to pay for treatment for victims of smoking-related illnesses. . . . In Santa Monica, California, Superior Court judge Alan Haber orders O. J. Simpson, who in October was acquitted of killing his former wife and her male friend, to turn over his financial records to the families of the murder victims as part of a civil lawsuit.	The Senate clears a $265.3 fiscal 1996 defense-authorization bill.	Pres. Clinton vetoes a $27.3 billion fiscal 1996 appropriations bill for the Departments of Commerce, Justice, and State and the federal judiciary. Clinton objects to the bill's alteration of a police hiring program. . . . Pres. Clinton vetoes a bill to curb the ability of stockholders to file securities-fraud suits and asks Congress to rewrite it. . . . The Federal Open Market Committee votes to reduce the federal funds rate, a key short-term interest rate, to 5.5% from 5.75%.	The FDA approves the nonprescription sale of the heartburn drug Zantac 75. It is the third of a new class of competing heartburn drugs to gain FDA approval for over-the-counter sale.	A Maryland priest, Alphonsus Smith, is sentenced to 16 years in prison after pleading guilty to molesting two boys.	Dec. 19
A three-judge panel of the U.S. Court of Appeals for the 11th Circuit orders the attorney general of Georgia, Michael Bowers, to show a "compelling" governmental interest for his 1991 withdrawal of a job offer to Robin Shahar, a lesbian who participated in a commitment ceremony with another woman. Bowers rescinded the offer to Shahar when he learned of the ceremony. The panel rules that the pair has "the fundamental right of intimate association."		House Republicans by voice vote approve a resolution requiring an agreement from Pres. Clinton to balance the budget in seven years using CBO economic projections before they will pass a continuing resolution. . . . The House votes, 319-100, to set aside the Dec. 19 veto of a bill to curb the ability of stockholders to file securities-fraud suits. . . . The California Public Utilities Commission votes in favor of a plan to deregulate the state's utilities market by 1998.			Dec. 20
The House approves, 245-178, a sweeping reform of the federal system of welfare distribution. . . . A Senate Judiciary subcommittee releases a report on a 1992 standoff between federal agents and white separatist Randall Weaver in Idaho's remote Ruby Ridge area. The report criticizes the conduct of the ATF, the FBI, and the U.S. Marshals Service, as well as that of Weaver.	The House and Senate approve, both by voice vote, a bill authorizing spending for intelligence operations in fiscal 1996. Although the exact amount is classified, estimates place it at $28 billion.	Occidental Chemical Corp. agrees to pay $129 million to the federal government to cover toxic waste cleanup costs in the Love Canal subdivision of Niagara Falls, New York. . . . The Senate approves by voice vote a bill to dissolve the Interstate Commerce Commission, effective Jan. 1, 1996.	Scientists report they have found a second major gene that, when mutated, causes breast cancer. . . . Researchers state that fossils of an 80-million-year-old nesting dinosaur found in Mongolia's Gobi Desert have yielded the first direct evidence that some dinosaurs cared for their offspring. . . . A study finds that the anti-AIDS drug AZT appears to significantly reduce the risk of transmission of HIV among health-care workers stuck with sharp objects.	Boerge Ousland of Norway reaches the South Pole after skiing about 800 miles (1,290 km) through Antarctica, becoming the first person to complete the trek alone and unassisted.	Dec. 21

F	G	H	I	J
Includes elections, federal-state relations, civil rights and liberties, crime, the judiciary, education, health care, poverty, urban affairs, and population.	*Includes formation and debate of U.S. foreign and defense policies, veterans' affairs, and defense spending. (Relations with specific foreign countries are usually found under the region concerned.)*	*Includes business, labor, agriculture, taxation, transportation, consumer affairs, monetary and fiscal policy, natural resources, and pollution.*	*Includes worldwide scientific, medical, and technological developments; natural phenomena; U.S. weather; natural disasters; and accidents.*	*Includes the arts, religion, scholarship, communications media, sports, entertainments, fashions, fads, and social life.*

	World Affairs	Europe	Africa & the Middle East	The Americas	Asia & the Pacific
Dec. 22		A car bomb explodes in León, Spain, killing Luciano Cortizo Alonso, a major in the Spanish army, and wounding his daughter, Beatriz Cortizo Alonso.... One of Lithuania's two largest commercial banks, Litimpeks Bank, is declared insolvent by the country's central bank.... James Edward Meade, 88, Nobel Prize–winning British economist who shared the 1977 economics prize, dies in Cambridge, England, of unreported causes.			
Dec. 23	The United Nations Human Rights Commission warns that widespread ethnic violence in Burundi is pulling the country into a "genocidal trend."	Andrzej Milczanowski is sworn in as Poland's president in Warsaw. Lech Walesa boycotts the inauguration.... French police discover the bodies of 16 people thought to have been members of an international religious cult known as the Order of the Solar Temple. In Oct. 1994, the cult orchestrated a similar mass suicide ritual, or mass execution, in Canada and Switzerland.	Hastings Kamuzu Banda, Malawi's ruler, 1964–94, is acquitted of conspiring in the 1983 murders of four political rivals. Also acquitted are John Tembo, Banda's former minister of police and state, and Cecilia Kadzamira, Tembo's niece and reportedly Banda's mistress, along with three senior police officers.		More than 500 people, over half of whom are children, die in a fire in the town of Mandi Dabwali, in the northern Haryana province in India. The hospital at Mandi Dabwali is unable to accommodate the large number of victims, and many are taken to hospitals as far as 125 miles (201 km) away.
Dec. 24		Kyrgyzstan's Pres. Askar Akayev is reelected to a second five-year term.... Turkey's Muslim fundamentalist Welfare Party, or Refah, emerges with the largest representation in Parliament in general elections.... Russian military commanders in the breakaway republic of Chechnya report they have regained control of Gudermes, the republic's second-largest city, which was seized Dec. 14.	Nigerian security forces arrest Nosa Igiebor, editor in chief of a newsmagazine, and seize the magazine's latest issue, with a story critical of Gen. Abacha, prior to its release.... For the first time in 29 years, Christmas is celebrated in Bethlehem under Palestinian control. Palestinian National Authority leader Yasser Arafat and his wife, Suha Arafat, attend Christmas eve mass at nearby St. Catherine's Roman Catholic Church.	The leftist Guatemalan National Revolutionary Union (URNG) guerrilla group begins a cease-fire to coincide with Christmas and runoff elections for president scheduled for Jan. 7, 1996.	
Dec. 25		Gen. Anatoly Shkirko, the commander of Russian forces at Gudermes, states that the bodies of 267 civilians have been found and that 70 Russian soldiers and more than 300 Chechen rebels have died in the worst fighting in Chechnya since a July truce. The figures place the death toll from the clashes that started Dec. 14 at more than 600.... Pope John Paul II does not attend Christmas High Mass in St. Peter's Basilica for the first time in his 17-year tenure and is forced to interrupt his Christmas Day address due to a bout of influenza.	In South Africa, at least 166 people die when the Umsunduzi River and several of its tributaries overflow and flood slum communities in the Edenvale valley in KwaZulu/Natal. Many others are reported missing. The floods, caused by torrential rains, leave more than 1,000 people homeless.		In India, 5,000 mourners gather outside Mandi Dabwali's hospital, protesting the lack of adequate facilities to care for victims of the Dec. 23 fire.
Dec. 26	Thailand, Vietnam, and the United Nations High Commissioner for Refugees sign an agreement under which some 5,000 Vietnamese people living in the Sikkiu refugee camp in northern Thailand will be repatriated.	Russian president Boris Yeltsin is released from full-time medical care for the first time since October, when he was hospitalized with a heart ailment for the second time in 1995.		Reports confirm that authorities in Ecuador have arrested Gloria Canales, a Peruvian-born woman who is allegedly the head of an international operation that smuggled at least 10,000 people a year into the U.S.	North Korea releases the five surviving crew members of a South Korean trawler, captured in May, in an effort to spur the resumption of rice aid from South Korea.
Dec. 27	France detonates a nuclear device under the Mururoa Atoll in the fifth of a series of tests. The blast measures 30 kilotons, roughly twice the explosive power of the bomb that destroyed the Japanese city of Hiroshima during World War II.	In Ireland, a so-called punishment killing is carried out when Martin McCrory is shot by an alleged republican gunman.... Shura Cherkassky, 84, Ukrainian-born pianist known for his interpretations of romantic music, dies in London, England, of unreported causes.	South African police disclose at least 135 people have been slain in strife in KwaZulu/Natal province. The recent wave of strife began with the Dec. 15 killings in Port Shepstone.... Israeli troops pull out of the city of Ramallah and the smaller city of Al-Bireh, completing of the pre-election transfer to PNA control of six large Palestinian cities and some 450 towns on the West Bank. That leaves Hebron as the only Palestinian city still under Israeli control.		A court in Seoul, the capital of South Korea, sentences Lee Joon, the owner of a Seoul department store that collapsed in June and killed scores of people, to 10 years in prison for criminal negligence.... Japan's former labor minister, Toshio Yamaguchi, is indicted on embezzlement, fraud, and other charges stemming from his alleged arrangement of illegal loans for family members.

A	B	C	D	E
Includes developments that affect more than one world region, international organizations, and important meetings of major world leaders.	Includes all domestic and regional developments in Europe, including the Soviet Union, Turkey, Cyprus, and Malta.	Includes all domestic and regional developments in Africa and the Middle East, including Iraq and Iran and excluding Cyprus, Turkey, and Afghanistan.	Includes all domestic and regional developments in Latin America, the Caribbean, and Canada.	Includes all domestic and regional developments in Asia and Pacific nations, extending from Afghanistan through all the Pacific Islands, except Hawaii.

U.S. Politics & Social Issues	U.S. Foreign Policy & Defense	U.S. Economy & Environment	Science, Technology, & Nature	Culture, Leisure, & Lifestyle	
The Senate approves, 52-47, a measure that will provide a sweeping reform of the federal system of welfare distribution.	Army officials reveal they have identified 22 soldiers in the 82nd Airborne linked to neo-Nazi skinhead groups or who hold extremist views. However, the officials state they have discovered no evidence of any formal ties with racist organizations.	The House passes, by unanimous consent, legislation that will abolish the ICC.... The Senate votes, 68-30, to override Pres. Clinton's veto of a bill to curb the ability of stockholders to file securities-fraud suits. It is the first time that Congress defeats a Clinton veto.... The White House hands over to the Senate Whitewater Committee notes the group had subpoenaed Dec. 8.... Congress approves and Pres. Clinton signs a spending measure that restores funding for various benefits while the government is shut down.	In the ongoing effort to map all of the approximately 100,000 human genes, researchers publish a map of 15,000 major landmarks, or sequence tagged sites, on human chromosomes.	(William) Thomas Pettit, 64, award-winning journalist, dies in New York City of complications after cardiac surgery.... Butterfly McQueen, 84, black actress best known for her role in *Gone With the Wind* (1939), dies in Augusta, Georgia, of burns suffered during a fire at her home.	Dec. 22
Pres. Clinton signs into law a bill that will increase sentences for child pornography and child prostitution.		Pres. Clinton signs into law a bill that will repeal a provision from the Clean Air Act of 1990 that requires businesses located in high-pollution areas to compel their workers to carpool to work.			Dec. 23
			Smoke inhalation from a fire at the Philadelphia Zoo in Pennsylvania kills 23 rare primates.		Dec. 24
Speaker of the House Newt Gingrich (R, Ga.) is named 1995's "Man of the Year" by *Time* magazine. According to *Time*, Gingrich has changed the focus of political debate in the U.S. by taking on difficult issues such as the federal budget deficit.				Nicolas Slonimsky, 101, musician, musicologist, and writer, dies in Los Angeles of unreported causes. ...Dean Martin (born Dino Paul Crocetti), 78, popular singer and comic considered a member of the "Rat Pack," who rose to stardom during the 1950s, dies in Beverly Hills, California, of acute respiratory failure.	Dec. 25
					Dec. 26
Federal agents arrest Ellis Edward Hurst and Joseph Martin Bailie, two suspects in the attempted bombing of an IRS office in Reno, Nevada. The bomb did not detonate because of a malfunction.	The Clinton administration reveals that the U.S. deported a record 51,600 criminal and illegal aliens in 1995. The INS reports that the number of illegal aliens turned away at U.S. borders increased in 1995 to 9,400, from 5,669 in 1994.			The National Gallery of Art in Washington, D.C., reopens an historic exhibit of paintings by Jan Vermeer in spite of the partial shutdown of the government that forced it to close Dec. 16. Gallery officials divert $30,000 in private donation money to keep the largest exhibition of Verneer's works open.	Dec. 27

F	G	H	I	J
Includes elections, federal-state relations, civil rights and liberties, crime, the judiciary, education, health care, poverty, urban affairs, and population.	Includes formation and debate of U.S. foreign and defense policies, veterans' affairs, and defense spending. (Relations with specific foreign countries are usually found under the region concerned.)	Includes business, labor, agriculture, taxation, transportation, consumer affairs, monetary and fiscal policy, natural resources, and pollution.	Includes worldwide scientific, medical, and technological developments; natural phenomena; U.S. weather; natural disasters; and accidents.	Includes the arts, religion, scholarship, communications media, sports, entertainments, fashions, fads, and social life.

	World Affairs	Europe	Africa & the Middle East	The Americas	Asia & the Pacific
Dec. 28					The trial of three U.S. servicemen charged with the September rape of a 12-year-old Japanese girl in Okinawa is suspended, pending a ruling on a motion to move the trial out of Okinawa.... China's National People's Congress approves a committee that will oversee preparations for Hong Kong's reversion to Chinese sovereignty, from British rule, in mid-1997.
Dec. 29	At the end of 1995 trading, world financial data shows that Switzerland's Zurich blue-chip Swiss Market Index surged to close 20.3% up from 1994's close, and, the British index climbed 16.9% to 3689.3, from its 1994 year-end close of 3065.5. Germany's DAX index gained 6.5% from the end of 1994. Japan's Nikkei average rose less than 1% to 19,868.15 points, from 19,723.06 at the close of 1994.	Russia's Central Electoral Commission releases the final results of Dec. 17 elections for the State Duma. The final tally shows that the Communist Party of the Russian Federation will hold 157 of the 450 seats in the Duma, nearly three times as many as any other party. . . . British prime minister John Major announces the recipients of public awards on the New Year's Honors List, which are made in the name of Queen Elizabeth II.			Philippine police in Manila, the capital, arrest nine men who are allegedly connected to an international terrorist ring. Among the nine arrested is Adel Anonn, who police assert is the brother of Ramzi Ahmed Yousef, the alleged mastermind behind the 1993 bombing of New York City's World Trade Center. . . . Former South Korean president Chun Doo Hwan, who has been on a hunger strike in protest of his arrest since Dec. 3, is found unconscious and put on life support.
Dec. 30		Army specialist Martin John Begosh becomes the first U.S. soldier to be wounded in Bosnia, suffering a fractured leg when his armored vehicle runs over a mine on a road near Bijela.			Activists calling for the ouster of P.M. Khaleda Zia cause the derailment of an express train near Dhaka, Bangladesh's capital. Some 25 people are injured. Protesters reportedly detonate bombs, set up barricades, and attack police as part of a national transportation strike. . . . A Sri Lankan army officer is wounded when a Tiger suicide bomber blows himself up in the Batticaloa district. . . . Former South Korean president Chun Doo Hwan ends the hunger strike started Dec. 3.
Dec. 31		U.S. Army engineers finish building a pontoon bridge across the Sava River, which forms the border between Croatia and northeastern Bosnia-Herzegovina. The river has been the principal obstacle along the main route by which 20,000 U.S. soldiers are to enter Bosnia to join a 60,000-member NATO force that will oversee implementation of a peace treaty.	Algerian president Lamine Zeroual names Ahmen Ouyahia as premier.... Reports suggest that renewed fighting in the western Liberian town of Tubmanburg threatens to destabilize a peace accord signed in August to end the country's civil war. The Economic Community of West African States (ECOWAS) sends reinforcements to the area.... The office of the Nigerian magazine *The News* is set ablaze in what the magazine claims is arson.		

A	B	C	D	E
Includes developments that affect more than one world region, international organizations, and important meetings of major world leaders.	*Includes all domestic and regional developments in Europe, including the Soviet Union, Turkey, Cyprus, and Malta.*	*Includes all domestic and regional developments in Africa and the Middle East, including Iraq and Iran and excluding Cyprus, Turkey, and Afghanistan.*	*Includes all domestic and regional developments in Latin America, the Caribbean, and Canada.*	*Includes all domestic and regional developments in Asia and Pacific nations, extending from Afghanistan through all the Pacific Islands, except Hawaii.*

U.S. Politics & Social Issues	U.S. Foreign Policy & Defense	U.S. Economy & Environment	Science, Technology, & Nature	Culture, Leisure, & Lifestyle	
Researchers report that the risk of contracting HIV through a blood transfusion is about half what it has been thought, with only 18–27 pints of the 12 million pints of blood donated in the U.S. each year infected with HIV.	Pres. Clinton vetoes the $265.3 fiscal 1996 defense-authorization bill, objecting to provisions that would have required development of a missile-defense system and would have limited his ability to deploy U.S. troops abroad. However, Clinton also issues an executive order giving military personnel a 2% pay raise, the most he is authorized to grant. . . . Pres. Clinton announces that he has suspended U.S. trade sanctions against what remains of the federation of Yugoslavia, which comprises Serbia and Montenegro.		Two studies find that a relatively common and easily cured infection, bacterial vaginosis, is to blame for about 6% of premature births in the U.S.	Virginius Dabney, 94, award-winning writer and historian known for his opposition to racial segregation, dies in Richmond, Virginia, of unreported causes.	Dec. 28
		Pres. Clinton signs legislation that will abolish the ICC. . . . The Dow closes at 5117.12, up 1282.68 points, or 33.5% from the 1994 year close of 3834.44. In a stunning year, the Dow twice passed 1000-point milestones. The NASDAQ rose 39.9% during the year to close at 1052.13. The ASE closes at 548.23, up 26.4% from its 1994 close of 433.67. The dollar finishes the year at 103.40 yen, up from 99.60 at the end of 1994, and at 1.4366 marks, down from the 1994 end of 1.5498 marks.	Researchers report they have located the molecular receptors in cells that receive the body's signal to stop eating. . . . Reports indicate that CompuServe Inc., an on-line computer service, has cut off all subscriber access to sexually oriented material. According to some accounts, no on-line service has ever before restricted access to its discussion groups.		Dec. 29
		The House passes by voice vote a measure to return employees to work by declaring all federal workers "essential," rather than by restoring funding to government agencies. The government has been partially shut down since Dec. 16.	NASA launches, on a Delta-2 rocket, the $195 million *X-ray Timing Explorer* satellite. The 6,700-pound XTE is designed to study astronomical phenomena.		Dec. 30
To date, 22 House members, 15 of them Democrats, have said they will not seek reelection in 1996.		The Senate rejects a measure that would return furloughed federal employees to work, which the House passed Dec. 30. The Senate objects to a provision that limits debate on the budget reconciliation bill to 10 hours.			Dec. 31

F	G	H	I	J
Includes elections, federal-state relations, civil rights and liberties, crime, the judiciary, education, health care, poverty, urban affairs, and population.	Includes formation and debate of U.S. foreign and defense policies, veterans' affairs, and defense spending. (Relations with specific foreign countries are usually found under the region concerned.)	Includes business, labor, agriculture, taxation, transportation, consumer affairs, monetary and fiscal policy, natural resources, and pollution.	Includes worldwide scientific, medical, and technological developments; natural phenomena; U.S. weather; natural disasters; and accidents.	Includes the arts, religion, scholarship, communications media, sports, entertainments, fashions, fads, and social life.

1996

U.S. soldiers view a blast-shattered building in the American military base in Dhahran, Saudi Arabia, June 1996.

	World Affairs	Europe	Africa & the Middle East	The Americas	Asia & the Pacific
Jan.	The international airlift of humanitarian supplies to Sarajevo in Bosnia-Herzegovina ends. The airlift, which began July 3, 1992, has been the longest such operation in history.	François Maurice Mitterrand, 79, French president for two terms from 1981 to 1995 who was among the most influential post–World War II leaders, dies in Paris of prostate cancer.	Saudi Arabia's King Fahd issues a royal decree in which he temporarily cedes power to his legal successor, Crown Prince Abdullah.	Some 300 student protesters storm the foreign ministry building in Managua, Nicaragua's capital, demanding increased government funding for their universities.	A suicide bomber rams a truck filled with explosives into the gates of the Central Bank of Sri Lanka in the financial district of Colombo, the capital, killing 86 people and injuring more than 1,400 others.
Feb.	NATO certifies that the Serbs have withdrawn all their military forces from a "separation zone" between Serb and Muslim-Croat territory. In response, the UN Security Council suspends its long-standing economic sanctions against Bosnia-Herzegovina's ethnic Serbs.	In Grozny, Chechnya, Russian troops destroy the presidential palace, a symbol of Chechen independence since Russia invaded the republic.	Two sons-in-law of Pres. Saddam Hussein who defected to Jordan return to Iraq and are slain, apparently by enraged family members.	Rene Preval is sworn in as president of Haiti, succeeding Pres. Jean-Bertrand Aristide. Preval's assumption of the presidency is the first peaceful transfer of power from one democratically elected president to another since Haiti gained independence from France in 1804.	In China, an earthquake measuring 7.0 on Richter scale strikes the sparsely populated southwestern province of Yunnan. The quake, centered near the town of Lijiang on the province's border with Tibet, kills at least 240 people and injures at least 14,000.
March	Despite objections from Britain, the European Commission, the executive arm of the EU, announces a worldwide ban on the export of British beef products amid fears that they pose a serious health risk.	In Bosnia-Herzegovina, Sarajevo and its environs are united under one government for the first time since Serbs began besieging the city in 1992.	In Benin, Mathieu Kerekou is the winner of a runoff presidential election. It is the first time that a sub-Saharan country has voted out a democratically elected leader.	Ruben Figueroa Alcocer, governor of the Mexican state of Guerrero, steps down while Mexico's Supreme Court investigates a June 1995 massacre of 17 peasants by police in Guerrero.	Taiwanese incumbent president Lee Teng-hui wins a resounding victory in Taiwan's first democratic presidential election. Lee's win is seen as a blow to mainland China, which regards Taiwan as a renegade Chinese province.
April	Representatives of 43 African countries sign a treaty that bans nuclear arms from the continent.	Turkish soldiers renew an army offensive against the separatist guerrilla group known as the Kurdistan Workers Party (PKK).	In Liberia, violence called the worst in at least three years breaks out despite an August 1995 peace plan to end the civil war.	At least 50,000 strikers riot in La Paz, prompting the Bolivian government to order in troops.	North Korea violates the 1953 armistice when hundreds of North Korean troops stage military exercises in the demilitarized zone between North and South Korea. In response, South Korea raises its intelligence monitoring to its highest level in 14 years.
May	The Council of Europe, a 39-nation intergovernmental body established in 1949 to promote democracy and human rights, postpones Croatia's admission to the council indefinitely. It is the first time in the history of the council that it overrules a vote by its parliamentary assembly in favor of membership.	Russian premier Viktor Chernomyrdin and Chechen rebel leader Zelimkhan Yandarbiyev sign a peace agreement establishing a cease-fire in the 17-month-long secessionist conflict.	South Africa's Constitutional Assembly votes overwhelmingly to approve a new democratic constitution. The new majority-rule charter, agreed upon after almost two years of negotiations, completes the transition to democracy from white-minority rule.	Officers of the Royal Canadian Mounted Police (RCMP) in Halifax, Nova Scotia, board a container ship registered in Taiwan, and arrest its captain and six officers on three charges of murder of stowaways during its voyage.	Vietnamese refugees riot at a detention center in Hong Kong's rural New Territories, setting ablaze 26 buildings and 53 cars.
June	The UN International Criminal Tribunal announces the indictment of eight Bosnian Serbs on charges of rape. It is the first time rape is treated as a war crime.	Ukraine completes its nuclear disarmament.	A powerful truck bomb explodes on the perimeter of a military complex near the eastern Saudi Arabian city of Dhahran, killing 19 U.S. servicemen and wounding several hundred people. It is called the most deadly guerrilla attack on Americans in the Middle East since 1983.	Colombia's House of Representatives, the lower chamber of Congress, votes to drop charges that Pres. Ernesto Samper Pizano accepted $6 million from the Cali drug cartel to finance his 1994 presidential election campaign.	Street riots break out in Jakarta, the Indonesian capital, as Pres. Suharto begins taking action to destabilize the PDI, one of two opposition groups officially sanctioned by the government.
July	The United Nations AIDS program estimates that at least 1.3 million people died from AIDS or AIDS-related illnesses in 1995 and that HIV is expected to cause more than 3.1 million new infections in 1996.	In the wake of violence surrounding traditional parades, a car bomb explodes in Enniskillen, Northern Ireland, injuring 17 people and virtually destroying a hotel. The blast is the first terrorist bombing in Northern Ireland, or Ulster, in 22 months.	Burundi's Tutsi-dominated military seizes power in a coup and names Major Pierre Buyoya, a Tutsi regarded as a moderate, as president. The action draws international condemnation.	Four police officers are indicted on charges of homicide for allegedly supplying the perpetrators with the van used in the 1994 bombing of a Jewish center in Buenos Aires, Argentina, that killed 87 people.	Chinese major general Liu Zhenwu visits Hong Kong, marking the first-ever visit to the British colony by a communist Chinese military general.
Aug.	India formally vetoes a draft of the multinational Comprehensive Test Ban Treaty (CTBT), which forbids its signatories to test nuclear weapons.	Pres. Boris Yeltsin is inaugurated as the first democratically elected Russian head of state.	Gen. Mohammed Farah Aidid, a Somali clan leader who fueled Somalia's civil war despite UN peacekeeping efforts, dies from gunshot wounds suffered in faction fighting.	At least 96 soldiers, policemen, rebels, and civilians, are killed in what Colombian officials call one of the deadliest series of attacks by left-wing rebels in decades. The rebels include factions from FARC and ELN.	The Seoul District Criminal Court in South Korea convicts and sentences to death former South Korean president Chun Doo Hwan for his role in the 1979 coup that brought him to power and the subsequent massacre of prodemocracy demonstrators in the southern city of Kwangju, as well as for accepting bribes. The three-judge panel also sentences Chun's successor, Roh Tae Woo, to 22 years and six months in prison for his support of the coup and for accepting bribes.
	A	B	C	D	E
	Includes developments that affect more than one world region, international organizations, and important meetings of major world leaders.	*Includes all domestic and regional developments in Europe, including the Soviet Union, Turkey, Cyprus, and Malta.*	*Includes all domestic and regional developments in Africa and the Middle East, including Iraq and Iran and excluding Cyprus, Turkey, and Afghanistan.*	*Includes all domestic and regional developments in Latin America, the Caribbean, and Canada.*	*Includes all domestic and regional developments in Asia and Pacific nations, extending from Afghanistan through all the Pacific Island, except Hawaii.*

U.S. Politics & Social Issues	U.S. Foreign Policy & Defense	U.S. Economy & Environment	Science, Technology, & Nature	Culture, Leisure, & Lifestyle	
James Watt, in an agreement with prosecutors, pleads guilty to a misdemeanor charge of attempting to mislead a federal grand jury. Watt, who served as interior secretary from 1981 until 1983, is the highest-ranking member of the Reagan administration to be charged in the HUD scandal.	The U.S. Army for the first time reveals the size and location of its chemical weapons arsenal, and it states that it is slowly destroying the 60-million-pound (27.12 million kg) stockpile.	First Lady Hillary Rodham Clinton testifies before a federal grand jury in Washington, D.C., concerning documents related to the investigation of the Whitewater affair. It is first time in U.S. history that a first lady testifies under oath before a grand jury.	A team of physicists in Geneva, Switzerland, announce that for the first time ever, they have created atoms of antimatter. Antimatter has the same mass as regular matter, but it has an opposite electric charge.	On a tour of the U.S., author Salman Rushdie, who is under a death threat from Muslim, militants, gives a lecture in Washington, D.C.	Jan.
Congress passes and Pres. Clinton signs the broadest overhaul of the nation's communications laws in 62 years. The reforms include the controversial Communications Decency Act. In Philadelphia, Pennsylvania, U.S. district judge Ronald Buckwalter grants a restraining order that will temporarily block enforcement of that provision.	Pres. Clinton signs a $265 billion defense-authorization bill with a controversial provision that requires all service members who test positive for HIV to be discharged.	The Dow closes at a record high of 5630.49, marking a 10th record high for the Dow in February and the 16th record high registered in 1996.	*Mir* marks the 10th anniversary of its 1986 launch. The Russian space station has been manned continuously since September 1989.	Gary Kasparov of Russia defeats the Deep Blue chess computer, designed by IBM, in the first multigame regulation match between a world champion and a computer.	Feb.
The U.S. Ninth Circuit Court of Appeals in San Francisco, California, strikes down a Washington State law that bars doctors from helping terminally ill patients to kill themselves, ruling that such patients have a constitutional right to a "dignified and humane death." The ruling is the first on doctor-assisted suicide by a full federal appeals court.	Pres. Clinton signs into law a bill that strengthens the U.S.'s economic embargo of Cuba by penalizing foreigners who invest in Cuba. The legislation draws protests from U.S. allies as an unacceptable extension of American law beyond U.S. territory.	As the debate over appropriations bills continues, Congress passes and Pres. Clinton signs the 12th continuing resolution enacted for the current fiscal year.	Shannon Lucid becomes the first of five U.S. astronauts to occupy *Mir* continuously through 1998. She is the second U.S. astronaut and the first U.S. woman to live on *Mir*.	When Michelle Kwan and Todd Eldredge win the women's and men's titles, respectively, at the World Figure Skating Championships, it is the first singles sweep for the U.S. since 1986.	March
Police take into custody a former university professor, Theodore Kaczynski, who is suspected of being the Unabomber, a serial bomber linked to a series of bombing incidents spanning 17 years in which three men have been killed and 23 other people wounded.	Congress clears and Pres. Clinton signs an antiterrorism bill, despite the fact that it excludes or weakens several provisions proposed by the president to combat terrorism.	Pres. Clinton signs into law a bill giving himself and future presidents a line-item veto, which permits presidents to invalidate particular spending items contained in appropriations bills.	The FDA approves the use of ultrasound equipment to determine whether lumps found in women's breasts are cancerous or benign.	Baylor University in Waco, Texas, the largest university in the world affiliated with the Baptist church, holds an on-campus dance for the first time in its 151-year history.	April
In *Romer v. Evans*, the Supreme Court rules, 6-3, to strike down an amendment to the Colorado constitution that prohibited any government body in the state from implementing policies that bar discrimination against homosexuals.	Admiral Jeremy M. (Mike) Boorda, 56, the highest ranking officer in the U.S. Navy, dies of a self-inflicted gunshot wound outside of his home at the Washington Navy Yard in Washington, D.C.	A federal jury in Little Rock, Arkansas, convicts James McDougal, Susan McDougal, and Gov. Jim Guy Tucker (D, Ark.) on fraud and conspiracy charges brought during an investigation of the Whitewater venture.	The FDA approves the drug Taxotere for use in treating breast cancer cases that do not respond to treatment with the drug doxorubicin, the standard initial chemotherapy treatment.	The religious group Pastors for Peace ends a 94-day hunger strike after the release of more than 300 computers bound for Cuba.	May
The last members of the militia the Freemen peacefully surrender from their complex near Jordan, Montana, after one of the longest-ever armed sieges in U.S. history.	A court-martial jury in Fort Bragg, North Carolina, convicts and sentences to death army sergeant William Kreutzer, 27, for opening fire on members of his own division, the 82nd Airborne Division, in an October 1995 sniper attack.	The Supreme Court rules, 7-2, in two separate cases involving free speech and political patronage issues, that independent government contractors cannot be fired for publicly criticizing the government bodies that hired them or for backing political candidates. The cases are *Board of County Commissioners, Wabaunsee County v. Umbehr* and *O'Hare Truck Service Inc. v. City of Northlake*.	The FDA reproductive health advisory panel unanimously rules that high doses of currently available birth-control pills are safe and effective when used soon after intercourse to prevent pregnancy.	In *Denver Area Educational Telecommunications Consortium Inc. v. FCC*, the Supreme Court, in a fragmented decision, rules that cable-TV operators may restrict access to indecent programs on certain commercial channels but not on public-access channels. The regulation at issue is known as the Helms Amendment.	June
Congress passes a sweeping overhaul of the welfare system that will give states unprecedented authority over the use of funding for poverty relief.	The Department of Defense indicates that 55% of women in the U.S. military reported some form of sexual harassment in the previous 12 months, including rape, assault, groping, and pressure for sexual favors. The figure is down from the 64% recorded in 1988.	Videotaped testimony by Pres. Clinton is played during a Whitewater-related fraud and conspiracy trial.	A Trans World Airlines (TWA) 747 jetliner bound for Paris crashes into the Atlantic Ocean about a half hour after taking off from Kennedy International Airport in New York City. All 230 people on board are killed in the crash.	A homemade pipe bomb goes off at an Olympic Games site in Atlanta, Georgia, killing one person and injuring 111 others. The park bombing is the first terrorist attack at the Olympics since the 1972 games in Munich, Germany.	July
California governor Pete Wilson (R) signs an executive order that bars state agencies and state-funded colleges and universities from providing benefits to illegal immigrants, effectively implementing part of Proposition 187, approved by California voters in a 1994 vote but not enforced because of legal challenges.	Pres. Clinton signs into law a bill that will impose economic sanctions on foreign companies that make large new investments in the energy sectors of Iran or Libya, which Clinton calls "two of the most dangerous supporters of terrorism in the world." The measure is opposed by U.S. trading partners in Europe, whose companies may be subject to the sanctions.	Pres. Clinton signs into law legislation that will allow workers who change or lose their jobs to retain their health-insurance coverage and will limit insurance companies' ability to withhold coverage because of preexisting medical conditions.	Computer hackers illegally enter the Department of Justice's site on the World Wide Web and post obscenities, sexually explicit pictures, and harsh criticisms of the Communications Decency Act.	The FCC approves new regulations, including one that requires TV stations to air three hours of children's educational programming each week.	Aug.
F	G	H	I	J	
Includes elections, federal-state relations, civil rights and liberties, crime, the judiciary, education, health care, poverty, urban affairs, and population.	*Includes formation and debate of U.S. foreign policy, veterans' affairs, and defense spending. (Relations with specific foreign countries are usually found under the region concerned.)*	*Includes business, labor, agriculture, taxation, transportation, consumer affairs, monetary and fiscal policy, natural resources, and pollution.*	*Includes worldwide scientific, medical, and technological developments; natural phenomena; U.S. weather; natural disasters; and accidents.*	*Includes the arts, religion, scholarship, communications media, sports, entertainments, fashions, fads, and social life.*	

	World Affairs	Europe	Africa & the Middle East	The Americas	Asia & the Pacific
Sept.	Britain announces that it will proceed with production of the Eurofighter, an advanced combat jet to be developed jointly with Britain, Germany, Italy, and Spain.	Voters in Bosnia-Herzegovina take part in the ethnically divided country's first nationwide elections since the end of its four-year-long civil war in 1995. Bosnian president Alija Izetbegovic, a Muslim, is elected the chair of a three-member collective presidency. He will be joined by Momcilo Krajisnik, a Bosnian Serb, and Kresimir Zubak, a Bosnian Croat.	U.S. forces direct cruise missiles toward Iraqi targets, prompting Iraqi troops to withdraw from the Kurdish city of Erbil.	The government and the leftist Guatemalan National Revolutionary Union (UNRG), an umbrella organization representing the country's main rebel groups, sign an accord hailed by both sides as a major breakthrough in efforts to end Guatemala's 35-year-long civil war.	Muslim fundamentalist Taliban forces take control of Kabul, Afghanistan's capital, after a siege that results in hundreds of deaths. The rebels announce that Islamic law will begin to apply nationwide, and they capture and execute former president Muhammad Najibullah. Mohammed Rabbani is the Taliban rebel named to serve as Kabul's provisional leader.
Oct.	The UN Security Council votes unanimously to lift the sanctions imposed on the federation of Yugoslavia, which consists of Serbia and Montenegro, that have been in place since 1992.	An unidentified gunman shoots and kills Bulgaria's first premier of its postcommunist era, Andrei Lukanov, 58, in Sofia, the Bulgarian capital.	An outbreak of fighting erupts between units of the Zairian army and the Banyamulenge, a 400,000-strong Tutsi community that has lived in the area south of Lake Kivu since the end of the 18th century.	The Mexican Congress approves a package of legislation that seeks to counter the U.S.'s Helms-Burton law, which attempts to force foreign companies to comply with the U.S.'s trade embargo of communist Cuba.	A court in Beijing, China, sentences prominent dissident Wang Dan to 11 years in jail. The sentencing is seen as a final blow to the Chinese dissident movement, whose key members are now all imprisoned or in exile.
Nov.	The UN General Assembly, in a secret ballot, elects candidates from France and New Zealand to the two vacant seats on a key UN budget committee. In an unprecedented move, the US loses its seat on the committee.	Belgrade's First District Court annuls the results of 33 Belgrade city council seats won by candidates from the Zajedno (Together) coalition, which opposes the party affiliated with Serbian president Slobodan Milosevic. The nullification prompts a series of rallies and protests.	An estimated 500,000 Hutu refugees return to Rwanda after spending more than two years in camps in eastern Zaire. The exodus averts a human catastrophe in Zaire's North Kivu province.	Pope John Paul II holds his first meeting with Cuban president Fidel Castro Ruz, leader of the last communist country in the West.	At least 1,000 people are killed when the deadliest cyclone to hit India since 1977 strikes the state of Andhra Pradesh. The cyclone destroys at least 500,000 homes and strands an estimated 500,000 people.
Dec.	The UN Security Council extends the mandate of the UN's peacekeeping mission to Angola until February 1997 and approves a plan to withdraw the 7,000-strong UN contingent by mid-1997.	Unknown gunmen kill six Red Cross workers in Chechnya. The slaying is reported to be the worst premeditated attack in the history of the Red Cross, and it prompts the UNHCR and the Doctors of the World to join the Red Cross and pull out of Chechnya.	At least 300 fighters and civilians die in less than a week during renewed factional fighting in Mogadishu, the capital of Somalia.	Some 25 members of the Tupac Amaru Revolutionary Movement, a Marxist guerrilla group, storm the Japanese ambassador's residence in Lima, Peru's capital, taking more than 600 hostages.	Muslim fundamentalist Taliban forces solidify their buffer zone around Kabul, the Afghanistan capital, retaking the strategic air base of Bagram, 30 miles (50 km) to the north, from the ousted government's coalition forces.

A	B	C	D	E
Includes developments that affect more than one world region, international organizations, and important meetings of major world leaders.	Includes all domestic and regional developments in Europe, including the Soviet Union, Turkey, Cyprus, and Malta.	Includes all domestic and regional developments in Africa and the Middle East, including Iraq and Iran and excluding Cyprus, Turkey, and Afghanistan.	Includes all domestic and regional developments in Latin America, the Caribbean, and Canada.	Includes all domestic and regional developments in Asia and Pacific nations, extending from Afghanistan through all the Pacific Island, except Hawaii.

U.S. Politics & Social Issues	U.S. Foreign Policy & Defense	U.S. Economy & Environment	Science, Technology, & Nature	Culture, Leisure, & Lifestyle	
California governor Pete Wilson (R) signs into law a bill requiring any adult convicted of two sexual assaults on minors to be injected with a drug that reduces their sex drive, unless they agree to voluntarily undergo surgical castration. California thereby becomes the first state in the nation to require "chemical castration" for repeat child molesters.	In the face of recent court decisions, the governing board of the Virginia Military Institute (VMI) votes to begin admitting women. VMI is the only remaining single-sex college in the U.S. that receives state funding.	Pres. Clinton signs an order that designates 1.7 million acres (690,000 hectares) of land in southern Utah as the Canyons of the Escalante National Monument.	The FDA declares that the abortion drug RU-486, also known as mifepristone, is safe and effective.	John F. Kennedy Jr. marries Carolyn Bessette in a secret ceremony on Cumberland Island, Georgia.	**Sept.**
Pres. Clinton signs a bill setting a 20-year sentence for using any illegal drug, including the date-rape drug Rohypnol, with intent to commit rape or other violent crimes.	The Defense Department notifies 20,000 U.S. soldiers that they may have been exposed to fallout from deadly chemical weapons in March 1991 after U.S. troops blew up an Iraqi munitions dump following the end of the Persian Gulf war. The announced total represents a sharp increase over the Pentagon's previous exposure estimates.	The Dow Jones industrial average of U.S. blue-chip securities closes above the 6000 level for the first time in its history. This marks the third time in some 20 months that the benchmark stock average broke through a so-called millennium level.	Researchers in Bangkok, Thailand, report they have discovered the world's largest known deposit of emeralds. A deposit in Madagascar is worth an estimated $54 million.	Christies auctions 8,000 pieces of art that German Nazis plundered from Jews during the Holocaust. The sale's proceeds of $14.5 million are to be donated to both Jewish and non-Jewish victims of the Holocaust.	**Oct.**
William J. Clinton is reelected president of the U.S., the first Democrat since Roosevelt to win a second presidential term. Clinton, 50, is also the youngest president to be reelected. Republicans maintain control of both chambers of Congress.	The army investigates allegations of sexual assault and harassment at the Aberdeen training center in Maryland.	Texaco agrees to a the largest-ever settlement—$176 million—in a race-discrimination suit brought in 1994 by black Texaco employees.	The FDA approves a new drug called Aricept to treat Alzheimer's disease.	The U.S. Court of Appeals for the Ninth Circuit in San Francisco, California, rules, 2-1, that the federal government cannot force the NEA to use standards of decency when giving grants to artists, arguing that such stipulations are an unconstitutional curb on freedom of speech.	**Nov.**
Pres. Clinton chooses Madeleine K. Albright as secretary of state. Albright will become the first woman to fill that post and the highest-ranking woman ever in the federal government.	Two freshman female cadets at the Citadel, a military academy in Charleston, South Carolina, allege that they were sprayed with nail-polish remover and set on fire by fellow students on three separate occasions.	The Dow Jones industrial average closes the year at 6448.27, up 1331.15 points, or 26.01%, from the 1995 year-end level of 5117.12.	*Mars Pathfinder*, an unmanned U.S. space vessel set to land on Mars on July 4, 1997, is launched from Cape Canaveral, Florida.	A panel composed of TV-industry representatives announce a planned system for rating TV programs based on their level of violent and sexual content, scheduled to take effect in January 1997.	**Dec.**

F	G	H	I	J
Includes elections, federal-state relations, civil rights and liberties, crime, the judiciary, education, health care, poverty, urban affairs, and population.	*Includes formation and debate of U.S. foreign and defense policies, veterans' affairs, and defense spending. (Relations with specific foreign countries are usually found under the region concerned.)*	*Includes business, labor, agriculture, taxation, transportation, consumer affairs, monetary and fiscal policy, natural resources, and pollution.*	*Includes worldwide scientific, medical, and technological developments; natural phenomena; U.S. weather; natural disasters; and accidents.*	*Includes the arts, religion, scholarship, communications media, sports, entertainments, fashions, fads, and social life.*

	World Affairs	Europe	Africa & the Middle East	The Americas	Asia & the Pacific
Jan. 1		A tenuous peace in the republic of Bosnia-Herzegovina is shaken when sporadic clashes begin in Mostar after Croat police shoot and kill a teenaged Muslim motorist.	Saudi Arabia's King Fahd issues a royal decree in which he temporarily cedes power to his legal successor, Crown Prince Abdullah. The move signals that the stroke suffered by Fahd in November 1995 was probably more serious than initially indicated.	Two buses collide near Sonoita, a town in the state of Sonora, Mexico, killing 26 people and injuring 22 others.... The Zapatista National Liberation Army (EZLN) rebel group, on the two-year anniversary of its armed uprising in the southern state of Chiapas, Mexico, announces it will form a civilian political organization, the Zapatista National Liberation Front (FZLN).	Some 1,500 government troops seize the stronghold of drug lord Khun Sa in eastern Myanmar.... Nineteen workers are killed and 37 are injured while trying to escape from a fire at a Christmas tree ornament factory in the Shenzhen free-trade zone, China.
Jan. 2				The Mexican stock market, the Bolsa, closes at a record high of 2929.43, up 150.96 points, or 5.4%.	India's tax commissioner, Somnath Pal, imposes a 7.99 billion rupee ($228 million) tax-evasion fine against the country's largest tobacco company, ITC. The commissioner also levies separate fines amounting to 32 million rupees against six ITC executives.
Jan. 3		In Bosnia-Herzegovina officials in the Serb-controlled Sarajevo suburbs of Ilidza and Lukavica release 18 civilian men and one woman imprisoned in late December 1995.... The British government orders the deportation of Mohammed al-Masaari, a leading Saudi Arabian dissident whose London-based Committee for the Defense of Legitimate Rights has castigated the Saudi monarchy as corrupt and autocratic and urged that it be replaced by an Islamic government.		The Mexican stock market, the Bolsa, reaches 3004.78, the first time ever that the market has risen above 3000.	At least six people are killed and another 31 are injured when a bomb explodes in a marketplace in New Delhi, the capital of India. The Jammu-Kashmir Islamic Front, a militant separatist group, claims responsibility for the bombing.
Jan. 4	Scientists tracking the Earth's temperature report that 1995 was the warmest year on record since researchers began keeping such records in 1866. The average temperature in 1995 was 58.72°F (14.84°C), according to the British data and 59.7°F in the U.S. figures. The previous record was in 1990. The data reinforces assertions that human activities—particularly the burning of fossil fuels—have contributed to a gradual warming of the Earth's climate.	Corporal Elio Sbordoni, an Italian soldier in the NATO force, is shot and wounded by a sniper in Serb-held territory near Vogosca, north of Sarajevo. The Vogosca clash is the first exchange of gunfire between NATO peacekeeping troops and Bosnian combatants, and Sbordoni is the first NATO casualty due to hostile fire, although several NATO troops were injured in December 1995 by land mines. In Mostar, shots from the Croat sector wound two Muslim policemen.		Sixty-eight Canadians are named recipients of the Order of Canada in the 1996 list.	
Jan. 5		The upper house of Russia's parliament, the Federation Council, gives final approval to the deployment of Russian troops as part of the NATO-led peacekeeping effort in the republic of Bosnia-Herzegovina.	Yahya Ayyash, a Hamas operative who topped Israel's most-wanted list, is killed in Beit Lahia in the northern Gaza Strip when his booby-trapped cellular phone explodes.	As U.S. troops, which number around 2,200, begin a gradual withdrawal from Haiti, President-elect René Préval formally requests that the UN extend the mandate of its troops in Haiti for six additional months, in light of a recent wave of violence in the country.	Japanese premier Tomiichi Murayama resigns abruptly after 18 months in office, citing the need to "inject fresh blood into the leadership."... Human Rights Watch charges that thousands of children have died in China's state-run orphanages due to deliberate medical neglect and starvation. China's State Council dismisses the allegations as "completely groundless."
Jan. 6	UN speakers confirm that two unidentified Pakistani members of the UN peacekeeping force were arrested in Haiti for allegedly raping a Haitian woman and later beating up a witness to the rape.	In the republic of Bosnia-Herzegovina, a Croat officer is shot dead, and the two sides begin exchanging small-arms fire and launching grenades at each other across the sector border.	Tens of thousands of Palestinians, many vowing revenge against Israel, attend the funeral and burial of Yahya Ayyash, a Hamas operative killed on Jan. 5 in Gaza City.		

A	B	C	D	E
Includes developments that affect more than one world region, international organizations, and important meetings of major world leaders.	Includes all domestic and regional developments in Europe, including the Soviet Union, Turkey, Cyprus, and Malta.	Includes all domestic and regional developments in Africa and the Middle East, including Iraq and Iran and excluding Cyprus, Turkey, and Afghanistan.	Includes all domestic and regional developments in Latin America, the Caribbean, and Canada.	Includes all domestic and regional developments in Asia and Pacific nations, extending from Afghanistan through all the Pacific Island, except Hawaii.

U.S. Politics & Social Issues	U.S. Foreign Policy & Defense	U.S. Economy & Environment	Science, Technology, & Nature	Culture, Leisure, & Lifestyle	
Lee Brown officially tenders his resignation, effective Jan. 14, as director of the Office of National Drug Control Policy.	Admiral Arleigh A(lbert) Burke, 94, highly decorated chief of U.S. naval operations, 1955–61, who became the first living person to have a ship named after him when the navy launched the *Arleigh Burke* in 1991, dies in Bethesda, Maryland, of pneumonia.		Arthur Rudolph, 89, German rocket scientist who joined the U.S. effort to develop a space program before he was accused in 1982 of having supervised concentration camp prisoners in forced labor during World War II, dies in Hamburg, Germany, after suffering from a heart condition.		Jan. 1
James Watt, in an agreement with prosecutors, pleads guilty to a misdemeanor charge of attempting to mislead a federal grand jury. By pleading guilty, Watt avoids a trial on 18 felony counts of perjury and influence peddling and brings an end to a nearly six-year-old, $20 million probe of the HUD scandal. Watt, who served as interior secretary from 1981 until 1983, is the highest-ranking member of the Reagan administration to be charged in the HUD scandal.		The Nature Conservancy reports that about one-third of some 20,000 native U.S. plant and animal species that it recently examined are rare or imperiled. The group's survey is reportedly the most comprehensive study on the state of U.S. plant and animal species ever conducted. According to the group, habitat degradation is the primary threat to the species studied.... AT&T announces plans to eliminate 40,000 of its 300,000 jobs, in what will be the largest downsizing ever in the U.S. telecommunications industry.			Jan. 2
					Jan. 3
	Doris Meissner, the INS commissioner, announces that new applications for political asylum fell 57% in 1995. The figures do not include 14,700 illegal aliens who filed asylum claims to avoid deportation, or 250,000 applications filed by Guatemalan and Salvadoran immigrants as a result of a 1990 federal court decision allowing them to file political asylum claims.... The National Academy of Science's Institute of Medicine concludes there is no evidence of a "previously unknown, serious illness among Persian Gulf veterans."	More than 30,000 maintenance workers walk off their jobs at some 1,000 office buildings in New York City. The action is the first work stoppage at commercial buildings in New York since 1948.	A team of physicists in Geneva, Switzerland, announce that for the first time ever they have created atoms of antimatter. Antimatter has the same mass as regular matter but an opposite electric charge.	A U.S. federal grand jury in Sherman, Texas, indicts three people in connection with the attempted sale of medieval objects that disappeared from Germany during World War II.	Jan. 4
	A car belonging to Jose Pertierra, a lawyer for U.S. attorney Jennifer Harbury, is firebombed in Washington, D.C. No one is injured in the attack. Harbury is the widow of a Guatemalan guerrilla leader, Efrain Bamaca Velasquez, whose death was linked to a Guatemalan colonel on the CIA's payroll.	The House, by voice vote, and the Senate, by unanimous consent, approve a stopgap spending measure that authorizes the federal government to resume full operations. In addition, Congress passes two other bills that will provide funding for certain federal agencies and programs through Sept. 30.... The White House releases records detailing First Lady Hillary Rodham Clinton's work for the Rose Law Firm in the mid-1980s to investigators studying the Whitewater affair.		Richard Versalle, 63, a tenor with the Metropolitan Opera in New York City, collapses on stage and is rushed to the hospital, where he is pronounced dead.... Lincoln Kirstein, 88, ballet promoter who won a 1984 Presidential Medal of Freedom and a 1985 National Medal of Arts, dies in New York City of unreported causes.	Jan. 5
		Pres. Clinton signs a stopgap spending measure that authorizes the federal government to resume full operations, ending the longest shutdown in U.S. history. The president also signs two other bills to provide funding for certain federal agencies and programs through Sept. 30.		Duane Hanson, 70, sculptor whose hyperrealistic depictions of people were often mistaken for real human beings, dies in Boca Raton, Florida, after suffering from lymphatic cancer.	Jan. 6

F	G	H	I	J
Includes elections, federal-state relations, civil rights and liberties, crime, the judiciary, education, health care, poverty, urban affairs, and population.	Includes formation and debate of U.S. foreign and defense policies, veterans' affairs, and defense spending. (Relations with specific foreign countries are usually found under the region concerned.)	Includes business, labor, agriculture, taxation, transportation, consumer affairs, monetary and fiscal policy, natural resources, and pollution.	Includes worldwide scientific, medical, and technological developments; natural phenomena; U.S. weather; natural disasters; and accidents.	Includes the arts, religion, scholarship, communications media, sports, entertainments, fashions, fads, and social life.

	World Affairs	Europe	Africa & the Middle East	The Americas	Asia & the Pacific
Jan. 7		In Bosnia-Herzegovina, to quell the small-arms fire started Jan. 5, Spanish troops under NATO command begin to patrol the factions. Reports indicate that Bosnian Serbs are exhuming and destroying bodies from mass graves. Observers contend the Serbs are trying to eradicate evidence of atrocities committed during ethnic-cleansing campaigns.... Karoly Grosz, 65, Hungary's communist premier, 1987–88, dies of kidney cancer in Hungary.		In Guatemala, Alvaro Arzu Irigoyen of the center-right National Advancement Party (PAN) party, wins in a presidential runoff vote. Arzu will succeed Pres. Ramiro de Leon Carpio.	
Jan. 8	The UN Security Council issues a statement condemning "violations of international humanitarian law" by Croatia in the Krajina region, which Croatian forces recaptured from Croatian Serb rebels in 1995.	François Maurice Mitterrand, 79, French president for two terms from 1981 to 1995 who was among the most influential post-World War II leaders, dies in Paris of prostate cancer.	A cargo plane crashes into an open-air market in Kinshasa, Zaire's capital, killing hundreds of people. A crowd of angry residents attack four of the Russian crew members at the hospital, and police take the crew into protective custody to prevent them from being lynched.... Algerian authorities reveal that they have killed 36 militants over the prior four days.	Leftist guerrillas wage two separate dynamite attacks on a main oil pipeline in the northeastern state of Arauca, Colombia.	The government of India's Maharashtra state approves a deal to restart development of an electrical power plant under construction by a U.S. business consortium led by Enron Corp.
Jan. 9	In Bosnia-Herzegovina, a French cargo plane lands at Sarajevo's airport with a shipment of wheat, marking the formal end of the international airlift of humanitarian supplies to the formerly besieged city. The airlift, which began July 3, 1992, has been the longest such operation in history.... China severs diplomatic ties with Senegal in retaliation for the African nation's earlier announcement that it is establishing official links with Taiwan.	A force of 250 Chechen commandos slip across the Dagestan-Chechnya border and stage a decoy attack on a regional airport in Kizlyar. As Russian soldiers respond, the Chechens seize the hospital, taking a total of 2,000 hostages. The attacks kill about 20 people.... A grenade attack in Sarajevo, Bosnia-Herzegovina, kills a civilian and wounds several others. The grenade is launched from Grbavica, a Serb-held suburb, and is the first in the capital since NATO troops began patrolling the area.		Brazilian president Fernando Henrique Cardoso signs a presidential decree that revokes a 1991 order barring non-Indians from appealing land allocations to indigenous peoples made by the government's Indian-protection agency, known as Funai.	South Korean president Kim Young Sam admits to wrongdoing in accepting political funds from businesses. However, he states he only did so before becoming president in 1993 and that the funds were not bribes. Kim's remarks are meant to rebut allegations that he received illicit money.
Jan. 10		The Chechen rebels who took over a hospital Jan. 9 release most of the hostages and return toward Chechnya with 150 captives in a convoy of buses. Russian troops abruptly stop the convoy at the village of Pervomayskoye, 6 miles (10 km) from Kizlyar. Army helicopters fire at the convoy, and the Chechens in response take over Pervomayskoye, occupying houses and taking more hostages, including a detachment of local militiamen.	The death toll from the crash of a cargo plane into an open-air market in Kinshasa, Zaire, on Jan. 8, is at least 350, with 470 injured. All the casualties were on the ground. Reports claim the plane took off without authorization and was hundreds of pounds overweight. Officials reveal the four crew members were arrested.... Israel frees 812 Palestinians from Israeli-administered jails.... Reports from Algeria indicate that the GIA has declared war on the AIS, the armed wing of the FIS.	Seventeen police officers and four state government officials in the western Mexican state of Guerrero are arrested in connection with a June 1995 massacre of 17 peasants who were on their way to a leftist antigovernment political rally.	
Jan. 11		Italian premier Lamberto Dini tenders his resignation for the second time in two weeks in order to avoid defeat in a parliamentary confidence motion. Pres. Oscar Luigi Scalfaro accepts the resignation "with reserve," allowing Dini to govern the country until elections are held or another government is established.... Greece's parliament defeats a motion to replace ailing premier Andreas Papandreou, who has been in the hospital for almost two months.		Lori Helene Berenson, 28, a U.S. woman who has been living in Peru since 1994, is convicted of treason by a military court in Peru and sentenced to life in prison. The secret trial is criticized by many observers.... Jose Santacruz Londoño, one of the three top leaders of the Cali drug cartel, escapes from the maximum-security La Picota prison in Bogota, Colombia's capital.... The U.S. releases $2.5 million in funds allocated to train Haiti's new civilian police force.	The Japanese Diet elects Ryutaro Hashimoto to succeed Japanese premier Tomiichi Murayama, who resigned Jan. 5.
Jan. 12					

A	B	C	D	E
Includes developments that affect more than one world region, international organizations, and important meetings of major world leaders.	Includes all domestic and regional developments in Europe, including the Soviet Union, Turkey, Cyprus, and Malta.	Includes all domestic and regional developments in Africa and the Middle East, including Iraq and Iran and excluding Cyprus, Turkey, and Afghanistan.	Includes all domestic and regional developments in Latin America, the Caribbean, and Canada.	Includes all domestic and regional developments in Asia and Pacific nations, extending from Afghanistan through all the Pacific Island, except Hawaii.

U.S. Politics & Social Issues	U.S. Foreign Policy & Defense	U.S. Economy & Environment	Science, Technology, & Nature	Culture, Leisure, & Lifestyle	
			A powerful snowstorm, dubbed the "Blizzard of '96," hits the U.S. Northeast.	Keiko, a killer whale featured in the 1993 movie *Free Willy*, is moved to the Oregon Coast Aquarium in Newport, Oregon. The popularity of the film brought attention to Keiko's overly warn living conditions in a park in Mexico, prompting a campaign to transfer him to a more suitable site.	Jan. 7
The Inner City Baptist Church in Knoxville, Tennessee, is set on fire in a high-profile attack. The racially integrated church's sanctuary is destroyed by firebombing, and racist graffiti is found elsewhere on the building.		In *Kurtz v. North Miami*, the Supreme Court rejects an appeal challenging the constitutionality of a Florida law that allows the city of North Miami to require job applicants to sign affidavits stating that they have not used tobacco products in the 12 months preceding their application.	Washington, D.C., receives a record 17 inches of snow, and the federal government and schools close. There is no postal service. Due to the blizzard in the Northeast, the New York Mercantile and Commodity exchanges are closed, and the New York Stock Exchange opens late.	Robert Dewey Hoskins, a homeless man accused of stalking pop singer Madonna, is found guilty by a Los Angeles jury of felony charges of stalking and making terrorist threats, and of a misdemeanor assault charge.	Jan. 8
Pres. Clinton vetoes a Republican-sponsored plan to reform the nation's system of welfare distribution. . . . A three-judge panel of the U.S. Eighth Circuit Court of Appeals in St. Louis, Missouri, overturns a lower court decision when it rules, 2-1, that a sexual harassment suit brought by Paula Corbin Jones against Pres. Clinton may proceed. . . . Mike Synar, 45, (D, Okla.), who served eight terms in the House after first being elected in 1978, dies in Arlington, Virginia, of brain cancer.	The Border Patrol begins constructing a 10 foot-high, 1.3-mile-long steel fence along the U.S.-Mexico border near the small town of Sunland Park, New Mexico.				Jan. 9
The Senate, by voice vote, approves legislation that will pass financial and managerial responsibilities for various public-housing programs to the states from the federal government. The measure is part of Republicans' ongoing campaign to cut federal spending and to give states increased authority over the administration of social welfare programs.			Data suggests that the "Blizzard of '96," which hit the Northeast on Jan. 7, caused at least 100 deaths across the region and an estimated $1 billion worth of damage.		Jan. 10
Gov. Mike Foster (R, La.) signs an executive order to end affirmative-action programs in the Louisiana state government. At the same time, he proclaims that Jan. 15 will be a state holiday in honor of slain black civil-rights leader Martin Luther King Jr., who Foster argues would have opposed affirmative action. . . . The CDC reports that the suicide rate among the elderly in the U.S. increased 9% from 1980 to 1992, after a drop in the rate over the previous four decades. There were 74,675 suicides reported among people age 65 and older in the study period. The rise was steepest among those in their early 80s.	The U.S. Air Force discloses that a flock of Canadian geese caused the September 1995 crash of an AWACS surveillance airplane at Elmendorf Air Force Base in Alaska, which killed 24 people. . . . Reports confirm that Judge Thomas Aquilino Jr. of the U.S. Court of International Trade has ruled that the U.S. Commerce Department must block shrimp imports from countries that fail to comply with regulations to safeguard sea turtles. Aquilino found that the Commerce Department had not complied fully with the Endangered Species Act, because it exempted some 70 countries that export shrimp to the U.S. from regulations intended to protect sea turtles.		The U.S. space shuttle *Endeavour* lifts off from Kennedy Space Center in Cape Canaveral, Florida, after a 20-minute delay caused by a communications problem. . . . Pres. Clinton promises federal disaster assistance to Washington, D.C., and Maryland in the wake of blizzards that hit the region on Jan. 7.	Eric Hebborn, 61, forger of Old Master works of art, dies in Rome, Italy, of undetermined causes. . . . Cigar wins horse-racing's Eclipse Award. . . . The doctrine commission of the Church of England urges the church to revise its concept of hell, asserting that its harsh descriptions of hell have left psychological scars on many churchgoers. The report suggests that the church describe hell as a "state of total nonbeing" rather than as a place of physical torment.	Jan. 11
A former postal worker, Bruce William Clark, pleads guilty to fatally shooting James Whooper III, his supervisor at a mail processing center in City of Industry, California, in July 1995. In an arrangement with prosecutors, Clark will serve a 22-year sentence.	Attorney General Janet Reno and INS commissioner Doris Meissner announce that the U.S. is increasing enforcement efforts along its border with Mexico.			Pop singer Janet Jackson signs a record contract worth an estimated $80 million with her current label Virgin Records. The four-album deal is reportedly the most lucrative in the history of the music industry.	Jan. 12

F	G	H	I	J
Includes elections, federal-state relations, civil rights and liberties, crime, the judiciary, education, health care, poverty, urban affairs, and population.	Includes formation and debate of U.S. foreign and defense policies, veterans' affairs, and defense spending. (Relations with specific foreign countries are usually found under the region concerned.)	Includes business, labor, agriculture, taxation, transportation, consumer affairs, monetary and fiscal policy, natural resources, and pollution.	Includes worldwide scientific, medical, and technological developments; natural phenomena; U.S. weather; natural disasters; and accidents.	Includes the arts, religion, scholarship, communications media, sports, entertainments, fashions, fads, and social life.

	World Affairs	Europe	Africa & the Middle East	The Americas	Asia & the Pacific
Jan. 13		Israeli president Ezer Weizman becomes only the second Israeli head of state ever to visit Germany.			
Jan. 14		Jorge Sampaio is elected Portugal's president. With Sampaio's victory, Portugal will have a president and a premier who are both from the Socialist Party for the first time since democracy was restored in 1974. . . . Bosnian Serb and Croat militias and the predominantly Muslim Bosnian government army begins to withdraw from their positions along the cease-fire line. At the same time, NATO troops reinforced by heavy armored vehicles continue their deployment in the zone of separation.		Mexican federal agents arrest Juan García Abrego, allegedly one of the Western Hemisphere's most powerful and violent drug traffickers, in a restaurant in the northern city of Monterrey.	China's religious authorities order all places of worship to register with the government.
Jan. 15	The UN Security Council votes to authorize a 5,000-member peacekeeping force to monitor the return of power in the region of Eastern Slavonia to the Croatian government from rebel Croatian Serbs. . . Delegates at a UN-backed conference in Bangkok, Thailand, announce a plan to expedite the repatriation to Vietnam of 38,000 Vietnamese boat people currently living in refugee camps in Southeast Asia.	Russian troops launch an all-out assault on separatist guerrillas from the breakaway republic of Chechnya who seized hundreds of hostages and occupied the village of Pervomayskoye in Russia's Dagestan region on Jan.10. . . . Ailing premier Andreas Papandreou resigns under pressure from officials who maintain that he is too sick to govern Greece.	Lesotho's King Moshoeshoe II, 57, dies when his car plunges off a cliff near Maseru, the capital. His chauffeur is also killed.	After the flyovers of Havana, the Cuban government reveals that it will take "all necessary measures" to halt future violations of its airspace.	Paul Keating becomes the first Australian prime minister to make an official visit to Malaysia since 1984.
Jan. 16		A group of Chechen gunmen led by Mohammed Tokcan seize a ferry with 209 passengers and crew, order the ship's pilot to sail toward Istanbul, and warn they will blow up the vessel unless fighters at Pervomayskoye are allowed to go free. . . . Anatoly Chubais, the architect of Russia's current economic policy and the last senior liberal in the cabinet, resigns under pressure from Pres. Boris Yeltsin. He is one of several Russian politicians to resign in January.	The leader of the military government in Sierra Leone, Captain Valentine E. M. Strasser, is overthrown by a group of army officers. Strasser, who seized power in a 1992 coup, is allowed safe passage to Guinea, and he is replaced as ruler by Brigadier Julius Maada Bio, previously the junta's second in command.	Nicaraguan national police chief Fernando Caldera announces that authorities have arrested 14 people suspected of involvement in a series of church bombings. Eighteen Roman Catholic Churches in four cities have been bombed since May 1995, causing minor damage and no injuries.	Indian police charge seven top political officials and seek the prosecution of three cabinet ministers for allegedly accepting bribes and participating in illegal foreign currency dealings. . . . The Chinese government announces that it will place limits on the flow of financial news into China from international news agencies. . . . The government of the Australian state of New South Wales removes many of the regal trappings that for 208 years have accompanied the office of state governor.
Jan. 17		Drawing condemnation, Russia launches a massive artillery and rocket bombardment against Pervomayskoye to crush the rebels. Reports suggest a group of Chechens broke out of Pervomayskoye and launched a counterattack in Sovetskoye. Data reveals that at least 26 Russian soldiers died and 93 others were wounded, while 135 Chechens died and 28 were captured. . . . A court in Oslo, Norway, convicts and sentences four men in connection with the theft of Edvard Munch's painting *The Scream* (1893).	Palestinian gunmen kill two Israeli soldiers in a drive-by shooting near Hebron in the West Bank. . . . The ousted leader of the military government in Sierra Leone, Captain Valentine E. M. Strasser, insists that he agreed to step down and that his Jan. 16 departure should not be termed a coup.		
Jan. 18		Russian president Boris Yeltsin announces that the Chechen separatists have been overcome and many of the hostages freed. Many of the Chechen rebels in Pervomayskoye reportedly escape under cover of darkness. . . . A fire that German police argue is likely an act of arson destroys a hostel in the northern port city of Luebeck, killing 10 foreigners seeking asylum in Germany. . . . Costas Simitis is selected as the new premier of Greece.		The Supreme Court of Honduras upholds the legality of a future civilian trial for eight military officers and two soldiers charged with the 1982 kidnapping and torture of six leftist students. . . . Colombian officials disclose that seven prison guards have been arrested on charges of aiding the Jan. 11 escape of Jose Santacruz Londoño, one of the three top leaders of the Cali drug cartel, from a maximum-security prison.	Seventeen boat people are injured when a riot breaks out at a refugee camp in Malaysia. . . . Dr. Zhang Shuyun, who accused a Shanghai orphanage of deliberately neglecting and starving children, reveals that Chinese officials have arrested her brother and charged him with subversion. . . . N(andamuri) T(araka) Rama Rao, 72, Indian movie actor and politician, dies in Hyderabad, India, after suffering a heart attack.

A	B	C	D	E
Includes developments that affect more than one world region, international organizations, and important meetings of major world leaders.	*Includes all domestic and regional developments in Europe, including the Soviet Union, Turkey, Cyprus, and Malta.*	*Includes all domestic and regional developments in Africa and the Middle East, including Iraq and Iran and excluding Cyprus, Turkey, and Afghanistan.*	*Includes all domestic and regional developments in Latin America, the Caribbean, and Canada.*	*Includes all domestic and regional developments in Asia and Pacific nations, extending from Afghanistan through all the Pacific Island, except Hawaii.*

U.S. Politics & Social Issues	U.S. Foreign Policy & Defense	U.S. Economy & Environment	Science, Technology, & Nature	Culture, Leisure, & Lifestyle	
	U.S. president Clinton travels to Bosnia to visit U.S. troops who will patrol the cease-fire zone as part of a 60,000-member NATO peacekeeping force. He calls the U.S. troops "warriors for peace" and tells them, "Your country is proud of you."	William P. Tavoulareas, 75, former president and chief operating officer of Mobil Corp., dies in Boca Raton, Florida, of complications from a stroke he suffered in 1995.			Jan. 13
		Graduate students who serve as teaching assistants at Yale University in New Haven, Connecticut, agree to submit undergraduate grades for the fall 1995 semester, ending a "grade strike" that began in December 1995. The students engaged in the strike action in an effort to persuade the university to recognize the Graduate Employees and Students Organization as an industrial union with collective-bargaining rights.		In professional football, the Dallas Cowboys win the NFC's championship with a 38-27 victory over the Green Bay Packers. The Pittsburgh Steelers win the AFC's championship over the Indianapolis Colts with a dramatic 20-16 victory in a game that comes down to the last play.	Jan. 14
Pres. Clinton speaks at the official Martin Luther King Jr. Day celebration at the Ebenezer Baptist Church in Atlanta, Georgia, using the same pulpit from which King preached.	Juan Garcia Abrego, allegedly one of the Western Hemisphere's most powerful and violent drug traffickers, who was arrested in Mexico on Jan. 14, is sent to the U.S., where he is on the FBI's list of the 10 most wanted criminals.		A corporate plane crashes 10 miles (16 km) northwest of Malad City, Idaho, killing all eight people on board. . . . Astronomers at a meeting of the American Astronomical Society report images from the *Hubble Space Telescope* indicate that the estimated number of galaxies in the universe is 50 billion, up from earlier estimates of 10 billion. . . . Astronauts Leroy Chiao and Daniel Barry leave the *Endeavour* to walk in space.	Leaders of five of the largest black churches in the U.S. announce that they are establishing a for-profit company to boost the buying power of black consumers.	Jan. 15
Illinois governor Jim Edgar (R) commutes the death sentence of Guinevere Garcia, convicted for the 1991 fatal shooting of her estranged husband, to life in prison without parole just hours before she is scheduled to be executed by lethal injection. Edgar denies that gender played a role in his decision to spare the inmate, who would have been the second woman to be executed in the U.S. since the Supreme Court allowed states to resume capital punishment in 1976.	In *Zicherman v. Korean Air Lines Co.,* the Supreme Court rules unanimously that survivors of victims of international air crashes cannot sue for compensation for the loss of companionship of their loved ones.	The Commerce Department reports that housing starts in November 1995 rose 5.7% from October, to a seasonally adjusted annual rate of 1.42 million units. This marks the indicator's first ascent after three straight monthly declines.	Astronomers report finding a halo of previously undetected objects around the Milky Way, which, if confirmed, will provide an explanation for half of the unexplained mass thought to make up the universe. . . . In *Lotus Development Corp. v. Borland International Inc.,* the Supreme Court deadlocks, leaving intact the lower court's opinion that Lotus's operating menu commands constitute a "method of operation," which is explicitly excluded from copyright-protection laws. John Paul Stevens, for undisclosed reasons, does not participate in the case.	Kaye Webb, 81, British editor of children's books, dies of unreported causes. . . . Cincinnati Bengals defensive lineman Dan Wilkinson is found guilty of domestic violence, a misdemeanor, for punching his pregnant girlfriend, Shawnda Lamarr, in the stomach. He is handed a six-month suspended sentence.	Jan. 16
Barbara Charline Jordan, (D, Tex.), 59, who in 1966 became the first black elected state senator in Texas and, in 1972, the first black and the first woman elected to Congress from Texas, dies in Austin, Texas, of pneumonia and complications from leukemia after suffering from multiple sclerosis for many years.	In New York City, U.S. District Court judge Michael Mukasey sentences 10 militant Muslims to terms ranging from 25 years to life in prison for their part in a failed plot to bomb the UN headquarters building and to assassinate political leaders. Sheik Omar Abdel Rahman, whom the government accused of plotting "a war of urban terrorism" against the U.S., is sentenced to life in prison. The sentencing is the culmination of the biggest terrorism trial in U.S. history.	In *Commissioner of Internal Revenue v. Lundy,* the Supreme Court rules, 7-2, that the IRS is justified in denying a tax refund to a Virginia man, Robert Lundy, because he waited too long to file his tax return.	Astronomers announce finding two planets outside the solar system, providing further evidence that extrasolar planet-like objects are not rare. . . . Astronauts Leroy Chiao and Koichi Wakata, the first Japanese astronaut to work full-time in the U.S. shuttle program, perform a space walk.	On a tour of the U.S., author Salman Rushdie, who is under a death threat by Muslim militants, gives a lecture in Washington, D.C. . . . Inductees to the Rock and Roll Hall of Fame include David Bowie, Gladys Knight and the Pips, Pink Floyd, and the Shirelles.	Jan. 17
In Chicago, federal judge George Marovich sentences a prominent equestrian, George Lindemann Jr., to 33 months in prison for three federal counts of wire fraud. The charges are part of a series of indictments against 23 people tied to the equestrian industry.		The former president of Perry County Bank in Perryville, Arkansas, Neal Ainley, is sentenced by federal judge Susan Webber Wright to two years' probation for failing to report to the IRS two large cash withdrawals that Pres. Clinton's campaign made from the bank in 1990.	Four people die when a fire breaks out in a federally subsidized apartment building in Chicago. At least 47 people are injured in the fire. . . . Two large studies indicate that the vitamin beta carotene is not effective at preventing cancer or heart disease when taken as a dietary supplement. . . . Reports confirm that studies for the first time have shown that mutation of the BRCA1 gene is often the cause of breast cancer among young women, especially Jewish women.	Minnesota Fats (born Rudolf Wanderone Jr.), 87 or 95, famous billiards player, dies in Nashville, Tennessee, of congestive heart failure. . . . Lisa Marie Presley-Jackson files for divorce from pop singer Michael Jackson. . . . Jenni Meno and Todd Sand successfully defend their pairs title at the U.S. Figure Skating Championships.	Jan. 18
F	G	H	I	J	
Includes elections, federal-state relations, civil rights and liberties, crime, the judiciary, education, health care, poverty, urban affairs, and population.	*Includes formation and debate of U.S. foreign and defense policies, veterans' affairs, and defense spending. (Relations with specific foreign countries are usually found under the region concerned.)*	*Includes business, labor, agriculture, taxation, transportation, consumer affairs, monetary and fiscal policy, natural resources, and pollution.*	*Includes worldwide scientific, medical, and technological developments; natural phenomena; U.S. weather; natural disasters; and accidents.*	*Includes the arts, religion, scholarship, communications media, sports, entertainments, fashions, fads, and social life.*	

	World Affairs	Europe	Africa & the Middle East	The Americas	Asia & the Pacific
Jan. 19	The World Bank approves a $280 million loan to help support Romania's efforts to privatize its state industries.	The nine gunmen who hijacked a ferry in the Black Sea on Jan. 16 surrender peacefully to Turkish authorities. Thousands of Muslims of Caucasian descent demonstrate in Istanbul and elsewhere in Turkey in support of the hijackers. . . . Armies of the opposing factions in Bosnia-Herzegovina comply with a deadline to withdraw their heavy weapons and most of their troops from a 2.5-mile-wide "zone of separation."	Israeli soldiers shoot dead three alleged Hamas members at a roadblock outside Jenin, in the northern West Bank. . . . Violence erupts in several Shi'ite Muslim villages in Bahrain.	Newly inaugurated Guatemalan president Alvaro Arzu Irigoyen discharges many military leaders linked to human-rights abuses and criminal enterprises.	A ferry carrying 210 people sinks off the northwestern tip of the Indonesian island of Sumatra. At least 54 people die, and more than 100 are missing.
Jan. 20			Yasser Arafat, the head of the PLO, easily wins the Palestinian presidency as Arab voters turn out in the Gaza Strip and West Bank to select a new self-rule Palestinian National Authority (PNA) government that includes a legislative council. In election violence, a suspected Hamas member wounds a young Israeli girl in a knife attack, sparking a brief round of clashes between settlers and Palestinians. . . . A car bomb explodes at a national guard base in Djebahia, east of Algiers, killing two people and injuring five others.	Haitian president Jean-Bertrand Aristide marries Mildred Trouillot, a U.S.-born Haitian-American lawyer, in Port-au-Prince.	
Jan. 21	A party of international war-crimes investigators led by U.S. assistant secretary of state John Shattuck inspect dozens of sites near Srebrenica, Bosnia, believed to be linked to a 1995 massacre of Muslims by Bosnian Serbs. Shattuck tells reporters after the tour that he believes he saw "overwhelming evidence" of "horrible crimes against humanity" at the sites.	Mufti Fatkhulla Sharipov, Tajikistan's highest-ranking Islamic cleric, is shot to death along with his wife, his son, and two other people by unknown assailants at his home near Dushanbe. . . . Bosnian premier Haris Silajdzic unexpectedly announces that he will leave his post before Bosnia's new central government is formed.	Reports suggest that Algerian authorities killed at least 33 Muslim militants in conflicts during the previous weekend.		
Jan. 22		The government of Greek premier Costas Simitis is sworn into office.	The Bahrain government reveals it has arrested nearly 200 protesters, including eight leading Shi'ite activists, who will face trial as part of "a subversive organization" due to the violence that started Jan. 19. . . . Israel Eldad (born Israel Scheib), 86, right-wing Israeli writer and former leader of the Jewish underground in Palestine, dies in Jerusalem, Israel, of unreported causes.	Argentine president Carlos Saul Menem announces that former Chilean secret police agent Enrique Arancibia Clavel was arrested in Buenos Aires, Argentina, in connection with the 1974 car bomb assassinations. The arrest sparks renewed tensions over the issue of human-rights abuses perpetrated by the former military dictatorship. . . . Former Colombian defense minister Fernando Botero Zea reveals from jail that Pres. Ernesto Samper Pizano solicited and knowingly accepted contributions for his 1994 campaign from the Cali drug cartel, renewing allegations against Samper.	
Jan. 23				In response to the Jan. 22 allegations made by Fernando Botero Zea, politicians from both the Liberal and the Conservative parties call for Pres. Samper's resignation. Thousands of students protest outside the presidential palace in Bogota, Colombia's capital, also demanding that Samper resign.	Prosecutors indict former South Korean president Chun Doo Hwan for sedition for his role in a May 1980 massacre of prodemocracy supporters in the southern city of Kwangju. Roh Tae Woo, a military general in charge of troops at the time of the Kwangju incident, is indicted for insurrection, although he is not accused of involvement in the massacre. Six former army generals are also indicted for treason.
Jan. 24		The Chechen rebels release 46 hostages taken when they escaped Jan. 18, but they hold on to 14 Russian policemen. . . . Poland's military prosecutor's office announces it will open a formal investigation into espionage allegations against Polish premier Jozef Oleksy, prompting Oleksy to resign in order to clear his name. . . . Spain's Supreme Court indicts Jose Barrionuevo, who is the highest-ranking former official charged for his alleged ties to antiterrorist death squads from the 1980s. . . . Three soldiers die in an accidental explosion at a NATO headquarters building in Bosnia.			

A	B	C	D	E
Includes developments that affect more than one world region, international organizations, and important meetings of major world leaders.	Includes all domestic and regional developments in Europe, including the Soviet Union, Turkey, Cyprus, and Malta.	Includes all domestic and regional developments in Africa and the Middle East, including Iraq and Iran and excluding Cyprus, Turkey, and Afghanistan.	Includes all domestic and regional developments in Latin America, the Caribbean, and Canada.	Includes all domestic and regional developments in Asia and Pacific nations, extending from Afghanistan through all the Pacific Island, except Hawaii.

U.S. Politics & Social Issues	U.S. Foreign Policy & Defense	U.S. Economy & Environment	Science, Technology, & Nature	Culture, Leisure, & Lifestyle	
		A barge strikes a sand bar off Point Judith, Rhode Island, and spills more than 828,000 gallons of oil into Block Island Sound. It is reportedly the worst spill in Rhode Island's history.... Figures show that the U.S. gross domestic product grew at a revised seasonally adjusted annual rate of 3.2% in the third quarter of 1995. It is the first time the number has been calculated with a new "chain-weighted" procedure for measuring the GDP.	Rain storms hit northeastern states.... Reports confirm that chemists have developed a process for breaking down freons and other gases containing chlorofluorocarbons (CFCs), ozone-damaging chemicals, into nonhazardous compounds.	Don Simpson, 52, who, with Jerry Bruckheimer, produced several blockbuster films, is found dead in Los Angeles; he reportedly died of natural causes.... Elizabeth Punsalan and Jerod Swallow win the ice-dancing medal at the U.S. National Skating Championships.	Jan. 19
	North Korea discloses that it is disbanding a team that had sought to recover the remains of American soldiers who had died in the Korean War, citing a disagreement over payments for remains already found.	Sidney R. Korshak, 88, labor lawyer and reputed fixer for organized-crime groups in Chicago who was subjected to investigations but was never indicted for any crime, dies in Beverly Hills, California, of unreported causes.	The U.S. space shuttle *Endeavour* touches down on the airstrip at Cape Canaveral after carrying out a mission during which members of its crew retrieved a Japanese satellite, deployed and retrieved a U.S. space probe, and twice walked in space. *Endeavour* traveled 3.7 million miles (6 million km) on its mission, circling the Earth completely 142 times.	Michelle Kwan wins the women's title at the U.S. National Skating Championships. Rudy Galindo captures the men's title.... Comedian and actor George Burns turns 100 years old.... Gerry Mulligan, 68, jazz saxophonist and composer, dies in Darien, Connecticut, from complications after knee surgery; he was suffering from liver cancer.	Jan. 20
		Pres. Clinton grants a request from Rhode Island governor Lincoln Almond (R) to make federal funds available to help clean up the Jan. 19 oil spill.	Northeastern states are hit by flooding caused by heavy rain that started Jan. 19 and by melting snow left over from a blizzard. At least 35 weather-related deaths are reported. The Potomac River rises to nearly 14 feet (4.3 m)—twice its usual level—causing flooding in some parts of Washington D.C. Pres. Clinton declares Pennsylvania, the hardest-hit state, a federal disaster area.	Golden Globe Awards for films are presented to *Sense and Sensibility* as the Best Drama and *Babe* as the Best Musical or Comedy. In television awards, *Party of Five* wins for Best Drama Series and *Cybill* wins the Best Comedy Series prize.	Jan. 21
Tens of thousands of abortion opponents protest in Washington, D.C.... Data shows that the percentage of student borrowers who default on their federal loans fell to 11.6% in the 1993 fiscal year That figure is the lowest student loan default rate reported by the department since it began keeping track in 1988....The Supreme Court rejects without comment a challenge, brought by Gov. Pete Wilson (R, Calif.), of the National Voter Registration Act of 1993, which requires states to offer voter registration forms at state motor vehicle offices and welfare agency offices.	The U.S. Army for the first time reveals the size and location of its chemical weapons arsenal and states that it is slowly destroying the 60-million-pound (27.12 million kg) stockpile. The army discloses that its largest stockpiles of chemical weapons are maintained at Tooele Army Depot in Utah, Pine Bluff Arsenal in Arkansas, and Hermiston Depot in Oregon. The existence of arsenals in five other states and on Johnston Atoll, a U.S. territory in the Pacific Ocean, are also revealed.	Cleanup crews are able to drain and stabilize the vessel that struck a sand bar off Point Judith, Rhode Island, and spilled more than 828,000 gallons of oil into Block Island Sound on Jan. 19....A White House official announces that a federal grand jury in Washington, D.C., has subpoenaed First Lady Hillary Rodham Clinton to testify about the handling of documents related to the Whitewater affair.	Scientists confirm that data relayed to Earth from a probe that in December 1995 plunged into the atmosphere of Jupiter has revealed less water on that planet than expected. ... Officials in Pennsylvania estimate that statewide flood losses have reached $700 million.	The Newbery Medal for the best children's book published in the U.S. in 1995 goes to Karen Cushman. The Caldecott Medal for the best illustrated children's book in 1995 is given to Peggy Rathmann.	Jan. 22
Pres. Clinton delivers his State of the Union address in which he declares an end to the "era of big government." Senate majority leader Robert J. Dole (R, Kans.) delivers the Republican Party's response.... The board of education in Hartford, Connecticut, votes to cancel an October 1994 contract that granted a private firm, Educational Alternatives Inc., control over Hartford's 32 public schools.				The Whitbread Book of the Year Award is given to first-time British novelist Kate Atkinson for *Behind the Scenes at the Museum*.	Jan. 23
	The House passes, 287-129, a $265 billion defense-authorization bill. Apart from the removal of three provisions, the bill is identical to one vetoed by Pres. Clinton in December 1995.... A military court at a U.S. Army base in Wurzburg, Germany, convicts U.S. soldier Michael New of disobedience for refusing to wear UN insignia on his uniform while serving on a UN-mandated peacekeeping mission in Macedonia.	The SEC charges financially troubled Orange County, California, with fraud connected to the issuance of $2.1 billion in bonds. Hours later, the SEC arrives at a settlement with county officials. The filing of civil charges by the SEC marks the first official action ever taken by the commission accusing a major municipality of financial wrongdoing.... Wells Fargo and Co. and First Interstate Bancorp. announce a merger valued at $10.9, the largest bank merger in U.S. history.	The FDA approves the use of the fat substitute olestra, despite protests from some scientists who express concern over its potentially harmful health effects.	Ellen F. Cooke, the former treasurer of the Episcopal Church, pleads guilty to embezzling more than $1.5 million of the church's assets. Cooke, who was national treasurer of the denomination from 1986 until 1995, also admits that she did not pay income tax on more than $300,000.	Jan. 24
F	G	H	I	J	
Includes elections, federal-state relations, civil rights and liberties, crime, the judiciary, education, health care, poverty, urban affairs, and population.	Includes formation and debate of U.S. foreign and defense policies, veterans' affairs, and defense spending. (Relations with specific foreign countries are usually found under the region concerned.)	Includes business, labor, agriculture, taxation, transportation, consumer affairs, monetary and fiscal policy, natural resources, and pollution.	Includes worldwide scientific, medical, and technological developments; natural phenomena; U.S. weather; natural disasters; and accidents.	Includes the arts, religion, scholarship, communications media, sports, entertainments, fashions, fads, and social life.	

	World Affairs	Europe	Africa & the Middle East	The Americas	Asia & the Pacific
Jan. 25	Delegates to the Council of Europe in Strasbourg, France, vote to admit Russia as the body's 39th member.	About 700 known prisoners of war from the fighting in the former Yugoslav republic remain in detention.		In an assassination attempt against rightist Nicaraguan presidential candidate Arnoldo Aleman, gunmen miss the politician but kill one of his bodyguards Three other people are injured. . . . Guatemalan officials announce that 118 police officers were dismissed because of involvement in criminal activities. . . . Canadian prime minister Jean Chrétien reorganizes his government in the first cabinet shuffle since 1993.	Police find seven people shot to death at a house in Brisbane, Australia, in what is believed to be a murder-suicide.
Jan. 26		Bosnian Croats, Muslims, and Serbs accelerate the release of prisoners of war.	Muslim militants break into several homes and cut the throats of six women and a girl in the eastern town of Ouagena, Algeria. The attacks reportedly are the first by fundamentalists on women who are not related to security personnel. . . . Tens of thousands of people climb the Thaba Bosiu plateau in a rainstorm to witness the ceremonial burial of King Moshoeshoe of Lesotho.		Two Russian-made rockets are fired into the village of Forward Kahuta, a Pakistani-controlled area of the disputed Kashmir region. The rockets hit a mosque and kill at least 19 worshipers. Pakistan officials blame India for the attack, although India denies responsibility. . . . Members of the Preparatory Committee, which will oversee Hong Kong's mid-1997 reversion to Chinese sovereignty, are installed in a ceremony attended by Chinese president Jiang Zemin at the Great Hall of the People in Beijing, the capital of China.
Jan. 27	France conducts the last of six controversial nuclear tests under the Fangataufa Atoll in the South Pacific.		Niger's first-ever democratically elected president, Mahamane Ousmane, is overthrown in a military coup and placed under house arrest. Col. Ibrahim Mainassara Bare declares himself chair of a temporary national council. Coup leaders outlaw political parties and suspend the constitution. Premier Hama Amadou is also arrested. Five people are reportedly killed.	In La Saline, a slum area of Port-au-Prince, Haiti, the body of activist Guy Jean-Pierre is discovered. Slum residents blame his death on robbers and go on a rampage against suspected thieves. At least nine people are killed, and more than 100 homes are destroyed by arson during mob violence.	India test-fires a ballistic missile, the Prithvi II, off its eastern coast into the Bay of Bengal. . . . A Vietnamese court sentences a U.S. man, Everett Sennholz, to five years in prison and fines him $12,700 for taking weapons and banned literature and videos into the country with him. Sennholz becomes the 12th U.S. citizen currently jailed in Vietnam.
Jan. 28	The Committee to Protect Journalists, an international advocacy group, finds that 51 journalists were killed in 1995. The total number of journalist deaths in 1995 represents a significant decline from the previous year's total of 73.	A group of Turkish journalists take down a Greek flag on an island known as Imia in Greece and Kardak in Turkey, and they replace it with a Turkish one, exacerbating an ongoing conflict over the island's ruler. . . . Three British soldiers are killed when their armored personnel carrier strikes a field mine near Mrkonjic Grad, Bosnia-Herzegovina. . . . J(ohn) Terence Reese, 82, who led Britain's bridge team to European championships five times and to a world title in 1955, dies in Hove, England, of unreported causes.	France suspends aid to Niger, its former colony, in the wake of the Jan. 27 coup there.		Clashes between Indian and Pakistani gunmen are reported at various points along the border. . . . Sonam Wangdu Lama, a four-year-old boy from Seattle, Washington, arrives in Nepal, where he is to become head of a Buddhist monastery outside Katmandu, the capital. Tibetan Buddhists call the boy Trulku-la, and in 1993 he was formally enthroned as the next head of the monastery, but he subsequently returned to Seattle with his mother. . . . San Yu, 78, president of Burma (now Myanmar), 1981–88, dies in Yangon, Myanmar, after reportedly suffering a heart ailment.
Jan. 29	French president Jacques Chirac announces "the definitive end" of France's nuclear-testing program in the South Pacific. The six tests were vigorously opposed by Japan, Australia, New Zealand, and most of France's fellow EU nations. The most violent protests were held in Tahiti, where demonstrators rioted in 1995, destroying an airport terminal and causing some $40 million in damage.	In response to the Jan. 28 Turkish flag-raising on Imia, Greece sends 12 commandos to plant the Greek flag on one side of the island and to guard it. . . . The renowned 204-year-old opera house, La Fenice, considered to be one of Venice's most beautiful monuments, is destroyed by a fire that rages for nine hours. . . . Swanee Hunt, U.S. ambassador to Austria, discloses the whereabouts of 79 weapons caches that the U.S. secretly planted in Austria in the 1950s.	Gunmen shoot and kill eight people and wound more than 20 others waiting in line for work at a factory in Alberton, a suburb southeast of Johannesburg, South Africa.	François Denis Gbetie of Benin becomes the first member of the UN contingent to be killed in a hostile attack in Haiti when gunmen fire at his motor vehicle in a Port-au-Prince suburb.	
Jan. 30		Gino Gallagher, leader of the militant Irish National Liberation Army, is shot and killed in Belfast, Northern Ireland, allegedly by feuding members within his group. . . . Turkey plants a flag on the other side of the disputed island known as Imia in Greece and Kardak in Turkey. . . . Bosnia's ruling SDA party elects Hasan Muratovic as the Bosnian premier. Separately, two senior Serb officers, Gen. Djordje Djukic and Col. Aleksa Krsmanovic, are arrested by Muslim authorities, posing a new threat to the republic's fragile peace.		Some 300 student protesters storm the foreign ministry building in Managua, Nicaragua's capital, demanding increased government funding for their universities. The students, most of whom are unarmed, hold more than 200 civil servants and foreign ambassadors captive, but they later release more than 100 of the hostages.	Chinese premier Li Peng states that the reunification of Taiwan, which China considers a renegade Chinese province, can no longer be delayed indefinitely.

A	B	C	D	E
Includes developments that affect more than one world region, international organizations, and important meetings of major world leaders.	Includes all domestic and regional developments in Europe, including the Soviet Union, Turkey, Cyprus, and Malta.	Includes all domestic and regional developments in Africa and the Middle East, including Iraq and Iran and excluding Cyprus, Turkey, and Afghanistan.	Includes all domestic and regional developments in Latin America, the Caribbean, and Canada.	Includes all domestic and regional developments in Asia and Pacific nations, extending from Afghanistan through all the Pacific Island, except Hawaii.

U.S. Politics & Social Issues	U.S. Foreign Policy & Defense	U.S. Economy & Environment	Science, Technology, & Nature	Culture, Leisure, & Lifestyle	
Billy Bailey, 49, convicted for the shotgun slayings of an elderly couple in Delaware in 1979, is executed by hanging in Smyrna, Delaware. He is the third inmate to be hanged since 1965 and the first in Delaware in 50 years. It is first time in the state's history that victims' family members are allowed to witness an execution. Bailey is the 316th person put to death in the U.S. and the sixth in Delaware since 1976.		The House passes, 371-42, a continuing resolution, or stopgap measure, that will fund government programs and agencies through Mar. 15.			Jan. 25
John Albert Taylor, 36, convicted of the 1989 rape and strangulation death of an 11-year-old girl, is executed by a firing squad in Point of the Mountain, Utah. He is the second inmate put to death by a firing squad since the Supreme Court reinstated capital punishment in 1976. Taylor is the fifth inmate executed in Utah and the 317th in the U.S. since 1976.	The U.S. Senate votes, 86-4, to ratify the second Strategic Arms Reduction Treaty (START II), which commits the U.S. and Russia to reducing their long-range nuclear arsenals to about one-third of their 1993 levels. START II will not take effect unless it is ratified by both houses of Russia's parliament. . . . The Senate approves, 56-34, a $265 billion defense-authorization bill.	First Lady Hillary Rodham Clinton testifies before a federal grand jury in Washington, D.C., concerning documents related to the investigation of the Whitewater affair. It is first time in U.S. history that a first lady testifies under oath before a grand jury. . . . The Senate approves, 82-8, a continuing resolution, or stopgap measure, that will fund government programs and agencies through Mar. 15. Pres. Clinton signs the measure.		Henry Jay Lewis, 63, who in 1968 became the first black conductor and musical director of a major U.S. orchestra, the New Jersey Symphony Orchestra, dies in New York City of a heart attack. . . . Harold Brodkey (born Aaron Roy Weintraub), 65, author who published in The New Yorker and American Poetry Review, dies in New York City of an AIDS-related illness.	Jan. 26
Police arrest Mark Berchard in the midst of a violent rampage at a convent in Waterville, Maine. Before being subdued, Berchard kills two nuns and wounds two others. . . . Ralph W(ebster) Yarborough, 92, (D, Tex.), 1957–71, the only senator from a state in the Deep South to vote for the landmark Civil Rights Act of 1964, dies in Austin, Texas, after suffering a series of illnesses.				At the Sundance Film Festival, in Utah, Welcome to the Dollhouse, written and directed by Todd Solondz, wins the Grand Jury Prize for the best dramatic film. . . . Monica Seles wins the women's tennis trophy at the Australian Open.	Jan. 27
After a 48-hour standoff at his Newtown Square, Pennsylvania, mansion, police capture John E. du Pont, an heir to the du Pont chemical fortune, for allegedly shooting and killing David Schultz, 36, a former Olympic wrestling champion.			Julian W(erner) Hill, 91, chemist who discovered nylon, dies in Hockessin, Delaware, of unreported causes.	Football's Dallas Cowboys win, 27-17, Super Bowl XXX over the Pittsburgh Steelers. . . . Boris Becker wins the men's tennis title at the Australian Open. . . . Jerry Siegel, 81, cocreator of the Superman character, dies in Los Angeles of heart ailments. . . . Joseph Aleksandrovich Brodsky, 55, Soviet born Nobel Prize–winning poet and the 1991 U.S. poet laureate, dies in New York City of a heart attack.	Jan. 28
In Chicago, Illinois, Juvenile Court judge Carol Kelly sentences two unidentified boys, ages 12 and 13, to state juvenile prison for dropping five-year-old Eric Morse to his death for refusing to steal candy for them. The 12-year-old will become the U.S.'s youngest inmate in a high-security prison.	A U.S. Navy F-14A Tomcat fighter jet crashes January 29 in Luna Heights, a suburb of Nashville, Tennessee, killing the two crewmen and three bystanders. . . . Russian premier Viktor Chernomyrdin meets with U.S. president Bill Clinton and vice president Al Gore in Washington, D.C.	A survey suggests that the cost of employee health-care benefits paid for by employers in the U.S. increased 2.1% in 1995, after a drop in 1994 that followed a decade of increases.	Research shows that a combination of indinavir, AZT, and ddl, a drug marketed by Bristol-Myers Squibb Co. as Videx, reduced HIV to undetectable levels in 13 of 22 patients after five months.	The Horse Whisperer, by Nicholas Evans, tops the bestseller list. . . . Data reveals a record 138.5 million people in the U.S. watched Super Bowl XXX, the largest total ever for a TV program. . . . Jamie Uys, 74, South African film director, dies in South Africa after suffering a heart attack.	Jan. 29
Ron Wyden (D, Oreg.) wins a special election held to fill the Senate seat vacated by Sen. Bob Packwood, (R), who resigned due to sexual misconduct. Wyden is the first Democrat elected to the Senate from Oregon since 1962. It is the first congressional election to be conducted entirely by mail. . . . William Henry Flamer, 40, convicted of murder in 1979, is executed by lethal injection in Smyrna, Delaware. Flamer is the 318th person executed in the U.S. and only the seventh in Delaware since 1976.			Scientist Francis Novembre reports that for the first time a chimpanzee developed AIDS, more than 10 years after it was injected with HIV-1, the strain that causes most AIDS cases.	Basketball star Earvin (Magic) Johnson plays in his first regular-season NBA game since announcing his retirement in 1991. . . . Rupert Murdoch announces that his company will begin broadcasting a 24-hour all-news TV channel by the end of 1996 with its U.S. television subsidiary, Fox Broadcasting Co.	Jan. 30
F	G	H	I	J	
Includes elections, federal-state relations, civil rights and liberties, crime, the judiciary, education, health care, poverty, urban affairs, and population.	Includes formation and debate of U.S. foreign and defense policies, veterans' affairs, and defense spending. (Relations with specific foreign countries are usually found under the region concerned.)	Includes business, labor, agriculture, taxation, transportation, consumer affairs, monetary and fiscal policy, natural resources, and pollution.	Includes worldwide scientific, medical, and technological developments; natural phenomena; U.S. weather; natural disasters; and accidents.	Includes the arts, religion, scholarship, communications media, sports, entertainments, fashions, fads, and social life.	

	World Affairs	Europe	Africa & the Middle East	The Americas	Asia & the Pacific
Jan. 31		In Tajikistan, two military commanders, Makhmud Khudoberdyev and Ibodullo Boimatov, lead their troops in a bloodless mutiny when they seize the industrial city of Tursun-Zade and march toward Dushanbe, the capital.... Greece and Turkey withdraw warships dispatched to an uninhabited island known as Imia in Greece and Kardak in Turkey in response to diplomatic efforts made by the UN, NATO and the U.S.		Police retake the foreign ministry building in Managua, Nicaragua's capital, and arrest 107 of the protesters who seized the area Jan. 30.	A suicide bomber rams a truck filled with explosives into the gates of the Central Bank of Sri Lanka in the financial district of Colombo, the capital, killing 86 people and injuring more than 1,400 others.... More than 11 tons (10 metric tons) of illegally stored dynamite explode in an apartment building in the city of Shaoyang in China, killing more than 100 people and injuring 400.... The U.S. warship *Fort McHenry* becomes the first such vessel to dock in Shanghai since 1989.
Feb. 1		French troops kill a sniper near Sarajevo in the first fatal exchange of fire between NATO troops and Bosnian combatants during a mission to transfer Serb suburbs to the Muslim-Croat federation.... More than 1 million coal miners in Russia and Ukraine strike, demanding that their respective governments pay them their overdue wages.... Italian president Oscar Luigi Scalfaro appoints Antonio Maccanico to form and head a new government, Italy's 55th since the end of World War II.		The Toronto Stock Exchange's TSE composite index surges 42.65 points to close at 5011.08. It is the first time that the Toronto index has ever topped the 5,000 mark.	
Feb. 2		A car belonging to Paddy Ashdown, leader of the Liberal Democratic Party, is destroyed in a suspected arson attack near the city of Yeovil, in southern England. Separately, a gunman fires 57 shots from an assault rifle at the home of a part-time member of the Royal Ulster Constabulary police force. No one is injured.... Albania's last communist president, Ramiz Alia, is arrested on charges of crimes against humanity.	In Guinea, mutinous soldiers surround and shell the palace of Pres. Lansana Conte after a dispute over pay.... Bahraini officials announce the arrests of 41 people on charges of rioting and acts of sabotage since the resurgence of Shi'ite-led opposition protests in January.	The Canadian Senate passes and Governor General Romeo Le Blanc approves legislation that will give five provinces and regions of Canada a veto over proposed changes to the Canadian constitution.	A Supreme Court judge from the Australian state of New South Wales rules that a woman has to pay her lesbian former partner to help support the two children they raised together. The decision represents the first time that a judge in Australia recognizes a same-sex couple as a family for the purpose of ruling on child support.
Feb. 3		Bosnian Serbs, Croats, and Muslims comply with a deadline to withdraw their armed forces from 1,500 square miles (3,900 sq km) of land in Bosnia-Herzegovina. The action effectively ends the Serb siege of Sarajevo. Separately, U.S. Army sergeant Donald Allen Dugan, 38, is killed in an explosion in northeastern Bosnia. Dugan is the ninth soldier slain during the NATO mission.... Coal miners in Russia suspend the strike started Feb. 1.... Turkish pres. Suleyman Demirel asks Mesut Yilmaz, leader of the conservative Motherland Party, to try to form a government.	In Guinea, the dispute that started Feb. 2 ends. Medical sources report that up to 50 people were killed in clashes between the mutinous soldiers and troops loyal to Pres. Lansana Conte and that Conte's residence was set ablaze before loyalist troops regained control.		In China, an earthquake measuring 7.0 on Richter scale strikes the sparsely populated southwestern province of Yunnan. The quake, centered near the town of Lijiang on the province's border with Tibet, kills at least 240 people and injures at least 14,000.
Feb. 4		More than 1,000 Chechen civilians begin a week-long rally outside the presidential palace in Grozny, the Chechen capital, to demand that Russian troops leave the republic.... Tajikistan pres. Imamali Rakhmanov dismisses several senior officials at the demand of Makhmud Khudoberdyev and Ibodullo Boimatov, who led a late-January mutiny.	Bahrain prevents eight members of the Kuwaiti parliament from entering Bahrain.	An unidentified man apparently attempts to assassinate Guatemalan president Alvaro Arzu Irigoyen by running him over with a car in the town of Antigua three times before being shot by Arzu's bodyguards. One of Arzu's bodyguards is injured in the attack.	
Feb. 5				Pope John Paul II starts his first tour of Central America since 1983.	In China, Yunnan officials report that more than 186,000, or around 80%, of the homes in Lijiang and surrounding areas were destroyed by the Feb. 3 earthquake. The effects of the quake are exacerbated by an aftershock measuring 6.0 on the Richter scale, and record low temperatures of around 10°F (–12°C).

A	B	C	D	E
Includes developments that affect more than one world region, international organizations, and important meetings of major world leaders.	Includes all domestic and regional developments in Europe, including the Soviet Union, Turkey, Cyprus, and Malta.	Includes all domestic and regional developments in Africa and the Middle East, including Iraq and Iran and excluding Cyprus, Turkey, and Afghanistan.	Includes all domestic and regional developments in Latin America, the Caribbean, and Canada.	Includes all domestic and regional developments in Asia and Pacific nations, extending from Afghanistan through all the Pacific Island, except Hawaii.

U.S. Politics & Social Issues	U.S. Foreign Policy & Defense	U.S. Economy & Environment	Science, Technology, & Nature	Culture, Leisure, & Lifestyle	
The Justice Department finds that the White House engaged in "ill-advised and erroneous actions" when in 1993 it ordered the dismissal of seven White House travel-office employees. However, its report does not conclude that aides to Pres. Clinton improperly pressured the FBI to investigate the travel office.	All the remaining Cuban refugees housed at a refugee camp at the U.S. Naval Base in Guantanamo Bay, Cuba, leave the base. Some 125 Cubans, many of whom have been living in the camp for over a year, are flown to South Florida. The U.S. then officially closes the Guantanamo refugee camps.	The Dow closes at a record high of 5395.30, marking a fourth consecutive record high for the Dow and the sixth record high registered in 1996. . . . The Federal Reserve Board announces that it will lower the federal funds rate to 5.25%, down from 5.5%, and the discount rate to 5%, down from 5.25%.	Astronomers announced the discovery of a galaxy that is 14 billion light years from Earth in the constellation Virgo, making it the most distant galaxy yet detected. . . . Officials at the London Zoo announce that the Polynesian tree snail has become extinct.		Jan. 31
The House, 414-16, and Senate, 91-5, approve the broadest overhaul of the nation's communications laws in 62 years. The reforms will eliminate many rules limiting competition in the radio, TV, and telephone-service markets, and will also impose criminal penalties for the distribution of pornographic materials to minors through the Internet computer network.	French president Jacques Chirac addresses a joint session of Congress.	The House, 396-0, and the Senate, by voice vote, pass a bill that permits the Treasury to borrow $29 billion to pay for Social Security checks to be sent out Mar. 1.	A cloud of toxic smoke fills the sky after a train carrying hazardous chemicals derails and bursts into flames at Cajon Summit, a mountain pass 15 miles (24 km) north of San Bernardino, California. Two crew members are killed, and 21 people are injured. . . . Scientists close the Third Conference on Retroviruses and Opportunistic Infections in Washington, D.C.	A misprinted commemorative stamp featuring the late President Richard Nixon sells for $16,675 at Christie's auction house.	Feb. 1
Thousands of feminists attend the opening of the "Feminist Expo '96 for Women's Empowerment" in Washington, D.C. The first-ever Feminist Expo is organized by the nonprofit Feminist Majority Foundation and cosponsored by 299 other organizations.			Ray McIntire, 77, former chemical engineer who invented Styrofoam, dies in Midland, Michigan, after suffering from interstitial fibrosis.	Gene Curran Kelly, 83, who was awarded a special Academy Award in 1951 and the National Medal of Arts in 1994, dies in Beverly Hills, California, after suffering strokes earlier. . . . Shamus Culhane, 87, pioneering film animator, dies in New York City of unreported causes.	Feb. 2
The Los Angeles Times prints portions of the 1,534-page transcript of a sworn deposition in a civil lawsuit brought by the victims' families against O. J. Simpson, who in October 1995 was acquitted of killing his former wife and a male friend of hers.				Audrey Meadows, 69, actress best known for her role as Alice Kramden on the 1950s television series The Honeymooners, dies in Los Angeles of lung cancer.	Feb. 3
	The U.S. Navy announces that Commander Fred Kilian has been relieved of his command of Navy Fighter Squadron 213. Three accidents have occurred in Squadron 213 in the past 10 months under Kilian's command, including a January accident in which five people died in Tennessee.			Jack Meador, Jane Meador Cook, and John Torigian are indicted in Sherman, Texas, in connection with the attempted sale of medieval objects that disappeared from Germany during World War II. . . . The National Football Conference defeats the American Football Conference, 20-13, in the all-star game.	Feb. 4
A Philadelphia, Pennsylvania, jury convicts Nicholas Pinero, 18, Thomas Crook, 19, and Anthony Rienzi, 18, of third-degree murder in the November 1994 beating death of Edward Polec, 16, on the steps of a church in a Fox Chase neighborhood. The case gained widespread attention because of accusations that 911 operators mishandled calls regarding Polec's beating. Three other youths are convicted on other charges related to the crime.		Judge George Howard Jr. of U.S. District Court in Little Rock, Arkansas, orders Pres. Clinton to testify in the fraud trial of Susan McDougal. . . . An FEC report finds that Malcolm S. (Steve) Forbes Jr. has spent over $14 million, which is more than any other GOP hopeful, in the last quarter of 1995. Senate majority leader Robert Dole (R, Kans.) spent $8.2 million in that period, and Sen. Phil Gramm (R, Tex.) spent $5.3 million. . . . Data shows that the Medicare Hospital Insurance Trust Fund lost money in 1995 for the first time since 1972, indicating that Medicare is in worse financial condition than expected.		Nancy Lieberman-Cline, George Gervin, David Thompson, Gail Goodrich, George Yardley, and the late Kresimir Cosic are elected into the Naismith Memorial Basketball Hall of Fame in Springfield, Massachusetts. . . . Actress Elizabeth Taylor files for divorce from her seventh husband, former construction worker Larry Fortensky, citing "irreconcilable differences."	Feb. 5

F	G	H	I	J
Includes elections, federal-state relations, civil rights and liberties, crime, the judiciary, education, health care, poverty, urban affairs, and population.	Includes formation and debate of U.S. foreign and defense policies, veterans' affairs, and defense spending. (Relations with specific foreign countries are usually found under the region concerned.)	Includes business, labor, agriculture, taxation, transportation, consumer affairs, monetary and fiscal policy, natural resources, and pollution.	Includes worldwide scientific, medical, and technological developments; natural phenomena; U.S. weather; natural disasters; and accidents.	Includes the arts, religion, scholarship, communications media, sports, entertainments, fashions, fads, and social life.

	World Affairs	Europe	Africa & the Middle East	The Americas	Asia & the Pacific
Feb. 6		Serb military leaders break off contact with the Muslims to protest the January arrests of Gen. Djordje Djukic and Col. Aleksa Krsmanovic.... Fernando Mugica Herzog, 62, the regional leader of the Socialist Party, is shot dead by two gunmen in San Sebastian. The radical Basque terrorist group ETA claims responsibility.		A Boeing 757 jetliner plunges into the Atlantic Ocean soon after taking off from Puerto Plata, on the northern coast of the Dominican Republic. All 176 passengers and 13 crew members die in the accident.... Pres. Jean-Bertrand Aristide, in his final official act as president, announces that Haiti has restored diplomatic relations with Cuba.	
Feb. 7		Wlodzimierz Cimoszewicz is sworn in as Poland's new premier.... Thousands of Basques in San Sebastian demonstrate against violence after the funeral of Fernando Mugica Herzog, killed Feb. 6.... The Swiss Bankers' Association announces it has uncovered $32.2 million in dormant bank accounts that could have belonged to victims of the Nazi Holocaust. The figure was estimated at $34 million in a preliminary report in 1995.... Lidiya Chukovskaya, 88, Russian writer who openly criticized oppressive policies of Joseph Stalin, dies in Moscow of unreported causes.	Crown Prince Letsie David Mohato assumes Lesotho's throne as King Letsie III, replacing his father, King Moshoeshoe II, who died in January in an automobile accident. He was king once before, when his father was exiled.... In the rural community of Potgietersrus, about 160 miles (260 km) north of Johannesburg, South Africa, 6,000 blacks stage a march, calling for a school to admit black students.	René Préval is sworn in as president of Haiti, succeeding Pres. Jean-Bertrand Aristide. Préval's assumption of the presidency is the first peaceful transfer of power from one democratically elected president to another since Haiti gained independence from France in 1804.... The Mexican army and riot police use tear gas and clubs in an unsuccessful attempt to dislodge protesters blocking state-owned oil wells in the southern state of Tabasco. The protesters have been blockading some 60 oil wells since late January. Reports indicate that at least 100 protesters have been arrested.	
Feb. 8	The UN Security Council renews the UN peacekeeping mission in Angola for three months.... The IMF announces that it will release the final $1.05 billion installment of a $6.8 billion loan it approved for Russia in 1995 to help advance reforms there.	Russian president Boris Yeltsin appoints Premier Viktor Chernomyrdin to head a commission to resolve the conflict in Chechnya.... The Serbs break off contact with NATO to protest the January arrests of senior officers.... In response to the Feb. 4 dismissals of senior officials, the premier of Tajikistan, Jamshed Karimov, resigns.... In the wake of a bank scandal, Lithuania's parliament ratifies a decree to dismiss Premier Adolfas Slezevicius.	The Bahraini government arrests Ahmad al-Shamlan, a well-known lawyer and writer, on charges of inciting sabotage. He is the first prominent Sunni Muslim detained by Bahraini authorities in connection with Shi'ite-led disturbances.... A Christian fundamentalist rebel group known as the Lord's Resistance Army (LRA) invades northern Uganda from neighboring Sudan.		
Feb. 9		A bomb explodes near a London office complex, killing two people and injuring about 100.... Reports indicate that Islamic rebels took advantage of the warlords' mutiny in Tajikistan to seize part of Tavil Dara, a strategically valuable town in the mountains about 90 miles east of Dushanbe.... General Adolf Joseph Ferdinand Galland, 83, who was regarded as one of the most successful German aviators of World War II, having shot down 104 airplanes, dies in Oberwinter, Germany, after suffering from a heart ailment.			
Feb. 10		Soldiers fire tear gas and bullets into a crowd of 1,000 Chechen civilians who started a protest Feb. 4 to demand that Russian troops leave the republic.... The Provisional IRA claims responsibility for the Feb. 9 explosion in London, ending an 18-month cease-fire.			A huge boulder breaks off from the side of a mountain and falls onto the Toyohama Tunnel, near the Japanese town of Furubira on the northern island of Hokkaido. One passenger car and a bus carrying 19 passengers are in the tunnel when the boulder falls.
Feb. 11		The independent Russian television network reports that six protesters were killed and 15 injured in the melees following the Feb. 10 police action against protesting Chechen civilians.	In Algeria, a bomb explodes in the busy Algiers quarter of Bab el Oued, an area known for Islamic fundamentalism, injuring 41 people. Another bomb, which kills 17 people and wounds 52, explodes in front of a building containing the offices of many independent journalists and photographers.... A bomb blast injures at least four people in the lobby of a luxury seaside hotel in Manama, Bahrain. The Islamic Front for the Liberation of Bahrain claims responsibility.	More than 1 million people attend an open-air mass conducted by Pope John Paul II at an airbase in Caracas, the capital of Venezuela.	

A	B	C	D	E
Includes developments that affect more than one world region, international organizations, and important meetings of major world leaders.	Includes all domestic and regional developments in Europe, including the Soviet Union, Turkey, Cyprus, and Malta.	Includes all domestic and regional developments in Africa and the Middle East, including Iraq and Iran and excluding Cyprus, Turkey, and Afghanistan.	Includes all domestic and regional developments in Latin America, the Caribbean, and Canada.	Includes all domestic and regional developments in Asia and Pacific nations, extending from Afghanistan through all the Pacific Island, except Hawaii.

U.S. Politics & Social Issues	U.S. Foreign Policy & Defense	U.S. Economy & Environment	Science, Technology, & Nature	Culture, Leisure, & Lifestyle	
The nation's governors endorse bipartisan policy statements for revamping federal Medicaid and welfare programs.		Energy Secretary Hazel R. O'Leary discloses that the U.S. inventory of plutonium, which includes amounts contained in nuclear weapons, totals some 99.5 metric tons. The plutonium is dispersed among 10 facilities in nine states.		Data from a study show that 57% of TV programs examined depict violence.... Guy Madison (born Robert Mos.), 74, actor from the TV series *The Adventures of Wild Bill Hickok*, dies in Palm Springs, California, of emphysema.	Feb. 6
		The Senate approves, 64-32, an agriculture bill that will sharply scale back the distribution of federal subsidies to farmers and save the government $13 billion over seven years. The overhaul is considered the most sweeping reform of U.S. farm policy in 60 years.... The Commerce Department reports that in November 1995 the U.S. recorded a seasonally adjusted $7.06 billion deficit in trade in goods and services. The November figure, the lowest since March 1994, marks the fifth consecutive monthly decline.	Preliminary tests indicate that baboon bone marrow cells transferred in December 1995 into the circulatory system of a patient with AIDS have largely failed to grow and function.		Feb. 7
Pres. Clinton signs the broadest overhaul of the nation's communications laws in 62 years. Civil-liberties and abortion-rights groups launch legal attacks against the measures that restrict on-line communications.... Attorney General Janet Reno announces that the Justice Department has undertaken a civil-rights investigation of a series of fires at predominantly black churches in Alabama and Tennessee.		Pres. Clinton signs a bill that permits the Treasury to borrow $29 billion to pay for Social Security checks to be sent out on Mar 1.... Felice N. Schwartz, 71, activist who in 1962 founded Catalyst, a group that helps women with their careers and pushes for increased participation by women in upper corporate management, dies in New York City of a heart ailment.	An analysis of seven prior studies finds no conclusive evidence that consumption of large amounts of fat raises a woman's risk of developing breast cancer.	Mercer Ellington, 76, trumpet player, composer and band leader who was presented with a Grammy Award in 1988, dies in Copenhagen, Denmark, of heart failure.	Feb. 8
Leo Jenkins Jr., 38, convicted of the 1988 fatal shootings of a brother and sister, is executed by lethal injection in Huntsville, Texas. Jenkins's execution marks the first time that victims' families are allowed to witness an execution in Texas. He is the 105th convict put to death in Texas and the 319th in the U.S. since the Supreme Court allowed states to resume executions in 1976.			Three people die and 162 others are injured when two commuter trains collide in Jersey City, New Jersey, due to either an error by the engineer or a signal malfunction.	The NFL approves the Cleveland Browns' proposed move to Baltimore, Maryland, after a compromise was reached among the league, team owner Art Modell, and the city of Cleveland, Ohio, which vigorously opposed the move.... Cigar is named 1995 horse of the year.	Feb. 9
	Pres. Clinton signs a $265 billion defense-authorization bill. The most controversial provision in the bill requires all service members who test positive for HIV to be discharged.				Feb. 10
				The Eastern Conference wins the NBA's All-Star Game, 129-118, over the Western Conference in San Antonio, Texas.	Feb. 11

F	G	H	I	J
Includes elections, federal-state relations, civil rights and liberties, crime, the judiciary, education, health care, poverty, urban affairs, and population.	*Includes formation and debate of U.S. foreign and defense policies, veterans' affairs, and defense spending. (Relations with specific foreign countries are usually found under the region concerned.)*	*Includes business, labor, agriculture, taxation, transportation, consumer affairs, monetary and fiscal policy, natural resources, and pollution.*	*Includes worldwide scientific, medical, and technological developments; natural phenomena; U.S. weather; natural disasters; and accidents.*	*Includes the arts, religion, scholarship, communications media, sports, entertainments, fashions, fads, and social life.*

	World Affairs	Europe	Africa & the Middle East	The Americas	Asia & the Pacific
Feb. 12		Representatives from Croatia, Bosnia, and Serbia agree that they will not arrest for war crimes any individuals who have not first been indicted by the tribunal in The Hague. As part of the compromise, Gen. Djordje Djukic and Col. Aleksa Krsmanovic, two senior Bosnian Serb military officers, fly to The Hague to face questioning. . . . In the wake of the Feb. 9 bombing in London, British prime minister John Major states his government has broken off all contact with Sinn Fein, the IRA's political wing.	Yasser Arafat, head of the Palestine Liberation Organization (PLO), is sworn in as president of the self-rule Palestine National Authority (PNA).		
Feb. 13				In Guatemala, a full-scale excavation of a suspected mass grave begins in the town of Rabinal, a military base from 1980 to 1987.	
Feb. 14	The European Parliament, the legislative branch of the EU, votes in favor of limiting the number of foreign-made productions broadcast on European television.	Francisco Tomas y Valiente, 63, a former president of Spain's highest court, is shot and killed by a single assailant in Madrid, the Spanish capital. The radical Basque terrorist group ETA claims responsibility.		Colombian prosecutors file formal charges against President Ernesto Samper Pizano that could eventually lead to his impeachment. The charges stem from allegations that Samper accepted money from the Cali drug cartel for his election campaign.	
Feb. 15		In Grozny, Chechnya, Russian troops destroy the presidential palace, which has been a symbol of Chechen independence since Russia invaded the republic. . . . The supertanker *Sea Empress* runs aground just off the southwest coast of Wales, slowly spilling more than 18 million gallons (70 million liters) of oil into the Celtic Sea. . . . French NATO troops capture three Iranian men and eight other Muslims in a raid in central Bosnia. . . . The parliament of Lithuania approves Mindaugas Stankevicius as the new premier.		Canadian federal and provincial officials in Vancouver, British Columbia, initial an agreement that settles land claims by the Nisga'a nation, an indigenous people whose native lands are in the northwestern corner of the province. The pact is the first of its kind between British Columbia and a native group.	Bangladeshi prime minister Khaleda Zia and her ruling Bangladesh National Party (BNP) wins an overwhelming victory in parliamentary elections that are marred by widespread violence, low voter turnout, and allegations of vote rigging. . . . A Chinese-made rocket carrying a U.S. telecommunications satellite crashes shortly after liftoff in China's Sichuan province.
Feb. 16		Leaders of Ukraine's coal-mining unions agree to suspend a strike they began Feb. 1. . . . Fighting in Chechnya spreads as Russian forces attack suspected guerrilla strongholds. . . . Italian president Oscar Luigi Scalfaro dissolves Italy's parliament, clearing the way for general elections in April.	South African Supreme Court judge Tjibbe Spoelstra orders an all-white school in the rural community of Potgietersrus, about 160 miles (260 km) north of Johannesburg, to admit black students who were turned away. Spoelstra's ruling is the first court decision on the racial integration of South African schools since majority rule began in 1994.	Representatives of the rebel Zapatista National Liberation Army (EZLN), the Mexican federal government, and the state government of Chiapas sign the first of six formal peace accords designed to resolve a two-year-old uprising. Separately, about 1,000 protesters end their blockades of state-owned oil wells in the southern Gulf Coast state of Tabasco. The protesters have been blockading some 60 oil wells since late January.	Sir William Deane, a former justice in Australia's High Court, is sworn in as the 22nd governor general of Australia, replacing Bill Hayden.
Feb. 17		In Bosnia-Herzegovina, reports indicate that at least three people have been injured, two of them seriously, in four separate attacks on buses linking Sarajevo with the suburb of Ilidza. . . . Herve Bazin (born Jean-Pierre Herve-Bazin), 84, French novelist who sharply criticized the institutions of his country's bourgeois society, dies in Angers, France, after suffering a stroke.			Rescuers in Japan recover the bodies of 20 people who were killed in the Feb. 10 accident in the Toyohama Tunnel, near the town of Furubira on the northern island of Hokkaido.

A	B	C	D	E
Includes developments that affect more than one world region, international organizations, and important meetings of major world leaders.	*Includes all domestic and regional developments in Europe, including the Soviet Union, Turkey, Cyprus, and Malta.*	*Includes all domestic and regional developments in Africa and the Middle East, including Iraq and Iran and excluding Cyprus, Turkey, and Afghanistan.*	*Includes all domestic and regional developments in Latin America, the Caribbean, and Canada.*	*Includes all domestic and regional developments in Asia and Pacific nations, extending from Afghanistan through all the Pacific Island, except Hawaii.*

U.S. Politics & Social Issues	U.S. Foreign Policy & Defense	U.S. Economy & Environment	Science, Technology, & Nature	Culture, Leisure, & Lifestyle	
			Gary Dockery, a Tennessee police officer who has been largely incommunicative since being shot in the forehead in 1988, becomes alert and speaks for the first time since being shot. His partial recovery calls attention to misperceptions commonly held by medical professionals and the public about comas and "vegetative states." . . . The FDA approves the nonprescription sale of the hair-growth drug minoxidil, which is made and marketed as Rogaine.	French Roman Catholic bishops for the first time approve the use of condoms to prevent individuals from contracting HIV. The move defies the doctrine of Pope John Paul II, who advocates abstinence. . . . Officials confirm that heavyweight boxer Tommy Morrison has tested positive for HIV.	Feb. 12
A Michigan appeals court clears the way for Dr. Jack Kevorkian, who has acknowledged attending the suicides of 26 people since June 1990, to stand trial for the 1993 deaths of Ali Khalili and Merian Frederick under an expired Michigan law banning assisted suicide.		Pres. Clinton signs an executive order barring companies that knowingly hire illegal aliens from competing for new federal contracts for one year.	CompuServe Inc., an on-line computer service, states that it will reverse a decision made in December 1995 in response to German pornography laws. The company announces it will remove most restrictions set in place in 1995 on the distribution of sex-related materials over the Internet.	Martin Henry Balsam, 76, actor who won the 1965 Academy Award for best supporting actor and a 1967 Tony Award, is found dead in a Rome, Italy, hotel after suffering a stroke. . . . Charlie Conerly, 74, football quarterback who led the New York Giants to the NFL title, dies in Memphis, Tennessee, of heart failure.	Feb. 13
		Deputy Interior Secretary John Garamendi states that a plan to build a dump site for low-level nuclear waste on federal land in the Mojave Desert will be delayed, pending further tests to determine the safety of the plan. The action temporarily blocks a May 1995 decision by Interior Secretary Bruce Babbitt. . . . A jury in Detroit, Michigan, finds that insurers of Dow Corning Corp. are liable for a total of $400 million in coverage pertaining to silicone breast-implant lawsuits.	A runaway freight train crashes into a railyard office building in St. Paul, Minnesota, injuring nine people.	The New York State Athletic Commission announces that it will implement mandatory annual HIV tests for boxers.	Feb. 14
In Philadelphia, Pennsylvania, U.S. district judge Ronald Buckwalter grants a restraining order that will temporarily block enforcement of the Communications Decency Act, a provision of the recent telecommunications bill. The provision would outlaw the transmission of "indecent" material to minors over on line computer networks, and Buckwalter rules that the legislation does not adequately define "indecent.". . . Contenders for the Republican presidential nomination participate in a televised debate held in Manchester, New Hampshire.				McLean Stevenson, 66, actor best known for his role as Lt. Col. Henry Blake in the TV series M*A*S*H, dies in Tarzana, California, of a heart attack.	Feb. 15
Three terminally ill patients in Florida are joined by Dr. Cecil McIver, the ACLU, and the Hemlock Society to file a suit to overturn the state's ban on doctor-assisted suicide. . . . Edmund G(erald) (Pat) Brown, 90, Democratic governor of California, 1959–67, who was largely credited with an economic boom in California during the 1960s, dies in Beverly Hills, Califronia, of a heart attack.		The Federal Reserve Board reports that its industrial-production index, which measures output at U.S. factories, mines, and utilities, plunged 0.6% in January, the sharpest decline since March 1991.	Eleven people are killed and 26 injured when an Amtrak passenger train collides with a Maryland Area Rail Commuter system train in Silver Spring, Maryland, less than 10 miles (16 km) outside of Washington, D.C.	Brownie (Walter Brown) McGhee, 80, black American blues vocalist and guitarist known for his smooth finger-picking style, dies in Oakland, California, of stomach cancer.	Feb. 16
	Jason Anthony Harloff, 22, a midshipman at the U.S. Naval Academy, is sentenced by a military court to four months in prison for possession, use and intent to distribute the drug LSD.		NASA launches a low-cost spacecraft on a four-year mission to study the asteroid 433 Eros. The Near Earth Asteroid Rendezvous (NEAR) craft is the first to orbit an asteroid.	Garry Kasparov of Russia defeats the Deep Blue chess computer, designed by IBM, in the first multigame regulation match between a world champion and a computer.	Feb. 17

F	G	H	I	J
Includes elections, federal-state relations, civil rights and liberties, crime, the judiciary, education, health care, poverty, urban affairs, and population.	*Includes formation and debate of U.S. foreign and defense policies, veterans' affairs, and defense spending. (Relations with specific foreign countries are usually found under the region concerned.)*	*Includes business, labor, agriculture, taxation, transportation, consumer affairs, monetary and fiscal policy, natural resources, and pollution.*	*Includes worldwide scientific, medical, and technological developments; natural phenomena; U.S. weather; natural disasters; and accidents.*	*Includes the arts, religion, scholarship, communications media, sports, entertainments, fashions, fads, and social life.*

	World Affairs	Europe	Africa & the Middle East	The Americas	Asia & the Pacific
Feb. 18		Pres. Alija Izetbegovic of Bosnia-Herzegovina, Croatian president Franjo Tudjman, and Serbian president Slobodan Milosevic reassert their commitment to fulfilling all the provisions of a December 1995 peace treaty.... A concealed bomb destroys a double-decker bus in London, killing one person and injuring at least eight others.			In the Philippines, a ferry carrying more than 200 passengers capsizes at the entrance to the port at Cadiz, a city some 300 miles (480 km) southeast of Manila, killing at least 50 people.
Feb. 19	Iraqi and UN officials end talks on terms under which Iraq would be allowed to resume limited oil sales for revenue to ameliorate a shortage of food and medical supplies that has reached crisis proportions among vast numbers of Iraqis. If enacted, the plan—Security Council Resolution 986—would permit Iraq to sell up to $2 billion of oil over a six-month period.	The Provisional IRA claims responsibility for the Feb. 18 blast on a double-decker bus in London.	WHO officials confirm that 13 people have died from the Ebola virus in Mayibout, a remote village in northeastern Gabon. WHO also confirms a total of 20 infections. ... A group of black secondary-school students in Trompsburg in South Africa's Orange Free State are barred from attending an all-white school.		
Feb. 20		Russian military officers claim the army captured Novogroznensky, Chechnya, about 40 miles (65 km) east of Grozny.... A joint Muslim-Croat police unit patrols in Mostar for the first time, amid exchanges of gunfire and incidents of rock-throwing.	A group of 400 black secondary students loot and protest in Trompsburg in Orange Free State in response to being barred Feb. 19 from attending an all-white school. ... Two sons-in-law of President Saddam Hussein who had defected to Jordan in August 1995, Lt. Gen. Hussein Kamel Hassan al-Majid and Lt. Col. Saddam Kamel Hassan al-Majid, return home to Iraq after receiving a pardon from the government. ... Qatar foils an antigovernment plot headed by supporters of the nation's deposed and exiled emir, Khalifa bin Hamad al-Thani, who was ousted in a June 1995 bloodless coup. Some 100 people are reported arrested.		Japan and South Korea in separate moves announce plans to declare so-called exclusive economic zones that encompass disputed islets located in waters off their shores.
Feb. 21	The European Court of Human Rights rules that the British government's power to detain juvenile offenders indefinitely violates their rights.	A flotilla of 12 British, French, and Dutch tugboats frees the *Sea Empress*, which ran aground Feb 15 off the southwest coast of Wales. The boats move it to a local inlet.			
Feb. 22	Michel Camdessus, the managing director of the International Monetary Fund, announces that the IMF will provide a package of $10.2 billion in loans over three years to help Russia implement free-market economic reforms.	Bosnian president Alija Izetbegovic is hospitalized in Sarajevo, the Bosnian capital, with an unspecified heart ailment.			Government prosecutors charge 14 high-ranking Indian politicians with accepting illegal payments. The charges are the latest to stem from a massive bribery probe based on information culled from the diaries of Surendra K. Jain, a former steel industrialist arrested on corruption charges in 1995. The scandal has caused a number of Indian politicians to resign in the past several weeks.
Feb. 23			Two sons-in-law of Pres. Saddam Hussein who defected to Jordan in August 1995 and returned to Iraq on Feb. 20 are slain, apparently by enraged family members. The two, Lt. Gen. Hussein Kamel Hassan al-Majid and Lt. Colonel Saddam Kamel Hassan al-Majid, die in a shoot-out along with a third brother and their father when members of the Majid clan, or extended family, storm their residence in a Baghdad suburb.... WHO officials declare that no new Ebola infections have been seen and that the Feb. 19 outbreak in northeastern Gabon is apparently under control.		

A	B	C	D	E
Includes developments that affect more than one world region, international organizations, and important meetings of major world leaders.	Includes all domestic and regional developments in Europe, including the Soviet Union, Turkey, Cyprus, and Malta.	Includes all domestic and regional developments in Africa and the Middle East, including Iraq and Iran and excluding Cyprus, Turkey, and Afghanistan.	Includes all domestic and regional developments in Latin America, the Caribbean, and Canada.	Includes all domestic and regional developments in Asia and Pacific nations, extending from Afghanistan through all the Pacific Island, except Hawaii.

U.S. Politics & Social Issues	U.S. Foreign Policy & Defense	U.S. Economy & Environment	Science, Technology, & Nature	Culture, Leisure, & Lifestyle	
		Sugar farmers and industry officials stage demonstrations in Miami, Florida, to protest potential increases in sugar taxes.		Picabo Street captures the downhill gold medal at the world skiing championships, becoming the first American woman ever to win an event there.... Dale Jarrett wins the Daytona 500 automobile race in Daytona Beach, Florida.	Feb. 18
Grant Sawyer, 77, Democratic governor of Nevada, 1959–67, who was known for his tough stance against organized crime, dies in Las Vegas, Nevada, of complications from a stroke.				Charles O(scar) Finley, 77, owner of the Athletics baseball team, 1960–80, dies in Chicago, Illinois, of heart and vascular ailments.	Feb. 19
Former representative Kweisi Mfume (D, Md.) is sworn in as the top officer of the NAACP in a ceremony at the Great Hall of the Justice Department in Washington, D.C.... Former TV commentator Patrick Buchanan edges out Senate majority leader Robert J. Dole (Kans.) to win the New Hampshire Republican presidential primary.		Kenneth W. Starr, the independent counsel investigating the Whitewater affair, indicts Robert M. Hill and Herby Branscum Jr. on fraud and conspiracy charges related to the handling of money donated to the 1990 reelection campaign of then-Arkansas governor Bill Clinton. Starr's indictment does not accuse Pres. Clinton of criminal wrongdoing.... FEC reports show that Sen. Robert Dole (R, Kans.) is in the best financial shape of the GOP candidates.	*Mir* marks the 10th anniversary of its 1986 launch. The Russian space station has been manned continuously since September 1989.... Solomon E. Asch, 88, Polish-born psychologist who served as director of the Institute for Cognitive Studies at Rutgers University, 1966–72, and as professor of psychology at the University of Pennsylvania, 1972–79, dies in Haverford, Pennsylvania, of unreported causes.	Rap singer Snoop Doggy Dogg (Calvin Broadus) and his former bodyguard are acquitted of first degree murder in connection with the 1993 shooting of Philip Woldemariam.... Toru Takemitsu, 65, who was the first Japanese composer to gain recognition in the West, dies in Tokyo of cancer.	Feb. 20
			A freight train carrying sulfuric acid derails while descending a snow-covered pass in the Rocky Mountains south of Red Cliff, Colorado, killing two crew members. Thousands of gallons of acid spill down a mountainside and across a main highway. The derailment is the fifth major U.S. train accident in the month of February.	Morton Gould, 82, composer and conductor who received a Kennedy Center Honors Award in 1994 and the Pulitzer Prize in 1995, dies in Orlando, Florida, of undetermined causes.	Feb. 21
		Pres. Clinton renominates Alan Greenspan for a third four-year term as chairman of the Federal Reserve Board. Clinton also picks Alice Rivlin to assume the Fed vice chairmanship and economic consultant Laurence Meyer to fill a vacated governor's seat on the seven-member board.	The U.S. space shuttle *Columbia* blasts off from Kennedy Space Center in Cape Canaveral, Florida.	A jury in Richmond, Texas, finds Warren Moon, a quarterback in the NFL, not guilty of beating his wife, Felicia Moon, during a July 1995 argument at their home in Missouri City, Texas.	Feb. 22
William G. Bonin, 49, known as the "Freeway Killer" for his serial slayings of boys and young men in 1979 and 1980, is put to death in San Quentin, California. Bonin is the first convict in California executed by lethal injection. He is also the third person to be executed in California and the 322nd in the U.S. since the Supreme Court reinstated capital punishment in 1976.		Data indicate that the U.S. gross domestic product grew at an annual rate of 2.1% in 1995. That is the lowest calendar-year growth rate since 1991, when the economy contracted just 1%.... The Dow closes at a record high of 5630.49, marking a 10th record high for the Dow in February and the 16th record high registered in 1996.			Feb. 23

F	G	H	I	J
Includes elections, federal-state relations, civil rights and liberties, crime, the judiciary, education, health care, poverty, urban affairs, and population.	Includes formation and debate of U.S. foreign and defense policies, veterans' affairs, and defense spending. (Relations with specific foreign countries are usually found under the region concerned.)	Includes business, labor, agriculture, taxation, transportation, consumer affairs, monetary and fiscal policy, natural resources, and pollution.	Includes worldwide scientific, medical, and technological developments; natural phenomena; U.S. weather; natural disasters; and accidents.	Includes the arts, religion, scholarship, communications media, sports, entertainments, fashions, fads, and social life.

	World Affairs	Europe	Africa & the Middle East	The Americas	Asia & the Pacific
Feb. 24		Russian artillery and warplanes shell villages where the army believes Chechen rebels are hiding in Ingushetia, a Russian republic that borders Chechnya. The attack sparks protests by officials in Ingushetia.		Two unarmed private planes belonging to a U.S.-based Cuban exile pilots organization called Brothers to the Rescue are shot down over waters between Cuba and the U.S. by Cuban MiG fighter jets, killing four airmen. The incident prompts international criticism of Cuba and moves by the U.S. toward tightening its economic embargo against the Caribbean island nation.	
Feb. 25	The U.S. calls an emergency meeting of the United Nations Security Council in response to the Feb. 24 attack on civilian planes by Cuba.		Two suicide bombers kill 27 people and injure scores of others in apparently coordinated attacks in West Jerusalem and the Israeli coastal town of Ashkelon. The military wing of the Islamic resistance organization Hamas cites revenge for the slaying of Yahya Ayyash, a former engineering student killed in January, when claiming responsibility. The attacks end a six-month lull in Palestinian bombings against Israeli targets and draw widespread condemnation.	Mexico's largest television network airs a videotape of a June 1995 massacre of 17 peasants by police in Guerrero. The tape shows police firing at unarmed peasants and confirms that guns were planted on the peasants after they were slain.	
Feb. 26	NATO certifies that the Serbs have withdrawn all their military forces from a "separation zone" between Serb and Muslim-Croat territory, in accordance with the 1995 treaty that halted the Bosnian civil war.	Russian forces withdraw from Ingushetia, a Russian republic that borders Chechnya.	In Jerusalem, Israel, armed Jewish civilians shoot to death an Arab-American motorist they suspect of being a terrorist after the rented car he is driving strikes and kills a Jewish woman waiting at a bus stop. More than 20 other people at the bus stop are injured in the incident. . . . Sierra Leone holds its first multiparty presidential election since 1967. Gunfire and rocket attacks disrupt the vote and cause voting to be extended for one day.	In Canada, more than 55,000 members of the Ontario Public Service Employees' Union (OPSEU) walk off their civil-service jobs in an effort to strengthen contract clauses related to their job security.	
Feb. 27	In response to the Feb. 26 certification by NATO, the UN Security Council suspends its long-standing economic sanctions against Bosnia-Herzegovina's ethnic Serbs. The rump federation of Yugoslavia, whose government is dominated by Serbs, lifts its own sanctions against the Bosnian Serbs as well.	George Iain Murray, 64, the 10th Duke of Atholl and one of the wealthiest landowners in Scotland, dies in Perth, Scotland, after suffering a stroke.	In Israel, the PNA police announce that some 140 suspected members of Hamas have been arrested in a crackdown following the Feb. 25 bombings. . . . Sierra Leone's first multiparty presidential election since 1967 results in no clear winner, and a second round of voting is scheduled for March.	Mario Polanco of the Guatemalan National Human Rights Coordinating Committee reveals that anthropologists have exhumed the burned remains of 167 people in the village of Agua Fria. Polanco asserts that the victims were killed during the army's hunt for suspected leftists and sympathizers in April 1982, under the rule of General Efrain Rios Montt. . . . Haiti's parliament ratifies the appointment of Rosny Smarth as premier.	
Feb. 28		Diana, the Princess of Wales, announces she has agreed to divorce her husband of 15 years, Charles, the Prince of Wales.			
Feb. 29	The UN Security Council unanimously approve a resolution extending the UN peacekeeping mission in Haiti.	Ilijas, a Serb suburb in Bosnia, passes into Muslim-Croat hands.			

A	B	C	D	E
Includes developments that affect more than one world region, international organizations, and important meetings of major world leaders.	Includes all domestic and regional developments in Europe, including the Soviet Union, Turkey, Cyprus, and Malta.	Includes all domestic and regional developments in Africa and the Middle East, including Iraq and Iran and excluding Cyprus, Turkey, and Afghanistan.	Includes all domestic and regional developments in Latin America, the Caribbean, and Canada.	Includes all domestic and regional developments in Asia and Pacific nations, extending from Afghanistan through all the Pacific Island, except Hawaii.

U.S. Politics & Social Issues	U.S. Foreign Policy & Defense	U.S. Economy & Environment	Science, Technology, & Nature	Culture, Leisure, & Lifestyle	
					Feb. 24
	Secretary of State Warren Christopher embarks on a largely symbolic nine-day tour of five countries in Latin America and the Caribbean region.		Astronauts aboard the space shuttle *Columbia* deploy 12.23 miles of a 12.8-mile-long cable attached to a satellite when the U.S.-made tether snaps, hurtling the satellite into space at about 100 miles per hour.	Dr. Haing S. Ngor, 45, a Cambodian refugee activist who won a best supporting actor Academy Award for his debut role in the 1984 film *The Killing Fields*, is found shot dead outside his home in Los Angeles. Ngor, a Cambodian-born physician, survived torture while a captive of his native country's Khmer Rouge government in the 1970s.	Feb. 25
	Defense Secretary William Perry and CIA director John Deutch announce they have asked National Reconnaissance Office (NRO) director Jeffrey Harris and deputy director Jimmie Hill to resign following allegations of fiscal mismanagement. Keith Hall is named the NRO's acting director. . . . In response to the Feb. 24 downing of private planes by Cuba, Pres. Clinton announces that all charter flights between the U.S. and Cuba will be suspended.			*Primary Colors*, by Anonymous, tops the bestseller list. . . . Fox Broadcasting Co. Chair Rupert Murdoch announces that the Fox TV network will offer the leading presidential candidates free airtime in the fall.	Feb. 26
Kevin Convey, 19, who pled guilty to third-degree murder in an agreement with prosecutors, is sentenced to 5–20 years in prison for the November 1994 beating death of Edward Polec, 16, on the steps of a church in the Fox Chase neighborhood of Philadelphia.	The independent Export-Import Bank, the U.S.'s chief export credit agency, states it will honor a request by Secretary of State Warren Christopher to defer for at least one month any new financing for American companies seeking to do business in China. The move, which heightens Sino-U.S. tensions, is prompted by CIA allegations of sales of nuclear technology to Pakistan by China.		AT&T Corp., the leading U.S. provider of long-distance telephone services, announces that it will offer its customers free access to the Internet global computer network through its new on-line service, known as WorldNet.		Feb. 27
Census Bureau officials state that for the first time the bureau will use sampling techniques in an official tabulation of the U.S. population when it conducts Census 2000.	A federal judge in Newark, New Jersey, throws out the deportation case against former Mexican deputy attorney general Mario Ruiz, who has been in U.S. custody since March 1995 and is wanted in Mexico on charges of embezzlement and conspiracy to commit murder. . . . Daiwa Bank Lth., a major Japanese commercial bank, pleads guilty to 16 counts of fraud and conspiracy and agrees to pay $340 million in fines in exchange for the U.S. government's agreement not to prosecute the bank or any of its affiliates.	The Commerce Department reports that the U.S. recorded a $111.04 billion deficit in trade in goods and services in 1995. That is up 4.5% from the 1994 deficit of $106.21 billion and is the largest calendar-year gap since 1988. . . . The FDIC informs Congress that it will not sue the Rose Law Firm, where First Lady Hillary Rodham Clinton was formerly a partner, for fraud or misconduct related to the collapse of the Madison Guaranty Savings and Loan thrift institution. The agency does not exonerate anyone.		At the Grammy Awards, Canadian singer Alanis Morissette, 21, is a big winner, picking up four Grammys, including best album of the year. Hootie and the Blowfish and Seal also win high-profile awards.	Feb. 28
The Senate by unanimous voice vote confirms a four-star army general, Barry R. McCaffrey, to serve as the director of the Office of National Drug Control Policy.	The Commission on Roles and Capabilities of the U.S. Intelligence Community, an expert advisory committee created in December 1994, releases the findings of its 16-month investigation into the government's intelligence agencies. The report suggests ways to make the intelligence community operate more efficiently, but it does not recommend any radical changes.	The House approves, 270-155, a bill that will eliminate many government subsidies paid to farmers and reduce federal spending by about $13 billion over seven years. . . . In Washington, D.C., U.S. district judge Louis Oberdorfer rules that GOPAC, a Republican political action committee headed by House Speaker Newt Gingrich (R, Ga.) from 1986 to 1995, did not make illegal campaign contributions to Gingrich and other Republicans prior to registering with the FEC in 1991.		Federal National Mortgage Association (Fannie Mae) chairman James A. Johnson is named to head the Kennedy Center for the Performing Arts. . . . The heads of large cable-TV companies and of the four major networks pledge to develop a system for rating programs based on their level of violent and sexual content.	Feb. 29

F	G	H	I	J
Includes elections, federal-state relations, civil rights and liberties, crime, the judiciary, education, health care, poverty, urban affairs, and population.	Includes formation and debate of U.S. foreign and defense policies, veterans' affairs, and defense spending. (Relations with specific foreign countries are usually found under the region concerned.)	Includes business, labor, agriculture, taxation, transportation, consumer affairs, monetary and fiscal policy, natural resources, and pollution.	Includes worldwide scientific, medical, and technological developments; natural phenomena; U.S. weather; natural disasters; and accidents.	Includes the arts, religion, scholarship, communications media, sports, entertainments, fashions, fads, and social life.

	World Affairs	Europe	Africa & the Middle East	The Americas	Asia & the Pacific
March 1	Leaders of 25 European and Asian nations hold a trade summit in Bangkok, Thailand, to lay out plans for strengthening Euro-Asian trade and investment ties. Participants avoid any substantive talks on Asia's human-rights record, drawing criticism from activists. . . . The UN International War Crimes Tribunal in The Hague charges Bosnian Serb general Djordje Djukic with war crimes related to his role in the civil war in Bosnia-Herzegovina.			In the waters off the South Georgia Islands, a British colony located some 800 miles (1,300 km) southeast of the Falkland Islands, a fishing vessel registered in Argentina is allegedly forced by a British warship to pay a $110,000 fee to fish in those waters. The incident renews tensions between Great Britain and Argentina.	
March 2					The Liberal Party-National Party coalition, led by John Howard, wins a decisive victory in Australian national elections, ending 13 years of political rule by the Australian Labor Party. Howard is expected to replace Paul Keating as Australia's prime minister.
March 3		Police in the republic of Serbia arrest Drazen Erdemovic, a former officer in the Bosnian Serb army, after he confesses that he took part in a mass execution near Srebrenica on July 20, 1995. Police also arrest another officer, Radoslav Kremenovic. . . . The Popular Party (PP) wins the most votes in general elections in Spain. . . . Turkey's two rival conservative parties agree to form a coalition government that excludes the Islamic Welfare (Refah) Party, which won a plurality in 1995 elections. . . . Marguerite Duras, 81, popular French writer, dies in Paris of unreported causes.	A suicide bomber carries out an attack on a bus in downtown West Jerusalem, The blast kills 19 people, including the bomber, and injures another 10. A communiqué that claims to represent the leadership of Hamas's military wing asserts that the attack is the last act of retaliation for the January slaying of Yahya Ayyash. . . . Pres. Nicephore Soglo and former president Mathieu Kerekou are the top two vote-getters in the first round of Benin's multiparty presidential elections.		Reports reveal that the rocket that crashed Feb. 15 in China's Sichuan province destroyed 80 homes, killing a family of six people and injuring 57.
March 4			A suicide attack at a busy intersection in Tel Aviv, Israel, outside the Dizengoff Center, the city's largest shopping mall, kills 14 people, including the bomber, who is affiliated with Hamas. About 130 are wounded. When combined the Mar. 3 assault, 33 people have died in Jerusalem and Tel Aviv, sending the Israeli-Palestinian peace process into disarray.		In Hong Kong, British prime minister John Major vows to ensure that the rights and freedoms of Hong Kong citizens will be protected after the territory reverts to Chinese sovereignty from British rule on June 30, 1997.
March 5	In response to the U.S. Senate's vote regarding Cuba, 14 Caribbean nations, along with Canada, release a joint statement condemning the bill as an unacceptable extension of American law beyond U.S. territory.		Israel Radio reports that four Israeli soldiers were killed in southern Lebanon after coming under fire from Hezbollah fighters. The South Lebanon Army, an Israeli proxy militia, states that two guerrillas were killed in the ambush.	Fugitive Colombian drug trafficker Jose Santacruz Londoño is killed in a shoot-out with police near Medellin, Colombia. . . . In Haiti, Pierre Denize is confirmed by the Senate as chief of the civilian police force. Denize is the first civilian to hold that position since Haiti gained independence in 1804. . . . Argentina lodges a complaint with Great Britain in response to the Mar. 1 incident off the South Georgia Islands.	
March 6	The International Civil Aviation Organization, a UN aviation agency, agrees to investigate the February downing of unarmed civilian planes by Cuba.	Russian troops clash with rebels in Grozny, the Russian-held capital of Chechnya. Russian news agencies report that Chechen guerrilla leader Salman Raduyev, who led a January raid on the Russian republic of Dagestan, has died of head wounds. . . . Hadzici, a suburb of Sarajevo, passes into Muslim-Croat hands. . . . Lord Douglas Patrick Thomas Jay, 88, prominent Labour Party member of Britain's Parliament, 1946–83, and trade minister under P.M. Harold Wilson, 1964–67, dies in Oxfordshire, England, of unreported causes.	In the West Bank city of Nablus, thousands of supporters of the Al-Fatah movement hold a rally supporting the Palestinian-Israeli peace process and denouncing terrorism. Israeli and PNA police conduct joint raids against suspected Islamic militants. PNA security forces reveal that they detained, found guilty, and sentenced Mohammed Abu Wardeh, 21, for recruiting three Hamas suicide bombers, one of whom allegedly detonated one of the recent blasts. Security officials state that Yasser Arafat approved a life prison term with hard labor for the Palestinian.		

A	B	C	D	E
Includes developments that affect more than one world region, international organizations, and important meetings of major world leaders.	Includes all domestic and regional developments in Europe, including the Soviet Union, Turkey, Cyprus, and Malta.	Includes all domestic and regional developments in Africa and the Middle East, including Iraq and Iran and excluding Cyprus, Turkey, and Afghanistan.	Includes all domestic and regional developments in Latin America, the Caribbean, and Canada.	Includes all domestic and regional developments in Asia and Pacific nations, extending from Afghanistan through all the Pacific Island, except Hawaii.

U.S. Politics & Social Issues	U.S. Foreign Policy & Defense	U.S. Economy & Environment	Science, Technology, & Nature	Culture, Leisure, & Lifestyle	
	The Clinton administration issues its annual report on the efforts of countries to combat the production and distribution of narcotics. Among those countries that the U.S. "decertified," or deemed uncooperative in the drug war, is Colombia, which the U.S. State Department claims is the world's leading producer and supplier of cocaine and a major supplier of heroin and marijuana. The decision will disqualify Colombia from receiving most U.S. economic aid. . . . An AH-1 Cobra helicopter crashes near Columbus, Georgia, killing both crewmen on board.		The FDA approves the AIDS drug ritonavir.		March 1
	Supporters of Brothers to the Rescue, the Cuban exile aviators' group to which the four pilots shot down by Cuba in late February belonged, organize a memorial. After civilian planes drop wreaths over the spot where the planes were downed, they fly over the Orange Bowl stadium in Miami, Florida, where some 60,000 people have gathered to commemorate the pilots.				March 2
Alan Keyes, a former State Department official and radio talk-show host who is running for the Republican Party presidential nomination, is arrested in Atlanta, Georgia, for attempting to enter a debate from which he had been excluded. Keyes is not among four candidates in the Georgia primary.				Lyle Talbot (born Lyle Henderson), 94, prolific actor, dies in San Francisco, California, of unreported causes. . . . Cardinal John Krol, 85, Roman Catholic archbishop of Philadelphia, Pennsylvania, 1961–88, dies in Philadelphia after suffering from various ailments. . . . Meyer Schapiro, 91, a preeminent art scholar, dies in New York City of unreported causes.	March 3
In *Bennis v. Michigan*, the Supreme Court rules, 5-4, that the government may seize property used for criminal activity even if the property owner does not participate in the illegal activity.	In *Hercules Inc. v. U.S.*, the Supreme Court rules, 6-2, that manufacturers of Agent Orange, a defoliating chemical used by the U.S. military during the Vietnam War, are not entitled to reimbursement from the federal government to recover costs incurred in settling lawsuits brought against them by veterans.	A survey that assesses some 35 industrial and service companies with average revenues of $21 billion finds that the average compensation received by chief executives jumped 23% in 1995, to $4.37 million. . . . The Commerce Department reports that personal pretax income increased 6.1% in 1995, the largest gain in five years. That compares with a revised 4.9% increase in 1994, and it outpaces 1995's inflation rate of 2.5%.	All 1,700 residents of the town of Weyauwega, Wisconsin, are evacuated after a train carrying liquid propane derails and the leaking fuel catches fire.	Minnie Pearl (born Sarah Ophelia Colley), 83, country comedian and storyteller who was among the most famous performers in "The Grand Ole Opry," dies in Nashville, Tennessee, of complications from a stroke.	March 4
California governor Pete Wilson (R) files a lawsuit against the federal government, demanding that the government reimburse his state for the cost of imprisoning nearly 20,000 illegal aliens convicted of felonies. . . . The federal government bans the importation of the sedative Rohypnol, a sedative 10 times more powerful than Valium that has been linked to cases of date rape.	The Senate passes, 74-22, a bill that strengthens the U.S.'s economic embargo of Cuba by penalizing foreigners who invest in Cuba. The legislation is prompted by Cuba's downing of two civilian planes in late February. . . . The House passes, 416-0, a bill that will grant federal income-tax exemptions to troops taking part in peacekeeping missions in the former Yugoslavia.	Some 3,200 members of the United Automobile Workers union walk off their jobs at two General Motors parts plants in Dayton, Ohio.		The Baseball Hall of Fame selects Earl Weaver, Jim Bunning, the late Ned Hanlon, and the late Bill Foster for induction.	March 5
The U.S. Ninth Circuit Court of Appeals in San Francisco, California, strikes down a Washington State law that bars doctors from helping terminally ill patients to kill themselves, ruling that such patients have a constitutional right to a "dignified and humane death." The ruling is the first on doctor-assisted suicide by a full federal appeals court.	The State Department releases its annual report on human rights. It singles out China for "widespread and well-documented human-rights abuses," and it criticizes many nations that maintain friendly relations with the U.S. for human-rights abuses while combating regional insurgencies or extremist groups. . . . The House approves, 336-86, a bill that penalizes foreigners who invest in Cuba. . . . The Senate passes, by unanimous voice vote, a bill to grant federal income-tax exemptions to troops in peacekeeping missions in the former Yugoslavia.	The Labor Department announces a six-month amnesty for companies that illegally diverted deposits for employees' 401(k) retirement-savings plans for the companies' own use. Labor Department officials estimate that as many as 1,000 employers will file for amnesty.			March 6

F	G	H	I	J
Includes elections, federal-state relations, civil rights and liberties, crime, the judiciary, education, health care, poverty, urban affairs, and population.	Includes formation and debate of U.S. foreign and defense policies, veterans' affairs, and defense spending. (Relations with specific foreign countries are usually found under the region concerned.)	Includes business, labor, agriculture, taxation, transportation, consumer affairs, monetary and fiscal policy, natural resources, and pollution.	Includes worldwide scientific, medical, and technological developments; natural phenomena; U.S. weather; natural disasters; and accidents.	Includes the arts, religion, scholarship, communications media, sports, entertainments, fashions, fads, and social life.

	World Affairs	Europe	Africa & the Middle East	The Americas	Asia & the Pacific
March 7		Two giant Swiss pharmaceutical firms, Sandoz AG and Ciba-Geigy AG, announce that they will merge, creating one of the largest drug companies in the world. By some accounts, the deal is the largest merger ever. . . . A Turkish court hands Yasar Kemal, considered Turkey's most famous living author, a 20-month suspended prison sentence for "fomenting enmity between peoples" by criticizing Turkey's restrictions on freedom of expression.	Yasser Arafat, president of the self-rule Palestine National Authority, convenes the inaugural session of the PNA's new 88-member Palestine Legislative Council.		A court in Naha, Okinawa, convicts three U.S. servicemen in the September 1995 rape of a 12-year-old Japanese girl in Okinawa. The court sentences two of the servicemen, Marine Pfc. Rodrico Harp and Navy Seaman Marcus D. Gill, to seven years in a Japanese prison. The third officer, Marine Pfc. Kendrick M. Ledet, is sentenced to 6 years. The case heightened tension between Japan and the U.S.
March 8		An unidentified gunman sympathetic with the Chechen rebels hijacks a North Cyprus Turkish Airlines jet with 101 passengers and eight crew members aboard. The hijacker takes control of the Boeing 727 after it leaves Cyprus for Istanbul, Turkey. . . . A representative for Ukraine's nuclear regulatory agency reveals that a minor accident had occurred at Chernobyl's No. 1 reactor in November 1995.	In the single most deadly reported raid by the Christian fundamentalist rebel group known as the Lord's Resistance Army (LRA) in Uganda, about 40 LRA rebels attack a military-escorted convoy of vehicles near Karuma Falls, northwest of Kampala, the capital. At least 130 people are killed in the ambush.		China fires unarmed surface-to-surface missiles at targets in the waters off the coasts of two Taiwanese ports in the first round of military exercises.
March 9		The gunman who hijacked a North Cyprus Turkish Airlines jet on Mar. 8 surrenders to German authorities in Munich. All the plane's occupants are released unharmed. . . . A small bomb explodes in West London, England, causing property damage but no injuries.			A "noncooperation" campaign is launched by opposition parties that boycotted February elections in Bangladesh with the goal of ousting Premier Khaleda Zia.
March 10			Hezbollah strikes Israeli troops in Lebanon with bomb and rocket attacks, killing at least one soldier. Israel responds by lobbing artillery shells at presumed Hezbollah positions in villages along the rim of the Israeli-occupied zone.	In the midst of controversy regarding a June 1995 massacre of 17 peasants by police in Guerrero, Mexico, Ruben Figueroa Alcocer, governor of the state of Guerrero, organizes several rallies on his own behalf.	
March 11		Russian interior minister Anatoly Kulikov reports that 170 Russian troops, about 300 rebels, and 100 civilians have been killed in the fighting that started Mar. 6 in Grozny, the Russian-held capital of Chechnya.			John Howard is sworn in as prime minister of Australia by Governor General Sir William Deane.
March 12		Renato Squillante, the chief examining magistrate in Rome, is arrested on corruption charges. Squillante is one of the most prominent officials to be implicated in Italy's sweeping anticorruption investigations. . . . Ilidza, a suburb of Sarajevo, the Bosnian capital, passes into Muslim-Croat hands. . . . Premier Mesut Yilmaz's government wins a vote of confidence in Turkey's parliament.		Ruben Figueroa Alcocer, governor of the Mexican state of Guerrero, steps down while Mexico's Supreme Court investigates a June 1995 massacre of 17 peasants by police in Guerrero. . . . The city council in Vancouver, British Columbia, passes a bylaw that bars smoking in most public restaurants. The ruling makes Vancouver the first major Canadian municipality to enact such a law.	China begins a series of live-ammunition tests off the coast of Taiwan.
March 13	Leaders of 27 nations and the Palestinians gather in Egypt to affirm support for the Arab-Israeli peace process, recently buffeted by a series of Palestinian suicide-bombings in Israel. . . . Canada discloses that it has lodged a formal protest against the bill signed by U.S. president Clinton on Mar. 12, arguing that it violates terms of NAFTA, which governs trade between the U.S., Canada, and Mexico.	In what is described as one of the worst mass murders in modern Britain, gunman Thomas Hamilton opens fire on a kindergarten class in Dunblane, Scotland, killing 16 children, the students' teacher, and then himself. . . . The IRA claims responsibility for the bomb that exploded in London on Mar. 9.			

A	B	C	D	E
Includes developments that affect more than one world region, international organizations, and important meetings of major world leaders.	Includes all domestic and regional developments in Europe, including the Soviet Union, Turkey, Cyprus, and Malta.	Includes all domestic and regional developments in Africa and the Middle East, including Iraq and Iran and excluding Cyprus, Turkey, and Afghanistan.	Includes all domestic and regional developments in Latin America, the Caribbean, and Canada.	Includes all domestic and regional developments in Asia and Pacific nations, extending from Afghanistan through all the Pacific Island, except Hawaii.

U.S. Politics & Social Issues	U.S. Foreign Policy & Defense	U.S. Economy & Environment	Science, Technology, & Nature	Culture, Leisure, & Lifestyle	
Senate Majority Leader Robert Dole (Kans.) emerges as the front-runner in the Republican presidential nomination race after winning decisive victories in a total of 11 primaries. . . . In Wilmington, Delaware, U.S. district judge Joseph Farnan grants a restraining order blocking a recently enacted law that orders cable-TV providers to block some sexually explicit channels.	Jennifer Harbury, a U.S. lawyer and the widow of slain Guatemalan rebel leader Efrain Bamaca Velasquez, files a $25 million lawsuit against various U.S. government officials. Bamaca was captured in Guatemala in March 1992 and was allegedly tortured and killed under the orders of a Guatemalan colonel, Julio Roberto Alpirez, who at the time was a paid informant for the CIA. . . . Two marines die when their F/A-18 jet crashes off the coast of Beaufort, South Carolina.	The House passes, 209-206, its version of the Fiscal 1996 Omnibus Appropriations bill, which will fund a host of federal departments and programs for the remainder of fiscal year 1996. The omnibus bill will authorize funding through Sept.30 for departments whose 1996 appropriations measures have yet to pass. . . . The House, 362-51, and the Senate, by voice vote, pass a bill increasing the federal debt limit through Mar. 29.			March 7
Dr. Jack Kevorkian, who advocates physician-assisted suicide, is acquitted by a Michigan jury of violating that state's since-expired ban on doctor-assisted suicide in two 1993 deaths. . . . Sen. Strom Thurmond (R, S.C.) becomes the oldest person ever to serve in the U.S. Senate. Thurmond, aged 93 years and 94 days, breaks the record achieved by Sen. Theodore F. Green (D, R.I.), who retired in 1961.	More than 100 garment workers, many of whom are illegal immigrants from Thailand and were discovered working under slave-like conditions for Thai supervisors in Los Angeles-area sweatshops in August 1995, receive $1.1 million in back wages.	The Dow closes at 5470.45, down 171.24 points, or 3.04%. That is the third-largest point loss in the index's history and the Dow's largest percentage decline since Nov. 15, 1991. . . . A Labor Department report indicates that more jobs were created in February than during any other month since September 1983.			March 8
			The U.S. space shuttle *Columbia* lands at Kennedy Space Center in Cape Canaveral, Florida. During its mission, an Italian-made satellite attached to the shuttle by a tether broke free and was lost in space.	George Burns (born Nathan Birnbaum), 100, actor and comedian famous for his ever-present cigar and his self-deprecating wit who won an Academy Award and a Kennedy Center Award for lifetime achievement, dies in Beverly Hills, California. He had been in failing health since he suffered a fall in 1994.	March 9
	Responding to China's planned live-ammunition exercises, Secretary of State Warren Christopher discloses that the will move an aircraft-carrier battle group closer to Taiwan to monitor the impending military training.				March 10
	The U.S. government files a complaint before the World Trade Organization, alleging that a Canadian excise tax unfairly bars American magazines from publishing Canadian editions. . . . The U.S.-based mining firm Battle Mountain Gold Co. reveals that it will purchase Canadian rival Hemlo Gold Mines Inc. The merged company, which will retain the Battle Mountain name, will become one of North America's largest gold-mining concerns.	The Dow soars 110.55 points, or 2%, to close at 5581.00 from the previous trading day's close of 5470.45. The gain is the Dow's third-largest single-day increase in its history.	America Online Inc., a company that provides access to the Internet, announces plans to distribute Netscape's Navigator software, a Web browser, to America Online users. In a separate deal, Microsoft Corp., the world's leading computer-software producer, announces it will collaborate with the DirecTV broadcasting service to transmit entertainment and information services over computers.	Vince Edwards (born Vincenzo Eduardo Zoino), 69, actor who starred in the TV series *Ben Casey*, dies in Los Angeles of pancreatic cancer.	March 11
Senate Majority Leader Robert Dole (R, Kans.) sweeps primaries in seven states, capturing 349 of the 362 delegates at stake in the "Super Tuesday" contests, which raises his total to 710, more than two-thirds the number needed to clinch the Republican presidential nomination. . . . As part of a plea bargain, U.S. district judge Royce Lamberth fines former interior secretary James Watt $5,000 and orders him to perform 500 hours of community service for withholding documents from a grand jury investigating a housing scandal.	Pres. Clinton signs into law a bill that strengthens the U.S.'s economic embargo of Cuba by penalizing foreigners who invest in Cuba. The legislation, prompted by Cuba's downing of two unarmed U.S. civilian planes in late February, has drawn protests from U.S. allies as an unacceptable extension of American law beyond U.S. territory.	President Clinton signs a bill increasing the federal debt limit through March 29. . . . The House passes, 226-172, a $13 billion State Department authorization bill.	After having agreed to offer Netscape's Navigator Web browser on its Internet service, America Online shocks many analysts when it announces that Internet Explorer, a similar program produced by Microsoft, will be America Online's primary Web-browsing software.	Denver Nuggets basketball guard Mahmoud Abdul-Rauf, a converted Muslim who refuses to stand during the playing of the U.S. and Canadian national anthems before games, is suspended without pay indefinitely. . . . In Alaska, Jeff King wins the 1,150-mile (1,850-km) Iditarod Trail Sled Dog Race with a time of nine days, five hours, and 43 minutes.	March 12
The Liggett Group Inc., the fifth-largest U.S. tobacco company, announces it has agreed to settle its part of the largest class-action suit pending against the tobacco industry. The settlement breaks the unified front that the tobacco industry has presented against decades of litigation as well as FDA efforts to regulate tobacco. It is the first time that a tobacco company has agreed to settle a smoking-related claim or pay money to a plaintiff.		A large tire dump catches fire, causing more than $6 million in damage to the surrounding area and forcing the closure of a stretch of Interstate 95 in the Philadelphia area.	A government-appointed panel calls for major changes in AIDS research and the management of the annual federal research budget of about $1.4 billion. The panel urges the strengthening of the NIH's Office of AIDS Research and rejects the idea of establishing a government institute dealing only with AIDS.	Krzysztof Kieslowski, 54, Polish film director best known for his *Three Colors* trilogy—*Blue, Red,* and *White*—dies in Warsaw, Poland, of a heart ailment.	March 13
F	G	H	I	J	
Includes elections, federal-state relations, civil rights and liberties, crime, the judiciary, education, health care, poverty, urban affairs, and population.	*Includes formation and debate of U.S. foreign and defense policies, veterans' affairs, and defense spending. (Relations with specific foreign countries are usually found under the region concerned.)*	*Includes business, labor, agriculture, taxation, transportation, consumer affairs, monetary and fiscal policy, natural resources, and pollution.*	*Includes worldwide scientific, medical, and technological developments; natural phenomena; U.S. weather; natural disasters; and accidents.*	*Includes the arts, religion, scholarship, communications media, sports, entertainments, fashions, fads, and social life.*	

	World Affairs	Europe	Africa & the Middle East	The Americas	Asia & the Pacific
March 14					Japanese health and welfare minister Naoto Kan and five drug companies agree to a proposed settlement with hemophiliacs who in the 1980s were infected with HIV, the virus that causes AIDS, through contaminated blood-clotting products.
March 15		The State Duma, the communist-dominated lower house of Russia's parliament, votes to annul the 1991 treaties that formally disbanded the Soviet Union. The Duma's action is not expected to have any immediate practical impact, but the vote draws condemnation from leaders in former Soviet states who fear that the resurgent communists may seek to reunite the USSR by force if their leader, Gennadi Zyuganov, wins Russia's presidential elections in June.	Sheik Gad al-Haq Ali Gad al-Haq, 78, Egyptian leader of the Al Azhar Muslim organization who was regarded as one of the world's leading authorities on conservative Islam, dies in Cairo, Egypt, of a heart attack.	Reports confirm that the Argentine has congress granted Pres. Carlos Saul Menem emergency economic powers.	
March 16		In Dortmund, Germany, 10,000 police attempt to prevent Kurds from attending a rally to celebrate the Kurdish new year. Some 2,000 demonstrators are able to enter the city, and 1,300 protesters are temporarily detained by police, sparking hundreds of Turkish Kurds to riot in several German cities, injuring 22 policemen.			In Taipei, Taiwan, 20,000 people take part in a rally for independence sponsored by the Democratic Progressive Party.
March 17		Italian NATO forces arrest some suspected arsonists in Grbavica, as many fleeing Serbs are setting their houses and apartments on fire. Separately, reports confirm that the Bosnian government has named a new Sarajevo city council from which Bosnian Serbs and Croats are virtually excluded. . . . René Clement, 82, award-winning French film director, dies in southern France of unreported causes.	Sierra Leone's electoral commission announces that Ahmad Tejan Kabbah has won a runoff presidential election, sparking celebrations in Freetown, the capital. . . . Final returns show that Sudan's Pres. Omar Hassan al-Bashir and his supporters dominated presidential and legislative elections. . . . Zimbabwe's Pres. Robert Mugabe is reelected to another six-year term in a one-man presidential election. Mugabe, 72, has ruled Zimbabwe since 1980.		
March 18	At a U.S.-sponsored summit in Geneva, leaders of Bosnia-Herzegovina, Serbia, and Croatia agree to step up their compliance with the 1995 accord that halted the Bosnian civil war. Serbian president Slobodan Milosevic agrees to hand over Drazen Erdemovic and Radoslav Kremenovic, arrested Mar. 3, to the UN-run tribunal investigating Bosnian war atrocities. Croatian president Franjo Tudjman agrees to arrange for Gen. Tihomir Blaskic, a Bosnian Croat indicted for his alleged connection to the killings of Muslims in 1993 near Vitez, to "submit himself" to the tribunal.	Zdravko Mucic, a Croat commander of the Celebici camp, is arrested in Vienna, Austria; and Zejnil Delalic, a Muslim officer who commanded the Bosnian army unit that oversaw the camp, is arrested in Munich, Germany. Police near Nuremberg, Germany, arrest Goran Lajic, a Bosnian Serb indicted in 1995 for war crimes against Muslims.		In Bolivia, state-employed teachers walk out in protest of low wages and the planned privatization of state companies. . . . At least four Ontario Public Service Employees' Union (OPSEU) demonstrators are injured when provincial police scuffle with union members blocking legislators from entering the Toronto Parliament building. The OPSEU has been striking since late February.	
March 19		The Muslim-dominated government of Bosnia-Herzegovina takes control of Grbavica, the last of five suburbs of Sarajevo transferred by Bosnian Serbs. With the hand-over, Sarajevo and its environs are united under one government for the first time since Serbs began besieging the city in 1992. But data shows that 90% of the area's Serb population fled their homes in a mass exodus before the transfer.	Judge Frikkie Eloff grants South African president Nelson Mandela a divorce from his estranged wife, Winnie Mandela, after a public trial that has transfixed the nation.		In the Philippines, more than 150 people are killed when a fire breaks out in an overcrowded nightclub in Quezon City, a suburb of Manila. Officials assert that it is the deadliest fire in the country's history.

A	B	C	D	E
Includes developments that affect more than one world region, international organizations, and important meetings of major world leaders.	Includes all domestic and regional developments in Europe, including the Soviet Union, Turkey, Cyprus, and Malta.	Includes all domestic and regional developments in Africa and the Middle East, including Iraq and Iran and excluding Cyprus, Turkey, and Afghanistan.	Includes all domestic and regional developments in Latin America, the Caribbean, and Canada.	Includes all domestic and regional developments in Asia and Pacific nations, extending from Afghanistan through all the Pacific Island, except Hawaii.

U.S. Politics & Social Issues	U.S. Foreign Policy & Defense	U.S. Economy & Environment	Science, Technology, & Nature	Culture, Leisure, & Lifestyle	
	The House passes, 229-191, its version of an antiterrorism bill. The measure is diluted form the one passed by the Senate in June 1995 and draws controversy.... A study conducted at the University of Houston estimates that 3,200 undocumented aliens drowned from 1985 to 1994 while attempting to enter the U.S. by crossing the Rio Grande, which runs along the border of Mexico. The figure is significantly higher than the one reported by Texas state officials.	The House, 238-179, and the Senate, by voice cote, pass a bill that extends a temporary spending measure for one week.... Data shows that the strike begun Mar. 5 in Dayton has forced the total or partial closure of 22 of GM's 29 car and truck assembly plants and 44 of its parts plants, idling at least 83,000 workers.	The FDA approves the AIDS drug indinavlr and a new diagnostic test for HIV that detects a part of the virus called an antigen.... Scientists at the National Center for Human Genome Research in Bethesda, Maryland, reveal that they have finished the first phase of a project whose ultimate goal is to create a complete map of human DNA.	The NBA lifts the Mar. 12 indefinite suspension against Denver Nuggets guard Mahmoud Abdul-Rauf, who refused to stand during the national anthem before games. Abdul-Rauf states that he will stand for the national anthem but will use those moments to pray "for those who are suffering."	March 14
The Liggett Group Inc., the fifth-largest U.S. tobacco company, announces it has reached a settlement with five states—Florida, Louisiana, Massachusetts, Mississippi, and West Virginia—that have filed suit against the tobacco industry to recoup money spent through Medicaid to care for victims of smoking-related illnesses.	Roswell L(eavitt) Gilpatric, 89, U.S. deputy secretary of defense, 1961–64, and a pivotal figure during the Cuban missile crisis of 1962, dies in New York City of prostate cancer.... Ray S(teiner) Cline, 77, who served as chief analyst for the CIA, 1962–66, and who was a leading decision maker during the Cuban missile crisis in 1962. dies in Arlington, Virginia, after suffering from Alzheimer's disease.	Pres. Clinton averts a shutdown of the federal government by signing a bill that extends a temporary spending measure for one week.			March 15
	Gerry Adams, leader of Sinn Fein, the political wing of the Provisional IRA, attends New York City's St. Patrick's Day parade, the oldest and largest celebration of its kind in the U.S.			Mike Tyson knocks out Frank Bruno of Great Britain to capture the World Boxing Council heavyweight crown. The title is Tyson's first since his 1995 release from prison after being convicted of rape.	March 16
Thomas O(strom) Enders, 64, former U.S. assistant secretary of state as the official in charge of economic and business affairs, 1974–76, and as the head of inter-American affairs, 1981–83, dies in New York City of melanoma.					March 17
In *Dalton v. Little Rock Family Planning*, the Supreme Court issues an unsigned opinion asserting that Arkansas Medicaid plans are required to provide funding for abortions in cases of rape and incest.... A superior court jury in Dedham, Mass., convicts John Salvi, 24, of murder and armed assault for a 1994 shooting spree at two abortion clinics in Brookline, Mass. Judge Barbara Dortch-Okara sentences Salvi to two consecutive life terms without parole and 18–20 years for the assault charges. The shootings were the worst violence ever at U.S. abortion clinics.	The INS launches a crackdown on illegal aliens in several different states.	The Dow closes at a record high of 5683.60, marking a second record high for the Dow in March and the 18th record high registered in 1996.		Odysseus Elytis (born Odysseus Alepoudelis), 84, Nobel Prize–winning Greek poet whose *Axion Esti (Worthy It Is)*, has been often regarded as one of the greatest pooms of the 20th century, dies in Athens, Greece, of a heart attack.	March 18
In New Orleans, Louisiana, Judge Jerry Smith strikes down a race-based admission policy at the University of Texas School of Law in Austin, Texas. In the ruling, the court suggests that race-based school admissions cannot be justified solely by an institution's intention to foster improved racial diversity.... Senate majority leader Robert Dole (R, Kans.) easily wins four primary contests in the Midwest.	The House approves, 369-14, a nonbinding measure saying that the U.S. should aid in the defense of Taiwan against Chinese aggression.... Haitian president Rene Preval makes his first trip to the U.S. since taking office in February.... A Marine CH-46 helicopter catches fire and burns at the Marine Corps Air Station in Yuma, Arizona. No one is seriously injured.	In *Varity Corp. v. Howe*, the Supreme Court rules, 6-3, that the Employee Retirement Income Security Act of 1974 permits workers to file lawsuits on their own behalf to gain direct compensation for lost benefits.... The Senate votes, 79-21, to pass its version of the Fiscal 1996 Omnibus Appropriations bill since only eight of the 13 regular appropriations bill for fiscal year 1996, which began Oct. 1, 1995, have been enacted.		Pop singer Michael Jackson and Saudi businessman Prince Walid bin Talal bin Abdulaziz Al Saud launch Kingdom Entertainment, a joint entertainment venture that will promote "family values" worldwide.	March 19

F	G	H	I	J
Includes elections, federal-state relations, civil rights and liberties, crime, the judiciary, education, health care, poverty, urban affairs, and population.	Includes formation and debate of U.S. foreign and defense policies, veterans' affairs, and defense spending. (Relations with specific foreign countries are usually found under the region concerned.)	Includes business, labor, agriculture, taxation, transportation, consumer affairs, monetary and fiscal policy, natural resources, and pollution.	Includes worldwide scientific, medical, and technological developments; natural phenomena; U.S. weather; natural disasters; and accidents.	Includes the arts, religion, scholarship, communications media, sports, entertainments, fashions, fads, and social life.

	World Affairs	Europe	Africa & the Middle East	The Americas	Asia & the Pacific
March 20		The British government unveils a scientific study reporting a link between bovine spongiform encephalopathy, (BSE), commonly known as mad-cow disease, and a similar ailment found in humans. Some observers suggest that the findings may completely devastate Britain's meat industry.			
March 21	In response to regarding BSE, Great Britain's Mar. 20 admission regarding BSE, France, Belgium, Sweden, the Netherlands, and Portugal ban the importation of British meat. Germany urges the EU to impose a complete ban on British beef products.	Press accounts suggest that Russian artillery and military aircraft have launched assaults on dozens of Chechen towns and villages suspected of harboring rebels.			
March 22	The tribunal prosecuting war crimes related to the civil war in Bosnia-Herzegovina indicts Zdravko Mucic, Hazim Delic, and Esad Landzo for committing atrocities at a Bosnian prison camp in 1992. It also indicts Zejnil Delalic for failing to prevent atrocities by his subordinates. The four suspects are the first Muslims to be charged by the tribunal for alleged crimes against Serbs. Separately, UN and U.S. diplomats release satellite photos indicating that Bosnian Serbs used a field on a farm near Pilice, Bosnia, as a mass grave for as many as 1,000 Muslims executed by Serbs. . . . South Africa, New Zealand, and Singapore join several EU nations in banning British beef after the Mar. 20 statement.	Pfc. Floyd Bright, 19, is killed and a second U.S. soldier is injured in a truck accident near Gornje Babine, south of Tuzla. Bright is the second U.S. soldier to be killed in Bosnia since the beginning of the NATO mission in December 1995.		In Canada, federal and provincial officials and leaders of the Nisga'a nation sign a groundbreaking land-claim agreement that will give the Nisga'a, a Native American people, control over resources and the right to limited self-government in part of their traditional homeland in British Columbia.	
March 23		Officials from Belarus and Russia announce plans for a union pact with each other's countries. . . . The Bosnian government releases 109 Bosnian Serbs who have been held in a jail in Tuzla since before the end of the war in late 1995.			Taiwanese incumbent president Lee Teng-hui wins a resounding victory in Taiwan's first democratic presidential election. Lee's win is seen as a blow to mainland China, which regards Taiwan as a renegade Chinese province. . . . Chang Hak Ro, a top aide to South Korean president Kim Young Sam, is arrested for alleged influence peddling.
March 24		As many as 30,000 people rally against the pact announced Mar. 23 in Minsk, the Belarussian capital, protesting that Russia will seek to suppress Belarussian independence and culture. Belarussian police disperse the crowd and beat several demonstrators.	Benin's constitutional court announces that the West African country's former Marxist military ruler, Mathieu Kerekou, is the winner of a runoff presidential election. Kerekou defeats Pres. Nicephore D. Soglo in the first time that a sub-Saharan country has voted out a democratically elected leader.		The Chinese-appointed Preparatory Committee votes to dissolve Hong Kong's democratically elected Legislative Council (LegCo) and install an appointed provisional body when the territory reverts to Chinese sovereignty from British rule in mid-1997.
March 25				In La Paz, Bolivia, police accidentally kill a worker watching the demonstrations that have escalated since a general strike started Mar. 18.	In Japan, the opposition New Frontier Party (NFP) ends a three-week sit-in during which party members physically blocked the doors to a budget committee room in the Diet building to protest the government's plan to use public funds to bail out seven housing-loan companies.

A	B	C	D	E
Includes developments that affect more than one world region, international organizations, and important meetings of major world leaders.	Includes all domestic and regional developments in Europe, including the Soviet Union, Turkey, Cyprus, and Malta.	Includes all domestic and regional developments in Africa and the Middle East, including Iraq and Iran and excluding Cyprus, Turkey, and Afghanistan.	Includes all domestic and regional developments in Latin America, the Caribbean, and Canada.	Includes all domestic and regional developments in Asia and Pacific nations, extending from Afghanistan through all the Pacific Island, except Hawaii.

U.S. Politics & Social Issues	U.S. Foreign Policy & Defense	U.S. Economy & Environment	Science, Technology, & Nature	Culture, Leisure, & Lifestyle	
A superior court jury in Van Nuys, California, finds brothers Lyle and Erik Menendez guilty of first-degree murder in the siblings' retrial on charges that they murdered their parents at their Beverly Hills mansion in 1989. . . . In *Wisconsin v. City of New York*, the Supreme Court rules unanimously that the federal government is not required to adjust its 1990 census figures to correct an undercount of some 4 million people, many of whom are believed to be minorities in urban areas.	Pres. Clinton signs legislation that will grant federal income-tax exemptions to U.S. troops taking part in peacekeeping missions in the former Yugoslavia.			Marina Eltsova and Andrei Bushkov of Russia win the pairs competition at the World Figure Skating Championships, Edmonton, Canada.	March 20
The Senate votes, 59-40, to adopt a compromise version of a bill that will for the first time impose nationwide limits on the awarding of punitive damages to consumers in product-liability lawsuits.	The House votes, 333-87, to approve legislation that increases efforts to prevent illegal immigration. . . . The Senate passes, 97-0, a resolution deploring China's military exercises near Taiwan.	The House, 244-180, and the Senate, by voice vote, pass the latest temporary spending bill, which provides funding through Mar. 29 for most of the agencies and programs that have yet to receive appropriations through the regular budgetary process.		The National Book Critics Circle presents awards to Robert Darnton, Robert Polito, Jonathan Harr, and the late Stanley Elkin. . . . At the World Figure Skating Championships, Todd Eldredge captures the men's title.	March 21
The House votes, 239-173, to repeal 1994 legislation that bans the manufacture, sale, or possession of 19 types of semiautomatic assault weapons. The ban was passed as part of a broad 1994 anticrime package. . . . The judicial panel that oversees the appointment of independent counsels gives Kenneth Starr, the counsel probing the Whitewater affair, formal authority to look into allegations of perjury surrounding the dismissal of aides at the White House travel office in 1993.	Colonel Robert Franklyn Overmyer, 59, astronaut who flew in the Apollo program and worked on the *Skylab* space station during the 1970s, dies near Duluth, Minnesota, in an airplane crash while conducting a test flight.	Members of United Auto Workers Local 696 vote overwhelmingly to end their strike against General Motors and return to their jobs at two brake-manufacturing plants in Dayton, Ohio. . . . Pres. Clinton signs the latest temporary spending bill, which provides funding through Mar. 29 for most of the agencies and programs that have yet to receive appropriations through the regular budgetary process.	The U.S. space shuttle *Atlantis* lifts off from Kennedy Space Center in Cape Canaveral, Florida, to dock with the Russian space station *Mir*. . . . The last of the 1,700 residents of the town of Weyauwega, Wisconsin, who were evacuated Mar. 4, after a train carrying liquid propane derailed, return to their homes.	Oksana Gritschuk and Yevgeny Platov of Russia win their third straight ice-dancing title at the World Figure Skating Championships.	March 22
			The U.S. space shuttle *Atlantis* docks with the Russian space station, *Mir*.	Michelle Kwan captures the women's title at the World Figure Skating Championships. With Todd Eldredge's Mar. 21 win, it is the first singles sweep for the U.S. since 1986.	March 23
	First Lady Hillary Rodham Clinton pays a visit to U.S. troops in Germany and Bosnia-Herzegovina involved with the NATO peacekeeping mission in Bosnia.		NASA mission controllers announce that Shannon Lucid, 53, a biochemist who has flown on the shuttle four times before, has joined the *Mir* crew. According to plan, Lucid will be the first of five U.S. astronauts to occupy *Mir* continuously through 1998. She is the second U.S. astronaut and the first U.S. woman to live on *Mir*.		March 24
Federal agents arrest the leaders of an antitax group known as the Freemen—LeRoy Schweitzer, 57, and Daniel Petersen, 53—on charges of fraud and of making death threats. Their arrests prompt a standoff between armed members of the group and the FBI in eastern Montana. . . . About 175 homosexual and lesbian couples are unofficially wed in a mass "domestic partnership ceremony" in San Francisco, California. Such same-sex unions have no legal weight because California does not recognize them.	An AV-8B from the Marine Corps Air Station in Yuma, Arizona, crashes after its engine catches fire. The pilot ejects to safety.	The Federal Reserve Board begins phasing new $100 bills into circulation, marking the first time in 68 years that the U.S. has issued a redesigned $100 bill. . . . The AFL-CIO labor federation endorses Pres. Clinton for reelection. . . . David Hale, who pled guilty to arranging fraudulent loans and is cooperating with federal independent counsels investigating the Whitewater affair, is sentenced to 28 months in prison for using his lending company to defraud the federal government out of more than $2 million.		Reports confirm that Fabian Bruskewitz, Roman Catholic bishop of the Lincoln, Nebraska, diocese, has threatened to excommunicate members of his diocese who belong to organizations he considers incompatible with the Catholic faith. . . . At the Oscars, *Braveheart* wins for Best Picture.	March 25

F	G	H	I	J
Includes elections, federal-state relations, civil rights and liberties, crime, the judiciary, education, health care, poverty, urban affairs, and population.	*Includes formation and debate of U.S. foreign and defense policies, veterans' affairs, and defense spending. (Relations with specific foreign countries are usually found under the region concerned.)*	*Includes business, labor, agriculture, taxation, transportation, consumer affairs, monetary and fiscal policy, natural resources, and pollution.*	*Includes worldwide scientific, medical, and technological developments; natural phenomena; U.S. weather; natural disasters; and accidents.*	*Includes the arts, religion, scholarship, communications media, sports, entertainments, fashions, fads, and social life.*

	World Affairs	Europe	Africa & the Middle East	The Americas	Asia & the Pacific
March 26			The government of Bahrain carries out its first official execution since 1977 when a firing squad executes Isa Ahmed Hassan Qambar, 29, a dissident convicted of killing a police officer. Qambar's execution sparks riots.	At least 40,000 people march in La Paz, Bolivia, in response to the Mar. 25 accidental death of a worker watching the demonstrations that have escalated since a general strike started Mar. 18.	
March 27	Despite objections from Britain, the European Commission, the executive arm of the EU, announces a worldwide ban on the export of British beef products amid fears that they pose a serious health risk.		A three-judge panel in Tel Aviv District Court finds Yigal Amir guilty of the premeditated murder of Israeli prime minister Yitzhak Rabin in November 1995. In announcing a mandatory life sentence for Amir, presiding judge Edmond Levy decries the 25-year-old former law student as someone who has "lost all semblance of humanity."		Bangladesh premier Khaleda Zia steps down from office and agrees to transfer power to a caretaker administration. Zia's action comes in response to unrelenting political violence throughout the country and a "noncooperation" campaign launched Mar. 9 by opposition parties that boycotted the February elections.
March 28		Allan Ford, Justin Fowler, and Geoffrey Pernell, three British soldiers stationed in Cyprus, are found guilty of kidnapping and killing Louise Jensen, a female Danish tour guide, in 1994.	Mohammed Sidqi Suleiman, 77, Egyptian prime minister under Pres. Gamal Abdel Nasser, 1966–67, dies in Cairo, Egypt, of unreported causes.	More than 100 people die when a ferry capsizes off the southwestern coast of Haiti.	A fire sweeps through a shopping mall in the city of Bogor, some 40 miles from Jakarta, Indonesia's capital city. The fire kills at least 78 people.... Shin Kanemaru, 81, deputy premier of Japan, 1986–87, and member of the Japanese Diet, 1958–92, dies in Shiranecho, Japan, of a stroke.
March 29	Leaders of the EU's 15 member states attend the launch of a year-long intergovernmental conference (IGC) in Turin, Italy.... Representatives from Russia, Belarus, Kazakhstan, and Kyrgyzstan sign a pact that commits them to increased economic cooperation.... The OECD admits Hungary as its 27th member and its second former communist state.	A court in Brescia, Italy, dismisses the third and final criminal charge against Antonio Di Pietro, who is considered one of Italy's most popular anticorruption magistrates.... The three British soldiers stationed in Cyprus who were found guilty on Mar. 28 of kidnapping and killing a female Danish tour guide are sentenced to life in prison for the murder, with additional sentences for abduction and conspiracy to rape.	The leaders of Sierra Leone's previous military government hand over power to Ahmad Tejan Kabbah who won a presidential runoff vote earlier in March. Tens of thousands of people crowd the streets of Freetown, Sierra Leone's capital, to celebrate Kabbah's swearing in.	The government and the Ontario Public Service Employees' Union (OPSEU) reach an agreement to end a five-week-old OPSEU strike.	
March 30			Israel's shelling of villages in south Lebanon kills two civilians, and Hezbollah retaliates with artillery attacks on northern Israel.	In Argentina, after a failed prison escape, some 1,000 inmates at the Sierra Chica maximum-security prison in the Buenos Aires province riot. They take a judge, Maria Malere, and her secretary hostage during negotiations mediated by the Malere.	In Bangladesh, Muhammad Habibur Rahman, a former chief justice, is sworn in as head of the interim government.... Police in Beijing disrupt a fund-raiser for Chinese orphans, barring best-selling Chinese-American author Amy Tan from giving a keynote speech. Police explain that the fund-raiser requires a permit. However, observers speculate the disruption is intended to quash potential public discussion of alleged abuses at China's state-run orphanages.
March 31		In a televised address, Russian president Boris Yeltsin unveils a plan to end the fighting in the breakaway Russian republic of Chechnya. He orders Russian troops stationed there to observe a unilateral cease-fire beginning at midnight local time.			

A	B	C	D	E
Includes developments that affect more than one world region, international organizations, and important meetings of major world leaders.	Includes all domestic and regional developments in Europe, including the Soviet Union, Turkey, Cyprus, and Malta.	Includes all domestic and regional developments in Africa and the Middle East, including Iraq and Iran and excluding Cyprus, Turkey, and Afghanistan.	Includes all domestic and regional developments in Latin America, the Caribbean, and Canada.	Includes all domestic and regional developments in Asia and Pacific nations, extending from Afghanistan through all the Pacific Island, except Hawaii.

U.S. Politics & Social Issues	U.S. Foreign Policy & Defense	U.S. Economy & Environment	Science, Technology, & Nature	Culture, Leisure, & Lifestyle	
Senate majority leader Robert Dole (R, Kans.) clinches the Republican presidential nomination after winning primaries in Washington, Nevada, and California.... Business leaders, governors, and education experts discuss strategies for improving the nation's school system at the second educational summit held in the U.S.... Edmund S(ixtus) Muskie, 81, governor of Maine, 1955–59, U.S. senator, 1959–80, and U.S. secretary of state, 1980–81, dies in Washington, D.C., after suffering a heart attack.	Marine Corps major general Carol Mutter is nominated for promotion to lieutenant general, a three-star general rank. No woman has ever attained that rank or its equivalent in the navy, vice admiral.... The INS states that immigrants abused by their spouses or parents may apply for legal residency without the sponsorship of their abusers. ...A Navy T-44 plunges into the Gulf of Mexico, killing the entire crew comprised of a Marine Corps flight instructor, a marine trainee, and a navy trainee.	The Interior Department partially opens the Glen Canyon Dam and begins a weeklong flooding of the Grand Canyon to stir up sediment and restore depleted beach areas in the canyon, which has not flooded since 1963, when the Glen Canyon Dam was built.... In *Barnett Bank v. Nelson*, the Supreme Court rules unanimously that federal law permits nationally chartered banks to sell insurance from branch offices in small towns, despite state laws that seek to prohibit them from doing so.	David Packard, 83, cofounder of the Hewlett-Packard Co. electronics and computer company, dies in Palo Alto, California, of pneumonia.		March 26
In *Seminole Tribe of Florida v. Florida*, the Supreme Court rules, 5-4, that the 1988 Indian Gaming Regulatory Act violates states' sovereignty rights granted under the Constitution's 11th Amendment. ... The House votes, 286-129, to give final congressional approval to a bill that will ban a particular abortion method used to end pregnancies in their late stages. It is the first attempt by Congress to ban an abortion procedure since 1973.		In the Senate, 19 Democrats join all but three Republicans to pass a so-called line-item veto bill that will give the president authority to veto certain parts of a spending bill without invalidating the entire measure.			March 27
The Tennessee Senate rejects legislation that would have allowed school boards to fire teachers who teach evolution as a scientific fact.	The DEA announces stricter controls on the export to Colombia of chemicals that can be used to process cocaine.	The House passes, 267-151, a health-insurance reform bill that will guarantee a right to continued coverage for people who lose, quit, or change their jobs.... The House, 328-91, and the Senate by unanimous consent pass a bill that raises the federal debt limit.... The Senate clears, 52-44, a $13 billion State Department authorization bill.... The House clears, 232-177, a so-called line-item veto bill..... The Senate passes, 74-26, a bill that will curtail many federal subsidies and price supports that benefit farmers.		The Central Conference of American Rabbis (CCAR) passes a resolution that endorses civil marriages for homosexuals. The CCAR represents some 1,750 rabbis from the Reform movement, the most liberal of the three main branches of Judaism.	March 28
The House Ethics Committee rules that Speaker Newt Gingrich (R, Ga.) violated House rules by allowing a telecommunications entrepreneur to work as a volunteer in his office. The panel imposes no punishment on Gingrich and does not advocate further investigation. ... The House approves, 259-159, a bill that will for the first time impose nationwide limits on punitive damages in product-liability suits.	U.S. district judge Emmet Sullivan prevents the navy from discharging Amy Barnes, a female sailor, for allegedly being homosexual.... In a separate case, U.S. judge Saundra Armstrong overturns the discharge of First Lieutenant Andrew Holmes for being homosexual and orders Holmes reinstated into the California Army National Guard.	The House passes, 318-89, a bill that will curtail many federal subsidies and price supports that benefit farmers.... Congress clears and Pres. Clinton signs the latest in a string of temporary spending bills to keep the federal government running. It is the 12th continuing resolution enacted for the current fiscal year.... Pres. Clinton signs a bill that raises the federal debt limit, narrowly avoiding a government loan default.			March 29
Richard Clark, a member of the Freemen organization involved in a standoff with FBI agents in Montana, surrenders peacefully to police about 100 miles (160 km) away from the farm, where other members of the group are holed up.				Rough Quest wins the Grand National steeplechase at Aintree racecourse in Liverpool, England.	March 30
	Sister Dianna Ortiz, a U.S. nun who was kidnapped, raped, and tortured in Guatemala in 1989, begins a silent vigil in Lafayette Park outside the White House in Washington, D.C. The vigil is intended to pressure the government to respond to her requests to release its files on the alleged involvement of U.S. intelligence agencies in her attack.		The U.S. space shuttle *Atlantis* touches down at Edwards Air Force Base, California, after docking with the Russian space station *Mir* and for the first time dropping off a U.S. astronaut for an extended stay on *Mir*. ... Hoiyan Wan, a 19-year-old U.S. college student, dies while participating in a medical experiment at the University of Rochester medical school.		March 31

F	G	H	I	J
Includes elections, federal-state relations, civil rights and liberties, crime, the judiciary, education, health care, poverty, urban affairs, and population.	Includes formation and debate of U.S. foreign and defense policies, veterans' affairs, and defense spending. (Relations with specific foreign countries are usually found under the region concerned.)	Includes business, labor, agriculture, taxation, transportation, consumer affairs, monetary and fiscal policy, natural resources, and pollution.	Includes worldwide scientific, medical, and technological developments; natural phenomena; U.S. weather; natural disasters; and accidents.	Includes the arts, religion, scholarship, communications media, sports, entertainments, fashions, fads, and social life.

	World Affairs	Europe	Africa & the Middle East	The Americas	Asia & the Pacific
April 1	Gen. Tihomir Blaskic, the only Bosnian Croat officer under indictment for war crimes has surrendered to the UN-sponsored tribunal investigating war crimes in Bosnia.	At least 28 Russian soldiers are killed, just after the cease-fire announced Mar. 31 takes effect, when their convoy is ambushed in the mountains of southern Chechnya, near the village of Vedeno.			
April 2	Russian president Boris Yeltsin and Pres. Aleksandr Lukashenko of Belarus sign a treaty that joins their respective former Soviet republics in a political and economic union called the Community of Sovereign Republics. Under the accord, the nations will continue to be independent, sovereign states, but they commit themselves to unspecified steps toward reintegration over the next several years.			At least 50,000 strikers riot in La Paz, Bolivia, throwing dynamite sticks at police and looting stores. . . . In Argentina, 30 prominent business and economic officials, including executives of IBM Argentina, a division of the U.S.-based IBM Corp., and former officials at Banco de la Nacion Argentina, a commercial bank owned by the government, are charged with fraud. . . . Peruvian premier Dante Cordova Blanco resigns amid disputes over the economic program.	
April 3		Despite Pres. Yeltsin's Mar. 31 call for a cease-fire, Russian troops continue to attack villages and suspected guerrilla strongholds throughout Chechnya. . . . A plane crashes in Croatia, killing 35 people. Among the dead is U.S. commerce secretary Ronald H. Brown. . . . Britain's parliament gives final approval to emergency legislation that will give police greater powers to search citizens under the Prevention of Terrorism Act.	U.S. defense secretary William Perry, in Cairo, states the U.S. will not permit Libya to complete an underground facility that the U.S. contends will be a chemical weapons factory. Libya maintains that the construction site is part of a water-irrigation system. . . . A South African judge sentences five white extremists to 26-year prison terms each for three bombings in 1994 that killed 21 people. The men are members of the right-wing AWB. Four suspects are acquitted, and five others are sentenced to terms ranging from three to six years.	Alberto Pandolfi is sworn in as Peru's premier.	
April 4		The *Royal Viking Sun*, a British luxury cruise liner with more than 500 passengers, hits a coral reef in the Red Sea. . . . Erich Priebke, a former Nazi special forces officer, is indicted in Rome for his alleged role in a massacre that took place in Italy during World War II. The forthcoming trial is widely expected to be the last in Italy involving Nazi war crimes.	The Constitutional Court, South Africa's highest judicial body, rules that schools cannot discriminate on the basis of language or religion, which are often cited as reasons for the exclusion of black students.	Reports reveal that the Bolivian government has ordered in troops to prevent more riots, which erupted Apr. 2 in La Paz. . . . Reports confirm that Vaughan Lewis has been sworn in as St. Lucia's new prime minister. . . . Argentina's justice ministry states that there have been riots in 18 prisons in four provinces and that inmates have taken control of five prisons since the Mar. 30 start of the ongoing Sierra Chica revolt.	North Korea declares that it will no longer maintain the demilitarized zone (DMZ) between North and South Korea. The DMZ was agreed to under the armistice that ended the Korean War in 1953.
April 5		Turkish soldiers renew an army offensive, reportedly after locating an army of up to 250 members of the separatist guerrilla group known as the Kurdistan Workers Party (PKK). . . . The *Royal Viking Sun*, a cruise liner that crashed Apr. 4, is towed to Sharm El-Sheikh, an Egyptian port on the southern tip of the Sinai peninsula. The 560 passengers, none of whom are injured, are evacuated.		Mark Vijay Chahal, 30, shoots and kills his estranged wife and eight members of her family at the wife's parents' home in Vernon, British Columbia. The gunman kills himself minutes later in a nearby hotel. The shooting is the second-worst multiple slaying in Canadian history.	North Korea violates the 1953 armistice when hundreds of North Korean troops stage military exercises in the demilitarized zone between North and South Korea. For several hours, some 130 armed North Korean troops enter the zone at the village of Panmunjom, where the armistice was signed. In response, South Korea raises its intelligence monitoring to its highest level in 14 years. . . . Reports state that Tibet is banning displays of photos of the Dalai Lama, the exiled leader of Tibetan Buddhists, in monasteries and in public areas.

A	B	C	D	E
Includes developments that affect more than one world region, international organizations, and important meetings of major world leaders.	Includes all domestic and regional developments in Europe, including the Soviet Union, Turkey, Cyprus, and Malta.	Includes all domestic and regional developments in Africa and the Middle East, including Iraq and Iran and excluding Cyprus, Turkey, and Afghanistan.	Includes all domestic and regional developments in Latin America, the Caribbean, and Canada.	Includes all domestic and regional developments in Asia and Pacific nations, extending from Afghanistan through all the Pacific Island, except Hawaii.

U.S. Politics & Social Issues	U.S. Foreign Policy & Defense	U.S. Economy & Environment	Science, Technology, & Nature	Culture, Leisure, & Lifestyle	
A TV news camera tapes two white Riverside County, California, sheriff's deputies beating two suspected Mexican illegal immigrants after an 80-mile (128-km) high-speed chase. The incident sparks protests from Hispanic and civil-rights groups, who argue that anti-immigrant rhetoric in the U.S. prompted the level of violence used against the two Mexicans, Enrique Funes Flores and Alicia Sotero Vasquez. . . . In New York City, Judge Harold Baer Jr. reverses his highly publicized decision to suppress evidence in a drug case because police did not have "probable cause" to conduct a search. Baer's initial ruling came under fire from members of Congress and from the White House.		In *O'Connor v. Consolidated Coin Caterers Corp.*, the Supreme Court rules unanimously that workers can sue for age discrimination even if they are replaced by individuals who are older than 40, the age at which workers are provided protection under the federal Age Discrimination in Employment Act of 1967. . . . Aetna Life and Casualty Co. reveals that it will purchase U.S. Healthcare Inc., which will make Aetna the U.S.'s largest company specializing in health insurance, with a total of 23 million policyholders, or one out of every 12 Americans.		*Primary Colors*, by Anonymous, is at the top of the bestseller list. . . . NFL star wide receiver Michael Irvin is indicted on two charges of possession of cocaine and marijuana.	April 1
	A Marine Corps F-18 fighter jet crashes in a desert region of southern California. The pilot ejects and suffers only minor cuts and bruises. . . . A Department of Defense study of 18,598 Persian Gulf war veterans finds no evidence of gulf war syndrome. . . . In response to the Apr. 1 taped attack on two Hispanics by the police, the Mexican government expresses its "indignation" at the "flagrant violation of human rights."			Data suggest that that the average salary for MLB players in 1996 was $1,176,967 per year, a 9.9% increase over 1995.	April 2
Police take into custody a former university professor, Theodore Kaczynski, who is suspected of being the Unabomber, a serial bomber linked to a series of bombing incidents spanning 17 years in which three men have been killed and 23 other people wounded. . . . Carl Burton Stokes, 68, mayor of Cleveland, Ohio, 1967–71, who was the first black American to become mayor of a major city and, in 1962, became the first black Democrat ever elected to the Ohio House of Representatives, dies in Cleveland of esophageal cancer.	*The New York Times* prints a letter signed by 15 retired U.S. generals and admirals from the Vietnam Veterans of America Foundation to Pres. Clinton that urges a ban on all land mines as militarily responsible.	The Dow closes at a record high of 5689.74, marking the 19th record high registered in 1996.			April 3
	Masahiro Tsuda, a former manager of Daiwa Bank Ltd., a Japanese commercial bank, pleads guilty to a U.S. federal charge that he helped cover up $1.1 billion in losses by a trader at the bank's New York offices. . . . Fugitive Venezuelan banker Orlando Castro Llanes is indicted in New York City on one count of conspiring to defraud more than $55 million from depositors in Banco Progreso Internacional de Puerto Rico.	In New York City, the U.S. Second Circuit Court of Appeals overturns a lower court's ruling when it finds that TV journalists and producers are "artistic professionals" and are therefore not entitled to earn overtime wages.		Barney Ewell (born Norwood H. Ewell), 78, record-breaking Olympic sprinter, dies in Lancaster, Pennsylvania, of complications from the partial amputation of his legs.	April 4
	The U.S. Fourth District Court of Appeals, 9-4, refuses to overturn the navy's dismissal of Lt. Paul G. Thomasson, a homosexual navy officer. In doing so, the court upholds the military's "don't ask, don't tell" policy, which bars the military from asking service members about their sexual orientation but permits it to discharge personnel based on their behavior or statements.	The EPA announces that Uniroyal Chemical Co. Inc. has agreed to stop selling the pesticide propargite for use on 10 different types of crops.			April 5

F	G	H	I	J
Includes elections, federal-state relations, civil rights and liberties, crime, the judiciary, education, health care, poverty, urban affairs, and population.	Includes formation and debate of U.S. foreign and defense policies, veterans' affairs, and defense spending. (Relations with specific foreign countries are usually found under the region concerned.)	Includes business, labor, agriculture, taxation, transportation, consumer affairs, monetary and fiscal policy, natural resources, and pollution.	Includes worldwide scientific, medical, and technological developments; natural phenomena; U.S. weather; natural disasters; and accidents.	Includes the arts, religion, scholarship, communications media, sports, entertainments, fashions, fads, and social life.

	World Affairs	Europe	Africa & the Middle East	The Americas	Asia & the Pacific
April 6			The Liberian Council of State orders that faction leader D. Roosevelt Johnson, who was recently fired as minister of rural development, be arrested on murder charges. The order sparks riots, which erupt into factional fighting. The violence, which observers call the worst in at least three years, breaks out despite the August 1995 peace plan to end the civil war.		Reports confirm that, in Bangladesh, Khaleda Zia and her main political rival, Awami League leader Sheik Hasina Wazed have separately appealed for an end to the political violence which has continued despite Zea's resignation.
April 7		Doku Zavgayev, the head of Chechnya's Russian-backed government, makes an unusual plea urging his Russian allies to ease their attacks, as shelling is killing or injuring scores of civilians.	The fighting that broke out Apr. 6 in Liberia spreads to Monrovia, the capital, where forces loyal to D. Roosevelt Johnson seize an army barracks and hold hostage members of a West African peacekeeping force and others, including Lebanese women and children.	An uprising started Mar. 30 by some 1,000 inmates at the Sierra Chica maximum-security prison in Buenos Aires province ends, and 17 hostages are released. Some 5,000 inmates at other jails across Argentina who revolted in sympathy with the Sierra Chica inmates surrender, releasing 10 more hostages. Officials call the revolts the worst in Argentina's history.	
April 8		Several hundred pro-unionist Protestant demonstrators clash with police in Northern Ireland, or Ulster, causing injuries to at least five people. The demonstration is part of Ulster's "marching season," during which sectarian groups hold a series of parades. . . . Turkish officials announce that 27 soldiers and 90 Kurdish rebels were killed in the Apr. 5 army offensive in the southeastern section of the country.		Twelve people die as a result of violence during a strike called for by the Revolutionary Armed Forces of Colombia (FARC) and two other leftist rebel groups. . . . Argentine officials reveal that seven prisoners at Sierra Chica, the site of the prison revolt that ended Apr. 7, are missing and believed dead.	
April 9			An explosion in the southern Lebanese village of Brashit kills a teenager and injures three other civilians, two of them children. Hezbollah, holding Israel responsible, fires rockets into Israel, wounding some 26 civilians. . . . U.S. forces begin evacuating the estimated 470 Americans and hundreds of other foreign nationals in Liberia.		
April 10		The UN arranges the release of 211 Bosnian Muslims who have been held in detention camps in Serbia since the siege of Zepa in July 1995.		A protester is shot to death during a clash between townspeople and armed police during a rally against the development of a golf course in Tepoztlan, a small town 30 miles (50 km) south of Mexico City, Mexico's capital. . . . In Para state, Brazil, 2,500 landless farmers begin a series of demonstrations.	The government of Australia's Northern Territory announces that voluntary euthanasia will be legal there as of July 1. . . . More than 3,000 Japanese who live near the U.S.'s Yokota air base file a lawsuit against the governments of the U.S. and Japan. The suit demands $30 million in damages stemming from noise from American jets and calls for a ban on their nighttime military flights. The suit is thought to be the first of its kind in Japan against the U.S. government.
April 11	Representatives of 43 African countries sign a treaty that bans nuclear arms from the continent. Similar nuclear-free zones have previously been established in other regions, including Latin America and the South Pacific.	A member of Spain's Civil Guard police force is killed when his helicopter crashes while in pursuit of alleged drug smugglers. . . . The Netherlands launches a program to slaughter 64,000 British cows imported into the country before the mad-cow disease scare. . . . Turkish officials state that 172 guerrillas and 33 soldiers have been killed in the fighting that started Apr. 5. . . . A fire at the Dusseldorf International Airport kills 16 people and injures more than 100 others.	Israel opens a large-scale military response against the Iranian-backed Shi'ite militants' shelling of Israel's northern settlements, dubbing it "Operation Grapes of Wrath."	Reports confirm that Susana Decibe has been appointed education minister, thereby becoming Argentina's first-ever female cabinet member.	A Singapore high court judge orders an American man, Christopher Lingle, to pay S$100,000 (US$71,000) in libel damages to former Singapore prime minister Lee Kuan Yew for 1994 articles that were critical of unidentified Asian governments and their judicial systems.

A	B	C	D	E
Includes developments that affect more than one world region, international organizations, and important meetings of major world leaders.	*Includes all domestic and regional developments in Europe, including the Soviet Union, Turkey, Cyprus, and Malta.*	*Includes all domestic and regional developments in Africa and the Middle East, including Iraq and Iran and excluding Cyprus, Turkey, and Afghanistan.*	*Includes all domestic and regional developments in Latin America, the Caribbean, and Canada.*	*Includes all domestic and regional developments in Asia and Pacific nations, extending from Afghanistan through all the Pacific Island, except Hawaii.*

U.S. Politics & Social Issues	U.S. Foreign Policy & Defense	U.S. Economy & Environment	Science, Technology, & Nature	Culture, Leisure, & Lifestyle	
Seven suspected Mexican illegal immigrants are killed and 18 others are injured when their bus overturns and crashes near Temecula, California. The truck crashes while it is being followed by U.S. Border Patrol agents, who claim they did not chase the truck when it suddenly accelerated.				Greer Garson, 92, actress who received seven Academy Award nominations and won an Oscar in 1942, dies in Dallas, Texas, after suffering from a heart ailment.	April 6
Some 6,000 people gather in Los Angeles to protest the Apr. 1 beatings of two suspected Mexican illegal immigrants by two white sheriff's deputies.				In Scottsdale, Arizona, Jack Nicklaus wins his 100th professional event, the Tradition Tournament on the senior circuit.	April 7
Georgia attorney general Michael Bowers asks the state's 34 government-sponsored colleges and universities to alter admissions policies that give preference to racial minorities. . . . A study shows that gunfire was the second leading cause of death in 1993 among Americans between the ages of 10 and 19.				Ben Johnson (born Francis Benjamin Johnson), 77, Academy Award-winning actor who appeared in several of director John Ford's westerns, dies in Mesa, Arizona, of an apparent heart attack.	April 8
Former representative Dan Rostenkowski (D, Ill.) pleads guilty to two counts of mail fraud as part of an agreement with federal prosecutors. In accordance with the plea-bargain deal, U.S. district judge Norma Johnson sentences Rostenkowski to 17 months in prison and fines him $100,000. . . . James W(ilson) Rouse, 81, developer who pioneered planned cities, urban marketplaces, and early shopping malls, dies in Columbia, Maryland, of ALS (Lou Gehrig's disease).	The U.S. government expels Ahmed Yousif Mohamed, a diplomat from Sudan's UN mission in New York City, arguing that he was linked to terrorist plots.	Pres. Clinton signs into law a bill giving himself and future presidents a line-item veto, which permits presidents to invalidate particular spending items contained in appropriations bills. . . . The EEOC files a lawsuit accusing Mitsubishi Motor Manufacturing of allowing widespread sexual harassment of female workers at a factory in Normal, Illinois.		Richard Thomas Condon, 81, bestselling novelist and political satirist, dies in Dallas, Texas, after suffering from heart and kidney ailments. . . . Columbia University announces the Pulitzer Prize winners, who include Jonathan Larson, Tina Rosenberg, George Walker, Jack Miles, and Richard Ford.	April 9
Pres. Clinton vetoes a bill that would have banned a particular abortion method used to end pregnancies in their later stages because it does not allow the procedure even in cases where the mother's health would otherwise be at risk. The bill would have been the first ban of an abortion procedure since 1973. . . . The California Supreme Court rules that landlords cannot refuse to rent to unmarried couples on the basis that such living arrangements violate their religious beliefs.		Reports indicate that more than 1,100 of the 1,700 graduate students attending the University of Michigan have walked off their jobs as teaching assistants as a result of a dispute with the university over wages and international students' pay.	The FDA warns consumers not to use products that contain the stimulant ephedrine and are often marketed as a "safe and natural" alternative to illegal drugs. . . . A study finds that alcoholics who smoke are more likely to die from the effects of cigarettes than from those of alcohol.		April 10
Seven-year-old Jessica Dubroff, while attempting to set a record for being the youngest person to pilot a plane across the U.S., crashes during a thunderstorm in Cheyenne, Wyoming. Also killed are Dubroff's flight instructor, Joe Reid, 52, and her father, Lloyd Dubroff, 57. The incident sparks debate on whether the girl should have been allowed to fly. . . . In the middle of the standoff that started Mar. 25 between the Freemen group and the FBI, two members, Agnes Stanton and her son, Ebert Stanton, surrender to the authorities.	A federal grand jury in Baltimore, Maryland, indicts two current and three former U.S. Naval Academy midshipmen on charges of orchestrating an elaborate scheme to steal automobiles.				April 11

F	G	H	I	J
Includes elections, federal-state relations, civil rights and liberties, crime, the judiciary, education, health care, poverty, urban affairs, and population.	Includes formation and debate of U.S. foreign and defense policies, veterans' affairs, and defense spending. (Relations with specific foreign countries are usually found under the region concerned.)	Includes business, labor, agriculture, taxation, transportation, consumer affairs, monetary and fiscal policy, natural resources, and pollution.	Includes worldwide scientific, medical, and technological developments; natural phenomena; U.S. weather; natural disasters; and accidents.	Includes the arts, religion, scholarship, communications media, sports, entertainments, fashions, fads, and social life.

	World Affairs	Europe	Africa & the Middle East	The Americas	Asia & the Pacific
April 12	An international pledging conference to aid the reconstruction of Bosnia-Herzegovina is held without the presence of representatives from the Bosnian Serb community, who refuse to join Muslims and Croats in a joint Bosnian delegation.		Widespread looting in Liberia prompts the withdrawal of most remaining international aid workers, including those with the Red Cross, the UN, and other groups. . . . Witnesses suggest that three Israeli helicopters conducted a rocket attack against a Syrian antiaircraft fortification near Beirut's international airport.	Lt. Col. Joseph Michel François, one of the three main leaders of the 1991 coup that ousted Pres. Jean-Bertrand Aristide, is arrested in the Dominican Republic. . . . After the Apr. 10 death of a protester, Mexico's Grupo KS cancels its plans to build a golf course in Tepoztlan, a small town 30 miles (50 km) south of Mexico City. In September 1995, the government suspended the project amid protests from residents that the golf course would damage the town's environment.	
April 13		George Mackay Brown, 74, Scottish poet and novelist whose writing centers around the culture of Scotland's Orkney Islands, dies in Kirkwall, Scotland, after suffering from cancer.	Israeli warships off the coast of Lebanon impose a virtual blockade on the country. Rockets from an Israeli helicopter gunship strike a Lebanese ambulance fleeing northward some 5 miles (8 km) south of the port city of Tyre. Six Lebanese civilians, including four children, are killed in the attack, and six others are injured. . . . Syria confirms that one of its soldiers was killed in the Apr. 12 incident.		
April 14		Ukrainian police capture a suspected serial killer, Anatoli Onoprienko, after a 3½ month manhunt.			A bomb explodes in the Shaukat Khanum Memorial Cancer Center in the city of Lahore, Pakistan, killing six people and wounding at least 25 others. More than 150 patients and relatives are in the center, Pakistan's only cancer hospital, at the time of the explosion. . . . Reports disclose that the Ministry of Public Security is requiring all Chinese users of the Internet and other international computer networks to register with the police.
April 15		About 6,000 Russian soldiers withdraw from northeastern Chechnya, in partial fulfillment of Pres. Yeltsin's March promise that forces will depart from "peaceful" areas of Chechnya. . . . Stavros Spyros Niarchos, 86, Greek tycoon best known for his rivalry with Aristotle Onassis in the shipping industry, dies in Zurich, Switzerland, after suffering a stroke.	In East London, South Africa's Truth and Reconciliation Commission opens its probe of human-rights abuses with its first public hearing, despite a bomb threat and legal challenges.	Leftist rebels ambush an army convoy near Colombia's border with Ecuador, killing 31 soldiers and injuring 18 others. The ambush is considered the worst rebel attack in at least three years.	The International Campaign for Tibet, a U.S.-based human-rights group, reports that the government of China has launched a crackdown on Buddhism in Tibet, which China considers a renegade province. . . . Representatives from the U.S. and Japan sign an agreement in Tokyo under which the whole or parts of 11 U.S. military installations in Okinawa will be returned to Japan within about seven years.
April 16		In one of the most damaging strikes against Russian forces in the 16-month-old war in Chechnya, more than 70 troops are killed when guerrillas ambush their convoy near the village of Yarysh-Mardy in the southern mountains. . . . Ukrainian police announced that Anatoli Onoprienko, captured on Apr. 14, has confessed to killing 52 people, including 10 children, during a six-year crime spree throughout Ukraine.	The Lebanese government states that at least 31 people have been killed since the Apr. 11 offensive started. They also assert that none of the dead were members of Hezbollah.		U.S. president Bill Clinton launches a visit to South Korea and Japan.
April 17		A bomb is detonated in West London, England. No one is injured in the blast, which causes minor property damage.		In Brazil, 100 Para state police arrive to disband 2,500 landless farmers blocking a highway near the town of Eldorado do Carajas as part of a series of demonstrations that started Apr. 10. Police open fire on the protesters, killing at least 19 people and injuring at least 50 others. . . . The last 82 U.S. soldiers in Haiti who are part of the UN peacekeeping force leave the country.	

A	B	C	D	E
Includes developments that affect more than one world region, international organizations, and important meetings of major world leaders.	Includes all domestic and regional developments in Europe, including the Soviet Union, Turkey, Cyprus, and Malta.	Includes all domestic and regional developments in Africa and the Middle East, including Iraq and Iran and excluding Cyprus, Turkey, and Afghanistan.	Includes all domestic and regional developments in Latin America, the Caribbean, and Canada.	Includes all domestic and regional developments in Asia and Pacific nations, extending from Afghanistan through all the Pacific Island, except Hawaii.

U.S. Politics & Social Issues	U.S. Foreign Policy & Defense	U.S. Economy & Environment	Science, Technology, & Nature	Culture, Leisure, & Lifestyle	
In a letter, Raul Yzaguirre, head of the National Council of La Raza, resigns from his post as chair of the President's Advisory Commission on Educational Excellence for Hispanic Americans. He argues that the 25-member group, created by then-President George Bush, is stymied by partisan politics.	Joseph H. Casey III, a senior midshipman at the Naval Academy, is sentenced to 20 months in prison for the possession, use, and distribution of illegal drugs.	Pres. Clinton names Trade Representative Mickey Kantor as the new head of the Commerce Department, succeeding Ronald H. Brown, who died Apr. 3 in a plane crash in Croatia. Clinton selects Charlene Barshefsky to replace Kantor on an acting basis. . . . Pres. Clinton vetoes a $13 billion State Department authorization bill.	The FDA approves the use of ultrasound equipment to determine whether lumps found in women's breasts are cancerous or benign. The new High-Definition Imaging equipment is the first ultrasound device powerful enough to show a clear picture of breast lumps. . . . Researchers report they have discovered a gene responsible for Werner's syndrome, a disorder that causes premature aging.		April 12
					April 13
Hundreds of people gather in Cheyenne, Wyoming, to commemorate the victims of the Apr. 11 crash of the plane piloted by seven-year-old Jessica Dubroff.		Data reveal that Pres. Clinton and his wife, First Lady Hillary Rodham Clinton, earned $316,074 and paid $75,437 in federal income taxes in 1995.		Nick Faldo of Great Britain wins the 60th Masters tournament at the Augusta (Georgia) National Golf Club in a stunning come-from-behind win over Greg Norman of Australia.	April 14
	Three crewmen are killed and a fourth is injured when two army helicopters crash at a training site in New Mexico.	Due to fears of BSE, or mad-cow disease, 21 states begin ordering the destruction of 113 British cows.	The FDA approves a two-drug combination of the antacid omeprazole with the antibiotic clarithromycin for use in curing and preventing the recurrence of duodenal ulcers. Clarithromycin is the first antibiotic backed for ulcer treatment.	Uta Pippig of Germany wins her record third straight women's title in the Boston Marathon, with a time of two hours, 27 minutes, and 12 seconds.	April 15
In *Cooper v. Oklahoma*, the Supreme Court rules unanimously that criminal defendants are not required to meet the exacting judicial standard of presenting "clear and convincing evidence" to prove their own mental incompetence or retardation. . . . Prosecutors charge Kathy Bush with child abuse for aggravating a digestive ailment that led her daughter, Jennifer Bush, eight, to be hospitalized 200 times and to undergo surgery 40 times, alleging that Kathy Bush suffers from Munchausen syndrome.	The superintendent of the U.S. Naval Academy in Annapolis, Maryland, orders a week-long cancellation of off-campus privileges for midshipmen in response to a spate of criminal charges against academy members.			The PEN/Faulkner Award for Fiction is awarded to author Richard Ford for *Independence Day*. Ford therefore becomes the first person to win both the PEN and the Pulitzer awards for the same novel.	April 16
A panel of three federal judges rules that Florida's black-majority Third District is unconstitutional on the grounds that the Florida legislature improperly used race as the chief criterion for determining the district's boundaries, and it orders that the district be redrawn.	The Justice Department reports that federal agents have arrested 1,176 foreign workers at more than 100 businesses in a campaign initiated Mar. 18 to halt employment of illegal aliens. . . . Two Marines who refused to supply DNA samples for a genetic registry—Lance Corporal John Mayfield III and Corporal Joseph Vlacovsky—are found guilty of disobeying a lawful order and sentenced to one week's confinement. . . . The Senate passes, 91-8, a weakened version of a compromise antiterrorism bill.	The Senate votes to reactivate the panel investigating the Whitewater affair, ending a seven-week standoff over extending the committee's authority. . . . Arnold Neustadter, 85, inventor of the popular Rolodex card file who sold his Zephyr American Corp. to Insilco Corp. in 1961, dies in New York City, after suffering several strokes.		Baylor University in Waco, Texas, the largest university in the world affiliated with the Baptist church, holds an on-campus dance for the first time in its 151-year history.	April 17

F	G	H	I	J
Includes elections, federal-state relations, civil rights and liberties, crime, the judiciary, education, health care, poverty, urban affairs, and population.	Includes formation and debate of U.S. foreign and defense policies, veterans' affairs, and defense spending. (Relations with specific foreign countries are usually found under the region concerned.)	Includes business, labor, agriculture, taxation, transportation, consumer affairs, monetary and fiscal policy, natural resources, and pollution.	Includes worldwide scientific, medical, and technological developments; natural phenomena; U.S. weather; natural disasters; and accidents.	Includes the arts, religion, scholarship, communications media, sports, entertainments, fashions, fads, and social life.

	World Affairs	Europe	Africa & the Middle East	The Americas	Asia & the Pacific
April 18		Boleslavs Maikovskis, 92, Latvian police officer during World War II who was later accused of war crimes in connection with the execution of 200 Latvian civilians dies in Munster, Germany, of a heart attack.	The Israeli army fires artillery shells at a UN camp housing hundreds of Lebanese refugees near Tyre, killing at least 107 civilians and wounding more than 100. The attacks bring the death toll to date to about 150. . . . Factional strife in Liberia ebbs with the announcement of a cease-fire. . . . Gunmen spray bullets into a crowd of Greek tourists in Cairo, Egypt, killing 18 people and wounding at least 15 others. The attack is the deadliest in the four years. . . . In the Central African Republic city of Bangui, about 400 mutinous soldiers rebel to demand back pay.	A videotape of the Apr. 17 killings in Brazil suggest that police began shooting at the protestors on arrival at the scene, sparking outrage across the nation.	Bill Clinton becomes the second U.S. president to address the Japanese Diet.
April 19	Leaders of the Group of Seven (G-7) nations meet in Moscow in a special summit hosted by Russian president Boris Yeltsin.	A speaker for the UN High Commissioner for Refugees states that 90% of requests made by Bosnians to cross from areas of Bosnia that are controlled by one ethnic group to another area have been denied.			
April 20			The Gamaa al-Islamiya (Islamic Group), claims responsibility for the Apr. 18 shooting in suburban Cairo, Egypt. Reports suggest that 1,500 people have been arrested since the attack during a sweep of three shantytown districts of Cairo for Muslim fundamentalist suspects. . . . U.S. ships carrying some 1,500 marines arrive off the coast of Monrovia, the capital of Liberia.	The Bolivian Workers Confederation, an umbrella labor organization that represents most of Bolivia's public-sector employees, signs an agreement with the government ending the general strike that began Mar. 18.	General Tran Van Tra, 77, Vietnamese army general who was instrumental in launching the Tet offensive during the Vietnam War, dies in Ho Chi Minh City, Vietnam, after suffering from a long illness.
April 21		Although it is not immediately confirmed, Chechnya's Pres. Dzhokhar Dudayev is slain in a rocket attack by Russian troops near the village of Gekhi-Chu. . . . A center-left alliance known as the Olive Tree coalition emerges as the largest bloc in Italy's upper and lower parliamentary houses in general elections. . . . Robert Hersant, 76, politician and publisher who controlled France's largest media company, the Hersant Group, dies in Saint-Cloud, France, after suffering from a long illness.	In the Central African Republic city of Bangui, the 400 mutinous soldiers who rebelled on Apr. 18 are offered amnesty and agree to return to their barracks. About a dozen people, half of them civilians, are reported killed in the fighting between the mutinous soldiers and the loyalist presidential guard. . . . A West African peacekeeping force, ECOMOG, begins to reassert control around Monrovia, the capital of Liberia.		
April 22		A Polish military prosecutor finds "no direct proof" that former Polish premier Jozef Oleksy was a Russian spy. . . . Eurotunnel PLC, the company that runs the Channel Tunnel between France and Britain, announces losses of £925 million ($1.4 billion) in 1995. Those losses during the Channel Tunnel's first full year of operation are much worse than predicted and are among the highest ever recorded in British corporate history.	Saudi authorities announce the arrest of four Saudi men in connection with the November 1995 bombings.	In Paraguay, Gen. Lino Cesar Oviedo refuses a presidential order to resign as army chief, threatening the possibility of a military coup. . . . Lt. Col. Joseph Michel François, who was arrested Apr. 12, is ordered to leave the Dominican Republic and finds political asylum in Honduras. Franck Romain, who was mayor of Port-au-Prince, Haiti's capital, in the 1980s under President Jean-Claude Duvalier, also is granted political asylum in Honduras.	A judge in the Australian state of Tasmania rules that a child developed from a frozen embryo has the right to inherit his father's estate, even if the embryo was implanted in the mother's womb after the father died. Based on the ruling, Tasmania will become one of the few places in the world where the legal inheritance rights of frozen embryos are acknowledged.
April 23	The EU confirms that an international ban on the sale of British beef will remain in place until Britain takes concrete measures to assure the safety of its beef products. . . . When discussing the Palestine Liberation Front's 1985 hijacking of the Italian ship *Achille Lauro*, Mohammed Abul Abbas, known as Abu Abbas, describes events surrounding his faction's violence as "a mistake." The incident, in which Leon Klinghoffer, an elderly wheelchair-bound U.S. Jew, was killed sparked international outrage.	A forest fire destroys the deserted village of Tovstiy Lis, Ukraine, 14 miles (22 km) west of the Chernobyl nuclear power plant.	Sierra Leone's government and rebel forces agree to a cease-fire and peace negotiations aimed at ending the country's five-year-old civil war. . . . Hundreds of Egyptian policemen stage a dawn raid on a village in southern Egypt in an effort to apprehend militants who they believe were involved in the Apr. 18 shooting. In an exchange of gunfire during the raid, two Muslim militants and four police officers are killed.	Mexico's Supreme Court finds that Ruben Figueroa Alcocer, the former governor of the state of Guerrero, and seven state officials took part in a cover-up of a June 1995 massacre by police of 17 peasants on their way to an antigovernment rally. The court also finds that Figueroa violated the peasants' civil rights by ordering the police to prevent them from attending the rally. . . . In Paraguay, Pres. Wasmosy announces that Gen. Lino Cesar Oviedo, who refused to step down Apr. 22, will be named defense minister, in return for Oviedo's resignation, prompting protests in Asuncion.	

A	B	C	D	E
Includes developments that affect more than one world region, international organizations, and important meetings of major world leaders.	*Includes all domestic and regional developments in Europe, including the Soviet Union, Turkey, Cyprus, and Malta.*	*Includes all domestic and regional developments in Africa and the Middle East, including Iraq and Iran and excluding Cyprus, Turkey, and Afghanistan.*	*Includes all domestic and regional developments in Latin America, the Caribbean, and Canada.*	*Includes all domestic and regional developments in Asia and Pacific nations, extending from Afghanistan through all the Pacific Island, except Hawaii.*

U.S. Politics & Social Issues	U.S. Foreign Policy & Defense	U.S. Economy & Environment	Science, Technology, & Nature	Culture, Leisure, & Lifestyle	
A federal judge in Los Angeles, California, sentences former representative Walter Tucker III (D, Calif.) to 27 months in prison for extortion and income-tax evasion. . . . Ronald Norwood Davies, 91, federal judge who issued a landmark decision ordering public schools in Little Rock, Arkansas, to integrate their white and black students, dies in Fargo, North Dakota, of unreported causes.	The House passes, 293-133, a weakened compromise version of an antiterrorism bill. . . . The U.S. administration dismisses Timothy Connolly, a Pentagon official who publicly questioned the military's opposition to banning land mines.				April 18
Thousands of mourners participate in a memorial service at the site of a 1995 bombing attack on a federal building in Oklahoma City, Oklahoma, on the anniversary of the explosion. . . . A federal appeals court in New Orleans, Louisiana, grants a stay blocking enforcement of a ruling that orders the Texas state university system to end race-based admissions policies.					April 19
A study finds that the regular use of child care provided by someone other than the child's mother does not harm the emotional bond between mother and child. Non-maternal child care may further undermine the maternal attachment if the mother has been insensitive to the child's needs, however.			Florida becomes the first state to ban products containing ephedrine.	Christopher Robin Milne, 75, who inspired the Christopher Robin character in the *Winnie the Pooh* books written by his father, A. A. Milne, dies of unreported causes.	April 20
		Senate majority leader Robert J. Dole (R, Kans.), asks the FEC to investigate allegations that Aqua-Leisure Industries, a sporting goods company, made illegal contributions to his campaign fund.		The British Academy of Film and Television Arts names *Sense and Sensibility* as best film and *The Madness of King George* as best British film. . . . Jimmy (the Greek) Snyder (born Demetrios Georgios Synodinos), 76, sports commentator who was fired in 1988 after making racist remarks, dies in Las Vegas, Nevada, of heart failure.	April 21
The Chicago Housing Authority (CHA) announces it has reached a settlement with Hispanic groups in a discrimination suit filed when the CHA did not provide Spanish-language instructions on forms. . . . Citing new evidence, Rep. George Miller (D, Calif.) files a new ethics complaint against House Speaker Newt Gingrich (R, Ga.) regarding allegations that a volunteer in Gingrich's office improperly advised the speaker on telecommunications legislation.	The FBI arrests Kurt G. Lessenthien, a U.S. Navy machinist, in Orlando, Florida, on charges of military espionage.	NYNEX Corp. and Bell Atlantic Corp., two of the seven "Baby Bell" telephone companies, announce that they will merge in a deal valued at $23 billion, based on the value of NYNEX stock. The deal will be the largest merger ever in the telecommunications industry and one of the largest corporate mergers in history.	A notorious computer hacker accused of stealing thousands of data files and credit-card numbers from computer systems, Kevin Mitnick, reaches a plea agreement with federal prosecutors in which 23 federal counts of computer fraud are dropped in exchange for Mitnick's admission to possession of stolen cellular telephone devices and violation of his probation, which stems from an earlier computer break-in conviction.	Erma Louise Bombeck, 69, humorist and writer whose column was published in as many as 600 newspapers, dies in San Francisco, California, of complications after kidney surgery.	April 22
U.S. district judge Joseph Tauro announces that the city of Boston, Massachusetts, has agreed to a $1 million settlement with the widow of Rev. Accelyne Williams, a black minister who died of heart failure after a 1994 mistaken drug raid on his apartment. . . . A jury in New York City orders Bernhard Goetz, the "subway vigilante," to pay $43 million in damages to Darrell Cabey, one of four black men he shot in 1984. . . . In *Markman v. Westview Instruments Inc.*, the Supreme Court rules unanimously that a judge's definition of what constitutes a patent takes precedence over that offered by a jury.		The Senate votes, 100-0, to pass a health-insurance reform bill that will guarantee continued health insurance coverage to people who lose, quit, or change their jobs. . . . Government data shows that Medicare's Hospital Insurance Trust Fund lost $4.2 billion in the first half of fiscal 1996. . . . The Commerce Department reports that in February the U.S. recorded a seasonally adjusted $8.19 billion deficit in trade in goods and services. That figure is down substantially from the revised deficit of $9.88 billion in January.		P(amela) L(yndon) Travers (born Helen Lyndon Goff), 96, British writer who created the popular children's book character Mary Poppins, dies in London, England, of unreported causes.	April 23

F	G	H	I	J
Includes elections, federal-state relations, civil rights and liberties, crime, the judiciary, education, health care, poverty, urban affairs, and population.	Includes formation and debate of U.S. foreign and defense policies, veterans' affairs, and defense spending. (Relations with specific foreign countries are usually found under the region concerned.)	Includes business, labor, agriculture, taxation, transportation, consumer affairs, monetary and fiscal policy, natural resources, and pollution.	Includes worldwide scientific, medical, and technological developments; natural phenomena; U.S. weather; natural disasters; and accidents.	Includes the arts, religion, scholarship, communications media, sports, entertainments, fashions, fads, and social life.

	World Affairs	Europe	Africa & the Middle East	The Americas	Asia & the Pacific
April 24	Bosnian Serb general Djordje Djukic is released for medical reasons from the custody of the international tribunal investigating war crimes in Bosnia on the condition that he return to The Hague to face charges if his health improves.... In response to the Apr. 23 EU announcement, British officials approve a selective slaughter plan intended to rid the country of so-called mad-cow disease.	Chechen vice president Zelimkhan Yandarbiyev reveals that he has succeeded Dzhokhar Dudayev as the rebels' leader.... The detonators on two bombs under London's Hammersmith Bridge explode, but the bombs themselves do not ignite.... Three trade unions representing French doctors strike to protest the government's plan on health-care reform.... Turkey's parliament approves the creation of a panel to investigate corruption charges against former premier Tansu Ciller.	The Palestine National Council (PNC), overwhelmingly rescinds clauses in its charter calling for the destruction of Israel and the waging of guerrilla warfare against the Jewish state. The vote fulfils a pledge that Yasser Arafat made in September 1995 on behalf of the PLO in a second-stage peace accord with Israel.	Thousands of protestors take to the streets of Asuncion, the capital of Paraguay, to protest Pres. Wasmosy's Apr. 23 decision regarding Oviedo.... Waterhen chief Harvey Nepinak and his supporters, accused of corruption and the embezzlement of more than C$1 million (US$730,000) from the tribe's accounts, flee the Waterhen Indian reservation, 300 miles (500 km) northwest of Winnipeg, Manitoba, Canada.	
April 25	Russian president Boris Yeltsin and Chinese president Jiang Zemin sign a number of agreements as part of what the two sides term a "strategic partnership."			Paraguay's president Juan Carlos Wasmosy announces he has reversed his decision to appoint former army commander Gen. Lino Cesar Oviedo as defense minister, thereby ending what is considered to be the country's worst constitutional crisis since a democratic government replaced a military dictatorship in 1989.... Prisoners at Headingley Correctional Institution, a prison in the province of Manitoba, Canada, begin to riot.	
April 26	Leaders from Russia, China, Kazakhstan, Kyrgyzstan, and Tajikistan sign a nonaggression pact.	Commercial bank creditors of the former Yugoslavia reach an agreement under which Croatia will be assigned 29.5% of the total $4.4 billion debt of the former Yugoslavia. ...The 10th anniversary of the 1986 Chernobyl nuclear disaster is marked by a candlelight vigil in Slavutych, Ukraine, 42 miles northeast of the plant.... The IRA takes responsibility for the two bombs placed under London's Hammersmith Bridge on Apr. 24.... Kidnapped German millionaire Jan Philipp Reemtsma is freed by his captors in exchange for $20 million, the largest ransom ever paid in Germany.	Israel and Lebanon agree to a cease-fire pact ending the Israeli bombardment of Lebanon that started Apr. 11 and the series of rocket volleys that Hezbollah guerrillas directed against northern Israel. Data indicates that during the violence, more than 150 Lebanese, almost all of them civilians, were killed.... The value of South Africa's currency, the rand, reaches an all-time low of 4.58 to the U.S. dollar.	The riot started Apr. 25 at the Headingley Correctional Institution in Manitoba ends. Seven guards and 30 inmates were injured in the clashes.	
April 27					
April 28					A gunman opens fire in Port Arthur, a town in Australia's island state of Tasmania, touching off a murderous rampage that results in 35 deaths. The incident, characterized as the worst massacre in Australia's history, also leaves 18 people injured.
April 29			Strife in Monrovia, the capital of Liberia, renews, marking the failure of a cease-fire reached on Apr. 18.	In Canada, one woman is slightly injured when a parcel bomb mailed to the Calgary Jewish Centre short-circuits and fails to explode with full force.	Police apprehend Martin Bryant, suspected of committing the Apr. 28 murders in Port Arthur, a town in Australia's island state of Tasmania.

A	B	C	D	E
Includes developments that affect more than one world region, international organizations, and important meetings of major world leaders.	*Includes all domestic and regional developments in Europe, including the Soviet Union, Turkey, Cyprus, and Malta.*	*Includes all domestic and regional developments in Africa and the Middle East, including Iraq and Iran and excluding Cyprus, Turkey, and Afghanistan.*	*Includes all domestic and regional developments in Latin America, the Caribbean, and Canada.*	*Includes all domestic and regional developments in Asia and Pacific nations, extending from Afghanistan through all the Pacific Island, except Hawaii.*

U.S. Politics & Social Issues	U.S. Foreign Policy & Defense	U.S. Economy & Environment	Science, Technology, & Nature	Culture, Leisure, & Lifestyle	
	Pres. Clinton signs an antiterrorism bill, despite the fact that it excludes or weakens several provisions that he proposed to combat terrorism.	Congress approves and Pres. Clinton signs a one-day stopgap measure. The stopgap bill is the 13th enacted since October 1995.... The management of the *Detroit Free Press* declares an impasse in a 10-month-old strike by its editorial employees.	A major fire is ignited near Bandelier National Monument in New Mexico.		April 24
Wisconsin governor Tommy Thompson (R) signs a bill that will end the distribution of welfare payments in that state starting in 1997. The bill, called Wisconsin Works, will replace the payments with work programs, child-care assistance, and subsidies. Observers characterize the legislation as the most dramatic overhaul of welfare policy approved in the U.S. in several decades.		The House, 399-25, and the Senate, 88-11, approve a $159.4 billion Omnibus Spending bill to provide funding for nine departments and dozens of federal agencies. The bill's passage ends a struggle over discretionary spending for fiscal 1996 that started Oct. 1, 1995.... Ford Motor Co. announces it will recall 8.7 million cars and trucks to replace ignition switches that may cause the vehicles to catch fire. The recall is the largest ever initiated by a single automobile maker.	Data show that the offspring of families living in areas affected by the Chernobyl disaster, including children born after the accident, have inherited genetic damage from their parents.... A study finds that women who eat diets rich in vitamin E are 62% less likely to die of heart disease.		April 25
		Pres. Clinton signs the omnibus spending bill that authorizes funding for nine cabinet-level departments and 38 agencies. The Congressional Budget Office indicates that non-defense-related discretionary spending in fiscal 1996 will decrease to $223.8 billion from $246.1 billion in the previous year.		Sotheby's closes its auction of items owned by Jacqueline Kennedy Onassis. The sale earns a total of $34.5 million, well above Sotheby's preliminary estimate..... Stirling Dale Silliphant, 78, Academy Award-winning screenwriter, dies in Bangkok, Thailand, of prostate cancer.... Olympic gold medalists Nadia Comaneci and Bart Conner get married in Bucharest, Romania.	April 26
Stewart Douglas Waterhouse, a sympathizer with the members of an antitax group known as the Freemen who have been engaged in a siege with FBI agents since March outside of Jordan, Montana, surrenders.	William Egan Colby, 76, CIA director, 1973–76, who was in charge of Operation Phoenix, a Vietnam War program under which 20,000 Vietnamese people were killed, apparently including many innocent civilians, disappears, sparking a highly publicized search.				April 27
		Pres. Clinton delivers three and a half hours of testimony in the fraud trial of his former Whitewater business partners, James McDougal and Susan McDougal, and Arkansas governor Jim Guy Tucker (D).... Pres. Clinton gives final approval to lifting a ban on the export of oil from Alaska's North Slope.			April 28
In *Janklow v. Planned Parenthood*, the Supreme Court refuses to hear an appeal from the state of South Dakota challenging a nullification of its law that requires teenage girls seeking abortions to notify their parents at least 48 hours before undergoing the procedure. In refusing the case, the justices let stand a decision by the U.S. 8th Circuit Court of Appeals in St. Louis, Missouri, that declared the South Dakota law unconstitutional.... In *Carlisle v. U.S.*, the Supreme Court rules, 7-2, that a federal district court in Michigan exceeded its authority when it set aside a jury's conviction in a criminal case.		Pres. Clinton announces he has approved the sale of some 12 million barrels of oil from the government's Strategic Petroleum Reserve in an effort to curb rising gasoline prices.	The FDA approves a new drug, called dexfenfluramine, used in the treatment of obesity. The FDA approval is the first for an antiobesity drug in 22 years.	Reports confirm that José Rafael Moneo is the first Spaniard to receive the annual Pritzker Architecture Prize for lifetime achievement.	April 29

F	G	H	I	J
Includes elections, federal-state relations, civil rights and liberties, crime, the judiciary, education, health care, poverty, urban affairs, and population.	Includes formation and debate of U.S. foreign and defense policies, veterans' affairs, and defense spending. (Relations with specific foreign countries are usually found under the region concerned.)	Includes business, labor, agriculture, taxation, transportation, consumer affairs, monetary and fiscal policy, natural resources, and pollution.	Includes worldwide scientific, medical, and technological developments; natural phenomena; U.S. weather; natural disasters; and accidents.	Includes the arts, religion, scholarship, communications media, sports, entertainments, fashions, fads, and social life.

	World Affairs	Europe	Africa & the Middle East	The Americas	Asia & the Pacific
April 30	Trade representatives from 53 nations agree to extend, until early 1997, talks aimed at easing restrictions on the global telecommunications market.	Justice Eduardo Moner of the Spanish Supreme Court rules that there is no firm evidence linking outgoing premier Felipe González to the killings of 27 supposed Basque nationalists by government "death squads" during the 1980s.	U.S. Marines open fire on Liberian fighters near the U.S. embassy compound, killing three and injuring at least one, after the embassy comes under fire.... U.S. president Bill Clinton and Israeli prime minister Shimon Peres sign an antiterrorism agreement that formally commits the U.S. and Israel to cooperate in enhancing their bilateral security.	Marcos Vinicius Borges Emmanuel, a former state police officer, is convicted of murder and sentenced to 309 years in prison for his part in a July 1993 massacre of eight homeless youths in Rio de Janeiro, Brazil's capital. The trial and harsh sentence are seen as a victory by human-rights advocates.	
May 1				Some 200,000 union members march in a May Day parade in Mexico City, Mexico's capital, despite the official cancellation of the annual event by Fidel Velazquez Sanchez, the leader of the government-allied Confederation of Mexican Workers.... Canadian deputy prime minister Sheila Copps resigns in the face of public pressure to abide by her 1993 campaign promise to quit if the Liberal Party did not repeal Canada's 7% goods and services tax.	
May 2		Swiss banking officials and Jewish leaders sign an agreement to search for funds deposited in Swiss banks during World War II by victims of the Nazi Holocaust.... Albania's first stock market open in Tirana, the capital.			
May 3	Delegates from 55 UN member states approve a treaty revision that extends existing limits on the use of land mines.	Reports confirm that Hazim Delic, and Esad Landzo, two Bosnian Muslim officials at the Celebici camp who have been charged by the war crimes tribunal at The Hague, are being detained by the Bosnian government.		Orlando Vasquez Velasquez, Colombia's attorney general, surrenders to authorities in Bogota, Colombia's capital, to face charges that he accepted money from the Cali drug cartel.	
May 4		The Spanish parliament approves Jose Maria Aznar, the leader of the center-right Popular Party (PP), as Spain's new premier.... General Jean Crepin, 87, commander of NATO forces in central Europe, 1963–66, dies in Seine-et-Marne, France, of unreported causes.			
May 5		Reports confirm that Kazakhstan authorities have detained two men for possession of more than 220 pounds (100 kg) of uranium-235, which could have been used as fuel for nuclear reactors or atomic bombs.... Voters in the central German state of Brandenburg reject a plan to unite with the neighboring city of Berlin. The vote is viewed as a victory for the former East German Communist Party, which had strongly opposed the proposal.... King Juan Carlos of Spain swears in Jose Maria Aznar to succeed Felipe Gonzalez, who has been premier since 1982.	In Bahrain, suspected Shi'ite activists set off nine bombs simultaneously in Manama, the capital, in homage to Isa Ahmed Hassan Qambar, a dissident who was executed Mar. 26.... Heavy fighting continues in Liberia.		

A	B	C	D	E
Includes developments that affect more than one world region, international organizations, and important meetings of major world leaders.	Includes all domestic and regional developments in Europe, including the Soviet Union, Turkey, Cyprus, and Malta.	Includes all domestic and regional developments in Africa and the Middle East, including Iraq and Iran and excluding Cyprus, Turkey, and Afghanistan.	Includes all domestic and regional developments in Latin America, the Caribbean, and Canada.	Includes all domestic and regional developments in Asia and Pacific nations, extending from Afghanistan through all the Pacific Island, except Hawaii.

U.S. Politics & Social Issues	U.S. Foreign Policy & Defense	U.S. Economy & Environment	Science, Technology, & Nature	Culture, Leisure, & Lifestyle	
	The State Department finds that the number of international terrorist attacks increased in 1995 from the previous year, although the number of casualties caused by those attacks decreased. There were 440 international terrorism attacks in 1995, up from 322 in 1994. Of those attacks, 99 were against U.S. interests, up from 66 in 1994. (The report does not include U.S. domestic attacks.) The report names the same seven countries as it had in 1995 to be sponsors of international terrorism: Cuba, Iran, Iraq, Libya, North Korea, Sudan, and Syria.	The Conference Board reports that its index of consumer confidence rose to 105.3 in April, from a revised level of 98.4 in March. The April figure marks the index's highest reading in almost six years. . . . The House fails to override Pres. Clinton's veto of a $13 billion State Department authorization bill. The vote is 234 to 188, 48 votes short of the two-thirds needed.			April 30
The House passes, 402-4, legislation that renews the federal program that provides money for state and local governments to care for people with AIDS or infected with HIV, the virus that causes AIDS. . . . Herbert Brownell Jr., 92, U.S. attorney general under Pres. Dwight Eisenhower, 1953–57, who was credited with engineering Eisenhower's victory in 1952, dies in New York City of cancer.		More than 5,000 truckers who service the ports of Los Angeles and Long Beach, California, begin a work stoppage that causes port-related trucking activity to plummet by between 50% and 90%.			May 1
Atty. Gen. Janet Reno announces the dismantling of a cocaine ring that resulted in the arrests of at least 130 people across the U.S. . . . The Senate, by voice vote, gives final congressional approval to legislation that renews the federal program that provides money to care for people with AIDS or infected with HIV. . . . Pres. Clinton vetoes a bill that would have set limits on the awarding of punitive damages in product-liability lawsuits.	The Board of Immigration Appeals holds a hearing to determine whether a Togolese woman, Fauziya Kasinga, 19, who fled her country because of the threat of forcible genital mutilation, should be granted political asylum in the U.S. Kasinga's story of her ordeal while in detention at Esmor and in prison has received much attention. . . . The Senate votes, 97-3, in favor of a bill that will impose tighter restrictions on illegal immigration to the U.S.	A grand jury in Washington, D.C., indicts Joseph P. Waldholtz, the estranged husband of Rep. Enid Greene (R, Utah), on 27 counts of bank fraud for a check-kiting scheme that generated $2.9 million in worthless checks.			May 2
	The White House confirms that prominent Chinese dissident Liu Gang has been admitted to the U.S. after escaping from China.			Timothy Edward Gullikson, 44, tennis player and coach who, with his identical twin brother Tom, won 10 titles as doubles partners during the 1970s and 1980s, dies in Wheaton, Illinois, of brain cancer.	May 3
Pres. Clinton announces that he will require states to deny welfare benefits to teenage mothers who do not attend school. . . . Reports confirm that former employees and patrons have filed a racial discrimination suit against Motel 6, one of the largest motel chains in the U.S.			A fire that has scorched 61,000 acres of the Tonto National Forest in central Arizona is brought under control.	Grindstone wins the 122nd running of the Kentucky Derby at Churchill Downs in Louisville, Kentucky.	May 4
The FBI reveals that overall serious crimes reported to the police decreased by 2% in 1995, compared with 1994. It is the fourth consecutive year that serious crimes have dropped in the U.S.			A wildfire starts from a trash fire in San Cristobal, New Mexico, which forces 2,000 residents of the villages of La Lama, Red River, and Questa to evacuate their homes.	Marge Schott, owner of baseball's Cincinnati Reds, causes an uproar when she says of Adolf Hitler, "Everybody knows he was good at the beginning but he just went too far," during an interview with ESPN.	May 5

F	G	H	I	J
Includes elections, federal-state relations, civil rights and liberties, crime, the judiciary, education, health care, poverty, urban affairs, and population.	*Includes formation and debate of U.S. foreign and defense policies, veterans' affairs, and defense spending. (Relations with specific foreign countries are usually found under the region concerned.)*	*Includes business, labor, agriculture, taxation, transportation, consumer affairs, monetary and fiscal policy, natural resources, and pollution.*	*Includes worldwide scientific, medical, and technological developments; natural phenomena; U.S. weather; natural disasters; and accidents.*	*Includes the arts, religion, scholarship, communications media, sports, entertainments, fashions, fads, and social life.*

	World Affairs	Europe	Africa & the Middle East	The Americas	Asia & the Pacific
May 6		Officials of Russia's domestic intelligence service, the Federal Security Service (FSB), disclose they have arrested a Russian citizen on charges of spying for Great Britain. . . . Cardinal Leo Jozef Suenens, 91, archbishop of Malines-Brussels, Belgium, 1962–79, who was an influential participant in the Second Vatican Council in the 1960s, dies in Brussels of unreported causes.	Charles Taylor, leader of one of the fighting factions in Liberia, announces a unilateral cease-fire to take effect, but fighting continues as U.S. troops and Liberian faction fighters exchange fire.	Representatives of the Guatemalan government and the rebel Guatemalan National Revolutionary Union (UNRG) sign a peace accord that brings the two sides closer to ending the country's 35-year-old civil war. The last Guatemalan peace accord was signed in March 1995. . . . A U.S. delegation attends the 13th annual meeting of the U.S.-Mexico Binational Commission, held in Mexico City, Mexico's capital.	
May 7	A UN-sponsored report contends that an Israeli artillery barrage that killed more than 100 civilians at a UN base in southern Lebanon on Apr. 18 did not appear to be accidental. . . . The trial of Dusan Tadic, a Bosnian Serb accused of torturing, raping, and killing Bosnian Muslims at three prison camps in Bosnia-Herzegovina, opens at the International Criminal Tribunal in The Hague, the Netherlands. The trial is the first to be held by the tribunal, which was set up in 1993.	The highway between Zagreb and Belgrade reopens to international traffic only. The 360-mile-long oil pipeline between the Croatian port of Rijeka on the Adriatic Sea and Pancevo also reopens. . . . Officials of Russia's Federal Security Service (FSB) link nine unidentified British diplomats to the spy arrested May 6 and threaten to expel them. Separately, the FSB reveals that a nuclear scientist was arrested for smuggling out of Russia materials that could be used to make nuclear weapons components.	Representatives from ECOWAS nations convene in Accra, Ghana's capital, for a meeting aimed at establishing peace in Liberia.	Representatives of Mexico and the U.S. sign 11 new agreements on issues such as the rights of immigrants, money laundering, and the environment.	In India, election polls close, with the Hindu nationalist Bharatiya Janata Party (BJP), winning an electoral plurality.
May 8		Thousands of antinuclear activists clash with German police to protest the storage of radioactive waste at a plant in Gorleben, south of Hamburg. Some 30 demonstrators are hurt, and another 30 are arrested. . . . Dominguin (born Luis Miguel Gonzales Lucas), 69, Spanish bullfighter during the 1940s and 1950s, dies in Sotogrande, Spain, of heart failure.	South Africa's Constitutional Assembly votes overwhelmingly to approve a new democratic constitution. The new majority-rule charter, agreed upon after almost two years of negotiations, provides for broad civil rights and officially completes the transition to democracy from white-minority rule. . . . Fighting in Monrovia, the capital of Liberia, spreads to Mamba Point as peace talks close in Ghana.		
May 9		Gary Rex Lauck, an American neo-Nazi, goes on trial in Germany on charges of disseminating Nazi material and inciting racial hatred.		Canada's House of Commons approves an amendment to the federal Human Rights Act that prohibits discrimination against homosexuals. The law's protections will apply only to the 10% of the Canadian workforce who work for the federal government or in government-regulated industries.	
May 10	The IMF approves a loan of $867 million to the Ukrainian government.				Vietnamese refugees riot at a detention center in Hong Kong's rural New Territories, setting ablaze 26 buildings and 53 cars. Dozens of police, wardens, and Vietnamese are injured in the disturbance. Detainees for a brief period take at least 15 prison wardens hostage. . . . Eight mountain climbers are believed dead when they are caught in a sudden blizzard near the summit of Nepal's Mount Everest. It is one of the worst-ever accidents on Mount Everest.
May 11			Electoral officials declare Ugandan president Yoweri Museveni the winner of a no-party presidential election. . . . Nnamdi Azikiwe, 91, first president of the republic of Nigeria, 1963–66, dies in Nigeria after suffering from a long illness.		Officials reveal that in the May 10 riot by Vietnamese refugees at a detention center in Hong Kong, 120 refugees escaped, and about 80 of them were subsequently caught.
May 12		The Bulgarian cabinet, after lengthy debate, adopts several privatization measures long sought by the international lending community.			

A	B	C	D	E
Includes developments that affect more than one world region, international organizations, and important meetings of major world leaders.	Includes all domestic and regional developments in Europe, including the Soviet Union, Turkey, Cyprus, and Malta.	Includes all domestic and regional developments in Africa and the Middle East, including Iraq and Iran and excluding Cyprus, Turkey, and Afghanistan.	Includes all domestic and regional developments in Latin America, the Caribbean, and Canada.	Includes all domestic and regional developments in Asia and Pacific nations, extending from Afghanistan through all the Pacific Island, except Hawaii.

U.S. Politics & Social Issues	U.S. Foreign Policy & Defense	U.S. Economy & Environment	Science, Technology, & Nature	Culture, Leisure, & Lifestyle	
	The State Department releases to the public several documents relating to alleged human-rights abuses perpetrated against U.S. citizens since 1984 by the Guatemalan military.... William Egan Colby, 76, CIA director, 1973–76, who was in charge of Operation Phoenix, a Vietnam War program under which 20,000 Vietnamese people were killed, is found dead in the Wicomico River, Maryland, ending a highly publicized search that started with his Apr. 27 disappearance.		Apple Computer reveals it has reached an agreement with IBM that will allow IBM to license Apple's Macintosh computer operating-system software.... The fire that started Apr. 24 near Bandelier National Monument in New Mexico is brought under control after charring more than 16,000 acres and damaging 800-year-old Anasazi Indian ruins.... The FDA approves the first nonsurgical treatment for enlarged prostates. The device uses microwaves.	*Moonlight Becomes You*, by Mary Higgins Clark, is at the top of the bestseller list.... The CBS network announces that it will offer free TV airtime to presidential candidates in the fall. Fox made a similar offer in February, and other networks are following suit.	May 6
The House approves, 418-0, legislation that will require state authorities to notify communities of the presence of convicted sex offenders in their areas.... A report indicates that the death rate from breast cancer among U.S. women continued to decline in 1993, but the breast-cancer death rate among black women increased in the same time period.			A wildfire that started May 5 in San Cristobal, New Mexico, is controlled after razing more than 7,500 acres in nearby Carson National Forest. Data shows that more than 142,000 acres (57,500 hectares) have been burned in New Mexico and Arizona in late April and early May.	Donald McNeill, 88, radio personality who hosted "Don McNeill's Breakfast Club," 1933–68, dies in Evanston, Illinois, of a respiratory ailment.	May 7
U.S. Circuit Court judge Robert Krupansky lifts a desegregation order that compelled the school district in Cleveland, Ohio, to integrate its public schools through the busing of students. The ruling ends 17 years of enforced busing in the Cleveland school system.		The Natural Resources Defense Council finds that the inhalation of fine airborne particles discharged primarily from smokestacks and automobiles causes or worsens heart and lung ailments and leads to more than 64,000 premature deaths a year in the U.S.		Julie Andrews announces she will not accept a Tony Award nomination for best actress since her musical, *Victor/Victoria*, was not nominated in any other category.... Garth Montgomery Williams, 84, illustrator of children's books, dies in Guanajuato, Mexico, of unreported causes.	May 8
The House approves, 315-107, a measure that will overhaul many of the policies and programs of the nation's public-housing system and will give state and local housing officials more power to decide how to allocate funds for housing programs managed by HUD.... The Senate by voice vote passes a bill that will require state authorities to notify communities of the presence of convicted sex offenders.	A CH-53E Super Stallion helicopter crashes at the Sikorsky Aircraft airfield in Stratford, Connecticut. The four crew members, all of them Sikorsky employees, are killed.... Lt. Gen. Calvin Agustine Hoffman Waller, 58, deputy commander of U.S. forces in the Persian Gulf war and one of the highest-ranking blacks in the U.S. Army when he retired in 1991, dies in Washington, D.C., of a heart attack.			The auction houses of Sotheby's and Christie's close their major spring NYC auctions. Revenues from the sales are down from the 1995 spring auctions.... Helen Kreis Wallenda, 85, last surviving member of the original Great Wallendas high-wire troupe, dies in Sarasota, Florida, of unreported causes.	May 9
In New Haven, Connecticut, Yale University announces that millionaire investor Robert Bass, a Yale graduate, has donated $20 million to the school.	Fourteen marines are killed when two helicopters collide during joint training exercises with British troops at Camp Lejeune, North Carolina. Two other marines on board the aircraft are injured in the mishap, one critically.	The House approves, 393-15, legislation granting a tax credit worth up to $5,000 to families that have adopted children.	Scientists report they have identified a protein that plays a crucial role in allowing the most common strain of HIV to infect human cells.	Designer Giorgio Armani announces that he has accepted a plea bargain in a sweeping corruption case aimed at Italy's fashion industry. He is ordered to pay a 101 million lire ($65,000) fine, the amount of his alleged 1990 bribes, and handed a nine-month suspended jail term.	May 10
		A ValuJet Airlines DC-9 jet crashes into the Everglades marsh region about 20 miles (32 km) west of Miami International Airport in Florida. The accident kills all 105 passengers and five crew members on board.			May 11
				A fire destroys part of a building in Atlanta, Georgia, where Margaret Mitchell wrote most of the 1936 novel *Gone With the Wind*.... Lance Armstrong successfully defends his title in the Tour DuPont cycling race in Blacksburg, Virginia.	May 12
F	G	H	I	J	
Includes elections, federal-state relations, civil rights and liberties, crime, the judiciary, education, health care, poverty, urban affairs, and population.	Includes formation and debate of U.S. foreign and defense policies, veterans' affairs, and defense spending. (Relations with specific foreign countries are usually found under the region concerned.)	Includes business, labor, agriculture, taxation, transportation, consumer affairs, monetary and fiscal policy, natural resources, and pollution.	Includes worldwide scientific, medical, and technological developments; natural phenomena; U.S. weather; natural disasters; and accidents.	Includes the arts, religion, scholarship, communications media, sports, entertainments, fashions, fads, and social life.	

	World Affairs	Europe	Africa & the Middle East	The Americas	Asia & the Pacific
May 13		In Norway, 37,000 mechanical-engineering workers go on strike over pay.... Germany's mail workers and garbage collectors hold a warning strike to protest proposed wage freezes and spending cuts.	Ghana turns away the *Bulk Challenge*, a leaking freighter carrying some 2,000 Liberian refugees. The move draws criticism, particularly since 200 passengers jump ship to board a medical-aid barge trailing the freighter.		A tornado hits Bangladesh, killing 600 people and injuring more than 34,000 others. The worst damage is in the Tangail district, 45 miles (70 km) north of Dhaka.... Reports confirm that rescuers have recovered the bodies of eight climbers caught in the May 10 blizzard on Mount Everest. U.S. climber Seaborn Beck Weathers and Makalu Gau of Taiwan are rescued by the Nepalese army at 19,000 feet (5,790 m) in the world's highest-ever helicopter rescue mission.... Reports reveal that Phoolan Devi, known as the Bandit Queen for allegedly robbing upper-caste villagers, has won a seat representing the town of Mirzapur in Uttar Pradesh state in India.
May 14	The Council of Europe, a 39-nation intergovernmental body established in 1949 to promote democracy and human rights, postpones Croatia's admission to the council indefinitely. It is the first time in the history of the council that it overrules a vote by its parliamentary assembly in favor of membership.	Germany's Constitutional Court, the country's highest tribunal, upholds controversial regulations restricting the number of foreigners allowed into the country.... Jacques Chirac becomes the first French president in more than 10 years to pay a state visit to Great Britain.	Authorities in Ghana, under pressure from foreign governments and aid groups, allows the *Bulk Challenge*, a leaking freighter carrying some 2,000 Liberian refugees, to dock in Takoradi. The authorities send the refugees to a nearby camp.... Heavy fighting in Monrovia, the capital of Liberia, renews.		
May 15		Radovan Karadzic, the hard-line leader of the Bosnian Serbs in Bosnia-Herzegovina, fires Rajko Kasagic, the moderate premier of the self-styled Serb Republic, Republika Srpska.			Indian president Shankar Dayal Sharma, facing general election results that has left India with the most fragmented parliament in its history, asks the Hindu nationalist Bharatiya Janata Party (BJP) to attempt to form a coalition government.... In Bangladesh, the government sends troops and medical teams to help with rescue and cleanup efforts in the wake of the May 13 tornado.
May 16		Russian president Boris Yeltsin announces a decree to abolish conscription into the Russian army.... Italian president Oscar Luigi Scalfaro appoints Romano Prodi as premier.		The Dominican Republic votes in the first round of presidential elections. Since no candidate garners more than 50% of the vote, the two leading candidates, José Francisco Peña Gómez and Leonel Fernández, will face each other in a runoff election. The elections mark the first time in 30 years that the incumbent president, Joaquín Balaguer, is not a candidate.	Indian president Shankar Dayal Sharma swears in BJP president Atal Bihari Vajpayee as prime minister, succeeding Congress (I) party leader P. V. Narasimha Rao.
May 17		Peter Caruana is elected leader of the British colony of Gibraltar.... Russian foreign ministry officials expel four British diplomats in the largest spy dispute since the end of the cold war in 1989. Britain retaliates by asking that four Russian embassy officials be withdrawn.... Italian premier-elect Romano Prodi unveils Italy's 55th government since the end of World War II.			Bob Bellear, a lawyer from Sydney, Australia, is sworn in as Australia's first aboriginal judge.

A	B	C	D	E
Includes developments that affect more than one world region, international organizations, and important meetings of major world leaders.	Includes all domestic and regional developments in Europe, including the Soviet Union, Turkey, Cyprus, and Malta.	Includes all domestic and regional developments in Africa and the Middle East, including Iraq and Iran and excluding Cyprus, Turkey, and Afghanistan.	Includes all domestic and regional developments in Latin America, the Caribbean, and Canada.	Includes all domestic and regional developments in Asia and Pacific nations, extending from Afghanistan through all the Pacific Island, except Hawaii.

U.S. Politics & Social Issues	U.S. Foreign Policy & Defense	U.S. Economy & Environment	Science, Technology, & Nature	Culture, Leisure, & Lifestyle	
	In *U.S. v. Armstrong*, the Supreme Court rules, 8-1, that a group of black defendants have insufficient evidence to support their claim that the federal government is unfairly targeting blacks for prosecution under stiff federal crack-cocaine penalties. . . . In *44 Liquormart v. Rhode Island*, the Supreme Court rules unanimously to strike down a Rhode Island statute that prohibits liquor retailers from including liquor prices in their advertisements.	In *United Food Workers v. Brown Group*, the Supreme Court rules unanimously that unions may seek back wages and other benefits on behalf of union members from companies that violate the Worker Adjustment and Retraining Act of 1988, which requires employers to give workers 60 days' notice before shutting down a facility and laying off staff.			May 13
Dr. Jack Kevorkian, a retired pathologist who has acknowledged attending more than two dozen suicides since 1990, is acquitted by a Michigan jury of violating that state's common-law ban on assisted suicide in the two 1991 deaths of Marjorie Wantz and Sherry Miller. . . . Edward J(ohn) Gurney, 82, (R, Fla.), member of the U.S. House, 1963–69, and Senate, 1969–75, dies in Winter Park, Florida, of undisclosed causes.			The FDA approves the first home screening test for infection with HIV, the AIDS-causing virus.		May 14
Senate Majority Leader Robert J. Dole (R, Kans.), the presumptive Republican presidential nominee, announces that he will resign from the Senate by June 11 in order to devote all his energies to his struggling campaign.	Reports suggest that the National Reconnaissance Office has accumulated nearly $4 billion in unspent congressional appropriations, up from a previous estimate of $2 billion. . . . The House passes, 272-153, a $266.7 billion defense authorization bill for the 1997 fiscal year. . . . The U.S. and China each list potential trade sanctions they will impose on each other as a result of a long-running dispute over what the U.S. sees as the Chinese government's inadequate steps to halt the widespread production of pirated goods in China.	Federal judge John Ryan accepts a plan designed to guide Orange County, California, out of the bankruptcy it declared in December 1994.	The FDA approves the drug Taxotere for use in treating breast cancer cases that do not respond to treatment with the drug doxorubicin, the standard initial chemotherapy treatment.	Richard M(ichael) Clurman, 72, journalist who served as a leading editor at *Time* magazine, 1949–55, 1959–72, dies in Quogue, New York, of a heart attack.	May 15
The Freemen, who have been staging a standoff with the FBI since Mar. 25 at a remote farm complex outside of Jordan, Montana, meet face-to-face with FBI agents for the first time.	Admiral Jeremy M. (Mike) Boorda, 56, the highest-ranking officer in the navy, dies of a self-inflicted gunshot wound outside of his home at the Washington Navy Yard in Washington, D.C. His suicide comes after reporters sought to question him about two combat decorations he received for service in Vietnam despite having never seen combat there. . . . Pres. Clinton states that his administration will curtail U.S. use of certain land mines.	The House, after rejecting Pres. Clinton's budget plan, 117-304, votes 226-195 to approve the Republican budget. The Senate rejects the president's budget, 45-53, in a straight party-line vote.			May 16
The president of the United Way of America, Elaine L. Chao, announces that she will step down by Sept. 1. . . . George Delury, 62, who acknowledges assisting in the 1995 death of his wife, Myrna Lebov, 52, who was crippled by multiple sclerosis, is sentenced to six months in prison after pleading guilty to attempted manslaughter. . . . Pres. Clinton signs into law a bill that requires state authorities to notify communities of the presence of convicted sex offenders.		The Commerce Department reports that the U.S. in March recorded a seasonally adjusted $8.92 billion deficit in trade in goods and services. That figure marks a sharp increase over the revised deficit of $7.04 billion registered in February.		Scott Brayton, 37, race-car driver, dies in a car accident at the Indianapolis (Indiana) speedway. . . . Johnny (Guitar) Watson, 61, rhythm-and-blues musician, dies in Yokohama, Japan, after suffering a heart attack during a performance. . . . Willis Conover, 75, disk jockey who broadcast over the Voice of America signal, 1955–96, dies in Alexandria, Virginia, of lung cancer.	May 17

F	G	H	I	J
Includes elections, federal-state relations, civil rights and liberties, crime, the judiciary, education, health care, poverty, urban affairs, and population.	Includes formation and debate of U.S. foreign and defense policies, veterans' affairs, and defense spending. (Relations with specific foreign countries are usually found under the region concerned.)	Includes business, labor, agriculture, taxation, transportation, consumer affairs, monetary and fiscal policy, natural resources, and pollution.	Includes worldwide scientific, medical, and technological developments; natural phenomena; U.S. weather; natural disasters; and accidents.	Includes the arts, religion, scholarship, communications media, sports, entertainments, fashions, fads, and social life.

	World Affairs	Europe	Africa & the Middle East	The Americas	Asia & the Pacific
May 18		The parliament in Bosnia-Herzegovina replaces Rajko Kasagic, fired May 15, with Gojko Klickovic, an economist and ally of Radovan Karadzic.... In the town of Izmit, 50 miles (80 km) east of Istanbul, Ibrahim Gumrukcuoglu points a gun at Turkish president Suleyman Demirel but is tackled before he can fire the weapon.... Gen. Djordje Djukic, 62, Bosnian Serb army officer charged by the UN war crimes tribunal for alleged atrocities during the war in Bosnia, dies in Belgrade, Yugoslavia, of pancreatic cancer.	A mutiny begins in the Central African Republic when soldiers demanding back pay surround the presidential palace in Bangui and take control of the city center, spurring riotous civilian protests and widespread looting.		
May 19		Radovan Karadzic, the hard-line leader of the Bosnian Serbs in Bosnia-Herzegovina, names Biljana Plavsic vice president and gives her responsibility for negotiations with the international community.... Reports confirm that that the government of Croatian president Franjo Tudjman will create a "memorial for all victims of war" at the Jasenovac concentration camp, the largest World War II-era concentration camp built in Yugoslavia.	French troops move into the downtown area to protect the 2,500 French citizens in Bangui, a city in the Central African Republic.	The Royal Canadian Mounted Police (RCMP) end a 3½ week armed standoff at the Waterhen Indian reservation, 300 miles (500 km) northwest of Winnipeg, Manitoba. A dissident faction of the tribe took control of the 4,500-acre (1,800-hectare) reserve and blockaded the road into the community after Waterhen chief Harvey Nepinak, accused of corruption and embezzlement, fled the reservation Apr. 24.	
May 20	Iraq and the UN sign an accord that allows Iraq to export oil on a limited basis so as to ease a shortage of food and medical supplies in Iraq. The deal marks the first easing of the broad trade sanctions imposed on Iraq following Iraq's 1990 invasion and subsequent occupation of Kuwait.	Giovanni Brusca, believed to be the top military figure in the Cosa Nostra, the Sicilian Mafia, is arrested by Italian police after spending six years avoiding arrest.... German public-sector workers launch a series of "warning" strikes to protest proposed wage freezes and spending cuts.	In the Central African Republic, French troops clash with rebels in Bangui, with a small number of casualties reported on both sides.... In response to the UN accord with Iraq, Iraqis in Baghdad, the capital, embrace each other and dance in the streets as fireworks explode overhead and as security officials fire AK-47 assault rifles into the air.	Reports confirm that one person has died in a clash between supporters of the Revolutionary and Liberation parties near the city of Santiago in the Dominican Republic.	Lee Teng-hui is sworn as Taiwan's president in Taipei, the capital.
May 21			More than 500 people die when an overcrowded Tanzanian ferry capsizes on Lake Victoria, Africa's largest lake. At least 114 people survive the accident, which is called the worst peacetime maritime disaster in Africa's history.		
May 22		In Norway, 37,000 mechanical-engineering workers end a crippling strike that started May 13.... Russian reports indicate that 40 Russian soldiers and 120 rebels have been killed in the battle to seize control of the hills around a former Soviet missile base near Bamut, 35 miles (56 km) southwest of Grozny in Chechnya.	Thousands of mourners, including Tanzanian president Benjamin Mkapa, gather in a soccer stadium in Mwanza for a memorial service for those who died May 21 in a ferry accident.		
May 23		A Russian army commander announces that his troops have taken control of a former Soviet missile base near Bamut, 35 miles (56 km) southwest of Grozny.... A report by the UNHCR describes the population movements after the 1991 collapse of the Soviet Union as "the largest, most complex and potentially most destabilizing" in Europe since the end of World War II in 1945.... (Edward Sydney) Patrick Cargill, 77, British actor known for TV comedies, dies in England of cancer.	In the Central African Republic, as fighting between rebels and French troops in Bangui escalates, several thousand protesters shouting anti-French slogans burn a French cultural center after being turned away from the French embassy. In response, French troops are reinforced, and France announces that it will evacuate all of its citizens.		A North Korean air force pilot, Captain Lee Chul Soo, defects to South Korea by plane. It is the first defection by a North Korean pilot in a plane since 1983.

A	B	C	D	E
Includes developments that affect more than one world region, international organizations, and important meetings of major world leaders.	Includes all domestic and regional developments in Europe, including the Soviet Union, Turkey, Cyprus, and Malta.	Includes all domestic and regional developments in Africa and the Middle East, including Iraq and Iran and excluding Cyprus, Turkey, and Afghanistan.	Includes all domestic and regional developments in Latin America, the Caribbean, and Canada.	Includes all domestic and regional developments in Asia and Pacific nations, extending from Afghanistan through all the Pacific Island, except Hawaii.

U.S. Politics & Social Issues	U.S. Foreign Policy & Defense	U.S. Economy & Environment	Science, Technology, & Nature	Culture, Leisure, & Lifestyle	
				In record-tying time, Louis Quatorze, a colt, wins the 121st running of the Preakness Stakes in Baltimore, Maryland. . . . Chet Forte, 60, born Fulvio Chester Fork Jr., sports broadcasting innovator who directed *Monday Night Football*, dies in San Diego, California, of a heart attack.	May 18
			The U.S. space shuttle *Endeavour* blasts off from Kennedy Space Center in Cape Canaveral, Florida, to conduct experiments regarding an inflatable antenna and a self-stabilizing satellite.		May 19
In *Romer v. Evans*, the Supreme Court rules, 6-3, to strike down an amendment to the Colorado constitution that prohibits any government body in the state from implementing policies that bar discrimination against homosexuals. The ruling is viewed as a major victory in homosexuals' ongoing battle to secure legal recourse against discrimination. . . . In *BMW of North America v. Gore*, the Supreme Court rules, 5-4, to overturn a $2 million punitive-damages award. It is the first time the Supreme Court invalidates a punitive-damages award.		Government officials project that the federal deficit for fiscal 1996 will be lowered to between $125 billion and $130 billion, down from the original estimate of $144 billion made by the Congressional Budget Office (CBO).	Russian cosmonauts carry out a five-hour space walk outside the Russian *Mir* space station. In a paid advertisement for PepsiCo Inc., the cosmonauts film a TV commercial during the space walk, posing with a four-foot-tall can of PepsiCo's Pepsi brand soda.	Jon (John Devon Roland Pertwee) Pertwee, 76, British actor best known for the TV series *Dr. Who*, dies of unreported causes. . . .At the Cannes (France) film festival, the Palme d'Or goes to *Secrets and Lies*, a film by British director Mike Leigh.	May 20
The assistant attorney general for civil rights, Deval Patrick, testifies before a congressional committee that there is no evidence linking a recent spate of suspected arson at predominantly black Southern churches to a regional or national conspiracy.	Pres. Clinton eulogizes Admiral Jeremy M. (Mike) Boorda, who committed suicide May 16, at funeral services held at the National Cathedral in Washington, D.C., that are attended by 3,900 people, including several members of the cabinet and Congress as well as numerous representatives from the military.	The Treasury Department reveals that it took in about $25 billion more in tax revenue in April than anticipated.		Lash (Alfred) LaRue, 78, star of more than 20 low-budget western movies in the 1940s and 1950s, dies in Burbank, California after suffering from heart disease and emphysema.	May 21
	Authorities in Atlanta, Georgia, find 34 suspected illegal Mexican immigrants locked inside a horse trailer in a motel parking lot. INS agents arrest the truck's driver, Kenneth Carnduff, for immigrant smuggling. Agents report that the immigrants had been denied food and water. . . . The House passes by voice vote a bill authorizing funds for the intelligence community for fiscal year 1997, which begins Oct. 1 The exact amount of the intelligence budget is classified, but estimates place it at more than $30 billion.	The Dow closes at a record high of 5778.00, marking the 21st record high registered in 1996.			May 22
A three-judge panel of the U.S. Fifth Circuit Court of Appeals in New Orleans, Louisiana, invalidates the largest class-action lawsuit pending against the tobacco industry. The ruling overturns a February 1995 decision that would have entitled virtually all smokers to join the lawsuit, which would have made it the largest class-action suit of any kind in U.S. history. . . . The CDC finds that an increasing proportion of U.S. high-school students, particularly among black males, smoke cigarettes.		The Senate passes its budget resolution for the 1997 fiscal year, 53-46, in a straight party-line vote. The measure proposes to balance the federal budget by reducing federal spending by some $700 billion over the next six years. . . . The House votes, 281-144, to approve a bill that will increase the federal minimum wage to $5.15, from $4.25.			May 23

F	G	H	I	J
Includes elections, federal-state relations, civil rights and liberties, crime, the judiciary, education, health care, poverty, urban affairs, and population.	Includes formation and debate of U.S. foreign and defense policies, veterans' affairs, and defense spending. (Relations with specific foreign countries are usually found under the region concerned.)	Includes business, labor, agriculture, taxation, transportation, consumer affairs, monetary and fiscal policy, natural resources, and pollution.	Includes worldwide scientific, medical, and technological developments; natural phenomena; U.S. weather; natural disasters; and accidents.	Includes the arts, religion, scholarship, communications media, sports, entertainments, fashions, fads, and social life.

	World Affairs	Europe	Africa & the Middle East	The Americas	Asia & the Pacific
May 24		Russian army sources report that 2,483 Russian soldiers and 16,843 Chechen rebels have been killed in the fighting in Chechnya since December 1994. Independent sources have estimated that between 30,000 and 40,000 people, most of them Chechen civilians, have died in the civil war.	More French troops arrive in Bangui in the Central Africa Republic, raising their number to about 3,000. Most of the 2,500 French citizens are evacuated, and two U.S. Marine Corps planes have evacuated 161 civilians to date, including 84 of the estimated 254 U.S. citizens in the country.		Reports confirm that military rulers in Myanmar, formerly Burma, have arrested more than 200 members of the National League for Democracy (NLD) in an attempt to block a major NLD party conference scheduled for May 26–28 at the home of NLD leader Aung San Suu Kyi.
May 25		Half a million Bulgarians gather in Sofia, the capital, to welcome the return of King Simeon II to Bulgaria, who last lived in Bulgaria in 1946.... Lord Margadale (born John Glanville Morrison), 89, British Conservative Party politician who was elevated to the peerage in 1964, dies of unreported causes.			
May 26		In Albania, the Socialist Party pulls out of parliamentary elections before polls close, accusing Pres. Sali Berisha's party of ballot rigging and intimidation.... The Greek Cypriot ruling coalition led by Pres. Glafcos Clerides wins a slim majority of parliamentary seats.... Reports confirm that thousands of Muslim refugees attempting to return to their homes in Bosnian Serb-controlled territory have been blocked. At least five refugees have been killed and 40 injured.	In the Central African Republic, mutinous soldiers release four senior civilian hostages, and Pres. Ange-Felix Patasse later agrees to offer them amnesty.		In Myanmar, because of the arrests reported May 24, only 18 NLD delegates are able to attend the party's conference, but the government allows some 10,000 NLD supporters to gather outside leader Aung San Suu Kyi's home.
May 27		Russian premier Viktor Chernomyrdin and Chechen rebel leader Zelimkhan Yandarbiyev sign a peace agreement establishing a cease-fire in the 17-month-long secessionist conflict.... Ukrainian Pres. Leonid Kuchma fires Yevhen Marchuk as premier.... Albanian Pres. Sali Berisha claims victory for his Democratic Party over his main opposition, the Socialist Party, in the May 26 elections.	At the request of the Central African Republic, French troops quell an uprising that began May 18 by mutinous soldiers demanding back pay.... Factional fighters complete a withdrawal from central Monrovia, the capital of Liberia.		China releases Bao Tong, the highest-ranking Chinese official imprisoned for offenses connected to June 1989 prodemocracy protests, after Bao served a seven-year jail term. A petition, signed by seven dissidents from Zhejiang province, demands that the government apologize for the 1989 massacre and release political prisoners.... In Myanmar, the State Law and Order Restoration Council stages rallies in Yangon, the capital, to denounce the NLD and Aung San Suu Kyi, who was released from house arrest in 1995.
May 28	In retaliation for the EU's refusal to ease the ban on British beef, Britain expands its noncooperation policy and blocks 12 EU measures that require unanimous approval.... The IMF, after prolonged negotiations, approves a $400 million standby loan to help support a new economic reform plan backed by Bulgarian premier Zhan Videnov.	Russian president Boris Yeltsin travels to Grozny, the capital of Chechnya, to address Russian soldiers and to sign a decree abolishing military conscription and limiting combat service to volunteer soldiers.... Ukrainian president Leonid Kuchma names Pavlo Lazarenko as premier.... At a rally in Tirana, the capital of Albania, police and paramilitary troops in riot gear beat protesters and arrest several leaders of the Socialist opposition.	Members of a West African peace-keeping force, ECOMOG, move into the eastern Sinkor district of Monrovia, the capital of Liberia, for the first time since strife had erupted in April.		Thai premier Banharn Silpa-archa shuffles his cabinet in the wake of a scandal involving mismanagement and fraud allegations against the Bangkok Bank of Commerce.... Indian prime minister Atal Bihari Vajpayee and his Hindu nationalist Bharatiya Janata Party (BJP) resign moments before facing defeat in a confidence vote.... The Chinese government detains one of the dissidents, Wang Donghai, who signed the May 27 petition.
May 29	The UN Population Fund estimates that, by the year 2005, half of the world's population will live in cities for the first time in history. The world's urban population is projected to rise to 3.3 billion from the current 2.6 billion, while the overall population will rise to 6.59 billion. More than 90% of urban population growth will occur in developing nations, mainly in Asia and Africa.	The Organization for Security and Cooperation in Europe (OSCE) confirms that ballots were altered and that armed men entered polling stations during the election in Albania. Socialist Party leaders continue their protests, holding rallies in five towns.	In what is widely regarded as Israeli's most momentous election, Benjamin Netanyahu of the rightist Likud bloc wins as prime minister over the incumbent, prime minister Shimon Peres. The Netanyahu win signals the electorate's concern for personal security over the program for regional peace that Peres and his Labor Party have championed.	Officers of the Royal Canadian Mounted Police (RCMP) in Halifax, Nova Scotia, board the *Maersk Dubai*, a container ship registered in Taiwan and arrest its captain and six officers, all Taiwanese citizens, on three charges of murder of stowaways during its voyage.	

A	B	C	D	E
Includes developments that affect more than one world region, international organizations, and important meetings of major world leaders.	Includes all domestic and regional developments in Europe, including the Soviet Union, Turkey, Cyprus, and Malta.	Includes all domestic and regional developments in Africa and the Middle East, including Iraq and Iran and excluding Cyprus, Turkey, and Afghanistan.	Includes all domestic and regional developments in Latin America, the Caribbean, and Canada.	Includes all domestic and regional developments in Asia and Pacific nations, extending from Afghanistan through all the Pacific Island, except Hawaii.

U.S. Politics & Social Issues	U.S. Foreign Policy & Defense	U.S. Economy & Environment	Science, Technology, & Nature	Culture, Leisure, & Lifestyle	
Kansas govenor Bill Graves (R) discloses that he will appoint Kansas lieutenant governor Sheila Frahm (R) to fill the Senate seat about to be vacated by Senate majority leader Robert Dole (R, Kans.).	San Diego County Superior Court judge William Howatt issues a ban on an anti-immigrant group called the U.S. Citizens Patrol, which has been patrolling San Diego's Lindbergh Field airport while wearing shirts similar to those worn by government agents.... The Treasury Department agrees to release more than 300 computers bound for Cuba that had been seized in February on the grounds that they violate the U.S. embargo against Cuba.			Joseph Mitchell, 87, staff writer for *New Yorker* magazine, 1938–64, who was known for his poetic stories about New York City, dies in New York of cancer.	May 24
				In response to the Treasury Department's May 24 release of more than 300 computers bound for Cuba that it had seized in February, three protesters from the religious group Pastors for Peace end a 94-day hunger strike.	May 25
			Searchers recover the cockpit voice recorder from ValuJet Airlines Flight 592, which crashed May 11. Evidence suggests that a fire in the jet's cargo hold contributed to the crash, although investigators state that they will not reach a final conclusion for several months.	Auto racer Buddy Lazier wins the 80th Indianapolis 500 at the Indianapolis Motor Speedway in Indiana.	May 26
					May 27
In *Ornelas v. U.S.*, the Supreme Court rules, 8-1, that defendants challenging convictions on the ground that they were victims of improper police searches are entitled to have appellate court judges conduct new reviews of their cases.	Pres. Clinton announces that he has ordered the Veterans Administration to provide benefits for Vietnam veterans who develop prostate cancer or peripheral neuropathy, a rare nerve disorder.	A federal jury in Little Rock, Arkansas, convicts James McDougal, Susan McDougal, and Gov. Jim Guy Tucker (D, Ark.) on fraud and conspiracy charges. Because they were Pres. Clinton's associates, the verdict is interpreted as politically damaging to the president. Reports indicate that the Clintons voluntarily paid $3,400 in back taxes and interest due to mistakes made when estimating the taxes on the Whitewater real-estate investment.	Texas Instruments Inc. announces it has developed new manufacturing technology that will facilitate the production of a computer chip with 20 times the processing power currently available in personal computers.... Pacific Telesis Group (PacTel) becomes the first Baby Bell telephone-service company to offer its customers access to the Internet global computer network.	Jimmy Rowles (born James George Hunter), 77, pianist renowned as a jazz accompanist and composer, dies in Burbank, California, of cardiac arrest.	May 28
			The U.S. space shuttle *Endeavour* touches down at Kennedy Space Center in Cape Canaveral, Florida, after conducting experiments that included the deployment of an inflatable antenna and a self-stabilizing satellite. . . . Jerry R. Junkins, 58, chairman and chief executive officer of Texas Instruments Inc., a computer-technology giant, dies of a heart attack while on a business trip in Stuttgart, Germany.	Tamara Toumanova, 77, Russianborn dancer considered one of the dominant ballerinas of the 1930s, dies in Santa Monica, California, after a brief illness.	May 29

F	G	H	I	J
Includes elections, federal-state relations, civil rights and liberties, crime, the judiciary, education, health care, poverty, urban affairs, and population.	Includes formation and debate of U.S. foreign and defense policies, veterans' affairs, and defense spending. (Relations with specific foreign countries are usually found under the region concerned.)	Includes business, labor, agriculture, taxation, transportation, consumer affairs, monetary and fiscal policy, natural resources, and pollution.	Includes worldwide scientific, medical, and technological developments; natural phenomena; U.S. weather; natural disasters; and accidents.	Includes the arts, religion, scholarship, communications media, sports, entertainments, fashions, fads, and social life.

	World Affairs	Europe	Africa & the Middle East	The Americas	Asia & the Pacific
May 30	Representatives of more than 80 countries attend an international conference on forced migration within the Commonwealth of Independent States. The meeting addresses problems related to the nearly 9 million people who have moved within the region since 1989.	Bulgarian premier Zhan Videnov announces new taxes and price increases, sparking protests in Sofia and in other towns. . . . In special elections to select negotiators for a round of peace talks, the Sinn Fein, the political wing of the Provisional IRA comes in fourth with 15.5% of the vote, which represents Sinn Fein's best showing ever in a province-wide election in Northern Ireland. . . . The divorce of Prince Andrew, the Duke of York, and Sarah Ferguson, the Duchess of York, is finalized.		Former president Carlos Andres Perez is convicted by Venezuela's Supreme Court of mismanaging government funds and is sentenced to 28 months in prison. . . . In Canada, a Saskatoon, Saskatchewan, jury convicts John Martin Crawford of three counts of murder in the 1992 deaths of three Indian women discovered near a Saskatoon-area golf course in October 1994.	
May 31		The center-left majority coalition led by Italian premier Romano Prodi wins a confidence vote. . . . In light of the May 30 election returns, the governments of Britain and Ireland reiterate that representatives of Sinn Fein may participate in the peace talks only if the IRA restores a previous cease-fire. Final results show that the Ulster Unionist Party led the voting, garnering 24.2% of all ballots cast.	In public beheadings in Riyadh, Saudi Arabia, authorities execute four men—Abdul-Aziz Fahd Nasser, Riyadh Hajri, Muslih Shamrani, and Khalid Ahmed Said—in connection with the November 1995 bombings.	In Saskatoon, Saskatchewan, Canada, serial killer John Martin Crawford, convicted May 30, is sentenced to three concurrent terms of 25 years with no chance of parole.	The ruling junta in Myanmar, the State Law and Order Restoration Council (SLORC), yields to international pressure and releases 81 of the recently arrested NLD members. . . . Neelam Sanjiva Reddy, 83, president of India, 1977–82, dies in Bangalore, India, of lung cancer.
June 1		Pres. Leonid Kuchma announces that Ukraine has transferred the last of its nuclear warheads to Russia. Under the terms of the 1994 agreement, Russia will destroy the weapons. . . . Russian reports indicate that Chechen rebels have attacked a roadblock near Shilani, capturing 26 soldiers and destroying an antiaircraft system. . . . Czech voters narrowly reject a new mandate for Premier Vaclav Klaus's Civic Democratic Party (ODS) and its center-right coalition partners.			H. D. Deve Gowda is sworn in as prime minister of India. . . . In the face of stricter gun legislation prompted by the Apr. 28 killings, the worst mass murder in Australia's history, more than 70,000 supporters of gun ownership take to the streets in Melbourne. An unidentified gunman opens fire on police officers near the town of Palmerston, wounding five people before he is shot and subdued. The incident draws wide attention in the Australian media.
June 2	At a summit in Geneva, Switzerland, U.S. secretary of state Warren Christopher meets with the presidents of Bosnia-Herzegovina, Croatia, and Serbia and with high-level officials from Western Europe to renew efforts to bring Bosnian Serb leaders and indicted war criminals Pres. Radovan Karadzic and Gen. Ratko Mladic to justice. Christopher threatens Serbian president Slobodan Milosevic with renewed economic sanctions and asks NATO troops stationed in Bosnia to begin hunting for war criminals.	Reports suggest that two mine explosions in Grozny, the capital of Chechnya, have killed six Russian soldiers and wounded 11 others. . . . Albania holds a second round of voting in 10 districts. The election is boycotted by the opposition.			In Australia, 7,000 gun supporters march in Adelaide. At the same time, a total of 25,000 backers of the gun ban march in Melbourne and Sydney. Relatives of victims of the Apr. 28 Port Arthur shooting speak at the Melbourne rally.
June 3	Foreign ministers of the 16 NATO countries agree on a proposal to strengthen the role of European armies in the alliance. . . . The World Bank estimates that, by 2010, some 1.4 billion people will be living without safe water and sanitation and that, currently, 220 million people lack access to safe water and 420 million lack adequate sanitation. . . . Representatives from more than 170 nations convene in Istanbul for the second UN Conference on Human Settlements, or Habitat II.		The government of Bahrain announces the arrest of 29 Bahraini suspects in connection with a purported Iranian-backed plot to overthrow Bahrain's ruling al-Khalifa family. . . . General Tito Okello, 82, military officer who was briefly Uganda's president after a July 1985 coup, dies near Kampala, Uganda.		A Japanese destroyer accidentally shoots down a U.S. Navy warplane during joint military maneuvers in the Pacific Ocean. The two crew members on the U.S. plane are not seriously injured. . . . Reports disclose that Chen Longde, a signatory of a May petition demanding that the Chinese government apologize for the 1989 massacre in Beijing's Tiananmen Square and release political prisoners, has been detained.
June 4	In a ceremony at the Pervomaisk missile base in Ukraine, Defense Minister Valery Shmarov, U.S. defense secretary William Perry, and Russian defense minister Gen. Pavel Grachev plant sunflowers on the site of a former Soviet missile silo to mark Ukraine's complete nuclear disarmament. . . . A new European satellite-delivery rocket is exploded by ground control officials when it veers from its course on its maiden voyage shortly after liftoff from Kourou, French Guiana.		Bahrain's interior minister, Mohammed bin Khalifa al-Khalifa, reveals that in addition to the June 3 arrests, 15 more suspects have been seized, bringing the coup-related arrest toll to 44 in connection with a purported Iranian-backed plot to overthrow Bahrain's ruling al-Khalifa family. . . . Three Swiss workers from the Red Cross are killed in an ambush in northern Cibitoke province in Burundi.		In response an apology by Japan's government regarding the June 3 incident, U.S. White House spokesman Michael McCurry explains that Pres. Clinton has accepted the "gracious expression of regret." . . . On the seventh anniversary of the massacre in Beijing's Tiananmen Square, an estimated 15,000–20,000 people gather in Hong Kong's Victoria Park for a candlelight vigil in memory of those who were killed.

A	B	C	D	E
Includes developments that affect more than one world region, international organizations, and important meetings of major world leaders.	*Includes all domestic and regional developments in Europe, including the Soviet Union, Turkey, Cyprus, and Malta.*	*Includes all domestic and regional developments in Africa and the Middle East, including Iraq and Iran and excluding Cyprus, Turkey, and Afghanistan.*	*Includes all domestic and regional developments in Latin America, the Caribbean, and Canada.*	*Includes all domestic and regional developments in Asia and Pacific nations, extending from Afghanistan through all the Pacific Island, except Hawaii.*

U.S. Politics & Social Issues	U.S. Foreign Policy & Defense	U.S. Economy & Environment	Science, Technology, & Nature	Culture, Leisure, & Lifestyle	
	The independent Export-Import Bank, the U.S.'s chief export-credit agency, refuses to finance U.S. companies seeking to work on China's Three Gorges Dam project.			Wendy Guey, 12, from West Palm Beach, Florida, wins the 69th National Spelling Bee by correctly spelling "vivisepulture."	May 30
	Pres. Clinton officially authorizes renewal of China's MFN status for an additional year.			South Korea and Japan are chosen as joint hosts for the 2002 World Cup soccer tournament. The U.S. will host the 1999 women's World Cup soccer tournament. . . . Timothy Leary, 75, clinical psychologist who became the world's best-known advocate of the use of hallucinogenic and psychedelic drugs, dies in Beverly Hills, California, of cancer.	May 31
				Jesse Hill Ford, 66, white novelist and screenwriter who depicted racial conflict in the American South, dies in Nashville, Tennessee, of a self-inflicted gunshot wound. . . . In horse-racing, Cigar takes his 15th straight victory in the Massachusetts Handicap at Suffolk Downs in Boston, Massachusetts.	June 1
			Amos Tversky, 59, cognitive psychologist whose findings became influential in the disciplines of economics, medicine and public policy, dies in Stanford, California, of complications from skin cancer.	At the Tony Awards, *Master Class* wins for best play, and *Rent* becomes the first musical since *A Chorus Line* in 1976 to capture both a Tony and a Pulitzer, which it received in April. . . . Ray Combs, 40, TV game-show host and stand-up comedian, is found dead at a hospital in Glendale, California, where he apparently hanged himself.	June 2
The Rising Star Baptist Church in Greensboro, Alabama, is destroyed by fire.	In *Loving v. U.S.*, the Supreme Court rules unanimously to uphold rules governing the implementation of capital punishment in the armed services. . . . U.S. officials arrest Julian Salazar Calero, who is wanted in Peru for his alleged involvement in a 1991 terrorist attack by the Shining Path guerrilla group.	In *Smiley v. Citibank*, the Supreme Court rules unanimously that nationally chartered banks may charge credit-card holders late-payment fees, regardless of whether card holders live in states that prohibit such fines.		Tommy Collins, 67, boxer whose severe beating in a 1953 fight prompted reforms in U.S. boxing, dies in Boston, Massachusetts. . . . Peter Glenville, 82, English-born theater and film director, dies in New York City of unreported causes. . . . *The Runaway Jury*, by John Grisham, tops the bestseller list.	June 3
A 32-year-old piano teacher is beaten almost to death in broad daylight in Central Park. The attack triggers an outpouring of concern, in which hundreds of New Yorkers send cards and gifts to the young woman's hospital room.					June 4

F	G	H	I	J
Includes elections, federal-state relations, civil rights and liberties, crime, the judiciary, education, health care, poverty, urban affairs, and population.	*Includes formation and debate of U.S. foreign and defense policies, veterans' affairs, and defense spending. (Relations with specific foreign countries are usually found under the region concerned.)*	*Includes business, labor, agriculture, taxation, transportation, consumer affairs, monetary and fiscal policy, natural resources, and pollution.*	*Includes worldwide scientific, medical, and technological developments; natural phenomena; U.S. weather; natural disasters; and accidents.*	*Includes the arts, religion, scholarship, communications media, sports, entertainments, fashions, fads, and social life.*

	World Affairs	Europe	Africa & the Middle East	The Americas	Asia & the Pacific
June 5	The Organization of American States (OAS) approves a measure condemning U.S. legislation known as the Helms-Burton law, which was passed in March to strengthen the economic embargo against Cuba, as a violation of international law.	In Bosnia-Herzegovina, a test trench is dug at Nova Kasaba and reveals six corpses, and the entire site is believed to contain the bodies of as many as 2,700 Muslims slaughtered while escaping from Srebrenica.	In the wake of the June 4 murders, the Red Cross suspends its operations in Burundi.		Hartono Reksono Dharsono, 70, Indonesian military officer who became a prominent dissident and was jailed for subversion, 1986–90, after he challenged the government's official account of a fatal 1984 riot, dies in Bandung, Indonesia, of lung cancer.
June 6		Turkish premier Mesut Yilmaz resigns from his post, effectively ending the rule of a conservative coalition plagued by bitter infighting since its rise to power in March. . . . Reports confirm that investigators have exhumed the remains of 20 Muslims in Jesovo, a town in central Bosnia. At least 63 bodies have been discovered in a mass grave in Jajce.			
June 7		Turkish president Suleyman Demirel asks the Islamic Welfare (Refah) Party, which holds the largest number of seats in Turkey's parliament based on December 1995 elections, to form a government. Opposition by Turkey's secular establishment has prevented Muslim parties from ever ruling the republic during its 73-year history. . . . One million Bulgarians protest the government's economic and social policies. . . . The running mate of Moscow's Mayor Yuri Luzhkov, Valery Shantsev, and two others are injured when a bomb goes off under Shantsev's car.	In response to the June 4 deaths in Burundi's Cibitoke province, 28 aid agencies start a one-week suspension of aid to Burundi.	Canadian immigration authorities order the deportation of Yelena Olshevskaya and Dmitry Olshevsky, two alleged Russian spies.	Zhang Xianliang, a Chinese dissident writer, is released from a labor camp after serving a three-year sentence for attempting to commemorate the 1989 prodemocracy crackdown in Beijing's Tiananmen Square.
June 8		Croatia arrests Zlatko Aleksovski, a Bosnian Croat, on charges of murder and mistreatment of Muslim prisoners in Bosnia's Lasva valley in 1993. Aleksovski's capture marks the first time Croatia arrests a suspect on war-crimes charges. . . . Human-rights advocates state that Turkish police are arresting hundreds of people at protests near the UN Conference on Human Settlements in Istanbul.			China announces that it has exploded a nuclear bomb in an underground test. It also reveals that the country will conduct only one more nuclear test before September, when it and 37 other nations will sign the nuclear test ban if an agreement is reached.
June 9					
June 10	Slovenia signs an association agreement with the EU and becomes the 10th country from Eastern and Central Europe to become an associate member of the group.	Russian nationalities minister Vyacheslav Mikhailov and Aslan Maskhadov, the chief of staff of the rebel forces in Chechnya, reach agreement on accords to withdraw Russian soldiers from Chechnya and end the conflict. . . . Amid a flurry of protests, historic negotiations aimed at bringing peace to Northern Ireland, or Ulster, begin in Belfast. . . . After hearing his appeal, an Italian court sentences tycoon Carlo De Benedetti to four years and six months in prison in connection with the 1982 collapse of Banco Ambrosiano, which was then Italy's largest private bank.	Hezbollah guerrillas kill five Israeli soldiers and wound eight others in an ambush in Israel's self-declared security zone in southern Lebanon. The attack is the deadliest since April, when Israel and Lebanon accepted U.S.-brokered terms for a cease-fire. Israel's armed forces respond by launching an artillery attack against the outskirts of the Lebanese town of Nabatiye. One Lebanese soldier is reportedly killed and one civilian wounded in the shelling.		In China, dissident Ren Wanding is released after serving a seven-year prison term for accusing the government of human-rights abuses, for urging that political prisoners be freed, and for his role in the 1989 protests in Tiananmen Square.

A	B	C	D	E
Includes developments that affect more than one world region, international organizations, and important meetings of major world leaders.	Includes all domestic and regional developments in Europe, including the Soviet Union, Turkey, Cyprus, and Malta.	Includes all domestic and regional developments in Africa and the Middle East, including Iraq and Iran and excluding Cyprus, Turkey, and Afghanistan.	Includes all domestic and regional developments in Latin America, the Caribbean, and Canada.	Includes all domestic and regional developments in Asia and Pacific nations, extending from Afghanistan through all the Pacific Island, except Hawaii.

U.S. Politics & Social Issues	U.S. Foreign Policy & Defense	U.S. Economy & Environment	Science, Technology, & Nature	Culture, Leisure, & Lifestyle	
A form letter revealing that White House staff sought confidential FBI files on Billy Dale, the former head of the White House travel office, seven months after he was fired, is made public.	Pres. Clinton nominates Admiral Jay Johnson to replace Admiral Jeremy (Mike) Boorda, who died in May, as director of naval operations. . . . The House passes, 268-153, a proposal to restrict aid to Turkey unless that country agrees to end its blockade against Armenia and to admit that the Turkish government participated in genocide against Armenians between 1915 and 1923.	The trustees of the Medicare Hospital Insurance Trust Fund confirm that the fund will be bankrupt by 2001, barring changes. . . . Joseph Waldholtz, pleads guilty in Washington, D.C., to bank, election and tax fraud. At the same time, a judge in Salt Lake City, Utah, grants Wadholtz and Rep. Enid Greene (R, Utah), a divorce. . . . More than 6,000 members of the International Association of Machinists at the St. Louis, Missouri, plant of McDonnell Douglas Corp. walk off their jobs.		Data reveal that ticket sales in New York City's Broadway district reached a record $436 million for the 1995–96 season. The ticket sales total is up 7.3% from the 1994–95 season, which set the previous record of $406 million.	June 5
The House votes, 289-136, to grant the state of Wisconsin waivers of some federal regulations, allowing the state to enact a welfare overhaul plan that will replace cash entitlements with work programs. . . . A family of four voluntarily leaves the Freemen compound outside of Jordan, Montana, the site of an ongoing standoff with the FBI that started in March. . . . A blaze destroys a building on the grounds of the Matthews-Murkland Presbyterian Church in Charlotte, North Carolina.	Jerry Plotkin, 62, who was the only nongovernment employee among the 52 Americans held hostage by Iranian militants from Nov. 4, 1979, to Jan. 20, 1981, at the U.S. embassy in Teheran, dies in Los Angeles after a long illness.	The Senate rejects, 64-35, a proposed amendment to the Constitution that would require Congress to balance the federal budget. Proponents of the measure fall three votes short of the two-thirds majority needed to send the proposal to state legislatures for approval.	George Davis Snell, 92, Nobel Prize-winning geneticist and biologist who identified groups of genes that control the body's rejection or acceptance of foreign tissues, dies in Bar Harbor, Maine.		June 6
In response to the form letter revealed on June 4, White House officials admit that the FBI files on Billy Dale, the former head of the White House travel office, along with 329 others, were improperly obtained as the result of a bureaucratic mix-up.	The Air Force's official report on the April crash of an Air Force jet near Dubrovnik, Croatia, that killed Commerce Secretary Ronald Brown and all 34 other people on board blames the accident on a combination of factors, including pilot error and the failure of air force commanders to carry out a mandated safety evaluation at the airport near Dubrovnik.			Max Factor (Francis Factor Jr.) 91, motion-picture makeup artist, cosmetics entrepreneur, and son of Max Factor, dies in Los Angeles after a heart attack.	June 7
Statistics suggest that only 27% of Republicans favor keeping the plank in the GOP platform that calls for a constitutional amendment banning abortion. Sixty-six percent state that the plank should be removed from the platform.		C(onrad) Arnholt Smith, 97, banker, businessman, and baseball-team owner who had a controlling interest in U.S. National Bank, which collapsed in 1973 with $400 million in debt—at the time the largest bank failure in U.S. history—dies in Del Mar, California, of unreported causes.		Steffi Graf of Germany retains her French Open women's tennis title by defeating Arantxa Sanchez Vicario of Spain. . . . In horse racing, Editor's Note wins the 128th running of the Belmont Stakes in Elmont, New York.	June 8
Black church leaders and civil-rights lawyers meet with Attorney General Janet Reno and Treasury Secretary Robert Rubin to discuss federal reaction to a spate of blazes of predominantly black churches.				Australian long-distance swimmer Susie Maroney, 21, claims a world record after swimming 88.5 miles (142 km) across the Florida Straits. . . . Yevgeny Kafelnikov of Russia beats Germany's Michael Stich to win the French Open men's tennis title.	June 9
Senate majority leader Robert J. Dole (R, Kans.) backs the inclusion of language supporting tolerance for abortion-rights supporters in a Republican Party platform plank that calls for a constitutional amendment outlawing abortion. . . . In *Whren v. U.S.*, the Supreme Court rules unanimously that police officers may stop motorists for minor traffic violations, even if the officers' primary intent in stopping drivers is to search their vehicles for drugs. . . . A fire burns a church with a predominantly black congregation in Greenville, Texas.		In *Lockheed v. Spin*, the Supreme Court rules unanimously that federal law does not prohibit companies from requiring employees to forfeit their rights to bring future lawsuits against them in exchange for special benefits linked to early-retirement packages.			June 10

F	G	H	I	J
Includes elections, federal-state relations, civil rights and liberties, crime, the judiciary, education, health care, poverty, urban affairs, and population.	*Includes formation and debate of U.S. foreign and defense policies, veterans' affairs, and defense spending. (Relations with specific foreign countries are usually found under the region concerned.)*	*Includes business, labor, agriculture, taxation, transportation, consumer affairs, monetary and fiscal policy, natural resources, and pollution.*	*Includes worldwide scientific, medical, and technological developments; natural phenomena; U.S. weather; natural disasters; and accidents.*	*Includes the arts, religion, scholarship, communications media, sports, entertainments, fashions, fads, and social life.*

	World Affairs	Europe	Africa & the Middle East	The Americas	Asia & the Pacific
June 11		In Russia, in explosion on a Moscow subway train kills four people and injures 12. . . . After peace talks regarding Chechnya conclude, mediators from the Chechen rebels and the OSCE are fired upon as they return to Grozny, the Chechen capital. Eight people are injured. . . . Slovenia issues new bonds, worth $812.5 million, for the first time since its secession from Yugoslavia in 1991.	In response to the June 4 killings, of three of its workers, the Red Cross removes its aid workers from Burundi.	An explosion in a shopping mall in Osasco, a suburb of Sao Paulo, Brazil, kills 39 people and injures some 470 others.	Reports reveal that 16 people have been killed in political violence in weeks leading up to elections in Bangladesh.
June 12		The Turkish government reports that renewed fighting in Turkey's predominantly Kurdish provinces has led to the deaths of 72 Kurdish rebels and six Turkish soldiers.		Colombia's House of Representatives, the lower chamber of Congress, votes 111-43 to drop charges that Pres. Ernesto Samper Pizano accepted $6 million from the Cali drug cartel to finance his 1994 presidential election campaign. Juan Carlos Gaviria, brother of former Colombian president and current OAS president Cesar Gaviria, is freed by police from kidnappers who threatened to kill him if Congress cleared Samper.	The liberal Awami League, Bangladesh's main opposition party, wins in general elections. Seven people are killed during polling. . . . Two Australian army helicopters collide in midair, explode, and crash during a training mission in Queensland state. The accident kills 18 people and wounds 10 others in the country's worst peacetime military incident in 32 years. . . . India's United Front coalition survives a confidence vote in the wake of May elections that left no party with a parliamentary majority. . . . Le Mai, 56, Vietnamese diplomat, dies after suffering a heart attack.
June 13	Esad Landzo and Hazim Delic, two Bosnian Muslims charges of multiple murders and rape at a camp in Celebici, are extradited by the Muslim-led Bosnian government to stand trial at the international war crimes tribunal regarding the war in Bosnia.		Foreign aid workers report that army troops have killed at least 70 civilians in northwestern Gitega province in Burundi.		Sumitomo Corp., Japan's largest trading company, reveals that its former head of copper trading may have caused the company losses of $1.8 billion over a 10-year period.
June 14	Delegates at the second UN Conference on Human Settlements, or Habitat II, approve by consensus a final conference declaration intended to serve as a blueprint for dealing with urban problems through the 21st century, when for the first time more than half of the world population is expected to live in urban areas.	An arms-control agreement that limits the weaponry to be possessed by each part of the former Yugoslavia is signed by Croatia, Bosnia, and Serbia.		Judicial authorities in Guerrero, Mexico, clear Guerrero's former governor, Ruben Figueroa Alcocer, who resigned in March, of involvement in the fatal shooting of 17 peasants in a politically motivated incident.	
June 15		A bomb explodes in Manchester, England, injuring more than 200 people. . . . Some 350,000 workers in Bonn, Germany's capital, hold a massive rally protesting austerity measures planned by the federal government. The demonstration is the largest protest rally in the nation since the end of World War II. . . . Haris Silajdzic, who has resigned as the premier of Bosnia, is attacked with a pipe at a rally in Cazin, Bosnia.			
June 16		Russian president Boris Yeltsin finishes first in a field of 10 candidates in the first round of presidential elections. He will face Communist Party leader Gennadi Zyuganov, who places second. . . . Albania's ruling Democratic Party wins all 17 districts contested in a partial rerun of nationwide parliamentary elections. The Socialist Party-led opposition boycotts the vote.	Reports reveal that UN and Somali leaders estimate some 9,000 people have been displaced over a six-week period due to food shortages and fighting in the Juba River valley.		

A	B	C	D	E
Includes developments that affect more than one world region, international organizations, and important meetings of major world leaders.	Includes all domestic and regional developments in Europe, including the Soviet Union, Turkey, Cyprus, and Malta.	Includes all domestic and regional developments in Africa and the Middle East, including Iraq and Iran and excluding Cyprus, Turkey, and Afghanistan.	Includes all domestic and regional developments in Latin America, the Caribbean, and Canada.	Includes all domestic and regional developments in Asia and Pacific nations, extending from Afghanistan through all the Pacific Island, except Hawaii.

U.S. Politics & Social Issues	U.S. Foreign Policy & Defense	U.S. Economy & Environment	Science, Technology, & Nature	Culture, Leisure, & Lifestyle	
Majority Leader Robert Dole (R, Kans.) resigns from the Senate, ending his 11-year tenure as the GOP leader in the chamber and his 35-year career as a legislator, to focus on his presidential campaign. . . . Wilson Watkins Wyatt, 90, (D, Ky.), who served as mayor of Louisville, 1941–45, and as lieutenant governor of Kentucky, 1959–63, dies in Louisville, Kentucky, of unreported causes.	A court-martial jury in Fort Bragg, North Carolina, finds an Army sergeant, William Kreutzer, 27, guilty of premeditated murder when he opened fire on members of his own division, in the 82nd Airborne Division, in an October 1995 sniper attack.			In hockey, the Colorado Avalanche wins their first NHL Stanley Cup title, over the Florida Panthers. . . . Lonne Elder III, 69, who was one of the first black American playwrights to enjoy major commercial success, dies in Woodland Hills, California, after a long illness.	June 11
A panel of three federal judges in Philadelphia, Pennsylvania, rules that the 1996 Communications Decency Act, which was partly designed to regulate the distribution of indecent material over the Internet global computer network, violates the First Amendment to the Constitution. . . . Pres. Clinton, speaking in Greeleyville, South Carolina, decries a recent rash of suspected arson at predominantly black southern churches. Data reveal that 33 possible arsons have occurred at southern black churches in the last 18 months.	A court-martial jury in Fort Bragg, North Carolina, sentences Army sergeant William Kreutzer, 27, convicted June 11, to the death penalty for killing an officer in an October 1995 sniper attack.	The House passes, 216-211, the final version of the fiscal 1997 budget resolution that is designed to keep federal spending on a track toward a balanced budget.		Marge Schott, owner of baseball's Cincinnati Reds, agrees to give up control of day-to-day operations of the team for two and a half years because of her recent inflammatory remarks. . . . The Southern Baptist Convention votes to censure Walt Disney Co. for offering health insurance benefits to the domestic partners of its employees.	June 12
NYC police disclose that they have arrested John Royster, who confessed to a string of attacks on women, including the June 4 near-fatal beating of a music teacher. . . . The last 16 members of the Freemen peacefully surrender from their complex near Jordan, Montana, after a standoff that started Mar. 25, one of the longest armed sieges in U.S. history. . . . In two separate cases involving race-based redistricting plans, the Supreme Court strikes down majority black and Hispanic congressional districts in Texas and North Carolina, asserting the districts are racial gerrymanders that violate the 14th Amendment's guarantee of equal protection.	The Board of Immigration Appeals, the highest immigration court in the U.S., grants political asylum to Fauziya Kasinga, 19, who fled her native country, Togo, to avoid forcible genital mutilation. The ruling sets a precedent for the 179 immigration judges in the U.S., imposing a uniform standard for future cases of women fleeing the rite, which is practiced in many African cultures.	A federal grand jury in Phoenix, Arizona, indicts state governor Fife Symington III (R) on 23 counts of fraud and extortion stemming from his business ventures and his filing for personal bankruptcy.	British and French researchers studying Creutzfeldt-Jakob disease (CJD) report they have uncovered the first empirical evidence of a connection between the human ailment and mad-cow disease.		June 13
		The Senate passes, 53-46, the Republican-backed budget resolution, which is designed to keep federal spending on a track toward a balanced budget.			June 14
				Ella Fitzgerald, 79, known as "the First Lady of Song," whose smooth voice and versatile improvising made her one of the most celebrated musicians of her era and who won at least 13 Grammy Awards, dies in Beverly Hills, California, of unreported causes.	June 15
				Basketball's Chicago Bulls win the NBA title, defeating the Seattle SuperSonics 87-75. . . . Mel (Melvin Allen Israel) Allen, 83, sports announcer, dies in Greenwich, Connecticut, after a long illness. . . . Steve Jones wins the U.S. Open golf tournament. . . . Mexico's soccer team wins the U.S. Cup title over the U.S., which places third in the round-robin event.	June 16

F	G	H	I	J
Includes elections, federal-state relations, civil rights and liberties, crime, the judiciary, education, health care, poverty, urban affairs, and population.	Includes formation and debate of U.S. foreign and defense policies, veterans' affairs, and defense spending. (Relations with specific foreign countries are usually found under the region concerned.)	Includes business, labor, agriculture, taxation, transportation, consumer affairs, monetary and fiscal policy, natural resources, and pollution.	Includes worldwide scientific, medical, and technological developments; natural phenomena; U.S. weather; natural disasters; and accidents.	Includes the arts, religion, scholarship, communications media, sports, entertainments, fashions, fads, and social life.

	World Affairs	Europe	Africa & the Middle East	The Americas	Asia & the Pacific
June 17	The international war crimes tribunal investigating the war in Bosnia frees Goran Lajic, a Bosnian Serb, who was mistakenly identified as a guard at the Keraterm concentration camp in northwestern Bosnia who has the same name.	Britain's Parliament approves, by a wide margin, a package of reforms to the nation's divorce laws. The overhaul legislation is regarded as the most significant divorce-reform bill to pass through Parliament since 1969.			
June 18	Following the June 14 signing of the arms accord by representatives from Bosnia, Croatia, and Serbia, the UN Security Council formally agrees to lift its 1991 heavy weapons embargo on the former Yugoslav republics.	In secret balloting, Latvia's parliament reelects Pres. Guntis Ulmanis for a new three-year term.			At a funeral in Perth, Western Australia, Australian prime minister John Howard, defense minister Ian McLachlan, and other dignitaries join 2,000 mourners to honor the victims of the June 12 crash of two army helicopters, that killed 18 people. Simultaneous services take place at other sites nationwide.
June 19		The Provisional Irish Republican Army (IRA) claims responsibility for the June 15 bombing in Manchester, England. Separately, Irish police raid a major explosives factory operated by IRA the near Clonaslee, Ireland.		Statscan estimates that Canada's population will be 29,955,000 on July 1, 1996.	
June 20				Walter Guevara Arce, 84, Bolivian revolutionary leader and politician who, in 1979, was appointed interim president of Bolivia but was ousted by a military coup after only 85 days in office, dies in La Paz, Bolivia, after a heart attack.	One person dies and at least 80 others are injured in street riots in Jakarta, the Indonesian capital, as Pres. Suharto begins taking action to destabilize the PDI, one of two opposition groups officially sanctioned by the government... In Bangladesh, the Awami League secures its victory in a second poll in 27 districts in which election voting irregularities were alleged.
June 21	Leaders of the 15 EU countries agree to a plan that will phase out the multinational ban on British beef, enacted to prevent the spread of BSE, or mad-cow disease. As part of the deal, British officials agree to institute a series of measures designed to gain control over the disease in British cattle and vow to end its month-long policy of refusing to cooperate with EU business.		In Somalia, fighting between clans loyal to Gen. Mohammed Farah Aidid and those supporting Usman Hasan Ali Ato erupts in a battle for control of a key Mogadishu road.	In Panama, Pres. Ernesto Perez Balladares admits that he inadvertently accepted $51,000 for his 1994 presidential campaign from a company allegedly owned by accused drug trafficker Jose Castrillon Henao.... During an investigation of 16 children who have been diagnosed with kidney failure over the last three weeks in Haiti, the CDC from the U.S. identifies a contaminant in a over-the-counter anti-fever medication as diethylene glycol, which is commonly used in antifreeze and lacquer.	
June 22	All Arab League members except Iraq, which is not invited, attend an emergency summit convened for the purpose of forging a broad-based Arab response to the Israeli electorate's selection of Benjamin Netanyahu, of the rightist Likud party, as prime minister.				James Leander Nichols, who served as an economic envoy in Myanmar for several European countries and was a close political ally of Aung San Suu Kyi, dies in a Myanmar prison while serving a three-year jail term for operating an unlicensed fax machine. His death causes controversy and angers many EU nations.
June 23		Andreas George Papandreou, 77, leftist premier of Greece, 1981–89, 1993–96, dies in Athens, Greece, of a heart attack.		In Brazil, Paulo Cesar Farias, the alleged mastermind of a massive influence-peddling scheme that brought about the resignation of Pres. Fernando Collor de Mello in 1992, is found shot to death in a beach house in Maceio, a town in Alagoas state.	Bangladesh's Sheik Hasina is sworn in as premier.

A	B	C	D	E
Includes developments that affect more than one world region, international organizations, and important meetings of major world leaders.	Includes all domestic and regional developments in Europe, including the Soviet Union, Turkey, Cyprus, and Malta.	Includes all domestic and regional developments in Africa and the Middle East, including Iraq and Iran and excluding Cyprus, Turkey, and Afghanistan.	Includes all domestic and regional developments in Latin America, the Caribbean, and Canada.	Includes all domestic and regional developments in Asia and Pacific nations, extending from Afghanistan through all the Pacific Island, except Hawaii.

U.S. Politics & Social Issues	U.S. Foreign Policy & Defense	U.S. Economy & Environment	Science, Technology, & Nature	Culture, Leisure, & Lifestyle	
The Supreme Court orders the 6th Circuit Court of Appeals in Cincinnati, Ohio, to reconsider a 1995 ruling to uphold an amendment prohibiting the city from adopting any measure to protect the civil rights of homosexuals.... In *Leavitt v. Jane L.*, the Supreme Court rules, 5-4, that the 10th Circuit Court of Appeals in Denver, Colorado, overreached its authority by striking down a 1991 Utah law that prohibits abortions from being performed after the 20th week of pregnancy in most cases.	The U.S. and China reach an agreement in a long-running dispute over what the U.S. sees as the Chinese government's failure to take adequate steps to halt the widespread production in China of so-called pirated goods. The agreement averts a trade war between the countries.	First Lady Hillary Rodham Clinton responds in writing to a new set of questions presented to her by the Senate panel investigating the so-called Whitewater affair.	The FAA shuts down ValuJet Airlines for an indefinite period after an intensive evaluation uncovers "serious deficiencies" in the airline's maintenance operations. The acts are prompted by the May crash of ValuJet Flight that killed all 110 people on board. . . . Thomas Samuel Kuhn, 73, professor and scientific historian whose theory of "paradigm shifts" was vastly influential, dies in Cambridge, Massachusetts, after suffering from cancer.		June 17
A federal grand jury in Sacramento, California, charges former university professor Theodore J. Kaczynski with 10 felony counts, stemming from two deaths and two injuries that authorities link to the so-called Unabomber . . . A superior court jury in San Jose, California, finds Richard Allen Davis, 42, guilty of kidnapping and murdering 12-year-old Polly Klaas in 1993 after abducting her from a slumber party.	Two army UH-60 Blackhawk helicopters collide in the air at Fort Campbell, Kentucky, killing six soldiers and injuring 30 people, including two civilians. It is the second helicopter crash at Fort Campbell in 1996.	The Republican majority and the Democratic minority on the Senate Whitewater Committee both issue their final reports. The Republican report concludes that White House officials, including First Lady Hillary Rodham Clinton, abused their power by monitoring and at times obstructing a federal probe into the Clintons' relation to Whitewater. The Democrats' report indicates the panel found no evidence of wrongdoing on the part of Pres. Clinton, his wife, or any senior White House officials.	Reports reveal that a new species of monkey, the Satere marmoset *(Callithrix saterei)*, has been discovered in the Amazon rain forest in Brazil. It is the sixth new monkey species to be discovered in Brazil since 1990.		June 18
G(erard) David Schine, 68, an investigative aide for Sen. Joseph R. McCarthy (R, Wis.) in the 1950s, dies in an airplane crash near Burbank, California.	The House votes, 415-0, to approve a bill that will impose economic sanctions against foreign companies that invest in Iran and Libya. The measure sparks debate.... A navy F/A-18 jet crashes in Bethalto, Illinois, killing the pilot, an employee of McDonnell Douglas Corp.				June 19
In *Lane v. Pena*, the Supreme Court rules, 7-2, that under some circumstances, individuals may not sue federal government agencies for damages for failing to comply with a law that bars discrimination against disabled people.... The California Supreme Court rules unanimously that judges who consider the tough prison sentences mandated under the state's "three strikes and you're out" law to be too severe in a case may hand down lighter sentences.		Prosecutors from the Whitewater independent counsel's office charge that Bruce R. Lindsey, one of Pres. Clinton's closest advisers, conspired to conceal a $30,000 bank withdrawal from federal regulators in 1990.... The Senate confirms, 91-7, Alan Greenspan for a third four-year term as chairman of the Federal Reserve Board. The Senate also approves Alice M. Rivlin and Laurence H. Meyer to vacant seats on the Fed board.	The U.S. space shuttle *Columbia* blasts off from Kennedy Space Center in Cape Canaveral, Florida, to carry out a medical and science mission.	Joseph Green (born Joseph Greenberg), 96, Polish-born director, dies in Great Neck, New York, after suffering from emphysema.... In *Brown v. Pro Football Inc.*, the Supreme Court rules, 8-1, that the NFL did not violate antitrust laws when it forced players to accept a salary cap after contract talks with the players' union reached an impasse in 1989.	June 20
A federal appeals court panel in Washington, D.C., grants independent counsel Kenneth W. Starr authority to investigate the White House's improper request for hundreds of confidential FBI files.... NYC police charge Heriberto Seda, 28, with murder and attempted murder in the so-called Zodiac killings, a double crime wave in 1990 and 1992–93 that terrorized the city.	The Department of Defense announces that a bunker at the Kamishiyah weapons storage site in Iraq contained chemical agents when it was blown up by U.S. troops in March 1991 after the end of the Persian Gulf war. Between 300 and 400 U.S. soldiers were nearby at the time of the detonation, which Pentagon officials theorize may have released deadly nerve gases.		A federal appeals panel dismisses all fraud charges against Thereza Imanishi-Kari, a former researcher at MIT who was found guilty of scientific misconduct in connection with a study published in 1986. The paper, coauthored by Nobel Prize-winning scientist David Baltimore, stirred controversy over the issue of scientific integrity.		June 21
Bill (William) Emerson, 58, Republican congressman from Missouri since 1981, dies in Bethesda, Maryland, of lung cancer.... Terrel H. Bell, 74, who served as a top U.S. education official under three Republican presidents, 1970–76, 1981–85, dies in Salt Lake City, Utah, of pulmonary fibrosis.					June 22
Elbert Parr Tuttle, 98, federal judge who played a pivotal role in the civil-rights struggle of the 1950s and 1960s in the South and was awarded the Presidential Medal of Freedom by Pres. Jimmy Carter in 1980, dies in Atlanta, Georgia, of unreported causes.					June 23
F	G	H	I	J	
Includes elections, federal-state relations, civil rights and liberties, crime, the judiciary, education, health care, poverty, urban affairs, and population.	Includes formation and debate of U.S. foreign and defense policies, veterans' affairs, and defense spending. (Relations with specific foreign countries are usually found under the region concerned.)	Includes business, labor, agriculture, taxation, transportation, consumer affairs, monetary and fiscal policy, natural resources, and pollution.	Includes worldwide scientific, medical, and technological developments; natural phenomena; U.S. weather; natural disasters; and accidents.	Includes the arts, religion, scholarship, communications media, sports, entertainments, fashions, fads, and social life.	

	World Affairs	Europe	Africa & the Middle East	The Americas	Asia & the Pacific
June 24		Irish police report they have found 130 pounds (60 kg) of Semtex—an explosive that the IRA has used for numerous bombings—in a factory and a nearby bunker.	Data show that the fighting that erupted June 21 in Mogadishu, Somalia, has left 11 people dead in a battle for control of a key Mogadishu road.	An estimated 2,000 people riot in Quebec City, Canada, breaking windows, looting shops, and damaging the National Assembly building. Police deploy 240 officers who use tear gas and a water cannon. Five officers are injured, and police make almost 100 arrests.	
June 25	Chile signs an agreement to become an associate member of South America's Southern Common Market (Mercosur), a customs union founded in January 1995.... At a summit, Burundian premier Antoine Nduwayo and Pres. Sylvestre Ntibantunganya appeal for assistance to help end their country's ethnic strife. The heads of state from six African countries agree to set up a committee to study an official request for "security assistance."		A powerful truck bomb explodes on the perimeter of a military complex near the eastern Saudi Arabian city of Dhahran, killing 19 U.S. servicemen and wounding several hundred people. It is called the most deadly guerrilla attack on Americans in the Middle East since 1983.... Mzawandile MacPherson Piliso, 73, South African activist in the ANC and long-time member of its national executive committee, dies of unreported causes.		
June 26		Rioting erupts in London and other English cities after England's football games loss to Germany. Some 200 people are arrested and 66 injured in rioting centered at London's Trafalgar Square.... Veronica Guerin, one of Ireland's leading crime reporters, is shot dead in her car near Clondalkin, a suburb of the Irish capital, Dublin.	FBI personnel from the U.S. arrive in Saudi Arabia to assist Saudi investigators in determining the identity of the assailants of the June 25 attack near Dhahran.... Three Israeli soldiers are killed an ambush near the West Bank city of Jericho.		Reports indicate that Chinese judges have convicted 1,725 people nationwide of drug charges, marking the UN-declared World Anti-Drugs Day. Of those convicted, 769 are sentenced to death or to life in prison, and at least 230 are executed.
June 27	The UN International Criminal Tribunal announces the indictment of eight Bosnian Serbs on charges of rape. It is the first time rape is treated as a war crime.... G-7 leaders hold an annual summit.... The International Civil Aviation Organization concludes that the U.S. planes downed by Cuba in February were over international waters, not Cuban airspace.	The three political parties that comprised the Czech Republic's previous government form a ruling coalition.... Italy's constitutional court overturns a 1995 decision and rules unanimously against allowing the extradition of Pietro Venezia, a suspect in the 1993 murder of a U.S. state tax official, to the U.S.... Iceland's parliament approves a bill allowing homosexuals to marry in civil ceremonies.			Final returns for all of the 300 parliamentary seats in Bangladesh show that the Awami League, led by Sheik Hasina Wazed, has won a majority with 147 seats.
June 28	The UN Security Council votes to extend the presence of an international peacekeeping force in Haiti through Nov. 30.	Turkish president Suleyman Demirel appoints Necmettin Erbakan to assume the role of premier. Separately, nine Turkish soldiers are killed and 20 others are wounded in Tunceli when a bomb carried by a Kurdish rebel explodes during a military parade.... Some 300 illegal immigrants from Africa occupy a Roman Catholic Church in Paris in an effort to avoid expulsion from France.... Ukraine's parliament votes to approve a new constitution. ... A bomb explodes at a British military installation in Osnabrueck, Germany.		In Canada's Ontario Court, Provincial Division, Judge Paul Belanger finds Andre Dallaire, 34, who broke into the prime minister's Ottawa residence in November 1995, guilty of the attempted murder of P.M. Jean Chrétien.... Some 50 armed guerrillas, identifying themselves as members of the previously unknown Popular Revolutionary Army, interrupt a memorial ceremony for 17 slain peasants a year earlier in the southern state of Guerrero. The guerrillas clash with police near Chilpancingo, Guerrero's capital, injuring three police officers.	

A	B	C	D	E
Includes developments that affect more than one world region, international organizations, and important meetings of major world leaders.	*Includes all domestic and regional developments in Europe, including the Soviet Union, Turkey, Cyprus, and Malta.*	*Includes all domestic and regional developments in Africa and the Middle East, including Iraq and Iran and excluding Cyprus, Turkey, and Afghanistan.*	*Includes all domestic and regional developments in Latin America, the Caribbean, and Canada.*	*Includes all domestic and regional developments in Asia and Pacific nations, extending from Afghanistan through all the Pacific Island, except Hawaii.*

U.S. Politics & Social Issues	U.S. Foreign Policy & Defense	U.S. Economy & Environment	Science, Technology, & Nature	Culture, Leisure, & Lifestyle	
A federal jury rules that the city of Philadelphia, Pennsylvania, used excessive force against the radical group MOVE in 1985. In that incident, police dropped a bomb on the group's headquarters, starting a blaze that killed 11 people, including five children. . . . . In *U.S. v. Ursery*, the Supreme Court rules, 8-1, that the government can both prosecute individuals for criminal activities and seize their property through civil forfeiture proceedings without violating the Constitution's double-jeopardy clause. . . . In *Lewis v. U.S.*, the Supreme Court rules, 5-4, that defendants who face a single trial for numerous petty criminal offenses are not entitled to a jury trial, even if they face a possible prison sentence that is longer than six months.					June 24
					June 25
Craig Livingstone resigns as head of the White House's personnel security office and accepts responsibility for the wrongful acquisition of FBI files but denies any malicious motives. . . . In *Medtronic v. Lohr*, the Supreme Court rules unanimously that a federal law regulating the manufacture of medical devices does not exempt manufacturers from suits in state courts brought by individuals. . . . J(ames) Lee Rankin, 88, lawyer who argued in *Brown vs. Board of Education* in 1954, a case which resulted in outlawing school segregation, dies in Santa Cruz, California, after a series of strokes.	In *U.S. v. Virginia*, the Supreme Court rules, 7-1, that Virginia Military Institute (VMI), a state-funded all-male military academy in Lexington, Virginia, violates women's 14th Amendment right to equal protection. The high court's ruling will affect The Citadel, the nation's only other state-funded all-male academy. . . . Pres. Clinton certifies that the Muslim-led government of Bosnia-Herzegovina has "ended its military and intelligence relationship" with Iran and expelled all Iranian military units from its territory. The certification allows the U.S. to send $70 million to Bosnia.	In *Colorado Republican Federal Campaign Committee v. FEC*, the Supreme Court rules, 7-2, that spending limits set out by federal campaign-financing laws do not apply to political parties if the parties are acting independently of their candidates in funding campaign advertisements.		Nearly 500 guests attend a New York City gala in celebration of the 100th anniversary of Adolph S. Ochs's purchase of *The New York Times* newspaper.	June 26
		Mollie H. Beattie, 49, the first woman to head the U.S. Fish and Wildlife Service, dies in Townsend, Vermont, of brain cancer.		Peter Adair, 53, documentary film director whose work examines social issues surrounding homosexuality, dies in San Francisco, California, of complications from AIDS. . . . Albert Romolo (Cubby) Broccoli, 87, producer of 16 of the 17 movies featuring James Bond, dies in Beverly Hills, California, after suffering from heart disease.	June 27
In *Felker v. Turpin*, the Supreme Court rules unanimously to uphold portions of recently passed federal legislation, the Antiterrorism and Effective Death Penalty Act of 1996, that impose new curbs on the rights of death-row inmates in state prisons to seek federal reviews of their convictions. The case is the first challenge of the new laws.		The Supreme Court rules, 7-2, in two separate cases involving free speech and political-patronage issues, that independent government contractors cannot be fired for publicly criticizing the government bodies that hired them or for backing political candidates. The cases are *Board of County Commissioners, Wabaunsee County v. Umbehr* and *O'Hare Truck Service Inc. v. City of Northlake*.	The FDA reproductive health advisory panel unanimously rules that high doses of currently available birth-control pills are safe and effective when used soon after intercourse to prevent pregnancy.	In *Denver Area Educational Telecommunications Consortium Inc. v. FCC*, the Supreme Court, in a fragmented decision, rules that cable-TV operators may restrict access to indecent programs on certain commercial channels but not on public-access channels. The regulation at issue is known as the Helms Amendment.	June 28
F	G	H	I	J	
Includes elections, federal-state relations, civil rights and liberties, crime, the judiciary, education, health care, poverty, urban affairs, and population.	Includes formation and debate of U.S. foreign and defense policies, veterans' affairs, and defense spending. (Relations with specific foreign countries are usually found under the region concerned.)	Includes business, labor, agriculture, taxation, transportation, consumer affairs, monetary and fiscal policy, natural resources, and pollution.	Includes worldwide scientific, medical, and technological developments; natural phenomena; U.S. weather; natural disasters; and accidents.	Includes the arts, religion, scholarship, communications media, sports, entertainments, fashions, fads, and social life.	

	World Affairs	Europe	Africa & the Middle East	The Americas	Asia & the Pacific
June 29		Olafur Ragnar Grimsson, one of Iceland's leading left-wing politicians, is elected president of Iceland.			
June 30		The Muslim-dominated List of Citizens for a United Mostar comes in first in elections to establish a unified government for the southern Bosnian city, which has been split between Muslims and Croats since the two factions' 1993 war. . . . The IRA claims responsibility for the June 28 bombing at a British military installation in Osnabrueck, Germany. The bombing reportedly is the first IRA attack on the British military in mainland Europe since 1990. No casualties resulted from the assault.		Leonel Fernandez Reyna wins a runoff election to become the new president of the Dominican Republic. Fernandez will replace Pres. Joaquin Balaguer, 89, who has served seven nonconsecutive terms as president in the past 30 years. . . . Fernando De la Rua of the opposition Radical Civic Union (UCR) wins the first-ever mayoral election in Buenos Aires, Argentina's capital. The mayor of Buenos Aires was in the past appointed by the president.	Mongolia's democratic opposition coalition wins a surprise landslide victory over the ruling formerly communist Mongolian People's Revolutionary Party (MPRP) in parliamentary elections.
July 1		A car bomb explodes in Bastia, a city on the French island of Corsica, killing a Corsican separatist and wounding two other nationalists and several bystanders. . . . Alfred Edward Marks (born Alfred Touchinsky), 75, actor, and singer who appeared on one of the first comedy sketch shows ever to run on British television, dies after suffering from cancer.			A new law takes effect in Australia's Northern Territory, making the Northern Territory's government the world's first to sanction voluntary euthanasia.
July 2			Israeli jets attack a base of the Fatah Uprising guerrilla organization in eastern Lebanon's Bekaa valley. Israel describes the attack as a retaliatory gesture for the June 26 ambush near the West Bank city of Jericho in which three Israeli soldiers were killed.		
July 3		In a runoff presidential election, Russian president Boris Yeltsin defeats the Communist Party's Gennadi Zyuganov by garnering 54% of the vote. . . . Hungary's cabinet and leaders of the country's Jewish community agree to set up a foundation to make restitution to Jews for property seized by the government during World War II. . . . . British prime minister John Major announces that the Stone of Scone, a symbol of Scottish nationalism that was removed from Scotland in 1296, will be returned to Scotland.	About 80 people are killed in an attack on a tea factory in Teza, just hours before Burundian government and army officials meet to discuss the proposed intervention in its civil strife.	Mexican authorities arrest Hilario Mesino Acosta, leader of the radical Southern Sierra Peasant Organization (OCSS), on charges of sedition for alleged ties to the Popular Revolutionary Army.	Amnesty International reports that China has executed at least 1,000 people since the nation began a crackdown on crime Apr. 28. According to Amnesty, the number of people executed in China since late April is the highest since 1983.
July 4		Ethnic Hungarians from throughout Central and Eastern Europe hold a meeting in Budapest, the Hungarian capital. . . . Ten of the 300 illegal immigrants from Africa occupying a Roman Catholic Church in Paris, France, since June 28 launch a hunger strike.			Reports confirm that Mongolia's democratic opposition coalition, which won a surprise landslide victory on June 30, has nominated its leader, Radnaasumberel Gonchigdorj, as the country's next premier.
July 5	The United Nations AIDS program estimates that at least 1.3 million people died from AIDS or AIDS-related illnesses in 1995 and that HIV is expected to cause more than 3.1 million new infections in 1996.	In Bosnia, Finnish investigators recover 30 bodies from a hillside near Srebrenica where they have been lying exposed since July 1995. . . . After a conference of ethnic Hungarians from throughout Central and Eastern Europe, delegates call for "autonomy" for ethnic Hungarians, or Magyars, living outside of Hungary.		Jorge Luis Ochoa Vasquez, the reputed second-in-command in the Medellin drug cartel, is released from prison after serving less than 5½ years of an 8½-year sentence.	A court in Hobart, the capital of the Australian state of Tasmania, indicts Martin Bryant on 34 counts of murder stemming from a shooting spree that killed 35 people and wounded 18 in April. The shooting incident was the worst mass killing in modern Australian history.

A	B	C	D	E
Includes developments that affect more than one world region, international organizations, and important meetings of major world leaders.	*Includes all domestic and regional developments in Europe, including the Soviet Union, Turkey, Cyprus, and Malta.*	*Includes all domestic and regional developments in Africa and the Middle East, including Iraq and Iran and excluding Cyprus, Turkey, and Afghanistan.*	*Includes all domestic and regional developments in Latin America, the Caribbean, and Canada.*	*Includes all domestic and regional developments in Asia and Pacific nations, extending from Afghanistan through all the Pacific Island, except Hawaii.*

U.S. Politics & Social Issues	U.S. Foreign Policy & Defense	U.S. Economy & Environment	Science, Technology, & Nature	Culture, Leisure, & Lifestyle	
				Steve Geppi, owner of Diamond Comics Distribution, pays $61,900 for a partly restored 10-cent comic book in which the character Superman made his 1938 debut.	June 29
	Captain David McCampbell, 86, U.S. Navy fighter pilot and officer who won the Medal of Honor for his exploits against Japanese forces during World War II and was credited with downing a total of 34 planes during the war, dies in Riviera Beach, Florida, of unreported causes.			Germany defeats the Czech Republic to win soccer's European Championship.	June 30
In *Texas v. Hopwood,* the Supreme Court lets stand a ruling issued in March by the U.S. Fifth Circuit Court of Appeals that struck down a race-based admissions policy at the University of Texas School of Law in Austin, Texas. . . . Federal authorities arrest 12 members of an Arizona paramilitary group known as the Viper Militia and charge them with conspiring to blow up several buildings. . . . William T. Cahill, 84, Republican governor of New Jersey (1970–74), dies in Haddonfield, New Jersey, of a circulatory ailment.		In *U.S. v. Winstar Corp.,* the Supreme Court rules, 7-2, that the federal government knowingly breached its contracts with savings and loan institutions when Congress revised several accounting laws in 1989. . . . Data show that the purchasing managers' index registered 54.3% in June, up from May's revised figure of 49.3%. The June level marks a 16-month high.		Margaux Hemingway, 41, granddaughter of Ernest Hemingway and a fashion model in the 1970s, is found dead in Santa Monica, California, in an apparent suicide. . . . Steve (Stoyan) Tesich, 53, who won an Oscar for screenwriting, dies of a heart attack while on vacation in Canada. . . . *The Runaway Jury,* by John Grisham, tops the bestseller list.	July 1
In Van Nuys, California, Superior Court judge Stanley Weisberg sentences the Menendez brothers—Lyle, 28, and Erik, 26—each to two consecutive life terms in prison without parole for the 1989 murders of their parents. . . . A Chicago judge dismisses rape and murder charges against Dennis Williams, William Rainge, and Kenneth Adams, who have spent 18 years in prison, when new genetic evidence shows that they did not commit those crimes.	The Department of Defense indicates that 55% of women in the U.S. military have reported some form of sexual harassment in the previous 12 months, including rape, assault, groping, and pressure for sexual favors. The figure is down from the 64% recorded in 1988. . . . An independent study of the high-tech aircraft and missiles used by the U.S. during the 1991 Persian Gulf war with Iraq finds that the claims made of the effectiveness of those weapons were overstated.				July 2
At least eight people die when fire sweeps through a busy fireworks store in Scottown, Ohio.			The FDA approves the sale of the first nonprescription nicotine patch designed to help smokers quit the habit.		July 3
					July 4
			Clyde E. Wiegand, 81, physicist who was a member of a team that discovered the antiproton in 1955, by using a high-energy accelerator, dies in Oakland, California, of prostate cancer.	Robert Ellis Dunn, 67, choreographer whose classes laid the foundations of postmodern dance and who received a Bessie (New York Dance and Performance Award) in 1985 an American Dance Guild conference award in 1988, dies in New Carrollton, Maryland, after a heart attack.	July 5

F	G	H	I	J
Includes elections, federal-state relations, civil rights and liberties, crime, the judiciary, education, health care, poverty, urban affairs, and population.	Includes formation and debate of U.S. foreign and defense policies, veterans' affairs, and defense spending. (Relations with specific foreign countries are usually found under the region concerned.)	Includes business, labor, agriculture, taxation, transportation, consumer affairs, monetary and fiscal policy, natural resources, and pollution.	Includes worldwide scientific, medical, and technological developments; natural phenomena; U.S. weather; natural disasters; and accidents.	Includes the arts, religion, scholarship, communications media, sports, entertainments, fashions, fads, and social life.

	World Affairs	Europe	Africa & the Middle East	The Americas	Asia & the Pacific
July 6					
July 7	More than 15,000 people from about 125 countries convene in Vancouver, Canada, for the 11th International Conference on AIDS.	Police and military officials bar the Orange Order, a pro-British Protestant group, from leading a parade through a Catholic area of Drumcree, Northern Ireland. The action sparks protests. . . . Polish premier Wlodzimierz Cimoszewicz marks the 50th anniversary of the Kielce pogrom, in which at least 42 Polish Jews who survived the Holocaust were beaten and killed.		Abdala Bucaram Ortiz of the center-left Roldosista Party defeats the center-right Social Christian Party's candidate Jaime Nebot Saadi in Ecuador's runoff presidential election.	
July 8	The International Court of Justice, the UN body that adjudicates international law, unanimously advises that the use of nuclear arms will be deemed unlawful in instances where their employment contravenes UN Charter provisions on territorial integrity and political independence. The judges also call on world leaders to pursue negotiations leading to nuclear disarmament.	In response to the parade halted July 7 in Northern Ireland, thousands of Protestant loyalists blockade roads and burn cars in several Ulster cities. . . . In Chechnya, rebels ignore an ultimatum to free an estimated 1,000 Russian prisoners of war. . . . A series of scuffles among legislators breaks out in Turkey's parliament chambers before the National Assembly confirms the recently formed ruling coalition. . . . Prince Luipold Ferdinand Michael Albrecht, Duke of Bavaria, 91, heir to the Bavarian throne, dies at the family's castle on Starnberg Lake.		Hurricane Bertha hits the eastern Caribbean Islands with winds gusting as high as 100 miles per hour (160 kmph).	In South Korea, opposition parties drop their boycott of the National Assembly's opening, and Parliament holds its inaugural session. . . . Kim Jong Il, the presumed leader of North Korea, appears at a memorial rally in Pyongyang, the capital, marking the second anniversary of the death of his father, North Korea's long-time leader Kim Il Sung. The ceremony is attended by tens of thousands of troops and civilians.
July 9		Because rebels ignored a July 8 deadline, Russian troops ignore a cease-fire and attack the village of Gekhi, 20 miles (32 km) southwest of Grozny, the Chechen capital. . . . Polish president Aleksander Kwasniewski presents a plan to ban commercial activity from the site of the Auschwitz-Birkenau concentration camp in Oswiecim. . . . Nelson Mandela becomes the first South African president to make a state visit to Britain.	Clashes between the factions supporting Gen. Mohammed Farah Aidid and those loyal to Ali Mahdi Mohammed erupt in Mogadishu, Somalia.	Hurricane Bertha strikes the Bahamas and Britain's Turks and Caicos Islands.	The Australian federal cabinet approves a package of measures designed to restrict public access to TV programs, films, videotapes, and videogames that depict extreme violence.
July 10	African heads of state close an annual summit of the OAU in Yaounde, Cameroon's capital, and strongly endorse a plan for a regional intervention force for Burundi.	Dalenergo, the state-run power company that serves Russia's Primorski region, halts regular distribution of electricity to its customers because of a shortage of funds. . . . A team of 15 forensic scientists report they have found the remains of more than 40 people during an excavation of a mass grave in Cerska, Bosnia. . . . Russian forces bomb Makhkety, where Chechen rebel leader Zelimkhan Yandarbiyev reportedly maintains his headquarters. Rebel sources assert that the bombing and shelling has killed up to 370 Chechen civilians and wounded 170 others.	Palestinian youths clash with Israeli soldiers in the West Bank city of Hebron in protest over delays in a scheduled Israeli troop pullback from the city.	Data suggests that six people have died in the Caribbean since Hurricane Bertha struck the region July 8. . . . Argentine justice minister Rodolfo Carlos Barra resigns amid charges that he once belonged to a 1960s rightist group that allegedly perpetrated attacks on Jews in Argentina. The charges caused an uproar, particularly since Barra was responsible for investigating the 1992 bombing of the Israeli embassy in Buenos Aires and the 1994 car bombing of a Jewish center in Buenos Aires that killed 87 people.	
July 11	The UN International Criminal Tribunal issues international arrest warrants for Radovan Karadzic and Gen. Ratko Mladic, the political and military leaders, respectively, of the self-styled Bosnian Serb republic. The tribunal calls for an investigation of Serbian president Slobodan Milosevic. . . . The OECD admits Poland as its 28th member and its third former communist state.	In an effort to stave off continuing violence from Protestant demonstrators, officials in Northern Ireland rescind the July 7 ban, against the Orange Order, prompting a wave of demonstrations by Catholic protesters. In Londonderry, Catholic protesters attack police, and more than 50 people are injured in what is described as the city's worst riots ever. . . . A bomb explodes near the end of the trolley line at Pushkin Square in Moscow, Russia, and injures five people.			

A	B	C	D	E
Includes developments that affect more than one world region, international organizations, and important meetings of major world leaders.	Includes all domestic and regional developments in Europe, including the Soviet Union, Turkey, Cyprus, and Malta.	Includes all domestic and regional developments in Africa and the Middle East, including Iraq and Iran and excluding Cyprus, Turkey, and Afghanistan.	Includes all domestic and regional developments in Latin America, the Caribbean, and Canada.	Includes all domestic and regional developments in Asia and Pacific nations, extending from Afghanistan through all the Pacific Island, except Hawaii.

U.S. Politics & Social Issues	U.S. Foreign Policy & Defense	U.S. Economy & Environment	Science, Technology, & Nature	Culture, Leisure, & Lifestyle	
The NAACP opens its convention in Charlotte, North Carolina.... Libertarian Party members nominate Harry Browne as their candidate for president.		Pres. Clinton reveals what is called the most sweeping reform of U.S. meat-safety guidelines since the Federal Meat Inspection Act of 1907. The new rules mandate, for the first time ever, that meat and poultry production facilities conduct scientific tests that detect disease-causing bacteria and allow the government to establish minimum quality standards for meat and poultry.	Two passengers are killed and five others are injured when the engine of a Delta Air Lines MD-88 plane explodes during takeoff from Pensacola, Florida.	At the All England Tennis Championship, Germany's Steffi Graf wins her seventh Wimbledon women's singles title.	July 6
	An officer in Cuba's national police force, Lt. Col. Jose Fernandez Pupo, hijacks a Cuban passenger jet and orders the pilot to fly to the U.S. Naval Base in Guantanamo Bay, Cuba, where he is detained by INS officials.... Polish president Aleksander Kwasniewski travels to the U.S. in his first visit to the U.S. since his inauguration in 1995.		The U.S. space shuttle *Columbia* lands at Kennedy Space Center in Cape Canaveral, Florida, after carrying out a successful medical and science mission in the longest flight ever for a shuttle.... Alexander G. Shulman, 81, Canadian surgeon who pioneered the treatment of burns with ice water and served as the chief of surgery at Los Angeles's Midway Hospital and director of the Lichtenstein Hernia Institute, dies in Los Angeles, California, of cancer.	Richard Krajicek of the Netherlands wins the men's singles title at the All England Tennis Championship at Wimbledon, in London.... Dave Stockton wins the U.S. Senior Open at the Canterbury Golf Club in Beachwood, Ohio.	July 7
Mary Fackler Schiavo, the Transportation Department's inspector general, tenders a letter of resignation to Pres. Clinton.					July 8
Two of Georgia's black House members—Cynthia McKinney and Sanford Bishop Jr.—win Democratic primaries in congressional districts redrawn in 1995.... In *Sheff v. O'Neill*, the Connecticut Supreme Court rules, 4-3, that racial segregation in public schools in and around Hartford violates the state constitution.... Melvin Mouron Belli, 88, lawyer whose clients included Jack Ruby and Lenny Bruce, dies in San Francisco, California.	Israel's P.M. Benjamin Netanyahu makes his first visit to U.S. president Bill Clinton since winning the Israeli premiership in late May.	The Senate votes, 74-24, to raise the federal minimum wage by 90 cents, to $5.15, from $4.25, by July 1997. The increase, the first in six years, will affect 10 million workers.... Prudential Insurance Co. reveals it has agreed to pay $35.3 million in fines and reimbursements to customers. The statement is issued shortly after a task force from 30 states and the District of Columbia conclude a 14-month probe of the company.		The leading pitcher for Cuba's Olympic baseball team, Rolando Arrojo, defects while the team is in Albany, Georgia.... The National League wins MLB's annual All-Star Game over the American League, 6-0, in Philadelphia, Pennsylvania.	July 9
		The Senate passes, 53-46, the Teamwork for Employees and Management Act, which will allow employers greater flexibility in creating worker-management teams.... The Commerce Department reports that the number of Hispanic-owned businesses in the U.S. increased by 76% between 1987 and 1992.... Federal prosecutors announce that Simon Fireman, a former official in Robert Dole's presidential campaign, has agreed to plead guilty to charges involving campaign finance laws.	In anticipation of Hurricane Bertha, 500,000 coastal residents of Florida are evacuated.	A statue of tennis player Arthur Ashe, the first black man to win the prestigious U.S. Open, Australian Open and Wimbledon tennis tournaments, is unveiled in his hometown of Richmond, Virginia.	July 10
	The U.S. government announces it has revoked Colombian president Ernesto Samper Pizano's visa, citing evidence that Samper accepted $6 million from the Cali drug cartel for his 1994 presidential campaign. It is the first time that the U.S. denies entry to a democratically elected foreign leader since 1987.... An air force F-16 fighter jet crashes into a Pensacola, Florida, house, setting it on fire and killing a four-year-old boy.		In response to the coming of Hurricane Bertha, 350,000 people in South Carolina and North Carolina are evacuated.	Riddick Bowe is declared the victor in a heavyweight boxing match against Andrew Golota of Poland at Madison Square Garden, after Golota is disqualified for delivering his fourth low blow of the fight. The disqualification sparks a brawl among fans, handlers, and managers.	July 11
F	G	H	I	J	
Includes elections, federal-state relations, civil rights and liberties, crime, the judiciary, education, health care, poverty, urban affairs, and population.	*Includes formation and debate of U.S. foreign and defense policies, veterans' affairs, and defense spending. (Relations with specific foreign countries are usually found under the region concerned.)*	*Includes business, labor, agriculture, taxation, transportation, consumer affairs, monetary and fiscal policy, natural resources, and pollution.*	*Includes worldwide scientific, medical, and technological developments; natural phenomena; U.S. weather; natural disasters; and accidents.*	*Includes the arts, religion, scholarship, communications media, sports, entertainments, fashions, fads, and social life.*	

	World Affairs	Europe	Africa & the Middle East	The Americas	Asia & the Pacific
July 12	Thirty-one countries, including the U.S. and Russia, agree to a new treaty intended to control sales of weapons and military technology. . . . The European Court of Justice, the EU's highest court, rules that the EU was justified in instituting a worldwide ban on British beef. . . . The UN Security Council votes unanimously to extend the mandate of the UN Observer Mission in Georgia until January 1997.	In Chechnya, Russian forces shell a rebel base near Shatoi, some 27 miles south of Grozny. Russian authorities claim that the attack kills 60 rebels. . . . A bomb injures 30 people when it explodes on one of Moscow's busiest streets. . . . Violence continues in Londonderry when a Catholic nationalist is struck and killed by a police security vehicle. In two separate incidents in Belfast, three police officers are wounded by gunfire. . . . In England, Charles and Diana, the Prince and Princess of Wales, reveal that they have agreed to the terms of their planned divorce.	A court rules that a main street in an Orthodox neighborhood of northern Jerusalem should remain open to traffic during the Jewish Sabbath. The ruling sparks clashes with police.		
July 13		The EU announces the official results in the June election of the divided city of Mostar in southwestern Bosnia-Herzegovina. The returns, disputed by the Croats, show that a Muslim-led party has taken the majority. . . . The Organization for Security and Cooperation in Europe, the group responsible for organizing the Bosnian elections, penalizes the ruling party in Bosnia, the Party for Democratic Action (SDA), for the June attack on Haris Silajdzic by removing the top seven names from the list of SDA candidates for municipal elections in Cazin.			
July 14		A car bomb explodes in Enniskillen, Northern Ireland, injuring 17 people and virtually destroying a hotel. The blast is the first terrorist bombing in Northern Ireland, or Ulster, in 22 months. . . . South African president Nelson Mandela is French president Jacques Chirac's guest of honor at the Bastille Day military parade in Paris.			
July 15		A military airplane crashes and catches fire while attempting to land in Eindhoven, the Netherlands. Of the 41 people aboard, 32 are killed and the other nine suffer serious injuries. . . . According to Ulster police, the July 7–14 riots resulted in 291 arrests, 149 injuries to police officers, 192 injuries to civilians, and two civilian deaths. . . . Some 10,000 coal miners in the Primorski region of Russia strike to demand back pay.		Canada's federal government agrees to extend medical and dental benefits to domestic partners of homosexual government employees.	
July 16		A remote-control bomb explodes in Kiev, Ukraine, slightly injuring Premier Pavlo Lazarenko and two guards. . . . Representatives of the government of Bosnia-Herzegovina, the Muslim-Croat federation in Bosnia, and the U.S. sign an agreement that will allow up to $360 million worth of military aid to be given to the Muslim-Croat federation's joint army. . . . Sir Geoffrey Alan Jellicoe, 95, British landscape architect who was one of the 20th century's leading practitioners in the field, dies in Devon, England, of unreported causes.	Reports suggest that some 40 people have died subsequently in clashes that started July 9 between two factions in Mogadishu, the capital of Somalia.	An army truck carrying 10 soldiers near the town of Tixtla in the Mexican state of Guerrero is ambushed. One civilian in a nearby delivery truck is killed in the attack.	Chinese major general Liu Zhenwu visits Hong Kong, marking the first-ever visit to the British colony by a Communist Chinese military general.
July 17		Paul Touvier, 81, the first Frenchman to be convicted of World War II-related crimes against humanity who, in 1994, was sentenced to life imprisonment for ordering the 1944 execution of seven Jews at Rillieux-la-Pape near Lyons, dies of prostate cancer at a prison hospital near Paris.	More than 400,000 Israeli workers take part in a 10-hour general strike that the Histadrut trade-union federation calls to protest sweeping budget-cut proposals approved by the rightist Likud party-led government of P.M. Benjamin Netanyahu.	Canadian lieutenant general Maurice Baril announces that disciplinary action will be taken against 34 Canadian soldiers, who were part of the UN peacekeeping mission in Bosnia, for their behavior while stationed at a mental hospital in Bakovici between October 1993 and April 1994.	More than 5,400 workers at the Australian Broadcasting Corp. stage a one-day protest strike. It is the first nationwide industrial action in 10 years.

A	B	C	D	E
Includes developments that affect more than one world region, international organizations, and important meetings of major world leaders.	Includes all domestic and regional developments in Europe, including the Soviet Union, Turkey, Cyprus, and Malta.	Includes all domestic and regional developments in Africa and the Middle East, including Iraq and Iran and excluding Cyprus, Turkey, and Afghanistan.	Includes all domestic and regional developments in Latin America, the Caribbean, and Canada.	Includes all domestic and regional developments in Asia and Pacific nations, extending from Afghanistan through all the Pacific Island, except Hawaii.

U.S. Politics & Social Issues	U.S. Foreign Policy & Defense	U.S. Economy & Environment	Science, Technology, & Nature	Culture, Leisure, & Lifestyle	
The House passes, 342-67, the Defense of Marriage Act, a bill that will let states choose to deny recognition to same-sex marriages performed in other states. It will also bar federal recognition of such unions.... John William Chancellor, 68, television news reporter and anchor, 1970–82, who, in 1975, hosted a joint appearance by Israeli prime minister Yitzhak Rabin and Egyptian president Anwar el-Sadat in their first-ever televised meeting, dies in Princeton, New Jersey, of stomach cancer.			Hurricane Bertha hits North Carolina's coast in full force, bringing heavy rain and 115 mph winds and causing four deaths and major damage.	Jonathan Melvoin, 34, a keyboardist for the popular rock group Smashing Pumpkins on their current world tour, is found dead in New York City of an apparent heroin overdose.... Gottfried von Einem, 78, prolific Austrian composer, dies near Vienna, Austria, of unreported causes.	July 12
Carl M. Shoffler, 51, one of three Washington, D.C., policemen whose arrest of five burglars at the Watergate complex in 1972 led to a scandal that forced the resignation of Pres. Richard M. Nixon, dies in Baltimore, Maryland, of pancreatitis.				Pandro Samuel Berman, 91, film producer who won the Irving G. Thalberg Award in 1977, dies in Beverly Hills, California, of undisclosed causes.... Cigar captures his 16th straight victory, tying a North American record for consecutive wins set by the racehorse Citation in 1950.	July 13
		Thomas Edwin Sandefur Jr., 56, chief executive of Brown and Williamson Tobacco Corp., 1993–95, who testified before Congress in 1994 that he did not believe nicotine is addictive, dies in Louisville, Kentucky, of aplastic anemia.		The Eastern Conference team defeats the Western Conference squad, 3-2, in the inaugural Major League Soccer All-Star Game at Giants Stadium in East Rutherford, New Jersey.... Ray Floyd wins the Senior Players Championship in Dearborn, Michigan.	July 14
Arkansas governor Jim Guy Tucker (D), convicted in May on fraud and conspiracy charges, resigns.... The White House admits that it has set up a special random drug-testing program to monitor 21 employees who have a history of drug use.		According to *Forbes* magazine, William H. Gates of the U.S. computer company Microsoft Corp. is the richest individual in the world, estimated at $18.0 billion.	U.S. astronaut Shannon W. Lucid, who has been on *Mir* since March, breaks the record for the longest stay in space by a U.S. astronaut, set by Norman E. Thagard in 1995.... The Insurance Information Institute sets preliminary losses due to Hurricane Bertha at $194 million.	Entertainment giant Walt Disney Co. announces plans to build a second theme park, Disney's California Adventure, in Anaheim, California, adjacent to Disneyland.	July 15
The International Commission of Jurists finds that the death penalty as applied in the U.S. is arbitrary and weighted against blacks and Hispanics. The commission's report describes application of the death penalty as "wanton and freakish" and "arbitrary and racially discriminatory."... Pres. Clinton states that he will direct the federal Department of HHS to institute new work requirements for people receiving welfare benefits. Under the new regulations, people on welfare will lose their benefits if they fail to find employment within two years.	U.S. president Clinton delays by six months the implementation of a controversial provision of the Helms-Burton law that would have allowed U.S. citizens whose property was expropriated after Cuba's 1959 communist revolution to sue users of those properties in U.S. courts. The Helms-Burton law passed in March and has drawn international criticism.	The House approves, by voice vote, the Federal Oil and Gas Royalty Simplification and Fairness Act of 1996, which revises the government's procedures for collecting royalty payments from companies that extract oil and gas from federal lands.... The Dow volume of shares traded reaches 683 million, the heaviest in the 204-year history of the New York Stock Exchange.		Judge Manny Alvarez accepts a plea bargain under which Michael Irvin, star wide receiver for the Dallas Cowboys, pleads no contest to second-degree felony cocaine possession charges in exchange for four years' probation.	July 16
The Senate passes, by voice vote, legislation that will establish a nine-member commission to examine the economic and social effects of gambling.... John J. Joubert, 33, a former U.S. airman condemned to die for murdering two boys in Bellevue, Nebraska, in 1983, is executed in the electric chair. He is the 332nd person executed in the U.S. and only the second in Nebraska since 1976.		A study questions assertions made by the EPA which claim that exposure to radon gas is responsible for up to 10% of lung cancer cases in the U.S.	A Trans World Airlines (TWA) 747 jetliner bound for Paris crashes into the Atlantic Ocean about a half hour after taking off from Kennedy International Airport in New York City. All 230 people on board are killed in the crash.	Chas (Bryan James) Chandler, 57, British rock musician and manager, dies in Newcastle, England, of a heart attack.... Joe Klein, a journalist, admits he is the author of *Primary Colors*, a bestselling novel loosely based on Pres. Clinton's 1992 election campaign.	July 17
F	**G**	**H**	**I**	**J**	
Includes elections, federal-state relations, civil rights and liberties, crime, the judiciary, education, health care, poverty, urban affairs, and population.	*Includes formation and debate of U.S. foreign and defense policies, veterans' affairs, and defense spending. (Relations with specific foreign countries are usually found under the region concerned.)*	*Includes business, labor, agriculture, taxation, transportation, consumer affairs, monetary and fiscal policy, natural resources, and pollution.*	*Includes worldwide scientific, medical, and technological developments; natural phenomena; U.S. weather; natural disasters; and accidents.*	*Includes the arts, religion, scholarship, communications media, sports, entertainments, fashions, fads, and social life.*	

	World Affairs	Europe	Africa & the Middle East	The Americas	Asia & the Pacific
July 18	Members of the Association of Southeast Asian Nations (ASEAN) gather in Jakarta, Indonesia, for their 29th annual conference and conduct meetings on regional trade and security issues.	A Chechen rebel officer claiming to be Salman Raduyev, a field commander reported slain in March, gives a news conference in Gudermes, Chechnya. He claims responsibility for two Moscow bus bombs earlier in July. . . . .The German government agrees to provide the estimated 320,000 Bosnian refugees in Germany with plane, bus, or train fares in order to return to their homes.	Israel's president, Ezer Weizman, announces he has issued pardons for two Palestinian women imprisoned in Israel on murder charges. The move appears to clear the way for the release of several dozen other Palestinian females, whose release from Israeli jails was stipulated in a second-stage accord signed by Israel and the PLO in September 1995.		Workers of the Australian Broadcasting Corp. hold demonstrations across the country.
July 19		Radovan Karadzic, leader of the Bosnian Serbs signs an agreement pledging to step down.	Burundian forces begin to forcibly repatriate 85,000 Rwandan refugees. . . . Palestinians in Karyut, in the north-central West Bank, fight with Jewish settlers whom they accuse of illegally seizing Palestinian land in the area. . . . . Mervyn Hugh Cowie, 87, British Kenyan who helped create national parks to protect East Africa's wildlife from extinction, dies in England of unreported causes.	The Popular Revolutionary Army, known by its Spanish initials EPR, claims responsibility for the July 16 ambush of an army truck carrying 10 soldiers near the town of Tixtla in the Mexican state of Guerrero. . . . Flooding and torrential rains strike the region around the Saguenay River in eastern Quebec, Canada.	Mongolia's parliament, the Great Hural, elects M. Enkhsaikhan as the nation's premier.
July 20		A bomb attributed to ETA terrorists explodes at an airport in Reus, Spain, injuring 35 people. Two other bombs explode in the Spanish resort towns of Cambrils and Salou, but no one is injured since warning calls prompted evacuations of those areas. . . . A U.S. Navy F/A-18 jet practicing bombing runs near Brcko, in Bosnia-Herzegovina, accidentally drops a bomb on the edge of a U.S. military base. No one is wounded. . . . Colin Mitchell, 70, British Army officer who served as a Conservative member of Parliament, 1970–74, dies in London.	More than 300 people, most of them women and children, are slain in an attack on a camp for displaced Tutsis in central Burundi. . . . Some 10,000 ultra-Orthodox Jews protest a July 12 court ruling that keeps a main street in an Orthodox neighborhood of northern Jerusalem open to traffic during the Jewish Sabbath.	Reports reveal that as many as 11 people have been arrested as EPR suspects since the group first appeared in Mexico, on charges ranging from illegal weapons possession to rebellion and conspiracy.	
July 21	Ministers of the seven member nations of ASEAN accept applications from Laos and Cambodia to become full ASEAN members in 1997. The ASEAN members also extend observer status to Myanmar, formerly Burma, despite protests from European Union (EU) countries and the U.S.	A bomb is found in a hotel in Salou, Spain, prompting authorities to evacuate about 500 tourists visiting from the Netherlands before the explosive is successfully defused. . . . Gerald McArthur, 80, British police investigator who helped solve the Great Train Robbery of 1963, one of the most notorious crimes in British history, dies of unreported causes.	Israel and the Iranian-backed Hezbollah (Party of God) guerrilla organization exchange several dozen prisoners and the bodies of fallen fighters in the largest such swap to date in their 13-year-old conflict in Lebanon.		Amid an epidemic of food poisoning, Japan's health ministry warns the public not to eat raw meat, a staple of the Japanese diet.
July 22	Franz Fischler, the EU agriculture commissioner, reveals laboratory research showing that mad-cow disease can be passed from cows to sheep, leading to widespread panic in the world's livestock markets.	Georgian and Abkhazi negotiators agree to grant police powers to Russian peacekeepers in the Gali district of Abkhazia.		Reports show that flooding and torrential rains that started July 19 in the region around the Saguenay River in eastern Quebec, Canada, have killed 10 people and left 2,000 others homeless. . . . A container loaded with 54 tons of Canadian two-dollar coins, worth a total of C$3 million (US$2.18 million), is stolen from a railroad yard in Canada. The theft is the most valuable shipment of Canadian coins to be stolen.	
July 23		French police arrest Julian Achurra Egurrola, a leading member of ETA, a Basque separatist group blamed for numerous terrorist attacks in Spain. . . . A team of business leaders and politicians from the Muslim-Croat federation in Bosnia-Herzegovina visit Belgrade, Serbia's capital. It is the first visit to Serbia by an official Bosnian delegation since the beginning of the Bosnian civil war in 1992.	Israel's new foreign minister, David Levy, meets with Palestinian leader Yasser Arafat. The meeting represents the two sides' first formal high-level talks since Israel's rightist Likud party, long a foe of Palestinian political aspirations, defeated the Labor Party-led government in Israeli elections in late May. . . . Burundian president Sylvestre Ntibantunganya takes refuge in the home of Morris Hughes, the U.S. ambassador in Bujumbura, Burundi's capital.		

A	B	C	D	E
Includes developments that affect more than one world region, international organizations, and important meetings of major world leaders.	Includes all domestic and regional developments in Europe, including the Soviet Union, Turkey, Cyprus, and Malta.	Includes all domestic and regional developments in Africa and the Middle East, including Iraq and Iran and excluding Cyprus, Turkey, and Afghanistan.	Includes all domestic and regional developments in Latin America, the Caribbean, and Canada.	Includes all domestic and regional developments in Asia and Pacific nations, extending from Afghanistan through all the Pacific Island, except Hawaii.

U.S. Politics & Social Issues	U.S. Foreign Policy & Defense	U.S. Economy & Environment	Science, Technology, & Nature	Culture, Leisure, & Lifestyle	
The House approves, 256-170, a sweeping overhaul of the nation's system of welfare distribution. The reforms will save an estimated $60 billion over six years, and states will gain unprecedented authority over the use of the funding for poverty relief. The bill also includes new work requirements for people on welfare. . . . Tommie J. Smith, 42, convicted of the 1980 slaying of an Indianapolis, Indiana, police officer, is executed by lethal injection. Smith is the 334th person put to death in the U.S. and only the fourth in Indiana since 1976.		The House passes by voice vote the Teamwork for Employees and Management Act, or Team Act, which will give employers broader discretion to set up worker-management teams to address workplace issues. . . . Videotaped testimony by Pres. Clinton is played during a Whitewater-related fraud and conspiracy trial.			July 18
Fred Kornahrens, 47, convicted of three 1985 murders, is executed by injection in Columbia, South Carolina. He is the 335th convict executed in the U.S. and only the seventh in South Carolina since 1976.	The Senate approves, 72-27, a $244.7 billion fiscal 1997 Defense Department appropriations bill.		A panel of advisers to the FDA recommends that the agency approve the abortion drug RU-486.	The 26th Summer Olympic Games opens in Atlanta, Georgia. The competition, marking the 100th anniversary of the games, draws more than 10,000 athletes from a record 197 countries.	July 19
	The U.S. hands Seaman First Class Terrence Michael Swanson, 20, who is accused of murder, over to Japan, making him the first U.S. military member surrendered to Japan under an October 1995 rule change on the custody of American servicemen suspected of serious crimes.			Markswoman Lida Fariman becomes the first woman ever to compete for Iran, an Islamic country, in the Olympic games when she takes part in the air rifle event.	July 20
				Claudia Cassidy, 96, arts critic for the *Chicago Tribune* newspaper, dies in Chicago, Illinois, of unreported causes. . . . Bjarne Riis becomes the first Dane to win the Tour de France cycling race. . . . Tom Lehman wins the 125th British Open Golf Title.	July 21
The House by voice vote gives final congressional approval to legislation that will establish a nine-member commission to examine the economic and social effects of gambling. . . . Former Rep. Dan Rostenkowski (D, Ill.) begins serving a 17-month sentence for mail fraud in a federal hospital prison in Rochester, Minnesota. . . . Leon Shenandoah, 81, leader of the Onondaga Indians of New York State and head of the Six Nations of the Iroquois Confederacy, dies on the Onondaga reservation just south of Syracuse, New York, of unreported causes.			Hundreds of relatives and friends of the 230 victims of the July 17 crash of a TWA plane attend an emotional oceanside memorial service on Fire Island, Long Island.	Vermont Connecticut Royster, 82, a reporter, 1936–58, and editor, 1958–71, of *The Wall Street Journal* and the winner of two Pulitzer Prizes, dies in Raleigh, North Carolina, of unreported causes.	July 22
The Senate passes, 74-24, a sweeping overhaul of the welfare system that will give states unprecedented authority over the use of the funding for poverty relief. . . . Robert Nathan Wilentz, 69, chief justice of the New Jersey Supreme Court, 1979–96, dies in New York City of cancer. . . . Hamilton Fish Jr., 70, moderate Republican congressman from New York who served 13 terms from 1969 to 1994 and supported liberal social causes, dies in Washington, D.C., of cancer.	The U.S. House by voice vote approves a bill that will impose economic sanctions on foreign companies that make large new investments in the energy sectors of Iran or Libya.	The House passes. 417-0, the Food Quality Protection Act, a measure that overhauls regulations covering the use of pesticides on foods.		Jean Muir, 85, actress who was blacklisted in the 1950s, dies in Mesa, Arizona. . . . At the Olympics, U.S. gymnast Kerri Strug lands a vault despite a dislocated ankle. . . . Jessica Mitford, 78, writer known for her irreverence, dies in Oakland, California, of cancer. . . . Senators Arlen Specter (R, Pa.) and Barbara Boxer (D, Calif.) present a $1 million federal grant to Steven Spielberg for his Holocaust documentation project.	July 23
F	G	H	I	J	
Includes elections, federal-state relations, civil rights and liberties, crime, the judiciary, education, health care, poverty, urban affairs, and population.	*Includes formation and debate of U.S. foreign and defense policies, veterans' affairs, and defense spending. (Relations with specific foreign countries are usually found under the region concerned.)*	*Includes business, labor, agriculture, taxation, transportation, consumer affairs, monetary and fiscal policy, natural resources, and pollution.*	*Includes worldwide scientific, medical, and technological developments; natural phenomena; U.S. weather; natural disasters; and accidents.*	*Includes the arts, religion, scholarship, communications media, sports, entertainments, fashions, fads, and social life.*	

	World Affairs	Europe	Africa & the Middle East	The Americas	Asia & the Pacific
July 24		The newspaper *Pravda*, once the official organ of the Soviet Union's Communist Party, suspends publication.... British agriculture minister Douglas Hogg announces stricter rules designed as a precaution against the remote possibility of mad-cow disease (BSE) in sheep and goats.... Reports state that Saudi Arabia will fund a $250,000 operation to return 1,000 Bosnian refugees to their homes.	General Mohammed Farah Aidid, a Somali clan leader suffers gunshot wounds in faction fighting. . . . In Burundi, the main Tutsi party in the coalition government, the Union for National Progress (UPRONA), rejects Pres. Ntibantunganya and the 1994 accord that established the coalition government.		
July 25	A military coup in Burundi is widely criticized, drawing denouncements from the UN, the U.S., the EU, South Africa, and the Organization of African Unity.	The Czech parliament votes to approve the new coalition government headed by Premier Vaclav Klaus.... Unidentified arsonists burn a mosque in the town of Prozor, in central Bosnia-Herzegovina.... Reports confirm that Russian president Boris Yeltsin has signed a decree creating a defense council with 18 high-level members.	Burundi's Tutsi-dominated military announces that it has seized power in a coup. The army names Major Pierre Buyoya, a Tutsi regarded as a moderate, as president. It also dissolves Parliament, declares political parties and demonstrations illegal, closes off the country's borders and airport, and institutes a curfew.	After 19 months of negotiations, Mexico's four major political parties sign a political and electoral reform pact.	
July 26	Germany, Italy, and the European Union urge the Turkish government to meet some of the demands made by prisoners who have been staging hunger strikes since May.... The UN Security Council adopts a resolution that mildly criticizes Cuba for shooting down two unarmed U.S. civilian planes in February.	Thousands of veterans of the four-year-long war in Bosnia-Herzegovina rally to demand that the government pay their pensions and those of fellow soldiers killed in the war. Separately, a bomb explosion in Bugojno damages the 120-year-old Church of St. Anton, the biggest Roman Catholic church in Bosnia.... Workers at Dalenergo, the state-run power company for Russia's far eastern Primorski region, launch a hunger strike to protest that their wages have not been paid since March.... Arthur William Bryant McDonald, 93, air marshal in Britain's Royal Air Force during World War II, dies of unreported causes.	Israel closes the border after suspected Palestinian militants kill two Israelis in a drive-by shooting in the village of Tirosh, southwest of Jerusalem.	A car bomb explodes outside a police station in Lima, Peru's capital, killing one person and injuring at least seven others.... In Buenos Aires, 30,000 protestors rally against proposed cutbacks.... Reports confirm that Bishop Hubert Patrick O'Connor was convicted of two sex-crime charges. He is the highest-ranking Roman Catholic official in Canada to be charged with sex crimes.... An explosion at one of state-owned oil facilities, near the town of Reforma in Chiapas Mexico state, kills at least six people and injures 39 others.... Tropical storm Cesar kills three people in Venezuela.	
July 27		Reports confirm that a panel of judges in Scotland has ruled that a homosexual man will be permitted to adopt a five-year-old disabled boy. The decision allows Britain's first known adoption by a gay man to take place.... Michael Penrose and Frederic Malardeau, two relief workers for International Action Against Hunger, are kidnapped in Grozny.	An estimated 50 civilians are killed in the Gitega province in central Burundi, as the Tutsi-dominated army retaliates against Hutu rebels thought to have set fire to a coffee farm in the town of Giheta.... Gen. Aidid's forces regain control of their main airbase, in Bale Dogle, 55 miles southwest of Mogadishu, Somalia.		Riots erupt in Jakarta, the Indonesian capital, when thousands of demonstrators protest a raid by military police on the headquarters of the opposition Indonesian Democratic Party (PDI). At least three people are killed and hundreds are injured in the riots.... Ivan Milat is convicted and sentenced to life in prison for the murders of seven backpackers, ending the biggest criminal inquiry in Australian history.
July 28		Left-wing inmates at prisons throughout Turkey end a 69-day hunger strike after reaching a settlement with the Turkish government. The strike, which resulted in the deaths of 12 prisoners and left dozens more critically ill, began in May after the Turkish government moved several leftist prisoners from the Bayrampasa prison in Istanbul to the Eskisehir prison in the central Anatolia region. Some 2,900 leftist prisoners, including about 900 inmates at Bayrampasa, supported or engaged in hunger strikes.		At least 30,000 farmers participate in protests in Putumayo, southern Colombia, opposing a government program to eradicate their coca plants, which are used to make cocaine, and their poppy plants, which can be used to make heroin.... Tropical storm Cesar, upgraded to a hurricane, continues to batter northern Colombia, Nicaragua, Costa Rica, and El Salvador, causing flooding and mudslides that kill at least 50 people.	Sporadic outbursts of violence continue in Jakarta, the capital of Indonesia, and military troops are stationed in the streets to deter further violence.
July 29	The UN Security Council votes to condemn the July 25 coup in Burundi.	A failed assassination attempt on Chechen rebel Gen. Aslan Maskhadov leaves one would-be assassin dead and one of Maskhadov's bodyguards injured near the village of Nozhay Yurt in southeast Chechnya.		A car bomb attack in Lima, the capital of Peru, targeting Gen. Manuel Valera Gamarra, head of the armed forces in the Huallaga region, kills one person and injures five others.	China declares a moratorium on future nuclear testing shortly after it conducts what it claims will be its final underground nuclear test.... Japanese premier Ryutaro Hashimoto visits a shrine for Japan's World War II dead in Tokyo, the nation's capital. The visit arouses controversy because among the dead honored at the shrine are wartime leader Hideki Tojo and six other executed war criminals.

A	B	C	D	E
Includes developments that affect more than one world region, international organizations, and important meetings of major world leaders.	Includes all domestic and regional developments in Europe, including the Soviet Union, Turkey, Cyprus, and Malta.	Includes all domestic and regional developments in Africa and the Middle East, including Iraq and Iran and excluding Cyprus, Turkey, and Afghanistan.	Includes all domestic and regional developments in Latin America, the Caribbean, and Canada.	Includes all domestic and regional developments in Asia and Pacific nations, extending from Afghanistan through all the Pacific Island, except Hawaii.

U.S. Politics & Social Issues	U.S. Foreign Policy & Defense	U.S. Economy & Environment	Science, Technology, & Nature	Culture, Leisure, & Lifestyle	
	The Senate Veterans' Affairs Committee votes to change date that the Vietnam War began to Feb. 28, 1961, from Aug. 5, 1964, thereby allowing some 16,500 veterans to gain benefits for wartime service they were previously denied.	The Senate by voice vote passes the Food Quality Protection Act, which will overhaul regulations covering the use of pesticides on foods.			July 24
		The House passes, 391-23, a $19.8 billion fiscal 1997 energy and water spending bill. . . . The House rejects, 259-162, legislation that would have placed various restrictions on House candidates' ability to raise campaign funds.	Investigators report that they have not uncovered the reason for the July 17 crash of a TWA jetliner into the Atlantic Ocean. Data shows that 126 bodies have been recovered from the crash site, and 111 have been identified.		July 25
Hector Perez Garcia, 82, physician who founded one of the nation's leading Mexican-American civil-rights organizations, the American GI Forum, and who, in 1968, was the first Mexican-American to serve on the U.S. Commission on Civil Rights, dies in Corpus Christi, Texas, of pneumonia and congestive heart failure after suffering from cancer.	The Senate passes, 93-7, its version of a $12.2 billion fiscal 1997 foreign operations bill. The measure includes a curb on U.S. investment in Myanmar and increases funding for an energy development program in North Korea.			Swimmer Amy Van Dyken of the U.S. becomes the first U.S. woman to win four gold medals in a single Olympics.	July 26
				A homemade pipe bomb goes off at an Olympic Games site in Atlanta, Georgia, killing one person and injuring 111 others. The park bombing is the first terrorist attack at the Olympics since the 1972 games in Munich, Germany.	July 27
			Roger Tory Peterson, 87, ornithologist who wrote *A Field Guide to the Birds* and who was given awards by the New York Zoological Society, the National Audubon Society, the World Wildlife Fund, and other organizations, dies in Old Lyme, Connecticut.	Harold C. Fox, 86, who popularized the zoot suit of the 1940s, dies in Siesta Key, Florida, of unreported causes. . . . Karch Kiraly and Kent Steffes of the U.S. win the first-ever men's Olympic beach volleyball competition. Ethiopian long-distance runner Fatuma Roba becomes the first African woman to win an Olympic or world championship marathon.	July 28
A panel of three federal judges in New York City rules unanimously that the Communications Decency Act of 1996, designed to censor indecent material on the Internet computer network, violates free-speech rights protected by the Constitution's First Amendment. The federal panel is the second to rule against the act.				Pres. Clinton announces an agreement that will require TV stations to broadcast a minimum of three hours of children's educational programming each week. Cable-TV stations, which are not federally licensed, will not be affected by the new rules.	July 29

F	G	H	I	J
Includes elections, federal-state relations, civil rights and liberties, crime, the judiciary, education, health care, poverty, urban affairs, and population.	Includes formation and debate of U.S. foreign and defense policies, veterans' affairs, and defense spending. (Relations with specific foreign countries are usually found under the region concerned.)	Includes business, labor, agriculture, taxation, transportation, consumer affairs, monetary and fiscal policy, natural resources, and pollution.	Includes worldwide scientific, medical, and technological developments; natural phenomena; U.S. weather; natural disasters; and accidents.	Includes the arts, religion, scholarship, communications media, sports, entertainments, fashions, fads, and social life.

	World Affairs	Europe	Africa & the Middle East	The Americas	Asia & the Pacific
July 30	Senior representatives of the Group of Seven (G-7) leading industrialized nations and Russia agree to step up measures aimed at stemming terrorism and prosecuting its practitioners.				
July 31	At a summit organized by the Organization of African Unity, African leaders agree to impose sanctions on Burundi that will create an economic blockade as a response to the July 25 coup.		The leaders of Liberia's rival factions announce they have agreed to cease fighting and to begin disarming their soldiers by the end of September.... At least 15 people are killed in a stampede at a railway station in Tembisa, a black township northeast of Johannesburg, South Africa, when guards block nonpaying passengers with electric-shock batons.... Major Pierre Buyoya names a Hutu, Pascal Firmin Ndimira, as Burundi's new premier.	Four police officers are indicted on charges of homicide for allegedly supplying the perpetrators with the van used in the 1994 bombing of a Jewish center in Buenos Aires, Argentina, that killed 87 people.	
Aug. 1		As a result of technical circumstances in the case, an Italian court orders the release from prison of Erich Priebke, 83, an officer in Nazi Germany's SS charged in connection with a World War II massacre.... Fertility clinics throughout Britain begin destroying 3,300 frozen embryos in compliance with a 1990 British law that limits storage time for frozen embryos to a maximum of five years.	Gen. Mohammed Farah Aidid, a Somali clan leader who fueled Somalia's civil war despite UN peacekeeping efforts, dies from gunshot wounds suffered in faction fighting on July 24. His age is variously reported to be between 59 and 61.		
Aug. 2		German officials confirm that they are extraditing Erich Priebke, 83, they who was charged in connection with a World War II massacre and released on a technicality in Italy Aug. 1.... Michel Debre, 84, French premier who served under Pres. Charles de Gaulle and who played a central role in drafting France's 1958 constitution, dies in Montlouis-sur-Loire.	Reports confirm that Burundi has formed a new 25-member government. Tanzania closes its border with Burundi to enforce the economic embargo enacted in response to the July coup. The UN Center for Human Rights reports that in attacks between April and July, the army killed 2,100–3,000 Hutus.... Thousands of mourners attend a funeral service in Mogadishu for Gen. Mohammed Farah Aidid, a Somali clan leader who died Aug. 1.	Two people are killed and 22 others wounded when 8,000 farmers in the Colombian town of Puerto Asis, in Putumayo, clash with government troops when they attempt to take over the airport.... In Peru, 200 guerrillas disguised as army soldiers occupy Aucayacu, a town in the Huallaga region, overwhelming the local police and killing at least one person.	
Aug. 3		A Royal Danish Air Force airplane crashes into a cliff as it approaches an airstrip in Denmark's Faroe Islands in the North Atlantic Ocean. All nine people aboard, including Admiral Hans Jorgen Garde, 57, the leader of Denmark's armed forces, are killed.		A convention of at least 2,000 foreign intellectuals and representatives of leftist organizations in Chiapas, Mexico, for the EZLN- sponsored "Conference for Humanity and Against Neoliberalism," closes.	
Aug. 4		Workers of Dalenergo, the state-run power company which serves Russia's far eastern Primorski region, end a hunger strike that started July 26.	An anticrime vigilante movement in Capetown, South Africa, called People Against Gangsterism and Drugs (PAGAD) shoots and burns to death reputed gang leader Rashaad Staggie in front of TV cameras and police.... The United Somali Congress-Somali National Alliance selects Hussein Mohamed Aidid to succeed his father, Gen. Mohammed Farah Aidid, as leader of the clan.		Japanese voters in the town of Maki, in the nation's first-ever referendum, oppose a federally backed proposal to build a nuclear power plant in their town.... Kiyoshi Atsumi (born Yasuo Tadokoro), 68, Japanese actor who played the character of Tora-san in a series of 48 films since 1969, dies of lung cancer.

A	B	C	D	E
Includes developments that affect more than one world region, international organizations, and important meetings of major world leaders.	*Includes all domestic and regional developments in Europe, including the Soviet Union, Turkey, Cyprus, and Malta.*	*Includes all domestic and regional developments in Africa and the Middle East, including Iraq and Iran and excluding Cyprus, Turkey, and Afghanistan.*	*Includes all domestic and regional developments in Latin America, the Caribbean, and Canada.*	*Includes all domestic and regional developments in Asia and Pacific nations, extending from Afghanistan through all the Pacific Island, except Hawaii.*

U.S. Politics & Social Issues	U.S. Foreign Policy & Defense	U.S. Economy & Environment	Science, Technology, & Nature	Culture, Leisure, & Lifestyle	
		Pres. Clinton vetoes the Teamwork for Employees and Management Act, or Team Act, a bill that would have given employers broader discretion to set up worker-management teams.... Conrail Inc. and the Brotherhood of Maintenance of Way Employees reach a contract settlement that averts a national rail strike and ends a nearly two-year-long negotiating battle.... Data show that the Conference Board's index surged to 107.2 in July, from a revised level of 100.1 in June. July's reading is the highest since May 1990.		The FEC files suit against the Christian Coalition, charging that the organization's distribution of millions of voter guides during the 1990, 1992, and 1994 elections amounted to illegal campaign contributions. . . . Claudette Colbert, 92, Paris-born American actress in films of the 1930s and 1940s, dies in Barbados.... In the first Olympic softball competition, the U.S. wins the gold medal.	July 30
Pres. Clinton reveals he will sign a measure that will radically alter the welfare system, sparking controversy.... The House passes, 328-101, a bill that will end the 61-year-old federal guarantee of cash assistance to poor families with children by eliminating Aid to Families with Dependent Children (AFDC) and by distributing welfare funds to the states in lump-sum payments known as "block grants."		The Senate votes, 63-37, to approve legislation that will require the federal government to set up an interim storage site for thousands of tons of civilian nuclear waste.... Former Rep. Joseph P. Kolter (D, Pa.) is sentenced to six months in prison for conspiracy to defraud taxpayers in connection with the 1992 House Post Office scandal.		British punk rock band the Sex Pistols perform in Denver, Colorado, in their first U.S. concert since 1978.... Iraqi weightlifter Raed Ahmed, who carried his country's flag at the Olympics' opening ceremonies, asks for political asylum in the U.S.	July 31
The Senate approves, 78-21, a bill to radically reform the welfare system... A U.S. District Court jury in Philadelphia, Pennsylvania, acquits Rep. Joseph M. McDade (R, Pa.) of bribery, racketeering, and conspiracy.... The House passes, 259-169, a bill that will make English the official language of the federal government. The measure sparks a heated debate on the House floor over the importance of the English language in defining U.S. citizenship and culture.	The House adopts, 285-132, the conference report on the $265.6 billion fiscal 1997 defense-authorization bill.	The House, 379-42, and the Senate, by unanimous consent, approve a $53.3 billion fiscal 1997 agriculture appropriations bill.... The House passes, 397-22, a $2.17 billion fiscal 1997 legislative branch appropriations bill. . . . The House approves, 421-2, a bill that will make health insurance more portable from job to job.... A jury in Little Rock, Arkansas, acquits Robert M. Hill and Herby Branscum Jr. on four felony counts in a Whitewater-related fraud and conspiracy trial.	Tadeus Reichstein, 99, Swiss chemist who shared the 1950 Nobel Prize in medicine for research on the anti-inflammatory agent cortisone, which is used in the treatment of arthritis, dies in Basel, Switzerland, of unreported causes.	In an Olympic debut, the U.S. women's soccer team wins the gold medal with a 2-1 victory over China.	Aug. 1
Rep. Jim Kolbe (R, Ariz.) publicly announces that he is a homosexual, becoming the fourth openly gay current member of the House.	The House passes, 389-22, a bill that will tighten airport security and impose other measures designed to fight terrorism.... Reports reveal that Mongolia has signed a security agreement with the U.S.... The Senate approves the appointment of Admiral Jay L. Johnson as chief of naval operations, succeeding Admiral Jeremy M. Boorda.... After two weeks of negotiations, trade representatives from the U.S. and Japan agree to an accord covering trade in computer chips.	The Senate passes, by unanimous consent, the Federal Oil and Gas Royalty Simplification and Fairness Act of 1996, which revises procedures for collecting payments from companies that extract oil and gas from federal lands.... The Senate, 76-22, and the House, 354-72, clear legislation that will raise the minimum hourly wage 90 cents, to $5.15 from $4.25.... The Senate approves, 98-0, a bill that will make health insurance more portable from job to job and limit insurance companies' ability to withhold coverage because of preexisting medical conditions.... The House, 392-30, and the Senate, 98-0, reauthorize the Safe Drinking Water Act of 1974.			Aug. 2
Pres. Clinton signs legislation that will establish a nine-member commission to examine the economic and social effects of gambling.				Nigeria wins the Olympic gold medal in soccer, 3-2, over Argentina, making Nigeria the first African nation to win a major international soccer competition.	Aug. 3
				Josia Thugwane becomes South Africa's first black Olympic gold medalist, coming in three seconds ahead of South Korea's Lee Bong-ju, the closest finish in Olympic marathon history. The 26th Summer Olympics close, and athletes from the U.S. won the most medals, 101. Germany came in second with 65, and Russia placed third with 63.	Aug. 4

F	G	H	I	J
Includes elections, federal-state relations, civil rights and liberties, crime, the judiciary, education, health care, poverty, urban affairs, and population.	Includes formation and debate of U.S. foreign and defense policies, veterans' affairs, and defense spending. (Relations with specific foreign countries are usually found under the region concerned.)	Includes business, labor, agriculture, taxation, transportation, consumer affairs, monetary and fiscal policy, natural resources, and pollution.	Includes worldwide scientific, medical, and technological developments; natural phenomena; U.S. weather; natural disasters; and accidents.	Includes the arts, religion, scholarship, communications media, sports, entertainments, fashions, fads, and social life.

	World Affairs	Europe	Africa & the Middle East	The Americas	Asia & the Pacific
Aug. 5		Reports disclose that Italian NATO troops discovered an unregistered Bosnian Serb arms depot in the village of Markovici. . . . Reports confirm that an unidentified pregnant British woman and her physician agreed that one of the woman's twin fetuses would be aborted, causing controversy. The procedure is reportedly Britain's first known abortion of a healthy fetus in a multiple pregnancy conceived without the use of fertility drugs.	In response to the July coup in Burundi, Kenya cuts off travel and suspends trade with the country.	Mexico's Congress gives final approval to a political and electoral reform pact hailed as one of the most significant measures of its kind ever enacted in Mexico. The legislation may eventually end the dominant standing that the ruling Institutional Revolutionary Party (PRI) has enjoyed in Mexican politics for 67 years.	
Aug. 6		Separatist rebels in the Russian republic of Chechnya launch a new attack on the region's capital, Grozny, and the two nearby towns of Gudermes and Argun. . . . Bosnian Muslims and Croats reach an agreement on the joint administration of the divided city of Mostar in southwestern Bosnia-Herzegovina, ending a boycott by Bosnian Croats of the unified city council, elected in June in an internationally monitored vote.	Imam Mohammed al-Badr, 67, last of the Zaydi dynasty in Yemen, which ruled the Arabian nation for 28 generations, dies in Kent, England, of unreported causes.	Catherine Callbeck, the first woman elected as a Canadian provincial premier, resigns as premier of Canada's smallest province, Prince Edward Island. . . . Hernan Siles Zuazo, 83, Bolivian president, 1956–60 and 1982–85, and a leader of the 1952 revolution that changed Bolivian society, dies in Montevideo, Uruguay, of unreported causes.	The Japanese government officially declares that a nationwide outbreak of food poisoning that has left more than 9,000 people ill and caused the deaths of seven people constitutes an epidemic caused by the rare bacterium E. coli O157:H7.
Aug. 7		In Athens, Croatian president Franjo Tudjman and Serbian president Slobodan Milosevic hold their first meeting since March 1991, before the onset of Croatia's secessionist war with Yugoslavia, and establish diplomatic ties. . . . A Russian armored convoy reaches Grozny in the Chechen republic and begins to attack rebel positions. . . . At least 83 campers are killed and about 150 injured when flash floods and mudslides in the Pyrenees mountains sweeps away the Virgen de las Nieves campsite near the town of Biescas, Spain.		In Guerrero, Mexico, one soldier is killed and two others are wounded in an ambush attributed to the EPR. . . . In Canada, Quebec premier Lucien Bouchard discloses the July 19–22 floods caused at least C$600 million (US$436 million) in damage, and that the Quebec government will provide C$400 million in disaster relief.	
Aug. 8	The European Union files a protest with the U.S. State Department in response to the U.S. law that imposes economic sanctions on foreign companies that make large new investments in the energy sectors of Iran or Libya. The law was signed on Aug. 5 by U.S. president Clinton.	Reports indicate that the offensive begun Aug. 6 in Chechnya has taken the lives of more than 70 Russian soldiers and has wounded 300 others.		Peru extends a state of emergency in 11 provinces, after several terrorist attacks in previous weeks killed nine people and injured 22 others. The attacks are attributed to the Sendero Luminoso (Shining Path) guerrillas. . . . Orlando Vasquez Velasquez, Colombia's attorney general imprisoned on charges of accepting money from the Cali cartel, is freed from prison on a legal technicality.	
Aug. 9		Pres. Boris Yeltsin is inaugurated as the first democratically elected Russian head of state. . . . Chechen rebel forces capture the main government building in Grozny. Russian officials evacuate civilians stationed at bases at the two airports near Grozny.	Zaire becomes the last of Burundi's neighboring countries to impose stringent economic sanctions on the central African nation in response to the July overthrow of Burundi's coalition government by its Tutsi-led army.	In Guatemala, about 200 militia members lay down their arms in Colotenango, the site of a bloody massacre of suspected rebel supporters in 1993.	
Aug. 10		In a special session, Russia's Parliament votes to reappoint Viktor S. Chernomyrdin as premier. . . . A national day of mourning for the victims of the fighting that was renewed Aug. 6 in Grozny, Bosnia, is marked. . . . Protestant unionist groups hold an annual march, which commemorates a 1689 victory by Protestant forces against the Catholic army of King James II.	At least 13 people are killed in a clash between Hussein Aidid's and Ali Mahdi's forces in the town of Warmohan, 28 miles (45 km) southwest of Mogadishu, Somalia.	Reports confirm that Colombia's former defense minister, Fernando Botero Zea, was sentenced to more than five years in jail and fined $1 million for his role in a drug-related scandal currently plaguing the government.	

A	B	C	D	E
Includes developments that affect more than one world region, international organizations, and important meetings of major world leaders.	Includes all domestic and regional developments in Europe, including the Soviet Union, Turkey, Cyprus, and Malta.	Includes all domestic and regional developments in Africa and the Middle East, including Iraq and Iran and excluding Cyprus, Turkey, and Afghanistan.	Includes all domestic and regional developments in Latin America, the Caribbean, and Canada.	Includes all domestic and regional developments in Asia and Pacific nations, extending from Afghanistan through all the Pacific Island, except Hawaii.

U.S. Politics & Social Issues	U.S. Foreign Policy & Defense	U.S. Economy & Environment	Science, Technology, & Nature	Culture, Leisure, & Lifestyle	
	Pres. Clinton signs into law a bill that will impose economic sanctions on foreign companies that make large new investments in the energy sectors of Iran or Libya, which Clinton calls "two of the most dangerous supporters of terrorism in the world." The measure is opposed by U.S. trading partners in Europe, whose companies may be subject to the sanctions.			*Cause of Death*, by Patricia Cornwell, tops the bestseller list. . . . Frank Marcus, 68, British playwright and critic who penned *The Killing of Sister George*, dies in London, England, of a pulmonary embolism.	Aug. 5
A panel of three federal judges redraws 13 of the 30 congressional districts in Texas, in response to a June Supreme Court ruling that the districts were drawn mainly on the basis of race and therefore unconstitutional.	The U.S. Air Force announces that 16 officers, including two generals, were reprimanded in connection with the Apr. 3 crash of a transport plane near Dubrovnik, Croatia, that had killed Commerce Secretary Ron Brown and 34 other passengers. . . . Loret Miller Ruppe, 60, the longest-serving director of the U.S. Peace Corps since its 1961 founding with her 1981–89 tenure, dies in Bethesda, Maryland, of ovarian cancer.	Pres. Clinton signs the $53.3 billion fiscal 1997 agriculture appropriations bill that will provide funding for the Department of Agriculture, the FDA, and other related agencies. . . . Pres. Clinton signs a bill reauthorizing the Safe Drinking Water Act of 1974. The new bill provides $7.6 billion over seven years to help states and municipalities make improvements to their water systems.	NASA administrator Daniel Goldin reveals that "NASA has made a startling discovery that points to the possibility that a primitive form of microscopic life may have existed on Mars more than three billion years ago." He adds that the evidence is "exciting, even compelling, but not conclusive."	Data shows that TV coverage of the Olympics by NBC drew an average rating of 21.6 for its nighttime telecasts. The numbers of viewers reportedly increased 25% over the 1992 Olympic Games in Barcelona.	Aug. 6
	An air force U-2 reconnaissance jet crashes in Oroville, California, killing the pilot and one civilian on the ground and injuring two other bystanders.	Pres. Clinton signs into law the Food Quality Protection Act, a measure that overhauls regulations covering the use of pesticides on foods.	America Online Inc. (AOL), which has 6 million subscribers and is the leading U.S. provider of on-line computer network access, experiences a 19-hour "blackout" that renders its services unavailable to customers. The blackout is described as the largest outage in the history of computer network services.	Ossie Clark (born Raymond Clark), 54, British fashion designer who invented the midi-skirt and designed clothes for Mick Jagger and Twiggy, is found stabbed to death at his home in London, England.	Aug. 7
	Data reveal that 22,140 U.S. Army soldiers are taking part in the Bosnia mission, 16,175 of whom are based in Bosnia.		Nevill Francis Mott, 90, British theoretical physicist who shared the 1977 Nobel Prize in physics for work in solid-state electronics that paved the way for the mass production of computers, dies of unreported causes. . . . Frank Whittle, 89, British inventor of the jet engine, which revolutionized military and civil aviation, dies in Columbia, Maryland, of lung cancer.	The FCC approves new regulations, including one that requires TV stations to air three hours of children's educational programming each week. . . . Herbert Huncke, 80, who inspired the writers of the Beat Generation, dies in New York City of congestive heart failure	Aug. 8
A federal appeals court in Philadelphia, Pennsylvania, rules that a New Jersey school district should not have laid off a white teacher, Sharon Taxman, in 1989 merely to promote racial diversity. . . . A jury in Jacksonville, Florida, orders Brown & Williamson Tobacco to pay $750,000 to Grady M. Carter. It is the only the second such order against a tobacco company; the first one was overturned on appeal. . . . John William King, 79, Democratic governor of New Hampshire, 1963–69, and chief justice of the New Hampshire Supreme Court, 1980–86, dies in Manchester of heart trouble.					Aug. 9
				The racehorse Cigar fails in his bid to win a record 17 consecutive races when he places second to Dare and Go in the Pacific Classic in Del Mar, California.	Aug. 10

F	G	H	I	J
Includes elections, federal-state relations, civil rights and liberties, crime, the judiciary, education, health care, poverty, urban affairs, and population.	Includes formation and debate of U.S. foreign and defense policies, veterans' affairs, and defense spending. (Relations with specific foreign countries are usually found under the region concerned.)	Includes business, labor, agriculture, taxation, transportation, consumer affairs, monetary and fiscal policy, natural resources, and pollution.	Includes worldwide scientific, medical, and technological developments; natural phenomena; U.S. weather; natural disasters; and accidents.	Includes the arts, religion, scholarship, communications media, sports, entertainments, fashions, fads, and social life.

	World Affairs	Europe	Africa & the Middle East	The Americas	Asia & the Pacific
Aug. 11		Some 7,000 Greek Cypriot bikers rally, along with 200 motorcycle riders from Europe and North America, to protest Turkey's occupation of the northern one-third of Cyprus. When Greek Cypriot motorcycle gangs cross into the buffer zone separating the Greek and Turkish sections of the island nation, a violent clash erupts, leaving one dead and injuring more than 60.... Catholics who favor Ulster's unification with Ireland march in Belfast, Northern Ireland's capital.	In Cape Town, South Africa, the Hard Livings gang stages a rally attended by some 1,000 people. The group was led by Rashaad Staggie, who was killed Aug. 4 by a Muslim-led vigilante organization, People Against Gangsterism and Drugs (PAGAD). Rioting erupts in Cape Town when police clash with 5,000 people marching in support of the Muslim vigilante group.	Peruvian justice minister Carlos Hermoza Moya admits that some 400 people may have been wrongly imprisoned under Peru's antiterrorism laws.	
Aug. 12		French police storm the Roman Catholic Church of St. Bernard de la Chapelle in Paris, which has been occupied by 300 illegal immigrants from Africa since June 28. The police forcibly transport the immigrants, who have been on hunger strikes since July 4, to area hospitals for treatment.... Sir Anthony Parsons, 73, British diplomat who was ambassador to the UN during the 1982 Falklands War with Argentina, dies in Ashburton, England, of unreported causes.	Because of violence between vigilante groups in Cape Town, South Africa, Western Cape provincial ANC leader Chris Nissen calls for a state of emergency to be declared in the region.		A series of illegal protests are launched by students at Yonsei University in Seoul, the capital of South Korea. The students are calling for South Korea's reunification with communist North Korea.
Aug. 13	The European Commission, the EU's executive body, approves a $5.3 million humanitarian aid package for the breakaway republic of Chechnya.	NATO troops finish an inspection of a Bosnian Serb-held bunker that was the headquarters of Gen. Ratko Mladic, the Bosnian Serb military commander, throughout the four-year-long war in Bosnia-Herzegovina.... Several gunmen stage an airplane robbery as the plane taxis on a runway in Perpignan, a town in southern France.... Antonio Sebastiao Ribeiro de Spinola, 86, Portuguese general who served briefly as the country's president after a coup in 1974, dies in Lisbon, Portugal, while receiving treatment for respiratory problems.			In Japan, 35,000 fans attend a farewell service for Kiyoshi Atsumi (born Yasuo Tadokoro), 68, the Japanese actor who died Aug. 4.
Aug. 14		At the funeral of Tassos Isaac, a protestor killed Aug. 11 on Cyprus, violence breaks out, leading to the death of another Greek Cypriot protester, Solomos Solomou, 26. The fighting leaves 11 others wounded.... Reports indicate that Georgia and Abkhazia have agreed to extend the mandate of CIS peacekeeping troops in Abkhazia.... Sergiu Celibidache, 84, Romanian conductor and composer, dies in Paris, France, after suffering from heart ailments.			
Aug. 15		The international airport in Sarajevo, the capital of Bosnia-Herzegovina, reopens for commercial traffic for the first time since 1992.			
Aug. 16			Riots erupt in Jordan when Muslim protestors in Kerak throw stones and set fires after police tear-gas the marchers during their peaceful protest. Reports indicate that 40 people were injured—some by police gunshots—in clashes.	Andre Dallaire, a schizophrenic found guilty in June of attempted murder of Canadian prime minister Jean Chrétien, is granted a conditional discharge.... Mexican attorney general Antonio Lozano Gracia discloses that he fired 17% of Mexico's 4,400-member federal judicial police force after an internal investigation revealed rampant corruption in the organization.	

A	B	C	D	E
Includes developments that affect more than one world region, international organizations, and important meetings of major world leaders.	Includes all domestic and regional developments in Europe, including the Soviet Union, Turkey, Cyprus, and Malta.	Includes all domestic and regional developments in Africa and the Middle East, including Iraq and Iran and excluding Cyprus, Turkey, and Afghanistan.	Includes all domestic and regional developments in Latin America, the Caribbean, and Canada.	Includes all domestic and regional developments in Asia and Pacific nations, extending from Afghanistan through all the Pacific Island, except Hawaii.

U.S. Politics & Social Issues	U.S. Foreign Policy & Defense	U.S. Economy & Environment	Science, Technology, & Nature	Culture, Leisure, & Lifestyle	
				Mark Brooks wins the PGA's Championship tournament at Valhalla Golf Club in Louisville, Kentucky. . . . (Jeronym) Rafael Kubelik, 82, Czech-born conductor known for his grand, personalized interpretations, dies in Lucerne, Switzerland, of unreported causes.	Aug. 11
The Republican Party opens its convention in San Diego, California. . . . Richard F. Upton, 81, New Hampshire lawyer and politician who turned the state's primary into a make-or-break test for presidential candidates, dies of unreported causes.		Pres. Clinton announces that representatives from Crown Butte Mines Inc. have agreed to halt their plans to construct a gold mine near Yellowstone National Park in Wyoming in exchange for $65 million worth of federal land. Activists charged that the mine could pollute rivers and streams in the national park.			Aug. 12
		Pres. Clinton signs into law the Federal Oil and Gas Royalty Simplification and Fairness Act of 1996. The measure revises the government's procedures for collecting royalty payments from companies that extract oil and gas from federal lands.		David Eugene Tudor, 70, composer and performer of avant-garde electronic music, dies in Tomkins Cove, New York, after a series of strokes.	Aug. 13
				Svetlana Masterkova of Russia sets a new world record in the women's mile, completing the distance in four minutes, 12.56 seconds in Zurich, Switzerland.	Aug. 14
In San Diego, California, Robert J. Dole accepts the Republican Party nomination for president. Jack F. Kemp accepts the vice-presidential nomination. . . . Frederick Martin Davidson, a graduate student at San Diego State University in California, is arrested after allegedly opening fire with a handgun while defending his engineering thesis, killing three professors—Chen Liang, 32; D. Preston Lowrey III, 44; and Constantinos Lyrintzis, 36.			Investigators report they have not found conclusive evidence supporting their suspicion that an explosive device caused the crash of TWA Flight 800 into the Atlantic Ocean in July. Divers have retrieved 201 of the 203 bodies from the crash site and have identified all but one of them.	Joe Seneca, theater, TV, and film actor who made a mystery of his age and was thought to have been in his late 70s or early 80s, dies in New York City after an asthma attack.	Aug. 15
	Pres. Clinton names Commerce Undersecretary Stuart E. Eizenstat as a special envoy to the EU, Canada, and Mexico to work with those countries on promoting democracy in Cuba.			The first-ever MLB regular-season game in Mexico is held in Monterrey between the San Diego Padres and the New York Mets.	Aug. 16

F	G	H	I	J
Includes elections, federal-state relations, civil rights and liberties, crime, the judiciary, education, health care, poverty, urban affairs, and population.	Includes formation and debate of U.S. foreign and defense policies, veterans' affairs, and defense spending. (Relations with specific foreign countries are usually found under the region concerned.)	Includes business, labor, agriculture, taxation, transportation, consumer affairs, monetary and fiscal policy, natural resources, and pollution.	Includes worldwide scientific, medical, and technological developments; natural phenomena; U.S. weather; natural disasters; and accidents.	Includes the arts, religion, scholarship, communications media, sports, entertainments, fashions, fads, and social life.

	World Affairs	Europe	Africa & the Middle East	The Americas	Asia & the Pacific
Aug. 17		General Witold Urbanowicz, 88, pilot who was Poland's most successful World War II fighter ace, dies in New York City of unreported causes.	West African leaders announce that they and Liberia's faction leaders have agreed on a peace plan under which Liberian senator Ruth Perry will serve as head of an interim government that will oversee a transition to democracy. . . . The Patriotic Union of Kurdistan (PUK), the dominant force in Erbil prior to Iraq's intervention, launches a new offensive in its ongoing conflict with the Kurdish Democratic Party (KDP) led by Massoud Barzani, a long-time enemy of Iraqi president Saddam Hussein. . . . In response to the Aug. 16 violence, Jordan's King Hussein suspends Parliament and inspects security emplacements in the city of Kerak.		South Korean police raid university campuses nationwide to search the offices of a radical student group, the Federation of Student Councils (Hanchongnyon), which has been blamed for encouraging the ongoing protests that started Aug. 12.
Aug. 18		Hugo Gabriel Gryn, 66, Eastern European rabbi and Holocaust survivor who was a leader of Britain's Reform Jews, dies in London, England, of brain cancer.	Jordanian security forces impose a curfew in several cities as riots over government-imposed price hikes for bread and other foodstuffs continue.		Tsutakiyokomatsu Asaji (born Haru Kato), 102, one of the last traditional Japanese geishas who went into service in 1910, dies of kidney failure in Tokyo.
Aug. 19			Burundi's army forces some 8,000 Rwandan refugees to return home.	At least one civilian is killed and a police officer is wounded in a drive-by shooting attack on the police headquarters in Port-au-Prince, Haiti's capital.	Thousands of protesters attend rallies in Australian cities, including Brisbane, Perth, and Adelaide, to express their opposition to proposed government spending cuts. Protesters in Canberra use sledgehammers and a makeshift battering ram to force their way into Parliament. Sixty police and demonstrators are injured in the clashes.
Aug. 20	India formally vetoes a draft of the multinational Comprehensive Test Ban Treaty (CTBT), which would forbid its signatories to test nuclear weapons. . . . The U.S. Congressional Research Service reports that Russian arms sales to the developing world grew by 62% in 1995, to $6 billion from $3.7 billion in 1994. The 1995 figure shows that Russia has surpassed France and the U.S. as the leading arms exporter to developing countries.	Hamid Hamidov, the finance minister of Dagestan, a Caucasian republic of Russia, is killed when a car bomb explodes in the city of Makhachkala, the republic's capital. Three other people are killed, and several dozen are injured.	In Liberia, a cease-fire takes effect.	In Haiti, Antoine Leroy, a leader of the rightist Mobilization for National Development (MDN) party, and Jacques Florival, also a member of the MDN, are assassinated.	Police quell protests by students at Yonsei University in Seoul, the capital of South Korea. The illegal protests, in which more than 1,000 students and police have been injured since they started Aug. 12, called for the South's reunification with communist North Korea. . . . Aboriginal protesters clash with police in Canberra, Australia. . . . In Calcutta, India, Mother Teresa is admitted to the intensive care unit at the Woodlands Nursing Home, suffering from malaria.
Aug. 21	IMF officials vote to release the July payout of a three-year, $10.2 billion loan the fund made to Russia.	Reports confirm that two aid workers who were kidnapped in Chechnya in July, Michael Penrose of Britain and Frederic Malardeau of France, have been released.			
Aug. 22		Gen. Aleksandr Lebed, Russia's security council secretary, signs a cease-fire agreement with Gen. Aslan Maskhadov, chief of staff of secessionist rebels in the breakaway republic of Chechnya. . . . In Moscow, Russia, a bomb explodes in front of the Marina Roscha synagogue, causing $15,000 worth of damage. . . . A German court convicts U.S. citizen Gary Rex Lauck for distributing neo-Nazi paraphernalia in Germany and sentences him to four years in prison.	Amnesty International reveals that 6,000 people were reported killed in the three weeks after the July coup in Burundi.		At least 239 Hindus on a pilgrimage to a remote mountain cave die in a sudden snowstorm during their 30-mile-long trek to the Amarnath Cave, located in the Himalaya mountains.

A	B	C	D	E
Includes developments that affect more than one world region, international organizations, and important meetings of major world leaders.	Includes all domestic and regional developments in Europe, including the Soviet Union, Turkey, Cyprus, and Malta.	Includes all domestic and regional developments in Africa and the Middle East, including Iraq and Iran and excluding Cyprus, Turkey, and Afghanistan.	Includes all domestic and regional developments in Latin America, the Caribbean, and Canada.	Includes all domestic and regional developments in Asia and Pacific nations, extending from Afghanistan through all the Pacific Island, except Hawaii.

U.S. Politics & Social Issues	U.S. Foreign Policy & Defense	U.S. Economy & Environment	Science, Technology, & Nature	Culture, Leisure, & Lifestyle	
Lester Cruzan, 62, who with his wife in 1990 won a legal battle to end the life of their daughter Nancy Beth Cruzan after she was left in a vegetative state following a 1983 road accident, is found dead in Carterville, Missouri, where he apparently hanged himself.	An air force cargo plane carrying a communications van used in Pres. Clinton's motorcades crashes in remote mountains in the Bridger-Teton National Forest, near Jackson, Wyoming. All those on board—eight air force crew members and a Secret Service agent—are killed in the crash.		Computer hackers illegally enter the Department of Justice's site on the World Wide Web and post obscenities, sexually explicit pictures, and harsh criticisms of the Communications Decency Act. . . . Russia's space agency launches a *Soyuz-U* rocket from Kazakhstan to replace the cosmonaut crew aboard *Mir.* . . . A memorial service is held at Montoursville (Pennsylvania) High School in honor of 16 students and their five chaperons killed in the July 17 crash of the Paris-bound TWA Flight 800. The service is attended by NYC mayor Rudolph Giuliani (R), Governor Tom Ridge (R, Pa.), and French dignitaries.	E(dward) Digby Baltzell, 80, sociologist who popularized the acronym WASP for white Anglo-Saxon Protestants in his 1964 book, dies in Boston, Massachusetts, of a heart attack.	Aug. 17
Texas billionaire Ross Perot accepts the Reform Party nomination for president at the party's national convention in Valley Forge, Pennsylvania. . . . Pres. Clinton celebrates his 50th birthday with a fund-raising gala in NYC expected to raise $10 million for the Democratic presidential campaign. . . . HUD secretary Henry Cisneros reveals that the national home ownership rate in 1995 was 65.4%, the highest in 15 years.				Geoffrey Dearmer, 103, British poet of World War I whose work was largely forgotten until the 1993 publication of an anthology of his work, dies in Birchington-on-Sea, England.	Aug. 18
Ralph Nader accepts the Green Party's nomination as its candidate for president in 1996 at the party's convention at the University of California at Los Angeles. . . . On Pres. Clinton's birthday, he and First Lady Hillary Rodham Clinton join Vice Pres. Al Gore and his wife, Mary (Tipper) Gore, to help churchgoers in rural Tennessee rebuild the Salem Missionary Baptist Church, which was destroyed by fire in 1995.		In Little Rock, Arkansas, U.S. district judge George Howard Jr. sentences former Arkansas governor Jim Guy Tucker (D) to four years' probation for fraud and conspiracy convictions. . . . Statistics reveal that the number of mortgage loans approved for blacks and Hispanics between 1993 and 1995 increased by 48% and 37%, respectively.			Aug. 19
An annual federal survey shows that drug use among U.S. teenagers more than doubled from 1992 through 1995, while overall drug usage among Americans remained flat during the same period. The survey reveals that 10.9% of 12- through 17-year-olds surveyed in 1995 reported using drugs in the preceding month, up from 1992's figure of 5.3%.		The Commerce Department reports that in June the U.S. recorded a seasonally adjusted $8.11 billion deficit in trade in goods and services. The June figure marks a significant decline from May's revised deficit of $10.55 billion. . . . Pres. Clinton signs legislation that will raise the minimum hourly wage 90 cents, to $5.15 from $4.25. . . . Judge George Howard Jr. sentences Susan McDougal, a former Whitewater partner, to two years in federal prison.			Aug. 20
The Supreme Court refuses, without comment, to force North Carolina to redraw its 12th Congressional District for the November general election, despite the fact that the court had ruled in June that the district was the product of an unconstitutional racial gerrymander. . . . In Alhambra, California, Rodney King, the victim of a widely publicized videotaped beating by the Los Angeles police in 1991, is sentenced to 90 days in jail and two years' probation for knocking down his wife, Crystal King, with his car in July 1995.		Pres. Clinton signs into law legislation that will allow workers who change or lose their jobs to retain their health-insurance coverage. The law will also limit insurance companies' ability to withhold coverage because of preexisting medical conditions.		The FCC approves a plan by several TV networks to grant free airtime to the major presidential candidates.	Aug. 21
Pres. Clinton signs a welfare reform bill that will end the federal guarantee of cash assistance to poor families with children and will instead distribute block grants to states. . . . The College Board reveals that scores on the mathematical portion of the SATs in 1996 were the highest in 24 years, with an average of 508, two points up from 1995. The average on the verbal section was 505, up one point.	The U.S. Army begins destroying its chemical weapons arsenal at Tooele Army Depot, a military installation 50 miles (80 km) southwest of Salt Lake City, Utah, that stores 44% of the U.S.'s chemical stockpile.				Aug. 22

F	G	H	I	J
Includes elections, federal-state relations, civil rights and liberties, crime, the judiciary, education, health care, poverty, urban affairs, and population.	*Includes formation and debate of U.S. foreign and defense policies, veterans' affairs, and defense spending. (Relations with specific foreign countries are usually found under the region concerned.)*	*Includes business, labor, agriculture, taxation, transportation, consumer affairs, monetary and fiscal policy, natural resources, and pollution.*	*Includes worldwide scientific, medical, and technological developments; natural phenomena; U.S. weather; natural disasters; and accidents.*	*Includes the arts, religion, scholarship, communications media, sports, entertainments, fashions, fads, and social life.*

	World Affairs	Europe	Africa & the Middle East	The Americas	Asia & the Pacific
Aug. 23		French police officers in riot gear storm St. Bernard de la Chapelle, a Roman Catholic church in Paris, and forcibly remove 300 illegal immigrants from Africa who were occupying the church in an effort to avoid expulsion from France.... Italian officials confirm that Giovanni Brusca, allegedly one of Italy's leading organized-crime figures, has agreed to provide information about people connected to the Sicilian Mafia, or "Cosa Nostra."		Reports confirm that at least three farmers protesting a government program to eradicate their coca plants, which were used to make cocaine, and poppy plants, used to make heroin, have died in clashes since Aug. 19 in Florencia, the provincial capital in southern Colombia.... Hurricane Dolly hits the port city of Tampico, Mexico, with 80-mph winds and heavy rains. Two people are killed.	
Aug. 24		Russian troops begin pulling out of southern Chechnya and Grozny.... Four immigrants who, in July, occupied the St. Bernard de la Chapelle, a Roman Catholic church in Paris, are deported to Africa.... Emile Noel, 73, French international civil servant who was regarded as one of the founding fathers of the European Union, dies in Viareggio, Italy, of unreported causes.			
Aug. 25		General Aleksandr Lebed, Russia's security council secretary, breaks off negotiations on a political agreement with separatist rebels in the Russian republic of Chechnya.			Officials begin a mass rescue operation for the survivors of the Aug. 22 snowstorm in India, taking tens of thousands of pilgrims to Pahalgam, a town at the base of the mountain.
Aug. 26			Seven unidentified Iraqi men hijack a Sudanese jet with 199 people on board and order the pilot to take the plane to London, England, reportedly to seek political asylum.	A tribunal in Havana, Cuba's capital, convicts fugitive U.S. financier Robert Vesco of illicit economic activity and fraud and sentences him to 13 years in prison. Vesco has been wanted in the U.S. for more than 20 years.... Gen. Alejandro Agustin Lanusse, 77, military ruler of Argentina, 1971–73, who oversaw a transition to civilian rule, dies in Buenos Aires after surgery to remove a blood clot near his brain.	The Seoul District Criminal Court in South Korea convicts and sentences to death former South Korean president Chun Doo Hwan for his role in the 1979 coup that brought him to power and the subsequent massacre of prodemocracy demonstrators in the southern city of Kwangju, as well as for accepting bribes. The three-judge panel also sentences Chun's successor, Roh Tae Woo, to 22 years and six months in prison for his support of the coup and for accepting bribes.
Aug. 27		Data reveal that more than 17,000 refugees from Chechnya have fled to the neighboring Russian republic of Ingushetia.... After eight hours of negotiations, police in Great Britain arrest the seven unidentified Iraqi men who hijacked a Sudanese jet on Aug. 26. All 199 people passengers and crew are released unharmed.	Israel's Likud party-led government approves plans to expand a Jewish settlement in the Israeli-occupied West Bank, lifting the freeze on Jewish settlement construction in the Palestinian territories imposed in 1992.... In South Africa, a high-ranking police official, Eugene de Kock, is convicted of a total of 89 of 121 criminal counts, including six counts of murder. He is the highest-ranking police official convicted to date for apartheid-era abuses.		
Aug. 28		Russian official sources report that 506 Russian soldiers were killed and 1,400 others injured in the offensive that began in early August in Chechnya.... The divorce of Charles, the Prince of Wales, and his wife, Princess Diana, is finalized in a decree absolute issued in London's High Court.... Phyllis Isobel Pearsall, 89, creator of the famous "A to Z" street guides of London, England, dies of unreported causes.		In Mexico, 50 masked rebels from the Popular Revolutionary Army (EPR) storm the town of Tlaxiaco in Oaxaca, killing two police officers.	

A	B	C	D	E
Includes developments that affect more than one world region, international organizations, and important meetings of major world leaders.	*Includes all domestic and regional developments in Europe, including the Soviet Union, Turkey, Cyprus, and Malta.*	*Includes all domestic and regional developments in Africa and the Middle East, including Iraq and Iran and excluding Cyprus, Turkey, and Afghanistan.*	*Includes all domestic and regional developments in Latin America, the Caribbean, and Canada.*	*Includes all domestic and regional developments in Asia and Pacific nations, extending from Afghanistan through all the Pacific Island, except Hawaii.*

U.S. Politics & Social Issues	U.S. Foreign Policy & Defense	U.S. Economy & Environment	Science, Technology, & Nature	Culture, Leisure, & Lifestyle	
Pres. Clinton announces the final approval of FDA regulations intended to curb the marketing and sale of tobacco products to young people. By approving the rules, Clinton establishes that the government classifies nicotine as an addictive drug and that, as such, it is for the first time subject to FDA rules.... Alberto Gonzalez, 33, the first person in the U.S. convicted of attempted murder for having unprotected sex while infected with HIV, dies in Salem, Oregon, of an AIDS-related illness.	The INS grants asylum to two leading opposition figures from Belarus, Zonon Poznyak and Sergel Naumchik, both of the Belarussian Popular Front (BPF).... A Marine Corps EA-6B Prowler radar-jamming jet crashes near Yuma, Arizona, killing all four crew members.		The FBI reports that chemists at an FBI crime laboratory in Washington, D.C., have found microscopic traces of a chemical explosive, pentaerythritol tetra nitrate (PETN), on a piece of wreckage from TWA Flight 800, which crashed into the Atlantic Ocean July 17. The discovery of PETN bolsters theories that the crash was caused by a bomb or a surface-to-air missile, while casting further doubt on the possibility that the incident was caused by a mechanical failure.		Aug. 23
	Four women—Petra Lovetinska, Nancy Mace, Jeanie Mentavlos, and Kim Messer—are admitted to The Citadel, a previously all-male state-supported military academy in Charleston, South Carolina.			Taiwan successfully defends its Little League World Series baseball title, 13-3 over a team from Cranston, Rhode Island, in Williamsport, Pennsylvania.	Aug. 24
				Eldrick (Tiger) Woods wins the U.S. Amateur Golf Tournament in Cornelius, Oregon, becoming the first player to win the stroke-and match-play tournament three times in a row.... Russian Olympic swimmer Aleksandr Popov is seriously wounded when he is stabbed in the stomach in Moscow.	Aug. 25
					Aug. 26
California governor Pete Wilson (R) signs an executive order that bars state agencies and state-funded colleges and universities from providing benefits to illegal immigrants, effectively implementing part of Proposition 187, approved by California voters in 1994 but not enforced because of legal challenges... In front of about 50 witnesses, off-duty officers in Indianapolis, Indiana, emerge from a downtown bar and beat a black motorist and a white man who goes to his aid. The episode prompts a grand jury investigation.				Greg Morris, 61, one of the first black actors to star in a hit TV series, dies in Las Vegas, Nevada, after suffering from lung and brain cancer.... Bernard B. Jacobs, 80, president of Shubert Organization Inc., the largest owner of theaters in the U.S., dies in Roslyn, New York, of complications after heart-bypass surgery.	Aug. 27
A federal judge in Martinsburg, West Virginia, sentences Kirtanananda Swami Bhaktipada, the former leader of a Hare Krishna religious community, to 20 years in prison for racketeering.	The U.S. Treasury Department bars Nation of Islam leader Louis Farrakhan from accepting a $250,000 award from a Libyan organization and from accepting $1 billion in aid promised to the Nation of Islam by Libyan leader Col. Muammar Gadhafi.... Reports confirm that 5,000 U.S. troops are training in Germany to assist in the withdrawal of NATO's peacekeeping troops in Bosnia-Herzegovina.		The National Interagency Fire Center reports that more than 18,000 firefighters are battling blazes across the West.		Aug. 28

F	G	H	I	J
Includes elections, federal-state relations, civil rights and liberties, crime, the judiciary, education, health care, poverty, urban affairs, and population.	Includes formation and debate of U.S. foreign and defense policies, veterans' affairs, and defense spending. (Relations with specific foreign countries are usually found under the region concerned.)	Includes business, labor, agriculture, taxation, transportation, consumer affairs, monetary and fiscal policy, natural resources, and pollution.	Includes worldwide scientific, medical, and technological developments; natural phenomena; U.S. weather; natural disasters; and accidents.	Includes the arts, religion, scholarship, communications media, sports, entertainments, fashions, fads, and social life.

	World Affairs	Europe	Africa & the Middle East	The Americas	Asia & the Pacific
Aug. 29		A Russian jet crashes into a mountain on the remote Spitsbergen Island in the Arctic Circle, killing all 141 passengers in the worst air disaster in Norway's history.... The Russian-Belarussian union treaty takes effect.... Some 60 Bosnian Serbs assault a group of Muslim refugees in Mahala, 8 miles (13 km) west of Zvornik. The Serbian gang is detained, which prompts a mob of Bosnian Serbs to hold several members of the UN International Police Task Force hostage for six hours until the Serbian group is released.	Palestinians stage a general strike across the West Bank, East Jerusalem, and the Gaza Strip to protest the plan approved Aug. 27 to expand a Jewish settlement in the Israeli-occupied West Bank.	In Mexico, squads of gunmen from the Popular Revolutionary Army (EPR) launch apparently coordinated attacks on government, police, and military buildings in several towns and cities, killing at least 11 people. Army troops are sent in and pursue the rebels into adjacent mountains.	
Aug. 30				At least 96 soldiers, policemen, rebels, and civilians are killed in what Colombian officials call one of the deadliest series of attacks by left-wing rebels in decades. The rebels, including factions from FARC and ELN, attack police and army installations in at least 13 regions.... José Toribio Merino Castro, 80, Chilean admiral who was a member of his nation's ruling military junta, 1973–90, dies in Valparaíso, Chile, of lymphatic cancer.	
Aug. 31		Gen. Aleksandr Lebed, Russian security council secretary, and Gen. Aslan Maskhadov, the commander of secessionist troops in the Russian republic of Chechnya, sign an agreement to end the 21-month conflict in the war-torn Russian region. Under the terms of the new agreement, the Chechen rebels will put aside their demands for independence from Russia for five years.	The Iraqis seize Erbil after a request for aid from the Kurdish Democratic Party (KDP) led by Massoud Barzani, a long-time enemy of Iraqi Pres. Saddam Hussein. The KDP has been locked in ongoing conflict that was renewed Aug. 17 when the Patriotic Union of Kurdistan (PUK), a rival faction, launched a new attack against the KDP.		
Sept. 1	In response to Iraq's Aug. 31 foray into the Kurdish sector, UN secretary general Boutros Boutros-Ghali freezes an agreement under which Iraq had been allowed to sell $2 billion in oil during a renewable, six-month period to ease a shortage of food and medical supplies in Iraq.	Serbian president Slobodan Milosevic agrees to allow ethnic Albanian children in the Serbian province of Kosovo to return to school.		Helmer Herrera Buitrago, a reputed leader of Colombia's Cali drug cartel, surrenders to authorities in Yumbo, a town near Cali.	
Sept. 2	British deputy prime minister Michael Heseltine and Defense Secretary Michael Portillo announce that Britain is prepared to proceed with production of the Eurofighter, an advanced combat jet that Britain, Germany, Italy, and Spain have agreed to develop jointly.	Scientists in Scotland uncover a small casket thought to hold the mummified heart of Robert the Bruce, the 14th-century Scottish king under whom Scotland gained independence from England.... Russian defense minister Igor Rodionov reveals that at least 2,837 Russian soldiers were killed throughout the fighting in Chechnya, and 13,270 were wounded.... Ukraine introduces the hryvna, a new currency, to replace the karbovanets. One hryvna is worth 100,000 karbovanets, or 57 U.S. cents.		In response to the Aug. 30 assaults, the Colombian government deploys more than 50,000 troops to pursue the rebels. FARC tells the International Committee of the Red Cross that they are holding 59 soldiers captive and that they will not release the hostages until the government agrees to negotiations.	
Sept. 3	The 22-member Arab League condemns the U.S. attack against Iraq.	Officials estimate that between 70,000 and 90,000 people lost their lives in the 21-month-long Chechen conflict.... Statistics indicate that Russia's inflation rate was close to zero in August, the lowest recorded monthly level of inflation since the onset of economic reforms in 1991.... French police defuse a bomb in the basilica of St. Laurent-sur-Sevre church in La Roche-sur-Yon, planted in what is considered a protest to the pope's upcoming visit.	Two U.S. Air Force bombers and two U.S. warships in the northern Persian Gulf direct the first of 27 cruise missiles toward Iraqi targets, prompting Iraqi troops to withdraw from the Kurdish city of Erbil, seized Aug. 31. The Iraqi regime states that five people have been killed and 19 others wounded.... Ruth Perry, a former Liberian senator, is inaugurated as the country's first female head of state.		

A	B	C	D	E
Includes developments that affect more than one world region, international organizations, and important meetings of major world leaders.	Includes all domestic and regional developments in Europe, including the Soviet Union, Turkey, Cyprus, and Malta.	Includes all domestic and regional developments in Africa and the Middle East, including Iraq and Iran and excluding Cyprus, Turkey, and Afghanistan.	Includes all domestic and regional developments in Latin America, the Caribbean, and Canada.	Includes all domestic and regional developments in Asia and Pacific nations, extending from Afghanistan through all the Pacific Island, except Hawaii.

U.S. Politics & Social Issues	U.S. Foreign Policy & Defense	U.S. Economy & Environment	Science, Technology, & Nature	Culture, Leisure, & Lifestyle	
Pres. Bill Clinton accepts the Democratic nomination for president at the party's convention in Chicago. Vice president Al Gore accepts the vice-presidential nomination. . . . President Clinton's top campaign strategist, Dick Morris, resigns in the face of allegations of personal indiscretions with Sherry Rowlands, a prostitute in the Washington, D.C., area.				Nielsen Media Research records 20.2 million viewers watching the final night of the Democratic convention on ABC, CBS, and NBC combined.	Aug. 29
		NationsBank Corp. agrees to acquire Boatmen's Bancshares Inc. for about $9.5 billion in a deal that analysts claim is the third-biggest U.S. banking merger ever. . . . The Commerce Department reports that personal pretax income rose 0.1% in July from June, to a seasonally adjusted annual figure of $6.47 trillion. The July figure is the 14th consecutive monthly income increase.			Aug. 30
Seven people drown when a truck rolls into John D. Long Lake near Union, South Carolina, the site where Susan Smith killed her two young sons in 1994 by allowing the car they were in to roll into the lake.					Aug. 31
				The daughter of former president Jimmy Carter, Amy Carter, 28, marries James Wentzel, 27, near Plains, Georgia.	Sept. 1
Charles Hughes Kirbo, 79, lawyer known as Pres. Jimmy Carter's "one-man kitchen cabinet," dies in Atlanta, Georgia, of complications from gall bladder surgery.			Russian cosmonauts Yuri I. Onufrienko and Yuri V. Usachev depart from *Mir* space station and land at Akmola, Kazakhstan.	*Executive Orders* by Tom Clancy, tops the bestseller list. . . . Ljuba Welitsch (born Velitchkova), 83, Bulgarian-born soprano known for her 1949 performance of Salome at the Metropolitan Opera in New York City, dies in Vienna, Austria. . . . Otto Clarence Luening, 96, composer, conductor, flutist, and teacher who was a tireless advocate for contemporary music, dies in New York City of unreported causes.	Sept. 2
		The Senate, by voice vote, approves the conference report for a $2.17 billion appropriations bill for fiscal 1997 to fund Congress's daily expenses; the Library of Congress; and the General Accounting Office (GAO), the investigative arm of Congress.			Sept. 3

F	G	H	I	J
Includes elections, federal-state relations, civil rights and liberties, crime, the judiciary, education, health care, poverty, urban affairs, and population.	*Includes formation and debate of U.S. foreign and defense policies, veterans' affairs, and defense spending. (Relations with specific foreign countries are usually found under the region concerned.)*	*Includes business, labor, agriculture, taxation, transportation, consumer affairs, monetary and fiscal policy, natural resources, and pollution.*	*Includes worldwide scientific, medical, and technological developments; natural phenomena; U.S. weather; natural disasters; and accidents.*	*Includes the arts, religion, scholarship, communications media, sports, entertainments, fashions, fads, and social life.*

	World Affairs	Europe	Africa & the Middle East	The Americas	Asia & the Pacific
Sept. 4		British troops that are part of the NATO peacekeeping force in Bosnia are challenged by a crowd of Bosnian Serb civilians as the soldiers attempt to halt the unauthorized movement of armored vehicles and heavy weapons through the Serb-controlled town of Banja Luka.... Reports confirm that Russian authorities have expelled two Swedes for alleged espionage.	The U.S. launches cruise-missile attack against Iraq as a follow-up to the Sept. 3 firing, bringing the two-day total to 44.... Israeli prime minister Benjamin Netanyahu meets with Yasser Arafat, the Palestinian National Authority leader. The meeting marks the formal reopening of long-stalled peace talks between the Palestinians and Israel.		
Sept. 5		Russian Security Council secretary Aleksandr Lebed becomes the first Russian politician to speak at a rally in Chechnya since December 1994.... Breaking with centuries of the Russian tradition of censoring news about the leader's health, Russian president Boris Yeltsin announces that he will undergo heart surgery at the end of September.... The largest synagogue in Europe, the Great Synagogue of Budapest, reopens after a five-year, $9 million reconstruction.	In response to parliamentary impeachment proceedings against him, Albert Zafy, the president of the African island nation of Madagascar, announces that he will resign from office, effective Oct. 10. The constitutional court appoints Premier Norbert Ratsirahonana to serve as interim president until elections can be held to replace Zafy.	Jules Wijdenbosch of the National Democratic Party (NDP), is elected Suriname's president, defeating incumbent Ronald Venetiaan of the New Front coalition.	
Sept. 6				In Colombia, FARC rebels attack a military base, killing 19 soldiers and injuring 13 others. The ELN blows up a section of the Cano Limon-Covenas oil pipeline in northeastern Colombia.	The Nobel Prize–winning Roman Catholic nun Mother Teresa is released from the Woodlands Nursing Home in Calcutta, India, after being admitted on Aug. 20 with malaria.
Sept. 7					
Sept. 8		In Chechnya, several hundred Russian army troops and tanks leave Grozny under the terms of the August settlement.... Unidentified gunmen kill a Turkish Cypriot soldier and severely wound another near the UN-patrolled buffer zone separating Cyprus's Greek and Turkish sections.... Police in the Belgian city of Liege arrest Alain Van der Biest, a former pensions minister in Belgium's cabinet, and charge him in connection with the July 1991 murder of Socialist Party leader and former deputy premier Andre Cools.	UN officials report that aid workers have found hundreds of women, children and elderly people starving in the town of Tubmanburg, Liberia.		Residents of the Japanese island of Okinawa, in a nonbinding resolution, register overwhelming support for a reduction in the U.S. military presence.
Sept. 9		Yugoslavia—which consists of Serbia and Montenegro—and the ex-Yugoslav republic of Croatia formally establish diplomatic relations.... Reports indicate that a Ukrainian soldier serving with NATO troops was shot and killed by an unidentified gunman in Bosnia-Herzegovina.	With the support of Iraqi military vehicles and troops, the KDP captures the town of Sulaymaniyah, considered the Kurdish cultural capital.		

A	B	C	D	E
Includes developments that affect more than one world region, international organizations, and important meetings of major world leaders.	Includes all domestic and regional developments in Europe, including the Soviet Union, Turkey, Cyprus, and Malta.	Includes all domestic and regional developments in Africa and the Middle East, including Iraq and Iran and excluding Cyprus, Turkey, and Afghanistan.	Includes all domestic and regional developments in Latin America, the Caribbean, and Canada.	Includes all domestic and regional developments in Asia and Pacific nations, extending from Afghanistan through all the Pacific Island, except Hawaii.

U.S. Politics & Social Issues	U.S. Foreign Policy & Defense	U.S. Economy & Environment	Science, Technology, & Nature	Culture, Leisure, & Lifestyle	
					Sept. 4
The Census Bureau reports that the high-school graduation rate for black Americans for the first time ever is roughly equal to the graduation rate for whites. However, the bureau also finds that graduation rates for Hispanic Americans continue to lag far behind the nation's overall graduation rate.	A federal jury in New York City convicts Abdul Hakim Murad, Wali Khan Amin Shah, and Ramzi Ahmed Yousef, the alleged mastermind of the 1993 bombing of World Trade Center, of all the charges against them stemming from a foiled plot to bomb 12 U.S. airliners in retaliation for the U.S.'s support of Israel.... The Senate passes, 92-6, an appropriations bill allocating $9.982 billion for military construction spending in the 1997 fiscal year.	The Senate approves, 83-15, a $5.156 billion fiscal 1997 appropriations bill for the District of Columbia.	Hurricane Fran goes ashore at Cape Fear, North Carolina, bringing 1 inch (2.5 cm) of rain per hour and 115-mph (185-kmph) winds.	Leonard Katzman, 69, TV producer, writer, and director who produced 356 episodes of the series Dallas, dies in Malibu, California, of an apparent heart attack.	Sept. 5
		The Labor Department reports that the seasonally adjusted unemployment rate in the U.S. dropped sharply in August to 5.1%, from 5.4% in July. The August unemployment rate is the lowest since March 1989 and marks only the second time since 1974 that the rate has dropped so low.	Hurricane Fran moves up the Atlantic coast, bringing heavy rain to Virginia, West Virginia, Maryland, Pennsylvania, Ohio, and New York.		Sept. 6
Arthur Sherwood Flemming, 91, U.S. secretary of health, education, and welfare, 1958–61, and chair of the U.S. Commission on Civil Rights, 1974–81, dies in Alexandria, Virginia, of acute renal failure.			U.S. astronaut Shannon W. Lucid completes her 169th full day in space, setting the world record for the longest space sojourn by a woman.... Flooding and widespread power outages are reported in Virginia due to Hurricane Fran. Flooding is also reported in West Virginia and Maryland. At least 22 people have died in North Carolina, South Carolina, Virginia, and West Virginia.	Boxer Mike Tyson knocks out WBA heavyweight champion Bruce Seldon to capture the WBA title.... Rap artist and actor Tupac Shakur, while driving with his entourage to a Las Vegas nightclub in a convoy of 10 cars, is shot four times in the chest.	Sept. 7
				Pete Sampras wins his second consecutive U.S. Open tennis title with a victory over Michael Chang. Germany's Steffi Graf wins her fifth career U.S. Open title with a victory over Monica Seles.... At the Emmys, E.R. wins for best drama while Frasier wins for best comedy.	Sept. 8
A Houston, Texas, judge sentences Wanda Webb Holloway, whose 1991 conviction for plotting a murder to secure a cheerleading squad spot for her daughter was overturned on a technicality, to 10 years in prison.... Pres. Clinton awards the Presidential Medal of Freedom, the nation's highest civilian honor, to 11 people.... A study finds that the "three-strikes" laws enacted by the federal government and more than 20 states since 1993 is rarely used, except in California.	Pres. Clinton proposes to Congress a set of antiterrorism and aviation security measures, at a cost of $1.1 billion.	Pres. Clinton signs a $5.156 billion fiscal 1997 appropriations bill for the District of Columbia.... Susan McDougal, a partner in the Whitewater Development Corp. real-estate venture, is sent to jail after refusing to answer prosecutors' questions about Pres. Clinton before a grand jury in Little Rock, Arkansas.		Robert A. Nisbet, 82, sociologist who specialized in the history of ideas, dies in Washington, D.C., of prostate cancer.... Bill Monroe (William Smith), 84, singer and mandolin player called the father of bluegrass, dies in Springfield, Tennessee, after suffering a stroke earlier in the year.	Sept. 9

F	G	H	I	J
Includes elections, federal-state relations, civil rights and liberties, crime, the judiciary, education, health care, poverty, urban affairs, and population.	Includes formation and debate of U.S. foreign and defense policies, veterans' affairs, and defense spending. (Relations with specific foreign countries are usually found under the region concerned.)	Includes business, labor, agriculture, taxation, transportation, consumer affairs, monetary and fiscal policy, natural resources, and pollution.	Includes worldwide scientific, medical, and technological developments; natural phenomena; U.S. weather; natural disasters; and accidents.	Includes the arts, religion, scholarship, communications media, sports, entertainments, fashions, fads, and social life.

	World Affairs	Europe	Africa & the Middle East	The Americas	Asia & the Pacific
Sept. 10	The UN General Assembly approves a draft version of the Comprehensive Test Ban Treaty (CTBT), which will forbid all testing of nuclear weapons.	A court in Berlin sentences six former East German generals for ordering guards to shoot people attempting to escape the communist state and enter West Germany. . . . The British government claims that Nazi Germany funneled some $550 million in gold into Swiss bank accounts, increasing the pressure on Swiss banks to release information on their holdings. . . . Due to health problems, Russian president Boris Yeltsin temporarily delegates most of his authority to Premier Viktor S. Chernomyrdin.	Since Iran claims that the number of Kurdish refugees along its border exceeds 200,000 and that it cannot provide them with the necessary humanitarian aid, tens of thousands of the Kurds begin to return to Sulamaniyah.	Colombian vice president Humberto de la Calle Lombana submits his resignation, claiming that the government of Pres. Ernesto Samper Pizano has lost credibility after allegations that the president accepted a $6 million donation from the Cali drug cartel for his 1994 presidential campaign emerged. . . . Hurricane Hortense hits Puerto Rico, with winds of up to 80 mph and 18 inches (45 cm) of rain. The storm kills 20 people. In the Dominican Republic, at least eight people died in flooding brought by Hurricane Hortense.	Japanese premier Ryutaro Hashimoto offers Okinawa a 5 billion yen ($45.4 million) economic development grant to garner support for the continuation of the U.S. military presence on the island. . . . In Australia, independent member of Parliament Pauline Hanson touches off a heated nationwide debate over the issue of race when she warns that if measures for a stricter immigration policy and for cutting social spending on the nation's aboriginal population are not passed, Australia is "in danger of being swamped by Asians."
Sept. 11	Reports indicate that nearly every Arab state with friendly ties to the U.S. has refused to allow the U.S. to base in their territory any military aircraft to be used against Iraq.		Iraq fires a missile at two U.S. jets surveying the so-called no-fly zone in northern Iraq, prompting the U.S. to step up its military presence in the Persian Gulf region. U.S. officials confirm the U.S. will airlift out of Iraq some 2,000 Iraqi dissidents employed by the U.S. in its Operation Provide Comfort project and other covert initiatives aimed at countering Pres. Hussein's control of the region.	Hurricane Hortense hits Grand Turk, in Britain's Turks and Caicos Islands, causing minor damage.	The Taliban, a militia group largely composed of former theology students, captures the city of Jalalabad, Afghanistan. At least 70 people are reportedly killed in fighting. . . . The Dalai Lama visits New Zealand, where he meets P.M. James Bolger.
Sept. 12		James Gerald Gulliver, 66, founder and chair of the Argyll Group PLC, whose 1985 bid to purchase drinks giant Distillers Co. led to one of the most hotly contested and controversial bidding wars of the 1980s, dies of a heart attack.	Iraq indiscriminately fires three missiles into the southern no-fly zone. No U.S. jets are endangered by the missiles.	Haitian president Rene Preval begins a purge of the Presidential Security Unit due to their suspected involvement in the Aug. 20 assassinations of Antoine Leroy and Jacques Florival, both members of the rightist Mobilization for National Development (MDN) party. . . . General Ernesto Geisel, 89, Brazilian president, 1974–79, and army general who paved the way for Brazil's return to democracy in 1985, dies in Rio de Janeiro of cancer.	
Sept. 13				At least two dozen U.S. State Department security agents arrive in Haiti to protect Pres. Rene Preval during a purge of Preval's Presidential Security Unit, which began Sept. 12. . . . Gen. Cesar Mendoza, 78, one of four commanders in the 1973 coup that installed Gen. Augusto Pinochet as a military leader in Chile, dies in Santiago, Chile, of pancreatic cancer.	The governor of the Japanese island of Okinawa, Masahide Ota, agrees to renew leases on land used by the U.S. military. . . . Data shows that Japan's gross domestic product shrunk at an annualized rate of 2.9% in the second quarter. The quarterly GDP figure marks the nation's first contraction in output since the 1994 fourth quarter.
Sept. 14		Voters in Bosnia-Herzegovina take part in the ethnically divided country's first nationwide elections since the end of its four-year-long civil war in 1995. Bosnian president Alija Izetbegovic, a Muslim, is elected the chair of a three-member collective presidency. He will be joined on the presidential panel by Momcilo Krajisnik, a Bosnian Serb, and Kresimir Zubak, a Bosnian Croat. . . . The Russian government warns separatist rebels from the republic of Chechnya that it is not prepared to grant them independence.		Jules Wijdenbosch of the National Democratic Party (NDP) is sworn in as Suriname's president.	
Sept. 15		In Venice, Italy, the Northern League political party stages a rally in which its leader, Umberto Bossi, declares the formation of an independent nation composed of many of Italy's northern provinces. Premier Romano Prodi calls the Venice rally "a ridiculous and artificial event."			Afghanistan government forces launch an aerial assault on Jalalabad in an effort to slow the advance of Taliban rebel troops toward Kabul. Afghan military jets drop bombs on the city, killing six people and prompting thousands to flee toward the Pakistan border 45 miles away.

A	B	C	D	E
Includes developments that affect more than one world region, international organizations, and important meetings of major world leaders.	*Includes all domestic and regional developments in Europe, including the Soviet Union, Turkey, Cyprus, and Malta.*	*Includes all domestic and regional developments in Africa and the Middle East, including Iraq and Iran and excluding Cyprus, Turkey, and Afghanistan.*	*Includes all domestic and regional developments in Latin America, the Caribbean, and Canada.*	*Includes all domestic and regional developments in Asia and Pacific nations, extending from Afghanistan through all the Pacific Island, except Hawaii.*

U.S. Politics & Social Issues	U.S. Foreign Policy & Defense	U.S. Economy & Environment	Science, Technology, & Nature	Culture, Leisure, & Lifestyle	
The Senate clears, 85-14, the Defense of Marriage Act, which denies federal marriage benefits to same-sex couples and allows states to deny recognition to same-sex marriages performed in other states. . . . Reform Party presidential nominee Ross Perot announces that he has selected Pat Choate, an economist best known for his opposition to free trade, as his running mate.	The Senate clears, 73-26, a $265.6 billion fiscal 1997 defense authorization bill.			Wal-Mart, the U.S.'s biggest retailer, states it will not sell singer Sheryl Crow's eponymous album because one of its songs suggests that the chain sells guns to children. . . . Joanne Dru (born Joanne LaCock), 73, film actress who specialized in westerns, dies in Beverly Hills, California, of a respiratory illness.	Sept. 10
Two assistant secretaries at the Department of Health and Human Services (HHS), Peter Edelman and Mary Jo Bane, resign, citing their opposition to the welfare overhaul bill signed in August by Pres. Clinton.		Machinists at the St. Louis, Missouri, plant of McDonnell Douglas Corp. overwhelmingly approve a four-year contract and end their 99-day-long strike against the military aircraft manufacturer.			Sept. 11
Indianapolis, Indiana, police chief Donald Christ resigns in the wake of allegations that 16 of his officers made lewd remarks to women and beat up two men during a drunken spree in August.		The House passes, 383-29, a $20.4 billion appropriations bill to fund energy, water-development, and nuclear-weapons programs in fiscal 1997.			Sept. 12
Election officials report that native Hawaiians participating in a mail-in referendum voted nearly 3 to 1 in favor of creating an indigenous government.			Officials reveal that divers have recovered two more bodies, bringing to 213 the total recovered from the July crash of TWA Flight 800 that killed 230 people.	Reform Party candidate Ross Perot addresses a convention of the Christian Coalition, the country's most powerful organization of politically active conservative Christians. . . . Rap artist and actor Tupac Shakur, 25, dies of wounds from the Sept. 7 drive-by shooting in Las Vegas, Nevada.	Sept. 13
The National Rifle Association (NRA) declines to endorse Republican presidential candidate Robert Dole and states it will not back a candidate in the current presidential race.				Republican presidential nominee Robert Dole addresses the Christian Coalition at their annual convention. . . . In Montreal, the U.S. defeats the Canadian team, 5-2, to win the first-ever World Cup of Hockey. . . . Juliet Prowse, 59, dancer whose scantily clad performance in 1959 offended Nikita Khrushchev, dies in Los Angeles of pancreatic cancer.	Sept. 14
				The defending champion U.S. team wins the second biennial Presidents Cup in Gainesville, Virginia, defeating a team of top non-European international golfers 16 points to 15 points.	Sept. 15

F	G	H	I	J
Includes elections, federal-state relations, civil rights and liberties, crime, the judiciary, education, health care, poverty, urban affairs, and population.	Includes formation and debate of U.S. foreign and defense policies, veterans' affairs, and defense spending. (Relations with specific foreign countries are usually found under the region concerned.)	Includes business, labor, agriculture, taxation, transportation, consumer affairs, monetary and fiscal policy, natural resources, and pollution.	Includes worldwide scientific, medical, and technological developments; natural phenomena; U.S. weather; natural disasters; and accidents.	Includes the arts, religion, scholarship, communications media, sports, entertainments, fashions, fads, and social life.

	World Affairs	Europe	Africa & the Middle East	The Americas	Asia & the Pacific
Sept. 16		Hungarian premier Gyula Horn and his Romanian counterpart, Nicolae Vacaroiu, sign a bilateral treaty that demarcates the two countries' common border and guarantees the rights of ethnic minority groups.... The Agency for International Development shuts down its Estonia operations, asserting that Estonia's economy is robust enough to "graduate" from U.S. development-assistance programs.... An Albanian court sentences four men arrested in connection with a car bombing in Tirana to prison terms ranging from 12 to 18 months for founding a communist party and trying to overthrow the government through violent means.			Australia's minister for primary industries, John Anderson, announces that all of Australia's states and territories have agreed to a controlled nation-wide release of a deadly rabbit virus to reduce the more than 200 million wild rabbit population.
Sept. 17	Delegates from the 185 member nations of the UN formally open the 51st General Assembly and elect Razali Ismail, Malaysia's ambassador to the UN, to the largely ceremonial office of assembly president.				
Sept. 18	China for the fourth consecutive year uses its power on the UN General Assembly agenda committee to block a bid by assembly members to vote on admitting Taiwan to the UN.	An appeals court in Bordeaux, France, orders Maurice Papon, a former minister in the French cabinet, to stand trial for his alleged role in the deportation and death of French Jews sent to concentration camps during World War II. Papon will be second Frenchman to stand trial in connection with the mass execution of Jews by Nazi Germany.		The Soufriere Hills volcano, also called Chances Peak, on the Caribbean island of Montserrat, erupts.	An abandoned North Korean submarine is found off the eastern coastal city of Kangnung, South Korea, 60 miles (100 km) across the border between the enemy nations. Searchers also find 11 North Koreans dead on a mountain-top clearing.

A	B	C	D	E
Includes developments that affect more than one world region, international organizations, and important meetings of major world leaders.	*Includes all domestic and regional developments in Europe, including the Soviet Union, Turkey, Cyprus, and Malta.*	*Includes all domestic and regional developments in Africa and the Middle East, including Iraq and Iran and excluding Cyprus, Turkey, and Afghanistan.*	*Includes all domestic and regional developments in Latin America, the Caribbean, and Canada.*	*Includes all domestic and regional developments in Asia and Pacific nations, extending from Afghanistan through all the Pacific Island, except Hawaii.*

U.S. Politics & Social Issues	U.S. Foreign Policy & Defense	U.S. Economy & Environment	Science, Technology, & Nature	Culture, Leisure, & Lifestyle	
Pres. Clinton receives an endorsement from the Fraternal Order of Police, a 270,000-member police union.	Pres. Clinton signs an appropriations bill allocating $9.982 billion for military construction spending in the 1997 fiscal year. . . . McGeorge Bundy, 77, foreign-policy adviser to Presidents John Kennedy and Lyndon Johnson who advocated expanding U.S. involvement in the Vietnam War, dies in Boston, Massachusetts, of a heart attack.	Pres. Clinton signs a $2.17 billion appropriations bill for Congress's daily expenses; the Library of Congress; and the General Accounting Office (GAO), the investigative arm of Congress, for fiscal 1997.	The U.S. space shuttle *Atlantis* takes off from Cape Canaveral, Florida, to link up with the Russian space station *Mir* and bring home U.S. astronaut Shannon W. Lucid, stationed on *Mir* since March.		Sept. 16
California governor Pete Wilson (R) signs into law a bill requiring any adult convicted of two sexual assaults on minors to be injected with a drug that reduces their sex drive, unless they agree to voluntarily undergo surgical castration. California thereby becomes the first state in the nation to require "chemical castration" for repeat child molesters. . . . The Commission on Presidential Debates unanimously recommends that Reform Party candidate Ross Perot be excluded from a planned series of presidential debates since he has no "realistic chance to win the election." . . . The Justice Department reports that violent crime in 1995 fell more than 9% compared with the preceding year. . . . Judge Hiroshi Fujisaki of Los Angeles County Superior Court opens the civil trial of O. J. Simpson, who was acquitted of criminal charges in the 1994 fatal stabbing of Nicole Brown Simpson, and Ronald Goldman. . . . The Senate clears a bill increasing penalties for possession and trafficking of methamphetamine, a drug known as speed or "crank." . . . Spiro Theodore Agnew, 77, 39th vice president of the U.S.,1969–73, who resigned in disgrace in 1973 when he pled no contest to an income-tax evasion charge, dies in Berlin, Maryland, of acute leukemia, which was undiagnosed until his death.		The Senate approves, 92-8, a $20.4 billion appropriations bill to fund energy, water-development, and nuclear-weapons programs in fiscal 1997.			Sept. 17
The House Committee on Government Reform and Oversight releases its final report on the firing of seven employees of the White House travel office, concluding that the firings were motivated by "political cronyism." . . . Congress clears a bill clarifying that the 1994 anticrime law includes stiffer penalties for sexual assault during a carjacking.		Pres. Clinton signs an order that designates 1.7 million acres (690,000 hectares) of land in southern Utah as the Canyons of the Escalante National Monument. . . . The Senate Ethics Committee clears Sen. Alfonse M. D'Amato (R, N.Y.) on charges that he violated Senate ethics rules when he profited $37,125 in a one-day stock trade in 1993. . . . The Commerce Department reports that the U.S. in July recorded a seasonally adjusted $11.68 billion deficit in trade in goods and services. The July figure, which represents a 42.7% increase over June's revised deficit of $8.19 billion, marks the highest deficit level since the government introduced its current system of measurement in January 1992. . . . The House, 395-19, and the Senate, 85-14, approve a $12.6 billion fiscal 1997 transportation appropriations bill.	The FDA declares that the abortion drug RU-486, also known as mifepristone, is safe and effective. . . . The U.S. shuttle *Atlantis* reaches *Mir* at the space station's orbital position 240 miles (385 km) above Earth.		Sept. 18

F	G	H	I	J
Includes elections, federal-state relations, civil rights and liberties, crime, the judiciary, education, health care, poverty, urban affairs, and population.	Includes formation and debate of U.S. foreign and defense policies, veterans' affairs, and defense spending. (Relations with specific foreign countries are usually found under the region concerned.)	Includes business, labor, agriculture, taxation, transportation, consumer affairs, monetary and fiscal policy, natural resources, and pollution.	Includes worldwide scientific, medical, and technological developments; natural phenomena; U.S. weather; natural disasters; and accidents.	Includes the arts, religion, scholarship, communications media, sports, entertainments, fashions, fads, and social life.

	World Affairs	Europe	Africa & the Middle East	The Americas	Asia & the Pacific
Sept. 19		Russian president Boris Yeltsin signs a decree giving Premier Viktor Chernomyrdin his full powers, including control of the launching codes for Russia's nuclear weapons, during Yeltsin's upcoming heart operation. . . . The British government announces it has called off a plan to slaughter 147,000 cows thought to be at risk of contracting bovine spongiform encephalopathy (BSE), or mad-cow disease. The move is widely seen as an act of defiance against the EU, which has banned British beef.		The government and the leftist Guatemalan National Revolutionary Union (UNRG), an umbrella organization representing the country's main rebel groups, sign an accord hailed by both sides as a major breakthrough in efforts to end Guatemala's 35-year-long civil war.	South Korean troops shoot to death seven North Korean infiltrators in an incident of heightened tensions between North and South Korea. The countries never signed a peace treaty in the 1950–53 Korean War and are technically still at war with each other.
Sept. 20		Max Manus, 81, Norwegian World War II resistance leader who during the war destroyed several German targets, including more than 100 planes, dies of unreported causes.		More than 8 pounds (3.6 kg) of heroin are discovered on Colombian president Ernesto Samper Pizano's official jet, just 12 hours before Samper is scheduled to fly to New York City.	The estranged brother of Pakistan's P.M. Benazir Bhutto, Mir Murtaza Bhutto, is killed in a gun battle with police in Karachi. Six of his followers in his Shaheed Bhutto faction of the Pakistan People's Party, the party of Benazir Bhutto, are also killed in the exchange.
Sept. 21					
Sept. 22		Armenian voters reelect incumbent president Levon Ter-Petrossian in the first round of balloting. Ter-Petrossian's reelection is marred by allegations of fraud. . . . Greece's ruling party, the Panhellenic Socialist Movement (PASOK), narrowly wins national parliamentary elections. As a result, PASOK chairman Costas Simitis will continue to serve as Greece's premier. . . . Voters in the Georgian autonomous republic of Ajaria return the ruling coalition to power in Parliament.			South Korean troops fatally shoot the captain and another infiltrator from the North Korean submarine detected Sept. 18. One other person is mistakenly killed. . . . A cancer patient, Bob Dent, becomes the first man to die legally under a new euthanasia law in Australia's Northern Territory. . . . Residents of Macao cast their votes in the territory's last direct elections under Portuguese rule.
Sept. 23		London police raid several suspected Provisional Irish Republican Army (IRA) hideouts, seizing 10 tons of homemade explosives. One suspected IRA member is killed by police, and five others are arrested. . . . In Armenia, protesters launch demonstrations outside the election commission building, alleging vote fraud and demanding that Pres. Ter-Petrossian resign.		In Canada, British Columbia premier Glen Clark names Cynthia Morton as the province's first independent children's commissioner.	
Sept. 24	U.S. president Bill Clinton and foreign ministers of the world's four other declared nuclear powers—Great Britain, China, France, and Russia—sign the Comprehensive Test Ban Treaty (CTBT), which will forbid all testing of nuclear weapons. Officials of more than 50 other countries also sign the pact, but the treaty will not become enforceable under international law until all 44 nations with nuclear potential sign it.	Chechen rebel representatives meet with the human-rights committee of the Council of Europe's parliamentary assembly. . . . Lt. Gen. Pavel Anatolievich Sudoplatov, 89, Soviet spymaster who claimed in his memoirs that American scientists leaked atomic secrets to the Soviet Union at the end of World War II, dies in Moscow, Russia, after suffering a stroke.	Israeli authorities open a second entrance to an archaeological tunnel at the Temple Mount in Jerusalem, a site sacred to both Muslims and Jews and the scene of a bloody incident in 1990 when Israeli police killed 19 Palestinian protesters. Palestinian youths gather at the new entrance and throw stones at Jews worshiping at the Wailing Wall, forcing a temporary evacuation until Israeli troops, using rubber bullets, disperse the crowd. Palestinians burn a car and a truck in East Jerusalem.		Taliban troops move into Kabul, the capital of Afghanistan, and begin to consolidate power.

A	B	C	D	E
Includes developments that affect more than one world region, international organizations, and important meetings of major world leaders.	Includes all domestic and regional developments in Europe, including the Soviet Union, Turkey, Cyprus, and Malta.	Includes all domestic and regional developments in Africa and the Middle East, including Iraq and Iran and excluding Cyprus, Turkey, and Afghanistan.	Includes all domestic and regional developments in Latin America, the Caribbean, and Canada.	Includes all domestic and regional developments in Asia and Pacific nations, extending from Afghanistan through all the Pacific Island, except Hawaii.

U.S. Politics & Social Issues	U.S. Foreign Policy & Defense	U.S. Economy & Environment	Science, Technology, & Nature	Culture, Leisure, & Lifestyle	
Sheriff Joe Arpaio of Maricopa County, Arizona, puts the nation's first female chain gang to work in Phoenix. . . . The House votes, 285-137, to override Pres. Clinton's April veto of a ban on a rarely used method of late-term abortion called intact dilation and evacuation. . . . The House ethics committee reprimands Newt Gingrich (R, Ga.) for allowing Donald Jones, a telecommunications executive, to work as a volunteer in his office.		The Senate passes, 100-0, a bill that seeks to curb the rapid depletion of U.S. fish stocks by preventing an overharvesting of U.S. fisheries. . . . IBM, the sixth largest corporation in the U.S., announces that beginning in January 1997 it will provide health-care coverage and other benefits to the partners of its U.S.-based homosexual and lesbian employees. It thereby becomes the largest company in the nation to offer benefits to same-sex partners.		Media conglomerate Time Warner, the nation's leading provider of cable TV announces that half of its cable systems will carry MSNBC, a new 24-hour news channel run by Microsoft and NBC. It also states that it has broken off negotiations with News Corp. to carry Fox News.	Sept. 19
A federal prosecutor reveals that Theodore Kaczynski kept detailed journals in his Montana cabin in which he admits to each of the bombings attributed to the Unabomber.	The State Department releases excerpts from manuals used by the School of the Americas—a U.S. Army-run training school for Latin American military and police officers in Fort Benning, Georgia—in which torture, blackmail, bribery, and other threats are recommended for use against suspected rebels. The manuals were used from 1982 to 1991 at the school, which was located in Panama from 1946 to 1984. The U.S. government claims that the controversial passages were mistakenly left over from the 1960s manuals.		Paul Erdos, 83, itinerant Hungarian-born mathematician who was regarded by his peers as one of the greatest mathematicians of the 20th century and who founded the field of discrete mathematics, which is the basis of computer science, dies of a heart attack while attending a conference in Warsaw, Poland.	Paul Draper, 86, tap dancer of the 1930s and 1940s known for his musicality and broad range, dies in Woodstock, New York, of emphysema.	Sept. 20
Pres. Clinton signs into law the Defense of Marriage Act, a bill that will deny federal recognition to same-sex marriages and deny federal benefits to partners in such marriages. The bill will also allow states to deny recognition to same-sex marriages performed in other states.	The governing board of the Virginia Military Institute (VMI), a state-funded, all-male military college in Lexington, Virginia, votes to begin admitting women. VMI is the only remaining single-sex college in the U.S. that receives state funding.		A team of Australian scientists announce they have discovered rock art that they believe to be between 50,000 and 75,000 years old, the oldest in the world. Previously, the oldest reliably dated human art was set at 32,000 years old. The scientists also uncovered artifacts suggesting that human beings lived in Australia far longer than previously thought.	John F. Kennedy Jr., 35, marries Carolyn Bessette, 30, in a secret ceremony on Cumberland Island, Georgia. . . . A 1910 Honus Wagner baseball card, considered the world's most prized baseball card, is sold at an auction for $640,500. . . . Metropolitan Spyridon is installed as the archbishop of the Greek Orthodox Church of America.	Sept. 21
				A team of U.S. women professional golfers defeats a European team to win the Solheim Cup in Chepstow, Wales. . . . Dorothy Lamour (Mary Leta Dorothy Slaton), 81, film actress who costarred with Bing Crosby and Bob Hope, dies in Los Angeles of unreported causes.	Sept. 22
A panel of three federal judges in Columbia, South Carolina, rule that nine of South Carolina's 170 legislative districts violate the Constitution because they were drawn solely on the basis of race. . . . Ross Perot, the Reform Party candidate, files a lawsuit in Washington, D.C., seeking to gain inclusion in presidential debates. . . . The Justice Department reveals it has reached a settlement with the owners of an apartment complex in Detroit, Michigan, charged with discriminating against blacks and families with children.	Pres. Clinton signs the $265.6 billion fiscal 1997 defense authorization bill.	The Dow closes at 5894.74, the 24th record high in 1996. . . . Federal financial regulators report that a legal document drafted by First Lady Hillary Rodham Clinton in 1986 in relation to Whitewater would "deceive federal bank examiners" about potentially fraudulent transactions. The report does not specifically accuse the first lady of wrongdoing, however.		*Forbes* magazine lists Oprah Winfrey, a TV host and producer, as the world's highest-paid entertainer with estimated earnings for 1995 and 1996 of $171 million.	Sept. 23
	Robert C. Kim, a civilian intelligence analyst for the U.S. Navy, is arrested by the FBI on spying charges in Fort Meyer, Virginia. Kim is charged with passing classified documents to South Korea, one of the U.S.'s closest allies.	The Senate, by unanimous consent, and the House, 388-25, pass a $84.8 billion fiscal 1997 appropriations bill for veterans affairs, housing, space, environmental agencies, and other departments. . . . The Patrolmen's Benevolent Association, the largest big-city police union in the country, endorses the Republican candidates Robert Dole and Jack Kemp in upcoming presidential elections.			Sept. 24

F	G	H	I	J
Includes elections, federal-state relations, civil rights and liberties, crime, the judiciary, education, health care, poverty, urban affairs, and population.	Includes formation and debate of U.S. foreign and defense policies, veterans' affairs, and defense spending. (Relations with specific foreign countries are usually found under the region concerned.)	Includes business, labor, agriculture, taxation, transportation, consumer affairs, monetary and fiscal policy, natural resources, and pollution.	Includes worldwide scientific, medical, and technological developments; natural phenomena; U.S. weather; natural disasters; and accidents.	Includes the arts, religion, scholarship, communications media, sports, entertainments, fashions, fads, and social life.

	World Affairs	Europe	Africa & the Middle East	The Americas	Asia & the Pacific
Sept. 25		Soldiers in Yerevan, the Armenian capital, beat several dozen protesters and arrest many more in an effort to stem protests over alleged vote fraud.	In response to the Sept. 24 opening of an entrance to a Temple Mount tunnel, armed Palestinian police and rock-throwing demonstrators battle Israeli soldiers in Palestinian self-rule zones in the West Bank and Gaza Strip in the worst outbreak of violence since the two sides agreed in 1993 to decide their future in peaceful talks.		Reports confirm that a Singapore court has fined Lai Chee Chuan S$61,500 for downloading sexual material from the Internet global computer network. Lai is the first person convicted of such an offense since Singapore announced Internet restrictions earlier in the year.
Sept. 26	Reports indicate that the NATO base in Gibraltar, at the mouth of the Mediterranean Sea, will close.... Russian defense minister Igor Rodionov and his U.S. and Norwegian counterparts, William Perry and Jorgen Kosmo, sign an agreement that will use $2 million in pledges from Norway and the U.S. to clean up radioactive waste around Russia's Kola peninsula left by the Soviet and Russian nuclear submarine fleet. An estimated two-thirds of all radioactive waste in the world's oceans is in Arctic Ocean waters.	Two journalists, Viktor Ivancic and Marinko Culic, are acquitted of charges of slander against Pres. Franjo Tudjman in a case that many international observers see as a test of media freedom in Croatia. ... Nicu Ceausescu, 45, playboy son of Romania's communist president Nicolae Ceausescu, dies in Vienna, Austria, of cirrhosis of the liver.	Palestinian security forces join protesters in conflicts that started Sept. 24. The Israeli military orders tanks and attack helicopters into the West Bank for the first time since the 1967 Six-Day War. At least 35 Palestinians and 11 Israelis are killed, and the total slain since Sept. 24 comes to at least 40 Palestinians and 11 Israelis.... Head of state Yahya Jammeh, who came to power in a 1994 military coup, is elected president of Gambia in a poll whose validity is questioned by foreign observers.	Argentina's largest labor federation, the Confederacion General del Trabajo (CGT), calls a 36-hour general strike, to protest Pres. Carlos Saul Menem's austere economic policies. Some 70,000 protesters gather outside Menem's office in Buenos Aires, Argentina's capital. ... Police in the Mexican town of San Augustin Loxicha arrest at least 11 people suspected of belonging to the EPR, including the mayor and other local officials.	Australian prime minister John Howard defies Chinese warnings by receiving the Dalai Lama, the exiled spiritual leader of Tibet, in Sydney. China regards the Dalai Lama as a political activist trying to split the country by seeking Tibet's independence from China. ... Statistics reveal that 20 North Korean infiltrators have either been killed or found dead since their ship ran aground on Sept. 18.
Sept. 27			Israeli border guards and police storm the Temple Mount in Jerusalem's Old City to battle stone-throwing Palestinian demonstrators. Three Palestinians are shot to death in the incident.		Muslim fundamentalist Taliban forces take control of Kabul, Afghanistan's capital, after a siege that resulted in hundreds of deaths. The rebels announce that Islamic law will begin to apply nationwide, and they capture and execute former president Najibullah, 49, who ruled the country from 1987 to 1992. Mohammed Rabbani is the Taliban rebel named to serve as Kabul's provisional leader.
Sept. 28	The UN Security Council votes to urge Israel to close the new entrance to the controversial Old City tunnel that was opened Sept. 24 and to resume peace negotiations.	Judge Mehdi Bici sentences nine communist-era Albanian officials to prison terms ranging from 15 to 20 years for crimes against humanity.... Reports indicate that Radio Free Europe, the U.S.-run broadcaster, falsely promised Hungarians that the West would support them in their fight against Soviet rule at the time of the Hungarian uprising of 1956. Radio Free Europe officials continue to deny any encouragement of the anti-communist uprising.			
Sept. 29		The Organization for Security and Cooperation in Europe (OSCE), certifies the results of Bosnia's elections, despite evidence of widespread fraud.			In the first local polls held since 1990, Farooq Abdullah is reinstalled as the chief minister of Kashmir state when his pro-India National Conference party wins 52 seats in the 87-member state assembly.... Shusako Paul Endo, 73, Japanese novelist, dies in Tokyo of respiratory complications caused by hepatitis.

A	B	C	D	E
Includes developments that affect more than one world region, international organizations, and important meetings of major world leaders.	Includes all domestic and regional developments in Europe, including the Soviet Union, Turkey, Cyprus, and Malta.	Includes all domestic and regional developments in Africa and the Middle East, including Iraq and Iran and excluding Cyprus, Turkey, and Afghanistan.	Includes all domestic and regional developments in Latin America, the Caribbean, and Canada.	Includes all domestic and regional developments in Asia and Pacific nations, extending from Afghanistan through all the Pacific Island, except Hawaii.

U.S. Politics & Social Issues	U.S. Foreign Policy & Defense	U.S. Economy & Environment	Science, Technology, & Nature	Culture, Leisure, & Lifestyle	
David Duke, a former Ku Klux Klan leader, squares off against civil-rights activist Joe Hicks in a debate at California State University at Northridge. Some 250 protesters on both sides of the issue clash briefly with police outside the debate hall.... Reports state that Johnathan Prevette, a six-year-old boy from Lexington, North Carolina, was suspended for a day from the first grade for kissing a female classmate on the cheek.	The House and Senate approve by voice votes the conference report on the fiscal 1997 intelligence authorization bill to provide funding for the CIA, the NRO, the NSA, and the DIA. The exact amount that Congress authorized is classified, but news reports estimate the amount to be some $30 billion.	The House passes a $221 million fiscal 1997 federal spending bill for child-abuse and treatment programs.			Sept. 25
The House passes by voice vote a bill to create a nationwide database on sex offenders.... The Senate fails to override Pres. Clinton's April veto of a ban on a method of late-term abortion called intact dilation and evacuation.... California judge Thomas Hastings imposes a death sentence on Richard Allen Davis, convicted in June of kidnapping and murdering Polly Klaas, 12, in 1993.... Walter Ridley, 86, educator who, in 1953, became the first black to earn a doctorate degree from a state-supported university in the South, dies in West Chester, Pennsylvania, of unreported causes.		Pres. Clinton signs an $84.8 billion fiscal 1997 appropriations bill for veterans affairs, housing, space, environmental, and other agencies.... The Senate passes by unanimous consent legislation that revises federal safety regulations for pipelines that carry oil, gas, and hazardous liquids.... The House clears by voice vote the Water Resources Development Act, legislation that provides $3.8 billion in funding for federal water projects.	The U.S. space shuttle *Atlantis* lands at Cape Canaveral, Florida, after carrying out a successful mission during which it linked up with the Russian space station *Mir* and brought home U.S. astronaut Shannon W. Lucid, who had been stationed on Mir since March. Lucid spent a total of 188 days in space, setting records for the longest stay in space by a woman and the longest stay by a U.S. astronaut.... Sir Geoffrey Wilkinson, 75, British inorganic chemist who shared a Nobel Prize in 1973 for his work on organometallic compounds, dies of unreported causes.		Sept. 26
Nation of Islam leader Louis Farrakhan and the Million Man March organizers open the first National Political Convention in St. Louis, Missouri.... Guards fire live ammunition to disperse a prison riot at a maximum-security facility in Represa, California. One inmate is killed and 13 others are injured, five critically.... Reports confirm that federal agencies have punished 28 agents for attending "Good Ol' Boys Roundups" where racist activity occurred.	The Senate Armed Services Committee informs the Defense Department that it has decided to relax curbs on the promotion process for officers implicated in the 1991 Tailhook scandal, in which dozens of women were sexually assaulted by naval aviators.	The House clears, 276-125, legislation that revises federal safety regulations covering pipelines that carry oil, gas, and hazardous liquids.... The Senate passes by unanimous consent the Water Resources Development Act, which provides $3.8 billion in funding for federal water projects.... The House passes, 384-30, a bill that seeks to curb the rapid depletion of U.S. fish stocks.... The House clears, 218-198, a bill to reauthorize $19.5 billion over two years for the FAA.	Researchers at the National Cancer Institute report they have discovered a genetic mutation common among Caucasians that slows the progress of AIDS and in rare cases even provides immunity from infection by HIV, the virus that causes AIDS.		Sept. 27
The House ethics subcommittee investigating Speaker Newt Gingrich (R, Ga.) dismisses three charges against Gingrich and one against Minority Leader Richard Gephardt (D, Mo.).... The House gives congressional approval to a bill increasing penalties for possession and trafficking of methamphetamine, a drug commonly known as speed or "crank."	Congress clears the Veterans Benefits Improvements Act.... The House approves legislation that will make it a federal crime to steal proprietary trade secrets with the intent to benefit a foreign or U.S. entity.	The House passes, 370-37, a massive omnibus bill that provides $380 billion for discretionary spending and $230 billion for mandatory spending. The bill includes controversial new curbs on illegal immigration.... The House, by voice vote, passes the National Securities Markets Improvement Act, which will largely end state regulators' oversight of the mutual fund industry.... The House passes, 404-4, a major package of legislation covering the nation's public lands and national parks.			Sept. 28
In the first televised debate among congressional leaders, House speaker Newt Gingrich (R, Ga.), Senate majority leader Trent Lott (R, Miss.), House minority leader Richard A. Gephardt (D, Mo.) and Senate minority leader Thomas A. Daschle (D, S.Dak.) are among those who discuss tax cuts, Medicare, education, and campaign-finance reform.				The U.S. wins the Fed Cup, a women's team tennis tournament, with a 5-0 sweep over defending champion Spain in Atlantic City, New Jersey. It is the U.S.'s first Fed Cup title since 1990.	Sept. 29

	World Affairs	Europe	Africa & the Middle East	The Americas	Asia & the Pacific
Sept. 30	Succeeding South African judge Richard Goldstone, Canadian judge Louise Arbour becomes the new chief prosecutor for the UN International Criminal Tribunal in The Hague, the Netherlands. Arbour calls on the international community to give the international troops in Bosnia-Herzegovina a new mandate to seek out and detain indicted war criminals.	Bosnia-Herzegovina's three presidents—Alija Izetbegovic, Kresimir Zubak, and Momcilo Krajisnik—meet for the first time since their election.	Bahrain's state security court sentences 15 men to prison sentences ranging from six months to five years as part of its crackdown on a two-year campaign of antigovernment unrest.... The National Electoral Commission of Nigeria announces the registration of five political parties for participation in elections slated for 1998. Other political groups—including all those opposed to Gen. Sani Abacha—are automatically dissolved on denial of registration.	In Haiti, police officials claim that they foiled a plot by former members of the pro-junta Haitian army, which was disbanded in April 1995. The plot was to create disorder by assassinating top government officials and launching attacks on Haiti's slum areas. The attacks allegedly were planned for the fifth anniversary of the 1991 military coup that ousted Jean-Bertrand Aristide.	In Afghanistan, Taliban rebels capture the key northern towns of Charikar and Jabal us Saraj, and other Taliban troops reach the southern end of the strategic Salang tunnel in the Hindu Kush mountains. Reports reveal that Pres. Burhanuddin Rabbani has fled and has been sentenced to death by the Taliban.... Chinese dissidents Liu Xiaobo and Wang Xizhe write a letter calling for China to stand by a 1945 promise to honor freedoms of speech and assembly. It also criticizes Pres. Jiang Zemin and insists he be impeached for violating the constitution.... The premier of Vanuatu, Maxine Korman-Carlot, is ousted by a vote of no confidence in Parliament.
Oct. 1	The International Monetary Fund and the World Bank hold the annual joint plenary session of their boards of governors in Washington, D.C.... The UN Security Council votes unanimously to lift the sanctions imposed on the federation of Yugoslavia, which consists of Serbia and Montenegro, that were enacted in 1992 in an attempt to punish Serbia for its support of Bosnian Serbs in the civil war in Bosnia-Herzegovina.	Some 125 miles (200 km) east of Reykjavik, Iceland's capital, a volcano begins erupting underneath the Vatnajokull glacier. The eruption causes the glacier to begin to melt, threatening severe flooding. ... Data show that more than 80 Albanians have been infected with polio since April and that 11 of them have died.... As many as 140,000 workers at automobile plants in Germany hold strikes and demonstrations to protest planned cuts.		The Mexican Congress approves a package of legislation that seeks to counter the U.S.'s Helms-Burton law, which attempts to force foreign companies to comply with the U.S.'s trade embargo of communist Cuba.	A South Korean diplomat, Choi Duck Keun, is slain in Vladivostok, Russia, leading to speculation that the killing was an assassination orchestrated by North Korea, as tensions between the two countries since the September discovery of a grounded submarine continue to rise.
Oct. 2	Yasser Arafat, president of the Palestinian National Authority (PNA), and Israeli prime minister Benjamin Netanyahu conclude a summit meeting in Washington, D.C., that sought to defuse an outbreak of Israeli-Palestinian clashes in the West Bank and Gaza Strip and to restart substantive negotiations.	An unidentified gunman shoots and kills Bulgaria's first premier of its postcommunist era, Andrei Lukanov, 58, in Sofia, the Bulgarian capital.... Reports disclose that, in an effort to combat tough economic times in Ukraine, 92 people died and more than 1,000 became sick from eating wild mushrooms.... Statistics reveal that the annual rate of drug-related crimes in Kyrgyzstan leapt 190% between 1990 and 1995, to 2,623 incidents from 904.	Israeli soldiers shoot dead a four-year-old Palestinian boy and wound at least two protesters during Palestinian demonstrations in a suburb of Hebron.	All 70 people on board a Peruvian jetliner die when the jet crashes into the Pacific Ocean.... A series of strikes is launched by the 26,000-member Canadian Auto Workers (CAW) labor union against General Motors.... Robert Bourassa, 63, premier of the Canadian province of Quebec, 1970–76, 1985–94, dies in Montreal of skin cancer.	
Oct. 3	The World Bank acknowledges that it funded projects that were harmful to the environment and that it needs to revise its environmental-impact methodology.	Presidents Alija Izetbegovic of Bosnia-Herzegovina and Slobodan Milosevic of Serbia meet in Paris to establish full diplomatic relations between Bosnia and Yugoslavia, the federation of Serbia and Montenegro.... The Romanian parliament ratifies a basic treaty with Yugoslavia.... Workers at Yugoslavia's Zastava arms factory in Kragujevac, Serbia, return to work after a 34-day strike.	Thousands of Somalis in Mogadishu celebrate the third anniversary of a battle in which 18 U.S. troops were killed.		
Oct. 4		Russian president Boris Yeltsin fires six top generals, including Gen. Yevgeni Podkolzin, the paratroop commander, and Gen. Vladimir Ivanov, chief of rocket forces. Defense Minister Igor N. Rodionov announces plans to reduce the size of the armed forces by some 300,000 servicemen before the end of 1997.... Princess Stephanie of Monaco is granted a divorce from her husband of 14 months, Daniel Ducruet.	In a goodwill gesture, the Israeli army pulls back tanks positioned on the outskirts of the West Bank city of Ramallah.		The New Zealand government agrees to settle a land claim made by members of the country's indigenous Maori population. The claimants will receive NZ$170 million (US$117 million) and some traditional fishing rights recognized by the government. The government will also recognize the Maori names of 78 localities currently known by their European names.... South Korea goes on a terrorist alert in response to North Korea's threats of retaliation for deaths of its commandos from the submarine that ran aground in September.
Oct. 5		A bomb explodes in the city hall of Bordeaux, France. The blast causes some damage to the building but does not lead to any casualties.			The Taliban initiates a major assault on the heavily defended Panjshir Gorge leading to the military stronghold of Gen. Ahmed Shah Massoud, the leader of the Tajik army, in the Panjshir Valley.

A	B	C	D	E
Includes developments that affect more than one world region, international organizations, and important meetings of major world leaders.	*Includes all domestic and regional developments in Europe, including the Soviet Union, Turkey, Cyprus, and Malta.*	*Includes all domestic and regional developments in Africa and the Middle East, including Iraq and Iran and excluding Cyprus, Turkey, and Afghanistan.*	*Includes all domestic and regional developments in Latin America, the Caribbean, and Canada.*	*Includes all domestic and regional developments in Asia and Pacific nations, extending from Afghanistan through all the Pacific Island, except Hawaii.*

U.S. Politics & Social Issues	U.S. Foreign Policy & Defense	U.S. Economy & Environment	Science, Technology, & Nature	Culture, Leisure, & Lifestyle	
Gun-control advocates line up an estimated 39,000 pairs of shoes, many of which belonged to victims of fatal shootings, outside the Capitol building in Washington, D.C., in a "Silent March" against firearm-related violence. . . . The Chicago school board places 109—or nearly one-fifth—of the city's 557 public elementary and high schools on academic probation. The official censure of Chicago schools is considered one of the nation's most aggressive recent actions to improve public education.		The Senate passes, 84-15, and Pres. Clinton signs a massive omnibus spending bill that provides $380 billion for discretionary spending and $230 billion for mandatory spending for fiscal 1997. It is the fourth time since 1974 that all regular appropriations have been completed before the start of the new fiscal year. . . . Pres. Clinton signs a $12.6 billion fiscal 1997 transportation bill and a $20.4 billion bill to fund energy, water-development, and nuclear-weapons programs in fiscal 1997.		*The Deep End of the Ocean*, by Jacquelyn Mitchard, tops the best-seller list. . . . Moneta Sleet Jr., 70, civil rights–era photographer who was the first black journalist to win a Pulitzer Prize, dies in New York City of cancer. . . . Frances Lear, 73, self-described Hollywood wife who founded *Lear's*, a magazine aimed at women over 40, dies in New York City of breast cancer.	Sept. 30
Pres. Clinton signs a bill clarifying that the 1994 anticrime law includes stiffer penalties for sexual assault during a carjacking. . . . A San Francisco, California, jury awards Tianna Ugarte, 14, an award of $500,000 after finding that officials at Antioch Unified School District ignored her sexual-harassment claim. . . . As per the welfare system's overhaul, the federal government begins to provide states with lump-sum payments to pay for cash benefits.	Defense Department officials reveal that senior commanders at the Pentagon plan to vaccinate all U.S. troops against the infectious disease anthrax due to fears of biological weapons.	The Senate, in a voice vote, clears the National Securities Markets Improvement Act, which will largely end state regulators' oversight of the mutual-fund industry and will direct the SEC to set up a database of investment advisers' disciplinary histories.	Francis Collins, head of the U.S. government's gene research project, retracts findings he published in 1995 on the genetics of leukemia. Collins says he learned that a student researcher who worked under him had fabricated the data on which his conclusions had been based.		Oct. 1
Detective Mark Fuhrman, who became notorious during the trial of O. J. Simpson, pleads no contest in State Superior Court in Los Angeles to one count of perjury for lying about his use of a racial epithet. Fuhrman is given three years' probation and ordered to pay a $200 fine.	The Senate gives final approval to legislation that will make it a federal crime to steal proprietary trade secrets with the intent to benefit a foreign or U.S. entity.	Peter Joseph Brennan, 78, New York City labor leader who was U.S. secretary of labor, 1973–75, under Presidents Richard Nixon and Gerald Ford, dies in Massapequa, New York, of lymphatic cancer.	Researchers in Bangkok, Thailand, report they have discovered the world's largest known deposit of emeralds. The researchers extracted a 167-pound (75-kg), or 380,000-carat, deposit of green emeralds from a rock found in Madagascar. The cluster is worth an estimated $54 million.		Oct. 2
Pres. Clinton signs into law a bill to create a nationwide database on sex offenders. . . . Pres. Clinton signs a bill increasing penalties for possession and trafficking of methamphetamine. . . . The Senate passes a bill to increase penalties for possession of flunitrazepam, a sedative linked to date rapes. Under the bill, using the drug in an attempt to commit rape will be punishable by up to 20 years in prison and fines of up to $2 million.	A $20 billion class-action lawsuit is filed in federal court in New York City on behalf of victims and survivors of the Nazi Holocaust accusing Union Bank of Switzerland and Swiss Bank Corp. of refusing to return assets deposited by Holocaust victims.	Pres. Clinton signs a bill setting fiscal 1997 federal spending for child-abuse and treatment programs at $221 million. . . . The Senate passes by unanimous consent a major package of legislation covering the nation's public lands and national parks. . . . The Senate passes, 92-2, legislation that reauthorizes $19.5 billion in funding over two years for the FAA.		The Swedish Academy of Letters awards the Nobel Prize in literature to Polish poet Wislawa Szymborska, the ninth woman to win the literature prize since it was created in 1901 and the fifth Polish-born writer to do so.	Oct. 3
The House clears by voice vote a bill to increase the penalty for possessing flunitrazepam,. Under the bill, using the drug in an attempt to commit date rape will be punishable by up to 20 years in prison and fines of up to $2 million. . . . Data reveals that the rate of births to unmarried women dropped in 1995 for the first time in nearly 20 years. . . . Larry Gene Bell, 47, convicted of killing two girls in separate incidents in 1985, is executed in Columbia, S.C. He is the ninth person in South Carolina and the 346th person executed in the U.S. since 1976.		The Social Security Administration reveals that it distributed insufficient benefits to some 300,000 people due to a computer fault. Officials declare that all underpaid benefit recipients will be compensated.			Oct. 4
	Reports suggest that Pres. Clinton has decided to sign the conference report on the fiscal 1997 intelligence authorization bill despite strong objections from Director of Central Intelligence John M. Deutch. The bill will fund the CIA, the NRO, the NSA, and the DIA. The exact amount that Congress authorized is classified, but reports estimate the amount to be $30 billion.		Seymour R. Cray, 71, who created the world's first supercomputers—the CDC 6600 (1963), CDC 7600 (1968), and Cray 1 (1976), each of which was the fastest computer of its day—dies in Colorado Springs, Colorado, of head injuries sustained in a Sept. 22 road accident.	Skip Away wins the Jockey Club Gold Cup horse race in Belmont, New York.	Oct. 5
F	G	H	I	J	
Includes elections, federal-state relations, civil rights and liberties, crime, the judiciary, education, health care, poverty, urban affairs, and population.	*Includes formation and debate of U.S. foreign and defense policies, veterans' affairs, and defense spending. (Relations with specific foreign countries are usually found under the region concerned.)*	*Includes business, labor, agriculture, taxation, transportation, consumer affairs, monetary and fiscal policy, natural resources, and pollution.*	*Includes worldwide scientific, medical, and technological developments; natural phenomena; U.S. weather; natural disasters; and accidents.*	*Includes the arts, religion, scholarship, communications media, sports, entertainments, fashions, fads, and social life.*	

	World Affairs	Europe	Africa & the Middle East	The Americas	Asia & the Pacific
Oct. 6		An antitank grenade explodes at the Hell's Angels motorcycle gang's headquarters in the Danish capital, Copenhagen, killing two people and wounding 19 others. . . . Hungarian premier Gyula Horn dismisses Industry and Trade Minister Tamas Suchman in connection with a scandal at the Hungarian privatization board.	Gunmen from the Banyamulenge, a 400,000-strong Tutsi community that has lived in the area south of Lake Kivu in Zaire since the end of the 18th century, attack a Swedish missionary hospital at Lemera, north of Uvira, killing four staff members and 38 patients. Twelve people die in an attack on a nearby Roman Catholic mission. . . . Israeli and Palestinian representatives resume negotiations.		Yao Wenyuan, 65, possibly the last surviving member of the "Gang of Four," which promoted revolution and class struggle under Chairman Mao Zedong during the 1966–76 Cultural Revolution, is freed from prison after 20 years. Separately, reports indicate that dissident and former student leader Guo Haifeng was sentenced to seven years in prison for hooliganism. . . . North Korea announces that it has charged Evan C. Hunziker, 26, an American and self-proclaimed missionary partly of South Korean ancestry, with espionage and illegal entry.
Oct. 7		Two car bombs explode at a British army base in Lisburn, Northern Ireland, injuring 21 soldiers and 10 civilians. . . . The largest Corsican terrorist group, the "historic" wing of the Corsican National Liberation Front (FLNC), claims responsibility for the Oct. 5 blast in the French city of Bordeaux.	In Laghouat, Algeria, 200 miles (320 km) south of Algiers, rebels force 20 passengers off a public bus and cut their throats, then kill 14 other people. . . . The number of Muslim fundamentalists holding seats in Kuwait's National Assembly declines as voters strengthen the progovernment bloc.		
Oct. 8		Reports confirm that Kyrgyzstan's first oil refinery has opened. . . . Poland approves an $88 million plan to develop the town of Oswiecim, site of the Auschwitz-Birkenau concentration camp. . . . Reports state that UN investigators have exhumed 200 bodies from a mass grave in Ovcara, Croatia. . . . Four Newfoundland fishermen caught on a 1995 videotape are convicted for inhumane killing of seals. . . . The IRA takes responsibility for the Oct. 7 bombings in Lisburn. It is the first attack in Northern Ireland that the IRA admits to staging since the 1994 cease-fire.	In response to the Oct. 6 violence, Lwasi Ngabo Lwabanji, deputy governor of South Kivu province, orders the Banyamulenge Tutsis to leave Zaire within one week or face expulsion by the Zairian military. . . . Renewed talks between Israel and the Palestine Liberation Organization (PLO) stall over terms for Israel's long-delayed military redeployment from the West Bank city of Hebron.	Gen. Jean Boyle, the head of Canada's armed forces, retires from the military.	
Oct. 9		A small pipe bomb explodes near the Great Synagogue of Budapest, Hungary's capital, but it does not damage the building or cause any injuries.	Under new guidelines, the first of 10,000 Palestinians are allowed to exit Gaza for day employment in Israel.		Farooq Abdullah is reinstalled as the chief minister of Kashmir state in India. . . . Chinese authorities sentence, without trial, prodemocracy activist Liu Xiaobo, to three years in a labor camp for a protest letter he coauthored Sept. 30.
Oct. 10	NATO officials reveal that the Bosnian Serbs possess far more heavy weaponry than a June arms-control agreement among Croatia, Bosnia-Herzegovina, and Yugoslavia allows. . . . Joseph Connor, the UN's undersecretary general for management and administration, states that he has had no funds since July for the UN's day-to-day costs, and he was forced to borrow money from the UN's peacekeeping account, resulting in a delayed reimbursement to a group of 90 countries owed money for peace-keeping operations.	Magda Trocme, 93, member of the French resistance during World War II who helped thousands of Jews escape persecution by the Nazis, dies in Paris after suffering a stroke.	An outbreak of fighting erupts between units of the Zairian army and the Banyamulenge, a 400,000-strong Tutsi community that has lived in the area south of Lake Kivu since the end of the 18th century. . . . Jan Hugo of Durban's Supreme Court in South Africa acquits six members of the Inkatha Freedom Party accused of carrying out a 1987 hit-squad attack that left 13 people dead.		In Afghanistan, opposition armies join forces when Uzbek commander Gen. Abdul Rashid Doestam signs a military alliance with his rival, Gen. Ahmed Shah Massoud, the leader of the Tajik army. Also joining their alliance is the small but powerful Hizb-i-Wahdat group, comprised mostly of members of the predominantly Shi'ite Hazara tribe of the central province of Bamiyan and led by Abdul Karim Khalili.

A	B	C	D	E
Includes developments that affect more than one world region, international organizations, and important meetings of major world leaders.	*Includes all domestic and regional developments in Europe, including the Soviet Union, Turkey, Cyprus, and Malta.*	*Includes all domestic and regional developments in Africa and the Middle East, including Iraq and Iran and excluding Cyprus, Turkey, and Afghanistan.*	*Includes all domestic and regional developments in Latin America, the Caribbean, and Canada.*	*Includes all domestic and regional developments in Asia and Pacific nations, extending from Afghanistan through all the Pacific Island, except Hawaii.*

U.S. Politics & Social Issues	U.S. Foreign Policy & Defense	U.S. Economy & Environment	Science, Technology, & Nature	Culture, Leisure, & Lifestyle	
Pres. Clinton and Republican presidential nominee Robert Dole square off in the first of two presidential debates scheduled for the 1996 campaign. In a poll conducted by CBS News immediately following the forum, 50% of respondents assert that Clinton won the debate, while 28% argue that Dole was the victor. Ninety-two percent maintain the debate did not change their minds about the candidates.				Golfer Eldrick (Tiger) Woods earns a spot on the 1997 PGA Tour when he wins the Las Vegas Invitational in Las Vegas, Nevada. . . . Ted Bessel, 57, TV actor best known for his role in the 1970s series *That Girl*, dies in Los Angeles of an aortic aneurysm.	Oct. 6
Kimberly Smartt, 14, files a suit against the school district in Fairborn, Ohio, alleging that racial bias affected her punishment for taking two Midol tablets from the school's clinic, ingesting one of the pills and giving the other to a white classmate Erica Taylor, 13, who did not swallow the pill. Smartt, who is black, was suspended for months, while Taylor's nine-day suspension was lifted when she agreed to attend drug counseling.	In Washington, D.C., U.S. District Court judge Royce C. Lamberth sentences Omar Mohammed Ali Rezaq to life in prison for the 1985 hijacking of an Egypt Air jetliner in which 60 of the 98 people aboard the jet were killed. Judge Lamberth also orders Rezaq to pay $264,000 in restitution to the survivors of the hijacking, one of the deadliest in history.		The Karolinska Institute for Medicine in Stockholm awards the Nobel Prize in Physiology or Medicine to Peter C. Doherty of Australia and Rolf M. Zinkernagel of Switzerland for discovering how the immune system identifies cells that are infected with viruses.		Oct. 7
Henry Cisneros, the outgoing secretary of HUD, authorizes the distribution of $716 million in grants for the demolition and reconstruction of dilapidated public-housing complexes in 74 communities, and for rental assistance programs for some 15,000 families who will be displaced by the demolition projects. . . . Antoine Jamar Dean, a 21-year-old black man, is sentenced in federal district court in Portland, Oregon, to five years in prison for the burning of a predominantly black church in June.		The Energy Department's inspector general who examined Energy Secretary Hazel O'Leary's travel expenditures concludes that poor planning and inefficient management led to the exorbitant expenses associated with foreign trade trips taken by O'Leary and other Energy Department officials. However, no individual is held responsible for the misuse of tax dollars.	The Royal Swedish Academy of Sciences awards the Nobel Memorial Prize in Economic Science to Canadian-born William S. Vickrey of Columbia University and Britain's James A. Mirrlees of Cambridge University for their separate contributions "to the economic theory of incentives under asymmetric information."	Pope John Paul II undergoes an appendectomy at the Gemelli Polyclinic in Rome, Italy.	Oct. 8
Vice president Al Gore and Republican vice-presidential nominee Jack Kemp meet in a nationally televised debate. . . . Federal civil-rights officials conclude that a recent wave of suspicious church fires reflect underlying racial tensions in the South.	Pres. Clinton signs into law the Veterans Benefits Improvements Act. . . . The Institute of Medicine, a branch of the federal National Academy of Sciences, reiterates its conclusion that there is no single cause for Gulf War syndrome, but it adds that its findings are affected in part by a lack of detailed research into the medical effects of low-level exposure to nerve gases.	Pres. Clinton signs legislation that reauthorizes $19.5 billion in funding over two years for the FAA. . . . Common Cause, a government watchdog group, alleges that both the Democratic and Republican parties committed "massive, knowing and willing" violations of campaign-finance laws by spending millions of dollars on TV advertisements for Clinton and Dole.	The Royal Swedish Academy of Sciences awards the Nobel Prize in Physics to three U.S. scientists, David M. Lee, Robert C. Richardson, and Douglas D. Osheroff, for their 1972 discovery of superfluidity in helium-3, a rare form of helium. The Nobel Prize in Chemistry goes to Americans Richard E. Smalley and Robert F. Curl Jr. and Briton Sir Harold W. Kroto for their 1985 discovery of a previously unknown class of carbon molecule.	Walter F. Kerr, 83, theater critic and author awarded a Pulitzer Prize in 1978 for his criticism, dies in Dobbs Ferry, New York, of congestive heart failure.	Oct. 9
Coya Knutson (born Coya Gjesdal), 82, member of Congress from Minnesota, 1955–59, who lost a reelection bid after her husband, whom she later divorced, publicly begged her to quit Congress, dies in Edina, Minnesota, of kidney failure.			William S. Vickrey, 82, economist who worked at Columbia University in New York City and received a Nobel Memorial Prize in Economic Science on Oct. 8, is found dead at the wheel of his car near Harrison, New York, apparently of a heart attack.		Oct. 10

F	G	H	I	J
Includes elections, federal-state relations, civil rights and liberties, crime, the judiciary, education, health care, poverty, urban affairs, and population.	*Includes formation and debate of U.S. foreign and defense policies, veterans' affairs, and defense spending. (Relations with specific foreign countries are usually found under the region concerned.)*	*Includes business, labor, agriculture, taxation, transportation, consumer affairs, monetary and fiscal policy, natural resources, and pollution.*	*Includes worldwide scientific, medical, and technological developments; natural phenomena; U.S. weather; natural disasters; and accidents.*	*Includes the arts, religion, scholarship, communications media, sports, entertainments, fashions, fads, and social life.*

	World Affairs	Europe	Africa & the Middle East	The Americas	Asia & the Pacific
Oct. 11	The Norwegian Nobel Committee awards the Nobel Peace Prize to Bishop Carlos Filepe Ximenes Belo and Jose Ramos Horta for their efforts to end abuses by Indonesian forces in East Timor, a former Portuguese colony annexed by Indonesia in 1976. Ramos Horta states that the award should rightfully have been presented to Jose Alexandre (Xanana) Gusmão, a military leader imprisoned since his 1992 capture by the Indonesian army.	In response to the Oct,. 6 attack in Copenhagen, the justice ministers of Denmark, Sweden, Norway, and Finland agree to work together to reduce the threat of motorcycle-gang violence.	Jan Hugo of Durban's Supreme Court in South Africa acquits former defense minister Magnus Malan and nine others of murder and conspiracy to murder in a 1987 hit-squad attack that killed 13 people. The acquittals end the seven-month trial that was South Africa's first attempt to bring senior apartheid-era officials to justice for atrocities committed against blacks.	A gravely ill leader of the leftist rebel Zapatista National Liberation Army (EZLN), Comandante Ramona, addresses an audience of 20,000 people at an international conference on Indian rights in Mexico City.	
Oct. 12		The government of Finland agrees to link its currency, the markka, to the European Union's exchange rate mechanism.			Neither New Zealand's ruling center-right National Party nor the main opposition Labour Party wins a majority in Parliament in general elections, which places the balance of political power in the hands of the third-place finisher, the nationalist New Zealand First (NZF) party.
Oct. 13		The right-wing Freedom Party registers significant gains in elections to determine Austria's representation in the European Parliament, the EU's legislative branch. . . Beryl Reid, 76, British actress, dies of unreported causes. . . . Henri Nannen, 82, cofounder and longtime editor of the German magazine *Stern*, dies in Hamburg after suffering from cancer.	Armed men believed to be Banyamulenge guerrillas open fire on Hutu camps in Zaire, killing at least one person. The attack causes some 20,000 Hutus to abandon the Runingo camp.		
Oct. 14		An article in a state-owned newspaper presents a Yugoslav army reservist's account of the 1991 beating and execution of more than 200 civilians in Croatia by the Serbian militia. . . . Turkish soldiers shoot and kill Petros Kakouli, a retired Greek Cypriot firefighter crossing the border separating Cyprus's Greek and Turkish sections. . . . Belgium's Supreme Court removes Judge Jean-Marc Connerotte as the chief magistrate investigating Marc Dutroux and a child pornography case linked to kidnappings and murders. The dismissal sparks widespread public protests.	Police in Niger arrest opposition leader Bello Tiousso Garba. Garba's Union for Democracy and Progress (UDP) is one of eight parties that formed the Front for the Restoration of Democracy to challenge a disputed presidential election won in July by coup leader Gen. Ibrahim Mainassara Bare.		Reports state that Wang Xizhe, who coauthored a letter critical of the Chinese government on Sept. 30, has escaped to Hong Kong, apparently fearing arrest. . . . McDonald's Corp., the world's largest fast-food and hamburger chain, opens its first franchise in India.
Oct. 15		Hungary's parliament passes a measure to establish a foundation to compensate Jewish groups for property that belonged to Jews who perished in the Nazi Holocaust. . . . People in Belgium stage a series of rallys to protest Judge Jean-Marc Connerotte's Oct. 14 dismissal. . . . Italy's highest appellate court orders a new trial for Erich Priebke, a former officer in Nazi Germany's SS who was released from his sentence in August on a technicality.	Jordan's King Hussein visits PNA head Yasser Arafat in Jericho, a West Bank city under Palestinian self-rule. The king's visit is his first to the West Bank since Israel seized the territory from Jordan in 1967. . . . In Somalia, Hussein Aidid, Ali Mahdi Mohammed, and Osman Hassan Ali (known as Ato) declare an end to hostilities and pledge to allow free movement of people in Mogadishu.		Australian researchers report that 130-million-year-old fossil footprints left during the Jurassic Age by a stegosaurus were stolen from a site north of Broome in Western Australia.
Oct. 16	The EU asks the WTO to rule on whether the U.S.'s Helms-Burton Act, which seeks to force foreign companies to comply with the U.S.'s trade embargo of communist Cuba, violates international trade rules. The U.S. attempts to block the EU's request, delaying the scheduled hearing on the issue until late November. . . . Croatia is admitted as the 40th member of the Council of Europe, a human-rights organization.	Figures suggest that 1,400 U.S. soldiers have left Bosnia to return to their bases in Germany.	Reports confirm that Mokrane Amouri, director of an independent Arabic-language weekly newspaper, was shot and killed while driving in Algiers. Nearly 70 Algerian journalists have been killed by militants since 1991.	At least 84 people die and 147 people are injured in a stampede before a qualifying game for the 1998 World Cup soccer tournament between Guatemala and Costa Rica at Mateo Flores National Stadium in Guatemala City, Guatemala.	

A	B	C	D	E
Includes developments that affect more than one world region, international organizations, and important meetings of major world leaders.	*Includes all domestic and regional developments in Europe, including the Soviet Union, Turkey, Cyprus, and Malta.*	*Includes all domestic and regional developments in Africa and the Middle East, including Iraq and Iran and excluding Cyprus, Turkey, and Afghanistan.*	*Includes all domestic and regional developments in Latin America, the Caribbean, and Canada.*	*Includes all domestic and regional developments in Asia and Pacific nations, extending from Afghanistan through all the Pacific Island, except Hawaii.*

U.S. Politics & Social Issues	U.S. Foreign Policy & Defense	U.S. Economy & Environment	Science, Technology, & Nature	Culture, Leisure, & Lifestyle	
	Pres. Clinton signs an intelligence-authorization bill, which provides funding for fiscal 1997 for the CIA and intelligence-related agencies in the Defense Department. . . . Pres. Clinton signs a bill that makes it a federal crime to steal proprietary trade secrets with the intent to benefit a U.S. or foreign entity.	Pres. Clinton signs the National Securities Markets Improvement Act, which will largely end state regulators' oversight of the mutual fund industry and will require the SEC to set up a database of investment advisers' disciplinary histories. . . . Pres. Clinton signs a bill that reauthorizes the 1976 Magnuson Fishery and Conservation Management Act, the primary law that regulates the management of U.S. fisheries.		Reports state that organizations representing black Americans have criticized the Christian Coalition for a brochure that suggests a fictitious black man opposes views espoused by the group. Christian Coalition officials state that they have stopped distribution of the pamphlets.	Oct. 11
		Pres. Clinton signs legislation that revises federal safety regulations covering pipelines that carry oil, gas, and hazardous liquids. . . . Pres. Clinton signs the Water Resources Development Act, legislation that provides $3.8 billion in funding for federal water projects.		(Jean) René Lacoste, 92, French tennis player who was one of the Four Musketeers, a group that dominated tennis in the 1920s, and who developed a clothing line with an alligator logo, considered a status symbol in the 1970s and 1980s, dies in St. Jean-de-Luz, France after recent surgery on a broken leg and after suffering from prostate cancer for years.	Oct. 12
Pres. Clinton signs a bill setting a 20-year sentence for using any illegal drug, including the date-rape drug Rohypnol, with intent to commit rape or other violent crimes. . . . Steve Stout and Patricia Stout of Fort Worth, Texas, end their three-month battle with doctors who want surgery performed on their daughter, Rachel Stout, 10, who has been hospitalized since July for an ulcerated colon.		General Motors announces that it has laid off more than 1,300 workers at its Cadillac assembly plant outside Detroit, Michigan, because of a series of strikes launched Oct. 2 at GM's Canadian plants, which manufacture many parts needed by GM's U.S. assembly plants.		Damon Hill of Great Britain captures the Formula One world championship motor racing title with a victory in the Japanese Grand Prix. . . . The U.S. golf team defeats New Zealand to win the Alfred Dunhill Cup.	Oct. 13
		The Dow Jones industrial average of U.S. blue-chip securities closes above the 6000 level for the first time in its history, rising 40.62 points to 6010. This marks the third time in some 20 months that the benchmark stock average broke through a so-called millennium level.		Pop singer Madonna, 38, gives birth to her first child, a girl named Lourdes Maria Ciccone Leon, in Los Angeles, California.	Oct. 14
The New York State Court of Appeals rules that doctors and dentists in that state cannot refuse to treat patients infected with HIV. . . . Robert F. Williams, 71, controversial black civil-rights leader who fled the U.S. after he was accused of kidnapping a white couple during an outbreak of racial violence in Monroe, North Carolina, dies in Grand Rapids, Michigan, of Hodgkin's disease.				Data suggests that the major TV networks showed fewer violent programs in the 1995–96 season than in the previous season. . . . Pierre Franey, 75, chef who popularized and simplified French cooking, dies in Southampton, England, after a stroke.	Oct. 15
Pres. Clinton and Robert Dole, the Republican presidential nominee, meet for the second and final presidential debate of the 1996 campaign, and they field questions from audience members in San Diego, California. . . . Tens of thousands of people gather outside UN headquarters in New York City for a "Day of Atonement" and to commemorate the one-year anniversary of the "Million Man March."	Accused Mexican drug cartel leader Juan Garcia Abrego is convicted by a jury in Houston, Texas, of 22 counts of drug trafficking and money laundering. Garcia Abrego, captured by Mexican authorities and expelled from Mexico to the U.S. in January, is the reputed leader of Mexico's Gulf cocaine cartel. . . . U.S. Sen. Alfonse D'Amato (R, N.Y.), claims that, in 1949, Switzerland made a deal with Poland under which it used assets stolen from Polish Jews to compensate Swiss citizens whose property had been seized.	Social Security Administrator Shirley Chater announces that beneficiaries receiving Social Security checks in 1997 will obtain a cost-of-living increase of 2.9%. That means that the average benefit paid will amount to $745 per month, up from $724 per month in 1996.		ABC News announces that veteran journalist David Brinkley will leave his job as host of *This Week With David Brinkley*, a show he has anchored since its creation in 1981, on Nov. 10.	Oct. 16

F	G	H	I	J
Includes elections, federal-state relations, civil rights and liberties, crime, the judiciary, education, health care, poverty, urban affairs, and population.	*Includes formation and debate of U.S. foreign and defense policies, veterans' affairs, and defense spending. (Relations with specific foreign countries are usually found under the region concerned.)*	*Includes business, labor, agriculture, taxation, transportation, consumer affairs, monetary and fiscal policy, natural resources, and pollution.*	*Includes worldwide scientific, medical, and technological developments; natural phenomena; U.S. weather; natural disasters; and accidents.*	*Includes the arts, religion, scholarship, communications media, sports, entertainments, fashions, fads, and social life.*

	World Affairs	Europe	Africa & the Middle East	The Americas	Asia & the Pacific
Oct. 17		Russian president Boris Yeltsin dismisses Gen. Aleksandr I. Lebed, Russian Security Council secretary and national security adviser, after Lebed was involved in several public feuds. . . . More than 1.5 million public-sector workers in France strike to protest the government's austere budget proposals. . . . In a highly publicized trial in Britain, a jury finds Learco Chindamo, 16, guilty of the 1995 murder of Philip Lawrence. . . . Berthold Goldschmidt, 93, British composer and conductor, dies in London, England.		At least eight people are killed by Hurricane Lili in coastal areas of Nicaragua, Costa Rica, and Honduras.	India's national government extends for six months its central rule over Uttar Pradesh state since local elections have failed to resolve a deadlock in the state assembly.
Oct. 18	The UN inaugurates the International Tribunal for the Law of the Sea, an international maritime court that will hand down judgments in disputes over a wide range of maritime issues.	The coalition government of secessionist rebels in the Russian republic of Chechnya name Gen. Aslan Maskhadov Chechnya's interim premier and defense minister. . . . Russian president Boris Yeltsin appoints Gen. Viktor Samsonov to the post of armed forces chief of staff.	Mauritania's ruling Republican Democratic and Social Party (PRDS) wins a total 70 of 79 parliamentary seats. . . . Armed men believed to be Banyamulenge guerrillas open fire on Hutu camps in Zaire. When combined with the Oct. 14 attack, the offensive has killed seven people.	Hurricane Lili hits Cuba, bringing winds of up to 114 mph and between 6 and 12 inches of rain. Some 4,300 homes are destroyed, and 430,000 others are damaged by winds and rain.	Hundreds of protesters riot outside the Taiwanese parliament in Taipei when a parliamentary vote restores funding for the construction of what will be the country's fourth nuclear power plant. The rioting antinuclear protesters are dispersed by 4,000 riot police. The unrest is considered the worst rioting to occur in Taiwan since it began its conversion to democracy in 1987.
Oct. 19		Russian president Boris Yeltsin names Ivan P. Rybkin as his new Security Council secretary. . . . The Bosnian Serb parliament, known as the National Assembly of the Republika Srpska, holds its first meeting. . . . The body of Jakub Fiszmann, 40, one of Germany's wealthiest businessmen, is found in the Taunus forest near Frankfurt after being kidnapped.	Attacks on Hutu camps continue in Zaire, and fighting breaks out between the Banyamulenge and the Hutu-allied Zairian military north of Uvira.		The combined forces of Uzbek commander Gen. Abdul Rashid Doestam and Gen. Ahmed Shah Massoud, the leader of the Tajik army, recapture the air base at Bagram and then move southward to Kalakan, some 20 miles (35 km) from Kabul, the capital of Afghanistan.
Oct. 20		In Brussels, Belgium, 300,000 demonstrators attend a rally to protest the Oct. 14 removal of Judge Jean Marc Connerotte from a case involving Marc Dutroux and a child pornography and prostitution ring that has been linked to recent kidnappings and murders.		Outside Buenos Aires, Argentina, 60 tombs in a Jewish cemetery are desecrated.	Japanese premier Ryutaro Hashimoto's conservative Liberal Democratic Party (LDP) falls just short of winning a majority in elections for the lower house of the Diet (parliament).
Oct. 21	The UN General Assembly, in a secret ballot to fill the five rotating seats on the 15-member Security Council, elects Costa Rica, Japan, Kenya, Portugal, and Sweden for two-year terms.		In Zaire, data show that heavy fighting between the Banyamulenge and the Zairian military north of Uvira has resulted in the deaths of at least 70 people. A UN official estimates that more than 220,000 Hutu refugees have fled their camps. . . . Former South African commissioner of police Johan van der Merwe becomes the highest-level official to admit he had a role in the covert campaign of violence against the antiapartheid movement. . . . The mayor of Algiers, Ali Boucetta, is shot and killed.	Rightist Liberal Alliance party candidate José Arnoldo Alemán Lacayo declares himself the winner of Nicaragua's presidential election. Alemán will replace current president Violeta Barrios de Chamorro. . . . Figures reveal that at least 51 members of the Toronto-based environmental group Earthroots have been arrested since Sept. 2 for leading antilogging protests in the Owain Lake forest near Lake Temagami, Canada.	Wang Li, 75, Chinese activist during the Cultural Revolution who helped Chinese leader Mao Zedong overthrow his rivals in the Communist Party, was jailed by Mao in 1967, and released from prison in 1982, dies in Beijing of heart failure.
Oct. 22			Burundian army soldiers kill between 258 and 435 returning Hutu refugees in a church in the village of Murambi in Cibitoke province.	At least 25 inmates at La Planta jail in Caracas, Venezuela's capital, die when a fire starts in their cell.	

A	B	C	D	E
Includes developments that affect more than one world region, international organizations, and important meetings of major world leaders.	Includes all domestic and regional developments in Europe, including the Soviet Union, Turkey, Cyprus, and Malta.	Includes all domestic and regional developments in Africa and the Middle East, including Iraq and Iran and excluding Cyprus, Turkey, and Afghanistan.	Includes all domestic and regional developments in Latin America, the Caribbean, and Canada.	Includes all domestic and regional developments in Asia and Pacific nations, extending from Afghanistan through all the Pacific Island, except Hawaii.

U.S. Politics & Social Issues	U.S. Foreign Policy & Defense	U.S. Economy & Environment	Science, Technology, & Nature	Culture, Leisure, & Lifestyle	
James Irons, 19, is convicted of a 1995 arson attack that fatally burned a NYC subway token clerk.... The City of New York sues the nation's major tobacco companies in New York State Supreme Court to recover the estimated $300 million a year that the city government spends treating people with smoking-related illnesses.		A study projects that spending for the 1996 presidential campaign will reach $800 million. That amount is three times greater than spending for the 1992 race. . . . The Dow closes at 6059.20, the 30th record high registered by the Dow in 1996.			Oct. 17
Florida circuit judge Harold J. Cohen rules that the 860,000 Florida Medicaid patients will remain anonymous in a $1 billion lawsuit that the state of Florida has filed against tobacco companies to recover the cost of treating the patients for smoking-related illnesses.... The Democratic National Committee reveals it has suspended John Huang, its vice chairman for finance operations, amid controversy over donations from associates of Indonesia's influential Riady family.	Ruth Farkas, 89, U.S. ambassador to Luxembourg, 1973–76, dies in New York after being treated for a heart problem at New York University Medical Center.	The Dow closes at a record high of 6094.23, marking the seventh record high of the month for the Dow and the 31st record high in 1996.... The Commerce Department reports that the U.S. in August recorded a seasonally adjusted $10.83 billion deficit in trade in goods and services. The August figure represents a 6.9% decline from July's revised record deficit of $11.60 billion.	A study uncovers evidence for the first time of a causal link between inhalation of a toxin found in tobacco smoke and the development of cancerous cells.	Authorities in Spain learn that artist Victor Ruiz Roizo mounted one of his own modern paintings amid a display of works by Rembrandt Harmenszoon van Rijn at the Prado Museum in Madrid. . . . The American Basketball League (ABL), a women's professional league, debuts with three games.	Oct. 18
					Oct. 19
J(oseph) Bracken Lee, 97, two-term Republican governor of Utah, 1949–57, and mayor of Salt Lake City, 1960–72, dies in Salt Lake City, Utah, of unreported causes.... Michael H. Cardozo, 86, a prominent lawyer who founded the Association of American Law Schools in 1963, dies in Washington, D.C., of chronic lung disease.				D.C. United wins the inaugural Major League Soccer (MLS) championship, defeating the Los Angeles Galaxy, 3-2, in Foxboro, Massachusetts. . . . Ernie Els of South Africa wins his third consecutive World Match Play Championship in Virginia Water, England. . . . Annika Sorenstam of Sweden wins her second straight World Championship of Women's Golf in Seoul, South Korea.	Oct. 20
In Reno, Nevada, federal judge Howard D. McKibben sentences Joseph Martin Bailie, 41, to 36 years in prison for a failed attempt to blow up an IRS office in Reno.	In *U.S. Department of State v. Legal Assistance for Vietnamese Asylum Seekers*, the Supreme Court vacates a lower court's 1995 ruling that the State Department violated federal immigration law by refusing to process the visa applications of Vietnamese immigrants housed at detention centers in Hong Kong.			Rap music entrepreneur Marion (Suge) Knight, 30, is arrested and jailed for violating his probation.	Oct. 21
A study finds that 31% of Americans either have no health insurance or have trouble getting medical care. . . . Pete Halat Jr., mayor of Biloxi, Mississippi, 1989–93, is indicted on federal charges of ordering the 1987 contract killing of Biloxi judge Vincent Sherry and his wife, Margaret Sherry, a former city councilwoman.	The Defense Department announces that it will notify 20,000 U.S. soldiers that they may have been exposed to fallout from deadly chemical weapons in March 1991 after U.S. troops blew up an Iraqi munitions dump following the end of the Persian Gulf war. The announced total represents a sharp increase over the Pentagon's previous exposure estimates.		Six firefighters are injured and some 100 houses are destroyed when wildfires, fanned by the Santa Ana winds, hit southern California.	Star cyclist Lance Armstrong, 25, who won the Tour DuPont in 1995 and 1996, reveals that he has testicular cancer that has spread to his abdomen and lungs.	Oct. 22

F	G	H	I	J
Includes elections, federal-state relations, civil rights and liberties, crime, the judiciary, education, health care, poverty, urban affairs, and population.	*Includes formation and debate of U.S. foreign and defense policies, veterans' affairs, and defense spending. (Relations with specific foreign countries are usually found under the region concerned.)*	*Includes business, labor, agriculture, taxation, transportation, consumer affairs, monetary and fiscal policy, natural resources, and pollution.*	*Includes worldwide scientific, medical, and technological developments; natural phenomena; U.S. weather; natural disasters; and accidents.*	*Includes the arts, religion, scholarship, communications media, sports, entertainments, fashions, fads, and social life.*

	World Affairs	Europe	Africa & the Middle East	The Americas	Asia & the Pacific
Oct. 23		Gro Harlem Brundtland announces she will resign as Norway's premier.... The Sejm votes not to charge Gen. Wojciech Jaruzelski, Poland's former leader, and other former communist officials with constitutional violations in connection with the declaration of martial law in 1981.... Czech authorities charge 25 people—among them former policemen, soldiers, and prison officers—with having fraudulently obtained unsecured loans from 10 banks.	Pres. Nelson Mandela appoints Judge Ismail Mohomed, deputy president of the Constitutional Court, as South Africa's first black chief justice.		
Oct. 24	The Convention on Nuclear Safety, a UN treaty on the safety of nuclear power plants, goes into effect.	Poland's Sejm (parliament) passes a law liberalizing the country's abortion laws, which are among the most restrictive in Europe.... More than 400,000 automobile engineers stage strikes in Germany.... Artur Axmann, 83, leader of Hitler Youth who claimed to have been the last person to see Adolf Hitler alive, dies at an undisclosed location of unreported causes.... Lord Gladwyn (born Hubert Miles Gladwyn Jebb), 96, British diplomat who played a key role in drafting the founding UN Charter, dies in Halesworth, England, of unreported causes.		Students in Quebec, Canada, launch a series of strikes to protest tuition costs.	
Oct. 25		Reports reveal that 30 bodies found in a mass grave near Ovcara have been identified as men executed in a 1991 massacre of hospital patients from the Croatian city of Vukovar.... Thorbjoern Jagland, the leader of Brundtland's Labor Party, is sworn in by King Harald V as premier of Norway.	In Zaire, members of the Banyamulenge capture Uvira, 60 miles south of Bukavu.... A U.S. helicopter on a training mission crashes into the Persian Gulf. One of the aircraft's 12 crew members is killed, and two are reported missing.	Protesters against the Progressive Conservative (Tory) government of Ontario disrupt routine activity in Toronto, Canada's largest city and the capital of Ontario.	Reports reveal that Taliban warplanes have killed 40 civilians in Kalakan, Afghanistan.
Oct. 26		An antitank rocket strikes a police barracks in Corsica, causing minor injuries to two police officers. The Corsican National Liberation Front (FLNC) claims responsibility for the attack.... Malta's socialist Labor Party wins a narrow majority over the ruling Nationalist Party in parliamentary elections.	In Zaire, unidentified gunmen fire machine guns on the Kibumba refugee camp north of Goma, killing at least six people. The incident causes the refugees to flee the camp.	In Canada, at least 75,000 people march to Queen's Park, site of the Ontario provincial legislature, to protest the Ontario government's recent cuts to social service programs.	Coalition warplanes launch a bomb campaign against the Taliban offensive in Kabul, the capital of Afghanistan.
Oct. 27		Unidentified gunmen in northern Corsica spray a police station with machine-gun fire. The attack causes no injuries. In a separate incident, a bomb explodes outside a prison in Casapianda, Corsica.... In Nazran, Russia, Security Council secretary Ivan P. Rybkin meets with leaders of the secessionist republic of Chechnya.	Reports confirm that the government of Zaire has declared a state of emergency in the country's eastern provinces of North and South Kivu as attacks on refugee camps continue.		
Oct. 28	The EU votes to allow Europeans sued under the U.S.'s Helms-Burton law, which seeks to tighten the U.S. economic embargo of Cuba by allowing Americans to sue foreign companies that were using property seized from them in Cuba's 1959 communist revolution, to countersue in European courts.	In Russia, RAO Gazprom, the world's largest natural-gas company, raises $429.3 million in an international share offering underwritten by investment banks Morgan Stanley Group Inc. of the U.S. and Kleinwort Benson, a unit of Germany's Dresdner Bank AG.... Alfred Sant, leader of Malta's socialist Labor Party, is sworn in as premier.	Carol Bellamy, the executive director of UNICEF, reports that 4,500 children under age five are dying per month of hunger and disease in Iraq because of a lack of humanitarian supplies ... The UNHCR evacuates all aid workers from camps around Uvira and Bukavu, in Zaire near the border with Rwanda and Burundi, which held 500,000 Hutu refugees. The Tutsi-led army of Burundi admits that its soldiers killed around 50 Hutu civilians accused of buying supplies for rebels. Aid workers claim that soldiers killed at least 100 people, mostly women and children, in the Oct. 13 shooting.		

A	B	C	D	E
Includes developments that affect more than one world region, international organizations, and important meetings of major world leaders.	Includes all domestic and regional developments in Europe, including the Soviet Union, Turkey, Cyprus, and Malta.	Includes all domestic and regional developments in Africa and the Middle East, including Iraq and Iran and excluding Cyprus, Turkey, and Afghanistan.	Includes all domestic and regional developments in Latin America, the Caribbean, and Canada.	Includes all domestic and regional developments in Asia and Pacific nations, extending from Afghanistan through all the Pacific Island, except Hawaii.

U.S. Politics & Social Issues	U.S. Foreign Policy & Defense	U.S. Economy & Environment	Science, Technology, & Nature	Culture, Leisure, & Lifestyle	
District judge Paul Brown dismisses charges against Jack Meador and Jane Meador Cook, the brother and sister of a U.S. soldier who stole medieval artifacts from Germany during World War II.... Harold E(verett) Hughes, 74, U.S. senator (D, Iowa), 1969–75, and governor, 1963-69, dies in Glendale, Arizona, of emphysema, pneumonia, and heart ailments.... Former state senator Chet Blaylock, 71, the Democratic candidate for governor in Montana, dies in Deer Lodge, Montana, after apparently suffering a heart attack.	The Senate Select Committee on Intelligence opens a hearing on allegations that the CIA had links with supporters of Nicaraguan contra rebels who sold cocaine in U.S. cities such as Los Angeles in the 1980s.	Simon Fireman, a former vice chairman of Robert Dole's campaign finance committee, pleads guilty in federal court in Boston, Massachusetts, to making illegal campaign donations. U.S. district judge William Young sentences Fireman to six months under house arrest and orders him to pay fines of $1 million; his company Aqua-Leisure is fined $5 million. The combined sentence is the most severe ever handed out for a campaign-finance violation.	A study in the *American Journal of Public Health* reports that the experience of racial discrimination may contribute to the high incidence of high blood pressure among black Americans.... The NHTSA confirms for the first time that a child who was properly belted into a car's front passenger seat was killed by the inflation force of an air bag.... Hugh James Davis, 69, gynecologist who in 1968 invented the Dalkon Shield birth-control device, dies in Gibson Island, Maryland, of pancreatic cancer.	Pope John Paul II states that "fresh knowledge leads to recognition of the theory of evolution as more than just a hypothesis.".... Cyclist Wayne Ross, 30, in his attempt to ride from one end of the globe to the other, is paralyzed after crashing into a bus in Guatemala City.... Diana Trilling (born Diana Rubin), 91, essayist, editor, and literary critic, dies in New York City of unreported causes.	Oct. 23
In St. Petersburg, Florida, two white police officers stop a speeding car in a predominantly black part of the city, and when the driver, Tyron Lewis, 18, refuses to get out of the car, they fatally shoot him through the windshield. The incident sparks riots, and a crowd of more than 200 people throw bricks and bottles and burn at least 26 buildings. Police reveal at least 11 people—including a police officer—are injured, none of them seriously.	A House Government Reform and Oversight subcommittee subpoenas the FBI files of more than 50,000 of the 986,000 immigrants naturalized between Aug. 31, 1995, and Sept. 30, 1996. The INS passes new regulations that allow the agency to immediately revoke the citizenship of anyone whose application was improperly approved. These measures come amid Republican allegations that the Clinton administration has allowed 100,000 criminal aliens to become citizens so they could register to vote in the Nov. 5 elections.		Reports confirm that British scientists have uncovered the strongest evidence yet connecting bovine spongiform encephalopathy (BSE), or mad-cow disease, to the fatal human brain ailment Creutzfeldt-Jakob disease (CJD), bolstering the theory that people with CJD may have contracted the disease by eating contaminated beef. . . . Data reveal that wildfires burned some 6 million acres (2.4 million hectares) in states in the western U.S. in 1996. Western states reportedly suffered the worst wildfire season since 1952.	Star cyclist Lance Armstrong, 25, who Oct. 8 revealed he had testicular cancer that had spread to his abdomen and lungs, undergoes surgery to remove cancerous lesions on his brain. Armstrong was a two-time stage winner of cycling's Tour de France and had won the Tour DuPont in 1995 and 1996.	Oct. 24
	A federal appeals court panel agrees to expand the investigative mandate of Kenneth Starr, the independent counsel looking into the Whitewater affair.				Oct. 25
				Baseball's New York Yankees win the 92nd World Series, 3-2, over the defending champion Atlanta Braves at Yankee Stadium. The Yankees are the first team in World Series history to lose the first two games at home and then win four consecutive games for the championship.... Alphabet Soup wins the Breeders' Cup Classic at Woodbine Racetrack in Toronto, Canada.	Oct. 26
		A survey of 400 nonprofit organizations finds that charitable contributions in the U.S. increased by 5% in 1995 from 1994.			Oct. 27
In a ruling considered the first of its kind, a jury in Laporte, Pennsylvania, convicts Rosa Marie Hartford, who drove an unidentified teen impregnated by Hartford's stepson from Pennsylvania to an abortion clinic in Binghamtom, New York, without the knowledge of the girl's mother, of interfering with the custody of a minor.... Data reveal that the birth rate for girls ages 15–19 dropped in 46 states from 62.1 per 100,000 in 1991 to 56.9 in 1995.	The Federal Security Service hands over to the U.S. Holocaust Memorial Museum copies of 15,000 pages of documents from the archives of the Soviet Union's secret police, the KGB, describing Nazi German atrocities during World War II.	The Treasury Department reveals the government's Medicare trust fund has a $4.2 billion shortfall for fiscal year 1996. In fiscal 1995, the shortfall was $35.7 million.		Morey Amsterdam, 81, a comedian whose career spanned the vaudeville era through the age of television, dies in Los Angeles after suffering a heart attack.... Golfer Tom Lehman wins the PGA Tour Championship in Tulsa, Oklahoma.	Oct. 28
F	G	H	I	J	
Includes elections, federal-state relations, civil rights and liberties, crime, the judiciary, education, health care, poverty, urban affairs, and population.	*Includes formation and debate of U.S. foreign and defense policies, veterans' affairs, and defense spending. (Relations with specific foreign countries are usually found under the region concerned.)*	*Includes business, labor, agriculture, taxation, transportation, consumer affairs, monetary and fiscal policy, natural resources, and pollution.*	*Includes worldwide scientific, medical, and technological developments; natural phenomena; U.S. weather; natural disasters; and accidents.*	*Includes the arts, religion, scholarship, communications media, sports, entertainments, fashions, fads, and social life.*	

	World Affairs	Europe	Africa & the Middle East	The Americas	Asia & the Pacific
Oct. 29			Ruth Marshall of the UNHCR describes the plight of 1.2 million Hutu refugees in eastern Zaire as "desperate," estimating that all but 400,000 of the refugees are cut off from UNHCR assistance, the region's only significant source of food and medicine.	In Canada, the 500 members of the Mushuau Innu Indian band vote overwhelmingly to relocate their community from Davis Inlet, Newfoundland, to a new site at Little Sango Pond, 5 miles (8 km) west of Davis Inlet.	A court in Seoul, the capital of South Korea, sentences 110 students for their roles in violent protests calling for reunification with communist North Korea at Seoul's Yonsei University in August.
Oct. 30	The Swiss government announces that it will join the Partnership for Peace initiative, a NATO program originally created to involve Eastern Europe and the former Soviet Union in NATO.	Russian nuclear scientist Vladimir Nechai 70, who headed the Chelyabinsk-70, one of Russia's top-secret nuclear research centers, commits suicide.	Hundreds of thousands of Rwandan Hutu refugees are stranded without aid in eastern Zaire as the Zairian army fights Tutsi rebels and trades mortar fire with Rwandan forces across the border..... Eugene de Kock, a former South African commander who acknowledged serving as an assassin in the security forces' campaign against antiapartheid activists, is sentenced to life in prison. Separately, the South African rand reaches an all-time low, hitting 4.74 to the U.S. dollar.		In Afghanistan, Taliban planes drop cluster bombs onto positions of Gen. Massoud's forces in the Panjshir Valley.... A court in Beijing, China, finds prominent dissident Wang Dan, who served four years in jail for his role as one of the top student leaders of 1989 prodemocracy demonstrations in Beijing's Tiananmen Square, guilty of plotting to subvert the government and sentences him to 11 years in jail. The sentencing is seen as a final blow to the Chinese dissident movement, whose key members are now all imprisoned or in exile.
Oct. 31	Reports reveal that Hungary is the 65th country to ratify the Chemical Weapons Convention, allowing the treaty to go into effect.	The French government discloses that the jobless rate has reached a record high of 12.6%.... Marcel Carne, 90, French film director best known for his 1945 classic *Les Enfants du Paradis*, dies in Paris of unreported causes.	Tutsi forces besiege Zairian army units at the southern and northern ends of Lake Kivu. Members of the Banyamulenge are on the verge of capturing Bukavu, capital of South Kivu. A UNHCR relief center in North Kivu swells to twice its normal capacity.... Charles Taylor, leader of the National Patriotic Front of Liberia, escapes an assassination attempt in Monrovia. At least three people are killed.	The Popular Revolutionary Army (EPR), a leftist rebel group based in the southern Mexican state of Guerrero, carries out attacks in two Mexican states that result in the deaths of six police officers.... A Fokker 100 passenger jet crashes into a crowded Sao Paulo neighborhood, killing all 96 people on board and two people on the ground.	
Nov. 1		A Danish court opens a hearing regarding allegations that Denmark's membership in the European Union violates the country's constitution.	In Sudan, three aid workers—John Early of the U.S., Moshen Raza of Kenya, and Mary Worthington of Australia—are taken prisoner while transporting wounded fighters loyal to John Garang, the enemy of rebel leader Kerubino Kwanyin Bol.		Junius R. Jayewardene, 90, former president of Sri Lanka, 1978–89, dies in Colombo of unreported causes.
Nov. 2			The UN High Commissioner for Refugees and other agencies evacuate the last foreign aid workers from the Goma region, ending all direct contact with more than 1 million refugees in eastern Zaire.		Thousands of Khmer Rouge rebels stationed along Cambodia's border with Thailand disclose their defection to the Cambodian government.
Nov. 3		Ukrainian member of Parliament Yevhen Shcherban is shot dead in an attack at Donetsk Airport that also kills two other people.... Voters in Montenegro and Serbia give the leftist coalition of Serbian president Slobodan Milosevic 64 seats in the federation's 138-seat parliament.... An unidentified gunman in Moscow kills U.S. hotelier Paul Tatum in the first killing of an American during a recent wave of gangland-style contract killings in Russia.... Voters in Romania elect a center-right parliament.... Bulgarians choose Petar Stoyanov of the opposition SDS party as their next president.... In Tajikistan, opposition troops move toward the Afghan border, capturing the villages of Sagirdasht and Kalai-Hussein.	Jean-Bedel Bokassa, 75, former ruler of the Central African Republic, 1964–79, known for brutality and greed during his reign, dies in Bangui of a heart attack.		Leaders of an estimated 4,000 Khmer Rouge rebel soldiers announce that their troops will unite with the government's Royal Cambodian Armed Forces beginning Nov. 6.

A	B	C	D	E
Includes developments that affect more than one world region, international organizations, and important meetings of major world leaders.	*Includes all domestic and regional developments in Europe, including the Soviet Union, Turkey, Cyprus, and Malta.*	*Includes all domestic and regional developments in Africa and the Middle East, including Iraq and Iran and excluding Cyprus, Turkey, and Afghanistan.*	*Includes all domestic and regional developments in Latin America, the Caribbean, and Canada.*	*Includes all domestic and regional developments in Asia and Pacific nations, extending from Afghanistan through all the Pacific Island, except Hawaii.*

U.S. Politics & Social Issues	U.S. Foreign Policy & Defense	U.S. Economy & Environment	Science, Technology, & Nature	Culture, Leisure, & Lifestyle	
U.S. District Court judge Emmet Sullivan declares a Washington, D.C., youth curfew violates the constitutional rights of minors and parents. . . . Reports disclose that police have arrested George Kobayashi, the head of a test-preparation school, for allegedly helping people cheat on standardized tests used to determine admission to graduate schools by taking advantage of time-zone differences.	The FBI arrests retired Russian spy Vladimir Galkin on charges of attempting to gather classified information on SDI, or "Star Wars." . . . INS commissioner Doris Meissner reports that a review has found "no evidence that significant numbers of unqualified individuals have been or are being granted citizenship," discrediting Republican allegations that 100,000 criminal aliens were allowed to become citizens in a push to register them as voters.	GM workers in Indianapolis, Indiana, and in Janesville, Wisconsin, walk off their jobs.		The Booker Prize is awarded to novelist Graham Smith for *Last Orders*. . . . Ewell Blackwell, 74, professional baseball pitcher in the 1940s and early 1950s, dies in Hendersonville, North Carolina, of cancer. . . . An estimated 3.5 million people attend a ticker-tape parade for the Yankees, winners of the World Series, in New York City.	Oct. 29
In Leland, Mississippi, around 400 marchers protest the death of Aaron White, 29, a black motorist who was shot and killed after he crashed his truck into a tree and then allegedly fled the scene. His death was later ruled a suicide. A riot breaks out after the mayor and the police chief state that they will speak only to the protesters' leaders. . . . FBI senior official Michael Kahoe admits to having destroyed an internal report critical of the FBI's performance in a 1992 siege in Idaho's remote Ruby Ridge area when he pleads guilty to one count of obstruction of justice in U.S. District Court.	Eleanor Lansing Dulles, 101, diplomat who founded the U.S. State Department's Berlin desk in 1952 and played a major role in the rehabilitation of West Berlin after World War II, dies in Washington, D.C., of complications from a stroke.	The Commerce Department reports that the GDP grew at a seasonally adjusted annual rate of 2.2% in the third quarter of 1996. That rate marks a sharp decline from the April-June quarter's heated economic expansion, when the total output of goods and services produced within U.S. borders grew at a robust rate of 4.7%.		Christie's closes a charitable auction in Vienna, Austria, featuring 8,000 pieces of art that German Nazis plundered from Jews who died during the World War II Holocaust. The sale's proceeds of $14.5 million are to be donated to both Jewish and non-Jewish victims of the Holocaust.	Oct. 30
Authorities declare a state of emergency in Leland, Mississippi, due to the riot that erupted Oct. 30. . . . Richard Thompson, the Oakland County, Michigan prosecutor, files charges against Dr. Jack Kevorkian in connection with 10 suicides that took place in that jurisdiction between June 20 and Sep. 7.	Frank Kurtz, 85, World War II pilot and Olympic high diver whose plane, the *Swoose*, was installed at the Smithsonian Institution in Washington, D.C., in 1960, dies in Toluca Lake, California, of complications from a head injury suffered in 1995.	The Commerce Department reports that personal pretax income increased by 0.6% in September from August, to a seasonally adjusted annual figure of $6.54 trillion. The September figure marks the 16th consecutive monthly income increase.		Notable racing horse Cigar is officially retired by his owner, Allen Paulson.	Oct. 31
A jury in Torrance, California, convicts freelance photographer Charles Rathbun of murder in the slaying of a model and former Los Angeles Raiders cheerleader, Linda Sobek, in November 1995.				Irving Gordon, 81, comedy writer and lyricist best known for the song "Unforgettable" and the sketch "Who's on First?" made famous by the comedy team of Bud Abbott and Lou Costello, dies of cancer.	Nov. 1
		General Motors Corp. announces that it has reached a three-year national labor contract with the United Auto Workers.		Marcenia Lyle (Toni) Stone, 75, black baseball player who was the first woman to play as a regular on a big-league professional team, dies in Alameda, California, of heart failure.	Nov. 2
		GM reaches a deal with the 2,750 workers who struck Oct. 29 at a metal-stamping parts plant in Indianapolis, Indiana.	British Telecommunications PLC and U.S. long-distance carrier MCI Communications Corp. announce plans to merge in a deal that will create the world's first transatlantic telephone carrier.	Ffyone Campbell, who in 1994 was named the first woman to walk around the world, admits that she did not actually accomplish the feat since she rode in trucks during a 1,000-mile stretch while she was pregnant. . . . Giacomo Leone of Italy wins the men's race in the 27th New York City Marathon. Anuta Catuna of Romania wins the women's title.	Nov. 3

F	G	H	I	J
Includes elections, federal-state relations, civil rights and liberties, crime, the judiciary, education, health care, poverty, urban affairs, and population.	Includes formation and debate of U.S. foreign and defense policies, veterans' affairs, and defense spending. (Relations with specific foreign countries are usually found under the region concerned.)	Includes business, labor, agriculture, taxation, transportation, consumer affairs, monetary and fiscal policy, natural resources, and pollution.	Includes worldwide scientific, medical, and technological developments; natural phenomena; U.S. weather; natural disasters; and accidents.	Includes the arts, religion, scholarship, communications media, sports, entertainments, fashions, fads, and social life.

	World Affairs	Europe	Africa & the Middle East	The Americas	Asia & the Pacific
Nov. 4		Armenian premier Hrant Bagratian resigns and is succeeded by Armen Sarkisyan.	Disenfranchised Zairian Tutsis led by two veteran Marxist guerrilla leaders capture three key towns from Zairian government troops, and they unilaterally declare a cease-fire.		
Nov. 5	The leaders of Rwanda, Kenya, Uganda, Tanzania, Zambia, Ethiopia, Eritrea, and Cameroon and the officers the Organization of African Unity (OAU) ask the UN Security Council to deploy a "neutral force" to set up temporary sanctuaries for the refugees and safe corridors for their repatriation to Rwanda and Burundi. . . . Croatian foreign minister Mate Granic agrees to an extension of the UN's authority in the Serb-held region of Eastern Slavonia until July 1997.	Spain's Supreme Court votes to clear former premier Felipe Gonzalez of involvement in the "death-squad" killings of Basque separatists in the 1980s. . . . A volcano under the Vatnajokull glacier in Iceland erupts, causing the Grimsvotn lake underneath the glacier to flood. . . . Russian president Boris Yeltsin undergoes multiple-bypass heart surgery in Moscow. . . . A German court convicts Birgit Hogefeld and sentences him to life in prison for killing two U.S. soldiers and one U.S. civilian and of attempting to murder a high-level official in the German government in the 1985 bombing of the U.S. Rhein-Main Air Base near Frankfurt.	Thousands of students commandeer dozens of vehicles in Kinshasa, Zaire, and call for Premier Leon Kengo wa Dondo, to step down as premier. The students denounce Kengo for not declaring war on Rwanda and Burundi, which, they maintain, are backing the rebels in eastern Zaire. . . . In Algeria, Muslim fundamentalist rebels kill 31 people in an attack on Sid el Kebir, a village south of Algiers. At least 228 Algerian civilians have been reported killed in bombings and massacres by rebels since July, mostly in the area south of Algiers.		South Korean troops kill two infiltrators from the submarine that ran aground off the South Korean coast in September in a gun battle. Four South Korean troops die in the attack. . . . Pakistani president Farooq Leghari dismisses prime minister Benazir Bhutto amid charges of corruption and economic mismanagement. He also dissolves the National Assembly and swears in Malik Meraj Khalid as interim prime minister.
Nov. 6		Tommy Lawton, 77, considered one of the all-time greats of English soccer, dies of unreported causes.	South African president Nelson Mandela signs a law guaranteeing equal school funding and a single syllabus for white and black children.		At least 1,000 people are killed when the deadliest cyclone to hit India since 1977 strikes the state of Andhra Pradesh. Local papers place the death toll at more than 2,000. The cyclone destroys at least 500,000 homes, and an estimated 500,000 people are stranded by floods. . . . Chinese dissident Chen Ziming, serving a 13-year sentence for his involvement in the 1989 Tiananmen Square prodemocracy protests, is released on medical parole from a jail in Beijing, China's capital.
Nov. 7			A Nigerian passenger jet crashes into a lagoon some 40 miles (65 km) southeast of Lagos, Nigeria's largest city, killing all 143 people on board.		The South Korean defense ministry calls off a massive manhunt for North Korean infiltrators from a submarine that ran aground off the South Korean coast in September. . . . Japanese premier Ryutaro Hashimoto is formally reelected by the Diet.
Nov. 8	The UN General Assembly, in a secret ballot, elects candidates from France and New Zealand to the two vacant seats on a key UN budget committee. The U.S. loses its seat on the committee, and U.S. officials attribute the unprecedented move to resentment over U.S. arrears to the UN.	Russian president Boris Yeltsin undergoes a quintuple-bypass operation. . . . A boycott by stockbrokers halts all operations at Greece's Athens Stock Exchange. The brokers start the boycott after learning that members of Delta Securities were charged with criminal fraud. . . . Serbian president Slobodan Milosevic states that he favors an extension of the UN authority in the Serb-held region of Eastern Slavonia until January 1998.	Jordan orders the release from prison of Islamic militant Laith Shubailat, arrested in late 1995 and sentenced to three years' imprisonment in March for "violating the king's dignity."	Employees of the Ontario Medical Association go on strike to protest February cuts to the province's health-care budget that involve turning away new patients seeking routine care.	

A	B	C	D	E
Includes developments that affect more than one world region, international organizations, and important meetings of major world leaders.	Includes all domestic and regional developments in Europe, including the Soviet Union, Turkey, Cyprus, and Malta.	Includes all domestic and regional developments in Africa and the Middle East, including Iraq and Iran and excluding Cyprus, Turkey, and Afghanistan.	Includes all domestic and regional developments in Latin America, the Caribbean, and Canada.	Includes all domestic and regional developments in Asia and Pacific nations, extending from Afghanistan through all the Pacific Island, except Hawaii.

U.S. Politics & Social Issues	U.S. Foreign Policy & Defense	U.S. Economy & Environment	Science, Technology, & Nature	Culture, Leisure, & Lifestyle	
The FBI reports that it received notification of nearly 8,000 hate-crime incidents in 1995. . . . An audiotape on which Texaco executives allegedly make racial slurs and discuss the destruction or alteration of documents pertinent to a lawsuit brought against the company in 1994 is made public.			Some 15 major fires that started over the summer in parts of western states are still burning.	*The Deep End of the Ocean*, by Jacquelyn Mitchard, tops the best-seller list.	Nov. 4
William J. Clinton is reelected president of the U.S., the first Democrat since Franklin D. Roosevelt to win a second presidential term. Clinton, 50, is also the youngest president to be reelected. Republicans maintain control of both chambers of Congress. The partisan balance of governorships remains at 32 Republicans and 17 Democrats. Preliminary data estimates that 48.8% of eligible voters cast ballots, the lowest turnout since 1924. Voters in California pass Proposition 209, which bars the state from using race- or gender-based preferences in public hiring and educational admissions. Nine states pass a measure that requires ballot forms to identify whether candidates favor or oppose term limits.				In San Francisco, California, the U.S. Court of Appeals for the Ninth Circuit rules, 2-1, that the federal government cannot force the NEA to use standards of decency when giving grants to artists, arguing that such stipulations are an unconstitutional curb on freedom of speech. The case stems from decency standards that Congress adopted for the endowment in 1990.	Nov. 5
A coalition of labor and civil-rights groups led by the ACLU file a lawsuit challenging California's Proposition 209 as unconstitutional. . . . A federal jury in Macon, Georgia, convicts three militia members—Robert Starr III, James McCranie Jr., and Troy Spain (also known as Troy Allen Kyser)—who are accused of planning to stockpile bombs for use in a war with the government. . . . Mario Savio, 53, student protest leader at UC Berkeley in the 1960s, dies in Sebastopol, California, of a heart attack.		Reports confirm that GM has reached a pact with 4,800 workers striking since Oct. 29 at its plant in Janesville, Wisconsin, its most profitable facility.		The National Book Foundation presents awards to Andrea Barrett, Victor Martinez, James Carroll, and Hayden Carruth. The Medal for Distinguished Contribution to American Letters is awarded to novelist Toni Morrison.	Nov. 6
Dr. Jack Kevorkian, a retired pathologist and leading advocate for physician-assisted suicide, and his associate, Janet Good, are arrested in Ionia, Michigan, and charged with participating in the Aug. 30 suicide of Loretta Peabody, 54, who suffered from multiple sclerosis. Peabody's death was the 46th suicide Kevorkian has acknowledged attending. . . . The CDC predicts that 16.6 million young people now under age 18 will become smokers in the future.	The U.S. Senate Select Committee on Intelligence finds that the Clinton administration broke no laws in refusing to stop Iranian weapons shipments to Bosnia in 1994. . . . U.S. Army officials disclose that the army is conducting a wide-ranging investigation into allegations of sexual assault and harassment at one of its training facilities in Maryland. . . . Pres. Clinton officially accepts the resignation of Secretary of State Warren Christopher.	Former representative Mel Reynolds (D, Ill.) and his wife, Marisol Reynolds, are indicted by a federal grand jury in Chicago on charges of bank fraud, illegal use of campaign funds, and making false statements to federal campaign regulators. . . . A U.S. District Court judge in Washington, D.C., sentences Joseph Waldholtz, the ex-husband of Rep. Enid Greene (R, Utah), to 37 months in prison for bank, election and tax fraud involving the source of $1.8 million that was funneled to Greene's 1994 reelection campaign.	A team of scientists report they have found material in sedimentary rock on Akilia Island in West Greenland that suggests life developed on earth more than 3.85 billion years ago. Scientists had previously argued, based on fossil evidence, that life originated 3.5 billion years ago. . . . As part of Mars 96, a $180-million cooperative effort among Russia and 20 other nations aimed at determining whether life has ever existed on Mars, the U.S. successfully sends the *Global Surveyor* into earth orbit.	The Distilled Spirits Council of the U.S. reveals that it will drop its voluntary ban on TV and radio commercials that advertise spirits. The nation's four primary TV networks—ABC, CBS, NBC, and Fox—state they will not begin airing national advertisements of hard-liquor products.	Nov. 7
Pres. Clinton names Erskine B. Bowles to replace White House chief of staff Leon Panetta. . . . A federal grand jury in Wheeling, West Virginia, indicts seven men who are part of a group known as the West Virginia Mountaineer Militia in an alleged plot to blow up a FBI computer complex.				An anonymous buyer purchases a 141-year-old rare Swedish stamp known as the Treskilling Yellow at an auction in Zurich, Switzerland, for a record 2.87 million Swiss francs ($2.3 million).	Nov. 8

F	G	H	I	J
Includes elections, federal-state relations, civil rights and liberties, crime, the judiciary, education, health care, poverty, urban affairs, and population.	*Includes formation and debate of U.S. foreign and defense policies, veterans' affairs, and defense spending. (Relations with specific foreign countries are usually found under the region concerned.)*	*Includes business, labor, agriculture, taxation, transportation, consumer affairs, monetary and fiscal policy, natural resources, and pollution.*	*Includes worldwide scientific, medical, and technological developments; natural phenomena; U.S. weather; natural disasters; and accidents.*	*Includes the arts, religion, scholarship, communications media, sports, entertainments, fashions, fads, and social life.*

	World Affairs	Europe	Africa & the Middle East	The Americas	Asia & the Pacific
Nov. 9		Bosnian Serb Republic president Biljana Plavsic fires Gen. Ratko Mladic, the leader of the Bosnian Serb armed forces during the four-year-long civil war in Bosnia-Herzegovina. . . . Lord Sherfield (born Roger Mellor Makins), 92, British ambassador to the U.S., 1953–56, who was knighted in 1949, dies in Basingstoke, England, of unreported causes.	Hutu militants start shelling rebel-held Goma, Zaire, from the Mugunga camp, killing at least two people.		
Nov. 10	Heads of state of most Latin American countries and the leaders of Spain and Portugal meet for the sixth annual Ibero-American Summit, held in Vina del Mar, Chile.	A bomb explodes in Moscow, Russia, killing 13 people at a memorial service for Afghan Veterans Invalids Fund head Mikhail Likhodei, who was killed, by a bomb in 1994. . . . A coalition of center-right parties wins 45.1% of the vote in Slovenian parliamentary elections. . . . Voters in Georgia's former autonomous region of South Ossetia elect Lyudvig Chibirov as president. . . . Marjorie Proops, British journalist known for her advice columns, dies of unreported causes.			
Nov. 11		Bosnian Serbs and Muslims battle in the town of Gajevi in northeast Bosnia-Herzegovina, in the separation zone between the Muslim-Croat federation and the Bosnian Serb Republic. Two Muslims are killed, and several other people are wounded. It is the worst ethnic fighting in Bosnia since a deployment of NATO forces in 1995 ended a four-year-long civil war. . . . The center-right Homeland Union party gains control of Lithuania's Seimas in a second round of parliamentary elections.	In Zaire, Kinshasa's shop owners and public transportation workers honor a strike called by students who denounce Premier Leon Kengo wa Dondo for not declaring war on Rwanda and Burundi, which they think are backing the rebels in eastern Zaire. The students block roads into the capital with burning tires.	In Mexico, a fuel-tank explosion at a storage plant in San Juan Ixhuatepec that belongs to the state oil monopoly results in the deaths of four people and the injury of at least 15 others. The explosion ignites two other tanks and sends a cloud of smoke over nearby Mexico City, the capital, forcing the evacuation of more than 3,000 people.	Some 300 of a group of 1,300 fishermen who were on an expedition in the Bay of Bengal when a cyclone hit on Nov. 6 return safely. The rest are presumed dead.
Nov. 12	In Cairo, Egypt, 4,000 people from some 70 countries attend the third annual Middle East-North Africa Economic Conference. . . . The UN General Assembly, for the fifth consecutive year, condemns the U.S. economic embargo of Cuba. For the first time all 15 EU countries condemn the act. . . . The European Court of Justice orders Britain to enforce an EU policy mandating a maximum 48-hour workweek and enacting other workplace rules.	Fighting continues between Bosnian Serbs and Muslims in the town of Gajevi. . . . French insurance company Groupe Axa announces that it will purchase Union des Assurances de Paris. The merger will create the world's largest insurance company in terms of the value of assets under management. . . . Serbian president Slobodan Milosevic sends Deputy Premier Nikola Sainovic to Pale to demand the ouster of Gen. Ratko Mladic, who has refused to step down.		At least 11 people are killed and some 560 others injured when a powerful earthquake hits southern Peru. The quake, measuring 6.4 on the Richter scale, also traps workers in remote gold mines in the Andes mountain range.	Two airplanes collide in midair some 60 miles (100 km) west of the airport in New Delhi, India, killing all 349 people aboard. The accident is the worst midair collision in aviation history, and the fourth-deadliest air crash ever.
Nov. 13	Some 10,000 delegates from 194 nations attend the World Food Summit, hosted by the UN Food and Agriculture Organization, and the delegates adopt a declaration enshrining "the right of everyone to have access to safe and nutritious food" and pledging to halve the number of the world's hungry—currently 840 million—by the year 2015.	Greece's stock exchange reopens after a boycott that started Nov. 8.		In Mexico, firefighters bring the blaze from the Nov. 11 explosion at a storage plant in San Juan Ixhuatepec under control. Another explosion at a Pemex plant in Dos Bocas in the southern state of Tabasco kills at least two workers.	

A	B	C	D	E
Includes developments that affect more than one world region, international organizations, and important meetings of major world leaders.	Includes all domestic and regional developments in Europe, including the Soviet Union, Turkey, Cyprus, and Malta.	Includes all domestic and regional developments in Africa and the Middle East, including Iraq and Iran and excluding Cyprus, Turkey, and Afghanistan.	Includes all domestic and regional developments in Latin America, the Caribbean, and Canada.	Includes all domestic and regional developments in Asia and Pacific nations, extending from Afghanistan through all the Pacific Island, except Hawaii.

U.S. Politics & Social Issues	U.S. Foreign Policy & Defense	U.S. Economy & Environment	Science, Technology, & Nature	Culture, Leisure, & Lifestyle	
David R. Hinson resigns as chief of the FAA.	Documents detailing the army's probe of sexual harassment charges reveal that Captain Derrick Robertson was charged with rape, forcible sodomy, conduct unbecoming an officer, adultery, obstruction of justice, and an improper relationship with a recruit. Staff Sergeant Delmar Simpson was charged with rape, forcible sodomy, adultery, and obstruction of justice. Sixteen other drill sergeants and instructors stationed at Aberdeen, Maryland, have been suspended as a result of the probe.			Evander Holyfield defeats Mike Tyson with a technical knockout in the 11th round to win the WBA heavyweight title in Las Vegas, Nevada. Holyfield becomes the second boxer to win three heavyweight championships in his career.	Nov. 9
				Auto racer Terry Labonte wins the NASCAR title, the Winston Cup, when he places fifth in the NAPA 500 in Hampton, Georgia.	Nov. 10
Police in New York City take 35 people into custody after a raid on three adjacent apartment buildings uncovers an arsenal of guns and explosives, including 26 rifles and two working replicas of machine guns.	Lloyd A. Free, 88, pioneer in international public-opinion polling who, during World War II, was director of the Foreign Broadcast Listening Service, which monitored Nazi German propaganda and who was head of what is now the U.S. Information Agency, dies in Bethesda, Maryland, of prostate cancer.				Nov. 11
The Supreme Court sets aside a lower-court ruling issued in March that upheld the constitutionality of Illinois's Fourth Congressional District, a majority-Hispanic district in the Chicago area. The justices, without comment, order the lower court to review its opinion in the context of two Supreme Court rulings issued in June that struck down race-based congressional districts in Texas and North Carolina.	Army officials at Fort Leonard Wood, a training installation in Missouri, reveal that three male sergeants stationed there—Staff Sergeant Anthony S. Fore, Sergeant George W. Blackley Jr., and Staff Sergeant Loren B. Taylor—have been charged with crimes ranging from improper consensual sex to assault and battery.	Pres. Clinton signs legislation that provides funds to create or preserve some 120 parks, rivers, and other historical sites in 41 states.		A Pontiac, Michigan, jury convicts Jonathan T. Schmitz, 26, for the fatal shooting of Scott Amedure, 32, who revealed his homosexual attraction to Schmitz on the *Jenny Jones Show*.	Nov. 12
A grand jury in St. Petersburg, Florida, clears James Knight, a white policeman, in the fatal shooting of Tyron Lewis, 18, a black motorist whose October death sparked riots. The ruling sets off more unrest. . . . An all-white jury in an Allegheny County, Pennsylvania, court acquits John Vojtas, a white police officer, of involuntary manslaughter in the October 1995 death of a black motorist, Jonny E. Gammage, 31, in Brentwood, Pennsylvania.		In New York City, U.S. District Court judge Jack Weinstein fines Susan Frank and Jane Frank Kresch $10,000 each for dumping toxic sludge into New York Harbor. Frank is sentenced to eight months' home confinement. Kresch is sentenced to one year and one day in prison.	A report in the *Journal of the American Medical Association* ties heavy smoking to the incidence of breast cancer among women.	Data show the Republican and Democratic parties broadcast 1,397 hours' worth of ads in the U.S.'s 75 top media markets between Apr. 1 and Nov. 4. The figure includes ads from the presidential campaigns. . . . Alma Kitchell, 103, who was a pioneer in radio and TV and a talk-show host in the 1940s, dies in Sarasota, Florida, of unreported causes.	Nov. 13

F	G	H	I	J
Includes elections, federal-state relations, civil rights and liberties, crime, the judiciary, education, health care, poverty, urban affairs, and population.	*Includes formation and debate of U.S. foreign and defense policies, veterans' affairs, and defense spending. (Relations with specific foreign countries are usually found under the region concerned.)*	*Includes business, labor, agriculture, taxation, transportation, consumer affairs, monetary and fiscal policy, natural resources, and pollution.*	*Includes worldwide scientific, medical, and technological developments; natural phenomena; U.S. weather; natural disasters; and accidents.*	*Includes the arts, religion, scholarship, communications media, sports, entertainments, fashions, fads, and social life.*

	World Affairs	Europe	Africa & the Middle East	The Americas	Asia & the Pacific
Nov. 14		Spain's parliament votes overwhelmingly in favor of the country's full participation in the military structure of NATO.... A crowd of Bosnian Muslims attack a 50-vehicle column of U.S. troops near the town of Brnjik. No U.S. soldiers are seriously injured.	Israel's Supreme Court grants permission to the nation's internal security service to employ methods that human-rights organizations characterize as "torture."... Zairian Tutsi rebels known as the Banyamulenge fire rockets into the camp at Mugunga, where Hutu militants take refuge behind a human shield of refugees.	In Canada, Quebec officials declare that French is the common language of communication in the province's public sector.... The Mexican Chamber of Deputies, the lower house of Congress, passes a watered-down version of a political-reform package approved by Mexico's four main political parties in July.	Four coal miners die in a mining accident at the Gretley Colliery in Wallsend, New South Wales. It is the state's worst mining disaster in 17 years.... Suresh Kumar, a member of the youth wing of the Communist Party of India, commits suicide by self-immolation to protest the planned Miss World beauty contest, which has been denounced as demeaning to Indian women and culture.
Nov. 15	The UN Security Council votes unanimously to authorize a Canadian-led force to take aid to the refugees in eastern Zaire and to help in their "voluntary, orderly repatriation." The council sets Mar. 31, 1997 as a deadline for completion of the mission.	In Tajikistan, opposition forces capture the town of Komsomolabad, 65 miles (100 km) east of Dushanbe.... The Stone of Scone, a sandstone used in the coronation of Scottish kings, is returned to Scotland after spending 700 years in England.	An estimated 500,000 Hutu refugees embark on a four-day trip to return to Rwanda after spending more than two years in camps in eastern Zaire. The exodus averts a human catastrophe in Zaire's North Kivu province, where fighting put the refugees at risk of death from starvation and disease. The refugees' departure from Mugunga is marred by the massacre of about 30 men, women, and children, allegedly by soldiers of the Rwandan army.... Units of the Central African Republic's army take up arms against the government of Pres. Ange-Felix Patasse for the third time in eight months.	Voters in Sao Paulo, Brazil's largest city, elect Celso Pitta of the conservative Partido Progressista Brasileiro (PPB) as the city's first black mayor.... In Canada, Michael Hopfner, a former provincial assemblyman, is convicted of fraud in Saskatchewan's largest-ever political scandal.	
Nov. 16		Doku Zavgayev, the head of the Russian government-aligned Chechen leadership, announces that the government of pro-Russian premier Nikolai Koshman has resigned.... A bomb blast in the Caspian Sea town of Kaspiysk, Dagestan, kills 68 people.	At least 25 cases of cholera are reported as refugees travel from the Mugunga camp in Zaire toward the Rwandan border.		Vietnamese president Le Duc Anh is hospitalized after reportedly suffering a stroke.
Nov. 17	As the World Food Summit draws to a close, protesters denounce the declaration adopted Nov. 13, enshrining "the right of everyone to have access to safe and nutritious food" and pledging to halve the number of the world's hungry—currently 840 million—by the year 2015, as a "farce" since the document is not legally binding and contains no financial commitments.	Romanians in a runoff election choose Emil Constantinescu, 56, of the reform-minded center-right Democratic Convention of Romania (CDR) party as president, ending the seven-year rule of former Communist Party official Ion Iliescu.... Between 5,000 and 10,000 demonstrators assemble in Minsk, the capital of Belarus, to protest Pres. Aleksandr Lukashenko's proposals on a new constitution. Police arrest 10 marchers, and a total of 20 are injured in clashes with police.			The Chart Thai (Thai Nation) party of incumbent premier Banharn Silpa-archa suffers a resounding defeat in parliamentary elections when the New Aspiration Party (NAP), led by Gen. Chavalit Yongchaiyudh, emerges with a narrow parliamentary plurality.

A	B	C	D	E
Includes developments that affect more than one world region, international organizations, and important meetings of major world leaders.	*Includes all domestic and regional developments in Europe, including the Soviet Union, Turkey, Cyprus, and Malta.*	*Includes all domestic and regional developments in Africa and the Middle East, including Iraq and Iran and excluding Cyprus, Turkey, and Afghanistan.*	*Includes all domestic and regional developments in Latin America, the Caribbean, and Canada.*	*Includes all domestic and regional developments in Asia and Pacific nations, extending from Afghanistan through all the Pacific Island, except Hawaii.*

U.S. Politics & Social Issues	U.S. Foreign Policy & Defense	U.S. Economy & Environment	Science, Technology, & Nature	Culture, Leisure, & Lifestyle	
Gerald Atkins, 29, allegedly opens fire on a cafeteria at the Ford Motor plant in Wixom, Michigan, killing a plant foreman and seriously injuring two people.... A report declares that Washington, D.C.'s public school system is unacceptable "by every important educational and management measure." .... Statistics suggest that cancer deaths in the U.S. have been declining at an average of 0.6% per year since 1990.	Officials at the Fort Jackson Army training center in South Carolina reveal that during the past year soldiers at the base were charged with 27 incidents of sexual misconduct. The air force discloses that, since 1994, eight male instructors have been punished for sexual harassment at Lackland Air Force Base in San Antonio, Texas. . . . Vladimir Galkin, a retired Russian spy arrested Oct. 29, is freed by CIA director John Deutch in a move criticized by FBI Persian agents.... Two studies find that Persian Gulf War veterans are no more likely to die from disease or to suffer from serious illness than are military personnel who did not serve in the war.	California passes legislation that requires companies with more than 10 employees to provide training and to redesign workstations for employees who sustain repetitive-stress injuries. The California law is the first in the nation to address the issue.		Cardinal Joseph Bernardin, 68, Roman Catholic archbishop of Chicago who was awarded the Presidential Medal of Freedom by Pres. Clinton in September, dies in Chicago of pancreatic cancer.	Nov. 14
CIA director John Deutch visits the Watts section of Los Angeles to answer questions from leaders in the predominantly black, inner-city community about allegations that the CIA was involved in drug trafficking in the neighborhood in the 1980s.... Ellis Wayne Felker, 48, convicted of murdering a college student in 1981, is executed in the electric chair in Jackson, Georgia, becoming the 350th person executed in the U.S. and the 22nd in Georgia since 1976.... In response to a lawsuit, the public-school system in Boston, Massachusetts, states it will end its use of racial preferences in the admission of students to its three top high schools.... Prompted by the Nov. 14 report, the federally appointed Washington, D.C., financial control board takes over the district's school system.... Alger Hiss, 92, diplomat in the State Department who in 1950 was convicted of perjury in what became a notorious communist espionage case that helped give validity to the anticommunist crusade launched by Sen. Joseph R. McCarthy (R, Wis.), dies in New York City of emphysema.	Four noncommissioned army officers assigned to Fort Leonard Wood, a training installation in Missouri, are charged with engaging in improper personal relationships with trainees.	Texaco agrees to a the largest-ever settlement—$176 million—in a race-discrimination suit brought in 1994 by black Texaco employees.... Amid allegations of illegal fund-raising by the Democratic Party, Clinton administration officials reveal that John Huang, while working for the Commerce Department, told the president that he would better serve him as a fund-raiser for the Democratic National Committee (DNC). The White House's disclosure provides the first evidence that both Clinton and Riady were involved in Huang's appointment to the DNC, which has since late September returned more than $1.5 million in contributions primarily solicited by Huang from foreign donors.... B(ob) J(ohn) Magness, 72, cable-TV company owner who has been ranked annually since 1985 by *Forbes* magazine as among the U.S.'s wealthiest people, dies in Charlottesville, Virginia, of lymphoma.	Pres. Clinton signs an executive order to ease restrictions on the export of data-scrambling technology. The plan is designed to improve U.S. companies' ability to compete in the lucrative market for encryption software, while continuing to allow law-enforcement officials to unscramble computer codes in the course of criminal investigations.... An international team of researchers report they have mapped the location of a gene they suspect of causing Parkinson's disease, a degenerative nerve condition.		Nov. 15
Delaware prosecutors charge Amy Grossberg, 18, and Brian C. Peterson Jr., 18, from Bergen County, New Jersey, with first-degree murder in the death of their newborn child. Peterson admitted to putting their baby in a plastic bag in a dumpster in freezing weather shortly after Grossman delivered their child in a motel. An autopsy, however, shows that the baby died of skull fractures.	Harold James Nicholson, a career CIA officer, is arrested for allegedly being involved in a conspiracy to commit espionage for Russia.... Mother Teresa is awarded honorary U.S. citizenship by the U.S. ambassador to India, Frank Wisner, in recognition of her lifelong dedication to helping the poor.	Although it is not immediately reported, a truck transporting two nuclear bombs to Ellsworth Air Force Base in Rapid City, South Dakota, slides off Interstate Highway 83 in western Nebraska during an ice storm. The incident is the first accident involving the transportation of "sensitive nuclear materials" in 13 years.	A 6-ton spaceship, *Mars 96*, is launched from Baikonur space center in Kazakhstan to study the atmosphere on the planet Mars.		Nov. 16
	At least four people among a group of 10 trying to enter the U.S. from Mexico by wading across the Rio Grande near the city of Brownsville, Texas, drown.	The Democratic National Committee announces that it has dismissed John Huang, a former senior DNC official at the center of the fund-raising controversy, from his post as part of normal, postelection cutbacks.	The Russian spacecraft bound for Mars that was launched Nov. 16 crashes into the Pacific Ocean 1,000 miles (1,600 km) east of Easter Island and 2,000 miles west of Santiago, Chile, damaging the credibility of the Russian space program.	Australian David Dicks, 18, becomes the youngest person to sail nonstop around the world.	Nov. 17

F	G	H	I	J
Includes elections, federal-state relations, civil rights and liberties, crime, the judiciary, education, health care, poverty, urban affairs, and population.	*Includes formation and debate of U.S. foreign and defense policies, veterans' affairs, and defense spending. (Relations with specific foreign countries are usually found under the region concerned.)*	*Includes business, labor, agriculture, taxation, transportation, consumer affairs, monetary and fiscal policy, natural resources, and pollution.*	*Includes worldwide scientific, medical, and technological developments; natural phenomena; U.S. weather; natural disasters; and accidents.*	*Includes the arts, religion, scholarship, communications media, sports, entertainments, fashions, fads, and social life.*

	World Affairs	Europe	Africa & the Middle East	The Americas	Asia & the Pacific
Nov. 18	NATO plans to deploy a 30,000-strong force in Bosnia for at least 12 months.	Belarus president Aleksandr Lukashenko accepts the resignation of Premier Mikhail Chigir, who quits when Lukashenko insists on holding a referendum regarding constitutional reforms that will give him more power. He is replaced by Sergei Ling. . . . Truckers, backed by several French labor unions, walk off their jobs. . . . Service on the English Channel rail tunnel connecting Britain and France is interrupted by a fire that breaks out, injuring 34 people.	Zambian president Frederick J. T. Chiluba and his ruling party win victory in general elections.		In respect to the Nov. 17 Thai elections, PollWatch, an election-monitoring group, reports that it has received more than 5,000 complaints of voting irregularities.
Nov. 19	The U.S. formally vetoes the reelection of UN secretary general Boutros Boutros-Ghali to a second five-year term, setting the stage for a leadership crisis. . . . The International Federation of Airline Pilots' Associations reveals that air-traffic control and radar facilities are inadequate over three-quarters of the African continent. . . . Reports disclose that the U.S.'s National Rifle Association (NRA) gun-rights organization has been accredited with the UN as a nongovernmental organization.	A court in Hamburg, Germany, sentences Suhaila Sayeh Andrawes to 12 years in prison for her role in the 1977 hijacking of a Lufthansa airliner and the slaying of the jet's pilot. . . . Kresimir Zubak, who represents the Croat community in Bosnia-Herzegovina's three-man presidency, orders the removal of Deputy Defense Minister Hasan Cengic from his post to fulfill a U.S. condition for delivery of an arms shipment. . . . In Romania, Emil Constantinescu names Victor Ciorbea to be premier.	Two Israeli border policemen are arrested after having been identified in an amateur videotape that shows them beating six Palestinians at a checkpoint near Jerusalem. . . . The Nigerian government releases three opposition figures—Gani Fawehinmi, Femi Falana, and Femi Aborishade—who have been jailed since the beginning of the year.	Pope John Paul II, who is credited with playing a key role in bringing down communism in Eastern Europe, holds his first meeting with Cuban president Fidel Castro Ruz, leader of the last communist country in the West. The pope accepts an invitation to visit Cuba in 1997, which will be the first visit to that country by any pope.	Bill Clinton becomes the third U.S. president to visit Australia. . . . China sentences without trial two pro-democracy campaigners, Fu Guoyong and Chen Ping, who authored articles demanding political reform, to labor camps for three years and one year, respectively.
Nov. 20	The WTO agrees to set up a three-member dispute panel to study whether the U.S.'s Helms-Burton law, which seeks to tighten the U.S. economic embargo of Cuba, violates international trade rules. . . . A U.S. study on science and math education in 41 nations finds that Singapore scores highest in both categories, while South Africa places last. On the science portion, the U.S. ranks 17th out of 41, and it comes in 28th out of 41 in math.	Poland's Pres. Aleksander Kwasniewski signs into law a bill that will liberalize the country's abortion laws, which are among the most restrictive in Europe. The new law allows women to have an abortion up to the 12th week of a pregnancy if they face financial or personal-health problems.			South Korean president Kim Young Sam becomes the first South Korean president to visit Vietnam since the two nations normalized diplomatic relations in 1992. . . . A fire in a 16-story commercial building kills 39 people and injures at least 80 others in a shopping district on the Kowloon Peninsula in Hong Kong.
Nov. 21		Estonia's coalition government collapses when the Reform Party, one of the junior parties in the government, announces that it will leave the coalition.	Frederick J. T. Chiluba is sworn in for a second term as Zambian president.	At least 29 people are killed and more than 80 others are injured when an explosion rips through a six-story building in a residential and shopping district in San Juan, Puerto Rico.	Masked assassins methodically shoot and kill a Taoyuan County magistrate, Liu Pang-yu, and seven others, in a suburb of Taipei. It is the worst criminal massacre ever in Taiwan. . . . The UN High Commissioner for Refugees shuts down operations in Kabul, the capital of Afghanistan, since the safety of its staff cannot be assured. . . . In Tasmanian Supreme Court, Australian chief justice William Cox in Tasmanian Supreme Court sentences Martin Bryant to 35 life prison terms for killing 35 people in a deadly shooting spree in April.
Nov. 22		Premier Vaclav Klaus's Civic Democratic Party (ODS) wins a plurality in parliamentary elections in the Czech Republic. . . . Maria Casares, 74, Spanish-born actress known for her legendary relationship with French writer Albert Camus, dies in France of unreported causes.			In Bangalore, India, protestors launch demonstrations against the Miss World beauty contest, denouncing the pageant as demeaning to Indian women and culture. . . . Nobel Peace Prize winner Mother Teresa undergoes heart surgery at a hospital in Calcutta, India, to clear two blocked arteries.

A	B	C	D	E
Includes developments that affect more than one world region, international organizations, and important meetings of major world leaders.	Includes all domestic and regional developments in Europe, including the Soviet Union, Turkey, Cyprus, and Malta.	Includes all domestic and regional developments in Africa and the Middle East, including Iraq and Iran and excluding Cyprus, Turkey, and Afghanistan.	Includes all domestic and regional developments in Latin America, the Caribbean, and Canada.	Includes all domestic and regional developments in Asia and Pacific nations, extending from Afghanistan through all the Pacific Island, except Hawaii.

U.S. Politics & Social Issues	U.S. Foreign Policy & Defense	U.S. Economy & Environment	Science, Technology, & Nature	Culture, Leisure, & Lifestyle	
In *Ohio v. Robinette*, the Supreme Court rules unanimously that police officers who stop drivers for traffic violations may secure permission to search cars for narcotics without telling motorists that they are free to go. . . . Judge Francis Egitto of Kings County Supreme Court sentences James Irons, 19, to 25 years to life in prison for a 1995 arson attack that fatally burned a subway token clerk. . . . Evelyn Hooker, 89, psychologist whose research shows that homosexuality is not a mental illness, dies in Santa Monica, California.	Eleven female House members meet with four U.S. Army generals in a closed-door session to discuss the revelations of sexual abuse at army installations. Reports confirm that officials at the Aberdeen training center received nearly 4,500 calls on a hotline established Nov. 7 to register complaints. Army officials report that about 580 of those complaints have been deemed credible. . . . U.S. administration officials announce a $140 million aid package for Rwanda.		Computer and electronics firm Hewlett-Packard Co. reveals that it has government approval to export new data-scrambling technology, known as the International Cryptography Framework, which incorporates several different encryption techniques.		Nov. 18
The Institute of Medicine reports that the U.S. has the highest rate of sexually transmitted diseases in the developed world. The report estimates that there are 12 million new cases of sexually transmitted diseases in the U.S. each year, including 3 million among teenagers.	Officials of the U.S. Department of Defense state that no more than 800 U.S. military personnel will participate in the UN mission. Pres. Clinton has pledged to send up to 4,000 U.S. troops to the Rwanda-Zaire region.	Judge J. Stephen Czuleger of California Superior Court sentences former Orange County treasurer Robert Citron, whose investment strategy lost $1.6 billion, pushing the county into one of the largest ever municipal bankruptcies, to one year in prison and fines him $100,000. . . . Energy Secretary Hazel O'Leary announces that the federal government will pay $4.8 million to the victims or their families to settle claims of 12 unwitting subjects in government-sponsored radiation experiments conducted during the cold war.	The U.S. space shuttle *Columbia* lifts off on a mission to launch two satellites that will conduct two experiments in space.		Nov. 19
Jamie Nabozny, a homosexual man who, as a middle-school and high-school student in the Ashland School District in northern Wisconsin, was beaten and mocked by classmates, wins a $900,000 out-of-court settlement, ending the first federal trial in which a school district is sued for not protecting a gay student.		Comptroller of the Currency Eugene A. Ludwig announces a newly adopted rule that will allow banks to pursue financial-service activities in areas from which they have been virtually barred since the 1930s.	Russia successfully launches a supply vehicle en route to astronauts on the *Mir* space station.	The auction houses of Sotheby's Holdings Inc. and Christie's International PLC close their NYC fall auctions with a combined sale total of $269 million, a slight increase over 1995's fall auction sales.	Nov. 20
The CDC reports that the number of babies born with the AIDS virus decreased steadily between 1992 and 1995. The number of newborn infants who contracted the disease fell by 27% to 663 in 1995, from 905 in 1992. . . . Walter Edward Hoffman, 89, U.S. district judge who presided over the trial that ended the political career of Vice Pres. Spiro Agnew, dies in Norfolk, Virginia, of unreported causes.	Harold James Nicholson, a career CIA officer, is indicted by a federal grand jury in Alexandria, Virginia, on one count of conspiracy to commit espionage for Russia. Nicholson is the highest-ranking CIA official ever to be charged with espionage.		Abdus Salam, 70, Pakistani physicist whose research on the unity of nature's fundamental forces helped him become, in 1979, the first Muslim to win a Nobel Prize, dies in Oxford, England, of a long-term neurological disorder.		Nov. 21
In a civil "wrongful-death" suit, O. J. Simpson, a former football star accused of stabbing his former wife and her friend to death in 1994, testifies in open court for the first time. . . . Ray Blanton, 66, governor of Tennessee, 1975–79, who was forced out of office in 1979 due to his suspected involvement in a "cash-for-clemency" scandal, dies in Jackson, Tennessee, of complications from liver disease.	Army Secretary Togo West Jr. announces that the army's inspector general will take over the investigation of charges of widespread sexual abuse at army training installations. . . . An air force search-and-rescue plane crashes into ocean waters 40 miles (65 km) off Cape Mendocino in northern California.	Amid allegations of illegal fundraising, the Democratic National Committee reveals that it has returned a $450,000 contribution, its largest refund to date. . . . Marisol Reynolds, the wife of former Rep. Mel Reynolds (D, Ill.), pleads guilty to falsifying loan applications, filing false reports to the FEC, and cashing campaign checks for the couple's personal use.	The crew of the spacecraft *Columbia* launches a satellite called the *Wake Shield* that is designed to grow semiconductor film.	Mark Lenard, 68, actor best known for his role as Dr. Spock's father on the TV series *Star Trek*, dies in New York City of multiple myeloma.	Nov. 22

F	G	H	I	J
Includes elections, federal-state relations, civil rights and liberties, crime, the judiciary, education, health care, poverty, urban affairs, and population.	*Includes formation and debate of U.S. foreign and defense policies, veterans' affairs, and defense spending. (Relations with specific foreign countries are usually found under the region concerned.)*	*Includes business, labor, agriculture, taxation, transportation, consumer affairs, monetary and fiscal policy, natural resources, and pollution.*	*Includes worldwide scientific, medical, and technological developments; natural phenomena; U.S. weather; natural disasters; and accidents.*	*Includes the arts, religion, scholarship, communications media, sports, entertainments, fashions, fads, and social life.*

	World Affairs	Europe	Africa & the Middle East	The Americas	Asia & the Pacific
Nov. 23		Russian president Boris Yeltsin signs a decree ordering the withdrawal of the last two remaining military brigades in Chechnya.	An Ethiopian Boeing 767 passenger jet is hijacked while en route from Addis Ababa, Ethiopia, to Nairobi, Kenya, and then to Abidjan, Ivory Coast. The jet runs out of fuel and crashes into the Indian Ocean near the Comoros, a small archipelago off the east coast of Africa, killing 123 of the 175 passengers and crew aboard in what is reportedly the second deadliest hijacking in history. . . . In Niger, the National Union of Independents for Democratic Renewal (UNIRD) and its allies wins 69 of 83 seats in the National Assembly.	Reports confirm that three lawsuits have been filed against Joaquin Balaguer, the former president of the Dominican Republic.	Police arrest more than 1,500 people staging violent street demonstrations to protest the Miss World beauty contest in Bangalore, India. The demonstrators denounce the pageant as demeaning to Indian women and culture.
Nov. 24	EU officials, after meeting with several of Europe's leading finance and bank officials, announce that Italy's currency, the lira, will be permitted to reenter the European exchange rate mechanism.	Despite rallies in Belgrade, the Serbian and Yugoslav capital, Belgrade's First District Court annuls the results of 33 Belgrade city council seats won by candidates from the Zajedno (Together) coalition which opposes the party affiliated with Serbian president Slobodan Milosevic. . . . Robert Kocharyan is reelected president of the breakaway region of Nagorno-Karabakh, with more than 85% of the vote.		Pres. Alberto Fujimori confirms that Peru has purchased Soviet-built MiG-29 fighter jets, a disclosure that heightens tensions with neighboring Ecuador.	
Nov. 25	Leaders of the 18 member nations of the Asia-Pacific Economic Cooperation (APEC) forum endorse a declaration under which the countries will eliminate almost all tariffs on computers and high-technology products by the year 2000. . . . The EU extends sanctions imposed on Nigeria by six months after the execution of nine minority-rights activists in November 1995.	In a Belarus referendum, voters approve a new constitution that increases presidential control over every branch of government. Opponents of Pres. Lukashenko claim that the vote was falsified and accuse the president of establishing a dictatorship. . . . In response to the Nov. 24 ruling on election results, more than 100,000 demonstrators peacefully march in Belgrade.	The death toll from the crash of the jet hijacked Nov. 23 rises to 125, as two more passengers die of injuries sustained in the crash.		King Bhumibol Adulyadej installs Gen. Chavalit Yongchaiyudh as Thailand's new premier.
Nov. 26	The UN's International Labor Organization reports that the number of unemployed and underemployed people worldwide rose to 1 billion in 1995, from 820 million in 1993 and 1994. . . . Canadian prime minister Jean Chretien and Chinese premier Li Peng sign a C$4 billion (US$3 billion) deal for the sale of two Canada Deuterium Uranium nuclear reactors by Atomic Energy Canada Ltd. to China.	Azerbaijan's president, Heydar A. Aliyev, confirms Artur Rasizade as premier. Azerbaijan also condemns the Nov. 24 elections in the breakaway region of Nagorno-Karabakh. . . . Michael Bentine, 72, British comedian who worked in radio and TV, dies in London of prostate cancer. . . . Secretary for Scotland Michael Forsyth announces that public health officials will investigate a food-poisoning epidemic in central Scotland.			The National Assembly approves South Korea's membership in the Organization for Economic Cooperation and Development (OECD). . . . North Korea releases Evan C. Hunziker, 26, an American detained in August and accused of spying for South Korea. . . . Dame Joan Hammond, 84, New Zealand-born opera singer, dies in New South Wales, Australia, of long-term ailments.
Nov. 27	The WHO reports that there were three million new AIDS cases worldwide in 1996. . . . The UN Security Council votes to extend the mission of a 23-member military observer group working with the ECOWAS peacekeepers in Liberia until Mar. 31, 1997. . . . The UN Security Council approves a six-month extension, to expire in May 1997, of the mandate of the UN Preventive Deployment Force in Macedonia.	Gen. Ratko Mladic formally resigns his leadership of the Bosnian Serb army.	Opposition leader Etienne Tshisekedi wa Mulumba returns to Zaire from a meeting with Pres. Mobutu Sese Seko in France and is greeted at the airport by more than 50,000 supporters. . . . The South African government announces that in December 1997 it will sever diplomatic ties with Taiwan.		Japan's Tokyo District Court decides in a landmark ruling that Shiba Shinkin Bank illegally denied promotions to 12 women employees due to their gender. The lawsuit marks the first time in Japan that a company is found guilty of gender discrimination in promotions. The court orders the bank to pay about 100 million yen ($890,000) in compensation to 12 women and to immediately promote 11 of them to management positions. One plaintiff had retired since the suit was filed in 1987.
Nov. 28		Greek farmers erect barricades throughout Greece to block major roads in an act of protest against the government's austere budget proposals. Public-sector workers stage a one-day strike. . . . In Belarus, Pres. Aleksandr Lukashenko signs a new constitution that increases his control over every branch of government.	In Lebanon, Premier Rafik al-Hariri deploys tanks and soldiers to curb nationwide demonstrations called by the Confederation of Trade Unions to protest the government's economic policies. . . . The United Arab Emirates and Britain sign a defense cooperation accord. . . . Algerians vote in a referendum to approve a new constitution extending the power of the presidency and effectively banning Islamic-based parties.	A former Rio de Janeiro state trooper, Nelson Oliveira dos Santos Cunha, is found guilty by a jury in Rio de Janeiro, Brazil, of eight counts of murder in connection with the massacre of eight homeless youths in July 1993. He is sentenced to 261 years in prison. . . . Naval officer Dean Marsaw ends a 29-day hunger strike when the Canadian navy restores him to his former rank of lieutenant commander. The military justice system will hear his appeal on his previous demotion in 1997.	

A	B	C	D	E
Includes developments that affect more than one world region, international organizations, and important meetings of major world leaders.	*Includes all domestic and regional developments in Europe, including the Soviet Union, Turkey, Cyprus, and Malta.*	*Includes all domestic and regional developments in Africa and the Middle East, including Iraq and Iran and excluding Cyprus, Turkey, and Afghanistan.*	*Includes all domestic and regional developments in Latin America, the Caribbean, and Canada.*	*Includes all domestic and regional developments in Asia and Pacific nations, extending from Afghanistan through all the Pacific Island, except Hawaii.*

U.S. Politics & Social Issues	U.S. Foreign Policy & Defense	U.S. Economy & Environment	Science, Technology, & Nature	Culture, Leisure, & Lifestyle	
	Coast Guard rescuers find two bodies and one survivor, Tech. Sergeant Robert Vogel, from the Nov. 22 crash off the coast of California. The other eight crew members are listed as missing and are presumed dead.				Nov. 23
				Golfer Karrie Webb of Australia wins the LPGA Tour Championship. . . . In football, the Toronto Argonauts win, 43-37, the Grey Cup over the Edmonton Eskimos. . . . Steffi Graf of Germany and Pete Sampras win the season-ending events on the women's and men's professional tennis tours.	Nov. 24
Dr. David A. Kessler, commissioner of the FDA, announces that he will quit his post, which he has held for six years, in 1997.		The Dow closes at a record high of 6547.79, marking the 12th record high of the month for the Dow and the 43rd record high in 1996.	The broadcasting, electronics, and computer industries reach an agreement setting national standards for the production of digital televisions, ending years of debate. . . . The FDA approves a new drug called Aricept to treat Alzheimer's disease.		Nov. 25
Vincent Ellerbe, 18, is found guilty of a 1995 arson attack that fatally burned a subway token clerk. . . . Almost 500 violent criminals and sexual offenders are freed from Florida prisons for good behavior because of an October court ruling regarding mandatory prison terms and time off for good behavior. . . . South Carolina governor David Beasley (R) calls for the removal of the Confederate States of America flag from the state capitol building in Columbia.		Interior Secretary Bruce Babbitt announces that the government is more than doubling the entrance fees at several of the country's most popular national parks, such as the Grand Canyon, Yosemite and Yellowstone. Fees in some areas will increase from $15 to $40 by May 23, 1997.		Major League Baseball team owners ratify a new five-year collective-bargaining agreement.	Nov. 26
In San Francisco, California, chief U.S. district judge Thelton Henderson temporarily blocks Proposition 209, a measure that will bar the California state government from relying on race or gender-based preferences in educational admissions, public hiring, and contracting, from going into effect. . . . Thomas Malik, 19, is found guilty of a 1995 arson attack that fatally burned a subway token clerk.		The Social Security Administration notifies the parents of 260,000 children that they may stop receiving disability payments covered by the Supplemental Security Income (SSI) program due to new federal welfare laws. . . . Carol Browner, administrator of the EPA, announces the agency's plans to impose stricter national air-quality standards.			Nov. 27
					Nov. 28

F	G	H	I	J
Includes elections, federal-state relations, civil rights and liberties, crime, the judiciary, education, health care, poverty, urban affairs, and population.	*Includes formation and debate of U.S. foreign and defense policies, veterans' affairs, and defense spending. (Relations with specific foreign countries are usually found under the region concerned.)*	*Includes business, labor, agriculture, taxation, transportation, consumer affairs, monetary and fiscal policy, natural resources, and pollution.*	*Includes worldwide scientific, medical, and technological developments; natural phenomena; U.S. weather; natural disasters; and accidents.*	*Includes the arts, religion, scholarship, communications media, sports, entertainments, fashions, fads, and social life.*

	World Affairs	Europe	Africa & the Middle East	The Americas	Asia & the Pacific
Nov. 29	Judge Claude Jorda of the UN international war crimes tribunal in The Hague, the Netherlands, sentences Drazen Erdemovic, 25, to a 10-year prison term. Erdemovic, a low-ranking soldier, pled guilty in May to participating in a massacre of Muslim civilians near the town of Srebrenica, Bosnia-Herzegovina, in 1995. His sentence is the first to be handed down by an international tribunal in the post-World War II era.	Reports confirm that the Lithuanian parliament has selected Gediminas Vagnorius to be premier of Lithuania. . . . French truck drivers end a national strike begun Nov. 18 that crippled several sectors of France's economy. . . . Reports reveal that marchers burned American flags in front of the U.S. embassy in Belgrade to protest alleged U.S. support of Serbian president Slobodan Milosevic.			Chinese president Jiang Zemin and Indian Prime Minister H. D. Deve Gowda sign several accords aimed at reducing tensions in Sino-Indian relations.
Nov. 30	Statistics show that at the close of the Atlantic hurricane season, 13 tropical storms, including nine hurricanes killed at least 135 people in the U.S., Central America, and the Caribbean.	Workers at the Sosnovyi Bor nuclear power station near St. Petersburg, Russia, begin a hunger strike to urge the government to pay 27 billion rubles worth of back wages.	Heavy fighting between the rebels and government forces breaks out in Bangui, the capital of the Central African Republic. . . . The government of Sierra Leone and rebel forces sign a peace agreement ending a five-year-long civil war.		Koji Kobayashi, 89, former chairman of Japan's NEC Corp., a computer and communications company, dies in Tokyo of unreported causes.
Dec. 1		In Tajikistan, opposition forces capture the town of Garm, 91 miles east of Dushanbe, as part of a intensified offensive. . . . As per the Nov. 23 decree, the last Russian military brigades in Chechnya begin their withdrawal. . . . Public-health workers begin vaccinating students at the University of Wales in an effort to stem a meningitis outbreak. . . . Moldova's voters choose Petru Lucinschi as their new president.	The UN World Food Program reports that the number of people being fed by aid agencies in Burundi has doubled in recent weeks, to 80,000.	Peter Bronfman, 67, Canadian businessman who, with his brother, Edward, headed what was once one of North America's largest corporate enterprises, Edper Investments Inc., dies in Toronto, Canada, of cancer.	The Chinese currency, the yuan, becomes fully convertible for purposes of international trade.
Dec. 2	The EU issues a policy statement that links trade and aid to Cuba to improvement in Cuba's human-rights record and progress toward democracy.	Czech Republic president Václav Havel undergoes surgery for lung cancer in a Prague hospital.		Mexican president Ernesto Zedillo Ponce de Leon fires Attorney General Antonio Lozano Gracia, the only opposition party member of his cabinet.	A committee made up of Japanese and American officials issue a finalized agreement between Japan and the U.S. under which the amount of land on the Japanese island of Okinawa used by the U.S. military will be reduced by 20%.
Dec. 3		A bomb explodes on a crowded commuter train in Paris, France, killing two people and injuring 88. . . . Serbian authorities shut down Radio B-92, which has reported extensively on the ongoing protests against Serbian president Slobodan Milosevic. . . . More than Russian 400,000 coal miners walk off their jobs at 180 mines nationwide to protest a delay in payment of their wages. . . . Reports suggest that Bosnia's military manufactured and used chlorine gas-filled mortar shells during the Bosnian civil war. Chlorine gas was banned by a 1925 treaty.	Burundi government soldiers allegedly kill more than 500 Hutu civilians in a massacre in the Butaganza commune.		Reports from India confirm that the Bombay High Court has rejected a suit aimed at blocking continued construction in Maharashtra state of a $2.5 billion power project by Enron Corp. of the U.S., a project that has been stalled since August 1995. . . . Babrak Karmal, 67, who was installed as head of state in Afghanistan after the 1979 Soviet invasion and replaced in 1986 by opposition guerillas supported by Iran and the West, dies in Moscow of liver cancer.
Dec. 4	A court in Athens, Greece, releases Mohammed Rashid, a Palestinian convicted of murder in the 1982 bombing of a Pan American World Airways jet over Hawaii that killed one person, from prison for good behavior. The U.S. criticizes the early release of Rashid, who in 1992 was sentenced to 15 years in prison.	Reports confirm that the British government has appointed Sir Richard Luce to serve as the first-ever civilian governor of Gibraltar. . . . In Belarus, three judges resign to protest Pres. Aleksandr Lukashenko's new constitution. . . . Eurotunnel PLC restarts limited passenger service after a November fire. . . . In Bulgaria, 1,000,000 people take part in a one-day strike to pressure the government to resign.		The Guatemalan government and leaders of the leftist Guatemalan National Revolutionary Union (UNRG) sign a definitive cease-fire.	A Japanese court sentences the U.S. Navy's Seaman First Class Terrence Michael Swanson, 20, to 13 years in prison for robbery and attempted murder of a Japanese woman. The U.S. handed Swanson over to Japan in July, making him the first American military member surrendered to Japan under an October 1995 rule change regarding custody of American servicemen suspected of serious crimes.

A	B	C	D	E
Includes developments that affect more than one world region, international organizations, and important meetings of major world leaders.	*Includes all domestic and regional developments in Europe, including the Soviet Union, Turkey, Cyprus, and Malta.*	*Includes all domestic and regional developments in Africa and the Middle East, including Iraq and Iran and excluding Cyprus, Turkey, and Afghanistan.*	*Includes all domestic and regional developments in Latin America, the Caribbean, and Canada.*	*Includes all domestic and regional developments in Asia and Pacific nations, extending from Afghanistan through all the Pacific Island, except Hawaii.*

U.S. Politics & Social Issues	U.S. Foreign Policy & Defense	U.S. Economy & Environment	Science, Technology, & Nature	Culture, Leisure, & Lifestyle	
John Salvi III, convicted of murdering two abortion clinic workers in a 1994 shooting spree in Brookline, Massachusetts, is found dead in his jail cell, an apparent suicide. . . Reports indicate that the Minnesota Supreme Court has upheld a lower-court ruling ordering tobacco companies that are being sued by the state and by the private firms of Blue Cross and Blue Shield of Minnesota to turn over to the court their secret formulas for making cigarettes.		The Justice Department rejects Republican lawmakers' request that an independent prosecutor be appointed to examine allegations of illegal fund-raising by the Democratic Party, arguing that the department found no credible evidence that Pres. Clinton, Vice Pres. Gore, or members of the president's cabinet engaged in illicit activity related to questionable donations to the party's national committee.	A study reports that scientists from the University of Wurzburg in Germany and from the U.S. National Institutes of Health have identified a gene that appears to influence the general level of anxiety a person experiences.		Nov. 29
				John Williamson, 44, basketball star who helped lead the New York Nets to two championships, in 1974 and 1976, dies in New Haven, Conn., of kidney problems. . . . Tiny Tim (born Herbert Khaury), 64, quirky singer who gained fame in the 1960s, dies in Minneapolis, Minn., of an apparent cardiac arrest.	Nov. 30
				France wins tennis's Davis Cup with a 3-2 victory over the Swedish team in Malmo, Sweden.	Dec. 1
	A navy training plane crashes near a runway at Maxwell Air Force Base in Montgomery, Alabama, killing both crew members.	In Los Angeles, U.S. district judge Mariana Pfaelzer throws out Charles Keating Jr.'s 1993 conviction on racketeering and securities fraud charges after ruling that several members of the 1993 jury became predisposed against Keating when they discussed details of Keating's related 1991 conviction. The decision leaves Keating at least temporarily free of all government cases brought against him in connection with the collapse of S&Ls in the 1980s and early 1990s.	U.S. astronaut Shannon W. Lucid, who spent a record 188 days in space, is awarded a Congressional Space Medal of Honor by Pres. Clinton.	*Silent Honor*, by Danielle Steel tops the bestseller list. . . . Heavyweight boxer Mike Tyson tops *Forbes* magazine's list of the 40 highest-paid athletes, earning $75 million in 1996, more than any athlete in history.	Dec. 2
In Honolulu, Hawaii, in a landmark ruling, Judge Kevin S. C. Chang rules that an existing state ban on same-sex marriages is unconstitutional and orders that the state grant marriage licenses to same-sex couples.	The U.S. Justice Department bars 16 Japanese World War II war crimes suspects from ever entering the U.S. The 16, who are not publicly identified, are the first Japanese put on the U.S. government's 60,000-name "watch list," which was established in 1979 to block U.S. entry by suspected war criminals from Nazi Germany or from Nazi-allied nations. The 16 are accused of forcing prisoners of war to undergo medical experiments or of making foreign women, known as "comfort women," provide sex for Japanese troops.	Florida governor Lawton Chiles (D) declares a fiscal emergency in Miami due to a budget crisis discovered in September after three officials resigned in a corruption scandal. He states that he will appoint a state oversight committee to help Miami authorities restore the city to financial health.		Canadian art student Jubal Brown, 22, admits that in November he intentionally vomited on modernist Piet Mondrian's Composition in White, Red and Black (1939) at New York City's Museum of Modern Art. Brown claims that he was making an artistic statement about what he calls "oppressively trite" and "banal" art.	Dec. 3
In Hawaii, Judge Kevin S. C. Chang awards a stay pending an appeal of his Dec. 3 decision so his ruling on same-sex marriages will not go into effect immediately.	The INS announces that it will tighten background checks on applicants for citizenship. Under the new rules, an applicant will not be granted citizenship until the fingerprint check is complete.	Officials state that they will permanently shut down the Connecticut Yankee nuclear power plant in Haddam Neck, Connecticut. . . . A Senate-appointed commission of economists reports that the nation's main gauge of inflation, the consumer price index (CPI), overestimates inflation by 1.1 percentage points annually. The commission argues that the correct figure for current inflation is about 1.9% per year, not the 3% reported by the CPI.	*Mars Pathfinder*, an unmanned U.S. space vessel set to land on Mars on July 4, 1997, is launched from Cape Canaveral, Florida.	In Oakland County, Michigan, Judge Francis O'Brien, sentences Jonathan Schmitz to 25–50 years in prison for the fatal shooting of a gay admirer, Scott Amedure, after a taping of the *Jenny Jones Show*.	Dec. 4

F	G	H	I	J
Includes elections, federal-state relations, civil rights and liberties, crime, the judiciary, education, health care, poverty, urban affairs, and population.	Includes formation and debate of U.S. foreign and defense policies, veterans' affairs, and defense spending. (Relations with specific foreign countries are usually found under the region concerned.)	Includes business, labor, agriculture, taxation, transportation, consumer affairs, monetary and fiscal policy, natural resources, and pollution.	Includes worldwide scientific, medical, and technological developments; natural phenomena; U.S. weather; natural disasters; and accidents.	Includes the arts, religion, scholarship, communications media, sports, entertainments, fashions, fads, and social life.

	World Affairs	Europe	Africa & the Middle East	The Americas	Asia & the Pacific
Dec. 5	The UN Security Council votes to extend its peacekeeping mission in Haiti through May 31, 1997. . . . The United Nations Education, Scientific and Cultural Organization (UNESCO) names the A-Bomb Dome building in Hiroshima, Japan, a structure that survived the atomic bomb dropped on the city by the U.S. in 1945, as a World Heritage site. The only other World War II-related place named a World Heritage site is a former Nazi concentration camp at Auschwitz in Poland.	Thousands of people continue to protest in Belgrade, and they call for Serbian president Slobodan Milosevic to step down. The government relents and allows Radio B-92 to start broadcasting again. . . . One man dies from injuries sustained in the Dec. 3 bombing in Paris, France, bringing the death toll to three.	The Tanzanian government, in a joint statement with the UN High Commissioner for Refugees (UNHCR), orders the refugees in its country to return to Rwanda by year's end. The Rwandan government begins an 80-day national campaign to build housing for an estimated 1 million returning refugees.	Bolivia sells Yacimientos Petroliferos Fiscales Bolivianos (YPFB), the state oil and gas company, to three groups of private investors in deals worth a combined $835 million. YPFB has been under government control for 59 years.	In response to the Nov. 27 declaration by South Africa that it is severing diplomatic ties, Taiwan announces that it is ending its aid to South Africa, suspending most of the treaties it has with that country, and recalling its ambassador.
Dec. 6		Daily protests continue in Belgrade, Serbia. . . . Nine oil companies and Kazakhstan, Russia, and Oman sign a $2 billion deal to build a pipeline stretching 900 miles (1,500 km) from western Kazakhstan to the Russian Black Sea port of Novorossiysk. . . . Sir John Gorst, a member of the British Parliament representing the ruling Conservative Party, withdraws his support for the party in an act of protest, causing the Tories to lose their one-seat majority in the House of Commons.			Vietnam receives pledges totaling $2.4 billion in aid for 1997, which is an increase of $100 million from 1996. . . . Japanese officials confirm that Nippon Telegraph and Telephone Corp. (NTT), the world's largest telephone company, will break up into three separate groups owned by a single holding company. . . . Crown Princess Masako of Japan speaks to the Japanese press for the first time without her husband, Crown Prince Naruhito, at her side.
Dec. 7			Pres. Jerry Rawlings, who has ruled Ghana since seizing power in 1981, is reelected in general elections that are declared free and fair by international observers.		Authorities in Tamil Nadu state in India arrest Jayalalitha Jayaram, former chief minister of the state, on charges of corruption. The arrest of Jayaram, a former film star who enjoys broad popular support, prompts massive street protests.
Dec. 8		Thirteen workers at the Sosnovyi Bor nuclear power station near St. Petersburg, Russia, end the hunger strike that started Nov. 30 when the government promises to pay 27 billion rubles worth of back wages. Separately, voters in Kostroma province reject a referendum proposal to complete a nuclear power station. . . . The death toll from the bomb that exploded in Paris Dec. 3 rises to four when an injured man dies.	Rebels in southern Sudan free three International Red Cross workers in a deal negotiated by U.S. representative Bill Richardson (D, N.Mex.) and Mahdi I. Mohamed, Sudan's ambassador to the U.S. The workers—John Early of the U.S., Moshen Raza of Kenya, and Mary Worthington of Australia—were taken prisoner Nov. 1.		
Dec. 9	UN secretary general Boutros Boutros-Ghali gives final approval to a deal that allows Iraq to resume its exports of oil. . . . Statistics reveal that more passengers—1,187—died in commercial airliner accidents in 1996 than in any other year. Airlines carried more than 1.5 billion passengers in 1996. . . . The WTO's annual report suggests that world trade slowed in 1996 because of reduced consumer demand in Western countries. The report predicts that 1996 will show a gain of 5% in merchandise exports, compared with an 8% increase in 1995 and a 10% gain in 1994.	The trial of 34 French Muslims linked to terrorist acts against the Moroccan government opens in Paris. Those on trial are allegedly part of the outlawed Moroccan Islamic Youth Movement, and only 21 of the accused are present in the courtroom. The remaining 13, who were imprisoned or are at large, are tried in absentia. . . . Alain Poher, 92, president of the French Senate for 24 years who also served as interim president of France in 1969 after the resignation of Charles de Gaulle and again in 1974 after the death of Pres. Georges Pompidou, dies in Paris of unreported causes.			In Nagaland state, near the India-Myanmar border, 34 people are killed and 24 wounded when separatist Naga tribesmen armed with guns and grenades attack a bus. . . . In Australia, parliament passes legislation that will nullify the Northern Territory's recently enacted euthanasia law, which is the first of its kind in the world. . . . Reports confirm that seven ministers in the government of Nepal's P.M. Sher Bahadur Deuba have resigned. . . . A North Korean family of 17 flies into Seoul, South Korea, in what is thought to be the largest single group defection from North Korea since the 1950–53 Korean War.
Dec. 10	Reports confirm that Britain will to pull out of the UN Industrial Development Organization at the end of 1997. . . . NATO ministers in Brussels agree to send between 25,000 and 30,000 troops to Bosnia-Herzegovina as part of the Stabilization Force (SFOR), which will replace the current 60,000-strong international contingent in the war-torn country on Dec. 20.		South African president Nelson Mandela signs into law a new democratic constitution. Separately, the Truth and Reconciliation Commission grants amnesty to Brian Mitchell, sentenced to death in 1992 for a 1988 police massacre of 11 people. . . . Reports indicate that government troops have abandoned the last major city they held in northeastern Zaire, Bunia. . . . Iraqi president Saddam Hussein turns on an oil pump to mark Iraq's reentry into the international oil market.	Mexico's Chamber of Deputies approves a measure that allows dual nationality for Mexicans living abroad.	The National Party and the New Zealand First Party agree to form a government together.

A	B	C	D	E
Includes developments that affect more than one world region, international organizations, and important meetings of major world leaders.	*Includes all domestic and regional developments in Europe, including the Soviet Union, Turkey, Cyprus, and Malta.*	*Includes all domestic and regional developments in Africa and the Middle East, including Iraq and Iran and excluding Cyprus, Turkey, and Afghanistan.*	*Includes all domestic and regional developments in Latin America, the Caribbean, and Canada.*	*Includes all domestic and regional developments in Asia and Pacific nations, extending from Afghanistan through all the Pacific Island, except Hawaii.*

U.S. Politics & Social Issues	U.S. Foreign Policy & Defense	U.S. Economy & Environment	Science, Technology, & Nature	Culture, Leisure, & Lifestyle	
Pres. Clinton announces that he has chosen Madeleine K. Albright as secretary of state. Albright will become the first woman to fill that post and the highest-ranking woman ever in the federal government.... Rosa Marie Hartford, convicted in October for driving a 13-year-old girl impregnated by Hartford's stepson into New York State for an abortion without the knowledge of the girl's mother, is sentenced to a year's probation.	CIA director John Deutch upholds the CIA's decision to revoke the security clearance of Richard Nuccio, a State Department official who in 1995 revealed to Rep. Robert Torricelli (D, N.J.), a member of the House Intelligence Committee, that Col. Julio Roberto Alpirez, a paid CIA informant, was allegedly involved in the murders in Guatemala of a U.S. citizen and a leftist Guatemalan rebel leader. The revelation caused a major scandal and led to the dismissal of two top CIA officials.				Dec. 5
In a landmark New Hampshire decision, Judge George Manias rules that the state did not violate the state constitution by relying primarily on property taxes to finance public education. The suit was brought by five relatively impoverished school districts that claim that the school-funding system deprives poorer districts of adequate funding.	U.S. authorities arrest Anwar Haddam, a speaker for Algeria's banned Islamic Salvation Front (FIS), after the INS denies his request for political asylum. Haddam is arrested a day after his "parole" period of legal residence in the U.S. expires, and he is wanted in Algeria on charges of involvement with the GIA.	The Labor Department finds that the seasonally adjusted unemployment rate in the U.S. rose to 5.4% in November.	Researchers report they have isolated the brain chemical that influences weight gain in experiments on mice. Removal of the chemical, called neuropeptide Y, is found to reverse the effects of a gene defect that causes obesity.	Pete Rozelle, 70, former NFL commissioner, 1960–89, dies in California of brain cancer.... Jules Davids, 75, professor at Georgetown University who helped Pres. John Kennedy research his Pulitzer-prize winning book *Profiles in Courage* (1956), dies in Rockville, Maryland, of Alzheimer's disease.	Dec. 6
Joseph Quinlan, 71, a pioneer of the patients' right-to-die movement after his daughter, Karen Ann Quinlan, lapsed into a drug-induced coma and he and his wife, Julia, objected to doctors' refusal to take their daughter off life support, dies in Wantage, New Jersey, of unreported causes.			The space shuttle *Columbia* touches down at Kennedy Space Center in Cape Canaveral, Florida, after carrying out the longest-ever shuttle flight.	The body of Eugene Izzi, 43, Chicago-based crime novelist, is found hanging from the window of his 14th-floor office wearing a bulletproof vest.... Retiring senator Nancy Kassebaum (R, Kans.) marries former senator Howard Baker (R, Tenn.) in Washington, D.C.	Dec. 7
Joseph Chagra, 50, Texas lawyer known for his involvement in the 1979 assassination of U.S. judge John H. Wood, dies in El Paso, Texas, of injuries sustained in a car accident.	The Virginia Military Institute, a state-funded college in Lexington, Virginia, announces that it has admitted four female applicants, who are the first women accepted into the traditionally all-male institution.... Evan C. Hunziker, who in November was released by North Korea after being detained and accused of espionage, is found dead in Tacoma, Wash., of an apparently self-inflicted gunshot wound.	John Langeloth Loeb Sr., 94, head of the Wall Street investment firm Loeb, Rhoades & Co., whose lifelong contributions to cultural, educational, and other charitable institutions are estimated to total $200 million, dies in his sleep in New York City.		Howard Rollins, 46, film and TV actor in "In the Heat of the Night," 1988–94, dies in New York City of a bacterial infection caused by the cancer lymphoma.	Dec. 8
A jury in Philadelphia, Pennsylvania, convicts Daniel Carr and Gerald Laarz of violating the Solid Waste Management Act through their mismanagement of a large tire dump that caught fire on Mar. 13, causing more than $6 million in damage to the surrounding area and forcing the closure of a stretch of Interstate 95.		Energy Secretary Hazel O'Leary announces a dual plan for disposing more than 52 tons of excess plutonium from the nation's nuclear arsenal.... Reports confirm that a jury in New York City awarded almost $6 million in compensatory and punitive damages to three women who developed repetitive-stress injuries through use of computer keyboards manufactured by Digital Equipment Corp. It is the first time that a computer keyboard manufacturer has been found liable for such injuries.... The NASDAQ index reaches a record high, closing at 1316.27.	Mary Leakey, 83, archaeologist best known for her discovery of prehistoric bones in East Africa that helped establish the earliest evidence of human existence, dies in Nairobi, Kenya, of unreported causes.	For the first time, the FBI plays publicly a tape recording of a 911 emergency phone call that warned of a bomb at Centennial Olympic Park, an Olympic Games site in Atlanta, Georgia. The agency requests for help from the public in investigating the July pipe-bomb explosion.	Dec. 9
Pres. Clinton urges the Senate to approve a 1979 UN treaty guaranteeing women's rights, which has been approved by 130 other nations.... A Marion County, Oregon, grand jury indicts Rep. Wes Cooley (R, Oreg.) on charges that he lied about his military service on voter guides during his 1994 campaign.... In Charleston, South Carolina, Arthur Haley and Hubert Rowell, formerly of the Ku Klux Klan, plead guilty to four counts related to the burning of a black church and a migrant labor camp.		The Commerce Department reports that the nation's current-account deficit expanded to a record $47.96 billion in the third quarter, up 10.3% over the revised second-quarter figure of $40.21 billion.... In *O'Gilvie v. U.S.*, the Supreme Court rules, 6-3, that punitive damages awarded to individuals in personal-injury cases are subject to federal income tax.		Faron Young, 64, country singer who enjoyed a string of hits from the 1950s to the 1970s, dies in Nashville, Tennessee, of a self-inflicted gunshot wound.	Dec. 10

F	G	H	I	J
Includes elections, federal-state relations, civil rights and liberties, crime, the judiciary, education, health care, poverty, urban affairs, and population.	Includes formation and debate of U.S. foreign and defense policies, veterans' affairs, and defense spending. (Relations with specific foreign countries are usually found under the region concerned.)	Includes business, labor, agriculture, taxation, transportation, consumer affairs, monetary and fiscal policy, natural resources, and pollution.	Includes worldwide scientific, medical, and technological developments; natural phenomena; U.S. weather; natural disasters; and accidents.	Includes the arts, religion, scholarship, communications media, sports, entertainments, fashions, fads, and social life.

	World Affairs	Europe	Africa & the Middle East	The Americas	Asia & the Pacific
Dec. 11	The UN Security Council extends the mandate of the UN's peace-keeping mission to Angola until February 1997 and approves a plan to withdraw the 7,000-strong UN contingent by mid-1997.... Russian foreign minister Yevgeny Primakov accepts an offer to negotiate a new Russia-NATO charter for the post–cold war era.	Switzerland's parliament grants final approval to the creation of a panel to search Swiss banks for funds that belonged to Nazi Holocaust victims.... Jawad Botmeh and Samar Alami are convicted of orchestrating two 1994 bombings of Jewish buildings in London. A third suspect, Mahmoud Abu Wardeh, is acquitted.... The Russian Coal Industry Workers' Union ends a strike that began Dec. 3.... William Rushton, 59, British humorist, dies in London of complications after heart surgery.	A 12-year-old Jewish boy and his mother are killed in a drive-by shooting near the Beit El settlement, 15 miles (25 km) north of Jerusalem.... A UN human-rights observer mission reports that at least 1,000 civilians were massacred by Burundi's Tutsi-led military from late October to November.... South African president Nelson Mandela signs a liberal abortion law.... Former premier Sadiq al-Mahdi reveals that he fled Sudan so that the government of Pres. Omar Hassan al-Bashir could not take him hostage.		Four UN aid workers arrested by Taliban authorities are released, prompting the UN High Commissioner for Refugees to resume its operations, suspended Nov. 21, in Kabul, the capital of Afghanistan.... The Indian Supreme Court issues a directive to the Indian government to implement measures to end child labor in the country.... Tung Chee-hwa is elected to the post of chief executive of Hong Kong, to succeed Christopher Patten when China takes over ruling the colony from Great Britain on June 30, 1997.
Dec. 12		Bosnia's presidents name Boro Bosic, a Serb, and Haris Silajdzic, a Muslim as joint premiers.... Data reveal that food poisoning caused by the rare bacterium *E. coli* 0157:H7 has left more than 300 people ill and 11 people dead in Scotland. It is Britain's worst *E. coli* epidemic on record.	In South Africa, Adriaan Vlok, a former minister of law and order, becomes the first apartheid-era cabinet minister to apply to the truth commission for amnesty.... Iraqi officials disclose that Pres. Saddam Hussein's eldest son, Uday Hussein, was wounded when his car was ambushed in Baghdad.... The Syrian-based Popular Front for the Liberation of Palestine (PFLP) claims responsibility for the Dec. 11 killings outside Jerusalem.		Indian prime minister H. D. Deve Gowda and Bangladeshi Premier Sheik Hasina Wazed sign a 30-year treaty under which the two countries will share water from the Ganges River.... An unidentified Tokyo police official states that the force recovered a bottle containing enough liquid VX nerve gas to kill 15,000 people.
Dec. 13	The UN Security Council votes to extend the UN Mission of Observers in Tajikistan for a further three-month period ending Mar. 15, 1997.... The EU agrees to a "stability pact" designed to promote budgetary discipline among countries that join the EU's planned single currency, the euro.... The WTO concludes its inaugural ministerial meeting with more than 30 countries signaling their intention to sign a trade pact whose implementation will reduce tariffs on information-technology items.	In Italy, 7 million workers in the manufacturing and transportation industries walk off their jobs for up to eight hours to show solidarity with 1.6 million metal workers involved in a labor dispute with employers.... Germany's parliament approves the deployment of 3,000 German peacekeepers to Bosnia. It will be the first time Germany deploys combat-ready ground troops beyond the borders of NATO countries since World War II.	Hamas (Islamic Resistance Movement) holds a mass rally in Khan Younis in the Gaza Strip and threatens suicide attacks against Israeli targets in retaliation for expanded Israeli settlements in the West Bank.		
Dec. 14		A group of Chechen fighters take hostages in an attack on a Russian border post on the Chechnya-Dagestan border.	Tanzanian soldiers and police start emptying camps in the Ngara area of northwestern Tanzania and order the refugees to march toward Rwanda. More than 460,000 Rwandan refugees begin a mass exodus as they depart for Rwanda.		
Dec. 15		In Tajikistan, government soldiers force two UN observer teams to participate in a mock execution, in which the observers are lined up and the soldiers shoot over their heads.... Sir Laurens Van Der Post, 90, South African writer, linguist, and anthropologist who was knighted in 1981, dies in London, England, of unreported causes.	In Somalia, at least 42 people are killed when three mortar rounds land on a market in an area controlled by Gen. Aidid.	After protests that started Nov. 8, the government of Ontario and the 20,000-member Ontario Medical Association reach an agreement intended to improve medical service in small towns and to boost doctors' incomes.	
Dec. 16	The U.S., European Union, and several other countries pledge $3.2 billion to Lebanon to accelerate reconstruction of the country's war-ravaged infrastructure and strengthen the government of Premier Rafik al-Hariri.... The presidents of South Africa, Eritrea, Kenya, Rwanda, Tanzania, Uganda, Zambia, and Zimbabwe and the premier of Ethiopia hold a summit to discuss the conflicts in eastern Zaire and in Burundi. Zaire declines to attend.	François Santoni, a leader of the militant separatist movement in Corsica, surrenders to police in the Corsican town of Bastia.... Jawad Botmeh and Samar Alami, convicted Dec. 11, are sentenced to 20 years each in prison for two 1994 bombings in London.... British agriculture minister Douglas Hogg states that the government will slaughter up to 100,000 cows at risk of contracting mad-cow disease (BSE). The planned cull is in addition to Britain's ongoing slaughter of 1.2 million cows.	Col. Muhammed Marwa, administrator of Lagos province and a close ally of military ruler Gen. Sani Abacha, escapes a bomb attack on his convoy in Lagos, Nigeria's commercial capital.	A car bomb explodes in Medellin, Colombia, outside the home of Juan Gomez Martinez, a prominent journalist and former politician who supports the antidrug legislation. The bomb kills one person and injures 48 others.	An appeals court in Seoul reduces the sentences of former South Korean presidents Chun Doo Hwan and Roh Tae Woo, both of whom were convicted in August of mutiny, sedition and corruption. Chun has his death sentence reduced to life imprisonment, while Roh has his 22½ year jail term reduced to 17 years. The appeals court suspends the sentences of or acquits 12 other defendants.

A	B	C	D	E
Includes developments that affect more than one world region, international organizations, and important meetings of major world leaders.	*Includes all domestic and regional developments in Europe, including the Soviet Union, Turkey, Cyprus, and Malta.*	*Includes all domestic and regional developments in Africa and the Middle East, including Iraq and Iran and excluding Cyprus, Turkey, and Afghanistan.*	*Includes all domestic and regional developments in Latin America, the Caribbean, and Canada.*	*Includes all domestic and regional developments in Asia and Pacific nations, extending from Afghanistan through all the Pacific Island, except Hawaii.*

U.S. Politics & Social Issues	U.S. Foreign Policy & Defense	U.S. Economy & Environment	Science, Technology, & Nature	Culture, Leisure, & Lifestyle	
The State University of New York at Stony Brook reports it has received a $25 million donation from businessman Charles B. Wang. The gift, which will be used to construct an Asian-American cultural center, is the most generous in the history of New York State school system.	VA officials disclose that they delayed an investigation into Persian Gulf war veterans' potential exposure to low levels of poisonous gases because the Defense Department had wrongly assured them that U.S. troops had not been exposed to chemical weapons during the 1991 war.	A study suggests that for the first time women hold more than 10% of directors' seats in the 500 largest companies in the U.S. As of March 31, women held 626 of 6,123 board seats, up 3% from 404 seats in 1995.			Dec. 11
The NIH recommends the continuation of its $2.4 million study of needle-exchange programs designed to help curb the spread of HIV. . . . Lem Tuggle, 44, one of six inmates who escaped in 1984 in the largest death-row breakout in U.S. history, is put to death by lethal injection in Jarratt, Virginia. Tuggle is the last escapee from the breakout to be executed, the 357th person put to death in the U.S., and the 36th in Virginia since 1976.	Staff Sergeant Anthony S. Fore, a drill instructor at Fort Leonard Wood, pleads guilty to charges of indecent assault, assault and battery, and failure to obey a general regulation.			Vance Oakley Packard, 82, sociologist and writer known for his works criticizing 20th-century American advertising, business practices, psychology, and social mobility, dies in Martha's Vineyard, Massachusetts, after suffering a heart attack.	Dec. 12
Pres. Clinton announces his choice for key members of his economic team, including his selection of William Daley as secretary of commerce, Charlene Barshefsky as the new U.S. trade representative, and Gene Sperling as the head of the White House's National Economic Council. He also states that he has reappointed Robert Rubin as secretary of the treasury, Franklin Raines as the director of the Office of Management and Budget, and Janet Reno as attorney general.	Staff Sergeant Anthony S. Fore, a drill instructor at Fort Leonard Wood convicted on a number of sexual harassment charges Dec. 12, is sentenced to 18 months in prison and a dishonorable discharge. . . . Reports reveal that Kim Messer and Jeanie Mentavlos, two freshman female cadets at the Citadel, a military academy in Charleston, S.C., were allegedly sprayed with nail-polish remover and set on fire by fellow students on three separate occasions. The victims of the alleged crimes were not hurt in the incidents.	A federal magistrate in Washington, D.C., sentences one current USDA employee and three former employees to two years' probation and fines them up to $2,500 each for pressuring other agency employees into contributing to a Democratic political action committee (PAC) during the 1992 presidential campaign.	The NTSB states that the explosion that caused the July crash of TWA Flight 800 into the Atlantic Ocean, killing all 230 people on board, may have resulted from a leak in a pipe connecting the plane's five main fuel tanks. . . . An FDA panel recommends the approval of a smokeless nicotine inhaler to help people quit smoking. . . . A Chilean official reveals that Mars 96, the Russian spacecraft that plunged out of orbit in November, crashed on Bolivian soil, not in the Pacific Ocean as originally reported.	Eulace Peacock, 82, track and field athlete who was the chief rival of 1936 Olympic gold medalist Jesse Owens, dies in Yonkers, New York, of Alzheimer's disease.	Dec. 13
	The Citadel suspends an unidentified sophomore cadet in connection with the allegations made by two freshman female cadets that were revealed Dec. 13.	Ron Carey declares that he has won reelection as president of the International Brotherhood of Teamsters labor union, over James P. Hoffa.	A 763-foot-long freighter carrying 64,000 tons of grain crashes into the Riverwalk, a mall on the bank of the Mississippi River in New Orleans, Louisiana, injuring 116 people. The crash destroys a 200-foot section of the Riverwalk, including many shops and a section of the Hilton Hotel.	University of Florida quarterback Danny Wuerffel is awarded the 62nd Heisman Trophy.	Dec. 14
		Members of Local 639 of the International Brotherhood of Teamsters strike against Giant Food Inc., the largest supermarket chain in the U.S.'s mid-Atlantic region.		St. John's University's men's soccer team wins its first-ever NCAA Division I title when it defeats Florida International University, 4-1, in Richmond, Virginia. . . . Harry Kemelman, 88, mystery novelist who wrote a series of 11 books about a rabbi turned sleuth, dies in Marblehead, Massachusetts, of renal failure.	Dec. 15
In M.L.B. v. S.L.J., the Supreme Court rules, 6-3, that the state of Mississippi cannot deny an appeal to a woman seeking to retain her parental rights because she cannot afford to pay legal fees associated with her appeal. . . . Ronald Lee Hoke Sr., 39, convicted of rape and murder, is put to death in Jarratt, Virginia. Hoke is the 358th person put to death in the U.S. and the 37th in Virginia since 1976. His death brings 1996's total number of executions to 45, the second most in a single year since 1976.	Judge Lewis Kaplan sentences Toshihide Iguchi, a former bond trader at the New York offices of Daiwa Bank Ltd. of Japan, to four years in prison for concealing from U.S. regulators $1.1 billion in losses over a period of more than a decade. . . . . Staff Sergeant George Blackley Jr., a drill instructor at Fort Leonard Wood, is acquitted of sexual misconduct charges. . . . The Citadel suspends an unidentified junior cadet in connection with the allegations revealed Dec. 13.	Reports confirm that the USW has approved a contract deal with tire manufacturer Bridgestone/Firestone Inc., ending 27 months of bitter contract talks. . . . Trustees for Pres. Clinton's legal defense fund report they have returned $639,000 in donations from Yah Lin (Charlie) Trie, an Arkansas businessman and Democratic fund-raiser, amid a controversy involving legally questionable donations to the Democratic National Committee (DNC).	Computer-chip producer Intel Corp. reports that it has developed the world's fastest computer, capable of performing 1 trillion operations per second. . . . Researchers report that depression sufferers are four times as likely as others to have heart attacks.	Quentin Bell, 86, British critic who was the son of Vanessa Bell, author and Virginia Woolf's older sister, dies in East Sussex, England, of a heart attack.	Dec. 16

F	G	H	I	J
Includes elections, federal-state relations, civil rights and liberties, crime, the judiciary, education, health care, poverty, urban affairs, and population.	Includes formation and debate of U.S. foreign and defense policies, veterans' affairs, and defense spending. (Relations with specific foreign countries are usually found under the region concerned.)	Includes business, labor, agriculture, taxation, transportation, consumer affairs, monetary and fiscal policy, natural resources, and pollution.	Includes worldwide scientific, medical, and technological developments; natural phenomena; U.S. weather; natural disasters; and accidents.	Includes the arts, religion, scholarship, communications media, sports, entertainments, fashions, fads, and social life.

	World Affairs	Europe	Africa & the Middle East	The Americas	Asia & the Pacific
Dec. 17	The United Nations General Assembly elects Kofi Annan of Ghana to become the seventh secretary general of the United Nations He will be the first sub-Saharan African to hold the top UN post.... South America's Southern Common Market (Mercosur) votes to admit Bolivia as an associate member.... NATO approves a mission in which the 31,000-strong Stabilization Force (SFOR), will replace the current 60,000-strong Implementation Force (IFOR) in Bosnia since 1995.	Unknown gunmen kill six Red Cross workers at a hospital in Novye Atagi, a village in Chechnya. The slaying is reported to be the worst premeditated attack in the history of the Red Cross.... Serbian president Slobodan Milosevic meets with a delegation of 17 student leaders who marched 148 miles (240 km) from Nis to Belgrade to ask Milosevic to restore the November municipal election results.... Stanko Todorov, 76, former communist premier of Bulgaria, 1971–90, dies of unreported causes.	Pres. Mobutu Sese Seko returns to Zaire after a four-month absence to undergo cancer treatment in Europe and is greeted by thousands of supportive Zairians at the airport outside the capital, Kinshasa.	Some 25 members of the Tupac Amaru Revolutionary Movement, a Marxist guerrilla group, storm the Japanese ambassador's residence in Lima, Peru's capital, taking more than 600 hostages. The group, known by its Spanish initials MRTA, threatens to kill hostages one by one unless the government releases the several hundred MRTA members imprisoned under Peru's harsh antiterrorism laws.	A Seoul court sentences recently dismissed South Korean defense minister Lee Yang Ho to four years in jail on charges of accepting bribes and leaking military secrets.... Employees of Sanyo Universal Electric PCL set fire to the company's Bangkok headquarters and a separate warehouse to protest the company's decision to reduce their year-end pay bonuses.... Sun Yaoting, 94, China's last surviving official eunuch, is found dead at the Guanghua temple where he was once the caretaker.
Dec. 18	The European Commission, the executive branch of the EU, grants formal approval to the sale of genetically modified corn on EU markets.	Chechen field commander Salman Raduyev releases 21 Russian soldiers who have been held as hostages since Dec. 14. Separately, in response to the Dec. 17 attack, the UNHCR and the Doctors of the World join the Red Cross and pull out of Chechnya.... Two elderly people in Scotland die of food poisoning caused by the rare bacterium *E. coli* 0157:H7. The deaths raise to 15 the total death toll from the food-poisoning outbreak, one of the world's deadliest *E. coli* epidemics ever.	UN officials report that at least 300 fighters and civilians died in less than a week during renewed factional fighting in the Mogadishu, the capital of Somali.... A bomb explodes on a military bus outside the office of Col. Muhammed Marwa, a close ally of Gen. Sani Abacha. The blast seriously injures 12 soldiers.... The PNA reveals its security court has convicted three 20-year-old Palestinians for the Dec. 11 murders, sentencing two of them to life imprisonment and the third to a 15-year prison term.	In Peru, the MRTA releases nine of the hostages taken Dec. 17 and begins to negotiate with the Peruvian government.... In Guatemala, the National Assembly passes a law of national reconciliation, which exempts from prosecution soldiers and guerrillas who took part in atrocities committed for political ends during the war. The law does not apply to genocide, torture, or forced disappearances.	Prosecutors charge Asif Ali Zardari, the husband of deposed Pakistani prime minister Benazir Bhutto, with the murder of Mir Murtaza Bhutto, Bhutto's younger brother and political rival.
Dec. 19	The Organization for Economic Cooperation and Development (OECD) predicts that average growth in its member countries in 1996 will be 2.4%, up from the 2.1% it forecast in its June report. At the same time, it lowers its 1997 growth prediction to 2.4%, from 2.5% and forecasts a 2.7% rate for 1998.	Figures suggest that a total of 73 Muslims have been evicted from the Croat-held west side of the Croat-Muslim divided town of Mostar since the start of 1996.... French police arrested 20 suspected Islamic terrorists.... Yuli B. Khariton, 92, Russian physicist who directed the building of the first Soviet atomic bomb, dies in Sarov, Russia, of unreported causes.		The death toll of a November building explosion in San Juan, Puerto Rico, is raised to 31 after two more bodies are discovered.... Reports confirm that the Ontario Court of Appeal has ruled that partners in same-sex couples have the same right to spousal support as heterosexuals.... Gabriel Galindo Lewis, 68, Panamanian diplomat recognized for his crucial role in the negotiation of the Panama Canal treaties, dies in Denver, Colo., of fibrosis of the lungs.	Former Indian prime minister P. V. Narasimha Rao, who is embroiled in three separate legal battles stemming from corruption charges, steps down as the parliamentary representative of the Congress (I) party at the urging of senior party members.... Nobel-prize-winning Roman Catholic nun Mother Teresa, 86, is released from a Calcutta hospital after spending a month there recovering from a severe heart attack.
Dec. 20	Delegates from 160 nations reach two landmark treaties designed to extend international copyright protections to material distributed by way of the Internet global computer network.... Gen. George A. Joulwan, NATO's supreme commander in Europe, launches the 31,000-strong Stabilization Force (SFOR), which will replace the current 60,000-strong Implementation Force (IFOR) deployed in Bosnia since 1995.	The governments of Germany and the Czech Republic approve a declaration of mutual reconciliation in which Germany apologizes for the 1939 invasion of Czechoslovakia, and the Czechs apologize for the expulsion of 2.5 million Germans in 1945 and 1946.... Two unidentified gunmen enter the Royal Belfast Hospital for Sick Children and fire at two police officers guarding Nigel Dodds, a loyalist visiting his ill son. One officer suffers a minor injury.	Israeli and Palestinian demonstrators in Jerusalem protest a plan to build 132 housing units in the Ras al-Amud neighborhood of Arab East Jerusalem.	Leftist rebels who are holding about 400 foreign and Peruvian dignitaries hostage at the Japanese ambassador's residence in Lima, Peru, release 38 captives.	Amata Kabua, 68, first and only president of the Republic of the Marshall Islands, dies in Honolulu, Hawaii.
Dec. 21		Bulgarian premier Zhan Videnov resigns as premier and leader of the Bulgarian Socialist Party (BSP).... Officials from Iran and Turkey sign several trade pacts that will double their current $1 billion in mutual trade.	Ethiopian troops advance on a border town in southeastern Somalia held by rebels of the fundamentalist Islamic Union.... A car bombing in Algiers, the capital of Algeria, kills at least one person and wounds dozens of others.		A China-backed special election committee selects the 60 members of a provisional legislature that will replace Hong Kong's Legislative Council (LegCo), a democratically elected body, when China resumes sovereignty over the colony from Great Britain at midnight on June 30, 1997.
Dec. 22		A remote-controlled land mine explodes in the village of Berkat-Yurt, Chechnya, killing five boys aged 10 to 12 years.... Greek farmers lift the barricades they erected Nov. 28 to protest the government's austere budget proposals. The blockades, which cut off entire regions of Greece, caused an estimated 25 billion drachmas ($100 million) in damage to the country's economy.... A car bomb explodes in Belfast, Northern Ireland, injuring Eddie Copeland, a prominent IRA supporter.		Leftist rebels holding about 400 foreign and Peruvian dignitaries hostage at the Japanese ambassador's residence in Lima, Peru, release 225 captives, most of whom have no ties to the government. The rebels, members of the Tupac Amaru Revolutionary Movement (MRTA), call the release, the largest since the siege began, "a gesture of ours for Christmas."	

A	B	C	D	E
Includes developments that affect more than one world region, international organizations, and important meetings of major world leaders.	Includes all domestic and regional developments in Europe, including the Soviet Union, Turkey, Cyprus, and Malta.	Includes all domestic and regional developments in Africa and the Middle East, including Iraq and Iran and excluding Cyprus, Turkey, and Afghanistan.	Includes all domestic and regional developments in Latin America, the Caribbean, and Canada.	Includes all domestic and regional developments in Asia and Pacific nations, extending from Afghanistan through all the Pacific Island, except Hawaii.

U.S. Politics & Social Issues	U.S. Foreign Policy & Defense	U.S. Economy & Environment	Science, Technology, & Nature	Culture, Leisure, & Lifestyle	
Judge Francis X. Egitto of Kings County Supreme Court in New York sentences Vincent Ellerbe and Thomas Malik to 25 years to life each, in prison for their role in a 1995 arson attack that fatally burned a subway token clerk.			Two large pieces of the wing of the space shuttle *Challenger* are discovered on a Florida beach, nearly 11 years after the *Challenger* exploded in flight, killing all seven people on board.	Irving Caesar, 101, lyricist who, with George Gershwin, published more than 1,000 songs, dies in New York of unreported causes. . . . Director Stephen Spielberg donates his recently purchased Oscar statue, awarded to Clark Gable in 1934, to the Academy of Motion Picture Arts and Science.	Dec. 17
The local school board in Oakland, California, decides in a unanimous vote that the school district will be the first in the nation to recognize "black English," a form of English spoken by some black Americans, as a distinct language rather than a dialect or a type of slang. . . . In Portland, Oregon, U.S. district judge Robert Jones bars plaintiffs from claiming that silicone breast implants caused impairment of their immune systems, on the grounds that scientific evidence offers no proof of such claims.	FBI agent Earl Edwin Pitts is arrested on charges of spying for Russia. Pitts is only the second agent to be arrested on espionage charges in the FBI's 88-year history.		In San Francisco, California, U.S. district judge Marilyn Hall Patel strikes down federal restrictions on the export of computer-encryption software by U.S. companies.	Reports confirm that philanthropist Brooke Astor, 94, plans to close the Vincent Astor Foundation by the end of 1997. The organization, named for her third husband, has donated $175 million to NYC cultural institutions and small nonprofit service programs since she became the administrator in 1959.	Dec. 18
The Department of Health and Human Services reports an increase in the use of illegal drugs by school-age children. The study finds that 40% of high-school seniors surveyed have used illegal drugs over the prior year, up from 39% in 1995.		Reports state that Arthur A. Coia was reelected as president of the Laborers International Union of North America (LIUNA). . . . The Dow gains 126.87 points, its second-largest point increase ever, to close at 6473.64.		A panel composed of TV-industry representatives announce a planned system for rating TV programs based on their level of violent and sexual content, scheduled to take effect in January 1997.	Dec. 19
Family court judge Nancy Wieben Stock of Orange County, California, awards O. J. Simpson full custody of his two young children. Simpson, who was acquitted of the murders of their mother and her friend in 1995, is currently on trial in a civil wrongful-death suit. . . . The Clinton administration announces it will join the legal challenge to California's Proposition 209, an anti-affirmative-action law. . . . Pres. Clinton announces four nominations as members of his cabinet.	Major Susan Gibson, deputy staff judge advocate at Aberdeen, reveals that Staff Sergeant Delmar Simpson, a drill instructor, has been charged with crimes involving 26 women. The army discloses that its hotline set up in November to help uncover abuse has received 942 calls that investigators consider worthy of further inquiry.	The Commerce Department reports that after-tax profits of U.S. corporations declined 1.4% in the 1996 third quarter from the previous quarter, to an annual rate of $402.2 billion. That marks an advance of 5.1% over after-tax profits in the 1995 third quarter.	Carl Sagan, 62, astronomer, physicist, and Pulitzer Prize–winning author known for his television series *Cosmos*, which appeared on public television in 1980 and was watched by 400 million people in 60 countries, dies in Seattle, Washington, of complications from the bone marrow disease myelodysplasia.		Dec. 20
Pres. Clinton announces that 20 college presidents have promised to assign half of their AmeriCorps participants to the tutoring of eight-year-old children in basic reading skills.		A House ethics subcommittee concludes that House Speaker Newt Gingrich (R, Ga.) violated House ethics rules by using tax-exempt donations for political purposes. The subcommittee also finds that Gingrich provided the House Ethics Committee with "inaccurate, incomplete and unreliable information" about the relationship between a college course that he had taught and GOPAC, a political action committee that Gingrich headed 1986–95.		Margaret Rey, 90, creator, with her husband, H. A. Rey, of the world-famous Curious George monkey character, dies in Cambridge, Massachusetts, of complications from a heart attack.	Dec. 21
Reports reveal that a state district court judge in New Orleans, Louisiana, has ruled that 4,000 women who accused Dow Corning Corp. of selling faulty breast implants in a class-action suit will be allowed only to ask for compensatory, not punitive, damages.		An explosion at a metal-fabricating plant in Cypress, Texas, kills eight workers.			Dec. 22

F	G	H	I	J
Includes elections, federal-state relations, civil rights and liberties, crime, the judiciary, education, health care, poverty, urban affairs, and population.	Includes formation and debate of U.S. foreign and defense policies, veterans' affairs, and defense spending. (Relations with specific foreign countries are usually found under the region concerned.)	Includes business, labor, agriculture, taxation, transportation, consumer affairs, monetary and fiscal policy, natural resources, and pollution.	Includes worldwide scientific, medical, and technological developments; natural phenomena; U.S. weather; natural disasters; and accidents.	Includes the arts, religion, scholarship, communications media, sports, entertainments, fashions, fads, and social life.

	World Affairs	Europe	Africa & the Middle East	The Americas	Asia & the Pacific
Dec. 23	Officials of the International Committee of the Red Cross (ICRC) reveal that the organization faces a financial crisis because governments failed to pay about $41 million of funds they promised for the fiscal 1996 year.	Russian president Boris Yeltsin returns to work after his heart surgery in November.... Tajik president Imamali Rakhmanov and United Tajik Opposition leader Said Abdullo Nuri sign a cease-fire to end the country's four-year-old civil war.... Ronnie Scott, 69, whose music club, Ronnie Scott's, is regarded as the birthplace of British jazz, dies in London of unreported causes.	The main Hutu rebel group in Burundi, the National Council for the Defense of Democracy (CNDD), announces an 11-day unilateral cease-fire in a Christmas and New Year message.		Philippine president Fidel V. Ramos undergoes surgery to clear a severe blockage in his carotid artery.... Reports disclose that six people were killed and hundreds were injured when 4,000 paramilitaries and police officers raided a prison in Jessore, in western Bangladesh, to bring an end to a week-long siege in which 2,000 inmates wrested control of the prison.
Dec. 24	Cuba's National Assembly approves a measure that counters the U.S.'s Helms-Burton law by declaring invalid any claim made under the U.S. law. The Helms-Burton law has drawn international condemnation.	A woman detonates two grenades in a Protestant church in the Sindlingen section of Frankfurt, Germany, killing herself and two others and injuring 13 people.... One man dies and 58 people are wounded as supporters of Serbian president Slobodan Milosevic stage a rally near another demonstration held by the opposition rally.... France discloses that it has received a letter from the Algeria-based Armed Islamic Group (GIA) that threatens to "destroy" France.	In South Africa, two bombs explode in a shopping area in Worcester, 60 miles (95 km) northeast of Cape Town, killing one adult and two children and injuring more than 50 other people.... UN officials report that Rwandan officials have arrested at least 2,350 Hutu refugees recently returned from Zaire and Tanzania, accusing them of involvement in the Tutsi massacres.	The government of Uruguay, in a move that draws criticism, releases two MRTA members, Sonia Silvia Gora Rivera and Luis Alberto Miguel Samaniego, who have been imprisoned since December 1995. The rebels holding hostages in Peru release the Uruguayan ambassador, Tabare Bocalandro Yapeyu. Despite Uruguay's denial that the two releases are connected, Peru recalls its chief of mission at the Peruvian embassy in Montevideo, Uruguay's capital.	Nguyen Huu Tho, 86, leader of the political arm of Vietnam's Vietcong guerrilla movement that fought for the unification, under communist rule, of North and South Vietnam, dies in Ho Chi Minh City of a heart ailment.
Dec. 25		Serbian authorities ban protest rallies in the centers of cities.			A remote-controlled bomb explodes outside government offices in Lhasa, the capital of the Chinese territory of Tibet, reportedly wounding five people.
Dec. 26	The Turkish parliament approves a six-month mandate for U.S. and British aircraft to keep flying patrols from Turkey to enforce a no-fly zone over northern Iraq.	In response to the Serbian government's Dec. 25 ban on protest rallies, 60,000 opposition protesters march through Belgrade's side streets, in a rally limited by the deployment of thousands of police in riot gear in central Belgrade. A march by 15,000 Serbian students earlier in the day is not hindered by police.... An avalanche in Georgia traps some 150 people in a 2½-mile-long tunnel under the Caucasus Mountains.	In Israel, protests against P.M. Benjamin Netanyahu to trim $1.87 billion from the budget begin. Separately, Israeli soldiers clash in Hebron with settlers protesting the government's slated redeployment from 85% of the city.... Michael Bruno, 64, governor of Israel's central bank, 1986–91, and chief economist at the World Bank, dies in Jerusalem, Israel, of cancer.	Reports confirm that leftist rebels at the Japanese ambassador's residence in Lima, Peru, are still holding more than 100 high-ranking officials hostage.	South Korea's ruling New Korea Party (NKP) clandestinely passes legislation that makes it easier for companies to lay off workers and replace striking employees. The move prompts hundreds of thousands of South Korean workers to launch a general strike.
Dec. 27		A fact-finding mission from the Organization for Security and Cooperation in Europe (OSCE) announces that opposition candidates won November municipal elections in 13 Serbian cities and towns as well as in the capital, Belgrade.... Czech Republic president Václav Havel, 60, is released from a Prague hospital after undergoing surgery for lung cancer.	The trials of Egide Gatanazi and Deo Bizimana, two Hutu men accused of participating in the 1994 massacres of ethnic Tutsis and moderate Hutus, opens in the city of Kibungo.		Muslim fundamentalist Taliban forces solidify their buffer zone around Kabul, the Afghanistan capital, retaking the strategic air base of Bagram, 30 miles (50 km) to the north, from the ousted government's coalition forces.... China announces that a court in Xigaze, Tibet, has sentenced Ngawang Choephel, a Tibetan music scholar, to 18 years in prison for spying.
Dec. 28		Some 10,000 protesters rally to mark the funeral of Predrag Starcevic, who died earlier in December after being beaten by Serbian president Slobodan Milosevic's supporters.	Reports indicate that Pres. Hafez al-Assad of Syria has exiled his younger brother, Jamil al-Assad, for unspecified illegal business activities.	MRTA rebels holding Peruvian and foreign dignitaries captive at the Japanese ambassador's residence in Lima, Peru, release 20 hostages, including the ambassadors of the Dominican Republic and Malaysia.	Riot police use tear gas on demonstrators protesting the labor legislation passed Dec. 26 in Seoul, the capital of South Korea.
Dec. 29		Mireille (born Mireille Hartuch), 90, French actress, composer, and singer who first earned recognition in 1932, dies in Paris of unreported causes.	The Algerian government passes a new weapons law that gives the defense ministry control over the manufacture, import, and export of all weapons and tightens restrictions on who may carry arms. Anyone violating the law will be subject to life imprisonment. Second-time offenders may face the death penalty. The legislation is aimed at curbing attacks by Islamic militants.	The Guatemalan government and leaders of the leftist Guatemalan National Revolutionary Union (UNRG) sign an accord ending the country's 36-year-long civil war, during which more than 100,000 people were killed, 40,000 others went missing, and an estimated 1 million civilians were driven from their homes or forced into exile.	North Korea, in an unprecedented sign of contrition, expresses its "deep regret" for a September incident in which a North Korean submarine filled with armed commandos ran aground off South Korea's coast.... About 20,000 strikers held a peaceful march on Seoul, the capital of South Korea.

A	B	C	D	E
Includes developments that affect more than one world region, international organizations, and important meetings of major world leaders.	Includes all domestic and regional developments in Europe, including the Soviet Union, Turkey, Cyprus, and Malta.	Includes all domestic and regional developments in Africa and the Middle East, including Iraq and Iran and excluding Cyprus, Turkey, and Afghanistan.	Includes all domestic and regional developments in Latin America, the Caribbean, and Canada.	Includes all domestic and regional developments in Asia and Pacific nations, extending from Afghanistan through all the Pacific Island, except Hawaii.

U.S. Politics & Social Issues	U.S. Foreign Policy & Defense	U.S. Economy & Environment	Science, Technology, & Nature	Culture, Leisure, & Lifestyle	
In San Francisco, California, chief U.S. district judge Thelton Henderson blocks the anti-affirmative-action Proposition 209 from going into effect until the courts decide on a lawsuit filed by a coalition of labor and civil-rights groups.... In New Haven, Connecticut, U.S. district judge Peter Dorsey dismisses a lawsuit filed by tobacco companies that would have blocked Connecticut's ability to proceed with a $1 billion lawsuit against them.		The Commerce Department reports that personal pretax income rose 0.5% in November from October, to a seasonally adjusted annual figure of $6.57 trillion. The November figure marks the 18th consecutive monthly income increase.	The FDA approves glatiramer acetate, a new drug for the treatment of a relapsing, remitting form of multiple sclerosis.	The Roman Catholic archdiocese of Los Angeles, California, announces plans to build a $45 million cathedral in downtown Los Angeles.	Dec. 23
The U.S. government announces that it has adopted stricter guidelines for health maintenance organizations (HMOs) that award bonuses to doctors who successfully control costs. The new policy will go into effect January 1, 1997.	Leonard K. Firestone, 89, U.S. ambassador to Belgium, 1974–76, dies in Pebble Beach, California, of unreported causes.				Dec. 24
Lee Alexander, 69, mayor of Syracuse, New York, 1970–85, who gained national attention as a champion of U.S. cities, dies in Syracuse of unreported causes.					Dec. 25
In a case that draws national attention, JonBenet Ramsey, a six-year-old girl who was named Little Miss Colorado 1995, is found dead in the basement of her home in Boulder, Colorado.... James Earl Ray, 68, convicted for the 1968 assassination of civil-rights leader Martin Luther King Jr., emerges from a coma caused by liver and kidney damage.		Reports confirm that the National Labor Relations Board has ordered Peoria, Illinois-based Caterpillar Inc. to compensate some 10,000 workers for perquisites they were denied during a nearly 18-month-long strike.	The FCC unanimously approves a proposed set of national standards for the production of digital television sets.		Dec. 26
	Reports confirm that Brigadier General Robert T. Newell was demoted to colonel after being accused of inappropriate contact with a female subordinate.	The Dow closes at a record high of 6560.91, marking the 44th record high in 1996.	William B(ertalan) Walsh, 76, medical doctor who, in 1958, founded Project HOPE, a worldwide medical assistance program and whose many awards include the U.S.'s Presidential Medal of Freedom and France's National Order of Merit, dies in Bethesda, Maryland, of prostate cancer.		Dec. 27
					Dec. 28
A study reveals that the gap in achievement between white and minority students has widened in recent years. The results are considered a major setback after years of improved achievement by black and Hispanic students.... Robert J. Morris, 82, counsel to a U.S Senate subcommittee that investigated communist activities in the U.S. during the 1950s, dies in Point Pleasant, New Jersey, of congestive heart failure related to a degenerative brain disease.			Computer hackers illegally alter the U.S. Air Force's official site on the World Wide Web, replacing much of the site's usual information with sexually explicit animation and antigovernment statements.		Dec. 29

F	G	H	I	J
Includes elections, federal-state relations, civil rights and liberties, crime, the judiciary, education, health care, poverty, urban affairs, and population.	Includes formation and debate of U.S. foreign and defense policies, veterans' affairs, and defense spending. (Relations with specific foreign countries are usually found under the region concerned.)	Includes business, labor, agriculture, taxation, transportation, consumer affairs, monetary and fiscal policy, natural resources, and pollution.	Includes worldwide scientific, medical, and technological developments; natural phenomena; U.S. weather; natural disasters; and accidents.	Includes the arts, religion, scholarship, communications media, sports, entertainments, fashions, fads, and social life.

	World Affairs	Europe	Africa & the Middle East	The Americas	Asia & the Pacific
Dec. 30	The U.S. reveals that North Korea has agreed for the first time to meet with the U.S. and South Korea to discuss engaging in talks to bring a permanent peace agreement in the 1950–53 Korean War.	The Turkish government sends 5,000 troops into Iraq to battle Kurdish rebels there in retaliation for a recent attack that the guerrillas launched against a military outpost in Turkey. More than 70 Kurds are reportedly killed in the action. . . . The British government releases the New Year's Honors List, which names the recipients of 1,035 knighthoods, peerages, and other honors.	In Israel, some 250,000 striking workers of the Histadrut trade-union federation shut down vital services across Israel as protests that began Dec. 26 continue against proposals by P.M. Benjamin Netanyahu to trim $1.87 billion from the budget. . . . Sporadic fighting breaks out in the Central African Republic.	Four leftist guerrillas break out of a maximum-security prison in Santiago, Chile's capital.	At least 26 people are killed and dozens are seriously injured when a passenger train is bombed in India's eastern state of Assam, some 130 miles (210 km) from Gauhati, the state capital. . . . South Korea returns to North Korea the remains of the 24 North Korean commandos killed after landing in South Korea in September. . . . India's Supreme Court orders the closure of 292 coal-industries located near the Taj Mahal in Agra as part of a conservation plan to restore the 17th-century palace.
Dec. 31	Data show that European stocks rose 20% on the average in 1996. The highest performers were the Amsterdam Stock Exchange, which surged 33.6%, and Germany's DAX index, which jumped 28.2% from the end of 1995. The London Stock Exchange 100 index climbed only 11.6%. The Tokyo Stock Exchange declined 2.6% from the previous year. Results in other Asian and South American markets indicate more fluctuations in emerging markets during 1996.	Protesters in Belgrade mark the 44th consecutive day of protests against the government's annulment of November municipal elections in 13 Serbian cities and towns. . . . A court in Sicily sentences 38 members of the Mafia to a combined 328 years in prison for a variety of crimes, ending a decade-long trial that examined several Mafia-related cases.		Leftist rebels holding Peruvian and foreign dignitaries hostage at the Japanese ambassador's residence in Lima, Peru, allow TV journalists and still photographers into the residence for the first time since the attack. The MRTA rebels free the Honduran ambassador, Jose Eduardo Martell, and the Argentine consul general, Juan Antonio Ibañez, leaving 81 captives in the building.	Indian officials report that the death toll from the Dec. 30 train bombing in Assam has climbed to 59 and that 63 people remain hospitalized. . . . Reports indicate that dissident and former student leader Li Hai was sentenced to nine years in jail for "prying into state secrets" in China.

A	B	C	D	E
Includes developments that affect more than one world region, international organizations, and important meetings of major world leaders.	Includes all domestic and regional developments in Europe, including the Soviet Union, Turkey, Cyprus, and Malta.	Includes all domestic and regional developments in Africa and the Middle East, including Iraq and Iran and excluding Cyprus, Turkey, and Afghanistan.	Includes all domestic and regional developments in Latin America, the Caribbean, and Canada.	Includes all domestic and regional developments in Asia and Pacific nations, extending from Afghanistan through all the Pacific Island, except Hawaii.

U.S. Politics & Social Issues	U.S. Foreign Policy & Defense	U.S. Economy & Environment	Science, Technology, & Nature	Culture, Leisure, & Lifestyle	
Prompted by the November passage of referendums in California and Arizona that legalize the use of marijuana for medicinal purposes, U.S. officials disclose the federal government will prosecute physicians who prescribe marijuana and other illegal drugs.			Dr. David Ho is named 1996's "Man of the Year" by *Time* magazine. Ho, a virologist and AIDS researcher, discovered a treatment that nearly eliminates the AIDS virus in infected patients.	*Airframe* by Michael Crichton tops the bestseller list. . . . Lew Ayres, 88, movie actor best known for his role in the 1930 film *All Quiet on the Western Front*, dies in Los Angeles of unreported causes. . . . Jack Nance (born Marvin John Nance), 53, actor known for his roles in director David Lynch's work, is found dead of a head injury.	Dec. 30
	The Justice Department files papers to strip Michael Kolnhofer, a 79-year-old resident of Kansas City, Kansas, of his U.S. citizenship, alleging that he concealed his past as a Nazi concentration camp guard while applying for a U.S. visa in 1952. Federal officials, citing Nazi documents, claim that Kolnhofer was a guard at the Sachsenhausen and Buchenwald camps. He is shot in the leg by police after brandishing a pistol from his front porch.	The U.S. dollar closes at 1.5400 marks, up from the 1995 year-end rate of 1.4366 marks, and at 115.85 yen, up from the previous year's final rate of 103.40 yen. The Dow Jones industrial average closes at 6448.27, up 1331.15 points, or 26.01%, from the 1995 year-end level of 5117.12. The NASDAQ index closes at 1291.03, rising 22.71% during the year. The American Stock Exchange closes at 583.28, up 6.39%. The S&P 500 closes at 740.74, rising 20.26% during 1995.			Dec. 31

F	G	H	I	J
Includes elections, federal-state relations, civil rights and liberties, crime, the judiciary, education, health care, poverty, urban affairs, and population.	Includes formation and debate of U.S. foreign and defense policies, veterans' affairs, and defense spending. (Relations with specific foreign countries are usually found under the region concerned.)	Includes business, labor, agriculture, taxation, transportation, consumer affairs, monetary and fiscal policy, natural resources, and pollution.	Includes worldwide scientific, medical, and technological developments; natural phenomena; U.S. weather; natural disasters; and accidents.	Includes the arts, religion, scholarship, communications media, sports, entertainments, fashions, fads, and social life.

1997

U.S. secretary of state Madeleine Albright shakes hands with Palestinian leader Yasser Arafat prior to holding talks aimed at restarting the Middle East peace process.

	World Affairs	**Europe**	**Africa & the Middle East**	**The Americas**	**Asia & the Pacific**
Jan.	In the UN Security Council, China exercises its veto power for the first time since 1972 when it refuses to pass a resolution to send 155 military observers to monitor a 1996 peace accord signed in Guatemala. China reverses its veto when Guatemala agrees not to support Taiwan's bid for UN membership in 1997.	Angered by failed pyramid schemes, 35,000 people riot in Tirana, Albania's capital. Parliament gives Pres. Sali Berisha emergency powers to deploy the military.	A Rwandan court sentences two Hutu men to death for their involvement in the massacres of half a million ethnic Tutsis and moderate Hutus during the country's 1994 civil war. The verdict is the first handed down in the Rwandan government's efforts to punish the organizers of the massacres.	Colombian antinarcotics police shut down a huge cocaine processing plant in the southeastern department of Guaviare. The plant, reported to be the largest ever seized by the Colombian government, is capable of processing 1.5 tons of raw cocaine per day.	Pakistan establishes a Council for Defense and National Security that expands the power of the country's military, giving it a formal role in setting national policy. It is the first time since 1988 that the military will be officially involved in government policy.
Feb.	The World Trade Organization sets up a panel to rule on a dispute between the EU and the U.S. over the U.S.'s Helms-Burton Act, which seeks to strengthen the U.S.'s economic embargo of Cuba by punishing foreign companies that invest in Cuba.	After staging three months of daily protests, the opposition Zajedno (Together) coalition takes control of the city council of Belgrade, the Serbian and Yugoslav capital.	Two Israeli military helicopters collide in midair just south of the Israel-Lebanon border, killing all 65 soldiers and eight crew members aboard. It is one of the worst air disaster in Israeli's history.	Ecuador's Congress votes to remove Pres. Abdala Bucaram Ortiz on the grounds of "mental incapacity." Fabian Alarcon, the president of Congress, is named interim president of Ecuador.	Deng Xiaoping, 92, China's paramount leader, dies in Beijing, China's capital, from respiratory failure.
March	The 22-member Arab League announces its decision to freeze relations with Israel in light of Israeli prime minister Benjamin Netanyahu's settlement policies.	Despite ongoing violent protests in Albania, Parliament reelects Pres. Sali Berisha to a second five-year term.	More than 450 Palestinians are wounded in street clashes.	Pamela Gordon becomes Bermuda's first female prime minister, as well as its youngest.	On Comoros, a three-island nation in the Indian Ocean, a strike turns into an open rebellion, and government troops move in.
April	The Chemical Weapons Convention (CWC), a multilateral treaty mandating disarmament of poison gas weapons, goes into effect.	Presidents Boris Yeltsin of Russia and Aleksandr Lukashenko of Belarus sign a treaty on closer integration between the two former Soviet states.	A group armed with hatchets and knives kill 93 villagers, including 43 women and girls, in Haouch Mokhfi, 12 miles (20 km) south of Algiers, Algeria. The attack, attributed to Islamic fundamentalists, is the biggest massacre of civilians reported since the strife began in 1992.	Peruvian commandos storm the Japanese ambassador's residence in Lima, the capital, freeing 72 hostages held by leftist rebels since December. The raid ends the longest guerrilla siege in Latin American history.	Pakistan's parliament votes unanimously to repeal a 12-year-old constitutional amendment that gives the president unilateral power to dismiss the prime minister, dissolve Parliament, and appoint armed forces chiefs.
May	Western and African nations condemn a coup in Sierra Leone that ousts Pres. Ahmed Tejan Kabbah, Sierra Leone's first freely elected ruler in three decades. The overthrow is also denounced by UN secretary general Kofi Annan and OAU leader Salim Ahmed Salim.	Turkish forces launch an offensive in northern Iraq against Kurdish rebels seeking autonomy for Turkey's Kurds.	Zairian president Mobutu Sese Seko relinquishes power, ending nearly 32 years of dictatorial rule over Africa's third-largest country. The Mobutu government crumbles as high-level officials flee across the Congo River to Brazzaville. Laurent Kabila declares himself head of state and changes the country's name to the Democratic Republic of the Congo.	Colombia's Constitutional Court votes to legalize euthanasia but imposes strict guidelines on the practice. The ruling makes Colombia the only country in the world to allow euthanasia.	Indian prime minister Inder Kumar Gujral and Pakistani prime minister Nawaz Sharif hold a landmark meeting in the Maldives on the disputed Kashmir region, over which the two countries have fought two wars since they were partitioned in 1947.
June	The territory of Hong Kong reverts to Chinese sovereignty at midnight on June 30, ending 156 years of British colonial rule. After a Sino-British handover ceremony, the territory becomes known as the Hong Kong Special Administrative Region (SAR) of China.	Caoimhghin O'Caolain, a candidate from Sinn Fein, the political arm of the Provisional IRA, wins a seat in the Dail for the first time in 16 years. He will be the first Sinn Fein member to join the Dail since the 1922 founding of the Republic of Ireland.	Rebellious soldiers in Sierra Leone's capital, Freetown, come under attack from Nigerian warships.	The Popocatepetl volcano near Mexico City, erupts, spewing lava and covering parts of the city with ash. Tens of thousands of people are placed on alert for evacuation during the eruption, which officials call the volcano's biggest in 72 years.	Pol Pot, allegedly responsible for more than 1 million deaths during the Khmer Rouge's rule of Cambodia from 1975 to 1979, is captured by forces loyal to Ta Mok, a popular leader among Khmer Rouge troops.
July	The U.S., Russia, and 28 European countries agree on revisions to the 1990 treaty governing Conventional Forces in Europe (CFE). The new accord will set country-by-country limits on nonnuclear arms and materiel deployed in Europe.	In Spain, the murder of councilman Miguel Angel Blanco by the separatist ETA sparks a series of both violent and peaceful protests.	After three months of political violence, the Kenyan government allows an opposition coalition to hold a rally in the port city of Mombasa.	In elections, Mexico's ruling Institutional Revolutionary Party (PRI) loses its near-absolute control over the government for the first time since the party's formation in 1929.	Fighting breaks out in Cambodia between the copremiers' forces, and First Premier Prince Norodom Ranariddh, is ousted by Hun Sen in a bloody coup.
Aug.	The UN Security Council votes to pass a resolution imposing air and travel sanctions against the National Union for the Total Liberation of Angola (UNITA), an armed rebel group in the southeast African nation of Angola.	Britain's Diana, Princess of Wales, 36, dies after suffering grave injuries in a car accident in an underpass in Paris, France. Emad Mohamed (Dodi) al-Fayed, 41, an Egyptian-born film producer to whom Diana was recently romantically linked, dies in the crash, along with driver Henri Paul, 41.	Former warlord Charles Taylor is sworn in as president of Liberia for a six-year term. Taylor is Liberia's first freely elected leader after seven years of civil war.	The Soufriere Hills volcano on the tiny Caribbean island of Montserrat erupts, forcing hundreds of people to evacuate areas previously declared safe.	In India, 15,000 people parade through the streets of New Delhi to mark the country's 50th year of independence in a "March of the Nation."

A	B	C	D	E
Includes developments that affect more than one world region, international organizations, and important meetings of major world leaders.	*Includes all domestic and regional developments in Europe, including the Soviet Union, Turkey, Cyprus, and Malta.*	*Includes all domestic and regional developments in Africa and the Middle East, including Iraq and Iran and excluding Cyprus, Turkey, and Afghanistan.*	*Includes all domestic and regional developments in Latin America, the Caribbean, and Canada.*	*Includes all domestic and regional developments in Asia and Pacific nations, extending from Afghanistan through all the Pacific Islands, except Hawaii.*

U.S. Politics & Social Issues	U.S. Foreign Policy & Defense	U.S. Economy & Environment	Science, Technology, & Nature	Culture, Leisure, & Lifestyle	
The House, votes, 395-28, to formally reprimand Speaker Newt Gingrich (R, Ga.) and fines him $300,000. The House's punishment of Gingrich is the first sanction imposed on a speaker in the House's 208-year history.	Videotapes depicting hazing rituals, in which medals are pounded into the chests of Marine paratroopers at Camp Lejeune, North Carolina, are broadcast on television.	The Dow volume of shares traded, 683.8 million, is the heaviest in the 204-year history of the New York Stock Exchange.	At a meeting of the American Astronomical Society, a team of U.S. scientists report they have found the first direct evidence of an event horizon, a defining characteristic of a black hole.	Boerge Ousland of Norway completes a 64-day-long trek across Antarctica, becoming the first person ever to cross the continent alone and unaided.	Jan.
In Los Angeles, California, two heavily armed bank robbers are shot and killed in a gun battle with police that is filmed by news helicopters and broadcast live on six Los Angeles TV stations.	The U.S. Ninth Circuit Court of Appeals in San Francisco, California, 2-1, upholds the military's "don't ask, don't tell" policy on homosexuals, rejecting arguments that the policy is unconstitutional because it treats homosexuals and heterosexuals differently.	Six labor unions end a bitter 19-month-long strike against the *Detroit Free Press* and the *Detroit News*, stopping the longest newspaper strike in U.S. history.	Researchers in Scotland create the first genetic clone of an adult animal, a Finn Dorset lamb named Dolly, which has a genetic makeup identical to that of her mother. The major scientific breakthrough prompts a flood of media reports and public speculation worldwide about the dangers of human cloning.	French sailor Christophe Auguin, 38, breaks the solo around-the-world sailing record with a time of 105 days, 20 hours, and 31 minutes.	Feb.
In California, 39 members of Heaven's Gate, a religious cult, are found dead. It is one of the largest mass suicides in U.S. history.	Former CIA officer Harold James Nicholson pleads guilty to selling top-secret information to Russia. Nicholson is the highest-ranking CIA officer ever to be convicted of espionage.	John G. Bennett Jr., the founder of the failed Foundation for New Era Philanthropy, pleads no contest to federal charges that he defrauded universities, churches, charities, and philanthropists of $135 million. The scheme is said to have been the largest charity fraud in U.S. history.	The Hale-Bopp comet, one of the largest and brightest comets to enter the solar system in centuries, reaches its closest proximity to Earth when it passes an estimated 122 million miles from the Earth's surface.	Sixteen-year-old Martina Hingis of Switzerland becomes the youngest women's tennis player ever to be ranked number one.	March
A three-judge panel of the U.S. Ninth Circuit Court of Appeals in San Francisco, California, unanimously upholds California's anti-affirmative-action Proposition 209.	Pres. Clinton imposes a ban prohibiting new U.S. investment in Myanmar, in response to reports of continued human-rights abuses.	Vice President Al Gore and Secretary of State Madeleine Albright issue the State Department's first annual "Environmental Diplomacy" report.	The Social Security Administration shuts down an information service operated on the Internet global computer network, citing concerns over the possibility of privacy violations.	In the TV series *Ellen*, the character played by Ellen DeGeneres reveals that she is a lesbian, becoming the first lead character in a TV series to openly acknowledge her homosexuality.	April
In *Clinton v. Jones*, the Supreme Court unanimously rejects Pres. Clinton's request to delay proceedings in a sexual-harassment suit until he leaves office. It is the first time that the high court rules that sitting presidents may be sued for actions outside the realm of their official duties.	The Senate unanimously agrees to ratify changes to the 1990 treaty governing Conventional Forces in Europe (CFE).	The White House and Republican congressional leaders reach an agreement to balance the federal budget by 2002. The historic deal includes tax cuts and reductions in discretionary spending favored by Republicans and funding increases for education, welfare, and health insurance for children backed by Pres. Clinton.	A team of Spanish paleontologists report the discovery in Spain of 800,000-year-old human fossils, the oldest human remains found in Europe.	Mattel introduces Share a Smile Becky, a Barbie doll that depicts a handicapped girl.	May
Timothy J. McVeigh, a decorated veteran of the 1991 Persian Gulf war, is convicted on all 11 charges before him by a U.S. federal jury in Denver, Colorado, of the Apr. 19, 1995, bombing of the Alfred P. Murrah Federal Building in Oklahoma City, Oklahoma. The bombing, which killed 168 people, was the deadliest act of terrorism ever committed on U.S. soil.	In New York City, Judge Jack B. Weinstein rules that the INS cannot retroactively apply an April 1996 antiterrorism law to automatically deport legal immigrants convicted of minor offenses.	Pres. Clinton approves new air-quality standards that tighten previous limits on soot and ground-level ozone, an element of smog.	A government-convened panel issues the first official guidelines on how doctors should administer newly developed drug treatments to effectively combat HIV, the virus that causes AIDS. A total of 11 so-called antiretroviral drugs that may be used in 320 different combinations are currently on the market.	The inaugural game of the Women's National Basketball Association (WNBA), a new U.S. women's professional league, is played, with the Los Angeles Sparks hosting the New York Liberty. The Liberty wins the game, 67-57.	June
The Senate unanimously approves Pres. Clinton's nomination of Eric H. Holder Jr. as deputy attorney general. Holder becomes the highest-ranking black law-enforcement official in U.S. history.	In a case that attracts intense media attention, police arrest seven alleged members of a nationwide ring that allegedly smuggled deaf people from Mexico into the U.S. and forced them to work selling trinkets.	The Dow Jones crosses the psychologically important 8000 mark for the first time ever.	After a 310 million-mile (500 million-km), seven-month-long journey, *Mars Pathfinder*, an unmanned spacecraft launched by NASA, lands on Mars. *Pathfinder* and *Sojourner*, a roving robotic explorer vehicle, explore the geology of the planet. *Pathfinder* is the first spacecraft to reach Mars since 1976.	Italian fashion designer Gianni Versace, 50, is shot and killed in Miami Beach, Florida. Andrew P. Cunanan, the suspect in the slaying of Versace and four other men, commits suicide, ending a manhunt that involved more than 1,000 law enforcement agents nationwide.	July
In response to the alleged beating and sodomizing of Abner Louima by NYC police, more than 2,000 demonstrators march through the precinct to the station house to protest what they denounce as a pattern of police brutality.	Female students enroll at the Virginia Military Institute in Lexington, Virginia, for the first time, ending 158 years of male-only education at the college.	OMB figures indicate that the federal budget deficit for fiscal 1997 will be $37 billion, the lowest in 23 years. The Congressional Budget Office (CBO) estimates that the 1997 deficit will be just $34 billion.	In New York City, Judge Sonia Sotomayor rules that publishers may transfer articles authored by freelance writers into electronic media, such as CD-ROM storage devices, without first obtaining the writers' permission. The decision is considered a landmark ruling in the evolving field of electronic publishing rights.	The Southern Baptist Convention, the nation's largest Protestant denomination, steps up its boycott of Walt Disney Co. to protest what it views as the company's shift to a "Christian-bashing, family-bashing, pro-homosexual agenda."	Aug.

F	G	H	I	J
Includes elections, federal-state relations, civil rights and liberties, crime, the judiciary, education, health care, poverty, urban affairs, and population.	*Includes formation and debate of U.S. foreign and defense policies, veterans' affairs, and defense spending. (Relations with specific foreign countries are usually found under the region concerned.)*	*Includes business, labor, agriculture, taxation, transportation, consumer affairs, monetary and fiscal policy, natural resources, and pollution.*	*Includes worldwide scientific, medical, and technological developments; natural phenomena; U.S. weather; natural disasters; and accidents.*	*Includes the arts, religion, scholarship, communications media, sports, entertainments, fashions, fads, and social life.*

	World Affairs	Europe	Africa & the Middle East	The Americas	Asia & the Pacific
Sept.	A haze caused by hundreds of raging forest fires blots out much of the sunlight in Indonesia, Malaysia, Singapore, the Philippines, Brunei, and southern Thailand. The U.S. and Canada authorize partial evacuations of their embassies in Kuala Lumpur, Malaysia's capital. The haze is widely called the worst ecological disaster on record in Southeast Asia.	Voters in Scotland, in a referendum, overwhelmingly approve plans to form a 129-member Scottish parliament with control over most local and regional affairs. The vote is regarded as a major landmark in the history of Scotland, which has been under British control for centuries.	An Israeli soldier is killed in southern Lebanon, raising to 865 the number of Israeli troops killed in Lebanon since Israel built a buffer zone abutting its northern border in 1982.	More than 400 Guatemalans who fled to Mexico during the civil war return to their country.	Mother Teresa (born Agnes Gonxha Bojaxhiu), 87, Roman Catholic nun who devoted her life to caring for the destitute and the sick in India and who won the 1979 Nobel Peace Prize for her work, dies in Calcutta, India, of a heart attack.
Oct.	Pres. Jiang Zemin of China meets with U.S. president Bill Clinton in Washington, D.C., in the first U.S.-China summit meeting since 1989.	Mary McAleese is declared the winner of the Republic of Ireland's presidential election. McAleese will be the country's first-ever president from Northern Ireland.	In the Congo Republic's capital, Brazzaville, Gen. Denis Sassou-Nguesso declares victory in his four-month-old civil war against Pres. Pascal Lissouba.	Paraguayan president Juan Carlos Wasmosy orders the arrest of Lino Cesar Oviedo, the ruling Colorado Party's candidate who is considered Wasmosy's likely successor.	Residents of Anjouan Island vote overwhelmingly to secede from the Comoros, a three-island nation in the Indian Ocean. The vote comes in the wake of an armed independence rebellion.
Nov.	Data indicates that more than a month of flooding has claimed at least 1,300 lives in Somalia, Ethiopia, and Kenya. UN officials state that East Africa has not experienced flooding as severe as current conditions since 1961.	In what is described as Germany's largest protest in at least 20 years, an estimated 40,000 university students march through Bonn, Germany's capital, in a demonstration of their discontent with the university system.	Iraq's Kurdistan Democratic Party (KDP) launches an all-out offensive against the Patriotic Union of Kurdistan (PUK) from Degala, east of the city of Irbil, to the town of Shaqlawah, some 30 miles (50 km) to the north.	The Peruvian government frees 83 people unjustly jailed on terrorism charges.	The State Law and Order Council (SLORC), Myanmar's ruling military junta, announces that it has dissolved itself and formed a new leadership council called the State Peace and Development Council (SPDC).
Dec.	The U.S. joins 101 other countries in signing the Global Financial Services Agreement, which essentially replaces a 1995 interim WTO pact.	A court in Milan, Italy, convicts former premier Silvio Berlusconi of fraud. He is given a 16-month suspended prison sentence.	Leaders of rival factions in Somalia's six-year-old civil war sign a landmark peace plan.	Cuban president Fidel Castro Ruz declares that Christmas (Dec. 25) will be a national holiday. Cuba, officially a communist, atheistic state, has not celebrated Christmas since 1969.	Jenny Shipley is sworn in as New Zealand's first woman prime minister.

A	B	C	D	E
Includes developments that affect more than one world region, international organizations, and important meetings of major world leaders.	Includes all domestic and regional developments in Europe, including the Soviet Union, Turkey, Cyprus, and Malta.	Includes all domestic and regional developments in Africa and the Middle East, including Iraq and Iran and excluding Cyprus, Turkey, and Afghanistan.	Includes all domestic and regional developments in Latin America, the Caribbean, and Canada.	Includes all domestic and regional developments in Asia and Pacific nations, extending from Afghanistan through all the Pacific Islands, except Hawaii.

U.S. Politics & Social Issues	U.S. Foreign Policy & Defense	U.S. Economy & Environment	Science, Technology, & Nature	Culture, Leisure, & Lifestyle	
The CDC reports that the number of new AIDS cases in the U.S. dropped for the first time in the epidemic's 16-year history when they fell by 6%.	The largest-ever investigation of sexual misconduct within Army ranks reveals evidence of widespread sexual harassment and discrimination.	The Forest Service imposes a ban on future oil and gas leasing along the Rocky Mountain Front in Montana, protecting a 100-mile-long stretch of land that runs along the eastern edge of the Lewis and Clark National Forest and borders the southern tip of Glacier National Park.	Officials at a marine-life observatory in the San Francisco, California, area report that the water surface there has warmed to 67°F (19.4°C), the highest temperature that the observatory has measured since it began keeping records in 1958.	The U.S. Catholic Conference of Bishops' committee on marriage and family attempts to provide spiritual guidance to the parents of homosexual children and urges parents not to reject their children on the basis of sexual orientation.	Sept.
The Supreme Court refuses to hear an appeal of a lower-court ruling that upholds an Oregon law permitting doctors in the state to prescribe lethal doses of medication to terminally ill patients. The court's action eliminates the last legal barrier to the implementation of the statute.	Tens of thousands of people turn out at Arlington National Cemetery in Virginia for the dedication of the Women in Military Service for America Memorial, a monument and exhibit hall commemorating the nearly 2 million women who have served in the U.S. armed forces during the past two centuries.	Reports confirm that a Pennsylvania landfill company has agreed to pay an $8 million fine for making illegal campaign contributions to 10 candidates. The fine is the largest penalty ever imposed for campaign-finance violations.	A jet-powered SuperSonic Car called Thrust becomes the first vehicle to break the sound barrier on land.	Jane Alexander states she will resign as head of the NEA, citing the hostility of conservative members of Congress as one of her reasons.	Oct.
Pres. Clinton becomes the first U.S. president to address a gay and lesbian organization when he speaks to the Human Rights Campaign, a leading gay-rights group, in Washington, D.C.	Pres. Clinton signs an executive order imposing new economic sanctions on Sudan for its alleged human rights abuses and sponsorship of terrorism.	For the first time in its history, the FERC orders the dismantling of a hydroelectric dam whose owner seeks its relicensing.	Two teams of astronomers report to a meeting of the American Astronomical Society in Estes Park, Colorado, that they have confirmed the prediction of Albert Einstein's theory of relativity that very large rotating astronomical objects will warp the surrounding fabric of space-time in an effect called "frame dragging."	Four of the five living U.S. presidents—Bill Clinton, George Bush, Gerald Ford, and Jimmy Carter—attend the dedication of the George Bush Presidential Library and Museum at Texas A&M University.	Nov.
The U.S. Ninth Circuit Court of Appeals in San Francisco upholds a California law established in a 1990 referendum that sets term limits for California state legislators.	Reports confirm that Pres. Clinton has issued new, classified nuclear-strike guidelines to top military officials, marking the first adjustment in U.S. nuclear defense strategy since 1981.	A survey of state governments' finances projects that the 50 states will have aggregate budget surpluses totaling $24 billion at the end of the current fiscal year. The states had a record surplus of $29.2 billion in the fiscal year that ended in 1997.	Astronomers present images taken by the *Hubble Space Telescope* showing the dying phases of stars in unprecedented detail.	A federal judge in Eugene, Oregon, orders the PGA to allow Casey Martin, who has Klippel-Trenaunay-Weber Syndrome, to use a golf cart in competitions.	Dec.

F	G	H	I	J
Includes elections, federal-state relations, civil rights and liberties, crime, the judiciary, education, health care, poverty, urban affairs, and population.	*Includes formation and debate of U.S. foreign and defense policies, veterans' affairs, and defense spending. (Relations with specific foreign countries are usually found under the region concerned.)*	*Includes business, labor, agriculture, taxation, transportation, consumer affairs, monetary and fiscal policy, natural resources, and pollution.*	*Includes worldwide scientific, medical, and technological developments; natural phenomena; U.S. weather; natural disasters; and accidents.*	*Includes the arts, religion, scholarship, communications media, sports, entertainments, fashions, fads, and social life.*

	World Affairs	Europe	Africa & the Middle East	The Americas	Asia & the Pacific
Jan. 1		Rescuers in Georgia free some 150 people trapped since Dec. 26, 1996, in a 2½-mile-long tunnel under the Caucasus Mountains. . . . Bomb-disposal officers in Belfast, Northern Ireland, conduct a controlled explosion of a suspected IRA land mine found in a van near Belfast Castle.	In Libya, eight suspected spies are sentenced to death for allegedly passing defense secrets to foreign governments. . . . Despite protests, Israel's Knesset passes a controversial budget package. . . . Reports confirm that a court in Tizi-Ouzou, Algeria, has sentenced 12 Islamic militants to death for "belonging to armed terrorist groups." . . . An Israeli soldier, Private Noam Friedman, opens fire on Palestinian civilians in a Hebron marketplace, wounding seven people, one of them critically.	The MRTA leftist rebels holding Peruvian and foreign dignitaries hostage inside the Japanese ambassador's residence free seven hostages before talks break down. The remaining 74 hostages include top Peruvian government officials, Pres. Fujimori's brother, the ambassadors of Japan and Bolivia, and several Japanese businessmen.	
Jan. 2			Libya executes the six senior military officers and two civilians who were sentenced Jan. 1. Foreign diplomats and area experts suspect that the men were not connected to espionage activities but to a failed 1993 military coup. . . . In Zaire, rebels claim they have captured the gold-mining region of Kilo-moto in northeastern Zaire, which is privately owned by Pres. Mobutu Sese Seko.	Some 200 inmates of Alberta's Drumheller Institution stage a prison riot, injuring 13 prisoners. . . . In a case that shocked many Canadians who revere hockey as a national pastime, Graham James, a junior hockey coach in western Canada, pleads guilty in Alberta Provincial Court to two counts of sexually assaulting two teenage former players and is sentenced to 3½ years in jail.	A Russian tanker carrying more than 19,000 tons of heavy fuel oil capsizes and sinks in the Sea of Japan, spilling at least 4,500 tons of its cargo. The spill, Japan's worst in more than 20 years, fouls some of the country's richest fishing grounds and large stretches of fragile beach areas. . . . Singapore's ruling People's Action Party (PAP) capture all but two seats in Parliament. . . . Police in Karachi, Pakistan, arrest Hakim Ali Zardari, the father-in-law of Benazir Bhutto, on charges of income-tax evasion and bank fraud.
Jan. 3	U.S. president Bill Clinton suspends for six months a provision of the Helms-Burton law that allows U.S. citizens whose properties were confiscated in Cuba's 1959 communist revolution to sue, in U.S. courts, foreign companies that use those properties. The law has angered many U.S. allies, and the EU, Canada, and Mexico have adopted retaliatory measures.	Thousands of Bulgarians launch a series of protests in Sofia to call for immediate new elections. . . . Russia reports that the number of new infections of HIV jumped to 1,031 in 1996, which surpasses the total number of HIV infections reported in Russia in the 10 years since the virus was first discovered there. . . . Bosnia-Herzegovina's parliament meets for the first time. Separately, a letter by Yugoslav foreign minister Milan Milutinovic disputes most of the findings of a December 1996 OSCE report that reaffirmed the opposition's claims of wins in November municipal elections.	A Rwandan court sentences Deo Bizimana and Egide Gatanazi, two Hutu men, to death for their involvement in the massacres of half a million ethnic Tutsis and moderate Hutus during the country's 1994 civil war. The verdict is the first handed down in the Rwandan government's efforts to punish the organizers of the massacres. . . . A previously unknown group, the Boer Attack Force, claims responsibility for the Dec. 24, 1996, fatal Worcester bombing.	Odín Gutiérrez Rico, a senior antidrug official, is killed in the northern city of Tijuana, Mexico, the eighth such killing in 11 months.	A raging bush fire breaks out in the barren countryside surrounding the city of Perth in Western Australia. The fire destroys 12 homes, kills livestock, and ruins 10,500 hectares (26,000 acres) of grazing land. . . . In South Korea, the Confederation of Trade Unions resumes strikes that started Dec. 26, 1996, in protest of new labor laws.
Jan. 4	The Greek Cypriot government signs an agreement to buy sophisticated S-300 surface-to-air missiles from Russia, drawing sharp criticism from Turkey, the U.S., Great Britain, and the United Nations.	Czech president Vaclav Havel marries actress Dagmar Veskrnova. . . . Reports confirm that an 11-day period of severely cold weather in Western Europe has resulted in 228 deaths.	Two unarmed French soldiers are shot and killed in a rebel-held suburb of Bangui, the capital of the Central African Republic, while escorting a mediation team led by officers from Chad and Burkina Faso. . . . A letter bomb is found at the headquarters of the Saudi-owned, Arabic-language *Al Hayat* newspaper in Riyadh, the capital of Saudi Arabia.		The bush fire that ignited Jan. 3 in Western Australia. Is brought under control by 500 firefighters. More than 1,000 residents have evacuated their homes in Wooroloo, Wundowie, and Bakers Hill, on the outskirts of Perth.
Jan. 5		Officials state that the Russian troop withdrawal from the separatist republic of Chechnya is complete. . . In Serbia, opposition supporters drive several thousand vehicles through Belgrade at a creeping pace, and many feign breakdowns in order to get around the December 1996 ban on street marches. . . . Prince Bertil Gustaf Oscar Carl Eugene, 84, third son born to King Gustaf VI of Sweden and Princess Margaret of Connaught, dies of unreported causes.	Three bombs explode in Rustenburg, South Africa, injuring two people and damaging a mosque. The Boer Attack Force claims responsibility. . . . In retaliation for the Jan 4 killings, French soldiers, backed by armored vehicles and helicopter gunships, attack positions held by mutineers in Bangui, Central African Republic. France's defense ministry reports that 10 rebel soldiers are killed and 30 others captured. Mutineers put their death toll at 21, and say 11 civilians also died.	In Mexico, federal officials arrest at least 25 people linked to the Juarez drug cartel in a raid of a ranch near the town of Navolato in Sinaloa state. . . . Health officials in Honduras predict that 65,000 of the 300,000 Hondurans currently suffering from Chagas disease, a deadly parasitic illness transmitted by insects, will die in the next two years.	Reports reveal that the 31-member crew of the *Nakhodka*, the Russian tanker that spilled at least 4,500 tons fuel oil in the Sea of Japan on Jan. 2, were rescued from waters near the vessel, but the ship's captain is missing and presumed dead.
Jan. 6		A live grenade is thrown from an automobile and strikes a security building on the grounds of the Northern Ireland High Court in Belfast. The explosion slightly wounds a police officer and a female pedestrian. The IRA claims responsibility . . . Data show that Poland's population in 1996 increased by 34,000, to 38.6 million. . . . Sandor Vegh, 91, violinist and conductor best known as the leader of the Vegh Quartet, dies in Freilassing, Germany, of unreported causes.		Justice Ross Wimmer of Saskatchewan Court of Queen's Bench sentences former Saskatchewan legislator Michael Hopfner to 18 months in jail for fraud. Hopfner is the sixth former Saskatchewan legislator to be convicted in connection with a fraud ring run by several deputies to the provincial legislature between 1986 and 1991.	Pakistan's senior political officials establish a Council for Defense and National Security that expands the power of the country's military, giving it a formal role in setting national policy. It is the first time since the 1988 death of Gen. Muhammad Zia ul-Haq, Pakistan's last military ruler, that the military will be officially involved in government policy. . . . In South Korea, protests against labor laws passed in December 1996 are significantly stepped up.
	A Includes developments that affect more than one world region, international organizations, and important meetings of major world leaders.	**B** Includes all domestic and regional developments in Europe, including the Soviet Union, Turkey, Cyprus, and Malta.	**C** Includes all domestic and regional developments in Africa and the Middle East, including Iraq and Iran and excluding Cyprus, Turkey, and Afghanistan.	**D** Includes all domestic and regional developments in Latin America, the Caribbean, and Canada.	**E** Includes all domestic and regional developments in Asia and Pacific nations, extending from Afghanistan through all the Pacific Islands, except Hawaii.

U.S. Politics & Social Issues	U.S. Foreign Policy & Defense	U.S. Economy & Environment	Science, Technology, & Nature	Culture, Leisure, & Lifestyle	
Data show that 117 federal, state, and local law-enforcement officers were killed in the line of duty in 1996. The number of police officers slain in 1996 is down 30% from 1995, when 162 were killed, and is the lowest since 1960. . . . Two containers of flammable liquid are thrown at an abortion clinic in Tulsa, Oklahoma, causing minor damage.			Reports confirm that workers for the expansion of the Los Angeles subway system have unearthed more than 2,000 fossils of prehistoric animals. Among the fossils found are those of 60 species of fish, as well as bones of a mastodon, a camel, and an extinct type of horse. Scientists estimate that the mammal bones are between 10,000 and 280,000 years old and that some of the fish fossils date back as many as 15 million years.	Townes Van Zandt, 52, country music singer-songwriter who influenced such singers as Roseanne Cash, Emmylou Harris, and Neil Young, dies of an apparent heart attack while recovering from hip surgery in Smyrna, Texas.	Jan. 1
Six lawmakers file a suit in federal court challenging the constitutionality of a new law known as the line-item veto that gives the president power to eliminate spending for specific items in an appropriations bill within five days after Congress passes the legislation. . . . The CDC reports that the rate of legal abortions in the U.S. fell 5% to 1.27 million in 1994, from 1.32 million in 1993. The 1994 rate is the lowest in 20 years.	Officials discover five letter bombs addressed to the Saudi newspaper *Al Hayat* bureau in Washington, D.C., and postmarked in Alexandria, Egypt.			The Roman Catholic Church formally excommunicates Rev. Tissa Balasuriya, a Sri Lankan priest under criticism for his books, which challenge such core tenets of the Roman Catholic faith as original sin and the immaculate conception.	Jan. 2
	Officials discover three letter bombs mailed to a federal penitentiary in Leavenworth, Kansas. Like the bombs discovered on Jan. 2, they are postmarked in Alexandria, Egypt.	Statistics show that the value of domestic mergers and acquisitions announced in 1996 reached an all-time high of $659 billion. The number of deals involving U.S. companies was 10,257, also a record. This figures compare to the total of 9,152 mergers announced in 1995, with a combined value of $519 billion.	Some 900 tourists are evacuated after being stranded in northern California's Yosemite National Park due to floods caused by heavy rains and melting snow from the Sierra Nevada mountains. . . . Wallace Broecker, a biochemist, reveals that he has resigned from his job as research coordinator of Biosphere 2, a six-year-old self-contained ecosystem experiment.	Jeffrey St. John, 66, TV and print journalist, dies in Randolph, Virginia, of lung cancer. . . . Marie Torre, 72, columnist who served 10 days in jail in 1959 for protecting a source, dies in Monroeville, Pennsylvania, of lung cancer. . . . The New Bedford (Massachusetts) Whaling Museum opens its first annual "Moby Dick: The Marathon," during which more than 150 volunteers read Herman Melville's *Moby Dick* (1851) over a 24-hour period.	Jan. 3
		Harry Helmsley, 87, billionaire real-estate mogul who, with his second wife, Leona Helmsley, was charged in 1988 with state and federal tax evasion, dies in Scottsdale, Arizona, of pneumonia.		Henk Angenent wins the Elfstedentocht, a 125-mile (200-km) skating race over a network of frozen waterways in the province of Friesland, the Netherlands. It is only the 15th time in the 20th century that the temperature has been cold enough for the race.	Jan. 4
				Burton Lane (born Burton Levy), 84, composer for Broadway musicals and Hollywood films, dies in New York City of a stroke.	Jan. 5
In the combined cases of *U.S. v. Watts* and *U.S. v. Putra*, the Supreme Court rules, 7-2, that federal judges may consider related criminal conduct of which a defendant has been found innocent in setting a sentence for crimes of which that defendant has been found guilty.		Chrysler Corp. unveils the Chrysler LHX, a new electric car design that runs on hydrogen fuel extracted from gasoline. . . . A federal advisory committee recommends that the nation's financially strained Social Security system invest some proportion of its assets in the stock market.		The Baseball Writers' Association of America elects pitcher Phil Niekro to the Baseball Hall of Fame in Cooperstown, New York.	Jan. 6

F	G	H	I	J
Includes elections, federal-state relations, civil rights and liberties, crime, the judiciary, education, health care, poverty, urban affairs, and population.	*Includes formation and debate of U.S. foreign and defense policies, veterans' affairs, and defense spending. (Relations with specific foreign countries are usually found under the region concerned.)*	*Includes business, labor, agriculture, taxation, transportation, consumer affairs, monetary and fiscal policy, natural resources, and pollution.*	*Includes worldwide scientific, medical, and technological developments; natural phenomena; U.S. weather; natural disasters; and accidents.*	*Includes the arts, religion, scholarship, communications media, sports, entertainments, fashions, fads, and social life.*

	World Affairs	Europe	Africa & the Middle East	The Americas	Asia & the Pacific
Jan. 7		A bomb explodes in Londonderry, Northern Ireland, as an armored police vehicle passes by.... The ruling Bulgarian Socialist Party (BSP) nominates Interior Minister Nikolai Dobrev as its candidate for premier.		Governor General Romeo LeBlanc appoints 73 Canadians to the Order of Canada.	
Jan. 8		An unidentified woman shoots and kills Spanish officer Lt. Col. Jesus Agustin Cuesta Abril in Madrid.... The IRA claims responsibility for the Jan. 7 attack, in Londonderry, Northern Ireland.... The Serbian government concedes that the Zajedno opposition coalition won November 1996 municipal elections in Nis, the second-largest city in Serbia.... Makhmud Khudoberdyev of the Tajik government attacks rebels in Tursunzade, a city on Tajikistan's border with Uzbekistan. No casualties are reported.		Strikes and protests begin in Ecuador, prompted by the government's announcement of large increases in the prices of basic utilities.	
Jan. 9	Prosecutors at the UN's Rwandan war-crimes tribunal open their case against Jean-Paul Akayesu, a former Hutu mayor accused of ordering the killings of 2,000 Tutsis during the 1994 civil war.... The UN-backed Pan American Health Organization reports that 16–18 million people living in Latin America have contracted Chagas disease, a deadly parasitic illness transmitted by insects.	Maliq Sheholli, an ethnic Albanian member of the ruling Socialist Party, is slain.... The Bulgarian Statistics Institute estimates 1996 inflation at 310.8%.... Police in the Kazakh capital, Almaty, discover the dead body of U.S. journalist Chris Gehring, 28.... Slovenia's parliament reelects Janez Drnovsek as premier.... Serbia's Supreme Court approves the opposition victory in November municipal elections in the town of Vrsac.	Two pipe bombs laden with nails explode in trash containers in Tel Aviv, Israel, wounding 13 people.... Zaire's Pres. Mobutu Sese Seko flies back to Europe just three weeks after returning to face a rebel uprising and political turmoil in his country.	Canadian prime minister Jean Chrétien, seven provincial premiers, the leaders of Canada's two territories, and some 400 business executives embark on a visit to South Korea, the Philippines, and Thailand on the Canadian government's largest-ever trade mission.	Ongoing protests that started in December in Seoul, South Korea, turn violent.... Tamil rebels attack the Elephant Pass and Paranthan military bases in Sri Lanka.... Tony Bullimore and Thierry Dubois, whose yachts capsized, are rescued by the Australian military after being exposed to four days of high winds, freezing temperatures, and wave swells of 50 feet (15 m).... The Bangladesh Supreme Court frees from prison Hossein Mohammed Ershad, the country's former military ruler.
Jan. 10	In the UN Security Council, China exercises its veto power for the first time since 1972 when it refuses to pass a resolution to send 155 military observers to monitor a peace accord signed in Guatemala in December 1996, ending a 36-year-long civil war.	Under pressure from the U.S., Georgian president Eduard Shevardnadze reveals that he will waive diplomatic immunity for Gueorgui Makharadze, a senior diplomat at Georgia's U.S. embassy alleged to have caused a car crash in Washington, D.C., which a teenage girl died.... In Bulgaria, protesters, angry because Parliament has avoided new elections, break into the parliament building, cause $1.1 million worth of damage, and blockade more than 100 legislators, many from the BSP, in the building.	Army soldiers kill 126 Hutu refugees trying to escape from a detention center. The refugees had been forcibly expelled from Tanzania, where an estimated 200,000 Burundians are still living in camps after fleeing the turmoil in their country.	Arnoldo Aleman Lacayo is sworn in as president of Nicaragua in Managua, the nation's capital.	Sri Lankan government officials and Tamil rebels give conflicting reports of losses suffered in the Jan. 9 clashes. Between 300 and 700 combatants are said to have been killed in the fighting.... In Seoul, a Hyundai Motor worker, Chung Jae Sung, is hospitalized after setting himself ablaze in protest of new labor laws. Hyundai Motor Co., South Korea's largest car manufacturer, shuts its assembly plant, saying it incurred $465 million in production losses linked to the strikes.
Jan. 11		In Bulgaria, police break through crowds of protestors to free the deputies trapped inside the parliament building Jan. 10. Some 100 demonstrators and police officers are injured.... Jill Summers, 89, British TV actress recognized for her comedic talents, dies in Selford, England, of kidney failure.	A letter bomb is found at the headquarters of the *Al Hayat* newspaper in the Saudi capital, Riyadh.		The Russian government contributes 1.5 billion rubles ($270,000) to help pay for the cleanup from the Jan. 2 oil spill in the Sea of Japan.
Jan. 12		Some 100,000 people hold protests in Sofia, the capital of Bulgaria, and other towns.... A high-speed train derails after rounding a sharp curve near the Italian town of Piacenza, killing eight people and injuring at least 29 others.... Jean-Edern Hallier, 60, controversial French writer known for his outspoken opinions, dies of a brain hemorrhage caused by a bicycle accident.	Britain's Diana, Princess of Wales, visits Angola to draw attention to the dangers of land mines.		

A	B	C	D	E
Includes developments that affect more than one world region, international organizations, and important meetings of major world leaders.	Includes all domestic and regional developments in Europe, including the Soviet Union, Turkey, Cyprus, and Malta.	Includes all domestic and regional developments in Africa and the Middle East, including Iraq and Iran and excluding Cyprus, Turkey, and Afghanistan.	Includes all domestic and regional developments in Latin America, the Caribbean, and Canada.	Includes all domestic and regional developments in Asia and Pacific nations, extending from Afghanistan through all the Pacific Islands, except Hawaii.

U.S. Politics & Social Issues	U.S. Foreign Policy & Defense	U.S. Economy & Environment	Science, Technology, & Nature	Culture, Leisure, & Lifestyle	
The 105th Congress convenes with the Republican Party retaining majorities in the House and Senate for the first time in 68 years. Rep. Newt Gingrich (R, Ga.), battling ethics charges, is narrowly reelected speaker of the House. . . . In *Old Chief v. U.S.*, the Supreme Court rules, 5-4, that in certain criminal cases prosecutors cannot disclose to juries details of a defendant's prior convictions, if that defendant agrees to acknowledge his past conviction in court.	A presidential panel examining the illnesses of Persian Gulf war veterans concludes that stress probably contributes to the veterans' health problems but states that there is little evidence that exposure to chemical weapons or pollutants does.	Reports confirm that the state of Illinois and the city of Chicago have agreed to turn Meigs Field, an airfield on a strip of landfill in Lake Michigan, into a park.	Reports indicate that Nevada governor Bob Miller (D) predicts that damage from flooding in that state could reach $500 million.	Judge Consuelo Marshall of U.S. District Court in Los Angeles sentences Hollywood madam Heidi Fleiss, who in 1995 was sentenced to three years in prison on state charges of procuring prostitutes, to 37 months in federal prison for tax evasion and money laundering.	Jan. 7
The State of Arkansas executes three convicted murderers—Earl Van Denton, 47; Paul Ruiz, 49; and Kirt Wainwright, 30—in one night at the state prison in Varner. It is the second time since 1976 that a state executes three prisoners in one day. . . . Residents of an impoverished section of Miami, Florida, pick up some $500,000 in cash and $149,000 in food stamps when a crashed Brink's Inc. armored truck spills money onto an interstate and a city street below.	A group of scientists report they have identified six separate clusters of ailments, or syndromes, from which Persian Gulf war veterans are suffering and found that exposure to certain combinations of chemicals encountered during the war appears linked to some of the syndromes. . . . Officials at The Citadel military academy reveal that 11 cadets have been disciplined for allegedly harassing Kim Messer and Jeanie Mentavlos, two female students who made sexual harassment allegations public in December.		Reports confirm that the U.S.-based computer-network access provider America Online Inc. (AOL) has cut off Russian subscribers' access to the company's service because of widespread credit card fraud. It is the first time that AOL has blocked off access to an entire country. . . . Melvin Calvin, 85, biochemist who won the 1961 Nobel Prize in Chemistry for his research on the phases of photosynthesis, dies in Alta Bates, California, of unreported causes.	The estate of Rev. Martin Luther King, Jr. and Time Warner Inc. plan to publish a series of books and other media products related to King's work. . . . Christies International PLC posts a 9% increase in its sales, to $1.602 billion in 1996 from $1.47 billion in 1995.	Jan. 8
Pres. Clinton discloses that the nation's college-loan default rate dropped to 10.7% in the 1994 fiscal year, from 11.6% the previous year. The 1994 rate represents a sharp decline in loan defaults from fiscal 1990, when the rate peaked at 22.4%. . . . Vice Pres. Al Gore, as president of the Senate, officially declares Pres. Clinton and himself the winners of the 1996 presidential election after Congress tallies the votes of the Electoral College.	Albert Wohlstetter, 83, adviser on nuclear-arms policy to several U.S. presidents who was awarded the Medal of Freedom in 1985, dies in Los Angeles, California, of unreported causes.	Federal authorities arrest 15 people for allegedly smuggling into the U.S. nearly 900 tons of illegal refrigerants that contain chlorofluorocarbons, or CFCs. That is the most arrests of such kind made by the federal government. . . . The Labor Department reports that the index of prices charged by manufacturers and farmers for finished goods rose 2.8% in 1996. That marks the largest annual gain since 1990 and compares with a 2.3% increase in 1995.	Comair Flight 3272 crashes in a snowstorm in Raisinville Township, Michigan, killing all 29 people on board. . . . In the largest study of its kind, research shows that women who had abortions in the first 18 weeks of pregnancy did not increase their risk of developing breast cancer. . . . Data confirms that 42 of California's 58 counties have been declared disaster areas due to floods. At least 29 deaths have been attributed to the floods.	Pres. Clinton confers National Medals of Arts and Charles Frankel Prizes for humanities on 16 American cultural figures and one arts organization. . . . Jesse White, 78, actor best known for his role as the lonely Maytag repairman in TV ads, dies in Los Angeles, California, of unreported causes.	Jan. 9
	Mary Bancroft, 93, U.S. spy during World War II, dies in New York City of unreported causes.		A study finds that resveratrol, a natural ingredient in grapes, wine, peanuts, and mulberries, successfully inhibits the formation of cancer tumors in mice. . . . Lord Todd (born Alexander Robertus Todd), 89, British chemist who won the Nobel Prize in Chemistry in 1957 for his advancements in the understanding of the constitution of genes, dies in Cambridge, England, of unreported causes.	Sheldon Leonard (born Sheldon Leonard Bershad), 89, actor and TV producer credited with giving actor Bill Cosby the first leading role for a black man in a U.S. television series, dies in Beverly Hills, California, of unreported causes.	Jan. 10
			Reports confirm that 12,800 homes in California have been damaged or destroyed as a result of ruptured levees.		Jan. 11
	Kim Messer and Jeanie Mentavlos, two of the four women attending The Citadel, a state-run military academy in Charleston, South Carolina, announce that they have dropped out of the formerly all-male institution after revealing allegations of harassment. Mentavlos's brother, Citadel senior Michael Mentavlos, states that he will leave the school as well and complete his course work at a different institution.		The space shuttle *Atlantis* blasts off from Kennedy Space Center in Cape Canaveral, Florida, on a mission to pick up a U.S. astronaut from the Russian *Mir* space station and deliver his replacement. . . . Charles Huggins, 95, surgeon who won the Nobel Prize for Medicine in 1966 for research that led to the use of drug therapy as a successful treatment for cancer, dies in Chicago, Illinois, of unreported causes.	Football's New England Patriots defeat the Jacksonville Jaguars, 20-6, to win the AFC title. The Green Bay Packers beat the Carolina Panthers, 30-13, to become the NFC champions. . . . Figure skater Oksana Baiul, a gold medalist in the 1994 Olympic Games, is hospitalized with a concussion after a car accident in Bloomfield, Connecticut.	Jan. 12
F	G	H	I	J	
Includes elections, federal-state relations, civil rights and liberties, crime, the judiciary, education, health care, poverty, urban affairs, and population.	*Includes formation and debate of U.S. foreign and defense policies, veterans' affairs, and defense spending. (Relations with specific foreign countries are usually found under the region concerned.)*	*Includes business, labor, agriculture, taxation, transportation, consumer affairs, monetary and fiscal policy, natural resources, and pollution.*	*Includes worldwide scientific, medical, and technological developments; natural phenomena; U.S. weather; natural disasters; and accidents.*	*Includes the arts, religion, scholarship, communications media, sports, entertainments, fashions, fads, and social life.*	

	World Affairs	Europe	Africa & the Middle East	The Americas	Asia & the Pacific
Jan. 13	The Council of Europe's parliamentary assembly suspends Belarus's special guest status in the organization, arguing that Belarus's new constitution does not respect human rights.	Four letter bombs are discovered in the London mail room of *Al Hayat*, a Saudi-owned Arabic-language newspaper, one of which explodes and seriously injures a mail clerk.... In Serbia, more than 300,000 protesters jam Belgrade's streets on the occasion of Orthodox New Year's Eve in the largest rally held to date in the capital. Separately, Fazli Hasani, who worked with the Serbian police near the town of Mitrovica, is slain.			A court in Shanghai, China, sentences a Chinese-American businessman, William Ping Chen, for smuggling garbage and medical waste into China. Chen is fined $60,000 and ordered expelled from China. He is also sentenced to 10 years in prison, although it appears that the expulsion order will effectively negate that sentence.
Jan. 14		The Belgrade election commission issues a preliminary ruling that the Zajedno coalition has won control of Belgrade's city assembly and that of Nis and 12 other cities and towns.... A Russian service association estimates that 4,379 Russian troops died in the 21-month-long Chechen war. More than 1,000 soldiers are still listed as missing.			
Jan. 15		Petru Lucinschi is sworn in as Moldova's second president since its independence from the Soviet Union in 1991.... Thousands of people across Albania begin a series of rallies urging the government to step in to protect their investments in failed pyramid schemes.	Israeli prime minister Benjamin Netanyahu and Yasser Arafat, leader of the self-rule Palestinian National Authority (PNA), conclude a long-delayed agreement on terms for Israel's withdrawal from most of the West Bank city of Hebron.	Leftist rebels holding 74 Peruvian and foreign dignitaries hostage inside the Japanese ambassador's residence in Lima, Peru, accept a government proposal for the creation of a guarantor commission to mediate a resolution to the standoff. It is the first significant progress in efforts to end the crisis since Jan. 1.	Riot police seal off the Myongdong Roman Catholic cathedral in Seoul, South Korea, where seven union leaders—including Confederation of Trade Unions head Kwon Young Kil—have camped out to avoid arrest.
Jan. 16	A World Trade Organization panel issues an interim ruling that a Canadian excise tax on "split-run" publications, which pair U.S.-produced editorial content with Canadian advertisements, violates international trade rules.	A bomb attack in Pristina, the Kosovar capital, wounds Radivoje Papovic, dean of Pristina University and a stalwart of Serbian president Slobodan Milosevic. His driver is also wounded.... In Azerbaijan, some 30 former members of the OPON elite police are sentenced to prison terms of up to 13 years in connection with a separate 1995 coup attempt.		A general strike is called in Haiti to protest austerity measures.... In Colombia, 10 marines are taken hostage by FARC rebels during a raid on a military base.	North Korea launches an official site on the World Wide Web. The launch of the Web site is considered remarkable because the communist country is one of the world's most reclusive and secretive nations.
Jan. 17		The High Court in Dublin, the Irish capital, grants the first divorce in the history of the Republic of Ireland.... Hundreds of disgruntled workers at Credit Foncier de France, a state-owned bank, occupy the company's Paris headquarters and prevent Jerome Meyssonnier, the bank's federally appointed governor, from leaving the premises.... A jury in London's Old Bailey courthouse decides that Szymon Serafinowicz, 86, the first person charged with World War II-era Nazi crimes under Britain's War Crimes Act, is unfit to stand trial due to his failing health.	Israel's military begins to withdraw from 80% of the West Bank city of Hebron.... A Rwandan court in southern Butare sentences three Hutus to death for helping to organize the 1994 massacres.... Retired South African Anglican archbishop and 1984 Nobel Peace Prize laureate Desmond Tutu announces that he has prostate cancer.... Crown Prince Asfa Wossen, 80, Ethiopian prince and son of the late Emperor Haile Selassie, dies in Oakton, Virginia.	Canadian army commander Lt. Gen. Maurice Baril reveals that 57 Canadian soldiers engaged in sexual misconduct, abuse, and drunkenness while guarding a mental hospital in Bakovici, Bosnia-Herzegovina during peacekeeping duty in 1993 and 1994.... A judge in Cali, Colombia, sentences the two reputed leaders of the Cali drug cartel, Gilberto Rodriguez Orejuela and his brother Miguel Rodriguez Orejuela, to 10½ years and nine years in prison, respectively.	
Jan. 18		Austrian chancellor Franz Vranitzky announces that he is stepping down from his post, effective immediately.... Danish police in Copenhagen, the capital, arrest seven suspected neo-Nazis who allegedly planned to deliver package bombs to targets in Britain.	Attackers kill 36 residents of Beni-Slimane, a village 45 miles (75 km) south of Algiers, Algeria, reportedly decapitating some of the victims. ... Hutu militiamen shoot and kill three Spanish aid workers and seriously wound an American in an attack on their compound in Ruhengeri, northwestern Rwanda. The attack is apparently coordinated with three other raids, in which three Rwandan soldiers die.		Twenty-five people, including Ziaur Rehman Farooqi, leader of a Sunni Muslim militant group, are killed and dozens of people are wounded when a bomb explodes near a courthouse in Lahore, Pakistan.

A	B	C	D	E
Includes developments that affect more than one world region, international organizations, and important meetings of major world leaders.	Includes all domestic and regional developments in Europe, including the Soviet Union, Turkey, Cyprus, and Malta.	Includes all domestic and regional developments in Africa and the Middle East, including Iraq and Iran and excluding Cyprus, Turkey, and Afghanistan.	Includes all domestic and regional developments in Latin America, the Caribbean, and Canada.	Includes all domestic and regional developments in Asia and Pacific nations, extending from Afghanistan through all the Pacific Islands, except Hawaii.

U.S. Politics & Social Issues	U.S. Foreign Policy & Defense	U.S. Economy & Environment	Science, Technology, & Nature	Culture, Leisure, & Lifestyle	
Judge John E. Sprizzo of U.S. District Court in New York City acquits retired bishop George E. Lynch and Franciscan friar Christopher Moscinski, two protesters who blocked access to an abortion clinic, because of what he calls their sincere religious beliefs.	Pres. Clinton awards seven black soldiers the Medal of Honor—the nation's highest award for bravery—for their heroism in World War II. Six of the awards are posthumous.... Four letter bombs are discovered at UN headquarters in NYC, addressed to the office of the *Al Hayat*, a Saudi-owned Arabic-language newspaper. Officials note that the bombs are similar to eight bombs discovered Jan. 2 and Jan. 3 in the U.S. and to the four discovered in London this same day.		At a meeting of the American Astronomical Society, a team of U.S. scientists report that they have found the first direct evidence of an event horizon, a defining characteristic of a black hole. A second group of U.S. scientists tells the conference they have found evidence of three new black holes within 50 million light years of Earth.... The FDA proposes a ban on the antihistamine drug Seldane due to the emergence of evidence that the drug may have fatal side effects.		Jan. 13
A group of physicians and patients file a class-action lawsuit against the federal government alleging that its plans to prosecute physicians who prescribe or discuss marijuana use as a treatment for their patients violates the Constitution's freedom-of-speech protections. California and Arizona passed referendums legalizing marijuana use for medicinal purposes in 1996.		The Labor Department reports that the government's index of consumer prices in 1996 rose 3.3%, up from the 2.5% rate registered in 1995. The 1996 inflation figure is the first in six years to surpass the 3.0% level.	U.S. astronomers report that, using the Hubble telescope, they have discovered an estimated 600 stars that are not part of any galaxy.... The U.S. spacecraft *Atlantis* successfully docks at the *Mir* space station.	Robert Irsay, 73, owner of the Indianapolis Colts football team since 1972, dies in Indianapolis, Indiana, of congestive heart failure related to a stroke suffered in November 1995.... Figure skater Oksana Baiul is charged with reckless and drunken driving for her Jan. 12 accident in Bloomfield, Connecticut.	Jan. 14
The American Civil Rights Institute, a national anti-affirmative-action group, is launched by Ward Connerly, a black California businessman.... In Wisconsin, Judge Paul Higginbotham issues a ruling blocking a state plan to use public money to send some students to religious schools. The plan would have allowed impoverished children in Milwaukee to attend such schools for free.... Darnell McGee, who is accused of knowingly exposing women to HIV, is shot at point-blank range and killed in Missouri.	Three years ahead of schedule, Mexico repays the remaining $3.5 billion of the $12.5 billion it borrowed from the U.S. in February 1995 in the wake of an economic crisis precipitated by a devaluation of Mexico's currency, the peso, in December 1994.		Oscar Auerbach, 92, pathologist who, in the 1960s, was the first researcher to demonstrate a physical link between smoking and lung cancer, dies in Livingston, New Jersey, of unreported causes.		Jan. 15
Two bombs explode at a building in Atlanta, Georgia, that houses an abortion clinic, injuring at least six people.	Data suggests that the following defense companies are the largest in the U.S.: Boeing Co., Lockheed Martin Corp., Raytheon Co., Northrop Grumman Corp., and General Dynamics Corp.	The Congressional Budget Office reports that it has reduced its projected estimate of the costs of Medicaid by $86 billion for the years 1997 through 2002.	The youngest person ever to receive a heart transplant dies in Miami, Florida, of complications from the procedure. The child, Cheyenne Pyle, was 67 days old when she died.	Ennis W. Cosby, the only son of TV comedian Bill Cosby, is shot to death on a freeway ramp in Los Angeles, California, while changing a flat tire.	Jan. 16
Reports confirm that antitobacco lawyers have filed a class-action lawsuit in a state court in Natchitoches, Louisiana, against the state's smokeless tobacco industry. It is the first to target makers of smokeless tobacco.... Data show that seven abortion clinics were bombed in 1996 and that at least 15 were bombed every year from 1993 to 1995.... Pres. Clinton presents former Sen. Robert J. Dole (R, Kans.) with the Presidential Medal of Freedom, the nation's highest civilian honor.			A single-engine Piper Dakota plane crashes near Alton, New Hampshire, killing the pilot, 46-year-old David Riach, and his mother, Dorothy Riach, 71.... Figures reveal that AOL customers spent a total of 102 million hours using the service in December 1996, up sharply from 45 million hours in September 1996.... Clyde William Tombaugh, 90, astronomer best known for his discovery of the planet Pluto in 1930, dies in Las Cruces, New Mexico, of unreported causes.	Chicago Bulls forward Dennis Rodman is suspended for at least 11 games and fined $25,000 by the NBA for kicking a cameraman during a Jan. 15 basketball game in Minneapolis, Minnesota. It is the second-harshest suspension in NBA history, and it costs Rodman more than $1 million in salary and incentives.	Jan. 17
Martin Luther King III, the oldest son of Rev. Martin Luther King Jr., announces he is forming a new national coalition to fight for affirmative action called Americans United for Affirmative Action.... Paul Efthemios Tsongas, 55, former Democratic senator from Massachusetts who made an unsuccessful bid for the presidency in 1992, dies in Boston of pneumonia caused by complications from his cancer treatments.				Boerge Ousland of Norway completes a 64-day-long trek across Antarctica, becoming the first person ever to cross the continent alone and unaided.... The Eastern Conference defeats the Western Conference, 11-7, in the National Hockey League's All-Star Game in San Jose, California.	Jan. 18
F	G	H	I	J	
Includes elections, federal-state relations, civil rights and liberties, crime, the judiciary, education, health care, poverty, urban affairs, and population.	*Includes formation and debate of U.S. foreign and defense policies, veterans' affairs, and defense spending. (Relations with specific foreign countries are usually found under the region concerned.)*	*Includes business, labor, agriculture, taxation, transportation, consumer affairs, monetary and fiscal policy, natural resources, and pollution.*	*Includes worldwide scientific, medical, and technological developments; natural phenomena; U.S. weather; natural disasters; and accidents.*	*Includes the arts, religion, scholarship, communications media, sports, entertainments, fashions, fads, and social life.*	

	World Affairs	Europe	Africa & the Middle East	The Americas	Asia & the Pacific
Jan. 19		Envoys of the Tajik government and the United Tajik Opposition sign a pact approving mutual amnesties and an election commission for the war-torn country.... Bulgaria's new president, Petar Stoyanov, takes the oath of office, replacing Zhelyu Zhelev.... Reports confirm that Austrian chancellor Franz Vranitzky has named Viktor Klima to replace him as chancellor and as head of the Social Democratic Party.	Reports confirm that a Rwandan court in Butare has sentenced the three Hutus convicted Jan. 17 to death for helping to organize the 1994 massacres.... Yasser Arafat, the Palestinian National Authority (PNA) president, returns to Hebron for the first time in more than 30 years. Armed Jewish settlers in Hebron march in protest.... At least 20 people are killed when a car bomb explodes in downtown Algiers, the capital of Algeria.		In response to the Jan. 18 bombing in Lahore, Pakistan, Sunni mourners set an Iranian cultural center ablaze.
Jan. 20	China reverses its Jan. 10 veto of a UN resolution to send 155 military observers to monitor a peace accord signed in Guatemala in December 1996, ending a 36-year-long civil war. Diplomats reveal that the Chinese reversal comes after Guatemala agreed not to support Taiwan's bid for UN membership in 1997.	Reports confirm that the Kosovo Liberation Army (UCK) has claimed responsibility for several violent incidents in January, including the Jan. 16 bomb attack that wounded two people.... Premier Andris Skele resigns, forcing the dissolution of Latvia's government.... The Serbian Supreme Court rules that the SPS won the city assembly of Sabac. Police with riot gear in Belgrade attack student demonstrators, injuring at least 12.	The Zairian military launches a counteroffensive, using Kisangani as a base. Reports confirm that Andre Ngandu Kissasse, the rebel alliance's military chief, was killed over a week ago.... News accounts indicate that nearly 100 Rwandans have been killed by Hutu militants in the past month, mostly in western Rwanda.		Japan launches a unified intelligence body, the Defense Intelligence Headquarters, which joins together five separate defense intelligence groups. The DIH has a 1,660-member staff, which far outnumbers that of Japan's next-largest intelligence agency, the 300-member Cabinet Research Information Bureau.... A study finds that 20% of Australian women revealed that they suffered sexual abuse before age 16.
Jan. 21		Reports confirm that a total of 31 mass graves, containing 1,462 bodies, and 466 single graves were discovered and exhumed in Bosnia in 1996.... Authorities free Todor Zhivkov, a former Bulgarian head of state under house arrest since 1992. ... Serbia's Supreme Court rules that the SPS won municipal elections in the city of Smederevska.... Svend Truelsen, 81, leader of the Danish resistance during World War II, dies in Copenhagen.			South Korean president Kim Young Sam, in an effort to end nearly a month of strikes and protests, agrees to send controversial labor laws back to the National Assembly for reconsideration.
Jan. 22	Reports confirm that multinational banks and foreign countries have promised Guatemala $1.9 billion to help the country rebuild after the devastation of the civil war.	The disgruntled workers who, on Jan. 17, took over Credit Foncier de France, a state-owned mortgage bank, release Jerome Meyssonnier, the bank's governor, but they continue to occupy the building.... Prompted by a confirmation that a cow died from BSE, or mad-cow disease, in December 1996, the German government announces a plan to kill 5,200 cows.... The lower house of the Duma approves a nonbinding resolution to oust Russian president Boris Yeltsin because of his poor health.		Pilar Barbosa de Rosario, 99, Puerto Rican historian and politician, dies in San Juan, Puerto Rico, of unreported causes.	
Jan. 23	The UN's Rwandan war-crimes tribunal in Arusha, Tanzania, gains custody of four former high-ranking officials suspected of organizing and inciting Rwanda's 1994 genocidal massacres of Tutsis and moderate Hutus.	As thousands of people in Albania continue to hold rallies, Parliament bans pyramid schemes and sets 20-year minimum prison sentences for those found guilty of operating them.... In response to claims that Swiss banks hold assets that rightly belong to Holocaust victims, Switzerland's government reaches an agreement with Swiss banks and businesses to create a fund to pay victims of the Nazi Holocaust.		A panel of the OAS condemns Mexico for the imprisonment of Gen. Jose Francisco Gallardo Rodriguez, detained since November 1993 for criticizing the armed forces' human-rights record.... Reports from Canada confirm that a vandal cut down a 300-year-old tree, known as the Golden Spruce, that is a cultural symbol of the Haida Indians and a tourist attraction near the village of Port Clement, British Columbia.	Due to financial woes stemmed from construction of a steel mill in Tangkin, Hanbo Steel Industry Co. files for court protection from its creditors in what is reported to be the largest bankruptcy case ever in South Korea.
Jan. 24		Moldova's legislature approves a new government led by Premier Ion Ciubuc.... Azerbaijani authorities reveal that 40 people were arrested in connection with a coup attempt planned for the fall of 1996.		In Canada, Ontario Attorney General Charles Harnick issues an apology and C$1.25 million (US$930,000) to Guy Paul Morin for Morin's 1992 wrongful murder conviction. The monetary award is the largest compensation ever awarded to a wrongfully convicted person in Canada.... Reports confirm that six more people were charged in connection with a fraud ring in Saskatchewan's Progressive Conservative (Tory) caucus.	In Seoul, South Korea, seven strike leaders staying on the grounds of the Myongdong cathedral since Jan. 15 leave the grounds when police drop charges against them and release four unionists arrested earlier in the month.

A	B	C	D	E
Includes developments that affect more than one world region, international organizations, and important meetings of major world leaders.	Includes all domestic and regional developments in Europe, including the Soviet Union, Turkey, Cyprus, and Malta.	Includes all domestic and regional developments in Africa and the Middle East, including Iraq and Iran and excluding Cyprus, Turkey, and Afghanistan.	Includes all domestic and regional developments in Latin America, the Caribbean, and Canada.	Includes all domestic and regional developments in Asia and Pacific nations, extending from Afghanistan through all the Pacific Islands, except Hawaii.

U.S. Politics & Social Issues	U.S. Foreign Policy & Defense	U.S. Economy & Environment	Science, Technology, & Nature	Culture, Leisure, & Lifestyle	
Two bombs explode behind an abortion clinic in Tulsa, Oklahoma, slightly damaging the building but causing no injuries.				James Dickey, 73, poet and author who won the 1966 National Book Award, dies in Columbia, South Carolina, of complications from lung disease.	Jan. 19
In a ceremony administered by Chief Justice William Rehnquist, William Jefferson Clinton is inaugurated to a second term as president of the United States. Addressing a crowd of more than 200,000 gathered at the Capitol in Washington, D.C., Clinton declares that the time has come to set aside racial animosity and partisan bickering and "to move on with America's mission."		Reports disclose that a coalition of 40 Native American tribes has joined with the National Wildlife Federation to lobby for a halt to a planned slaughter of bison to prevent the spread of brucellosis, a disease that caused spontaneous abortions in cattle. The tribes petition the government to allow the bison—even those that carry brucellosis—to roam freely on the tribes' reservation lands.	Archaeologists remove a 2,000-year-old Roman sculpture that was discovered in November 1996 from the bed of the River Almond near Edinburgh, Scotland.	Edith Haisman, 100, oldest survivor of the 1912 *Titanic* tragedy, dies in London. . . . Curt Flood, 59, All-Star baseball player, dies in Los Angeles of pneumonia after suffering from throat cancer. . . . In a failed bid to become the first person to sail around the world nonstop in a balloon, Steve Fossett lands in India after setting world records for endurance and distance.	Jan. 20
The House, 395-28 votes to formally reprimand House Speaker Newt Gingrich (R, Ga.) and fines him $300,000. The House's punishment of Gingrich is the first sanction imposed on a speaker in the House's 208-year history. . . . In *Babbitt v. Youpee*, the Supreme Court rules, 8-1, that a 1984 federal law that bars Native American from passing on to their heirs small parcels of reservation land that they own is unconstitutional.		The Dow Jones closes at a record high of 6883.90. . . . In response to accusations that the Democratic Party skirted fund-raising laws in collecting more than a million dollars from Asian businesses and Asian foreign nationals, Don Fowler, the outgoing national chairman of the DNC, announces that the committee will no longer accept donations from foreign nationals or from American subsidiaries of foreign companies.	The FDA approves the first home drug-testing kit.	The Whitbread Book of the Year Award is given to Irish poet Seamus Heaney. . . . Colonel Tom Parker (born Andreas Cornelius van Kuijk), 87, who represented rock singer Elvis Presley, 1955–77, dies in Las Vegas, Nevada, of complications from a stroke.	Jan. 21
The Senate confirms, 99-0, Madeleine K. Albright as secretary of state. . . . First Lady Hillary Rodham Clinton affirms her support for abortion rights at a NARAL luncheon to mark the 24th anniversary of the 1973 *Roe v. Wade* decision. Tens of thousands of abortion opponents march on Washington in protest. . . . A study of 14 issues debated in Congress between 1995 and 1996 finds a strong correlation between the voting records of legislators and the amount of money they received from industries with an interest in those issues.	William S. Cohen, the nominee for defense secretary, is confirmed by the Senate in a 99-0 vote. . . . In New York City, U.S. district judge Shira Scheindlin rules that a 1996 law banning the sale or rental of sexually explicit magazines and videotapes at U.S. military bases is unconstitutional.		The space shuttle *Atlantis* touches down at Kennedy Space Center in Cape Canaveral, Florida, after carrying out a mission to pick up John Blaha, who has been on *Mir* since September 1996, and replace him with U.S. Navy captain Jerry L. Linenger. . . . The U.S. Fourth Court of Appeals in Richmond, Virginia, overturns a lower court's ruling against four scientists accused of stealing a colleague's work. In the first case, the plaintiff, Pamela Berge, was awarded $1.9 million in damages in May 1995.	Mollie Panter-Downes, 90, the London correspondent for *The New Yorker* magazine, 1939–87, dies of unreported causes.	Jan. 22
Madeleine K. Albright is sworn in as the 64th secretary of state, thereby becoming the first woman to fill the post and the highest-ranking woman ever in the U.S. government. . . . Randy Greenawalt, 47, convicted of murder after escaping from prison, is executed by lethal injection in Florence, Arizona. Greenawalt is only the seventh person executed in Arizona and the 363rd in the U.S. since 1976.		The Dow volume of shares traded, 683.8 million, is the heaviest in the 204-year history of the New York Stock Exchange.	An NIH-sponsored panel does not recommend mammograms for women between the ages of 40 and 49 as an effective means of reducing deaths from breast cancer. . . . Scientists report they have discovered the skeleton of a previously unknown species of flesh-eating dinosaur. . . . Reports reveal that between 1992 and 1994 archaeologists discovered 2.5 million-year-old stone tools in Ethiopia. The tools are 200,000 years older than previously believed and predate fossils of genus *Homo*, an ancestor of the modern human being.	Richard Berry, 61, singer and songwriter, dies in Los Angeles, California, of possible complications from an aneurysm. . . . Stuntwoman Laura (Dinky) Patterson, 43, dies as she practices a bungee jump for what was to be the finale of the Super Bowl halftime show.	Jan. 23
At an AIDS conference, New York City health officials tell attendees that AIDS death rates in the city fell in 1996, down 30% from the previous year. Dr. Paul Denning of the CDC reports that the number of AIDS cases nationwide among people between the ages of 13 and 25 rose between 1990 and 1995. AIDS rates in that age group increased 18%, to 2,800 cases in 1995, from 2,300 cases in 1990.			Dr. Mark R. Hughes, a geneticist at Washington, D.C.'s Georgetown University, resigns as head of the university's Institute for Molecular and Human Genetics in response to a controversy over his acknowledgement that he conducted unauthorized research on human embryos. . . . Reports state that wheat seeds planted in December 1996 on board the Russian space station *Mir* have produced sterile offspring.		Jan. 24

F	G	H	I	J
Includes elections, federal-state relations, civil rights and liberties, crime, the judiciary, education, health care, poverty, urban affairs, and population.	Includes formation and debate of U.S. foreign and defense policies, veterans' affairs, and defense spending. (Relations with specific foreign countries are usually found under the region concerned.)	Includes business, labor, agriculture, taxation, transportation, consumer affairs, monetary and fiscal policy, natural resources, and pollution.	Includes worldwide scientific, medical, and technological developments; natural phenomena; U.S. weather; natural disasters; and accidents.	Includes the arts, religion, scholarship, communications media, sports, entertainments, fashions, fads, and social life.

	World Affairs	Europe	Africa & the Middle East	The Americas	Asia & the Pacific
Jan. 25		During ongoing rallies in Albania that urge the government to step in to protect their investments in failed pyramid schemes, protesters in the southern town of Lushnja beat Deputy Premier Tritan Shehu.... Former Bosnian Serb vice president Nikolai Koljevic, 60, dies after having shot himself in the head on Jan. 16.	Pres. Ange-Felix Patasse of the Central African Republic, his political opponents, and a group of army mutineers sign a peace agreement aimed at ending the mutineers' 10-week-long uprising and the tribal violence that accompanied it.... Hutu militants reportedly massacre at least 20 Tutsi civilians in the village of Kinigi in Ruhengeri.		The Chinese-appointed Preparatory Committee, which will replace Hong Kong's current, democratically elected Legislative Council (LegCo), holds its first session.
Jan. 26		Angered by failed pyramid schemes, 35,000 rioters in Tirana, Albania's capital, throw rocks at police, injuring 84 officers. Mobs set fire to government buildings in the towns of Lushnja Berat, Vlora, Fier, and Korca. Parliament gives Pres. Sali Berisha emergency powers to deploy the military, and Premier Aleksandr Meksi announces the government will repay investors . . . Serbian police arrest Avni Klinaku, who allegedly heads the UCK, as they launch a crackdown in Kosovo.	Government soldiers reportedly kill at least 100 people while searching for militants in the village of Kinigi in Ruhengeri.		
Jan. 27		More than 100,000 people join a St. Sava's Day parade in what is reported as the largest religious procession in Serbia since World War II.... Inmates of the Barwhor prison in Albania end a riot, during which two convicts die.... In Chechnya, voters elect Gen. Aslan Maskhadov, the republic's premier, as president.... Cecil Lewis, 98, British fighter pilot, author, and film director, dies in London.			
Jan. 28		A Socialist-dominated city council holds its first meeting in the town of Smederevska Palanka, where the Zajedno party claims a victory. At least 15 demonstrators are injured when police break up an opposition rally protesting the meeting.... Lord Rippon (of Hexam) (born Aubrey Geoffrey Frederick Rippon), 72, politician from Britain's Conservative Party, dies near Bridgewater, England, after a long illness.... Cardinal Mikel Koliqi, 94, Albanian priest who in 1994 became the first-ever cardinal from his nation, dies in Shkoder of unreported causes.	Algeria's top labor union leader, Abdelhak Benhamouda, is shot and killed by gunmen in Algiers.... South Africa's Truth and Reconciliation Commission reveals that former policemen admitted killing Steve Biko, a black antiapartheid activist whose death while in police custody in 1977 sparked international outrage, particularly since an official inquest at the time ruled that Biko's death from a massive brain hemorrhage was an accident.		
Jan. 29		In Bulgaria, the country's three main trade unions call warning strikes. Road and rail traffic to Greece is halted for several days.... Reports confirm that Azerbaijan's Supreme Court has sentenced three high-level police officials to prison terms for treason in connection with a 1994 coup attempt.			Pakistan's Supreme Court rules to uphold Pres. Farooq Leghari's November 1996 decision to dissolve the government of Benazir Bhutto and call new elections for Feb. 3.
Jan. 30	The Council of Europe's parliamentary assembly votes to end its monitoring of Estonia, which signals that human rights are well established there.		Three Israeli soldiers are killed in occupied southern Lebanon by a booby-trapped roadside bomb set by the Shi'ite Muslim Hezbollah militia.... Thousands of Algerians attend a state funeral for labor leader Abdelhak Benhamouda, slain Jan. 28. Separately, reports confirm that Habib Khelil, a retired army general, was killed by Islamic militants in Oran, western Algeria.	Colombian officials disclose that antinarcotics police have shut down a huge cocaine processing plant in the southeastern department of Guaviare. The plant, reported to be the largest ever seized by the Colombian government, is capable of processing 1.5 tons of raw cocaine per day.	

A	B	C	D	E
Includes developments that affect more than one world region, international organizations, and important meetings of major world leaders.	Includes all domestic and regional developments in Europe, including the Soviet Union, Turkey, Cyprus, and Malta.	Includes all domestic and regional developments in Africa and the Middle East, including Iraq and Iran and excluding Cyprus, Turkey, and Afghanistan.	Includes all domestic and regional developments in Latin America, the Caribbean, and Canada.	Includes all domestic and regional developments in Asia and Pacific nations, extending from Afghanistan through all the Pacific Islands, except Hawaii.

U.S. Politics & Social Issues	U.S. Foreign Policy & Defense	U.S. Economy & Environment	Science, Technology, & Nature	Culture, Leisure, & Lifestyle	
Noel Keane, 58, attorney best known for brokering a 1986 adoption agreement that led to the "Baby M" case, dies in Dearborn, Michigan.	Reports confirm that Col. David C. Rauhecker, a high-ranking Air Force officer stationed at Hurlburt Field in Florida, has been charged with fondling and kissing a female captain against her will. . . . John Mohr, high-level official of the FBI under the leadership of J. Edgar Hoover, dies in Arlington, Virginia, of renal failure.			Werner Aspenstrom, 78, Swedish poet who served on the committee that chooses the Nobel Prize for Literature, is reported dead. . . . At the Australian Open, Martina Hingis of Switzerland win the women's tennis title . . . . Jeane Dixon, 79, popular astrologer, dies in Washington, D.C., after a heart attack.	Jan. 25
		More than 4,000 workers go on strike at a General Motors Corp. assembly plant in Moraine, Ohio.	Janet Pasaye, 35, gives birth to the second of a pair of twins 92 days after the first child was born. Doctors at the Chicago hospital where the child is delivered claim that the birth sets a world record for the number of days between the birth of twins.	The Green Bay Packers defeat the New England Patriots, 35-21, in New Orleans, Louisiana, to capture Super Bowl XXXI. The victory gives the Packers their first NFL title since 1968. . . . Pete Sampras wins the men's tennis title at the Australian Open.	Jan. 26
New York becomes the 19th state in the U.S. to sue the tobacco industry to recover public health-care costs for smoking-related illnesses. . . . Louis E. Martin, 84, black political activist who was an adviser to Presidents John Kennedy, Lyndon Johnson, and Jimmy Carter, dies in Orange, California, of pneumonia.			A team of MIT scientists announce they have created the first atom laser.		Jan. 27
		Data shows that U.S. stock mutual funds attracted a record $222.08 billion during the 1996 calendar year, easily surpassing the previous inflow record of $128.22 billion, set in 1993.			Jan. 28
The Senate confirms, 99-0, Andrew M. Cuomo as secretary of housing and urban development. . . . In Charlotte, North Carolina, Judge Robert Johnston sentences Henry Louis Wallace, 31, to death for killing and raping nine women between June 1992 and March 1994. The case drew publicity when critics charged that police did not give it their full attention because the victims were black and female.		The Treasury Department auctions inflation-indexed securities for the first time in its history. Investors brave uncertainties over the new instrument, a 10-year note, and responded enthusiastically to the offering, oversubscribing by better than a five-to-one ratio.	The FAA announces that it will release information on the safety records of U.S. airlines, making the data public on the Internet global computer network. Such information previously was made public only upon filing a Freedom of Information Act request with the federal government.		Jan. 29
Frank Tejeda, 51, a decorated veteran and Democratic congressman from Texas who was elected to a third term in November 1996, in San Antonio, Texas, of pneumonia brought on by treatment for a brain tumor.	CNN broadcasts a 1991 videotape depicting a hazing ritual, in which medals are pounded into the chests of U.S. Marine paratroopers at Camp Lejeune, North Carolina. . . . Officials confirm that 28 soldiers at Fort Leonard Wood, in Missouri, are under investigation for alleged sexual abuses. . . . The State Department releases its annual report on human rights around the world. Critics note that the U.S. is involved in trade with countries cited for human rights violations, such as China. The report singles out the Islamic government of the Taliban in Afghanistan as particularly oppressive toward women.	The Senate confirms, 95-2, William M. Daley as commerce secretary. . . . Federal officials declare that they will curb a program to trap and send to slaughterhouses bison that stray outside Yellowstone National Park. The program was launched to prevent the spread of brucellosis, a disease that causes spontaneous abortions in cattle.	The FDA gives final approval to the drug company Parke-Davis Co. Inc. to market Rezulin, a new drug treatment for victims of adult onset, or Type II, diabetes. The generic name for the new diabetes drug is troglitazone.		Jan. 30
F	G	H	I	J	
Includes elections, federal-state relations, civil rights and liberties, crime, the judiciary, education, health care, poverty, urban affairs, and population.	*Includes formation and debate of U.S. foreign and defense policies, veterans' affairs, and defense spending. (Relations with specific foreign countries are usually found under the region concerned.)*	*Includes business, labor, agriculture, taxation, transportation, consumer affairs, monetary and fiscal policy, natural resources, and pollution.*	*Includes worldwide scientific, medical, and technological developments; natural phenomena; U.S. weather; natural disasters; and accidents.*	*Includes the arts, religion, scholarship, communications media, sports, entertainments, fashions, fads, and social life.*	

	World Affairs	Europe	Africa & the Middle East	The Americas	Asia & the Pacific
Jan. 31	The European Investment Bank (EIB), the EU's lending institution, launches its first sale of bonds denominated in the euro, the common European currency that the EU is scheduled to launch in 1999.	The crackdown that began Jan. 26 in Kosovo culminates in a shootout near the town of Vucitrn in which three UCK members, including top official Zahir Pajaziti, are killed. Three Serbian policemen are injured.	Official returns show that Didier Rat-siraka has won the presidential election in Madagascar.... Human-rights monitors report that Hutu militias are killing Tutsis in an apparent attempt to stop them from testifying at genocide trials.... South African president Nelson Mandela names his long-time political rival, Chief Mangosuthu Buthelezi, as acting president for one day in February when he and Deputy President Thabo Mbeki will be out of the country.		In Vietnam's biggest corruption case ever, a court in Ho Chi Minh City sentences four people to death for their roles in a bribery and extortion scandal that caused at least $27 million in losses at Tamexco, a state-run import-export firm.... An independent panel rules against a Japanese government proposal to outlaw the Aum Shinrikyo cult, the group held responsible for a fatal 1995 nerve-gas attack on Tokyo's subway system.
Feb. 1	Peruvian president Alberto Fujimori meets with Japanese prime minister Ryutaro Hashimoto in Toronto, Canada, to discuss an ongoing siege in which leftist rebels took 72 hostages at the Japanese ambassador's residence in Lima, Peru, in December 1996.		Algerians observe a day of mourning for Algeria's top labor union leader, Abdelhak Benhamouda, slain on Jan. 28. An Islamic group, the Algerian Jihad Islamic Front, claims responsibility for the shooting.... Chief Mangosuthu Buthelezi is sworn in as acting president of South Africa. He is to hold the post from 12:01 A.M. Feb. 2 until Deputy president Thabo Mbeki's return on Feb. 3.	Clashes between leftist guerrillas of the Revolutionary Armed Forces of Colombia (FARC) and the government erupt after troops inadvertently happen upon what is believed to be FARC's headquarters near San Juanito, some 30 miles (50 km) outside Bogota, the capital of Colombia.	The Chinese-appointed Preparatory Committee, the body overseeing China's resumption of sovereignty over the colony from Great Britain, votes to repeal or amend laws protecting civil liberties in Hong Kong.
Feb. 2		Militant separatists in Corsica explode 60 bombs in a rural section of the island. The FLNC's historic wing claims responsibility.... Protesters calling for parliamentary elections set up roadblocks in Sofia, the capital of Bulgaria.... Serbian police, armed with batons, tear gas, and a water cannon, attack political protesters at Belgrade's Brankov Bridge. Some 100 protesters are injured.	The AP reports that some 310 people have died in Algeria in attacks attributed to Islamic extremists since the Muslim holy month of Ramadan began Jan. 10.... Rev. Guy Pinard, a Canadian missionary said to have witnessed atrocities committed by Hutu extremists during the 1994 civil war, is shot and killed while he celebrates mass in a Roman Catholic church in Ruhengeri district in northwestern Rwanda.	Chico Science (born Fernando de Assis Franca), 30, Brazilian songwriter and band leader, dies near Recife, Brazil, of injuries sustained in a car accident.	
Feb. 3	U.S. officials declare that the U.S. government, along with those of Britain and France, will freeze the distribution of $68 million in gold bars to countries looted by Nazi Germany in World War II. The move is prompted by claims by Jewish advocacy groups, led by the World Jewish Congress (WJC), that much of the gold rightly belongs to individual victims of the Nazi Holocaust and their heirs.	Sofia's public-transit workers go on strike in Bulgaria.... A bomb explosion damages the automobile of Russian first deputy finance Minister Andrei Vavilov.... Bohumil Hrabal, 82, Czech writer whose work was severely restricted during the 21-year Soviet occupation of his country, dies after falling from a window in a Prague hospital while trying to feed pigeons on the sill; he was under treatment for arthritis at the hospital.			The Pakistan Muslim League party, led by former prime minister Nawaz Sharif, secures a landslide victory in parliamentary elections.... North Korea, in an unusual statement, reveals that due to severe floods, farms have only produced 2.5 million tons of grain, half of that needed by the nation.
Feb. 4		In Bulgaria, an agreement is reached on holding fresh parliamentary elections, prompting 100,000 protesters to end 32 days of protests as well as strikes.... Serbian president Slobodan Milosevic calls for legislation to seat opposition-led city councils.... Tajik renegades loyal to mercenaries Bakhran Sadirov and his brother Rizvon Sadirov take hostage four UN military observers and a Tajik interpreter.	Two Israeli military helicopters collide in midair just south of the Israel-Lebanon border, killing all 65 soldiers and eight crew members aboard. It is one of the worst air disaster in Israeli's history.... Four UN human-rights monitors are killed when unidentified gunmen ambush their unarmed convoy in southwestern Rwanda. A fifth member of the UN team is critically wounded.		Benjamin de Jesus, the Roman Catholic bishop in Jolo, on the Philippine island of Sulu, is shot and killed near his cathedral on the predominantly Muslim island. The bishop's murder prompts army officials to impose a ban on firearms on the island.
Feb. 5		Tajik renegades and Bakhran Sadirov and his brother Rizvon Sadirov seize two Red Cross workers and four Russian reporters.... A thousand opposition protesters rally to hold the Serbian president to promises made Feb. 4 about the municipal elections.... Tens of thousands of Albanians launch a series of daily protests in Vlora to demand that the government repay lost investments.... Switzerland's three largest banks announce that they have established a compensation fund for Holocaust victims.	UN officials state that they will evacuate all UN personnel from western Rwanda in the wake of recent attacks.	Ecuador's labor unions, business leaders, and opposition parties call a general strike that brings the country to a standstill. Some 2 million workers protest the economic program and corruption and nepotism in Pres. Bucaram's government and call for the president's ouster. In response, Bucaram mobilizes army troops to patrol the capital, Quito.... Clashes that started Feb. 1 between leftist guerrillas of the Revolutionary Armed Forces of Colombia (FARC) and government troops begin to cease. The fighting has left at least 28 people dead.	Muslim separatists riot in Yining, a city in China's remote northwestern Xinjiang Uighur Autonomous Region. The rioting is considered some of the worst antigovernment violence to hit the tense region in decades.

A	B	C	D	E
Includes developments that affect more than one world region, international organizations, and important meetings of major world leaders.	Includes all domestic and regional developments in Europe, including the Soviet Union, Turkey, Cyprus, and Malta.	Includes all domestic and regional developments in Africa and the Middle East, including Iraq and Iran and excluding Cyprus, Turkey, and Afghanistan.	Includes all domestic and regional developments in Latin America, the Caribbean, and Canada.	Includes all domestic and regional developments in Asia and Pacific nations, extending from Afghanistan through all the Pacific Islands, except Hawaii.

U.S. Politics & Social Issues	U.S. Foreign Policy & Defense	U.S. Economy & Environment	Science, Technology, & Nature	Culture, Leisure, & Lifestyle	
	Army spokesmen confirm that an army sexual-harassment hotline set up in November 1996 has received nearly 7,000 calls. Of that number, 1,025 involve allegations of criminal sexual conduct.... NBC broadcasts the 1991 tape aired by CNN on Jan. 30, and another tape depicting a similar hazing incident in 1993 at the same camp.	A coalition of state agencies and nuclear-power companies file suit against the Department of Energy, asking the U.S. Circuit Court of Appeals for the District of Columbia to order the federal government to begin accepting spent fuel rods and nuclear waste from the states by Jan. 31, 1998.		Reports confirm that cosmetics tycoon Ronald Lauder bought a Paul Cezanne painting in Paris for $50 million. The painting, *Nature Morte: Rideau a Fleur et Fruits*, drew the fifth-highest price ever for a work of art.	Jan. 31
Statistics reveal that the number of people receiving welfare through AFDC payments stood at 11,864,000 in October 1996, down nearly 18% from the March 1994 peak of 14,398,286.... A jury in State District Court in Kerrville, Texas, convicts Darlie Routier, 27, for the June 1996 stabbing death of her five-year-old son, Damon Routier. She also faces murder charges in the death of an older son, Devon, aged six.	Data shows that 52 U.S. Marines have been court-martialed for their role in hazing incidents since 1994, and 34 were given nonjudicial punishments.			Herb Caen, 80, San Francisco journalist well known for his long-running column on the city, dies in San Francisco, California, of lung cancer.... Marjorie Reynolds (born Marjorie Goodspeed), 79, actress who began her career as a child in silent films, dies in Manhattan Beach, California, of unreported causes.	Feb. 1
An intruder breaks into an abortion clinic in Tulsa, Oklahoma, and fires shots at medical equipment.				The AFC defeats the NFC, 26-23, in overtime to win the Pro Bowl, the National Football League's all-star game.... Sanford Meisner, 91, director of the Neighborhood Playhouse School in New York City, 1935–94, dies in Sherman Oaks, California.	Feb. 2
The policy-making body of the American Bar Association (ABA) votes to seek a moratorium on executions until the federal government and the 38 states with the death penalty can ensure greater fairness and due process for defendants.		The Commerce Department reports that personal income rose 0.8% in December 1996 from the previous month, to a seasonally adjusted annual rate of $6.639 trillion. The percent increase, the largest in six months, marks the 19th consecutive month that incomes have grown.		The World Alpine Ski Championships open in Sestiere, Italy.... Seven people—Don Haskins, Pete Carril, Alex English, Bailey Howell, Denise Curry, Joan Crawford, and Antonio Diaz-Miguel—are elected to the Basketball Hall of Fame in Springfield, Massachusetts.... *Hornet's Nest*, by Patricia Cornwell, tops the bestseller list.	Feb. 3
Pres. Clinton delivers his State of the Union address. Rep. J. C. Watts (R, Okla.), issues the GOP's response.... A civil jury in Santa Monica, Calif., finds O. J. Simpson liable in the 1994 stabbing deaths of Nicole Brown Simpson Ronald Goldman.... A jury in Kerrville, Texas, sentences Darlie Routier to death for killing her five-year-old son in June 1996. Routier is one of only five women in the U.S. on death row for murdering their children.	In the midst of sexual harassment scandals in the army, reports reveal that Sergeant Major Gene C. McKinney, a member of a panel examining the Army's sexual-harassment policies, was accused of sexual assault by his former assistant. Staff Sergeant Vernell Robinson Jr. becomes the seventh drill instructor at the Aberdeen Proving Ground in Maryland to be charged with sexual misconduct.			Cigar wins the Eclipse Award as the 1996 horse of the year.... The American Bowling Congress confirms that Jeremy Sonnenfeld, 20, is the first bowler ever to roll a 900 series, or three consecutive perfect games, in competition.	Feb. 4
Pamela Harriman, (born Pamela Beryl Digby), 76, Democratic Party activist, fund-raiser, and socialite, dies in Paris, France, of complications from a stroke.	Officials reveal that a navy antisubmarine aircraft crashed during a training mission about 90 miles (145 km) off the coast of Haifa, Israel. All four crewmen were killed. ... The U.S. Circuit Court of Appeals votes to censure Elliott Abrams, a former assistant secretary of state, for unlawfully withholding information from Congress in 1986 about the Reagan administration's plan to arm Nicaraguan contras.... Dorothy Fosdick, 83, foreign policy expert who was instrumental in the formation of the U.S. Marshall Plan, the UN, and NATO, dies in Washington, D.C., of cardiac arrest.	Morgan Stanley Group Inc., one of Wall Street's elite investment banks, announces plans to merge with retail broker Dean Witter, Discover & Co., in a stock swap valued at $10.2 billion. The merger—the biggest in Wall Street history—will create a securities giant that will displace Merrill Lynch & Co. as the U.S.'s biggest securities firm in terms of market capitalization and assets under management.			Feb. 5

F	G	H	I	J
Includes elections, federal-state relations, civil rights and liberties, crime, the judiciary, education, health care, poverty, urban affairs, and population.	*Includes formation and debate of U.S. foreign and defense policies, veterans' affairs, and defense spending. (Relations with specific foreign countries are usually found under the region concerned.)*	*Includes business, labor, agriculture, taxation, transportation, consumer affairs, monetary and fiscal policy, natural resources, and pollution.*	*Includes worldwide scientific, medical, and technological developments; natural phenomena; U.S. weather; natural disasters; and accidents.*	*Includes the arts, religion, scholarship, communications media, sports, entertainments, fashions, fads, and social life.*

	World Affairs	Europe	Africa & the Middle East	The Americas	Asia & the Pacific
Feb. 6		Tajik mercenaries Bakhran Sadirov and his brother Rizvon Sadirov abduct four employees of the UN High Commissioner for Refugees. . . . Truck drivers demanding improved benefits and access to cheaper fuel begin a work stoppage and block major highways in Spain.	Residents of mixed-race suburbs of Johannesburg block roads with burning tires and fight running battles with police in some of the worst racial violence since South African president Nelson Mandela took office in 1994. At least four people, including a seven-year-old boy, are reported to have been killed in exchanges of gunfire between police and the rioters.	Ecuador's Congress votes to remove Pres. Abdala Bucaram Ortiz on the grounds of "mental incapacity." . . . Gen. Jesus Gutierrez Rebollo is forced to resign as head of the National Institute to Combat Drugs, Mexico's top antidrug agency, amid allegations of bribery. Gutierrez's removal indicates that corruption has reached the highest levels of Mexico's government.	In Pakistan, some 20,000 Muslims riot in the Christian-dominated villages of Khaniwal and Shantinagar in Punjab state. Thousands of Pakistani Christians are driven from their homes in the riots, which are prompted by false rumors that Christians desecrated a copy of the Koran and threw it into a mosque.
Feb. 7		Tajik interior minister Saidamir Zukhurov is taken hostage when he meets with mercenaries Bakhran Sadirov and his brother Rizvon Sadirov to bargain for the release of other captives. The Sadirovs free two Red Cross workers.		In Mexico, prosecutors drop murder charges against Claudia Rodriguez Ferrando, who has spent a year in jail after being charged with murder for shooting a man who she claims was trying to rape her. The case received attention when prosecutors and judges criticized Rodriguez for being out late at night without her husband and asserted that she was responsible for the attack because she was sober while her attacker was drunk. The comments prompted a public outcry and rallying from feminist groups, which, in turn, led prosecutors to drop the murder charges.	
Feb. 8		Police in Tirana, the capital of Albania, detain and beat several opposition figures, including Socialist Party leaders Rexhep Mejdani and Kastriot Islami.			A gunman goes on a shooting spree at a ski resort in the village of Raurimu, New Zealand. He fires his weapon indiscriminately, leaving six people dead and five others wounded.
Feb. 9		In Albania, one man dies of a heart attack and more than 40 others are injured in clashes with police in the southern port town of Vlora during protests sparked by the bankruptcy of the Gjallica pyramid scheme. Authorities arrest Fitim Gerxhalliu, the director of the Gjallica fund, and 11 of the fund's managers. In Tirana, Albania's capital, a uniformed gang beats several prominent members of Albania's opposition Democratic Alliance party, including its leader, Neritan Ceka.	Seven Israeli soldiers are wounded in the western sector of the security zone when Hezbollah guerrillas ambush their patrol. Israeli warplanes launch two attacks against presumed guerrilla targets near the Lebanese village of Zibqine, just north of the zone. No casualties are reported. . . . Didier Ratsiraka, a former longtime president of the African island republic of Madagascar, takes office.		
Feb. 10		Some 700 Bosnian Croats in the town of Mostar attack 500 Muslim pilgrims visiting family graves, killing one man and injuring 22. The incident is one of the most violent in Bosnia-Herzegovina since the end of the civil war in 1995 . . . In Vlora, Albania, two people die and 81 people are injured when protests turn violent. . . . In Madrid, Spain, Supreme Court judge Rafael Martinez Emperador is shot and killed. A car bomb is detonated in Granada, killing one person and wounding at least seven others. Both attacks are attributed to the ETA.			Reports of the violence from the Feb. 5 riots in Yining, a city in China's remote northwestern Xinjiang Uighur, surface in the West, and details are sketchy. The reported death toll in the rioting varies from four to almost 300. . . . The U.S. military acknowledges that U.S. jets inadvertently fired uranium bullets during military exercises near the Japanese island of Okinawa in late 1995 and early 1996, and then authorities waited a year to inform Japan of the incident.
Feb. 11		Serbia's parliament votes to pass a law approving the opposition's victories in the 1996 municipal elections in Belgrade and 13 other cities. . . . Tajik mercenaries Bakhran Sadirov and Rizvon Sadirov release one of the four UN military observers taken hostage on Feb. 4. . . . Croat police set up roadblocks to prevent Muslims from returning to west Mostar, a violation of freedom-of-movement guarantees in the 1995 peace agreement.	Israel frees 31 Palestinian women prisoners, originally slated for release under the September 1995 accord. The release was delayed since 28 of the women refused to accept their freedom in a gesture of solidarity with two of the women prisoners—convicted of murdering Israeli Jews—who were not granted pardons. . . . Data show that South African gold mines produced 16 million ounces (494 metric tons) of gold in 1996, the lowest output since 1956.	After much political maneuvering since the Feb. 6 ouster of Pres. Abdala Bucaram Ortiz, Fabian Alarcon, the president of Congress, is named interim president of Ecuador until August 1998. . . . Colombia's public-sector workers launch the largest Colombian strike in 20 years. . . . Reports confirm that a Cuban court has handed out prison sentences ranging from eight to 20 years to six Cubans for attempting to flee to the U.S. in a hijacked tugboat in April 1996.	Police arrest two prominent parliament members from the ruling New Korea Party (NKP), Hong In Kil and Chung Jae Chul, for taking a total of 900 million won in bribes in a political corruption scandal.

A	B	C	D	E
Includes developments that affect more than one world region, international organizations, and important meetings of major world leaders.	Includes all domestic and regional developments in Europe, including the Soviet Union, Turkey, Cyprus, and Malta.	Includes all domestic and regional developments in Africa and the Middle East, including Iraq and Iran and excluding Cyprus, Turkey, and Afghanistan.	Includes all domestic and regional developments in Latin America, the Caribbean, and Canada.	Includes all domestic and regional developments in Asia and Pacific nations, extending from Afghanistan through all the Pacific Islands, except Hawaii.

U.S. Politics & Social Issues	U.S. Foreign Policy & Defense	U.S. Economy & Environment	Science, Technology, & Nature	Culture, Leisure, & Lifestyle	
The CDC reports that the U.S. has the highest rates of childhood homicide and suicide out of the world's 26 richest countries. The U.S. accounts for 73% of children 14 and younger murdered in the industrialized countries surveyed.		Pres. Clinton presents a $1.69 trillion budget proposal to Congress for the 1998 fiscal year, which begins Oct. 1. The amount is a 3% increase over the current year. . . . The Senate confirms, 98-0, Rodney E. Slater as transportation secretary.		Sotheby's announces it earned $1.599 billion in sales in 1996, a 5% decrease from 1995. . . . Data suggest that the three leading TV networks devoted a total of 2,768 minutes of their weeknight newscasts to the O. J. Simpson case between June 17, 1994, and Jan. 31, 1997.	Feb. 6
	The U.S. Air Force suspends flight training operations on the East Coast following two incidents in which F-16 fighter jets flew too close to civilian airliners. . . . The INS estimates that the number of illegal immigrants in the U.S. rose to 5 million in October 1996, from 3.9 million in October 1992.		Interior Secretary Bruce Babbitt announces government plans to spend $32.8 million on the controlled burning of forest lands in fiscal year 1998.	Rap artist Snoop Doggy Dogg (Calvin Broadus) pleads guilty to weapons charges in a Los Angeles court. As part of a plea-bargain deal, Broadus agrees to perform on a series of antiviolence radio messages. . . . Lennox Lewis of Great Britain becomes the WBC's heavyweight champion after a technical knockout of Oliver McCall for the vacant title.	Feb. 7
Congressional Quarterly report that Rep. Sidney R. Yates (D, Ill.), the longest-serving current member of the House, will not seek a 25th term. At 87, Yates is the oldest House member. He was first elected in 1948 and has served in every Congress since then, except the 88th, which was in session from 1963 to 1965.			Pres. Clinton and Vice Pres. Gore announce that the Education Department has released $14.3 million in grants to help public schools connect to the Internet computer network. Clinton notes that 65% of U.S. schools have Internet connections, up from 35% in 1994.		Feb. 8
	A Marine Corps F/A-18 fighter-attack jet crashes in the Yellow Sea between South Korea and China. The plane's two crewmen, Captain Mark R. Nickles and Major Dany A. D'Eredita, are reported missing and presumed dead.			In basketball, the Eastern Conference defeats the Western Conference, 132-120, to win the NBA's 47th annual All-Star Game, in Cleveland, Ohio. In celebration of the NBA's 50th anniversary, the league's 50 greatest players of all time are honored at halftime.	Feb. 9
A civil jury orders O. J. Simpson to pay $25 million in punitive damages to the families of Nicole Brown Simpson, and Ronald L. Goldman, bringing the total damages against Simpson to $33.5 million . . . A federal jury in NYC convicts two black men, Lemrick Nelson Jr. and Charles Price, of violating the civil rights of Yankel Rosenbaum, a Hasidic Jew killed during racial rioting in 1991 . . . Alabama judge William Rhea sentences Walter Leroy Moody Jr. to death for the 1989 mail-bomb killing of a federal judge, Robert S. Vance.	Gen. Dennis J. Reimer, the U.S. Army chief of staff, announces that Sergeant Major Gene C. McKinney, the highest-ranking enlisted person in the army, has been suspended after another woman alleged that he sexually harassed her. . . . Three air force F-16s come close to civilian passenger planes over New Mexico and Texas.	In New York City, U.S. district judge Milton Pollack approves a final settlement of civil lawsuits against former financier Ivan Boesky, Martin Siegel, and Robert Freeman and others implicated in insider-trading frauds in the 1980s. . . . In Newark, New Jersey, Judge Harold Ackerman sentences Eddie Antar to 82 months in prison for defrauding shareholders of more than $74 million in a stock-manipulation scheme.	An international team of scientists agree that early human remains discovered in Chile provide conclusive evidence that human ancestors lived in the Americas 1,300 years prior to previous estimates. . . . The Russian space capsule *Soyuz* blasts off from the Baikonur space center in Kazakhstan. . . . Conrad Arensberg, 86, anthropologist who pioneered the study of modern cultures in his field in 1937, dies in Hazlet, New Jersey, of respiratory failure brought on by a long illness.	Hollywood madam Heidi Fleiss pleads guilty in Los Angeles Superior Court to one count of attempted pandering and is sentenced to 18 months in prison.	Feb. 10
	The Senate, 100-0, confirms Rep. Bill Richardson (D, N.Mex.) as U.S. ambassador to the United Nations.	The air force resumes training operations suspended Feb. 7 due to incidents in which F-16 fighter jets flew too close to civilian airliners.	The space shuttle *Discovery* blasts off from Kennedy Space Center in Cape Canaveral, Florida, on a mission to repair and service the *Hubble Space Telescope*, deployed by NASA in 1990.	At the Westminster Kennel Club Dog Show, held in NYC and considered the premier competition for dog breeders, a five-year-old standard schnauzer, Ch. Parsifal Di Casa Netzer, is judged best in show.	Feb. 11

F	G	H	I	J
Includes elections, federal-state relations, civil rights and liberties, crime, the judiciary, education, health care, poverty, urban affairs, and population.	*Includes formation and debate of U.S. foreign and defense policies, veterans' affairs, and defense spending. (Relations with specific foreign countries are usually found under the region concerned.)*	*Includes business, labor, agriculture, taxation, transportation, consumer affairs, monetary and fiscal policy, natural resources, and pollution.*	*Includes worldwide scientific, medical, and technological developments; natural phenomena; U.S. weather; natural disasters; and accidents.*	*Includes the arts, religion, scholarship, communications media, sports, entertainments, fashions, fads, and social life.*

	World Affairs	Europe	Africa & the Middle East	The Americas	Asia & the Pacific
Feb. 12	Reports indicate that the U.S., Britain, and Spain are withholding their 1997 contributions to the UN Environment Program because the troubled agency failed to adopt long-delayed reforms.... Officials reveal that the strategic town of Brcko in Bosnia-Herzegovina will remain under international supervision until 1998.	A British soldier is shot and killed by an unidentified gunman at a military base in Bessbrook, Northern Ireland.... A policeman is shot dead in Vlora, Albania, as clashes over pyramid schemes continue.... Gen. Aslan Maskhadov is sworn in as Chechnya's president.... Stefan Sofiyanskii is sworn in as a caretaker premier of Bulgaria.... Nora Beloff, 78, who, in 1964, became the first female political correspondent at Britain's *Observer*, dies in London	In Egypt, nine young Coptic Christians are killed and four are wounded when gunmen burst into a church near the town of Abu Qurqas, located about midway between Cairo and Ezbet Dawoud.	In an apparent assassination attempt, a bomb explodes on a runway in the city of Barranquilla as the plane of Colombian president Ernesto Samper Pizano is preparing to land.	Reports confirm that a prominent North Korean official, Hwang Jang Yop, entered the South Korean consulate in Beijing, China, and asked for asylum in South Korea. The reported move represents the highest-level defection ever from North Korea.
Feb. 13		During the strike started Feb. 6 by Spanish truck drivers, a protestor is killed in Villaquiran de los Infantes when an angry French driver steers his vehicle into a crowd of strikers. ... Latvia's parliament approves a new government led by Premier Andris Skele.... Brigadier Dame Mary Joan Caroline Tyrwhitt, 93, founder of Britain's Women's Royal Army Corps (WRAC), dies of unreported causes.	Alphonse-Marie Nkubito, 42, justice minister of Rwanda, 1994–95, known for his advocacy of human rights and his moderate stance on the ethnic divisions between Rwanda's Hutu and Tutsi tribes, dies in Kigali, Rwanda, of unspecified natural causes after suffering from diabetes and hypertension.	Data confirms that the MRTA leftist rebels who took over the Japanese ambassador's residence in Lima, the capital of Peru, in December still have 72 hostages.	Reports from Pakistan reveal that 25 Christian girls are missing and 13 churches were destroyed in the Feb. 6 riots, which were among the most violent attacks on Christians since Pakistan declared itself an Islamic republic in 1956.... Three prominent politicians are arrested in the scandal involving the case of the Hanbo Steel Industry Co., which is said to be the largest bankruptcy case ever in South Korea.
Feb. 14		Tajik mercenaries Bakhran Sadirov and Rizvon Sadirov release the last two of four UN military observers taken hostage Feb. 4. The brothers continue to hold other captives.	Three Hutu militants suspected of the Feb. 4 killings are slain in a clash with Rwandan security forces trying to arrest them in Karengera. Separately, a Kigali court sentences a former politician, Froduald Karamira, to death for helping lead the 1994 massacres and orders him to pay $380,000 in compensation to the victims' families. UN officials estimate that more than 200 people died in January in massacres by Hutu militants and reprisals by Rwandan security forces.	Two of Canada's top paper makers, Abitibi-Price Inc. and Stone-Consolidated Corp., announce a C$2.3 billion (US$1.7 billion) merger that will create the world's biggest newsprint producer, to be known as Abitibi-Consolidated Inc. ... Clashes between rival drug gangs erupt in Cité Soleil, a slum section of Haiti's capital, Port-au-Prince.	
Feb. 15	More than 65 countries have agreed to a breakthrough global telecommunications accord negotiated under the auspices of the World Trade Organization by which they consent to open their telephone markets to foreign as well as domestic competition.	The Tajik government flies in from Afghanistan some of the forces loyal to mercenaries Bakhran Sadirov and Rizvon Sadirov, who are holding about a dozen hostages.... In Bulgaria, the Zajedno party holds its 89th and last daily protest rally in the streets of Belgrade.... More than 8,000 people, mostly women, march in Ankara, the capital of Turkey, to protest the government's recent efforts to enact laws based on the teachings of Islam.	Guyana's Pres. Cheddi B. Jagan, 78, suffers a serious heart attack and is flown to Washington, D.C., for treatment.... Rwandan Supreme Court justice Vincent Nkezabaganwa is killed when three gunmen open fire on his car in the driveway of his house in Kigali. Nkezabaganwa's driver and a neighbor are also killed in the attack.		A prominent North Korean defector, Lee Han Yong, formerly known as Li Il Nam, is shot by apparent assassins in South Korea. The incident is the first shooting of a North Korean defector in the South.
Feb. 16		Tajik mercenaries Bakhran Sadirov and Rizvon Sadirov free their remaining hostages in response to the government's Feb. 15 act.... The Liberal Union (UL) party wins national parliamentary elections in Andorra, a small country located between France and Spain in the Pyrenees Mountains.			Data show that South Korea's current account deficit nearly tripled in 1996 to a record $23.72 billion. The nation's current account deficit is second in size only to that of the U.S.... North Korea celebrates Kim Jong Il's 55th birthday.
Feb. 17	The U.S. and South Korea announce that they will resume emergency food aid to the North in response to a new U.N. appeal for $41.6 million in famine relief.	A car bomb explodes in Bilbao, the largest city in Spain's Basque region, killing an officer in the national police force. The slaying is the year's sixth in which authorities suspected the ETA terrorist group, whereas only five terrorist killings were attributed to ETA in all of 1996. ... Several thousand teachers rally in Belgrade, the Yugoslav and Serbian capital, to protest a new collective-bargaining agreement.... Tajik mercenaries Bakhran Sadirov and Rizvon Sadirov declare their loyalty to the government of Tajik president Imamali Rakhmanov.	An army court convicts two Tutsi soldiers who are sentenced to eight years and five months in prison for killing 78 civilians at Kizuka in southern Bururi province in Dec. 1996. Three other soldiers are sentenced to between eight and 10 years for the Oct. 1996 killings of 50 people in a southern village. Separately, rebels attack Mugara, near the shore of Lake Tanganyika 45 miles (70 km) south of the capital, Bujumbura.... The Zairian military bombs three rebel-held towns in eastern Zaire. At least six people are reported killed and more than 20 others wounded in one of the towns, Bukavu.		Nawaz Sharif is sworn in as Pakistan's new prime minister.

A	B	C	D	E
Includes developments that affect more than one world region, international organizations, and important meetings of major world leaders.	Includes all domestic and regional developments in Europe, including the Soviet Union, Turkey, Cyprus, and Malta.	Includes all domestic and regional developments in Africa and the Middle East, including Iraq and Iran and excluding Cyprus, Turkey, and Afghanistan.	Includes all domestic and regional developments in Latin America, the Caribbean, and Canada.	Includes all domestic and regional developments in Asia and Pacific nations, extending from Afghanistan through all the Pacific Islands, except Hawaii.

U.S. Politics & Social Issues	U.S. Foreign Policy & Defense	U.S. Economy & Environment	Science, Technology, & Nature	Culture, Leisure, & Lifestyle	
The Population Council announces that it has settled a legal dispute that was delaying its plans to market mifepristone, a drug that induces abortion known as RU-486, once it receives final FDA approval.... Thomas B. Stoddard, 48, homosexual-rights advocate who directed the Lambda Legal Defense and Education Fund, 1986-1992, dies in New York City of complications from AIDS.	The Clinton administration states it will allow U.S. news organizations to set up bureaus in Cuba.... Reports disclose that three male instructors at an Army installation near Frankfurt, Germany, were suspended after 11 women accused them of sexual harassment.... A commission to improve aviation security causes controversy when it recommends that airlines single out travelers whose profiles match those of potential terrorists for more rigorous security checks.			Pres. Clinton states that he has chosen the Little Rock campus of the University of Arkansas as the site for his presidential library.... At the U.S. National Figure Skating Championships in Nashville, Tennessee, Elizabeth Punsalan and Jerod Swallow become the first U.S. ice-dance team win two perfect 6.0 scores.	Feb. 12
An NIH panel endorses needle-exchange programs and safe-sex education as effective means of combating the spread of the AIDS virus.... The lower house of the Mississippi state legislature passes a bill that would impose a jail term on doctors who perform certain kinds of late-term abortions. The law would also enable the fetuses' fathers to sue those doctors for "psychological and physical damages." The bill is similar to one passed by the Mississippi state Senate.	The House approves, 220-209, a request by Pres. Clinton for the early release of foreign aid for U.S. family-planning programs overseas.	A Senate committee votes to issue 52 subpoenas in fund-raising controversies surrounding Democrats and Republicans.... A U.S. District Court jury acquits two former executives of making illegal campaign donations to Henry Espy, the brother of former Agriculture Secretary Mike Espy. The acquittal is the first significant legal defeat for Donald Smaltz, who has won seven convictions or pleas of guilty or no contest in the case.... The Dow closes above 7000 for the first time.	California governor Pete Wilson (R) estimates that damage from the December 1996 and January 1997 floods caused in California by heavy rains and melting snow from the Sierra Nevada mountains will top $1.8 billion.... R(obert) K(lark) Graham, 90, optometrist who invented the first shatterproof eyeglass lens, dies in a hotel in Seattle, Washington, after falling down in the bathtub.	Reports confirm that Omus Hirshbein, program director of music, opera, and presentation at the NEA, plans to leave his post.	Feb. 13
Montana's State Senate votes to reject a numerical speed limit for daytime driving on the state's interstate highways. Montana thereby maintains its status as the only state in the U.S. that has no set daytime speed limit. Instead of setting legal limits, Montana requires daytime motorists to drive in a "reasonable and prudent" manner.	The Clinton administration orders the release of 53 illegal Chinese immigrants who have been detained since 1993 when an immigrant smuggling ship, the *Golden Venture*, ran aground in June 1993 near NYC.... The U.S. Ninth Circuit Court of Appeals in San Francisco, Calif., 2-1, upholds the military's "don't ask, don't tell" policy on homosexuals, rejecting arguments that the policy is unconstitutional because it treats homosexuals and heterosexuals differently.	The IRS rules that it will not allow residents of California and Arizona to deduct the costs of marijuana purchased for medicinal use from their federal taxes.		At the U.S. National Figure Skating Championships, Kyoko Ina and Jason Dungjen win the pairs' title, upsetting two-time defending champions Jenni Meno and Todd Sand. In the ice-dancing competition, defending champions Elizabeth Punsalan and Jerod Swallow place first.	Feb. 14
Oscar Adams, 72, former justice of the Alabama Supreme Court who, in 1982, became the first black person ever elected to statewide office in Alabama and pioneered the way as the first black member of other associations, dies in Birmingham, Alabama, of cancer.	Madeleine K. Albright embarks on her first world tour as U.S. secretary of state.	Pres. Clinton invokes emergency powers granted to the office of the president under the Railway Labor Act of 1926 and blocks a strike called by pilots employed by American Airlines Inc. Clinton's move marks the first time since 1966 that a president takes action to block an airline strike.... Reports confirm that the Treasury Department has paid about $500,000 in legal fees to seven former employees of the White House travel office who were fired in 1993.		Tara Lipinski upsets defending champion Michelle Kwan to win the women's title at the U.S. National Figure Skating Championships in Nashville, Tennessee. Lipinski, 14, is the U.S.'s youngest-ever figure-skating champion. Todd Eldredge wins his fourth men's title, followed by Michael Weiss.	Feb. 15
			Chien-Hsiung Wu, 84, physicist who was best known for a 1957 experiment in which she was able to defy physics' law of symmetry and who won the National Medal of Science, dies in New York City from a stroke.	Actress Elizabeth Taylor attends a gala to celebrate her 65th birthday at the Pantages Theater in Los Angeles.... Jeff Gordon wins the 39th annual Daytona 500 automobile race at Daytona International Speedway in Daytona Beach, Florida.	Feb. 16
		A federal court jury in Jackson, Mississippi acquits Norris Faust Jr., the former state executive director of the federal Farm Service Agency, of lying to a federal grand jury examining farm-subsidy fraud.		French sailor Christophe Auguin, 38, breaks the solo around-the-world sailing record with a time of 105 days, 20 hours, and 31 minutes.	Feb. 17

F	G	H	I	J
Includes elections, federal-state relations, civil rights and liberties, crime, the judiciary, education, health care, poverty, urban affairs, and population.	*Includes formation and debate of U.S. foreign and defense policies, veterans' affairs, and defense spending. (Relations with specific foreign countries are usually found under the region concerned.)*	*Includes business, labor, agriculture, taxation, transportation, consumer affairs, monetary and fiscal policy, natural resources, and pollution.*	*Includes worldwide scientific, medical, and technological developments; natural phenomena; U.S. weather; natural disasters; and accidents.*	*Includes the arts, religion, scholarship, communications media, sports, entertainments, fashions, fads, and social life.*

	World Affairs	Europe	Africa & the Middle East	The Americas	Asia & the Pacific
Feb. 18	The UN Security Council passes a resolution proposing a five-point peace plan for Zaire.		A tribunal in Gikongoro in Rwanda acquits Israel Nemeyimana. It is reportedly the first acquittal since Rwanda's genocide trials started in December 1996. More than 90,000 genocide suspects are awaiting trial.... Reports confirm that Israel has forcibly evicted the Jahalin, a seminomadic Bedouin tribe, from their long-term encampment near the West Bank town of Al Eizariya, ending a years-long dispute between the tribe and Israeli legal authorities.	At least 250 people are killed when a mudslide in Peru buries two villages, Ccocha and Pumaranra.... A strike started Feb. 11 by Colombia's public-sector workers ends when government and union negotiators reach an agreement. The job action was supported by some 800,000 workers, making it the largest Colombian strike in 20 years.	The Indonesian government formally approves a joint venture to develop the Busang gold lode in East Kalimantan province.
Feb. 19		Truck drivers end a strike started Feb. 6 that had blocked major highways in Spain.			Deng Xiaoping, 92, China's paramount leader, dies in Beijing, China's capital, from respiratory failure. Deng, a founder of communist China, was credited with bringing about China's current economic boom but was condemned for ordering the use of force in a 1989 crackdown on prodemocracy protesters in Beijing's Tiananmen Square. A six-day period of mourning is declared.... Prosecutors indict 10 senior politicians and businessmen in a loans scandal involving Hanbo Steel Industry Co. in South Korea.
Feb. 20	The World Trade Organization sets up a panel to rule on a dispute between the EU and the U.S. over the U.S.'s Helms-Burton Act, which seeks to strengthen the U.S.'s economic embargo of Cuba by punishing foreign companies that invest in Cuba.	In downtown Tirana, the capital of Albania, police scuffle with a crowd of 1,000 people protesting pyramid schemes. Four people are injured. A peaceful demonstration of 7,000 people is staged in a Tirana suburb. Several dozen students in Vlora, Albania, begin hunger strikes to call for the resignation of the government.... Poland's parliament approves a bill that will allow the country's small Jewish community to attempt to recover assets stolen by the Nazi regime during World War II.	Data suggests that 5,000 Palestinian males remain imprisoned in Israel.	In El Salvador, two FMLN campaign workers are killed and three others are injured in a machine-gun attack by masked men in the town of Nejapa.	A vessel carrying Sri Lankan Tamils sinks as it heads to India. Officials reveal that 165 people aboard are presumed dead.... Seven people are killed in an attack on an Iranian cultural center in Multan, in Punjab state, Pakistan.... Hong Kong's designated chief executive, Tung Chee-hwa, reveals that he will retain Hong Kong's current top civil servants after the colony reverts to Chinese sovereignty.
Feb. 21		After staging three months of daily protests when the ruling Socialist coalition nullified November 1996 municipal election returns, the opposition Zajedno (Together) coalition takes control of the city council of Belgrade, the Serbian and Yugoslav capital. The Belgrade council is the last of the 14 cities where Zajedno won to come under opposition control.... Britain's High Court frees three men who were in prison for more than 17 years for a murder they claim not to have committed.	Foreign aid workers in Burundi report that the army has killed more than 100 civilians in retaliation for the Feb. 17 rebel attack in Mugara, near the shore of Lake Tanganyika, 45 miles (70 km) south of the capital, Bujumbura. The aid workers also reveal that the army had killed 51 people in reprisal for a rebel attack at Burambi in northwestern Burundi. The government contests those reports, arguing that troops killed no civilians in reprisal and that the rebels killed 13 people and destroyed a health center.		North Korea announces the replacement of Premier Kang Song San with his deputy, Hong Song Nam, who will serve as acting premier. North Korean defense minister Choe Kwang, 78, dies of a heart attack.
Feb. 22		At least 20,000 demonstrators march in Paris to protest proposed new immigration laws in France.		A judge in Bogota, Colombia's capital, extends convicted drug lord Miguel Rodriguez Orejuela's prison sentence from a relatively lenient term of nine years to 23 years. The earlier sentence for Rodriguez, one of the reputed leaders of the Cali cartel, had prompted an angry reaction from the U.S.	Reports confirm that members of the Warriors of Jhangvi, a militant Sunni Muslim group, have claimed responsibility for the Feb. 20 attack in Multan, in Punjab state.
Feb. 23		Oscar Lewenstein, 80, British theatrical and film producer best known for the 1956 stage production of John Osborne's play *Look Back in Anger*, dies of unreported causes.			Pakistan's prime minister, Nawaz Sharif, announces the adoption of a Monday-through-Friday work week. Since 1977, businesses and government offices have shut down on Fridays so that devout Muslims in the largely Islamic country could attend religious services.

A	B	C	D	E
Includes developments that affect more than one world region, international organizations, and important meetings of major world leaders.	*Includes all domestic and regional developments in Europe, including the Soviet Union, Turkey, Cyprus, and Malta.*	*Includes all domestic and regional developments in Africa and the Middle East, including Iraq and Iran and excluding Cyprus, Turkey, and Afghanistan.*	*Includes all domestic and regional developments in Latin America, the Caribbean, and Canada.*	*Includes all domestic and regional developments in Asia and Pacific nations, extending from Afghanistan through all the Pacific Islands, except Hawaii.*

U.S. Politics & Social Issues	U.S. Foreign Policy & Defense	U.S. Economy & Environment	Science, Technology, & Nature	Culture, Leisure, & Lifestyle	
		In *U.S. v. Brockamp*, the Supreme Court rules unanimously that a time limit for claiming IRS refunds should not be extended to account for a taxpayer's mental incompetence.... In *Robinson v. Shell Oil Co.*, the Supreme Court rules unanimously that a federal law that prohibits employers from retaliating against employees. who bring discrimination claims against them so extends to former employees.... The Dow closes at 7067.46, marking the 13th record high in 1997.	Daniel Carleton Gajdusek, a winner of the 1976 Nobel Prize in Medicine, pleads guilty to sexually abusing one of dozens of boys he brought back from Micronesia to live with him in the U.S. Under the plea agreement, he will serve between nine months and one year in prison and spend five years on probation.	Actor Al Pacino is named a member of the artistic directorate of London's Globe Theatre. . . . Emily Hahn, 92, author who published 54 books and more than 200 articles, dies in New York City of unreported causes.	Feb. 18
In *Schenck v. Pro-Choice Network*, the Supreme Court rules, 6-3, to uphold a court-ordered imposition of buffer zones that ban antiabortion protesters from staging demonstrations within 15 feet (4.6 m) of abortion clinic entrances in upstate New York. . . . In *Maryland v. Wilson*, the Supreme Court rules, 7-2, that police officers may order all occupants of an automobile to get out of the car during a routine traffic stop.	The U.S. Army drops criminal charges of sexual misconduct against Staff Sergeant Nathanael C. Beach, a drill instructor at the Aberdeen Proving Ground in Maryland.	The Commerce Department reports that the U.S. recorded a $114.23 billion deficit in trade in goods and services in 1996. That is up 8.7% from the revised 1995 deficit of $105.06 billion and the largest calendar-year gap since 1988. . . . Six labor unions end a bitter 19-month-long strike against the *Detroit Free Press* and the *Detroit News*, the two major daily newspapers in Detroit, Michigan The agreement ends the longest newspaper strike in U.S. history.	Reports reveal that users of on-line services on the Internet were bilked out of thousands of dollars through a scam that reroutes connections to overseas telephone numbers. The connections reportedly were transferred to the Eastern European nation of Moldova after the Internet sites, at the request of users, began to download pornographic pictures.	Leo Rosten, 88, writer and language expert best known for his book *The Joys of Yiddish* (1968), dies in New York City of unreported causes.	Feb. 19
	Justin C. Elzie, an openly homosexual Marine Corps sergeant, is given an honorable discharge and a $30,000 early retirement bonus as part of a lawsuit settlement filed after the Marine Corps in March 1993 attempted to discharge Elzie without benefits.	U.S. District Court judge Norma Holloway Johnson sentences Robert V. Rota, the former postmaster of the House Post Office, to four months in prison for permitting former Reps. Dan Rostenkowski (D, Ill.) and Joseph P. Kolter (D, Pa.) to exchange stamps for cash.	The National Transportation Safety Board announces that the Boeing 737 jet is less safe than other planes. Unlike other jets, the 737's rudder is controlled by a single valve. . . . A panel of experts called together by the NIH recommends further study into marijuana's medicinal benefits.	Ruth Clark, 80, pollster best known for her 1979 survey that sparked the emergence of what was dubbed the "news you can use" format, dies in New York City of lung cancer.	Feb. 20
	Army officials confirm that 10 more women have come forward with allegations of sexual misconduct against the instructors in Frankfurt, Germany.	The USDA reports that it found traces of bone, bone marrow, and spinal cord in ground beef produced by a newly adopted mechanical deboning system, known as advanced meat recovery (AMR), which uses hydraulic pressure to separate meat from the bone. The USDA states it will tighten the regulations for AMR processing.	The space shuttle *Discovery* lands at Kennedy Space Center in Cape Canaveral, Florida, after carrying out its mission to repair and service the *Hubble Space Telescope*, deployed by NASA in 1990. . . . The NTSB reveals that a total of 380 people died in large-carrier air accidents in 1996, the greatest number of such air deaths since 1985. A total of 1,070 people were killed in 2,040 civil aviation accidents in 1996, an 11% increase in deaths from the 962 reported in 1995.		Feb. 21
A fire destroys the Oak Grove Christian Methodist Episcopal Church in rural Elko, Georgia. . . . In Jacksonville, Florida, children attending a bar mitzvah find a bomb behind a wall in a synagogue where former Israeli prime minister Shimon Peres gave a speech a week earlier. Federal and local law-enforcement teams and Israeli security personnel had searched the synagogue after a threat had been phoned in, but had failed to find the bomb.		Albert Shanker, 68, president of the American Federation of Teachers, 1974–97, a labor organization that represents 900,000 teachers, dies in New York City of bladder cancer.		Robert William Sarnoff, 78, former president of RCA Corp., 1965–75, and former president of NBC, 1956–65, dies in New York City of cancer.	Feb. 22
The former head of the NAACP, Benjamin F. Chavis Jr., announces that he is converting to Islam and joining the controversial Nation of Islam group.	A gunman identified as Ali Abu Kamal opens fire with a semiautomatic handgun on the 86th-floor observation deck of the Empire State Building, killing a tourist from Denmark and injuring six others before committing suicide.		Researchers in Scotland report they have created the first genetic clone of an adult animal, a Finn Dorset lamb named Dolly, which has a genetic makeup identical to that of her mother. The major scientific breakthrough prompts a flood of media reports and public speculation worldwide about the dangers of human cloning.	Tony Williams, 51, jazz drummer known for helping to pioneer jazz-rock fusion, dies in Daly City, California, while recovering from a gall bladder operation. . . . Frank Launder, 89, screenwriter and film director who directed the St. Trinian's movie series, dies in Monaco of unreported causes.	Feb. 23

F	G	H	I	J
Includes elections, federal-state relations, civil rights and liberties, crime, the judiciary, education, health care, poverty, urban affairs, and population.	Includes formation and debate of U.S. foreign and defense policies, veterans' affairs, and defense spending. (Relations with specific foreign countries are usually found under the region concerned.)	Includes business, labor, agriculture, taxation, transportation, consumer affairs, monetary and fiscal policy, natural resources, and pollution.	Includes worldwide scientific, medical, and technological developments; natural phenomena; U.S. weather; natural disasters; and accidents.	Includes the arts, religion, scholarship, communications media, sports, entertainments, fashions, fads, and social life.

	World Affairs	Europe	Africa & the Middle East	The Americas	Asia & the Pacific
Feb. 24			Reports suggest that Burundi's Tutsi-dominated military has set up more than a dozen "protection zones" for Hutu civilians while soldiers battle Hutu rebels.		Chinese officials pay final respects to Deng Xiaoping, China's late paramount leader, in a ceremony in Beijing attended by 10,000 Communist Party members. In accordance with tradition, no foreign dignitaries are invited to the service.... The Taliban breaks a military stalemate when their forces north of Kabul displace Hizb-i-Wahdat fighters from the strategic Shibar Pass, which is considered a gateway to northern Afghanistan.
Feb. 25		Estonian premier Tiit Vahi, who has been linked to a privatization scandal, resigns.... The British government announces plans to sell London's subway system, the London Underground, to private investors.... Nenad Dusan Popovic, 87, economist who in 1961 became one of the highest-ranking Yugoslav officials to defect to the West, dies in New York City of bone cancer.... Andrei Sinyavsky, 71, Russian author and dissident, dies in Paris, France, of cancer.		Mexico announces that 36 officers who served at the National Institute to Combat Drugs have been fired and states that more dismissals are imminent.	Three bus bombs explode simultaneously in Xinjiang's capital, Urumqi, killing nine people and wounding 74. A fourth bomb does not explode. Some reports speculate that the bombs were timed to coincide with president Jiang Zemin eulogy for Deng Xiaoping, China's late paramount leader.... South Korean president Kim apologizes for the Hanbo Steel bankruptcy scandal, although he has not been directly linked to the controversy .... Lee Han Yong, a prominent North Korean defector shot Feb. 15, dies of his wounds in South Korea.
Feb. 26	A UN spokesman reveals that Secretary General Kofi Annan has dismissed two top officials at the war crimes tribunal after an internal investigation found widespread mismanagement, incompetence and financial abuses.	Giuseppe (Nuccio) Bertone, 82, Italian sports car designer, dies in Turin, Italy, of unreported causes.	The cabinet of Israeli prime minister Benjamin Netanyahu approves the development of a large Jewish neighborhood in East Jerusalem despite Palestinian warnings that any such construction in the traditionally Arab sector of the city may prove fatal to the peace process. The decision sparks international condemnation.	In clashes between rival drug gangs that started Feb. 14 in Cité Soleil, a slum section of Haiti's capital, Port-au-Prince, at least 70 shacks are destroyed in fires.	In the midst of the the Hanbo steel scandal in South Korea, which has included the arrest of three prominent politicians on Feb. 13, the entire cabinet tenders resignations.
Feb. 27		After weeks of debate and protests, France's National Assembly approves a bill that will increase the government's power to deport immigrants.... Estonian president Lennart Meri names Mart Siiman premier.... An amendment ending the Irish constitution's divorce ban goes into effect, making divorce universally available for the first time in the history of the Irish Republic.... Restrictions on the ownership of handguns in Britain goes into effect.	In response to the Israeli government's Feb, 26 decision to develop a Jewish neighborhood in East Jerusalem, hundreds of Palestinians, many carrying Palestinian flags and olive branches, march toward the slated site, known to Israelis as Har Homa. When Israeli soldiers prevent them from reaching the location, the protesters hold a peaceful demonstration nearby.		Soldiers from Myanmar, formerly Burma, cross into Thailand and attempt to attack an encampment that houses ethnic Karens from Myanmar. The Thai military prevents the Myanmar troops from reaching the refugee camp.... Kim Kwang Jin, 69, North Korea's first vice minister of the armed forces, dies of an "incurable disease."
Feb. 28		In Albania, residents of Vlora, Fier, Gjirokaster, and Sarande take up arms. In Vlora, members of the Shik secret police attempt to storm the building where hunger strikers are housed. In response, townspeople surround the Shik headquarters begin a gun battle that results in 10 dead, most of them police.... In Belgium, Renault workers protest plans to close a factory, and they block finished cars from leaving the plant.	The province of Ardabil in northwest Iran is struck by a powerful earthquake. The official death toll is set at close to 1,000. The quake is reported to measure between 5.5 and 6.1 on the Richter scale An estimated 2,600 people are injured and 40,000 others left homeless by the quake.	Reports confirm that at least 18 people have been killed in clashes between rival drug gangs that began Feb. 14 in Cité Soleil, a slum section of Haiti's capital, Port-au-Prince.	A powerful earthquake hits western Pakistan, killing at least 100 people. The quake, centered in Baluchistan province, measures 7.3 on the Richter scale.
March 1		In Albania, Pres. Sali Berisha asks the government of Premier Aleksandr Meksi to resign, in an effort to mollify protesters.... Neo-Nazis and rightist politicians hold a rally in Munich, Germany, to protest an exhibition depicting German soldiers' participation in World War II-era atrocities. The groups opposing the exhibit include the Christian Social Union (CSU), a junior partner of the Christian Democratic Party in Germany's ruling coalition.	Rwandan Hutu refugees flee the Tingi Tingi camps on the Zaire River when they are overrun by the rebels.		

A	B	C	D	E
Includes developments that affect more than one world region, international organizations, and important meetings of major world leaders.	Includes all domestic and regional developments in Europe, including the Soviet Union, Turkey, Cyprus, and Malta.	Includes all domestic and regional developments in Africa and the Middle East, including Iraq and Iran and excluding Cyprus, Turkey, and Afghanistan.	Includes all domestic and regional developments in Latin America, the Caribbean, and Canada.	Includes all domestic and regional developments in Asia and Pacific nations, extending from Afghanistan through all the Pacific Islands, except Hawaii.

U.S. Politics & Social Issues	U.S. Foreign Policy & Defense	U.S. Economy & Environment	Science, Technology, & Nature	Culture, Leisure, & Lifestyle	
	New York City police commissioner Howard Safir says police believe the Feb. 23 attack atop the Empire State Building was the work of a "deranged individual" with no links to terrorist groups. . . . Reps. Lamar S. Smith (R, Tex.) and J. Dennis Hastert (R, Ill.) disclose that 180,000 applicants were granted U.S. citizenship from August 1995 to September 1996 before required fingerprint checks for criminal records were completed by the FBI.	Justice Department officials disclose that SmithKline Beecham PLC has agreed to pay $325 million to settle allegations that one of its subsidiaries overbilled government-funded health-care programs. It is the largest civil health-care settlement in U.S. history.			Feb. 24
Police in Jacksonville, Florida, have charged an Orthodox Jewish man, Harry Shapiro, 31, with planting the pipe bomb found in a synagogue on Feb. 22.	Reports reveal that the CIA warned the army about the possible presence of chemical weapons at an Iraqi ammunition depot days before U.S. troops demolished the site. Since Pentagon officials had previously maintained that the army learned that poisonous gases may have been present at the depot only after its destruction, the report causes controversy. . . . Statistics reveal that the number of servicemen and women discharged from the military for homosexual conduct has increased since the Defense Department adopted its "don't ask, don't tell" policy in 1994.	Internal White House documents reveal that in 1995 Pres. Clinton enthusiastically endorsed plans to reward big contributors to the Democratic Party by offering them various perquisites, including golf games and morning outings with the president and overnight stays in the White House's Lincoln Bedroom. The report sparks controversy.		John E. du Pont, an heir to the du Pont chemical fortune, is convicted by a Media, Pennsylvania, jury of fatally shooting Olympic wrestler David Schultz in January 1996. The jury also rules that he is mentally ill. . . . Cal Abrams, 72, baseball player for the Brooklyn Dodgers and other teams in the 1950s, dies in Fort Lauderdale, Florida, after suffering a heart attack.	Feb. 25
	In response to the Feb. 25 report regarding knowledge of poison gases in Iraq, Pres. Clinton orders his Presidential Advisory Committee on Gulf Veterans' Illnesses to investigate the matter and to report its findings within 60 days.	FDIC officials announce that the Rose Law Firm, where First Lady Hillary Clinton once worked, has agreed to pay more than $250,000 to the government as part of a billing dispute settlement. . . . The House votes, 347-73, to reinstate a package of aviation taxes through Sept. 30.	The Vatican appeals for a global ban on human cloning.	David Doyle, 67, popular TV actor, dies in Los Angeles of a heart attack. . . . At the Grammys, LeAnn Rimes, 14, becomes the first country artist ever to win the best new artist award. The Record of the Year award goes to "Change the World," by Eric Clapton.	Feb. 26
A federal jury convicts a plastic surgeon, Jose Castillo, for performing surgery on a fugitive drug dealer to help him elude police. . . . The CDC reports that AIDS deaths nationwide have declined for the first time since 1981. Deaths from AIDS fell 12% in the first six months of 1996. . . . A jury in Rochester, N.Y., convicts John Horace, a nurse's aide, of raping an unidentified woman who was in a coma-like state in 1995. The woman became pregnant and gave birth while still in a vegetative state before dying.	A Fayetteville, North Carolina, jury convicts James N. Burmeister, a white former army soldier, of murder in the slaying of a black couple, Jackie Burden, 27, and Michael James, 36, in 1995. Prosecutors argued that the soldier is a neo-Nazi skinhead who targeted the couple because of their race in a case that prompted the army to investigate the activity of extremist groups in its ranks.	The Senate approves by voice vote a bill that renews a package of aviation taxes through Sept. 30.			Feb. 27
In Los Angeles, California, two heavily armed bank robbers are shot and killed in a gun battle with police that is filmed by news helicopters and broadcast live on six Los Angeles TV stations. The men fire hundreds of rounds at police and bystanders. Eleven police officers and six civilians are injured. . . . Charles Dederich, 83, founder of a successful drug-rehabilitation program, Synanon, which was later criticized for allegedly violent tactics, dies of cardiorespiratory failure.	Former FBI agent Earl Edwin Pitts pleads guilty to conspiracy to commit espionage and attempted espionage in federal court in Alexandria, Virginia. Pitts is only the second FBI agent ever to be convicted of espionage. . . . The Clinton administration issues its annual report on antidrug efforts of countries receiving U.S. aid. A notable point is that the U.S. "certifies" Mexico. The U.S. decertifies Colombia for the second straight year.	President Clinton signs a bill that renews a package of aviation taxes through Sept. 30. . . . In Oxford, Mississippi, Judge L. T. Senter acquits Henry Espy, the brother of former Agriculture Secretary Mike Espy, on five counts of making false statements in connection with his 1993 election campaign. . . . DNC officials plan to return an additional $1.5 million in contributions, bringing the total amount returned by the committee since October 1996 to more than $3 million.	The federal Office of Research Integrity (ORI) clears Bernard Fisher, a prominent research physician, of 1994 charges of misconduct related to a major study of breast-cancer treatments that he led.	Los Angeles Superior Court judge Stephen Czuleger sentences rap music entrepreneur Marion (Suge) Knight to nine years in prison for violating his probation.	Feb. 28
			Scientists in Beaverton, Oregon, announce that they have created two monkey clones from embryo cells. The team's success marks the first time that close relatives of humans has been cloned. . . . Tornadoes hit Arkansas.		March 1

F	G	H	I	J
Includes elections, federal-state relations, civil rights and liberties, crime, the judiciary, education, health care, poverty, urban affairs, and population.	Includes formation and debate of U.S. foreign and defense policies, veterans' affairs, and defense spending. (Relations with specific foreign countries are usually found under the region concerned.)	Includes business, labor, agriculture, taxation, transportation, consumer affairs, monetary and fiscal policy, natural resources, and pollution.	Includes worldwide scientific, medical, and technological developments; natural phenomena; U.S. weather; natural disasters; and accidents.	Includes the arts, religion, scholarship, communications media, sports, entertainments, fashions, fads, and social life.

	World Affairs	Europe	Africa & the Middle East	The Americas	Asia & the Pacific
March 2		Violence continues in Albania as gangs loot Pres. Sali Berisha's summer home near Vlora. Townspeople in Sarande ransack security forces' headquarters, and armed civilians in Gjirokaster burn down the police station. The Albanian parliament decrees a nationwide state of emergency.	The province of Ardabil in northwest Iran is hit by strong aftershocks from the Feb. 28 earthquake, some measuring as high as 5.1, causing further damage to the region.		
March 3		Students in Vlora, Albania, end hunger strikes that started Feb. 20. Despite the violent protests, Parliament reelects Pres. Sali to a second five-year term. . . . Several thousand environmental protesters hold a demonstration, erect blockades, and sabotage rail lines in an effort to block a massive delivery of nuclear waste to a facility in the town of Gorleben in Germany. . . . More than 4,000 Renault employees hold a protest march in Brussels, Belgium. . . . Stanislav S. Shatalin, 62, Soviet economist who, during the perestroika era, advocated the breakup of the Soviet Union, dies in Moscow of unreported causes.	Palestinians stage a five-hour general strike in East Jerusalem, the West Bank, and Gaza Strip to protest the settlement plan announced in late February.		At least 125 people are killed and another 175 people are injured when a 17-car passenger train derails while en route to Karachi, Pakistan, from Peshawar. . . . Cambodia's opposition leader Sam Rainsy holds a rally in which at least 16 of Sam's supporters are killed and another 100, including Sam, are wounded in a grenade attack on the protest.
March 4	A new international economic group known as the Six Market Group, or the Group of Six (G-6), holds its inaugural meeting in Tokyo, Japan. The G-6 nations are Japan, China, Hong Kong, Singapore, Australia, and the U.S.	Some 10,000 demonstrators gather in Dannenberg, Germany, to protest the transfer of nuclear material. Some protestors erect blockades and throw firebombs at police officers. . . . Albanian army tanks enter the town of Gjirokaster. . . . A bomb damages a Sarajevo church.			In an effort to distance the government from a loans scandal involving Hanbo Steel Industry Co., South Korean president Kim Young Sam appoints Koh Kun, as the new premier, succeeding Lee Soo Sung. . . . Data reveals that more than 1,500 people have died in railway accidents in Pakistan in recent years.
March 5		Belarussian president Aleksandr Lukashenko decrees a ban on public demonstrations against the 1996 constitution. . . . A massive delivery of nuclear waste arrives in the northern German town of Gorleben after several protests, during which the government deployed 30,000 police officers in the country's biggest security operation in over 50 years. . . . The Swiss government announces plans to create a fund that will provide financial compensation to victims of the Nazi Holocaust and of other catastrophes and human-rights violations. . . . Reports suggest that Albanian government jets attacked the village of Delvina, near Sarande.			South Korean president Kim Young Sam implements a major shuffle of his cabinet in a move aimed at distancing the government from a loans scandal involving Hanbo Steel Industry Co.
March 6	Justice Michael MacDonald of Nova Scotia Supreme Court rules that he has no authority to extradite to Romania six Taiwanese sailors accused in the 1996 deaths of three Romanian stowaways on the high seas. Stephen Hsia, a Taiwanese government attaché in Canada, declares that the six will be arrested upon their return to Taiwan.	Reports suggest that at least 25 people have died since Feb. 28, when residents of towns across southern Albania took up arms and confronted authorities. . . . Armenia's premier, Armen Sarkisyan, resigns in poor health. . . . Data confirm an outbreak of E. coli has resulted in 20 deaths since November 1996, making it Britain's worst epidemic ever.		Cheddi B. Jagan, 78, the president of Guyana, dies in Washington D.C., of a heart attack suffered Feb. 15. Samuel Hinds is sworn in as Guyana's interim president. . . . Michael Norman Manley, 72, three-term prime minister of Jamaica, 1972–80, 1989–92, dies near Kingston, Jamaica, of prostate cancer.	Nepal's Premier Sher Bahadur Deuba resigns after his government loses a confidence vote. . . . Although it is not immediately reported, a car bomb explodes in Beijing, China. No one is injured.
March 7		Coal miners in Germany launch a series of strikes and demonstrations to protest the government's plan to reduce subsidies on the price of coal.		Ecuador's Supreme Court charges former president Abdala Bucaram Ortiz, who was ousted by Congress in February, and four of his former aides with corruption.	A home-made bomb explodes on a public bus in a busy shopping area of Beijing, the Chinese capital, wounding 11 people.

A	B	C	D	E
Includes developments that affect more than one world region, international organizations, and important meetings of major world leaders.	Includes all domestic and regional developments in Europe, including the Soviet Union, Turkey, Cyprus, and Malta.	Includes all domestic and regional developments in Africa and the Middle East, including Iraq and Iran and excluding Cyprus, Turkey, and Afghanistan.	Includes all domestic and regional developments in Latin America, the Caribbean, and Canada.	Includes all domestic and regional developments in Asia and Pacific nations, extending from Afghanistan through all the Pacific Islands, except Hawaii.

U.S. Politics & Social Issues	U.S. Foreign Policy & Defense	U.S. Economy & Environment	Science, Technology, & Nature	Culture, Leisure, & Lifestyle	
Leanne Katz, 65, free-speech advocate who served as the executive director of the National Coalition against Censorship since its founding in 1974, dies in New York City of cancer.		Judi Bari, 47, environmental activist who gained recognition in the 1990s for her protests against the destruction of California's redwood trees, dies in Willits, California, of cancer.	A spate of tornadoes kill a total of at least 25 people in Arkansas. . . . J. Carson Mark, 83, Canadian-born mathematician who played a key role in the development of the hydrogen bomb, dies in Los Alamos, New Mexico, after a year-long battle with nerve paralysis.		March 2
In *U.S. v. Gonzales*, the Supreme Court rules, 7-2, that individuals sentenced to a mandatory five-year federal prison sentence for using a gun in the commission of a narcotics crime should serve that sentence after they complete their state prison terms. . . . In *Arizonans for Official English v. Arizona*, the Supreme Court rules unanimously to set aside a lower court's decision that struck down an amendment to the Arizona state constitution requiring all government employees to speak only English while at work. . . . U.S. district judge Simeon T. Lake declares a mistrial in the case of Dr. Stanislaw Burzynski, who is charged with dispensing a cancer drug not yet approved by the FDA.	Former CIA officer Harold James Nicholson pleads guilty to selling top-secret information to Russia. Nicholson is the highest-ranking CIA officer ever to be convicted of espionage. . . . A study by the U.S.-based American Association for World Health finds that the U.S. economic embargo of Cuba is having a negative effect on the health of the Cuban people. Since 1992, when the embargo was tightened under the Cuban Democracy Act, doctors have been forced to work without adequate equipment, and patients often are unable to obtain necessary drugs.		In *Warner-Jenkinson Co. Inc. v. Hilton Davis Chemical Co.*, the Supreme Court rules unanimously to uphold the "doctrine of equivalents," a principle of patent law that the high court established in 1950. Under the principle, patented products, as well as the processes by which they are created, are provided patent protection from products that are not only identical but also those that are deemed substantially equivalent to them.	*Sole Survivor* by Dean Koontz tops the bestseller list.	March 3
		For the third time in three years, the Senate rejects a proposed amendment to the Constitution requiring the federal government to balance its budget. The 66-34 vote is one vote short of the two-thirds needed.	Pres. Clinton imposes a ban on the federal funding of human cloning research. . . . Robert Henry Dicke, 80, physicist who earned recognition for his challenges to physicist Albert Einstein's theory of relativity, dies in Princeton, New Jersey, of complications from Parkinson's disease.	Roger William Brown, 54, professional basketball player for the Indiana Pacers in the late 1960s and early 1970s, dies in Indianapolis, Indiana, of liver cancer.	March 4
The two heavily armed bank robbers who were shot and killed Feb. 28 during a televised gun battle with police are identified as Larry Eugene Phillips Jr., 26, and Emil Dechebal Matasareanu, 30.	Pres. Clinton orders the ATF to tighten a regulation requiring legal immigrants to prove they resided in a state for at least 90 days before buying a firearm. . . . The Senate votes, 99-1, to approve Pres. Clinton's appointment of Charlene Barshefsky as U.S. trade representative.	Arthur A. Gross, the IRS's chief information officer, admits that the agency has wasted about $400 million over the past 10 years in attempts to modernize its computer systems.		Reports confirm that the 1997 John M. Templeton Prize for Progress in Religion will be awarded to Pandurang Shastri Athavale, an Indian spiritual leader who espouses the belief that God is present in everyone, regardless of one's class or caste. . . . The Baseball Hall of Fame selects Tommy Lasorda, Nelson (Nellie) Fox, and Willie Wells Sr. for induction.	March 5
A Washington, D.C., Superior Court jury awards $1.7 million in damages to Martha Dixon Martinez, whose husband, a FBI agent, was killed in 1994 when Bennie Lee Lawson Jr. opened fire with an assault pistol at the D.C. police headquarters.	Presiding judge Coy Brewer Jr. of Cumberland County Superior Court sentences former soldier James Burmeister, convicted Feb. 27 on two counts of first-degree murder and conspiracy in the deaths of Jackie Burden, 27, and Michael James, 36, to two consecutive life terms in prison without parole.	In Charlotte, North Carolina, U.S. district judge Robert Potter awards $601 million in damages to franchisees of Meineke Discount Muffler Shops Inc., whose parent company is alleged to have skimmed $31 million over a 10-year period from an advertising fund set up by the chain's 2,500 U.S. franchises.		Long Island (New York) University announces the 11 winners of the annual George Polk Memorial Award for excellence in journalism in 1996.	March 6
	In Honduras, U.S. drug-enforcement agents arrest Joseph Michel François, the former police chief of Port-au-Prince, Haiti's capital, on charges of drug smuggling.	Judge Robert W. Sweet of U.S. District Court in New York City sentences Steven Hoffenberg, the former chairman of Towers Financial Corp., to 20 years in prison for defrauding thousands of investors in one of the largest Ponzi schemes in U.S. history. The sentence is reportedly one of the longest ever imposed for securities fraud. . . . UPS flies its first charter passenger flight, carrying 115 passengers from Pittsburgh, Pennsylvania, to Orlando, Florida.	Floods are affecting tens of thousands of residents of the Ohio River Valley in Indiana, Kentucky, Ohio, Tennessee, and West Virginia. The city of Louisville, Kentucky, is saved from heavy damage by flood walls when the river crests at 16 feet (5 m) above flood level. . . . Edward Mills Purcell, 84, scientist who won the Nobel Prize in Physics in 1952 for his discovery of a method to detect the magnetic waves emanating from the nuclei of atoms, dies in Cambridge, Massachusetts, of respiratory failure.	Chuck Green, 78, one of the most acclaimed tap dancers of the 20th century, dies in Oakland, California, after a long illness. . . . Pernilla Wiberg of Sweden clinches the women's overall title for the alpine skiing World Cup when she places third in the super giant slalom at Mammoth Mountain, California. . . . Roman Catholic cardinals in seven U.S. cities send a letter to Pres. Bill Clinton urging him to outlaw a method of late-term abortion.	March 7

F	G	H	I	J
Includes elections, federal-state relations, civil rights and liberties, crime, the judiciary, education, health care, poverty, urban affairs, and population.	*Includes formation and debate of U.S. foreign and defense policies, veterans' affairs, and defense spending. (Relations with specific foreign countries are usually found under the region concerned.)*	*Includes business, labor, agriculture, taxation, transportation, consumer affairs, monetary and fiscal policy, natural resources, and pollution.*	*Includes worldwide scientific, medical, and technological developments; natural phenomena; U.S. weather; natural disasters; and accidents.*	*Includes the arts, religion, scholarship, communications media, sports, entertainments, fashions, fads, and social life.*

	World Affairs	Europe	Africa & the Middle East	The Americas	Asia & the Pacific
March 8		Violence in Albania continues, and Gjirokaster, site of the country's largest military base in the south, falls to the rebels.			In South Korea, the ruling and opposition parties reach an agreement on a labor bill to replace the legislation passed earlier that led to a month of protests and strikes.
March 9		In Albania, looters break into a Kalashnikov assault-rifle factory in Polican, 89 miles (140 km) south of Tirana, and make off with up to 40,000 firearms.... Jean-Dominique Bauby, 44, French journalist best known for his recently published book about his experience of being paralyzed, dies near Paris of unreported causes.... Dame C(icely) V(eronica) Wedgwood, 86, British historian and author who, in 1968, received the Order of Merit, dies in London of unreported causes.	King Hussein of Jordan tells Israeli prime minister Benjamin Netanyahu that planned construction of a new Jewish settlement in Arab East Jerusalem will lead to an "inevitable violent (Palestinian) resistance" and may trigger a bloody Israeli crackdown that could "bury the peace process for all time."		Taiwan's state-funded Central News Agency reports that ethnic Uighur separatists have claimed responsibility for the Mar. 7 Beijing bus attack.
March 10	The war-crimes trial of three Muslims and a Serb opens in The Hague. The four—Hazim Delic, Esad Landzo, and Zejnil Delalic, all Muslims, and Zdravko Mucic, a Croat—are the first people to be tried at the tribunal for atrocities against Serbs.	In Albania, gangs capture an air base in Kucove, 37 miles south of Tirana, where 19 MiG fighter aircraft are based.... Thousands of coal miners protest in Bonn and Berlin.	Ibrahim Maqadmeh, regarded by Israel as a leader of a secret Hamas military cell, is reportedly released from jail by PLO authorities. ... The Vatican establishes full diplomatic relations with Libya.	The Mexican government appoints Mariano Herran Salvatti as the new head of the National Institute to Combat Drugs, the nation's top antidrug agency.	King Birendra of Nepal names Lokendra Bahadur Chand as the new premier.... South Korea's National Assembly approves a new labor bill that replaces a controversial law, passed clandestinely in December 1996, that set off nearly a month of strikes and protests.... A Lahore, Pakistan, court rules to uphold the marriage of an Islamic couple who wed in February 1996 without first receiving permission from the woman's parents.
March 11		Reports confirm that Serb gangs have destroyed and burned 15 prefabricated houses built by Muslim returnees in the village of Gajevi, which is in the zone of separation between Muslim-Croat and Serb territory.... Russian president Boris Yeltsin dismisses most of his cabinet and asks Premier Viktor Chernomyrdin to restructure the cabinet. ... In Albania, Parliament passes an amnesty. Pres. Sali Berisha names Bashkim Fino as premier and forms a new government.			Although it is not immediately reported, the PNC nuclear-waste reprocessing center in Tokaimura experiences what is considered Japan's worst-ever nuclear accident when a fire breaks, followed by an explosion 10 hours later. The accident exposes at least 37 workers to low-level radiation—although none are immediately harmed—and releases radioactivity into the atmosphere.
March 12		In Russia, the Duma passes a bill granting an amnesty for Chechen. ... The Albanian government loses control of Ballsh, 50 miles south of Tirana.... Russian coast guard ships fire on nine Turkish fishing boats in the Black Sea that are allegedly poaching in Georgian waters. One fisherman is killed.... In Poland, 2,000 shipyard workers block roads to protest the impending closing of a shipbuilding company.	Nigeria's military government charges 1986 Nobel literature laureate Wole Soyinka and 11 other dissidents with treason in connection with a recent series of bombings around the country.	The Constitutional Court, Colombia's highest court, rules that a state of economic emergency declared by Pres. Ernesto Samper Pizano in January was unconstitutional.... Talks between the Peruvian government and leftist rebels holding 72 hostages inside the Japanese ambassador's residence in Lima, Peru, collapse.	On Comoros, a three-island nation in the Indian Ocean, a general strike is launched on the island of Anjouan.
March 13	The UN General Assembly approves a nonbinding resolution that urges Israel to refrain from implementing its East Jerusalem housing plans.	Desperate to flee the violence, thousands of Albanians mass at Durres for passage to Italy, while U.S. and European troops begin to airlift foreigners to safety. Guards at the central prison in Tirana free hundreds of prisoners, including former premier Fatos Nano and Ramiz Alia, Albania's last communist president.	In Egypt, masked gunmen shoot to death 13 men in the predominantly Coptic Christian hamlet of Ezbet Dawoud, 300 miles (480 km) south of Cairo, the capital. Nine of those killed are Copts. Bullets are fired into a station in Nag Hammadi. One woman dies, and seven other people are wounded ... A lone Jordanian soldier armed with an automatic rifle, Ahmed Daqamseh, 23, fires on a group of 80 seventh- and eighth-grade Israeli schoolgirls at a border site in the northern Jordan Valley, killing seven of the girls and wounding six other group members, including a teacher.		Fighting between Taliban forces and troops loyal to the displaced government continue north of Kabul. Afghanistan, as a consequence, currently has no functioning government.... A group of 130 senior nuns from the Missionaries of Charity elect Sister Nirmala Joshi to succeed Mother Teresa as head of their order.... President Kim Young Sam names former premier Lee Hoi Chang as chairman of the ruling New Korea Party. Kim's choice of Lee is a surprise, because the two men are considered political rivals.

A	B	C	D	E
Includes developments that affect more than one world region, international organizations, and important meetings of major world leaders.	Includes all domestic and regional developments in Europe, including the Soviet Union, Turkey, Cyprus, and Malta.	Includes all domestic and regional developments in Africa and the Middle East, including Iraq and Iran and excluding Cyprus, Turkey, and Afghanistan.	Includes all domestic and regional developments in Latin America, the Caribbean, and Canada.	Includes all domestic and regional developments in Asia and Pacific nations, extending from Afghanistan through all the Pacific Islands, except Hawaii.

U.S. Politics & Social Issues	U.S. Foreign Policy & Defense	U.S. Economy & Environment	Science, Technology, & Nature	Culture, Leisure, & Lifestyle	
Pres. Clinton announces that he has ordered all departments of the federal government to begin training and hiring welfare recipients.					March 8
Michael Kolnhofer, 79, a Kansas City, Kansas, man accused of being a Nazi death camp guard, dies 10 weeks after being wounded in a shoot-out with police.				The Notorious B.I.G., who performed rap songs about his past as a drug dealer, is shot and killed in a drive-by shooting in Los Angeles.	March 9
The Los Angeles Police Commission announces that it will not reappoint the city's police chief, Willie L. Williams, to a second five-year term.	The Citadel, a state-run military academy in Charleston, South Carolina, announces that 10 cadets have been disciplined for harassing female students. The school reveals that one of the students has been suspended for at least one year.			LaVern Baker (born Delores Williams), 67, rhythm-and-blues singer best known for her 1954 hit song "Tweedlee Dee," dies in New York City of heart complications.	March 10
Police in Detroit, Michigan, shoot and kill a gunman, Allen Lane Griffin Jr., 21, after he kills three people and wounds at least two others in a shooting spree at a bank.	Five women who were recruits at the Army's Aberdeen Proving Ground in Maryland indicate that military investigators tried to coerce them into making accusations of rape against their superiors. The five women speak at press conference organized by the NAACP, which notes that all of the men facing criminal charges are black.	The Senate votes, 99-0, to widen its probe of fund-raising practices to include improper as well as illegal activities during the 1996 election campaigns. The Senate also approves, 99-0, a resolution setting a $4.35 million budget for the investigation and a Dec. 31 deadline for the probe's completion. . . . A grand jury in U.S. District Court in Atlanta, Georgia, indicts James Wardlaw and Eric Turpin, executives of Atlanta Coca-Cola Bottling Co., on corruption charges related to their alleged efforts to quash a union-organizing effort.	Estimates suggest that the March 1–2 tornadoes in Arkansas caused damage in the hundreds of millions of dollars.	Reports confirm that the family of Victor Hugo have called the 1996 Walt Disney film The Hunchback of Notre Dame a "commercial pillage of heritage.". . . Hugo Weisgall, 84, composer, dies in Manhassett, New York, after a fall. . . . The Columbus Quest captures the first championship of the ABL, a women's professional league . . . Martin Buser wins the Iditarod dog-sledding race in Alaska.	March 11
	Federico F. Pena is confirmed as energy secretary by the Senate, 99-1. . . . The National Association of Securities Dealers (NASD) announces that $5.6 million in refunds are due to more than 15,700 investors who were charged commissions for redeeming mutual-funds shares by Smith Barney Shearson Inc. and Lehman Brothers Inc.			Reports confirm that Charles S. Olton has been named president and chief executive officer of the American Symphony Orchestra League.	March 12
Cleve McDowell, 56, a civil-rights lawyer, is found shot to death in Drew, Mississippi.	The House votes, 251-175, to "decertify" Mexico as an ally in the drug war unless Pres. Clinton demonstrates within 90 days that Mexico has made significant progress in fighting drug trafficking,	Figures suggest that the percentage of credit card accounts that are more than 30 days past due increased to 3.72% in the fourth quarter of 1996. The delinquency rate is the highest recorded since 1973, when the association began keeping track. The rate for the corresponding period in 1995 was 3.34%.	Reports reveal that floods brought on by the overflowing of the Ohio River caused the deaths of at least 30 people in late February and early March.	Robert Saudek, 85, producer remembered for his cultural contributions to television, dies in Baltimore, Maryland, of unreported causes.	March 13

F	G	H	I	J
Includes elections, federal-state relations, civil rights and liberties, crime, the judiciary, education, health care, poverty, urban affairs, and population.	Includes formation and debate of U.S. foreign and defense policies, veterans' affairs, and defense spending. (Relations with specific foreign countries are usually found under the region concerned.)	Includes business, labor, agriculture, taxation, transportation, consumer affairs, monetary and fiscal policy, natural resources, and pollution.	Includes worldwide scientific, medical, and technological developments; natural phenomena; U.S. weather; natural disasters; and accidents.	Includes the arts, religion, scholarship, communications media, sports, entertainments, fashions, fads, and social life.

	World Affairs	Europe	Africa & the Middle East	The Americas	Asia & the Pacific
March 14		Armed gangs aiming to depose Pres. Sali Berisha for his role in the collapse of investment schemes take control of Tirana, the capital of Albania. For the first time since World War II, German troops open fire in "hostile conditions" during an airlift of 120 people, including 20 Germans, from Albania.	In Kisangani, Zaire, fleeing government soldiers riot, stripping shops of their goods and destroying them with hand grenades.	Four peasants die and several others are injured in a clash between state police officers and supporters of the rebel Zapatista National Liberation Army (EZLN) in the village of San Pedro Nixtalucum in Chiapas state, Mexico.... The ruling Free National Movement (FNM) captures 34 seats in the legislature in parliamentary elections in the Bahamas.	China's congress approves legislation that will revise the nation's criminal code. The revisions are the first major changes to the code since 1979.
March 15		In Albania, Tirana's main hospital reports that gunshot wounds have killed 27 people and injured more than 200 since Mar. 12.... An estimated 10,000 people rally in Minsk to mark the anniversary of the adoption of Belarus's now superseded 1994 constitution.	Rebels in Zaire capture Kisangani, the country's third-largest city and the headquarters for the army's counteroffensive. The rebels immediately start cracking down on looting by residents and army stragglers. Some of Kisangani's residents cheer the rebel soldiers as they enter the city.... Algerian security troops kill 43 GIA fighters in Relizane, 180 miles south of Algiers. Three policemen are slain, allegedly by a group of militants in the Casbah district of Algiers.		On Comoros, a three-island nation in the Indian Ocean, the strike that started Mar. 12 turns into an open rebellion, and government troops move in, killing four demonstrators and arresting 200 others.
March 16		Thousands of workers from several European countries hold a march in Brussels, the Belgian capital, to protest a wave of job cuts throughout the continent. Estimates of the march's total number of participants range from 40,000 to 120,000.... Albanian government militia restore some order to Tirana, and several thousand people rally in the capital for peace.	Jordan's King Hussein, in a gesture considered unprecedented in modern Arab-Israeli relations, travels to Israel to offer condolences to the grieving families of the seven girls slain Mar. 13.... Reports suggest there are 70,000 Rwandan Hutu refugees in Ubundu, a town 80 miles south of Kisangani on the Zaire River.... Zaire's Pres. Mobutu Sese Seko Mobutu is admitted to a hospital in Monaco to undergo cancer treatment.... At least 10 militants are killed in a shoot-out with security forces in the Casbah district of Algiers, Algeria.	Venezuela demolishes the notorious Catia prison that has been criticized by human-rights organizations for its inhumane conditions and rampant corruption.... Colombian defense minister Guillermo Alberto Gonzalez resigns amid charges that he accepted a contribution from a drug trafficker for his 1989 Senate election campaign.	
March 17	UN secretary general Kofi Annan outlines a detailed reform package that involves cutting 1,000 staff jobs and reducing the UN's budget for the first time ever.		Reports from Zaire suggest that more than 500 soldiers have emerged from the forests around Kisangani and turned themselves in to the rebels.	Janet Jagan, the widow of the late Pres. Cheddi Jagan, is sworn in as Guyana's new prime minister.	
March 18			Despite international pleas, Israeli bulldozers, protected by some 1,000 troops, begin clearing ground for construction of the controversial Har Homa settlement on land known to Arabs as Jabal Abu Ghneim, in East Jerusalem.... Zaire's parliament votes to dismiss Premier Leon Kengo wa Dondo and to hold talks with the rebels.	In Canada, a bomb blast outside a Montreal-area bar linked to the Hells Angels kills two men. These deaths raise the death toll from a three-year-old conflict between Hells Angels and Rock Machine, rival biker gangs in Quebec, to 32.	
March 19		Shipyard workers in Poland continue to protest the yard's closing, and 70 workers occupy several government buildings in Warsaw, the capital, before they are removed by police.... Reports state that more than 10,000 Albanian refugees have reached Italy, which calls a state of emergency in order to deal with the refugee flow.... Jacques Foccart, 83, diplomat who served as France's secretary general for African affairs, 1959–74, dies in Luzarches, France, after suffering from Parkinson's disease.	King Hussein dismisses Abdul Karim al-Kabariti as Jordanian prime minister and replaces him with Abdel Salem al-Majali.... Retired South African archbishop Desmond Tutu reveals that his prostate cancer has spread.	David Saul, the prime minister of Bermuda, a British colony, unexpectedly announces his resignation, effective Mar. 27.	

A	B	C	D	E
Includes developments that affect more than one world region, international organizations, and important meetings of major world leaders.	Includes all domestic and regional developments in Europe, including the Soviet Union, Turkey, Cyprus, and Malta.	Includes all domestic and regional developments in Africa and the Middle East, including Iraq and Iran and excluding Cyprus, Turkey, and Afghanistan.	Includes all domestic and regional developments in Latin America, the Caribbean, and Canada.	Includes all domestic and regional developments in Asia and Pacific nations, extending from Afghanistan through all the Pacific Islands, except Hawaii.

U.S. Politics & Social Issues	U.S. Foreign Policy & Defense	U.S. Economy & Environment	Science, Technology, & Nature	Culture, Leisure, & Lifestyle	
A jury in State Supreme Court in NYC awards $37 million in damages to Felix Rivera, a mentally retarded man shot by police in 1983 after he brandished a toy gun at them.... Pres. Clinton suffers major damage to his right knee and has to have torn quadriceps tendon reattached to his kneecap in surgery.... Cyril Francis Brickfield, 78, lawyer and former executive director of the AARP, 1967–87, dies in Bethesda, Maryland, of cancer.		The National Highway Traffic Safety Administration (NHTSA) ruled that automobile makers may reduce the force at which air bags inflate.	Researcher in Melbourne, Australia, report that they have created 470 identical cattle embryos. The specimens, however, have not yet resulted in pregnancies.	An unidentified man strikes the America's Cup yachting trophy repeatedly with a sledgehammer in Auckland, New Zealand.... Fred Zinnemann, 89, film director who won Oscars in 1938, 1953, and 1966, dies in London of unreported causes.... Joey Mullen scores his 500th career goal, becoming the first U.S.-born hockey player to do so.	March 14
	A U.S. jury in Houston, Texas, rules that $7.9 million of a total of $9 million held in a bank account belonging to former top Mexican official Mario Ruiz Massieu came from bribes paid by drug traffickers. The jury's decision allows the U.S. government to seize the $7.9 million.			Victor Vasarely (born Gyozo Vasarhelyi), 88, who pioneered the Op Art movement in the 1960s, dies in Paris, France, of prostate cancer.... Gail Davis, (born Betty Jeanne Grayson) 71, actress known for the TV series *Annie Oakley* (1955–58), the first western to star a woman, dies in Burbank, California, of cancer.	March 15
				The World Cup alpine ski season concludes, and Luc Alphand of France clinches the men's overall title.	March 16
In St. Louis, Missouri, two men rob a bank and open fire with assault rifles, killing a guard. One suspect is arrested, but the other escapes. ... Reports state that a woman, identified only as Kathy, who gave birth after being raped while in a coma-like state, died a few days before her son's first birthday at the age of 30 without regaining consciousness.	Anthony Lake withdraws his nomination to be the director of central intelligence, asserting that he has "lost patience" with the nomination process, which he calls "nasty and brutish without being short." ... The U.S.-based Cable News Network (CNN) airs its first broadcast from Cuba.	Statistics show that the number of U.S. households filing for personal bankruptcy rose to 1.125 million in 1996, a record high.		Ford Motor Co. announces that in 1997 it will end production of its Thunderbird sports coupe, an American icon since it first went on sale in 1954.	March 17
The House passes, 418-9, the Victims' Rights Clarification Act, which bars federal courts from excluding victims from a courtroom on the basis that they intend to testify in the penalty phase..... Former representative Wes S. Cooley (R, Oreg.) is convicted by Salem, Oregon, circuit court judge Albin Norblad for lying about his military service in a 1994 voters' pamphlet. He is sentenced to two years' probation, 100 hours of community service, and a $7,110 fine.		The Senate rejects, 61-38, a proposed constitutional amendment that would have set spending and contribution limits on federal election campaigns. The vote falls well short of the two-thirds majority needed.		The National Book Critics Circle presents its awards to Robert Hass, Frank McCourt, Gina Berriault, William Gass, and Jonathan Raban.	March 18
The Senate passes, by voice vote, and Pres. Clinton signs the Victims' Rights Clarification Act, which bars federal courts from excluding victims from a courtroom on the grounds that they intend to testify in the penalty phase ... Earl Carroll of U.S. District Court in Phoenix, Arizona, sentences six defendants to prison terms ranging from 12 to 37 months. The defendants are members of a paramilitary group known as the Viper Militia and have pled guilty to charges of conspiracy to make and possess unregistered destructive devices in a bombing plot.	Pres. Clinton names George J. Tenet as his new nominee for the post of director of central intelligence.	In *Bennett v. Spear*, the Supreme Court rules unanimously that people whose economic interests are affected by the enforcement of the Endangered Species Act have a right to legally challenge the federal government's enforcement of the law.		Jessie Lee Brown Foveaux, 98 sells her memoir to Warner Books for reportedly more than $1 million.... Willem De Kooning, 92, a preeminent 20th-century American artist, dies in East Hampton, New York, after a long illness.... At the World Figure Skating Championships in Lausanne, Switzerland, Mandy Wotzel and Ingo Steuer of Germany win the pairs' title.	March 19

F	G	H	I	J
Includes elections, federal-state relations, civil rights and liberties, crime, the judiciary, education, health care, poverty, urban affairs, and population.	Includes formation and debate of U.S. foreign and defense policies, veterans' affairs, and defense spending. (Relations with specific foreign countries are usually found under the region concerned.)	Includes business, labor, agriculture, taxation, transportation, consumer affairs, monetary and fiscal policy, natural resources, and pollution.	Includes worldwide scientific, medical, and technological developments; natural phenomena; U.S. weather; natural disasters; and accidents.	Includes the arts, religion, scholarship, communications media, sports, entertainments, fashions, fads, and social life.

	World Affairs	Europe	Africa & the Middle East	The Americas	Asia & the Pacific
March 20	Russian president Boris Yeltsin and U.S. president Bill Clinton meet in Helsinki, the capital of Finland, for their first summit together in 11 months. The two leaders discuss the expansion of NATO to include former Soviet-bloc countries in Eastern Europe, as well as nuclear disarmament and economic aid to Russia.	Authorities in the Croat section of the ethnically split city of Mostar hand out suspended sentences to three police officers accused of shooting at unarmed civilians in a February incident in which one person died and 34 were wounded.... Pres. Levon Ter-Petrossian names Robert Kocharyan Armenia's new premier.... Sir V(ictor) S(awdon) Pritchett, 96, acclaimed British writer who was knighted in 1975, dies in London of unreported causes.	Palestinian protests swell, and Israeli troops fire tear-gas canisters in street battles with stone-throwing Palestinian students on the outskirts of Bethlehem, in the West Bank.	Gerardo Bedoya Borrero, the chief editorial writer at a conservative daily newspaper, is gunned down in the city of Cali, Colombia.	
March 21	U.S. president Clinton and Russian president Yeltsin come to an agreement on the future of the START pact, under which Yeltsin promises to submit START II, signed in 1993 and ratified by the U.S. Senate in 1996, to the Duma for ratification. In exchange, the U.S. agrees to postpone a deadline for dismantling nuclear warheads by one year, to the end of the year 2003, and to postpone from that year until the year 2007 the new deadline for the destruction of nuclear missile silos and bombers.		A Palestinian belonging to the military wing of Hamas ends a 12-month lull in Palestinian suicide attacks by detonating an explosive on the patio of a crowded cafe in Tel Aviv, Israel's largest city. The bomber and three Israeli women die in the blast, which injures some 40 other people. Ensuing street clashes spread to Hebron.... After virtually ignoring Zaire's troubles for months, Zairian president Mobutu Sese Seko returns from Europe and starts asserting control.	An ammonia leak in a Montreal meat-packing plant kills one man and injures 24 others. Six firefighters are also injured.	
March 22	The Canadian Security Intelligence Service reveals that Canadian immigration officials have arrested a Saudi man, Hani Abdel Rahim al-Sayegh, on suspicion of involvement in a June 1996 truck bombing of a U.S. military complex near Dhahran, Saudi Arabia. The blast killed 19 U.S. servicemen and injured 384 people.	Spain's Supreme Court orders the government to declassify secret documents related to the so-called Dirty War, in which 27 suspected Basque terrorists were killed under mysterious circumstances in the 1980s.	Villagers in Nigeria's southern Delta State seize 127 employees of the Royal Dutch/Shell Group oil conglomerate in a protest over local government policies.	Reports disclose that a wave of violence in Port-au-Prince, Haiti's capital, killed more than 50 people in February and March.... Five members of the Order of the Solar Temple sect are found dead in Canada. The incident is apparently the third mass suicide carried out by the cult since 1994.... An estimated 8,000 people rally to protest the closing of Hopital Montfort, an Ottawa hospital that serves the French-speaking community.	Tibet's exiled spiritual leader, the Dalai Lama, pays his first-ever visit to Taiwan.
March 23	The 54-member Organization of the Islamic Conference closes a summit in Islamabad, Pakistan, by approving a declaration in support of Palestinian claims to Jerusalem.	Some 70 protesters, including two opposition leaders, are arrested at an antigovernment rally that draws 10,000 people in Minsk to commemorate of the 69th anniversary of the Belarussian People's Republic. One of those arrested is U.S. diplomat Serge Alexandrov.			
March 24		Reports reveal that the ancient ruins at Butrint, considered to be Albania's most important archeological site, were pillaged in the recent unrest.... Belarussian authorities expel U.S. diplomat Serge Alexandrov, accusing him of spying and of fomenting antigovernment sentiment. Alexandrov, the first secretary at the U.S. embassy in Minsk, the Belarussian capital, was arrested for taking part in the Mar. 23 rally against Belarussian president Aleksandr Lukashenko.	The Palestine National Authority (PNA) formally suspends security ties with Israel.... A speaker for Shell states that the Mar. 22 dispute in Nigeria has nothing to do with Shell and that the villagers are using the company to raise the profile of their protest.... Zairian president Mobutu Sese Seko accepts the resignation of his unpopular premier, Leon Kengo wa Dondo.		The Tokyo High Court overturns a lower court's ruling when it convicts Takao Fujinami, a former chief of Japan's cabinet, for bribery. The court sentences Fujinami to a three-year suspended prison sentence and fines him 42.7 million yen.
March 25		A judge in Spain, Baltasar Garzon, issues an international arrest warrant for Gen. Leopoldo Galtieri, who led the military junta that ruled Argentina from December 1981 to July 1982. Garzon orders Galtieri's arrest in connection with the general's alleged involvement in the murders of three Spaniards during Argentina's "dirty war" against suspected leftists from 1976 to 1983.... Reports confirm that the coalition government of Czech premier Vaclav Klaus has obtained a parliamentary majority.	Algerian government forces kill Abdelkadur Seddouki, the suspected leader of the Jihad Armed Islamic Front, a group said to have carried out bombing attacks on prominent government figures.	Election returns show that the FMLN has won 27 seats in El Salvador's 84-seat National Assembly, up from the 21 seats it won in the previous election.... The United Bermuda Party (UBP) elects Pamela Gordon as the new prime minister.... Roberto Sanchez Vilella, 84, former governor of Puerto Rico elected governor in 1964 whose 1967 plan to divorce his wife of 30 years and marry his young assistant, kept him from winning reelection, dies in San Juan, Puerto Rico, of cancer.	Taiwan launches an emergency assistance package for the nation's pig industry, hit by an outbreak of hoof-and-mouth disease. The government orders farmers to slaughter all of their pigs even if only one animal in a herd is found to have the virus.

A	B	C	D	E
Includes developments that affect more than one world region, international organizations, and important meetings of major world leaders.	Includes all domestic and regional developments in Europe, including the Soviet Union, Turkey, Cyprus, and Malta.	Includes all domestic and regional developments in Africa and the Middle East, including Iraq and Iran and excluding Cyprus, Turkey, and Afghanistan.	Includes all domestic and regional developments in Latin America, the Caribbean, and Canada.	Includes all domestic and regional developments in Asia and Pacific nations, extending from Afghanistan through all the Pacific Islands, except Hawaii.

U.S. Politics & Social Issues	U.S. Foreign Policy & Defense	U.S. Economy & Environment	Science, Technology, & Nature	Culture, Leisure, & Lifestyle	
The House passes, 295-136, a measure that will outlaw a method of late-term abortion. . . . Liggett Group agrees to settle lawsuits brought by 22 states seeking to recover the cost of treating smoking-related illnesses. Liggett agrees to admit that smoking cigarettes is addictive and causes cancer—which the industry has never before conceded. . . . In Phoenix, Arizona, Judge Earl Carroll sentences Gary Bauer, an alleged leader of the Viper Militia, to nine years in prison.	Army captain Derrick Robertson, a company commander at the Aberdeen Proving Ground in Maryland, is sentenced to four months in prison after pleading guilty to having consensual sex with a private. . . . The Senate approves, 94-5, a resolution that gives Pres. Clinton until Sept. 1 to report to Congress that Mexico has made progress in fighting drugs. Unlike the House bill, the measure does not threaten to decertify Mexico.	A federal jury in Houston, Texas, awards damages totaling $222.7 million in a libel case against *The Wall Street Journal*. MMAR had accused the newspaper of contributing to its collapse through a 1993 article that criticized the firm's business practices. The libel award is the largest in U.S. history.	An independent group of computer scientists announce that new digital cellular telephones may be nearly as susceptible to electronic eavesdropping as the analog wireless phones, in use for some 15 years.	At the World Figure Skating Championships in Lausanne, Switzerland, Elvis Stojko of Canada wins the men's title for the third time in his career. . . . Tony Zale (born Anthony Florian Zaleski), 83, the world middleweight champion, 1940–48, dies in Portage, Indiana, after suffering from Alzheimer's and Parkinson's diseases.	March 20
Liggett Group, in accordance with its Mar. 20 agreement, issues a statement declaring that its executives "know and acknowledge" that "nicotine is addictive" and that smoking cigarettes "causes health problems, including lung cancer, heart and vascular disease and emphysema." . . . A federal judge in White Plains, New York, approves Texaco's $176.1 million settlement of a 1994 federal discrimination lawsuit brought by black Texaco employees. It is the largest ever in a race-discrimination suit.	The U.S. suspends its annual foreign aid to Belarus, which totals $40 million, on account of Belarus's poor human-rights record.			In Lausanne, Switzerland, at the World Figure Skating Championships, Oksana Gritschuk and Yevgeny Platov of Russia win the ice-dancing title. . . . Rev. W(ilbert) (Vere) Awdry, 85, British Anglican minister and children's author, dies in Gloucestershire, England, after a long illness.	March 21
	Reports indicate that a U.S. District Court in Uniondale, New York, has awarded $2.1 million to the family of Alice Ephraimson-Abt, who was killed in the 1983 downing of Korean Air Lines Flight 007 by a Soviet military jet. It is the largest amount so far awarded to a Flight 007 victim's family.	Data suggests that Chicago's O'Hare International Airport remained the world's busiest airport in 1996, serving 69.1 million passengers, 2.8% more than in the previous year. Hartsfield airport in Atlanta, Georgia, is in second place, with 63.3 million passengers, followed by Los Angeles, with 57.9 million passengers.	The Hale-Bopp comet, one of the largest and brightest comets to enter the solar system in centuries, reaches its closest proximity to the Earth when it passes an estimated 122 million miles from the Earth's surface. Astronomers estimate that Hale-Bopp is 25 miles (16 km) in diameter, making it four times as large as the well-known Halley's comet, and that it is traveling at a speed of nearly 100,000 mph (160,000 kmph).		March 22
				Tara Lipinski wins the women's title at the World Figure Skating Championships in Lausanne, Switzerland. Lipinski, 14, is the youngest person ever to win the title.	March 23
Michigan health officials contact the federal CDC when hepatitis A cases begin to proliferate in the towns of Marshall and Battle Creek.	U(ral) Alexis Johnson, 88, U.S. diplomat best known for helping to broker the first strategic-arms limitation treaty between the U.S. and the Soviet Union, dies in Raleigh, North Carolina, of unreported causes.			At the Academy Awards, *The English Patient* wins nine of the 12 honors for which it is nominated, including best picture and best director. . . . Harold Melvin, 57, singer who headed the Blue Notes, a 1950s rhythm-and-blues group, dies in Philadelphia, Pennsylvania, after suffering a stroke.	March 24
A malfunction in Florida's 74-year-old electric chair causes flames to burst from the leather face mask of convicted murderer Pedro L. Medina, seconds after the lethal current is turned on. The accident prompts Florida governor Lawton Chiles to state that Florida will consider using other methods of execution. Of the 38 states with the death penalty, only four, including Florida, still use the electric chair exclusively.	Army officials announce that criminal sexual-misconduct charges were brought against two more instructors—Staff Sergeant Wayne Gamble and Sergeant First Class Ronald Moffett—at the Aberdeen Proving Ground. . . . Pres. Clinton nominates Major General Claudia J. Kennedy to become the army's first female lieutenant general, a three-star rank.	The Federal Reserve Board announces that it will increase the federal-funds rate, the interest rate banks charge on overnight loans made to one another, to 5.5%, from 5.25%.		Former president George Bush safely completes a 12,500-foot (3,800-meter) parachute jump at Yuma Proving Ground, Arizona. Bush, who made a similar jump in 1944 as a World War II Navy pilot, reportedly is the only U.S. president ever to have parachuted from an airplane.	March 25

F	G	H	I	J
Includes elections, federal-state relations, civil rights and liberties, crime, the judiciary, education, health care, poverty, urban affairs, and population.	*Includes formation and debate of U.S. foreign and defense policies, veterans' affairs, and defense spending. (Relations with specific foreign countries are usually found under the region concerned.)*	*Includes business, labor, agriculture, taxation, transportation, consumer affairs, monetary and fiscal policy, natural resources, and pollution.*	*Includes worldwide scientific, medical, and technological developments; natural phenomena; U.S. weather; natural disasters; and accidents.*	*Includes the arts, religion, scholarship, communications media, sports, entertainments, fashions, fads, and social life.*

	World Affairs	Europe	Africa & the Middle East	The Americas	Asia & the Pacific
March 26	The heads of state of 15 African nations hold a summit in Lome, the capital of Togo, aimed at finding a way to end the Zairian conflict.	Two bombs explode near a train station in Wilmslow, a city south of Manchester, England. Later, an unidentified attacker shoots an explosive device at a police station in Coalisland, a town in Northern Ireland. Police fire at the attacker and wound him.... Otto John, 88, German official who played an important role in the Nazi resistance during World War II and was later at the center of a cold war–era espionage controversy, dies in Innsbruck, Austria, of unreported causes.	Street clashes spread in Ramallah, Israel, just north of Jerusalem.... Three Ijaw tribesmen are killed in rioting related to the dispute that started Mar. 22 when rebels took over a Shell station in Nigeria.	Workers at the 79 Alberta stores of Canada Safeway Ltd. launch a strike.... The Canadian government charges Fahad Sheheri, 21, a Saudi citizen currently under detention in Canada, with being a member of a terrorist group.	
March 27		In Russia, 1.8 million workers hold a strike, joining in some 1,000 demonstrations across the country to protest unpaid wages and pensions.... In the central Albanian village of Levan, 16 members of a gang assassinate the chair of the local council of elders. Villagers attack the gang in response, killing them all. It is the most violent single incident of the recent unrest.... Ella Maillart, 94, Swiss travel writer, dies in Chandolin, Switzerland, of unreported causes.	In Nigeria, protesters begin to free the hostages taken Mar. 22 at a Shell station.	Pamela Gordon becomes Bermuda's first female prime minister, as well as its youngest.	Japan's Sapporo District Court rules that the regional government of Hokkaido island acted illegally in constructing a dam on land held sacred by the Ainu ethnic minority. The ruling marks the first official recognition of an aboriginal minority in Japan.... Australian governor general William Deane signs a bill that will strike down a law in the Northern Territory legalizing euthanasia, the world's only law of its kind.
March 28	The UN Security Council agrees to an Italian plan to approve the deployment of a multinational force to oversee relief efforts in Albania.	The IRA claims responsibility for the Mar. 26 bombings but does not mention the Ulster attack.... The Italian navy warship Sibilla, on patrol in the Adriatic Sea, rams an Albanian vessel filled with refugees from the southern port of Vlore. Italian searchers rescue 34 survivors and pick up four dead bodies from the sinking ship.	Abdullah Khalil Abdullah, 20, a Palestinian college student, is killed by Israeli soldiers in clashes at a roadblock near Ramallah.		
March 29		Some 40,000 demonstrators hold a rally in Strasbourg, France, to protest proposals of the National Front party regarding immigration laws. The protests are staged during a convention of France's right-wing National Front party in Strasbourg.... Reports confirm that Muslim and Croat leaders in Sarajevo have reached a power-sharing deal under which the city will be allowed to elect a new mayor. Sarajevo's last mayor, Tarik Kupusovic, quit a year earlier when the Bosnian government named 45 Muslims to the 47-member city council.			
March 30		While holding a family hostage, a suspected IRA gunman shoots and wounds a police officer in Forkhill, Northern Ireland.... The Albanian ambassador to Italy, Pandeli Pasko, reveals that 83 people aboard the Albanian vessel that crashed Mar. 28 are missing and presumed dead.... During demonstrations in Strasbourg, France, several protestors clash with riot police.	Palestinian officials report that the number of Palestinians wounded since street clashes that began Mar. 20 is at 460.		
March 31	The 22-member Arab League announces its decision to freeze relations with Israel in light of Israeli prime minister Benjamin Netanyahu's settlement policies. The league's resolution, which is nonbinding, also reinstitutes the Arab states' economic boycott of Israel.... U.S. president Clinton nominates U.S. Army general Wesley K. Clark to be the next commander of NATO and the supreme allied commander in Europe.	Albanian president Sali Berisha declares a national day of mourning for the Mar. 28 boat accident. Pope John Paul II calls for all Roman Catholics to pray for the victims.... Eighteen people are killed and 50 others are injured when a train derails while entering the station at Huarte Arakil in northern Spain.		A videotape that shows military police officers in Sao Paulo brutalizing drivers at a roadblock set up to catch drug traffickers is broadcast on TV Globo. The highly publicized tape causes an outcry in Brazil.	

A	B	C	D	E
Includes developments that affect more than one world region, international organizations, and important meetings of major world leaders.	*Includes all domestic and regional developments in Europe, including the Soviet Union, Turkey, Cyprus, and Malta.*	*Includes all domestic and regional developments in Africa and the Middle East, including Iraq and Iran and excluding Cyprus, Turkey, and Afghanistan.*	*Includes all domestic and regional developments in Latin America, the Caribbean, and Canada.*	*Includes all domestic and regional developments in Asia and Pacific nations, extending from Afghanistan through all the Pacific Islands, except Hawaii.*

U.S. Politics & Social Issues	U.S. Foreign Policy & Defense	U.S. Economy & Environment	Science, Technology, & Nature	Culture, Leisure, & Lifestyle	
In California, 39 members of Heaven's Gate, a religious cult, are found dead. It is one of the largest mass suicides in U.S. history. The cult's leader, Marshall Herff Applewhite, 66, is among the dead.	In response to the Mar. 24 expulsion of Serge Alexandrov, the State Department orders Vladimir Gramyka, the first secretary at the Belarussian embassy in Washington, to leave the U.S. . . . Reports reveal that Staff Sergeant Nathanael Beach, a drill sergeant at Aberdeen, was acquitted of sexual misconduct charges. . . . NYC mayor Rudolph W. Giuliani (R) files suit against the federal government, charging that provisions in the 1996 welfare-reform bill violate immigrants' rights.	John G. Bennett Jr., the founder of the failed Foundation for New Era Philanthropy, pleads no contest to federal charges that he defrauded universities, churches, charities, and philanthropists of $135 million. The foundation was revealed as a huge pyramid scheme after it declared bankruptcy in 1995. The scheme is said to have been the largest charity fraud in U.S. history.		Researchers conducting a study commissioned by the National Cable Television Association find that the new national television-ratings system often attracts children to adult-oriented programs.	March 26
Judge Donald Mark sentences John Horace, 53, to a minimum of eight years and four months and a maximum of 25 years in prison for raping and sexually abusing a woman who was in a coma-like state in August 1995. . . . San Diego County medical examiner Brian Blackbourne reveals that many of the Heaven's Gate cultists found dead on March 26 carried out their suicides in three shifts over several days.	U.S. House speaker Newt Gingrich (R, Ga.) leads a bipartisan delegation of 11 other Congress members on a tour of Hong Kong, China, Japan, and Taiwan. . . . The ACLU files suit in U.S. District Court in Washington, D.C., seeking to delay the implementation of the new welfare rules regarding immigrants for 30 days. A group representing some of the 40,000 Nicaraguan refugees living in the Miami, Florida, area files suit in U.S. District Court in Miami.		The National Cancer Institute announces that it has changed its position and now recommends that women between the ages of 40 and 49 who are at average risk of contracting breast cancer undergo mammogram screenings every one to two years.		March 27
A Justice Department report concludes that Howard M. Shapiro, the general counsel for the FBI, did not violate professional standards in his dealings with the White House at a time when the White House was being investigated for improperly acquiring confidential FBI files. However, the report states that Shapiro exercised "very poor judgment" in the incident.		The Commerce Department reports that after-tax profits of U.S. corporations rose 7% in 1996 to $406.8 billion, from the revised 1995 level of $380.2 billion.			March 28
			The University of North Dakota Fighting Sioux defeats the Boston University Terriers, 6-4, to win the NCAA Division I hockey title.		March 29
				Jon Stone, 65, one of the creators of the children's public TV program *Sesame Street*, dies in New York City of complications from Lou Gehrig's disease. . . . Golfer Betsy King wins the Nabisco Dinah Shore tournament, the first major event on the LPGA Tour.	March 30
In *Lambert v. Wicklund*, the Supreme Court rules unanimously to reinstate a 1995 Montana law requiring teenage girls to notify at least one parent before having an abortion. . . . An autopsy concludes that Pedro Medina, executed in Florida Mar. 25, died painlessly before the fire in his face mask broke out. . . . In *U.S. v. Lanier*, the Supreme Court rules unanimously that a case against David Lanier, a former Tennessee judge charged with sexually assaulting five women in his courtroom chambers, should be reinstated. . . . Marvin Liebman, 73, noted conservative who shocked his colleagues in 1990 when he revealed that he was homosexual, dies in Washington, D.C., of heart disease.	Eugenie M. Anderson (born Helen Eugenie Moore), 87, who was the first female U.S. ambassador when she was named ambassador to Denmark in 1949 by Pres. Harry Truman, dies in Red Wing, Minnesota, of unreported causes.	When combined with points dropped on the last trading day, Mar. 27, the Dow closes down a total of 297.22 points, the biggest two-session point decline since the 1987 crash. On a percentage basis, however, the 4.3% decline is only the 20th-largest two-session drop during that 10-year period. . . . The Commerce Department reports that personal pretax income rose 0.9% in February from January, to a seasonally adjusted annual figure of $6.71 trillion. The February increase, the largest since June 1996, marks the 21st consecutive month that incomes have grown.		In *TBS v. FCC*, the Supreme Court rules, 5-4, to uphold the "must-carry" law, a provision in a 1992 package of cable-TV legislation that requires operators of cable-TV systems to carry the signals of local broadcast-TV stations. . . . Sixteen-year-old Martina Hingis of Switzerland becomes the youngest women's tennis player ever to be ranked number one.	March 31
F	G	H	I	J	
Includes elections, federal-state relations, civil rights and liberties, crime, the judiciary, education, health care, poverty, urban affairs, and population.	Includes formation and debate of U.S. foreign and defense policies, veterans' affairs, and defense spending. (Relations with specific foreign countries are usually found under the region concerned.)	Includes business, labor, agriculture, taxation, transportation, consumer affairs, monetary and fiscal policy, natural resources, and pollution.	Includes worldwide scientific, medical, and technological developments; natural phenomena; U.S. weather; natural disasters; and accidents.	Includes the arts, religion, scholarship, communications media, sports, entertainments, fashions, fads, and social life.	

	World Affairs	Europe	Africa & the Middle East	The Americas	Asia & the Pacific
April 1		German authorities repatriate some 30 orphans aged between five and nine on a flight to Sarajevo, the Bosnian capital, from Berlin, Germany, claiming that their guardians repeatedly sought their return.	Two Palestinians are killed in separate exchanges with Israeli troops in the West Bank cities of Hebron and Nablus. . . . Zaire's parliament chooses Etienne Tshisekedi as premier.	Paramilitary groups raid the Panamanian village of La Bonga, killing four peasants in their pursuit of rebels and refugees.	Pakistan's parliament votes unanimously to repeal a 12-year-old constitutional amendment that gives the president unilateral power to dismiss the prime minister, dissolve Parliament, and appoint armed forces chiefs. The amendment had been invoked four times in the past decade, during which none of Pakistan's civilian prime ministers have completed a full five-year term.
April 2		Presidents Boris Yeltsin of Russia and Aleksandr Lukashenko of Belarus sign a treaty on closer integration between the two former Soviet states. Police in Minsk, the Belarussian capital, beat dozens of protesters rallying to preserve their country's independence in the face of the treaty. Around 4,000 people are estimated to have taken part in the rally, and more than 100 are arrested.	An Israeli military bus transporting 12 soldiers to guard Jewish settlements in the West Bank comes under attack near the Jalazoun refugee camp, located some 12 miles (20 km) north of Jerusalem. No one is injured or killed. Palestinian police round up about 30 presumed Islamic militants, most of whom are reportedly tied to Islamic Jihad. . . . in Zaire, Pres. Mobutu Sese Seko approves Etienne Tshisekedi as premier.		China confirms that a prominent Chinese journalist, Wei Guoqiang, committed suicide in Beijing, the Chinese capital, after his plans to defect were foiled.
April 3	The UN Security Council announces that its multinational peacekeeping force will remain in Haiti until July 31.	Amnesty International reports that Russian police routinely torture, abuse, and asphyxiate suspects and prisoners. . . . In England, a jury at London's central courthouse convicts shipping magnate Abbas Gokal of defrauding customers of the failed BCCI of £750 million ($1.2 billion). . . . Eight players and a trainer from Albania's national soccer team ask for political asylum in Madrid, Spain. . . . British police find two bombs under a highway near Birmingham.		Brazil's Senate unanimously passes a bill that makes torture a crime, punishable by four to 16 years in prison. Separately, reports disclose that 10 Sao Paulo officers have been arrested in connection with the beatings shown on a videotape that was broadcast Mar. 31. . . . After a failed escape attempt, 10 heavily armed inmates kill three guards and a police officer, and they take 13 people hostage at a prison in Valledupar, a town in northern Colombia.	
April 4			Israeli prime minister Benjamin Netanyahu states that, despite international pressure, his government will proceed with settlement construction in historically Arab East Jerusalem and the occupied West Bank. . . . In Zaire, the rebel alliance captures Zaire's principal diamond-trading city, Mbuji-Mayi, in East Kasai province, 600 miles east of Kinshasa. The government troops loot the city and terrorize residents before fleeing ahead of the rebel advance.		
April 5		Albanian premier Bashkim Fino is barred from traveling to the northern town of Shkoder from Tirana by a group of 15 armed men, who set off two grenades to force the premier to turn back. . . . In Kraljeva Sutjeska, a Roman Catholic monastery is struck by three rifle grenades. . . . The 150th running of Great Britain's Grand National Steeplechase is postponed due to two bomb threats from the Provisional IRA.	In Zaire, the leader of the rebel ADFL group, Laurent Kabila, approves a plan by the UN to airlift some 80,000 Rwandan Hutu refugees to safety. . . . Jordan's King Hussein undergoes prostate surgery at the Mayo Clinic in Rochester, Minnesota.	Heberto Castillo Martinez, 68, Mexican political leader who was an outspoken opponent of the long-ruling Institutional Revolutionary Party (PRI), dies in Mexico City of heart failure.	
April 6			Delegates from the Zairian government and the ADFL hold talks in the South African capital, Pretoria.	In the first-round voting for nine Senate seats and two seats in the Chamber of Deputies in Haiti, the Lavalas Family party wins outright two Senate seats and one seat in the Chamber of Deputies. The other seats will be decided in run-off elections.	A bomb explodes at the home of Lt. Gen. Tin Oo, who is the second secretary and army chief of staff of Myanmar's ruling military junta, the State Law and Order Restoration Council (SLORC). The bomb kills his eldest daughter, Cho Lei Oo.

A	B	C	D	E
Includes developments that affect more than one world region, international organizations, and important meetings of major world leaders.	*Includes all domestic and regional developments in Europe, including the Soviet Union, Turkey, Cyprus, and Malta.*	*Includes all domestic and regional developments in Africa and the Middle East, including Iraq and Iran and excluding Cyprus, Turkey, and Afghanistan.*	*Includes all domestic and regional developments in Latin America, the Caribbean, and Canada.*	*Includes all domestic and regional developments in Asia and Pacific nations, extending from Afghanistan through all the Pacific Islands, except Hawaii.*

U.S. Politics & Social Issues	U.S. Foreign Policy & Defense	U.S. Economy & Environment	Science, Technology, & Nature	Culture, Leisure, & Lifestyle	
New restrictions on the distribution of food stamps, as mandated by the 1996 welfare bill, go into effect.... In Sacramento, California, U.S. district judge Lawrence Karlton issues a temporary injunction to block a provision of California's new welfare law restricting benefit payments to newcomers to the state.	Many rules contained in a law passed in September 1996 that impose new restrictions on legal and illegal immigrants, called the Illegal Immigrant Reform and Immigrant Responsibility Act, take effect. The implementation of the rules has elicited legal challenges from civil-rights groups.... The Air Force's radar-evading B-2 Stealth bomber becomes operational.			Nancy J. Woodhull, 52, journalist who was the first managing editor for news at *USA Today*, dies in Pittsford, New York, of cancer.... Jolie Gabor, 97, socialite best known as the mother of Eva and Zsa Zsa Gabor, dies in Rancho Mirage, California, of unreported causes.	April 1
Dean Pleasant, a member of the paramilitary group involved in a bomb-making plot, is ordered to serve 71 months in prison.... Tennessee becomes the last state in the union to ratify the 15th Amendment, which guarantees citizens of the U.S. the right to vote regardless of "race, color or previous condition of servitude."... A federal jury in Spokane, Washington, deadlocks in the case of Verne Jay Merrell, Charles H. Barbee, and Robert S. Berry, white separatists accused of three bombings and two bank robberies in 1996. The jury convicts them on lesser charges, including conspiracy, and possession of hand grenades	A U.S. Air Force A-10 attack jet disappears in the mountains of Colorado when its pilot, Captain Craig Button, mysteriously breaks away from formation during a training mission.			Secretary of State Madeleine Albright throws out the first pitch at the Baltimore Orioles' home opener baseball game against the Kansas City Royals.... Tomoyuki Tanaka, 86, Japanese film producer who created the Godzilla monster featured in a series of internationally popular movies, dies in Tokyo of a stroke.	April 2
Six handcuffed, shackled prisoners burn to death when the van they are riding in burst into flames on a Tennessee highway.					April 3
FBI data suggests that bank robberies in 1996 increased nearly 10% over the previous year. The FBI recorded 7,562 bank heists in 1996, compared with 6,915 in 1995. Both years' totals are well below the 1991 record of 9,388 bank robberies.... Reports estimate that 185 people in Saginaw and Calhoun counties in Michigan are exhibiting symptoms of hepatitis A, as the virus spreads among school employees and students due to tainted frozen strawberries served in school lunches.			The space shuttle *Columbia* blasts off from Kennedy Space Center in Cape Canaveral, Florida, to study the effects of the absence of gravity on combustion.		April 4
	Henry Baldwin Hyde, 81, spymaster for the U.S. Office of Strategic Services during World War II who was awarded two Bronze Stars, dies in New York City after a long illness.			Allen Ginsberg, 70, poet who helped define the Beat Generation with his poem "The Howl," and who won numerous literary honors, including the 1974 National Book Award, dies in New York City of liver cancer.	April 5
			NASA officials order the crew of the space shuttle *Columbia* to return to Earth 12 days ahead of schedule after one of the shuttle's fuel cells shows signs of malfunctioning.	Federal Reserve Board chairman Alan Greenspan marries NBC News reporter Andrea Mitchell in Washington, Virginia.... Jack Kent Cooke, 84, businessman who owned the Washington Redskins football team and pioneered the practice of pay-per-view sporting events, dies in Washington, D.C., of congestive heart failure.	April 6

F	G	H	I	J
Includes elections, federal-state relations, civil rights and liberties, crime, the judiciary, education, health care, poverty, urban affairs, and population.	*Includes formation and debate of U.S. foreign and defense policies, veterans' affairs, and defense spending. (Relations with specific foreign countries are usually found under the region concerned.)*	*Includes business, labor, agriculture, taxation, transportation, consumer affairs, monetary and fiscal policy, natural resources, and pollution.*	*Includes worldwide scientific, medical, and technological developments; natural phenomena; U.S. weather; natural disasters; and accidents.*	*Includes the arts, religion, scholarship, communications media, sports, entertainments, fashions, fads, and social life.*

	World Affairs	Europe	Africa & the Middle East	The Americas	Asia & the Pacific
April 7	Chinese president Jiang Zemin announces that China will sign the UN International Covenant on Economic, Social, and Cultural Rights by the end of 1997.		Supporters of Zaire's Premier Etienne Tshisekedi clash with police in Kinshasa and attack the houses and vehicles of members of Parliament who oppose Tshisekedi's appointment as premier. In Lubumbashi, several hundred troops reportedly lay down their arms and don white headbands as a symbol of solidarity with the rebels.	In Brazil, TV Globo broadcasts a tape that shows six police officers forcing 11 residents of a slum area of Rio de Janeiro to line up against a wall and then beating them for an hour. The tape prompts outrage.	
April 8	Ronald Freeman, a U.S. investment banker, states he will resign as first vice president of the European Bank for Reconstruction and Development (EBRD).		Zairian president Mobutu Sese Seko declares a nationwide state of emergency and appoints military governors for the provinces still under government control.	The six Rio de Janeiro officers depicted on the tape aired in Brazil Apr. 7 are arrested.	
April 9	An Iraqi aircraft flies more than 100 passengers to Saudi Arabia for a Muslim religious pilgrimage. The U.S. immediately condemns the flight as a violation of the UN air embargo imposed on Iraq shortly after its invasion of Kuwait in 1990.	Striking miners block the tracks of the trans-Siberian railroad in a 16-hour protest in Russia. . . . Chechen separatist rebel Salman Raduyev is reportedly injured when a bomb explodes beneath his car. . . . A court in Turin, Italy, convicts Cesare Romiti, chair of automaker Fiat SpA, making him one of the most prominent Italians to face a criminal conviction since the 1992 crackdown on corruption in politics and business.	Zairian president Mobutu Sese Seko orders army chief of staff General Likulia Bolongo to form a military government. The move effectively ousts Premier Etienne Tshisekedi. In Kinshasa, tens of thousands of Tshisekedi's supporters clash with troops loyal to Mobutu. . . . . In Angola, 70 UNITA legislators—elected in 1992 during the earlier peace effort—are sworn in as members of Angola's 220-seat parliament.	The Mexican government announces that more than 100 children in that country contracted hepatitis A one month prior to the outbreak in Michigan. Reports confirm that Mexican strawberry farmers have suspended their harvests in the wake of the U.S. hepatitis cases.	Hong Kong's designated future leader, Tung Chee-hwa, reveals specific proposals that will place restrictions on political groups and public protests when China assumes control of the colony from Britain after midnight on June 30. The document, entitled Civil Liberties and Social Order, provides the first details regarding rights limits after the handover.
April 10	A court in Berlin, Germany, concludes that a committee of top government officials in Iran orchestrated the 1992 killing of four Iranian Kurds in a Berlin restaurant. The court sentences four of the accused—three from Lebanon, one from Iran—to prison terms ranging from life to five years. Germany suspends its policy of critical dialogue with Iran. Iranian militants launch a series of demonstrations to protest the German court decision.	An unidentified gunman in Londonderry, Northern Ireland, shoots and wounds Alice Collins, an officer of the Royal Ulster Constabulary (RUC) police force. The Provisional IRA claims responsibility.	Israeli and PNA security forces cooperate to uncover a West Bank cell of the military wing of the Islamic militant group Hamas. Israel arrests two suspected members of the cell in Surif, a town under direct Israeli jurisdiction. Palestinian police in Hebron take three other cell members into custody.		
April 11	Negotiators from the EU and the U.S. reach a tentative agreement that delays a likely confrontation over the U.S.'s Helms-Burton Act, which seeks to strengthen the U.S.'s economic embargo of Cuba by punishing foreign companies that invest in Cuba. . . . The IMF approves a new $658 million loan to Bulgaria.	Royal Ulster Constabulary officers raid a farmhouse in Crossmaglen, Northern Ireland, and seize a cache of weapons believed to belong to the IRA. Police arrest seven suspected terrorists. . . . In Italy, a fire damages Turin's San Giovanni Cathedral and its Guarini Chapel, which houses the Shroud of Turin, believed to be the burial cloth of Jesus Christ. The shroud, kept inside a silver urn, is not damaged.	The two sides in Angola's long-running civil war inaugurate a national-unity government after 19 years of fighting and two and a half years of uneasy peace. Members of the rebel UNITA are sworn in as ministers along with Pres. Jose Eduardo dos Santos's ruling MPLA.		The 10-month-old government of Indian prime minister H. D. Deve Gowda collapses after losing a confidence vote. . . . The last operating British naval base in Asia, a ship located off Stonecutter's Island in Hong Kong Harbor, is closed in advance of the colony's handover from Britain to China.
April 12		A London (England) rally organized by dockworkers and environmentalists erupts into a riot as protesters hurl bottles, sticks, and smoke bombs at police officers. Some 200 riot police are deployed to control the crowd. Eight demonstrators are arrested, and four police officers suffer injuries. . . . In Bosnia-Herzegovina, authorities discover a cache of 23 recently planted mines along the planned route for Pope John Paul II's upcoming visit.			Hong Kong's provisional legislature, a Chinese-appointed body, begins the lawmaking process for the first time. . . . Some 3,000 people gather at a demonstration in Sydney, Australia, to protest the recent formation of a political group, One Nation, founded by Pauline Hanson, a member of Parliament known for her right-wing views on race and immigration.

A	B	C	D	E
Includes developments that affect more than one world region, international organizations, and important meetings of major world leaders.	Includes all domestic and regional developments in Europe, including the Soviet Union, Turkey, Cyprus, and Malta.	Includes all domestic and regional developments in Africa and the Middle East, including Iraq and Iran and excluding Cyprus, Turkey, and Afghanistan.	Includes all domestic and regional developments in Latin America, the Caribbean, and Canada.	Includes all domestic and regional developments in Asia and Pacific nations, extending from Afghanistan through all the Pacific Islands, except Hawaii.

U.S. Politics & Social Issues	U.S. Foreign Policy & Defense	U.S. Economy & Environment	Science, Technology, & Nature	Culture, Leisure, & Lifestyle	
	Judge Stanley Sporkin of U.S. District Court in Washington, D.C., rules that the military violated the free speech and religious rights of its chaplains by barring them from asking members of their congregations to support antiabortion legislation.			Pulitzer Prizes are awarded to novelist Steven Millhauser and nonfiction writer Richard Kluger.... At the 150th running of Great Britain's Grand National Steeplechase, longshot Lord Gyllene wins.... *The Partner*, by John Grisham, tops the bestseller list.	April 7
A three-judge panel of the U.S. Ninth Circuit Court of Appeals in San Francisco, California, unanimously upholds the state's anti-affirmative-action Proposition 209. The voter-approved proposition will bar the state government from relying on race- or gender-based preferences in school admissions, public hiring, and contracting.... An Illinois man, John E. Ewing, 37, allegedly throws a Molotov cocktail at Judge George Miller, who dismissed his 1988 lawsuit against a grocery-store chain. The bomb explodes and sets fire to the judge's courtroom in Urbana, Illinois, injuring four people.	Army officials reveal that two sergeants stationed in Germany—Sergeant First Class Julius Davis and Sergeant Paul Fuller—will face courts-martial on charges of rape and sodomy against 18 female recruits at the Darmstadt military training center near Frankfurt, Germany.	The Justice Department and the FTC announce revised merger guidelines that outline how the agencies will weigh mergers' potential cost savings against antitrust concerns.... Reports by the IRS and GAO show that efforts by the IRS to stop its employees from browsing through taxpayers' income-tax returns have been largely unsuccessful.	The space shuttle *Columbia* touches down at Cape Canaveral, Florida, curtailing its slated 16-day mission due to equipment problems.... Due to concerns over U.S. antiabortion groups' threats to boycott Hoechst products, French pharmaceutical company Roussel Uclaf S.A. announces that it has donated the non-U.S. patent rights to the drug RU-486, or mifepristone, to Edouard Sakiz, a scientist who helped create the drug. Sakiz states that any profits earned will be invested in medical research.	Pope John Paul II names Francis E. George as the new leader of the Roman Catholic Archdiocese of Chicago.... Laura Nyro (born Laura Nigro), 49, singer and songwriter, dies in Danbury, Connecticut, of ovarian cancer.	April 8
A congressional study finds that many of the guns used in crimes in states with tough gun-control laws are acquired in other states with comparatively lax controls, especially four southern states: Florida, Texas, South Carolina, and Georgia.	Four drill sergeants at the Army's Fort Jackson basic training post in Columbia, South Carolina, are suspended from duties pending investigation of alleged sexual misconduct.		Shell Oil Co. unveils a robotic gas pump in Sacramento, California, that allows automobile drivers to fill their gas tanks without leaving their vehicle.... The Social Security Administration shuts down an information service operated on the Internet global computer network, citing concerns over the possibility of privacy violations.	James (Yank) Rachell, 87, one of the few blues musicians who specialized in playing the mandolin, dies in Indianapolis, Indiana, of unreported causes.... Helene Hanff, 80, writer best known for her 1970 book *84 Charing Cross Road*, dies in New York City.	April 9
Judge Thomas P. Jackson of U.S. District Court in Washington, D.C., strikes down a law that gave the president authority to cancel portions of spending bills after they were passed by Congress, ruling that the line-item veto violates the law-making procedure established by the Constitution.... Pres. Clinton announces that the government plans to hire at least 10,000 welfare recipients over the next four years.	Judge David Coar of U.S. District Court in Chicago, Illinois, rules that Bronislaw Hajda, a Polish-born resident of Chicago, participated in the killings of hundreds of Jews as a guard at a Nazi labor camp during World War II. The judge strips Hajda of his U.S. citizenship, clearing the way for federal authorities to begin deportation proceedings.	The dollar reaches a 55-month high against the Japanese yen, closing at 127.14 yen.... The AFL-CIO establishes a site on the Internet that lets computer users compare their salary with the compensation packages of 100 top CEOs.... The House Government Reform and Oversight Committee approves a set of procedural rules granting Rep. Dan Burton (R, Ind.), the committee chairman, virtually unchecked authority to determine the direction of the panel's inquiry into campaign finance abuses.			April 10
	Army officials disclose that Sergeant First Class Tony Cross faces 13 criminal charges of sexual misconduct, including adultery and sodomy, against four women.				April 11
			George Wald, 90, biologist whose discoveries first explained the process of human vision and who won the Nobel Prize in 1967, dies in Cambridge, Massachusetts, of unreported causes.	The Hollywood Women's Political Committee, a fund-raising group whose members are involved in the entertainment industry, votes to disband in protest against the growing influence of money in politics.	April 12

F	G	H	I	J
Includes elections, federal-state relations, civil rights and liberties, crime, the judiciary, education, health care, poverty, urban affairs, and population.	*Includes formation and debate of U.S. foreign and defense policies, veterans' affairs, and defense spending. (Relations with specific foreign countries are usually found under the region concerned.)*	*Includes business, labor, agriculture, taxation, transportation, consumer affairs, monetary and fiscal policy, natural resources, and pollution.*	*Includes worldwide scientific, medical, and technological developments; natural phenomena; U.S. weather; natural disasters; and accidents.*	*Includes the arts, religion, scholarship, communications media, sports, entertainments, fashions, fads, and social life.*

	World Affairs	Europe	Africa & the Middle East	The Americas	Asia & the Pacific
April 13	In response to the Apr. 10 decision by a German court that Iranian officials had arranged a killing, more than 100,000 Iranian militants rally outside the German embassy in Teheran, the Iranian capital. The protesters shout, "Death to America!" and "Death to Israel!"	Pope John Paul II holds an outdoor mass in Sarajevo, the capital of Bosnia-Herzegovina, appealing to a crowd of some 35,000 to reconcile with their neighbors and to repudiate the religious hatreds that ignited the civil war that ravaged Bosnia from 1992 through 1995. . . . Candidates of the ruling Croatian Democratic Union (HDZ) win election to 41 of the 63 seats in Croatia's upper house of Parliament, up from the 37 they had previously.	The World Health Organization reveals that a proposed UN airlift of Rwandan Hutu refugees from Zaire will be delayed because 120 cases of cholera, five of them fatal, were recorded at one site, which houses about half of the 100,000 refugees. . . . Mustafa Amin, 83, Egyptian journalist and outspoken critic of Pres. Gamal Abdel Nasser, dies in Cairo of unreported causes.	Eleven hostages who were taken captive Apr. 3 during a prison riot are released from the prison in Valledupar, a town in northern Colombia.	
April 14	The World Bank pledges to make $6 billion in loans available to Russia over a two-year period in order to smooth the transition to a free-market economy.	A military tribunal convening in Rome's Rebibbia prison begins a second trial against accused Nazi war criminal Erich Priebke.	Zairian president Mobutu Sese Seko's political opposition shuts down Zaire's capital, Kinshasa, in a general strike called by supporters of Etienne Tshisekedi, a popular pro-democracy politician who served as premier for nearly a week in April. Rebel leader Laurent Kabila claims that his forces have taken Kananga, the capital of West Kasai province.	Ten heavily armed inmates at a prison in Valledupar, a town in northern Colombia, lay down their weapons, ending a standoff that began April 3 with a failed escape attempt.	
April 15	Chinese diplomats, for the seventh consecutive year, succeed in blocking a draft resolution by the UN Human Rights Commission expressing concern over China's human-rights record.	Bosnia-Herzegovina's joint presidency agrees on terms for a new currency to be used in both the Bosnian Serb Republic and the Muslim-Croat federation. . . . Some 1,200 Italian, Spanish, and French peacekeeping troops land at the Albanian port of Durres and at the airport in Albania's capital, Tirana.	A fire and an ensuing stampede in a crowded tent city at Mina, seven miles (11 km) outside Mecca, the Muslim holy city, kills more than 300 pilgrims. At least 1,300 people are injured in the fire, and the death toll is expected to rise as the more seriously injured pilgrims die. . . . In Zaire, supporters of Etienne Tshisekedi shut down the capital, Kinshasa, in a general strike.		Officials report that radioactive tritium, or heavy water, leaked from a nuclear facility on the Fugen grounds in Japan. The facility is shut down. The corporation did not report the incident until 30 hours after it occurred. . . . In a highly publicized case, Miyuki Monobe, an eight-year-old Japanese girl, dies while awaiting a heart transplant in the U.S. since such surgeries are forbidden in Japan. The only heart transplant operation known to have been carried out in Japan occurred in 1968.
April 16	The UN Security Council, after vigorous behind-the-scenes diplomacy, issues a unanimous statement that refrains from either condemning the flight taken by Iraqi aircraft on Apr. 9 or categorizing it as a clear-cut violation of UN sanctions.	Prosecutors in Bavaria announce they have filed a criminal indictment against Felix Somm, the top executive at CompuServe Corp.'s German unit, for distributing pornography and racist propaganda. The indictment against Somm is considered a landmark in Bavaria's long-running effort to control the distribution of information over the Internet.		Emilio Azcarraga Milmo, 66, Mexican billionaire who owned Grupo Televisa SA, the world's largest producer of Spanish-language television programs, dies in Miami, Florida, of cancer.	
April 17			Chaim Herzog, 78, president of Israel, 1983–93, dies in Tel Aviv, Israel, of heart failure.	A two-month-long march by landless workers ends when the marchers reach Brasilia, the capital of Brazil. The march and a subsequent demonstration, organized by the Landless Movement (MST), is the largest protest against Pres. Fernando Henrique Cardoso since he took office in 1995.	Japan's state-run PNC admits to having failed to report 11 radiation leaks over the past three years at the Fugen plant, located in the town of Tsuruga. . . . Reports confirm that the South Pacific island of Tokelau, a territory of New Zealand with a population of 1,500, has become the last locale in the world to acquire telephone service. . . . Biju Patnaik, 81, Indian politician and daredevil pilot who was a key participant in India's struggle for independence from Great Britain, dies in New Delhi of unreported causes.
April 18		A Swiss military court acquits Goran Grabez, 32, of charges of war crimes committed at the Serbian Omarska camp. The court orders that Grabez, arrested in 1995 upon seeking asylum in Switzerland, be paid $68,000 in compensation.			

A	B	C	D	E
Includes developments that affect more than one world region, international organizations, and important meetings of major world leaders.	Includes all domestic and regional developments in Europe, including the Soviet Union, Turkey, Cyprus, and Malta.	Includes all domestic and regional developments in Africa and the Middle East, including Iraq and Iran and excluding Cyprus, Turkey, and Afghanistan.	Includes all domestic and regional developments in Latin America, the Caribbean, and Canada.	Includes all domestic and regional developments in Asia and Pacific nations, extending from Afghanistan through all the Pacific Islands, except Hawaii.

U.S. Politics & Social Issues	U.S. Foreign Policy & Defense	U.S. Economy & Environment	Science, Technology, & Nature	Culture, Leisure, & Lifestyle	
The Justice Department indicates that in 1995 violent crime—not including murder—fell more than 12% from the previous year.	Dorothy Frooks, political activist who became the highest-ranking woman in the U.S. military during World War I and who was a persistent advocate for the poor, dies in New York City.			Golfer Eldrick (Tiger) Woods wins the 61st Masters tournament in Augusta, Georgia, with a score of 270, the lowest in the tournament's history. He is the first black to win the Masters. . . . Michael Dorris, 52, writer best known for his 1989 book *The Broken Cord*, dies in Concord, New Hampshire, after apparently suffocating himself with a plastic bag.	April 13
Pres. Clinton orders the Justice Department to establish procedures to extend the reach of the 1989 Whistleblower Protection Act to FBI employees. . . . In *Edwards v. U.S.*, the Supreme Court rejects an appeal asserting that the equal-protection rights of blacks are violated by the stiffer federal sentencing guidelines set for crimes involving crack cocaine, versus those set for powder cocaine offenses.		Statistics suggest that the chief executive officers of large U.S. companies earned record gains in pay in 1996. The average of the chiefs' total compensation in 1996 was $5.78 million, an unprecedented 54% leap over year-earlier levels. . . . In Little Rock, Arkansas, U.S. district judge George Howard Jr. sentences James B. McDougal, a former partner of Pres. Clinton in Whitewater Development Corp., to three years in prison for his role in obtaining some $3 million in fraudulent loans during the mid-1980s.		The NHL reports that attendance in the 1996-97 season averaged 16,548 people per game, a 3.5% increase over the previous season. NHL games drew a record total of 17,640,529 fans.	April 14
In *Chandler v. Miller*, the Supreme Court rules, 8-1, to strike down a Georgia statute that requires political candidates to undergo drug tests before their names appear on ballots. It is the first time that the high court strikes down a government-backed drug-testing program. . . . The Justice Department finds that FBI scientists performed sloppy analytical work and gave "tilted" testimony in a number of high-profile cases. . . . Reports confirm that health officials in St. Louis, Missouri, have identified 62 women and girls between the ages of 12 and 22 who were exposed to HIV by Darnell McGee, who was killed in January.		The Senate approves, 65-34, a bill that will require the federal government to build in Nevada an interim storage facility for thousands of tons of nuclear waste currently held at 80 nuclear facilities across the country. . . . The House, 412-0, and Senate, 97-0, pass bills making unauthorized browsing through confidential taxpayer returns a crime. . . . The dollar climbs to 1.7374 marks, registering a 38-month high against the German currency. . . . The House rejects, 233-190, a proposed constitutional amendment that would have mandated a two-thirds majority vote by Congress to raise taxes.			April 15
The Connecticut Senate and House of Representatives approve a measure transferring control over the school system in Hartford, the capital, from local authorities to the state government. The takeover of Hartford schools represents the first time the state has taken control of a local school system.		A U.S. District Court jury in Chicago finds former Rep. Mel Reynolds (D, Ill.) guilty on 15 of 16 counts of bank and mortgage fraud. He is also convicted of violating FEC campaign finance laws.			April 16
House Speaker Newt Gingrich (R, Ga.), in an announcement that surprises Republicans and Democrats alike, reveals that he will pay his $300,000 fine for violating House rules with a loan from former Senate majority leader Robert J. Dole (R, Kans.).	Pres. Clinton approves a plan to merge two independent foreign policy agencies—the Arms Control and Disarmament Agency (ACDA) and the U.S. Information Agency (USIA)—with the U.S. State Department over two years.				April 17
The North Carolina vacation home of Andrew J. Schindler, president of R. J. Reynolds Tobacco Co., is destroyed by a fire that officials suspect was caused by a cigarette butt.					April 18

F	G	H	I	J
Includes elections, federal-state relations, civil rights and liberties, crime, the judiciary, education, health care, poverty, urban affairs, and population.	*Includes formation and debate of U.S. foreign and defense policies, veterans' affairs, and defense spending. (Relations with specific foreign countries are usually found under the region concerned.)*	*Includes business, labor, agriculture, taxation, transportation, consumer affairs, monetary and fiscal policy, natural resources, and pollution.*	*Includes worldwide scientific, medical, and technological developments; natural phenomena; U.S. weather; natural disasters; and accidents.*	*Includes the arts, religion, scholarship, communications media, sports, entertainments, fashions, fads, and social life.*

	World Affairs	Europe	Africa & the Middle East	The Americas	Asia & the Pacific
April 19		The anticommunist United Democratic Forces (ODS) wins a decisive victory in elections to Bulgaria's National Assembly.			
April 20					In response to planned restrictions on freedom in Hong Kong when the colony reverts to Chinese authority on June 30, hundreds of activists hold a street march in protest.
April 21	Iraq announces that it will fly helicopters to the Saudi border to pick up "sick and exhausted" pilgrims returning from their hajj, even though the flights violate a U.S.-backed ban on airborne Iraqi aircraft in southern Iraq.			The 750 residents of Emerson, a Canadian town that borders the U.S. along the Red River, are ordered to evacuate in anticipation of flooding. . . . General Andres Rodriguez Pedotti, 72, politician who led a 1989 coup that ended 35 years of military rule in Paraguay, dies in New York City of complications from liver cancer.	Inder Kumar Gujral is sworn in as prime minister by Indian president Shankar Dayal Sharma. . . . A small advance contingent of China's People's Liberation Army arrives in Hong Kong, marking the first time in 150 years that Chinese troops have taken up position in the colony. . . . Diosdado P. Macapagal, 86, president of the Philippines, 1961–65, dies in Manila after suffering a heart attack.
April 22		Ante Klaric, a Croatian government ombudsman, acknowledges that many Serb refugees have been blocked from going home or have found ethnic Croats living in their homes. It is the first time a Croatian government official admits that rights abuses are taking place in the recaptured areas.	In Algeria, a group armed with hatchets and knives kill 93 villagers, including 43 women and girls in Haouch Mokhfi, 12 miles (20 km) south of Algiers. The attack, attributed to Islamic fundamentalists, is the biggest massacre of civilians reported since the strife began in 1992. . . . Rebel soldiers and local villagers armed with machetes reportedly attack the camps for Rwandan Hutu refugees, sending them fleeing to a deep forest along the Congo River south of Kisangani, a city in the northeast.	Peruvian commandos storm the Japanese ambassador's residence in Lima, the capital, freeing 72 hostages held by leftist rebels since December. The raid ends the longest guerrilla siege in Latin American history. All 14 rebels, members of the MRTA, are killed in the raid. One hostage, Peruvian Supreme Court justice Carlos Giusti Acuna, is struck by a stray bullet during the raid and dies after suffering a heart attack on the way to the hospital. Two Peruvian soldiers, Lt. Col. Juan Valer Sandoval and Lt. Raul Jimenez Chavez, are also killed in the raid.	A nine-year-old illegal immigrant girl, Chung Yeuk-lam, is handcuffed and taken from her Hong Kong home in a televised raid before being deported to China along with her mother. The raid apparently is meant to warn parents seeking to smuggle their Chinese children into Hong Kong before the colony reverts to Chinese sovereignty, from British rule, after midnight on June 30.
April 23	Chinese president Jiang Zemin and Russian president Boris Yeltsin sign a declaration pledging to promote a new world order in which no single country will monopolize international affairs. . . . The European Commission forecasts that, of the EU's 15 members, only Italy and Greece will have deficits above 3% of GDP in 1997. The IMF, though, predicts six EU countries will have deficits above 3% of GDP for 1997. The IMF projects that Canada's economy will lead the G-7 countries in growth in 1997 and that Italy will trail the group. IMF statistics place world growth at 4.0% in 1996, and it predicts 4.4% for 1997 and 1998.	A bomb explodes on southern Russia's rail network in the town of Armavir, killing two people and wounding eight. . . . Denis Charles Scott Compton, 78, widely considered one of the best British cricket players ever, dies in Windsor, England, of complications after hip surgery. . . . Iris Margaret Elsie Lemare, 94, the first professional female conductor in Britain, dies of unreported causes.	Some 10,000 supporters of the Shas movement, comprised predominantly of Jews from North Africa and Arab countries of the Middle East, rally in Jerusalem in defense of the head of the fundamentalist Shas party, Arye Deri, who faces fraud and bribery charges in a scandal involving the appointment of an attorney general.	The Toronto Stock Exchange closes its 145-year-old trading floor. The bourse, Canada's largest, will henceforth use an automated trading system that links brokers' computer terminals. . . . All residents of the Red River Valley south of Winnipeg, some 17,000 people, are ordered to evacuate due to flooding.	
April 24	The presidents of Russia, China, Kazakhstan, Kyrgyzstan, and Tajikistan sign an agreement to reduce military forces on the former Soviet-Chinese border, which stretches some 5,000 miles (8,000 km).	Ivan Kostov is sworn in as premier of Bulgaria. . . . A court in the Bosnian Serb town of Zvornik sentences three Muslims to 20-year prison terms on charges of murdering four Serbs. Four other Muslims charged with illegal possession of firearms receive one-year sentences. A UN official asserts that the trial presented no conclusive evidence against the accused.	The South African health ministry reports that, at the end of 1996, an estimated 2.4 million people, or 6% of the population, were infected with HIV, the virus that causes AIDS. The infection rate is up one-third from 1995 year-end figures, which indicated that 1.8 million South Africans, or 4.6% of the population, were HIV-positive.		In China, at least three people are executed and 27 others are sentenced to prison terms for participating in February riots in the remote Xinjiang Uighur Autonomous Region. . . . Prompted by the Apr. 15 death of Miyuki Monobe, the lower house of Japan's Diet passes a bill that will make heart transplants possible in Japan.

A	B	C	D	E
Includes developments that affect more than one world region, international organizations, and important meetings of major world leaders.	*Includes all domestic and regional developments in Europe, including the Soviet Union, Turkey, Cyprus, and Malta.*	*Includes all domestic and regional developments in Africa and the Middle East, including Iraq and Iran and excluding Cyprus, Turkey, and Afghanistan.*	*Includes all domestic and regional developments in Latin America, the Caribbean, and Canada.*	*Includes all domestic and regional developments in Asia and Pacific nations, extending from Afghanistan through all the Pacific Islands, except Hawaii.*

U.S. Politics & Social Issues	U.S. Foreign Policy & Defense	U.S. Economy & Environment	Science, Technology, & Nature	Culture, Leisure, & Lifestyle	
	Reports confirm that Denver, Colorado, will be the first of 26 cities to receive antiterrorism training from the U.S. Army. The city, which has the largest concentration of federal workers outside Washington, D.C., was reportedly chosen because of an upcoming summit of the heads of eight leading industrialized nations.		The Red River of the North floods Grand Forks, North Dakota, and East Grand Forks, Minnesota, the two worst-hit towns along the swelled river. All 50,000 residents of Grand Forks are ordered to evacuate. A fire destroys at least six buildings and damages at least 11 others in downtown Grand Forks.		April 19
	Henry A. Mucci, 88, World War II U.S. Army colonel, dies in Melbourne, Florida, of unreported causes.			Jean Louis (born Jean Louis Berthault), 89, Hollywood costume designer whose gowns include the one worn by Marilyn Monroe when she sang her famous rendition of "Happy Birthday" to Pres. John F. Kennedy in 1962, dies in Palm Springs, California, of unreported causes.	April 20
In *Blessing v. Freestone*, the Supreme Court rules unanimously that a group of women from Arizona cannot sue that state for its ineffective enforcement of federal child-support laws.... Police in rural Sussex County, New Jersey, arrest two teenagers in what appears to be a thrill-seeking slaying of two pizza delivery men in a carefully planned ambush near a deserted house in the hamlet of Franklin, New Jersey.				The ashes of 24 people, including the creator of the TV series *Star Trek*, Gene Roddenberry, and 1960s drug guru Timothy Leary, are launched into space.... Lameck Aguta of Kenya wins the men's title at the Boston Marathon. In the women's race, Fatuma Roba of Ethiopia wins.	April 21
In Pittsburgh, Pennsylvania, Judge David R. Cashman dismisses involuntary manslaughter charges against Milton Mulholland and Michael Albert, two white police officers accused of killing a black motorist during a 1995 traffic stop.... FBI agents in Fort Worth, Texas, arrest four people in an alleged plot to blow up a natural-gas plant and rob an armored car to fund further terrorist activities.	The INS announces that legal immigration rose 27% in 1996.... Pres. Clinton imposes a ban prohibiting new U.S. investment in Myanmar, in response to reports of continued human-rights abuses.... In a report by Justice Department inspector general Michael Bromwich regarding the Aldrich H. Ames spy case, Bromwich criticizes the FBI and CIA for not cooperating in investigations into the deaths of Russian agents working for both agencies in 1985 and 1986. Ames, sentenced to life in prison in 1994, is believed to have caused the deaths of at least 10 agents spying on Russia for the U.S.	Vice Pres. Al Gore and Secretary of State Madeleine Albright issue the State Department's first annual "Environmental Diplomacy" report to mark Earth Day.... The Dow closes at 6833, up 173.38 points, which, in terms of single-session point gains, is surpassed only by a rise on Oct. 21, 1987. On a percentage basis, the 2.60% gain is the largest since Dec. 23, 1991.... Whitewater independent counsel Kenneth Starr gains a six-month extension of a grand jury investigation after claiming that the panel uncovered "extensive evidence" of possible obstruction of justice.	The Red River crests in Grand Forks, North Dakota, at 54.1 feet (16.5 m).	A jury in Hollidaysburg, Pennsylvania, convicts Dennis and Lorie Nixon, a couple who belong to a Christian faith-healing sect, for allowing their 16-year-old daughter, Shannon Nixon, to die of treatable diabetes. The ruling marks the second such conviction for the couple.	April 22
The third-highest-ranking member of the New York City-based Genovese crime family, James (Little Jimmy) Ida, is convicted on racketeering and murder conspiracy charges in U.S. District Court in Manhattan.	U.S. Air Force officials confirm that they found wreckage from a missing air force A-10 attack jet that disappeared in the mountains of Colorado Apr. 2.				April 23
Opening statements are heard in the trial of Timothy J. McVeigh, the federal government's chief suspect in the Apr. 19, 1995, bombing of a federal Building in Oklahoma City, Oklahoma, in which a total of 168 people were killed, including 19 children, and more than 500 people were wounded.	The U.S. Senate votes, 74-26, to ratify the Chemical Weapons Convention (CWC), a multilateral treaty mandating disarmament of poison-gas weapons. The ratification makes the U.S. a charter member of the treaty.	The campaign committee for Sen. Frank Lautenberg (D, N.J.) admits that it improperly accepted $20,895 from the Mercer County Democratic Committee during a 1994 reelection bid and states that it will pay the same amount to the FEC in restitution.	Doctors at a fertility clinic at UCLA reveal that they ignore successfully performed in vitro fertilization on a 63-year-old woman, who became the oldest-known mother when she gave birth to a healthy baby girl in November 1996.... A House committee approves a bill providing $5.5 billion in disaster relief for 22 regions in states affected by flooding.	Pat (Layton) Paulsen, 69, comedian best known for his farcical campaigns for the U.S. presidency that began in 1968, dies in Tijuana, Mexico, while reportedly undergoing treatment for cancer of the brain and colon.	April 24
F	G	H	I	J	
Includes elections, federal-state relations, civil rights and liberties, crime, the judiciary, education, health care, poverty, urban affairs, and population.	*Includes formation and debate of U.S. foreign and defense policies, veterans' affairs, and defense spending. (Relations with specific foreign countries are usually found under the region concerned.)*	*Includes business, labor, agriculture, taxation, transportation, consumer affairs, monetary and fiscal policy, natural resources, and pollution.*	*Includes worldwide scientific, medical, and technological developments; natural phenomena; U.S. weather; natural disasters; and accidents.*	*Includes the arts, religion, scholarship, communications media, sports, entertainments, fashions, fads, and social life.*	

	World Affairs	Europe	Africa & the Middle East	The Americas	Asia & the Pacific
April 25	The UN General Assembly, convening in an emergency session, votes to condemn Israeli plans to construct the Har Homa settlement in Arab East Jerusalem.	Pope John Paul II visits the Czech Republic on a trip marking the 1,000th anniversary of the martyrdom of St. Adalbert, a missionary who introduced Christianity to Bohemia. . . . Nikolai D. Yegorov, 45, a former Russian nationalities minister who was a proponent of the ultimately unsuccessful strategy to use military force to crush the Chechen uprising, dies after a long illness.	In Algeria, a bomb explodes under a train 10 miles (16 km) south of Algiers, killing 21 passengers.		China ratifies the Chemical Weapons Convention (CWC), a multilateral treaty mandating disarmament of poison-gas weapons.
April 26		Turkish premier Necmettin Erbakan agrees to enact 18 measures to preserve secularism in Turkey.			Peng Zhen, 95, hard-line elder of China's Communist Party who was one of the last surviving "eight immortals," leaders of the 1949 communist revolution, dies in Beijing of an unspecified illness.
April 27			The government reports that 410,000 Algerians have fled the country since 1992. . . . Yemen's ruling General People's Congress (GPC) party of Pres. Ali Abdullah Saleh retains solid control of Parliament in elections. A soldier guarding a ballot station in the town of Mukayras, 150 miles (240 km) southeast of Sanaa, the capital, indiscriminately opens fire just prior to the opening of polls, killing five other guards and three civilians.	Gabriel Figueroa Mateos, 89, Mexican cinematographer who established a definitive style for Mexican films and made some 200 films during his career, dies in Mexico City after suffering a stroke.	Former British prime minister Margaret Thatcher presides over a ceremony opening a suspension bridge leading to Hong Kong's new airport. The 1.3-mile-long, US$900 million structure, the Tsing-Ma Bridge, is the world's longest road and rail link.
April 28		A bomb explodes on Southern Russia's rail network in Pyatigorsk, killing two people and wounding 20 others. . . . Business and labor-union leaders formally sign an agreement on national labor reforms in Spain. . . . Peter Murray Taylor (Lord of Gosforth), 66, chief justice of Britain's second-highest court, the Court of Appeals, 1992–96, dies in Guildford, England, reportedly of cancer.		The Panamanian government announces that it has granted political asylum to former Ecuadoran president Abdala Bucaram Ortiz.	A court in Jakarta, the capital of Indonesia, convicts Budiman Sudjatmiko, leader of the small leftist Indonesian Democratic Party, which is not recognized by the government, of subversion and sentences him to 13 years in prison.
April 29	The Chemical Weapons Convention (CWC), a multilateral treaty mandating disarmament of poison gas weapons, goes into effect. A total of 165 countries have signed the CWC since it was opened for signing in 1993.			In Rio de Janeiro, Brazil, more than 1,000 protesters demonstrate against the sale of Companhia Vale do Rio Doce SA, the state-owned mining company. At least 25 people are injured when protesters clash with police. . . . The Canadian town of Ste. Agathe, which has a population of 500, is flooded when water enters overland as floods along the U.S.-Canadian border continue.	At least 60 people are killed and more than 260 others are injured when a crowded passenger train crashes into another train stopped at a station in Rongjiawan, in China's central Hunan province. . . . Reports confirm that Chinese police opened fire on a crowd of Muslim protesters trying to block buses that were carrying the rioters who were convicted Apr. 24. Police reportedly killed two Muslims in the incident.
April 30	The U.S. finds that domestic terrorism is "probably a more widespread phenomenon than international terrorism today." The report cites civil strife in Sri Lanka, Algeria, India, and Pakistan, as well as in the U.S. The report notes that 296 international terrorist attacks were recorded in 1996, the lowest in 24 years. However, 311 people were killed in the 1996 attacks, nearly twice as many as in 1995. The Tamil Tigers and Hamas are the groups that killed the most people in 1996.	Italy's cabinet approves a plan to end the forced exile of heirs to the Italian throne. The government in 1946 barred heirs to the House of Savoy from entering Italy.	In Yemen, a journalist is shot to death and four other people are wounded outside a vote-counting location. . . . Samir Mutawe, Jordan's information minister, reveals that King Hussein will provide haven for Mousa Mohammed Abu Marzook, the leader of the political wing of Hamas. . . . The UN begins an airlift aimed at repatriating 80,000 Rwandan Hutu refugees stranded in deep forest along the Congo River south of Kisangani, a city in the northeast of Zaire.	Mexico abolishes the National Institute to Combat Drugs, the government's main antidrug agency, amid allegations that it is corrupt and inefficient.	Reports from China confirm that the highest-ranking official imprisoned for offenses related to 1989 prodemocracy protests in the capital city of Beijing, Bao Tong, has been released and allowed to go home.

A	B	C	D	E
Includes developments that affect more than one world region, international organizations, and important meetings of major world leaders.	Includes all domestic and regional developments in Europe, including the Soviet Union, Turkey, Cyprus, and Malta.	Includes all domestic and regional developments in Africa and the Middle East, including Iraq and Iran and excluding Cyprus, Turkey, and Afghanistan.	Includes all domestic and regional developments in Latin America, the Caribbean, and Canada.	Includes all domestic and regional developments in Asia and Pacific nations, extending from Afghanistan through all the Pacific Islands, except Hawaii.

U.S. Politics & Social Issues	U.S. Foreign Policy & Defense	U.S. Economy & Environment	Science, Technology, & Nature	Culture, Leisure, & Lifestyle	
Judge William Osteen Sr. rules that the FDA has authority to regulate the distribution, sale, and use of tobacco products. The ruling deals a severe blow to the tobacco industry in its four-decade-long battle to avoid closer government scrutiny of its practices. However, the court rejects the FDA's assertion that it has jurisdiction over tobacco advertising.	The army discloses that three officers at Fort Bliss in El Paso, Texas—Second Lieutenant Trevor Gordon, Major Eddie Brenham, and Captain Ivan Brown—were discharged and sentenced to prison terms for sexual misconduct.... The U.S. indicates it will provide the same treatment to Hong Kong residents who hold the colony's post-handover passports as it does for those who hold the current British passports.	According to the Justice Department, the federal government spent nearly $60,000 to reimburse lawyers hired by White House employees who testified before Congress in 1996 concerning the firing of seven travel office employees and its improper requisition of confidential FBI files.	*Time* magazine settles a $3.5 million lawsuit against on-line service provider CompuServe Corp., filed when the computer service dropped its *Time Online* magazine service. ... An FCC auction for wireless-service licenses closes after raising only $13.6 million. FCC officials characterize the event as the most disappointing auction held in recent years.	Nancy Claster, 82, best known as Miss Nancy from the long-running children's TV program *Romper Room*, 1953–64, dies in Baltimore, Maryland, of unreported causes.	April 25
				Joey Faye (born Joseph Palladino), 87, comedian and actor known for his part in vaudeville duos, dies in Englewood, New Jersey, of unreported causes.	April 26
Three members of the Republic of Texas, a group that claims Texas was illegally annexed by the U.S. in 1845, begin a standoff by taking Joe and Margaret Ann Rowe hostage.... In Philadelphia, Pennsylvania, the President's Summit for America's Future, a series to promote volunteerism nationwide, opens. Several thousand people protest the summit, arguing that, although volunteerism is noble, it cannot make up for federal cutbacks.	Scientists at the Armed Forces Institute of Pathology in Washington, D.C., confirm that human remains found at the crash site of an A-10 attack jet are those of Captain Craig Button, who broke formation during a training exercise on Apr. 2.		Arceli Keh, a resident of Highland, California, identifies herself as the 63-year-old woman who became the oldest-known mother ever in November 1996.		April 27
The Republic of Texas group releases the Rowes, taken hostage Apr. 27, when negotiators agree to hand over Robert Scheidt, a member arrested on trespassing and weapons charges.... In *Timmons v. Twin Cities Area New Party*, the Supreme Court rules, 6-3, that the state of Minnesota may bar individuals from running for political office as candidates on more than one party ticket.... In *Bryan County Board of Commissioners v. Brown*, the Supreme Court rules, 5-4, that a county in Oklahoma is not liable to pay damages to a woman who was a victim of police brutality there.		Data from *Fortune 500* suggests that the 500 largest U.S. companies in 1996 recorded their fourth straight year in which earnings grew faster than revenues, 23.3% and 8.3%, respectively, Aggregate profits for the 500 top companies came to $300.911 billion, while aggregate revenues were $5.077 trillion.		An NCAA study finds that funding for women's collegiate athletic programs increased over the last five years but has not gained full equity with men's programs.... *Pretend You Don't See Her* by Mary Higgins Clark tops the bestseller list.	April 28
Pres. Clinton names three people to a nine-member commission that will examine the economic and social effects of gambling.... The U.S. Sentencing Commission recommends narrowing the discrepancy between federal sentences for crack cocaine offenses and those for crimes involving powdered cocaine, which is a retreat from its 1995 position.	An army court-martial jury convicts a former drill instructor, Staff Sergeant Delmar G. Simpson, of raping six women trainees under his command in 1995 and 1996. The rape convictions are the first in an investigation into alleged widespread sexual misconduct by instructors at the army's Ordnance Center and School at the Aberdeen Proving Ground in Maryland.	Judge Jack B. Weinstein of U.S. District Court in Brooklyn, New York, throws out a verdict against Digital Equipment Corp. that awarded $5.3 million to Patricia Geressy, who suffers from repetitive-stress injury, and orders a new trial in the case. He also throws out a $302,000 award to a third coplaintiff, Jill Jackson, because the statute of limitations has expired.... The Dow closes at 6962.03 up 179.01 points, the second-highest gain on record.	Judge Jim Dwyer of Frederick County Court in Maryland sentences Daniel Carleton Gajdusek, a Nobel Prize–winning scientist, to 18 months in prison for sexually abusing a teenage boy he brought from Micronesia to live with him in the U.S.	Mike Royko, 64, Chicago-based journalist known for championing the causes of working people and the poor, dies in Chicago Illinois, after suffering a brain aneurysm.	April 29
Judge Barrington D. Parker Jr. of U.S. District Court in White Plains, New York, sentences Rita Gluzman to life imprisonment without parole on federal spousal-abuse charges for the 1996 axe slaying of her husband, Yakov Gluzman. Rita Gluzman is the first woman tried under the 1994 Violence Against Women Act, designed primarily to prosecute abusive husbands who travel across state lines. She is the first defendant of either sex tried under the law in a homicide case.	The U.S. State Department's report on terrorism lists seven countries that it alleges support terrorism and are therefore not eligible for U.S. military or economic aid. The countries are Iran, Iraq, Cuba, Libya, North Korea, Sudan, and Syria.	The Senate votes, 85-13, to confirm Alexis Herman as secretary of labor.... The Treasury Department, after tallying 1996 tax-return revenues, predicts that the federal deficit for fiscal 1997 will fall to $75 billion—the lowest budget deficit relative to the size of the economy since 1974.... The Commerce Department reports that the U.S. gross domestic product grew at a seasonally adjusted annual rate of 5.6% in the first quarter of 1997.		In the TV series *Ellen*, the character played by Ellen DeGeneres reveals that she is a lesbian, becoming the first lead character in a TV series to openly acknowledge her homosexuality.... Residents of Concord, Massachusetts, vote to contribute $160,000 toward the purchase of the birthplace of Henry David Thoreau from a private owner.	April 30

F	G	H	I	J
Includes elections, federal-state relations, civil rights and liberties, crime, the judiciary, education, health care, poverty, urban affairs, and population.	*Includes formation and debate of U.S. foreign and defense policies, veterans' affairs, and defense spending. (Relations with specific foreign countries are usually found under the region concerned.)*	*Includes business, labor, agriculture, taxation, transportation, consumer affairs, monetary and fiscal policy, natural resources, and pollution.*	*Includes worldwide scientific, medical, and technological developments; natural phenomena; U.S. weather; natural disasters; and accidents.*	*Includes the arts, religion, scholarship, communications media, sports, entertainments, fashions, fads, and social life.*

	World Affairs	Europe	Africa & the Middle East	The Americas	Asia & the Pacific
May 1		Britain's opposition Labour Party routs the ruling Conservative (Tory) Party, winning a 179-seat majority in the House of Commons. Labour Party leader Tony Blair will replace P.M. John Major, ending 18 years of Tory rule.... Miners in the eastern Russian city of Vladivostok strike to protest their growing wage arrears.... Bo Widerberg, 66, Swedish film director, dies in Angelholm, Sweden, after a long illness.		In Canada, the Red River crests in Winnipeg, the provincial capital, but the city is saved from major damage due to a floodway built in 1968 and the recently constructed Brunkild dike.	
May 2		In Turkey, about 50 unidentified gunmen enter the Istanbul studios of a television station and fire dozens of shots while berating employees for broadcasting an interview critical of Deputy Premier Tansu Ciller. No injuries are reported.		Reports confirm that Peru has charged five generals and 14 other police officials with negligence and disobedience for intelligence and security lapses that led to the rebels' successful takeover of the ambassador's residence.... Some 200 leftist rebels of the Guatemalan National Revolutionary Union (UNRG) in the Sacol disarmament camp turn in their weapons, as agreed in a December 1996 peace agreement. The weapons turnover ends a two-month-long rebel disarmament program.	Reports indicate that more than 700,000 of Taiwan's pigs have died of hoof-and-mouth disease.... Statistics reveal that Japan's average monthly unemployment rate in the 1996–97 fiscal year marked a post–World War II high.
May 3		Prince Napoleon (Louis Jerome Victor-Emmanuel Leopold Marie Bonaparte), 83, great-great nephew of Emperor Napoleon I, dies in Switzerland of unreported causes.... Sir John Junor, 78, renowned British newspaper editor and columnist, dies in London of unreported causes.... Narciso Garcia Yepes, 69, Spanish guitarist, dies in Murcia, Spain, of cancer.... Hugh Hughes (Hughie) Green, 77, British entertainer and child star, dies in London, England, of cancer.		The village of Grande Pointe, near Winnipeg, Canada, floods.	
May 4		Chechen separatist rebel Salman Raduyev, who states he was injured in a Apr. 9 bomb, claims responsibility for the Apr. 23 and Apr. 28 bombings in Russia.... A presidential commission finds that Russia faces a demographic crisis caused by a decline in the number of births and a rise in the death rate. Only 1.4 million Russians were born in 1995, while 2.2 million died. Russia's death rate is the highest in Europe and surpasses that of many Asian and African countries.	Ninety-one Rwandan refugees suffocate or are crushed to death on an overcrowded train to Kisangani, Zaire.		An official from Calgary, Canada-based Bre-X Minerals Ltd. reveals that an independent report shows that the highly touted Busang gold lode in Indonesia's East Kalimantan province is a hoax.... More than 50,000 demonstrators lay down on the boulevard in front of the presidential office in Taipei, the capital of Taiwan, to protest what they call the government's failure to protect its citizens from crime. The protesters demand Premier Lien Chan's resignation.
May 5			PNA justice minister Freih Abu Medein reveals that Palestinians convicted of land sales to Jews will be sentenced to death.... World Food Program officials report that some 50,000 Hutu refugees emerged near the Congo River town of Mbandaka, close to the western border with the Republic of the Congo. The previously unknown group traversed the breadth of Zaire on foot, a distance of more than 800 miles (1,300 km).	U.S. president Bill Clinton makes his first visit as president to Mexico, Costa Rica, and the Caribbean island nation of Barbados.	In response to the May 4 disclosure in Indonesia, Freeport-McMoRan Copper and Gold Inc. of the U.S. and Indonesia's PT Nusantara Ampera Bakti (Nusamba), partners with Bre-X in the development of the alleged Busang lode, withdraw from the joint venture. The Royal Canadian Mounted Police and Bre-X announce separate probes into the Busang hoax.
May 6			At the town of Kenge, 120 miles (190 km) east of Kinshasa, Zaire, government troops and UNITA fighters battle ADFL forces in some of the fiercest fighting of the rebellion.	Despite protests, Brazil sells a controlling stake in Companhia Vale do Rio Doce SA, the state-owned mining company, to a consortium led by Brazilian steelmaker Companhia Siderurgica Nacional SA. The privatization is the largest ever in Latin America.... U.S. president Bill Clinton, in an unprecedented move, meets with leaders of the conservative National Action Party (PAN) and the left-wing Democratic Revolutionary Party (PRD), Mexico's two main opposition parties.	Former Indian prime minister P. V. Narasimha Rao is charged with criminal conspiracy and bribery in a four-year-old vote-buying scandal. The ruling makes Rao the first Indian prime minister ever to be indicted on criminal charges.... Wijayananda Dahanayake, 94, prime minister from September 1959 to March 1960 of what was then Ceylon (now Sri Lanka), dies of unreported causes.

A	B	C	D	E
Includes developments that affect more than one world region, international organizations, and important meetings of major world leaders.	Includes all domestic and regional developments in Europe, including the Soviet Union, Turkey, Cyprus, and Malta.	Includes all domestic and regional developments in Africa and the Middle East, including Iraq and Iran and excluding Cyprus, Turkey, and Afghanistan.	Includes all domestic and regional developments in Latin America, the Caribbean, and Canada.	Includes all domestic and regional developments in Asia and Pacific nations, extending from Afghanistan through all the Pacific Islands, except Hawaii.

U.S. Politics & Social Issues	U.S. Foreign Policy & Defense	U.S. Economy & Environment	Science, Technology, & Nature	Culture, Leisure, & Lifestyle	
The Ohio District Court of Appeals rules that a program of distributing vouchers that poor families may use to send children to private religious schools is unconstitutional. . . . John Ramsey and Patricia Ramsey strongly deny any involvement in the 1996 death of their daughter, JonBenet Ramsey. The murder of JonBenet Ramsey, who was named Little Miss Colorado in 1995, has received much media attention.		Abraham J. Hirschfeld, a NYC millionaire, is charged with numerous counts of tax fraud for failing to pay more than $2.2 million in state income taxes between 1988 and 1995. . . . The House approves, 262-157, a bill authorizing $149.9 million to fund 18 of the chamber's 20 committees. . . . The CBO estimates that spending shortfalls will be about $225 billion less over the next five years than predicted.			May 1
Robert Allen Stillman, a 25-year-old white man, becomes the first person convicted under a 1996 federal law targeting racially motivated church arson when he pleads guilty in U.S. District Court in Dallas, Texas. His codefendant, Randall Elliott Moore, 22, pleads guilty to charges of arson and conspiracy to violate civil rights. . . . Hundreds of youths in Boulder, Colorado, clash with police after firefighters arrive to put out a bonfire reportedly set by University of Colorado students. . . . Audley Eloise (Queen Mother) Moore, 98, civil-rights activist, dies in New York City of unreported causes.	A former army soldier and alleged neo-Nazi, Malcolm Wright Jr., is convicted of two counts of first-degree murder in the deaths of a black couple, Jackie Burden and Michael James, in Fayetteville. North Carolina, in 1995.	The White House and Republican congressional leaders announce that they have reached an agreement to balance the federal budget by 2002. The historic deal includes tax cuts and reductions in discretionary spending favored by Republicans and funding increases for education, welfare, and health insurance for children backed by Pres. Clinton. . . . The Labor Department reports that the seasonally adjusted unemployment rate in the U.S. plunged to 4.9% in April, from the previous month's 5.2% rate. The April figure is the nation's lowest unemployment rate since December 1973.	Sir John Carew Eccles, 94, Australian neurophysiologist who shared the Nobel Prize in Medicine in 1963 for research that explained how electrical currents stimulate human nerve cells, dies in Contra, Switzerland.		May 2
The Republic of Texas, an armed separatist group founded on the belief that Texas was illegally annexed by the U.S. in 1845, ends the standoff started Apr. 27 in the remote Davis Mountains of southwestern Texas. A total of six members of the group, including its leader, Richard L. McLaren, surrender to police. Two group members flee into the mountains.				Silver Charm wins the 123rd running of the Kentucky Derby at Churchill Downs in Louisville, Kentucky.	May 3
The confrontation that started May 2 between hundreds of youths in Boulder, Colorado, and police calms. During the incident, 11 people were arrested and 20 were injured.			FBI director Louis J. Freeh reveals that the evidence uncovered so far in the 1996 downing of TWA Flight 800 off Long Island, New York, points to "catastrophic mechanical failure."		May 4
A state circuit court jury in Jacksonville, Florida, finds that R. J. Reynolds Tobacco Co. does not owe punitive and compensatory damages to the family of Jean Connor, a woman who smoked for 34 years and died in 1995 at the age of 49 of lung cancer.	The Virginia Military Institute announces that at least 24 women offered places at the school will attend. They will be the first female cadets in the military academy's 157-year history. . . . Responding to Jordan's Apr. 30 decision to provide haven, the U.S. deports Mousa Mohammed Abu Marzook, the leader of the political wing of Hamas, to Jordan, after having held him for more than 21 months in a federal prison in New York City.	Statistics suggest that the net incomes of large U.S. companies rose 17.6% in the first quarter of 1997, compared with results from the corresponding period a year earlier. Net income in the January–March period for the 707 firms surveyed totaled $86.262 billion.		Murray Kempton, 79, Pulitzer Prize–winning journalist best known for his socially conscious commentary, dies in New York City of a heart attack; he also suffered from pancreatic cancer.	May 5
Mike Matson, 48, who fled when the Republic of Texas, an armed group, ended its standoff with police May 3, is killed in a shoot-out with police. . . . A jury in Winston-Salem, North Carolina, spares Thomas R. Jones from the death penalty in what is believed to be the first case in which prosecutors sought a death sentence for homicides caused by impaired driving. Judge William H. Freeman sentences him to two concurrent life terms without parole for the September 1996 deaths of Maia Witzl and Julie Hansen, both aged 19.	A military jury sentences Staff Sergeant Delmar G. Simpson to 25 years in prison for raping six trainees under his charge at the army's Ordnance Center and School at the Aberdeen Proving Ground in Maryland.	The American Federation of Teachers (AFT), the nation's largest teachers' union after the National Education Association, elects Sandra Feldman to succeed the late Albert Shanker as president.		Inductees to the Rock and Roll Hall of Fame include the Bee Gees, Buffalo Springfield, the Jackson Five, Joni Mitchell, the Rascals, and Crosby, Stills and Nash. . . . Sydney J(oseph) Freedberg, 82, who, in 1988, became the first and, to date, the only art historian to receive a National Medal of Arts, dies of cardiac arrest and renal failure in Washington, D.C.	May 6
F	G	H	I	J	
Includes elections, federal-state relations, civil rights and liberties, crime, the judiciary, education, health care, poverty, urban affairs, and population.	*Includes formation and debate of U.S. foreign and defense policies, veterans' affairs, and defense spending. (Relations with specific foreign countries are usually found under the region concerned.)*	*Includes business, labor, agriculture, taxation, transportation, consumer affairs, monetary and fiscal policy, natural resources, and pollution.*	*Includes worldwide scientific, medical, and technological developments; natural phenomena; U.S. weather; natural disasters; and accidents.*	*Includes the arts, religion, scholarship, communications media, sports, entertainments, fashions, fads, and social life.*	

	World Affairs	Europe	Africa & the Middle East	The Americas	Asia & the Pacific
May 7	The International Criminal Tribunal for the Former Yugoslavia convicts Dusan Tadic, a Bosnian Serb, of 11 counts of war crimes and crimes against humanity, including the slaying of two Muslim policemen. It is the tribunal's first contested conviction, and Tadic is the first person to be tried on war-crimes charges since Drazen Erdemovic, a Croat, pled guilty in November 1996 to atrocity charges.				Two 18-year-old twins, Sarah Ingham and Joanne Ingham, who stowed away on a container ship and later jumped overboard to avoid arrest on an array of charges, are discovered alive by police in the Australian town of Coen after reportedly surviving for 18 hours in shark-infested waters and 17 days in the wilderness.
May 8	The heads of state of the U.S., Costa Rica, El Salvador, Nicaragua, Honduras, Guatemala, Belize, and the Dominican Republic hold a summit.	Russian president Boris Yeltsin lays the foundation for the reconstruction of the chapel of St. Boris and St. Gleb, which, in 1930, was torn down under the rule of Joseph Stalin . . . . The eastern Russian city of Vladivostok declares a state of emergency amid power cuts and a lack of fuel after miners struck on May 1. . . . Pakistani shipping magnate Abbas Gokal is sentenced to 14 years in prison for defrauding BCCI customers of £750 million ($1.2 billion). It is the largest prison sentence ever handed down by a British court in a corporate fraud case.	Jordanian and Israeli leaders, meeting in the Jordanian Red Sea coastal city of Aqaba, overcome a dispute that erupted between the two countries over water-sharing agreements.	More than 200 Mexico City police officers riot in the streets of that city, protesting impending transfers and a recent increase in the use of the military in police functions. The officers throw rocks and bottles at a force of some 1,000 fellow officers, who respond with clubs and tear gas. At least 17 people are arrested, and dozens of others are injured in the riots.	A China Southern Airlines Boeing 737 crash-lands on a runway at Huangtian Airport in the southern city of Shenzhen, killing at least 30 people and injuring more than 20 others. . . . In Japan, the lower house of the Diet unanimously adopts legislation that will protect and promote the culture and traditions of the Ainu ethnic minority.
May 9		Officials reveal that Russian president Boris Yeltsin has approved a new Russian nuclear policy that allows Russia to respond with nuclear weapons in case of an attack by conventional forces. . . . Armed separatist rebels advocating political independence for Venice, in northern Italy, occupy a bell tower in the city's St. Mark's Square for seven hours. . . . Marco Ferreri, 68, Italian film director known for his bizarre sense of humor, dies in Paris France, of a heart attack.	Lebanon's Judicial Council, the country's highest court, sentences Samir Geagea, who commanded the Christian Lebanese Forces during the civil war, to death. The court immediately commutes Geagea's sentence to life imprisonment. Geagea, who is already serving two life sentences, is the only militia leader from the war to be prosecuted. . . . In the West Bank city of Ramallah, land dealer Farid Bashiti, 70, is found dead by a roadside with his skull crushed and his hands tied behind his back.		
May 10			A powerful earthquake kills an estimated 2,400 people and injures at least 6,000 others in northeastern Iran. The quake measures 7.1 on the Richter scale and is centered near the town of Qayen in Khorasan Province, a remote mountainous farming region near the border with Afghanistan. . . . Pope John Paul II visits Lebanon, marking his first trip to the Middle East as pope and the first to the region by any pope since Pope Paul VI visited Israel and Jordan in 1964.		
May 11		An estimated 300,000 people gather in Sultanahmet Square in Istanbul, Turkey's capital, to rally in defense of Islamic fundamentalism.	Pope John Paul II holds an outdoor mass near Beirut, the capital of Lebanon, on a landfill of rubble from war-ravaged buildings. The service draws the largest gathering in Lebanon's history as more than 300,000 people reportedly attend.		
May 12		Russian president Boris Yeltsin and Chechen president Aslan Maskhadov sign a peace treaty that sidesteps the question of independence for the secessionist-minded Chechen republic. . . . Ethnic Croat mobs in central Croatia begin beating and forcing Serbs out of their homes. . . . The Switzerland-based Bank for International Settlements (BIS) confirms that it had held at least 13.5 tons (12.2 metric tons) of gold that Nazi Germany looted from the central banks of European countries. The BIS claims it gave the looted gold to allied nations responsible for returning stolen World War II-era gold.		In Haiti, the closing of a school prompts teachers to go on strike. The teachers, who are employed by the government, also protest that they have not been paid in some 14 months.	Indian prime minister Inder Kumar Gujral and Pakistani prime minister Nawaz Sharif hold a landmark meeting in the Maldives on the disputed Kashmir region, over which the two countries have fought two wars since they were partitioned in 1947.

A	B	C	D	E
Includes developments that affect more than one world region, international organizations, and important meetings of major world leaders.	Includes all domestic and regional developments in Europe, including the Soviet Union, Turkey, Cyprus, and Malta.	Includes all domestic and regional developments in Africa and the Middle East, including Iraq and Iran and excluding Cyprus, Turkey, and Afghanistan.	Includes all domestic and regional developments in Latin America, the Caribbean, and Canada.	Includes all domestic and regional developments in Asia and Pacific nations, extending from Afghanistan through all the Pacific Islands, except Hawaii.

U.S. Politics & Social Issues	U.S. Foreign Policy & Defense	U.S. Economy & Environment	Science, Technology, & Nature	Culture, Leisure, & Lifestyle	
	Robert C. Kim, a former civilian intelligence analyst for the U.S. Navy, pleads guilty in U.S. District Court in Arlington, Virginia, to a charge of conspiracy to commit espionage. . . . Sergeant Major Gene McKinney, the army's highest-ranking enlisted soldier, is formally charged with sexual misconduct and indecent assault involving three enlisted women in the army and one in the navy.	The Labor Department reports that the nation's overall productivity in nonfarm business sectors jumped by a seasonally adjusted annual rate of 2% in the first quarter of 1997 from the fourth quarter of 1996. The first-quarter growth marks the highest productivity rate in three years. . . . The AMEX begins quoting share prices in increments of one-sixteenth of a dollar, or 6.25 cents, rather than in one-eighths of a dollar, or 12.5 cents.		Former Detroit Tigers pitcher Denny McLain, who won the Cy Young award in 1968 and 1969, is sentenced to eight years in jail for stealing $3 million from the pension plan of a company he owned.	May 7
In McAlester, Oklahoma, Scott Dawn Carpenter, 22, becomes the youngest person executed in the U.S. since 1976. He is the 379th pers on executed in the U.S. and the ninth in Oklahoma since 1976. . . . The U.S. House votes, 286-132, to pass a bill allocating $1.5 billion over three years as an incentive for states to try violent juvenile offenders as adults. . . . Arthur J. Hanes Sr., 80, attorney known for representing whites accused of committing racially motivated crimes, dies in Birmingham, Alabama, of unreported causes.	A military judge at Fort Leonard Wood in Missouri sentences Staff Sergeant Steve A. Holloway, 32, to a bad-conduct discharge, reduction in rank to private, and four months' confinement for forcing a kiss on a female trainee, engaging in consensual sex with another, and making sexual comments.	The Senate approves, 78-22, an $8.4 billion emergency spending bill that includes $5.5 billion for disaster relief and $2 billion for international peace-keeping efforts. . . . Reports confirm that the late millionaire Jack Kent Cooke left the bulk of his estimated $825 million fortune to be used to create the Jack Kent Cooke Foundation, which will reward youths "for unusual intelligence, application, deportment and character."	A study links the high incidence of asthma among inner-city children to their allergies to proteins found in cockroach excretions.		May 8
		Eugene K. H. Lum and his wife, Nora T. Lum sign a plea bargain under which they plead guilty to charges that they participated in a scheme to funnel some $50,000 to Democratic candidates in 1994 and 1995.		Robert Simon Devaney, 82, football coach who built the University of Nebraska Cornhuskers into a powerhouse, dies in Lincoln, Nebraska, of cardiac arrest. He had suffered a stroke in March 1995.	May 9
				Joanie Weston, 62, famed star of the popular Roller Derby roller skating competitions in the 1950s and 1960s, dies in Hayward, California, of Creutzfeldt-Jakob disease, a rare brain disorder.	May 10
				Russian chess grandmaster Garry Kasparov is defeated in a rematch with IBM's Deep Blue chess computer in New York City. It is the first time that a chess champion is beaten by a computer in a traditional match.	May 11
A jury in Wilmington, North Carolina, sentences a white former army soldier and alleged neo-Nazi, Malcolm Wright Jr., to life in prison without parole for his part in the slaying of a black couple, Jackie Burden and Michael James, in Fayetteville, North Carolina, in 1995.	In *Inter-Modal Rail Employees Association v. Atchison, Topeka and Santa Fe Railway Co.*, the Supreme Court rules unanimously that employers cannot discharge staff and contract out their jobs in order to cut down on the costs of health insurance and other employee benefits.	The FAA announces that it will require ice-detection equipment to be installed on all 220 Embraer EMB-120 turboprop aircraft flying in the U.S. It is the first time the FAA mandates ice-detection equipment for any aircraft model.	Australian long-distance swimmer Susie Maroney completes a swim across the Florida Straits, from Cuba to Fort Zachary Taylor Beach on the U.S.'s Key West. Maroney, 22, claims to be the first person to accomplish the 110-mile (180-km) swim unassisted.		May 12

F	G	H	I	J
Includes elections, federal-state relations, civil rights and liberties, crime, the judiciary, education, health care, poverty, urban affairs, and population.	*Includes formation and debate of U.S. foreign and defense policies, veterans' affairs, and defense spending. (Relations with specific foreign countries are usually found under the region concerned.)*	*Includes business, labor, agriculture, taxation, transportation, consumer affairs, monetary and fiscal policy, natural resources, and pollution.*	*Includes worldwide scientific, medical, and technological developments; natural phenomena; U.S. weather; natural disasters; and accidents.*	*Includes the arts, religion, scholarship, communications media, sports, entertainments, fashions, fads, and social life.*

	World Affairs	Europe	Africa & the Middle East	The Americas	Asia & the Pacific
May 13					A bomb explodes in Beijing, the Chinese capital, in a park located near top leaders' offices. The blast kills one person. Police contend that the bombing was a suicide by the person killed, a migrant worker.
May 14	Russian foreign minister Yevgeny M. Primakov and Javier Solana Madariaga, secretary general of NATO, agree on terms of a new treaty between the alliance and Russia. The pact will permit NATO to add Central and Eastern European states to its current roster of 16 members. In a concession, Solana promises not to deploy nuclear weapons on new members' soil. . . . Trade ministers of 34 countries hold the Americas Business Forum to discuss the future of the Free Trade Area of the Americas (FTAA), first proposed in 1994.	Turkish forces launch an offensive in northern Iraq against Kurdish rebels seeking autonomy for Turkey's Kurds. . . . Reports confirm that that more than 100 Serbs have been beaten by ethnic Croat mobs in central Croatia and forced out of their homes since May 12.			Taiwanese president Lee Teng-hui implements a partial reshuffle of his cabinet in response to a public uproar over crime in the nation. . . . In New Zealand, Parliament's select privileges committee finds Deputy Prime Minister Winston Peters guilty of assaulting MP John Banks during a dispute in March. The committee report calls on Peters to apologize to Parliament for his actions but does not conclude that Peters is in contempt of Parliament.
May 15	Reports confirm that the World Bank has lent $93 million to Croatia in order to help the country's banks restructure.	The Soros Foundation, an international group that supports educational, medical, and ecological programs, announces that it will cease operating in Belarus after a series of tax disputes.	The remains of Juvenal Habyarimana, the former Hutu president of Rwanda who died in 1994, are cremated in Kinshasa, Zaire, on orders from Zairian president Mobutu Sese Seko—reportedly to stop rebels from desecrating the body. . . . Saadallah Wannous, 56, Syrian playwright whose work often includes commentary on the Arab-Israeli conflict, dies in Damascus, Syria, of cancer.	In Port-au-Prince, Haiti's capital, riots break out between students and police. More than 300 students, protesting a teachers' strike that began on May 12, occupy the school, and rioters vandalize cars and set fires, forcing the closure of businesses. Five people are seriously injured in the riots.	Hong Kong's chief executive designate, Tung Chee-hwa, announces revisions that ease his future government's planned restrictions on political groups and public protests when China assumes control of the colony from Britain after midnight on June 30.
May 16		The U.S. drug company G. D. Searle and Co. launches the first pharmaceutical factory in Russia to be built to international standards. The $30 million factory, in Izvarino outside Moscow, will open in 1999.	Zairian president Mobutu Sese Seko, facing a final rebel assault on the capital, Kinshasa, relinquishes power, ending nearly 32 years of dictatorial rule over Africa's third-largest country. Mobutu, 66, who is stricken by cancer, quietly leaves Kinshasa after three senior generals tell him they can no longer defend the city. The Mobutu government crumbles as high-level officials flee across the Congo River to Brazzaville, capital of the neighboring Republic of the Congo.		
May 17		Reports disclose that a court in Moscow has convicted Moisei Finkel of treason for spying for the U.S. and sentenced him to a 12-year prison term.	Laurent Kabila, a veteran guerrilla fighter who led the rebels' seven-month offensive in Zaire, declares himself head of state and changes the country's name to the Democratic Republic of the Congo. The first columns of rebel troops, numbering up to 1,500 men, enter Kinshasa, where some residents express jubilation at Mobutu's overthrow. . . . The body of Harbi Abu Sara, a Palestinian purportedly involved in land deals, is found dead in Ramallah in the West Bank after being shot in the head.		Reports indicate that a court in Dalian, China, has sentenced four people for their roles in a gun-smuggling operation in which some 2,000 fully automatic AK-47 rifles were shipped illegally to the U.S. The court gave Qi Feng, accused of being the ringleader, a 14-year jail sentence. The other three defendants, all Norinco employees, received jail sentences ranging from three to four years.
May 18	The Organization of African Unity (OAU) acknowledges Laurent Kabila's May 17 victory in Zaire. UN secretary general Kofi Annan urges Kabila to respect the "choice and voice" of the people.				Natsagiin Bagabandi, chair of the opposition Mongolian People's Revolutionary Party (MPRP), ousts the incumbent, Punsalmaagiyn Ochirbat, in presidential elections.

A	B	C	D	E
Includes developments that affect more than one world region, international organizations, and important meetings of major world leaders.	Includes all domestic and regional developments in Europe, including the Soviet Union, Turkey, Cyprus, and Malta.	Includes all domestic and regional developments in Africa and the Middle East, including Iraq and Iran and excluding Cyprus, Turkey, and Afghanistan.	Includes all domestic and regional developments in Latin America, the Caribbean, and Canada.	Includes all domestic and regional developments in Asia and Pacific nations, extending from Afghanistan through all the Pacific Islands, except Hawaii.

U.S. Politics & Social Issues	U.S. Foreign Policy & Defense	U.S. Economy & Environment	Science, Technology, & Nature	Culture, Leisure, & Lifestyle	
The Indiana Court of Appeals rules unanimously that incarcerating juveniles with adults violates the state's constitution and orders prison authorities to transfer a 16-year-old girl, Donna Ratliff, to a facility for juveniles. . . . The House passes, 420-3, a bill designed to improve the teaching of disabled students and to increase schools' power to discipline such students.	Randy Lee Meadows Jr., who served at Fort Bragg, North Carolina, with Malcolm Wright Jr. and James N. Burmeister, is sentenced to three years' probation as part of a plea bargain for his part in the killing of Jackie Burden and Michael James, a black couple, in Fayetteville, North Carolina, in 1995.	In Washington, D.C., U.S. district judge Ricardo M. Urbina fines California-based Sun Diamond Growers, the nation's largest food cooperative, $1.5 million for giving illegal gifts to former agriculture secretary Mike Espy and making illegal campaign donations to his brother, Henry Espy.		In Media, Pennsylvania, Judge Patricia Jenkins sentences chemicals-fortune heir John E. du Pont to 13–30 years in prison for the January 1996 slaying of Olympic wrestler Dave Schultz. Du Pont, 58, will serve some of the sentence in prison and some in a mental hospital.	May 13
The House votes, 293-132, to approve a measure that will overhaul the nation's public housing system.	The U.S. Senate unanimously agrees to ratify changes to the 1990 treaty governing Conventional Forces in Europe (CFE). The new changes will allow Russia to shift more of its forces to its northern and southern flanks.	The FTC rejects a proposed merger between Northern States Power Co. of Minneapolis, Minnesota, and Wisconsin Energy Corp. of Milwaukee, Wisconsin, citing concern that they will dominate the upper midwestern power market. It is the first time the commission rejects a utilities merger for such a reason. . . . The Labor Department reports that the federal government's index of prices charged by manufacturers and farmers for finished goods dropped a seasonally adjusted 0.6% in April from March. It is the largest one-month drop in nearly four years.		Canada wins the world hockey championship, defeating Sweden, 2-1, in the final game of a best-two-of-three-games series in Helsinki, Finland. . . . Harry Blackstone Jr., 62, magician who followed in the footsteps of his father, the "Great Blackstone," dies in Loma Linda, California, of pancreatic cancer.	May 14
The House Ethics Committee announces that House Speaker Newt Gingrich (R, Ga.) will pay with his own money half of a $300,000 fine levied against him for violating ethics rules. The remaining amount may be paid with a loan from former senator Robert J. Dole (R, Kans.). Gingrich's April plan of allowing Dole to pay the entire fine came under criticism from both parties.		The House passes, 244-178, an $8.4 billion emergency spending bill that includes $5.5 billion for disaster relief and $2 billion for international peace-keeping efforts. . . . The Clinton administration announces that federal minimum-wage laws will apply to welfare recipients participating in work programs.	The space shuttle *Atlantis* blasts off from Kennedy Space Center in Cape Canaveral, Florida, on a mission to deliver essential supplies and equipment to the Russian *Mir* space station.	Thelma Carpenter, 77, singer who fronted jazz bands in the 1930s and 1940s, dies in New York City of unreported causes. . . . Laurie Lee, 82, British poet and novelist, dies in Gloucestershire, England, of unreported causes.	May 15
Pres. Clinton makes an official apology to survivors and family members of the 399 black men from Tuskegee, Alabama, whose syphilis went untreated for decades as part of a federally funded study. Clinton states that the government will attempt to compensate by providing a $200,000 grant to Tuskegee University to establish a bioethics research center. . . . Harry Charles Moore, 56, condemned for two 1992 murders, is put to death by lethal injection in Salem, Oregon. He is only the second person in Oregon and the 381st person in the U.S. to be executed since 1976.	Elbridge C. Durbrow, 93, diplomat whose 38-year career was distinguished by service in hostile communist regions, dies in Walnut Creek, California, after suffering a stroke.		*Atlantis* successfully docks at the *Mir* space station.		May 16
				The PEN/Faulkner Award for Fiction is awarded to Gina Berriault, author of *Women in Their Beds*, who, in March, won the National Book Critics Circle fiction award. . . . Silver Charm wins the 122nd running of the Preakness Stakes at Pimlico Race Course in Baltimore, Maryland.	May 17
A second-floor balcony collapses at a graduation ceremony at the University of Virginia in Charlottesville, killing one spectator and injuring 18 others.				Golfer Chris Johnson wins the LPGA Championship at the Dupont Country Club in Rockland, Delaware. . . . In France, the 50th annual Cannes Film Festival awards the Palme d'Or to two films: *Taste of Cherries*, by Iranian director Abbas Kiarostami; and *Unagi (The Eel)*, by Japanese director Shohei Imamura.	May 18

F	G	H	I	J
Includes elections, federal-state relations, civil rights and liberties, crime, the judiciary, education, health care, poverty, urban affairs, and population.	*Includes formation and debate of U.S. foreign and defense policies, veterans' affairs, and defense spending. (Relations with specific foreign countries are usually found under the region concerned.)*	*Includes business, labor, agriculture, taxation, transportation, consumer affairs, monetary and fiscal policy, natural resources, and pollution.*	*Includes worldwide scientific, medical, and technological developments; natural phenomena; U.S. weather; natural disasters; and accidents.*	*Includes the arts, religion, scholarship, communications media, sports, entertainments, fashions, fads, and social life.*

	World Affairs	Europe	Africa & the Middle East	The Americas	Asia & the Pacific
May 19		Reports suggest that, in the offensive launched May 14 by Turkish forces against Kurdish rebels, the KDP seized PKK offices in the southern town of Irbid and executed a number of the separatists that they initially detained there. . . . The Croatian Democratic Union (HDZ) party takes control of the city council of Zagreb, the Croatian capital, when two members of the Peasants Party defect to the HDZ, giving it 26 of the 50 council seats.	The local Red Cross reveals that 222 people, mostly soldiers loyal to former Zairian president Mobutu Sese Seko, were killed during the May 17–18 rebel takeover of Zaire.	Statistics show that 28,000 residents of the Red River Valley in Manitoba, Canada, were evacuated in late April due to the region's worst floods of the century. Three people died and more than 800 properties suffered damage. . . . Canada's federal government partly reopens commercial cod fisheries off Newfoundland's south coast and in the northern Gulf of St. Lawrence for the first time in five years.	A powerful cyclone with winds reaching 125 miles per hour (200 kmph) hits the southern coast of Bangladesh. . . . A court in Thailand orders that Li Yung Chung be extradited to the U.S., where he faces drug-smuggling charges. . . . Jerry Wolf Stuchiner. who held the top-ranking U.S. immigration post in Hong Kong until 1994, is sentenced in Hong Kong to three months in jail for possessing material to make false passports.
May 20	China declares that countries that do not have diplomatic relations with the mainland government will not be allowed to keep consulates in Hong Kong after the sovereignty shift. The move is directed at the approximately 30 countries that recognize Taiwan, which China considers a renegade Chinese province.	A Turkish military report claims that 1,300 rebels and only 14 government troops have been killed to date in the fighting that started May 14.		Colombia's Constitutional Court votes to legalize euthanasia but imposes strict guidelines on the practice. The ruling makes Colombia the only country in the world to allow euthanasia. . . . In Argentina, thousands of laid-off sugar workers block a major highway, demanding jobs and government aid. Some 100 protesters are injured when police fire rubber bullets and tear gas into the crowd. . . . Virgilio Barco Vargas, 75, former president of Colombia, 1986–90, dies in Bogota of stomach cancer.	The death toll from the May 19 cyclone on the southern coast of Bangladesh reaches 108 people, with some 1,500 fishermen reported missing. More than 8,000 people were injured in the cyclone, and an estimated 400,000 homes were destroyed.
May 21		Representatives of the British government meet with leaders of Sinn Fein, the political wing of the Provisional IRA, for the first time since February 1996.		In Mexico, thousands of dissident members of the teachers' union protest in the streets of Mexico City against a wage agreement between union leadership and the ruling Institutional Revolutionary Party (PRI). . . . The Brazilian Senate gives preliminary approval to a constitutional amendment that will allow presidents, state governors, and mayors to run for second consecutive terms.	Reports suggest that Australia's Human Rights and Equal Opportunity Commission condemned the government for instituting policies from 1910 to 1970 that resulted in the forced removal of as many 100,000 aborigine children from their families.
May 22		Russian president Boris Yeltsin fires Defense Minister Igor Rodionov and Viktor N. Samsonov, the chief of the Russian army's general staff. He names First Deputy Premiers Anatoly B. Chubais and Boris Y. Nemtsov to his Security Council.	Laurent Kabila, self-appointed president of the newly named Democratic Republic of the Congo, names 13 ministers to a new transitional government.	The Colombian Senate passes a watered-down version of a bill that will amend the constitution to allow for the extradition of citizens to face trial in foreign countries. . . . The Venezuelan Supreme Court decides to extradite fugitive Colombian drug lord Justo Pastor Perafan to the U.S. after the U.S. stipulated that he will not face sentences of the death penalty or life imprisonment, in accordance with Venezuelan law.	
May 23		Gen. Igor Sergeyev is named the head of Russia's strategic rocket forces.	Mohammed Khatami, a moderate cleric, is elected president in Iran by a surprising landslide margin. . . . In the newly named Democratic Republic of the Congo, 1,000 supporters of Etienne Tshisekedi march in Kinshasa to protest Laurent Kabila's May 22 cabinet appointments. . . . Daoud Kuttab, a noted Palestinian print and broadcast journalist, begins a hunger strike to protest being detained by Palestinian police in the West Bank on unspecified charges.	The opposition St. Lucia Labor Party (SLP) wins 16 of the 17 seats in St. Lucia's Parliament, ousting the United Workers' Party (UWP), which has been in power since 1982, and its leader, P.M. Vaughan Lewis. It is the biggest electoral landslide in the history of the tiny eastern Caribbean island. Kenny Anthony, leader of the SLP, will be the island's new prime minister. . . . The Haitian government and teachers reach an agreement to end the strike that started May 12.	Amid one of the most violent campaigns for parliamentary elections in Indonesia's recent history, members of the Golkar party clash with PPP supporters in Banjarmasin, southern Borneo.
May 24			In Congo, 200 opposition supporters demonstrate, but the protest is broken up by troops and 70 people rallying in support of Laurent Kabila's government. . . . Mohammed Fadhil al-Jamali, 94, Iraqi statesman who was the country's foreign minister in the 1940s and 1950s, dies in Tunis, Tunisia, while being treated for a heart condition.	In Mexico, suspected leftist rebels in the southern state of Guerrero skirmish with government troops.	The Taliban seizes the major northern city of Mazar-i-Sharif and stands poised to complete their goal of controlling the entire country of Afghanistan.

A	B	C	D	E
Includes developments that affect more than one world region, international organizations, and important meetings of major world leaders.	Includes all domestic and regional developments in Europe, including the Soviet Union, Turkey, Cyprus, and Malta.	Includes all domestic and regional developments in Africa and the Middle East, including Iraq and Iran and excluding Cyprus, Turkey, and Afghanistan.	Includes all domestic and regional developments in Latin America, the Caribbean, and Canada.	Includes all domestic and regional developments in Asia and Pacific nations, extending from Afghanistan through all the Pacific Islands, except Hawaii.

U.S. Politics & Social Issues	U.S. Foreign Policy & Defense	U.S. Economy & Environment	Science, Technology, & Nature	Culture, Leisure, & Lifestyle	
Data reveals that the University of California and University of Texas—both of which abandoned admissions policies that consider the race of applicants—have seen dramatic declines in the admission of minority students. . . . Aaron E. Henry, 74, civil rights leader who was president of the Mississippi branch of the NAACP, 1960–93, dies in Clarksdale of congestive heart failure.				Sportscaster Marv Albert is indicted by a grand jury in Arlington, Virginia, on charges of sodomy and assault. . . . Millie, the English springer spaniel of former president George Bush and former first lady Barbara Bush, dies in Kennebunkport, Maine.	May 19
The Senate passes, 64-36, a measure that will outlaw a method of late-term abortion known as intact dilation and extraction (IDE). . . . A Trenton, New Jersey, appellate court throws out part of the 1993 convictions of three former high school football players, Christopher Archer and twins Kevin and Kyle Scherzer, found guilty of sexually assaulting a retarded girl in 1989. The court overturns the men's convictions of first-degree sexual assault by force, but it upholds the other charges and orders their resentencing.	The Senate confirms Major General Claudia J. Kennedy as the U.S. Army's first female lieutenant general, a three-star rank. . . . Ezequiel Hernandez Jr., 18, is shot by a member of a Marine Corps antidrug patrol in Texas. Hernandez is the first U.S. civilian killed by military antidrug patrols on the Mexico-U.S. border since their inception in 1989.	The White House agrees to hand over thousands of pages of documents subpoenaed by the House committee investigating campaign finance abuses.	Paleontologists announce the discovery in Argentina's Patagonia region of a fossil of a dinosaur that they believe is more closely related to birds than any previously known dinosaur species. The creature, named *Unenlagia comahuensis*, could not fly, but its shoulder bones are oriented in a bird-like way. The fossil, which at 90 million years old is from a later date than the earliest known birds, is not itself a bird ancestor but a surviving intermediate species.		May 20
		The House adopts, 333-99, a resolution to balance the federal budget by the year 2002. . . . The SEC and the American Institute of Certified Public Accountants set up the Independence Standards Board, a new group to set standards for company auditors.		Mattel introduces Share a Smile Becky, a Barbie doll that depicts a handicapped girl. . . . Lorenzo (Piper) Davis, 79, baseball player in the U.S. Negro leagues who, in 1950, was the first black player to be signed by the Boston Red Sox, dies in Birmingham, Alabama, of a heart attack.	May 21
	First Lieutenant Kelly Flinn, the air force's first female B-52 pilot, discloses that she will accept a general discharge from the military rather than face a court martial for adultery, disobeying an order, and lying to investigators.	Democratic senators accuse the Republican majority on the Senate Governmental Affairs Committee of leading a partisan investigation into campaign finances despite recent allegations regarding campaign funds to the RNC.	Alfred D. Hershey, 88, chemist who shared the 1969 Nobel prize for his work in molecular biology and the study of viruses, dies in Syosset, New York, of unreported causes.		May 22
	Robert Stephen Lipka, 51, pleads guilty in U.S. District Court in Philadelphia, Pennsylvania, to conspiracy to commit espionage while working for the NSA in the 1960s. . . . The INS states that it will seek to strip U.S. citizenship from 4,946 people wrongly naturalized since late 1995. In the past, the INS never issued more than two dozen revocations in a year. . . . The CIA releases 1,400 pages of recently declassified documents that reveal the agency's plan to assassinate 58 Guatemalan political leaders as part of a June 1954 coup that toppled the leftist Guatemalan president Jacobo Arbenz Guzman.	The Senate passes, 78-22, a resolution to balance the federal budget by the year 2002. . . . In Charlotte, North Carolina, U.S. district judge Robert Potter cuts the damages awarded to franchisees of Meineke Discount Muffler Shops Inc. by 34%, to $390 million from $591 million.	In a race that started May 19, an electric car sets a new distance record for production models by traveling 249 miles (400 km) without a recharge. The winner is a Geo Metro that uses a newly developed nickel metal-hydride battery to win the race, the American Tour de Sol.		May 23
			The space shuttle *Atlantis* lands at Kennedy Space Center in Cape Canaveral, Florida, after completing a mission to deliver essential supplies and equipment to the Russian *Mir* space station and to pick up U.S. astronaut Jerry L. Linenger, who has been on board *Mir* since January, and deliver his replacement, C. Michael Foale.	Edward Mulhare, 74, television, film, and stage actor, dies in Van Nuys, California, of lung cancer.	May 24

F	G	H	I	J
Includes elections, federal-state relations, civil rights and liberties, crime, the judiciary, education, health care, poverty, urban affairs, and population.	Includes formation and debate of U.S. foreign and defense policies, veterans' affairs, and defense spending. (Relations with specific foreign countries are usually found under the region concerned.)	Includes business, labor, agriculture, taxation, transportation, consumer affairs, monetary and fiscal policy, natural resources, and pollution.	Includes worldwide scientific, medical, and technological developments; natural phenomena; U.S. weather; natural disasters; and accidents.	Includes the arts, religion, scholarship, communications media, sports, entertainments, fashions, fads, and social life.

	World Affairs	Europe	Africa & the Middle East	The Americas	Asia & the Pacific
May 25		Polish voters in a referendum approve a new constitution that will codify Poland's adoption of a democratic system.... At a spa in Jesenik, Czech Republic, an explosion injures 20 people. The blast is a result of the apparent suicide of Bohumil Sole, 63, a Czech scientist who, as a member of a team of researchers, helped develop the plastic explosive known as Semtex.	In Sierra Leone, junior officers in the army stage a coup, toppling Pres. Ahmad Tejan Kabbah, Sierra Leone's first freely elected ruler in three decades. Kabbah flees to Guinea. The rebels free 600 inmates, including soldiers imprisoned for previous coup attempts. After clashing with Nigerian peacekeepers, the rebels capture the parliament building and burn the national treasury. Johnny Paul Koromah, 33, a major who was jailed for earlier coup attempts, announces on state radio that he has taken control of the country.	Ecuador's interim president, Fabian Alarcon, appointed by Congress in February, wins an endorsement from 65% of voters in a referendum on his presidency.	In Banjarmasin, in southern Borneo in Indonesia, officials report that they have recovered 130 bodies from a shopping mall that the rioters looted and then set ablaze on May 23. They also state that several other shopping centers, more than 100 houses, and at least seven churches were torched during the unrest. Police report that four other people were killed in election-related violence in other parts of the city.... Pakistan becomes the first nation to formally recognize the Taliban government of Afghanistan.
May 26	Western and African nations condemn the May 25 coup in Sierra Leone. UN secretary general Kofi Annan and OAU leader Salim Ahmed Salim also denounce Ahmad Tejan Kabbah's overthrow.	In response to the first round of parliamentary election returns, which show that France's two main leftist parties collectively outpolled the right-of-center ruling coalition, Premier Alain Juppe, in an effort to boost his coalition's chances in runoff voting, vows to step down if his party maintains control of Parliament.	The independent Palestinian Human Rights Monitoring Group suggests that security forces of the self-rule Palestine National Authority (PNA) have tortured or otherwise abused numerous prisoners in their custody. ... The new government in Congo bans public demonstrations and suspends all political party activity.		
May 27	Leaders of the 16 member countries of NATO and Pres. Boris Yeltsin of Russia sign the Founding Act on Mutual Relations, Cooperation and Security, a mutual cooperation agreement that will create a permanent NATO-Russia council in which Russia can bring up issues of concern with the Atlantic alliance. It also eases Russian objections to enlargement of NATO to include former Soviet bloc states.		Palestinian police in the West Bank city of Ramallah release Daoud Kuttab, who has been on a hunger strike since May 23, after having held him a week for unspecified reasons.... In Sierra Leone, fighters from the Revolutionary United Front (RUF), who since 1991 have waged a civil war that has cost tens of thousands of lives, begin streaming into Freetown to back up the rebellious troops who seized power May 25.	Suspected leftist rebels in the southern state of Guerrero skirmish with Mexican government troops. ... The Royal Canadian Mounted Police (RCMP) arrest 31 people allegedly involved in a hashish smuggling ring.	The severed head and the body of Jun Hase, an 11-year-old retarded boy, is discovered in Kobe, Japan, in a crime that police suspect was perpetrated by an at-large serial killer. The boy's murder causes alarm and increased vigilance in Japan, where violent crime is rare.... Abdul Malik's Uzbek troops and Hizb-i-Wahdat militiamen reverse their allegiances and take up arms against the Taliban in Afghanistan.
May 28	At a celebration of the 50th anniversary of the proposal of the Marshall Plan, the American economic assistance program that helped European nations recover from World War II, held in The Hague, the Netherlands, U.S. president Bill Clinton states that the West "must complete the noble journey that Marshall's generation began" and integrate former communist Eastern European nations with the rest of Europe.	Poland's Constitutional Court strikes down major provisions of an abortion-rights law that President Aleksander Kwasniewski endorsed in October 1996.... Ukrainian premier Pavlo Lazarenko and Russian premier Viktor Chernomyrdin reach agreement on the future status of Sevastopol and the Black Sea fleet.	The PNA announces that application of the May 5 policy of sentencing Palestinians convicted of land sales to Jews to death will be extended to Israel's 1 million Arab citizens.... In Sierra Leone, tribal militias known as the Kamajors declare that they will fight to restore the government of Pres. Ahmad Tejan Kabbah. Nigeria lands a total of 900 troops in Freetown's port to reinforce the 600 troops already in the capital of Sierra Leone.... In Congo, an opposition march of about 800 people is dispersed by soldiers.	Mexican officials aver that in the May 24 and May 27 skirmishes, five soldiers and four rebels died. The rebel Popular Revolutionary Army (EPR) claims that the clashes were instigated by the troops and that the army suffered more than 30 casualties, many of whom died. The clashes are considered the most significant involving the rebels since November 1996.	Malik's Uzbek troops and Hizb-i-Wahdat militiamen drive the Taliban from Mazar-i-Sharif and kill a number of senior Taliban officials.
May 29			Rebel leader Laurent Kabila is sworn in as president of the newly renamed Congo.	The Peruvian Congress votes to dismiss three Constitutional Court judges who in December 1996 ruled that Pres. Alberto Fujimori's bid for a third consecutive term was unconstitutional.	Indonesia's ruling Golkar Party routs opposition parties in parliamentary elections. Data shows more than 200 people were killed during campaigning.... China executes eight Muslim separatists convicted of crimes that left 18 people dead, including the February bombings in Urumqi.... A Singapore High Court judge awards a record S$8.08 million (US$5.6 million) in libel damages to P.M. Goh Chok Tong and 10 other members of the ruling People's Action Party.... In Afghanistan, forces loyal to Ahmed Shah Massoud capture the towns of Golbahar and Sherqat, about 60 miles (100 km) north of Kabul.
May 30		The Bosnia Peace Implementation Council names former Spanish foreign minister Carlos Westendorp to replace Carl Bildt as the international community's representative in Bosnia. Westendorp's job will be to ensure that Bosnia's civilian authorities fulfill the 1995 peace accords.	U.S. Marines, defying an order by the coup leaders closing Sierra Leone's borders, land helicopters at a Freetown hotel to evacuate about 900 people, including 330 American citizens, to the USS *Kearsarge* warship, anchored 12 miles (19 km) offshore. Britain, Sierra Leone's former colonial ruler, evacuates 400 Westerners, including 200 Britons, aboard a passenger jet.		In Indonesia, thousands of opposition supporters, largely in areas favoring the opposition PPP, hold demonstrations to protest the Golkar Party's May 29 victory. Protestors in Madura, an island off the coast of Java, attack government buildings.... South Korean president Kim Young Sam, whose administration is embroiled in a number of corruption scandals, refuses to reveal how much he spent on his 1992 election campaign.

A	B	C	D	E
Includes developments that affect more than one world region, international organizations, and important meetings of major world leaders.	*Includes all domestic and regional developments in Europe, including the Soviet Union, Turkey, Cyprus, and Malta.*	*Includes all domestic and regional developments in Africa and the Middle East, including Iraq and Iran and excluding Cyprus, Turkey, and Afghanistan.*	*Includes all domestic and regional developments in Latin America, the Caribbean, and Canada.*	*Includes all domestic and regional developments in Asia and Pacific nations, extending from Afghanistan through all the Pacific Islands, except Hawaii.*

U.S. Politics & Social Issues	U.S. Foreign Policy & Defense	U.S. Economy & Environment	Science, Technology, & Nature	Culture, Leisure, & Lifestyle	
Sen. Strom Thurmond (R, S.C.), elected in 1954, becomes the longest-serving senator in U.S. history, with a tenure of 41 years, nine months, and 31 days, which breaks the 1969 record set by Sen. Carl Hayden (D, Ariz.). Thurmond, 94, is also the oldest person to have served in the Senate.		Some 3,500 General Motors Corp. workers end the strike that started Apr. at the company's Oklahoma City, Oklahoma, plant.		Former White House press secretary Dee Dee Myers and *New York Times* reporter Todd Purdum marry at a church ceremony in Chicago, Illinois.	May 25
	Reports confirm that a military jury at Fairchild Air Force Base in Washington State has sentenced Master Sergeant Napolean Bailey, 39, to 30 years in prison after finding him guilty of sexually assaulting three women and convicting him of 15 of the 17 charges against him, which include one charge of rape and two of forcible sodomy.				May 26
In *Clinton v. Jones*, the Supreme Court unanimously rejects Pres. Clinton's request to delay proceedings in a sexual-harassment suit until he leaves office. It is the first time that the high court rules that sitting presidents may be sued for actions outside the realm of their official duties.... Dr. Stanislaw Burzynski is cleared of the last criminal charge against him regarding his use of cancer-treatment drugs not approved by the FDA.		The Conference Board states its index of consumer confidence leaped to 127.1 in May, the highest level in 27 years.... In *Suitum v. Tahoe Regional Planning Agency*, the Supreme Court rules unanimously that a Nevada landowner whose residential property was declared unfit for future development due to environmental concerns may sue a state planning agency.... The Dow closes at 7383.41, the 20th record high in 1997.	At least six tornadoes sweep through central Texas, killing 30 people and causing widespread damage. It is the most destructive series of tornadoes in the state since 1987. Twenty-seven of the deaths occur in Jarrell, Texas, a small town of about 1,000 residents.	Arie Luyendyk wins the 81st Indianapolis 500 at the Indianapolis Motor Speedway in Indiana.	May 27
	The CIA admits that most of its records on the 1953 CIA-backed coup in Iran were destroyed in the 1960s.			Sydney Guilaroff, 89, the first hair stylist ever credited on the screen who worked on 1,000 films, dies in Beverly Hills, California, of pneumonia.... John Herman Henry Sengstacke, 84, black newspaper publisher who owned the *Chicago Defender*, at one time the U.S.'s largest black daily newspaper, dies in Chicago, Illinois, of complications from a stroke.	May 28
A NYC transit police officer, Paolo Colecchia, is convicted of committing homicide while on duty in the shooting of an unarmed man, Nathaniel Levi Gaines Jr., 25, on a subway platform in July 1996. Colecchia is only the second NYC police officer convicted of homicide since 1977.... Judge Everett Dickey grants Elmer (Geronimo) Pratt, a former leader of the Black Panthers, a new trial after ruling that prosecutors withheld crucial evidence in his 1972 trial.	A military jury convicts Staff Sergeant Vernell Robinson Jr., a drill instructor at the Aberdeen Proving Ground in Maryland, on 19 criminal counts involving adultery, improper relations with female trainees, sodomy, obstruction of justice, and disobeying orders. He is found guilty of having improper consensual sex with five female trainees and of interfering with an investigation into his conduct.	The price of coffee rises to its highest level since April 1977 amid concerns that subpar global supplies will further dwindle before the end of the year. In U.S. trading on the Coffee, Sugar and Cocoa Exchange in New York City, coffee slated for July delivery closes at $3.15 a pound, up 19.25 cents, after selling for as high as $3.18 earlier in the day.	The National Weather Service attests the May 27 twister that hit Jarrell, Texas, was an F-5 tornado, the most severe on the five-level tornado-power scale. The tornado's winds blew up to 260 miles per hour (420 kmph).	Jeff Buckley, 30, folk-rock musician who cultivated a loyal following in the early 1990s, drowns in Memphis, Tennessee, while swimming in the Mississippi River.... George Fenneman, 77, entertainer best known as the serious sidekick to comedian Groucho Marx, dies in Los Angeles of emphysema.	May 29
The NTSB announces that it will set up a privately funded national airline disaster response center by the end of 1997.	Staff Sergeant Vernell Robinson Jr., convicted on 19 counts May 29, is sentenced to six months in prison and a dishonorable discharge from the Army.		A team of Spanish paleontologists report the discovery in Spain of 800,000-year-old human fossils, the oldest human remains found in Europe.		May 30

F	G	H	I	J
Includes elections, federal-state relations, civil rights and liberties, crime, the judiciary, education, health care, poverty, urban affairs, and population.	Includes formation and debate of U.S. foreign and defense policies, veterans' affairs, and defense spending. (Relations with specific foreign countries are usually found under the region concerned.)	Includes business, labor, agriculture, taxation, transportation, consumer affairs, monetary and fiscal policy, natural resources, and pollution.	Includes worldwide scientific, medical, and technological developments; natural phenomena; U.S. weather; natural disasters; and accidents.	Includes the arts, religion, scholarship, communications media, sports, entertainments, fashions, fads, and social life.

	World Affairs	Europe	Africa & the Middle East	The Americas	Asia & the Pacific
May 31		P.M. Tony Blair expresses regret for Britain's role in Ireland's cataclysmic potato famine in the 1840s. The statement is considered the strongest admission ever by a British prime minister that the British government was partially responsible for the tragedy.... Russian president Boris Yeltsin and Ukrainian president Leonid Kuchma sign a friendship treaty.	The body of Ali Mohammed Jumhour, 34, is found near Ramallah, a PNA-administered West Bank town. Jumhour's death marks the third apparent assassination in May of Palestinians suspected in the sale of land to Israelis.... At an opposition rally in the capital of Kenya, Nairobi, hundreds of riot police use tear gas, rubber bullets, and clubs to disperse the crowd of more than 1,000 demonstrators.	Reports reveal that protests involving thousands of activists broke out across Argentina in May in response to the government's austere economic policies.... The Confederation Bridge, which links Prince Edward Island to Canada's mainland, opens.	Some 10,000 students riot in Seoul, South Korea, protesting Pres. Kim Young Sam's May 30 refusal to reveal how much he spent on his 1992 election campaign.... East Timorese separatists attack a police vehicle with grenades, killing 17 officers. It is the latest in a string of attacks that have claimed 41 lives in a week.... Massoud's forces drive five miles southward and capture the town of Jabal Siraj, a strategic point in Afghanistan.
June 1		The French left, led by the Socialist Party, wins a decisive victory over the center-right ruling coalition in legislative elections.... Premier Necmettin Erbakan, Turkey's first Islamist leader, states he will resign by the end of the month in response to a recent collapse of the ruling coalition.... An off-duty officer of the Royal Ulster Constabulary police is beaten to death by at least seven men in County Antrim.... Nikolai Alexandrovich Tikhonov, 92, Soviet premier, 1980–85, dies in Moscow, Russia, of pneumonia.	Four opposition legislators who helped organize the May 31 rally in Kenya are detained for several hours.	Retired general Hugo Banzer Suarez, who ruled Bolivia from 1971 to 1978 after seizing power in a military coup, leads a field of presidential candidates in a popular vote. Juan Carlos Duran of the governing Nationalist Revolutionary Movement (MNR) places second. In the second round of the presidential voting, Bolivia's Congress will choose between the two front-runners.	
June 2		Presidents Emil Constantinescu of Romania and Leonid Kuchma of Ukraine sign a treaty to normalize the two countries' relations.... Two separate bomb blasts in Tirana, the capital of Albania, injure 28 people.	Rebellious soldiers in Sierra Leone's capital, Freetown, come under attack from Nigerian warships. The Nigerian bombardment sets off fighting between the rebels and Nigerian peacekeeping troops stationed in Freetown since 1994 under the auspices of ECOMOG. Several hundred Sierra Leoneans attend a demonstration organized by the rebels to protest the Nigerian offensive.	Canada's voters elect a new Parliament, giving the ruling Liberal Party, led by P.M. Jean Chrétien, 155 seats in the House of Commons, down from 174 before the vote.	As riots that began May 31 in Seoul, the capital of South Korea, continue, police officer Yoo Ji Woong is killed amid a clash. Separately, South Korean judge Son Yi Jol convicts and sentences the founder of the Hanbo Group conglomerate, Chung Tae Soo, and 10 others in a loans scandal involving the group's Hanbo Steel Industry Co. subsidiary to jail sentences ranging from a suspended term to 15 years.
June 3	Pope John Paul II addresses a meeting of six Central European presidents: Poland's Aleksander Kwasniewski, Hungary's Arpad Goncz, Vaclav Havel of the Czech Republic, Slovakia's Michal Kovac, Leonid Kuchma of Ukraine, and Algirdas Brazauskas of Lithuania. German president Roman Herzog also attends the meeting.	In France, Socialist Party leader Lionel Jospin takes office as premier, replacing the unpopular incumbent, Alain Juppe.	U.S. troops fly 1,200 foreigners, including around 30 Americans, from Freetown, Sierra Leone, to a U.S. warship off the coast.		
June 4		Albanian president Sali Berisha escapes injury in an attempt on his life at a rally in the town of Shkallnuer.... A clubhouse of the Bandidos motorcycle gang in Drammen, Norway, is destroyed by a bomb. The attack kills one person, Irene Astrid Bekkevold, 51. Four others are wounded. Bekkevold is the first innocent bystander killed in the Scandinavian motorcycle-gang war between the Bandidos and the Hells Angels.			In Seoul, protests that started May 31 lead to the death of a factory worker, Lee Seok. The student group suspends the protests after admitting demonstrators beat Lee to death after wrongly suspected him of being a police informer.... More than 50,000 people gather in Hong Kong's Victoria Park for an annual candlelight vigil in memory of those killed in a June 4, 1989, government crackdown on prodemocracy protesters in Tiananmen Square in Beijing, China.
June 5		A captain in Croatian president Franjo Tudjman's presidential guard attacks a presidential candidate, Vlado Gotovac of the Liberals, during a campaign rally, striking him several times with a belt buckle. Gotovac is forced to suspend his campaign to recuperate.	Fighting breaks out in Brazzaville, capital of the Republic of the Congo, between soldiers loyal to Pres. Pascal Lissouba and militia forces supporting his predecessor, Gen. Denis Sassou-Nguesso.... In Algeria's first legislative elections since January 1992, parties supporting Algeria's military-backed government win a majority in a new lower house of Parliament.	A rally described as the largest march in years takes place in Lima, the capital of Peru, in protest of Pres. Fujimori's increasingly authoritarian style of governing.	China appoints Ma Yuzhen, a former Chinese ambassador to Britain, to be foreign ministry commissioner in Hong Kong after the colony reverts to Chinese sovereignty, from British rule, at midnight June 30. Ma's ascension to the new post will make him China's top civilian official in the colony.... Ships from North Korea and South Korea exchange fire after North Korean fishing boats, accompanied by a military vessel, enter South Korean waters. Neither side's vessels are hit.

A	B	C	D	E
Includes developments that affect more than one world region, international organizations, and important meetings of major world leaders.	Includes all domestic and regional developments in Europe, including the Soviet Union, Turkey, Cyprus, and Malta.	Includes all domestic and regional developments in Africa and the Middle East, including Iraq and Iran and excluding Cyprus, Turkey, and Afghanistan.	Includes all domestic and regional developments in Latin America, the Caribbean, and Canada.	Includes all domestic and regional developments in Asia and Pacific nations, extending from Afghanistan through all the Pacific Islands, except Hawaii.

U.S. Politics & Social Issues	U.S. Foreign Policy & Defense	U.S. Economy & Environment	Science, Technology, & Nature	Culture, Leisure, & Lifestyle	
				The IAAF suspends runner Mary Decker Slaney from competition, due to suspicious results of a drug test taken at the trials for the 1996 Olympics.... Rose Will Monroe, 77, who portrayed "Rosie the Riveter," dies in Clarkesville, Indiana, of complications related to kidney failure.	May 31
			Robert Serber, 88, physicist who played a key role in the birth of the atomic bomb and who won the 1972 J. Robert Oppenheimer Prize for physics, dies in New York City of complications after surgery for brain cancer.	Canadian Donovan Bailey beats Michael Johnson in a one-on-one, 150-meter (164-yard) race to claim the unofficial title of "world's fastest man."... At the Tony Awards, the musicals *Titanic* and *Chicago* dominate the major award categories. For Best Play, *The Last Night of Ballyhoo* wins, and *A Doll's House* wins for Best Play Revival.	June 1
Timothy J. McVeigh, a decorated veteran of the 1991 Persian Gulf war, is convicted on all 11 charges before him by a U.S. federal jury in Denver, Colorado, of the Apr. 19, 1995, bombing of the Alfred P. Murrah Federal Building in Oklahoma City, Okla. The bombing, which killed 168 people, was the deadliest act of terrorism ever committed on U.S. soil.... The body of Jonathan M. Levin, 31, a high school teacher and the son of prominent corporate chief executives, Gerald Levin of Time Warner Inc., is found in his New York apartment.	Pentagon officials reveal that Major Gen. John E. Longhouser, commander of the U.S. Army's Aberdeen Provings Ground in Maryland, decides to retire after admitting that he had an adulterous affair five years earlier while he was separated from his wife.	In *Boggs v. Boggs*, the Supreme Court rules that the Employee Retirement Income Security Act of 1974 (Erisa), a federal law that protects workers' pension benefits, takes precedence over states' community property laws that protect married couples' property interests.		Helen Hull Jacobs, 88, top tennis player in the 1930s, dies in East Hampton, New York, of heart failure.... Adolphus Anthony (Doc) Cheatham, 91, jazz trumpeter whose career spanned more than 70 years, dies in Washington, D.C., after suffering a stroke.... *The Partner*, by John Grisham, tops the bestseller list.	June 2
Harvey Johnson is elected as the first black mayor of Jackson, Mississippi.		David E. Kendall, First Lady Hillary Rodham Clinton's personal attorney, accuses Whitewater independent counsel Kenneth Starr of employing a "leak-and-smear" campaign against the White House.		Dennis James, 79, TV host of variety and game shows, dies in in Palm Springs, California, of lung cancer.	June 3
Two convicts—Dorsie Johnson-Bey and Davis Losada—are executed in Huntsville, Texas. With their deaths, Texas has executed 20 prisoners in 1997, more than any state has put to death in a single year since 1976, when the Supreme Court reintroduced the death penalty. Texas set the record in 1995, executing 19 inmates. Johnson and Losada are the 390th and 391st in the U.S. and the 126th and 127th in Texas to be put to death since 1976, respectively.	The U.S. Army confirms that Sergeant Major Gene C. McKinney, charged with sexual assault and indecent assault involving four women, has asked for early retirement.			Ronnie Lane, 51, British guitarist and songwriter, dies in Colorado of multiple sclerosis.	June 4
A U.S. District Court jury in Buffalo, New York, awards $4 million in damages to Frank Smith, a former inmate tortured by prison guards in the aftermath of a 1971 prison uprising in Attica, New York. Smith is the first of 1,281 former inmates to win damages in a $2.8 billion suit filed in 1974.... The F. W. Olin Foundation announces that it will contribute $200 million to the building of a new engineering college, the Franklin W. Olin College of Engineering in Needham, Massachusetts. The donation is the largest gift ever to a U.S. college or university.	In Alexandria, Virginia, Judge James C. Cacheris sentences former CIA officer Harold Nicholson to 23 years and seven months in prison for selling top-secret information to Russia.... Sergeant First Class Julius Davis, an army instructor in Darmstadt, Germany, is convicted of 11 counts of sexual misconduct. He is sentenced to two years in prison, reduction in rank, and a bad-conduct dismissal. Davis is the first army soldier stationed in Europe to be convicted of sexual misconduct since a wide-ranging investigation into sex abuse began in November 1996.	Congress gives final approval to a plan to balance the federal budget by the year 2002.... In U.S. Bankruptcy Court in Boston, Massachusetts, retailer Sears, Roebuck & Co. presents a settlement to the attorneys general of 39 states as part of its accord with the FTC regarding refunds to bankrupt credit card customers from whom Sears improperly collected debts. Sears will pay out at least $138 million, the largest FTC refund settlement ever.... The New York City Council approves a $33.4 billion budget for the fiscal 1997–98 year, which begins July 1.		J(ay) Anthony Lukas, 64, journalist and author who won a Pulitzer in 1968, the National Book Award in 1985, and the National Book Critics Circle Award in 1986, dies in New York, an apparent suicide.	June 5

F	G	H	I	J
Includes elections, federal-state relations, civil rights and liberties, crime, the judiciary, education, health care, poverty, urban affairs, and population.	*Includes formation and debate of U.S. foreign and defense policies, veterans' affairs, and defense spending. (Relations with specific foreign countries are usually found under the region concerned.)*	*Includes business, labor, agriculture, taxation, transportation, consumer affairs, monetary and fiscal policy, natural resources, and pollution.*	*Includes worldwide scientific, medical, and technological developments; natural phenomena; U.S. weather; natural disasters; and accidents.*	*Includes the arts, religion, scholarship, communications media, sports, entertainments, fashions, fads, and social life.*

	World Affairs	Europe	Africa & the Middle East	The Americas	Asia & the Pacific
June 6	The 138-nation Convention on International Trade in Endangered Species (CITES) opens in Harare, the capital of Zimbabwe.	Ireland's ruling political coalition, headed by P.M. John Bruton, loses its parliamentary majority in elections. Caoimhghin O'Caolain, a candidate from Sinn Fein, the political arm of the Provisional IRA, wins a seat in the Dail for the first time in 16 years. He will be the first Sinn Fein member to join the Dail since the 1922 founding of the Republic of Ireland.			
June 7		Reports confirm that four Russian journalists captured in March were released from captivity in the republic of Chechnya.... Automatic-weapon fire from a car in Liseleje, Denmark, kills a member of the Bandidos motorcycle gang and wounds three others. The death toll from the gang war in Scandanavia is 10 since early 1996.			
June 8		Protestant rioters break into a Catholic church in Ballymena, Northern Ireland, prompting a clash with police that leaves 27 officers injured. Six people are arrested in the fighting.... Voters in a referendum in Switzerland reject a measure that would have outlawed Swiss arms exports.	The Cobras, a 5,000-strong militia maintained by Gen. Denis Sassou-Nguesso, seize the center of Brazzaville, the capital of the Republic of the Congo.... Amos Tutuola, 76 or 77, Nigerian novelist of Yoruban descent whose first novel was the first widely disseminated English-language publication by an African author, dies in Ibadan, Nigeria.	Workers at the 79 Alberta stores of Canada Safeway Ltd., a unit of U.S.-based Safeway Inc., end a strike that started March 26 and involved 10,000 workers.	
June 9		Two Turkish men surrender to authorities in Cologne, Germany, after hijacking an Air Malta jet en route to Istanbul, Turkey, from Valetta, Malta. None of the passengers or crew on board are injured.	France, Congo's former colonial ruler, sends 550 troops to Brazzaville, the capital, to reinforce a 450-strong force already there. French troops evacuate 2,000 foreigners.	Haitian premier Rosny Smarth resigns, alleging that supporters of former president Jean-Bertrand Aristide rigged April 6 legislative elections in a bid to force the premier's ouster.... Stanley Howard Knowles, 88, left-wing member of Canada's Parliament for four decades, dies in Ottawa, Canada, of complications related to pneumonia.	
June 10	The U.S. Department of Education releases the results of an international survey designed to measure the mathematics and science performance of primary-school students. Singapore registers the strongest overall performance on the math test, followed by South Korea and Japan. Kuwait receives the lowest score. South Korea receives the highest mark on the science exam, followed by Japan. The U.S. ranks third, tying Austria. Kuwait has lowest mark.	Presidents Boris Yeltsin of Russia and Aleksandr Lukashenko of Belarus sign a union treaty into law. ... Reports indicate that Chechen president Aslan Maskhadov has imposed Islamic law, or sharia, in the breakaway republic in a bid to restore order.	A U.S. Air Force transport plane flies 30 Americans and 24 other foreigners from Brazzaville, the capital of the Republic of the Congo.		In a scandal that alleges that Dai-Ichi Kangyo Bank Ltd. (DKB), one of Japan's largest banks, has links to racketeers, 21 DKB directors—just over half the board—resigns. That is the largest mass board resignation ever in Japan.... Reports state that Pol Pot, the leader of the Khmer Rouge guerrillas in Cambodia, caused dissension when he ordered the killing of the Khmer Rouge's defense chief, Son Sen, and his family.
June 11	The International Federation of Red Cross and Red Crescent Societies urge the adoption of universal quality standards for aid agencies, noting that, of 170 aid agencies registered during the 1994 Rwandan crisis, nearly one-third had disappeared by 1997. The Red Cross estimates that $120 million of the $1.4 billion in aid sent to the region remains unaccounted for, largely due to substandard accounting procedures.	An unidentified gunman in Belfast, Northern Ireland, shoots and kills Robert Bates, a prominent former member of a pro-British Protestant death squad who was freed in 1996 after spending 19 years in prison.... Officials confirm that Swiss banks found far more accounts belonging to potential Holocaust victims than previously revealed, up from 37.8 million Swiss francs ($26 million) to 49.4 million francs.... Jill Neville, 65, a popular member of the London literary elite in the post-World War II era, dies in London, England, of lymphoma.			The Taliban loses control of Pul-e-Khumri, 90 miles north of Kabul, the capital of Afghanistan. The town is recaptured by alliance forces in a three-pronged attack, with Ahmed Shah Massoud's troops moving in from the south, Hizb-i-Wahdat fighters attacking from the east and Abdul Malik's Uzbek forces closing in from the north. The defeat marks the loss of the Taliban's last remaining stronghold in northern Afghanistan.

A	B	C	D	E
Includes developments that affect more than one world region, international organizations, and important meetings of major world leaders.	*Includes all domestic and regional developments in Europe, including the Soviet Union, Turkey, Cyprus, and Malta.*	*Includes all domestic and regional developments in Africa and the Middle East, including Iraq and Iran and excluding Cyprus, Turkey, and Afghanistan.*	*Includes all domestic and regional developments in Latin America, the Caribbean, and Canada.*	*Includes all domestic and regional developments in Asia and Pacific nations, extending from Afghanistan through all the Pacific Islands, except Hawaii.*

U.S. Politics & Social Issues	U.S. Foreign Policy & Defense	U.S. Economy & Environment	Science, Technology, & Nature	Culture, Leisure, & Lifestyle	
Henry Francis Hays, 42, formerly of the Ku Klux Klan, is executed in Atmore, Alabama, for killing a black teenager, Michael Donald, in a 1981 lynching. The slaying led to a 1987 civil suit that bankrupted the United Klans of America, the largest of several rival Klan groups. Hays is the first white man executed in Alabama for killing a black person since 1913. Hays is the 392nd person in the U.S. and the 16th in Alabama executed since 1976.	Reports indicate that Rear Admiral R. M. Mitchell Jr. was relieved as commander of the Navy Supply Systems Command in Mechanicsburg, Pennsylvania, for allegedly making repeated advances toward a female subordinate. Mitchell asks the navy for permission to retire.	The Dow Jones industrial average goes up 130.49 points, to close at a record 7435.78. . . . Federal authorities in New York City arrest political consultant Martin Davis on charges of mail fraud for allegedly embezzling from the International Brotherhood of Teamsters union to fund the 1996 reelection campaign of Teamsters president Ron Carey.		Pres. Clinton speaks to the graduating class, which includes his daughter Chelsea, at Sidwell Friends school in Washington, D.C. . . . Magda Gabor, 78, Hollywood actress and socialite, dies in Rancho Mirage, California, of kidney failure. . . . Reports from Ontario, Canada, state that Roman Catholic bishop Anthony Tonnos denied a church funeral service to slain mobster John Papalia.	June 6
New Hampshire governor Jeanne Shaheen (D) signs legislation making the state the 11th to give legal protection against discrimination to homosexuals. The law, effective Jan. 1, 1998, will give gay men and lesbians protection in employment and housing.			The National Bioethics Advisory Commission writes to Pres. Clinton, calling for the government to impose a short-term legal ban on the cloning of human beings. . . . A report notes that some 14,000 medical emergencies occur each year on the nine major U.S. airlines and calls for more aircraft to carry heart defibrillators.	Hockey's Detroit Red Wings defeat the Philadelphia Flyers, 2–1, to win the NHL's Stanley Cup championship. . . . Ninth-seeded Iva Majoli of Croatia wins the women's tennis title at the French Open. . . . In horse racing, Touch Gold wins the 129th running of the Belmont Stakes.	June 7
		Pres. Clinton vetoes an emergency spending bill that would provide funds for disaster aid and for U.S. peacekeeping missions overseas because he opposes amendments in the bill that seek to avoid government shutdowns such as those that occurred in late 1995 and early 1996.		Reid Shelton, 72, stage and TV actor who played Daddy Warbucks in the original three-year Broadway run of the musical *Annie*, dies in Portland, Oregon, after undergoing a heart bypass operation. . . . At the French Open, unseeded Gustavo Kuerten of Brazil wins the men's tennis title.	June 8
	U.S. Air Force general Joseph W. Ralston withdraws his name from consideration to become the nation's military chief after concluding that controversy over an admitted adulterous affair will make his confirmation process too contentious and will compromise his ability to lead the military.	In *Gilbert v. Homar*, the Supreme Court rules unanimously that public institutions are not required to hold hearings before they suspend an employee without pay.			June 9
After a late May ruling that ordered a new trial by Judge Everett W. Dickey of Orange County Superior Court, Elmer (Geronimo) Pratt, a former leader of the militant Black Panther Party, is freed on bail after serving 27 years for a murder he always maintained he did not commit. Pratt in 1972 was convicted of killing a Los Angeles woman during a 1968 robbery attempt in Santa Monica, California.	The U.S. House of Representatives reaffirms Jerusalem as Israel's undivided capital and calls for relocating the U.S. embassy to Jerusalem from Tel Aviv by May 1999.			In Hollidaysburg, Pennsylvania, Judge Norman Callan sentences Dennis and Lorie Nixon, who belong to a Christian faith-healing sect, to at least 2½ years in prison for allowing their daughter, Shannon Nixon, 16, to die of treatable diabetes.	June 10
A state parole board in Alabama pardons former Alabama governor Guy Hunt (R), declaring he is innocent of the ethics violations that he was convicted of in 1993. The unanimous decision effectively exonerates Hunt of all charges and restores all of his civil rights. . . . The Mashantucket Pequot Indians of Connecticut launch the *Sassacus*, the first ferryboat built at the Pequot River Shipworks in New London, Connecticut. . . . Pres. Clinton names Jane Garvey as the new administrator of the FAA, succeeding Linda Hall Daschle.		Thomas J. Donohue Jr. is named the next president of the U.S. Chamber of Commerce, replacing Richard L. Lesher.	The FDA sends letters to thousands of U.S. doctors warning them that the newly developed protease-inhibitor drugs may cause diabetic symptoms in AIDS patients.	The Christian Coalition announces that Pat Robertson, will be the association's new board chairman. Donald P. Hodel, will be the new president, and Randy Tate will be executive director. . . . Thalassa Cruso, 88, amateur horticulturalist, author and columnist, dies of Alzheimer's disease in Wellesley, Massachusetts.	June 11

F	G	H	I	J
Includes elections, federal-state relations, civil rights and liberties, crime, the judiciary, education, health care, poverty, urban affairs, and population.	Includes formation and debate of U.S. foreign and defense policies, veterans' affairs, and defense spending. (Relations with specific foreign countries are usually found under the region concerned.)	Includes business, labor, agriculture, taxation, transportation, consumer affairs, monetary and fiscal policy, natural resources, and pollution.	Includes worldwide scientific, medical, and technological developments; natural phenomena; U.S. weather; natural disasters; and accidents.	Includes the arts, religion, scholarship, communications media, sports, entertainments, fashions, fads, and social life.

	World Affairs	Europe	Africa & the Middle East	The Americas	Asia & the Pacific
June 12	Pres. Bill Clinton states that the U.S. will back only Poland, Hungary, and the Czech Republic as new NATO members. As NATO decisions are made by consensus, Clinton's statement effectively vetoes offers of membership to any other nation.... The UN's 1997 Human Development Report asserts that extreme poverty can feasibly be eradicated by the first or second decade of the 21st century, claiming that a lack of "political commitment, not financial resources" is the real obstacle to reducing poverty.	Bulat Okudzhava, 73, Russian poet, songwriter, and singer who was a voice of political dissent in post–World War II Russia, dies in Paris, France, of complications from pneumonia and kidney failure. ... Vittorio Mussolini, 81, son of the Fascist ruler of Italy, 1922–43, Benito Mussolini, dies in Rome after a long illness.	Firefights, looting, and summary killings continue in Brazzaville, the capital of the Republic of the Congo.	In Colombia, at least five inmates are killed and 30 others are injured in riots at the Modelo prison in Bogota, the capital, and the Picalena prison in Ibague in the province of Tolima.	Members of India's embattled Congress Party (I) reelect Sitaram Kesri as the party's president. It is only the third election held by the party in its 112-year history.
June 13	The UN General Assembly votes to urge Israel to pay $1.7 million in damages for its artillery attack on a UN camp near Tyre, Lebanon, that killed more than 100 people in April 1996.	Officials announce the closing of Russia's main Antarctic base, Molodyozhnaya, by the year 2000 due to budget cuts.... Police in southwestern France arrest Ira Einhorn, a former New Age guru convicted in absentia in the U.S. in 1993 for the 1977 beating death of his girlfriend, Holly Maddux.			Sixty people are killed and 200 others injured when a fire sweeps through a crowded movie theater in New Delhi, India's capital.
June 14		Queen Elizabeth II marks the official celebration of her 71st birthday by awarding several hundred peerages, knighthoods, and other honors. ... The Italian government creates an independent committee to probe claims that Italian soldiers tortured Somali civilians during a peacekeeping mission in 1993. Army generals Bruno Loi and Carmine Flore, who commanded Italian troops in Somalia, resign over the abuse allegations.	Palestinians demonstrate against a resolution passed June 10 by the U.S. House of Representatives that reaffirmed Jerusalem as Israel's undivided capital and called for relocating the U.S. embassy to Jerusalem from Tel Aviv by May 1999. The demonstration will lead to a series of nearly daily conflicts.		Hong Kong's provisional legislature, a Chinese-appointed body, passes controversial legislation that will place restrictions on political groups and public protests when China assumes control of the colony from Britain at midnight on June 30.... In Japan, the Diet approves legislation that will bar discrimination against women in the workplace and relax rules governing which hours women are permitted to work.
June 15		Croatians reelect Pres. Franjo Tudjman to a third term with 61.41% of the vote.		Colombia's main leftist rebel group, FARC, frees 70 soldiers and marines being held in remote jungle locations in Caqueta department in southern Colombia. The rebels agree to release the soldiers after the government temporarily withdraws its troops from a part of the area. FARC captured 60 of the 70 soldiers in August 1996, and the other 10 hostages, who are marines, were taken in January.	
June 16	French and German leaders at an EU summit meeting in Amsterdam, the Netherlands, reach a compromise plan to allow the projected European currency union to go forward. Prototypes of eight coins designed by Luc Luycx of the Belgian Royal Mint for the new currency, known as the euro, are unveiled.	Unidentified gunmen in Lurgan, Northern Ireland, shoot and kill two officers of the Royal Ulster Constabulary (RUC) police force. The Provisional IRA claims responsibility. British prime minister Tony Blair halts indefinitely all contact between his government and the IRA's political wing, Sinn Fein. The attack represents the first IRA murders of RUC officers since 1994.... International monitors criticize the June 15 voting in Croatia as "fundamentally flawed."			The benchmark Hang Seng index to track "red chips," or mainland Chinese-backed companies, begins operating in Hong Kong.
June 17	Hani Abdel Rahim al-Sayegh, a Saudi dissident accused of involvement in a deadly 1996 truck bombing of a U.S. military complex near Dhahran, Saudi Arabia, is deported to the U.S. from Canada. Officials reveal that he will tell the U.S. what he knows about the attack in exchange for reduced charges and a guarantee that he will not be extradited to Saudi Arabia, where he may face execution.... The UN General Assembly approves the appointment of Irish president Mary Robinson as UN High Commissioner for Human Rights.	Federal police officers throughout France conduct a series of raids in which they arrest more than 600 people suspected of possessing or selling child pornography. The discovery of an intricate child-sex network contradicts a long-standing misconception within France that child pornography is virtually non-existent in the country.			Both houses of the Japanese Diet pass a compromise bill that will make heart transplants possible in Japan.... In Phnom Penh, the capital of Cambodia, a gun battle between bodyguards loyal to Hun Sen and Prince Ranariddh kills two of the prince's guards.

A	B	C	D	E
Includes developments that affect more than one world region, international organizations, and important meetings of major world leaders.	*Includes all domestic and regional developments in Europe, including the Soviet Union, Turkey, Cyprus, and Malta.*	*Includes all domestic and regional developments in Africa and the Middle East, including Iraq and Iran and excluding Cyprus, Turkey, and Afghanistan.*	*Includes all domestic and regional developments in Latin America, the Caribbean, and Canada.*	*Includes all domestic and regional developments in Asia and Pacific nations, extending from Afghanistan through all the Pacific Islands, except Hawaii.*

U.S. Politics & Social Issues	U.S. Foreign Policy & Defense	U.S. Economy & Environment	Science, Technology, & Nature	Culture, Leisure, & Lifestyle	
Michigan circuit court judge Charles Miel declares a mistrial in the prosecution of Dr. Jack Kevorkian on charges of helping Loretta Peabody, a terminally ill woman, commit suicide in August 1996. It is Kevorkian's fourth trial on charges related to his alleged participation in the death of a terminally ill person.... Pres. Clinton names seven people to a presidential advisory board on race relations.... Alex Kelly, who spent eight years as a fugitive in European resorts, is convicted by a Stamford, Connecticut, jury of raping a 16-year-old girl in 1986.	Sergeant First Class Paul Fuller, 25, is found guilty of violations involving five women, including one count of rape, one count of kidnapping, three counts of forcible sodomy, and three counts of cruelty. A military court sentences Fuller to five years in prison, a dishonorable discharge, reduction in rank to private, and forfeiture of all pay.	The Senate, 78-21, and the House, 348-74, approve an $8.6 billion emergency spending bill that provides $5.6 billion in disaster aid to 35 states, including flood-stricken states in the Upper Midwest. The measure also includes $1.9 billion for U.S. peacekeeping missions overseas. Since the bill is stripped of amendments the president objected to in his June 8 veto, Clinton signs the bill.		The National Basketball Association fines Dennis Rodman $50,000 for derogatory remarks he made about Mormons, members of the Church of Jesus Christ of Latter-Day Saints. The fine is the largest ever handed out to a player by the NBA and Rodman's third NBA fine in the 1996-97 season..... In the first-ever interleague baseball game between the National League and American League, the San Francisco Giants defeat the Texas Rangers, 4-3.	June 12
A federal jury in Denver, Colo., unanimously recommends that Timothy J. McVeigh, a 29-year-old former soldier, be sentenced to death for the Apr. 19, 1995 bombing of the Alfred P. Murrah Federal Building in Oklahoma City, Okla., that killed 168 people and injured 850 others.... Thomas Coleman, 86, who in 1965 was acquitted, on grounds of self-defense, of manslaughter in the shotgun slaying of civil-rights activist Jonathan Daniels, dies in Alabama of unreported causes.				Basketball's Chicago Bulls defeat the Utah Jazz, 90-86, in the sixth game of a best-of-seven series to win their fifth NBA championship in seven years.... Two players from hockey's Detroit Red Wings, Vladimir Konstantinov and Slava Fetisov, and the team's masseur are injured in a car accident in Royal Oak, Michigan.	June 13
In a high-profile commencement address at the University of California at San Diego, Pres. Clinton calls for racial reconciliation, defends affirmative action, and launches a planned yearlong effort to spur a "great and unprecedented conversation about race."				Richard Jaeckel, 70, film and TV actor best known for his role in The Dirty Dozen (1967), dies in Woodland Hills, California, of cancer.... Oscar De La Hoya successfully defends his WBC welterweight title with a second-round knockout of David Kamau of Kenya.	June 14
				Ernie Els of South Africa wins the U.S. Open Golf Tournament in Bethesda, Maryland.... Kim Casali, 55, cartoonist whose work appeared in newspapers in 60 countries during the 1960s and 1970s, dies in Surrey, England, of unreported causes.	June 15
New York governor George Pataki (R) announces that state legislators have reached an agreement to extend the state's system of rent restrictions, which will leave intact the bulk of the current regulations for another six years.... The John D. and Catherine T. MacArthur Foundation of Chicago awards its annual MacArthur Fellowships, honoring 23 individuals in a wide range of fields.	The U.S. Senate expresses its support for adding Romania, Bulgaria, and the three Baltic republics—Lithuania, Latvia and Estonia—to NATO.			Actor Tim Allen, known for the ABC comedy Home Improvement, pleads guilty in a Bloomfield Hills, Michigan, court to a charge of driving while impaired and is sentenced to one year of probation and a $500 fine.	June 16
The U.S. Circuit Court of Appeals for the District of Columbia rules that the White House has to hand over all documents subpoenaed by independent counsel Donald Smaltz that "might reasonably be relevant" to his investigation of former agriculture secretary Mike Espy. However, the appeals court's ruling also extends the president's constitutional right to confidential communication with his staff.	The FBI announces that the agency has captured Mir Aimal Kansi, a Pakistani native suspected of opening fire outside the Langley, Virginia, headquarters of the CIA in 1993, killing two CIA employees. ... The U.S. Senate votes, 90-5, to approve a State Department authorization bill that includes a plan to pay a total of $819 million in delinquent UN dues over three years.				June 17

F	G	H	I	J
Includes elections, federal-state relations, civil rights and liberties, crime, the judiciary, education, health care, poverty, urban affairs, and population.	Includes formation and debate of U.S. foreign and defense policies, veterans' affairs, and defense spending. (Relations with specific foreign countries are usually found under the region concerned.)	Includes business, labor, agriculture, taxation, transportation, consumer affairs, monetary and fiscal policy, natural resources, and pollution.	Includes worldwide scientific, medical, and technological developments; natural phenomena; U.S. weather; natural disasters; and accidents.	Includes the arts, religion, scholarship, communications media, sports, entertainments, fashions, fads, and social life.

	World Affairs	Europe	Africa & the Middle East	The Americas	Asia & the Pacific
June 18	The 15 EU leaders agree on a treaty to update the 1992 Maastricht pact.... At the Convention on International Trade in Endangered Species (CITES), delegates vote to restrict trade in sturgeon and to maintain existing controls on the trade of rhinoceros horn. Reports confirm that CITES also rejected a request by Norway and Japan to lift curbs on commercial whaling.	Premier Necmettin Erbakan, Turkey's first-ever leader from a fundamentalist Muslim party, resigns under military pressure.... Multinational troops in Albania kill a man who opens fire on Greek soldiers in the town of Elbasan. He is the first person killed by the multinational force since its April deployment.... Lev Z. Kopelev, 85, Russian writer and dissident during the Soviet era, dies in Cologne, Germany, of heart disease.			
June 19	At the Convention on International Trade in Endangered Species (CITES), delegates grant approval for three southern African countries—Botswana, Namibia and Zimbabwe—to sell a limited amount of stockpiled ivory to Japan. The transaction would be the first legal sale of ivory since January 1990, when CITES's worldwide ban on ivory trading went into effect.	Ukraine president Leonid Kuchma issues a decree removing Premier Pavlo Lazarenko from office, ostensibly due to a "severe cold."... In the longest trial in British history, McDonald's is awarded £60,000 ($98,000) in damages. In the three-year-long libel case known as the "McLibel" trial, the judge rules that British environmentalists David Morris and Helen Steel defamed the company.... Julia Smith, 87, producer of a popular British soap opera, dies in London, England, of unreported causes.	In Kenya, police use violence to prevent Nairobi University students from marching on Parliament. The march is reportedly sparked by state broadcasters' decision to halt live TV and radio coverage of Finance Minister Musalia Mudavadi's budget speech after a disruption led to scuffles on the parliament floor between opposition figures and members of Pres. Daniel T. arap Moi's KANU party.		British governor Chris Patten holds his last monthly question-and-answer session before the Legislative Council, the democratically elected body that will be dissolved when control of the colony changes hands. Francis Cornish is named Britain's first consul-general in post-handover Hong Kong.... Pol Pot, allegedly responsible for more than 1 million deaths during the Khmer Rouge's rule of Cambodia from 1975 to 1979, is captured by forces loyal to Ta Mok, a popular leader among Khmer Rouge troops.
June 20	At a summit in Denver, Colorado, Russia's entry into what has been the Group of Seven (G-7) leading industrial democracies is formalized, prompting commentators to dub the new assemblage the Group of Eight (G-8). Other items on the summit's agenda include discussions on pollution, implications of the handover of Hong Kong to China, aid to Africa, and the expansion of NATO into Eastern Europe.	Alexander Zakharov, an arms researcher, dies less than a week after being exposed to neutron rays at the Arzamas-16 nuclear center. Zakharov is reported to be the first Russian seriously injured in an atomic energy accident since the 1986 Chernobyl nuclear disaster.			
June 21	Traditionally neutral Switzerland becomes the 28th country to join the NATO Partnership for Peace program.	Three people are injured when a car bomb explodes in Belfast, Northern Ireland.... Russian television broadcasts a videotape of Justice Minister Valentin Kovalev, nude with two naked young women at a sauna reportedly controlled by Russian organized crime.		Fidel Velazquez Sanchez, 97, Mexican labor leader known as Don Fidel who ran the country's largest union alliance, the Confederation of Mexican Workers, for more than 50 years, dies in Mexico City of cardiac arrest and respiratory failure.	In Cambodia, Prince Ranariddh and Hun Sen jointly announce the capture of Pol Pot. Ranariddh reveals that Pol Pot is being held by the Khmer Rouge rebels in Anlong Veng, a jungle stronghold near the Thai border.
June 22		In response to the video aired June 21, Russian premier Viktor Chernomyrdin states that he has suspended Justice Minister Valentin Kovalev.... In separate incidents, police in two Northern Ireland towns prevent a Protestant organization from marching through predominantly Catholic neighborhoods.			Taiwan begins to conduct live-fire military exercises, which are interpreted as a signal to China that it will resist reunification planned for June 30.
June 23	High-level delegates from nearly 180 countries, including about 60 heads of state, attend a special session of the UN General Assembly to assess the state of the global environment five years after the landmark 1992 UN Conference on Environment and Development, or Earth Summit, in Rio de Janeiro, Brazil.			The British Commonwealth's sovereign, Queen Elizabeth II, and her husband, Prince Philip, make a visit to Canada. It is the queen's first visit to Canada, a member of the Commonwealth, since 1992.	Indian foreign secretary Salman Haider and Pakistani foreign secretary Shamshad Ahmed conclude talks in Islamabad, Pakistan's capital, on the disputed Kashmir region. The ministers reveal that their governments are committed to launching continuing negotiations on the region, over which the two countries have fought two wars since they were partitioned in 1947.... Great Britain agrees to allow some 500 more Chinese soldiers into Hong Kong ahead of the colony's handover to China from Britain at midnight on June 30.

A	B	C	D	E
Includes developments that affect more than one world region, international organizations, and important meetings of major world leaders.	Includes all domestic and regional developments in Europe, including the Soviet Union, Turkey, Cyprus, and Malta.	Includes all domestic and regional developments in Africa and the Middle East, including Iraq and Iran and excluding Cyprus, Turkey, and Afghanistan.	Includes all domestic and regional developments in Latin America, the Caribbean, and Canada.	Includes all domestic and regional developments in Asia and Pacific nations, extending from Afghanistan through all the Pacific Islands, except Hawaii.

U.S. Politics & Social Issues	U.S. Foreign Policy & Defense	U.S. Economy & Environment	Science, Technology, & Nature	Culture, Leisure, & Lifestyle	
	Irineo Tristan Montoya, a 30-year-old Mexican citizen who confessed to murdering U.S. motorist John Kilheffer in 1985, is executed in Huntsville, Tex. His death sentence provoked protests from Mexico. Montoya is the 397th person executed in the U.S. and the 131st in Texas since 1976.... In Hammond, Ind., Judge James Moody orders that U.S. citizenship be stripped from Kazys Ciurinskas, 79, who is accused of World War II–era atrocities.	The Labor Department reports that the nation's overall productivity in nonfarm sectors rose by a revised seasonally adjusted 2.6% annual rate in the first quarter of 1997. That marks the indicator's most robust showing since the final quarter of 1993.		Some 12,000 delegates at the Southern Baptist Convention, the nation's largest Protestant group, vote overwhelmingly to boycott Disney to protest what it views as the company's shift to a "Christian-bashing, family-bashing, pro-homosexual agenda."	June 18
In *Abrams v. Johnson*, the Supreme Court rules, 5-4, to uphold an electoral districting map for the state of Georgia that leaves the state with just one black-majority congressional district. The state's previous districting plan was struck down by the Supreme Court's 1995 decision in *Miller v. Johnson*.	The Mexican foreign ministry delivers a diplomatic protest to the U.S. embassy in Mexico City calling the June 18 execution of Irineo Tristan Montoya "cruel and inhuman." Mexican officials argue that Montoya's arrest violated the Vienna Convention because Texas police failed to inform him of his right to contact Mexican authorities for legal help. Mexico has no civilian death penalty.	In *U.S. v. Alaska*, the Supreme Court rules that the federal government has complete rights to a tract of oil-rich seabed off the northeast coast of Alaska.... Merrill Lynch & Co. Inc. announces that it has agreed to pay $30 million to settle a criminal investigation into the firm's role in underwriting bond issues for Orange County, California, before the county's 1994 bankruptcy. Merrill Lynch still faces a civil suit filed by the county and a probe by the SEC.	A government-convened panel issues the first official guidelines on how doctors should administer newly developed drug treatments to effectively combat HIV, the virus that causes AIDS. A total of 11 so-called antiretroviral drugs that may used in 320 different combinations are currently on the market.		June 19
The tobacco industry and their legal opponents reach an unprecedented $368.5 billion settlement that, if implemented, will require tobacco companies to pay billions of dollars in damages, impose strict rules on the marketing of cigarettes, and assure the FDA regulatory authority over tobacco products. In exchange, cigarette makers will win immunity from many of the legal claims against them, including actions by attorneys general in 39 states and the Commonwealth of Puerto Rico as well as several suits filed by smokers.	Reports confirm that that Amnesty International sent a letter to Texas Gov. George W. Bush (R) contending that Irineo Tristan Montoya, a Mexican citizen who was executed June 18, was not allowed a lawyer during his police interrogation and that the confession he signed was in English, a language he did not understand.	The Dow closes at a record high of 7796.51, marking the seventh record high in June and the 27th registered in 1997.... Judge Thomas Wilks rules that the *Detroit News* and the *Detroit Free Press* engaged in unfair labor practices that forced a 19-month-long strike, the longest newspaper walkout in U.S. history. Since many workers were not rehired after the strike ended in February, the court orders the Detroit papers to rehire those employees, even if that requires laying off replacement workers.			June 20
				The inaugural game of the Women's National Basketball Association (WNBA), a new U.S. women's professional league, is played, with the Los Angeles Sparks hosting the New York Liberty. The Liberty wins the game, 67-57.	June 21
Data shows that the state and federal prison population increased by nearly 56,000 inmates in 1996, reaching a record high of 1.18 million at the end of the year, up 5% from year-end 1995. The prison population has more than doubled since year-end 1985, when just 502,500 inmates were held in federal and state penitentiaries.			Two trains collide head-on in Devine, Texas, killing two Union Pacific workers and two trespassing riders and injuring two other people.		June 22
In *Agostini v. Felton*, the Supreme Court rules, 5-4, to overturn a 12-year-old Supreme Court precedent that bars public school teachers in New York City from providing remedial tutoring to students at religious schools.... In *Kansas v. Hendricks*, the Supreme Court upholds, 5-4, a Kansas statute that allows the state to commit violent sex offenders to mental institutions, even after the offenders served prison terms for their crimes.... In *Idaho v. Coeur d'Alene Tribe*, the Supreme Court rules, 5-4, that the Coeur d'Alene tribe can not bring a federal lawsuit against the state of Idaho to claim ownership of a portion of a lake bed located partially on the tribe's reservation.	Former FBI agent Earl Edwin Pitts is sentenced by a federal judge in Alexandria, Virginia, to 27 years in prison for spying for the former Soviet Union and Russia.... In *Lindh v. Murphy*, the Supreme Court rules, 5-4, that the Antiterrorism and Effective Death Penalty Act of 1996 does not apply retroactively to writs of habeas corpus pending in federal courts when the law took effect.	The Dow closes down 192.25 points, or 2.47%, which, in terms of single session point declines, is surpassed only by the drop of 508.32 points recorded on Oct. 19, 1987. ... In *Metro-North v. Buckley*, the Supreme Court rejects claims brought by a group of rail workers exposed to high levels of asbestos while employed by New York's Metro-North commuter railroad.... In *Richardson v. McKnight*, the Supreme Court rules, 5-4, that guards working for privately run prisons are not entitled to the same protection against inmates' lawsuits as prison guards employed by a state or the federal government.		Betty Shabazz (born Betty Sanders), 61, college administrator and widow of slain black nationalist leader Malcolm X, dies in New York City after suffering extensive burns in a fire allegedly set by her 12-year-old grandson, Malcolm Shabazz.	June 23

F	G	H	I	J
Includes elections, federal-state relations, civil rights and liberties, crime, the judiciary, education, health care, poverty, urban affairs, and population.	Includes formation and debate of U.S. foreign and defense policies, veterans' affairs, and defense spending. (Relations with specific foreign countries are usually found under the region concerned.)	Includes business, labor, agriculture, taxation, transportation, consumer affairs, monetary and fiscal policy, natural resources, and pollution.	Includes worldwide scientific, medical, and technological developments; natural phenomena; U.S. weather; natural disasters; and accidents.	Includes the arts, religion, scholarship, communications media, sports, entertainments, fashions, fads, and social life.

	World Affairs	Europe	Africa & the Middle East	The Americas	Asia & the Pacific
June 24			In Egypt, a lower court temporarily lifts the ban on the genital cutting of girls and women.	In Canada, some 140 revelers are arrested in Quebec City and Montreal when celebrations of St. Jean Baptiste Day, Quebec's national holiday, turn violent. One police officer and three youths are injured. It is the fourth straight year that violence mars the festivities.... Reports from Chile state floods and mudslides over the past three weeks have caused 17 deaths and $200 million in infrastructure damage.	Jerry Wolf Stuchiner, a former top U.S. immigration official in Hong Kong sentenced to three months in jail for possessing material to make false passports, gains early release from a colony jail.... Justice Murray Wilcox of Australia's Federal Court finds that pesticide maker ICI Australia, a unit of Britain's Imperial Chemical Industries PLC, manufactured and distributed contaminated cattle feed.
June 25	The first-ever report from the UN International Drug Control Program estimates that the global drug trade generates $400 billion a year in revenue, equivalent to 8% of all international trade, and that about 140 million people worldwide smoke marijuana or hashish, 30 million take amphetamines and other stimulants, and 8 million use heroin. At least 13 million are said to use the various forms of cocaine.	Swiss banks agree to waive Swiss bank secrecy laws and to publish the names on unclaimed accounts that dated back to the Nazi Holocaust era..... Christies International PLC auctions 79 gowns that belonged to Diana, Princess of Wales. The proceeds, which total some $3.25 million, will go to two British charities, the Royal Marsden Hospital Cancer Fund, and the AIDS Crisis Trust.	Algerian premier Ahmed Ouyahia, in an apparent effort to attract Islamic support to Liamine Zéroual's government, names seven Islamic moderates to the cabinet he is forming.	A special government commission frees 116 prisoners after finding that they were wrongly convicted under Peru's strict terrorism laws.... At least 19 people are dead or missing after the Soufriere Hills volcano on the tiny Caribbean island of Montserrat erupts, spewing streams of hot rock and ash over surrounding villages. The deaths are the first caused by the volcano, which began erupting in July 1995.	East Timor resistance leader David Alex dies after being wounded in a battle with Indonesian troops in Baucau. The military states Alex died from the wounds suffered during the clash, but resistance leaders claim that he died under torture by military interrogators.
June 26		The Dail, the 166-seat lower chamber of Ireland's parliament, elects Bertie Ahern as the country's new taoiseach, or prime minister, defeating incumbent John Bruton.... Albanian president Berisha's campaign entourage is attacked in the southern town of Lushnja. Eight people are wounded.... Turkey ends a six-week offensive against Iraq-based PKK fighters, which reportedly resulted in the deaths of more than 3,000 guerrillas and 113 Turks.... Cecil Victor (Charlie) Chester, 83, British comedian, dies of unreported causes.	Congolese opposition leader Etienne Tshisekedi is arrested and held overnight after he addresses a rally of students at the University of Kinshasa.		The family of prominent Chinese dissident Wei Jingsheng, who was sentenced in 1995 to 14 years in prison for plotting to subvert the government, report that Wei was severely beaten by other inmates at a prison camp in China.... Statistics reveal the number of Japanese senior citizens exceeds the number of children in the nation for the first time.
June 27	Investigators from the international criminal tribunal in The Hague and UN peacekeepers arrest a Croatian Serb, Slavko Dokmanovic, on war crimes related to a massacre of 61 civilians near the town of Ovcara, Croatia.... Delegates to the conference on the global environment that started June 23 are unable to agree on concrete measures or even a political statement to combat environmental problems as the summit closes.	A bomb blast on a Russian train near Torbino station kills three people and injures seven others.... Tajik president Imamali Rakhmanov and United Tajik Opposition (UTO) leader Said Abdullo Nuri sign a peace pact ending a five-year-long civil war. Since the 1991 breakup of the Soviet Union, 20,000–40,000 people have died in civil strife in Tajikistan.		Angry residents of El Cayo, a remote village on the Usumacinta River in the Mexican state of Chiapas, attack archaeologists who try to remove an ancient Mayan altar to take to a museum in the town of Palenque, some 80 miles (130 km) away. Around 100 villagers rob and beat the archaeologists, who flee into the Mexican jungle.	Hong Kong's Hang Seng stock index closes at a record high 15,196.79, up 68.77 points, on the last day of trading under British rule. Hong Kong's government-in-waiting announces plans to send in 4,000 soldiers, many in armored personnel carriers.
June 28					In Hong Kong, the Legislative Council ends its final session, marked by the passage of a number of measures, including public housing and communications privacy legislation and amendments to the bill of rights. It is anticipated that most of those laws will be rolled back by the provisional legislature. An estimated 70,000 people attend a "Say No to China" antireunification rally in Taiwan.... Japanese police state they have arrested a 14-year-old boy for the May decapitation murder of an 11-year-old boy in Kobe, a murder which caused alarm and increased vigilance in Japan, where violent crime is rare.
June 29		Albania's Socialist Party, led by communist-era premier Fatos Nano, wins a sizeable majority in the first round elections for Parliament. In a parallel ballot, voters turn down a referendum proposal on restoring the monarchy. A Democratic Party official is shot dead in election-related violence.			Hundreds of thousands of people head to Tiananmen Square in Beijing, China, for a spontaneous celebration of the June 30 handover of Hong Kong to China from Britain. Prince Charles knights industrialist Gordon Wu, Financial Secretary Donald Tsang, and Executive Council member Jimmy McGregor in the last such ceremony in the colony.

A	B	C	D	E
Includes developments that affect more than one world region, international organizations, and important meetings of major world leaders.	Includes all domestic and regional developments in Europe, including the Soviet Union, Turkey, Cyprus, and Malta.	Includes all domestic and regional developments in Africa and the Middle East, including Iraq and Iran and excluding Cyprus, Turkey, and Afghanistan.	Includes all domestic and regional developments in Latin America, the Caribbean, and Canada.	Includes all domestic and regional developments in Asia and Pacific nations, extending from Afghanistan through all the Pacific Islands, except Hawaii.

U.S. Politics & Social Issues	U.S. Foreign Policy & Defense	U.S. Economy & Environment	Science, Technology, & Nature	Culture, Leisure, & Lifestyle	
Judge Ralph Nimmons Jr. of U.S. District Court in Jacksonville, Florida, sentences Harry Shapiro, a 31-year-old Orthodox Jew, to 10 years' imprisonment for planting a pipe bomb at a synagogue in Jacksonville before an appearance by former Israeli prime minister Shimon Peres in February. The bomb did not explode.	In New York City, Judge Jack B. Weinstein rules that the INS cannot retroactively apply an April 1996 antiterrorism law to automatically deport legal immigrants convicted of minor offenses.... In Miami, Florida, Judge James Lawrence King issues an injunction against the deportation of tens of thousands of refugees from Nicaragua and other Central American countries living in three southern states.	The Conference Board reports that its index of consumer confidence ascended to 129.6 in June, marking the index's fourth-consecutive monthly gain and its highest level in 28 years.... The Financial Accounting Foundation announces its choice of Edmund L. Jenkins as chair of the seven-member Financial Accounting Standards Board.	The U.S. Air Force issues a report debunking claims that an alien spacecraft landed near Roswell, New Mexico, in 1947.	(Robert) Brian Keith Jr., 75, TV actor known for his role on *Family Affair* (1966–71), is found dead in Malibu, California, of an apparent suicide; he reportedly was suffering from cancer.	June 24
In *Amchem Products v. Windsor*, the Supreme Court rules, 6-2, to affirm a 1996 lower-court ruling that overturned a $1.3 billion settlement in a massive class-action suit brought against 20 asbestos manufacturers.... William Woratzeck, 51, convicted of a 1981 murder, is put to death by lethal injection in Florence, Arizona. He is the 398th person in the U.S. and only the eighth in Arizona to be executed since 1976.	The House votes, 304-120, to approve a $268.2 billion defense authorization bill for fiscal 1998.... The U.S. House votes, 278-148, to cut off funding for the Bosnia mission by June 30, 1998, as scheduled.	In *U.S. v. O'Hagan*, the Supreme Court rules, 6-3, that federal restrictions against insider trading may be applied to individuals who profit from confidential securities information, even if they are not directly affiliated with the companies whose shares are being traded.... Pres. Clinton approves new air-quality standards that tighten previous limits on soot and ground-level ozone, an element of smog.... The House, 270-162, and the Senate, 73-27, approve their versions of spending bills to balance the federal budget by the year 2002.	The Russian space station *Mir* loses between 40% and 50% of its power supply in a crash with an unmanned cargo craft during a practice docking maneuver. It is the worst collision ever involving a manned spacecraft and the second accident to involve the 11-year-old *Mir* in 1997.... Jacques-Yves Cousteau, 87, renowned French marine explorer who wrote or cowrote more than 80 books, produced 100 films, and hosted a popular TV series, (1968–77), dies in Paris of a heart attack, after a long hospitalization for a respiratory ailment.	In *Department of Human Resources of Oregon v. Smith*, the Supreme Court rules, 6-3, to overturn the 1993 Religious Freedom Restoration Act, asserting that Congress exceeded its authority when it attempted to define the level of protection that the Constitution affords to religious expression.	June 25
In *Raines v. Byrd*, the Supreme Court rejects, 7-2, a challenge of the 1996 Line-Item Veto Act..... In *Washington v. Glucksberg* and in *Vacco v. Quill*, the Supreme Court rules unanimously that the 14th Amendment's due process guarantee does not endow terminally ill individuals with a right to physician-assisted suicide.... In *Reno v. ACLU*, the Supreme Court overturns the Communications Decency Act, a bill that made it a crime to display or distribute "indecent" or "patently offensive" material to minors over on-line computer networks.	FBI agent Jerome R. Sullivan is indicted in Miami, Florida, on charges of stealing more than $400,000, including some $100,000 of cash confiscated from a loansharking ring allegedly run by reputed crime boss Nicholas Corozzo. Sullivan, a 25-year veteran of the FBI, headed an investigation that led to Corozzo's arrest in December 1996.	The House votes, 253-179, to pass its version of a tax bill that seeks to balance the federal budget by the year 2002.		Don (Donald Montgomery) Hutson, 84, who was a charter member of both the College Football Hall of Fame (1951) and the Pro Football Hall of Fame (1963), dies in Rancho Mirage, California, of unreported causes.	June 26
In *Printz v. U.S.*, the Supreme Court rules, 5-4, to strike down a central provision of the 1993 Brady Handgun Violence Prevention Act. The court argues that the requirement that local law-enforcement officials conduct background checks on potential gun purchasers is an unconstitutional incursion on states' sovereignty rights.	Federal agents in Miami, Florida, arrest two immigrants from the former Soviet Union—Aleksandr Progrebovsky, 28, and Aleksandr Darichev, 36, both of Lithuania—on charges of conspiring to sell nuclear warheads and other weapons to undercover federal agents posing as drug traffickers.	The Senate passes, 80-18, its version of a tax bill that seeks to balance the federal budget by the year 2002.... The Democratic National Committee states that it has returned an additional $1.4 million in questionable donations.			June 27
				Evander Holyfield retains his WBA heavyweight title in a bout with former champion Mike Tyson after Tyson is disqualified in the third round for biting Holyfield on both ears. Tyson's actions are widely condemned in the boxing community.	June 28
				Golfer Graham Marsh of Australia wins the U.S. Senior Open in Olympia Fields, Illinois ... William Hickey, actor who was nominated for an Oscar in 1986, dies in New York City of complications of emphysema and bronchitis.	June 29

F	G	H	I	J
Includes elections, federal-state relations, civil rights and liberties, crime, the judiciary, education, health care, poverty, urban affairs, and population.	*Includes formation and debate of U.S. foreign and defense policies, veterans' affairs, and defense spending. (Relations with specific foreign countries are usually found under the region concerned.)*	*Includes business, labor, agriculture, taxation, transportation, consumer affairs, monetary and fiscal policy, natural resources, and pollution.*	*Includes worldwide scientific, medical, and technological developments; natural phenomena; U.S. weather; natural disasters; and accidents.*	*Includes the arts, religion, scholarship, communications media, sports, entertainments, fashions, fads, and social life.*

	World Affairs	Europe	Africa & the Middle East	The Americas	Asia & the Pacific
June 30	The territory of Hong Kong reverts to Chinese sovereignty at midnight, ending 156 years of British colonial rule. After a Sino-British handover ceremony, the territory becomes known as the Hong Kong Special Administrative Region (SAR) of China.... Officials at the international criminal tribunal in The Hague states it will no longer make its indictments public.... At the annual summit of CARICOM, members agrees to admit Haiti as its 15th member.	Turkish president Suleyman Demirel grants formal approval to a new government headed by three of the country's secular parties.	Nasser al-Abed Radwan, a 28-year-old devout Muslim who was arrested by the PNA on June 23, dies from complications of a fractured skull. He is the 14th Palestinian to die while in PNA custody.	The Popocatepetl volcano near Mexico City, erupts, spewing lava and covering parts of the city with ash. Tens of thousands of people are placed on alert for evacuation during the eruption, which officials call the volcano's biggest in 72 years.... A team of archaeologists reaches safety after being attacked June 27 by angry residents of El Cayo, a remote village on the Usumacinta River in the southern state of Chiapas, Mexico.	In Beijing's Tiananmen Square, 70,000–100,000 people celebrate and watch a clock count down to the handover of Hong Kong to China from Britain. In Hong Kong, Chinese authorities do not attempt to suppress the peaceful rallies that take place outside the Legislative Council building as LegCo is officially dissolved at midnight.
July 1	Romania becomes the sixth member of the Central European Free Trade Agreement.... Britain rejoins the UN Educational, Scientific and Cultural Organization (UNESCO), 12 years after following the U.S.'s lead by quitting the body in protest of its alleged mismanagement and anti-Western bias.	In Spain, two hostages held by ETA are freed in unrelated circumstances.... In Sandormokh, 143 miles (230 km) north of St. Petersburg, a group finds a mass grave dating from 1937 that holds the bodies of at least 1,111 people executed in purges led by Joseph Stalin.... Annie Fratellini, 64, French founder of the National Circus School, dies in Paris of cancer.... Sir Joshua Abraham (Salvador) Hassan, 81, mayor, 1964–69, and chief minister, 1972–87, of the British colony of Gibraltar, dies in Gibraltar.	Thousands of Palestinian demonstrators in Gaza City protest the June 30 death of Nasser al-Abed Radwan, who was allegedly beaten to death by members of Force 17, an elite Palestinian security service.	At least 10 people are injured during a series of strikes when protesters clash with security forces in the northeastern Dominican Republic. The strikers demand improvements to the mainly agricultural region's infrastructure.	Tung Chee-hwa, a shipping magnate, is sworn in as Hong Kong's first chief executive, succeeding British governor Chris Patten. The China-backed provisional legislature is also sworn in. About 2,500 protesters march in a peaceful demonstration organized by the prodemocracy Hong Kong Alliance. In what is considered a show of military force, an advance unit of 4,000 additional armed Chinese troops enter the colony by land, sea, and air.
July 2	Roberto Garreton reports to the UN Security Council that he has evidence of 134 alleged massacres of Hutu refugees by troops loyal to Congolese president Laurent Kabila during the rebellion in the former Zaire. Garreton recommends that the UN probe should focus on "whether a genocide was planned and executed" and whether those guilty should be tried before an international tribunal.	In Russia, a defense ministry official, Valeri Sintsov, is sentenced to 10 years in a labor camp for passing secrets to Britain.		Officials report that a team of Cuban, Argentine, and Bolivian forensic scientists have found seven sets of remains in Vallegrande, Bolivia.... The Commission of Inquiry into the Deployment of Canadian Forces to Somalia accuses the Canadian military of poor leadership and cover-ups in the Canadian armed forces' Somalia humanitarian mission in 1992 and 1993.	Fighting breaks out in Cambodia between the copremiers' forces. ... Thailand devalues its currency, the baht, which, in offshore trading, closes at a record low of 29.55 per U.S. dollar, down 16.4% from the previous day's close of 24.70 baht.
July 3	Iraqi and UN negotiators reach revised terms for distributing food, medical, and other humanitarian supplies to Iraqis in accordance with UN Security Council Resolution 986, the so-called oil-for-food agreement originally put into effect in December 1996.	One person reportedly dies and five others are wounded by gunfire at a monarchist rally in Tirana, Albania's capital, led by pretender King Leka I, the son of King Zog, who ruled Albania from 1928 to 1939.... Two British aid workers—CamillaICarr and Jon James—are taken hostage in Dzhokhar-Ghala (formerly Grozny), the capital of Chechnya.			
July 4					In Afghanistan, Taliban jets bomb Maimana, the capital of Fariab province.... Cambodia's First Premier Prince Norodom Ranariddh departs for an unannounced visit to France.
July 5					In Afghanistan, opposition jets retaliate for the July 4 Taliban attack by bombing Kabul's airport. At least three Taliban rebels are reported killed in the attack.... Fighting breaks out between forces loyal to rival Cambodian premiers, Hun Sen, and Prince Norodom Ranariddh.

A	B	C	D	E
Includes developments that affect more than one world region, international organizations, and important meetings of major world leaders.	Includes all domestic and regional developments in Europe, including the Soviet Union, Turkey, Cyprus, and Malta.	Includes all domestic and regional developments in Africa and the Middle East, including Iraq and Iran and excluding Cyprus, Turkey, and Afghanistan.	Includes all domestic and regional developments in Latin America, the Caribbean, and Canada.	Includes all domestic and regional developments in Asia and Pacific nations, extending from Afghanistan through all the Pacific Islands, except Hawaii.

U.S. Politics & Social Issues	U.S. Foreign Policy & Defense	U.S. Economy & Environment	Science, Technology, & Nature	Culture, Leisure, & Lifestyle	
		Pres. Clinton releases his own tax-cutting plan, setting the stage for a final round of negotiations over spending and tax bills designed to balance the federal budget by 2002.		Harry A. McQuillen III, 51, media mogul and magazine publisher, is found dead in Darien, Connecticut, of an apparently self-inflicted gunshot wound to the head.	June 30
The state of Kentucky carries out its first execution in 35 years when it puts convicted murderer Harold McQueen to death in the electric chair at the Kentucky State Penitentiary in Eddyville. McQueen, 44, is the 399th person executed in the U.S. since 1976.... A new welfare bill that ends the federal guarantee of assistance for the poor and shifts most poverty-relief responsibilities to the states goes into effect.	The Justice Department's Office of Special Investigations files deportation papers in Philadelphia, Pennsylvania, against alleged war criminal Jonas Stelmokas, an 80-year-old retired architect who served in a Lithuanian police unit that helped Nazi German forces brutalize and kill Jews during World War II.... Jesse Brown resigns as secretary of Veterans Affairs (VA).	The Postal Service's board of governors proposes a one-cent increase in the price of first-class postage, a move that will raise the cost of mailing a domestic letter to 33 cents.	The space shuttle *Columbia* blasts off from Kennedy Space Center in Cape Canaveral, Florida, to study the effects of the absence of gravity on combustion.	Many provisions of the 1996 Professional Boxing Safety Act go into effect.... Robert (Charles) Mitchum, 79, actor whose Hollywood career stretched from the 1940s to the 1990s and included appearances in more than 100 films, dies in Santa Barbara, California, after suffering from emphysema and lung cancer.	July 1
Flint Gregory Hunt, 38, convicted of killing a Baltimore, Maryland, police officer in 1985, is executed by lethal injection in Baltimore. Hunt is the 400th person executed in the U.S. and the second in Maryland since 1976.			In Kenefick, Kansas, a Union Pacific train rams the side of a passing train, killing one crew member. A leak of hazardous materials from one of the trains prompts local authorities to evacuate hundreds of nearby residents.	Jimmy (James Maitland) Stewart, 89, one of the U.S.'s most beloved actors who, in 1984, received an honorary Oscar for lifetime achievement, dies in Beverly Hills, California, of heart failure associated with a pulmonary blood clot.	July 2
Mississippi attorney general Michael Moore announces an agreement with the nation's four major tobacco companies that will settle the state's liability lawsuit against the industry. The cigarette makers will pay Mississippi more than $3 billion over 25 years to compensate for the public costs of treating smoking-related illnesses.		Data reveals that the cost of an average car dipped below 50% of the average U.S. family's annual pretax income for the first time since 1981.... The Dow closes at a record 7895.81, up 100.43 points, or 1.29%, from the previous day's close.			July 3
			After a 310 million-mile (500 million-km), seven-month-long journey, *Mars Pathfinder*, an unmanned spacecraft launched by the NASA, lands on Mars. *Pathfinder* and *Sojourner*, a roving robotic explorer vehicle, will explore the geology of a region of the planet known as Ares Vallis. *Pathfinder* is the first spacecraft to reach Mars since two NASA *Viking* missions landed there in 1976.	Miguel Najdorf (born Moishe Najdorf), 87, Polish-born international chess grandmaster, dies in Malaga, Spain, after a long illness.... Charles Bishop Kuralt, 62, prize-winning journalist and author who won three Peabody Awards and 12 Emmy Awards, dies in New York City of heart failure; he was recently diagnosed with lupus.	July 4
The National Organization for Women (NOW) elects Patricia Ireland to her second term as president at the group's annual convention in Memphis, Tennessee. Ireland launches NOW's Victory 2000 campaign, the goal of which is to elect 2,000 feminist women to political office by the year 2000.			The *Mars Pathfinder* sends to Earth the first close-up images of Mars's landscape seen by space observers in 21 years. Scientists assert that the pictures support the theory that the landing region was flooded by water over a distance of hundreds of miles 1–3 billion years ago. NASA officials announce that the *Pathfinder* lander has been renamed the *Carl Sagan Memorial Station*, after the well-known astronomer who died in December 1996.	Martina Hingis of Switzerland wins the women's singles title at the All England Tennis Championship at Wimbledon, in London. Hingis, 16, is the youngest Wimbledon champion since 1887.	July 5

F	G	H	I	J
Includes elections, federal-state relations, civil rights and liberties, crime, the judiciary, education, health care, poverty, urban affairs, and population.	Includes formation and debate of U.S. foreign and defense policies, veterans' affairs, and defense spending. (Relations with specific foreign countries are usually found under the region concerned.)	Includes business, labor, agriculture, taxation, transportation, consumer affairs, monetary and fiscal policy, natural resources, and pollution.	Includes worldwide scientific, medical, and technological developments; natural phenomena; U.S. weather; natural disasters; and accidents.	Includes the arts, religion, scholarship, communications media, sports, entertainments, fashions, fads, and social life.

	World Affairs	Europe	Africa & the Middle East	The Americas	Asia & the Pacific
July 6		Some 2,000 members of the Orange Order, a pro-British Protestant group, conducts its traditional parade in Portadown, Northern Ireland. Police remove 200 Catholic protestors. Some of the demonstrators launch gasoline bombs at police, who retaliate with night sticks and plastic bullets, resulting in 19 injuries. A gunman in Coalisland shoots and seriously wounds a police officer. The IRA claims responsibility.... In a second round of elections, Albania's Socialist Party solidifies its parliamentary majority. Three people are killed in election violence.		In elections, Mexico's ruling Institutional Revolutionary Party (PRI) loses its majority in the Chamber of Deputies, the lower house of Congress, and the mayoralty of Mexico City, the capital. The elections mark the first time since the party's formation in 1929 that the PRI loses its near-absolute control over the government. Violence is reported at polling places in the southern state of Chiapas, the site of the EZLN uprising in 1994.	Cambodian second premier Hun Sen ousts First Premier Prince Norodom Ranariddh from power after the fighting that erupted July 5 in Phnom Penh, the capital, between army factions loyal to the rival premiers.
July 7		Catholics continue to protest the Orange Order's July 6 parade in Northern Ireland. Police report that 80 Orange Order's people, including 46 RUC officers, are wounded. Other observers report more than 100 injuries. Rioters clash with police in several cities and set fire to cars, trucks, buses, and trains.... Mate Boban, 57, Croatian nationalist who in 1992 helped form an independent enclave and was believed to have ordered mass killings in central Bosnia in 1993, dies in Mostar, Bosnia-Herzegovina, after suffering a stroke.	Nine people die as police break up pro-reform rallies across Kenya. In Nairobi, several coalition leaders are beaten by police.	The Chilean government grants permission to a wealthy U.S. conservationist, Douglas Tompkins, to create a nature park on a 677,000-acre (274,000-hectare) swath of land that he owns in southern Chile.	Mumeo Oku, 101, Japanese activist who founded the Housewives' Association, a consumer-rights group, during World War II, dies in Tokyo of unreported causes.
July 8	At a summit meeting in Madrid, Spain, leaders of the 16 NATO member states formally invite Poland, Hungary, and the Czech Republic to join the military alliance in 1999. Inclusion of the three countries will mark the largest expansion of NATO since its founding in 1949 and the first since the admission of Spain in 1982. The trio will be the first former members of the Warsaw Pact, NATO's cold war adversary, to join the Atlantic alliance.	A bomb blast in Dagestan kills nine Russian border police traveling by truck. Three other bombs are found on the same road.	In Kenya, opposition leaders call for more protests.	Allan Kupcis, the CEO of Ontario Hydro, North America's largest electric utility, admits that Hydro released almost 2,000 tons of the common metals arsenic, copper, iron, lead, tin, and zinc into the Great Lakes as part of the effluent at six Canadian power stations.	Reports suggest the fighting that started July 5 in Phnom Penh, the capital of Cambodia, has left 32 people dead and at least 75 wounded. Hun Sen's forces begin arresting Prince Norodom Ranariddh's political opponents .... The North Korean government declares an end to the three-year mourning period for North Korea's longtime leader, Kim Il Sung.
July 9	Pres. Leonid Kuchma of Ukraine and NATO leaders sign a charter of cooperation, similar to a Russia-NATO accord reached in May. Separately, 16 NATO leaders and representatives of 28 other European and former Soviet countries meet for the first session of the Euro-Atlantic Partnership Council. The new council, which includes members of the NATO Partnership for Peace program, replaces the North Atlantic Cooperation Council.	An experimental bomb explodes at a military airfield in Craiova, Romania, killing 16 workers.... A court in Italy sentences eight Venetian separatists to prison terms of up to six years for illegally occupying a bell tower in May.... Greek Cypriot president Glafcos Clerides and Turkish Cypriot leader Rauf Denktash meet for the first time in three years.... A dispute started by Rufi Osmani, an ethnic Albanian and the mayor of Gostivar, leads to a violent protest in which three people die and 40 are wounded.	After Nairobi University students clash with police in Kenya, officials order the closure of the university's four campuses and of Jomo Kenyatta University, north of the capital.	An earthquake strikes Sucre province on Venezuela's northeastern coast, killing at least 82 people and injuring more than 500 others. The quake measures 6.9 on the Richter scale and is the country's worst earthquake in 30 years.... A bomb explodes on a TAM Airlines jet, blowing a hole in the side of the airliner and killing one man who is sucked out of the cabin. The plane later lands safely in the city of Sao Paulo, Brazil.... A fire ignites in a plastics-recycling plant in Hamilton, Ontario, Canada.	Hong Kong's provisional legislature, in its first formal meeting, votes to tighten controls on child immigrants from mainland China. Prodemocracy forces hold a noisy rally outside the provisional legislature building to protest the dissolution of the LegCo.... An aide to Prince Ranariddh, Chau Sambath, is found dead in Cambodia.
July 10	In response to the July 6 takeover in Cambodia, ASEAN members vote to indefinitely postpone the country's entrance, which was approved in May, into their powerful trade group.... British troops under NATO command in Bosnia-Herzegovina kill Simo Drljaca, a Bosnian Serb accused of committing war crimes and wanted by the international tribunal. One soldier is injured in the raid. In a separate incident, they arrest Milan Kovacevic, accused of war crimes.	Miguel Angel Blanco, a member of Spanish premier Jose Maria Aznar's ruling Popular Party, is kidnapped. The ETA states he will be executed on July 12 unless the government transfers 500 imprisoned ETA rebels to prisons in the Basque region. Protests are held in Barcelona and Madrid.... In London, 100,000 British hunters hold a rally to protest a planned ban on hunting with hounds.... Due to the July 6 violence in Portadown, Northern Ireland, the Orange Order states it will reroute or cancel four parades scheduled for July 12.		Mexican officials confirm that billionaire drug lord Amado Carrillo Fuentes died nearly a week earlier. Carrillo reportedly suffered a heart attack after undergoing liposuction and extensive facial reconstructive surgery.	Several opposition members and at least 10 members of Cambodia's royal family reportedly flee the country.

A	B	C	D	E
Includes developments that affect more than one world region, international organizations, and important meetings of major world leaders.	Includes all domestic and regional developments in Europe, including the Soviet Union, Turkey, Cyprus, and Malta.	Includes all domestic and regional developments in Africa and the Middle East, including Iraq and Iran and excluding Cyprus, Turkey, and Afghanistan.	Includes all domestic and regional developments in Latin America, the Caribbean, and Canada.	Includes all domestic and regional developments in Asia and Pacific nations, extending from Afghanistan through all the Pacific Islands, except Hawaii.

U.S. Politics & Social Issues	U.S. Foreign Policy & Defense	U.S. Economy & Environment	Science, Technology, & Nature	Culture, Leisure, & Lifestyle	
				Pete Sampras wins his fourth Wimbledon men's title. . . . Dorothy Buffum Chandler, 96, philanthropist who used her family's newspaper-publishing fortune to promote arts programs in Los Angeles, dies in Hollywood, California, of unreported causes.	July 6
		Figures show that merger and acquisition activity reached a new high in the first half of 1997. Merger volume in the U.S. was $366 billion in deals announced, up 16% from 1996's first-half total of $314 billion. At least 74 of those transactions were valued at $1 billion or more, compared with 49 in the first half of 1996.		*Plum Island*, by Nelson DeMille, tops the bestseller list.	July 7
Jeffrey Locke, the Norfolk County, Massachusetts, district attorney, ends the agency's criminal investigation of Michael Kennedy, suspected of committing statutory rape when he allegedly had sexual relations with his family baby-sitter beginning when she was 14. Locke is terminating the investigation because the former baby-sitter refuses to assist authorities.	The House passes, 395-14, a $9.183 billion for military construction spending in fiscal year 1998.	Christine Varney, one of five members of the FTC, announces that she will leave her post for private law practice. . . . The U.S. Senate Governmental Affairs Committee opens hearings on campaign-finance practices in the 1996 election.	NASA reveals that the first-ever chemical analysis of a rock on Mars shows it is similar to andesite, a volcanic rock found on Earth that contains large amounts of quartz, feldspar, and orthopyroxene. Soil samples contain large amounts of iron. NASA officials estimate that 15 million people have visited their website since July 4. . . . Doctors at the Mayo Clinic reveal that in 24 cases, women taking the diet drug fen/phen developed heart-valve disease.	The American League beats the National League, 3-1, in MLB's All-Star Game in Cleveland, Ohio.	July 8
Reports confirm that Yale University has rejected homosexual playwright Larry Kramer's offer to donate several million dollars to fund a gay-studies professorship at the school. Alison Richard, Yale's provost, states that only the university's faculty has the power to determine curriculum and establish tenured teaching positions. Richard adds that the field of gay studies is too limited in scope to justify devoting a permanent professorship to it.			NASA releases images of Mars's hilly terrain, including a close-up view of a shallow channel and a cluster of tilted rocks.	The Eastern Conference wins the Major League Soccer (MLS) All-Star Game, 5-4, over the Western Conference. . . . The Nevada State Athletic Commission revokes heavyweight boxer Mike Tyson's license to fight in that state for one year and fines him $3 million for twice biting Evander Holyfield's ears on June 28.	July 9
The FBI reveals that it is reinvestigating the 1963 bombing of a church in which four black girls were killed in Birmingham, Alabama. Only one man—Robert Chambliss, who was convicted in 1977 and died in 1985—had been charged in the crime, despite evidence implicating at least three others. . . . R.J. Reynolds Tobacco Co. announces that it will eliminate the Joe Camel character from its ads. . . . The CDC reports the first known case of a person who contracted HIV through kissing.	The Senate confirms by voice vote the appointment of George J. Tenet as director of central intelligence.				July 10

F	G	H	I	J
Includes elections, federal-state relations, civil rights and liberties, crime, the judiciary, education, health care, poverty, urban affairs, and population.	*Includes formation and debate of U.S. foreign and defense policies, veterans' affairs, and defense spending. (Relations with specific foreign countries are usually found under the region concerned.)*	*Includes business, labor, agriculture, taxation, transportation, consumer affairs, monetary and fiscal policy, natural resources, and pollution.*	*Includes worldwide scientific, medical, and technological developments; natural phenomena; U.S. weather; natural disasters; and accidents.*	*Includes the arts, religion, scholarship, communications media, sports, entertainments, fashions, fads, and social life.*

	World Affairs	Europe	Africa & the Middle East	The Americas	Asia & the Pacific
July 11	The British Commonwealth, a grouping of Britain and its former colonies, suspends Sierra Leone pending the restoration of the government of ousted president Ahmad Tejan Kabbah.	Unidentified gunmen in a Catholic section of Belfast, Northern Ireland, shoot and wound two police officers and three British soldiers. The attackers also throw a homemade bomb at the patrol.		All 39 passengers and five crew members die when a plane crashes in the Caribbean Sea off the southern city of Santiago de Cuba.... Reports reveal that the Panamanian government has sent a force of more than 1,200 armed police officers to the Darien region, on Panama's border with Colombia, to repel recent incursions by leftist Colombian rebels, right-wing paramilitary groups and refugees.	In Pattaya, a coastal resort town in Thailand, 90 people die in a fire that rages through a hotel.... In a poor area in Mumbai, formerly Bombay, India, a riot breaks out when Dalits—who were once referred to as "untouchables"—discover that a statue of Bhimrao Ambedkar, a Dalit politician who became the chief architect of India's constitution in 1950, was vandalized. Ten Dalits are shot to death by police called in to quell the violence.
July 12		A march is held in the Basque city of Bilbao, Spain. Hours later, Miguel Angel Blanco, who was kidnapped July 10, is found gravely wounded by gunshots near the northern coastal city of San Sebastian.... Bill Clinton becomes the first U.S. president to visit Denmark while in office.... Reports confirm that the last independent national Russian newspaper lost its editorial control when it was sold.		Bombs explode almost simultaneously in two popular tourist hotels in Havana, Cuba's capital. Cuba's official news agency reveals that three people were slightly injured in the blasts... The Bolivian government confirms that the remains of leftist guerrilla leader Ernesto (Che) Guevara, executed by the Bolivian army in October 1967, are in the mass grave near an airstrip in Vallegrande discovered on July 2.	In India, as the riots that erupted July 11 in an impoverished neighborhood in Mumbai, formerly Bombay, continue, two Dalits die.
July 13		Miguel Angel Blanco, 29, a Spanish council member kidnapped July 10, dies from gunshot wounds. In Pamplona, a town in Spain's Basque region, officials cancel the annual running of the bulls festivities in recognition of Blanco's murder. Protests in Pamplona turn violent, leaving both ETA opponents and sympathizers injured.... In the town of Banja Luka, Bosnia-Herzegovina, 3,000 people attend the funeral of Simo Drljaca, killed July 10 by NATO soldiers trying to arrest him. Separately, an OSCE truck is destroyed by a bomb in the town of Zvornik.		A TV station airs an exposé charging that Peru's intelligence services secretly wiretapped telephone conversations of prominent Peruvians. Hours later, the Peruvian government revokes the citizenship of Baruch Ivcher Bronstein, the Israeli-born majority owner of the TV station..... The fire that started July 9 in a plastics-recycling plant in Hamilton, Ontario, Canada, is extinguished after forcing 650 of the plant's neighbors to leave their homes. Some 200 tons of polyvinyl chloride from recycled car bumpers burned in the blaze, spreading toxic chemicals.	In Hong Kong, hundreds of demonstrators protest the proposed suspension of social welfare laws.
July 14	The International Criminal Tribunal for the former Yugoslavia sentences Dusan Tadic, a Bosnian Serb convicted in May of crimes against humanity, to a 20-year prison term. Tadic is sentenced on 11 counts to a total of 97 years in prison; the sentences will run concurrently.... Reports confirm that the African state of Sao Tome and Principe has established diplomatic relations with Taiwan, prompting China to sever its Sao Tome ties.	Nearly 1 million people participate in marches in Spain in response to Miguel Angel Blanco's July 13 death.... Waters begin to recede from Wroclaw, Poland's fourth-largest city, one of the more than 1,000 areas in Poland that are flooded.... Czech president Vaclav Havel bestows the Order of the White Lion, the Czech Republic's highest state honor, on U.S. secretary of state Madeleine Albright.	Israeli and PNA security officials in the West Bank city of Hebron forge an agreement to end month-long clashes between Palestinian youths and Israeli troops.... Students at the Kenya Polytechnic University in Nairobi riot in protest over government repression.	The July 13 revelations of wiretapping and action against Baruch Ivcher Bronstein prompts thousands of people to take to the streets in protests that continue throughout the week in Peru.	State and federal legislators elect Kocheril Raman Narayanan as India's 11th president. Narayanan is the first member of Hinduism's lowest caste—the Dalits, or "oppressed," who were once referred to as "untouchables"—to become president of the country.
July 15	The UN General Assembly condemns Israel's construction of settlements on occupied Palestinian land.	The Yugoslav parliament elects Slobodan Milosevic president of Yugoslavia, a federation of Serbia and Montenegro. Opposition legislators boycott the session.... Reports confirm that Gerda Christian (born Gerda Daranowski), 83, personal secretary to Nazi German leader Adolf Hitler during World War II, has died of cancer of the lungs, stomach and intestines.	In Algeria, FIS leader Abassi Madani is paroled after serving five years of a 12-year sentence for undermining state security.	Benjamin Flores Gonzalez, a newspaper editor who led a crusade against drug traffickers, is shot to death in broad daylight in San Luis Rio Colorado, a Mexican town in Sonora state across the border from the U.S. state of Arizona.	Japan's securities industry watchdog completes its investigation of Nomura Securities Co., recommending that the brokerage firm be penalized for its alleged links to corporate racketeers.... An unidentified UN official states that, in Cambodia, such high-ranking officials as Interior Minister Ho Sok and Chau Sambath were shot dead by Hun Sen's troops. Krouch Yoeum and Sam Norin, generals in the royalist forces, also were executed.
July 16	UN secretary general Kofi Annan announces a plan to restructure the organization's numerous agencies into a cabinet-style administration.... For the third time, U.S. president Bill Clinton suspends for six months Title III of the 1996 Helms-Burton Act, which seeks to tighten the U.S.'s embargo on Cuba.... The European Commission, the executive arm of the EU, names six nations that will have the opportunity to negotiate for EU membership.	Four hand grenades are thrown at a British army compound in Banja Luka, Bosnia-Herzegovina. Roberto Ducato, a U.S. Army officer liaison with the Bosnian Serb military near Vlasenica, is wounded by an unknown assailant.... Ukraine's parliament approves Pres. Leonid Kuchma's nomination of Valery Pustovoitenko as premier.... Reports confirm that Dora Maar (born Henriette Theodora Markovitch), 89, French-born artist's model and painter, has died in Paris, France.	Physicians for Human Rights reports that "widespread atrocities" are continuing against civilians in eastern Congo and estimates that more than 2,000 civilians have died at the hands of marauding Rwandan soldiers in recent months.		Hong Kong's provisional legislature suspends a series of social welfare laws passed by LegCo before the handover. The debate is interrupted when a small group of protesters bursts into the legislative gallery.... North and South Korean troops exchange mortar and machine-gun fire along the DMZ. North Korea claims some of its soldiers are wounded by the exchange.... In an effort to mollify critics, Hun Sen names Ung Huot as first premier of Cambodia.
	A	**B**	**C**	**D**	**E**
	Includes developments that affect more than one world region, international organizations, and important meetings of major world leaders.	*Includes all domestic and regional developments in Europe, including the Soviet Union, Turkey, Cyprus, and Malta.*	*Includes all domestic and regional developments in Africa and the Middle East, including Iraq and Iran and excluding Cyprus, Turkey, and Afghanistan.*	*Includes all domestic and regional developments in Latin America, the Caribbean, and Canada.*	*Includes all domestic and regional developments in Asia and Pacific nations, extending from Afghanistan through all the Pacific Islands, except Hawaii.*

U.S. Politics & Social Issues	U.S. Foreign Policy & Defense	U.S. Economy & Environment	Science, Technology, & Nature	Culture, Leisure, & Lifestyle	
In Los Angeles, California, Judge Alan Buckner issues an order barring 18 members of a street gang from gathering in public in groups of three or more, arguing that there is sufficient evidence that the defendants are involve, in crimes such as robbery, drug dealing, and urinating in public. The order is the fourth such injunction granted to Los Angeles authorities against gangs.	In Alexandria, Virginia, U.S. district judge Leonie Brinkema sentences Robert C. Kim, a former civilian intelligence analyst for the U.S. Navy who in May pled guilty to a charge of passing classified information to South Korea, to nine years in prison for conspiracy to commit espionage.	The Labor Department reports that the federal government's index of prices charged by manufacturers and farmers for finished goods dropped a seasonally adjusted 0.1% in June from May. That is the sixth straight month in which wholesale prices declined, marking the longest monthly string since the government began compiling the figure some 50 years earlier.	Doctors in Florida perform the first-ever transplant of nerve tissue from a fetus into the damaged spinal cord of a 43-year-old patient suffering from syringomyelia, a degenerative disease. . . . A study reports some of the most conclusive DNA evidence ever that modern humans and Neanderthals did not interbreed and that the evolutionary split between the two species occurred much earlier than previously believed.	Joseph John Hauser, 98, the only person in the history of professional baseball to twice hit more than 60 home runs in one season, dies in Sheboygan, Wisconsin, of unreported causes. . . . John Spano cedes control of the NHL's New York Islanders to former owner John O. Pickett.	July 11
				Lennox Lewis of Great Britain retains his WBC heavyweight title when Britain's Henry Akinwande is disqualified for repeatedly holding his opponent. . . . Andrew Schiff marries Karenna Gore, daughter of Vice Pres. Al Gore Jr. and his wife Mary (Tipper) Gore.	July 12
	Cuban exiles based in South Florida lead a flotilla near the edge of Cuban territorial waters to mark the third anniversary of the deaths of 41 Cuban refugees in the sinking by the Cuban navy of a tugboat on its way to the U.S.			Golfer Larry Gilbert wins the Senior Players Championship. . . . Stuart Jewell, 84, cinematographer known for nature films made for Walt Disney, his dies in Costa Mesa, California, of cancer. . . . Alexandra Danilova, 93, Russian-born ballet dancer and teacher, dies in New York City after suffering from a heart ailment.	July 13
The CDC reports new evidence of the first-ever overall decline in AIDS death rates since the epidemic began. According to the new CDC figures, there were 19% fewer AIDS fatalities in the first nine months of 1996 than during the same period in 1995.					July 14
		Judge Charles R. Norgle of U.S. District Court in Chicago, Illinois, sentences former Rep. Mel Reynolds (D, Ill.) to 6½ years in prison for bank and mortgage fraud and campaign finance violations. Reynolds, who is already in jail serving a five-year state term for having sex with a minor, was convicted of the federal fraud charges in April.		Italian fashion designer Gianni Versace, 50, is shot and killed in the South Beach section of Miami Beach, Florida. Police identify Andrew Phillip Cunanan, a reputed homosexual gigolo wanted in connection with four other killings in three states, as the chief suspect in Versace's murder.	July 15
		Federal authorities conclude that the Medicare health-insurance program paid an estimated $23 billion in unnecessary benefits in fiscal 1996. The inspector general's revelations mark the third consecutive year that investigators have raised concerns about Medicare's accounting and record-keeping procedures. . . . The Dow Jones crosses the psychologically important 8000 mark for the first time ever.	Pres. Clinton, after meeting with legislators and industry representatives, reveals that his administration will work with the computer industry to help parents shield their children from on-line material that may be considered inappropriate for them. Clinton's plan relies on voluntary self-regulation by the industry, rather than forced restrictions imposed by Congress.	William Henry Reynolds, 87, film editor whose career spanned some six decades during which he won Academy Awards in 1966 and in 1973, dies in South Pasadena, California, of cancer.	July 16
F	G	H	I	J	
Includes elections, federal-state relations, civil rights and liberties, crime, the judiciary, education, health care, poverty, urban affairs, and population.	Includes formation and debate of U.S. foreign and defense policies, veterans' affairs, and defense spending. (Relations with specific foreign countries are usually found under the region concerned.)	Includes business, labor, agriculture, taxation, transportation, consumer affairs, monetary and fiscal policy, natural resources, and pollution.	Includes worldwide scientific, medical, and technological developments; natural phenomena; U.S. weather; natural disasters; and accidents.	Includes the arts, religion, scholarship, communications media, sports, entertainments, fashions, fads, and social life.	

	World Affairs	Europe	Africa & the Middle East	The Americas	Asia & the Pacific
July 17		In Ukraine, Valery Pustovoitenko is sworn in as premier.			
July 18		In Bosnia, an unidentified U.S. soldier is slightly injured when a bomb explodes outside his house in the town of Doboj. He is the fourth U.S. soldier injured in hostile action since the deployment of U.S. troops in Bosnia in December 1995. . . . Sir James Michael Goldsmith 64, French-born financier known as a staunch opponent of further European integration, dies in Torre de Tamores, Spain, of a heart attack; he was also suffering from pancreatic cancer.			The Hong Kong government issues guidelines for police that will allow them to crack down on demonstrations that either threaten peace or back independence for Taiwan or Tibet.
July 19		The outlawed Provisional IRA declares a cease-fire in its 28-year-old armed campaign to end British rule in Northern Ireland, or Ulster.	Former warlord Charles Taylor is elected president of Liberia in a peaceful and democratic vote that follows seven years of a bloody civil war in which than 150,000 of Liberia's 2.4 million people died and the country was in ruins. Taylor, 49, started the war in 1989 by leading an armed incursion against then-president Samuel Doe.		Cambodia's de facto leader, Hun Sen, rejects a plan proffered by ministers of the Association of Southeast Asian Nations (ASEAN) to mediate negotiations between himself and former first premier Prince Norodom Ranariddh, whom Hun Sen ousted in a bloody coup July 6.
July 20		The Serb Democratic Party (SDS) ousts the president of Bosnia-Herzegovina's Serb-ruled entity, Biljana Plavsic, from its ranks and urges her to step down as president.			In the wake of Hun Sen's July 19 rejection of the ASEAN plan, fighting reportedly resumes in earnest around Samrong, near the Thai border. UN officials report that some 30 soldiers loyal to Prince Ranariddh were tortured by government authorities earlier in July.
July 21		Two of Germany's largest banks, Bayerische Vereinsbank AG and Bayerische Hypotheken-und-Wechsel-Bank AG (Hypobank), announce that they will merge to form Bayerische Hypo-und-Vereinsbank AG, which, with 743 billion German marks ($415 billion) in assets, will be Europe's second largest bank behind Germany's Deutsche Bank AG, in terms of assets held.		Reports confirm that more than 30 people were killed in a massacre allegedly perpetrated by a right-wing paramilitary group in a remote village in eastern Colombia. In response, the military evacuates hundreds of residents of the village of Mapiripan in Meta province.	Human-rights workers reveal they documented 40 cases of coup-related executions in Cambodia.
July 22	The UN Children's Fund (UNICEF) estimates that more than half of the world's population does not have access to sanitary toilet facilities, which leads to the deaths of 2.2 million children each year. . . . The UN Security Council creates the Dag Hammarskjold Medal in honor of the 1,500 people killed in UN peacekeeping operations since 1948, when the first mission was established in the Middle East.	An Italian military court in Rome convicts Nazi war criminal Erich Priebke, along with a codefendant, Karl Hass, for their participation in a World War II massacre of 335 civilians in the Ardeatine Caves near Rome. Priebke, 83, is given a 15-year sentence, but the prison term is reduced to five years in accordance with a long-standing amnesty law. Hass is sentenced to 10 years and eight months in prison, but his entire sentence is suspended under the amnesty law.			

A	B	C	D	E
Includes developments that affect more than one world region, international organizations, and important meetings of major world leaders.	Includes all domestic and regional developments in Europe, including the Soviet Union, Turkey, Cyprus, and Malta.	Includes all domestic and regional developments in Africa and the Middle East, including Iraq and Iran and excluding Cyprus, Turkey, and Afghanistan.	Includes all domestic and regional developments in Latin America, the Caribbean, and Canada.	Includes all domestic and regional developments in Asia and Pacific nations, extending from Afghanistan through all the Pacific Islands, except Hawaii.

U.S. Politics & Social Issues	U.S. Foreign Policy & Defense	U.S. Economy & Environment	Science, Technology, & Nature	Culture, Leisure, & Lifestyle	
The Senate unanimously approves Pres. Clinton's nomination of Eric H. Holder Jr. as deputy attorney general. Holder becomes the highest-ranking black law-enforcement official in U.S. history. . . . Robert C. Weaver, 89, who in 1966 was the first-ever black U.S. cabinet member, dies in New York City of unreported causes. . . . Arthur L. Liman, 64, attorney known for his roles in the investigations of the 1971 Attica prison uprising and the Iran-contra arms scandal in the 1980s, dies in NYC of bladder cancer.	Pres. Clinton nominates army general Henry (Hugh) Shelton, commander of U.S. Special Operations, to be the next chairman of the Joint Chiefs of Staff.	The nonpartisan CBO reports that the budget deficit for the first nine months of fiscal 1997 was just $11 billion, compared with $74 billion for the first nine months of fiscal 1996. Analysts estimate that the full-year deficit for fiscal 1997 (which ends Sept. 31) may be as low as $30 billion.	An employee error at Network Solutions Inc. results in hours of disrupted Internet service in the U.S. and overseas. It is considered one of the most serious disruptions of Internet service ever. . . . The space shuttle *Columbia* lands at Kennedy Space, Center in Cape Canaveral, Florida, after completing a study on the effects of the absence of gravity on combustion. . . . Due to a mishap aboard *Mir*, the vessel's batteries do not recharge, forcing astronauts to temporarily retreat into the *Soyuz* capsule.	The 200-member board of the National Baptist Convention U.S.A. Inc., one of the nation's largest black denominations, votes unanimously to retain the Rev. Henry J. Lyons as president. The confidence vote is taken in the midst of a scandal involving criminal charges against Lyons's wife, Deborah Lyons.	July 17
Frederick Martin Davidson, 37, a former graduate student at San Diego State University in California, is sentenced to three consecutive life terms without parole for shooting to death three professors at an August 1996 meeting to defend his master's thesis in engineering.		The U.S. Eighth Circuit Court of Appeals in St. Louis, Missouri, strikes down several key rules that the FCC had formulated to control prices as long-distance telephone markets open to competition, arguing that the proposed regulations violate provisions of the Telecommunications Act of 1996.	Eugene Merle Shoemaker, 69, planetary geologist and astronomer who, with his wife Carolyn, held the world record for discovering the most comets, dies from injuries he suffered in a car accident near Alice Springs, Australia.		July 18
	Police in New York City discover some 60 Mexican immigrants, most of whom are deaf and speech-impaired, living in two apartments in Queens. The immigrants were smuggled into the U.S. illegally and forced to work in slave-like conditions. . . . A group of 190 Canadian fishing boats, angered by the overfishing of sockeye salmon as the fish migrate through U.S. waters, block a ferry owned by Alaska in the harbor of Prince Rupert, British Columbia.			John E. Hines, 86, former presiding bishop of the Episcopal Church, 1965–74, dies after suffering a stroke earlier in July.	July 19
	In a case that attracts intense media attention in Mexico and the U.S., police arrest seven members of a nationwide ring uncovered July 19 that allegedly smuggled deaf people from Mexico into the U.S. and forced them to work selling trinkets. Authorities believe that the ring is run by members of the Mexican-based Paoletti family, some of whom are deaf themselves.			Justin Leonard wins the 126th British Open golf championship in Troon, Scotland.	July 20
	The blockade of Alaskan vessels started July 19 by a group of 190 Canadian fishing boats is lifted after representatives of the fishermen on the blockade meet with Canadian fisheries minister David Anderson.		The Russian space agency announces that repairs to the beleaguered space station *Mir* will be undertaken by a new crew and not by the station's current occupants, who have been confronted with a series of problems following the crash of an unmanned cargo vehicle in June.		July 21
	In response to a the July 19 blockade by 190 Canadian fishing boats, Alaska suspends ferry service to Prince Rupert in British Columbia. . . . The Justice Department files a complaint seeking to revoke the citizenship of Walter Berezowskyj, 73, of Guilford, Connecticut. The department claims Berezowski is a former Nazi labor-camp guard who concealed his role in the persecution of civilians during World War II on applications for a visa in 1949 and for citizenship in 1981.	An automated highway stretching 7.6 miles (12 km) opens to test vehicles near San Diego, California The roadway, which uses magnets, video cameras, and radar to guide specially equipped vehicles along its course without human intervention, easing congestion, is set up along Interstate Highway 15. . . . The Dow Jones industrial average closes at a record high of 8061.65 points.			July 22

F	G	H	I	J
Includes elections, federal-state relations, civil rights and liberties, crime, the judiciary, education, health care, poverty, urban affairs, and population.	*Includes formation and debate of U.S. foreign and defense policies, veterans' affairs, and defense spending. (Relations with specific foreign countries are usually found under the region concerned.)*	*Includes business, labor, agriculture, taxation, transportation, consumer affairs, monetary and fiscal policy, natural resources, and pollution.*	*Includes worldwide scientific, medical, and technological developments; natural phenomena; U.S. weather; natural disasters; and accidents.*	*Includes the arts, religion, scholarship, communications media, sports, entertainments, fashions, fads, and social life.*

	World Affairs	Europe	Africa & the Middle East	The Americas	Asia & the Pacific
July 23	The U.S., Russia, and 28 European countries agree on revisions to the 1990 treaty governing Conventional Forces in Europe (CFE). The new accord will set country-by-country limits on nonnuclear arms and materiel deployed in Europe.	Slobodan Milosevic is sworn in as president of Yugoslavia, a federation of Serbia and Montenegro. Some 1,000 demonstrators rally across the street from the parliament building and throw shoes at the new president's departing car. . . . The British government announces a plan to begin charging university students tuition for the first time. . . . As part of an effort to return Holocaust victims' assets, the Swiss Bankers' Association publishes a list of nearly 2,000 names that appear on dormant Swiss bank accounts opened during or before World War II.			
July 24		Albania's Socialist Party-dominated Parliament elects Rexhep Mejdani as the country's new president succeeding Sali Berisha. Mejdani picks Fatos Nano, the Socialist leader, to succeed caretaker Bashkim Fino as premier. . . . Brian Glover, 63, British stage, screen, and television actor, dies in London of a brain tumor.			Saw Maung, 68, Burmese general who became leader of the country's military junta after orchestrating a coup, 1988–92, dies in Yangon, Myanmar (formerly Burma), of a heart attack.
July 25		Despite the July 24 political changeover in Albania, bombings and gun battles continue, and a total of 20 people die in violent incidents. . . . In Ireland, Judge Cyril Kelly sentences a Roman Catholic priest, Rev. Brendan Smyth, to 12 years in prison for sexually abusing children 74 times over a 36-year period. Smyth, who pled guilty to the charges, recently completed a four-year prison term in Northern Ireland for similar crimes.	Congolese government soldiers open fire on an opposition demonstration in Kinshasa, killing at least three people.	Ricardo Cesareo Vazquez Tafolla, a key government witness against Gen. Jesus Gutierrez Rebollo, former head of Mexico's antidrug agency, is attacked.	Kocheril Raman Narayanan takes the oath of office as India's president. . . . Pol Pot, the deposed leader of what is widely acknowledged to be the 20th-century's deadliest guerrilla group, Cambodia's Khmer Rouge, and was sentenced to death in absentia by the Cambodian government in 1979, is condemned to "life imprisonment" at a carefully staged tribunal held by his former comrades at the group's jungle stronghold in Anlong Veng.
July 26		Lt. Gen. Jaime Milans del Bosch, 82, Spanish general who supported dictator Gen. Francisco Franco in 1930s and who, in 1981, helped lead a failed military coup, dies of unreported causes.	After three months of political violence, the Kenyan government allows an opposition coalition to hold a rally in the port city of Mombasa demanding that constitutional reforms be instituted prior to upcoming elections.	Hector Ixtlahuac Gaspar, a retired military officer in Guadalajara and a witness in the case against Gen. Jesus Gutierrez Rebollo, former head of Mexico's antidrug agency, is murdered. . . . Colombian officials reveal that Werner Mauss, a German intelligence operative jailed since November 1996, and his wife, Michaela, were released.	
July 27		Some 20,000 Basque separatists march in the Basque town of San Sebastian, Spain, in a show of support for the region's militant rebels known as the ETA. . . . Isabel Dean, 79, British stage, screen, and television actress, dies of unreported causes. . . . Raymond Allen Jackson, 70, British cartoonist best known as "Jak," dies in London of complications from heart-bypass surgery.			
July 28		Latvian president Guntis Ulmanis designates Guntars Krasts as premier, succeeding Andris Skele. . . . Officials of the British government meet with members of Sinn Fein, the political arm of the IRA. . . . Reports state that the government of Czech premier Vaclav Klaus has promised a 12 billion koruna ($350 million) relief package for areas hit by intense flooding. . . . An appeals court in Lyons rules that the controversial Church of Scientology has the legal right to regard itself as a religion in France.		The Mexican defense ministry confirms that 34 current and former military officers are under arrest for alleged involvement in drug trafficking.	Seni Pramoj, 92, three-time Thai premier and diplomat who, as ambassador to the U.S. during World War II, refused to follow the orders of the Japanese occupation government to declare war on the U.S. and Great Britain. dies in Bangkok, Thailand, of kidney failure and complications from heart disease.

A	B	C	D	E
Includes developments that affect more than one world region, international organizations, and important meetings of major world leaders.	Includes all domestic and regional developments in Europe, including the Soviet Union, Turkey, Cyprus, and Malta.	Includes all domestic and regional developments in Africa and the Middle East, including Iraq and Iran and excluding Cyprus, Turkey, and Afghanistan.	Includes all domestic and regional developments in Latin America, the Caribbean, and Canada.	Includes all domestic and regional developments in Asia and Pacific nations, extending from Afghanistan through all the Pacific Islands, except Hawaii.

U.S. Politics & Social Issues	U.S. Foreign Policy & Defense	U.S. Economy & Environment	Science, Technology, & Nature	Culture, Leisure, & Lifestyle	
Joseph Roger O'Dell III, 55, is put to death by lethal injection in Richmond, Virginia, for the 1985 rape and murder of a Virginia Beach, Virginia, woman. His execution receives wide publicity particularly since he was the subject of *Dead Man Walking*, a book by Sister Helen Prejean. . . . In a highly publicized case, John B. Ramsey, the father of JonBenet Ramsey, a six-year-old girl killed in 1996, vows to intensify the family's to independent investigation into the slaying.			The California Department of Transportation reopens the highway that collapsed in the 1989 earthquake that hit the San Francisco Bay area. The new, single-decked road, part of Interstate Highway 880, cost more than $1 billion to construct, making it the most expensive thoroughfare on a per-mile basis in the U.S.	Andrew P. Cunanan, a 27-year-old fugitive accused of killing fashion designer Gianni Versace and four other men, commits suicide as a police investigation closes in on the houseboat where he is holed up in Miami Beach, Florida. Cunanan's suicide ends a manhunt that had involved more than 1,000 law enforcement agents nationwide.	July 23
In Spokane, Washington, a jury convicts three white separatists—Verne Jay Merrell, Charles Barbee, and Robert Berry—of a series of bombings and bank robberies in 1996. . . . Judge Kevin Tierney sentences former fugitive Alex Kelly to 16 years in prison for raping a 16-year-old girl in 1986. . . . William J. Brennan Jr., 91, U.S. Supreme Court Justice, 1956–90, who was a strong advocate of individual rights and profoundly impacted U.S. public policy, dies in Arlington, Virginia, after being in poor health for several years.	The Department of Defense and the CIA announce that a new study indicates nearly 100,000 U.S. troops may have been exposed to nerve-gas fallout from an Iraqi ammunition depot destroyed by U.S. forces in March 1991, shortly after the Persian Gulf war ended. That figure represents a substantial increase over past estimates of troops' exposure to chemical toxins in the Persian Gulf, which placed the number of affected soldiers at around 20,000.		Scottish scientists reveal that they have produced the first cloned animal whose cells contain human genes. The animal is called Polly, a Poll Dorset sheep created through the fusing of human genes with the skin cells of sheep embryos. The breakthrough is considered a major advance in geneticists' quest to produce animals whose biological products may be used to treat human diseases.	A jury in Dallas, Texas, orders the Roman Catholic diocese of Dallas and Rev. Rudolph Kos to pay $120 million in compensatory and punitive damages to 10 former altar boys who were sexually abused by Kos, a former priest in the diocese. It is the largest fine ever levied against the Roman Catholic Church in a child-abuse case.	July 24
A federal jury in New York City convicts organized-crime boss Vincent (The Chin) Gigante of racketeering and conspiracy to commit murder but acquits him of three murder charges. The trial of Gigante, described by prosecutors as head of the Genovese crime family, is the biggest U.S. Mafia trial since that of John Gotti in 1992.		Police arrest 250 people during a monthly protest by bicyclists that clogs traffic in San Francisco, California. Some riders jump on cars and spit on drivers in a protest known as "Critical Mass," which is held regularly to rally for better bicycling conditions on the nation's roads.	John A. McLachlan, a researcher from Tulane University in New Orleans, Louisiana, retracts the results of a June 1996 study linking pesticides to large increases in the hormone estrogen in humans.	Ben W. Hogan, 84, one of only five golfers ever to win all four major tournaments, dies in Fort Worth, Texas, after suffering from colon cancer. . . . Elvis Presley's Memphis, a theme nightclub, opens in Memphis, Tennessee. . . . A federal jury in New York City convicts Autumn Jackson, 22, of trying to extort $40 million from Bill Cosby.	July 25
		Pres. Clinton announces that the federal government will double between 1997 and 1999 the amount of funding allocated to preserve Lake Tahoe, Nevada.		Boxer Steve Johnson retains his WBC lightweight title, winning a split decision over Hiroyuki Sakamoto in Yokohama, Japan.	July 26
		A new terminal designed to resemble Les Halles food market in Paris, which cost $450 million, opens at Washington, D.C.'s National Airport.		Jan Ullrich of Germany wins the Tour de France cycling race, which ends in Paris. Ullrich is the first German to win the Tour de France.	July 27
	Massachusetts governor William F. Weld (R) announces that he is resigning, effective July 29, in order to focus his attention on gaining the ambassadorship to Mexico. . . . Gen. Ronald R. Fogleman, 56, the air force chief of staff, resigns in protest over the anticipated government sanctioning of Brigadier General Terryl J. Schwalier, a senior air force officer who allegedly provided inadequate protection for U.S. troops killed in a June 1996 terrorist bombing in Dhahran, Saudi Arabia.	The White House and congressional Republicans agree on a final version of legislation to balance the federal budget by the year 2002. . . . The House, passes, 214-203, a $2.2 billion 1998 fiscal-year appropriations bill for legislative branch spending. . . . *Forbes* magazine lists William H. Gates, of Microsoft Corp., as the world's richest person, with assets totaling $36.4 billion.			July 28

F	G	H	I	J
Includes elections, federal-state relations, civil rights and liberties, crime, the judiciary, education, health care, poverty, urban affairs, and population.	*Includes formation and debate of U.S. foreign and defense policies, veterans' affairs, and defense spending. (Relations with specific foreign countries are usually found under the region concerned.)*	*Includes business, labor, agriculture, taxation, transportation, consumer affairs, monetary and fiscal policy, natural resources, and pollution.*	*Includes worldwide scientific, medical, and technological developments; natural phenomena; U.S. weather; natural disasters; and accidents.*	*Includes the arts, religion, scholarship, communications media, sports, entertainments, fashions, fads, and social life.*

	World Affairs	Europe	Africa & the Middle East	The Americas	Asia & the Pacific
July 29		About 15,000 Islamic fundamentalists hold a rally in Ankara, the capital of Turkey, to protest a government plan to reduce access to religious schooling. The protest, which was not officially authorized, turns violent, and at least 13 people are injured.		Reports confirm that the Mexican city of Juarez has been wracked by drug-related violence since the death of drug lord Amado Carrillo Fuentes. Separately, Irma Lizzete Ibarra Navejat, a former beauty queen who allegedly had ties to General Jesus Gutierrez Rebollo, the former head of Mexico's antidrug agency, is gunned down in her car in the city of Guadalajara in Jalisco state. Her murder marks the third attack on individuals preparing to testify or talk to the media about the military's alleged links to drug traffickers.	The Hong Kong Court of Appeals rules unanimously that the China-backed provisional legislature is legal. . . . In Cambodia, Hun Sen dismisses the July 25 trial of Pol Pot as a farce.
July 30	The UN Security Council votes to extend its peacekeeping mission in Haiti for four months. . . . . The European Commission, the executive arm of the EU, formally accepts the $14 billion merger of U.S. aerospace firms Boeing Co. and McDonnell Douglas Corp.		Two suicide bombers working in tandem detonate powerful explosives in a crowded West Jerusalem outdoor market, killing at least 13 bystanders as well as themselves and injuring more than 150 others. Hamas, a militant Palestinian Islamic organization, claims responsibility.		Twenty people are trapped when a landslide buries two lodges at a popular ski resort in the town of Thredbo in New South Wales, Australia. . . . Four members of a Cambodian government helicopter crew report that Khmer Rouge soldiers have executed a team of 11 negotiators whom they flew to Khmer Rouge territory in February. The crew claims they had been held hostage since February.
July 31	The IMF suspends its three-year, $216 million loan package to Kenya after the Kenyan government fails to satisfy IMF concerns over official corruption.	Greek Cypriot president Glafcos Clerides and Turkish Cypriot leader Rauf Denktash reach a landmark agreement to exchange information on 2,000 Turkish and Greek Cypriots reported missing as a result of their conflict. . . . Security officers discover and defuse a bomb in an automobile abandoned near a hotel in Lisbellaw, a Northern Ireland town near the border with the Irish Republic.			Bao Dai (born Nguyen Vinh Thuy), 83, the last emperor of Vietnam, 1926–45, dies in Paris, France, of unreported causes.
Aug. 1				The Canadian Red Cross Society, a charitable organization that came under fire because of its role in a tainted-blood scandal in the 1980s, decides to withdraw entirely from participation in Canada's blood-collection system, which it has managed since 1939.	Some 6,000 civilians flee into Thailand to escape fighting that flared between Hun Sen's troops and forces loyal to Prince Ranariddh in northwestern Cambodia.
Aug. 2		Croat mobs drive away some 500 Bosnian Muslims who returned to their prewar homes in villages near the town of Jajce, Bosnia-Herzegovina. One man dies when his house is burned down. . . . Chechen hostage takers seize four Frenchmen in the Russian republic of Dagestan. . . . British prime minister Tony Blair appoints 47 prominent figures in politics, business, and the arts as life peers, or eligible members of the House of Lords, the nonelected upper house of Parliament.	Former warlord Charles Taylor, whose National Patriotic Party won an overwhelming victory in July elections, is sworn in as president of Liberia for a six-year term. Taylor, 49, is Liberia's first freely elected leader after seven years of civil war. . . . Fela Anikulapo-Kuti (born Fela Ransome-Kuti), 58, Nigerian singer, saxophonist and political dissident, dies in Lagos, Nigeria, of complications related to AIDS.		In Australia, rescuers save ski instructor Stuart Diver, 27, who is the apparent lone survivor of the July 30 landslide in the town of Thredbo in New South Wales. He survives after being buried under some 35 feet (10 m) of rubble.
Aug. 3		Reports confirm that the overflowing Oder River in central Europe has caused more than 100 deaths in Poland and the Czech Republic since early July. The flooding is called the worst in the region in 200 years.	Mohammed Khatami, a who scored a surprising landslide win in May, is confirmed as Iran's president. . . . Israeli prime minister Benjamin Netanyahu insists that he will not honor agreements that Israel's previous, Labor Party government negotiated with the Palestinians unless the self-rule PNA takes stern measures to control Islamic militants. The Israeli cabinet votes to halt payment of the taxes and customs fees it collects for the PNA.	The Soufriere Hills volcano on the tiny Caribbean island of Montserrat erupts, forcing hundreds of people to evacuate areas previously declared safe. . . . Peruvian television reveals that the telephone of former UN secretary general Javier Perez de Cuellar was tapped while he was running for president in 1995. The revelation widens a scandal that hit the government in July. . . . Two gunmen open fire in a restaurant in Juarez, Mexico, killing six people and wounding three others.	On Comoros, a three-island nation in the Indian Ocean, more than 7,000 Anjouan islanders march in Mutsamudu, to demand independence and a return to French rule. Soldiers and police—whose recent clashes with prosecessionist demonstrators left four people dead—do not attempt to break up the protest. . . . Maha Ghosananda, Cambodia's Buddhist patriarch, leads more than 1,000 people on a peace march in Phnom Penh, the capital.
	A	B	C	D	E
	Includes developments that affect more than one world region, international organizations, and important meetings of major world leaders.	Includes all domestic and regional developments in Europe, including the Soviet Union, Turkey, Cyprus, and Malta.	Includes all domestic and regional developments in Africa and the Middle East, including Iraq and Iran and excluding Cyprus, Turkey, and Afghanistan.	Includes all domestic and regional developments in Latin America, the Caribbean, and Canada.	Includes all domestic and regional developments in Asia and Pacific nations, extending from Afghanistan through all the Pacific Islands, except Hawaii.

U.S. Politics & Social Issues	U.S. Foreign Policy & Defense	U.S. Economy & Environment	Science, Technology, & Nature	Culture, Leisure, & Lifestyle	
	The Department of Defense announces that all military antidrug activity along the Mexico-U.S. border will be suspended indefinitely while the practice is reviewed. The suspension is prompted by the May death of Ezequiel Hernandez Jr., a Texas teenager shot by a member of a Marine Corps antidrug patrol.	Financial services firm Smith Barney Inc. agrees to pay the government $1.05 million to settle a lawsuit in connection with an alleged donation to former agriculture secretary Mike Espy.	A study finds that the addition of ammonia compounds to cigarette tobacco may dramatically increase the amount of nicotine inhaled by smokers.	Thomas K. Welch, the chief organizer of the 2002 Winter Olympics in Salt Lake City, Utah, resigns after being charged with domestic abuse. . . . Chuck Wayne (born Charles Jagelka), 74, jazz guitarist who helped to pioneer the genre's bebop style in the 1940s, dies in Jackson, New Jersey, of emphysema.	July 29
The Chicago City Council passes an ethics ordinance that for the first time sets out a code of conduct for its 50 members.	Secretary of State Madeleine K. Albright discloses that the U.S. will lift its 10-year-old ban on travel by Americans to Lebanon.	The House votes, 346-85, to pass the balanced-budget bill unveiled July 28. . . . The Dow closes at a record high of 8254.89, marking the tenth record high in July and the 37th registered in 1997.			July 30
Reports confirm that Gladys Holm, a retired secretary who died in 1996, left a will donating $18 million to the Children's Memorial Hospital in Chicago. Holm's gift is the largest single donation to the hospital in its 115-year history.	NYC police raid an apartment where they find two powerful pipe bombs and a note threatening violence against U.S. and Jewish targets. Two Palestinians who live in the apartment—Ghazi Ibrahim Abu Maizar and Lafi Khalil—are taken into custody after being wounded by police fire. . . . Defense Secretary William Cohen voids the Senate-approved promotion of Brigadier General Terryl Schwalier, who allegedly provided inadequate protection for U.S. troops killed in a June 1996 terrorist bombing in Dhahran. Schwalier states that he has requested retirement.	The House votes, 389-43, to pass the tax bill to achieve a balanced budget by 2002. The Senate clears both bills, voting 85-15 to approve the budget bill and 92-8 for the tax bill. . . . The Senate confirms Robert Stanton as director of the Interior Department's National Park Service.			July 31
	The U.S. ends a 20-year-old ban on the sale of most advanced weapons to Latin America. . . . Colombia and the U.S. sign an agreement on U.S. assistance in fighting drug trafficking, under which the U.S. agrees to send $70 million worth of military equipment for the Colombian military's antidrug operations, in return for assurances that steps will be taken to improve the military's human-rights record.	The Commerce Department reports that personal pretax income rose 0.6% in June from May, to a seasonally adjusted figure of $6.866 trillion. The June increase marks the 25th consecutive month that incomes have grown. . . . Data suggests that between 10,000 and 75,000 people are at risk of contracting thyroid cancer as a result of 90 nuclear bomb tests conducted in Nevada between 1951 and 1962. Residents of 23 counties in Colorado, Montana, Idaho, South Dakota, and Utah are particularly at risk.		Syatoslav Teofilovich Richter, 82, Russian classical pianist considered one of the greatest musicians of his era, dies in Moscow of a heart attack. . . . The World Track & Field Championships open in Athens, Greece.	Aug. 1
				The U.S. Postal Service unveils a stamp in honor of the actor Humphrey Bogart. . . . William S(eward) Burroughs, 83, writer who, along with Jack Kerouac and Allen Ginsberg, came to define the Beat Generation cultural movement, dies in Lawrence, Kansas, after suffering a heart attack.	Aug. 2
				Manager Tommy Lasorda and players Phil Niekro, Nelson (Nellie) Fox, and Willie Wells Sr. are inducted into the Baseball Hall of Fame in Cooperstown, New York.	Aug. 3

F	G	H	I	J
Includes elections, federal-state relations, civil rights and liberties, crime, the judiciary, education, health care, poverty, urban affairs, and population.	*Includes formation and debate of U.S. foreign and defense policies, veterans' affairs, and defense spending. (Relations with specific foreign countries are usually found under the region concerned.)*	*Includes business, labor, agriculture, taxation, transportation, consumer affairs, monetary and fiscal policy, natural resources, and pollution.*	*Includes worldwide scientific, medical, and technological developments; natural phenomena; U.S. weather; natural disasters; and accidents.*	*Includes the arts, religion, scholarship, communications media, sports, entertainments, fashions, fads, and social life.*

	World Affairs	Europe	Africa & the Middle East	The Americas	Asia & the Pacific
Aug. 4		Water levels drop in areas of eastern Germany for the first time after three weeks of serious floods. . . . Using an OSCE formula, Chechen authorities report that the region's 21-month-long civil war with Russian troops, which ended in 1996, caused some $258 billion in damage, of which more than half is "moral damage." . . . Jeanne Louise Calment, 122, native of France who was recognized as the world's oldest person and had held that distinction since 1986, dies in Arles of unreported causes.	Israel commandos set off a series of bombs in Hezbollah-controlled territory in Lebanon just north of Israel's self-declared security enclave, killing five guerrillas, including at least two field commanders. Lebanese officials claim that three of the dead are civilians.	The Panamanian labor ministry decides not to renew the work permit of prize-winning Peruvian journalist Gustavo. Media members throughout Panama allege that Gorriti's expulsion amounts to an attack on freedom of expression.	
Aug. 5				Bolivia's Congress elects former military ruler Hugo Banzer Suarez as the country's new president. . . . Two people die from asphyxiation and 107 others are injured during an overcrowded outdoor concert at the Home Show park in Lima, Peru's capital.	On Comoros, a three-island nation in the Indian Ocean, demonstrators on Moheli island stage a protest and state that they want to join Anjouan island in seceding from the Comoros republic.
Aug. 6			Five peacekeepers of the UN Interim Force in Lebanon die when their helicopter crashes in Israel's southern occupation zone.	Hugo Banzer Suarez is sworn in as Bolivia's new president in La Paz, the capital.	A Korean Air jet carrying 254 people crashes on its approach to Guam's Agana International Airport, killing at least 225 people. . . . In Cambodia, Hun Sen successfully consolidates his rule as the Cambodian parliament in Phnom Penh, the capital, approves his appointment of Foreign Minister Ung Huot to succeed Prince Ranariddh as first premier.
Aug. 7		Romanian premier Victor Ciorbea announces the immediate closing of 17 factories that operate at a loss. . . . Latvia's parliament votes to approve a new government headed by Premier Guntars Krasts. . . . The managers of Britain's last active tin mine, the South Crofty mine in the county of Cornwall, announce that the mine will close permanently, ending Britain's 2,500-year-old tin-mining industry.	A roadside explosive planted by unidentified assailants kills a woman and her two children in southern Lebanon. An SLA militiaman dies in a Hezbollah car bombing. Retaliatory Israeli artillery shelling kills a Lebanese farmer. The violence brings the death toll to 13 people, at least seven of whom were civilians, in the Israeli-Hezbollah clashes that started Aug. 4.	A surprise snowstorm hits the Andes mountain range, trapping hundreds of motorists on a mountain highway some 10,000 feet (3,000 m) above sea level.	King Norodom Sihanouk, who is undergoing cancer treatments in Beijing, China, permits Hun Sen's Aug. 6 appointment, and Ung Huot is formally seated as Cambodia's new first premier. . . . There are 29 survivors of the Aug. 6 plane crash in Korea, but the death toll is expected to rise as many are critically wounded.
Aug. 8		Workers across Romania demonstrate to protest the factory closures announced on Aug. 7. Some 5,000 people rally in the oil-refining town of Ploiesti, and two policemen are injured. . . . The Italian government confirms that Italian soldiers tortured Somali civilians during a UN mission in Somalia. Their report suggests that nonmilitary observers should accompany soldiers on future peacekeeping missions and claims that the attacks were isolated incidents.	Opposition demonstrators beat two policemen to death in Nairobi, the capital of Kenya, and in a nearby village. . . . Hezbollah responds to the Aug. 7 attack by launching rockets against Qiryat Shemona, marking the first time that the Upper Galilee town has been hit by rockets since the signing of the April 1996 pact. Israel retaliates by dispatching two warplanes, which fire rockets at guerrilla positions nine miles (15 km) south of Beirut, Lebanon, where the radical Popular Front for the Liberation of Palestine maintains bases.	Colombian senator Jorge Cristo, a prominent political ally of Pres. Samper, is shot and killed in the city of Cucuta, near Colombia's northern border with Venezuela. . . . In a highly publicized murder case, a judge in Kingstown, the capital of St. Vincent and the Grenadines, acquits a wealthy U.S. couple, James and Penella (Penny) Fletcher, who were criticized by residents for their ostentatious lifestyle, of murdering Jerome (Jolly) Joseph, a black water-taxi driver.	The executive director of UNICEF, Carol Bellamy, estimates that 80,000 children in North Korea are in immediate danger of dying and another 800,000 are suffering from severe malnutrition.
Aug. 9		In Tajikistan, Makhmud Khudoberdyev, a renegade government colonel who opposes the terms of the June peace deal, launches a military campaign against government forces and rival warlords. . . . Protestant unionists in Londonderry, Northern Ireland, march in the annual Apprentice Boys parade. The event ends the summer parade season, which in recent years has been marred by terrorism and rioting. A few scuffles break out after the parade is finished.			

A	B	C	D	E
Includes developments that affect more than one world region, international organizations, and important meetings of major world leaders.	Includes all domestic and regional developments in Europe, including the Soviet Union, Turkey, Cyprus, and Malta.	Includes all domestic and regional developments in Africa and the Middle East, including Iraq and Iran and excluding Cyprus, Turkey, and Afghanistan.	Includes all domestic and regional developments in Latin America, the Caribbean, and Canada.	Includes all domestic and regional developments in Asia and Pacific nations, extending from Afghanistan through all the Pacific Islands, except Hawaii.

U.S. Politics & Social Issues	U.S. Foreign Policy & Defense	U.S. Economy & Environment	Science, Technology, & Nature	Culture, Leisure, & Lifestyle	
	A federal advisory panel, the U.S. Commission on Immigration Reform, recommends that the INS be shut down, citing "mission overload."	Figures suggest that net incomes of large U.S. companies grew by 4.9% in the second quarter of 1997, compared with the corresponding term in the previous year. . . . The International Brotherhood of Teamsters union launches a strike against UPS, the nation's largest shipping company. . . . Robert Stanton is sworn in, becoming the National Park Service's first black director.	Reports state that wildfires have charred some 2,800 acres (1,100 hectares) in southern California in the summer months.	*Unnatural Exposure* by Patricia Cornwell tops the bestseller list. . . . Horace Bristol, 88, photojournalist known for his stark images of poverty and war, dies in Ojai, California, of unreported causes. . . . Luise King Rey, 83, big-band singer and television entertainer, dies in Sandy, Utah, of unreported causes.	Aug. 4
	Pres. Clinton signs a measure that restores some welfare benefits to legal immigrants. . . . Clarence M(arion) Kelley, 85, head of the FBI, 1973–78, dies emphysema in Kansas City, Kansas.	Pres. Clinton signs twin bills enacting a plan to balance the federal budget by the year 2002. The bill includes provisions for a federal rescue plan for the nation's financially troubled capital, and the District of Columbia's federally appointed control board replaces four of the district's department heads. . . . In Albany, New York, U.S. district judge Lawrence Kahn upholds a state rule mandating that electric vehicles account for 2% of all vehicles sold in New York State in the 12 months beginning Oct. 1.			Aug. 5
In West Palm Beach, Florida, circuit court judge Harold Cohen orders the release of internal tobacco industry files containing new evidence that cigarette makers over the previous 30 years had used legal advisers to deliberately mislead the public about the health risks of smoking.		Pres. Clinton cites new figures from the OMB indicating that the federal budget deficit for fiscal 1997 will be $37 billion, the lowest in 23 years. The Congressional Budget Office (CBO) estimates that the 1997 deficit will be just $34 billion. . . . The Senate Governmental Affairs Committee announces it has issued 39 subpoenas in an effort to determine whether major Democratic donors received favorable treatment from Pres. Clinton's administration.			Aug. 6
School officials in Washington, D.C., announce that the start of the 1997–98 school year, scheduled for Sept. 2, will be delayed until Sept. 22 to make repairs on dozens of school buildings. It is the third delay of the school year in that area in four years.			Five people die when a DC-8 cargo plane crashes into a heavily trafficked commercial area of Miami, Florida, after taking off from Miami International Airport. . . . The space shuttle *Discovery* blasts off from Kennedy Space Center in Cape Canaveral, Florida, on a mission to gather environmental data and test new equipment designed for use on the planned international space station.	Popular country music singer Garth Brooks gives a free concert in New York City's Central Park that is attended by approximately 250,000 people.	Aug. 7
Malcolm Shabazz, 12, is sentenced to 18 months in a psychiatric home after admitting that he set a fire in June that led to the death of his grandmother, Betty Shabazz, the widow of the slain black nationalist leader Malcolm X.	The INS grants a stay of deportation to Emmanuel (Toto) Constant, a former leader of the right-wing paramilitary group in Haiti accused of numerous human-rights atrocities.		NASA officials reveal that in its first 30 days on Mars, *Pathfinder* has transmitted 10,000 pictures of the planet to Earth, while the roving vehicle *Sojourner* has taken 384 pictures and followed 114 commands from mission control since its arrival on Mars. Officials note that the vehicles have outlasted their expected life spans and are continuing to gather new data about the geography and atmosphere of Mars, and they proclaim the mission a complete success.	The FDA relaxes restrictions on radio and TV advertising of prescription drugs. . . . A bomb blast destroys sections of the Olympic Stadium in Stockholm, Sweden, a finalist for the host of the 2004 games. . . . Paul Rudolph, 78, architect and former chairman of the School for Architecture at Yale University, 1957–65, dies in New York City of mesothelioma, or asbestos cancer.	Aug. 8
Pres. Clinton issues an executive order banning smoking in federal office buildings, including visitor's centers at national parks.	U.S. civil-rights groups and Haitian Americans protest the Aug. 8 ruling in New York City, where Emmanuel (Toto) Constant lives, that has granted him a stay of deportation.		An Amtrak train carrying 309 people partially derails near Kingman, Arizona, injuring more than 100 people, 16 of whom are hospitalized, with one in serious condition.		Aug. 9

F	G	H	I	J
Includes elections, federal-state relations, civil rights and liberties, crime, the judiciary, education, health care, poverty, urban affairs, and population.	Includes formation and debate of U.S. foreign and defense policies, veterans' affairs, and defense spending. (Relations with specific foreign countries are usually found under the region concerned.)	Includes business, labor, agriculture, taxation, transportation, consumer affairs, monetary and fiscal policy, natural resources, and pollution.	Includes worldwide scientific, medical, and technological developments; natural phenomena; U.S. weather; natural disasters; and accidents.	Includes the arts, religion, scholarship, communications media, sports, entertainments, fashions, fads, and social life.

	World Affairs	Europe	Africa & the Middle East	The Americas	Asia & the Pacific
Aug. 10		British government officials announce that recently proposed university tuition fees will be waived for students eligible to enter a university in the coming fall but who have chosen to take a year off.	Mohammed Mahdi al-Jawahri, 97, Iraqi poet and journalist, dies in Damascus, Syria, of unreported causes.	The snowstorm that began Aug. 7 in the Andes mountain range starts to abate, allowing rescue workers to plow the roadway and free many of the motorists. In Peru, the storm killed six people trapped in their cars. . . . Conlon Nancarrow, 84, an eccentric yet innovative composer, dies in Mexico City, Mexico, of unreported causes,	
Aug. 11	Asian nations and the IMF pledge $16 billion in loans to Thailand to help the country stabilize its economy, which has been in upheaval since the Thai currency, the baht, was devalued in July.	The last 60 soldiers from a multinational force in Albania depart. . . . The international SFOR in Bosnia-Herzegovina bans the deployment of paramilitary forces. . . . Credit Suisse Group, Switzerland's second-largest bank, announces that it will purchase a Swiss insurance company to create one of the world's largest financial-services companies. . . . Reports state that 46 people have been diagnosed with typhoid in Dagestan.		Some 700 inmates escape from two prisons in northern Honduras after rioting and setting fire to the facilities in Santa Barbara and Trujillo. One prisoner is killed in the Santa Barbara riot.	
Aug. 12	Taiwan announces that it has established diplomatic relations with Chad, which previously recognized the government of China. The Chad ties bring the number of countries officially recognizing Taiwan to 31.	Reports reveal that Turkish president Suleyman Demirel has signed legislation banning gambling at casinos. . . . Reports confirm that Moscow's Christ the Savior Cathedral, originally demolished by Soviet leader Joseph Stalin in the 1930s, has been rebuilt.		In Brasilia, Brazil's capital, federal judge Sandra Mello clears four youths of the murder of Galdino Jesus dos Santos, chief of the Pataxo tribe, who they burned to death in April. The judge rules that the youths did not intend to kill dos Santos and reduces the charges to committing bodily harm. . . . Ontario Hydro, North America's largest electric utility, announces it will shut down the seven oldest of its 19 nuclear reactors, as recommended. The state-owned company's chief executive, Allan Kupcis, resigns.	Popular film producer and businessman Gulshan Kumar, 41, is shot to death while leaving a Hindu temple just north of Bombay, India. Kumar's murder is the latest in a series of attacks on leading figures in India's film industry.
Aug. 13			More than 100 men, armed with machetes and firearms, storm two police stations in the port city of Mombasa, Kenya. Seven police officers, three civilians, and five attackers are killed. . . . A panel that includes a U.S. representative from the CIA as well as Israeli and Palestinian security officials is established to facilitate security cooperation between Israel and the PNA and to enable the U.S. to monitor goodwill efforts of Israeli and Palestinian participants.	The majority of the inmates who escaped from two prisons in northern Honduras on Aug. 11 surrender or are recaptured.	
Aug. 14	Jose Bustani, director general of the UN Organization for the Prohibition of Chemical Weapons, reveals that more than six nations—most of which will not disclose their names—have acknowledged to his organization that they possess chemical weapons or the technology to produce them.	Albanian interior minister Neritan Ceka announces that the army and police have retaken control of Vlore, southern Albania's most important port, which has been under the control of gangs since February. . . . Turkey's parliament approves and president Suleyman Demirel signs an amnesty for editors jailed under the country's harsh press restrictions.		Two prisoners are killed during a riot in a prison in Santa Rosa de Copan, Honduras. . . . Officials from the Guinness Book of World Records rule that Marie-Louise Meilleur, 116, of Corbeil, Canada, is the world's oldest living person.	Fifteen thousand people parade through the streets of New Delhi, India's capital, to rally at midnight, marking the country's 50th year of independence in a "March of the Nation." Crowds gather in the streets and listen to recordings of India's first prime minister, Jawaharlal Nehru, and Mohandas K. Gandhi, who led a nonviolent campaign for India's independence.
Aug. 15		In the continuation of fighting in Tajikistan that erupted Aug. 9, government troops drive Makhmud Khudoberdyev from his main base, some 60 miles (100 km) south of Dushanbe.	Kenyan police, security troops, and navy sailors exchange fire with the rioters from the Aug. 13 violence as they pursue them south of Mombasa.	Leftist guerrillas take 29 oil workers hostage in a remote jungle area of central Peru.	

A	B	C	D	E
Includes developments that affect more than one world region, international organizations, and important meetings of major world leaders.	*Includes all domestic and regional developments in Europe, including the Soviet Union, Turkey, Cyprus, and Malta.*	*Includes all domestic and regional developments in Africa and the Middle East, including Iraq and Iran and excluding Cyprus, Turkey, and Afghanistan.*	*Includes all domestic and regional developments in Latin America, the Caribbean, and Canada.*	*Includes all domestic and regional developments in Asia and Pacific nations, extending from Afghanistan through all the Pacific Islands, except Hawaii.*

U.S. Politics & Social Issues	U.S. Foreign Policy & Defense	U.S. Economy & Environment	Science, Technology, & Nature	Culture, Leisure, & Lifestyle	
		Data shows that the value of U.S. orders for machine tools leaped 38.9% in June to $894 million, from the revised May figure of $644 million.	A flash flood hits an area southwest of the Grand Canyon in Arizona, prompting the evacuation of some 300 tourists and more than 350 residents of the Havasupai Indian Reservation.	In Athens, Greece, the World Track & Field Championships close, with the U.S. topping the medals standings by winning a total of 18. Germany places second with 10 medals, and Russia is third with eight. Ukrainian pole vaulter Sergei Bubka becomes the first person to win a gold medal in each of the six world championships.	**Aug. 10**
	Judge Lenore Nesbitt of U.S. District Court in Miami, Florida, sentences a Palestinian hijacker, Saad'o Mohammed Ibrahim Intissar, to 20 years in prison, the maximum term for air piracy, for diverting an Iberia Airlines DC-10 to Miami on July 26, 1996.	Pres. Clinton becomes the first U.S. chief executive to exercise the presidential right to veto items in spending bills after their passage by Congress when he strikes three special-interest provisions from balanced-budget legislation cleared in July. . . . Rep. Jay C. Kim (R, Calif.) and his wife, June Kim, plead guilty in Los Angeles to charges stemming from more than $250,000 in illegal campaign contributions between 1992 and 1997.		Sweden's national news agency receives a letter claiming responsibility for the Aug. 8 bombing of the Olympic Stadium in Stockholm, Sweden, from an extremist group that opposes the city's Olympic bid.	**Aug. 11**
A local newspaper in Angleton, Texas, publishes a detailed account of a videotape which depicts prison guards kicking inmates and prodding them with stun guns at the Brazoria County Detention Center. . . . Bernard Parks is sworn in as the new chief of the Los Angeles Police Department.				Lava from the Kilauea volcano in Hawaii destroys the 700-year-old Wahaula Heiau temple. . . . Officials reach an agreement that will allow St. Peter's Roman Catholic Church to enlarge its parish in Boerne, Texas, ending a four-year dispute that prompted the Supreme Court to strike down the Religious Freedom Restoration Act of 1993 in June.	**Aug. 12**
NYC police officer Justin A. Volpe is arrested and charged with aggravated sexual abuse and first-degree assault for allegedly beating and sodomizing Abner Louima, 30, a Haitian immigrant who arrested earlier in the week. . . . Robert Louis Leggett, 71, California congressman, 1963–78, who was a target of the 1976 "Koreagate" investigation, dies in Orange, California, of a heart attack.		The Labor Department reports that the federal government's index of prices charged by manufacturers and farmers for finished goods dropped a seasonally adjusted 0.1% in July from June, the seventh consecutive month in which wholesale prices declined.	Twelve hikers are swept away by a flash flood in Arizona with an 11-foot-high wall of water. One person survives by clinging to a ledge. . . . In NYC, Judge Sonia Sotomayor rules that publishers may transfer articles authored by freelance writers into electronic media, such as CD-ROM storage devices, without first obtaining the writers' permission. The decision is considered a landmark ruling in the evolving field of electronic publishing rights.	An official from the Southern Baptist Convention, the nation's largest Protestant denomination, states the group will step up its boycott of Walt Disney Co., launched in June to protest what it views as the company's shift to a "Christian-bashing, family-bashing, pro-homosexual agenda."	**Aug. 13**
U.S. district judge Richard P. Matsch formally sentences Timothy J. McVeigh to death for the 1995 bombing of the Alfred P. Murrah Federal Building in Oklahoma City, Okla., that killed 168 people and injured hundreds of others. . . . Officials confirm that the government will stop distributing Supplemental Security Income (SSI) benefits to 95,180 disabled children due to provisions in the 1996 welfare law.		The FCC formally approves a $23.7 billion merger between so-called Baby Bell telecommunications companies Bell Atlantic Corp. and NYNEX Corp. The merged firm, to take Bell Atlantic's name, will provide local telephone service to 40 million customers along the East Coast between Maine and Virginia.	Scientists report the discovery of the oldest footprint ever found of an anatomically modern human. The two prints, measuring 8.5 inches (21.6 cm) long, are 117,000 years old and probably belonged to a woman about 5 feet, 4 inches (1.63 m) tall.	Hugo Boss AG, an upscale men's clothing manufacturer, confirms that it made uniforms for Nazi police and soldiers during the Third Reich. . . . Pres. Clinton announces new federal guidelines aimed at protecting the rights of government employees to express their religious views in the workplace.	**Aug. 14**
NYC police officer Charles Schwarz, 31, is charged, reportedly for holding Abner Louima, a 30-year-old Haitian immigrant, while officer Justin A. Volpe allegedly assaulted him. . . . A Louisiana law authorizing carjacking victims to use deadly force against attackers goes into effect. The legislation is apparently the first of its kind in the nation.	Pres. Clinton signs a bill that seeks to protect dolphins from fishing nets used to catch tuna, revising the system for labeling packaged tuna cans as "dolphin safe" and lifting an embargo on tuna imports from Latin America.	The Dow closes down 247.37 points, or 3.1%, which, in terms of single-session point declines, is surpassed only by a drop of 508.32 points recorded on Oct. 19, 1987.	The Suffolk County, New York, medical examiner completes the genetic identification of the last two bodies of the 230 victims of the 1996 crash of TWA Flight 800 off Long Island, New York.	John F. Kennedy Jr. refers to his cousins Joseph Kennedy and Michael Kennedy as "poster boys for bad behavior" in an "Editor's Letter" prefacing an issue of his political magazine *George*, causing a ruckus.	**Aug. 15**

F	G	H	I	J
Includes elections, federal-state relations, civil rights and liberties, crime, the judiciary, education, health care, poverty, urban affairs, and population.	*Includes formation and debate of U.S. foreign and defense policies, veterans' affairs, and defense spending. (Relations with specific foreign countries are usually found under the region concerned.)*	*Includes business, labor, agriculture, taxation, transportation, consumer affairs, monetary and fiscal policy, natural resources, and pollution.*	*Includes worldwide scientific, medical, and technological developments; natural phenomena; U.S. weather; natural disasters; and accidents.*	*Includes the arts, religion, scholarship, communications media, sports, entertainments, fashions, fads, and social life.*

	World Affairs	Europe	Africa & the Middle East	The Americas	Asia & the Pacific
Aug. 16		German police arrest about 200 neo-Nazis who assemble in various parts of the country to mark the 10th anniversary of the death of Rudolf Hess, a deputy to Adolf Hitler.... Turkey's parliament approves legislation that will curb access to Islam-based education. In the run-up to the parliamentary vote, fundamentalist activists opposing the education reform held several demonstrations throughout the country, during which more than 100 people were arrested.	In Kenya, armed gangs attack two villages in the Mombasa area, killing at least eight people and burning dozens of houses and hundreds of roadside stalls.		
Aug. 17		Chechen rebels begin to release some of the Russian journalists being held hostage.	The PNA formally announces its phased boycott of Israeli products imported into the West Bank and Gaza.	Reports confirm that the leftist National Liberation Army (ELN), the smaller of Colombia's two main guerrilla groups, has kidnapped at least 12 town council members in Bolivar province in northern Colombia in apparent attempt to sabotage municipal elections.	Burnum Burnum (born Harry Penrith), 61, Australian aboriginal rights activist, dies in Woronora, Australia, of a heart attack.
Aug. 18		The reform-minded deputy governor of St. Petersburg, Mikhail Manevich, is killed by a sniper. His wife is also injured by the gunfire.... More Russian journalists being held hostage in the separatist republic of Chechnya are released, bringing the total freed to five.... In Tajikistan, 50 of Mukhmud Khudoberdyev's men are killed by government troops in fighting for control of a bridge over the Vakhsh River, 95 miles south of Dushanbe.	SLA militiamen shell Sidon, Lebanon, a stronghold of Muslim militancy, killing at least 10 civilians and wounding dozens of others. Three youths, die in a roadside bomb blast outside Jezzine, a predominantly Christian town just north of the so-called security zone in southern Lebanon.... Israel announces a partial release of frozen PNA funds as a response to the PNA's timely arrest and conviction of three Palestinians for the slaying of an Israeli taxi driver and its "partial cooperation" in the July bombing investigation.... In Sierra Leone, the National Union of Students protest against the rebel regime is forcibly dispersed by fighters from the Revolutionary United Front (RUF).	Reports from Peru confirm that the leftist guerrillas who took 29 oil workers hostage Aug. 15 were released after CGG agreed to give food, medicine and clothing to the rebels.... Konrad Kalejs, an alleged World War II-era war criminal, is deported to Australia from Canada.	High winds and torrential rains from Typhoon Winnie hit the eastern Chinese province of Zhejiang, killing 242 people. Before striking the mainland, typhoon Winnie killed at least 24 people in neighboring Taiwan, and more than 28 inches (70 cm) of rain has fallen on northern Taiwan since Aug. 16.
Aug. 19		Reports indicate that Chechen president Aslan Maskhadov has declared Chechen as the republic's official language ... St. Petersburg's Church of the Savior of Spilt Blood, built on the site of the 1881 assassination of Czar Alexander II, opens for services for the first time in 60 years.... Tajik government sources reveal that Makhmud Khudoberdiyev and 40 of his troops have fled to Uzbekistan.	Hezbollah guerrillas fire dozens of rockets into northern Israel in response to the Aug. 18 shelling that SLA militiamen carried out against Sidon in Lebanon.... Two people die in an attack in Malindi, a tourist resort in Kenya, 75 miles (120 km) north of Mombasa.	In Jamaica, prison guards go on strike after being angered by a plan to combat the spread of AIDS in Jamaica's jails by distributing condoms to prisoners and guards. The guards reportedly take offense, believing it implies that they engage in homosexual relations with prisoners.... Clare Short, an official from Great Britain, announces a voluntary evacuation plan for residents of the Caribbean island of Montserrat, a British dependency, to help them flee an erupting volcano.	A ground-breaking ceremony is held in the remote town of Kumho, on North Korea's east coast, to mark the official launch of an internationally funded project to construct two light-water nuclear power plants nearby.
Aug. 20		The international Stabilization Force (SFOR) seizes control of six police buildings in Banja Luka, the largest city in the Serb part of Bosnia-Herzegovina, from secret-police forces loyal to former Bosnian Serb Pres. Radovan Karadzic. The troops confiscate thousands of grenades, rocket launchers, booby traps, and rifles from the premises.	Israeli warplanes launch strikes against targets in Lebanon, hitting Hezbollah bases in eastern Lebanon's Bekaa valley near Syria, injuring two children. The raids are Israel's largest since April 1996.... Reports state that, in Kenya, the police have arrested more than 300 people in connection with recent violence. Those arrested include two local KANU leaders, Karisa Maitha and Omar Masumbuko.	In Jamaica, at the General Penitentiary in Kingston and the St. Catherine District Prison in Spanish Town, prisoners riot, prompted by a prison guard strike started Aug. 19.	
Aug. 21	Reports suggest that St. Lucia's cabinet has decided to establish relations with China instead of Taiwan.	Croatia apologizes to Jews for the anti-Semitic actions of its World War II-era Ustashe regime, which sided with the Nazis and killed tens of thousands of Jews.... Pope John Paul II visits France to help celebrate the 12th World Youth Days festival, an event which draws as many as 500,000 young people. ... Yuri Vladimirovich Nikulin, 75, Russian clown and actor, dies in Moscow, Russia, while undergoing emergency heart surgery.	A truck driver in southern Lebanon is killed by a roadside bomb apparently planted by Hezbollah, whose fighters also exchange artillery fire in the region with Israeli soldiers and militiamen of the South Lebanon Army (SLA), Israel's Lebanese proxy army.	In Jamaica, prison guards who went on strike August 19 return to work, but the violence in the penitentiaries continues.... Bertrand Osbourne, the chief minister of the Caribbean island of Montserrat, resigns amid protests over his handling of the volcanic eruptions.... Misael Pastrana Borrero, 73, Colombian president, 1970–74, dies in Bogota, Colombia, of stomach cancer.	Premier Lien Chan resigns in the face of criticism over a surge in Taiwan's crime rate. Vincent Siew will replace Lien.... A plane crash in central Afghanistan kills everyone on board, including seven senior officials of the anti-Taliban opposition. Among the dead is Abdul Rahim Ghafurzai, the coalition's new premier.

A	B	C	D	E
Includes developments that affect more than one world region, international organizations, and important meetings of major world leaders.	Includes all domestic and regional developments in Europe, including the Soviet Union, Turkey, Cyprus, and Malta.	Includes all domestic and regional developments in Africa and the Middle East, including Iraq and Iran and excluding Cyprus, Turkey, and Afghanistan.	Includes all domestic and regional developments in Latin America, the Caribbean, and Canada.	Includes all domestic and regional developments in Asia and Pacific nations, extending from Afghanistan through all the Pacific Islands, except Hawaii.

U.S. Politics & Social Issues	U.S. Foreign Policy & Defense	U.S. Economy & Environment	Science, Technology, & Nature	Culture, Leisure, & Lifestyle	
In response to the alleged beating and sodomizing of Abner Louima by NYC police, more than 2,000 demonstrators, including neighborhood residents and Caribbean immigrants, march through the precinct to the station house to protest what they denounce as a pattern of police brutality. The Rev. Al Sharpton, a Democratic candidate for mayor, addresses a smaller rally that is later joined by the marchers.				Nusrat Fateh Ali Khan, 48, Pakistani singer who won worldwide acclaim for his renditions of qawwali, traditional Islamic music adapted from Sufi devotional poetry, dies in London, England, of a heart attack.	Aug. 16
Reports reveal that financier and philanthropist George Soros plans to donate $1 million to needle-exchange programs throughout the U.S. in an attempt to curb the spread of HIV, the virus that causes AIDS.				Golfer Davis Love III wins the PGA Championship in Mamaroneck, New York. . . . Karrie Webb of Australia wins the Women's British Open golf championship in Sunningdale, England.	Aug. 17
In the first-ever class-action suit against breast implant makers to go to trial, a New Orleans, Louisiana, jury finds Dow Chemical Co., a co-owner of Dow Corning, guilty of deliberately misleading women about the health risks of silicone breast implants. . . . Jean Westwood, 73, who, in 1972, became the first woman ever to head a major U.S. political party when she chaired the Democratic National Committee, dies in American Fork, Utah, of complications from a pituitary tumor.	Female students enroll at the Virginia Military Institute in Lexington, Virginia, for the first time, ending 158 years of male-only education at the college. . . . An army jury sentences Sergeant Herman Gunter to a reprimand and two-rank demotion for sexually abusing a female subordinate. Gunter, who is the eighth of 12 soldiers at Aberdeen Proving Ground in Maryland to be disciplined for sexual misconduct, was convicted earlier of only three of the score of charges originally leveled against him.		Reports confirm that nine bodies have been recovered from the Aug. 13 flash flood in Arizona.	The Evangelical Lutheran Church in America, the nation's largest Lutheran denomination, votes to forge closer ties with three other Protestant denominations—the Presbyterian Church (USA), the United Church of Christ, and the Reformed Church in America.	Aug. 18
A gunman involved in a zoning dispute, Carl C. Drega, goes on a shooting spree in the town of Colebrook, New Hampshire, killing four people and wounding four others before being shot to death by police officers near Bloomfield, Vermont. . . . Former Rep. Dan Rostenkowski (D, Ill.), who pled guilty to two counts of mail fraud in 1996, is released from a federal prison in Oxford, Wisconsin, after serving 13 months of a 17-month prison term.		The International Brotherhood of Teamsters union reaches a tentative five-year contract agreement with the United Parcel Service of America Inc. (UPS), ending a strike begun Aug. 4 by some 185,000 unionized workers. The strike was the largest walkout in the U.S. in more than a decade and nearly shut down UPS, the world's largest package-delivery company.	Reports confirm that Dutch scientist Marc Van Roosmalen has identified a previously unknown species of monkey living in the rain forests of Brazil. The animal, which is the size of a mouse and has a greenish-gray coat with a black tail and crown, is called the black-headed Saguinus dwarf. . . . The space shuttle Discovery lands in Cape Canaveral, Florida, after carrying out a mission to gather environmental data and test new equipment.		Aug. 19
The U.S. Third Circuit Court of Appeals in Philadelphia, Pennsylvania, upholds the constitutionality of New Jersey's 1994 sex-offender notification law, known as "Megan's Law." The measure requires local police departments to inform residents when a convicted sex offender begins living in a community.	A federal grand jury in NYC hands down an 11-count indictment against 20 people who allegedly led a ring that smuggled deaf Mexican immigrants into the U.S. and forced them to work selling trinkets. . . . A state prosecutor in Charleston, S.C., David Schwacke, states he will not pursue criminal charges against male cadets at The Citadel, a military academy in Charleston, accused of harassing and abusing two female cadets in 1996.		In Fort Worth, Texas, two engineers are killed when four unmanned locomotives roll 10 miles (16 km) off a siding and into the path of an oncoming train, igniting a fire.	Leo Jaffe, 88, chair of Columbia Pictures, 1973–81, and philanthropist, dies in New York City after a long illness.	Aug. 20
Judge Fredric Block rules that former New York mayor David N. Dinkins and former police commissioner Lee P. Brown cannot be held personally liable for their handling of 1991 riots in the city's Crown Heights neighborhood. . . . Department of Education officials estimate that the total enrollment at U.S. schools will increase to a record 52.2 million students for the 1997–98 school year, up 800,000 from the previous year.		Hudson Foods, a meat-processing company based in Rogers, Arkansas, announces a nationwide recall of 25 million pounds (11 million kg) of beef after state health officials in Colorado link an outbreak of E. coli bacteria poisoning to hamburgers produced by the company. It is the largest meat recall in U.S. history. . . . Barbara Zack Quindel invalidates the December 1996 International Brotherhood of Teamsters election in which Ronald Carey had won a second term as the powerful labor union's president and orders a new election.			Aug. 21

F	G	H	I	J
Includes elections, federal-state relations, civil rights and liberties, crime, the judiciary, education, health care, poverty, urban affairs, and population.	Includes formation and debate of U.S. foreign and defense policies, veterans' affairs, and defense spending. (Relations with specific foreign countries are usually found under the region concerned.)	Includes business, labor, agriculture, taxation, transportation, consumer affairs, monetary and fiscal policy, natural resources, and pollution.	Includes worldwide scientific, medical, and technological developments; natural phenomena; U.S. weather; natural disasters; and accidents.	Includes the arts, religion, scholarship, communications media, sports, entertainments, fashions, fads, and social life.

	World Affairs	Europe	Africa & the Middle East	The Americas	Asia & the Pacific
Aug. 22				David Brandt, a member of Montserrat's parliament, is sworn in as the chief minister of Montserrat, a tiny island in the Caribbean.	Reports confirm that 242 people in China died in Typhoon Winnie Aug. 18. The typhoon, which flooded some 2 million acres (800,000 hectares) of farmland and forced the evacuation of 1.3 million people, is described as the worst in China in more than a decade.
Aug. 23		The Swedish government admits to conducting a program from 1935 to 1976 of coerced sterilizations for women deemed mentally inferior or ethnically impure.	Former Zambian president Kenneth D. Kaunda is shot and slightly wounded by police after trying to address an opposition rally in the central Zambian town of Kabwe. . . . Scheduled commercial flights between Saudi Arabia and Iran resume for the first time since Iran's Islamic revolution in 1979.	Data confirm that 16 inmates died in two prisons during riots at the General Penitentiary in Kingston and the St. Catherine District Prison in Spanish Town that were prompted by the Aug. 19 walkout by guards. . . . Reports disclose that residents of Montserrat are protesting daily in the streets, criticizing the British and Montserratian governments' response to the crisis and demanding greater compensation from Britain . . . . Sir Eric M. Gairy, 75, first prime minister of Grenada, 1974–79, dies in Grand Anse, Grenada, of unreported causes.	
Aug. 24			Israeli security forces prevent tour buses carrying 600 Christian pilgrims from Italy from entering Bethlehem.	The riots that started Aug. 20 at the General Penitentiary in Kingston and the St. Catherine District Prison in Spanish Town are quieted after the Jamaican government sends army troops to help guards subdue the prisoners.	
Aug. 25		A court in Berlin sentences Egon Krenz, the former East Germany's last hard-line communist leader, to six years and six months in prison for his role in the deaths of people shot by border guards. . . . Robert Pinget, 78, innovative Swiss-born novelist and playwright considered part of the late-1950s Nouveau Roman literary movement in France, dies in Tours, France, after a stroke.		Banco Industrial Colombiano announces it will acquire Banco de Colombia to form a bank with assets of $5.3 billion, making it Colombia's largest bank. . . . Reports confirm that the ELN and the FARC abducted 50 local officials in the previous week in Colombia. . . . Clodomiro Almeyda Medina, 74, Chilean statesman and Socialist Party official, dies in Santiago, Chile, of colon cancer.	
Aug. 26	The UN-affiliated World Climate Research Program (WCRP) opens an international conference, and weather experts predict that "El Nino," a periodic warming of ocean waters off the west coast of South America, may cause disastrous weather conditions in the U.S., Africa and Asia during the first half of 1998.	Italian police in Rome arrest Musbah Abulgasem Eter, a Libyan man suspected of involvement in a 1986 bombing that killed three people in Berlin, Germany. He is the last of five suspected participants in the attack to be apprehended.	Former president F. W. de Klerk, South Africa's last apartheid-era ruler, announces that he is resigning as head of the National Party and retiring from politics.	The Chamber of Deputies, the lower house of Haiti's parliament, votes to reject Pres. Rene Preval's nominee for premier, Ericq Pierre. . . . Mauricio Guzman Cuevas, the mayor of Cali, Colombia's second-largest city and home base of the powerful Cali drug cartel, is arrested on charges of accepting money from the cartel for his 1994 election campaign. . . . Reports state that guerrillas in Colombia have destroyed campaign headquarters and local offices of the electoral authority in several towns.	Amnesty International attests that in 1996 Chinese authorities imposed 6,100 death sentences and executed 4,367 prisoners. Many of the executions were for minor crimes, including indecency, drug possession, and cattle rustling.
Aug. 27		Reports confirm that the Norwegian government has admitted its participation in the program of coerced sterilizations for women who were deemed mentally inferior or ethnically impure, which the Swedish government disclosed on Aug. 23.	Israel lifts its 28-day siege of Bethlehem, making the city the last on the West Bank to be freed from an Israeli blockade imposed following a suicide bombing in late July.		

A	B	C	D	E
Includes developments that affect more than one world region, international organizations, and important meetings of major world leaders.	Includes all domestic and regional developments in Europe, including the Soviet Union, Turkey, Cyprus, and Malta.	Includes all domestic and regional developments in Africa and the Middle East, including Iraq and Iran and excluding Cyprus, Turkey, and Afghanistan.	Includes all domestic and regional developments in Latin America, the Caribbean, and Canada.	Includes all domestic and regional developments in Asia and Pacific nations, extending from Afghanistan through all the Pacific Islands, except Hawaii.

U.S. Politics & Social Issues	U.S. Foreign Policy & Defense	U.S. Economy & Environment	Science, Technology, & Nature	Culture, Leisure, & Lifestyle	
Prospective Republican candidates for the 2000 presidential election address a GOP conference in Indianapolis, Indiana.... NYC police officers Thomas Wiese and Thomas Bruder are charged with participating in the alleged beating of Abner Louima, a 30-year-old Haitian immigrant.... Mary Louise Smith, 82, who was the first woman ever to serve as Republican National Committee chair, 1974–77, dies in Des Moines, Iowa, of lung cancer.			A revitalized crew carries out the first phase of repairs on *Mir* to mend damage caused in June when a cargo vessel crashed into the space station.		**Aug. 22**
			Sir John Cowdery Kendrew, 80, British biochemist who shared the 1962 Nobel Prize in chemistry for research on the molecular structure of myoglobin and hemoglobin, dies in Cambridge, England, of unreported causes.	A team from Guadalupe, Mexico, defeats Mission Viejo, CA, 5-4, to win the Little League World Series title in Williamsport, Pennsylvania.	**Aug. 23**
					Aug. 24
The state of Florida and five major tobacco companies reach an agreement that will settle the state's lawsuit to recover the costs of treating smoking-related illnesses. The companies agree to pay the state $11.3 billion over 25 years.		A state jury in New Orleans, Louisiana, awards 20 plaintiffs compensatory damages of some $2 million in their claim against CSX Transportation, a unit of CSX Corp., and four other companies for a 1987 fire in a railroad car containing a hazardous chemical.	NASA officials and the Texas election board announce the creation of a computer program that will enable astronauts to vote in U.S. elections while traveling in outer space.	A bomb explodes in the New Ullevi Stadium in Goteborg, Sweden. The stadium, Sweden's largest, was included in Stockholm's proposal for the 2004 Olympics as the site of soccer matches.	**Aug. 25**
In a case that draws attention, Benjamin Wynne, a student at LSU in Baton Rouge, Louisiana, dies of alcohol poisoning and three other students are hospitalized after a drinking binge celebrating pledge week with fraternity Sigma Alpha Epsilon.... The College Board releases the 1997 results for the Scholastic Assessment Test (SAT). The average score on the math section of the test improved to 511, from 508 the previous year, while the average verbal score was unchanged at 505. The average math score is the highest recorded in 26 years.	The U.S. announces that it will grant political asylum to Chang Sung Gil, North Korea's ambassador to Egypt who defected to the U.S., and his brother, also a diplomat. Chang is the only North Korean at the ambassador level ever to defect and is the highest-ranking North Korean ever to seek political asylum in the U.S. North Korea, in protest, pulls out of talks with the U.S. on missile proliferation scheduled to commence Aug. 27.			U.S. track star Carl Lewis, 36, runs in what he states is his last competitive race, ending a 15-year career highlighted by nine Olympic gold medals.... The organizing committee of the 2002 Winter Olympic Games in Salt Lake City, Utah, elects Frank Joklik as its new president.... Allen Iverson, a basketball guard for the Philadelphia 76ers, is sentenced to three years' probation for carrying a concealed weapon.	**Aug. 26**
	A federal grand jury indicts former agriculture secretary Mike Espy on charges that he accepted more than $35,000 in gifts from companies that he was in charge of regulating, and that he later tried to deceive investigators about his activities.		NASA scientists note that an analysis of four different Martian rocks yielded confusing results, indicating that Mars's geology is "more complicated" than previously believed.... The FDA states it will require drug makers to print labels on the diet medication fen/phen, warning users that the product may damage heart valves.	A group claims responsibility for the bombings at Olympic venues in Sweden and threatens to launch further attacks if Stockholm's bid to host the games is approved.... Brandon Tartikoff, 48, president of the NBC entertainment division, 1980–91, dies in Los Angeles, California, of complications from treatment for Hodgkin's disease.	**Aug. 27**

F	G	H	I	J
Includes elections, federal-state relations, civil rights and liberties, crime, the judiciary, education, health care, poverty, urban affairs, and population.	*Includes formation and debate of U.S. foreign and defense policies, veterans' affairs, and defense spending. (Relations with specific foreign countries are usually found under the region concerned.)*	*Includes business, labor, agriculture, taxation, transportation, consumer affairs, monetary and fiscal policy, natural resources, and pollution.*	*Includes worldwide scientific, medical, and technological developments; natural phenomena; U.S. weather; natural disasters; and accidents.*	*Includes the arts, religion, scholarship, communications media, sports, entertainments, fashions, fads, and social life.*

	World Affairs	Europe	Africa & the Middle East	The Americas	Asia & the Pacific
Aug. 28	The UN Security Council votes to pass a resolution imposing air and travel sanctions against the National Union for the Total Liberation of Angola (UNITA), an armed rebel group in the southeast African nation of Angola. UN speakers claim that UNITA has ignored UN demands that the movement demobilize and disarm its troops and has not disclosed information about the size of its armed forces.	U.S. soldiers monitoring an attempt by pro-Plavsic forces to take control of the police station in Brcko are menaced by mobs of Bosnian Serbs loyal to former president Radovan Karadzic. Two soldiers are injured in the melee, the most violent confrontation between Bosnian Serbs and SFOR peacekeepers since 1995. Separately, U.S. troops surround a TV broadcast tower in Udrigovo while NATO peacekeeping officials decide which faction of Bosnian Serbs should legitimately control it.	Israeli warplanes strike a suspected Hezbollah target just north of the security zone. Five Israeli soldiers are killed by Muslim guerrillas who attack their patrol in Israel's self-declared security zone in southern Lebanon.		
Aug. 29	In response to the Aug. 21 report that the Caribbean island nation of St. Lucia is establishing diplomatic relations with China, Taiwan announces that it has severed relations with St. Lucia.	The offices of a newspaper in the Bosnian town of Doboj are destroyed by a bomb.	Hundreds of civilians are slain by unknown assailants in a predawn attack on Rais, a village 15 miles (25 km) south of the Algerian capital, Algiers. The attack was the bloodiest yet in a 5½-year-long insurgency by Islamic fundamentalists against the military-backed government of Pres. Liamine Zeroual. More than 1,500 people are estimated to have been killed since legislative elections were held in June.	After protests that the planned expulsion from Panama of prize-winning Peruvian journalist Gustavo Gorriti amounts to an attack on freedom of expression, the Panamanian government relents, stating that Gorriti may stay in Panama until the Supreme Court rules on his case.	
Aug. 30	The Economic Community of West African States (ECOWAS) formally imposes a trade embargo on Sierra Leone to put pressure on the leaders of the May military coup to restore power to the civilian government of Pres. Ahmad Tejan Kabbah. . . . In response to the Aug. 29 attack in Algeria, UN secretary general Kofi Annan argues that the situation in Algeria has reached the point at which the international community should no longer "leave the Algerian people to their lot."	About 100 people riot in the predominantly Roman Catholic neighborhood of Ballymurphy, in West Belfast, Northern Ireland. The rioters attack the New Barnsley police station and throw gasoline bombs at officers who respond with plastic bullets. No injuries are reported		In Mexico, a coalition of four opposition parties in a special session of the Chamber of Deputies elects Porfirio Muñoz Ledo of the leftist Democratic Revolutionary Party (PRD) as speaker of the house. It is the first time in 68 years that the Institutional Revolutionary Party (PRI) does not lead the chamber. PRI legislators boycott the special session.	
Aug. 31	People around the world are shocked by the death of Britain's Princess Diana, and reports of mourning come from every region of the globe.	Britain's Diana, Princess of Wales, 36, dies after suffering grave injuries in a car accident in an underpass in Paris. Emad Mohamed (Dodi) al-Fayed, 41, an Egyptian-born film producer to whom Diana was recently romantically linked, dies in the crash, along with driver Henri Paul, 41. The Fayed family bodyguard is seriously injured. British prime minister Tony Blair calls Diana "the people's princess," and says, "We are today a nation in a state of shock."			
Sept. 1	Delegates from 89 countries meet at a conference in Oslo, Norway, to discuss a treaty to ban the use, production, transfer, and stockpiling of antipersonnel land mines.	Reports confirm that Miro Bajramovic confessed to killing 72 civilians and to running a concentration camp during Croatia's 1991 war. Bajramovic is arrested. . . . A mob of 300 Serbs attack the U.S. soldiers blockading the broadcasting tower in the Serb town of Udrigovo in northeast Bosnia-Herzegovina since Aug. 28. . . . . Officials reveal that Henri Paul, Diana's driver in the fatal Aug. 31 crash, was legally drunk at the time of the accident. The paparazzi are widely accused of causing the accident by pursuing Diana relentlessly.	Iran's official news agency discloses that Iran has hanged an Iranian man, Siavash Bayani, for spying for the U.S. Central Intelligence Agency (CIA). . . . Israel begins to ease its closure of its borders, allowing entry to 4,000 of the 80,000 Palestinian laborers who hold jobs in Israel.	In an unprecedented move in Mexico, Porfirio Muñoz Ledo delivers a response to PRI president Ernesto Zedillo Ponce de Leon's annual State of the Nation speech, which traditionally has been looked upon as a demonstration of the near-imperial power of the president. Muñoz's speech marks the first time that a member of the opposition publicly responds to the address.	
Sept. 2		Three accomplices of Miro Bajramovic, who confessed to running a concentration camp in Croatia in 1991, are arrested. . . . Officials in the town of Udrigovo in Bosnia-Herzegovina return a TV broadcast tower surrounded by troops since Aug. 28 to Serbs led by former president Radovan Karadzic, who agree to moderate their propaganda. . . . A jury in Copenhagen, Denmark, finds three neo-Nazis guilty of attempting to send package bombs to targets in Britain.			

A	B	C	D	E
Includes developments that affect more than one world region, international organizations, and important meetings of major world leaders.	*Includes all domestic and regional developments in Europe, including the Soviet Union, Turkey, Cyprus, and Malta.*	*Includes all domestic and regional developments in Africa and the Middle East, including Iraq and Iran and excluding Cyprus, Turkey, and Afghanistan.*	*Includes all domestic and regional developments in Latin America, the Caribbean, and Canada.*	*Includes all domestic and regional developments in Asia and Pacific nations, extending from Afghanistan through all the Pacific Islands, except Hawaii.*

U.S. Politics & Social Issues	U.S. Foreign Policy & Defense	U.S. Economy & Environment	Science, Technology, & Nature	Culture, Leisure, & Lifestyle	
California's Proposition 209, a controversial anti-affirmative-action measure approved by state voters in 1996, officially goes into effect. Civil-rights leader Rev. Jesse Jackson and San Francisco mayor Willie L. Brown Jr. (D) lead thousands of anti-Proposition 209 protesters in a march across San Francisco's landmark Golden Gate Bridge.		Michael Brown, son of the late commerce secretary Ronald Brown, pleads guilty to a misdemeanor charge that he used "straw donors" to funnel $4,000 from an Oklahoma company to the 1994 reelection campaign of Sen. Edward Kennedy (D, Mass.).		British writer Salman Rushdie weds a British-born editor identified only as Elizabeth. Rushdie has been under police protection since 1989, when Iran's leader at the time, Ayatollah Ruhollah Khomeini, issued a public call for the writer's death.	Aug. 28
A coalition of the ACLU and other groups file emergency requests with the Supreme Court to block enforcement of Proposition 209, a controversial anti-affirmative-action measure that went into effect on Aug. 28.		NationsBank Corp. of North Carolina announces that it will buy Florida's largest bank, Barnett Banks Inc., in a deal initially worth $15.5 billion. The stock-only transaction will be the largest banking merger in U.S. history and will boost NationsBank's assets to some $290 billion, making it the third-largest bank in the U.S., behind Chase Manhattan Corp. and Citicorp.	Because thousands of dead fish are being discovered in the Pocomoke River, Maryland governor Parris Glendening (D) orders the Pocomoke River closed.		Aug. 29
				The Houston Comets win the inaugural Women's National Basketball Association (WNBA) title over the New York Liberty, 65-51.... Controversial film director Leni Riefenstahl, who made propaganda films for Nazi German leader Adolf Hitler during the 1930s, accepts a film achievement award in Los Angeles from Cinecon.	Aug. 30
				A bomb explodes outside the office of the Greek Olympic Committee in Athens, damaging the building's entrance.	Aug. 31
				Cold Mountain by Charles Frazier tops the bestseller list.... A leftist group that opposes Athens's bid to host the Olympics claims responsibility for the Aug. 31 attack.... Data shows that the average attendance of the inaugural WNBA season, which was projected to be 4,000 fans per game, turned out to be 9,669 fans per game, making the debut of women's professional basketball a success.	Sept. 1
A Miami Beach, Florida, postal worker, Jesus Antonio Tamayo, shoots his ex-wife and another woman and then kills himself while on duty at the local post office. The two women are wounded and hospitalized.		The Dow closes at 7879.78, up 257.36 points, setting a record single-session point increase. The day's 3.4% gain is the Dow's highest percentage rise since early 1991.... Figures reveal that the purchasing managers' index declined to 56.8 in August, from July's figure of 58.6. The August index marks the 15th consecutive month that the indicator surpasses the 50 level indicative of expansion in the manufacturing sector.	Viktor Emil Frankl, 92, Austrian psychiatrist who founded logotherapy, the study of how individuals find meaning within a particular set of life circumstances, dies in Vienna, Austria, of heart failure.	Sir Rudolf Bing, 95, general manager of the New York Metropolitan Opera, 1950–72, who brought the world's finest directors, designers, and performers to the organization, dies in Yonkers, New York, of respiratory ailments.	Sept. 2

F	G	H	I	J
Includes elections, federal-state relations, civil rights and liberties, crime, the judiciary, education, health care, poverty, urban affairs, and population.	*Includes formation and debate of U.S. foreign and defense policies, veterans' affairs, and defense spending. (Relations with specific foreign countries are usually found under the region concerned.)*	*Includes business, labor, agriculture, taxation, transportation, consumer affairs, monetary and fiscal policy, natural resources, and pollution.*	*Includes worldwide scientific, medical, and technological developments; natural phenomena; U.S. weather; natural disasters; and accidents.*	*Includes the arts, religion, scholarship, communications media, sports, entertainments, fashions, fads, and social life.*

	World Affairs	Europe	Africa & the Middle East	The Americas	Asia & the Pacific
Sept. 3		The Soros Foundation, once Belarus's largest nongovernmental organization, announces that it will shut down its operations in the country, claiming it was hounded out of Belarus by tax officials. . . . Data shows that 95 people died while climbing in the French Alps over the summer. Of that number, 36 were killed on Mont Blanc, Europe's highest peak.		In Canada, one person dies and 65 others are injured when a Via Rail passenger train derails near Biggar, Saskatchewan. Some 193 passengers and 29 crew members are on the train when it derails.	Officials in the Comoran capital, Moroni, on the biggest island of the chain in the Indian Ocean, Grande Comore, sends a force of 300 heavily armed soldiers to reestablish government control on Anjouan, where secessionist protests in August turned into revolt. . . . At least 65 people die when a Vietnam Airlines plane crashes in Phnom Penh, Cambodia's capital. Two children survive, and locals loot the site while rescuers search for bodies.
Sept. 4		Three unidentified photographers who took pictures of the crash that killed Princess Diana in Paris on Aug. 31 turn themselves in to police, as, under French law, failure to provide assistance at an accident scene is a crime punishable by fines and up to five years in prison. They join seven other members of the paparazzi, who were charged earlier. . . . Jeffrey Bernard, 65, British journalist and author, dies of kidney failure.	Three suicide bombers kill four Israeli civilians in a coordinated attack on West Jerusalem. An estimated 190 people are injured. Hamas claims responsibility. Israel immediately reinstates its border closure with the West Bank and Gaza Strip. . . . ECOWAS troops fire on ships unloading rice at the Freetown harbor in Sierra Leone, reportedly killing more than 30 civilians. . . . Congolese troops forcibly remove hundreds of refugees from a camp and return them to Rwanda.	Three tourist hotels and a restaurant in Havana, Cuba's capital, are hit by explosions. One person is killed in the blasts. The explosions mark the third time since April that hotels in Havana have been bombed.	In Malaysia, High Court judge Low Hop Bing sentences correspondent Murray Hiebert to a three-month jail term for contempt of the judiciary. The sentence stems from an article Hiebert wrote that Judge Low considers offensive. It is the first time that a Malaysian court sentences a journalist to prison for contempt of court. . . . The government of the Comoros, a three-island nation in the Indian Ocean, finds significant resistance to the troops deployed Sept. 3 on Anjouan.
Sept. 5	Mother Teresa (born Agnes Gonxha Bojaxhiu), 87, Roman Catholic nun of Albanian parentage who devoted her life to caring for the destitute and the sick in India and whose work was internationally recognized and earned her the 1979 Nobel Peace Prize, dies in Calcutta, India, of a heart attack.	Daniel Villar Enciso, a member of Spain's police force, is killed by a car bomb in Basauri, near Bilbao. . . . In Russia, the city of Moscow launches a three-day celebration of the 850th anniversary of its founding.	As violence continues in Algeria, four people die in a bomb attack on a bus near Blida, 30 miles south of Algiers, and 20 others are murdered in the region. At least 80 people are killed in a raid on Beni Messous, a suburb 12 miles west of Algiers. . . . Lebanese Shi'ite Muslims ambush Israeli commandos, and 12 Israelis and two Lebanese civilians die near Insariye, nine miles south of Sidon. The Israeli death toll is the highest Israel has sustained in an armed clash in Lebanon since its protracted 1982 invasion of the country.	At least 36 people die when a powerful storm causes a stadium to collapse during a political rally in Ciudad del Este, Paraguay, located along the Parana River in Alto Parana state. More than 100 people are injured.	
Sept. 6		Britain's Princess Diana is memorialized at London's Westminster Abbey. The funeral is attended by 2,000 guests, while more than 1 million mourners gather near the abbey and listen to the service on loudspeakers. In an unprecedented move, Britain's national flag, the Union Jack, flies at half-mast atop Buckingham Palace, which traditionally displays only the monarch's royal standard.		More than 400 Guatemalans who fled to Mexico during the civil war return to their country in a convoy of buses escorted by the UN High Commission for Refugees and the International Committee of the Red Cross.	The government of Comoros, a three-island nation in the Indian Ocean, admits its troops have failed to recapture Anjouan from separatists fighting for reunion with France. . . . To acknowledge the late Mother Teresa, the Indian government breaks with tradition by calling for the honor of state rites. She is the first person in a nongovernmental role to be given the honor since Mohandas Karamchand Gandhi in 1948.
Sept. 7	Hundreds of foreign diplomats and businesspeople gather in Panama for a conference on the future of the Panama Canal. The canal, currently controlled by the U.S., is scheduled to come under Panamanian control on Dec. 31, 1999.		An Israeli soldier is killed in southern Lebanon, raising to 865 the number of Israeli troops killed in Lebanon since 1982, when Israel created a buffer zone abutting its northern border. . . . Mobutu Sese Seko (born Joseph Desire Mobutu), 66, Zairian president, 1965–97, who was the last of Africa's cold war–era dictators and was ousted in May by Laurent Kabila, dies in Rabat, Morocco, of prostate cancer. . . . Abdullah Ibn Hamoud al-Tariki, 80, Saudi Arabia's first oil minister and a founder of OPEC, dies in Cairo, Egypt, of a heart attack.		
Sept. 8		Reports reveal that the Princess of Wales Memorial Fund, set up Sept. 2 by Princess Diana's lawyers, has received about £100 million ($160 million) in donations so far.		A ferry sinks some 50 yards (45 m) offshore from Montrouis, on Haiti's western coast. At least 200 people die in the accident. Between 30 and 60 people survive. . . . A forest fire threatens to destroy the Machu Picchu ruins, known as the Lost City of the Incas, in the Andes mountains in southern Peru. The area is closed to tourists when the fire comes within 1,000 feet (300 m) of the ruins. . . . About 1,100 unarmed EZLN fighters in Chiapas, Mexico, launch a trek to Mexico City for a rally.	Reports indicate that 40 government soldiers have been killed and 100 have been captured by members of an Anjouan island secessionist group during fighting in Comoros, a three-island nation in the Indian Ocean.

A	B	C	D	E
Includes developments that affect more than one world region, international organizations, and important meetings of major world leaders.	*Includes all domestic and regional developments in Europe, including the Soviet Union, Turkey, Cyprus, and Malta.*	*Includes all domestic and regional developments in Africa and the Middle East, including Iraq and Iran and excluding Cyprus, Turkey, and Afghanistan.*	*Includes all domestic and regional developments in Latin America, the Caribbean, and Canada.*	*Includes all domestic and regional developments in Asia and Pacific nations, extending from Afghanistan through all the Pacific Islands, except Hawaii.*

U.S. Politics & Social Issues	U.S. Foreign Policy & Defense	U.S. Economy & Environment	Science, Technology, & Nature	Culture, Leisure, & Lifestyle	
		A federal jury in Phoenix, Arizona's capital, convicts the state's Republican governor, J. Fife Symington III, of seven felony counts for defrauding lenders who provided millions of dollars to his ailing real-estate empire. Under Arizona law, a governor convicted of any felony is required to step down. Symington is the third governor in the 1990s forced to resign because of a criminal conviction. The other two are Guy Hunt (R, Ala.) and Jim Guy Tucker (D, Ark.).	Officials at a marine-life observatory in the San Francisco, California, area report that the water surface there has warmed to 67°F (19.4°C), the highest temperature the observatory has measured since it began keeping records in 1958. The water's normal temperature is 50°F.		Sept. 3
The Supreme Court refuses to hear an emergency appeal of Proposition 209, the controversial anti-affirmative-action measure that officially went into effect Aug. 28.	The House passes, 375-49, a $12.3 billion appropriations bill for fiscal 1998 for foreign operations. It includes a controversial antiabortion provision.	Poultry producer Tyson Foods Inc. announces the acquisition of Hudson Foods Inc., which in August was forced to recall 25 million pounds (11 million kg) of ground beef in the largest meat recall in U.S. history, for $681.75 million in cash and Tyson stock.	Meteorological experts confirm that temperatures are warmer than normal in the Pacific Ocean.... Hans Jurgen Eysenck, 81, German-born behavioral psychologist known for his controversial theories of intelligence, dies in London, England, after suffering from a brain tumor.	MTV presents British funk band Jamiroquai with the award for best video of the year for "Virtual Insanity."... Aldo Rossi, 66, Italian architect who, in 1990, received the Pritzker Architecture Prize, dies in Milan, Italy, of injuries sustained in an car accident the previous week.	Sept. 4
				The International Olympic Committee picks Athens, Greece, as the host for the 2004 Olympics.... Sir Georg Solti (born Gyorgy Stern), 84, Hungarian-born conductor of the Chicago Symphony, 1969–91, dies in Antibes, France, after suffering a heart attack earlier.... Leon (Joseph) Edel, 89, literary critic and Pulitzer Prize–winning biographer, dies in Honolulu, Hawaii, of a heart attack.	Sept. 5
			Astronomers at California's Mount Palomar observatory discover two tiny moons orbiting the planet Uranus. The discovery brings to 17 the number of known moons of Uranus. The newly found moons have diameters of 50 miles and 100 miles (80 km and 160 km), respectively.... Russian cosmonaut Anatoly Solovyev and U.S. astronaut Mike Foale conduct a six-hour space walk to inspect damage done to *Mir* by the June collision.	The memorial service for Princess Diana is one of the most widely viewed broadcasts in TV history, with an estimated 2 billion viewers worldwide.	Sept. 6
George William Crockett Jr., 88, Democratic U.S. congressman from Michigan, judge and attorney known for his outspoken stands on civil rights, dies in Washington, D.C., of cancer.				In tennis, Martina Hingis of Switzerland wins the women's title at the U.S. Open, and Australia's Patrick Rafter wins the men's title.... Edgar Kaplan, 72, champion bridge player, dies in New York City of cancer.... Derek Wyn Taylor, 65, publicist for several 1960s rock groups, most notably the Beatles, dies in Suffolk, England, of esophagus cancer.	Sept. 7
	The Justice Department announces that it will drop federal criminal charges against Hani Abdel Rahim al-Sayegh, a Saudi Arabian man, in connection to the fatal 1996 truck bombing of a U.S. military complex near Dhahran, Saudi Arabia, because investigators cannot obtain sufficient evidence to prove Sayegh's guilt in a U.S. court of law	A jury in New Orleans, Louisiana, orders CSX Transportation and four other companies to pay $3.4 billion in punitive damages for a 1987 fire in a railroad car containing a hazardous chemical. It is the largest award ever against a railroad company.... The Clinton administration approves a bid to begin exploratory oil and gas drilling at a site in the Red Rock region of Utah, where Clinton established the Grand Staircase-Escalante National Monument in 1996.		James R. Phelan, 85, investigative journalist and author, dies in Temecula, California, of lung cancer.	Sept. 8
F	G	H	I	J	
Includes elections, federal-state relations, civil rights and liberties, crime, the judiciary, education, health care, poverty, urban affairs, and population.	*Includes formation and debate of U.S. foreign and defense policies, veterans' affairs, and defense spending. (Relations with specific foreign countries are usually found under the region concerned.)*	*Includes business, labor, agriculture, taxation, transportation, consumer affairs, monetary and fiscal policy, natural resources, and pollution.*	*Includes worldwide scientific, medical, and technological developments; natural phenomena; U.S. weather; natural disasters; and accidents.*	*Includes the arts, religion, scholarship, communications media, sports, entertainments, fashions, fads, and social life.*	

	World Affairs	Europe	Africa & the Middle East	The Americas	Asia & the Pacific
Sept. 9	The World Bank predicts that China, Russia, India, Brazil, and Indonesia, spurred by their size and potential for market integration, will emerge as economic powerhouses. It forecasts that, by the year 2020, those so-called Big Five nations' combined share of world output will grow to 16.1%, from 7.8% in 1992.	Russia and the separatist republic of Chechnya agree on terms to reopen an oil pipeline that stretches 93 miles (150 km) through the war-damaged region.	Sadako Ogata, the UN high commissioner for refugees, discloses that the agency is suspending its aid operations for the Rwandan refugees dispersed across Africa's Great Lakes region because of the host governments' failure to observe "the principles and standards of law."		Forty-nine of India's leading Hindu politicians are charged with inciting massive riots in Uttar Pradesh in 1992 in which hundreds of people died and a 16th-century Muslim mosque was destroyed. . . . The Chinese Communist Party's Central Committee announces that it has revoked the party membership of Chen Xitong, a long-time rival of Communist Party general secretary and Chinese president Jiang Zemin, and handed him over to prosecutors.
Sept. 10				Some 1,000 survivors of those killed in the Sept. 8 ferry disaster block Haiti's main highway to protest the delay in the recovery of the bodies, which are trapped in the hull of the sunken ship.	
Sept. 11		United Tajik Opposition (UTO) leader Said Abdullo Nuri returns to Dushan from Iran after five years in exile. . . . Voters in a referendum in Scotland overwhelmingly approve plans to form a 129-member Scottish parliament with control over most local and regional affairs. The vote is regarded as a major landmark in the history of Scotland, which has been under British control for centuries. . . . In Ploiesti, Romania, four officers are injured in rallies protesting the closing of 17 factories announced Aug. 7.		An unexpected rainstorm helps firefighters extinguish the blaze in Peru, which has burned some 1,500 acres (600 hectares) of forest around the Machu Picchu ruins, known as the Lost City of the Incas, in the Andes mountains.	Japanese premier Ryutaro Hashimoto names a new cabinet that includes Takayuki (Koko) Sato, 69, a convicted felon. . . . Fighting between Taliban forces and troops loyal to the displaced Afghanistan government continue north of Kabul.
Sept. 12				The leftist rebel Zapatista National Liberation Army (EZLN) holds a rally that draws tens of thousands of people in Mexico City, the capital of Mexico. The rally is the culmination of a journey that started Sept. 8 in the southern state of Chiapas, the rebels' stronghold.	
Sept. 13	Mother Teresa, a Nobel Peace Prize–winning Roman Catholic nun who spent nearly 70 years tending to thousands of the impoverished and ill in Calcutta, India, is given a state funeral and laid to rest in the courtyard of the convent she founded in 1952. Eulogies are delivered by representatives of seven faiths—Roman Catholicism, Protestantism, Sikhism, Islam, Hinduism, Buddhism, and Zoroastrianism. In attendance are dignitaries from 24 nations, including former Canadian p.m. Jean Chrétien, British deputy p.m. John Prescott, and Bangladeshi p.m. Sheikh Hasina Wazed.	Bosnia-Herzegovina holds internationally monitored municipal elections for 142 local councils. . . . Roger Frey, 84, French politician who served as minister of the interior under Pres. Charles de Gaulle, dies in Paris, France, of unreported causes.			
Sept. 14			Israeli prime minister Benjamin Netanyahu announces that he will release half the remaining PNA tax funds frozen by Israel after a suicide bombing in West Jerusalem in late July. As a further goodwill gesture, Israeli will ease restrictions placed on the movement of West Bank Palestinians.		At least 77 people die when a train derails while crossing a bridge in Madhya Pradesh state and several cars plunge into a river bed in central India. It is the 27th disaster on India's heavily traveled railway system since 1985.

A	B	C	D	E
Includes developments that affect more than one world region, international organizations, and important meetings of major world leaders.	Includes all domestic and regional developments in Europe, including the Soviet Union, Turkey, Cyprus, and Malta.	Includes all domestic and regional developments in Africa and the Middle East, including Iraq and Iran and excluding Cyprus, Turkey, and Afghanistan.	Includes all domestic and regional developments in Latin America, the Caribbean, and Canada.	Includes all domestic and regional developments in Asia and Pacific nations, extending from Afghanistan through all the Pacific Islands, except Hawaii.

U.S. Politics & Social Issues	U.S. Foreign Policy & Defense	U.S. Economy & Environment	Science, Technology, & Nature	Culture, Leisure, & Lifestyle	
An Oklahoma couple, Eugene K.H. Lum and Nora T. Lum, are sentenced to 10-month federal prison terms and a $30,000 fine each for using "straw donors" to funnel $50,000 to Democratic candidates in 1994 and 1995.		A coalition of trade and industry groups launch a $13 million advertising campaign aimed at deterring the Clinton administration from supporting a UN-sponsored global-warming treaty that will be discussed at a December conference in Kyoto, Japan.		Mario Lemieux is elected to the Hockey Hall of Fame.... Richie (Don Richard) Ashburn, 70, broadcaster and Hall of Fame baseball player, dies in New York City of a heart attack.... Burgess (Oliver) Meredith, 89, stage, film, and TV actor whose career spanned the 1930s to the 1990s, dies in Malibu, California, of unreported causes.	Sept. 9
		William S. Hussey, a Columbia/HCA Healthcare Corp. executive who supervised three managers indicted in July for Medicare fraud, resigns, although he has not been charged in the ongoing investigation of the firm.	Maryland governor Parris Glendening (D) orders the closure of King's Creek, a tributary to the Manokin River, after sick and dead fish are observed there.	George Louis Schaefer, 76, director and producer whose awards include a Tony, Pulitzer, Emmy, and four Directors Guild Awards, dies in Los Angeles after a long illness.	Sept. 10
In Miami, Florida, Judge Stanley Marcus rules that American Airlines Inc., a division of AMR Corp., is guilty of "willful misconduct" in a December 1995 crash near Cali, Colombia, that killed 159 people. It is the first time that such a ruling has been made before an airline has had a chance to present its case to a jury, and observers note that it sets a precedent that is potentially damaging for the airline industry.... The CDC releases new figures showing that the number of AIDS deaths in the U.S. has continued to decline. The AIDS mortality rate dropped 26%, to 11.6 per 100,000 people in 1996, from 15.6 per 100,000 in 1995.	Army officials at a Pentagon news conference release the findings of the largest-ever investigation of sexual misconduct within army ranks. The report, based on a survey of 30,000 army soldiers stationed worldwide, finds evidence of widespread sexual harassment and discrimination. It also faults the military's leadership and complaint procedure for allowing sexual improprieties to go on unacknowledged. The strongly worded document, compiled by a panel of nine senior officers, recommends 128 ways to improve gender relations within the U.S. Army.		The *Mars Global Surveyor* enters Mars's orbit to begin a two-year mission to study the planet's geology and atmosphere.		Sept. 11
Pres. Clinton nominates Dr. David Satcher, director of the federal CDC, to fill the post of surgeon general, which has been vacant for nearly three years.... Roger O(laf) Egeberg, 93, senior health official under Pres. Richard Nixon, dies in Washington, D.C., of pneumonia.			Maryland state environmental officials report that they have discovered in the Chicamacomico River thousands of fish afflicted with lesions typical of poisoning associated with exposure to the *Pfiesteria piscicida* microorganism. Virginia officials also disclose that they have discovered fish in the Rappahannock River that appear to be sickened by *Pfiesteria*.	Judith Merril, (born Juliet Grossman) 74, science fiction writer who was one of the first women to achieve popularity in the genre, dies in Toronto, Canada, of unreported causes.	Sept. 12
	An air force C-141 cargo plane carrying nine passengers disappears off the coast of Africa, near Namibia. The plane is believed to have crashed into a German military transport that disappeared at nearly the same time and place.			Elton John's recorded single "Candle in the Wind 1997," a version to commemorate Princess Diana, goes on sale in Britain. Some 250,000 copies sell within four hours, and a record 600,000 within a day.... Oscar De La Hoya wins a unanimous decision over Hector (Macho) Camacho to retain his WBC welterweight boxing title.	Sept. 13
	A U.S. Navy fighter plane crashes near Raysut, Oman, during a routine training exercise, killing the lone pilot.... An air force fighter loses part of its wing while performing at the Chesapeake Air Show. The plane crash injures four civilians; the pilot ejects unharmed. ... Wiliam Itoh, the U.S. ambassador in Thailand, dedicates a memorial to the 365 U.S. troops from World War II who died when their Japanese captors forced them to rebuild a railway bridge, an event made famous in the film *The Bridge on the River Kwai* (1957).		In response to the Sept. 12 reports, Maryland governor Parris Glendening (D) orders the closure of a six-mile-long stretch of the Chicamacomico River.	At the Emmys, *Law and Order* wins for best drama while *Frasier* wins for best comedy. The President's Award goes to *Miss Evers' Boys*.	Sept. 14

F	G	H	I	J
Includes elections, federal-state relations, civil rights and liberties, crime, the judiciary, education, health care, poverty, urban affairs, and population.	*Includes formation and debate of U.S. foreign and defense policies, veterans' affairs, and defense spending. (Relations with specific foreign countries are usually found under the region concerned.)*	*Includes business, labor, agriculture, taxation, transportation, consumer affairs, monetary and fiscal policy, natural resources, and pollution.*	*Includes worldwide scientific, medical, and technological developments; natural phenomena; U.S. weather; natural disasters; and accidents.*	*Includes the arts, religion, scholarship, communications media, sports, entertainments, fashions, fads, and social life.*

	World Affairs	Europe	Africa & the Middle East	The Americas	Asia & the Pacific
Sept. 15		Sinn Fein, the political wing of the Provisional Irish Republican Army (IRA), takes part for the first time ever in broad-based, multiparty peace talks aimed at achieving peace in Northern Ireland.... Norway's right-wing parties register significant gains in elections for members of the Storting, the country's parliament.... U.S. paratroopers begin a weeklong peacekeeping exercise in Kazakhstan.		In Peru, separate courts reaffirm the revocation of Baruch Ivcher Bronstein's citizenship and strip him of control of a TV station that had aired reports critical of the government.	
Sept. 16	The UN opens its 52nd General Assembly. The delegates elect Hennady Udovenko, Ukraine's foreign minister, to the office of president of the General Assembly.... Due to a haze caused by hundreds of raging forest fires in Indonesia that blots out much of the sunlight in Indonesia, Malaysia, Singapore, the Philippines, Brunei, and southern Thailand, Indonesian president Suharto apologizes to those countries for the crisis.	A large bomb explodes in a parked van in Markethill, a predominantly Protestant town southwest of Belfast in County Armagh, Northern Ireland.			Vietnam's Communist Party Central Committee closes a conference during which they named Tran Duc Luong to replace 77-year-old Le Duc Anh, who is in failing health, as president. The party selected Phan Van Khai to succeed Vo Van Kiet, 74, as premier.
Sept. 17	Delegates from 89 countries approve a treaty to ban the use, production, transfer, and stockpiling of antipersonnel land mines. Some nations do not sign, including the U.S., Russia, China, India, Pakistan, Iran, and Iraq.... Russia joins the Paris Club of 18 creditor nations.... The IMF, in its semiannual World Economic Outlook, projects that Canada, followed by the U.S. and Britain, will lead the G-7 countries in growth in 1997. The IMF reports that world growth in 1996 was 4.1% and projects that will be 4.2% in 1997 and 4.3% in 1998.	A helicopter crash near the town of Bugojno in central Bosnia claims the lives of 12 passengers, including Gerd Wagner, a deputy to Carlos Westendorp, the international community's representative in Bosnia. The four Ukrainians who crew the Russian-made aircraft escape alive.... A Macedonian court sentences Rufi Osmani, mayor of Gostivar, to almost 14 years in jail for inciting protests on July 9 that caused a riot in which three people died.	Settlers in the 17 Ras al-Amud neighborhood of Arab East Jerusalem refuse to leave the premises, prompting some 300 Palestinian protesters to demonstrate at the site.		
Sept. 18	Delegates from 89 countries formally adopt a treaty to ban the use, production, transfer, and stockpiling of antipersonnel land mines.	Two convicted murderers are publicly executed by firing squad in the separatist republic of Chechnya.... Fifty people are injured when a car bomb explodes in Croat-controlled West Mostar. It is believed to be the largest explosion in Bosnia-Herzegovina since 1995.... In a referendum, Welsh voters narrowly approve plans to create a 60-member Welsh assembly that will control some decisions concerning government spending in Wales.	At least two men attack a tourist bus with gunfire and gasoline bombs in downtown Cairo, the Egyptian capital, killing nine German passengers and the bus's Egyptian driver. The assault is the first deadly attack on foreign tourists in Egypt since April 1996. Some 20 other people are wounded. Egyptian officials identify the assailants and state that the attack was not politically motivated.... A crisis that threatened to erupt in violence is defused when an agreement is reached with Israeli officials and Jewish settlers in disputed residence in two homes in the Ras al-Amud neighborhood of Arab East Jerusalem.		Prosecutors in Tokyo, Japan's capital, and officials of the Securities and Exchange Surveillance Commission (SESC) raid the offices of Daiwa, Japan's second-largest brokerage house, and homes of Daiwa executives.... Ganesh Man Singh, 81, leader of Nepal's 1990 prodemocracy movement, dies in Katmandu, Nepal, of a heart attack.
Sept. 19		A crowded passenger train collides with a freight train in West London, killing six people and injuring more than 170 others. It is the worst rail crash in Britain since 1988.	A policeman is killed and three others are wounded in separate shooting attacks in southern Egypt.	Progovernment minority shareholders of the Frecuencia Latina television station in Lima, the capital of Peru, seize control of the station. The government in July revoked the citizenship of the Israeli-born majority owner, Baruch Ivcher Bronstein, in a move that observers call a retaliation for reports critical of the government.	
Sept. 20		Reports confirm that Russian president Boris Yeltsin plans to export part of Russia's 1997 grain harvest. It will be the first grain exported from Russia in 50 years.... The Continuity Army Council, an extremist republican group that split off from the IRA, claims responsibility for two bombing attacks that have threatened to derail the Northern Ireland peace process. The first bomb was discovered and defused in July; the second exploded Sept. 16 in Markethill.			

A	B	C	D	E
Includes developments that affect more than one world region, international organizations, and important meetings of major world leaders.	*Includes all domestic and regional developments in Europe, including the Soviet Union, Turkey, Cyprus, and Malta.*	*Includes all domestic and regional developments in Africa and the Middle East, including Iraq and Iran and excluding Cyprus, Turkey, and Afghanistan.*	*Includes all domestic and regional developments in Latin America, the Caribbean, and Canada.*	*Includes all domestic and regional developments in Asia and Pacific nations, extending from Afghanistan through all the Pacific Islands, except Hawaii.*

U.S. Politics & Social Issues	U.S. Foreign Policy & Defense	U.S. Economy & Environment	Science, Technology, & Nature	Culture, Leisure, & Lifestyle	
	Former Massachusetts governor William F. Weld (R) abandons his bid to become ambassador to Mexico, ending a five-month-long showdown with Senate Foreign Relations Committee chairman Jesse Helms (R, N.C.), who refused to hold a confirmation hearing for Weld's appointment.... A Marine Corps F/A-18 fighter crashes off the coast of North Carolina, killing its two-man crew.	Pres. Clinton announces plans to impose new federal regulations designed to curb Medicare fraud.	A 370-pound (170-kg) U.S. military satellite comes within 500 to 1,000 feet (150 to 300 m) of crashing into *Mir*.... Two pharmaceutical companies announce that they will remove the appetite suppressants fenfluramine and dexfenfluramine from the market due to evidence that the drugs can cause serious heart ailments.... Scientists in two studies report they have observed the parthenogenesis, or birth without mating, of male offspring to snakes.	Raymond L. Flynn announces his resignation as ambassador to the Vatican, a post he has held since 1993. Pres. Clinton nominates Lindy (Corinne C.) Boggs as his successor.	Sept. 15
	The Senate, by voice vote, confirms Gen. Henry (Hugh) Shelton as chairman of the Joint Chiefs of Staff. He is the first commander of U.S. Special Operations ever to head the joint chiefs.... The House, approves, 413-12, a $9.183 billion appropriations bill for military construction in the 1998 fiscal year. ... Two Air National Guard fighter jets collide in midair off the coast of Atlantic City, New Jersey, during a night training exercise.	The Dow closes at 7895.92, up 174.78 points, or 2.3%, the fifth-highest single-session point gain in the history of the Dow.	A team of researchers reports evidence that young broccoli seedlings contain high concentrations of chemicals known to stimulate the body's resistance to cancer.	William N. Oatis, 83, Associated Press (AP) reporter who was imprisoned in Czechoslovakia during the cold war, dies in New York City after a long illness.	Sept. 16
	The Department of Defense, responding to a series of recent accidents involving military aircraft, orders all branches of the armed services to suspend their training flights for 24 hours and review aviation safety methods. It is the first time that each branch of the armed forces is simultaneously ordered to halt their flights.... The Senate clears, 97-3, a $9.183 billion fiscal 1998 spending bill for military construction.	The Interior Department reports that nearly 1.2 million acres (500,000 hectares) of wetlands were lost between 1985 and 1995, despite legislative efforts to protect the vulnerable ecosystems. The report notes, however, that the loss is just over a third of the wetlands loss suffered in the previous decade.		Comedian Martin Lawrence is sentenced to community service and two years' probation on a battery charge.... Red (Richard Bernard) Skelton, 84, comedian and actor who hosted popular radio and TV comedy programs and was inducted into the Academy of Television Arts and Sciences Hall of Fame in 1989, dies in Rancho Mirage, California.	Sept. 17
The CDC reports that the number of new AIDS cases in the U.S. dropped for the first time in the epidemic's 16-year history when they fell by 6%... The House votes, 258-154, to adopt new ethics rules in the wake of an inquiry involving Speaker Newt Gingrich (R, Ga.).... The FBI reports that agents recovered most of the $18.8 million stolen in March from a vault at Loomis, Fargo and Co. The heist was the largest of its kind in U.S. history.		Three people who worked as campaign officials for the December election of Ronald Carey as president of the International Brotherhood of the Teamsters plead guilty in federal court in New York City to conspiracy charges for their involvement in the illegal fund-raising scheme.... Accounting firms Coopers & Lybrand and Price Waterhouse & Co. announce that they will merge to form the world's largest accounting and consulting firm. The merged firm will have 8,600 partners and some $12 billion in global revenue annually.	Governors George Allen (R, Va.) and Parris Glendening (D, Md.) state that they will coordinate efforts to fight the outbreaks of the *Pfiesteria piscicida* microorganism that has infected fish in rivers.	Jimmy Witherspoon, 74, blues and jazz singer known for his deep voice and shouting vocal delivery, dies in Los Angeles.	Sept. 18
	An air force B-1 bomber on a training mission crashes in southeast Montana, killing its four-person crew.	The Senate confirms Pres. Clinton's nomination of Kenneth S. Apfel, a White House adviser on social security issues, as social security commissioner.	Scientists reveal they have found a ring of 11 earthen mounds in Louisiana to be the oldest such complex in the Americas. Construction of the mounds, at a site called Watson Brake near Monroe, is determined to have begun about 5,400 years ago, predating by 1,900 years the mounds previously known as the oldest, at Poverty Point, Louisiana.	The daughter of Pres. Clinton and First Lady Hillary Rodham Clinton, Chelsea Clinton, arrives with her parents at Stanford University in Palo Alto, California, to begin her college orientation.	Sept. 19
		Amid Senate hearings regarding campaign finances, the Justice Department announces that it has begun an initial inquiry into Pres. Clinton's efforts to solicit contributions for his 1996 reelection campaign and for the Democratic National Committee.			Sept. 20

F	G	H	I	J
Includes elections, federal-state relations, civil rights and liberties, crime, the judiciary, education, health care, poverty, urban affairs, and population.	*Includes formation and debate of U.S. foreign and defense policies, veterans' affairs, and defense spending. (Relations with specific foreign countries are usually found under the region concerned.)*	*Includes business, labor, agriculture, taxation, transportation, consumer affairs, monetary and fiscal policy, natural resources, and pollution.*	*Includes worldwide scientific, medical, and technological developments; natural phenomena; U.S. weather; natural disasters; and accidents.*	*Includes the arts, religion, scholarship, communications media, sports, entertainments, fashions, fads, and social life.*

	World Affairs	Europe	Africa & the Middle East	The Americas	Asia & the Pacific
Sept. 21		In parliamentary elections for Serbia, which is part of Yugoslavia, along with Montenegro, the Socialist Party and its left-wing allies, led by Yugoslav president Slobodan Milosevic, takes 110 seats, not enough for a majority in the 250-seat body.... Poland's voters give the 36-party anticommunist Solidarity Electoral Action (AWS) coalition a victory in elections to the Sejm, Poland's parliament.			Hundreds of thousands of Filipinos gather in Luneta Park in Manila, the Philippine capital, to voice their opposition to Pres. Fidel Ramos's recent moves to seek reelection to the presidency after his current term ends in May 1998.
Sept. 22		Reports confirm that Polish prosecutors have cleared Col. Ryszard Kuklinski, who served as spy for the CIA until November 1981, was convicted in 1984 in absentia, and sentenced to death..... Viscount Tonypandy, (born Thomas George Thomas) 88, Welsh-born parliamentarian who served as speaker of the British House of Commons, 1976–83, dies in Cardiff, Wales, of unreported causes.	In Algeria, a band of armed men slaughter as many 200 people and wound as many as 100 others in the Bentalha neighborhood of Baraki, a suburb of Algiers, the capital.... Two Israeli embassy security guards suffer gunfire wounds in a drive-by attack in the Jordanian capital, Amman. Abdul Aziz al-Rantisi, a Gaza Strip-based political leader of Hamas, insists that "this attack was not carried out by our movement."	The government of Bolivia declares a formal state of emergency after the manifestations of the El Nino weather system caused three deaths across the country.... Former army chief Gen. Lino César Oviedo, who in 1996 caused a constitutional crisis by defying Pres. Juan Carlos Wasmosy's order to step down, is named the winner of the ruling Colorado Party's primary for Paraguay's May 1998 presidential elections.	Shoichi Yokoi, 82, Japanese soldier who, rather than surrender to U.S. forces during World War II, hid in the jungles of Guam for 27 years, dies in Nagoya, Japan, of a heart attack.
Sept. 23	The IMF and the World Bank, its sister organization, hold the annual joint plenary session of their boards of governors.	More than 10,000 Turkish troops supported by 100 tanks and numerous war planes cross into northern Iraq to renew Turkey's military offensive against PKK guerrillas seeking to establish a separate Kurdish entity in Turkey.... Irish rock group U2 performs a benefit concert in front of some 45,000 Bosnians at the newly rebuilt Kosevo Stadium in Sarajevo, the capital of Bosnia-Herzegovina. The concert is the city's most widely attended entertainment event since the 1984 Winter Olympic Games.		Canadian prime minister Jean Chrétien announces four appointments to fill vacancies in the Senate, the upper house of Canada's Parliament, which will increase the Liberals' standing in the unelected chamber to 52 members.	Officials from Japan and the U.S. announce that they have approved a new cooperative regional security agreement.... Ne Win, a hard-line military leader who had ruled Myanmar from 1962 until 1988 and still exercises significant influence over the junta leaders, visits Indonesia in his first public appearance since 1989.
Sept. 24	Due to a haze caused by hundreds of raging forest fires in Indonesia that blots out much sunlight in Indonesia, Malaysia, Singapore, Brunei, the Philippines, and southern Thailand, the U.S. and Canada authorize partial evacuations of their embassies in Kuala Lumpur, Malaysia's capital. The haze, which has forced the closure of schools and caused respiratory ailments in tens of thousands of people, is widely called the worst ecological disaster on record in Southeast Asia.	Two Basque separatist guerrillas—Salvador Gaztelumendi Gil and Jose-Miguel Bustinza—are killed in a gun battle with police in downtown Bilbao, a city in Spain's north-central Basque region. The rebels are members of ETA, the main Basque guerrilla group.	Israeli prime minister Benjamin Netanyahu declares that his government will build 300 new homes at the West Bank settlement of Efrat, just south of the Palestinian town of Bethlehem.... In Algeria, Madani Mezerag, the commander of the Army of Islamic Salvation, the military wing of the FIS, declares a cease-fire as of Oct. 1.		Indonesian officials state that, in addition to the deaths related to the haze caused by hundreds of fires, some 271 people in the Irian Jaya region have died from famine and disease.... Australian prime minister John Howard announces the resignations of Transportation Minister John Sharp and Administrative Services Minister David Jull for alleged travel expense improprieties amid one of the most devastating scandals faced by an Australian prime minister in 20 years.
Sept. 25	The International Court of Justice rules that both Slovakia and Hungary have violated a 1977 treaty in which they agreed to build two hydroelectric dams using water from the Danube River, which divides the countries, but only one dam was ever built, at Gabcikovo, Slovakia.... The OAS amends its charter to condemn governments that come to power through a coup.	The Press Complaints Commission releases guidelines designed to prevent paparazzi, or free-lance photographers, from aggressively and intrusively pursuing public figures. The move is prompted largely by Princess Diana's Aug. 31 car accident in France.	Two operatives of Israel's foreign spy agency Mossad attempt to assassinate Khaled Meshal, the Jordanian-based political leader of Hamas. The act draws international condemnation, and Jordan's King Hussein is reportedly outraged that the incident is perpetrated on Jordanian soil.	A judge in the northern city of Tijuana, Mexico, frees former federal police agent Ricardo Cordero Ontiveros, who was jailed in 1996 after exposing drug corruption in Mexican law enforcement.	Former Indian prime minister P. V. Narasimha Rao is formally charged with corruption and bribery in connection with an alleged 1993 vote-buying scheme. Rao is India's first former head of state to face trial on criminal charges.... Due to the ecological crisis over Indonesia, Malaysia sends more than 1,000 firefighters to help fight the forest fires, and the World Bank and several Southeast Asian nations offer various forms of assistance.
Sept. 26	Foreign ministers from NATO's 16 member countries and Russia hold the first meeting of the NATO-Russia Permanent Joint Council.... The U.S. and Russia agree to delay implementation of the Strategic Arms Reduction Treaty (START II) for four years. Representatives of the U.S., Belarus, Kazakhstan, Russia, and Ukraine sign an accord to modify the 1972 Antiballistic Missile (ABM) Treaty.... French president Jacques Chirac confirms that France, like Russia, the U.S., and Britain, no longer keeps its nuclear missiles aimed at specific targets.	Russian president Boris Yeltsin signs a bill that will restrict religious practice in Russia.... At least 11 people are killed and more than 120 injured when two earthquakes strike Italy. Separately, a seven-judge panel in Italy convicts and sentences 24 leading figures in the Cosa Nostra, the Sicilian mafia.... A court in Dusseldorf, Germany, convicts Nikola Jorgic of war crimes offenses in Bosnia and sentences him to life in prison. The UN international war crimes tribunal, citing a heavy case load, asked Germany to try Jorgic.			A jet crash in Indonesia kills 234 people. The crash is the most deadly air disaster in Indonesia's history. Separately, a supertanker collides with an Indian cargo vessel in the Strait of Malacca, killing 29 people. The accidents may be caused by the haze over Indonesia due to fires.... Hong Kong announces that schools using English as their teaching language will be required to switch to Cantonese in 1998.... Hundreds of workers take to the streets of Bangkok, Thailand's capital, in support of the proposed constitution.

A	B	C	D	E
Includes developments that affect more than one world region, international organizations, and important meetings of major world leaders.	*Includes all domestic and regional developments in Europe, including the Soviet Union, Turkey, Cyprus, and Malta.*	*Includes all domestic and regional developments in Africa and the Middle East, including Iraq and Iran and excluding Cyprus, Turkey, and Afghanistan.*	*Includes all domestic and regional developments in Latin America, the Caribbean, and Canada.*	*Includes all domestic and regional developments in Asia and Pacific nations, extending from Afghanistan through all the Pacific Islands, except Hawaii.*

U.S. Politics & Social Issues	U.S. Foreign Policy & Defense	U.S. Economy & Environment	Science, Technology, & Nature	Culture, Leisure, & Lifestyle	
	Timothy Wadsworth Stanley, 69, who, from the 1950s to the 1970s, held key defense posts under a succession of U.S. presidents, dies in Washington, D.C., of pancreatic cancer.	The Federal Highway Administration finds that the number of cars on U.S. roads between 1969 and 1995 grew six times faster than the U.S. population. The report notes that there were 176 million vehicles in the U.S. in 1995, up 144% from 1969 levels. Just 7.9% of all households had no vehicle, down from 20.1% in 1969.			Sept. 21
In Roby, Illinois, Shirley Allen starts a standoff with authorities when she refuses to go with sheriff's deputies and her brother, Byron Dugger, for a court-ordered mental evaluation. . . . In Chicago, Illinois, U.S. district judge Ruben Castillo announces that families of 27 victims of a 1994 Indiana air crash settled with the carrier and manufacturer to receive a total of $110 million.		In Philadelphia, Pennsylvania, U.S. district judge Edmund Ludwig sentences John Bennett Jr. to 12 years in prison for defrauding charity organizations of millions of dollars. . . . The FEC shows that the Republicans raised $21.7 million in the first six months of 1997, while Democrats raised $13.7 million. By comparison, the GOP raised $16.6 million, while the Democrats raised $10.8 million over the same period in 1995.	The Albert and Mary Lasker Foundation presents its Medical Research Awards to Dr. Alfred Sommer and Dr. Mark S. Ptashne. Dr. Victor A. McKusick receives a special achievement award for his role in the NIH's Human Genome Project. . . . Mir's aging computer breaks down for the fifth time in two months. NASA officials announce that the spacecraft Atlantis will deliver a new computer to Mir.	Forbes magazine places Steven Spielberg at the top of its annual list of the world's highest-paid entertainers, with an estimated earning of $313 million for 1996 and 1997.	Sept. 22
		The Senate opens hearings into alleged abuses by tax collectors and mismanagement at the IRS. . . . Smith Barney Inc. agrees to pay $5.1 million to settle an SEC charge tied to a Dade County, Florida, municipal bond issue. . . . The Forest Service imposes a ban on future oil and gas leasing along the Rocky Mountain Front in Montana, protecting a 100-mile-long stretch of land that runs along the eastern edge of the Lewis and Clark National Forest and borders the southern tip of Glacier National Park.		A speaker for IBM announces that the Deep Blue chess computer, which made headlines in May when it defeated chess grandmaster Garry Kasparov, has been retired. . . . Shirley Clarke, 72, Academy Award-winning filmmaker, dies in Boston, Massachusetts, after suffering a stroke two weeks earlier.	Sept. 23
The College Board reports that tuition at public and private four-year universities for the 1997–98 academic year rose by 5% over the previous year. That increase compares with a 2.5% rise in inflation in 1996. The average yearly tuition at a four-year private university is currently $13,664; at four-year public schools, the annual cost is $3,111.	Robert Lipka, 51, a former Army clerk at the NSA who pled guilty in May to selling secrets to the Soviet Union in the 1960s, is sentenced in Philadelphia, Pennsylvania, to 18 years in prison for conspiracy to commit espionage.	The House, 309-107, and the Senate, 90-10, approve a fiscal 1998 spending bill allocating $2.25 billion for the legislative branch, a 2% increase over fiscal 1997 spending levels.	The Senate votes, 98-2, to pass legislation that will allow the FDA to approve new drugs and medical devices more quickly.	Data shows that "Candle in the Wind 1997," a song that British singer Elton John adapted as a tribute to Princess Diana, has sold a record 8 million copies in its initial U.S. shipment.	Sept. 24
President Clinton attends a ceremony in Little Rock, Arkansas, marking the 40th anniversary of the integration of public schools when nine black students entered Little Rock's Central High School under a military escort amid threats and taunts from white citizens. The state and local chapters of the NAACP boycott the ceremony, asserting that little progress has been made in race relations in the 40 years since then.	The House, 356-65, and the Senate, 93-5, vote to approve a $247.7 billion defense spending bill for fiscal 1998. . . . The U.S. military's Southern Command, which coordinates U.S. military operations in Latin America and the Caribbean, closes its headquarters in Panama after 80 years in the country. The Southern Command will move to Miami, Florida.		The space shuttle Atlantis lifts off from Kennedy Space Center in Cape Canaveral, Florida, to deliver essential supplies to the Russian Mir space station and to assist with repairs to the beleaguered craft.	Reports state that the FBI has released all but 10 pages of its 300-page surveillance file on deceased rock singer John Lennon. . . . In the middle of a highly publicized criminal trial, sportscaster Marv Albert pleads guilty in Arlington, Virginia, to assaulting a woman in February during a sexual encounter.	Sept. 25
		The U.S. Senate, prompted by an ongoing scandal over Democratic fund-raising activities during the 1996 election cycle, opens debate on legislation to revamp the nation's campaign-finance laws.			Sept. 26

F	G	H	I	J
Includes elections, federal-state relations, civil rights and liberties, crime, the judiciary, education, health care, poverty, urban affairs, and population.	Includes formation and debate of U.S. foreign and defense policies, veterans' affairs, and defense spending. (Relations with specific foreign countries are usually found under the region concerned.)	Includes business, labor, agriculture, taxation, transportation, consumer affairs, monetary and fiscal policy, natural resources, and pollution.	Includes worldwide scientific, medical, and technological developments; natural phenomena; U.S. weather; natural disasters; and accidents.	Includes the arts, religion, scholarship, communications media, sports, entertainments, fashions, fads, and social life.

	World Affairs	Europe	Africa & the Middle East	The Americas	Asia & the Pacific
Sept. 27			In Algeria, eight armed men shoot and slash to death 11 female schoolteachers and one male instructor at the Ain Adden School in Sfisef, a village located 260 miles (420 km) south of Algiers. . . . Bantu Holomisa and Roelf Meyer, former political rivals, announce the formation of a new multiracial political party, the United Democratic Movement, in South Africa.		The Thai parliament approves a new constitution aimed at reforming Thailand's political system and electoral process. . . . Reports confirm that at least 35,000 Indonesians and 16,000 Malaysians have been treated for smoke inhalation and respiratory ailments due to the haze caused by forest fires. The smoke is also cited as the cause of five deaths in Indonesia.
Sept. 28		Voters in a referendum in Switzerland overwhelmingly reject a curtailment of the government's liberal drug policies, including a program that distributes heroin to addicts at state-run clinics.	Israel's Histadrut labor federation stages a one-day strike involving about 500,000 workers to protest economic policies.	An estimated 600,000 Protestants gather for an outdoor religious rally in Sao Paulo, prompting the Catholic clergy in Brazil to express concern over the increasing popularity of Protestant faiths in Brazil.	Reports reveal that Indonesian president Suharto has ordered some 50,000 soldiers to assist the firefighting efforts. . . . Hong Kong's provisional legislature passes a law severely limiting the number of people eligible to vote for two-thirds of the seats in a new legislative council.
Sept. 29		Turkey carries out air raids against Kurdish rebels inside northern Iraq as part of a continuing Turkish air and ground operation against Iraq-based guerrillas of the Kurdistan Workers Party (PKK), which seeks to establish Kurdish self-rule in southeastern Turkey.	Iranian war planes cross into Iraqi air space and strike two outposts of an Iraq-based Iranian opposition group.	A fire in a Colima, Chile, home for the mentally handicapped kills 30 residents.	In Singapore, a High Court judge awards damages of S$20,000 (US$13,150) to P.M. Goh Chok Tong in a libel suit against J. B. Jeyaretnam, leader of the opposition Workers Party. The suit is one of eight brought by members of Goh's People's Action Party (PAP) against Jeyaretnam.
Sept. 30	Reports reveal that the effects of the El Nino weather system are impacting Latin America, South America, and the Caribbean. The weather patterns range from heavy rains and floods in Peru, Brazil, Venezuela, Colombia, Ecuador, Chile, and Bolivia to droughts in Mexico, Guatemala, Honduras, El Salvador, and Nicaragua. Floods have caused the declaration of a state of emergency in 14 departments in Peru.	A coalition of the Socialist Party and the Serbian Renewal Movement forces Zoran Djindjic from his post as mayor of Belgrade, which he took in February. Police loyal to Pres. Slobodan Milosevic break up a demonstration of 20,000 protesters in Belgrade who are denouncing Djindjic's ouster. . . . In what is considered its most forthright and unequivocal acknowledgment of remorse, the Roman Catholic Church in France issues a formal apology to Jews for the church's silence during the holocaust.			At least 15 people are killed and more than 30 others are wounded by artillery fire in Kashmir when a hospital and mosque are hit by fire that Indian officials allege comes from Pakistani troops stationed in the disputed area. The attack is the most deadly on a civilian target in India in recent years.
Oct. 1	NATO defense ministers agree that the alliance should maintain some military presence in Bosnia-Herzegovina beyond the scheduled pullout of peacekeeping troops in June 1998.	SFOR troops, led by NATO, seize four TV transmitters located in the Serb part of Bosnia-Herzegovina to halt broadcasts that NATO leaders describe as inflammatory. . . . Serb police in Pristina, the capital of the Kosovo region, spray tear gas and beat protesters with clubs to break up a rally of 20,000 ethnic Albanian students calling for Albanian-language education at Pristina University.	Israel frees Hamas spiritual leader Sheik Ahmed Yassin from a life sentence.		The government announces presidential pardons for seven conglomerate executives found guilty in 1996 of bribing former president Roh Tae Woo. The executives are given suspended sentences.
Oct. 2	EU nations sign the Treaty of Amsterdam, an updated version of the 1992 Maastricht pact, which introduced greater economic unity to the EU and contained provisions for the admittance of new members.		In Kharrouba, a village more than 200 miles west of Algiers, 20 people are killed when armed men storm a wedding ceremony.	Gen. Manuel Jose Bonett, the head of Colombia's armed forces, emerges unharmed from a bomb attack on the car he was riding in near the city of Santa Marta. One civilian dies in the incident. . . . Pope John Paul II begins a tour of Brazil to preside over the Second Annual Conference on Families.	A bomb explodes during a Hindu religious procession in New Delhi, India, wounding 27 people. . . . South Korea suspends the import of beef from the U.S. state of Nebraska after detecting a strain of E. coli bacteria in a shipment of frozen beef from U.S. meatpacker IBP Inc.

A	B	C	D	E
Includes developments that affect more than one world region, international organizations, and important meetings of major world leaders.	*Includes all domestic and regional developments in Europe, including the Soviet Union, Turkey, Cyprus, and Malta.*	*Includes all domestic and regional developments in Africa and the Middle East, including Iraq and Iran and excluding Cyprus, Turkey, and Afghanistan.*	*Includes all domestic and regional developments in Latin America, the Caribbean, and Canada.*	*Includes all domestic and regional developments in Asia and Pacific nations, extending from Afghanistan through all the Pacific Islands, except Hawaii.*

U.S. Politics & Social Issues	U.S. Foreign Policy & Defense	U.S. Economy & Environment	Science, Technology, & Nature	Culture, Leisure, & Lifestyle	
			The spacecraft *Atlantis* successfully docks at the *Mir* space station.	Singer Bob Dylan perform for an estimated 250,000 spectators, including Pope John Paul II, at the World Eucharistic Congress in Bologna, Italy.	Sept. 27
			Wildfires in the area near the Sierra Nevada mountains in northern California force the evacuation of some 1,000 residents.	Veteran TV news commentator David Brinkley retires from broadcasting after 54 years when he gives his final commentary on ABC's *This Week*. . . . A European team of golfers in Spain defeats a U.S. team to retain the Ryder Cup.	Sept. 28
	The House passes, 355-57, a bill that effectively issues a three-week reprieve of a strict new policy on illegal immigration contained in a September 1996 immigration law. The reprieve, which lasts until Oct. 23, is part of a larger measure providing funding for federal agencies for the start of fiscal 1998, which begins Oct. 1.	The House, 355-57, passes a stopgap measure to maintain federal spending at fiscal 1997 levels for all programs and agencies until Congress finishes its work on the budget. . . . The Census Bureau reports that the median household income in the U.S. rose for the second consecutive year in 1996, while the number of people living in poverty remained about the same.		Pres. Clinton, confers the National Medal of Arts and National Humanities Medal on 20 cultural figures and one arts organization. . . . Roy Lichtenstein, 73, American painter who was a seminal figure in the 1960s Pop Art movement, dies in New York City of complications from pneumonia.	Sept. 29
Scott Krueger, an 18-year-old pledge at Phi Gamma Delta fraternity at MIT, dies of alcohol poisoning following a drinking binge three days earlier. He reportedly had a blood alcohol level of 0.41%— more than five times Massachusetts's legal limit for driving. The case sparks attention about drinking and fraternity hazing at universities and colleges.	Pres. Clinton signs a $9.183 billion appropriations bill for military construction in the 1998 fiscal year. . . . The Senate, 99-0, passes a bill that effectively issues a three-week reprieve of a strict new policy on illegal immigration when it clears a measure providing funding for federal agencies for the start of fiscal 1998, which begins Oct. 1.	The CBO reveals that the four main independent counsel investigations launched against Pres. Clinton and members of his administration cost a total of more than $44 million as of Mar. 31. . . . The Senate passes, 99-0, and Pres. Clinton signs a stopgap measure. . . . The House, 404-17, and the Senate, 99-0, clear the final version of the fiscal 1998 energy and water appropriations bill. . . The House, 220-207, passes a fiscal 1998 spending bill allocating $25.6 billion to fund the Treasury Department, the U.S. Postal Service, the White House, and other government costs.	Fire officials disclose that 83 homes and 65 barn and storage buildings were destroyed in the fires reported Sept. 28. . . . A statement signed by 1,500 scientists, 102 of whom are Nobel laureates, urges governments to support an upcoming UN conference on environmental issues to be held in December in Kyoto, Japan. . . . British scientists unveil the most compelling evidence yet that mad-cow disease (BSE) can be transferred to humans, and that it is related to Creutzfeldt-Jakob disease.	The U.S. Catholic Conference of Bishops' committee on marriage and family attempt to provide spiritual guidance to the parents of homosexual children and urge parents not to reject their sons or daughters on the basis of their sexual orientation.	Sept. 30
The Senate Rules and Administration Committee votes to end an inquiry into the November 1996 election of Sen. Mary Landrieu (D, La.), reporting that it found no evidence of systematic vote fraud that may have affected the outcome of the race. . . . Luke Woodham, 16, kills his mother at home and two other people at Pearl High School in Pearl, Mississippi Seven other students are wounded, and police take Woodham into custody.		The Senate clears, 55-45, a fiscal 1998 spending bill allocating $25.6 billion to fund the Treasury Department, the U.S. Postal Service, the White House, and other government costs. For the first time in five years, the annual spending bill does not contain a provision blocking congressional pay raises. . . . Union Pacific Railroad Co. announces plans to ease unprecedented congestion on the 36,700 miles (60,000 km) of railroad operated by the company.		Gul Mohammed, 40, the world's shortest man with a height of 22.5 inches (57 cm), dies in New Delhi, India, of a heart attack.	Oct. 1
Attorney General Janet Reno reveals that the annual juvenile arrest rate for violent crime declined for the second consecutive year in 1996. Juvenile arrests fell 9.2% in 1996 to 464.7 per 100,000 youths from 511.9 per 100,000 in 1995.				Figures show that that "Candle in the Wind 1997," a song that British singer Elton John adapted as a tribute to Princess Diana, sold 3.45 million copies in the U.S. in six days, shattering the previous record of 632,000 copies in the same period set in 1992.	Oct. 2

F	G	H	I	J
Includes elections, federal-state relations, civil rights and liberties, crime, the judiciary, education, health care, poverty, urban affairs, and population.	Includes formation and debate of U.S. foreign and defense policies, veterans' affairs, and defense spending. (Relations with specific foreign countries are usually found under the region concerned.)	Includes business, labor, agriculture, taxation, transportation, consumer affairs, monetary and fiscal policy, natural resources, and pollution.	Includes worldwide scientific, medical, and technological developments; natural phenomena; U.S. weather; natural disasters; and accidents.	Includes the arts, religion, scholarship, communications media, sports, entertainments, fashions, fads, and social life.

	World Affairs	Europe	Africa & the Middle East	The Americas	Asia & the Pacific
Oct. 3		An earthquake hits central Italy, injuring at least 20 people. The tremor, which measures 5.1 on the Richter scale, damages the renowned Basilica of St. Francis in Assisi, which was badly damaged by two earthquakes in late September.... A(lfred) L(eslie) Rowse, 93, controversial British scholar of Shakespeare and Elizabethan history, dies in St. Austell.... George Urban, 76, Hungarian-born scholar who served as director of both Radio Free Europe (RFE) and Britain's Centre for Policy Studies, dies of unreported causes.	In Algeria, several schools and apartment buildings in Blida, 30 miles south of Algiers, are bombed with explosives. According to hospital estimates, five people are killed and 30 others are injured. Assailants murder 26 adults and 12 children in Mahelma, a village near Blida. Attackers take the lives of 37 people, many of them children, in a massacre in the village of Ouled Benaissa, 30 miles south of Blida.	Paraguayan president Juan Carlos Wasmosy orders the arrest of Lino Cesar Oviedo, the ruling Colorado Party's candidate in the May 1998 presidential election who is considered Wasmosy's likely successor. ... In Mexico City, Mexico, 19 members of an elite police force known as the Jaguares, or Jaguars, are arraigned in connection with the September murders of six youths after their arrests.	The Indian government bans the Bodoland Liberation Tigers Front, a militant separatist group in the northern state of Assam.
Oct. 4		Around 700 passengers and crew members are rescued from a cruise ship that has caught fire in the Mediterranean Sea some 60 miles (95 km) from Cyprus. No fatalities or injuries are reported.... Princess Cristina of Spain marries Inaki Urdangarin, a professional athlete from the nation's Basque region, in an internationally televised ceremony. The wedding service, which employs three languages—Spanish, Basque, and Catalan—is seen as a symbolic unification of the nation's often antagonistic regions.			Nepalese prime minister Lokendra Bahadur Chand resigns after his coalition government loses a confidence motion in the House of Representatives, the lower house of Nepal's Parliament.
Oct. 5		Just 48.97% of Serbia's 3.2 million voters turn out at the polls for the second round of presidential elections, invalidating the vote and leaving the republic without a president until new elections can be held.	Iran criticizes the U.S. administration's Oct. 3 deployment of the *Nimitz* to the Persian Gulf, saying that the U.S.'s presence in the area is "illegitimate."		
Oct. 6		A group of 10 Bosnian Croats in the town of Split, Croatia, surrender to a representative of the UN war crimes tribunal. The 10 are accused of having massacred Muslim civilians in April 1993 in the Lasva Valley of central Bosnia-Herzegovina. Their surrender raises the number of suspects in the tribunal's custody from 10 to 20.	Hamas spiritual leader Sheik Ahmed Yassin returns to his Gaza City home and is greeted by a cheering throng of some 20,000 supporters. Jordan flies the two Mossad agents who attempted to assassinate a Hamas leader in Jordan in September to Israel, where they are released. Twenty-two other Palestinian and Jordanian prisoners are also freed.	Orlando Agosti, 72, Argentine air force commander who helped overthrow the democratically elected government of Isabel Peron in 1976 and who, from 1976 to 1983, participated in a violent campaign against leftist guerrillas and sympathizers, in which an estimated 30,000 people died or disappeared, dies in Buenos Aires of cancer.	In Nepal, King Birendra names Surya Bahadur Thapa to succeed Chand as prime minister.
Oct. 7		Turkish military officials state that more than 500 guerrillas have been killed to date in the clashes that started in September against the PKK.... Belarussian authorities free Pavel Sheremet, a reporter for Russia's ORT television network imprisoned since July. He is the last of seven ORT employees arrested in July and August to be freed.		Former navy captain Adolfo Francisco Scilingo is arrested in Spain after voluntarily testifying in a Madrid court about his actions in Argentina's "dirty war" against suspected leftists in the 1970s.	
Oct. 8		A court in the Palace of Justice in Bordeaux, France, begins proceedings in the trial against Maurice Papon, a former government minister accused of delivering more than 1,500 Jews to Nazi death camps during World War II.		Hurricane Pauline hits Puerto Angel in Oaxaca state, a town on Mexico's Pacific coast some 310 miles (500 km) southeast of Mexico City, the capital. Pauline brings winds of 115 miles per hour (185 kmph), as well as heavy rains and tidal waves reaching as high as 30 feet (9 m).	Kim Jong Il, who is the son of North Korean founder Kim Il Sung and who has been North Korea's presumed leader since the 1994 death of his father, formally takes over the country's top political post, that of general secretary of the ruling communist Korean Workers' Party. Some 20,000 people reportedly gather in the streets of Pyongyang, the capital, to celebrate.

A	B	C	D	E
Includes developments that affect more than one world region, international organizations, and important meetings of major world leaders.	Includes all domestic and regional developments in Europe, including the Soviet Union, Turkey, Cyprus, and Malta.	Includes all domestic and regional developments in Africa and the Middle East, including Iraq and Iran and excluding Cyprus, Turkey, and Afghanistan.	Includes all domestic and regional developments in Latin America, the Caribbean, and Canada.	Includes all domestic and regional developments in Asia and Pacific nations, extending from Afghanistan through all the Pacific Islands, except Hawaii.

U.S. Politics & Social Issues	U.S. Foreign Policy & Defense	U.S. Economy & Environment	Science, Technology, & Nature	Culture, Leisure, & Lifestyle	
	Thai officials extradite to the U.S. Lee Peng Fei, 47, the Taiwanese man alleged to be the mastermind of a failed 1993 attempt to smuggle nearly 300 Chinese immigrants into the U.S. aboard the *Golden Venture* cargo vessel, which had run aground off the coast of New York City.... In response to the Sept. 29 incident involving Iraq and Iran, U.S. Defense Department officials announced that the U.S. has ordered the immediate deployment of aircraft carrier USS *Nimitz* to the Persian Gulf.			Reports state that the National Organization for Women and Equal Partners in Faith, a coalition of 60 religious groups, has criticized the all-male, evangelical Promise Keepers for its exclusion of women and for its conservative political agenda. ... Millard Lampell, 78, songwriter, screenwriter, and novelist known for his dedication to social causes, dies in Ashburn, Virginia, of lung cancer.	Oct. 3
The FBI reveals that serious crimes reported to the police decreased by 3% in 1996 from the 1995 level. It is the fifth consecutive decline in the annual crime rate.			Several hundred demonstrators rally at Cape Canaveral to protest the planned launch of the *Cassini*, an unmanned spacecraft powered by plutonium, arguing that the plutonium will be hazardous if the rocket explodes upon launch or reentry.... The Field Museum of Natural History in Chicago acquires the largest fossil of a *Tyrannosaurus rex* dinosaur ever discovered for a bid of $8.36 million, which is believed to be the highest price ever paid for a fossil, at a Sotheby's auction.	Hundreds of thousands of members of Promise Keepers, an all-male, evangelical Christian group, converge on the National Mall in Washington, D.C., to pray for spiritual renewal, pledge their faith in Jesus Christ, and repent for their failure to uphold their personal commitments to their families and communities.	Oct. 4
				Mary Jane Gold, 88, Chicago heiress who helped Jewish and anti-Nazi intellectuals and artists flee Europe during World War II, dies near St. Tropez, France, after suffering from pancreatic cancer.... David Francis Marr, 63, golfer and sportscaster, dies in Houston, Texas, of cancer.	Oct. 5
	Pres. Clinton uses his line-item veto power to eliminate 38 proposed spending items from a military construction appropriations bill he signed earlier. The vetoed items total $287 million of the $9.183 billion fiscal 1998 bill and include projects from both Republican and Democratic districts nationwide. The president's choice of projects to cut draws criticism.	Unsealed portions of an FBI affidavit allege that Columbia/HCA executives and managers took part in a scheme to defraud several of the federal government's health-care programs, including Medicare and Medicaid.... The House passes, 399-18, a $49.7 billion agriculture appropriations bill for fiscal 1998 to provide funding for the Department of Agriculture, the FDA, and related agencies.	The Nobel Prize in Physiology for Medicine is awarded to Dr. Stanley B. Prusiner for his controversial research concerning disease-causing proteins called prions.... The space shuttle *Atlantis* lands at Kennedy Space Center in Cape Canaveral, Florida, after helping to repair *Mir* and picking up U.S. astronaut C. Michael Foale, who was replaced by David A. Wolf.	Robert Hector O'Brien, 93, president of MGM, 1963–69, dies in Seattle, Washington. ... John Samuel (Johnny) Vander Meer, 82, Major League Baseball player, 1937–43, 1946–51, dies in Tampa, Florida, of an abdominal aneurysm.... *Flood Tide*, by Clive Cussler, tops the best-seller list.	Oct. 6
A panel of three federal judges from the U.S. Ninth Circuit Court of Appeals in San Francisco, California, strike down a State law setting term limits for state legislators. The judges rule that the 1990 referendum on which the law was based did not clearly state that the limits will apply throughout a legislator's lifetime.	The INS announces plans to extend the range of "Operation Gatekeeper," an effort geared at halting the flow of illegal aliens from Mexico into Southern California.	Pres. Clinton signs a $2.25 billion fiscal 1998 spending bill for the legislative branch.... The House passes, 229-197, a measure to limit a president's authority to protect environmentally threatened lands by designating them as national monuments.... Reports confirm that a Pennsylvania landfill company agreed to pay an $8 million fine for making illegal campaign contributions to 10 candidates. The fine is the largest penalty ever imposed for campaign-finance violations.... The Senate, by voice vote, approves a $13.1 billion fiscal 1998 transportation bill.	The Space Telescope Science Institute and the University of California at Los Angeles announce the *Hubble Space Telescope*'s detection of the brightest star ever observed, called the Pistol Star, which burns with energy 10 million times greater than the Sun's and is located some 25,000 light years from Earth, near the center of the Milky Way. Astronomers believe that it formed 1–3 million years ago.	Yevgeny Khaldei, 80, Russian photographer known for the images he captured at the finale of World War II, dies in Moscow of unreported causes.	Oct. 7
The House clears, 296-132, a measure banning a controversial abortion procedure.... William Belser Spong 77, U.S. Democratic senator from Virginia, 1967–73, dies in Portsmouth, Va., of a ruptured aneurysm.... A South Carolina jury finds Chrysler Corp. liable in the death of Sergio Jimenez II, a six-year-old boy, in a 1994 accident and fines the company $12.5 million in compensatory damages and $250 million punitive damages.	Pres. Clinton signs the $247.7 billion defense-spending bill for fiscal 1998.... The U.S. Army announces that Sergeant Major of the Army Gene McKinney, that military branch's highest-ranking enlisted person, will face a court-martial on charges of sexual harassment.... Secretary of State Madeleine Albright designates 30 foreign organizations as terrorist groups.	The House clears, 405-21, a $90.7 fiscal 1998 appropriations bill for veterans affairs, housing, space, environmental protection, and other independent agencies.... The House passes, 401-21, a $13.1 billion fiscal 1998 appropriations bill for transportation.... A U.S. District Court jury in Alexandria, Virginia, rules that Anthony Cerullo, a male employee of the Defense Intelligence Agency, was sexually harassed by a female coworker and awards him $850,000.	A plane crashes in a densely wooded area of southwestern Colorado, killing eight employees of the federal Bureau of Reclamation, the part of the Interior Department that oversees federal dams and other water projects.	Jane Alexander states she will resign as head of the NEA, citing the hostility toward the agency displayed by conservative members of Congress as one of her reasons ... Bertrand Goldberg, 84, Chicago architect known for designing Marina City, consisting of two towers in downtown Chicago, dies in Chicago, Illinois, of complications from a stroke.	Oct. 8
F	G	H	I	J	
Includes elections, federal-state relations, civil rights and liberties, crime, the judiciary, education, health care, poverty, urban affairs, and population.	*Includes formation and debate of U.S. foreign and defense policies, veterans' affairs, and defense spending. (Relations with specific foreign countries are usually found under the region concerned.)*	*Includes business, labor, agriculture, taxation, transportation, consumer affairs, monetary and fiscal policy, natural resources, and pollution.*	*Includes worldwide scientific, medical, and technological developments; natural phenomena; U.S. weather; natural disasters; and accidents.*	*Includes the arts, religion, scholarship, communications media, sports, entertainments, fashions, fads, and social life.*	

	World Affairs	Europe	Africa & the Middle East	The Americas	Asia & the Pacific
Oct. 9		The OSCE finds that the Muslim Party for Democratic Action (SDA) won a slim majority in municipal elections in Srebrenica, a town inhabited exclusively by Serbs since 1995 after they executed many of their 40,000 Muslim neighbors in one of the Bosnian civil war's worst episodes of genocide. Observers believe that Muslims voted mostly by absentee ballot.		Hurricane Pauline strikes the Mexican resort town of Acapulco, in Guerrero state, Mexico, with 115 mph winds. Sixteen inches (40 cm) of rain falls on Acapulco in a period of three hours. After hitting Acapulco, Pauline continues to travel up the coast, hitting resorts at Zihuatanejo and Ixtapa with winds that decrease to 70 mph. At least 230 people have been killed, hundreds of others injured, and some 20,000 people left homeless since Oct. 8.	
Oct. 10	The Norwegian Nobel Committee awards the Nobel Peace Prize to the International Campaign to Ban Landmines and its coordinator, Jody Williams, for efforts to eradicate the use of land mines worldwide. Some 110 million land mines are currently deployed in several dozen countries around the world, killing an estimated 9,600 civilians and injuring 14,000 others each year. . . . Reports reveal that Liberia has moved to recognize Taiwan as well as China.	Kazakhstan president Nursultan Nazarbayev appoints Nurlan Balgimbayev as premier, replacing Akezhan Kazhegeldin. . . . The Swedish government officially rules out pursuing membership in the European Union's economic and monetary union (EMU) in time for the launch of the unified European currency, scheduled for January 1, 1999. . . . Reports confirm that a French court of appeals has fined actress Brigitte Bardot $1,600 for inciting racial hatred in comments made about Muslims in 1996.	Angolan jets start flying bombing missions against government positions in Brazzaville. Angolan troops clash with Congo government forces on Congo's southern border with the Angolan enclave of Cabinda.	An Argentine jetliner crashes in neighboring Uruguay, killing all 74 people on board.	Three bomb blasts in New Delhi, the capital of India, wound 16 people and kill one child.
Oct. 11		During World Cup qualifying match between England and Italy in Rome, spectators turn violent, and numerous British fans are jailed.		Cubans launch a weeklong celebration to mark the 30th anniversary of the death of Ernesto (Che) Guevara, an Argentine revolutionary who fought alongside Pres. Fidel Castro Ruz in Cuba's 1959 communist revolution. An estimated 250,000 Cubans begin to flock to Havana to pay tribute.	
Oct. 12			In Cameroon, local and foreign journalists note that polling stations are virtually deserted on election day due to a boycott by the country's three major opposition parties since Pres. Paul Biya refused to create an independent commission to oversee the voting process.	U.S. president Bill Clinton launches a tour of South America.	After leaving Pakistan, where she marked the country's 50th anniversary of its independence, Britain's Queen Elizabeth II and her husband, Prince Philip, the Duke of Edinburgh, visit India in a tour that is part of a year-long celebration of the 50th anniversary of India's independence.
Oct. 13		In Spain, a policeman is wounded by gunfire when he and his partner interrupt two ETA guerrillas planting bombs at the new Guggenheim Museum in Bilbao. . . . Turkey winds down a three-week incursion against the Kurdish group, the PKK. . . . Merita Ltd., the largest bank in Finland, announces that it will merge with Nordbanken AB, Sweden's fourth-largest bank. The merged Scandinavian bank will be the largest such institution in the Nordic region, with a total market value of about 80 billion Swedish krona ($10.6 billion). . . . Adil Carcani, 75, who from 1982 to 1991, was the last of Albania's communist-era premiers, dies in Tirana, Albania, of a brain hemorrhage.	Suspected Islamic gunmen kill nine police officers and two Coptic Christians in two separate incidents in southern Egypt. . . . Israel frees nine Arab prisoners to Jordan as part of the Oct. 6 Israeli-Jordanian prisoner exchange.	A chartered bus crashes into a ravine near Saint-Joseph-de-la-Rive, Quebec, killing 43 people. Five people survive the accident, the worst road crash in Canada's history.	Kim Hyun Chul, the second son of South Korean president Kim Young Sam, is sentenced to three years in prison on charges of bribery and tax evasion.
Oct. 14	In a secret ballot to fill five rotating seats on the UN Security Council, Bahrain, Brazil, Gabon, Gambia, and Slovenia are elected to two-year terms, beginning in January 1998. Slovenia, which defeats Macedonia for the Eastern European seat, is the first former Yugoslav republic elected to the Security Council.	In Spain, Jose Maria Aguirre, the policeman wounded Oct. 13 in a gunfight with ETA members, dies. . . . The dome of a 15th-century bell tower in Foligno collapses due to damages sustained recent earthquakes throughout central Italy.	The Congo Republic's Pres. Pascal Lissouba flees the presidential palace, and his government troops withdraw from the capital, Brazzaville.	An earthquake measuring 6.8 on the Richter scale strikes north-central Chile, killing at least eight people and injuring 100 others. . . . Lawmakers in Nevis, the smaller of the two islands that comprise St. Christopher (St. Kitts) and Nevis, vote to secede from the federation. The succession still has to be ratified by voters. . . . Officials in Brazil reveal that hundreds of people have been left homeless by floods.	In India, British queen Elizabeth II pays a silent, 30-second tribute to those slain at Amritsar, where a 1919 massacre of unarmed Indians ordered by British brigadier Reginald Dyer resulted in as many as 2,000 deaths. . . . In Tokyo, Japan's Toyota Motor Corp. introduces a gasoline-electric hybrid car, the first of its kind on the market.

A	B	C	D	E
Includes developments that affect more than one world region, international organizations, and important meetings of major world leaders.	Includes all domestic and regional developments in Europe, including the Soviet Union, Turkey, Cyprus, and Malta.	Includes all domestic and regional developments in Africa and the Middle East, including Iraq and Iran and excluding Cyprus, Turkey, and Afghanistan.	Includes all domestic and regional developments in Latin America, the Caribbean, and Canada.	Includes all domestic and regional developments in Asia and Pacific nations, extending from Afghanistan through all the Pacific Islands, except Hawaii.

U.S. Politics & Social Issues	U.S. Foreign Policy & Defense	U.S. Economy & Environment	Science, Technology, & Nature	Culture, Leisure, & Lifestyle	
The White House announces that Pres. Clinton has chosen Kevin Gover, a 42-year-old Pawnee Indian, as the new head of the Bureau of Indian Affairs, succeeding Ada Deer.... A U.S. District Court jury in Greenbelt, Maryland, orders apparel retailer Eddie Bauer Inc. to pay a total of $1 million in damages to three young black men who in 1995 were falsely accused of shoplifting at a Bauer store in Fort Washington, Maryland.	The U.S. Army strips Sergeant Major of the Army Gene McKinney, that military branch's highest-ranking enlisted person, of his title due to charges of sexual harassment.... A study indicates that illegal immigrants from Mexico make up 40% of the current farm workforce in California, compared with 10% in 1990. The study finds that a greater percentage of illegal immigrants are staying in the U.S. rather than returning to Mexico because of wariness of increased Border Patrol security.	The Senate clears, by voice vote, a $90.7 billion fiscal 1998 appropriations bill for veterans affairs, housing, space, environmental protection, and other independent agencies.... The National Association of Securities Dealers names the 27 members of the new board of governors to take office in 1998.... NASDAQ reaches a record high of.... Reports confirm that the NHTSA will allow drivers to deactivate air bags in their own cars without the NHTSA's express approval.	A scientist in Hong Kong identifies an influenza virus that killed a three-year-old boy in May as the first instance of the strain in humans. The virus, H5N1, is common in waterfowl and chickens.	The Nobel Prize in Literature is awarded to Dario Fo, an Italian playwright-performer. The choice sparks protest as Fo's work frequently ridicules the authority of such institutions as the Italian government and the Roman Catholic Church.... The Senate confirms Lindy (Corinne C.) Boggs as ambassador to the Vatican.	Oct. 9
Pres. Clinton vetoes a bill that would have banned a controversial late-term abortion method.... Judge Ricardo M. Urbina sentences E. Michael Kahoe to 18 months in federal prison for concealing information about the 1992 standoff in Ruby Ridge, Idaho.... Four major tobacco companies announce they have reached a $349 million settlement with flight attendants exposed to secondhand smoke. It is the first class-action suit against the tobacco industry to reach trial and the first linking liability to secondhand smoke.... In the high profile investigation of JonBenet Ramsey's 1996 death in Boulder, Colorado, Commander Mark Beckner is named the new lead investigator.		Pres. Clinton signs a fiscal 1998 spending bill allocating $25.6 billion to fund the Treasury Department, the U.S. Postal Service, the White House, and other general government costs. For the first time in five years, the spending bill does not contain a provision blocking congressional pay raises.... Whitewater counsel Kenneth Starr reaffirms that the 1993 death of White House deputy counsel Vincent Foster Jr. was a suicide that was not linked to the Whitewater scandal. Four previous probes had reached the same conclusion.... Data show that highway death rates have increased an average of 12% in 12 states that have raised speed limits.	Data suggests that organic molecules, another precondition for life, are present on two small moons of Jupiter, Callisto and Ganymede.		Oct. 10
				James Wesley (Wes) Gallagher, 86, chief executive of the Associated Press (AP), 1962–76, dies in Santa Barbara, California, of congestive heart failure.	Oct. 11
				In a ceremony at the Vatican, Pope John Paul II beatifies five people who served the Roman Catholic Church. Beatification is the final rite in the process toward canonization, or sainthood.	Oct. 12
Gary Lee Davis, 53, is put to death by lethal injection in Canon City, Colorado, for the 1986 murder of 33-year-old Virginia May. Davis and his wife, Rebecca Fincham, kidnapped May in front of her young children before raping and killing her. Davis's execution is the first in Colorado in 30 years, although it has been legal in that state since 1978. He is the 417th person executed in the U.S. since the Supreme Court reinstated the death penalty in 1976.	Robert Hall, command sergeant major at MacDill Air Force Base in Florida, is named to succeed Sergeant Major of the Army Gene McKinney, who was that military branch's highest-ranking enlisted person before being stripped of the title Oct. 9.	President Clinton signs a fiscal 1998 energy and water-development appropriations bill.	A jet-powered supersonic car called Thrust becomes the first vehicle to break the sound barrier on land. The Thrust team's achievement nearly coincides with the 50th anniversary of U.S. test pilot Chuck Yeager's first-ever supersonic flight.	John Denver (born Henry John Deutschendorf Jr.), 53, singer and songwriter whose sincere, acoustic guitar-based recordings include 14 gold and eight platinum albums that sold more than 100 million copies, dies off Monterey, California, when the single-passenger plane he was piloting crashes into Monterey Bay.	Oct. 13
The Supreme Court refuses to hear an appeal of a lower-court ruling that upholds an Oregon law permitting doctors in the state to prescribe lethal doses of medication to terminally ill patients. The court's action eliminates the last legal barrier to the implementation of the statute.	Pres. Clinton uses his line-item veto power to eliminate 13 proposed projects from a defense appropriations bill signed Oct. 8. The vetoed items comprise $144 million of the $247.7 billion bill.	Attorney General Janet Reno extends an investigation into allegations that Pres. Clinton made improper fund-raising calls from his White House office during the 1996 election campaign.	The Royal Swedish Academy of Sciences awards the Nobel Memorial Prize in Economic Science to Robert C. Merton and Myron S. Scholes for their groundbreaking work in creating a formula for measuring the worth of stock options.	The Booker Prize is awarded to an Indian first-time novelist, Arundhati Roy, for The God of Small Things.... Harold Robbins, 81, bestselling author whose novels typically feature a cast of cosmopolitan characters, dies in Palm Springs, California, of pulmonary arrest.	Oct. 14

F	G	H	I	J
Includes elections, federal-state relations, civil rights and liberties, crime, the judiciary, education, health care, poverty, urban affairs, and population.	*Includes formation and debate of U.S. foreign and defense policies, veterans' affairs, and defense spending. (Relations with specific foreign countries are usually found under the region concerned.)*	*Includes business, labor, agriculture, taxation, transportation, consumer affairs, monetary and fiscal policy, natural resources, and pollution.*	*Includes worldwide scientific, medical, and technological developments; natural phenomena; U.S. weather; natural disasters; and accidents.*	*Includes the arts, religion, scholarship, communications media, sports, entertainments, fashions, fads, and social life.*

	World Affairs	Europe	Africa & the Middle East	The Americas	Asia & the Pacific
Oct. 15	The European Commission, the EU's executive arm, approves the planned £23.8 billion ($38 billion) merger of British food-and-drinks companies Guinness PLC and Grand Metropolitan PLC (Grand Met).		Militia fighters loyal to Congo's former president, Gen. Denis Sassou-Nguesso, gain control of the Congo Republic's capital, Brazzaville, and, with the help of Angolan troops, of the second-largest city, Pointe-Noire.... In Egypt, a military court sentences three Jihad militants, including Adel Ali Bayoomi Sudani, the leader of Jihad's military wing, to death and another 53 to prison terms for their roles in planned subversive acts.	The Panamanian government allows Peruvian journalist Gustavo Gorriti to remain in Panama, despite previous attempts to have him deported. Those attempts were criticized by international media and human-rights groups as an attack on freedom of the press.... Peru abolishes the system of so-called faceless judges for trials of suspected terrorists. Under that system, judges' identities are concealed.	A truck bomb explodes in the central business district of Colombo, the capital of Sri Lanka. The bomb and ensuing gunfights between government security forces and rebels in the streets of the capital kill 18 people and wound more than 100 others. The blast is the first major bomb attack in the capital since January 1996. Despite the substantial power of the blast, which reportedly leaves a 10-feet-deep crater in the street, the death toll is relatively low as many Sri Lankan businesses are closed for a Buddhist holiday.
Oct. 16		Dozens of masked gunmen raid the headquarters of the presidential guard in Dushanbe, the Tajikistan capital, killing 14 guard members, Three members of the marauders are reported killed.... An estimated 300,000 people led by Basque political leaders march silently through the streets of Bilbao, Spain, to protest recent acts of violence attributed to ETA.	In the Congo Republic's capital, Brazzaville, Gen. Denis Sassou-Nguesso declares victory in his four-month-old civil war against Pres. Pascal Lissouba. The rebel victory is the third violent overthrow of an African government since May. France, Congo's former colonial ruler and an ally of Sassou-Nguesso, immediately recognizes his victory.	Health officials note that eight cases of cholera, caused by contaminated drinking water due to Hurricane Pauline's heavy rains, have been reported in Acapulco in Guerrero state, Mexico.	Pol Pot, the deposed leader of Cambodia's Khmer Rouge guerrilla army whose actions are said to have led to the deaths of the deaths of as many as 2 million Cambodians during the period of Khmer Rouge rule between 1975 and 1979, gives his first interview in 18 years, in which he denies that the death toll was in the millions and asserts that his " conscience is clear."
Oct. 17	China makes public an agreement in principle to discontinue aiding Iran's nuclear energy program and to halt sales of antiship cruise missiles to Iran.... The UN and the Organization of African Unity (OAU) calls for the withdrawal of foreign forces from the Congo Republic in apparent condemnations of Angola's role in the Oct. 16 takeover.	Scores of Gypsy immigrants from the Czech Republic and Slovakia begin to arrive in Dover, a port in southern England.... Poland's parliament, the Sejm, names Jerzy Buzek as the country's new premier.		The chief of police in Mexico City, the capital of Mexico, disbands an elite police force known as the Jaguares, or Jaguars, after several members of the force were linked to murders of six youths following their arrests in a September raid.	In a case that received publicity in Japan, an unidentified teenage boy charged with the decapitation murder of a boy and the fatal beating of a girl is convicted of those murders and three other assaults and sentenced to a juvenile correctional institution with psychiatric treatment facilities until he turns 26.
Oct. 18		Despite the Oct. 13 gunfire incident, King Juan Carlos I of Spain inaugurates the new Guggenheim Museum. . . . Gyorgy von Habsburg, 32, the grandson of the last of Hungary's kings, marries Princess Eilika von Oldenburg, 24, at a ceremony in Budapest, Hungary. The Habsburgs were one of Europe's most powerful families, ruling the Holy Roman Empire for nearly 400 years. The wedding is the first between members of the Roman Catholic Habsburg and the Lutheran Oldenburg royal families.			
Oct. 19		Voters in Montenegro, which with its much larger neighbor Serbia makes up the Yugoslav federation, elects Milo Djukanovic as president of their republic in a runoff against incumbent president Momir Bulatovic.... The United Tajik Opposition (UTO) frees 80 government troops held as prisoners of war.		Three antidrug police officers are killed and another is wounded in an ambush by gunmen in the Amazon jungle in Peru.	Jun-ichi Ueno, 87, co-owner of Japan's second-largest newspaper, dies in Tokyo, Japan, of pneumonia.
Oct. 20		Albania's Supreme Court drops charges of genocide against Ramiz Alia, the country's last communist-era president, and similar charges against former justice officials.... Hungarian-born U.S. financier and philanthropist George Soros announces that he will donate between $300 million and $500 million to Russia over the next three years.... Harold Albert (born Harold Kemp), 88, biographer who, under the pseudonym of Helen Cathcart, chronicled Britain's royal family, dies in Midhurst, England, of unreported causes.			Fourteen environmental activists are arrested after staging a three-hour demonstration on the roof of Australian prime minister John Howard's home in Sydney.

A	B	C	D	E
Includes developments that affect more than one world region, international organizations, and important meetings of major world leaders.	Includes all domestic and regional developments in Europe, including the Soviet Union, Turkey, Cyprus, and Malta.	Includes all domestic and regional developments in Africa and the Middle East, including Iraq and Iran and excluding Cyprus, Turkey, and Afghanistan.	Includes all domestic and regional developments in Latin America, the Caribbean, and Canada.	Includes all domestic and regional developments in Asia and Pacific nations, extending from Afghanistan through all the Pacific Islands, except Hawaii.

U.S. Politics & Social Issues	U.S. Foreign Policy & Defense	U.S. Economy & Environment	Science, Technology, & Nature	Culture, Leisure, & Lifestyle	
Former representative Dan Rostenkowskl (D, Ill.) is released from federal custody after serving 15 months of a 17-month sentence for mail fraud.... The CDC reports that in the period 1988–94, 5.6% of people between the ages of 12 and 19 were infected with the sexually transmitted disease herpes, compared with 1.6% in the period 1976–80.	As a result of a lawsuit filed under the Freedom of Information Act, the director of central intelligence, George Tenet, makes the amount of the fiscal 1997 intelligence budget public for the first time ever when he reveals that the budget for that fiscal year was $26.6 billion.		*Cassini*, an unmanned spacecraft, is launched from Cape Canaveral Air Force Station in Florida to orbit the planet Saturn.... The Nobel Prize in Chemistry is awarded to John E. Walker, Paul D. Boyer, and Jens C. Skou for advances in the study of how living cells store and release energy. The Nobel Prize in Physics goes to Steven Chu, William D. Phillips, and Claude Cohen-Tannoudji for developing a method to trap atoms.... The jet-powered Thrust, a supersonic car, measures an average speed of 763.035 mph to set the official record.	A New York State Supreme Court jury finds boxer Mike Tyson liable for injuries sustained by former boxer Mitch Green in a 1988 brawl in New York City and awards Green $45,000.	Oct. 15
The second anniversary of the "Million Man March," a rally of black men in Washington, D.C., is marked with rallies around the country, most of which are sparsely attended.... The National Archives releases 154 hours of recordings pertaining to abuses of governmental power in the Watergate scandal.	Six Marine Corps members and seven civilians are arrested in connection with the theft and attempted sale of weapons and explosives from Camp Lejeune military base in North Carolina.	Pres. Clinton uses his line-item veto power to eliminate a provision from a bill signed Oct. 10 that would have allowed 1.1 million federal employees and postal workers to switch to a stock-based retirement plan. In response, the National Treasury Employees Union files a lawsuit. Officials in NYC file a separate suit ... Kenneth Apfel, SSA commissioner, reveals that Social Security checks in 1998 will increase for cost-of-living by 2.1%, raising the average benefit to $765 per month from $749 per month in 1997.	A study finds that excessive doses of acetaminophen may cause liver damage, including acute liver failure, especially in heavy drinkers.	Folk rock musician Bob Dylan is awarded the fourth annual Dorothy and Lillian Gish Prize.... James Albert Michener, 90, best-selling author known for his lengthy, heavily researched historical novels and for his generous support of literature and the arts, dies in Austin, Texas, of kidney failure.	Oct. 16
	Although it is not immediately reported, a powerful army laser from a military base in New Mexico strikes an air force satellite orbiting the Earth at an altitude of 260 miles (420 km).	Pres. Clinton, exercising his line-item veto, eliminates eight projects from the fiscal 1998 energy and water-development appropriations bill signed Oct. 13. The vetoed items, which total $19.3 million, include five water projects, two Department of Energy research programs, and one Bureau of Reclamation science project.	Reports confirm that an unidentified 39-year-old Georgia woman gave birth in August to twin boys in the first birth in the U.S. resulting from the fertilization of eggs that had been frozen. Separately, scientists reveal the birth of a girl to an Italian woman whose eggs were frozen.	Judge Lawrence Mira revokes the probation of actor Robert Downey Jr., 32, after receiving evidence that Downey had slipped back into drug use. She allows the actor to finish a film he is shooting, however.	Oct. 17
	Tens of thousands of people turn out at Arlington National Cemetery in Virginia for the dedication of the Women in Military Service for America Memorial, a monument and exhibit hall commemorating the nearly 2 million women who have served in the U.S. armed forces during the past two centuries.	Roberto Crispulo Goizueta, 65, chair and CEO, 1981–97, of the Coca-Cola Co., dies in Atlanta, Georgia, of complications from lung cancer treatment.		Nancy Hanschman Dickerson, 70, TV news reporter and producer who, in 1960, became the first woman correspondent for CBS, dies in New York City of complications from a stroke suffered in 1996.	Oct. 18
				Pope John Paul II declares Saint Terese of Lisieux, a 19th-century Carmelite nun from Siena, Italy, a doctor of the church.... Ecumenical patriarch Bartholomew I, the spiritual leader of Orthodox Christianity, makes his first visit to the U.S. since his 1991 enthronement.	Oct. 19
In Richmond, Virginia, the U.S. Fourth Circuit Court of Appeals denies a request to temporarily stay a Virginia law that requires parental notification before a teenage girl may obtain an abortion, which went into effect July 1.... The Florida Supreme Court votes to reject a claim that use of the electric chair for the death penalty in the state constitutes cruel and unusual punishment.		A federal panel recommends changes to the Bankruptcy Code, as personal bankruptcy filings are expected to hit a record 1.3 million in 1997, seven times as many as in 1978, when the code was enacted. ... The Energy Department reveals that the U.S.'s emissions of carbon dioxide and other greenhouse gases rose by 3.4% in 1996.... The California Public Employees' Retirement System (Calpers), the biggest public pension fund in the U.S., joins a shareholder suit against Columbia/HCA led by New York comptroller H. Carl McCall.	The Justice Department files a petition in U.S. District Court in Washington, D.C., accusing Microsoft Corp., the world's leading computer software company, of illegally coercing computer manufacturers to equip computers with a Microsoft "browser," which is used to retrieve data from the Internet. The petition filing is the latest chapter in a long-running Justice Department probe into alleged anticompetitive behavior by Microsoft.	In an address to a Jewish community, ecumenical patriarch Bartholomew I condemns the Nazi Holocaust as "the singular icon of our century's evils." He is reportedly the first ecumenical patriarch to denounce the Holocaust, in which some 6 million Jews died.	Oct. 20

F	G	H	I	J
Includes elections, federal-state relations, civil rights and liberties, crime, the judiciary, education, health care, poverty, urban affairs, and population.	*Includes formation and debate of U.S. foreign and defense policies, veterans' affairs, and defense spending. (Relations with specific foreign countries are usually found under the region concerned.)*	*Includes business, labor, agriculture, taxation, transportation, consumer affairs, monetary and fiscal policy, natural resources, and pollution.*	*Includes worldwide scientific, medical, and technological developments; natural phenomena; U.S. weather; natural disasters; and accidents.*	*Includes the arts, religion, scholarship, communications media, sports, entertainments, fashions, fads, and social life.*

	World Affairs	Europe	Africa & the Middle East	The Americas	Asia & the Pacific
Oct. 21					In the Uttar Pradesh state assembly during their debate on a confidence vote, members from centrist and leftist opposition parties brawl with and hurl chairs at members of the Hindu nationalist Bharatiya Janata Party (BJP) party. The incident prompts the cabinet of Indian prime minister Inder Kumar Gujral to ask Pres. Kocheril Raman Narayanan to dismiss the state government of Uttar Pradesh and to place it under direct federal rule.
Oct. 22	Four health agencies warn that drug-resistant strains of the infectious disease tuberculosis (TB) are spreading in many countries. One-third of the countries surveyed have significant levels of TB strains that are resistant to the two main drugs used to treat the disease. Latvia, Estonia, Argentina, the Dominican Republic, Russia, and Ivory Coast are identified as "hot spot" countries with levels of drug-resistant TB that threaten to overwhelm their TB control programs.		Four members of the Islamic Group are hanged in a prison in Cairo for attacks on security or tourist targets in 1993 and 1994.... South African president Nelson Mandela arrives in the Libyan capital, Tripoli, for talks with Col. Muammar Gadhafi, the Libyan leader. Diplomats consider Mandela's visit significant because Libya has become increasingly isolated from the international community in recent years.		The South Korean government announces that it will take over Kia Motors Corp., the country's third-largest automobile maker and the core of the debt-ridden Kia Group conglomerate.... Indian president Kocheril Raman Narayanan denies the Oct. 21 request to dismiss the state government of Uttar Pradesh. ... Statistics show that a quarterly drop in Australia's CPI brought national inflation below zero for the first time since 1962.
Oct. 23	The ELN draws international attention by kidnapping two election observers from the Organization of American States (OAS) in northwestern Colombia.	A Greek naval ship and a Turkish warship collide in international waters in the Aegean Sea. Each country blames the other for the collision, which causes no injuries.	A military junta that seized power in a May coup in Sierra Leone agrees to a peace plan that will return Ahmad Tejan Kabbah, the ousted president, to power by April 1998.... The Supreme Court of Cameroon declares Pres. Paul Biya the winner of the country's Oct. 12 presidential election. Opposition leaders accuse the government of fabricating the results. ... Parties supporting Algeria's military-backed government dominate the country's first local elections since 1990.		The opposition coalition's leaders choose Gen. Abdul Rashid Doestam, an Uzbek warlord, as leader of the anti-Taliban forces in Afghanistan.
Oct. 24	The British Commonwealth, a 54-nation association of Britain and its former colonies, holds its biennial summit in Edinburgh, Scotland.	Unidentified gunmen shoot dead Zoran Todorovic, a high-level adviser to Slobodan Milosevic's wife, Mirjana Markovic, who leads the hard-line Yugoslav United Left party. Todorovic, the general secretary of Markovic's party, is the third member of Milosevic's circle to die violently in 1997.		Reports reveal that at least 20,000 people have been left homeless due to flooding caused by two weeks of storms and torrential rains in southern Brazil.... Luis Aguilar Manzo, 79, Mexican actor who appeared in more than 150 Spanish-language films over a span of five decades, dies in Mexico City of a heart attack.	
Oct. 25		A pipeline stretching 870 miles (1,400 km) between Baku, the capital of Azerbaijan, and Novorossiysk, a Russian Black Sea port, opens.... A bomb explodes under a car in the Northern Ireland town of Bangor, County Down, killing the car's driver, Glen Greer.	General Denis Sassou-Nguesso is sworn in as president of the Congo Republic.	Rebels fail in an apparent attempt to assassinate Alvaro Uribe Velez, governor of the state of Antioquia, in Colombia, instead killing Rev. Antonio Bedoya, a Roman Catholic priest.	Residents of Anjouan island vote overwhelmingly to secede from Comoros, a three-island nation in the Indian Ocean. The vote is prompted by an armed independence rebellion staged in August that called for Anjouan to reunite with France, the former colonial ruler of Comoros.... King Norodom Sihanouk of Cambodia leaves his country after failing to reconcile the country's two feuding rulers, de facto leader Hun Sen and Prince Norodom Ranariddh, whom Hun Sen ousted in a July coup.
Oct. 26	Italy formally joins the Schengen group, an open-border zone in the EU that now includes eight EU nations.			Argentina's ruling Justicialist (Peronist) Party loses its majority in the Chamber of Deputies. The defeat of the Peronists by a center-left coalition of opposition parties, is the party's first since 1983. It is also the first time in the party's 51-year history that it has been defeated in a nationwide vote while in power.... Suriname president Jules Wijdenbosch states that government security forces have foiled a coup plot in Paramaribo.	

A	B	C	D	E
Includes developments that affect more than one world region, international organizations, and important meetings of major world leaders.	Includes all domestic and regional developments in Europe, including the Soviet Union, Turkey, Cyprus, and Malta.	Includes all domestic and regional developments in Africa and the Middle East, including Iraq and Iran and excluding Cyprus, Turkey, and Afghanistan.	Includes all domestic and regional developments in Latin America, the Caribbean, and Canada.	Includes all domestic and regional developments in Asia and Pacific nations, extending from Afghanistan through all the Pacific Islands, except Hawaii.

U.S. Politics & Social Issues	U.S. Foreign Policy & Defense	U.S. Economy & Environment	Science, Technology, & Nature	Culture, Leisure, & Lifestyle	
Results of a nationwide exam show that about two in three U.S. students have a basic understanding of science.	Louis Freeh, director of the FBI, names Donald Kerr Jr., a nuclear physicist, to head the bureau's crime laboratory.... Pres. Clinton nominates Daryl Jones as secretary of the U.S. Air Force. Jones will replace Sheila Widnall and will be both the first black man and the first ex-pilot to head the air force.	Figures suggest that large U.S. firms created an average of 110 new jobs in the 12 months ending in June and cut only 57 jobs.	Scientists present detailed images sent by the Earth-orbiting *Hubble Space Telescope* of a collision of two galaxies and the resulting formation of hundreds of millions of new stars.... Researchers announce a breakthrough in producing electricity from gasoline. The new system turns gasoline into hydrogen gas, which is then used to power an electricity-generating fuel cell.		Oct. 21
In New Jersey, Bergen County Superior Court judge Sybil R. Moses rules that gay parents Michael Galluccio and Jon Holden may jointly adopt their two-year-old foster son. New Jersey becomes the first state to explicitly expand its adoption policy to gay and unmarried parents.	USDA officials announce that inspectors in Montana have discovered *E. coli* bacteria in a nearly 35,000-pound shipment of Canadian beef, marking the first time that that bacterium has been found in imported beef.	President Clinton announces a proposal to fight global warming.... In Washington, D.C., Judge Royce C. Lamberth approves a $58.5 million settlement in a 1994 age-discrimination case against First Union, a North Carolina bank. Lawyers for the plaintiffs, who include job applicants, state that it is the largest the age-discrimination settlement ever. ... The House passes by voice vote a stopgap bill, extending the deadline for enacting fiscal 1998 spending bills until Nov. 7.			Oct. 22
The U.S. Sixth Circuit Court of Appeals upholds a 1993 resolution by voters in Cincinnati, Ohio, that bars the city from protecting homosexuals' civil rights.... A survey shows that graduating students have an average of $18,800 each in college debts. That compares to a 1991 study, which found an average debt load of $8,200 per student.	The U.S. Army announces that it is raising the physical fitness standards for women, marking the first change in the branch's conditioning requirements since 1984.... The Defense Department reports that the powerful army laser fired from a military base Oct. 17 that struck an air force satellite was designed to assess the vulnerability of U.S. satellites to laser weapons, but it did not provide enough data to assess the weapon's destructive power in space.	The Senate confirms Ellen Seidman as director of the Treasury Department's Office of Thrift Supervision. The office has not had a permanent director in five years.... The Senate clears, 100-0, and Pres. Clinton signs a stopgap measure extending the deadline for enacting fiscal 1998 spending bills until Nov. 7. Congress has cleared only seven of the 13 annual spending bills.	A study finds that the antidepressant prescription drug bupropion may help people quit smoking.		Oct. 23
		The House approves, 233-171, a fiscal 1998 appropriations bill that allocates $13.8 billion for the Department of the Interior and related agencies.		Arlington County, Virginia, circuit court judge Benjamin Kendrick places sportscaster Marv Albert on probation and defers for one year Albert's sentencing for misdemeanor assault.	Oct. 24
Black women from across the U.S. gather in Philadelphia, Pennsylvania, for the "Million Woman March," a rally encouraging unity among women of African descent. Unofficial estimates suggest that between 300,000 and 500,000 people hear from speakers that include Winnie Madikizela-Mandela—the ex-wife of South African president Nelson Mandela—and California representative Maxine Waters (D).			Four employees of Union Pacific Railroad are injured in a head-on collision in Houston, Texas, that destroys four locomotives.		Oct. 25
				Baseball's Florida Marlins defeat the Cleveland Indians, 3-2, to win the 93rd World Series.... D.C. United wins, 2-1, their second MLS championship, over the Colorado Rapids.... Jacques Villeneuve of Canada captures the Formula One world auto-racing title.	Oct. 26

F	G	H	I	J
Includes elections, federal-state relations, civil rights and liberties, crime, the judiciary, education, health care, poverty, urban affairs, and population.	*Includes formation and debate of U.S. foreign and defense policies, veterans' affairs, and defense spending. (Relations with specific foreign countries are usually found under the region concerned.)*	*Includes business, labor, agriculture, taxation, transportation, consumer affairs, monetary and fiscal policy, natural resources, and pollution.*	*Includes worldwide scientific, medical, and technological developments; natural phenomena; U.S. weather; natural disasters; and accidents.*	*Includes the arts, religion, scholarship, communications media, sports, entertainments, fashions, fads, and social life.*

	World Affairs	Europe	Africa & the Middle East	The Americas	Asia & the Pacific
Oct. 27		Thousands of Scientologists stage a march in Berlin, protesting the German government's treatment of the church. . . . Reports confirm that some 300 Gypsy immigrants from the Czech Republic and Slovakia have arrived in Dover, a port in southern England, since Oct. 17, touching off a refugee crisis.		In Canada, five unions representing Ontario's 126,000 elementary and high school teachers stage a walk-out.	
Oct. 28			The Zambian army quells a coup attempt led by Captain Steven Lungu against the government of Pres. Frederick Chiluba. One officer is killed, and at least 15 others, including Lungu, are arrested.	Reports confirm that the overflow of the Uruguay River, which borders Brazil, Argentina, and Uruguay, has caused flooding in Argentina and Uruguay.	Naoharu Yamashina, 79, founder of Bandai Co., Japan's largest toy manufacturer, dies of respiratory ailments after a long illness.
Oct. 29	Pres. Jiang Zemin of China meets with U.S. president Clinton in Washington, D.C., in the first U.S.-China summit meeting since 1989. . . . Iraq orders all U.S. members of a UN arms inspection team to leave the country within seven days and demands that the UN bar flights of U.S. U-2 spy planes, which are monitoring Iraqi weapons programs. . . . The UN Security Council votes to impose air and travel sanctions on UNITA, a rebel group in Angola.				In Pakistan, the Supreme Court strikes down the Sharif-sponsored constitutional amendment that mandates party loyalty sponsored by P.M. Nawaz Sharif. That ruling is extraordinary because Pakistani law bars courts from striking down constitutional amendments. . . . Herbert Cole (Nugget) Coombs, 91, head of Australia's central bank, 1949–68, dies in Sydney, Australia, of unreported causes.
Oct. 30		A bomb explodes in an office of the British government in Londonderry, Northern Ireland. No one is injured. . . . The Republic of Ireland holds presidential elections.	A military court sentences to death Sabir Abu al-Ila and Mahmoud Abu al-Ila, brothers who attacked a tourist bus in Cairo, Egypt's capital, in September, killing nine Germans and the bus's Egyptian driver. . . . Yemeni tribesmen take Steve Carpenter, a U.S. oil executive, hostage near Sanaa, the capital.	The Supreme Court of Canada rules that authorities cannot force a pregnant woman addicted to solvent-sniffing into treatment in order to save her fetus.	The Japanese government announces that it has reached an agreement to liberalize the country's port practices. . . . Reports reveal that Ta Mok, the Khmer Rouge's military leader, has admitted that "hundreds of thousands" of Cambodians died during the group's rule in the 1970s. Ta Mok is the first Khmer Rouge leader to make such specific comments about the scale of the movement's atrocities.
Oct. 31	The IMF announces a three-year, $33 billion loan package to stabilize Indonesia's economy.	Mary McAleese is declared the winner of the Republic of Ireland's presidential election. McAleese, 46, will be the country's first-ever president from Northern Ireland. . . . A series of severe mudslides leave at least 26 people dead in the Portuguese Azores, an archipelago off the Iberian Peninsula in the central Atlantic Ocean.	King Letsie III is formally coronated as the monarch of Lesotho before some 25,000 spectators at a stadium in the capital, Maseru. King Letsie assumed the throne in 1996 after his father, King Moshoeshoe II, died in a car accident.		
Nov. 1	The ELN releases the two election observers from the Organization of American States (OAS) kidnapped Oct. 23 in northwestern Colombia.	Italian premier Romano Prodi discloses that his government has reached an agreement with trade-union leaders over pension reforms.		A Panamanian jury acquits three men charged with the 1992 murder of U.S. Army sergeant Zak A. Hernandez, who was gunned down while driving near Panama City, the capital. Since one of the defendants, Pedro Miguel Gonzalez, is the son of the anti-American president of the country's congress and ruling party, Gerardo Gonzalez, the U.S. criticizes the verdict as politically motivated.	The government of Indonesian president Suharto closes 16 ailing banks.

A	B	C	D	E
Includes developments that affect more than one world region, international organizations, and important meetings of major world leaders.	Includes all domestic and regional developments in Europe, including the Soviet Union, Turkey, Cyprus, and Malta.	Includes all domestic and regional developments in Africa and the Middle East, including Iraq and Iran and excluding Cyprus, Turkey, and Afghanistan.	Includes all domestic and regional developments in Latin America, the Caribbean, and Canada.	Includes all domestic and regional developments in Asia and Pacific nations, extending from Afghanistan through all the Pacific Islands, except Hawaii.

U.S. Politics & Social Issues	U.S. Foreign Policy & Defense	U.S. Economy & Environment	Science, Technology, & Nature	Culture, Leisure, & Lifestyle	
The South Carolina Supreme Court upholds the criminal prosecution of Cornelia Whitner, who was convicted of child neglect in 1992 for using cocaine while pregnant.... Health officials in Chautauqua County, New York, have identified Nushawn J. Williams as the man they believe infected at least 10 people with HIV, the virus that causes AIDS.	The U.S. Coast Guard arrests four Cuban Americans on a boat in waters near the U.S. territory of Puerto Rico on suspicion of conspiracy to commit murder and illegal possession of firearms.... Three Japanese shipping companies reach a settlement with the U.S. Federal Maritime Commission (FMC) over fines imposed in September, ending a dispute in which the U.S. had threatened to ban Japanese ships from its ports in retaliation against restrictive Japanese harbor practices.	The Dow Jones plunges 554.26 points, to 7161.15, down 7.18% from the previous day's close. It is the largest one-day point decline in the Dow's history, though it is only the index's 12th-largest drop in percentage terms.... Pres. Clinton reveals that the federal government's budget deficit for fiscal 1997 was $22.6 billion, the lowest annual deficit since 1974. ... Pres. Clinton signs a $13.1 billion transportation appropriations bill for fiscal 1998. He also signs $90.7 billion fiscal 1998 appropriations bill for veterans affairs, housing, space, environmental protection, and other independent agencies.		First Lady Hillary Rodham Clinton celebrates her 50th birthday with a visit to her hometown, Park Ridge, Illinois.	Oct. 27
The Senate confirms Pres. Clinton's three other nominees fill vacancies on the FCC. They are Michael Powell, Harold Furchtgott-Roth, and Gloria Tristani.... Walter Holden Capps, 63, Democratic U.S. congressman from California (1997) whose 1996 victory over Republican representative Andrea Seastrand marked the first time that a Democrat had won control of the seat since World War II, dies in Washington, D.C., of a heart attack.	The House votes, 286-123, to pass a $268.2 billion fiscal 1998 defense-authorization bill.... Sergeant Marvin Kelley is sentenced to a suspended three-month jail term and a dishonorable discharge for sexual misconduct. Army officials report that they will not pursue criminal charges against Sergeant First Class William Jones but will discharge him from the army. Kelley and Jones are the final 11th and 12th, respectively, Aberdeen soldiers facing sexual misconduct charges.	The Dow rebounds from its Oct, 27 fall, climbing 337.17 points to 7498.32, a record single-session gain in point terms. It is 70th best on the basis of percentage, at 4.7%. ... The Senate clears, 84-14, the final version of the fiscal 1998 interior appropriations bill that allocates $13.8 billion for the Department of the Interior and related agencies.		The Baltimore Symphony Orchestra states that Yuri Temirkanov will be its new music director.... The National Basketball Association hires the first female referees in any of the U.S.'s four major all-male sports league: Dee Kantner and Violet Palmer.... Paul Jarrico, 82, screenwriter who was blacklisted in 1951, dies in Ojai, California, in a car accident.	Oct. 28
The Senate confirms William Kennard as the new chair of the FCC.		The Senate clears, by voice vote, a $49.7 billion agriculture appropriations bill for fiscal 1998.	A Union Pacific train carrying toxic chemicals along with other freight rams the rear of another train and bursts into flames in Navasota, Texas.		Oct. 29
The CDC reports that the incidence of diabetes in the U.S. is at an all-time high as 10 million residents have been diagnosed with diabetes, compared with 1.6 million in 1958..... A standoff that started Sept. 22 in Roby, Illinois, ends when police apprehend Shirley Allen, 51, by pelting her with rubber bullets and take her to a hospital where she will undergo psychiatric testing.	Louise Woodward, a 19-year-old British au pair, is found guilty by a jury in Middlesex County, Massachusetts, of second-degree murder in the death of Matthew Eappen, her eight-month-old ward. Hundreds of her supporters stage protests in her hometown of Elton, England, and in Middlesex.... Data shows the U.S. deported a record 112,000 illegal immigrants in the 1997 fiscal year. The previous record of 69,000 was set in fiscal 1996.	The House, 242-182, passes a bill to revise federal livestock grazing policy.... The House votes, 307-120, to approve a bill that will require the Department of Energy to fund the construction of an interim storage site for high-level nuclear waste by the year 2002.... The Senate, by voice vote, confirms two nominees—Roger Ferguson and Edward Gramlich—to the Federal Reserve Board of Governors.	The European Space Agency (ESA) successfully test-launches its new unmanned Ariane-5 satellite-delivery rocket, which failed in its debut launch in 1996.	Samuel Michael Fuller, 85, motion picture director, producer, and screenwriter, dies in Hollywood Hills, California, of unreported causes.	Oct. 30
A Texas District Court jury convicts Richard McLaren and Robert Otto—members of a group known as the Republic of Texas, which argues that Texas was illegally annexed by the U.S. in 1845—of organized criminal activity for the August abduction of Joe and Margaret Ann Rowe.... A state circuit court jury in Jacksonville, Florida, finds that R.J. Reynolds Tobacco Co. does not owe damages to JoAnn Karbiwnyk, 59, who developed lung cancer.	Louise Woodward, a 19-year-old British au pair convicted of second-degree murder on Oct. 30, is sentenced to life in prison, causing controversy.... The House passes by voice vote a bill that will bar veterans convicted of federal capital crimes from being buried in national veterans' cemeteries.... The House by voice vote passes a bill extending the annual cost-of-living increase to veterans' benefits.	Senate Governmental Affairs Committee Chairman Fred Thompson (R, Tenn.) suspends the panel's public hearings into campaign-finance abuses that allegedly occurred during the 1996 elections, unless new evidence becomes available. The probe has cost $2.6 million.... The Surface Transportation Board, a federal agency, declares that persistent delays on the Union Pacific Railroad's tracks constitutes "a transportation emergency" in the Houston, Texas, area.	Two teams of scientists report that they have genetically engineered mice to mimic the human blood disease sickle cell anemia. The mice, the first animal models of the disease, will greatly assist research by enabling animal testing of drug treatments and gene therapies.		Oct. 31
In Kansas City, Missouri, Texas billionaire and two-time presidential candidate Ross Perot appears as the featured speaker before 800 delegates at the inaugural convention of the Reform Party, which he founded in 1995.	President Jiang Zemin of China gives a speech at Harvard University, where around 1,500 protesters rally while 1,200 Jiang's supporters stage counterdemonstrations. The closest Jiang comes to acknowledging human-rights violations is in response to a question about Tiananmen Square, when he admits, "We may have shortcomings and even make some mistakes in our work."	President Clinton invokes his line-item veto authority to eliminate seven projects from a $90.7 billion fiscal 1998 appropriations bill signed Oct. 27 for veterans affairs, housing, space, environmental protection, and other independent agencies. He also cuts three projects from a $13.1 billion fiscal 1998 transportation bill.... Judge Susan Webber Wright grants Kenneth Starr's request to extend the grand jury investigating the Whitewater affair to May 7, 1998, two years after it first convened.		Southern Christian Leadership Conference delegates unanimously approve the selection of Martin Luther King III, the eldest son of slain civil-rights leader Martin Luther King Jr., as the group's president. He will replace the retiring president, Rev. Joseph E. Lowery Jr., who took the post in 1977.	Nov. 1
F	G	H	I	J	
Includes elections, federal-state relations, civil rights and liberties, crime, the judiciary, education, health care, poverty, urban affairs, and population.	*Includes formation and debate of U.S. foreign and defense policies, veterans' affairs, and defense spending. (Relations with specific foreign countries are usually found under the region concerned.)*	*Includes business, labor, agriculture, taxation, transportation, consumer affairs, monetary and fiscal policy, natural resources, and pollution.*	*Includes worldwide scientific, medical, and technological developments; natural phenomena; U.S. weather; natural disasters; and accidents.*	*Includes the arts, religion, scholarship, communications media, sports, entertainments, fashions, fads, and social life.*	

	World Affairs	Europe	Africa & the Middle East	The Americas	Asia & the Pacific
Nov. 2	At the close of a summit meeting in Siberia, Japanese premier Ryutaro Hashimoto and Russian president Boris Yeltsin pledge to sign a peace treaty by the year 2000, ending a diplomatic freeze that has lasted since the end of World War II.	Some 250,000 French truck drivers launch a massive strike, blockading major roads and ports as part of an effort to secure pay raises and a reduction in working hours.... Baron Edmond Adolphe Maurice Jules Jacques de Rothschild, 71, believed to be the wealthiest member of the renowned French Rothschild banking dynasty, dies in Geneva, Switzerland, of emphysema.		Police in Guerrero state, Mexico, discover the mutilated bodies of at least two doctors believed to have participated in ultimately fatal cosmetic surgery on Amado Carrillo Fuentes, who allegedly headed the powerful Juarez drug cartel, in July.	
Nov. 3	The UN's International Labor Organization (ILO) finds that union membership fell in most industrialized countries between 1985 and 1995. Union membership declined most rapidly during the 10-year period in Central and Eastern Europe. However, union membership increased dramatically in South Africa (127%), Spain (92%) and Chile (90%), during the same period. About 164 million of the world's 1.3 billion workers are unionized.	Nearly 1,000 refugees, mostly Turkish Kurds, arrive in southern Italy from Albania, reportedly fleeing persecution by the Turkish government.... Greek premier Costas Simitis and Turkish premier Mesut Yilmaz agree to work toward improving relations between their countries.... Reports confirm that five people are still missing from the Oct. 31 mudslides in the Portuguese Azores that have left at least 26 people dead.			Typhoon Linda, with winds of more than 80 miles per hour (130 kmph), batters Vietnam's coast, killing more than 100 people and devastating several villages in Ca Mau province. It is the worst storm to hit Vietnam in nearly a century.... Thai premier Chavalit Yongchaiyudh states that he will resign.... New Zealand prime minister Jim Bolger, under pressure from the ruling National Party, reveals he will resign.
Nov. 4			Progovernment independents emerge as the dominant force in Jordan's parliament in elections boycotted by the Islamic bloc and eight smaller, mainly leftist political parties.	Gunmen allegedly belonging to a right-wing paramilitary group in Chiapas, Mexico, open fire on the car of Roman Catholic bishop Samuel Ruiz, a chief mediator between the EZLN and the government. Ruiz is unharmed.... George Michael Chambers, 69, prime minister of Trinidad and Tobago, 1981–86, dies in Port of Spain, Trinidad, of a heart attack.	Although only 120 deaths have been confirmed, more than 1,000 other people are presumed to have perished aboard some 1,300 fishing vessels that sank Nov. 3 due to Typhoon Linda.... Five violent offenders escape from their cells at the high-security Sir David Longland Correctional Centre in Brisbane, Australia.
Nov. 5		Russia's parliament ratifies a global treaty banning chemical weapons. Russia has the world's largest poison gas arsenal.... The Spanish city of Badajoz reportedly receives as much as 5.5 inches (14 cm) of rain during the night.			
Nov. 6		At least 21 people drown in and near Badajoz, Spain, where rain since Nov. 5 has caused several rivers to overflow. Also hard hit by the floods are the Algarve and Alentejo regions of Portugal, where 10 other victims drown.... Yugoslav authorities arrest Slobodan Misic, a former paramilitary who has confessed to torture and killing.... Paul Ricard, 88, French liquor manufacturer, dies in Signes, France.		In Cuba, 56 people are killed and six others are injured when a passenger train collides with an overcrowded bus near the town of San German in Holguin province.	
Nov. 7	The seventh annual Ibero-American Summit opens on Venezuela's Margarita Island.			Colombia's Constitutional Court rules that armed citizens' groups, which formed to combat leftist rebels, are legal.... In Canada, five unions representing Ontario's 126,000 elementary and high school teachers end a walkout started Oct. 27. Although the strike was the largest teachers' walkout ever in North America, it did not force the province to delay or rework draft legislation to alter the Ontario educational system.	In Thailand, former premier Chuan Leekpai, leader of the opposition Democrat Party, emerges the successor to Chavalit Yongchaiyudh, who announced his resignation as premier on Nov. 3.

A	B	C	D	E
Includes developments that affect more than one world region, international organizations, and important meetings of major world leaders.	*Includes all domestic and regional developments in Europe, including the Soviet Union, Turkey, Cyprus, and Malta.*	*Includes all domestic and regional developments in Africa and the Middle East, including Iraq and Iran and excluding Cyprus, Turkey, and Afghanistan.*	*Includes all domestic and regional developments in Latin America, the Caribbean, and Canada.*	*Includes all domestic and regional developments in Asia and Pacific nations, extending from Afghanistan through all the Pacific Islands, except Hawaii.*

U.S. Politics & Social Issues	U.S. Foreign Policy & Defense	U.S. Economy & Environment	Science, Technology, & Nature	Culture, Leisure, & Lifestyle	
				David Duval wins the PGA Tour Championship in Houston, Texas. . . . Franziska Rochat-Moser of Switzerland wins the women's race in the 28th New York City Marathon, becoming the first Swiss runner ever to win a major marathon. John Kagwe of Kenya wins the men's race.	**Nov. 2**
The Supreme Court refuses without comment to hear a challenge to Proposition 209, a California law that bars the state government from relying on race- or gender-based preferences in school admissions, public hiring, and public contracting decisions. . . . Opening statements are delivered in the trial of Terry Nichols, accused of collaborating with Timothy McVeigh in the Apr. 19, 1995, bombing of a federal building in Oklahoma City, Oklahoma.	Pres. Clinton signs an executive order imposing new economic sanctions on Sudan for its alleged human-rights abuses and sponsorship of terrorism.	The Senate votes, 92-0, to confirm the appointment of Charles O. Rossotti as commissioner of the IRS. . . . Data shows that the purchasing managers' index rose to 56 in October, from September's figure of 54.2. The October index marks the 17th consecutive month that the indicator has surpassed the 50 level indicative of expansion in the manufacturing sector.	Warner-Lambert Co., the U.S. maker of troglitazone, a diabetes drug marketed as Rezulin, issues a warning to doctors that in rare cases the popular drug may cause serious liver damage.	*Cold Mountain*, by Charles Frazier, tops the bestseller list. . . . Wallace C. (Wally) Bruner, 66, television host, dies near Indianapolis, Indiana, of liver cancer.	**Nov. 3**
In elections, Republicans maintain their lead over Democrats in Congress and among the nation's governors. Residents of Houston, Texas, reject a measure that would have barred city agencies from relying on affirmative-action targets in hiring and contracting. Voters in Washington defeat a bill that would have required all handguns sold in the state to be equipped with a trigger guard. Oregon voters decide to keep the nation's only law that allows physician-assisted suicide. . . . Texas separatists Richard McLaren and Robert Otto, convicted Oct. 31, are sentenced to 99 years and 50 years in prison, respectively.	Immigration officials disclose that they deported Pedro Antonio Andrade, a former Salvadoran guerrilla suspected of involvement in the killing of six Americans in El Salvador in 1985. The U.S. in 1990 granted Andrade and his family a visa despite its apparent knowledge of his role in the murders, and Andrade agreed to work as a CIA informant in return. . . . Amanda Kaufman quits the VMI, a military academy in Lexington, Virginia, that has started enrolling female students. Four of the 30 female first-year students have quit to date, as have 42 of the 430 male freshmen.	In *State Oil Co. v. Khan*, the Supreme Court rules unanimously that manufacturers and wholesalers may set ceilings on the prices that retailers may charge for their products. The ruling, which is considered a landmark decision in U.S. antitrust law, overturns a 1968 Supreme Court precedent.	Jet Propulsion Laboratory scientists officially announce the end of the Mars lander's mission. Scientists believe that *Pathfinder* has frozen in Mars's cold atmosphere and that the craft's batteries have died. . . . The FTC reveals that it has reached two settlements with companies that illegally rerouted the on-line connections of Internet computer network users to Moldova, causing the users to accumulate large long-distance phone charges. Under the agreement, several firms and individuals will pay a total of $2.74 million in refunds to about 38,000 consumers.	Ralph Burton Rogers, 87, founder of PBS and philanthropist, dies in Dallas, Texas. . . . Samantha Geimer, 33, makes her identity public for the first time in 20 years when she discusses her underage sexual relationship with film director Roman Polanski, which started when she was 13 years old.	**Nov. 4**
	The Senate clears, by voice vote, a bill extending the annual cost-of-living increase to veterans' benefits. . . . The House begins passing a series of measures, largely considered symbolic, that penalize China for human-rights violations.	The House passes, 426-4, an extensive overhaul of the IRS. . . . Roger Ferguson Jr. and Edward Gramlich are sworn in as new members of the Federal Reserve Board. . . . Edgar Swaab resigns as managing director of FTC in the midst of an investigation of a scandal involving the Dutch brokerage firm Leemhuis & Van Loon. He denies wrongdoing.	Scientists reveal that the use of milder, filtered cigarettes since the 1950s has increased the incidence of adenocarcinoma, a type of lung cancer. . . . A 12-member panel convened by the NIH concludes that the ancient Chinese practice of acupuncture is effective in treating some forms of pain and nausea and recommends that appropriate uses of acupuncture be covered by medical insurers.	Sir Isaiah Berlin, 88, Russian-born scholar of intellectual history and political thought, dies in Oxford, England, of a heart attack.	**Nov. 5**
U.S. district judge James Ware withdraws his nomination to the U.S. Ninth Circuit Court of Appeals after confessing that he fabricated a story that he was the brother of Virgil Lamar Ware, a teenager murdered in Birmingham, Alabama, in 1963. Ware, who is black, often recounted how the racially motivated murder of his brother inspired him to become a lawyer. . . . The Massachusetts state assembly defeats, 80-80, a bill to legalize the death penalty. Under the state's parliamentary rules, a tie effectively defeats the legislation. Massachusetts is one of 12 states in which the death penalty is barred.	The Senate confirms 23 U.S. ambassadors. . . . The Senate clears, 90-10, a $268.2 billion defense authorization bill for fiscal 1998. . . . The Senate passes by a voice vote the fiscal 1998 intelligence authorization bill. Although the exact funding level is technically classified, the amount is reported to be nearly $27 billion.	A federally mandated overseer in charge of investigating corruption within the Laborers' International Union of North America (LIUNA) files charges against union president Arthur Coia, accusing him of having ties to organized crime and improperly accepting gifts from a union service provider. . . . Data suggests that in 1996 U.S. companies increased spending on research for the second straight year. Spending grew to $118.65 billion, up 9% from 1995 levels. Federal research subsidies fell slightly, to $20.9 billion.	Two teams of astronomers report to a meeting of the American Astronomical Society in Estes Park, Colorado, that they have confirmed the prediction of Albert Einstein's theory of relativity that very large rotating astronomical objects will warp the surrounding fabric of space-time in an effect called "frame dragging."	Four of the five living U.S. presidents—Bill Clinton, George Bush, Gerald Ford, and Jimmy Carter—attend the dedication of the George Bush Presidential Library and Museum at Texas A&M University. . . . Lillian Adele Rogers Parks, 100, White House seamstress and maid whose memoir became a bestseller, dies in Washington, D.C., of a heart attack.	**Nov. 6**
The House approves, 367-57, a bill that will increase federal funding for "charter schools," publicly funded schools that operate independently of school district supervision and that are encouraged to experiment with teaching strategies.	The House votes, 385-36, to adopt the fiscal 1998 intelligence authorization bill. The bill authorizes funding for the CIA and other intelligence-related agencies. Although the exact funding level is classified, the amount is estimated to be nearly $27 billion.	The House votes, 352-65, to pass a fiscal 1998 measure that allocates $80.4 billion in discretionary spending for the Departments of Labor, Education, and Health and Human Services (HHS). . . . The Labor Department reports that the seasonally adjusted unemployment rate in the U.S. fell to 4.7% in October from September's revised rate of 4.9% the lowest since October 1973.			**Nov. 7**

F	G	H	I	J
Includes elections, federal-state relations, civil rights and liberties, crime, the judiciary, education, health care, poverty, urban affairs, and population.	*Includes formation and debate of U.S. foreign and defense policies, veterans' affairs, and defense spending. (Relations with specific foreign countries are usually found under the region concerned.)*	*Includes business, labor, agriculture, taxation, transportation, consumer affairs, monetary and fiscal policy, natural resources, and pollution.*	*Includes worldwide scientific, medical, and technological developments; natural phenomena; U.S. weather; natural disasters; and accidents.*	*Includes the arts, religion, scholarship, communications media, sports, entertainments, fashions, fads, and social life.*

	World Affairs	Europe	Africa & the Middle East	The Americas	Asia & the Pacific
Nov. 8		After reaching an agreement, some 250,000 French truck drivers end a massive strike that started Nov. 2, during which major roads and ports were blockaded.	Iraq's Kurdistan Democratic Party (KDP) launches an all-out offensive against the Patriotic Union of Kurdistan (PUK) from Degala, which is east of the city of Irbil, to the town of Shaqlawah, some 30 miles (50 km) to the north. Both Iraqi Kurdish factions are vying for supremacy in U.N.-protected northern Iraq.	Nine people are killed and more than 3,000 people are left homeless in southern Ecuador because heavy rains have caused a number of rivers to overflow. Some 20,000 acres (8,000 hectares) of crops are also destroyed in the floods.	Fifteen Japanese-born women who live in North Korea with their Korean husbands are permitted to make their first visit to Japan since moving to North Korea in the late 1950s and early 1960s. . . . Chinese workers complete the diversion of the Yangtze River into a side channel, clearing the site of the Three Gorges Dam, an enormous hydroelectric power project to be completed in 2009.
Nov. 9	Russian president Boris Yeltsin visits China to hold a summit with Chinese president Jiang Zemin.		Iran ratifies the Chemical Weapons Convention, which bans the manufacture and storage of nerve-gas weapons.	Hurricane Rick hits Mexico's southern coast. Winds and rains from the hurricane destroy buildings, power lines, and roads but cause no deaths.	King Bhumibol Adulyadej of Thailand formally appoints Chuan Leekpai as premier.
Nov. 10	Russian president Boris Yeltsin and Chinese president Jiang Zemin sign a pact codifying the 2,800-mile-long border between their countries from Mongolia to North Korea. A 1991 deal between China and the Soviet Union established much of the border, but geographical complexities have kept some territory in dispute.	In Bosnia-Herzegovina, Danish troops from the NATO force seize the headquarters of the branch of the Serb special paramilitary police in the town of Doboj, which is under the control of former Bosnian Serb president Radovan Karadzic.	Israel and the Vatican sign an agreement that defines the Roman Catholic Church's legal status in Israel. Under terms of the pact, church institutions are accorded internal autonomy, while their outside activities fall under the purview of Israeli law.		
Nov. 11	The EU's European Court of Justice rules in favor of a law in Germany's North Rhine-Westphalia state under which women are given preference for public-sector jobs. The decision effectively upholds the practice of affirmative action in hiring in EU nations. . . . Members of the UNESCO adopt by unanimous consent a declaration outlining ethical standards for human genetic research, including cloning.	Mary McAleese is sworn in as president of the Republic of Ireland. McAleese, 46, is the country's first president to hail from Northern Ireland, a British-controlled province, and succeeds Mary Robinson, who resigned to become the UN High Commissioner for Human Rights. . . . The lower house of the Czech parliament approves the creation of a securities and exchange commission.	Egyptian president Hosni Mubarak announces Egypt's boycott of the Middle East-North Africa Economic Conference (MENA) in a speech to members of his ruling National Democratic Party.	One person is reported killed during clashes that break out between government troops and protesters in Santo Domingo, the capital of the Dominican Republic, during a strike. . . . An international team of police arrest alleged Australian sex offender Robert (Dolly) Dunn in the Honduran capital, Tegucigalpa. Dunn, 56, is one of the most wanted alleged criminals in Australia, where he faces 85 charges.	
Nov. 12	The UN Security Council imposes a travel ban on Iraqi officials who do not cooperate with UN arms inspections.	Reports confirm that Belgian authorities have detained Eli Ndayambaje and Joseph Kanyabashi, former mayors of two Rwandan villages, at the request of the Rwandan war-crimes tribunal. . . . The regional parliament of Saratov, in the Volga River region, passes the first formal Russian law to legalize the buying and selling of land. The right to buy and sell property was guaranteed in the 1993 Russian constitution, but no regulations have existed outlining the legal structure of such deals.		More than 2,000 leftist demonstrators take to the streets of Brasilia, the capital of Brazil, to voice their opposition to economic austerity measures.	Gunmen shoot to death four U.S. businessmen and their Pakistani driver in Karachi, Pakistan's largest city and business hub. . . . Officials state that Malaysian prime minister Mahathir bin Mohamad will face a vote of confidence in response to international condemnation of his comments made in October. Mahathir said, "We are Muslims, and the Jews are not happy to see the Muslims progress. The Jews robbed the Palestinians of everything, but in Malaysia they could not do so, hence they do this, depress the ringgit."

A	B	C	D	E
Includes developments that affect more than one world region, international organizations, and important meetings of major world leaders.	*Includes all domestic and regional developments in Europe, including the Soviet Union, Turkey, Cyprus, and Malta.*	*Includes all domestic and regional developments in Africa and the Middle East, including Iraq and Iran and excluding Cyprus, Turkey, and Afghanistan.*	*Includes all domestic and regional developments in Latin America, the Caribbean, and Canada.*	*Includes all domestic and regional developments in Asia and Pacific nations, extending from Afghanistan through all the Pacific Islands, except Hawaii.*

U.S. Politics & Social Issues	U.S. Foreign Policy & Defense	U.S. Economy & Environment	Science, Technology, & Nature	Culture, Leisure, & Lifestyle	
Pres. Clinton becomes the first U.S. president to address a gay and lesbian organization when he speaks to the Human Rights Campaign, a leading gay rights group, in Washington, D.C. . . . The House approves, by voice vote, a bill designed to improve literacy among children.	A report on Gulf War Syndrome criticizes the Department of Defense for failing to adequately address the health problems suffered by veterans of the 1991 conflict. In response, Pres. Clinton announces that his administration will spend $13.2 million and appoint an independent panel to oversee government investigations into the syndrome. . . . The House passes, 352-64, legislation that would have overturned Pres. Clinton's recent use of the presidential line-item veto power to strike 38 items from a military construction spending bill for fiscal 1998.	The Senate confirms Nancy-Ann Min DeParle as head of the Health Care Financing Administration, which operates the Medicare and Medicaid programs. . . . The Senate approves by voice vote a bill reauthorizing the Export-Import Bank through Sept. 30, 2001. . . . The Senate approves, 91-4, a fiscal 1998 bill appropriating $80.4 billion in discretionary spending for the Departments of Labor, Education, and Health and Human Services (HHS).		Reports state that Pres. Clinton has selected a site in the new River Market district of Little Rock, Arkansas, for his presidential library. . . . Skip Away wins the Breeders' Cup Classic in Inglewood, California. . . . WBA heavyweight champion Evander Holyfield defeats Michael Moorer, the IBF heavyweight champion, in Las Vegas, Nevada.	Nov. 8
The Senate confirms Kevin Gover as head of the Bureau of Indian Affairs.	The Senate, by voice vote, clears legislation that will overturn Pres. Clinton's recent use of the presidential line-item veto power to strike 38 items from a military construction spending bill for fiscal 1998. . . . The Senate passes a bill intended to punish China for its human-rights practices, arms sales, and policy toward Taiwan. It is the ninth such measure passed by the House since Nov. 5.	The House approves, by voice vote, a bill reauthorizing the Export-Import Bank through Sept. 30, 2001. . . . The Senate passes, by voice vote, a bill to create a gold-colored dollar coin and a series of quarters commemorating the 50 states.	The House and Senate both pass, by voice vote, legislation that reforms the approval process for drugs and other medical products by the FDA. . . . Researchers report that genes injected into the legs of patients with blocked leg arteries stimulated the growth of new blood vessels. The results are seen as a major advance in the medical use of gene therapies.	Pope John Paul II beatifies Vilmos Apor, a Hungarian bishop who resisted Nazi and Soviet forces; Giovanni Battista Scalabrini, an Italian bishop who died in 1905; and Dorotea Chavez, a Mexican nun who died in 1949.	Nov. 9
Pres. Clinton opens a daylong conference on hate crimes at George Washington University in Washington, D.C. . . . A three-judge panel of the U.S. Fourth Circuit Court of Appeals in Richmond, Virginia, rules that a book that provides instructions for carrying out contract murders is not protected by the Constitution's First Amendment.	The Senate clears a bill barring veterans convicted of federal or state capital crimes from being buried in national veterans' cemeteries. . . . Judge Hiller Zobel reduces the conviction of Louise Woodward, the British au pair found guilty Oct. 30, to manslaughter and sentences her to 279 days in jail, which she has already served. . . . A Virginia jury convicts Mir Aimal Kasi of 10 charges, including one count of capital murder, in connection with the January 1993 shooting deaths of CIA employees Frank Darling and Lansing Bennett outside CIA headquarters in Langley, Virginia.	The Senate passes, by voice vote, a six-month stopgap bill authorizing $9.8 billion in funding for the nation's mass-transit systems and highways.	The Senate passes legislation to criminalize the "cloning" of cellular telephones, in which the electronic serial number of a cellular phone is transferred to other phones for illegitimate use. . . . The House passes, by voice vote, legislation exempting the National Academy of Sciences (NAS) from openness rules of the 1972 Federal Advisory Committee Act. The NAS is a body chartered by Congress to provide scientific advice to the government.	French author Patrick Rambaud is awarded the Goncourt Prize, France's most coveted literary award, for his novel *La Bataille* (*The Battle*). . . . Pop artist Peter Max, 60, pleads guilty to single counts of conspiracy and tax evasion in U.S. District Court in New York City.	Nov. 10
				Rod(ney) Milburn Jr., 47, track star who won a gold at the 1972 Olympics in Munich, is found dead in Port Hudson, Louisiana, after an apparent workplace accident in which he fell into a bleach-filled rail car.	Nov. 11
Data suggest that the nation's college-loan default rate fell to 10.4% for the 1995 fiscal year, from 10.7% the previous year. The latest drop continues a decline in the rate that began after 1990, when it reached a peak of 22.4%. . . . A Delaware political operative, Thomas J. Capano, is arrested and charged with the murder of Anne Marie Fahey, an aide to Gov. Thomas Carper (D, Del.) with whom Capano had a secret affair.	A federal jury in New York City convicts Muslim fundamentalist Ramzi Ahmed Yousef and his codefendant, Eyad Ismoil, of conspiracy and explosives-related charges for the 1993 bombing of the World Trade Center. Four other Islamic militants have also been convicted of charges related to the bombing. . . . A measure in the District of Columbia appropriations bill that the House passes grants permanent resident status to some 150,000 Nicaraguans and 5,000 Cubans who arrived in the U.S. before Dec. 1, 1995.	The House passes, by voice vote, a package of technical changes to the bankruptcy code. . . . The House clears, by voice vote, a six-month stopgap bill authorizing $9.8 billion in funding for the nation's mass-transit systems and highways. . . . The House passes, by voice vote, a fiscal 1998 appropriations bill allocating $855 million for the District of Columbia. The House had passed the bill by voice vote on November 12, and the Senate cleared it the following day, also by acclamation		Lindy (Corinne C.) Boggs is sworn in as ambassador to the Vatican. . . . James Laughlin, 83, publisher and poet who founded New Directions Publishing Corp., dies in Norfolk, Connecticut, after a stroke.	Nov. 12

F	G	H	I	J
Includes elections, federal-state relations, civil rights and liberties, crime, the judiciary, education, health care, poverty, urban affairs, and population.	*Includes formation and debate of U.S. foreign and defense policies, veterans' affairs, and defense spending. (Relations with specific foreign countries are usually found under the region concerned.)*	*Includes business, labor, agriculture, taxation, transportation, consumer affairs, monetary and fiscal policy, natural resources, and pollution.*	*Includes worldwide scientific, medical, and technological developments; natural phenomena; U.S. weather; natural disasters; and accidents.*	*Includes the arts, religion, scholarship, communications media, sports, entertainments, fashions, fads, and social life.*

	World Affairs	Europe	Africa & the Middle East	The Americas	Asia & the Pacific
Nov. 13	Iraq expels six U.S. arms inspectors who are member of the UN Special Commission (UNSCOM), prompting other inspectors to leave and sparking a dispute over the future of seven-year-old UN economic sanctions on Iraq.	The German Bundestag, the lower house of Parliament, passes legislation rescinding a 1950 law that allowed Nazi war criminals to receive war-victim pension payments.			
Nov. 14	Mexican president Zedillo and U.S. president Clinton, along with representatives of 26 other member nations of the Organization of American States (OAS), sign an accord to fight trafficking in illegal weapons.... La Francophonie, a loose alliance of 49 French-speaking nations, holds its seventh summit in Hanoi, Vietnam.		Progovernment and opposition parties win nearly equal numbers of seats in legislative elections in Morocco. The vote is the first since 1996 constitutional reforms that provided for the direct election of all members of the lower house of the federal parliament.		Indonesian police clash with student protesters outside the University of East Timor in Dili, the provincial capital. The protesters claim that two students were killed when police fired shots into the air to disperse the activists. A military spokesman counters that police fired only warning shots and that no students were killed.
Nov. 15			The UN World Food Program estimates that 148,200 acres of Somalian cropland are waterlogged. CARE International in Somalia suggests that the death toll there is at least 2,000 due to torrential rains and floods.		The State Law and Order Council (SLORC), Myanmar's ruling military junta, announces that it has dissolved itself and formed a new leadership council called the State Peace and Development Council (SPDC).... Chinese authorities grant medical parole to Wei Jingsheng, a prominent political dissident imprisoned in China for most of the previous 18 years. He will leave for the U.S., and if he returns to China, he will be arrested.
Nov. 16		A majority of Hungarian voters approve an offer to join NATO.... Italy's ruling center-left Olive Tree coalition registers several major victories in local elections.... Georges René-Louis Marchais, 77, leader of the French Communist Party, 1972–94, dies in Paris after suffering with heart and lung ailments.			
Nov. 17	Five new judges are sworn in at the international war crimes tribunal at The Hague, starting its second four-year term.		More than 300 people die in clashes between Hutu guerrillas and the Rwandan army when rebels try to free Hutu prisoners jailed on genocide charges northwest of Kigali, the capital.... The Juba and Shabelle rivers merge, covering almost 60 square miles (155 sq km) with water in Somalia..... Six gunmen ambush visitors at an Egyptian tourist site in Luxor, killing some 65 foreign tourists and wounding 24 others.		
Nov. 18	The annual Middle East-North Africa Economic Conference (MENA), boycotted for the first time by Egypt and other key pro-U.S. Arab nations, closes with a declaration calling on Israel to exchange occupied Arab land for peace.	The Swiss Fund for Needy Victims of the Holocaust distributes its first payments to 80 Jewish Holocaust survivors in Riga, Latvia.... An employee of the UN Commissioner for Refugees, Karine Mane, and a male friend, Franck Janier-Dubry of the EU, are kidnapped by forces loyal to mercenary Tajik commander Rizvon Sadirov.	Egypt's largest and most violent militant Islamic organization, Gamaa al Islamiya (Islamic Group), claims responsibility for the Nov, 17 shootings, which were by far the deadliest in a five-year-old insurgency campaign launched against foreign tourists and Egyptian government officials in an attempt to topple the government of Pres. Hosni Mubarak.	The Canadian federal Parliament's lower house, the House of Commons, votes to amend Canada's 1982 constitution in order to allow Quebec to replace its religious-based school board system with one drawn along linguistic lines.	At least 29 schoolchildren are killed when their school bus plunges into the Yamuna River near New Delhi, the capital of India. More than 60 other children are injured, and another 20 are missing and presumed dead.... Chen Chin-hsing, a man wanted for the murder of a teenager in April, takes a South African military attaché, Edward Alexander, and his family hostage. Over the next 24 hours, he releases two of them, both wounded, before setting them all free.

A	B	C	D	E
Includes developments that affect more than one world region, international organizations, and important meetings of major world leaders.	Includes all domestic and regional developments in Europe, including the Soviet Union, Turkey, Cyprus, and Malta.	Includes all domestic and regional developments in Africa and the Middle East, including Iraq and Iran and excluding Cyprus, Turkey, and Afghanistan.	Includes all domestic and regional developments in Latin America, the Caribbean, and Canada.	Includes all domestic and regional developments in Asia and Pacific nations, extending from Afghanistan through all the Pacific Islands, except Hawaii.

U.S. Politics & Social Issues	U.S. Foreign Policy & Defense	U.S. Economy & Environment	Science, Technology, & Nature	Culture, Leisure, & Lifestyle	
The House, 406-7, and the Senate, by voice vote, pass a bipartisan bill aimed at speeding up and increasing the permanent adoption of the 500,000 abused and neglected children in the nation's foster care system.... In the Justice Department's first annual survey of stalking, figures show that more than 1 million women and some 370,000 men are stalked each year in the U.S.	By passing the appropriations for the District of Columbia and the Commerce-Justice-State departments, Congress approves measures in those bills that reform the 1996 immigration law.... Pres. Clinton vetoes legislation that would have overturned his recent use of the presidential line-item veto power to strike 38 items from a military construction spending bill for fiscal 1998.... The House, 333-76, and the Senate, by voice vote, clear a $13.1 billion fiscal 1998 foreign operations appropriations bill.	The Senate passes, by voice vote, a $855 million fiscal 1998 bill for the District of Columbia.... The House passes, by voice vote, a bill to create a gold-colored dollar coin and a series of quarters honoring the 50 states.... Congress clears a bill authorizing funds for Amtrak through 2002.... Congress clears a $31.8 billion bill for the Departments of Commerce, Justice, and State and related agencies in fiscal 1998.... Pres. Clinton signs an $80.4 billion fiscal 1998 bill for the Departments of Labor, Education, and HHS.	The FDA, NIH, and CDC recommend medical examinations for heart or lung disease for all people who took either of two popular diet medications withdrawn from the market in September, fenfluramine and dexfenfluramine.... The Senate clears legislation exempting the National Academy of Sciences (NAS) from openness rules of the 1972 Federal Advisory Committee Act. The NAS is a body chartered by Congress to provide scientific advice to the government.		Nov. 13
Judge Sandra Silver orders Nathaniel Jamal Abraham, 11, to stand trial as an adult for the sniper shooting of Ronnie Green Jr. He will be the youngest person ever tried as an adult for murder in Michigan... Judge Mariana Pfaelzer rules that major sections of California's controversial Proposition 187 are both unconstitutional and in violation of 1996's federal welfare-reform law. The measure seeks to deny education, health, and welfare benefits to illegal immigrants.	A Fairfax County (Virginia) Circuit Court jury recommends the death penalty for Mir Aimal Kasi, who was convicted Nov. 10 for the shooting deaths of two CIA employees in 1993.... Sara Lister, the army's top personnel official, resigns amid a furor over comments that she made about the Marine Corps in October.	The U.S. Court of Appeals in Washington, D.C., rules that utility companies may seek financial compensation from the government if the government does not make good on its legal obligation, beginning Jan. 31, 1998, to ship and store the companies' nuclear waste.... Pres. Clinton signs the $13.8 billion fiscal 1998 appropriations bill for the Department of the Interior and related agencies.	Reports confirm that three separate studies have located HIV, the virus that causes AIDS, resting dormant in infected patients whose blood levels of the virus have become undetectably low with a widely used combination of drugs. The studies showed, however, that the surviving viruses, which hide inside resting immune-system cells, do not develop resistance to the drugs, which prevent the virus from replicating.	George Edward (Eddie) Arcaro, 81, preeminent jockey who was the only rider to twice win thoroughbred racing's Triple Crown, dies in Miami, Florida, after a long bout with liver cancer.	Nov. 14
The Justice Department finds that violent crime fell by 10% and property crimes by 8%. The figures on violent crime do not include homicide.					Nov. 15
				In tennis, Pete Sampras wins the ATP Championship, over Russia's Yevgeny Kafelnikov in Germany.... In football, the Toronto Argonauts win the Grey Cup championship, 47-23, over the Saskatchewan Roughriders.... Jamaica qualifies for soccer's World Cup with a 0-0 tie against Mexico. Jamaica is only the third Caribbean nation ever to qualify and the first since 1974.	Nov. 16
	Nebraska state Agriculture Director Larry Sitzman reveals South Korea will lift the ban instituted Oct. 2 against from U.S. beef from Nebraska after finding an illness-causing strain of E. coli bacteria in a shipment.	A federally appointed overseer disqualifies Ronald Carey, president of the International Brotherhood of Teamsters, from participating in a 1998 rerun election against rival James P Hoffa.... Thomas Frist Jr., chair of Columbia/HCA Healthcare Corp., which is under investigation for possible Medicare fraud, unveils a restructuring plan that will lead to the sale of 108 of the company's 340 hospitals.		Because of Jamaica's Nov. 16 qualification for soccer's World Cup, the government declares a national holiday.	Nov. 17
Nathan Thill, 19, a self-proclaimed racist skinhead, shoots and kills Oumar Dia, 38, an African immigrant, in Denver, Colorado. He also wounds Jeannie VanVelkinburgh, a 36-year-old white woman. This follows other violent incidents linked to racism in the area... The U.S. Sixth Circuit Court of Appeals in Cincinnati, Ohio, strikes down an Ohio law banning IDE, a late-term abortion method. A total of 17 states have passed laws banning the method. The Ohio law is the first to be tested at the appeals level.	Pres. Clinton signs a $268.2 billion defense authorization bill for fiscal 1998.	Pres. Clinton signs a $49.7 billion agriculture appropriations bill for fiscal 1998.	The FBI announces that it is ending its 16-month-long investigation of the 1996 crash of TWA Flight 800 off Long Island, New York, and asserts that the crash was not caused by a criminal act of sabotage.... Norman H. Topping, 89, viral researcher and university president credited with turning USC into a major national research institution, dies in Los Angeles, California, of pneumonia.	National Book Awards are presented to Charles Frazier, Joseph Ellis William Meredith, and Han Nolan. Historian Studs Terkel receives the Medal for Distinguished Contribution to American Letters.... Joyce Wethered, 96, who was considered one of the greatest women golfers of all time, dies of unreported causes.	Nov. 18

F	G	H	I	J
Includes elections, federal-state relations, civil rights and liberties, crime, the judiciary, education, health care, poverty, urban affairs, and population.	Includes formation and debate of U.S. foreign and defense policies, veterans' affairs, and defense spending. (Relations with specific foreign countries are usually found under the region concerned.)	Includes business, labor, agriculture, taxation, transportation, consumer affairs, monetary and fiscal policy, natural resources, and pollution.	Includes worldwide scientific, medical, and technological developments; natural phenomena; U.S. weather; natural disasters; and accidents.	Includes the arts, religion, scholarship, communications media, sports, entertainments, fashions, fads, and social life.

	World Affairs	Europe	Africa & the Middle East	The Americas	Asia & the Pacific
Nov. 19	Heavy monsoon rains begin dousing lingering forest fires in Indonesia, clearing a thick haze that has blanketed much of Southeast Asia since July. The monsoon rains fell on the islands of Sumatra, Borneo, and Irian Jaya, where fires have consumed thousands of acres of forest lands. The fires, many of which were set deliberately to clear land for farming, have been blamed for creating severe air pollution throughout Southeast Asia.		Protestors opposed to Ayatollah Ali Montazeri, who has openly challenged the legitimacy of Ayatollah Ali Khamenei's reign, demonstrate against him in the city of Qom, Iran.	The Canadian Union of Postal Workers (CUPW), goes on strike.	A car bomb explodes near a movie studio on the outskirts of the city of Hyderabad, killing 23 people and wounding at least 20 others. . . . Malaysian prime minister Mahathir bin Mohamad survives a confidence vote called in response to remarks he made about currency speculators perceived as anti-Semitic.
Nov. 20	In a joint statement, Iraq and Russia announce that UN arms inspectors are free to return to Iraq. Most of the inspectors, members of UNSCOM, left the country Nov. 14, the day after Iraq expelled six of their U.S. colleagues. . . . Reports confirm that Judge Gabrielle Kirk McDonald, a native of the U.S. state of Texas, has been elected president of the UN international criminal tribunal in The Hague, the Netherlands.	England's monarch, Queen Elizabeth II, and her husband, Prince Philip, celebrate their golden wedding anniversary at Westminster Abbey in London, where they were married 50 years earlier.	Palestinian militants in the Muslim quarter of the walled Old City of Jerusalem shoot to death an Israeli studying at a nearby yeshiva. . . . Officials estimate that 20,000 people in northern Kenya have been affected by floods. Other relief groups claim that at least 200 people in Ethiopia have died due to flooding.		South Korea's intelligence agency announces that it has uncovered a ring of North Korean spies in Seoul, the capital. . . . The composite index of Malaysia's Kuala Lumpur Stock Exchange plunges 11% to 536.62, its lowest level since 1991.
Nov. 21	Data indicates that more than a month of flooding has claimed at least 1,300 lives in Somalia, Ethiopia, and Kenya. Torrential rains have destroyed crops and left thousands homeless, prompting fears of famine in the region. Weather experts blame the current flooding on the periodic warming of coastal waters near Chile known as El Nino, which is causing abnormal weather patterns around the world.	A court in the Polish city of Katowice acquits 22 former riot policemen of charges of killing nine miners at a 1981 protest rally.	Armed men in northern Somalia kidnap five aid workers who represent UN agencies and the European Union.		
Nov. 22				Statistics reveal that seven journalists were killed in Colombia in 1997.	
Nov. 23		Voters in the Serb part of Bosnia-Herzegovina vote for a parliament split between supporters of former Bosnian Serb president Radovan Karadzic and current president Biljana Plavsic. . . . Slovenes reelect Pres. Milan Kucan for a second five-year term.	The UN reports that Somalis trapped by flooding received long-awaited aid when two boats carrying medical and food supplies reached Buaale and Jamame in southern Somalia after traveling 120 miles (195 km) down the Juba River.		UN and Taliban officials agree on a five-year plan aimed at virtually eradicating the cultivation and production of opium poppies, the plant from which heroin is made, in Afghanistan.
Nov. 24	Leaders of the 18-member Asia-Pacific Economic Cooperation (APEC) trade group convenes in Vancouver, Canada, for their annual meeting.	A Paris court begins a trial of 38 Islamic fundamentalists charged with helping Algerian terrorists carry out a wave of bombings in 1995.	The hostages from the UN and EU taken Nov. 21 in Somalia arrive unharmed at a UN office in Bossasso after being released by their captors. . . . South Africa's Truth and Reconciliation Commission opens hearings on allegations linking Winnie Madikizela-Mandela, the former wife of Pres. Nelson Mandela, to killings and other human-rights abuses during the 1980s.	John Sopinka, 64, justice of the Supreme Court of Canada appointed in 1988, dies in Ottawa, Ontario, of a blood disease.	In Sri Lanka, P.M. Inder Kumar Gujral refuses to expel the Dravida Munnetra Kazagham (DMK) from the coalition. The DMK, a Tamil party based in the southern state of Tamil Nadu, has been linked to a Tamil separatist group in Sri Lanka blamed for the assassination of India's Rajiv Gandhi. . . . Yamaichi Securities Co., the smallest of Japan's "Big Four" securities firms, announces that it will shut down after weeks of rumors about its financial health.
	A	B	C	D	E
	Includes developments that affect more than one world region, international organizations, and important meetings of major world leaders.	*Includes all domestic and regional developments in Europe, including the Soviet Union, Turkey, Cyprus, and Malta.*	*Includes all domestic and regional developments in Africa and the Middle East, including Iraq and Iran and excluding Cyprus, Turkey, and Afghanistan.*	*Includes all domestic and regional developments in Latin America, the Caribbean, and Canada.*	*Includes all domestic and regional developments in Asia and Pacific nations, extending from Afghanistan through all the Pacific Islands, except Hawaii.*

U.S. Politics & Social Issues	U.S. Foreign Policy & Defense	U.S. Economy & Environment	Science, Technology, & Nature	Culture, Leisure, & Lifestyle	
Pres. Clinton signs a bill aimed at speeding up and increasing the permanent adoption of the 500,000 abused and neglected children in the nation's foster-care system. . . . In Joilet, Illinois, both Walter Stewart, 42, convicted of killing two people during an armed robbery, and Durlyn Eddmonds, 45, convicted of raping and murdering a nine-year-old boy, are put to death by lethal injection. They are the 424th and 425th inmates executed in the U.S. and the 9th and 10th in Illinois since 1976.	Pres. Clinton signs a bill extending the annual cost-of-living increase to veterans' benefits.	Pres. Clinton signs a fiscal 1998 appropriations bill allocating $855 million for the District of Columbia. . . . Pres. Clinton signs a bill to create a gold-colored dollar coin and a series of quarters commemorating the 50 states.	The space shuttle *Columbia* lifts off from Kennedy Space Center in Cape Canaveral, Florida, to carry out a mission to conduct materials science experiments in microgravity and to test equipment. . . . Bobbi McCaughey, 29, who underwent treatment with fertility drugs, gives birth to septuplets in Des Moines, Iowa. McCaughey is the first American woman to deliver seven live children and the second known woman in the world to do so.		Nov. 19
The CDC reports that the number of children in the U.S. who contracted AIDS from their mothers at birth declined by 43% between 1992 and 1996. . . . A Piscataway, New Jersey, school board settles an affirmative-action lawsuit brought by Sharon Taxman, a white teacher fired in 1989, ending the case weeks before it is scheduled for argument in the Supreme Court. . . . Gary Burris, 40, convicted of murder, is put to death in Michigan City, Indiana. He is the 427th person executed in the U.S. and only the fifth in Indiana since 1976.	Pres. Clinton signs a bill authorizing intelligence spending for fiscal 1998. . . . The U.S. Coast Guard seizes a boat carrying 417 Haitians attempting to flee to the U.S. All of the passengers are sent back to Haiti. It is the largest contingent of so-called boat people—refugees from political and economic turmoil in Haiti—since 1995.	Pres. Clinton uses his line-veto authority to strike five projects totaling $1.9 million from the agriculture spending bill. . . . Pres. Clinton uses his line-veto authority to strike two projects totaling $6.2 million from the interior spending bill.		The auction houses of Sotheby's Holdings Inc. and Christie's Inc. close their major fall New York City sales. Overall combined sales for the two houses total $535.4 million, nearly double the amount taken in during the fall auctions in the previous year.	Nov. 20
	The U.S. Second Circuit Court in New York City rules, 2-1, that the Defense Department may enforce a law prohibiting the sale of sexually explicit material on U.S. military bases. The ruling overturns a January lower court decision. . . . Pres. Clinton signs into law a bill barring veterans convicted of federal or state capital crimes from being buried in national veterans' cemeteries.	Harold S. Geneen, 87, president and CEO of International Telephone and Telegraph Corp. (ITT), 1959–77, dies in New York City of a heart attack.	Pres. Clinton signs into law a bill reforming the FDA's approval process for new medications.	Robert Wilfred Levick Simpson, 76, British composer, dies of unreported causes. . . . Grayson Louis Kirk, 94, president of Columbia University in New York City, 1953–68, dies in Bronxville, New York, of unreported causes.	Nov. 21
A Justice Department survey finds that an estimated 500,000 people either were threatened or had force used against them by law-enforcement officers in 1996. The 500,000 people are only 1% of the 45 million people over age 12 who, the survey estimates, had face-to-face contact annually with the police. Hispanics and blacks—only one-fifth of the population covered by the survey—were 70% more likely to have contact with the police than whites.				Michael Hutchence, 37, lead singer of the Australian rock group INXS who was considered Australia's best-known popular musical personality, is found dead in a Sydney, Australia, hotel room after apparently hanging himself. . . . A sale of famed baseball player Mickey Mantle memorabilia brings in $541,880.	Nov. 22
	Jorge Mas Canosa, 58, Cuban exile who, as the founder and chair of the Cuban-American National Foundation, was one of the most influential individuals in shaping U.S. policy toward Cuba, dies in Miami, Florida, of lung cancer.			Robert Lewis, 88, actor, director, and teacher who helped found the prestigious Actors Studio in New York City, dies in New York of a heart attack. . . . Annika Sorenstam of Sweden wins the Ladies PGA Tour Championship, the final event of the golf season, in Las Vegas, Nevada.	Nov. 23
		The nonpartisan Center for Responsive Politics reports that the 1996 election campaigns were the most expensive ever, with overall spending at $2.2 billion. The largest overall political donor in the 1996 elections was tobacco giant Philip Morris. Republicans received 79% of the company's $4.2 million in contributions, and Democrats received the rest. . . . The International Brotherhood of Teamsters agrees to a Justice Department request that an independent financial auditor monitor closely the union's day-to-day expenditures for any possible improprieties.			Nov. 24

F	G	H	I	J
Includes elections, federal-state relations, civil rights and liberties, crime, the judiciary, education, health care, poverty, urban affairs, and population.	Includes formation and debate of U.S. foreign and defense policies, veterans' affairs, and defense spending. (Relations with specific foreign countries are usually found under the region concerned.)	Includes business, labor, agriculture, taxation, transportation, consumer affairs, monetary and fiscal policy, natural resources, and pollution.	Includes worldwide scientific, medical, and technological developments; natural phenomena; U.S. weather; natural disasters; and accidents.	Includes the arts, religion, scholarship, communications media, sports, entertainments, fashions, fads, and social life.

	World Affairs	Europe	Africa & the Middle East	The Americas	Asia & the Pacific
Nov. 25	The UN Program on HIV/AIDS estimates that 30.6 million people have HIV, compared with 22.6 million estimated in 1996. The UN suggests that about 16,000 new infections occur every day, compared with 8,200 estimated in 1996. It approximates that 11.7 million people have died of AIDS since the epidemic's beginning, including some 2.3 million people in 1997.		UN officials state that East Africa has not experienced flooding as severe as current conditions since 1961.... Hastings Kamuzu Banda, first president of the African nation of Malawi, 1966–94, who was either 101 or 99 years old at the time of his death, dies in Johannesburg, South Africa, of respiratory failure.	Sixteen inmates die in a fire in the Sabaneta prison near Maracaibo in northwest Venezuela.... The House of Representatives gives final approval to a constitutional amendment lifting a six-year-old ban on extradition. The amendment will not apply to imprisoned leaders of the Cali drug cartel wanted for trial in the U.S.	
Nov. 26				Nicaragua's National Assembly passes a law resolving how to manage more than 2,470,000 acres (1 million hectares) of property seized and redistributed during the 1980s. ... Reports confirm that a court in Havana, Cuba, has sentenced Walter K. Van der Veer, a U.S. citizen, to 15 years in prison for plotting to overthrow the communist government of Pres. Fidel Castro Ruz.... A commission investigating the 1908s distribution of blood tainted with the viruses that cause AIDS and hepatitis C, calls for the Canadian government to compensate all past and future victims of infection from blood transfusions.	Chinese president Jiang Zemin makes a state visit to Canada. He is the most powerful Chinese leader ever to visit Canada.
Nov. 27	The IMF releases $100 million to the Ukrainian government.	An estimated 40,000 university students march through Bonn, Germany's capital, in a demonstration of their discontent with the university system. The student protest is described as the country's largest in at least 20 years.	Yemeni tribesmen release Steve Carpenter, a U.S. oil executive they kidnapped Oct. 30 near Sanaa, the capital.... Iran's supreme leader Ayatollah Ali Khamenei, an ideological conservative, calls for treason charges to be brought against Ayatollah Ali Montazeri, one of his fiercest critics.	Gunmen in the northern Mexican city of Tijuana attack newspaper editor Jesus Blancornelas, who has written numerous articles about drug traffickers and related official corruption in Mexico. Blancornelas is seriously wounded in the attack, in which one of his bodyguards and a gunman are killed.	Cambodia's opposition leader Sam Rainsy returns to Phnom Penh, Cambodia's capital, after spending several months of self-imposed exile in Thailand.
Nov. 28	The UN approves a mandate for a multinational force of 300 civilian police to remain in Haiti for one year in order to train and assist the new police force.	British prime minister Tony Blair makes his first visit to Bosnia-Herzegovina.... Turkey's State Security Court in Ankara, the capital, sentences 33 Islamic fundamentalists to death for staging a 1993 attack in which 37 secular activists were killed. The executions, if carried out, will be the country's first since the early 1980s.	The government of Pres. Robert Mugabe publishes a list of commercial farms that it plans to appropriate from private owners as part of a land-reform initiative.... Witnesses reveal that at least 11 people are killed when gunfire erupts between two rival factions of forces loyal to Pres. Laurent Kabila in Kinshasa, the capital of the Democratic Republic of the Congo.	The Peruvian government frees 83 people unjustly jailed on terrorism charges.... In Rio de Janeiro, Brazil, Judge Jose Geraldo Antonio sentences former police officer Arlindo Maginario Filho to 441 years and four months in jail for participating in the massacre of 21 people in Rio's Vigario Geral shantytown in 1993.	India's seven-month-old United Front government collapses when the Congress Party (I) withdraws from the coalition after one of the coalition's parties is implicated in the 1991 assassination of former prime minister Rajiv Gandhi. P.M. Inder Kumar Gujral tenders his resignation to Pres. K.R. Narayanan at midnight, but the president asks Gujral to retain his post in a caretaker capacity. Gujral's coalition is the third government to collapse in 18 months.... The United Liberation Front of Assam (ULFA) bombs portions of an oil pipeline to mark the seventh anniversary of the day that the ULFA was banned by the Indian government.
Nov. 29					Taiwan's Nationalist Party suffers set backs in municipal elections.
Nov. 30		Karine Mane, a UN employee abducted Nov. 18, and five of her captors are killed during a botched hostage rescue in Tajikistan's capital, Dushanbe. The other hostage, Franck Janier-Dubry, was freed earlier.... British cattle farmers dump 40 metric tons of hamburger meat imported from Ireland into the harbor in Holyhead, a port in northwestern Wales, to protest the importation of cheap Irish beef.		Carlos Roberto Flores Facusse, the candidate for the ruling Liberal Party, wins presidential elections in Honduras.... Voters in Ecuador elect 70 members to a temporary National Assembly that will reform the 1978 constitution.	Two bombs explode in a marketplace in New Delhi, the capital of India, killing three people and wounding 62 others.

A	B	C	D	E
Includes developments that affect more than one world region, international organizations, and important meetings of major world leaders.	Includes all domestic and regional developments in Europe, including the Soviet Union, Turkey, Cyprus, and Malta.	Includes all domestic and regional developments in Africa and the Middle East, including Iraq and Iran and excluding Cyprus, Turkey, and Afghanistan.	Includes all domestic and regional developments in Latin America, the Caribbean, and Canada.	Includes all domestic and regional developments in Asia and Pacific nations, extending from Afghanistan through all the Pacific Islands, except Hawaii.

U.S. Politics & Social Issues	U.S. Foreign Policy & Defense	U.S. Economy & Environment	Science, Technology, & Nature	Culture, Leisure, & Lifestyle	
Larry D. Soulsby, the Washington, D.C., chief of police, resigns amid allegations of impropriety.		The FERC, for the first time in its history, orders the dismantling of a hydroelectric dam whose owner was seeking its relicensing. The commission, in a 2-1 decision, orders Edwards Manufacturing Co. to submit a plan for removing the dam on the Kennebec River in Augusta, Maine, in order to clear the way for the passage of migratory fish.			Nov. 25
	Pres. Clinton signs into law an appropriations measure for foreign operations in fiscal 1998.	Pres. Clinton signs into law a fiscal 1998 appropriations bill to fund the Departments of Commerce, Justice, and State.... Pres. Clinton signs into law a bill reauthorizing the Export-Import Bank for four years.... The Commerce Department reports that U.S. gross domestic product grew at a revised, seasonally adjusted annual rate of 3.3% in the third quarter. That is equal to the rate registered in the April-June quarter.... The Florida Supreme Court rules that all polluters of the Everglades should share in the cost of restoring the region, not merely the sugar growers.			Nov. 26
	Army sergeant Robert McLean, a former drill instructor at Fort Jackson in Columbia, South Carolina, is sentenced to eight years in prison and a bad-conduct discharge for having engaged in sexual improprieties with female trainees.		Four spectators at the Macy's Thanksgiving Day Parade in New York City are injured when a balloon knocks over a lamppost.	Walter Fenner (Buck) Leonard, 90, Hall of Fame Negro league baseball player, 1933–50, who was considered the best first baseman in the history of the Negro Leagues, dies in Rocky Mount, North Carolina, of unreported causes.	Nov. 27
					Nov. 28
Coleman Alexander Young, 79, first black mayor of Detroit, Michigan, 1974–93, dies in Detroit of respiratory failure.				Iran qualifies for the World Cup for the second time ever, prompting a celebration in Teheran that is reportedly the largest since before the 1979 Islamic Revolution.... Some 15,000 couples who are members of Rev. Sun Myung Moon's Unification Church gather for a mass wedding ceremony in Washington, D.C.	Nov. 29
				Sweden wins tennis's Davis Cup over the U.S., 5-0, in Goteborg, Sweden.	Nov. 30

F	G	H	I	J
Includes elections, federal-state relations, civil rights and liberties, crime, the judiciary, education, health care, poverty, urban affairs, and population.	Includes formation and debate of U.S. foreign and defense policies, veterans' affairs, and defense spending. (Relations with specific foreign countries are usually found under the region concerned.)	Includes business, labor, agriculture, taxation, transportation, consumer affairs, monetary and fiscal policy, natural resources, and pollution.	Includes worldwide scientific, medical, and technological developments; natural phenomena; U.S. weather; natural disasters; and accidents.	Includes the arts, religion, scholarship, communications media, sports, entertainments, fashions, fads, and social life.

	World Affairs	Europe	Africa & the Middle East	The Americas	Asia & the Pacific
Dec. 1	A UN summit on global warming, the Conference of the Parties to the United Nations Framework Convention on Climate Change, convenes in Kyoto, Japan, drawing delegates from more than 150 nations. . . . Representatives of the Caribbean Community and Common Market (CARICOM) and Cuban officials meet in Havana, Cuba's capital, to discuss strengthening economic ties between the trade group and Cuba.	Spain's Supreme Court jails the 23 leading members of Herri Batasuna, the political wing of ETA, the Basque region's main separatist guerrilla group. The politicians, who make up the party's entire governing body, are sentenced to seven years in prison for collaborating with ETA terrorists. . . . Stephane Grappelli, 89, French violinist known for his masterful jazz improvisations, dies in Paris of complications from hernia surgery.	An apartment in West Jerusalem inhabited by two Israeli-Arab women is fire-bombed for the second time in six weeks. No one is injured in either of the incidents. . . . In South Africa, Matthews Phosa, a legal adviser to the ruling African National Congress, reveals that investigators working for the Truth and Reconciliation Commission have discovered mass graves containing the bodies of more than 100 antiapartheid activists who disappeared during the 1980s.		
Dec. 2	The NATO defense ministry orders the alliance's military commanders to prepare a set of options for extending the ongoing military deployment in Bosnia-Herzegovina. . . . Delegates from 41 nations participate in the first international conference focusing on the theft of gold from Holocaust victims and on Holocaust survivors' efforts to recover funds hidden in Swiss banks during World War II.	In Dushanbe, Tajikistan's capital, forces kill mercenary commander Rizvon Sadirov in a shoot-out. . . . A methane gas explosion in a Siberian coal mine kills 68 miners. Six other miners are injured. It is one of the deadliest Russian mine accidents ever. . . . In the southwestern Welsh port of Fishguard, hundreds of farmers gather to block the unloading of six trucks carrying Irish beef and lamb.	Hutu rebels free 103 inmates from a prison in Rwerere, near Rwanda's border with Congo.	In Jamaica, 12 people are injured in a gunfight between rival parties in the August Town area of Kingston, the capital.	Pakistan president Farooq Leghari resigns, and the chief justice of the Supreme Court, Sajjad Ali Shah, is demoted, capping an ongoing power struggle with P.M. Nawaz Sharif. . . . In Japan, Ryuichi Koike, a sokaiya racketeer, pleads guilty to receiving 12 billion yen ($93 million) in loans from DKB and 700 million yen ($5.4 million) in payoffs from securities firms. . . . The Bangladeshi government signs a peace pact with Chakma rebels waging a 22-year-long separatist campaign in the Chittagong Hill Tracts.
Dec. 3	Diplomats from 121 countries worldwide gather in Ottawa, Canada, to sign a treaty banning the use and manufacture of antipersonnel land mines. Russia, China, and the U.S. send observers to the signing ceremony but do not agree to the treaty. . . . The South Korean government formally agrees to terms for a $57 billion financial bailout coordinated by the IMF in response to the country's severe debt crisis.	A court in Milan, Italy, convicts former premier Silvio Berlusconi, leader of Italy's center-right opposition coalition, of fraud. Judge Edoardo D'Avossa hands Berlusconi a 16-month suspended prison sentence. . . . The German defense ministry reveals that it will discipline six soldiers who in 1993 held a party in a room decorated with Nazi symbols and pictures of Nazi leader Adolf Hitler.	Hutu rebels storm a prison in Bulinga, 30 miles (50 km) northwest of Kigali, the capital of Rwanda, freeing 507 Hutu inmates there. . . . Israel's Histadrut labor federation launches a nationwide strike, involving some 700,000 predominantly public-sector workers, over pension rights and privatization.	The 1,400 Canadian and Pakistani troops of a UN force in Haiti begin leaving the island, turning control over to Haiti's newly trained police force. . . . The Canadian Parliament passes legislation ordering the 45,000 CUPW members, who form the post office's largest union, to return to work. . . . The federal cabinet and the National Energy Board approve plans to construct Canada's first offshore natural-gas project, known as Sable Island.	Ajmal Mian is sworn in as Sajjad Ali Shah's successor as Pakistan's chief justice of the Supreme Court.
Dec. 4	The UN Security Council unanimously approves a six-month extension to a program that allows Iraq to sell $2 billion of oil during a six-month period so as to ease its domestic shortage of food, medical supplies, and other essential items.	The latest available figures show that a total of 22 people in Britain have died of the Creutzfeldt-Jakob strain linked to BSE, or mad-cow disease.		In the wake of the Dec. 3 legislation, the Canadian Union of Postal Workers (CUPW), ends the strike that started Nov. 19. . . . According to incomplete results form the Nov. 30 election in Ecuador, the right-wing Social Christian Party (PSC) will hold a plurality in the assembly that will reform the 1978 constitution.	
Dec. 5		Turkey launches an attack against the PKK, sending 10,000 soldiers backed by warplanes and heavy artillery across the border into northern Iraq. . . . In response to the Dec. 1 sentences, gunmen in the Basque town of San Sebastian shoot and wound a bodyguard for Elena Aspiroz, a member of the ruling Popular Party. . . . Russia's Federal Security Service (FSB) charges Richard L. Bliss, a U.S. telecommunications engineer, with spying on military facilities near the town of Rostov-on-Don in southern Russia.		Data reveals that massacres by right-wing paramilitary groups in Colombia killed at least 57 people in November. More than 41,000 people have fled their homes as a result of the attacks. . . . Cuauhtemoc Cardenas Solorzano of the leftist Democratic Revolutionary Party (PRD) is sworn in for a three-year term as mayor of Mexico City, the capital. Cardenas, elected in July, is the first democratically elected mayor of the city.	
Dec. 6		An Antonov AN-124 military cargo jet crashes into an apartment complex in the Siberian city of Irkutsk 20 seconds after takeoff, killing all crew members and passengers and scores of others on the ground.			Reports confirm that police have rounded up four of five dangerous convicts who escaped from a Brisbane, Australia, prison in November.

A	B	C	D	E
Includes developments that affect more than one world region, international organizations, and important meetings of major world leaders.	*Includes all domestic and regional developments in Europe, including the Soviet Union, Turkey, Cyprus, and Malta.*	*Includes all domestic and regional developments in Africa and the Middle East, including Iraq and Iran and excluding Cyprus, Turkey, and Afghanistan.*	*Includes all domestic and regional developments in Latin America, the Caribbean, and Canada.*	*Includes all domestic and regional developments in Asia and Pacific nations, extending from Afghanistan through all the Pacific Islands, except Hawaii.*

U.S. Politics & Social Issues	U.S. Foreign Policy & Defense	U.S. Economy & Environment	Science, Technology, & Nature	Culture, Leisure, & Lifestyle	
Michael Carneal, 14, opens fire on classmates in West Paducah, Kentucky, killing three girls and injuring five others. He is arrested. . . . The U.S. Conference of Mayors releases a survey in which 276 of 347 responding cities said they have night curfews for youth. That is up from 1995, when 270 of 387 cities in a similar survey claimed to have night curfews. About 90% of the respondents believe that enforcement of youth curfews is a worthwhile use of police power.		A federal jury in Washington, D.C., convicts Ronald Blackley, the former chief of staff to former agriculture secretary Mike Espy, of concealing $22,025 he received from two associates seeking farm subsidies in 1993. . . . Pres. Clinton signs into a law a measure providing for a six-month stopgap bill to fund the nation's highways and mass-transit systems. . . . Pres. Clinton signs into law a bill that will create a gold-colored dollar coin and quarters to commemorate the 50 states.	Government officials meet with executives from the computer and media industries at a Washington, D.C., conference focused on forming strategies to prevent children from viewing excessively sexual and violent material on the Internet computer network.	A federal judge in Eugene, Oregon, orders the PGA to allow Casey Martin, who has Klippel-Trenaunay-Weber Syndrome, to use a golf cart in competitions. . . . Edwin Rosario (Chapo), 34, boxer who won three world championships, dies in Toa Baja, Puerto Rico, of pulmonary edema. . . . *Cold Mountain*, by Charles Frazier, tops the bestseller list.	Dec. 1
Robert E. Williams, 61, convicted of killing two women in 1977, is put to death by electrocution in Lincoln, Nebraska. Williams is the 429th person in the U.S. and only the third in Nebraska to be executed since 1976. . . . Judge Yada Magee rules that a lawsuit brought against Dow Chemical Co. for allegedly misleading women about the dangers of silicone breast implants cannot proceed as a class action. . . . Endicott Peabody, 77, Democratic governor of Massachusetts, 1963–65, dies in Hollis, New Hampshire, of leukemia.	Pres. Clinton nominates Army Secretary Togo D. West Jr. as secretary of Veterans Affairs.	Pres. Clinton signs into law a bill authorizing funding for Amtrak through 2002. . . . Pres. Clinton uses his newly won line-item veto power to eliminate one item from the Commerce-Justice-State bill. Overall, he has vetoed 79 items from nine of the 13 spending bills for fiscal 1998.	The FDA approves the use of radiation to kill illness-causing microorganisms in red meat.		Dec. 2
A study reveals wide disparities in life expectancies based on locality and ethnicity. The longest male life expectancy for all races, 77.5 years, is found in Utah's Cache and Rich counties, and the longest for women of all races, 83.5, in Stearns County, Minnesota. However, Native American men living in South Dakota have a life expectancy of 56.5 years, and black men in Washington, D.C., have an expectancy of 57.9 years. Asian men living in wealthier counties in Massachusetts and New York have a life expectancy of 89.5 years.		The IRA and Columbia/HCA agree to a $71 million settlement in a dispute over stock options.			Dec. 3
The CDC reports that 1.21 million legal abortions were recorded in 1995, continuing a steady decline from 1.43 million in 1990. . . . P. John Seward, executive vice president of the American Medical Association (AMA), resigns from the organization, citing his responsibility for a controversial August announcement that the AMA would endorse a line of home health-care products made by Sunbeam Corp.		FEC staff members recommend that the Republican Party reimburse $3.7 million to the U.S. Treasury after a regular FEC audit uncovers irregularities in the funding of the GOP's 1996 national convention in San Diego, California. . . . The Surface Transportation Board extends for three months a rail "transportation emergency" declared on Union Pacific's Texas tracks.	Three scientists dispute the hypothesis that formations observed on a Martian meteorite might be fossils of microscopic life.		Dec. 4
Four tobacco manufacturers hand over to the House Commerce Committee 864 internal documents relating to their research on cigarette health hazards and to their alleged efforts to market tobacco to minors. . . . John Emerson Moss, 82, Democratic U.S. congressman from California, 1953–78, dies in San Francisco, California, of complications from pneumonia and asthma.		Derivatives based on the Dow Jones industrial average of blue-chip stocks begin being traded for the first time in the average's 101-year history. . . . The Labor Department reports that the seasonally adjusted unemployment rate in the U.S. fell to 4.6% in November, from October's revised rate of 4.7%. The November jobless figure is the lowest rate registered since October 1973.	The space shuttle *Columbia* lands at Cape Canaveral, Florida, after carrying out a mission during which the crew manually retrieved a satellite intended to gather information about the sun's atmosphere that had failed to deploy properly.	Critics of the Church of Scientology hold a candlelight vigil in Clearwater, Florida, to mark the second anniversary of the death of Lisa McPherson, a Scientologist who died while in the care of church members.	Dec. 5
Voters in Houston, Texas, elect Lee Brown (D), a veteran law-enforcement official and former national "drug czar," as the city's first black mayor.		The U.S. administration and the state of Florida, in an effort to protect Florida's Everglades National Park from further pollution, agree to buy more than 50,000 acres (20,000 hectares) of sugar-cane fields near the park.		Three skydivers die during a jump over the South Pole after their parachutes fail to open properly. . . . ABC News anchor Peter Jennings, marries Kayce Freed. . . . Willie Pastrano, 62, light-heavyweight boxer, dies in New Orleans, Louisiana of liver cancer.	Dec. 6

F	G	H	I	J
Includes elections, federal-state relations, civil rights and liberties, crime, the judiciary, education, health care, poverty, urban affairs, and population.	*Includes formation and debate of U.S. foreign and defense policies, veterans' affairs, and defense spending. (Relations with specific foreign countries are usually found under the region concerned.)*	*Includes business, labor, agriculture, taxation, transportation, consumer affairs, monetary and fiscal policy, natural resources, and pollution.*	*Includes worldwide scientific, medical, and technological developments; natural phenomena; U.S. weather; natural disasters; and accidents.*	*Includes the arts, religion, scholarship, communications media, sports, entertainments, fashions, fads, and social life.*

	World Affairs	Europe	Africa & the Middle East	The Americas	Asia & the Pacific
Dec. 7		Police officials disclose that youths firebombed and damaged three bank branches in San Sebastian and Azpeitia, Spain, in an apparent response to the Dec. 1 sentences. . . . Woodrow Wyatt (Lord Wyatt of Weeford), 79, British political figure, newspaper columnist, and television personality, dies in London of unreported causes.	Israel's Histadrut labor federation signs a compromise agreement with the Treasury, ending a nationwide strike begun Dec. 3 over pension rights and privatization that had paralyzed the country.		Cambodia's opposition leader Sam Rainsy holds a peace march in Phnom Penh, the capital, that draws an estimated 3,000 supporters.
Dec. 8	Mexico signs an agreement for greater political and economic cooperation with the EU. . . . The U.S. formally agrees to provide $531 million in materials and services to aid in the construction of what will be the world's most powerful atom smasher. The particle accelerator, the Large Hadron Collider (LHC), is being built in Geneva, Switzerland at the European Laboratory for Particle Physics (CERN). Other non-European nations participating in the accelerator project are Japan, Canada, Russia, and India.	German defense minister Volker Ruehe announces that he has suspended Lt. Gen. Hartmut Olboeter and ordered disciplinary proceedings for Col. Norbert Schwarzer for their roles in allowing Manfred Roeder, a prominent neo-Nazi, to speak at a military academy in Hamburg in 1995. . . . Union Bank of Switzerland and Swiss Bank Corp., Switzerland's second- and third-largest banks, respectively, confirm that they plan to merge. The combined company will replace Credit Suisse Group as the country's biggest bank and will be the world's second-largest financial institution, with some $590 billion in total assets.	A team of UN human-rights investigators begin their long-awaited inquiry into allegations that rebel forces under the command of Pres. Laurent Kabila massacred thousands of Rwandan Hutu refugees during the seven-month rebellion that had brought Kabila to power. . . . Shehu Musa Yaradua, 54, Nigerian dissident who once was a general in the armed forces and served as vice president, dies in prison. . . . Cardinal Laurean Rugambwa, 85, Tanzanian Roman Catholic churchman who became Africa's first cardinal in 1960, dies in Dar-es-Salaam.	Peru authorizes representatives of the International Committee of the Red Cross to resume visits to people jailed on terrorism charges. . . . Carlos Rafael Rodriguez, 84, Cuban communist intellectual who held a number of top posts in Pres. Fidel Castro's government, dies in Havana, Cuba, after suffering from Parkinson's disease and a heart condition.	The Thai government announces that it will close 56 of 58 suspended nonbank finance companies, which loan money to private firms. It is the first time Thailand allows licensed lenders to fail. The closing is applauded by international observers, including the IMF which approves a second payment, of $810 million. . . . Jenny Shipley is sworn in as New Zealand's first woman prime minister. . . . A Chinese-appointed committee selects 36 delegates to represent Hong Kong in China's parliament, the National People's Congress, in 1998.
Dec. 9	The Organization of the Islamic Conference (OIC) opens a summit in Tehran, Iran, attended by some 28 heads of state, premiers, and crown princes. . . . North and South Korean diplomats meet in Geneva, Switzerland, for the first session of talks intended to reach a formal end to the 1950–53 Korean War.	Reports confirm that Chechen war hero Shamil Basayev was named Chechnya's premier by Pres. Aslan Maskhadov.	U.S. secretary of state Madeleine K. Albright embarks on a tour of seven African nations: Ethiopia, Uganda, Rwanda, Congo, Angola, South Africa, and Zimbabwe.	Four homeless people are killed by a gunman while they are sleeping on a street in Rio. . . . In protest of increased fuel prices, thousands of workers take to the streets of La Paz, the capital of Bolivia.	
Dec. 10	The Federal Supreme Court of Switzerland rules that Swiss banks should return to the Philippine government some $100 million in assets linked to late Philippine president Ferdinand Marcos, capping an 11-year-long legal battle. . . . U.S. attorney general Janet Reno and high-level ministers from Britain, Canada, France, Germany, Italy, Japan, and Russia sign an agreement to combat crime committed over computer networks.	Kazakhstan's parliament votes formally to move the capital to Akmola, a city of 300,000 that is 750 miles (1,200 km) north of the old capital, Almaty. . . . Officials reveal that the death toll from the Dec. 6 plane crash in the Siberian city of Irkutsk is 67 people, 23 of whom were on board the jet.	Jordan orders the expulsion of two Iraqi diplomats in protest over Iraq's recent hanging of four Jordanians accused of smuggling some $850 worth of automotive parts.		The Chinese government announces that it has cleared Australia as an "approved destination" for Chinese tourists, making Australia the first non-Asian nation to receive that status.
Dec. 11	A UN summit on global warming closes with the adoption of the first international treaty that sets binding limits on nations' emissions of carbon dioxide and five other so-called greenhouse gases. . . . The Organization of the Islamic Conference (OIC) concludes with a joint declaration condemning terrorism as incompatible with Islam and denouncing Israeli settlement activities in East Jerusalem and other Arab territories occupied since 1967.	British prime minister Tony Blair holds a historic meeting in London with Gerry Adams, head of Sinn Fein, the IRA's political wing. It is the first time in 76 years that a leader of Northern Ireland's republican movement has visited Britain's official prime ministerial residence at 10 Downing Street in London. . . . Eddie (Arnold Edward) Chapman, 83, British double agent during World War II, dies in Brickett Wood, near London.	Hutus wielding guns and machetes kill at least 231 people and wound some 200 others in Rwanda.	Chile's ruling center-left Concertacion coalition takes a majority in midterm legislative elections.	
Dec. 12	An international team of legal experts completes preliminary negotiations on the creation of an international criminal court that will adjudicate cases of genocide and other crimes against humanity.	In an apparent response to the Dec. 1 sentences in Spain, Jose Luis Caso, a Popular Party councilor, is shot to death in Renteria, Spain.		In Paraguay, the former armed forces head and the ruling Colorado Party's candidate in presidential elections, retired general Lino Cesar Oviedo, surrenders to authorities after spending more than a month as a fugitive.	

A	B	C	D	E
Includes developments that affect more than one world region, international organizations, and important meetings of major world leaders.	Includes all domestic and regional developments in Europe, including the Soviet Union, Turkey, Cyprus, and Malta.	Includes all domestic and regional developments in Africa and the Middle East, including Iraq and Iran and excluding Cyprus, Turkey, and Afghanistan.	Includes all domestic and regional developments in Latin America, the Caribbean, and Canada.	Includes all domestic and regional developments in Asia and Pacific nations, extending from Afghanistan through all the Pacific Islands, except Hawaii.

U.S. Politics & Social Issues	U.S. Foreign Policy & Defense	U.S. Economy & Environment	Science, Technology, & Nature	Culture, Leisure, & Lifestyle	
	Reports confirm that Pres. Clinton has issued new, classified nuclear strike guidelines to top military officials, marking the first adjustment in U.S. nuclear defense strategy since 1981. The guidelines reportedly recommend diminishing military attention on Russia and focusing on threats posed by smaller, nonnuclear nations.				Dec. 7
A survey that asked political figures to rank the most influential groups shows that the American Association of Retired Persons (AARP) tops a list of the nation's most powerful interest groups. The AARP is followed by the American Israel Public Affairs Committee, the AFL-CIO labor federation, the National Federation of Independent Business, and the Association of Trial Lawyers of America.		June Gibbs Brown, the inspector general of the Department of HHS, concludes that the Medicare program's method of reimbursement for prescription drugs resulted in overpayments of $447 million for 22 major drugs in 1996. The study estimates that total Medicare overspending for all drugs in 1996 amounted to $667 million.... Michael H. Sutton, the chief accountant at the SEC, announces his resignation, effective in January 1998.		New York City's Metropolitan Museum of Art holds a gala tribute to murdered fashion designer Gianni Versace.... In Malibu, California, Judge Lawrence Mira sentences actor Robert Downey Jr., 32, to 180 days in jail for violating his 1996 probation by using drugs.... MOMA announces that Japanese architect Yoshio Taniguchi has won a competition for designs of an extension for the museum.	Dec. 8
			Bright flashes illuminate the night sky around the southern tip of Greenland in what scientists believe is an enormous meteor impact. Three boat crews scattered around southern Greenland observe the bright light at 5:11 A.M. local time, and seismic tremors are detected shortly thereafter at observation stations in Europe.	Actor Christian Slater, 28, enters a no-contest plea on battery and substance-abuse charges and is sentenced to three months in jail, followed by three months in a residential drug-treatment facility.	Dec. 9
In *Hudson v. U.S.*, the Supreme Court rules, 9-0, that the Constitution's protection against double jeopardy does not prohibit the government from imposing both criminal and civil fines for the same offense.... A federal jury in Kansas City, Kansas, awards $1.56 million in damages to Paula Hampton, a black woman who claims that she was stopped and searched at a Dillard's department store because of her race.... U.S. District Court judge George O'Toole issues an injunction against enforcement of a 1996 Massachusetts law requiring tobacco makers to disclose the ingredients of cigarette brands.		The Nuclear Regulatory Commission fines Northeast Utilities $2.1 million, the largest penalty ever assessed by the agency, for safety flaws at the company's Millstone nuclear power plant in Waterford, Connecticut.... Data reveals that the Postal Service recorded profits of $1.26 billion during fiscal year 1997, marking the third consecutive year that the historically cash-strapped institution's profits have exceeded the billion-dollar mark. The 1997 revenues help reduce the Postal Service's overall debt to $2.7 billion.		Singer Elton John donates £20 million to the Princess of Wales Memorial Fund as the first installment of proceeds from his single that pays homage to Diana.	Dec. 10
Thomas H. Beavers, 26, convicted of rape and murder, is put to death in Jarratt, Virginia. He is the 432nd person in the U.S. and the 46th in Virginia executed since 1976. He is also the 74th and final inmate executed in 1997, the largest number of executions since 1976.... A grand jury hands down an indictment against Henry Cisneros, former HUD secretary, charging that he lied in his 1993 confirmation hearings about payments to his former mistress, Linda Medlar.	The remains of M. Larry Lawrence, the former U.S. ambassador to Switzerland, are removed from Arlington National Cemetery in Virginia and transferred to a cemetery in San Diego, California, following discoveries that Lawrence lied about having served in the military.	The Office of the Comptroller of the Currency for the first time allows a national bank to underwrite municipal bonds through an existing subsidiary, rather than requiring it to create a separate holding company.... William W. Winpisinger, 73, U.S. labor leader, Democratic Party official, and self-described "seat-of-the-pants socialist," dies of cancer in Columbia, Maryland.	In Washington, D.C., Judge Thomas Penfield Jackson issues a preliminary injunction ordering Microsoft to stop requiring computer manufacturers who ship their machines with Microsoft's Windows operating systems to install Microsoft's Internet browsing software.... A team of biologists report that they have fully decoded the genetic sequence of *Borrelia burgdorferi*, the bacterium that causes Lyme disease.		Dec. 11
Federal prosecutors in Little Rock, Arkansas, indict three white separatists—Chevie Kehoe, Daniel Lewis, Lee and Faron Lovelace—on murder and racketeering charges in connection with a plot to revolt against the U.S. government.	The U.S. government enacts a ban on cattle and sheep imports from Europe out of concern for the possible spread of bovine spongiform encephalopathy (BSE), or mad-cow disease.	A survey finds that the percentage of female corporate officers at the U.S.'s largest 500 companies in 1997 grew to 10.6% from 10% in 1996. The number with no female officers grew to 120 from 105.... The Labor Department states that two NYC factories that make clothes for nationwide chains—MSL Sportswear and Laura and Sarah Sportswear—have flagrantly violated federal minimum-wage and overtime laws.... Judge William Downes rules that a 1995 wolf reintroduction program in Yellowstone Park is illegal.	Reports reveal that thousands of seals and sea lions have died off the coast of the U.S. state of California because unusually warm weather has driven away fish and squid that the animals feed upon.	A federal judge sentences Autumn Jackson, 23, to 26 months in prison for trying to extort $40 million from entertainer Bill Cosby.... Roman Catholic bishops from the Western Hemisphere conclude a conference at the Vatican that had focused on the social and political challenges facing the church in North and South America.	Dec. 12

F	G	H	I	J
Includes elections, federal-state relations, civil rights and liberties, crime, the judiciary, education, health care, poverty, urban affairs, and population.	*Includes formation and debate of U.S. foreign and defense policies, veterans' affairs, and defense spending. (Relations with specific foreign countries are usually found under the region concerned.)*	*Includes business, labor, agriculture, taxation, transportation, consumer affairs, monetary and fiscal policy, natural resources, and pollution.*	*Includes worldwide scientific, medical, and technological developments; natural phenomena; U.S. weather; natural disasters; and accidents.*	*Includes the arts, religion, scholarship, communications media, sports, entertainments, fashions, fads, and social life.*

	World Affairs	Europe	Africa & the Middle East	The Americas	Asia & the Pacific
Dec. 13	The U.S. joins 101 other countries in signing the Global Financial Services Agreement, which essentially replaces an interim WTO pact that was concluded in July 1995.... The EU lays the groundwork for inviting six nations—including five former members of the Soviet bloc—to join the 15-nation body. EU leaders specifically exclude Turkey from the candidates, creating a major diplomatic rift.		South African authorities arrest three Congolese men who were high-ranking officials in the government of the late Mobutu Sese Seko, Congo's former ruler.... The UN Children's Fund (UNICEF), using Iraqi government sources for much of its relevant statistics, claims that one-third of Iraqi children are malnourished and that the infant mortality rate in Iraq has doubled to 117 per thousand between 1991 and 1997.	In Colombia, FARC kidnaps four journalists in the northwest Antioquia province.... Cuban president Fidel Castro Ruz declares that Christmas (Dec. 25) will be a national holiday. The move is made at the request of Pope John Paul II, who is scheduled to visit Cuba in January 1998. Cuba, officially a communist, atheistic state, has not celebrated Christmas since 1969.	
Dec. 14	Members of the Association of Southeast Asian Nations (ASEAN) convene in Kuala Lumpur, Malaysia, for their annual trade summit and to mark the 30th anniversary of the group.	In response to the EU's Dec. 13 decision, Turkish premier Mesut Yilmaz states that his government will sever all political contacts with the EU, telling reporters in Ankara, the capital, "We will have no political dialogue with the [European] Union anymore."	Reports indicate that violence concentrated in Rwanda's northwest region has claimed an estimated 6,000 lives since April.		
Dec. 15	The UN General Assembly adopts a resolution that pledges international cooperation in the prosecution of terrorists.	In Moscow, Russia, temperatures of –26°F (–35°C) cause the death of five people with hypothermia and send another 138 to the hospital. It is the capital city's coldest December 15 since 1882.		Guyana holds presidential elections.	
Dec. 16	Foreign ministers from NATO countries agree to back an extension of NATO's mission to Bosnia. Foreign ministers of the three Central and Eastern European countries invited to join NATO—Poland, the Czech Republic, and Hungary—sign documents to amend the 1949 Treaty of Washington, which created the Atlantic alliance.... The UN Children's Fund (UNICEF) reveals that malnutrition is related to more than half of child deaths worldwide. Six million children under the age of five die each year due to malnutrition.	A court in the Albanian-majority province of Kosovo hands 15 ethnic Albanians jail sentences of between four and 20 years for terrorism offenses. Two others are found not guilty.... Czech president Vaclav Havel names Josef Tosovsky as interim premier, replacing Vaclav Klaus, who has led the government since 1992.	The African National Congress (ANC), South Africa's ruling party, holds its 50th annual conference in Mafeking.		A UN team investigating reports that some 2,000 Taliban fighters held captive in 1996 were killed reveals it has found hundreds of bodies in shallow graves about 90 miles (140 km) east of Mazar-i-Sharif.... In Japan, some 729 people, mostly children, are taken to hospitals after suffering violent reactions to a flashing explosion scene in a popular animated TV series, *Pocket Monsters,* or "Pokemon" for short. Some neurologists claim the seizures and other health problems are likely to be optically stimulated epilepsy.
Dec. 17	Thirty-four countries sign a convention in Paris designed to combat bribery in international business.	Czech president Vaclav Havel swears in Josef Tosovsky as interim premier.... A Russian-built Yakovlev-42 airliner with 62 passengers en route to Odessa loses contact with air-traffic controllers.... Poland's legislature votes to reimpose a strict abortion ban, in accordance with a May Constitutional Court ruling.			
Dec. 18	The IMF releases $3.5 billion in loan aid under its bailout agreement with South Korea, following a favorable review of South Korea's performance under the agreement so far.	A squad of elite Dutch soldiers in central Bosnia-Herzegovina capture two Croats alleged to be war criminals. Both men—Vlatko Kupreskic and Anto Furundzija—have been linked to the massacres of dozens of Muslim civilians in the Lasva Valley in 1993.		In Guyana, hundreds of people demonstrate in Georgetown, the capital, in support of allegations of fraud in the Dec, 15 elections made by the People's National Congress (PNC).... In Jamaica, the ruling People's National Party (PNP), led by P.M. Percival Patterson, wins 49 of the 60 seats in Jamaica's Parliament. The PNP will control the government for an unprecedented third consecutive term.	South Koreans end five decades of one-party rule by electing veteran opposition leader Kim Dae Jung president. He succeeds Pres. Kim Young Sam, who is prohibited by law from seeking another term.... Japan's finance ministry announces penalties against Daiwa Securities Co. and Nikko Securities Co. for making illegal payments to racketeers.

A	B	C	D	E
Includes developments that affect more than one world region, international organizations, and important meetings of major world leaders.	*Includes all domestic and regional developments in Europe, including the Soviet Union, Turkey, Cyprus, and Malta.*	*Includes all domestic and regional developments in Africa and the Middle East, including Iraq and Iran and excluding Cyprus, Turkey, and Afghanistan.*	*Includes all domestic and regional developments in Latin America, the Caribbean, and Canada.*	*Includes all domestic and regional developments in Asia and Pacific nations, extending from Afghanistan through all the Pacific Islands, except Hawaii.*

U.S. Politics & Social Issues	U.S. Foreign Policy & Defense	U.S. Economy & Environment	Science, Technology, & Nature	Culture, Leisure, & Lifestyle	
				In response to the suggestion that Vice Pres. Al Gore and his wife, Mary (Tipper) Gore were the models for the young lovers in Erich Segal's 1970 novel *Love Story*, Segal explains that Gore was one of two real-life models for the book's hero, but its heroine was not based on Tipper Gore at all. The other model for the hero was actor Tommy Lee Jones, Gore's roommate at Harvard College.	Dec. 13
Edna Kelly, 91, longtime Democratic member of Congress, 1949–69, and the first woman elected to Congress from Brooklyn, dies in Alexandria, Virginia, of undisclosed causes.		The U.S. Conference of Mayors reports that the demand for emergency food and housing is rising in spite of the strong economy and low jobless rates. According to a survey of 29 cities, demand for emergency food jumped 16% over the past year. That is the largest increase reported since 1992.		Stubby Kaye, 79, actor known for his role in the classic Broadway musical *Guys and Dolls*, dies of lung cancer in Rancho Mirage, California.	Dec. 14
The New Jersey senate narrowly overrules Gov. Christine Todd Whitman's (R) June veto of a bill to ban partial-birth abortion. . . . Pres. Clinton defies Senate Republicans by appointing Bill Lann Lee as assistant attorney general for civil rights in an acting capacity. Lee was nominated in June, but Republicans on the Senate Judiciary Committee, unhappy with his support for affirmative action, blocked his confirmation.	The Department of Defense announces that it will vaccinate all U.S. soldiers against anthrax bacteria, one of the deadliest biological agents known, over the next six years.	The Clinton administration announces that employers will have to comply with a new law mandating parity for mental health-care coverage for at least six months before applying for an exemption.	Officials of the CDC and WHO state that scientists with both institutions are working to develop a vaccine for a strain of influenza virus that has infected six people in Hong Kong since May, killing two of them. The virus, H5N1, was not previously been found in humans but is common in waterfowl and chickens.	*Forbes* magazine's list of the 40 highest-paid athletes puts basketball star Michael Jordan of the Chicago Bulls at the top, with $78.3 million in earnings in 1997, $31.3 million of which comes from his salary and the rest is mainly from endorsements.	Dec. 15
In response to the Dec. 15 vote in New Jersey, U.S. district judge Anne Thompson issues a temporary restraining order barring enforcement of the ban on the late-term abortion method known by its critics as partial-birth abortion.	A panel commissioned by Defense Secretary William S. Cohen, after conducting a six-month study of military training procedures, recommends that male and female recruits be separated during a significant portion of their basic training.	A survey of state governments' finances indicates that states' revenues are rising and allowing modest tax cuts. The report projects that the 50 states will have aggregate budget surpluses totaling $24 billion at the end of the current fiscal year. The states had a record surplus of $29.2 billion in the fiscal year that ended in 1997. . . . In Helena, Montana, Judge Charles C. Lovell refuses to block government officials from slaughtering bison that stray outside the boundaries of Yellowstone National Park, as per a plan adopted in 1996.		Thanking the public for submitting hundreds of names for his new dog, Pres. Clinton states that he will call the Labrador retriever puppy Buddy. . . . Lillian B. Disney (born Lillian Bounds), 98, widow of Walt Disney and a philanthropist who helped found the California Institute of the Arts, dies in Los Angeles after suffering a stroke.	Dec. 16
State child welfare officials in New Jersey agree to allow homosexual couples to jointly adopt children in the same way as heterosexual married couples. . . . The City Council of New York votes in favor of the nation's tightest restrictions on outdoor cigarette advertising. . . . Anthony T. Ulasewicz, 79, key witness at the U.S. Senate's Watergate hearings, which led to the resignation of U.S. president Richard Nixon, dies in Glens Falls, New York.	In Laredo, Texas, Judge Marcel C. Notzon releases from prison Elizaphan Ntakirutimana, a Rwandan man charged with genocide, because the U.S. and the tribunal do not have an extradition treaty with one another. . . . A judge in Miami, Florida, orders Cuba to pay $187.6 million in punitive and compensatory damages to the families of three of the four U.S. pilots shot down in February 1996 by Cuban fighter jets in international waters. The suit is the first to be tried under the U.S.'s Anti-Terrorism and Effective Death Penalty Act.		Pres. Clinton signs a bill exempting the National Academy of Sciences from openness rules of the 1972 Federal Advisory Committee Act. . . . Astronomers present images taken by the *Hubble Space Telescope* showing the dying phases of stars in unprecedented detail. . . . R(eginald) V(ictor) Jones, 86, British physicist who, during World War II, came up with various ways to thwart Nazi military technology, dies of a heart attack in Aberdeen, Scotland.		Dec. 17
In Washington, D.C., Judge Royce C. Lamberth fines the government $285,864 for misrepresenting the nature of the federal task force that developed Pres. Clinton's failed health care reform proposals during his first term. . . . A federal judge in New York City sentences organized-crime boss Vincent (The Chin) Gigante, convicted in July, to 12 years in prison.	Pres. Clinton announces that U.S. troops will remain in Bosnia after the withdrawal of the current Stabilization Force (SFOR), led by NATO.	In New York City, Judge David Edelstein orders the International Brotherhood of Teamsters union to pay for the 1998 rerun of its 1996 presidential election with its own funds, arguing that the Teamsters are "merely being called upon to pay the price for undoing the harm they caused." The order removes the federal government, which has financed the union's elections since 1989, from financial responsibility for the upcoming race.		Chris Farley, 33, portly comedian and actor known for playing likable, buffoonish characters, is found dead in his Chicago, Illinois, apartment. . . . Pres. Clinton makes public his nomination of William Ivey to head the NEA.	Dec. 18

F	G	H	I	J
Includes elections, federal-state relations, civil rights and liberties, crime, the judiciary, education, health care, poverty, urban affairs, and population.	*Includes formation and debate of U.S. foreign and defense policies, veterans' affairs, and defense spending. (Relations with specific foreign countries are usually found under the region concerned.)*	*Includes business, labor, agriculture, taxation, transportation, consumer affairs, monetary and fiscal policy, natural resources, and pollution.*	*Includes worldwide scientific, medical, and technological developments; natural phenomena; U.S. weather; natural disasters; and accidents.*	*Includes the arts, religion, scholarship, communications media, sports, entertainments, fashions, fads, and social life.*

	World Affairs	Europe	Africa & the Middle East	The Americas	Asia & the Pacific
Dec. 19	The UN General Assembly approves the establishment of a new deputy secretary general post.	Judges of the International Criminal Tribunal for the Former Yugoslavia agree to free three suspected war criminals—Marinko Katava, Pero Skopljak, and Ivan Santic—on the recommendation of the tribunal's chief prosecutor, Louise Arbour, who cites insufficient evidence against the three men.	Hutu rebels attack a Tutsi refugee camp and an army barracks in Gisenyi, a town near Rwanda's border with Congo. At least 52 people die. In the another incident, Hutu rebels kill about 30 civilians in the village of Bugogwe, near Gisenyi. . . . South Africa's Truth and Reconciliation Commission files criminal charges against former president P. W. Botha for ignoring an order that he testify before the panel. . . . WHO reveals that a cholera epidemic in East Africa has affected 61,534 people and killed 2,687.	Interim prime minister Janet Jagan, the widow of late Pres. Cheddi Jagan, is declared the winner of presidential elections held Dec. 15 in Guyana. She is sworn in amid charges of election fraud by her main opponent, former president Desmond Hoyte. Jagan is the first white president of Guyana, a small nation in northern South America populated mainly by people of East Indian and African descent.	A Boeing jet crashes on the Indonesian island of Sumatra, killing all 104 passengers and crew aboard. . . . Masaru Ibuka, 89, Japanese engineer who, with Akio Morita, cofounded Tokyo Telecommunications Engineering Corp. in 1946, which was renamed Sony Corp. in 1958, dies in Tokyo, Japan, of congestive heart failure.
Dec. 20	The Gulf Cooperation Council of six oil-rich Persian Gulf states holds its annual summit in Kuwait City, the capital of Kuwait.	Rescue teams searching mountainous terrain near Salonika, Greece, uncover the wreckage of a Russian-built Yakovlev-42 airliner that had lost contact with air-traffic controllers Dec. 17. All 62 passengers and eight crew members are found dead at the crash site. . . . A Greek C-130 military plane crashes near Athens, the Greek capital, in foggy conditions, killing all five officers on board.			South Korean president Kim Young Sam and President-elect Kim Dae Jung agree on granting pardons to Chun Doo Hwan and Roh Tae Woo, two of the former military presidents who persecuted President-elect Kim Dae Young in the past. . . . Juzo Itami (born Yoshihiro Ikeuchi), 64, Japanese film director known for his satirical comedies, leaps to his death from a Tokyo rooftop amid allegations that he is having an affair.
Dec. 21		Lithuanians give Arturas Paulauskas the largest number of votes in the Baltic state's second presidential election since independence in 1991. Paulauskas will face a runoff with Valdas Adamkus. . . . Voters in Serbia, which along with Montenegro makes up the Yugoslav federation, in a runoff vote elect the ruling Socialist Party's Milan Milutinovic as president.	Nigeria's military government discloses that 11 senior army officers have been arrested after a failed coup attempt.	Leftist rebels of the Revolutionary Armed Forces of Colombia (FARC) attack a remote military base atop Mount Patascoy in the southwest province of Narino.	Laos holds parliamentary elections in which 159 candidates are running for spots in the 99-member National Assembly. All but four of the candidates are members of the ruling communist People's Revolutionary Party. . . . Citizens of the town of Nago on the island of Okinawa vote in a referendum against the opening of an offshore U.S. helicopter base near the town.
Dec. 22	The UN General Assembly approves a UN budget that calls for $2.53 billion in spending over two years.	The Turkish government discloses that it is expelling Greek diplomat Efstratios Haralambous, accused of spying. . . . Bruce Woodcock, 76, British heavyweight boxing champion, 1945–50, dies in Doncaster, England.	Leaders of rival factions in Somalia's six-year-old civil war sign a landmark peace plan after more than a month of negotiations.	Gunmen raid the Tzotzil Indian village of Acteal in the southern Mexican state of Chiapas, killing 45 men, women, and children and wounding at least 25 others. It is the worst violence in Chiapas since January 1994. The victims of the Acteal attack reportedly sympathize with, but are not members of, the EZLN. . . . At least seven people, mainly soldiers and police, are killed across Colombia in attacks by the FARC and the National Liberation Army rebel group.	Chun Doo Hwan and Roh Tae Woo, two of the former South Korean military presidents who persecuted President-elect Kim Dae Young in the past, are released from prison after being pardoned by current president Kim Young Sam in an agreement reached Dec. 20. . . . The International Commission of Jurists (ICJ) finds that there has been an "escalation of repression" in Tibet in the past two years and describes the actions as China's "total war" on Tibet's exiled leader, the Dalai Lama.
Dec. 23		In retaliation for Turkey's Dec. 22 expulsion of a Greak diplomat, Greece expels a Turkish diplomat. . . . Juergen Schneider, a well-known German property developer, is sentenced by Judge Heinrich Gehrke to six years and nine months in prison for bilking some of the country's largest banks out of millions of German marks. The verdict ends a 3½-year effort by German prosecutors.		In Guyana, reports confirm that continued protests by opposition supporters have led to incidents of sporadic violence. Police defuse two bombs found near President-elect Janet Jagan's official residence. Jagan names Samuel Hinds, who was acting president, as prime minister.	
Dec. 24	The IMF, the U.S., Japan, and 11 other countries agree to the early release to South Korea of $10 billion of the $57 billion IMF-led rescue package set earlier in the month. . . . Ilich Ramirez Sanchez, a Venezuelan-born terrorist better known as "Carlos" and "the Jackal," is convicted by a Paris court of the 1975 slaying of two French intelligence agents and a Lebanese informant. A 12-member panel sentences the self-styled "professional revolutionary" to life in prison. The murders constitute one of several terrorist acts in the 1970s and 1980s to which Carlos has been linked.	A violent storm carrying winds of up to 80 miles per hour (130 kmph) strikes southern Britain, killing 13 people and cutting off power to thousands of homes.		Data shows that heavy rains and flooding linked to the El Nino weather system has killed nine people and destroyed 6,820 acres (2,763 hectares) of crops in north and central Peru in December. . . . Reports confirm that Celso Pitta, the mayor of the Brazilian city of Sao Paulo, and 16 other defendants were convicted of fraud for an illegal bond issue while Pitta was Sao Paulo's finance secretary. . . . Pierre Peladeau, 72, Canadian newspaper publisher, dies in Montreal three weeks after lapsing into a coma induced by a heart attack.	Toshiro Mifune, 77, Japanese film actor who embodied the heroic qualities of the samurai warrior in numerous films, dies of organ failure in Mitaka, Japan.
	A	**B**	**C**	**D**	**E**
	Includes developments that affect more than one world region, international organizations, and important meetings of major world leaders.	*Includes all domestic and regional developments in Europe, including the Soviet Union, Turkey, Cyprus, and Malta.*	*Includes all domestic and regional developments in Africa and the Middle East, including Iraq and Iran and excluding Cyprus, Turkey, and Afghanistan.*	*Includes all domestic and regional developments in Latin America, the Caribbean, and Canada.*	*Includes all domestic and regional developments in Asia and Pacific nations, extending from Afghanistan through all the Pacific Islands, except Hawaii.*

U.S. Politics & Social Issues	U.S. Foreign Policy & Defense	U.S. Economy & Environment	Science, Technology, & Nature	Culture, Leisure, & Lifestyle	
The U.S. Ninth Circuit Court of Appeals in San Francisco upholds a California law established in a 1990 referendum that sets term limits for California state legislators. The 9-2 ruling overturns two earlier rulings.	Gueorgui Makharadze, a diplomat from the former Soviet republic of Georgia, receives a prison sentence of seven to 21 years in connection with the January death of teenager Joviane Waltrick in a District of Columbia car crash. Makharadze was drinking before the crash.	The USDA agrees to open a six-month mediation process to settle a backlog of nearly 1,000 discrimination complaints brought by black farmers, some dating back to the early 1980s. The agreement heads off a $2 billion class-action lawsuit brought in August by more than 200 of those farmers. . . . Data shows that the IRS withheld a record $1.1 billion in delinquent child support from deadbeat parents in 1996. In each case, the money was returned to the parent supporting children or, if a family was receiving welfare, to the state.			Dec. 19
A study shows that nearly half of graduating seniors have reported that they smoked marijuana, up from 45% in 1996. Among eighth graders, 29.4% report use of illegal drugs, down from 31.2% the previous year.		The White House announces the reversal of Pres. Clinton's Oct. 16 line-item veto of a plan to allow 1.1 million federal workers to switch to a stock-based pension plan. . . . Esther Peterson, 91, labor movement and women's rights lobbyist, dies in Washington, D.C., after a stroke.		Dawn Steel, 51, the first woman to head a major Hollywood studio when she was appointed president of Columbia Pictures in 1987, dies of brain cancer in Los Angeles. . . . Denise Levertov, 74, British-born poet, essayist, and political activist, dies of complications of lymphoma in Seattle, Washington.	Dec. 20
				Brazil wins the Federation Internationale de Football Association (FIFA) Confederations Cup, beating Australia, 6-0, in Riyadh, Saudi Arabia.	Dec. 21
Federal archivists release a 1963 memorandum supporting the theory that Pres. John F. Kennedy intended to end the U.S.'s military involvement in Vietnam during his second term. . . . The Mississippi Supreme Court upholds the conviction of Byron De La Beckwith, who was found guilty in 1994 of the slaying of civil-rights leader Medgar Evers in 1963.	The Department of Energy releases hundreds of thousands of declassified documents as well as numerous films, including 1960s footage of a pair of groundbreaking, portable nuclear weapons—eventually discontinued—that were capable of being transported and operated by individual soldiers. . . . The Defense Department admits that botulinum toxoid, a vaccine with unknown side effects, was given to 8,000 Persian Gulf War soldiers. The vaccine, intended to protect soldiers against chemical and biological weapons, is being investigated as a possible cause of veterans' health problems.		The FDA approves the sale of Propecia, a prescription pill treatment for male pattern baldness made by Merck & Co. Inc. . . . Time magazine names Andrew Steven Grove as 1997's "Man of the Year." Grove, the 61-year-old chairman and chief executive officer of Intel Corp., is described as "the person most responsible for the amazing growth in the power and innovative potential of microchips."	A Los Angeles jury awards actress Hunter Tylo, 34, nearly $5 million in a pregnancy-discrimination lawsuit against the producers of the TV show Melrose Place. Tylo was fired in 1996 after revealing that she was pregnant. . . . Cold Mountain, by Charles Frazier, remains at the top of the bestseller list.	Dec. 22
A federal jury in Denver, Colorado, convicts Terry L. Nichols of conspiracy and involuntary manslaughter for his role in the 1995 bombing of the Alfred P. Murrah Federal Building in Oklahoma City, Oklahoma, that killed 168 people. . . . Pres. Clinton grants Christmas-week pardons to 21 people convicted of federal crimes ranging from petty theft to bank robbing to bootlegging to cocaine dealing.	Pres. Clinton signs an executive order that allows thousands of illegal immigrants from Haiti who are seeking political asylum to remain in the U.S. for at least one year.	The insurance department of New York State fines Connecticut-based Oxford Health Plans Inc., one of the largest health maintenance organizations in the New York City area, $3 million, for violating state regulations. . . . The probation of Michael Milken, a convicted former junk bond financier, is extended to Jan. 23, 1998.		Filmmaker and actor Woody Allen, 62, marries Soon-Yi Previn, 27, in Venice, Italy. Previn was the adopted daughter of actress Mia Farrow, Allen's former companion, and composer-conductor Andre Previn, Farrow's second husband.	Dec. 23
		Thirty brokerage firms agree to pay $910 million to settle a class-action lawsuit that investors brought against them in July 1994.	FEMA notes that it spent $1.38 billion in aid for relief from natural disasters in 1997. . . . EarthWatch Inc. of the U.S. launches EarlyBird 1, the world's first commercial spy satellite, from a site in eastern Russia.		Dec. 24

F	G	H	I	J
Includes elections, federal-state relations, civil rights and liberties, crime, the judiciary, education, health care, poverty, urban affairs, and population.	Includes formation and debate of U.S. foreign and defense policies, veterans' affairs, and defense spending. (Relations with specific foreign countries are usually found under the region concerned.)	Includes business, labor, agriculture, taxation, transportation, consumer affairs, monetary and fiscal policy, natural resources, and pollution.	Includes worldwide scientific, medical, and technological developments; natural phenomena; U.S. weather; natural disasters; and accidents.	Includes the arts, religion, scholarship, communications media, sports, entertainments, fashions, fads, and social life.

	World Affairs	Europe	Africa & the Middle East	The Americas	Asia & the Pacific
Dec. 25		Giorgio Strehler, 76, Italian theater director who, with Paolo Grassi in 1947, founded one of Europe's most important theaters, the Piccolo Teatro in Milan, Italy, dies of a heart attack in Lugano, Switzerland.	Government security forces arrest Kenneth Kaunda, Zambia's former president.....The members of newly elected municipal councils in Algeria choose representatives to the upper house of Parliament. Mustapha Benmansour, the interior minister, announces that the ruling National Democratic Rally won 80 of the 96 seats up for election.	A group of mourners from Acteal, Mexico, the village that was the site of the Dec. 22 massacre, and from neighboring villages stop a truck filled with some 24 men, charging that they were responsible for the killings.	
Dec. 26		Jean-Marie Le Pen, leader of the National Front, a right-wing, anti-immigrant political party, is convicted by a French court of denying Nazi crimes against humanity, a criminal offense under French law. The court fines him 300,000 francs ($50,000).		Mexican attorney general Jorge Madrazo Cuellar announces that 16 people have been charged with first-degree murder in connection with the Dec. 22 massacre in Acteal, Chiapas.... Simone Duvalier, 73, 83 or 84, widow of François (Papa Doc) Duvalier, who ruled Haiti, 1957–71, dies in the Parisian suburb of St.-Cloud, France.	
Dec. 27		Billy Wright, one of the most notorious leaders of Northern Ireland's Protestant militants, is shot and killed by Roman Catholic extremist inmates inside the high-security Maze Prison near Lisburn, Northern Ireland. Police claim that the killers belong to the Irish National Liberation Army (INLA), a Catholic guerrilla group that broke off from the Provisional IRA. Later, Seamus Dillon, a Catholic and former IRA member, is shot and killed at the Dungannon Hotel in County Tyrone.... A boatload of 825 refugees, also mostly Kurds, arrived in Italy.	In Egypt, a pro-tenant organization claims that six farmers were killed and 50 others injured in confrontations with law-enforcement officials in the month of November.	Mexican authorities arrest Jacinto Arias Cruz, the PRI mayor of Chenalho, the municipality where the Dec. 22 attack occurred. Twenty-three others are also charged, almost all of whom are Tzotzil Indians. An estimated 3,000 Tzotzil Indians begin to flee to a refugee center in Polho, near Acteal.	
Dec. 28			An estimated 97 people are killed in a series of raids on villages and at fake roadblocks in Algeria. In one such attack, assailants slit the throats of 34 civilians, including 11 children, in a village in the Medea region, south of Algiers, the capital.... The supreme administrative court, Egypt's highest court, upholds a health ministry ban on the genital cutting of girls and women, a ban that was temporarily lifted in June.	At the maximum-security Sorocaba prison, 50 miles (80 km) west of the city of Sao Paulo, Brazil, inmates take some 650 guards and visiting relatives hostage after a failed escape attempt. Two people—an inmate and a female visitor—are killed during the takeover.	
Dec. 29		Turkey reveals that its military forces have completed their most recent offensive against guerrillas of the Iraq-based Kurdistan Workers Party (PKK), a separatist group that seeks to establish self-rule in southeastern Turkey.... Members of the Loyalist Volunteer Force claim that the Dec. 27 attack on Seamus Dillon was in reprisal for Billy Wright's Dec. 27 death.... In France, jobless protesters occupy nine employment offices and demand bonus payments of $500 to supplement their benefits.	Palestine National Authority (PNA) leader Yasser Arafat agrees to accept the resignation of his cabinet in the face of a looming no-confidence vote by the elected Palestinian Legislative Council (PLC).	Argentina and Chile sign an accord on mining along the countries' shared border.	Lt. Gen. La Kha Phieu is appointed secretary general of Vietnam's ruling Communist Party, the country's most powerful post.... Hong Kong authorities and poultry vendors begin the destruction of the territory's 1.2 million chickens in an effort to prevent the further spread to humans of a fowl-borne strain of influenza virus.
Dec. 30	The Population Institute warns that, although worldwide birth rates are declining, they remain high in countries "least able to support their growing millions." The report projects that 74 countries, including Nigeria, Iran, and Pakistan, will double their populations in 30 years.... South Africa and China establish formal diplomatic relations. With the recognition of China, South Africa severs its official relations with Taiwan.	The British government releases its list of New Year's honors, which names 976 recipients of knighthoods, life peerages, and other honors.... The Antwerp Bourse, which has been operating since 1531, shuts down permanently.... Danilo Dolci, 73, Italian social activist, labor organizer, and literary figure twice nominated for the Nobel Peace Prize, dies of heart failure in Sicily.	Armed assailants kill 21 civilians in the village of Ouled Kherarba, Algeria.... Police shoot and kill three demonstrators outside a location where votes are being counted in Kenya.	The Venezuelan government states that 282 inmates were killed and 1,294 others injured in prison violence in 1997. Venezuela's total prison population is 24,262 at the end of 1997, but the prison system is designed to hold 15,361 inmates.... Colombian army commander Mario Hugo Galan reports that some 4,000 troops were sent to a remote military base atop Mount Patascoy that was attacked by FARC guerillas Dec. 21.	

A	B	C	D	E
Includes developments that affect more than one world region, international organizations, and important meetings of major world leaders.	*Includes all domestic and regional developments in Europe, including the Soviet Union, Turkey, Cyprus, and Malta.*	*Includes all domestic and regional developments in Africa and the Middle East, including Iraq and Iran and excluding Cyprus, Turkey, and Afghanistan.*	*Includes all domestic and regional developments in Latin America, the Caribbean, and Canada.*	*Includes all domestic and regional developments in Asia and Pacific nations, extending from Afghanistan through all the Pacific Islands, except Hawaii.*

U.S. Politics & Social Issues	U.S. Foreign Policy & Defense	U.S. Economy & Environment	Science, Technology, & Nature	Culture, Leisure, & Lifestyle	
				Denver Pyle, 77, television character actor, dies in Burbank, California, of lung cancer. . . . Pope John Paul II delivers his "Urbi et Orbi" ("To the City and the World") annual Christmas message from St. Peter's Basilica in Rome. His address is televised live in some 70 countries.	Dec. 25
					Dec. 26
James M. Nabrit Jr., 97, lawyer in civil-rights cases and educator who served as president of Howard University, 1960–69, dies in Washington, D.C.				Brendan Gill, 83, author whose association with the *New Yorker* magazine dated back to 1936, dies in New York City.	Dec. 27
					Dec. 28
		Arkansas-based poultry processor Tyson Foods Inc. pleads guilty to making more than $12,000 in illegal gifts to former agriculture secretary Mike Espy in 1993. As part of a plea agreement obtained by independent counsel Donald Smaltz, the company agrees to pay $4 million in fines and $2 million toward the cost of the investigation. . . . Pres. Clinton authorizes pay raises that range between 2.3% and 2.8% for all federal workers except himself.	A total of 83 passengers and crew are injured and one passenger dies when United Airlines Flight 826 hits severe air turbulence midway between Tokyo's Narita airport and Honolulu, Hawaii.		Dec. 29
		The Conference Board reports that its index of consumer confidence leaped in December to 134.5, from a revised November reading of 128.1. The December figure marks the confidence index's highest level in 28 years.		Reports confirm that the Church of Scientology paid $12.5 million to the IRS in October 1993 as part of a deal under which the IRS grants the church tax-exempt status. . . . Warren Mehrtens, 77, jockey made famous during races in 1946, dies in Sarasota, Florida.	Dec. 30

F	G	H	I	J
Includes elections, federal-state relations, civil rights and liberties, crime, the judiciary, education, health care, poverty, urban affairs, and population.	*Includes formation and debate of U.S. foreign and defense policies, veterans' affairs, and defense spending. (Relations with specific foreign countries are usually found under the region concerned.)*	*Includes business, labor, agriculture, taxation, transportation, consumer affairs, monetary and fiscal policy, natural resources, and pollution.*	*Includes worldwide scientific, medical, and technological developments; natural phenomena; U.S. weather; natural disasters; and accidents.*	*Includes the arts, religion, scholarship, communications media, sports, entertainments, fashions, fads, and social life.*

	World Affairs	Europe	Africa & the Middle East	The Americas	Asia & the Pacific
Dec. 31	Year-end data shows that stock markets worldwide rose 12.3%. Analysts note that strong market performances in the Americas and Europe enabled the global index to record double-digit returns despite a financial crisis that affected much of Southeast Asia during the last half of 1997. The London Stock Exchange 100 in Britain climbed 24.7% in 1997. Japan's market plunged in 1997, as the Nikkei average on the Tokyo Stock Exchange fell 30.2% from the previous year.	Turkey reports that 86 Kurd separatists and four KDP troops were killed in the most recent offensive against guerrillas of the Iraq-based Kurdistan Workers Party (PKK), a separatist group that sought to establish self-rule in southeastern Turkey. . . . Unidentified masked gunmen fire on New Years revelers at a pub in Belfast frequented largely by Catholics, killing one person and wounding five others. . . . France's New Year's Eve celebrations in Strasbourg and in the suburbs of Paris erupt into violence due to frustration over joblessness. Revelers in Strasbourg throw firebombs, set more than 50 cars on fire, and destroy telephone booths and bus shelters. In Yvelines and Seine-Saint-Denis, near Paris, cars are set ablaze, and responding firefighters are pelted with stones.	Although counting continues, Kenyan president Daniel T. arap Moi appears poised to win national elections. The police reveal that rioters beat and burned to death five suspected Moi supporters during the election period. . . . The Algerian government discloses that 78 people were killed and 68 others wounded in three separate massacres during the first 24 hours of the Islamic holy month of Ramadan. In the village of Ouled Selma, 29 people are killed, and, in the village of Ouled Taieb, 28 people die.	Some 250 riot troops storm the maximum-security Sorocaba prison, 50 miles (80 km) west of the city of Sao Paulo, Brazil, freeing some 650 people held hostage by 20 inmates. The troops reclaim control of the prison without firing a shot.	Pakistan's electoral college elects Mohammad Rafiq Tarar as the country's new president by an overwhelming majority.

A	B	C	D	E
Includes developments that affect more than one world region, international organizations, and important meetings of major world leaders.	*Includes all domestic and regional developments in Europe, including the Soviet Union, Turkey, Cyprus, and Malta.*	*Includes all domestic and regional developments in Africa and the Middle East, including Iraq and Iran and excluding Cyprus, Turkey, and Afghanistan.*	*Includes all domestic and regional developments in Latin America, the Caribbean, and Canada.*	*Includes all domestic and regional developments in Asia and Pacific nations, extending from Afghanistan through all the Pacific Islands, except Hawaii.*

U.S. Politics & Social Issues	U.S. Foreign Policy & Defense	U.S. Economy & Environment	Science, Technology, & Nature	Culture, Leisure, & Lifestyle	
		Judge Joe Kendall of U.S. District Court in Wichita Falls, Texas, strikes down a central provision of the 1996 Telecommunications Act when he rules unconstitutional a provision of the act that prohibits regional "Baby Bell" phone companies from entering the long-distance market until they convince the FCC that their markets are open to competition. . . . The dollar closes at 1.7980 marks, up from the 1996 year-end rate of 1.5400 marks. The dollar closes at 130.57 yen, up from the previous year's final rate of 115.85 yen. The Dow Jones closes at 7908.25, up 1459.98 points, or 22.64%, from the 1996 year-end level of 6448.27. The NASDAQ rose 21.64% during the year to close at 1570.37. The Nasdaq closed at 1291.03 in 1996. The AMEX closes at 684.61, up 19.62% from its close of 583.28 in 1996. The Dow global index shows the U.S. market up 31.7%, while the more inclusive Dow Jones industrial average shows a 22.6% rise for U.S. blue-chip stocks.		Michael LeMoyne Kennedy, 39, sixth of the 11 children of the late Sen. Robert Kennedy (D, N.Y.) who served as campaign manager for his uncle, Sen. Edward Kennedy (D, Mass.) and his brother Rep. Joseph Kennedy II (D, Mass.), and whose career was marred by allegations that he had an affair with an underage baby-sitter, dies in Aspen, Colorado, of head and neck injuries sustained from crashing into a tree while skiing and simultaneously playing a makeshift game of football with members of his family. . . . Dominique De Menil, 89, art collector and philanthropist, dies in Houston, Texas.	Dec. 31

F	G	H	I	J
Includes elections, federal-state relations, civil rights and liberties, crime, the judiciary, education, health care, poverty, urban affairs, and population.	Includes formation and debate of U.S. foreign and defense policies, veterans' affairs, and defense spending. (Relations with specific foreign countries are usually found under the region concerned.)	Includes business, labor, agriculture, taxation, transportation, consumer affairs, monetary and fiscal policy, natural resources, and pollution.	Includes worldwide scientific, medical, and technological developments; natural phenomena; U.S. weather; natural disasters; and accidents.	Includes the arts, religion, scholarship, communications media, sports, entertainments, fashions, fads, and social life.

1998

The Taliban gather in the streets of Kandahar to protest against U.S. air strikes, Afghanistan, 1998.

	World Affairs	Europe	Africa & the Middle East	The Americas	Asia & the Pacific
Jan.	The UN World Food Program launches an appeal for $378 million to provide emergency food aid to North Korea in the largest such effort in the program's history.	Turkey's highest court, the Constitutional Court, imposes a ban on the Welfare (Refah) Party, the country's largest party. The court finds that the party, which supports adherence to Islamic teachings in the formation of laws, violates provisions in the Turkish constitution mandating a secular political system.	The Algerian government's first-ever official count of 26,536 deaths in the civil war contrasts with reports by the media and human-rights organizations, which place the death toll at more than 75,000.	Pope John Paul II makes an unprecedented tour of Cuba. The tour is the pope's first visit to Cuba—the only major Latin American country he has not previously visited.	A court in Poonamallee, in the southern state of Tamil Nadu, India, condemns 26 people to death by hanging for their roles in the 1991 assassination of former prime minister Rajiv Gandhi. The sentencing of the defendants ends the longest assassination trial in India's history.
Feb.	Iraq and the UN sign an accord that affirms the right of UN arms inspectors to immediate and unconditional access to suspected Iraqi weapons sites. The deal averts an imminent U.S.-led campaign of retaliatory air strikes against Iraq.	The Albanian separatist Kosovo Liberation Army launches attacks across Kosovo, raising fears of a new ethnic conflict in the Balkans.	Nigerian-led peacekeeping troops under the banner of an alliance of West African nations known as ECOMOG oust Sierra Leone's military government from power.	A team of more than 200 human-rights observers alleges that the Mexican government is targeting foreigners as "a way of distracting from the conflict" in Chiapas and finds that the standoff between the EZLN and government supporters in the state is growing more dangerous.	Kim Dae Jung of the National Congress for New Politics party is inaugurated as South Korea's president. Kim's inauguration marks the first transfer of power from the ruling party to an opposition in South Korea's history.
March	Floods and mudslides from El Niño storms in Peru have resulted in 200 fatalities, left 80,000 people homeless, and caused at least $700 million in damage. In Bolivia, 130 people have died and 70,000 others have been left homeless as a result of El Niño. In Ecuador, at least 135 people have died, and 30,000 others have been left homeless by El Niño.	As violence continues, Serbian police launch a large-scale assault against the Albanian separatist Kosovo Liberation Army in Kosovo.	King Hassan of Morocco appoints Morocco's first opposition-led government since the country gained independence in 1956.	Gen. Augusto Pinochet Ugarte, Chile's former president, is sworn in as a senator for life. In response, a fistfight breaks out on the Senate floor between legislators who oppose and support Pinochet. Thousands of people protest Pinochet in the streets of Santiago and Valparaiso.	Reports confirm that fighting has erupted for control of the major northern city of Mazar-i-Sharif in Afghanistan.
April	Britain and France ratify the Comprehensive Test Ban Treaty (CTBT), becoming the first nations with nuclear-weapons capabilities to do so.	Political leaders tentatively agree to a groundbreaking settlement aimed at ending the long-running sectarian conflict in Northern Ireland. The settlement proposes fundamental changes in the way Northern Ireland was governed and requires approval by the Irish people and the British and Irish Parliaments.	Iran and Iraq begin a prisoner of war (POW) exchange of captives taken during the two nations' 1980–88 war.	Roman Catholic bishop Juan Gerardi Conedera, who heads the human rights office of the Guatemala City archdiocese, presents a harsh critique of the Guatemalan army's human-rights record during the country's 36-year-long civil war. When he is found dead soon after, thousands of mourners gather in Guatemala City for a march and a candlelight vigil.	Pol Pot (born Saloth Sar), leader of the Khmer Rouge whose age is reportedly between 73 and 76, dies of heart failure at a jungle outpost near the Dangrek mountains in Cambodia. Pol Pot was charged with overseeing the deaths of as many as 2 million people from 1975 to 1979 and evaded international efforts to capture him and try him for genocide.
May	India detonates five underground nuclear devices, and Pakistan conducts six underground nuclear tests. The actions draw international condemnation and raise concerns about an escalating nuclear arms race in South Asia.	Tajikistan's secular government and Islamist opposition forces agree to withdraw their troops from Dushanbe, the capital, and its surrounding areas.	Clashes erupt between Ethiopia and Eritrea in a disputed region, touching off an intense armed conflict.	Hundreds of thousands of people across Colombia stop work to protest the recent upsurge in political violence.	Amid widespread protests and rioting, Indonesian president Suharto resigns, ending his 32 years of nearly autocratic rule over Indonesia. Vice Pres. Bacharuddin Jusuf (B.J.) Habibie, is sworn in as his successor.
June	About 80 military aircraft from NATO countries conduct airborne exercises near the Yugoslav border over Albania and Macedonia in an effort to pressure the Yugoslav republic of Serbia to stop using military force against ethnic Albanian separatists in the province of Kosovo.	Voters in Northern Ireland cast ballots in the first election for the British-controlled province's new 108-seat local legislature. Candidates who favor the peace plan capture a large majority of seats in the new Northern Ireland Assembly.	Brigadier General Ansumane Mane, Guinea-Bissau's former army chief of staff, leads a mutiny against the government, launching waves of violence.	Reports reveal that Brazil's Federal Indian Bureau has discovered a previously unknown Indian tribe living in a remote region of the Amazon rain forest, near the border with Peru. Little is known about the customs, language, or name of the tribe, which is believed to comprise about 200 people who rely on fishing and hunting for sustenance.	A powerful cyclone, packing winds of up to 95 miles per hour (150 km per hour), lashes India's western coastal state of Gujarat. Officials state that the cyclone is the most severe storm to hit the state since 1973.
July	UN member states vote in favor of a treaty authorizing the creation of a permanent international court for the adjudication of war crimes.	Spain's Supreme Court sentence 12 government officials for illegal acts connected to the government's effort to silence the Basque separatist movement. The ruling rekindles the long-running controversy over the "Dirty War," in which the government allegedly sponsored death squads in the 1980s.	Moshood K. O. Abiola, 60, who claimed to be Nigeria's rightful head of state since his apparent victory in 1993 presidential elections, dies suddenly, reportedly of a heart attack, while imprisoned in Abuja, the capital. His death, which comes as Nigeria's military government appears poised to announce his release from prison, sets off violent ethnic rioting in several major cities.	To mark the 100th anniversary of the landing of U.S. troops on the island of Puerto Rico, the Puerto Rican Independence Party holds a pro-independence rally in Guanica. At the same time, the pro-commonwealth Popular Democratic Party holds a rally in the capital, San Juan, marking the 46th anniversary of the creation of Puerto Rico's commonwealth.	Chen Xitong is convicted and sentenced to 16 years in prison on charges of corruption and dereliction of duty. Chen, a former member of the party's Politburo, is the highest-ranking Chinese leader to be imprisoned since 1978.
Aug.	The Iraqi government of Pres. Saddam Hussein states that it is freezing cooperation with UN weapons inspectors to underscore its insistence that crippling UN sanctions imposed against Iraq since 1991 must end.	A car bomb explodes in the town of Omagh, in County Tyrone, Northern Ireland, killing 28 people and wounding 220 others. The blast is widely regarded as the worst act of violence yet in the long-running conflict between the British-controlled province's Roman Catholic and Protestant residents.	Two bombs explode within minutes of each other near the U.S. embassies in Nairobi, Kenya, and Dar es Salaam, Tanzania, killing more than 250 people. U.S., Kenyan, and Tanzanian officials assert that the bombings are most likely aimed at the U.S.	Colombia's two main rebel groups—FARC and the ELN—launch a fierce nationwide offensive that is widely seen as an intended reminder of the guerrillas' strength in advance of planned peace talks.	Hun Sen wins in Cambodia's national election, but thousands of demonstrators march through the streets of Phnom Penh soon after, calling for his ouster. The demonstrators argue that the election was tainted by fraud and voter intimidation.
	A *Includes developments that affect more than one world region, international organizations, and important meetings of major world leaders.*	**B** *Includes all domestic and regional developments in Europe, including the Soviet Union, Turkey, Cyprus, and Malta.*	**C** *Includes all domestic and regional developments in Africa and the Middle East, including Iraq and Iran and excluding Cyprus, Turkey, and Afghanistan.*	**D** *Includes all domestic and regional developments in Latin America, the Caribbean, and Canada.*	**E** *Includes all domestic and regional developments in Asia and Pacific nations, extending from Afghanistan through all the Pacific Islands, except Hawaii.*

U.S. Politics & Social Issues	U.S. Foreign Policy & Defense	U.S. Economy & Environment	Science, Technology, & Nature	Culture, Leisure, & Lifestyle	
Allegations that Pres. Clinton had a sexual relationship with Monica Lewinsky, a 21-year-old White House intern, almost instantaneously balloon into what is called the greatest crisis the Clinton White House has ever faced.	In Washington, D.C., Judge Stanley Sporkin orders the U.S. Navy to cease its efforts to discharge Senior Chief Petty Officer Timothy R. McVeigh, who had listed himself as homosexual in a personal profile on the America Online (AOL) computer service.	The first-ever public disclosure detailing the Senate's spending on oversight activities reveals that Senate committees spent nearly $190 million on investigations and regular operating costs, such as staff salaries and office expenses, since Republicans took control of Congress in January 1995.	A team of scientists reports that it discovered seven 92-million-year-old ant fossils preserved in amber in Cliffwood Beach, New Jersey.	*The Times* of London begins serializing previously unpublished poems by British poet laureate Ted Hughes about his late wife, American poet Sylvia Plath. It is the first time he has written at length about Plath since her 1963 suicide.	Jan.
Dr. David Satcher is sworn in as U.S. surgeon general, filling a post vacant for more than three years.	The U.S. ends a 35-year ban on the sale of weapons and weapons technology to South Africa.	The Standard & Poor's index of 500 stocks closes above the 1000-point mark.	A total solar eclipse is visible in parts of South America and the Caribbean The event is to be the last total solar eclipse appearing in the Western Hemisphere until the year 2017.	Tara Lipinski of the U.S. wins the gold medal in the women's figure skating competition at the Winter Olympics. Lipinski, 15, is the youngest person ever to win an Olympic gold medal in figure skating.	Feb.
Data shows that the number of organized hate groups in the U.S. rose in 1997 to 474. The report notes that 163 hate-group websites have appeared on the Internet since the first such site was posted in 1995.	In a ceremony at the Vietnam Veterans' Memorial in Washington, D.C., the army honors Hugh Thompson, Lawrence Colburn, and Glenn Andreotta, three former servicemen who 30 years earlier risked their lives to halt a massacre in My Lai, Vietnam, in which U.S. troops killed hundreds of unarmed civilians.	Democratic fund-raiser Johnny Chung pleads guilty to using "conduit" donors to funnel $20,000 in illegal contributions to the 1996 reelection campaign of Pres. Clinton and Vice Pres. Al Gore. He is the first person charged in a Justice Department investigation of fund-raising abuses in the 1996 election cycle who agrees to cooperate with prosecutors.	Astronomers reveal that they have observed a complete "Einstein ring" created by gravitational lensing. It is the first time the image of a complete Einstein ring has been captured in the infrared or visible light wavelengths. Einstein rings are named after physicist Albert Einstein, whose general theory of relativity predicted their existence.	In a long-awaited statement on the actions of the Roman Catholic Church during the Holocaust of World War II, the Vatican apologizes to Jews for the Roman Catholic Church's failure to take decisive action to prevent Nazi Germany's extermination of more than 6 million Jews.	March
The Arizona Supreme Court strikes down Arizona's English-only law, which required state and local governments to use only English in all official business.	Jose Villafuerte, 45, a Honduran convicted of murder, is executed by lethal injection in Florence, Arizona, despite Honduran pleas for clemency since Villafuerte was denied his right, under the Vienna Convention, to contact the Honduran consulate after his arrest.	The Dow closes above the 9000 mark for the first time.	Two teams of astronomers announce they have independently observed evidence of the early formation of a group of planets around a young star.	Rudolph Kos, a former Roman Catholic priest in Dallas, Texas, is sentenced to life in prison for sexually assaulting altar boys an estimated 1,350 times over five years.	April
Federal judge Norma Holloway Johnson orders members of the Secret Service to testify before a grand jury investigating whether Pres. Clinton illegally tried to cover up an affair with Monica Lewinsky.	Military representatives exhume the unidentified Vietnam War soldier buried in the Tomb of the Unknowns in Arlington National Cemetery in Virginia. The remains are to undergo previously unavailable genetic tests in an effort to determine the soldier's identity and thus address the hopes of those who believe that the remains might belong to a member of their family.	The Clinton administration forecasts a $39 billion budget surplus in the current fiscal year. The surplus, if achieved, will be the federal government's first surplus since 1969. The OMB forecasts an aggregate surplus of $495 billion over the next five years and $1.477 trillion over 10 years.	Astronomers announce that a picture taken by the *Hubble Space Telescope* appears to include the first image ever of a planet outside the Earth's solar system.	Frank (Francis Albert) Sinatra, 82, American icon and one of the most popular entertainers of the 20th century, dies of a heart attack in Los Angeles, California.	May
In *Clinton v. City of New York*, the Supreme Court rules, 6-3, that the Line Item Veto Act is unconstitutional.	Congress passes and Pres. Clinton signs a bill that will create a 21-member panel to look for assets of Holocaust victims in the coffers of government agencies.	Pres. Clinton extends by 10 years an existing ban on offshore oil drilling along most of the U.S. coastline. Clinton also places an indefinite moratorium on oil exploration in several marine sanctuaries, including California's Monterey Bay and the Florida Keys.	Researchers report they have captured the first-ever images of HIV, the virus that causes AIDS, in the process of attacking a human cell.	In *National Endowment for the Arts v. Finley*, the Supreme Court rules, 8-1, that the federal government is allowed to consider standards of decency when awarding federal arts grants.	June
In a shoot-out, Russell E. Weston Jr., 41, allegedly kills two Capitol police officers. The attack is the deadliest at the Capitol since Congress first met there in 1800 and the first shooting at the building since 1954.	The House votes, 264-166, to defeat a resolution that would have rejected Pres. Clinton's decision to renew China's so-called most-favored nation (MFN) trading status.	Pres. Clinton signs a bill enacting a major overhaul of the Internal Revenue Service (IRS).	Reports confirm that that scientists at the University of Hawaii have created more than 50 clones of adult mice.	Pope John Paul II issues an apostolic letter urging Catholics to attend Sunday Mass each week. About one-third of the U.S.'s 60 million Catholics currently do so.	July
Pres. Clinton testifies to a federal grand jury about his relationship with former White House intern Monica Lewinsky.	In the wake of bombings in Africa, the U.S. orders nonessential diplomatic personnel and dependents in Pakistan and Albania to return to the U.S. for fear of other strikes.	Some 6,170 pilots employed by Northwest Airlines go on strike, stranding thousands of passengers worldwide. The pilots' strike is the first at Northwest since 1978.	An unmanned Delta 3 rocket carrying a private communications satellite blows up about 80 seconds after launch at Cape Canaveral, Florida. The launch is the first flight of the newest version of the Delta rocket.	American Steve Fossett is the first person to cross the South Atlantic Ocean in a balloon.	Aug.

F	G	H	I	J
Includes elections, federal-state relations, civil rights and liberties, crime, the judiciary, education, health care, poverty, urban affairs, and population.	*Includes formation and debate of U.S. foreign and defense policies, veterans' affairs, and defense spending. (Relations with specific foreign countries are usually found under the region concerned.)*	*Includes business, labor, agriculture, taxation, transportation, consumer affairs, monetary and fiscal policy, natural resources, and pollution.*	*Includes worldwide scientific, medical, and technological developments; natural phenomena; U.S. weather; natural disasters; and accidents.*	*Includes the arts, religion, scholarship, communications media, sports, entertainments, fashions, fads, and social life.*

	World Affairs	Europe	Africa & the Middle East	The Americas	Asia & the Pacific
Sept.	Saudi Arabia suspends diplomatic ties to protest the Taliban's harboring of Osama bin Laden, a Saudi dissident accused in August terrorist attacks on U.S. embassies in Kenya and Tanzania. That moves leaves Pakistan and the United Arab Emirates as the only countries that recognize Taliban rule in Afghanistan.	The State Duma confirms former foreign minister Yevgeny Primakov as Russia's new premier, ending a period of political paralysis in the face of a collapsing economy.	In the face of a military mutiny in Lesotho, South Africa sends in troops and meets unexpectedly fierce resistance.	Gunmen suspected of being affiliated with the Tijuana drug cartel drag 20 members of three families from their homes and shoot them, killing 18. The massacre is described as the most violent drug-related incident in Mexico's history.	In Malaysia, an estimated 40,000 people attend the largest antigovernment protest ever staged during the 17-year tenure of prime minister Mahathir bin Mohamad.
Oct.	Gen. Augusto Pinochet Ugarte, the former military leader of Chile, is arrested in London after Spain requests his extradition on charges of ordering the murder of hundreds of Spanish citizens during his rule. The arrest sparks protests and a string of court decisions.	Serbian police and army troops begin to withdraw en masse from Kosovo, as per a NATO deadline.	The U.S. holds its first bilateral military exercise with Algeria since that country gained its independence in 1962.	Hurricane Mitch, the deadliest hurricane to strike Central America since 1988, causes more than 9,000 deaths and leaves another 1 million people homeless.	The Supreme Court of the Philippines overturns a 1993 corruption conviction against Imelda Marcos. The ruling overturns the only conviction won against Marcos in several corruption suits brought against her.
Nov.	The UN AIDS Program reveals that in 1998 the number of people infected with HIV rose to 33.4 million, from 27.6 million in 1997. Some 95% of the new infections in 1998 occurred in Africa, Asia, and Eastern Europe.	Amid allegations of corruption and links to organized crime, the government of Premier Mesut Yilmaz collapses when it loses a vote of confidence in Turkey's parliament. It is the first time a government in Turkey has been brought down over allegations of corruption.	According to the final results of the Palestine National Authority's first official census, Palestinians in the West Bank, including East Jerusalem, and the Gaza Strip number 2,895,683.	The Cuban foreign ministry gives the Associated Press permission to open a permanent bureau in Havana, the capital of Cuba.	In Indonesia, police open fire on demonstrators in an effort to stop a mass march on the Parliament building.
Dec.	Prompted by Iraq's failure to cooperate with UN weapons inspectors, the U.S. and Great Britain launch a campaign of air strikes against Iraq.	Violence continues to besiege Kosovo.	Nigeria holds local elections, marking a major step in its transition to democracy.	Reports confirm that three former progovernment fighters in Guatemala have been sentenced to death for their role in a March 1982 massacre. The convictions are the first war-crimes convictions since Guatemala's civil war.	Khieu Samphan and Nuon Chea, senior leaders of Cambodia's Khmer Rouge guerrillas, surrender to the government after negotiating an amnesty deal. The two leaders were among the chief architects of the Khmer Rouge's radical communist regime, responsible for the deaths of more than 1 million Cambodians when it ruled the country from 1975 to 1979.

A	B	C	D	E
Includes developments that affect more than one world region, international organizations, and important meetings of major world leaders.	*Includes all domestic and regional developments in Europe, including the Soviet Union, Turkey, Cyprus, and Malta.*	*Includes all domestic and regional developments in Africa and the Middle East, including Iraq and Iran and excluding Cyprus, Turkey, and Afghanistan.*	*Includes all domestic and regional developments in Latin America, the Caribbean, and Canada.*	*Includes all domestic and regional developments in Asia and Pacific nations, extending from Afghanistan through all the Pacific Islands, except Hawaii.*

U.S. Politics & Social Issues	U.S. Foreign Policy & Defense	U.S. Economy & Environment	Science, Technology, & Nature	Culture, Leisure, & Lifestyle	
Independent counsel Kenneth Starr delivers to the House of Representatives a report on his investigation of Pres. Clinton's relationship with former White House intern Monica Lewinsky. Many newspapers publish the full text of the report after the House votes to release it to the public.	The Defense Department orders that sensitive information that may compromise national security or place personnel at risk be pulled from its roughly 1,000 Pentagon Internet computer network sites accessible by the public.	Pres. Clinton announces that the 1998 fiscal year resulted in the first federal budget surplus since 1969. Clinton reports the surplus to amount to about $70 billion.	The FDA approves Herceptin, a drug for the treatment of some forms of metastatic breast cancer. Herceptin is the first genetically engineered drug to be approved for the treatment of breast cancer.	The John F. Kennedy Center for the Performing Arts announces that comedian Richard Pryor will be the first-ever recipient of its Mark Twain Prize, an annual award to honor humor in the U.S.	Sept.
The Senate confirms the appointments of 17 federal judges nominated by Pres. Clinton. The confirmations bring the number of new federal judges the Senate confirmed in 1998 to 65. That number compares with 36 in 1997.	The Department of Defense merges three cold war defense agencies—the Defense Special Weapons Agency, the On-Site Inspection Agency, and the Defense Technology Security Administration—into one, the Defense Threat Reduction Agency, that will respond to threats posed by nuclear, chemical, and biological weapons.	The world's seven biggest manufacturers of diesel engines for heavy trucks agree to pay $83 million in fines and $1 billion in corrective actions to avoid a federal civil lawsuit on environmental charges. The settlement is the largest financial penalty imposed in an environmental-enforcement action in U.S. history.	The *Discovery* lifts off from Cape Canaveral, Florida, with a crew that includes retiring senator John Glenn (D, Ohio), who, at 77, is the oldest space traveler ever.	A 10th-century manuscript of a work by the mathematician Archimedes is sold at Christies for $2 million. The text is the oldest surviving copy of a work by Archimedes.	Oct.
Michigan prosecutors charge Dr. Jack Kevorkian with first-degree murder for the videotaped euthanasia of Thomas Youk, 52, who was suffering from ALS, or Lou Gehrig's disease. While Kevorkian has assisted in more than 120 suicides since 1990, this marks the first time in which he directly killed his patient.	A grand jury issues an indictment against Saudi millionaire Osama bin Laden, charging him and five members of his alleged terrorist group, al-Qaeda, in the August bombings of U.S. embassies in Kenya and Tanzania. The State Department offers a reward of $5 million—the largest ever offered by the U.S. for the capture of a terrorist—for information leading to his conviction or arrest.	A General Accounting Office (GAO) report finds that the U.S. Postal Service has lost $84.7 million on new products it developed to compete with electronic bill-payment systems.	Reports indicate that U.S. scientists succeeded for the first time in isolating and cultivating human embryonic stem cells.	Pope John Paul II states that Roman Catholics may earn "indulgences." The granting of indulgences prompted Martin Luther to rebel against the papacy, which led to the Protestant Reformation.	Nov.
In near-party-line votes, the House votes to impeach Pres. Clinton for his conduct in the Monica Lewinsky scandal.	U.S. secretary of defense William Cohen and Colombian defense minister Rodrigo Lloredo sign an agreement that establishes a permanent committee for consultation on issues of defense and security in the two countries.	The FEC finds that both the Democrats and the Republicans violated federal campaign finance rules in 1996.	Two teams of scientists report that they have completed a map of the entire genome, or genetic code, of a microscopic worm. It is the first time that scientists have deciphered the entire genetic map of a multicellular animal.	Allegations that International Olympic Committee (IOC) officials accepted bribes in exchange for their votes on which cities will host the Olympic Games touches off the biggest ethics scandal in the century-old organization's history.	Dec.

F	G	H	I	J
Includes elections, federal-state relations, civil rights and liberties, crime, the judiciary, education, health care, poverty, urban affairs, and population.	*Includes formation and debate of U.S. foreign and defense policies, veterans' affairs, and defense spending. (Relations with specific foreign countries are usually found under the region concerned.)*	*Includes business, labor, agriculture, taxation, transportation, consumer affairs, monetary and fiscal policy, natural resources, and pollution.*	*Includes worldwide scientific, medical, and technological developments; natural phenomena; U.S. weather; natural disasters; and accidents.*	*Includes the arts, religion, scholarship, communications media, sports, entertainments, fashions, fads, and social life.*

	World Affairs	Europe	Africa & the Middle East	The Americas	Asia & the Pacific
Jan. 1		Russia redenominates the ruble to make 1,000 old rubles equal to one new ruble. Russia also reintroduces the kopeck coin, of which 100 are worth one ruble.	A band of Hutu rebels in Burundi kill at least 150 civilians in a predawn attack on a military camp near Bujumbura, the capital. It is called one of the largest assaults since 1993. The attack leads to more clashes, in which at least 300 people are killed. . . . An Israeli woman sustains critical head and neck wounds during a drive-by shooting northwest of the West Bank city of Ramallah.	EZLN supporters mark the three-year anniversary of the uprising in Chiapas, Mexico.	
Jan. 2		In the Czech Republic, a new caretaker government headed by Premier Josef Tosovsky takes office. . . . Frank Muir, 77, British comedy writer and broadcasting personality, dies in Egham, England, of unreported causes.	A rocket-propelled grenade crashes through the window of UNSCOM headquarters in Baghdad, Iraq, causing minor damage to the interior of the facility. No injuries are reported. . . . Authorities in Niger arrest Hama Amadou, the former premier, for his alleged involvement in a plot to assassinate Pres. Ibrahim Mainassara Bare.	Judge Maria Claudia Campuzano releases without trial five men charged with the kidnapping and murder of U.S. businessman Peter Zarate in Mexico City in December 1997. Campuzano's ruling prompts objections from Mexico City prosecutors and the U.S. It also sparks a public outcry in Mexico City.	
Jan. 3		Police in Sweden arrest 314 youths at a rock concert outside Stockholm that focuses on neo-Nazi themes after a worker at the venue is hit by a thrown bottle. . . . Britain and Ireland are struck by severe storms that are blamed in at least two deaths.	Algerian newspapers report that more than 400 people died in a group of massacres on the night of Dec. 30, 1997, the first day of the Islamic holy month of Ramadan. The Algerian government stands by its original death toll of 78. Separately, 117 people are slashed to death in the Relizane village of Remka.	In the wake of a December 1997 massacre of 45 Tzotzil Indians in Acteal in Chiapas, Mexican president Ernesto Zedillo Ponce de Leon replaces Emilio Chuayffet, the interior minister responsible for overseeing peace talks with the EZLN. He is succeeded by Francisco Labastida Ochoa. It is widely believed that Chuayffet is forced out because he allowed peace talks with the EZLN to stall and allegedly ignored evidence of mounting violence in the state. The Mexican army begins operations near the town of La Realidad, an EZLN stronghold in Chiapas. . . . Reports confirm that Rafael Caldera, the president of Venezuela, has signed a law reforming the electoral system.	
Jan. 4		In a Lithuanian runoff election, voters select Valdas Adamkus, a Lithuanian American, as president. . . . Storms sweep through western and northern Britain, bringing winds of up to 100 miles per hour (160 kmph). . . . Two police stations are bombed in Kumanovo and Prilep in Macedonia.			In Hong Kong, some 700 poultry workers hold a protest march to demand compensation after the chicken slaughter prompted by an outbreak of a bird-borne strain of influenza.
Jan. 5		Data suggests that crime in Moscow fell by about 20% in 1997. . . . Tickets to visit the grave site of Diana, Princess of Wales, go on sale to the public.	Pres. Daniel T. arap Moi is sworn in for a fifth five-year term as Kenya's ruler after December 1997 national elections. . . . Algerian newspapers report that "several hundred" people were burned alive in Had Chekala, a village in Relizane.	A severe winter storm rages across Eastern Canada, lashing Ontario, New Brunswick, and Quebec.	
Jan. 6	The UN World Food Program launches an appeal for $378 million to provide emergency food aid to North Korea beginning Apr. 1, in the largest such effort in the program's history.		According to Algerian press reports, which had estimated that hundreds of people had died during the previous several days, the death toll is raised to more than 1,000 since the beginning of Ramadan.		The Roman Catholic Church in Australia releases a preliminary draft of a professional conduct code aimed at curbing the sexual abuse of parishioners by members of the clergy.

A	B	C	D	E
Includes developments that affect more than one world region, international organizations, and important meetings of major world leaders.	Includes all domestic and regional developments in Europe, including the Soviet Union, Turkey, Cyprus, and Malta.	Includes all domestic and regional developments in Africa and the Middle East, including Iraq and Iran and excluding Cyprus, Turkey, and Afghanistan.	Includes all domestic and regional developments in Latin America, the Caribbean, and Canada.	Includes all domestic and regional developments in Asia and Pacific nations, extending from Afghanistan through all the Pacific Island, except Hawaii.

U.S. Politics & Social Issues	U.S. Foreign Policy & Defense	U.S. Economy & Environment	Science, Technology, & Nature	Culture, Leisure, & Lifestyle	
A California ban on smoking in bars, casinos, and nightclubs goes into effect.			The largest study ever of the health consequences of obesity finds that obesity moderately increases the risk of premature death. The risk declines with age, disappearing by age 74. The study shows obesity to be less dangerous than many thought, and possibly less dangerous than some attempts to treat it.	Peter Treseder, Keith Williams, and Ian Brown become the first Australians to reach the South Pole unassisted.... Helen Wills Moody (Rourke), 92, preeminent female tennis player of the 1920s and 1930s, dies in Carmel, California.	Jan. 1
Former elementary school teacher Mary Kay Letourneau, 35, is released from prison on parole with the condition that she will not contact the 14-year-old boy with whom she had sexual relations in 1996. In the highly publicized case, Letourneau gave birth to a daughter fathered by her former pupil, and she pled guilty to rape charges in August 1997.		Data suggests that U.S. firms announced a record 10,700 mergers and acquisitions worth $919 billion in 1997. That figure is up 47% from the $626 billion in deals announced in 1996.	Scientists report they discovered a powerful new kind of painkiller when isolating a painkilling but toxic chemical from the poison of a South American frog, Epipedobates tricolor. The painkiller is called ABT-594.		Jan. 2
		William Russell Kelly, 92, who was credited with founding the temporary work—or "temp"—profession when, in 1946, he opened Kelly Services Inc., dies in Fort Lauderdale, Florida, of unreported causes.			Jan. 3
A prison inmate, Teshome Abate, dies in Arizona after a five-month hunger strike launched to protest his prison diet that he claimed conflicted with the food restrictions prescribed by his Ethiopian Orthodox faith.			Thomas F. Frist Sr., 87, founder of the for-profit system of hospital administration who cofounded Hospital Corp. of America in the 1960s, dies in Nashville, Tennessee, of pneumonia.		Jan. 4
Sonny (Salvatore) Bono, 62, (R, Calif.) congressman since 1995 after a career as a popular singer and television host, dies in South Lake Tahoe, California, in a skiing accident.				The Baseball Writers Association of America elects pitcher Don Sutton to the Baseball Hall of Fame in Cooperstown, New York.	Jan. 5
		In Washington, D.C., Judge Thomas F. Hogan approves an agreement in one of three lawsuits challenging Pres. Clinton's use of the line-item veto in 1997. The pact, between the Justice Department and the National Treasury Employees Union, invalidates Clinton's October 1997 veto of a pension-switching plan for 1.1 million federal employees.... The 10th annual North American International Auto Show in Detroit, Michigan, closes after U.S. automobile makers introduce several new cars with advanced fuel-efficient technology.... Data suggests that U.S. filings for personal bankruptcy increased 19.5% in 1997, to a record annual high of 1.3 million.	NASA launches the *Lunar Prospector*, an unmanned spacecraft that will orbit the Moon, on an Athena-2 rocket from Cape Canaveral, Florida. The year-long mission to search for concentrations of hydrogen on the Moon, which may indicate the presence of frozen water there, and to complete a geographical survey of the entire Moon is NASA's first lunar venture since the *Apollo 17* mission of 1972. At a cost of $63 million, it is reportedly the cheapest-ever mission to another body in space.	R. Alan Eagleson, a former agent and head of the National Hockey League Players Association (NHLPA), pleads guilty in U.S. District Court in Boston, Massachusetts, to three counts of felony mail fraud. He is sentenced to one year of probation and fined $697,810.	Jan. 6

F	G	H	I	J
Includes elections, federal-state relations, civil rights and liberties, crime, the judiciary, education, health care, poverty, urban affairs, and population.	Includes formation and debate of U.S. foreign and defense policies, veterans' affairs, and defense spending. (Relations with specific foreign countries are usually found under the region concerned.)	Includes business, labor, agriculture, taxation, transportation, consumer affairs, monetary and fiscal policy, natural resources, and pollution.	Includes worldwide scientific, medical, and technological developments; natural phenomena; U.S. weather; natural disasters; and accidents.	Includes the arts, religion, scholarship, communications media, sports, entertainments, fashions, fads, and social life.

	World Affairs	Europe	Africa & the Middle East	The Americas	Asia & the Pacific
Jan. 7		Data shows that within 24 hours following the Jan. 5 announcement, 40,000 of the 152,500 tickets available to visit the grave site of Diana, Princess of Wales, were sold.		Following the December 1997 massacre of 45 Tzotzil Indians in Acteal, the governor of Chiapas, Julio Cesar Ruiz Ferro, resigns amid an effort by Pres. Ernesto Zedillo Ponce de Leon to avoid any hint of a cover-up in the massacre.... The Canadian federal government apologizes to native Indian peoples for its support of programs that have harmed them and allocates C$600 million (US$420 million) to native "healing" and to economic development of native communities.	
Jan. 8		Reports reveal that an ethnic Albanian separatist group, the Kosovo Liberation Army (UCK), has claimed responsibility for the Jan. 4 police-station bombings in Macedonia. The attacks, as well as a bomb planted outside a courthouse in Gostivar in December 1997, are the first operations on Macedonian soil claimed by the UCK.... The governments of Italy and Turkey agree to coordinate efforts to stem the flow of Kurdish refugees into Western Europe.... Sir Michael Kemp Tippett, 93, British composer, dies in London.		Hutu rebels allegedly kill nine Roman Catholic nuns in the Rwandan village of Rwerere near the border with Congo (formerly Zaire).	
Jan. 9		In Spain, a car bomb explodes in Zarauz, killing Jose Ignacio Iruretagoyena, a town councilor and member of Premier Jose Maria Aznar's ruling Popular Party.... In response to several weeks of demonstrations throughout France, Premier Lionel Jospin announces plans to create an emergency relief fund of 1 billion French francs ($166 million) for the most impoverished of France's unemployed citizens.		Eight prisoners are killed in a riot among inmates at a facility in southeastern Brazil.... At least 25 deaths across Eastern Canada are attributed to the winter storm that started Jan. 5. The storm has caused an estimated C$2 billion (US$1.4 billion) in damage along a corridor that stretches from Ottawa to Montreal, prompting officials to call it the most costly natural disaster on record in Canada.	Hong Kong's legislature approves $97 million in compensation for losses incurred by the territory's poultry industry during the chicken slaughter prompted by a bird-borne strain of influenza.... Record-breaking rains begin to cause severe flooding along parts of Australia's northeast coast.
Jan. 10		A letter bomb explodes in Vitoria, a town in Spain's Basque region, wounding two women.... Police in eight French cities remove jobless protesters who have been occupying 21 unemployment offices for as long as a month. Five such buildings remain occupied.... Polish police beat a 13-year-old basketball fan to death in connection with allegations of hooliganism.	The government of Zambia formally charges ex-president Kenneth Kaunda with plotting to overthrow Pres. Frederick T. J. Chiluba.		An earthquake measuring 6.2 on the Richter scale strikes the Chinese province of Hebei. The quake, centered between the rural counties of Shangyi and Zhangbei, kills 50 people and injures some 11,400 others.... Reports confirm that, in the midst of a currency crisis in Indonesia, military troops are stationed in Bandung in West Java to stem rioting among local merchants.... The Australian city of Townsville is hit with 21.45 inches (55 cm) of rain, and one man dies in the flooding.
Jan. 11		A Roman Catholic doorman, Terry Enright, 28, is shot and killed in Belfast, Northern Ireland. Members of the Loyalist Volunteer Force (LVF), a militant Protestant group, claim responsibility for the attack, which is the latest killing in apparent retaliation for the 1997 death of Billy Wright, a Protestant leader murdered in prison.... John Campbell Wells, 61, British comic writer, actor, and stage director, dies in London, England, of lymphoma.	A bomb reportedly explodes in the Algerian village of Sidi Hamed. Armed men attack people with spades and axes when they flee the explosion. In a separate incident, people leaving a mosque in the Algerian village of Haouche Sahraoui are ambushed and killed. Reports estimate that at least 100 are killed in the two attacks.	Hundreds of women gather in the Mexican town of Altamirano, demanding that troops cease conducting raids of their homes in search of illegal weapons.... At the San Isidro prison in Popayan, Colombia, more than 300 inmates take control of the institution. They are joined by some 450 female visitors in a protest of conditions in the prison.	Unidentified gunmen open fire on Shi'ite Muslim mourners at the Mominpura cemetery in Lahore, the capital of Punjab state in Pakistan, killing at least 24 Shi'ites and seriously wounding 40 others. It is one of the worst incidents of sectarian violence in the region.... Sonia Gandhi, widow of slain former prime minister Rajiv Gandhi, launches a campaign to support the Congress (I) party with an emotional tribute to her husband at the site of his 1991 assassination.

A	B	C	D	E
Includes developments that affect more than one world region, international organizations, and important meetings of major world leaders.	*Includes all domestic and regional developments in Europe, including the Soviet Union, Turkey, Cyprus, and Malta.*	*Includes all domestic and regional developments in Africa and the Middle East, including Iraq and Iran and excluding Cyprus, Turkey, and Afghanistan.*	*Includes all domestic and regional developments in Latin America, the Caribbean, and Canada.*	*Includes all domestic and regional developments in Asia and Pacific nations, extending from Afghanistan through all the Pacific Island, except Hawaii.*

U.S. Politics & Social Issues	U.S. Foreign Policy & Defense	U.S. Economy & Environment	Science, Technology, & Nature	Culture, Leisure, & Lifestyle	
Terry Nichols, convicted in December 1997 for his role in the 1995 bombing of a federal building in Oklahoma City, Oklahoma, escapes the death penalty when the federal jury in Denver, Colorado, charged with his sentencing declare they cannot reach consensus.... Data suggests that students attending urban public schools performed far more poorly on standardized tests than nonurban public-school students in 1994.	Nathan Hill, a U.S. native who was indicted in Chicago, Illinois, on charges of murder and cocaine dealing and placed on the U.S. Marshals Service's "15 Most Wanted List" in 1996, is arrested by authorities in the West African nation of Guinea.	The Congressional Budget Office (CBO) estimates that the 1998 deficit will be just $5 billion, a figure seen as practically insignificant in a $1.7 trillion budget.	A research team announces it has found evidence that it is possible to escape the powerful gravitational pull of a black hole.... Vladimir Prelog, 91, Swiss chemist who shared the 1975 Nobel Prize in chemistry for insights into the designs of various complex molecules, dies in Zurich, Switzerland, of unreported causes.	Owen Bradley, 82, record producer who was instrumental in transforming Nashville, Tennessee, into the center of the country music industry, dies in Nashville where he was receiving treatment for influenza symptoms.	Jan. 7
A study finds that 80% of adults in U.S. prisons are incarcerated due to offenses related to drug and alcohol abuse.	In New York City, U.S. district judge Kevin Thomas Duffy sentences Ramzi Ahmed Yousef to life in prison for playing a central role in the 1993 bombing of the World Trade Center that killed six people and injured at least 1,000 others. ... Clyde Lee Conrad, 50, former U.S. Army sergeant convicted of treason and sentenced to life in prison in 1990, dies in a prison in Koblenz, Germany, apparently of a heart attack.	Statistics reveal that the government's index of prices charged by manufacturers and farmers for finished goods fell 1.2% in 1997, the largest yearly decline since 1986. The index recorded a 2.8% increase for 1996.	An ice storm batters the Northeast, knocking out power to hundreds of thousands of people in Maine, New Hampshire, New York, and Vermont. Seven deaths in New York and another four in Maine are attributed to the storm.... Several teams of astronomers present research showing that the universe is about 15 billion years old—much older than many scientists estimated—and that it will continue to expand forever.... Astronomer David Gray states he cannot reproduce his 1997 observations that disproved the discovery of a planet orbiting the star 51 Pegasi.	Walter E. Diemer, 93, inventor of bubble gum, dies in Lancaster, Pennsylvania. ... At the U.S. Figure Skating Championships in Philadelphia, Pennsylvania, Todd Eldredge, 26, wins his fifth men's U.S. title.	Jan. 8
Marlene Corrigan is convicted of misdemeanor child abuse after the death of her 13-year-old daughter from heart failure caused by obesity. The daughter, Christina Corrigan, reportedly weighed 680 pounds (310 kg) at the time of her death in 1996.	The INS plans to raise 30 of the 40 fees it charges for processing applications for various services.		Scientists announce they have used data collected by an infrared-detecting satellite to quantify for the first time the total amount of light energy emitted by almost all of the stars that have ever existed in the universe.... Kenichi Fukui, 79, Japanese chemist who shared the 1981 Nobel Prize for his work in helping uncover the complex rules that determine when and why chemical reactions take place, dies in Kyoto, Japan, of an intestinal ailment.	At the U.S. Figure Skating Championships in Philadelphia, Pennsylvania, Kyoko Ina and Jason Dungjen win their second straight pairs' title. ... Russia's Anatoly Karpov successfully defends his World Chess Federation title, over India's Viswanathan Anand in Switzerland.	Jan. 9
		The Washington Post reveals that Senate committees have spent nearly $190 million on investigations and regular operating costs, such as staff salaries and office expenses, since Republicans took control of Congress in January 1995. The data comes from a report by the secretary of the Senate in compliance with new reporting rules adopted in 1995. It is the first-ever public disclosure detailing the body's spending on oversight activities.	Due to the ice storm that hit the eastern United States on Jan. 8, Pres. Clinton declares five counties in upstate New York a federal disaster area. Disaster areas are also declared in Maine, New Hampshire, and Vermont.	Michelle Kwan wins the women's title at the U.S. Figure Skating Championships in Philadelphia, Pennsylvania. Elizabeth Punsalan and Jerod Swallow successfully defend their ice-dancing title and win their fifth U.S. championship.... Mona May Karff, 86, Russian-born U.S. women's chess champion, dies in New York City of a heart attack.	Jan. 10
				Football's Green Bay Packers defeat the San Francisco 49ers, 23-10, to win the NFC title. The Denver Broncos beat the Pittsburgh Steelers, 24-21, to win the AFC title.... Klaus Tennstedt, 71, German conductor known for his intense style, dies in Kiel, Germany, of throat cancer.	Jan. 11

F	G	H	I	J
Includes elections, federal-state relations, civil rights and liberties, crime, the judiciary, education, health care, poverty, urban affairs, and population.	Includes formation and debate of U.S. foreign and defense policies, veterans' affairs, and defense spending. (Relations with specific foreign countries are usually found under the region concerned.)	Includes business, labor, agriculture, taxation, transportation, consumer affairs, monetary and fiscal policy, natural resources, and pollution.	Includes worldwide scientific, medical, and technological developments; natural phenomena; U.S. weather; natural disasters; and accidents.	Includes the arts, religion, scholarship, communications media, sports, entertainments, fashions, fads, and social life.

	World Affairs	Europe	Africa & the Middle East	The Americas	Asia & the Pacific
Jan. 12	UN secretary general Kofi Annan announces the appointment of Canadian Louise Frechette to the newly established post of deputy secretary general.... Nineteen member nations of the 40-member Council of Europe sign an agreement to prohibit human cloning.	Some 1,000 teenagers in the Polish city of Slupsk riot to protest a Jan. 10 incident of alleged police brutality. During the violence, 20 police officers are injured and 42 protesters arrested.... Data suggests that Russia's gross domestic product (GDP) rose by 0.4% in 1997. The rise is the first since 1989, before the collapse of the USSR.		In Mexico, some 100,000 people rally in the streets of Mexico City to show support for the people of Chiapas. During a demonstration in the town of Ocosingo in Chiapas, a Tzeltal Indian woman is killed and two others are injured when police open fire. The new governor of Chiapas, Roberto Albores Guillen, calls in army troops to arrest at least 26 police officers allegedly involved in the shooting.... The prison standoff that started Jan. 11 in Colombia ends after an agreement is reached on improving conditions at the prison.	In response to the Jan. 11 killings, thousands of Shi'ite Muslims riot in Lahore, Pakistan, setting fire to buildings, smashing cars, and vowing revenge.... An unidentified Chinese official discloses that 16 people were executed in late Dec. 1997. The executions are said to be connected to the Feb. 1997 separatist riots.... Japanese premier Ryutaro Hashimoto, in a meeting in Tokyo with British prime minister Tony Blair, offers the government's official expression of "deep remorse" for Japan's treatment of British prisoners of war during World War II.
Jan. 13	Iraq, for the second time in two months, prevents a U.S.-led team of UN inspectors from continuing their search for Iraqi chemical- and biological-weapons depots. The move prompts renewed U.S. warnings of an armed response.	Demonstrations against the government's employment policies and against its Jan. 10 eviction of protesters breaks out throughout France. Hundreds of people occupy the chamber of commerce in Paris. Riot police use tear gas to remove the protesters and to break up a sit-in at Paris's commodities exchange building.... The lower house of the Czech parliament overrules the Senate to create a securities markets oversight agency.		Following weeks of protests by opposition supporters who allege that U.S.-born president Janet Jagan used fraud to win December 1997 presidential elections, the government of Guyana bans street demonstrations in Georgetown, the capital. Some 10,000 supporters of Desmond Hoyte, Jagan's opponent in the election, ignore the ban and take to the streets of Georgetown, prompted by a high court's dismissal of a challenge to the legality of Jagan's inauguration.	An Afghan aircraft crashes in Pakistan's Baluchistan province, which borders Afghanistan, killing at least 51 passengers.... Reports confirm that Warriors of Jhangvi, a militant Sunni Muslim organization, has claimed responsibility for the Jan. 11 massacre in Lahore, Pakistan, and threatened additional attacks.... Records show that there have been nearly 350 aftershocks, 10 of which have measured higher than 4.0 on the Richter scale, since the Jan. 10 earthquake in China.
Jan. 14		The Rada, Ukraine's parliament, ratifies a Ukrainian-Russian friendship treaty.... British agriculture minister Jack Cunningham announces the government's plan for the creation of the Food Standards Agency, an independent body that will monitor food safety.... Some 8,000 supporters of former president Momir Bulatovic hold a violent rally in Podgorica, the present-day capital of Montenegro. Around 40 police officers are injured in the violence.	A 40-year-old Saudi Arabian woman, Hasna Mohammed Humair, gives birth to seven babies, four boys and three girls, in the southern city of Abha. Humair's caesarean section operation is the third known delivery of live septuplets and the second in Saudi Arabia.		A veteran Chinese dissident, Qin Yongmin, sends an open letter to the state security ministry refusing its offer to allow him to leave China. Qin, 45, a member of the 1978–79 Democracy Wall movement who has been imprisoned several times since 1970, states that he will risk his security and his life to work for "a legal opposition party and free workers' unions."
Jan. 15	The UN returns control of Eastern Slavonia, an enclave on Croatia's border with Yugoslavia, to Croatia.	Montenegro's new president, Milo Djukanovic, takes office in the former capital, Cetinje.... Reports emerge that Elizabeth Buttle, 60, in November 1997 had a baby, making her Britain's oldest woman to give birth without using fertility drugs.... EMI Records chairman Sir Colin Southgate is confirmed as the new chair of the Royal Opera House in London.	Israeli and Palestinian troops engage in an armed standoff in the southern Gaza Strip city of Khan Younis after some 400 Palestinian protesters block traffic on a main road, leaving several Israeli drivers stranded.	The Argentine navy arrests retired captain Alfredo Astiz after the publication of an interview in which he boasts about his actions as a member of a death squad in Argentina's "dirty war" against suspected leftists during the rule of a military regime from 1976 to 1983.	Indonesian president Suharto signs a pact with the IMF under which he pledges to implement sweeping economic reforms aimed at stabilizing the country's faltering economy.... A cargo ship sinks off the South Korean coast. The bodies of two Philippine sailors and two empty lifeboats are found ashore. Eighteen others are missing.
Jan. 16	The presidents of the three Baltic republics and the U.S. sign a "Charter of Partnership" between their nations.... U.S. president Clinton delays for six months the implementation of Title III of the 1996 Helms-Burton Act, a law to which U.S. allies in Europe, Canada, and Latin America strongly object.... The European Commission, the executive branch of the EU, states the EU should "participate alongside the U.S." in all Middle East peace talks and should act as "key coordinator" of global economic-assistance programs in the peace process.	A cargo ship sinks 50 miles (80 km) off the French islands of St. Pierre and Miquelon. The bodies of 15 crew members are recovered; six others are missing and presumed dead. Four sailors are rescued from the waters.... Turkey's highest court, the Constitutional Court, imposes a ban on the Welfare (Refah) Party, the country's largest party. The court finds that the party, which supports adherence to Islamic teachings in the formation of laws, violates provisions in the Turkish constitution mandating a secular political system.		Although it is not immediately reported, five students from St. Mary's College in the U.S. are raped after gunmen stop the bus they are traveling in near the southwestern town of Santa Lucia Cotzumalguapa in Guatemala.	Four former executives of Dai-Ichi Kangyo Bank Ltd. (DKB), including former chair Tadashi Okuda, plead guilty in Tokyo District Court to making illegal payments to Ryuichi Koike, a so-called sokaiya racketeer.
Jan. 17			The International Red Cross reports that about 450 people in Kenya and western Somalia have died from an epidemic of Rift Valley fever.... Police in Kenya reveal that at least 86 people have died in flooding that has washed out major roads and bridges and left hundreds of people homeless.	Janet Jagan, the president of Guyana, and opposition leader Desmond Hoyte reach an agreement on ending protests by Hoyte's supporters of alleged fraud in the December 1997 elections that brought Jagan to power.	

A	B	C	D	E
Includes developments that affect more than one world region, international organizations, and important meetings of major world leaders.	*Includes all domestic and regional developments in Europe, including the Soviet Union, Turkey, Cyprus, and Malta.*	*Includes all domestic and regional developments in Africa and the Middle East, including Iraq and Iran and excluding Cyprus, Turkey, and Afghanistan.*	*Includes all domestic and regional developments in Latin America, the Caribbean, and Canada.*	*Includes all domestic and regional developments in Asia and Pacific nations, extending from Afghanistan through all the Pacific Island, except Hawaii.*

U.S. Politics & Social Issues	U.S. Foreign Policy & Defense	U.S. Economy & Environment	Science, Technology, & Nature	Culture, Leisure, & Lifestyle	
Pres. Clinton signs a federal directive that requires states to track and report statistics on drug use by prison inmates.... Martha Farnsworth Riche, the director of the Census Bureau, announces that she is resigning, effective Jan. 30.		The Department of Health and Human Services reports that U.S. spending on health care grew in 1996 at the lowest rate since 1960, 4.4%, to $1.04 trillion from $991.4 billion in 1995. After adjustment for inflation, the rate was 1.9%. Retail spending on prescription drugs grew by 9.2% to $62 billion.... Robert Townsend, 77, president and chair of car-rental company Avis Inc., 1962–65, whose books on business were bestsellers, dies of a heart attack while vacationing on the island of Anguilla in the Caribbean.		The American Library Association announces that Karen Hesse and Paul O. Zelinsky have won the Newbery Medal and the Caldecott Medal, respectively.... The Eagles, Fleetwood Mac, Santana, and the Mamas and the Papas are among the inductees to the Rock and Roll Hall of Fame.	Jan. 12
Louisiana state judge Yada Magee rules that a 1996 jury verdict of negligence against Dow Chemical Co. will be binding on individual lawsuits filed by 1,800 women with complaints of injury from breast implants.		The Labor Department reports that the government's index of consumer prices in 1997 rose 1.7%, about half the 3.3% increase registered in 1996. The 1997 rate, which is the lowest yearly rate since 1986, indicates that inflation remains in check.... The Department of Energy awards contracts to six private companies to help the government cut energy costs and decrease greenhouse gas emissions at federal buildings in the southeastern U.S. and U.S. islands in the Caribbean.	Scientists report they have genetically altered adult human cells to bypass a natural limit on their lifetimes.		Jan. 13
Gay Men's Health Crisis (GMHC), the nation's largest AIDS advocacy group, reverses a policy and recommends that doctors in New York State report cases of people infected with HIV to the health department.... NYC Mayor Rudolph Giuliani (R) signs a bill restricting outdoor tobacco advertising.... Internal documents from the R.J. Reynolds Tobacco Corp. that provide evidence of efforts to market cigarettes to minors as young as 12 years old are made public.	Five people plead guilty in U.S. District Court in Lubbock, Texas, to charges related to visa fraud and alien smuggling in connection with a ring that smuggled some 500 nurses from the Philippines and South Korea into the U.S. beginning in 1993. Federal prosecutors allege that the nurses, after entering the U.S. with fraudulent visas, worked for substandard wages in hospitals and nursing homes in Texas and several other states.	For the first time, Pres. Clinton's advisory board on race relations addresses the economic gap between whites and most racial minorities, especially blacks. Several experts state that minority applicants still face discrimination in hiring.... A conference designed to promote greater diversity in the financial-services industry on Wall Street opens at the World Trade Center in New York City.	A study reveals that smoking and breathing secondhand smoke speeds up atherosclerosis, or hardening of the arteries.... The FDA approves the sale of the over-the-counter painkiller extra-strength Excedrin as the first nonprescription treatment for migraine headaches.	NBC agrees to pay $13 million per episode for the next three years to continue broadcasting ER. It is the highest per-episode price ever paid for a TV series.... FINA bans Chinese swimmer Yuan Yuan from national and international competition for four years after she tests positive in drug tests.	Jan. 14
Democrats and Republicans in the Virginia House of Delegates announce a power-sharing agreement that ends more than 100 years of Democratic control over the state legislature. Under the agreement, which will last for four years, Republicans will have equal representation on all but one of the House's 21 committees.		Commonwealth Edison, the nation's largest private operator of nuclear power, announces that it will permanently close its Zion, Illinois, nuclear plant, stating it is prohibitively expensive to run and can no longer compete with lower-priced energy brought about by increasing deregulation.		Rev. Tissa Balasuriya, a priest who was excommunicated from the Roman Catholic Church in 1997, signs a statement of reconciliation with the Vatican.... Junior Wells (born Amos Blakemore), 63, blues harmonica player, dies in Chicago, Illinois, after being in a coma since a 1997.	Jan. 15
The Maryland Senate votes, 36-10, to expel state senator Larry Young (D) for misusing his office for private gain.... Pres. Clinton, Senate majority leader Trent Lott (R, Miss.) and House speaker Newt Gingrich (R, Ga.) name Sen. John Breaux (D, La.) chair of the National Bipartisan Commission on the Future of Medicare.... The tobacco industry agrees to a $15.3 billion settlement of a lawsuit brought by the state of Texas. The settlement, to be paid over 25 years, is larger than the total of two previous ones the industry reached with the states of Florida and Mississippi.			NASA Administrator Daniel Goldin announces that Sen. John Glenn (D, Ohio), the first American to orbit the Earth, will return to space aboard the space shuttle Discovery. ... Two studies report that much of the organic material found on a Martian meteorite in 1996 is of terrestrial origin and not evidence of possible past life on Mars.... Researchers report that they shifted the internal "body clock" of human subjects by shining light onto the backs of knees. It is the first indication that light may affect the body's 24-hour cycle through parts of the body other than the eyes.		Jan. 16
Pres. Clinton is deposed by lawyers for Paula Corbin Jones in a six-hour session in the sexual-harassment suit brought by Jones.	Secretary of Defense William Cohen embarks on a tour of several Asian countries.			The Times of London begins serializing previously unpublished poems by British poet laureate Ted Hughes about his late wife, American poet Sylvia Plath. It is the first time he has written at length about Plath since her 1963 suicide.	Jan. 17

F	G	H	I	J
Includes elections, federal-state relations, civil rights and liberties, crime, the judiciary, education, health care, poverty, urban affairs, and population.	Includes formation and debate of U.S. foreign and defense policies, veterans' affairs, and defense spending. (Relations with specific foreign countries are usually found under the region concerned.)	Includes business, labor, agriculture, taxation, transportation, consumer affairs, monetary and fiscal policy, natural resources, and pollution.	Includes worldwide scientific, medical, and technological developments; natural phenomena; U.S. weather; natural disasters; and accidents.	Includes the arts, religion, scholarship, communications media, sports, entertainments, fashions, fads, and social life.

	World Affairs	Europe	Africa & the Middle East	The Americas	Asia & the Pacific
Jan. 18		The Bosnian Serb Republic's parliament, meeting in the city of Bijeljina, elect Milorad Dodik, a moderate, as the region's new premier.... The body of a Catholic man, Fergal McCusker, who was shot to death, is found in Maghera, County Londonderry, Northern Ireland. The Loyalist Volunteer Force (LVF), a Protestant militant group, claims responsibility.			
Jan. 19	The European Union's finance council endorses Italy's ongoing efforts at reforming government finances.	Jim Guiney, a hard-line Protestant who supported British rule in Northern Ireland, is shot dead in South Belfast. The Irish National Liberation Army, a militant republican guerrilla group, claims responsibility. Later, Catholic taxi driver Larry Brennan is shot and killed in Belfast, in apparent retaliation.... Russian president Boris Yeltsin returns to the Kremlin, Russia's seat of government, for the first time in more than a month after illnesses and vacations.	A European Union (EU) delegation arrives in Algeria to emphasize the international community's concern over the escalating violence in the country.... A PNA military court sentences two bomb makers of Hamas's military wing—Jasser Samaru and Nassim Abu al-Rous—to 15 years' imprisonment with hard labor for their involvement with suicide attacks in West Jerusalem in July and September 1997.		
Jan. 20		The Czech parliament elects Pres. Vaclav Havel to a second five-year term.	Reports disclose that Hutu rebels killed 34 people and injured 25 others when they doused a bus with gasoline and set it on fire outside the town of Gisenyi, Rwanda.	A judge in Lima, Peru's capital, orders Aeroperu airline to pay $29 million to the families of 58 of the 70 victims of an October 1996 jet crash. Families of the 12 other victims are pursuing separate legal action.	
Jan. 21	Iraq freezes all weapons inspections, heightening tensions.	Benedict Hughes, a Catholic, is killed by unidentified gunmen in Belfast.	Algerian premier Ahmed Ouyahia issues the government's first-ever official death toll for the civil war. He estimates that 26,536 people died and an additional 21,137 were injured in the conflict. His data contrasts with reports by the media and human-rights organizations, which place the death toll at more than 75,000.	Pope John Paul II makes an unprecedented tour of Cuba. The tour is Pope John Paul's first visit to Cuba—the only major Latin American country he has not previously visited.	

A	B	C	D	E
Includes developments that affect more than one world region, international organizations, and important meetings of major world leaders.	Includes all domestic and regional developments in Europe, including the Soviet Union, Turkey, Cyprus, and Malta.	Includes all domestic and regional developments in Africa and the Middle East, including Iraq and Iran and excluding Cyprus, Turkey, and Afghanistan.	Includes all domestic and regional developments in Latin America, the Caribbean, and Canada.	Includes all domestic and regional developments in Asia and Pacific nations, extending from Afghanistan through all the Pacific Island, except Hawaii.

U.S. Politics & Social Issues	U.S. Foreign Policy & Defense	U.S. Economy & Environment	Science, Technology, & Nature	Culture, Leisure, & Lifestyle	
Data from the Justice Department reveals that the number of inmates incarcerated in city and county jails increased by 9.4%, or 48,587, during the period of July 1, 1996, to June 30, 1997. The increase amounts to nearly twice the average annual rise in county and city inmates since 1990.				The world swimming championships, held in New Zealand, close. The U.S. collected the most gold medals—14—while Australia finished second with seven, and China won three gold medals. . . . At the Golden Globe Awards for films, *Titanic* wins for Best Drama, and *As Good as It Gets* wins as Best Musical or Comedy. . . . In basketball, the Western Conference routs the Eastern Conference, 102-73, to win the women's ABL All-Star Game.	Jan. 18
		After nearly a week of negotiations presided over by the National Mediation Board, United Parcel Service of America Inc. (UPS) and officials of the company's Independent Pilots Union reach a tentative agreement on a six-year contract for the package-delivery company's 2,100 pilots.	Acting FDA commissioner Michael Friedman asserts that the FDA has the authority under law to regulate human cloning and that its approval will be required for anyone who wishes to try to clone a person.	In Washington, D.C., Israeli prime minister Benjamin Netanyahu addresses 500 evangelical Christians, including Jerry Falwell, who calls Netanyahu "the Ronald Reagan of Israel" and vows to crusade against the return of Israeli-held territory to Palestinians. . . . Carl Lee Perkins, 65, songwriter and one of the first practitioners of rockabilly music, dies in Jackson, Tennessee, of complications from a stroke.	Jan. 19
Allegations that Pres. Clinton had a sexual relationship with Monica Lewinsky, a 21-year-old White House intern, are leaked to news agencies in the late evening. . . . In Phoenix, Arizona, Judge Roger Strand orders an acquittal on one of the seven fraud counts of which former Arizona governor J. Fife Symington III (R) was convicted.			James Robl and Steven Stice of the University of Massachusetts in Amherst report that they have created three Holstein calves that are the first cows cloned from a genetically altered cell.	Sir Anthony Glyn (born Geoffrey Leo Simon Davson), 75, British biographer and novelist known for his 1955 biography of his grandmother, 19th-century novelist Elinor Glyn, dies in the south of France of congestive heart failure.	Jan. 20
Pres. Clinton denies allegations that he had a sexual relationship with Monica Lewinsky, 21, a White House intern, and that he asked her to lie under oath about the affair. The allegations came to light after Whitewater independent counsel Kenneth Starr learned of audio-tapes on which Lewinsky allegedly describes the affair and cover-up to her confidante, Linda Tripp. The story almost instantaneously balloons into what is called the greatest crisis the Clinton White House has ever faced. . . . The Supreme Court rules, 6-3, that the Constitution does not require a judge to advise a jury during the sentencing phase of a capital trial to consider mitigating evidence that may persuade the jury to impose on the defendant a life-imprisonment sentence rather than a death sentence. With their ruling, the justices uphold the death sentence imposed on Virginia inmate Douglas Buchanan. . . . Federal authorities arrest 44 police and corrections officers in northern Ohio for selling protection to suspected cocaine traffickers in one of the largest sting operations in U.S. history. . . . Jose Jesus Ceja, 42, convicted of the 1974 murder of a couple in Phoenix, Arizona, is put to death by lethal injection in Florence, Arizona. Ceja is the 434th person to be executed in the U.S. and only the ninth in Arizona since 1976. . . . Mary Ingraham Bunting-Smith, 87, president of Radcliffe College, 1959–72, dies in Hanover, New Hampshire, of unreported causes.	The INS orders Saudi Arabian dissident Hani Abdel Rahim al-Sayegh deported from the U.S. In 1997, Sayegh reneged on a pledge to plead guilty to involvement in aborted terrorist plots against the U.S. in 1994 and 1995. He also withdrew a promise to provide U.S. authorities with information about the 1996 truck bombing of Khobar Towers, a U.S. military complex in Dharan, Saudi Arabia.	Former representative Mary Rose Oakar (D, Ohio) is fined $32,000 and sentenced to two years' probation for using false contributor names to funnel funds from her House bank account to her unsuccessful 1992 reelection campaign. . . . In *Lunding v. New York Tax Appeals Tribunal*, the Supreme Court rules, 6-3, to strike down a provision in a New York State tax law that bars nonresidents from deducting alimony payments from their New York income tax, a deduction that the state allows. . . . In *LaChance v. Erickson*, the Supreme Court rules unanimously to overturn a lower-court ruling that protected federal workers under investigation for job-related misconduct from facing additional charges for lying about that alleged misconduct.		Jack Lord (born John Joseph Patrick Ryan), 77, actor best known for his role in the TV series *Hawaii Five-O*, 1968–80, dies in Honolulu, Hawaii, of congestive heart failure.	Jan. 21

	World Affairs	Europe	Africa & the Middle East	The Americas	Asia & the Pacific
Jan. 22	The newly approved commander of the Russian air force, Gen. Anatoly Kornukov, publicly acknowledges that he gave the 1983 order to shoot down a South Korean commercial airplane that had entered Soviet airspace. All of the plane's 269 passengers were killed in the incident, and Russian authorities claimed that the jet was on a U.S.-sponsored mission to spy on Sakhalin Island in the Sea of Japan.	A group of U.S.-led troops from the NATO force in Bosnia-Herzegovina arrests alleged Bosnian Serb war criminal Goran Jelisic in the northeastern town of Bijeljina. It is the first time that U.S. troops on the NATO force have arrested a war crimes suspect.	Mwai Kibaki, who finished second to Pres. Daniel T. arap Moi in the December 1997 presidential election, files a petition before the High Court of Kenya in Nairobi, the capital, requesting the nullification of the poll's results.	Sixty-eight Canadians are named recipients of the Order of Canada. Separately, Thousands of homes in Canada remain without power due to the severe winter storm started Jan. 5.	Health authorities report that 111 patients in a Hong Kong hospital were given medical tests that could have infected them with Creutzfeldt-Jakob disease, the human counterpart to bovine spongiform encephalopathy, (BSE), or mad-cow disease, and that seven of those patients died.... Chinese news media report that the Jan. 10 earthquake in Hebei province left cracks in the nearby Great Wall.... The Australian government bans Japanese fishing boats from the nation's waters after Japan refuses to limit its fishing of southern bluefin tuna, a possibly endangered species.
Jan. 23		An avalanche strikes the French Alps near Les Orres ski resort, killing 11 hikers and injuring about 20 others.... The Albanian separatist Kosovo Liberation Army (UCK) assassinates a local Serbian official, Desimir Vasic.... The Ulster Freedom Fighters disclose that they have broken a cease-fire enacted in October 1994 and that they have murdered three Catholics since Dec. 31, 1997. Hours later, an unidentified gunman shoots and kills Liam Conway, a Catholic, in Belfast, but no group claims responsibility.	Hilla Limann, 64, president of the African nation of Ghana, 1979–81, dies in Accra, Ghana, of a heart ailment.	Pres. Carlos Saul Menem expels retired captain Alfredo Astiz from the Argentine navy for "provoking.a grave situation" with his Jan. 15 remarks about Argentina's "dirty war" against suspected leftists.... Royal Bank of Canada and Bank of Montreal, Canada's largest and third-largest banks, respectively, announce plans to merge. The deal, valued at more than C$40 billion (US$28 billion), will create the largest bank in Canada and the second-largest bank in North America in terms of assets.	Japan unilaterally withdraws from a 1965 treaty with South Korea governing fishing rights in the waters between the two countries.... The Hong Kong government declares that an outbreak of a bird-borne strain of influenza that killed six people is over since no new cases of the disease have been reported since Dec. 28, 1997.
Jan. 24		Neo-Nazis hold demonstrations in Dresden, Germany, to protest an exhibit displaying atrocities committed during World War II by the Wehrmacht, Nazi Germany's regular army. Leftist activists stage a rival protest against neo-Nazism.... A Catholic taxi driver is shot dead in Belfast, Northern Ireland.		The governor of the Mexican state of Chiapas, Roberto Albores Guillen, orders the release of some 300 Indians, in an effort to ease tensions in the state and to revive stalled peace talks with the EZLN.... Pope John Paul II holds a coronation ceremony to honor a statue of Our Lady of Charity, declared Cuba's patron saint in 1916, in Santiago de Cuba. The coronation ceremony is an emotional gesture for Cubans, who revere the statue as a cherished symbol of spiritual and national identity.	
Jan. 25		Britain's Queen Elizabeth, the Queen Mother, fractures her left hip in a fall at the royal family's estate in Sandringham, England.		At the Plaza of the Revolution in Havana, Cuba, an enthusiastic crowd of at least 250,000, including Pres. Fidel Castro and senior government officials, attend a 2½-hour mass held by Pope John Paul II.	Severe rains from Cyclone Les hit the Northern Territory town of Katherine, Australia.
Jan. 26	In a 20-year campaign with the World Health Organization (WHO), British pharmaceutical manufacturer SmithKline Beecham PLC announces that it will donate antiparasite drugs to treat about 1 billion people in Africa, Asia, the Pacific and Central and South America at risk of being infected by a mosquito-borne disease, lymphatic filariasis, or elephantiasis. Some 120 million people currently suffer from elephantiasis, an infection by parasitic worms of the lymphatic system.... A UN human-rights mission begins a visit of five high-security jails in Peru that house some 4,000 people detained on terrorism charges.	Reports from Northern Ireland confirm that the LVF has claimed responsibility for the Jan. 24 attack in Belfast.... Some 300 picketing former dockworkers in Liverpool, England, accept a cash settlement to end a two-year-long protest against Mersey Docks and Harbour Co.... A separatist group seeking greater autonomy from France, the outlawed "historic wing" of the Corsican National Liberation Front, declares an end to a seven-month-long truce.... A comprehensive ban on the possession of handguns goes into effect in Britain.		Brazil's government reports that deforestation in the Amazon rain forest in the 1994–95 burning season was the worst ever recorded. During that period some 11,196 square miles (29,000 sq km) of rain forest were destroyed.... TransCanada Pipelines Ltd. and Nova Corp., two of Canada's largest energy firms, announce plans to merge. The deal, valued at some C$14 billion (US$9.7 billion), will be the largest ever in Canada's energy sector and the second-largest merger ever in Canada.	A judge rules that a law denying Hong Kong residency to children born to a Hong Kong parent in China but outside of the territory is unconstitutional. The law was passed by the China-appointed legislature that took office when Hong Kong reverted to Chinese sovereignty in 1997.

A	B	C	D	E
Includes developments that affect more than one world region, international organizations, and important meetings of major world leaders.	*Includes all domestic and regional developments in Europe, including the Soviet Union, Turkey, Cyprus, and Malta.*	*Includes all domestic and regional developments in Africa and the Middle East, including Iraq and Iran and excluding Cyprus, Turkey, and Afghanistan.*	*Includes all domestic and regional developments in Latin America, the Caribbean, and Canada.*	*Includes all domestic and regional developments in Asia and Pacific nations, extending from Afghanistan through all the Pacific Island, except Hawaii.*

U.S. Politics & Social Issues	U.S. Foreign Policy & Defense	U.S. Economy & Environment	Science, Technology, & Nature	Culture, Leisure, & Lifestyle	
Theodore J. Kaczynski, the alleged Unabomber, pleads guilty in a federal court in Sacramento, California, to charges linking him to a series of bombings that killed three people and injured two others. The California case covers 10 of 13 federal counts against him. Under the deal, Kaczynski will not face the death penalty. . . . The office of Kenneth Starr begins serving subpoenas on several White House employees, including Clinton's personal secretary, Betty Currie, and former interns who worked with Monica Lewinsky and Vernon Jordan.		Michael P. Dombeck, head of the U.S. Forest Service, announces that the Clinton administration is imposing a ban on the building of new logging roads into some 33 million acres (13 million hectares) of pristine forest lands in 130 federal forests.	A study finds that premenstrual syndrome (PMS), widely regarded as an emotional disorder, has a physiological cause in the effect on the brain of fluctuating hormone levels. . . . Microsoft Corp. reaches a partial out-of-court settlement in an antitrust suit brought by the Justice Department, agreeing to modify its Windows 95 operating system in compliance with a federal judge's December 1997 order. . . . Some 2,000 Maine residents remain without power due to the Jan. 8 ice storm. . . . The U.S. space shuttle *Endeavour* lifts off from Kennedy Space Center in Cape Canaveral, Florida, on a mission to deliver U.S. astronaut Dr. Andrew S.W. Thomas to the Russian space station *Mir* and to collect from it another U.S. astronaut, Dr. David A. Wolf.		Jan. 22
DNA Plant Technology Corp. pleads guilty in U.S. District Court in Washington, D.C., to one misdemeanor count of conspiracy to illegally export specially bred high-nicotine tobacco seeds. . . . A jury in Brownsville, Texas, overturns the 1988 conviction of Susie Mowbray, accused of killing her husband, Bill Mowbray. Mowbray, who served nine years of a life sentence, won the right to a new trial in 1996 after an appeals court ruled that prosecutors had suppressed a forensic report.	Fairfax County circuit court judge J. Howe Brown Jr. formally sentences Pakistani immigrant Mir Aimal Kasi to death for murdering two CIA employees in 1993. . . . In response to the scandal involving Pres. Clinton and Monica Lewinsky, foreign commentators note the seriousness of the obstruction of justice allegations, but the overwhelming tone—especially in Europe and Latin America—is that Clinton is a victim of what they see as Americans' puritanical attitude toward sex.		Researchers find that high levels of the hormone insulinlike growth factor-1 (IGF-1) increases men's risk of cancer of the prostate gland.	The Alabama Supreme Court dismisses a lawsuit that sought to allow Judge Roy Moore to continue to hold prayer sessions and display the Ten Commandments in his courtroom. . . . Victor (Edward John) Pasmore, 89, British painter who in 1937 cofounded the Euston Road School, dies on the island of Malta.	Jan. 23
		Reports confirm that ASARCO Inc., one of the largest mining companies in the U.S., has settled charges that it illegally discharged toxic waste at its copper mine near Kelvin, Arizona, and at its lead smelting site in East Helena, Montana. Under the terms of the settlement, ASARCO agrees to spend $50 million to clean up the sites and to establish pollution-monitoring programs at its 38 facilities in seven states. ASARCO also agrees to pay $6 million for violating environmental statutes.	The U.S. spacecraft *Endeavour* successfully docks with the Russian space station *Mir*.	Five former players—Mike Singletary, Anthony Munoz, Dwight Stephenson, Tommy McDonald, and Paul Krause—are named to the Pro Football Hall of Fame in Canton, Ohio.	Jan. 24
				The Denver Broncos upset the Green Bay Packers, 31-24, to win football's Super Bowl XXXII in San Diego, California. It is the first AFC victory in 13 years. Denver police use tear gas to disperse a near-riot by 10,000 Broncos fans.	Jan. 25
In his strongest remarks to date on the sex scandal that broke Jan. 21, Pres. Clinton states, "I want you to listen to me. I'm going to say this again: I did not have sexual relations with that woman, Miss Lewinsky. I never told anybody to lie, not a single time—never. These allegations are false. And I need to go back to work for the American people.". . . In *Brogan v. United States*, the Supreme Court rules, 7-2, that individuals who falsely claim their innocence while under questioning by a federal investigator may be prosecuted under the federal false-statements statute.	Judge Stanley Sporkin of U.S. District Court in Washington, D.C., orders the U.S. Navy to cease its efforts to discharge Senior Chief Petty Officer Timothy R. McVeigh, who listed himself as homosexual in a personal profile on the America Online (AOL) computer service. Navy administrators in November 1997 recommended that McVeigh—no relation to the man convicted of the bombing in Oklahoma City—be dismissed due to his sexual orientation.	Environmental officials release three Mexican wolves into the Apache National Forest, which straddles the New Mexico-Arizona border. It is the first step in a reintroduction program. . . . Data shows that sales of existing homes in 1997 totaled 4.21 million units, a new record that surpasses the previous high of 4.09 million homes resold in 1996. . . . Officials of the nation's two largest teachers' unions, the NEA and the AFT, release plans for a proposed merger. If approved, the merger will create the largest labor union in U.S. history, with some 3.2 million members nationwide.		Statistics reveal that the Super Bowl's Nielsen rating was 44.5, which means it drew an audience of 133.4 million people in the U.S., tying it for the third-most watched program in TV history. . . . Shinichi Suzuki, 99, Japanese violinist who developed the internationally used "Suzuki Method" of childhood music instruction, dies in Matsumoto, Japan, of a heart attack.	Jan. 26

F	G	H	I	J
Includes elections, federal-state relations, civil rights and liberties, crime, the judiciary, education, health care, poverty, urban affairs, and population.	*Includes formation and debate of U.S. foreign and defense policies, veterans' affairs, and defense spending. (Relations with specific foreign countries are usually found under the region concerned.)*	*Includes business, labor, agriculture, taxation, transportation, consumer affairs, monetary and fiscal policy, natural resources, and pollution.*	*Includes worldwide scientific, medical, and technological developments; natural phenomena; U.S. weather; natural disasters; and accidents.*	*Includes the arts, religion, scholarship, communications media, sports, entertainments, fashions, fads, and social life.*

	World Affairs	Europe	Africa & the Middle East	The Americas	Asia & the Pacific
Jan. 27	The executive board of the World Health Organization (WHO) nominates former Norwegian premier Gro Harlem Brundtland to be the next director general of the WHO.	A letter is made public, in which Pope John Paul II asks Germany's Catholic bishops to end the church's role in issuing certificates showing that women have undergone counseling before undergoing an abortion. Women in Germany are required to obtain proof that they had counseling before they can legally have an abortion. In response to the letter, bishops of the Roman Catholic Church in Germany announce that church-sponsored counseling centers will stop issuing such certificates.	Military firing squads in Kinshasa, the capital of the Democratic Republic of the Congo, publicly execute 21 people convicted of murder and armed robbery.	Reports confirm that the government of Guatemala has restored diplomatic relations with Cuba and plans to open an embassy in Havana, Cuba's capital, in 1998.... Carlos Flores Facusse is sworn in as the president of Honduras in Tegucigalpa, the capital.	The severe rains from Cyclone Les that hit the Northern Territory town of Katherine, Australia, on Jan. 25 have killed at least three people and forced the evacuation of most of the town's 9,000 residents. During the three-day deluge, about 17 inches (42 cm) of rain fell on the town. The resultant flooding temporarily shuts down power and causes tens of millions of dollars in damage to homes and businesses.
Jan. 28		The Turkish government releases a report confirming widespread suspicions that government officials were partially responsible for several assassinations and kidnappings in the mid-1990s, frequently targeting Kurdish separatists.	A helicopter crash kills Lt. Col. Firmin Sinzoyiheba, the defense minister of Burundi, as well as the pilot, a bodyguard, a military commander, and the personal secretary to Burundian president Pierre Buyoya. The officials were en route to peace talks with Hutu rebels.	In Mexico, Rubicel Ruiz Gamboa, a peasant leader and supporter of the leftist opposition Democratic Revolutionary Party (PRD), is shot dead outside his home in Tuxtla Gutiérrez, the capital of the southern state of Chiapas. The killing is the latest in a wave of violence that began with the massacre of 45 Tzotzil Indians in December 1997.... Brazil's Congress passes a bill giving Brazil's federal environmental agency power to impose fines for environmental damage.	A court in Poonamallee, in the southern state of Tamil Nadu, India, condemns 26 people to death by hanging for their roles in the 1991 assassination of former prime minister Rajiv Gandhi. The defendants are among 41 people charged with orchestrating the assassination plot; 12 other suspects have committed suicide or died in gun battles with police. The sentencing of the defendants ends the longest assassination trial in India's history.
Jan. 29	The Central African Republic establishes diplomatic ties with China, severing its relations with Taiwan. It is the Central African Republic's third resumption of relations with China since 1964.	British prime minister Tony Blair announces that the government will launch a new investigation into "Bloody Sunday," a 1972 incident in Londonderry, Northern Ireland, in which British troops shot and killed 14 unarmed Roman Catholic protesters. The announcement, which comes a day before the 26th anniversary of the killings, is seen as a potential boost for peace talks under way in London and in Belfast, Northern Ireland.			
Jan. 30		Thousands of people throughout Northern Ireland participate in peace rallies to mark the 26th anniversary of the Bloody Sunday massacre.	Eight people are killed and some 40 are wounded in the eastern Bekaa Valley city of Baalbek when the Lebanese army tries to take control of a Hezbollah (Party of God) religious school seized by supporters of Sheik Sobhi al-Tufaili's Hunger Revolution movement.		The finance ministry shuts down 10 of South Korea's 30 merchant banks, saying that they have insufficient capital and excessive borrowing.
Jan. 31		Milorad Dodik is sworn in as the Bosnian Serb Republic's new premier in Banja Luka, the republic's new capital.			
Feb. 1				Miguel Angel Rodriguez of the conservative opposition Social Christian Unity Party is elected Costa Rica's new president. The Social Christian Unity Party wins a slim majority in the Legislative Assembly, the country's single-chamber legislative body.	

A	B	C	D	E
Includes developments that affect more than one world region, international organizations, and important meetings of major world leaders.	Includes all domestic and regional developments in Europe, including the Soviet Union, Turkey, Cyprus, and Malta.	Includes all domestic and regional developments in Africa and the Middle East, including Iraq and Iran and excluding Cyprus, Turkey, and Afghanistan.	Includes all domestic and regional developments in Latin America, the Caribbean, and Canada.	Includes all domestic and regional developments in Asia and Pacific nations, extending from Afghanistan through all the Pacific Island, except Hawaii.

U.S. Politics & Social Issues	U.S. Foreign Policy & Defense	U.S. Economy & Environment	Science, Technology, & Nature	Culture, Leisure, & Lifestyle	
In his State of the union address, Pres. Clinton proclaims that the closing years of the 20th century are "a time to build" for the future. Clinton states that expected budget surpluses should be utilized to ensure that the Social Security system will meet Americans' needs. Senate majority leader Trent Lott (R, Miss.) delivers the Republican response.... Jerome R. Sullivan, a former FBI agent, pleads guilty to 10 counts of embezzlement for stealing more than $400,000 from the FBI from 1992 to 1997.		Reports find that federal wildlife officials have observed that a deadly toxin plaguing American bald eagles and American coots has migrated to three lakes in central Arkansas.... The Conference Board reports that its index of consumer confidence plunged in January to 127.3, from a revised December 1997 reading of 136.2. The January drop is the largest in eight years.		The Whitbread Book of the Year Award, considered one of Britain's most prestigious literary prizes, is given to British poet Ted Hughes.... Some 400,000 fans turn out for a parade to celebrate the Broncos' Jan. 25 win in the Super Bowl in Denver, Colorado.	Jan. 27
Dr. Barbara A. DeBuono, the New York State health commissioner, discloses that two women thought to have contracted HIV, the virus that causes AIDS, from Nushawn J. Williams gave birth to HIV-positive babies. Williams is accused of knowingly infecting as many as 13 women in the Chautauqua County region.... A CBS News poll puts Pres. Clinton's approval rating at 73%, the highest of his presidency and up from 58% earlier in the week.					Jan. 28
A bomb explodes outside an abortion clinic in Birmingham, Alabama, killing Robert Sanderson, 35, an off-duty police officer working as a security guard, and seriously injuring a nurse. It is the first time ever that the bombing of an abortion clinic results in a fatality.... Robert Smith, 47, convicted of the 1995 murder of an Indiana prison inmate, is put to death by lethal injection in Michigan City, Indiana. He is the 435th person to be executed in the U.S. and only the sixth in Indiana since 1976.	CIA inspector general Frederick Hitz releases the first volume of a report on his 15-month-long investigation into the 1996 allegations that the CIA condoned the cocaine sales in the U.S. in the 1980s that raised funds for U.S.-backed Nicaraguan contra rebels. Hitz's report finds that the CIA had no knowledge of such activities.		A team of scientists report that it discovered seven 92-million-year-old ant fossils preserved in amber in Cliffwood Beach, New Jersey. The discovery confirms the existence of socially organized, varied ant species some 40 million years before their populations suddenly began to flourish.	Singer Bobby Brown is convicted on two counts of driving while under the influence of alcohol, a misdemeanor, and is sentenced to five days in jail, 30 days in a residential substance-abuse treatment facility, and 100 hours of community service.	Jan. 29
	The State Department issues its annual report on the status of human rights around the world. The report tones down the criticisms of China made in 1997. Human-rights groups disagree with that assessment. Women in both Algeria and Afghanistan are found to have suffered serious abuses. Other countries cited for abuses include Cambodia, Indonesia, Pakistan, Sudan, and Vietnam. The report names U.S. allies such as Saudi Arabia, Turkey, and Mexico, for human-rights violations as well.	Judge Ricardo Urbina fines Republican lobbyist James Lake $150,000 for his part in an illegal scheme to pay off the campaign debts incurred by Henry Espy in an unsuccessful run for Congress in 1993.... Data reveal that the total membership of U.S. unions in 1997 was 12.9 million individuals, about the same number as the previous year.	A study identifies the gene responsible for a severe form of hair loss.... Two scientists—Vittorio Sgaramella of the University of Calabria, Italy, and Norton D. Zinder of New York City's Rockefeller University—express skepticism over the "lack of any confirmation" of the cloning of an adult sheep by Scottish scientists, reported in 1997.		Jan. 30
			The U.S. space shuttle *Endeavour* touches down at the Kennedy Space Center after delivering U.S. astronaut Dr. Andrew S.W. Thomas to the Russian space station *Mir* and collecting from it another U.S. astronaut, Dr. David A. Wolf. Thomas is the seventh and expected to be the final U.S. astronaut to stay on *Mir*.	Top-seeded Martina Hingis of Switzerland for the second straight year wins the women's tennis title at the Australian Open in Melbourne, defeating Spain's Conchita Martinez.	Jan. 31
		Hundreds of employees of the Frontier Hotel-Casino in Las Vegas, Nevada, end a more than six-year-long strike against the resort, with a pledge from the new owner to restore most of their jobs and compensate their lost pay.		Judge Robert Altman finds that Giles Harrison and Andrew O'Brien, two British paparazzi, trapped actor Arnold Schwarzenegger and his wife, journalist Maria Shriver, while trying to obtain pictures in May 1997.... The AFC defeats the NFC, 29-24, to win the National Football League's all-star game.... At the Australian Open, Petr Korda of the Czech Republic beats Chile's Marcelo Rios to win the men's tennis title.	Feb. 1

F	G	H	I	J
Includes elections, federal-state relations, civil rights and liberties, crime, the judiciary, education, health care, poverty, urban affairs, and population.	*Includes formation and debate of U.S. foreign and defense policies, veterans' affairs, and defense spending. (Relations with specific foreign countries are usually found under the region concerned.)*	*Includes business, labor, agriculture, taxation, transportation, consumer affairs, monetary and fiscal policy, natural resources, and pollution.*	*Includes worldwide scientific, medical, and technological developments; natural phenomena; U.S. weather; natural disasters; and accidents.*	*Includes the arts, religion, scholarship, communications media, sports, entertainments, fashions, fads, and social life.*

	World Affairs	Europe	Africa & the Middle East	The Americas	Asia & the Pacific
Feb. 2					A plane crashes near Mt. Sumagaya on the Philippine island of Mindanao, killing all 99 passengers and five crew members.... Three rockets are fired into a cargo section of the Narita International Airport near Tokyo, Japan, injuring one worker.... Australia's Industrial Relations Commission rules that nearly 300 miners fired in 1997 are entitled to as much as A$8 million (US$5.2 million) in compensation from their former employer, Gordonstone Coal Management. It is the nation's largest-ever unfair-dismissal case.
Feb. 3		Armenian president Levon Ter-Petrossian resigns after disagreements with Premier Kocharyan over policy toward the region of Nagorno-Karabakh in Azerbaijan.... In the Dolomite Mountains in Italy, a U.S. military aircraft severs a cable carrying ski-lift cars, causing one car to plummet 300 feet (90 m). All 20 people on board the car are killed.... Berlin's landmark preservation office confirms the discovery of the bunker used by Josef Goebbels, the now-deceased former Nazi propaganda chief.	Kenya's political opposition stages a protest at the opening of the first session of Parliament since Daniel T. arap Moi was reelected president.		South Korea's defense ministry states that Byun Yong Kwan, a North Korean army captain, defected to South Korea through the neutral village of Panmunjom in the demilitarized zone between the two countries.
Feb. 4				Six inmates die and 37 others are injured in a riot at the overcrowded Modelo prison in the city of Cucuta in northeastern Colombia.	An earthquake measuring 6.1 on the Richter scale strikes Afghanistan, killing an estimated 4,500 people and leaving thousands of others injured or homeless. The quake is centered in the vicinity of Rostaq, 200 miles (320 km) north of Kabul.... Kim Dong Su, a North Korean delegate to the UN Food and Agriculture Organization based in Rome, Italy, seeks political asylum at South Korea's Rome embassy.
Feb. 5		The German government announces that the national unemployment rate, not adjusted for seasonal variations, rose to 12.6% in January, from 11.8% in December 1997. The release of the figures prompts tens of thousands of unemployed workers to stage massive demonstrations in more than 100 cities.	ECOMOG peacekeeping troops launch an offensive against Sierra Leone's military junta after it failed to meet a December 1997 deadline for disarming its troops.... Kenyan Pres. Daniel T. arap Moi imposes a curfew in the Rift Valley region after weeks of ethnic violence that has led to at least 100 deaths.... Iraq's Pres. Hussein orders the release of all non-Iraqi Arab prisoners in Iraqi jails or awaiting trial.... Authorities in Lagos, Nigeria, rename the street where the U.S. embassy is located after Louis Farrakhan.		Sonia Gandhi, the widow of slain former prime minister Rajiv Gandhi, draws a crowd of some 120,000 supporters at a rally in Calcutta, India.... A radical leftist group, the Revolutionary Workers Association, claims responsibility for the Feb. 2 rocket attack on Narita International Airport near Tokyo, Japan's capital.
Feb. 6		Claude Erignac, the prefect of the Mediterranean island of Corsica, a French possession, is killed by two gunmen on a street in Ajaccio, the capital. Erignac, 60, was the French government's top official on the island.... Germany's parliamentary upper chamber, the Bundesrat, passes by a one-vote margin a bill to amend the constitution to allow electronic surveillance of homes and businesses by police in many circumstances.	Nazem el-Kodsi, 91, president of Syria, 1961–63, who was ousted in a bloodless coup by Col. Ziad Hariri in 1963, dies in Jordan of unreported causes.	Myles Neuts, a 10-year-old Ontario, Canada, student, is found hanging in a school washroom at St. Agnes Roman Catholic school in Chatham.	South Korea's labor unions reach agreement with business leaders and the government on legislation that will legalize layoffs by troubled companies and companies involved in mergers and acquisitions. Reform of South Korea's labor laws is a condition of the 1997 bailout agreement with the IMF.... Gov. Masahide Ota of Japan's Okinawa prefecture rejects a plan agreed to in 1996 to build an offshore helicopter base for the U.S. military near the town of Nago, Okinawa.

A	B	C	D	E
Includes developments that affect more than one world region, international organizations, and important meetings of major world leaders.	Includes all domestic and regional developments in Europe, including the Soviet Union, Turkey, Cyprus, and Malta.	Includes all domestic and regional developments in Africa and the Middle East, including Iraq and Iran and excluding Cyprus, Turkey, and Afghanistan.	Includes all domestic and regional developments in Latin America, the Caribbean, and Canada.	Includes all domestic and regional developments in Asia and Pacific nations, extending from Afghanistan through all the Pacific Island, except Hawaii.

U.S. Politics & Social Issues	U.S. Foreign Policy & Defense	U.S. Economy & Environment	Science, Technology, & Nature	Culture, Leisure, & Lifestyle	
The CDC notes that U.S. AIDS deaths decreased in the first half of 1997 by 44% from the same period in 1996. It also reports that 12,040 people in the U.S. died of AIDS in the first half of 1997, down from 21,460 the previous year.... Reports state that a group called the Army of God has taken responsibility for the Jan. 29 bombing of an abortion clinic in Birmingham, Alabama.... Judge Roger Strand sentences former Arizona governor J. Fife Symington III (R) to two and half years in prison and five years' probation on federal fraud charges.		Pres. Clinton presents to Congress the first balanced federal budget in nearly 30 years. Clinton's $1.73 trillion proposal for the fiscal 1999 year, which begins Oct. 1, represents a 3.9% increase over the current year.... The Standard & Poor's index of 500 stocks for the first time ends a trading day above the 1000-point mark, closing up 20.99, or 2.14%, at 1001.27.	The FDA issues new regulations requiring doctors who conduct tests of new drugs and medical devices to disclose financial links to the products' makers.... South Florida is hit by tornadoes, bringing high winds and heavy rains.	Roger L(acey) Stevens, 87, Broadway producer and founding chair of the Kennedy Center for the Performing Arts, dies in Washington, D.C., of pneumonia; he had suffered a stroke in 1993.... Paradise, by Toni Morrison, tops the bestseller list.	Feb. 2
Convicted murderer Karla Faye Tucker is put to death by lethal injection in Huntsville, Texas. She is the second woman executed in the U.S. since 1976. The state of North Carolina executed convicted murderer Margie Velma Barfield in 1984. Texas last executed a woman in 1863. Tucker is the 437th person executed in the U.S. and the 145th in Texas since 1976.	Reports state that an accidental 1979 release of anthrax bacterial spores from a military facility in the Soviet Union included at least four strains of the bacteria. The finding suggests the possibility that Soviet scientists devised the strains in order to render useless the anthrax vaccine used by the U.S. military.	A panel of the U.S. Ninth Circuit Court of Appeals unanimously rules that the Lawrence Berkeley National Laboratory may have violated the constitutional privacy rights of its employees by conducting genetic tests without their permission on the blood and urine obtained in employment physical examinations.... Yah Lin (Charlie) Trie, a friend of Pres. Clinton wanted in connection with alleged political fund-raising offenses, surrenders to federal agents at Dulles International Airport.	David Ho and Tuofu Zhu of the Aaron Diamond AIDS Research Center report the discovery of the oldest known case of HIV infection in a human being. The researchers found the virus in a blood sample taken in 1959 from a Bantu man in what was then the Belgian Congo, now the Democratic Republic of the Congo. Comparisons of the 1959 virus with more recent samples indicate that the different subtypes of HIV share a common ancestor in the late 1940s or early 1950s.		Feb. 3
The Senate passes, 76-22, a bill to rename Washington National Airport in honor of former president Ronald Reagan.... Alan Keith Campbell, 74, architect of civil service reform who, in 1977, was named to head the Civil Service Commission, dies in Haverford, Pennsylvania, of complications from emphysema.... Mary Kay Letourneau, 35, is arrested for violating her Jan. 2 parole by contacting the 14-year-old boy with whom she had sexual relations.	Prime Minister Tony Blair makes his first official visit to the U.S. as head of the British government.		Pres. Clinton creates, by executive order, a White House council that will coordinate the administration's efforts to tackle computer problems related to the arrival of the year 2000.... An official reports that scientists have discovered the remains of a duck-billed dinosaur in Antarctica. It is the first discovery of such a creature outside the Americas and supports the theory that South America and Antarctica were connected by land.	Jean Blackwell Hutson, 83, curator and head of the Schomburg Center for Research in Black Culture in New York City who helped increase the collection's holdings to roughly 75,000 volumes, dies in New York.	Feb. 4
The House gives final congressional approval to a bill that will rename Washington National Airport in honor of former president Ronald Reagan.... Roderick Ferrell, 17, the professed leader of a vampire cult, pleads guilty to murdering Richard Wendorf and his wife, Naoma Ruth Queen, in their home in Eustis, Florida, in 1996. The couple's 17-year-old daughter, Heather Wendorf, a former member of Ferrell's cult, was cleared by a grand jury in 1997 of any involvement in the murders.	The House votes, 347-69, to override Pres. Clinton's line-item veto of 38 items from the fiscal 1998 military construction appropriations bill.	Astra USA Inc., the U.S. subsidiary of a Swedish pharmaceuticals company, agrees to pay a record $9.9 million to settle sexual-harassment charges brought by the EEOC. In an unusual move, Astra USA publicly acknowledges it has a hostile workplace environment for its female employees.... The Long Island Sound Policy Committee approves a plan to reduce the release of nitrogen into the waters of Long Island Sound from sewage-treatment plants along the New York and Connecticut shoreline.	A study suggests that carotid endarterectomy, a common operation intended to prevent strokes in patients with blocked carotid arteries, is not effective in many patients and may even cause strokes in others.... Two teams of paleontologists reveal they have discovered rich troves of well-preserved early animal and plant fossils in phosphate deposits in China's Guizhou province. The fossils date back as far as 580 million years, about 40 million years before the Cambrian explosion.		Feb. 5
Pres. Clinton signs a bill to rename Washington National Airport in honor of former president Ronald Reagan, a move that coincides with Reagan's 87th birthday.... When asked if he will resign in face of allegations involving Monica Lewinsky, Pres. Clinton answers, "Never. You know, I was elected to do a job. And I'm just going to keep showing up for work.".... Mary Kay Letourneau's 7½ year prison sentence for rape is reinstated after her Feb. 4 arrest. In the highly publicized case, Letourneau pled guilty to rape charges in August 1997 and was paroled on Jan. 2.	Marine Corps officials admit for the first time that the plane that cut a ski lift cable in Italy Feb. 3, causing it to plummet more than 300 feet (90 m) and kill all 20 people inside the car, was flying too low.... Two U.S. Marine Corps F/A-18C Hornet single-seat jet fighters collide over the Persian Gulf during a training mission about 80 miles (125 km) east of Kuwait. One of the pilots is killed and the other is rescued at sea.	The Labor Department reports that the seasonally adjusted unemployment rate in the U.S. in January remained at the 4.7% revised level recorded for December 1997. That rate is just a step above November's 24-year low of 4.6%.		Australian medical officials rule that the November 1997 death of Michael Hutchence, the former lead singer of the rock group INXS, was the result of a suicide, precipitated by severe psychological depression.	Feb. 6

F	G	H	I	J
Includes elections, federal-state relations, civil rights and liberties, crime, the judiciary, education, health care, poverty, urban affairs, and population.	Includes formation and debate of U.S. foreign and defense policies, veterans' affairs, and defense spending. (Relations with specific foreign countries are usually found under the region concerned.)	Includes business, labor, agriculture, taxation, transportation, consumer affairs, monetary and fiscal policy, natural resources, and pollution.	Includes worldwide scientific, medical, and technological developments; natural phenomena; U.S. weather; natural disasters; and accidents.	Includes the arts, religion, scholarship, communications media, sports, entertainments, fashions, fads, and social life.

	World Affairs	Europe	Africa & the Middle East	The Americas	Asia & the Pacific
Feb. 7			A bomb explodes at a crowded cafe in central Algiers, the capital of Algeria, killing three people and injuring eight others. A second blast occurs in the town of Blida, south of Algiers, causing two deaths and injuring 12 people.... A pro-Iraq rally in the Palestinian West Bank city of Bethlehem turns violent.... The U.S.'s Rev. Jesse Jackson launches a visit to Kenya, Congo, and Liberia on behalf of the Clinton administration.	At least 14 civilians suspected of being rebel sympathizers in and around the Colombian city of Puerto Asis are murdered by paramilitary gunmen.... Haiti reopens its embassy in Havana, Cuba, more than 30 years after diplomatic relations between the two Caribbean nations was cut off by then Haitian president François (Papa Doc) Duvalier.	Reports from Afghanistan confirm that Taliban leader Sheik Mohammed Omar has ordered his forces to suspend military operations in the vicinity of the Feb. 4 earthquake.... Chinese dissidents in the U.S. and Hong Kong claim that police in the eastern city of Bengbu have arrested Wang Bingzhang, an exiled Chinese prodemocracy activist, after a nationwide manhunt.
Feb. 8		Enoch Powell, 85, British member of Parliament, 1950–87, known for his staunchly nationalistic, right-wing political stance, dies in London after suffering from Parkinson's disease.	Nine members of the European Parliament embark on a peace mission to Algeria.	Historians disclose that mudslides have damaged parts of the historic Nazca Lines in Peru's southern desert. The Nazca Lines, a major tourist attraction, are mysterious symbols and animal figures etched into the ground by Peru's indigenous peoples more than 1,000 years ago.	In Afghanistan, despite the Feb. 7 order, clashes between the Taliban and opposition forces erupt in the region of the Feb. 4. earthquake.
Feb. 9		Georgian president Eduard Shevardnadze survives an assassination attempt in which an estimated 24 rebels open fire on his motorcade in Tbilisi, the capital. Three people are killed and four are wounded in the attack, the second attempt on Shevardnadze's life in 30 months.... Brendan Campbell, a suspected drug dealer, is killed in Belfast, Northern Ireland. Although he was a Roman Catholic, the Catholic-dominated IRA is suspected in the slaying. ... The American Jewish Committee, a U.S.-based Jewish advocacy group, opens an office in Berlin, Germany, for the first time since the fall of the Nazi regime in 1945.	ECOMOG forces bombard Freetown, the capital of Sierra Leone, with artillery fire.	In Canada, three teenaged girls plead guilty to assault charges in connection with the death of Reena Virk, a 14-year-old girl who was beaten by a group of teenagers and subsequently drowned in November 1997.	Tokyo prosecutors raid Industrial Bank of Japan Ltd., widening their investigation of Japanese banks' alleged bribery of government bureaucrats.... Reports reveal that two prodemocracy activists, Yang Qinheng and Zhang Rujuan, were arrested in Shanghai, China.
Feb. 10	Australian prime minister John Howard announces that his cabinet has agreed to offer military support to a U.S.-led coalition of nations, should any conflict erupt over Iraq's blockade of UN arms inspectors. The decision marks Australia's first commitment of ground forces to a foreign military scenario since the Vietnam War. The Canadian government also announces that it is willing to take part in a military campaign against Iraq.	Robert Dougan, a Protestant who supported British rule in Northern Ireland, is shot dead near Belfast.... Maurice Schumann, 86, French radio broadcaster, statesman, and a key member of the resistance to the Nazis during World War II, dies in Paris, France, of unreported causes.	The UN High Commissioner for Refugees estimates that 7,000 Sierra Leoneans in recent weeks fled the country for neighboring Guinea in makeshift boats.... In response to the Feb. 7 violent rally in the Palestinian West Bank city of Bethlehem, Major General Ghazi Jabali, the head of the PNA police, bans all such demonstrations in areas under PNA jurisdiction.	Reports state that winter storms have caused 13 deaths in and around the Mexican city of Tijuana. Separately, the Mexican government expels Maria Bullitt Darlington of the U.S. because she participated in a pro-EZLN demonstration in April 1997, in violation of her tourist visa.	
Feb. 11		Turkey's legal gambling halls, which number nearly 80, close down permanently as a national ban on casino gambling takes effect.... In response to the Feb. 6 assassination of prefect Claude Erignac, 40,000 people march in peace rallies throughout the Mediterranean island of Corsica, a French possession.	About 50 Sierra Leonean refugees fleeing the country for neighboring Guinea drown when a boat packed with more than 100 people capsizes.	Some 80 miners die when the Mocotoro gold mine in Bolivia is buried by a mudslide caused by heavy rains.	Reports disclose that Wang Bingzhang, an exiled Chinese prodemocracy activist, was deported and flown to Los Angeles from Shanghai.... Thousands of Taiwanese farmers demonstrate outside the American Institute, the U.S. government's representative office in Taipei, the capital, to protest U.S. demands for lowered tariffs on imported agricultural products and for an end to Taiwan's ban on rice imports.

A	B	C	D	E
Includes developments that affect more than one world region, international organizations, and important meetings of major world leaders.	*Includes all domestic and regional developments in Europe, including the Soviet Union, Turkey, Cyprus, and Malta.*	*Includes all domestic and regional developments in Africa and the Middle East, including Iraq and Iran and excluding Cyprus, Turkey, and Afghanistan.*	*Includes all domestic and regional developments in Latin America, the Caribbean, and Canada.*	*Includes all domestic and regional developments in Asia and Pacific nations, extending from Afghanistan through all the Pacific Island, except Hawaii.*

U.S. Politics & Social Issues	U.S. Foreign Policy & Defense	U.S. Economy & Environment	Science, Technology, & Nature	Culture, Leisure, & Lifestyle	
				The XVIII Winter Olympic Games open in Nagano, Japan. The competition draws 2,450 athletes from 72 nations. . . . Carl (Dean) Wilson, 51, founding member of the rock-and-roll band the Beach Boys, dies in Los Angeles, California, of complications from lung cancer.	Feb. 7
William G. Lambert, 78, Pulitzer-prize winning investigative reporter whose articles exposed shady business dealings by Supreme Court justice Abe Fortas before he resigned from the court and contributed to a Senate investigation of the Teamsters and conviction of the union's president, Dave Beck, dies in Bryn Mawr, Pennsylvania, of respiratory problems after a long illness.			Reports confirm that Dr. Johan Hultin has isolated a specimen of the virus that killed some 21 million people worldwide in a 1918 influenza epidemic.	Halldor Laxness, 95, Icelandic writer who won the 1955 Nobel Prize in literature, dies in Reykjavik. . . . The Eastern Conference wins the National Basketball Association's All-Star Game over the Western Conference, 135-114, in New York City.	Feb. 8
The FTC states it will require the U.S.'s five largest cigar companies to furnish detailed reports of their annual sales and their spending on advertising and promotions. The order comes amid reports that cigar sales reached 5.2 billion in 1997, up 53% from 1993. . . . A survey of HIV-infected patients at two hospitals in Boston, Massachusetts, and Providence, Rhode Island, finds that some 40% of them failed to inform sex partners about their infection. Two-thirds of those who did not reveal their condition had not always used condoms during sex.		The financially troubled District of Columbia reports a budget surplus of $185.9 million for the fiscal year ending Sept. 30, 1997. The district—which last recorded a surplus in 1993—had projected a $74 million deficit for 1997.			Feb. 9
The Senate votes, 63-35, to confirm Dr. David Satcher as surgeon general, filling a post vacant for over three years.		The year's first record high is registered when the Dow closes at 8295.61. . . . The CEA notes that 1997 "saw the nation's economy turn in its best performance in a generation." But the CEA forecasts that the U.S.'s 1997 growth rate of 3.9% will trail off to around 2% during the years 1998 to 2000. . . . An EPA report finds that women in California who drink five or more glasses of tap water a day have a higher rate of miscarriage than women who drink less tap water.	Procter & Gamble Co. announces that it has begun shipping its synthetic fat substitute, olestra, to snack-food maker Frito-Lay Co. for use in products nationwide. . . . Reports reveal that winter storms have caused seven deaths in California.	Two-year-old racehorse Favorite Trick wins the Eclipse Award as 1997's horse of the year.	Feb. 10
Maine's House of Representatives rejects, 99-42, a bill that would have allowed physicians to prescribe medications to commit suicide to terminally ill patients. . . . In a racial-discrimination suit, U.S. district judge Harvey E. Schlesinger of Jacksonville, Florida, orders a Domino's Pizza franchise in Fernandina Beach, Florida, to start making home deliveries in a black community within the boundaries of its delivery area. The franchise did not deliver to homes in American Beach, where 71 of 75 residents were black, telling customers that that area was unsafe.		New York governor George E. Pataki (R) announces that New York State has purchased Sterling Forest, a 15,800-acre (6,400-hectare) parcel of land northwest of New York City. . . . The EPA announces a policy that would require all of the 56,000 community water agencies in the U.S. to send to their customers annual reports on the safety of local drinking water.		In Eugene, Oregon, U.S. district judge Thomas Coffin rules that disabled golfer Casey Martin, who suffers from a rare circulatory disorder called Klippel-Trenaunay-Weber syndrome, which restricts blood flow in his right leg, may use a cart in PGA Tour events.	Feb. 11

F	G	H	I	J
Includes elections, federal-state relations, civil rights and liberties, crime, the judiciary, education, health care, poverty, urban affairs, and population.	Includes formation and debate of U.S. foreign and defense policies, veterans' affairs, and defense spending. (Relations with specific foreign countries are usually found under the region concerned.)	Includes business, labor, agriculture, taxation, transportation, consumer affairs, monetary and fiscal policy, natural resources, and pollution.	Includes worldwide scientific, medical, and technological developments; natural phenomena; U.S. weather; natural disasters; and accidents.	Includes the arts, religion, scholarship, communications media, sports, entertainments, fashions, fads, and social life.

	World Affairs	Europe	Africa & the Middle East	The Americas	Asia & the Pacific
Feb. 12			ECOMOG forces capture the junta's headquarters in Freetown, the capital of Sierra Leone, after the artillery fire campaign that began Feb. 9.... At least eight senior Sudanese political and military leaders and about 42 others die in a plane crash in southern Sudan. Major General al-Zubayr Muhammad Salih, 54, Sudan's first vice president who played a key role in the 1989 coup that brought the current Islamic government to power, dies in the crash.	Colombian officials reveal that paramilitary troops killed at least 48 civilians—including those slain Feb. 7—who were suspected of being rebel sympathizers in and around the southern city of Puerto Asis in recent weeks.... The Cuban government announces that it will free at least 200 inmates, including some political prisoners, "on humanitarian grounds."	
Feb. 13			Nigerian-led peacekeeping troops under the banner of an alliance of West African nations known as ECOMOG oust Sierra Leone's military government from power, concluding the offensive launched Feb. 5.... Jordanian riot police arrest 80 people in Amman, the capital, when they try to hold a pro-Iraq demonstration.	Three Canadian girls, ages 14, 15, and 16, are found guilty in a Victoria, British Columbia, court of assault causing bodily harm to Reena Virk, a 14-year-old girl beaten and drowned in November 1997. Three other teenage girls pled guilty to assault charges on Feb. 9.	As Indonesia's currency, the rupiah, continues to plunge, hundreds of people loot and set fire to local shops in western Java, the country's main island. Reports confirm that rioters in previous incidents set Chinese-owned stores ablaze and ransacked churches.... Delegates to Australia's Constitutional Convention vote in favor of severing ties to the British monarchy and establishing a republic with an Australian head of state. P.M. John Howard promises a referendum on the issue before the year 2000.
Feb. 14			A train collision followed by an explosion in Yaounde, Cameroon, kills at least 100 people.	In contrast with the death toll reported Feb. 12, the Cuban government claims that 26 people died in a recent crackdown against leftist sympathizers.	In Coimbatore in the Indian state of Tamil Nadu, dozens are killed in a string of bombings that explode just before Lal Krishna Advani, a hard-line Hindu nationalist of the Bharatiya Janata Party (BJP), is scheduled to hold a rally there.... An explosion goes off on an electric-powered bus in the Chinese city of Wuhan, in Hubei province. Official Chinese news states that 16 people have been killed and 30 others injured in the explosion. However, sources in Wuhan place the death toll at 30.
Feb. 15		Greek Cypriot president Glafcos Clerides wins a second five-year term in the second round of a presidential election.			
Feb. 16	Iraq permits a UN survey team in Baghdad to begin mapping the eight presidential sites that Saddam Hussein previously declared off-limits to UNSCOM inspectors.		Data suggests that at least 118 people had been killed and an estimated 700 wounded in the fighting by ECOMOG forces and the military junta in Sierra Leone. Most of the injured are apparently civilians.		A China Airlines jet crashes near Taipei, the Tawainese capital, killing all 196 passengers and crew aboard and seven people on the ground. Among the passengers killed is the governor of Taiwan's central bank, Sheu Yuan-dong, and three other bank officials. In an emergency session, Taiwan's cabinet names Patrick Liang Cheng-chin as acting governor, to replace Sheu.
Feb. 17	Pres. Bill Clinton warns that he is ready to order a campaign of air strikes against Iraq unless Iraq soon agrees to allow UN arms inspectors to resume their "free, full, unfettered access" to potential Iraqi storage and production facilities for weapons of mass destruction. While Britain also is ready to use "all necessary means," the other three members of the Security Council—France, Russia, and China—have voiced opposition to a military solution to the conflict. UN secretary general Kofi Annan announces that he will travel to Baghdad in an effort to defuse the crisis through diplomatic means.	Ernst Junger, 102, German writer best known for works about war, dies in Wilflingen, Germany.	Officials of the Roman Catholic Church report that bands of armed men who support the ousted military government in Sierra Leone are terrorizing the northeastern region of the country and have kidnapped five European missionaries in the town of Lunsar, some 35 miles (60 km) northeast of Freetown.	A U.S. citizen, Robert Edwin Schweitzer, is expelled from Mexico for violating his tourist visa when he allegedly met with EZLN leaders.... Statistics Canada (Statscan) releases the results of the first-ever direct question on race in an attempt to determine the size of Canada's "visible minority" population. According to Statscan, 3,197,480 people, or 11.2% of Canada's population, identified themselves as visible minorities in the 1996 census, a sharp increase from a 1986 estimate of 6.3%.... Nicaragua's 3,000 government-employed doctors go on strike, prompting a crisis in the health-care system.	

A	B	C	D	E
Includes developments that affect more than one world region, international organizations, and important meetings of major world leaders.	Includes all domestic and regional developments in Europe, including the Soviet Union, Turkey, Cyprus, and Malta.	Includes all domestic and regional developments in Africa and the Middle East, including Iraq and Iran and excluding Cyprus, Turkey, and Afghanistan.	Includes all domestic and regional developments in Latin America, the Caribbean, and Canada.	Includes all domestic and regional developments in Asia and Pacific nations, extending from Afghanistan through all the Pacific Island, except Hawaii.

U.S. Politics & Social Issues	U.S. Foreign Policy & Defense	U.S. Economy & Environment	Science, Technology, & Nature	Culture, Leisure, & Lifestyle	
In Washington, D.C., Judge Thomas Hogan declares Pres. Clinton's line-item veto power unconstitutional, setting the stage for a definitive Supreme Court decision. . . . The House votes, 378-33, to end its investigation of the 1996 victory of Rep. Loretta Sanchez (D, Calif.) over Robert Dornan, the nine-term Republican incumbent. A House task force found evidence that 748 votes for Sanchez were cast by noncitizens, but that number is not enough to invalidate her victory.		In Montgomery, Alabama, Circuit Court judge Sally Greenhaw adds five years' probation to the sentence of former governor Guy Hunt (R) of Alabama, convicted of ethics charges in 1993 for stealing from his 1987 inaugural fund.	Pres. Clinton makes federal disaster aid available to three counties in Florida hit by tornadoes on Feb. 2. Those storms caused one fatality, power outages, and flooding. . . . Scientists disclose that airborne radar surveys of the ancient city of Angkor in Cambodia revealed remains of temples older than any previously known at the site. The ruins of Angkor, the capital of the ancient Khmer empire, date from the eighth to the 13th centuries A.D.		Feb. 12
Dr. David Satcher is sworn in as U.S. surgeon general, filling a post vacant for more than three years.			Pres. Clinton names Rita R. Colwell, president of the University of Maryland Biotechnology Institute, to head the National Science Foundation. If confirmed by the Senate, Colwell, 63, will be the science foundation's first female director.		Feb. 13
Federal prosecutors name Eric Robert Rudolph a suspect in the Jan. 29 bombing of a Birmingham, Alabama, abortion clinic that killed one person and seriously injured another. The FBI offers a $100,000 reward for information leading to the capture and conviction of Rudolph, who has been missing since the bombing.					Feb. 14
				Dale Earnhardt wins the Daytona 500 automobile race. . . . In soccer, Mexico defeats the U.S., 1-0, to win its third consecutive Gold Cup, the championship of the international CONCACAF. . . . Martha Ellis Gellhorn, 89, renowned war journalist who for a short time was married to writer Ernest Hemingway, dies in London, England, of cancer.	Feb. 15
	Reports confirm that declassified U.S. Army intelligence reports show that the U.S. tracked the whereabouts of hundreds of its troops held in China after being taken prisoner in the 1950–53 Korean War.		A 44-year-old woman in Los Angeles gives birth to a boy who developed from the oldest known frozen embryo to result in a birth. The embryo had been frozen in 1989. A hospital in Philadelphia, Pennsylvania, disputes the claim, revealing that one of its patients in December 1997 delivered a baby from an embryo frozen for longer than the one in California.	At the Olympics, Russia's Pasha Grishuk and Yevgeny Platov become the first ice-dancing duo to repeat as Olympic champions since the event was introduced in 1976.	Feb. 16
	A federal grand jury in Alexandria, Virginia, indicts three former student radicals—Theresa Marie Squillacote, Kurt Alan Stand, and James M. Clark—on espionage-related charges. . . . In a publicized case, Diane Zamora, a 20-year-old former midshipman at the U.S. Naval Academy in Annapolis, Maryland, is convicted in Fort Worth, Texas, of capital murder. Prosecutors accuse Zamora of helping her boyfriend, David Graham, kill Adrianne Jones, 16, in December 1995 after Graham admitted that he had a single sexual encounter with Jones the month before.	Statistics reveal that large companies' net incomes were 1.3% higher in the fourth quarter of 1997 than in the year-earlier period.		Bob Merrill (born H. Robert Merrill Levan), 77, award-winning songwriter, dies in Los Angeles of a self-inflicted gunshot wound. . . . Ch. Fairewood Frolic, a three-year-old female Norwich terrier, wins best-in-show honors at the Westminster Kennel Club Dog Show. . . . At the Olympics, the U.S. beats Canada, 3-1, to win the first-ever women's Olympic ice hockey tournament.	Feb. 17

F	G	H	I	J
Includes elections, federal-state relations, civil rights and liberties, crime, the judiciary, education, health care, poverty, urban affairs, and population.	Includes formation and debate of U.S. foreign and defense policies, veterans' affairs, and defense spending. (Relations with specific foreign countries are usually found under the region concerned.)	Includes business, labor, agriculture, taxation, transportation, consumer affairs, monetary and fiscal policy, natural resources, and pollution.	Includes worldwide scientific, medical, and technological developments; natural phenomena; U.S. weather; natural disasters; and accidents.	Includes the arts, religion, scholarship, communications media, sports, entertainments, fashions, fads, and social life.

	World Affairs	Europe	Africa & the Middle East	The Americas	Asia & the Pacific
Feb. 18		A court in Paris, France, convicts and sentences 36 militant Moslems for their involvement in a wave of bombings in 1995 that resulted in nine deaths and more than 200 injuries. Punishments range from suspended sentences to a 10-year jail term for Ali Touchent, considered a central figure in the bombings. Four other defendants are acquitted.			Financial Secretary Donald Tsang unveils Hong Kong's first budget since its reversion to Chinese sovereignty in 1997. The budget includes the largest package of tax cuts in Hong Kong's history, totaling HK$100 billion (US$12.9 billion) over four years. Tsang predicts that 1998 gross domestic product growth will fall to 3.5%, from 5.2% in 1997.
Feb. 19		An armed gang attacks a UN office in western Georgia and takes four UN observers and six civilians hostage. The group demands that the Georgian government release seven suspects held for the Feb. 9 assassination attempt on Pres. Eduard Shevardnadze.... The Swiss government rejects a claim by Charles Sonabend, a survivor of the Nazi Holocaust, for compensation for the deportation of his parents, who later died in a Nazi death camp. The suit is the first of its kind in Switzerland.		A U.S. citizen, Thomas Hansen of the human-rights group Pastors for Peace, is deported from Mexico.... Canada's Senate votes to suspend without pay Sen. Andrew Thompson, who has attended only 12 sessions since 1990, for his poor attendance record. He is the first senator ever suspended without pay in the 130-year history of the legislative chamber.... Cuban officials report that 299 prisoners have been released since Feb.12. One of the prisoners set free is Hector Palacios Ruiz, the leader of the outlawed Democratic Solidarity Party.	The North Korean government, in a rare conciliatory gesture toward South Korea, sends letters to some 70 South Korean political and civic leaders, including President-elect Kim Dae Jung, urging dialogue between the two countries.
Feb. 20	The UN Security Council unanimously approves a resolution that raises Iraq's quota of oil sales under the UN's oil-for-food program to $5.2 billion, from $2.14 billion, during any six-month period.	A bomb explodes in the Northern Ireland village of Moira, outside a station of the Royal Ulster Constabulary (RUC) police force, wounding 11 people. Separately, in response to the Feb. 9–10 deaths, the British and Irish governments suspend Sinn Fein, the political wing of the Provisional IRA from participating in the Northern Ireland peace talks until at least Mar. 9.			A power blackout hits the central business and financial district of Auckland, New Zealand's largest city with about 1 million people, crippling commerce and effectively shutting down much of the city's most important commercial activity.... Reports indicate that five people died in sporadic rioting spurred by an economic crisis in Indonesia. In response to escalating tensions, three ethnic Chinese millionaires begin to distribute food to impoverished Indonesians.
Feb. 21			Algeria's largest pipeline is bombed.		
Feb. 22	Iraq and the UN sign an accord that affirms the right of UN arms inspectors to immediate and unconditional access to suspected Iraqi weapons sites. The deal, brokered by UN secretary general Kofi Annan, defuses an explosive crisis over Iraq's barring of the UN inspections team and averts an imminent U.S.-led campaign of retaliatory air strikes against Iraq.	The kidnappers who attacked a UN office in western Georgia Feb. 19, release one of the UN hostages.... Jose Maria de Areilza, 88, Spanish statesman who fought for Gen. Francisco Franco during the Spanish Civil War in the 1930s, dies in Madrid, Spain, of unreported causes.			
Feb. 23		The Turkish government formally begins dissolving the Welfare (Refah) Party, a fundamentalist Islamic party that has controlled a plurality of seats in Parliament.... British drug companies SmithKline Beecham PLC and Glaxo Wellcome PLC abandon plans for a widely anticipated merger. The proposed deal would have been the world's largest corporate merger ever.... A car bomb explodes in Portadown, Northern Ireland, a town noted for its fervent support of British rule.	In Algeria, a bomb explodes under a moving train on the outskirts of Algiers, killing 18 people and wounding 25 others.		

A	B	C	D	E
Includes developments that affect more than one world region, international organizations, and important meetings of major world leaders.	*Includes all domestic and regional developments in Europe, including the Soviet Union, Turkey, Cyprus, and Malta.*	*Includes all domestic and regional developments in Africa and the Middle East, including Iraq and Iran and excluding Cyprus, Turkey, and Afghanistan.*	*Includes all domestic and regional developments in Latin America, the Caribbean, and Canada.*	*Includes all domestic and regional developments in Asia and Pacific nations, extending from Afghanistan through all the Pacific Island, except Hawaii.*

U.S. Politics & Social Issues	U.S. Foreign Policy & Defense	U.S. Economy & Environment	Science, Technology, & Nature	Culture, Leisure, & Lifestyle	
Ocean County, New Jersey, Family Court judge Robert Fall orders Samuel Manzie, 15, to stand trial as an adult for the 1997 murder of Edward P. Werner, an 11-year-old boy. Manzie is accused of abducting, sexually assaulting, and then fatally strangling Werner..... Chicago mayor Richard Daley names Terry Hillard the new superintendent of the Chicago police department.	Secretary of Defense William Cohen, Secretary of State Madeleine Albright, and Pres. Clinton's national security adviser Samuel Berger face an audience of 6,000 people to discuss the crisis in Iraq at Ohio State University in a town hall meeting broadcast live worldwide by CNN.	The Labor Department reports that the government's index of prices charged by manufacturers and farmers for finished goods fell a seasonally adjusted 0.7% in January from December 1997. That figure marks the indicator's steepest monthly decline since August 1993.	A study suggests that a woman's risk of developing breast cancer increases with the amount of alcohol she consumes.... One of a controversial series of studies shows that a shortened, relatively inexpensive regimen of the drug AZT helps prevent transmission of HIV from pregnant women to their fetuses.... A cardiac defibrillator is used to restart the heart of an airline passenger in what is thought to be the first time on a U.S. airplane.	Walter Reich, director of the U.S. Holocaust Museum in Washington, D.C., tenders his resignation, effective March 31.... Harry Caray, baseball announcer inducted into the Baseball Hall of Fame in 1989, dies in Rancho Mirage, California, of heart failure; his age is variously reported to be in the 70s or 80s.	Feb. 18
The Mississippi legislature becomes the last in the nation to pass a "motor-voter" law allowing people to register to vote in federal and state elections when they apply for a driver's license or welfare benefits.... Lawyers for Pres. Clinton formally start negotiations on whether White House aides are protected from testifying about allegations that Clinton tried to cover up an alleged affair with Monica Lewinsky.	U.S. forces in the Persian Gulf area available for potential action against Iraq include 133 attack jets and other fighter aircraft, 15 combat vessels (including two aircraft carriers), and 13 support ships, and 5,000 army troops in Kuwait and 2,000 marines aboard four ships in the gulf.	Data reveals that concentrations of radon gas inside homes contributed to an estimated 15,400–21,800 lung cancer deaths in the U.S. in 1995.... The Commerce Department reports that the U.S. recorded a $113.7 billion deficit in trade in goods and services in 1997. That amount is up 2.4% from the revised 1996 deficit of $111 billion and is the largest calendar-year trade gap since 1988.	Russian cosmonauts Anatoly Solovyev and Pavel Vinogradov and French astronaut Leopold Eyharts depart the Russian station Mir and return to Earth in the Soyuz capsule that carried the two Russians to the station in August 1997.	Leaders of the Promise Keepers, an all-male revivalist Christian group, state that the group will lay off its entire 345-member staff on Mar. 31 due to a financial crisis.... Grandpa Jones (Louis Marshall), 84, country music banjo player known for his longtime role on the TV show Hee Haw, dies in Nashville, Tennessee, after suffering a series of strokes.	Feb. 19
Self-proclaimed white supremacist Chevie Kehoe pleads guilty to felonious assault, attempted murder, and carrying a concealed weapon. The charges stem from a 1997 shoot-out with Ohio police.... A Florida jury finds Lawrence Singleton, 70, guilty of first-degree murder in the 1997 stabbing death of Roxanne Hayes, a 31-year-old prostitute. Singleton was convicted in 1979 of raping and cutting off the forearms of a teenaged girl in California and committed the 1997 murder while on parole.	In Cleveland, Ohio, U.S. district judge Paul Matia restores U.S. citizenship to John Demjanjuk, 77, who was cleared of charges that he was a Nazi concentration camp guard known as "Ivan the Terrible." ... Federal authorities in New York City arrest Cheng Yong Wang and Xingqi Fu, who offered to sell organs of executed Chinese prisoners to Americans for transplants.		Researchers reveal that they have identified a hormone that plays an important role in triggering hunger in humans. The hormone is produced by nerve cells in the lateral hypothalamus, a part of the brain already known to influence the appetite.	Tara Lipinski of the U.S. wins the gold medal in the women's figure skating competition at the Olympics. Lipinski, 15, is the youngest person ever to win an Olympic gold medal in figure skating, as Sonja Henie of Norway was two months older than Lipinski when she won the first of her three gold medals in 1928.	Feb. 20
Julian Bond, a longtime civil-rights leader, is elected chairman of the NAACP. Bond will succeed Myrlie Evers-Williams, who resigned.					Feb. 21
Donald Stuart Russell, 92, (D, S.C.), U.S. governor, senator, and federal judge dies in Spartanburg, South Carolina, of unreported causes.... Abraham Alexander Ribicoff, 87, (D, Conn.) U.S. representative, senator, governor, and cabinet member, dies in New York City.	An internal report by the CIA on the 1961 Bay of Pigs invasion of Cuba is released to the public. The 150-page report, written by then-CIA Inspector General Lyman Kirkpatrick in 1961, levels scathing criticism at the CIA, blaming the agency for the disastrous attempt by CIA-trained Cuban commandos to oust the communist government of Cuban president Fidel Castro Ruz.	Thousands of employees of Caterpillar Inc. vote to reject a six-year contract their union officials recently negotiated with the company. The employees, represented by the United Auto Workers union (UAW), have been without a contract since 1991.	Several tornadoes hit central Florida, carrying winds ranging from 158 to 206 miles per hour (254–332 kmph).	The XVIII Winter Olympic Games in Nagano, Japan, conclude. German athletes won the most medals of any country, taking home a total of 29 medals. Norway is second in the medal count, with a total of 25, and Russia is third with 18. The U.S. earned 13 medals, tying its record for the most ever in the Winter Games, set in 1994.	Feb. 22
			Tornadoes continue to sweep through central Florida, killing a total of 42 people and injuring more than 260 others. The tornadoes are described as the worst ever to hit the state.... Major winter storms hit coastal regions of California. The severity of the California and Florida storms is attributed to the periodic weather phenomenon known as El Niño, which causes abnormal climate conditions throughout the Western Hemisphere by warming ocean currents near the Pacific coast of Peru.	William (Billy) Hallissey Sullivan Jr., 82, founder of the New England Patriots professional football team, dies in Atlantis, Florida, after a bout with colon cancer.	Feb. 23

F	G	H	I	J
Includes elections, federal-state relations, civil rights and liberties, crime, the judiciary, education, health care, poverty, urban affairs, and population.	Includes formation and debate of U.S. foreign and defense policies, veterans' affairs, and defense spending. (Relations with specific foreign countries are usually found under the region concerned.)	Includes business, labor, agriculture, taxation, transportation, consumer affairs, monetary and fiscal policy, natural resources, and pollution.	Includes worldwide scientific, medical, and technological developments; natural phenomena; U.S. weather; natural disasters; and accidents.	Includes the arts, religion, scholarship, communications media, sports, entertainments, fashions, fads, and social life.

	World Affairs	Europe	Africa & the Middle East	The Americas	Asia & the Pacific
Feb. 24	The Third International Mathematics and Science Study (TIMSS), an evaluation of student achievement in mathematics and science worldwide, shows that the Netherlands registered the highest score on the 1995 test. South Africa registered the poorest performance. The highest composite score on the science portion was achieved by Sweden, and South Africa registered the lowest score.	Thousands of demonstrators launch a series of marches in Istanbul, Turkey, to protest a government-enforced ban on religious apparel in schools.	Race riots erupt at a high school in Vryburg, a rural town in North West province in South Africa, after white parents attack black students with whips and sticks.	Cuba's newly elected National Assembly reelects Fidel Castro Ruz to another five-year term as president of the ruling Council of State. Castro has ruled Cuba since 1959. . . . Canadian finance minister Paul Martin introduces the government's first balanced budget in nearly 30 years.	The National Assembly of Laos votes to appoint Premier Khamtai Siphandon of the Lao People's Revolutionary Party to the presidency. The legislature also names Sisavat Keobounphan as premier. . . . Reports indicate that two members of the Aum Shinrikyo cult—Satoshi Matsushita and Zenji Yagisawa—were sentenced to four years in prison for a May 1995 attempted gas attack on a Tokyo subway station.
Feb. 25		A letter bomb detonates in a mail-sorting office in Belfast, Northern Ireland, wounding four employees. . . . Reports reveal more than 100 of the 150 lawmakers in the Islamic Fundamentalist Welfare (Refah) Party, which the Turkish government dissolved Feb. 23, have joined a new Islamist political group, the Virtue Party. . . . The standoff, begun Feb. 19 when an armed gang attacked a UN office in western Georgia, ends when the gunmen release the remaining hostages. Three kidnappers escape, and the remaining gunmen surrender.		Colombian authorities indict two Colombians and four former officers in the Israeli army on charges of training right-wing paramilitary terrorist units in the late 1980s.	Kim Dae Jung of the National Congress for New Politics party is inaugurated as South Korea's president. Kim's inauguration marks the first transfer of power from the ruling party to an opposition in South Korea's history. . . . Perng Fai-nan is named governor of Taiwan's central bank, the Central Bank of China.
Feb. 26		Valdas Adamkus is sworn in as president of Lithuania.		Mexico deports Michel Henri Jean Chanteau, a French Roman Catholic priest who had worked in Chiapas for 32 years, for criticizing the government's handling of the December 1997 massacre of 45 Tzotzil Indians. . . . Canada announces that it will admit 19 Cuban political prisoners and their families.	
Feb. 27	The International Court of Justice, a UN body in The Hague, the Netherlands, rules that it has jurisdiction over an extradition dispute related to the 1988 bombing of Pan Am Flight 103 over Lockerbie, Scotland. Libya has refused to release two suspects, both Libyans, to stand trial in the U.S. or Britain.	Lord Williams of Mostyn, a junior minister in the British Home Office, reveals that Queen Elizabeth II has endorsed plans to incorporate gender equality in the succession to the throne. The endorsement is seen as a major step toward ending royal primogeniture.		Human-rights activist Jesús María Valle Jaramillo is slain in the northeastern city of Medellín. Valle reportedly is the 11th human rights worker killed in Colombia since early 1997.	Singapore's Parliament passes a ban on political television advertisements.
Feb. 28		The Albanian separatist Kosovo Liberation Army (UCK) attacks a Serbian police patrol near the village of Likosane, killing four policemen. Serbian police respond by killing at least 24 ethnic Albanians from Likosane. Other such attacks occur across Kosovo. The clashes spark ongoing violence in the region, raising fears of a new ethnic conflict in the Balkans.	Roman Catholic Church officials disclose that rebels have released seven hostages, most of them European missionaries, held for two weeks in Sierra Leone.	A team of more than 200 human-rights observers from Europe and Canada complete a fact-finding mission in Chiapas, Mexico. The team alleges that the government is targeting foreigners as "a way of distracting from the conflict" in Chiapas and finds that the standoff between the EZLN and government supporters in the state is growing more dangerous.	
March 1		At least 250,000 people from rural sections of Britain hold a massive march in London, the capital, to protest government policies that they claim disregard rural interests. The demonstration is Britain's largest since the early 1980s.			

A	B	C	D	E
Includes developments that affect more than one world region, international organizations, and important meetings of major world leaders.	*Includes all domestic and regional developments in Europe, including the Soviet Union, Turkey, Cyprus, and Malta.*	*Includes all domestic and regional developments in Africa and the Middle East, including Iraq and Iran and excluding Cyprus, Turkey, and Afghanistan.*	*Includes all domestic and regional developments in Latin America, the Caribbean, and Canada.*	*Includes all domestic and regional developments in Asia and Pacific nations, extending from Afghanistan through all the Pacific Island, except Hawaii.*

U.S. Politics & Social Issues	U.S. Foreign Policy & Defense	U.S. Economy & Environment	Science, Technology, & Nature	Culture, Leisure, & Lifestyle	
Mississippi governor Kirk Fordice (R), vetoes a "motor-voter" law passed Feb. 19.... Terry Allen Langford, 31, convicted of murder, is executed by lethal injection in Deer Lodge, Montana. Langford confessed to murder nine years earlier. He is the 441st person put to death in the U.S. and only the second in Montana since 1976.... The results of the TIMSS show the U.S. scored below average in both the science and math portions of the test.		The Conference Board business-research organization reports that its index of consumer confidence soared in February to 138.3, a 30-year high.	The winter storms that struck California Feb. 23 continue to rage, causing at least nine deaths and some $475 million in damage.	Antonio Prohias, 77, Cuban-born cartoonist who published in *Mad* magazine, dies in Miami, Florida, of lung cancer.... Henny Youngman, 91, comedian known as the "King of the One-Liners," dies in New York City while being treated for pneumonia.	Feb. 24
A Florida jury recommends the death sentence for convicted murderer Lawrence Singleton, convicted Feb. 20 of first-degree murder in the 1997 stabbing death of Roxanne Hayes, a 31-year-old prostitute.	The Senate votes, 78-20, to override Pres. Clinton's line-item veto of 38 items from the fiscal 1998 military construction appropriations bill. The House overrode the veto Feb. 5.	In *Alaska v. Native Village of Venetie*, the Supreme Court rules unanimously that the state of Alaska has tax and regulatory control of a remote village of Athabaskan Indians.... In *National Credit Union Administration v. First National Bank & Trust Co.*, the Supreme Court rules, 5-4, that individuals employed in a variety of occupations cannot be members of the same federally chartered credit union. With their ruling, the justices overturn a policy adopted in 1982 by the National Credit Union Administration (NCUA).	Figures show that the cities of Los Angeles and San Francisco set 20th-century records for rainfall in the winter of 1997–98.... Pres. Clinton visits some of the areas of central Florida hardest hit by tornadoes. He states that he will make federal disaster aid available to 34 counties, and that the Labor Department will contribute an additional $3 million to hire cleanup workers.	Prosecutors in Tampa, Florida, charge Rev. Henry Lyons, leader of the National Baptist Convention USA, with two counts of grand theft and one count of racketeering.... At the Grammys, veteran folk-rock singer Bob Dylan wins three awards, including Album of the Year. "Sunny Came Home," by Shawn Colvin, wins for Song of the Year.	Feb. 25
Oregon's Health Services Commission, which governs the state's health plan for low-income residents, votes to cover lethal drug doses prescribed under the assisted-suicide law as a "medical service."... Federal prosecutors indict four NYC police officers for allegedly violating the civil rights of Abner Louima and Patrick Antoine in August 1997 when they allegedly assaulted the two Haitian immigrants in their custody.	In its annual report to Congress on the antidrug efforts of countries receiving U.S. aid, the Clinton administration "certifies" Mexico. It decertifies Colombia but issues the country a "national interest" waiver that would allow it to receive U.S. aid. Pakistan, Paraguay, and Cambodia are also decertified but given national interest waivers. The report decertifies Afghanistan, Myanmar, Nigeria, and Iran.... FBI agents in Laredo, Texas, arrest Elizaphan Ntakirutimana, a Rwandan Seventh-day Adventist minister charged with committing genocide during Rwanda's 1994 civil war.	Michael Milken, a convicted former junk-bond financier, agrees to pay $47 million to settle an SEC suit.... The FBI reaches a partial settlement with Frederic Whitehurst, a chemist who was suspended from his job at the FBI's crime laboratory after calling attention to improper practices at the facility. The FBI agrees to give Whitehurst $1.166 million in compensation over seven years, and he, in exchange, will resign.... Theodore W. Schultz, 95, winner of the Nobel Prize in Economic Science in 1979 for his work in agricultural economics, dies in Evanston, Ill., of pneumonia.	A total solar eclipse visible in parts of South America and the Caribbean occurs when the moon begins to occlude the sun over the Pacific Ocean southeast of Hawaii at 3:46 P.M. Greenwich mean time, or 10:46 A.M. eastern standard time. The eclipse path proceeds across northern Colombia and Venezuela and several Caribbean islands. The event is to be the last total solar eclipse appearing in the Western Hemisphere until the year 2017.	A federal jury in Amarillo, Texas, clears talk-show host Oprah Winfrey of charges that she illegally slandered U.S.-produced beef in a 1996 segment of her show when discussing bovine spongiform encephalopathy (BSE), or mad-cow disease.	Feb. 26
Judge Jerry Lockett sentences Roderick Ferrell to death for the 1996 murder of a Florida couple. Ferrell, 17, a self-proclaimed vampire, confessed to the killings.	The U.S. ends a 35-year ban on the sale of weapons and weapons technology to South Africa.		George Herbert Hitchings, 92, who shared the 1988 Nobel Prize in Medicine for decades of pioneering pharmaceutical research, dies in Chapel Hill, North Carolina.	In New York City, Sotheby's concludes its auction of more than 40,000 items from the Paris home of Britain's late Duke and Duchess of Windsor. Revenues from auctions total $23 million, well above the $6 million projection.	Feb. 27
	Arkady Nikolayevich Shevchenko, 67, top Russian diplomat who defected to the U.S., dies in Bethesda, Maryland, of a heart attack.			Todd (Robert) Duncan, 95, baritone who sang more than 2,000 recitals in 56 countries, dies in Washington, D.C., of a heart ailment.	Feb. 28
A report finds that the 1968 prediction by a presidential commission that the U.S. is "moving toward two societies, one black, one white—separate and unequal" has largely come true 30 years later. The report notes that, while some progress has been made, racial minorities suffer disproportionately from a widening gap between the rich and the poor in the U.S. The report states that 40% of minority children attend urban schools, where more than half the students fail to achieve "basic" levels of education, and notes that one in three black American males is in prison, on parole, or on probation.					March 1

F	G	H	I	J
Includes elections, federal-state relations, civil rights and liberties, crime, the judiciary, education, health care, poverty, urban affairs, and population.	Includes formation and debate of U.S. foreign and defense policies, veterans' affairs, and defense spending. (Relations with specific foreign countries are usually found under the region concerned.)	Includes business, labor, agriculture, taxation, transportation, consumer affairs, monetary and fiscal policy, natural resources, and pollution.	Includes worldwide scientific, medical, and technological developments; natural phenomena; U.S. weather; natural disasters; and accidents.	Includes the arts, religion, scholarship, communications media, sports, entertainments, fashions, fads, and social life.

	World Affairs	Europe	Africa & the Middle East	The Americas	Asia & the Pacific
March 2	The UN Security Council unanimously approves a weapons-inspection accord brokered by UN secretary general Kofi Annan with Iraqi leaders. While the council refuses to give the U.S. an automatic green light to launch a military strike against Iraq if Iraq reneges on the accord's terms, it warns Iraq that it will face "the severest consequences" if it again obstructs UN inspectors.	Serbian riot police use clubs and tear gas to quell a protest by tens of thousands of ethnic Albanians in Pristina, Kosovo's capital. The government reports that 16 Albanians and four Serbian policemen were killed in Feb. 28 attacks.... The Polish government authorizes the return of a synagogue near Auschwitz to the local Jewish community. It is the first such action under a 1997 program.	Italian foreign minister Lamberto Dini declares in Teheran, the Iranian capital, that Iran has severed all links with terrorist groups.	Leftist rebels of the Revolutionary Armed Forces of Colombia (FARC) ambush an elite army battalion in the jungle near Cartagena del Chaira in the southern Caqueta province, sparking days of fighting. At least 62 of the approximately 150 soldiers in the battalion are killed. The attack is called the worst single defeat the army has ever suffered at the hands of leftist rebels in more than 30 years of civil strife.	Reports confirm that a cargo plane operated by Hong Kong's Cathay Pacific Airways has made the first flight over North Korea by an airline from a noncommunist country since the 1950–53 Korean War.... Reports reveal that Australian federal and state ministers have decided that thousands of sacred aboriginal relics housed in museums nationwide will be returned to their traditional owners.
March 3	Reports from Peru show that floods and mudslides from El Niño storms have resulted in 200 fatalities, left 80,000 people homeless, and caused at least $700 million in damage. In Bolivia, 130 people have died and 70,000 others have been left homeless as a result of El Niño. In Ecuador, at least 135 people have died and 30,000 others have been left homeless by El Niño.	Thousands of ethnic Albanians attend a funeral for those killed Feb. 28 in Likosane.... Unidentified gunmen open fire on a bar in Poyntzpass, Northern Ireland, killing two people and wounding two others. The apparent terrorist attack is unusual since one of those killed is Protestant while the other is Roman Catholic.... Latvian police in Riga, the capital, use force to break up a demonstration held by thousands of elderly members of the Russian-speaking minority protesting the high cost of living and demanding that Latvia recognize their Soviet-era passports.		Zoilamerica Narvaez Murillo, the stepdaughter of former president Daniel Ortega Saavedra, publicly accuses him of sexually abusing her as a child. The charges stun Nicaragua.	Taiwan's transport ministry announces that it will allow a Chinese shipping company to sail directly between the northern Taiwanese port of Keelung and Shanghai, China. The route will be the first economically meaningful direct shipping link between China and Taiwan since 1949.
March 4		A former Bosnian Serb paramilitary leader indicted in 1996, Dragoljub Kunarac, turns himself in to French-led NATO peacekeeping forces in the southeastern Bosnian town of Filipovici.	Ezer Weizman wins reelection in the Knesset as president of Israel.		In Phnom Penh, the capital of Cambodia, ousted first premier Prince Norodom Ranariddh is convicted, in absentia, of weapons smuggling and sentenced to five years' imprisonment. The ousted leader is charged with forging a covert alliance with Khmer Rouge guerrillas and attempting to supply them with ammunition.
March 5	The UN war-crimes tribunal reduces by half the jail sentence for Drazen Erdemovic, a 26-year-old Bosnian Croat who in January was convicted of killing at least 70 unarmed Bosnian Moslems in 1995. The ruling reduces Erdemovic's sentence to five years. The presiding judge, Florence Mumba, reveals that Erdemovic's young age and displays of remorse were factors in the decision.	Data shows that some 50 people have been killed in clashes between Serbian police and the Albanian separatist Kosovo Liberation Army (UCK) in the volatile Kosovo province since Feb. 28. The clashes are described as the worst outbreak of violence in the separatists' nine-year-old campaign in the region, and raise fears of a new ethnic conflict in the Balkans on the scale of the recent Bosnian civil war. Serbian police launch a large-scale assault against the UCK in Kosovo. At least 20 ethnic Albanians and two policemen are killed in the fighting.		Colombian air force jets bomb the site of the Mar. 2 ambush in a jungle near Cartagena del Chaira, in the southern Caqueta province, in an attempt to open up an escape route for the remainder of the battalion. The army also dispatches at least 600 reinforcements to the region.	A bomb explodes outside a department store in the Mei Foo district in Hong Kong.... Fighting between Taliban forces and troops loyal to the displaced government continue north of Kabul in Afghanistan.
March 6		Serbian special police forces continue a large-scale assault on the Drenica valley region of Kosovo, attacking villages with mortar rounds, armored vehicles, and helicopter gunships. The Serbian government claims that it has "destroyed the core" of the UCK.			

A	B	C	D	E
Includes developments that affect more than one world region, international organizations, and important meetings of major world leaders.	*Includes all domestic and regional developments in Europe, including the Soviet Union, Turkey, Cyprus, and Malta.*	*Includes all domestic and regional developments in Africa and the Middle East, including Iraq and Iran and excluding Cyprus, Turkey, and Afghanistan.*	*Includes all domestic and regional developments in Latin America, the Caribbean, and Canada.*	*Includes all domestic and regional developments in Asia and Pacific nations, extending from Afghanistan through all the Pacific Island, except Hawaii.*

U.S. Politics & Social Issues	U.S. Foreign Policy & Defense	U.S. Economy & Environment	Science, Technology, & Nature	Culture, Leisure, & Lifestyle	
A three-judge appellate panel in New Jersey rules, 2-1, that the Boy Scouts' expulsion of an Eagle Scout because he is a homosexual violates the state's antidiscrimination laws. The court rules that the Boy Scouts group is a public accommodation and argues that the Boy Scouts produced "absolutely no evidence" that gay Scoutmasters are unfit to lead young Scouts.			NASA releases images taken by the spacecraft *Galileo* of Jupiter's moon Europa. The pictures provide further evidence that a liquid water ocean existed beneath the moon's cratered icy surface. . . . Researchers report they have found the first evidence of a physiological difference between lesbian and heterosexual women when noting a disparity in otoacoustic emissions—tiny echoes produced by the ear in response to a clicking sound.	*The Street Lawyer*, by John Grisham, tops the bestseller list. . . . Henry Steele Commager, 95, scholar of U.S. history known for his writings that defended the Constitution as a hallmark of political achievement, dies in Amherst, Massachusetts, of unreported causes.	March 2
In *Bogan v. Scott-Harris*, the Supreme Court rules unanimously that officials from local or municipal government bodies cannot be sued for actions related to their legislative duties. The ruling extends to local lawmakers the legal immunity provided to federal legislators by the Constitution. . . . Data shows that the number of organized hate-groups in the U.S. rose in 1997 to 474. The report notes that 163 hate-group websites have appeared on the Internet since the first such site was posted by former Ku Klux Klan member Don Black in 1995.	The Department of Defense announces that U.S. troops stationed in the Persian Gulf area will begin receiving inoculations against anthrax bacteria within one week. The program, which represents the first time that the U.S. military has been routinely vaccinated against a germ warfare agent, was originally scheduled to begin in the summer.			A Santa Monica, California, jury convicts Jonathan Norman, 31, for an alleged plot to attack film director Steven Spielberg. . . . Outfielder Larry Doby, the first black to play in the American League, is elected to the Baseball Hall of Fame. George Davis, Joe Rogan, and Lee MacPhail are also elected. . . . Fred W. Friendly 82, pioneering news producer and executive for CBS, dies in New York City of a stroke.	March 3
The House votes, 209-208, to approve a plebiscite in the Caribbean island of Puerto Rico, a U.S. commonwealth, on its political future. . . . A jury in Yreka, California, awards $95.1 million to Reba Gregory, 69, a nursing home patient who sued Beverly Enterprises, Inc., the U.S.'s largest nursing home operator. The award is a record for a suit against a nursing home.		The Supreme Court rules unanimously in *Oncale v. Sundowner Offshore Services* that same-sex harassment in the workplace is a violation of federal civil-rights law.	Federal prosecutors in NYC charge owners and managers of six overseas companies with illegally using U.S. telephone lines to take bets on sporting events from U.S. gamblers. The case is the first-ever prosecution of gambling operations on the Internet global computer network. . . . The FDA approves the use of hydroxyurea, a cancer drug, to control the symptoms of sickle-cell anemia.	Reports confirm that the 1998 John M. Templeton Prize for Progress in Religion will be awarded to Sir Sigmund Sternberg, a British philanthropist who promotes understanding among different religious faiths.	March 4
A state court of appeals in Sacramento, California, strikes down provisions of a gun-control law that banned 62 kinds of assault rifles. The legislation has been in effect since 1989.		Republicans and Democrats on the Senate Governmental Affairs Committee issue separate reports on the panel's year-long inquiry into alleged fund-raising abuses in the 1996 federal election campaigns. Observers note that the reports' sharply different conclusions will undermine the impact of the committee's findings on the debate over how to reform the nation's campaign finance laws. . . . Johnny Chung, a central figure in the Democratic fund-raising controversy, agrees to plead guilty to two instances of campaign finance abuse.	U.S. Air Force lieutenant colonel Eileen M. Collins is appointed the first female commander of a U.S. space shuttle mission when she is scheduled to command a Columbia mission in December. . . . NASA scientists announce that the unmanned spacecraft *Lunar Prospector* has detected the presence of frozen water mixed in with the soil of the moon.		March 5
A New York State Supreme Court jury convicts John J. Royster, 23, of 18 criminal counts, including murder, attempted rape, robbery, and assault. The charges stem from the murder of one woman and brutal attacks on two others during an eight-day spree of violence in New York City in June 1996. . . . A disgruntled employee of the Connecticut Lottery, Matthew Beck, fatally stabs and shoots four coworkers in a rampage in Newington, Connecticut. Beck, 35, commits suicide after the killings.	In a ceremony at the Vietnam Veterans' Memorial., the U.S. Army honors Hugh Thompson, Lawrence Colburn, and Glenn Andreotta, three former servicemen who 30 years earlier risked their lives to halt a massacre in My Lai, Vietnam, in which U.S. troops killed hundreds of unarmed civilians. . . . Three Union County, New Jersey, prison guards are convicted for actions related to the brutalization of immigrants seeking asylum in the U.S. who were transferred to the county facility in 1995 after a disturbance at a federal detention center.	The Labor Department reports that the seasonally adjusted unemployment rate in the U.S. in February declined to 4.6%, from January's revised rate of 4.7%. With the decline, the February rate matches the 24-year low registered in November 1997.		Baseball pitcher Orlando Hernandez, who defected from Cuba in December 1997 and settled in Costa Rica in January, agrees to a four-year, $6.6 million contract with the New York Yankees.	March 6

F	G	H	I	J
Includes elections, federal-state relations, civil rights and liberties, crime, the judiciary, education, health care, poverty, urban affairs, and population.	Includes formation and debate of U.S. foreign and defense policies, veterans' affairs, and defense spending. (Relations with specific foreign countries are usually found under the region concerned.)	Includes business, labor, agriculture, taxation, transportation, consumer affairs, monetary and fiscal policy, natural resources, and pollution.	Includes worldwide scientific, medical, and technological developments; natural phenomena; U.S. weather; natural disasters; and accidents.	Includes the arts, religion, scholarship, communications media, sports, entertainments, fashions, fads, and social life.

	World Affairs	Europe	Africa & the Middle East	The Americas	Asia & the Pacific
March 7				Thousands of people protest against Gen. Augusto Pinochet Ugarte, Chile's former president, in the streets of Santiago and Valparaiso.... Reports suggest that the leftist rebel group FARC in Colombia has kidnapped at least 15 mayors, in addition to other intimidation tactics, in the weeks leading to Mar. 8 elections.	India conducts the final poll in its four-stage national elections. The results of the election show that no party has come close to drawing a parliamentary majority. Thirty-eight parties will be represented in the country's Parliament, the highest number ever.
March 8		Serbian authorities reveal that 26 people, whom it accused of terrorist acts, were killed during an assault on the village of Prekaz. Local leaders put the number of deaths at 38.	In Algeria, two leaders of the Armed Islamic Group, a fundamentalist rebel organization, and 22 others die in a skirmish with government forces.	Colombia's ruling Liberal Party retains a majority in both houses of Congress in balloting held amid threats of violence from leftist rebels. Eleven soldiers and eight rebels die in clashes.	
March 9	Ministers from the U.S., Britain, France, Italy, and Germany announce sanctions against Yugoslavia, intended to pressure it to end a violent crackdown on ethnic Albanians in the province of Kosovo. The minister from Russia does not agree to adopt all the sanctions.... Former Bosnian Serb paramilitary leader Dragoljub Kunarac pleads guilty to one count of crimes against humanity. Kunarac admits he raped at least three Muslim women during the 1992–95 civil war. It is the first time that an international court treats rape as a crime against humanity. Kunarac pleads innocent to several other charges.	Serbian authorities take the bodies of 51 ethnic Albanians to a garage in the Kosovo town of Srbica, bringing to 77 the known number of ethnic Albanian civilians killed since fighting began Feb. 28.... The administration of Polish president Aleksander Kwasniewski announces that it will make efforts to restore citizenship to thousands of Jews who fled the country during an anti-Semitic campaign in 1968.	Reports disclose that PNA police in the Gaza Strip have arrested 10 people in raids on seven bomb-making factories that allegedly belong to Hamas's military wing.	In Paraguay, a five-member military tribunal sentences retired general Lino Cesar Oviedo to 10 years in prison for leading a failed coup attempt in April 1996.... Native Innu protesters, whose ancestral lands include the Churchill River basin, protest a new power project to be developed in the part of the Labrador peninsula in Canada.	Assembly delegates pass a decree that broadens the powers of Indonesian president Suharto... The Vatican announces that it has named Jean-Baptiste Pham Minh Man, 64, as the new archbishop of Ho Chi Minh City, formerly Saigon.
March 10		Turkish military officials disclose that the army killed 32 Kurdish separatists in the southeastern part of the country. Two Turkish soldiers are reported to have been killed in the fighting.... Mortar shells are fired at a Royal Ulster Constabulary (RUC) police force station in Armagh, Northern Ireland.	Pres. Ahmad Tejan Kabbah returns to office in Sierra Leone after nearly 10 months in exile.... Statistics show that the number of foreign tourists visiting Egypt in December 1997 was down more than 50% from the year-earlier period. It is the lowest monthly figure since February 1995 and follows a November 1997 terrorist attack that killed 58 tourists.	Gen. Augusto Pinochet Ugarte, Chile's former president, resigns as head of the armed forces. In a ceremony in Santiago, the capital, he hands over control of Chile's military to Gen. Ricardo Izurieta, who was named his successor in October 1997.	Six Tibetans in New Delhi, India, launch a hunger strike, vowing to fast until the UN General Assembly addresses the question of China's rule over Tibet.
March 11		The International Committee of the Red Cross, the only outside aid group operating in Kosovo, pulls its workers out of the province , claiming that it received "repeated anonymous death threats.".... The Social Democratic Party, Denmark's ruling center-left coalition, wins a slim victory in a general election.... A court in Manisa, Turkey, acquits 10 police officers accused of torturing and sexually abusing 14 teenagers detained in December 1995. In the controversial ruling, a three-judge panel finds that prosecutors failed to produce "definitive and convincing evidence" that the abuse took place.	An independent Algerian newspaper reports that government troops killed 146 Muslim rebels during an ongoing offensive in western Algeria.	Gen. Augusto Pinochet Ugarte, Chile's former president, is sworn in as a senator for life, a privilege awarded to all former presidents who served more than six years under a constitution written during his presidency. In response, several legislators demonstrate on the Senate floor, holding up pictures of those allegedly killed or "disappeared" by Pinochet's security forces. Rightist supporters of Pinochet attempt to shield him from the protesters, and a fistfight breaks out between members of the two groups. Thousands of people protest against Pinochet in the streets of Santiago and Valparaiso.	Indonesian president Suharto is sworn in for a seventh consecutive five-year term. Hitherto peaceful protests turn violent, and as many as 10,000 students burn an effigy of the president at a rally at Gadjah Mada University in Yogyakarta, on the main island of Java. More than a dozen students are injured in the town of Surabaya in a clash with troops.... An ongoing investigation of alleged bribery of Japanese government officials by banks and other financial institutions spreads to the Bank of Japan, the central bank, when Tokyo prosecutors arrest Yasuyuki Yoshizawa, head of its capital markets division.
March 12	Chinese foreign minister Qian Qichen announces that China will sign the International Covenant on Civil and Political Rights, a UN treaty that guarantees citizens freedom of expression, movement, and religion, as well as participation in elections and equality under law.			Manuel Piñeiro Losada, 63, Cuban security and intelligence director who served as deputy minister of the interior, 1961–74, dies in a car crash in Havana, Cuba.	

A	B	C	D	E
Includes developments that affect more than one world region, international organizations, and important meetings of major world leaders.	Includes all domestic and regional developments in Europe, including the Soviet Union, Turkey, Cyprus, and Malta.	Includes all domestic and regional developments in Africa and the Middle East, including Iraq and Iran and excluding Cyprus, Turkey, and Afghanistan.	Includes all domestic and regional developments in Latin America, the Caribbean, and Canada.	Includes all domestic and regional developments in Asia and Pacific nations, extending from Afghanistan through all the Pacific Island, except Hawaii.

U.S. Politics & Social Issues	U.S. Foreign Policy & Defense	U.S. Economy & Environment	Science, Technology, & Nature	Culture, Leisure, & Lifestyle	
				Hermann Maier of Austria wins the men's overall title for alpine skiing's World Cup. . . . Leonie Rysanek, 71, operatic soprano who gave more than 2,100 performances at the world's leading opera houses from 1949 to 1996, dies in Vienna, Austria, after suffering from bone cancer.	March 7
		James B. McDougal, 57, former business partner of Pres. Clinton and First Lady Hillary Rodham Clinton and a central figure in the four-year-old Whitewater investigation, dies of a heart attack in Fort Worth, Tex., while serving a three-year sentence for a 1996 fraud conviction relating to illegal operations at Madison Guaranty Savings & Loan.		Ray Nitschke, 61, professional football player voted into the Pro Football Hall of Fame in 1978, dies in Naples, Florida, of a heart attack.	March 8
Brian Peterson, 19, charged with first-degree murder in the death of his newborn baby who was found dead in a trash container shortly after his girlfriend Amy Grossberg, 19, gave birth, pleads guilty to manslaughter and agrees to testify against Grossberg.	The Senate passes, 93-1, a bill that will prevent intelligence agencies from punishing employees who reveal classified information to Congress if that information contains evidence of wrongdoing at the agencies. . . . In Quality King Distributors Inc. v. L'anza Research International Inc., the Supreme Court rules unanimously that U.S. companies that sell their products at a discount abroad cannot invoke federal copyright law to bar the goods' importation back into the U.S.	In Los Angeles, California, U.S. district judge Richard A. Paez sentences Rep. Jay C. Kim (R, Calif.) to two months of home detention and a year's probation for accepting more than $250,000 in illegal campaign contributions.			March 9
	Pres. Clinton waives a trade curb that the U.S. imposed on Vietnam under a cold war–era law that limited U.S. trade with communist countries that restrict emigration.			Lloyd Vernet Bridges Jr., 85, TV actor who also had prominent roles in a number of acclaimed motion pictures, dies in Los Angeles, California, of unreported causes.	March 10
	In Washington, D.C., U.S. district judge Royce Lamberth orders the government of Iran to pay $247.5 million to the family of Alisa M. Flatow, a 20-year-old Jewish exchange student from the U.S. killed in a 1995 suicide bombing near a Jewish settlement in the Israeli-occupied Gaza Strip. The decision is the second issued under the Antiterrorism and Effective Death Penalty Act.	The Justice Department agrees to pay Frederic Whitehurst, a former FBI employee, $300,000 to settle claims that the government tried to discredit him publicly with false and derogatory information. Whitehurst was suspended in 1997 from his job at the crime laboratory after calling attention to shoddy practices there. The Justice Department agreed in February to pay Whitehurst $1.16 million to settle other aspects of his suit against them.	U.S. astronomer Brian Marsden announces that an asteroid is likely to pass within 30,000 miles (48,000 km) of the Earth on October 26, 2028. . . . A study finds that blacks and some Hispanics in the U.S. have a higher risk than whites of developing Alzheimer's disease.		March 11
Data shows the incidence of new cancer cases in the U.S. declined slightly between 1990 and 1995, the first drop since such statistics began to be collected in the 1930s. . . . Police in Boulder, Colorado, ask the local district attorney to convene a grand jury to investigate the highly publicized 1996 murder of JonBenet Ramsey. . . . David Bowman, a former DEA budget analyst, is indicted on charges of theft, mail fraud, and money laundering for stealing funds from the DEA.	The House votes, 233-186, to endorse the African Growth and Opportunity Act, legislation designed to encourage trade and investment in Africa.	The Senate votes, 96-4, to pass a $214.3 billion, six-year reauthorization bill for the nation's mass-transit systems and highways.	Astronomers at the W. M. Keck Observatory announce they have sighted a galaxy in the constellation Triangulum that is the most distant object yet seen from Earth. . . . Scientists report they have found evidence of the existence in humans of pheromones—chemicals produced by an individual of a species that affects the physiology or behavior of another. The influence of pheromones has been documented in animals and insects, but not conclusively in humans.	Beatrice Wood, 105, ceramist known for her associations with the Dadaist art movement of the 1910s and 1920s, dies in Ojai, California, of unreported causes.	March 12

F	G	H	I	J
Includes elections, federal-state relations, civil rights and liberties, crime, the judiciary, education, health care, poverty, urban affairs, and population.	Includes formation and debate of U.S. foreign and defense policies, veterans' affairs, and defense spending. (Relations with specific foreign countries are usually found under the region concerned.)	Includes business, labor, agriculture, taxation, transportation, consumer affairs, monetary and fiscal policy, natural resources, and pollution.	Includes worldwide scientific, medical, and technological developments; natural phenomena; U.S. weather; natural disasters; and accidents.	Includes the arts, religion, scholarship, communications media, sports, entertainments, fashions, fads, and social life.

	World Affairs	Europe	Africa & the Middle East	The Americas	Asia & the Pacific
March 13	The World Bank agrees to grant a $100 million emergency loan to Kenya.	The Greek government confirms that it has begun procedures for incorporating the country's currency, the drachma, into the European Union's Exchange Rate Mechanism (ERM).			Pres. Kim Dae Jung approves an amnesty freeing some 2,300 prisoners, including 74 political prisoners, and clearing millions more of their traffic violations. South Korean human-rights groups sharply criticize the amnesty for failing to include more of the inmates they consider to be prisoners of conscience.... A British-registered ship unloads a cargo of nuclear waste at the Japanese port of Mutsu-Ogawara after a standoff between the local governor and the central government.
March 14		Reports reveal that 30 Kurdish rebels have died in separate clashes in Turkey. Those killings are reportedly retaliation for the slaying of the two army soldiers.	King Hassan of Morocco appoints Morocco's first opposition-led government since the country gained independence in 1956.... Ariel Sharon, Israel's infrastructure minister, vows that Israel will assassinate Khaled Meshal, the Jordan-based leader of Hamas's political wing.... Sheikh Abdul Rahman al-Iryani, 86, president of the Republic of North Yemen, 1967–74, dies in Damascus, Syria.		
March 15		Grece's entry into the European Union's Exchange Rate Mechanism (ERM) is finalized.			
March 16	Agriculture ministers from European Union member nations approve plans to allow the export of some beef from cattle herds in the British province of Northern Ireland. The move is the most significant step yet toward easing the EU's worldwide ban on British beef exports enacted in March 1996.	Northern Ireland prison inmate David Keys, 26, an apparent member of the LVF and a suspect in the March 3 Poyntzpass killings, is found dead in his cell at the Maze Prison.... In Chechnya, a government soldier and a kidnapper are killed during a failed attempt by Chechen antiterrorist forces to free two British hostages being held outside of Grozny. Eight others are injured during the raid.			
March 17		A Turkish appeals court rules that former premier Tansu Ciller will not be tried on charges that she misused public funds.	Zambian president Frederick Chiluba lifts a national state of emergency in effect since October 1997.... Reports reveal that rebels loyal to the ousted junta in Sierra Leone have executed more than 50 civilians in the mining district of Kono.		Reports confirm that fighting has erupted for control of the major northern city of Mazar-i-Sharif in Afghanistan. Ethnic Uzbek forces loyal to Gen. Abdul Rashid Doestam challenged the Hezb-i-Wahdat militia, and an exchange of rocket-propelled grenades and mortar shells between the two sides reportedly left some 100 dead and more than 300 wounded. Doestam's forces were joined by the Hizb-i-Islami faction headed by former premier Gulbuddin Hekmatyar in the battle for Mazar-i-Sharif.
March 18		Serbian police open fire on a gathering of ethnic Albanian demonstrators in Pec, Kosovo's second-largest city, killing one man and injuring several others. A speaker for the province's Serbian government denies the casualty report.... Chechen security officials report that two hostages, aid workers Jon James and Camilla Carr, were apparently unharmed in the Mar. 16 raid to free them. The pair had been kidnapped by unidentified assailants in July 1907.	The South African Ministry of Health estimates that 50,000 people nationwide are infected each month with HIV, the virus that causes AIDS.	Workers at Venezuela Aluminum Corp. end nearly a week-long strike, after the government agrees to the union's demand for a $961 productivity bonus for each of the company's more than 9,000 employees.	Ousted first premier Prince Norodom Ranariddh is convicted, in absentia, of attempting to overthrow the Cambodian government. The trial is conducted by a military court in Phnom Penh, the capital.... A Formosa Airlines Saab 340 turboprop airplane crashes into the Taiwan Strait, killing all eight passengers and five crew members aboard.... The Singapore government announces it has dropped charges against Kevin Wallace, a former employee of Merrill Lynch in Singapore who was arrested in Hong Kong in July 1997.
	A Includes developments that affect more than one world region, international organizations, and important meetings of major world leaders.	B Includes all domestic and regional developments in Europe, including the Soviet Union, Turkey, Cyprus, and Malta.	C Includes all domestic and regional developments in Africa and the Middle East, including Iraq and Iran and excluding Cyprus, Turkey, and Afghanistan.	D Includes all domestic and regional developments in Latin America, the Caribbean, and Canada.	E Includes all domestic and regional developments in Asia and Pacific nations, extending from Afghanistan through all the Pacific Island, except Hawaii.

U.S. Politics & Social Issues	U.S. Foreign Policy & Defense	U.S. Economy & Environment	Science, Technology, & Nature	Culture, Leisure, & Lifestyle	
	A military jury acquits Sergeant Major Gene McKinney of all charges that he engaged in sexual misconduct with six female accusers. The jury convicts McKinney of only one of the 19 charges brought against him, determining that he is guilty of obstructing justice for having tried to coach one of his accuser's responses to army investigators.	A federal grand jury indicts Texas entrepreneur Nolanda Hill and her chief financial adviser, Kenneth White, on charges stemming from an independent counsel investigation of late Commerce Secretary Ronald H. Brown.	Hans Joachim Pabst von Ohain, 86, German aeronautical engineer who built the engine for the first jet-powered flight and who, in 1947, became chief scientist at the U.S. Air Force Base in Dayton, Ohio, dies in Melbourne, Florida, of congestive heart failure.	Katja Seizinger of Germany wins the women's overall title, for alpine skiing's World Cup. . . . A jury of the United Methodist Church acquits Jimmy Creech, a Nebraska minister, of charges that he violated church law by performing a commitment ceremony for a lesbian couple in September 1997.	March 13
Geoffrey Fieger, the lawyer for physician-assisted suicide advocate Dr. Jack Kevorkian, reveals Kevorkian has assisted in a total of 100 suicides. . . . A lawyer for Mary Kay Letourneau, a former lteacher convicted of statutory rape for having a sexual relationship with a 14-year-old boy, confirms that Letourneau is pregnant. She gave birth to a daughter fathored by the youth in 1997 and is currently serving a seven-year prison term for violating a court order that she refrain from contact with the teenager.					March 14
				In basketball, the Columbus Quest beat the Long Beach StingRays, 86-81, to win their second consecutive women's ABL championship. . . . Dr. Benjamin McLane Spock, 94, whose highly influential book *Baby and Child Care* (1946), sold 50 million copies worldwide, dies in San Diego, California, after months of failing health.	March 15
The Presidential Advisory Council on HIV/AIDS passes a unanimous vote of no confidence in the Clinton administration's efforts to stop the spread of HIV, the virus that causes AIDS. . . . New York City district judge Denny Chin imposes temporary restrictions on provisions in New York State's sex-offender notification law when he temporarily bars the state from publishing details about a sex offender's age, address, and criminal history.	Sergeant Major Gene McKinney, convicted March 13 on one charge of sexual harassment, is sentenced to a one-rank demotion and a reprimand. . . . In the wake of a sexual-harassment scandal at the Aberdeen Proving Ground in Maryland, Defense Secretary William Cohen rejects a panel's recommendation that male and female military recruits be housed in separate barracks during basic training.	Democratic fund-raiser Johnny Chung pleads guilty to using "conduit" donors to funnel $20,000 in illegal contributions to the 1996 reelection campaign of Pres. Clinton and Vice Pres. Al Gore. He is the first person charged in a Justice Department investigation of fund-raising abuses in the 1996 election cycle who agrees to cooperate with prosecutors.	Sir Derek Henry Richard Barton, 79, British cowinner of the 1969 Nobel Prize for Chemistry for his understanding of organic molecules, dies of a heart attack in College Station, Texas.	In a long-awaited statement on the actions of the Roman Catholic Church during the Holocaust of World War II, the Vatican apologizes to Jews for the church's failure to take decisive action to prevent Nazi Germany's extermination of more than 6 million Jews.	March 16
The state of Mississippi releases documents relating to the work of a now-defunct state agency that used spy tactics and intimidation in an effort to preserve the state's system of racial segregation during the civil-rights era of the 1950s and 1960s. . . . The Senate confirms Susan Graber as justice of the Ninth Circuit Court of Appeals in San Francisco, California, and Jeremy Fogel as a justice in San Francisco's District Court. Despite these confirmations, 80 of the 842 federal judgeships remain vacant.		Washington Mutual Inc., the nation's largest savings and loan company in terms of assets, announces the acquisition of the nation's second-largest thrift, H. F. Ahmanson & Co. of Irwindale, California, in a stock swap worth $10.03 billion. The combined company will control assets worth $149.5 billion.		Jeff King wins the 26th Iditarod Trail Sled Dog Race from Anchorage to Nome, Alaska. It is King's third victory in the Iditarod.	March 17
Public Citizen, an advocacy group, reports that tobacco companies in 1997 spent $19.3 million on outside lobbying firms. The industry had spent $5.8 million on outside lobbyists in 1996. The increase is attributed chiefly to lobbying efforts related to the proposed 1997 settlement. . . . Gov. Zell Miller (D, Ga.) announces an agreement with federal authorities that calls for the state to make major reforms to its juvenile justice system.		A federal judge in Washington, D.C., sentences Ronald Blackley, former agriculture secretary Mike Espy's chief of staff, to 27 months in prison for concealing $22,025 he received from farmers seeking government subsidies. The sentence is the longest yet given in independent counsel Donald Smaltz's investigation of whether Espy and his aides accepted illegal gratuities from agricultural companies.		In New York City, Guernsey's Auction House auctions 600 personal artifacts, documents, and other memorabilia that belonged to members of the Kennedy family. The auction goes forward despite strong objections from the late president's children, John F. Kennedy Jr. and Caroline B. Kennedy Schlossberg.	March 18
F	G	H	I	J	
Includes elections, federal-state relations, civil rights and liberties, crime, the judiciary, education, health care, poverty, urban affairs, and population.	*Includes formation and debate of U.S. foreign and defense policies, veterans' affairs, and defense spending. (Relations with specific foreign countries are usually found under the region concerned.)*	*Includes business, labor, agriculture, taxation, transportation, consumer affairs, monetary and fiscal policy, natural resources, and pollution.*	*Includes worldwide scientific, medical, and technological developments; natural phenomena; U.S. weather; natural disasters; and accidents.*	*Includes the arts, religion, scholarship, communications media, sports, entertainments, fashions, fads, and social life.*	

	World Affairs	Europe	Africa & the Middle East	The Americas	Asia & the Pacific
March 19		Some 30,000 ethnic Albanians assemble in Pec, Kosovo, to mourn the demonstrator slain Mar. 18. . . . In Turkey, five police officers are sentenced for the beating death of journalist Metin Goktepe.			Hindu nationalist leader Atal Bihari Vajpayee is sworn in for a five-year term as India's new prime minister. . . . A passenger jet belonging to Afghanistan's state-run Ariana airlines crashes about 20 miles (32 km) south of Kabul, the capital, killing all 22 people on board. . . . Hideo Shima, 96, developer of Japan's bullet train who was presented with the Order of Cultural Merit in 1994, dies of a stroke in a hospital in Tokyo.
March 20		Thousands of antinuclear power demonstrators attempt to prevent the progress of a train carrying radioactive nuclear waste to a storage facility in northern Germany. Some 450 protesters are arrested, and seven are injured.			
March 21			Pope John Paul II makes his second visit to Nigeria in 16 years.		After receiving approval from Cambodian copremier Hun Sen, King Norodom Sihanouk issues a royal pardon in which he grants full amnesty to his son, Prince Norodom Ranariddh, who was convicted in absentia Mar. 4 and Mar. 18. Separately, some 3,000 troops loyal to Khmer Rouge strongman Ta Mok splinter, and two divisions take control of an area near Anlong Veng.
March 22	Saudi Arabia, Venezuela, and Mexico announce that they will cut their petroleum production in an effort to raise plunging oil prices.	The Communist Party captures more votes than any other single party, 30.1%, in Moldova's parliamentary elections.	At an outdoor mass that draws an estimated 1 million people in the Nigerian village of Oba, near the predominantly Roman Catholic southern city of Onitsha, Pope John Paul beatifies Michael Iwene Tansi, a Nigerian ascetic priest who died in 1964. Tansi is the first Nigerian ever beatified.	Connie Jacobs, 37, and her son Ty, nine, are killed in a shoot-out with a Royal Canadian Mounted Police (RCMP) officer on the Tsuu T'ina reserve outside Calgary, Alberta, inciting anger in native communities across Canada.	
March 23	Iran, Kuwait, the United Arab Emirates, Oman, Algeria, and Libya announce that they will cut their petroleum output, alongside the Mar. 22 pledge. . . . Chilean diplomat Juan Somavia is chosen as the next director general of the International Labor Organization (ILO), a United Nations agency.	Russian president Boris Yeltsin announces that he has dismissed his entire cabinet, including Premier Viktor Chernomyrdin, in an effort to revitalize the policy-making initiative within his government. . . . Government officials and ethnic Albanian leaders in Kosovo have signed an agreement that grants ethnic Albanian students readmittance to the national school system after several years of exile. The accord sparks protests and angry condemnation from the Serb population of Pristina.		Leftist rebels of the Revolutionary Armed Forces of Colombia (FARC) kidnap five foreigners and at least nine Colombians at a FARC roadblock on the Via al Llano highway, some 30 miles (50 km) southeast of Bogota, the capital.	
March 24		Ethnic Albanian separatists ambush a Serbian police patrol in the Kosovo village of Dubrava, killing a police officer. Another police officer is seriously injured in the attack. Gunfights between police and ethnic Albanian militants go on for several hours. Heavily armed Serbian paramilitary units launch a counterattack on several small villages in the area, injuring one ethnic Albanian man and forcing many residents to flee.	In a brief speech to more than 1,000 schoolchildren outside Kampala, the capital of Uganda, U.S. president Bill Clinton states that the U.S. was historically guilty of both neglect and ignorance in its relations with Africa. He also admits that the U.S. was wrong to participate in the slave trade. Clinton's remarks on slavery are unscripted, taking observers by surprise since the Clinton administration in 1997 considered issuing an official apology for slavery, but ultimately decided against it.		South Korean officials announce that Pres. Kim Dae Jung has fired 24 of the 38 highest officials of the Agency for National Security Planning. . . . The UN suspends operations in Kandahar province in Afghanistan, citing physical harassment of its workers and interference by the Taliban militia. . . . In India, at least 105 people are killed and another 1,100 are injured when a tornado devastates villages in the eastern states of Orissa and West Bengal. The death toll is expected to climb, as another 500 people are reported missing.

A	B	C	D	E
Includes developments that affect more than one world region, international organizations, and important meetings of major world leaders.	Includes all domestic and regional developments in Europe, including the Soviet Union, Turkey, Cyprus, and Malta.	Includes all domestic and regional developments in Africa and the Middle East, including Iraq and Iran and excluding Cyprus, Turkey, and Afghanistan.	Includes all domestic and regional developments in Latin America, the Caribbean, and Canada.	Includes all domestic and regional developments in Asia and Pacific nations, extending from Afghanistan through all the Pacific Island, except Hawaii.

U.S. Politics & Social Issues	U.S. Foreign Policy & Defense	U.S. Economy & Environment	Science, Technology, & Nature	Culture, Leisure, & Lifestyle	
A jury in Muncie, Indiana, finds that the tobacco industry was not liable for the death of Mildred Wiley, a nonsmoker who died of lung cancer after working for 17 years as a nurse in the psychiatric ward where she was exposed to second hand smoke. . . . A Detroit, Michigan, jury convicts former police officer Walter Budzyn of involuntary manslaughter in the 1992 beating death of black motorist Malice Green. Budzyn's 1993 conviction in the case was overturned in 1997.		The Commerce Department reports that in January the U.S. recorded a seasonally adjusted $12.04 billion deficit in trade in goods and services, up from December 1997's revised deficit of $10.90 billion. January's trade gap is the highest level registered since late 1987.	A study finds that regular cigar smoking nearly doubles a person's risk of death from cancer and from cardiovascular disease.		March 19
The CDC reports that the suicide rate for black teenagers rose dramatically in the past two decades. The suicide rate for blacks ages 15–19 rose to 8.1 per 100,000 in 1995, more than double the 1980 rate of 3.6 per 100,000. The rate for young blacks was approaching the higher suicide rate found among their white peers. In 1980, the suicide rate for white teenagers ages 10–19 was two and a half times greater than for their black peers; in 1995, the rate for white teenagers was only 42% higher than for blacks.	The Clinton administration confirms reports that the U.S. will ease restrictions on cash remittances and travel to Cuba. The changes, however, do not alter the U.S.'s 36-year-old economic embargo of Cuba. . . . Director of Central Intelligence George Tenet reveals that the U.S.'s intelligence budget for fiscal 1998 was $26.7 billion. It is the first voluntary disclosure of the intelligence budget to the public. The 1997 budget—$26.6 billion—was made public in October 1997 after Tenet was compelled by the Freedom of Information Act.	The Dow closes at a record high of 8906.43. That marks the 17th record high of 1998.	Twelve people are killed when a tornado sweeps through a rural area of northeast Georgia. At least 120 people are injured, 12,000 residents are left without power, and more than 170 homes are destroyed or damaged. Two people are killed and at least 19 others were injured when another tornado sweeps through the town of Stoneville, North Carolina.		March 20
				Galina Sergeyevna Ulanova, 88, Russian dancer known as one of the greatest ballerinas of the 20th century, dies in Moscow.	March 21
		More than 13,000 Caterpillar employees at 14 plants in Illinois, Colorado, Michigan, Pennsylvania, and Tennessee who are members of the United Auto Workers (UAW) labor union vote to approve a six-year contract with Caterpillar Inc.			March 22
Several dozen Native Americans disrupt a meeting of Pres. Clinton's advisory board on race in Denver, Colorado, protesting that the seven-member panel does not include any indigenous Americans. . . . In *Voinovich v. Women's Medical Professional Corp.*, the Supreme Court lets stand a lower-court ruling that struck down an Ohio statute banning a late-term abortion method known as IDE. It is the first case regarding IDE procedures to reach the high court. . . . The California Supreme Court rules that the Boy Scouts of America can bar homosexuals, agnostics, and atheists because it is a private membership organization.			An independent audit of spending on a planned international space station finds that the project's costs could reach $24 billion, some $3 billion more than previously projected.	At the Oscars, *Titanic* wins 11 of the 14 Oscars for which it is nominated, including best picture. The 14 nominations tie the record set by *All About Eve* in 1950, and the 11 wins tie the record set by *Ben-Hur* in 1959.	March 23
Mitchell Johnson, 13, and Andrew Golden, 11, open fire on Westside Middle School in Jonesboro, Arkansas, killing four students and one teacher. Ten other people are wounded in the shooting. The incident is among the deadliest school shootings in U.S. history. . . . New York State Supreme Court judge Leslie Crocker Snyder sentences convicted murderer John Royster to life in prison with no possibility of parole for a string of attacks on women in New York City in 1996.		In *Cohen v. De La Cruz*, the Supreme Court rules unanimously that federal bankruptcy law does not relieve a Hoboken, New Jersey, landlord of his obligation to pay punitive damages to a group of low-income tenants he overcharged.		The National Book Critics Circle present awards to Penelope Fitzgerald, Anne Fadiman, and Charles Wright. Literary critic Leslie Fiedler receives a lifetime achievement award. Writer and critic Thomas Mallon wins a special award for excellence in reviewing.	March 24

F	G	H	I	J
Includes elections, federal-state relations, civil rights and liberties, crime, the judiciary, education, health care, poverty, urban affairs, and population.	*Includes formation and debate of U.S. foreign and defense policies, veterans' affairs, and defense spending. (Relations with specific foreign countries are usually found under the region concerned.)*	*Includes business, labor, agriculture, taxation, transportation, consumer affairs, monetary and fiscal policy, natural resources, and pollution.*	*Includes worldwide scientific, medical, and technological developments; natural phenomena; U.S. weather; natural disasters; and accidents.*	*Includes the arts, religion, scholarship, communications media, sports, entertainments, fashions, fads, and social life.*

	World Affairs	Europe	Africa & the Middle East	The Americas	Asia & the Pacific
March 25	A six-nation committee monitoring internal strife in the Baltic region announces that it will postpone considering the sanctions announced Mar. 9 against Yugoslavia for one month.... The European Commission, the EU's executive branch, officially recommends that 11 of the EU's 15 nations be permitted to join the European economic and monetary union (EMU).				
March 26	A letter from Switzerland's three largest banks, which pledges to negotiate a global settlement with victims of the Nazi Holocaust who claim to have lost money held in Swiss bank accounts, is made public.		Bill Clinton becomes the first U.S. president ever to visit South Africa.		In Cambodia, Ta Mok executes Generals Sarouen, San, and Khon, the three aides who were tried with Pol Pot in 1997, because the troops that mutinied on Mar. 21 were loyal to them.... Eight illegal immigrants from Indonesia are killed in a clash with police at the Semenyih Detention Camp near Kuala Lumpur, Malaysia's capital. The immigrants were protesting their planned deportation to Indonesia.
March 27	NATO announces that it will send a small number of advisers to Albania to help train Albanian security forces who patrol the Yugoslav border. The move is intended to protect Albania from becoming embroiled in violent conflicts that have recently flared up between the Yugoslav government and ethnic Albanian separatists in the southern Yugoslav province of Kosovo.	Two masked gunmen shoot and killed Cyril Stewart, 52, a retired police officer, in Armagh, Northern Ireland.... Russian president Boris Yeltsin officially nominates interim premier Sergei Kiriyenko to assume the post on a permanent basis, pending the approval of Parliament.... Baroness Joan of Eccles Lestor, 66, British member of Parliament, 1966–83, 1987–98, dies in London after suffering from a disease of the nervous system.			Electrical power is restored to the downtown area of Auckland, New Zealand's largest city, after the Feb. 20 blackout.... Aid workers report that thousands of people in Irian Jaya, Indonesia, have died from starvation and malaria since January.
March 28		The Irish National Liberation Army (INLA), a hard-line republican group that broke off from the IRA, claims responsibility for the Mar. 27 killing in Armagh, Northern Ireland.	Israeli police open fire with rubber-coated bullets on Palestinian protesters outside a Jewish settlement near the West Bank city of Nablus. Six Palestinians, including at least one member of the PLO executive committee, are wounded in the shooting.		Malaysian authorities deport more than 1,100 of the 10,000 immigrants from Indonesia in detention camps.... The East Kalimantan Environmental Impact Agency reports that some 3,400 people in Indonesia have become ill due to a noxious haze caused by fires, which have been burning since January, set to clear land for farming.... India's Hindu nationalist Bharatiya Janata Party (BJP) survives a vote of confidence in Parliament.
March 29		The Communist Party wins the largest share of the vote in Ukraine's parliamentary elections.	An unidentified man is found dead near an exploded automobile outside the Palestinian-ruled West Bank city of Ramallah.		
March 30	The European Union, at a ceremony in Brussels, Belgium, officially launches negotiations expected to lead to the largest expansion of the grouping's membership in its 40-year history.	Armenian premier Robert Kocharyan defeats Karen Demirchyan in a runoff for the nation's presidency.... Romanian premier Victor Ciorbea resigns under heavy pressure from junior parties in his coalition government.... Thousands of employees of the Polish mining company KGHM go on strike to protest a corporate restructuring plan.			Taiwanese transport minister Tsai Chao-yang resigns to accept responsibility for a recent series of aviation disasters.

A	B	C	D	E
Includes developments that affect more than one world region, international organizations, and important meetings of major world leaders.	*Includes all domestic and regional developments in Europe, including the Soviet Union, Turkey, Cyprus, and Malta.*	*Includes all domestic and regional developments in Africa and the Middle East, including Iraq and Iran and excluding Cyprus, Turkey, and Afghanistan.*	*Includes all domestic and regional developments in Latin America, the Caribbean, and Canada.*	*Includes all domestic and regional developments in Asia and Pacific nations, extending from Afghanistan through all the Pacific Island, except Hawaii.*

U.S. Politics & Social Issues	U.S. Foreign Policy & Defense	U.S. Economy & Environment	Science, Technology, & Nature	Culture, Leisure, & Lifestyle	
Compassion in Dying states that the U.S.'s first known legal physician-assisted suicide took place when an unidentified 80-year-old Portland woman suffering from terminal breast cancer killed herself with an overdose of barbiturates. . . . Steven Harvey Schiff, 51, Republican congressman from New Mexico, 1989–98, dies in Albuquerque, N.Mex., of squamous cell carcinoma.		The Treasury Department estimates that smoking-related illnesses cost the U.S. $130 billion a year in medical expenses and lost productivity. The Treasury report argues that meeting a goal of reducing teenage smoking by 60% will produce an annual economic gain of $78 billion within 10 years.	Norway announces that it will join the U.S. in building a tracking station that will monitor orbiting space debris.	R. Alan Eagleson, former head of the NHL Players Association convicted for defrauding the union and players, resigns from the Hockey Hall of Fame. It is the first time that a member has ever resigned from a major North American professional sport's hall of fame.	March 25
The CDC urges more widespread testing for infection by HIV and estimates that 250,000 people in the U.S. are unknowingly infected. . . . The Department of Health and Human Services orders the United Network for Organ Sharing (UNOS) to devise a new system of assigning priority to patients waiting for transplants. It is the first move by the federal government to regulate organ distribution.	The House approves, by voice vote, a fiscal 1998–99 State Department authorization bill. The bill authorizes $819 million for the U.S. to pay its debts to the UN, merges several foreign-policy agencies, and bars family-planning organizations overseas that perform abortions from receiving U.S. funding.	The Commerce Department reports that U.S. gross domestic product (GDP) grew at a revised annual rate of 3.7% in the 1997 fourth quarter.	Italian scientists describe a fossil of a baby dinosaur containing rare fossilized internal dinosaur organs. The dinosaur's intestines, liver, muscles, and windpipe are among the parts visible in the fossil. . . . A study conclusively shows that widely used drug combinations designed to combat HIV, the virus that causes AIDS, dramatically reduces mortality rates among AIDS patients.		March 26
A federal jury in NYC finds that a divorced Tennessee couple and the seven gun-making companies that they own are not responsible for a fatal shooting attack on a group of Hasidic Jewish students in 1994. Gun-control advocates in recent years have filed similar legal actions against gun makers nationwide. The current case marks the first time that such a lawsuit has gone to trial. . . . Tennessee authorities state that a third official inquiry into the 1968 assassination of civil-rights activist Rev. Martin Luther King Jr. concluded that James Earl Ray was guilty of King's murder.	Rep. Tom DeLay (R, Tex.), criticizes Pres. Clinton for the comments he made Mar. 24 in Africa about slavery. . . . Army officials reveal that Major General David Hale, the former deputy inspector general of the army, was allowed to retire honorably from the service despite being under investigation for allegedly coercing a subordinate's wife to have a sexual relationship with him. Hale, who retired in February, was the Army's second in command for investigating personnel-related improprieties.	The Commerce Department reports that personal pretax income rose 0.6% in February from January, to a seasonally adjusted figure of $7.135 trillion. The February gain marks the 16th consecutive month in which personal income increased.	The FDA approves a prescription pill made by Pfizer Inc. to treat male impotence. Pfizer will market the drug, sildenafil citrate, under the name Viagra.	Ferdinand (Ferry) Porsche Jr., 88, car designer, dies in Zell am See, Austria.	March 27
				In horse racing, Silver Charm wins the Dubai World Cup. . . . A jury convicts him Rudolph Kos, a former Roman Catholic priest in Dallas, Texas, on five counts of sexually assaulting altar boys.	March 28
			Israeli archaeologists reveal that they have uncovered the oldest ruins of a Jewish synagogue ever found. The synagogue, which dates from between 70 B.C. and 50 B.C., is outside the town of Jericho in the West Bank in the ruins of a Maccabean palace.	Pat Hurst wins the Dinah Shore golf tournament in Rancho Mirage, California.	March 29
Convicted murderer Judias Buenoano, 54, is put to death by execution in Starke, Florida. Buenoano is the 450th person executed in the U.S. and the 42nd in Florida since 1976. Florida last executed a woman in 1848. . . . Alfred U. McKenzie, 80, civil-rights pioneer and World War II pilot, dies in Clinton, Maryland, of complications from prostate cancer.			Astronomers report they have observed a complete "Einstein ring" created by gravitational lensing. It is the first time the image of a complete Einstein ring has been captured in the infrared or visible light wavelengths. Einstein rings are named after physicist Albert Einstein, whose general theory of relativity predicted their existence.	Pandora, by Anne Rice, tops the bestseller list.	March 30

F	G	H	I	J
Includes elections, federal-state relations, civil rights and liberties, crime, the judiciary, education, health care, poverty, urban affairs, and population.	Includes formation and debate of U.S. foreign and defense policies, veterans' affairs, and defense spending. (Relations with specific foreign countries are usually found under the region concerned.)	Includes business, labor, agriculture, taxation, transportation, consumer affairs, monetary and fiscal policy, natural resources, and pollution.	Includes worldwide scientific, medical, and technological developments; natural phenomena; U.S. weather; natural disasters; and accidents.	Includes the arts, religion, scholarship, communications media, sports, entertainments, fashions, fads, and social life.

	World Affairs	Europe	Africa & the Middle East	The Americas	Asia & the Pacific
March 31	The UN Security Council votes to impose an arms embargo on Yugoslavia, where a recent government crackdown on ethnic Albanian separatists in the Kosovo province has left more than 80 people dead. . . . The 11-nation OPEC agrees to reduce its total crude-oil production by 1.25 million barrels a day as part of a broad effort to stem plunging oil prices.	Jozef Krawczyk, the mayor of the southern city of Oswiecim, approves the construction of a visitors' center for Auschwitz, the infamous World War II-era Nazi death camp. . . . Zhu Rongji, China's newly selected premier, meets Queen Elizabeth II, becoming the first Chinese premier to do so since Zhao Ziyang in 1986.	The UNHCR states that an estimated 180 Somalis died when their boat sank off the coast of Yemen. . . . Sir Ketumile Masire voluntarily steps down as president of Botswana. Masire, 72, the second president in Botswana's history, served for 18 years. . . . The rand, South Africa's currency, drops to its lowest value ever in relation to the U.S. dollar, closing at 5.0375 to the dollar.		Australian prime minister John Howard appoints Judge Murray Gleeson, the chief justice of the state of New South Wales, to be the next chief justice of the Australian High Court. Gleeson will be the first person in 34 years to serve as the High Court's chief justice without prior High Court experience.
April 1		Romanian president Emil Constantinescu names Radu Vasile to replace Victor Ciorbea as premier.	At least 280 people die when a boat carrying an estimated 300 passengers overturns in stormy waters off the Nigerian coast while en route to Gabon. . . . Festus Mogae is sworn in as Botswana's new president. . . . Arab-Israeli tensions rise when the man found dead Mar. 29 near an exploded automobile outside the Palestinian-ruled West Bank city of Ramallah is identified as Muhyideen al-Sharif, a suspected master bomb-maker of the Islamic militant group Hamas.		
April 2	UNSCOM inspectors complete their first-ever search for weapons-related materials in Iraq's eight presidential compounds.	In Bordeaux, France, a jury finds Maurice Papon, a former French budget minister, guilty of complicity in Nazi crimes against humanity and sentences him to 10 years in prison.	In the west Bank, thousands of Palestinians, many calling for revenge, march at a funeral for Muhyideen al-Sharif in Ramallah. . . . Iran and Iraq begin a prisoner of war (POW) exchange when Iran hands over 800 Iraqi prisoners and Iraq releases 62 Iranian captives. The POWs were captured during the two nations' 1980–88 war.	The Supreme Court of Canada rules that the nation's Charter of Rights and Freedoms requires the province of Alberta to extend its law banning discrimination to protect homosexuals.	
April 3	UNSCOM inspectors report that they found no prohibited weapons-related materials in their search of the 1,058 buildings comprising Iraq's eight presidential compounds.	The British government offers an official apology to survivors of the Nazi Holocaust who were unable to recover money deposited in British banks during World War II.	Thousands of Palestinians march in a pro-Hamas demonstration in Gaza City.		
April 4		A methane gas explosion at a Ukrainian coal mine in the city of Donetsk kills 63 miners and hospitalizes at least 45 others. The accident brings the death toll from mining disasters in 1998 to more than 220, which compares with some 290 miners who died in 1997.	Gholamhossein Karbaschi, the mayor of Teheran, the capital of Iran, is placed in "temporary detention" on orders of the public prosecutor's office.		Reports suggest that Chinese dissident Shen Liangqing, arrested in February, has been sentenced to two years in a labor camp.

A	B	C	D	E
Includes developments that affect more than one world region, international organizations, and important meetings of major world leaders.	Includes all domestic and regional developments in Europe, including the Soviet Union, Turkey, Cyprus, and Malta.	Includes all domestic and regional developments in Africa and the Middle East, including Iraq and Iran and excluding Cyprus, Turkey, and Afghanistan.	Includes all domestic and regional developments in Latin America, the Caribbean, and Canada.	Includes all domestic and regional developments in Asia and Pacific nations, extending from Afghanistan through all the Pacific Island, except Hawaii.

U.S. Politics & Social Issues	U.S. Foreign Policy & Defense	U.S. Economy & Environment	Science, Technology, & Nature	Culture, Leisure, & Lifestyle	
In *U.S. v. Scheffer*, the Supreme Court rules, 8-1, that state and federal courts can bar evidence from polygraph tests from trials. . . . A judge in New York City sentences Lemrick Nelson Jr. to 19½ years in prison for violating the civil rights of Yankel Rosenbaum, a Jewish rabbinical student killed in 1991. . . . A jury in Billings, Montana, convicts five members of the Montana Freemen on charges resulting from a 1996 standoff with federal authorities. . . . Bella Savitzky Abzug, 77, (D, N.Y.), the first Jewish woman elected to the U.S. Congress, 1970–76, and a feminist leader, dies after complications following heart surgery in New York City.		The Treasury releases the first-ever comprehensive audit of the federal government. The GAO audit finds widespread record-keeping and accounting problems that left the government unable to account for billions of dollars in property. . . . In *U.S. v. U.S. Shoe Corp.*, the Supreme Court rules unanimously that the federal Harbor Maintenance Tax violates the Constitution's so-called export clause, which prohibits taxes on exports.	A study suggests that short-term use of the diet medication dexfenfluramine does not cause damage to heart valves. Dexfenfluramine, sold as Redux, was withdrawn from the market in 1997 at the request of the FDA. The study does not examine the effects of the widely prescribed "fen/phen" combination of fenfluramine and another drug, phentermine.		March 31
Judge Susan Webber Wright of U.S. District Court in Little Rock, Arkansas, throws out Paula Corbin Jones's sexual-harassment lawsuit against U.S. Pres. Clinton, ruling that the case is "without merit." . . . Former vampire-cult member Howard Scott Anderson, 17, is sentenced to two life prison terms for his role in the 1996 murder of Richard Wendorf and Naoma Queen, who were killed during a robbery.		The House votes, 337-80, to pass a $217 billion, six-year reauthorization bill for the nation's highways, mass-transit systems, and other transportation infrastructure The bill is the largest public works measure in U.S. history, providing for a 42% increase in spending over six years.	The FDA approves a calorie-free artificial sweetener called sucralose. . . . A woman and her infant son are killed when a tornado rips through their house in the farming community of Coatesville, Virginia. The tornado destroys or damages 35 homes and cuts off power to some 4,500 people in the town.	In Dallas, Texas, Rudolph Kos, a former Roman Catholic priest is sentenced to life in prison for sexually assaulting altar boys an estimated 1,350 times over five years. . . . At the World Figure Skating Championships, in Minneapolis, Minnesota, Russia's Yelena Berezhnaya and Anton Sikharulidze win the pairs competition.	April 1
The City of New York announces it has reached an out-of-court settlement with members of a Hasidic Jewish community who accused the city of failing to protect some residents during four days of racially charged rioting in the Crown Heights section of Brooklyn in 1991. . . . The CDC finds that cigarette smoking among U.S. high school students rose by about a third between 1991 and 1997. Of 12,262 students surveyed in grades nine through 12 in 1997, 36.4% reported having smoked cigarettes during the previous month, up from 27.5% in 1991.	Former CIA officer Douglas F. Groat is arrested on espionage charges.		Reports revel that an international group of archaeologists have discovered an ancient array of stones and slabs in Egypt that appear to be constructed in alignment with astronomical events. The archaeologists state that different parts of the complex range in age from 5,000 to 7,000 years old.	The NCAA agrees to pay Fresno State basketball coach Jerry Tarkanian $2.5 million to settle the coach's claim that it harassed him and manufactured evidence of rules violations, closing a more than five-year-old suit. . . . At the World Figure Skating Championships in Minneapolis, Minnesota, Russia's Alexei Yagudin wins the men's title.	April 2
The UN Commission on Human Rights condemns the U.S. for arbitrary and racist use of the death penalty. . . . The Republican National Committee announces plans to broadcast Spanish-language responses to Pres. Clinton's weekly radio address as part of an effort to build GOP support among Hispanic voters in the run-up to the November elections. . . . A three-judge panel of the U.S. Fourth Circuit Court of Appeals in Richmond, Virginia, rules that the 12th Congressional District in North Carolina is an unconstitutional racial gerrymander.	U.S. district judge Kevin Duffy sentences Eyad Ismoil to 240 years in prison for his role in the 1993 bombing of the World Trade Center in New York City. Ismoil is the last of six suspects convicted on charges related to the bombing.	The Senate, by voice vote, approves the reappointment of Arthur Levitt Jr. as chairman of the Securities and Exchange Commission (SEC).		At the World Figure Skating Championships in Minneapolis, Minnesota, Russian couple of Anjelika Krylova and Oleg Ovsyannikov win the ice-dancing title. . . . John Sweeterman, 91, publisher of *The Washington Post*, 1961–68, dies in Chevy Chase, Maryland, of unreported causes.	April 3
				Michelle Kwan wins her second career women's title at the World Figure Skating Championships in Minneapolis, Minnesota. . . . Earth Summit wins the 151st running of Great Britain's Grand National Steeplechase in Liverpool, England.	April 4

F	G	H	I	J
Includes elections, federal-state relations, civil rights and liberties, crime, the judiciary, education, health care, poverty, urban affairs, and population.	*Includes formation and debate of U.S. foreign and defense policies, veterans' affairs, and defense spending. (Relations with specific foreign countries are usually found under the region concerned.)*	*Includes business, labor, agriculture, taxation, transportation, consumer affairs, monetary and fiscal policy, natural resources, and pollution.*	*Includes worldwide scientific, medical, and technological developments; natural phenomena; U.S. weather; natural disasters; and accidents.*	*Includes the arts, religion, scholarship, communications media, sports, entertainments, fashions, fads, and social life.*

	World Affairs	Europe	Africa & the Middle East	The Americas	Asia & the Pacific
April 5			Israeli troops wound six Palestinians near Jerusalem in demonstrations protesting the Mar. 29 slaying of Muhyideen al-Sharif.		
April 6	Britain and France ratify the Comprehensive Test Ban Treaty (CTBT), becoming the first nations with nuclear-weapons capabilities to do so. The treaty, which prohibits all nuclear weapons test explosions, has been ratified by 13 nations and requires the ratification of the 44 nations that possess either civilian or military nuclear power before it can officially take effect.	An antipersonnel mine explodes outside the Russian embassy in Riga, the capital of Latvia.	The International Committee of the Red Cross discloses that some 4,000 prisoners have been repatriated in the exchange between Iraq and Iran since April 2.		Pakistan successfully tests its domestically produced "Ghauri" medium-range missile, which has a range of approximately 900 miles (1,500 km) and is capable of hitting targets deep within the territory of neighboring India.
April 7				Twelve Cuban political prisoners, who were freed on the condition that they leave Cuba, arrive in Toronto, Canada.	Hong Kong's provisional legislature passes a law exempting the territorial government and the Chinese central government from certain laws, including privacy and antidiscrimination laws. The legislation transfers the exemptions granted to "the Crown" under British colonial rule to "the State," in what government officials describe as a routine aspect of decolonization.
April 8	Indonesia announces that it has reached agreement with the IMF on a new financial-rescue package. The pact, the third the country has reached in six months, will allow the resumption of an earlier $43 billion loan package offered to Indonesia by the IMF in late 1997. ... A British NATO force arrests two Bosnian Serbs wanted for alleged war crimes and crimes against humanity. The suspects, Miroslav Kvocka and Mladen Radic, were indicted in 1995 by the UN International Criminal Tribunal for the former Yugoslavia in The Hague, the Netherlands.				
April 9		Tens of thousands of workers across Russia hold demonstrations to protest economic conditions. ... Thousands of employees of Polish mining company KGHM return to work after a strike that started Mar. 30. ... Russia announces that it will reduce the amount of oil it channels through Latvia in response to the Latvian government's mistreatment of Russian-speaking citizens there.	At least 56 Tanzanian miners die due to severe flooding in the northern Arusha province that causes a number of mine shafts to collapse. ... Some 150 Islamic pilgrims die when they are crushed or suffocated as a rush to perform a holy ritual turns into a deadly stampede in the town of Mina in Saudi Arabia, near the holy city of Mecca.		
April 10	Reports confirm that the World Bank and the International Monetary Fund (IMF) have approved a $650 million debt-relief package for Uganda.	Political leaders tentatively agree to a groundbreaking settlement aimed at ending the long-running sectarian conflict in Northern Ireland. The settlement proposes fundamental changes in the way Northern Ireland is governed and requires approval by the Irish people and the British and Irish Parliaments. ... Torrential rains begin fall in central and eastern England.		Taniperlas, a farming cooperative founded by pro-EZLN Indians in Mexico, declares itself independent from the local government.	The Bank of Japan, the central bank, announces that it has disciplined 98 of its officials following an internal corruption investigation. ... Nguyen Co Thach, 75, Vietnamese foreign minister, 1980–91, dies in Hanoi, Vietnam.

A	B	C	D	E
Includes developments that affect more than one world region, international organizations, and important meetings of major world leaders.	*Includes all domestic and regional developments in Europe, including the Soviet Union, Turkey, Cyprus, and Malta.*	*Includes all domestic and regional developments in Africa and the Middle East, including Iraq and Iran and excluding Cyprus, Turkey, and Afghanistan.*	*Includes all domestic and regional developments in Latin America, the Caribbean, and Canada.*	*Includes all domestic and regional developments in Asia and Pacific nations, extending from Afghanistan through all the Pacific Island, except Hawaii.*

U.S. Politics & Social Issues	U.S. Foreign Policy & Defense	U.S. Economy & Environment	Science, Technology, & Nature	Culture, Leisure, & Lifestyle	
			(Frederick) Charles Frank, 87, British physicist who was the first scientist to suggest the notion of cold nuclear fusion, dies in Bristol, England, of unreported causes.	Golfer Gil Morgan, for the second year in a row, wins the Tradition, the first major competition of the year on the Senior PGA.	April 5
Reports confirm that a virulent strain of streptococcus bacteria infected 134 people in Texas and killed 33 of them between Dec. 1, 1997, and Mar. 20, 1998. . . . Pres. Clinton imposes a permanent ban on U.S. imports of certain types of assault weapons.		The Dow closes at 9033.23, above the 9000 mark for the first time. . . . Energy Secretary Federico F. Pena, citing personal and family reasons, announces that he will resign at the end of June. . . . Travelers Group Inc. and Citicorp announce that they will combine to form a new holding company, to be called Citigroup Inc. The merger is valued between $70 billion and $83 billion. If completed, the deal will be the largest merger in history and will create the world's biggest financial services company.	Federal health officials announce that a study conclusively shows that the drug tamoxifen may prevent breast cancer in women at high risk for the disease. . . . NASA releases a new image of a rock formation on the planet Mars that in a 1976 previous photograph resembled a human face and had prompted speculation that the formation had been constructed by an ancient civilization on Mars. In the new image, which is more detailed, the formation no longer resembles a face.	Tammy Wynette (born Virginia Wynette Pugh), 55, country music singer best known for her 1968 song "Stand by Your Man," dies in Nashville, Tennessee.	April 6
	A Defense Department study finds that discharges for homosexuality have risen by 67% since 1994, the first full year in which the Clinton administration's "don't ask, don't tell" policy was in effect. According to the study, 997 members of the military were discharged for being homosexual in 1997, compared with 597 in 1994.		A researcher studying arthritis patients suggests that women are more sensitive to pain than men are, but that women are more likely to find ways to cope with pain. . . . The National Academy of Sciences increases the recommended intake of folic acid and vitamin B6 for all people and of vitamin B12 for many groups.		April 7
A ban on a rarely performed late-term abortion procedure known medically as intact dilation and extraction (IDE) is signed in West Virginia. . . . The nation's major tobacco companies state they will no longer cooperate with Congress and the Clinton administration in seeking to implement a nationwide settlement of smoking-related lawsuits.		Reports suggest that two 20-year-old computer errors caused a $1.2 billion shortfall in Los Angeles County's pension fund.	A series of storms and tornadoes sweep from Mississippi through Alabama and Georgia. . . . Scientists assert that at least one of every eight known plant species on Earth is considered threatened or nearly extinct. The scientists cite continuing habitat destruction and the introduction of nonnative species into various regions of the world as the two chief causes of species endangerment.		April 8
The CDC reports that cases of tuberculosis (TB) in the U.S. declined in 1997 for the fifth straight year. There were 19,855 cases of TB in 1997, down 7% from the previous year and down 26% from 1992.	The Census Bureau reveals that 25.8 million U.S. residents, or 9.7% of the population, were born in foreign nations, the highest percentage since 1930. . . . Thousands of war veterans turn out in Andersonville, Georgia, for the dedication of the National Prisoner of War Museum. The center honors the roughly 800,000 Americans held as POWs in conflicts dating back to the American Revolution in 1776. Andersonville is the site of an infamous Civil War prison in which 13,000 of the 45,000 Union soldiers interned there died of starvation or disease.	Vice Pres. Al Gore announces that 31 departments and agencies of the federal government, under a program launched in 1997, have hired a total of 3,688 welfare recipients. . . . Reports state that two-time presidential candidate Ross Perot has ended his computer services company's policy of extending health-care benefits to same-sex partners of its employees. The company, Perot Systems Inc., is reportedly the first U.S. corporation to abandon such a policy after adopting it. Perot claims he ended the policy because it is unfair to unmarried heterosexual couples.	A series of storms and tornadoes sweeps through Mississippi, Alabama, and Georgia, killing at least 39 people since Apr. 8. Jefferson County, Alabama, is hit the hardest, when a tornado with winds reaching 250 miles per hour (400 kmph) blows through the area. Pres. Clinton declares parts of Alabama and Georgia disaster areas and makes federal aid available. . . . Researchers find that excessive doses of vitamin C may cause damage to a person's genetic material.	John Tate, 43, heavyweight boxing champion, 1979–80, who won a bronze medal in boxing at the 1976 Olympics in Montreal, Canada, dies in an automobile accident in Knoxville, Tennessee.	April 9
The National Cancer Institute reports that smoking cigars may be as dangerous to a person's health as smoking cigarettes.			Reports confirm that the U.S.'s EarthWatch Inc.'s *EarlyBird 1* satellite, the world's first commercial spy satellite, has been lost.	Archbishop Seraphim (born Vissarion Tikas), 84, leader of the Greek Orthodox Church since 1974, dies in Athens, Greece, after suffering from a viral infection and a kidney ailment.	April 10

F	G	H	I	J
Includes elections, federal-state relations, civil rights and liberties, crime, the judiciary, education, health care, poverty, urban affairs, and population.	Includes formation and debate of U.S. foreign and defense policies, veterans' affairs, and defense spending. (Relations with specific foreign countries are usually found under the region concerned.)	Includes business, labor, agriculture, taxation, transportation, consumer affairs, monetary and fiscal policy, natural resources, and pollution.	Includes worldwide scientific, medical, and technological developments; natural phenomena; U.S. weather; natural disasters; and accidents.	Includes the arts, religion, scholarship, communications media, sports, entertainments, fashions, fads, and social life.

	World Affairs	Europe	Africa & the Middle East	The Americas	Asia & the Pacific
April 11		Torrential rains lead to record-setting flooding in much of central and eastern England. The floods, regarded as the regions' worst such disaster in at least 50 years, result in at least five deaths.	Nicholas Steyn, a white farmer, shoots and kills a black infant and wounds another child as they cross his property in the rural town of Benoni, near Johannesburg. It is the latest in a string of incidents in recent months that exposes lingering racial tensions in South Africa. . . . PNA police arrest Adel Awadallah, the top West Bank military commander of Hamas, during a sweep of suspects involved in the death of Muhyideen al-Sharif, an alleged bomb maker wanted by Israel.	More than 500 state and federal police officers raid Taniperlas, a Mexican farming cooperative founded by pro-EZLN Indians that declared itself independent from the local government on Apr. 10. . . . The Colombian military renews ground offensives against leftist rebels of the Revolutionary Armed Forces of Colombia (FARC).	In Beijing, the capital of China, the governments of North Korea and South Korea hold their first direct talks since 1994.
April 12				Twelve foreigners of various nationalities are accused of interfering in Mexico's internal political affairs and of sympathizing with the leftist rebel Zapatista National Liberation Army (EZLN), and they are expelled from Mexico.	
April 13	In its World Economic Outlook, the IMF forecasts a global economic expansion of 3.1% in 1998—the slowest growth rate in five years—and of 3.7% in 1999.	Turkish armed forces attack Kurdish rebels in northern Iraq and capture Semdin Sakik, the former second-highest-ranking official in the Kurdistan Workers' Party (PKK), the main Kurdish separatist group. . . . Sir Ian Kinloch MacGregor, 85, chairman of British Steel PLC, 1980–83, and Britain's National Coal Board, 1983–86, dies in Somerset, England.	Reports state that that 21 people have been rescued from the Apr. 9 flooding in mines in the Tanzanian Arusha province. Companies estimate that as many as 100 workers were trapped inside when the flooding occurred. . . . Bahi Ladgham, 85, prime minister of Tunisia, 1969–70, dies of a heart attack in Paris, France.		
April 14		The Irish government releases nine members of the IRA from prison ahead of schedule. . . . Hans Hermann Groer, an Austrian cardinal accused of sexually molesting young boys, agrees to surrender all his duties in the Roman Catholic Church and go into exile, as requested by Pope John Paul II. . . . Dorothy Squires (born Edna May Squires), 83, popular British singer, dies of lung cancer near Trebanog, South Wales.	Riot police in Teheran, the capital of Iran, break up a demonstration by as many as 4,000 students calling for the release of the mayor, Gholamhossein Karbaschi.	German Emilio Ornes, 78, publisher of a Dominican Republic newspaper and an advocate of press freedoms, dies of a heart attack in Santo Domingo, Dominican Republic.	Reports reveal that a "red tide," a flourishing of toxic algae, appeared in the waters off Hong Kong, devastating the territory's fishery stocks and forcing the closure of its beaches. . . . Reports confirm that India will lift import restrictions on 340 items.
April 15	The finance ministers and central bankers of the Group of Seven (G-7) wealthiest industrialized nations call on Japan to take timely steps to shore up its troubled economy.	Turkish military officials disclose that 75 people—64 PKK rebels and 11 Turkish soldiers—have been killed over the previous two days in fighting along the border between Turkey and Iraq.	In Iran, Ayatollah Ali Khamenei orders the mayor of Teheran, Gholamhossein Karbaschi, free on bail. . . . In Somalia, ten relief workers are taken hostage by heavily armed men in Mogadishu, the capital. . . . Israel frees Ahmed Qatamesh, 46, a reputed leader of the militant Popular Front for the Liberation of Palestine (PFLP), and permits him to return to the West Bank city of Al-Bireh.		Pol Pot (born Saloth Sar), leader of the Khmer Rouge whose age is reportedly between 73 and 76, dies of heart failure at a jungle outpost near the Dangrek mountains in Cambodia. Pol Pot, charged with overseeing the deaths of as many as 2 million people from 1975 to 1979 while his Khmer Rouge guerrilla army ruled Cambodia, had evaded international efforts to capture him and try him for genocide.
April 16		Unidentified gunmen attack a Russian military convoy in the North Ossetia section of the Caucasus region, killing a general and three other officers. Seven soldiers are wounded. . . . Sir Ronald Graeme Millar, 78, British playwright and speechwriter for Conservative prime minister Margaret Thatcher, dies in London, England.	A Rwanda court convicts Rev. Jean-François Kayiranga and Rev. Edouard Nkurikiye of organizing the execution of 2,000 Tutsis seeking refuge in a Catholic church in the town of Kivumu. The priests are the first church officials convicted on charges related to the massacres. . . . The Egyptian government's Supreme Press Council initiates a widespread purge of independent-minded editors on state-owned publications, replacing them with staunch backers of the regime of Pres. Hosni Mubarak.	Reports confirm that leftist rebels of the Revolutionary Armed Forces of Colombia (FARC) still hold four of the 14 hostages kidnapped Mar. 23. . . . Marie-Louise Meilleur, 117, a Canadian woman listed as the oldest living person in the world, dies.	Workers at Kia Motors Corp., which was placed into court receivership, go on strike.

A	B	C	D	E
Includes developments that affect more than one world region, international organizations, and important meetings of major world leaders.	Includes all domestic and regional developments in Europe, including the Soviet Union, Turkey, Cyprus, and Malta.	Includes all domestic and regional developments in Africa and the Middle East, including Iraq and Iran and excluding Cyprus, Turkey, and Afghanistan.	Includes all domestic and regional developments in Latin America, the Caribbean, and Canada.	Includes all domestic and regional developments in Asia and Pacific nations, extending from Afghanistan through all the Pacific Island, except Hawaii.

U.S. Politics & Social Issues	U.S. Foreign Policy & Defense	U.S. Economy & Environment	Science, Technology, & Nature	Culture, Leisure, & Lifestyle	
					April 11
Marvin Eugene Wolfgang, 73, leading criminologist whose work was revolutionary when it focused on patterns of criminal violence that emerge from great masses of data, dies in Philadelphia, Pennsylvania, of pancreatic cancer.				Mark O'Meara wins the 62nd Masters tournament at the Augusta National Golf Club. . . . James B. Conkling, 83, president of Columbia Records, 1951–56, who became the first president of Warner Bros. Records in 1958, dies in Sacramento, California, of pneumonia and diabetes.	**April 12**
A law banning a rarely performed late term abortion procedure known medically as intact dilaton and extraction (IDE) is signed in Virginia. . . . Maryland's General Assembly passes a bill allowing the state to present statistical evidence in its lawsuit seeking compensation from the tobacco industry for the cost of treating smoking-related illnesses. . . . The Supreme Court lets stand the Apr. 3 lower-court ruling that orders North Carolina to redraw its 12th Congressional District.		BankAmerica Corp. announces plans to merge with NationsBank Corp., in a stock transaction valued at $60 billion. If successful, the merger will create the nation's largest bank in terms of deposits. . . . Banc One Corp. reveals plans to merge with First Chicago NBD Corp., in a stock swap worth an estimated $30 billion. . . . William Burwell Fitzgerald, 65, cofounder of what became the Independence Federal Savings bank, one of the U.S.'s largest black-owned businesses, dies in Washington, D.C., of complications from pneumonia.	Researchers report that the world's first clone of an adult mammal, a sheep named Dolly, has given birth to a female lamb, Bonnie. The birth confirms that Dolly can "breed normally and produce healthy offspring."		**April 13**
Eight members of the Republic of Texas separatist group are convicted in Dallas, Texas, on federal fraud charges. One member is acquitted. Richard McLaren, the group's leader, is serving 99 years in prison on state charges related to a 1997 kidnapping and standoff. . . . A Tampa, Florida, judge formally sentences convicted murderer Lawrence Singleton, found guilty of first-degree murder in the 1997 fatal stabbing of Roxanne Hayes, to death.	Despite protests from the U.S. State Department, the government of Paraguay, and the World Court, convicted murderer Angel Francisco Breard, 32, is put to death by lethal injection in Jarratt, Virginia, after the Supreme Court votes, 6-3, to deny requests for a stay. The protests stem from the fact that Breard was denied his right to contact the Paraguayan consulate after his arrest. Breard is the 452nd person executed in the U.S. and the 50th in Virginia since 1976.	The director of the White House OMB, Franklin D. Raines, announces his resignation. Pres. Clinton appoints OMB deputy director Jacob J. Lew to replace Raines. . . . The New York State legislature passes a $71.5 billion budget for the 1998–99 fiscal year, which began Apr. 1. . . . Maurice Hubert Stans, 90, U.S. secretary of commerce, 1969–72, and finance chair for Pres. Richard Nixon's reelection committee, 1972–73, dies in Pasadena, California, after suffering a heart attack.	Two teams of scientists report they have discovered a key clue to how the rhinovirus, the virus that causes colds, enters human cells.	Pres. Clinton hosts a televised discussion on the role of race in American sports. . . . Pulitzer Prizes are awarded to playwright Paula Vogel, writer Jared Diamond, and novelist Philip Roth. The late composer George Gershwin receives a special citation for his enduring contributions to music in the U.S.	**April 14**
The San Francisco Superior Court orders the closure of the Cannabis Cultivators Club, a medical-marijuana club. . . . A law banning a rarely performed late-term abortion procedure known as intact dilaton and extraction (IDE) is signed in Oklahoma. . . . Ordway Hilton, 84, leading authority on detecting forged documents, dies in Spartanburg, South Carolina, of unreported causes.			A New York City jury convicts Columbia University graduate student Oliver Jovanovic of kidnapping and assaulting a woman he met over the Internet. The case received national attention because it is one of the first Internet-related crimes of its kind to go to trial. . . . Researchers estimate that between 76,000 and 137,000 hospital patients in the U.S. die each year from adverse reactions to medications.	The annual George Polk Memorial Awards are presented to journalists Laurie Garrett and Keith Bradsher journalists. Pennsylvania's *Pittsburgh Courier* receives a special Polk Career Award as the most influential source of news geared toward black readers.	**April 15**
Independent counsel Kenneth W. Starr reveals that he has withdrawn his agreement to become dean of the schools of law and of public policy at Pepperdine University in Malibu, California, claiming that his latest investigation of Pres. Clinton "has expanded considerably and the end is not yet in sight." . . . Massachusetts authorities arrest Stephen Fagan, a Florida man accused of kidnapping his two young daughters in 1979 during a weekend custody visit.			Tornadoes kill 10 people in Arkansas, Tennessee, and Kentucky. . . . A study finds that women who undergo mammogram examinations every year for 10 years have a 50% chance of getting a result indicating the presence of breast cancer that later turns out to be false. . . . Alberto Calderon, 77, Argentine-born mathematician and a pioneer in the field of mathematical analysis who received Israel's Wolf Prize in 1989 and won the U.S.'s National Medal of Science, in 1991, dies in Chicago, Illinois, of unreported causes.	Three separate juries in Los Angeles, California, render guilty verdicts for Tak Sun Tan, 21, Jason Chan, 20, and Indra Lim, 21, who were charged with the 1996 murder of Dr. Haing S. Ngor. Ngor, a trained gynecologist and a Cambodian refugee activist, won a best supporting actor Academy Award in 1985 for his debut role in *The Killing Fields*.	**April 16**

F	G	H	I	J
Includes elections, federal-state relations, civil rights and liberties, crime, the judiciary, education, health care, poverty, urban affairs, and population.	*Includes formation and debate of U.S. foreign and defense policies, veterans' affairs, and defense spending. (Relations with specific foreign countries are usually found under the region concerned.)*	*Includes business, labor, agriculture, taxation, transportation, consumer affairs, monetary and fiscal policy, natural resources, and pollution.*	*Includes worldwide scientific, medical, and technological developments; natural phenomena; U.S. weather; natural disasters; and accidents.*	*Includes the arts, religion, scholarship, communications media, sports, entertainments, fashions, fads, and social life.*

	World Affairs	Europe	Africa & the Middle East	The Americas	Asia & the Pacific
April 17		An unidentified man is shot and killed in a Catholic section of Belfast, Northern Ireland.	UN secretary general Kofi Annan announces that a UN human-rights team investigating allegations that rebel forces under the command of Pres. Laurent Kabila massacred thousands of Rwandan Hutu refugees during the seven-month rebellion that brought Kabila to power in May 1997 will withdraw from the Democratic Republic of the Congo since it is facing repeated obstacles that has delayed the probe.... Three members of an English family are taken hostage in Yemen.	The Canadian Imperial Bank of Commerce (CIBC) and the Toronto-Dominion Bank, Canada's largest and fifth-largest banks in terms of assets, respectively, announce plans to merge. The deal, which is a stock transaction valued at C$46.7 billion (US$32.2 billion), will create the second-largest Canadian bank and the ninth-largest bank in North America in terms of assets.	Thousands of workers demonstrating against mass layoffs in Seoul, the capital of South Korea, clash with riot police wielding tear gas.... Thai military officials, in the presence of a group of journalists, confirm that Pol Pot has died. King Norodom Sihanouk of Cambodia, who in the past aligned himself with the Khmer Rouge states, "We have been liberated from Pol Pot Now our nation can be very peaceful."
April 18	Leaders of 34 Western Hemisphere countries meet in Santiago, Chile, for the second Summit of the Americas. At the summit, the leaders agree to begin formal negotiations on creating the Free Trade Area of the Americas (FTAA), a free-trade zone that will stretch throughout the entire hemisphere, by the year 2005. If created, the FTAA will be the world's largest trading bloc, containing some 800 million people.		Rwandan radio reports that Rev. Jean-François Kayiranga and Rev. Edouard Nkurikiye, two Roman Catholic priests convicted on Apr. 16, have been sentenced to death by a Rwandan court for their roles in the 1994 massacres.	Paraguay's electoral tribunal bars retired general Lino Cesar Oviedo, the former head of the armed forces convicted of attempting to lead a 1996 military coup, from running in May presidential elections as the ruling Colorado Party's candidate.... Unidentified gunmen murder lawyer Eduardo Umana Mendoza, a leading human-rights advocate, in his office in Bogota, the capital of Columbia.	
April 19		Austrian voters elect conservative president Thomas Klestil to a second six-year term.... Lord Denis Herbert Howell, 74, British member of Parliament, 1955–59, 1961–98, dies of a heart attack in Birmingham, England.	One Jewish settler is killed and one member of an unarmed group of Palestinian goatherds is seriously wounded in a clash over disputed farmland near the West Bank city of Hebron.	Sergio Roberto Viera da Motta, 57, Brazil's communications minister, dies after a lengthy battle with lung disease.	Chinese authorities grant medical parole to Wang Dan, a prominent dissident imprisoned for most of the previous nine years, and place him on a flight to the U.S. Wang, 29, was a leader of the 1989 pro-democracy demonstrations in Tiananmen Square in Beijing, the capital of China.
April 20		Germany's Red Army Faction (RAF), a left-wing guerrilla group that waged a terror campaign in Germany during the 1970s and 1980s and is held responsible for 50 killings, announces that it has disbanded.	The Peace Corps states that it has withdrawn all of its volunteers and suspended funding for its program in Chad due to violent incidents associated with ongoing civil unrest in the central African nation. ... Archbishop Ernest Urban Trevor Huddleston, 84, British-born opponent of apartheid who helped found the Anti-Apartheid Movement in the late 1950s, dies in England after suffering from diabetes.	A passenger jet carrying 53 people crashes into a mountain in dense fog near Bogota, the capital of Columbia, killing everyone on board.... In protest of the Apr. 18 killing of Eduardo Umana Mendoza, many of Colombia's public-sector unions hold a day-long strike. At least 5,000 people gather in Bogota for his funeral.	UN-Taliban tensions are heightened when Taliban officials refuse to meet with UN aid coordinator Alfredo Witschi-Cestari of Venezuela.
April 21	The UN Commission on Human Rights passes a resolution condemning Nigeria for egregious human-rights abuses within the country's justice system. Separately, it rejects a U.S. proposal to renew the UN's mandate to monitor human rights in Cuba. The vote means that the UN will end its seven-year-old practice of retaining a human rights investigator specifically for Cuba.	A state security court in Diyarbakir, Turkey, convicts Recep Tayyip Erdogan, the mayor of Istanbul, and sentences him to 10 months in jail on charges of "inciting hatred" in a 1997 speech in which he mentioned Islam in the context of political reform.	Shi'ite cleric Sheik Morteza Ali Mohammed Ibrahim Borujerdi, an Iranian, is slain by a gunman after leading prayers at a mosque in Najaf, a Shi'ite holy city in Iran.	Luis Eduardo Magalhaes, 43, the leader of Brazilian president Fernando Henrique Cardoso's party in the lower house of Congress, dies unexpectedly of a heart attack.	
April 22		Yugoslav army forces kill at least 19 ethnic Albanians in clashes near the Albanian border.		The New Brunswick Court of Appeals vote unanimously to overturn a lower-court decision that granted the province's native population the right to harvest and sell timber from state-owned land in Canada.	

A	B	C	D	E
Includes developments that affect more than one world region, international organizations, and important meetings of major world leaders.	Includes all domestic and regional developments in Europe, including the Soviet Union, Turkey, Cyprus, and Malta.	Includes all domestic and regional developments in Africa and the Middle East, including Iraq and Iran and excluding Cyprus, Turkey, and Afghanistan.	Includes all domestic and regional developments in Latin America, the Caribbean, and Canada.	Includes all domestic and regional developments in Asia and Pacific nations, extending from Afghanistan through all the Pacific Island, except Hawaii.

U.S. Politics & Social Issues	U.S. Foreign Policy & Defense	U.S. Economy & Environment	Science, Technology, & Nature	Culture, Leisure, & Lifestyle	
A Detroit, Michigan, judge sentences former police officer Walter Budzyn to four to 15 years in prison for involuntary manslaughter in the 1992 beating death of black motorist Malice Green. Budzyn was convicted in 1993 of second-degree murder and sentenced to 18 years in prison for the same crime. However, in 1997 the Michigan State Supreme Court overturned the initial conviction and ordered a new trial.		The Labor Department states that CoreStates Financial Corp. has agreed to pay nearly $1.5 million in back wages and salary adjustments to 142 female and minority managers. The settlement is the largest ever in a case brought by the compliance program.... The Commerce Department reports that in February the U.S. recorded a seasonally adjusted $12.11 billion deficit in trade in goods and services, up 4.2% from January's revised deficit of $11.62 billion. February's trade gap is the highest level registered in a decade.	The space shuttle *Columbia* lifts off from Kennedy Space Center in Cape Canaveral, Florida, on a mission devoted entirely to experiments investigating the effects of microgravity on the brain and nervous system.	Officials from the *Guinness Book of Records* inform Sarah Clark Knauss, 117, of Allentown, Pennsylvania, that she is now listed as the world's oldest living person.... Linda Eastman McCartney (born Linda Louise Eastman), 56, wife of Paul McCartney and an advocate of animal rights and vegetarianism, dies near Tucson, Arizona, of breast cancer that spread to her liver.	April 17
Terry Sanford, 80, Democratic governor of North Carolina, 1961–65, and U.S. senator, 1986–92, dies in Durham, North Carolina, of complications from cancer.			Data reveals that a series of severe tornadoes that swept through the southeast U.S. in late March and early April killed more than 60 people.		April 18
		A 12,000-gallon (45,480-liter) shipment of napalm gel arrives for storage at California's China Lake Naval Weapons Center, one week after Pollution Control Industries of East Chicago, Indiana, reneged on a deal to recycle the potentially dangerous substance.		Golfer Hale Irwin wins the PGA Seniors' Championship.... Kenya's Tegla Loroupe sets a world record of 2:20:47 in a marathon.... Italian architect Renzo Piano wins the 1998 Pritzker Architecture Prize.... Octavio Paz, 84, Mexican poet and essayist who won the 1990 Nobel Prize in literature, dies in Mexico City.	April 19
A federal jury in Chicago, Illinois, finds that antiabortion activists Joseph Scheidler, Timothy Murphy, and Andrew Scholberg violated a federal racketeering law by conducting a campaign to intimidate abortion providers and patients.... The Clinton administration reveals that scientific studies have shown that needle-exchange programs for intravenous drug users reduces the spread of HIV, the virus that causes AIDS, and that they do not promote drug use.			The American Society of Clinical Oncology reports that two preliminary studies have shown that the drug raloxifene may prevent breast cancer.	Moses Tanui of Kenya wins the men's race at the Boston Marathon. Ethiopia's Fatuma Roba wins the women's race.	April 20
		The Dow closes at a record high of 9184.94. That marks the 23rd record high of 1998 and the sixth record high registered in April 1998.	Two teams of astronomers announce that they have independently observed evidence of the early formation of a group of planets around a young star. Using a recently developed kind of infrared camera, the astronomers saw a disk of dust and gas around the star HR 4796. HR 4796, about 10 million years old, is located 220 light years from Earth, in the constellation Centaurus.	Helen Ward, 81, jazz singer in the 1930s, dies in Arlington, Virginia, of unreported causes.... Jean-François Lyotard, 73, French philosopher of a loosely defined movement known popularly as post-modernism, or deconstructionism, dies in Paris, France, of leukemia.	April 21
Amy Grossberg, 19, pleads guilty in Delaware Superior Court to manslaughter in the 1996 death of her infant son, who was found dead in a trash container. Brian Peterson, 19, the baby's father, pled guilty to manslaughter on Mar. 9.... In *California v. Deep Sea Research*, the Supreme Court rules unanimously that federal courts have authority to rule in cases stemming from disputes over property rights to ships that sunk in state waters.	In *Miller v. Albright*, the Supreme Court rules, 6-3, to uphold a lower-court ruling that denied U.S. citizenship to a woman whose mother is Filipino and whose father is a U.S. citizen.... Jose Villafuerte, 45, a Honduran convicted of murder, is executed by lethal injection in Florence, Arizona, despite pleas by Honduran foreign minister Fernando Martinez for clemency since Villafuerte was denied his right, under the Vienna Convention, to contact the Honduran consulate after his arrest. He is the 454th person executed in the U.S. and the 10th in Arizona since 1976.	The House votes, 238-186, in favor of a constitutional amendment that would make it more difficult to raise taxes. The vote is 45 votes short of the two-thirds majority required for passage. It marks the third time in three years that the measure has failed in the House.			April 22

F	G	H	I	J
Includes elections, federal-state relations, civil rights and liberties, crime, the judiciary, education, health care, poverty, urban affairs, and population.	Includes formation and debate of U.S. foreign and defense policies, veterans' affairs, and defense spending. (Relations with specific foreign countries are usually found under the region concerned.)	Includes business, labor, agriculture, taxation, transportation, consumer affairs, monetary and fiscal policy, natural resources, and pollution.	Includes worldwide scientific, medical, and technological developments; natural phenomena; U.S. weather; natural disasters; and accidents.	Includes the arts, religion, scholarship, communications media, sports, entertainments, fashions, fads, and social life.

	World Affairs	Europe	Africa & the Middle East	The Americas	Asia & the Pacific
April 23		A group of U.S. security agents and scientists remove several pounds of weapons-grade uranium and spent fuel from a poorly protected nuclear plant outside of Tbilisi, Georgia's capital. The uranium is transported to a nuclear facility in Dounreay, Scotland, where it will be more safely stored.... Constantine Karamanlis, 91, Greek premier, 1955–63, 1974–80, and president, 1980–85, 1990–95, dies in Athens, Greece, after suffering from a respiratory infection and heart and kidney ailments.			The Great Hural, Mongolia's 76-member parliament, elects Tsakhiagiin Elbegdorj as the country's new premier.... Taiwanese and Chinese officials meet in Beijing, China's capital, to reopen talks broken off in 1995.... Reports suggest that some 1,500 troops have defected from Khmer Rouge strongman Ta Mok, widely known as "the Butcher" for his role in the 1970s genocide, since Mar. 21.
April 24	The Geneva, Switzerland–based World Economic Forum (WEF) announces that the 1998 annual meeting of the Middle East–North Africa Economic Conference (MENA) has been suspended because of the continued impasse in Arab-Israeli peace negotiations.	The lower house of the Russian legislature, the Duma, confirms Sergei Kiriyenko as the country's premier.	The 10 relief workers taken hostage Apr. 15 in Mogadishu, the capital of Somalia, are freed.... The Rwandan government executes by firing squad 22 people convicted of committing genocide during the nation's 1994 civil war.	Roman Catholic bishop Juan Gerardi Conedera, who heads the human rights office of the Guatemala City archdiocese, presents a harsh critique of the Guatemalan army's human-rights record during the country's 36-year-long civil war that ended in December 1996.	Hundreds of people in Zhangjiajie in China's Hunan province protest a ban against direct marketing recently enacted in China.
April 25		A dam at southern Spain's Los Frailes zinc mine bursts, releasing some 150 million cubic feet of toxic sludge into the nearby Guadiamar River. The mine waste spreads to farmland adjoining the river, contaminating thousands of acres and imperiling local wildlife.	Fewer than 10% of registered voters turn out for legislative elections in Nigeria.	A faction of the leftist rebel Revolutionary Armed Forces of Colombia (FARC) releases the final two hostages whom they captured in late March.	Fighting erupts north of Kabul, the capital of Afghanistan.
April 26				Roman Catholic bishop Juan Gerardi Conedera, who on Apr. 24 presented a harsh critique of the Guatemalan army's human rights record, is found dead in the garage of his house in Guatemala City, the capital. He apparently was beaten to death with a concrete block.	Police in New Delhi, India, begin to halt a 48-day hunger strike by six Tibetans appealing to the UN to take up the issue of Chinese rule over Tibet, by forcibly putting the protestors in the care of a hospital. ... The Taliban and the Northern Alliance, comprised of ethnic Uzbek and Tajik forces and the Muslim Shi'ite group Hizb-i-Wahdat, open talks.
April 27		Some 500,000 Danish workers— about 10% of the country's population and 20% of its workforce—go on strike.... Yugoslav army forces kill at least three ethnic Albanians. Their deaths bring the total number killed in clashes between ethnic Albanians and Yugoslav government forces to more than 120 since February.... The body of an unidentified man is found in County Louth, Ireland. Security officials suspect that hardline Catholic guerrillas killed the man, and that he may have been an informer.		John White Hughes Bassett Jr., 82, Canadian newspaper publisher and broadcasting executive, dies in Toronto, Ontario, while suffering the effects of a major heart attack in 1994.	Japan's finance ministry announces that it has disciplined 112 officials following an internal corruption investigation.... Thupten Ngodup, a former Tibetan monk who was not among the hunger strikers forced into hospitalized care in India, sets himself on fire in protest of the Apr. 26 breakup of the fast. ... Nguyen Van Linh (born Nguyen Van Cuc), 82, general secretary of the Vietnamese Communist Party, 1986–91, dies in Ho Chi Minh City, Vietnam, after suffering from liver cancer.
April 28			A military tribunal in the Nigerian town of Jos condemns the former deputy head of state and five other men to death for attempting to overthrow the military government of Gen. Sani Abacha.	An attack on a Colombian village near the northern city of Urrao leaves at least 22 civilians dead.	Authorities in Hong Kong complete a seizure of US$90 million worth of pirated audio and video compact discs, along with equipment used to manufacture them, in what was reportedly the world's largest such confiscation ever.... The government reports that Japan's unemployment rate rose in March to 3.9%, from 3.6% in February. The March jobless rate was the country's highest since the current method of calculating unemployment began in 1953.

A	B	C	D	E
Includes developments that affect more than one world region, international organizations, and important meetings of major world leaders.	*Includes all domestic and regional developments in Europe, including the Soviet Union, Turkey, Cyprus, and Malta.*	*Includes all domestic and regional developments in Africa and the Middle East, including Iraq and Iran and excluding Cyprus, Turkey, and Afghanistan.*	*Includes all domestic and regional developments in Latin America, the Caribbean, and Canada.*	*Includes all domestic and regional developments in Asia and Pacific nations, extending from Afghanistan through all the Pacific Island, except Hawaii.*

U.S. Politics & Social Issues	U.S. Foreign Policy & Defense	U.S. Economy & Environment	Science, Technology, & Nature	Culture, Leisure, & Lifestyle	
The first nationwide survey seeking to determine how often physicians provide assistance to terminally ill patients who wish to commit suicide shows that some 6% of the doctors who respond to a 1996 survey provided such assistance at least once either by prescribing medication or administering a lethal injection, or both. . . . James Earl Ray, 70, convicted killer of civil-rights activist Rev. Martin Luther King Jr., dies in Nashville, Tennessee, after suffering from liver disease and kidney ailments.	A federal grand jury in Fort Pierce, Florida, indicts a group of Mexicans for operating a prostitution ring in the U.S. using illegal immigrants from Mexico. The 52-count indictment charges 16 defendants with forcing at least 20 women to work as prostitutes over an 18-month period in rural Florida and South Carolina. Some of the women involved are as young as 14.	The CDC reports that homicide is the second-leading cause of U.S. job-related deaths, surpassing injuries caused by machinery. Murders account for 13.5% of such deaths between 1980 and 1994. The leading cause is motor vehicle accidents, accounting for 23.1% of work-related deaths. . . . The Senate approves, 56-43, a Republican-authored bill that provides a tax break for families saving money to pay for primary and secondary education.		An unidentified family donates eight 19th-century documents related to slavery to the Underground Railroad Freedom Center in Cincinnati, Ohio.	April 23
The Florida State Senate passes a package of electoral reforms designed to prevent the types of voter fraud that had tarnished the 1997 Miami elections. . . . Andrew Wurst, a 14-year-old middle-school student, allegedly opens fire at a school dance near Edinboro, Pennsylvania, killing a teacher and wounding two students and a second teacher.				Mel Powell (born Melvin Epstein), 75, composer and jazz musician who won the Pulitzer Prize in 1990, dies in Sherman Oaks, California, reportedly of liver cancer.	April 24
				Wright Morris, 88, who wrote 33 books as well as short stories and essays and who won the 1957 National Book Award, dies in Mill Valley, California, of unreported causes.	April 25
				Dominique Aury (born Anne Desclos), 90, French author who wrote the 1954 erotic novel *The Story of O*, dies in Paris, France, of unreported causes.	April 26
A federal appeals court in Cincinnati, Ohio, rules that the city cannot impose spending limits on candidates running in municipal elections.		Data suggests that the 500 largest U.S. companies in 1997 saw their aggregate profit growth rate fall to 7.8% from 23.3% in 1996. The median stock-market return of ranked firms in 1997 was 30.5%, up from 20.9% in 1996. . . . Michael Cherkasky, a federally appointed election overseer, rules that James P. Hoffa's 1996 campaign for the Teamsters union presidency broke several fund-raising rules, but that the violations were not sufficient to disqualify Hoffa from participating in a rerun election.	Daniel Carleton Gajdusek, a Nobel Prize-winning scientist, is released from a Maryland prison after serving almost one year for molesting a teenaged boy whom he had brought to the U.S. from a Micronesian island where Gajdusek conducted field research.	Carlos Cesar Arana Castaneda, whose age was reported to be 67 or 73 and who wrote the best-selling book series that present the teachings of a native American shaman named Don Juan Matus whose existence was never verified, dies in Los Angeles, California, of liver cancer. . . . *Black and Blue*, by Anna Quindlen, tops the bestseller list.	April 27
The Arizona Supreme Court strikes down Arizona's English-only law, which required state and local governments to use only English in all official business. . . . The Florida State House passes a package of electoral reforms designed to prevent the types of voter fraud that had tarnished the 1997 Miami elections. . . . In *Edwards v. United States*, the Supreme Court rules unanimously to give federal judges broader discretion in setting prison sentences in cocaine-trafficking cases.	The General Accounting Office (GAO), the investigative arm of Congress, reports that a U.S.-led international embargo against arms sales to China is not preventing the country from acquiring weapons abroad. . . . The Senate, by voice vote, confirms former army secretary Togo D. West Jr. as the secretary of the Department of Veterans Affairs (VA). . . . Congress clears a bill to pay $1 billion that the U.S. owes the UN in back dues. However, the bill also contains antiabortion provisions.	The Senate gives final congressional approval to the fiscal 1998–99 State Department authorization bill in a close 51-49 vote.	Scientists report that early human species may have been capable of speech much earlier than previously thought. The claim is based on studies of Neanderthal skulls, which suggest speech capability about 400,000 years ago, some 10 times earlier than previously thought.		April 28

F	G	H	I	J
Includes elections, federal-state relations, civil rights and liberties, crime, the judiciary, education, health care, poverty, urban affairs, and population.	Includes formation and debate of U.S. foreign and defense policies, veterans' affairs, and defense spending. (Relations with specific foreign countries are usually found under the region concerned.)	Includes business, labor, agriculture, taxation, transportation, consumer affairs, monetary and fiscal policy, natural resources, and pollution.	Includes worldwide scientific, medical, and technological developments; natural phenomena; U.S. weather; natural disasters; and accidents.	Includes the arts, religion, scholarship, communications media, sports, entertainments, fashions, fads, and social life.

	World Affairs	Europe	Africa & the Middle East	The Americas	Asia & the Pacific
April 29	The six-nation "contact group" monitoring internal strife in the Balkan region declares an international freeze on all the Yugoslav government's foreign assets in an attempt to pressure the government of Pres. Slobodan Milosevic to reach a peaceful settlement with ethnic Albanian separatists in Kosovo. . . . A summit meeting of leaders from the Commonwealth of Independent States (CIS) names Boris Berezovsky as the organization's executive secretary.		Lieutenant General Siphiwe Nyanda, a former leader in the armed struggle against apartheid, is appointed to head South Africa's armed forces. Nyanda will be the first black to head the South African military and will replace Gen. Georg Meiring, who announced his resignation in April amid accusations that he gave the government a false report of an impending coup.	Thousands of mourners gather in Guatemala City for a march and a candlelight vigil to honor Roman Catholic bishop Juan Gerardi Conedera, who was found dead April 26.	Escalating protests by Indonesians in the city of Medan in northern Sumatra prompt the closure of the University of North Sumatra. . . . Bai Baoshan, named "Public Enemy Number One" by the Chinese government in 1997, is executed in the northwestern province of Xinjiang.
April 30	Argentine police arrest Dinko Sakic, a Croatian World War II veteran and suspected war criminal. He drew international attention in April after he admitted on Argentine television that he commanded a notorious World War II death camp in Nazi-controlled Croatia.		U.S. vice president Al Gore, during a tour of the Middle East, attends the official ceremony in West Jerusalem marking Israel's 50th anniversary as a modern state. . . . Nizar Qabbani, 75, Syrian poet considered one of the greatest writers of verse in Arab literature, dies in London, England, of a heart attack.		Reports from China reveal that the Apr. 24 protests in Zhangjiajie, Hunan province, and protests in Hengyang turned into riots resulting in 10 deaths. Separately, riot police in Chengdu, in Sichuan province, clash with some 3,000 street market vendors when police attempt to shut down their stalls.
May 1	Former Rwandan premier Jean Kambanda pleads guilty to six counts of genocide before the UN International Criminal Tribunal for Rwanda that is investigating charges that Rwandans participated in the massacre of some 500,000 ethnic Tutsis and moderate Hutus during the central African country's 1994 civil war. Kambanda is the first Hutu official to acknowledge the extent of the government's role in the 1994 massacres, and his plea marks the first conviction for the three-year-old tribunal.	In Leipzig, some 3,000 neo-Nazis attend one of Germany's largest neo-Nazi rallies in recent years. Some 5,000 leftists hold a counterdemonstration. Police use water cannons to keep the neo-Nazis and leftists apart, and 27 people from both sides are arrested. . . . Unidentified armed assailants kidnap Valentin Vlasov, Russian president Boris Yeltsin's personal envoy to the separatist republic of Chechnya. . . . A suspected republican activist is killed in a shootout with police in County Wicklow, Ireland.	Police in the Nigerian city of Ibadan open fire on a crowd of demonstrators after an antigovernment rally escalates into a riot. An estimated 5,000 protesters, mostly from the Yoruba ethnic group, march through the city when some set fire to cars, shops and houses. At least seven people are reportedly killed by police gunfire.	Mexican police raid an autonomous township run by EZLN supporters near Amparo Agua Tinta, a village located on the Guatemalan border, arresting 47 people.	At a May Day rally in Seoul's Chongro park, riot police in armored cars fire tear gas at demonstrators. Some protesters charge the police, wielding pipes, iron bars, and chunks of sidewalk. . . . Hundreds of thousands of workers and unemployed people march in Tokyo, Japan's capital, to protest rising joblessness in the first May Day demonstration staged there in seven years. . . . In Dharmsala, India, 5,000 Tibetans attend the funeral of Thupten Ngodup, a former Tibetan monk who set himself on fire Apr. 27.
May 2		Tajikistan's secular government and Islamist opposition forces agree to withdraw their troops from Dushanbe, the capital, and its surrounding areas, ending an armed conflict during which some 45 people were killed and 80 others were wounded. Prior to the agreement, observers expressed fears that the violence would reignite the country's 1992–97 civil war. . . . Four neo-Nazi skinheads attack a black U.S. Marine in Moscow, the capital of Russia, punching and kicking him unconscious.			Tens of thousands of students hold protests on university campuses across Indonesia. At least four police officers and seven students are injured in what is reportedly the most violent day of protesting in the capital since demonstrations began in January. . . . Police apprehend Australia's most wanted fugitive, Brendan Abbott, in the Northern Territory city of Darwin. Abbott is the last of four fugitives who escaped from a Queensland prison in November 1997 to be captured.
May 3	Top EU officials formally launch plans to institute an economic and monetary union (EMU) among 11 of the EU's 15 member nations. The long-anticipated project will center on the 1999 launch of the euro, a unified European currency to replace the respective currencies of participating nations. They appoint Wim Duisenberg as head of the European Central Bank (ECB).	Gojko Susak, 53, Croatian defense minister, 1991–98, considered the second-most-powerful person in Croatia, dies in Zagreb, Croatia, while suffering from lung cancer.	Nigerian authorities complete their arrests of 20 people in the wake of the May 1 unrest, including opposition leaders Bola Ige and Lam Adesina.		Negotiations aimed at ending nearly two decades of civil war in Afghanistan break down after differences surfaced between the Taliban militia and the opposition Northern Alliance. . . . Reports confirm that police in Beijing, China, had detained Wang Youcai, a leader of the 1989 student protests in Beijing's Tiananmen Square who came for the May 4 celebration of Beijing University's 100th anniversary.

A	B	C	D	E
Includes developments that affect more than one world region, international organizations, and important meetings of major world leaders.	*Includes all domestic and regional developments in Europe, including the Soviet Union, Turkey, Cyprus, and Malta.*	*Includes all domestic and regional developments in Africa and the Middle East, including Iraq and Iran and excluding Cyprus, Turkey, and Afghanistan.*	*Includes all domestic and regional developments in Latin America, the Caribbean, and Canada.*	*Includes all domestic and regional developments in Asia and Pacific nations, extending from Afghanistan through all the Pacific Island, except Hawaii.*

U.S. Politics & Social Issues	U.S. Foreign Policy & Defense	U.S. Economy & Environment	Science, Technology, & Nature	Culture, Leisure, & Lifestyle	
Wisconsin governor Tommy Thompson (R) signs a law banning a rarely performed late-term abortion procedure known medically as intact dilation and extraction (IDE).... Frank McFarland, 34, convicted of murder, is executed by lethal injection in Huntsville, Texas. He is the 458th person executed in the U.S. and the 150th in Texas since 1976.	Samuel Cummings, 71, the world's leading small-arms trader and a former CIA weapons specialist, dies in Monaco after suffering several strokes.	The House votes, 413-8, to pass a bill that will create a bipartisan commission on Social Security reform.			April 29
A jury in Hannibal, Missouri, convicts James Scott of deliberately breaking a Mississippi River levee during severe flooding in 1993, causing the destruction of some 14,000 acres (5,700 hectares) of farmland. Scott's 1994 conviction was overturned in 1997.... Data shows that the proportion of teenaged girls giving birth fell by 12% between 1991 and 1996. The teenage birthrate in 1996 was 54.7 for every 1,000 females ages 15–19, down from 62.1 in 1991.	The Senate votes, 80-19, to grant NATO membership to three former Soviet bloc adversaries—Poland, Hungary, and the Czech Republic. ... The State Department reports that international terrorist activity in 1997 continued a general trend of decline, finding that a total of 304 terrorist incidents occurred in 1997, up eight from 1996. The 1997 figure is one of the lowest since 1971. It identifies seven countries—Cuba, Iran, Iraq, Libya, North Korea, Sudan, and Syria—as sponsors of terrorism.	The Commerce Department reports that the gross domestic product (GDP) grew at a seasonally adjusted annual rate of 4.2% in the first quarter. The rate compares with a revised economic expansion of 3.7% in the October-December 1997 quarter.... The House, 242-163, and the Senate, 88-11, pass a $6 billion supplemental spending request from Pres. Clinton.	A published study finds that an abortion-inducing pill known as RU-486, or mifepristone, terminates pregnancies in 92% of 859 U.S. women ages 18–35 who are no more than 49 days pregnant. The study's results are similar to those achieved in previous studies in France on the pill's effectiveness.		April 30
Eldridge (Leroy) Cleaver, 62, black political activist who was the Black Panthers' minister of information before he became a born-again Christian and a Republican, dies in Pomona, California; his family declines to disclose the cause of death.	Reports confirm that the CIA has determined that 13 of China's CSS-4 long-range nuclear missiles are aimed at the U.S. Officials note, however, that China keeps its nuclear warheads in storage and not on the missiles.... The U.S. reveals that it will keep Hong Kong on its watch list, known as the Special 301 list, of countries producing counterfeit copyrighted materials.	Pres. Clinton signs a $6 billion supplemental spending bill.... The Commerce Department reports that personal pretax income rose 0.3% in March from February, to a seasonally adjusted figure of $7.158 trillion. March's gain marks the 17th consecutive month in which income increased. Personal income in February was revised to $7.134 trillion, a gain of 0.6% from January.	Guy Altmann, 20, a student at Texas A&M University in College Station, becomes the first known person to survive a heart autotransplant operation on a heart with a malignant tumor.	Otto Ludwig Bettmann, 94, German-born founder of the Bettmann Archive, the world's largest collection of photographs and illustrations, dies in Boca Raton, Florida, of unreported causes.	May 1
Emily Hartshorne Mudd, 99, who in 1933 cofounded the Philadelphia Marriage Council and served as the organization's executive director, 1936–67, dies in Haverford, Pennsylvania.				Real Quiet wins the 124th running of the Kentucky Derby at Churchill Downs in Louisville, Kentucky.	May 2
			Reports disclose that a combination of two drugs discovered by Dr. Judah Folkman of Children's Hospital in Boston, Massachusetts, completely eliminated cancerous tumors in mice.... The space shuttle *Columbia* lands at Kennedy Space Center after carrying out experiments investigating the effects of microgravity on the brain and nervous system. The flight was the 25th for the *Columbia* orbiter.		May 3

F	G	H	I	J
Includes elections, federal-state relations, civil rights and liberties, crime, the judiciary, education, health care, poverty, urban affairs, and population.	*Includes formation and debate of U.S. foreign and defense policies, veterans' affairs, and defense spending. (Relations with specific foreign countries are usually found under the region concerned.)*	*Includes business, labor, agriculture, taxation, transportation, consumer affairs, monetary and fiscal policy, natural resources, and pollution.*	*Includes worldwide scientific, medical, and technological developments; natural phenomena; U.S. weather; natural disasters; and accidents.*	*Includes the arts, religion, scholarship, communications media, sports, entertainments, fashions, fads, and social life.*

	World Affairs	Europe	Africa & the Middle East	The Americas	Asia & the Pacific
May 4		Reports confirm that genetic tests have proved that remains uncovered in Berlin in 1972 are indeed those of Martin Bormann, Nazi German leader Adolf Hitler's private secretary.	Nigerian security forces detain Olusegun Maiyegun, a researcher for the Committee for the Defense of Human Rights.	A band of some 200 gunmen kill at least 21 people, reportedly targeting suspected leftist rebel supporters, in the remote village of Puerto Alvira in eastern Colombia.	The Indonesian government announces price increases just hours before the IMF states it will release $1 billion in aid to Indonesia. The IMF suspended disbursement of aid to Indonesia because of Pres. Suharto's refusal to implement substantial economic reforms. Riot police reportedly take at least 94 protesters into custody during protests that escalate once the increases are announced. . . . Beijing University celebrates its 100th anniversary with ceremonies that include the opening of a new library and a speech by Pres. Jiang Zemin.
May 5	Reports confirm that the Bahamas has established diplomatic relations with China after cutting ties to Taiwan.		Three members of an English family held hostage in Yemen since Apr. 17 return safely to England after negotiations secured their release. . . . Nigerian authorities arrest opposition leader Ayo Opadokun at his office in Lagos.	Nicaraguan president Arnoldo Aleman Lacayo suspends seven high-ranking members of the government in the wake of revelations that Aleman and other top Nicaraguan officials unknowingly flew aboard a jet loaded with smuggled cocaine. The suspended officials include Mario Rivas, the civil aviation director; Carlos Palacios, the chief of Nicaragua's antidrug operations; and immigration chief Carlos Garcia.	Indonesians in the city of Medan in northern Sumatra riot and loot, and students across the country hold rallies to protest steep fuel and energy price increases. The price hikes are part of a larger economic reform package that Pres. Suharto reached with the IMF in April. . . . Four naval personnel are killed in a fire on board the Australian navy tanker *Westralia*. Five other personnel are injured. It is Australia's worst naval disaster since 1964.
May 6		Severe mudslides set off by torrential rain sweep southern Italy, killing scores of people and destroying hundreds of homes. The mudslides are described as the region's worst in decades. . . . Tomas Caballero, a town councilor in Pamplona, Spain, is shot and killed. He is the fifth local politician believed to be killed by the ETA in less than a year. . . . In the Netherlands, parliamentary elections keep the left-of-center Labor Party and Premier Wim Kok in power.	Clashes erupt between Ethiopia and Eritrea in a disputed region, a 150-square-mile (390-sq-km) area known as Badame on Ethiopia's northern border. The skirmish touches off an intense armed conflict. . . . South Africa's Truth and Reconciliation Commission announces its first decision to award reparations to victims of human-rights abuses during the apartheid era. . . . A Nigerian official reveals that the government released 142 political prisoners during the previous week.	In Mexico, some members of a group of 134 Italian human-rights observers visiting Chiapas break through an immigration checkpoint in order to travel to Taniperlas. The Mecian government authorized only 10 members to enter the town. Upon entering Taniperlas, the Italians clash with progovernment Indians who took over the town in April.	Six people are reported killed and another 100 injured in Medan, Indonesia, either by gunfire from riot police or in buildings set ablaze by rioters. . . . Chatichai Choonhavan, 76, Thai premier, 1988–91, dies in London, England, after suffering from liver cancer.
May 7		The Danish parliament enacts legislation that forcibly ends the strike begun Apr. 27, the country's largest in over a decade as it involved 20% of its workforce.			Crowds estimated at 25,000–50,000 people gather at Honganji Temple in Tokyo, the Japanese capital, for the funeral of Japanese rock-and-roll star Hideto Matsumoto, 33, who hanged himself May 2.
May 8			The Cape High Court in Cape Town, South Africa, overturns the blanket amnesties that an arm of the Truth and Reconciliation Commission had granted to high-ranking officials of the ruling African National Congress (ANC). Separately, a high court judge in Johannesburg throws out apartheid-era statutes that outlawed homosexual sex on grounds that they are unconstitutional.		

A	B	C	D	E
Includes developments that affect more than one world region, international organizations, and important meetings of major world leaders.	*Includes all domestic and regional developments in Europe, including the Soviet Union, Turkey, Cyprus, and Malta.*	*Includes all domestic and regional developments in Africa and the Middle East, including Iraq and Iran and excluding Cyprus, Turkey, and Afghanistan.*	*Includes all domestic and regional developments in Latin America, the Caribbean, and Canada.*	*Includes all domestic and regional developments in Asia and Pacific nations, extending from Afghanistan through all the Pacific Island, except Hawaii.*

U.S. Politics & Social Issues	U.S. Foreign Policy & Defense	U.S. Economy & Environment	Science, Technology, & Nature	Culture, Leisure, & Lifestyle	
In Sacramento, California, U.S. district judge Garland Burrell Jr. sentences Theodore J. Kaczynski to four life prison terms plus 30 years for carrying out four bombings between 1982 and 1995 that killed three people and injured two others. . . . . In a sealed ruling, Judge Norma Holloway Johnson in Washington, D.C., finds that Pres. Clinton cannot invoke executive privilege or attorney-client privilege to protect his aides from testifying in a criminal obstruction-of-justice probe against him, according to officials. It is considered a victory for Kenneth Starr.		Susan McDougal, one of the partners of Pres. Clinton and First Lady Hillary Rodham Clinton in the failed Whitewater Development Corp. who is already serving a prison term, is indicted on charges of criminal contempt and obstruction of justice for refusing to cooperate with independent counsel Kenneth Starr's investigation of the matter. . . . Merrill Lynch & Co. announces that it has agreed to pay eight female brokers a total of $600,000 to settle their claims of sexual discrimination.		Reports confirm that William Gates paid $30 million for *Lost on the Grand Banks* (1885), a seascape by Winslow Homer. It is the highest price ever paid for the work of a U.S.-born artist. . . . A jury in Kansas City, Kansas, orders the NCAA to pay nearly $67 million in damages to assistant coaches whose earnings the NCAA restricted under a 1991 rule.	**May 4**
Ohio voters reject, 80%-20%, a ballot proposition to add a penny to the state's sales tax to raise funds for education. . . . Pres. Clinton and former first lady Nancy Reagan formally dedicate the Ronald Reagan Building and International Trade Center. . . . Alan Simpson, 85, president of Vassar College, 1964–77, who oversaw the first admission of male students to the college, dies in Lake Forest, Illinois, of pneumonia.				Reports confirm that French art collector François Pinault has purchased 29% of Christie's, which has been under British ownership since founded in 1766. Separately, Sotheby's and Christie's open their spring New York City sales, and Christie's reclassifies its art into three historic eras.	**May 5**
		The Congressional Budget Office (CBO) forecasts a surplus in 1998 of between $43 billion and $63 billion.	Astronomers from institutions in several countries announce at a news conference that they recently detected a burst of gamma rays coming from the constellation Ursa Major, energy emanating from an enormous explosion that took place some 12 billion years ago at a far edge of the universe. The scientists note that current theories cannot explain how such an intense burst of energy, which they argue outshone all of the rest of the universe for a matter of seconds, could be created.		**May 6**
The New York State Court of Appeals unanimously rules that a divorced couple must abide by a signed contract that requires the consent of both parties before either of them may use frozen embryos placed in storage. . . . Three people linked to the white-supremacist movement—Brian Picket, Christopher Norris, and Deena Wanzie—are charged with conspiring to set off pipe bombs in busy tourist areas near Orlando, Florida, in 1997.	Delia Lemus Ruiz de Paoletti and Adriana Paoletti Lemus, leaders of a forced-labor ring exploiting deaf illegal Mexican immigrants, are sentenced to 14 years in prison. . . . In Tallahassee, Florida, Customs Service officials reveal they have arrested six people in an international fraud scheme to steal some $60 million from more than 400 people in at least 10 countries. It the largest money-laundering scheme unrelated to drugs ever investigated by the Customs Service.	The Labor Department reports that the nation's overall productivity in nonfarm business sectors rose by a seasonally adjusted annual rate of 0.2% in the first quarter of 1998 from the fourth quarter of 1997. It is the weakest rate in more than a year. . . . The Senate votes, 97-0, to pass a bill proposing far-reaching reforms for the IRS in the wake of Senate hearings. . . . The Whitewater grand jury in Little Rock, Arkansas, expires after four and a half years of operation.	A series of tornadoes sweeps through South Carolina, Georgia, North Carolina, and Virginia. . . . Allan MacLeod Cormack, 74, physicist who established the mathematical basis of the computerized axial tomographic (CAT) scan and cowinner of the 1979 Nobel prize for medicine, dies in Winchester, Massachusetts, of cancer.	William Louther, 56, U.S. dancer and choreographer who helped popularize modern dance in England. dies in London of esophageal cancer.	**May 7**
The tobacco industry agrees to pay some $6.6 billion to the state of Minnesota and Blue Cross & Blue Shield of Minnesota to settle a suit. . . . Reports confirm Rep. Cynthia McKinney, (D, Ga.), who is black, has complained that White House security personnel gave her and two Pakistani Americans "disparate treatment" because of their race. . . . Jennings Randolph, 96, (D, W.Va.), representative, 1933–46, and senator, 1958–85, who wrote the amendment that lowered the legal voting age to 18, dies in St. Louis, Missouri.		The Labor Department reports that the seasonally adjusted unemployment rate in April dropped to 4.3%, its lowest level since February 1970. A survey of business payroll indicates that the economy created 262,000 new jobs during the month, more than reversing a small decline in jobs in March. . . . Charles Gregory (Bebe) Rebozo, 85, self-made multimillionaire and longtime friend of Pres. Richard Nixon who was an informal financial adviser to Nixon, dies in Miami, Florida, of a brain aneurysm.	The series of tornadoes that began sweeping through South Carolina, Georgia, North Carolina, and Virginia on May 7, ebbs after causing the deaths of two people. At least 20 others were injured. . . . Researchers suggest that a genetic mutation that protects some people against infection by HIV, the virus that causes AIDS, may have been inherited from 14th-century survivors of bubonic plague.	Reports state that the U.S. Library of Congress plans to purchase the archives of the late dancer and choreographer Martha Graham for $500,000.	**May 8**

F	G	H	I	J
Includes elections, federal-state relations, civil rights and liberties, crime, the judiciary, education, health care, poverty, urban affairs, and population.	*Includes formation and debate of U.S. foreign and defense policies, veterans' affairs, and defense spending. (Relations with specific foreign countries are usually found under the region concerned.)*	*Includes business, labor, agriculture, taxation, transportation, consumer affairs, monetary and fiscal policy, natural resources, and pollution.*	*Includes worldwide scientific, medical, and technological developments; natural phenomena; U.S. weather; natural disasters; and accidents.*	*Includes the arts, religion, scholarship, communications media, sports, entertainments, fashions, fads, and social life.*

	World Affairs	Europe	Africa & the Middle East	The Americas	Asia & the Pacific
May 9			Rwandan authorities order Jose Luis Herrero, a UN human-rights official who in April spoke out against the government's execution of 22 people convicted of war crimes, to leave the country.... Reports confirm that Herrero Olisa Agbakoba, head of the opposition group United Action for Democracy, is arrested at Lagos airport as he returns to Nigeria from a human-rights conference in the U.S.		North Korean foreign minister Kim Yong Nam announces that the government has suspended its implementation of a 1994 agreement with the U.S. under which North Korea was to halt its nuclear energy program.... Chinese authorities release from prison Zeng Jingmu, a bishop of the outlawed "underground" Roman Catholic Church that maintains allegiance to the pope. Zeng was sentenced without trial in 1996 to three years of "reeducation through labor."
May 10	UN secretary general Kofi Annan ends a tour of Africa, during which he visited Ethiopia, Rwanda, Kenya, Djibouti, Tanzania, Uganda, Burundi, and Eritrea.	Reports confirm that 100 died in the Italian town of Sarno in the Campania region, hit hardest by the May 6 mudslides. Some 15,000 mourners, among them Premier Romano Prodi and President Oscar Luigi Scalfaro, attend a funeral mass in Sarno for the victims.... Sinn Fein, the political wing of the Provisional Irish Republican Army (IRA), overwhelmingly endorses a Northern Ireland peace agreement that negotiators reached in April.		Raul Cubas Grau of Paraguay's ruling Colorado Party wins presidential elections.... Jose Francisco Peña Gomez, 61, longtime head of the opposition Dominican Revolutionary Party (PRD), dies of stomach cancer.	Reports from China surface regarding the Apr. 30 clash with riot police in Chengdu, in Sichuan province surface, and they state that four people died and 30 others were seriously injured in the incident.
May 11	India detonates three underground nuclear devices at the Pokharan test site, located near the Pakistan border. The international community condemns India's actions.		Israel officially acknowledges that Jonathan Pollard, an American Jew jailed for life in the U.S. for spying for Israel, "acted as an Israeli agent."	The strike started Feb. 17 by doctors in Nicaragua escalates into violent street clashes between protesters and police, as students and other citizens join the doctors' cause. Nineteen doctors are arrested for blocking roads in Managua, the capital.... In response to the May 6 clash, the Mexican government deports 40 Italian human-rights observers investigating alleged abuses in the southern state of Chiapas.	Voters in the Philippines cast ballots in nationwide elections for president, vice president, members of Congress, and more than 17,000 other provincial and local posts.
May 12				In Nicaragua, 25 people are arrested after seven officers are injured as clashes that started May 11 continue.... Retired general Fernando Landazabal Reyes, a former right-wing defense minister, is slain in Bogota, the capital of Colombia.	In Jakarta, the capital of Indonesia, riot police open fire on students at Trisakti University, killing six student protesters. The killings unleash violent rioting in Jakarta.
May 13	India detonates two underground nuclear devices near the village of Khetlai in the Thar Desert. The government states that the exercise "completes the planned series of tests." U.S. president Bill Clinton announces that the U.S. will impose economic sanctions against India. Japan cancels $30 million in grants to India, and Germany, Sweden, and Denmark suspend some development. None of those nations agree to implement sanctions.... Gro Harlem Brundtland is confirmed as director general of the WHO.	Yugoslav president Slobodan Milosevic agrees to open talks with ethnic Albanian leader Ibrahim Rugova. Violence between government forces and ethnic Albanian separatists in Kosovo province have claimed more than 150 lives since late February.... A bomb explodes at the Lubavitch Marina Roscha synagogue in Moscow, the capital of Russia, destroying the building's outer wall and injuring construction workers at an adjacent building.	Israeli jets bomb a training camp of the Syrian-backed Fatah Uprising in eastern Lebanon's Bekaa Valley, killing at least eight people.		
May 14					Riots continue in Indonesia, and 200 people die when they are trapped in four shopping malls set ablaze.

A	B	C	D	E
Includes developments that affect more than one world region, international organizations, and important meetings of major world leaders.	Includes all domestic and regional developments in Europe, including the Soviet Union, Turkey, Cyprus, and Malta.	Includes all domestic and regional developments in Africa and the Middle East, including Iraq and Iran and excluding Cyprus, Turkey, and Afghanistan.	Includes all domestic and regional developments in Latin America, the Caribbean, and Canada.	Includes all domestic and regional developments in Asia and Pacific nations, extending from Afghanistan through all the Pacific Island, except Hawaii.

U.S. Politics & Social Issues	U.S. Foreign Policy & Defense	U.S. Economy & Environment	Science, Technology, & Nature	Culture, Leisure, & Lifestyle	
		The U.S. Court of Appeals for the District of Columbia Circuit rules, 6–5, that employers are liable for punitive damages for sexual discrimination only in "particularly egregious" cases in which they ignore victims' civil rights with "reckless indifference."		Alice Faye (born Alice Jeanne Leppert), lead actress in Hollywood movie musicals of the 1930s and 1940s whose age is variously reported as 83 and 86, dies in Rancho Mirage, California, of cancer.	May 9
	Ronald Lee Ridenhour, 52, U.S. journalist and Vietnam War veteran who brought the infamous My Lai massacre to public attention, dies in Metairie, Louisiana, of a heart attack.		The FAA pulls 179 U.S.-registered Boeing 737 jetliners out of service to inspect the planes' fuel-pump wiring. The FAA also gives U.S. airline companies two weeks to examine and service the wiring in 118 later-model 737s from the 300, 400, and 500 series with 40,000–50,000 flight hours. Its grounding order will affect about 100,000 U.S. air passengers.		May 10
Blanche Revere Long, 93, wife of three-term Louisiana government Earl K. Long who committed her husband to a Texas mental institution in 1959 after he made a rambling, incoherent speech to the Louisiana legislature, dies in Covington, Louisiana, of unreported causes.					May 11
The U.S. Postal Service's nine-member board of governors unanimously select William J. Henderson as the nation's 71st postmaster general. . . . The House passes, 402-16, a bill increasing penalties for parents who refuse to pay child support.	The Senate approves, 92-8, an agriculture bill that will restore food-stamp benefits to 250,000 of the 935,000 legal immigrants who lost eligibility under a welfare overhaul bill enacted in 1996. . . . A key army missile-defense system known as the Theater High-Altitude Area Defense (THAAD) fails its fifth consecutive flight test during a trial run at the White Sands Missile Range in New Mexico.	Financial disclosure forms reveal that Pres. Clinton and his family had assets worth between $1.26 million and $5.76 million at the end of 1997. . . . In response to repeated attacks for its labor practices in Asia and Latin America, Nike Inc., an athletic shoe and apparel manufacturer, states the company will raise the minimum-age requirements for its overseas workers and will adopt healthier air-quality standards at its overseas production plants.	The U.S. Court of Appeals in Washington, D.C., rules that a December 1997 ruling, in which a lower court forced Microsoft to offer a version of its Windows operating system not equipped with Internet Explorer, does not require the company to similarly separate Internet Explorer from the new Windows 98 operating system.		May 12
Dr. E. Ratcliffe Anderson is named the new executive vice president of the American Medical Association (AMA). . . . The Senate passes, by voice vote, a bill allowing churches and charities to keep contributions from donors who go bankrupt.		The Dow closes at a record high of 9211.84. That marks the 25th record high of 1998 and the second record high registered in May. . . . The House passes, 214-213, a bank-reform bill that will dismantle Depression-era barriers separating the banking, insurance, and securities industries.	A study finds that the drug raloxifene may lower blood levels of low-density lipoprotein (LDL), a kind of cholesterol harmful to the heart, in postmenopausal women.		May 13
Doctors at abortion clinics in Wisconsin stop performing all types of abortions because they claim that the Apr. 29 law banning IDE abortions is so vaguely worded that it may apply to all abortions. . . . Pres. Clinton issues an executive order setting out nine circumstances under which federal intervention is justified. It revokes two earlier presidential orders on federalism—issued by Clinton in 1993 and by Pres. Reagan in 1987—that stress deference to state and local governments.	Military representatives exhume the unidentified Vietnam War serviceman buried in the Tomb of the Unknowns in Arlington National Cemetery in Virginia. The remains are to undergo previously unavailable genetic tests in an effort to determine the soldier's identity. Defense Secretary William S. Cohen states that he felt obligated to do whatever he could to address the hopes of the families who believe that the remains might belong to one of their members.	Marjory Stoneman Douglas, 108, author and environmentalist who fought to preserve the Everglades, Florida's unique wetlands, and was presented with the Presidential Medal of Freedom in 1993, in Miami, Florida, of natural causes.		Frank (Francis Albert) Sinatra, 82, American icon and one of the most popular entertainers of the 20th century, winner of the Academy Award for his supporting role in the 1953 film *From Here to Eternity*, and founder of his own record company, Reprise, dies of a heart attack in Los Angeles, California.	May 14
F	**G**	**H**	**I**	**J**	
Includes elections, federal-state relations, civil rights and liberties, crime, the judiciary, education, health care, poverty, urban affairs, and population.	*Includes formation and debate of U.S. foreign and defense policies, veterans' affairs, and defense spending. (Relations with specific foreign countries are usually found under the region concerned.)*	*Includes business, labor, agriculture, taxation, transportation, consumer affairs, monetary and fiscal policy, natural resources, and pollution.*	*Includes worldwide scientific, medical, and technological developments; natural phenomena; U.S. weather; natural disasters; and accidents.*	*Includes the arts, religion, scholarship, communications media, sports, entertainments, fashions, fads, and social life.*	

	World Affairs	Europe	Africa & the Middle East	The Americas	Asia & the Pacific
May 15	Leaders of the world's seven wealthiest industrialized nations and Russia, collectively known as the Group of Eight (G-8), meet for their 24th annual summit.	Reports reveal that, after the May 6 mudslides in southern Italy near Naples, the bodies of 147 victims have been found, and another 200 people remain missing. Some 1,000 people are left homeless. . . . (Patrick Palles) Lorne (Elphinstone) Welch, 81, British Royal Air Force pilot in World War II who participated in several escape attempts from Nazi prisoner-of-war camps, dies in Farnham, England, of unreported causes.		Argentina reveals that it will expel seven of the eight officials at the Iranian embassy in Buenos Aires, the capital, claiming that the government has proof that Iran was behind two previously unsolved anti-Jewish bomb attacks in the city. The attacks were the 1992 bombing of the Israeli embassy, which killed 29 people, and the 1994 bombing of a Jewish community center, in which 87 people died.	An estimated 500 people are reported to have died since May 13 in rioting in Jakarta, the capital of Indonesia. In an effort to quell the unrest, Pres. Suharto restores the fuel subsidies. Despite the president's action, students continue to call for his ouster. . . . Reports suggest that Chinese antiquities are being looted from historic sites surrounding the construction site of the Three Gorges Dam on the Yangtze River.
May 16				In the Colombian town of Barrancabermeja, 11 people die and 25 people are kidnapped during a raid by a paramilitary group.	
May 17		Lord Hugh Cudlipp (born Hubert Kinsman Cudlipp), 84, British newspaperman credited with creating modern British tabloid journalism, dies in Chichester, England, while suffering from lung and prostate cancer.	In response to Argentina's May 15 decision, the Iranian government expels the Argentine commercial attaché from Teheran, the capital, and threatens to impose trade sanctions against Argentina.	In the Dominican Republic, the opposition Dominican Revolutionary Party (PRD) registers an overwhelming victory in midterm legislative elections.	
May 18	Amid protests, the World Trade Organization (WTO) holds a meeting in Geneva, Switzerland. . . . The UN World Food Program announces that it will reduce food aid to North Korea because the North Korean government has restricted the agency's ability to monitor the use of the donated food. . . . The U.S. and the EU resolve a dispute over U.S. sanctions against foreign companies doing business with Cuba, Iran, and Libya.	The British Foreign Office announces that the six-nation "contact group" monitoring civil strife in the Balkan region will cease certain economic sanctions against Yugoslavia because of Yugoslav president Slobodan Milosevic's May 13 agreement to open talks with ethnic Albanian leader Ibrahim Rugova. . . . The upper house of the Yugoslav parliament passes a vote of no confidence in Premier Radoje Kontic, effectively dismissing him from the position.	Ezer Weizman takes the oath for his second five-year term as president of Israel.	The Bahamas repatriate 65 Cuban refugees, including three baseball players and a coach banned from baseball in Cuba.	In Indonesia, government troops allow thousands of students to launch a massive sit-in protest in the parliament building. The students march peacefully into the government building, vowing to remain there until Pres. Suharto resigns.
May 19		Pres. Slobodan Milosevic nominates Momir Bulatovic to replace Radoje Kontic as premier of Yugoslavia. . . . Armed gunmen break into the National Gallery of Modern Art in Rome, Italy, and steal three valuable paintings, valued at a total of $34 million. . . . At a rock concert organized by peace-plan advocates in Belfast, Catholic leader John Hume and David Trimble, Northern Ireland's leading Protestant politician, appear on stage, making their first joint public appearance in the current round of peace initiatives.	Lebanon carries out its first public execution in 15 years when Wissam Nayef Issa, 25, and Hassan Abu Jabal, 24, are hanged at dawn in front of 1,200 spectators in the coastal resort of Tabarja, located 15 miles (25 km) north of Beirut, the capital. The two executed men had killed two men during a 1995 robbery attempt in Tabarja.	Hundreds of thousands of people across Colombia stop work to protest the recent upsurge in political violence.	Sosuke Uno, 75, Japanese premier who resigned after two months in office in 1989 after he was accused of having had an extramarital affair, dies in Moriyama, Japan, of lung cancer.
May 20				Reports state that at least 50 people have been killed and dozens others are missing as a result of politically motivated attacks across Colombia since late April.	As protests continue, Indonesia's parliament announces that it will begin impeachment proceedings against Pres. Suharto.

A	B	C	D	E
Includes developments that affect more than one world region, international organizations, and important meetings of major world leaders.	Includes all domestic and regional developments in Europe, including the Soviet Union, Turkey, Cyprus, and Malta.	Includes all domestic and regional developments in Africa and the Middle East, including Iraq and Iran and excluding Cyprus, Turkey, and Afghanistan.	Includes all domestic and regional developments in Latin America, the Caribbean, and Canada.	Includes all domestic and regional developments in Asia and Pacific nations, extending from Afghanistan through all the Pacific Island, except Hawaii.

U.S. Politics & Social Issues	U.S. Foreign Policy & Defense	U.S. Economy & Environment	Science, Technology, & Nature	Culture, Leisure, & Lifestyle	
			A study finds that mentally ill people who do not abuse drugs or alcohol are no more likely to be violent than other people.	The Library of Congress plans to establish a permanent exhibition on Bob Hope, 95, and his decades-long career in entertainment. . . . Earl Manigault, 53, legendary NYC playground basketball star, nicknamed "the Goat," dies in New York City of congestive heart failure.	May 15
Christopher Sercye, a 15-year-old boy shot in the chest in Chicago, Illinois, dies after lying untreated near the door of Ravenswood Hospital for some 20 minutes. According to policy, hospital staff refused to leave the premises to treat the boy as he bled 35 feet (11 m) away from the hospital door. Ravenswood staff tell Sercye's friends that the hospital does not possess a trauma center equipped to treat a serious gunshot wound.				Real Quiet wins the 123rd running of the Preakness Stakes in Baltimore, Maryland. . . . The PEN/Faulkner Award for Fiction is awarded to first-time novelist Rafi Zabor for *The Bear Comes Home*.	May 16
The FBI reports that the incidence of serious crime has dropped 4% nationwide, marking the sixth consecutive annual decline. The incidence of violent crimes, including murder, rape, robbery, and aggravated assault, fell 5% overall. The sharpest decrease was in the murder rate, with a 9% decline nationwide.				Rookie golfer Se Ri Pak of South Korea wins the LPGA Championship in Wilmington, Delaware. . . . Pitcher David Wells of the New York Yankees pitches the 15th perfect game in MLB history in a 4-0 victory over the Minnesota Twins.	May 17
In light of criticism stemming from the May 16 death of Christopher Sercye, Ravenswood Hospital rescinds rules that prohibited treating the boy as he bled outside the hospital doors. . . . In *Bousley v. United States*, the Supreme Court rules, 7-2, that a prisoner who in 1990 pled guilty to a federal charge of using a firearm in connection with a drug offense may reopen the gun-use case. . . . In *Arkansas Educational Television Commission v. Forbes*, the Supreme Court rules, 6-3, that an Arkansas public television station may exclude lesser-known candidates from participating in its televised political debates.	Treasury Secretary Robert E. Rubin and Attorney General Janet Reno announce the indictment of three Mexican banks, scores of Mexican bankers, and operatives in two international drug cartels in what officials call the largest case of drug-money laundering ever investigated by U.S. law enforcement.		The first large-scale effort to investigate whether routine screening using the prostate-specific antigen (PSA) examination cuts prostate cancer deaths, data reveals that routine screening of men for prostate cancer may cut prostate cancer deaths by some 69% annually. . . . The Justice Department and attorneys general from 20 states file two separate antitrust lawsuits in U.S. District Court in Washington, D.C., against Microsoft Corp., accusing Microsoft of violating antitrust laws by using its near-monopoly in the market for personal computer (PC) operating systems to attempt to dominate other segments of the software market.	French investor and art collector François Pinault announces that he will buy the 71% of the London-based Christie's auction house that he does not already own, in a deal that values the company at £720 million ($1.2 billion).	May 18
The House passes, by voice vote, a bill that will authorize $750 million in compensation for hemophiliacs infected with HIV, the virus that causes AIDS, through blood transfusions.				Comedian Bob Hope state he will donate his personal papers, recordings, and an archive of some 90,000 jokes to the Library of Congress. . . . Judge J. D. Smith sentences Tak Sun Tan, Indra Lim, and Jason Chan to prison sentences ranging from 26 years to life for the 1996 murder of Academy Award-winning actor Dr. Haing S. Ngor.	May 19
The five abortion clinics in Wisconsin that stopped performing all types of abortions May 14, resume practicing certain procedures after local prosecutors assure them that they will not pursue cases against doctors performing first-trimester abortions, which have been legal since 1973.	Federal authorities announce the indictment of four high-ranking Venezuelan bank officials in the same probe that ensnared the Mexicans in a drug-money laundering case revealed May 18.	The Commerce Department reports that in March the U.S. registered its second record trade deficit in three months, reaching a seasonally adjusted $13.03 billion gap in trade in goods and services. That is up from February's revised deficit of $12.18 billion.			May 20
F	G	H	I	J	
Includes elections, federal-state relations, civil rights and liberties, crime, the judiciary, education, health care, poverty, urban affairs, and population.	Includes formation and debate of U.S. foreign and defense policies, veterans' affairs, and defense spending. (Relations with specific foreign countries are usually found under the region concerned.)	Includes business, labor, agriculture, taxation, transportation, consumer affairs, monetary and fiscal policy, natural resources, and pollution.	Includes worldwide scientific, medical, and technological developments; natural phenomena; U.S. weather; natural disasters; and accidents.	Includes the arts, religion, scholarship, communications media, sports, entertainments, fashions, fads, and social life.	

	World Affairs	Europe	Africa & the Middle East	The Americas	Asia & the Pacific
May 21	U.S. Pres. Clinton ratifies a resolution to expand NATO membership to include Poland, Hungary, and the Czech Republic, making the U.S. the fifth nation to do so.		Jacob Katz, 93, Hungarian-born scholar of Jewish history who joined the faculty at the Hebrew University in Jerusalem in 1950, dies in Jerusalem of unreported causes.	Fighting continues in Colombia when at least 19 people are killed in clashes between the army and the leftist rebel ELN, the smaller of Colombia's two major rebel groups. Three policemen are also killed that day in clashes with FARC.	Amid widespread protests and rioting, Indonesian president Suharto resigns, ending his 32 years of nearly autocratic rule over Indonesia, the world's fourth-most-populous nation. His longtime protégé, Vice Pres. Bacharuddin Jusuf (B. J.) Habibie, is sworn in as his successor.
May 22		Serbian special police units commence a major offensive against ethnic Albanian separatists in the southern region of Kosovo province. . . . Voters in the Irish Republic and in Northern Ireland back a peace agreement reached in April by Northern Ireland's main political parties and the British and Irish governments in two separate referenda. The plan is designed to enact the most sweeping changes in Northern Ireland's governmental structure since 1922.			In Indonesia, several thousand Muslim students march onto the Parliament grounds to declare their support for the newly sworn-in Pres. Habibie. However, some 2,000 students remain in the parliament building where they have been protesting since May 18, until they are forcibly removed by military troops in an overnight operation. While the hundreds of soldiers are armed with tear gas and automatic weapons, no injuries are reported. In the wake of the political turmoil, the IMF postpones indefinitely the disbursement of a $1 billion installment of the loan package scheduled for release on June 4.
May 23			The political opposition in the southern African nation of Lesotho wins its first-ever parliamentary seat in elections. . . . Several thousand students and other Iranians gather at Teheran University to mark the first anniversary of Mohammed Khatami's election as president.		
May 24		The center-right Fidesz-Hungarian Civic Party defeats the ruling Socialist Party in Hungary's second and final round of parliamentary elections, capturing 148 seats in the 386-member federal legislature.			In what is viewed as a gesture to convey new openness in Indonesia, TV reporters and photographers are permitted to enter Cipinang, Jakarta's main jail for political prisoners. It is the first time that cameras are permitted in the prison. . . . Hong Kong holds its first legislative elections since the former British colony reverted to Chinese sovereignty in July 1997. Prodemocracy parties, excluded from the provisional legislature appointed by China at the 1997 handover, make a strong showing.
May 25		Japanese emperor Akihito arrives in London amid protests by British war veterans who were imprisoned and, in many cases, tortured by the Japanese army during World War II.			Indonesia releases two well-known political dissidents—Muchtar Pakpahan and Sri Bintang Pamungkas—from Cipinang Prison, Jakarta's main jail for political prisoners.
May 26					Ikuo Hayashi, a principal member of the Aum Shinrikyo religious cult, is sentenced to life in prison for his role in the cult's March 1995 nerve-gas attack on the Tokyo subway system. Twelve people were killed in the attack, and thousands more were made ill.

A	B	C	D	E
Includes developments that affect more than one world region, international organizations, and important meetings of major world leaders.	Includes all domestic and regional developments in Europe, including the Soviet Union, Turkey, Cyprus, and Malta.	Includes all domestic and regional developments in Africa and the Middle East, including Iraq and Iran and excluding Cyprus, Turkey, and Afghanistan.	Includes all domestic and regional developments in Latin America, the Caribbean, and Canada.	Includes all domestic and regional developments in Asia and Pacific nations, extending from Afghanistan through all the Pacific Island, except Hawaii.

U.S. Politics & Social Issues	U.S. Foreign Policy & Defense	U.S. Economy & Environment	Science, Technology, & Nature	Culture, Leisure, & Lifestyle	
Kipland Kinkel, a 15-year-old student in Springfield, Oregon, opens fire with a semiautomatic rifle in his high school's crowded cafeteria, killing one student and wounding 23 others. Kinkel had fatally shot his parents before the rampage.... Statistics show that at least 28 states have passed laws banning a rarely performed, controversial late-term procedure, known as intact dilation and extraction (IDE).				The Senate votes unanimously to confirm William J. Ivey as chair of the National Endowment for the Arts (NEA).	May 21
In Washington, D.C., federal judge Norma Holloway Johnson orders members of the Secret Service to testify before a grand jury investigating whether Pres. Clinton illegally tried to cover up an affair with a former White House intern, Monica Lewinsky.... A student shot May 21 by Kipland Kinkel, 15, in Thurston High School in Springfield, Oregon dies, bringing the death toll to two.	Pres. Clinton nominates Louis Caldera to become the next secretary of the army.... The Senate passes, 90-4, legislation that will mandate imposing sanctions on companies and research laboratories anywhere in the world that supply Iran with missile technology.	The House, 297-86, and the Senate, 88-5, clear the final version of a six-year surface-transportation bill that will authorize $216 billion in federal funding for the nation's highways, mass-transit systems, and highway-safety programs. The bill, the Transportation Equity Act for the 21st Century, is one of the largest public-works programs in U.S. history.... The FEC reveals that former agriculture secretary Mike Espy has paid a $50,000 fine for improperly using campaign funds from his days as a Mississippi congressman to pay legal bills stemming from his actions as a cabinet official.	Pfizer Inc., the maker of Viagra, a popular impotence drug approved by the FDA in March, discloses that six people died after taking the drug.	John Derek (born Derek Harris), 71, motion-picture actor and director who appeared in dozens of films from the 1940s to the 1960s, dies in Santa Maria, California, of a heart ailment.	May 22
	Telford Taylor, 90, U.S. Army lawyer who was a leading prosecutor of Nazi officials and German industrialists at the Nuremberg war crimes trials after World War II, dies in New York City of a stroke.				May 23
Samuel William Yorty, 88, Democratic mayor of Los Angeles, 1961–73, and member of the House representing California, 1951–55, dies in Los Angeles after suffering a stroke.				At the Cannes (France) Film Festival, the Palme d'Or goes to Greek director Theo Angelopoulos for *Eternity and a Day*. The Grand Prix goes to Italian comic actor Roberto Benigni for *Life Is Beautiful*.... Eddie Cheever wins the 82nd running of the Indianapolis 500 auto race.... The Swedish yacht *EF Language* becomes the official winner of the Whitbread Round the World yacht race.	May 24
A bomb explodes outside a church in Danville, Illinois, injuring 33 worshipers.	North Korea hands over to U.S. military officials remains believed to be those of two U.S. soldiers killed in the 1950–53 Korean War. The identities of the soldiers are not known.			*A Widow for One Year* by John Irving tops the bestseller list.	May 25
In *New Jersey v. New York*, the Supreme Court rules, 6-3, that most of Ellis Island, in New York Harbor, is part of the territory of New Jersey rather than that of New York.... In *Sacramento County v. Lewis*, the Supreme Court rules unanimously that a Sacramento, California, county sheriff's deputy cannot be held liable for a death caused by a high-speed car chase because he did not act with "a purpose to cause harm." The justices overturn a 1996 decision by the U.S. Ninth Circuit Court of Appeals in San Francisco, California.	Pres. Clinton authorizes the U.S. Defense Department to reduce by half the U.S.'s military presence in the Persian Gulf region.	President Clinton announces that his administration has forecast a $39 billion budget surplus in the current fiscal year. The surplus, if achieved, will be the federal government's first surplus since 1969. The OMB forecasts an aggregate surplus of $495 billion over the next five years and $1.477 trillion over 10 years.			May 26

F	G	H	I	J
Includes elections, federal-state relations, civil rights and liberties, crime, the judiciary, education, health care, poverty, urban affairs, and population.	Includes formation and debate of U.S. foreign and defense policies, veterans' affairs, and defense spending. (Relations with specific foreign countries are usually found under the region concerned.)	Includes business, labor, agriculture, taxation, transportation, consumer affairs, monetary and fiscal policy, natural resources, and pollution.	Includes worldwide scientific, medical, and technological developments; natural phenomena; U.S. weather; natural disasters; and accidents.	Includes the arts, religion, scholarship, communications media, sports, entertainments, fashions, fads, and social life.

	World Affairs	Europe	Africa & the Middle East	The Americas	Asia & the Pacific
May 27	The European Commission, the EU's executive arm, authorizes the resumption of some beef exports from the British province of Northern Ireland. Since March 1996 Britain has been barred by the EU from exporting beef products because of claims that bovine spongiform encephalopathy (BSE), or mad-cow disease, prevalent in British herds, may be related to Creutzfeldt-Jakob disease in humans.		Reports confirm that President Laurent Kabila of the Democratic Republic of the Congo (formerly Zaire) has ordered the creation of a 300-member transitional legislative assembly.		The Korean Confederation of Trade Unions (KCTU) stages a general strike to protest growing unemployment and a recently passed law legalizing mass layoffs in South Korea.
May 28	Pakistan conducts five underground nuclear tests at the Chagai Hills test site near the country's borders with Afghanistan and Iran, provoking international condemnation and concerns about an escalating nuclear arms race in South Asia. As they did following India's tests on May 11 and May 13, wealthy donor nations, including Japan Germany, Canada, and Australia, state they will curb their aid to Pakistan.	The German parliament enacts legislation that grants a blanket pardon to Germans persecuted by the Nazi justice system before and during World War II. . . . A court in Munich convicts Felix Somm, the former head of U.S. company CompuServe Inc.'s German subsidiary CompuServe Deutschland, of disseminating illegal forms of pornography over the Internet computer network. The conviction marks the first time that the head of a German Internet-service provider is held criminally responsible for illegal material accessible through the provider.	Two Israeli soldiers are killed and two others are wounded by a remote-controlled bomb while on a patrol in southern Lebanon some 50 yards (55 m) from the Israeli border. Hezbollah claims responsibility for the action, which follows intense clashes that have taken the lives of at least five Hezbollah fighters and four militiamen of the South Lebanon Army (SLA), Israel's proxy militia in the contested zone. . . . Eritrea deploys thousands of armed troops on the border, where Ethiopian troops were already stationed, as fighting that started May 6 escalates.		
May 29	UN secretary general Kofi Annan approves a food-distribution plan that Iraq has set as a precondition for renewal of the UN's oil-for-food program. . . . The IMF agrees to release the latest installment of a three-year, $9.2 billion loan to Russia by the end of June.				The Philippine congress officially declares Joseph Estrada, a former film actor and the current vice president, the winner of the presidential election held May 11. . . . Pakistani president Mohammad Rafiq Tarar declares a state of emergency following the country's May 28 nuclear tests.
May 30	Pakistan detonates what it states is its sixth in a series of underground nuclear tests at its Chagai Hills test site, defying international appeals for restraint following its first round of tests May 28.				A powerful earthquake measuring 6.9 on the Richter scale strikes northeastern Afghanistan, leaving an estimated 3,000–5,000 people dead and injuring an additional 2,000 others. The quake destroys dozens of remote villages, and an additional 45,000 people are reported homeless. An earthquake of comparable magnitude killed an estimated 4,500 in the same mountainous region in February.
May 31		A coalition of reform parties led by Montenegrin president Milo Djukanovic defeats the Socialist People's Party (SPP) in parliamentary elections in Montenegro, the smaller of Yugoslavia's two republics.		Candidates from Colombia's two largest political parties—Serpa Uribe and Andres Pastrana Arango—register a virtual tie in a presidential election, setting the stage for a runoff vote on June 21.	In response to the May 30 earthquake, the UN Office for the Coordination of Humanitarian Assistance to Afghanistan and the UN World Food Program begin to coordinate a joint airlift of food, medical supplies and tents. Other agencies, including France's Doctors Without Borders and the International Committee for the Red Cross, are also reportedly transporting aid to the devastated areas.
June 1		Most of the 3,200 pilots employed by Air France, the country's state-owned airline, go on strike to protest planned changes in their salary structure.	Former Zambian president Kenneth Kaunda is freed from house arrest after the government withdraws charges of treason against him.		

A	B	C	D	E
Includes developments that affect more than one world region, international organizations, and important meetings of major world leaders.	Includes all domestic and regional developments in Europe, including the Soviet Union, Turkey, Cyprus, and Malta.	Includes all domestic and regional developments in Africa and the Middle East, including Iraq and Iran and excluding Cyprus, Turkey, and Afghanistan.	Includes all domestic and regional developments in Latin America, the Caribbean, and Canada.	Includes all domestic and regional developments in Asia and Pacific nations, extending from Afghanistan through all the Pacific Island, except Hawaii.

U.S. Politics & Social Issues	U.S. Foreign Policy & Defense	U.S. Economy & Environment	Science, Technology, & Nature	Culture, Leisure, & Lifestyle	
U.S. district judge G. Thomas Van Bebber sentences Michael Fortier to 12 years in prison for withholding information from authorities about his knowledge of a plan that resulted in the April 1995 bombing in Oklahoma City, Oklahoma.... Dana Landers and Emmett Clark, members of the Montana Freemen, plead guilty to charges stemming from an armed standoff with federal authorities in 1996.		Louisiana-Pacific Corp., a forest-products manufacturer, pleads guilty in U.S. District Court in Denver, Colorado, to committing fraud and conspiracy and to violating the federal Clean Air Act. As part of a plea agreement with federal authorities, the company agrees to pay $37 million in fines and penalties.	A study finds that Lovastatin, a cholesterol-lowering drug, substantially lowers the risk of heart attacks in patients who have average blood levels of cholesterol.	Frank Capaci, 67, of Carol Stream, Illinois, accepts a $104.3 million prize from organizers of the multistate Powerball lottery. Officially, the prize is worth $195 million, the world's largest-ever lottery prize that could be won by one person.	May 27
Authorities in Hattiesburg, Mississippi, arrest Samuel Bowers, Charles Noble, and Deavours Nix, three Ku Klux Klan (KKK) members on charges related to the 1966 murder of civil-rights activist Vernon F. Dahmer Sr.... Richard White, 39, is killed by an explosion in his home while authorities are en route to question him about the May 25 church bombing in Danville, Illinois. ... Law enforcement officials in Miami, Florida, arrest Humberto Hernandez, a member of the Miami City Commission, on charges of fabricating evidence in a state investigation of voter fraud in the city's 1997 municipal elections.		The Commerce Department reports that U.S. gross domestic product (GDP) grew at a revised, seasonally adjusted annual rate of 4.8% in the first quarter. That compares with an annualized GDP gain of 3.7% in the October–December 1997 quarter.... Philip Lord Carret, 101, financial investor and founder of one of the nation's first mutual funds, the Pioneer Fund, which he managed from 1928 to 1983, dies in Mount Vernon, New York, where he was recovering from hip surgery.	Astronomers announce that a picture taken by the *Hubble Space Telescope* in August 1997 appears to include the first image ever of a planet outside the Earth's solar system. The object is believed to be a planet near a binary star system in the constellation Taurus. The apparent planet, called TMR-1C, is about 450 light years from Earth.... A study suggests that the EPA has overestimated the lung-cancer risk from breathing relatively low amounts of asbestos.	Phil Hartman, 49, popular actor and a regular on *Saturday Night Live* for eight seasons, dies in Encino, California; he is allegedly shot to death by his wife, Brynn Hartman, who then commits suicide.... Jody-Anne Maxwell, 12, wins the 71st National Spelling Bee by correctly spelling "chiaroscurist." Maxwell, from Kingston, Jamaica, is the first foreign contestant ever to win the contest.	May 28
Barry Morris Goldwater, 89, Republican senator from Arizona, 1953–64, 1969–87, and 1964 presidential candidate considered a founder of modern conservative politics, dies in Paradise Valley, Arizona, of natural causes.		The Commerce Department reports that personal pretax income rose 0.4% in April from March, to a seasonally adjusted figure of $7.184 trillion. April's gain marks the 18th consecutive month in which income increased.... Pres. Clinton states he has chosen Alice Rivlin, vice chair of the Federal Reserve Board, to head the federally appointed financial control board for the District of Columbia.		The government of the Philippines files a lawsuit against Christie's International PLC in U.S. District Court in New York City to recover a Pablo Picasso painting, *Head of a Woman* (1954), that was allegedly stolen from the Philippines government.	May 29
			A tornado destroys the small farming town of Spencer, South Dakota, killing six people and injuring some 150 others.		May 30
			Sixteen countries participating in the construction of a planned international space station release a new schedule that calls for the station to be completed in the year 2004.		May 31
In *Federal Election Commission v. Akins*, the Supreme Court rules, 6-3, that a group of voters have a right to sue the FEC for its refusal to impose financial disclosure requirements on a pro-Israel lobbying group. Such disclosure requirements are imposed on political action committees under federal election law.... The John D. and Catherine T. MacArthur Foundation of Chicago awards 29 annual MacArthur Fellowships, honoring individuals in a wide range of fields.		The Financial Accounting Standards Board unanimously approves an accounting proposal that will force U.S. companies to list the fair-market value of derivatives that they own on their balance sheets.... Maryland-based Browning-Ferris Inc. pleads guilty in U.S. District Court in Washington, D.C., to criminal violations of the federal Clean Water Act and agrees to pay $1.5 million in fines.	Pres. Clinton declares Spencer, South Dakota, destroyed by a tornado on May 30, eligible for federal disaster assistance.... The FDA approves a urine-based test for infection by HIV, the virus that causes AIDS.	Australian marathon swimmer Susie Maroney is the first person to swim across the Yucatan Channel between Mexico and Cuba. Maroney's 123-mile (200-km) swim sets an unofficial record for distance swimming at sea. She completes the crossing in 38 hours and 33 minutes.	June 1

F	G	H	I	J
Includes elections, federal-state relations, civil rights and liberties, crime, the judiciary, education, health care, poverty, urban affairs, and population.	*Includes formation and debate of U.S. foreign and defense policies, veterans' affairs, and defense spending. (Relations with specific foreign countries are usually found under the region concerned.)*	*Includes business, labor, agriculture, taxation, transportation, consumer affairs, monetary and fiscal policy, natural resources, and pollution.*	*Includes worldwide scientific, medical, and technological developments; natural phenomena; U.S. weather; natural disasters; and accidents.*	*Includes the arts, religion, scholarship, communications media, sports, entertainments, fashions, fads, and social life.*

	World Affairs	Europe	Africa & the Middle East	The Americas	Asia & the Pacific
June 2	Directors of the World Bank disclose that they will postpone disbursement of $206.4 million in loans to India because of the nation's recent nuclear tests.	Reports reveal that Serbian armored vehicles and helicopters are systematically assaulting ethnic Albanian enclaves by firing on villages and burning houses. The offensive that started May 22 has resulted in the deaths of at least 37 ethnic Albanians as well as two Serbian police officers. At least a dozen villages have reportedly been reduced to rubble and abandoned.		An audit team from the Caribbean Community (CARICOM) concludes that Guyana's 1997 presidential election of Janet Jagan was fair. . . . In Canada, a Quebec court finds Progressive Conservative senator Michel Cogger guilty of influence peddling.	
June 3		A high-speed passenger train crashes in northern Germany, killing scores of people and injuring at least 300 others. The accident is described as Germany's worst railroad crash in at least 50 years and Western Europe's worst in nearly 25 years. . . . Three Holocaust survivors file a class-action lawsuit in New York City against Germany's two largest banks, Deutsche Bank AG and Dresdner Bank AG, accusing the banks of trafficking in gold that the Nazi German regime stole from Holocaust victims. The suit is the first seeking compensation for looted gold that specifically targeted banks outside Switzerland.	Mohammed Rashid, a Palestinian man suspected of carrying out a deadly midair bombing of a U.S. airliner in 1982, is transported to the U.S. from Egypt to face charges. The blast killed one passenger and wounded 15 others.	Reports confirm that Suzy Camelia-Romer of the People's National Party has been sworn in as the new premier of the Netherlands Antilles, ending a five-month-long political stalemate in the self-governing Dutch territory, which comprises five Caribbean islands.	
June 4	Representatives from the world's five recognized nuclear powers—the U.S., Russia, China, France, and Britain—hold emergency talks on security issues tied to the South Asian nuclear tests. The five nations call for India and Pakistan to halt their development of nuclear weapons and to refrain from testing nuclear missiles. In exchange, the five nations pledge to assist Pakistan and India in resolving their dispute over the Kashmir region.	The official death toll from the June 3 train crash in Germany stands at 93, but many officials predict that the toll may rise above 100 as additional bodies are found in the wreckage. . . . Reports suggest that between 5,000 and 10,000 ethnic Albanian refugees from Kosovo have poured into Albania since May 31.		The Colombian government announces that a right-wing paramilitary group, the United Self-Defense Group of Colombia, has claimed responsibility for the slaughter of 36 people in the oil town of Barrancabermeja. The group states that it killed 11 people during a raid on the town May 16–17 and kidnapped and later killed 25 others and burned their bodies. . . . Peruvian president Alberto Fujimori appoints Javier Valle Riestra, a liberal and longtime advocate of human rights in Peru, as premier.	Tens of thousands of people attend a candlelight vigil in Hong Kong's Victoria Park in memory of those killed in a June 4, 1989, government crackdown on prodemocracy protesters in Tiananmen Square in Beijing, China. The annual vigil is held for the first time since Hong Kong reverted to Chinese sovereignty in July 1997. . . . South Koreans vote for local and regional government officials in the first elections since Pres. Kim Dae Jung was elected in December 1997.
June 5			In the border dispute between Ethiopia and Eritrea that erupted May 6, Eritrean forces carry out an air raid on the northern Ethiopian town of Mekele, killing at least 40 people, many of whom are civilians. Ethiopia retaliates with air attacks on the Eritrean capital, Asmara.	The province of Alberta announces that it will compensate 504 people sterilized without their permission under a provincial policy intended to prevent mentally handicapped people from reproducing.	In the Philippines, more than 600 pilots launch a strike against Philippine Airlines (PAL), the nation's most widely used airline, to protest the institution of a new early-retirement policy.
June 6		A court in Florence, Italy, finds 24 people guilty of orchestrating a series of 1993 car bombings linked to the Mafia. Of those convicted, 14 receive life prison sentences, while the others receive prison terms ranging from 12 to 28 years. Three reputed bosses of the Sicilian Mafia, or Cosa Nostra—Leoluca Bagarella, Filippo Graviano, and Bernardo Provenzano—are among those sentenced to life.	Guinea-Bissau president João Bernardo Vieira dismisses Brigadier General Ansumane Mane in the wake of revelations that a group of senior army officers smuggled arms to separatist rebels in neighboring Senegal.		
June 7		Violence in Kosovo spreads to Pristina, the provincial capital, where police officers break up an independence rally. . . . Voters in Switzerland reject a ballot measure that would have sharply restricted research involving genetically altered animals and barred the patenting of genetically engineered plants.	Brigadier General Ansumane Mane, Guinea-Bissau's former army chief of staff, leads a mutiny against the government in Bissau, the capital. The mutiny launches weeks of fighting.		Statistics show that 2,518 people have died since a heat wave struck India in May. The eastern state of Orissa reportedly has suffered over 1,200 deaths related to the heat wave since May 12. . . . A bomb explodes on a train in southern Pakistan, killing at least 23 people and injuring at least 45 others. . . . In the Philippines, PAL fires the pilots striking since June 5 after they defy a government order to return to work.

A	B	C	D	E
Includes developments that affect more than one world region, international organizations, and important meetings of major world leaders.	*Includes all domestic and regional developments in Europe, including the Soviet Union, Turkey, Cyprus, and Malta.*	*Includes all domestic and regional developments in Africa and the Middle East, including Iraq and Iran and excluding Cyprus, Turkey, and Afghanistan.*	*Includes all domestic and regional developments in Latin America, the Caribbean, and Canada.*	*Includes all domestic and regional developments in Asia and Pacific nations, extending from Afghanistan through all the Pacific Island, except Hawaii.*

U.S. Politics & Social Issues	U.S. Foreign Policy & Defense	U.S. Economy & Environment	Science, Technology, & Nature	Culture, Leisure, & Lifestyle	
California voters approve, 61%-39%, a ballot proposal to eliminate the state's bilingual education system adopted in the 1960s. Under the bilingual system, non-English-speaking students are taught basic subjects in their native tongue while they learn English.	Oran K. Henderson, 77, U.S. Army colonel in the Vietnam War who was the highest-ranking officer to be tried in connection with the infamous 1968 My Lai massacre, dies in Lebanon, Pennsylvania, while suffering from pancreatic cancer.	Merrill Lynch & Co. Inc. agrees to pay $400 million to settle a civil lawsuit brought by Orange County, California, in connection with the county's bankruptcy in 1994.... California's voters reject, 53%-47%, a "paycheck protection" measure to require labor unions to secure written permission from their members before using their dues for political contributions.	The U.S. space shuttle *Discovery* lifts off from Kennedy Space Center in Cape Canaveral, Florida, on a mission to retrieve U.S. astronaut Andrew Thomas from the Russian space station *Mir*.	A U.S. District Court judge sentences artist Peter Max to two months in prison and 800 hours of community service for tax evasion and conspiracy.... Dorothy Stickney, 101, theater actress of the 1930s and 1940s, dies in New York City of unreported causes.	June 2
The House, by voice vote, passes a bill allowing churches and charities to keep contributions from donors who go bankrupt.... George Soros, a billionaire investor and philanthropist, announces plans to help fund a grant program for U.S. public-interest lawyers serving low- and moderate-income communities.	James M. Clark, a former student radical accused of spying for the former East Germany, pleads guilty to conspiracy to commit espionage in U.S. District Court in Alexandria, Virginia.... Lucien E. Conein, 79, who began working for U.S. intelligence in the 1940s and was in charge of covert operations for the DEA, 1973–84, dies in Bethesda, Maryland, of heart ailments.		VaxGen Inc. announces that the FDA gave the company approval to conduct the first full-scale human trial of a vaccine designed to prevent infection with HIV, the virus that causes AIDS.... The FDA approves a combination therapy of two antiviral drugs—ribavirin and injected interferon—to treat hepatitis C, a chronic viral infection of the liver.	Sara Lee Corp. announces that it will donate 40 works of art worth approximately $100 million to 20 different U.S. museums.... Sotheby's and Christie's close their major spring New York City sales. Total revenues for both auction houses fell below spring 1997 earnings. Sotheby's took in a total of $113.5 million, a 7% drop from 1997. Christie's sales totaled $113.2 million, down 57% from 1997.	June 3
The House votes, 224-203, for a constitutional amendment allowing prayer in schools and religious symbols in federal buildings falling 61 votes short of the two-thirds majority needed. It is the first time a school prayer bill has reached the House floor since 1971.... Judge Richard Matsch sentences Terry L. Nichols to life in prison with no possibility of parole for conspiring in the 1995 bombing of a federal building in Oklahoma City, Oklahoma.	The House approves, 364-50, an agriculture bill that will restore food-stamp benefits to 250,000 of the 935,000 legal immigrants who lost eligibility under a welfare overhaul bill enacted in 1996.	The House approves, 410-1, a bill designed to encourage some recipients of Social Security disability benefits to return to the workforce.	Reports confirm that the NIH has lowered the weight threshold at which a person will be considered overweight or obese, adding some 29 million people to the 68 million already considered overweight. The guidelines use the "body mass index" to define overweight and obesity.	Shirley Povich, 92, sports columnist for *The Washington Post*, dies in Washington, D.C., of a heart attack.... Former heavyweight boxing world champion Riddick Bowe pleads guilty in U.S. District Court in Charlotte, North Carolina, to a single felony charge of interstate domestic violence.	June 4
The Senate clears, by voice vote, a bill increasing penalties for parents who refuse to pay child support. ... Attorney General Janet Reno states that the Justice Department will not prosecute doctors for prescribing drugs for the purpose of suicide under an Oregon law permitting physician-assisted suicide. ... Samuel William Yorty, 88, Democratic mayor of Los Angeles, 1961–73, and member of the House representing California, 1951–55, dies in Los Angeles after suffering a stroke in May.		Members of UAW Local 659 walk off their jobs at the Flint Metal Center, a GM metal-stamping plant.... Attorney General Janet Reno states she has named David Vicinanzo, an assistant U.S. attorney from New Hampshire, to take over the Justice Department task force investigating the 1996 fund-raising scandals.	Scientists announce their finding that neutrinos, by far the most common kind of subatomic particles and ones that had long been assumed to have no mass, do in fact have mass. The discovery is expected to force physicists to revise what is known as the "standard model" explaining the behavior of particles and physical forces.	Alfred Kazin, 83, author, literary critic, and intellectual, dies in New york City while suffering from prostate and bone cancer.	June 5
A New York City jury sentences Darrel K. Harris, a former city corrections officer, to death for the 1996 murders of three people at a social club, imposing the death penalty for the first time since New York State reenacted it in 1995.				Arantxa Sanchez Vicario of Spain wins her third French Open women's tennis title... Victory Gallop wins the 130th running of the Belmont Stakes in Elmont, New York.... High-Rise wins the 219th Derby at Epsom Downs racetrack in England.	June 6
James Byrd Jr., a 49-year-old black man, is beaten and then dragged for 2 miles (3 km) while chained to the back of a pick-up truck in a remote area near the rural town of Jasper, Texas. Byrd dies from his injuries. The incident draws nationwide media attention, fueling public concern about the threat of racially motivated crimes.			Reports confirm that surgeons at Cleveland Clinic in Cleveland, Ohio, performed the world's first successful larynx transplant operation.	South Korean president Kim Dae Jung Kim dedicates a new gallery of Korean art at New York's Metropolitan Museum of Art.... At the French Open, Spain's Carlos Moya wins the men's tennis title.... At the Tonys, the musicals *The Lion King*, *Ragtime*, and *Cabaret* dominate the major award categories, and *Art* wins for best play.	June 7

F	G	H	I	J
Includes elections, federal-state relations, civil rights and liberties, crime, the judiciary, education, health care, poverty, urban affairs, and population.	*Includes formation and debate of U.S. foreign and defense policies, veterans' affairs, and defense spending. (Relations with specific foreign countries are usually found under the region concerned.)*	*Includes business, labor, agriculture, taxation, transportation, consumer affairs, monetary and fiscal policy, natural resources, and pollution.*	*Includes worldwide scientific, medical, and technological developments; natural phenomena; U.S. weather; natural disasters; and accidents.*	*Includes the arts, religion, scholarship, communications media, sports, entertainments, fashions, fads, and social life.*

	World Affairs	Europe	Africa & the Middle East	The Americas	Asia & the Pacific
June 8		Reports suggest that the death toll from an ongoing Serbian offensive along the province's southwestern border reached at least 50.	Gen. Sani Abacha, 54, Nigerian military leader and president since 1993, dies in Abuja, Nigeria, reportedly of a heart attack.		
June 9	Officials of the Belarus government issue a formal order for several diplomats to leave their residences, located in a wooded compound outside of the capital, Minsk, so that important repairs can be undertaken. Only the ambassador from Bulgaria agrees to leave, prompting negotiations to commence between the U.S., EU nations, and Belarus.	The final official death toll from the June 3 train accident in Germany is set at 95. . . . Cardinal Agostino Casaroli, 83, former Vatican secretary of state, 1979–90, who played a leading role in a reconciliation of the Roman Catholic Church with communist states in Eastern Europe, dies in Rome, Italy, of an infection after minor surgery.	General Abdulsalam Abubakar, the army's chief of staff, is sworn in as Nigeria's new military ruler.	Reports reveal that in April, officials of Brazil's Federal Indian Bureau discovered a previously unknown Indian tribe living in a remote region of the Amazon rain forest, near the border with Peru. Little is known about the customs, language, or name of the tribe, which is believed to comprise about 200 people who rely on fishing and hunting for sustenance.	A powerful cyclone, packing winds of up to 95 miles per hour (150 kph), lashes India's western coastal state of Gujarat. Officials state that the cyclone is the most severe storm to hit the state since 1973.
June 10	The UN General Assembly endorses a UN International Drug Control Program (IDCP) plan to end the worldwide cultivation of coca and poppy leaves within 10 years. The plants are used in the production of cocaine and heroin, respectively.	The pilots employed by Air France, the country's state-owned airline, who struck in June, reach a settlement. . . . Sir David English, 67, British newspaperman considered one of the most influential journalists in England, dies in London after suffering a stroke a day earlier.		An official of the Colombian Red Cross states that in recent weeks, dozens of members of leftist rebel groups and right-wing paramilitary groups have died in clashes in the northwest Uraba region.	
June 11	The defense ministers from NATO's 16 member nations approve plans to conduct military maneuvers near Serbia.	Unidentified European military officials report that the Yugoslav army has begun planting land mines in Kosovo along the province's border with Albania.	In Nigeria, Colonel Muhammad Marwa, the military administrator of Lagos—the hub of political opposition to the military government—bans planned demonstrations.		
June 12		The British government publishes a list of several hundred people receiving peerages, knighthoods and other honors to mark the official birthday celebration of Queen Elizabeth II.	Heavily armed police and government troops disperse antigovernment demonstrators with tear gas and warning shots in Lagos, Nigeria. The protest marks the fifth anniversary of nullified elections in which jailed political leader Moshood K. O. Abiola was the apparent victor. Fifty-five people are arrested at the gathering. . . . Thousands of Guinea-Bissau refugees begin arriving in Senegal. Some 200 refugees die when their boat capsizes off the coast of Bissau.	Reports confirm that in Guyana, 25 legislators from the People's National Congress (PNC) were expelled from the 65-member Parliament after refusing to take their seats in protest of the 1997 election.	
June 13			Serbian forces kill at least four ethnic Albanians in raids on villages.	Lucio Costa, 96, Brazilian architect and urban planner, dies in Rio de Janeiro of unreported causes.	Data shows that 36 Taiwanese children have died from an intestinal virus epidemic of the enterovirus type 71. Another 200 were hospitalized in serious condition.

A	B	C	D	E
Includes developments that affect more than one world region, international organizations, and important meetings of major world leaders.	*Includes all domestic and regional developments in Europe, including the Soviet Union, Turkey, Cyprus, and Malta.*	*Includes all domestic and regional developments in Africa and the Middle East, including Iraq and Iran and excluding Cyprus, Turkey, and Afghanistan.*	*Includes all domestic and regional developments in Latin America, the Caribbean, and Canada.*	*Includes all domestic and regional developments in Asia and Pacific nations, extending from Afghanistan through all the Pacific Island, except Hawaii.*

U.S. Politics & Social Issues	U.S. Foreign Policy & Defense	U.S. Economy & Environment	Science, Technology, & Nature	Culture, Leisure, & Lifestyle	
In *New Mexico v. Reed*, the Supreme Court rules unanimously that states must extradite fugitives to other states upon request. . . . In *Muscarello v. U.S.*, the Supreme Court rules, 5-4, to uphold a broad reading of a federal gun law that imposes a mandatory five-year prison sentence on individuals who carry guns while committing narcotics crimes.	Navy Secretary John Dalton resigns, ending a five-year tenure as the U.S. Navy's civilian leader.	In *U.S. v. Bestfoods*, the Supreme Court rules unanimously that parent companies may be required to help pay for cleaning up pollution caused by their subsidiaries' facilities if they were directly involved in operating the polluting facilities. . . . American Honda Motor Co. and Ford Motor Co. agree to pay millions of dollars in fines for violations of the Clean Air Act.	The FTC files a lawsuit against Intel Corp., accusing it of using its near-monopoly in the microprocessor market to coerce three computer makers to sign patent agreements that favor Intel. . . . Hoffmann-LaRoche Inc. complies with an FDA request to withdraw mibefradil, a popular blood-pressure medicine, because it interacts adversely with 25 other drugs.	The NRA elects actor Charlton Heston as its new president. . . . Former Beatles Ringo Starr, Paul McCartney, and George Harrison appear together in public for the first time in nearly three decades when they attend a memorial service for Linda McCartney.	June 8
Police charge three white men—Shawn Berry, 23; Lawrence Brewer, 31; and John King, 23—with the murder of James Byrd Jr., 49, who died June 7.	The House passes, 392-22, legislation that will mandate imposing sanctions on companies and research laboratories anywhere in the world that supply Iran with missile technology. . . . The House approves, by voice vote, a bill that will create a 21-member panel to look for assets of Holocaust victims in the coffers of government agencies. . . . The U.S. Army unveils plans to revamp most of its basic combat units, known as divisions, in order meet the changing needs of contemporary warfare.	AMEX and the Philadelphia Stock Exchange, the nation's oldest exchange, agree to merge. . . . Pres. Clinton signs a six-year, $216 billion surface-transportation bill passed by Congress in May.		Delegates to the Southern Baptist Convention approve a statement declaring that wives should "submit graciously" to their husbands. . . . Lois Mailou Jones, 92, a pioneer for and a mentor to new generations of black painters, dies in Washington, D.C., of a heart attack. . . . Data reveals that a record 11.5 million people attended shows in New York City's Broadway theater district during the 1997–98 season.	June 9
A jury in Jacksonville, Florida, finds Brown & Williamson Tobacco Corp. liable for the death of Roland Maddox from lung cancer and awards $950,000 in damages to Maddox's family. . . . The Wisconsin Supreme Court rules, 4-2, that state funds may be used to send children in Milwaukee to religious schools. The landmark decision is expected to pave the way for the U.S. Supreme Court's first-ever consideration of the constitutionality of such voucher programs.	The Senate passes by voice vote a bill that will create a 21-member panel to look for assets of Holocaust victims in the coffers of government agencies. Hidden assets include funds looted by the Nazis and later seized by the U.S., as well as the contents of unclaimed bank accounts in which Holocaust victims may have concealed money.			(Ralph) Hammond Innes, 84, British author of adventure and suspense novels who wrote more than 30 books and sold some 40 million copies of his works, dies in Kersey, England, of unreported causes.	June 10
The Washington State Supreme Court, 5-4, strikes down a 1984 state law barring false political advertising, arguing that the law is unconstitutional because it violates First Amendment free speech rights.	Reports confirm that the U.S. Navy and Timothy R. McVeigh, an officer whom the service tried unsuccessfully to discharge after learning that he anonymously declared himself a homosexual on the Internet global computer network, reach a settlement that will allow McVeigh to retire early with full benefits. In a separate agreement, AOL has volunteered to pay McVeigh an undisclosed amount of money for violating his privacy by revealing to naval investigators that he was the subscriber in question.	Mitsubishi Motor Manufacturing of America Inc. agrees to pay a record $34 million to settle a sexual harassment lawsuit brought by the EEOC in April 1996. The $34 million award is the largest sum ever to be paid to settle a sexual harassment suit, according to the EEOC. . . . Some 5,800 GM workers at a Flint, Michigan, plant, Delphi East, walk off their jobs.	Reports reveal that astronomers have discovered a new class of small, cool stellar objects called L dwarfs, gaseous bodies that did not gather enough mass to start the nuclear fusion process that makes stars hot and bright.	Dame Catherine Ann Cookson, 91, British author of best-selling historical novels, dies in Newcastle, England, while suffering from a blood disorder and a heart ailment.	June 11
Middlesex County (Massachusetts) Superior Court judge Isaac Borenstein grants a new trial to Cheryl Amirault LeFave, convicted in 1987 of sexually abusing children at a day-care center in Malden, Massachusetts. . . . A jury in Hattiesburg, Mississippi, convicts Luke Woodham, 17, on multiple charges of murder and aggravated assault for opening fire on his classmates in October 1997. Two students were killed and seven others were wounded in the shooting. . . . Baron Manning, a 17-year-old black youth, reports being dragged alongside a vehicle driven by three white youths in Belleville, Illinois.	The Justice Department announces it has settled a class-action lawsuit filed on behalf of 1,200 Latin Americans of Japanese descent forcibly placed in U.S. internment camps during World War II. The U.S. had interred 2,264 people of Japanese descent from 13 Latin American countries, along with some 120,000 Japanese Americans, during the war. The current settlement offers $5,000 to each Latin American plaintiff and an apology from the U.S. government.	Pres. Clinton announces that he has extended by 10 years an existing ban on offshore oil drilling along most of the U.S. coastline. Clinton also places an indefinite moratorium on oil exploration in several marine sanctuaries, including California's Monterey Bay and the Florida Keys.	The U.S. space shuttle *Discovery* lands at Kennedy Space Center in Cape Canaveral, Florida, after carrying out its mission to retrieve U.S. astronaut Andrew Thomas from the Russian space station *Mir*.	Eric Marcel Guy Tabarly, 66, French yachtsman, goes missing when he falls overboard while sailing off the coast of Wales.	June 12
A crowd of about 1,000 people attend the funeral of James Byrd, Jr., killed June 7 in Jasper, Texas, by being dragged by a car driven by white youths. . . . A jury in Fauquier County, Virginia, convicts arms heiress Susan Cummings of voluntary manslaughter in the 1997 death of her boyfriend, polo player Roberto Villegas. She is sentenced to 60 days in jail and fined $2,500.			At least 11 people are injured when they are struck by lightning while attending the Tibetan Freedom Concert at Robert F. Kennedy Memorial Stadium in Washington, D.C.	Reg Smythe (Reginald Smyth), 80, British cartoonist who created the Andy Capp character, dies in Hartlepool, England, from cancer.	June 13

F	G	H	I	J
Includes elections, federal-state relations, civil rights and liberties, crime, the judiciary, education, health care, poverty, urban affairs, and population.	Includes formation and debate of U.S. foreign and defense policies, veterans' affairs, and defense spending. (Relations with specific foreign countries are usually found under the region concerned.)	Includes business, labor, agriculture, taxation, transportation, consumer affairs, monetary and fiscal policy, natural resources, and pollution.	Includes worldwide scientific, medical, and technological developments; natural phenomena; U.S. weather; natural disasters; and accidents.	Includes the arts, religion, scholarship, communications media, sports, entertainments, fashions, fads, and social life.

	World Affairs	Europe	Africa & the Middle East	The Americas	Asia & the Pacific
June 14		Ethnic Albanian separatists in Kosovo ambush Serbian police officers and Yugoslav soldiers, killing two officers and wounding seven officers and soldiers.	Lebanon concludes its first municipal elections in 35 years. No party, faction, or alliance emerges with a clear hold on overall local power.		
June 15	About 80 military aircraft from NATO countries conduct airborne exercises near the Yugoslav border over Albania and Macedonia in an effort to pressure the Yugoslav republic of Serbia to stop using military force against ethnic Albanian separatists in the province of Kosovo, the population of which is 90% ethnic Albanian. Since February, fighting in the region has led to more than 250 deaths, including several civilian casualties, and has prompted the exodus of tens of thousands of ethnic Albanians.		General Abdulsalam Abubakar, Nigeria's newly appointed military ruler, orders the release of nine prominent critics of the late General Sani Abacha's military regime from their detention in prison.	Voters in the Caribbean nation of St. Vincent and the Grenadines re-elect Prime Minister James Mitchell to a fourth five-year term.	Philippine Airlines (PAL) announces that it will lay off more than 5,000 of its 13,000 employees amid an ongoing pilots' strike that started June 5. The layoff is the largest by a Philippine company since the 1980s. . . . The Federal Supreme Court of Switzerland rules that some $270 million in assets of the late president Ferdinand Marcos may be transferred to the Philippine government.
June 16		In an apparent response to the June 15 NATO maneuvers, Yugoslav president Slobodan Milosevic agrees to make some concessions over the Kosovo conflict, but he categorically refuses to withdraw Serbian military personnel from the province. Separately, a shepherd, Adem Bajram Selmani, is shot to death in Albania near the border with Kosovo, in a slaying blamed on Serbian security forces.	Senegalese troops launch an artillery attack on Casamance rebel units inside Guinea-Bissau. . . . Israeli warplanes fire missiles at suspected military outposts of the Hezbollah movement near the village of Sojod, located just north of Israel's self-declared security zone in southern Lebanon. No casualties are reported in the attack, the latest in an ongoing deadly exchange. . . . Jafar Sharif-Emami, 87, Iranian premier, 1960–61, 1978, dies in NYC of unreported causes.		The Taliban orders the closure of more than 100 private schools educating girls in Afghanistan. . . . Chung Ju Yung, the founder of South Korea's Hyundai Group conglomerate, leads a convoy of 50 trucks carrying 500 cattle from South Korea to its long-time enemy North Korea. The cattle are to be used to pull plows on farmland in North Korea, which is suffering from a severe food shortage.
June 17		The parliament of Montenegro appoints 20 members of the reformist Democratic Socialist Party (DPS) to serve as the republic's representatives to the upper chamber of the federal Yugoslav legislature in Belgrade, the capital of Yugoslavia.	Sheik Mohammed Mutwali el-Sharawi, 87, Egyptian cleric and Islamic scholar who served as Egypt's minister of religious endowments, 1976–78 dies near Giza, Egypt, of unreported causes.	In Guyana, supporters of the People's National Congress (PNC) riot in the streets of Georgetown, the capital, virtually shutting down the city.	Data reveals that the June 9 cyclone in India's western coastal state of Gujarat resulted in 1,320 deaths. That figure is expected to climb, because officials estimate that between 10,000 and 14,000 people are missing in the wake of the storm.
June 18				On the Caribbean island of Puerto Rico, a U.S. commonwealth, telephone workers begin an island-wide strike, prompting several violent confrontations between riot police and union members. . . . A commuter plane crashes at Mirabel International Airport, some 50 km (30 miles) north of Montreal, Quebec, Canada, as it attempts an emergency landing. The nine passengers—all employees of General Electric Canada Inc.—and the plane's two crew members are killed in the crash.	
June 19	Frustrated by the protracted discussion among the governments of the U.S., Belarus, and EU nations regarding Belarus's June 9 order that diplomats leave their residences in a compound outside of Minsk, Belarus officials cut off the compound's water, electricity, and telephone service without warning. Turkey recalls its ambassador.	Pope John Paul II makes his first visit to Austria since 1988. . . . Switzerland's three largest banks offer to pay $600 million to victims of the Nazi Holocaust to settle the victims' claims that they were unable to recover assets deposited in the banks before and during World War II. Leaders of Jewish advocacy groups attack the settlement offer as inadequate.	Ayatollah Mirza Ali al-Gharawi, a senior Iraqi Shi'ite cleric, is shot to death while traveling by car between the cities of Karbala and Najaf. . . . A car bomb explodes, killing two people in the Dawra section of east Beirut, Lebanon, a predominantly Christian area. . . . Forces loyal to Brigadier General Ansumane Mane, Guinea-Bissau's former army chief of staff who led a mutiny against the government June 7, launch an artillery strike on Bissau, the capital.		
	A	**B**	**C**	**D**	**E**
	Includes developments that affect more than one world region, international organizations, and important meetings of major world leaders.	*Includes all domestic and regional developments in Europe, including the Soviet Union, Turkey, Cyprus, and Malta.*	*Includes all domestic and regional developments in Africa and the Middle East, including Iraq and Iran and excluding Cyprus, Turkey, and Afghanistan.*	*Includes all domestic and regional developments in Latin America, the Caribbean, and Canada.*	*Includes all domestic and regional developments in Asia and Pacific nations, extending from Afghanistan through all the Pacific Island, except Hawaii.*

U.S. Politics & Social Issues	U.S. Foreign Policy & Defense	U.S. Economy & Environment	Science, Technology, & Nature	Culture, Leisure, & Lifestyle	
Some members of the Montana Freemen, a right-wing antitax group, who are charged in connection with an 81-day armed standoff with federal authorities in 1996, launch a hunger strike.... At a commencement address at the University of California in San Diego by House speaker Newt Gingrich (R, Ga.), some 40 of the graduates walk out in protest of his appearance and of the 1997 anti-affirmative action measure, Proposition 209.				Basketball's Chicago Bulls win their third consecutive NBA championship, over the Utah Jazz, 87-86.... Eric Marcel Guy Tabarly, 66, who fell overboard off the coast of Wales on June 12, is declared dead by drowning.... Ginette Mathiot, 91, French cooking expert whose book sold more than 5 million copies, dies in Paris.	June 14
In Richmond, Virginia, Quinshawn Booker, 15, allegedly fires an automatic handgun in his high school, injuring two people.... In *Pennsylvania Department of Corrections v. Yeskey*, the Supreme Court rules unanimously that state prisoners are protected by the 1990 Americans With Disabilities Act (ADA).... In *Phillips v. Washington Legal Foundation*, the Supreme Court rules, 5-4, that programs currently used in every state to fund legal services for poor people may be unconstitutional.		The Dow closes at 8627.93, down 207.01 points, the fifth-largest single-session point decrease on record.	Leptin, a human hormone that helps regulate appetite and metabolism, may be effective in assisting weight loss, according to research.		June 15
	The Supreme Judicial Court of Massachusetts, 4-3, upholds the manslaughter conviction of Louise Woodward, a British au pair accused of killing Matthew Eappen, an eight-month-old infant who died while in her care. The case sparked international attention with the 1997 decision to reduce Woodward's second-degree murder conviction to manslaughter.			Hockey's Detroit Red Wings defeat the Washington Capitals, 4-1, in Washington, D.C., to win their second consecutive Stanley Cup.... The American Film Institute (AFI) announces the winners of a poll for the 100 best U.S. films of all time, and *Citizen Kane* (1941) tops the list.	June 16
Dr. Nancy Dickey of College Station, Texas, takes office as the American Medical Association's first female president. Delegates elect Dr. Thomas Reardon of Portland, Oregon, as the next president of the organization, to begin a one-year term in June 1999.... The National Cancer Institute estimates that 50% fewer white men ages 18–27 were infected with HIV, the virus that causes AIDS, in 1993 than in 1988.					June 17
The House approves, 225-197, legislation that will allow parents to save money for their children's education costs, including private-school tuition fees, in new tax-sheltered accounts.... A jury in Fort Stockton, Texas, convicts Richard Frank Keyes III, a member of the Republic of Texas, separatist group, of burglary and assault charges stemming from the group's 1997 armed standoff with federal authorities.	Pres. Clinton names Richard C. Holbrooke as the U.S. ambassador to the United Nations.	Pres. Clinton names Bill Richardson as energy secretary.... The Commerce Department reports that the U.S. trade deficit expanded 9.5% in April to register its third record high in four months, logging a seasonally adjusted $14.46 billion gap in trade in goods and services. That is up from March's revised record deficit of $13.21 billion.	Researchers report they have captured the first-ever images of HIV, the virus that causes AIDS, in the process of attacking a human cell.		June 18
Pres. Clinton signs a bill allowing churches and charities to keep contributions from donors who go bankrupt.	The INS announces that 49 illegal Mexican immigrants caught up in a forced-labor smuggling ring in New York City will be allowed to remain in the U.S. INS officials state that the immigrants—almost all of whom are deaf—will be released within 30 days from a hotel where they have been held in federal custody for about 11 months. Agustin Rodriguez-Torres, an accomplice, is sentenced to 10 months in prison, the amount of time he has already served.				June 19
F	G	H	I	J	
Includes elections, federal-state relations, civil rights and liberties, crime, the judiciary, education, health care, poverty, urban affairs, and population.	*Includes formation and debate of U.S. foreign and defense policies, veterans' affairs, and defense spending. (Relations with specific foreign countries are usually found under the region concerned.)*	*Includes business, labor, agriculture, taxation, transportation, consumer affairs, monetary and fiscal policy, natural resources, and pollution.*	*Includes worldwide scientific, medical, and technological developments; natural phenomena; U.S. weather; natural disasters; and accidents.*	*Includes the arts, religion, scholarship, communications media, sports, entertainments, fashions, fads, and social life.*	

	World Affairs	Europe	Africa & the Middle East	The Americas	Asia & the Pacific
June 20		The center-left Czech Social Democratic Party (CSSD) tops the balloting in parliamentary elections in the Czech Republic, capturing 32.3% of the vote.	Riots erupt in Yemen as demonstrators protest cuts in bread and fuel subsidies prompted by lost oil income.	In an apparent attempt to intimidate voters, leftist rebels, reportedly of the FARC and the ELN, seize at least 14 hostages near the town of Lejanias in northwest Colombia.	
June 21		French security officials institute emergency powers allowing them to deport so-called Category C hooligans on the basis that such soccer rowdies pose a marked potential danger to public order. Daniel Nivel, 43, a French police officer, is clubbed into a coma by German hooligans in Lens. . . . Pope John Paul II beatifies three former clerics of the church, including Restituta Kafka, a nun beheaded by the Nazis during World War II. . . . Ernst Brugger, 84, Swiss president, 1974, dies in Grueningen, Switzerland, after suffering a stroke two years earlier.	Warring factions in Burundi's five-year-old civil conflict agree to call a temporary truce and commit to further peace negotiations after a week of talks in Arusha, Tanzania. . . . Togo holds presidential elections. . . . Heavy exchanges of fire that started June 19 in Bissau, the capital of Guinea-Bissau, subside, giving way to isolated street skirmishes between the opposing factions. . . . Iran's Majlis, or parliament, votes to impeach Interior Minister Abdullah Nouri, a member of Agatollah Ali Khatami's inner leadership circle.	Colombians elect Andres Pastrana Arango of the Conservative Party as the country's new president in a second-round runoff vote. He will succeed current president Ernesto Samper Pizano of the Liberal Party, ending 12 consecutive years of Liberal Party rule in Colombia.	
June 22	Ambassadors from the U.S., Japan, and five European nations return indefinitely to their native countries to protest ongoing attempts by the government of Belarus to evict them from their local diplomatic residences. Britain expels the Belarus ambassador to Britain. . . . The European Union formally approves a broad-based ban on tobacco advertising.		A spokesman for the United Nations High Commissioner for Refugees projects that an outbreak of famine is imminent in Guinea-Bissau because fighting has prevented aid workers from transporting adequate food and medical supplies.	Reports confirm that rebels have attacked army and police stations, kidnapped three election officials, and torched 32 buses in the northern and northeastern regions of Columbia in preelection violence. . . . In Guyana, bombs and fires, apparently set by rioters who turned violent on June 17, damage buildings that house several government ministries.	A small North Korean submarine on an apparent infiltration mission to South Korea becomes entangled in a fishing net some 11 miles (20 km) off the South Korean coast.
June 23	The UN finds that in 1997, some 5.8 million people worldwide were newly infected with HIV, and 2.3 million people died from AIDS. A total of 30.6 million people worldwide carried the virus in 1997. Twenty-one million of the world's infected people are in Africa. Some 860,000 people infected with HIV live in North America. A total of 11.7 million people have died of AIDS since the epidemic began. . . . Data suggest that the current global oversupply of oil caused OPEC nations' collective oil revenues to drop by nearly $50 billion during the previous 12 months.	Ethnic Albanian separatists have taken control of the strategic Belacevac coal mine in the embattled Kosovo province, marking the first seizure of a major industrial facility by the rebels in their conflict with the Serb government.		Government officials disclose that attackers believed to belong to the leftist rebel National Liberation Army (ELN) set off six bombs along the Cano Limon-Covenas oil pipeline in northeast Colombia, forcing the its second-largest oil-field to halt production. The latest bombings were the worst of 32 such attacks to occur on the pipeline to date in 1998.	The small North Korean submarine entangled June 22 in a fishing net some 11 miles (20 km) off the South Korean coast sinks to the ocean floor after a towing cable breaks.
June 24	The 11-nation Organization of Petroleum Exporting Countries (OPEC) cartel institutes its second round of oil-production cutbacks in three months, reducing the cumulative output quotas of OPEC members by about 1.36 million barrels a day for a full year.		Togo president Gnassingbe Eyadema is declared the official winner of elections held June 21, despite widespread allegations of voter fraud.	In Puerto Rico, police report that a bomb planted at the Banco Popular de Puerto Rico exploded in an officer's hands, tearing off one of his fingers and injuring his leg. . . . In El Salvador, Judge Gloria Platero orders the release on parole of three of the five national guardsmen convicted of the 1980 abduction, rape, and murder of three U.S. Roman Catholic nuns and a church lay worker in El Salvador. Platero rules that the three guardsmen—Daniel Canales Ramirez, Jose Roberto Moreno Canjura, and Luis Antonio Colindres Aleman—are eligible for parole because they served two-thirds of their 30-year sentences, including time off for good behavior.	

A	B	C	D	E
Includes developments that affect more than one world region, international organizations, and important meetings of major world leaders.	Includes all domestic and regional developments in Europe, including the Soviet Union, Turkey, Cyprus, and Malta.	Includes all domestic and regional developments in Africa and the Middle East, including Iraq and Iran and excluding Cyprus, Turkey, and Afghanistan.	Includes all domestic and regional developments in Latin America, the Caribbean, and Canada.	Includes all domestic and regional developments in Asia and Pacific nations, extending from Afghanistan through all the Pacific Island, except Hawaii.

U.S. Politics & Social Issues	U.S. Foreign Policy & Defense	U.S. Economy & Environment	Science, Technology, & Nature	Culture, Leisure, & Lifestyle	
			Seven people are killed and 18 others are injured when a Greyhound Lines bus crashes into a parked tractor-trailer on the Pennsylvania Turnpike near Fulton Township, Pennsylvania.		June 20
				Lee Janzen wins his second career U.S. Open golf championship.... Al(exander) Sebastian Campanis (born Alessandro Campani), 81, Greek-born general manager of the Los Angeles Dodgers Major League Baseball team who was fired in 1987, dies in Fullerton, California, of coronary artery disease.	June 21
In *U.S. v. Bajakajian*, the Supreme Court rules, 5-4, that the government's seizure of an individual's property as a punishment for criminal conduct is unconstitutional if the value of the property is "grossly disproportional" to the seriousness of the crime.... In *Gebser v. Lago Vista Independent School District*, the Supreme Court limits the circumstances under which students who claim to have been sexually harassed by teachers may sue school districts for monetary damages.			Scientists report they have discovered a planet orbiting a star 15 light-years from Earth, the closest extrasolar planet yet found. The planet is believed to be a cold, gaseous body at least 1.6 times the size of Jupiter. It orbits the star Gliese 876 once every 61 days.... In response to four deaths and eight liver transplants among users, Wyeth-Ayerst withdraws from the market a prescription painkilling drug, Duract, approved by the FDA in July 1997. It is the second such recall in the month.	*Fortune* magazine suggests that NBA star Michael Jordan has had an estimated $10 billion impact on the world's economy since he entered the league in 1984.	June 22
Two Amish men—Abner Stoltzfus, 24, and Abner King Stoltzfus, 23—are charged in Philadelphia, Pennsylvania, with dealing cocaine.	Pres. Clinton signs into law an agriculture bill that will restore food-stamp benefits to 250,000 of the 935,000 legal immigrants who lost eligibility under a welfare overhaul bill enacted in 1996.... Pres. Clinton vetoes U.S. legislation that would mandate imposing sanctions on companies and research laboratories anywhere in the world that supply Iran with missile technology.... Pres. Clinton signs a bill that will create a panel to look for assets of Holocaust victims in the coffers of government agencies.	The SEC announces that it will stop forcing securities workers to take discrimination claims to the industry's mandatory arbitration panels.	A three-judge panel reverses a December 1997 injunction that ordered Microsoft Corp. to sell its Windows 95 operating system separately from Internet Explorer, its "browsing" software.... A study suggests two recently discovered dinosaur fossils show that birds descended from dinosaurs.... Pres. Clinton nominates Dr. Jane E. Henney as commissioner of the FDA.... The House passes, by voice vote, legislation barring state and local governments from imposing new taxes on on-line commerce for three years.	Maureen O'Sullivan, 87, actress who appeared in more than 60 films, dies in Scottsdale, Arizona, of unreported causes.... Mark Iredell Hampton Jr., 58, interior decorator and fabric designer, dies of liver cancer in New York City.	June 23
A jury in New York City convicts Heriberto Seda, the so-called Zodiac killer, of fatally shooting three people and wounding a fourth in a string of attacks from 1990 to 1993.... The House votes, 223-202, to block the FDA from testing or approving drugs to induce abortions, including a French-made pill, RU-486. The measure, sponsored by Rep. Tom Coburn (R, Okla.), is attached to the 1999 agriculture appropriations bill.... Pres. Clinton signs into law a bill increasing penalties for parents who refuse to pay child support.... The Senate passes, 59-36, legislation that will allow parents to save money for their children's education costs, including private-school tuition fees, in new tax-sheltered accounts.			NASA scientists lose contact with a spacecraft launched in 1995 to observe the sun. The craft, the *Solar and Heliospheric Observatory* (SOHO), is a joint project of NASA and the European Space Agency.		June 24

F	G	H	I	J
Includes elections, federal-state relations, civil rights and liberties, crime, the judiciary, education, health care, poverty, urban affairs, and population.	*Includes formation and debate of U.S. foreign and defense policies, veterans' affairs, and defense spending. (Relations with specific foreign countries are usually found under the region concerned.)*	*Includes business, labor, agriculture, taxation, transportation, consumer affairs, monetary and fiscal policy, natural resources, and pollution.*	*Includes worldwide scientific, medical, and technological developments; natural phenomena; U.S. weather; natural disasters; and accidents.*	*Includes the arts, religion, scholarship, communications media, sports, entertainments, fashions, fads, and social life.*

	World Affairs	Europe	Africa & the Middle East	The Americas	Asia & the Pacific
June 25		Voters in Northern Ireland cast ballots in the first election for the British-controlled province's new 108-seat local legislature. The body was created as part of a peace agreement unveiled by political leaders in April. Candidates who favor the peace plan capture a large majority of seats in the new Northern Ireland Assembly. . . . In Spain, Manuel Zamarreno, a councilor in the Basque town of Renteria, is killed when a bomb attached to a motorcycle explodes as he walks past. The attack is blamed on the Basque separatist group ETA. Zamarreno, a member of Aznar's ruling Popular Party, is the party's sixth town councilor killed over the past year in an attack attributed to ETA.	Two Israeli soldiers are killed and four others injured when two roadside bombs explode in Israel's occupation zone in South Lebanon. Separately, after 10 months of intense negotiations, Israel and Lebanon begin a major trade of prisoners and bodies of slain soldiers and guerrillas. . . . Matoub Lounes, 42, a popular singer and outspoken critic of Algeria's civil war, is murdered in a hail of gunfire when his car, en route to his home village in eastern Algeria, is ambushed at a roadblock.		Bill Clinton makes the first visit by a U.S. president to China since 1989.
June 26		U.S. special envoy Richard C. Holbrooke calls the village of Kijevo, Kosovo, situated halfway between Pristina and the city of Pec, "the most dangerous place in Europe," due to fears that fighting among ethnic Albanians and Serbians will spark a wider rebellion . . . . Andrew Croft, 91, British explorer of Greenland and other Arctic regions, dies of undisclosed causes. . . . Lord Derek George Rayner, 72, fomer British chair of Marks & Spencer PLC, 1984–91, dies in London of unreported causes.	Israel and Lebanon complete a major trade of prisoners and bodies of slain soldiers and guerrillas. . . . Some 2,000 youths march in the streets of Tizi-Ouzou, the principal city in the Berber Kabylia region east of Algiers, the capital of Algeria, to protest the June 25 death of singer Matoub Lounes. Rioting erupts outside Algiers in response to the murder . . . . The plane of UN diplomat Alioune Blondin Beye, 59, crashes outside Abidjan, the capital of the Ivory Coast.		South Korean forces cut open the North Korean submarine that became entangled in a fishing net on June 22 and find the bodies of nine crew members, all of whom died of gunshot wounds.
June 27	U.S. president Bill Clinton holds a summit with Chinese president Jiang Zemin in Beijing, China's capital, during the first visit by a U.S. president to that country since 1989. Pres. Clinton is welcomed by a military honor guard in Tiananmen Square.	An earthquake strikes southern Turkey in and around the city of Adana, killing 144 people and injuring more than 1,000 others.			
June 28	Some 13,200 people from 177 countries convene in Geneva, Switzerland, for the 12th International Conference on AIDS. It is the largest such meeting to date.		Authorities in the West African nation of Ivory Coast confirm that UN diplomat Alioune Blondin Beye was killed on June 26 when his plane went down outside Abidjan, the capital.		
June 29	At the UN War Crimes Tribunal for the Former Yugoslavia in The Hague, the Netherlands, indicted Serb war criminal Slavko Dokmanovic, 48, is found hanged in his prison cell. Dokmanovic was arrested in Croatia in June 1997 and charged with six counts of war crimes and crimes against humanity for his alleged accessory role in a 1991 siege and massacre in the town of Vukovar His verdict was expected in early July. . . . The UN AIDS Program announces that it will launch a pilot program to treat 30,000 pregnant women infected with HIV in an effort to prevent the transmission of the virus to their newborn children.	Serb forces kill about 10 ethnic Albanian separatists in the battle to retake the strategic Belacevac coal mine in the embattled Kosovo province seized by rebels June 23. . . . Union Bank of Switzerland and Swiss Bank Corp., Switzerland's second- and third-largest banks, respectively, officially merge as UBS AG and begin operations. The new bank, with more than $700 billion in total assets, is the world's second largest, after Japan's Bank of Tokyo-Mitsubishi Ltd.		The Guyanese army is called out to help police quell the riots that began June 17.	Reports confirm that China's Supreme People's Procuratorate in 1997 published the first official statistics on the number of people killed or seriously injured by police torture. Published after the 1996 passage of a revised Criminal Procedure Law prohibiting the use of torture by police to obtain confessions, the book finds that 241 people were killed by torture under police interrogation in 1993 and 1994, and 64 others were seriously injured in the same period. . . . The South Korean government orders that five small troubled commercial banks be closed and merged with five of South Korea's largest commercial banks. The move is an effort to stabilize the country's banking system, struck by a debt crisis in late 1997.

A	B	C	D	E
Includes developments that affect more than one world region, international organizations, and important meetings of major world leaders.	Includes all domestic and regional developments in Europe, including the Soviet Union, Turkey, Cyprus, and Malta.	Includes all domestic and regional developments in Africa and the Middle East, including Iraq and Iran and excluding Cyprus, Turkey, and Afghanistan.	Includes all domestic and regional developments in Latin America, the Caribbean, and Canada.	Includes all domestic and regional developments in Asia and Pacific nations, extending from Afghanistan through all the Pacific Island, except Hawaii.

U.S. Politics & Social Issues	U.S. Foreign Policy & Defense	U.S. Economy & Environment	Science, Technology, & Nature	Culture, Leisure, & Lifestyle	
In *Clinton v. City of New York*, the Supreme Court rules, 6-3, that the Line Item Veto Act is unconstitutional. . . . In *Swidler & Berlin and Hamilton v. U.S.*, the Supreme Court rules, 6-3, that the confidentiality privilege enjoyed by attorneys and their clients endures after a client's death. . . . In *Bragdon v. Abbott*, the Supreme Court rules, 5-4, that people infected with HIV, the virus that causes AIDS, are entitled to protections provided by the 1990 Americans with Disabilities Act (ADA). The justices' decision marks the high court's first major review of the ADA, which bars discrimination on the basis of disability, and the first significant extension, of legal protection afforded by the high court to individuals with HIV. . . . Reports confirm that at least nine children were infected with a dangerous strain of the *E. coli* O157:H7 bacterium in a Marietta, Georgia, swimming pool. . . . Data shows that a food-poisoning outbreak caused by an illness-causing strain of the E. coli O157:H7 bacterium earlier in the month in Cook County, Illinois, made some 4,500 people sick.	In *U.S. v. Balsys*, the Supreme Court rules, 7-2, that the Constitution's protection against self-incrimination does not extend to defendants in deportation proceedings who express concern about prosecution in foreign countries. . . . A judge in U.S. District Court in New York City sentences Felix Rolando Peterson-Coplin to 6½ years in prison after the defendant pleads guilty to hijacking a plane to Cuba in 1969. Peterson-Coplin was apprehended by federal agents in December 1997 when he tried to enter the U.S. from Canada, where he had been living since 1990.	In Little Rock, Arkansas, U.S. district judge George Howard Jr. orders Whitewater figure Susan McDougal freed from prison and releases her to the custody of her parents for three months of home detention. . . . In *Eastern Enterprises v. Apfel*, the Supreme Court rules, 5-4, to strike down a provision in the 1992 Coal Industry Retiree Health Benefit Act that required companies to bear retroactive liability for the payment of health-care benefits to retired miners and their families. . . . The House approves, 402-8, a bill intended to overhaul the IRS.		In *National Endowment for the Arts v. Finley*, the Supreme Court rules, 8-1, that the federal government is allowed to consider standards of decency when awarding federal arts grants. . . . The Vatican announces that it will sign an accord with the Lutheran World Federation resolving a theological dispute between Roman Catholics and Lutherans over "justification," or how humans achieve salvation. The accord declares that justification is achieved solely by God's grace, from which faith and good works naturally follow.	June 25
In *Monge v. California*, the Supreme Court rules, 5-4, that California prosecutors may pursue a second sentencing proceeding of a convicted criminal under the state's so-called three-strikes law. . . . Former NYC police officer, Francis Livoti, whose illegal choke hold on Anthony Baez resulted in Baez's death in 1994, is convicted of federal charges that he violated Baez's civil rights.	Canada and Washington State announce a one-year agreement restricting the catch of two threatened salmon species, coho and chinook.	The Supreme Court hands down decisions in two cases regarding sexual harassment in the workplace. In *Burlington Industries Inc. v. Ellerth*, the justices rule, 7-2, that an employee who rebuffs a supervisor's sexual advances may pursue a sexual-harassment suit, even though the employee suffered no retaliation for rejecting the advances. In *Faragher v. City of Boca Raton*, the justices hold, 7-2, that an employer may be held liable for sexual harassment by supervisory staff, even if the employer does not know of its supervisors' misconduct.			June 26
A group of about 20 Ku Klux Klan members stage a rally outside the courthouse in the town of Jasper, Texas.					June 27
					June 28
				I Know This Much Is True by Wally Lamb is at the top of *Publishers Weekly*'s bestseller list.	June 29

F	G	H	I	J
Includes elections, federal-state relations, civil rights and liberties, crime, the judiciary, education, health care, poverty, urban affairs, and population.	*Includes formation and debate of U.S. foreign and defense policies, veterans' affairs, and defense spending. (Relations with specific foreign countries are usually found under the region concerned.)*	*Includes business, labor, agriculture, taxation, transportation, consumer affairs, monetary and fiscal policy, natural resources, and pollution.*	*Includes worldwide scientific, medical, and technological developments; natural phenomena; U.S. weather; natural disasters; and accidents.*	*Includes the arts, religion, scholarship, communications media, sports, entertainments, fashions, fads, and social life.*

	World Affairs	Europe	Africa & the Middle East	The Americas	Asia & the Pacific
June 30	In what is called an isolated incident, a U.S. fighter jet fires a missile at an Iraqi antiaircraft battery after the site's radar focused on a British warplane involved in a routine patrol of southern Iraq's "no-flight" zone. The missile misses its target, and no injuries are reported. . . . The EU announces the implementation of new antipollution rules aimed at reducing toxic emissions from automobiles. . . . Several European governments agree to surrender most of their claims to gold looted by Nazi Germany and to donate it to Holocaust survivors.	Serb special police units recapture the strategic Belacevac coal mine in the embattled Kosovo province.	In Algeria, thousands of protesters shout antigovernment and anti-Islamist slogans. At least one person is killed by police gunfire in the demonstration. . . . Reports suggest that troops loyal to Congolese president Laurent Kabila have massacred as many as 500 people at a time. Authors of the report were poorly received by Kabila's government, and they acknowledge that their report is incomplete.	Data show that at least 285 people have died in El Niño's torrential rains and floods in Ecuador. In addition, some 5,000 homes have been destroyed, and widespread damage to bridges, roads, and croplands have been reported. The government estimates that reconstruction in the region will cost $3 billion.	Joseph Estrada is sworn in as the 13th president of the Philippines . . . . In Afghanistan, aid agencies refuse an order by the Taliban to move their Kabul offices of aid organizations into one centralized location, the Kabul Polytechnic, a heavily war-damaged building without water or electricity. . . . Officials of Tibet's government in exile reveal that seven Tibetans were shot dead and 60 others wounded in early May by Chinese authorities in Lhasa, Tibet. The victims, reportedly including a Buddhist monk and five nuns, were prisoners in a Lhasa jail peacefully demonstrating for Tibetan independence.
July 1		Ten Catholic churches in Northern Ireland are set on fire overnight. . . . Princess Diana's grave, on the grounds of Althorp House, the ancestral home of her family in Northamptonshire, England, open to the public for the first time on the day that would have been Diana's 37th birthday.	The Congolese government frees Etienne Tshisekedi, the political opposition's most prominent leader, from internal exile.		The South Korean government states it will release political prisoners to mark the 53rd anniversary of the end of Japanese rule in Korea, which will fall on August 15. . . . Hong Kong stages a series of events marking the first anniversary of Hong Kong's 1997 reversion to Chinese sovereignty. However, a group of anti-China protesters attempts to march to the Hong Kong Convention Center, where they are stopped by police.
July 2	The UN Security Council imposes a new set of sanctions on the National Union for the Total Independence of Angola (UNITA), a rebel movement, in response to the group's lagging compliance with the terms of the 1994 peace plan.	The Loyalist Volunteer Force, a hard-line Protestant guerrilla group opposed to ongoing peace efforts, is suspected in the July 1 arson attacks on 10 Catholic churches in Northern Ireland. A Catholic primary school and three buildings linked to Protestant groups are set ablaze in possible retaliation by Catholics for the church fires.	Abd al-Aziz Shahin, a PNA cabinet minister, and other Palestinians engage in a sit-down demonstration, blocking the major access routes to the Jewish settlements of Gush Qatif and Netzarim. The move prompts a standoff between Israeli soldiers and Palestinian police in the Gaza Strip. . . . UN secretary general Kofi Annan reveals that Nigeria plans to release Moshood K. O. Abiola, who apparently won 1993 presidential elections, and numerous other political figures in the near future.		U.S. president Bill Clinton makes the first visit to Hong Kong by a sitting U.S. president, and he meets with Hong Kong chief executive Tung Chee-hwa. The flight of Air Force One, the presidential jet, is the first to land at Hong Kong's new Chek Lap Kok airport.
July 3	The 12th International Conference on AIDS closes in Geneva, Switzerland, and, in contrast to the last such gathering, held in 1996 in Canada, reports presented at the conference offered little evidence of significant breakthroughs in the search for a cure or vaccine for AIDS.	In Kosova, Serbian forces end a siege of the village of Kijevo, situated halfway between Pristina and the city of Pec. One soldier is reported killed, and 60 rebels are wounded; no casualties are acknowledged by Yugoslav authorities.	The armed standoff that began July 2 between Israeli soldiers and Palestinian police in the Gaza Strip is defused when a deal is brokered that allows Palestinian cars to travel along the road.		Australia's House of Representatives approves the Native Title Bill, a controversial measure that restricts aboriginal land rights. . . . Mohammad Alam Channa, 42, a Pakistani farmer recognized as the world's tallest man with a height of 7 feet, 7¼ inches (2.32 m), dies in New York State while suffering from kidney disease, diabetes, and hypertension.
July 4	Kazakhstan president Nursultan Nazarbayev and Chinese president Jiang Zemin sign a treaty demarcating the 1,200-mile (1,900-km) border between the two countries.	Measuring 5.1 on the Richter scale, an aftershock of the June 27 earthquake strikes southern Turkey It is the largest in a series of more than 70 aftershocks recorded since June 27.		Reports confirm that the relatives of 45 victims of a massacre in Chiapas, Mexico in December 1997 have received $3,900 per family from the state government. The victims were supporters of the Zapatista National Liberation Army, and the suspected perpetrators were members of a paramilitary group that supports the government.	
July 5		Violence erupts throughout Northern Ireland, as Protestant supporters of British rule protest the blocking of a traditional parade. The Orange Order, the province's largest Protestant organization, conducts its annual parade in Portadown, commemorating the victory of Protestant forces over Roman Catholics in the 1690 Battle of the Boyne. Youths in Belfast, the provincial capital, throw gasoline bombs at police, who respond by firing plastic bullets at their attackers.			

A	B	C	D	E
Includes developments that affect more than one world region, international organizations, and important meetings of major world leaders.	Includes all domestic and regional developments in Europe, including the Soviet Union, Turkey, Cyprus, and Malta.	Includes all domestic and regional developments in Africa and the Middle East, including Iraq and Iran and excluding Cyprus, Turkey, and Afghanistan.	Includes all domestic and regional developments in Latin America, the Caribbean, and Canada.	Includes all domestic and regional developments in Asia and Pacific nations, extending from Afghanistan through all the Pacific Island, except Hawaii.

U.S. Politics & Social Issues	U.S. Foreign Policy & Defense	U.S. Economy & Environment	Science, Technology, & Nature	Culture, Leisure, & Lifestyle	
Linda Tripp, whose secret tapes of former White House intern Monica Lewinsky led to an obstruction-of-justice investigation of Pres. Clinton, appears before independent counsel Kenneth Starr's federal grand jury in Washington, D.C. . . . The National Center for Health Statistics finds that the overall 1996 birth rate was 14.7 births per 1,000 total population, down from 14.8 in 1995. The report shows that out-of-wedlock births declined to 44.8 per 1,000 unmarried women, from a peak rate of 46.9 per 1,000 in 1994.	Defense Secretary William S. Cohen announces that genetic tests ordered in May on the remains of the Vietnam War representative in the Tomb of the Unknowns indicate that they belong to U.S. Air Force lieutenant Michael J. Blassie.	The Conference Board reports that its index of consumer confidence rose to a 29-year high of 137.6 in June, from May's revised reading of 136.3. . . . Data shows the aggregate value of U.S. mergers announced in the first six months of 1998 exceeded the total for all of 1997. U.S. companies announced 5,623 deals worth $962.1 billion from January 1 to June 30. In 1997, U.S. firms announced 10,700 deals worth $919 billion. In the first six months of 1997, the value of all announced deals was $366 billion. Both the six-month and year-end figures for 1997 are record totals.	The FDA approves the use of a new artificial sweetener, acesulfame potassium, in soft drinks. The sweetener, known also as Ace-K, is marketed as Sunett by Germany's Hoechst AG. . . . The FDA approves a prescription drug for migraine headaches manufactured by Merck & Co. Inc. The drug, rizatriptan, is to be marketed as Maxalt.	Pope John Paul II issues an apostolic letter that codifies the Roman Catholic Church's opposition to the ordination of women, euthanasia, and sex outside of marriage as "divinely revealed truths" that cannot be challenged.	June 30
The U.S. 10th Circuit Court of Appeals in Denver, Colorado, rules that it is illegal for federal prosecutors to offer witnesses leniency in exchange for testimony. . . . The CDC reveals that AIDS-related deaths among whites fell by 54% from the first half of 1997. AIDS deaths among blacks fell 37% in the first half of 1997. Deaths also fell further among men, by 47%, than among women, by 37%	Representatives of about 800 U.S. state and local governments plan to impose economic sanctions against Swiss banks in an effort to secure a settlement more substantial than the one offered June 19 to compensate Holocaust victims who lost assets deposited in Swiss accounts before and during World War II.	James Robertson of U.S. District Court throws out independent counsel Kenneth Starr's tax-evasion case against Whitewater figure Webster Hubbell.	Doctors at the University of Pittsburgh Medical Center report they have implanted human nerve cells grown in a laboratory into the brain of a stroke patient. It is the first time laboratory-grown cells have been implanted into a patient's brain.	Martin Seymour-Smith, 70, British author of more than 40 books, dies in Bexhill-on-Sea, England, of a heart attack.	July 1
A federal jury in Billings, Montana, convicts LeRoy Schweitzer, Daniel Petersen, and Richard Clark, members of the Montana Freeman, on two counts each of threatening to kill Montana's chief federal judge, Jack Shanstrom. The three are also convicted on various other charges.	The U.S. State Department discloses that it has asked Cuba to extradite about 90 people to the U.S.			Kay Thompson, children's book author who created the successful Eloise book series and was reportedly between 92 and 95 years old, dies in New York City of unreported causes.	July 2
The Texas Supreme Court rules, 6-3, that court-ordered buffer zones around abortion clinics violate the First Amendment free-speech rights of antiabortion protesters. . . . The Michigan state legislature passes a bill that will ban assisted suicide. A temporary ban expired in 1994.	Canada and the U.S. state of Washington announce a one-year accord that restricts the catch of a lucrative species of salmon, sockeye, that migrates between Canadian and U.S. waters.		Astronomers report they have discovered the first asteroid to orbit the sun entirely within Earth's orbit, a claim that is disputed by other researchers.	Reverend Bernhard Haering, 85, liberal Roman Catholic theologian, dies in Germany. . . . George Lloyd, 85, British composer best known for his 12 symphonies, dies in London. . . . A British powerboat breaks the 1960 around-the-world record when it makes the trip in 74 days, 20 hours, and 58 minutes.	July 3
			Planet-B, an unmanned spacecraft set to orbit the planet Mars, is launched from Kagoshima on Kyushu, Japan's southernmost island. Planet-B is Japan's first interplanetary space mission.	Third-seeded Jana Novotna of the Czech Republic wins the women's singles title at the All England Tennis Championship at Wimbledon, England.	July 4
		National Education Association (NEA) convention delegates in New Orleans, Louisiana, vote to reject a proposed merger of the NEA and the American Federation of Teachers (AFT). The merger, which required a two-thirds majority vote for approval, would have combined the two largest teachers organizations in the U.S.		At the All England Tennis Championship in Wimbledon, England, top-seeded Pete Sampras wins his fifth career men's title, tying the record set by Sweden's Bjorn Borg in 1980 for the most Wimbledon men's titles. . . . Sid Luckman, 81, Hall of Fame professional football player, dies in North Miami Beach, Florida, of unreported causes.	July 5
F	G	H	I	J	
Includes elections, federal-state relations, civil rights and liberties, crime, the judiciary, education, health care, poverty, urban affairs, and population.	*Includes formation and debate of U.S. foreign and defense policies, veterans' affairs, and defense spending. (Relations with specific foreign countries are usually found under the region concerned.)*	*Includes business, labor, agriculture, taxation, transportation, consumer affairs, monetary and fiscal policy, natural resources, and pollution.*	*Includes worldwide scientific, medical, and technological developments; natural phenomena; U.S. weather; natural disasters; and accidents.*	*Includes the arts, religion, scholarship, communications media, sports, entertainments, fashions, fads, and social life.*	

	World Affairs	Europe	Africa & the Middle East	The Americas	Asia & the Pacific
July 6	Britain and Spain reach an agreement under which NATO may expand operations in Gibraltar. . . . The trial of Milan Kovacevic, allegedly responsible for the deaths of at least 2,000 people, opens in The Hague. . . . According to *Forbes* magazine, U.S. natives account for 70 of the 200 richest people or families in the world; 52 are from Europe, and 44 are from Asia. U.S. citizen William Gates, of Microsoft Corp., tops the list with $51 billion.	As protests in Ireland continue, some 3,000 members of the Orange Order surround the official residence of Britain's Northern Ireland secretary. . . . Russian president Boris Yeltsin and Kazakh president Nursultan Nazarbayev sign an agreement to divide the northern part of the oil-rich Caspian Sea bed. The pact is the first to address legal rights to the Caspian Sea's resources since the 1991 breakup of the Soviet Union.	In Angola, 16 police officers, who are reportedly the survivors of an explosion of three newly laid antitank mines, are killed in Lunda Norte, on the road between the villages of Camaxilo and Cuangula, in an ambush attributed to UNITA rebels.		Hong Kong's 73-year-old Kai Tak Airport ceases operating, and some 1,100 trucks, 14 barges, and 31 planes transport equipment from Kai Tak to the new Hong Kong International Airport on Chek Lap Kok island, which begins operations.
July 7	The UN General Assembly votes to upgrade the observer status of the Palestine Liberation Organization (PLO), or Palestine, to a "nonvoting" role that accords the PLO the right to participate in General Assembly debates and cosponsor resolutions.	A jury in Milan convicts Silvio Berlusconi, Italy's premier in 1994, of bribing government tax inspectors. Berlusconi is sentenced to two years and nine months in prison. . . . German automobile manufacturer Volkswagen AG states that it will create a fund to compensate workers forced to perform slave labor for the company during World War II. . . . Europe's two largest stock exchanges, Britain's London Stock Exchange and Germany's Deutsche Börse, sign an agreement to create a common electronic-trading system.	Moshood K. O. Abiola, 60, who claimed to be Nigeria's rightful head of state since his apparent victory in 1993 presidential elections, dies suddenly, reportedly of a heart attack, while imprisoned in Abuja, the capital. His death, which comes as Nigeria's military government appeared poised to announce his release from prison, sets off violent ethnic rioting in several major cities.	Hundreds of thousands of workers on the Caribbean island of Puerto Rico, a U.S. commonwealth, hold a 48-hour general strike to protest the pending privatization of state-owned Puerto Rico Telephone Co. The workers support more than 6,400 Puerto Rico Telephone employees who walked off their jobs on June 18.	
July 8		Officials in Northern Ireland state that police and army troops have been attacked in 400 separate incidents since the July 5 parade. The attacks reportedly wounded 44 police officers. . . . Serbian forces kill at least five rebels in a raid on the town of Morina, which borders Albania. Several rebels are also injured in the fighting, in which Serbian artillery shells four other villages.	USAID announces that it will provide nearly 10,000 tons of food worth some $16 million to Sudan's famine victims. . . . As unrest continues in Nigeria from the July 7 death of Moshood K. O. Abiola, Gen. Abdulsalam Abubakar reiterates his vow to restore democratic government. He dissolves the military-appointed cabinet, leaving a Provisional Ruling Council, also dominated by the military, with sole authority.	Under criticism from the Chinese community, the province of Alberta, Canada, renames Chinaman's Peak, an 8,793-foot (2,680-m) peak in the Rocky Mountains chain near Banff National Park, to Ha Ling Peak in honor of a railroad worker who in 1896 climbed to the peak's summit to win a $50 bet.	Australia's Senate approves the Native Title Bill, a controversial measure that restricts aboriginal land rights.
July 9	The United Nations Children's Fund (UNICEF) estimates that as many as one-third of infants worldwide do not have their births registered, barring them from receiving essential social services in some countries.		Algerian security forces reveal they have shot and killed Khalifi Athmane, a GIA leader. Authorities state that a total of 11 Muslim rebels were killed in the encounter. . . . Nigeria's Provisional Ruling Council states it has commuted the death sentences of Lt. Gen. Oladipo Diya and several other former military officials convicted of participating in a failed coup in 1997. According to accounts, as many as 45 people have been killed in Lagos in violent clashes between unemployed Yoruba youths and Hausa merchants.		Reports disclose that a court in Vietnam has imposed prison sentences on more than 30 people who participated in violent protests in Thai Binh province in November 1997. During the unrest, some 300 villagers raided the offices of the local party officials and took hostage more than 20 police officers.
July 10		Police in Britain and in the Irish Republic conduct coordinated raids in which they arrest 10 people allegedly plotting to detonate bombs in central London.			Police in China's eastern Province of Zhejiang detain nine prodemocracy activists involved in efforts to found an opposition political party, the China Democracy Party.
July 11		Octav Botnar, 84, British businessman who built Nissan UK into the largest Japanese car franchise in Britain, dies in Villars, Switzerland, while suffering from stomach cancer.	An international team of medical experts attest that an autopsy on the late Nigerian opposition leader Moshood K. O. Abiola shows that he died on July 7 of complications from heart disease.		State-run Chinese Central Television conducts its first live broadcast of a trial when it airs a civil copyright case held in the Intermediate People's Court in Beijing, the capital.

A	B	C	D	E
Includes developments that affect more than one world region, international organizations, and important meetings of major world leaders.	Includes all domestic and regional developments in Europe, including the Soviet Union, Turkey, Cyprus, and Malta.	Includes all domestic and regional developments in Africa and the Middle East, including Iraq and Iran and excluding Cyprus, Turkey, and Afghanistan.	Includes all domestic and regional developments in Latin America, the Caribbean, and Canada.	Includes all domestic and regional developments in Asia and Pacific nations, extending from Afghanistan through all the Pacific Island, except Hawaii.

U.S. Politics & Social Issues	U.S. Foreign Policy & Defense	U.S. Economy & Environment	Science, Technology, & Nature	Culture, Leisure, & Lifestyle	
Data shows that five abortion clinics were attacked in New Orleans, Louisiana, over the July 4 weekend and that 10 Florida clinics were attacked in May.... Philip Morris, R.J. Reynolds, Brown & Williamson, and Lorillard announce that they will pay the state of Mississippi an additional $550 million under their 1997 settlement of the state's lawsuit seeking compensation for the costs of treating smoking-related illnesses.			Scientists in Japan announce they have cloned two calves from adult cows, but their research has not yet been published in a scientific journal.	South Korea's Se Ri Pak wins the U.S. Women's Open in Kohler, Wisconsin.... Roy Rogers (born Leonard Franklin Slye), 86, motion picture and television star and an icon of the American West, dies in Apple Valley, California, of congestive heart failure.	July 6
A federal appeals panel in Washington, D.C., upholds a previous decision when it orders members of the Secret Service to testify about their knowledge of the relationship between Pres. Clinton and Monica Lewinsky.... Susan Lynn Rodriguez is the first female officer from the Border Patrol killed in the line of duty when she assists local police pursuing a suspect in murders unrelated to the U.S.-Mexico border.... Dow Corning and lawyers for 170,000 women who claim they were made ill by silicone breast implants agree to a tentative $3.2 billion settlement.		Pres. Clinton states that the federal government will punish insurance companies that fail to comply with the 1996 Health Insurance Portability and Accountability Act, which guarantees access to health insurance to people who lose or change employment.	Japan's National Space Development Agency successfully docks two Earth-orbiting satellites without the aid of astronauts. The first-ever unmanned satellite docking is an experiment in preparation for the construction of a planned international space station, set to begin later in the year.	A jury in Los Angeles, California, convicts Mikail Markhasev, 19, in the 1997 killing of Ennis Cosby, the son of TV entertainer Bill Cosby.... The American League defeats the National League, 13-8, to win MLB's All-Star Game in Denver, Colorado.... Pope John Paul II issues an apostolic letter urging Catholics to attend Sunday Mass each week. About one-third of the U.S.'s 60 million Catholics currently do so.	July 7
At least three Houston clinics are targeted in a series of acid attacks on abortion clinics, and three people are hospitalized with breathing difficulties. The attacks are similar to the ones in Louisiana in July and Florida in May.... A federal jury in Billings, Montana, convicts LeRoy Schweitzer, Daniel Petersen, Dale Jacobi, and Russell Landers—four leads of the Montana Freemen—on 11 counts of conspiring to defraud four U.S. banks.		D. Wayne Calloway, 62, chair and chief executive officer of Pepsico Inc., 1986–96, dies of prostate cancer in New York City.	Two studies find that, on average, black smokers inhaled more nicotine than white smokers.		July 8
Wilmington, Delaware, Superior Court judge Henry duPont Ridgely sentences Amy Grossberg, 19, to 30 months in prison on manslaughter charges in the 1996 death of her newborn son. Brian Peterson, 20, Grossberg's former boyfriend and the child's father, is sentenced to a 24-month prison term for the death of the baby. Authorities found the dead child wrapped in a plastic bag in a trash receptacle behind a Newark, Delaware, motel where Grossberg gave birth.		The Senate votes, 96-2, to give final approval to a bill intended to overhaul the IRS.... Harold Butler, 77, founder of the Denny's fast-food restaurant chain, dies of a heart attack in La Paz, Mexico.		Pitcher Ila Borders is the first woman to start for a minor-league professional baseball team, pitching five innings for the Northern League's Duluth-Superior Dukes in a game in Duluth, Minnesota.	July 9
Health and Human Services Secretary Donna Shalala names Jeffrey Koplan director of the Centers for Disease Control and Prevention (CDC).	Lt. Gen. Peter Pace, commander of the Marine Corps's Atlantic fleet, orders a court-martial for the pilot and navigator of a military jet that severed a ski-lift cable in a February accident in Italy. The mishap caused a cable car to plummet more than 300 feet (90 m) to the ground, killing all 20 people inside. ... The U.S. Senate approves, 92-0, a nonbinding resolution reaffirming the 1979 Taiwan Relations Act, which authorizes arms sales to Taiwan for defensive purposes and which calls for the peaceful resolution of Taiwan's status.				July 10
					July 11

F	G	H	I	J
Includes elections, federal-state relations, civil rights and liberties, crime, the judiciary, education, health care, poverty, urban affairs, and population.	Includes formation and debate of U.S. foreign and defense policies, veterans' affairs, and defense spending. (Relations with specific foreign countries are usually found under the region concerned.)	Includes business, labor, agriculture, taxation, transportation, consumer affairs, monetary and fiscal policy, natural resources, and pollution.	Includes worldwide scientific, medical, and technological developments; natural phenomena; U.S. weather; natural disasters; and accidents.	Includes the arts, religion, scholarship, communications media, sports, entertainments, fashions, fads, and social life.

	World Affairs	Europe	Africa & the Middle East	The Americas	Asia & the Pacific
July 12		Three Roman Catholic brothers are killed in a fire in their home in the Northern Ireland town of Ballymoney. Police blame the fire on arson by Protestant extremists.		Jamil Mahuad Witt, the mayor of Quito, Ecuador's capital, is elected president in a second-round run-off vote.	Japan's ruling Liberal Democratic Party (LDP) suffers losses in elections to the House of Councillors, the upper house of the Diet, but it remains in power in the more powerful lower house of the Diet. . . . In Seoul, the capital of South Korea, tens of thousands of workers protest rising unemployment. . . . A man in Donghae, on the eastern coast of South Korea, finds the dead body of a diver whom the government claims is a North Korean commando.
July 13	In response to moves by the Belarussian government to evict ambassadors of some 12 foreign governments from their residences in Belarus's Drozdy diplomatic quarter, the 15 member states of the European Union (EU) ban some 130 high-level Belarussian officials, including Pres. Aleksandr Lukashenko, from traveling to EU countries. . . . IMF officials and the Russian government agree on a plan to lend an additional $17.1 billion to Russia before the end of 1999.	Silvio Berlusconi, the leader of Italy's center-right opposition coalition, is convicted in Milan in connection with illegal political contributions. Former premier Bettino Craxi Craxi, currently in hiding in Tunisia, is convicted in absentia, sentenced to a four-year prison term, and fined $10 million. . . . An Italian judge throws out a manslaughter case against the crew of the plane that severed a ski-lift cable in a February accident in Italy and killed all 20 people inside, explaining that Italy has no jurisdiction over the matter under a NATO pact.	A small bomb explodes in East Jerusalem near Orient House, the unofficial headquarters of the Palestine Liberation Organization in the Arab portion of the city. One Palestinian man is injured slightly by the blast.	In Colombia, authorities state that at least 25 FARC rebels were killed recently in a military raid on a camp and drug laboratory in the Meta province. Separately, reports confirm that a group believed to be right-wing paramilitaries killed nine people and forced 250 others to flee their homes near the town of Sabanalarga in the northwest Antioquia province. . . . The aboriginal Nisga'a people sign a treaty with the Canadian government that will give the group title to an area of land in northwest British Columbia.	Japanese premier Ryutaro Hashimoto announces that he will resign as premier and as president of the ruling Liberal Democratic Party (LDP) to take responsibility for the LDP's losses in July 12 elections.
July 14				Jorge Rafael Videla, one of the military leaders who waged the "dirty war" against suspected leftists after seizing power in Argentina in 1976, is indicted on charges of child abduction as he is alleged to be have been involved from 1976 to 1978 in a system under which the newborn infants of female political prisoners were given up for adoption to military couples. Many of the women were then killed.	Zhu Lilan, China's minister of science and technology, is the first Chinese government minister to visit Taiwan since the Communist Party took power in China in 1949 . . . . Labor unions stage nationwide strikes to protest layoffs in South Korea. . . . Nguyen Ngoc Loan, 67, South Vietnamese general and national police commander during the Vietnam War, dies of cancer in Burke, Virginia.
July 15		British troops and Northern Ireland police raid the encampment in Portadown where Orange Order members have been protesting the blocking of the July 5 parade. Police arrest at least 20 people and seize weaponry. . . . Spanish police close down a Basque separatist newspaper linked to the outlawed ETA. . . . Karl Schirdewan, 91, Communist Party functionary in the former East Germany who for a time during the 1950s was considered the second most powerful government official in that country, dies in Berlin, Germany.	The Sudan People's Liberation Army, a separatist rebel group, declares a three-month cease-fire in its campaign against the government in order to allow shipments of food to reach famine victims in the country's southwestern region. The Sudanese government responds by declaring a one-month suspension of hostilities.	Royal Canadian Mounted Police (RCMP) officers in Woodbridge, Ontario, arrest Alfonso Caruana, 52, allegedly the head of an organized-crime family that specializes in drug smuggling and money laundering.	
July 16	U.S. president Bill Clinton for the fifth time implements a six-month waiver blocking a controversial provision of the 1996 Helms-Burton Act, which seeks to tighten the U.S.'s economic embargo of Cuba. The Helms-Burton Act angered the U.S.'s allies in Europe and Latin America whose firms do business in Cuba, and Clinton has waived the provision every six months since the passage of the law.	Syria's president Hafez al-Assad visits France on his first trip to a Western country in 22 years.	Members of the United Nations Human Rights Committee state that Israel's state-sanctioned use of torture is in violation of the International Covenant on Civil and Political Rights (ICCPR), which Israel had signed in 1991. . . . British officials confirm that the Sudanese government has extended the truce announced on July 15 to three months.		A letter in which 79 Chinese dissidents from 19 provinces call on Pres. Jiang Zemin and Premier Zhu Rongji to release the dissidents arrested July 10 who are still in detention is made public. Some of those arrested July 10 have been released. . . . Mahbubul Haq, 64, Pakistani economist who devised the Human Development Index, which was adopted by the UN to assess the wealth of nations, dies in New York City of pneumonia.

A	B	C	D	E
Includes developments that affect more than one world region, international organizations, and important meetings of major world leaders.	Includes all domestic and regional developments in Europe, including the Soviet Union, Turkey, Cyprus, and Malta.	Includes all domestic and regional developments in Africa and the Middle East, including Iraq and Iran and excluding Cyprus, Turkey, and Afghanistan.	Includes all domestic and regional developments in Latin America, the Caribbean, and Canada.	Includes all domestic and regional developments in Asia and Pacific nations, extending from Afghanistan through all the Pacific Island, except Hawaii.

U.S. Politics & Social Issues	U.S. Foreign Policy & Defense	U.S. Economy & Environment	Science, Technology, & Nature	Culture, Leisure, & Lifestyle	
		Charles J. Givens, 57, author of best-selling books who was found guilty in 1996 of defrauding thousands of Californians and ordered to repay them $14.1 million, dies of prostate cancer in Orlando, Florida.		France wins the 1998 World Cup soccer tournament, 3-0, over Brazil, in St.-Denis. . . . Jimmy Driftwood (born James Corbett Morris), 91, folk singer and songwriter, dies in Fayetteville, Arkansas, after a stroke and heart attack. . . . Golfer Gil Morgan wins the Senior Players Championship in Dearborn, Michigan.	July 12
A jury in Poughkeepsie, New York, finds black activist Rev. Al Sharpton and two black former civil-rights attorneys—Alton Maddox Jr. and C. Vernon Mason—liable in a civil defamation case brought by a white former county prosecutor, Steven Pagones. The three accused Pagones of participating in a gang rape of a black teenager, Tawana Brawley, 10 years earlier. . . . Watkins M. Abbitt, 90, (D, Va.), who served in the U.S. House of Representatives, 1948–73, dies in Lynchburg, Virginia, while suffering from leukemia.		A federal grand jury in Washington, D.C., indicts Thai businesswoman Pauline Kanchanalak on charges of illegally funneling foreign contributions to the Democratic Party between 1992 and 1996. The indictment brings to 10 the number of people indicted in a Justice Department investigation of fund-raising abuses in the 1996 elections.		Polo Ralph Lauren Corp. reveals it will donate $13 million to the Smithsonian Institution. . . . A coalition of 15 conservative religious groups launch an advertising campaign against homosexuality. . . . Red Badgro (Morris Hiram), 95, oldest member of the Pro Football Hall of Fame, dies in Kent, Washington, after a fall.	July 13
	The House and Senate clear, by voice vote, a measure that will waive agricultural export credits from a raft of economic sanctions that the U.S. imposed on India and Pakistan after the two countries detonated nuclear devices in May. Pres. Clinton signs the measure.	Richard McDonald, 89, fast-food restaurant pioneer who, with his brother Maurice McDonald, laid the foundation for the McDonald's hamburger empire, dies in Manchester, New Hampshire.		Miroslav Holub, 74, Czech poet whose Collected Poems was not published in his homeland until after the fall of communism, dies in Prague, the Czech Republic. . . . Beryl Audrey Bryden, 78, British jazz singer whose career spanned five decades, dies in London, England, of cancer.	July 14
Judge Charles Legge of U.S. District Court in San Francisco, California, refuses to block implementation of Proposition 227, a statewide ballot measure barring bilingual education in California schools. . . . The House votes, 276-150, to pass a bill that will make it a crime for an adult to transport a minor across state lines for an abortion.				A New York City cable-TV company states it has rehired sportscaster Marv Albert, who pled guilty in 1997 to a misdemeanor assault on a woman with whom he had had a decade-long sexual relationship, to anchor a nightly studio sports show.	July 15
Pres. Clinton signs a bill that allows a planned memorial to Rev. Martin Luther King Jr. to be sited within the Mall area in Washington, D.C. . . . Blue Cross and Blue Shield of Illinois, also known as Health Care Service Corp. (HCSC), pleads guilty in U.S. District Court in East St. Louis, Illinois, to defrauding Medicare. The company agrees to pay $144 million in fines and civil penalties.		The NASDAQ index of over-the-counter stocks, considered the benchmark of smaller stocks' performance, closes above the 2000 level for the first time, at 2000.56 points.	The FDA approves the use of the drug thalidomide to treat a painful symptom of leprosy. . . . Astronomers report that, by using a new kind of infrared camera, they could observe the formation of galaxies in an area of the sky some 11 billion light-years from Earth.		July 16

F	G	H	I	J
Includes elections, federal-state relations, civil rights and liberties, crime, the judiciary, education, health care, poverty, urban affairs, and population.	Includes formation and debate of U.S. foreign and defense policies, veterans' affairs, and defense spending. (Relations with specific foreign countries are usually found under the region concerned.)	Includes business, labor, agriculture, taxation, transportation, consumer affairs, monetary and fiscal policy, natural resources, and pollution.	Includes worldwide scientific, medical, and technological developments; natural phenomena; U.S. weather; natural disasters; and accidents.	Includes the arts, religion, scholarship, communications media, sports, entertainments, fashions, fads, and social life.

	World Affairs	Europe	Africa & the Middle East	The Americas	Asia & the Pacific
July 17	UN member states vote in favor of a treaty authorizing the creation of a permanent international court for the adjudication of war crimes.	The Russian government buries the remains of Czar Nicholas II, the last member of the imperial Romanov dynasty to rule Russia, and his family in a ceremony at the 18th-century St. Peter and Paul Cathedral in St. Petersburg. The somber service is held 80 years to the day after the family was executed by the Bolsheviks during the Russian Revolution. . . . Rebel forces launch an offensive in Orahovac, a town of 20,000 people located 30 miles (50 km) southwest of Pristina in Kosovo.	The South African government announces that it will begin releasing some 9,000 prison inmates in honor of Pres. Nelson Mandela's July 18 birthday.		An earthquake measuring 6.2 on the Richter scale strikes southern Taiwan. The quake, centered in the mountainous area of Alishan, triggers rock slides and blocks highways and tunnels. Five people are killed, and 27 are injured. It is Taiwan's worst earthquake since 1964. . . . A series of three giant ocean waves, the first as high as 30 feet (9 m), crashes onto the northern coast of Papua New Guinea, washing away several villages. An estimated 8,000–10,000 people reside in the affected areas.
July 18		Betty Marsden, 79, British actress whose comic talents were highlighted in two popular 1960s radio shows, dies of unreported causes.	South African president Nelson Mandela celebrates his 80th birthday by marrying Graca Machel, his longtime romantic companion.		Reports confirm that some 400 aftershocks have been recorded since the July 17 earthquake in southern Taiwan.
July 19			Senior Israeli and Palestinian officials hold their first direct talks in a half-year in the latest attempt to salvage a peace process now in its 17th month of stalled negotiations. Just hours before the initial session, an apparent car bomb misfires in a van in downtown West Jerusalem, hospitalizing the driver with extensive burns but causing no other injuries. . . . Saudi Arabian warships bombard a Yemen-controlled island in the Red Sea, killing three Yemeni coast guard personnel and wounding nine others. The attack is part of a continuing border dispute between the two countries.		After aid organizations refused an ultimatum to relocate their offices into one centralized location outside the capital, Kabul, or shut down their operations and leave Afghanistan, Taliban authorities order their operations closed. . . . Supporters and opponents of Pauline Hanson, head of the far-right, anti-immigrant One Nation Party, engage in a violent confrontation outside a town hall in Melbourne, Australia, where Hanson had scheduled a meeting.
July 20		Spanish judge Baltasar Garzon imprisons eight people associated with the Basque separatist newspaper that was shut down July 15, citing the paper's apparent links to terrorism.	General Abdulsalam Abubakar, Nigeria's military ruler, pledges to end 15 years of military rule by May 29, 1999.		After the July 19 closures, some 200 aid workers leave Kabul, as CARE International, Doctors without Borders, and 36 other agencies suspend their activities in Afghanistan. The UN and the Red Cross are exempted from the Taliban's directive and maintain a presence in Kabul. . . . The government announces that Hong Kong's unemployment rate in the second quarter reached a 15-year high of 4.5%, up from 4.1% in the March–May period.
July 21	The UN Security Council votes to add 350 troops to the 700-strong UN Preventive Deployment Force in Macedonia and to extend the force's mandate until February 1999.			Despite an ongoing strike, the Puerto Rican government accepts an enhanced bid from the GTE-led group for a controlling stake in Puerto Rico Telephone.	Chinese activist Fan Yiping is sentenced to three years in prison for helping a dissident leave the country. . . . Workers at Hyundai Motor Co. and Daewoo Motor Co. go on strike to protest plans for the first mass layoffs by South Korean conglomerates since the onset of a nationwide financial crisis in 1997. . . . At the end of a tour of Victoria, Australia, by Pauline Hanson, head of the far-right, anti-immigrant One Nation Party, some 100 protesters in the town of Echuca clash with her supporters, and a demonstration by some 2,000 protesters forces Hanson to flee the town of Bendigo.
July 22		In Kosovo, Serb forces report that they have countered the July 17 rebel attack on Orahovac, 30 miles (50 km) southwest of Pristina. Serbian police acknowledge that four Serb civilians and two policemen died in the battle; Albanian refugees in Malisevo report that 37 Albanian civilians were killed. . . . Britain's public records office releases World War II-era documents detailing plans to assassinate Adolf Hitler,.	More than 200 civilians die in a massacre by unknown assailants in Angola's northern diamond-mining province of Lunda Norte.	In Colombia, the ELN and the little-known Popular Liberation Forces rebel group claim responsibility for the simultaneous detonation of at least 12 bombs outside banks in the city of Medellin, killing one person.	Prominent Chinese dissident Zhang Shanguang is arrested after attempting to organize a group of laid-off workers. Separately, Pres. Jiang Zemin orders China's People's Liberation Army (PLA) to shut down its many business operations as part of a government campaign to curb the rampant smuggling of goods into China.

A	B	C	D	E
Includes developments that affect more than one world region, international organizations, and important meetings of major world leaders.	*Includes all domestic and regional developments in Europe, including the Soviet Union, Turkey, Cyprus, and Malta.*	*Includes all domestic and regional developments in Africa and the Middle East, including Iraq and Iran and excluding Cyprus, Turkey, and Afghanistan.*	*Includes all domestic and regional developments in Latin America, the Caribbean, and Canada.*	*Includes all domestic and regional developments in Asia and Pacific nations, extending from Afghanistan through all the Pacific Island, except Hawaii.*

U.S. Politics & Social Issues	U.S. Foreign Policy & Defense	U.S. Economy & Environment	Science, Technology, & Nature	Culture, Leisure, & Lifestyle	
The state of Texas reaches a final settlement of its lawsuit seeking compensation from the tobacco industry for the costs of treating smoke-related illnesses. The companies agree to pay $17.6 billion instead of the $15.3 billion agreed to in their original settlement with Texas, reached in January.		The Dow closes at 9337.97, the 28th record high of 1998 and the third record high registered in July.... Judge William Osteen Sr. invalidates most of an influential 1993 EPA report that asserted that second-hand smoke causes cancer.... The White House's OMB announces that the administration will release $197 million in federal funding for 40 projects that Pres. Clinton vetoed from spending bills in 1997. The announcement follows a June decision by the Supreme Court that line-item veto power is unconstitutional.	Reports reveal that scientists have mapped the genome, or sequence of genetic code, of the microbe that causes syphilis.		July 17
					July 18
				The fourth Goodwill Games open, in the New York City area, attracting some 1,500 athletes from more than 60 countries.... Golfer Mark O'Meara wins the British Open.	July 19
	Senate majority leader Trent Lott (R, Miss.) states that it is "not practical" for the Senate to consider confirming the nomination of James Hormel, an openly homosexual California philanthropist, as ambassador to Luxembourg.... A federal jury in Miami, Florida, convicts Michael Abbell, a former Justice Department official, and Miami defense lawyer William Moran of performing criminal acts for their clients in a Colombian drug cartel.			At the Goodwill Games, Bill May becomes the first man to win a medal in international synchronized swimming. The Olympics and most other international competitions bar men from the sport.	July 20
Pres. Clinton vetoes legislation that would have allowed parents to save money for their children's education costs, including private-school tuition fees, in new tax-sheltered accounts.... The Senate votes down, 61-39, a Democratic-sponsored proposal to require all guns sold in the U.S. to have trigger locks, designed to prevent accidents.		An SEC administrative-law judge, Carol Fox Foelak, finds Joseph Jett not guilty of fraud in a 1994 trading scandal that ultimately caused Kidder, Peabody & Co. to cease operations.... Representatives from the petroleum company Unocal Corp. announce that the company has agreed to pay a $43.8 million fine for polluting a stretch of California coastline with millions of gallons of petroleum. The fine is among the largest environmental claims ever won by the state.	Alan Bartlett Shepard Jr., 74, one of the first seven U.S. astronauts, known collectively as the Mercury Seven, who, on May 5, 1961, became the first American launched into space and, in 1971, became the fifth man to walk on the moon and the first to play golf there, dies near Monterey, California. He was reportedly suffering from leukemia.	The Liverpool, England, home where British rock musician Paul McCartney lived from 1955 to 1964 opens as a museum.... Robert Young, 91, U.S. actor who won three Emmy Awards, dies in Westlake Village, California.	July 21
Senators reject, 69-31, a Democratic-backed measure that would have allowed the prosecution of adults who did not take adequate steps to secure guns taken by a child to commit a crime. The legislation would have made such negligence a misdemeanor.... New York State Supreme Court justice Robert Hanophy sentences Heriberto Seda, the so-called Zodiac killer, to life in prison for murder and attempted murder.	The House votes, 264-166, to defeat a resolution that would have rejected Pres. Clinton's June decision to renew China's so-called most-favored nation (MFN) trading status. Separately, Pres. Clinton signs a bill containing a provision changing the name of MFN status to "normal trade relations."	Pres. Clinton signs a bill enacting a major overhaul of the Internal Revenue Service (IRS).	Reports confirm that a French magistrate has indicted three officials of the ministry of culture on charges of falsifying documents related to the 1994 discovery of the oldest known prehistoric cave paintings.	Don Dunphy, 90, U.S. radio and TV announcer whose career lasted from 1939 to the 1980s, dies in Roslyn, New York.... (John) Michael terence wellesley Denison, 82, British actor who epitomized the English gentleman in several roles, dies of cancer in Amersham, England.	July 22

F	G	H	I	J
Includes elections, federal-state relations, civil rights and liberties, crime, the judiciary, education, health care, poverty, urban affairs, and population.	Includes formation and debate of U.S. foreign and defense policies, veterans' affairs, and defense spending. (Relations with specific foreign countries are usually found under the region concerned.)	Includes business, labor, agriculture, taxation, transportation, consumer affairs, monetary and fiscal policy, natural resources, and pollution.	Includes worldwide scientific, medical, and technological developments; natural phenomena; U.S. weather; natural disasters; and accidents.	Includes the arts, religion, scholarship, communications media, sports, entertainments, fashions, fads, and social life.

	World Affairs	Europe	Africa & the Middle East	The Americas	Asia & the Pacific
July 23	Delegates to the Association of Southeast Asian Nations (ASEAN) trade group convene in Manila, the capital of the Philippines, for their 31st annual series of ministerial meetings on regional economic and security issues.	Vladimir Dudintsev, 79, Russian writer, dies near Moscow after suffering a stroke several years earlier. . . . Henri Ziegler, 91, French aviation industry leader, dies in Paris. . . . Hermann Prey, 69, German baritone who excelled as an opera singer, dies near Munich, Germany, after a heart attack.	An Iranian court sentences Gholamhossein Karbaschi, the reform-minded mayor of Teheran, the capital, to five years in prison on charges of embezzlement and mismanagement. Separately, an Iranian appeals court upholds a lower court's decision ordering the immediate closure of a pro-reform daily newspaper which, since its founding in February, has openly challenged the political line of the conservative elite.		The official death toll from the July 17 tsunamis in Papua New Guinea stands at some 1,300. Thousands are still missing. . . . Chinese dissident Wang Donghai is freed from prison and placed under house arrest.
July 24		Yugoslav army units and Serbian soldiers launch an offensive intended to reopen the roads linking Pristina, the Kosovo region's capital; Pec, its second-largest city; and Prizren, a large town in southwest Kosovo. . . . Roland W. (Tiny) Rowland (born Roland Walter Fuhrhop), 80, British businessman of the Lonrho Group, a huge international trading empire, dies of cancer in London, England.	The Angolan government reveals that 215 bodies have been recovered from the site of the July 22 massacre in the province of Lunda Nore.		In Myanmar, police stop the car of dissident Aung San Suu Kyi approximately 20 miles (32 km) west of the capital, blocking her from meeting members of her NLD party. She refuses to turn back to Yangon and remains in her car. . . . Mongolia's Great Hural calls for the resignation of Premier Tsakhiagiin Elbegdorj and his cabinet in the wake of a stalemate over a bank merger. Elbegdorj and his cabinet resign but remain in office in an acting capacity
July 25			Iranian defense minister Ali Shamkhani confirms that Iran successfully has test-fired a Shehab-3 medium-range ballistic missile capable of reaching distances of about 800 miles (1,300 km). The missile theoretically may strike U.S. forces in the Persian Gulf region, as well as targets in Israel, Saudi Arabia, and Turkey. Separately, the editorial staff of a pro-reform paper shut down by the government launches a new paper with a similar format and sells 100,000 copies within an hour.	To mark the 100th anniversary of the landing of U.S. troops on the island of Puerto Rico, the Puerto Rican Independence Party holds a pro-independence rally in Guanica. The pro-commonwealth Popular Democratic Party holds a rally in the capital, San Juan, marking the 46th anniversary of the creation of the commonwealth.	UN human-rights observers in Cambodia reveal they have received reports of more than 400 instances in which voters have been murdered, beaten, or threatened by security forces or local CPP officials during the election campaign. . . . In the Japanese city of Wakayama, four people die and 60 are sickened from cyanide poisoning after eating curry at a community festival. . . . Reports confirm that the Vietnamese Red Cross has established a fund for victims with ailments linked to exposure to Agent Orange.
July 26					North Korea holds elections to the Supreme People's Assembly for the first time since 1990, and Kim Jong II is elected to an assembly seat, in what is widely seen as a sign that he will soon be elevated to the country's supreme post. . . . Cambodia holds national elections.
July 27					Lin Ti-chuan of Kaohsiung City Council in Taiwan is kidnapped in Dalian. . . . A Supreme Court justice in Brisbane, the capital of the state of Queensland, Australia, orders a freeze on A$500,000 (US$310,000) in election reimbursement funds designated for the One Nation Party, a 15-month-old far-right political party.
July 28		Reports confirm that Serb forces have recaptured the town of Malisevo and several surrounding villages in the offensive that started July 24. . . . German automaker BMW announces that it has purchased the Rolls-Royce luxury automobile brand name, along with Rolls-Royce's "Spirit of Ecstasy" emblem for £40 million ($66 million). . . . Zbigniew Herbert, 73, Polish poet and essayist, dies in Warsaw, Poland, while suffering from asthma and circulatory ailments.	The Congolese government announces that all Rwandan, Ugandan, and Angolan troops on Congolese soil have been withdrawn, a gesture that observers interpret as meaning that Pres. Laurent Kabila no longer trusts the foreign allies who helped install him in 1997.	Some 6,400 telephone workers on the Caribbean island of Puerto Rico, a U.S. commonwealth, vote to end a 41-day-old strike against their employer, Puerto Rico Telephone Co.	

A	B	C	D	E
Includes developments that affect more than one world region, international organizations, and important meetings of major world leaders.	Includes all domestic and regional developments in Europe, including the Soviet Union, Turkey, Cyprus, and Malta.	Includes all domestic and regional developments in Africa and the Middle East, including Iraq and Iran and excluding Cyprus, Turkey, and Afghanistan.	Includes all domestic and regional developments in Latin America, the Caribbean, and Canada.	Includes all domestic and regional developments in Asia and Pacific nations, extending from Afghanistan through all the Pacific Island, except Hawaii.

U.S. Politics & Social Issues	U.S. Foreign Policy & Defense	U.S. Economy & Environment	Science, Technology, & Nature	Culture, Leisure, & Lifestyle	
The House votes, 296-132, to override Pres. Clinton's 1997 veto of legislation to restrict a controversial late-term abortion procedure known as intact dilation and extraction (IDE).... Juice maker Odwalla Inc. pleads guilty to violating federal food safety laws in connection with a shipment of tainted apple juice that killed one child and made 70 other people ill in 1996. Odwalla also agrees to pay a $1.5 million fine, which federal officials call the largest criminal penalty ever imposed in a food-injury case.	A federal jury in New York City convicts Palestinian immigrant Ghazi Ibrahim Abu Maizar of plotting to set off a bomb in the New York City subway system in 1997. Lafi Khalil, a second defendant in the case, is acquitted on charges related to the bombing plot.	Ralph Geoffrey Newman, 86, bookseller who, in 1975, was convicted on two counts of lying about his role in helping former president Richard Nixon claim an illegal income-tax deduction, dies in Chicago, Illinois, of unreported causes.	Reports confirm that scientists at the University of Hawaii have created more than 50 clones of adult mice. The cloned mice are the first confirmed instance of the cloning of adult mammals since the creation of Dolly, a sheep cloned from an adult ewe by Scottish scientists, reported in February 1997.		July 23
In a shoot-out, Russell E. Weston Jr., 41, allegedly kills two Capitol police officers. The attack is the deadliest at the Capitol since Congress first met there in 1800 and the first shooting at the building since 1954.... The House passes, 216-210, a bill establishing protections for patients enrolled in managed-care health insurance plans run by HMOs.... In Indianapolis, Indiana, Judge Gerald Zore of issues the first dismissal of a suit filed by a state seeking compensation from five tobacco companies.	In a case that drew intense media attention, a jury in New Braunfels, Texas, convicts former Air Force Academy cadet David Graham of capital murder in the 1995 slaying of 16-year-old Adrianne Jones. Graham, 21, allegedly killed Jones with his girlfriend, Diane Zamora, after Graham told Zamora that he had had a sexual encounter with Jones.			Tazio Secchiaroli, 73, photographer whose stalking of celebrities inspired the character of Paparazzo in a Fellini film, which became the standard term for celebrity-hounding photographers, dies in Rome, Italy, after an apparent heart attack.	July 24
				Tal Farlow, 77, jazz guitarist who recorded a series of notable albums in the 1950s, dies of esophageal cancer in New York City.	July 25
				Don Sutton, Larry Doby, George Davis, (Bullet) Joe Rogan, former American League president Lee MacPhail, and media workers Jaime Jarrin and Sam Lacy are inducted into the Baseball Hall of Fame in Cooperstown, New York.	July 26
		Reports from New York City confirm that Judge Constance Baker Motley has given final approval to a $15 million settlement of a sexual-harassment and discrimination suit against Salomon Smith Barney Inc. announced in November 1997.... William McChesney Martin Jr., 91, chair of the U.S. Federal Reserve, 1951–70, dies in Washington, D.C.	The U.S. State Department suspends the work of Sea Launch, an international joint venture formed to launch commercial satellites from a platform floating at sea.	Binnie Barnes (born Gertrude Maude Barnes), 95, English actress who appeared in dozens of Hollywood films, dies in Beverly Hills, California.... Point of Origin, by Patricia Cornwell, tops the bestseller list.	July 27
In an honor usually reserved for high-ranking government and military officials, the flag-draped coffins of Officer Jacob Chestnut, 58, and Special Agent John Gibson, 42, killed in the July 24 shooting at the Capitol, lie in state at the Great Rotunda of the Capitol building. They are the first Capitol police officers killed while on duty.		The Senate approves, 92-6, the Credit Union Membership Access Act, a bill that expands consumers' access to credit unions.	NASA announces that it has determined the position of SOHO, a spacecraft launched in 1995 to observe the sun with which they had lost contact in June.		July 28

F	G	H	I	J
Includes elections, federal-state relations, civil rights and liberties, crime, the judiciary, education, health care, poverty, urban affairs, and population.	*Includes formation and debate of U.S. foreign and defense policies, veterans' affairs, and defense spending. (Relations with specific foreign countries are usually found under the region concerned.)*	*Includes business, labor, agriculture, taxation, transportation, consumer affairs, monetary and fiscal policy, natural resources, and pollution.*	*Includes worldwide scientific, medical, and technological developments; natural phenomena; U.S. weather; natural disasters; and accidents.*	*Includes the arts, religion, scholarship, communications media, sports, entertainments, fashions, fads, and social life.*

	World Affairs	Europe	Africa & the Middle East	The Americas	Asia & the Pacific
July 29	Indian prime minister Atal Bihari Vajpayee and Pakistani prime minister Nawaz Sharif meet in Colombo, the Sri Lankan capital, for their first talks since the May nuclear tests.	Spain's Supreme Court sentences 12 government officials, including former interior minister Jose Barrionuevo, for illegal acts connected to the government's effort to silence the Basque separatist movement. Barrionuevo, Julian Sancristobal, and Rafael Vera receive 10-year sentences. The ruling rekindles the long-running controversy over the "Dirty War," in which the government allegedly sponsored death squads that kidnapped and killed dozens of suspected Basque terrorists in the 1980s.		In Brazil, 2,000 military police in riot gear battle thousands of protesters outside the venue where the auction in the privatization of Telecomunicacoes Brasileiras SA (Telebras), the national telephone company, is taking place. . . . A three-person tribunal rules that the federal government owes back wages plus interest to almost 200,000 victims of unfair pay policies. If it stands, the tribunal's decision will be one of the largest pay-equity monetary awards ever in North America. Officials estimate the total amount to be as high as C$5 billion (US$3.3 billion).	
July 30		Lord Bingham, chief justice of Britain's highest court, the Court of Appeal, overturns the controversial conviction of Derek Bentley, who was hanged for murder in 1953. Bingham states that Bentley did not receive "the fair trial which is the birthright of every British citizen."	UN officials disclose that they found mass graves in the village of Mbula, Angola, that contain the bodies of 105 of the victims of the July 22 massacre in Angola's northern diamond-mining province of Lunda Norte.		Japan's Diet names Keizo Obuchi as Japan's new premier, succeeding Ryutaro Hashimoto. . . . Lin Tichuan, a local Taiwanese councilor kidnapped July 27, is found dead at a mortuary in Haicheng. . . . Officials of Myanmar's ruling military junta state that they have forced prodemocracy dissident Aung San Suu Kyi to end her standoff with police that began July 24 near Yangon. . . . A West Australian District Court jury acquits three U.S. sailors of charges that they raped a 15-year-old girl.
July 31	The IMF and the Ukrainian government agree on a three-year, $2.2 billion loan intended to help the country improve its macroeconomic outlook.	Six inmates linked to the IRA are released from Ireland's Portlaoise Prison under the terms of the April peace agreement.	The United Nations Commission on Human Rights (UNCHR) condemns the Algerian government's human-rights record, citing allegations made by Algerians of systematic torture, secret detentions, and disappearances.		Japan's Financial Supervisory Agency imposes penalties on several banks and securities brokerages for their involvement in a widespread bribery scandal. . . . Chen Xitong, the former mayor and Communist Party secretary of Beijing, China's capital, is convicted and sentenced to 16 years in prison on charges of corruption and dereliction of duty. Chen, a former member of the party's Politburo, is the highest-ranking Chinese leader to be imprisoned since 1978.
Aug. 1	Milan Kovacevic, 57, allegedly responsible for the deaths of at least 2,000 people in three concentration camps near the Bosnian town of Prijedor—Omarska, Keraterm, and Trnopolje—in 1992, dies of a heart attack while in custody during his trial for war crimes in The Hague, the Netherlands.	Four illegal immigrants from Africa, along with five activists who support their plight, occupy the residence of the papal nuncio in Paris, France, demanding legal residence papers for the immigrants and for 13 others. . . . A car bomb explodes in the predominantly Protestant town of Banbridge, wounding 35 people.			Hun Sen, the de facto ruler of Cambodia and likely winner of the July elections, announces that police captured Nuon Paet, a Khmer Rouge rebel commander wanted for the 1994 kidnapping and murder of three Western tourists. Separately, reports suggest that a growing number of villagers who voted against the CPP in July are fleeing their homes for refuge in Phnom Penh, the capital.
Aug. 2		Fighting breaks out in the Drenica valley region between Pristina, the Kosovo region's capital, and Pec, its second-largest city. . . . A pub and two stores in Belfast, the provincial capital of Northern Ireland, are struck by firebombs.	Rebellious soldiers of the Congolese army begin an insurrection by taking control of the eastern cities Goma and Bukavu, some 900 miles (1,500 km) east of Kinshasa. Sylvain Mbuchi, who commands the army's 10th battalion, announces that the army "had decided to remove Pres. Kabila from power." In Kinshasa, scattered fighting breaks out, reportedly between Rwandan troops stationed in the city and Congolese government forces loyal to Kabila.		
Aug. 3	Officials of the United Nations High Commissioner for Refugees (UNHCR) estimate that 20,000–30,000 ethnic Albanians have fled their homes in Kosovo in the past three days alone, pushing the region's refugee problem to the brink of a humanitarian crisis. As many as 180,000 civilians have been displaced since fighting began in February.		The government restores order in Kinshasa, the Congolese capital.	Colombia's two main rebel groups—FARC and the ELN—launch a fierce nationwide offensive that is widely seen as an intended reminder of the guerrillas' strength in advance of planned peace talks. Reports reveal that the ELN has kidnapped Sen. Carlos Espinosa of the opposition Liberal Party.	

A	B	C	D	E
Includes developments that affect more than one world region, international organizations, and important meetings of major world leaders.	Includes all domestic and regional developments in Europe, including the Soviet Union, Turkey, Cyprus, and Malta.	Includes all domestic and regional developments in Africa and the Middle East, including Iraq and Iran and excluding Cyprus, Turkey, and Afghanistan.	Includes all domestic and regional developments in Latin America, the Caribbean, and Canada.	Includes all domestic and regional developments in Asia and Pacific nations, extending from Afghanistan through all the Pacific Island, except Hawaii.

U.S. Politics & Social Issues	U.S. Foreign Policy & Defense	U.S. Economy & Environment	Science, Technology, & Nature	Culture, Leisure, & Lifestyle	
Pres. Clinton agrees to give video-taped testimony about his relationship with former White House intern Monica Lewinsky. . . . In Poughkeepsie, New York, state supreme court justice S. Barrett Hickman orders black activist Rev. Al Sharpton, Alton Maddox Jr., and C. Vernon Mason to pay $345,000 in damages in a civil defamation lawsuit brought by Steven Pagones, a former county prosecutor.	The House passes, 417-1, an appropriations bill allocating $8.45 billion for military construction spending in fiscal 1999.	Members of United Auto Workers (UAW) Locals 659 and 651 vote to ratify a labor agreement, ending strikes at two GM auto-parts factories in Flint, Michigan, that began in early June. The work stoppages produced an immense ripple effect that extended to GM plants throughout North America. . . . The House passes, 305-317, a three-state agreement to dispose of low-level nuclear waste at a site in western Texas near the Mexican border. The three states represented in the bill are Texas, Vermont, and Maine		Jerome Robbins (born Jerome Rabinowitz), 79, choreographer, dies in New York City of complications from a stroke suffered July 25. . . . In Westerville, Ohio, 13 machinists win the lottery with a $295.7 million jackpot, the largest lottery prize in U.S. history. . . . New York City's Whitney Museum of American Art names Maxwell Anderson as director.	July 29
Ruthann Aron, a onetime Republican candidate for the U.S. Senate, pleads no contest to charges that she tried to hire a contract killer to murder her husband, Barry Aron, and Arthur G. Kahn, one of her political rivals.		Data suggests that net investments in equity funds totaled $126.2 billion for the first six months of 1998. That is up from the $108.3 billion recorded during the comparable period of 1997's record year. . . . The Senate, by voice vote, passes a bill that will provide $5.5 billion in early crop-support payments to farmers hurt by bad weather and a worldwide decline in commodities prices. . . . The Senate approves, by unanimous consent, a bill consolidating many federal job-training programs.		"Buffalo Bob" Smith (born Robert Schmidt), 80, whose *Howdy Doody* show was a staple of U.S. children's television, 1947–60, dies of cancer in Henderson, North Carolina. . . . The Senate passes, by voice vote, a bill that will overturn MLB's exemption from antitrust laws in regard to labor relations.	July 30
Vice Pres. Al Gore announces that the Clinton administration will delay plans to implement a nationwide system of identification numbers for medical patients until Congress passes legislation to protect patients' privacy rights. . . . Leroy Edgar Burney, 91, U.S. surgeon general, 1956–61, and the first federal official to implicate smoking as a cause of lung cancer, dies in Arlington Heights, Illinois.		The Senate confirms, by voice vote, Pres. Clinton's nomination of Jacob Lew as director of the White House's OMB. Lew will succeed Franklin Raines. . . . The Senate confirms, by voice vote, Pres. Clinton's appointment of Bill Richardson as energy secretary, succeeding Federico Pena. . . . The House approves, by voice vote, legislation that will consolidate dozens of the 163 job-training programs run by the federal government.		ABC names Patricia Fili-Krushel, 44, as president of the ABC Television Network, making her the highest-ranking woman executive in the television industry.	July 31
White House officials agree to suspend a controversial executive order on federalism issued May 14 by Pres. Clinton. The order sets out nine circumstances under which federal intervention is justified. It revokes two earlier presidential orders on federalism—issued by Clinton in 1993 and by Pres. Reagan in 1987—that stressed deference to state and local governments.	Joel Barr, 82, U.S. electronics expert who, after his defection to Czechoslovakia in 1950, was linked to the Julius and Ethel Rosenberg spy ring, dies in Moscow, Russia, of complications related to diabetes.			Anthony Munoz is the first Hispanic player inducted into the Football Hall of Fame. Four other players are inducted as well. . . . Eva Bartok, 72, Hungarian-born actress who appeared in nearly 40 films, dies in London, England, while suffering from a heart ailment.	Aug. 1
				In an upset, the U.S. All-Stars wins, 6-1, over the World All-Stars in MLS's third annual All-Star Game. . . . Shari Lewis, 65, who had delighted children for four decades with her puppet Lamb Chop, dies in Los Angeles, California, of pneumonia while suffering from uterine cancer. . . . Marco Pantani of Italy wins the Tour de France, which was marred by charges that several teams used performance-enhancing drugs.	Aug. 2
	Capts. Richard Ashby and Joseph Schweitzer, the pilot and navigator of a Marine Corps jet that severed a ski-lift cable at an Italian resort, killing 20 people, are indicted in a U.S. military court in Italy.	The House, by voice vote, passes a bill that will provide $5.5 billion in early crop-support payments to farmers hurt by bad weather and a worldwide decline in commodities prices.		Alfred Schnittke, 63, Russian composer whose works include eight symphonies, more than 60 film scores, and a satirical opera, dies in Hamburg, Germany of a stroke; earlier had strokes had left him severely handicapped.	Aug. 3

F	G	H	I	J
Includes elections, federal-state relations, civil rights and liberties, crime, the judiciary, education, health care, poverty, urban affairs, and population.	Includes formation and debate of U.S. foreign and defense policies, veterans' affairs, and defense spending. (Relations with specific foreign countries are usually found under the region concerned.)	Includes business, labor, agriculture, taxation, transportation, consumer affairs, monetary and fiscal policy, natural resources, and pollution.	Includes worldwide scientific, medical, and technological developments; natural phenomena; U.S. weather; natural disasters; and accidents.	Includes the arts, religion, scholarship, communications media, sports, entertainments, fashions, fads, and social life.

	World Affairs	Europe	Africa & the Middle East	The Americas	Asia & the Pacific
Aug. 4		In Kosovo, Serb forces capture the Drenica valley town of Lausa, one of the UCK's strongholds.	Rebels use an air convoy to transport some 600 troops from Goma, in the east, to Kitona, a Congolese military base 190 miles (300 km) southwest of Kinshasa, Congo's capital.	In Colombia, 500 FARC fighters overrun a U.S.-supported police antinarcotics base in Milaflores, Guaviare province. Out of the estimated 150–200 soldiers and police officers stationed at the base, at least 30 are killed, 50 are wounded, and the rest are taken hostage.	
Aug. 5	The Iraqi government of Pres. Saddam Hussein states that it is freezing cooperation with UN weapons inspectors to underscore its insistence that crippling UN sanctions imposed against Iraq since 1991 must end. Iraq reveals that it is discontinuing its relations with the International Atomic Energy Agency' (IAEA), which was responsible for monitoring Iraq's nuclear weapons programs.	Todor Zhivkov, 86, Bulgarian communist who ruled his country for 35 years, 1954–89, longer than any other leader in the former Soviet bloc, dies in Sofia, Bulgaria.	Two Jewish men are shot to death near the small West Bank settlement of Yitzhar, located some 4 miles (6 km) south of Nablus.	Data shows that more than 40 rebels and government soldiers have been killed in La Uribe in Colombia's Meta province since fighting broke out Aug. 3.	Cambodia's de facto leader, Hun Sen, is declared the winner of the country's July 26 national election. . . . Foreign ministers from Indonesia and Portugal announce they have agreed on a general outline of an autonomy plan for the disputed territory of East Timor. The accord is the first major breakthrough in the two nations' dispute over the region. Since Indonesia annexed East Timor in 1976, more than 100,000 people are thought to have been killed.
Aug. 6		Thomas McMahon, a former IRA member convicted in the 1979 bombing death of Britain's Lord Mountbatten, is freed from an Irish prison as part of a prisoner-release plan in the April Northern Ireland peace agreement. . . . Reports from kosovo state that Serb forces have destroyed more than a dozen villages in the Drenica region, bombarding them with artillery and then using gasoline to burn farms and fields.	Rebel troops capture the Congolese western town of Moanda, an oil depot, and the nearby city of Banana.		
Aug. 7		Slobodan Miljkovic, an accused Serb war criminal, is shot dead by a Serb policeman during a bar brawl in Kragujevac, Yugoslavia. Two others are also killed in an argument which is allegedly prompted when Miljkovic allegedly insults the officer's girlfriend. Miljkovic was accused of murder, war crimes, and crimes against humanity that allegedly took place in Bosanski Samac, a northeastern Bosnian town, in 1992.	Two bombs explode within minutes of each other near the U.S. embassies in Nairobi, Kenya, and Dar es Salaam, Tanzania. The Nairobi blast kills at least 247 people—including 12 U.S. citizens—and wounds approximately 5,000 thousand others. In Dar es Salaam, 10 people are killed, and some 75 people are reported wounded. U.S., Kenyan, and Tanzanian officials asserts that the bombings are most likely unrelated to political conditions within the two African countries and are aimed at the U.S.	Andres Pastrana Arango is inaugurated as Colombia's president in Bogota, the capital. The Red Cross reveals that 100 people have been killed in attacks since Aug. 3 and that some 75 police and soldiers are missing and presumed to be held captive. A FARC leader discloses that the offensive that began Aug. 3 was intended as a parting shot at the government of outgoing president Samper. . . . Peruvian president Alberto Fujimori accepts the resignation of Premier Javier Valle Riestra, a liberal who, since his June appointment, has repeatedly clashed with hard-liners.	
Aug. 8		The four illegal immigrants from Africa, along with five activists who support their plight, end their occupancy of the residence of the papal nuncio in Paris, France, which began Aug. 1.	In the Angolan town of Kunda-Dya-Base, 250 miles (400 km) east of Luanda, the capital, 150 people die in a massacre by unknown assailants. . . . Rescue and medical teams from the U.S., Israel, France, Britain, and other countries arrive in Nairobi, Kenya, in the wake of the Aug. 7 bomb. U.S. officials suspect the involvement of groups linked to Osama bin Laden, a Saudi-born multimillionaire believed to support militant Islamic followers.		In Afghanistan, the Taliban captures the opposition's capital, Mazar-i-Sharif, the base of operations for ousted president Burhanuddin Rabbani and ethnic Uzbek militia leader Gen. Abdul Rashid Doestam.
Aug. 9					Police arrest 18 foreigners who are handing out leaflets commemorating the Aug. 8 anniversary of a violent crackdown on prodemocracy demonstrators in Yangon and expressing support for Myanmar's prodemocracy movement.

A	B	C	D	E
Includes developments that affect more than one world region, international organizations, and important meetings of major world leaders.	Includes all domestic and regional developments in Europe, including the Soviet Union, Turkey, Cyprus, and Malta.	Includes all domestic and regional developments in Africa and the Middle East, including Iraq and Iran and excluding Cyprus, Turkey, and Afghanistan.	Includes all domestic and regional developments in Latin America, the Caribbean, and Canada.	Includes all domestic and regional developments in Asia and Pacific nations, extending from Afghanistan through all the Pacific Island, except Hawaii.

U.S. Politics & Social Issues	U.S. Foreign Policy & Defense	U.S. Economy & Environment	Science, Technology, & Nature	Culture, Leisure, & Lifestyle	
Pres. Clinton directs the Department of Health and Human Services to allow states to eliminate a rule that bars Medicaid coverage for some poor families with two working parents.	The U.S. Air Force announces that it will replace its cold war–era structure by reorganizing its staff and aircraft into 10 expeditionary units that will take turns being deployed to troubled areas worldwide.	The House by voice vote approves the Credit Union Membership Access Act, a bill that expands consumers' access to credit unions.			Aug. 4
A Philadelphia, Pennsylvania, woman, Marie Noe, is arrested and charged with fatally smothering eight of her 10 children from 1949 to 1968.				Anglican bishops attending a worldwide church conference, overwhelmingly approve a resolution calling homosexuality "incompatible with Scripture."	Aug. 5
Before a federal grand jury in Washington, D.C., former White House intern Monica Lewinsky, 25, testifies that she and Pres. Clinton had a sexual affair inside the White House and that they discussed ways of keeping it secret.		Interior Secretary Bruce Babbitt announces that the Interior Department will open more than 4 million acres (1.62 million hectares) of the Alaska National Petroleum Reserve to oil and gas leasing.... The House votes, 252-179, to approve a proposal to overhaul the nation's campaign-finance laws.... Dorothy Carnegie Rivkin (born Dorothy Price), 85, wife of Dale Carnegie who turned Dale Carnegie Training into a multinational operation, dies in New York City.	Andre Weil, 92, French-born mathematician who made fundamental contributions to areas of mathematics ranging from number theory to algebraic geometry, dies in Princeton, New Jersey.	Jack (John Beasley) Brickhouse, 82, baseball announcer who, between 1940 and 1981, broadcast a total of more than 5,000 regular-season games for the Chicago Cubs and the Chicago White Sox, dies in Chicago, Illinois, of cardiac arrest.	Aug. 6
U.S. district judge Norma Holloway Johnson unseals a June ruling in which she ordered Kenneth Starr's office to demonstrate that it did not leak grand jury information to the media.... The House attaches an antigay measure to a spending bill for the District of Columbia, which passes, 214-206. It is the third House measure seen as antigay that has been attached to other bills since July 29.		Pres. Clinton signs legislation that will consolidate dozens of the 163 job-training programs run by the federal government.... Pres. Clinton signs a bill expanding consumers' access to credit unions.... The Labor Department reports that the economy, hindered by Southeast Asia's financial crisis, created only 66,000 jobs in July. This marks the lowest monthly job expansion in 30 months.... Rose Blumkin, 104, furniture industry magnate whose 1937 store grew into one of the U.S.'s largest home-furnishings stores, dies in Omaha, Nebraska.			Aug. 7
Scores of demonstrators mark the 100th anniversary of the U.S. annexation of Hawaii by staging a march in Washington, D.C. The protesters aim to highlight the growing support for sovereignty among native Hawaiians, who make up a small minority of the island state's population.				Reverend Raymond E. Brown, 70, Roman Catholic biblical scholar and author of historically oriented works on the New Testament, dies in Redwood City, California, of a heart attack.	Aug. 8
Two boys, ages seven and eight, are charged in a Chicago juvenile court with murdering an 11-year-old girl, Ryan Harris, in late July. According to crime experts, the defendants are among the youngest children in U.S. history ever to be charged with murder.	Some 1,500 U.S. and Mexican citizens complete a 76-mile (120-km) march from El Paso, Texas, to Sierra Blanca to protest the construction of the Sierra Blanca waste-storage site. Marchers express fears that the nuclear waste stored at the site may leak into the nearby Rio Grande river and contaminate water supplies in both the U.S. and Mexico.	Some workers affiliated with the Communications Workers of America (CWA), a union that represents 73,000 Bell Atlantic employees, walk off their jobs at Bell Atlantic. The CWA and BellSouth Corp., a Baby Bell based in Atlanta, Georgia, agree on the terms of a tentative three-year labor contract covering 48,000 workers.		Yugoslavia wins the men's world basketball championships for a record fourth time by edging out Russia, 64-62, in Athens, Greece.	Aug. 9

F	G	H	I	J
Includes elections, federal-state relations, civil rights and liberties, crime, the judiciary, education, health care, poverty, urban affairs, and population.	*Includes formation and debate of U.S. foreign and defense policies, veterans' affairs, and defense spending. (Relations with specific foreign countries are usually found under the region concerned.)*	*Includes business, labor, agriculture, taxation, transportation, consumer affairs, monetary and fiscal policy, natural resources, and pollution.*	*Includes worldwide scientific, medical, and technological developments; natural phenomena; U.S. weather; natural disasters; and accidents.*	*Includes the arts, religion, scholarship, communications media, sports, entertainments, fashions, fads, and social life.*

	World Affairs	Europe	Africa & the Middle East	The Americas	Asia & the Pacific
Aug. 10	U.S. vice president Al Gore announces that the earth's average temperature for July was 61.7°F (16.5°C), the highest ever recorded. It was 1.26°F hotter than average.		Sultan Hassanal Bolkiah installs his 24-year-old son, Prince al-Muhtadee Billah, as Brunei's crown prince.	Jamil Mahuad Witt is inaugurated as president of Ecuador, succeeding acting president Fabian Alarcon.	Taliban troops intensify their assault on the Panjshir Valley stronghold of Gen. Ahmed Shah Massoud's ethnic Tajik forces. Separately, Iran demands that the Taliban leadership provide a full accounting of 11 Iranian diplomats whom Taliban troops allegedly seized upon entering Mazar-i-Sharif. . . . Ten people are hospitalized in the Japanese city of Niigata after drinking coffee and tea apparently containing an unidentified poisonous substance.
Aug. 11	Oil industry giant British Petroleum PLC (BP) announces a planned merger with the U.S.-based Amoco Corp. in a stock transaction valued at $48.2 billion. If completed, the deal will be the largest oil-industry merger ever, the largest transnational merger, the largest combination of industrial companies, and the largest foreign takeover of a U.S. firm—displacing the May merger of Daimler-Benz AG and Chrysler Corp.				In Afghanistan, Gen. Ahmed Shah Massoud's ethnic Tajik forces pull out of Taloqan, the capital of Takhar province, to consolidate their position in the Panjshir Valley, some 25 miles (40 km) north of Taliban-controlled Kabul, the capital.
Aug. 12		The British government reports that the national unemployment rate, seasonally adjusted, fell to 4.7% in July, from 4.8% in June. The July figure is the lowest recorded since 1980. . . . In a landmark settlement, officials from Swiss banks and representatives of victims of the Nazi Holocaust announce they have reached an accord under which the banks will pay a total of $1.25 billion to compensate Holocaust victims who lost assets deposited in Swiss accounts before and during World War II.			The Taliban ousts the opposition Northern Alliance from the town of Hayratan, extending Taliban rule to 90% of Afghanistan's territory. The Taliban also seizes Pol-i-Khomri. . . . In Indonesia, a military court hands down jail terms of less than a year each to two officers whose troops opened fire on student demonstrators in May, killing four. . . . In Myanmar, police stop Aung San Suu Kyi as she attempts to meet with her NLD party. She refuses to return to Yangon. . . . A Chinese court convicts four Taiwanese men of espionage.
Aug. 13		Eve Boswell (born Eva Keleti), 76, Hungarian-born singer who rose to the top of British pop charts in the 1950s, dies in Durban, South Africa, after suffering a heart attack.	A Tutsi-led rebel group called the Congolese Democratic Movement announces that it has captured the Inga hydroelectric dam, which supplies power to the Congolese capital, Kinshasa, in its quest to topple the government of Pres. Laurent Kabila.	Officials of Citizenship and Immigration Canada announce that four Filipino seamen will be allowed to stay in Canada on humanitarian grounds. The men told Halifax, Nova Scotia, authorities in 1996 that they witnessed six Taiwanese officers force three Romanian stowaways off the vessel and onto rafts in the middle of the Atlantic Ocean.	
Aug. 14			Reports reveal that Israel paid some $335,000 in compensation to a Palestinian mother whose son, Abd al-Samed Harizat, purportedly a member of Hamas, was tortured to death by Shin Bet.		The 18 foreigners arrested Aug. 9 in Yangon, Myanmar, are convicted of attempting to incite unrest and sentenced to five years' hard labor. However, the Home Affairs Ministry suspends the sentences and orders the activists deported.
Aug. 15		A car bomb explodes in the town of Omagh, in County Tyrone, Northern Ireland, killing 28 people and wounding 220 others. The blast is widely regarded as the worst act of violence yet in the long-running conflict between the British-controlled province's Roman Catholic and Protestant residents.		Raul Cubas Grau is inaugurated as president of Paraguay in Asuncion, the capital. Cubas succeeds Juan Carlos Wasmosy. . . . In Colombia, FARC guerrillas attack the 17th army brigade in the northwestern Uraba region.	

A	B	C	D	E
Includes developments that affect more than one world region, international organizations, and important meetings of major world leaders.	*Includes all domestic and regional developments in Europe, including the Soviet Union, Turkey, Cyprus, and Malta.*	*Includes all domestic and regional developments in Africa and the Middle East, including Iraq and Iran and excluding Cyprus, Turkey, and Afghanistan.*	*Includes all domestic and regional developments in Latin America, the Caribbean, and Canada.*	*Includes all domestic and regional developments in Asia and Pacific nations, extending from Afghanistan through all the Pacific Island, except Hawaii.*

U.S. Politics & Social Issues	U.S. Foreign Policy & Defense	U.S. Economy & Environment	Science, Technology, & Nature	Culture, Leisure, & Lifestyle	
June Gibbs Brown, the inspector general of the Department of Health and Human Services (HHS), argues that Medicare, the federal program that provides health insurance to the nation's elderly and disabled, overpaid health maintenance organizations (HMOs) by as much as $1.9 billion in 1996. Her report claims that Medicare overpaid HMOs by as much as $1.3 billion in 1995 and $1 billion in 1994.		CWA members set up picket lines outside Bell Atlantic offices in several cities in the Northeast, and 12 strike-related arrests are reported.			Aug. 10
A juvenile-court judge in Jonesboro, Arkansas, finds Andrew Golden, 12, and Mitchell Johnson, 14, guilty of carrying out a fatal shooting spree at their junior high school in March. Five people—four students and a teacher—were killed in the gunfire, and 10 others were wounded. . . . New England's Mashantucket Pequot Tribal Nation opens its Mashantucket Museum and Research Center, located near Mashantucket, Connecticut.	The attorney for the family of Ezequiel Hernandez Jr., 18, who was fatally shot by a member of a Marine Corps antidrug patrol near the U.S.-Mexico border in 1997, reveals that the U.S. government will pay a $1.9 million settlement to the teen's family.	Bell Atlantic reaches a tentative agreement on a two-year contract with the CWA, ending a strike that started Aug. 9. . . . The Labor Department reports that the nation's overall productivity in nonfarm business sectors dropped by a seasonally adjusted annual rate of 0.2% in the second quarter from the January-through-March quarter. That marks the indicator's first decline since the first quarter of 1995.		Steve Fossett is the first person to cross the South Atlantic Ocean in a balloon. . . . Benny Waters, 96, jazz musician, dies in Columbia, Maryland, of cardiac arrest. . . . The United Methodist Church rules that ministers who perform marriage rites for homosexuals violate church law.	Aug. 11
The U.S. Ninth Circuit Court of Appeals in San Francisco, California, upholds a lower court's decision when it rules that Medicare beneficiaries enrolled in health maintenance organizations (HMOs) are entitled to a broader set of legal protections than currently enforced by the federal government.	Trading company Sumitomo Corp. agrees to pay $99 million to settle six class-action lawsuits filed against it in the state of New York. The lawsuits were filed on behalf on copper futures and options traders who, between 1993 and 1996, suffered losses due to illegal copper price manipulation by a Sumitomo trader, Yasuo Hamanaka.	Pres. Clinton signs into law a bill that will provide $5.5 billion in early crop-support payments to farmers hurt by bad weather and a worldwide decline in commodities prices.	An Air Force rocket carrying a U.S. spy satellite explodes just after its launch from Cape Canaveral, Florida.		Aug. 12
The Oakland, California, City Council designates staff members of a local club that distributes marijuana for medical uses as officers of the city. The move is intended to shield the club, the Oakland Cannabis Buyers' Cooperative, from prosecution under federal drug laws.		Former Democratic fund-raiser Eugene K. H. Lum, convicted of campaign finance violations in 1997, pleads guilty to unrelated tax violations. . . . A federal judge in Phoenix, Arizona, approves a $100 million settlement between the state of Arizona and three copper-mining companies regarding underground pollution threatening Pinal Creek, a major source of drinking water in east-central Arizona.	Three Russian cosmonauts bound for the Mir space station blast off in Kazakhstan. They are scheduled to be the next-to-last crew to inhabit Mir. . . . The FTC and GeoCities, a popular site on the Internet computer network, disclose they have reached an agreement settling charges that the site violated users' right to privacy. The settlement represents the first time that the government used federal law to enforce privacy protections for Internet users.	Julian Green, 97, French-American novelist and playwright who, as a U.S. citizen, became the first foreigner elected to the Academie Francaise in 1971 but renounced his membership in 1996 on the grounds that he felt "exclusively American." dies in Paris, France, of unreported causes.	Aug. 13
An appeals court in Richmond, Virginia, rules that the FDA does not have the authority to regulate cigarettes or smokeless tobacco products. . . . A jury finds Miami Commissioner Humberto Hernandez guilty of one misdemeanor count related to election fraud . . . NYC mayor Rudolph Giuliani (R) orders five city hospitals to wean 2,000 patients in their methadone programs from the drug. . . . Chalmers Pangburn Wylie, 77, (R, Ohio) who served in the House of Representatives, 1967–93, dies in Columbus, Ohio of a heart attack.	Pres. Clinton grants waivers allowing three of the U.S. civilians killed Aug. 7 in the Nairobi, Kenya, bombing to be buried in Arlington National Cemetery in Virginia.			Jerry Loftis, a pioneer in the sport of sky surfing, falls to his death during a skydiving exhibition at an airfield near Quincy, Illinois.	Aug. 14
					Aug. 15

F	G	H	I	J
Includes elections, federal-state relations, civil rights and liberties, crime, the judiciary, education, health care, poverty, urban affairs, and population.	Includes formation and debate of U.S. foreign and defense policies, veterans' affairs, and defense spending. (Relations with specific foreign countries are usually found under the region concerned.)	Includes business, labor, agriculture, taxation, transportation, consumer affairs, monetary and fiscal policy, natural resources, and pollution.	Includes worldwide scientific, medical, and technological developments; natural phenomena; U.S. weather; natural disasters; and accidents.	Includes the arts, religion, scholarship, communications media, sports, entertainments, fashions, fads, and social life.

	World Affairs	Europe	Africa & the Middle East	The Americas	Asia & the Pacific
Aug. 16					
Aug. 17		In an effort to prevent a collapse of the Russian economy, the Russian government takes a series of drastic measures, including a de facto devaluation of the ruble, the national currency; restructuring of the domestic bond market; and a moratorium on foreign-debt repayment.		In Colombia, Defense Minister Rodrigo Lloreda reveals that 36 soldiers and an estimated 63 rebels have been killed since the Aug. 15 assault began.... Puerto Rico governor Pedro Rossello signs a bill authorizing a nonbinding referendum on whether the Caribbean island should become the 51st U.S. state.	Due to ongoing torrential summer rains, the third of three dikes protecting the Daqing oil field in northeastern China, which produces a third of the country's petroleum output, bursts.... South Korea's parliament approves the appointment of Kim Jong Pil as premier.... Chinese students' and women's groups hold events in Beijing, the capital, to protest the anti-Chinese violence in Indonesia. Groups of students visit Indonesia's Beijing embassy to register their protest.
Aug. 18		An IRA splinter group calling itself the Real IRA claims responsibility for the Aug. 15 bombing in the town of Omagh, in County Tyrone, Northern Ireland.		In Paraguay, Pres. Cubas commutes a jail sentence against retired general Lino Cesar Oviedo, the original presidential candidate of Cubas's Colorado Party sentenced to prison in March.	
Aug. 19		Assicurazioni Generali SpA, Italy's largest insurance company, tentatively agrees to pay $100 million to victims of the Nazi Holocaust and victims' heirs, who were denied access to benefits from policies they purchased from Generali before and during World War II.... In rare appearance together, Gerry Adams, head of Sinn Fein, the IRA's political wing, and Northern Ireland Protestant leader David Trimble attend a funeral service in Buncrana, Ireland, for three victims of the Aug. 15 Omagh bombing.		Canadian justice Robert Blair approves the sale of the Canadian Red Cross's national blood-collection and distribution services. The planned sale is part of a major reorganization of the not-for-profit humanitarian agency, which faces more than 200 lawsuits filed by people who contracted the hepatitis C virus or HIV, the virus that causes AIDS, from transfusions of tainted blood.	Two unidentified men attack and severely hurt popular Hong Kong radio talk-show host Albert Cheng with carving knives. Cheng is well-known for his sharp criticisms of the territorial and Chinese governments and of powerful interest groups in Hong Kong society.
Aug. 20	The U.S. fires some 75 Tomahawk cruise missiles at facilities in Afghanistan and Sudan thought to have links to terrorist activities. U.S. president Bill Clinton states the strikes are a response to an "imminent threat" to the U.S. posed by a terrorist network backed by Saudi-born multimillionaire Osama bin Laden, who currently lives in Afghanistan.		Kenyan authorities announce that the deaths of six Kenyans injured in the Aug. 7 blast in Nairobi brings the death toll in that bombing to 253. The total death toll from the twin embassy bombings now stands at 263.... Shlomo Raanan, 63, becomes the third Jewish settler killed in August by suspected Palestinians when he is fatally stabbed in the divided West Bank city of Hebron. The Israeli army immediately seals off Hebron and imposes a curfew on Palestinians in the Israeli-controlled part of the city.	The Supreme Court of Canada issues a ruling stating that under both Canadian and international law, the province of Quebec will not be free to secede from Canada without first negotiating terms with the other provinces and with the federal government.	In Cambodia, opposition party leader Sam Rainsy narrowly escapes a drive-by shooting and grenade blast that kills a driver for Japanese journalists.... The Nen River swamps parts of the Daqing oil field in northeastern China, which produces a third of the country's petroleum output.... Vu Van Mau, 84, South Vietnam's premier in the last days before the communists declared victory in the Vietnam War in 1975, dies in Paris, France.
Aug. 21	Representatives from 16 Caribbean nations open a summit meeting in Santo Domingo, Dominican Republic.		Some 50 settlers go on a rampage in Hebron and beat two Palestinian passersby, hospitalizing one of them. The attack prompts clashes between Palestinians, settlers, and Israeli soldiers.... A court in the South African town of George finds former president P. W. Botha guilty of contempt for refusing to testify before the Truth and Reconciliation Commission and orders him to pay a fine of about $1,600 or to serve one year in prison.	Reports confirm that former president Juan Carlos Wasmosy, has taken refuge in the Argentine embassy in Asunción, Paraguay's capital, in what is seen as a move to avoid arrest on corruption charges.	An Italian army officer who works for the UN Special Mission to Afghanistan is shot in Kabul, Afghanistan's capital, in an apparent act of retaliation for the Aug. 20 U.S. missile strikes.... Australia's federal court rules that the Northern Territory government has the right to grant a lease to Energy Resources of Australia (ERA) to mine uranium at Jabiluka, an area in the custody of the Mirrar aboriginal people.... The Indonesian government shuts down three commercial banks and takes control of four others in an effort to restructure the nation's ailing banking system.

A	B	C	D	E
Includes developments that affect more than one world region, international organizations, and important meetings of major world leaders.	Includes all domestic and regional developments in Europe, including the Soviet Union, Turkey, Cyprus, and Malta.	Includes all domestic and regional developments in Africa and the Middle East, including Iraq and Iran and excluding Cyprus, Turkey, and Afghanistan.	Includes all domestic and regional developments in Latin America, the Caribbean, and Canada.	Includes all domestic and regional developments in Asia and Pacific nations, extending from Afghanistan through all the Pacific Island, except Hawaii.

U.S. Politics & Social Issues	U.S. Foreign Policy & Defense	U.S. Economy & Environment	Science, Technology, & Nature	Culture, Leisure, & Lifestyle	
	The U.S. orders nonessential diplomatic personnel and dependents in Pakistan to return to the U.S. The order comes partially in response to threats of retaliation for the recent arrest in Pakistan of a suspect in the Aug. 7 African embassy bombings. The U.S. evacuates its diplomats from Tirana, the capital of Albania, in response to threats of an attack on its embassy there by Islamic militants.	Some 34,000 CWA members employed by US West Inc., a Baby Bell headquartered in Denver, Colorado, go on strike.		Dorothy West, 91, member of the Harlem Renaissance circle of black writers, dies in Boston, Massachusetts. . . . Jim (James Patrick) Murray, 78, nationally syndicated Pulitzer Prize–winning sportswriter, dies in Los Angeles of cardiac arrest. . . . D.C. United defeats Mexican soccer champion Toluca, 1-0, to become the first U.S. team to win the CONCACAF Champions' Cup. . . . Golfer Vijay Singh of Fiji wins the PGA Championship in Redmond, Washington.	Aug. 16
Pres. Clinton testifies to a federal grand jury about his relationship with former White House intern Monica Lewinsky. In a televised address, the president acknowledges that he and Lewinsky had had a relationship that was "not appropriate." While he asserts that "at no time did I ask anyone to lie, to hide or destroy evidence, or to take any other unlawful action," he admits he "misled" the public and his wife, First Lady Hillary Rodham Clinton.				CBS names Nancy Tellem the head of its entertainment division, making her the second woman to head a network's entertainment division. . . . An estimated 10 million TV viewers tune in to coverage regarding the scandal involving Pres. Clinton and Monica Lewinsky.	Aug. 17
The first official tally of terminally ill people who died in Oregon from lethal medications prescribed under a state law permitting physician-assisted suicide stands at eight since the law took effect in November 1997. Two other patients received state authorization to take lethal drugs but died from their illnesses before doing so.		Bill Richardson is sworn in as energy secretary. . . . The Commerce Department reports that the U.S. trade deficit contracted 8.9% in June, following a string of four record highs in five months. The department records a seasonally adjusted $14.15 billion gap in trade in goods and services for June. May's revised record deficit stood at $15.54 billion.		World War II researchers in Amsterdam, the Netherlands, claim that they found five handwritten pages of Anne Frank's diary that were previously not known to exist.	Aug. 18
In Miami, Florida, Circuit Court judge Roberto Pineiro sentences suspended Miami commissioner Humberto Hernandez to the maximum 364 days in jail for trying to cover up vote fraud in the city's 1997 municipal elections.	A statement published in the London-based Arabic newspaper *Al Hayat* by a coalition of militant Islamic groups assembled by Osama bin Laden warns of more terrorist attacks against the U.S. The group, the World Islamic Front for Holy War Against Jews and Crusaders, threatens that the U.S. will "face a black fate." The statement also attributes the Aug. 7 embassy bombings to the previously unknown Islamic Army for the Liberation of Holy Shrines in retaliation for the U.S.'s actions in Somalia in 1993.				Aug. 19
A committee recommends that the federal government's system of ensuring food safety be brought under the control of a single authority. . . . Monica Lewinsky testifies before a grand jury regarding her involvement with Pres. Clinton when she was an intern at the White House. . . . . Melissa Drexler, 20, pleads guilty to aggravated manslaughter in the killing of her newborn son after giving birth in the bathroom at her senior prom in 1997 when she was 18.	Pres. Clinton signs an executive order freezing any U.S. assets held by Osama bin Laden, two of his top lieutenants, or his Islamic Army group. The order also prohibits financial transactions between those entities and U.S. companies and individuals.				Aug. 20
A jury in Hattiesburg, Mississippi, convicts former Ku Klux Klan (KKK) leader Samuel Bowers of murder for ordering and planning the 1966 killing of civil-rights activist Vernon Dahmer Sr., who died from severe burns after a group of Klansmen firebombed his home and business. Dahmer apparently was targeted because he allowed his store to be used as a voter-registration venue for fellow blacks. Judge Richard McKenzie sentences Bowers to a life prison term immediately after the verdict is announced.	U.S. lawyers file a lawsuit in U.S. District Court in Newark, New Jersey, against Germany's Degussa AG, a chemicals and metals company, on behalf of Holocaust victims, contending that Degussa willingly worked with the Nazis to produce Zyklon B, a fatal gas used in death camps during World War II.			Data reveals that attendance at 1998 Women's National Basketball Association (WNBA) games rose by 12% a game to an average of 10,869 spectators. . . . Wanda Toscanini Horowitz, 90, daughter of classical musician Arturo Toscanini and wife of pianist Vladimir Horowitz, dies in New York City.	Aug. 21

F	G	H	I	J
Includes elections, federal-state relations, civil rights and liberties, crime, the judiciary, education, health care, poverty, urban affairs, and population.	Includes formation and debate of U.S. foreign and defense policies, veterans' affairs, and defense spending. (Relations with specific foreign countries are usually found under the region concerned.)	Includes business, labor, agriculture, taxation, transportation, consumer affairs, monetary and fiscal policy, natural resources, and pollution.	Includes worldwide scientific, medical, and technological developments; natural phenomena; U.S. weather; natural disasters; and accidents.	Includes the arts, religion, scholarship, communications media, sports, entertainments, fashions, fads, and social life.

	World Affairs	Europe	Africa & the Middle East	The Americas	Asia & the Pacific
Aug. 22		In memory of the Aug. 15 bombing, at least 40,000 people gather in the town of Omagh, Northern Ireland, to observe a minute of silence, along with thousands of others at memorials throughout the country. Some 12,000 demonstrators gather for a peace rally in Dundalk. The Irish National Liberation Army (INLA), a hard-line Roman Catholic guerrilla group, announces an end to its use of violent tactics.	Gen. Abdulsalami Abubakar appoints an interim cabinet to prepare Nigeria for transition to civilian rule by May 1999.		An official radio broadcast of the Taliban militia that controls most of Afghanistan reports that 21 people were killed by the Aug. 20 U.S. missile attack on camps in that country. Lt. Col. Carmine Calo, the Italian army officer shot Aug. 21, dies in Afghanistan.
Aug. 23		Russian president Boris Yeltsin dismisses reformist premier Sergei Kiriyenko and reinstates Kiriyenko's predecessor, Viktor Chernomyrdin.			
Aug. 24					Officials announce that Lt. Gen. Prabowo Subianto, son-in-law of former Indonesian president Suharto, was dismissed from the military in response to his alleged role in the abduction and torture of political dissidents in 1997 and early 1998. . . . About 200 students stage a demonstration in support of the NLD in Yangon, the capital of Myanmar, in the first street protest there since 1996. The SPDC reports that prodemocracy dissident Aung San Suu Kyi voluntarily ended a standoff with police that started Aug. 12 near Yangon. . . . In Cambodia, protestors begin a round-the-clock demonstration near Parliament. . . . In South Korea, Hyundai Motor and its workers' labor union reach an agreement, ending a strike that started in July.
Aug. 25	Reports reveal that the UN international war crimes tribunal has begun to investigate war crimes committed in Kosovo.	The Russian government announces details of a bond restructuring that will cost Russian banks and foreign investors billions of dollars. In response, the ruble plummets to 7.86 to the dollar from 7.14, a 9% drop that is the Russian currency's biggest one-day decline in four years.	A bomb explodes in a restaurant in Cape Town, South Africa, killing one person and injuring 27 others.		The New South Wales Health Department warns residents of Sydney, Australia, that the city's tap water has been contaminated by two parasite strains, giardia and cryptosporidium. The same parasites were found in municipal tap water in July. Separately, officials state Australia will accept fewer refugee immigrants from Asia in the fiscal year that began June 30 than in the previous fiscal year. The number of refugee immigrants accepted from Europe—particularly those from nations that made up the former Yugoslavia—will increase.
Aug. 26		Russia's central bank suspends the trading of rubles for U.S. dollars as the Russian currency, devalued Aug. 17 by the government of Pres. Boris Yeltsin, continues to lose value.			China announces that 3,004 people have died since June in severe floods along several Chinese rivers. The floods, an annual product of torrential summer rains, are the worst in China since 1954. China's state-run Xinhua news agency estimates the economic losses resulting from the floods at 166.6 billion yuan ($20 billion).
Aug. 27	The financial crisis in Russia unleashes investor fears worldwide, as economists and traders express alarm that Asia's year-old economic upheaval will envelop Latin American emerging markets and bring growth among major industrialized nations to a halt. Waves of stock selling jars markets in most of Asia, Europe, and the Americas. . . . The UN Security Council passes a resolution stipulating that economic sanctions against Libya will be removed when Abdel Basset Ali al-Megrahi and Lamen Khalifa Fhimah, suspects in the 1988 Pan Am 103 bombing, are delivered to the international tribunal.	Russia's central bank shuts down the Moscow Interbank Currency Exchange, the nation's main currency exchange, after 10 minutes of trading shows the ruble falling further. The Russian Trading System index of stocks plunges by 17% to close at 63.2 points, the index's lowest level since it was created in September 1995. The Russian stock market has dropped by 84% since the beginning of 1998. . . . Bob Arnold, 87, actor on a British radio serial for several years, dies.	A small pipe bomb crammed with nails explodes in a trash can in central Tel Aviv, Israel, injuring more than 20 people.		The government reports that Malaysia has slipped into its first recession in 13 years.

A	B	C	D	E
Includes developments that affect more than one world region, international organizations, and important meetings of major world leaders.	*Includes all domestic and regional developments in Europe, including the Soviet Union, Turkey, Cyprus, and Malta.*	*Includes all domestic and regional developments in Africa and the Middle East, including Iraq and Iran and excluding Cyprus, Turkey, and Afghanistan.*	*Includes all domestic and regional developments in Latin America, the Caribbean, and Canada.*	*Includes all domestic and regional developments in Asia and the Pacific nations, extending from Afghanistan through all the Pacific Island, except Hawaii.*

U.S. Politics & Social Issues	U.S. Foreign Policy & Defense	U.S. Economy & Environment	Science, Technology, & Nature	Culture, Leisure, & Lifestyle	
				Elena Garro, 78, Mexican novelist and playwright, dies of emphysema in Cuernavaca, Mexico.... Woody Stephens, 84, U.S. horse trainer, dies in Miami Lakes, Florida, of complications of emphysema.	Aug. 22
	Francisco Salveron, 88, Philippine-born aide to General Douglas MacArthur during World War II, dies of lung cancer in Bladensburg, Maryland.				Aug. 23
A special three-judge federal panel unanimously rejects the Census Bureau's proposed use of statistical sampling in conducting the national census in the year 2000, finding that such a use of sampling is in direct violation of existing federal law.... Charles Coles Diggs Jr., 75, (D, Mich.), who served in the U.S. House of Representatives, 1955–80, dies in Washington D.C., of a stroke. ... John R(ichard) Williams, 88, (R, Ariz.) who, after serving two terms as mayor of Phoenix, became governor of Arizona, 1967–75, dies in Phoenix, Arizona.	U.S. officials confirm that a federal grand jury has issued a sealed indictment against Osama bin Laden for terrorist attacks against the U.S. prior to the embassy bombings in Africa.			E. G. Marshall, stage, screen, and television actor who won two Emmy Awards, dies in Mount Kisco, New York. His age is variously reported at 88 and 84.	Aug. 24
Pres. Clinton orders the creation of a Council on Food Safety.... Lewis Franklin Powell Jr., 90, associate justice of the Supreme Court, 1972–87, who generally sided with the court's conservative bloc on business and crime issues but often provided the swing vote on social issues that allowed the court's liberal bloc to prevail, dies of pneumonia in Richmond, Virginia.... Floyd K. Haskell, 82, (D, Colo.), who served one term in the Senate, 1973–79, dies of pneumonia while being transported to a Washington, D.C., hospital from Maine.	A U.S. grand jury in San Juan, Puerto Rico, indicts seven Cuban Americans on charges that they plotted to kill Cuban president Fidel Castro Ruz during a visit to Venezuela's Margarita Island in 1997.			Reports confirm that the Wortham Foundation and the Houston Endowment have each donated $3.65 million to the Houston Symphony Orchestra in one of the largest arts grants of 1998.	Aug. 25
Judge Lewis A. Kaplan of U.S. District Court orders New York City to allow a rally, billed as the "Million Youth March," to take place. NYC mayor Rudolph W. Giuliani has refused to grant a permit for the has planned event, which he called a "hate march."			An unmanned Delta 3 rocket carrying a private communications satellite blows up about 80 seconds after its launch from Cape Canaveral, Florida. The launch is the first flight of the newest version of the Delta rocket.... Frederick Reines, 80, U.S. physicist who received a 1995 Nobel Prize in physics for his mid-1950s discovery of the subatomic particle known as the neutrino, dies in Orange, California.		Aug. 26
	Mohamed Rashed Daoud al-Owhali, a suspect in the Aug. 7 bombing of the U.S. embassy in Nairobi, Kenya, is flown from Nairobi to New York City, where he is arraigned in U.S. District Court on charges related to the bombing.	Some 935 million shares are traded on the New York Stock Exchange, second in volume only to the record registered in October 1997. ... The Commerce Department reports that gross domestic product (GDP) grew at a revised, seasonally adjusted annual rate of 1.6% in the second quarter. That compares with an annualized GDP expansion of 5.5% in the January-March quarter.	An intense five-minute wave of radiation emanating from a faraway star disturbs the Earth's upper atmosphere.		Aug. 27

F	G	H	I	J
Includes elections, federal-state relations, civil rights and liberties, crime, the judiciary, education, health care, poverty, urban affairs, and population.	Includes formation and debate of U.S. foreign and defense policies, veterans' affairs, and defense spending. (Relations with specific foreign countries are usually found under the region concerned.)	Includes business, labor, agriculture, taxation, transportation, consumer affairs, monetary and fiscal policy, natural resources, and pollution.	Includes worldwide scientific, medical, and technological developments; natural phenomena; U.S. weather; natural disasters; and accidents.	Includes the arts, religion, scholarship, communications media, sports, entertainments, fashions, fads, and social life.

	World Affairs	Europe	Africa & the Middle East	The Americas	Asia & the Pacific
Aug. 28				Reports confirm that Colombia's Supreme Court will open an investigation into a 1996 decision by Congress to clear former president Ernesto Samper of the charges that drug cartels financed his 1994 presidential campaign.	Japan's Nikkei 225 stock index is pushed down to 13,915.63 points, a 12-year low. . . . Vietnam's government announces that it will soon free more than 5,000 prisoners in a mass amnesty deal. Among the inmates to be released are Doan Viet Hoat and Nguyen Dan Que, two of the country's most prominent political dissidents.
Aug. 29	Minerva Bernardino, 91, one of the four women to sign the UN Charter in 1945 and one of the feminists who helped to create the UN Commission on the Status of Women, dies in the Dominican Republic.		Sudanese news media report that one person was killed in the Aug. 20 strike by the U.S. on the Al Shifa plant, and nine others were injured.	A Cuban airliner crashes and explodes at the international airport in Quito, Ecuador, after a failed take-off attempt. The plane skids off the end of the runway and slams through a fence into an adjacent field where several children are playing soccer. Score of people are killed.	
Aug. 30		To mark the first anniversary of the Aug. 31 death of Diana, Princess of Wales, a service is held for the royal family at a church near Balmoral Castle, Queen Elizabeth II's retreat in Scotland. Thousands of people gather near Kensington Palace, Diana's residence in London, to remember her.		The official death toll from the Aug. 29 crash in Ecuador stands at 79. Ten of those killed, including five children, were on the ground when the plane crashed. . . . Voters in Panama overwhelmingly reject a constitutional change that would have allowed Panamanian president Ernesto Perez Balladares to seek a second five-year term in 1999.	Thousands of demonstrators march through the streets of Phnom Penh, Cambodia's capital, calling for the ouster of Hun Sen, the country's recently elected premier. The demonstrators argue that the election was tainted by fraud and voter intimidation. The march is held as demonstrators continue a round-the-clock protest that started Aug. 24. . . . Authorities release from prison Wang Youcai, one of several founders of the China Democracy Party arrested in July, and place him under house arrest.
Aug. 31	The Dow Jones World Stock Index, a measure of overall movement in stock markets worldwide, closes at 164.75 points. That represents a decline of 7.9% in the average weighted value of securities in global stock markets since Aug. 26, when the Dow's world index stood at 178.91.	The communist-dominated Russian parliament overwhelmingly rejects Pres. Boris Yeltsin's bid to reinstate his longtime premier, Viktor Chernomyrdin. Rather than consider another candidate, Yeltsin immediately renominates Chernomyrdin. . . . Sir (Leslie) Gordon Newton, 90, British journalist who was knighted in 1966, dies.			North Korea fires a medium-range ballistic missile toward Japan. The launch prompts concern among other countries that North Korea's introduction of a new, longer-range missile may spur new missile proliferation in Asia. . . . In Indonesia, rioters attack ethnic Chinese and burn buildings in Lhokseumawe, in the northern province of Aceh.
Sept. 1	Russian president Boris Yeltsin and U.S. president Bill Clinton hold a summit, their first meeting since March 1997.	Lord Rothermere (born Vere Harold Esmond Harmsworth), 73, British newspaper magnate who turned the *Daily Mail* into a highly successful tabloid, dies of a heart attack in London, England.	Iran begins conducting military exercises known as Ashura 3 about 40 miles (65 km) from the Afghanistan border.		In response to the Aug. 31 missile launch, Japan puts off a planned resumption of talks with North Korea on establishing diplomatic relations. Japan also suspends food aid to famine-stricken North Korea.
Sept. 2				Swissair Flight 111 plunges into the Atlantic Ocean about 5 miles (8 km) off the southeastern shore of Nova Scotia, Canada. Apparently all 229 people aboard the plane are killed. . . . Pilots employed by Air Canada go on strike.	Thousands of students in Yangon, the capital of Myanmar, stage protests against the ruling State Peace and Development Council (SPDC). The protests are the largest since December 1996. . . . An Australian justice refuses to extend a two-month-long freeze on A$500,000 (US$300,000) in election reimbursement funds designated for the far-right One Nation Party.

A	B	C	D	E
Includes developments that affect more than one world region, international organizations, and important meetings of major world leaders.	Includes all domestic and regional developments in Europe, including the Soviet Union, Turkey, Cyprus, and Malta.	Includes all domestic and regional developments in Africa and the Middle East, including Iraq and Iran and excluding Cyprus, Turkey, and Afghanistan.	Includes all domestic and regional developments in Latin America, the Caribbean, and Canada.	Includes all domestic and regional developments in Asia and Pacific nations, extending from Afghanistan through all the Pacific Island, except Hawaii.

U.S. Politics & Social Issues	U.S. Foreign Policy & Defense	U.S. Economy & Environment	Science, Technology, & Nature	Culture, Leisure, & Lifestyle	
The U.S. Court of Appeals for the District of Columbia Circuit reinstates a lawsuit challenging a law barring gun ownership by people convicted of domestic abuse.	Mohammed Saddiq Odeh, a suspect accused of helping plot the Aug. 7 bombing of a U.S. embassy in Kenya, is charged in U.S. District Court on charges related to the blast.	The Dow Jones falls 357.36 points, or 4.2%, to 8165.99. That marks the average's worst trading day to date in 1998.			Aug. 28
		Some 6,170 pilots employed by Northwest Airlines go on strike, grounding all 400 of Northwest's airplanes and also the airplanes owned by the company's commuter affiliates. Thousands of Northwest passengers are stranded worldwide. The pilots' strike is the first at Northwest since 1978. It is also the first at any U.S. carrier since February 1997, when pilots employed by American Airlines Inc. staged a brief stoppage.		A Toms River, New Jersey, baseball team wins the Little League World Series, 12-9, over defeated a team from Kashima, Japan, in Williamsport, Pennsylvania.	Aug. 29
					Aug. 30
		US West Inc. reaches a tentative three-year contract agreement with the Communications Workers of America (CWA) labor union, ending a strike that started Aug. 16. . . . The Dow Jones closes at 7539.07, or some 19.3% down from its record high set July 17. It is down 6.37%, or 512.61 points, the second largest single-session point decline on record. The drop is not among top-20 historic declines in percentage terms.	Reports suggest that an international team of scientists have discovered a strain of HIV, the virus that causes AIDS, that is not detectable by current blood tests for the virus. . . . The ashes of late hurricane researcher Jose Fernandez Partagas, who died in 1996, are scattered from an airplane into the winds of Hurricane Danielle as the storm travels over the Atlantic Ocean. Six scientists and 11 airplane crew members attend the ash-scattering ceremony.	*Rainbow Six* by Tom Clancy tops the bestseller list.	Aug. 31
The College Board reports that the average score on the math section of the 1998 Scholastic Assessment Test (SAT) was 512, one point higher than in the previous year, while the average verbal score was unchanged at 505. The average math score is the highest recorded in 27 years.	The Senate votes, 87-3, to clear an appropriations bill allocating $8.45 billion for military construction spending in fiscal 1999. It is the first of the 13 annual appropriations bills to clear Congress. . . . Law enforcement agents in the U.S. and 13 other countries begin raiding the property of nearly 200 people suspected of membership in a child pornography ring known as the Wonderland Club on the Internet global computer network. More than 40 people worldwide are arrested. Investigators call it the largest Internet child pornography ring ever uncovered.	A record 1.205 billion shares are traded on the New York Stock Exchange, surpassing the previous record set in October 1997.		In basketball, the Houston Comets win their second straight WNBA title, defeating the Phoenix Mercury, 80-71, in Houston, Texas. . . . (Emmett) Cary Middlecoff, 77, golfer who won the U.S. Open in 1949 and 1956, dies of congestive heart failure in Memphis, Tennessee.	Sept. 1
Judge Daniel Eismann rejects Idaho's lawsuit against the tobacco industry seeking compensation for state money spent on treating smoking-related illnesses. . . . Kendall Francois, 27, is arrested in Poughkeepsie, New York, after police find the bodies of three women in his house.		The Senate votes, 78-15, to approve a three-state agreement to dispose of low-level nuclear waste at a site in western Texas near the Mexican border. The three states in the agreement are Texas, Vermont, and Maine.	The FDA approves the marketing of a kit of "morning-after" contraceptive pills intended to help prevent pregnancy soon after unprotected sexual intercourse. . . . Dr. Jonathan Max Mann, 51, the founder and first director of the WHO's Global Program on AIDS, 1986–90, dies in the crash of Swissair Flight 111 off the coast of Nova Scotia, Canada.	Allen Stuart Drury, 80, U.S. writer and journalist who won a Pulitzer Prize in 1960, dies of cardiac arrest in San Francisco, California.	Sept. 2

F	G	H	I	J
Includes elections, federal-state relations, civil rights and liberties, crime, the judiciary, education, health care, poverty, urban affairs, and population.	*Includes formation and debate of U.S. foreign and defense policies, veterans' affairs, and defense spending. (Relations with specific foreign countries are usually found under the region concerned.)*	*Includes business, labor, agriculture, taxation, transportation, consumer affairs, monetary and fiscal policy, natural resources, and pollution.*	*Includes worldwide scientific, medical, and technological developments; natural phenomena; U.S. weather; natural disasters; and accidents.*	*Includes the arts, religion, scholarship, communications media, sports, entertainments, fashions, fads, and social life.*

	World Affairs	Europe	Africa & the Middle East	The Americas	Asia & the Pacific
Sept. 3				The Supreme Court of Canada rules that people who know they have dangerous sexually transmitted diseases will face criminal sanctions if they fail to disclose their condition to a partner before having unprotected sex. Such a failure to disclose constitutes a criminal act whether or not that partner actually contracts the disease.	Amnesty International estimates that 3,000 people were executed in China in 1997. That is down from 4,367 people thought to have been executed in 1996. . . . In Malaysia, thousands of supporters of former deputy prime minister Anwar Ibrahim, dismissed earlier by P.M. Mahathir bin Mohamad, gather around Anwar's residence. . . . In Australia, Lindsey Robert Rose is sentenced to life in prison for a series of five murders that police have been attempting to solve for more than 15 years. . . . A speaker for the Taliban reveals that the group has no information on the 10 Iranians missing since Aug. 8, but he acknowledges that they may have been killed.
Sept. 4					North Korea reveals that a ballistic missile fired over Japan in late August has launched the country's first satellite into orbit.
Sept. 5		In Northern Ireland, protesting the blocking by police of a traditional parade in Portadown's Drumcree section, Protestants riot. Separately, Sean McGrath, 61, critically wounded in the Omagh blast in August, dies from his injuries in Belfast, bringing the blast's death toll to 29. Another 29 people wounded in the attack remain hospitalized, two of them in critical condition.			Reports confirm that torrential rains in India caused the Ganges River to flood, killing more than 1,000 people. . . . North Korea announces that Kim Jong Il, son of the late North Korean paramount leader Kim Il Sung, was reelected chair of the National Defense Commission. The announcement calls that position "the highest post of the state," indicating that Kim Jong Il, 56, has officially succeeded Kim Il Sung as head of state four years after the former leader's death. Kim Jong Il's official elevation is the first instance of hereditary succession in a communist country.
Sept. 6	Mary Robinson, the United Nations High Commissioner for Human Rights, makes the first trip to China by a holder of that post.				North Korea announces that the country's constitution will be amended so that the title of president will remain reserved for Kim Il Sung. The government also announces that Kim Yong Nam, formerly the foreign minister, will become president of the presidium of the Supreme People's Assembly, the country's rubber-stamp parliament, and will represent North Korea in diplomatic functions. . . . Fenech Adami is named premier of Malta when returns from parliamentary elections show his Nationalist Party is the winner.
Sept. 7		The Russian Duma rejects Pres. Boris Yeltsin's nominee for premier, former premier Viktor Chernomyrdin for the second time. . . . Protestant unionist leader David Trimble and Gerry Adams, head of Sinn Fein, the political wing of the IRA, talk directly to each other for the first time during a meeting of the Northern Ireland Assembly,			Iran completes conducted military exercises known as Ashura 3, which began Sep. 1 about 40 miles (65 km) from the Afghanistan border.

A	B	C	D	E
Includes developments that affect more than one world region, international organizations, and important meetings of major world leaders.	Includes all domestic and regional developments in Europe, including the Soviet Union, Turkey, Cyprus, and Malta.	Includes all domestic and regional developments in Africa and the Middle East, including Iraq and Iran and excluding Cyprus, Turkey, and Afghanistan.	Includes all domestic and regional developments in Latin America, the Caribbean, and Canada.	Includes all domestic and regional developments in Asia and Pacific nations, extending from Afghanistan through all the Pacific Island, except Hawaii.

U.S. Politics & Social Issues	U.S. Foreign Policy & Defense	U.S. Economy & Environment	Science, Technology, & Nature	Culture, Leisure, & Lifestyle	
					Sept. 3
Cook County, Illinois, prosecutors withdraw murder charges against two boys under the age of 10 accused of sexually molesting and killing Ryan Harris, an 11-year-old girl. Laboratory tests found semen stains in Harris's underwear, and authorities believe that neither of the suspects, aged seven and eight, are physically capable of producing semen.			Alan Binder, the chief scientist of the unmanned *Lunar Prospector* spacecraft orbiting the moon, theorizes that the moon may hold as much as 10 billion tons (9 billion metric tons) of water frozen in its polar regions.		**Sept. 4**
Police reveal that they have found the bodies of five more women in the house of Kendall Francois, who was arrested Sep. 2.... The "Million Youth March," a controversial rally for black youths held in Harlem, New York City, ends in a clash when police officers rush the stage as Khallid Abdul Muhammad, the chief organizer of the event, concludes a speech in which he denounces the police and the city's mayor, Rudolph Giuliani (R). Demonstrators pelt the police with chairs and bricks.				Leo Penn, 77, actor who made his mark as a director, primarily in television, dies of cancer in Santa Monica, California.	**Sept. 5**
	An Israeli judge in West Jerusalem rules that Samuel Sheinbein, an 18-year-old American wanted for murder in Maryland, may be extradited to the U.S. to stand trial.			Akira Kurosawa, 88, Japanese filmmaker widely regarded as one of the giants of world cinema who, in 1990, was honored with an Oscar for lifetime achievement, dies in Tokyo after a stroke.... Auto racer Alex Zanardi of Italy clinches his second PPG Cup in the CART world series. It is the earliest point in a CART season that a driver clinches the league title.	**Sept. 6**
About 1,000 people attend a rally for black youths in Atlanta, Georgia, which draws prominent civil-rights leaders, including Rev. Jesse Jackson and Kweisi Mfume, the president of the NAACP.				In baseball, Mark McGwire of the St. Louis Cardinals hits his 61st home run in the Cardinals' 144th game of the season. The homer ties the record set by Roger Maris in 1961.	**Sept. 7**

F	G	H	I	J
Includes elections, federal-state relations, civil rights and liberties, crime, the judiciary, education, health care, poverty, urban affairs, and population.	*Includes formation and debate of U.S. foreign and defense policies, veterans' affairs, and defense spending. (Relations with specific foreign countries are usually found under the region concerned.)*	*Includes business, labor, agriculture, taxation, transportation, consumer affairs, monetary and fiscal policy, natural resources, and pollution.*	*Includes worldwide scientific, medical, and technological developments; natural phenomena; U.S. weather; natural disasters; and accidents.*	*Includes the arts, religion, scholarship, communications media, sports, entertainments, fashions, fads, and social life.*

	World Affairs	Europe	Africa & the Middle East	The Americas	Asia & the Pacific
Sept. 8		Serbian forces launch attacks against villages in northern and central Kosovo, where the Albanian Kosovo Liberation Army (UCK) remains in control.... In Northern Ireland, the so-called Real IRA, an extremist IRA splinter group that claimed responsibility for the August bombing in Omagh, declares a permanent cease-fire.			In South Korea, Hana Bank and Boram Bank announce that they will merge in January 1999, creating the seventh-largest commercial bank in the country in terms of assets.... New Zealand prime minister Jenny Shipley's government wins a vote of confidence in Parliament. It is the first such vote ever conducted in New Zealand.... Malaysia's Kuala Lumpur Stock Exchange plunges 21.5%, the largest single-day percentage drop ever recorded on the exchange.
Sept. 9		In a last-ditch attempt to solve its serious financial problems, Britain's Royal Opera House announces a shutdown, canceling all opera and most ballet performances in 1999.	Amnesty International chides both Israel and the self-rule Palestinian National Authority (PNA) for their arrests and unlawful detentions of thousands of Palestinians on politically motivated grounds as part of an effort to deter terrorism.		Thousands of civilians and troops work to fortify an embankment protecting Dhaka, Bangladesh's capital, from surging floodwaters. Ongoing monsoon rains have caused the worst floods on record in Bangladesh.... An elaborate parade in Pyongyang, the capital of North Korea, marks the 50th anniversary of the North Korean state.
Sept. 10		UN officials estimate the conflict in Kosovo that started Sep. 8 has sent 265,000 people fleeing from their homes, of whom 50,000 are living without suitable shelter.... Russian president Boris Yeltsin nominates former foreign minister Yevgeny Primakov, as premier.... In Northern Ireland, Protestant unionist leader David Trimble and Gerry Adams, head of Sinn Fein, the political wing of the IRA, hold face-to-face talks for the first time ever. Separately, the British government announces that British troops will halt regular patrols of Belfast.	In a surprise raid near the West Bank city of Hebron, Israeli commandos kill two brothers, Adel and Imad Awadallah, who are leaders of the military wing of Hamas and long wanted by both Israel and the self-rule Palestinian National Authority (PNA) for allegedly orchestrating several deadly bombings against Israeli civilians.	Drug lord Rafael Muñoz Talavera is found shot to death in his car in Ciudad Juárez, Mexico.... Brazil's São Paulo Bovespa stock index falls a record 15.8%.	Taliban officials disclose that the bodies of nine of the 10 Iranians missing since Aug. 8 have been found. Iran responds by announcing that it will hold another round of war maneuvers along the border.... In Bangladesh, more than 850 deaths are attributed to the floods, which have also left homeless approximately one quarter of the country's population of 124 million.
Sept. 11		The State Duma confirms former foreign minister Yevgeny Primakov as Russia's new premier, ending a three-week-long period of political paralysis in the face of a collapsing economy.... Northern Ireland initiates a release inmates from prison in the province to benefit from the terms of a peace plan reached in April..... In Germany, Volkswagen AG announces the creation of a $12 million fund to compensate surviving former slave laborers who had worked for the automaker during World War II.	In the midst of ongoing protests in Lesotho over the results of the country's May parliamentary elections, pro-opposition members of the army arrest several senior officers.... Hamas supporters stage demonstrations across the West Bank and Gaza Strip, demanding revenge for the Sep. 10 killings of Adel and Imad Awadallah.... In a surprise move, Algerian president Liamine Zeroual announces that he will step down from office in February 1999 and calls for early elections.	Ricardo Ramirez, 67, one of the four top leaders of Guatemala's former guerrilla factions better known to his countrymen as Commander Rolando Moran, dies of a heart attack in Guatemala City.	Fighting between Taliban forces and troops loyal to the displaced government continue north of Kabul, the capital of Afghanistan.
Sept. 12		Nikola Poplasen, the leader of the Serb Radical Party, is elected president of the Serb republic in Bosnia-Herzegovina. The vote is perceived as a setback to international efforts to restore peace in Bosnia because international officials strongly backed the incumbent president, Biljana Plavsic.... In Albania, Democratic Party aide to former president Sali Berisha, Azem Hajdari, and a bodyguard are shot by unidentified gunmen.			Authorities in Beijing detain Shi Binhai, an newspaper editor and coeditor of a recent book on political changes in China.

A	B	C	D	E
Includes developments that affect more than one world region, international organizations, and important meetings of major world leaders.	*Includes all domestic and regional developments in Europe, including the Soviet Union, Turkey, Cyprus, and Malta.*	*Includes all domestic and regional developments in Africa and the Middle East, including Iraq and Iran and excluding Cyprus, Turkey, and Afghanistan.*	*Includes all domestic and regional developments in Latin America, the Caribbean, and Canada.*	*Includes all domestic and regional developments in Asia and Pacific nations, extending from Afghanistan through all the Pacific Island, except Hawaii.*

U.S. Politics & Social Issues	U.S. Foreign Policy & Defense	U.S. Economy & Environment	Science, Technology, & Nature	Culture, Leisure, & Lifestyle	
Jeremy Strohmeyer pleads guilty to the May 1997 murder of seven-year-old Sherrice Iverson. The killing received national attention because Strohmeyer's then-friend, David Cash, saw Strohmeyer struggling with Iverson but did not take action. . . . The U.S. 10th Circuit Court of Appeals in Denver, Colorado, upholds the conviction and death sentence of Timothy J. McVeigh for the 1995 bombing of the Alfred P. Murrah Federal Building in Oklahoma City, Oklahoma.		The U.S. stock market surges 380.53 points, or nearly 5%, to 8020.78, marking its largest-ever point gain.		Mark McGwire of the St. Louis Cardinals hits his 62nd home run of 1998, breaking the single-season home-run record in the MLB. The record is considered by many to be the most celebrated mark in all of U.S. sports. The previous record holder, Roger Maris, hit 61 home runs in 1961.	Sept. 8
Independent counsel Kenneth Starr delivers to the House of Representatives a report on his investigation of Pres. Clinton's relationship with former White House intern Monica Lewinsky. Citing the terms of the 1978 independent counsel law under which he was appointed, Starr attests that he has referred the matter to the House because he found "substantial and credible information. . . that may constitute grounds for an impeachment" of the president.					Sept. 9
The House Rules Committee recommends that the full House vote to immediately release to the public the 445-page report delivered Sep. 9 by independent counsel Kenneth Starr.		In Washington, D.C., Judge Paul Friedman dismisses five of six charges the Justice Department had brought against Democratic fund-raiser Maria Hsia. . . . The Commerce Department reports that the nation's current-account deficit jumped 21% to a record $56.53 billion in the second quarter, up from the revised first-quarter figure of $46.74 billion.			Sept. 10
The House votes, 363-63, to release to the public the entire text of the 445-page report presented Sep. 9 by Kenneth Starr. The report accuses the president of having a sexual affair with a former White House intern, Monica Lewinsky, and of lying, obstructing justice, and abusing his presidential power in an effort to keep it quiet.			Kenneth Starr's 445-page report on the scandal involving Pres. Clinton and Monica Lewinsky is published in its entirety on the Internet global computer network. America Online (AOL) Inc., the U.S.'s biggest Internet service provider, reveals that its 13 million users are spending a record 10.1 million hours logged on to AOL, and that a single file containing the report was downloaded 750,000 times during the first 24 hours.	U.S. film director Steven Spielberg, whose 1993 Academy Award–winning film Schindler's List deals at length with the Holocaust, is honored in Germany by being presented with a national medal of merit.	Sept. 11
Many newspapers publish the full text of the Kenneth Starr report. Pres. Clinton's lawyers issue a rebuttal accusing Starr of pursuing a "smear campaign," noting that, after a four-year-long probe that cost $40 million, Starr barely mentions Whitewater, the original subject of his investigation, in his report. . . . George E. Danielson, 83, (D, Calif.), who served in the House, 1971–82, dies in Monterey, California, after a heart attack.		A negotiating team representing Northwest Airlines pilots ratifies a four-year contract agreement between the carrier and the Air Line Pilots Association (ALPA), ending a two-week-old strike against the airline by its some 6,170 pilots. The work stoppage was the longest at any U.S. airline since a 1989 strike by machinists at Eastern Airlines that lasted through that company's closure and liquidation in 1991.		John Holliman Jr., 49, CNN correspondent who was one of three reporters to broadcast live coverage of the allied air raids on Baghdad during the 1991 Persian Gulf war, dies in a car crash in Snellville, Geogia. . . . Lindsay Davenport wins the women's tennis title at the U.S. Open in New York City.	Sept. 12

F	G	H	I	J
Includes elections, federal-state relations, civil rights and liberties, crime, the judiciary, education, health care, poverty, urban affairs, and population.	Includes formation and debate of U.S. foreign and defense policies, veterans' affairs, and defense spending. (Relations with specific foreign countries are usually found under the region concerned.)	Includes business, labor, agriculture, taxation, transportation, consumer affairs, monetary and fiscal policy, natural resources, and pollution.	Includes worldwide scientific, medical, and technological developments; natural phenomena; U.S. weather; natural disasters; and accidents.	Includes the arts, religion, scholarship, communications media, sports, entertainments, fashions, fads, and social life.

	World Affairs	Europe	Africa & the Middle East	The Americas	Asia & the Pacific
Sept. 13		Angered by the Sep. 12 deaths of Democratic Party politician Azem Hajdari and a bodyguard, supporters of the opposition Democratic Party besiege government buildings in Tirana, the capital of Albania, forcing Premier Fatos Nano and his cabinet to flee amid flames and gunfire. One protester is killed and four of the premier's guards are wounded during gun battles at his offices.			The Taliban militia captures the town of Bamiyan, one of the last remaining strongholds of the anti-Taliban alliance in Afghanistan.
Sept. 14		The new Northern Ireland Assembly convenes for its first working session at the Stormont parliamentary building in Belfast, the province's capital. . . . In Albania, armed supporters of former president Sali Berisha seize government buildings and commandeer at least four government tanks. The government retakes the buildings, killing three people and wounding 14. Clashes between opposition supporters and the government since Sep. 13 are described as the worst violence in Albania since 1997 riots over fraudulent investment schemes.	In Lesotho, protestors grow increasingly angry when a report by the 14-nation Southern African Development Community (SADC) acknowledges "serious concerns" about the May voting but concludes that the elections should not be nullified. . . . Data shows that 123 Palestinians have been injured in the violent exchanges since Sep. 11.	Unidentified gunmen shoot and kill Jorge Humberto Gonzalez, a Liberal congressional deputy, in Medellin, Colombia. . . . Air Canada's 2,100 pilots vote to ratify a two-year contract with the airline, ending a strike that started Sep. 2 and cost Air Canada an estimated C$200 million (US$133 million).	Yang Shangkun, 91 or 92, veteran of China's historic Long March of 1934–35 who was named in 1988 to the largely ceremonial post of president and was replaced as president in 1993, dies in Beijing. . . . The U.S. discloses that a North Korean rocket launch in late August failed to send a small satellite into space. . . . Feminist writer Taslima Nasreen returns to Bangladesh after four years of self-imposed exile in Europe and the U.S. Nasreen faces blasphemy charges, and her return renews Islamic militants' demands that she be put to death.
Sept. 15		Three Norwegian banks announce plans to merge, in a deal that will create the country's largest financial-services company, with a total market value as high as 28 billion kroner ($3.6 billion). . . . Some 3,000 opposition supporters defy a government ban and hold a peaceful march in Tirana, the capital of Albania.			Thailand's health minister, Rakkiat Sukthana, resigns after his ministry comes under scrutiny for corruption involving the misuse of 1.4 billion baht ($60 million) in ministry funds.
Sept. 16		In Spain, ETA, the main Basque separatist group, declares a ceasefire, to take effect Sep. 18.	A UN panel finds that antigovernment Islamic radicals are responsible for an overwhelming number of the estimated 75,000 deaths that have occurred since the conflict began in 1992. However, the panel acknowledges that the government was guilty of "excesses" against civilians. Amnesty International characterizes the panel's findings as a "whitewash" of government abuses.		
Sept. 17			The two dominant Kurd factions in northern Iraq end their long-running feud in a U.S.-brokered agreement signed by Massoud Barzani of the Kurdistan Democratic Party and Jalal Talabani of the Patriotic Union of Kurdistan. . . . Jewish settlers spray Palestinian high-school students with gunfire in a drive-by shooting in the West Bank town of Beitunya, near Ramallah. A Palestinian teenager is killed. A settler, Avshalom Ladani, surrenders to Israeli police, claiming that he opened fire after stones were thrown at his car.	At a ranch compound outside Ensenada, Baja California, gunmen suspected of being affiliated with the Tijuana drug cartel drag 20 members of three families from their homes and shoot them, killing 18. The massacre is described as the most violent drug-related incident in Mexico's history.	
Sept. 18		Five men serving sentences for murder are the first convicted murderers set free in Northern Ireland under the terms of the April prisoner-release program. Their release brings the number of inmates freed in the province under the program to 24.	Funerals in Iran for seven of the Iranians killed in Afghanistan prompt mass protests across the country. In Teheran, thousands of protestors chant "Death to the Taliban. Death to Pakistan. Death to America.". . . Some 3,000 Hamas supporters attend a memorial rally for the Awadallahs in the town of Al-Bireh. Later, 32 Palestinians are injured when Israeli soldiers fire rubber-coated bullets to disperse several hundred stone throwers.		

A	B	C	D	E
Includes developments that affect more than one world region, international organizations, and important meetings of major world leaders.	Includes all domestic and regional developments in Europe, including the Soviet Union, Turkey, Cyprus, and Malta.	Includes all domestic and regional developments in Africa and the Middle East, including Iraq and Iran and excluding Cyprus, Turkey, and Afghanistan.	Includes all domestic and regional developments in Latin America, the Caribbean, and Canada.	Includes all domestic and regional developments in Asia and Pacific nations, extending from Afghanistan through all the Pacific Island, except Hawaii.

U.S. Politics & Social Issues	U.S. Foreign Policy & Defense	U.S. Economy & Environment	Science, Technology, & Nature	Culture, Leisure, & Lifestyle	
George Corley Wallace, 79, former governor of Alabama, who became a national symbol of segregation in the South when he personally blocked the path of two black students trying to enroll at the University of Alabama in 1963 and who reached out to black voters in the latter part of his political career, dies of cardiac and respiratory arrest in Montgomery, Alabama. He had been confined to a wheelchair since being shot in a 1972 assassination attempt, and his health had steadily deteriorated				Cubs outfielder Sammy Sosa hits his 62nd homer of the season, making him the second player in MLB history to pass the 1961 record set by Roger Moris. . . . At the Emmys, *Frasier* wins best comedy series for a fifth consecutive year, setting a record. *The Practice* wins for best drama series. . . . At the U.S. Open, Patrick Rafter of Australia wins the men's tennis title.	Sept. 13
The Health Care Financing Administration (HCFA) predicts that total annual spending on health care in the U.S. will rise to $2.1 trillion in the year 2007, from the 1996 level of $1 trillion.			Faced with competition, the National Human Genome Research Institute, which is directing a worldwide effort to decode the entire human genome, or genetic sequence, announces an accelerated timetable for the completion of the project, projecting that it will be finished by the year 2003, two years sooner than the goal set by the NIH when it began the project in 1990.	The Michigan Court of Appeals overturns the 1996 murder conviction and orders a new trial of Jonathan Schmitz, who allegedly killed Scott Amedure for admitting he had a crush on him during a taping of the *Jenny Jones Show*.	Sept. 14
The House passes, 401-1, a bill that will reauthorize for four years a program of inspecting and accrediting mammography facilities for the detection of breast cancer. The program was instituted by a 1992 law that expired in 1997. . . . Statistics suggest that Kenneth Starr's eight-month-old probe of the scandal involving Pres. Clinton and Monica Lewinsky matter cost taxpayers $4.4 million.	Gen. Zhang Wannian, senior vice chairman of China's Central Military Commission, and U.S. defense secretary William Cohen sign a military cooperation pact addressing environmental problems caused by the two countries' armed forces.		Reynold B. Johnson, 92, engineer who, while working for IBM, invented the world's first commercial computer disk drive in the 1950s and who, when he retired from IBM in 1971, held dozens of patents, dies of malignant melanoma in Palo Alto, California.	The John F. Kennedy Center for the Performing Arts in Washington, D.C., announces that comedian Richard Pryor will be the first-ever recipient of its Mark Twain Prize, an annual award to honor humor in the U.S.	Sept. 15
		The Federal Reserve Board reports that its industrial production index, which measures output at U.S. factories, mines, and utilities, rose 1.7% in August from July. The rise is the largest since January 1984, and it follows two consecutive monthly declines.		Junius Kellogg, 71, college and professional basketball player who, after a 1954 car accident left him paralyzed, coached and helped popularize wheelchair basketball, dies of respiratory failure in New York City.	Sept. 16
Florida governor Lawton Chiles (D) announces that the state will receive an additional $1.7 billion under the August 1997 settlement of its suit against the tobacco industry. . . . Pres. Clinton announces new regulations guaranteeing protections for patients who receive Medicaid benefits through health maintenance organizations (HMOs).	U.S. authorities in New York City unseal a criminal complaint charging Haroun Fazil of Comoros with a key role in an August bomb attack on the U.S. embassy in Nairobi, Kenya. Wadih el Hage of Arlington, Texas, is charged in New York City with lying to investigators in connection with the case.	The House passes, 421-0, a stop-gap spending measure to keep the federal government operating from Oct. 1, the start of the 1999 fiscal year, through Oct. 9. The Senate clears the stopgap measure by voice vote. Congress so far has cleared only one of the 13 appropriations bills for fiscal 1999.	NASA and ESA scientists report that a sun-observing satellite was successfully realigned so that its solar panels once again face the sun. The craft, the *Solar and Heliospheric Observatory* (SOHO), spun out of control and lost power in June. . . . Scientists report they have found that the height of the thermosphere, the outer layer of the earth's atmosphere, has dropped by some 5 miles (8 km) over the past 40 years.		Sept. 17
The Senate fails to override Pres. Clinton's 1997 veto of legislation banning intact dilation and extraction (IDE) abortions when the 64-36 ballot falls three votes short of the two-thirds majority required.	Harvard University presents South African president Nelson Mandela with an honorary law doctorate. Mandela is the third individual ever to receive an honorary degree from Harvard outside the university's annual commencement ceremony. . . . INS agents take into custody some 150 Chinese migrants from aboard a fishing boat at a San Diego, California, pier. The migrants reportedly planned to enter the U.S. via the Mexican border.				Sept. 18

F	G	H	I	J
Includes elections, federal-state relations, civil rights and liberties, crime, the judiciary, education, health care, poverty, urban affairs, and population.	Includes formation and debate of U.S. foreign and defense policies, veterans' affairs, and defense spending. (Relations with specific foreign countries are usually found under the region concerned.)	Includes business, labor, agriculture, taxation, transportation, consumer affairs, monetary and fiscal policy, natural resources, and pollution.	Includes worldwide scientific, medical, and technological developments; natural phenomena; U.S. weather; natural disasters; and accidents.	Includes the arts, religion, scholarship, communications media, sports, entertainments, fashions, fads, and social life.

	World Affairs	Europe	Africa & the Middle East	The Americas	Asia & the Pacific
Sept. 19		Susan Barrantes, the mother of Britain's Duchess of York, Sarah Ferguson, dies in an automobile accident outside Tres Lomas, Argentina. . . . Patricia Hayes, 88, comedic British actress who worked on stage, screen, television and radio, dies in London, England.	Government opposition leader Roosevelt Johnson takes refuge in the U.S. embassy in Monrovia, Liberia's capital. Authorities are trying to arrest Johnson, a former militia leader who fought against now-Pres. Charles Taylor in Liberia's 1989–96 civil war, Fighting during the attempted arrest leaves 50 people dead.		In a goodwill gesture toward Iran, the Taliban frees five Iranian "military drivers" captured in Mazar-i-Sharif. . . . In Australia, the New South Wales Health Department announces that Sydney's tap water is safe to drink for the first time since Aug. 25. . . . In the Philippines a ferry carrying more than 400 passengers sinks in stormy waters in Manila Bay.
Sept. 20		Kidnappers release two British aid workers held hostage in Chechnya for nearly 15 months. . . . Premier Goran Persson's ruling Social Democratic Party (SDP) wins a plurality of seats in Sweden's parliament. . . . To protest plans to remove a cross used in a 1979 mass at Auschwitz, radical Roman Catholics erect four crosses in a field there. More than 200 crosses have been planted since the campaign began in June.		In Colombia, seven people are killed in El Rosario in a shootout between government troops and FARC rebels. Separately, a bomb planted inside a corpse undergoing an inquest explodes, killing one person. . . . Hurricane Georges, the fourth hurricane of the 1998 Atlantic Ocean hurricane season, reaches Antigua and Barbuda, St. Christopher (St. Kitts) and Nevis, Guadeloupe, and Montserrat.	In Afghanistan, the Taliban comes under fire as opposition forces under Gen. Ahmed Shah Massoud rain rockets on Kabul, killing 180 people. . . . In Malaysia, an estimated 40,000 people attend the largest antigovernment protest ever staged during the 17-year tenure of P.M. Mahathir bin Mohamad. Malaysian police arrest recently ousted Deputy P.M. Anwar Ibrahim on charges of sexual indecency hours after he addresses the rally.
Sept. 21	A working group comprised of the U.S., Russia, Iran, Pakistan, China, Tajikistan, Uzbekistan, and Turkmenistan meets in New York City with the aim of forging a diplomatic initiative that will avert the possibility of armed conflict between Iran and the Taliban. . . . The 53rd session of the UN General Assembly opens at the UN's headquarters in NYC. South African president Nelson Mandela delivers what he calls a farewell address to the General Assembly as he plans to "retire to some rest and tranquillity" in his home village.	Reports claim that 212 villages in Kosovo have been burned by Serbian forces. . . . Ahmet Krasniqi, a member of Kosovo's self-styled ethnic Albanian government, is shot dead in Albania. . . . Russian authorities announce that they have annulled the Soviet-era treason conviction of late ballet star Rudolf Nureyev, under a law protecting victims of political reprisals. . . . Margaret Jennings, 89, who, driving under her maiden name, Margaret Allan, won a number of car races on the male-dominated European circuit in the 1930s, dies.	Mustafa Mahmoud Said Ahmed of Egypt and Rashid Saleh Hemed, a Tanzanian, are charged with 11 counts each of murder in a court in Dar es Salaam, Tanzania, in connection with the August bombing of the U.S. embassy there.	Since Hurricane Georges struck on Sep. 20, two people in Antigua and Barbuda have died, and St. Kitts and Nevis has suffered four fatalities.	As many as 143 people are reported dead from the Sep. 29 ferry accident in Manila Bay, the Philippines.
Sept. 22	Saudi Arabia, one of the three countries that recognizes Taliban rule in Afghanistan, suspends diplomatic ties to protest the Taliban's harboring of Osama bin Laden, a Saudi dissident accused in August terrorist attacks on U.S. embassies in Kenya and Tanzania. That moves leaves Pakistan and the United Arab Emirates as the only countries that recognize Taliban rule in Afghanistan.	Amnesty International reports that both Serbian and Albanian forces committed war crimes during the Kosovo conflict. Amnesty cites the Serbian side as responsible for the majority of deaths and missing persons since the start of the fighting.	South Africa sends about 600 troops into neighboring Lesotho in an attempt to put an end to a military mutiny there. The South African forces meet unexpectedly fierce resistance from Lesotho's rebellious army around Maseru, the capital. Nine South Africans and some 40 Lesotho troops are killed in fighting. The South Africans are joined later by 200 soldiers from Botswana.	Reports confirm that at least 25 people have been killed in another wave of attacks by leftist and rightwing forces in Colombia. . . . Hurricane Georges is blamed for at least 94 deaths in Haiti and at least 210 in the Dominican Republic. The region hardest hit is the island of Hispaniola. The hurricane also strikes Puerto Rico, stirring up winds of 130 mph (210 kph). Five people are killed. The storm forces 300,000 Dominicans to evacuate their homes.	Iran masses more than 200,000 troops on its border with Afghanistan as it opens military exercises in a threat of force against Afghanistan's ruling Muslim fundamentalist Taliban militia. . . . In Myanmar, an antigovernment demonstration is held.
Sept. 23	The UN Security Council endorses a resolution calling for a cease-fire in the troubled Yugoslav province of Kosovo. . . . The European Court of Human Rights in Strasbourg, France, rules that Britain's law on corporal punishment in the home includes inadequate protection of children's rights.	Siemens AG, a German company facing a slave labor lawsuit, announces that it will set up a $12 million fund to compensate surviving former workers from the World War II-era forced labor.	South African soldiers gain effective control over Maseru in Lesotho.	Hurricane Georges passes Cuba, prompting the evacuation of 200,000 people. Three people lose their lives. . . . South African president Nelson Mandela visits Canada for the first time since June 1990.	Malaysian police ban political rallies.
Sept. 24			Ugandan security minister Muruli Mukasa reveals that Ugandan authorities and U.S. agents from the FBI have thwarted an attempt to bomb the U.S. embassy in Kampala, the Ugandan capital. Authorities report that 20 people have been arrested in the plot. . . . The British and Iranian foreign ministers indicate they have reached a compromise on the issue of Iran's decade-old death sentence against British author Salman Rushdie, and their countries will reestablish diplomatic relations.		An unidentified assailant launches a rocket at a motorcade, narrowly missing the car of Cambodia premier Hun Sen. One bystander is killed.
	A	**B**	**C**	**D**	**E**
	Includes developments that affect more than one world region, international organizations, and important meetings of major world leaders.	*Includes all domestic and regional developments in Europe, including the Soviet Union, Turkey, Cyprus, and Malta.*	*Includes all domestic and regional developments in Africa and the Middle East, including Iraq and Iran and excluding Cyprus, Turkey, and Afghanistan.*	*Includes all domestic and regional developments in Latin America, the Caribbean, and Canada.*	*Includes all domestic and regional developments in Asia and Pacific nations, extending from Afghanistan through all the Pacific Island, except Hawaii.*

U.S. Politics & Social Issues	U.S. Foreign Policy & Defense	U.S. Economy & Environment	Science, Technology, & Nature	Culture, Leisure, & Lifestyle	
			The Albert and Mary Lasker Foundation announces the winners of the 1998 Albert Lasker Medical Research Awards. Awards for clinical research go to Dr. Alfred Knudson Jr., Dr. Peter Nowell, and Dr. Janet Rowley. Awards for basic medical research go to Lee Hartwell, Paul Nurse, and Yoshio Masui. The award for special achievement is presented to Daniel Koshland Jr.	Reynald Herren, 38, wins $14 million in Reno, Nevada, the largest jackpot ever won on a slot machine.... A new opera based on Tennessee Williams's 1947 play *A Streetcar Named Desire* opens at the San Francisco Opera.... Boxer Evander Holyfield, the IBF and WBA heavyweight champion, successfully defends his IBF title, over challenger Vaughn Bean.	Sept. 19
Muriel Humphrey Brown, 86, (D, Minn.), who served in the Senate, 1978–79, dies in Minneapolis, Minnesota.	Pres. Clinton signs an appropriations bill allocating $8.45 billion for military construction spending in fiscal 1999. The military construction bill is the first of the 13 annual appropriations bills to clear Congress.	Pres. Clinton signs into law a bill that codifies a three-state agreement to dispose of low-level nuclear waste at a site in western Texas near the Mexican border. Texas, Vermont, and Maine are the three states represented in the bill.		Grupo Televisa SA shuts down its internationally known Cultural Center for Contemporary Art in Mexico City in an attempt to cut costs.	Sept. 20
The House releases a videotape of testimony that Pres. Clinton gave before a federal grand jury investigating his relationship with former White House intern Monica Lewinsky. Clinton's testimony is part of the evidence independent counsel Kenneth Starr submitted to Congress Sep. 9 as possible grounds for impeaching the president. The House also releases 3,183 pages of evidence that Starr appended to his report.	Hundreds of U.S. farmers block a Canadian Pacific rail line near the town of Portal, North Dakota, just south of the Canadian border, to protest the influx of Canadian agricultural products. The incident is one of a series of actions taken in northern U.S. states by farmers and officials angry over Canadian trade policies.... Reports confirm that the U.S. State Department recently listed Iran as the world's leading state sponsor of terrorist activities.		More than 1 million people view video portions of Pres. Clinton's testimony on the Internet global computer network.	Some 22.5 million viewers watch parts of Pres. Clinton's testimony. ...Florence Griffith Joyner, 38, U.S. sprinter who won three gold medals at the 1988 Summer Olympics, dies in Mission Viejo, California; the cause of her death is being investigated.... *Forbes* lists Jerry Seinfeld, with earnings estimated at $225 million, as the world's highest paid entertainer.	Sept. 21
The FCC announces that its chief of staff, John Nakahata, will step down at the end of October.... The Justice Department announces that DNA Plant Technology Corp. may be fined $100,000 for violating federal law by exporting specially bred high-nicotine tobacco seeds.	Japanese premier Keizo Obuchi meets informally for the first time with U.S. president Bill Clinton in New York City.				Sept. 22
Joan Kroc, the widow of fast-food restaurateur Ray Kroc, donates $80 million to the San Diego, California, division of the Salvation Army. It is the largest donation in the Salvation Army's 133-year history.... Kenneth Stewart, 44, convicted of murder, is executed by electrocution in Jarratt, Virginia. It is the first time since 1994 that the electric chair is used in Virginia. Stewart, who chose execution over lethal injection, is the 479th person to be executed in the U.S. and the 55th in Virginia since 1976.	A three-judge panel of the U.S. Second Circuit Court of Appeals upholds the military's "don't ask, don't tell" policy on homosexuals and the military's long-standing ban on homosexual activity.... Clark Clifford and Robert Altman agree to settle the remaining civil lawsuits related to the fraud-ridden Bank of Credit and Commerce International (BCCI), which folded in 1991.... Officials confirm that 18 people have been charged with smuggling in the Sep. 18 incident in San Diego, California.	The House passes, by voice vote, legislation that will guarantee Supplemental Security Income (SSI) and Medicaid benefits to certain immigrants whose eligibility was cut off by a 1996 welfare reform measure. ... A jury in Dedham, Mass., orders Ground Round Restaurants Inc. to pay $6.7 million in damages in an age discrimination suit.... The SEC adopts guidelines that for the first time ever spell out what constitutes professional misconduct for accountants involved in auditing corporate financial statements.	Surgeons in Lyons, France, attach the hand and forearm of an anonymous brain-dead donor to the arm of a patient whose forearm was amputated years before. A successful hand transplant has never before been carried out.	The U.S. Hockey Hall of Fame in Eveleth, Minnesota, inducts Lou Nanne, Joe Mullen, Mike Curran, and the late Bruce Mather.	Sept. 23
George Soros, a Hungarian-born philanthropist, announces that he will donate $1.2 million over the next four years to the Maryland State Department of Education's Correctional Educational Program.	Reports reveal that the state governments of South Dakota, North Dakota, Montana, Minnesota, and Idaho have instructed local authorities to step up inspections of trucks hauling Canadian farm products. The action is prompted by anger over Canadian trade policies.... The House passes, 373-50, the fiscal 1999 defense authorization bill.	The House passes, 356-65, a $2.35 billion fiscal 1999 appropriations bill for the legislative branch.... The Census Bureau finds that the median household annual income, adjusted for inflation, was $37,005 in 1997, a 1.9% gain over 1996.... The EPA orders 22 states in the Northeast and the Midwest to curb smog-causing emissions of nitrogen oxides... GE reaches an agreement with the EPA to clean up a contaminated stretch of the Housatonic River.... The Treasury introduces a redesigned $20 bill into circulation.	Scientists report that they found coelacanths, a species of fish dating back some 380 million years, in Indonesia. Coelacanths, which only in 1938 were discovered not to be extinct, have so far been previously believed to inhabit only the waters off the eastern coast of southern Africa.	Jeffrey Moss, 56, Emmy and Grammy Award–winning head writer and composer-lyricist for the children's educational television show *Sesame Street*, dies of colon cancer in New York City.	Sept. 24

F	G	H	I	J
Includes elections, federal-state relations, civil rights and liberties, crime, the judiciary, education, health care, poverty, urban affairs, and population.	*Includes formation and debate of U.S. foreign and defense policies, veterans' affairs, and defense spending. (Relations with specific foreign countries are usually found under the region concerned.)*	*Includes business, labor, agriculture, taxation, transportation, consumer affairs, monetary and fiscal policy, natural resources, and pollution.*	*Includes worldwide scientific, medical, and technological developments; natural phenomena; U.S. weather; natural disasters; and accidents.*	*Includes the arts, religion, scholarship, communications media, sports, entertainments, fashions, fads, and social life.*

	World Affairs	Europe	Africa & the Middle East	The Americas	Asia & the Pacific
Sept. 25			The U.S. airlifts government opposition leader Roosevelt Johnson out of Liberia after he took refuge in the U.S. embassy in Monrovia on Sep. 19. The airlift ends a standoff in which the U.S. evacuated most of the embassy staff and suspended regular embassy operations.		Explosions and fire in a gas-processing plant in the southern Australian state of Victoria kill two people and seriously injure eight others. The explosions leave more than 1 million households and 100,000 businesses without gas.
Sept. 26	Seven southeastern European countries—Albania, Bulgaria, Greece, Italy, Macedonia, Romania, and Turkey—sign an agreement creating a southern European multinational force of 2,000–3,000 troops.	A massacre kills more than 60 ethnic Albanians, many of them children, in the towns of Plocic, Golubova, and Gornje Obrinje.			
Sept. 27	NATO troops arrest alleged Bosnian Serb war criminal Stevan Todorovic. The arrest marks the first time that NATO has seized a suspected war criminal in Serbia.	Gerhard Schroeder of the left-of-center Social Democratic Party (SPD) ousts Helmut Kohl as German chancellor when his party wins a plurality in a national parliamentary election. Kohl has served as chancellor for 16 years, an unrivaled tenure in the country's modern history, and he is the first German or West German chancellor since before World War II to be ousted in an election.... Four opposition parties announce that they will form a coalition government, after results from Slovakia's national elections show that they won 58% of the vote. Together, the parties will control enough seats to oust Premier Vladimir Meciar's ruling party, Movement for a Democratic Slovakia (HZDS).	South Africa sends an additional 450 soldiers and 100 armored vehicles to Lesotho to help quell the spreading disorder.		The Sri Lankan government launches an offensive to retake a strategic highway in northern Sri Lanka, where Tamil rebels have been waging a secessionist campaign since 1983.
Sept. 28		Albanian premier Fatos Nano announces his resignation after telling Pres. Rexhep Mejdani that disagreement within Nano's five-party coalition makes it impossible for him to put together an acceptable cabinet.... Yugoslav president Slobodan Milosevic announces a unilateral cease-fire in the Kosovo campaign, declaring victory over the Albanian Kosovo Liberation Army (UCK).			
Sept. 29	Reports confirm that the IMF has approved an $850 million loan to Bulgaria.	Albania's ruling Socialist Party nominates Pandeli Majko as premier.... Diplomats estimate that during the seven-month campaign against the UCK, Serb forces damaged or obliterated more than 200 villages in Kosovo.			The fighting between the Sri Lankan government and rebel forces launched on Sep. 27 eases, after leaving as many as 1,300 troops and rebels dead.... The Paris-based Doctors Without Borders charity group announces that it is suspending its operations in North Korea because the government has denied access to some of the country's neediest and hungriest children.

A	B	C	D	E
Includes developments that affect more than one world region, international organizations, and important meetings of major world leaders.	*Includes all domestic and regional developments in Europe, including the Soviet Union, Turkey, Cyprus, and Malta.*	*Includes all domestic and regional developments in Africa and the Middle East, including Iraq and Iran and excluding Cyprus, Turkey, and Afghanistan.*	*Includes all domestic and regional developments in Latin America, the Caribbean, and Canada.*	*Includes all domestic and regional developments in Asia and Pacific nations, extending from Afghanistan through all the Pacific Island, except Hawaii.*

U.S. Politics & Social Issues	U.S. Foreign Policy & Defense	U.S. Economy & Environment	Science, Technology, & Nature	Culture, Leisure, & Lifestyle	
The Census Bureau reports that the percentage of people in the U.S. who lack health insurance rose to 16.1% in 1997 from 15.6% in 1996. The That increase is much sharper than the average increase a year over the previous decade.... The Senate, by voice vote, clears a bill that will reauthorize for four years a program of inspecting and accrediting mammography facilities for the detection of breast cancer.	The Senate confirms Richard J. Danzig as the next secretary of the navy.... Former CIA employee Douglas Groat is sentenced to five years in prison after pleading guilty to one count of attempted extortion.... The Defense Department orders sensitive information that may compromise national security or place personnel at risk pulled from its roughly 1,000 Pentagon Internet computer network sites accessible by the public.	The Senate passes, by voice vote, a $2.35 billion fiscal 1999 appropriations bill the for legislative branch. ... Pres. Clinton signs the stopgap bill passed by Congress Sep. 17.... The House approves, 240-188, legislation that will reserve 90% of the budget surplus in a special Treasury account until a long-term plan is in place for Social Security. ... The Senate passes, 92-1, a bill that will provide $5.6 billion in funding in fiscal 1999 for the FAA.	Hurricane Georges hits Key West, Florida, with winds of 105 mph (170 kph). Many of the Florida Keys are flooded in the storm, whose passing coincides with high tide. One Key West resident dies.... The FDA approves Herceptin, a drug for the treatment of some forms of metastatic breast cancer. Herceptin is the first genetically engineered drug to be approved for the treatment of breast cancer.	France's Benoit Lecomte, 31, is the first person to swim across the Atlantic Ocean, reaching France's Brittany coast after a 72-day-long journey from Hyannis, Massachusetts.	Sept. 25
Tens of thousands of people gather on the National Mall in Washington, D.C., for a rally calling for increased funding for cancer research. Among the speakers at the rally are Vice Pres. Al Gore, civil-rights leader Rev. Jesse Jackson and retired general H. Norman Schwarzkopf.				Betty Carter (born Lillie Mae Jones), 69, jazz vocalist who was presented with a National Medal of Arts award in 1997, dies of pancreatic cancer in New York City.	Sept. 26
				Baseball's Mark McGwire of the St. Louis Cardinals hits two home runs in the team's final game of the season to raise his record total to 70.	Sept. 27
The House passes, by voice vote, a bill reauthorizing the 1965 Higher Education Act for five years. The legislation includes a provision that will lower the interest rate on new student loans to its lowest level in 17 years.... California governor Pete Wilson (R) signs a law moving the date of the state's presidential primary up to the first Tuesday in March.	The House passes, 369-43, a $250.5 billion defense appropriations bill for fiscal 1999.	The house passes, 389-25, a bill that will provide $20.9 billion in funding for energy, water-development, and nuclear weapons programs in fiscal 1999.	Hurricane Georges hits the Gulf Coast of Mississippi. Some 15 inches (40 cm) of rain falls in the Gulf Coast region, which comprises parts of Louisiana, Mississippi, Alabama, and Florida. Four people die.... The Senate, by voice vote, passes legislation intended to encourage companies to share information about solving the Year 2000 computer glitch by shielding them from lawsuits based on the data they disclose.	*Publishers Weekly* lists *Rainbow Six*, by Tom Clancy, as the top bestseller.... Fiamma di San Giuliano Ferragamo, 57, women's shoe designer, dies of cancer in Florence, Italy.	Sept. 28
The Senate clears, 96-0, a bill reauthorizing the 1965 Higher Education Act for five years. The legislation includes a provision that will lower the interest rate on new student loans to its lowest level in 17 years.... Tom (Thomas) Bradley, 80, (D) five-term mayor of Los Angeles, 1973–93, whose tenure as the first black mayor of Los Angeles oversaw the city as it became the U.S.'s second-largest metropolis, dies of a heart attack in Los Angeles. He suffered a stroke after undergoing coronary bypass surgery in March 1996.	The Senate clears, 94-2, a $250.5 billion defense appropriations bill for fiscal 1999.	The Federal Reserve Board announces a reduction in the federal-funds rate to 5.25%, from 5.5%. The discount rate is left unchanged at 5%.... California governor Pete Wilson (R) signs into law a bill intended to protect California from oil spills.... The Senate, by voice vote, passes a bill that will provide $20.9 billion in funding for energy, water-development, and nuclear weapons programs in fiscal 1999.	Scientists report that the intense five-minute wave of radiation emanating from a faraway star on Aug. 27 came from a star some 20,000 light-years away. They argue the energy burst is a possible indication of the existence of "magnetars," a kind of neutron star believed to emit repeated gamma ray pulses.	The Corcoran Gallery of Art in Washington, D.C., announces that photographer Gordon Parks has donated 227 of his original prints to the museum. Parks, 85, worked as a photo-essayist for *Life* magazine for 20 years.	Sept. 29

F	G	H	I	J
Includes elections, federal-state relations, civil rights and liberties, crime, the judiciary, education, health care, poverty, urban affairs, and population.	Includes formation and debate of U.S. foreign and defense policies, veterans' affairs, and defense spending. (Relations with specific foreign countries are usually found under the region concerned.)	Includes business, labor, agriculture, taxation, transportation, consumer affairs, monetary and fiscal policy, natural resources, and pollution.	Includes worldwide scientific, medical, and technological developments; natural phenomena; U.S. weather; natural disasters; and accidents.	Includes the arts, religion, scholarship, communications media, sports, entertainments, fashions, fads, and social life.

	World Affairs	Europe	Africa & the Middle East	The Americas	Asia & the Pacific
Sept. 30	The IMF forecasts a global economic expansion of 2% in 1998 and of 2.5% in 1999. The fund's unusually gloomy projections stem from the impact of eastern Asia's economic crisis. The IMF predicts that the U.S. in 1998 will register 3.5% economic growth but slow to a 2% expansion in 1999. EU economies will expand 2.9% in 1998 and 2.5% in 1999. The comparable figures for Latin America are 2.8% for 1998 and 2.7% in 1999. African growth is predicted at 3.7% in 1998, up from 3.2% the previous year, and at 4.7% in 1999.	A Red Cross vehicle runs over a land mine in central Kosovo and explodes, killing one doctor and injuring three aid workers. . . . Marius Goring, 86, British stage, screen, and television actor, dies of cancer in West Sussex, England.		Pauline Julien, 70, French-Canadian vocalist and the musical standard-bearer of the separatist movement in her native Quebec, commits suicide in Montreal; she is said to have grown despondent over an illness that had eroded her language skills.	
Oct. 1	Hungarian-born financier and philanthropist George Soros states he will donate $300,000 to a fund administered by the International Campaign to Ban Landmines. The governments of several nations, including those of Canada, Norway, and Ireland, also pledged contributions to the fund.		Prince Jefri Bolkiah returns to Brunei after five months of self-imposed exile.		China implements a ban on the sale of blood in an effort to stem the rapid spread of HIV, the virus that causes AIDS. . . . The Dalai Lama's Tibetan government in exile acknowledges that during the 1960s their movement received $1.7 million a year from the U.S.'s Central Intelligence Agency (CIA).
Oct. 2	A UN court convicts and sentences to life in prison Jean-Paul Akayesu, the former Hutu mayor of the village of Taba, for his role in the deaths of 2,000 ethnic Tutsis during a 1994 genocide campaign led by Rwanda's Hutu government. It is the first genocide ruling by an international court. The conviction of Akayesu, accused of having incited others to rape Tutsi women, also marks the first time that rape and sexual violence are ruled as tools of genocide.		Addressing opposition accusations that the May election reinstating the Lesotho Congress for Democracy (LCD) was rigged, the LCD and opposition leaders agree to hold new elections in the following 18 months, quelling an army mutiny that started in September.	A Canadian Forces helicopter crashes and explodes on impact, killing all six crew members, a team from the 413 Search and Rescue Squadron. . . . Fermin Castro, said to be the primary target of the Sep. 17 executions in Ensenada, Baja California, dies after having been in a coma since the attack. His death brings the death toll from the massacre to 19.	Mongolia's outgoing minister of infrastructure and telecommunications, Sanjaasuren Zorig, is axed and stabbed to death by unidentified attackers.
Oct. 3		Former Latvian premier Andris Skele regains the premiership when his People's Party wins the largest percentage of the vote in national parliamentary elections. In a national referendum, Latvians also pass amendments that will ease restrictive immigration laws. . . . An armed group of men attack a house in Grozny, the capital of the separatist republic of Chechnya, and kidnap three British men and a New Zealander.			Australian prime minister John Howard's governing Liberal Party–National Party coalition emerges victorious in Australia's national elections, defeating Kim Beazley's Australian Labor Party by a narrow margin.
Oct. 4		In France, secondary-school students begin to stage demonstrations to protest classroom overcrowding, inadequate classroom equipment, and crumbling school buildings. . . . The death of Jean-Pascal Delamuraz, 62, long-time Swiss cabinet member who in 1996 served as Switzerland's president in the rotating Swiss presidency, is reported.	The U.S. holds its first bilateral military exercise with Algeria since that country gained its independence in 1962. The move ends U.S. president Clinton's policy of refraining from involvement with Algeria. . . . Reports disclose that ethnic fighting over rights to an oil deposit in the Akpata region east of Lagos, Nigeria, has left hundreds of people dead and thousands more homeless.	Brazilian president Fernando Henrique Cardoso wins reelection to a second four-year term.	Reports confirm that Mou Paet, a former Khmer Rouge commander, has admitted responsibility for the kidnapping of three Western backpackers in July 1994. However, he asserts another Khmer Rouge officer is responsible for their murders. . . . Demonstrators protesting the Sep. 14 return of feminist writer Taslima Nasreen to Bangladesh clash with police in the capital, Dhaka.

A	B	C	D	E
Includes developments that affect more than one world region, international organizations, and important meetings of major world leaders.	Includes all domestic and regional developments in Europe, including the Soviet Union, Turkey, Cyprus, and Malta.	Includes all domestic and regional developments in Africa and the Middle East, including Iraq and Iran and excluding Cyprus, Turkey, and Afghanistan.	Includes all domestic and regional developments in Latin America, the Caribbean, and Canada.	Includes all domestic and regional developments in Asia and Pacific nations, extending from Afghanistan through all the Pacific Island, except Hawaii.

U.S. Politics & Social Issues	U.S. Foreign Policy & Defense	U.S. Economy & Environment	Science, Technology, & Nature	Culture, Leisure, & Lifestyle	
		Pres. Clinton announces that the 1998 fiscal year resulted in the first federal budget surplus since 1969. Clinton reports the surplus to amount to about $70 billion.... NationsBank Corp. and BankAmerica Corp. complete their merger, holding 8.1% of U.S. bank deposits, more than any other bank.... A federal grand jury indicts Mark Jimenez on charges that he made $39,500 in illegal contributions to Democratic campaigns. Jimenez is the 12th person indicted as part of a Justice Department investigation of fund-raising abuses in the 1996 elections.		Dan (Daniel Raymond) Quisenberry, 45, one of MLB's most successful relief pitchers during the 1980s, dies of brain cancer in Leawood, Kansas.... Robert Lewis Taylor, 88, journalist, novelist and biographer who won the 1959 Pulitzer Prize for fiction, dies in Southbury, Connecticut.	Sept. 30
Prompted by a letter from the Health Care Financing Administration (HCFA), which runs Medicare, refusing an HMO request to increase premiums or reduce benefits for their Medicare plans in 1999, several HMOs announce that they plan to drop insurance coverage for hundreds of thousands of Medicare beneficiaries in 1999.	The Senate votes, 96-2, to clear the fiscal 1999 defense authorization bill.... The Department of Defense merges three cold war defense agencies—the Defense Special Weapons Agency, the On-Site Inspection Agency, and the Defense Technology Security Administration—into one, the Defense Threat Reduction Agency, which will respond to threats posed by nuclear, chemical and biological weapons.	Figures reveal that the purchasing managers' index was 49.4 in September, the same figure as recorded in August. A reading below 50 is interpreted as an indication of a contracting manufacturing sector.	The House passes, by voice vote, legislation intended to encourage companies to share information about solving the so-called Year 2000 computer glitch by shielding them from lawsuits based on the data they disclose.		Oct. 1
The state of Washington accepts an out-of-court $2 million settlement of its lawsuit against U.S Tobacco Co. of UST Inc.... The Senate votes, 68-28, to confirm the elevation of U.S. district judge Sonia Sotomayor to the U.S. Second Circuit Court of Appeals.... New York City agrees to pay $2.94 million to the family of Anthony Baez, who died during an arrest by police officer Francis Livoti in 1994. Officials claim it is the largest settlement the city ever made in a civil wrongful-death case involving police brutality.	Reports confirm that the Boeing Co. has agreed to pay a $10 million fine for failing to protect U.S. technology secrets when the company shared technical information with a Russian and a Ukrainian company without an official from the State Department present.... A federal grand jury in Miami, Florida, formally indicts 10 people, charging them with conspiracy to spy and acting illegally as foreign agents in an alleged plot to kill Cuban president Fidel Castro.	The House passes, 333-53, a $55.9 billion fiscal 1999 spending bill for the USDA; the FDA; and federal nutrition programs such as food stamps, school lunches, and Women, Infants and Children (WIC). The bill calls for 12% more funding than in fiscal 1998.	Scientists report evidence that worm-like animals lived more than one billion years ago.	Gene Autry (Orvon Gene), 91, whose career as a singing cowboy made him an emblem of the American West, dies in Los Angeles, California.... Roger Vivier, 90, French designer of women's shoes who invented the stiletto heel (1954), dies in Toulouse, France.	Oct. 2
				Roddy McDowall (Roderick Andrew Anthony Jude), 70, actor best known in his adult career for roles in *Planet of the Apes* (1968) and several sequels, dies of cancer in Los Angeles, California.	Oct. 3
	Some of the ashes of Nobuo Fujita, the only Japanese pilot to have bombed the U.S. mainland during World War II, are scattered at the site in Oregon where the lone bomb landed. Since the end of World War II, Fujita had made four visits as a peace activist to Brookings, Oregon, whose city council named him an honorary citizen in 1997.				Oct. 4

F	G	H	I	J
Includes elections, federal-state relations, civil rights and liberties, crime, the judiciary, education, health care, poverty, urban affairs, and population.	*Includes formation and debate of U.S. foreign and defense policies, veterans' affairs, and defense spending. (Relations with specific foreign countries are usually found under the region concerned.)*	*Includes business, labor, agriculture, taxation, transportation, consumer affairs, monetary and fiscal policy, natural resources, and pollution.*	*Includes worldwide scientific, medical, and technological developments; natural phenomena; U.S. weather; natural disasters; and accidents.*	*Includes the arts, religion, scholarship, communications media, sports, entertainments, fashions, fads, and social life.*

	World Affairs	Europe	Africa & the Middle East	The Americas	Asia & the Pacific
Oct. 5	China signs the International Covenant on Civil and Political Rights, a UN treaty that guarantees citizens freedom of expression, movement, and religion, as well as participation in elections and equality before the law. China is not expected to ratify the treaty for several years.	Swisscom, a formerly state-owned telephone-service company, debuts on stock exchanges in Zurich and New York City. The initial public offering, the year's largest yet in Europe, is valued at 7.5 billion Swiss francs ($5.6 billion).	Armed youths seize oil-pumping stations owned by the Royal Dutch/Shell Group, an Anglo-Dutch company, in the Niger Delta region in southern Nigeria.		In Lahore, Pakistani general Jehangir Karamat calls for the creation of a military-dominated national security council, which will increase the military's role in setting government policy.
Oct. 6		Frank O'Reilly, a policeman injured when a bomb exploded during Sep. 5 rioting by Protestants in Portadown, Northern Ireland, dies.			The Supreme Court of the Philippines overturns a 1993 corruption conviction against Imelda Marcos. The ruling overturns the only conviction won against Marcos in several corruption suits brought against her. . . . Gas resumes flowing to businesses and residences in the state of Victoria, Australia, nearly two weeks after an explosion at a gas processing plant.
Oct. 7		Communists and workers stage strikes and protest marches throughout Russia to demand the resignation of Pres. Boris Yeltsin and the immediate payment of back wages.	Armed youths again seize oil-pumping stations owned by the Royal Dutch/Shell Group, an Anglo-Dutch company, in the Niger Delta region in southern Nigeria.	More than 650,000 public-sector workers go on strike to protest the government's proposed austerity package, still under consideration in Colombia's Congress.	The government of Myanmar reports that 54 people, including 23 NLD members, have been arrested for staging antigovernment demonstrations. . . . U.S. Marine Corps corporal Randall Eskridge is arrested in Okinawa in connection with a hit-and-run automobile accident. . . . Pakistani general Jehangir Karamat resigns as head of the Pakistani armed forces in the wake of his Oct. 5 call for a national security council. Karamat's resignation marks the first time in the 51-year history of independent Pakistan that an army chief has resigned instead of seizing power after a dispute.
Oct. 8	The IMF and the World Bank end an annual joint plenary session of their boards of governors. . . . Five members—Argentina, the Netherlands, Canada, Namibia, and Malaysia—are elected to fill half of the 10 rotating slots on the 15-member UN Security Council. The new countries will replace outgoing members Japan, Costa Rica, Sweden, Portugal, and Kenya.				Japanese premier Obuchi offers South Korean president Kim an official apology for Japan's colonial and World War II atrocities in Korea. Obuchi's apology carries the weight of an official declaration.
Oct. 9		The government of Italian premier Romano Prodi collapses as it loses a vote of confidence held in the Chamber of Deputies, the lower house of Parliament.	The Constitutional Court, the highest court in South Africa, strikes down sodomy laws left on the books from before the country's 1994 post-apartheid provisional constitution. . . . Israeli prime minister Benjamin Netanyahu names Ariel Sharon as foreign minister. . . . An international arbitration panel finds that the Hanish islands in the Red Sea, over which Yemen and Eritrea clashed in 1995, belong partly to both countries.	The lower house of Pakistan's Parliament votes to pass legislation that will give the government authority to impose sharia law, which is based on the Koran, the holy text of Islam.	

A	B	C	D	E
Includes developments that affect more than one world region, international organizations, and important meetings of major world leaders.	Includes all domestic and regional developments in Europe, including the Soviet Union, Turkey, Cyprus, and Malta.	Includes all domestic and regional developments in Africa and the Middle East, including Iraq and Iran and excluding Cyprus, Turkey, and Afghanistan.	Includes all domestic and regional developments in Latin America, the Caribbean, and Canada.	Includes all domestic and regional developments in Asia and Pacific nations, extending from Afghanistan through all the Pacific Island, except Hawaii.

U.S. Politics & Social Issues	U.S. Foreign Policy & Defense	U.S. Economy & Environment	Science, Technology, & Nature	Culture, Leisure, & Lifestyle	
The Supreme Court begins its 1998–99 term, and about 1,000 civil-rights activists hold a rally, protesting the lack of minority law clerks employed by the justices. Kweisi Mfume, president of the NAACP, is among 19 protesters arrested. . . . David Schippers, the House Judiciary Committee's chief GOP investigative counsel, presents to the panel a list of 15 potentially impeachable offenses by Pres. Clinton. . . . Roderick Abeyta, 46, convicted of murder, is executed in Carson City, Nevada. Abeyta is the 482nd person executed in the U.S. and the seventh in Nevada since 1976.	The House passes, 360-38, a bill to give $97 million in U.S. military aid to help prodemocracy forces in Iraq mount an armed insurrection against Iraqi president Saddam Hussein.		The House, by voice vote, passes a bill intended to encourage more commercial involvement in space exploration and promote competition in the development of space-related industrial products. . . . Reports confirm that NASA has agreed to buy Russia's research time aboard the planned international space station for $60 million. The deal is intended to prevent the Russian Space Agency's current lack of funding, due to an economic crisis in Russia, from causing further delays in the launch of the space station.	A photographic work by surrealist photographer Man Ray, *Noire et Banche* (1926), sells for a, world record $607,500 at a Christie's auction in NYC. The previous record for a work of photography was set in 1993, when Alfred Stieglitz's *Georgia O'Keeffe: A Portrait-Hands and Thimble* (1920), sold for $398,500 at a Christie's auction.	Oct. 5
Joseph Neale allegedly shoots five people in Riverside, California, including Mayor Ron Loveridge and two City Council members. All the injured people are expected to survive. . . . In its first study of an industrialized nation, Amnesty International accuses the U.S. of maintaining a double standard by attacking other countries' abuses without complying with human rights ideals itself.	Seven Midwestern and Western U.S. states formally suspend, for 90 days, strict inspections of Canadian agricultural exports that the states imposed in September. The inspections, which effectively blocked exports of Canadian grain and livestock, are een by Canadian farmers and officials as a violation of NAFTA.	The Senate clears, 55-43, a $55.9 billion fiscal 1999 spending bill for the USDA; the FDA; and federal nutrition programs such as food stamps, school lunches, and WIC. . . . The House passes, 409-14, an appropriations bill that provides $93.4 billion in funding for the VA, HUD, NASA, EPA, and other independent agencies for the 1999 fiscal year.	Joseph Sandler, 71, British psychoanalyst who championed a scientific approach to his subject that takes neurobiology into account, dies of lung cancer in London.	Jerome Weidman, 85, novelist and playwright who, in 1960, won a Pulitzer Prize as coauthor of the musical *Fiorello!*, dies in New York City. . . . Mark Henry Belanger, 54, one of MLB's best fielding shortstops of the 1970s, dies of lung cancer in New York City	Oct. 6
Matthew Shepard, 21, a homosexual student at the University of Wyoming, is found hanging on fence after suffering a beating that put him in a coma. . . . The House passes, by voice vote, legislation outlawing identity theft. . . . Congress approves legislation extending existing U.S. copyrights by 20 years. . . . The Senate passes by unanimous consent a five-year reauthorization of the WIC and other nutrition programs. . . . Pres. Clinton signs a bill reauthorizing the 1965 Higher Education Act for five years. . . . Data show that nation's death rate in 1997 was the lowest ever recorded.	Nilo and Linda Hernandez plead guilty to charges of serving as illegal foreign agents to Cuba. . . . The Senate clears, by voice vote, a bill to give $97 million in U.S. military aid to help prodemocracy forces in Iraq mount an armed insurrection against Iraqi president Saddam Hussein. . . . The House passes, 337-83, a bill reauthorizing the nation's intelligence programs for fiscal 1999. Although the details of the bill are classified, its spending total is reportedly slightly higher than $26.7 billion, the amount authorized for fiscal 1998.	President Clinton vetoes a $55.9 billion fiscal 1999 spending bill for the USDA, the FDA, and other federal nutrition programs. The final bill called for 12% more funding than in fiscal 1998. . . . Pres. Clinton signs a bill that will provide $20.9 billion in funding for energy, water-development, and nuclear weapons programs in fiscal 1999.		The House clears, by voice vote, a bill that will overturn MLB's exemption from antitrust laws in regard to labor relations. The exemption will remain in effect with regard to franchise relocation, league expansion, and the operation of the minor leagues.	Oct. 7
The House approves, 258-176, an open-ended impeachment investigation of Pres. Clinton's conduct in the Monica Lewinsky matter. Clinton is the third president in U.S. history to face a formal impeachment inquiry. . . . After a delay of more than three years, the Senate confirms, 57-41, William Fletcher to the U.S. Ninth Circuit Court of Appeals. . . . The Senate passes, by voice vote, legislation to expand aid to "charter schools," public schools exempted from some regulations. . . . The Senate, by voice vote, passes a five-year reauthorization of the Head Start program.	The Senate clears, by voice vote, legislation that will guarantee Supplemental Security Income (SSI) and Medicaid benefits to certain immigrants whose eligibility was cut off by a 1996 welfare reform measure. . . . The Senate clears by voice vote a bill reauthorizing the nation's intelligence programs for fiscal 1999. Although the details of the bill are classified, its spending total is reportedly slightly higher than $26.7 billion, the amount authorized for fiscal 1998.	The Senate, by voice vote, passes legislation overhauling federal vocational programs. . . . The Senate clears, 96-1, an appropriations bill that provides $93.4 billion in funding for the VA, HUD, NASA, EPA, and other independent agencies for the 1999 fiscal year. . . . Travelers Group Inc. and Citicorp complete their merger and officially combine to form Citigroup Inc., the world's largest financial-services company in terms of assets, which stand at $697.5 billion in combined 1997 assets.	The Senate, by voice vote, passes legislation updating copyright provisions for computer software and other works created in digital media. The measure will implement the provisions of two treaties adopted in 1996 by the UN World Intellectual Property Organization. . . . The Senate approves, 96-2, legislation barring state and local governments from imposing new taxes on on-line commerce for three years. . . . The Senate, by unanimous consent, clears a bill intended to encourage more commercial involvement in space exploration.	The Swedish Academy of Letters awards the Nobel Prize in Literature to Portuguese writer Jose Saramago, the first Portuguese-language writer and one of only a few communists to win the prize.	Oct. 8
The House, by voice vote, clears a five-year reauthorization of the Head Start preschool program. . . . The House votes, 422-1, to pass a five-year reauthorization of the WIC program and other nutrition programs. . . . Pres. Clinton signs a bill that will reauthorize for four years a program of inspecting and accrediting mammography facilities for the detection of breast cancer.	Congress clears a GOP-sponsored bill designed to deter persecution of religious minorities in foreign countries.	The House, by voice vote, clears legislation overhauling federal vocational programs. . . . The House ethics committee reveals that Rep. Jay Kim (R, Calif.), who will leave Congress at the end of the term, has violated House rules and campaign finance laws. . . . Judge Paul Friedman rules that federal laws barring foreign nationals from contributing to U.S. political campaigns apply only to direct, "hard money" donations.			Oct. 9

F	G	H	I	J
Includes elections, federal-state relations, civil rights and liberties, crime, the judiciary, education, health care, poverty, urban affairs, and population.	*Includes formation and debate of U.S. foreign and defense policies, veterans' affairs, and defense spending. (Relations with specific foreign countries are usually found under the region concerned.)*	*Includes business, labor, agriculture, taxation, transportation, consumer affairs, monetary and fiscal policy, natural resources, and pollution.*	*Includes worldwide scientific, medical, and technological developments; natural phenomena; U.S. weather; natural disasters; and accidents.*	*Includes the arts, religion, scholarship, communications media, sports, entertainments, fashions, fads, and social life.*

	World Affairs	Europe	Africa & the Middle East	The Americas	Asia & the Pacific
Oct. 10			At least 700 people are killed after a fire erupts at a ruptured gasoline pipeline in the Niger Delta region of southern Nigeria. The pipeline was spewing gas after being sabotaged Oct. 7. . . . An Iranian appeals court reaffirms a death sentence imposed on German national Helmut Hofer, 57, for having had sex with a 27-year-old unmarried Muslim female. . . . Rebels capture the town of Kindu, a river port 235 miles (365 km) inside Congo, near the Rwandan border.		Reports confirm that China has revised the official death toll from summer floods to 3,656, up from the 3,004 deaths reported in September. Other revised flood-damage figures include 5.6 million homes destroyed, 64 million acres (26 million hectares) of farmland inundated, and economic losses totaling $30 billion.
Oct. 11		A human-rights investigator discloses that a team has exhumed as many as 274 bodies from a mass grave discovered in the village of Donja Glumina, 20 miles (30 km) east of Tuzla. The grave is reportedly the largest mass grave in Bosnia discovered to date.	Rebel troops shoot down a Congolese airliner in eastern Congo, outside Kindu. The plane's wreckage is discovered with no apparent survivors among the 41 passengers and crew aboard.		
Oct. 12	NATO authorizes the use of air strikes against the Yugoslav republic of Serbia if Yugoslav president Slobodan Milosevic does not end his crackdown against ethnic Albanians in the Serbian province of Kosovo. . . . The WTO's appellate body rules that the U.S. violated international trade law by applying arbitrary and discriminatory standards in banning shrimp imports from countries that utilize nets which trap sea turtles.	Azerbaijan president Heydar Aliyev, a former Communist Party official, declares victory in a disputed presidential election marked by opponents' allegations of fraud and a boycott of the balloting.	A military court sentences at least 24 to death after finding them guilty of treason for their roles in a May 1997 coup that ousted Pres. Ahmad Tejan Kabbah. . . . The government and rebel Sudan People's Liberation Army agree to extend a cease-fire for three months to allow humanitarian relief in the famine-hit southwest. . . . Protesters seize four Chevron Corp. workers, thereby shutting down a quarter of the company's Nigerian production.		Japan's Diet passes legislation designed to overhaul Japan's ailing banking system.
Oct. 13					The body of murdered Saudi Arabian diplomat Abdullah Jamaan Al-Ghamadi, 54, is discovered in his apartment in Canberra, Australia's capital. The murder is the first suspicious death of a foreign diplomat in Australia since 1981.
Oct. 14	The UN General Assembly passes a nonbinding resolution calling for the U.S. to end its 36-year-old embargo against Cuba. . . . The WTO offers membership to Latvia and Kyrgyzstan, the first former Soviet republics to be invited into the WTO. . . . A UN report estimates that peacekeeping missions lost more than $23 million worth of equipment between 1993 and 1995. It finds that theft accounts for almost three-fifths of that loss.		The embattled government of Lesotho and the country's opposition leaders agree upon a transitional structure to sustain the kingdom until new elections in 2000 and to guide the electoral process.	Pres. Andres Pastrana Arango orders troops to begin pulling out of five townships in southeast Colombia, comprising more than 16,000 square miles (40,000 sq km) of land, so that the Revolutionary Armed Forces of Colombia (FARC) will have control of the area. The withdrawal of troops, which will last for 90 days, is intended as a major step toward peace negotiations.	Koo Chen-fu, Taiwan's chief official for relations with China, visits China, marking the highest-level contacts between Taiwan and China since 1949. . . . Australian law-enforcement authorities seize 180 pounds (400 kg) of pure heroin, three times the amount Australian authorities seized in all of 1997 and by far the largest in Australia's history. Police arrest 18 people, 11 of whom are Indonesian and seven of whom are Hong Kong Chinese.
Oct. 15		Some 500,000 secondary-school students march in cities in France to protest classroom overcrowding and inadequate equipment and buildings. The protests are the culmination of smaller ones begun Oct. 4. In Paris, a march attended by more than 25,000 students erupts into violence, as protesters vandalize cars and loot shops. . . . The upper house of Russia's parliament passes legislation that will reestablish a public holiday commemorating the defeat of Japan in World War II on Sep. 3, 1945.	Lebanon's pro-Syrian, unicameral National Assembly, the country's parliament, unanimously elects Gen. Emile Lahoud, the military chief of staff, as president, succeeding Elias Hrawi.		

A	B	C	D	E
Includes developments that affect more than one world region, international organizations, and important meetings of major world leaders.	Includes all domestic and regional developments in Europe, including the Soviet Union, Turkey, Cyprus, and Malta.	Includes all domestic and regional developments in Africa and the Middle East, including Iraq and Iran and excluding Cyprus, Turkey, and Afghanistan.	Includes all domestic and regional developments in Latin America, the Caribbean, and Canada.	Includes all domestic and regional developments in Asia and Pacific nations, extending from Afghanistan through all the Pacific Island, except Hawaii.

U.S. Politics & Social Issues	U.S. Foreign Policy & Defense	U.S. Economy & Environment	Science, Technology, & Nature	Culture, Leisure, & Lifestyle	
The House ethics committee drops the last three of 84 ethics charges Democratic representatives filed against House Speaker Newt Gingrich (R, Ga.) since he led the Republican takeover of Congress in 1994. . . . The House clears, 369-50, legislation to expand federal aid to "charter schools," public schools exempted from some local regulations. . . . Clark McAdams Clifford, 91, lawyer, government official and adviser to four Democratic presidents, dies of respiratory failure in Bethesda, Maryland.	The House, by voice vote, passes a bill aimed at deterring persecution of minority religious groups overseas. . . . Declassified documents show that the CIA ignored reports that some 50 Nicaraguan contras or their supporters had links to drug trafficking during the war against Nicaragua's Sandinista government in the 1980s.				Oct. 10
Spottswood W(illiam) Robinson III, 82, civil-rights lawyer who helped persuade the Supreme Court to declare racial segregation in public schools unconstitutional in the 1954 landmark case *Brown v. Board of Education*, dies in Richmond, Virginia, of an apparent heart attack.				Pope John Paul II canonizes Edith Stein, an Orthodox Jew who became a Roman Catholic nun and was killed in Auschwitz. The action draws anger from Jewish groups, who criticize the decision to declare Stein a Christian martyr of the Holocaust in which 6 million Jews died.	Oct. 11
Matthew Shepard, 21, an openly homosexual student at the University of Wyoming who was beaten into a coma and left hanging on a ranch fence, dies at a Colorado hospital. Police charge Russell Henderson, 21, and Aaron McKinney, 22, with his murder.			The Nobel Prize in Physiology or Medicine is awarded to Robert Furchgott, Louis Ignarro, and Ferid Murad, all of the U.S., for their pioneering research in the early 1980s into the wide-reaching internal biological role of naturally produced nitric oxide. . . . The House, by voice vote, passes legislation updating copyright provisions for computer software and other works created in digital media.	Kenny Brack of Sweden wins the Indy Racing League (IRL) points title at the Las Vegas 500 in Nevada, where he finishes sixth.	Oct. 12
In San Francisco, California, Judge Charles Breyer orders shut the Oakland Cannabis Buyers' Cooperative, which provided marijuana for medical use. . . . Jeremy Sagastegui, 27, convicted of the 1995 murders of a three-year-old boy, his mother, and another woman, is executed in Walla Walla, Washington. Sagastegui is the 484th person executed in the U.S. and only the third in Washington State since 1976.	The INS institutes higher fees for most immigration services, claiming that they will help the agency modernize and speed up the citizenship process.	The Senate, by unanimous consent, and the House, 319-82, clear legislation that will make federal courts the sole arbiter of class-action lawsuits involving fraud allegations against companies with volatile stocks.	The Nobel Prize in Chemistry is awarded to Walter Kohn and John Pople, both of the U.S., for using quantum theory to calculate the behavior of atoms and molecules. The Nobel Prize in Physics is awarded to to three U.S. university professors—Daniel Tsui, Horst Stoermer, and Robert Laughlin—for their work in studies of a phenomenon called the fractional quantum.	Writer Isabel Allende receives the fifth annual Dorothy and Lillian Gish Prize for the arts. . . . The NBA announces the cancellation of the first two weeks of the 1998-99 basketball season due to a labor dispute for the first time in the league's 51-year history. The NBA had been the only major U.S. professional sports league that had not canceled games due to labor disputes.	Oct. 13
Dwayne Allen Wright, 26, convicted of killing a woman when he was 17, is executed in Jarratt, Virginia. Wright is the first juvenile offender and the 56th person executed in Virginia since 1976. He is 485th person since 1976 and the 12th juvenile offender since 1985 to be executed in the U.S. . . . The Senate clears, by voice vote, legislation outlawing identity theft. . . . In Nevada, Jeremy Strohmeyer is sentenced to life in prison for the May 1997 murder of seven-year-old Sherrice Iverson.	The House clears a bill passed by the Senate in 1997 that requires the State Department to report to Congress each year the number of foreign diplomats suspected of committing a serious crime in the U.S.		The Nobel Memorial Prize in Economic Sciences is awarded to to Indian-born Amartya Sen for his work in welfare economics, which addresses the economic theory behind famines and poverty.	Frank Yankovic, 83, accordionist and singer known as the "Polka King," dies in New Port Richey, Florida.	Oct. 14
Frank Caruso Jr., 19, is sentenced to eight years in prison for the beating of Lenard Clark, 13, a black teenager who rode his bicycle into a mostly white Chicago area in 1997. . . . The Senate passes legislation create a national strategy to combat money laundering. . . . The CDC issues recommendations for the testing for hepatitis C of patients who may have contracted the disease through tainted blood transfusions.	Reports confirm that the family of Joviane Waltrick, an American teenager killed in a 1997 traffic accident in the U.S. caused by Georgian diplomat Gueorgui Makharadze, has agreed to settle a civil lawsuit against the Republic of Georgia and two other defendants for more than $250,000. Makharadze who had been speeding in Washington, D.C., when he caused the accident, is serving seven to 21 years in prison.	In a surprise move, The Federal Reserve Board, cuts the federal-funds rate, the interest rate banks charge one another on overnight loans, to 5%, from 5.25%. The discount rate, the largely symbolic rate the Fed charges on loans it makes to commercial banks, is lowered to 4.75%, from 5%. A number of commercial banks quickly cut their prime rate to 8%, from 8.25%.		Pope John Paul II issues his 13th encyclical, in which he urges Roman Catholics to affirm that the union of religious faith and rational thought is possible and essential for the perpetuation of a vibrant faith. . . . Cleveland Amory, 81, writer and animal-rights advocate, dies in New York City of an aneurysm.	Oct. 15

F	G	H	I	J
Includes elections, federal-state relations, civil rights and liberties, crime, the judiciary, education, health care, poverty, urban affairs, and population.	Includes formation and debate of U.S. foreign and defense policies, veterans' affairs, and defense spending. (Relations with specific foreign countries are usually found under the region concerned.)	Includes business, labor, agriculture, taxation, transportation, consumer affairs, monetary and fiscal policy, natural resources, and pollution.	Includes worldwide scientific, medical, and technological developments; natural phenomena; U.S. weather; natural disasters; and accidents.	Includes the arts, religion, scholarship, communications media, sports, entertainments, fashions, fads, and social life.

	World Affairs	Europe	Africa & the Middle East	The Americas	Asia & the Pacific
Oct. 16	NATO extends by 10 days a deadline for the withdrawal of Serbian forces from Kosovo.... Gen. Augusto Pinochet Ugarte, the former military leader of Chile, is arrested in London after Spain requests his extradition on charges of ordering the murder of hundreds of Spanish citizens during his rule. ... The Nobel Peace Prize is presented to John Hume and David Trimble for their work to bring an end to sectarian violence in Northern Ireland, which has claimed nearly 3,600 lives since 1969.	Macedonia holds a round of national parliamentary elections.			The foreign secretaries of India and Pakistan meet for the first extended negotiations on the disputed Himalayan region of Kashmir, to which both countries have laid claim, since 1963.
Oct. 17	Reports confirm that Russian and Belarussian defense ministers plan to enhance military ties to counter eastward expansion by NATO.... The Chilean government demands the release of Gen. Pinochet, claiming that he is protected by diplomatic immunity as a member of the Chilean Senate. His Oct. 16 arrest is considered to have wide-ranging implications for the prosecution of human-rights abuses.	The ethnic Albanian Kosovo Liberation Army (UCK) kills three Serbian police officers.... Joan Bogle Hickson, 92, British actress known for her portrayal of Agatha Christie's sleuth, Miss Marple, in a BBC television series, 1984–92, dies in Colchester, England.			
Oct. 18		The Yugoslav government deploys two battalion-sized armored units in central Kosovo after reports of the Oct. 17 killings by the ethnic Albanian Kosovo Liberation Army (UCK).	Nine people are killed by rebels in Hamma Bouziane, a village 212 miles east of Algiers.	A pipeline explodes in the northern Antioquia province of Colombia, killing some 40 people and leaving at least 60 injured.	
Oct. 19	Judge Baltasar Garzon of Spain, who issued the Oct 16 arrest warrant for Gen. Augusto Pinochet Ugarte, expands the accusations to human-rights abuses involving 94 people, including citizens of Chile, Argentina, Britain, and the U.S. The judge bases his arrest request on the European Convention on Terrorism, which requires member nations to assist each other in the apprehension of terrorists.	Soldiers opposed to the rule of Georgian president Eduard Shevardnadze stage a revolt as they block roads with tanks and clash with government troops sent to put down the rebellion. They surrender after talks with government negotiators.	Sierra Leone executes by firing squad 24 soldiers, sentenced Oct. 12 for their roles in a May 1997 coup that ousted Pres. Ahmad Tejan Kabbah.... Africa's biggest airline, South African Airways (SAA), reveals that it has suspended its flights to Congo pending the results of an investigation into the Oct. 11 incident in which an airliner was shut down by rebel troops.... A West Bank Palestinian man carries out a grenade attack against Israeli soldiers in a crowded public bus station in Beersheba, wounding some 60 people.		Vietnamese premier Phan Van Khai visits China, making the first such trip by a Vietnamese head of government since 1991.
Oct. 20	To mark the 50th anniversary of the Universal Declaration of Human Rights, China hosts an international conference.... Officials in Switzerland announce they have seized about $90 million controlled by Raul Salinas de Gortari, brother of former Mexican president Carlos Salinas de Gortari. Salinas allegedly received the money for protecting the passage of drugs to the U.S. during his brother's 1988–94 term.	In France, about 300,000 students demonstrate for better learning conditions, and 25,000 march in Paris alone. Parents and teachers march with students for the first time. Riot police spray tear gas to break up a wave of vandalism in Paris, where about 100 people are arrested.... Reports reveal that 50 people were injured in the Oct. 19 rebellion in Georgia. At least one government soldier and four of the rebel soldiers were killed.	The military wing of Hamas takes responsibility for the Oct. 19 attack. ... Reports confirm that the government's commission is paying reparations to victims of apartheid in South Africa.... John Mowbray Didcott, 67, South African judge known for his commitment to human rights, dies in Durban, South Africa, of leukemia.	Jorge Ortega, who was vice president of the Unitary Workers' Federation, Colombia's largest labor organization, is assassinated by an unidentified gunman.... The Oct, 16 arrest of Gen. Pinochet in London continues to escalate tensions in Chile, and police arrest 117 people after violent clashes in Santiago, the capital.	
Oct. 21	Leaders of Turkey and Syria state they have signed an agreement aimed at staving off a possible military confrontation over Syria's alleged support for Kurds in Turkey, easing tensions that have been rising since September.	Massimo D'Alema, head of the Democratic Party of the Left (PDS), is sworn in to succeed Romano Prodi as Italy's premier. D'Alema is the first former communist to become Italy's premier.... In response to student protests, French officials announce that the government will appropriate an extra four billion francs ($730 million) in funding for schools.... Lord (Alan John) Sainsbury, 96, chair, 1956–67, and joint president, 1967–98, of J. Sainsbury PLC, a leading British supermarket chain, dies.	The governments of Angola, Zimbabwe, and Namibia announce an agreement to support Pres. Laurent Kabila's offensive in eastern Congo. The UN Children's Fund states that it will pull out of the areas of Congo held by the rebels, as it lost $1 million worth of equipment due to pillaging.... A judge in Sierra Leone sentences 11 people to death for treason for their involvement in a May 1997 coup that ousted Pres. Ahmad Tejan Kabbah.	Alberta's provincial government announces that a Royal Canadian Mounted Police (RCMP) officer who shot and killed a native woman and her nine-year-old son in March will not face criminal charges in connection with the incident.	In South Korea, Kim Sun Hong, the former chairman of the Kia conglomerate, is sentenced to seven years in prison for embezzlement and dereliction of duty.

A	B	C	D	E
Includes developments that affect more than one world region, international organizations, and important meetings of major world leaders.	*Includes all domestic and regional developments in Europe, including the Soviet Union, Turkey, Cyprus, and Malta.*	*Includes all domestic and regional developments in Africa and the Middle East, including Iraq and Iran and excluding Cyprus, Turkey, and Afghanistan.*	*Includes all domestic and regional developments in Latin America, the Caribbean, and Canada.*	*Includes all domestic and regional developments in Asia and Pacific nations, extending from Afghanistan through all the Pacific Island, except Hawaii.*

U.S. Politics & Social Issues	U.S. Foreign Policy & Defense	U.S. Economy & Environment	Science, Technology, & Nature	Culture, Leisure, & Lifestyle	
The House passes a bill to create a national strategy to combat money laundering.		The Social Security Administration announces that beneficiaries receiving social security checks in 1999 will obtain a cost-of-living increase of 1.3%, the smallest rise since 1987. That means that the average benefit paid will increase by about $10, to $780 per month.	Jon(athan) B. Postel, 55, Internet pioneer who helped create its address system and worked at the federally funded Internet Assigned Numbers Authority for 30 years, dies of complications from heart surgery in Santa Monica, California.	Maynard Michael Parker, 58, *Newsweek* editor since 1982 who joined the magazine's staff in 1966, dies in New York City of complications from leukemia.	Oct. 16
			Flooding and deadly tornadoes begin to sweep through central, southern, and eastern Texas.	Joseph Machlis, 92, music author and educator whose book sold more than 2 million copies, dies in New York of unreported causes. . . . Marvin P. Gay Sr., 84, who shot and killed his son, late soul music singer Marvin Gaye, in 1984, dies of pneumonia in Los Angeles, California.	Oct. 17
					Oct. 18
Incumbent state senator Tommy Burks (D, Tenn.), 58, is found dead, shot in the forehead. . . . Victor Jasas, 18, and Michael Kwidzinski, 21, accused of beating black teenager Lenard Clark, 13, who rode his bicycle into their mostly white Chicago neighborhood, plead guilty to reduced charges and are sentenced to probation and community service. . . . Two black health organizations file a class-action lawsuit against the tobacco industry in U.S. District Court in Philadelphia, claiming that cigarette companies violated federal civil-rights laws by targeting menthol cigarettes at black customers.			Pres. Clinton signs legislation intended to encourage companies to share information about solving the so-called Year 2000 (Y2K) computer glitch by shielding them from lawsuits based on the data they disclose.	The Nevada State Athletic Commission votes to restore former heavyweight champion Mike Tyson's boxing license, which was revoked in 1997 after he bit both of opponent Evander Holyfield's ears in a championship bout in Las Vegas. The ruling causes controversy, especially since Tyson is still on probation after serving three years in an Indiana prison for a rape conviction.	Oct. 19
	Pres. Clinton signs the intelligence authorization bill for fiscal 1999. . . . The House passes, by voice vote, a bill bringing U.S. law into line with an international antibribery treaty signed in 1997 by the U.S. and other major industrial countries that make up the Organization for Economic Cooperation and Development (OECD).	The Commerce Department reports that the U.S. trade deficit expanded by 15.3% in August from July, recording a seasonally adjusted $16.77 billion gap in trade in goods and services. The August gap is the largest recorded since the department began tracking it in its present format. . . . The House passes, 333-95, an omnibus bill that will provide more than $500 billion for federal spending in the fiscal 1999 year.	The SEC formally charges 37 small brokerage firms with failing to file adequate reports on the Y2K glitch, the problems anticipated with computer systems in the year 2000. . . . Flooding continues in Texas, and in Victoria the Guadalupe River crests at almost 36 feet, breaking a record set in 1936 by nearly 5 feet.	The UN appoints Geri Halliwell, a former member of the Spice Girls, a British popular music group, as a goodwill ambassador for the UN Population Fund.	Oct. 20
The Senate confirms the appointments of 17 federal judges nominated by Pres. Clinton. The confirmations bring the number of new federal judges the Senate confirmed in 1998 to 65. That number compares with 36 in 1997. . . . The Senate clears by unanimous consent a bill that will authorize $750 million in compensation for hemophiliacs infected with HIV, the virus that causes AIDS, through blood transfusions. . . . The Senate confirms Kenneth Prewitt as director of the Census Bureau.	Pres. Clinton vetoes a bill to pay $1 billion that the U.S. owes the UN in back dues because it contains antiabortion provisions. However, part of the omnibus spending bill includes a dues payment of some $200 million to the UN that will allow the U.S. to retain its General Assembly voting rights. . . . The Senate passes, by voice vote, a bill bringing U.S. law into line with an international antibribery treaty signed in 1997. . . . Joseph Santos and Amarylis Silverio Santos plead guilty to charges of serving as illegal foreign agents to Cuba.	The Senate clears, 65-29, and Pres. Clinton signs an omnibus bill that will provide more than $500 billion for the fiscal 1999 year, which began Oct. 1. The bill incorporates eight of the 13 annual appropriations measures, as well as legislation authorizing $18 billion in new financing for the IMF and $20.8 billion dollars in emergency spending for farmers, the military and other uses. . . . Pres. Clinton signs a measure enacting a major overhaul of the nation's public housing system. . . . Pres. Clinton signs an $93.4 fiscal 1999 bill for the VA, HUD, EPA, NASA, and other independent agencies.	The Senate ratifies by voice vote two treaties adopted in 1996 by the UN World Intellectual Property Organization. . . . The Senate confirms Pres. Clinton's appointment of Dr. Jane Henney as commissioner of the FDA. . . . Arianespace, the commercial arm of the ESA, successfully completes its third and last test launch of the Ariane-5 rocket from Kourou, French Guiana.	The New York Yankees defeat the San Diego Padres, 3-0, to win 94th World Series in San Diego, California.	Oct. 21

F	G	H	I	J
Includes elections, federal-state relations, civil rights and liberties, crime, the judiciary, education, health care, poverty, urban affairs, and population.	Includes formation and debate of U.S. foreign and defense policies, veterans' affairs, and defense spending. (Relations with specific foreign countries are usually found under the region concerned.)	Includes business, labor, agriculture, taxation, transportation, consumer affairs, monetary and fiscal policy, natural resources, and pollution.	Includes worldwide scientific, medical, and technological developments; natural phenomena; U.S. weather; natural disasters; and accidents.	Includes the arts, religion, scholarship, communications media, sports, entertainments, fashions, fads, and social life.

	World Affairs	Europe	Africa & the Middle East	The Americas	Asia & the Pacific
Oct. 22		Yugoslav army soldiers fire on a group of 16 ethnic Albanians as the refugees cross the border from Albania to return to their village in southern Kosovo. Two men and three young children die in the shooting.	In Sierra Leone, a judge sentences five people to 10 years in prison for their involvement in a May 1997 coup that ousted Pres. Ahmad Tejan Kabbah.		Pakistan's carpet makers sign an agreement with the International Labor Organization seeking to end child labor in the industry.... In Japan an initial public offering of stock in NTT Mobile Communications Network Inc. raises some 2.13 trillion yen ($18 billion). The sale is the largest IPO ever.... Kazuaki Okazaki, 38, a founding member of the Aum Shinrikyo religious cult, which released deadly sarin gas into Tokyo's subway system in March 1995, is sentenced to death for the killings of four people in a separate incident.
Oct. 23	In Washington, D.C., Israeli prime minister Benjamin Netanyahu and Yasser Arafat, president of the self-rule Palestinian National Authority (PNA), sign a long-delayed interim agreement on conditions for an Israeli military withdrawal from 13.1% of the West Bank.	Christopher Gable, 58, British ballet star and film and stage actor, dies near Halifax, England, of cancer.	In response to the interim agreement between Israel and the PNA signed in Washington, D.C., some 2,000 supporters of Hamas and the smaller Islamic Jihad burn Israeli and U.S. flags at a rally in the southern Gaza Strip.... Iranian voters elect conservatives to a majority of seats in the Assembly of Experts, which may select and advise Iran's supreme leader.... In Sierra Leone, Foday Sankoh, founder and one leader of the RUF, is sentenced to death for treason for the1997 coup.		
Oct. 24					A protest by some 2,000 people in Kuala Lumpur, the capital of Malaysia, turns violent as demonstrators clash with riot police. Several police officers and protesters suffer injuries, but no fatalities are reported. At least 240 of the protesters are arrested.... One of Japan's largest financial institutions, Daiwa Bank, announces that it will close all of its overseas branches over the next 18 months.
Oct. 25		The moderate Basque Nationalist Party wins the largest number of seats in a legislative election held in Spain's Basque region.	In the PNA-controlled city of Ramallah on the West Bank, one Palestinian youth is killed when PNA military intelligence officers open fire on protest marchers.	Reports confirm that, in Peru, three protesters have been killed and eight seriously injured in clashes with police over the upcoming treaty designed to a 50-year-old border dispute that brought Peru and Ecuador to war in 1995.	
Oct. 26		Serbian police and army troops begin to withdraw en masse from Kosovo, just before the latest NATO deadline for Yugoslav president Slobodan Milosevic to comply with the terms of an agreement reached earlier. Thousands of refugees begin returning to their homes.... Reports confirm that Chechnya's top official in charge of combating kidnapping, Shadid Bargishev, was killed in a bomb explosion outside of his office. Two bodyguards and several people in the area were injured.	Danny Vargas, a Jewish security guard from a settlement near Hebron, is shot to death. Later, a caller speaking in Hebrew tells Israeli police that he killed a Palestinian near Nablus in revenge for the Vargas slaying. Israeli authorities find the body of olive farmer Mohammed Suleiman Zalmut, 68.	Pres. Alberto Fujimori of Peru and Pres. Jamil Mahuad of Ecuador sign a treaty ending a 50-year-old border dispute that brought their countries to war in 1995.... Hurricane Mitch intensifies into a Category Five hurricane—the most powerful on the Saffer-Simpson hurricane scale—before hitting Central America.	Authorities raid and close down the China Development Union, an independent policy research organization founded earlier in the year by Peng Ming, a businessman and former government official.
Oct. 27	Reports confirm that foreign ministers of the European Union have agreed to increase sanctions against Myanmar's ruling junta.... NATO suspends the immediate threat of air strikes against Yugoslavia, after determining that Yugoslav president Slobodan Milosevic is in "substantial compliance" with NATO demands to withdraw Serbian police and military forces from the province of Kosovo.	In Kosova, in a booby trap left by Serbian forces, a 19-year-old man is killed.... The Bundestag votes to install Gerhard Schroeder as Germany's chancellor. Schroeder and his cabinet are sworn in by Pres. Roman Herzog, formally ending the 16-year tenure of outgoing Chancellor Helmut Kohl.... Pres. Carlos Saul Menem of Argentina arrives in Britain, making the first official visit to Britain by an Argentine leader since 1960.... Rosamund John (born Nora Rosamund Jones), 85, 1940s-era British actress, dies in London, England.			

A	B	C	D	E
Includes developments that affect more than one world region, international organizations, and important meetings of major world leaders.	Includes all domestic and regional developments in Europe, including the Soviet Union, Turkey, Cyprus, and Malta.	Includes all domestic and regional developments in Africa and the Middle East, including Iraq and Iran and excluding Cyprus, Turkey, and Afghanistan.	Includes all domestic and regional developments in Latin America, the Caribbean, and Canada.	Includes all domestic and regional developments in Asia and Pacific nations, extending from Afghanistan through all the Pacific Island, except Hawaii.

U.S. Politics & Social Issues	U.S. Foreign Policy & Defense	U.S. Economy & Environment	Science, Technology, & Nature	Culture, Leisure, & Lifestyle	
A consortium of 17 advocacy groups, led by the ACLU, files a lawsuit in U.S. District Court challenging the constitutionality of the Internet-pornography law passed Oct. 21 as part of the omnibus fiscal 1999 spending bill. Under the measure, operators of commercial websites are required to limit access to material deemed pornographic or "harmful to minors.". . . Pres. Clinton signs a bill expanding federal aid to "charter schools." . . . Francis W. Sargent, 83, (R, Mass.), governor of Massachusetts, 1969–75, dies in Dover, Massachusetts, of unreported causes.	Reports confirm that Alejandro Alonso has pled guilty to charges of being an illegal foreign agent to Cuba. . . . Declassified documents reveal that the CIA continued to support anticommunist forces in Honduras in the 1980s even though the agency knew of humans-rights abuses by the Honduran military.	A commission of Texas environmental regulators votes unanimously to deny a license for a low-level radioactive waste dump to be built on the outskirts of Sierra Blanca. . . . The world's seven biggest manufacturers of diesel engines for heavy trucks agree to pay $83 million in fines and $1 billion in corrective actions to avoid a federal civil lawsuit on environmental charges. The settlement, brokered after nearly a year of negotiations, is the largest financial penalty imposed in an environmental-enforcement action in U.S. history.	Scientists report new evidence that oceans of liquid water exists below the frozen surfaces of two of Jupiter's moons, Europa and Callisto.	Reports state that the death of Olympic track star Florence Griffith Joyner, 38, was caused by suffocation that resulted from a seizure. . . . Frank Bidart receives the 1998 Rebekah Johnson Bobbitt National Prize for Poetry. . . . Eric Ambler, 89, British author whose early works are credited with legitimizing the thriller, dies in London, England.	Oct. 22
An unidentified sniper shoots and kills Barnett Slepian, 52, an obstetrician in Amherst, New York, who performed abortions as a small part of his practice. He is the third abortion doctor killed in the U.S. since 1993 . . . Police in Cookeville, Tennessee, arrest Byron (Low Tax) Looper, a Republican candidate for the state senate, on charges of murdering his Democratic opponent, popular incumbent Tommy Burks.	Two former University of Wisconsin radicals, Kurt Stand and his wife Theresa Squillacote, are found guilty of espionage in U.S. District Court in Alexandria, Virginia, for spying for East Germany in the 1970s and 1980s.		James Lee Witt, director of FEMA, and Texas governor George Bush (R) visit Cuero, Texas, the site of recent flooding. Twenty counties have been declared federal disaster areas, and Witt states that five more counties are slated for the federal disaster designation. . . . Scientists report they have found that rhesus monkeys are capable of placing objects in serial order.	Data shows that the television ratings for the 1998 World Series averaged a record low of 14.1. . . . Winnie Ruth Judd, 93, infamous 1930s-era criminal known as the "trunk murderess," dies in Phoenix, Arizona, of unreported causes.	Oct. 23
Mary Steichen Calderone, 94, preeminent advocate of sex education who in 1964 cofounded the Sex Information and Education Council of the United States, dies in Kennet Square, Pennsylvania, while suffering from Alzheimer's disease.	INS officials estimate that 100,000 Chinese nationals arrive illegally in the U.S. each year.		*Deep Space 1*, an unmanned spacecraft that is to fly past an asteroid, is launched on a Delta rocket from Cape Canaveral Air Force Station in Florida. *Deep Space 1* is the first spacecraft to use an ion engine as its primary source of propulsion, allowing it to carry much less fuel than it would otherwise have to carry.		Oct. 24
	Admiral John Joseph Hyland Jr., 86, U.S. Navy admiral who commanded the Pacific Fleet from 1967 to 1971, dies in Honolulu, Hawaii, of unreported causes.			The Chicago Fire, an expansion team, defeats D.C. United, 2-0, in the championship game of the Major League Soccer playoffs in Pasadena, California. The win marks the first time that an expansion team in a major U.S. sport has won the championship in its first season.	Oct. 25
A jury in Richmond, Virginia, finds that Columbus, Ohio–based Nationwide Mutual Insurance Co. discriminated against black homeowners in Richmond by refusing to sell them home insurance policies, and it orders the company to pay $100 million in punitive damages and $500,000 in compensation to Housing Opportunities Made Equal Inc., a Richmond-based housing group.	Two Washington, D.C., think tanks, the Center for Strategic and International Studies (CSIS) and the Henry L. Stimson Center, release separate reports criticizing the U.S.'s foreign policy apparatus. Both reports find that U.S. diplomacy suffers from outdated computer technology and inefficient organization.			Mike Piazza, catcher for the New York Mets, announces that he will stay with the Mets after signing a seven-year contract worth a record $91 million. Piazza will average $13 million a season, making him the highest-paid baseball player in the major leagues.	Oct. 26
Pres. Clinton signs a five-year reauthorization of the Head Start preschool program. . . . Pres. Clinton signs a measure extending U.S. copyrights by 20 years. . . . Pres. Clinton signs a measure barring close relatives from serving as judges on the same federal court. . . . Two independent counsels release a final report on their extensive probe into corruption and influence peddling, finding "a pattern of greed, criminal conduct and systematic corruption of the government process by HUD officials" during the 1980s.	Pres. Clinton signs a bill aimed at deterring persecution of religious groups overseas.		The flooding and deadly tornadoes that have swept through central, southern and eastern Texas since Oct. 17 begin to subside. The floods in 60 counties have caused 31 deaths and prompted the evacuation of 14,000 people.	Pres. Clinton signs a bill to overturn MLB'S exemption from antitrust laws in regard to labor relations. . . . The Booker Prize is awarded to novelist Ian McEwan for *Amsterdam*. . . . The White House reveals the 19 cultural figures, a corporation, and a theater company that will receive National Medals of Arts or National Humanities Medals.	Oct. 27

F	G	H	I	J
Includes elections, federal-state relations, civil rights and liberties, crime, the judiciary, education, health care, poverty, urban affairs, and population.	Includes formation and debate of U.S. foreign and defense policies, veterans' affairs, and defense spending. (Relations with specific foreign countries are usually found under the region concerned.)	Includes business, labor, agriculture, taxation, transportation, consumer affairs, monetary and fiscal policy, natural resources, and pollution.	Includes worldwide scientific, medical, and technological developments; natural phenomena; U.S. weather; natural disasters; and accidents.	Includes the arts, religion, scholarship, communications media, sports, entertainments, fashions, fads, and social life.

	World Affairs	Europe	Africa & the Middle East	The Americas	Asia & the Pacific
Oct. 28	A UN report forecasts a global population of 8.9 billion in the year 2050, down from the 1996 prediction of a 2050 population of 9.4 billion.... Britain's High Court rules that Chilean general Augusto Pinochet Ugarte is immune from arrest in Britain and extradition to Spain, nullifying the Oct. 16 warrant. ... Reports confirm that Belarus has rescinded a June eviction order that forced foreign diplomats from their diplomatic residences and prompted several countries to recall their ambassadors from Belarus.	Argentine president Carlos Saul Menem lays a wreath at a memorial to British victims of the Falklands War in London.... A Kremlin speaker announces that Russian president Boris Yeltsin will relinquish the day-to-day running of the government to focus on securing an orderly succession at the end of his current term..... Thomas Harold Flowers, 92, British engineer who developed a machine that decoded German military communications during World War II, dies in London, England, of a heart attack.		The 650,000 public-sector workers who struck Oct. 7 in Colombia end the job action when government officials agree to implement a 15% wage increase.... Winnipeg, the capital of Manitoba, becomes the first major Canadian city to elect an openly homosexual mayor, Glen Murray.	
Oct. 29	Alleged Bosnian Serb war criminal Goran Jelisic pleads guilty to killing 12 Moslems and Croats in Brcko, northern Bosnia, but maintains that he is not guilty of genocide. Because Jelisic is charged with genocide, he will go on trial at the court in The Hague and will not be sentenced for the other crimes until that trial is completed.... The World Bank and the Inter-American Development Bank announce a $2 billion loan package for Colombia.	Judge Sergei Golets in St. Petersburg dismisses the case of Alexander Nikitin, a retired Russian navy captain accused of espionage for his work on a report on the environmental risks posed by Russia's nuclear submarines. It is the first time in Soviet and Russian history that charges of treason have been dismissed.	A Palestinian suicide bomber kills one Israeli soldier and himself in the Gaza Strip.... In its final report on human-rights violations during apartheid, South Africa's Truth and Reconciliation Commission finds that the white-minority government sustained institutionalized violence and committed most of the apartheid era's severe human-rights violations. However, the report also criticizes opposition groups, most notably the ANC, finding that it too was responsible for killings and torture.	Hurricane Mitch is downgraded to a tropical storm, but it continues to dump as much as 2 feet (0.6 m) of rain daily on parts of Central America.	
Oct. 30	Reports reveal that Japan has agreed effectively to forgive 90% of the debts incurred by 10 African countries over the previous decade. ... A consortium of UN agencies, including the World Bank, UNICEF, and the UN Development Fund, announce the launch of an anti-malaria campaign coordinated by the World Health Organization. ... Despite the Oct. 29 ruling in Britain, Spain's National Court rules unanimously that Spain has the right to charge and extradite General Augusto Pinochet Ugarte, the former military ruler of Chile.	In Slovakia, Mikulas Dzurinda is sworn into office as premier, officially ending the tenure of Premier Vladimir Meciar.... Fire tears through a discotheque in Goteborg, Sweden, killing 60 people and injuring about 180 others. The fire is Sweden's deadliest in decades.	South Africa states that it will withdraw 1,400 of its 3,500 troops stationed in Lesotho since the September violence.	In western Nicaragua, the crater on top of the 4,610-foot (1,405 m) Casitas volcano collapses, causing a slide of rock, mud, and debris down its slopes that buries at least four communities and up to 2,000 people.	
Oct. 31	To protest mounting Iraqi deaths as a result of the UN's embargo, Iraqi Pres. Saddam Hussein halts Iraq's cooperation with the United Nations Special Commission on Iraq (UNSCOM), which is overseeing the dismantlement of Iraq's missiles and its chemical and biological weapons programs.... Taiwan announces it will break diplomatic ties with Tonga, which plans to formally recognize China.	Brian Service, a Roman Catholic, is shot and killed by unidentified assailants in a Catholic section of Belfast, Northern Ireland. The murder is the year's 55th slaying linked to the conflict between Catholics and Protestants in British-ruled Northern Ireland.	While on a shuttle diplomacy tour to seven African countries, U.S. assistant secretary of state for African affairs Susan Rice warns that the Congo fighting may reach genocidal proportions.	Data reveal that Hurricane Mitch, the deadliest hurricane to strike Central America since 1988, has caused more than 9,000 deaths in the region and left another one million people homeless since Oct. 26. Though most of the deaths are recorded in Honduras and Nicaragua, hurricane-related deaths are also reported in El Salvador, Guatemala, Mexico, Panama, Jamaica, and Costa Rica.	
Nov. 1	Denis Halliday resigns as coordinator of the UN's oil-for-food program in Iraq in protest over the impact of UN economic sanctions on Iraqi civilians, arguing that the sanctions are responsible for the deaths of 6,000–7,000 Iraqi children each month.	In Macedonia, the Coalition for Changes soundly defeats the ruling Social-Democratic Union of Macedonia party (SDSM). Ljupco Georgievski is named premier.... A Protestant guerrilla group called the Red Hand Defenders claims responsibility for the Oct. 31 attack in Belfast, Northern Ireland. ... Norbert Wollheim, 85, survivor of the Auschwitz Nazi concentration camp who, in 1951, sued the I. G. Farben company for payment for labor he was forced to perform, dies in New York City of a heart ailment.	The government of Guinea-Bissau signs a peace agreement with army mutineers, ending a civil war that has racked the West African country for five months.	Data reveals that Hurricane Mitch was the fourth-strongest hurricane of the 20th century. An estimated 7,000 people were killed and 600,000 people left homeless in Honduras, which bore the brunt of the storm's force. Mayor Cesar Castellanos of Tegucigalpa, the capital of Honduras, is killed in a helicopter crash while surveying the damage.... In Colombia, FARC begins an assault on Mitu, the capital of Vaupes province.	

A	B	C	D	E
Includes developments that affect more than one world region, international organizations, and important meetings of major world leaders.	Includes all domestic and regional developments in Europe, including the Soviet Union, Turkey, Cyprus, and Malta.	Includes all domestic and regional developments in Africa and the Middle East, including Iraq and Iran and excluding Cyprus, Turkey, and Afghanistan.	Includes all domestic and regional developments in Latin America, the Caribbean, and Canada.	Includes all domestic and regional developments in Asia and Pacific nations, extending from Afghanistan through all the Pacific Island, except Hawaii.

U.S. Politics & Social Issues	U.S. Foreign Policy & Defense	U.S. Economy & Environment	Science, Technology, & Nature	Culture, Leisure, & Lifestyle	
Officials in Miami, Florida, arrest 18 people as part of a probe of vote fraud in the city's 1997 municipal elections. . . . More than 400 historians claim that Pres. Clinton's actions do not meet the impeachment criteria envisioned by the Constitution's framers. A group of 200 constitutional scholars releases a similar petition.	Pres. Clinton signs a bill restoring Supplemental Security Income (SSI) and Medicaid benefits to certain legal immigrants. . . . Pres. Andres Pastrana Arango and Pres. Clinton sign a pact to cooperate in combating drug trafficking in the U.S. and Colombia. The state visit is the first by a Colombian president to the U.S. in 23 years. . . . General James L. Day, 73, retired Marine Corps general who, in January, belatedly received the Medal of Honor, dies in Cathedral City, California, of a heart attack.	President Clinton announces a final, official budget surplus figure of $70 billion for fiscal 1998, which ended Sep. 30. It is the first federal budget surplus since 1969.	President Clinton signs a measure to encourage commercial involvement in space exploration. . . . Pres. Clinton signs a bill updating copyright protections for digital products such as computer software and compact discs.	The National Basketball Association announces the cancellation of two weeks of the season in addition to the games canceled Oct. 13. . . . Ted (Edward James) Hughes, 68, British poet laureate since 1984 and the winner of the the 1997 Whitbread Book of the Year Award, dies in North Tawton, England, of cancer.	Oct. 28
A New Jersey judge sentences Melissa Drexler, 20, to 15 years in prison for killing her newborn son after giving birth in the bathroom at her senior prom in 1997. . . . Harry Mohr Weese, 83, Chicago-based architect who designed Washington, D.C.'s Metro subway system, dies in Manteno, Illinois, after a stroke.			Scientists report they have discovered for the first time new brain cells being generated in adults. . . . The FDA approves use of tamoxifen to help reduce the risk of breast cancer in women at high risk of the disease. Tamoxifen is the first drug approved by the FDA as a preventive measure against breast cancer. . . . The Discovery lifts off from Cape Canaveral, Florida, with a crew that includes retiring senator John Glenn (D, Ohio), who, at 77, is the oldest space traveler ever.	Reports confirm that a fisherman has discovered a bracelet believed to have belonged to Antoine de Saint-Exupéry, the French author, near Marseilles. . . . A 10th-century manuscript of a work by the mathematician Archimedes is sold at Christie's for $2 million. The text is the oldest surviving copy of a work by Archimedes.	Oct. 29
Pres. Clinton signs bills to make identity theft a federal crime and to create a national strategy to combat money laundering. . . . Five abortion clinics in three states receive letters that claim to contain the deadly anthrax virus. . . . In the first government suit filed against the firearms industry, the city of New Orleans alleges that gun makers knowingly omit safety devices from weapons. . . . Anthony J. Celebrezze, 88, mayor of Cleveland, 1953–62, who, in 1962, was the first Italian-American appointed to a presidential cabinet, dies in Cleveland, Ohio, of esophageal cancer.	Judge Carlos Cuevas of the federal immigration court in Chicago orders the deportation of Bronislaw Hajda, who served as a guard at a Nazi concentration camp in Trawniki, Poland, during World War II. Some 60 people have been stripped of U.S. citizenship in the Justice Department's efforts to find Nazi war criminals in the U.S.			The World Boxing Council (WBC) votes to extend accreditation to women's boxing. . . . Clyde (Bulldog) Turner, 79, Hall of Fame linebacker and center elected to the Pro Football Hall of Fame in 1966, dies in Gatesville, Texas, while suffering from lung cancer.	Oct. 30
Pres. Clinton signs a bill reauthorizing the Women, Infants and Children (WIC) nutrition program.	Pres. Clinton signs a bill providing U.S. military aid to opposition groups in Iraq.	Pres. Clinton signs a bill overhauling federal vocational training programs. . . . Figures show that political parties and outside special-interest groups spent between $260 million and $330 million on issue advertising during the 1997–98 midterm election cycle. That amount—a record—is roughly twice as much as was spent on issue ads in the 1995–96 presidential election cycle.	Scientists report they have succeeded in isolating neural stem cells from a human fetus. In a separate study, scientists injected human fetal brain cells into the brains of rat embryos that have a genetic disorder causing their neurons to lack their protective myelin sheath. . . . The Royal Greenwich Observatory, founded in 1675 and the oldest scientific institution in Britain, closes due to government budget cuts.	Boxer Prince Naseem Hamed of England defeats Ireland's Wayne McCullough in Atlantic City, New Jersey, to retain his WBO featherweight title.	Oct. 31
Reports confirm that, according to genetic evidence, it is likely that Thomas Jefferson, the third President of the U.S., fathered a son by Sally Hemings, a slave who belonged to him. The new genetic evidence follows years of disputes among historians and adds a twist to discussions of the history of slavery and race relations in the U.S.				Golfer Hal Sutton wins the PGA's Tour Championship in Atlanta, Georgia. . . . John Kagwe of Kenya wins his second consecutive New York City Marathon. Franca Fiacconi of Italy clinches the women's title. . . . Auto racer Jeff Gordon clinches his third NASCAR Winston Cup title.	Nov. 1

F	G	H	I	J
Includes elections, federal-state relations, civil rights and liberties, crime, the judiciary, education, health care, poverty, urban affairs, and population.	Includes formation and debate of U.S. foreign and defense policies, veterans' affairs, and defense spending. (Relations with specific foreign countries are usually found under the region concerned.)	Includes business, labor, agriculture, taxation, transportation, consumer affairs, monetary and fiscal policy, natural resources, and pollution.	Includes worldwide scientific, medical, and technological developments; natural phenomena; U.S. weather; natural disasters; and accidents.	Includes the arts, religion, scholarship, communications media, sports, entertainments, fashions, fads, and social life.

	World Affairs	Europe	Africa & the Middle East	The Americas	Asia & the Pacific
Nov. 2	Delegates from more than 160 nations open a conference in Argentina's capital, Buenos Aires, to work out plans for implementing the Kyoto Protocol, a 1997 international accord that seeks to curb global warming.		In the southwestern city of Bulawayo, Zimbabwe, protesters demonstrate against poor economic conditions; 27 people are arrested and 20 injured when they confront police.	Nicaraguan president Arnoldo Alemán Lacayo calls Hurricane Mitch the worst disaster to strike his country since 1972, as the storm killed an estimated 2,000 people and left 400,000 homeless. The International Committee of the Red Cross states it is tripling the amount of assistance it seeks for the area to $7.4 million. U.S. president Clinton pledges $3.5 million to airlift food, water, blankets, and plastic sheeting to Central America.	The corruption and sodomy trial of former deputy prime minister Anwar Ibrahim in Malaysia's High Court in Kuala Lumpur, the capital. Malaysian prime minister Mahathir bin Mohamad ousted Anwar in early September, prompting weeks of street protests unprecedented in Mahathir's 17-year tenure. Some 200 Anwar supporters gather outside the courthouse.... Wang Youcai, a China Democracy Party leader, is detained by the Chinese government.
Nov. 3		Ilich Ramirez Sanchez, a self-styled, "professional revolutionary" known as "Carlos the Jackal," launches a hunger strike in prison. Carlos, jailed in 1997 on murder charges, contends that he was unfairly placed in solitary confinement.... A court in Milan, Italy, convicts Patrizia Reggiani Martinelli and sentences her to 29 years in prison for hiring hit men to kill her former husband, Maurizio Gucci, the former chair of Guccio Gucci SpA, in 1995.... The official death toll from the Oct. 30 fire in Goteborg, Sweden, climbs to 62.		The Cerro Negro volcano erupts in Nicaragua, covering 90 square miles (240 square km) with lava and ash and causing $20 million in agricultural damage.... Reports confirm that Esperanza Luburic (formerly Nada Luburic), believed to have run a women's detention camp during World War II, was extradited to Croatia from Argentina.	
Nov. 4	Reports suggest that Pres. Laurent Kabila's 30,000-strong Congolese army is being supported by some 4,000 troops from Angola, 3,500 from Zimbabwe, more than 1,000 from Sudan, 1,000 from Chad, and some 8,000 Rwandan Hutu extremists. The rebels are backed by several thousand Rwandan troops and 4,000 soldiers from Uganda.	In Tajikistan, rebel forces led by former army colonel Makhmud Khudoberdyev launch an offensive by marching on the city of Khudzhand and taking over buildings and an airport.... The Yugoslav government turns down visa requests for investigators from the International Criminal Tribunal for the Former Yugoslavia.	A judge in Sierra Leone finds former president Joseph Momoh guilty of conspiracy in relation to the May 1997 coup that ousted Pres. Ahmad Tejan Kabbah.... Riots break out in Harare, the capital of Zimbabwe, over economic concerns. Police, who break up the march, estimate that they arrested more than 50 people on suspicion of looting during the riots.	In Colombia, the offensive started Nov. 1 by FARC is subdued after about 500 reinforcements are called in. During the assault on Mitu, the capital of Vaupes province, an estimated 150 soldiers and police officers were killed, and 45 police officers were taken prisoner.	
Nov. 5		Several demonstrations are held by secondary-school students throughout France to protest classroom overcrowding, inadequate classroom equipment, and crumbling school buildings.		Helmer (Pacho) Herrera Buitrago, considered by officials to be a leading member of the Cali drug cartel, is shot dead in a maximum security prison outside the city of Cali, Colombia.	The UN Commission on Human Rights reports that the Taliban, the militant Islamic movement that rules most of Afghanistan, systematically executed from 4,000 to 5,000 civilians when it overran the northern city of Mazar-i-Sharif in August.... The Philippines formally complains to China, asserting that China is attempting to increase its territorial claims on the disputed Spratly Islands chain in the South China Sea by constructing piers on Mischief Reef.
Nov. 6	The U.S. is denied a seat on the Advisory Committee on Administrative and Budgetary Questions, a UN committee responsible for financial oversight. Diplomats reveal that the denial is mostly due to negative sentiment regarding the sizable U.S. debt of more than $1 billion to the UN.		Paul Kagame, Rwanda's vice president and minister of defense, admits that Rwandan troops are aiding a rebellion in neighboring Congo aimed at ousting Pres. Laurent Kabila.... A car driven by two suicide bombers apparently explodes prematurely near West Jerusalem's Mahane Yehuda marketplace, killing the attackers and injuring 24 bystanders.	Members of the Nisga'a nation, a native tribe of about 5,400 people whose ancestral lands are located in the province of British Columbia, Canada, vote to ratify a treaty that will give the tribe title to 745 square miles (1,930 sq km) of land in British Columbia's Upper Nass Valley.	The Indian government allows private companies to compete against the state-run VSNL online service. ... A senior U.S. official announces that U.S. president Clinton has decided to remove some sanctions on India and Pakistan imposed after nuclear tests in May to reward their progress on nuclear arms control and to encourage further progress.... Mohamed Taki Abdulkarim, 62, president since 1996 of the Federal Islamic Republic of the Comoros, dies in Moroni, Comoros, of unreported causes.
Nov. 7			The military wing of Islamic Jihad takes responsibility for the Nov. 6 bombing.		

A	B	C	D	E
Includes developments that affect more than one world region, international organizations, and important meetings of major world leaders.	Includes all domestic and regional developments in Europe, including the Soviet Union, Turkey, Cyprus, and Malta.	Includes all domestic and regional developments in Africa and the Middle East, including Iraq and Iran and excluding Cyprus, Turkey, and Afghanistan.	Includes all domestic and regional developments in Latin America, the Caribbean, and Canada.	Includes all domestic and regional developments in Asia and Pacific nations, extending from Afghanistan through all the Pacific Island, except Hawaii.

U.S. Politics & Social Issues	U.S. Foreign Policy & Defense	U.S. Economy & Environment	Science, Technology, & Nature	Culture, Leisure, & Lifestyle	
		The parent company of the NASDAQ Stock Market, the National Association of Securities Dealers (NASD), and the American Stock Exchange (AMEX) complete their merger. Under the terms of the deal, the AMEX is folded into a new NASD unit, the Nasdaq-Amex Market Group, which also oversees NASDAQ. The two securities markets continue to operate independently, and their tables appear separately in newspapers.		The Los Angeles Opera names Spanish-born tenor Placido Domingo to the post of artistic director, starting in the year 2000. . . . *The Path of Daggers* by Robert Jordan tops the bestseller list.	Nov. 2
In midterm elections, Republicans lose five seats to the Democrats in the House, reducing the GOP's edge in the body to six seats—the smallest majority since 1953. Republican governors lose one of their 32 state when independent Jesse (the Body) Ventura, a former wrestler, wins in Minnesota. Voters in Washington State pass an anti-affirmative action initiative. Michigan rejects a measure to allow physician-assisted suicide. Voters back a measure that makes Oregon the first state in the nation to conduct elections solely by mail.		President Clinton signs a bill curbing class-action lawsuits involving allegations of securities fraud. . . . The television corporation ABC locks out 1,600–1,800 off-camera employees after they walked off their jobs for a 24-hour strike.		Christie's sells sports memorabilia for a total of $1.3 million. Included in the auction were mementos of "Shoeless" Joe Jackson, who in 1920 was banned from baseball for allegedly fixing the World Series. . . . Bob Kane, 83, cartoonist who, in 1938, at the age of 18, created Batman the Caped Crusader with his partner, Bill Finger, dies in Los Angeles.	Nov. 3
Vice Pres. Al Gore announces new rules designed to make it easier for victims of domestic violence to get new social security numbers to help them evade their abusers. . . . Wendell Chino, 74, president of the Mescalero Apache Nation of New Mexico since 1964, dies in Los Angeles, California, of a heart attack.	A U.S. grand jury in New York issues an indictment against Saudi millionaire Osama bin Laden, charging him and five members of his alleged terrorist–group, al-Qaeda, in the August bombings of U.S. embassies in Kenya and Tanzania. The State Department offers rewards of $5 million—the largest ever offered by the U.S. for information leading to the conviction or arrest of bin Laden and Muhammed Atef, described as bin Laden's top military commander.	A federal grand jury in Washington, D.C., returns a 42-count indictment charging Franklin Haney with illegally funneling $80,000 of his own money to Democratic campaigns. Haney is the 14th person charged in the Justice Department's campaign finance investigation.	Tropical storm Mitch hits the Florida Keys, southwest Florida, and Cuba, with heavy rain and high winds. Twenty storm-related injuries are reported.		Nov. 4
The Justice Department files a lawsuit against Louisiana for what it charges are inadequacies in the state's juvenile prison system.		Data from the Center for Responsive Politics finds that higher-spending candidates won in 95% of the 1998 congressional races.		Pres. Clinton presents the National Medal of Arts and National Humanities Medal to 19 American cultural figures, a corporation, and a theater company.	Nov. 5
In the wake of unexpected losses by the Republican Party in the Nov. 3 elections, House speaker Newt Gingrich (R, Ga.) announces that he is stepping aside as speaker and leaving Congress. . . . A federal grand jury in Baton Rouge, Louisiana, indicts former Louisiana governor Edwin Edwards (D), his son Stephen Edwards, and four others in an alleged racketeering conspiracy to extort bribes from casino companies seeking riverboat gaming licenses.			Reports indicate that U.S. scientists have succeeded for the first time in isolating and cultivating human embryonic stem cells.		Nov. 6
			A study suggests that women infected with HIV, the virus that causes AIDS, suffer more damage to their immune systems than infected males with similar blood levels of the virus. . . . The *Discovery* touches down at Cape Canaveral, Florida, after carrying out its mission with a crew that includes retiring Sen. John Glenn (D, Ohio), the first American to orbit the Earth.	Awesome Again wins the 15th Breeders' Cup Classic, the richest horse race in history, in Louisville, Kentucky.	Nov. 7

F	G	H	I	J
Includes elections, federal-state relations, civil rights and liberties, crime, the judiciary, education, health care, poverty, urban affairs, and population.	*Includes formation and debate of U.S. foreign and defense policies, veterans' affairs, and defense spending. (Relations with specific foreign countries are usually found under the region concerned.)*	*Includes business, labor, agriculture, taxation, transportation, consumer affairs, monetary and fiscal policy, natural resources, and pollution.*	*Includes worldwide scientific, medical, and technological developments; natural phenomena; U.S. weather; natural disasters; and accidents.*	*Includes the arts, religion, scholarship, communications media, sports, entertainments, fashions, fads, and social life.*

	World Affairs	Europe	Africa & the Middle East	The Americas	Asia & the Pacific
Nov. 8		Gerald Long, 75, general manager of Britain's Reuters news agency, 1963–81, and the principal architect of its transformation into a highly successful international news organization, dies in Paris. . . . Jean Marais (born Jean Villain-Marais), 84, French stage and film actor, dies in Cannes, France. . . . Lord (Henry Cecil John) Hunt, 88, British Army colonel who led the 1953 expedition in which Sir Edmund Hillary and Tenzing Norgay became the first people to climb to the top of Mount Everest, dies in Henley, England, while suffering from a heart ailment.	Unidentified gunmen attack an Angolan diamond mine in the village of Yetwene, some 350 miles (560 km) east of the capital, Luanda. Eight people die in the attack.		A Bangladeshi judge convicts and sentences to death 15 people in the 1975 assassination of Sheik Mujibur Rahman, the country's independence leader and the father of current prime minister Sheik Hasina Wazed. He acquits four other people. Five of the accused assassins are present for the verdict. The rest are believed to be out of the country. After the verdict, thousands of Mujibur supporters celebrate the convictions on the streets of Dhaka. In Chittagong, dozens of stores and vehicles are damaged by people on a rampage after hearing the verdict.
Nov. 9	At an emergency summit in San Salvador, Honduran president Carlos Flores Facusse, Nicaraguan president Arnoldo Aleman Lacayo, Salvadoran president Armando Calderon Sol, and Costa Rican president Miguel Angel Rodriguez, along, with Guatemalan foreign minister Eduardo Stein, appeal for international aid in the wake of hurricane Mitch.	The Tajik government, with the assistance of former opposition groups, drives a large band of antigovernment rebels into the mountains, ending an uprising in northern Tajikistan that was launched Nov. 4. A presidential speaker declares that 40 rebel soldiers and 10 government soldiers were killed during the uprising. However, other estimates put that figure at more than 200.	Rebels attack the town of Pendembu in the northern section of Sierra Leone.	Jennifer Smith, the leader of Bermuda's Progressive Labour Party, is elected prime minister after Labour wins 26 of the 40 seats in the parliamentary assembly.	At least two people die in Dhaka, Bangladesh, during a strike called in response to the Nov. 8 verdict for the assassins of Sheik Mujibur Rahman.
Nov. 10	In response to the Nov. 11 appeal, the French government cancels debts owed by Nicaragua and Honduras, and other nations soon follow suit. The World Bank reveals it will redirect $200 million earmarked for other projects to Honduras, Nicaragua, El Salvador, and Guatemala, and other international aid groups make similar moves.	The British government frees the 200th inmate at the Maze prison to be released ahead of schedule in the government's early-release program. It also announces that it will close the infamous Maze prison near Belfast, Northern Ireland. . . . Svetlana Beriosova, 66, a former leading ballerina with London's Royal Ballet, dies of cancer in London.		Jennifer Smith is sworn in as prime minister of Bermuda.	Reports suggest that Chinese authorities have detained some 140 members of illegally unregistered Protestant groups and severely beaten some of them.
Nov. 11	At an international conference to discuss the Kyoto Protocol, Argentine president Carlos Saul Menem agrees to set binding targets for reducing emissions of carbon dioxide and other greenhouse gases. Argentina thus becomes the first of nearly 120 developing nations to commit to any emissions reductions. Kazakhstan follows with a similar pledge. . . . U.S. president Clinton warns Iraqi president Saddam Hussein that the U.S. is ready to attack Iraq without further notice unless Iraq permits the immediate and unconditional resumption of UN weapons inspections, halted Oct. 31.	Japanese premier Keizo Obuchi visits Russia, marking the first time that a Japanese premier has made an official visit to the country in 25 years. . . . Unidentified abductors kidnap a U.S. missionary, Herbert Gregg, 51, in Makhachkala, the capital of the southern Russian region of Dagestan.	Workers stage the first of planned weekly general strikes across Zimbabwe. Zimbabwean soldiers in the eastern city of Mutare kill a 20-year-old man.	Reports estimate that 11,000 people died from damage incurred by Hurricane Mitch, a storm described as the deadliest Atlantic hurricane in 200 years.	The Philippine navy is ordered to block any other Chinese vessels from entering Mischief Reef in the disputed Spratly Islands chain in the South China Sea. . . . Dozens of dissident Buddhist monks and their supporters occupy the Chogye Temple in Seoul, the capital of South Korea, to protest a move by its leader, Song Wol Ju, to seek a third term. The Chogye order limits its leaders to two terms.
Nov. 12			Reports reveal that the Nov. 9 attack in Sierra Leone left approximately 100 people dead.	The Cuban foreign ministry gives the Associated Press permission to open a permanent bureau in Havana, the capital. Only one other U.S.-based news organization, Cable News Network (CNN), has a permanent bureau in Cuba.	A court in Guangzhou convicts a Hong Kong organized crime boss, Cheung Tze-keung, of kidnapping, armed robbery, and smuggling explosives, and sentences him and four associates to death. The court also hands down jail terms to some 30 other gangsters linked to Cheung, nicknamed "Big Spender" for his lavish tastes.

A	B	C	D	E
Includes developments that affect more than one world region, international organizations, and important meetings of major world leaders.	Includes all domestic and regional developments in Europe, including the Soviet Union, Turkey, Cyprus, and Malta.	Includes all domestic and regional developments in Africa and the Middle East, including Iraq and Iran and excluding Cyprus, Turkey, and Afghanistan.	Includes all domestic and regional developments in Latin America, the Caribbean, and Canada.	Includes all domestic and regional developments in Asia and Pacific nations, extending from Afghanistan through all the Pacific Island, except Hawaii.

U.S. Politics & Social Issues	U.S. Foreign Policy & Defense	U.S. Economy & Environment	Science, Technology, & Nature	Culture, Leisure, & Lifestyle	
	A U.S. Navy crew member, Lt. Brendan Duffy, is killed, and three others—Lt. Commander Kurt Barich, Lt. Meredith Loughran, and Lt. Charles Woodard—are missing and presumed dead after an EA-6B Prowler airplane crashes into a Viking S-3 plane on the flight deck of the USS *Enterprise*, 120 miles (200 km) off the coast of Virginia.			In tennis, Greg Rusedski of Britain defeats top-ranked Pete Sampras to win the Paris Open. . . . (Margaret) Rumer Godden, 90, British author who wrote novels and children's stories, dies in Dumfriesshire, Scotland.	Nov. 8
	U.S. Customs officials seize 1,600 pounds (500 kg) of cocaine from a detained Colombian air force cargo plane in Fort Lauderdale, Florida. . . . An air force pilot, Major Gregory Martineac, is killed when his F-16 jet crashes 65 miles (105 km) west of Hill Air Force Base. . . . Reports reveal that three army officers—Sergeant William Westgate and Chief Warrant Officers David Guido and Daniel Riddell—have been charged with involuntary manslaughter for a crash that killed two of the officers' wives.	In New York City, Judge Robert Sweet in N.Y.C. approves a $1.03 billion settlement in a class-action lawsuit that investors brought in 1997 against 37 major brokerage houses. The settlement is called "the largest ever in an antitrust class action." . . . A federal grand jury in Little Rock, Arkansas, indicts Yah Lin (Charlie) Trie on charges of obstructing the Senate Governmental Affairs Committee's investigation of 1996 fund-raising abuses.	Several teams of researchers report that a gene injected into the hearts of patients with blocked blood vessels enables the heart to grow its own bypasses.	French author Paule Constant is awarded the Goncourt Prize, France's most coveted literary honor.	Nov. 9
A state appeals court in Santa Ana, California, overturns a 1996 ruling that gave former football star O. J. Simpson custody of his two young children, Sydney, 13, and Justin, 10. . . . A jury in New York City convicts Corey Arthur, 20, of second-degree murder in the 1997 torture and murder of Jonathan Levin, his former high-school English teacher. However, the jury acquits Arthur of first-degree murder charges.	Pres. Clinton signs a measure bringing U.S. law into line with a 1997 international antibribery treaty. . . . Vice Pres. Al Gore announces the creation of a Vietnam Veterans Memorial website, which will list the 58,196 names of U.S. service members cited on the Vietnam Memorial in Washington, D.C. . . . In response to the Nov. 9 seizure in Fort Lauderdale, officials report that drugs have never before been discovered aboard Colombian government planes.		Ground controllers turn on *Deep Space 1*'s ion engine, but the engine shuts down after running for only 4½ minutes.	A group of several hundred conservative Baptists votes to sever ties with the Baptist General Convention of Texas. . . . Hal (Harold) Newhouser, 77, Hall of Fame baseball pitcher, dies in Southfield, Michigan, while suffering from emphysema and heart ailments.	Nov. 10
		Pennzoil Co., an oil company based in Houston, Texas, announces it has agreed to pay $6.75 million to settle an employment-discrimination lawsuit brought on behalf of 700 blacks who had worked at the company between 1994 and 1998.	Advanced Cell Technology Inc. announces it has fused a human cell with a cow egg to create hybrid embryonic stem cells. The possible creation of such a cell with a nonhuman species intensifies the ethical debate surrounding stem-cell research.	Kurt Masur, the music director of the New York Philharmonic, announces that, in the year 2000, he will also be the conductor for the London Philharmonic. . . . National Public Radio (NPR) names Kevin Klose its president and chief executive. . . . Patrick (Paddy) Clancy, 76, a member of the Clancy Brothers, a group that popularized traditional Irish music, dies of cancer in Carrick-on-Suir, Ireland.	Nov. 11
Pres. Clinton signs a bill providing $750 million in compensation for hemophiliacs infected with HIV, the virus that causes AIDS, through blood transfusions. . . . Lewis Merletti, the director of the Secret Service, announces that he will step down. . . . The city of Chicago and Cook County, Illinois, sue gun manufacturers, distributors, and stores for $433 million, accusing them of knowingly flooding the city with illegal guns.	Pres. Clinton signs a bill requiring the State Department to report to Congress each year the number of foreign diplomats suspected of committing a serious crime in the U.S.	Chrysler Corp. and Daimler-Benz AG merge to form DaimlerChrysler AG, the world's third-largest automaker in terms of revenue and the fifth-largest in terms of unit sales. The deal, valued at $38.3 billion in May, creates the world's fourth-largest company overall in terms of revenue.	Reports conclude that scientists have not been able to replicate a dramatic reduction of cancer tumors in mice reported by a researcher in May.		Nov. 12
F	**G**	**H**	**I**	**J**	
Includes elections, federal-state relations, civil rights and liberties, crime, the judiciary, education, health care, poverty, urban affairs, and population.	*Includes formation and debate of U.S. foreign and defense policies, veterans' affairs, and defense spending. (Relations with specific foreign countries are usually found under the region concerned.)*	*Includes business, labor, agriculture, taxation, transportation, consumer affairs, monetary and fiscal policy, natural resources, and pollution.*	*Includes worldwide scientific, medical, and technological developments; natural phenomena; U.S. weather; natural disasters; and accidents.*	*Includes the arts, religion, scholarship, communications media, sports, entertainments, fashions, fads, and social life.*	

	World Affairs	Europe	Africa & the Middle East	The Americas	Asia & the Pacific
Nov. 13	The IMF and the U.S. announce a $42 billion aid package designed to stave off the collapse of Brazil's beleaguered economy.	Chechen abductors free Valentin Vlasov, Russian president Yeltsin's personal envoy who was kidnapped in May. . . . Both the minority government and the largest opposition party lose seats in Senate elections in the Czech Republic. . . . Edwige Feuillere (born Edwige Caroline Cunati), 91, French actress, dies in Paris. . . . Valerie Babette Louise Hobson, 81, British actress, dies of a heart attack in London.		Canada reports that in the first nine months of 1998, it accepted 604 refugees displaced within the borders of their home countries by war or terrorism. . . . Michel Trudeau, 23, the youngest of former Prime Minister Pierre Trudeau's three sons, drowns after being swept into a frigid mountain lake by an avalanche in Kokanee Glacier Provincial Park in British Columbia, Canada.	In Indonesia, police open fire on demonstrators in an effort to stop a mass march on the Parliament building in Jakarta. Sixteen students are killed at the National Monument.
Nov. 14	Representatives from the 21 member nations of the Asia-Pacific Economic Cooperation (APEC) trade group gather in Malaysia for a summit. . . . Delegates from more than 160 nations endorse the "Buenos Aires Action Plan," under which they agree to devise, by the year 2000, strategies for carrying out the emissions reductions called for in the Kyoto treaty.	The England rugby team defeats the Netherlands, 110-0, at the European World Cup qualifying match. The score sets a new English record for points in an international match, breaking a record set in 1881.	Laurence Owen Vine Gandar, 82, South African journalist who was one of the first prominent journalists to challenge his country's apartheid policies, dies in Pietermaritzburg, South Africa, while suffering from Parkinson's disease.		
Nov. 15	U.S. president Clinton announces that Iraq has "backed down" and promised to cooperate unconditionally with UN weapons inspectors, ending a crisis that started Oct. 31. U.S. and British forces, which aborted a planned air strike against Iraq, remain on combat readiness in the region. The Security Council instructs UNSCOM inspectors to return to Iraq.				
Nov. 16	The International Tribunal for the Former Yugoslavia convicts Hazim Delic and Esad Landzo and Zdravco Mucic for crimes committed while running the Celebici prison camp in 1992. Delic and Landzo are the first alleged war criminals charged with committing crimes against Serbs and the first Moslems accused of war crimes. . . . Data reveal that record global temperatures were set from January through September. October was the first month of the year to fall short with an average global temperature was 58.14° F (15°C), just short of the record of 58.15°F set in October 1997.		Rebels claim to have seized the port of Moba on Lake Tanganyika, on Congo's eastern border.		
Nov. 17	The UN Security Council adopts a resolution calling on Yugoslav president Slobodan Milosevic to allow international investigators into the Serbian province of Kosovo to gather evidence of war crimes.	German chancellor Gerhard Schroeder meets with Russian president Boris Yeltsin during his first visit to the country as the leader of Germany. . . . Kurdish groups orchestrate several demonstrations in Rome to protest the arrest of Kurdish separatist Abdullah Ocalan in Italy. . . . A court in Versailles disqualifies right-wing politician Jean-Marie Le Pen from holding political office for one year for assaulting a legislative candidate. . . . Jacques Medecin, 70, former mayor of Nice, France, dies in Uruguay.	George Saadeh, 67, the leader since 1986 of the right-wing Phalange Party, Lebanon's largest Christian political faction, dies of colon cancer in a suburb of Beirut.		Reports indicate that Christian leaders have cited about 40 violent attacks in the Indian state of Gujarat during the year.
Nov. 18			Reports confirm that the South African Parliament has passed legislation that will institute strict limits on smoking in public places and allow the health ministry to ban tobacco advertising. . . . As part of a series of weekly protests planned by the Zimbabwe Congress of Trade Unions (ZCTU), workers stage general strikes across Zimbabwe, shutting down almost all of the country's business and industry.	Tara Singh Hayer, a prominent member of Canada's large Sikh population, is shot dead in Surrey, a suburb of Vancouver, British Columbia. . . . The Roman Catholic Church in Cuba states the government has authorized the arrival of 19 foreign priests, bringing the number of Catholic priests working on the island to 305.	A UN report finds that 62% of North Korean children suffer from stunted growth due to undernourishment and that 16% of children are acutely malnourished. North Korea has been undergoing a food crisis for years. . . . In Indonesia, students are permitted to hold a memorial for the victims of the Nov. 13 protest at the National Monument in which police killed 16 people.

A	B	C	D	E
Includes developments that affect more than one world region, international organizations, and important meetings of major world leaders.	Includes all domestic and regional developments in Europe, including the Soviet Union, Turkey, Cyprus, and Malta.	Includes all domestic and regional developments in Africa and the Middle East, including Iraq and Iran and excluding Cyprus, Turkey, and Afghanistan.	Includes all domestic and regional developments in Latin America, the Caribbean, and Canada.	Includes all domestic and regional developments in Asia and Pacific nations, extending from Afghanistan through all the Pacific Island, except Hawaii.

U.S. Politics & Social Issues	U.S. Foreign Policy & Defense	U.S. Economy & Environment	Science, Technology, & Nature	Culture, Leisure, & Lifestyle	
Pres. Clinton agrees to pay $850,000 to settle Paula Corbin Jones's sexual-harassment lawsuit against him. Clinton admits no wrongdoing and offers no apology to Jones.... In Little Rock, Arkansas, Judge Jerry Cavaneau voids a 1997 state Arkansas law banning the late-term abortion procedure known as IDE. Cavaneau states the law is so broadly worded that it could be used to bar all abortions in the state.... A court approves a $115.5 million settlement of two shareholders' class-action lawsuits against Philip Morris, the nation's largest cigarette producer.		Independent counsel Kenneth Starr's Whitewater grand jury indicts Webster Hubbell, First Lady Hillary Rodham Clinton's former law partner, for the third time.	Paleontologists report the discovery of a new species of spinosaur, *Suchomimus tenerensis*, in the Tenere desert region of Niger. It is the most complete spinosaur fossil ever found.	Charges of criminal neglect or abuse of a disabled adult and unlicensed practicing of medicine are filed against the Church of Scientology, stemmed from the 1995 death of Lisa McPherson.... Red Holzman (born William Holzman), 78, basketball coach inducted into the Hall of Fame in 1991, dies in New York of complications from leukemia.	Nov. 13
A New York City law requiring safety locking devices for handguns takes effect.	Reports reveal that Clinton administration officials have acknowledged that one of the unspoken objectives of an August bombing raid on Afghanistan was to kill suspected terrorist Osama bin Laden and his associates.			Reports confirm that Carolyn Kizer and Maxine Kumin have resigned as chancellors of the Academy of American Poets to protest the "insularity" and "elitism" of the academy's 12-member board of chancellors.	Nov. 14
Kwame Ture (born Stokely Carmichael), 57, 1960s-era civil-rights activist whose stance on racial issues grew increasingly radical as the decade progressed, dies in Conakry, Guinea, of prostate cancer.					Nov. 15
A California jury acquits gun manufacturer Beretta U.S.A. Corp. of negligence stemming from the death of Kenzo Dix, 15, who was accidentally shot by a friend in 1994.... Tyrone. Gilliam, 32, convicted of murder, is executed in Baltimore, Maryland. Gilliam is the 487th person in the U.S. and only the third in Maryland to be executed since 1976.... The attorneys general of eight states disclose the terms for a proposed $206 billion settlement of all outstanding state lawsuits against the tobacco industry.		In *Wright v. Universal Maritime Service Corp.*, the Supreme Court rules unanimously that a union member has a right to pursue a discrimination claim in federal court, despite the fact that a clause in the union member's labor agreement suggests that disputes should be resolved by arbitration.		New York City honors 77-year-old Sen. John Glenn (D, Ohio) and the other six crew members of the U.S. space shuttle *Discovery* with a ticker tape parade in lower Manhattan.	Nov. 16
A grand jury in NYC indicts six men on charges relating to a melee that broke out at the end of a September rally known as the "Million Youth March."....U.S. Supreme Court chief justice William Rehnquist issues a letter to three black members of Congress in which he rejects assertions that Supreme Court justices discriminate against minorities when hiring law clerks.... Reports state that three states—Arizona, Iowa, and Arkansas—have agreed to join the settlement terms disclosed Nov. 16 in suits against the tobacco industry.		The Federal Reserve Board reduces the federal-funds rate to 4.75% from 5%. The discount rate, the largely symbolic rate the Fed charges on loans it makes to commercial banks, is reduced to 4.5% from 4.75%. It is the Fed's third such cut in seven weeks. A number of commercial banks cut their prime rate to 7.75% from 8%.	Paleontologists announce the discovery of a dinosaur nesting site in Argentina that contains the richest trove of dinosaur eggs ever found. ...In San Jose, California, U.S. district judge Ronald Whyte orders Microsoft to stop distributing the company's version of Java, a computer-programming language created by Sun Microsystems Inc.... The Earth passes through a storm of meteors, most of which are the size of a grain of sand, trailing comet 55P/Tempel-Tuttle.	Esther Rolle, 78, actress known for 1970s TV shows, dies in Los Angeles, California, after suffering from diabetes and receiving dialysis.... Yefim Petrovich Geller, 73, Soviet-born chess grandmaster, dies in Moscow, Russia.... Weeb (Wilbur Charles) Ewbank, 91, pro football Hall of Fame coach, dies in Oxford, Ohio, of unreported causes.	Nov. 17
		The Bureau of Labor Statistics announces that it will change the way the CPI is calculated in January 1999. The change, which will likely increase inflation calculations slightly, will involve the method the agency uses to assess the impact of pollution-control modifications on prices.		The National Book Foundation presents its fiction award to Alice McDermott and the nonfiction prize to Edward Ball. John Updike receives the 1998 National Book Foundation Medal for Distinguished Contribution to American Letters.	Nov. 18

F	G	H	I	J
Includes elections, federal-state relations, civil rights and liberties, crime, the judiciary, education, health care, poverty, urban affairs, and population.	Includes formation and debate of U.S. foreign and defense policies, veterans' affairs, and defense spending. (Relations with specific foreign countries are usually found under the region concerned.)	Includes business, labor, agriculture, taxation, transportation, consumer affairs, monetary and fiscal policy, natural resources, and pollution.	Includes worldwide scientific, medical, and technological developments; natural phenomena; U.S. weather; natural disasters; and accidents.	Includes the arts, religion, scholarship, communications media, sports, entertainments, fashions, fads, and social life.

	World Affairs	Europe	Africa & the Middle East	The Americas	Asia & the Pacific
Nov. 19		Officials at the Paris Bourse, France's main stock exchange, reveal the market will participate in an electronic-trading alliance announced by Britain's London Stock Exchange and Germany's Deutsche Bourse in July.			A cruise ship carrying the first South Korean tourists to visit North Korea since 1950 docks in Changjon. . . . Two medical studies find that some 2,000 people die daily in China due to smoking-related illnesses, and they predict that if present trends in smoking continue, the number will increase to 8,000 by the year 2050.
Nov. 20	Reports conclude that several international organizations and foreign governments, including Brazil, France, the U.S., Austria, Sweden, Britain, Canada, Spain, the IMF, the World Bank, and the UN World Food program, have pledged relief in the form of debt forgiveness, emergency funds, supplies, and military support for the countries ravaged by Hurricane Mitch in late October.	The ethnic Albanian Kosovo Liberation Army (now known under the acronym KLA) allegedly ambushes a Serbian police vehicle, killing two Serbian officers and wounding three others. . . . Two unidentified assailants shoot and kill Russia's leading female politician, Galina Starovoitova, in St. Petersburg. Her aide, Ruslan Linkov, is critically wounded in the attack.	Israeli occupation forces pull back from 9.1% of the Palestinian West Bank in the first of a three-tiered redeployment outlined in the Wye Memorandum, an interim agreement signed by Israel and the PNA in late October. In keeping with the accord, Israel also releases 250 Palestinian prisoners. . . . Reports confirm that the government of Zimbabwe's Pres. Robert Mugabe has sent some 1,500 military police officers to control its approximately 6,000 troops in Congo.		The Pakistani government declares a state of emergency in the southern province of Sindh in an attempt to stop violence between ethnic rivals that has left as many as 1,000 people dead in 1998.
Nov. 21		Italian officials release Kurdish separatist leader Abdullah Ocalan, who was arrested earlier in Rome. Ocalan is the head of the Kurdistan Workers' Party (PKK), the main Kurdish rebel group, which operates largely in Turkey, Iraq, and Syria. His arrest has been the subject of many protests.	Kenyan officials announce that the government has instituted a 2-billion-shilling (US$34 million) bailout of the National Bank of Kenya Ltd. (NBK), one of the country's largest commercial banks. . . . Israel and Britain commit to increased cooperation in weapons research.		
Nov. 22			In Iran, veteran nationalist dissident, Dariush Foruhar, and his wife, Parvaneh are discovered stabbed to death in their home in Teheran, the capital. . . . College students demonstrate in West Jerusalem in continuation of a month-long strike for lower tuition costs and higher priority for education. . . . Senior Iraqi leader Izzat Ibrahim escapes injury during an attempt on his life in the city of Karbala, some 60 miles (100 km) south of Baghdad, the capital.		
Nov. 23	The UN AIDS Program reveals that in 1998 the number of people infected with HIV rose to 33.4 million, from 27.6 million in 1997. The report predicts that some 2.5 million people will die of AIDS in 1998. Some 14 million people have died of AIDS since the disease was recognized. Some 95% of the new infections in 1998 occurred in Africa, Asia, and Eastern Europe. . . . The EU partially lifts a 1996 ban on British exports of beef off the bone from relatively young cattle.	Ilich Ramirez Sanchez, a self-styled "professional revolutionary" known as "Carlos the Jackal," announces that he is ending a hunger strike begun in prison on November 3. Carlos, who was jailed in 1997 on murder charges, contended that he was unfairly placed in solitary confinement.		Some 200 policemen in Mexico City, Mexico, are arrested on various criminal charges in a crackdown on police corruption by newly appointed police chief Alejandro Gertz.	U.S. president Bill Clinton concludes a trip to Asia that included stops in Japan and South Korea.
Nov. 24		Thousands of mourners wait in the bitter cold for as long as five hours to view the coffin of Galina Starovoitova, murdered Nov. 20, as it lays in state. Starovoitova is buried on the grounds of the Alexander Nevsky monastery—one of the highest honors St. Petersburg accords to prominent citizens—and her funeral is attended by three former premiers—Sergei Kiriyenko, Yegor Gaidar, and Viktor Chernomyrdin.	Israel allows the self-rule Palestinian National Authority (PNA) to open the Gaza International Airport in the southern Gaza Strip. . . . General Emile Lahoud takes the oath of office as the president of Lebanon.	Retired Argentine admiral Emilio Eduardo Massera is arrested in connection with the abduction of babies from the Navy Mechanics School, which he had commanded in the 1970s. He was allegedly part of a system under which the newborn infants of female political prisoners were taken from them immediately following birth and given up for adoption to military couples. Many of the women were then killed.	Australian federal justice Malcolm Lee rules that the Miriuwung Gajerrong, an aboriginal group, holds native title over more than 4,350 square miles (7,000 sq km) of land across northern portions of Western Australia and the Northern Territory. Justice Lee's decision marks the first determination of native title on the Australian mainland.
	A	**B**	**C**	**D**	**E**
	Includes developments that affect more than one world region, international organizations, and important meetings of major world leaders.	*Includes all domestic and regional developments in Europe, including the Soviet Union, Turkey, Cyprus, and Malta.*	*Includes all domestic and regional developments in Africa and the Middle East, including Iraq and Iran and excluding Cyprus, Turkey, and Afghanistan.*	*Includes all domestic and regional developments in Latin America, the Caribbean, and Canada.*	*Includes all domestic and regional developments in Asia and Pacific nations, extending from Afghanistan through all the Pacific Island, except Hawaii.*

U.S. Politics & Social Issues	U.S. Foreign Policy & Defense	U.S. Economy & Environment	Science, Technology, & Nature	Culture, Leisure, & Lifestyle	
A three-judge panel rules that an admission policy based on race at a Boston public school is unconstitutional. It is the first time that a federal court rules on the constitutionality of race-based policies in a public school.... Independent counsel Kenneth Starr testifies before the House Judiciary Committee about his investigation of Pres. Clinton's conduct in the Monica Lewinsky scandal.... The Postal Service plans to issue a stamp bearing the image of the late civil-rights activist Malcolm X.		Members of the Jersey City Education Association go on strike.... The National Labor Relations Board rules that the Nov. 3 ABC lockout, which affects a total of 2,200 workers, is legal.... William J. McCarthy, 79, labor leader who served as last president of the International Brotherhood of Teamsters not to be chosen by the union's rank and file, 1988–91, dies in Arlington, Massachusetts.	Tetsuya (Ted) Fujita, 78, Japanese-born meteorologist who, with his wife, Sumiko Fujita, devised the standard scale for measuring the strength of tornadoes, dies in Chicago, Illinois.	Alan J. Pakula, 70, respected film producer and director whose films include *Klute* (1971), *All the President's Men* (1976), and *Sophie's Choice* (1982), dies in Suffolk County, New York, after a metal pipe crashed through the windshield of his vehicle, striking him in the head.	Nov. 19
In Washington, D.C., the FBI opens the $20 million Strategic Information and Operations Center at FBI headquarters.... Forty-six states, the District of Columbia, and four U.S. territories agree to the tobacco industry's proposed $206 billion settlement, the largest civil settlement in U.S. history. The deal calls for the country's four largest tobacco companies to pay the states $206 billion over 25 years to repay public health costs related to smoking.	U.S. government officials announce that INS agents arrested 21 suspects in connection with an international immigrant-smuggling ring that smuggled as many as 12,000 illegal immigrants into the U.S. in the course of three years. Officials claim the case is the largest in U.S. history and that it is the first time that such an operation completely uncovers and breaks up, from top to bottom, all those involved.... Data reveals that Mexico is the U.S.'s second-largest trading partner, behind only Canada.	Elmer H. Wavering, 91, who developed the prototype for the first commercial car radio and later became Motorola's president, 1964–72, dies in Naples, Florida.	*Zarya*, an unmanned Russian Proton booster rocket carrying a module of a planned international space station, lifts off from Baikonur Cosmodrome in Kazakhstan.	Christie's and Sotheby's close their NYC fall auctions with combined sales totaling $495 million, slightly lower than 1997 totals.... Israeli police state that they have found 10 of 75 members of Concerned Christians, an apocalyptic sect that left Denver, Colorado, in October in an attempt to escape an earthquake prophesied by their leader.	Nov. 20
					Nov. 21
The television show *60 Minutes* airs footage of Dr. Jack Kevorkian administering lethal injections to Thomas Youk, 52, suffering from ALS, or Lou Gehrig's disease. Youk gave signed consent to the killing. Kevorkian has assisted in more than 120 suicides since 1990, but it was the first time he had directly killed his patient.... A FBI report shows that 13.2 million serious crimes were reported to authorities in 1997, a 2% drop from 1996 and a 7% drop from 1993. It is the sixth consecutive decrease. The country's murder rate of 6.8 per 100,000 residents in 1997 is lower than it has been for 30 years.				Henry Eugene Hampton, 58, documentary filmmaker best known for *Eyes on the Prize*, dies in Boston, Massachusetts, of bone-marrow complications stemming from lung cancer treatment.... Martina Hingis of Switzerland defeats Lindsay Davenport to win the season-ending Chase Championships.... Golfer Laura Davies of England wins the LPGA's Pagenet Tour Championship in Las Vegas, Nevada..... The English team captures England's first World Cup of Golf title.	Nov. 22
The Georgia Supreme Court strikes down, 6-1, the state's 1883 anti-sodomy law on grounds that it violates privacy rights guaranteed by the state constitution. The Georgia court's ruling leaves 18 states with some form of antisodomy law on their books.... Maryland politician Ruthann Aron, 55, is sentenced to three years in jail for her attempt to hire a hit man in June 1997 to kill her husband, Barry Aron, and a Baltimore lawyer, Arthur G. Kahn.		A jury in Santa Monica, California, acquits Susan McDougal in an embezzlement case unrelated to Whitewater.... The Dow closes at a record high of 9374.27. That marks the 29th record high of 1998 and is a 24.3% rise in the Dow from its to-date 1998 low of 7539.07, recorded Aug. 31.	Judge Leonie Brinkema of U.S. District Court in Alexandria, Virginia, issues a permanent injunction forcing Loudon County, Virginia, to stop using filtering software to restrict access to Internet sites on computers in public libraries. The decision is the first ruling barring public libraries from restricting Internet access on terminals available to the general public.		Nov. 23
In Miami, Florida, Judge Donald Graham strikes down a ban against a late-term abortion procedure, ruling that it has "the unconstitutional effect of placing a substantial obstacle in the path of women seeking an abortion prior to the fetus attaining viability."	In New York City, Judge Michael Mukasey sentences Mohammed Abouhalima to eight years in prison for his role in the 1993 World Trade Center bombing.... New York City judge Whitman Knapp sentences Ahmad Suleiman to 10 months in prison for his role in the 1993 World Trade Center bombing.	In Washington, D.C., Judge Henry Kennedy orders Democratic fund-raiser Howard Glicken to pay a fine of $80,000 and perform 500 hours of community service. Glicken, a supporter and friend of Vice Pres. Al Gore, pled guilty in July to illegally soliciting a $20,000 contribution to the Democratic Senatorial Campaign Committee in 1993.	The ion engine that propels *Deep Space 1*, an unmanned spacecraft, is successfully restarted by a signal from ground controllers.... America Online Inc. (AOL), which provides access to the Internet, announces plans to acquire software firm Netscape Communications Corp. AOL also reveals that it has entered into a three-year marketing alliance with Sun Microsystems Inc., which owns a widely used computer-programming language called Java.	John Chadwick, 78, British classicist who in the early 1950s collaborated with Michael Ventris in deciphering the ancient Greek script known as Linear B, dies.... Rod McGeoch, who led the bid to bring the 2000 Summer Olympic Games to Sydney, Australia, resigns from the Olympic organizing committee.	Nov. 24
F	G	H	I	J	
Includes elections, federal-state relations, civil rights and liberties, crime, the judiciary, education, health care, poverty, urban affairs, and population.	*Includes formation and debate of U.S. foreign and defense policies, veterans' affairs, and defense spending. (Relations with specific foreign countries are usually found under the region concerned.)*	*Includes business, labor, agriculture, taxation, transportation, consumer affairs, monetary and fiscal policy, natural resources, and pollution.*	*Includes worldwide scientific, medical, and technological developments; natural phenomena; U.S. weather; natural disasters; and accidents.*	*Includes the arts, religion, scholarship, communications media, sports, entertainments, fashions, fads, and social life.*	

	World Affairs	Europe	Africa & the Middle East	The Americas	Asia & the Pacific
Nov. 25	In a reversal of an Oct. 11 decision by Britain's High Court, Britain's highest court, the Appellate Committee of the House of Lords, rules that Gen. Augusto Pinochet Ugarte, Chile's former military leader, is not immune from arrest. Pinochet was arrested in London in October after Spanish officials requested his extradition to face charges of torture, terrorism, and genocide.... The IMF announces that it has approved a financial aid package for Pakistan valued at $5.5 billion.	Amid allegations of corruption and links to organized crime, the government of Premier Mesut Yilmaz collapses when it loses a vote of confidence in Turkey's parliament, the Grand National Assembly. It is the first time a government in Turkey has been brought down over allegations of corruption.		The British court's ruling this day regarding the arrest of Gen. Augusto Pinochet Ugarte sparks protests by pro- and anti-Pinochet demonstrators in Santiago, Chile's capital, and in the city of Concepcion. Police, who use water cannons and riot shields to control the crowds, arrest some 120 people.	Chinese president Jiang Zemin makes the fist visit to Japan by a president of communist China.... Reports confirm that Premier Tofilau Eti Alesana, 74, the longest-serving head of government in the South Pacific, has resigned 16 years after first taking office as Samoa's leader. Samoa's legislative assembly elected Tuilaepa Sailele Malielegaoi as premier.... Cambodia's National Assembly elects Prince Norodom Ranariddh as its president.... Reports reveal that a UN human-rights investigator was blocked entry to Myanmar by the government.
Nov. 26		Tony Blair becomes the first British prime minister ever to address the Irish Parliament.... A Bosnian Serb team exhumes 55 bodies from two sites in a cemetery in Sarajevo. There is disagreement as to whether these sites represent a mass grave from the Bosnian war of 1992–95. It is the first suspected mass grave opened in Sarajevo, the Bosnian capital.	Two members of the UN World Food Program are shot to death, and another one is wounded in northern Angola.... In Iran, thousands of people attend the funeral of dissident Dariush Foruhar and his wife, Parvaneh, who were found dead on Nov. 22. Mourners chant "Down with despotism," in an oblique accusation that the killings were politically motivated.		The Singapore government states it will lift restrictions imposed on Chia Thye Poh, an opposition politician who, since 1989, has been allowed to live on the island of Sentosa but is barred from any political activity.
Nov. 27		In Dublin, Ireland, a three-judge panel convicts admitted drug dealer Paul Ward of participating in a plot to murder investigative journalist Veronica Guerin in 1996. Ward, 34, is sentenced to life in prison.... German chancellor Gerhard Schroeder states that his government will not seek the extradition of Abdullah Ocalan, a Kurdish rebel leader arrested in Italy and wanted in Germany on charges of arson and incitement to murder.... A Turkish military helicopter crashes, killing 15 soldiers and injuring one.			
Nov. 28		Thousands of ethnic Turks demonstrate throughout Germany to protest the decision made Nov. 28 by German chancellor Gerhard Schroeder to not seek the extradition of Abdullah Ocalan, a Kurdish rebel leader, from Italy.... The National Liberation Army of Kurdistan, the military wing of the PKK, claims that it shot down the helicopter that crashed Nov. 27. The incident is widely linked to Ocalan's detention.		A court in Rio de Janeiro, Brazil, acquits 10 policemen charged with the killings of 21 residents of the Vigario Geral neighborhood in Rio in 1993.	
Nov. 29		Swiss voters overwhelmingly reject a proposal that would have legalized narcotics including marijuana, heroin, and cocaine.			The Chinese government decrees that state organizations and the ruling Communist Party will be required to relinquish their business enterprises.... In a dispute that has been escalating since Nov. 11, the Philippine navy seizes a group of 20 Chinese fishermen near Mischief Reef, an area in the disputed Spratly Islands chain in the South China Sea.
Nov. 30	The UN World Heritage Committee calls on the Australian government to shut down the Jabiluka mine, located within Kakadu National Park, while the government compiles a report to decide whether to list Kakadu, on the UN's list of world heritage sites, as a "world heritage in danger" site.... Delegates representing 44 nations gather in Washington, D.C., for the second annual conference on efforts to recover missing assets from the Nazi Holocaust era.		According to the final results of the Palestine National Authority's first official census, Palestinians in the West Bank, including East Jerusalem, and the Gaza Strip number 2,895,683. The report projects that the Palestinian population of the occupied territories will grow to 3.2 million in the year 2000 and to 7.4 million by 2025.		Chinese authorities arrest five activists involved in attempting to form an independent political party, the China Democracy Party. Two of those arrested, Xu Wenli and Qin Yongmin, are leading members of the party and among China's most prominent dissidents.... Cambodia's National Assembly approves a coalition government, electing Hun Sen as its premier.

A	B	C	D	E
Includes developments that affect more than one world region, international organizations, and important meetings of major world leaders.	Includes all domestic and regional developments in Europe, including the Soviet Union, Turkey, Cyprus, and Malta.	Includes all domestic and regional developments in Africa and the Middle East, including Iraq and Iran and excluding Cyprus, Turkey, and Afghanistan.	Includes all domestic and regional developments in Latin America, the Caribbean, and Canada.	Includes all domestic and regional developments in Asia and Pacific nations, extending from Afghanistan through all the Pacific Island, except Hawaii.

U.S. Politics & Social Issues	U.S. Foreign Policy & Defense	U.S. Economy & Environment	Science, Technology, & Nature	Culture, Leisure, & Lifestyle	
Michigan prosecutors charge Dr. Jack Kevorkian with first-degree murder for the videotaped euthanasia of Thomas Youk, 52, who was suffering from ALS, or Lou Gehrig's disease. Youk's death was nationally televised in a Nov. 22 airing of the CBS news program *60 Minutes*. Kevorkian has assisted in more than 120 suicides since 1990, but this marks the first time in which he had directly killed his patient.			Kenneth C. Brugger, 80, an amateur naturalist who in 1975 discovered the location southwest of Mexico City, Mexico, where migrating North American monarch butterflies spend the winter months, dies in Austin, Texas, of unreported causes.	Flip (Clerow) Wilson, 64, the first black host of a successful weekly variety show on network TV, dies of liver cancer in Malibu, California. . . . The Anaheim Angels sign Mo Vaughn to a six-year, $80 million deal that gives him the highest annual salary of any professional baseball player. The New York Yankees match the largest contract in baseball history, signed by Mike Piazza with the New York Mets, in an offer to Bernie Williams.	Nov. 25
					Nov. 26
Pres. Clinton responds to a list of 81 questions asked by a House panel regarding the evidence Kenneth Starr gathered in the scandal involving Monica Lewinsky. . . . Martin Gurule, a death-row inmate, escapes from a Texas prison complex in Huntsville, 50 miles (80 km) north of Houston. He is the first person to escape from death row in Texas since 1934. . . . An unidentified man shoots and kills a Seattle, Washington, bus driver, Mark McLaughlin, causing his bus with 35 passengers to fall 50 feet, crashing through the edge of a building roof.		A General Accounting Office (GAO) report finds that the U.S. Postal Service lost $84.7 million on new products it developed to compete with electronic bill-payment systems.	Scientists report the discovery of a fossil that may be the oldest flowering plant ever found. The 142-million-year-old fossil, found in northeastern China, preserves the woody stem and pea-pod-like fruit of an early flowering plant.	Pope John Paul II announces that Roman Catholics may earn "indulgences," grants of amnesty from punishment for sinful acts, by performing charitable works or by refraining from minor vices. The granting of indulgences prompted Martin Luther to rebel against the papacy, which ultimately led to the Protestant Reformation of the 16th century.	Nov. 27
Dante B. Fascell, 81, (D, Fa.), who served in the U.S. House of Representatives, 1955–93, dies of cancer in Clearwater, Florida.		Pres. Clinton announces that HUD will allocate $822 million to nonprofit and housing agencies that help provide housing to low-income people who are elderly or disabled.		Theodore Newhouse, 95, cofounder of a family-owned publishing empire whose properties include several dozen U.S. newspapers, dies in New York City.	Nov. 28
		Members of the Jersey City Education Association, a union that represents more than 3,500 public-school teachers, secretaries, and teachers' aides in Jersey City, New Jersey, votes to approve a new three-year contract, ending a strike that started Nov. 19.		Tennis player Alex Corretja of Spain wins the season-ending ATP Tour World Championship in Hanover, Germany.	Nov. 29
Vanderbilt University in Nashville, Tennesee, announces that it has received a gift of stock, currently valued at more than $300 million, from Martha Ingram, the chairwoman of Ingram Industries Inc. Observers suggest the Ingram bequest is perhaps the largest private donation ever made to a college or university in the U.S. . . . Police in Seattle, Washington, confirm that Silas Cool, a homeless man originally from Plainfield, New Jersey, shot bus driver Mark McLaughlin on Nov. 27 with a handgun and then shot himself.				*A Man in Full*, by Tom Wolfe tops the bestseller list.	Nov. 30

F	G	H	I	J
Includes elections, federal-state relations, civil rights and liberties, crime, the judiciary, education, health care, poverty, urban affairs, and population.	Includes formation and debate of U.S. foreign and defense policies, veterans' affairs, and defense spending. (Relations with specific foreign countries are usually found under the region concerned.)	Includes business, labor, agriculture, taxation, transportation, consumer affairs, monetary and fiscal policy, natural resources, and pollution.	Includes worldwide scientific, medical, and technological developments; natural phenomena; U.S. weather; natural disasters; and accidents.	Includes the arts, religion, scholarship, communications media, sports, entertainments, fashions, fads, and social life.

	World Affairs	Europe	Africa & the Middle East	The Americas	Asia & the Pacific
Dec. 1	Environment Minister Robert Hill reveals that the Australian government will defy an order issued Nov. 30 by the UN to close down the Jabiluka uranium mine in Kakadu National Park.		Police in Cairo, the capital of Egypt, arrest Hafez Abu Saada, the secretary general of the Egyptian Organization for Human Rights (EOHR), the country's main independent human-rights group.	The ruling Communist Party in Cuba recommends that Christmas, banned in 1969, may again become a permanent holiday in the country.	
Dec. 2	U.S. and NATO troops arrest Gen. Radislav Krstic, a Bosnian Serb who allegedly committed crimes against humanity during a 1995 Serbian campaign against Srebrenica, a Muslim enclave. Krstic is the highest-ranking official, and the first active military officer, arrested on war-crimes charges to date. . . . The World Bank projects that the average per capita income in the developing world will rise by only 0.4% in 1998, down from the 3.2% gain registered in 1997.	In Kosovo, three ethnic Albanians are killed in what is called an ambush. In a separate incident, one Serb is shot and killed at a KLA roadblock.	Lebanese president Gen. Emile Lahoud names Selim al-Hoss to serve as his premier. . . . Palestinian protests over Israeli-held Palestinian prisoners erupt, prompting days of clashes with Israeli troops on the West Bank.	The Supreme Court in Paraguay orders Gen. Lino Cesar Oviedo back to prison for his role in a 1996 military coup, ruling the presidential decree that freed him was unconstitutional. . . . Reports confirm that three former progovernment fighters in Guatemala were sentenced to death for their role in a March 1982 massacre in which 130 civilians were killed. The convictions are the first war-crimes convictions since Guatemala's civil war, which ended in 1996.	A letter signed by 191 dissidents demanding the release of Chinese Democracy Party leaders Xu Wenli, Qin Yongmin, and Wang Youcai—arrested in November—is made public.
Dec. 3	The WTO reveals that world trade in 1998 slowed to 4%–5%, from the previous year's historic high of 10%. . . . The central banks of 11 European countries cut their benchmark interest rates, bringing nearly all of their rates to an identical level of 3%. . . . Nearly 1,000 delegates from Protestant and Orthodox churches worldwide meet in Harare, Zimbabwe, to mark the 50th anniversary of the World Council of Churches.	In the worst violation of the cease-fire to date, Yugoslav border guards kill eight ethnic Albanians.		In Mexico, the minimum wage is increased by 14% to $3.40 a day. The increase compares to the projected 16% inflation rate.	China demands the release of 20 Chinese fishermen seized Nov. 29 by the Philippine navy near Mischief Reef, an area in the disputed Spratly Islands chain in the South China Sea.
Dec. 4	NATO approves the creation of a so-called rapid reaction extraction force to evacuate cease-fire monitors in the Serbian province of Kosovo in case of emergency. . . . At a Franco-British summit, British prime minister Tony Blair and French president Jacques Chirac sign an agreement to work toward the creation of a unified European Union defense policy.		Reports confirm that Pres. Hafez al-Assad's ruling National Progressive Front coalition has won all 167 seats its candidates ran for in Syrian legislative elections. The remaining 83 seats were captured by independent candidates.		In India, tens of thousands of Christians hold nationwide street demonstrations to protest a rise in attacks on Christians by Hindus. . . . South Korea's armed forces accidentally launch an antiaircraft missile over the city of Inchon. The Nike Hercules missile self-destructs automatically soon after launch, showering a residential area with fragments that injure three people. . . . Two organizers of the of the letter released Dec. 2 in China, Wang Zechen and Wang Wenjiang, are detained in Qishan.
Dec. 5	Reports indicate that Cambodian premier Hun Sen's coalition government has been given Cambodia's seat, vacant since September 1997, in the UN.		Some 700 Palestinian prisoners held in Israeli jails begin a hunger strike to protest their continued incarceration. Protests over their jailings continue. . . . Nigeria holds local elections, marking a major step in its transition to democracy. The country's three biggest political parties take the top slots in the race for seats on 774 local councils.	Reports confirm that Honduras has declared a national state of alert due to widespread epidemics resulting from damage incurred by Hurricane Mitch. Some 20,000 people are suffering from cholera, 31,000 from malaria, and 208,000 from diarrhea. . . . Juan Ramon Hernandez, one of Honduras's most notorious alleged drug traffickers, escapes from jail by walking out of the front gate of the National Penitentiary to a waiting car.	In Taiwan, the Nationalists win 124 seats in the legislature. Citizens in the city of Tainan vote "no" in an unprecedented, nonbinding plebiscite asking whether they wish Taiwan to be ruled by Communist China. . . . Convicted Hong Kong organized-crime boss Cheung Tzekeung and four associates are executed. . . . The last remaining forces of the Khmer Rouge surrender to the Cambodian government. The troops' surrender, broadcast on national TV, is presented as the end of the 30-year-old Khmer Rouge movement.

A	B	C	D	E
Includes developments that affect more than one world region, international organizations, and important meetings of major world leaders.	Includes all domestic and regional developments in Europe, including the Soviet Union, Turkey, Cyprus, and Malta.	Includes all domestic and regional developments in Africa and the Middle East, including Iraq and Iran and excluding Cyprus, Turkey, and Afghanistan.	Includes all domestic and regional developments in Latin America, the Caribbean, and Canada.	Includes all domestic and regional developments in Asia and Pacific nations, extending from Afghanistan through all the Pacific Island, except Hawaii.

U.S. Politics & Social Issues	U.S. Foreign Policy & Defense	U.S. Economy & Environment	Science, Technology, & Nature	Culture, Leisure, & Lifestyle	
In *Minnesota v. Carter*, the Supreme Court rules, 5-4, that individuals who are temporary guests in someone else's home are not entitled to challenge the constitutionality of a police search conducted at the home in which they are staying.... The House Judiciary Committee expands its impeachment investigation of Pres. Clinton by voting to subpoena materials relating to fund-raising practices in his 1996 reelection campaign.	U.S. secretary of defense William Cohen and Colombian defense minister Rodrigo Lloreda sign an agreement that establishes a permanent committee for consultation on issues of defense and security in the two countries.... In Brooklyn, New York, Judge Reena Raggi sentences Lee Peng Fei, a Taiwanese citizen who tried to smuggle hundreds of Chinese immigrants into the U.S. in 1993, to 20 years in prison. Lee is the 22nd and last person to be convicted in the case.	The FEC finds that both the Democrats and the Republicans violated federal campaign finance rules in 1996.... Exxon Corp., the largest energy company in the U.S., announces plans to buy Mobil Corp., the nation's second-largest energy company, in a stock transaction valued at $75.3 billion. If completed, the deal will be the largest merger in history and will create the largest corporation in the world in terms of annual revenue.		Freddie Young, 96, British cinematographer who won the Oscar for cinematography three times, dies in London, England.... Janet Lewis, 99, poet and historical novelist, dies in Los Altos, California.	Dec. 1
In one of the most highly publicized and still unsolved case of the 1950s, the Ohio Supreme Court clears the way for the son of Sam Sheppard, convicted and then acquitted of the 1954 killing of his wife, to proceed to trial with a wrongful-imprisonment suit filed on behalf of his father, who died at age 46 in 1970.... Microsoft chairman William Gates announces a $100 million donation to the Program for Appropriate Technology in Health (PATH) to help accelerate the delivery of vaccines to children in developing countries.	Pakistani prime minister Nawaz Sharif meets with U.S. president Clinton, marking the prime minister's first visit to the U.S. since taking office in February 1997.... Kim Jong Che and Jiang Yong Zhu are convicted for an immigrant-smuggling incident in which a boat carrying 23 illegal Chinese immigrants ran aground in May.... Navy officials announce that Rear Admiral John Scudi was found guilty of violating Defense Department ethics rules and of several other charges including obstruction of justice and adultery.	A federal jury in Washington, D.C. acquits former agriculture secretary Mike Espy of 30 corruption charges involving his acceptance of gifts and favors from businesses regulated by his agency. The jury's decision ends the four-year-long investigation into Espy's conduct by independent counsel Donald Smaltz.			Dec. 2
Rep. Henry Hyde (R, Ill.), the Judiciary Committee's chair, abandons plans to extend the impeachment probe to allegations of Democratic fund-raising abuses in the 1996 elections.... Martin Gurule, the first person to have escaped from death row in Texas since 1934 with his Nov. 27 breakout, is found dead in a river, approximately one mile from the death row complex. Officials suspect that he drowned.		Pres. Clinton announces new regulations aimed at cleaning up the nation's drinking water supply, the first rules to be mandated under the Safe Drinking Water Act of 1996.		Australian Olympic Committee (AOC) Pres. John Coates states that the AOC will have the right to search Australian Olympic athletes' possessions for banned drugs at the 2000 Olympic Games in Sydney.	Dec. 3
In Washington, D.C., Judge Emmet Sullivan reveals that a psychiatrist has found Russell Weston Jr., the alleged gunman in a July shooting spree at the Capitol building, mentally unfit for trial.... A sealed ruling made by Judge Norma Holloway Johnson in April is made public. The judge cleared Kenneth Starr's investigators of allegations that they improperly prevented Monica Lewinsky from telephoning her lawyer when they confronted her with evidence of her relationship with Pres. Clinton in January.	James M. Clark, a former student radical at the University of Wisconsin who had admitted in June to spying for East Germany from 1976 to 1989, is sentenced to 12 years and seven months in prison.... A report by the General Accounting Office (GAO) concludes that officers at Citibank violated internal money-laundering controls by aiding in the transfer of funds belonging to Raul Salinas de Gortari, the brother of a former Mexican president, without investigating the source of his funds.		The U.S. space shuttle *Endeavour* lifts off from Kennedy Space Center in Cape Canaveral, Florida, to launch the second component of an international space station currently undergoing assembly in orbit, and to link the module to a unit put into orbit in November.		Dec. 4
In a rare speaking engagement, Supreme Court justices Anthony Kennedy and Stephen Breyer address a conference of the American Bar Association (ABA).... Albert Arnold Gore Sr., 90, (D, Tenn.), who served in the U.S. Senate, 1953–71, and the House of Representatives, 1939–53, and who is the father of Vice Pres. Al Gore, dies in Carthage, Tennessee.		James Hoffa wins a mail-in election for the presidency of the International Brotherhood of Teamsters labor union after his main rival, Tom Leedham, concedes defeat.			Dec. 5

F	G	H	I	J
Includes elections, federal-state relations, civil rights and liberties, crime, the judiciary, education, health care, poverty, urban affairs, and population.	Includes formation and debate of U.S. foreign and defense policies, veterans' affairs, and defense spending. (Relations with specific foreign countries are usually found under the region concerned.)	Includes business, labor, agriculture, taxation, transportation, consumer affairs, monetary and fiscal policy, natural resources, and pollution.	Includes worldwide scientific, medical, and technological developments; natural phenomena; U.S. weather; natural disasters; and accidents.	Includes the arts, religion, scholarship, communications media, sports, entertainments, fashions, fads, and social life.

	World Affairs	Europe	Africa & the Middle East	The Americas	Asia & the Pacific
Dec. 6			In Yemen, tribesmen abduct four German tourists.... Police in Cairo, the capital of Egypt, release on bail Hafez Abu Saada, the secretary general of the Egyptian Organization for Human Rights (EOHR), the country's main independent human-rights group, who was arrested Dec. 1.... Omar Bongo wins another term as president of Gabon in an election that many electoral observers call unfair.	Hugo Chavez Frias of the Patriotic Pole coalition, is elected president of Venezuela. Chavez had led an unsuccessful coup attempt against the presidency of Carlos Andres Perez Rodriguez in February 1992. ... Reports confirm that Cuban president Fidel Castro Ruz has signed a decree declaring that Christmas Day be restored as a national public holiday, as recommended by the ruling Communist Party on Dec. 1.	
Dec. 7					
Dec. 8		The heads of four foreigners abducted from their residence in Grozny, the capital of Chechnya, in October are discovered on the side of a road in the separatist republic. ... The Estonian parliament votes to amend Estonia's citizenship laws, making it easier for Estonia's Russian-speaking minority—roughly 30% of the population—to obtain Estonian citizenship.			
Dec. 9	British home secretary Jack Straw rules that the extradition case against Gen. Augusto Pinochet Ugarte, Chile's former military leader, may proceed, drawing angry responses from Chile. At a summit of the Southern Common Market (Mercosur), member nations Argentina, Brazil, Paraguay, and Uruguay, along with associate members Bolivia and Chile, sign a declaration that backs Chile's position by supporting state sovereignty.	Switzerland's parliament votes to install Interior Minister Ruth Dreifuss, a member of the Social Democratic Party, as the country's first female president. Dreifuss will succeed Pres. Flavio Cotti.	Sudanese state radio reports that Pres. Omar Hassan al-Bashir has signed a law restoring a multiparty system effective January 1, 1999.... Reports confirm that missing dissident poet Mohammed Mokhtari was found dead in Iran. Mokhtari was involved in efforts to reestablish a banned writers union and to end censorship.	Riot police clash with demonstrators in Vancouver, British Columbia, Canada, where P.M. Jean Chrétien is speaking. At least four demonstrators are injured.... Shaughnessy Cohen, 50, who headed the Commons justice committee since 1995, collapses in the House of Commons and dies in Ottawa, Canada, of a massive brain hemorrhage.... In response to the British ruling regarding Gen. Pinochet, hundreds of demonstrators burn British flags, while police use water cannons to control the crowd in Santiago, the capital of Chile.	In Indonesia, state prosecutors formally question former president Suharto about the source of his vast personal wealth. It is the first such action in Indonesian history.... The Great Hural approves the appointment of Janlaviin Narantsatsralt as Mongolia's new premier.... In Thailand, demonstrators protesting the construction of three power plants clash with police, injuring at least 70 people. Deputy Interior Minister Pinit Charusombat states he will not allow the plants to be built.
Dec. 10	The UN International Criminal Tribunal for the Former Yugoslavia convicts Anto Furundzija, a Bosnian Croat paramilitary leader, of allowing a subordinate to rape a Bosnian Muslim woman and sentences him to 10 years in prison. It is the first time the Yugoslav court has considered war-crimes charges stemming exclusively from rape.... Judge Baltasar Garzon of Spain formally indicts Gen. Augusto Pinochet Ugarte, Chile's former military leader.	Reports confirm that Bulgaria has voted to abolish the death penalty.	The U.S. Committee for Refugees reports that 1.9 million civilians have died in Sudan as a result of the 15-year-old civil war.	Police in Santiago, Chile's capital, reveal they have arrested 51 Pinochet supporters who were trying to reach the residences of the Spanish and British ambassadors on Dec. 9.	Australia's Parliament passes the Antipersonnel Mines Convention Bill 1998, which implements a UN treaty banning the use, production, transfer, and stockpiling of land mines.
Dec. 11		Former dissident and Nobel Prize-winning author Alexander I. Solzhenitsyn declines to accept the Order of St. Andrew, Russia's most prestigious cultural award from Russian president Boris Yeltsin, claiming that he cannot accept the award "from the supreme authority which brought Russia to its current disastrous state."	Reports confirm that Muslim militants killed 81 people in an attack on three northern Algerian villages near Tadjena, approximately 125 miles (200 km) west of Algiers, the capital. The attack is one of the deadliest incidents to occur in the conflict over the past year.... Palestinian protests over Israeli-held Palestinian prisoners, that started Dec. 2 begin to ease after sweeping through Bethlehem, East Jerusalem, Ramallah, and Qalqilyah, leaving four Palestinians dead.	The Canadian government announces that it will pay a total of C$18 million to compensate Canadian veterans who labored in Japanese prisoner-of-war camps during World War II.	A Thai airliner crashes into a swamp and catches fire near the airport in Surat Thani, killing scores of people.

A	B	C	D	E
Includes developments that affect more than one world region, international organizations, and important meetings of major world leaders.	*Includes all domestic and regional developments in Europe, including the Soviet Union, Turkey, Cyprus, and Malta.*	*Includes all domestic and regional developments in Africa and the Middle East, including Iraq and Iran and excluding Cyprus, Turkey, and Afghanistan.*	*Includes all domestic and regional developments in Latin America, the Caribbean, and Canada.*	*Includes all domestic and regional developments in Asia and Pacific nations, extending from Afghanistan through all the Pacific Island, except Hawaii.*

U.S. Politics & Social Issues	U.S. Foreign Policy & Defense	U.S. Economy & Environment	Science, Technology, & Nature	Culture, Leisure, & Lifestyle	
	Protesting farmers in Minnesota, North Dakota, and Montana block several entry points for Canadian trucks hauling farm products for several hours.			The Kennedy Center presents awards to Bill Cosby, Andre Previn, Willie Nelson, Shirley Temple Black, John Kander, and Fred Ebb. . . . Cesar (Cesar Baldaccini), 77, French sculptor who worked in scrap metal, dies in Paris, France, of cancer. . . . The Swedish team wins golfing's Davis Cup.	Dec. 6
A letter by the Supreme Court's chief justice, William Rehnquist, is made public. The letter, addressed to three black members of Congress, rejects assertions that Supreme Court justices discriminate against minorities when hiring law clerks. . . . Reports confirm that former Rep. Michael R. Huffington, (R, Calif.), who in 1994 made a failed bid for the U.S. Senate, admits that he is homosexual.	Pres. Clinton removes Iran from his government's list of major drug-producing countries. . . . A Defense Department assessment finds that satellite maker Hughes Electronics Corp. revealed sensitive technological information to the Chinese, damaging U.S. national security.		Martin Rodbell, 73, biochemist and cowinner of the 1994 Nobel Prize in medicine and physiology for research during the 1960s and 1970s into the communications system that regulates cellular activity, dies in Chapel Hill, North Carolina, of cardiovascular disease.		Dec. 7
In Trenton, New Jersey, Judge Anne Thompson strikes down a 1997 New Jersey law banning a late-term abortion procedure, ruling that the law is too vaguely written. . . . In *Knowles v. Iowa*, the Supreme Court rules unanimously that police officers do not have a right to conduct a full search of motorists' vehicles after ticketing motorists for minor traffic violations. . . . White House lawyers begin to present their defense of Pres. Clinton to the House Judiciary Committee, which is considering whether to recommend impeaching the president.	Hamilton Hawkins Howze, 89, mastermind of helicopter warfare tactics pioneered by the U.S. in the Vietnam War, dies in Fort Worth, Texas.			The FBI releases nearly all of its 1,300-page file on the entertainer Frank Sinatra, who died in May at the age of 82.	Dec. 8
		The Conservation Fund, a nonprofit environmental group, agrees to purchase nearly 300,000 acres (120,000 hectares) of forests and wetlands located in New Hampshire, New York State, and Vermont.	Scientists in South Africa announce they have discovered a skeleton believed to belong to a member of the genus of human forerunners known as australopithecines. The nearly intact skeleton, estimated to be between 3.2 and 3.6 million years old, is among the oldest australopithecine remains ever found . . . . Scientists in Japan reveal they have created eight calves cloned from a single adult cows. It is the third confirmed instance of the cloning of an adult mammal.	Archie Moore (born Archibald Lee Wright), 84, boxer who won the world light heavyweight title in 1952 and successfully defended it nine times, dies in San Diego, California.	Dec. 9
Prosecutors charge NYC real-estate developer Abe Hirschfeld, 79, with hiring a hit man to kill his longtime business associate, Stanley Stahl. . . . In New York City, Judge Marcy Kahn sentences Corey Arthur, 20, to 25 years in prison for killing his former teacher, Jonathan Levin in May 1997. . . . The House Judiciary Committee debates the articles of impeachment against Pres. Clinton.	The U.S. Army charges Major General David Hale with 17 counts of misconduct for his "improper relationships" with the wives of four army officers under his command. . . . president Clinton announces increased funding for nongovernmental human-rights organizations and a new Genocide Early Warning Center in Washington, D.C. The announcement marks the 50th anniversary of the Universal Declaration of Human Rights, adopted by the UN in 1948.	The six-member Federal Election Commission (FEC) rejects recommendations by its own campaign auditors to take action against the Democratic and Republican 1996 presidential campaigns over their use of so-called issue advertising.			Dec. 10
The House Judiciary Committee approves three articles of impeachment against Pres. Clinton, accusing him of lying under oath and obstructing justice in an effort to conceal a sexual relationship with Monica Lewinsky. . . . A study finds the number of abortion providers in the U.S. dropped by 14% between 1992 and 1996. About 650 late-term abortions were performed in the U.S. in 1996, out of an estimated 1.4 million procedures.		Former Rhode Island governor Edward DiPrete (R) pleads guilty to 18 charges of corruption for extorting bribes from contractors while he was in office between 1985 and 1991. Judge Francis Darigan sentences the former governor to one year in prison.	NASA launches the *Mars Climate Orbiter*, an unmanned spacecraft, atop a Delta-2 rocket from Cape Canaveral, Florida. The craft is to orbit the planet Mars and collect data on its weather patterns. . . . Two teams of scientists report they have completed a map of the entire genome, or genetic code, of a microscopic worm. The mapping of the genome of the worm, *Caenorhabditis elegans*, marks the first time that scientists have deciphered the entire genetic map of a multicellular animal.		Dec. 11

F	G	H	I	J
Includes elections, federal-state relations, civil rights and liberties, crime, the judiciary, education, health care, poverty, urban affairs, and population.	*Includes formation and debate of U.S. foreign and defense policies, veterans' affairs, and defense spending. (Relations with specific foreign countries are usually found under the region concerned.)*	*Includes business, labor, agriculture, taxation, transportation, consumer affairs, monetary and fiscal policy, natural resources, and pollution.*	*Includes worldwide scientific, medical, and technological developments; natural phenomena; U.S. weather; natural disasters; and accidents.*	*Includes the arts, religion, scholarship, communications media, sports, entertainments, fashions, fads, and social life.*

	World Affairs	Europe	Africa & the Middle East	The Americas	Asia & the Pacific
Dec. 12	China severs its ties to the Marshall Islands, which in November switched recognition to Taiwan from China. Currently, 27 countries, including the Marshall Islands, recognize Taiwan.	Russian forces rescue Vincent Cochetel, a French UN official seized by masked gunmen in the southern region of North Ossetia Three of the kidnappers are killed and two of the Russian troops are injured in the raid.			Thai officials report that, of the 146 passengers and crew aboard the plane that crashed on Dec. 11, 101 were killed.
Dec. 13		Lord (Lew) Grade (born Louis Winogradsky), 91, British television and film producer, dies in London of a heart attack.	Reports reveal that Mohammed Jafar Pouyandeh, 45, a writer who criticized the censorship in Iran, was found dead. . . . In Algeria, reports state that the bodies of some 110 people were found in a mass grave in the Mefta region southwest of Algiers, the capital. . . . PNA security officials arrest Abdullah Sharni, a Gaza-based Islamic Jihad leader, after Sharni stated on Palestinian television that he welcomed U.S. president Bill Clinton's assassination.	In a plebiscite on Puerto Rico's future relationship with the U.S., residents reject statehood as an option. It is the third plebiscite on statehood status in Puerto Rico's history.	The Japanese government announces that it will take over Nippon Credit Bank Ltd., one of Japan's largest banks. Nippon Credit is the second bank to be temporarily nationalized under a recently enacted plan to prevent a collapse of Japan's ailing banking system.
Dec. 14	Hutu death-squad leader Omar Serushago pleads guilty to genocide and crimes against humanity at the UN war crimes tribunal.	Serbian border guards kill 36 members of the Kosovo Liberation Army (KLA)—the ethnic Albanian group fighting for Kosovo's independence—during a five-hour gun battle. In apparent retaliation for the border killings, masked gunmen open fire on a cafe in the southwestern Kosovo town of Pec, killing six Serbs and wounding about 15 others. The victims are among the first civilians targeted in the conflict since the cease-fire began.	The Palestine National Council (PNC), with U.S. president Clinton in attendance, votes with a near-unanimous show of hands to reaffirm its cancellation of all articles in the 1964 Palestinian charter that called for the destruction or nonacceptance of Israel. . . . Heavy fighting between Angolan troops and rebels in northern and central Angola leads UN secretary general Kofi Annan to declare that Angola has reverted to all-out war. . . . Algerian premier Ahmed Ouyahia resigns.	Statistics Canada reports that an ice storm that lashed eastern Canada in January caused economic losses of C$585 million (US$380 million) in Montreal, Quebec, and of C$114 million in Ottawa, the nation's capital. An Environment Department official indicates that the ice storm was the most destructive storm in Canadian history.	
Dec. 15	In a report to the UN, UNSCOM chairman Richard Butler reveals that, since inspectors resumed work after the November agreement, Iraq has failed to "provide the full cooperation it promised" and "initiated new forms of restrictions" on inspectors. . . . Leaders of the nine member countries of the Association of Southeast Asian Nations (ASEAN) meet in Hanoi, Vietnam.		Algerian president Liamine Zeroual names Smail Hamdani as the country's interim premier.	Haiti's Senate ratifies the nomination of Jacques-Edouard Alexis as premier. Haiti has not had a premier since June 1997, when Rosny Smarth resigned.	
Dec. 16	Prompted by Iraq's failure to cooperate with UN weapons inspectors, the U.S. and Great Britain launch a campaign of air strikes against Iraq. Two permanent members of the UN Security Council, Russia and China, express fury at the U.S. decision to act without consulting the council.	Reports reveal that the government in the separatist republic of Chechnya has declared a one-month state of emergency to try to stem the growing lawlessness and kidnappings in the region.	West Bank Palestinians denounce the U.S. and British assault on Iraq.	The body of U.S. journalist Philip True is found hanging in western Mexico.	

A	B	C	D	E
Includes developments that affect more than one world region, international organizations, and important meetings of major world leaders.	*Includes all domestic and regional developments in Europe, including the Soviet Union, Turkey, Cyprus, and Malta.*	*Includes all domestic and regional developments in Africa and the Middle East, including Iraq and Iran and excluding Cyprus, Turkey, and Afghanistan.*	*Includes all domestic and regional developments in Latin America, the Caribbean, and Canada.*	*Includes all domestic and regional developments in Asia and Pacific nations, extending from Afghanistan through all the Pacific Island, except Hawaii.*

U.S. Politics & Social Issues	U.S. Foreign Policy & Defense	U.S. Economy & Environment	Science, Technology, & Nature	Culture, Leisure, & Lifestyle	
The House Judiciary Committee approves a fourth article of impeachment against Pres. Clinton, a watered-down version of Kenneth Starr's abuse-of-power allegations. . . . Lawton Mainor Chiles Jr., 68, governor of Florida (D) since 1991, who previously served in the Senate, 1971–89, dies at the governor's mansion in Tallahassee, Florida, of an apparent heart attack. . . . Morris King Udall, 76, (D, Ariz.), congressman from Arizona, 1961–91, dies in Washington, D.C., of complications from Parkinson's disease.				Marc Hodler, an International Olympic Committee (IOC) official, reports of bribes accepted in exchange for their votes on which cities will host the Olympic Games, touching off the biggest ethics scandal in the century-old organization's history. . . . Kevin Brown signs the biggest contract in MLB history with the Los Angeles Dodgers.	Dec. 12
The FBI reveals that serious crimes in the U.S. were down 5% in the first half of 1998. It is the sixth consecutive year in which a drop in serious crime has been reported.	William D. Denson, 85, U.S. Army lawyer who, from 1945 to 1947, was the chief prosecutor of those accused of committing atrocities at Nazi concentration camps in Germany, dies in Lawrence, New York, of unreported causes.			Reports state that the John D. and Catherine T. MacArthur Foundation, an organization that supports public-television programming and awards "genius" grants to individuals who excelled in academics, the arts and other areas, has named Jonathan Fanton as its president.	Dec. 13
In *Calderon v. Coleman*, the Supreme Court rules, 5-4, to narrow the discretion that federal judges may exercise in deciding whether a trial error warrants the reversal of a state death-row inmate's sentence. . . . A. Leon Higginbotham Jr., 70, federal judge and legal scholar known as a defender of social justice and civil rights who was only the third black jurist to preside over one of the 12 U.S. Circuit Courts, dies in Boston, Massachusetts, after a stroke.		Judge Manuel Real sentences Democratic fund-raiser Johnny Chung to five years' probation for using "straw donors" to funnel illegal contributions to Democratic campaigns in 1996, including the reelection effort of Pres. Clinton and Vice Pres. Gore. . . . In Washington, D.C., Judge Stanley Sporkin approves a settlement under which the Department of Energy agrees to allocate $6.25 million to private groups conducting independent monitoring of federal nuclear waste cleanup programs.		Norman Fell, 74, TV actor best known for his role on the situation comedy *Three's Company*, dies in Woodland Hills, California, of cancer.	Dec. 14
Judge Deborah Batts strikes down a New York City law banning most outdoor advertisements for tobacco products and restricting tobacco advertisements in stores, arguing that federal cigarette-labeling law prohibits cities and states from imposing further restrictions on cigarette advertising.	The State Department warns U.S. citizens in seven nations in the Persian Gulf area of the possibility of terrorist attacks. Unidentified Clinton administration officials state that Osama bin Laden has ordered an attack on U.S. targets in the Persian Gulf to take place sometime in the following weeks. . . . Data shows that almost 300,000 immigrants have been deported by federal authorities since the passage of the 1996 Immigration Reform and Immigrant Responsibility Act. In both years, the INS exceeded its deportation goals.	A report by Congress's Joint Committee on Taxation estimates that 47.8 million Americans will pay no federal income tax in the 1998 tax year, up from 46 million in 1997. The panel estimates that wealthier households with annual incomes above $100,000 will account for 62% of income taxes paid in 1998, compared with 56% in 1997. . . . The Nature Conservancy announces that it will purchase 185,000 acres (75,000 hectares) of Maine forestland from International Paper Co.			Dec. 15
Judge Jeff Hines in Paducah, Kentucky, sentences Michael Carneal, 15, to life in prison for killing three fellow students at a prayer session and wounding five others.	Federal prosecutors in the U.S. charge five suspects—Khalfan Khamis Mohamed, Ahmed Khalfan Ghailani, Fahad Mohammed Ali Msalam, Sheikh Ahmed Salim Swedan, and Mustafa Mohammed Fadhil—with murder and conspiracy in the August bombing of the U.S. embassy in Dar es Salaam, Tanzania. All of the new suspects are at large.			William Gaddis, 75, U.S. author whose books were thought by some critics to be among the most important literary works of their time, dies of prostate cancer in East Hampton, New York.	Dec. 16

F	G	H	I	J
Includes elections, federal-state relations, civil rights and liberties, crime, the judiciary, education, health care, poverty, urban affairs, and population.	Includes formation and debate of U.S. foreign and defense policies, veterans' affairs, and defense spending. (Relations with specific foreign countries are usually found under the region concerned.)	Includes business, labor, agriculture, taxation, transportation, consumer affairs, monetary and fiscal policy, natural resources, and pollution.	Includes worldwide scientific, medical, and technological developments; natural phenomena; U.S. weather; natural disasters; and accidents.	Includes the arts, religion, scholarship, communications media, sports, entertainments, fashions, fads, and social life.

	World Affairs	Europe	Africa & the Middle East	The Americas	Asia & the Pacific
Dec. 17	The U.S. and Britain begin the campaign's second wave of attacks against Iraq when almost 100 cruise missiles are launched from B-52 bombers. . . . Data shows that 1998, which ended Dec. 1 on the meteorological calendar, was the warmest year on record, with a global average surface temperature about 58°F (14°C). . . . A committee of the House of Lords voids a court decision that denied Gen. Augusto Pinochet Ugarte, Chile's former military leader, immunity from arrest in Britain.	Serbian police launch an assault on the kosovo village of Glodjane, 6 miles (10 km) south of Pec. Two KLA members are killed and 34 are arrested. The KLA denies involvement in the Dec. 14 attack in Pec. Five masked assailants abduct and shoot to death Zvonko Bojanic, mayor of Kosovo Polje. . . . In protest of the U.S. strikes against Iraq, Russia recalls its ambassador in the U.S., Yuli Vorontsov . . . Britain announces that it will ease an arms embargo on Argentina imposed since the Falkland Islands war in 1982.	Iraqi officials reveal that 25 Iraqis have been killed and 75 wounded in the first two rounds of attacks by U.S. and British forces.		Some 4,000 protesters clash with Indonesian security forces outside the Parliament building in Jakarta, the capital of Indonesia. The demonstration is among the most violent of the protests that have crippled areas of the capital on a daily basis for more than a month. More than 100 demonstrators and 14 soldiers are wounded in the clashes. One student is shot dead.
Dec. 18		The Polish parliament passes a bill that will open up Poland's communist-era secret police files. . . . Parties in Northern Ireland attempting to implement an April peace accord reach a major agreement on the structure of governmental bodies in the province. . . . Reports disclose that the Latvian parliament has voted to approve Latvia's membership in the World Trade Organization.		Mexican lieutenant colonel Hildegardo Bacilio Gomez leads a group of dissident soldiers in a march in Mexico City to protest alleged abuses in military courts and economic conditions in Mexico. . . . The parliament in Haiti votes to approve the nomination of Jacques-Edouard Alexis as premier. The Senate ratified the nomination on Dec. 15. Haiti has not had a premier since June 1997, when Rosny Smarth resigned.	South Korean naval forces sink a small North Korean submarine in the waters off South Korea's southern coast. . . . India expels an official from Pakistan's embassy in New Delhi, India's capital, on charges of espionage.
Dec. 19	U.S. and British forces end their 70-hour-long air bombardment of Iraq, and U.S. president Clinton expresses confidence that the strikes, dubbed Operation Desert Fox, "achieved our mission," as Pentagon leaders argue the bombardment weakened the government of Iraqi president Saddam Hussein and set back his long-range missile program by at least a year. In response to the attacks, Iraqi officials reveal that Iraq will not permit UN weapons inspectors to reenter the country.	Bulent Ecevit, head of the Democratic Left Party, states he has ended his effort to form a new government in Turkey.	In Damascus, Syria's capital, mobs angered by the attack on Iraq storm U.S. and British diplomatic buildings before being brought under control by Syrian security personnel and U.S. Marines.	In Mexico, the army's top prosecutor and others in command of the military denounce the Dec. 18 march of dissident soldiers and the movement, called the Patriotic Command to Raise the People's Consciousness. The internal division in the military is described as being without precedent in modern Mexican history.	In response to India's Dec. 18 expulsion of a Pakistani official, Pakistan expels an Indian official from India's mission in Islamabad, Pakistan's capital.
Dec. 20	U.S. and British military sources reveal that aircraft from the two countries flew 650 sorties, including 250 bombing runs, as part of the Dec. 16–19 attack on some 100 designated targets in Iraq. Reports confirm that anti-U.S. protests have erupted in Syria, Lebanon, Egypt, Jordan, Libya, and the West Bank and Gaza Strip since the assault started. Morocco permits an officially outlawed Islamic movement to lead a demonstration of 100,000 protesters in Rabat, the capital.	Andre Lucien Charles Daniel Dewavrin, 87, director of intelligence operations for the French Resistance under Charles de Gaulle during World War II, dies in Paris.			China releases imprisoned labor activist Liu Nianchun on medical parole.
Dec. 21	The IMF revises its projections and forecasts 2.2% global economic expansion for 1999, down from the earlier prediction of 2.5%. The economies hardest hit by Southeast Asia's financial crisis—Indonesia, Thailand, Malaysia, and the Philippines—are expected to contract by a combined 10.6% in 1998 and by 1.4% in 1999. Japan's economy will contract 0.5% in 1999. The U.S. economy will grow 1.8% in 1999, rather than 2%. Growth in the EU nations is revised downward, to 2.2% for 1999 from the earlier estimate of 2.5%.		In raucous proceedings, the Israeli Knesset votes to dissolve the rightist Likud party-led government of Prime Minister Benjamin Netanyahu. The vote sets the stage for new general elections sometime in the spring of 1999.		The Indonesian government admits that dozens of women—most of whom are ethnic Chinese—were gang-raped in the May rioting that preceded Pres. Suharto's ouster. . . . As many as 1,000 people flee the Cambodian town of Sihanoukville after becoming alarmed that a mound of some 3,000 tons of waste from a Taiwanese plastics company is toxic. . . . Nepal's premier, Girija Prasad Koirala, resigns. . . . Prominent Chinese dissidents Xu Wenli and Wang Youcai are sentenced to prison terms of 13 years and 11 years, respectively.

A	B	C	D	E
Includes developments that affect more than one world region, international organizations, and important meetings of major world leaders.	*Includes all domestic and regional developments in Europe, including the Soviet Union, Turkey, Cyprus, and Malta.*	*Includes all domestic and regional developments in Africa and the Middle East, including Iraq and Iran and excluding Cyprus, Turkey, and Afghanistan.*	*Includes all domestic and regional developments in Latin America, the Caribbean, and Canada.*	*Includes all domestic and regional developments in Asia and Pacific nations, extending from Afghanistan through all the Pacific Island, except Hawaii.*

U.S. Politics & Social Issues	U.S. Foreign Policy & Defense	U.S. Economy & Environment	Science, Technology, & Nature	Culture, Leisure, & Lifestyle	
As many as 3,000 people attend a rally outside the Capitol urging Republicans to halt the drive toward the impeachment of Pres. Clinton. . . . The CDC reports that hot dogs and cold cuts may have caused an outbreak of food poisoning that killed four people and sickened more than 35 others in nine states.	The U.S. announces that it has temporarily closed 38 of its embassies in Africa as a precaution against possible terrorist reprisals for the operation against Iraq.	Future Tech International Inc., a Miami, Florida-based computer sales company, agrees to plead guilty to two counts of tax evasion relating to illegal contributions it had made to the Democratic National Committee (DNC) in 1994 and to Pres. Clinton's reelection effort in 1995. The company will pay a $1 million fine, which will also repay back taxes and penalties it owes for falsely claiming the reimbursement costs as deductible payroll expenses.			Dec. 17
The House debates the impeachment articles against Pres. Clinton for 13 hours. . . . South Carolina executes Andrew Lavern Smith, 38, by lethal injection in Columbia. Smith is the 500th convict executed in the U.S. since 1976. Texas has executed 164 inmates since 1977, more than any other state. Following Texas are Virginia, Florida, Missouri, Louisiana, and Georgia. Smith is the 20th convict executed in South Carolina since 1976. The most executions performed in any year since 1976 was 74, in 1997.	Francisco Gomez and Pedro Guevara, Cubans who reside in Florida, are arrested on charges of attempted immigrant smuggling after they are rescued along with seven other Cubans from a capsized boat in the Atlantic Ocean, 30 miles (50 km) from Miami. Officials believe the rest of the 23 passengers on board are dead. . . . David Sheldon Boone, a former cryptologist for the NSA, pleads guilty to conspiracy to commit espionage when he sold classified documents to the KGB from 1988 to 1991.	Figures reveal that U.S. banks' credit losses on derivatives reached a new quarterly high in the July-through-September period. Losses in the third quarter rose to $445 million, up from the previous quarter's $94 million in write-offs. Profits from derivatives in the third quarter dropped to $614 million, from the $2.6 billion figure recorded in April through June.		Data shows that attendance at NCAA football games surpassed 37 million for the first time during the 1998 season.	Dec. 18
The House votes to impeach Pres. Clinton for his conduct in the Monica Lewinsky scandal. In near-party-line votes, the House's Republican majority wins passage of two articles of impeachment accusing Clinton of committing perjury and obstruction of justice in an effort to conceal his sexual affair with Lewinsky. . . . Rep. Robert Livingston (R, La.), stuns his House colleagues by withdrawing his candidacy for speaker after admitting to extramarital affairs.					Dec. 19
Nkem Chukwu, 27, a Houston, Texas, woman who underwent fertility treatment, delivers seven children. Because she gave birth to a daughter on Dec. 8, the frail infants are the first known set of octuplets born alive in the U.S.	Germany extradites to the U.S. Mamdouh Mahmud Salim, accused of playing a key role in the organization led by Osama bin Laden, al-Qaeda, which the U.S. believes was behind the August embassy bombings in Tanzania and Kenya.		NASA loses contact with the *Near Earth Asteroid Rendezvous* (NEAR) spacecraft, an unmanned probe launched in 1996 to orbit the asteroid 433 Eros. . . . Sir Alan Lloyd Hodgkin, 84, British neurophysiologist and cowinner of the 1963 Nobel prize for research on the electrochemical mechanism through which nerve cells transmit information, dies in Cambridge, England.		Dec. 20
In Des Moines, Iowa, Judge Robert Pratt strikes down the state's ban on a late-term abortion procedure, ruling that the law is unconstitutional because its vague wording will likely lead doctors to "steer far wider of the unlawful zone" than the law intends.			The FDA approves the first vaccine against Lyme disease, a bacterial infection transmitted by tick bites. The FDA warns that the vaccine does not provide complete immunity from the disease. . . . NASA controllers relocate the *Near Earth Asteroid Rendezvous* (NEAR) spacecraft, lost Dec. 20.	*A Man in Full* by Tom Wolfe tops the bestseller list.	Dec. 21

F	G	H	I	J
Includes elections, federal-state relations, civil rights and liberties, crime, the judiciary, education, health care, poverty, urban affairs, and population.	Includes formation and debate of U.S. foreign and defense policies, veterans' affairs, and defense spending. (Relations with specific foreign countries are usually found under the region concerned.)	Includes business, labor, agriculture, taxation, transportation, consumer affairs, monetary and fiscal policy, natural resources, and pollution.	Includes worldwide scientific, medical, and technological developments; natural phenomena; U.S. weather; natural disasters; and accidents.	Includes the arts, religion, scholarship, communications media, sports, entertainments, fashions, fads, and social life.

	World Affairs	Europe	Africa & the Middle East	The Americas	Asia & the Pacific
Dec. 22		Rev. Lord (Donald Oliver) Soper, 95, minister of the Methodist Church in Britain who was known for his open-air preaching at Tower Hill and Hyde Park in London, dies in London of unreported causes.	Israeli warplanes kill a woman and six of her seven children during an air raid in eastern Lebanon against suspected guerrilla bases.... About 100 UN relief workers return to Iraq to resume their aid activities.	Pierre Vallieres, 60, whose 1968 book, *White Niggers of America*, was considered a manifesto of the early French-Canadian separatist movement in Quebec, dies in Montreal, Canada, after having slipped into a coma a week earlier; he never recovered from a heart attack suffered in 1997.	Prominent Chinese dissident Qin Yongmin is sentenced to a 12-year prison term.... The Cambodian government begins cleanup efforts in Sihanoukville and states that the waste from a Taiwanese plastic company will be returned to Taiwan.
Dec. 23	Reports confirm that Kyrgyzstan is the first former Soviet republic to officially become a member of the World Trade Organization (WTO).	Reports reveal that the Lithuanian parliament has abolished the death penalty in Lithuania.... Some 170 inmates implicated in acts of sectarian violence are released from Maze prison outside Belfast, Northern Ireland, on a 10-day Christmas leave. The release draws protests.... The Cour de Cassation, Belgium's highest court, convicts former NATO secretary general Willy Claes and 11 other defendants in connection with a bribery scandal. All of the defendants receive suspended sentences.	In retaliation for the Dec. 22 Israeli attack, Lebanon's Shi'ite movement Hezbollah fires dozens of rockets into northern Israel, wounding about 15 Israelis.		Some 4,500 police officers wielding batons and tear gas raid Chogye Temple in Seoul, the capital of South Korea, and oust dozens of dissident Buddhist monks and their supporters, who have been occupying the temple since Nov. 11 to protest a move by its leader, Song Wol Ju, to seek a third term. Song states he will withdraw his reelection bid.... An Indonesian military court charges 11 soldiers in an elite army unit with kidnapping democracy activists between February and April.
Dec. 24			Fighting in Kuito, Angola, the capital of the central Bie province, leaves 30 people dead and 37 wounded.... The PNA frees Hamas spiritual leader Sheik Ahmed Yassin from house arrest in Gaza City.... An appeals court in Teheran, the capital of Iran, reduces the jail sentence of Gholamhossein Karbaschi, formerly mayor of Teheran, to two years from five years.		
Dec. 25		Russian president Boris Yeltsin and Belarussian president Aleksandr Lukashenko sign a declaration of cooperation that will more closely bind Russia and the former Soviet republic of Belarus. Separately, Russia's lower house of parliament, the Duma, ratifies a friendship treaty with Ukraine, pledging closer ties between the two countries.			Khieu Samphan and Nuon Chea, senior leaders of Cambodia's Khmer Rouge guerrillas, surrender to the government after negotiating an amnesty deal with Cambodian premier Hun Sen. The two leaders were among the chief architects of the Khmer Rouge's radical communist regime, responsible for the deaths of more than 1 million Cambodians when it ruled the country from 1975 to 1979.... Militant Hindus launch a campaign against Christians in India.
Dec. 26	Iraqi vice president Taha Yasin Ramadan warns that a squadron of U.S. and British warplanes on patrol constitutes a violation of Iraq's airspace and will "be met by Iraqi fire." Iraq later fires antiaircraft artillery near two British Tornado fighter jets flying in the southern zone.	Cathal Goulding, reported variously as 75 or 76, chief of staff of the Irish Republican Army (IRA), 1962–70, when a more violent wing of the organization, the Provisional IRA, split off from his "Official" IRA branch, dies in Dublin, Ireland, of unreported causes.			
Dec. 27				A state investigator in Mexico City reveals that two men—Chivarrer Lopez and Miguel Hernandez de la Cruz Juan—were arrested in connection with the death of U.S. journalist Philip True, whose body was found Dec. 16. The two men reportedly admitted to killing True.	A Chinese court convicts Zhang Shanguang, a prominent labor activist, of "providing intelligence to hostile foreign organizations" and sentences him to 10 years in prison.

A	B	C	D	E
Includes developments that affect more than one world region, international organizations, and important meetings of major world leaders.	*Includes all domestic and regional developments in Europe, including the Soviet Union, Turkey, Cyprus, and Malta.*	*Includes all domestic and regional developments in Africa and the Middle East, including Iraq and Iran and excluding Cyprus, Turkey, and Afghanistan.*	*Includes all domestic and regional developments in Latin America, the Caribbean, and Canada.*	*Includes all domestic and regional developments in Asia and Pacific nations, extending from Afghanistan through all the Pacific Island, except Hawaii.*

U.S. Politics & Social Issues	U.S. Foreign Policy & Defense	U.S. Economy & Environment	Science, Technology, & Nature	Culture, Leisure, & Lifestyle	
Northern Brands International, a North Carolina-based marketing unit of R.J. Reynolds Tobacco Co., pleads guilty to aiding cigarette distributors in a smuggling plan designed to evade excise taxes in the U.S. and Canada in the mid-1990s. It is the first time that a tobacco company in the U.S. is convicted of a federal crime. Northern Brands is fined $5 million and directed to pay $10 million to the U.S. Treasury.		The New York Stock Exchange (NYSE), located on Wall Street in New York City, reveals that it has reached a preliminary agreement with the city and state of New York on terms for its remaining in the city for at least 50 years.		An official of the American Basketball League (ABL) states the league will file for bankruptcy, leaving the Women's National Basketball Association (WNBA) as the only remaining U.S. league for professional female basketball players.	Dec. 22
Chastity Pasley, 22, pleads guilty in Laramie, Wyoming, to the charge that she was an accessory after the fact to first-degree murder in the October beating death of Matthew Shepard, a homosexual Wyoming college student. . . . In Stamford, Connecticut, Judge Martin Nigro sentences former fugitive Alex Kelly, who pleads no contest and is serving a 16-year sentence for the rape, to 10 years in prison for the rape of a 17-year-old girl in 1986.	The State Department announces that three Cuban diplomats stationed at the UN who are allegedly part of a spy ring have been ordered to leave the U.S. . . . Jewish Holocaust survivors and their relatives file a class-action lawsuit in New York City, accusing the U.S.'s Chase Manhattan Corp. and J.P. Morgan & Co., as well as seven French banks, of helping the Nazi German regime steal the assets of Jewish customers in France. The action is the first to name institutions based in the U.S. in connection with the theft of assets.	The Commerce Department reports that U.S. gross domestic product (GDP) grew at a seasonally adjusted annual rate of 3.7% in the third quarter of 1998. That compares with an annualized gain of 1.8% in the second quarter.		Anatoly Rybakov, 87, Russian writer whose 1987 book *Children of the Arbat* went two decades without a publisher due to censorship in the former USSR, dies in New York City while suffering from heart ailments.	Dec. 23
Pres. Clinton, in a Christmas Eve act of executive clemency, pardons 33 people convicted of nonviolent crimes.			Data reveal that since Dec. 21, freezing temperatures in the high teens and low 20s Fahrenheit—the most severe freeze in the area since 1990—have seriously damaged California's lemon and orange crops. . . . A study finds that women tend to live longer if they bear fewer children and if they bear them later in life. . . . Raemer E. Schreiber, 88, physicist who helped the U.S. develop the atom bomb and the hydrogen bomb, dies in Los Alamos, New Mexico, of unreported causes.		Dec. 24
					Dec. 25
					Dec. 26
The smallest of the octuplets born Dec. 20 to Nkem Chukwu in Houston, Texas, dies of heart and lung failure.	William Andrew Lee, 98, U.S. Marine Corps colonel known as "Ironman" who won three Navy Crosses during campaigns to subdue leftist rebels in Nicaragua in the early 1930s, dies in Fredericksburg, Virginia, of cancer.				Dec. 27

F	G	H	I	J
Includes elections, federal-state relations, civil rights and liberties, crime, the judiciary, education, health care, poverty, urban affairs, and population.	*Includes formation and debate of U.S. foreign and defense policies, veterans' affairs, and defense spending. (Relations with specific foreign countries are usually found under the region concerned.)*	*Includes business, labor, agriculture, taxation, transportation, consumer affairs, monetary and fiscal policy, natural resources, and pollution.*	*Includes worldwide scientific, medical, and technological developments; natural phenomena; U.S. weather; natural disasters; and accidents.*	*Includes the arts, religion, scholarship, communications media, sports, entertainments, fashions, fads, and social life.*

	World Affairs	Europe	Africa & the Middle East	The Americas	Asia & the Pacific
Dec. 28	U.S. jets fire Harm antiaircraft missiles north of Mosul in the northern no-flight zone of Iraq, in retaliation for several missiles the Iraqi battery had fired at the patrol.		In Yemen, 16 foreign tourists are kidnapped.	Retired admiral Ruben Franco is arrested in connection with the kidnapping of infants born to political prisoners during Argentina's "dirty war" against suspected leftists from 1976 to 1983. Franco is alleged to be the force behind the kidnapping ring and is the sixth senior officer arrested in connection with the investigation.	Although Khieu Samphan and Nuon Chea, leaders of the Khmer Rouge who surrendered Dec. 25, are targets of a possible international tribunal for genocide, Cambodian premier Hun Sen discloses that he will not force the men to face an international tribunal or a Cambodian criminal court.... South Korea's composite index ends its trading year with a gain of 49.5% for 1998.... A severe storm with winds of 90 mph (144 kmph) strikes in the Tasman Sea off the southeastern coast of Australia, killing sailors competing in the 54th annual Sydney-to-Hobart yacht race. The storm forces the rescue of nearly 60 people by Royal Australian Navy helicopters.
Dec. 29	Iraqi vice president Taha Yasin Ramadan reveals that Iraq considers the restrictions placed on fly zones by the U.S., Britain, and France in 1991 to be null and void.		Three Britons and one Australian die in southern Abyan province when Yemeni security forces apparently botch an attempt to free 16 foreign tourists kidnapped Dec. 28. Three kidnappers are also slain.		Riotous mobs of villagers attack military posts and soldiers in Indonesia's Aceh province, on the northern tip of Sumatra. Eight troops are killed.... The National People's Congress passes China's first law governing securities markets.... Chinese officials reveal that Zhang Lin and Wei Quanbao, New York City-based Chinese dissidents who secretly entered China, have been sentenced to three years in a labor camp.
Dec. 30	U.S. fighter jets attack an Iraqi air-defense site in Iraq's southern "no-flight" zone after Iraq fires surface-to-air missiles (SAMs) at a squadron of U.S. and British warplanes on patrol.... Data reveals that at the end of the trading year, Italy's MIBtel Index surged 41%; Spain's IBEX 35 index was up 35.6%; the French CAC 40 index closes up 31.5%; Germany's DAX index shows a gain of 17.7%; and the London Stock Exchange 100 ends up 14.5%. Japan's Nikkei average ends down 9.3%. Canada's Toronto Stock Exchange composite index ends down 4%.	The British government releases its list of New Year's honors, which identifies 981 recipients of knighthoods, life peerages, and other honors.	Yemeni tribesmen release four German tourists abducted Dec 16 after the German government intervenes in negotiations.	Mexican legislators pass one of the most austere budgets in the country's recent history.	Reports confirm that Indonesian government investigators have linked former Pres. Suharto, members of his family, and some close associates to corrupt schemes involving hundreds of millions of dollars.
Dec. 31	The EU's executive arm, the European Commission, announces conversion rates that place one euro, the new EU currency, as equal to 6.56 French francs, 1.96 German marks, and 1,936.27 Italian lire. The euro is scheduled to come into existence on Jan. 1, 1999, although euro bills and coins will not be circulated until 2002.... The Dow global index shows the U.S. market up 26.34% from 1997. Data shows that, for the 1998 year, Mexico's Bolsa index plunged nearly 40%; Brazil's Bovespa index ended 1998 down 33.5%; Chilean stocks fell 28.1%; and Argentina's Merval index finished down 37.5%. Hong Kong's Hang Seng index showed a 6.3% year-on-year decline, and Australia's All-Ordinaries index closed the year up 7.5%.				Reports reveal that 25 people were arrested after the Dec. 29 attack in Indonesia.... Reports confirm that Japan's well-known high-speed "bullet" trains will be withdrawn from service in 1999.... Reports reveal that 12 churches, schools, and prayer halls in India have been demolished in fires set by Hindu mobs since Dec. 25.... Reports confirm that six yachtsmen died in the Dec. 27 storm off the coast of Australia.

A	B	C	D	E
Includes developments that affect more than one world region, international organizations, and important meetings of major world leaders.	Includes all domestic and regional developments in Europe, including the Soviet Union, Turkey, Cyprus, and Malta.	Includes all domestic and regional developments in Africa and the Middle East, including Iraq and Iran and excluding Cyprus, Turkey, and Afghanistan.	Includes all domestic and regional developments in Latin America, the Caribbean, and Canada.	Includes all domestic and regional developments in Asia and Pacific nations, extending from Afghanistan through all the Pacific Island, except Hawaii.

U.S. Politics & Social Issues	U.S. Foreign Policy & Defense	U.S. Economy & Environment	Science, Technology, & Nature	Culture, Leisure, & Lifestyle	
	Robert Samuel Johnson, 78, U.S. Air Force pilot who shot down 27 German planes in an 11-month period during World War II, the second-highest total of all U.S. pilots flying in Europe and the third-highest total among all American pilots in World War II, dies in Tulsa, Oklahoma, of unreported causes.	Pres. Clinton announces that the Social Security Administration (SSA) has resolved potential computer problems related to the arrival of the year 2000, the anticipated Y2K glitch.			Dec. 28
The Pizza Hut restaurant chain announces that it has settled for an undisclosed amount a precedent-setting case in which a black family sued the chain for racial harassment committed by its employees at an outlet in Godfrey, Illinois, in 1997. In the case, the presiding judge, William Hart of U.S. District Court in Chicago, ruled for the first time that a corporation may be held liable for hate crimes committed by its employees.		The FEC reports that overall congressional campaign spending in the 1998 election cycle fell to $617.1 million, $9.2 million less than in 1996. The FEC attributes the drop to fewer closely fought House races in 1998 than in 1996.			Dec. 29
The House Ethics Committee announces that outgoing Speaker Newt Gingrich (R, Ga.) has completed payment of a $300,000 fine for ethics violations. . . . The Justice Department announces it has joined a second lawsuit against the nation's largest hospital company, Columbia/HCA Healthcare Corp., alleging fraud in the company's claims for reimbursement from federal health programs.	INS officials announce that the U.S. will not deport illegal immigrants from Honduras and Nicaragua for at least 18 months, extending a January 1999 deadline announced in November in the wake of Hurricane Mitch.	A semiannual survey finds that the U.S. states are generally in fine fiscal health, largely because of the nation's strong economy and prudent economic management by governors and state legislatures. The survey predicts that "virtually all states" will have a budget surplus in fiscal 1999, which for most states ends June 30, 1999. Fiscal 1999 will be the fifth straight year in which the states report healthy surpluses.		Jean-Claude Forest, 68, French cartoonist who, in 1962, created the comic-strip character Barbarella, which inspired the 1968 film, dies near Paris of a respiratory ailment. . . . Reports confirm that the body of U.S. movie producer David MacLeod was found in Montreal, Quebec, in early December.	Dec. 30
	In a deal was valued at $52.41 billion, oil producer British Petroleum PLC (BP) completes its acquisition of the U.S.-based energy company Amoco Corp. . . . At the end of the trading year, the dollar closes at 1.6685 marks, down from the 1997 year-end rate of 1.7980, and at 113.45 yen, down from 1997's final rate of 130.57. It finishes at $1.6595 per pound sterling, down slightly from the $1.6508 level in 1997. The dollar rose to 9.908 pesos from 8.07 pesos at the close of 1997. The Dow Jones industrial average closes at 9181.43, up 1273.18 points, or 16.1%, from the 1997 year-end level of 7908.25. The NASDAQ leapt 39.63% during the year to close at a record high of 2192.69. The ASE closes at 688.99, up 0.64% from its 1997 close of 684.61. The S&P 500 rose 26.67% during 1998, closing at 1229.23.	The FDA approves Celebrex, an arthritis pain reliever. . . . Official national timekeeping agencies around the world delay their clocks by one second to keep their atomic clocks synchronous with the slightly less regular rotation of the Earth. The "leap second" is added at 7:00 P.M. eastern standard time. . . . Reports confirm that 20,000 dead fish were found floating in Maryland's Patapsco River. It is the largest fish kill in Maryland since an outbreak of the toxic microbe Pfiesteria piscicida killed thousands of fish in 1997.		Dec. 31

F	G	H	I	J
Includes elections, federal-state relations, civil rights and liberties, crime, the judiciary, education, health care, poverty, urban affairs, and population.	Includes formation and debate of U.S. foreign and defense policies, veterans' affairs, and defense spending. (Relations with specific foreign countries are usually found under the region concerned.)	Includes business, labor, agriculture, taxation, transportation, consumer affairs, monetary and fiscal policy, natural resources, and pollution.	Includes worldwide scientific, medical, and technological developments; natural phenomena; U.S. weather; natural disasters; and accidents.	Includes the arts, religion, scholarship, communications media, sports, entertainments, fashions, fads, and social life.

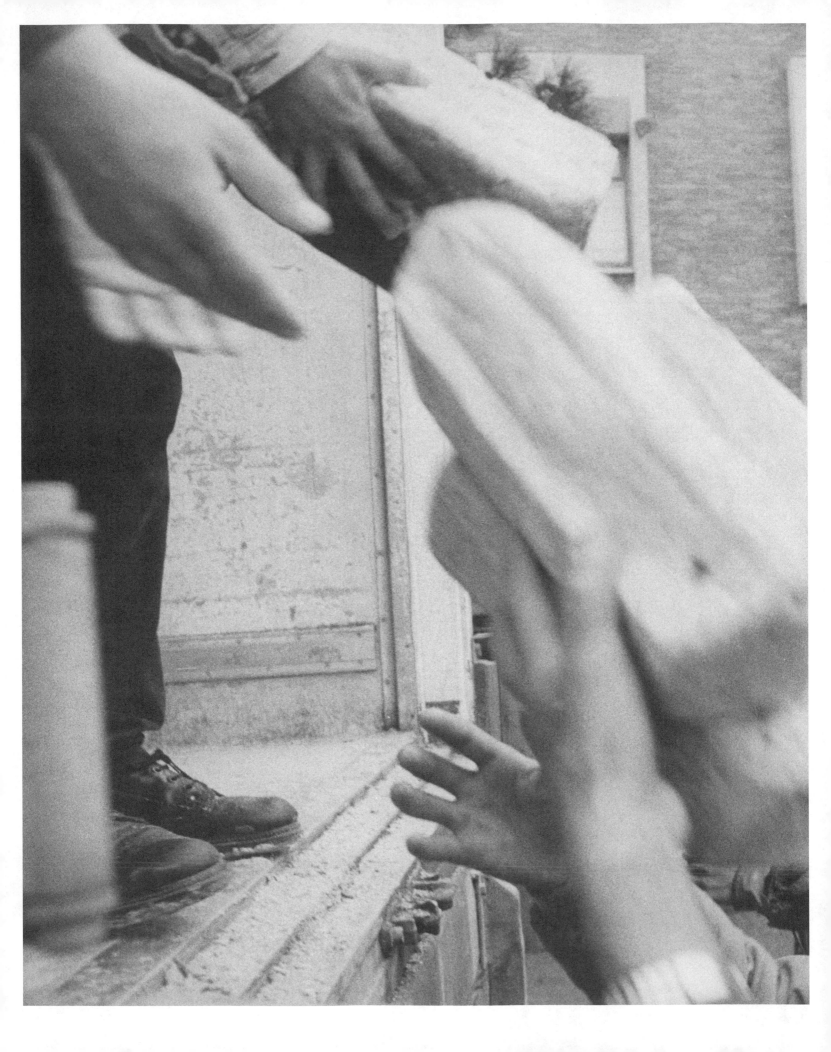

1999

Loaves of bread are handed out to Kosovar refugees in Albania, 1999.

	World Affairs	Europe	Africa & the Middle East	The Americas	Asia & the Pacific
Jan.	The EU's new unified currency, the euro, comes into existence, and the ECU ceases to exist. The euro is launched in Austria, Belgium, Italy, Finland, France, Spain, Germany, Ireland, Luxembourg, Portugal, and the Netherlands.	Pope John Paul II holds a private meeting at the Vatican with Italian premier Massimo D'Alema, a former communist who took office in October 1998. The event garners significant attention because the pope was a pivotal figure in bringing about the collapse of communism in Eastern Europe.	Fighting erupts in Freetown, the capital of Sierra Leone.	In Honduras, Brigadier General Mario Hung Pacheco formally hands over control of the armed forces to civilian Pres. Carlos Flores.	Indonesia reveals that it is prepared to grant full independence in East Timor if the East Timorese reject the government's autonomy plan. It is the first time that Indonesia indicates that it will recognize an independent East Timor.
Feb.	In reaction to the arrest of Kurdish rebel leader Abdullah Ocalan, Kurdish separatists stage demonstrations in many nations, including Armenia, Belgium, Denmark, Italy Sweden, Australia, and Canada.	Russia's Constitutional Court bans capital punishment until all of Russia's 89 regions adopt a system of trial by jury. Because only nine of Russia's regions operate a jury system, the ruling effectively abolishes the death penalty in Russia.	In his 46th year as Jordan's monarch, King Hussein, 63, dies in Amman, the capital, of non-Hodgkins lymphoma. Prince Abdullah, 37, Hussein's eldest son, takes the oath as monarch, becoming King Abdullah II.	Reports reveal that Cuba's National Assembly has passed legislation strengthening penalties against criminals and against political activists opposed to the ruling Communist Party who "collaborated" with the U.S.	Indian prime minister Atal Bihari Vajpayee visits Pakistan, meeting with Pakistani prime minister Nawaz Sharif in an effort to reduce tensions between their nations. The meeting draws protests in Pakistan.
March	NATO launches air strikes against Yugoslavia, prompted by the Serbian refusal to sign a peace accord with ethnic Albanians fighting for the independence of Kosovo and by Serbian violence against ethnic Albanians. The strikes are NATO's first assault on a sovereign nation in its 50-year history.	A bomb explodes in Vladikavkaz, capital of the Russian republic of North Ossetia, killing at least 53 people and severely wounding more than 100 others.	Jailed leaders of Gamaa al-Islamiyya (Islamic Group), Egypt's largest Islamic guerrilla organization, announce a permanent cease-fire, ending their seven-year-old armed campaign to replace the secular government of Pres. Hosni Mubarak with an Islamic regime.	Four unidentified gunmen assassinate Vice Pres. Luis Maria Argana in Asuncion, the capital of Paraguay. The killing prompts protests, and the lower house of Paraguay's Congress votes to begin impeachment proceedings against pres. Raul Cubas Grau, who resigns. Senate president Luis Angel Gonzalez Macchi is sworn in as Paraguay's president.	Afghanistan's two warring sides—the ruling Islamic fundamentalist Taliban militia and the opposition Northern Alliance—announce that they have agreed in principle to form a coalition government.
April	British and U.S. fighter planes resume attacks against targets in northern Iraq.	As fighting continues in Kosovo under NATO fire, a UNHCR report claims that killings and numerous atrocities have been committed by both the ethnic Albanian KLA and the Serbs.	Niger president Ibrahim Mainassara Bare, 49, is assassinated, apparently by members of his presidential guard. An army junta led by Daouda Malam Wanke assumes power in the wake of Bare's death.	Canada officially redraws its map to include the new territory of Nunavut, an Arctic area that was the eastern part of the Northwest Territories. It is the first time Canada has altered its map since 1949. The new territory has a population of only 25,000 people, roughly 85% of whom are Inuit.	The Cormoran army overthrows the government of the Comoros, a three-island nation in the Indian Ocean, in a bloodless coup. Col. Azaly Assoumani is named the country's new leader.
May	The International Criminal Tribunal for the Former Yugoslavia indicts Yugoslav president Slobodan Milosevic for "crimes against humanity" stemming from the forced deportation of hundreds of thousands of ethnic Albanians from Kosovo. Louise Arbour is the first tribunal prosecutor to indict a sitting head of state.	The newly elected members of the Scottish parliament are sworn in, and the newly elected Welsh Assembly meets for the first time.	Former military ruler Olusegun Obasanjo is sworn in as Nigeria's democratically elected president, making him the country's first civilian leader in more than 15 years.	Mireya Moscoso de Gruber is the first woman elected president of Panama.	India launches a series of air strikes on a band of Islamic militants encamped in an Indian-controlled area of the disputed Kashmir region.
June	NATO formally ends its bombing campaign against Yugoslavia after verifying that the government has withdrawn all of its forces from the Serbian province of Kosovo.	Chechen rebels fire on Russian outposts along Chechnya's border with the Russian republic of Dagestan.	Israeli warplanes pound Lebanon's civilian infrastructure, and the Shi'ite Muslim guerrilla group Hezbollah fires rockets into northern Israel in the heaviest battles involving the two sides since 1996 in their continuing conflict along the Israel-Lebanon border.	For the first time since Brazil returned to democracy in 1985, the military is under civilian control.	More than 100 million Indonesians go to the polls to vote in the country's first fully democratic election in 44 years.
July	Zambian president Frederick Chiluba criticizes the UN for spending 11 cents on each African refugee from the Congo conflict while spending $1.50 on each refugee from the conflict in Kosovo, a Serbian province, calling the difference in spending "discrimination of the worst kind."	Spanish police, customs, and naval officials seize a ship in the mid-Atlantic Ocean carrying about 10 tons of cocaine. The operation is believed to be the biggest cocaine seizure ever by European authorities.	King Hassan II of Morocco, 70, the longest-ruling monarch in the Arab world, who played a key role in the Middle East peace process, dies of a heart attack in Rabat. He is immediately succeeded by his eldest son, Sidi Mohammed, who takes the official title of King Mohammed VI.	Off the coast of Vancouver Island in British Columbia, 123 Chinese illegal immigrants are found smuggled aboard a fishing boat. The human-smuggling case is one of the biggest in Canadian history.	Commanders of military operations from India and Pakistan lay out a plan for ending the heaviest fighting in Kashmir in nearly 30 years.
Aug.	Japan and the U.S. sign an agreement to conduct joint research on developing a missile defense system. That proposal is vigorously criticized by China, North Korea, and Russia.	A powerful earthquake strikes northwestern Turkey, killing more than 15,000 people and devastating several major cities.	The two rival factions of one of the Democratic Republic of the Congo's main rebel groups sign a peace agreement aimed at ending the country's civil war.	Venezuela's constitutional assembly approves measures that effectively strip the opposition-controlled Congress of the last of its powers. Venezuela's constitutional assembly declares a "judicial emergency" and grants itself the power to assess and purge members of the nation's judiciary, including Supreme Court justices.	Three major Japanese banks announce that they will merge to form what will be the world's largest financial institution in terms of assets.

A	B	C	D	E
Includes developments that affect more than one world region, international organizations, and important meetings of major world leaders.	Includes all domestic and regional developments in Europe, including the Soviet Union, Turkey, Cyprus, and Malta.	Includes all domestic and regional developments in Africa and the Middle East, including Iraq and Iran and excluding Cyprus, Turkey, and Afghanistan.	Includes all domestic and regional developments in Latin America, the Caribbean, and Canada.	Includes all domestic and regional developments in Asia and Pacific nations, extending from Afghanistan through all the Pacific Islands, except Hawaii.

U.S. Politics & Social Issues	U.S. Foreign Policy & Defense	U.S. Economy & Environment	Science, Technology, & Nature	Culture, Leisure, & Lifestyle	
The Supreme Court rules, 5-4, that the Census Bureau cannot use statistical sampling when it conducts the official national census, upholding a lower court decision in *Clinton v. Glavin*.	The Department of the Navy announces that it is lowering educational standards for recruits in an attempt to reverse a decline in enlistments. The navy will now require only 90% of its recruits to have high school diplomas, down from 95%.	The Commerce Department reports that the U.S. growth domestic product (GDP) grew at an inflation-adjusted annual rate of 3.9% in 1998. That matches 1997's revised GDP gain, equaling the fastest growth rate since 1984.	The NIH states that a federal ban on research on human embryos does not apply to human embryonic stem cells because the cells do not have the capacity to develop into human beings.	Pope John Paul II arrives in St. Louis, Missouri, and the pontiff addresses some 20,000 teenagers at the Kiel Center sports arena.	Jan.
In general party lines, the Senate votes to acquit Pres. Clinton of impeachment charges in the Monica Lewinsky scandal, ending the second presidential impeachment in U.S. history.	Pres. Clinton pardons Henry Ossian Flipper, the first black to graduate from West Point. In 1882, Flipper was given a dishonorable discharge, and an army review board found that Flipper was unfairly prosecuted because of his race. Nonetheless, the U.S. Army did not formally exonerate Flipper until 1976, 36 years after his death. Clinton's action is the first posthumous presidential pardon in U.S. history.	A cargo ship called the *New Carissa*, holding 400,000 gallons of oil, runs aground in stormy weather at Coos Bay, Oregon.	Reports disclose that scientists have succeeded in slowing the speed of light to about 38 miles per hour (61 kph) from its normal speed through empty space, 186,282 miles per second (299,792.458 km per second). The feat is seen as having potential for the advanced study of quantum mechanics and for the development of a variety of high-precision technologies.	In *National Collegiate Athletic Association v. Smith*, the Supreme Court rules unanimously that the NCAA cannot be sued for sex discrimination under Title IX of the Education Amendments of 1972 simply because it receives dues from federally funded member schools.	Feb.
Congress passes and Pres. Clinton signs a bill that will prohibit nursing homes from evicting patients solely because their bills were paid by Medicaid, the health-insurance program for the nation's poor that the federal government and states fund jointly.	Major General David Hale, a two-star army general who retired in 1998 while under investigation for allegations of sexual misconduct, pleads guilty to eight counts of misconduct. He is the first army general to undergo a court-martial since 1952 and the first general ever to be court-martialed in retirement.	The Dow Jones Industrial Average closes above the 10,000 level for the first time ever. It is the seventh time in just over four years that the benchmark stock average breaks through a so-called millennium level.	As Y2K fears persist, the White House reveals that 92% of the federal government's critical computer systems have been repaired and updated in preparation for the year 2000 (Y2K) computer glitch. The Senate votes, 99-0, in favor of a bill that will provide $900 million worth of loans for small businesses to make Y2K computer repairs.	Joe (Joseph Paul) DiMaggio, 84, star center fielder for baseball's New York Yankees who became an icon of an idealized America, dies in Hollywood, Florida, after suffering from lung cancer and pneumonia.	March
Eric Harris, 18, and Dylan Klebold, 17, storm Columbine High School in Littleton, Colorado, and, in a five-hour rampage, use guns and bombs to kill 13 people and wound more than 30 others before killing themselves. The attack is the deadliest such incident in U.S. history.	The House passes, 249-180, a measure that will force Pres. Clinton to secure approval from Congress before sending ground troops to Yugoslavia.	Recent statistics show that women on average earned 74% as much as men in 1997.	In a landmark observation, two teams of astronomers announce the first discovery of a system of multiple planets orbiting a star other than the sun. Three large planets are orbiting Upsilon Andromedae, about 44 light years away in the constellation Andromeda.	Eric Ross donates $5 million to the Holocaust Memorial Museum in Washington, D.C., and helps dedicate its administration building to his parents, Albert and Regina Rosenberg, both of whom died at Auschwitz. It is the largest gift to the institution since its opening in 1993.	April
The Senate approves, 73-25, a juvenile crime bill that includes several amendments aimed at strengthening gun-control laws. It is the first major gun-control initiative to gain legislative approval since 1994.	In *INS v. Aguirre-Aguirre*, the Supreme Court rules unanimously that foreigners are ineligible for refugee protection in the U.S. if they committed a "serious nonpolitical crime" in their own country, regardless of whether they might face political persecution if deported.	The Justice Department files an antitrust lawsuit against American Airlines that accuses the carrier of using predatory pricing. The suit is the first predatory pricing action brought against a U.S. carrier by the government since 1978.	The FBI shuts down its sites on the World Wide Web after computer hackers illegally enter the site.	Three spectators are killed by flying debris from a car crash at an Indy Racing League event. The deaths are the first fatalities in the 40-year car racing history of Lowe's Motor Speedway.	May
Congress awards its highest honor, the Congressional Gold Medal, to Rosa Parks, whose 1955 refusal to give up her seat on a segregated bus in Montgomery, Alabama, sparked a 381-day-long bus boycott that ended when the Supreme Court found bus-segregation unconstitutional.	Pres. Clinton invokes a seldom-used provision of the Constitution to directly appoint James Hormel, as ambassador to Luxembourg. The confirmation makes Hormel the first openly gay ambassador in U.S. history.	In *West v. Gibson*, the Supreme Court rules, 5-4, that the Equal Employment Opportunity Commission (EEOC) possesses the authority to award federal employees compensatory damages in cases of discrimination by other government employers.	A study finds that Raloxifene, a drug prescribed for the bone disease osteoporosis, significantly reduces the risk of developing breast cancer in women past menopause.	The Women's Basketball Hall of Fame opens in Knoxville, Tennessee. It is the first hall of fame dedicated to any women's sport.	June
The Senate, 53-45, reinstates Senate Rule XVI, which bans adding unrelated legislative "riders" to appropriations bills.	Pres. Clinton imposes economic sanctions on the Taliban militia in Afghanistan for allegedly harboring Saudi Arabian exile Osama bin Laden.	On his tour of some of the nation's most economically depressed areas, Pres. Clinton visits the Oglala Lakota Sioux reservation in Pine Ridge, South Dakota, the nation's second-largest Indian reservation. He is the first sitting president to visit an Indian reservation since 1936.	A study finds that by the end of 1998, more than 40% of U.S. homes had a computer, 25% were connected to the Internet, and 94.1% had phones. The report also notes a growing "digital divide" in information access drawn along financial and racial lines.	John F. Kennedy Jr., 38, the only surviving son of former president John F. Kennedy and the editor of the political magazine *George*, dies in an airplane crash with his wife, Carolyn Bessette Kennedy, and his sister-in-law Lauren Bessette.	July
California enacts a ban on the sale and manufacture of "unsafe" handguns. The law is primarily aimed at cheap, powerful handguns called "Saturday night specials."	Pres. Clinton offers to commute the sentences of 16 members of the Armed Forces of National Liberation (FALN), a Puerto Rican independence group that waged a bombing campaign in the U.S. from 1974 to 1983. The move sparks controversy.	The Department of the Interior removes the peregrine falcon from the endangered-species list, due to its steady population growth. There are currently more than 1,650 peregrine breeding pairs in North America, up from 39 breeding pairs at the peregrines' low point in 1970.	The final crew of the Russian space station *Mir* departs the station in a *Soyuz* capsule. *Mir*, the Russian space program's only remaining independent manned flight project, has been in space for 13 years, longer than any other space station, and it is scheduled to fall from its orbit and burn up in the lower atmosphere in the year 2000.	In a historic pact, the Evangelical Lutheran Church in America approves a proposal to unite with the Episcopal Church.	Aug.

F	G	H	I	J
Includes elections, federal-state relations, civil rights and liberties, crime, the judiciary, education, health care, poverty, urban affairs, and population.	*Includes formation and debate of U.S. foreign and defense policies, veterans' affairs, and defense spending. (Relations with specific foreign countries are usually found under the region concerned.)*	*Includes business, labor, agriculture, taxation, transportation, consumer affairs, monetary and fiscal policy, natural resources, and pollution.*	*Includes worldwide scientific, medical, and technological developments; natural phenomena; U.S. weather; natural disasters; and accidents.*	*Includes the arts, religion, scholarship, communications media, sports, entertainments, fashions, fads, and social life.*

	World Affairs	Europe	Africa & the Middle East	The Americas	Asia & the Pacific
Sept.	The UN Security Council votes unanimously to authorize the deployment of a multinational force to restore peace and security in the Indonesian territory of East Timor.	Russia's air force begins bombing targets on the outskirts of Grozny, the capital of Russia's separatist republic of Chechnya.	Iranian officials announce the discovery of the country's largest oil find in 30 years.	A series of powerful explosions rip through a central section of the Mexican city of Celaya, killing at least 56 people and injuring 348 others.	Referendum returns show that residents of East Timor have overwhelmingly voted for independence from Indonesia. In response to the official results, pro-Indonesia militias launch an assault on the East Timorese capital, Dili, killing independence leaders and forcing thousands of East Timorese to flee into the neighboring Indonesian province of West Timor.
Oct.	According to UN experts, the global population reaches 6 billion, doubling since 1960.	Five gunmen open fire on a session of Armenia's parliament in Yerevan, the capital, killing Premier Vazgen Sarkisyan, 40, and seven other government officials.	An Israeli official announces the end of a policy under which Palestinians had to prove they lived in East Jerusalem for seven consecutive years in order to maintain their residency rights.	Buenos Aires mayor Fernando de la Rua of the center-left Alianza coalition is elected president of Argentina. It is the first time that the Peronists lose a presidential election since the party was founded in the 1940s.	The People's Consultative Assembly, Indonesia's national legislature, elects Abdurrahman Wahid as the nation's new president. Wahid's election is the first democratic transfer of power in the nation's 49-year history.
Nov.	The UN issues a report in which it assumes considerable blame for failing to stop the massacre of thousands of Bosnian Muslim men and boys in the town of Srebrenica in July 1995. The UN report breaks new ground by condemning an international organization for attempting to remain neutral in a civil conflict.	Pope John Paul II visits Georgia. It is the first trip to the Caucasus region by a pope and only the second time that a pope has visited a predominantly Eastern Orthodox nation in more than 1,000 years.	Some 2,000 Nigerian troops begin deploying in the Niger River Delta region to quell ongoing clashes between members of the Hausa and Yoruba ethnic groups.	The foreign ministers of Chile and Peru sign a pact that settles the last territorial dispute between the two nations.	Pakistan's military rulers charge ousted prime minister Nawaz Sharif with treason, kidnapping, hijacking, and attempted murder, incidents which they claim sparked the recent bloodless coup.
Dec.	Leaders of the EU member nations agree to create a European rapid-reaction military force of about 60,000 troops that can respond to regional and international military crises.	Britain's Parliament officially devolves political power over the province of Northern Ireland to a new provincial government, granting Northern Ireland home rule for the first time in decades.	Members of the military oust Pres. Henri Konan Bedie in a largely nonviolent coup in Ivory Coast. Gen. Robert Guei takes over as the new president.	Panama assumes control of the Panama Canal and the surrounding canal zone from the U.S., culminating a transfer of sovereignty outlined in a 1977 treaty.	Foreign ministers from Vietnam and China sign a treaty that resolves outstanding border disputes between their two countries.

A	B	C	D	E
Includes developments that affect more than one world region, international organizations, and important meetings of major world leaders.	*Includes all domestic and regional developments in Europe, including the Soviet Union, Turkey, Cyprus, and Malta.*	*Includes all domestic and regional developments in Africa and the Middle East, including Iraq and Iran and excluding Cyprus, Turkey, and Afghanistan.*	*Includes all domestic and regional developments in Latin America, the Caribbean, and Canada.*	*Includes all domestic and regional developments in Asia and Pacific nations, extending from Afghanistan through all the Pacific Islands, except Hawaii.*

U.S. Politics & Social Issues	U.S. Foreign Policy & Defense	U.S. Economy & Environment	Science, Technology, & Nature	Culture, Leisure, & Lifestyle	
Health officials in New York City confirm that an ongoing outbreak of a mosquito-borne viral illness in the city, initially identified as St. Louis encephalitis, is in fact caused by the West Nile virus, never before found in the Western Hemisphere.	In the wake of allegations about massacres in South Korea during the Korean War, Secretary of Defense William Cohen orders the U.S. Army to open a new investigation. South Korea states it will open an investigation as well.	Northeast Nuclear Energy Co. pleads guilty in Hartford, Connecticut, to 23 federal felony counts of falsifying environmental records. The company agrees to pay $10 million in fines, the largest penalty ever levied against a U.S. nuclear plant. Northeast is only the second nuclear power company in the U.S. to be charged with felonies.	Smithsonian Institution officials announce that Steven Udvar-Hazy, a Hungarian-American businessman, has pledged $60 million to the National Air and Space Museum, which will be the largest grant the Smithsonian has ever received.	The Smithsonian reveals that its Arthur M. Sackler Gallery has received a collection of Chinese artifacts—donated by New Jersey psychologist Paul Singer—worth between $50 million and $60 million.	Sept.
A prosecutor in Milwaukee County, Wisconsin, files charges against a rapist known only by his DNA, which was found in semen samples from three separate 1993 rapes.	In a largely partisan vote, the Senate rejects, 48-51, ratification of the Comprehensive Test Ban Treaty (CTBT), which would prohibit nuclear weapons testing. It is the first time since 1920—when the Senate failed to ratify the Treaty of Versailles—that the U.S. Senate defeats a major international security agreement supported by the president. The vote draws international criticism.	Pres. Clinton signs a bill creating a new national park in Colorado, known as Black Canyon of the Gunnison National Park.	EgyptAir Flight 990, a Boeing 767 jetliner bound for Cairo, Egypt, crashes into the Atlantic Ocean about 30 minutes after taking off from John F. Kennedy International Airport in New York City, apparently killing all passengers and crew aboard.	A controversial exhibition of contemporary British art opens at the Brooklyn Museum of Art in New York City, despite the opposition of and threats to cut the museum's funding by the city's mayor, Rudolph Giuliani.	Oct.
Nathaniel Abraham, 13, is convicted for a killing he committed when he was 11. He is the first person tried under Michigan's new juvenile justice law, which allows a juvenile of any age to be tried as an adult, and he is thought to be the youngest person ever tried as an adult in the U.S. for first-degree murder.	A six-year-old Cuban refugee, Elian Gonzalez, is found off the coast of Florida in a case that sparks extended controversy.	United Parcel Service Inc. (UPS) issues shares to the public for the first time in its 92-year history. The sale, worth $5.47 billion, is the largest initial public offering (IPO) ever in the U.S.	Astronomers announce the discovery of six new extrasolar planets, or planets orbiting stars other than the sun. The discoveries bring the total known number of extrasolar planets to 28.	Golfer Tiger Woods caps the most successful season by a PGA player in 25 years when he wins the World Championship.	Nov.
In Washington, D.C., Judge Royce Lamberth rules that the government mismanaged a trust fund that held $500 million belonging to 300,000 Native Americans.	More than 400 people protesting the ongoing World Trade Organization (WTO) talks in Seattle, Washington, are arrested.	Texas governor George W. Bush's campaign reports that it has raised more than $67 million since January, far more than any presidential candidate has ever raised in the entire final 18 months of the nomination process.	An international group of researchers announce that for the first time they have established the chemical sequence of about 97% of chromosome 22, the second-smallest human chromosome.	Footballer Rae Carruth of the Carolina Panthers faces first-degree murder charges in the death of his pregnant girlfriend, Cherica Adams, 24. He is reportedly the first active NFL player to be charged with murder.	Dec.

F	G	H	I	J
Includes elections, federal-state relations, civil rights and liberties, crime, the judiciary, education, health care, poverty, urban affairs, and population.	*Includes formation and debate of U.S. foreign and defense policies, veterans' affairs, and defense spending. (Relations with specific foreign countries are usually found under the region concerned.)*	*Includes business, labor, agriculture, taxation, transportation, consumer affairs, monetary and fiscal policy, natural resources, and pollution.*	*Includes worldwide scientific, medical, and technological developments; natural phenomena; U.S. weather; natural disasters; and accidents.*	*Includes the arts, religion, scholarship, communications media, sports, entertainments, fashions, fads, and social life.*

	World Affairs	Europe	Africa & the Middle East	The Americas	Asia & the Pacific
Jan. 1	The EU's new unified currency, the euro, comes into existence, and the ECU ceases to exist. The initial value of one euro is equal to the value of one ECU. The EU countries in which the euro is launched are Austria, Belgium, Italy, Finland, France, Spain, Germany, Ireland, Luxembourg, Portugal, and the Netherlands. Greece is the only EU country that failed to qualify for participation. Although coins and bills denominated in euros will not begin circulating until the year 2002, the euro is legal tender dispensed through personal checks, travelers' checks, and credit cards.		A car bomb injures two people in Cape Town, South Africa.	The Mexican government ends its subsidy on tortillas, its last remaining control on food prices. . . . An avalanche crashes into a school gymnasium where 400–500 people have gathered for a New Year's Eve celebration in Kangiqsualujjuaq, a small Inuit village in northern Quebec, Canada. Snow slides from a 250-foot (75-m) hill above the gymnasium, tears through a wall of the building, and kills nine people, five of whom are children under the age of eight. Twenty-five people are injured in the incident.	In the face of criticism, Cambodian premier Hun Sen asserts that he is not opposed to having former Khmer Rouge leaders face trial for crimes against humanity.
Jan. 2	Iraq notifies UN officials in Baghdad, the capital, that it will not renew visas or issue entry permits to U.S. or British citizens working for UN aid agencies in Iraq.	Rolf Liebermann, 88, Swiss-born opera house director and composer credited with revitalizing the Paris Opera as its general administrator, 1973–80, dies in Paris, France, of unreported causes.	Reports find that an estimated 200,000 troops are stationed along the 600-mile (970-km) border between Ethiopia and Eritrea. . . . The UN states that one of its chartered cargo planes, transporting seven UN workers from the embattled central city of Huambo to Luanda, crashed in war-torn Angola.		In response to killings in late December, the Indonesian military launches security sweeps in search of Ahmed Kandang, leader of the separatist Free Aceh movement.
Jan. 3				Peruvian president Alberto Fujimori appoints Victor Joy Way Rojas, a long-time ally and the leader of Congress, as premier, touching off an extensive cabinet reshuffle.	In response to the military's Jan. 2 security sweeps, some 3,000 separatist supporters set fire to police stations and other buildings in the Indonesian village of Kandang. Indonesian security forces open fire on demonstrators in Aceh, a province located on the northern tip of Sumatra. . . . In Pakistan, a bomb explodes under a bridge across which P.M. Nawaz Sharif is scheduled to travel, killing four people and injuring three others. The blast, in a suburb of Lahore, the capital of Punjab province, is widely viewed as an attempt to assassinate the prime minister.
Jan. 4					In Pakistan, a group of gunmen open fire on worshipers at Shi'ite Muslim mosque in Quereshi More in Punjab province, killing 16 people and wounding 25 others. No group claims responsibility for the attack, which is among the deadliest incidents in an ongoing sectarian rivalry between Pakistan's Sunni and Shi'ite Muslim communities.
Jan. 5	Two U.S. warplanes fire missiles at, but fail to hit, Iraqi MIG jets that enter the "no-fly" zone in southern Iraq which the U.S. and its allies have declared off-limits to Iraqi military aircraft. The Iraqi jets do not return the fire. A second, similar air confrontation occurs some 15 minutes later about 60 miles (100 km) away, also in the southern no-fly zone. It is the third armed clash involving the U.S. and Iraq since Dec. 28, 1998, and the first to directly involve U.S. and Iraqi jet fighters in six years.	Romanian coal miners go on strike to protest low wages and government plans to close loss-making mines.			Reports reveal that 16 people died when Indonesian security forces opened fire on demonstrators in Aceh on Jan. 3. About 170 people were arrested. . . . Reports disclose that the Indira Gandhi International Airport in New Delhi, the capital of India, has been shut down every night since mid-December 1998, due to air pollution. Separately, Reports indicate that 12 people were killed in a fire sparked when a girl committed suicide by self-immolation in Madras, the provincial capital of Tamil Nadu. Eight victims were children.
Jan. 6		Henrietta Moraes (born Audrey Wendy Abbott), 67, British model who posed for several well-known artists working in London in the 1950s, dies in London while suffering from a liver ailment.	Reports indicate that 500 people have been killed in the remote eastern Congo village of Makobola. The rebels insist that the victims were 400 Hutu militiamen killed in battle. . . . Rebels force their way into Freetown, the capital of Sierra Leone, and set fire to sections of the city. . . . British prime minister Tony Blair makes his first visit to South Africa since he took office in 1997. . . . Ntsu Mokhehle, 80, prime minister of Lesotho, 1993–98, dies in Bloemfontein, South Africa.		

A	B	C	D	E
Includes developments that affect more than one world region, international organizations, and important meetings of major world leaders.	Includes all domestic and regional developments in Europe, including the Soviet Union, Turkey, Cyprus, and Malta.	Includes all domestic and regional developments in Africa and the Middle East, including Iraq and Iran and excluding Cyprus, Turkey, and Afghanistan.	Includes all domestic and regional developments in Latin America, the Caribbean, and Canada.	Includes all domestic and regional developments in Asia and Pacific nations, extending from Afghanistan through all the Pacific Island, except Hawaii.

U.S. Politics & Social Issues	U.S. Foreign Policy & Defense	U.S. Economy & Environment	Science, Technology, & Nature	Culture, Leisure, & Lifestyle	
					Jan. 1
Reports indicate that the Nevada Supreme Court has eliminated the $10 million in punitive damages awarded in a 1995 breast implant lawsuit to plaintiff Charlotte Mahlum of Las Vegas.					**Jan. 2**
			NASA launches *Mars Polar Lander*, an unmanned spacecraft intended to look for signs of water on the surface of the planet Mars. The 639-pound (290-kg) spacecraft lifts off aboard a Delta-2 rocket at Cape Canaveral, Florida	The National Society of Film Critics selects the film *Out of Sight*, directed by Steven Soderbergh, for best picture honors.... Jerry Quarry, 53, heavyweight boxer who tallied a career record of 53 wins, dies in Templeton, California, after experiencing complications of pneumonia brought on by boxing-induced brain damage, a condition known as dementia pugilistica.	**Jan. 3**
A federal jury in Washington, D.C., awards $10 million in damages to Brenda Meister, who claims she was made ill by silicone breast implants.... Elizabeth Dole, 62, the wife of former Sen. Robert Dole (R, Kans.), announces her resignation as president of the American Red Cross, a nonprofit aid organization she led since 1991.	Officials announce a plan to dispose of millions of gallons of napalm stored at a naval base in California since the early 1970s.	Figures reveal that U.S. firms announced 11,652 mergers and acquisitions worth a record $1.61 trillion in 1998, 78% more than the $919 billion announced in 1997. Worldwide, announced merger volume was $2.49 trillion, up 54% from 1997's $1.63 trillion in deals. It is the fourth consecutive year that U.S. and worldwide merger volume has reached record levels.		Iron Eyes Cody, 94, Native American actor who appeared in some 100 films and numerous TV shows and was best known for a 1970 public service announcement in which he looked stoically upon a polluted American landscape and shed a tear, dies in Los Angeles, California.	**Jan. 4**
	U.S. president Clinton announces measures designed to ease the U.S. economic embargo on Cuba by increasing contact with the communist country without directly supporting the government of Cuban leader Fidel Castro Ruz.	The USDA announces that it has reached a settlement with a group of black farmers who in 1997 filed a lawsuit charging the agency with race-based discrimination.	The FDA announces the approval of the use of two drugs to treat mental-health problems in dogs.... Paul Maurice Zoll, 87, heart specialist whose research in the early 1950s led to the development of heart monitors, pacemakers, and defibrillators, dies in Chestnut Hill, Massachusetts, of respiratory failure.	Nolan Ryan, George Brett, and Robin Yount are elected to the Baseball Hall of Fame in Cooperstown, New York.	**Jan. 5**
The 106th Congress convenes, and eight new senators are sworn in, four Republicans and four Democrats. House Representatives approve, by voice vote, a change easing the rules governing the gifts they may receive. The new change, effective immediately, allows members to accept noncash gifts worth up to $50 and up to $100 in total gifts from a single source in one year. Gifts worth less than $10 do not count toward the annual total.		The Dow closes at a record high of 9544.97. That marks the first record high of 1999.	Astronomers suggest that dim "dwarf galaxies" may far outnumber the more commonly detected bright "giant galaxies."	National Basketball Association team owners and players reach a tentative collective bargaining agreement that will end a player lockout that started in July 1998.	**Jan. 6**

F	G	H	I	J
Includes elections, federal-state relations, civil rights and liberties, crime, the judiciary, education, health care, poverty, urban affairs, and population.	*Includes formation and debate of U.S. foreign and defense policies, veterans' affairs, and defense spending. (Relations with specific foreign countries are usually found under the region concerned.)*	*Includes business, labor, agriculture, taxation, transportation, consumer affairs, monetary and fiscal policy, natural resources, and pollution.*	*Includes worldwide scientific, medical, and technological developments; natural phenomena; U.S. weather; natural disasters; and accidents.*	*Includes the arts, religion, scholarship, communications media, sports, entertainments, fashions, fads, and social life.*

	World Affairs	Europe	Africa & the Middle East	The Americas	Asia & the Pacific
Jan. 7	A U.S. fighter jet patrolling the no-fly zone in northern Iraq fires a missile at an Iraqi antiaircraft battery that locks its radar on the American fighter.		The London-based Iraqi opposition group Center for Human Rights reports that 81 political detainees suspected of plotting to overthrow Pres. Hussein were slain in Baghdad in mid-December 1998. . . . Sierra Leone president Ahmad Tejan Kabbah states that he and jailed rebel leader Foday Sankoh have agreed upon a cease-fire and on plans for subsequent negotiations. Active rebel field commander Sam Bockarie, however, contends that the fighting will continue.	Members of the Revolutionary Armed Forces of Colombia (FARC) and the government of Pres. Andres Pastrana Arango begin negotiations aimed at setting an agenda for peace talks, the first such talks in seven years. The United Self-Defense Forces launches a series of attacks across several provinces in northern Colombia for allegedly sympathizing with FARC.	Indian police arrest Sayed Abu Nasir, a 27-year-old Bangladeshi reportedly carrying four pounds (1.8 kg) of explosives and five detonators, in New Delhi, the capital. . . . The inspector general of Malaysia's national police resigns, taking responsibility for the injuries that ousted deputy prime minister Anwar Ibrahim suffered while in police custody. . . . Cambodians celebrate Victory Day, marking the 20th anniversary of the invasion by Vietnam that ended the Khmer Rouge regime.
Jan. 8		The KLA takes eight Yugoslav army troops hostage near the northern town of Podujevo. . . . Pope John Paul II holds a private meeting at the Vatican with Italian premier Massimo D'Alema, a former communist who took office in October 1998. The event garners significant attention because the pope was a pivotal figure in bringing about the collapse of communism in Eastern Europe.	Reports reveal that four mining personnel were killed in an ambush on a diamond mine in Angola's Lunda Norte province. . . . At a rally in Cape Town, South Africa, hundreds of protesters demonstrate against recent U.S. and British air strikes in Iraq. A conflict with police leaves one man dead and several others injured. The protest is timed to coincide with a visit by British prime minister Tony Blair. . . . Abdel-Latif Baghdadi, 81, Egyptian military officer and politician, dies in Cairo, Egypt, of liver cancer.		One farmer is reportedly killed by an exploding tear-gas canister during a battle with police in ongoing protests against local taxation in China. . . . Malaysian prime minister Mahathir bin Mohamad appoints Abdullah bin Ahmad Badawi to succeed Anwar Ibrahim as deputy prime minister. The post has been vacant since September 1998, when Anwar was ousted by Mahathir and subsequently arrested on charges of illegal sex acts and abuse of power.
Jan. 9	French NATO troops shoot and kill a Bosnian Serb war-crimes suspect, Dragan Gagovic, while attempting to arrest him in the eastern Bosnian town of Foca. Gagovic was accused of raping and torturing Muslim women during a Serb campaign to "ethnically cleanse" eastern Bosnia of all Muslims in 1992–93. After he is shot, a crowd of roughly 100 people gathers outside the office of the UN International Police Task Force in Foca and attacks UN monitors. Five monitors are injured, two seriously.		Nigeria holds state elections, the second of three scheduled rounds of voting in the transition to civilian rule.		The Indonesian military mounts further security raids on Aceh villages.
Jan. 10		In Kazakhstan, voters reelect Nursultan Nazarbayev as president in early general elections.	Progovernment allies reportedly bomb Kisangani, the third-largest city in Congo and the rebels' military headquarters.		Reports state that during the Jan. 9 raid in Aceh, the Indonesian military beat to death four people who were taken into custody; 20 others were injured.
Jan. 11			The South African Truth and Reconciliation Commission denies amnesty to Gideon Nieuwoudt, who in 1997 killed antiapartheid activist Steve Biko while Biko was in police custody. . . . U.S. State Department officials reveal that, according to unconfirmed reports by Iraqi opposition sources, the Hussein regime in the previous two months carried out some 500 summary executions of suspect military officers in Baghdad, the capital, and of dissidents in the Shi'ite-dominated region of the country.	Lt. Col. Hildegardo Bacilio Gomez, who in December 1998 led a march of some 50 dissident soldiers in Mexico City, is charged with sedition. . . . Haitian president Rene Preval announces that he will bypass the legislature and establish a new government by decree. Haiti has not had a functioning government or a budget since the resignation of Premier Rosny Smarth in June 1997.	Indonesian military leaders disclose that some 30 soldiers have been arrested in connection with the Jan. 9 deaths in Aceh. . . . Australian minister of foreign affairs Alexander Downer announces what he describes as "an historic shift" in Australia's policy on East Timor, a former Portuguese colony annexed by Indonesia in 1976, when he reveals that Australia will now urge Indonesia to agree to "an act of self-determination" by the East Timorese.
Jan. 12			Conflicting reports put the death toll from the Jan. 12 attack on Kisangani, the third-largest city in Congo, at 17 civilians and 40 people.	Reports confirm that the United Self-Defense Forces have killed some 140 people in Columbia since Jan. 7 for allegedly sympathizing with FARC. . . . Unidentified gunmen on a motorcycle fire on a car carrying the sister of Haitian president Rene Preval, Marie-Claude Calvin, wounding her and killing her driver . . . . Reports confirm that a new autopsy has found the death of U.S. journalist Philip True was caused by blows to the head and chest. That report supports officials' original assertions that True fell to his death in a canyon in Mexico.	

A	B	C	D	E
Includes developments that affect more than one world region, international organizations, and important meetings of major world leaders.	Includes all domestic and regional developments in Europe, including the Soviet Union, Turkey, Cyprus, and Malta.	Includes all domestic and regional developments in Africa and the Middle East, including Iraq and Iran and excluding Cyprus, Turkey, and Afghanistan.	Includes all domestic and regional developments in Latin America, the Caribbean, and Canada.	Includes all domestic and regional developments in Asia and Pacific nations, extending from Afghanistan through all the Pacific Island, except Hawaii.

U.S. Politics & Social Issues	U.S. Foreign Policy & Defense	U.S. Economy & Environment	Science, Technology, & Nature	Culture, Leisure, & Lifestyle	
U.S. Supreme Court chief justice William Rehnquist formally opens Pres. Clinton's impeachment trial in the U.S. Senate.			Astronomers present a new estimate of the number of galaxies in the observable universe, 125 billion, based on images taken by the Earth-orbiting *Hubble Space Telescope*.		Jan. 7
The U.S. 10th Circuit Court of Appeals in Denver, Colorado, reverses a ruling that made it illegal to offer witnesses leniency in exchange for testimony. . . . Brian Stewart, 32, convicted in December 1998 of injecting his son with the HIV virus so that he would not have to pay child support, is sentenced to life in prison. His son, now seven, was diagnosed with AIDS in 1998.		The Labor Department reports that the seasonally adjusted unemployment rate in the U.S. dropped to 4.3% in December 1998, matching April 1998's rate as the lowest since 1970. . . . The Dow closes at a record high of 9643.32. That marks the second record high of 1999.			Jan. 8
Carl A. Elliott, 85, (D, Ala.), who served in Congress, 1949–65, and in 1990 received the first Profiles in Courage Award, an honor that recognizes members of Congress who take principled stands despite the risk of political defeat, dies in Jasper, Alabama, of unreported causes.		Researchers report that contraceptive pills pose no long-term danger to women's health. . . . Astronomers report the discovery of three more nearby stars orbited by planets. The newly found planets bring the total number of known extrasolar planets to 17.			Jan. 9
		The U.S. Postal Service raises the price of a first-class stamp one penny to 33 cents.			Jan. 10
In Seattle, Washington, Judge Barbara Jacobs Rothstein dismisses a lawsuit filed against the tobacco industry by a consortium of Blue Cross & Blue Shield of America health insurance plans, seeking compensation for the costs of treating smoking-related illnesses.	In Washington, D.C., the U.S. and China hold their first talks devoted exclusively to human rights since 1995.	The dollar reaches a 28-month low value of 108.21 yen during trading in New York City, down 27% from August 1998, when it stood at an eight-year high.		Naomi Mitchison (born Naomi Mary Margaret Haldane), 101, British author who produced more than 70 books and numerous articles and papers, dies on the Mull of Kintyre, Scotland. . . . Brian Moore, 77, Irish-born writer who published 19 novels, dies in Malibu, California, of pulmonary fibrosis.	Jan. 11
In *Buckley v. American Constitutional Law Foundation*, the Supreme Court rules, 6-3, that the state of Colorado unconstitutionally hindered free speech in its efforts to regulate the process by which initiatives were placed on state ballots. . . . Data reveals that the income gap between male and female doctors in many specialties had widened between 1996 and 1997. . . . Pres. Clinton sends a check for $850,000 to Paula Corbin Jones, settling a sexual-harassment lawsuit she filed against him in 1994.	Leo Cherne, 86, chair of the International Rescue Committee, 1951–91, who was awarded the Presidential Medal of Freedom in 1984, dies in New York while suffering from a pulmonary ailment. . . . The U.S. imposes economic sanctions on three Russian scientific institutions after concluding that they exported technology to Iran that may help Iran develop nuclear weapons and ballistic missiles.	Figures suggest that the net income at major U.S. corporations was $86.4 billion in the third quarter of 1998, falling 5% when compared with a year-earlier figure of $90.7 billion.		The 70th home run baseball hit by St. Louis Cardinal first baseman Mark McGwire during the 1998 baseball season is auctioned for a record $3,005,000 at Guernsey's auction house. . . . William Hollingsworth Whyte Jr., 81, author and urbanologist, dies in New York City of unreported causes.	Jan. 12

F	G	H	I	J
Includes elections, federal-state relations, civil rights and liberties, crime, the judiciary, education, health care, poverty, urban affairs, and population.	*Includes formation and debate of U.S. foreign and defense policies, veterans' affairs, and defense spending. (Relations with specific foreign countries are usually found under the region concerned.)*	*Includes business, labor, agriculture, taxation, transportation, consumer affairs, monetary and fiscal policy, natural resources, and pollution.*	*Includes worldwide scientific, medical, and technological developments; natural phenomena; U.S. weather; natural disasters; and accidents.*	*Includes the arts, religion, scholarship, communications media, sports, entertainments, fashions, fads, and social life.*

	World Affairs	Europe	Africa & the Middle East	The Americas	Asia & the Pacific
Jan. 13		The KLA releases the eight Yugoslav army troops taken hostage Jan. 8 near the northern town of Podujevo, Kosovo.		The mayor of Toronto, Ontario, Canada, Mel Lastman, declares a 72-hour snow emergency after the city is hit by its fourth major snowstorm in less than two weeks. Toronto has already received 44 inches (113 cm) of snowfall in 1999, far more than the city's historical average for the entire month of January.	A report released by the Australian government on the effects of prawn trawling in the Great Barrier Reef finds that illegal trawlers have inflicted serious damage on the reef's environment. The reef is listed as a United Nations world heritage site.
Jan. 14	Efforts to oust all 20 members of the EU's European Commission evaporate as two motions to censure the body fail to pass in the European Parliament, the EU's legislative arm. Instead, the members vote to investigate the commission for widespread mismanagement and corruption.	German chancellor Gerhard Schroeder discloses that Germany's two ruling parties have reached an agreement on altering German law to accommodate a planned phasing-out of the use of nuclear power to generate electricity.... Jerzy Grotowski, 65, Polish-born theater director, dies in Pontedera, Italy, while suffering from leukemia and a heart ailment.	ECOMOG troops regain control of the center of Freetown, the capital of Sierra Leone, and secure surrounding areas as well.... In South Africa, Bennie Lategan, one of the chief investigators in a police operation to infiltrate the vigilante group People Against Gangsterism and Drugs, is assassinated.	Human Rights Watch accuses Mexican authorities of human-rights abuses such as condoning the use of torture, illegal arrests and detentions, forced confessions, and fabricated evidence.... Reports confirm that former army chief Cristino Nicolaides was arrested after refusing to testify in an investigation into the kidnapping of infants born to political prisoners during Argentina's "dirty war" against suspected leftists.	A landslide and stampede kills 51 pilgrims near the popular Sabarimila shrine in Kerala state in India.... Japan's ruling Liberal Democratic Party (LDP) and the Liberal Party, a small opposition party, form a coalition government.
Jan. 15	U.S. president Bill Clinton for the sixth time implements a six-month waiver blocking a controversial provision of the 1996 Helms-Burton Act, which seeks to tighten the U.S.'s economic embargo of Cuba. Clinton has waived the provision every six months since the law's passage, which was opposed by several nations.	Serbian forces kill 45 ethnic Albanian civilians in southern Kosovo, delivering the most serious blow yet to a cease-fire agreement between the Yugoslav government and ethnic Albanians fighting for the independence of Kosovo, a Serbian province. In a separate incident, unidentified gunmen shoot and wound a British observer and his translator near the southwestern town of Decani.... Betty Evelyn Box, 83, British film producer who made some 50 films, dies of unreported causes.		Pres. Pastrana makes a state visit to Cuba, the first such visit by a Colombian president in some 40 years.... The British Columbia Supreme Court rules that a six-year-old law prohibiting the possession of child pornography violates Canada's Charter of Rights and Freedoms.	Reports from China reveal that thousands of farmers in the southern province of Hunan clashed with police during protests against local taxation.
Jan. 16	The UN condemns the Jan. 15 killings in southern Kosovo.	The Italian government reports that Abdullah Ocalan, a Kurdish rebel leader whose November arrest spurred protests and nearly led to a major diplomatic crisis, has left the country.			
Jan. 17		Fighting between KLA and Serbian forces erupts in Racak, Kosovo, and surrounding villages, halting the burial of the victims of the Jan. 15 attacks.... A new government headed by Democratic Left Party head Bulent Ecevit wins a confidence vote in Turkey's parliament, the Grand National Assembly. The vote formally installs Ecevit as premier.... Russian president Boris Yeltsin is admitted to a Moscow hospital for the third time since October 1998.	Armed tribesmen in northern Yemen kidnap four Dutch and two British citizens.		A bomb explodes aboard a bus in Changsha, China, injuring four people.
Jan. 18	A seven-member appellate committee of Britain's highest court, the Law Lords, opens a hearing to determine whether Gen. Augusto Pinochet Ugarte, Chile's former military leader, should be granted immunity from arrest. The question has touched off protests since his arrest in 1998.	Romanian coal miners who have been striking since Jan. 5, march on Bucharest, the capital, to protest low wages and government plans to close loss-making mines.... Serbian forces remove 40 bodies of the 45 victims from the Jan. 15 attacks and transport them to Pristina for autopsies. Yugoslav Pres. Slobodan Milosevic refuses to allow the chief prosecutor for the UN war crimes tribunal, Louise Arbour, entry into Yugoslavia to investigate the Racak killings.	Zimbabwe's former president, Rev. Canaan Banana, is sentenced to 10 years in prison for sodomy and indecent assault.	The New National Party in Grenada wins all 15 seats in the country's Parliament, returning Prime Minister Keith Mitchell to his position.	
Jan. 19	Officials from North Korea, South Korea, the U.S., and China meet in Geneva, Switzerland, for the latest round of four-way talks aimed at reaching a peace treaty to formally end the 1950–53 Korean War.	Russian officials reveal that Russian industry currently emits 35% less air pollution than it had in 1991, and 15%–18% less waterborne and other kinds of pollutants.	King Hussein, Jordan's ruler since 1952 and a key player in Arab-Israeli peace efforts, returns home to a tumultuous welcome following six months of cancer treatment in the U.S.	In Grenada, returning prime minister Keith Mitchell is sworn in.	

A	B	C	D	E
Includes developments that affect more than one world region, international organizations, and important meetings of major world leaders.	*Includes all domestic and regional developments in Europe, including the Soviet Union, Turkey, Cyprus, and Malta.*	*Includes all domestic and regional developments in Africa and the Middle East, including Iraq and Iran and excluding Cyprus, Turkey, and Afghanistan.*	*Includes all domestic and regional developments in Latin America, the Caribbean, and Canada.*	*Includes all domestic and regional developments in Asia and Pacific nations, extending from Afghanistan through all the Pacific Island, except Hawaii.*

U.S. Politics & Social Issues	U.S. Foreign Policy & Defense	U.S. Economy & Environment	Science, Technology, & Nature	Culture, Leisure, & Lifestyle	
		Sen. Pete Domenici (R, N.Mex.), chair of the Senate Budget Committee, names Dan Crippen to replace June O'Neill as director of the Congressional Budget Office (CBO), effective Feb. 1.		Michael Jordan, considered by many to be the greatest player in the history of the NBA, announces his retirement from professional basketball.	Jan. 13
The 13 House Republicans acting as "managers" for the House's impeachment case against Pres. Clinton open their arguments to the Senate. . . . Daniel Leroy Crocker, 38, who confessed to killing Tracy Fresquez, 19, in 1979 in Kansas, is sentenced to serve a minimum of 10 years in prison.	Deputy Defense Secretary John Hamre reveals that 81% of the Defense Department's critical computer systems are prepared for glitches associated with the coming of the year 2000, or the Y2K problem.	The Labor Department's consumer price index (CPI) report finds that the government's index of consumer prices in 1998 rose 1.6%, incrementally down from the 1.7% increase registered in 1997. The 1998 rate is the lowest yearly rate since 1986, as inflation continues at historically low levels.	A study finds that women considered to be at risk for developing breast cancer who have both of their still-healthy breasts surgically removed reduce their risk of the disease by 90%. The study confirms for the first time the effectiveness of the operation, called a bilateral prophylactic mastectomy.	Alfredo LaMont, director of international relations for the U.S. Olympic Committee, resigns amidst reports that he had a business relationship with the Salt Lake bid committee.	Jan. 14
A panel of the U.S. Court of Appeals for the District of Columbia in Washington, D.C., rules that the administrators of the mental hospital treating John W. Hinckley Jr., who in 1981 shot Pres. Ronald Reagan and three other men, has the authority to grant him supervised outings away from the hospital. . . . NYC mayor Rudolph Giuliani (R) discloses that he has abandoned a goal of shifting all the heroin addicts receiving methadone treatment at city hospitals to abstinence programs.	The Department of the Navy announces that it is lowering educational standards for recruits in an attempt to reverse a decline in enlistments. The navy will now require only 90% of its recruits to have high school diplomas, down from 95%.		Data shows that the U.S. Patent and Trademark Office issued a record 151,024 patents for inventions in 1998, up 33% from the 113,720 issued in 1997. IBM, for the sixth consecutive year, led all other companies in U.S. patents received, with a record 2,657 patents in 1998, 54% more than in 1997.		Jan. 15
				Mike Tyson knocks out South African heavyweight Francois Botha in the fifth round of a match held in Las Vegas, Nevada. It is Tyson's first match after being suspended for biting the ears of opponent Evander Holyfield during a bout in June 1997.	Jan. 16
A jury in Wilmington, Delaware, convicts prominent Delaware attorney Thomas J. Capano of killing his mistress, Anne Marie Fahey, 30, and disposing of her body at sea.			A chain of tornadoes strikes western Tennessee, killing nine people and injuring at least 100.	In professional football, the Denver Broncos defeats the New York Jets, 23-10, to win the AFC title. The Atlanta Falcons upsets the Minnesota Vikings, 30-27, to win the NFC title.	Jan. 17
				Lucille Kallen, 76, one of the few female television writers and the only one in a group writing for a 1950s show, dies in Ardsley, New York, of cancer.	Jan. 18
Lawyers open their defense in Pres. Clinton's impeachment trial. . . . Pres. Clinton delivers the annual State of the Union address to both houses of Congress. He avoids any direct mention of his ongoing impeachment trial in the Senate. Republican representatives Jennifer Dunn (Wash.) and Steve Largent (Okla.) deliver the Republican response. . . . The Supreme Court rejects an appeal by a convicted killer from Florida that electrocution is a cruel and outdated execution method	Gerland Squires, 21, a female army private based at Aberdeen Proving Ground in Maryland, pleads guilty to aggravated assault for having unprotected sex even though she knows she is infected with HIV, the virus that causes AIDS. Squires is sentenced to three years in a military prison, demoted, and receives a bad-conduct discharge from the army, which will deprive her of her pay and her benefits.	In Pres. Clinton's State of the Union address, he proposes investing some Social Security funds—for the first time ever—in the U.S. stock market.	The NIH states that a federal ban on research on human embryos does not apply to human embryonic stem cells, which scientists in 1998 isolated and cultivated for the first time, because the cells do not have the capacity to develop into human beings. . . . Charles Gordon Zubrod, 84, physician who pioneered the use of chemotherapy as a treatment for cancer patients, dies while suffering from spinal meningitis and pneumonia in Washington, D.C..	Pirjo Haeggman of Finland is the first International Olympic Committee (IOC) member to step down in ongoing bribery scandal about the selection of Salt Lake City as the host of the 2000 games.	Jan. 19

F	G	H	I	J
Includes elections, federal-state relations, civil rights and liberties, crime, the judiciary, education, health care, poverty, urban affairs, and population.	Includes formation and debate of U.S. foreign and defense policies, veterans' affairs, and defense spending. (Relations with specific foreign countries are usually found under the region concerned.)	Includes business, labor, agriculture, taxation, transportation, consumer affairs, monetary and fiscal policy, natural resources, and pollution.	Includes worldwide scientific, medical, and technological developments; natural phenomena; U.S. weather; natural disasters; and accidents.	Includes the arts, religion, scholarship, communications media, sports, entertainments, fashions, fads, and social life.

	World Affairs	Europe	Africa & the Middle East	The Americas	Asia & the Pacific
Jan. 20	In response to fighting between the Yugoslav government and ethnic Albanians in Kosovo, NATO stages a show of force by sending a U.S. Navy aircraft carrier to the Adriatic Sea and ordering several other warships to the Italian port of Brindisi, at the mouth of the Adriatic. NATO also reduces a deadline to 48 hours from 96 hours before it may launch air strikes.		Police announce that they recaptured one of the most wanted fugitives in South Africa, Colin Chauke, a former antiapartheid guerrilla fighter, who escaped from prison in late 1997.	The Barbados Labour Party wins 26 of 28 seats in the country's Parliament, the largest electoral margin of victory in the history of the nation. The election returns P.M. Owen Arthur to his post. . . . Former military president General Reynaldo Bignone is arrested in the kidnapping of infants born to political prisoners during Argentina's "dirty war" against suspected leftists.	Indian police and U.S. officials announce that four men have been arrested in India as suspects in a plot to bomb U.S. consulates in Madras and Calcutta. . . . Reports confirm that Indian and Pakistani troops clashed in the disputed territory of Kashmir, leaving four Pakistani soldiers dead. . . . A Shanghai court sentences Lin Hai, 30, to two years in prison for giving 30,000 Chinese e-mail addresses to a U.S.-based dissident on-line publication. It is the first sentence handed down in China for alleged dissident political activity conducted over the Internet.
Jan. 21	The UN Security Council unanimously votes to seek to continue its mission in war-torn Angola, despite UN secretary general Kofi Annan's recommendation that the organization withdraw its forces from the country because he believes that the recently shattered peace in Angola is the fault of both UNITA and the government.	Reports confirm that clashes between striking Romanian coal miners marching on Bucharest, the capital, have injured more than 150 people since the protest march started Jan. 18. . . . The KLA abducts a group of five elderly Serbians.	Two Zimbabwean journalists—Mark Chavunduka, 34, and Ray Choto, 36—are released from military custody on bail, and they allege that they were tortured by authorities in an attempt to force them to reveal their sources for an article about an alleged plot by members of the army to overthrow Pres. Robert Mugabe.	In Nicaragua, a military plane crashes, killing all 28 people aboard. . . . Raul Salinas de Gortari, brother of former Mexican president Carlos Salinas de Gortari, is convicted of masterminding the killing of politician Jose Francisco Ruiz Massieu in 1994. Judge Ricardo Ojeda Bohorquez sentences Salinas to 50 years in prison without parole, the maximum sentence allowed. Salinas is the highest-ranking official charged with and convicted of such a crime in modern Mexico.	
Jan. 22		Reports confirm that Russian premier Yevgeny Primakov has launched a government crackdown on corruption.	In Zimbabwe, police detain Clive Wilson, 62, a newspaper publisher who printed the article on an alleged military plot to overthrow Pres. Robert Mugabe. The article's authors were released from custody Jan. 21.	The government of Nicaragua declares a nationwide day of mourning in memory of the victims of the Jan. 21 crash of a military plane. . . . Government officials announce that Barbados will seek to end the monarchical system on the island, replacing it with a republican constitution presided over by a president. The head of government will remain the prime minister. . . . Pope John Paul II makes his fourth visit to Mexico before traveling to the U.S. in the 85th foreign tour of his pontificate.	Pres. Lee Teng-hui reappoints Vincent Siew as Taiwan's premier.
Jan. 23		Canadian prime minister Jean Chrétien embarks on a visit to Europe that includes stays in Poland and Ukraine, marking the first time that a Canadian prime minister has made official visits to those countries. . . . The government releases a group of nine KLA members taken hostage while crossing the border from Albania in December 1998, and KLA forces release a group of five elderly Serbians kidnapped Jan. 21. . . . Lord Lewin (Terence Thornton), 78, British Royal Navy admiral, dies in Woodbridge, England, of cancer.	Sifiso Nkabinde, a high-level official of the United Democratic Movement (UDM), a multiracial political party, is assassinated in KwaZulu-Natal province in South Africa, which is facing its second democratic elections since the abolition of apartheid. Hours later, 11 people are murdered in Richmond township in what is widely seen as a revenge killing. . . . Reports confirm that West African forces have rescued Freetown's Roman Catholic archbishop and four missionaries kidnapped by rebels earlier in January in Sierra Leone.		
Jan. 24			In South Africa, a group of ANC officials are ambushed in the center of Richmond, but no one is injured. The deputy chair of the UDM, Valindlela Matiyase, is shot to death by two gunman near Capetown. . . . Jordan's King Hussein unexpectedly names his eldest son, Abdullah, as his designated successor. . . . In Sierra Leone, rebels kidnap 11 Indian businessmen, including Kishoie Shakandas, Japan's honorary consul.		
Jan. 25	U.S. jets fire missiles that strike one or more civilian sites around the city of Basra in southeastern Iraq. Iraqi general Ahmed Ibrahim Hammash, Basra's governor, claims that U.S. missiles killed 11 civilians and wounded 50 others.	Polish farmers barricade nearly 100 roads and border crossing points to protest falling produce prices.	In Zimbabwe, police release Clive Wilson, a publisher detained since Jan. 22, after the attorney general's office states there is insufficient evidence to arrest him. Wilson's newspaper published a story about an alleged military plot to overthrow Pres. Robert Mugabe.	An earthquake measuring 6.0 on the Richter scale strikes western Colombia, killing hundreds of people. In the chaos, inmates at Armenia's San Bernardo prison set fire to the structure and prevent firefighters from entering to extinguish the blaze. . . . Pope John Paul II holds a mass to a crowd of 100,000 at Mexico City's Aztec Stadium.	An explosion in a farmers' market in Yizhang, in Hunan province, China, kills eight people and injures some 65 others. Separately, reports reveal that a township in Sichuan province held China's first direct election for a township chief in December 1998. Tan Xiaoqiu won the election with 50.19% of the vote.

A	B	C	D	E
Includes developments that affect more than one world region, international organizations, and important meetings of major world leaders.	*Includes all domestic and regional developments in Europe, including the Soviet Union, Turkey, Cyprus, and Malta.*	*Includes all domestic and regional developments in Africa and the Middle East, including Iraq and Iran and excluding Cyprus, Turkey, and Afghanistan.*	*Includes all domestic and regional developments in Latin America, the Caribbean, and Canada.*	*Includes all domestic and regional developments in Asia and Pacific nations, extending from Afghanistan through all the Pacific Island, except Hawaii.*

U.S. Politics & Social Issues	U.S. Foreign Policy & Defense	U.S. Economy & Environment	Science, Technology, & Nature	Culture, Leisure, & Lifestyle	
A California state jury awards $116 million in punitive damages to Teresa Goodrich, the widow of a cancer patient, in a suit against health insurer Aetna Inc. Together with compensatory damages of $4.5 million awarded earlier, the verdict is believed to be the largest ever against a HMO.... In *Humana Inc. v. Forsyth*, the Supreme Court rules unanimously that health insurers are not immune from prosecution under the federal Racketeer Influenced and Corrupt Organizations Act (RICO).				The National Basketball Association and the players' union sign a six-year collective bargaining agreement, formally ending a 204-day player lockout.... Eugene Smith Pulliam, 84, newspaperman based in Indiana, dies in Indianapolis, Indiana, of unreported causes.	Jan. 20
Opening presentations in Pres. Clinton's impeachment trial close. ... The nation's four largest tobacco companies announce that they will establish a $5.15 billion fund to aid tobacco farmers who face a reduced market following the industry's settlement of states' tobacco-related lawsuits.... Federal authorities announce they made one of the largest seizures of cocaine in U.S. history. The cocaine, found concealed in a freighter under a load of iron ore, carries a street value of $186 million.		The FEC fines longtime Democratic fund-raiser Howard Glicken $40,000 for illegally soliciting a donation from German national Thomas Kramer. The FEC penalty is in addition to an $80,000 fine Glicken was ordered to pay in 1998 in a criminal case brought by the Justice Department's task force.	As many as 38 tornadoes strike central and eastern Arkansas and western Tennessee, killing seven people in Arkansas and one person in Tennessee. Meteorologists reveal it is the highest number of tornadoes ever recorded in one state on one day....A study of some 88,000 women suggests that a diet high in fiber does not lower the risk of developing colon cancer, as is widely believed .... The FDA requests the voluntary recall of dietary supplements containing the substance gamma butyrolactone (GBL).	Susan Strasberg, 60, actress and daughter of renowned acting instructors Lee Strasberg and Paula Miller, dies in NYC of breast cancer.	Jan. 21
In the impeachment trial of Pres. Clinton, senators begin to question both sides.	Kurt Stand and his wife, Theresa Squillacote, are sentenced to 17 and 21 years in prison, respectively, for spying for East Germany. The couple was found guilty in October 1998.... Defense Department officials reveal that the number of recruits discharged for being homosexual came to 1,145 in 1998, which is nearly double the total in 1993, the year before the Clinton administration's "don't ask, don't tell" policy was implemented. It is the fifth consecutive increase.			I. Michael Heyman, the secretary of the Smithsonian Institution in Washington, D.C., states he will retire by the end of 1999.	Jan. 22
		Jay A. Pritzker, 76, U.S. businessman who founded the Hyatt hotel chain and who, in 1979, endowed the Pritzker Architecture Prize, dies in Chicago, Illinois, after a heart attack.	A gamma ray burst, an immense eruptions of energy in space whose exact sources remain unknown to scientists, occurs near the constellation Bootes.		Jan. 23
			Pres. Clinton surveys damage from the Jan. 21 tornadoes in Little Rock, Arkansas, and declares at least five counties natural disaster areas, making them eligible for federal aid.	At the Golden Globes Awards, the film *Saving Private Ryan* wins as Best Drama while *Shakespeare in Love* wins for Best Musical or Comedy.... The International Olympic Committee recommends the expulsion of six of its members on bribery charges. At least three members of the IOC under investigation already resigned.	Jan. 24
In *AT&T Corp. et al. v. Iowa Utilities Board*, the Supreme Court overturns, 5-3, a lower court ruling that curbed the authority of the FCC to set policy on opening the $100 billion local telephone market to competition..... The Supreme Court rules, 5-4, that the Census Bureau cannot use statistical sampling when it conducts the official national census, upholding a lower court decision in *Clinton v. Glavin*.		Statistics suggest that sales of existing homes in 1998 jumped 13.5% from the previous year to 4.8 million units, marking a third consecutive yearly record.	Surgeons in Louisville, Kentucky, complete the first hand transplant to be performed in the U.S.... Pharmaceutical maker Eli Lilly & Co. agrees to pay $4 million to settle a lawsuit challenging its patent on the popular antidepressant drug Prozac.	Sarah Louise (Sadie) Delany, 109, bestselling coauthor of the 1993 book, *Having Our Say*, dies in Mount Vernon, New York.... Robert (Lawson) Shaw, 82, conductor whose recorded performances garnered him 14 Grammy Awards, dies of a stroke in New Haven, Connecticut.	Jan. 25

F	G	H	I	J
Includes elections, federal-state relations, civil rights and liberties, crime, the judiciary, education, health care, poverty, urban affairs, and population.	Includes formation and debate of U.S. foreign and defense policies, veterans' affairs, and defense spending. (Relations with specific foreign countries are usually found under the region concerned.)	Includes business, labor, agriculture, taxation, transportation, consumer affairs, monetary and fiscal policy, natural resources, and pollution.	Includes worldwide scientific, medical, and technological developments; natural phenomena; U.S. weather; natural disasters; and accidents.	Includes the arts, religion, scholarship, communications media, sports, entertainments, fashions, fads, and social life.

	World Affairs	Europe	Africa & the Middle East	The Americas	Asia & the Pacific
Jan. 26	Rescue teams from the U.S. and Japan travel to Colombia to assist local efforts. Reports confirm that the European Commission has committed $1.1 million in aid to Colombia in the wake of the Jan. 25 earthquake.	A human-rights advocacy group estimates that paramilitary groups in Ireland have been responsible for 37 punishment beatings and shootings since the beginning of the year.	Reports indicate that rebels in Sierra Leone have abducted 12 foreigners.... In Angola, UNITA captures Mbanza Congo, 190 miles north of Luanda.... Jordan's King Hussein surprises Jordanians by publicly changing the line of succession and swearing in his eldest son, Prince Abdullah, as crown prince and regent. Minutes later, the king departs for the U.S. for medical treatment.... In Zimbabwe, police break up a demonstration by lawyers and journalists protesting the alleged use of torture during the detention of journalists who were released Jan. 21.	Legislators vote to approve constitutional changes that will put the Honduran military under civilian control.... Reports reveal that three military officers have been charged with organizing a plot to kill Guatemalan anthropologist Myrna Mack Chang, who was investigating human-rights violations by the military before being stabbed to death in 1990. Sergeant Noel de Jesus Beteta was convicted in 1993 of carrying out the murder.... Some 15 aftershocks of the Jan. 25 earthquake are recorded in Colombia.	
Jan. 27	Taiwan reveals that it has established diplomatic ties with Macedonia. That brings the number of countries that formally recognize Taiwan to 28.	The body of Eamon Collins, a former member of the Provisional Irish Republican Army (IRA), is found near the town of Newry, Northern Ireland.		In Honduras, Brigadier General Mario Hung Pacheco formally hands over control of the armed forces to civilian president Carlos Flores.... In Colombia, residents of Armenia and Pereira loot stores and clash with police and soldiers in the wake of the Jan. 25 tremor.... The British Privy Council grants a reprieve to two inmates on death row in Trinidad and Tobago, pending a ruling by the Interamerican Commission on Human Rights.	Indonesian foreign minister Ali Alatas announces that the government of Pres. B. J. Habibie is prepared to grant the province full independence if the East Timorese reject the government's autonomy plan. It is the first time that Indonesia indicates that it will recognize an independent East Timor.... Reports disclose that feminist author Taslima Nasreen returned to exile in Sweden after Islamic militants in Bangladesh renewed death threats against her.
Jan. 28		Britain's Prince Charles and his longtime companion, Camilla Parker Bowles, make their first public appearance as a couple.	A bomb explodes outside the main police station in Cape Town, injuring 11 people. It is the third bomb to explode in the city over the past five months.	Data shows that at least 878 people died in the Jan. 25 quake in Colombia and that more than 3,410 have been injured. Military police use tear gas to control looters in Armenia, and Pres. Pastrana reveals that some 2,700 soldiers and police will be sent to the city to restore order.... Cuban foreign ministry official Alejandro Gonzalez confirms that two Cuban men, Sergio Antonio Duarte Scull and Carlos Rafael Pelaez Prieto, have been sentenced to death by firing squad for the 1998 killings of two Italian tourists.	Chinese authorities in the predominantly Muslim province of Xinjiang execute two leaders of a separatist movement, Yibulayin Simayi and Abudureyimu Aisha. They were convicted of planning and carrying out riots and bombings that took place in 1997.
Jan. 29	A contact group of six nations orders the Yugoslav government and KLA forces to participate in peace talks under threat of military action.	Serbian forces attack a suspected KLA stronghold in Rogovo, southwestern Kosovo, killing 24 men—mostly civilians.	Authorities disclose that more than 4,000 people have died in Freetown, the capital of Sierra Leone, since the start of fighting in early January.... Data shows that Ethiopia has forcibly deported some 52,000 Eritreans since May 1998, when fighting broke out in a border dispute between Ethiopia and Eritrea.		Reports indicate that more than 200,000 Bangladeshi women have been smuggled into Pakistan to serve as prostitutes since the late 1980s.... The Court of Final Appeal, Hong Kong's highest court, unanimously rules that children born in China to parents who are Hong Kong residents have the right to live in Hong Kong. The ruling overturns a law, passed by Hong Kong's China-appointed legislature in 1997.
Jan. 30	The UN Security Council agrees to a plan to review all aspects of Iraq's relations with the UN, with the aim of reformulating the UN's Iraq policy.				About 1,000 supporters of Malaysia's ousted deputy prime minister, Anwar Ibrahim, gather outside the courthouse in Kuala Lumpur.
Jan. 31		Some 200,000 people march in Paris, France, to protest legislation that would create new rights for unmarried couples. The demonstrators argue that the law will effectively legalize homosexual marriages, which they claim will endanger traditional family values.			

A	B	C	D	E
Includes developments that affect more than one world region, international organizations, and important meetings of major world leaders.	Includes all domestic and regional developments in Europe, including the Soviet Union, Turkey, Cyprus, and Malta.	Includes all domestic and regional developments in Africa and the Middle East, including Iraq and Iran and excluding Cyprus, Turkey, and Afghanistan.	Includes all domestic and regional developments in Latin America, the Caribbean, and Canada.	Includes all domestic and regional developments in Asia and Pacific nations, extending from Afghanistan through all the Pacific Island, except Hawaii.

U.S. Politics & Social Issues	U.S. Foreign Policy & Defense	U.S. Economy & Environment	Science, Technology, & Nature	Culture, Leisure, & Lifestyle	
		A court of appeals in Washington, D.C., reinstates independent counsel Kenneth Starr's tax fraud case against Whitewater figure Webster Hubbell. A federal court dismissed Starr's case against Hubbell in July 1998.		Pope John Paul II arrives in St. Louis, Missouri, where he is welcomed by tens of thousands of cheering supporters. The pontiff addresses some 20,000 teenagers at the Kiel Center sports arena.... The Whitbread Award is given to British poet Ted Hughes. Hughes is the first person to win the award posthumously and the first to win it twice.	Jan. 26
The Senate votes to proceed with the impeachment trial of Pres. Clinton and to summon three witnesses, including Monica Lewinsky. The identical 56-44 votes are split by party lines.... Florida's Miami-Dade County files a suit against the gun industry seeking compensation for the costs of treating gun-related injuries and of investigating gun-related crimes. A similar suit is filed by Bridgeport, Connecticut.			NASA reports that for the first time scientists have photographed light emitted by the gamma ray burst caught Jan. 23 near the constellation Bootes.... Two studies find that many ordinary daily activities may improve physical fitness as much as structured exercise regimens.	Ben Margolis, 88, lawyer known for defending Hollywood personalities accused in the 1950s of belonging to the Communist Party, dies in Portland, Oregon.	Jan. 27
Missouri governor Mel Carnahan (D) commutes the death sentence of a convicted triple murderer, Darrell Mease, 52, after a personal request by Pope John Paul II, who is visiting St. Louis, Missouri.					Jan. 28
A Florida state appeals court vacates a June 1998 $1 million jury verdict in a smoking-related liability lawsuit against Brown & Williamson Tobacco Corp. and orders that the case be retried in either Palm Beach County or Broward County.	Louise Woodward, a British au pair convicted in 1997 of killing the baby in her charge, settles a civil wrongful-death lawsuit brought by the baby's parents. The settlement bars Woodward from profiting from the case.	The Commerce Department reports that the U.S. growth domestic product (GDP) grew at an inflation-adjusted annual rate of 3.9% in 1998. That matches 1997's revised GDP gain, equaling the fastest growth rate since 1984.... The CBO projects there will be $2.67 trillion in budget surpluses over the years 2000 to 2009. The CBO predicts that surpluses in non-Social Security accounts will total $787 billion over the years 2000–2009.	An analysis suggests that women with HIV can nearly eliminate the risk of transmitting the virus to their newborn babies by taking AZT during pregnancy and undergoing a Caesarean section delivery.	Lili St. Cyr (born Willis Marie Van Schaack), 80, striptease artist who, in 1951, was acquitted of indecent exposure in a well-publicized case, dies in Hollywood, California, of a heart attack.	Jan. 29
Mills Edwin Godwin Jr., 84, Virginia's only two-term governor since the Civil War, who served his first term, 1966–70, as a Democrat and his second term, 1974–78, as a Republican, dies in Newport News, Virginia.				Huntz (Henry) Hall, 78, one of a group of young actors who appeared in the 1935 play Dead End, dies in Los Angeles after a heart attack.... Lawrence Taylor, Eric Dickerson, Tom Mack, Ozzie Newsome, and Billy Shaw are named to the Pro Football Hall of Fame.... At the Australian Open, Martina Hingis of Switzerland wins her third consecutive tennis title.	Jan. 30
	Customs agents near Niagara Falls, on the New York State-Canadian border, foil an attempt to smuggle four Chinese women into the U.S. from Canada.	Claude Vealey, 55, convicted of the 1969 shooting murders of United Mine Workers of America reformer Joseph Yablonski and Yablonski's wife and daughter in Clarksville, Pennsylvania, dies at a prison in Laurel Highlands, Pennsylvania, of cancer.	Scientists report they have discovered the origin of the predominant strain of HIV, the virus that causes AIDS. They argue that it spread to humans from a subspecies of chimpanzee, Pan troglodytes troglodytes, that lives in western Africa.	The Denver Broncos trounce the Atlanta Falcons, 34-19, to win pro football's Super Bowl XXXIII. Police in Denver, Colorado, have to use tear gas for the second year in a row to disperse violent Broncos fans.... At the Australian Open, Yevgeny Kafelnikov of Russia wins the men's title.... At the Sundance Film Festival, Three Seasons, directed by Tony Bui, wins the Grand Jury Prize.	Jan. 31

F	G	H	I	J
Includes elections, federal-state relations, civil rights and liberties, crime, the judiciary, education, health care, poverty, urban affairs, and population.	Includes formation and debate of U.S. foreign and defense policies, veterans' affairs, and defense spending. (Relations with specific foreign countries are usually found under the region concerned.)	Includes business, labor, agriculture, taxation, transportation, consumer affairs, monetary and fiscal policy, natural resources, and pollution.	Includes worldwide scientific, medical, and technological developments; natural phenomena; U.S. weather; natural disasters; and accidents.	Includes the arts, religion, scholarship, communications media, sports, entertainments, fashions, fads, and social life.

	World Affairs	Europe	Africa & the Middle East	The Americas	Asia & the Pacific
Feb. 1		In Moldova, Premier Ion Ciubuc resigns, citing political divisions that have hindered his reform efforts.... Marion Boyars (born Marion Asmus), 71, British independent book publisher, dies in London of pancreatic cancer.	Some 146 Israeli writers, artists, and intellectuals issue a statement in support of a Palestinian state in all of the West Bank and Gaza Strip, with its capital located in East Jerusalem.... Police officer Rifat Joudah is shot and killed while trying to arrest Hamas suspect Raed al-Attar.		
Feb. 2		Alleged World War II criminal Esperanza Luburic, arrested in Argentina in July 1998, is released from custody. Croatian officials disclose that a trial found no evidence proving the allegations that Luburic committed war crimes while allegedly running a women's block at the Stara Gradiska detention camp in Nazi-controlled Croatia from 1942 to 1945.		Populist Hugo Chavez Frias is sworn in as president of Venezuela in Caracas, the capital.	Chee Soon Juan, leader of the small opposition Singapore Democratic Party, is convicted of making a public speech in December 1998 without a police permit. Chee is ordered to pay a fine of S$1,400 (US$827) or face a week in prison.... A survey reveals that only 19% of Australia's working-age population is adequately literate to cope with the needs of their jobs.
Feb. 3		Reports confirm that Russia's Constitutional Court has banned capital punishment until all of Russia's 89 regions adopt a system of trial by jury. Because only nine of Russia's regions operate a jury system, the ruling effectively abolishes the death penalty in Russia.			
Feb. 4		Deutsche Bank AG, the largest bank in Germany, confirms that it helped finance the Nazi German regime's construction of Auschwitz, a World War II-era death camp in Poland.		Canada's federal government, nine of its 10 provinces, and both of its territories sign a "Framework to Improve the Social Union for Canadians," creating a partnership between federal and provincial governments in the implementation of social programs.	A Chinese court in Hangzhou hands down a four-year prison sentence to Wang Ce, a Chinese dissident who had resided abroad but slipped back into the country in 1998. Separately, the official Chinese newspaper reports that 1,000 soldiers were transferred in January to the city of Yining in Xinjiang, where they arrested hundreds of suspected separatists.
Feb. 5	The International Criminal Tribunal for Rwanda in Arusha, Tanzania, sentences Omar Serushago, a Rwandan militia leader, to 15 years in prison for participating in the deaths of 37 people. He is the third person sentenced for genocide by the tribunal. Serushago cooperated with prosecutors and is the only one of the three to receive less than a life sentence.	Serbian officials announce that after reviewing a 1991 sale, they have determined that the government actually owns a 65% stake in ICN Yugoslavia, a subsidiary of U.S.-based ICN Pharmaceuticals Inc. In 1991, Milan Panic, who was premier in 1992, purchased a 75% stake in Galenika, a state-owned company that then became ICN Yugoslavia. They claim that Panic paid only $50 million of the agreed $270 million purchase price, and they have reduced his stake accordingly.		The Supreme Court in Paraguay demands that Pres. Raul Cubas Grau return Gen. Lino Cesar Oviedo to prison, repeating a request made in December 1998.	The Philippines executes by lethal injection Leo Echegaray, a man convicted in 1994 of repeatedly raping his stepdaughter. Echegaray is the first person executed in the Philippines since 1976. The country outlawed capital punishment in 1987, but it restored the death penalty in 1993.... Neville Thomas Bonner, 76, Australia's first aboriginal parliamentarian who served in the federal Senate, 1971–83, dies of lung cancer.
Feb. 6		Representatives from ethnic Albanian political and military groups and the Serbian government, under heavy pressure from the West, attend peace talks at the chateau of Rambouillet, France, some 32 miles (50 km) outside of Paris. Separately, armed Serbian police seize ICN Yugoslavia, a subsidiary of U.S.-based ICN Pharmaceuticals Inc., in which the government claimed a 65% share Feb. 5. Serbian Deputy Health Minister Marija Krstajic appoints herself general manager of the company and orders the police to evict ICN's previous management.	Heavy fighting breaks out between Eritrea and Ethiopia in an ongoing border dispute.... Zimbabwe's Pres. Robert Mugabe claims that four of the country's top judges should resign and threatens action against the independent press. Mugabe's comments are prompted by a letter by three of the justices that address the January arrest and apparent torture of two journalists. Representatives of the EU, Canada, Japan, Australia, and the U.S. have protested the treatment of the two detained journalists.		Isao Sasaki, a retired Japanese electronics executive, is arrested in connection with the alleged illegal sale to China of equipment that can be used in the development of nuclear weapons.

A	B	C	D	E
Includes developments that affect more than one world region, international organizations, and important meetings of major world leaders.	Includes all domestic and regional developments in Europe, including the Soviet Union, Turkey, Cyprus, and Malta.	Includes all domestic and regional developments in Africa and the Middle East, including Iraq and Iran and excluding Cyprus, Turkey, and Afghanistan.	Includes all domestic and regional developments in Latin America, the Caribbean, and Canada.	Includes all domestic and regional developments in Asia and Pacific nations, extending from Afghanistan through all the Pacific Island, except Hawaii.

U.S. Politics & Social Issues	U.S. Foreign Policy & Defense	U.S. Economy & Environment	Science, Technology, & Nature	Culture, Leisure, & Lifestyle	
In Philadelphia, Pennsylvania, Judge Lowell Reed grants a preliminary injunction against a law aimed at preventing children from viewing sexually explicit images on the World Wide Web.... The New Jersey Supreme Court upholds the state's capital punishment law and rejects the contention that the state's sentencing process is racially biased.		Pres. Clinton presents to Congress a $1.77 trillion budget proposal for the 2000 fiscal year, an increase of 2.2%, or $39 billion from the current year.... A natural gas buildup at a Ford power station in Dearborn, Michigan, causes an explosion, killing one employee and injuring 16 others.... Paul Mellon, 91, one of the U.S.'s most generous patrons of the arts and of environmentalist causes, dies in Upperville, Virginia, after suffering from cancer.	A study shows that a new short-term drug treatment might substantially reduce the risk that pregnant women infected with HIV, the virus that causes AIDS, will transmit the virus to their newborn children.	*Southern Cross*, by Patricia Cornwell, tops the bestseller list.... The Caldecott Medal is awarded to Mary Azarian, and the Newbery Medal goes to Louis Sachar.... A crowd of 375,000 celebrate the Super Bowl victory at a parade in Denver, Colorado.	Feb. 1
A civil jury in Portland, Oregon, finds that the creators of an Internet site that features "wanted" posters listing the names of abortion providers made what amounts to a "hit list" that threatens deadly violence. The jury awards $107 million in damages to the Planned Parenthood Foundation of America and a group of doctors who brought the lawsuit.					Feb. 2
	John Stewart Service, 89, Foreign Service officer who was the first of a group of experts on China purged from the State Department during the "Red Scare" of the late 1940s and early 1950s, dies of heart disease in Oakland, California.	Officials reveal that the IRS has cleared a conservative foundation of charges that it violated tax laws by funding a college course taught by former Rep. Newt Gingrich (R, Ga.) before he became House speaker in 1995.	Research indicates that there is an apparent link between certain antibiotic drugs and a lowered risk of heart disease. Scientists assert that the study does not prove that antibiotics cause the reduced risk, but it adds to current evidence that chronic infections might be a cause of heart disease.		Feb. 3
The Senate votes, 70-30, against calling Monica Lewinsky or any other witness to testify in person at Pres. Clinton's impeachment trial. Instead, the House prosecution team may present videotaped excerpts from depositions by Lewinsky and two other witnesses, Vernon Jordan Jr. and Sidney Blumenthal.... Atlanta, Georgia, seeks monetary reimbursement for the costs of gun-related violence in a lawsuit filed against 15 gun makers and two trade associations.	NYC police officers kill Amadou Diallo, 22, an unarmed West African immigrant, hitting him with 19 of 41 shots fired at him. The incident draws national and international attention and triggers protests across the country as well as in the victim's native country, Guinea. Because Diallo had no criminal record and was shot in the vestibule of his apartment building, the circumstances of the shooting are under investigation.	A cargo ship called the *New Carissa*, holding 400,000 gallons of oil, runs aground in stormy weather at Coos Bay, Oregon.	Several teams of scientists report that new testing techniques show that drug-resistant strains of HIV, the virus that causes AIDS, are more widespread than previously thought.... Cosmonauts aboard the Russian space station *Mir* attempt to deploy a mirror intended to illuminate a portion of the dark side of Earth. However, the mirror's panels become stuck in a cargo module.		Feb. 4
The board of fellows at the University of Notre Dame vote to continue to exclude sexual orientation as a basis for protection under its policy against discrimination.... Anthony Porter, 43, a convicted killer who has been on death row for 16 years, is freed on bond after an investigation by Northwestern University journalism students reveals his probable innocence. He is the 75th death row inmate since 1976 to be freed on appeal or to be proven innocent and the 10th death-row inmate released in Illinois since its 1977 reinstatement of capital punishment.		An employee of Ford Motor Co. dies from burns sustained in the Feb. 1 blast at Ford's River Rouge complex in Dearborn, Michigan, bringing the death toll to two.	After the Feb. 4 mishap, Russian space officials abandon the mirror project and send the *Progress* supply ship into the Earth's atmosphere, where it burns up.... Wassily Leontief, 93, Russian-born economist and winner of the 1973 Nobel prize in economic science for developing a method adopted by most industrialized nations for planning and predicting economic progress, dies in New York City.	Former heavyweight boxing champion Mike Tyson is sentenced to one year in jail in Maryland for assaulting two motorists after a traffic accident in August 1998. Legal analysts suggest that the sentence may cause the revocation of Tyson's probation in Indiana, where he served only three years of a six-year term on a rape conviction.	Feb. 5
				Reports confirm that the Chinese government has given the U.S.'s Walt Disney Co. permission to distribute the animated film *Mulan*, based on a legend about a Chinese warrior heroine, in China. The country had previously rebuffed Disney films and business ventures after the company distributed *Kundun*, a film about the Dalai Lama, the exiled Tibetan leader.	Feb. 6

F	G	H	I	J
Includes elections, federal-state relations, civil rights and liberties, crime, the judiciary, education, health care, poverty, urban affairs, and population.	Includes formation and debate of U.S. foreign and defense policies, veterans' affairs, and defense spending. (Relations with specific foreign countries are usually found under the region concerned.)	Includes business, labor, agriculture, taxation, transportation, consumer affairs, monetary and fiscal policy, natural resources, and pollution.	Includes worldwide scientific, medical, and technological developments; natural phenomena; U.S. weather; natural disasters; and accidents.	Includes the arts, religion, scholarship, communications media, sports, entertainments, fashions, fads, and social life.

	World Affairs	Europe	Africa & the Middle East	The Americas	Asia & the Pacific
Feb. 7	The death of King Hussein of Jordan prompts international response, particularly as he was a longtime mainstay in the Arab-Israeli peace process.		In his 46th year as Jordan's monarch, King Hussein, 63, dies of non-Hodgkins lymphoma in Amman. His eldest son, Prince Abdullah, takes the oath as monarch, becoming King Abdullah II. . . . Ethiopia accuses Eritrea of shelling civilians in an attack on the town of Adigrat, wounding seven. . . . Marius Schoon, 61, one of a small number of Afrikaners prominent in the antiapartheid movement in South Africa, dies of lung cancer in Johannesburg.		
Feb. 8	An array of world leaders—many of whom are at odds with each other—attend the funeral of Jordan's King Hussein. They include Palestinian leader Yasser Arafat; Israeli prime minister Benjamin Netanyahu; former Israeli prime minister Shimon Peres; Khaled Meshal, the Hamas political leader whom Israel attempted to assassinate in 1997; and Syria's president, Hafez al-Assad, who has never before attended an event at which Israeli officials are present. Other leaders include U.S. president Clinton British prime minister Blair, Sudanese president Omar Hassan Bashir, French president Chirac, and German chancellor Schroeder.	Nearly all of the Polish farmers who erected barricades on Jan. 25 end their protest . . . The first trial to be held under the 1991 War Crimes Act, which provides for the prosecution of alleged World War II criminals living in Britain, opens in London. The defendant is Anthony Sawoniuk, charged with murdering Jews in four separate incidents in 1942. . . . Serbian police arrest six executives and detain three vice presidents of ICN Yugoslavia, seized on Feb. 6. An estimated 1,000–2,000 ICN workers storm through police lines around the plant in protest.	Ethiopian warplanes attack Tsorona, approximately 100 miles east of Badme. Fighting also reportedly breaks out near Burie.	A three-judge panel in Esquintla, Guatamala, convicts three men—Cosbi Gamaliel Urias Ortiz, Rony Leonel Polanco Sil, and Reyes Guch Ventura—in the robbery and rape of a group of college students from St. Mary's College in the U.S. The convictions come as a surprise to many observers, who note that similar crimes against Guatamalans are rarely punished. . . . Reports indicate that five police officers have been charged in the November 1998 death of U.S. graduate student Frederick McPhail Jr. in Mexico City, Mexico.	
Feb. 9	In response to the establishment of diplomatic ties between Taiwan and Macedonia announced Jan. 27, China discloses that it has cut its diplomatic relations with Macedonia.	Heavy snows cause a series of avalanches to strike the region around Chamonix in France.	An Ethiopian plane bombs the Eritrean village of Laili Deda, killing at least five civilians.	Reports confirm that Cuba has approved the country's first 100% foreign-owned venture. Panama-based Genpower Cuba SA will build, own, and operate the venture, a diesel electric power plant valued at some $15 million, on Cuba's Youth Island, off the main island's southwest coast.	Four districts in southeastern Queensland, Australia, are declared disaster areas after nearly a week of heavy rains that are causing widespread flooding.
Feb. 10		ICN Pharmaceuticals, a U.S. parent company of the firm seized by Serbia on Feb. 6, files a $500 million lawsuit against the Yugoslav government of Pres. Slobodan Milosevic and the state health ministry of Serbia. . . . Italy's highest appeals court, the Court of Cassation, sparks controversy when it overturns a rape conviction handed down in 1998, asserting that the alleged rape victim's blue jeans were too tight to be removed without her assistance.	Police break up an antigovernment demonstration by students at the University of Zimbabwe in Harare, the capital. The students are protesting Pres. Mugabe's crackdown on journalists, the government's corruption, Zimbabwe's participation in the Congo conflict, and delays in student grant payments.		Taiwan reveals that China deployed more than 100 new ballistic missiles within firing range of Taiwan. . . . Heavy rains in Queensland, Australia, cause the Mary River to peak at 72 feet (21.95 m), its highest level in more than a century. The flooding results in seven deaths. . . . An armed gang shoots and kills 12 low-caste, or "untouchable," villagers in Narayanpur in the Indian state of Bihar. It is the second such caste-related massacre in less than three weeks.
Feb. 11		Data reveals that a series of avalanches that struck Chamonix, France, on Feb. 9 left at least 10 people dead. Twenty people buried under snow were pulled out alive, and two people are missing. . . . Austria reveals it will return to the Rothschild family about 250 works of art stolen by Nazi forces between 1938 and 1945. . . . In response to the Feb. 10 Italian court ruling-overturning a rape conviction many female members of Italy's parliament wear jeans to parliament in a demonstration.	The Ethiopian government apologizes for killing Eritrean civilians in a Feb. 9 bombing raid. The U.S. State Department orders nonessential employees at U.S. embassies in both Ethiopia and Eritrea to leave. It also advises U.S. citizens to depart.		A powerful storm, cyclone Rona, crosses over northern Queensland, Australia, bringing heavy rains that flood much of the region, forcing more than 1,800 people from their homes.

A	B	C	D	E
Includes developments that affect more than one world region, international organizations, and important meetings of major world leaders.	*Includes all domestic and regional developments in Europe, including the Soviet Union, Turkey, Cyprus, and Malta.*	*Includes all domestic and regional developments in Africa and the Middle East, including Iraq and Iran and excluding Cyprus, Turkey, and Afghanistan.*	*Includes all domestic and regional developments in Latin America, the Caribbean, and Canada.*	*Includes all domestic and regional developments in Asia and Pacific nations, extending from Afghanistan through all the Pacific Island, except Hawaii.*

U.S. Politics & Social Issues	U.S. Foreign Policy & Defense	U.S. Economy & Environment	Science, Technology, & Nature	Culture, Leisure, & Lifestyle	
	Reports confirm that U.S. Border Patrol officials arrested 162 illegal immigrants in San Diego, California, in a dilapidated 1,500-square-foot (140-sq-m) house.		NASA launches *Stardust*, an unmanned spacecraft, atop a Delta-2 rocket at Cape Canaveral, Florida. *Stardust* is intended to collect samples of dust from the comet Wild-2 and return them to Earth for study.	The AFC defeats the NFC, 23-10, to win the Pro Bowl, the National Football League's annual all-star game.	Feb. 7
The impeachment trial of Pres. Clinton enters its final phase as the Senate hears final arguments from the House prosecutors and the president's White House defense team. . . . The U.S. Fourth Circuit Court of Appeals in Richmond, Virginia, rules, 2-1, that prosecutors may use a suspect's voluntary confession even if that suspect has not been read his or her Miranda rights.				Dame (Jean) Iris Murdoch, 79, British novelist whose more than two dozen novels reflect her training in philosophy, dies in Oxford, England, after a five-year battle with Alzheimer's disease. . . . Todd McFarlane, creator of a best-selling comic book, reveals that he was the anonymous buyer who paid a record $3 million for the 70th home run baseball hit by Mark McGwire during the 1998 season.	Feb. 8
Statistics reveal that only 36% of eligible voters participated in the 1998 midterm elections—the lowest turnout for a nationwide election since 1942. . . . Georgia governor Roy Barnes (D) signs a bill barring a liability suit that the city of Atlanta filed Feb. 4 against gun makers. The law, which allows only the state to bring such a suit, is the first of its kind in the country.	Richard Holbrooke, a veteran diplomat named by Pres. Clinton in June 1998 as his choice for U.S. ambassador to the UN, agrees to pay a $5,000 fine to settle charges brought by the Justice Department that he broke conflict-of-interest laws.	June Gibbs Brown, the inspector general of the Department of Health and Human Services, reports that overpayments to health-care providers by Medicare totaled an estimated $12.6 billion in 1998. That is a decline from the estimated 1997 total of $20.3 billion in excess payments. Spending by Medicare totaled $211 billion in 1998.		A panel investigating ethics violations in the bid to hold the 2002 Winter Olympics in Salt Lake City, Utah, releases a 300-page report . . . . Ch. Loteki Supernatural Being, a papillon, wins best-in-show at the Westminster Kennel Club Dog Show.	Feb. 9
Statistics show that 19 fatal shootings by police occurred in New York City in 1998, the lowest number since 1985. . . . A jury awards $50 million in punitive damages to Patricia Henley in a lawsuit against Philip Morris. When combined with compensatory damages awarded earlier, the total damages are by far the largest ever in such a case. . . . Truong Van Tran, who sparked controversy by hanging a picture of the late North Vietnamese communist leader Ho Chi Minh in his shop, is attacked by a group of 150 protesters in Orange County, California.		Crews from the U.S. Navy and U.S. Coast Guard set fire to the *New Carissa*, which ran aground in Oregon on Feb. 4, in an attempt to burn away thousands of gallons of oil over several days. . . . In Dallas, Texas, Judge Joe Kendall issues a temporary restraining order against the APA, requiring the union's members to end a sick-out, which started Feb. 6 when an inordinate number of pilots at AMR Corp.'s American Airlines called in sick.		Reports confirm that former Moral Majority leader Rev. Jerry Falwell has argued that Tinky Winky, a character on the children's TV show *Teletubbies*, is homosexual and therefore a poor role model for children.	Feb. 10
A NYC jury finds a group of gun manufacturers liable for shootings carried out with illegally purchased handguns. The jury bases its unprecedented decision on the gun companies' marketing practices, which it claims give youths and criminals access to illegal firearms. . . . A NYC jury acquits Montoun Hart, 27, in the 1997 torture and murder of teacher Jonathan Levin.		Despite the Feb. 10 order, some 2,400 pilots call in sick, the most since the disruption at American Airlines began. Due to the shortage of pilots, American cancels 1,170 flights, more than 50% of the carrier's daily total. . . . Agriculture Secretary Dan Glickman announces an 18-month moratorium on road building in more than 33 million acres (13 million hectares) of national forest lands in the Northwest, Alaska, and the Southeast.			Feb. 11

F	G	H	I	J
Includes elections, federal-state relations, civil rights and liberties, crime, the judiciary, education, health care, poverty, urban affairs, and population.	Includes formation and debate of U.S. foreign and defense policies, veterans' affairs, and defense spending. (Relations with specific foreign countries are usually found under the region concerned.)	Includes business, labor, agriculture, taxation, transportation, consumer affairs, monetary and fiscal policy, natural resources, and pollution.	Includes worldwide scientific, medical, and technological developments; natural phenomena; U.S. weather; natural disasters; and accidents.	Includes the arts, religion, scholarship, communications media, sports, entertainments, fashions, fads, and social life.

	World Affairs	Europe	Africa & the Middle East	The Americas	Asia & the Pacific
Feb. 12			The Angolan government states it has recaptured Mbanza Congo, a provincial capital 190 miles north of Luanda, from the rebels.		The Thai Senate votes to pass legislation that will establish a new bankruptcy court. . . . Due to floods, Queensland Emergency Services Minister Merri Rose declares a state of disaster in the regions of Cairns and Innisfail in northern Queensland, Australia.
Feb. 13					Reports confirm that British author Salman Rushdie has been granted a visa permitting him to visit India, his native country.
Feb. 14			Eritrea reveals that it shot down an Ethiopian helicopter gunship over the front line, killing the crew. It also states that Ethiopian planes have killed 16 civilians and wounded 20 since the latest round of fighting began in early February. An Ethiopian plane bombs an area sparsely populated by civilians just outside the Eritrean port city of Assab. . . . Two separate Jewish groups, one composed of some 250,000 ultra-Orthodox Jews and the other comprised of some 50,000 secular liberal Jews, stage separate protests near the Supreme Court building in West Jerusalem.	A fire at an electrical substation in Buenos Aires, the Argentine capital, causes a power outage.	
Feb. 15	Delegates of some 170 nations meet in Cartagena, Colombia, to draft and adopt a treaty governing international trade in genetically modified products. . . . Turkish intelligence operatives seize Kurdish rebel leader Abdullah Ocalan in Nairobi, Kenya, and fly him to Turkey for trial.	Romania's supreme court sentences coal-mining labor leader Miron Cozma in absentia to 18 years in prison on the charge of undermining state authority during a 1991 protest march. Cozma led miners through Bucharest and forced the resignation of then-Premier Petre Roman.		Nineteen candidates win election to the legislative assembly of Nunavut, a Canadian territory that will officially come into existence April 1. The creation of Nunavut will represent the first redrawing of the map of Canada since 1949.	Chinese authorities release Gao Yu, 55, a journalist imprisoned for her political writings, on medical parole some seven months before the end of her six-year sentence.
Feb. 16	In reaction to the Feb. 15 arrest of Kurdish rebel leader Abdullah Ocalan, Kurdish separatists stage demonstrations in many nations, including Armenia, Belgium, Denmark, Italy Sweden, Australia, and Canada. Some 1,000 Kurds hold a march in a Kurdish section of Istanbul, Turkey, setting cars on fire. Meanwhile, other people in Turkey celebrate his capture. At least three Kurdish nationalists in European cities set themselves on fire. They all survive. Kurds in Vienna take the Greek ambassador to Austria and four other people hostage. Kurds also take hostages in Bonn, Leipzig, The Hague, London, and Paris. All hostages are peacefully released within hours.	A Paris court convicts Hawa Greou and sentences him to eight years in prison for performing genital mutilation on 48 girls in France. The case is the largest ever of its kind in France. . . . At least six car bombs explode in Tashkent, Uzbekistan's capital, killing at least 13 people and injuring about 120 others. . . . In response to the Feb. 15 sentencing of Miron Cozma, more than 2,000 miners begin marching towards Bucharest, Romania's capital . . . . Northern Ireland's provincial legislature formally approves a plan for the new government's structure of the . . . . German chancellor Gerhard Schroeder announces the creation of a $2 billion fund to compensate victims of the Nazi Holocaust.	South Africa's Truth and Reconciliation Commission denies amnesty to four former police officers implicated in the 1977 death of Steve Biko, an antiapartheid leader who died after an interrogation by the officers.		
Feb. 17	Protests over the Feb. 15 arrest of Kurdish rebel leader Abdullah Ocalan continue. Three Kurdish protesters are killed and 16 are wounded when Israeli troops guarding Israel's consulate in the Berlin suburb of Wilmersdorf, Germany, fire on demonstrators forcibly entering the building.	Romanian police arrest militant coal-mining labor leader Miron Cozma, sentenced in absentia Feb. 15, amid violent clashes between police and miners that leave one miner dead and scores injured.	In Congo, rebels backed by Rwandan fighters near Kabinda, the last government-held position on the route to Mbuji-Mayi, launch a three-front offensive. . . . South Africa's Truth and Reconciliation Commission grants amnesty to police officer Jeffrey Benzien, who was convicted of torturing antiapartheid activists.	Jaime Hurtado, a founding member of the opposition Popular Democratic Movement, is murdered in Quito, the capital of Ecuador. Hurtado's aide and his driver are also killed. . . . Reports confirm that the national map of Honduras will be redrawn to reflect changes in river routes and village locations that resulted In 1998 from Hurricane Mitch.	Pakistan's Supreme Court rules unanimously that civilians cannot be tried in special military courts that P.M. Nawaz Sharif established in December 1998.

A	B	C	D	E
Includes developments that affect more than one world region, international organizations, and important meetings of major world leaders.	Includes all domestic and regional developments in Europe, including the Soviet Union, Turkey, Cyprus, and Malta.	Includes all domestic and regional developments in Africa and the Middle East, including Iraq and Iran and excluding Cyprus, Turkey, and Afghanistan.	Includes all domestic and regional developments in Latin America, the Caribbean, and Canada.	Includes all domestic and regional developments in Asia and Pacific nations, extending from Afghanistan through all the Pacific Island, except Hawaii.

U.S. Politics & Social Issues	U.S. Foreign Policy & Defense	U.S. Economy & Environment	Science, Technology, & Nature	Culture, Leisure, & Lifestyle	
The Senate votes to acquit Pres. Clinton of impeachment charges in the Monica Lewinsky scandal, ending the second presidential impeachment in U.S. history. The 45-55 tally for Article I, the perjury charge, is 22 votes short of the 67 needed for conviction. Article II, the obstruction charge, fails in a 50-50 vote, 17 short of the two-thirds majority. The fact that neither charge gains even a simple majority of 51 votes is seen as a humiliating defeat for the 13 House Republicans who presented the case to the Senate.	Kelly Therese Warren, a former U.S. Army clerk convicted in 1998 on espionage charges, is sentenced to 25 years in prison.	The Oregon Department of Agriculture places a ban on oyster harvesting until Mar. 4 because of the threat of contamination from the *New Carissa*, which ran aground off the Oregon coast on Feb. 4. . . . A worker dies of burns from a Feb. 1 fire at a Ford Motor Co. power station in Ford's River Rouge complex in Dearborn, Michigan, bringing the death toll from the accident to three.		At the U.S. Figure Skating Championships, in Salt Lake City, Utah, Danielle and Steve Hartsell win their first title in the pairs competition and become the first brother and sister pair to win the title since 1984. In the ice-dancing competition, Naomi Lang and Peter Tchernyshev win the gold medal for the first time.	Feb. 12
		In Dallas, Texas, Judge Joe Kendall finds the APA and its two highest-ranking officers, Pres. Richard LaVoy and Vice Pres. Brian Mayhew, guilty of contempt of court for failing to abide by his Feb. 10 return-to-work order. Kendall also rules that the union should reimburse American Airlines for its losses resulting from the sick-out.		Michelle Kwan, 18, wins her third U.S. Figure Skating Championship women's title, becoming the first woman to win the title two years in a row since Jill Trenary in 1989–90. Michael Weiss, 22, wins the men's title for the first time in the U.S. championships.	Feb. 13
John D(aniel) Ehrlichman, 73, top aide to Pres. Richard Nixon and a crucial figure in the Watergate scandal that led to Nixon's 1974 resignation as president, dies in Atlanta, Georgia, while suffering from diabetes.		An employee dies from injuries sustained during a Feb. 1 fire at a Ford Motor Co. power station at Ford's River Rouge complex in Dearborn, Michigan, bringing the accident's death tally to four.		In Colorado, the World Alpine Ski Championships close, and Lasse Kjus of Norway becomes the first skier in the history of alpine skiing to win five medals in one world championship competition. . . . Jeff Gordon wins the 41st annual Daytona 500 automobile race in Daytona Beach, Florida.	Feb. 14
			Henry Way Kendall, 72, physicist who shared the 1990 Nobel prize in Physics for works that confirmed the existence of the quark, dies while making an underwater photography dive in Florida's Wakulla Springs State Park.		Feb. 15
The San Francisco, California, public school system and representatives of racial minority groups reach a settlement that will end the city's 15-year-old race-based school desegregation program designed to guarantee racial diversity in every public school.	Figures suggest that the net income at major U.S. companies rose 3% in the fourth quarter of 1998 from the corresponding period a year earlier. The rise in profits is a reversal from 1998's third quarter, when corporate earnings declined 5%.		Seventy members of the House of Representatives send a letter to Health and Human Services (HHS) secretary Donna Shalala protesting a decision to allow federal funds to be used for research on human embryonic stem cells.	Five-year-old racehorse Skip Away wins the Eclipse Award for 1998's horse of the year.	Feb. 16
Oregon's Health Division reports that 15 people died in the state in 1998 by legal physician-assisted suicide. Oregon is the only jurisdiction in the world where assisted suicide is officially legalized. Thirteen of those who died suffered from cancer, one had a lung disease, and one had heart disease.			A study suggests that the consumption of tomatoes helps cut the risk of developing some kinds of cancer. . . . Kurt Robert Eissler, 90, psychoanalyst who cofounded the Sigmund Freud Archives after World War II, dies in New York City of unreported causes.		Feb. 17

F	G	H	I	J
Includes elections, federal-state relations, civil rights and liberties, crime, the judiciary, education, health care, poverty, urban affairs, and population.	*Includes formation and debate of U.S. foreign and defense policies, veterans' affairs, and defense spending. (Relations with specific foreign countries are usually found under the region concerned.)*	*Includes business, labor, agriculture, taxation, transportation, consumer affairs, monetary and fiscal policy, natural resources, and pollution.*	*Includes worldwide scientific, medical, and technological developments; natural phenomena; U.S. weather; natural disasters; and accidents.*	*Includes the arts, religion, scholarship, communications media, sports, entertainments, fashions, fads, and social life.*

	World Affairs	Europe	Africa & the Middle East	The Americas	Asia & the Pacific
Feb. 18		A French court rules that 1960s antiwar campaigner Ira Einhorn may be extradited to the U.S., where he faces murder charges, provided that he will receive a new trial and will not face the death penalty. . . . The AP reports that Turkish troops have been crossing the border into northern Iraq in pursuit of PKK rebels since Feb. 15.	Reports confirm that rebels in Congo have resumed their drive to topple Pres. Laurent Kabila after months of reduced fighting in the conflict, which started in August 1998. . . . Israeli troops and an allied Lebanese militia seize the village of Arnoun, located on the northern rim of Israel's security belt.	Reports reveal that Cuba's National Assembly has passed legislation strengthening penalties against criminals and against political activists opposed to the ruling Communist Party who "collaborated" with the U.S.	
Feb. 19			Unidentified assailants shoot to death Iraq's leading Shi'ite Muslim cleric, Grand Ayatollah Mohammed Sadeq al-Sadr, in the Shi'ite holy city of Najaf, located 100 miles (160 km) south of Baghdad, the capital of Lebanon. Sadr is the third Iraqi Shi'ite cleric killed in the past year.		In India, at least 20 Hindus are slain by Muslim rebels in the disputed state of Kashmir. . . . Officials in Australia confirm that the resignations of four members of Queensland Parliament has lowered the representation of right-wing nationalist One Nation party to under 10 seats, thereby terminating the political party status of the group. . . . Reports confirm that communist rebels in the southern Philippines have kidnapped Brigadier General Victor Obillo and one of his officers. Obillo is the highest-ranking military official ever seized by the rebels.
Feb. 20	Finance ministers and central-bank governors from the Group of Seven (G-7) major industrialized nations agree to establish a twice-yearly forum aimed at averting the kind of economic crisis that has shaken southeast Asia for the past two years.	Turkish military officials disclose that some 10 guerrillas have been killed during the attacks against PKK positions in northern Iraq that started Feb. 15. . . . Sarah Kane, 27, British playwright, dies an apparent suicide at a hospital in London while being treated for depression.	As part of the country's transition to democracy, Nigeria holds elections for the National Assembly. The People's Democratic Party (PDP) emerges as the dominant party. . . . Iran's supreme court overturns a 1998 ruling that sentenced German national Helmut Hofer to death by stoning for allegedly having had sexual relations with an unmarried Muslim female. It orders a retrial.		Indian prime minister Atal Bihari Vajpayee visits Pakistan, meeting with Pakistani prime minister Nawaz Sharif in an effort to reduce tensions between their nations. Activists from Jamaat-i-Islami, Pakistan's largest militant Muslim group, hold mass street demonstrations and stage a general strike in Lahore to protest Vajpayee's visit.
Feb. 21		An avalanche strikes the town of Evolene in Switzerland. . . . Turkish troops end nearly a week of air and ground attacks on PKK positions in northern Iraq.	Embattled president Robert Mugabe attacks Zimbabwe's white minority, the press, the judiciary, Western embassies, and the International Monetary Fund (IMF).		In Pakistan, to protest the visit of Indian prime minister Atal Bihari Vajpayee, protestors rally, and Pakistani police arrest about 100 activists, including several party leaders, in Lahore. . . . Gerry Adams, the leader of the political wing of the Provisional IRA, Sinn Fein, makes his first trip to Australia . . . . Walter Lini, 57, first prime minister of the 83 Melanesian islands of Vanuatu, dies in Port Vila, Vanuatu, of unreported causes. He had suffered a stroke in 1987.
Feb. 22		Heavy fighting occurs in northern Kosovo as Serbian security forces and the KLA fight for control of the town of Bukos, populated by both Serbs and ethnic Albanians. . . . The German government announces that plans to ban the export of nuclear waste for processing have been dropped. The proposed ban was part of a controversial plan to phase out Germany's use of nuclear power to generate electricity.	In response to the Feb. 18 attack in Arnoun, Lebanon, Hezbollah guerrillas kill three members of an Israeli commando unit in a three-hour battle.		
Feb. 23	Turkish authorities formally charge Kurdish rebel leader Abdullah Ocalan with treason and "seeking to undermine the indivisible unity of the Turkish state." Ocalan, head of the Kurdistan Workers' Party (PKK), was seized by Turkish intelligence operatives in Nairobi, Kenya, and his arrest prompted worldwide demonstrations by Kurds.	Serb and ethnic Albanian representatives agree in principle to an accord that will end a year-old conflict in Kosovo. . . . An avalanche strikes a resort region of the Austrian Alps. Nine people are confirmed dead. At least 30 people buried in the snow have been rescued, and about 30 more remain missing. . . . Sir Anthony Nutting (Harold), 79, British minister of state for foreign affairs, 1954–56, dies in London of a heart attack.	Ethiopian troops launch an offensive on Badme. . . . South Africa's Truth and Reconciliation Commission grants amnesty to four former police officers who in 1981 kidnapped and killed Sizwe Kondile, a leading antiapartheid activist.		

A	B	C	D	E
Includes developments that affect more than one world region, international organizations, and important meetings of major world leaders.	Includes all domestic and regional developments in Europe, including the Soviet Union, Turkey, Cyprus, and Malta.	Includes all domestic and regional developments in Africa and the Middle East, including Iraq and Iran and excluding Cyprus, Turkey, and Afghanistan.	Includes all domestic and regional developments in Latin America, the Caribbean, and Canada.	Includes all domestic and regional developments in Asia and Pacific nations, extending from Afghanistan through all the Pacific Island, except Hawaii.

U.S. Politics & Social Issues	U.S. Foreign Policy & Defense	U.S. Economy & Environment	Science, Technology, & Nature	Culture, Leisure, & Lifestyle	
		A study suggests that, in most cases, U.S. produce has higher levels of pesticide residue than imported fruits and vegetables have.	Reports disclose that scientists have succeeded in slowing the speed of light to about 38 miles per hour (61 kph) from its normal speed through empty space, 186,282 miles per second (299,792.458 km per second). The feat is seen as having potential for the advanced study of quantum mechanics and for the development of a variety of high-precision technologies.		Feb. 18
Reports confirm that at least 14 letters that claim to contain deadly anthrax bacteria have been received by abortion clinics and Planned Parenthood Federation of America centers across the country since Feb. 18. They were mailed from Lexington, Kentucky.	Pres. Clinton pardons Henry Ossian Flipper, the first black to graduate from West Point. In 1882 Flipper was given a dishonorable discharge after a court-martial convicted him of conduct unbecoming an officer, even though it acquitted him on embezzlement charges. That same year an army review board found that Flipper had been unfairly prosecuted because of his race. Nonetheless, the army did not formally exonerate Flipper until 1976, 36 years after his death. Clinton's action is the first posthumous presidential pardon in U.S. history.	The Commerce Department reports that the U.S. recorded a $168.6 billion deficit in trade in goods and services in 1998. That amount represents a 53% leap from the revised 1997 deficit of $110.2 billion and sets a new record for a calendar-year trade gap in the U.S. . . . Curtis L. Carlson, 84, founder in 1938 of a trading-stamp business that later became Carlson Cos., dies in Minneapolis, Minnesota, of unreported causes.		The policy council of the U.S. Holocaust Museum in Washington, D.C., selects Sara Jane Bloomfield as the institution's executive director.	Feb. 19
Truong Van Tran, who had sparked protests by hanging a picture of the late North Vietnamese communist leader Ho Chi Minh in his video-rental shop, wades through a crowd of 300 demonstrators with the help of a police escort and puts the poster of Ho Chi Minh and the flag up. The store is in California's back Orange County, home to more than 35,000 Vietnamese Americans, the largest Vietnamese community outside of Asia.		Two employees of Ford Motor Co. die from injuries sustained in the Feb. 1 fire at Ford's River Rouge complex in Dearborn, Michigan, bringing the death toll from the accident to six.		Gene Siskel, 53, who, with Roger Ebert, formed what was considered the most influential pair of film reviewers in the U.S., dies in Evanston, Illinois. He had had a brain tumor removed in 1998 . . . Willard R. Espy, 88, author of books about word games and rhymes, dies in New York City.	Feb. 20
Wilmer David Mizell (Vinegar Bend), 68, professional baseball player and three-term Republican congressman from North Carolina, 1969–75, dies in Kerrville, Texas He had suffered a heart attack in October 1998.			Gertrude Belle Elion, 81, Nobel Prize-winning research chemist who developed drugs used to treat a variety of conditions and was awarded a National Medal of Science in 1991, dies of a cerebral hemorrhage in Chapel Hill, North Carolina.		Feb. 21
In Washington, D.C., Judge Royce Lamberth cites Interior Secretary Bruce Babbitt, Treasury Secretary Robert Rubin, and Assistant for Interior Secretary Kevin Gover for contempt of court, claiming they did not ensure that their departments produced documents in a lawsuit alleging mismanagement of American Indians' trust funds. . . Some 10,000 protesters gather in an area known as Little Saigon in Orange County, California, near the store of Truong Van Tran, who is displaying a picture of Ho Chi Minh.		Interior Secretary Bruce Babbitt announces the creation of a scientific panel that will monitor a restoration plan for Florida's Everglades.	The National Cancer Institute announces that chemotherapy, when combined with the standard radiation treatment for cervical cancer, may significantly reduce deaths from the disease.		Feb. 22
A Jasper county, Texas, jury convicts John William King, a self-proclaimed white supremacist, of capital murder for chaining a black man, James Byrd Jr., to a pickup truck and dragging him to his death in 1998.			David Hamilton Smith, 67, scientist and pediatrician who in the 1980s helped develop a vaccine that immunizes children against a bacterium, known as Hib, that causes meningitis, dies in New York City of malignant melanoma.	In National Collegiate Athletic Association v. Smith, the Supreme Court rules unanimously that the NCAA cannot be sued for sex discrimination under Title IX of the Education Amendments of 1972 simply because it receives dues from federally funded member schools.	Feb. 23

F	G	H	I	J
Includes elections, federal-state relations, civil rights and liberties, crime, the judiciary, education, health care, poverty, urban affairs, and population.	Includes formation and debate of U.S. foreign and defense policies, veterans' affairs, and defense spending. (Relations with specific foreign countries are usually found under the region concerned.)	Includes business, labor, agriculture, taxation, transportation, consumer affairs, monetary and fiscal policy, natural resources, and pollution.	Includes worldwide scientific, medical, and technological developments; natural phenomena; U.S. weather; natural disasters; and accidents.	Includes the arts, religion, scholarship, communications media, sports, entertainments, fashions, fads, and social life.

	World Affairs	Europe	Africa & the Middle East	The Americas	Asia & the Pacific
Feb. 24		In the Austrian Alps, an avalanche strikes Valzur. One person is confirmed dead. . . . The KLA announces plans to form an unofficial provisional government in Kosovo. . . . Reports confirm that Bulgaria now recognizes the Macedonian language. . . . Viscount Eccles (David MacAdam), 94, British parliamentarian, 1943–62, 1970–73, dies of unreported causes. . . . Derek Robert Nimmo, 66, British actor and comedian, dies in London of pneumonia and complications from a December 1998 fall.			A China Southwest Airlines jet crashes in Zhejiang province, killing all 61 passengers and crew. . . . Chee Soon Juan, leader of the opposition Singapore Democratic Party, is convicted of making a public speech without an official permit. This is his second such conviction in February.
Feb. 25	China uses its veto power as a permanent member of the UN Security Council to block extension of the mission in Macedonia to prevent the spread of fighting from Yugoslavia. China argues that the force is no longer needed because the situation seems to have stabilized.	Data reveals that nine people have been confirmed dead from the Feb. 21 avalanche in Evolene in Switzerland. The death toll from the Feb. 9 avalanche in the region around Chamonix, France, has risen to 18.	The Israeli Supreme Court rules that Samuel Sheinbein, 18, who is charged with murder in the U.S., cannot be extradited. He will stand trial in Israel. . . Four Hezbollah fighters are killed by Israeli forces. . . . King Otumfuo Opoku Ware II (born Matthew Poku), 79, leader of the Ashanti, a West African people whose centuries-old kingdom is now an administrative region in Ghana, dies of unreported causes in Kumasi, Ghana.	The first comprehensive investigation by an international panel into alleged abuses by the Guatemalan government its 36-year civil war estimates that 200,000 people, mostly civilians, have died. It blames the government and allied paramilitary groups for the majority of the killings and charges the government received support from the U.S. agencies, including the CIA. . . . Some 10,000 people are still without power due to the Feb. 14 fire in Buenos Aires, the Argentine capital.	Woo Yong Gak, 71, believed to be the world's longest-serving political prisoner, is released in an amnesty marking the first anniversary of Pres. Kim Dae Jung's inauguration. Woo had been jailed for 41 years after he was captured along with other members of a North Korean reconnaissance unit in South Korean waters. . . . . In a letter, a paramilitary group makes threats against Australian government officials and journalists, prompting at least 15 Australian aid workers to flee East Timor.
Feb. 26	The UN Security Council votes to withdraw peacekeepers from Angola in the wake of resumed fighting there. The UN will continue its humanitarian relief work in Angola.		According to the Sierra Leone social welfare ministry, some 2,000 children between the ages of five and 14 vanished after the rebel invasion of Freetown, the capital in January. . . . Political reformers and other center-left candidates win all 15 seats on the city council of Teheran and score widespread victories in balloting nationwide in Iran's first local elections since its 1979 Islamic revolution. . . . South Africa's Truth and Reconciliation Commission denies amnesty to the members of the AWB who fatally shot four black people and wounded six others in December 1993.	Reports confirm that a federal jury in San Jaun, Puerto Rico, has convicted Angel Rodriguez, the mayor of Toa Alta, and contractor Jose Orlando Figueroa on charges of conspiracy and bribery.	Police in Hangzhou, China, detain Wu Yilong, a student and a founding member of a fledgling opposition political party, the China Democracy Party. Authorities in Beijing, the capital, inform the wife of Peng Ming, an academic arrested in January, that Peng has been sentenced to 18 months in a labor camp.
Feb. 27		The KLA kidnaps two Serbs near the town of Orahovac, Kosovo, sparking a new spate of fighting. . . . In the Austrian Alps, the death toll from the Feb. 23 avalanche in Galtuer rises to 31. The death toll from the Feb. 24 Valzur avalanche is at seven.	Former military ruler Gen. Olusegun Obasanjo is elected president of Nigeria, implementing the country's transition to democratic rule. Obasanjo, the candidate of the dominant People's Democratic Party (PDP), will be Nigeria's first civilian leader in more than 15 years. . . . Eritrea states that it will agree to an Organization of African Unity (OAU) peace plan that Ethiopia has already accepted.		
Feb. 28	A U.S. air strike damages a pumping station along the pipeline between Iraq and Turkey, halting the main channel for oil flow in Iraq's oil-for-food program.	Serbs begin rooting out the KLA in villages near Kosovo's border with Macedonia. . . . Data reveals that the latest avalanches made the 1998–99 winter one of Europe's deadliest ever, with more than 70 people killed in avalanches.	A series of 14 bombs explode in Lusaka, the capital of Zambia, killing one person and cutting off the city's water supply. . . . Ethiopia declares that it has achieved "total victory" over Eritrea after winning a decisive battle in the Badme region, the sovereignty of which is at the core of their border dispute. . . . A Hezbollah bomb kills an Israeli general in Israel's self-declared security zone in southern Lebanon. Israeli warplanes retaliate by striking Hezbollah bases deep in Lebanon.		Doctors in Osaka perform Japan's first legal organ transplant, a type of surgery approved in Japan in 1997.
March 1	The UN officially ends its 1,100-member peacekeeping mission in Macedonia after China's Feb. 25 veto of an extension of the mission's mandate. . . . An international treaty banning the use and production of antipersonnel land mines goes into effect.	Turkey launches an attack against PKK rebels in Hatay province, located near Turkey's border with Syria. Premier Bulent Ecevit announces that the government will provide $90 million in aid for the southeastern area of Turkey, which is dominated by Kurds.	Rwandan Hutu rebels kidnap and kill eight foreign tourists in a national park on the border with the Democratic Republic of Congo. Two of the dead were Americans, four were Britons, and two were New Zealanders. . . . A PNA-Hamas agreement ends a 36-day-old hunger strike by prisoners affiliated with Hamas and the more hard-line Islamic Jihad.	Leftist senator Jean-Yvon Toussaint is fatally shot by an unidentified assailant in a suburb of Port-au-Prince, the capital of Haiti.	

A	B	C	D	E
Includes developments that affect more than one world region, international organizations, and important meetings of major world leaders.	Includes all domestic and regional developments in Europe, including the Soviet Union, Turkey, Cyprus, and Malta.	Includes all domestic and regional developments in Africa and the Middle East, including Iraq and Iran and excluding Cyprus, Turkey, and Afghanistan.	Includes all domestic and regional developments in Latin America, the Caribbean, and Canada.	Includes all domestic and regional developments in Asia and Pacific nations, extending from Afghanistan through all the Pacific Island, except Hawaii.

U.S. Politics & Social Issues	U.S. Foreign Policy & Defense	U.S. Economy & Environment	Science, Technology, & Nature	Culture, Leisure, & Lifestyle	
Census Bureau director Kenneth Prewitt announces plans to conduct two separate census counts in the year 2000: a traditional "head count" of the U.S. population to determine apportionment of seats in the House; and a second count, using controversial "statistical sampling" methods to determine the distribution of federal dollars and to redraw legislative districts. The Supreme Court ruled in January that sampling cannot be used in the apportionment of House seats.	The Senate approves 91-8, legislation that will provide the largest military pay raise since 1982. . . . A lawyer for former premier Pavlo Lazarenko, who left Ukraine amid charges of corruption, announces that Lazarenko has requested political asylum in the U.S.			At the Grammy Awards, Lauryn Hill wins five awards, setting a record for a female artist. The song and record of the year go to Celine Dion for "My Heart Will Go On."	Feb. 24
John William King, a self-proclaimed white supremacist convicted of capital murder, is sentenced to death by lethal injection for chaining James Byrd Jr. to a pickup truck and dragging him to his death. Only one white man has ever been executed in Texas for killing a black person. . . . Data reveal that the number of people using food stamps fell to about 19 million as of November 1998, from nearly 28 million four years earlier.		The Service Employees International Union (SEIU), a fast-growing unit of the AFL-CIO labor federation, wins the right to represent 74,000 home health-care workers in Los Angeles County, California. Union officials note the SEIU victory is the U.S. labor movement's largest successful organizing drive since 1937. . . . The SEC sues 13 companies and individuals for on-line investment activities that allegedly misrepresent the prospects of 56 companies.	The FCC rules that calls placed to access the Internet computer network are interstate calls and thus are subject to federal regulations. Internet service providers will continue to be exempt from paying per-minute access charges to regional phone companies. . . . Glenn Theodore Seaborg, 86, Nobel Prize-winning scientist who led the research team that discovered plutonium and had element 106 named seaborgium in his honor, dies in Lafayette, California, of complications of a stroke suffered in 1998.		Feb. 25
The U.S. 10th Circuit Court of Appeals in Denver, Colorado, upholds the conviction and life sentence of Oklahoma City bombing conspirator Terry Nichols. Nichols was convicted in December 1997. . . . An estimated 15,000 people hold a vigil in Westminster, California, to denounce what they call continuing human rights violations in Vietnam. It is the largest of a series of protests prompted by controversy started when Truong Van Tran hung a picture of Ho Chi Minh in his shop.	Pres. Clinton states that his administration will again "certify" Mexico and Colombia in the war against drugs. . . . An annual report by the State Department sharply criticizes China and, citing Sierra Leone, Congo, Angola, Serbia, Afghanistan, and Colombia, notes "the disturbing trend toward the widespread abuse of civilians trapped in conflict." The report singles out the Taliban for "perhaps the most severe abuse of women's human rights in the world.". . . David Sheldon Boone, a former NSA cryptologist, is sentenced to 24 years in prison for conspiring to commit espionage.			Jose Benjamin Quintero, 74, Panamanian-born theater director who won a Tony Award in 1974, dies in New York City of cancer. . . . John L. Goldwater, 83, writer who in 1941 created Archie, a teenaged comic-book character, with partner Bob Montana, dies in New York City of a heart attack.	Feb. 26
				Rev. Henry J. Lyons, president of the National Baptist Convention USA, is convicted in Largo, Florida, on state charges of racketeering and grand theft.	Feb. 27
					Feb. 28
A study finds that the development of young children whose mothers work outside the home is not harmed by their mothers' absence. . . . The American Academy of Pediatrics revises its position on the benefits and drawbacks of circumcising newborn boys, finding that "potential medical benefits" of circumcision are "not sufficient to recommend routine neonatal circumcision."	Reports reveal that U.S. prosecutors have charged a Chinese citizen and a Chinese-born Canadian with attempting to purchase missile-guidance equipment in the U.S. and smuggle it to China.	Pacific Lumber Co. agrees to sell 10,000 acres (4,000 hectares) of a redwood forest tract in northern California for $480 million. The U.S. will contribute $250 million, and California will pay $230 million. The deal concludes years of negotiations between the federal and California governments and Pacific Lumber, as well as more than a decade of protests and protracted legal action over the logging of the forests.		An independent panel criticizes a "culture of improper gift-giving" among members of the International Olympic Committee (IOC) in an investigation of the worst ethics scandals in the history of the Olympic Games. . . . The Testament by John Grisham tops the bestseller lists.	March 1
F	G	H	I	J	
Includes elections, federal-state relations, civil rights and liberties, crime, the judiciary, education, health care, poverty, urban affairs, and population.	*Includes formation and debate of U.S. foreign and defense policies, veterans' affairs, and defense spending. (Relations with specific foreign countries are usually found under the region concerned.)*	*Includes business, labor, agriculture, taxation, transportation, consumer affairs, monetary and fiscal policy, natural resources, and pollution.*	*Includes worldwide scientific, medical, and technological developments; natural phenomena; U.S. weather; natural disasters; and accidents.*	*Includes the arts, religion, scholarship, communications media, sports, entertainments, fashions, fads, and social life.*	

	World Affairs	Europe	Africa & the Middle East	The Americas	Asia & the Pacific
March 2					Taiwan's legislature defeats a motion of no confidence in Premier Vincent Siew brought by opposition parties. It is the first no-confidence vote to take place in Taiwan since the constitution was amended to permit such motions in 1997.
March 3	Jordan and Kuwait reestablish diplomatic relations, severed during the 1990–91 Persian Gulf conflict.		In Zimbabwe, Judge Yunus Omerjee rules that the government cannot prevent two journalists tortured while in detention from leaving the country for medical treatment.		Reports reveal that hundreds of East Timorese have fled the region as violent clashes between supporters and opponents of independence escalate.
March 4	Russian president Boris Yeltsin demands the dismissal of Boris Berezovsky, a politically powerful Russian tycoon, from his post as executive secretary of the Commonwealth of Independent States (CIS).		Jordan's King Abdullah II, in his first major political move, forms a new government, appointing Abdul-Raouf Rawabdeh as prime minister and Abdul Karim al-Kabariti as chief of the royal court. . . . Reports state that Ugandan and Rwandan forces have killed 15 rebels in Congo, south of the site of the Mar. 1 kidnapping and murders of civilians. . . . South Africa's Truth and Reconciliation Commission rejects a collective amnesty application by 27 senior ANC members, including Thabo Mbeki, the ANC president.	Mexico's Institutional Revolutionary Party (PRI), the longest-ruling political party in the world, celebrates 70 years in power. . . . The bodies of the three Americans kidnapped Feb. 25 in northeast Colombia are found on the Venezuelan side of the Arauca River.	
March 5	Carlos Westendorp, the international community's top representative in Bosnia-Herzegovina, dismisses the hard-line president of Bosnia's Serb Republic, Nikola Poplasen. Another international arbitrator decides to remove the disputed town of Brcko from Serb control, placing it under neutral administration. The dual decisions spark protests and violence. A U.S. soldier shoots and kills one protester after the soldier and three others allegedly are attacked by a larger group of Serbs.	Unidentified armed assailants kidnap Major General Gennadi Shpigun, the interior ministry's representative in the separatist republic of Chechnya. . . . Swiss authorities report they have found the bodies of three people killed by a February avalanche in the town of Evolene, raising the death toll from the snowslide to 12. . . . Lord Denning (Alfred Thompson), 100, British judge who served as Master of the Rolls, the head of Britain's Court of Appeals, 1962–82, dies in Winchester, England.			
March 6	The Mar. 5 decisions by international representatives continues to spark protests and violence throughout the Bosnian Serb Republic, including an attack on a Western-funded radio station and attacks on UN vehicles.		Amnesty International estimates that more than 3,000 people have disappeared since 1993 after detention by security forces in Algeria. . . . Sheik Isa bin Salman al-Khalifa, 65, who was named crown prince of Bahrain in 1958 and assumed the title emir in 1971, the year Bahrain gained independence, dies in Manama, Bahrain, of a heart attack.	Reports from Canada indicate that the legislative assembly of Nunavut, an Arctic territory that will officially come into existence on April 1, has selected Paul Okalik, a 34-year-old Inuit attorney, as Nunavut's first premier.	Cambodian military troops arrest Ta Mok, the last Khmer Rouge leader still at large, north of Anlong Ven. Ta Mok is the first senior member of the Khmer Rouge arrested for his activities in the group, which is blamed for the deaths of more than 1 million Cambodians in the late 1970s.
March 7	The Bosnian Serb parliament votes to reject both Mar. 5 rulings by international arbitrators. After the votes, Carlos Westendorp, the international community's top representative in Bosnia-Herzegovina, calls Nikola Poplasen's dismissal "irrevocable," and also states that the ruling on Brcko will not be overturned.	Estonians elect a new government led by a coalition of three center-right parties—the Fatherland Party, the Reform Party, and the Moderates. . . . The right-wing Freedom Party wins a regional election in Carinthia, one of Austria's nine states. The election marks the first time that the anti-immigration party gains a plurality of votes in a statewide vote.	In South Africa, ANC councilor Zwelinzima Hlazo is shot to death en route to Nyanga. UDM member Mncedisi Mpongwana is shot and killed in nearby Guguletu, in what police think is a revenge attack. . . . Reports confirm that, as a goodwill gesture, rebels from Sierra Leone have released 31 children whom they had kidnapped. . . . Zimbabwean authorities arrest three Americans—John Dixon, Gary Blanchard, and Joseph Pettijohn—on charges of espionage, sabotage, and terrorism.	Francisco Flores Perez of the ruling Nationalist Republican Alliance (ARENA) party is elected president of El Salvador, succeeding Pres. Armando Calderon Sol.	

A	B	C	D	E
Includes developments that affect more than one world region, international organizations, and important meetings of major world leaders.	Includes all domestic and regional developments in Europe, including the Soviet Union, Turkey, Cyprus, and Malta.	Includes all domestic and regional developments in Africa and the Middle East, including Iraq and Iran and excluding Cyprus, Turkey, and Afghanistan.	Includes all domestic and regional developments in Latin America, the Caribbean, and Canada.	Includes all domestic and regional developments in Asia and Pacific nations, extending from Afghanistan through all the Pacific Island, except Hawaii.

U.S. Politics & Social Issues	U.S. Foreign Policy & Defense	U.S. Economy & Environment	Science, Technology, & Nature	Culture, Leisure, & Lifestyle	
		The EEOC announces that a nursing home in Gladstone, Missouri, has agreed to pay $2.1 million to 65 Filipino nurses who complained that they were paid less than their U.S.-born counterparts.... The House passes, by voice vote, a bill that frees $470 million in reserved funds for use as federal farm-loan guarantees in time for the spring planting season.	A Senate committee examining the year 2000 (Y2K) computer glitch reports that the U.S. health care industry and many small businesses are lagging behind other domestic entities in their efforts to address the problem. The Senate votes, 99-0, in favor of a bill that will provide $900 million worth of loans for small businesses to make Y2K computer repairs.	Dusty Springfield, 59, singer whose career spanned three decades, dies in England of breast cancer. . . . Orlando Cepeda, Nestor Chylak, Frank Selee, and Smokey Joe Williams are elected to the Baseball Hall of Fame.... Thomas E. Hitchings, 52, publisher of Facts On File News Services who oversaw the company as it expanded into electronic publishing, dies in New York City of colon cancer.	March 2
In *Cedar Rapids Community School District v. Garret F.*, the Supreme Court rules, 7-2, that public schools must accommodate disabled students who need special assistance during the school day, as long as the necessary assistance can be provided by an individual who is not a physician.	Prosecutors with the U.S. Attorney's Office file charges of manslaughter against Pedro Guevara and Francisco Gomez of Florida in the December 1998 smuggling deaths of 14 Cuban refugees. The boat, owned by Gomez, capsized 12 miles (20 km) from the Florida shore.		Gerhard Herzberg, 94, German-born Canadian scientist who won the 1971 Nobel Prize in Chemistry for his research in molecular spectroscopy, dies in Ottawa of unreported causes. . . . The House approves, by voice vote, a bill that will ban Concorde, the supersonic jet, from landing at U.S. airports.	Monica Lewinsky appears in a TV interview. An estimated 70 million or more viewers watch at least part of the interview, making it by far the most-watched news program ever.	March 3
Police in Coosa County, Alabama, reveal that Steven Mullins and Charles Butler have admitted to the February murder of a homosexual man, Billy Jack Gaither.... Harry A(ndrew) Blackmun, 90, associate justice of the U.S. Supreme Court, 1970–94, who wrote the opinion for the majority in *Roe v. Wade* and who, by the time of his retirement, was regarded as a defender of the rights of society's less privileged, dies in Arlington, Virginia, of complications after hip-replacement surgery.	Judge William Hoeveler reduces the prison sentence of Gen. Manuel Antonio Noriega, a former military president of Panama, to 30 years from 40 years. Noriega may be eligible for release in 2007 if he earns time off for good behavior.... A court-martial jury acquits U.S. Marine captain Richard Ashby of all charges related to a February 1998 incident in which a U.S. jet severed a ski-lift cable in Italy, sending 20 people plunging to their deaths. Ashby's acquittal sparks outrage in Italy.		The NASA launches the *Wide-Field Infrared Explorer* (WIRE), an unmanned spacecraft intended to study the formation of stars and galaxies, from Vandenberg Air Force Base in California.		March 4
		The Labor Department reports that the seasonally adjusted unemployment rate in the U.S. in February edged up slightly to 4.4%, from 4.3% in January. The February climb is the first increase since November 1998.	NASA reveals that a malfunction has caused WIRE, an unmanned spacecraft launched Mar. 4, to overheat and its supply of frozen hydrogen to melt and disperse too quickly, causing the $79 million craft to spin out of control.... Scientists reveal they have detected a so-called blind thrust fault underneath Los Angeles that has the potential to cause a major earthquake. It is the first proof of the existence of that kind of fault beneath the city.	Richard Paul Kiley, 76, actor best known for his starring performances in the musical *Man of La Mancha*, dies in Warwick, New York, of a blood disorder.	March 5
	Three Haitian refugees are rescued from a boating accident about 30 miles (50 km) from Palm Beach, Florida, when crewmen aboard a passing freighter hear calls for help and contact the U.S. Coast Guard. An unknown number of Haitians drown in the accident.... Reports disclose that China obtained secret information from the U.S.'s Los Alamos National Laboratory in the 1980s that allowed it to develop advanced nuclear warheads.			Alexandra Meissnitzer of Austria clinches the women's overall World Cup alpine skiing title.	March 6
	Sidney Gottlieb, 80, chemist who oversaw mind-control experiments for the CIA in the 1950s and 1960s, during which the agency created poisonous devices intended for use in assassination plots and administered mind-altering drugs, including lycergic acid diethylamide (LSD), to hundreds of unwitting subjects, dies in Washington, Virginia, of unreported causes.			In Seville, Spain, the World Indoor Track and Field Championships close after two unprecedented double gold-medal wins by Haile Gebrselassie of Ethiopia and Gabriela Szabo of Romania.... Stanley Kubrick, 70, film director considered one of the most talented and uncompromising artists in his field, dies in Hertfordshire, England.	March 7

F	G	H	I	J
Includes elections, federal-state relations, civil rights and liberties, crime, the judiciary, education, health care, poverty, urban affairs, and population.	*Includes formation and debate of U.S. foreign and defense policies, veterans' affairs, and defense spending. (Relations with specific foreign countries are usually found under the region concerned.)*	*Includes business, labor, agriculture, taxation, transportation, consumer affairs, monetary and fiscal policy, natural resources, and pollution.*	*Includes worldwide scientific, medical, and technological developments; natural phenomena; U.S. weather; natural disasters; and accidents.*	*Includes the arts, religion, scholarship, communications media, sports, entertainments, fashions, fads, and social life.*

	World Affairs	Europe	Africa & the Middle East	The Americas	Asia & the Pacific
March 8	The IMF and Brazil formally agree on revised terms for the release of the remainder of a $42 billion aid package for Brazil assembled in November 1998.	Reports reveal that Russia has removed all of its official representatives from Chechnya.	The UDM's chair in Nyanga, Bhabha Dyonise, and UDM party member Zolile Tyandela are shot to death in Nyanga, South Africa. . . . Ugandan and Rwandan forces report they have killed 10 more rebels suspected in the Mar. 1 kidnapping and murder eight foreign tourists.		
March 9		A French court acquits former French premier Laurent Fabius and his former social affairs minister, Georgina Dufoix, of manslaughter and negligence charges in connection with the accidental contamination of France's blood supply with HIV in the mid-1980s. A third defendant, former health minister Edmond Herve, is convicted on two charges in the trial, although he receives no prison sentence Separately, police in Paris arrest six members of ETA, Spain's main Basque separatist guerrilla group. . . . Sir Arnold Machin, 87, British sculptor who designed the image of Queen Elizabeth II that has appeared on every British definitive stamp since 1967, dies in Staffordshire, England.	Iran's President Mohammed Khatami begins a visit to Italy and the Vatican, marking the first visit to the West by an Iranian leader in 20 years. . . . An article that discusses Zambia's state of military readiness in the case of a war against Angola is published. In response to the article, police begin arresting the journalists who wrote the story, arguing that they exposed military secrets. . . . An official of the local branch of the UDM, Patata Nqwaru, is killed March 9 in the Cape Town area of South Africa. His death is the fifth murder of politicians in the Cape Town area since Mar. 7.	Prince Charles of Britain makes the first visit to Argentina by a prince of Wales since 1931. He lays a wreath at a memorial in Buenos Aires honoring some 650 Argentine soldiers who died during the war with Britain over the Falkland Islands in 1982. His visit sparks protests that result in the injury of two police officers and the arrest of 27 civilians. . . . The ruling Antigua Labour Party (ALP) retains power in Antigua and Barbuda, enabling P.M. Lester Bird to stay in office. It is the ALP's sixth consecutive term of rule.	
March 10	A Paris court convicts five Libyan intelligence agents and a Libyan diplomat of orchestrating the 1989 bombing of a French airliner over Africa that killed all 156 passengers and 14 crew. The defendants, tried in absentia, are sentenced to life in prison. The conviction is symbolic, because the French legal system does not officially recognize trials conducted without the defendants present. The defendants include Abdallah Senoussi, the deputy head of Libya's secret services and the brother-in-law of Libyan leader Col. Muammar Gadhafi.	Spanish officials reveal they have arrested nine members of ETA in the area around San Sebastian, a Basque nationalist stronghold in northern Spain.	A PNA military court sentences Raed al-Attar, a suspected member of Hamas, to death by firing squad for the Feb. 1 killing of police captain Rifat Joudah. The court sentences the two other suspects to terms of life and 15 years. The ruling sparks street clashes in the Gaza border town of Rafah. . . . Because of the killings that have taken place since Mar. 7, the South African government sends troops of the South African National Defense Force and 300 additional police to Nyanga. . . . A British diplomat is expelled when Congo accuses him of spying.	In Ecuador, a general strike is held to protest the economic changes Pres. Jamil Mahuad made in the 1999 budget. . . . Pres. Bill Clinton travels to Guatemala, making the first visit by a U.S. president to the country in some 30 years. . . . In Colombia, in response to the Mar. 4 discovery of the bodies of kidnapped U.S. citizens, a FARC speaker admits that a low-level commander within FARC captured and executed the three Americans without the knowledge of senior commanders.	In the midst of a spate of religious violence, Indonesian troops fire on thousands of rioters in Ambon, killing at least two people and wounding about 50 others. . . . Some 4,000 exiled Tibetans hold demonstrations in Dharmsala, India, to mark the 40th anniversary of a revolt against Chinese rule in Tibet. Other marches of similar size are held in New Delhi, India's capital, and in Katmandu, the capital of Nepal.
March 11	The UN Security Council votes to extend until June 13 the mandate of its observer mission in Sierra Leone. . . . UN secretary general Kofi Annan announces that Indonesia and Portugal have agreed to allow East Timor to decide whether it wants status as an autonomous region of Indonesia or full independence. East Timor, a former Portuguese colony, was invaded by Indonesia in 1975.		Four British officials and a U.S. State Department official on temporary assignment with the British government are expelled from the Democratic Republic of Congo after its government accused them of spying.	In Ecuador, the general strike that began Mar. 10 continues. Figures show that 19 people have been injured and 235 arrested during the strikes. Pres. Jamil Mahuad Witt announces a package of emergency austerity measures designed to lower the country's inflation rate and stabilize the economy. . . . Thousands of students shut down Mexico's largest state university, National Autonomous University, to protest a planned tuition hike.	Reports reveal that, since fighting in a religious conflict erupted in January in Indonesia, nearly 10,000 people have fled Ambon to escape the violence there.

A	B	C	D	E
Includes developments that affect more than one world region, international organizations, and important meetings of major world leaders.	*Includes all domestic and regional developments in Europe, including the Soviet Union, Turkey, Cyprus, and Malta.*	*Includes all domestic and regional developments in Africa and the Middle East, including Iraq and Iran and excluding Cyprus, Turkey, and Afghanistan.*	*Includes all domestic and regional developments in Latin America, the Caribbean, and Canada.*	*Includes all domestic and regional developments in Asia and Pacific nations, extending from Afghanistan through all the Pacific Island, except Hawaii.*

U.S. Politics & Social Issues	U.S. Foreign Policy & Defense	U.S. Economy & Environment	Science, Technology, & Nature	Culture, Leisure, & Lifestyle	
The Urban Institute, a think tank, concludes that noncitizens' use of cash welfare benefits dropped by 35% between 1994 and 1997, compared with a 15% decline among citizens. A similar pattern is reportedly observed in a decline in the use of food stamps and Medicaid.	In light of the Mar. 6 reports that China obtained secret information from the U.S. in the 1980s, the Department of Energy, which runs the national lab in Los Alamos, New Mexico, fires the suspected scientist, identified as Wen Ho Lee.... Pres. Clinton embarks on a visit to Nicaragua, Honduras, El Salvador, and Guatemala to survey damage wrought by Hurricane Mitch in October 1998.	The Senate, by voice vote, clears a bill that frees $470 million in reserved funds for use as federal farm-loan guarantees in time for the spring planting season.... Navy demolition experts haul the bow of the oil tanker that ran aground Feb. 4, the *New Carissa*, nearly 300 miles (480 km) from the Oregon coast. A third of the vessel remains partially submerged just off the coast.	A federal court sentences Larry Matthews Jr., a veteran broadcast reporter, to 18 months in prison for distributing child pornography via the Internet in 1996. He is the first journalist prosecuted for trafficking pornography on the Internet under federal child pornography laws, and the case is seen as a test of the limits of the First Amendment for journalism on the Internet.... NASA reports indicate that WIRE's hydrogen supply ran out, putting an end to the mission, which was launched Mar. 4 and planned to last four months.... The FTC states it has reached a tentative settlement of its antitrust case against computer microprocessor maker Intel Corp. The specific terms of the settlement are not released to the public.	The National Book Critics issue awards that for the first time considered authors who are not U.S. citizens. The awards go to Marie Ponsot, Gary Giddins. Sylvia Nasar, Alice Munro, and Philip Gourevitch. The Nona Balakian Citation for Excellence in reviewing goes to Albert Mobilio.... Joe (Joseph Paul) DiMaggio, 84, star center fielder for baseball's New York Yankees who became an icon of an idealized America and of dignified, graceful celebrity, dies in Hollywood, Florida, after suffering from lung cancer and pneumonia. . . In *Time Warner Entertainment Co. L.P. v. Byers*, the Supreme Court lets stand a ruling by a Louisiana State appeals court that permits a shooting victim's family to sue the makers of the film *Natural Born Killers*.... In Philadelphia, Pennsylvania, Judge Ronald Buckwalter rules against the use of minimum test scores by the NCAA as a requirement for eligibility to play collegiate sports.	March 8
Outside police headquarters in New York City, a series of daily demonstrations begins in protest of the February killing of an unarmed African immigrant, Amadou Diallo, 22.			An international team of scientists reveal they have found a way to predict coronal mass ejections, the most violent kind of magnetic storm on the sun.	William Ivey, chairman of the NEA, cancels the foundation's grant for a children's book written by a Mexican rebel leader, Subcomandante Marcos, one of the top leaders of the leftist Zapatista National Liberation Army (EZLN), for fear that some of the money might go to the Zapatistas.... George Polk Memorial Awards for excellence in journalism in 1998 go to Tracy Wilkinson, Donald L. Barlett, and James B. Steele.... The NCAA agrees to settle a class-action lawsuit challenging NCAA salary rules filed on behalf of some 1,900 assistant coaches.	March 9
The House passes, 398-12, a bill that will prohibit nursing homes from evicting patients solely because their bills are paid by Medicaid, the health-insurance program for the nation's poor funded by both the federal and state governments.... In response to complaints over the dearth of minority and female law clerks employed by the high court, Supreme Court justices David H. Souter and Clarence Thomas defends the court's hiring practices in testimony before a House subcommittee.			A study finds no evidence that a diet high in fat increases a woman's risk of breast cancer.	The Lannan Foundation states it will fund the U.S. publication of a book written by a Mexican rebel leader who was denied NEA funding on Mar. 9.... Reports confirm that the 1999 John M. Templeton Prize for Progress in Religion will be awarded to Ian G. Barbour, a physicist and theologian who seeks to bridge the gap between science and religion.	March 10
The House, 330-90, and the Senate, 98-1, approve legislation giving states more flexibility to decide how to spend federal funding for schools.... Independent counsel Kenneth Starr reveals that he has asked the Justice Department to take over an investigation of improper leaks from his office.	U.S. Defense Department officials report that the navy has demoted and fined a group of 23 sailors after they refused to take a vaccination against anthrax bacteria, one of the deadliest biological agents known, for fear that it has not been adequately tested and may have serious unforeseen negative effects.... The House approves, 219-191, Pres. Clinton's plan to contribute 4,000 U.S. troops to a potential NATO force for Kosovo.	The crew of a navy destroyer sinks the hull of a cargo ship stranded off the Oregon coast since Feb. 4. The ship, the *New Carissa*, has spilled some 70,000 gallons (265,000 liters) of fuel and bunker oil since it ran aground. Officials estimates that the New Carissa is holding 130,000 gallons of fuel oil when the crews sink the vessel in waters where temperatures never rise above 34°F (1°C), keeping the oil in a semisolid state.	A study finds that the incidence of the most common form of liver cancer, hepatocellular carcinoma, rose by 71% between the mid-1970s and the mid-1990s.		March 11

F	G	H	I	J
Includes elections, federal-state relations, civil rights and liberties, crime, the judiciary, education, health care, poverty, urban affairs, and population.	*Includes formation and debate of U.S. foreign and defense policies, veterans' affairs, and defense spending. (Relations with specific foreign countries are usually found under the region concerned.)*	*Includes business, labor, agriculture, taxation, transportation, consumer affairs, monetary and fiscal policy, natural resources, and pollution.*	*Includes worldwide scientific, medical, and technological developments; natural phenomena; U.S. weather; natural disasters; and accidents.*	*Includes the arts, religion, scholarship, communications media, sports, entertainments, fashions, fads, and social life.*

	World Affairs	Europe	Africa & the Middle East	The Americas	Asia & the Pacific
March 12	The Czech Republic, Hungary, and Poland officially join NATO. The three Eastern European nations are the first former members of the Soviet-allied Warsaw Pact to join NATO.	Moldova's parliament approves a new premier, Ion Sturza.	In Zambia, the six journalists arrested Mar. 9 and Mar. 10 on espionage charges are released on orders from the High Court in Lusaka, Zambia's capital.... The British government calls Douglas Scrafton, its ambassador in Kinshasa, Congo, back to Britain in response to the March 10 and March 11 expulsions.		
March 13		Unidentified assailants hurl gasoline bombs into a crowded department store in Istanbul, Turkey, causing explosions and a fire that kills 13 people and wounds three others.... In Kosovo, three bombs explode in marketplaces in the towns of Podujevo and Kosovska Mitrovica, killing six people and wounding 58 others. A seventh victim is shot and killed at the time of the bombings. Both towns have predominantly ethnic Albanian populations.		Britain's Prince Charles travels to the Falkland Islands, where he lays a wreath at a memorial marking the Falkland Islands war.	Reports confirm that that Taiwanese authorities have indicted Cheng Shiou, the captain of a Taiwanese container ship, on charges that he put three Romanian stowaways overboard in the middle of the Atlantic Ocean in 1996 before docking in Canada.... The Indonesian government shuts down 38 debt-ridden banks in an effort to revive the country's devastated financial sector and meet IMF loan conditions.
March 14		Two militant Kurdish separatist groups claim responsibility for the Mar. 13 attack in Istanbul, Turkey.			Afghanistan's two warring sides—the ruling Islamic fundamentalist Taliban militia and the opposition Northern Alliance—announce they have agreed in principle to form a coalition government that will include shared executive, legislative, and judicial branches at an unspecified future date. Separately, UN relief workers return to the country for the first time since July 1998.
March 15	A report by a five-member independent panel states that several members of the European Commission, EU's executive branch, mismanaged programs under their control and hired friends for EU jobs. The panel adds that it found no evidence that commissioners were "directly and personally involved" in fraudulent activities, or had profited from fraud.... A UN helicopter crashes about 35 miles (56 km) northeast of Port-Au-Prince, the capital of Haiti. The 13 crew members and U.N. personnel are presumed dead. The team included six Russians, six Argentines, and an American.	A car bombing in Lurgan, Northern Ireland, kills prominent Roman Catholic attorney Rosemary Nelson. Members of the Red Hand Defenders, a hard-line Protestant guerrilla group that opposes the Northern Ireland peace process, claims responsibility.... The PKK warns tourists to stay away from Turkey in order to avoid being caught in a violent "war" between Kurdish separatists and the government.	A state security court sentences two Jordanians to death for killing an Iraqi diplomat, Hikmet al-Hajou, and 11 other people in two separate incidents in 1998. Two other defendants receive 20-year sentences.	Four prominent dissidents in Cuba are convicted of sedition and sentenced to jail terms ranging from three and a half to five years. The dissidents—Vladimiro Roca, 56, Rene Gomez Manzano, 55, Felix Bonne, 59, and Marta Beatriz Roque, 53—have been held in custody since August 1997 despite repeated international calls for their release.... Despite protests, Mexico's largest state university, National Autonomous University, approves a tuition hike.	
March 16	The U.S. bombs air-defense installations in northern Iraq.... Prompted by the Mar. 15 report, all 20 members of the EU's executive branch, the European Commission, announce that they will resign. It is the first time since the commission's formation in 1958 that any commissioner has been compelled to resign, and the move is regarded as the most serious internal crisis ever in the EU.	The Turkish government announces that it is tightening security measures in response to an ongoing wave of bombings.		In Canada, a judge of the Saskatchewan Court of Queen's Bench sentences federal senator Eric Berntson to one year in jail for defrauding taxpayers while serving as Saskatchewan's deputy premier in the late 1980s.	North Korea agrees to allow U.S. officials to inspect a large underground site that the U.S. suspects is intended to become a nuclear weapons facility. The development of such a facility would violate an agreement signed by North Korea in 1994.
March 17		A Finnish forensic team that examined the bodies of 40 victims killed in January by Serbian forces in the town of Racak concludes that the killings were an organized massacre of unarmed civilians.... An automobile explodes on a road in southern Turkey, killing both of its occupants.... Jean Pierre-Bloch, 93, French Resistance organizer during World War II, close aide to Gen. Charles de Gaulle, and president of the International League Against Racism and Anti-Semitism, 1068 02, dies in Paris, France.	Allan Boesak, a former church leader who served as a high official of the antiapartheid ANC, is convicted by a High Court judge in Cape Town, South Africa, of theft and fraud involving more than US$400,000.... A three-judge panel of the Jerusalem District Court unanimously holds that Arye Deri, a key power broker in P.M. Benjamin Netanyahu's ruling rightist coalition and leader of an ultra-Orthodox group, is guilty of bribery, fraud, and breach of public trust.	Lt. Col. Hildegardo Bacilio Gomez, who in December 1998 led a march of some 50 dissident soldiers in Mexico City, Mexico, is arrested by military police.	The group Human Rights in China claims that Chinese authorities have charged Fang Jue, a former government official who in 1998 called for democratic political reforms, with embezzlement and illegal business activities. Fang has been held since July 1998.

A	B	C	D	E
Includes developments that affect more than one world region, international organizations, and important meetings of major world leaders.	Includes all domestic and regional developments in Europe, including the Soviet Union, Turkey, Cyprus, and Malta.	Includes all domestic and regional developments in Africa and the Middle East, including Iraq and Iran and excluding Cyprus, Turkey, and Afghanistan.	Includes all domestic and regional developments in Latin America, the Caribbean, and Canada.	Includes all domestic and regional developments in Asia and Pacific nations, extending from Afghanistan through all the Pacific Island, except Hawaii.

U.S. Politics & Social Issues	U.S. Foreign Policy & Defense	U.S. Economy & Environment	Science, Technology, & Nature	Culture, Leisure, & Lifestyle	
Pres. Clinton visits Hope, Arizona, the town where he was born, to officially dedicate his boyhood home as an historical site.		Cleanup costs in the effort to dispose of the *New Carissa*, which ran aground Feb. 4, and its oil are estimated at $14 million. . . . The Labor Department reports that the government's index of prices charged by manufacturers and farmers for finished goods fell a seasonally adjusted 0.4% in February from January. That is the index's biggest drop since January 1998, and it follows a 0.5% rise in January and a gain of 0.4% in December 1998.		Bidu Sayao, 96, Brazilian soprano who made her U.S. debut at Carnegie Hall in 1934, dies in Rockport, Maine. . . . Sir Yehudi Menuhin, 82, violinist and conductor of worldwide renown who was involved with hundreds of charities and cultural groups, dies in Berlin, Germany, after suffering a heart attack.	March 12
A bomb explodes outside an Asheville, North Carolina, abortion clinic. No injuries are reported. . . . Reports disclose that Ravenswood Hospital Medical Center in Chicago, Illinois, whose rules barred its staff from aiding a teenaged gunshot victim who died steps from its doors in 1998, has agreed to pay $40,000 to settle a federal complaint of "patient dumping."				Garson Kanin, 86, Academy Award–winning director and writer, dies in New York City. . . . A fight between WBA and IBF heavyweight champion Evander Holyfield and WBC heavyweight champion Lennox Lewis ends in a draw, prompting an international outcry.	March 13
The Justice Department reveals that the number of people in U.S. federal, state, and local jails and prisons reached 1,802,496 as of June 30, 1998. The population of incarcerated people increased by 4.4%, or more than 76,700, during the period of July 1, 1997, to June 30, 1998. The 1998 increase is less than the average yearly increase of 7.3% registered in the period from 1985 to 1998.			Robert Quarles Marston, 76, medical educator and director of the NIH, 1968–73, dies in Gainesville, Florida, of cancer.	Lasse Kjus of Norway clinches the men's overall World Cup alpine skiing title.	March 14
The Senate clears, by voice vote, a bill that will prohibit nursing homes from evicting patients solely because their bills were paid by Medicaid, the health-insurance program for the nation's poor that the federal government and states jointly fund.	George Tenet, director of the CIA, announces the appointment of an independent panel to review the damage to national security caused by China's alleged theft of nuclear secrets from the Los Alamos National Laboratory in New Mexico in the 1980s. . . . In New York City, Judge Deborah Batts dismisses charges against two Chinese men accused of conspiring to sell human organs allegedly taken from executed Chinese prisoners. . . . The Marine Corps drops manslaughter charges against Captain Joseph Schweitzer, the navigator of a jet involved in a fatal 1998 ski-lift mishap in Italy that led to the death of 20 people.	Pres. Clinton signs into law a bill that frees $470 million in reserved funds for use as federal farm-loan guarantees in time for the spring planting season.	Eleven passengers are killed and more than 100 are injured when an Amtrak train crashes in Bourbonnais, Illinois, some 50 miles (80 km) south of Chicago. Officials state it is among the deadliest crashes in Amtrak's 26-year history. . . . The U.S. National Human Genome Research Institute announces an accelerated timetable, estimating that the year 2000 will mark the completion of the project to decode the entire human genome, or genetic sequence.	Chess player Maurice Ashley becomes the first black person to attain the rank of grandmaster. . . . Billy Joel, Bruce Springsteen, Paul McCartney, Curtis Mayfield, Del Shannon, the Staple Singers, and Dusty Springfield are inducted into the Rock and Roll Hall of Fame. . . . Harry Morey Callahan, 86, photographer considered one of the most talented and influential artists in his field, dies in Atlanta, Georgia, of cancer.	March 15
In Billings, Montana, Judge John Coughenour sentences LeRoy Schweitzer, the leader of the Freemen, to 22 years and six months in prison for trying to damage the nation's banking system. Four other Freemen also receive sentences that range from probation to 15 years in prison. . . . A national panel appointed to devise ways to reform Medicare, disbands without endorsing any proposals.			A genetic study concludes that the lineages of African and non-African humans split apart 189,000 years ago, some 70,000 years earlier than previously estimated. The researchers base their conclusion on their study of a gene controlling the production of an enzyme that plays a key role in glucose metabolism.	Rev. Henry J. Lyons, charged with federal fraud and tax evasion, resigns as president of the Baptist Convention.	March 16
In Los Angeles, California, Gaby Vernoff gives birth to a baby girl after having been artificially inseminated with sperm from her deceased husband. It is the first known instance of such a birth in the U.S., and it sparks debate over the ethics of allowing the use of sperm to create a child without the consent of the father.	The Senate approves, 97-3, a Republican-sponsored bill that expresses a commitment to deploy "as soon as technologically possible" a national missile defense system to protect the U.S. against a limited missile attack. . . . Major General David Hale, a two-star army general who retired in 1998 while under investigation for allegations of sexual misconduct, pleads guilty to eight counts of misconduct. He is the first army general to undergo a court-martial since 1952 and the first general ever to be court-martialed in retirement. Hale is reprimanded and ordered to pay a $10,000 fine.		A panel investigating the medical benefits of marijuana finds that the drug is moderately useful in treating such symptoms as the pain and nausea associated with AIDS. However, the report argues that the benefits of marijuana in its smoked form are extremely limited because of the toxicity of the smoke. . . . The FTC votes to accept a settlement it had reached in an antitrust lawsuit against computer microprocessor maker Intel Corp.	Doug Swingley of Lincoln, Montana, wins the Iditarod Trail Sled Dog Race in Alaska. He is the only non-Alaskan ever to win the race. . . . The IOC votes to expel six members who allegedly took gifts and cash payments in return for their votes in favor of holding the 2002 Winter Olympics in Salt Lake City, Utah. . . . Rev. Henry J. Lyons pleads guilty to federal fraud and tax evasion charges in Tampa, Florida.	March 17

F	G	H	I	J
Includes elections, federal-state relations, civil rights and liberties, crime, the judiciary, education, health care, poverty, urban affairs, and population.	*Includes formation and debate of U.S. foreign and defense policies, veterans' affairs, and defense spending. (Relations with specific foreign countries are usually found under the region concerned.)*	*Includes business, labor, agriculture, taxation, transportation, consumer affairs, monetary and fiscal policy, natural resources, and pollution.*	*Includes worldwide scientific, medical, and technological developments; natural phenomena; U.S. weather; natural disasters; and accidents.*	*Includes the arts, religion, scholarship, communications media, sports, entertainments, fashions, fads, and social life.*

	World Affairs	Europe	Africa & the Middle East	The Americas	Asia & the Pacific
March 18		Ethnic Albanian representatives sign a peace accord aimed at ending a year-old conflict between Yugoslavia and the ethnic Albanian Kosovo Liberation Army (KLA). Separately, officials report that the fighting has spread along a nine-mile (15-km) front in northern Kosovo.		Pres. Jamil Mahuad Witt reaches a compromise with opposition parties that enables the government to decrease a heavy surcharge on gasoline that exacerbated economic turmoil in Ecuador.... Reports indicate that former interim president Fabian Alarcon Rivera has been jailed on corruption charges.	
March 19		Fiona Jones, a Labour Party member of the British Parliament, is stripped of her seat after being convicted for campaign malpractice. It is the first conviction of a sitting MP for electoral malpractice in 75 years.... A bomb explodes in Vladikavkaz, the capital of the Russian republic of North Ossetia, killing at least 53 people and severely wounding more than 100 others.... The Serbs reject the peace proposal accepted by the KLA Mar. 18. Officials estimate the conflict has forced 240,000 ethnic Albanians to flee.	Some 18,000 Iraqis, in defiance of UN travel and other restrictions, cross into Saudi Arabia for the annual Muslim pilgrimage to Mecca after Saudi king Fahd agrees to pay the pilgrims' expenses.	Jaime Sabines Gutierrez, 72, Mexican poet who was one of his country's best-loved and most widely read writers and the winner of Mexico's highest literary award, the National Prize for Letters, in 1983, dies in Mexico City of cancer.	Japanese premier Keizo Obuchi visits South Korea in the first trip to that country by a Japanese premier in five years.... Reports indicate that Chinese authorities have ordered an academic magazine known for its discussions of political reform to close.... Tofilau Eti Alesana, 74, prime minister of the Independent State of Samoa (formerly Western Samoa), from 1982 to 1985 and for some months in 1988, dies in Apia, Samoa, of cancer.
March 20		International cease-fire monitors begin withdrawing from Kosovo because of intensifying violence. Serbian forces launch a renewed offensive against ethnic Albanians in Kosovo's central Drenica region, a KLA stronghold. In one incident, Serbian forces reportedly detain and kill 10 men in the village of Srbica.... Sir Michael Harris Caine, 71, British businessman who spearheaded the founding in 1968 of the Booker Prize, Britain's most prestigious literary award, and who was knighted in 1988, dies in London of cancer.	Most of the pilgrims who crossed into Saudi Arabia on Mar. 19, return to Iraq, some citing Saudi mistreatment.		
March 21		The left-of-center Social Democrats, the largest party in Finland's ruling coalition, wins a plurality of parliamentary seats in a general election.... Ernie Wise (born Ernest Wiseman), 73, British comedian who with Eric Morecambe made up the comedy duo Morecambe and Wise, dies of heart failure and a chest infection.	Reports from Zambia confirm that three reporters have been charged with espionage.		Reports reveal that the UN Committee on the Elimination of Racial Discrimination has called on the Australian government to suspend its implementation of the 1998 Native Title Amendments Act, which restricts aboriginal land rights.
March 22			In Zambia, newspaper editor Fred Mmembe is charged with espionage.		In Australia, P.M. John Howard's cabinet approves a draft of a new constitutional preamble, which among other features will recognize the aborigines' prior occupation of the land. Australians will vote on the preamble in November.... A powerful storm, Cyclone Vance, sweeps across Western Australia's Pilbara coast, destroying infrastructure and hundreds of buildings.
March 23	NATO secretary general Javier Solana announces NATO's decision to launch air strikes directed at stopping the Serb attacks on ethnic Albanians and "weakening their ability to cause further humanitarian catastrophe."		Nicholas Steyn, a white farmer convicted of murdering a young black girl, is sentenced to five years in prison, but the presiding judge suspends the sentence, ruling that Steyn had no intention of harming the child. The case raises racial tensions in South Africa.	Four unidentified gunmen assassinate Vice Pres. Luis Maria Argana in Asuncion, the capital of Paraguay. His driver is also killed, but his bodyguard survives the attack.... The Cuban government reveals that Raul Ernesto Cruz Leon, 27, has been convicted of terrorism and sentenced to execution for planting bombs at Cuban tourist locations in 1997.	Japanese warships fire warning shots at two suspected North Korean boats that have entered Japanese waters, in Japan's first naval engagement since 1953.... Australia's stock market, the Australian Stock Exchange (ASX), breaks through the 3000-point mark for the first time in its existence.

A	B	C	D	E
Includes developments that affect more than one world region, international organizations, and important meetings of major world leaders.	*Includes all domestic and regional developments in Europe, including the Soviet Union, Turkey, Cyprus, and Malta.*	*Includes all domestic and regional developments in Africa and the Middle East, including Iraq and Iran and excluding Cyprus, Turkey, and Afghanistan.*	*Includes all domestic and regional developments in Latin America, the Caribbean, and Canada.*	*Includes all domestic and regional developments in Asia and Pacific nations, extending from Afghanistan through all the Pacific Island, except Hawaii.*

U.S. Politics & Social Issues	U.S. Foreign Policy & Defense	U.S. Economy & Environment	Science, Technology, & Nature	Culture, Leisure, & Lifestyle	
	The House passes, 317-105, a bill that expresses a commitment to deploy a national missile defense system to protect the U.S. against a limited missile attack.... The parents of six men held by the INS begin a hunger strike... In Miami, Florida, Judge James King rules that payments owed to U.S. telephone companies to a Cuban-Italian phone company may be used to pay damages awarded to the families of four Cuban-American pilots killed by the Cuban military in 1996.	The Commerce Department reports that the U.S. trade deficit ballooned in January, registering a record $16.99 billion gap in trade in goods and services, up from December 1998's revised $14.06 billion deficit. The gap exceeds economists' expectations.... A federal jury in Akron, Ohio, rules that the nation's four largest tobacco companies are not liable for the costs of treating smoking-related illnesses incurred by 114 union health plans in the state.			March 18
House Republicans and Democrats attend a bipartisan retreat in Hershey, Pennsylvania, designed to foster greater civility in Congress after four years of partisan attack politics that culminated in Pres. Clinton's impeachment in December 1998.					March 19
	Roy Lee Johnson, 93, admiral of the U.S. Navy who commanded the Seventh Fleet in 1964, when U.S. ships fired on North Vietnamese gunboats in the Gulf of Tonkin, dies in Virginia Beach, Virginia, of respiratory failure.			Dr. Bertrand Piccard of Switzerland and Brian Jones of Britain complete the first-ever nonstop circumnavigation of the earth in a balloon, achieving what is regarded as one of the last major challenges in aviation.... Patrick Heron, 79, British abstract painter and art commentator, dies near St. Ives, Cornwall, England, of unreported causes.	March 20
	Brigadier General Henry V. Graham, 82, National Guard general who in 1963 ordered Alabama governor George Wallace (D) to step aside and allow the entry of the University of Alabama's first black students into a school building, dies in Birmingham, Alabama, while suffering from Parkinson's disease.			At the Academy Awards ceremony in Los Angeles, the romantic comedy *Shakespeare in Love* wins seven Oscars, including the one for best picture.	March 21
The General Accounting Office (GAO) reports that federal and state officials often ignore complaints of abuse of nursing-home residents.		James P. Hoffa is sworn in as president of the International Brotherhood of Teamsters union.... In *Central State University v. American Association of University Professors*, the Supreme Court rules, 8-1, that the state of Ohio may exempt from its contract negotiations with public university professors a policy that allows the state to determine the amount of time that professors are required to spend in the classroom.	Arthur Emmons Raymond, 99, engineer who led the team that designed the DC-3 twin-engine airplane for Douglas Aircraft Co. in the early 1930s, dies in Santa Monica, California.		March 22
In *Kumho Tire Co. Ltd. et al. v. Carmichael et al.*, the Supreme Court rules unanimously to expand the role of trial judges to act as "gatekeepers" in preventing unreliable or irrelevant expert testimony from reaching a jury.	The Senate passes, 58-41, a resolution supporting U.S. participation in the impending NATO strikes in Kosovo.			A United Methodist bishop lodges an official complaint against 69 ministers who, in an act of defiance of church law, jointly officiated at a union ceremony for a female homosexual couple in Sacramento, California, in January.	March 23

F	G	H	I	J
Includes elections, federal-state relations, civil rights and liberties, crime, the judiciary, education, health care, poverty, urban affairs, and population.	Includes formation and debate of U.S. foreign and defense policies, veterans' affairs, and defense spending. (Relations with specific foreign countries are usually found under the region concerned.)	Includes business, labor, agriculture, taxation, transportation, consumer affairs, monetary and fiscal policy, natural resources, and pollution.	Includes worldwide scientific, medical, and technological developments; natural phenomena; U.S. weather; natural disasters; and accidents.	Includes the arts, religion, scholarship, communications media, sports, entertainments, fashions, fads, and social life.

	World Affairs	Europe	Africa & the Middle East	The Americas	Asia & the Pacific
March 24	NATO launches air strikes against Yugoslavia, prompted by the Serbian refusal to sign a peace accord with ethnic Albanians fighting for the independence of Kosovo and by Serbian violence against ethnic Albanians. The strikes are NATO's first assault on a sovereign nation in its 50-year history. Yugoslavia uses MiG jets in defense. . . . Britain's highest court rules that the 1998 arrest of Gen. Augusto Pinochet Ugarte, Chile's former military ruler, was lawful. . . . German chancellor Gerhard Schroeder announces that EU member nations have unanimously decided to nominate Romano Prodi, a former premier of Italy, as the president of the European Commission.	A deadly fire breaks out near the middle of a vehicular tunnel that connects France and Italy under Mont Blanc, the highest mountain in the Alps. The blaze traps dozens of cars and trucks in the seven-mile (11-km) tunnel.	A train traveling from Nairobi, the capital of Kenya, to the port of Mombasa derails in a safari park, killing 32 people and injuring 254. . . . Allan Boesak, a former church leader convicted Mar. 17 of theft and fraud, is sentenced to six years in prison.	In the wake of the Mar. 23 assassination of Luis Maria Argana, the lower house of Paraguay's Congress votes to begin impeachment proceedings against Pres. Raul Cubas Grau. . . . In response to Britain's decision about the arrest of Chilean general Pinochet, several hundred anti-Pinochet demonstrators celebrate in Santiago, the capital of Chile. Police use water cannons on students who stage demonstrations, and some 20 people are arrested. . . . in Guatemala, Judge Henry Monroy, presiding over the case of the April 1998 killing of Roman Catholic bishop Juan Gerardi Conedera, becomes the third official to resign from the case, citing acts of intimidation.	
March 25	NATO cruise missile and aerial bombardments strike some 50 targets in Yugoslavia. Yugoslav authorities report that 10 Yugoslav civilians were killed and 60 people were injured in the Mar. 24 attacks. Yugoslavia announces it is severing diplomatic relations with the U.S., Britain, France, and Germany. . . . EU heads of government approve a trade pact with South Africa.	In Macedonia, thousands of demonstrators launch protests at the U.S., British, and German embassies, denouncing the NATO strikes. Police use tear gas to dispel the protesters after they break windows and set fire to embassy cars. . . . In Estonia, Mart Laar of the Fatherland Party is sworn in as the new premier.	Jailed leaders of Gamaa al-Islamiyya (Islamic Group), Egypt's largest Islamic guerrilla organization, announce a permanent cease-fire, ending their seven-year-old armed campaign to replace the secular government of Pres. Hosni Mubarak with an Islamic regime.		
March 26	The 15-nation EU declares in a summit communiqué that it stands ready to recognize a Palestinian state "in due course." It is the first time that the EU explicitly recognizes the Palestinians' "unqualified right" to statehood and other forms of self-determination. . . . NATO planes shoot down two Yugoslav MiG fighter jets over Bosnia–Herzegovina.	The deadly fire that broke out March 24 in a vehicular tunnel that connects France and Italy is brought under control.	The PNA frees Mahmoud al-Zohar, a Hamas leader in Gaza who was jailed in February.	In Paraguay, protesters clash with police and military troops outside the Congress building, where the Senate is debating Pres. Cubas's impeachment. As many as 150 demonstrators are injured in the protests. . . . Haitian president René Préval installs a new, 15-member cabinet by decree in an effort to end a political stalemate that has left Haiti without a functioning government since the resignation of Premier Rosny Smarth in 1997.	
March 27	The Serbs for the first time shoot down a NATO plane, a U.S. F-117 stealth fighter, near Budjenovci, 35 miles (50 km) northwest of Belgrade. The plane's unidentified pilot is rescued six hours later.				
March 28		In Vienna, Austria, roughly 9,000 Serbs rally in a demonstration against NATO and the U.S. . . . A masked gunman tries to launch a grenade at the U.S. embassy in Moscow, sparking a gun battle with Russian authorities. No one is injured.		Reports reveal that four protestors injured in the Mar. 26 demonstrations died from their wounds. In response, Pres. Raul Cubas Grau resigns. Senate president Luis Angel Gonzalez Macchi is sworn in as Paraguay's president.	
March 29	NATO begins the second phase of its campaign against Yugoslavia, launching strikes around the clock and expanding targets to include military support infrastructure such as headquarters and barracks, equipment, supply lines and depots, and munitions factories.		In Israel, the finance ministry and the Histadrut trade-union federation signs a compromise wage agreement, ending a public-sector strike that has halted garbage collection and mail delivery, closed schools, and slowed public transportation and state utilities.	A protester dies from wounds received during the Mar. 26 demonstrations in Paraguay, bringing the death toll to 5. . . . Statistics Canada finds that 62% of reported Canadian sexual-assault victims in 1997 were under the age of 18, and that about one-third of all victims were younger than 12 years old. There were 30,735 incidents of sexual assault reported to the police in 1997, the fourth consecutive year that the number of such offenses had decreased.	

A	B	C	D	E
Includes developments that affect more than one world region, international organizations, and important meetings of major world leaders.	Includes all domestic and regional developments in Europe, including the Soviet Union, Turkey, Cyprus, and Malta.	Includes all domestic and regional developments in Africa and the Middle East, including Iraq and Iran and excluding Cyprus, Turkey, and Afghanistan.	Includes all domestic and regional developments in Latin America, the Caribbean, and Canada.	Includes all domestic and regional developments in Asia and Pacific nations, extending from Afghanistan through all the Pacific Island, except Hawaii.

U.S. Politics & Social Issues	U.S. Foreign Policy & Defense	U.S. Economy & Environment	Science, Technology, & Nature	Culture, Leisure, & Lifestyle	
A pair of separate studies link the growth of managed-care health insurance plans to a decline in academic medical research funding and in free physician care provided to the poor. . . . San Jose, California, police announce that the department will require officers to record the race, sex, and age of every motorist they pulled over. By doing so, San Jose becomes the second city in California to announce such a program, joining San Diego.	The U.S. and Russia sign an agreement to restart a $12 billion program under which Russia will convert uranium from dismantled nuclear warheads into fuel for U.S. nuclear power plants.	In *Minnesota v. Mille Lacs Band of Chippewa Indians*, the Supreme Court rules, 5-4, that several bands of Chippewa Indians in Minnesota retain fishing and hunting rights guaranteed to them in an 1837 treaty with the U.S. government.		In Helsinki, Finland, at the World Figure Skating Championships, Russians Yelena Berezhnaya and Anton Sikharulidze, the defending world champions, win the gold medal for pairs.	March 24
Pres. Clinton signs a bill that will prohibit nursing homes from evicting patients solely because their bills were paid by Medicaid, the health-insurance program for the nation's poor that the federal government and states jointly fund.		The House, 221-208, and the Senate, 55-44, pass a Republican budget blueprint for the fiscal 2000 year and the coming decade.		At the World Figure Skating Championships, Russian Alexei Yagudin, 19, wins the men's title. . . . Calvin Edwin Ripken Sr., 63, professional baseball player, coach and manager, dies in Baltimore, Maryland, of lung cancer.	March 25
A Michigan jury convicts assisted-suicide advocate Dr. Jack Kevorkian of second-degree murder for killing Thomas Youk, 52, a terminally ill man suffering from ALS, by lethal injection in 1998. The death, which Kevorkian videotaped, was broadcast on the CBS television news program *60 Minutes* in November 1998.		A state jury in Little Rock, Arkansas, convicts Whitewater figure David Hale of lying to state regulators about the financial health of a company he owned, National Savings Life Insurance Co.	Astronomers report that a gamma ray burst detected by scientists in January occurred some 9 billion light-years away.	A United Methodist Church jury in Downers Grove, Illinois, convicts Rev. Gregory Dell of breaking church law by officiating at the union of two homosexual men in 1998. He is the first minister convicted under the Methodists' rule. . . . At the World Figure Skating Championships, Anjelika Krylova and Oleg Ovsyannikov of Russia win the ice-dancing gold.	March 26
				At the World Figure Skating Championships, Mariya Butyrskaya clinches the gold medal, becoming the first Russian to win that event at the World Championships. With her win, it is the first time that one country has swept all four events.	March 27
			Sea Launch Co., an international joint venture formed to send commercial satellites into space from a platform at sea, conducts its first test launch when a Ukrainian- and Russian-built Zenit-3SL rocket carrying a dummy satellite blasts off from a converted oil-drilling platform in the Pacific Ocean. The dummy satellite successfully enters its planned geosynchronous orbit.	Baseball's Baltimore Orioles win, 3-2, in a game against a team of Cuban players in Havana, the capital of Cuba. It is the first time a U.S. professional baseball team has played in Cuba since March 1959. Leader Fidel Castro Ruz attends the event.	March 28
Data shows that, in the daily protests that have been taking place outside police headquarters in New York City since Mar. 9, more than 1,200 people have been peaceably arrested, including prominent public figures. . . . Lawyers for Donna and Richard Fasano reveal the couple will give up one of two twins recently born to Donna Fasano after she was mistakenly impregnated with another couple's embryo by a fertility clinic. The Fasanos, who are white, will allow the child, who is black, to be raised by its apparent biological parents, Deborah Perry-Rogers and Robert Rogers.	A Marine Corps navigator, Captain Joseph Schweitzer, pleads guilty to obstruction of justice and conspiracy charges in the case of a 1998 military jet flight in Italy that resulted in a fatal ski-lift accident in which 20 people died. . . . A missile-defense system being developed for the Army known as the Theater High-Altitude Area Defense (THAAD) program fails its sixth consecutive interception test.	The Dow Jones Industrial Average closes above the 10,000 level for the first time ever, streaking 184.54 points, or 1.88%, from the previous day's close to 10006.78. It is the seventh time in just over four years that the benchmark stock average has broken through a so-called millennium level.	More than 100,000 workplace computers are affected by a virus contained in computer documents attached to e-mail messages.	*The Testament* by John Grisham tops the bestseller list.	March 29

F	G	H	I	J
Includes elections, federal-state relations, civil rights and liberties, crime, the judiciary, education, health care, poverty, urban affairs, and population.	Includes formation and debate of U.S. foreign and defense policies, veterans' affairs, and defense spending. (Relations with specific foreign countries are usually found under the region concerned.)	Includes business, labor, agriculture, taxation, transportation, consumer affairs, monetary and fiscal policy, natural resources, and pollution.	Includes worldwide scientific, medical, and technological developments; natural phenomena; U.S. weather; natural disasters; and accidents.	Includes the arts, religion, scholarship, communications media, sports, entertainments, fashions, fads, and social life.

	World Affairs	Europe	Africa & the Middle East	The Americas	Asia & the Pacific
March 30			The opposition headed by former Pres. Nicephore Soglo's Renaissance of Benin (RB) party wins a majority in the 83-seat National Assembly. The legislative election is Benin's third since the advent of a multiparty political system in 1990.		Reports indicate that Chinese authorities have charged Wang Yingzheng, a 19-year-old prodemocracy activist, with attempting to subvert state power. . . . A Hong Kong court rules that 17 residents of mainland China who overstayed their temporary visas in Hong Kong have to return to China.
March 31	NATO members respond to the refugee crisis in Kosovo with an outpouring of aid.	Serb forces capture three U.S. soldiers patrolling the Yugoslav-Macedonia border. . . . Finnish president Martti Ahtisaari appoints current premier Paavo Lipponen to serve as caretaker premier while negotiations continue on the formation of a new government.	Zambia's High Court rules that the founder and former president of Zambia, Kenneth Kaunda, is not a citizen of the country because, although he was born in the country, his parents were Malawian missionaries. Kaunda had voluntarily given up his Malawian citizenship years before.	Reports reveal that a Cuban court has sentenced Otto Rene Rodriguez Llerena, a Salvadoran charged with terrorism in a bombing campaign, to death by firing squad.	
April 1	Iraq tells the UN Security Council that in the first two weeks of March, Britain and the U.S. flew 195 sorties over Iraq's northern no-flight zone and 511 missions over the southern no-flight zone.	Monitors in Kosovo state they have received reports of at least 800 ethnic Albanian executions in the past week. A UNHCR report claims that killings and numerous atrocities have been committed by both the ethnic Albanian KLA fighting for Kosovo's independence and the Serbs. . . . A jury in London, England, convicts Anthony Sawoniuk of two counts of murder for his involvement in World War II–era Nazi war crimes. Sawoniuk, 78, receives two life sentences. His trial is the first held under Britain's War Crimes Act of 1991.	In light of the Mar. 31 ruling by Zambia's High Court, founder and former president of Zambia Kenneth Kaunda is granted a court order preventing his arrest pending his appeal. . . . Businessman Nana Kwaku Dua is chosen as the new Ashanti king, succeeding King Otumfuo Opoku Ware II, who died in February. The Ashanti are a West African people whose centuries-old kingdom is now an administrative region in Ghana.	Canada officially redraws its map to include the new territory of Nunavut, an Arctic area that was the eastern part of the Northwest Territories. It is the first time Canada has altered its map since 1949. The new territory covers some 772,000 square miles (2 million sq km) and has a population of only 25,000 people, roughly 85% of whom are Inuit. . . . In Mexico, protesters attempt to impede the inauguration of Rene Juarez Cisneros as governor of Guerrero by blocking the entry to the government palace.	
April 2					
April 3	In its first assault on Belgrade, NATO fires seven cruise missiles at the Serbian and Yugoslav interior ministry buildings at 1:00 A.M. local time. NATO states it will send 6,000–8,000 troops to Albania to ensure the security of the refugees and assist in the emergency relief effort.				
April 4	In the face of the worsening refugee crisis in Kosovo, several NATO member nations state that they will airlift as many as 110,000 refugees out of the region. More than 400,000 ethnic Albanians have fled Kosovo since NATO started its bombing campaign on Mar. 24.		In Israel, clashes erupt between Muslims and Christians in Nazareth on Easter Sunday, amid Christian fears that Muslims will build a towering mosque with a minaret that might overshadow the Church of the Annunciation.		

A	B	C	D	E
Includes developments that affect more than one world region, international organizations, and important meetings of major world leaders.	*Includes all domestic and regional developments in Europe, including the Soviet Union, Turkey, Cyprus, and Malta.*	*Includes all domestic and regional developments in Africa and the Middle East, including Iraq and Iran and excluding Cyprus, Turkey, and Afghanistan.*	*Includes all domestic and regional developments in Latin America, the Caribbean, and Canada.*	*Includes all domestic and regional developments in Asia and Pacific nations, extending from Afghanistan through all the Pacific Island, except Hawaii.*

U.S. Politics & Social Issues	U.S. Foreign Policy & Defense	U.S. Economy & Environment	Science, Technology, & Nature	Culture, Leisure, & Lifestyle	
An Oregon jury awards $81 million in damages to the family of Jesse Williams, a deceased smoker, in a lawsuit against Philip Morris. It is the largest award in such a case.... Green Party candidate Audie Bock wins a seat in the California State Assembly, becoming the first Green Party member elected to a state legislature in the U.S.... Olsten Corp., a home health-care company, states it has agreed to pay $61 million to settle a federal investigation of alleged fraudulent Medicare billing practices.... Democrats in the Alabama State Senate end a dispute with Lt. Gov. Steve Windom (R) that shut down the chamber for a month.	Two of Mexico's largest banks, Grupo Financiero Bancomer SA and Grupo Financiero Serfin SA, plead guilty in Los Angeles to criminal charges of international drug-money laundering. It is said to be one of the largest money-laundering cases ever investigated by U.S. law enforcement.	New forecasts predict that Social Security and Medicare, the nation's two biggest social programs, will remain solvent longer than expected. Social Security is predicted to be unable to meet its obligations beginning in 2034, two years later than previously forecast. Medicare is forecast to run short of funds in 2015, seven years later than the last estimate.	Researchers reveal they have found that a popular fertility treatment alters the ordinary process by which DNA from a sperm cell and an egg combine to form the genetic makeup of an embryo.	The U.S. Third Circuit Court of Appeals in Philadelphia, Pennsylvania, grants the NCAA a stay of a lower court order that abolished its eligibility rules for freshman athletes.	March 30
Four NYC police officers—Sean Carroll, Edward McMellon, Richard Murphy, and Kenneth Boss—who are charged with murder in the February shooting death of Amadou Diallo, an unarmed African immigrant, are arraigned in the Bronx.			The White House reveals that 92% of the federal government's critical computer systems have been repaired and updated in preparation for the year 2000 (Y2K) computer glitch.	In Largo, Florida, Judge Susan Schaeffer sentences Rev. Henry J. Lyons to five and a half years in prison for bilking money from the National Baptist Convention, a leading black denomination in the U.S.	March 31
The CDC reports that in the year after Florida adopted an aggressive antismoking educational campaign, the smoking rate among middle-school students declined by 19%. That drop is larger than any national decline observed among youth groups since 1980.... In Lubbock, Texas, Judge Sam Cummings deems that a federal law prohibiting any person under a restraining order from owning a gun is unconstitutional when he dismisses charges against Dr. Timothy Emerson.	U.S. officials state that the soldiers captured in Serbia on March 31 are Staff Sergeant Andrew Ramirez, 24; Staff Sergeant Christopher Stone, 25; and Specialist Steven Gonzales, 24.... The Arms Control and Disarmament Agency (ACDA) officially becomes part of the State Department, ending its 38-year existence as an independent arms-control agency within the federal government.		An unusual snowstorm hits the mountains and canyons in and around the Cleveland National Forest, some 40 miles (65 km) east of San Diego, California.	Jesse Stone, 97, songwriter, arranger and producer, dies who in Altamonte Springs, Florida, of heart and kidney ailments.	April 1
	A Marine jury at Camp Lejeune, North Carolina, sentences Joseph Schweitzer, who Mar. 29, pled guilty to obstruction of justice and conspiracy charges, to dismissal from the Marine Corps.... Reports confirm that the unusual snowstorm in California on Apr. 1 resulted in the deaths of at least 12 Mexicans attempting to cross the U.S.-Mexican border and illegally enter the U.S.		New Jersey law-enforcement officials arrest David Smith, 30, a computer programmer, and charge him with creating and sending out a computer virus that spread to more than 100,000 computers around the world.	The administrative board of the National Conference of Catholic Bishops calls for the public, especially Roman Catholics, to seek an end to capital punishment.	April 2
			A tornado estimated to be 300 yards (275 m) wide strikes the small town of Benton, Louisiana, 10 miles (16 km) north of Shreveport, destroying two mobile-home parks and killing six people. More than 100 people are injured, and some 200 are left homeless.	Helen Aberson Mayer, 91, writer who created the cartoon character Dumbo, dies in New York City.	April 3
				Early (Gus) Wynn, 79, baseball pitcher who won 300 games in a 23-year career in the American League, dies in Venice, Florida, of complications of a stroke.... Lucille Lortel (born Lucille Wadler), 98, theatrical producer whose Lucille Lortel Theater provided a forum for innovative theatrical talent, dies in New York City.	April 4

F	G	H	I	J
Includes elections, federal-state relations, civil rights and liberties, crime, the judiciary, education, health care, poverty, urban affairs, and population.	*Includes formation and debate of U.S. foreign and defense policies, veterans' affairs, and defense spending. (Relations with specific foreign countries are usually found under the region concerned.)*	*Includes business, labor, agriculture, taxation, transportation, consumer affairs, monetary and fiscal policy, natural resources, and pollution.*	*Includes worldwide scientific, medical, and technological developments; natural phenomena; U.S. weather; natural disasters; and accidents.*	*Includes the arts, religion, scholarship, communications media, sports, entertainments, fashions, fads, and social life.*

	World Affairs	Europe	Africa & the Middle East	The Americas	Asia & the Pacific
April 5	Two Libyans charged in the U.S. and Britain with the 1988 bombing of Pan Am Flight 103 over Scotland—Abdel Basset Ali al-Megrahi and Lamen Khalifa Fhimah—arrive in the Netherlands for trial there. . . . As many as three NATO bombs fall on two residential areas in the town of Aleksinac, 100 miles (160 km) southwest of Belgrade. It is the first time in the bombing campaign that NATO strikes have hit civilian buildings.				Reports confirm that 34 people have been killed in several days of clashes between Christians and Muslims in the eastern Moluccas archipelago, which forms Indonesia's Maluku Province.
April 6	NATO focuses its attacks on Serbian troops and armored vehicles in an area near the Kosovo-Albanian border. NATO also launches a series of attacks against the Yugoslav Third Army, which is leading the offensive against ethnic Albanians in Nis and Pristina.		Violence flares between Muslims and Christians in Nazareth. . . . South Africa's Truth and Reconciliation Commission denies a collective amnesty application submitted by 79 senior ANC members.	An arrest warrant is issued for for Mario Villanueva Madrid, outgoing governor of the Mexican state of Quintana Roo. He is the highest-ranked elected official in Mexico to be investigated on drug charges. . . . Pierre Lebrun, a former employee of a bus company based in Ottawa, Ontario, Canada, shoots and kills four workers and wounds one other before committing suicide.	As many as 57 people are killed in an attack on a church in Liquica in Indonesia.
April 7	NATO loses an unmanned U.S. reconnaissance plane, apparently due to Serbian fire. It is the second NATO aircraft downed since the bombing campaign started. . . . The UN condemns Macedonia for forcibly relocating an estimated 30,000–45,000 refugees from a camp on the border with Kosovo.	Yugoslavia closes Kosovo's borders with Albania and Macedonia. Officials report that Serbs have set fire to 50 villages since April 4. . . . Edgar Pearce pleads guilty at London's Central Criminal Court to 20 charges related to a 3½-year bombing campaign known as the "Mardi Gra" bombings.	South Africa's Truth and Reconciliation Commission denies amnesty to Janusz Walus and Clive Derby-Lewis, who killed Chris Hani, an antiapartheid leader who headed the South African Communist Party.		
April 8	Iraq rejects the recommendations of three UN special panels established in January to end the impasse over the UN's U.S.-led arms monitoring and sanctions regimes on Iraq. . . . The European Central Bank (ECB) lowers its main lending rate, the refinancing rate, to 2.5% from 3%. The ECB rate cut is the first interest rate change ever implemented by the institution, which controls monetary policy in European Union countries that adopted the EU's new currency, the euro.	The death toll from the Mar. 24 fire in a vehicular tunnel that connects France and Italy stands at 40.	Reports reveal that Libyan Airlines has made its first international flight since the suspension of U.N. sanctions imposed in 1992. The flights come after the Apr. 5 handover of two Libyans charged in the U.S. and Britain with the 1988 bombing of Pan Am Flight 103 over Scotland.		
April 9		The Yugoslav republic of Serbia reopens Kosovo's borders with Albania and Macedonia, allowing refugees to once again flee Kosovo. Serbian forces begin a daily campaign of firing artillery at the KLA over the border.	Niger president Ibrahim Mainassara Bare, 49, is assassinated, apparently by members of his presidential guard in an ambush at the international airport. . . . Ismail Omar Guelleh is elected president of Djibouti.		
April 10		Yugoslav officials disclose that since the NATO bombings began in March, more than 300 civilians have been killed and nearly 3,000 more have been wounded in the attacks.	Iran's deputy chief of staff of the armed forces, Brigadier General Ali Sayyad Shirazi, 55, is shot to death in Teheran, the capital. The Iraq-based Iranian opposition group People's Mujahedeen claims responsibility for the assassination.		A boat carrying 54 illegal Chinese immigrants runs aground on the north coast of New South Wales, Australia.

A	B	C	D	E
Includes developments that affect more than one world region, international organizations, and important meetings of major world leaders.	Includes all domestic and regional developments in Europe, including the Soviet Union, Turkey, Cyprus, and Malta.	Includes all domestic and regional developments in Africa and the Middle East, including Iraq and Iran and excluding Cyprus, Turkey, and Afghanistan.	Includes all domestic and regional developments in Latin America, the Caribbean, and Canada.	Includes all domestic and regional developments in Asia and Pacific nations, extending from Afghanistan through all the Pacific Island, except Hawaii.

U.S. Politics & Social Issues	U.S. Foreign Policy & Defense	U.S. Economy & Environment	Science, Technology, & Nature	Culture, Leisure, & Lifestyle	
Russell Henderson, 21, pleads guilty in the 1998 kidnapping and beating death of Matthew Shepard, a homosexual Wyoming college student. Judge Jeffrey Donnell sentences him to two consecutive life terms in prison..... In *Wyoming v. Houghton*, the Supreme Court rules, 6-3, that police officers have the authority to search the belongings of automobile passengers even if the officers suspect only the driver of illegal activity.... The Supreme Court rules unanimously in *Mitchell v. U.S.* that defendants who plead guilty to criminal charges do not forfeit their right to remain silent at their sentencing hearings.	Reports reveal that three Mexicans have been arrested on federal charges of immigrant smuggling in connection with the immigrants who died in the Apr. 1–2 snowstorm.	Pulaski County circuit judge David Bogard formally imposes the jury's recommended sentence of 21 days' imprisonment on Whitewater figure David Hale.			April 5
Missouri voters reject a proposal that would have lifted a century-old ban on the carrying of concealed weapons. The vote, which receives nationwide attention, is the first referendum ever held in the U.S. on the issue.... In San Francisco, California, Judge John Munter in cuts in half the $50 million in punitive damages awarded by a jury in February to Patricia Henley in her suit against cigarette maker Philip Morris.			Archaeologists announce they have discovered the frozen mummies of three Inca children atop a volcano in northern Argentina.	Red Norvo (born Kenneth Norville), 91, xylophone and vibraphone player credited with helping popularize and legitimize both instruments in the jazz community, dies in Santa Monica, California.	April 6
				Michael Cunningham, author of *The Hours*, is named the winner of the PEN/Faulkner Award for Fiction.	April 7
		On Equal Pay Day, recent statistics show that women on average earned 74% as much as men in 1997.	A working group of an advisory panel to the NIH releases its draft version of rules governing federal funding for research on human embryonic stem cells.	Julie Krone, the most successful female jockey in North American horse racing, announces that she will retire from the sport, effective Apr. 19.	April 8
	The U.S. announces plans to impose 100% tariffs on $191.4 million worth of European products in retaliation for what U.S. officials call unfair European Union restrictions on Latin American bananas.	The U.S. Second Circuit Court of Appeals in New York City rules that two labor-union health funds cannot proceed with a lawsuit against cigarette makers over smoking-related illnesses suffered by their members.... Federal judge Loren Smith orders the U.S. government to pay $908.9 million to Glendale Federal Bank, a California thrift, for the government's failure to honor financial promises made at the beginning of the savings and loan crisis in the early 1980s.	The FDA approves the use of eye implants called Intacs to correct mild nearsightedness.... A missile warning satellite is launched from Cape Canaveral aboard a Titan rocket but is put into the wrong orbit.		April 9
				Bobbyjo wins the 152nd running of Great Britain's Grand National Steeplechase in Liverpool, England.	April 10

F	G	H	I	J
Includes elections, federal-state relations, civil rights and liberties, crime, the judiciary, education, health care, poverty, urban affairs, and population.	*Includes formation and debate of U.S. foreign and defense policies, veterans' affairs, and defense spending. (Relations with specific foreign countries are usually found under the region concerned.)*	*Includes business, labor, agriculture, taxation, transportation, consumer affairs, monetary and fiscal policy, natural resources, and pollution.*	*Includes worldwide scientific, medical, and technological developments; natural phenomena; U.S. weather; natural disasters; and accidents.*	*Includes the arts, religion, scholarship, communications media, sports, entertainments, fashions, fads, and social life.*

	World Affairs	Europe	Africa & the Middle East	The Americas	Asia & the Pacific
April 11	NATO states it has disabled half of Serbia's air force, damaged all of its airfields, and destroyed roughly half of Serbia's air defenses and two of Serbia's three main army headquarters.	Serbian shelling of the northern Albanian town of Tropoja kills two Albanian civilians and wounds 12 others. Two masked men shoot and kill Slavko Curuvija, one of Yugoslavia's most prominent independent journalists and a vocal critic of Pres. Slobodan Milosevic.	Niger president Ibrahim Mainassara Bare, assassinated April 9, is buried in his home village 125 miles (200 km) south of Niamey. An army junta led by the head of the presidential guard, Daouda Malam Wanke, assumes power in the wake of Bare's death.		India conducts a test launch of an intermediate-range ballistic missile capable of carrying a nuclear warhead and of striking targets in Pakistan.
April 12		Two NATO missiles strike a passenger train as it crosses a bridge in southeastern Serbia, killing at least nine civilians and injuring 16. . . . Truck drivers throughout Britain blockade streets and highways to protest recent increases in fuel levies and vehicle registration taxes.	Tens of thousands of Iranians attend the military funeral of Brigadier General Ali Sayyad Shirazi, assassinated Apr. 10. . . . Niger's 11 opposition parties express support for the new military junta.	In Colombia, a plane with 46 passengers and crew aboard is hijacked en route to Bogota, the capital, from the northeast city of Bucaramanga.	Hutomo (Tommy) Mandala Putra, son of former Indonesian president Suharto, is formally charged with corruption in connection with a real estate deal.
April 13	NATO begins escalating its air strikes against Yugoslavia.	French investigators blame Italian officials for exacerbating the effects of a tunnel fire in March that killed at least 41 people. . . . An estimated 60–100 Serbian troops raid an Albanian border post in the town of Kamenica, just inside Albania's northern border. It is the first time since the NATO bombing began that Serbian troops enter Albania. . . . Willi Stoph, 84, premier of East Germany 1964–73, 1976–89, dies in Berlin of unreported causes.	Local newspapers report that 29 people were killed in Mascara province—some 250 miles (400 km) southwest of Algiers—a few days earlier by suspected Islamic rebels.	In Colombia, five elderly people and an infant—six of the hostages aboard the plane hijacked Apr. 12—are released to Red Cross workers. . . . In Venezuela, supporters of Pres. Hugo Chavez Frias rally outside the Congress building, calling for the dissolution of Congress. . . . In one of the most exhaustive investigations in Toronto's history, a jury convicts Francis Roy, 41, of first-degree murder in the 1986 killing of 11-year-old Alison Parrott.	
April 14	NATO launches missiles and bombs at targets throughout Yugoslavia in what NATO describes as its most intensive attacks since the bombing campaign began more than three weeks earlier. . . . The European Union meets to discuss diplomatic means of ending the conflict in Kosovo.	Yugoslav officials reveal that NATO bombed two convoys of ethnic Albanian refugees, killing between 64 and 85 people and injuring 25 others. . . . Edgar Pearce, labeled the "Mardi Gra" bomber, is sentenced in London's Central Criminal Court to 21 years in prison for a series of bombings and threatened bombings perpetrated in the mid-1990s.			Anwar Ibrahim, Malaysia's former deputy prime minister, is found guilty of four charges of corruption and sentenced to a six-year prison term. Anwar's 1998 arrest and subsequent trial sparked unprecedented protests against the government of P.M. Mahathir bin Mohamad. Riot police arrest 18 demonstrators and use water cannons and tear gas to break up protests that draw several thousand people. . . . In response to India's April 11 tests, Pakistan conducts a test-launch of an intermediate-range ballistic missile that can carry a nuclear warhead.
April 15	British home secretary Jack Straw rules that the extradition case against General Augusto Pinochet Ugarte, Chile's former military leader, will be allowed to proceed.	Latvia's parliament abolishes capital punishment. . . . A coalition of five political parties, headed by Premier Paavo Lipponen, is sworn in as the government of Finland.	Abdelaziz Bouteflika, who has the support of the army, is elected president of Algeria. He is the only candidate on the ballot. . . . Arye Deri, leader of the ultra-Orthodox Shas Party of Jews of Middle Eastern and North African origin, is sentenced to four years in prison for corruption. . . . Israeli soldiers and the Israel-allied SLA seize the village of Arnoun, effectively absorbing it into Israel's self-declared security zone in southern Lebanon.	At least 40 people are killed when two separate torrents of mud and rock triggered by weeks of rain bury several blocks of the western town of Argelia, 150 miles (240 km) west of Bogotá, the capital of Colombia. Separately, the ELN releases three of the 41 remaining hostages taken during the Apr. 12 hijacking of a commercial airplane.	Pakistan test-fires a missile able to carry nuclear warheads. Separately, former Pakistani prime minister Benazir Bhutto and her husband, Asif Ali Zardari, are convicted of corruption charges by a panel of two Lahore High Court judges in Rawalpindi. Both Bhutto and Zardari are sentenced to five years in prison.
April 16		The ethnic Albanian Kosovo Liberation Army (KLA) turns over to Albanian authorities a Yugoslav army officer captured overnight near the town of Junik, in Kosovo. . . . Sir (Archibald) Laurence Patrick Kirwan, 91, director and secretary of Britain's Royal Geographical Society, 1947–75, dies in London of unreported causes.	Thousands of demonstrators in Algiers and other cities protest the Apr. 15 election results.	An increase of some 30% in fuel prices, along with several other new taxes, prompts protests all over Jamaica.	Former prime minister Benazir Bhutto's Pakistan People's Party (PPP) calls for a strike in Bhutto's home province, Sindh, in protest of her Apr. 15 conviction for corruption.

A	B	C	D	E
Includes developments that affect more than one world region, international organizations, and important meetings of major world leaders.	Includes all domestic and regional developments in Europe, including the Soviet Union, Turkey, Cyprus, and Malta.	Includes all domestic and regional developments in Africa and the Middle East, including Iraq and Iran and excluding Cyprus, Turkey, and Afghanistan.	Includes all domestic and regional developments in Latin America, the Caribbean, and Canada.	Includes all domestic and regional developments in Asia and Pacific nations, extending from Afghanistan through all the Pacific Island, except Hawaii.

U.S. Politics & Social Issues	U.S. Foreign Policy & Defense	U.S. Economy & Environment	Science, Technology, & Nature	Culture, Leisure, & Lifestyle	
		Data reveals that the IRS audited 20% fewer tax returns in the fiscal 1998 year than it had in fiscal 1997. Of the 120 million individual tax returns filed in fiscal 1998, one in 217 was audited.	At the Denver International Airport in Colorado, the FAA concludes full-scale test of its Y2K computer repairs and finds that the system "worked as it should, smoothly, efficiently and safely."	José María Olazabal of Spain wins the 63rd Masters golf tournament in Augusta, Georgia. . . . British architect Sir Norman Foster is named the winner of the 1999 Pritzker Architecture Prize for lifetime achievement. . . . *Shakespeare in Love* wins for best film at Britain's annual motion-picture awards.	**April 11**
In Little Rock, Arkansas, Judge Susan Webber Wright holds Pres. Clinton in contempt of court for giving "intentionally false" testimony about his relationship with former White House intern Monica Lewinsky in the Paula Jones sexual-harassment case. She orders Clinton to pay Jones "any reasonable expenses" incurred as a result of his false testimony. . . . The GAO reports that health maintenance organizations (HMOs) often give Medicare beneficiaries inaccurate and incomplete information on costs and benefits.		A federal jury in Little Rock, Arkansas, acquits Susan McDougal of obstruction of justice for refusing to testify about the roles of Pres. Clinton and First Lady Hillary Rodham Clinton in the Whitewater land development and other Arkansas business deals. The presiding judge, George Howard Jr., declares a mistrial on the criminal contempt charges. . . . In Washington, D.C., Judge Stanley Sporkin sentences Nolanda Hill, a former business partner of late commerce secretary Ronald Brown, to four months in prison for failing to report some $140,000 of income on her federal tax returns.	Researchers suggest that lycopene, a nutrient found in tomatoes, helps shrink prostate tumors and prevents them from spreading beyond the prostate gland.	Pulitzer Prizes are awarded to Michael Cunningham, John McPhee, and Margaret Edson, among others. Musician Duke Ellington receives a posthumous citation for his work in jazz during a career that lasted more than 50 years. . . . Boxcar Willie (born Lecil Travis Martin), 67, country-music singer and self-styled railroad hobo, dies in Branson, Missouri, of leukemia.	**April 12**
Judge Jessica Cooper sentences assisted-suicide advocate Dr. Jack Kevorkian to 10–25 years in prison for his role in the euthanasia death of Thomas Youk, 52, a terminally ill man he was convicted of killing in September 1998. The death, which Kevorkian videotaped, aired on the CBS television program *60 Minutes* in November 1998.				Eric Ross donates $5 million to the Holocaust Memorial Museum in Washington, D.C., and helps dedicate its administration building to his parents, Albert and Regina Rosenberg, both of whom died at Auschwitz. It is the largest gift to the institution since its opening in 1993.	**April 13**
Independent counsel Kenneth Starr tells the Senate Governmental Affairs Committee that he opposes renewing the 1978 law under which he was appointed. Starr defends his 4½-year-old investigation of Pres. Clinton—which led to the president's impeachment in the Monica Lewinsky matter—but argues that the independent counsel law itself is flawed.		The House approves, 220-208, vote the Republican majority's budget resolution for fiscal 2000. The nonbinding resolution will serve as a blueprint for congressional appropriators during their negotiations with Pres. Clinton on the final terms of the 2000 budget.			**April 14**
		Figures reveal that Vice Pres. Al Gore and Texas governor George W. Bush (R) have raised far more campaign money than their rivals for presidential nominations in 2000. Gore raised $8.9 million in the first quarter of 1999; Bush received $7.6 million in contributions in 28 days without holding a single fund-raising event. . . . The Senate approves, 54-44, the budget blueprint for fiscal 2000. It is the first time since 1994 that lawmakers have passed the budget resolution in time for the Apr. 15 deadline.	In a landmark observation, two teams of astronomers announce the first discovery of a system of multiple planets orbiting a star other than the sun. Three large planets are orbiting Upsilon Andromedae, about 44 light years away in the constellation Andromeda. . . . Four studies suggest that a treatment of high doses of chemotherapy and a bone-marrow transplant does not help patients with advanced breast cancer live longer than they would with chemotherapy alone.		**April 15**
			Scientists report they have discovered a species of bacterium that is larger by far than any previously known. The bacterium, named Thiomargarita namibiensis, was discovered in 1997 in sediment from the ocean floor off Namibia, is spherical in shape, and ranges in size from about 750 to 100 micrometers, visible to the naked eye.	Wayne Gretzky, considered by many to be the greatest player in the history of the National Hockey League, announces his retirement. . . . Skip Spence, 52, a member of rock bands Moby Grape and Jefferson Airplane, dies in Santa Cruz, California, of lung cancer. . . . Rap-music producer Sean (Puffy) Combs is arrested in the beating of record executive Steven Stoute.	**April 16**

F	G	H	I	J
Includes elections, federal-state relations, civil rights and liberties, crime, the judiciary, education, health care, poverty, urban affairs, and population.	*Includes formation and debate of U.S. foreign and defense policies, veterans' affairs, and defense spending. (Relations with specific foreign countries are usually found under the region concerned.)*	*Includes business, labor, agriculture, taxation, transportation, consumer affairs, monetary and fiscal policy, natural resources, and pollution.*	*Includes worldwide scientific, medical, and technological developments; natural phenomena; U.S. weather; natural disasters; and accidents.*	*Includes the arts, religion, scholarship, communications media, sports, entertainments, fashions, fads, and social life.*

	World Affairs	Europe	Africa & the Middle East	The Americas	Asia & the Pacific
April 17	British and U.S. fighter planes resume attacks against targets in northern Iraq.	The KLA discloses that it captured two Yugoslav army officers and a soldier described as a Russian mercenary near Kosovo's border with Albania.... A 515-mile (830-km) oil pipeline running through Azerbaijan and Georgia to the Black Sea opens. A consortium of 11 companies from eight countries spent $1.5 billion over two years to build the pipeline.... An explosion wounds at least 40 people in the Brixton section of South London.			The 13-month-old government of P.M. Atal Behari Vajpayee collapses when it loses a vote of confidence in the Lok Sabha, the lower house of India's parliament.
April 18		The Yugoslav government breaks off diplomatic relations with Albania.... Premier Bulent Ecevit's Democratic Left Party wins a plurality of votes cast in Turkey's national parliamentary election.	A military tribunal in Cairo, the capital of Egypt, sentences nine militants of the outlawed Islamic Jihad (Islamic Holy War) group to death for conspiring to overthrow the secular government of Pres. Hosni Mubarak and replace it with a strict Islamic regime. In other tribunal decisions, some 11 defendants are given life sentences at hard labor; 67 are sentenced to prison terms ranging from one to 15 years; and 20 are found not guilty.		
April 19	NATO for the first time admits that it hit a column of refugees near the town of Djakovica, in southeastern Kosovo, the previous week.	The Bundestag, the lower house of Germany's parliament, holds its inaugural session in the recently renovated Reichstag building in Berlin. It is a major step in the ongoing transfer of the German government to Berlin, the country's capital throughout most of its early history, from Bonn.		Two U.S. Marine Corps F-18 jets drop 500-pound (225-kg) bombs off target in Vieques, Puerto Rico, leaving one civilian security guard dead. The accident prompts Puerto Ricans to protest the U.S. Navy presence on the island.... In Jamaica, rioters block roads by burning tires, trees, and appliances, and they clash with police who try to remove the roadblocks.... Argentine farmers and ranchers carry out a three-day strike to protest new economic policies.	Britain's Queen Elizabeth II travels to South Korea in the first visit by a British monarch to the country since Britain established diplomatic relations with the former Korean kingdom in 1883.
April 20				Students of the National Autonomous University of Mexico (UNAM), the country's largest university, launch a strike to protest a tuition increase. ... Retired colonel Bernardo Ruiz, the former commander of the 20th Intelligence Brigade, which was disbanded in 1998, is arrested on murder charges in Bogota, Colombia.	In Peshawar, Pakistan, more than 20 people are arrested after police use tear gas to break up a demonstration protesting the Apr. 15 convictions of former Pakistani prime minister Benazir Bhutto and her husband, Asif Ali Zardari.
April 21				In response to the protests that started April 16 in Jamaica, Prime Minister P. J. Patterson announces that he will appoint a committee to suggest alternatives to the fuel tax.	Forces of the opposition Northern Alliance in Afghanistan's civil war capture Bamiyan, a city 60 miles (100 km) west of the capital, Kabul, held by the ruling Taliban militia. The Taliban, which espouses a fundamentalist brand of Sunni Islam, controls some 90% of the country.

A	B	C	D	E
Includes developments that affect more than one world region, international organizations, and important meetings of major world leaders.	Includes all domestic and regional developments in Europe, including the Soviet Union, Turkey, Cyprus, and Malta.	Includes all domestic and regional developments in Africa and the Middle East, including Iraq and Iran and excluding Cyprus, Turkey, and Afghanistan.	Includes all domestic and regional developments in Latin America, the Caribbean, and Canada.	Includes all domestic and regional developments in Asia and Pacific nations, extending from Afghanistan through all the Pacific Island, except Hawaii.

U.S. Politics & Social Issues	U.S. Foreign Policy & Defense	U.S. Economy & Environment	Science, Technology, & Nature	Culture, Leisure, & Lifestyle	
					April 17
				Golfer Allen Doyle wins the 60th PGA Seniors' Championship.... Raghubir Singh, 56, Indian photographer whose pictures were published in Indian and U.S. periodicals and are on display at a retrospective exhibition at the Art Institute of Chicago, Illinois, dies in New York City of an apparent heart attack.	**April 18**
In *ApolloMedia Corp. v. Reno*, the Supreme Court denies a First Amendment challenge of a provision in the Telecommunications Act of 1996 that makes it a crime to send obscene electronic-mail messages or faxes.... A federal rule requiring federal prosecutors to comply with ethics standards set by state bar associations in the states where they are operating goes into effect. The rule was mandated by a provision in the fiscal 1999 appropriations bill for the Justice Department.		A study suggests that the chief executive officers (CEOs) of large U.S. companies earned an average pay of $10.6 million in 1998. The 1998 average represents a 36% increase over the corresponding figure in 1997, and a 442% hike over the average CEO compensation of $2 million in 1990.		Joseph Chebet of Kenya and Fatuma Roba of Ethiopia win the men's and women's races, respectively, in the Boston Marathon.... Actor Danny Glover donates $1 million to the TransAfrica Forum, a group that monitors U.S. government policies toward Africa and the Caribbean and seeks to promote democracy in Africa.	**April 19**
Eric Harris, 18, and Dylan Klebold, 17, storm Columbine High School in Littleton, Colorado, and, in a five-hour rampage, use guns and bombs to kill 13 people and wound more than 30 others before killing themselves. The attack is the deadliest such incident in U.S. history.... New Jersey governor Christine Todd Whitman (R) and New Jersey attorney general Peter Verniero admit that some state troopers have practiced racial profiling, pulling over black and Hispanic motorists solely because of their race.		In *Unum Life Insurance Co. of America v. Ward*, the Supreme Court rules unanimously that California state law regulating insurance supersedes a provision in the federal Employee Retirement Income Security Act (ERISA) pertaining to insurance-claims deadlines.... The Commerce Department reports that the U.S. trade deficit soared in February, rising to register a record $19.44 billion gap in trade in goods and services. That is up from January's revised $16.81 billion deficit.		Señor Wences (born Wenceslao Moreno), 103, Spanish-born ventriloquist who was a popular guest on U.S. television programs in the 1950s and 1960s, dies in New York City.	**April 20**
In the wake of the Apr. 20 attack at Columbine High School in Littleton, Colorado, lawmakers withdraw two pending bills that would eliminate local gun controls and liberalize state rules for carrying concealed handguns. In Florida and Alabama, lawmakers postpone bills that would protect gunmakers from liability lawsuits arising from shootings. Arizona governor Jane Dee Hull (R) vetoes similar legislation .... The House, 368-57, and the Senate, 98-1, approve the "Ed-Flex" bill, giving states flexibility in using federal education funds.	The Senate confirms Timothy Geithner as undersecretary for international affairs and Edwin Truman as assistant secretary for international affairs.	The Senate confirms Gary Gensler as undersecretary for domestic finance.		Buddy Rogers (born Charles Edward Rogers), 94, motion picture actor and band leader, dies in Rancho Mirage, California.... Liz Tilberis (born Elizabeth Kelly), 51, British-born magazine editor who became president of the Ovarian Cancer Research Fund in 1997, dies in New York City of cancer.	**April 21**

F	G	H	I	J
Includes elections, federal-state relations, civil rights and liberties, crime, the judiciary, education, health care, poverty, urban affairs, and population.	*Includes formation and debate of U.S. foreign and defense policies, veterans' affairs, and defense spending. (Relations with specific foreign countries are usually found under the region concerned.)*	*Includes business, labor, agriculture, taxation, transportation, consumer affairs, monetary and fiscal policy, natural resources, and pollution.*	*Includes worldwide scientific, medical, and technological developments; natural phenomena; U.S. weather; natural disasters; and accidents.*	*Includes the arts, religion, scholarship, communications media, sports, entertainments, fashions, fads, and social life.*

	World Affairs	Europe	Africa & the Middle East	The Americas	Asia & the Pacific
April 22	NATO bombs a Belgrade residence of Yugoslav president Slobodan Milosevic at 4:00 A.M. local time, as NATO attacks on Yugoslavia enter their second month. . . . U.S. Pres. Clinton presents the Presidential Medal of Freedom, the U.S.'s highest civilian honor, to former German chancellor Helmut Kohl, who oversaw the reunification of East and West Germany.			In Venezuela, Congress approves legislation granting Pres. Hugo Chávez sweeping powers to reform the country's economy. . . . Hernando Santos Castillo, 76, considered one of the most politically influential journalists in Colombia and an adviser to a number of Colombian presidents, dies in Bogotá of complications of a cerebral hemorrhage.	
April 23	The heads of state and government of the 19 NATO member nations meet in Washington, D.C., to mark the alliance's 50th anniversary. The leaders of more than 20 other nations that hope to join NATO also attend the ceremonies, Separately, NATO attacks the headquarters of Serbian state television at 2:00 A.M. local time, killing an estimated 16–20 people.			A Via Rail passenger train derails at a switching station in Thamesville, Ontario, Canada, and crashes into a set of stationary freight cars. The train's engineer and a trainee engineer are killed in the accident. Six other crewmen and more than 90 passengers are injured.	The agriculture minister for the state of New South Wales, Australia, approves the slaughter of an estimated 1.5 million chickens afflicted with Newcastle disease.
April 24		An explosion injures seven people in London's Brick Lane neighborhood, which has a large population of Bangladeshi residents.		Figures show that nine people have been killed and at least 70 people arrested in connection with the violence that started April 16 in Jamaica. Authorities acknowledge that police officers are responsible for seven of the deaths.	Arthur Merric Bloomfield Boyd, 78, painter considered one of the greatest Australian artists of the century, dies in Melbourne, Australia, after suffering from heart ailments.
April 25				Venezuelans vote overwhelmingly in favor of the creation of a national assembly to write a new constitution for the country.	More than 10,000 members of a quasi-religious sect gather for a silent protest outside Zhongnanhai, the compound where China's highest-ranking officials live and work in Beijing, the capital of China. The protesters demand recognition from the government for their movement, known as Falun Gong or Falun Dafa.
April 26	Finance ministers and central-bank governors from the Group of Seven (G-7) major industrialized nations meet in Washington, D.C. . . . The foreign ministers of the EU approve a voluntary embargo on oil shipments to Yugoslavia by the 15 EU nations.	Jill Dando, 37, a nationally known television news host who appeared on several BBC programs, is shot and killed outside her London home. . . . The head of the International Committee of the Red Cross, Cornelio Sommaruga, is allowed for the first time to visit three U.S. soldiers taken captive by Serbian forces nearly a month earlier.	Businessman Nana Kwaku Dua is installed as the new Ashanti king, succeeding King Otumfuo Opoku Ware II, who died in February. He takes for his title King Osei Tutu II. . . . Officials disclose that Egyptian authorities have freed some 1,000 imprisoned members of the Gamaa al-Islamiyya (Islamic Group), the country's largest Islamic guerrilla organization.		Indian president K. R. Narayanan dissolves the Lok Sabha, the lower house of India's Parliament, and calls for a general election. . . . Anti-Anjouan protests are unleashed in Moroni, located on Grande Comore on Comoros, a three-island nation in the Indian Ocean. . . . Man Mohan Adhikary, 78, the first Communist prime minister of Nepal, 1994–95, dies in Katmandu, Nepal, of unreported causes.
April 27	NATO launches an attack on a transmitter on an office building housing the party headquarters of Slobodan Milosevic's ruling Socialist Party of Serbia. Separately, NATO commander General Wesley Clark estimates that since NATO began its bombing campaign over a month earlier, Serbian forces have driven more than 700,000 ethnic Albanians out of Kosovo.	A NATO laser-guided bomb misses a target and hits a residential complex in the Serbian town of Surdulica, killing an estimated 16–20 civilians, including 11 children.		The Supreme Court in Paraguay rules that Pres. Luis Gonzalez Macchi, who took office when former Pres. Raul Cubas Grau fled the country in March, will remain in office until 2003, through the end of Cubas's term.	

A	B	C	D	E
Includes developments that affect more than one world region, international organizations, and important meetings of major world leaders.	Includes all domestic and regional developments in Europe, including the Soviet Union, Turkey, Cyprus, and Malta.	Includes all domestic and regional developments in Africa and the Middle East, including Iraq and Iran and excluding Cyprus, Turkey, and Afghanistan.	Includes all domestic and regional developments in Latin America, the Caribbean, and Canada.	Includes all domestic and regional developments in Asia and Pacific nations, extending from Afghanistan through all the Pacific Island, except Hawaii.

U.S. Politics & Social Issues	U.S. Foreign Policy & Defense	U.S. Economy & Environment	Science, Technology, & Nature	Culture, Leisure, & Lifestyle	
North Carolina becomes the first state to enact a law requiring the collection of race data at all traffic stops. . . . Billboard ads for cigarettes are taken down across the country under the terms of a November 1998 settlement of state lawsuits against the tobacco industry. . . . In Washington, D.C., Judge Emmet Sullivan rules that Russell Weston Jr. is incompetent to stand trial for killing two Capitol police officers in July 1998. Sullivan orders Weston to be placed in a mental health facility.	A Black Hawk helicopter engaged in practice exercises crashes in Fort Campbell, Kentucky, killing seven people aboard and injuring the remaining four passengers.				April 22
Thomas Koskovich is convicted for his role in the 1997 murder of Jeremy Giordano, 22, and Giorgio Gallara, 24. The murders of the two pizza deliverymen are called "thrill killings" by authorities who attest that Koskovich committed the murders to feel what it was like to kill someone. . . . The Maine Supreme Court upholds a previous ruling when it finds, 5-1, that state-funded school vouchers cannot be used to send children to parochial schools.			Scientists reveal they cannot confirm the findings of researchers who claimed to have found a genetic link to homosexuality in males. . . . A team of paleontologists disclose the discovery of a fossil skull in Ethiopia that they think belonged to a previously unknown species of human ancestor. The scientists name the new species *Australopithecus garhi*. Their claim that it is a possible immediate predecessor of humans is disputed.		April 23
Officials confirm that four 14-year-old students in Wimberley, Texas, have been charged as juveniles for allegedly plotting to kill students and teachers at their junior high school.					April 24
A memorial service attended by some 70,000 people—twice the population of Littleton, Colorado—is held for the victims of the Apr. 20 school attack. Local, state and national officials attend, including Vice Pres. Al Gore. . . . Roman Lee Hruska, 94, Republican congressman, 1952–54, and senator, 1954–76, from Nebraska, dies in Omaha, Nebraska, of complications from injuries suffered in a fall.				Lord Killanin (born Michael Morris), 84, president of the International Olympic Committee (IOC), 1972–80, dies in Dublin, Ireland.	April 25
		Figures show that the 500 largest U.S. companies saw their aggregate profit fall in 1998 for the first time in seven years. Excluding a large one-time gain at Ford Motor Co., total profit at 500 companies fell 1.8% to $318 billion, from $324 billion in 1997. Aggregate revenue was $5.741 trillion, up 4% from $5.519 trillion a year earlier. The gain in total revenue, however, was down from 1997, when the rate of revenue growth was 8.7%.	The FDA approves the first of a new class of diet drugs that work by blocking the body's absorption of fat from food. The drug is called orlistat. . . . A computer virus affects hundreds of thousands of computers around the world. The virus is called the Chernobyl virus because it is designed to strike on the anniversary of the 1986 accident at the Chernobyl nuclear power plant in the former Soviet republic of Ukraine.		April 26
A federal grand jury in Little Rock, Arkansas, hands down a 133-count corruption indictment against several members of the state's Democratic establishment. The indictment names 10 people, including two current and two former state senators and two former senior education officials. The defendants face charges of money laundering, racketeering, mail fraud, and other crimes.			A satellite intended to take high-resolution photographs of the Earth for commercial use is launched from Vandenberg Air Force Base in California. Ground controllers lose contact with the satellite minutes late.	Reports confirm that poet Robert Pinsky has been named to a third term as poet laureate of the U.S. . . . Al(ois) Maxwell Hirt, 76, trumpeter whose music came to symbolize the New Orleans sound and who recorded 55 albums, dies in New Orleans, Louisiana, after suffering from liver ailments.	April 27

F	G	H	I	J
Includes elections, federal-state relations, civil rights and liberties, crime, the judiciary, education, health care, poverty, urban affairs, and population.	Includes formation and debate of U.S. foreign and defense policies, veterans' affairs, and defense spending. (Relations with specific foreign countries are usually found under the region concerned.)	Includes business, labor, agriculture, taxation, transportation, consumer affairs, monetary and fiscal policy, natural resources, and pollution.	Includes worldwide scientific, medical, and technological developments; natural phenomena; U.S. weather; natural disasters; and accidents.	Includes the arts, religion, scholarship, communications media, sports, entertainments, fashions, fads, and social life.

	World Affairs	Europe	Africa & the Middle East	The Americas	Asia & the Pacific
April 28	NATO launches its most intense air attacks to date against targets in Montenegro, Serbia's junior partner in the Yugoslav federation, as it continues its air campaign against Yugoslavia.	Sir Alf(red) Ernest Ramsey, 79, manager of England's national soccer team, 1963–74, dies.		The Peruvian General Workers' Federation (CGTP) leads a nationwide general strike, criticizing the government's failure to improve living standards in Peru and protesting Pres. Alberto Fujimori's intention to run for a third term despite a constitutional ban. It is the first general strike in the country since Fujimori took office in 1990. . . . A 14-year-old boy shoots two students at a high school in Taber, Alberta, Canada, before he is subdued and arrested. One of the students is killed in the attack.	
April 29	Yugoslavia files cases against 10 NATO members, including the U.S., in the World Court, claiming that NATO's air strikes contravene international law.	NATO planes hit Yugoslavia's defense ministry headquarters in downtown Belgrade for the first time. . . . Russian president Boris Yeltsin endorses a blueprint planning for "the development and use of nonstrategic nuclear weapons."	The Central Council of the PLO endorses Palestinian leader Yasser Arafat's recommendation to delay a decision on Palestinian statehood, originally scheduled to be declared May 4, until after the outcome of Israeli national elections.		The Cormoran army overthrows the government of Comoros, a three-island nation in the Indian Ocean, in a bloodless coup.
April 30	Since Apr. 29, NATO flies the most bombing runs in a 24-hour period than it has flown since the campaign against Yugoslavia started in late March. . . . Cambodia is inducted as the 10th member of the Association of Southeast Asian Nations (ASEAN) regional trade organization.	More than 11,000 ethnic Albanians enter Albania. . . . A nail bomb explodes in a bar in central London, killing two people and wounding more than 70 others. At least 13 people sustain serious injuries in the blast, including two people who lose limbs.		The Nicaraguan government yields to the demands of university students after nearly two months of protests when it agrees to raise the budget for the country's universities.	The Tokyo Stock Exchange holds its last trading session. Face-to-face trading on the floor of the exchange is to be replaced by electronic trading systems. . . . The Cormoran army reveals that the military coup on Apr. 29 against the government of Pres. Tadjiddine Ben Said Massounde was launched to quell violence on the main island of Grande Comore and to prevent the country from falling into anarchy. Col. Azaly Assoumani is named the country's new leader.
May 1		Yugoslav president Slobodan Milosevic orders the release of three captured U.S. soldiers—Specialist Steven Gonzales and Staff Sgts. Andrew Ramirez and Christopher Stone—following an appeal by U.S. civil-rights activist Rev. Jesse Jackson to make such a "bold diplomatic move." . . . The death toll from the Apr. 30 nail bomb in central London climbs to three when one of the wounded dies from his injuries.			Thailand detonates 1,000 land mines in compliance with an international treaty that bans use of the devices. . . . A group of American mountain climbers on Nepal's Mount Everest finds the body of a man identified as George Mallory, who died in June 1924 during an attempt to be the first person to reach the summit of Everest, the world's highest mountain.
May 2	NATO admits that a NATO missile struck a bus as it passed over a bridge in Luzane, Serbia. The missile cut the bus in half, killing an estimated 34–47 civilian passengers.	NATO hits transformers at five separate locations in Serbia, disrupting electricity in much of Yugoslavia. NATO also bombs a hydroelectric plant in Obrenovac, cutting power to all of Belgrade and other parts of Serbia. . . . Pope John Paul II beatifies Padre Pio, a Franciscan Capuchin friar said to have borne stigmata, or marks resembling the wounds of Jesus Christ. The ceremony is attended by 200,000 people, among the largest crowds ever assembled at the Vatican. . . . A political crisis erupts in Turkey when member of Parliament Merve Kavakci arrives at the legislature's swearing-in ceremony wearing a traditional Islamic head scarf.		Mireya Moscoso de Gruber of the conservative opposition Arnulfista Party is elected president or Panama. Moscoso is the first woman ever elected to the position.	

A	B	C	D	E
Includes developments that affect more than one world region, international organizations, and important meetings of major world leaders.	Includes all domestic and regional developments in Europe, including the Soviet Union, Turkey, Cyprus, and Malta.	Includes all domestic and regional developments in Africa and the Middle East, including Iraq and Iran and excluding Cyprus, Turkey, and Afghanistan.	Includes all domestic and regional developments in Latin America, the Caribbean, and Canada.	Includes all domestic and regional developments in Asia and Pacific nations, extending from Afghanistan through all the Pacific Island, except Hawaii.

U.S. Politics & Social Issues	U.S. Foreign Policy & Defense	U.S. Economy & Environment	Science, Technology, & Nature	Culture, Leisure, & Lifestyle	
The National Center for Health Statistics finds that the overall 1997 birth rate was 14.5 births per 1,000 total population, down from 14.7 in 1996. The 1997 rate is the lowest since the government began keeping such records in 1909. The teenage birth rate fell 4% in 1997, to 52.3 births per 1,000 girls ages 15–19. That is the sixth consecutive annual drop in the rate, reflecting a 16% decrease from its peak level of 62.1 in 1991.	The House passes, 249-180, a measure that will force Pres. Clinton to secure approval from Congress before sending ground troops to Yugoslavia.	The Clinton administration eases food and medicine sanctions against Iran, Libya, and Sudan, stating that sales of such commodities to the three countries will henceforth be determined on a case-by-case basis.	Arthur Leonard Schawlow, 77, physicist who played a key role in the development of the laser and cowinner of the 1981 Nobel Prize in physics for his contributions to the field of laser spectroscopy, dies in Palo Alto, California, of congestive heart failure resulting from leukemia.	Rory Calhoun (born Francis Timothy Durgin), 76, film and television actor who appeared in scores of westerns in the 1940s and 1950s, dies in Burbank, California, while suffering from diabetes and emphysema.	April 28
Pres. Clinton signs into law the "Ed-Flex" bill, giving states flexibility in using federal education funding.	Japanese premier Keizo Obuchi visits the U.S. It is the first official visit to the U.S. by a Japanese premier in 11 years.	New Hampshire resolves a school-funding crisis without resorting to creating a statewide income tax. New Hampshire is one of only two states, with Alaska, that has no statewide income or sales tax. . . . The Labor Department reports that the employment-cost index, the broadest measure of labor costs, rose 0.4% in the first quarter, the smallest increase since the department introduced the index in 1982. . . . The Dow closes at a record high of 10,878.38. That marks the 13th record high of the month and the 21st record high of 1999.	Scientists reveal that the *Mars Global Surveyor* spacecraft has detected strong magnetic fields on the planet Mars, suggesting that the planet once had a molten core.		April 29
The National Rifle Association (NRA) holds its annual convention in Denver, Colorado. The gathering has been scaled back to a one-day event in the wake of the Littleton attack at Columbine High School. Several thousand people protest the convention in a rally on the steps of the nearby state capitol building.	The U.S. State Department's annual terrorism survey characterizes Iran as a country that plans and executes terrorist acts, but the survey drops its year-earlier designation of Iran as "the most active state sponsor of terrorism." In addition to Iran, Libya, and Sudan, the State Department continues to identify Cuba, Syria, Iraq, and North Korea as sponsors of international terrorism.		A U.S. military communications satellite is launched by the U.S. Air Force from Cape Canaveral, Florida, but it is stranded thousands of miles below its intended orbit.	A federal jury in New York City convicts document dealer Lawrence X. Cusack III of mail and wire fraud for forging more than 200 documents that he attributed to Pres. John F. Kennedy. Cusack sold the forged documents to more than 100 investors for a total of $7 million.	April 30
			An amphibious tour boat sinks on Lake Hamilton in Hot Springs, Arkansas, killing 13 of the 21 passengers on board. . . . . J. John Sepkoski Jr., 50, paleontologist who, with a colleague, uncovered evidence supporting catastrophism, a theory that sees evolution as a series of mass species extinctions rather than a gradual process, dies in Chicago, Illinois, of heart failure related to high blood pressure.	Charismatic wins the 125th running of the Kentucky Derby in Louisville, Kentucky. . . . Three spectators are killed by flying debris from a car crash at an Indy Racing League event in Charlotte, North Carolina, Eight fans are injured. The deaths are the first fatalities in the 40-year car racing history of Lowe's Motor Speedway.	May 1
			Underwater explorers reveal they have found the Mercury space capsule that carried astronaut Virgil (Gus) Grissom back to Earth in 1961. The capsule sank when a hatch accidentally opened, and Grissom was rescued.	John Elway, considered by many to be one of the best quarterbacks in the history of the NFL, announces his retirement from professional football. . . . (Robert) Oliver Reed, 61, British film and television actor known for his formidable screen presence, dies in Valletta, Malta, of unknown causes after becoming ill while drinking at a bar.	May 2

F	G	H	I	J
Includes elections, federal-state relations, civil rights and liberties, crime, the judiciary, education, health care, poverty, urban affairs, and population.	Includes formation and debate of U.S. foreign and defense policies, veterans' affairs, and defense spending. (Relations with specific foreign countries are usually found under the region concerned.)	Includes business, labor, agriculture, taxation, transportation, consumer affairs, monetary and fiscal policy, natural resources, and pollution.	Includes worldwide scientific, medical, and technological developments; natural phenomena; U.S. weather; natural disasters; and accidents.	Includes the arts, religion, scholarship, communications media, sports, entertainments, fashions, fads, and social life.

	World Affairs	Europe	Africa & the Middle East	The Americas	Asia & the Pacific
May 3	U.S. and British planes continue their near-daily targeting of Iraqi air defense sites in the so-called northern and southern no-fly zones. . . . NATO reports that, in unrelated incidents, two NATO planes were struck by Serbian fire in May. The crews were not harmed. . . . Mohammed Daoud Odeh, a former PLO guerrilla who is known by his code name Abu Daoud and who is tied to the massacre of Israeli athletes at the 1972 summer Olympic Games, is denied entry into France and put on a return flight to Tunisia.	Lithuanian premier Gediminas Vagnorius, steps down after Pres. Valdas Adamkus accuses him of being too authoritarian in handling the country's privatization program.			
May 4		French premier Lionel Jospin fires Bernard Bonnet, prefect of the French-controlled Mediterranean island of Corsica, in connection with allegations that the island's police set fire to a restaurant frequented by Corsican nationalists. The controversy is regarded as France's first major government scandal since Jospin came to power in 1997.	Kuwait's emir, Sheik Jabir al-Ahmad al-Sabah, dissolves Parliament after lawmakers seek a no-confidence vote against the minister of Islamic affairs, Ahmed al-Kulaib. . . . Iraqi officials claim that seven members of one family were killed in late April during an air attack by U.S. and British forces near Mosul, located 220 miles (350 km) north of Baghdad, the capital.	The Nicaraguan government of Pres. Arnoldo Aleman Lacayo accedes to the demands of an estimated 10,000 transportation workers who have been striking for two months and who have set up roadblocks and clashed with police to protest an increased fuel tax and other government changes to the industry.	Reports confirm that a newly identified form of viral encephalitis that experts believe spread from pigs to humans have killed at least 101 people in Malaysia. The epidemic led the Malaysian government to embark on a mass slaughter of nearly 1 million pigs in the affected region, which is the largest pig-breeding area in Southeast Asia. About 200 pig farmers protest in Kuala Lumpur, calling for an increase in the planned amounts of compensation.
May 5	Indonesia and Portugal sign a UN-brokered agreement to allow citizens of East Timor to vote on whether to officially become an autonomous region within Indonesia. . . . The European Parliament votes to approve the nomination of former Italian premier Romano Prodi as president of the European Commission. . . . NATO experiences its first casualties of the mission against Yugoslavia when a U.S. helicopter crashes during a training flight in Albania, killing two U.S. soldiers, Chief Warrant Officers David Gibbs, 38, and Kevin Reichert, 28.	Macedonia closes its borders to ethnic Albanian refugees, saying it will take in only as many refugees as are airlifted out of Macedonia each day. . . . Major John Howard, 86, British commander of a glider-borne light infantry unit that seized two strategically important bridges in the first battle of the Allies' June 1944 D-Day invasion of Normandy, dies in Surrey, England, of unreported causes.	In Nigeria, Gen. Abdulsalami Abubakar, who took power in June 1998, signs a new constitution that will take effect with the May 29 handover to civilian rule. . . . A court in Yemen issues death sentences to three Islamic militants for their role in the abduction and killing of Western tourists in Yemen in December 1998. A fourth man is sentenced to 20 years' imprisonment. Ten others are acquitted.	Police find and destroy three cocaine-processing laboratories capable of producing eight tons of cocaine a month in Colombia.	Col. Azaly Assoumani is sworn in as president of Comoros, a three-island nation in the Indian Ocean.
May 6	The foreign ministers of the Group of Eight (G-8) industrialized countries—Britain, Canada, France, Germany, Italy, Japan, Russia, and the U.S.—agree on general principles for a diplomatic solution to the conflict in Kosovo.	British prime minister Tony Blair's ruling Labour Party wins the largest number of seats in the first elections for the new Scottish Parliament and Welsh Assembly. Although Labour will not hold a majority of seats in either body, the elections are seen as a victory by the party over nationalist parties that advocate greater home rule for Scotland and Wales.	Doctors identify a disease that recently killed 63 people in northeastern Congo as the Marburg virus.		Reports reveal that since the beginning of May, a number of small clashes that erupted between militants and Indian military troops in the disputed Kashmir region have left some 300 people dead.
May 7	Three Chinese citizens staying in the Chinese embassy in Belgrade, Yugoslavia's capital, are killed when a NATO plane drops at least three precision-guided bombs on the embassy. The dead are identified as journalists Shao Yunhuan and Xu Xinghu, and Xu's wife, Zhu Ying. Another 20 people are wounded in the bombing, six seriously. The bombing sparks massive protests throughout China and strains the ongoing diplomatic effort to end the conflict in Kosovo.	NATO bombs hit hospital grounds and a marketplace in Nis, Yugoslavia's third-largest city, killing 15 people and injuring as many as 70. . . . The Bundestag approves an overhaul of laws on the attainment of citizenship. . . . Pope John Paul II visits Romania, becoming the first pope to travel to a predominantly Orthodox Christian country since the Eastern and Western branches of Christianity split in the Great Schism of 1054.	In Guinea-Bissau, a rebel military junta ousts Pres. João Bernardo Vieira. Renegade troops led by former army chief Brigadier General Ansumane Mane attack the presidential palace in Bissau, the capital city. Some 70 people die during the fighting.	The National Liberation Army (ELN), a leftist rebel guerrilla group, releases seven more hostages whom the group has held since hijacking a commercial airplane in April.	

A	B	C	D	E
Includes developments that affect more than one world region, international organizations, and important meetings of major world leaders.	*Includes all domestic and regional developments in Europe, including the Soviet Union, Turkey, Cyprus, and Malta.*	*Includes all domestic and regional developments in Africa and the Middle East, including Iraq and Iran and excluding Cyprus, Turkey, and Afghanistan.*	*Includes all domestic and regional developments in Latin America, the Caribbean, and Canada.*	*Includes all domestic and regional developments in Asia and Pacific nations, extending from Afghanistan through all the Pacific Island, except Hawaii.*

U.S. Politics & Social Issues	U.S. Foreign Policy & Defense	U.S. Economy & Environment	Science, Technology, & Nature	Culture, Leisure, & Lifestyle	
In Colorado, Jefferson County authorities arrest Mark Manes, 22, a recent graduate of Columbine High School, in the town of Littleton, on a charge that he provided one of the guns used by two students in a deadly attack on the school in April.	In *INS v. Aguirre-Aguirre*, the Supreme Court unanimously rules that foreigners are ineligible for refugee protection in the U.S. if they committed a "serious nonpolitical crime" in their own country, regardless of whether they might face political persecution if deported. . . . The parents of men held by the INS end the hunger strike they started March 18. . . . Japanese premier Keizo Obuchi and U.S. president Bill Clinton announce a series of measures to deregulate the Japanese economy.		As many as 76 huge tornadoes strike Oklahoma, Kansas, Nebraska, Texas, and South Dakota, causing severe destruction and leaving at least 47 people dead. The two hardest-hit states are Oklahoma and Kansas, where most of the deaths occur. The tornadoes injure more than 700 people in those states and damage or destroy more than 2,000 homes.	The Baltimore Orioles host the Cuban national baseball team in Baltimore, Maryland. It is the first time a Cuban team plays a professional baseball team in the U.S. since Fidel Castro Ruz took power in Cuba in 1959. The Cuban team defeats the Orioles, 12-6. . . . *We'll Meet Again*, by Mary Higgins Clark, tops the bestseller list.	May 3
			An unmanned Delta 3 rocket carrying a communications satellite malfunctions shortly after liftoff from Cape Canaveral, Florida. The rocket enters space, but fails to place the satellite in its intended orbit. It is the fourth U.S. satellite launch failure to occur within a month. . . . Pres. Clinton declares 11 counties in Oklahoma and one in Kansas to be disaster areas. Officials in Oklahoma and Kansas estimate $200 million and $140 million in damages, respectively.	Cuban pitching coach Rigoberto Herrera Betancourt, 54, seeks asylum in a Baltimore, Maryland, police station after the May 3 game.	May 4
The governors of 10 states announce plans for a joint effort to improve middle-school students' performance in mathematics, through the development of a common curriculum and standardized tests.			The storm system that hit Oklahoma and Kansas May 3 spawns destructive thunderstorms and high winds across Arkansas, Kentucky, and Tennessee.		May 5
	Wen Ho Lee, dismissed in March from his job at Los Alamos National Laboratory in New Mexico for allegedly divulging U.S. nuclear secrets to China, makes the first detailed rebuttal of the widely reported allegations through his lawyer. . . . The House votes, 311-105, to approve $13 billion in emergency defense spending.		The May 5 storms begin to subside after damaging homes and power lines and leaving four dead in Tennessee. . . . The U.S. Ninth Circuit Court of Appeals in San Francisco, California, upholds a lower court ruling that federal restrictions on the export of encryption technology violates constitutional free-speech guarantees.		May 6
A jury in Newton, New Jersey, sentences to death Thomas Koskovich, 21, convicted Apr. 23 of murdering Jeremy Giordano and Giorgio Gallara. In a move called unprecedented, Judge Reginald Stanton imposes a five-year deadline for the state to carry out the execution. . . . A federal judge in Alexandria, Virginia, declares a mistrial in Kenneth Starr's obstruction of justice case against Julie Hiatt Steele, a peripheral figure in the Monica Lewinsky case and the only person prosecuted in the investigation.	A Marine Corps jury finds marine captain Richard Ashby, the pilot of a Marine jet that caused a fatal ski lift crash in Italy in 1998, guilty of obstructing justice by helping destroy a videotape made during the flight. Ashby was acquitted in March of manslaughter charges in the accident that sent 20 people plunging to their death.	Leon Hess, 85, founder of the Amerada Hess Corp. oil company and owner of the NFL's New York Jets, whose personal fortune was estimated at $720 million in 1998, dies in New York City of complications of a blood disease.		A Michigan jury orders *The Jenny Jones Show* to pay $25 million to the family of Scott Amedure, a homosexual man murdered by Jonathan Schmitz after Amedure admitted on a 1995 episode of the talk show that he was sexually attracted to Schmitz. Schmitz's criminal retrial is pending.	May 7

F	G	H	I	J
Includes elections, federal-state relations, civil rights and liberties, crime, the judiciary, education, health care, poverty, urban affairs, and population.	*Includes formation and debate of U.S. foreign and defense policies, veterans' affairs, and defense spending. (Relations with specific foreign countries are usually found under the region concerned.)*	*Includes business, labor, agriculture, taxation, transportation, consumer affairs, monetary and fiscal policy, natural resources, and pollution.*	*Includes worldwide scientific, medical, and technological developments; natural phenomena; U.S. weather; natural disasters; and accidents.*	*Includes the arts, religion, scholarship, communications media, sports, entertainments, fashions, fads, and social life.*

	World Affairs	Europe	Africa & the Middle East	The Americas	Asia & the Pacific
May 8	In response to the May 7 bombings on the Chinese embassy in Belgrade, Yugoslavia, U.S. president Bill Clinton and NATO secretary general Javier Solana apologize for what they both describe as a "tragic mistake."	Polish president Aleksander Kwasniewski signs a law that will limit development and public gatherings within 100 yards (90 m) of former Nazi concentration camps. . . . The ruling center-right coalition of Premier David Oddsson wins a majority of seats in Iceland's 63-seat unicameral parliament, the Althing. . . . Sir Dirk Bogarde (born Derek Jules Gaspard Ulric Niven Van Den Bogaerde), 78, British actor, writer, and the biggest male sex symbol in the late 1950s, dies in London of a heart attack.			In response to the May 7 bombings, thousands of people launch daily demonstrations in front of the U.S. embassy in Beijing, effectively trapping U.S. ambassador James Sasser and his staff. . . . The first group of UN representatives acting as advisers arrive in East Timor in anticipation of a vote on the future status of the region. . . . Pakistani authorities arrest prominent journalist Najam Sethi, whose editorials were highly critical of the government of P.M. Nawaz Sharif.
May 9		Brendan Fegan, reputed to be one of Northern Ireland's leading drug dealers, is shot and killed at a bar in the town of Newry.			The Cambodian government detains under protective custody Kang Kek Ieu, who served as a prison camp commander and chief of the secret service for the Khmer Rouge. Known as Duch, he had been presumed dead since he fled Phnom Penh, the capital, after the fall of the Khmer Rouge regime in 1979. . . . Authorities seize 54 people of apparent Middle Eastern origin on an island off Australia's northwestern coast.
May 10	NATO resumes its intensified attacks throughout Yugoslavia and in Belgrade.	A report by the U.S. State Department reveals evidence of mass executions committed by Serbian forces in at least 70 towns and villages. According to the report, more than 4,000 ethnic Albanians have been killed and more than 300 villages burned. . . . German prosecutors reveal that Barbara Meyer, 42, a member of the defunct Red Army Faction (RAF) left-wing guerrilla group, has turned herself in to police. The RAF is held responsible for the deaths of 50 people in the 1970s and 1980s, and it disbanded in April 1998.			
May 11	The World Health Organization (WHO) sets its goal, and it makes combating malaria and reducing deaths from smoking top priorities. The report also lists the top causes of death worldwide in 1998: heart disease, stroke, and respiratory diseases. AIDS moves up to fourth place among all causes of death, from seventh in 1997.	The KLA and Yugoslav forces are reported to be engaged in fierce fighting. . . . Sir Ian Fraser, 98, British doctor who led a medical team that administered penicillin to wounded soldiers in World War II, dies in Belfast.			India's Supreme Court affirms the death sentences of four people convicted of conspiracy in the 1991 assassination of former Indian prime minister Rajiv Gandhi. The high court commutes the death sentences of three defendants to life in prison. Two people are acquitted. . . . Protests that started May 7 in Beijing begin to break up. . . . Liu Lixian of Beijing is sentenced to four years in prison. Liu attempted to publish writings by China Democracy Party leaders.
May 12		Russian president Boris Yeltsin dismisses Premier Yevgeny Primakov, threatening to plunge Russia into a new political and economic crisis Primakov is the third premier Yeltsin has fired in 14 months. . . . The newly elected members of the Scottish parliament are sworn in and vote to appoint Lord Steel as presiding officer in Edinburgh, Scotland's capital. The newly elected Welsh Assembly meets for the first time. The body votes to install as presiding officer Plaid Cymru's Lord Dafydd Elis-Thomas.	An Iraqi military spokesman contends that U.S. warplanes killed 12 civilians, including two children, in attacks on sites in Iraq's northern no-fly zone.		An estimated 3,000 Indonesians gather in four cities across Indonesia to commemorate the deaths of four students killed during antigovernment protests a year earlier.

A	B	C	D	E
Includes developments that affect more than one world region, international organizations, and important meetings of major world leaders.	Includes all domestic and regional developments in Europe, including the Soviet Union, Turkey, Cyprus, and Malta.	Includes all domestic and regional developments in Africa and the Middle East, including Iraq and Iran and excluding Cyprus, Turkey, and Afghanistan.	Includes all domestic and regional developments in Latin America, the Caribbean, and Canada.	Includes all domestic and regional developments in Asia and Pacific nations, extending from Afghanistan through all the Pacific Island, except Hawaii.

U.S. Politics & Social Issues	U.S. Foreign Policy & Defense	U.S. Economy & Environment	Science, Technology, & Nature	Culture, Leisure, & Lifestyle	
	Nancy Mace becomes the first woman to graduate from the Citadel, a state-run military college in Charleston, South Carolina.		Sir Edward Penley Abraham, 85, British biochemist who, with his colleagues, discovered the enzyme penicillinase and aided the development of cephalosporins, a group of antibiotics that provide an alternative for patients allergic to penicillin, dies in Oxford, England, of unreported causes.	Dana Plato, actress who starred in the sitcom *Diff'rent Strokes* from 1978 to 1984, dies of an overdose of painkillers and Valium in Moore, Oklahoma.	May 8
	Reports suggest that Peter Lee, a scientist working on U.S. weapons programs, disclosed classified information about a U.S. laser device used to simulate nuclear explosions to Chinese scientists in 1985.		A chartered bus en route from La Place, Louisiana, to Bay St. Louis, Mississippi, crashes in New Orleans, Louisiana, killing 22 of the 46 passengers on board and severely injuring at least 17 others.	Shel(by) Silverstein, 66, children's book author and illustrator whose three classics of children's literature sold more than 14 million copies and were translated into 20 languages, dies in Key West, Florida, of a heart attack.	May 9
A Tennessee jury clears three tobacco companies of liability in the deaths of three smokers. It is the first court victory by the tobacco industry in such a case after decisions against cigarette companies in California and Oregon. . . . Amy Fisher, 24, who pled guilty to shooting her former lover's wife in 1992, leaves a state prison in Albion, New York, on parole. Fisher was the subject of a storm of media attention at the time of her guilty plea. . . . Reports confirm that William Gates has donated $50 million to Columbia University's School of Public Health.	A Marine Corps jury sentences Captain Richard Ashby, found guilty of obstruction of justice on May 7, to six months in prison, as well as dismissal from the corps.		The FDA releases a report concluding that changes made by a 1992 law in its procedures for approving new drugs and medical devices have not resulted in a decrease in the safety of such products on the market.		May 10
Eqbal Ahmad, 67, scholar and political activist who taught at Hampshire College in Amherst, Massachusetts, dies in Islamabad, Pakistan when his heart fails after undergoing surgery for colon cancer.		The Labor Department reports that the nation's overall productivity in nonfarm business sectors rose by a seasonally adjusted annual rate of 4% in the first quarter from the October-through-December 1998 quarter. That marks the indicator's 11th consecutive quarterly increase and exceeds analysts' expectations. A revised 4.3% gain was registered for the 1998 fourth quarter.			May 11
Virginia governor James Gilmore III (R) commutes the death sentence of Calvin Swann, 44, a convicted murderer, a few hours before the execution is scheduled to occur. Citing concerns about the inmate's mental illness, Gilmore commutes his sentence to life in prison without parole. It is the first time that Gilmore has granted clemency to a death-row inmate, and the sixth time since the death penalty was reinstated in 1976 that a Virginia governor has commuted a death sentence.	The INS orders the release of five Cuban-born felons detained according to provisions of the 1996 Immigration Reform and Immigrant Responsibility Act. Their release is ordered after the INS reviewed their cases; the reviews were prompted by a hunger strike carried out from Mar. 18 to May 3 by parents of the five detainees.	Treasury Secretary Robert E. Rubin announces that he is resigning. Pres. Clinton plans to nominate Lawrence H. Summers to succeed him. . . . The SEC charges 26 companies and individuals with trying to defraud investors through "outrageous or baseless promises" made over the Internet global computer network.		Saul Steinberg, 84, Romanian-born artist whose drawings often recast popular imagery to comment on urban life and life in the U.S., dies in New York City of unreported causes.	May 12

F	G	H	I	J
Includes elections, federal-state relations, civil rights and liberties, crime, the judiciary, education, health care, poverty, urban affairs, and population.	Includes formation and debate of U.S. foreign and defense policies, veterans' affairs, and defense spending. (Relations with specific foreign countries are usually found under the region concerned.)	Includes business, labor, agriculture, taxation, transportation, consumer affairs, monetary and fiscal policy, natural resources, and pollution.	Includes worldwide scientific, medical, and technological developments; natural phenomena; U.S. weather; natural disasters; and accidents.	Includes the arts, religion, scholarship, communications media, sports, entertainments, fashions, fads, and social life.

	World Affairs	Europe	Africa & the Middle East	The Americas	Asia & the Pacific
May 13		Three U.S. F-16 jets drop two laser-guided bombs and six gravity bombs on Korisa, a village in southwestern Kosovo.... Italian treasury and budget minister Carlo Azeglio Ciampi, a former premier, is elected president by Italy's lawmakers and regional political leaders. Ciampi will succeed Pres. Oscar Luigi Scalfaro.	Sheik Abdelaziz Bin Baz, Saudi Arabia's highest religious authority, who was believed to be in his late 80s, dies in Taif, Saudi Arabia, of cancer.	Presidents Alberto Fujimori of Peru and Jamil Mahuad Witt of Ecuador dedicate the last boundary stone along a disputed area of the Peru-Ecuador border, formally resolving an issue that has plagued the two nations for more than 50 years.... King Abdullah II of Jordan visits Canada on his first trip to North America since he was sworn in as Jordan's monarch following the death of his father, King Hussein, in February.	
May 14	According to Swiss police, Saudi billionaire Osama bin Laden financed the 1997 killings of 58 tourists in Egypt. The slayings, which took place in an attack at Luxor, were carried out by Gamaa al Islamiya (Islamic Group), an Egyptian fundamentalist group.	British prime minister Tony Blair's ruling Labour Party and the opposition Liberal Democrats agree to form a ruling coalition in the newly elected Scottish Parliament. The alliance is the first coalition to rule a major branch of the British government in more than 50 years.... The Yugoslav government returns the bodies of 10 local army conscripts killed in NATO's attacks.	Abdulbagi al-Saadun, a deputy to the Iraqi army chief in the south of the country, discloses that antigovernment riots occurred in the city of Basra in March.		
May 15	Finance ministers from the 21-member Asia-Pacific Economic Cooperation (APEC) trade group meet in Langkawi, Malaysia.... NATO and the U.S. confirm that NATO dropped eight bombs on a village in the Serbian province of Kosovo on May 13, killing as many as 100 ethnic Albanian refugees. NATO states it was targeting military forces and installations in the area and was unaware civilians were in the village at the time.	Russia's State Duma, votes not to launch impeachment proceedings against Pres. Boris Yeltsin.... Turkish premier Bulent Ecevit announces that Merve Kavakci, an Islamic activist elected to Parliament, is being stripped of her Turkish citizenship because she accepted U.S. citizenship without first informing Turkish officials, a rarely enforced requirement under Turkish law. Kavakci caused an uproar May 2 and never took her oath of office.	Iran's Pres. Mohammed Khatami visits Saudi Arabia, becoming the highest-level Iranian official to visit the country since Iran's 1979 Shi'ite Muslim revolution.	Canada's largest copper mine, the Highland Valley mine in British Columbia, shuts down because of a contract dispute between the mine's owners and its unionized workforce.	In Fiji, an opposition coalition led by the Fiji Labour Party (FLP) wins 54 of 71 seats in legislative elections.... A committee appointed by China's central government votes to name Edmund Ho chief executive of Macao when the territory, currently a Portuguese colony, reverts to Chinese sovereignty in December.
May 16		Thousands of women launch a series of demonstrations in the Serbian villages of Krusevac and Aleksandrovac, demanding that the government settle the conflict in Kosovo and release their sons and husbands from service in the Yugoslav army. The protests are sparked by the May 14 return of the bodies of 10 local army conscripts. While anti-NATO protests have been prevalent in Serbia, the current protest is the first directed against the government.		Guatemalan voters, in a national referendum, reject 47 constitutional changes that would have given more rights to indigenous Guatemalans and changed the role of the military and of the judicial and executive branches of government.	Five civilians are killed in their homes in the rural village of Atara in East Timor.
May 17		Queen Elizabeth II formally confirms Donald Dewar as Scotland's first minister.	In Israel, Ehud Barak, of the Labor Party-led center-left One Israel coalition, scores a resounding victory over incumbent prime minister Benjamin Netanyahu. In balloting for the Knesset, centrist parties score substantial gains, shifting the swing vote in the balance of power to Russian immigrants and others. That means that Barak, in the 45 days allotted him to form a new government, will not need the support of the ultra-Orthodox Jewish parties that wielded a near-veto over Netanyahu's decision making.	Mexico's ruling Institutional Revolutionary Party (PRI) votes overwhelmingly in favor of holding a nationwide primary to choose a presidential candidate for the national election in 2000. The vote officially ends the traditional method of choosing the party candidate, routinely hand-picked by the sitting president. The PRI has been in power in Mexico since 1929.... The ruling Virgin Islands Party (VIP) wins seven of 13 seats in the Legislative Council in elections in the British Virgin Islands. The VIP has been in power for 13 years on the islands, a British territory.	Authorities seize 69 illegal Chinese immigrants off the south coast of New South Wales.... In the final round of balloting, voters in Nepal elect members of the Nepali Congress Party to a majority of the seats in the House of Representatives, the lower house of Nepal's parliament.
May 18	The U.S. releases two Serbian soldiers captured by the KLA and handed over to U.S. custody in April.... Iran and Britain agree to exchange ambassadors, normalizing their diplomatic relations for the first time since the establishment of Iran's Islamic government in 1979.	Parliament confirms Rolandas Paksas as premier of Lithuania.			

A	B	C	D	E
Includes developments that affect more than one world region, international organizations, and important meetings of major world leaders.	*Includes all domestic and regional developments in Europe, including the Soviet Union, Turkey, Cyprus, and Malta.*	*Includes all domestic and regional developments in Africa and the Middle East, including Iraq and Iran and excluding Cyprus, Turkey, and Afghanistan.*	*Includes all domestic and regional developments in Latin America, the Caribbean, and Canada.*	*Includes all domestic and regional developments in Asia and Pacific nations, extending from Afghanistan through all the Pacific Island, except Hawaii.*

U.S. Politics & Social Issues	U.S. Foreign Policy & Defense	U.S. Economy & Environment	Science, Technology, & Nature	Culture, Leisure, & Lifestyle	
The U.S. Ninth Circuit Court of Appeals in San Francisco, California, rules that Border Patrol agents may use ethnicity as a factor in determining which cars to pull over at traffic stops. . . . A U.S. District Court jury in Kansas City, Missouri, decides that the tobacco company Brown & Williamson is not liable for the death of former smoker Charles Steele, who died in 1995 from lung cancer. . . . An Oregon state judge reduces to $32 million the punitive damages awarded in March to the family of a deceased smoker in a suit against Philip Morris.	In New York City, Judge Peter Leisure orders the release of thousands of pages of grand jury testimony in the case of Alger Hiss, a State Department official accused in 1948 of being a Soviet spy. Hiss was convicted of perjury in the case in 1950, but debate over whether he was a communist spy continues.	The Dow closes at a record 11,107.19. It the third record high of the month and the 24th record high in 1999. . . . The Justice Department files an antitrust lawsuit against American Airlines that accuses the carrier of using predatory pricing and other illegal means to drive smaller competitors from its hub at Dallas–Fort Worth Airport in the mid-1990s. The suit is the first predatory-pricing action brought against a U.S. carrier by the government since 1978, when the airline industry was deregulated.	A study finds that a federal nutritional requirement has nearly eliminated folic acid deficiency in the U.S.	Gene Sarazen (born Eugene Saraceni), 97, considered one of the finest golfers during the 1920s and 1930s, dies in Naples, Florida, of complications of leukemia. . . . Meg Greenfield (born Mary Ellen Greenfield), 68, *Washington Post* editorial page editor since 1979 who won a 1978 Pulitzer Prize, dies in Washington, D.C., of cancer.	May 13
A Justice Department report finds that 18- to 20-year-olds—which make up 4% of the population—commit some 24% of gun-related murders. . . . Reports confirm that Wal-Mart Stores has decided not to dispense Preven, a morning-after contraceptive approved for sale in 1998, in its pharmacies. . . . Republicans in the Texas Senate block a bill aimed at protecting members of racial minorities and other specified groups, including homosexuals, from hate crimes.		The South Coast Air Quality Management District in California adopts strict rules designed to remove 22 tons (20 metric tons) of paint pollutants from the air.			May 14
John Minor Wisdom, 93, judge of the U.S. Fifth Circuit Court of Appeals in New Orleans, Louisiana, 1957–99, who, in 1966, wrote a ruling *In U.S. v. Jefferson County (Alabama) Board of Education* that is considered to have established the first legal basis for affirmative-action policies, dies in New Orleans while suffering from a heart ailment.	Chih-Yuan Ho and Melissa Graham become the first women to graduate from the Virginia Military Institute (VMI), a state-funded military college in Lexington, Virginia.			Charismatic wins the 124th running of the Preakness Stakes in Baltimore, Maryland.	May 15
An FBI report discloses that serious crimes reported to the police in 1998 declined by 7% from the previous year. It is the seventh consecutive year that serious crimes have declined in the U.S.—the longest uninterrupted downward trend since the 1950s.				Robert (Bobby) Goldman, 60, World Bridge Federation Grand Master, dies of a heart attack while en route to a hospital in Lewisville, Texas. . . . The Czech Republic defeats Finland, 4-1, to win hockey's World Championships in Lillehammer, Norway.	May 16
In *Saenz v. Roe*, the Supreme Court rules, 7-2, that states cannot pay lower welfare benefits to newly arrived state residents than those paid to longtime residents. . . . In *Florida v. White*, the Supreme Court rules, 7-2, that police do not need to get a search warrant before seizing a vehicle from a public place if they believe it was used in the commission of a crime. . . . In *Hunt v. Cromartie*, the Supreme Court rules unanimously that a lower court erred by declaring North Carolina's 12th Congressional District an unconstitutional racial gerrymander without evaluating the motivations of state legislators who drew the district's boundaries.	U.S. authorities charge Jean-Philippe Wispelaere, 28, a former employee of the Australian Defense Intelligence Organization (DIO), with attempted espionage and criminal forfeiture for his alleged efforts to sell top-secret U.S. documents to an unidentified foreign country.	According to financial disclosure forms, Pres. Clinton and First Lady Hillary Rodham Clinton had assets worth between $1.2 million and $5.57 million in 1998. The president's legal bills soared in 1998 because of his impeachment in the Monica Lewinsky scandal. According to media estimates, the president ran up as much as $10 million in legal fees in the Lewinsky case and the Paula Jones sexual-harassment case. In their financial disclosure, the Clintons report that the president's legal defense fund paid $2.6 million of his legal fees in 1998.			May 17
	The House passes, 269-158, an emergency spending measure releasing $14.5 billion for the Kosovo air war, hurricane relief for Central America, and numerous other military and civilian projects added by members of Congress.		The American Society of Clinical Oncology recommends that doctors consider prescribing the drug tamoxifen to help prevent breast cancer in healthy women with increased risk of developing the disease.	Betty Robinson Schwartz (born Elizabeth Robinson), 87, sprinter and the first woman to receive an Olympic gold medal in her sport, dies in Colorado while suffering from cancer and Alzheimer's disease.	May 18
F	G	H	I	J	
Includes elections, federal-state relations, civil rights and liberties, crime, the judiciary, education, health care, poverty, urban affairs, and population.	*Includes formation and debate of U.S. foreign and defense policies, veterans' affairs, and defense spending. (Relations with specific foreign countries are usually found under the region concerned.)*	*Includes business, labor, agriculture, taxation, transportation, consumer affairs, monetary and fiscal policy, natural resources, and pollution.*	*Includes worldwide scientific, medical, and technological developments; natural phenomena; U.S. weather; natural disasters; and accidents.*	*Includes the arts, religion, scholarship, communications media, sports, entertainments, fashions, fads, and social life.*	

	World Affairs	Europe	Africa & the Middle East	The Americas	Asia & the Pacific
May 19	The British Commonwealth, which primarily consists of Britain's former colonies, states that it will readmit Nigeria on May 29. The Commonwealth suspended Nigeria's membership in 1995 after Gen. Abacha's military regime executed nine minority-rights and environmental activists, including the writer Ken Saro-Wiwa.	The government of Dutch premier Wim Kok collapses over a conflict concerning the proposed introduction of the use of popular referenda in the Netherlands. . . . The Russian Duma confirms Sergei V. Stepashin as premier.			Thousands of people gather at an election rally in Jakarta, Indonesia's capital, as campaigning for June 7 parliamentary elections officially commences. All 48 parties launch campaigns in Indonesia's first free elections since the 1950s. . . . Mahendra Chaudhry is sworn in as prime minister by Pres. Kamisese Mara, becoming Fiji's first ethnic Indian prime minister.
May 20		Unidentified gunmen shoot and kill Massimo D'Antona, top advisor to Italian labor minister Antonio Bassolino. . . . In Germany, Alfons Goetzfried, 79, formerly a member of Nazi Germany's Gestapo, is convicted and sentenced to 10 years in prison. . . . Thousands of women end the protests that began May 16 in Serbia as the soldiers begin to return home. . . . In Turkey, a three-judge panel sentences Kurdish rebel Semdin Sakik and his brother, Arif Sakik, to death for their role in the separatist campaign. . . . Albanian president Rexhep Mejdani approves the dismissal of Interior Minister Petro Koci, averting a constitutional crisis.		Victor Ricardo, the government's chief negotiator with FARC, announces that a region in southwest Colombia ceded to FARC in November 1998 will remain demilitarized indefinitely. . . . In Toronto, Ontario, an escaped convict, Tyrone Conn, shoots and kills himself, ending a two-hour standoff with police and a nationwide manhunt. . . . The Supreme Court of Canada strikes down a definition of the term "spouse" in the Ontario Family Law Act under which homosexuals are denied the right to sue for spousal support.	Police discover the remains of eight people in six drums of acid stored in an old bank vault in Snowtown, South Australia.
May 21	During heavy attacks on Belgrade, Yugoslavia, a stray NATO bomb at 1:00 A.M. local time hits a hospital, killing three people. The bombing also damages the nearby residences of the ambassadors of Hungary, India, Norway, Spain, and Sweden, as well as the Libyan and Israeli embassies. Swedish premier Goran Persson lodges a formal protest, and NATO secretary general Javier Solana apologizes to those countries. . . . The UN Security Council votes unanimously to extend by six months the relief program that allows Iraq to raise money for its citizens' humanitarian needs through the sale of exported oil.	In a mistaken attack, 20 NATO planes launch two strikes against Dubrava prison in Kosovo, killing 19 people, mostly prison inmates, including members of the KLA and political prisoners. . . . Germany's Bundesrat approves an overhaul of laws on the attainment of citizenship. . . . Three Catholic nationalists are convicted and sentenced to prison terms ranging from 22 to 25 years in connection with a foiled plot to detonate bombs in London in 1998.	South Africa's Truth and Reconciliation Commission grants amnesty to 13 former members of the police or army for several killings in 1986, including the murder of ANC member Fabian Ribeiro and of a black homeland minister, Piet Ntuli.	Sen. Piedad Cordoba of the opposition Liberal Party is kidnapped by Colombia's main right-wing paramilitary group in the northwestern city of Medellin.	
May 22	In response to the May 21 strikes against Dubrava prison, NATO explains that it targeted the facility in the belief that it was no longer being used as a prison. NATO confirms that it mistakenly bombed a base held by the KLA in the town of Kosare. The number of the dead from the attack vary from one to seven, and the number of wounded vary from 15 to 25.	Roughly 1,000 ethnic Albanian men, most in their late teens and early twenties, cross Kosovo's border into Albania.			
May 23		In Germany, Johannes Rau, a moderate member of Chancellor Gerhard Schroeder's Social Democratic Party (SPD), is elected by lawmakers to serve as the country's next president.			Australian police find the body of a person in a yard in Adelaide, and they connect that victim with the eight others unearthed May 20 in Snowtown, South Australia.
May 24	The International Criminal Tribunal for the Former Yugoslavia indicts Yugoslav president Slobodan Milosevic for "crimes against humanity" stemming from the forced deportation of hundreds of thousands of ethnic Albanians from Kosovo. Louise Arbour is the first tribunal prosecutor to indict a sitting head of state. . . . The World Health Assembly, WHO's governing body, votes to delay the destruction of the world's known remaining samples of the smallpox virus until 2002.				South Korean president Kim Dae Jung carries out the first broad reshuffle of his cabinet since taking office in February 1998, replacing 11 of the 18 members of the cabinet. . . . The upper house of Japan's Diet clears bills expanding Japan's military cooperation with the U.S. in Asia.

A	B	C	D	E
Includes developments that affect more than one world region, international organizations, and important meetings of major world leaders.	*Includes all domestic and regional developments in Europe, including the Soviet Union, Turkey, Cyprus, and Malta.*	*Includes all domestic and regional developments in Africa and the Middle East, including Iraq and Iran and excluding Cyprus, Turkey, and Afghanistan.*	*Includes all domestic and regional developments in Latin America, the Caribbean, and Canada.*	*Includes all domestic and regional developments in Asia and Pacific nations, extending from Afghanistan through all the Pacific Island, except Hawaii.*

U.S. Politics & Social Issues	U.S. Foreign Policy & Defense	U.S. Economy & Environment	Science, Technology, & Nature	Culture, Leisure, & Lifestyle	
	Former U.S. Army sergeant Ali Mohamed is indicted in New York City on charges that he trained members of a terrorist organization called al-Qaeda. The indictment marks the first time that the U.S. officially accuses al-Qaeda of responsibility for the 1998 bombings of the U.S. embassies in Kenya and Tanzania.			Reports confirm that poet Andrew Motion has been selected as Britain's new poet laureate.... James Blades, 97, British percussionist and writer on the history of percussion instruments, dies in Cheam, England.	May 19
The Senate approves, 73-25, a juvenile crime bill that includes several amendments aimed at strengthening gun-control laws. It is the first major gun-control initiative to gain legislative approval since 1994. ... Thomas (T. J.) Solomon, 15, opens fire on an indoor commons area at Heritage High School in Conyers, Georgia, injuring six students before surrendering to school officials.... Pres. Clinton and First Lady Hillary Rodham Clinton address a crowd of almost 2,000 students, teachers and families in Littleton, Colorado, about the tragic school shooting that took place there in April.	The INS announces that the rules for granting permanent residency status to refugees from Guatemala and El Salvador will be eased, allowing as many as 240,000 immigrants from those countries to remain in the U.S. legally.... The Senate clears, 64-36, an emergency spending measure releasing $14.5 billion for the Kosovo air war, hurricane relief for Central America, and numerous other military and civilian projects added by members of Congress.	The Commerce Department reports that the U.S. trade deficit leapt in March, registering a $19.70 billion gap in trade in goods and services. That marks a third straight record high, and it is up from February's revised $19.15 billion deficit.	A study finds that antibiotics given to animals raised for food are contributing to a rise in drug-resistant strains of disease in humans.	Stuntman Robbie Knievel, 37, makes a successful 228-foot (70-m) motorcycle jump over the mouth of a 2,500-foot-deep gorge of the Grand Canyon, setting a world distance record for motorcycle jumps.... Sir Robert Vidal Rhodes James, 66, British historian, biographer, and politician whose written works chronicle 19th- and 20th-century British history, dies of cancer.	May 20
The publisher of an instruction manual for hired assassins agrees to settle a civil lawsuit brought against it by relatives of three people killed by a man who consulted the book in the crime. The case raises the issue of free-speech rights, and many journalists' organizations support the publisher, Paladin Press of Boulder, Colorado.	Pres. Clinton signs an emergency spending measure releasing $14.5 billion for the Kosovo air war, hurricane relief for Central America, and numerous other military and civilian projects added by members of Congress.	Yah Lin (Charlie) Trie, a longtime friend of Pres. Clinton, pleads guilty to two charges relating to his fundraising for Clinton's 1996 reelection campaign and other Democratic causes. Trie is the second suspect in the fund-raising probe to agree to cooperate with prosecutors, after Johnny Chung.	The Clinton administration discloses that it will allow privately funded scientists studying the medical uses of marijuana to use marijuana grown for research purposes by the federal government.	Norman Rossington, 70, British actor who appeared in more than 40 motion pictures, dies in Manchester, England, of cancer.	May 21
					May 22
				At the Cannes (France) Film Festival, the Palme d'Or goes to Belgian brothers Jean-Pierre and Luc Dardenne for *Rosetta*.... Canadian-born professional wrestler Owen Hart, 33, falls 50 feet (15 m) to his death during a World Wrestling Federation (WWF) performance in Kansas City, Missouri.	May 23
In *Davis v. Monroe County Board of Education*, the Supreme Court rules, 5-4, that a Georgia school board may be sued for damages under Title IX of the Education Amendments of 1972 for failing to stop a student from sexually harassing a classmate.... In *Hanlon v. Berger* and *Wilson v. Layne*, the Supreme Court rules unanimously that police violate individuals' privacy rights by allowing journalists and photographers to accompany them into private residences as they conduct searches or attempt to make arrests.		In *Cleveland v. Policy Management Systems Corp.*, the Supreme Court rules unanimously that a Texas woman's acceptance of Social Security disability payments does not preclude her from pursuing a discrimination case against her employer under the Americans With Disabilities Act.... In *California Dental Association v. FTC.*, the Supreme Court rules unanimously that authority over the practices of nonprofit organizations is within the jurisdiction of the FTC.		Former heavyweight boxing champion Mike Tyson is released from a Rockville, Maryland, prison after having served 3½ months of a 14-month sentence.	May 24
F	G	H	I	J	
Includes elections, federal-state relations, civil rights and liberties, crime, the judiciary, education, health care, poverty, urban affairs, and population.	*Includes formation and debate of U.S. foreign and defense policies, veterans' affairs, and defense spending. (Relations with specific foreign countries are usually found under the region concerned.)*	*Includes business, labor, agriculture, taxation, transportation, consumer affairs, monetary and fiscal policy, natural resources, and pollution.*	*Includes worldwide scientific, medical, and technological developments; natural phenomena; U.S. weather; natural disasters; and accidents.*	*Includes the arts, religion, scholarship, communications media, sports, entertainments, fashions, fads, and social life.*	

	World Affairs	Europe	Africa & the Middle East	The Americas	Asia & the Pacific
May 25	The Inter-American Development Bank agrees to grant some $3.5 billion to countries in Central America hardest hit by Hurricane Mitch in October 1998.... NATO's 19 members approve a plan for an expanded peacekeeping force that will enter Kosovo once Yugoslav president Slobodan Milosevic withdraws his troops from the province.	Data suggests that as many as 25,000 ethnic Albanians have fled into Macedonia since May 22 as Serbian forces accelerate their expulsion of ethnic Albanians from Kosovo, a province of Yugoslavia's republic of Serbia.... The U.S. agrees to give Uzbekistan $32.3 million in aid to bolster the country's economic reforms.	A UN report finds that a drought currently affecting Iraq is the worst on record in the country.		Former U.S. defense secretary William Perry, serving as a special presidential envoy, visits North Korea. Perry is the highest-level U.S. official to visit North Korea, a highly isolated communist country that has long had bitter relations with the U.S.
May 26		Queen Elizabeth II formally inaugurates the Welsh Assembly, a newly elected body with the power to legislate certain isolated matters within Wales. The legislature is Wales's first-ever independent law-making body.		Great Britain's Privy Council, which serves as the Supreme Court for many former British colonies in the Caribbean, rejects a final appeal by nine men convicted of murder in Trinidad and Tobago, clearing the way for the men to be hanged.	India launches a series of air strikes on a band of Islamic militants encamped in an Indian-controlled area of the disputed Kashmir region. The strikes come because Indian aerial surveillance discovered that a force of some 500 heavily armed militants have taken up strategic positions in Kashmir.... Australian police locate a body of a victim connected to the eight corpses found May 20.... The Australian Senate passes a bill intended to shield children from pornography and violence on the Internet. In response, hundreds of people in Australia protest what they describe as censorship.
May 27	High Court justice Harry Ognall blocks an attempt by Gen. Augusto Pinochet Ugarte, a former military ruler of Chile, to appeal British home secretary Jack Straw's April 15 ruling that Pinochet's extradition case may proceed.... The International Criminal Tribunal for the Former Yugoslavia's May 24 indictment of Yugoslav president Slobodan Milosevic is made public.				Pakistan's military forces shoot down two Indian jet fighters flying over the Pakistani-controlled area of Kashmir. Flight Lt. K. Nachiketa, a pilot of one of the downed Indian jets, is captured by Pakistani forces.... In China, Zhang Youjou is sentenced to four years in prison. Zhang was arrested in 1998 after posting fliers demanding that the government reevaluate its official position on the 1989 violent crackdown in Tiananmen Square.
May 28		The Belgian health ministry bans the retail sale of domestically produced chicken and eggs, which they believe may contain high levels of dioxin, a cancer-causing chemical.... About 200 Polish troops and police officers remove 300 crosses that radical Roman Catholics erected near Auschwitz. The police also arrest Kazimierz Switon, who claims to have planted explosive devices at the site.... Three parties, headed by Premier Bulent Ecevit's Democratic Left Party, sign a coalition agreement to govern Turkey for five years.	General Abdulsalami Abubakar, who took power in Nigeria in June 1998 after the sudden death of Pres. Sani Abacha, announces the repeal of a 1984 decree that the military government used to detain hundreds of people without trial.	Suriname president Jules Wijdenbosch fires his entire cabinet in an effort to stem mounting protests and strikes, which began earlier in May in response to a steep drop in the value of Suriname's currency, the gilder.	
May 29		Rudolf Schuster, a member of Slovakia's ruling four-party coalition, wins Slovakia's first direct presidential elections.... A Yugoslav court sentences three aid workers accused of espionage to prison terms that vary from four to 12 years. The workers are Australians Steve Pratt and Peter Wallace and Yugoslav Branko Jelen.... A vehicular crash in Austria's Tauern tunnel touches off explosions and a massive fire, killing at least 12 people and injuring about 50.	Former military ruler Olusegun Obasanjo is sworn in as Nigeria's democratically elected president, making him the country's first civilian leader in more than 15 years. Obasanjo's assumption of the presidency completes a transition to civilian rule outlined in July 1998 by Gen. Abdulsalami Abubakar, who took power in June 1998 after the sudden death of Pres. Sani Abacha.		
May 30		In Belarus, 52 people attending an outdoor concert in Minsk are killed and another 150 are injured when concertgoers rush into an underground passageway to escape a rain and hail storm.	In Nigeria despite the pledge of a truce by some of the militias engaged in ongoing conflict over ethnic rivalries and rights to oil revenues, fighting between the rival Itsekiri and Ijaw ethnic groups in the volatile oil-rich Niger River Delta region renews.	Leftist rebels in Colombia kidnap more than 100 churchgoers during a Roman Catholic mass in the southwestern city of Cali.	

A	B	C	D	E
Includes developments that affect more than one world region, international organizations, and important meetings of major world leaders.	*Includes all domestic and regional developments in Europe, including the Soviet Union, Turkey, Cyprus, and Malta.*	*Includes all domestic and regional developments in Africa and the Middle East, including Iraq and Iran and excluding Cyprus, Turkey, and Afghanistan.*	*Includes all domestic and regional developments in Latin America, the Caribbean, and Canada.*	*Includes all domestic and regional developments in Asia and Pacific nations, extending from Afghanistan through all the Pacific Island, except Hawaii.*

U.S. Politics & Social Issues	U.S. Foreign Policy & Defense	U.S. Economy & Environment	Science, Technology, & Nature	Culture, Leisure, & Lifestyle	
Justin Volpe, a NYC police officer charged in the 1997 torture of Abner Louima, a Haitian immigrant, in the restroom of a police station, pleads guilty to six federal charges against him. Volpe admits that he sodomized Louima with a stick after Louima's arrest outside a Brooklyn nightclub. The incident received international attention and highlighted the issue of police brutality.	In a report, the U.S. House select committee investigating evidence of Chinese has espionage activities in the U.S. suggests that for some 20 years China has engaged in wide-ranging and successful efforts to obtain secret data from U.S. nuclear weapons laboratories. The report recommends 38 measures to strengthen counterintelligence and the security of secret information.		A team of astronomers announces that observations by the *Hubble Space Telescope* suggest that the "Big Bang" explosion, believed to have created the universe, happened at least 12 billion years ago. However, the astronomers also note that the universe may be as old as 15 billion years, depending on certain facts about the universe's composition that remain unknown.		May 25
		In a civil lawsuit brought in a New York City federal court, the SEC charges 25 people with insider trading.	The FBI shuts down its sites on the World Wide Web after computer hackers illegally enter the site. The FBI starts to execute a string of search warrants at the homes of suspected hackers in several states. . . . Waldo Lonsbury Semon, 100, chemist and inventor who, as an employee of B.F. Goodrich Co., invented vinyl in 1928, dies in Hudson, Ohio.	Paul Sacher, 93, Swiss conductor, businessman, and founder of the Basel Chamber Orchestra, the Schola Cantorum Basiliensis, and the Paul Sacher Foundation, who used his wealth to commission some 200 new compositions, dies in Zurich, Switzerland. . . . In soccer, Manchester United wins the European Champions Cup, defeating Bayern Munich, 2-1, in Barcelona, Spain.	May 26
	The Senate approves a series of measures to improve security at the U.S.'s national laboratories, where nuclear weapons research is conducted, and to restrict the export of sensitive technology. Separately, in a letter to Pres. Clinton, more than 80 members of Congress demand the resignation of National Security Adviser Samuel (Sandy) Berger.	Berek Don, a New Jersey lawyer who chaired the Bergen County Republican Party in 1996, pleads guilty to helping to illegally funnel a client's contributions to the successful 1996 Senate campaign of Democrat Robert Torricelli, then a congressman. Don is the 18th person charged by the Justice Department's Campaign Financing Task Force.	NASA scientists unveil the first three-dimensional map of the entire planet of Mars, revealing that its surface exhibits more extreme contrasts in elevation than previously known. . . . The U.S. space shuttle *Discovery* lifts off from Kennedy Space Center in Cape Canaveral, Florida, on a mission to load supplies onto the international space station under construction in orbit . . . . The Senate shuts down its website after hackers illegally enter the site.	Alice Adams, 72, novelist and short-story writer praised for her artful depictions of women's lives, dies May 27 in San Francisco, California. She had recently undergone treatment for a heart ailment.	May 27
					May 28
				Joao Carlos De Oliveira, 45, Brazilian track and field athlete who, at the 1975 Pan American Games in Mexico City, set a triple-jump world record of 58 feet, 8¼ inches (17.89 m), dies in Sao Paulo, Brazil, while suffering from pneumonia, hepatitis, and cirrhosis of the liver.	May 29
				Auto racer Jeff Burton wins the NASCAR Coca-Cola 600 at Lowe's Motor Speedway in Concord, North Carolina. . . . Kenny Brack of Sweden wins the 83rd running of the Indianapolis 500 automobile race at the Indianapolis Motor Speedway in Indiana.	May 30

F	G	H	I	J
Includes elections, federal-state relations, civil rights and liberties, crime, the judiciary, education, health care, poverty, urban affairs, and population.	*Includes formation and debate of U.S. foreign and defense policies, veterans' affairs, and defense spending. (Relations with specific foreign countries are usually found under the region concerned.)*	*Includes business, labor, agriculture, taxation, transportation, consumer affairs, monetary and fiscal policy, natural resources, and pollution.*	*Includes worldwide scientific, medical, and technological developments; natural phenomena; U.S. weather; natural disasters; and accidents.*	*Includes the arts, religion, scholarship, communications media, sports, entertainments, fashions, fads, and social life.*

	World Affairs	Europe	Africa & the Middle East	The Americas	Asia & the Pacific
May 31		At the opening of his trial on treason charges, Kurdish rebel leader Abdullah Ocalan stuns many observers by offering to work toward ending Kurdish separatist violence. Turkey's government blames Ocalan for some 30,000 deaths in the PKK's 15-year-old struggle for Kurdish independence.... Russian president Boris Yeltsin makes final appointments to the new government headed by Premier Sergei Stepashin.			Krishna Prasad Bhattarai takes office as Nepal's premier.... Reports confirm that a group of 105 Chinese citizens, most of them relatives of people killed in the 1989 crackdown, petitioned the Supreme People's Procuratorate, or national prosecutor's office, to open an investigation into the Tiananmen Square killings. The relatives' two petitions are the first effort to seek an inquiry into the crackdown through official legal channels.
June 1		Sir Christopher Sydney Cockerell, 88, British engineer who, in 1959, developed a hovercraft prototype that crossed the English Channel in 20 minutes, dies in Hythe, England.	An appeals court in Cape Town, South Africa, overturns former president Pieter W. Botha's contempt conviction, which he received for refusing to testify before the Truth and Reconciliation commission.	Pres. Francisco Flores Perez of the ruling Nationalist Republican Alliance (ARENA) party is sworn in as the 34th president of El Salvador.... After the National Assembly, Suriname's parliament, passes a no-confidence vote, Pres. Jules Wijdenbosch offers to cut short his five-year term, due to end in 2001, and lead the country until new elections can be held.	South Korean president Kim concludes a trip to Mongolia, the first visit there by a South Korean president since the two countries established diplomatic ties in 1990.
June 2	In response to the May 28 ban by the Belgian health ministry, the EU bans the sale and export of Belgian-produced chicken and eggs and of products containing Belgian chicken or eggs, in the EU's 15 member nations.... The International Court of Justice rules against suits brought against NATO members by Yugoslavia calling for an immediate suspension of the bombing. The court does not rule on the legality of NATO's bombing campaign but claims it has no jurisdiction in the case.	A UN official notes that in some parts of Kosovo, 80% of the homes are destroyed.	South Africa's ruling African National Congress (ANC) wins an overwhelming victory in the country's second multiracial democratic election since the end of apartheid in 1994. Two people are killed in KwaZulu-Natal just before polling stations open.... Figures indicate that the fighting between the rival Itsekiri and Ijaw ethnic groups in the volatile oil-rich Niger River Delta region have killed some 200 people in Nigeria since May 30.	A judge in Victoria, British Columbia, Canada, finds Warren Glowatski, 18, guilty of second-degree murder in the November 1997 death of Reena Virk, a 14-year-old girl. The Virk case attracted much media attention because of the youth of Virk's assailants and as an example of seemingly motiveless violence .... Paramilitary groups mount sporadic offensives in Colombia.	The Pakistani government frees from prison newspaper editor Najam Sethi, who was detained after delivering a controversial speech in India.... The Information Center of Human Rights and Democratic Movement in China states that, in the month before the June 4 anniversary of the 1989 crackdown against prodemocracy students in Beijing, the Chinese government has detained about 80 democracy advocates, and that 28 remain in detention.
June 3	Yugoslav president Slobodan Milosevic and the Serbian parliament accept a peace accord that will end the 10-week-old NATO bombing campaign.... The EU expands its June 2 ban to include beef and pork. U.S. agriculture officials ban imports of chicken and pork from all EU nations.... Leaders of the EU's 15 member nations agree to develop a common defense policy and to endow the EU with military capabilities.	Turkish human-rights activist Akin Birdal is sentenced to nine months in prison on charges of uttering subversive statements.... Russian president Boris Yeltsin signs a decree commuting all death sentences in Russia to life sentences or 25-year prison terms. The decree will affect 716 people sentenced to death.... Peter Brough, 83, British ventriloquist on a popular BBC radio series from 1950 to 1960, dies.	Nigeria's new parliament, elected in a landmark vote that ended more than 15 years of military rule, convenes for the first time.	In clashes that started June 2 in Colombia, about 20 soldiers and rebels are killed.	North Korea's second-ranking leader and other senior officials visit China. The visit marks the two countries' highest-level contact since the late North Korean president Kim Il Sung visited China in 1991.
June 4	EU leaders name NATO secretary general Javier Solana of Spain as its first security and foreign policy czar.... NATO and the U.S. Defense Department estimate that the alliance has killed or wounded between 10,000 and 15,000 Serbian soldiers during NATO's air campaign against Yugoslavia. An IMF study projects that in the six countries surrounding Yugoslavia, the costs caused by the conflict will range from $1.25 billion to $2.25 billion.			Trinidad and Tobago execute by hanging three gang members convicted in 1996 of killing a family of four in 1994. They are three of nine condemned prisoners. Prior to the hangings, only one prisoner had been executed in the nation since 1979, and none since 1994.... The leader of Colombia's right-wing paramilitary forces release a senator kidnapped in May, Piedad Cordoba of the opposition Liberal Party.	The 10th anniversary of China's violent crackdown on mass prodemocracy activists in Tiananmen Square passes with little incident in mainland China. However, 70,000 people gather in Hong Kong's Victoria Park for a vigil commemorating the crackdown. The crowd for the annual vigil is much larger than it has been in recent years.... Flight Lt. K. Nachiketa, an Indian pilot captured May 27 by Pakistani forces, is released to Indian custody.
June 5		Pope John Paul II visits his native Poland. The trip is the pontiff's eighth visit to Poland.... A pipe bomb explodes in Portadown, Northern Ireland, killing Protestant Elizabeth O'Neill.		Trinidad and Tobago execute three members of a drug gang convicted in 1996 of killing a family of four in 1994.... In addition to the 80 churchgoers already released by the ELN, the guerrilla group frees five more of the hostages taken after a Roman Catholic mass in Colombia.	India surrenders the bodies of three Pakistani soldiers to Pakistani officials.

A	B	C	D	E
Includes developments that affect more than one world region, international organizations, and important meetings of major world leaders.	Includes all domestic and regional developments in Europe, including the Soviet Union, Turkey, Cyprus, and Malta.	Includes all domestic and regional developments in Africa and the Middle East, including Iraq and Iran and excluding Cyprus, Turkey, and Afghanistan.	Includes all domestic and regional developments in Latin America, the Caribbean, and Canada.	Includes all domestic and regional developments in Asia and Pacific nations, extending from Afghanistan through all the Pacific Island, except Hawaii.

U.S. Politics & Social Issues	U.S. Foreign Policy & Defense	U.S. Economy & Environment	Science, Technology, & Nature	Culture, Leisure, & Lifestyle	
	The speaker for China's State Council sharply criticizes the U.S. House committee report released May 25, known as the Cox report after the chair of the panel, Rep. Christopher Cox (R, Calif.)... Cuba files a lawsuit against the U.S. in Cuban civil court, seeking $181.1 billion in compensation for deaths and injuries incurred during what it terms a "dirty war" against Cuba. The suit also charges that U.S. aggression and anti-Castro plots have caused the deaths of 3,478 Cuban citizens.		Websites for the Interior Department and the Idaho National Engineering and Environmental Laboratory in Idaho Falls, a federal computer facility, are invaded by hackers.	*Star Wars: Episode I—The Phantom Menace*, by Terry Brooks, tops the bestseller lists.	May 31
In *Richardson v. U.S.*, the Supreme Court rules, 6-3, that prosecutors must prove that a defendant committed each in a series of drug offenses in order to convict the defendant of operating a drug-trafficking business.... Reports reveal that women claiming Dow Corning implants made them seriously ill, or who want their implants removed, have voted to accept a proposed $3.2 billion settlement of their claims against the company.		Loewen Group Inc., North America's second-largest funeral home and cemetery operator, files for bankruptcy protection in the U.S. and Canada after accumulating C$3.4 billion (US$2.3 billion) in debt.	In Little Rock, Arkansas, an American Airlines MD-80 jet crashes and bursts into flames, killing nine people, including the pilot. They are the first deaths on a U.S. passenger flight since 1997.... Reports reveal that scientists have created a clone of a male adult mouse, succeeding for the first time in cloning a male adult mammal. Previous cloned adult mammals were created using genetic material from female reproductive cells.... Due to a spate of invasions by computer hackers, the Defense Department temporarily closes its website.		June 1
A group of 20 Native American tribes file a federal lawsuit against the U.S.'s four largest tobacco companies, arguing that they were unfairly excluded from a November 1998 settlement of 46 states' suits against the companies.... A state jury in Ellisville, Mississippi, rules that tobacco companies are not liable for the cancer death of Burl Butler, a barber who claimed that his illness was caused by inhaling his customers' secondhand cigarette smoke.		Microsoft Corp. chairman William Gates and his wife, Melinda Gates, announce a donation of $5 billion to the William H. Gates Foundation, which funds programs to improve child and maternal health in developing countries. The gift is reported to be the largest-ever donation by living persons to a foundation.			June 2
John Julian McKeithen, 81, Democratic governor of Louisiana, 1964–72, dies in Columbia, Louisiana. His health had been declining since he underwent heart surgery in 1997.	Several leaders of the 1989 pro-democracy movement in China's Tiananmen Square who live in exile gather at Harvard University in the U.S. Those present include Li Lu, Wang Dan, Wang Juntao, Wu'er Kaixi, and Wei Jingsheng.... Ending a protracted dispute, Canada and the U.S. announce a comprehensive treaty governing the conservation and sharing of Pacific Ocean salmon that migrate between the two nations' waters.	Federal Reserve Board vice chair Alice Rivlin announces that she will leave her post July 16.... The NYSE, the largest U.S. stock market, decides to delay until the second half of the year 2000 offering extended trading hours to individual investors.			June 3
Three Illinois sheriff's deputies—Thomas Vosburgh, James Montesano, and Dennis Kurzawaand—and a former prosecutor, Thomas Knightare, are acquitted of conspiring to frame Rolando Cruz, who was sent to death row for the killing of a 10-year-old girl. Cruz is one of 12 men on death row in Illinois who was found innocent and freed since that state legalized the death penalty in the 1970s. Judge William Kelly also acquits police officer Robert Winkler in a bench trial.	Pres. Clinton invokes a seldom-used provision of the Constitution to directly appoint James Hormel as ambassador to Luxembourg. The confirmation of Hormel, an open homosexual, was blocked by conservative Republican senators. Hormel is the first openly gay ambassador in U.S. history.	Zachary Fisher, 88, a top executive with Fisher Brothers, a family construction business whose many office and residential buildings helped shape the NYC skyline who, in the 1970s, donated more than $25 million and set up a foundation to establish New York's Intrepid Sea-Air-Space Museum, dies in New York City of cancer.		Ruth Whitney (born Ruth Reinke), 70, editor of *Glamour*, a women's fashion magazine, 1967–98, dies in Irvington, New York, of amyotrophic lateral sclerosis (ALS), also known as Lou Gehrig's disease.	June 4
				The Women's Basketball Hall of Fame opens in Knoxville, Tennessee. It is the first hall of fame dedicated to any women's sports.... Mel(vin) Howard Tormé, 73, popular jazz singer dubbed the Velvet Fog, dies in Los Angeles of complications of a 1996 stroke.... In horse racing, Lemon Drop Kid wins the Belmont Stakes.... Steffi Graff wins her sixth French Open women's title.	June 5
F	**G**	**H**	**I**	**J**	
Includes elections, federal-state relations, civil rights and liberties, crime, the judiciary, education, health care, poverty, urban affairs, and population.	*Includes formation and debate of U.S. foreign and defense policies, veterans' affairs, and defense spending. (Relations with specific foreign countries are usually found under the region concerned.)*	*Includes business, labor, agriculture, taxation, transportation, consumer affairs, monetary and fiscal policy, natural resources, and pollution.*	*Includes worldwide scientific, medical, and technological developments; natural phenomena; U.S. weather; natural disasters; and accidents.*	*Includes the arts, religion, scholarship, communications media, sports, entertainments, fashions, fads, and social life.*	

	World Affairs	Europe	Africa & the Middle East	The Americas	Asia & the Pacific
June 6		Turkish officials reveal that 20 Kurdish rebels and one Turkish soldier were killed in fighting in the provinces of Van, Diyarbakir, and Bingol. . . . Ilya Aleksandrovich Musin, 95, Russian conductor and teacher who was prevented by anti-Semitism from leading a major orchestra in the Soviet Union, dies in St. Petersburg, Russia.			
June 7	British NATO troops serving in Bosnia-Herzegovina apprehend alleged Bosnian Serb war criminal Dragan Kulundzija, indicted in 1995 for crimes committed against Muslims and Croats while he was commander of a detention camp in Bosnia during the war there in 1992–95.		Armed youths take over the center of the southern town of Warri, the scene of ethnic clashes in the previous days. Warri is the main town in Nigeria's oil-producing Niger River Delta region.	Trinidad and Tobago execute the last three of nine members of a drug gang convicted in 1996 of killing a family of four in 1994. . . . Officials at the National Autonomous University of Mexico (UNAM), the country's largest university, back down on a proposed tuition increase in the face of student strikes that started Apr. 20, the longest strike in the school's 89-year history.	More than 100 million Indonesians go to the polls to vote in the country's first fully democratic election in 44 years. . . . Nuon Paet, a former commander of the Khmer Rouge guerrilla regime, is sentenced to life in prison for his role in the 1994 kidnapping and murder of three backpackers from Australia, France, and Britain. He is the first senior Khmer Rouge officer to be tried for crimes committed as a member of the guerrilla group.
June 8		A political crisis in the Netherlands eases as Premier Wim Kok and the members of his cabinet retract their resignations, tendered in May. . . . More than 30 children are treated at a hospital in the Belgian town of Bornem after having consumed Coca-Cola's most popular product, Coke. . . . Christina Agnes Lilian Foyle, 88, owner of W. & G. Foyle Ltd., a massive London bookstore founded in 1904 by her father and an uncle, dies near Maldon, England, of unreported causes.	Two gunmen fire into a crowded courtroom in the southern coastal city of Sidon in Lebanon, leaving three judges and the prosecutor dead and wounding three other people. At the time of the shooting, eight men—four Lebanese and four Palestinians—were about to be sentenced for crimes including murder. . . . Iran's state-run radio reports that 13 people, later identified as Iranian Jews from the southern part of the country, were arrested on spying charges.	Reports state that an attack in the Colombian province of Cesar has left eight policemen and 10 civilians dead.	A tense naval standoff begins when North Korean military and fishing boats start a series of incursions across a demarcation line, drawn by the UN, that runs between the North Korean coast and a group of South Korean islands. . . . In Australia, an inquiry into Queensland's orphanages and juvenile-detention facilities concludes that there has been widespread neglect and physical and sexual abuse of children in those institutions over the past 80 years.
June 9	Yugoslavia signs an agreement with NATO, pledging to withdraw all of its forces from the Serbian province of Kosovo.	Reports confirm that the government of Croatia has stated that it will turn over alleged Bosnian Croat war criminal Vinko Martinovic to the International Criminal Tribunal for the Former Yugoslavia. . . . The Turkish National Assembly backs Premier Bulent Ecevit's new coalition government in a confidence vote.	Jordan's King Abdullah II is crowned at a ceremony in Amman, the capital. Abdullah inherited the throne Feb. 7, taking the oath hours after the death of his father, King Hussein. . . . A truck bomb attack on the Iraq-based Iranian opposition group Mujahedeen kills seven people, including one Iraqi, and wounds more than 20 others.		
June 10	NATO secretary general Javier Solana announces that NATO is suspending its 78-day bombing campaign against Yugoslavia. The UN Security Council adopts a resolution authorizing an international military force to enter Kosovo. NATO generals also officially authorize NATO forces to enter Kosovo (KFOR). . . . Louise Arbour, the chief prosecutor for the UN International Criminal Tribunal. is named to the Supreme Court of Canada.	Britain's central bank, the Bank of England, lowers its base interest rate for the seventh time in eight months. The bank cuts its benchmark rate, the repurchase (repo) rate, to 5% from 5.25%, the lowest level since October 1977. . . . Henry Grunfeld, 95, German-born investment banker who helped form one of London's most successful and innovative merchant banks, dies in London, England, of unreported causes.	Reports suggest that ECOMOG arrested two journalists during a raid on a newspaper in Freetown, the capital of Sierra Leone.	Elcio Alvarez, a former conservative senator, is sworn in as Brazil's first defense minister. The occasion marks the first time since Brazil returned to democracy in 1985 that the military is under civilian control.	In China, Fang Jue, a former government official who in 1998 called for democratic political reforms, is sentenced to four years in prison on charges of illegal business activities. Reports reveal that in late May Li Zhiyou was sentenced to three years in prison. Li was arrested in 1998 after protesting a prison sentence given to a prodemocracy leader. . . . India concludes its series of air strikes, which began May 26 in the disputed Kashmir region.
June 11	The U.S., citing a contamination of dioxin, suspends the import of eggs, egg products, animal feed, and game meats from Belgium, France, and the Netherlands.	Pope John Paul II addresses the Sejm, Poland's parliament. It is the first time the pontiff speaks to a national parliament during his 20-year papacy. . . . Reports reveal that, in response to the June 8 illnesses, in Belgium, Coca-Cola has ordered the recall of 2.5 million bottles of Coke produced in Antwerp. . . . Britain announces nearly 1,000 recipients of peerages, knighthoods, and other honors to mark the birthday celebration of Queen Elizabeth II. . . . About 200 Russian troops enter Pristina in Kosovo. The troops are not part of the international KFOR.	Iraq holds Iran responsible for three surface-to-surface missiles allegedly fired across their common border, hitting an Iranian opposition base in Iraq.	Reports indicate that at least eight police officers and a civilian were killed after FARC attacked a small town in the Colombian province of Boyaca.	Authorities in China's Hunan province arrest two of the leaders of an antitax demonstration staged by thousands of farmers in January. . . . South Korean ships ram four North Korean vessels in an episode that nearly erupts into gunfire.

A	B	C	D	E
Includes developments that affect more than one world region, international organizations, and important meetings of major world leaders.	*Includes all domestic and regional developments in Europe, including the Soviet Union, Turkey, Cyprus, and Malta.*	*Includes all domestic and regional developments in Africa and the Middle East, including Iraq and Iran and excluding Cyprus, Turkey, and Afghanistan.*	*Includes all domestic and regional developments in Latin America, the Caribbean, and Canada.*	*Includes all domestic and regional developments in Asia and Pacific nations, extending from Afghanistan through all the Pacific Island, except Hawaii.*

U.S. Politics & Social Issues	U.S. Foreign Policy & Defense	U.S. Economy & Environment	Science, Technology, & Nature	Culture, Leisure, & Lifestyle	
The National Blood Data Resource Center in Bethesda, Maryland, reports that between 1992 and 1997, blood donations declined to 13.2 million pints while the number of blood transfusions performed increased to 11.5 million. The center predicts that if the trend continues, the need for donated blood will outstrip supply in the year 2000.			The U.S. space shuttle *Discovery* touches down at Cape Canaveral, Florida, in a rare nighttime landing after carrying out a mission to load supplies onto the international space station currently under construction in orbit.	Andre Agassi wins his first French Open tennis title.... Golfer Juli Inkster wins the U.S. Women's Open.... At the Tonys, *Side Man* wins for Best Play and *Fosse* wins for Best Musical.... Edward (Eddie) Raymond Stanky, 82, baseball player from the 1940s and 1950s, dies in Fairhope, Alabama, of a heart attack.	June 6
Texas governor George W. Bush (R) signs a Texas law requiring that parents of unmarried teenage girls be notified if their daughters seek an abortion.... Illinois enacts a law requiring that any gun accessible to children under 14 either have a safety lock or be stored in a child-proof location. Sixteen other states have similar laws.... In *O'Sullivan v. Boerckel*, the Supreme Court rules, 6-3, that state prisoners who want to challenge their cases in federal court must first make their appeals in the state supreme court, even if that court is unlikely to hear their case.		In *Amoco Production Co. v. Southern Ute Tribe*, the Supreme Court rules, 7-1, that a Native American tribe's rights to massive coal deposits in the Western U.S. do not include rights to methane gas contained in those coalbeds.	A computer program designed to erase stored data is found in Israel.		June 7
Los Angeles citizens vote to replace the city's 1925 charter with one that gives greater power to the mayor.... Voters in Las Vegas, Nevada, elect Oscar Goodman, an attorney who defended notorious organized-crime figures, as their mayor.... A jury convicts Officer Justin Volpe, who pled guilty in May, of assault charges stemming from the 1997 station-house torture of Abner Louima, a Haitian immigrant. The jury finds Officer Charles Schwarz guilty on three charges, It acquits Thomas Bruder, Thomas Wiese, and Michael Bellomo.					June 8
Pres. Clinton orders federal law-enforcement agencies to collect data on the race, ethnicity, and sex of individuals they detain for questioning, in order to determine the validity of allegations of racial profiling.... Giles S(utherland) Rich, 95, federal judge known as the foremost authority on U.S. patent law who, in 1997, became the oldest active federal judge in U.S. history, dies in Washington, D.C., of lymphoma.			A study finds that hormone-replacement therapy does not increase the risk of the most common kinds of breast cancer in postmenopausal women.... The computer program designed to erase stored data found in Israel on June 7 has affected thousands of computers in Europe and the U.S.		June 9
In *Chicago v. Morales*, the Supreme Court rules, 6-3, that an antiloitering ordinance that seeks to prevent gang members from gathering on Chicago streets is unconstitutional.	An army missile defense system known as the Theatre High-Altitude Area Defense (THAAD) succeeds for the first time in intercepting a test missile after it had failed six previous tests.... A jury in Los Angeles convicts three Mexican businessmen and bankers of conspiring to launder money for drug traffickers. The jury acquits three other people. The defendants are among 167 suspects indicted in the investigation.	Federal government accounting regulators approve new rules designed to improve the accounting standards of state and local governments. The new rules are to take effect from 2001.... Patrick Bennett, a former chief financial officer of Bennett Funding Group Inc., is convicted of 42 counts of fraud and money laundering by a jury in New York City. The trial is Bennett's second in what prosecutors call the largest pyramid-scheme case in U.S. history.	The death toll in the June 1 plane crash in Little Rock, Arkansas, rises to 10 people when a man who suffered a head injury in the accident dies.... A study shows that people who regularly smoke cigars are twice as likely as nonsmokers to develop cancer of the mouth, throat, or lungs.... In *Dickinson v. Zurko*, the Supreme Court rules, 6-3, that a lower court improperly evaluated a decision by the Patent and Trademark Office to reject an application for a patent on a computer-security device.	The Christian Coalition, the most powerful political organization on the religious right, announces that it has dropped its 10-year-old bid for tax-exempt status.	June 10
A jury in Arenac County, Michigan, convicts Timothy Boomer, 25, of violating an 1897 Michigan law that prohibits swearing in front of children.... The Vermont Supreme Court rules that the use of vouchers to pay parochial-school tuition would violates the state's constitution.				A jury in Nashville, Tennessee, awards former heavyweight boxer Randall (Tex) Cobb $2.2 million in punitive damages for a 1993 article that accused Cobb of fixing a fight and using cocaine.... DeForest Kelley, 79, actor in the science-fiction series *Star Trek*, a show that garnered a cult following, dies in Woodland Hills, California.	June 11

F	G	H	I	J
Includes elections, federal-state relations, civil rights and liberties, crime, the judiciary, education, health care, poverty, urban affairs, and population.	*Includes formation and debate of U.S. foreign and defense policies, veterans' affairs, and defense spending. (Relations with specific foreign countries are usually found under the region concerned.)*	*Includes business, labor, agriculture, taxation, transportation, consumer affairs, monetary and fiscal policy, natural resources, and pollution.*	*Includes worldwide scientific, medical, and technological developments; natural phenomena; U.S. weather; natural disasters; and accidents.*	*Includes the arts, religion, scholarship, communications media, sports, entertainments, fashions, fads, and social life.*

	World Affairs	Europe	Africa & the Middle East	The Americas	Asia & the Pacific
June 12		The first NATO troops of the peace-keeping force enter the Serbian province of Kosovo in Yugoslavia, hours after Russian troops unexpectedly occupied the airport in Pristina, Kosovo's capital. Ethnic Albanians begin returning to Kosovo from Albania and Macedonia.		Former Mexican president Carlos Salinas de Gortari returns from self-imposed exile in Ireland to visit Mexico. It is his first visit since he left the country in 1995.	Ethnic violence erupts on Guadalcanal, the main island of the Solomon Islands, when a group of militant Guadalcanal residents attack a plantation, killing three people. The attack follows months of increasing tension between indigenous Guadalcanalese and settlers from Malaita, the country's most heavily populated island.
June 13		Swiss voters approve a ballot measure tightening restrictions on refugees' attainment of permanent asylum. . . . Pope John Paul II beatifies 108 Roman Catholics who died in concentration camps under the Nazi regime. . . . The KLA takes over control of the Morini border crossing point into Albania. Aid agencies and journalists return to Kosovo. In sporadic violence, four people die. . . . Luxembourg's Socialist Party, one of two parties in the country's ruling coalition, suffers heavy losses in a general election.	Libyan leader Colonel Muammar Gadhafi visits South Africa in a his first trip outside Libya since UN sanctions against the country were suspended in April.		
June 14	Election returns show that the European People's Party, an alliance of right-of-center parties from several of the EU's 15 member nations, has won the largest number of seats of any bloc in elections for the membership of the European Parliament, the EU's legislative arm. As before the election, no political bloc controls a majority of seats in the 626-member legislature.	Nearly complete election returns are released in Belgium, showing that Premier Jean-Luc Dehaene's Flemish-speaking Christian People's Party captured 14% of the vote, down from about 17% in 1995. The poor showing prompts Dehaene to resign. . . . The government of Belgium indefinitely bans the sale of bottled and canned beverages made by Coca-Cola, after those drinks are blamed for health problems in about 100 children.	The South African National Assembly elects Thabo Mbeki as president.	A federal jury convicts three former officials of the San Juan AIDS Institute in Puerto Rico of stealing $2.2 million in U.S. AIDS funds intended for AIDS patients.	
June 15		In reaction to the June 14 ban, on Coca-Cola in Belgium, three of its neighboring countries—France, Luxembourg, and the Netherlands—issue broad recalls of Coca-Cola products.	Voters reelect Pres. Bakili Muluzi of the United Democratic Front in Malawi. . . . South Africa's Truth and Reconciliation Commission grants amnesty to Eugene Terre'Blanche, who headed the right-wing Afrikaner Resistance Movement (AWB). Terre'Blanche's amnesty covers his role in a 1991 gun battle, but not other crimes attributed to him.	An earthquake measuring 6.7 on the Richter scale shakes central Mexico, killing at least 16 people and injuring more than 200. Seismologists report the epicenter of the quake is near the town of Tehuacan in the southeast state of Oaxaca, about 135 miles (220 km) from Mexico City, the capital. . . . The National Liberation Army (ELN), Colombia's second-largest leftist guerrilla group, releases 33 hostages kidnapped in May from La Maria Church in Cali. The ELN retains some 20 hostages from the church.	In East Timor, UNAMET officials observe members of one prominent militia, the Besar Mera Puti (Red and White Flag), beating a man in the village of Leotela. . . . Amid a tense naval standoff that begun June 8, South Korean naval forces sink a North Korean torpedo boat during a firefight in disputed waters in the Yellow Sea. South Korean officials report that at least 20 North Koreans are killed in the clash, including the sunken ship's 17 crew members. Seven South Koreans are reportedly injured.
June 16	U.S. president Bill Clinton addresses the International Labor Organization. He is the only U.S. president besides Franklin Delano Roosevelt to do so.	Pope John Paul II confers sainthood on 13th-century Polish queen Kinga. . . . The price of gold is fixed on the London market at $258.70 per troy ounce, its lowest price in 20 years. . . . Some 15,000 NATO peacekeeping troops are currently deployed in Kosovo. . . . . (Screaming) Lord Sutch (born David Edward Sutch), 58, British political candidate and sometime rock-and-roll musician, is found hanged in London in an apparent suicide.	Thabo Mbeki is inaugurated as South Africa's second democratically elected president, succeeding Nelson Mandela. . . . . Saudi King Fahd shuffles his cabinet for only the second time in some 25 years.		Japan's health and welfare ministry officially approves the sale of the oral contraceptive pill, nine years after pharmaceutical companies first applied for approval. . . . North Korea states it will suspend diplomatic contacts with South Korea.
June 17	The International Labor Organization (ILO) adopts a treaty that institutes a ban on the harshest forms of child labor. It includes a controversial provision that allows children under 18 to enlist in the military voluntarily.	According to NATO, some 95 suspected mass grave sites have been discovered in Kosovo. Officials estimate that 10,000 ethnic Albanians were killed in more than 100 massacres. . . . Chechen rebels fire on Russian outposts along Chechnya's border with the Russian republic of Dagestan. Separately, Chechen rebels kill four Russian policemen. . . . The Latvian parliament chooses former Canadian citizen Vaira Vike-Freiberga as president. . . . Cecilia Danieli, 56, Italian steel magnate, dies in Udine, Italy, of cancer.	In a surprise move, South African president Thabo Mbeki names Jacob Zuma his deputy president.		Justice Terrence Higgins of the Australian Capital Territory Supreme Court sentences former senator Bob Woods to a suspended 18-month jail term for making fraudulent travel expense claims in 1994–95.

A	B	C	D	E
Includes developments that affect more than one world region, international organizations, and important meetings of major world leaders.	*Includes all domestic and regional developments in Europe, including the Soviet Union, Turkey, Cyprus, and Malta.*	*Includes all domestic and regional developments in Africa and the Middle East, including Iraq and Iran and excluding Cyprus, Turkey, and Afghanistan.*	*Includes all domestic and regional developments in Latin America, the Caribbean, and Canada.*	*Includes all domestic and regional developments in Asia and Pacific nations, extending from Afghanistan through all the Pacific Island, except Hawaii.*

U.S. Politics & Social Issues	U.S. Foreign Policy & Defense	U.S. Economy & Environment	Science, Technology, & Nature	Culture, Leisure, & Lifestyle	
The Center for Responsive Politics finds that the senators who received the top contributions from the NRA over the five previous years all voted against the gun controls approved by the Senate in May.					June 12
The Justice Department finds that drunk-driving arrests fell to some 1.5 million in 1997, from some 1.8 million in 1986. That difference is a decline of almost 18%. Between 1986 and 1997, the number of drivers on the road increased nearly 15%. Taking that increase into account, the rate of arrests per 100,000 drivers declined by 28% between 1986 and 1997.					June 13
In *Greater New Orleans Broadcasting Association v. U.S.*, the Supreme Court rules unanimously to overturn a 1934 federal statute that bans television and radio advertising for casino gambling in states where the activity is legal.	The Foreign Intelligence Advisory Board submits a report on the security conditions at U.S. nuclear weapons laboratories to Pres. Clinton. The report includes a review of the measures taken to counter security threats.	In *West v. Gibson*, the Supreme Court rules, 5-4, that the Equal Employment Opportunity Commission (EEOC) possesses the authority to award federal employees compensatory damages in cases of discrimination by other government employers.	Reports confirm that the computer program designed to erase stored data first discovered June 7 in Israel has spread to more than 12 countries and affected tens of thousands of computers.		June 14
Congress awards its highest honor, the Congressional Gold Medal, to Rosa Parks, whose 1955 refusal to give up her seat on a segregated bus in Montgomery, Alabama, sparked a 381-day-long bus boycott that ended when the Supreme Court found bus segregation unconstitutional. Parks, 86, is the 121st person to receive the honor. . . . Maria Lydia Hernandez Lopez, 25, who recently woke from a six-week coma, gives birth to healthy twin daughters. . . . Jack M. Campbell, 82, (D, N.Mex.) governor of New Mexico, 1963–67, dies in Santa Fe, New Mexico.					June 15
Former leftist radical Kathleen Soliah is arrested on a 1976 indictment that includes charges of conspiracy to murder police officers and possession of explosives. Soliah, a fugitive since 1976, is arrested in Minnesota, where she has been living under the name Sara Jane Olson.	The Senate confirm four-star army general Eric Shinseki as the U.S. Army's chief of staff. . . . Prosecutors indict two men on charges that they assisted in the 1998 bombings of the U.S. embassies in Kenya and Tanzania. The two men, Ayman al-Zawahri and Khalid al-Fawwazare, said to be leaders of al-Qaeda, an organization linked to Osama bin Laden, a Saudi Arabian exile charged in U.S. court with masterminding the embassy attacks.	The Senate votes, 99-0, to approve a bill that will allow disabled people to retain their government healthcare benefits when they become employed. . . . Energy Secretary Bill Richardson appoints retired air force general Eugene Habiger as the department's first security czar. . . . At the end of a three-year probe, 85 stockbrokers are indicted in three separate cases on federal charges of stock manipulation, money laundering, mail fraud, and racketeering.	The death toll in the June 1 plane crash in Little Rock, Arkansas, rises to 11 when another victim dies. . . . A study finds that Raloxifene, a drug prescribed for the bone disease osteoporosis, significantly reduces the risk of developing breast cancer in women past menopause.	Lawrence Stone, 79, British-born social historian whose work ranges over many centuries of English history, dies in Princeton, New Jersey, of Parkinson's disease.	June 16
The Supreme Court rules that charitable organizations, even those that do not behave negligently, may be held liable if children in their care are sexually abused. . . . The CDC finds that during, the years 1987–96, for every 100,000 live births, 7.7 mothers died. However, for black women, the rate was 19.6; for white women, it was 5.3. . . . The New Jersey Supreme Court throws out Superior Court judge Reginald Stanton's five-year time limit on carrying out the death sentence of convicted murderer Thomas Koskovich.	Canadian citizen Joseph Stanley Faulder, 61, is executed by lethal injection in Huntsville, Texas. Faulder is the first Canadian executed in the U.S. since 1952, and his case received international attention and raised diplomatic tensions between the U.S. and Canada. He is the 14th person executed in Texas since the beginning of the year, and the 178th executed there since the reinstatement of the state's death penalty in 1982.		Scientists reviewing seven long-term studies of chimpanzees report that the wide diversity of social customs and tool uses observed in the chimpanzees suggests that there are cultural variations among populations of the animal.	Cardinal Basil Hume (born George Haliburton Hume), 76, Roman Catholic archbishop of Westminster, dies in London, England, of cancer.	June 17

F	G	H	I	J
Includes elections, federal-state relations, civil rights and liberties, crime, the judiciary, education, health care, poverty, urban affairs, and population.	Includes formation and debate of U.S. foreign and defense policies, veterans' affairs, and defense spending. (Relations with specific foreign countries are usually found under the region concerned.)	Includes business, labor, agriculture, taxation, transportation, consumer affairs, monetary and fiscal policy, natural resources, and pollution.	Includes worldwide scientific, medical, and technological developments; natural phenomena; U.S. weather; natural disasters; and accidents.	Includes the arts, religion, scholarship, communications media, sports, entertainments, fashions, fads, and social life.

	World Affairs	Europe	Africa & the Middle East	The Americas	Asia & the Pacific
June 18	NATO and Russia reach agreement on Russia's role in the Kosovo force (KFOR). . . . Leaders from the Group of Eight (G-8) industrialized nations meet in Cologne, Germany, to formulate a global economic agenda as NATO ends its bombing campaign to expel Serbian troops from the Yugoslav province of Kosovo. The G-8 leaders agree to an enhanced plan for cutting the debt obligations of the world's poorest nations.	Attacks that started June 17 along the borders of the Russian republic of Chechnya leave seven Russian police officers and interior ministry troops dead. At least 14 others are wounded. Russia closes 50 of its 60 checkpoints along the border. . . . A demonstration against capitalism in the City of London financial district erupts into violence. As many as 100 people are injured in the melee, and 15 protesters are arrested. . . . Count of Paris (Henri Robert Ferdinand Marie Louis Philippe d'Orleans), 90, pretender to the French throne since 1940, dies in Dreux, France, of prostate cancer.			The Chinese official news media reports that the nine-year-old child designated by the government as the Panchen Lama, Gyaincain Norbu, has appeared in Lhasa, the capital of Tibet, for the first time. The child is not the one chosen by the Dalai Lama, the exiled spiritual leader of Tibet whom China condemns as a separatist.
June 19		Some 20,000 people gather in Cologne, Germany, to protest the G-7 plan announced June 18. . . . Prince Edward, the youngest child of Queen Elizabeth II, marries Sophie Rhys-Jones. Edward, the seventh in line for the throne, is the last of the queen's four children to marry. . . . Mario Soldati, 92, Italian author and film director, dies in Tellaro, Italy.	Kamal Eddin Hussein, 77, Egyptian army officer who helped Gamal Abdel Nasser topple Egypt's King Farouk in 1952, dies of liver cancer in Cairo.		
June 20	NATO formally ends its bombing campaign against Yugoslavia after verifying that the government has withdrawn all of its forces from the Serbian province of Kosovo.	In Kosovo, the KLA signs a disarmament pact, committing them to disarm completely within 90 days.		Some 100,000 people gather in Havana's Revolution Square to take part in a Protestant celebration, culminating a month of Protestant festivities across the island of Cuba. Cuban leader Fidel Castro Ruz and other officials from the ruling Communist Party attend the event.	
June 21		NATO suffers its first casualties since it entered Kosovo when two British peacekeepers and two civilians are killed in a munitions-clearing accident.	Hezbollah launches a mortar attack on northern Israel, sending some 250,000 people fleeing to the safety of bomb shelters. . . . Pres. Bakili Muluzi is inaugurated in Malawi.		In Australia, the cabinet of the Queensland government approves a plan that will legalize and strictly regulate brothels in Queensland.
June 22		IRA member Patrick Magee is released early from Northern Ireland's Maze prison, under a provision in the 1998 peace accord calling for the ahead-of-schedule release of inmates linked to paramilitary groups.		In Colombia, rebel soldiers attempt to attack the jungle hideout of Carlos Castaño, the leader of a coalition of right-wing paramilitary groups. Government soldiers are called in to stop the attack.	
June 23	Congo files an appeal with the International Court of Justice in The Hague, the Netherlands, claiming that Uganda, Rwanda, and Burundi are violating international law and Congo's sovereignty in their support of the rebels. The appeal also accuses Uganda, Rwanda, and Burundi of human rights violations in Congo.	A group of Serbian civilians fire on U.S. NATO peacekeepers in the southeastern village of Zegra. In the ensuing gunfight, U.S. troops shoot and kill one Serb and wound two others. In the first arrest by NATO troops of a Serbian paramilitary suspected of participating in Serbia's ethnic cleansing campaign against ethnic Albanians, Dragisa Peica is taken into custody. . . . Belgium lifts its ban on Coca-Cola products.		The fighting that started June 22 in Colombia continues, leaving at least 60 soldiers and left-wing guerrillas dead in clashes in the northern province of Cordoba. A military spokesman reveals as many as 32 government soldiers have been killed in the fighting, the largest number of army fatalities in a single clash since the government held brief peace talks with FARC in January.	In a retrial, South Korea's Supreme Court sentences Kim Hyun Chul, a son of former president Kim Young Sam, to two years in prison and a $1.31 million fine for bribery and tax evasion. . . . Australia's High Court rules that Heather Hill of the One Nation Party is ineligible to hold a seat in the Federal Parliament because she holds dual citizenship. Hill is the only member of the controversial party to have won such a seat.

A	B	C	D	E
Includes developments that affect more than one world region, international organizations, and important meetings of major world leaders.	*Includes all domestic and regional developments in Europe, including the Soviet Union, Turkey, Cyprus, and Malta.*	*Includes all domestic and regional developments in Africa and the Middle East, including Iraq and Iran and excluding Cyprus, Turkey, and Afghanistan.*	*Includes all domestic and regional developments in Latin America, the Caribbean, and Canada.*	*Includes all domestic and regional developments in Asia and Pacific nations, extending from Afghanistan through all the Pacific Island, except Hawaii.*

U.S. Politics & Social Issues	U.S. Foreign Policy & Defense	U.S. Economy & Environment	Science, Technology, & Nature	Culture, Leisure, & Lifestyle	
Gov. George W. Bush (R, Tex.) signs a law effectively banning Texas cities and counties from filing liability lawsuits against gun manufacturers. Thirteen other states have adopted similar laws. . . . Gov. George Pataki (R, N.Y.) states he will use his executive authority to require that vendors at gun shows on state property perform background checks on all buyers. . . . Three Sacramento, California, synagogues are burned in what authorities call a hate crime. . . . Robert D. (Bob) Bullock, 69, (D, Tex.) state comptroller, 1975–90, and lieutenant governor, 1991–99, dies of congestive heart failure in Austin, Texas.					June 18
According to the Anti-Defamation League, there have been 39 cases of arson at U.S. synagogues in the past five years.				Best-selling horror-fiction author Stephen King, 51, is hit by a minivan in Lovell, Maine. King suffers a broken hip, a punctured lung, and multiple breaks to his ribs and right leg.	June 19
			Reports confirm that doctors at, Vanderbilt University Medical Center in Nashville, Tennessee, performed the first brain surgery on a fetus in March.	Golfer Payne Stewart wins the U.S. Open in Pinehurst, North Carolina. . . . In professional hockey, the Dallas Stars beat the Buffalo Sabres, 2-1, to win the Stanley Cup. . . . Clifton Paul Fadiman, 95, author, editor, and radio and TV personality, dies in Florida of pancreatic cancer.	June 20
In *Jones v. United States*, the Supreme Court rules, 5-4, that jurors do not need to be informed that, if they cannot decide between a death sentence and life imprisonment, a 1994 law requires judges to impose a life sentence. . . . Judge Jacqueline Connor sentences Juan Chavez, 35, to five life terms in prison without the possibility of parole for killing five homosexual men in what he calls an attempt to stop the spread of AIDS. . . . Florida governor. Jeb Bush (R) signs into law a bill creating a school voucher program for students throughout the state. It is the nation's first statewide school voucher program.	U.S. forest-products company Weyerhaeuser Co. announces plans to buy MacMillan Bloedel Ltd., a longtime icon of the Canadian forestry industry, in a stock transaction valued at US$2.36 billion (C$3.47 billion). If completed, the deal will make Weyerhaeuser one of the largest forest-products companies in North America, with estimated annual sales of $13.3 billion. . . . Four-star army general Eric Shinseki is sworn in as the U.S. Army's 34th chief of staff.	In *Jefferson County v. Acker*, the Supreme Court rules, 7-2, that Alabama's Jefferson County has the right to impose an occupational license tax on its public officials and other county workers. . . . Joseph Hazelwood, the former captain of the *Exxon Valdez* tanker, which ran aground in Alaska in 1989, begins to fulfill a sentence of 1,000 hours of community service by picking up litter along roadsides in Anchorage, Alaska. The *Exxon Valdez*, under Hazelwood's command, spilled an estimated 11 million gallons (42 million liters) of oil into Prince William Sound.			June 21
In *Olmstead v. L.C.*, the Supreme Court rules, 6-3, that the state of Georgia violated the 1990 Americans With Disabilities Act by keeping two mentally disabled women in institutions, although they requested to be placed in less restrictive residential facilities. . . . A three-judge panel overturns the 1997 fraud conviction of former Arizona governor J. Fife Symington III (R). . . . In *Kolstad v. American Dental Association*, the Supreme Court rules, 7-2, that a lower court set too high a standard for individuals to prove they are entitled to punitive damages after violations of Title VII of the Civil Rights Act of 1964.		The Supreme Court rules, 7-2, in three job-discrimination cases that the 1990 Americans With Disabilities Act is not intended to protect individuals who have physical impairments that are corrected with medication or simple remedial devices such as eyeglasses. The cases are *Sutton v. United Airlines*, *Albertson's Inc. v. Kirkingburg*, and *Murphy v. United Parcel Service Inc.* . . . The Commerce Department concludes that information-technology companies were responsible for more than one-third of the U.S.'s economic growth between 1995 and 1998.		The Boston Symphony Orchestra announces that its music director and conductor, Seiji Ozawa, will leave In August 2002 to become music director of the Vienna State Opera in Austria. . . . The John D. and Catherine T. MacArthur Foundation of Chicago awards its annual MacArthur Fellowships, or "genius grants," to 32 individuals in a wide range of fields.	June 22
The Supreme Court issues three vigorously contested 5-4 decisions in which the majority justices significantly curb individuals' rights to sue states for their alleged failure to comply with federal laws. . . . A Hillsville, Virginia, jury convicts Barry Black, a Ku Klux Klan leader, of burning a cross with the intent to intimidate a group or individual.		In *Amchem Products v. Windsor*, the Supreme Court rules, 7-2, to set aside a landmark $1.5 billion class-action settlement against asbestos maker Fibreboard Corp. . . . Delegates to a meeting of the American Medical Association (AMA), the nation's largest doctors' group, vote in favor of supporting the formation of a labor union for some doctors.		Wayne Gretzky, Andy Van Hellemond, and Ian (Scotty) Morrison are elected to the Hockey Hall of Fame. . . . The Naismith Memorial Basketball Hall of Fame elects John Thompson, Kevin McHale, Wayne Embry, the late Fred Zollner, and Billie Moore.	June 23
F	G	H	I	J	
Includes elections, federal-state relations, civil rights and liberties, crime, the judiciary, education, health care, poverty, urban affairs, and population.	*Includes formation and debate of U.S. foreign and defense policies, veterans' affairs, and defense spending. (Relations with specific foreign countries are usually found under the region concerned.)*	*Includes business, labor, agriculture, taxation, transportation, consumer affairs, monetary and fiscal policy, natural resources, and pollution.*	*Includes worldwide scientific, medical, and technological developments; natural phenomena; U.S. weather; natural disasters; and accidents.*	*Includes the arts, religion, scholarship, communications media, sports, entertainments, fashions, fads, and social life.*	

	World Affairs	Europe	Africa & the Middle East	The Americas	Asia & the Pacific
June 24	The International Bank for Reconstruction and Development, the World Bank, approves a controversial $160 million antipoverty loan package for China. However, the World Bank decides to delay the funding of the disputed portion of the package, a $40 million plan to resettle nearly 58,000 farmers from northeastern Qinghai province to an area further west in the province.	The Yugoslav parliament votes unanimously to officially end the state of war declared when NATO began bombing Mar. 24. The government announces that it is lifting 31 decrees imposed during the state of war that limited personal freedoms.... The French government authorizes the resumption of production at the Dunkirk Coca-Cola bottling plant.	Hezbollah fighters and troops of the South Lebanon Army (SLA), Israel's proxy militia in the area, exchange fire in the security zone. Hezbollah retaliates with a rocket attack against Israeli civilians, prompting Israel's caretaker prime minister, Benjamin Netanyahu, to order large-scale Israeli air strikes.... Human Rights Watch claims that battles earlier in the year for control of Freetown, the capital of Sierra Leone, saw the worst human-rights violations in the conflict thus far.		
June 25		For security reasons, Britain temporarily closes its embassies in Gambia, Madagascar, Senegal, and Namibia.... The Bundestag, Germany's lower house of parliament, approves plans for the construction in Berlin of a memorial to victims of the Nazi Holocaust.... The Netherlands and Luxembourg lift their bans on Coca-Cola.... Arthur Katz, 91, maker of the Corgi line of toy cars, dies in London, England.... Angus MacDonald, 60, preeminent Scottish bagpiper, dies of cancer in Edinburgh, Scotland.	Israeli warplanes pound Lebanon's civilian infrastructure, and the Shi'ite Muslim guerrilla group Hezbollah fires rockets into northern Israel in the heaviest battles involving the two sides since 1996 in their continuing conflict along the Israel-Lebanon border. The fighting leaves eight Lebanese and two Israelisall civilians dead and scores of others injured.		A lower Hong Kong court issues rulings against the government's efforts to deport mainland Chinese citizens.... Sir (Emil Herbert) Peter Abeles, 75, trucking magnate who founded TNT Ltd. after surviving a Nazi work camp during World War II, dies in Sydney, Australia, of cancer.
June 26		Jiri Pelikan, 76, head of Czechoslovakia's state-run television system in the 1960s, dies in Rome, Italy.		About 47,500 nurses in Quebec, Canada, go on strike.	The Standing Committee of the National People's Congress, China's parliament, overturns a controversial ruling by a Hong Kong court on immigration from China. Pro-democracy and legal activists demonstrate in Hong Kong against China's ruling, arguing that it sets a dangerous precedent for judicial interference by China.... East Timorese independence leader Jose Ramos Horta returns to Indonesia after a 24-year-long exile.
June 27		Italy's political left loses a mayoral election in Bologna for the first time in more than 50 years.... George Papadopoulos, 80, Greek army colonel who helped overthrow Greece's King Constantine in 1967, dies in Athens of a heart attack.... Lord Robens of Woldingham (born Alfred Robens), 88, British Labour Party politician and chair of Britain's National Coal Board, 1961–71, dies.	Reports suggest that 100,000 people have been killed in Algeria since 1992.		
June 28		The Swedish government announces that it will pay 175,000 kronor ($20,800) to each victim of a forced-sterilization program that the government operated from 1936 to 1976.... The Supreme Court of Uzbekistan sentences to death six men who orchestrated a series of bombings in February that killed 16 people and wounded 120 others. The court sentences 16 other people involved in the attacks to prison terms of between 10 and 20 years.	Reports indicate that Ethiopian forces have captured Garba Harre, a Somali regional capital 250 miles (400 km) northwest of Mogadishu. Winning the city gives Ethiopia control over much of the southern area of Somalia.	Vere Cornwall Bird Sr., 89, prime minister, 1981–94, regarded as the father of Antigua and Barbuda's independence from Britain, dies in St. Johns, Antigua, of unreported causes.	A ship spills 70,000 gallons (270,000 liters) of oil off the coast of Adelaide, South Australia.... In the Soloman Islands, after two weeks of violence, which has forced as many as 20,000 Malaitans to flee, the federal government and the provincial governments of Guadalcanal and Malaita sign an accord setting out principles for ending the unrest. Those include the surrender of weapons by the militants and a review of the land question.
June 29	Leaders of the 15-nation European Union (EU) and 33 Latin American and Caribbean countries conclude their first-ever summit with a vague commitment to forge "gradual and reciprocal trade liberalization."	A court on Turkey's Imrali Island convicts Kurdish nationalist leader Abdullah Ocalan for committing acts of treason and separatism and sentences him to death by hanging. Ocalan's execution, if carried out, will be the country's first since 1984.... Herbert Gregg, a U.S. missionary abducted in the Russian republic of Dagestan and taken to Chechnya in November 1998, is freed.... Karekin I (born Neshan Sarkissian), 66, leader of the Armenian Apostolic Church since 1995, dies in Etchmiadzin, Armenia, of throat cancer.			Two organizers of the China Democracy Party's branch in Beijing, Zha Jianguo and Gao Hongming, are arrested.... More than 100 members of a pro-integrationist militia attack a recently opened UN office in Maliana, near the West Timor border. An unidentified diplomat from South Africa and at least a dozen East Timorese are wounded in the attack.

A	B	C	D	E
Includes developments that affect more than one world region, international organizations, and important meetings of major world leaders.	Includes all domestic and regional developments in Europe, including the Soviet Union, Turkey, Cyprus, and Malta.	Includes all domestic and regional developments in Africa and the Middle East, including Iraq and Iran and excluding Cyprus, Turkey, and Afghanistan.	Includes all domestic and regional developments in Latin America, the Caribbean, and Canada.	Includes all domestic and regional developments in Asia and Pacific nations, extending from Afghanistan through all the Pacific Island, except Hawaii.

U.S. Politics & Social Issues	U.S. Foreign Policy & Defense	U.S. Economy & Environment	Science, Technology, & Nature	Culture, Leisure, & Lifestyle	
The United Network for Organ Sharing approves new rules giving the sickest patients higher priority for receiving livers. . . . James Kopp, a fugitive suspect in the slaying of Dr. Barnett Slepian, who performed abortions, is indicted by an Erie County, New York, grand jury. . . . The House approves, 305-124, a constitutional amendment that will allow Congress to ban burning or other desecration of the U.S. flag.	The U.S. State Department shuts six U.S. embassies in Togo, Gambia, Namibia, Liberia, Senegal, and Madagascar for security reasons. . . . Judge Joyce Hens Green orders Sheik Abdul Raouf Khalil, a wealthy Saudi businessman tied to the Bank of Credit and Commerce International (BCCI) fraud, to pay nearly $1.2 billion in damages to investors.		The FTC notes it has identified 800 sites on the World Wide Web that promote unproven medical treatments.	Geoff Lawson, 54, British automobile designer and styling director of Jaguar Cars since 1984, dies in Coventry, England, after suffering a stroke.	June 24
Data shows that, since November 1998, some 1,700 people banned by law from buying guns have been able to purchase them anyway.	Vietnamese and U.S. trade negotiators announce they have reached an agreement to normalize trade between the U.S. and Vietnam.	Former Democratic fund-raiser Yogesh Gandhi pleads guilty in San Francisco, California, to violating federal election law by funneling a contribution to the Democratic National Committee (DNC) from a foreign source. . . . Frederick Christ Trump, 93, who made his fortune building residential housing in the New York City's outer boroughs and who was the father of developer Donald Trump, dies in New York after suffering from Alzheimer's disease.		The San Antonio Spurs win their first NBA title over the New York Knicks, 78-77, in the deciding game of the basketball league's championship series. . . . Leaders of the 2.6-million-member Presbyterian Church vote to prohibit the church's regional governing bodies from voting on the ordination of homosexuals.	June 25
					June 26
				Golfer Juli Inkster wins the LPGA Championship, becoming only the second woman in modern LPGA history to win a career Grand Slam. . . . Marion Motley, 79, who in 1968 became only the second black player inducted into the Pro Football Hall of Fame, dies in Cleveland, Ohio, while suffering from prostate cancer.	June 27
New Jersey governor Christine Todd Whitman, a moderate Republican known nationally for her support of abortion rights, signs a law requiring parental notification for teenage abortions. The law is the first significant abortion restriction enacted in New Jersey in more than 20 years. . . . In Philadelphia, Pennsylvania, Judge William Mazzola sentences Marie Noe, 70, to 20 years of probation for murdering eight of her young children between 1949 and 1968.	The U.S. State Department reopens the embassies in Togo, Gambia, Namibia, Liberia, and Senegal. The embassy in Madagascar remains closed.	Pres. Clinton unveils new economic projections that add $1 trillion to earlier forecasts of the federal budget surplus over 15 years. Based on assumptions that the nation's economy will continue to grow, Clinton projects that the surplus will allow the government to pay off the national debt by 2015.		Hannibal, by Thomas Harris, tops the bestseller lists. . . . Sir John Woolf, 86, British film producer whose films won 13 Academy Awards, dies in London, England.	June 28
Pres. Clinton unveils a plan to restructure Medicare, the federal health-care program for the nation's elderly and disabled.	A group of independent oil producers based in the U.S. state of Oklahoma lodge the first antidumping complaint ever filed in the U.S. against foreign oil producers. In a petition to the Commerce Department, the independents allege that the oil-producing nations of Saudi Arabia, Iran, Venezuela, and Mexico are attempting to put U.S. producers out of business by selling oil in the U.S. at unfairly low prices.			Data suggests that the NBA finals recorded an average Nielsen television rating of 11.3, their lowest since 1981. . . . Allan Carr, 62, film and stage producer whose most successful film was Grease (1978), dies of liver cancer in Beverly Hills, California.	June 29

F	G	H	I	J
Includes elections, federal-state relations, civil rights and liberties, crime, the judiciary, education, health care, poverty, urban affairs, and population.	Includes formation and debate of U.S. foreign and defense policies, veterans' affairs, and defense spending. (Relations with specific foreign countries are usually found under the region concerned.)	Includes business, labor, agriculture, taxation, transportation, consumer affairs, monetary and fiscal policy, natural resources, and pollution.	Includes worldwide scientific, medical, and technological developments; natural phenomena; U.S. weather; natural disasters; and accidents.	Includes the arts, religion, scholarship, communications media, sports, entertainments, fashions, fads, and social life.

	World Affairs	Europe	Africa & the Middle East	The Americas	Asia & the Pacific
June 30	UN undersecretary general Sergio Vieira de Mello swears in the first panel of judges in Kosovo as the UN sets up a court system for the province. The panel—consisting of five ethnic Albanians, three Serbs and one ethnic Turk—will hear the cases of people arrested by NATO. The courts will operate on the basis of the Yugoslav penal code, although NATO troops will make arrests based on their national laws.			In Canada, Tyrell Dueck, 13, a 13-year-old Saskatchewan boy whose refusal of treatment for bone cancer ignited a nationwide ethical debate, dies of his illness. Dueck refused treatment because he believed God and alternative medicine would cure him of his disease.	A fire sweeps through a three-story summer camp building in Hwasung on South Korea's western coast, killing 19 children and four adults.
July 1	The Inter-American Human Rights Court (IAHRC), the legal arm of the Organization of American States, orders a retrial for four Chilean political prisoners convicted of terrorist acts and sentenced to life in prison in Peru.	The Bundestag holds its final session in Bonn before moving to Berlin. . . . Viscount Whitelaw (born William Stephen Ian Whitelaw), 81, British politician, dies. . . . Viktor Mikhailovich Chebrikov, 76, head of the KGB, 1982–88, dies in Moscow. . . . Queen Elizabeth II opens the Scottish Parliament. Scotland's last legislature was dissolved by Britain in 1706. . . . A cable car in the French Alps plunges 260 feet (80 m), killing all 20 people on board. It is the worst such accident in French history.	Joshua Mqabuko Nyongolo Nkomo, 82, African nationalist who played a key role in Zimbabwe's struggle for independence, dies in Harare, Zimbabwe, of prostate cancer.	Sola Sierra, 63, Chilean human-rights activist, dies in Santiago, Chile, of a heart attack during surgery for a recently sustained back injury.	Japan's National Police Agency reports that 32,863 people committed suicide in 1998, up 35% from 1997. The 1998 figure is the highest since Japanese police began keeping such records in 1947 and also represents a record per-capita suicide rate.
July 2	A large majority of the 179 participating nations in a UN conference approve a plan to limit global population growth, although a small group of conservative Muslim and Roman Catholic countries object to provisions on abortion services and family planning.	French NATO troops arrest Dragan Marjanovic, suspected of committing atrocities against ethnic Albanians during NATO's bombing campaign.		Canada's National Assembly passes back-to-work legislation aimed at forcing the nurses who struck June 26 off the picket lines by penalizing their union leadership.	China Democracy Party member Liu Xianbin of Sichuan is arrested.
July 3		British NATO soldiers kill two members of the ethnic Albanian Kosovo Liberation Army (KLA) and injure two others.	In elections for Kuwait's parliament, Islamist candidates from both the Shi'ite and Sunni branches of Islam and Liberal candidates together win 34 seats of the 50 seats contested.		Former Singapore-based futures trader Nicholas Leeson of Britain, whose market losses led to the 1995 collapse of Barings Bank PLC, is released from a prison in Singapore after serving a little more than half of a 6½-year sentence for fraud and forgery related to his trading losses, valued at £875 million ($1.4 billion).
July 4		In Turkey, a bomb in a garbage can at an Istanbul park explodes, killing one person and wounding 25 others. . . . A traditional Protestant parade in the Drumcree section of Portadown, Northern Ireland, proceeds peacefully. In previous years, the Drumcree march had frequently erupted in sectarian violence.			In, East Timor, a humanitarian-aid, convoy is attacked by armed militiamen. At least three people are injured, and another five are reported missing. . . . India claims that its troops have taken Tiger Hill, a strategic point that overlooks a military supply route in the disputed Himalayan region of Kashmir.
July 5	Russia and NATO agree on outstanding details of Russian participation in NATO's peacekeeping force in Kosovo, easing tensions in Russian-NATO relations, which were strained by Russia's opposition to NATO's 78-day bombing campaign in Yugoslavia. . . . Papua New Guinea establishes diplomatic relations with Taiwan, bringing to 29 the number of nations recognizing Taiwan as a country.	A suicide bomber, apparently linked to the Kurdish separatist movement, kills herself and wounds 14 bystanders when she detonates a bomb in Adana. . . . An estimated 10,000–20,000 Serbs gather in Leskovac, a traditional base of support for Pres. Slobodan Milosevic, in a spontaneous protest against the Yugoslav president. The protest in Leskovac is one of many recent demonstrations against Milosevic throughout Serbia.	The Algerian government releases thousands of jailed Islamic militants under the terms of an amnesty peace deal.		UN officials announce that they are withdrawing staff from the town of Liquica, some 28 miles (45 km) west of Dili, East Timor's capital city, following a July 4 attack on a humanitarian-aid convoy.

A	B	C	D	E
Includes developments that affect more than one world region, international organizations, and important meetings of major world leaders.	*Includes all domestic and regional developments in Europe, including the Soviet Union, Turkey, Cyprus, and Malta.*	*Includes all domestic and regional developments in Africa and the Middle East, including Iraq and Iran and excluding Cyprus, Turkey, and Afghanistan.*	*Includes all domestic and regional developments in Latin America, the Caribbean, and Canada.*	*Includes all domestic and regional developments in Asia and Pacific nations, extending from Afghanistan through all the Pacific Island, except Hawaii.*

U.S. Politics & Social Issues	U.S. Foreign Policy & Defense	U.S. Economy & Environment	Science, Technology, & Nature	Culture, Leisure, & Lifestyle	
The Massachusetts Supreme Judicial Court in Boston rules that the state attorney general's office is allowed to regulate handgun safety according to consumer protection laws. The unanimous decision is the first such ruling in the country.... California judge John Ryan sentences serial killer Charles Ng to death for murders committed in 1984 and 1985.... The 1978 independent counsel statute expires.		Texas governor George W. Bush announces that his presidential campaign raised an unprecedented $36.25 million in the first half of 1999.... Webster Hubbell, a friend of Pres. Clinton and First Lady Hillary Rodham Clinton, enters guilty pleas in two cases brought against him by independent counsel Kenneth Starr, who asserts that the pleas close the Whitewater aspect of his five-year-old investigation of the Clintons. Judge James Robertson orders Hubbell to pay $125.			June 30
The Justice Department releases new rules that will govern outside prosecutors appointed after the demise of the 1978 independent counsel statute.... The American Association of Health Plans states that many health maintenance organizations (HMOs) that serve Medicare beneficiaries will raise premiums or reduce benefits in the year 2000.	Robert Polhill, 65, U.S. professor of business at Beirut University College in Lebanon who, with three colleagues, was held hostage kidnapped by Lebanese militias, 1987–90, dies in Washington, D.C., of complications of chemotherapy he was receiving for bladder cancer.	The Senate votes, 97-2, to confirm Lawrence H. Summers as secretary of the treasury.... A jury in Washington, D.C., acquits Franklin Haney, a longtime supporter of Vice Pres. Al Gore, of charges that he used "straw donors" to evade federal fund-raising limits.... Forrest Mars Sr., 95, candy magnate who helped build Mars Inc., dies in Miami, Florida, of unreported causes.... The CBO projects the 10-year total surplus at $2.895 trillion, or $1 trillion without Social Security.	A study finds that a heart condition known as mitral valve prolapse is less common and less dangerous than widely believed.... The House, 404-24, and Senate, 81-18, adopt legislation that will protect businesses from lawsuits stemming from problems caused by the year 2000 (Y2K) computer glitch. Many computers, if not reprogrammed, are expected to recognize the year 2000 as 1900, resulting in potentially severe disruptions.	Sylvia Sidney (born Sophia Kosow), 88, actress of the 1930s and 1940s, dies in New York City of throat cancer.... Edward Dmytryk, 90, film director best known for The Caine Mutiny (1954), who was jailed for refusing to answer questions during the McCarthy era, dies of heart and kidney failure in Encino, California.	July 1
A gunman wounds six Orthodox Jewish men in Chicago, Illinois, and then kills Ricky Byrdsong, 42, who is black, in Skokie, a Chicago suburb. Later he fires four shots at two Asian Americans.... A federal jury in Florida finds Jay Jarrell and Robert Whiteside, two executives at Columbia/HCA Healthcare Corp., guilty of defrauding Medicare and other federal health-care programs of some $3 million. They are the first jury verdicts to result from a probe that started in 1997.... Data shows that almost a quarter of the 182,545 handguns sold in 1988 in California, 40,722, were bought as part of a purchase of two or more handguns by the same buyer.	South Korean president Kim Dae Jung visits the U.S., his third trip to the States since he was elected in 1997.	Pres. Clinton announces that the North American bald eagle will be removed from the list of endangered species, due to steady growth in the bald eagle population. There are currently 5,800 bald eagle pairs in the U.S., up from 417 in 1963.		Mario Puzo, 78, novelist and screenwriter who wrote The Godfather (1969), one of the most successful novels of all time, and cowrote the screenplays for the movies of the same name, dies in Bay Shore, New York, of heart failure.	July 2
The gunman who went on a rampage July 2 continues the violence when he shoots a black man in Springfield, Illinois, and another black person in Decatur. That night in Urbana, east of Springfield, he fires at a group of six Asian students, and one is wounded.					July 3
The gunman who went on a shooting rampage July 2 fires four shots into a crowd at the Korean United Methodist Church in Bloomington, Illinois. A 26-year-old Korean-American graduate student is killed. The suspected killer, Benjamin Nathaniel Smith, 21, kills himself during a police chase. Smith is a member of the white-supremacist World Church of the Creator, one of the fastest-growing hate groups in the U.S. His July 2–4 rampage leaves two people dead and nine wounded.			A heat wave rolls across states in the Northeastern and mid-Atlantic regions of the U.S., causing temperatures to soar in several cities on the East Coast, including Washington, D.C.; New York City; and Atlantic City, New Jersey.	Pete Sampras wins his sixth men's singles title at the All England Tennis Championship at Wimbledon. Third-seeded Lindsay Davenport wins her first Wimbledon singles title.	July 4
	According to Forbes, William Gates of Microsoft Corp. is the richest person still working with his assets in the world, with a fortune estimated at $90 billion.		In Kazakhstan, a Russian Proton rocket carrying a satellite crashes soon after liftoff.... C(larence) Walton Lillehei, 80, surgeon who while teaching at the University of Minnesota in 1952, performed the first successful open-heart surgery, dies in St. Paul, Minnesota, of cancer.		July 5

F	G	H	I	J
Includes elections, federal-state relations, civil rights and liberties, crime, the judiciary, education, health care, poverty, urban affairs, and population.	*Includes formation and debate of U.S. foreign and defense policies, veterans' affairs, and defense spending. (Relations with specific foreign countries are usually found under the region concerned.)*	*Includes business, labor, agriculture, taxation, transportation, consumer affairs, monetary and fiscal policy, natural resources, and pollution.*	*Includes worldwide scientific, medical, and technological developments; natural phenomena; U.S. weather; natural disasters; and accidents.*	*Includes the arts, religion, scholarship, communications media, sports, entertainments, fashions, fads, and social life.*

	World Affairs	Europe	Africa & the Middle East	The Americas	Asia & the Pacific
July 6	British NATO troops apprehend Radoslav Brdjanin on charges of war crimes committed against Bosnian Muslims and Croats during the 1992–95 war in Bosnia-Herzegovina. Brdjanin, a deputy premier of Bosnia's Serb Republic, is the highest-level Bosnian Serb politician NATO has arrested on war crimes charges.	In accordance with the July 5 agreement with NATO, a contingent of Russian troops enter the Serbian province of Kosovo. . . . Joe Hyman, 77, British textile magnate, dies of unreported causes.	Ehud Barak takes the oath as Israel's prime minister.		Indian and Pakistani officials exchange allegations that their embassy staff members have been abducted and tortured. India claims it has retaken several peaks in the Batalik area of Kashmir. . . . Nearly 1,000 Falun Gong followers hold a rally inside the Communist Party headquarters in Nanchang, the capital of Jiangxi province. The protesters demand that a provincial party publication retract an article denouncing their movement. . . . Dancer and film star Piseth Pelika is shot on a street in Phnom Penh, the capitol of Cambodia.
July 7	Britain announces that it is resuming normal diplomatic relations with Libya due to Libya's agreement to cooperate with an investigation into the 1984 shooting death of British police officer Yvonne Fletcher. The British government severed all diplomatic ties with Libya five days after that incident.	Spanish police, customs, and naval officials seize a ship in the mid-Atlantic Ocean carrying about 10 tons of cocaine. The operation is believed to be the biggest cocaine seizure ever by European authorities.	Pres. Ahmad Tejan Kabbah and rebel leader Foday Sankoh sign a pact to end Sierra Leone's eight-year-old civil war. . . . In Iran, the conservative Special Court for Clergy that bans Iran's leading moderate daily paper. The conservative-led Majlis parliament votes to restrict the reformist press. . . . In Bahrain, Sheik Abdul Amir al-Jamri is sentenced to a 10-year prison term. He has been imprisoned since January 1996.	Peru's Congress votes to ignore the July 1 rulings of the Inter-American Human Rights Court (IAHRC), the legal arm of the OAS, that called for a retrial of four Chilean political prisoners.	Bill Skate resigns as prime minister of Papua New Guinea. . . . The Indonesian government states that it will send 1,200 additional police officers to East Timor to prevent further attacks on UN staff. . . . Leaders of 16 Islamic militant groups vow to continue fighting in Kashmir and reject recent claims made by Indian military officials that India had recaptured strategic positions in the region.
July 8		Latvia's parliament approves a controversial law that requires the use of the Latvian language at most public and business functions.	Members of Ansar-e Hezbollah, an Islamic vigilante group, attack students protesting the July 7 rulings at Teheran University in Iran. Riot police storm a dormitory, and students claim that as many as eight people are killed and scores injured . . . . A speaker for the Congolese Rally for Democracy (RCD) reports heavy fighting in Kabinda, a government-held town . . . . In Bahrain, Sheik Abdul Amir al-Jamri, sentenced July 7, is issued an amnesty and freed from jail. . . . Shafik al-Wazzan, 74, premier of Lebanon, 1980–84, dies in Beirut of a heart attack.	In Colombia, FARC forces begin a series of raids against more than 20 towns and installations, including one on an army encampment only about 27 miles (40 km) from Bogota, the capital. Rebels kill 38 government soldiers in the attack on the military camp.	
July 9				The Supreme Court of Canada rules that children cannot sue their mothers for injuries suffered while in the womb.	In an interview with a German radio station, Taiwanese president Lee Teng-hui states that Taiwan should henceforth conduct its relations with China on a "state-to-state" basis.
July 10	The heads of six African nations with troops in the Democratic Republic of Congo sign a cease-fire agreement aimed at ending the civil war in that country. The signers are Congo and its allies—Zimbabwe, Angola, and Namibia—and the two main rebel allies, Rwanda and Uganda. However, a representative for the Movement for the Liberation of Congo, one main rebel group, asserts, "We have not signed so we are not bound." The UNHCR reports that 200,000 people have left Congo since August 1998.				
July 11	Zambian president Frederick Chiluba criticizes the U.N. for spending 11 cents on each African refugee from the Congo conflict while spending $1.50 on each refugee from the conflict in Kosovo, a Serbian province, calling the difference in spending "discrimination of the worst kind."	A bomb explodes in Van, a city in Turkey's predominantly Kurdish southeastern region. The blast injures 16 people.	Iran's government officials claim that only one person was killed in the July 8 raid on a student dorm at Teheran University. At least one person has been killed in the ongoing unrest.	A powerful earthquake strikes Guatemala, injuring at least 37 people and damaging homes and buildings. The quake registers between 6.1 and 6.6 on the Richter scale. The epicenter is about 20 miles (30 km) east of the city of Puerto Barrios on Guatemala's Caribbean coast. . . . Colombia's military states its troops have effectively put down the FARC attacks that started July 8, the largest guerrilla offensive in 40 years.	Commanders of military operations from India and Pakistan meet at a border point and lay out a plan for ending the current crisis, which has brought the heaviest fighting in Kashmir in nearly 30 years. . . . The Chinese foreign ministry calls Taiwan's July 9 remarks regarding its relations with Chiha "an extremely dangerous step" and warns Taiwan's government to "rein in at the brink of the precipice."
	A	B	C	D	E
	Includes developments that affect more than one world region, international organizations, and important meetings of major world leaders.	Includes all domestic and regional developments in Europe, including the Soviet Union, Turkey, Cyprus, and Malta.	Includes all domestic and regional developments in Africa and the Middle East, including Iraq and Iran and excluding Cyprus, Turkey, and Afghanistan.	Includes all domestic and regional developments in Latin America, the Caribbean, and Canada.	Includes all domestic and regional developments in Asia and Pacific nations, extending from Afghanistan through all the Pacific Island, except Hawaii.

U.S. Politics & Social Issues	U.S. Foreign Policy & Defense	U.S. Economy & Environment	Science, Technology, & Nature	Culture, Leisure, & Lifestyle	
Mark Potok, of the Southern Poverty Law Center, notes that members of the World Church of the Creator, the white supremacist group connected to alleged killer Benjamin Nathaniel Smith, who went on a rampage in Illinois July 2–4, has also been linked to a 1993 plot to bomb a Los Angeles African Methodist Episcopal church and to the 1993 bombing of a Tacoma, Washington, office of the NAACP.	Pres. Clinton imposes economic sanctions on the Taliban militia in Afghanistan for allegedly harboring Saudi Arabian exile Osama bin Laden. . . . Gay soldier Pfc. Barry Winchell dies after being beaten with a baseball bat at Fort Campbell army base in Kentucky. . . . Judge Joyce Hens Green closes U.S. forfeiture proceedings against the BCCI, stating that the U.S. government gained clear title to $1.2 billion in U.S.-based assets that BCCI forfeited. BCCI folded in 1991 after disclosures of many kinds of fraud around the world.	BankAmerica Corp. announces the creation of a $500 million "catalyst fund" to make equity investments in businesses in poor areas.	A power failure in Washington Heights, a section of New York City that is home to a mostly low-income, minority population lasts 18 hours and cuts off electric power to 200,000 people and 700 businesses. . . . In response to the July 5 crash of a Russian Proton rocket, Kazakhstan suspends space launches from the Baikonur cosmodrome, from which Russia regularly launches capsules to *Mir*.	Joaquin Rodrigo, 97, Spanish composer best known for his *Concierto de Aranjuez*, dies in Madrid. . . . Thor Axel Appfjell, 32, who made daredevil jumps from buildings including the Eiffel Tower and the Empire State Building, dies in a jump from a cliff near Stavanger, Norway.	July 6
Reports confirm that Philip Morris, the nation's largest cigarette company, ended its financial support of the National Smokers Alliance. . . . A Florida jury finds that the nation's largest tobacco companies conspired to conceal the addictiveness and health hazards of smoking, and that they may be held liable for causing a variety of illnesses in smokers. It is the first class-action suit on behalf of injured smokers to reach trial.	Pres. Clinton imposes import restrictions on steel from Brazil and on lamb from Australia and New Zealand.	On his tour of some of the nation's most economically depressed areas, Pres. Clinton visits the Oglala Lakota Sioux reservation in Pine Ridge, South Dakota, the nation's second-largest Indian reservation. He is the first sitting president to visit an Indian reservation since Franklin D. Roosevelt visited a Cherokee reservation in 1936. The Pine Ridge reservation's 38,000 residents suffer from 73% unemployment.			July 7
The American Red Cross, the U.S.'s largest blood supplier, names Dr. Bernadine Healy as its next president, effective September 1.			A study finds that by the end of 1998, more than 40% of U.S. homes had a computer, 25% were connected to the Internet and 94.1% had phones. The report also notes a growing "digital divide" in information access drawn along financial and racial lines. . . . Researchers report they have developed a vaccine that, in mice, prevents and reverses the accumulation of protein deposits in the brain associated with Alzheimer's disease. . . . (Charles) Pete Conrad Jr., 69, the third man to walk on the moon, dies after a motorcycle accident in Ojai, California.	Christie's International PLC holds an $89.5 million auction of art and antiques owned by the Rothschild family in London. The sale is Britain's highest-grossing art auction ever.	July 8
A jury in Baton Rouge, Louisiana, clears two cigarette companies of responsibility for the death of Robert Gilboy, a longtime smoker who had lung cancer. . . . James Leonard Farmer, 79, U.S. civil-rights leader who spearheaded the integration of public facilities throughout the South during the 1950s and 1960s, advocating nonviolent protest, dies in Fredericksburg, Virginia, while suffering from complications of diabetes.		A Louisiana jury orders GM to pay $4.9 billion to six people burned when the fuel tank of their 1979 Chevrolet Malibu exploded when it was hit from behind in 1993. It is the largest damages award ever in a product-liability lawsuit. . . . In Chicago, Illinois Judge Blanche Manning sentences three former Archer Daniels Midland Co. executives to prison terms for their roles in a conspiracy to fix the price of lysine, a livestock-feed additive.			July 9
Cyrano Marks shoots six people to death in an Atlanta, Georgia, house before killing himself. The incident is the deadliest mass shooting in Atlanta in the 20th century.				The U.S. defeats China, 5-4, to win the quadrennial Women's World Cup championship in Pasadena, California. The tournament sets an attendance record of 90,185 for women's sports and sparks soccer fever throughout the U.S. . . . American John McEnroe and Australian Ken McGregor are inducted into the International Tennis Hall of Fame.	July 10
The Justice Department releases the first comprehensive survey of mental illness among inmates in the nation's prisons. The study finds that there are 283,800 inmates with mental illness, or about 16% of the total state and local prison population. Slightly more than 7% of federal prison inmates are found to suffer from mental illness.				Golfer Dave Eichelberger wins his first U.S. Senior Open. . . . Helen Forrest (born Helen Fogel), 81, big band singer in the 1940s who recorded her last album in 1983, dies of congestive heart failure in Los Angeles, California.	July 11

F	G	H	I	J
Includes elections, federal-state relations, civil rights and liberties, crime, the judiciary, education, health care, poverty, urban affairs, and population.	Includes formation and debate of U.S. foreign and defense policies, veterans' affairs, and defense spending. (Relations with specific foreign countries are usually found under the region concerned.)	Includes business, labor, agriculture, taxation, transportation, consumer affairs, monetary and fiscal policy, natural resources, and pollution.	Includes worldwide scientific, medical, and technological developments; natural phenomena; U.S. weather; natural disasters; and accidents.	Includes the arts, religion, scholarship, communications media, sports, entertainments, fashions, fads, and social life.

	World Affairs	Europe	Africa & the Middle East	The Americas	Asia & the Pacific
July 12	The UN World Heritage votes not to place World Heritage–listed Kakadu National Park, Australia, on a list of sites "in danger.". . . The UN Human Development Program urges tougher regulations to combat the negative effects of globalization. . . . A WTO arbitration panel authorizes the U.S. to impose $116.8 million in tariffs to penalize the EU for failing to lift its 11-year-old ban on the import of beef treated with growth hormones. The panel also rules that Canada is entitled to impose $7.5 million in tariffs.	Guy Verhofstadt, head of the free-market Liberal party based in Belgium's Flemish-speaking region, is sworn in by King Albert II as the country's new premier. The king also swears in Verhofstadt's government. . . . In Northern Ireland, several marches to commemorate a Protestant victory over Catholic forces in 1690 take place without incident. In previous years, the parades were often flashpoints of sectarian violence.	In Iran, protests that started Jul. 8 spread from Teheran, the capital, to the provinces, with demonstrations reported in 18 cities. Pres. Mohammed Khamenei appeals for calm in a speech broadcast on television and the radio.		
July 13	The World Economic Forum's annual global competitiveness report finds that Singapore remains the most competitive country among 59 surveyed. It is followed by the U.S., Hong Kong, Taiwan, and Canada. . . . Officials from Europe and the U.S. agree with a World Bank finding indicating that the damage wreaked on Kosovo is not as extensive as previously thought.	In Moscow, Russia, Nikita Krivchun, 20, repeatedly stabs a prominent Russian rabbi, Leopold Kaimovsky, 52, who is in "very serious" condition after the anti-Semitic attack.	Tens of thousands of riot police, government troops, and Islamic militants launch the most concerted crackdown against the protesters in Iran, sparking clashes that close down most businesses in Teheran. Paramilitary and vigilante groups fire tear gas into the crowd, discharge weapons in the air, and beat protesters. The unrest is reported to be Iran's worst civil disturbance since the country's Islamic revolution in 1979.	General Fernando Tapias, the chief of Colombia's armed forces, reveals that government troops have killed more than 300 guerrillas since the July 8 rebel offensive began.	The office of the UN High Commissioner for Refugees estimates that militias have driven some 50,000 East Timorese—approximately 5% of the province's population—from their homes. . . . Thousands of Cambodians gather in Phnom Penh, the capital, to mourn the July 6 death of dancer and film star Piseth Pelika. The massive outpouring of public grief is reportedly unusual in Cambodia.
July 14	In Algiers, 42 African leaders close the 35th annual summit of the Organization of African Unity (OAU). Among the attendees is Libyan leader Col. Muammar Gadhafi, whose last OAU summit appearance was in 1977. . . . The European Commission votes to end its ban on beef exports from Britain . . . Argentina and Britain agree to reinstate commercial flights between Argentina and the Falkland Islands, known as the Malvinas in Argentina, for the first time since 1982.	Latvian president Vaira Vike-Freiberga vetoes a controversial law that requires the use of the Latvian language at most public and business functions, sending it back to Parliament for revision. . . . Reports indicate that Murat Bozlak, head of Hadep, the largest Kurdish party in Turkey, has been released from prison.	After the July 13 violence, student leaders state that they ended the protest, but. they insist that the hard-line police chief, Hedayat Lotfian, be dismissed, and that the two officers fired July 11 be put on public trial. They also demand the release of the bodies of the students killed in the July 8 raid. Tens of thousands of Iranians—as many as 100,000 by some estimates—participate in a march in Teheran staged by conservative factions in Parliament, in support of the Islamic government.	Peruvian armed forces capture Oscar Ramirez Durand (known by the nom de guerre Comrade Feliciano), a guerrilla leader whom the government describes as the last remaining commander of Sendero Luminoso (Shining Path), a Maoist insurgency group.	In Papua New Guinea, Parliament elects Sir Mekere Morauta, leader of the opposition People's Democratic Movement (PDM) party, as the country's new prime minister.
July 15	Israeli prime minister Ehud Barak in talks with U.S. president Clinton, outlines a 15-month deadline for peace in the Middle East.	Bernard Kouchner, the UN's newly appointed administrator in the Yugoslav province of Kosovo, arrives in the province to officially take up his duties. Investigators report that, with the investigation not yet concluded, they have discovered 280 mass grave sites containing a total of more than 6,100 bodies.			Statistics New Zealand reports that prices in New Zealand in the year to June 30 were 0.4% lower than in the previous year. The decline places inflation at its lowest level since the 1930s.
July 16	A court in The Hague, the Netherlands, convicts Suriname's former military leader Desi Bouterse in absentia on charges of cocaine trafficking. Bouterse, 54, who led military coups in Suriname in 1980 and 1990, was chief adviser to Suriname president Jules Wijdenbosch until the president dismissed him in April. The court sentences Bouterse to 16 years in prison and fines him $2.18 million.	Latvia's parliament, the Saeima, elects former premier Andris Skele as the country's new premier. . . . A UN-sponsored council comprised of ethnic Albanians, Serbs, and other ethnic groups—the Kosovo Transitional Council—holds its first meeting.	In Sierra Leone, rebels hand over 192 civilians abducted during the civil war. More than half of the civilians are children.	An appellate court judge in Toluca, Mexico, reduces the prison sentence of Raul Salinas de Gortari, the brother of former Mexican president Carlos Salinas de Gortari, to 27½ years, from a maximum sentence of 50 years.	Japan receives the first legal shipment of ivory since 1990, when a worldwide ban on ivory trading went into effect. In 1997, the Convention on International Trade in Endangered Species approved the one-time sale of 50 tons of ivory to Japan by Namibia, Botswana, and Zimbabwe.
July 17		Donal McCann, 56, widely seen as Ireland's greatest actor, dies in Dublin, Ireland, of pancreatic cancer.	Israel releases its longest-held Palestinian prisoner, Osama Barham, after he spent nearly six years in prison without being formally charged or brought to trial.		

A	B	C	D	E
Includes developments that affect more than one world region, international organizations, and important meetings of major world leaders.	Includes all domestic and regional developments in Europe, including the Soviet Union, Turkey, Cyprus, and Malta.	Includes all domestic and regional developments in Africa and the Middle East, including Iraq and Iran and excluding Cyprus, Turkey, and Afghanistan.	Includes all domestic and regional developments in Latin America, the Caribbean, and Canada.	Includes all domestic and regional developments in Asia and Pacific nations, extending from Afghanistan through all the Pacific Island, except Hawaii.

U.S. Politics & Social Issues	U.S. Foreign Policy & Defense	U.S. Economy & Environment	Science, Technology, & Nature	Culture, Leisure, & Lifestyle	
		The Justice Department files a lawsuit against Toyota Motor Co., alleging that Toyota violated regulations under the Clean Air Act when it installed faulty emissions-control equipment in 2.2 million vehicles in its 1996-through-1998 model years.			July 12
A suspected serial killer who allegedly murdered eight people in Kentucky, Texas, and Illinois surrenders to authorities in Texas, ending a weeks-long nationwide manhunt. The suspect is known by the name Rafael Resendez-Ramirez but uses a variety of aliases. His real name is said to be Angel Maturino Resendez.	A bipartisan congressional commission criticizes the U.S. for failing to take adequate measures to combat the proliferation of nuclear, chemical, and biological weapons.	In response to the July 12 suit filed by the Justice Department, Toyota refuses an out-of-court settlement that would have required a recall of the vehicles. Toyota is the first carmaker to refuse to settle a pollution case with the U.S. government.		The Vatican orders Rev. Robert Nugent and Sister Jeannine Gramick, a Maryland-based Roman Catholic priest and nun, to halt their national ministry for homosexuals. . . . The American League defeats the National League, 4-1, to win Major League Baseball's All-Star Game at Fenway Park in Boston, Massachusetts.	July 13
The school committee in Boston, Massachusetts, votes, 5-2, to stop using race as a factor in determining which schools public-school students may attend. The decision means that school busing in Boston is to end in the year 2000. . . . John Roy Steelman, 99, longtime aide to Pres. Harry S. Truman, dies in Naples, Florida, of pneumonia.			U.S. and Ugandan scientists announce they have discovered a cheaper and more effective method of reducing mother-to-child birth transmission of HIV, the virus that causes AIDS, in developing countries. The researchers reveal that a single dose of the drug nevirapine given to HIV-positive mothers during labor and to their newborns cuts the transmission rate to 13% of children four months after birth. . . . Kazakhstan agrees to allow the launch of a supply ship to Mir.	In basketball, the Western Conference beats the Eastern Conference, 79-61, to win the inaugural WNBA All-Star Game before a sell-out crowd of 18,649 in New York City. . . . During construction of a stadium for baseball's Milwaukee Brewers, a crane collapses, killing three workers and injuring five others.	July 14
After intense debate on a rival Democratic bill, the Senate passes, 53-47, a Republican-sponsored bill establishing consumer protections for patients enrolled in health maintenance organizations (HMOs) and other health insurance plans. . . . George E. Brown Jr., 79, (D, Calif.) serving his 18th term in the U.S. House of Representatives and the oldest House member in the current Congress, dies of a post-surgical infection at Bethesda Naval Hospital. He had had a heart valve replaced in May.	China releases a report rebutting allegations by a U.S. congressional committee that China has stolen U.S. nuclear and other weapons technology. The report contains China's first acknowledgment that it possesses the capability to build a neutron bomb.	Energy Secretary Bill Richardson recommends that Congress compensate thousands of workers sickened while making nuclear weapons. Richardson's report to Congress marks the first time the government acknowledges a link between workers' exposure to radioactive materials and cancer or other diseases. . . . Gov. George W. Bush (R, Tex.) announces he will not seek federal matching funds for his presidential primary campaign, releasing him from federal and state spending caps.		The House votes, 306-118, to pass legislation aimed at protecting individuals' religious freedoms, even if the practice of those beliefs breaches local laws.	July 15
	The House votes, 234-163, to endorse legislation that will institute trade benefits for Africa.	The Dow closes at a record high of 11,209.84. That marks the fifth record high of the month and the 29th record high in 1999.	A jury in Bridgeport, Connecticut, dismisses claims in an antitrust lawsuit filed against Microsoft by a small software firm, Bristol Technology Inc. Bristol filed the lawsuit in August 1998, accusing Microsoft of seeking to gain a monopoly for its Windows NT system. . . . Neil Armstrong, Buzz Aldrin, and others attend the 30th anniversary of the launch of Apollo 11 at a reunion of mission personnel at the launch site at Cape Canaveral, known as Cape Kennedy in 1969.	John F. Kennedy Jr., 38, only surviving son of former president John F. Kennedy and editor of the political magazine George, dies in an airplane crash with his wife, Carolyn Bessette Kennedy, and his sister-in-law Lauren Bessette. The plane, piloted by John Kennedy, plunges into the Atlantic Ocean near Martha's Vineyard.	July 16
Rep. Michael Forbes, a third-term Republican from New York, switches his allegiance from the GOP to the Democrats, criticizing the Republicans as an "angry, narrow-minded, intolerant and uncaring majority, incapable of governing." Forbes's shift narrows the Republicans' slim majority, boosting the Democrats' chances of retaking the House in 2000.				The Western Conference defeats the Eastern Conference, 6-4, in the 1999 MLS All-Star Game at Qualcomm Stadium in San Diego, California.	July 17

F	G	H	I	J
Includes elections, federal-state relations, civil rights and liberties, crime, the judiciary, education, health care, poverty, urban affairs, and population.	Includes formation and debate of U.S. foreign and defense policies, veterans' affairs, and defense spending. (Relations with specific foreign countries are usually found under the region concerned.)	Includes business, labor, agriculture, taxation, transportation, consumer affairs, monetary and fiscal policy, natural resources, and pollution.	Includes worldwide scientific, medical, and technological developments; natural phenomena; U.S. weather; natural disasters; and accidents.	Includes the arts, religion, scholarship, communications media, sports, entertainments, fashions, fads, and social life.

	World Affairs	Europe	Africa & the Middle East	The Americas	Asia & the Pacific
July 18	The U.S. Census Bureau's International Programs Center estimates that the world's population has reached the 6 billion mark.	Two U.S. soldiers taking part in NATO's Kosovo force—Specialist Sherwood Brim, 30, and Sergeant William Wright, 27—die in an accident while on patrol near Gnjilane. The incident marks the first U.S. fatalities since the alliance entered Kosovo a month earlier.	Dozens of people are killed during ethnic rioting in the town of Shagamu, 36 miles (60 km) north of Lagos, Nigeria. The rioting reportedly occurs after a woman from the Hausa ethnic group violates a taboo by watching a ceremony of the Yoruba people. . . . According to Iraqi military officials, U.S. fighter planes kill 14 civilians and injure 17 others in Iraq's southern no-fly zone.		
July 19	The U.S. announces that it will impose tariffs of 100% on several high-priced items imported from Europe, in retaliation for the European Union's refusal to lift its 11-year-old ban on the import of beef treated with growth hormones.		The Iraqi News Agency reports that 17 people were killed and 18 wounded in the Jul. 18 attack in southern Iraq.	A court in San Cristobal de las Casas, Mexico, sentences 20 people convicted of participating in a December 1997 massacre in the Tzotzil Indian village of Acteal in the southern state of Chiapas. In the massacre, gunmen from neighboring Indian villages killed 45 people in Acteal. The court sentences each of the defendants to 35-year prison terms.	The Chinese government starts a roundup of dozens of leaders of the quasi-religious Falun Gong spiritual movement, prompting protests.
July 20	The EU's legislative arm, the European Parliament, elects French conservative Nicole Fontaine as its president. . . . Inspectors from the European Commission, the EU's executive arm, raid European offices of U.S.-based Coca-Cola Co. and its affiliated bottling companies in Austria, Britain, Denmark, and Germany, seeking evidence of anticompetitive practices.	Turkish premier Bulent Ecevit declares that Turkish Cyprus must maintain independence from the rest of the divided nation. . . . The Constitutional Court, Spain's highest appeals court, rules that 22 imprisoned members of Herri Batasuna, ETA's political wing, should be released. . . . A Russian military journalist accused of passing naval secrets to Japan, navy captain Grigori Pasko, is released from prison after a military court drops a charge of treason against him.	In response to the July 18–19 claims, U.S. defense secretary William Cohen states that there is no evidence that the U.S. attack in southern Iraq killed any civilians.	Off the coast of Vancouver Island in British Columbia, 123 Chinese illegal immigrants are found smuggled aboard a fishing boat. The human-smuggling case, one of the biggest in Canadian history, sparks a national controversy over Canada's immigration and refugee laws.	In India, Muslim fighters kill 20 Hindus in three predawn attacks in the Himalayan foothills in the Doda and Punch districts of Kashmir. . . . Indonesian election officials postpone the release of an official tally of the country's June 7 general election results. It is the latest in a string of delays following the historic June vote, the country's first fully democratic election in 44 years.
July 21	The new prime minister of Papua New Guinea, Sir Mekere Morauta, announces that he has reversed his predecessor's decision to establish diplomatic ties with Taiwan.	Turkish premier Bulent Ecevit announces that Turkish forces have arrested Kurdish separatist Cevat Soysal in Moldova. . . . David MacKenzie Ogilvy, 88, British-born founder of Ogilvy & Mather, a major international advertising agency, dies near Bonnes, France, of unreported causes.		Nurses in Quebec, Canada, vote to reject a labor agreement with the government and resume their 24-day-old strike. Separately, data shows that Canada's overall crime rate in 1998 declined for the seventh consecutive year, down by 4.1% from 1997. The crime rate is at its lowest level since 1979.	Despite the July 11 agreement, Kashmiri guerrillas bombard an Indian army headquarters in Kashmir. India responds with artillery fire against some 150 guerrillas. Some 16 people are reported killed in several gun battles in Indian-held territory. . . . Tens of thousands of Falun Gong members gather in 30 cities in protest of the July 19 detentions in China. Hundreds of followers converging on the Communist Party compound Beijing are stopped by police and put onto buses.
July 22	The World Trade Organization (WTO) officially appoints New Zealander Mike Moore, an economist and former prime minister, as its director general.	Claudio Rodriguez, 65, who was regarded as one of the best Spanish poets of the century and who published five books of verse, dies in Madrid, Spain, of colon cancer.			In Mongolia, the Great Hural passes a no-confidence vote in the government of Premier Janlaviin Narantsatsralt. It is the third government to collapse in 15 months. . . . Japan's Diet passes legislation granting official status to Japan's de facto national flag and anthem. . . . The Chinese government issues a ban on the quasi-religious Falun Gong spiritual movement. Followers of the movement gather in Beijing before being hustled away by police.

A	B	C	D	E
Includes developments that affect more than one world region, international organizations, and important meetings of major world leaders.	Includes all domestic and regional developments in Europe, including the Soviet Union, Turkey, Cyprus, and Malta.	Includes all domestic and regional developments in Africa and the Middle East, including Iraq and Iran and excluding Cyprus, Turkey, and Afghanistan.	Includes all domestic and regional developments in Latin America, the Caribbean, and Canada.	Includes all domestic and regional developments in Asia and Pacific nations, extending from Afghanistan through all the Pacific Island, except Hawaii.

U.S. Politics & Social Issues	U.S. Foreign Policy & Defense	U.S. Economy & Environment	Science, Technology, & Nature	Culture, Leisure, & Lifestyle	
The Justice Department announces that the 1998 violent-crime rate decreased 7% from the 1997 rate. The 1998 level, 8.1 million violent crimes, is the lowest recorded since the figure was first measured in 1973. The data does not include homicides.				Pitcher David Cone of the New York Yankees pitches the 16th perfect game in Major League Baseball history in a 6-0 win over the Montreal Expos.... Golfer Paul Lawrie of Scotland wins the 128th British Open.	July 18
California governor Gray Davis (D) signs into law the nation's strictest ban on assault weapons. He also signs a bill that makes it illegal for someone to buy more than one gun per month. Maryland, South Carolina, and Virginia have passed similar laws.... An arbitration panel sets the value of Abraham Zapruder's famous home movie of Pres. John F. Kennedy's 1963 assassination at $16 million when it rules that the federal government should pay that sum to Zapruder's family in return for ownership of the 26-second film. The Assassination Records Review Board awarded the government permanent ownership of the film in 1997.		Hewlett-Packard Co., the world's second-largest computer maker, announces that Carleton Fiorina, 44, has been named the company's president and chief executive. Fiorina is the first woman to run one of the U.S.'s 20 largest publicly held companies.	A heat wave rolls across the midwestern, southern, and eastern states.... Ludwik Gross, 94, cancer researcher who won the prestigious Albert and Mary Lasker Foundation prize in 1974 for his discovery in the 1950s of a virus that induced cancer in mice, dies in New York City of stomach cancer.	A(aron) Stanley Tretick, 77, photographer best known for his candid White House photographs of Pres. John F. Kennedy and his family, dies in Gaithersburg, Maryland, of pneumonia after suffering several strokes in recent years.	July 19
The House approves, 239-185, Republican-sponsored legislation that will authorize $2 billion in annual spending for five years, starting in fiscal 2000, on teacher hiring and training. It will also give states and school districts significant control over how to spend the funding.		The Commerce Department reports that the U.S. trade deficit in May rose to a record high, registering a $21.335 billion gap in trade in goods and services. That is up from April's revised $18.591 billion deficit.	Vice Pres. Al Gore presents the Langley Medal to Neil Armstrong, Buzz Aldrin, and Michael Collins, the crew of *Apollo 11*, the first mission to land men on the moon. The ceremony takes place on the 30th anniversary of the mission's moon landing.... Ocean explorers recover the *Mercury* space capsule that had carried astronaut Virgil (Gus) Grissom to earth after he became the second American to travel in space in 1961.	Public TV officials tell a House subcommittee that many public-TV stations have shared donor information with political organizations, including the Democratic Party. The revelations give new life to efforts by some Republicans to end federal support for public television.	July 20
	The Senate votes, 96-1, to approve legislation that would create a semiautonomous agency within the Energy Department to oversee the nation's nuclear weapons research programs.	Royal Caribbean Cruises Ltd., the world's second-largest cruise line, announces that it will plead guilty to illegally dumping oil and hazardous chemicals at sea and lying about it to the U.S. Coast Guard. The cruise line agrees to pay $18 million in fines in the largest settlement ever recorded against a cruise line.... General Motors recalls 3.5 million pickup trucks, vans and sport-utility vehicles (SUVs) because of potential problems with antilock brakes.		The bodies of John F. Kennedy Jr., his wife Carolyn Bessette Kennedy, and his sister-in-law Lauren Bessette are found and recovered from the Atlantic Ocean following the July 16 plane crash near Martha's Vineyard. More than 10,000 mourners stage a vigil outside the Kennedys' apartment in New York City.	July 21
In Mobile, Alabama, Judge Robert Kendall rejects a class-action settlement by cigarette maker Liggett Group Inc. intended to resolve claims against the company by people made ill by its cigarettes.		The House votes, 223-208, to approve a Republican-sponsored major tax-cutting package that will reduce federal taxes by $792 billion over 10 years.	Data shows that hundreds of thousands of people have lost electrical power in New York City and that 31 of the city's residents have died from the heat wave that started July 4.... As many as 500,000 dead fish are found floating in Virginia's Bullbegger Creek, a tributary of Maryland's Pocomoke River, in the Chesapeake Bay area's worst fish kill in the past decade. Biologists attribute it to oxygen deprivation caused by drought conditions and algae.	The ashes of John and Carolyn Kennedy and of Lauren Bessette are committed to the sea in a private ceremony aboard the U.S. Navy destroyer *Briscoe*.	July 22

F	G	H	I	J
Includes elections, federal-state relations, civil rights and liberties, crime, the judiciary, education, health care, poverty, urban affairs, and population.	Includes formation and debate of U.S. foreign and defense policies, veterans' affairs, and defense spending. (Relations with specific foreign countries are usually found under the region concerned.)	Includes business, labor, agriculture, taxation, transportation, consumer affairs, monetary and fiscal policy, natural resources, and pollution.	Includes worldwide scientific, medical, and technological developments; natural phenomena; U.S. weather; natural disasters; and accidents.	Includes the arts, religion, scholarship, communications media, sports, entertainments, fashions, fads, and social life.

	World Affairs	Europe	Africa & the Middle East	The Americas	Asia & the Pacific
July 23	The foreign ministers of member countries of the Association of Southeast Asian Nations (ASEAN) convene in Singapore for the 32nd annual conference on regional economic and security issues.	British NATO peacekeepers in the Serbian province of Kosovo discover the bodies of 14 Serbian farmers in a field when they investigate the sound of gunfire. The attack on the farmers marks the single worst incidence of violence in Kosovo since NATO entered the province six weeks earlier.	King Hassan II of Morocco, 70, the longest-ruling monarch in the Arab world, who played a key role in the Middle East peace process, dies of a heart attack in Rabat. He is immediately succeeded by his eldest son, Sidi Mohammed, who takes the official title of King Mohammed VI. . . . Sierra Leone officials state that the government has pardoned 98 leaders of a rebel military junta that temporarily held power after a 1997 coup. Those pardoned include a former president, Joseph Momoh.	A U.S. Army reconnaissance plane crashes in southern Colombia.	In Japan, six former executives of the failed Nippon Credit Bank Ltd. are arrested for allegedly concealing bank losses of more than $830 million. Separately, a hijacker reported to be Yuji Nishizawa, 28, fatally stabs Naoyuki Nagashima, the pilot of an All Nippon Airways domestic flight. The pilot disarms the hijacker before dying, and the plane is landed safely by the copilot. Nagashima's death is the first to occur in a hijacking of a domestic Japanese flight. . . . Some 200 Falun Gong followers gather in Beijing's Tiananmen Square to protest the July 22 ban.
July 24			In an offshoot of the July 18 violence in Shagamu, Nigeria, more clashes between the Hausa and Yoruba occur in the northern city of Kano, Nigeria.	In Canada, Quebec nurses end their 26-day-old strike and decide to return to work.	Reports suggest that Chinese authorities have detained more than 4,000 people in Beijing alone since the July 19 beginning of the crackdown. Most of those arrested have been released after being held in stadiums used as detention centers, but some have been charged with serious crimes.
July 25	Several world leaders, including U.S. president Clinton, French president Jacques Chirac, Egyptian president Hosni Mubarak, Jordan's King Abdullah, Israeli president Ezer Weizman, former Israeli prime minister, Shimon Peres, and Palestinian leader Yasser Arafat, attend a funeral procession for King Hassan II of Morocco. Hundreds of thousands of mourners march in Hassan's funeral procession in Rabat.				Thousands of Muslim fundamentalists demonstrate in the streets of Lahore, Pakistan, to protest the Sharif administration's agreement to retreat from Kashmir. . . . Raul S. Manglapus, 80, Filipino politician, dies in Alabang, the Philippines, of cancer.
July 26		Shares of Freeserve PLC, a provider of service on the Internet computer network, debuts on the London Stock Exchange as the first initial public offering (IPO) of a large European Internet company. . . . General Phaidon Gizikis, 82, president of Greece, 1973–74, dies in Athens, Greece, of unreported causes.	Ahmed Qurie, speaker of the Palestinian Legislative Council, makes an historic visit to the Knesset. He is the highest-ranking Palestinian ever to visit Israeli's parliament. . . . Reports confirm that, in the continuing unrest in the Niger River Delta region, youths have taken hostage 64 Shell workers and seized a drilling rig. Separately, the Nigerian government sends troops to restore calm to the clashes that started July 24 in Kano.	Brazilian truck drivers launch a nationwide strike to protest increased roadway tolls, inadequate protections against cargo thieves, recent hikes in fuel prices and what they call draconian penalties for traffic violations.	Indian military officials reveal that their forces have driven Pakistan-backed Muslim insurgents from Indian-held territory in the disputed region of Kashmir. The officials state that they are restoring the 1972 Line of Control that divides Kashmir between India and Pakistan. . . . A human-rights group claims that some 1,200 Chinese government officials who are Falun Gong practitioners were rounded up over the previous weekend.
July 27		In Switzerland, a flash flood kills 21 people engaging in the adventure sport of "canyoning" in the Saxeten Brook near Interlaken. Six survivors of the incident are injured. . . . Amaryllis Fleming, 73, British cellist who became a leading soloist in the 1950s and early 1960s, dies in Nettlebed, England, of unreported causes.	Simon (Mahlathini) Nkabinde, 61, South African musician and singer in a popular Zulu music group during the 1960s and 1970s, dies in Johannesburg, South Africa, of diabetes.		New South Wales premier Bob Carr announces the opening of Australia's first legal heroin-injecting room for a 12-month trial period. The government of the Australian Capital Territory also announces that it will open a trial injecting room.
July 28	The European Court of Human Rights finds France guilty of torturing Ahmed Selmouni, a drug dealer, while in police custody. It is the court's first-ever conviction of a Western European nation on torture charges. The court orders France to pay the victim 613,000 francs ($100,000) in compensation. . . . Nearly 100 countries, international organizations, and aid agencies pledge a total of $2.1 billion to help rebuild Kosovo.			Rescue teams in southern Colombia recover the bodies of four U.S. military personnel from the U.S. reconnaissance plane that crashed July 23. The U.S. soldiers, who were based at Fort Bliss in El Paso, Texas, are the first U.S. military personnel to be killed in an antidrug operation in Colombia. . . . Eight Chinese boys from the group of 123 illegal immigrants found July 20 off of Vancouver Island, Canada, are released to child-welfare authorities.	The Muslim fundamentalist Taliban militia, which controls 90% of Afghanistan, launches an offensive aimed at taking control of the remaining 10% of the country. . . . Reports confirm that Indian Pres. K. R. Narayanan has issued a declaration that bars Balasaheb K. Thackeray, leader of the Hindu nationalist Shiv Sena party, from voting or seeking public office for six years. The start of the ban is backdated to Dec. 11, 1995.

A	B	C	D	E
Includes developments that affect more than one world region, international organizations, and important meetings of major world leaders.	Includes all domestic and regional developments in Europe, including the Soviet Union, Turkey, Cyprus, and Malta.	Includes all domestic and regional developments in Africa and the Middle East, including Iraq and Iran and excluding Cyprus, Turkey, and Afghanistan.	Includes all domestic and regional developments in Latin America, the Caribbean, and Canada.	Includes all domestic and regional developments in Asia and Pacific nations, extending from Afghanistan through all the Pacific Island, except Hawaii.

U.S. Politics & Social Issues	U.S. Foreign Policy & Defense	U.S. Economy & Environment	Science, Technology, & Nature	Culture, Leisure, & Lifestyle	
Frank M(inis) Johnson Jr., 80, U.S. District Court judge in Alabama, 1955–79, and member of the U.S. Fifth Circuit Court of Appeals, 1979–92, dies in Montgomery, Alabama, of pneumonia that developed after a fall a week earlier.			The U.S. space shuttle *Columbia* lifts off from Kennedy Space Center in Cape Canaveral, Florida, to deploy the *Chandra X-ray Observatory*, an orbiting X-ray telescope.		July 23
The Cherokee Nation, the second-largest Native American tribe in the U.S., elects Chad Smith as its new chief.... Reports confirm that Children Requiring a Caring Kommunity (CRACK), a group that claims to want to stop the birth of unwanted children to drug-addicted mothers, is offering $200 to female addicts who undergo sterilization or obtain long-term contraception.			Reports disclose that federal investigators found that the author of two 1997 studies purporting to show a link between electric power lines and cancer had falsified the studies' results.		July 24
The Reform Party chooses Jack Gargan of Florida as chair. Gargan is backed by Minnesota governor Jesse Ventura rather than by the party's founder, Texas billionaire Ross Perot.	Russian premier Sergei Stepashin visits the U.S. in a trip aimed at repairing strained relations between the two countries. The visit is Stepashin's first to the U.S. since he replaced Yevgeny Primakov as premier in May.			In a remarkable comeback, U.S. cyclist Lance Armstrong wins the Tour de France after battling testicular cancer in 1996.... Nolan Ryan, George Brett, Robin Yount, Orlando Cepeda, and Smokey Joe Williams are inducted into the Baseball Hall of Fame.... Martin Zama Agronsky, 84, host of a public affairs program, 1969–97, dies in Washington, D.C. of congestive heart failure.	July 25
The Senate, 53–45, reinstates Senate Rule XVI, which bans adding unrelated legislative "riders" to appropriations bills. The bill is passed in a near-partyline vote.... Cary Stayner, 37, is charged with the murder of Joie Armstrong in California's Yosemite National Park. Stayner reportedly confesses to the February murders of three other tourists in the park.			Data shows that the number of near collisions on airport runways in 1998 has increased by 11%, to 325, since 1997. The figure has risen 75% since 1993.	Walter Jackson Bate, 81, Harvard University English professor who won Pulitzer prizes for his biographies, dies in Boston, Massachusetts, of unreported causes.	July 26
Federal grand juries in Indiana and Georgia indict Jay Ballinger, 36, on charges that he set fire to 17 churches in several states. Ballinger has already been charged with setting fire to 12 other churches.	The House votes, 260-170, to defeat a resolution that would have rejected Pres. Clinton's June decision to renew "normal trade relations" with China for another year.		The U.S. space shuttle *Columbia* lands at Kennedy Space Center in Cape Canaveral, Florida, after carrying out a mission to deploy the *Chandra X-ray Observatory*, an orbiting X-ray telescope. It is the first shuttle mission commanded by a woman, air force colonel Eileen Collins.... The FDA approves the sale of Relenza, a new prescription drug to treat influenza, despite the fact that an advisory panel earlier in the year had recommended the agency reject it. Relenza is the first drug approved to treat both the A and B strains of the flu.	Harry (Sweets) Edison, 83, jazz trumpeter and a key member of the Count Basie Orchestra, 1938–50, dies in Columbus, Ohio, of prostate cancer.	July 27
Carnival Cruise Lines reveals that it recorded 108 accusations of sexual assault and sexual misconduct aboard its ships during a five-year period ending in August 1998.... In a wrongful-death suit, a Philadelphia, Pennsylvania, jury orders fugitive 1960s antiwar activist Ira Einhorn to pay $907 million to the family of Holly Maddux, whom he was convicted of killing in 1997 in absentia. Einhorn is currently fighting extradition from France.			Researchers report that for the first time they have turned healthy human cells into cancer cells by altering their genes.... Russian cosmonauts Viktor Afanasyev and Sergei Avdeyev conduct the last spacewalk from *Mir*.		July 28

F	G	H	I	J
Includes elections, federal-state relations, civil rights and liberties, crime, the judiciary, education, health care, poverty, urban affairs, and population.	*Includes formation and debate of U.S. foreign and defense policies, veterans' affairs, and defense spending. (Relations with specific foreign countries are usually found under the region concerned.)*	*Includes business, labor, agriculture, taxation, transportation, consumer affairs, monetary and fiscal policy, natural resources, and pollution.*	*Includes worldwide scientific, medical, and technological developments; natural phenomena; U.S. weather; natural disasters; and accidents.*	*Includes the arts, religion, scholarship, communications media, sports, entertainments, fashions, fads, and social life.*

	World Affairs	Europe	Africa & the Middle East	The Americas	Asia & the Pacific
July 29	The Financial Reconstruction Commission imposes sanctions on Credit Suisse Group of Switzerland for helping Japanese companies hide losses and for obstructing regulators' investigation of Credit Suisse's practices. Among the penalties leveled against the Swiss banking group, the commission revokes the banking license of its derivatives unit, Credit Suisse Financial Products. It is the first time that Japan has revoked a banking license in the post–World War II era.		In South Africa, hundreds of thousands of state workers stage a two-day strike, the largest public-sector strike since the end of apartheid in 1994. . . . Salisu Buhari, the former speaker of Nigeria's House of Representatives, is convicted of forgery and perjury.	After winning some government concessions, Brazilian truck drivers end a nationwide strike that started July 26. During the strike, in Sao Paulo state, truckers blocking roads clashed with riot police. . . . Rescuers are unable to locate the three other passengers—two Colombian air force officers and a fifth U.S. serviceman—from the U.S. Army reconnaissance plane that crashed July 23. in southern Colombia. They are presumed dead.	A suicide bomber in Colombo, the capital of Sri Lanka, kills Neelam Tiruchelvam, a moderate Tamil politician seeking a legislative solution to the country's 16-year-old conflict. . . . China's public security ministry issues an arrest warrant for Li Hongzhi, the founder of the Falun Gong spiritual movement banned July 22.
July 30	The leaders of 39 Western countries converge in Sarajevo, the capital of Bosnia-Herzegovina, to attend a summit on bolstering political and economic stability in the Balkans. . . . The U.S. and China agree that the U.S. will pay $4.5 million in compensation for the victims of the embassy bombing during an air campaign conducted against Yugoslavia by NATO.	Charles Bennett, 22, a Catholic man, is found murdered in Belfast, Northern Ireland.	In Nigeria, fighting between ethnic Ijaws and Yoruba-speaking Ilajes renews.	FARC guerrillas begin to bombard the western town of Narino, Colombia, with homemade missiles.	Parliament approves the appointment of former foreign minister Rinchinnyamiin Amarjargal, 38, as the new premier of Mongolia.
July 31	A study finds that global carbon emissions declined 0.5% in 1998, marking the first drop in carbon emissions since 1993. Global economic growth expanded by 2.8% in 1998, disproving claims by some governments and private industries that reducing carbon emissions will hinder economic growth. The greatest drop in emissions in 1998 was in China, where emissions declined 3.7%, despite economic growth of 7.2%.				China's coast guard seizes a Taiwanese ship carrying supplies to military forces stationed on a small Taiwan-held island near the coast of China.
Aug. 1				Data show that FARC guerrillas have killed at least 17 people in an attack on the Colombian town of Narino that started July 30, using homemade missiles.	In the Philippines, severe rains begin to fall. . . . Taliban forces seize the opposition's only air base at Bagram in Afghanistan. . . . Nirad Chandra Chaudhuri, 101, Indian writer who in 1951 published *The Autobiography of an Unknown Indian* a massive memoir that received wide praise in the West, dies in Oxford, England, after a stroke.
Aug. 2	NATO troops in Bosnia-Herzegovina arrest alleged Bosnian Serb war criminal Radomir Kovac, 38, in the southeastern town of Foca. The UN International Criminal Tribunal for the Former Yugoslavia indicted Kovac in 1996 for allegedly enslaving and sexually assaulting several Muslim women in Foca in 1992–93, during the Bosnian war.	In a Turkish village in Diyarbakir province, gunmen fire on a bus carrying farm workers, killing six people. Two children are among those killed by gunfire.			Two passenger trains collide head-on in eastern India, killing nearly 300 people and wounding at least 500 others. . . . South Korea and Japan hold joint naval exercises for the first time. . . . In China, democracy advocate Gao Hongming is sentenced to nine years in prison, and Zha Jianguo is given an eight-year sentence. . . . In Afghanistan, the Taliban captures the towns of Charikar, the capital of Parwan province, and Mahmud-i-Raqi, the capital of Kapisa province. . . . Gen. Sunthorn Kongsompong, 68, Thai military commander who led a 1991 coup that toppled the government of Gen. Chatichai Choonhavan, dies in Bangkok, Thailand, of lung cancer.

A	B	C	D	E
Includes developments that affect more than one world region, international organizations, and important meetings of major world leaders.	Includes all domestic and regional developments in Europe, including the Soviet Union, Turkey, Cyprus, and Malta.	Includes all domestic and regional developments in Africa and the Middle East, including Iraq and Iran and excluding Cyprus, Turkey, and Afghanistan.	Includes all domestic and regional developments in Latin America, the Caribbean, and Canada.	Includes all domestic and regional developments in Asia and Pacific nations, extending from Afghanistan through all the Pacific Island, except Hawaii.

U.S. Politics & Social Issues	U.S. Foreign Policy & Defense	U.S. Economy & Environment	Science, Technology, & Nature	Culture, Leisure, & Lifestyle	
California governor Gray Davis (D) announces that the state has agreed to drop its appeals of court rulings that invalidate nearly every provision of Proposition 187, a 1994 ballot measure that denied illegal aliens access to government services. . . . Judge Susan Webber Wright orders Pres. Clinton to pay about $89,000 to cover legal expenses that came from "intentionally false" testimony given concerning his relationship with Monica Lewinsky. It is the first time a sitting president is punished on contempt-of-court charges.	The House passes, 412-8, an appropriations bill allocating $8.4 billion for military construction spending in fiscal 2000.	In the deadliest spree at a U.S. workplace, day trader Mark Barton kills nine people and injures 13 others in two buildings during a shooting rampage in Atlanta, Georgia. It is the third mass shooting in the Atlanta area since May. Barton kills himself, and the bodies of his wife and children are found in his apartment.	*Deep Space 1*, an unmanned spacecraft, flies within 10 miles (16 km) of the asteroid Braille (formerly known as 1992 KD), in the closest encounter of a spacecraft with an asteroid. While the craft fails to aim its camera correctly and sends back to Earth photographs of empty space, the probe successfully collects other data on the asteroid, including observations of heat, infrared light, and charged particles.	(Ina) Anita Carter, 66, Member of the Carter Family music group, dies in Goodlettsville, Tennessee, while suffering from rheumatoid arthritis.	July 29
A Maryland grand jury indicts Linda Tripp, whose secret tapes of her telephone conversations with former White House intern Monica Lewinsky led to Pres. Clinton's 1998 impeachment, on two criminal charges of illegal wiretapping. Tripp is the only central figure in the Lewinsky scandal to be criminally charged.		James Hoffa, president of the International Brotherhood of Teamsters union, hires Edwin Stier, a former state and federal prosecutor, to oversee the Teamsters' anticorruption initiative. . . . The Senate votes, 57-43, to approve a tax-relief package. In contrast to the House's July 22 bill, the Senate's bill is weighted less heavily toward a reduction in personal income taxes. . . . United Air Lines announces it will extend benefits to its employees' same-sex and opposite-sex domestic partners.	The FDA announces measures intended to combat the illegal sale of prescription drugs over the Internet.		July 30
Officials disclose that all 50 states are in compliance with the 1996 welfare act's welfare-to-work requirements.			NASA scientists intentionally crash *Lunar Prospector*, an unmanned spacecraft launched in 1998, onto the moon's surface in an attempt to throw up lunar debris that telescopes can analyze for evidence of water vapor. . . . According to the National Weather Service, rainfall in all of the eastern U.S. during June and July was the lowest in more than a decade.	In Winnipeg, Canada, at the Pan-American Games, heads of 42 delegations issue a statement denouncing the media's and sports agents' treatment of the Cuban delegation, who have been allegedly hounded by sports agents trying to lure Cuban athletes into defecting.	July 31
			Agriculture Secretary Dan Glickman notes that a drought in the East Coast farm belt is the worst in the U.S. since the Great Depression of the 1930s. . . . Data show that the heat wave that started July 19 has resulted in at least 200 deaths and contributed to severe drought conditions in several states. Many cities have recorded temperatures of 100°F (38°C) and above.	Ervin Duggan, president of the Public Broadcasting Service (PBS), tells a meeting of the Television Critics Association that all of the nation's public television stations will immediately stop sharing donor information with political groups.	Aug. 1
The Clinton administration discloses that the number of people on welfare nationwide stands at 7.3 million, down from 14.1 million in 1993, when Pres. Clinton took office, and from 12.2 million in 1996, when the welfare bill was enacted. Separately, a study on the 2.1 million women who left the welfare rolls between 1995 and 1997 finds that welfare reform was largely successful at reducing the welfare rolls but left many of the poor still trapped in poverty.		The EPA places restrictions on two pesticides widely used to protect fruits and vegetables commonly consumed by children. The action is the first major initiative under the 1996 Food Quality Protection Act, which charges the EPA with reassessing its pesticide safety standards.	Agriculture Secretary Dan Glickman declares West Virginia a disaster area due to drought and prolonged heat that scorched fields and ruined crops. The declaration automatically applies also to all 33 counties in Maryland, Virginia, Kentucky, Ohio, and Pennsylvania that borders West Virginia. Pres. Clinton declares six states—Kentucky, Maryland, Ohio, Pennsylvania, Virginia, and West Virginia—agricultural disaster areas due to the drought.	*Hannibal* by Thomas Harris tops the bestseller list. . . . Willie Morris, 64, writer and magazine editor credited with revitalizing *Harper's* in the late 1960s and early 1970s, dies in Jackson, Mississippi, of a heart attack.	Aug. 2

F	G	H	I	J
Includes elections, federal-state relations, civil rights and liberties, crime, the judiciary, education, health care, poverty, urban affairs, and population.	Includes formation and debate of U.S. foreign and defense policies, veterans' affairs, and defense spending. (Relations with specific foreign countries are usually found under the region concerned.)	Includes business, labor, agriculture, taxation, transportation, consumer affairs, monetary and fiscal policy, natural resources, and pollution.	Includes worldwide scientific, medical, and technological developments; natural phenomena; U.S. weather; natural disasters; and accidents.	Includes the arts, religion, scholarship, communications media, sports, entertainments, fashions, fads, and social life.

	World Affairs	Europe	Africa & the Middle East	The Americas	Asia & the Pacific
Aug. 3		Jailed Kurdish leader Abdullah Ocalan calls on his fellow PKK members to "end the armed struggle and withdraw their forces outside the borders of Turkey" starting September 1. It is Ocalan's first-ever formal endorsement of an end to the armed campaign.	Salisu Buhari, convicted July 29 in Nigeria, is sentenced to one year in prison, although he will be able to pay a fine of 2,000 naira ($19) instead.... Abdul Wahab al- Bayati, 73, Iraqi poet known for his innovative style, which departs from classical Arabic poetry in both form and content, dies in Damascus, Syria, of a heart attack after being hospitalized following an asthma attack.		Pres. B. J. Habibie formally ratifies the results of Indonesia's June elections, in which his Golkar party was outpolled by the Indonesian Democratic Party of Struggle (PDI-P), the party of his rival, Megawati Sukarnoputri.... In Afghanistan, a speaker for the Northern Alliance claims as many as 200,000 civilians have fled since July 28.... Dozens of people are killed in a landslide in the Philippines.... A tanker spills 80,000 gallons (300,000 liters) of light crude oil into Sydney Harbor in Australia.
Aug. 4	NATO appoints British defense secretary George Robertson as its secretary general, the organization's highest civilian post.	The German government announces that it will continue to ban the import of British beef while it studies whether the beef is safe to eat.	Rebels take more than 30 hostages, including aid workers and UN observers, during a meeting in which they were to negotiate the release of up to 200 women and children seized during Sierra Leone's civil war.... Iran's conservative Special Court for Clergy orders the country's leading moderate newspaper, *Salam*, closed for five years and suspends its publisher from journalism for three years. The July closure of the paper sparks violent protests.		China Democracy Party member She Wanbao is sentenced to 12 years in prison.... Heavy rains and Typhoon Olga cause the deaths of 42 people in North Korea, at least 63 people in South Korea, 24 people in Vietnam, and five in Thailand.... Officials report that the death toll from the Aug. 2 train collision in India stands at 282.
Aug. 5		In response to the Aug. 3 appeal by Abdullah Ocalan, the Kurdistan Workers' Party (PKK), the main Kurdish rebel group, states that it will end its armed struggle and pull its paramilitary forces out of Turkey. ... Montenegro, Yugoslavia's smaller republic, presents the Yugoslav government with a draft plan that will accord greater independence to Montenegro and place it on equal footing with the country's main republic, Serbia.	P.M. Ehud Barak appoints Nawaf Masalha, an Israeli Arab, to the post of deputy foreign minister, the highest political position attained by an Arab in Israel.... South Africa's Truth and Reconciliation Commission grants amnesty to 17 people for a 1998 bombing in Johannesburg. Included in the pardon are Eugene de Kock, Adriaan Volk, and Gen. Johan van der Merwe. It also grants amnesty to Ontlametse Bernstein Menyatsoe, a member of a black homeland police force whose killing of three white extremists in April 1994 was televised around the world.	Immigration officials free 78 of 123 Chinese illegal immigrants found July 20 smuggled aboard a fishing boat off the coast of Vancouver Island in British Columbia, Canada.	In Afghanistan, the forces of the opposition Northern Alliance, led by Ahmed Shah Massoud, launch a counteroffensive to drive the Taliban out of Parwan and Kapisa provinces, back to within 35 miles (55 km) of Kabul, Afghanistan's capital.
Aug. 6					Liu Xianbin is sentenced to 13 years in prison, the harshest term given to a China Democracy Party member since December 1998.
Aug. 7		Russia launches an air assault against militants seeking an independent Islamic state in Dagestan.			Reports confirm that China's Yangtze River Valley has flooded, causing some 725 deaths and leaving 5.5 million people homeless since June.... In Afghanistan, the opposition Northern Alliance reclaims the Bagram air base and key towns in the provinces of Kunduz and Takhar, recapturing most of the territory it had lost in the Taliban offensive that started July 28.
Aug. 8				In Guyana, Pres. Janet Jagan announces that she is resigning because of illness. P.M. Samuel Hinds of the Civic Group becomes temporary president.	

A	B	C	D	E
Includes developments that affect more than one world region, international organizations, and important meetings of major world leaders.	*Includes all domestic and regional developments in Europe, including the Soviet Union, Turkey, Cyprus, and Malta.*	*Includes all domestic and regional developments in Africa and the Middle East, including Iraq and Iran and excluding Cyprus, Turkey, and Afghanistan.*	*Includes all domestic and regional developments in Latin America, the Caribbean, and Canada.*	*Includes all domestic and regional developments in Asia and Pacific nations, extending from Afghanistan through all the Pacific Island, except Hawaii.*

U.S. Politics & Social Issues	U.S. Foreign Policy & Defense	U.S. Economy & Environment	Science, Technology, & Nature	Culture, Leisure, & Lifestyle	
A study finds that children who participate in the Drug Abuse Resistance Education (DARE) program widely used by elementary schools are about as likely to use drugs and alcohol 10 years later as students who received drug education in ordinary classes.	The Senate unanimously clears an appropriations bill allocating $8.4 billion for military construction spending in fiscal 2000. It is the first of the 13 annual appropriation bills to clear Congress.			Utah businessman David Simmons pleads guilty to a misdemeanor tax violation. The criminal case is the first to stem from a federal probe into allegations that the IOC accepted bribes to vote in favor of Salt Lake City's bid to host the 2002 Olympics.... Richard Olney, 71, who wrote more than 35 cookbooks, is found dead in Sollies-Toucas, France.	Aug. 3
The New Jersey Supreme Court rules that the Boy Scouts of America's exclusion of homosexuals violates the state's antidiscrimination law. The New Jersey court is the first state high court to rule against the Boy Scouts' exclusion of gays.... Data shows that 1.8 million children of single mothers live in families with annual incomes that were less than half the poverty line in 1997, up 374,000, or 26%, from the 1996 figure.				Victor John Mature, 86, film actor who starred in numerous Hollywood movies of the 1940s and 1950s, dies in San Diego County, California, of cancer.	Aug. 4
Alan Eugene Miller allegedly kills three employees at two firms where he worked in Pelham, Alabama.	The Senate confirms Richard Holbrooke as ambassador to the United Nations.	The House, 221-206, and the Senate, 50-49, approve a Republican-designed tax initiative that will reduce federal taxes by $792 billion over 10 years.... The House, 367-49, and Senate, by voice vote, clear a $2.5 billion fiscal 2000 appropriations bill for the legislative branch... The SEC fines brokerage firm Bear Stearns $38.5 million for fraud with now-defunct A.R. Baron & Co. ... American Airlines states it will extend benefits to its employees' same-sex and opposite-sex domestic partners.	New Jersey governor Christine Todd Whitman (R) declares a drought emergency in New Jersey and imposes statewide mandatory restrictions on outdoor water use.	St. Louis Cardinals first baseman Mark McGwire hits his 500th career home run in a game against the San Diego Padres in St. Louis, Missouri. He is the 16th player to have hit at least 500 home runs, and he reaches the milestone in fewer at-bats—5,487—than anyone else in Major League Baseball history.	Aug. 5
A Texas jury orders American Home Products Corp. to pay $23.3 million in damages to Debbie Lovett, who claims that the company failed to warn doctors and patients of a risk of heart damage from a diet drug commonly known as Fen/Phen, it sold until 1997.		The U.S. Ninth Circuit Court of Appeals in San Francisco, California, invalidates a $4.3 billion judgment against Charles Keating Jr. former chair of Lincoln Savings & Loan and a central figure in the S&L scandals of the 1980s.... Edward L. Morgan, 61, who in 1974 pled guilty in a scheme to obtain a fraudulent $576,000 tax deduction for Pres. Nixon, dies in Santa Monica, California, of heart failure.	The CDC reports that death rates from cardiovascular disease fell by 60% between 1950 and 1996.	Kathryn Murray, 92, ballroom dancer who, with her husband Arthur Murray, built a successful chain of dance studios in the 1940s, dies in Honolulu, Hawaii, of unreported causes.	Aug. 6
				Eric Dickerson, Tom Mack, Ozzie Newsome, Billy Shaw, and Lawrence Taylor are inducted into the Pro Football Hall of Fame in Canton, Ohio.	Aug. 7
	John Dortch Lewis, 84, World War II pilot whose repeated, and ultimately successful, attempts to escape from a Nazi German prisoner of war camp are dramatized in the film *The Great Escape* (1963), dies in Goldsboro, North Carolina, of pancreatic cancer.			The Pan-American Games, which attracted more than 5,000 athletes representing 42 countries, close. The U.S. won the most medals, followed by Canada and Cuba.	Aug. 8

F	G	H	I	J
Includes elections, federal-state relations, civil rights and liberties, crime, the judiciary, education, health care, poverty, urban affairs, and population.	Includes formation and debate of U.S. foreign and defense policies, veterans' affairs, and defense spending. (Relations with specific foreign countries are usually found under the region concerned.)	Includes business, labor, agriculture, taxation, transportation, consumer affairs, monetary and fiscal policy, natural resources, and pollution.	Includes worldwide scientific, medical, and technological developments; natural phenomena; U.S. weather; natural disasters; and accidents.	Includes the arts, religion, scholarship, communications media, sports, entertainments, fashions, fads, and social life.

	World Affairs	Europe	Africa & the Middle East	The Americas	Asia & the Pacific
Aug. 9	A Yemeni court in the southern port city of Aden convicts eight Britons—all of Pakistani or Arab origin—and two Algerians for their roles in bomb attacks on the British consulate in Yemen and an Anglican church and hotel in 1998. The trial has strained relations between Yemen and Britain.	Russian president Boris Yeltsin unexpectedly dismisses Premier Sergei Stepashin, less than three months after Stepashin was confirmed in the position. Stepashin is the fourth premier Yeltsin has fired in the past 17 months. Yeltsin names Vladimir Putin, a loyal supporter and 15-year veteran of the Soviet-era KGB intelligence agency, as Stepashin's successor.	Figures confirm that dozens of people have been killed since July 30 in fighting that erupted between ethnic Ijaws and Yoruba-speaking Ilajes in Nigeria. Much of the violence, which occurs 100 miles (160 km) east of Lagos, is sparked over rights to an oil deposit.	In Canada, two workers are killed in a fire at Hub Oil Co. Ltd., a Calgary oil-recycling plant. The blaze forces 2,000 local residents to evacuate their homes.	Hong Kong's Roman Catholic bishop, Joseph Zen, announces that Hong Kong's government has rejected a proposed visit there by Pope John Paul II.
Aug. 10		Lieutenant Colonel Ernesto de Melo Antunes, 66, Portuguese military officer who was the chief architect of a nearly bloodless 1974 coup, known as the "carnation revolution," that ultimately restored democracy in Portugal, dies in Sintra, Portugal, of cancer.	A Palestinian man drives his car into a group of Israeli soldiers outside of Jerusalem, injuring as many as 12 people. Israeli police shoot and kill the driver.... Rebels in Sierra Leone release an estimated 200 civilian hostages—half of whom are children— seized during the war. They also release the last of more than 30 hostages taken Aug. 4.		An Indian fighter jet shoots down a Pakistani naval aircraft, killing all 16 people aboard. The incident occurs in a border area near Pakistan's southern state of Sindh and India's Gujarat state.
Aug. 11	The UN Security Council approves the appointment of Swiss lawyer Carla Del Ponte as chief prosecutor for the international war crimes tribunals for Rwanda and the former Yugoslavia.... A total solar eclipse visible in Europe and in western and southern Asia occurs. The moon's shadow traces a path—112 kilometers (70 miles) wide at its widest point—across the Atlantic and then to the southeast over Europe, Turkey, Iraq, Iran, Pakistan, and India.			An unmarked ship unloads 131 smuggled Chinese immigrants on a remote beach in the Queen Charlotte Islands before being seized by the RCMP. It is the second major case of Chinese migrant smuggling in Canada in three weeks.... Bharrat Jagdeo, 35, is sworn in as president of Guyana. He is the youngest head of state in the Americas.	Pakistan fires surface-to-air missiles at Indian aircraft flying to the crash site of the Pakistani plane downed Aug. 10. No casualties are reported.... Data shows that at least 160 people have died in floods and landslides caused by nearly two weeks of torrential rains in the Philippines.
Aug. 12	UN officials announce that the International Criminal Tribunal for Rwanda in Arusha, Tanzania, has indicted a woman, Pauline Nyiramasuhuko, for rape. Nyiramasuhuko was the minister of family and women's affairs during the 1994 massacres of Tutsis and moderate Hutus in Rwanda and is accused of allowing her subordinates to rape Tutsi women. She is the first woman to be tried in an international tribunal for a rape charge as a crime against humanity.	Turkey's predominantly secular parliament approves legislation that will allow prominent Islamist Necmettin Erbakan to reenter politics. The government in January 1998 banned Erbakan from politics for five years.... David Maurice Graham, 87, BBC broadcaster and commentator, 1939–71, dies at an undisclosed location of unreported causes.	UNICEF finds that child mortality rates for children under the age of five have nearly doubled since the mid-1980s in areas under the control of Iraqi president Saddam Hussein.	Jean Drapeau, 83, mayor of Montreal, Canada, 1954–57, 1960–86, dies in Montreal of unreported causes.	
Aug. 13		Ignatz Bubis, 72, whose father, brother, and sister died in a Nazi concentration camp during World War II and who was elected president of the Central Council of Jews in Germany in 1992, dies in Frankfurt, Germany, of unreported causes.		Jaime Garzon, 39, Colombia's most popular political satirist, is shot and killed by two motorcycle-riding gunmen on a street in Bogota, the capital.	South Korean president Kim Dae Jung grants amnesty to some 3,000 convicts, including Kim Hyun Chul, the son of former president Kim Young Sam. The amnesty includes 56 political prisoners and is granted to mark the 54th anniversary of the end of Japanese rule over the Korean peninsula.
Aug. 14		Violent protests erupt throughout Northern Ireland as Protestant activists hold traditional parades in Londonberry, Belfast, and Lurgan. The controversial parades commemorate Protestants' victories in 17th-century battles that determined the sovereignty of Northern Ireland. In Londonderry, Catholic protesters hurl bottles, bricks, and gasoline bombs at riot police. In Belfast, scuffles injure several people, including 19 officers. Five people are arrested in Lurgan.... Russia announces that it has bombed suspected rebel bases inside Chechnya.	In Iran, a group of five armed men and women abduct four European tourists—two Spanish priests, another Spaniard, and an Italian—and an Iranian citizen from a hotel in the southeastern city of Kerman.	Thousands of mourners gather in Bogota's Plaza de Bolivar to pay their respects to Jaime Garzon, killed Aug. 13, and to display indignation at the rising tide of violence in Colombia.	
	A Includes developments that affect more than one world region, international organizations, and important meetings of major world leaders.	**B** Includes all domestic and regional developments in Europe, including the Soviet Union, Turkey, Cyprus, and Malta.	**C** Includes all domestic and regional developments in Africa and the Middle East, including Iraq and Iran and excluding Cyprus, Turkey, and Afghanistan.	**D** Includes all domestic and regional developments in Latin America, the Caribbean, and Canada.	**E** Includes all domestic and regional developments in Asia and Pacific nations, extending from Afghanistan through all the Pacific Island, except Hawaii.

U.S. Politics & Social Issues	U.S. Foreign Policy & Defense	U.S. Economy & Environment	Science, Technology, & Nature	Culture, Leisure, & Lifestyle	
Pres. Clinton awards the Presidential Medal of Freedom to former president Jimmy and his wife, Rosalynn Carter, at the Carter Center, a human rights organization in Atlanta, Georgia, founded by the Carters.	The Department of Commerce decides it will not proceed with a formal investigation of oil-dumping allegations lodged in June against Mexico, Venezuela, Saudi Arabia, and Iraq. . . . A van carrying 15 farmworkers home from tomato fields near Five Points, California, crashes, killing 13 of the van's passengers and injuring the other two. All of the crash victims are Mexican nationals. The accident raises concerns about dangerous working conditions faced by migrant workers from Mexico and other Latin American nations.	US Airways Group Inc. announces that it will extend benefits to its employees' same-sex and opposite-sex domestic partners.			Aug. 9
Buford Furrow Jr., a white supremacist gunman, wounds three children and two staff members at a Jewish community center in Los Angeles. He then kills Joseph Ileto, a letter carrier. . . . A study suggests that the current decline in crime is linked to the legalization of abortion. The authors argue that women who had abortions in the 1970s came from demographic groups that suggest that, based upon statistics, their children would have been more likely to commit crimes.				Jennifer Mary Paterson, 71, British cook and cohost of a cooking show syndicated in 10 countries, dies in London, England, of lung cancer. . . . Whitney Darrow Jr., 89, cartoonist who published more than 1,500 cartoons in the *New Yorker* magazine, dies in Burlington, Vermont, of unreported causes.	Aug. 10
The Kansas Board of Education votes to remove the theory of evolution from the state's science curriculum. The decision neither outlaws the teaching of evolution nor requires the teaching of creationism. . . . Buford Furrow Jr., the white supremacist who went on a shooting spree Aug. 10, surrenders in Las Vegas, Nevada. . . . A judge in Georgia rules that Thomas (T. J.) Solomon 15, who allegedly shot six students during a high-school shooting spree, will be tried as an adult.	Pres. Clinton offers to commute the sentences of 16 members of the Armed Forces of National Liberation (FALN), a Puerto Rican independence group that waged a bombing campaign in the U.S. from 1974 to 1983.		A tornado strikes Salt Lake City, Utah, killing one person and injuring more than 100 others. The lone fatality is the first tornado-related death ever reported in the state. . . . R(obert) T(homas) Jones, 89, aerospace scientist who designed innovative swept-back airplane wings in 1944 and who, in 1981, received the Smithsonian Institution's Langley medal, dies in Los Altos Hills, California, of unreported causes.	Pres. Clinton awards the Presidential Medal of Freedom, the nation's highest civilian honor, to eight recipients in a ceremony at the White House.	Aug. 11
	Energy Secretary Bill Richardson requests punishment for Siegfried Hecker, Terry Craig, and Robert Vrooman, three senior officials of Los Alamos National Laboratory, New Mexico, for failing to adequately enforce security at the lab, where nuclear weapons secrets were allegedly stolen and given to China.	Former Democratic National Committee (DNC) fund-raiser John Huang pleads guilty to a single felony count of conspiring to defraud the FEC in relation to two improper donations he arranged for California Democrats. U.S. district judge Richard Paez sentences Huang to one year's probation and orders him to pay a $10,000 fine and to perform 500 hours of community service.		Sir John Hale, 75, British historian of the Renaissance, dies in London, England, after suffering a debilitating stroke in 1992.	Aug. 12
John Hinckley Jr., the man who shot Pres. Ronald Reagan in 1981, takes a day trip escorted by Secret Service agents from the mental hospital in Washington, D.C., where he has been confined for the past 17 years.	The Defense Department unveils guidelines to enhance compliance with the Clinton administration's "don't ask, don't tell" policy, which permits homosexuals to serve in the military as long as they do not reveal their sexual orientation. The number of service members dismissed annually for being homosexual—which was 1,145 in 1998—has nearly doubled since the policy went into effect in 1994.	Alaska files a civil suit against the cruise-ship line Royal Caribbean for dumping chemicals in the environmentally sensitive Inside Passage and other Alaskan waters.	Nathaniel Kleitman, 104, pioneering sleep researcher who, with a colleague in 1953, discovered a stage of sleep, rapid eye movement (REM), that has close associations with dreaming, dies in Los Angeles, California.	Steffi Graf, a 22-time Grand Slam champion, announces her retirement from tennis, ending an illustrious 17-year career.	Aug. 13
		(Joseph) Lane Kirkland, 77, president of the AFL-CIO labor federation, 1979–95, who was awarded the Presidential Medal of Freedom in 1994, dies in Washington, D.C., of lung cancer.		Harold Henry (Pee Wee) Reese, 81, Hall of Fame baseball player considered a consummate team leader, dies in Louisville, Kentucky, while suffering from lung cancer.	Aug. 14

F	G	H	I	J
Includes elections, federal-state relations, civil rights and liberties, crime, the judiciary, education, health care, poverty, urban affairs, and population.	*Includes formation and debate of U.S. foreign and defense policies, veterans' affairs, and defense spending. (Relations with specific foreign countries are usually found under the region concerned.)*	*Includes business, labor, agriculture, taxation, transportation, consumer affairs, monetary and fiscal policy, natural resources, and pollution.*	*Includes worldwide scientific, medical, and technological developments; natural phenomena; U.S. weather; natural disasters; and accidents.*	*Includes the arts, religion, scholarship, communications media, sports, entertainments, fashions, fads, and social life.*

	World Affairs	Europe	Africa & the Middle East	The Americas	Asia & the Pacific
Aug. 15		Chechen president Aslan Maskhadov declares a month-long state of emergency.... At least 10,000 people gather in Omagh, Northern Ireland, to commemorate the first anniversary of a bombing that killed 29 people.... Patrick Joseph (Paddy) Devlin, 74, Northern Ireland politician who, in 1970, cofounded the Social Democratic and Labour Party (SDLP), dies of complications of diabetes.... Sir Hugh Maxwell Casson, 89, British architect and president of the Royal Academy of Arts, 1976–84, dies in London.	Rebel allies Uganda and Rwanda begin fighting each other over control of the northern Congolese city of Kisangani.		Chinese authorities in Qinghai province arrest Daja Meston of the U.S. and Gabriel Lafitte of Australia, both Tibetan-rights advocates.
Aug. 16	Japan and the U.S. sign an agreement to conduct joint research on developing a missile-defense system. That proposal is vigorously criticized by China, North Korea, and Russia.... The IMF demands that Indonesian president B. J. Habibie conduct a probe of a banking scandal involving one of Indonesia's largest private banks and the ruling Golkar Party. The scandal threatens the continued distribution of more than $40 billion in loans from the IMF.	Russia's parliament confirms Vladimir V. Putin as premier.	Ali Hassan Deeb, also known as Abu Hassan, is killed outside the southern port city of Sidon, Lebanon, when two roadside bombs are detonated simultaneously, striking his vehicle. The Israeli media reports that Deeb was on Israel's "most wanted" list for his role in Hezbollah attacks against Israeli forces in Lebanon.		
Aug. 17		A powerful earthquake strikes northwestern Turkey, killing thousands of people and devastating several major cities. The tremor measures 7.4 on the Richter scale, and the quake's epicenter is located just south of Izmit, an industrial city of nearly 1 million people about 55 miles (90 km) east of Istanbul. The earthquake touches off a massive fire at Turkey's largest oil refinery. Turkish premier Bulent Ecevit characterizes the quake as the worst natural disaster he has ever seen.	Rebel allies Uganda and Rwanda agree to a cease-fire in the fighting that started Aug. 15. During the battle, dozens of people were killed, and Rwanda reportedly seized control of the Congolese town of Kisangani.... The Shi'ite Muslim guerrilla group Hezbollah (Party of God) launches a raid against Israeli forces in Israel's self-declared security zone in southern Lebanon.		Singapore's Presidential Elections Committee announces that S. R. Nathan, 75, is the only candidate eligible for an election scheduled for Aug. 28, and that the election is therefore canceled.
Aug. 18			The UN discloses that Somalia, which has no working government, has become a "black hole" of anarchy.		In light of the Aug. 17 declaration regarding the canceled election, S. R. Nathan, a former diplomat, is proclaimed Singapore's new president.... The Australian Supreme Court rules that the leadership of One Nation, a controversial ultranationalist party, fraudulently registered the party in 1997.
Aug. 19	In response to the Aug. 17 earthquake in Turkey, at least 15 foreign countries, including the U.S., Algeria, Egypt, Israel, Japan, Jordan, and Pakistan have sent workers, equipment, or financial assistance. Several European countries, even Greece, a country with a bitter historical rivalry with Turkey, have sent aid as well.	An estimated 50,000–150,000 Serbs attend a rally in Belgrade, the capital of both Yugoslavia and Serbia, to demand the resignation of Yugoslav president Slobodan Milosevic. It is the largest rally in the capital since protests held in 1996–97 against Milosevic, who was then the president of Serbia.... In Turkey, initial estimates state that the Aug. 17 earthquake caused some $40 billion in damage. In Izmit, 1,700 people are confirmed dead, and another 3,000 are wounded. The massive fire at Turkey's largest oil refinery begins to be brought under control by firefighters.		Venezuela's constitutional assembly declares a "judicial emergency" and grants itself the power to assess and purge members of the nation's judiciary, including Supreme Court justices. Under the decree, the assembly assumes the right to suspend or dismiss judges accused of corruption or other misdeeds. Roughly half of Venezuela's 4,700 judges face such allegations.	In light of the Australian Supreme Court's Aug. 18 ruling, One Nation, a controversial ultranationalist party, is officially decertified as a political party in the state of Queensland.
Aug. 20	The International Criminal Tribunal for Rwanda in Arusha, Tanzania, charges a Rwandan Roman Catholic bishop, Augustin Misago, 56, for his alleged role in the 1994 genocide in Rwanda.	Data reveals that the total number of people confirmed dead from the Aug. 17 earthquake in Turkey stands at 10,059. More than 45,000 people were injured in the quake, and as many as 35,000 others remain missing.			Three major Japanese banks, DaiIchi Kangyo Bank Ltd. (DKB), Fuji Bank Ltd., and Industrial Bank of Japan Ltd. (IBJ), announce that they will merge to form what will be the world's largest financial institution in terms of assets.....Tens of thousands of people demonstrate in Manila, the Philippines, to protest Pres. Estrada's attempts to remove a constitutional provision that limits a president to one six-year term.

A	B	C	D	E
Includes developments that affect more than one world region, international organizations, and important meetings of major world leaders.	*Includes all domestic and regional developments in Europe, including the Soviet Union, Turkey, Cyprus, and Malta.*	*Includes all domestic and regional developments in Africa and the Middle East, including Iraq and Iran and excluding Cyprus, Turkey, and Afghanistan.*	*Includes all domestic and regional developments in Latin America, the Caribbean, and Canada.*	*Includes all domestic and regional developments in Asia and Pacific nations, extending from Afghanistan through all the Pacific Island, except Hawaii.*

U.S. Politics & Social Issues	U.S. Foreign Policy & Defense	U.S. Economy & Environment	Science, Technology, & Nature	Culture, Leisure, & Lifestyle	
Data shows that the federal and state prison population increased 4.8% during 1998, lower than the average rate of 6.7% per year since 1990. At the end of 1998, there were 1,302,019 inmates in state and federal prisons. There were also 592,462 adult inmates in local jails. Thus, the total number of people incarcerated in federal, state, and local facilities was more than 1.8 million.				Golfer Tiger Woods wins the PGA Championship at Medinah in Medinah, Illinois, in a thrilling one-stroke, victory over Spaniard Sergio García. García, 19, is the youngest person ever to play in the championship. Woods, 23, is the youngest player to have won two major tournaments.	Aug. 15
		DaimlerChrysler AG recalls more than 2 million vehicles for faulty doors and fuel pumps.			Aug. 16
	Pres. Clinton signs an appropriations bill allocating $8.4 billion for military construction spending in fiscal 2000. It is the first of the 13 annual appropriation bills to clear Congress and become law.		*Cassini*, an unmanned spacecraft launched to orbit the planet Saturn, flies within 727 miles (1,170 km) of Earth at a speed of 35,000 miles per hour (56,000 kmph) in a maneuver that boosts the craft's speed for its journey to Saturn. *Cassini*, a joint U.S.-European mission, was launched in 1997 and is scheduled to reach Saturn in 2004.		Aug. 17
		Metropolitan Life Insurance Co. agrees to pay as much as $1.7 billion to compensate millions of customers who allege that its agents used deceptive sales practices, including providing misleading information about the cost of policies. The fund settles more than a dozen lawsuits and three class-action suits brought against Met Life.			Aug. 18
Texas governor George W. Bush, the front-runner for the Republican presidential nomination in 2000, indicates that he has not used illegal drugs at any time in the past 25 years. Bush makes the statement in response to a growing media storm over rumors that he used cocaine. It is the first major controversy in Bush's campaign. . . . The CDC reveals that a drug-resistant strain of staph bacterium has killed four children and made more than 200 other people sick in Minnesota and North Dakota since 1997. The drug-resistant bacterium previously was thought to be confined to hospitals and other medical facilities.	Reports disclose that federal investigators are examining whether Russian criminals laundered billions of dollars of illegally obtained money through accounts at the Bank of New York Co. The case is believed to be one of the largest money-laundering operations ever uncovered in the U.S.	The Commerce Department reports that the U.S. trade deficit in June rose to a new high, recording a $24.62 billion gap in trade in goods and services. That marks an increase of $3.45 billion from May's revised $21.17 billion deficit. . . . A state court in Raleigh, North Carolina, approves the creation of a fund to aid tobacco farmers who face a reduced market following cigarette makers' 1998 settlement of states' smoking-related lawsuits.		In a historic pact, the Evangelical Lutheran Church in America approves a proposal to unite with the Episcopal Church. . . . Archbishop Spyridon resigns as leader of the Greek Orthodox Church of America. Metropolitan Demetrios Trakatellis is selected to succeed him. . . . Kim Perrot, 32, a WBNA point guard, dies of lung cancer in Houston, Texas.	Aug. 19
Washington, D.C., adopts a plan to track the number of new cases of HIV infection by anonymous numbers rather than the patients' names.	Director of Central Intelligence George Tenet reveals that he has suspended the security clearance of his predecessor, John Deutch, for improperly storing classified documents on his personal computer during his tenure as director. It is the first time in the 52-year history of the CIA that a former director has lost the right to access the agency's classified data.	The Department of the Interior removes the peregrine falcon from the endangered-species list, due to its steady population growth. There are currently more than 1,650 peregrine breeding pairs in North America, up from 39 breeding pairs at the peregrines' low point in 1970.	A study of 160 patients treated in various ways with pig tissue finds that the patients are not infected with a virus commonly found in pigs. The results are seen as evidence that the transplant of pig organs into humans may not result in infection by pig-borne viruses not previously found in humans.		Aug. 20
F	G	H	I	J	
Includes elections, federal-state relations, civil rights and liberties, crime, the judiciary, education, health care, poverty, urban affairs, and population.	Includes formation and debate of U.S. foreign and defense policies, veterans' affairs, and defense spending. (Relations with specific foreign countries are usually found under the region concerned.)	Includes business, labor, agriculture, taxation, transportation, consumer affairs, monetary and fiscal policy, natural resources, and pollution.	Includes worldwide scientific, medical, and technological developments; natural phenomena; U.S. weather; natural disasters; and accidents.	Includes the arts, religion, scholarship, communications media, sports, entertainments, fashions, fads, and social life.	

	World Affairs	Europe	Africa & the Middle East	The Americas	Asia & the Pacific
Aug. 21					An antiterrorism court convicts and sentences to death Ahmed Saeed, 29, and Muhammad Saleem, 39, for the shooting deaths of four U.S. businessmen and their Pakistani driver in a November 1997 ambush in Karachi, Pakistan. Two other gunmen believed to have participated in the ambush reportedly remain at large.... Tibetan-rights advocate Gabriel Lafitte of Australia, who was arrested Aug. 15 in China, is released and put onto a plane to Australia.
Aug. 22		Patrick Lowry Cole Holwell Rance, 81, British cheese merchant and author of the definitive work on his nation's traditional raw-milk cheeses, dies in London, England.	Pres. Ali Abdullah Saleh announces that Yemen's first direct presidential elections will be held in September.		In severe winds and rain caused by a typhoon, a China Airlines jet flips over and burst into flames after crash landing at Hong Kong International Airport, killing two people and injuring more than 200 others.
Aug. 23		In Kosovo, hundreds of ethnic Albanians block roads leading to the town of Orahavoc to prevent Russian troops from taking up assigned positions.... Rebels announce that they are withdrawing from Dagestan to redeploy their troops.... German chancellor Gerhard Schroeder formally inaugurates Berlin as Germany's capital for the first time since the end of World War II.... Hundreds of Islamic militants enter Kyrgyzstan from Tajikistan and take 13 hostages, the start of an offensive in which they seize several villages.			South Korean defense minister Cho Sung Tae visits Beijing, China's capital, for talks with his Chinese counterpart, Chi Haotian. The talks are the first between defense ministers of the two countries, enemies during the 1950–53 Korean War.
Aug. 24		Alexandre Lagoya, 70, French classical guitarist who achieved renown both as a soloist and as part of a duo, dies in Paris, France, after a long illness.			In the southern town of Kandahar, Afghanistan, a truck bomb explodes near the home of Sheik Mohammed Omar, the leader of the Taliban militia, which controls most of Afghanistan. The blast kills between seven and 10 soldiers and civilians and injures scores of other people.
Aug. 25	Austrian police arrest the chief of staff of the Bosnian Serb army, Gen. Momir Talic, on allegations that he committed war crimes during the 1992–95 war in Bosnia-Herzegovina. His capture marks the first time that a suspected Bosnian war criminal is arrested outside the territory of the former Yugoslavia.	The official death toll from the Aug. 17 earthquake in Turkey stands at 12,514.... The Russian military states that it has driven Islamic militants out of Dagestan, ending nearly three weeks of fighting. Russia claims that 47 of its soldiers and 12 policemen were killed. A Chechen official contends that 38 rebel fighters died. Each camp claims that the other lost as many as 1,000 troops.		In Venezuela, a power struggle between Congress and the constitutional assembly begins when the assembly declares a "legislative emergency" and takes over most of Congress's functions.	
Aug. 26	The leaders of Russia, China, Kazakhstan, Kyrgyzstan, and Tajikistan pledge to bolster cooperation, economic integration, and regional security along their borders.	The official death toll from the Aug. 17 earthquake in Turkey reaches 13,009. The number of people confirmed injured stands at about 26,000, and another 35,000 are thought to be missing.... Four Northern Ireland teenagers are ordered, through an intermediary, to leave the province by the end of Aug. 28, or they will be killed. The order and the death threats are widely attributed to the IRA.		Tens of thousands of demonstrators marched in Brasilia, the capital of Brazil, to call for the resignation of Pres. Fernando Henrique Cardoso.	In Dili, East Timor's capital, at least six people are killed in clashes with militias. Separately, the Habibie administration states it will release from house arrest East Timorese independence leader Jose Alexandre Gusmão, popularly known as Xanana.... Tibetan-rights advocate Daja Meston of the U.S., who was arrested Aug. 15, is allowed to leave China after consenting to a confession.... Australia's Parliament approves an historic motion that expresses regret for mistreatment of Australia's aborigines and Torres Strait Islanders. It is the first such national expression.

A	B	C	D	E
Includes developments that affect more than one world region, international organizations, and important meetings of major world leaders.	Includes all domestic and regional developments in Europe, including the Soviet Union, Turkey, Cyprus, and Malta.	Includes all domestic and regional developments in Africa and the Middle East, including Iraq and Iran and excluding Cyprus, Turkey, and Afghanistan.	Includes all domestic and regional developments in Latin America, the Caribbean, and Canada.	Includes all domestic and regional developments in Asia and Pacific nations, extending from Afghanistan through all the Pacific Island, except Hawaii.

U.S. Politics & Social Issues	U.S. Foreign Policy & Defense	U.S. Economy & Environment	Science, Technology, & Nature	Culture, Leisure, & Lifestyle	
A study indicates that the poorest Americans may have grown poorer since the enactment of federal welfare-reform legislation. The study finds that, on average, the poorest 20% of those households had annual incomes of $8,047 in 1997, down $577 from 1995. The poorest 10% of families in the study saw their annual incomes drop by an average of $814 over the same period.		Pres. Clinton announces the completion of a deal to acquire roughly 9,000 acres (3,600 hectares) of land adjacent to Yellowstone National Park's northern border. The government purchased control of the land from a church for $13 million.		Leo Castelli (born Leo Krause), 91, art dealer who greatly influenced contemporary American art and helped U.S. artists gain international acclaim, dies in New York City of unreported causes.	Aug. 21
Statistics show that the combined federal, state, and local adult correctional population reached a record high of 5.9 million people in 1998. The figure includes all people incarcerated, on probation, or on parole. At the end of 1998, the number of adults on probation, or parole was greater than 4 million for the first time. The 1998 figure of 4.1 million is an increase from 3.2 million at the end of 1990.			U.S. boaters and Japanese drivers encounter navigational problems when the Global Positioning System's current calendar resets back to week zero.	Minnesota governor Jesse Ventura referees a televised World Wrestling Federation match in Minneapolis, Minnesota. Ventura, a former professional wrestler, responds to critics of his appearance at the event by saying, "I'm proud of wrestling. I'm proud I was a wrestler, and I'm proud to be here tonight."	Aug. 22
The California Supreme Court overturns a ballot initiative that backs expanding legalized gambling on Indian lands. . . . Judge Allen Yenior orders Timothy Boomer, who violated an 1897 Michigan law against swearing in front of children, to four days of community service and to either spend three days in jail or pay a $75 fine. . . . Reports indicate that Microsoft chair William Gates and his wife, Melinda Gates, donated $6 billion to the Bill and Melinda Gates Foundation, increasing its endowment to more than $17 billion as the U.S.'s largest charitable foundation.	The money-laundering investigation revealed Aug. 19 widens with a report that some of the money may have been diverted from International Monetary Fund (IMF) loans intended to bolster Russia's economy.			Martha Rountree, 87, television producer and a cocreator of *Meet the Press*, dies in Washington, D.C., while suffering from Alzheimer's disease. . . . Norman Wexler, 73, screenwriter whose film credits include *Serpico* (1973) and *Saturday Night Fever* (1977), dies in Washington, D.C., after a heart attack.	Aug. 23
Judge Solomon Oliver Jr. issues a temporary injunction suspending a state-funded school voucher program in Cleveland, Ohio, arguing that the program might violate the constitutionally mandated separation of church and state because it allows the use of government funds to pay for tuition at parochial schools. The decision is considered particularly notable because it temporarily blocks a voucher program in place for several years.		The Federal Reserve Board's Open Market Committee votes to raise the federal-funds rate by a quarter of a percentage point, to 5.25% from 5%. The panel also boosts the discount rate by a quarter of a percentage point, to 4.75% from 4.5%. In response, three of the nation's largest banks—First Union Corp., Bank of America Corp., and Bank One Corp.—announce that they will increase their prime lending rate to 8.25% from 8%.			Aug. 24
The FBI admits that the agency used military-type pyrotechnic tear gas canisters during a 1993 assault on the compound of the Branch Davidian cult, near Waco, Texas. However, officials affirm that the canisters did not start the deadly fire that ended the assault in which some 80 cult members died.	After a pair of two-year investigations, federal agents arrest dozens of American Airlines employees who work at Miami International Airport in Florida for allegedly participating in a smuggling ring. Authorities indict 58 people in the investigation.	The Dow closes at a record high of 11,326.04. That marks the second record high of the month and the 31st record high in 1999.	A study finds that women infected with HIV, the virus that causes AIDS, have a 10% chance of transmitting the virus to an infant through breastfeeding over two years. It is the first study to show that HIV can be passed on through milk for as long as a mother breast-feeds, although the risk is greater in the child's earlier months.		Aug. 25
NYC mayor Rudolph Giuliani (R) announces that the city is denying the organizers of the Million Youth March, a rally for black youth which erupted in violence in 1998, a permit because they failed to submit a proper application on time.		In Los Angeles, California, Judge Ernest Williams reduces a punitive damages judgment that a jury handed down against General Motors in July to $1.09 billion, from $4.8 billion. . . . Raymond Vernon (born Raymond Visotsky), 85, U.S. economist who worked for the federal government on such projects as the Marshall Plan, which guided the economic revival of Europe after World War II, dies of cancer in Cambridge, Massachusetts.		A Michigan jury convicts Jonathan Schmitz, who killed Scott Amedure, a fellow male guest on *The Jenny Jones Show*, of second-degree murder. Schmitz was convicted in 1996, but that verdict was overturned on appeal.	Aug. 26

F	G	H	I	J
Includes elections, federal-state relations, civil rights and liberties, crime, the judiciary, education, health care, poverty, urban affairs, and population.	*Includes formation and debate of U.S. foreign and defense policies, veterans' affairs, and defense spending. (Relations with specific foreign countries are usually found under the region concerned.)*	*Includes business, labor, agriculture, taxation, transportation, consumer affairs, monetary and fiscal policy, natural resources, and pollution.*	*Includes worldwide scientific, medical, and technological developments; natural phenomena; U.S. weather; natural disasters; and accidents.*	*Includes the arts, religion, scholarship, communications media, sports, entertainments, fashions, fads, and social life.*

	World Affairs	Europe	Africa & the Middle East	The Americas	Asia & the Pacific
Aug. 27				Hundreds of supporters of Pres. Hugo Chavez Frias gather in front of the Congress building in Caracas, the capital of Venezuela, to prevent members of Congress from convening a special session.... Archbishop Helder Pessoa Camara, 90, Brazilian cleric who was in the vanguard of the Roman Catholic liberation theology movement in Latin America in the 1960s and 1970s, dies in Olinda, Brazil.	
Aug. 28		The four Northern Ireland teenagers ordered Aug. 26 to leave the province depart on a ferry bound for Scotland.	Hutu rebels attack Bujumbura, Burundi's capital, killing 38 civilians. Many of the victims are children.		
Aug. 29		The IRA allegedly orders two teenagers to leave the province, under threat of execution.... Russian forces begin a campaign against the Wahhabis, a puritanical Islamic sect with headquarters in central Dagestan.	Hutu rebels clash with the army in fighting that results in 20 Hutu fatalities. The Hutu rebels target the minority Tutsi population in Bujumbura, Burundi's capital, burning houses and shooting civilians. Government troops drove the rebels from the capital.		
Aug. 30			Jordanian security forces raid and close the offices of three senior Hamas leaders in Amman, Jordan's capital, and arrest 12 members of the group.... An orthodox Jewish couple is found stabbed to death near the Israeli-West Bank border.	Venezuela's constitutional assembly, a body dominated by supporters of Pres. Hugo Chavez Frias, approves measures that effectively strip the opposition-controlled Congress of the last of its powers.	Hundreds of thousands of East Timorese turn out for a UN-sponsored referendum that will determine whether East Timor becomes an autonomous region within Indonesia or an independent nation. More than 98% of the eligible voters reportedly turn out for the poll, defying intimidation and threats of retaliation from pro-Indonesia militias. The only election-day death occurs in the village of Ermera, where Joel Lopez Gomes, an East Timorese UN worker, is stabbed to death.
Aug. 31		In Russia, an explosion in Moscow's Manezh shopping mall injures 41 people but causes no fatalities.... Two moderate earthquakes strike the area hit by the August 17 quake in Turkey, killing at least one person. In Izmit, seven buildings collapse, and 166 people are treated for injuries.... A small crowd gathers outside Kensington Palace in London to mark the second anniversary of Princess Diana's death.	The two rival factions of one of the Democratic Republic of the Congo's main rebel groups sign a peace agreement aimed at ending the country's civil war. Infighting among members of the group, the Congolese Rally for Democracy (RCD), had prevented both the RCD and the Movement for the Liberation of Congo (MLC), the other main rebel group, from signing an international peace accord in July.... The group of four European tourists abducted Aug. 14 in Iran are released unharmed.	A passenger jet crashes just after takeoff at Jorge Newberry Airport in Buenos Aires, the capital of Argentina, killing at least 74 people. It is one of the deadliest aviation disasters in Argentina's history.	In Indonesia, militia members resume their campaign of violence, signaling that they will not accept a vote for independence in East Timor. Eurico Guterres, commander of the Aitarak militia, states that his group will block those who voted for independence from leaving the territory.
Sept. 1		Yugoslav president Slobodan Milosevic pardons and frees Peter Wallace and Steve Pratt, Australian aid workers convicted as spies in May.... An Italian magistrate indicts four military generals and five other people in connection with a 1980 airplane crash.... A French magistrate rules that Alois Brunner, a convicted Nazi war criminal, will be tried for a third time in 2000.	Ethiopia and Eritrea fight a nine-hour battle at Zalambessa, some 220 miles (350 km) north of Addis Ababa.... The military wing of Hamas claims responsibility for the killing of a Jewish couple found stabbed to death Aug. 30.... An airplane carrying 10 U.S. tourists, a Tanzanian tour guide, and a pilot crashes on Mount Meru, Tanzania, killing all those on board.	Mireya Moscoso de Gruber is sworn in as Panama's new president at National Stadium in Panama City, the capital. Moscoso is the first female president in Panama's history.... Reports reveal that at least 10 of the fatalities from the Aug. 31 plane crash in Argentina were motorists and pedestrians caught in the path of the skidding jet.	In Indonesia, militia members attack a neighborhood near a UN compound in Dili, East Timor, indiscriminately firing automatic weapons and burning houses. UN workers, foreign journalists and some 200 local villagers flee into the compound. At least one person is killed before Indonesian security forces arrive and regain control of the area.

A	B	C	D	E
Includes developments that affect more than one world region, international organizations, and important meetings of major world leaders.	Includes all domestic and regional developments in Europe, including the Soviet Union, Turkey, Cyprus, and Malta.	Includes all domestic and regional developments in Africa and the Middle East, including Iraq and Iran and excluding Cyprus, Turkey, and Afghanistan.	Includes all domestic and regional developments in Latin America, the Caribbean, and Canada.	Includes all domestic and regional developments in Asia and Pacific nations, extending from Afghanistan through all the Pacific Island, except Hawaii.

U.S. Politics & Social Issues	U.S. Foreign Policy & Defense	U.S. Economy & Environment	Science, Technology, & Nature	Culture, Leisure, & Lifestyle	
Organizers of the Million Youth March, a rally for black youth, sue New York City in federal court, alleging that a refusal to grant a permit for the demonstration is a violation of their First Amendment free-speech rights. . . . California enacts a ban on the sale and manufacture of "unsafe" handguns. The law is primarily aimed at cheap, powerful handguns called "Saturday night specials."	Reports suggest that several federal agencies, including the FBI, have flatly turned down petitions for clemency brought since Pres. Clinton's August 11 offer to commute the sentences of 16 members of the Armed Forces of National Liberation (FALN), a Puerto Rican independence group that waged a bombing campaign in the U.S. from 1974 to 1983.		Scientists reveal they have found liquid water embedded in a meteorite, the first discovery of water in an extraterrestrial object. . . . The final crew of the Russian space station *Mir* departs the station in a *Soyuz* capsule. *Mir*, the Russian space program's only remaining independent manned flight project, has been in space for 13 years, longer than any other space station, and it is scheduled to fall from its orbit and burn up in the lower atmosphere in the year 2000.		Aug. 27
				A baseball team from Osaka, Japan, defeats Phenix City, Alabama, 5-0, to win the Little League World Series in Williamsport, Pennsylvania.	Aug. 28
				The World Track and Field Championships close in Seville, Spain. The U.S. won the most medals with 17. Russia won 13 medals, and Germany won 12. . . . Tiger Woods wins the World Golf Championships NEC Invitational, becoming the fifth golfer to win five PGA events in one year.	Aug. 29
The CDC reports that 17,047 people died of AIDS in 1998, down 20% from 1997. That decline is less than half the decline of 42% in AIDS deaths between 1996 and 1997.		Common Cause reports that the Democratic and Republican parties raised a record $55 million in soft money in the first half of 1999, up 80% from the first half of 1995. GOP committees raised nearly $31 million by June 30, compared with $24 million raised by Democratic committees.	Hurricane Dennis skirts the coastal areas of North Carolina.	*Black Notice* by Patricia Cornwell tops the bestseller list.	Aug. 30
Judge Denny Chin orders NYC to allow the Million Youth March, a rally for black youth, to proceed. . . . NYC mayor Rudolph Giuliani (R) serves as foreman on a New York State Supreme Court jury. Giuliani is the first New York City mayor to sit on a jury while in office. . . . A study finds that a youth in a two-parent family who has a poor relationship with the father is 68% more likely to smoke, drink alcohol, or use drugs than one in an "average two-parent household." The same teenager is at more than 60% greater risk of substance abuse than a child reared by a single mother who has an "excellent relationship" with the mother.		The Detroit Federation of Teachers, which represents 7,200 teachers, strikes, defying a 1994 Michigan law that makes it illegal for teachers to walk out. . . . Henry Earl Singleton, 82, engineer who cofounded and was chief executive of Los Angeles-based Teledyne Inc., 1960–91, dies of brain cancer in Los Angeles, California.			Aug. 31
		Federal regulators close the First National Bank of Keystone (NBK) in West Virginia after finding evidence of alleged fraud. NBK, with $1.1 billion in assets and $880.9 million in deposits, is the fourth U.S. bank to fail in 1999. The collapse is expected to cost the federal government $500–$800 million, making it one of the costliest bank failures ever.		In the Olympic bribery scandal, Kim Jung Hoon, also known as John Kim, is indicted on federal charges of fraud relating to a sham employment arrangement as a favor for the IOC to vote in favor of Utah's bid to host the 2002 Winter games.	Sept. 1

F	G	H	I	J
Includes elections, federal-state relations, civil rights and liberties, crime, the judiciary, education, health care, poverty, urban affairs, and population.	*Includes formation and debate of U.S. foreign and defense policies, veterans' affairs, and defense spending. (Relations with specific foreign countries are usually found under the region concerned.)*	*Includes business, labor, agriculture, taxation, transportation, consumer affairs, monetary and fiscal policy, natural resources, and pollution.*	*Includes worldwide scientific, medical, and technological developments; natural phenomena; U.S. weather; natural disasters; and accidents.*	*Includes the arts, religion, scholarship, communications media, sports, entertainments, fashions, fads, and social life.*

	World Affairs	Europe	Africa & the Middle East	The Americas	Asia & the Pacific
Sept. 2		A Bosnian Muslim official announces the discovery of two mass graves containing 28 bodies each. One site is near Sarajevo, the Bosnian capital. The other grave is near the northern Bosnian town of Teslic. The 56 victims are believed to have been of Bosnian Muslim and Croat civilians.	Reports reveal that Ethiopia shot down a civilian jet near the border with Eritrea, killing both men on board.... Tel Aviv District Court convicts Samuel Sheinbein, 18, of the U.S. of premeditated murder after he pleads guilty to 10 charges in the slaying of Alfredo Enrique Tello Jr., 19, in the U.S.	In Canada, about 700 relatives of victims of Swissair Flight 111 attend memorial services in Halifax, Nova Scotia, marking the first anniversary of the plane crash that killed 229 people.... Reports disclose that, of the 131 Chinese migrants discovered on Aug. 11 in Canada, 57 have been ordered deported.	In Indonesia, the militias seize control of the western towns of Maliana, Gleno, and Liquica.
Sept. 3	The eighth biennial summit of La Francophonie, an alliance of 52 French-speaking states, opens in Moncton, New Brunswick, in Canada.	Two French magistrates dismiss all charges against press photographers under investigation for their role in a Paris automobile accident that killed Britain's Diana, Princess of Wales, in 1997. The magistrates conclude that the crash occurred largely because French driver Henri Paul, who died in the crash, was legally drunk.... The UN Mission in Kosovo (UNMIK) declares that Kosovo will now use the German mark as its official currency, although the Yugoslav dinar will still be considered legal tender. The UN mission also inaugurates a customs service.		In Canada, Dave Stupich, a former British Columbia finance minister, is sentenced to two years' house arrest for orchestrating a bingo and lottery scam—dubbed Bingogate—that led to the 1996 resignation of then-British Columbia premier Michael Harcourt. Separately, seven people are killed and 45 are injured in one of the worst highway collisions in Ontario history. The disaster includes an 82-car pileup and an intense fire that melts parts of the pavement and burns 29 cars.	UN officials confirm that the militias who seized control of the western Indonesian towns of Maliana, Gleno, and Liquica burned 200 houses in Maliana and killed more than 20 people in the town, including at least two UN local employees. Indonesia's military commander, General Wiranto, sends extra battalions to East Timor.
Sept. 4	At the summit of La Francophonie in New Brunswick, Canada, the delegation from Congo leads a demonstration against protesters who criticize Congo president Laurent Kabila's regime. One unidentified diplomat is arrested, as are two Canadians.	A car bomb is detonated outside an apartment complex in Russia's southern region of Dagestan, killing at least 64 people and wounding more than 100.... Police in Hamburg, Germany, arrest fugitive U.S. financier Martin Frankel, who disappeared in May with hundreds of millions of dollars of insurance companies' money. Frankel's arrest ends a four-month-long international manhunt.			The UN reveals that the residents of East Timor overwhelmingly voted for independence from Indonesia in the Aug. 30 referendum. Pro-Indonesia police launch an assault on the East Timorese capital, Dili, killing independence leaders and forcing thousands of East Timorese to flee into the neighboring Indonesian province of West Timor.
Sept. 5	The foreign ministers of the EU's 15 member states unanimously agree to provide Turkey with 30 million euros ($31.5 million) in aid to help the country recover from the August 17 earthquake.	In an unexpected incursion of Islamic militants into western Dagestan from the republic of Chechnya, an estimated 1,000–2,000 Chechen militants surge across the border and seize six villages and a town.... Alan Kenneth McKenzie Clark, 71, British Conservative Party politician who served in Parliament, 1974–92, and won reelection to Parliament in 1997, dies at Saltwood Castle, Kent, England, after having undergone surgery for a brain tumor three months earlier.	Israeli prime minister Ehud Barak and Palestinian leader Yasser Arafat sign an accord that sets a February 2000 deadline for completing a broad framework for a permanent peace accord. Separately, two car bomb explosions occur nearly simultaneously in the towns of Haifa and Tiberias, in northern Israel. Several passers-bys are injured and the occupants of both vehicles are killed.		
Sept. 6	The International Labor Organization (ILO), a UN agency, reports a study, the first of its kind, that examines productivity, unemployment, and other facets of the labor market in more than 230 countries between 1980 and 1997. The ILO concludes that U.S. citizens worked the most when compared to any other industrialized nation. Americans worked an average of 1,966 hours in 1997.	Russian troops participating in KFOR shoot and kill three Serbs attacking a group of ethnic Albanians in eastern Kosovo.	Jordan's King Abdullah II visits Kuwait. It is the first time a Jordanian leader has traveled to Kuwait since the Persian Gulf war in 1990–91.... An assailant attacks Egyptian president Hosni Mubarak in Port Said, slightly wounding him with a knife. The assailant is shot and killed.... Israel's Supreme Court unanimously bars the use of prisoner interrogation methods that critics claim amount to torture.	Reports confirm that Panamanian president Moscoso has annulled presidential pardons granted to Eduardo Herrera, the former governor of the province of Panama, and 33 former government officials who served under Manuel Noriega's regime in the 1980s. Moscoso's predecessor, Perez Balladares, issued the pardons on his last day in office.	China's Pres. Jiang Zemin visits Australia, marking the first trip ever by a Chinese president to the country.... UN officials reveal e that 25,000 people are seeking refuge from the militias in Dili, East Timor. Militias attack the home of Bishop Carlos Belo, a cowinner of the 1996 Nobel Peace Prize. Belo escapes unharmed, but the 5,000 refugees at his home are taken to an unknown site. Reports suggest that 120 people have been killed in the towns of Suai and Atsabe.

A	B	C	D	E
Includes developments that affect more than one world region, international organizations, and important meetings of major world leaders.	Includes all domestic and regional developments in Europe, including the Soviet Union, Turkey, Cyprus, and Malta.	Includes all domestic and regional developments in Africa and the Middle East, including Iraq and Iran and excluding Cyprus, Turkey, and Afghanistan.	Includes all domestic and regional developments in Latin America, the Caribbean, and Canada.	Includes all domestic and regional developments in Asia and Pacific nations, extending from Afghanistan through all the Pacific Island, except Hawaii.

U.S. Politics & Social Issues	U.S. Foreign Policy & Defense	U.S. Economy & Environment	Science, Technology, & Nature	Culture, Leisure, & Lifestyle	
The White House announces that Pres. Clinton and First Lady Hillary Rodham Clinton have signed a deal to purchase a $1.7 million house in New York's Westchester County. The purchase will establish New York residency for the first lady, who is considering running for one of the state's U.S. Senate seats in 2000. The home will be the first the Clintons will own since Bill Clinton's second election as Arkansas governor in 1982.			Scientists report they have genetically engineered a strain of mouse that consistently performs better than ordinary mice in a series of learning and memory tests. The creation of the "smarter" mice confirms a long-held theory about the brain's basic mechanism for forming memories.		Sept. 2
In White Plains, New York, Judge Barrington Parker Jr. sentences John Gotti, the alleged acting boss of the Gambino crime family, to six years and five months in prison. . . . NYC mayor Rudolph Giuliani (R) reveals that at least one city resident has died of St. Louis encephalitis, a viral disease spread by mosquitoes, and that several other cases are suspected. The city sprays malathion, an insecticide, over Queens. . . . A Florida state appeals court rules that the jury in a class-action lawsuit brought against cigarette makers has to determine damages in the suit on a case-by-case basis.		Workers at the Department of Energy's uranium plant in Paducah, Kentucky, file a class-action lawsuit against three government contractors—Lockheed Martin Corp., Union Carbide Corp., and General Electric Co.—charging that they have deliberately exposed the workers to radioactive and toxic materials since 1952. The class-action suit seeks $10 billion in compensation, including $5 billion in punitive damages. It is reportedly one of the largest damage claims ever filed by workers.			Sept. 3
The Million Youth March, a rally for black youth in New York City that turned violent in 1998, takes place without incident.		A study finds that the U.S. income gap in 1999 is the widest it has been since 1977. The top 20% of households are projected to receive half of all after-tax income in 1999, while households in the other income brackets are expected to receive a share of the national after-tax income that is as small as or smaller than it has been at any point since 1977.	Hurricane Dennis brings torrential downpours in the eastern part of North Carolina and spawns two tornadoes in southeastern Virginia.		Sept. 4
				The Western Conference basketball champion Houston Comets win their third straight WNBA title, defeating the Eastern Conference champion New York Liberty, 59-47, in Houston, Texas. . . . Allen Funt, 84, creator of the TV show *Candid Camera*, dies in Pebble Beach, California, from complications of a 1993 stroke.	Sept. 5
Gregory Smith, 10, begins his freshman year at Randolph-Macon College in Ashland, Virginia. Smith entered the second grade in 1996 and completed a high-school curriculum in 22 months before being awarded a full, four-year scholarship to Randolph-Macon.					Sept. 6

F	G	H	I	J
Includes elections, federal-state relations, civil rights and liberties, crime, the judiciary, education, health care, poverty, urban affairs, and population.	*Includes formation and debate of U.S. foreign and defense policies, veterans' affairs, and defense spending. (Relations with specific foreign countries are usually found under the region concerned.)*	*Includes business, labor, agriculture, taxation, transportation, consumer affairs, monetary and fiscal policy, natural resources, and pollution.*	*Includes worldwide scientific, medical, and technological developments; natural phenomena; U.S. weather; natural disasters; and accidents.*	*Includes the arts, religion, scholarship, communications media, sports, entertainments, fashions, fads, and social life.*

	World Affairs	Europe	Africa & the Middle East	The Americas	Asia & the Pacific
Sept. 7	Reports reveal that, as violence in Indonesia continues, Australia, Canada, New Zealand, France, Malaysia, Bangladesh, Pakistan, and Thailand have offered to contribute peacekeeping troops.	The government of Bosnia's Serb Republic bars ousted president Nikola Poplasen from using Bosnian presidential offices, cars, telephones, and security. . . . A strong earthquake strkes Greece, killing scores of people in and around Athens and injuring hundreds more. The quake, which measures 5.9 on the Richter scale, is the most powerful tremor to hit the Athens area in over 80 years.	Mcwayizeni Ka Dinizulu, 67, prince of the Zulu people of South Africa and a close ally of the Zulu monarch, King Goodwill Zwelithini, dies in Johannesburg, South Africa, of unreported causes.		In Myanmar, British activist Rachel Goldwyn, 28. is arrested when she ties herself to a lamp post and shouts prodemocracy slogans in Yangon, the capital. . . . A UN speaker estimates that the violence in Indonesia has caused as many as 200,000 East Timorese—nearly one-quarter of the province's 850,000 people—to flee their homes. Pres. Habibie imposes martial law in East Timor. Indonesian authorities release Jose Alexandre (Xanana) Gusmao, who is expected to become East Timor's first leader after independence, into UN protection in Jakarta.
Sept. 8	African leaders meet for a special Organization of African Unity (OAU) summit in Sirte, Libya. . . . In response to international offers, Indonesian foreign minister Ali Alatas rejects any foreign intervention, saying that East Timor is Indonesia's responsibility.	The Turkish government announces that the death toll in the Aug. 17 earthquake has reached 15,303. According to current totals, 23,954 people were injured, and some 250,000 survivors remain homeless. . . . The government of Lithuania plans to shut down the first of two nuclear reactors at the Ignalina nuclear power plant by 2005. International safety experts in 1997 recommended closing the plant until improvements were made.		Adrienne Clarkson is named as Canada's new governor general and ceremonial representative of Queen Elizabeth II of Britain. Clarkson, a former Chinese refugee who fled Hong Kong during World War II, will be the second woman and first immigrant to hold the nation's top ceremonial post.	Reports reveal that at least four East Timorese working for UNAMET have been killed by militiamen. Five other UNAMET local employees have disappeared. The UN states it will evacuate almost all of its remaining staff from the province, leaving a skeleton presence at the Dili headquarters. Some 1,000 refugees who gathered at the UNAMET compound in Dili flee.
Sept. 9	Representatives from the 21 member nations of the Asia-Pacific Economic Cooperation (APEC) trade group gather in Auckland, New Zealand, for the group's annual summit.	A bomb explodes in a Moscow apartment complex, killing 94 people. . . . The official death toll from the Sept. 7 earthquake in Greece stands at 75, and some 1,600 people have been treated for injuries. About 45 people are thought to be trapped in the rubble. . . . Ethnic rioting between Serbian and ethnic Albanian residents of the town of Mitrovica, Kosovo, erupts. Nine French peacekeepers and 37 civilians are injured slightly.	Israel releases 199 Palestinian prisoners.	The Canadian navy intercepts a ship carrying scores of smuggled Chinese migrants off the coast of British Columbia, bringing the total of detained Chinese boat people to more than 600 in less than two months. The discovery continues a public outcry over Canadian immigration laws since the first boat was intercepted in July.	The efforts by pro-Indonesia militias, often supported by government troops, to destroy East Timor's infrastructure begins to ebb, and militia violence is estimated to have left hundreds dead. Dili is largely deserted.
Sept. 10		Violence flares again in Mitrovica, Kosovo, when a group of 300 ethnic Albanian youths attempt to cross the Ibar River, renewing the Sep. 9 clashes. . . . Alfredo Kraus, 71, Spanish lyric tenor known for his refined phrasing, dies in Madrid, Spain, of pancreatic cancer.	In Uganda, the army steps in to halt fighting between members of the Bokora, Jie, and Tien ethnic groups and the Matheniko ethnic group. The ongoing violence is occurring some 150 miles (250 km) north of Kampala, the capital. . . . Zimbabwe's High Court convicts three Americans—John Dixon, Gary Blanchard, and Joseph Pettijohn—of illegal arms possession and attempting to smuggle guns onto an airplane.	In Canada, the Nova Scotia Court of Appeal overturns a stay of nine sex-related charges against former Nova Scotia premier Gerald Regan. The decision allows provincial Crown prosecutors to proceed with indecent assault charges against Regan, who was acquitted in December 1998 of eight counts of sex-related offenses, including rape, attempted rape, and indecent assault.	About 300 UNAMET staff are evacuated from their compound in Dili, East Timor's capital. Some 80 UN staff and several foreign journalists remain in the compound with nearly 1,000 East Timorese who sought refuge there.
Sept. 11		NATO troops and ethnic KLA forces restore order in Mitrovica, in the Serbian province of Kosovo after ethnic rioting erupted Sep. 9. Altogether, 184 people were injured in the rioting. . . . Momcilo Djujic, 92, Serbian priest who commanded a group of Serbian fighters in World War II, dies in San Diego, California, of unreported causes.	Madzorera Meki, Zimbabwe's vice consul in South Africa, is shot to death in a Johannesburg suburb by thieves stealing his car.	Eight employees of Edmonton-based United Pipeline Systems, and four tourists are abducted from a job site near the Ecuador-Colombia boarder by suspected Colombian guerillas.	An appeals court in Kuala Lumpur, the capital of Malaysia, upholds a 1997 contempt conviction against Canadian journalist Murray Hiebert and sentences him to a six-week jail term. The court's ruling in the closely watched case draws sharp criticism from human-rights groups and foreign leaders.
Sept. 12	The 11th International Conference on AIDS and Sexually Transmitted Diseases in Africa opens in Lusaka, Zambia's capital. The forum is the largest AIDS conference ever held in Africa. . . . Indonesian Pres. B. J. Habibie yields to international pressure and agrees to permit foreign troops to enter East Timor.		Field Marshal Mohammed Ali Fahmy, 77, Egyptian military commander who served as commander in chief of the armed forces, 1975–78, dies in London, England, of kidney failure.		Some 3,000 antigovernment demonstrators stage a protest in Dhaka, the capital of Bangladesh, calling for the resignation of P.M. Sheikh Hasina Wazed and for early elections. Demonstrators explode bombs, set vehicles ablaze, and attack government offices. At least 150 people are injured in the melee.

A	B	C	D	E
Includes developments that affect more than one world region, international organizations, and important meetings of major world leaders.	*Includes all domestic and regional developments in Europe, including the Soviet Union, Turkey, Cyprus, and Malta.*	*Includes all domestic and regional developments in Africa and the Middle East, including Iraq and Iran and excluding Cyprus, Turkey, and Afghanistan.*	*Includes all domestic and regional developments in Latin America, the Caribbean, and Canada.*	*Includes all domestic and regional developments in Asia and Pacific nations, extending from Afghanistan through all the Pacific Island, except Hawaii.*

U.S. Politics & Social Issues	U.S. Foreign Policy & Defense	U.S. Economy & Environment	Science, Technology, & Nature	Culture, Leisure, & Lifestyle	
Alstory Simon pleads guilty to killing Marilyn Green and Jerry Hillard and is sentenced to concurrent prison terms of 37 and 15 years. Anthony Porter has spent almost 17 years on death row for committing those murders. . . . Ambrose Harris, a death-row inmate at the New Jersey State Prison in Trenton, beats to death fellow inmate Robert Simon. Some people believe that it is the first incident in which one death-row inmate has killed another since 1976. . . . Los Angeles County bans sales of weapons or ammunition on county property.	The White House announces that 12 jailed members of a militant Puerto Rican independence group has accepted the terms of a clemency offer made by Pres. Clinton. The offer has been supported by Hispanic leaders and human rights groups but opposed by law-enforcement agencies and many Democratic and Republican politicians.	Former housing secretary Henry Cisneros pleads guilty to one misdemeanor count of lying to the FBI about payments that he made to Linda Jones between 1989 and 1994. His plea ends a four-year-long independent counsel investigation. . . . Ford Motor Co. reveals it has settled a sexual-harassment complaint brought by the EEOC on behalf of 19 female workers at two factories in Illinois. . . . Eighteen current and former employees of First Union Corp., the nation's sixth-largest bank, sue the bank over its administration of its 401(k) retirement program.		Viacom Inc. announce plans to acquire CBS Corp. If completed, the merger will create the world's second-largest media and entertainment company in terms of market capitalization after Time Warner Inc. The deal will also be the largest-ever media merger.	Sept. 7
Atty. Gen. Janet Reno names former Sen. John Danforth (R, Mo.) to head an independent investigation into the 1993 assault by federal agents on a compound of the Branch Davidian cult near Waco, Texas. Reno orders the outside investigation after the recent emergence of evidence that the FBI used pyrotechnic tear gas during the compound assault. . . . A report finds that about 70% of users of illegal drugs hold full-time jobs, in contrast to the popular perception of drug users as poor and unemployed.		Pres. Clinton is questioned under oath in an investigation of allegations that Labor Secretary Alexis Herman was involved in an influence-peddling scheme. Herman is accused of illegally soliciting $250,000 in contributions to Clinton's 1996 campaign. . . . The Detroit Federation of Teachers ratifies a new three-year contract, ending a strike that started Aug. 31. . . . Herbert Stein, 83, economist who chaired the President's Council of Economic Advisers,1972–74, dies in Washington, D.C., of a heart ailment.		The Smithsonian reveals that its Arthur M. Sackler Gallery has received a collection of Chinese artifacts—donated by New Jersey psychologist Paul Singer—worth between $50 million and $60 million.	Sept. 8
Federal agents arrest 13 workers employed at Miami International Airport, and two others on charges of conspiracy to import cocaine. . . . Pres. Clinton announces an initiative that will make $15 million in federal grants available to police and local officials for gun buyback programs. States have instituted similar programs in the past, but this is the first federal effort.	The House passes, 311-41, a GOP-sponsored resolution condemning Pres. Clinton's clemency offer to the FALN members. . . . The State Department issues its first annual report on global religious freedom and persecution. The report, which includes data on 194 countries, lists Afghanistan, China, Cuba, Iran, and Iraq among the nations where religious persecution is most severe. The report also cites U.S. allies Saudi Arabia and Egypt for religious persecution.	The House, 208-206, approves an appropriations bill allocating $429 million for the District of Columbia in fiscal 2000.		James Augustus (Catfish) Hunter, 53, Hall of Fame baseball pitcher who, in effect, became MLB's first free agent, dies in Hertford, North Carolina, of amyotrophic lateral sclerosis, or Lou Gehrig's disease . . . . Ruth Roman, 75, actress who appeared in more than 30 films from 1948 to 1965, dies in Laguna Beach, California.	Sept. 9
Judge Robert Potter orders the school district in Charlotte, North Carolina, to halt the use of student busing to achieve racial balance in schools, arguing that the school district "eliminated, to the extent practicable, the vestiges of past discrimination in the traditional areas of school operations." Charlotte's busing program, launched in 1969, was one of the first in the nation. . . . The Denver Classroom Teachers Association, a union representing 4,300 teachers in Denver, Colorado, overwhelmingly accepts a two-year merit pay plan that will, for the first time in the U.S., link some teachers' pay to the performance of their students.	The Los Alamos National Laboratory in New Mexico states that it has disciplined Siegfried (Sig) Hecker, Terry Craig, and Robert Vrooman for failing to adequately enforce security at the lab. The lab is the center of alleged Chinese espionage at U.S. nuclear weapons facilities. . . . Eleven members of the Armed Forces of National Liberation (FALN), which carried out more than 130 bombings in the U.S. between 1974 and 1983, are released from prison as part of a controversial clemency deal offered by Pres. Clinton. None of the 11 were convicted in attacks that resulted in deaths or injuries.	Energy Secretary Bill Richardson and the governors of four states with nuclear weapons plants sign an agreement in which they pledge cooperation to clean up the nation's nuclear waste. The four governors who sign the pact are Bill Owens (R, Colo.), Jim Hodges (D, S.C.), Don Sundquist (R, Tenn.) and Gary Locke (D, Wash.).			Sept. 10
				In tennis, Serena Williams wins her first Grand Slam singles title, at the U.S. Open. . . . Otto A. Silha, 80, president and publisher of the Minneapolis newspapers during the 1970s and 1980s, dies in Minneapolis, Minnesota, of complications of a heart attack.	Sept. 11
				At the Emmys, *The Practice* wins for best drama, and *Ally McBeal* wins for best comedy. David E. Kelley is the first person in the history of the awards to have produced shows that win both awards. . . . At the U.S. Open, Andre Agassi wins the men's singles tennis championship. Sisters Venus and Serena Williams win the doubles title.	Sept. 12

F	G	H	I	J
Includes elections, federal-state relations, civil rights and liberties, crime, the judiciary, education, health care, poverty, urban affairs, and population.	*Includes formation and debate of U.S. foreign and defense policies, veterans' affairs, and defense spending. (Relations with specific foreign countries are usually found under the region concerned.)*	*Includes business, labor, agriculture, taxation, transportation, consumer affairs, monetary and fiscal policy, natural resources, and pollution.*	*Includes worldwide scientific, medical, and technological developments; natural phenomena; U.S. weather; natural disasters; and accidents.*	*Includes the arts, religion, scholarship, communications media, sports, entertainments, fashions, fads, and social life.*

	World Affairs	Europe	Africa & the Middle East	The Americas	Asia & the Pacific
Sept. 13		An earthquake hits northwestern Turkey, killing at least seven people and injuring more than 300. The epicenter of the quake, which measures 5.8 on the Richter scale, is in the province of Kocaeli.... A bomb in a Moscow apartment building kills at least 118 people. The explosion reduces an eight-story building to rubble, and it occurs on a day of national mourning for victims of previous bomb blasts.	In Uganda, a senior army official reveals that up to 400 people have been killed in ethnic fighting some 150 miles (250 km) north of Kampala, the capital.... Jordan's King Abdullah II visits Lebanon, in the first visit to that country by a Jordanian head of state since 1969.... In Zimbabwe, a judge sentences the three U.S. nationals convicted Sept. 10 to six months for weapons possession and 21 months for attempting to take the weapons on a plane. The sentences are unusually light.		
Sept. 14	The UN General Assembly's 54th session opens, and delegates elect Theo-Ben Gurirab, Namibia's minister of foreign affairs, as president of the General Assembly.... The World Bank announces a $3 billion program to help fight AIDS in Africa, where 11.5 million people have died of the disease, accounting for about 80% of the world's total AIDS deaths.	Greek deputy foreign minister Yannos Kranidiotis and five other people are killed when a government airplane plunges 18,000 feet (5,500 m) while flying over Romania. The plane subsequently levels off and lands in Bucharest, Romania's capital. Three of the seven survivors on the plane are injured.... Charles Ainslie Crichton, 89, British film director, dies in London.		Hurricane Floyd passes directly over several Bahamian islands.	Reports confirm that China court-martialed and executed two military officers—Major General Liu Liankun and Colonel Shao Zhengzhong—for selling state secrets to Taiwan.... In East Timor, Indonesia, the UN abandons its Dili headquarters. Several dozen UN workers and some 1,500 displaced East Timorese are flown to Darwin, Australia, some 400 miles (640 km) southeast of East Timor.
Sept. 15	The European Parliament, the EU's legislative arm, approves the proposed new membership of the European Commission, the EU's executive panel.... The UN Security Council votes unanimously to authorize the deployment of a multinational force to restore peace and security in the Indonesian territory of East Timor. Australia will lead the multinational force. ... Swiss lawyer Carla Del Ponte takes office as chief prosecutor for the international war crimes tribunals for Rwanda and the former Yugoslavia.	Reports confirm that the death toll of the Sept. 7 earthquake centered near Athens, the Greek capital, has risen to 137, with six people believed to be missing and presumed dead.	Israeli police arrest Maher Dasuki, a Palestinian talk show host, shortly after guests on his show criticized Palestinian leader Yasser Arafat.... At a roadblock near Jowhar, some 60 miles (100 km) north of Mogadishu, the capital of Somalia, gunmen mortally wound the chief health officer of UNICEF when they open fire on a vehicle carrying six of the fund's workers. The five other workers are wounded in the attack, which appears to be an attempted robbery.	Reports confirm that Jacinto Arias Cruz, the former mayor of Acteal, a town in Chiapas, Mexico, where 45 unarmed Indians were massacred in 1997, and 23 of his associates have been sentenced to 35 years in prison.... Quebec's Roman Catholic Church refuses to compensate or apologize to 3,000 former orphans in Quebec, Canada, who claim they were physically and sexually abused for years in church-run institutions. Separately in Canada, a lockout that shuts down an Inco Ltd., a nickel mine in Thompson, Manitoba, begins	China's state-run news media announce that authorities have arrested 100,000 criminals in an effort to ensure "social stability and safety" during the 50th-anniversary celebrations of the establishment of communist rule in China.
Sept. 16	NATO commander General Wesley Clark presents the results of a three-month study of NATO's military successes during its recent 78-day bombing campaign against Yugoslavia. The study shows that NATO damaged or destroyed roughly a third of the Yugoslav army's weapons and vehicles.	A bomb explosion in a Volgodonsk, Russian, apartment building kills at least 17 people. Volgodonsk is located 200 miles (320 km) south of Moscow. With those deaths, 229 people have been killed in bombings in Russia since Sept. 9.... Viktor Gonchar, the vice speaker of the Belarussian parliament that Pres. Aleksandr Lukashenko disbanded in 1996, and publisher Anatoli Krasovsky disappear from Belarus.	Sibusiso Madubela, a black South African army lieutenant, shoots to death six white soldiers and a white civilian at a South African army base outside of Bloemfontein. A fellow soldier then kills the lieutenant.... Ayub Sheikh Yarow, 41, the chief health officer of UNICEF shot Set. 15, dies of his wounds.... In a nationwide referendum, Algerians overwhelmingly approve a government plan that will provide amnesty to many Islamic rebels fighting in the country's civil war.		In Myanmar, British activist Rachel Goldwyn, arrested Sept. 7, is sentenced to seven years in prison for staging a solitary democracy protest in Yangon, the capital.
Sept. 17		Frankie Vaughan (born Frank Abelson), 71, British popular singer who at the peak of his career as a teenage idol in the mid-1950s became known as "Mr. Moonlight," dies in Buckinghamshire, England, after having recently undergone surgery for a heart ailment.	In Zambia, a high court sentences 59 soldiers to death for their roles in a failed 1997 coup. One soldier is sentenced to 21 years in jail for failing to disclose his knowledge about treason. Eight officers are acquitted.	In Canada, the Supreme Court rules that a 1760 treaty between Britain and the Micmac Indians guarantees the band's right to make a living by fishing, hunting, and logging year round. The decision sparks controversy because it allows the Micmacs to fish out of season and because it is seen as a landmark victory for natives' commercial fishing and hunting rights.	During a month-long poll in India, a leader of Kashmir's ruling National Conference party is killed and 26 people are injured in attacks allegedly carried out by separatists.

A	B	C	D	E
Includes developments that affect more than one world region, international organizations, and important meetings of major world leaders.	*Includes all domestic and regional developments in Europe, including the Soviet Union, Turkey, Cyprus, and Malta.*	*Includes all domestic and regional developments in Africa and the Middle East, including Iraq and Iran and excluding Cyprus, Turkey, and Afghanistan.*	*Includes all domestic and regional developments in Latin America, the Caribbean, and Canada.*	*Includes all domestic and regional developments in Asia and Pacific nations, extending from Afghanistan through all the Pacific Island, except Hawaii.*

U.S. Politics & Social Issues	U.S. Foreign Policy & Defense	U.S. Economy & Environment	Science, Technology, & Nature	Culture, Leisure, & Lifestyle	
In Denver, Colorado, Judge Richard Matsch refuses to grant convicted Oklahoma City bombing conspirator Terry Nichols a new trial. . . . The U.S. Ninth Circuit Court of Appeals in San Francisco, California, orders a U.S. district judge to review his 1998 ruling shutting the Oakland Cannabis Buyers' Cooperative, which provides marijuana for medical use.		IBM agrees to pay $15.5 million to a group of former employees in Louisville, Kentucky, who sued the company in 1992 for converting pension plans without informing them.	The National Bioethics Advisory Commission recommends that the government allow federal funds to be used to support research on human embryonic stem cells.	The Smithsonian Institution's Board of Regents unanimously selects Lawrence Small as the museum complex's next secretary.	Sept. 13
		The House votes, 252-177, to pass a bill overhauling the nation's campaign finance laws.		Judge Wendy Potts sentences Jonathan Schmitz to 25–50 years in prison for killing acquaintance Scott Amedure, a homosexual man who admitted during a 1995 taping of *The Jenny Jones Show* that he had a crush on Schmitz.	Sept. 14
The Los Angeles Police Department (LAPD) states that one of its former officers, Rafael Perez, admitted that in October 1996 he and his partner, Nino Durden, shot and framed Javier Ovando, an unarmed gang member who was subsequently sentenced to a long prison term. Bernard Parks, the chief of the LAPD, announces that 12 officers were either suspended or dismissed. . . . Larry Ashbrook shoots to death seven people and wounds seven more in a Baptist church in Fort Worth, Texas. Immediately following the rampage, Ashbrook commits suicide by shooting himself in the head.	The House approves, 375-45, a $288.8 billion fiscal 2000 defense authorization bill. . . . Mexico's former chief antinarcotics official, Mario Ruiz Massieu, is found dead at his home in Palisades Park, New Jersey, where he was under house arrest for the past four years. Ruiz Massieu, 48, was scheduled to be arraigned Sept. 17 in federal court in Houston, Texas, on charges of money laundering. The Justice Department announces that Ruiz Massieu died "of an apparent overdose of antidepressants" in a likely suicide.	Local 54 of the Hotel Employees and Restaurant Employees International, which represents about 14,000 workers in Atlantic City, New Jersey, goes on strike.	Hurricane Floyd brings heavy rainfall and strong winds to states along the East Coast of the U.S. The storm prompts the largest mass evacuation in U.S. history, as more than 3 million people in coastal regions are ordered to move inland.		Sept. 15
Javier Ovando, the gang member whom former LAPD officers admitted Sept. 15 that they framed, is released from prison at the request of the Los Angeles District Attorney's Office. It is the first time in the history of Los Angeles County that prosecutors ask a judge to free a convicted man. . . . W(endell) Arthur Garrity Jr., 79, federal judge who in 1974 mandated busing in Boston as a means of desegregating the city's schools, dies of cancer in Wellesley, Massachusetts.		DaimlerChrysler reaches an agreement with the UAW after 48 hours of around-the-clock negotiations. . . . The Senate votes, 52-39, to clear an appropriations bill allocating $429 million for the District of Columbia in fiscal 2000. . . . The Senate votes, 54-38, to clear a $28.2 billion appropriations bill to fund the Treasury Department, the U.S. Postal Service, the Executive Office of the President, and other agencies. The measure includes the first presidential pay raise in 32 years, the fifth presidential pay increase in U.S. history.	Hurricane Floyd comes ashore near Wilmington, North Carolina, and pours as much as 2 feet (60 cm) of rain in some areas as it moves to southeastern Virginia and north through the mid-Atlantic states.		Sept. 16
	The U.S. and South Africa reach an agreement ending a trade dispute over drugs to treat AIDS.	Local 54 of the Hotel Employees and Restaurant Employees International, which represents about 14,000 workers in Atlantic City, New Jersey, tentatively agrees to a new five-year contract, ending a strike started Sept. 15.	Rainfall from Hurricane Floyd causes scores of rivers and creeks in eastern North Carolina to overflow, flooding thousands of homes and making roadways impassable.	In New York City, Judge Denise Cote sentences Lawrence X. Cusack III to nine years in prison for selling forged documents that he claimed were written or signed by Pres. John F. Kennedy. The judge orders him to pay $7 million in restitution to those who purchased the papers.	Sept. 17

F	G	H	I	J
Includes elections, federal-state relations, civil rights and liberties, crime, the judiciary, education, health care, poverty, urban affairs, and population.	*Includes formation and debate of U.S. foreign and defense policies, veterans' affairs, and defense spending. (Relations with specific foreign countries are usually found under the region concerned.)*	*Includes business, labor, agriculture, taxation, transportation, consumer affairs, monetary and fiscal policy, natural resources, and pollution.*	*Includes worldwide scientific, medical, and technological developments; natural phenomena; U.S. weather; natural disasters; and accidents.*	*Includes the arts, religion, scholarship, communications media, sports, entertainments, fashions, fads, and social life.*

	World Affairs	Europe	Africa & the Middle East	The Americas	Asia & the Pacific
Sept. 18	Reports confirm that Iraq's air force commander has stated that 187 civilians have been killed in the U.S. and British strikes against Iraq since they began in December 1998, and another 494 people were wounded. The disclosure marks the first time Iraq gives a full casualty toll for the strikes. . . . The new European Commission approves plans to overhaul its administrative structure. It also enacts a code of conduct aimed at preventing the kinds of missteps that led the previous commission to resign.	Leo Valiani (born Leo Weiczen), 90, Italian antifascist who helped lead the resistance in Italy during World War II and who, in 1980, was awarded the title of life senator of the Italian Republic, dies in Milan, Italy, of cancer.			In a month-long poll in India, election-related violence erupts in the disputed state of Jammu and Kashmir and in Bihar. At least 40 people are killed, and dozens of others are injured. . . . An antiterrorism court in the southern port city of Karachi acquits three men—Saulat Mirza, Arif Tutu, and Pervez Salman Haider—charged in connection with the March 1995 murders of two U.S. diplomats. Despite their acquittal, Mirza, Tutu, and Haider remain jailed in connection with other crimes.
Sept. 19		Pope John Paul II beatifies Anton Martin Slomsek, a 19th-century Slovene bishop who championed Slovene language and cultural identity under the Austro-Hungarian Empire. The pontiff's stop in Slovenia, a former republic of Yugoslavia, marks his second visit to the predominantly Roman Catholic nation since it gained its independence in 1991.			Some 10,000 protesters demonstrate in Kuala Lumpur, the capital of Malaysia, demanding an investigation into recent assertions by Anwar Ibrahim, the country's jailed former deputy prime minister, that he is being poisoned in prison.
Sept. 20		The ethnic Albanian Kosovo Liberation Army (KLA), signs an agreement with NATO. . . . Raisa Maximovna Gorbachev, 67, wife of Mikhail Gorbachev, the last president of the former Soviet Union, dies of leukemia in Muenster, Germany.	Austrian president Thomas Klestil visits Iran, marking the first time a leader from a European Union member country has visited Iran since the Islamic Revolution in 1979. . . . Due to generally dangerous conditions for aid workers in the area, UNICEF has suspended its operations in Somalia.		Reports confirm that authorities in Myanmar have sentenced a British-Australian activist, James Mawdsley, 26, to 17 years in prison. . . . The first contingent of a UN peacekeeping force arrives in the Indonesian province of East Timor to help end to violence launched by pro-Indonesia militias after East Timorese voted at the end of August to declare independence from Indonesia.
Sept. 21	NATO defense ministers meet in Toronto, Ontario, Canada.	The protesters, organized by Serbian opposition parties, begin holding daily rallies to demand the resignation of Yugoslav president Slobodan Milosevic. Separately, the KLA, which for more than a year has fought for the independence of Kosovo, formally disbands. . . . Israeli prime minister Ehud Barak visits Germany, making the first official state visit to Berlin since the German government moved there from Bonn in August. The visit is regarded as symbolically significant because Berlin was the capital of the Nazi German regime, which carried out the executions of millions of European Jews in the 1930s and 1940s.	Due to the Sept. 15 UNICEF attack and what they cite as dangerous conditions for aid workers, international aid agencies suspend operations in Somalia.		A major earthquake strikes Taiwan, killing thousands of people and devastating towns and villages. The earthquake also causes significant damage in the western coastal city of Taichung. . . . In the Philippines, more than 100,000 demonstrators hold street rallies in Manila and several other major cities to protest Pres. Estrada's attempts to remove a constitutional provision that limits a president to one six-year term. Transit strikes disrupt business in four cities. . . . Reports confirm that Chinese police have detained Yongyi Song, a U.S.-based Chinese scholar who was visiting China to conduct research on the Cultural Revolution.
Sept. 22	The UN Population Fund projects that the global population will reach 6 billion people on Oct. 12—declared "The Day of Six Billion"—and will likely near 8.9 billion by the year 2050. That is 500 million fewer people than the fund predicted for that year in 1994 and 1996. . . . The IMF predicts that Malaysia's economy will grow by 2.4% in 1999, and some economists put that figure at 5.5%.	Serbian leaders announce that they will no longer participate in the multiethnic Kosovo Transitional Council, a civilian advisory group, claiming that it is essentially the same rebel army under a different name.	Jordanian police arrest Khaled Meshal, Ibrahim Ghosheh, and Mousa Abu Marzook—three senior leaders of the militant Islamic group Hamas.		An aftershock measuring 6.8 on the Richter scale shakes Taiwan. . . . Vice Pres. Hu Jintao, the youngest of China's senior leaders, is named vice chair of the Central Military Commission. The appointment is widely seen as a confirmation of Hu's status as designated successor to Jiang, who is chair of the commission.
Sept. 23		Russia's air force begins bombing targets on the outskirts of Grozny, the capital of Russia's separatist republic of Chechnya.	Pres. Ali Abdullah Saleh is reelected in Yemen's first direct presidential election. He is the only candidate. Political opposition groups boycotted the election because Yemen's parliament did not approve the nomination of their candidate for president.	In Brazil, Hildebrando Pascoal, a first-term congressman accused of heading a death squad in his home state of Acre surrenders to federal authorities.	The total number of people confirmed dead from the Sept. 21 earthquake in Taiwan is 2,103. Nearly 8,000 people are injured, about 1,600 people are believed to be trapped, and 210 others are listed as missing. . . . The Indonesian parliament passes a bill that will broaden the power of the military during "emergency situations." Passage of the measure sparks massive street protests in major cities across Indonesia. . . Ri Jon Ok, 83, North Korea's premier for six years and its vice president, 1984–88, dies.

A	B	C	D	E
Includes developments that affect more than one world region, international organizations, and important meetings of major world leaders.	*Includes all domestic and regional developments in Europe, including the Soviet Union, Turkey, Cyprus, and Malta.*	*Includes all domestic and regional developments in Africa and the Middle East, including Iraq and Iran and excluding Cyprus, Turkey, and Afghanistan.*	*Includes all domestic and regional developments in Latin America, the Caribbean, and Canada.*	*Includes all domestic and regional developments in Asia and Pacific nations, extending from Afghanistan through all the Pacific Island, except Hawaii.*

U.S. Politics & Social Issues	U.S. Foreign Policy & Defense	U.S. Economy & Environment	Science, Technology, & Nature	Culture, Leisure, & Lifestyle	
				Metropolitan Demetrios Trakatellis is enthroned as head of the Greek Orthodox Church in the U.S.	Sept. 18
A memorial service for the victims of the Sept. 15 shooting spree at a Baptist church in Fort Worth, Texas, is attended by more than 10,000 people, including Gov. George W. Bush (R).			Data shows, that, due to Hurricane Floyd. numerous counties in states from Florida to New York State have been declared disaster areas by the federal government, making residents and local authorities eligible for federal emergency funds.	In a publicized boxing match, Oscar De La Hoya loses his WBC welterweight title to challenger Felix Trinidad Jr., by a majority decision. . . . Lindsay Davenport clinches tennis's 1999 Federation Cup championship for the U.S.	Sept. 19
New Jersey governor Christine Todd Whitman (R) names Carson Dunbar, a former FBI agent, as head of the state police. . . . A jury in Bryan, Texas, convicts Lawrence Brewer, 32, a white supremacist, of beating and dragging James Byrd Jr., a black man, to death.			One of several companies working to decode the entire human genome, or sequence of genes reveals that human cells have about 140,000 genes. Previous estimates ranged from about 70,000 to 100,000 genes. . . . North Carolina officials estimate that Hurricane Floyd caused damage in the state of at least $6 billion.		Sept. 20
Connecticut officials reveal that mosquitoes trapped at two sites in that state are carrying the St. Louis encephalitis virus. The state plans to begin insecticide spraying in some areas the following week.	Pres. Clinton, in a letter read at a congressional hearing, defends his offer to commute the sentences of 16 members of the FALN, a Puerto Rican independence group that carried out a series of deadly bombings in the U.S. in the late 1970s and early 1980s.	The Commerce Department reports that the seasonally adjusted U.S. deficit in trade in goods and services in July reached a record $25.18 billion. The July figure marks a $579 million increase from June's revised $24.6 billion trade deficit. . . . US Airways Group Inc. reaches a tentative labor agreement with its 7,000 mechanics and cleaners after four years of negotiations. . . . The U.S. Third Circuit Court of Appeals in Philadelphia, Pennsylvania, finds that, even under the ERISA, patients may sue HMOs in state courts for medical malpractice, on the grounds that the insurers' control over treatment amounts to the provision of medical care.	The FDA approves the use of an antibiotic drug that can kill a strain of bacterium resistant to currently used antibiotics. The drug, Synercid, is the first of a new class of antibiotics known as streptogramins to be approved in the U.S. . . . Tropical Storm Harvey, formed in the Gulf of Mexico, brings heavy rains and some flooding to Florida's Gulf Coast.		Sept. 21
The Justice Department files a lawsuit against the U.S.'s major tobacco have companies, alleging that the firms have conspired since the 1950s to defraud their customers and mislead them about the addictiveness and health hazards of smoking cigarettes.	The Senate votes, 93-5, to clear the $288.8 billion fiscal 2000 defense authorization bill.		North Carolina officials report that 30,000 homes have been flooded statewide, and 10,000 residences are still without electrical power. . . . The FTC announces it has obtained a preliminary injunction against three individuals who operated a scheme that forcibly redirects World Wide Web users to pornographic sites and holds them captive by disabling their browser functions. FTC officials refer to the activities as "page-jacking" and "mouse-trapping."	NYC mayor Rudolph Giuliani threatens to end city subsidies to the Brooklyn Museum of Art because of a planned controversial exhibit. . . . George C(ampbell) Scott, 71, best known for starring in *Patton* (1970), dies in Westlake Village, California, of a ruptured abdominal aortic aneurysm.	Sept. 22
A jury in Bryan, Texas, sentences Lawrence Brewer, 32, to death for murder in the beating and dragging death of a black man, James Byrd. . . . Senate majority leader Trent Lott (R, Miss.) announces the creation of the task force to investigate the Justice Department. . . . Stanley Fleishman, 79, lawyer who specialized in First Amendment cases, successfully arguing a number of them before the U.S. Supreme Court, dies in Los Angeles, California, after surgery for a benign tumor; he contracted pneumonia.		Pres. Clinton vetoes a Republican-backed plan for a $792 billion tax cut over 10 years, arguing that it will jeopardize the future of Social Security and Medicare. . . . Former Connecticut state treasurer Paul Silvester (R) pleads guilty in Hartford, Connecticut, to accepting kickbacks for steering state pension funds to private equity funds. . . . The antitrust division of the Justice Department gives its approval to a long-discussed plan to convert U.S. stock trading to decimals from fractions.	Due to Hurricane Floyd, 42 people in North Carolina are confirmed dead. . . . Officials at the Jet Propulsion Laboratory in Pasadena, California, reveal they lost contact with *Mars Climate Orbiter*, an unmanned spacecraft. . . . Reports reveal that archaeologists in China have discovered what is to believed to be the oldest still-playable musical instrument, a flute made from the wing bone of a crane that is about 9,000 years old.		Sept. 23
F	G	H	I	J	
Includes elections, federal-state relations, civil rights and liberties, crime, the judiciary, education, health care, poverty, urban affairs, and population.	*Includes formation and debate of U.S. foreign and defense policies, veterans' affairs, and defense spending. (Relations with specific foreign countries are usually found under the region concerned.)*	*Includes business, labor, agriculture, taxation, transportation, consumer affairs, monetary and fiscal policy, natural resources, and pollution.*	*Includes worldwide scientific, medical, and technological developments; natural phenomena; U.S. weather; natural disasters; and accidents.*	*Includes the arts, religion, scholarship, communications media, sports, entertainments, fashions, fads, and social life.*	

	World Affairs	Europe	Africa & the Middle East	The Americas	Asia & the Pacific
Sept. 24		Tens of thousands of farmers and workers march through Warsaw, the capital of Poland, to protest the government's restrictive economic policies.... Former Italian premier Giulio Andreotti is acquitted of conspiring in the murder of Mino Pecorelli, a journalist, in 1979. The verdict concludes one of the most widely publicized trials in Italian history. Andreotti remains on trial in Palermo on charges of associating with the Cosa Nostra, the Sicilian Mafia.			The total number of people confirmed killed by the Sept. 21 earthquake in Taiwan stands at 2,160, with 8,432 people injured. A six-year-old boy is freed from a collapsed apartment building in the town of Dali.
Sept. 25	Finance ministers and central-bank governors from the Group of Seven (G-7) major industrialized nations meet in Washington, D.C. The G-7 financial leaders reveal they have agreed to establish a new Group of 20 (G-20) nations that will include both industrialized and developing countries.	In Chechnya, Russia attacks Grozny's oil refinery and its gas distribution facility.			Gunmen kill nine people, including Roman Catholic clerics, in a rural area near the town of Los Palos in East Timor.... Pres. Lee Teng-hui declares a state of emergency in response to the Sept. 21 earth quake in Taiwan.
Sept. 26		In Chechnya, Russian attacks destroy Grozny's oil refinery and severely damage its gas distribution facility.... Violence erupts at the Ulucanlar prison in Ankara, Turkey, when prisoners attack guards. The guards retaliate, killing 10 prisoners. In the riots, 23 other inmates and seven guards are injured. News of the deaths in Ankara sparks similar violence in seven prisons across the nation.	Egyptian president Hosni Mubarak is reelected to a fourth six-year term as president in a referendum in which he ran unopposed.	In central Mexico, a series of powerful explosions rip through a central section of the city of Celaya, killing at least 56 people and injuring 348 others. Celaya is located 120 miles (195 km) northwest of Mexico City, the capital of Mexico.... One of the 12 people taken hostage Sept. 11 by suspected Colombian guerillas is released.	Reports confirm that six demonstrators and one police officer died in the protests sparked by legislation passed Sept. 23 in Indonesia. Separately, aid workers and UN officials find that pro-Indonesia forces are systematically laying waste to villages as they withdraw from the region.... An aftershock measuring 6.8 on the Richter scale strikes Taiwan, killing at least three people and injuring 58 others.
Sept. 27	The European Court of Human Rights rules that a law barring homosexuals from serving in the British armed forces violates the privacy rights of military personnel.... The board of the World Bank reappoints former U.S. investment banker James D. Wolfensohn as the bank's president. Wolfensohn will be only the second World Bank president—out of a total of nine since the organization was formally established in 1946—to serve a second term.	French peacekeepers in the town of Kosovska Mitrovica announce they have arrested four suspects after unearthing a mass grave containing 28 ethnic Albanian men earlier in the week.... The Turkish military launches an incursion into northern Iraq to attack PKK guerillas there.	A bus carrying British tourists crashes near Lydenburg, a town northeast of Johannesburg, killing 26 of the passengers. Reports indicate that this is the fifth fatal bus accident in South Africa in a week.... Israeli forces fire a barrage of missiles at a Hezbollah stronghold in Iqlim al-Tuffah after a top official of the pro-Israeli militia in Lebanon dies in a roadside bombing.		Indonesia turns over security in East Timor to the International Force for East Timor (INTERFET), a UN peacekeeping force deployed there a week earlier.... A court in Bombay, India, finds Harshad Mehta, a former stockbroker, guilty of securities fraud in connection with a 1992 Bombay stock market scandal. Mehta is convicted of siphoning $9 million from an Indian automobile company.
Sept. 28		Two people are killed and roughly 40 are wounded when two grenades explode in a Serbian marketplace in Kosovo Polje, Kosovo.... Reports confirm that voters in Tajikistan have approved a change to the country's constitution extending the president's term to seven years from five.... Sir Nigel Broackes, 65, chair of the Trafalgar House conglomerate, 1969–92, dies in London, England, of unreported causes.	Iranian officials announce the discovery of the country's largest oil find in 30 years. The oil is in an onshore oil field in Khuzestan province, roughly 6 miles (10 km) from Iran's border with Iraq.		In Bombay, India, Harshad Mehta, a former stockbroker found guilty Sept. 27, is sentenced to a five-year jail term.

A	B	C	D	E
Includes developments that affect more than one world region, international organizations, and important meetings of major world leaders.	Includes all domestic and regional developments in Europe, including the Soviet Union, Turkey, Cyprus, and Malta.	Includes all domestic and regional developments in Africa and the Middle East, including Iraq and Iran and excluding Cyprus, Turkey, and Afghanistan.	Includes all domestic and regional developments in Latin America, the Caribbean, and Canada.	Includes all domestic and regional developments in Asia and Pacific nations, extending from Afghanistan through all the Pacific Island, except Hawaii.

U.S. Politics & Social Issues	U.S. Foreign Policy & Defense	U.S. Economy & Environment	Science, Technology, & Nature	Culture, Leisure, & Lifestyle	
A jury in Annapolis, Maryland, acquits former Maryland state senator Larry Young (D) of corruption charges. . . . CDC officials identify the West Nile virus as the virus that has killed an unusual number of birds in New York City, raising the possibility that it is that virus, rather than St. Louis encephalitis, which may be infecting people in the area. . . . The eighth Circuit appeals court in St. Louis, Missouri, strikes down bans in Arkansas, Iowa, and Nebraska of a controversial abortion method known medically as intact dilation and evacuation (IDE).			Reports confirm that doctors have implanted a woman with parts of her ovaries, which were removed earlier in her life and frozen. The woman, who was made infertile by the previous operation, has reportedly ovulated and menstruated normally since the ovarian tissue was reimplanted.	Judith Campbell Exner (born Judith Eileen Katherine Immoor), 65, who gained notoriety when she claimed she had been romantically involved with both Pres. John F. Kennedy and Chicago Mafia boss Sam Giancana, testimony that was later challenged, dies in Duarte, California, of breast cancer.	Sept. 24
			A twin-engine sightseeing airplane crashes into a slope of the Mauna Loa volcano on the island of Hawaii, killing all 10 people aboard.		Sept. 25
Oseola McCarty, 91, Mississippi woman who in 1995 attracted attention when she gave away $150,000, most of what she had saved working as a washerwoman, to endow a scholarship fund at the University of Southern Mississippi in Hattiesburg, dies of cancer in Hattiesburg. . . . Donald Gilbert Sanders, 69, lawyer who played a key role in events leading to the 1974 resignation of Pres. Richard Nixon, dies of cancer in Columbia, Missouri.			The 1999 Albert Lasker Medical Research Award for clinical research goes to David Cushman and Miguel Ondetti for finding a way to design drugs based on protein structure. The award for basic medical research goes to Clay Armstrong, Bertil Hille, and Roderick MacKinnon for their work on ion channel proteins. The award for special achievement goes to Seymour Kety for his groundbreaking contributions to neuroscience.	In golf, the U.S. Ryder Cup team mounts a record comeback, overcoming a four-point deficit to defeat the two-time defending champion European team in Brookline, Massachusetts, sparking a celebration on the golf course that the Europeans criticize as unsportsmanlike.	Sept. 26
California passes a law expanding patients' ability to sue insurers in state court. . . . Alexander Pogosyan, 18, is sentenced to five consecutive life terms in prison for the September 1998 shooting deaths of five people in Aurora, Colorado. . . . Health officials in New York City confirm that an ongoing outbreak of a mosquito-borne viral illness in the city, initially identified as St. Louis encephalitis, is in fact caused by the West Nile virus, never before found in the Western Hemisphere. The total number of confirmed cases in the area is 37, and four people have died of the West Nile disease.	Texas governor George W. Bush's service in the Texas Air National Guard during the Vietnam War comes under scrutiny when Ben Barnes, former speaker of the Texas House of Representatives, reveals that in late 1967 or early 1968 he personally asked the senior official in the Texas Air National Guard to help secure a pilot's slot for Bush, exempting Bush from being drafted to serve in Vietnam.	Pres. Clinton announces that the surplus for fiscal 1999 is a record $115 billion. The surplus is an off-budget surplus that required borrowing from Social Security. . . . The House passes, 327-87, an appropriations bill for energy, water, and nuclear weapons programs for fiscal 2000. . . . Northeast Nuclear Energy Co. pleads guilty in Hartford, Connecticut, to 23 federal felony counts of falsifying environmental records. The company agrees to pay $10 million in fines, the largest penalty ever levied against a U.S. nuclear plant. Northeast is only the second nuclear power company in the U.S. to be charged with felonies.		Spanish-born tenor Placido Domingo opens the Metropolitan Opera House's season for the 18th time since 1971, breaking the record set by the late Enrico Caruso for the most opening-night performances at the Met.	Sept. 27
The National Assessment of Educational Progress finds that 22% of fourth-graders, 26% of eighth-graders and 21% of 12th-graders demonstrated strong proficiency in writing, and 1% of students in each grade were judged to be writing at an "advanced" level in the 1998 tests. Some 16% of students in the fourth and eighth grades and 22% of high-school seniors demonstrated a lack of the most basic writing skills. The remainder are found to have basic, though not sophisticated, writing skills.		Pres. Clinton vetoes the District of Columbia fiscal 2000 appropriations bill because it contains "unwarranted intrusions into local citizens' decisions about local matters.". . . The House, 421-2, and the Senate, 98-1, passe a stopgap spending measure to keep the federal government running after the 2000 fiscal year begins Oct 1. . . . The Senate clears, 96-3, a fiscal 2000 appropriations bill for energy, water and nuclear weapons programs. . . . The SEC files charges against 68 individuals at 15 public companies, accusing them of accounting fraud. . . . GM and the UAW reach a tentative four-year agreement.		In a controversy over an exhibit of contemporary British art, the Brooklyn Museum of Art files a preemptive lawsuit, claiming that cutting off city funding will violate the museum's free-speech rights. However, the administration of NYC mayor Rudolph Giuliani (R) freezes the city's contributions to the museum's operating budget. . . . A groundbreaking is held for the National Museum of the American Indian, the last museum run by the Smithsonian Institution to be constructed along the Mall in Washington, D.C.	Sept. 28

F	G	H	I	J
Includes elections, federal-state relations, civil rights and liberties, crime, the judiciary, education, health care, poverty, urban affairs, and population.	*Includes formation and debate of U.S. foreign and defense policies, veterans' affairs, and defense spending. (Relations with specific foreign countries are usually found under the region concerned.)*	*Includes business, labor, agriculture, taxation, transportation, consumer affairs, monetary and fiscal policy, natural resources, and pollution.*	*Includes worldwide scientific, medical, and technological developments; natural phenomena; U.S. weather; natural disasters; and accidents.*	*Includes the arts, religion, scholarship, communications media, sports, entertainments, fashions, fads, and social life.*

	World Affairs	Europe	Africa & the Middle East	The Americas	Asia & the Pacific
Sept. 29		Serbian police forcefully disperse an estimated 30,000 protesters in Belgrade, Yugoslavia's capital, as they attempt to march to the residence of Yugoslav president Slobodan Milosevic. It is the first time that the daily protests, which started Sept. 21, have been broken up by police.		Nortel Networks Corp., becomes the first Canadian company to reach a market value of more than C$100 billion when its stock temporarily reaches an all-time high of C$74.30 (US$50.60) a share on the Toronto Stock Exchange. The company's stock closes at C$74 a share, reducing Nortel's market capitalization to C$99.84 billion. . . . Gen. Gustavo Leigh Guzman, 79, Chilean air force general who was a member of the four-man military junta led by Gen. Augusto Pinochet Ugarte and who broke with the junta when Pinochet proclaimed himself president in 1978, dies in Santiago, Chile, of a vascular ailment.	INTERFET forces discover the charred remains of at least nine bodies piled in the bed of a torched pickup truck on the outskirts of Dili in East Timor. . . . Aum Shinrikyo, a religious cult linked to the March 1995 nerve-gas attack in the Tokyo subway system, announces that it will suspend its recruitment of new members, close its branches, and discontinue the use of the Aum Shinrikyo name.
Sept. 30		Russian ground forces enter Chechnya to secure a buffer zone that will prevent Islamic militant incursions into other areas. Russian officials estimate that 78,000 people have fled Chechnya in the past week. . . . The violence that spread to seven prisons in Turkey after the Sept. 26 riots calms when inmates release the 93 guards seized in the uprisings. . . . Dmitri Sergeievich Likhachev, 92, Russian intellectual who survived four years in a Soviet labor camp and the 900-day Nazi German siege of Leningrad, dies in St. Petersburg, Russia.	Mustafa Zubari, the deputy chief of the Popular Front for the Liberation of Palestinians, returns to Israel for the first time in 32 years.	A powerful earthquake strikes southern Mexico, killing at least 20 people. The quake's epicenter is located between the resort towns of Puerto Escondido and Huatulco, about 275 miles (445 km) southeast of Mexico City, the capital, and it registers a 7.5 on the Richter scale. . . . Peruvian president Alberto Fujimori signs into law a bill that makes military service voluntary. . . . Canadian mining technology specialist Manley Guarducci is abducted by Nicaraguan rebels in Bonanza, Nicaragua.	Workers at a Japanese nuclear fuel-processing plant in Tokaimura accidentally set off an uncontrolled nuclear chain reaction, causing radiation levels to skyrocket in the plant and releasing radioactive gas into the surrounding area. The IAEA gives the accident a preliminary rating of four on a scale of seven used to measure the magnitude of nuclear mishaps. Separately, Masato Yokoyama, 35, a member of the Aum Shinrikyo religious cult, is sentenced to death by hanging for his role in a 1995 nerve-gas attack in Tokyo.
Oct. 1		Kazakhstan premier Nurlan Balgimbayev, resigns amid criticism of his handling of the country's slumping economy. . . . France's Food Safety Agency decides to continue the country's long-standing ban on the import of beef from Britain, prompting a sustained trade dispute between Britain and France. . . . Russian premier Vladimir Putin appoints Chechnya's pro-Russian parliament as the "sole legitimate authority" in Chechnya.		Heavy rains and massive mudslides begin to wreak havoc in several Mexican states along the nation's Gulf Coast and in the Sierra Madre Oriental Mountain range.	The Chinese government stages an elaborate parade in Beijing's Tiananmen Square to mark the 50th anniversary of the proclamation of communist rule over China. The anniversary pageantry is dominated by an unprecedented public display of Chinese military equipment. . . . Japanese officials reveal that at least 55 people were exposed to radiation in the Sept. 30 incident in Tokaimura. Three plant workers were hospitalized.
Oct. 2		Assailants throw two grenades at a rally for leftist presidential candidate Natalya Vitrenko in Inguletsk, southeastern Ukraine. Vitrenko and 33 other people are injured in the explosions. . . . Reports confirm that a group of nine Kurdish rebels from the nationalist Kurdistan Workers Party (PKK) surrendered to Turkish forces near Turkey's border with northern Iraq.	Reports indicate that King Mohammed VI has allowed well-known political exile Abraham Serfaty, a Marxist leader banished by Hassan, to return to Morocco after eight years of exile.		
Oct. 3		The Freedom Party, an extreme right-wing anti-immigration party led by Joerg Haider, registers the second-largest share of votes in elections for Austria's lower house of parliament. It is the strongest electoral showing by a far-right party in Western Europe since the end of World War II. . . . In what he calls an assassination attempt, Serbian opposition leader Vuk Draskovic suffers minor injuries in a car crash that kills Draskovic's brother-in-law and three bodyguards. . . . (Hector) Alastair Hetherington, 79, British editor of *The Guardian* newspaper, 1956–75, dies in Stirling, Scotland.	Foday Sankoh, the leader of the rebel Revolutionary United Front, returns to Sierra Leone from Togo, where he has been since May.	In reaction to a Sept. 17 ruling by the Canadian Supreme Court that allows the Micmacs to fish out of season, nonnative fishermen in about 150 boats damage more than 2,000 of the natives' 4,200 lobster traps by cutting the lines or breaking trap doors to free the catch in Miramichi Bay, off the coast of New Brunswick. About 100 nonnative fishermen and supporters allegedly cause C$25,000 (US$17,000) in damage to a fish plant in Pointe-Sapin, New Brunswick, where native-caught lobster is sold.	Akio Morita, 78, who cofounded Tokyo Telecommunications Engineering Corp., renamed Sony Corp. in 1958, dies of pneumonia in Tokyo, Japan.

A	B	C	D	E
Includes developments that affect more than one world region, international organizations, and important meetings of major world leaders.	Includes all domestic and regional developments in Europe, including the Soviet Union, Turkey, Cyprus, and Malta.	Includes all domestic and regional developments in Africa and the Middle East, including Iraq and Iran and excluding Cyprus, Turkey, and Afghanistan.	Includes all domestic and regional developments in Latin America, the Caribbean, and Canada.	Includes all domestic and regional developments in Asia and Pacific nations, extending from Afghanistan through all the Pacific Island, except Hawaii.

U.S. Politics & Social Issues	U.S. Foreign Policy & Defense	U.S. Economy & Environment	Science, Technology, & Nature	Culture, Leisure, & Lifestyle	
A California appeals court reinstates a lawsuit against a gun maker that manufactured the weapons used in a 1993 mass shooting at a San Francisco, California, office building, leaving nine dead and six injured. The 2-1 ruling is the first by an appellate court to approve a liability lawsuit against a gun maker. . . . Applications from Housing Works stages a public rally and files a class-action lawsuit against NYC mayor Rudolph Giuliani (R) and two administration officials on behalf of homeless people living with AIDS. . . . The Chicago Community Trust, the third-largest U.S. foundation and the nation's second-oldest community foundation, names Donald Stewart as its next president and chief executive. . . . Walter Bergman, 100, Michigan civil-rights advocate who was one of the first Freedom Riders, a group of blacks and whites that rode buses through the South in the early 1960s in order to desegregate interstate bus travel, dies in Grand Rapids, Michigan.	The AP reports that a dozen U.S. veterans of the 1950–53 Korean War described in interviews the killing of a group of South Korean civilian refugees by U.S. troops early in the war. If the massacre occurred as described, it would be one of two known orchestrated killings of civilians by U.S. ground troops in the 20th century. . . . Pres. Clinton announces a plan to write off all of the remaining $5.7 billion owed to U.S. federal aid agencies by the world's poorest nations. The plan will require debtor nations to prove that they are using the money for poverty-reduction efforts.	Pres. Clinton signs the fiscal 2000 Treasury-postal spending bill. . . . Pres. Clinton signs the fiscal 2000 legislative branch appropriations bill. . . . The Senate confirms, by voice vote, the appointment of Roger Ferguson to the post of vice chair of the Federal Reserve Board. . . . Pres. Clinton signs an appropriation's bill for energy, water, and nuclear weapons programs in fiscal 2000 . . . . The House passes, by voice vote, a bill to overhaul the nation's crop insurance program.	Smithsonian Institution officials announce that Steven Udvar-Hazy, a Hungarian-American businessman, pledged $60 million to the National Air and Space Museum, which will be the largest grant the Smithsonian has ever received.	Pres. Clinton, in a White House ceremony, presents the National Medal of Arts and National Humanities Medal to 18 American cultural figures and one performing-arts school. . . . The Senate passes a nonbinding resolution that calls for a stop to the Brooklyn Museum's federal funding if the museum does not cancel a controversial exhibition of contemporary British art. . . . Rev. Cotesworth Pinckney Lewis, 86, longtime rector of the Bruton Parish Episcopal Church in Williamsburg, Virginia, dies in Williamsburg of unreported causes.	Sept. 29
The House votes, 254-172, to approve legislation that will grant limited federal protection to a human fetus. Under the bill, it will be a federal crime to harm or kill a fetus during the commission of another crime. Although the measure does not criminalize consensual abortion procedures, pro-choice activists attack the bill for treating fetuses as humans with rights independent of the wishes of the women carrying the fetuses.	In the wake of Sept. 29 reports about alleged massacres in South Korea during the Korean War, Secretary of Defense William Cohen orders the army to open a new investigation. South Korea states it will open an investigation also. . . . A federal grand jury in New York City indicts investment adviser Martin Armstrong on 14 counts of securities fraud, wire fraud, and conspiracy in connection with the disappearance of as much as $950 million in Japanese corporate investments.	Pres. Clinton signs the stopgap measure. . . . The GAO reports that Kenneth Starr's probe cost $47 million through Mar. 31. Starr's office spent $7.2 million from October 1998 through March 1999, the period covering Pres. Clinton's impeachment. . . . The Illinois Supreme Court issues a decision that suggests that, even under ERISA, patients can sue HMOs in state courts for medical malpractice, on the grounds that the insurers' control over treatment amounts to the provision of medical care.		The Swedish Academy of Letters awards the Nobel Prize in Literature to German novelist Guenter Grass.	Sept. 30
		The House passes, 304-91, a $49.5 billion fiscal 2000 appropriations bill for the Department of Transportation. . . . Data shows the purchasing managers' index reached 57.8 in September, a five-year high. . . . The House passes, 240-175, a $69 billion fiscal 2000 appropriations bill a for agriculture and food programs. . . . Ted Arison, 75, American Israeli who founded Carnival Cruise Lines in 1972, dies in Tel Aviv, Israel, of a heart attack.	A study fails to confirm a link between fen/phen use and heart valve damage.	The Naismith Memorial Basketball Hall of Fame in Springfield, Massachusetts, inducts John Thompson, Kevin McHale, Wayne Embry, Billie Moore, and the late Fred Zollner.	Oct. 1
Francis Cutler Turner, 90, engineer and administrator considered by many to be the chief architect of the U.S.'s interstate highway system, dies in Goldsboro, North Carolina, while suffering from cancer and dementia.	A ground-based interceptor missile successfully hits and destroys a target missile in the first major test of a limited national missile defense system. The system is a smaller-scale version of the Strategic Defense Initiative that Pres. Ronald Reagan pursued in the 1980s.	In the midst of an ongoing dispute over whether subsistence fishers, including native Eskimos, Indians, and Aleut, should be given priority over sport and commercial anglers in gaining access to Alaska's rich fish stock, federal officials take partial control of Alaska's fisheries.		A controversial exhibition of contemporary British art opens at the Brooklyn Museum of Art in New York City, despite the opposition of the city's mayor, Rudolph Giuliani, and the U.S. Senate.	Oct. 2
The Census Bureau reports that the number of people in the U.S. who did not have health insurance rose in 1998 by 833,000 from the previous year, to 44.3 million. That is 16.3% of the country's population, up from 16.1% in 1997.					Oct. 3

F	G	H	I	J
Includes elections, federal-state relations, civil rights and liberties, crime, the judiciary, education, health care, poverty, urban affairs, and population.	Includes formation and debate of U.S. foreign and defense policies, veterans' affairs, and defense spending. (Relations with specific foreign countries are usually found under the region concerned.)	Includes business, labor, agriculture, taxation, transportation, consumer affairs, monetary and fiscal policy, natural resources, and pollution.	Includes worldwide scientific, medical, and technological developments; natural phenomena; U.S. weather; natural disasters; and accidents.	Includes the arts, religion, scholarship, communications media, sports, entertainments, fashions, fads, and social life.

	World Affairs	Europe	Africa & the Middle East	The Americas	Asia & the Pacific
Oct. 4		A Croatian court convicts Dinko Sakic, a commander of a World War II death camp in Nazi-controlled Croatia, on charges of committing war crimes. A seven-judge panel sentences Sakic to the maximum 20 years in prison. Sakic, 78, is the only known Nazi concentration camp commander still living. . . . Bernard Buffet, 71, prolific French painter, is found dead in the Var region of southern France in an apparent suicide; he was suffering from Parkinson's disease.	Israeli police release a Palestinian talk-show host, Maher Dasuki, arrested Sept. 15, without filing charges against him. . . . Sir de Villiers Graaff, 85, leader of South Africa's United Party (UP), 1956–77, dies outside Cape Town, South Africa.	As the violence that started Oct. 3 against the native population in New Brunswick, Canada, continues, a cabin is burned.	In South Korea, a leak of radioactive water at a nuclear power plant exposes 22 workers to radiation.
Oct. 5		In Kosovo, one Serb is killed and roughly 20 other people, including NATO peacekeepers, are injured in ethnic fighting in Kosovska Mitrovica. . . . Chechen president Aslan Maskhadov declares martial law in the republic. . . . Two commuter trains collide in London, England, killing dozens of people and injuring scores more. It is described as Britain's worst railroad accident in at least 40 years.	Palestinian and Israeli negotiators sign an agreement to open a transportation corridor through Israel, allowing Palestinians to travel between the Palestinian-controlled West Bank and Gaza Strip. . . . Egyptian president Hosni Mubarak retakes his oath of office, and he names Atef Obeid as his new prime minister, replacing Kamal al-Ganzouri.	As violence that started Oct. 3 against the Mimac in Canada continues, a gazebo-like structure used by natives as a religious shrine is set on fire, and a boat belonging to a nonstatus Micmac is partially sunk. . . . Due to heavy rains that started Oct. 1 in Mexico, an avalanche of mud buries people and houses in the Puebla town of Teziutlan.	
Oct. 6	More than 600 delegates from 25 nations attend the first International Conference on Federalism in the Quebec, Canada, resort of Mont-Tremblant Village.	Sir (D'arcy) Patrick Reilly, 90, British ambassador to the Soviet Union, 1957–60, and to France, 1965–68, dies in Oxford, England, of unreported causes. . . . Amalia da Piedade Rebordão Rodrigues, 79, Portuguese singer considered the queen of fado, a traditional musical style, dies in Lisbon, Portugal, of unreported causes.		Native leaders from 35 bands in Atlantic Canada ask natives to observe a 30-day moratorium on lobster fishing beginning Oct. 9, to ease tensions that started Oct. 3.	Police raid the Tokyo offices of JCO Co. Ltd., operator of a nuclear fuel-processing plant in Tokaimura, the site of Japan's worst nuclear accident on Oct. 1. The police raid the plant and JCO's Tokaimura office, searching for evidence of possible negligence and violation of regulations by the company.
Oct. 7		The confirmed death toll from the Oct. 5 train collision in London, England, stands at 33.		Celvin Galindo Lopez, the prosecutor investigating the April 1998 murder of Roman Catholic bishop Juan Gerardi Conedera, resigns and flees with his family to the U.S. after receiving death threats. He is one of several officials who have resigned from the case, in which Gerardi was killed two days after releasing a report that accused the Guatemalan military of widespread human-rights abuses during the country's long-running civil war.	A 24-party coalition led by Indian prime minister Atal Bihari Vajpayee's Hindu nationalist Bharatiya Janata Party (BJP) is declared the winner of India's parliamentary elections. Its newly formed National Democratic Alliance coalition will enjoy a solid parliamentary majority, with 294 seats.
Oct. 8	A magistrate at London's Bow Street Magistrates' Court rules that former Chilean military ruler Gen. Augusto Pinochet Ugarte can be extradited to Spain, where he faces charges of torture and conspiracy. The decision, the latest in a series of British court rulings concerning Pinochet, is praised by human-rights groups and condemned by the general's many supporters.			In response to the heavy rains and massive mudslides that are wreaking havoc in several Mexican states along the nation's Gulf Coast and in the Sierra Madre Oriental Mountain range, Pres. Ernesto Zedillo Ponce de Leon describes the devastation as the "tragedy of the decade" for Mexico. . . . Peruvian premier Victor Joy Way Rojas resigns in order to run for reelection to Congress.	Reports suggest that China has released Liu Xiaobo, a dissident sentenced to a labor camp in 1996 for writing a letter in which he called for the impeachment of Pres. Jiang Zemin.
Oct. 9				João Cabral de Melo Neto, 79, Brazilian poet widely regarded as one of the major Portuguese-language poets of the 20th century, dies in Rio de Janeiro, Brazil, after a long illness.	

A	B	C	D	E
Includes developments that affect more than one world region, international organizations, and important meetings of major world leaders.	Includes all domestic and regional developments in Europe, including the Soviet Union, Turkey, Cyprus, and Malta.	Includes all domestic and regional developments in Africa and the Middle East, including Iraq and Iran and excluding Cyprus, Turkey, and Afghanistan.	Includes all domestic and regional developments in Latin America, the Caribbean, and Canada.	Includes all domestic and regional developments in Asia and Pacific nations, extending from Afghanistan through all the Pacific Island, except Hawaii.

U.S. Politics & Social Issues	U.S. Foreign Policy & Defense	U.S. Economy & Environment	Science, Technology, & Nature	Culture, Leisure, & Lifestyle	
		The Senate clears, 88-3, a $49.5 billion fiscal 2000 appropriations bill for the Department of Transportation. . . . State Farm Mutual Automobile Insurance Co. is ordered to pay $456 million to policyholders for requiring body shops to use lower-priced generic parts when making repairs. . . . About 400 labor unions and environmental concerns unveil an alliance. . . . Leonard S. Shoen, 83, who in 1945 founded the company that became U-Haul International Inc., dies after driving his car into a utility pole in Las Vegas, Nevada, in what is called a suicide.		Martin S. Davis, 72, CEO of what became media giant Paramount, 1983–94, dies in New York City of a heart attack. . . . Art Stewart Farmer, 71, pioneering jazz musician, dies in of cardiac arrest in New York City. . . . At the top of the bestseller list is *Hearts in Atlantis*, by Stephen King. . . . In a nonbinding resolution, the House of Representatives calls for a stop of federal finds to Brooklyn Museum if it does not cancel the show opened Oct. 2.	Oct. 4
Data shows that the average annual cost of tuition and fees at four-year colleges and universities in 1999–2000 is $3,356, up 3.4% from the previous year. It is the smallest percentage increase in four years. . . . The Senate rejects Pres. Clinton's nomination of Judge Ronnie White to sit on the U.S. District Court in St. Louis, Missouri. It is the first time the full Senate rejects a judicial nomination since 1987.	The House passes, 214-21, a $12.7 billion fiscal 2000 foreign operations spending bill. . . . Officials reveal that a grand jury has indicted three people—Lucy Edwards, Peter Berlin, and Aleksey Volkov—on charges of illegally transmitting and receiving money. It is the first indictment handed down during a probe of whether Russian criminals laundered billions of dollars through accounts at the Bank of New York.	MCI WorldCom Inc. and Sprint Corp., the nation's second- and third-largest long-distance telephone companies, respectively, announce plans to merge in a stock transaction valued at $115 billion. If completed, the deal will be the largest merger in history, eclipsing the pending $75 billion combination of oil companies Exxon Corp. and Mobil Corp.		Alex(ander) Stewart Lowe, 40, whose unmatched record in mountain ranges all over the world has made him the best-known American mountaineer of his generation, disappears in an avalanche in the Tibetan Himalayas.	Oct. 5
A survey shows that life expectancy for children born in 1998 was 76.7 years, up from 76.5 years in 1997. AIDS was not among the top 15 causes of death in the U.S. in 1998, for the first year since 1987. Heart disease remains the nation's leading cause of death.	The Senate clears, 51-49, the $12.7 billion fiscal 2000 foreign operations spending bill.				Oct. 6
The House passes, 275-151, a bipartisan bill establishing consumer protections for patients enrolled in HMOs and other health-insurance plans. It offers more consumer protections than the one passed by the Senate July 15. . . . Judge Robert Ruehlman dismisses a liability case filed by the city of Cincinnati, Ohio, against the gun industry. The case is one of 28 such lawsuits filed in courts across the country. . . . Reports confirm that a prosecutor in Milwaukee County, Wisconsin, has filed charges against a rapist known only by his DNA, which was found in semen samples from three separate 1993 rapes.	A federal grand jury in Bridgeport, Connecticut, indicts Martin Frankel, a U.S. financier who fled to Germany, where he is currently facing extradition. Frankel is indicted on 36 counts of money laundering, fraud, conspiracy and racketeering.	A jury in New York City finds American Airlines Inc., of AMR Corp., liable for passengers' emotional distress on a turbulent flight in 1995 and awards the plaintiffs $2 million in damages, the highest amount ever awarded by a jury for primarily emotional, rather than physical, injuries. . . . American Home Products Corp. agrees to pay a total of $3.75 billion to settle thousands of lawsuits brought by people claiming that they were injured by two diet drugs known as fen/phen.		Richard Hough, 77, British historian and novelist who penned more than 90 books, dies in London, England, while suffering from a heart ailment. . . . Rev. Bruce Ritter (born John Ritter), 72, Franciscan friar who in 1969 founded Covenant House, a shelter for runaways, and who was later accused of sexual misconduct, dies near Decatur, New York, of Hodgkin's disease.	Oct. 7
The New Mexico Board of Education votes, 14-1, to end the state science curriculum's requirement that teachers teach alternative theories to the theory of evolution. New Mexico is the first state in years to move to discourage the teaching of creationism in science classes. . . . In Oklahoma, in a resentencing mandated by an appellate court, Judge G. Thomas Van Bebber again sentences Michael Fortier to 12 years in prison for failing to inform officials about his knowledge of a plan that resulted in the 1995 bombing in Oklahoma City, which killed 168 people.	Prosecutors in New York City charge a Tanzanian man, Khalfan Khamis Mohamed, with murder and conspiracy in the 1998 bombings of the U.S. embassies in Kenya and Tanzania. Mohamed is the first suspect in custody believed to have had "direct operational responsibility" for the bombing in Tanzania.			Laila Ali, daughter of boxing great Muhammad Ali, knocks out opponent April Fowler in just 31 seconds in Ali's professional boxing debut in Verona, New York.	Oct. 8
The director of the National Institutes of Health (NIH), Dr. Harold Varmus, announces that he will leave the post at the end of the year.		Pres. Clinton signs the fiscal 2000 appropriations bill for the Department of Transportation and other federal transportation programs.		Morris Langlo West, 83, Australian author who wrote 27 novels, dies in Sydney, Australia, of a heart ailment. . . . Milt(on) Jackson, 76, jazz musician known for his technical virtuosity and his warm, bluesy tone dies, in New York City of liver cancer.	Oct. 9
F	G	H	I	J	
Includes elections, federal-state relations, civil rights and liberties, crime, the judiciary, education, health care, poverty, urban affairs, and population.	*Includes formation and debate of U.S. foreign and defense policies, veterans' affairs, and defense spending. (Relations with specific foreign countries are usually found under the region concerned.)*	*Includes business, labor, agriculture, taxation, transportation, consumer affairs, monetary and fiscal policy, natural resources, and pollution.*	*Includes worldwide scientific, medical, and technological developments; natural phenomena; U.S. weather; natural disasters; and accidents.*	*Includes the arts, religion, scholarship, communications media, sports, entertainments, fashions, fads, and social life.*	

	World Affairs	Europe	Africa & the Middle East	The Americas	Asia & the Pacific
Oct. 10		Portuguese premier Antonio Guterres's ruling Socialist Party wins a second consecutive term in government in a general election. . . . A St. Petersburg arbitration court orders foreign shareholders to give up their stakes in Russia's Lomonosov Porcelain Factory, in the first decision of its kind since Russia launched its privatization program in 1992.		Three of the 11 remaining captives from the Sept. 11 abduction by suspected Colombian guerrillas are freed. . . . In Mexico, unofficial tallies of the death toll from heavy rains and mudslides exceed 400 people, with some reports putting the total as high as 600. Flood victims protest perceived government incompetence. Police in Villahermosa clash with a group of protesters, beating them with batons and arresting about 100 people. . . . Peruvian president Alberto Fujimori appoints Alberto Bustamante Belaúnde as premier.	
Oct. 11	South Africa signs a free-trade agreement with the EU that will eliminate tariffs on most trade between the two partners.	A Bulgarian member of the UN Mission in Kosovo (UNMIK) is shot to death in the city of Pec. He is the first member of UNMIK killed since the UN began operating in Kosovo in July.	Reports confirm that the Israeli government has deported 26 members of the "Concerned Christians" cult, after they tried to enter Haifa without visas. The group is suspected of being a "doomsday cult" that authorities fear may incite violence or mass suicides in the year 2000.		Canadian journalist Murray Hiebert is released from a Malaysian prison after serving four weeks of a six-week prison sentence. His case raised international concern over freedom of the press. . . . Reports suggest that Chinese police beat to death a woman who refused to refrain from practicing Falun Gong meditation exercises while in custody.
Oct. 12	UN secretary general Kofi Annan attends a ceremony in Sarajevo, the capital of Bosnia-Herzegovina, to mark the day that the global population reaches 6 billion, according to experts. Annan congratulates a Bosnian Muslim woman, Helac Fatima, on giving birth to a baby boy designated as the earth's 6 billionth human inhabitant. According to experts, the global population has doubled since 1960.	Kazakhstan's parliament confirms Foreign Minister Kasymzhomart Tokayev as the country's new premier.	Israeli officials reveal the Supreme Court has ruled that Mohammed Abul Abbas, the alleged mastermind of the 1985 seizure of the Italian ship *Achille Lauro*, is immune from prosecution in Israel. . . . Hutu rebels attack members of a UN aid convoy in southern Burundi, killing nine people. The attack takes place at the Muzye refugee camp, 90 miles (140 km) southeast of Bujumbura, Burundi's capital.		Pakistan's armed forces stage a bloodless coup d'état, toppling the democratically elected government of P.M. Nawaz Sharif. Soldiers seize control of airports, television stations, and other communications facilities, and place Sharif and several cabinet ministers under house arrest in Islamabad, the capital. The military takeover is the fourth coup in Pakistan's 52-year history.
Oct. 13		The National Assembly, France's lower house of parliament, approves legislation that will give legal status to unmarried couples, regardless of their sexual orientation. France is the first predominantly Roman Catholic nation to formally recognize same-sex unions. . . . In the Czech Republic town of Usti nad Labem, the city council builds a barrier to protect Czechs from what they claim is lawless behavior from the town's Gypsy residents. . . . In London, England, a delegation of aborigines meets privately with Queen Elizabeth II. It is the first such meeting in 200 years.	Israeli prime minister Ehud Barak reaches agreement with settlers in the Palestinian-controlled West Bank to close 10 of 42 settlements that Israelis have established since late 1998, when the Wye land-for-peace agreement was approved.		Atal Bihari Vajpayee is sworn in for his third term as prime minister of India. . . . In response to plans to deregulate Australia's universities, students begin to stage demonstrations across Australia. . . . Reports from China reveal that Liu Janguo, the leader of an outlawed religious cult called Supreme Deity, was executed in Hunan province. Liu, 44, was convicted in June of raping 11 women—two of them under age 14—and of defrauding cult members.
Oct. 14	Many world leaders express dismay at the Oct. 13 failure of the U.S. Senate to ratify the Comprehensive Test Ban Treaty (CTBT). Nations expressing concern include Japan, France, China, Russia, and Germany. . . . Germany's Daimler-Benz Aerospace AG (DASA) and Aerospatiale Matra SA of France agree to merge their aerospace businesses, creating Europe's largest aerospace and military contractor.	A NATO-led force raids a building in Bosnia-Herzegovina that NATO officials claim is a base of operations for Croatian intelligence agents attempting to influence local politics and undermine the Bosnian peace accords signed in Dayton, Ohio. . . . Josef Locke (born Joseph McLaughlin), 82, Irish singer who became one of Britain's most popular entertainers of the 1940s and 1950s, dies in Clane, Ireland, of unreported causes.	Julius Kambarage Nyerere (born Kambarage Nyerere), president of Tanzaniai, 1964–85, dies in London, England; he had leukemia and also suffered a major stroke in the week before his death.	Hurricane Irene, bearing high winds and heavy rains, strikes western Cuba, flooding roads, destroying buildings, and flattening tobacco fields. The storm passes over the Bahamas, where it causes the deaths of four people. . . . Canadian immigration officials reveal that 22 smuggled Chinese migrants—six of whom tested positive for tuberculosis—were found at Toronto's Pearson International Airport one week earlier.	Police in Karachi, Pakistan, arrest more than a dozen demonstrators chanting support for ousted prime minister Nawaz Sharif. A small protest staged by Sharif supporters in Lahore is also broken up by police. . . . Two major Japanese banks, Sumitomo Bank Ltd. and Sakura Bank Ltd., announce their plans to merge by April 2002. The resulting combined bank will be the second-largest in the world.

A	B	C	D	E
Includes developments that affect more than one world region, international organizations, and important meetings of major world leaders.	*Includes all domestic and regional developments in Europe, including the Soviet Union, Turkey, Cyprus, and Malta.*	*Includes all domestic and regional developments in Africa and the Middle East, including Iraq and Iran and excluding Cyprus, Turkey, and Afghanistan.*	*Includes all domestic and regional developments in Latin America, the Caribbean, and Canada.*	*Includes all domestic and regional developments in Asia and Pacific nations, extending from Afghanistan through all the Pacific Island, except Hawaii.*

U.S. Politics & Social Issues	U.S. Foreign Policy & Defense	U.S. Economy & Environment	Science, Technology, & Nature	Culture, Leisure, & Lifestyle	
			Sea Launch Co., an international joint venture formed to launch private satellites from a platform at sea, conducts its first commercial launch when a Ukrainian-and Russian-built rocket lifts a satellite for U.S. satellite-television company DirecTV Inc. into orbit.	Margaret MacGregor defeats male opponent Loi Chow in boxing's first sanctioned mixed-gender bout in Seattle, Washington.	Oct. 10
Reports confirm that California governor Gray Davis (D) has signed a bill establishing required nurse-to-patient staffing ratios in all departments of hospitals. California is the first state to set such requirements. . . . Reports indicate that Colt's Manufacturing Co. has decided to discontinue production of its seven cheapest civilian handgun models and to concentrate on so-called smart-gun technology. Smart guns are designed to fire only when used by their authorized owners.	The U.S. Justice Department announces that it has deported Saudi Arabian dissident Hani Abdel Rahim al-Sayegh to Saudi Arabia, where he is expected to stand trial for his alleged role in the 1996 truck bombing of Khobar Towers, a U.S. military complex in that country. The bombing killed 19 U.S. servicemen.		The Karolinska Institute for Medicine in Stockholm awards the Nobel Prize in Physiology or Medicine to German-born U.S. scientist Guenter Blobel for his research into mechanisms used by proteins to locate their correct places within a cell.		Oct. 11
The Supreme Court refuses two appeals challenging the constitutionality of a Maine voucher program that subsidizes students in private schools but bars subsidies to students attending religious schools. . . . New Jersey governor Christine Todd Whitman (R) signs a gun-safety law requiring all new handguns to be sold with trigger locks that, when enabled, will prevent them from firing. New Jersey is the fourth state to pass such a law.			The Nobel Prize in Chemistry is awarded to Ahmed Zewail for developing a technique to photograph steps in chemical reactions that occur too quickly to be observed any other way. The Nobel Prize in Physics is awarded to Gerardus 't Hooft and Martinus Veltman for their work on a mathematical description of the link between two of the four fundamental forces believed to exist in the universe.	Wilt(on) Norman Chamberlain, 63, Hall of Fame basketball player considered by many to be the most dominant player in the history of the NBA, dies in Los Angeles of an apparent heart attack. He had suffered ill health and dramatic weight loss in the weeks leading up to his death.	Oct. 12
The Massachusetts Governor's Council votes to approve the elevation of Justice Margaret Marshall to chief justice of the Supreme Judicial Court. Marshall is the first woman to head the court. . . . Reports confirm that cigarette maker Philip Morris has acknowledged for the first time that scientific evidence shows smoking is addictive and can cause cancer and other deadly diseases. . . . Colorado prosecutors announce that they will not file charges in the 1996 murder of six-year-old JonBenet Ramsey, a child beauty-pageant winner whose murder was covered extensively by the media.	In a largely partisan vote, the Senate rejects, 48-51, ratification of the Comprehensive Test Ban Treaty (CTBT), which would prohibit nuclear weapons testing. It is the first time since 1920—when the Senate failed to ratify the Treaty of Versailles—that the U.S. Senate defeats a major international security agreement supported by the president. . . . The House passes, 372-55, a $267.8 billion fiscal 2000 defense appropriations bill. . . . Judge Kevin Duffy resentences four men convicted in a 1993 bombing at New York City's World Trade Center to more than 100 years in prison each.	Pres. Clinton announces a new initiative that will ban the building of roads in at least 40 million acres (16 million hectares) of federal forest land, in a move aimed at preventing the commercial development of those lands. . . . Vice Pres. Al Gore wins a key endorsement from the AFL-CIO labor federation in his bid for the Democratic presidential nomination in 2000. . . . The Senate clears, 74-26, an appropriations bill allocating $69 billion for agriculture and food programs in fiscal 2000.	Scientists report that they did not detect signs of water vapor in the debris kicked up by the crash of an unmanned probe, Lunar Prospector, into the moon in July. . . . The Nobel Memorial Prize in Economics is awarded to Canadian-born economist Robert Mundell for his study of how the international flow of capital affects the economies of individual countries.		Oct. 13
Senate Republican leaders agree to disband a controversial task force assembled on Sept. 23 to investigate the Justice Department.	In response to the Oct. 13 vote against the CTBT, Pres. Clinton states, "By this vote, the Senate majority has turned its back on 50 years of American leadership against the spread of weapons of mass destruction.". . . The Senate clears, 87-11, a $267.8 billion defense appropriations bill for fiscal 2000. . . . U.S. investigators find that the U.S. military failed to return valuables seized during the war to victims of the Nazi Holocaust.	The House passes, 406-18, a $99.5 billion appropriations bill allocating fiscal 2000 funding for the Department of Veterans Affairs (VA), the Department of Housing and Urban Development (HUD), and 17 independent agencies.	The U.S. Geological Survey states there is a 70% probability that a large earthquake will strike the San Francisco Bay area sometime in the next 30 years.	Playwright Arthur Miller is awarded the sixth annual Dorothy and Lillian Gish Prize at a ceremony in New York City.	Oct. 14

F	G	H	I	J
Includes elections, federal-state relations, civil rights and liberties, crime, the judiciary, education, health care, poverty, urban affairs, and population.	Includes formation and debate of U.S. foreign and defense policies, veterans' affairs, and defense spending. (Relations with specific foreign countries are usually found under the region concerned.)	Includes business, labor, agriculture, taxation, transportation, consumer affairs, monetary and fiscal policy, natural resources, and pollution.	Includes worldwide scientific, medical, and technological developments; natural phenomena; U.S. weather; natural disasters; and accidents.	Includes the arts, religion, scholarship, communications media, sports, entertainments, fashions, fads, and social life.

	World Affairs	Europe	Africa & the Middle East	The Americas	Asia & the Pacific
Oct. 15	Jamaica, Mali, Tunisia, Bangladesh, and Ukraine are elected as temporary members to the UN Security Council, replacing Bahrain, Brazil, Gabon, Gambia, and Slovenia. . . . The Nobel Peace Prize is awarded to the aid organization Doctors Without Borders, a group of medical personnel that responds to health crises around the world. . . The UN approves a resolution to impose economic sanctions on the Taliban militia unless the group hands over after alleged terrorist Osama bin Laden to the U.S. by Nov. 14.	Russian military commanders announce they have established a security zone in the separatist republic of Chechnya, concluding the first phase of a campaign against Islamic militants in the republic. . . . Reports from Germany confirm that construction workers accidentally dug up the concrete bunker in which Adolf Hitler, the World War II-era ruler of Nazi Germany, committed suicide at the end of the war.	South Africa's Truth and Reconciliation Commission grants amnesty to nine former South African security policemen in the 1982 bombing of the London offices of the ANC. Included in the amnesty are Eugene de Kock, Craig Williamson, and Gen. Johannes Coetzee. . . . Israel releases 151 Palestinian prisoners, bringing to 350 the total of prisoners freed since September signing of an accord. . . . Yosef Burg, 90, German-born Israeli politician known for his efforts to heal rifts between religious and secular Jews in Israel, dies in Jerusalem.	Cuban officials confirm that two people have died from electrocution in Havana and a handful of other victims are missing and feared drowned from the Oct. 13 storm. . . . Canadian fisheries minister Herb Dhaliwal appoints James MacKenzie as mediator in discussions to broker a permanent fishing agreement between the federal and provincial governments and the native bands of Atlantic Canada.	
Oct. 16			Voters reelect the ruling Botswana Democratic Party (BDP) as the majority party in Botswana's National Assembly.		
Oct. 17		Police and antigovernment protesters clash in Minsk, Belarus's capital. Scores of people are injured in the incident, which occurs when some 5,000 protestors break off from an authorized demonstration of 20,000 and begin an unauthorized march toward the presidential palace. The demonstrators are protesting a proposed reunification of Belarus and Russia.	Yemen executes by firing squad Islamic militant Zain al-Abdin Abu Bakar al-Mehdar (known as Abu Hassan) for his role in the abduction of 16 Western tourists in Yemen in December 1998. Four of the hostages died in a failed rescue attempt. Yemen's Supreme Court commutes the death sentence of another of the kidnappers to 20 years. . . . An Israeli official announces the end of a policy under which Palestinians had to prove they lived in East Jerusalem for seven consecutive years in order to maintain their residency rights.		Gen. Pervez Musharraf outlines his plans for governing Pakistan in a nationally televised address. Musharraf states he will replace Parliament with a six-member national security council made up of civilian and military leaders. The general also reveals that Pakistan will return to civilian rule, but he specifies no timetables for this return. . . . A Chinese ferry burns and sinks near Dalian, resulting in three deaths.
Oct. 18		Chinese president Jiang Zemin makes the first state visit to Britain by a Chinese president.	South Africa's Truth and Reconciliation Commission rejects an appeal by Eugene Terre'Blanche, who headed the right-wing Afrikaner Resistance Movement (AWB), for amnesty in a 1997 attempted murder conviction. . . . Reports disclose that thousands of settlers are protesting the Oct. 13 agreement with rallies outside Israeli prime minister Ehud Barak's home in Jerusalem.		Australian prime minister John Howard announces that the government will not implement plans to deregulate Australia's universities, following strong opposition voiced by universities and students since Oct. 13.
Oct. 19	The UN International Criminal Tribunal for the Former Yugoslavia convicts alleged Bosnian war criminal Goran Jelisic on 31 counts of torture and murder but acquits him of genocide charges.		Madeleine Albright becomes the first U.S. secretary of state to visit Nigeria in almost 13 years.	The Federal Court of Canada rules against the federal government in a 15-year-old pay-equity dispute. The decision is seen as a major victory for the women's movement and is expected to have far-reaching implications on pay structures in Canada and in the neighboring U.S.	Peace forces recover the remains of as many as 20 people from a site near Liquica in East Timor.
Oct. 20	Koichiro Matsuura, Japan's ambassador to France, is nominated as the new director general of the United Nations Educational, Scientific and Cultural Organization (UNESCO).	In an ongoing trade war between Britain and France, hundreds of British farmers in Poole, England, confront two truck drivers transporting French beef to British markets. The protesters blockade the road in front of the trucks, forcing them to return to the ferry. . . . Jack (John) Mary Lynch, 82, prime minister of Ireland, 1966–73, 1977–79, dies in Dublin.	Israeli police raid the home and office of former prime minister Benjamin Netanyahu, seizing dozens of expensive items that they suspect him of keeping illegally after being voted out of office in May.	In Canada, Quebec court judge Danielle Cote overturns parts of a law stipulating that French must be the predominant language on signs in the province. Cote's ruling touches upon a major focus of the Quebec sovereignty movement, the contentious issue of preserving the French language to promote cultural identity. Separately, the Quebec Court of Appeal unanimously overturns the conviction of Michel Jette, a deceased man, marking the first time Canadian courts clear a convicted killer posthumously.	The People's Consultative Assembly, Indonesia's national legislature, elects Abdurrahman Wahid as the nation's new president. Wahid's election caps 17 months of political uncertainty that followed the collapse of rule by former president Suharto. It is the first democratic transfer of power in the nation's 49-year history. Violent street protests erupt in Jakarta, the capital, moments after Wahid's victory is announced. At least one person dies, and dozens of others are injured. Rioting is also reported in several other cities.

A	B	C	D	E
Includes developments that affect more than one world region, international organizations, and important meetings of major world leaders.	*Includes all domestic and regional developments in Europe, including the Soviet Union, Turkey, Cyprus, and Malta.*	*Includes all domestic and regional developments in Africa and the Middle East, including Iraq and Iran and excluding Cyprus, Turkey, and Afghanistan.*	*Includes all domestic and regional developments in Latin America, the Caribbean, and Canada.*	*Includes all domestic and regional developments in Asia and Pacific nations, extending from Afghanistan through all the Pacific Island, except Hawaii.*

U.S. Politics & Social Issues	U.S. Foreign Policy & Defense	U.S. Economy & Environment	Science, Technology, & Nature	Culture, Leisure, & Lifestyle	
In Los Angeles, California, Judge Richard Paez strikes down a ban on gun sales that Los Angeles County enacted in September. Paez argues that the ban was an attempt by county officials to circumvent state law, which allows firearms to be sold under certain restrictions.	In New York City, Judge Michael Mukasey sentences Siddig Ibrahim Siddig Ali to 11 years in prison for participating in a failed plot to bomb New York City landmarks, including the United Nations building. Siddig Ali receives a reduced sentence for aiding prosecutors in the case—which resulted in the conviction of 10 people in 1995	The Senate clears, 93-5, a $99.5 billion appropriations bill allocating fiscal 2000 funding for the Department of Veterans Affairs (VA), the Department of Housing and Urban Development (HUD), and 17 independent agencies.	Hurricane Irene goes ashore in southwestern Florida, downing power lines and spawning a small tornado in Fort Lauderdale. The storm leaves more than a million people without electricity in Miami-Dade and Martin counties. Five people perish. . . . Scientists reveal they have found evidence that adult monkeys' brains regularly produce new cells. If the finding proves true in humans as well, it will challenge the long-held view that adult brains do not generate new cells.	An Olympic official reveals that some 250,000 tickets to premium Olympic events in Sydney have been withheld with the intent of selling them to companies willing to pay at least 300% more than normal prices for the tickets, and they were not included in a random national ticket ballot, as previously claimed.	Oct. 15
The national board of the NAACP unanimously approves a tourism boycott of the state of South Carolina to protest the state's continued flying of the Confederate States of America flag over the state capitol building in Columbia.			A powerful earthquake rocks the Mojave Desert area of California. No serious injuries are reported, and there is relatively little property damage considering the size of the temblor, which registers a 7.0 on the Richter scale. . . . A plane evacuates Dr. Jerri Nielsen from Amundsen-Scott South Pole Research Station. Nielsen, unable to leave Antarctica, has been treating herself for suspected breast cancer at the science station.	Jean Shepherd, radio performer and author described as the "first radio novelist" whose age is variously given as 70 and 78, dies in Sanibel Island, Florida, of unreported causes.	Oct. 16
Orville Lynn Majors, a former nurse, is convicted of killing six patients at a rural Indiana hospital where he worked. Judge Ernest Yelton sentences Majors to six prison terms of 60 years each, amounting to a sentence of life in prison without parole. . . . An FBI report shows that violent and property crimes were each down 6% in 1998 from the year before. Homicides in 1998 decreased 7% from 1997, a drop entirely accounted for by a decline in killings with guns.			The U.S. Geological Survey reveals that the Oct. 16 earthquake in California's Mojave Desert exposed a 25-mile-long fault line, dubbed the Lavic Lake, that seismologists had previously considered inactive. . . . Hurricane Irene moves out to sea after dumping a half-foot (15 cm) of rain on southeastern North Carolina.	American Greg Ray clinches his first Indy Racing League (IRL) title by finishing third in the season-ending Mall.com 500 at Texas Motor Speedway in Fort Worth, Texas.	Oct. 17
In *Flippo v. West Virginia*, the Supreme Court rules unanimously that police officers must obtain warrants before conducting searches of murder scenes. . . . Independent counsel Kenneth Starr resigns his post. Starr's five-year investigations—which culminated in Pres. Clinton's impeachment—cost more than $47 million. Robert Ray is sworn in as Starr's successor.	Pres. Clinton vetoes the $12.7 billion fiscal 2000 foreign aid appropriations bill, saying that it contains too little funding and reflects growing isolationism on the part of congressional Republicans.				Oct. 18
Members of the white supremacist Ku Klux Klan sues NYC on grounds that it is violating their First Amendment free-speech rights by denying the group a permit to rally. . . . The American Medical Association (AMA) withdraws its endorsement of legislation outlawing intact dilation and evacuation (IDE) abortions, arguing that it cannot support legislation that will make doctors criminally liable for performing a medical procedure.		Senate Republicans block campaign finance-reform legislation for the fourth year in a row. . . . Groups of college students launch an anti-sweatshop campaign against Nike, a major maker of sportswear that has licenses with five large U.S. colleges to produce their athletic wear.	The Florida Department of Agriculture reports that Hurricane Irene caused estimated crop damage in the state of at least $100 million.	Penelope Mortimer (born Penelope Ruth Fletcher), 81, English novelist, dies in London of cancer. . . . Nathalie Sarraute (born Natasha Tcherniak), 99, Russian-born French novelist who prefigured and profoundly influenced a 1950s French literary movement, dies in Paris.	Oct. 19
Florida's Third District Court of Appeal reverses a September ruling in which it held that damages in a class-action lawsuit brought against cigarette makers have to be determined on a case-by-case basis. . . . In response to the lawsuit against New York City filed by the Ku Klux Klan on Oct. 19, black civil-rights activist Rev. Al Sharpton reveals that his National Action Network has filed a brief supporting the Klan's right to demonstrate.	In Newark, New Jersey, Judge William Walls rules that the use in court of classified terrorism as evidence against immigrants is unconstitutional, and he orders an immigrant, Hany Kiareldeen, to be released. Kiareldeen has been held by the INS for 18 months because government agencies claim to have evidence that he associated with terrorists but refuse to release the evidence to Kiareldeen or his lawyers. . . . Reports reveal that the U.S. secretly deployed some 12,000 nuclear weapons in 18 countries and nine territories during the height of the cold war.	The Senate, by voice vote, and the House, 215-213, pass a $39 billion fiscal 2000 appropriations measure for the Departments of Commerce, Justice, and State. . . . Pres. Clinton signs a $99.5 billion appropriations bill allocating fiscal 2000 funding for the Department of Veterans Affairs (VA), the Department of Housing and Urban Development (HUD), and 17 independent agencies.	The FTC releases new rules designed to prevent commercial child-oriented World Wide Web sites from collecting personal data from children under age 13 without "verifiable parental consent."	The John F. Kennedy Center for the Performing Arts awards its Mark Twain Prize for humor to comedian Jonathan Winters. . . . Calvin Griffith, 87, longtime baseball team owner known for his old-fashioned, tight-fisted approach to the business of baseball, dies in Melbourne, Florida, of heart ailments and a kidney infection.	Oct. 20
F	G	H	I	J	
Includes elections, federal-state relations, civil rights and liberties, crime, the judiciary, education, health care, poverty, urban affairs, and population.	Includes formation and debate of U.S. foreign and defense policies, veterans' affairs, and defense spending. (Relations with specific foreign countries are usually found under the region concerned.)	Includes business, labor, agriculture, taxation, transportation, consumer affairs, monetary and fiscal policy, natural resources, and pollution.	Includes worldwide scientific, medical, and technological developments; natural phenomena; U.S. weather; natural disasters; and accidents.	Includes the arts, religion, scholarship, communications media, sports, entertainments, fashions, fads, and social life.	

	World Affairs	Europe	Africa & the Middle East	The Americas	Asia & the Pacific
Oct. 21	The U.S. National Oceanic and Atmospheric Administration (NOAA) reveals that the Earth's ozone layer appears to be in the first stages of recovery because NASA readings show that the 1999 hole in the ozone layer above Antarctica is slightly smaller than in 1998.	Roughly 150 people are killed in a series of explosions in a marketplace in Grozny, the capital of the separatist republic of Chechnya.			Much of the street violence that started Oct. 20 in Indonesia subsides when the legislature elects Megawati Sukarnoputri, the sole rival of Abdurrahman Wahid in the presidential election, as vice president. The appointments mark the first time in Indonesian history that the Golongan Karya (Golkar), or Functional Group party—the party of former president Suharto and his successor, B. J. Habibie—have not headed the nation's government.
Oct. 22	The UN votes to send 6,000 peacekeeping troops to Sierra Leone to oversee a controversial peace plan signed in July.				East Timorese independence leader Jose Alexandre (Xanana) Gusmão returns to Dili, the capital of East Timor, after seven years of exile. In an address to 3,000 supporters, Gusmao urges East Timorese to work together to rebuild their communities, devastated by violence in the wake of the August referendum.
Oct. 23		A three-judge panel in Palermo, Italy, finds former premier Giulio Andreotti not guilty of collusion with the Mafia, ending a four-year trial. . . . Andras Hegedus, 76, Hungarian premier, 1955–56, dies after suffering from heart disease in recent years.			
Oct. 24		In Kosovo, roughly 4,000 ethnic Albanians in the town of Orahovac hold a rally to protest the deployment of Russian peacekeeping forces in the town. . . . The Swiss People's Party, a far-right, nationalist party, makes significant gains in parliamentary elections. . . . Islamic militants free four Japanese geologists and an interpreter after holding them captive since Aug. 23. Since then, the militants who entered Kyrgyzstan from Tajikistan have released seven of the hostages, and one has been killed.	Tunisian voters reelect Pres. Zine el-Abidine Ben Ali to a third term in office by an overwhelming margin. . . . A three-judge panel in Tel Aviv sentences Samuel Sheinbein, 18, a U.S. teenager convicted of murder, to a 24-year prison term for killing Alfredo Enrique Tello, Jr., 19, in the U.S.	Buenos Aires mayor Fernando De la Rua of the center-left Alianza coalition is elected president of Argentina. It is the first time that the Peronists have lost a presidential election since the party was founded in the 1940s. . . . Millions of Colombians march in antiwar protests in hundreds of cities across the nation. The marches coincide with the resumption of formal peace talks, and they are part of a series of peace demonstrations begun in May.	
Oct. 25	The UN Security Council approves a resolution establishing a UN force that will assume administrative authority over East Timor. The force—the UN Transitional Administration for East Timor (UNTAET)—will replace the INTERFET. . . . Delegates from more than 170 nations open a conference on global warming held in Bonn, Germany. . . . Health officials from 109 nations open the first round of talks on creating an international treaty to regulate tobacco.	Albanian premier Pandeli Majko resigns, two weeks after losing a vote to retain the leadership of his governing Socialist Party.	Israel officially opens a safe passage route for Palestinians traveling between the occupied territories of the West Bank and Gaza Strip. Separately, an Israeli soldier shoots and kills a Palestinian street vendor near a Jewish holy site in Bethlehem, sparking three days of clashes between Palestinians and Israeli troops guarding the site.		Pakistan's military rulers announce the appointment of seven civilian leaders to the government of Gen. Pervez Musharraf, who seized power in an Oct. 12 bloodless coup. . . . Followers of the banned Falun Gong spiritual movement begin to gather in small groups in Tiananmen Square in Beijing, the capital of China, to protest the drafting of a new anticult law aimed at their group. Police detain the protesters as they trickle into the square.
Oct. 26		In retaliation for protests and boycotts in Britain, French farmers blockade the French exit of the English Channel tunnel, which links the two countries. . . . Members of the House of Lords, Britain's upper chamber of Parliament, approves a bill that will abolish the right of hereditary peers to sit and vote in the chamber.			

A	B	C	D	E
Includes developments that affect more than one world region, international organizations, and important meetings of major world leaders.	Includes all domestic and regional developments in Europe, including the Soviet Union, Turkey, Cyprus, and Malta.	Includes all domestic and regional developments in Africa and the Middle East, including Iraq and Iran and excluding Cyprus, Turkey, and Afghanistan.	Includes all domestic and regional developments in Latin America, the Caribbean, and Canada.	Includes all domestic and regional developments in Asia and Pacific nations, extending from Afghanistan through all the Pacific Island, except Hawaii.

U.S. Politics & Social Issues	U.S. Foreign Policy & Defense	U.S. Economy & Environment	Science, Technology, & Nature	Culture, Leisure, & Lifestyle	
The House approves, 358-67, a bill that will reauthorize the Title I program, which provides federal aid to disadvantaged students. The House also passes, 213-208, a bill that will allow some states to convert Title I funding into lump-sum payments. . . . The Senate passes, 63-34, a bill outlawing a controversial procedure known medically as intact dilation and evacuation (IDE). . . . A District Court panel orders New York City to allow a Ku Klux Klan rally to proceed.		The Senate, by voice vote, and the House, 225-200, clear a $14.5 billion interior spending bill for fiscal 2000. . . . Pres. Clinton signs a second continuing resolution. . . . Pres. Clinton signs a bill creating a new national park in Colorado, known as the Black Canyon of the Gunnison National Park. . . . A federal jury in Miami, Florida, convicts former Miami-Dade County Commissioner James Burke for accepting a $5,000 bribe from financier Howard Gary.		John Bromwich, 80, Australian tennis star who won the Australian Open twice (1939, 1946) but especially excelled in doubles play, dies of a heart attack in Geelong, Australia.	Oct. 21
Texas governor George W. Bush, the front-runner for the Republican presidential nomination in 2000, misses the first televised debate of the 2000 presidential campaign, held in New Hampshire.		Pres. Clinton signs into law a fiscal 2000 appropriations bill for the Department of Agriculture and other agricultural programs.	Scientists report they have identified an enzyme that possibly plays a role in the development of Alzheimer's disease. The enzyme, beta-secretase, is involved in the creation of protein fragments that form deposits, known as amyloid plaques, that are associated with Alzheimer's disease.		Oct. 22
Members of the white supremacist Ku Klux Klan hold the first-ever Klan rally in New York City The 18 Klan members at the rally wear no masks, because of an 1845 state law prohibiting masks at public demonstrations. The Klan members are vastly outnumbered by an estimated 6,000 protesters, 2,000 onlookers, and hundreds of riot police. At least three police officers are injured in scuffles with counterdemonstrators, and 14 of the protesters are arrested. One Klan member is injured. . . . The Cystic Fibrosis Foundation announces that it has received a $20 million gift from the Bill and Melinda Gates Foundation, the largest gift in the foundation's history.				Rev. Jerry Falwell and 200 of his evangelical Christian supporters meet with gay minister Mel White and a group of homosexual Christians. The meeting draws dozens of protestors, including Rev. Fred Phelps, who gained attention when members of his congregation harassed homosexuals at the funeral of Matthew Shepard, a gay college student killed in 1998.	Oct. 23
John Lester Hubbard Chafee, 77, Republican governor of Rhode Island, 1963–69, and senator, 1976–99, dies in Bethesda, Maryland, of congestive heart failure.		The Teamsters union begins a strike against Overnite Transportation Co., the nation's largest nonunion trucking firm, to pressure the company into granting union recognition to its 8,200 workers.		Moroccan Khalid Khannouchi runs the fastest marathon in history, winning the Chicago Marathon in two hours, five minutes, and 42 seconds.	Oct. 24
The National Center for Health Statistics reports that the rate of births to teenage mothers fell from 1997 to 1998. It is the seventh consecutive annual decline.	Pres. Clinton signs the $267.8 billion fiscal 2000 defense appropriations bill.	Pres. Clinton vetoes the fiscal 2000 appropriations measure for the Departments of Commerce, Justice, and State.		(William) Payne Stewart, 42, golfer who won U.S. Open titles in 1991 and 1999, dies aboard a plane that crashes near Mina, South Dakota. Five others are also killed in the crash. . . . The Booker Prize is awarded to J. M. Coetzee of South Africa. Coetzee is the first author in the history of the prize to win it twice.	Oct. 25
The U.S. Seventh Circuit Court of Appeals rules, 5-4, that bans on intact dilation and evacuation (IDE) abortions in Illinois and Wisconsin are constitutional. . . . Stanford University announces a $150 million donation from James H. Clark, a former faculty member now involved in high-technology companies. Clark's gift is the largest ever given to a university by a former faculty member.		Dow Jones & Co. announces that four companies—Microsoft, Intel, Home Depot, and SBC Communications—will be new components of the Dow Jones Industrial Average. The four outgoing companies are Chevron, Goodyear Tire & Rubber, Sears, Roebuck & Co., and Union Carbide. With the reshuffle to take effect Nov. 1, the Dow the first time will include stocks that are not traded on the NYSE.		Abraham Lincoln Polonsky, 88, screenwriter who was blacklisted during the 1950s, dies in Beverly Hills, California, after a heart attack. . . . Hoyt Axton, 61, songwriter whose biggest hit was "Joy to the World" (1971), dies near Victor, Montana, after recently suffering two heart attacks.	Oct. 26

F	G	H	I	J
Includes elections, federal-state relations, civil rights and liberties, crime, the judiciary, education, health care, poverty, urban affairs, and population.	*Includes formation and debate of U.S. foreign and defense policies, veterans' affairs, and defense spending. (Relations with specific foreign countries are usually found under the region concerned.)*	*Includes business, labor, agriculture, taxation, transportation, consumer affairs, monetary and fiscal policy, natural resources, and pollution.*	*Includes worldwide scientific, medical, and technological developments; natural phenomena; U.S. weather; natural disasters; and accidents.*	*Includes the arts, religion, scholarship, communications media, sports, entertainments, fashions, fads, and social life.*

	World Affairs	Europe	Africa & the Middle East	The Americas	Asia & the Pacific
Oct. 27		The Russian air force bombs Grozny, the capital of Chechnya. The bombing kills 116 people, according to Chechen officials. . . . Five gunmen open fire on a session of Armenia's parliament in Yerevan, the capital, killing Premier Vazgen Sarkisyan, 40, and seven other government officials. The gunmen hold dozens of people hostage in the parliament. . . . Iranian president Mohammed Khatami makes the first trip to France and only the second visit to Western Europe by an Iranian head of state since 1979.	Reports suggest that fighting broke out in Sierra Leone in mid-October.	In Canada, tensions between aboriginal and commercial fishermen over out-of-season fishing rights flares when nonnative fishermen set fire to Micmac natives' clothing and boots on shore in an attempt to disrupt their fishing expedition.	
Oct. 28		The five gunmen who killed Premier Vazgen Sarkisyan and seven other government officials in Armenia Oct. 27 release their hostages and surrender to police. . . . Rafael Alberti, 96, Spanish poet who was awarded the Cervantes Prize, Spain's highest literary honor, dies in El Puerto de Santa Maria, Spain.	Israel begins deporting a group of foreign-born Christians suspected of being involved in "doomsday cults," which authorities fear may incite violence or mass suicides in the year 2000.		Reports reveal that in recent months, Australian officials have seized 28 ships—all bound from Indonesia—carrying nearly 1,000 people.
Oct. 29		In Chechnya, Russian forces bomb a convoy of civilians, killing 25 people and wounding 70 others near the village of Shami-Yurt, west of Grozny. The Russian military denies the incident. . . In Belfast, Northern Ireland, Garfield Gilmore is convicted and sentenced to life for murdering three boys in a gas bomb attack in July 1998.		In Colombia, Luis Alfredo Garavito, 42, tells prosecutors that he killed 140 boys between ages eight and 16 over a five-year period that ended in April with his incarceration on an unrelated rape charge. If Garavito's claims prove true, he will be among the most prolific serial murderers on record.	A powerful cyclone packing winds of 160 miles per hour (260 kmph) slams into India's eastern coast, devastating the state of Orissa and killing thousands of people. The cyclone destroys hundreds of thousands of dwellings, leaving millions of people homeless.
Oct. 30		In face of the Russian military's denial of the Oct. 29 incident in Chechnya, the Red Cross confirms reports of civilian deaths.	Five Israelis are injured when gunmen fire on a bus traveling through the West Bank, near the crossing point for a newly opened safe-passage route between the West Bank and Gaza Strip.		The Standing Committee of the National People's Congress, China's parliament, approves a new anticult law. Reports suggest that some 3,000 people have been arrested across Beijing since Falun Gong practitioners renewed protests on Oct. 25. Most of them were forcibly returned to their home provinces.
Oct. 31		Georgia's ruling Citizens Union party wins a majority in parliamentary elections. . . . In Armenia, funerals are held for Premier Vazgen Sarkisyan and seven other officials killed on Oct. 27. . . . Lord Jakobovits (Rabbi Immanuel), 78, chief rabbi of the United Hebrew Congregations of the British Commonwealth (1967–91) and the leading spokesman for British Jews, dies in London, England, of a brain hemorrhage.		Tabare Vazquez, the candidate of the opposition leftist Broad Front coalition, wins the most votes in Uruguay's presidential election, garnering 39% of the ballots cast. However, because Vazquez falls short of a majority, he will face the second-place finisher, Sen. Jorge Batlle of the ruling Colorado Party, in a runoff election.	Chinese state media reports that authorities have charged four leading Falun Gong members—Li Chang, Wang Zhiwen, Ji Liewu, and Yao Jie—under the new anticult law passed Oct. 30. . . . A fire sweeps through a three-story building in Inchon, South Korea, killing at least 54 people. At least 71 other people are injured.
Nov. 1			Saudi Arabia's finance ministry announces that the country will for the first time open its stock market to investment by foreigners. . . . An Israeli-developed Arrow-2 missile successfully hits and destroys a target missile over the Mediterranean Sea in its first major test.		The ruling military regime in Myanmar free British activist Rachel Goldwyn, who was sentenced to seven years in prison on Sept. 16. . . . Torrential rains and flooding begins in central Vietnam.

A	B	C	D	E
Includes developments that affect more than one world region, international organizations, and important meetings of major world leaders.	Includes all domestic and regional developments in Europe, including the Soviet Union, Turkey, Cyprus, and Malta.	Includes all domestic and regional developments in Africa and the Middle East, including Iraq and Iran and excluding Cyprus, Turkey, and Afghanistan.	Includes all domestic and regional developments in Latin America, the Caribbean, and Canada.	Includes all domestic and regional developments in Asia and Pacific nations, extending from Afghanistan through all the Pacific Island, except Hawaii.

U.S. Politics & Social Issues	U.S. Foreign Policy & Defense	U.S. Economy & Environment	Science, Technology, & Nature	Culture, Leisure, & Lifestyle	
Congress awards Congressional Gold Medals to former president Gerald Ford and his wife, Betty Ford. . . . The House votes, 271-156, to make it a federal crime for doctors to prescribe drugs for the purpose of helping terminally ill patients commit suicide. . . . Vice Pres. Al Gore and former senator Bill Bradley (D, N.J.) face each other in the first televised debate in their contest for the Democratic presidential nomination in 2000.		Pres. Clinton, citing final figures from the White House's Office of Management and Budget (OMB), announces that the federal government posted a $123 billion budget surplus in fiscal 1999.	Robert L(aurence) Mills, 72, U.S. physicist who, with colleague Chen Ning Yang in 1953, developed a mathematical theory explaining the behavior of nuclear forces that came to be known as the Yang-Mills theory, dies of prostate cancer in East Charleston, Vermont.	The New York Yankees defeat the Atlanta Braves, 4-1, to win MLB's 95th World Series. By sweeping the Braves, the Yankees post the first back-to-back World Series sweeps since the Yankees accomplished the feat in 1938 and 1939.	Oct. 27
Texas governor George W. Bush, the front-runner for the Republican presidential nomination in 2000, misses a debate held in New Hampshire. The other five GOP presidential contenders attend the forum. Bush's absence causes some New Hampshire Republicans to question whether he is taking their support for granted.	Lieutenant Commander Kieron O'Connor, 35, and Lieutenant Kevin Colling, 32, members of the U.S. Navy's Blue Angels precision flying team, die when their jet crashes while making a routine landing at Moody Air Force Base in Georgia. Their deaths raise the number of Blue Angels pilots who have died during air shows or training since the team's 1946 founding to 23. The accident is the first Blue Angels crash since 1990, and the first fatal incident involving the team since 1985.	The Commerce Department announces that it has adopted new methods for calculating economic data. . . . The House passes, 218-211, an appropriations bill for the Departments of Labor, Education, and Health and Human Services (HHS) in fiscal 2000. The $317 billion Labor-HHS measure is the biggest of the 13 annual spending bills.			Oct. 28
A three-judge panel of the U.S. 11th Circuit Court of Appeals in Atlanta, Georgia, overturns the federal death sentence of David Chandler, the first person sentenced to death under the 1998 AntiDrug Abuse Act. . . . Police arrest and charge four students in an alleged plan to bomb their Cleveland, Ohio, high school.		Pres. Clinton signs a third continuing resolution keeping money flowing to government agencies at fiscal 1999 levels.		The Senate approves, by voice vote, the authorization of funds for the Library of Congress's planned $20 million purchase of the private papers of the late civil-rights leader Rev. Martin Luther King Jr. If the House concurs, the purchase price will be the highest ever paid by the Library of Congress for a single collection.	Oct. 29
					Oct. 30
		EgyptAir Flight 990, a Boeing 767 jetliner bound for Cairo, Egypt, crashes into the Atlantic Ocean about 30 minutes after taking off from John F. Kennedy International Airport in New York City. Hours after the accident, U.S. Coast Guard ships and U.S. military aircraft locate debris from the 767 floating in an area about 50 miles (80 km) south of the Massachusetts island of Nantucket, but they find no survivors.		Australian Jesse Martin, 18, becomes the youngest person to sail around the globe unassisted and nonstop. . . . Golfer Tiger Woods wins the PGA Tour Championship in Houston, Texas. . . . Leaders from the Roman Catholic and Lutheran churches sign an accord ending a centuries-old doctrinal dispute over the nature of faith and salvation that sparked the Protestant Reformation in the 16th century.	Oct. 31
	The Iraqi National Congress (INC), an umbrella group of exiles opposed to Pres. Saddam Hussein, closes a conference in New York City. The New York assembly is the INC's first in seven years. . . . The U.S. Air Force entirely vacates Howard Air Force Base in Panama.	Yah Lin (Charlie) Trie, a friend of Pres. Bill Clinton, is sentenced to four months of home detention and three years of probation for violating political fund-raising laws. Democrats returned more than $600,000 in donations after learning that Trie might have collected the money from foreign donors. . . . Lobbyists Vernon Clark and Ann Eppard plead guilty to misdemeanor charges over illegal payments made in connection with a construction project in Boston, Massachusetts. The pleas end a long-running federal investigation.	After an intensive search, authorities state that all 217 people on board Egypt Air Flight 990, which crashed in the Atlantic after taking off from New York City Oct. 31, are presumed dead. . . . Theodore Alvin Hall, 74, scientist who worked on the U.S.'s World War II atom-bomb project at Los Alamos, New Mexico, dies in Cambridge, England, of kidney cancer.	In Brooklyn, New York, Judge Nina Gershon issues a preliminary injunction ordering New York City to restore $7.2 million in funding to the Brooklyn Museum of Art that the city cut over objections to a controversial exhibition that opened in October. . . . Walter Jerry Payton, 45, Football Hall of Fame running back who set at least three NFL career records, dies in Barrington, Illinois, of bile duct cancer. . . . *Pop Goes the Weasel*, by James Patterson, is at the top of the bestseller list.	Nov. 1

F	G	H	I	J
Includes elections, federal-state relations, civil rights and liberties, crime, the judiciary, education, health care, poverty, urban affairs, and population.	*Includes formation and debate of U.S. foreign and defense policies, veterans' affairs, and defense spending. (Relations with specific foreign countries are usually found under the region concerned.)*	*Includes business, labor, agriculture, taxation, transportation, consumer affairs, monetary and fiscal policy, natural resources, and pollution.*	*Includes worldwide scientific, medical, and technological developments; natural phenomena; U.S. weather; natural disasters; and accidents.*	*Includes the arts, religion, scholarship, communications media, sports, entertainments, fashions, fads, and social life.*

	World Affairs	Europe	Africa & the Middle East	The Americas	Asia & the Pacific
Nov. 2	Israeli prime minister Ehud Barak, Palestinian leader Yasser Arafat and U.S. president Bill Clinton meet in Oslo, Norway, in the first Israeli-Palestinian-U.S. meeting in 11 months. It is the first official visit to Norway by a U.S. president, and Clinton attends ceremonies commemorating the fourth anniversary of the assassination of Israeli prime minister Yitzak Rabin. . . . A Spanish judge issues an international arrest warrant for 98 former Argentine military officers, whom he indicts on charges of torture, terrorism, and genocide. The charges relate to the officers' actions during Argentina's so-called dirty war against left-wing activists from 1976 to 1983. The judge, Baltasar Garzon, brought the criminal charges that led to the arrest in Britain of former Chilean military leader Gen. Augusto Pinochet Ugarte.	French author Jean Echenoz is awarded the Goncourt Prize, France's most coveted literary award. . . . The Swedish government announces that more than 500 victims of the government's forced sterilization program, which operated from 1936 to 1976, have applied for compensation. An official reveals that 178 people have been compensated with $21,250 each.	In Lamontville, south of Durban, South Africa, unidentified gunmen shoot to death Cyril Zulu, 35, a Zulu prince and an African National Congress (ANC) leader. The slain prince was a key figure in peace negotiations between warring political factions in the volatile KwaZulu-Natal province. . . . An apparent missile attack against the Iraq-based Iranian opposition group People's Mujahedeen kills at least five Iranians and wounds 78 others.	Scouts Canada establishes a new scouting troop in Toronto for homosexuals ages 18 to 26. The troop is believed to be the first of its kind in North America. . . . The Alberta, Canada, provincial government announces that it will compensate 247 people sterilized against their will. The C$82 million (US$55 million) package includes an "expression of regret" by the government. . . . The Honduran congress ratifies an accord with Colombia that divides between them sovereignty over 12,000 square miles (31,000 sq km) of Caribbean coastal waters . . . . Demetrio Lakas, 74, president of Panama, 1972–78, dies in Panama City of a heart ailment.	An earthquake measuring 6.1 on the Richter scale strikes off the eastern coast of Taiwan, causing little reported damage. . . . Australian authorities seize an Indonesian ship carrying 352 illegal immigrants—the most people ever apprehended at one time in Australia. . . . Guerrillas from the Liberation Tigers of Tamil Elam rebel group launch a surprise offensive in northern Sri Lanka. . . . The Hong Kong government announces that it has struck a $4.1 billion deal with the U.S.'s Walt Disney Co. to jointly develop a theme park on Lantau Island, west of central Hong Kong.
Nov. 3	The appeals chamber of the war crimes court, located at The Hague, the Netherlands, orders that genocide suspect Jean-Bosco Barayagwiza be released because his rights were violated by a prolonged detention. Barayagwiza, charged in February 1998 with six counts of genocide and crimes against humanity, was arrested in Cameroon in November 1997.	Lithuania's parliament, the Seimas, confirms Andrius Kubilius as the country's new premier, succeeding Rolandas Paksas, who resigned in October in protest over a deal to privatize the state-owned Mazheikiu Nafta oil refinery. . . . Armenian president Robert Kocharyan appoints Aram Sarkisyan as the country's new premier . . . . . The government of Montenegro designates the German mark as its official currency, replacing the Yugoslav dinar.	In Zambia, unidentified gunmen shoot to death Wezi Kaunda, 47, an opposition leader and a son of former Zambian president Kenneth Kaunda.	P.M. Jean Chrétien appoints Justice Beverley McLachlin as the first female chief justice of the Supreme Court of Canada. . . . Mining technology specialist Manley Guarducci is released after 34 days in captivity in Nicaragua. Guarducci was abducted by Nicaraguan rebels at a mine site operated by Hemco Nicaragua SA in Bonanza, near Nicaragua's Caribbean coast.	Hyundai Securities Co. chairman Lee Ik Chi is convicted on charges of manipulating the stock price of Hyundai Electronics, and given a suspended two-year prison sentence. . . . Keizo Saji, 80, president, 1961–90, and chair since 1990 of Japan's Suntory Ltd., one of the world's foremost alcoholic beverage companies, dies in Osaka, Japan, of pneumonia.
Nov. 4	The European Central Bank (ECB) raises its benchmark interest rate to 3.0% from 2.5%. It is the first interest hike in the brief history of the ECB, which controls monetary policy in the European nations that have adopted the euro, the European Union's new currency.	Police in Northern Ireland seize weapons, ammunition, and pipe bombs from Protestant paramilitary groups that oppose the peace process. The police also arrest six men in a local office of the Orange Order, the province's largest Protestant organization. . . . Charles Wintour, 82, British editor of London's *Evening Standard*, 1959–76 and 1978–80, dies.	Iran marks the 20-year anniversary of the 1979 seizure of the U.S. embassy in Teheran, the capital, that is attended by about 7,000 people.	Health Canada, a government agency, approves the sale of Preven, a contraceptive pill intended to prevent unwanted pregnancy hours after unprotected sexual intercourse. The approval touches off a heated debate between prochoice and antiabortion groups. . . . Malcolm Denzil Marshall, 41, cricket player considered largely responsible for the ascendancy of the West Indian team that dominated the sport for more than a decade in the mid-1970s, dies in Bridgetown, Barbados, of colon cancer.	While there is no official death toll from the cyclone that slammed into India's eastern coast on Oct. 29, several government speakers estimate that at least 3,000 people perished in the storm. D. N. Pandhi, Orissa's special relief commissioner, states that food and aid supplies have not yet reached some 60% of the people affected by the cyclone.
Nov. 5	NATO officials disclose that NATO will delay its planned reduction of troops from Bosnia until after municipal elections scheduled for April 2000.	The Russian Federal Security Service (FSB) charges Igor Sutyagin, an arms-control researcher at the Institute for the Study of the U.S. and Canada, with spying for the U.S.			Pope John Paul II visits India for the first time since 1986. The pontiff lays a wreath at the national memorial site for legendary Indian pacifist Mohandas Karamchand Gandhi.
Nov. 6	The Rwandan government suspends cooperation with the UN war crimes court because of the court's Nov. 3 decision to release genocide suspect Jean-Bosco Barayagwiza, who was detained for two years without a trial.				Voters choose to retain the British monarch as Australia's head of state, in a national referendum on whether the country should become a republic. Voters reject a new preamble to the country's constitution which would have, among other things, recognized Australia's aborigines as the country's prior occupants and honored them for their "deep kinship" with their lands.

	A	B	C	D	E
	Includes developments that affect more than one world region, international organizations, and important meetings of major world leaders.	Includes all domestic and regional developments in Europe, including the Soviet Union, Turkey, Cyprus, and Malta.	Includes all domestic and regional developments in Africa and the Middle East, including Iraq and Iran and excluding Cyprus, Turkey, and Afghanistan.	Includes all domestic and regional developments in Latin America, the Caribbean, and Canada.	Includes all domestic and regional developments in Asia and Pacific nations, extending from Afghanistan through all the Pacific Island, except Hawaii.

U.S. Politics & Social Issues	U.S. Foreign Policy & Defense	U.S. Economy & Environment	Science, Technology, & Nature	Culture, Leisure, & Lifestyle	
State and local elections produce no clear partisan trend. Republicans capture control of both houses of the Virginia legislature for the first time in the state's history. However, Democrats prevail in several key mayoral races. Paul Patton, Kentucky's Democratic governor, becomes the first governor of that state to win reelection in 200 years. Residents of Maine defeat a proposed ban on late-term abortion and approve a measure that will legalize the use of marijuana for certain medical conditions. Residents of Mississippi reject a measure that would have instituted term limits on members of the state legislature. Mississippi is the first state to reject such a referendum proposal. . . . The House, by voice vote, passes a bill that will set penalties for companies that distribute deceptive notices of sweepstakes and other contests through the mail.	The People's Provincial Court in Havana, the capital of Cuba, orders the U.S. government to pay Cuba $181 billion in compensatory and punitive damages to redress the effects of a U.S. policy that Cuban agencies claim was devoted to "destroying the Cuban revolution." Observers note that it is unlikely that Cuba can compel the U.S. to pay the award, especially because there are no U.S. funds or assets in Cuba that the government might seize.	Abbott Laboratories agrees to pay a $100 million civil penalty to the federal government to settle accusations that it violated quality standards for manufacturing medical testing kits for years, despite warnings from the FDA. It is the largest fine ever imposed by the FDA. . . . A copier repairman, Byran Uyesugi, shoots to death seven coworkers at a Xerox Corp. office in Honolulu, Hawaii. He is captured after an hours-long standoff with police at a nearby nature preserve. . . . The Senate passes, 49-48, a $317 billion fiscal 2000 appropriations bill for the Departments of Labor, Education, and Health and Human Services (HHS) The. Labor-HHS measure is the biggest of the 13 annual spending bills. . . . In a referendum, residents of Washington State approve a measure abolishing the state's system of taxing automobiles, replacing it with an annual fee of $30 per car. Washington is the only state to have approved such a mandate, which observers argue marks a fundamental change in tax-writing power.		Three Dutch Old Master paintings stolen in 1978 from the M. H. de Young Memorial Museum in San Francisco, California, are anonymously left at the William Doyle Galleries in New York City. One painting stolen in the heist is still unaccounted for.	Nov. 2
A jury in Laramie, Wyoming, convicts Aaron McKinney, 22, in the October 1998 beating death of a homosexual college student, Matthew Shepard. . . . A gunman kills two men and injures two more in an office building in Seattle, Washington. . . . Real-estate developer Herman J. Russell states he will donate $1 million apiece to four colleges to boost entrepreneurship programs. It is the largest donation ever given by a black American to expand such programs.	The Senate approves, 76-19, a bill promoting trade with African, Caribbean and Central American nations. . . . Seven of the world's largest pharmaceutical firms agree to pay $1.17 billion to settle a class-action lawsuit that charges the companies with fixing vitamin prices. It brings to a close the largest price-fixing case ever pursued by the U.S. government. The companies are based in Switzerland, Germany, France, and Japan.	Pres. Clinton vetoes the $317 billion fiscal 2000 Labor-HHS spending bill. . . . The Justice Department, on behalf of the EPA, files lawsuits against seven large utilities for violating the 1970 Clean Air Act. . . . The families of four victims who died in a 1994 USAir crash reach a collective $48 million settlement. The sum includes a $25.2 million payment to the family of Marshall Berkman, the largest single settlement in U.S. commercial-aviation history.			Nov. 3
In Laramie, Wyoming, Judge Barton Voigt sentences Aaron McKinney, 22, to two consecutive life terms in prison for the October 1998 beating death of a homosexual college student, Matthew Shepard. . . . The CDC reports that 24.7% of U.S. adults smoked in 1997, the same as the 1995 rate. . . . Daisy Bates, 84, civil-rights leader who, in 1957, gained national attention when she counteracted attempts by Arkansas governor Orval Faubus (R) to prevent black students from entering Little Rock's Central High School, dies in Little Rock. She had had a number of strokes.		The Senate, 90-8, and the House, 362-57, pass a bill that will overhaul federal regulations governing the financial services sector. The bill is known as the Financial Services Modernization Act. . . . Congress passes a fourth stopgap measure.	The National Federation for the Blind files a lawsuit against Internet service provider America Online Inc. (AOL) under the Americans With Disabilities Act (ADA) of 1990. The group claims that AOL discriminates against the blind because its system is not compatible with special computer programs used by the blind to help convert written text into synthesized speech or Braille. . . . FBI officials test its main computer database and find that the system is ready for the year 2000.		Nov. 4
The Supreme Court grants a request to permit the state of Ohio to continue its school-voucher program until a federal appeals court rules on the program's constitutionality. . . . The U.S. Civil Rights Commission decides to hold a hearing into the recent deaths of Native Americans in South Dakota. . . . Kristen Price pleads guilty to a misdemeanor in the 1998 death of Matthew Shepard. Judge Jeffrey Donnell sentences Price to 180 days in jail, 120 of which are suspended and 60 of which are credited to time served.	The Senate, by voice vote, ratifies the treaty signed by the International Labor Organization in June. The treaty bans the harshest forms of child labor, including slavery, forced labor, prostitution, and pornography. It also bans forced recruitment of children into the military, but it allows voluntary military enlistment by those under 18.	Pres. Clinton signs a fourth stopgap measure.	Judge Thomas Penfield Jackson, in preliminary findings in an antitrust lawsuit against computer software maker Microsoft Corp., finds that the company enjoyed "monopoly power," which it used to the detriment of its competitors and consumers. The judge presents his findings following a year-long nonjury trial pursued by the Justice Department and 19 states.		Nov. 5
				In horse racing, Cat Thief wins the 16th annual Breeders' Cup Classic at in Hallandale, Florida . . . . George V(incent) Higgins, 59, U.S. author best known for a series of crime novels set in and around Boston, Massachusetts, is found dead in Milton, Massachusetts. His death is attributed to natural causes.	Nov. 6
F	G	H	I	J	
Includes elections, federal-state relations, civil rights and liberties, crime, the judiciary, education, health care, poverty, urban affairs, and population.	*Includes formation and debate of U.S. foreign and defense policies, veterans' affairs, and defense spending. (Relations with specific foreign countries are usually found under the region concerned.)*	*Includes business, labor, agriculture, taxation, transportation, consumer affairs, monetary and fiscal policy, natural resources, and pollution.*	*Includes worldwide scientific, medical, and technological developments; natural phenomena; U.S. weather; natural disasters; and accidents.*	*Includes the arts, religion, scholarship, communications media, sports, entertainments, fashions, fads, and social life.*	

	World Affairs	Europe	Africa & the Middle East	The Americas	Asia & the Pacific
Nov. 7		Tajik president Imamali Rakhmanov is elected to a second term, receiving 96% of the vote in an election that Western diplomats claim is marred by electoral irregularities.	Three bomb explosions in the Israeli town of Netanya causes minor injures to 14 people.	In Peru, a landslide sweeps over the remote Andean village of La Púcara, 400 miles (640 km) northwest of Lima. At least 34 people are missing. . . . Alfonso Portillo Cabrera wins the most votes in Guatemala's first peacetime presidential election in more than 30 years. However, because Portillo does not capture a majority, he will face a runoff against second-place finisher Oscar Berger. . . The British Columbia Maritime Employers Association locks out 2,000 workers when they refuse to vote on a final contract offer.	A human-rights group claims that about 500 Falun Gong members have recently been sent to labor camps in Hebei, a northern province in China.
Nov. 8		Pope John Paul II visits Georgia. It is the first trip to the Caucasus region by a pope and only the second time that a pope has visited a predominantly Eastern Orthodox nation in more than 1,000 years. . . . A federal appeals court in Leipzig upholds the 1997 conviction of former East German leader Egon Krenz on manslaughter charges for his role in the shootings of East Germans trying to escape to the West.			Reports suggest that, in the offensive launched Nov. 2, guerrillas from the Liberation Tigers of Tamil Elam captured 10 key military bases in northern Sri Lanka. The rebels claim they killed more than 1,000 soldiers; official government figures put the loss at 101 troops. . . . An estimated 1 million people rally peacefully in Banda Aceh to call for independence from Indonesia.
Nov. 9	Michel Camdessus, the head of the IMF, reveals he will step down in 2000. . . . Germans gather in Berlin, the capital, to celebrate the 10th anniversary of the collapse of the Berlin Wall. Speakers at the ceremony include German chancellor Gerhard Schroeder, former German chancellor Helmut Kohl, former U.S. president George Bush, and former Soviet leader Mikhail Gorbachev.	Russia imposes a ban on foreign trade with Chechnya and bans flights between southern Russia and Azerbaijan, Georgia, and several Middle Eastern countries. . . . Reports confirm that Moldova's parliament have given the ruling coalition a vote of no confidence, ousting Premier Ion Sturza.		A plane crashes west of Mexico City, the Mexican capital, killing all 18 people on board.	Fighting in the disputed border region of Kashmir flares. . . . A court in Hangzhou convicts four founding members of the China Democracy Party, a small illegal opposition party, of subversion and sentences them to prison sentences ranging from five to 11 years. . . . Human-rights groups estimate that nearly 2,800 civilians have been killed in Aceh province in Indonesia in the past decade.
Nov. 10	A report by the UN International Criminal Tribunal for the Former Yugoslavia claims that 2,108 bodies in 195 grave sites were found throughout the province before exhumation work stopped for the winter. There were a total of 529 known grave sites at the time of the report.		The Israeli cabinet approves the transfer of 5% of the West Bank to Palestinian control. Israeli soldiers and police forcibly remove a group of Israeli settlers from the Havat Maon settlement in the West Bank.		Indian military officials reveal that 21 people have been killed in the fighting in the disputed border region of Kashmir that renewed Nov. 9.
Nov. 11		Russia denies the OSCE access to a "security zone" in northern Chechnya. . . . Britain's House of Lords grants final approval to a bill that strips the right of almost all of the chamber's "hereditary peers" to sit and vote in the House. . . . At least 52 people are killed in Italy when a building collapses. Officials blame the disaster on poor construction. . . . Sir Vivian Ernest Fuchs, 91, British explorer who led the team that in 1957–58 made the first surface crossing of Antarctica, dies in Cambridge, England.		Venezuela's National Constituent Assembly suspends 75 judges and dismisses five others, bring to 200 the number of judges removed from the bench since the constitutional assembly declared a "judicial emergency" in August. . . . Jacobo Timerman, 76, Argentine journalist whose open criticism of the human-rights abuses perpetrated by his country's military regime during the latter part of the 1970s led to his imprisonment and torture, dies in Buenos Aires, Argentina, of a heart attack.	Pakistan's military rulers charge ousted prime minister Nawaz Sharif with treason, kidnapping, hijacking, and attempted murder in connection with an incident that sparked an October military coup led by armed forces chief Gen. Pervez Musharraf. Sharif has been in military custody since the army seized control of the country. . . . Reports reveal that Australian authorities have seized six ships carrying a total of 717 attempted illegal immigrants off the northwestern coast of Western Australia since Nov. 2.
Nov. 12	Members of the Commonwealth, a 54-nation association of Britain and its former colonies, opens its biennial meeting in Durban, South Africa. During the summit, the organization votes to suspend Pakistan's membership in response to an October military coup in that country.	A powerful earthquake hits Turkey, killing hundreds of people. The epicenter is just south of Duzce, about 115 miles (185 km) northwest of Ankara. The quake measures 7.2 on the Richter scale. . . . A plane chartered by the UN World Food Program crashes in the Serbian province of Kosovo, killing all 24 passengers and crew aboard. . . . Russia takes control of Gudermes, Chechnya's second-largest city. . . . Gaby Casadesus (born Gaby L'Hote), 98, French pianist, dies in Paris, France.			The death toll from a cyclone that devastated the Indian state of Orissa in late October rises to nearly 9,400. The storm, the worst to hit the region in a century, also caused some $3.94 billion in crop damage. . . . Several rockets are launched at U.S. and UN offices in Islamabad, the capital of Pakistan. One person is injured in the attacks. . . . A court in Haikou, in Hainan province in China sentences four Falun Gong followers to prison terms ranging from two to 12 years.

A	B	C	D	E
Includes developments that affect more than one world region, international organizations, and important meetings of major world leaders.	Includes all domestic and regional developments in Europe, including the Soviet Union, Turkey, Cyprus, and Malta.	Includes all domestic and regional developments in Africa and the Middle East, including Iraq and Iran and excluding Cyprus, Turkey, and Afghanistan.	Includes all domestic and regional developments in Latin America, the Caribbean, and Canada.	Includes all domestic and regional developments in Asia and Pacific nations, extending from Afghanistan through all the Pacific Island, except Hawaii.

U.S. Politics & Social Issues	U.S. Foreign Policy & Defense	U.S. Economy & Environment	Science, Technology, & Nature	Culture, Leisure, & Lifestyle	
		The Labor Department reports that the seasonally adjusted unemployment rate in October dipped to 4.1%, down from the 4.2% recorded the previous month. The October jobless rate is the lowest recorded since January 1970 and is coupled with a meager one-cent increase in hourly wages for the month.		Golfer Tiger Woods caps the most successful season by a PGA player in 25 years when he wins the World Championship. . . . Kenyan Joseph Chebet and Adriana Fernandez of Mexico win the men's and women's titles, respectively, in the New York City Marathon. . . . Primo Nebiolo, 76, president of the International Amateur Athletic Federation since 1981, dies in Rome, Italy, of a heart attack.	Nov. 7
Amid a series of lawsuits against managed-care companies, United-Health Group, a large managed-care health insurance company, announces that it will no longer require its member physicians to obtain prior approval from the company for treatment decisions.	Republicans on the House Government Reform Committee accuse Pres. Clinton of being affected by political considerations when he offered to commute the prison sentences of 16 members of the Armed Forces of National Liberation (FALN), a Puerto Rican separatist group responsible for several bombings between 1974 and 1983.			Leaders from four Jewish seminaries send a letter to Rev. Paige Patterson, president of the Southern Baptist Convention, asking him to stop recent attempts to convert Jews. . . . . Lester Bowie, 58, jazz trumpeter whose career spans at least 30 years, dies in New York City of liver cancer.	Nov. 8
Angela Wood pleads guilty in Indianapolis, Indiana, to arson and conspiracy in the burning of seven churches in that state. In her plea, Wood, 24, agrees to testify against former boyfriend Jay Scott Ballinger, 37, in exchange for immunity from prosecution for her part in church burnings in 19 other states.	The House, by voice vote, reauthorizes fiscal 2000 funding for the CIA, NSA, and the intelligence-gathering activities of nine other federal agencies, including the FBI. Historically, the funding levels of the intelligence authorization bill are not released to the public. However, Director of Central Intelligence George Tenet in 1998 disclosed the fiscal 1998 intelligence budget to be $26.7 billion.	United Parcel Service Inc. (UPS) issues shares to the public for the first time in its 92-year history. The sale, worth $5.47 billion, is the largest initial public offering (IPO) ever in the U.S. . . . New York State governor George Pataki (R) tightens restrictions on a widely used gasoline additive that makes gasoline burn more cleanly.			Nov. 9
In Eugene, Oregon, Judge Jack Mattison sentences Kipland Kinkel, 17, to 112 years in prison without parole for killing two students during a shooting spree at a Springfield, Oregon, high school in 1998. Kinkel, who was 15 at the time of the murders, shot his parents to death before the school killings. He pled guilty in September.	The Senate confirms former Sen. Carol Moseley-Braun (D, Ill.) as ambassador to New Zealand and Samoa, and retired Admiral Joseph Prueher as ambassador to China. The confirmations clear the Senate as part of a deal between Republicans and Democrats to end blocks that each side had placed against nominees favored by the other.	Pillowtex Corp., the parent company of Fieldcrest Cannon Inc., drops a 25-year legal challenge and accepts its 5,200 workers' vote to unionize.		Felix Galimir, 89, violinist and music teacher affiliated with such prestigious music schools as the Juilliard School and the Curtis Institute, dies in New York City.	Nov. 10
		Amid pressure from students from more than 100 colleges, Nike Inc. agrees to take college students to its overseas factories to show that they do not operate under sweatshop-like conditions. Students had launched the anti-sweatshop campaign on Oct. 19.		An art auction at Sotheby's totals $144.2 million, the house's most profitable since 1990.	Nov. 11
Judge Allen Schwartz rules that the administration of NYC mayor Rudolph Giuliani improperly downgraded grant applications from Housing Works, a nonprofit community group that provides services to people with AIDS.		Pres. Clinton signs into law a bill that codifies a sweeping overhaul of the regulatory framework governing the financial services industry.			Nov. 12

F	G	H	I	J
Includes elections, federal-state relations, civil rights and liberties, crime, the judiciary, education, health care, poverty, urban affairs, and population.	Includes formation and debate of U.S. foreign and defense policies, veterans' affairs, and defense spending. (Relations with specific foreign countries are usually found under the region concerned.)	Includes business, labor, agriculture, taxation, transportation, consumer affairs, monetary and fiscal policy, natural resources, and pollution.	Includes worldwide scientific, medical, and technological developments; natural phenomena; U.S. weather; natural disasters; and accidents.	Includes the arts, religion, scholarship, communications media, sports, entertainments, fashions, fads, and social life.

	World Affairs	Europe	Africa & the Middle East	The Americas	Asia & the Pacific
Nov. 13	Jacques Diouf is reelected head of the United Nations Food and Agriculture Organization (FAO).	Peter Wildeblood, 76, British homosexual-rights pioneer, dies in Vancouver, Canada, of complications of a stroke.		The foreign ministers of Chile and Peru sign a pact that settles the last territorial dispute between the two nations. Under the agreement, Peru will gain the exclusive use of a pier in the Chilean port of Arica, a port that Peru had controlled prior to the 1879–83 War of the Pacific. Chile agrees to construct the pier and a Peruvian customs office there. The facilities will remain under Chilean sovereignty.	
Nov. 14	The UN imposes economic sanctions on the fundamentalist Taliban militia that controls most of Afghanistan, after the Taliban refuses to hand over alleged terrorist Osama bin Laden to the U.S. Tens of thousands of Afghanis participate in demonstrations against the UN and the U.S. throughout the country. Demonstrators throw stones at UN offices, and in some cases raid them and destroy equipment. A UN office in Farah is set on fire.	Macedonian deputy foreign minister Boris Trajkovski, a Methodist minister trained in the U.S., is elected to the largely ceremonial post of president in a runoff election. . . . Ukraine's Pres. Leonid Kuchma is reelected to a second five-year term in a runoff presidential election.		Hurricane Lenny, a powerful late-season hurricane packing heavy rains and high winds, strikes the Caribbean islands.	
Nov. 15	The UN issues a report in which it assumes considerable blame for failing to stop the massacre of thousands of Bosnian Muslim men and boys in the town of Srebrenica in July 1995. The fall of Srebrenica became a major symbol of the UN's failure to prevent bloodshed in conflicts worldwide. The UN report breaks new ground by condemning an international organization for attempting to remain neutral in a civil conflict. . . . The ninth annual Ibero-American Summit opens in Havana, Cuba.		Queen Elizabeth II flies to Mozambique, becoming the first British monarch to visit that country.	In Canada, the port of Vancouver, British Columbia, and other Canadian Pacific ports reopen when 2,000 longshoremen return to work, ending the Nov. 7 lockout that cost about C$90 million (US$60 million) per day in lost trade.	
Nov. 16				In Canada, British Columbia Supreme Court judge William Stewart sentences five self-proclaimed skinheads to 12- to 15-year prison sentences for their roles in the 1998 beating death of Nirmal Singh Gill, 65, an Indo-Canadian caretaker of a Sikh temple. It marks the first time in Canadian history that a court has been asked to rule that a killing is a hate crime and to issue a more severe prison sentence as a result.	An Islamic woman is executed by being shot three times by a Taliban soldier before a crowd of thousands. It is the first time a woman is publicly executed in Afghanistan since the Islamic fundamentalist Taliban militia took over control of most of the country in 1996. . . . In China, police quickly round up some 20 Falun Gong followers who unfurl a banner in Beijing's Tiananmen Square.
Nov. 17	U.S. Court of Appeals judge Patricia Wald, 70, becomes a judge on the Yugoslav war crimes tribunal.	Several thousand people gather in the town of Memici for a funeral for victims exhumed from the largest mass grave so far discovered in Bosnia. A total of 274 bodies were unearthed from the site. . . . The Russian navy's Arctic Fleet test-fires two ballistic missiles from a submarine in the Barents Sea, striking targets on the Kamchatka Peninsula in Russia's Far East.			In Pakistan, military police arrest at least 21 business leaders and politicians who failed to meet a deadline to pay delinquent taxes and other debts.

A	B	C	D	E
Includes developments that affect more than one world region, international organizations, and important meetings of major world leaders.	Includes all domestic and regional developments in Europe, including the Soviet Union, Turkey, Cyprus, and Malta.	Includes all domestic and regional developments in Africa and the Middle East, including Iraq and Iran and excluding Cyprus, Turkey, and Afghanistan.	Includes all domestic and regional developments in Latin America, the Caribbean, and Canada.	Includes all domestic and regional developments in Asia and Pacific nations, extending from Afghanistan through all the Pacific Island, except Hawaii.

U.S. Politics & Social Issues	U.S. Foreign Policy & Defense	U.S. Economy & Environment	Science, Technology, & Nature	Culture, Leisure, & Lifestyle	
		The New York Department of Environmental Conservation orders GF to clean up PCBs in the soil around one of its defunct factories along the Hudson River, in the village of Hudson Falls. The cleanup, of 700,000 cubic feet (19,800 cubic meters) of soil, will cost GE an estimated $28.4 million.	The Earth-orbiting *Hubble Space Telescope* shuts down when one of its three remaining working gyroscopes—which maintains its orientation—fails.	Lennox Lewis defeats Evander Holyfield by unanimous decision in Las Vegas, Nevada, to become the undisputed heavyweight champion of the world. . . . Donald Mills, 84, last surviving member of the Mills Brothers singing group, dies in Los Angeles, California, of complications of pneumonia.	Nov. 13
		The USDA seeks to quarantine 365 sheep in Vermont because they may have come in contact with bovine spongiform encephalopathy (BSE), or mad-cow disease.	Reports confirm that U.S. researchers have found examples of alphabetic writing in Egypt at least 200 years older than the earliest previously known examples. The inscriptions are believed to have been written between 1900 and 1800 B.C.	Golfer Se Ri Pak of South Korea wins a three-way playoff to capture the LPGA PageNet Tour Championship in Las Vegas, Nevada. . . . Dale Jarrett clinches his first NASCAR Winston Cup title when he finishes fifth in the inaugural Pennzoil 400 in Miami, Florida.	Nov. 14
In Waco, Texas, Judge Walter Smith orders the Justice Department and the FBI to reenact the last day of its 1993 siege of the Waco compound of the Branch Davidian religious sect in order to determine whether FBI agents fired at the Davidians during the standoff, which ended in a fatal fire.	Pres. Clinton embarks on a nine-day tour encompassing several Western and Eastern European countries. . . . China and the U.S. sign a wide-ranging agreement in which China agrees to significantly reduce obstacles to imported goods and foreign investments.	New York attorney general Eliot Spitzer files a lawsuit against General Electric Co. (GE) over PCBs polluting the Hudson River.			Nov. 15
A Michigan jury convicts Nathaniel Abraham, 13, for a killing he committed when he was 11 when he murdered Ronnie Greene, 18, in a Detroit suburb. Abraham is the first person tried under Michigan's new juvenile justice law, which allows a juvenile of any age to be tried as an adult. Abraham is thought to be the youngest person ever tried as an adult in the U.S. for first-degree murder.	The House passes, by voice vote, a bill intended to improve long-term health care for veterans.	The Federal Reserve Board votes to raise the federal funds rate to 5.5% from 5.25%. The committee also boosts the largely symbolic discount rate by a quarter of a percentage point, to 5% from 4.75%. In response to the Fed's action, commercial banks begin raising their prime lending rates by a quarter of a percentage point, to 8.5%. . . . Energy Secretary Bill Richardson announces the permanent closing of a nuclear reactor at the Brookhaven National Laboratory in Upton, New York.	Daniel Nathans, 71, molecular biologist who developed a cutting technique for analyzing DNA for which he was awarded a share of the 1978 Nobel Prize for Medicine, dies in Baltimore, Maryland, of leukemia.		Nov. 16
Data shows that at least 44 states have passed juvenile justice laws that allow juveniles to be tried as adults in a greater number of cases. . . . A lawsuit accusing a developer and a transportation authority in western New York State of race-based negligence in the 1995 death of a black teenager, Cynthia Wiggins, is settled. The agreement gives $2.55 million to Wiggins's son, Taquilo Castellanos. . . . A study finds that, between 1986 and 1996, the number of women jailed for drug crimes rose by 888%. Over the same period, the increase in incarcerations of women for nondrug crimes stood at 129%.			Research indicates that an ice mass floating in the Arctic Ocean appears to be about 40% thinner than it was 20–40 years previously.	The National Conference of Catholic Bishops call for tighter church control over Roman Catholic colleges and universities in the U.S. . . . The United Methodist Church defrocks Nebraska minister Jimmy Creech for officiating at a wedding ceremony of two homosexual men. . . . National Book Awards are presented to Ha Jin, John Dower, a poet known as Ai, and Kimberly Willis Holt. In addition, Oprah Winfrey receives a special 50th Anniversary Gold medal for encouraging people to read through her televised book club. . . . Time Warner Inc., one of the world's largest media and entertainment companies, announces that it will no longer make "soft money" donations to political parties.	Nov. 17

F	G	H	I	J
Includes elections, federal-state relations, civil rights and liberties, crime, the judiciary, education, health care, poverty, urban affairs, and population.	*Includes formation and debate of U.S. foreign and defense policies, veterans' affairs, and defense spending. (Relations with specific foreign countries are usually found under the region concerned.)*	*Includes business, labor, agriculture, taxation, transportation, consumer affairs, monetary and fiscal policy, natural resources, and pollution.*	*Includes worldwide scientific, medical, and technological developments; natural phenomena; U.S. weather; natural disasters; and accidents.*	*Includes the arts, religion, scholarship, communications media, sports, entertainments, fashions, fads, and social life.*

	World Affairs	Europe	Africa & the Middle East	The Americas	Asia & the Pacific
Nov. 18		The official death toll from the Nov. 12 earthquake in Turkey stands at more than 600. . . . Rescue workers are still pulling bodies from the building that collapsed Nov. 11 in Foggia, Italy, killing at least 52 people. . . . Russian forces take control of the town of Achkhoi-Martan in the separatist republic of Chechnya. . . . Gladys Yang (born Gladys Taylor), 80, British translator of Chinese literature, dies in Beijing, China, of unreported causes.			Australia's state Parliament of New South Wales passes legislation that will establish an operating license for Australia's first legalized heroin-injecting room.
Nov. 19	At the close of a summit in Istanbul, Turkey, the 54-member Organization for Security and Cooperation in Europe (OSCE) adopts new limits on conventional arms in Europe.	Reports reveal that Russia's shelling has killed more than 4,100 civilians, according to Chechen officials. Reports also suggest that the campaign has caused more than 200,000 Chechens to flee their homes.	Some 2,000 Nigerian troops begin deploying in the Niger River Delta region to quell ongoing clashes between members of the Hausa and Yoruba ethnic groups. In addition, local youths have been waging armed protests against a government economic policy that they claim returns too little oil revenue to the area.	Data shows that Hurricane Lenny, a powerful late-season hurricane that struck the Caribbean on Nov. 14, has wreaked havoc on its course over more than 16 Caribbean islands. The storm killed at least 12 people and inflicted property damage estimated in the tens of millions of dollars.	
Nov. 20		Amintore Fanfani, 91, one of the most prominent figures in post-World War II Italian politics, dies in Rome after a month's hospitalization for flu-related health problems.	Algerian security forces report that 15 people were killed and eight more wounded at a false roadblock 37 miles (75 km) south of Algiers.		A bomb blast in Lahore, the capital of Pakistan's Punjab province, kills at least five people and injures nearly 20 others.
Nov. 21		Quentin Crisp (born Denis Pratt), 90, British-born author and actor, dies in Manchester, England.	Jordan releases some two dozen members of the militant Islamic group Hamas that it detained in a crackdown in August. . . . Reports suggest that some 20 people were slain in the previous week in Algeria.		A militant group of ousted p.m. Nawaz Sharif's supporters claims responsibility for the Nov. 20 bombing in Pakistan. The militants call themselves the Al-Nawaz group. Sharif's Pakistan Muslim League denounces the group's action. . . . China announces that it test-launched an unmanned space capsule, and that the craft returned to Earth and was retrieved. It is the first time that China has lofted and recovered a craft designed for manned space flight.
Nov. 22	The Rwandan government refuses an entrance visa to the chief prosecutor of the International Criminal Tribunal for Rwanda, Carla Del Ponte. The action follows a controversial decision by the court to release a genocide suspect, Jean-Bosco Barayagwiza.	A crowd of more than 10,000 people gather in Nevsky Square in Sofia, Bulgaria's capital, to welcome U.S. president Bill Clinton.	Due to plans to build a mosque next to the Christian Church of the Annunciation in Nazareth, several Christian churches throughout Israel close in protest. . . . Abdelkader Hachani, one of the leaders of the banned Islamic Salvation Front (FIS), is assassinated in Algiers, the capital of Algeria.	Convicted serial rapist Larry Fisher is found guilty of first-degree murder in the 1969 rape and slaying of Gail Miller, a nurse's aid in Saskatchewan, Canada. The verdict ends a 30-year legal saga during which another man, David Milgaard, now 46, was wrongly imprisoned for the crime for nearly 23 years.	The South Korean government grants official recognition to the Korea Confederation of Trade Unions (KTCU), the more militant of South Korea's two main trade union umbrella groups.
Nov. 23	The Joint UN Program on HIV/AIDS estimates that by year's end, 5.6 million people will have become infected with HIV, the virus that causes AIDS, bringing the total number of infected people to 33.6 million. The report projects that 2.6 million people will die of the disease in 1999, raising the total number of deaths from AIDS to about 16.3 million.	The Constitutional Court, Russia's highest court, strikes down part of a law that prevented some religions from legally operating in Russia.	In Nigeria's Niger River Delta region, reports claim that 43 people have died since the army moved in. Military officials reject that figure as too high. . . . Kuwait's parliament rejects a May decree issued by Sheikh Jabir al-Ahmad Al-Sabah that would have extended political rights to women. . . . Muslims lay the cornerstone for a mosque next to the Christian Church of the Annunciation in Nazareth. . . . Reports suggest that, since the beginning of November, more than 100 people have died in Algeria.	U.S. president Bill Clinton declares a disaster area in the U.S. Virgin Islands, allowing the disbursement of federal aid to the territory. Virgin Islands officials estimate losses from Hurricane Lenny to be at $31.5 million, mostly on the island of St. Croix.	Reports confirm that Iran has reopened the Iran-Afghanistan border, which was closed in response to the August 1998 slaying of nine Iranians in an offensive by the Taliban. . . . Thailand executes a woman, Samai Pan-intara, 59, convicted of numerous drug-trafficking offenses. She is the first woman executed in Thailand in more than 20 years. Her execution brings the number of death sentences carried out in Thailand in 1999 to 16, a record for a single year.
	A *Includes developments that affect more than one world region, international organizations, and important meetings of major world leaders.*	**B** *Includes all domestic and regional developments in Europe, including the Soviet Union, Turkey, Cyprus, and Malta.*	**C** *Includes all domestic and regional developments in Africa and the Middle East, including Iraq and Iran and excluding Cyprus, Turkey, and Afghanistan.*	**D** *Includes all domestic and regional developments in Latin America, the Caribbean, and Canada.*	**E** *Includes all domestic and regional developments in Asia and Pacific nations, extending from Afghanistan through all the Pacific Island, except Hawaii.*

U.S. Politics & Social Issues	U.S. Foreign Policy & Defense	U.S. Economy & Environment	Science, Technology, & Nature	Culture, Leisure, & Lifestyle	
A jury in Jasper, Texas, convicts Shawn Allen Berry of capital murder in the dragging death of a black man, James Byrd, and the jury sentences him to life in prison.... A preliminary report by the FBI reveals that it received reports of 7,755 hate-crime incidents in 1998.... A tower of logs stacked for a ritual bonfire collapses on the campus of Texas A&M University, killing 11 students and one recent graduate and injuring 27 others.... The House passes, 418-2, a bill that that will allow disabled people to retain their government health-care benefits when they become employed.		The House approves, 296-135, a year-end omnibus spending bill for fiscal 2000, which began Oct. 1. The legislation allocates $385 billion in federal spending and incorporates five of the 13 appropriation bills. It allocates $14.9 billion for the Interior Department and related agencies and $6 billion for the State Department.... By voice vote, the House and the Senate pass a fifth stopgap measure.... Boeing agrees to pay $4.5 million to settle a government case claiming that the company discriminated against female and minority workers. The settlement is the largest ever reached under an affirmative-action compliance program operated by the Labor Department.	Research indicates that the drug thalidomide may slow or reverse multiple myeloma, a kind of bone cancer, in some patients.	Sotheby's and Christie's close their major fall New York City sales, raising $334 million and $252 million, respectively.... Doug(las Wayne) Sahm, 58, versatile Texas musician and singer, is found dead in Taos, New Mexico. He reportedly died of natural causes.... Horst P. Horst (born Horst Paul Albert Bohrmann), 93, photographer often referred to simply as Horst, dies in Palm Beach Gardens, Florida.... Paul Bowles, 88, U.S.-born author and composer, dies in Tangier, Morocco, after a heart attack.	Nov. 18
The Senate clears, 95-1, a bill that will allow disabled people to retain their government health-care benefits when they become employed.... The Senate clears, by voice vote, a bill that will set penalties for companies that distribute deceptive notices of sweepstakes and other contests through the mail.... The Senate approves, by voice vote, a bill that will create a new federal agency to administer truck and bus safety programs.... In Deming, New Mexico, Victor Cordova Jr., 13, allegedly shoots to death classmate Araceli Tena, 13.	The Senate, by voice vote, clears a bill reauthorizing the nation's intelligence programs for fiscal 2000. Historically, the funding levels of the intelligence authorization bill are not released to the public. However, in 1998 Director of Central Intelligence George Tenet disclosed that the intelligence budget for fiscal 1998 was $26.7 billion.... The Senate, by voice vote, clears a bill intended to improve long-term health care for veterans.	The Senate approves, 74-24, a year-end omnibus spending bill for fiscal 2000, which began Oct. 1. The bill incorporates five of the 13 appropriation bills and allocated $385 billion in federal spending.... Pres. Clinton signs the stopgap resolution.... A federal grand jury in New York City convicts William Hamilton Jr., the former political director of the International Brotherhood of Teamsters union, on charges that he illegally funneled $885,000 in union money into the 1996 reelection campaign of former Teamsters president Ron Carey.		Alexander Liberman, 87, editorial director of Conde Nast Publications, 1962-94, dies in Miami Beach, FL.	Nov. 19
				Officials in California auction items recovered from the Heaven's Gate cult, whose members committed suicide in March 1997. The sale draws approximately $33,000.	Nov. 20
The FBI reveals that the number of serious crimes reported to law-enforcement agencies in the U.S. fell 10% in the first half of 1999 from the same period in 1998. It is the seventh consecutive year in which a decline in serious crime has been reported.... Four of a caravan of six buses carrying hundreds of students back to Pennsylvania State University crash into each other on a Pennsylvania highway, killing two people and injuring 106 others.				D.C. United wins the MLS title, defeating the Los Angeles Galaxy, 2-0, in Foxboro, Massachusetts.	Nov. 21
	A major survey of race relations in the U.S. military finds that. although race relations are better in the military than elsewhere in American society, there are significant gaps between the views of whites and blacks on how they are treated. Approximately 75% of blacks and other minorities reported experiencing racially offensive behavior. At the same time, however, large majorities of respondents report that they are comfortable establishing friendships across racial boundaries.			The Synod of the Northeast lets stand a New Jersey church's decision to admit an openly gay man to a ministerial post and upholds a New York State church's authority to hold marriage ceremonies for gay couples.... Wayne Gretzky is inducted into the Hockey Hall of Fame in Toronto, Canada.	Nov. 22
Alex Witmer, 18, and Jason Powell, 19, white teenagers in Indiana, are charged with murder for the shooting death of black teenager Sasezley Richardson, 19. Reports indicate that that Powell committed the murder to qualify for membership in the Aryan Brotherhood, a white-supremacist prison gang.... The Justice Department finds that juvenile crime rates declined 30% between 1994 and 1998. It is the fourth decline in a row, and the 1998 rate is the lowest since 1987.					Nov. 23

F	G	H	I	J
Includes elections, federal-state relations, civil rights and liberties, crime, the judiciary, education, health care, poverty, urban affairs, and population.	Includes formation and debate of U.S. foreign and defense policies, veterans' affairs, and defense spending. (Relations with specific foreign countries are usually found under the region concerned.)	Includes business, labor, agriculture, taxation, transportation, consumer affairs, monetary and fiscal policy, natural resources, and pollution.	Includes worldwide scientific, medical, and technological developments; natural phenomena; U.S. weather; natural disasters; and accidents.	Includes the arts, religion, scholarship, communications media, sports, entertainments, fashions, fads, and social life.

	World Affairs	Europe	Africa & the Middle East	The Americas	Asia & the Pacific
Nov. 24	Trade officials from Mexico and the EU sign a tentative free-trade accord that will apply to industrial and agricultural goods and services as well as to issues of public procurement, investment, and dispute-settlement policies.	Montenegrin authorities declare the airport, which is also used as a Yugoslav air base, to be property of the republic. The declaration is the latest in a string of unilateral decisions by Montenegro to increase its autonomy from Yugoslavia. . . . In the face of criticism, the city council of Usti nad Labem demolishes a wall erected Oct. 13 to separate Gypsy residents from their ethnically Czech neighbors. . . . Sir John Foster Wilson, 80, British founder of the organization that became Sight Savers International, dies in Brighton, England.		In Canada, Jack Ramsay, a Reform Party member of Parliament (MP) from Alberta, is convicted of attempting to rape a 14-year-old girl in 1969 when he was a Royal Canadian Mounted Police officer on a northern Saskatchewan Indian reserve.	A ferry traveling across Bo Hai bay in northeastern China catches fire and sinks, killing scores of people. . . . Four miners die in an accident at the Northparkes gold and copper mine near Parkes, New South Wales, in Australia.
Nov. 25			In Niger, voters elect Pres. Tandja Mamadou, a retired army colonel. The election ends a period of military rule in place since an April coup. . . . Li Peng, a former Chinese premier and the current speaker of China's parliament, visits Israel. Li, the second-highest-ranking official in China, is the most senior Chinese official to make a diplomatic visit to Israel since 1992.	The Supreme Court of Canada upholds a law protecting the confidentiality of a sexual-assault complainant's counseling documents. The court also states for the first time that the sensitive nature of sexual assault puts victims at a greater disadvantage to claim redress than victims of other crimes.	
Nov. 26		Ukrainian authorities restart the only working reactor in Chernobyl, the site of a major nuclear accident in 1986, after five months of repairs. . . . The Constitutional Court, Croatia's highest court, declares Pres. Franjo Tudjman "temporarily incapacitated," transferring his powers to the speaker of parliament, Vlatko Pavletic, for a renewable 60-day term. Tudjman, 77, has been hospitalized since Nov. 1 for complications from stomach cancer.	Reports find that Iran's intelligence ministry has arrested 34 religious extremists accused of planning to assassinate Pres. Mohammed Khatami and other major Iranian political leaders. Twenty members of the group, the Shi'ite Muslim Mahdaviat movement, have been subsequently released on bail. . . . Sudanese president Omar Hassan Ahmed al-Bashir and the Umma party, a major Islamic opposition group, reaches an agreement on a peace proposal aimed at ending the country's ongoing civil war.	In Canada, Alberta's Court of Queen's Bench rules in favor of two lesbian couples adopting the sons they have raised since birth. The decision, seen as a controversial challenge of the province's adoption law, allows same-sex partners to become parents. . . . The smoldering Guagua Pinchincha volcano, just west of Quito, Ecuador, belches out a column of gases and ash, which coat the capital and force authorities to close schools and the airport. It is the latest in a series of eruptions from the volcano, which awakened from 339 years of inactivity in 1998.	Indonesian investigators exhume the bodies of 25 East Timorese from a site in West Timor. The victims are believed to have been killed in a Sept. 6 raid in the town of Suai. . . . The death toll from the Nov. 24 ferry accident in Bo Hai bay in northeastern China stands at 118. Twenty-two of the vessel's 302 passengers and crew have reached safety. Authorities state that there is little hope that any of the missing people missing to have survived. It is China's worst maritime disaster since 1994.
Nov. 27	Members of the Association of Southeast Asian Nations (ASEAN) trade group meet in Manila, the capital of the Philippines.	Macedonia's Supreme Court orders that a presidential election between Boris Trajkovski and Tito Petkovski be rerun, due to irregularities in the runoff. . . . Alain Antoine Peyrefitte, 74, French statesman, author and journalist, dies in Paris, France, of cancer.	Iran's Special Court for the Clergy sentences Abdullah Nouri, a reform-minded cleric and newspaper publisher, to five years in prison on charges of insulting Islam and defaming Ayatollah Ali Khamenei, Iran's spiritual leader and supreme political ruler. The charges are among the most serious a senior politician has ever faced in Iran. In another trial, Iran's Press Court sentences publisher Mashallah Shamsolvaezine to three years in prison on the charge of questioning Islam.		Labour Party leader Helen Clark is elected prime minister of New Zealand, ending nine years of conservative National Party government rule. Clark is the country's first elected woman prime minister. Georgina Beyer, a member of the Labour Party, is elected to a seat in Parliament, becoming New Zealand's first transsexual member of Parliament.
Nov. 28		Reports confirm that the French government plans to compensate Jewish children orphaned during the Holocaust with either an undisclosed lump sum or a monthly pension of about $484. . . . The Basque separatist group ETA announces that it will end a 14-month cease-fire. . . . The Russian government announces that a safe-passage route for Chechen citizens to flee from Grozny will be opened.	A pipe bomb explodes in a restaurant near Cape Town, South Africa, injuring at least 43 people.	Sen. Jorge Batlle of the ruling Colorado Party wins the Uruguayan presidency in a runoff election.	
Nov. 29	Bosnian Serb Maksim Sokolovic, 59, is sentenced to nine years in prison by a war crimes court in Düsseldorf, Germany. Sokolovic led a paramilitary unit during the Bosnian conflict. His trial was held in Germany to ease the caseload of the UN tribunal in The Hague, the Netherlands.	A group of ethnic Albanians attack three Serbs and kill one of them, amid celebrations of a major nationalist holiday in Pristina, the capital of the Serbian province of Kosovo. Ethnic Albanians reportedly watch the attack and obstruct police and NATO forces from intervening. . . . International authorities announce they have dismissed 22 officials for obstructing the enforcement of the Bosnian peace accords.	Guinea-Bissau completes the first presidential and parliamentary elections since a military coup ousted Pres. João Bernardo Vieira in May. Voters elect opposition parties to the majority of seats in Parliament. . . . Palestinian authorities detain a total of 11 people who were among 20 signers of a letter denouncing Palestinian leader Yasser Arafat. . . . Reports state that in Lagos, Nigeria, clashes between members of the Hausa and Yoruba ethnic groups have left nearly 100 dead.		Malaysia's ruling coalition of P.M. Mahathir bin Mohamad scores a decisive victory in snap parliamentary elections. The win will extend the 18-year tenure of Mahathir by another five years.

A	B	C	D	E
Includes developments that affect more than one world region, international organizations, and important meetings of major world leaders.	Includes all domestic and regional developments in Europe, including the Soviet Union, Turkey, Cyprus, and Malta.	Includes all domestic and regional developments in Africa and the Middle East, including Iraq and Iran and excluding Cyprus, Turkey, and Afghanistan.	Includes all domestic and regional developments in Latin America, the Caribbean, and Canada.	Includes all domestic and regional developments in Asia and Pacific nations, extending from Afghanistan through all the Pacific Island, except Hawaii.

U.S. Politics & Social Issues	U.S. Foreign Policy & Defense	U.S. Economy & Environment	Science, Technology, & Nature	Culture, Leisure, & Lifestyle	
		The Commerce Department reports that gross domestic product (GDP) grew at a revised, seasonally adjusted annual rate of 5.5% in the third quarter of 1999. The rate compares with an economic expansion of 1.9% in the second quarter.... Native American farmers and ranchers file a class-action lawsuit accusing the Agriculture Department of discriminating against Native Americans in the approval of loans.			Nov. 24
Reports confirm that Golda and Gilmore Reynolds, a local couple from the town of Osgood, Indiana, willed their $23 million estate to benefit Osgood's schools, libraries, and other public institutions. The couple lived in Osgood, population 1,688, for their entire lives and amassed their fortune through shrewd stock picks and a modest lifestyle.	Elián González, a six-year-old Cuban refugee, is found with two adult survivors clinging to inner tubes off the coast of Florida. Their boat had sunk a few days earlier, and all of the other passengers, including González's mother, drowned. The case receives much media attention.				Nov. 25
		The National Labor Relations Board (NLRB) rules, 3-2, that medical interns, fellows, and residents working in private hospitals are employees, not students, and are therefore permitted to form or join labor unions. The NLRB's decision overturns the board's 1976 ruling.	A single-engine aircraft crashes in a Newark, New Jersey, neighborhood, killing all three people aboard and injuring 25 people on the ground.	Ashley Montagu (Montague Francis) (born Israel Ehrenberg), 94, anthropologist, author, and commentator, dies in Princeton, New Jersey, while suffering from a heart ailment.	Nov. 26
					Nov. 27
	Cuba's foreign ministry announces that it has asked the U.S. government to return Elián González, recently found off the coast of Florida. If returned, he will live with his father, Juan Miguel González Quintana, who was divorced from his mother. Elián González is currently living with relatives of his father in Miami, Florida.			Hsing-Hsing, a male giant panda given to the U.S. in 1972 by former Chinese leader Mao Zedong, dies. His companion, Ling-Ling, died in 1992... Golfer Aaron Baddeley, 18, wins the Australian Open, the youngest champion in the event's 95-year history and the first amateur champion in 39 years.	Nov. 28
Data shows that errors made by health-care providers cause between 44,000 and 98,000 deaths per year in the U.S. The report's authors call for a nationwide system for collecting and analyzing data on medical errors and their consequences.	An Egyptian man, Nasser Ahmed, is freed from a NYC jail where he has been held for three and a half years on secret evidence that the FBI claims links him to terrorist activity. He is one of some 20 Arab or Islamic suspects held in U.S. prisons on the basis of secret evidence.... Pres. Clinton signs a bill that will allow the U.S. to provide food aid to rebels in southern Sudan who are trying to overthrow the Islamic government.	Pres. Clinton signs a massive omnibus spending bill for fiscal 2000, which began Oct. 1. The bill incorporates five of the 13 annual appropriations bills that the government is required to enact each year. Prior to signing the bill, Clinton signes five continuing resolutions to keep government departments operating after the fiscal year began.	Astronomers announce the discovery of six new extrasolar planets, or planets orbiting stars other than the sun. The discoveries bring the total known number of extrasolar planets to 28. The newly found planets orbit stars ranging from 65 to 192 light-years from Earth.	Timeline by Michael Crichton tops the bestseller list.... The Grawemeyer Award for Music Composition is given to British composer Thomas Ades, 28, the youngest such winner.... Gene Rayburn (born Gene Rubessa), 81, television game-show host dies in Gloucester, Massachusetts, of congestive heart failure.	Nov. 29
F	G	H	I	J	
Includes elections, federal-state relations, civil rights and liberties, crime, the judiciary, education, health care, poverty, urban affairs, and population.	*Includes formation and debate of U.S. foreign and defense policies, veterans' affairs, and defense spending. (Relations with specific foreign countries are usually found under the region concerned.)*	*Includes business, labor, agriculture, taxation, transportation, consumer affairs, monetary and fiscal policy, natural resources, and pollution.*	*Includes worldwide scientific, medical, and technological developments; natural phenomena; U.S. weather; natural disasters; and accidents.*	*Includes the arts, religion, scholarship, communications media, sports, entertainments, fashions, fads, and social life.*	

	World Affairs	Europe	Africa & the Middle East	The Americas	Asia & the Pacific
Nov. 30	Trade ministers from the 135 member nations of the World Trade Organization (WTO) meet in the U.S. city of Seattle, Washington. Tens of thousands of demonstrators gather in Seattle to protest unfettered trade and the power of the WTO. The protests delay the formal opening of the WTO when tens of thousands of protesters prevent delegates from entering the convention center.		The first soldiers of a UN peacekeeping force arrives in Freetown, the capital of Sierra Leone. Amnesty International reports that killings, rapes, and kidnappings have increased in Sierra Leone since the cease-fire was signed. Reports indicate that two formerly allied rebel factions have started fighting in the north. . . . Kuwait's parliament narrowly rejects a bill that would have given the country's women the same political rights as men, including the right to vote.	Mexican authorities estimate that 208 people, including 18 U.S. citizens, have disappeared in the Juarez area since 1994. . . . German Arciniegas, 98, Colombian historian, newspaper columnist, and social critic, dies in Bogota, Colombia, of a lung ailment.	
Dec. 1	The UN AIDS program and UNICEF report that more than 11 million children have been orphaned by AIDS since the epidemic was recognized in 1981. The UN projects that the number will reach 13 million by the end of the year 2000. The report defines AIDS orphans as children under 15 years of age whose mother or whose mother and father have died of the disease.	Ukrainian authorities shut down the only working reactor in Chernobyl, the site of a major nuclear accident in 1986, because of a cooling system leak. Despite international pressure to shut it down, the reactor, labeled No. 3, was restarted on Nov. 26.	In Namibia, voters overwhelmingly elect Pres. Sam Nujoma to his third term in office. . . . Italian premier Massimo D'Alema becomes the first Western leader to visit Libya since 1991. . . . Unidentified gunmen shoot and wound Muawiya Masri, a member of the Palestinian Legislative Council (PLC).	A jury in Dangriga, Belize, convicts Alan Cal and Estevan Sho of killing Anna Lightfoot, a British aid worker, in 1998. They are sentenced to death by hanging.	Independence leader Jose Ramos Horta returns to East Timor after spending 24 years in exile and is greeted by thousands of supporters in Dili, East Timor's capital.
Dec. 2		Britain's Parliament officially devolves political power over the province of Northern Ireland to a new provincial government, granting Northern Ireland home rule for the first time in decades. The province's new cabinet, the Northern Ireland Executive, holds its first meeting. Membership in the cabinet is divided equally between the province's Protestant and Roman Catholic factions. The Republic of Ireland renounces the goal, stated in its constitution, of uniting Northern Ireland with the republic. . . . Mike (Michael Robert) Ockrent, 53, British stage director, dies in New York City of leukemia.		Matt Cohen, 56, Canadian author who, in November, won the Governor General's Award, Canada's most prestigious literary prize, dies in Toronto of lung cancer.	In Australia, a commuter train collides with a transcontinental express train in the Blue Mountains, west of Sydney, New South Wales's capital, killing seven people and injuring 51 others. . . . In Thailand, a group of 572 skydivers from 39 countries hold a jump in Bangkok, the capital, to honor King Bhumibol Adulyadej for his 72nd birthday. Among those who participate in the jump is Gen. Henry Shelton, the chairman of the U.S. joint chiefs of staff. . . . A wave of torrential rains causes more flooding in Vietnam, which has been deluged with rainfall since November.
Dec. 3	The Rwandan government agrees to allow the chief prosecutor of the International Criminal Tribunal for Rwanda, Carla del Ponte, to enter the country, reversing a Nov. 22 decision. The move comes after del Ponte asked a judicial appeals panel of the war crimes court to reconsider the release of Jean-Bosco Barayagwiza, founding member of the Hutu extremist party coalition for the Defense of the Republic.	Russian military forces encircle Argun, the third-largest city in Chechnya. . . . Some 50,000 people gather in Prague to call for the removal of Premier Milos Zeman and Speaker of Parliament Vaclav Klaus. It is one of the largest street protests in the Czech Republic in 10 years. Similar rallies are held in more than 20 cities. . . . Nilde Iotti, 79, who in 1979 became the first woman president of the lower house of Italy's parliament, dies outside Rome after a heart attack. . . . Edmond J. Safra, 67, billionaire and philanthropist, dies of smoke inhalation in an apparent arson at his home in Monaco.		Statistics reveal that Canada's unemployment rate for November hit 6.9%, an 18-year low.	The Court of Final Appeal, Hong Kong's highest court, reverses a controversial January ruling on immigration from mainland China. The ruling is widely seen as an acknowledgement that the central government has the power to overrule the Hong Kong court. Hundreds of mainland Chinese, who protested regularly during the court case, attempt to storm the Hong Kong government headquarters, but they are repelled by riot police. . . . Reports from China confirm that U.S. scholar Hua Di has been convicted and sentenced to 15 years in prison.
Dec. 4		Russian television and Radio Liberty, a U.S. government-funded service, broadcast interviews with refugees from Chechnya who claim that Russian troops gunned down some 40 civilians trying to flee Grozny. Russian military officials deny the reports, claiming that, while 30 vehicles were destroyed, all of the cars contained rebels, not civilians.			Indonesian troops open fire on activists rallying for an independence referendum in Aceh province. At least 12 people are wounded in the incident, which occurs in the town of Sigli, where thousands of people gathered to mark the 23rd anniversary of an Islamic-based independence movement in Aceh.
Dec. 5		Boris Trajkovski is elected president of Macedonia in a partial rerun of the presidential runoff election held in November.		Cuban president Fidel Castro Ruz demands that Elián González, a six-year-old Cuban refugee found off the coast of Florida in November, be returned to Cuba from the U.S. within 72 hours. Tens of thousands of Cuban demonstrators march on the streets of Havana, the Cuban capital, in ongoing rallies to demand that the U.S. release González to his father's custody.	Transit officials open the Skytrain, a 16-mile-long elevated rail system in Bangkok, the capital of Thailand. . . . The chief minister of the Indian state of Orissa, Giridhar Gamang, is dismissed by Congress (I) party leader Sonia Gandhi. Party leaders criticized Gamang's handling of relief efforts in the wake of a devastating cyclone that hit Orissa in October. The storm killed nearly 10,000 people.

A	B	C	D	E
Includes developments that affect more than one world region, international organizations, and important meetings of major world leaders.	*Includes all domestic and regional developments in Europe, including the Soviet Union, Turkey, Cyprus, and Malta.*	*Includes all domestic and regional developments in Africa and the Middle East, including Iraq and Iran and excluding Cyprus, Turkey, and Afghanistan.*	*Includes all domestic and regional developments in Latin America, the Caribbean, and Canada.*	*Includes all domestic and regional developments in Asia and Pacific nations, extending from Afghanistan through all the Pacific Island, except Hawaii.*

U.S. Politics & Social Issues	U.S. Foreign Policy & Defense	U.S. Economy & Environment	Science, Technology, & Nature	Culture, Leisure, & Lifestyle	
Supreme Court justice John Paul Stevens issues an order that will temporarily block the enforcement of laws in Illinois and Wisconsin that prohibit late-term abortions medically known as intact dilation and extraction (IDE).	The U.S. hands over its last military base in Panama, the army's Fort Clayton. The event effectively ends the U.S.'s 95-year control over the canal zone. . . . Pres. Clinton signs a waiver lifting restrictions on federal funding to foreign-aid organizations that perform abortions or advocate abortion rights. . . . Pres. Clinton signs a bill expanding the availability of long-term health care to veterans.	The FTC approves Exxon Corp.'s $81 billion acquisition through stock transactions of Mobil Corp. The acquisition creates the world's largest company in revenue, combining Exxon, the U.S.'s largest oil producer, with Mobil, the second-largest. Upon the deal's approval, the two companies close their deal. The newly formed company is called Exxon Mobil Corp.	Sam Bard Treiman, 74, physicist who, with his colleague Marvin Goldberger in 1958, deduced a relationship between strong and weak forces, previously thought of as distinct, a relationship that came to be known as the Goldberger-Treiman Relation, dies in New York City of leukemia.	MLB owners unanimously approve a business merger between baseball's New York Yankees and basketball's New Jersey Nets. NBA owners unanimously approved the deal in September. The business merger is the first of its kind in North American professional sports and is expected to generate as much as $600 million a year in revenue.	Nov. 30
The findings of a five-month study of airport security reveal lax security controls at major U.S. airports.	More than 400 people protesting the ongoing World Trade Organization (WTO) talks in Seattle, Washington, are arrested. . . . Judge Hector Laffitte dismisses all charges against Alfredo Otero, a Cuban exile accused of plotting to assassinate Cuban president Fidel Castro Ruz in 1997.		An international group of researchers announce that for the first time they have established the chemical sequence of about 97% of chromosome 22, the second-smallest human chromosome.		Dec. 1
The National Education Goals Panel, created in 1989, announces that none of the eight goals it set for the year 2000 have been achieved. One member, Gov. Tommy Thompson (R, Wis.), observes, "We're going in the right direction, but we're going at a very slow speed." . . . The six candidates for the Republican presidential nomination in 2000 square off in a debate in Manchester, New Hampshire. The nationally televised forum marks the first time in the election campaign that Texas governor George W. Bush participates in a debate with his rivals. Bush failed to attend the first three televised GOP debates.	Energy Secretary Bill Richardson reveals that he will start reissuing waivers allowing foreign scientists to visit U.S. nuclear weapons laboratories. A moratorium was declared on visits to major labs following allegations of Chinese nuclear espionage.	The nonpartisan Congressional Budget Office (CBO) finds that the fiscal 2000 appropriations bills signed earlier in the year will require the federal government to use $17 billion of the Social Security Surplus, from which lawmakers vowed not to draw. The CBO also reports that the government's fiscal 2000 spending commitments exceed by $37 billion the spending limits set by a balanced-budget agreement enacted in 1997. . . . The NYSE votes to begin quoting stock prices in dollars and cents, abandoning the existing fractional system.	The National Institutes of Health (NIH) publishes draft guidelines governing federally financed research on human embryonic stem cells.	Charlie (Charles Lee) Byrd, 74, American jazz guitarist who recorded more than 100 albums, dies in Annapolis, Maryland, of cancer. . . . Joey Adams, 88, stand-up comedian, dies in New York City of heart failure.	Dec. 2
	Pres. Clinton orders a permanent end to live-fire military exercises on the island of Vieques and the closure of the Vieques bombing range within five years unless Puerto Rico's residents agree to allow the military to continue using the land. . . . Mexican naval vessels and U.S. Coast Guard ships seize a fishing boat off Mexico's Pacific Coast transporting nine tons of cocaine. . . . A charter airplane carrying 138 passengers is the first direct passenger flight leaving New York for Havana, the Cuban capital, since 1961. . . . Pres. Clinton signs a bill authorizing the nation's intelligence programs for fiscal 2000.		NASA officials lose radio contact with *Mars Polar Lander*, an unmanned spacecraft intended to look for signs of frozen water on the planet Mars.	Madeline (Gail) Kahn, 57, U.S. stage and screen actress nominated for several Oscar and Tony awards, dies in New York City. . . . Tori Murden, the first American to ski to the geographic South Pole in 1988, becomes the first American and the first woman ever to row across the Atlantic Ocean alone.	Dec. 3
Six firefighters in Worcester, Massachusetts, die in a burning warehouse. It is said to be the deadliest blaze for U.S. firefighters since 1994. . . . A van carrying 17 people crashes near Albuquerque, New Mexico, killing 13 passengers and injuring the other four. . . . Rose Elizabeth Bird, 63, first woman to serve on California's Supreme Court, dies in Stanford, California, of breast cancer.					Dec. 4
				Australia defeats France, three matches to two, in the finals of the 100th Davis Cup tennis competition. . . . The 22nd Annual Kennedy Center Honors are awarded to Stevie Wonder, Sean Connery, Jason Robards, Victor Borge, and Judith Jamison. Wonder, 49, is the youngest person ever to receive the honor.	Dec. 5

F	G	H	I	J
Includes elections, federal-state relations, civil rights and liberties, crime, the judiciary, education, health care, poverty, urban affairs, and population.	*Includes formation and debate of U.S. foreign and defense policies, veterans' affairs, and defense spending. (Relations with specific foreign countries are usually found under the region concerned.)*	*Includes business, labor, agriculture, taxation, transportation, consumer affairs, monetary and fiscal policy, natural resources, and pollution.*	*Includes worldwide scientific, medical, and technological developments; natural phenomena; U.S. weather; natural disasters; and accidents.*	*Includes the arts, religion, scholarship, communications media, sports, entertainments, fashions, fads, and social life.*

	World Affairs	Europe	Africa & the Middle East	The Americas	Asia & the Pacific
Dec. 6	The UN court convicts former Hutu militia leader Georges Rutaganda of genocide and crimes against humanity in a 1994 war in which more than 500,000 people, mainly Tutsis, were killed. The court sentences Rutaganda to life in prison. . . . Two reports by the OSCE provide overwhelming evidence of a Serbian campaign, organized by the state, to drive nearly 1 million Albanians from Kosovo. It also shows that continued violence and terrorism in Kosovo was at times perpetrated by ethnic Albanians motivated by revenge against Serbs.	Russian military forces shower the city of Grozny, the capital of the breakaway republic of Chechnya, with leaflets warning residents to flee the city by Dec. 11 or risk death. . . . Ted Maher, the U.S. nurse of Edmond Safra, who died Dec. 3 in a fire at his home in Monaco, confesses to lighting the fire, hoping that he would rescue Safra from the fire and be considered a hero.	The Sudanese government pardons and frees two Roman Catholic priests, Hilary Boma and Lino Sebit, along with at least 18 other men. All of the men, arrested in August 1998, were accused of planting bombs in Khartoum, the capital.		In the Indian state of Orissa, Hemananda Biswal is sworn in to succeed Giridhar Gamang, who was dismissed Dec. 5 in the midst of criticism over his handling of a devastating cyclone that killed nearly 10,000 people. . . . Reports from Vietnam suggest that more than 100 people have been killed in rains that started Dec. 2.
Dec. 7				Inco Ltd., Canada's largest nickel producer, reaches a tentative contract agreement with 1,100 mine workers after a lockout that started Sept. 15.	Data reveals that nearly 600 people have been killed in the torrential rains and flooding that began Nov. 1 in central Vietnam. The flooding, said to be the worst ever recorded in the country, has caused $50 million in damage and left millions homeless.
Dec. 8		Russian president Boris Yeltsin and Belarussian president Aleksandr Lukashenko sign an agreement to form a political and economic confederation between their nations. . . . In response to Montenegro's Nov. 24 declaration, armed Yugoslav troops seize control of the airport in Podgorica, the capital. . . . France announces that it will retain its ban on British beef indefinitely, despite a round of negotiations in which Britain made concessions regarding meat inspections and labeling.	Pres. Omar Hassan Ahmed al-Bashir of Sudan and Pres. Yoweri Museveni of Uganda sign a peace pact in which each agree not to support rebel groups trying to overthrow the other's government. The deal also restores diplomatic ties between the two nations that were broken in 1995.		Prosecutors formally charge Pakistan's ousted prime minister, Nawaz Sharif, with hijacking, kidnapping, attempted murder, and conspiracy to wage war against the state. Sharif and six others are indicted in a special antiterrorism court in Karachi.
Dec. 9		A Serbian court sentences Flora Brovina, a poet and women's rights advocate, to 12 years in prison on charges of terrorism during the NATO bombing campaign in Kosovo. . . . The U.S. State Department claims that an estimated 10,000 ethnic Albanians were killed by Serbs between March and June in Kosovo. . . . Yugoslav troops reopen Montenegro's airport, ending a standoff started Dec. 8 with Montenegrin police.	Heavy fighting flares in the Israeli security zone in southern Lebanon when Lebanon's Shi'ite Muslim Hezbollah movement attack Israeli fighters. . . . Reports confirm that Mengistu Haile Mariam, a former military ruler of Ethiopia accused of genocide, has returned to Zimbabwe from South Africa.	Thirty-seven people are arrested in Canada and the U.S. in an international police operation intended to bring down an Eastern European organized crime ring based in Toronto. The suspects face more than 100 charges, including fraud and drug trafficking.	
Dec. 10	Leaders from the 15 member nations of the EU meet for discussions in Helsinki and invited seven nations—Bulgaria, Romania, Slovakia, Latvia, Lithuania, Malta, and Turkey—to apply for membership, expanding its list of current applicants to 13. . . . The 15-member UN Security Council unanimously votes to extend for six months its existing "oil-for-food" program, which lets Iraq raise money for its citizens' humanitarian needs through the sale of exported oil.	Pres. Franjo Tudjman, 77, who had led Croatia's secession from Yugoslavia and served as its first president since 1990, dies in Zagreb of stomach cancer. . . . Niccolo Tucci, 91, Italian-born author who wrote in Italian and English and was known for his autobiographical fiction, dies in New York City.	The Vatican announces that Iraq has rejected plans for Pope John Paul II to travel to Iraq in 2000 because of current sanctions on Iraq and UN no-fly zones in the north and south of the country.	Fernando De la Rua of the center-left Alianza coalition is sworn in as president of Argentina. . . . In what is called the largest demonstration in Cuba since Castro took power in 1959, an estimated 2 million protesters march to demand that the U.S. release Elián González, a six-year-old Cuban refugee found off the coast of Florida in November, to his father's custody in Cuba.	Labour Party leader Helen Clark is sworn in as New Zealand's prime minister.
Dec. 11	Leaders of the EU member nations agree to create a European rapid-reaction military force of about 60,000 troops that can respond to regional and international military crises.			Former army commander Lino Cesar Oviedo, who fled to Argentina in March after he and then-Pres. Raul Cubas Grau were accused of plotting the assassination of Vice Pres. Luis Maria Argana, reveals he has returned to Paraguay.	

A	B	C	D	E
Includes developments that affect more than one world region, international organizations, and important meetings of major world leaders.	Includes all domestic and regional developments in Europe, including the Soviet Union, Turkey, Cyprus, and Malta.	Includes all domestic and regional developments in Africa and the Middle East, including Iraq and Iran and excluding Cyprus, Turkey, and Afghanistan.	Includes all domestic and regional developments in Latin America, the Caribbean, and Canada.	Includes all domestic and regional developments in Asia and Pacific nations, extending from Afghanistan through all the Pacific Island, except Hawaii.

U.S. Politics & Social Issues	U.S. Foreign Policy & Defense	U.S. Economy & Environment	Science, Technology, & Nature	Culture, Leisure, & Lifestyle	
An unidentified 13-year-old boy shoots four schoolmates, none of them fatally, when he opens fire in Fort Gibson, Oklahoma. . . . Reports from Chicago confirm that Judge Jennifer Duncan-Brice has ruled that a private liability lawsuit against the gun industry may proceed. . . . A federal jury in Miami, Florida, convicts SabreTech Inc., an airline maintenance company, of improperly packaging and handling hazardous materials linked to the fatal 1996 crash of ValuJet Flight 592 in the Florida Everglades. Two SabreTech employees are acquitted.	Despite ongoing protests in Cuba, the State Department rejects Fidel Castro's Dec. 5 demand that the U.S. immediately return Elián González, a six-year-old Cuban refugee found off the coast of Florida in November.	A federal advisory panel argues that the government is underestimating how long future Social Security beneficiaries are likely to live in their budget forecasts. . . . A Michigan environmental group and six Michigan residents file a lawsuit in Kalamazoo seeking an injunction to stop a plutonium shipment from passing through the state. . . . Robert A. Swanson, 52, cofounder, chief executive, 1976–90, and chair, 1990–96, of biotechnology company Genentech Inc., dies in Hillsborough, California, after a yearlong battle with brain cancer.			Dec. 6
In the wake of a report finding that medical mistakes cause as many as 98,000 deaths a year, Pres. Clinton orders a series of measures intended to reduce the number of such injuries and deaths. . . . In *LAPD v. United Reporting Publishing Corp.*, the Supreme Court rules, 7-2, to uphold a California statute that prohibits the release of information contained in police records to companies that seek to use the information for commercial purposes.		In response to the suit filed Dec. 6 in Michigan, Judge Richard Enslen issues a 10-day restraining order blocking the shipment of plutonium. . . . Cendant Corp., a U.S. franchising and direct marketing company, announces that it has agreed to pay $2.83 billion to settle a class-action lawsuit over a 1998 accounting scandal. The settlement is said to be the largest ever reached in a shareholder class action.			Dec. 7
A jury in Memphis, Tennessee, rules that the 1968 slaying of civil-rights leader Rev. Martin Luther King Jr. was part of a conspiracy involving a former Memphis restaurant owner, Lloyd Jowers, and "others, including governmental agencies." It awards $100 in damages to the King family. The trial received little publicity, and some observers question the reliability of the proceedings.	FBI counterintelligence agents in Washington, D.C., arrest Stanislav Borisovich Grusev, a Russian diplomat believed to have been spying for Russia. . . . A federal jury in San Juan, Puerto Rico, acquits five Cuban exiles accused of plotting to assassinate Cuban president Fidel Castro Ruz in 1997. . . . A U.S. military jury convicts Private Calvin Glover for the fatal beating of a gay infantryman, Barry Winchell, 21, with a baseball bat while Winchell slept.	The SEC unanimously approves plans to provide all trading firms access to trade New York Stock Exchange (NYSE) stocks. The proposed move will be accomplished by opening up the Intermarket Trading System (ITS), an electronic order-routing system that links the NYSE with the NASDAQ Stock Market and regional markets.	A committee of the National Institutes of Health (NIH) meets to discuss the safety of clinical trials of experimental gene therapies.	Sir Rupert Charles Hart-Davis, 92, British publisher, editor, and writer, dies in North Yorkshire, England.	Dec. 8
Pres. Clinton signs a bill creating a new agency that will administer truck and bus safety programs. . . . Hawaii's Supreme Court rules that a 1998 amendment to the state constitution banning gay marriages is legitimate and enforceable. . . . Tens of thousands of firefighters from around world travel to Worcester, Massachusetts, to attend a memorial service for the six who died in the Dec. 4 blaze there. Pres. Clinton and Vice Pres. Al Gore also attend the service.	A U.S. military jury sentences Private Calvin Glover to life in prison with the possibility of parole for the fatal beating of a gay infantryman, Barry Winchell, 21, with a baseball bat while Winchell slept.	The National Association of Securities Dealers (NASD), which runs the NASDAQ Stock Market, announces that it will adopt an electronic trading system.	David Smith, 31, of Aberdeen Township, New Jersey, pleads guilty to state and federal charges that he created and sent out the "Melissa" computer virus in March. Melissa spread to more than 1 million computers worldwide and was called the most rapidly spreading, costly, and disruptive computer virus ever.		Dec. 9
Connecticut Superior Court judge Robert McWeeny dismisses a gun liability lawsuit filed by Bridgeport, arguing that victims of gun violence rather than municipalities are the proper plaintiffs to bring such lawsuits.	A federal grand jury in New Mexico indicts Wen Ho Lee, the chief suspect in a government investigation into alleged Chinese espionage at U.S. nuclear weapons laboratories.		Scientists report new evidence that there was a large ocean in the northern region of the planet Mars some 2 billion years ago. Scientific opinion remains divided on the issue, however.	Early Wright, 84, Southern black disk jockey, dies in Clarksdale, Mississippi, after a heart attack. . . . In Inglewood, California, Panamanian jockey Laffit Pincay Jr. wins his 8,834th race, surpassing the record set in 1970. . . . Rick Danko, 56, who was inducted into the Rock and Roll Hall of Fame in 1994, dies in Marbletown, New York.	Dec. 10
	The State Department issues a warning to Americans abroad that they may be the target of attacks around the millennial new year. . . . Pres. Clinton admits that the "don't ask, don't tell" policy toward homosexuals in the military has failed to end discrimination and harassment against gays in the armed forces. He pledges to work with the Defense Department to find a way to revise military policy toward gays.			In the wake of scandals, the International Olympic Committee (IOC) overwhelmingly approves 50 reform measures aimed at overhauling the IOC's practices and restoring public faith in the 105-year-old Olympic governing body.	Dec. 11
F	G	H	I	J	
Includes elections, federal-state relations, civil rights and liberties, crime, the judiciary, education, health care, poverty, urban affairs, and population.	*Includes formation and debate of U.S. foreign and defense policies, veterans' affairs, and defense spending. (Relations with specific foreign countries are usually found under the region concerned.)*	*Includes business, labor, agriculture, taxation, transportation, consumer affairs, monetary and fiscal policy, natural resources, and pollution.*	*Includes worldwide scientific, medical, and technological developments; natural phenomena; U.S. weather; natural disasters; and accidents.*	*Includes the arts, religion, scholarship, communications media, sports, entertainments, fashions, fads, and social life.*	

	World Affairs	Europe	Africa & the Middle East	The Americas	Asia & the Pacific
Dec. 12		In France, a tanker carrying about 8 million gallons of oil breaks up during a storm off the Brittany coast, spilling 1.5 million gallons (5.7 million liters) of oil into the ocean. The 26 crew members are rescued.	Sudanese president Omar Hassan Ahmed al-Bashir declares a three-month state of emergency and dissolves the parliament.	Socialist Ricardo Lagos, the candidate of the governing Concertacion coalition, is locked in a virtual tie with conservative challenger Joaquin Lavin after first-round voting in Chile's presidential election. The results mean that Lagos and Lavin will compete in a runoff in January 2000.	
Dec. 13		Unprecedented peace negotiations between Corsican nationalists and the French government begin. . . . Romanian president Constantinescu dismisses Premier Radu Vasile. . . . Croatian president Franjo Tudjman, who died Dec. 10, is buried in Zagreb. An estimated 100,000 people watch the funeral procession. . . . Stane Dolanc, 74, second in command to Josip Broz Tito during most of the 1970s and a member of the joint presidency that assumed control of Yugoslavia, 1984–89, dies in Ljubljana, Slovenia, several months after suffering a stroke.	Israeli forces kill two men they claim are members of the Palestinian militant Hamas group during a raid in the West Bank town of Beit Awwa.	Canada's House of Commons votes, 217-48, in favor of a bill that will give the native Nisga'a people in northwestern British Columbia the right to self-government. If cleared, the legislation will turn into law the Nisga'a Final Agreement, a land treaty negotiated over a period of 20 years between the aboriginals and the British Columbia and federal governments. The agreement will give the Nisga'a people the powers of self government they have sought for over 100 years.	João Tavarres, leader of pro-Indonesia militias, orders the groups to formally disband. . . . A court in Osaka, Japan, orders Isamu Yamada, governor of Osaka prefecture, to pay $107,000 damages to a 21-year-old woman in what is Japan's largest sexual-harassment verdict ever.
Dec. 14	The International Criminal Tribunal for the Former Yugoslavia sentences Goran Jelisic, a Bosnian Serb shift commander at a prison camp in northern Bosnia in 1992, to 40 years in prison for war crimes and crimes against humanity. The sentence is the stiffest imposed by the six-year-old UN court.	German government officials and industry representatives agree to establish a fund of 10 billion marks ($5.1 billion) to compensate people forced into slave labor during the Nazi regime.		The U.S. hands over control of the Panama Canal to Panama in a public ceremony held at the canal's Miraflores Locks. Former U.S. president Jimmy Carter heads the U.S. delegation, and he states, "Today we come together with mutual respect to acknowledge without question the complete sovereignty of Panama."	Japan states that it will lift its ban on food aid to famine-stricken North Korea, and open negotiations with North Korea on establishing diplomatic relations.
Dec. 15	Iraq fails to meet a deadline to allow inspectors from the International Atomic Energy Agency (IAEA) to examine the country's uranium supply, raising questions about its commitment to disarmament.	A court in Bavaria, Germany sentences Djurdadj Kusljic, 44, a Bosnian Serb police chief, to life in prison for ordering the killing of Muslims in Bosnia.	Israeli prime minister Ehud Barak and Syrian foreign minister Farouk al-Sharaa meet in the first direct meeting between the two countries in nearly four years. . . . A Lebanese court acquits popular Arab singer Marcel Khalife on all charges of blasphemy for including a verse of the Koran, the Muslim holy text, in a song.	Venezuelan voters overwhelmingly approve a new national charter drafted by the country's constitutional assembly and aggressively supported by Pres. Hugo Chavez Frias. The new charter—Venezuela's 26th constitution since it gained its independence from Spain in 1821—includes 350 articles that drastically reshape state institutions and their assigned powers. Separately, torrential downpours begin in Venezuela's coastal region.	Hong Kong's highest court reverses a lower court's ruling that overturned the convictions of two men under a law prohibiting the desecration of the flags of Hong Kong and China.
Dec. 16	A UN panel faults the UN and major powers, especially the U.S., for failing to take action to prevent the 1994 genocide in Rwanda, despite signs that it was imminent. In the 1994 genocide, some 800,000 people—mainly ethnic Tutsis—were killed. . . . Data shows the 1990s were the warmest decade on record, and the 1900s the warmest century in 1,000 years. . . . . The U.S. agrees to pay China $28 million for the May bombing of the Chinese embassy in Yugoslavia by NATO forces. China agrees to pay the U.S. $2.87 million for damage done to the U.S. embassy during demonstrations after the bombing.	Padraic Wilson, a leader in the IRA, is released from Northern Ireland's Maze Prison, where he completed eight years of a 24-year sentence for possessing explosives. . . . Romanian president Emil Constantinescu appoints Mugur Isarescu as premier.	As many as 20 children are wounded when an Israeli mortar shell explodes near a school in Arab Salim as fighting that flared Dec. 9 in the Israeli security zone in southern Lebanon continues.		
Dec. 17	Representatives from more than 50 nations and international groups meet in Tokyo and pledge $520 million in aid to East Timor to fund reconstruction and humanitarian projects there. . . . A divided UN Security Council approves a resolution creating a new arms-monitoring regime for Iraq, ending a year-long deadlock. The new body is called the UN Monitoring, Verification and Inspection Commission (UNMOVIC).	Gunmen hurl grenades and open fire on a cafe in a Serbian enclave in the town of Orahovac in southwestern Kosovo. One man is killed and at least eight people are injured in the attack. The incident is the latest in a string of revenge attacks apparently perpetrated by Kosovo Albanians on Serbs in Kosovo. . . . In a move that ends a 500-year link, the Swedish government states that on Jan. 1, 2000, it will officially divorce from the Lutheran Church of Sweden. . . . Cardinal Paolo Dezza, 98, Italian Roman Catholic churchman and interim head of the Jesuit order, 1981–83, dies in Rome, Italy.		Reports reveal that, since Dec. 15, torrential downpours have caused widespread flooding and numerous mudslides throughout Venezuela's northwestern coastal region, leaving thousands of people dead and 150,000 homeless. The devastation is described as Venezuela's worst natural disaster in modern times. . . . Luis Alfredo Garavito, who admitted in October to having killed 140 children since 1992, is found guilty of murdering an 11-year-old boy in 1996 in Tunja, Colombia, and of raping another victim. He is sentenced to 52 years in prison.	Police kill five men in a gunfight following an unsuccessful bank robbery attempt in Port Moresby, the capital of Papua New Guinea.

A	B	C	D	E
Includes developments that affect more than one world region, international organizations, and important meetings of major world leaders.	*Includes all domestic and regional developments in Europe, including the Soviet Union, Turkey, Cyprus, and Malta.*	*Includes all domestic and regional developments in Africa and the Middle East, including Iraq and Iran and excluding Cyprus, Turkey, and Afghanistan.*	*Includes all domestic and regional developments in Latin America, the Caribbean, and Canada.*	*Includes all domestic and regional developments in Asia and Pacific nations, extending from Afghanistan through all the Pacific Island, except Hawaii.*

U.S. Politics & Social Issues	U.S. Foreign Policy & Defense	U.S. Economy & Environment	Science, Technology, & Nature	Culture, Leisure, & Lifestyle	
Pres. Clinton signs into law a bill barring companies from mailing deceptive notices of sweepstakes and other contests.				Paul Cadmus, 94, painter who generated controversy in the 1930s by depicting military personnel in compromising situations, dies in Weston, Conn. . . . Joseph Heller, 76, author best known for *Catch-22* (1961), a classic U.S. novel about World War II, dies in East Hampton, N.Y., after a heart attack.	Dec. 12
In Miami, Florida, Judge Amy Dean dismissed a liability lawsuit filed by Miami-Dade County against the firearms industry. . . . Data shows that states have executed a record 96 prisoners since the beginning of 1999. That is more executions than in any other year since 1976. . . . In Brooklyn New York Judge Eugene Nickerson sentences former city police officer Justin Volpe to 30 years in prison for the 1997 station-house torture of Abner Louima, a Haitian immigrant.	At a jail in Louisiana, four Cuban inmates and a Bahamian detainee take over the warden's office and the jail's command post. . . . The U.S. reveals that approximately 12 suspects allegedly linked to Osama bin Laden were arrested in the Middle East during the previous two weeks. The suspects are accused of planning attacks on Americans celebrating the new year.		Scientists report that a house cat gave birth to a rare wildcat in the first successful transfer of an embryo to the womb of an animal of a different species. The scientists suggest that the procedure might be used to bolster the population of endangered species.		Dec. 13
	U.S. customs officials arrest Ahmed Ressam, an Algerian-born man caught entering the U.S. at Port Angeles, Wash., from Victoria, British Columbia, with over 130 pounds (60 kg) of bomb-making materials in the trunk of his car. . . . The Cuban inmates who took control of a prison in Louisiana Dec. 13 demand that they be freed from detention in the U.S. and sent back to Cuba.	The Department of Agriculture announces that food processors will be allowed to irradiate raw beef, pork, and lamb to eliminate potentially deadly microbes, such as the *E. coli* O157:H7 bacterium.	A federal judicial committee bars the posting of federal judges' financial statements on the Internet computer network.	Cartoonist Charles M. Schulz, 77, the creator of the "Peanuts" comic strip, reveals that he is retiring because of ill health. "Peanuts" currently appears in roughly 2,600 newspapers in 75 countries and has an estimated 355 million readers.	Dec. 14
	Jordanian officials announce the arrest of 11 Jordanians, an Algerian, and an Iraqi suspected of planning attacks on Americans and other nationals in Jordan. U.S. officials reveal that those arrested are believed to be followers of suspected Saudi terrorist Osama bin Laden.	New York City's Metropolitan Transportation Authority (MTA) reaches a tentative three-year contract agreement with the Transport Workers Union Local 100, which represents the city's 33,000 bus and subway workers. The deal, brokered after five days of around-the-clock negotiations, narrowly averts a strike of the nation's largest mass-transit system, which serves 3.5 million riders daily.			Dec. 15
	The INS reveals that the inmates in the standoff that started Dec. 14 at a prison in Louisiana had been convicted of committing crimes in the U.S. and had completed serving their sentences. Normally, foreign criminals who served their time are deported, but the U.S. has no repatriation agreement with Cuba. Currently, there are about 2,400 Cuban convicts under INS detention in the U.S. Of those, about 1,400 are incarcerated in local jails.	The Commerce Department reports that the U.S. trade deficit swelled in October, to a seasonally adjusted $25.94 billion, a record. That marks the seventh time since January that the deficit reaches a record high. The rise follows a revised deficit figure of $24.15 billion in September. . . . The Justice Department files a class-action lawsuit against the St. Louis-based Adam's Mark hotel chain, accusing it of discriminating against black customers by charging them higher rates than white customers and renting them inferior rooms.		Carolina Panthers football coach George Seifert releases wide receiver Rae Carruth, who is a suspect in the shooting death of his pregnant girlfriend. The NFL also suspends him indefinitely from the league.	Dec. 16
Pres. Clinton signs into law a bill allowing disabled people to keep their government health-care benefits when they become employed. . . . Ken W. Clawson, 63, director of communications during the final months of the administration of Pres. Richard M. Nixon, dies in New Orleans, Louisiana, after a heart attack.	The U.S. announces that it will close indefinitely its embassy in Quito, the capital of Ecuador, along with two consulates because the offices received unspecified threats against their security.	Pres. Clinton appoints NLRB member Sara Fox to another five-year term. . . . In San Francisco, California, Judge Susan Illston entences former Democratic fund-raiser Yogesh K. Gandhi to one year in prison on charges of using foreign money to contribute to the Democratic Party, mail fraud, and tax evasion. . . . A federal judge lifts a temporary restraining order issued Dec. 10 regarding a shipment of plutonium. . . . The EPA orders 392 power plants and other facilities in the South and Midwest to reduce their emissions of nitrogen oxide by nearly half.		Grover Washington Jr., 56, jazz saxophonist who pioneered a form of crossover jazz, dies in New York City, after collapsing from a heart attack at a TV studio. . . . C(omer) Vann Woodward, 91, historian who win the 1982 Pulitzer Prize, dies in Hamden, Connecticut.	Dec. 17
F Includes elections, federal-state relations, civil rights and liberties, crime, the judiciary, education, health care, poverty, urban affairs, and population.	**G** Includes formation and debate of U.S. foreign and defense policies, veterans' affairs, and defense spending. (Relations with specific foreign countries are usually found under the region concerned.)	**H** Includes business, labor, agriculture, taxation, transportation, consumer affairs, monetary and fiscal policy, natural resources, and pollution.	**I** Includes worldwide scientific, medical, and technological developments; natural phenomena; U.S. weather; natural disasters; and accidents.	**J** Includes the arts, religion, scholarship, communications media, sports, entertainments, fashions, fads, and social life.	

	World Affairs	Europe	Africa & the Middle East	The Americas	Asia & the Pacific
Dec. 18	Iraq rejects the new weapons monitoring regime formed Dec. 17, the UN Monitoring, Verification and Inspection Commission (UNMOVIC).	Serbia's Alliance for Change opposition group, which for 89 consecutive days has held rallies to protest Yugoslav president Slobodan Milosevic's regime, announces that it will end its daily protests.			At a campaign rally in Colombo, the capital of Sri Lanka, a suicide bombing kills more than 20 people and injures more than 100 others., including Pres. Chandrika Kumaratunga. . . . In Bhutan, 200 prisoners are released from prison in a mass amnesty by King Jigme Singye Wangchuck. The monarch releases all prisoners regarded by human-rights groups as political detainees.
Dec. 19		Russian voters favor centrist and progovernment parties over left- and right-wing parties in elections to the State Duma, the lower house of the Russian parliament.	Palestinian leader Yasser Arafat releases six people arrested in November for signing a letter that criticized him. Two other signers of the letter remain in jail.	Eight people are freed after being abducted Sept. 11 near the Ecuador-Colombia boarder by suspected Colombian guerilas.	The territory of Macao reverts to Chinese sovereignty at midnight local time, ending 442 years of Portuguese colonial rule. A ceremony is attended by Portuguese president Jorge Sampaio and Chinese president Jiang Zemin. Some 30,000 people gather in Tiananmen Square in Beijing, China's capital, to celebrate the occasion. Macao police break up a gathering of about 40 members of Falun Gong, a spiritual movement banned in China. . . . Hisashi Ouchi, 35, one of three workers made seriously ill by exposure to radiation in a September nuclear accident in Japan, dies.
Dec. 20	British NATO troops in northwestern Bosnia-Herzegovina arrest Major General Stanislav Galic, a former Bosnian Serb general charged with war crimes committed in the 1992–95 war in Bosnia.	During a routine traffic stop in the town of Calatayud, Spanish police discover 950 kilograms (one ton) of explosives and a detonator in a van reportedly bound for Madrid, Spain's capital. . . . In Serbia, Judge Zoran Ivosevic of the Supreme Court and Judge Bozidar Prelevic of a municipal court are ousted for their membership in a nongovernmental union.		A Cubana de Aviacion plane crashes into a low-income neighborhood located next to the airport in Guatemala City, Guatemala. Six passengers, eight crew members, and nine people on the ground are killed. . . . The Revolutionary Armed Forces of Colombia (FARC) rebel group declares a cease-fire scheduled to last through Jan. 10, 2000. The announcement comes after intense fighting between FARC guerrillas and government forces that reportedly led to the deaths of more than 230 government soldiers and guerrillas. . . . Panamanian president Moscoso signs an executive order that abrogates two 1978 laws that restrict journalistic freedom.	International peacekeepers discover two mass graves in East Timor that they predict will contain the bodies of more than 100 victims killed in rampages launched by militias that oppose East Timor's independence referendum.
Dec. 21		The Serbian parliament fires Judge Slobodan Vucetic for criticizing the Yugoslav government. . . . Gordon Brown, Britain's chancellor of the exchequer, announces that Britain will forgive the debt owed to the government by 41 of the world's poorest countries.	Israeli prime minister Ehud Barak and Palestinian leader Yasser Arafat meet in the West Bank city of Ramallah. The meeting marks the first time an Israeli prime minister attends peace negotiations in the Palestinian-controlled occupied territories. . . . Israeli and Hezbollah forces observe a cease-fire to allow Red Cross workers to retrieve the bodies of five Hezbollah fighters killed in recent clashes in the security zone in Lebanon.	In regard to the floods from rains that started Dec. 15, Angel Rangel, Venezuela's civil defense director, notes that "there are unfortunately thousands of people buried in the mud, and the final number [of deaths] we will never know. The forecast is that we could have maybe 25,000 or 30,000 [fatalities]." . . . A group of protesters throw rocks and bags of paint at the U.S. embassy in Panama City to mark the 10th anniversary of the U.S. invasion of Panama.	Sri Lankan president Chandrika Kumaratunga of the ruling People's Alliance coalition is reelected to a second six-year term in office. In an outbreaks of poll-related violence, at least five people are killed.

A	B	C	D	E
Includes developments that affect more than one world region, international organizations, and important meetings of major world leaders.	Includes all domestic and regional developments in Europe, including the Soviet Union, Turkey, Cyprus, and Malta.	Includes all domestic and regional developments in Africa and the Middle East, including Iraq and Iran and excluding Cyprus, Turkey, and Afghanistan.	Includes all domestic and regional developments in Latin America, the Caribbean, and Canada.	Includes all domestic and regional developments in Asia and Pacific nations, extending from Afghanistan through all the Pacific Island, except Hawaii.

U.S. Politics & Social Issues	U.S. Foreign Policy & Defense	U.S. Economy & Environment	Science, Technology, & Nature	Culture, Leisure, & Lifestyle	
	In response to the standoff that started Dec. 13 at a prison in Louisiana, Cuba and the U.S. State Department agree to a deal under which seven Cuban detainees involved in the hostage crisis will be allowed to be deported to Havana. The Cuban inmates—now numbering five—and one Bahamian detainee release their seven remaining hostages and surrender to authorities.			Joe Higgs, 59, pioneering reggae performer, dies in Los Angeles of cancer. . . . Robert Bresson, 98, French film director and screenwriter, dies in Droue-sur-Drouette, southwest of Paris.	Dec. 18
In an interview, former first lady Nancy Reagan reveals that the condition of her husband, former president Ronald Reagan—who suffers from Alzheimer's disease—has deteriorated to the point that he is no longer able to hold a coherent conversation.	Authorities in Beecher Falls, Vermont, arrest an Algerian man and a Canadian woman—Bouabide Chamchi, 20, and Lucia Garofalo, 35—as they try to enter the U.S. from Canada when dogs smell residue of explosives in their car. No explosives are found. . . . Reports confirm that the VA has documented almost 3,000 medical errors that occurred in department hospitals in the previous two years. The department noted that 710 deaths resulted from medical mistakes in that period.		The space shuttle *Discovery* lifts off from Kennedy Space Center in Cape Canaveral, Florida, to repair and replace equipment on the Earth-orbiting *Hubble Space Telescope*, which shut down Nov. 13.	Desmond Llewelyn, 85, British actor in 17 James Bond films, dies in East Sussex after being involved in a car crash. . . . After fleeing the state, football player Rae Carruth, of the Carolina Panthers, returns to Charlotte, North Carolina, to face first-degree murder charges in the death of his pregnant girlfriend, Cherica Adams, 24. He is reportedly the first active NFL player to be charged with murder.	Dec. 19
The Vermont Supreme Court orders the state government to offer homosexual couples the same benefits and legal rights afforded to heterosexual married couples. . . . In Denver, Colorado, Judge Jeffrey Bayless sentences Nathan Thill, 21, a white supremacist, to life in prison without parole for the 1997 shooting death of Oumar Dia, an African immigrant. . . . Housing Secretary Andrew Cuomo reveals that HUD will seize control of a program that allocates federal grant money for NYC homeless programs in response to a November court ruling that city officials had unfairly denied grant money to a group critical of NYC mayor Rudolph Giuliani (R). . . . In Cleveland, Ohio, Judge Solomon Oliver Jr. rules that Cleveland's school-voucher program Is unconstitutional because it violates the separation of church and state. . . . Sen. James Inhofe (R, Okla.) states that he will block every nominee that Pres. Clinton offers for federal judgeships until Clinton leaves office in 2001, as a protest against the Dec. 17 appointment of NLRB member Sara Fox.	In a letter, Senate majority leader Trent Lott (R, Miss.) and five other senators ask Pres. Clinton to delay any INS action in the case of Elián González, a six-year-old Cuban refugee rescued off the coast of Florida in November, until Congress returns in January. . . . Six Cuban inmates involved in the Dec. 13 hostage standoff at a jail in St. Martinville, Louisiana, are deported to Havana, the Cuban capital. . . . Wen Ho Lee, a physicist indicted for mishandling nuclear weapons information, files a lawsuit against three U.S. agencies for violating his privacy and wrongfully portraying him as a spy in the news media.	Pres. Clinton authorizes the largest pay raise for federal workers since 1981. Beginning January 2000, white-collar federal civil servants nationwide will receive a 3.8% wage increase. Local government workers will receive a an increase that varies by metropolitan area and falls between 4.69% and 5.59%. . . . The NYSE issues its largest fine ever against a firm for day-trading violations when it levies $1.5 million against Schonfeld Securities LLC and several of its officers. . . . Burlington Northern Santa Fe Corp. (BN) of the U.S. and Canadian National Railway Co. (CN) announce plans to merge in a US$6 billion (C$8.8 billion) transaction that will create the largest railroad company in North America. The new company, to be called North American Railways Inc. (NAR), will provide nonstop freight service across Canada and to every U.S. state west of the Mississippi River.		Hank (Clarence Eugene) Snow, 85, Canadian-born country music legend who recorded more than 80 albums, dies in Madison, Tennessee, after recently being treated for pneumonia.	Dec. 20
In Washington, D.C., Judge Royce Lamberth rules that the government mismanaged a trust fund that held $500 million belonging to 300,000 Native Americans. Lamberth characterizes the mishandling of funds by the Interior and Treasury departments as "fiscal and governmental irresponsibility in its purest form." . . . American Home Products agrees to pay at least $350 million to settle 1,400 injury cases over the diet drug combination fen/phen.	The Clinton administration gives a $51 million check to the UN With the check, the U.S. pays enough of its back dues to the UN to save its vote in the General Assembly. . . . The U.S. government reports that the Bahamian detainee involved in the Dec. 13–18 standoff at a Louisiana prison will be repatriated to the Bahamas under routine procedures.	Pres. Clinton announces new EPA standards that require the oil industry to produce cleaner gasoline and that tighten emissions regulations for the "light truck" category of vehicles.			Dec. 21

F	G	H	I	J
Includes elections, federal-state relations, civil rights and liberties, crime, the judiciary, education, health care, poverty, urban affairs, and population.	Includes formation and debate of U.S. foreign and defense policies, veterans' affairs, and defense spending. (Relations with specific foreign countries are usually found under the region concerned.)	Includes business, labor, agriculture, taxation, transportation, consumer affairs, monetary and fiscal policy, natural resources, and pollution.	Includes worldwide scientific, medical, and technological developments; natural phenomena; U.S. weather; natural disasters; and accidents.	Includes the arts, religion, scholarship, communications media, sports, entertainments, fashions, fads, and social life.

	World Affairs	Europe	Africa & the Middle East	The Americas	Asia & the Pacific
Dec. 22	UN investigators call on the UN Security Council to set up an international war crimes tribunal to investigate the military's role in human-rights abuses committed in East Timor. Indonesian president Abdurrahman Wahid states his administration will not sanction the trial of military officers by an international tribunal. . . . A three-member WTO panel rules that Section 301 of U.S. trade law, which allows the U.S. to take unilateral action against trading partners it accuses of unfair trade practices, does not violate international trade agreements.	Ukraine's parliament approves Victor Yushchenko as premier.			
Dec. 23		Four militant separatist groups on the French-controlled island of Corsica announce an unconditional cease-fire. In the past 10 years, Corsica has seen more than 4,000 bombings, most of them attributed to nationalist organizations that favor Corsica's official separation from France. . . . Italy's parliament gives Italian premier Massimo D'Alema's new, slightly different government coalition a vote of confidence.	A military uprising ignites when troops, upset over their pay, rampages through Abidjan, the capital of Ivory Coast.		A ferry carrying 650 passengers and crew members sinks after its hull strikes a rock in shallow waters. Some 590 people are rescued from waters near Bantayan Island, about 300 miles (480 km) southeast of Manila, the capital of the Philippines. At least nine people are killed, and 58 others are missing.
Dec. 24			In Ivory Coast, members of the military oust Pres. Henri Konan Bedie in a largely nonviolent coup, which comes after the Dec. 23 military uprising. Gen. Robert Guei, a former armed forces chief of staff, takes over as the new president and announces that democratic rules will be "closely respected.". . . The Dec. 21 cease-fire in Lebanon ends when Hezbollah begins firing on Israeli forces.		Five heavily armed men commandeer an Indian passenger jet en route from Katmandu, Nepal, to New Delhi, India. The hijackers reroute the jet to Afghanistan.
Dec. 25		Russian military forces advance into Grozny, the capital of the breakaway republic of Chechnya. The civilian population still remaining in Grozny is estimated at around 50,000. . . . Due to rough weather conditions, the oil slick from the Dec. 12 tanker accident near Brittany reaches the French coast, trapping about 10,000 sea birds.		A jet operated by Cubana de Aviacion, Cuba's government-run airline, crashes into the side of a mountain near Valencia, Venezuela, killing all 22 people on board. It is the second deadly accident in less than a week involving planes operated by Cubana de Aviacion.	The heavily armed men who hijacked a plane on Dec. 24 land at an airport in Kandahar, Afghanistan. There, the hijackers threaten to kill more than 150 passengers and crew members unless India frees imprisoned Pakistani militants, including Masood Azhar. Militants in Kashmir kill at least 10 people, in several raids viewed as expressions of support for the hijackers. . . . Reports confirm that some 230 bodies have been recovered in East Timor since international peacekeepers were deployed in the region in September.
Dec. 26		A storm sweeps hurricane-force winds of up to 125 miles per hour (200 kmph) across France.		Alfonso Portillo Cabrera of the opposition rightist Guatemalan Republican Front (FRG) wins the Guatemalan presidency in a runoff. He will be the first president elected in Guatemala since the end of the nation's 36-year-long civil war in 1996.	A court in Beijing, China's capital, sentences four followers of the outlawed Falun Gong spiritual movement to prison terms ranging from seven to 18 years. The sentences, handed down to the four—Li Chang, Wang Zhiwen, Ji Liewu, and Yao Jie—are among the longest given to any political or religious dissidents in China in recent years.
Dec. 27			Israel releases five Lebanese prisoners, including four members of the Shi'ite Muslim guerilla group Hezbollah, in the first release of Lebanese prisoners since mid-1998. The freed prisoners have been held without trial for between 10 and 13 years. The release is widely seen as a gesture of goodwill before Israel enters into a further round of peace talks with Syria in January 2000.	Government-owned BC Rail Ltd., Canada's third-largest freight transporter, locks out 1,600 unionized staff and shut down operations to preempt a walkout by workers.	Indian foreign minister Jaswant Singh leads a 52-member team to Kandahar, Afghanistan, to negotiate with the hijackers who took control of a plane Dec. 24.

A	B	C	D	E
Includes developments that affect more than one world region, international organizations, and important meetings of major world leaders.	Includes all domestic and regional developments in Europe, including the Soviet Union, Turkey, Cyprus, and Malta.	Includes all domestic and regional developments in Africa and the Middle East, including Iraq and Iran and excluding Cyprus, Turkey, and Afghanistan.	Includes all domestic and regional developments in Latin America, the Caribbean, and Canada.	Includes all domestic and regional developments in Asia and Pacific nations, extending from Afghanistan through all the Pacific Island, except Hawaii.

U.S. Politics & Social Issues	U.S. Foreign Policy & Defense	U.S. Economy & Environment	Science, Technology, & Nature	Culture, Leisure, & Lifestyle	
A Boston, Massachusetts, grand jury indicts former FBI agent John Connolly on charges that he conspired to commit crimes with two Boston mob leaders who were FBI informers. The indictment also charges the two mob leaders, James Bulger and Stephen Flemmi. . . . A jury in Newton, New Jersey, convicts Jayson Vreeland, 20, for his role in the 1997 murders of two pizza delivery men, Georgio Gallara, 24, and Jeremy Giordano, 22. . . . The Justice Department announces it will appoint a monitor to oversee the New Jersey State Police, due to evidence of discrimination by the use of racial profiling.	The INS reveals that it has postponed its inspection interview with a six-year-old Cuban refugee, Elián González, whose case has given rise to a tense dispute between the U.S.'s Cuban exile community and the Cuban government, which demands the boy's return.			A federal appeals court in Philadelphia, Pennsylvania, reverses a lower-court decision and rules that the NCAA may use minimum test scores to determine which students are eligible to compete in collegiate athletics and receive athletic scholarships.	Dec. 22
					Dec. 23
					Dec. 24
Pres. Clinton announces $900 million in new grant money to fund programs for the country's homeless.					Dec. 25
					Dec. 26
			The space shuttle *Discovery* touches down at Kennedy Space Center in Cape Canaveral, Florida, after carrying out a mission to repair and replace equipment on the earth-orbiting *Hubble Space Telescope*.		Dec. 27

F	G	H	I	J
Includes elections, federal-state relations, civil rights and liberties, crime, the judiciary, education, health care, poverty, urban affairs, and population.	Includes formation and debate of U.S. foreign and defense policies, veterans' affairs, and defense spending. (Relations with specific foreign countries are usually found under the region concerned.)	Includes business, labor, agriculture, taxation, transportation, consumer affairs, monetary and fiscal policy, natural resources, and pollution.	Includes worldwide scientific, medical, and technological developments; natural phenomena; U.S. weather; natural disasters; and accidents.	Includes the arts, religion, scholarship, communications media, sports, entertainments, fashions, fads, and social life.

	World Affairs	Europe	Africa & the Middle East	The Americas	Asia & the Pacific
Dec. 28		Turkmenistan's parliament votes unanimously to allow Pres. Sapar-murad Niyazov to serve as leader of the country for life. Niyazov, 59, was first elected president in 1990. . . . A storm sweeps through France. When coupled with the Dec. 26 storm, the winds killed 68 people and damage several historical landmarks. The storms also kill about 40 other people in neighboring nations.	Israel hands over to Hezbollah the bodies of two of their members slain in recent fighting in Israel's security zone in southern Lebanon.		Reports reveal that Pakistan's military government has ordered the arrests of 33 bureaucrats and politicians for financial corruption. . . . South Korea's composite index closes up 82.8% for 1999.
Dec. 29	UN secretary general Kofi Annan announces that Major General Jaime de los Santos of the Philippines will serve as commander of a 9,000-member UN peacekeeping force for East Timor.	Judge Sergei Golets of the St. Petersburg city court in Russia acquits retired naval captain Alexander Nikitin of charges relating to his leaking state secrets about nuclear pollution to a Norwegian environmental group. Separately, officials claim that Russian troops have captured all of Grozny's suburbs in Chechnya.	Israel releases 26 Palestinian prisoners in an apparent gesture of goodwill at the start of Ramadan, the Muslim holy month. Separately, the Israeli army tears down a shrine erected at the grave of Baruch Goldstein, a U.S.-born Israeli settler who killed scores of Palestinians in an attack on a mosque in Hebron in 1994.		The Indonesian military takes over security on Ambon island, where religious violence has flared sporadically throughout the year.
Dec. 30	Germany's Frankfurt DAX 30 exchange closes up 39% for the year. The London Stock Exchange 100 closes with a year-end gain of 17.8%. Finland's HEX 20 shows a 162% surge in 1999, the biggest rise of any market. Mexico's Bolsa index in Mexico City rose a record 80% for the year. In Japan, the Nikkei average on the Tokyo Stock Exchange closes up 36.8% from one year earlier. . . . Taiwan reveals that it has agreed to establish diplomatic relations with Palau, an island nation in the Pacific Ocean. That brings the number of countries that recognize Taiwan to 29.	Russian officials claim that Chechen rebels have given up key positions in Grozny and the southern mountains of Chechnya. Reports place the number of rebels still holed up in the capital at between 2,000 and 5,000.	A car bomb is detonated on Lebanon's Qlaia highway, killing the driver of the van carrying the bomb and injuring 12 Lebanese civilians and an Israeli soldier. Hezbollah claims responsibility for the attack. . . . Israel releases seven Palestinian prisoners—most of whom are allied with Yasser Arafat's Fatah faction of the PLO. The seven prisoners are from Israeli-occupied East Jerusalem, marking the first time since 1994 that an Israeli prisoner release includes residents of East Jerusalem.	The foreign ministers of Honduras and Nicaragua sign an agreement to defuse military tensions pending a World Court decision regarding sovereignty over 12,000 square miles (31,000 sq km) of Caribbean coastal waters.	Foreign ministers from Vietnam and China sign a treaty that resolves outstanding border disputes between their two countries. . . . Javed Iqbal, the target of a mass manhunt in connection with the alleged rape and murder of 100 boys, surrenders in Lahore, the capital of Punjab province in Pakistan.
Dec. 31		Russian president Boris Yeltsin unexpectedly announces his resignation, naming Premier Vladimir Putin acting president. Yeltsin was first elected president of Russia, then a Soviet republic, in 1991, and subsequently presided over the dismantling of the Soviet Union.		Panama assumes control of the Panama Canal and the surrounding canal zone from the U.S., culminating a transfer of sovereignty outlined in a 1977 treaty between the two nations. Thousands of Panamanians attend a ceremony held inside the zone in front of the headquarters of the Panama Canal Commission, a U.S. government agency that oversaw the operation of the canal. The commission is succeeded as canal administrator by the Panama Canal Authority, an autonomous corporation. . . . In Canada, the Toronto Stock Exchange composite index closes with a 29.7% increase from 1998's closing figure.	The crisis that started Dec. 24 when five men hijacked an Indian passenger jet ends when the Indian government releases three jailed Pakistani militants, Mushtaq Ahmed Zargar, Ahmed Umar Saeed Sheik, and Masood Azhar. . . . Reports reveal that some 300 people have been killed in several days of clashes between Christians and Muslims in the Moluccas island chain, which forms Indonesia's Maluku Province.

A	B	C	D	E
Includes developments that affect more than one world region, international organizations, and important meetings of major world leaders.	*Includes all domestic and regional developments in Europe, including the Soviet Union, Turkey, Cyprus, and Malta.*	*Includes all domestic and regional developments in Africa and the Middle East, including Iraq and Iran and excluding Cyprus, Turkey, and Afghanistan.*	*Includes all domestic and regional developments in Latin America, the Caribbean, and Canada.*	*Includes all domestic and regional developments in Asia and Pacific nations, extending from Afghanistan through all the Pacific Island, except Hawaii.*

U.S. Politics & Social Issues	U.S. Foreign Policy & Defense	U.S. Economy & Environment	Science, Technology, & Nature	Culture, Leisure, & Lifestyle	
					Dec. 28
		Data shows that, in fund-raising totals for the year, Sen. John McCain (R, Ariz.), has raised about $13.6 million since January, including $6.1 million in the final quarter. The campaign of Democratic vice president Al Gore states that Gore raised $4 million in the fourth quarter of 1999, increasing his annual total to nearly $29 million. Former senator Bill Bradley (D, N.J.) raised more than $8 million in the quarter and about $27 million since January.		Reports confirm that Thailand's censorship board has barred the release of a U.S.-made film, *Anna and the King*, claiming that the film's depiction of 19th-century Thai king Mongkut is insulting.	**Dec. 29**
	The last U.S. flag over the Panama Canal is lowered in a small ceremony at the Panama Canal commission headquarters.	Texas governor George W. Bush's campaign reports that it has raised more than $67 million since January, far more than any presidential candidate has ever raised in the entire final 18 months of the nomination process. Former senator Robert J. Dole (R, Kans.) had held the previous record, raising $31.3 million in that period.	Technicians with the FAA scramble to fix a previously undetected Y2K bug in systems at its 21 en-route air-traffic-control centers.	In England, former Beatle George Harrison is stabbed twice in the chest by an intruder in Harrison's Henley-on-Thames mansion. Harrison is wounded by the attack.	**Dec. 30**
Data shows that a total of 24 members of the U.S. House of Representatives do not plan to run for reelection in the year 2000.		Silvio Izquierdo-Leyva shoots to death four fellow workers and one other person at the Radisson Bay Harbor Inn, in Tampa, Florida. He wounds three people. . . . The U.S. dollar ends 1999 at 1.9423 marks, up from the 1998 year-end rate. The dollar closes 1999 at 102.12 yen, down from the previous year's final rate. The Dow Jones Industrial Average closes at 11497.12, up 2315.69 points, or 25.22%, from the 1998 year-end level of 9181.43. The 1999 closing figure also marks the Dow's highest trading-day close over the 12-month period. NASDAQ closes at a record 4069.31, an 85.5% increase from 1998. AMEX closes at 876.97, up 27.28% from its 1998 close of 688.99. The Dow global index shows the U.S. market up 18.9%. The S&P 500 closes at 1469.25, a 19.5% increase for the year, the fifth consecutive year it has double-digit percentage gains.		In England, news reports identify Michael Abram, 33, as the man who stabbed George Harrison on Dec. 30. He reportedly believed the Beatles to be witches.	**Dec. 31**

F	G	H	I	J
Includes elections, federal-state relations, civil rights and liberties, crime, the judiciary, education, health care, poverty, urban affairs, and population.	*Includes formation and debate of U.S. foreign and defense policies, veterans' affairs, and defense spending. (Relations with specific foreign countries are usually found under the region concerned.)*	*Includes business, labor, agriculture, taxation, transportation, consumer affairs, monetary and fiscal policy, natural resources, and pollution.*	*Includes worldwide scientific, medical, and technological developments; natural phenomena; U.S. weather; natural disasters; and accidents.*	*Includes the arts, religion, scholarship, communications media, sports, entertainments, fashions, fads, and social life.*

NAME INDEX

The index is arranged alphabetically letter-by-letter. Entries are arranged both alphabetically and chronologically. Every index entry contains the year, month, day, and column location (e.g., Allen, Woody 1997 Dec 23J). The year is 1997, the month is December, the day is 23, and the column is J.

Gandhi—1363

Fegan, Brendan 1999 May 9B
Feighan, Michael Aloysius 1992 Mar 19F
Feinstein, Diane 1992 Jun 2F
  gubanatorial campaign of, fines assessed for 1992 Dec 25H
  Riordan, Richard, on 1994 Oct 30F
  1994 Senate race 1995 Feb 7F
Feinstein, Martin 1994 Mar 14J
Feldman, Avigdor 1991 Nov 21G
Feldman, Sandra 1997 May 6H
Feliciano, Comrad *see* Ramirez Durand, Oscar
Felix, Mary 1995 Oct 19G
Felker, Ellis Wayne 1996 Nov 15F
Fell, Norman 1998 Dec 14J
Fender, Clarence Leo 1991 Mar 21J
Fendick, Patty 1991 Jan 27J
Feng Congde 1990 Mar 26B
Fennerman, George 1997 May 29J
Fensterwald, Bernard W., Jr 1991 Apr 2F
Fenwick, Millicent 1992 Sep 16F
Ferguson, Colin 1995 Feb 17F/Mar 22F
Ferguson, Roger, Jr. 1997 Oct 30H/Nov 5H; 1999 Sep 29H
Ferguson, Sarah *see* Sarah (duchess of York)
Ferlinghetti, Lawrence 1994 May 19J
Fernandez, Adriana 1999 Nov 7J
Fernandez, Clarisa 1991 Jan 27J
Fernandez, Emiliano 1992 Jan 4F
Fernandez, Gigi 1990 Sep 9J; 1991 Jun 9J
Fernandez, Jose B. 1994 Jun 19E
Fernandez, Joseph 1992 Dec 1F
Fernandez, Joseph F. 1990 Sep 6G/Oct 12G
  in Iran-contra arms scandal 1990 Sep 6G/Oct 12G
Fernandez Ordoñez, Francisco 1992 Aug 7B
Fernandez Partagas, Jose 1998 Aug 31I
Fernandez Pupo, Jose 1996 Jul 7G
Fernandez Reyna, Leonel 1996 May 16D/Jun 30D
Ferragamo, Fiamma di San Giuliano 1998 Sep 28J
Ferrari, Francisco Amico 1990 Feb 15D/Feb 19D
Ferrell, Rick 1995 Jul 27J
Ferrell, Roderick 1998 Feb 5F/Feb 27F
Ferrer, Jose 1992 Jan 26J
Ferreri, Marco 1997 May 9B
Ferri, Gian Luigi 1995 Apr 10F
Ferry, Charles Hugh Owen *see* Charles, Hugh
Fetisov, Slava 1997 June 13J
Feuille, Jean-Hubert 1995 Nov 7D/Nov 11D
Feuillere, Edwige 1998 Nov 13B
Fhimah, Lamen Khalifa 1992 Feb 18A; 1998 Aug 27A; 1999 Apr 5A
  and Lockerbie disaster 1991 Nov 14A
Fiacconi, Franca 1998 Nov 1J
Fiedler, Leslie 1998 Mar 24J
Fieger, Geoffrey 1998 Mar 14F
Field, Michael 1990 Nov 27E
Field, Ted 1995 Sep 27J
Fields, Cleo 1995 Nov 18F
Fields, Craig I. 1990 May 7G
Fiennes, Ralph 1994 Apr 24J
Fiers, Alan D., Jr. 1991 Jul 9G; 1992 Jan 31G/Dec 24G
Figueres Ferrer, Jose 1990 Jun 8D
Figueres Olsen, Jose Maria 1994 Feb 6D
Figueroa Mateos, Gabriel 1997 Apr 27D
Figueros Alcocer, Ruben 1996 Mar 10D/Mar 12D/Apr 23D/Jun 14D
Filho, Arlindo Maginario 1997 Nov 28D
Filho, Hermogenes Almeida 1994 Jun 14D
Fili-Krushel, Patricia 1998 Jul 31J
Filipov, Georgi Stanchev 1992 Jul 14B
Finca, Bongani Blessing 1994 Mar 23C
Fincham, Rebecca 1997 Oct 13F
Fine, Larry 1994 Dec 6J
Finger, Bill 1998 Nov 3J
Fingers, Rollie 1992 Jan 7J
Finkel, Moisei 1997 May 17B
Finks, Jim 1995 Jan 28J/Jul 29J
Finley, Charles O(scar) 1996 Feb 19J
Finley, Karen 1990 Jun 29J; 1991 Jan 4J
Finn, Kelly 1997 May 22G
Finney, John 1992 Apr 23F
Fino, Bashkim 1997 Mar 11B/Apr 5B/July 24B
Finsel, Paul T., Jr. 1990 May 4G
Finta, Imre 1990 May 25D
Fiorina, Carleton 1999 Jul 19H
Fireman, Simon 1996 Jul 10H/Oct 23H
Firestone, Leonard K. 1996 Dec 24G
Firkusny, Rudolf 1994 Jul 19J
Fischer, Edmond 1992 Oct 12I
Fischer, Kristie 1992 Jul 7F
Fischer, Tim 1990 Apr 10D
Fischler, Franz 1996 Jul 22A
Fish, Hamilton 1991 Jan 18F
Fish, Hamilton, Jr. 1996 Jul 23F
Fisher, Amy 1992 Sep 23F; 1994 Mar 23F; 1995 Jun 8F/Jul 7F/Sep 15F; 1999 May 10F
  sentencing of 1992 Dec 1F
Fisher, Avery Robert 1994 Feb 26I
Fisher, Bernard 1997 Feb 28I
Fisher, Christopher 1994 Jan 13F
Fisher, Cynthia J. 1995 Sep 7F
Fisher, Larry 1999 Nov 22D
Fisher, Max Henry (Fredy) 1993 Aug 29B
Fisher, Zachary 1999 Jun 4H
Fisk, Carlton 1990 Aug 17J
Fiske, Robert B., Jr., in Whitewater investigation 1994 Jan 20H/Mar 4H/Jun 30H
  dismissal of 1994 Aug 5H/Aug 10H
Fiszmann, Jakub 1996 Oct 19B
Fitzgerald, Daniel P. 1995 Feb 7J
Fitzgerald, Ella 1994 Apr 11J; 1996 Jun 15J
Fitzgerald, John 1991 Jun 8J/Jul 6J/Jul 7J
Fitzgerald, Marta 1994 May 27J
Fitzgerald, Penelope 1998 Mar 24J
Fitzgerald, William Burwell 1998 Apr 13H
Fitzwater, Marlin 1990 Mar 27G/Apr 4G; 1991 Jan 16G
Fiuza, Ricardo 1994 May 11D
Fivaz, George 1995 Jan 29C
Flade, Klaus-Dietrich 1992 Mar 17I
Flake, Flake 1991 Apr 3F
Flake, Floyd H. 1990 Aug 2F
Flamer, William Henry 1996 Jan 30F
Flatow, Alisa M. 1998 Mar 11G
Fleck, John 1990 Jun 29J
Fleet, Preston 1995 Jan 31H
Fleishman, Stanley 1999 Sep 23F
Fleiss, Heidi 1995 May 24J; 1997 Jan 7J/Feb 10J
  conviction of 1994 Dec 2J
  indictment of 1994 Jul 28J
Fleming, Amaryllis 1999 Jul 27B
Fleming, Art Fazzin 1995 Apr 25J
Fleming, Patricia 1994 Nov 10F
Fleming, Peter 1992 Mar 25F
Flemming, Arthur Sherwood 1994 Aug 8F; 1996 Sep 7F
Flemmmi, Stephen 1999 Dec 22F
Fletcher, James 1997 Aug 8D
Fletcher, James Chipman 1991 Dec 22I
Fletcher, Penella (Penny) 1997 Aug 8D
Fletcher, Penelope Ruth *see* Mortimer, Penelope
Fletcher, William 1998 Oct 8F
Fletcher, Yvonne 1999 Jul 7A
Flipper, Henry Ossian 1999 Feb 19G
Flood, Curt 1997 Jan 20J
Flood, Daniel 1994 May 28F
Flore, Carmine 1997 June 14B
Florenzie, Dwayne Howard 1995 Aug 2E/Aug 3E
Flores, Carlos 1999 Jan 27D
Flores, Enrique Funes 1996 Apr 1F
Flores, Lola (Dolores) 1995 May 16B
Flores Facusse, Carlos Roberto 1997 Nov 30D; 1998 Jan 27D/Nov 9A
Flores Gonzalez, Benjamin 1997 July 15D
Flores Montiel, Ignacio 1994 Jan 26D
Flores Perez, Francisco 1999 Mar 7D/Jun 1D
Florival, Jacques 1996 Aug 20D/Sep 12D
Flowers, Gennifer, and Bill Clinton
  rumors of affair with 1992 Jan 23F
  tapes released by 1992 Oct 23F
Flowers, Thomas Harold 1998 Oct 28B
Floyd, Ray 1996 Jul 14J
Flynn, Raymond L. 1997 Sep 15J
Fo, Dario 1997 Oct 9J
Foale, C. Michael 1995 Feb 9I; 1997 May 24I/Sep 6I/Oct 6I
Foda, Faraq 1993 Dec 1C
Fodor, Eugene 1991 Feb 18J
Foelak, Carol Fox 1998 Jul 21H
Fogarty, Mary Jane 1995 Dec 18D
Fogel, Helen *see* Forrest, Helen
Fogel, Jeremy 1998 Mar 17F
Fogerty, Tom 1990 Sep 6J
Fogleman, Ronald R. 1995 Aug 15G; 1997 July 28G
Foisie, Philip M. 1995 Apr 18J
Fokin, Vitold P. 1992 Sep 30B
Foley, James Thomas 1990 Aug 17F
Foley, Thomas (Tom) 1991 Jan 12G; 1992 Jan 28F/Mar 20H/Mar 28F
Folkman, Judah 1998 May 3I
Fonda, Jane 1991 Dec 21J
Fontaine, Nicole 1999 Jul 20A
Fontaine, Philip 1990 Oct 30D
Fonteyn, Margot 1991 Feb 21J
Foote, Horton 1995 Apr 18J
Forbes, Malcolm S. (Steve), Jr. 1996 Feb 5H
Forbes, Malcolm Stevenson 1990 Feb 24J
Forbes, Michael 1999 Jul 17F
Ford, Allan 1996 Mar 28B
Ford, Betty 1999 Oct 27F
Ford, Ernest Jennings *see* Ford, Tennessee Ernie
Ford, Gerald 1990 Jul 19J; 1997 Nov 6J; 1999 Oct 27F
  at dedication of Ronald Reagan Presidential Library 1991 Nov 4J
Ford, Harold E. 1990 Apr 27F
Ford, Jesse Hill 1996 Jun 1J
Ford, John 1993 Jun 9E
Ford, Richard 1996 Apr 9J/Apr 16J
Ford, Tennessee Ernie 1991 Oct 17J
Ford, Wendell H. 1990 Nov 13F
Fordice, Kirk 1994 Apr 8F; 1998 Feb 24F
Fore, Anthony S. 1996 Nov 12G/Dec 12G/Dec 13G
Foreman, George 1994 Nov 6J
Forcot, Jean Claude 1990 Dec 30J
Fork, Fulvio Chester, Jr. *see* Forte, Chet
Forrest, Helen 1999 Jul 11J
Forsyth, Michael 1996 Nov 26B
Fortas, Abe 1998 Feb 8F
Forte, Chet 1996 May 18J
Fortensky, Larry 1996 Feb 5J
Fortier, Michael 1998 May 27F; 1999 Oct 8F
Fortune, Gabriel 1995 Nov 7D
Foruhar, Dariush 1998 Nov 22C/Nov 26C
Foruhar, Parvaneh 1998 Nov 22C
Fosdick, Dorothy 1997 Feb 5G
Fossett, Steve 1997 Jan 20J; 1998 Aug 11J
Foster, Bill 1996 Mar 5J
Foster, Greg 1991 Aug 29J
Foster, Henry W., Jr. 1995 Feb 2F/Feb 8F/Jun 22F
Foster, Jodie 1992 Jan 18J
Foster, Mike 1995 Nov 18F; 1996 Jan 11F
Foster, Norman 1999 Apr 11J
Foster, Vincent, Jr. 1997 Oct 10H
Foveaux, Jessie Lee Brown 1997 Mar 19J
Fowler, April 1999 Oct 8J
Fowler, Don 1997 Jan 21H
Fowler, Justin 1996 Mar 28B
Fowler, Norman 1990 Jan 3B; 1992 May 10B
Fowler, Susan 1992 Oct 11I/Oct 12I
Fowler, William Alfred 1995 Mar 14I
Fox, Harold C. 1996 Jul 28J
Fox, Nelson (Nellie) 1997 Mar 5J/Aug 3J
Fox, Susan 1999 Dec 17H/Dec 20F
Fox Quesada, Vicente 1995 May 28D
Foxx, Redd (John Elroy Sanford) 1991 Oct 11J
Foyle, Christina Agness Lillian 1999 Jun 8B
Fraenckel, Alan 1995 Sep 12B
Frahm, Herbert Ernst Karl *see* Brandt, Willy
Frahm, Sheila 1996 May 24F
Franca, Fernando de Assis 1997 Feb 2D
Francisco, Jerry 1994 Sep 29J
Franco, Francisco 1997 July 26B
Franco, Itamar 1993 Mar 5D/Aug 27D/Sep 15D; 1995 Jan 1D
Franco, Ruben 1998 Dec 28D
François, Joseph Michel 1994 Oct 4D; 1996 Apr 12D/Apr 22D; 1997 Mar 7G
Francois, Kendall 1998 Sep 2F/Sep 5F
Franey, Pierre 1996 Oct 15J
Frank, Anne 1998 Aug 18J
Frank, Anthony 1992 Jan 7F/Jan 9J
Frank, Barney 1990 Jul 26F
Frank, Charles 1998 Apr 5I
Frank, Ilya M. 1990 Jun 22I
Frank, Patrick Lee 1992 Feb 13F
Frank, Susan 1996 Nov 13H
Frankel, Martin 1999 Sep 4B/Oct 7G
Frankl, Viktor Emil 1997 Sep 2I
Franklin, Aretha 1991 Feb 9J; 1994 Mar 1J/Dec 4J
Franklin, Barbara H. 1991 Dec 26H; 1992 Feb 27H
Franklin, Melvin 1995 Feb 23J
Frankovich, Mike 1992 Jan 1J
Fraser, Ian 1999 May 11B
Frasure, Robert C. 1995 Aug 19B
Fratellini, Annie 1997 July 1B
Frazier, Charles 1997 Sep 1J/Nov 3J/Nov 18J/Dec 1J/Dec 22J
Frazier, Joe 1995 Sep 6J
Frechette, Louise 1998 Jan 12A
Frederick, Merian 1996 Feb 13F
Frederick, Pauline 1990 May 9F
Fredette, John S. 1990 May 4E
Free, Lloyd A. 1996 Nov 11G
Freed, Kayce 1997 Dec 6J
Freedberg, Sydney Joseph 1997 May 6J
Freeh, Louis J. 1995 Jul 14F/Aug 8F/Aug 11F; 1997 May 4I/Oct 21G
  European tour by 1994 Jun 28G
  on FBI office in Poland 1994 Jul 1G
  travel, to Moscow 1994 Jul 3B/Jul 4B
Freeman, Brenda 1995 Dec 7F
Freeman, Bryan 1995 Dec 7F/Dec 15F
Freeman, David 1995 Dec 15F
Freeman, Dennis 1995 Dec 15F
Freeman, Robert 1997 Feb 10H/Apr 8A
Freeman, William H. 1992 Nov 12F; 1997 May 6F
Frei Ruiz-Tagle, Eduardo 1993 Dec 11D; 1994 Mar 11D
Freitas do Amaral, Diogo 1995 Sep 19A
Freleng, Isadore (Friz) 1995 May 26J
French, Kristen 1995 Sep 1D
French, Melinda 1994 Jan 1J
Fresquez, Tracy 1999 Jan14F
Frey, Roger 1997 Sep 13B
Frick, Gottlob 1994 Aug 18J
Fricker, Peter Racine 1990 Feb 1J
Friedman, Jerome 1990 Oct 8I/Oct 17I
Friedman, Maurice Harold 1991 Mar 8I
Friedman, Michael 1998 Jan 19I
Friedman, Noam 1997 Jan 1C
Friedman, Paul 1995 Aug 9H; 1998 Sep 10H/Oct 9H
Friedrich, Ralf Baptist 1992 Jun 22B
Friedrichs, Hanns Joachim 1995 Mar 27B
Friendly, Fred W. 1998 Mar 3J
Frist, Thomas, Jr. 1997 Nov 17H
Frist, Thomas F. 1998 Jan 4I
Frohnmayer, John 1991 Nov 5J
Frondizi, Arturo 1995 Apr 18D
Frooks, Dorothy 1997 Apr 13G
Frye, Northrop (Herman) 1991 Jan 23J
Fryers, Robert 1995 Jan 20B
Fu, Xingqi 1998 Feb 20G
Fuchs, Klaus 1990 Jan 3I
Fuchs, Vivian Ernest 1999 Nov 11B
Fuentes, Norberto 1994 Aug 16J/Aug 26J
Fuentes, Severiano 1993 May 24D
Fu Guoyong 1996 Nov 19E
Fuhrman, Mark 1995 Nov 27F; 1996 Oct 2F
Fujimori, Alberto
  and drug traffic 1990 Sep 12D
  human rights violations by 1993 Apr 22D
  political life of 1990 Apr 8D/Jun 10D/Jul 28D; 1991 Feb 14D; 1995 Feb 5D/Apr 9D/Jul 27D; 1997 Jan 1D/Jan 31E/May 29D/June 5D; 1998 Oct 26D; 1999 Oct 10D; cabinet of 1994 Feb 17D; 1999 Jan 3D; constitutional reforms by 1993 Dec 28D; contraception program of 1990 Oct 23D; economic policies of 1990 Aug 21D; 1999 Apr 28D; foreign relations 1999 May 13D; second term of 1995 Jul 28D; voluntary military service plan and 1999 Sep 30D
  repressive measures of 1993 Apr 7D
  wife of, in opposition party challenge 1994 Sep 12D
Fujinami, Takao 1997 Mar 24E
Fujisaki, Hiroshi 1996 Sep 17F
Fujita, Nobuo 1998 Oct 4G
Fujita, Sumiko 1998 Nov 19I
Fujita, Tetsuya (Ted) 1998 Nov 19I
Fukuda, Takeo 1995 Jul 5E
Fukui, Kenichi 1998 Jan 9I
Fulani, Lenora 1992 Jan 19A
Fulbright, (James) William 1995 Feb 9F
Fuller, Charles 1994 Dec 1J
Fuller, Paul 1997 Apr 8G/June 12G
Fuller, Samuel Michael 1997 Oct 30J
Fullerton, Eddie 1991 May 25B
Funk, Sherman 1992 Nov 18F
Funston, G(eorge) Keith 1992 May 15H
Funt, Allen 1999 Sep 5J
Furchgott, Robert 1998 Oct 12I
Furchtgott-Roth, Harold 1997 Oct 28F
Furcolo, Foster 1995 Jul 4F
Furness, Betty 1994 Apr 2J
Furrow, Buford, Jr. 1999 Aug 10F/Aug 11F
Furundzija, Anto 1997 Dec 18B; 1998 Dec 10A
Fussell, Stephen 1990 Nov 17G
Fyodorov, Boris 1994 Jan 26B

G

Gabelmann, Colin 1993 Oct 12D
Gable, Christopher 1998 Oct 23B
Gable, Clark 1996 Dec 17J
Gabor, Eva 1995 Jul 4J; 1997 Apr 1J
Gabor, Jolie 1997 Apr 1J
Gabor, Magda 1997 June 6J
Gabor, Zsa Zsa 1997 Apr 1J
Gabrish, Joseph 1992 Nov 28F
Gachot, Bertrand 1991 Jun 23J
Gacy, John Wayne 1994 May 9F/May 10F
Gad al-Haq, Gad al-Haq Ali 1996 Mar 15C
Gaddis, William 1994 Nov 16J; 1998 Dec 16J
Gadhafi, Muammar 1990 Mar 6C/Mar 11C/Apr 4C; 1991 May 17G/Jun 11C; 1997 Oct 22C; 1999 Jul 14B
  and expulsion of Palestinians from Libya 1995 Sep 1C/Oct 25C
  and Iraqi invasion of Kuwait 1990 Aug 20C
  and Nation of Islam 1996 Aug 28G
  South Africa and 1999 Jan 13C
Gaffney, Martin 1991 Nov 1G
Gagovic, Dragan 1999 Jan 9A
Gah Chok Tong 1997 Sep 29E
Gaidar, Yegor 1993 Sep 18B
Gaines, Ernest J. 1994 Feb 13J
Gaines, James E. 1992 Mar 6G
Gaines, Nathaniel Levi, Jr. 1997 May 29F
Gairy, Eric M. 1997 Aug 23D
Gaither, Billy Jack 1999 Mar 4F
Gajdusek, Daniel Carleton 1997 Feb 18I/Apr 29I; 1998 Apr 27I
Galan, Mario Hugo 1997 Dec 30D
Galic, Stanislav 1999 Dec 20A
Galimir, Felix 1999 Nov 10J
Galindo, Rudy 1996 Jan 20J
Galindo Lewis, Gabriel 1996 Dec 19D
Galindo Lopez, Ceivin 1999 Oct 7D
Galinski, Heinz 1992 Jul 19B
Galkin, Vladimir 1996 Oct 29G/Nov 14G
Gallagher, Gino 1996 Jan 30B
Gallagher, James Wesley (Wes) 1997 Oct 11J
Galland, Adolf Joseph Ferdinand 1996 Feb 9B
Gallara, Giorgio 1999 Apr 23F/May 7F/Dec 22G
Gallardo Rodriguez, Jose Francisco 1997 Jan 23D
Gallego, Hector 1993 Nov 21D
Galligan, Thomas B. 1990 Sep 11F
Gallina, Juliane 1991 Apr 26G
Gallo, Dean Anderson 1994 Nov 6F
Gallo, Robert 1992 Dec 30I
Galluccio, Michael 1997 Oct 22F
Galtieri, Leopoldo 1997 Mar 25B
Galvin, William M. 1990 Mar 28G
Gamang, Giridhar 1999 Dec 5E
Gambarov, Isa 1993 Jun 13B
Gamble, Wayne 1997 Mar 25G
Gammage, Jonny E. 1996 Nov 13F
Gamsakhurdia, Zviad 1990 Nov 14B; 1991 Apr 14B/May 26B/Sep 2B/Sep 16B/Sep 24B/Dec 22B
  arrest warrant issued for 1993 Oct 27B
  besieged by rebel forces 1992 Jan 5B/Jan 6B
  death of 1994 Jan 5B
  Georgian civil war and 1993 Oct 10B/Oct 18B
  Georgian elections and 1993 Oct 31B
  grave of 1994 Feb 24B
  recall from exile of 1993 Sep 2B
  resignation rejected by 1992 Jan 8B
  return of, to Georgia 1992 Jan 16B
  successor to: attempted coup by 1992 Jun 24B; selection of 1992 Mar 10B
  supporters of: demonstrations by 1992 Jan 16B; military action against 1992 Jan 23B/Jan 28B; rallies by 1992 Jan 3B
Gandar, Laurence Owen Vine 1998 Nov 14C
Gandhi, Mohandas K. 1997 Aug 14E/Sep 6E

SUBJECT INDEX

The index is arranged alphabetically letter-by-letter. Entries are arranged both alphabetically and chronologically. Every index entry contains the year, month, day, and column location (e.g., Adriatic Sea 1997 Mar 28B). The year is 1997, the month is March, the day is 28, and the column is B.

B

H